The New College
SPANISH & ENGLISH
Dictionary

The New College
SPANISH & ENGLISH Dictionary

EDWIN B. WILLIAMS
Professor of Romance Languages
University of Pennsylvania

Dedicated to serving
AMSCO
our nation's youth

AMSCO SCHOOL PUBLICATIONS, INC.
315 HUDSON STREET / NEW YORK, N.Y. 10013

THE NEW COLLEGE SPANISH & ENGLISH DICTIONARY

ISBN 0-87720-511-6

Published by Amsco School Publications, Inc., by arrangement with the copyright owners.

The cover photograph shows the cloister of San Cugat del Valles, Barcelona. Courtesy of Trans World Airlines, Inc.

Printed in the United States of America

10th printing

EDWIN B. WILLIAMS, A.B., A.M., Ph.D., Doct. d'Univ., LL.D., L.H.D., has been Chairman of the Department of Romance Languages, Dean of the Graduate School, and Provost of the University of Pennsylvania. He is a member of the American Philosophical Society and the Hispanic Society of America and the author of the Holt *Spanish and English Dictionary* and many other works on the Spanish, Portuguese, and French languages. Dr. Williams is General Editor of The New College Dictionary Series.

The New College Spanish & English Dictionary is the most modern, most usefully organized Spanish and English dictionary in print, and the most extensive one in a paperback edition. There are more than 70,000 entries, based on spoken and written sources, and organized to achieve the utmost clarity, precision, and convenience.

Important features:

1. Shows, on both English and Spanish sides, which of two or more words is appropriate →

   temple ['tɛmpəl] *s* (*place of worship*) templo; (*side of forehead*) sien *f*; (*sidepiece of spectacles*) gafa

   chinche *mf* (coll) bore, tiresome person || *m* (*clavito de cabeza chata*) thumbtack || *f* (*insecto*) bedbug; **caer** or **morir como chinches** to die like flies

2. Transitive verbs translated strictly by transitive verbs and expressions →

   embragar §44 *tr* (*el motor*) to engage || *intr* to throw the clutch in

3. Centered period shows where endings are to be added →

   car·ry ['kæri] *v* (*pret & pp* **-ried**) *tr*

   lá·piz *m* (*pl* **-pices**) (*grafito*) black lead;

4. Gender of Spanish nouns shown also on English side →

   mind [maɪnd] *s* mente *f*, espíritu *m*;

5. Spanish American words and meanings designated by regional labels →

   chacare·ro -ra *mf* (SAm) farm laborer, field worker; (Col) quack doctor; (Urug) gossip

   jaula *f* cage; (*embalaje de listones de madera*) crate; (Mex) open freight car; (Cuba, P-R) police wagon; **jaula de locos** insane asylum, madhouse

Contents

Preface vi
Prólogo vii
Labels and Grammatical Abbreviations x
Calificativos y abreviaturas gramaticales x

Part One **Spanish-English**

Spanish Pronunciation 3
SPANISH-ENGLISH 5-344
Model Verbs 345

Part Two **Inglés-Español**

La pronunciación del inglés 3
INGLÉS-ESPAÑOL 5-370

Preface

This book is based on primary spoken and written sources. It is designed for speakers of either language who wish to find words or the meanings of words in the foreign language. Its purpose is, therefore, fourfold. It gives to the English-speaking user (1) the Spanish words he needs to express his thoughts in Spanish and (2) the English meanings of Spanish words he needs to understand Spanish, and to the Spanish-speaking user (3) the English words he needs to express his thoughts in English and (4) the Spanish meanings of English words he needs to understand English.

In order to accomplish the purpose of (1) and (3), discriminations are provided in the source language except that, because of the special facility with which the subject of the verb can be shown in Spanish and because of the convenience of showing the object with personal **a,** discriminations in the form of subject and/or object are given in Spanish on the English-Spanish side as well as on the Spanish-English side. For the purpose of (2) and (4) discriminations are not needed and are not given because the user will always have the context of what he hears or reads to guide him. However, some glosses whose purpose is not to show discrimination but rather to elaborate on the meaning of what may be judged to be an unfamiliar or obscure word or expression in the user's native language are provided in that language.

All words are treated in a fixed order according to the parts of speech and the functions of verbs; and meanings with subject, usage, and regional labels come after more general meanings.

In order to facilitate the finding of the meaning and use sought for, changes within a vocabulary entry in part of speech and function of verb, in irregular inflection, in the gender of Spanish nouns, and in the pronunciation of English words are marked with parallels instead of the usual semicolons.

Periods are omitted after labels and grammatical abbreviations and at the end of vocabulary entries.

The feminine form of a Spanish adjective used as a noun (or a Spanish feminine noun having identical spelling with the feminine form of an adjective) which falls alphabetically in a separate position from the adjective is treated in that position and is listed again as a cross reference under the adjective.

Prólogo

Hemos basado este libro en fuentes originales del lenguaje hablado y escrito. Está destinado a los hablantes de uno u otro idioma que buscan palabras o significados de palabras en el idioma extranjero. Tiene, por lo tanto, los cuatro siguientes propósitos: al usuario de habla inglesa le suministra (1) las palabras españolas que necesita para expresar su pensamiento en español y (2) los significados ingleses de las palabras españolas que necesita para comprender el español; y al usuario de habla española le suministra (3) las palabras inglesas que necesita para expresar su pensamiento en inglés y (4) los significados españoles de las palabras inglesas que necesita para comprender el inglés.

Para lograr los propósitos indicados bajo los números (1) y (3), se suministran diferenciaciones (es decir, distinciones entre dos o más significados de una palabra) en la lengua-fuente; pero, dada la facilidad con que el sujeto del verbo puede indicarse en español y dada la conveniencia de destacar el objeto del verbo con la preposición **a**, las diferenciaciones consistentes en el sujeto o el objeto, o ambos, se dan en español tanto en la parte de inglés-español como en la parte de español-inglés. Para los propósitos indicados bajo los números (2) y (4) no se necesitan diferenciaciones y no se dan, porque el usuario siempre tendrá como guía el contexto de lo que oye o lee. Con todo, algunas glosas que no tienen por objeto indicar diferenciaciones sino más bien dilucidar el sentido de lo que parece ser una palabra o expresión raras u obscuras en la lengua nativa del usuario, se indican en esta lengua.

Los vocablos se tratan consecutivamente de acuerdo con las partes de la oración y las funciones verbales; y los significados marcados con calificativos de tema, uso y país van después de los significados más generales.

Para facilitar la búsqueda del significado y el uso deseados, los cambios en la parte de la oración y función verbal, en la flexión, en el género de los nombres españoles y en la pronunciación de las palabras inglesas van señalados con doble raya vertical, en vez del punto y coma de costumbre.

Se han omitido los puntos después de los calificativos y abreviaturas gramaticales y al fin de los artículos.

La forma femenina de un adjetivo español usado como sustan-

The gender of Spanish nouns is shown on both sides of the Dictionary except that the gender of masculine nouns ending in **-o,** feminine nouns ending in **-a, -dad, -tad, -tud, -ión,** and **-umbre,** masculine nouns modified by an adjective ending in **-o,** and feminine nouns modified by an adjective ending in **-a** is not shown on the English-Spanish side.

Numbers referring to the model conjugations of Spanish verbs are placed before the abbreviations indicating the part of speech. The complete list of model verbs includes models of all verbs that show a combination of two types of irregularity, e.g., **esforzar, seguir, teñir.**

Proper nouns and abbreviations are listed in their alphabetical position in the main body of the Dictionary. Thus **España** and **español** do not have to be looked up in two different parts of the book. And all subentries are listed in strictly alphabetical order.

The centered period is used in vocabulary entries of irregularly inflected words to mark off the final syllable that has to be detached before the syllable showing the inflection is added, e.g., **lá·piz** *m* (*pl* **-pices**) and **falsi·fy** [ˈfɔlsɪˌfaɪ] *v* (*pret & pp* **-fied**).

There are three kinds of compound words in English: (1) solid, e.g., **steamboat,** (2) hyphenated, e.g., **long-range,** and (3) spaced, e.g., **high school.** In this Dictionary the pronunciation of all English simple words is shown in a new adaptation of the symbols of the International Phonetic Alphabet and in brackets. The pronunciation of English compound words is not shown provided the pronunciation of the components is shown where they appear as independent vocabulary entries, except that the accentuation of solid and hyphenated compounds is indicated in the vocabulary entry itself, e.g., **fall′out′,** the IPA pronunciation of **fall** and **out** being shown where these words appear as independent vocabulary entries.

Since vocabulary entries are not determined on the basis of etymology, homographs are included in a single entry. When the pronunciation of an English homograph changes, this is shown in the proper place after parallels.

E.B.W.

The author wishes to express his gratitude to many persons who have worked with him in lexicographical research and development and who helped him directly in the compilation of this book and particularly to the following: Paul Aguilar, William Beigel, Henry H. Carter, Eugenio Chang-Rodríguez, R. Thomas Douglass, David Louis Gold, Allison Gronberg, James E. Iannucci, Christopher Stavrou, Roger J. Steiner, John C. Traupman, and José Vidal.

tivo (o de un sustantivo femenino que se escribe lo mismo que la forma femenina de un adjetivo), que cae alfabéticamente en lugar apartado del adjetivo, se trata en este lugar y se consigna otra vez bajo el adjetivo con una referencia a la palabra traducida anteriormente.

El género de los nombres españoles aparece en ambas partes del Diccionario; pero no aparece en la parte de inglés-español el género de los nombres masculinos que terminan en **-o,** los nombres femeninos que terminan en **-a, -dad, -tad, -tud, -ión** y **-umbre,** los nombres masculinos modificados por un adjetivo que termina en **-o** ni los nombres femeninos modificados por un adjetivo que termina en **-a.**

Los números que se refieren a los modelos de conjugación de los verbos españoles van antes de las abreviaturas que indican la parte de la oración. La lista completa de los modelos de conjugación incluye muchos que muestran una combinación de dos irregularidades, p.ej., **esforzar, seguir, teñir.**

Los nombres propios y las abreviaturas se consignan en su propio lugar alfabético en el texto del Diccionario. No hay, pues, que buscar **España** y **español** en dos partes distintas del libro. Y todos los artículos secundarios van colocados en riguroso orden alfabético.

Se usa el punto divisorio en los artículos de palabras de flexión irregular para señalar la sílaba final que debe separarse antes de agregar la sílaba que denota la flexión, p.ej., **lá·piz** (*pl* **-pices**) y **falsi·fy** ['fɔlsɪˌfaɪ] *v* (*pret & pp* **-fied**).

Hay tres clases de palabras compuestas en inglés: (1) las sólidas, p.ej., **steamboat,** (2) las escritas con guión, p.ej., **long-range** y (3) las separadas en dos o más elementos, p.ej., **high school.** En este Diccionario se muestra la pronunciación de todas las palabras inglesas simples por medio de una nueva adaptación de los símbolos del Alfabeto fonético internacional y entre corchetes. No se muestra la pronunciación de las palabras inglesas compuestas cuando la pronunciación de los componentes consta en los lugares donde aparecen como artículos independientes, si bien la acentuación de las palabras compuestas sólidas y las escritas con guión se indica en la voz alfabetizada misma, p.ej., **fall'out',** pues la pronunciación de **fall** y **out** va indicada según el Alfabeto fonético internacional en los lugares donde estas palabras aparecen como artículos independientes.

Como la constitución de los artículos no se ha determinado a base de su etimología, se incluyen bajo un mismo artículo todos los homógrafos de una palabra. Cuando varía la pronunciación de un homógrafo inglés, se indica en su propio lugar después de la doble raya vertical.

E.B.W.

Labels and Grammatical Abbreviations
Calificativos y abreviaturas gramaticales

abbr abbreviation—abreviatura
(acronym) acrónimo—a word formed from the initial letters or syllables of a series of words—palabra formada de las letras o sílabas iniciales de una serie de palabras
adj adjective—adjetivo
adv adverb—adverbio
(aer) aeronautics—aeronáutica
(agr) agriculture—agricultura
(alg) algebra—álgebra
(Am) Spanish American—hispanoamericano
(anat) anatomy—anatomía
(archaic) arcaico
(archeol) archeology—arqueología
(archit) architecture—arquitectura
(Arg) Argentine—argentino
(arith) arithmetic—aritmética
art article—artículo
(arti) artillery—artillería
(astr) astronomy—astronomía
(aut) automobiles—automóviles
(bact) bacteriology—bacteriología
(bb) bookbinding—encuadernación
(Bib) Biblical—bíblico
(billiards) billar
(biochem) biochemistry—bioquímica
(biol) biology—biología
(Bol) Bolivian—boliviano
(bowling) bolos
(bot) botany—botánica
(box) boxing—boxeo
(Brit) British—británico
(CAm) Central American—centroamericano
(cards) naipes
(carp) carpentry—carpintería
(chem) chemistry—química
(chess) ajedrez
(Chile) Chilean—chileno
(Col) Colombian—colombiano
(coll) colloquial—familiar
(com) commercial—comercial
comp comparative—comparativo
cond conditional—condicional
conj conjunction—conjunción
(C-R) Costa Rican—costarriqueño
(Cuba) Cuban—cubano
(culin) cooking—cocina
def definite—definido
dem demonstrative—demostrativo
(dent) dentistry—odontología
(dial) dialectal—dialectal
(eccl) ecclesiastical—eclesiástico
(econ) economics—economía
(Ecuad) Ecuadorian—ecuatoriano
(educ) education—educación
(elec) electricity—electricidad
(electron) electronics—electrónica
(El Salv) El Salvador
(ent) entomology—entomología
f feminine noun—nombre femenino
(fa) fine arts—bellas artes
fem feminine—femenino
(fencing) esgrima
(feud) feudalism—feudalismo
(fig) figurative—figurado
fpl feminine noun plural—nombre femenino plural
fsg feminine noun singular—nombre femenino singular
fut future—futuro
(geog) geography—geografía
(geol) geology—geología
(geom) geometry—geometría
ger gerund—gerundio
(gram) grammar—gramática
(Guat) Guatemalan—guatemalteco
(heral) heraldry—heráldica
(hist) history—historia
(Hond) Honduran—hondureño
(hort) horticulture—horticultura
(hum) humorous—jocoso
(hunt) hunting—caza
(ichth) ichthyology—ictiología
imperf imperfect—imperfecto
impers impersonal—impersonal
impv imperative—imperativo
ind indicative—indicativo
indecl indeclinable—indeclinable
indef indefinite—indefinido
inf infinitive—infinitivo
(ins) insurance—seguros
interj interjection—interjección
interr interrogative—interrogativo
intr intransitive verb—verbo intransitivo
invar invariable—invariable
(iron) ironical—irónico
(Lat) Latin—latín
(law) derecho
(letterword) a word in the form of an abbreviation which is pronounced by sounding the names of its letters in succession and which functions as a part of speech—palabra en forma de abreviatura la cual se pronuncia haciendo sonar el nombre de cada letra consecutivamente y que funciona como parte del discurso
(log) logic—lógica
m masculine noun—nombre masculino
(mach) machinery—maquinaria
(mas) masonry—albañilería
masc masculine—masculino
(math) mathematics—matemática
(mech) mechanics—mecánica
(med) medicine—medicina
(metal) metallurgy—metalurgia
(meteor) meteorology—meteorología
(Mex) Mexican—mejicano
mf masculine or feminine noun according to sex—nombre masculino o nombre femenino según el sexo
(mil) military—militar
(min) mining—minería
(mineral) mineralogy—mineralogía
(mountaineering) alpinismo
(mov) moving pictures—cine
mpl masculine noun plural—nombre masculino plural
msg masculine noun singular—nombre masculino singular
(mus) music—música
(myth) mythology—mitología

m & f masculine and feminine noun without regard to sex—nombre masculino y femenino sin tener en cuenta el sexo
(naut) nautical—náutico
(nav) naval—naval militar
neut neuter—neutro
(obs) obsolete—desusado
(obstet) obstetrics—obstetricia
(opt) optics—óptica
(orn) ornithology—ornitología
(paint) painting—pintura
(Pan) Panamanian—panameño
(Para) Paraguayan—paraguayo
(pathol) pathology—patología
pers personal—personal
(Peru) Peruvian—peruano
(pharm) pharmacy—farmacia
(philol) philology—filología
(philos) philosophy—filosofía
(phonet) phonetics—fonética
(phot) photography—fotografía
(phys) physics—física
(physiol) physiology—fisiología
pl plural—plural
(poet) poetical—poético
(pol) politics—política
poss possessive—posesivo
pp past participle—participio pasado
(P-R) Puerto Rican—puertorriqueño
prep preposition—preposición
pres present—presente
pret preterit—pretérito
pron pronoun—pronombre
(psychol) psychology—sicología
(rad) radio—radio
ref reflexive verb—verbo reflexivo
reflex reflexive—reflexivo
rel relative—relativo
(rhet) rhetoric—retórica
(rr) railway—ferrocarril
s substantive—substantivo
(SAm) South American—sudamericano
(scornful) despreciativo
(sculp) sculpture—escultura
(S-D) Santo Domingo—República Dominicana
(sew) sewing—costura
sg singular—singular
(slang) jerga
spl substantive plural—substantivo plural
ssg substantive singular—substantivo singular
subj subjunctive—subjuntivo
super superlative—superlativo
(surg) surgery—cirugía
(surv) surveying—agrimensura
(taur) bullfighting—tauromaquia
(telg) telegraphy—telegrafía
(telp) telephony—telefonía
(telv) television—televisión
(tennis) tenis
(theat) theater—teatro
(theol) theology—teología
tr transitive verb—verbo transitivo
(typ) printing—imprenta
(Urug) Uruguayan—uruguayo
v verb—verbo
var variant—variante
v aux auxiliary verb—verbo auxiliar
(Ven) Venezuelan—venezolano
(vet) veterinary medicine—veterinaria
(vulg) vulgar—grosero
(W-I) West Indian—antillano
(zool) zoology—zoología

PART ONE

Spanish-English

Spanish Pronunciation

The Spanish alphabet has twenty-eight letters. Note that **ch, ll,** and **ñ** are considered to be separate single letters and are so treated in the alphabetization of Spanish words. While **rr** is considered to be a distinct sign for a particular sound, it is not included in the alphabet and, except in syllabification—notably for the division of words at the end of a line—, is not treated as a separate letter, perhaps because words never begin with it.

These twenty-eight letters plus the sign **rr** are listed below with their names and a description of their sounds.

LETTER	NAME	SOUND
a	a	Like **a** in English **father,** e.g., **casa, fácil.**
b	be	When initial or preceded by **m,** like **b** in English **book,** e.g., **boca, combate.** When standing between two vowels and when preceded by a vowel and followed by **l** or **r,** like **v** in English **voodoo** except that it is formed with both lips, e.g., **saber, hablar, sobre.** It is generally silent before **s** plus a consonant and often dropped in spelling, e.g., **oscuro** for **obscuro.**
c	ce	When followed by **e** or **i,** like **th** in English **think** in Castilian and like **c** in English **cent** in American Spanish, e.g., **acento, cinco.** When followed by **a, o, u,** or a consonant, like **c** in English **come,** e.g., **cantar, como, cubo, acto, creer.**
ch	che	Like **ch** in English **much,** e.g., **escuchar.**
d	de	Generally, like **d** in **dog,** e.g., **diente, rendir.** When standing between two vowels, when preceded by a vowel and followed by **r,** and when final, like **th** in English **this,** e.g., **miedo, piedra, libertad.**
e	e	At the end of a syllable, like **a** in English **fate,** but without the glide the English sound sometimes has, e.g., **beso, menos.** When followed by a consonant in the same syllable, like **e** in English **met,** e.g., **perla, selva.**
f	efe	Like **f** in English **five,** e.g., **flor, efecto.**
g	ge	When followed by **e** or **i,** like **h** in English **home,** e.g., **gente, giro.** When followed by **a, o, u,** or a consonant, like **g** in English **go,** e.g., **gato, gota, agudo, grande.**
h	hache	Always silent, e.g., **hombre, alcohol.**
i	i	Like **i** in English **machine,** e.g., **camino, ida.** When preceded or followed by another vowel, it has the sound of English **y,** e.g., **tierra, reina.**
j	jota	Like **h** in English **home,** e.g., **jardín, junto.**
k	ka	Like English **k,** e.g., **kilociclo.**
l	ele	Like **l** in English **laugh,** e.g., **lado, ala.**
ll	elle	Somewhat like **lli** in **William** in Castilian and like **y** in English **yes** in American Spanish, e.g., **silla, llamar.**
m	eme	Like **m** in English **man,** e.g., **mesa, amar.**
n	ene	Generally, like **n** in English **name,** e.g., **andar, nube.** Before **v,** like **m** in English **man,** e.g., **invierno, enviar.** Before **c** [k] and **g** [g], like **n** in English **drink,** e.g., **finca, manga.**

LETTER	NAME	SOUND
ñ	eñe	Somewhat like **ni** in English **onion,** e.g., **año, enseñar.**
o	o	At the end of a syllable, like **o** in English **note,** but without the glide the English sound sometimes has, e.g., **boca, como.** When followed by a consonant in the same syllable, like **o** in English **organ,** e.g., **poste, norte.**
p	pe	Like **p** in English **pen,** e.g., **poco, aplicar.** It is often silent in **septiembre** and **séptimo.**
q	cu	Like **c** in English **come.** It is always followed by **ue** or **ui,** in which the **u** is silent, e.g., **querer, quitar.** The sound of English **qu** is represented in Spanish by **cu,** e.g., **frecuente.**
r	ere	Strongly trilled, when initial and when preceded by **l, n,** or **s,** e.g., **rico, alrededor, honra, israelí.** Pronounced with a single tap of the tongue in all other positions, e.g., **caro, grande, amar.**
rr	erre	Strongly trilled, e.g., **carro, tierra.**
s	ese	Generally, like **s** in English **say,** e.g., **servir, casa, este.** Before a voiced consonant (**b, d, g** [g], **l, r, m, n**), like **z** in English **zero,** e.g., **esbelto, desde, rasgar, eslabón, mismo, asno.**
t	te	Like **t** in English **stamp,** e.g., **tiempo, matar.**
u	u	Like **u** in English **rude,** e.g., **mudo, puño.** It is silent in **gue, gui, que,** and **qui,** but not in **güe** and **güi,** e.g., **guerra, guisa, querer, quitar,** but **agüero, lingüístico.** When preceded or followed by another vowel, it has the sound of English **w,** e.g., **fuego, deuda.**
v	ve or uve	Like Spanish **b** in all positions, e.g., **vengo, invierno, uva, huevo.**
x	equis	When followed by a consonant, like **s** in English **say,** e.g., **expresar, sexto.** Between two vowels, like **gs,** e.g., **examen, existencia, exótico;** and in some words, like **s** in **say,** e.g., **auxilio, exacto.** In **México** (for **Méjico**), like Spanish **j.**
y	ye or i griega	In the conjunction **y,** like **i** in English **machine.** When standing next to a vowel or between two vowels, like **y** in English **yes,** e.g., **yo, hoy, vaya.**
z	zeda or zeta	Like **th** in English **think** in Castilian and like **c** in English **cent** in American Spanish, e.g., **zapato, zona.**

A

A, a (a) *f* first letter of the Spanish alphabet
a *prep* at; for, to; on, upon; in, into; by; from; **a decir verdad** to tell the truth; **a la española** in the Spanish manner; **a lo que parece** as it seems; **a no ser por** if it weren't for; **a saberlo yo** if I had known it; **oler a** to smell of
abacería *f* grocery store
abace•ro -ra *mf* grocer
abad *m* abbot
abadejo *m* codfish; (orn) kinglet; (ent) Spanish fly
abadesa *f* abbess
abadía *f* abbacy; abbey
abaje•ño -ña *adj* (Mex) coastal, lowland || *mf* (Mex) lowlander
abaje•ro -ra *adj* (Arg) lower, under || *f* (Arg) bellyband, bellystrap; (Arg) saddlecloth
abaji•no -na *adj* (Col, Chile) northern || *mf* (Col, Chile) northerner
abajo *adv* down, underneath; downwards; downstairs; **abajo de** down; **más abajo** lower down; **río abajo** downstream || *interj* down with . . .!
abalanzar **§60** *tr* to hurl || *ref* to rush; to venture; (*un caballo*) to rear
abalizar **§60** *tr* to mark with buoys || *ref* (naut) to take bearings
abalorio *m* glass bead
abaluartar *tr* to bulwark
abanderado *m* colorbearer
abanderar *tr* (*un buque*) to register
abanderizar **§60** *tr* to organize into bands || *ref* to band together; (Chile, Peru) to join up
abandonar *tr* to abandon, to forsake || *intr* to give up || *ref* to abandon oneself; to give up
abandonismo *m* defeatism
abandonista *adj & mf* defeatist
abandono *m* abandon, abandonment; neglect; forlornness; yielding, giving up
abanicar **§73** *tr* to fan
abanico *m* fan; fanlight; (coll) sword; **abanico de chimenea** fire screen
abaniquear *tr* to fan
abaniqueo *m* fanning; gesticulations
abanto *adj* skittish (*bull*)
abaratar *tr* to cheapen; (*precios*) to lower || *intr & ref* to get cheap
abarca *f* sandal
abarcar **§73** *tr* to embrace; to encompass; to surround; (Am) to corner, monopolize
abarloar *tr* (naut) to bring alongside || *ref* to snuggle up
abarquillar *tr & ref* to curl up
abarrotar *tr* to bar; to bind, to fasten; to jam, to pack, to stuff; to overstock || *ref* (Am) to become a glut on the market
abarrote *m* (naut) packing; **abarrotes** (Am) groceries; (Am) hardware
abarrotería *f* (Guat) grocery store; (CAm) hardware store
abarrote•ro -ra *mf* (Am) grocer
abastecer **§22** *tr* to supply, to provide
abastecimiento *m* supplying; supplies, provisions
abasto *m* supply; abundance; **dar abasto** to be sufficient
abatanar *tr* to full
abatí *m* (Arg, Para) corn; (Arg, Para) corn whiskey
abati•do -da *adj* downcast; abject, contemptible || *f* abatis
abatir *tr* to lower; to knock down; to shoot down; to take apart; to humble; to discourage || *intr* (aer) to drift; (naut) to have leeway || *ref* to be discouraged; to be humbled; to drop, fall; to swoop down
abdicar **§73** *tr & intr* to abdicate
abdomen *m* abdomen
abecé *m* A B C
abecedario *m* A B C's
abedul *m* birch
abeja *f* bee; **abeja maestra** or **abeja reina** queen bee
abejar *m* apiary, beehive
abejarrón *m* bumblebee
abeje•ro -ra *mf* beekeeper
abejorro *m* bumblebee
abertura *f* aperture; opening; crack, slit; cove; openness, frankness
abeto *m* fir tree; hemlock; **abeto del Norte, abeto falso** spruce tree
abier•to -ta *adj* open; frank
abigarra•do -da *adj* motley, variegated
abigeo *m* horse thief, cattle thief
abijar *tr* (Col) to sic
abiselar *tr* to bevel
abismar *tr* to cast down; to humble; to spoil, ruin || *ref* to sink; to cave in; to be humbled; to give in; to lose oneself; (Am) to be surprised
abismo *m* abyss, chasm
ablandabre•vas *m* (*pl* **-vas**) or **ablandahi•gos** *m* (*pl* **-gos**) good-for-nothing
ablandar *tr* to soften; to soften up; to soothe; to loosen || *intr* (*el tiempo*) to moderate || *ref* to soften; to relent; (*el tiempo*) to moderate
ablativo *m* ablative
aboba•do -da *adj* stupid, stupid-looking
abobar *tr* to make stupid || *ref* to grow stupid

aboca•do -da *adj* (*vino*) mild, smooth; vulnerable; **abocado a** verging on
abocar §73 *tr* to bite; to pour; to bring near || *intr* to enter || *ref* to approach; to have an interview
abocinar *tr* to give a flare to || *intr* to fall on the face || *ref* to flare
abochornar *tr* to overheat; to make blush || *ref* to blush; to wilt
abofetear *tr* to slap in the face
abogacía *f* law, legal profession
abogaderas *fpl* (CAm) specious arguments
abogado *m* lawyer; **abogado de secano** quack lawyer; **abogado firmón** lawyer who will sign anything; **abogado trampista** shyster
abogar §44 *intr* to plead; **abogar por** to advocate, to back
abolengo *m* ancestry, descent; inheritance
abolir §1 *tr* to revoke, to repeal
abolladura *f* dent; bump, bruise; embossing
abollar *tr* to bump, to bruise; to dent; to stun; to emboss || *ref* to get bumped, get bruised; to dent, be dented
abollonar *tr* to emboss
abombar *tr* to make convex; (coll) to stun, confound || *ref* to rot, to decompose
abominación *f* abomination
abominar *tr* to detest, abominate || *intr* — **abominar de** to abominate
abona•do -da *adj* trustworthy; apt, likely || *mf* subscriber; (*al gas, electricidad, etc.*) consumer; (*a una localidad en el teatro*) season-ticket holder; (*al ferrocarril*) commuter
abonanzar §60 *intr* (*el tiempo*) to clear up; (*el viento*) to abate
abonar *tr* to vouch for; to certify; to improve; to fertilize; **abonar en cuenta a** to credit to the account of || *intr* (*el tiempo*) to clear up || *ref* to subscribe
abonaré *m* promissory note
abono *m* subscription; credit; installment; voucher; fertilizer, manure
abordar *tr* to approach; to accost; to undertake, to plan; (naut) to board; (naut) to run afoul of; (naut) to dock || *intr* to run afoul; (naut) to put into port
aborígenes *mpl* aborigines
aborrascar §73 *ref* to get stormy
aborrecer §22 *tr* to abhor, detest, hate; to bore || *ref* to get bored
aborrecible *adj* abhorrent, hateful
aborrega•do -da *adj* (*nubes*) fleecy; (*cielo*) mackerel
abortar *tr & intr* to abort
aborto *m* abortion
abotagar §44 *ref* to become bloated, to swell up
abotonador *m* buttonhook
abotonar *tr* to button || *intr* to bud
abovedar *tr* to arch, to vault
abozalar *tr* to muzzle
abra *f* cove; vale; fissure; (Mex) clearing
abrasar *tr* to set fire to, to burn; to parch; to nip; to squander; to shame || *intr* to burn || *ref* to burn; to become parched; (fig) to be burning up
abrasi•vo -va *adj & m* abrasive
abrazadera *f* clasp, clip, clamp; (typ) bracket
abrazar §60 *tr* to embrace, to clasp; to include; to take in || *ref* (*dos personas*) to embrace
abrazo *m* embrace, hug
abrebo•cas *m* (*pl* **-cas**) mouth prop, mouth gag
abrebote•llas *m* (*pl* **-llas**) bottle opener
abrecar•tas *m* (*pl* **-tas**) knife, letter opener
abreco•ches *m* (*pl* **-ches**) doorman
abrela•tas *m* (*pl* **-tas**) can opener
abreos•tras *m* (*pl* **-tras**) oyster knife
abrevadero *m* watering place, drinking trough
abrevar *tr* to water; to wet, soak; to irrigate; to size || *ref* to drink
abreviación *f* abridgment, abbreviation, shortening; hastening
abreviar *tr* to abridge; to abbreviate; to shorten; to hasten || *intr* to be quick; **abreviar con** to make short work of
abreviatura *f* abbreviation; **en abreviatura** (coll) in a hurry
abridor *m* opener; grafting knife; **abridor de guantes** glove stretcher
abrigadero *m* windbreak
abrigar §44 *tr* to shelter; to protect; (*esperanzas, sospechas*) to harbor || *ref* to take shelter; to wrap oneself up
abrigo *m* shelter; aid, support; cover, wrap; overcoat; (naut) harbor; **abrigo antiaéreo** air-raid shelter; **abrigo de entretiempo** topcoat, spring-and-fall coat; **al abrigo de** sheltered from, protected from; sheltered by, protected by; (*ropa*) **de mucho abrigo** heavy
abril *m* April
abrir *m* opening; **en un abrir y cerrar de ojos** (coll) in the twinkling of an eye || §83 *tr* to open; to unlock, unfasten; (*el apetito*) to whet; (*el bosque*) (Am) to clear || *intr* to open || *ref* to open; **abrirse a** or **con** to unbosom oneself to
abrochador *m* buttonhook
abrochar *tr* to button, to hook, to fasten
abrojo *m* thistle, thorn; **abrojos** reef, hidden rocks
abrótano *m* southernwood
abruma•dor -dora *adj* crushing, oppressing; overwhelming
abrumar *tr* to crush, oppress; to overwhelm; to annoy || *ref* to become foggy
abrup•to -ta *adj* abrupt, steep; rough, rugged
absceso *m* abscess
absenta *f* absinth
ábsida *f* or **ábside** *m* apse
absoluta *f* dogmatic statement; (mil) discharge

absolutamente *adv* absolutely; (Am) by no means
absolu•to -ta *adj* absolute; (coll) arbitrary || *m* absolute; **en absoluto** absolutely not || *f* see **absoluta**
absolvederas *fpl* — **tener buenas absolvederas** (coll) to be an indulgent confessor
absolver §47 & §83 *tr* to absolve; to solve, to answer
absorbente *adj* absorbent; (*interesante*) absorbing
absorber *tr* to absorb; to use up; to attract
absor•to -ta *adj* absorbed; entranced
abste•mio -mia *adj* abstemious
abstener §71 *ref* to abstain
abstinente *adj* abstinent
abstracción *f* abstraction; absorption, deep thought; **hacer abstracción de** to leave out, to disregard
abstrac•to -ta *adj* abstract
abstraer §75 *tr* to abstract || *intr* — **abstraer de** to do without, leave aside || *ref* to be abstracted or absorbed; **abstraerse de** to do without, leave aside
abstraí•do -da *adj* absorbed in thought; withdrawn
abstru•so -sa *adj* abstruse
absurdidad *f* absurdity
absur•do -da *adj* absurd || *m* absurdity
abuchear *tr* & *intr* to boo, to hoot
abuela *f* grandmother; **cuénteselo a su abuela** (coll) tell that to the marines
abuelo *m* grandparent; grandfather; **abuelos** grandparents; ancestors
abulta•do -da *adj* bulky, massive
abultar *tr* to enlarge; to exaggerate || *intr* to be bulky
abundamiento *m* abundance; **a mayor abundamiento** with greater reason
abundante *adj* abundant
abundar *intr* to abound
abur *interj* (coll) good-bye!, so long!
aburri•do -da *adj* bored; tiresome
aburrir *tr* to bore, tire || *ref* to become bored
abusar *intr* to go too far; **abusar de** to abuse; to impose on; to overindulge in
abusión *f* superstition
abusi•vo -va *adj* abusive
abuso *m* abuse; imposition
abyec•to -ta *adj* abject
A.C. *abbr* **año de Cristo**
acá *adv* here, around here; **acá y allá** here and there; **de ayer acá** since yesterday; **¿de cuándo acá?** since when?; **desde entonces acá** since then; **más acá** here closer; **muy acá** right here
acaba•do -da *adj* complete, perfect; worn-out, exhausted || *m* finish
acabar *tr* to end, finish, complete || *intr* to end; to die; **acabar con** to put an end to; to end in; **acabar de** to finish; to have just, e.g., **acaba de salir** he has just left; **acababa de salir** he had just left; **acabar por** to end in; to end by; **no acabar de decidirse** to be unable to make up one's mind || *ref* to end; to be exhausted; to be all over; to run out of, e.g., **se me acabó el café** I have run out of coffee
acabóse *m* (coll) limit, last straw
acacia *f* acacia; **acacia falsa** locust tree
academia *f* academy
académi•co -ca *adj* academic || *mf* academician
acaecer §22 *intr* to happen, to occur
acaecimiento *m* happening, occurrence
acalora•do -da *adj* heated; warm; fiery, excited
acalorar *tr* to heat, to warm; to incite, to encourage; to stir up || *ref* to become heated; to warm up
acallar *tr* to quiet, to silence; to pacify
acampada *f* camp
acamar *tr* (*las mieses la lluvia o el viento*) to beat down, to blow over
acampamento *m* camp, encampment
acampana•do -da *adj* bell-shaped
acampar *tr, intr* & *ref* to encamp
acanalar *tr* to groove; to flute; to channel; to corrugate
acantila•do -da *adj* rocky; steep, precipitous || *m* cliff, bluff
acantonamiento *m* cantonment
acantonar *tr* to canton, to quarter || *ref* to be quartered; **acantonarse en** to limit one's activities to
acaparar *tr* to corner; to monopolize; to hoard
acaramela•do -da *adj* candied; (coll) smooth, honey-tongued
acarar *tr* to bring face to face
acarear *tr* to bring face to face; to face, to brave
acariciar *tr* to caress; (*una ilusión*) to cherish
acarraladura *f* (Chile, Peru) run (*in stockings*)
acarreadi•zo -za *adj* transportable
acarrear *tr* to cart, transport, carry along; to cause, occasion || *ref* to incur, to bring upon oneself
acarreo *m* cartage, drayage; conveyance
acartonar *ref* (coll) to shrivel up, become wizened
acasera•do -da *adj* (Chile, Peru) home-loving; (*parroquiano*) (Chile, Peru) regular || *mf* (Chile, Peru) stay-at-home, homebody; (Chile, Peru) regular customer
acaso *m* chance, accident; **al acaso** at random || *adv* maybe, perhaps; **por si acaso** in case of need, just in case
acatar *tr* to respect, to hold in awe; to observe
acatarrar *tr* to chill, give a cold to; (Chile, Mex) to bother, annoy || *ref* to catch cold; (Am) to get tipsy
acaudala•do -da *adj* rich, well-to-do
acaudalar *tr* to acquire, to accumulate
acaudillar *tr* to lead, to command; to direct
acceder *intr* to accede; to agree
accesible *adj* accesible
accesión *f* accession; acquiescence; access, entry
accésit *m* second prize, honorable mention

acceso *m* access, approach; attack, fit, spell; **acceso prohibido** no admittance
acceso·rio -ria *adj* accessory || *m* accessory, fixture, attachment; **accesorios** (theat) properties
accidenta·do -da *adj* agitated; restless; rough, uneven || *mf* victim, casualty
accidental *adj* accidental; acting, pro-tempore, temporary
accidentar *tr* to injure, hurt || *ref* to faint
accidente *m* accident; (*del terreno*) roughness, unevenness; fainting spell
acción *f* action; gesture; (*parte del capital de una sociedad*) share; stock certificate; **acción crecedera** growth stock; **acción de gracias** thanksgiving; **acción liberada** stock dividend
accionar *tr* to drive || *intr* to gesticulate
accionista *mf* shareholder, stockholder
acebo *m* holly tree
acebuche *m* wild olive
acecinar *tr* to dry-cure, to dry-salt; (*el salmón o el arenque*) to kipper || *intr* to shrivel up
acechar *tr* to watch, to spy on
acecho *m* watching, spying; **al acecho** or **en acecho** on the watch, spying
acedar *tr* to turn sour; to embitter || *ref* to turn sour; to wither
acedía *f* sourness; crabbedness; heartburn
ace·do -da *adj* sour, tart; crabbed
aceitar *tr* to oil; to grease
aceite *m* oil; olive oil; **aceite de hígado de bacalao** cod-liver oil; **aceite de linaza** linseed oil; **aceite de pie de buey** neat's-foot oil; **aceite de ricino** castor oil; **aceite mineral** coal oil
aceite·ro -ra *adj* oil || *mf* oiler; oil dealer || *f* oilcan; oil cup; **aceiteras** cruet stand
aceito·so -sa *adj* oily, greasy
aceituna *f* olive
aceituno *m* olive tree
acelerador *m* accelerator
acelerar *tr & ref* to accelerate; to hasten, hurry
acelga *f* Swiss chard
acémila *f* beast of burden, pack animal; (coll) dolt; (coll) drudge
acendra·do -da *adj* refined; stainless, spotless
acendrar *tr* to refine; to purify, make stainless
acento *m* accent; **acento de altura** pitch accent; **acento ortográfico** written accent, accent mark; **acento prosódico** stress accent, tonic accent
acentuar **§21** *tr* to accent; to accentuate, emphasize
aceña *f* water-driven flour mill
acepción *f* meaning
acepillar *tr* to plane; to brush; to smooth
aceptable *adj* acceptable
aceptación *f* acceptance
aceptar *tr* to accept; to agree
acequia *f* irrigation ditch; (Bol, Col, Peru) stream, rivulet
acera *f* sidewalk
acera·do -da *adj* steel, steely; (fig) cutting, biting, sharp
acerar *tr* to steel, to harden; to line with a sidewalk || *ref* to harden; to steel oneself
acer·bo -ba *adj* sour, bitter; harsh
acerca *adv* — **acerca de** about, with regard to
acercamiento *m* approach, rapprochement
acercar **§73** *tr* to bring near or nearer || *ref* to approach, to come near or nearer
acería *f* steel mill
acerico *m* small cushion; pincushion
acero *m* steel; sword; courage, spirit
acérri·mo -ma *adj* all-out; (*enemigo*) bitter
acerrojar *tr* to bolt
acerta·do -da *adj* fit, right; skillful, sure; well-aimed
acertante *mf* winner
acertar **§2** *tr* to hit; to hit upon; to figure out correctly; to find; to do right || *intr* to be right; to succeed; to guess right; **acertar a** to happen to; to succeed in; **acertar con** to come upon; to find
acertijo *m* conundrum, riddle
acervo *m* heap; assets, estate; shoal; store, fund, hoard
acetato *m* acetate
acéti·co -ca *adj* acetic
acetificar **§73** *tr & ref* to acetify
acetileno *m* acetylene
acetona *f* acetone
acia·go -ga *adj* unlucky, ill-fated, evil
acíbar *m* aloes; bitterness, sorrow
acicalar *tr* to polish, to burnish; to dress, to dress up || *ref* to get all dressed up
acicate *m* long-pointed spur; incentive, stimulus
acidez *f* acidity
acidificar **§73** *tr & ref* to acidify
áci·do -da *adj* acid, tart, sour || *m* acid
acierto *m* lucky hit, good shot; good guess; tact, prudence; ability, skill; accuracy; success
aci·mut *m* (*pl* **-muts**) azimut
aclamación *f* acclaim, applause
aclamar *tr & intr* to acclaim, to hail, to cheer
aclarar *tr* to brighten, to clear; to rinse; to explain || *intr* to get bright; to clear up; to dawn
aclarato·rio -ria *adj* explanatory
aclimatar *tr & ref* to acclimate
acobardar *tr* to cow, intimidate || *ref* to be frightened
acocear *tr* to kick; to trample upon, to ill-treat
acocil *m* Mexican crayfish; **estar como un acocil** (Mex) to blush, to be abashed
acoda·do -da *adj* elbow-shaped
acodar *tr* (*el brazo*) to lean; to prop; (hort) to layer || *ref* to lean
acodillar *tr* to bend at an angle || *ref* to double up; to bend, to crumple
acoger **§17** *tr* to receive, to welcome;

to accept || *ref* to take refuge; to resort
acogida *f* reception, welcome; meeting place, confluence; refuge, shelter; **dar acogida a** (com) to honor
acolada *f* accolade
acolchar *tr* to quilt, to pad
acolchí *m* (Mex) red-winged blackbird
acólito *m* acolyte; altar boy
acollador *m* (naut) lanyard
acomedi•do -da *adj* (Am) obliging
acometer *tr* to attack; to undertake; (*el sueño, la enfermedad, el deseo a una persona*) to overcome
acometida *f* attack; (*p.ej., de una línea eléctrica*) house connection
acomodación *f* accommodation
acomodadi•zo -za *adj* accommodating, obliging
acomoda•do -da *adj* convenient, suitable; comfort-loving; well-to-do
acomoda•dor -dora *adj* accommodating, obliging || *mf* usher
acomodar *tr* to accommodate; to usher; to reconcile; to suit; to furnish, to supply || *intr* to be suitable, be convenient || *ref* to comply; to come to terms; to hire out; to make oneself comfortable
acomodo *m* arrangement, adjustment; lodgings; job, position; (Chile) neatness, tidiness
acompañamiento *m* accompaniment; escort, retinue; (theat) extras, supernumeraries
acompañanta *f* female companion or escort; accompanist
acompañante *m* companion; accompanist
acompañar *tr* to accompany; to escort; to enclose; to sympathize with
acompasa•do -da *adj* rhythmic; slow; easy-going; cautious
aconchar *tr* to push to safety; (naut) to beach, run aground || *ref* to take shelter; (naut) to run aground; (Chile) to form a deposit
acondiciona•do -da *adj* conditioned; **bien acondicionado** well-disposed; in good condition; **mal acondicionado** ill-disposed; in bad condition
acondicionador *m* conditioner; **acondicionador de aire** air conditioner
acondicionamiento *m* conditioning; **acondicionamiento del aire** air conditioning
acondicionar *tr* to condition; to put in condition; to repair; to season || *ref* to qualify; to find a job
acongojar *tr* to grieve, to afflict || *ref* to grieve
aconsejable *adj* advisable
aconsejar *tr* to advise, to counsel, to warn || *ref* to seek advice, to get advice
acontecer **§22** *intr* to happen, to occur
acontecimiento *m* happening, event
acopiar *tr* to gather together
acopio *m* gathering; stock; abundance
acoplado *m* (Arg, Chile, Urug) trailer trolley car
acoplamiento *m* coupling; joint; connection
acoplar *tr* to couple; to join; to connect; to hitch; to reconcile || *ref* to be reconciled; to mate; to be intimate
acoquinar *tr* to intimidate
acoraza•do -da *adj* armored, armor-plated; (coll) contrary || *m* battleship
acorazar **§60** *tr* to armor-plate
acorchar *tr* to line with cork; to turn into cork || *ref* to get spongy; to wither, shrivel; to become corky or pithy; to get numb
acorchetar *tr* to bracket
acordar **§61** *tr* to agree upon; to authorize; to reconcile; to make level or flush; to remind of; to tune || *intr* to agree; to blend || *ref* to be agreed, come to an agreement; to remember; **acordarse de** to remember
acorde *adj* agreed, in accord; in tune || *m* accord; (mus) chord
acordeón *m* accordion
acordonar *tr* to cord, to lace; (*monedas*) to knurl, to mill; to rope off
acornar **§61** *tr* gore; to butt
acornear *tr* to gore; to butt
acorralar *tr* to corral, to corner; to intimidate
acortar *tr* to shorten; to reduce; to slow down; to check, to stop || *ref* to become shorter; to hold back; to be timid; to slow down; to shrink
acosar *tr* to harass; to pester
acostar **§61** *tr* to lay down; to put to bed; (naut) to bring alongside || *ref* to lie down; to go to bed
acostumbra•do -da *adj* accustomed; customary, usual
acostumbrar *tr* to accustom || *intr* to be accustomed || *ref* to accustom oneself; to become accustomed
acotación *f* boundary mark; marginal note; elevation mark
acotamiento *m* boundary mark; marginal note; elevation mark; stage direction
acotar *tr* to mark off, to map; to annotate; to admit, to accept; to check; to vouch for; to select; to mark elevations on
acotillo *m* sledge hammer
acre *adj* acrid; austere; biting, mordant
acrecentamiento *m* increase, growth; promotion
acrecentar **§2** *tr* to increase; to promote || *ref* to increase; to bud, to blossom
acreditar *tr* to accredit; to credit; to get a reputation for || *ref* to get a reputation, to prove oneself
acree•dor -dora *adj* accrediting; deserving || *mf* creditor; **acreedor hipotecario** mortgagee
acribar *tr* to sift; to riddle
acribillar *tr* to riddle; (coll) to harass, to plague, to pester
acriminar *tr* to incriminate; to exaggerate
acrimonio•so -sa *adj* acrid; acrimonious

acriollar *ref* (Am) to acquire Spanish American ways
acrisolar *tr* to purify, to refine; to reveal, to bring out
acrobacia *f* acrobatics
acróbata *mf* acrobat
acrobatismo *m* acrobatics
acrónimo *m* acronym
acrópo•lis *f* (*pl* **-lis**) acropolis
acróstico *m* acrostic
acta *f* minutes; certificate; **acta notarial** affidavit; **actas** proceedings, transactions; **levantar acta** to write up the minutes
actitud *f* attitude; **en actitud de** getting ready to
activar *tr* to activate; to hasten, to expedite
actividad *f* activity
acti•vo -va *adj* active || *m* (com) assets; (com) credit side
acto *m* act; ceremony, function; commencement; thesis; **acto continuo** right afterward; **acto seguido** right afterward; **acto seguido de** right after; **hacer acto de presencia** to honor with one's presence
actor *m* actor; agent; **primer actor** leading man
ac•triz *f* (*pl* **-trices**) actress; **primera actriz** leading lady
actuación *f* acting, performance; action; operation; behavior
actual *adj* present, present-day; up-to-date || *m* current month
actualidad *f* present time; timeliness; **actualidades** current events; newsreel; **actualidad escénica** theater news; **actualidad gráfica** news in pictures
actualizar **§60** *tr* to bring up to date
actualmente *adv* at present, at the present time
actuante *mf* participant
actuar **§21** *tr* to actuate || *intr* to act; to perform
actua•rio -ria *mf* actuary
acuaplano *m* aquaplane
acuarela *f* water color
acuario *m* aquarium
acuartelar *tr* to billet, to quarter
acuáti•co -ca *adj* aquatic
acuatizaje *m* (aer) alighting on water; (*de nave espacial*) splashdown
acuatizar **§60** *intr* (aer) to alight on water
acucia *f* zeal, diligence; yearning
acuciar *tr* to goad, to prod; to harass; to yearn for
acuclillar *ref* to squat, to crouch
acuchilla•do -da *adj* knife-shaped; schooled by experienced; (*vestido*) slashed
acuchillar *tr* to stab; to stab to death; to slash
acudir *intr* to come up, to respond; to apply; to hang around; to come to the rescue
acueducto *m* aqueduct
acuerdo *m* accord; agreement; memory; **de acuerdo con** in accord with; **de común acuerdo** with one accord; **estar en su acuerdo** to be in one's right mind; **ponerse de acuerdo** to come to an agreement; **recobrar su acuerdo** to come to; **tomar un acuerdo** to make a decision; **volver en su acuerdo** to come to; to change one's mind
acuitar *tr & intr* to grieve
acullá *adv* yonder, over there
acumulador *m* storage battery
acumular *tr* to accumulate, to gather; to store up || *intr & ref* to accumulate, to gather
acunar *tr* to rock; to cradle
acuñación *f* coining, minting; wedging
acuñar *tr* to coin, to mint; to wedge; to key, to lock; (typ) to quoin
acuo•so -sa *adj* watery; juicy
acurrucar **§73** *ref* to squat, to crouch; to huddle
acusación *f* accusation
acusa•do -da marked || *mf* accused
acusar *tr* to accuse; to show; (*recibo de una carta*) to acknowledge || *ref* to confess
acusati•vo -va *adj & m* accusative
acuse *m* acknowledgment
acústi•co -ca *adj* acoustic || *f* acoustics
achacar **§73** *tr* to impute, to attribute
achaco•so -sa *adj* ailing, sickly
achaparra•do -da *adj* stocky; stubby; chubby
achaparrar *ref* to become stunted
achaque *m* sickliness, indisposition; excuse, pretext; matter, subject; weakness; (coll) monthlies
achatar *tr* to flatten
achica•do -da *adj* childish; abashed, disconcerted
achicador *m* scoop
achicar **§73** *tr* to make smaller; to humble; to bail, to bail out
achicoria *f* chicory
achicharrar *tr* to scorch; to bedevil || *ref* to get scorched
achispa•do -da *adj* tipsy
achispar *tr* to make tipsy || *ref* to get tipsy
achuchar *tr* to incite; to crumple, crush; to jostle || *ref* (Arg, Urug) to shiver, have a chill
adagio *m* adage
adalid *m* chief; guide, leader; champion
adama•do -da *adj* womanish; chic, stylish
adamar *ref* to become effeminate
adán *m* (coll) dirty, ragged fellow, lazy, careless fellow || **Adán** *m* Adam
adaptación *f* adaptation
adaptar *tr* to adapt
adarga *f* oval or heart-shaped leather shield
adarvar *tr* to bewilder, to stun
A. de C. *abbr* **año de Cristo**
adecentar *tr* to clean up, to tidy up || *ref* (coll) to put on a clean shirt, to dress up
adecua•do -da *adj* fitting, suitable
adecuar *tr* to fit, to adapt
adefesio *m* (coll) nonsense; (coll) outlandish outfit; (coll) queer-looking fellow

adehala *f* gratuity, extra
adehesar *tr* to convert into pasture
adelanta·do -da *adj* precocious; bold, forward; (*reloj*) fast; **por adelantado** in advance || *m* provincial governor
adelantamiento *m* anticipation; advancement, promotion, progress
adelantar *tr* to move forward; to outstrip, get ahead of; to advance; to promote; to improve || *intr* to advance; to improve; to be fast || *ref* to move forward; to gain, be fast
adelante *adv* ahead; forward; **más adelante** farther on; later || *interj* go ahead!; come in!
adelanto *m* advance, progress, improvement; advancement; payment in advance
adelfa *f* oleander
adelgazar **§60** *tr* to make thin; to taper; to purify; to argue subtly about; to weaken, lessen || *intr & ref* to get thin; to taper
ademán *m* attitude; gesture; **ademanes** manners; **en ademán de** getting ready to; **hacer ademán de** to make a move to
además *adv* moreover, besides; **además de** in addition to, besides
adentellar *tr* to sink one's teeth into
adentrar *intr & ref* to go in; **adentrarse en el mar** to go farther out to sea
adentro *adv* inside; **mar adentro** out at sea; **ser muy de adentro** to be like a member of the family; **tierra adentro** inland || **adentros** *mpl* inmost being, inmost thoughts; **en** or **para sus adentros** to oneself, to himself, etc.
adep·to -ta *adj* initiated || *mf* follower
aderezar **§60** *tr* to dress, adorn; to cook; (*una tela*) to starch; to season; to repair; to lead; (*bebidas*) to mix; (*vinos*) to blend || *ref* to dress, get ready
aderezo *m* dressing; seasoning, condiment; starch; finery; equipment; set of jewelry
adestrar **§2** *tr & ref* var of **adiestrar**
adeuda·do -da *adj* indebted, in debt
adeudar *tr* to owe; to be liable for; to charge || *intr* to become related by marriage || *ref* to run into debt
adeudo *m* debt, indebtedness; customs duty; charge, debit
adherencia *f* adhesion; **tener adherencias** to have connections
adherente *adj* adherent || *m* adherent; **adherentes** accessories
adherir **§68** *intr & ref* to adhere; to stick
adhesión *f* adherence, adhesion
adhesi·vo -va *adj* adhesive
adición *f* addition; (*en un café o restaurante*) check
adicionar *tr* to add; to add to
adic·to -ta *adj* devoted; supporting || *mf* supporter, follower
adiestrar *tr* to train; to teach; to lead, to guide || *ref* to train, to practice
adietar *tr* to put on a diet
adinera·do -da *adj* wealthy, well-to-do
adiós *m* adieu, good-bye || *interj* adieu!, good-bye!
aditamento *m* addition; accessory
aditi·vo -va *adj & m* additive
adivinación *f* prophecy; guessing, divination; **adivinación del pensamiento** mind reading
adivina·dor -dora *mf* guesser; good guesser; **adivinador del pensamiento** mind reader
adivinaja *f* (coll) riddle, puzzle
adivinanza *f* riddle; guess
adivinar *tr* to prophesy; to guess, to divine; (*un enigma*) to solve; (*el pensamiento ajeno*) to read
adivi·no -na *mf* fortuneteller; guesser
adjetivo *m* adjective
adjudicar **§73** *tr* to adjudge, to award || *ref* to appropriate
adjuntar *tr* to join, connect; to add; to enclose
adjun·to -ta *adj* added, attached; enclosed || *mf* associate || *m* adjunct; adjective
adminículo *m* aid, auxiliary; gadget; meddler; **adminículos** emergency equipment
administración *f* administration, management; headquarters
administra·dor -dora *mf* administrator, manager; **administrador de correos** postmaster
administrar *tr* to administer, to manage
admiración *f* admiration; wonder; exclamation mark
admira·dor -dora *mf* admirer
admirar *tr* to admire; to surprise || *ref* to wonder; **admirarse de** to wonder at
admisible *adj* admissible
admisión *f* admission; (mach) intake
admitir *tr* to admit; to allow; to accept, recognize; to agree to
adobar *tr* to repair, restore; to dress, prepare; to cook, stew; (*carne, pescado*) to pickle; (*pieles*) to tan
adobe *m* adobe
adobo *m* repairing; dressing; cooking; pickling; tanning; pickled meat or fish
adocena·do -da common, ordinary
adoctrinar *tr* to indoctrinate, to teach, to instruct
adolecer **§22** *intr* to fall sick; **adolecer de** to suffer from || *ref* — **adolecerse de** (archaic) to sympathize with, feel sorry for
adolescencia *f* adolescence
adolescente *adj & mf* adolescent
adonde *conj* where, whither
adónde *adv* where, whither
adopción *f* adoption
adoptar *tr* to adopt
adoquín *m* paving stone, paving block; (coll) blockhead
adoquina·do -da *adj* paved with cobblestones || *m* cobblestone paving
adorable *adj* adorable
adoración *f* adoration, worship; **Adoración de los Reyes** Epiphany

adora•dor -dora *mf* adorer, worshiper || *m* suitor
adorar *tr & intr* to adore, to worship
adormecer §22 *tr* to put to sleep || *ref* to go to sleep; to get sleepy
adormeci•do -da *adj* sleepy, drowsy; numb; calm
adormilar *ref* to doze, to drowse
adornar *tr* to adorn; (*un cuento*) to embroider
adornista *mf* decorator
adorno *m* adornment, decoration; **adorno de escaparate** window dressing
adosar *tr* to lean; to push close
adquirir §40 *tr* to acquire; **adquirir en propiedad** to buy, to purchase
adquisición *f* acquisition
adrede *adv* on purpose
Adriáti•co -ca *adj & m* Adriatic
adscribir §83 *tr* to attribute; to assign
adscripción *f* attribution; assignment
aduana *f* customhouse; **aduana seca** inland customhouse
aduane•ro -ra *adj* customhouse; customs || *m* customhouse officer, customs inspector
aduar *m* Arab settlement; gipsy camp; Indian ranch
adueñar *ref* to take possession
adujar *tr* (naut) to coil || *ref* (naut) to curl up
adular *tr* to flatter, to fawn on
adu•lón -lona *adj* (coll) fawning, groveling || *mf* (coll) fawner
adúltera *f* adulteress
adulterar *tr* to adulterate || *intr* to commit adultery || *ref* to become adulterated, to spoil
adulterio *m* adultery
adúlte•ro -ra *adj* adulterous || *m* adulterer || *f* see **adúltera**
adul•to -ta *adj & mf* adult
adulzar §60 *tr* to sweeten; (*metales*) to soften
adunar *tr* to join, bring together
adus•to -ta *adj* grim, stern, gloomy; scorching hot
advenedi•zo -za *adj* strange; foreign || *mf* stranger; foreigner; outsider; parvenu, upstart; nouveau riche
advenimiento *m* advent, coming; accession; **esperar el santo advenimiento** (coll) to wait in vain
advenir §79 *intr* to come, arrive; to happen
adverbio *m* adverb
adversa•rio -ria *mf* adversary
adversidad *f* adversity
advertencia *f* observation; notice, remark; warning; preface
adverti•do -da *adj* capable, clever, wide-awake
advertir §68 *tr* to notice, observe; to notify, warn; to point out || *ref* to become aware
Adviento *m* (eccl) Advent
adyacente *adj* adjacent
aeración *f* aeration; ventilation; air conditioning
aére•o -a *adj* air, aerial; overhead, elevated; airy, light, fanciful
aéroatómi•co -ca *adj* air-atomic
aerodinámi•co -ca *adj* aerodynamic || *f* aerodynamics
aeródromo *m* aerodrome, airdrome; **aeródromo de urgencia** emergency landing field
aeroespacial *adj* aerospace
aerofumigación *f* crop dusting
aeromedicina *f* aviation medicine
aeromodelismo *m* model-airplane building
aeromodelista *mf* model-airplane builder
aeromodelo *m* model airplane
aeromotor *m* windmill; airplane motor
aeromoza *f* air hostess, stewardess
aeronauta *mf* aeronaut
aeronáuti•co -ca *adj* aeronautic || *f* aeronautics
aeronave *f* airship; **aeronave cohete** rocket ship
aeropista *f* landing strip
aeroplano *m* aeroplane
aeroposta *f* air mail
aeropostal *adj* air-mail
aeropropulsor *m* airplane engine; **aeropropulsor por reacción** jet engine
aeropuerto *m* airport
aeroscala *f* transit point
aerosol *m* aerosol
aeroste•ro -ra *adj* aviation || *m* flyer; airman
aeroterrestre *adj* air-ground
aerovía *f* airway
afable *adj* affable, friendly, agreeable
afama•do -da *adj* noted, famous
afamar *tr* to make famous || *ref* to become famous
afán *m* hard work; eagerness, zeal; task; worry
afanar *tr* to press, hurry || *intr* to strive, toil || *ref* to strive, toil; to busy oneself
afano•so -sa *adj* hard, laborious; hard-working
afarolar *ref* (Am) to make a fuss, to get excited
afear *tr* to deface, to disfigure; to blame
afeblecer §22 *intr* to grow feeble, to get thin
afección *f* affection, fondness; (med) affection
afectación *f* affectation
afecta•do -da *adj* affected; **estar afectado de** (*p.ej., los riñones*) to have (*e.g., kidney*) trouble
afectar *tr* to affect; (Am) to hurt, to injure || *ref* to be moved, be stirred
afecti•vo -va *adj* emotional
afec•to -ta *adj* fond; kind; affected; **afecto a** fond of; (*un empleo, un servicio, etc.*) attached to; **afecto de** suffering from || *m* affection, fondness; emotion
afectuo•so -sa *adj* affectionate; kind
afeitado *m* shave; **afeitado a ras** close shave
afeitar *tr* to shave; to adorn; (*la cara*) to paint || *ref* to shave; to paint
afeite *m* cosmetics, rouge, make-up
afeminación *f* effeminacy
afemina•do -da *adj* effeminate

afeminar *tr* to effeminate || *ref* to become effeminate
aferra•do -da *adj* stubborn, obstinate
aferrar *tr* to seize; to catch; to hook; (naut) to moor; (naut) to furl || *ref* to interlock, hook together; to cling; to insist
Afganistán, el Afghanistan
afga•no -na *adj & mf* Afghan
afianzar §60 *tr* to guarantee, vouch for; to bail; to fasten; to prop up; to grasp; to support || *ref* to hold fast, to steady oneself
afición *f* fondness, liking, taste; ardor, zeal; fans, public
aficiona•do -da *adj* fond; amateur; **aficionado a** fond of || *mf* amateur; fan, follower
aficionar *tr* to win, to win the attachment of || *ref* — **aficionarse a** or **de** to become fond of; to become a follower of, become a fan of
afiebra•do -da *adj* feverish
afi•jo -ja *adj* affixed || *m* affix
afila•do -da *adj* sharp; tapering; pointed; peaked
afilador *m* grinder, sharpener; razor strop
afilalápi•ces *m* (*pl* **-ces**) pencil sharpener
afilar *tr* to grind, to sharpen; (*una navaja de afeitar*) to strop; (Arg & Urug) to flirt with || *ref* to sharpen, get sharp; to taper, get thin
afiliar §77 & regular *tr* to affiliate, take in || *ref* — **afiliarse a** to join
afiligranar *tr* to filigree; to adorn, embellish
afilón *m* knife sharpener; razor strop
afín *adj* near, bordering; like, similar; related || *mf* relative by marriage
afinador *m* tuner; tuning hammer, tuning key
afinar *tr* to purify, refine, perfect; to trim; to tune
afincar §73 *intr & ref* to buy up real estate
afinidad *f* affinity; **por afinidad** by marriage
afirmar *tr* to strengthen, secure, fasten; to assert || *ref* to hold fast; to steady oneself
afirmati•vo -va *adj & f* affirmative
aflicción *f* affliction; sorrow, grief
afligir §27 *tr* to afflict, to grieve || *ref* to grieve
aflojar *tr* to slacken, to let go; to loosen || *intr* to slacken, to slow up; to abate, lessen || *ref* to come loose; to slacken
aflora•do -da *adj* flour; fine, elegant
aflorar *tr* to sift || *intr* to crop out
afluencia *f* flowing; affluence, abundance; crowd, jam, rush; fluency
afluente *adj* flowing; abundant; fluent || *m* tributary
afluir §20 *intr* to flow; to pour, to flock
afmo. *abbr* **afectísimo**
afofar *tr* to make fluffy, make spongy
afonizar §60 *tr & ref* to unvoice
aforar *tr* to gauge, to measure; to appraise
aforismo *m* aphorism
afortuna•do -da *adj* fortunate; happy
afrancesa•do -da *adj & mf* Francophile
afrecho *m* bran
afrenta *f* affront
afrentar *tr* to affront || *ref* to be ashamed
Africa *f* Africa
africa•no -na *adj & mf* African
afrodisía•co -ca *adj & m* aphrodisiac
afrontar *tr* to bring face to face; to defy || *ref* — **afrontarse con** to confront, to meet face to face
afuera *adv* outside || *interj* clear the way!, look out! || **afueras** *fpl* outskirts, environs
agachadiza *f* snipe; **hacer la agachadiza** (coll) to duck
agachar *tr* to lower, bend down || *ref* to crouch, to squat; to cower; (SAm) to give in, yield
agalla *f* gallnut; (*de pez*) gill; (*de ave*) ear lobe; **agallas** (coll) courage, guts
ágape *m* banquet, love feast
agarrada *f* (coll) brawl, fight, scrap
agarra•do -da *adj* (coll) stingy, tight || *f* see **agarrada**
agarrar *tr* to grab, to grasp; to take hold of; (coll) to get, obtain || *intr* to take hold; to take root; to stick || *ref* to grapple; to have a good hold; to worry; **agarrarse a** to take hold of, to cling to
agarrochar *tr* to jab with a goad
agarrotar *tr* to garrote; to bind, to tie up || *ref* to become numb
agasajar *tr* to regale, to lionize, to make a fuss over
agasajo *m* kindness, attention; lionization; favor, gift; treat; party
agavillar *tr* to bind or tie in sheaves || *ref* to band together
agazapar *tr* (coll) to grab, to nab || *ref* (coll) to crouch; (coll) to hide
agencia *f* agency; bureau; (Chile) pawn shop; **agencia de noticias** news agency
agenciar *tr* to manage to bring about; to promote || *ref* to manage
agenda *f* notebook
agente *m* agent; policeman; **agente de policía** policeman; **agente viajero** traveling salesman, commercial traveler
agigantar *tr* to make huge || *ref* to become huge
ágil *adj* agile; flexible, light
agilitar *tr & ref* to limber up
agita•do -da *adj* agitated, excited; (*mar*) rough; exalted
agitar *tr* to agitate; to shake; to wave; to stir || *intr* to agitate || *ref* to be agitated; to shake; to wave; to get excited; (*el mar*) to get rough
aglomeración *f* agglomeration; crowd; built-up area
aglomerado *m* briquet, coal briquet
aglutinar *tr* to stick together || *ref* to cake
agnósti•co -ca *adj & mf* agnostic
agobiar *tr* to overburden; to exhaust, oppress

agolpar *ref* to flock, to throng
agonía *f* agony, throes of death; agony, anguish; yearning; craving
agonizar **§60** *tr* (*al moribundo*) to assist, to attend; (coll) to harass || *intr* to be in the throes of death
agorar **§3** *tr* to augur, foretell
agore•ro **-ra** *adj* fortunetelling; ill-omened; superstitious || *mf* fortuneteller
agostar *tr* to burn up, to parch || *ref* to dry up; (*la esperanza, la felicidad*) to fade away
agostero *m* harvest helper
agosto *m* August; harvest; harvest time; **hacer su agosto** to make hay while the sun shines
agota•do **-da** *adj* exhausted; sold out; out of print
agotar *tr* to exhaust, to wear out, to use up || *ref* to become exhausted, to be used up; to go out of print; to run out
agracia•do **-da** *adj* charming, graceful; nice, pretty || *mf* winner
agradable *adj* agreeable
agradar *tr* to please || *intr* to be pleasing || *ref* to be pleased
agradecer **§22** *tr* to thank; **agradecerle a uno una cosa** to thank someone for something
agradeci•do **-da** *adj* thankful, grateful; rewarding
agradecimiento *m* thanks, gratitude
agrado *m* agreeableness, graciousness; pleasure, liking
agrandar *tr* to enlarge || *ref* to grow larger
agranelar *tr* (*cuero*) to grain, to pebble
agrapar *tr* to clamp
agrariense *adj* & *mf* agrarian
agra•rio **-ria** *adj* agrarian
agravar *tr* to weigh down; to aggravate; to exaggerate; to oppress || *ref* to get worse
agraviar *tr* to wrong, offend || *ref* to take offense
agravio *m* wrong, offense; **agravios de hecho** assault and battery
agravio•so **-sa** *adj* offensive, insulting
agraz *m* (*pl* **agraces**) sour grape; sourgrape juice; (coll) bitterness, displeasure; **en agraz** prematurely
agredir **§1** *tr* to attack, assault
agregado *m* aggregate; concrete block; attaché; (Arg) tenant farmer
agregar **§44** *tr* to add; to attach; to appoint || *ref* to join
agremiado *m* union member
agremiar *tr* to unionize
agresión *f* aggression
agresi•vo **-va** *adj* aggressive
agre•sor **-sora** *adj* aggressive || *mf* aggressor
agreste *adj* country, rustic; wild, rough; uncouth
agriar **§77 & regular** *tr* to make sour; to exasperate || *ref* to turn sour; to become exasperated
agrícola *adj* agricultural || *mf* farmer
agricultura *f* agriculture
agridulce *adj* bittersweet
agriera *f* (Chile) heartburn; **agrieras** (Col) cruet stand
agrietar *tr* & *ref* to crack
agrimensor *m* surveyor
agrimensura *f* surveying
agringar **§44** *ref* (Am) to act like a gringo
a•grio **-gria** *adj* sour, acrid; uneven, rough; brittle || **agrios** *mpl* citrus fruit
agronomía *f* agronomy
agropecua•rio **-ria** *adj* land-and-cattle, farm
agrumar *tr* & *ref* to curd, to clot
agrupar *tr* & *ref* to group, to cluster
agrura *f* sourness; unpleasantness; **agruras** citrus fruit
agua *f* water; (*de un tejado*) slope; **agua abajo** downstream; **agua arriba** upstream; **agua bendita** holy water; **agua corriente** running water; **agua de Colonia** eau de Cologne; **agua de marea** tidewater; **agua gaseosa** carbonated water; **agua oxigenada** hydrogen peroxide; **aguas** mineral springs; (*de sedas; de piedras preciosas*) water, sparkle; **aguas mayores** equinoctial tide; feces; **aguas menores** ordinary tide; urination; **cubrir aguas** to have under roof; **entre dos aguas** under water, under the surface of the water; (coll) undecided
aguacate *m* avocado, alligator pear
aguacero *m* shower
aguada *f* source of water; water color; watering station
aguade•ro **-ra** *adj* water || *m* watering place
agua•do **-da** *adj* watery; thin, watered; (Am) weak, washed out, limp; (Am) dull, insipid || *f* see **aguada**
agua•dor **-dora** *mf* water carrier || *m* paddle, bucket
aguafies•tas *mf* (*pl* **-tas**) kill-joy, wet blanket, crapehanger
aguafortista *mf* etcher
aguafuerte *f* etching; **grabar al aguafuerte** to etch
aguaje *m* watering place; tidal wave; strong current; (*de buque*) wake
aguamala *f* jellyfish
aguamanil *m* ewer, wash pitcher; washstand
aguama•nos *m* (*pl* **-nos**) water for washing hands; washstand
aguamarina *f* aquamarine
aguanie•ves *f* (*pl* **-ves**) wagtail
aguano•so **-sa** *adj* watery, soaked
aguantar *tr* to hold up, sustain; to bear, endure, tolerate; to hold back, control || *intr* to last, to hold out || *ref* to restrain oneself; to keep quiet; **aguantarse las lágrimas** to swallow one's tears
aguante *m* patience, endurance; strength, vigor
aguar **§10** *tr* to water; to spoil, to mar || *ref* to become watery; to fill up with water; to be spoiled
aguardar *tr* to await, to wait for; to grant time to || *intr* to wait; **aguardar a que** to wait until

aguardentera *f* liquor bottle, brandy flask
aguardentería *f* liquor store
aguardento·so -sa *adj* brandy; (*voz*) whiskey
aguardiente *m* brandy; spirituous liquor; **aguardiente de caña** rum; **aguardiente de manzana** applejack
aguardo *m* hunter's blind
aguasar *ref* (Arg & Chile) to become countrified
aguazal *m* swamp, pool
agudeza *f* acuteness, acuity; sharpness; witticism; **agudeza visual** visual acuity
agu·do -da *adj* acute; sharp; keen; witty
agüero *m* augury; omen; forecast
aguerri·do -da *adj* inured, hardened
aguijada *f* goad, spur; prod
aguijar *tr* to goad, spur, prod || *intr* to hurry along
aguijón *m* goad, spur; sting; thorn; stimulus; **dar coces contra el aguijón** to kick against the pricks
aguijonear *tr* to goad, incite; to sting
águila *f* eagle; **ser un águila** to be wide-awake, be a wizard
aguile·ño -ña *adj* aquiline; sharp-featured
aguilón *m* (*de grúa*) boom, jib; (*del tejado*) gable
aguinaldo *m* Christmas gift, Epiphany gift; Christmas carol
aguja *f* needle; hatpin; steeple, spire; (*del reloj*) hand; **aguja de gancho** crochet needle; **aguja de hacer media** knitting needle; **aguja de zurcir** darning needle; **agujas** (rr) switch; **buscar una aguja en un pajar** to look for a needle in a haystack
agujerear *tr* to make a hole in, to pierce, to perforate
agujero *m* hole; pincushion
agujeta *f* (*de la jeringa*) needle; shoestring; **agujetas** stitches, twinges
agusanar *ref* to get wormy; to become worm-eaten
aguzanie·ves *f* (*pl* **-ves**) wagtail
aguzar §60 *tr* to sharpen; to incite, stir up; to stare at; (*las orejas*) to prick up
ah-chís *interj* kerchoo!
aherrojar *tr* to fetter, to shackle; to oppress
aherrumbrar *tr & ref* to rust
ahí *adv* there; **de ahí que** hence; **por ahí** that way
ahija·do -da *mf* godchild; protégé || *m* godson || *f* goddaughter
ahilar *ref* to faint from hunger; to waste away; to grow poorly; to turn sour
ahincar §73 *tr* to urge, press; to importune || *ref* to hasten
ahinco *m* earnestness, zeal, eagerness
ahitar *tr* to cloy, to surfeit, to stuff
ahi·to -ta *adj* surfeited, stuffed; fed up, disgusted || *m* surfeit; indigestion
ahoga·do -da *adj* drowned; smothered; sunk; close, unventilated; **mate ahogado** stalemate; **perecer ahogado** to drown; **verse ahogado** (coll) to be swamped
ahogar §44 *tr* to drown; to suffocate, smother; (*cal*) to slake; (*plantas*) to soak; to oppress; to extinguish; to stalemate || *ref* to drown; to suffocate; to drown oneself
ahogo *m* shortness of breath; great sorrow; stringency
ahondar *tr* to make deeper; to go deep into || *intr* to go deep, go deeper
ahora *adv* now; presently; **ahora bien** now then, so then; **ahora mismo** right now; **por ahora** for the present
ahorcajar *ref* to sit astride
ahorcar §73 *tr* to hang || *ref* to hang, be hanged; to hang oneself
ahorra·do -da *adj* saving, thrifty
ahorrar *tr* to save; to spare || *ref* to save or spare oneself
ahorrati·vo -va *adj* saving, thrifty; stingy || *f* economy
ahorro *m* economy; **ahorros** savings
ahuchar *tr* to hoard
ahuecar §73 *tr* to hollow, hollow out; to loosen, fluff up; **ahuecar la voz** to speak in deep and solemn tones || *ref* to be puffed up
ahumar *tr* to smoke || *intr* to be smoky || *ref* to get smoked up; to look or taste smoky; (coll) to get drunk
ahusar *tr & ref* to taper
ahuyentar *tr* to put to flight; to scare away || *ref* to flee, run away
aira·do -da *adj* angry; wild; depraved
airar §4 *tr* to anger || *ref* to get angry
aire *m* air; **al aire libre** in the open air; **darse aires** to put on airs
airear *tr* to air, aerate, ventilate || *ref* to get aired; to catch cold
airón *m* aigrette, panache; gray heron
airo·so -sa *adj* airy; drafty; graceful, light; resplendent; successful
aislación *f* insulation
aislacionista *adj & mf* isolationist
aislador *m* insulator
aislamiento *m* isolation; (elec) insulation
aislar §4 *tr* to isolate; to detach, separate; (elec) to insulate || *ref* to live in seclusion
ajar *m* garlic field || *tr* to crumple, to muss; (*marchitar*) to wither; to tamper with; to abuse, ill-treat || *ref* to get mussed; to wither
ajedrea *f* (bot) savory
ajedrecista *mf* chess player
ajedrez *m* chess; chess set
ajenjo *m* (*Artemisia*) wormwood; (*licor*) absinthe; (*sinsabores y penas*) (fig) wormwood, bitterness; **ajenjo del campo** or **ajenjo mayor** (*Artemisia absinthium*) wormwood
aje·no -na *adj* another's; extraneous, foreign; different; contrary; free; insane; uninformed; **lo ajeno** what belongs to someone else
ajetrear *tr* to drive, harass || *ref* to bustle about; to fidget
ajetreo *m* bustle, fuss
ají *m* (*pl* **ajíes**) chili; chili sauce; **po-**

nerse como un ají (Chile) to turn red as a tomato
aji·mez *m* (*pl* **-meces**) mullioned window
ajo *m* garlic; garlic clove; garlic sauce
ajorca *f* bracelet, anklet
ajornalar *tr* to hire by the day || *ref* to hire out by the day
ajuar *m* housefurnishings; trousseau
ajuiciar *tr* to bring to one's senses || *ref* to come to one's senses
ajusta·do -da *adj* just, right; tight, close-fitting
ajustar *tr* to adapt, to fit, to adjust; to hire; to arrange; to reconcile; to fasten; to settle || *intr* to fit || *ref* to fit; to hire out; to be hired; to come to an agreement
ajuste *m* fit; fitting, adjustment; hiring; arrangement; reconciliation; settlement; agreement
ajusticiar *tr* to execute, to put to death
ala *f* wing; (*del sombrero*) brim; (*de puerta, mesa, etc.*) leaf; (*de pez*) fin; (*de hélice*) blade; (football) end; **ahuecar el ala** (coll) to beat it; **ala en flecha** (aer) sweptback wing; **alas** boldness, courage; **volar con sus propias alas** to stand on one's own feet
Alá *m* Allah
alabanza *f* praise
alabar *tr* to praise || *ref* to boast
alabarda *f* halberd
alabardero *m* halberdier; hired applauder, claqueur
alabastro *m* alabaster
álabe *m* drooping branch; bucket, paddle; cog
alabear *tr & ref* to warp
alacena *f* cupboard, wall closet; (naut) locker; (Mex) booth, stall
alacrán *m* scorpion
ala·do -da *adj* winged
alamar *m* frog (*button and loop on a garment*)
alambica·do -da *adj* precious, oversubtle, fine-spun; begrudged
alambicar §73 *tr* to distill; to refine to excess
alambique *m* still, alembic; (*de laboratorio*) retort; **por alambique** sparingly
alambrada *f* chicken wire; wire mesh; (mil) barbed wire; (elec) wiring
alambrado *m* chicken wire; wire mesh; wire fence; (elec) wiring; (mil) wire entanglement
alambraje *m* (elec) wiring
alambrar *tr* to fence with wire; to string with wire; to wire
alambre *m* wire; **alambre cargado** live wire; **alambre de púas** barbed wire; **alambre sin aislar** bare wire
alambrera *f* wire screen; wire cover
alameda *f* poplar grove; mall, shaded walk
álamo *m* poplar; **álamo de Italia** Lombardy poplar; **álamo negro** black poplar; **álamo temblón** aspen
alampar *ref* to have a craving
alancear *tr* to lance, to spear
alano *m* mastiff, great Dane
alarde *m* display, ostentation; (mil) review; **hacer alarde de** to make a show of; to boast of
alardear *intr* to boast, brag, show off
alardo·so -sa *adj* showy, ostentatious
alargar §44 *tr* to extend, lengthen, stretch; to hand; to increase; to let out || *ref* to go away, withdraw; to grow longer; to be long-winded
alarido *m* howl, shout, yell, whoop
alarma *f* alarm; (aer) alert; **alarma aérea** air-raid warning; **alarma de incendios** fire alarm; **alarma de ladrones** burglar alarm
alarmar *tr* to alarm; to alert || *ref* to become alarmed
alarmista *mf* alarmist
alastrar *tr* (*las orejas*) to throw back; (naut) to ballast || *ref* to lie flat, to cower
ala·zán -zana *adj* sorrel, reddish-brown || *mf* sorrel horse
alba *f* dawn, daybreak
albacea *m* executor || *f* executrix
albahaquero *m* flowerpot
alba·nés -nesa *adj & mf* Albanian
albañal *m* sewer, drain
albañil *m* mason, bricklayer
albañilería *f* masonry
albarán *m* rent sign; bulletin; (com) check list
albarca *f* sandal
albarda *f* packsaddle
albardilla *f* (*tejadillo sobre los muros*) coping; shoulder pad
albaricoque *m* apricot
albaricoquero *m* apricot tree
alba·tros *m* (*pl* **-tros**) albatross
albayalde *m* white lead
albear *intr* to turn white; (Arg) to get up at dawn
albedrío *m* free will; fancy, caprice, pleasure; **libre albedrío** free will
albéitar *m* veterinarian
alberca *f* pond, pool; tank, reservoir; **en alberca** roofless
albérchigo *m* clingstone peach
albergar §44 *tr* to shelter, to harbor; to house || *intr & ref* to take shelter; to take lodgings
albergue *m* shelter, refuge; lodging; den, lair
albero *m* dishcloth, dishrag; white earth
al·bo -ba *adj* (poet) white || *f* see **alba**
albóndiga *f* meat ball, fish ball
albor *m* whiteness; dawn
alborada *f* dawn; morning serenade; reveille
alborear *intr* to dawn
albor·noz *m* (*pl* **-noces**) terry cloth; burnoose; cardigan; beach robe
alborota·do -da *adj* hasty, rash; noisy; rough
alborota·dor -dora *mf* agitator, rioter
alborotapue·blos *mf* (*pl* **-blos**) (coll) rabble rouser; (coll) gay noisy person
alborotar *tr* to agitate, arouse, stir up || *intr* to make a racket || *ref* to get excited; to riot; (*la mar*) to get rough
alboroto *m* agitation, disturbance;

noise, riot; **alborotos** (CAm) candied popcorn; **armar un alboroto** to raise a racket
alborozar **§60** *tr* to gladden, to cheer, to overjoy, to elate
alborozo *m* joy, merriment, elation
albricias *fpl* reward for good news; reward given on the occasion of some happy event; **en albricias de** as a token of || *interj* good news!, congratulations!
albufera *f* saltwater lagoon
ál•bum *m* (*pl* **-bumes**) album; **álbum de recortes** scrapbook
albumen *m* albumen
albúmina *f* albumin
albuminar *tr* (phot) to emulsify
albur *m* risk, chance
alcachofa *f* artichoke
alcahue•te -ta *mf* bawd, procurer, gobetween; screen, fence; (coll) schemer; (coll) gossip
alcahuetear *tr* to procure; to harbor || *intr* to pander
alcaide *m* governor, warden, jailer
alcalde *m* mayor, chief burgess; **alcalde de monterilla** small-town mayor; **tener el padre alcalde** to have a friend at court
alcaldesa *f* mayoress
álcali *m* alkali
alcali•no -na *adj* alkaline
alcallería *f* pottery
alcana *f* henna
alcance *m* reach, scope, extent; range; pursuit; capacity; late news; import; coverage; brains, intelligence; **al alcance de** within reach of, within range of; **alcance de la vista** eyesight, eyeshot; **alcance del oído** earshot; **dar alcance a** to catch up with
alcancía *f* child's bank; bin, hopper
alcanfor *m* camphor
alcantarilla *f* sewer; culvert
alcantarillar *tr* to sewer
alcanza•do -da *adj* needy, hard up
alcanzar **§60** *tr* to reach; to overtake, catch up to; to grasp; to obtain; to understand; to live through || *intr* to succeed; (*un arma de fuego*) to carry; to manage; to suffice
alcaravea *f* caraway
alcázar *m* fortress; castle, royal palace; quarterdeck
alce *m* elk, moose
alcista *adj* bullish || *mf* (fig) bull
alcoba *f* bedroom; **alcoba de respeto** master bedroom
alcohol *m* alcohol
alcohóli•co -ca *adj & mf* alcoholic
alcor *m* hill, elevation, eminence
alcornoque *m* cork oak; (coll) blockhead
alcorque *m* cork-soled shoe; trench for water around a tree
alcorza *f* sugar paste, sugar icing; **ser una alcorza** (Arg) to be highly emotional
alcurnia *f* ancestry, lineage
alcuza *f* olive-oil can
aldaba *f* knocker, door knocker; bolt, crossbar; latch; hitching ring; **aldaba dormida** deadlatch; **tener buenas aldabas** to have pull
aldabonazo *m* knock on the door
aldea *f* village, hamlet
aldea•no -na *adj* village; rustic || *mf* villager
aleación *f* alloy
alear *tr* to alloy || *intr* to flap the wings; to flap one's arms; to convalesce
aleccionar *tr* to teach, instruct; to train, to coach
aleda•ño -ña *adj* bordering || *m* border, boundary
alegar **§44** *tr* to allege; to declare, assert || *intr* (Col, Hond) to quarrel
alegoría *f* allegory
alegóri•co -ca *adj* allegoric(al)
alegrar *tr* to cheer, gladden; (*un fuego*) to stir || *ref* to be glad, to rejoice; (coll) to get tipsy
alegre *adj* glad; bright, gay; cheerful, light-hearted; careless; fast, spicy; **alegre de cascos** scatterbrained
alegría *f* cheer, joy, gladness; brightness, gaiety
aleja•do -da *adj* distant, remote
alejandri•no -na *adj & mf* Alexandrine
alejar *tr & ref* to move aside, to move away
alelar *tr* to make stupid || *ref* to grow stupid
aleluya *m & f* hallelujah || *m* Easter time || *f* doggerel; daub; **aleluya navideña** Christmas card || *interj* hallelujah!
ale•mán -mana *adj & mf* German
Alemania *f* Germany
alenta•do -da *adj* brave, spirited; proud, haughty; (Am) well, healthy || *f* deep breath
alentar **§2** *tr* to encourage, to cheer up || *intr* to breathe || *ref* to take heart; to get well, to recover
alerce *m* larch
alergia *f* allergy
alero *m* eaves
alerón *m* aileron
alerta *adv* on the alert || *interj* watch out!, look out! || *m* (mil) alert; (mil) watchword
alertar *tr* to alert
aler•to -ta *adj* alert, watchful, vigilant
alesaje *m* bore
alesna *f* awl
aleta *f* small wing; (*de pez*) fin; (*de hélice*) blade
aletargar **§44** *tr* to benumb; to put to sleep || *ref* to get drowsy, fall asleep
aletear *intr* to flap the wings; to flap, flip, flutter
aleve *adj* treacherous, perfidious
alevosía *f* treachery, perfidy
alevo•so -sa *adj* treacherous, perfidious
alfabetizar **§60** *tr* to alphabetize; to teach reading and writing to
alfabeto *m* alphabet
alfaneque *m* buzzard
alfanje *m* cutlass
alfarería *f* pottery
alfarero *m* potter

alféizar *m* splay; embrasure

alfeñicar §73 *tr* to candy, to ice || *ref* (coll) to grow thin; (coll) to be affected, to be finical

alfeñique *m* almond-flavored sugar paste; (coll) affectation, prudery; (coll) thin, delicate person, weakling

alfé•rez *m* (*pl* **-reces**) (mil) second lieutenant; (mil) subaltern (Brit); **alférez de fragata** (nav) ensign; **alférez de navío** (nav) lieutenant (j.g.)

alfil *m* bishop

alfiler *m* pin; **alfiler de corbata** stickpin, scarfpin; **alfiler de madera** clothespin; **alfiler de seguridad** safety pin; **alfileres** pin money

alfilerar *tr* to pin, to pin up

alfiletero *m* pincase, needlecase

alfombra *f* carpet; rug

alfombrar *tr* to carpet

alforfón *m* buckwheat

alforja *f* shoulder bag; traveling supplies; **pasarse a la otra alforja** (coll) to go too far, take too much liberty

alforza *f* pleat, tuck

al•foz *m* (*pl* **-foces**) outskirts; dependence; mountain pass

alga *f* alga; **alga marina** seaweed; **algas** algae

algaida *f* brush, thicket; sandbank

algalia *f* civet; catheter

algarabía *f* Arabic; (coll) gibberish, jabber; (coll) hubbub, uproar

algarada *f* outcry; uproar

algarroba *f* carob bean

algarrobo *m* carob

algazara *f* Moorish battle cry; din, uproar

álgebra *f* algebra

algebrai•co -ca *adj* algebraic

álgi•do -da *adj* cold, icy, frigid

algo *pron indef* something; anything; **algo por el estilo** something of the sort || *adv* somewhat, a little, rather

algodón *m* cotton; **algodón pólvora** guncotton; **estar criado entre algodones** to be brought up in comfort

algodoncillo *m* milkweed

algodono•so -sa *adj* cottony

alguacil *m* bailiff; mounted police officer at the head of the processional entrance of the bullfighters

alguien *pron indef* somebody, someone

algún *adj indef* apocopated form of **alguno,** used only before masculine singular nouns and adjectives

algu•no -na *adj indef* some, any; not any; **alguna vez** sometimes; ever || *pron indef* someone; **algunos** some

alhaja *f* jewel, gem; **buena alhaja** a bad egg, a sly fellow

alharaca *f* fuss, ado, ballyhoo; **hacer alharacas** to make a fuss

alharaquien•to -ta *adj* fussy, noisy

alhe•lí *m* (*pl* **-líes**) gillyflower (*Matthiola incana*); wallflower (*Cheiranthus*)

alheña *f* henna; blight, mildew

alheñar *tr* to henna; to blight, mildew || *ref* (*el pelo*) to henna

alhucema *f* lavender

alhumajo *m* pine needles

alia•do -da *adj* allied || *mf* ally

aliaga *f* furze, gorse

alianza *f* alliance; wedding ring; (Bib) covenant

aliar §77 *tr* to ally || *ref* to ally, become allied; to form an alliance

alias *adv & m* alias

alicaí•do -da *adj* failing, weak; (coll) crestfallen, discouraged

alicates *mpl* pliers

aliciente *m* inducement, incentive

alienar *tr* to alienate; to enrapture

aliento *m* breath, breathing; courage, spirit; **dar aliento a** to encourage; **de mucho aliento** arduous, difficult, endless; **nuevo aliento** second wind; **sin aliento** out of breath

alifafe *m* (coll) complaint, indisposition

aligerar *tr* to lighten; to alleviate, to ease; to hasten; to shorten

aligustre *m* privet

alijador *m* lighter; lighterman; sander

alijar *tr* to unload, to lighten; to sandpaper

alimaña *f* varmint, small predacious animal

alimentar *tr* to feed, nourish; (*p.ej., esperanzas*) to cherish, foster || *ref* to feed, to nourish oneself

alimenti•cio -cia *adj* alimentary, nourishing

alimento *m* food, nourishment; encouragement; **alimentos** foodstuffs; allowance; alimony

alindar *tr* to mark off; to embellish, to prettify || *intr* to border, be contiguous

alinear *tr & ref* to align, to line up

aliñar *tr* to dress, to season

aliño *m* dressing, seasoning

aliquebra•do -da *adj* (coll) crestfallen

alisar *tr* to smooth; to polish, to sleek; to iron lightly

aliso *m* alder tree

alistar *tr* to list; to enlist, to enroll; to stripe || *ref* to enlist, to enroll; to get ready

aliteración *f* alliteration

aliviar *tr* to alleviate, to relieve, to soothe; to remedy; to lighten; to hasten || *ref* to get better, to recover

alivio *m* alleviation, relief; remedy

aljaba *f* quiver

aljama *f* mosque; synagogue; Moorish quarter; ghetto

aljamía *f* Spanish of Moors and Jews; Spanish written in Arabic characters

aljez *m* gypsum

aljibe *m* water tender, tank barge; oil tanker; cistern

aljófar *m* imperfect pearl; (fig) dewdrops

aljofifa *f* floor mop

aljofifar *tr* to mop

alma *f* soul, heart, spirit; (*persona*) living soul; crux, heart; sweetheart; (*de carril*) web; (*de cañón*) bore; (*de escalera*) newel; **dar el alma,**

entregar el alma, rendir el alma to give up the ghost
almacén *m* warehouse; store, department store; storehouse; (phot) magazine
almacenaje *m* storage
almacenar *tr* to store; to store up, to hoard
almacenista *mf* storekeeper || *m* warehouseman
almáciga *f* seedbed, tree nursery
almádana *f* spalling hammer
almagre *m* red ocher
almajara *f* (hort) hotbed
almanaque *m* almanac; calendar
almeja *f* clam
almena *f* merlon
almenaje *m* battlement
almendra *f* almond; (*de cualquier fruto drupáceo*) kernel; **almendra amarga** bitter almond; **almendra de Málaga** Jordan almond; **almendra tostada** burnt almond
almendrado *m* macaroon
almendro *m* almond tree
almiar *m* haystack, hayrick
almíbar *m* simple syrup; fruit juice; **estar hecho un almíbar** (coll) to be as sweet as pie
almibarar *tr* to preserve in syrup; (*sus palabras*) to honey || *intr* to candy
almidón *m* starch; (Am) paste; **almidón de maíz** cornstarch
almidona•do -da *adj* starched; (coll) spruce, dapper; (coll) stiff, prim
almidonar *tr* to starch
alminar *m* minaret
almiranta *f* admiral's wife; flagship
almirante *m* admiral
almi•rez *m* (*pl* **-reces**) brass mortar
almizcle *m* musk
almizclera *f* muskrat
almizclero *m* musk deer
almohada *f* pillow; **consultar con la almohada** to sleep it over
almohadilla *f* cushion; pad; (Chile) pincushion
almohaza *f* currycomb
almohazar §60 *tr* to currycomb
almoneda *f* auction; clearance sale
almonedar *tr* to auction
almorranas *fpl* piles, hemorrhoids
almorta *f* grass pea
almorzar §35 *tr* to lunch on || *intr* to lunch, have lunch
almuecín *m* or **almuédano** *m* muezzin
almuerzo *m* lunch
alna•do -da *mf* stepchild
aloca•do -da *adj* mad, wild, reckless || *mf* madcap
alocar §73 *tr* to drive crazy
alocución *f* address, speech
áloe *m* or **aloe** *m* aloe; aloes
alojar *tr* to lodge; to quarter, billet || *intr & ref* to lodge; to be quartered or billeted
alondra *f* lark
aloquecer §22 *ref* to go crazy, to lose one's mind
alosa *f* shad
alpargata *f* hemp sandal, espadrille
alpende *m* tool shed; lean-to, penthouse
Alpes *mpl* Alps
alpestre *adj* alpine
alpinismo *m* mountain climbing
alpi•no -na *adj* alpine
alpiste *m* canary seed, birdseed; **quedarse alpiste** (coll) to be disappointed
alquería *f* farmhouse
alquibla *f* kiblah
alquiladi•zo -za *adj & mf* hireling
alquilar *tr* to rent, to let, to hire || *ref* to hire out; to be for rent
alquiler *m* rent, rental, hire; **alquiler de coches** car-rental service; **alquiler sin chófer** drive-yourself service; **de alquiler** for rent, for hire
alquilona *f* cleaning woman, charwoman
alquimia *f* alchemy
alquitarar *tr* to distill
alquitrán *m* tar; **alquitrán de hulla** coal tar
alquitranado *m* tarpaulin
alquitranar *tr* to tar
alrededor *adv* around; **alrededor de** around; about, approximately || **alrededores** *mpl* environs, surroundings, outskirts
Alsacia *f* Alsace
alsacia•no -na *adj & mf* Alsatian
alta *f* discharge from hospital; (mil) certificate of induction into active service; **dar de alta** to discharge from the hospital; **darse de alta** to join, be admitted; (mil) to report for duty
altane•ro -ra *adj* towering; arrogant, haughty
altar *m* altar; **altar mayor** high altar; **conducir al altar** to lead to the altar
alta•voz *m* (*pl* **-voces**) loudspeaker
altea *f* (bot) marsh mallow
alteración *f* alteration; disturbance; uneven pulse; altercation, quarrel
alterar *tr* to alter; to disturb; to agitate, upset; to falsify; to lessen || *ref* to alter; to be disturbed; to be agitated; to lessen; (*el pulso*) to flutter
altercación *f* or **altercado** *m* argument, wrangle, bickering
altercar §73 *intr* to argue, bicker, wrangle
alternar *tr & intr* to alternate; **alternar con** to go around with
alternativa *f* choice, option; admission as a matador; **no tener alternativa** to have no choice
alter•no -na *adj* alternate
alteza *f* sublimity || **Alteza** *f* (*tratamiento*) Highness
altibajo *m* downward thrust; **altibajos** uneven ground; ups and downs
altillo *m* hillock; (*oficina en una tienda o taller*) balcony; (Arg, Ecuad) attic, garret
altimetría *f* altimetry
altiplanicie *f* tableland
altitud *f* altitude; height
altivez *f* or **altiveza** *f* arrogance, haughtiness, pride
alti•vo -va *adj* haughty, proud; high, lofty
al•to -ta *adj* high; upper; top; loud;

(*horas*) late; **ponerse tan alto** to take offense, to be hoity-toity || *m* height, altitude; story, floor; stop, halt; **de alto a bajo** from top to bottom; **hacer alto** to stop; **pasar por alto** to overlook, disregard || *f* see **alta** || **alto** *adv* high up; loud; aloud || **alto** *interj* halt!

altoparlante *m* loudspeaker

altozanero *m* (Col) public errand boy

altozano *m* hill, knoll; upper part of town; (CAm, Col, Ven) parvis

altruísta *adj* altruistic || *mf* altruist

altura *f* height, altitude; high seas; juncture, point, stage; (mus) pitch; (naut) latitude; **a estas alturas** at this juncture; **a la altura de** (naut) off; **estar a la altura de** to be up to, to be equal to; to be abreast of; **por estas alturas** (coll) around here

alucinación *f* hallucination

alud *m* avalanche

aludi•do -da *adj* above-mentioned

aludir *intr* to allude

alumbra•do -da *adj* lighted; enlightened; (coll) tipsy || *m* lighting; lighting system

alumbramiento *m* lighting; childbirth, accouchement

alumbrar *tr* to light, illuminate; (*a los ciegos*) to give sight to; to enlighten; (*aguas subterráneas*) to discover and bring to the surface || *intr* to have a child || *ref* (coll) to get tipsy

alumbre *m* alum

aluminio *m* aluminum

alumnado *m* student body

alum•no -na *mf* (*niño criado como si fuera hijo*) foster child; (*discípulo*) pupil, student; **alumno mimado** teacher's pet

alunizaje *m* lunar landing

alunizar **§60** *intr* to land on the moon

alusión *f* allusion

álveo *m* bed of a stream, river bed

alvéolo *m* alveolus; (*de diente*) socket; (*de rueda de agua*) bucket

alza *f* rise, advance, increase; **jugar al alza** to bull the market

alzada *f* height (*e.g., of a horse*)

alzado *m* lump sum, cash settlement; front elevation; (bb) quire, gathering

alzapaño *m* curtain holder; tieback

alzapié *m* snare, trap

alzaprima *f* crowbar, lever; (*de instrumento de arco*) (mus) bridge

alzaprimar *tr* to pry, pry up; to arouse, stir up

alzapuer•tas *m* (*pl* **-tas**) (archaic) dumb player, supernumerary

alzar **§60** *tr* to raise, lift, hoist; to pick up; (*la hostia*) to elevate; to hide, lock up; (*naipes*) to cut; (bb) to gather || *ref* to rise, to get up; to revolt; **alzarse con** to abscond with

alzaválvu•las *m* (*pl* **-las**) tappet

allá *adv* there, over there; back there; **allá en** over in; back in; **el más allá** the beyond; **más allá** farther on, farther away; **más allá de** beyond; **por allá** thereabouts; that way

allanar *tr* to level, smooth, flatten; (*una dificultad*) to iron out, to overcome, to get around; (*una casa*) to break into; the subdue || *intr* to level off || *ref* to tumble down; to yield, to submit; to humble oneself

allega•do -da *adj* near, close; related; partisan || *mf* relative; partisan

allegar **§44** *tr* to collect, gather; to reap || *intr* to approach || *ref* to approach; to be attached, be a follower, agree

allende *adv* beyond; **allende de** besides, in addition to || *prep* beyond

allí *adv* there; **allí dentro** in there; **por allí** that way; around there

ama *f* housekeeper; housewife, lady of the house; landlady, proprietress; **ama de casa** housewife; **ama de cría** or **de leche** wet nurse; **ama de llaves** housekeeper; **ama seca** dry nurse

amable *adj* amiable, kind, obliging; (*digno de ser amado*) lovable

ama•do -da *adj & mf* beloved

ama•dor -dora *adj* fond, loving || *mf* lover

amadrigar **§44** *tr* to welcome, receive with open arms || *ref* to burrow; to go into seclusion

amaestrar *tr* to teach, to coach; (*a los animales*) to train

amagar **§44** *tr* to show signs of, to threaten; to feint || *intr* to look threatening

amago *m* threat, menace; sign, indication; feint

amainar *tr* to lessen; (naut) to lower, shorten || *intr* to subside, die down; to lessen; to yield || *ref* to lessen; to yield

amalgama *f* amalgam

amalgamar *tr & ref* to amalgamate

amamantar *tr* to nurse, to suckle

amancebamiento *m* cohabitation, concubinage, liaison

amancebar *ref* to cohabit, to live in concubinage

amancillar *tr* to stain, spot; to sully, to tarnish

amanecer *m* dawn, daybreak || *v* **§22** *intr* to dawn, to begin to get light; to begin to appear; to get awake, to start the day

amanecida *f* dawn, daybreak

amanera•do -da *adj* mannered, affected

amansar *tr* (*a un animal*) to tame; (*a un caballo*) to break; to soothe, to appease

amante *adj* fond, loving || *mf* lover

amaño *m* skill, cleverness, dexterity; trick; **amaños** tools, implements

amapola *f* poppy

amar *tr* to love

amaraje *m* alighting on water

amarar *intr* to alight on water

amargar **§44** *tr* to make bitter; to embitter; (*una tertulia, una velada*) to spoil || *intr & ref* to become bitter; to become embittered

amar•go -ga *adj* bitter; sour; distressing || **amargos** *mpl* bitters

amargura *f* bitterness; sorrow, grief

amarillear *intr* to turn yellow, to show yellow

amarillecer §22 *intr* to become yellow
amarillen•to -ta *adj* yellowish
amarillez *f* yellowness
amari•llo -lla *adj & m* yellow
amarra *f* mooring cable; **amarras** support, protection; **soltar las amarras** (naut) to cast off
amarrar *tr* to moor; to lash, to tie up; (*las cartas*) to stack
amartelar *tr* to make love to; to make jealous || *ref* to fall in love; to become jealous
amartillar *tr* to hammer; (*un arma de fuego*) to cock
amasar *tr* to knead; to mix; to massage; (*dinero*) to amass; to concoct
amatista *f* amethyst
Amazonas *m* Amazon
ambages *mpl* ambiguity, quibbling; **sin ambages** straight to the point
ámbar *m* amber
Amberes *f* Antwerp
ambición *f* ambition
ambicionar *tr* to strive for, to be eager for
ambicio•so -sa *adj* ambitious; eager; **ambicioso de figurar** social climber
ambiente *m* atmosphere
ambi•gú *m* (*pl* **-gúes**) buffet supper; bar, refreshment bar
ambigüedad *f* ambiguity
ambi•guo -gua *adj* ambiguous; (*género*) (gram) common
ámbito *m* boundary, limit; compass, scope
ambladura *f* amble
amblar *intr* to amble
am•bos -bas *adj & pron indef* both; **ambos a dos** both, both together
ambrosía *f* ragweed
ambulancia *f* ambulance; **ambulancia de correos** mail car, railway post office
ambulante *adj* itinerant, traveling || *m* railway mail clerk
amedrentar *tr* to frighten, to scare
amelona•do -da *adj* melon-shaped; (coll) mentally retarded; (coll) lovesick
amén *interj* amen! || *m* amen || *adv* — **amén de** (coll) aside from; (coll) in addition to
amenaza *f* threat, menace
amenazar §60 *tr* to threaten, menace
amenguar §10 *tr* to lessen, to diminish; to belittle; to dishonor
amenidad *f* amenity
amenizar §60 *tr* to make pleasant, to brighten, to cheer
ame•no -na *adj* agreeable, pleasant
amento *m* catkin
América *f* America; **la América Central** Central America; **la América del Norte** North America; **la América del Sur** South America; **la América Latina** Latin America
americana *f* sack coat, jacket
americanizar §60 *tr* to Americanize
america•no -na *adj & mf* American; Spanish American || *f* see **americana**
amerizar §60 *intr* to alight on water
ametralladora *f* machine gun
ametrallar *tr* to machine-gun
amiba *f* amoeba
amiga *f* friend; mistress; schoolmistress; girls' school
amigable *adj* amicable, friendly
amigacho *m* (coll) chum, crony, pal
amígdala *f* tonsil
amigdalitis *f* tonsillitis
ami•go -ga *adj* friendly; fond || *mf* friend; sweetheart; **amigo del alma** bosom friend || *f* see **amiga**
amigote *m* (coll) chum, crony, pal
amilanar *tr* to terrify, intimidate
aminorar *tr* to lessen, to diminish
amistad *f* friendship; liaison; **hacer las amistades** (coll) to make up; **romper las amistades** (coll) to fall out, become enemies
amistar *tr* to bring together || *ref* to become friends
amisto•so -sa *adj* friendly
amnistía *f* amnesty
amnistiar §77 *tr* to amnesty, to grant amnesty to
amo *m* head of family; landlord, proprietor; boss; **ser el amo del cotarro** (coll) to rule the roost
amoblar §61 *tr* to furnish
amodorrar *ref* to get drowsy; to fall asleep; to grow numb
amohinar *tr* to annoy, irritate, vex
amojonar *tr* to mark off with landmarks
amoladera *f* grindstone, whetstone
amolar §61 *tr* to grind, sharpen; (coll) to bore, to annoy
amoldar *tr* to mold; to model, to pattern, to fashion; to adjust, adapt
amonestación *f* admonition; marriage banns
amonestar *tr* to admonish, to warn; to publish the banns of
amoníaco *m* ammonia
amontonar *tr* to heap, pile; to accumulate; to hoard || *ref* to collect, to gather; to crowd; (coll) to get angry; (Mex) to gang up
amor *m* love; **al amor del agua** with the current; obligingly; **al amor de la lumbre** by the fire, in the warmth of the fire; **amores** love affair; **amor propio** amour-propre; conceit; **por amor de** for the sake of
amorata•do -da *adj* livid, black-and-blue
amordazar §60 *tr* to muzzle; to gag
amorío *m* (coll) love-making; (coll) love affair
amoro•so -sa *adj* loving, affectionate, amorous
amortajar *tr* to shroud; (carp) to mortise
amortecer §22 *tr* to deaden, to muffle || *ref* to die away, become faint
amortiguador *m* shock absorber; door check; (*de automóvil*) bumper; **amortiguador de luz** dimmer; **amortiguador de ruido** muffler
amortiguar §10 *tr* to deaden, to muffle; to soften, tone down; to dim; to damp; (*un golpe*) to cushion; (*ondas electromagnéticas*) to damp

amortizar §60 *tr* to amortize; (*una deuda*) to pay off
amoscar §73 *ref* (coll) to get peeved; (Mex) to blush, be embarrassed
amotina·do -da *adj* mutinous, rebellious || *mf* mutineer, rebel, rioter
amotinar *tr* to stir up; to incite to mutiny || *ref* to rise up, mutiny, rebel
amover §47 *tr* to discharge, dismiss
amovible *adj* removable, detachable
amparar *tr* to shelter, protect || *ref* to seek shelter; to protect oneself
amparo *m* shelter, protection, refuge; stall; aid, favor
amperio *m* ampere
amperio-hora *m* (*pl* **amperios-hora**) ampere-hour
ampliación *f* amplification; (phot) enlargement
ampliar §77 *tr* to amplify, enlarge; to widen; (phot) to enlarge
amplificador *m* amplifier
amplificar §73 *tr* to amplify; to expand, enlarge; to magnify
am·plio -plia *adj* ample; spacious, roomy
amplitud *f* amplitude; roominess
ampo *m* dazzling white; snowflake
ampolla *f* blister; bubble; cruet; bulb, light bulb
ampollar *tr & ref* to blister
ampolleta *f* vial; sandglass, hourglass; bulb, light bulb; cruet
ampulosidad *f* bombast, pomposity
ampulo·so -sa *adj* bombastic, pompous
amputar *tr* to amputate
amueblar *tr* to furnish
amujera·do -da *adj* effeminate
amuleto *m* amulet, charm
amurallar *tr* to wall, to wall in
amurcar §73 *tr* to gore
amusgar §44 *tr* (*las orejas* **el** *toro*, **el** *caballo*) to throw back
anacardo *m* cashew; cashew nut
anacronismo *m* anachronism
ánade *mf* duck
anadear *intr* to waddle
anadeo *m* waddle, waddling
anales *mpl* annals
analfabetismo *m* illiteracy
analfabe·to -ta *adj & mf* illiterate
análi·sis *m & f* (*pl* **-sis**) analysis; **análisis gramatical** parsing; **análisis ocupacional** job analysis
analista *mf* analyst; annalist
analíti·co -ca *adj* analytic(al)
analizar §60 *tr* to analyze; **analizar gramaticalmente** to parse
analogía *f* analogy; similarity
análo·go -ga *adj* analogous; similar
ana·ná *m* (*pl* **-naes**) pineapple
ananás *m* pineapple
anaquel *m* shelf
anaranja·do -da *adj & m* (*color*) orange
anarquía *f* anarchy
anárqui·co -ca *adj* anarchic(al)
anarquista *mf* anarch, anarchist
anatema *m & f* anathema; curse
anatomía *f* anatomy
anatómi·co -ca *adj* anatomic(al) || *mf* anatomist
anatomista *mf* anatomist
anca *f* croup, haunch; buttock, rump; **a ancas** or **a las ancas** mounted behind another person
ancianidad *f* old age
ancia·no -na *adj* old, aged || *m* old man; (eccl) elder || *f* old woman
ancla *f* anchor; **echar anclas** to cast anchor; **levar anclas** to weigh anchor
anclar *intr* to anchor
anclote *m* kedge, kedge anchor
ancón *m* bay, cove
áncora *f* anchor
ancorar *intr* to anchor
an·cho -cha *adj* wide, broad; full, ample; loose, loose-fitting || *m* width, breadth
anchoa *f* anchovy
anchura *f* width, breadth; fullness, ampleness; looseness; comfort, ease
anchuro·so -sa *adj* wide, broad; spacious, roomy
andada *f* thin, hard-baked cracker; **andadas** (*de conejos y otros animales*) tracks; **volver a los andadas** to revert to one's old tricks
andaderas *fpl* gocart, walker
anda·do -da *adj* gone by, elapsed; frequented, trodden; worn, used; ordinary || *m* (Am) gait || *f* see **andada**
andadores *mpl* leading strings
andadura *f* pace, gait; amble; (Mex) mount
Andalucía *f* Andalusia
anda·luz -luza *adj & mf* Andalusian
andaluzada *f* (coll) tall story, exaggeration, fish story
andamiaje *m* scaffolding
andamio *m* scaffold; platform
andanada *f* (naut) broadside; (taur) covered upper section; (coll) scolding; (fig) fusillade
andante *adj* walking; errant, wandering
andanza *f* wandering, rambling; fate, fortune
andar *m* gait, pace, walk || §5 *tr* (*p.ej., dos millas*) to go; (*un camino*) to go down or up || *intr* to go, to walk; to run; to travel; to act, to behave; (*p.ej., un reloj*) to go, to run, to work; to be, to feel; to go by, to pass, to elapse; to go (*to bear up, to last*), e.g., **anduve diez horas sin comer** I went ten hours without eating || *ref* to go by, to pass, to elapse; to go away; **andarse sin** to go without
andarie·go -ga *adj* wandering, roving; swift, fleet
andas *fpl* litter; stretcher; bier
andén *m* railway platform; quay; footpath
Andes *mpl* Andes
andi·no -na *adj* Andean
andraje·ro -ra *mf* ragpicker
andrajo *m* rag, tatter; ragamuffin, scalawag
andrajo·so -sa *adj* ragged, raggedy, in tatters

andurriales *mpl* byways, out-of-the-way place
anea *f* cattail, bulrush
aneblar §2 *tr* to cloud; to becloud || *ref* to become clouded; to get dark
anécdota *f* anecdote
anegar §44 *tr* to flood; to drown || *ref* to become flooded; to drown
ane•jo -ja *adj* annexed; accessory || *m* annex; dependency; supplement
anemia *f* anaemia
anémi•co -ca *adj* anaemic
anestesia *f* anaesthesia
anestesiar *tr* anaesthetize
anestési•co -ca *adj & m* anaesthetic
aneurisma *m & f* aneurysm
anexar *tr* to annex
ane•xo -xa *adj* annexed; accessory || *m* annex; dependency
anfi•bio -bia *adj* amphibious
anfiteatro *m* amphitheater
anfitrión *m* (coll) host
anfitriona *f* (coll) hostess
ánfora *f* (Am) voting urn, ballot box
anfractuo•so -sa *adj* winding, tortuous
angarillas *fpl* handbarrow; panniers; cruet stand
ángel *m* angel; **ángel custodio** or **de la guarda** guardian angel; **ángel patudo** (coll) wolf in sheep's clothing; **tener ángel** to have great charm
angelical or **angéli•co -ca** *adj* angelic(al)
angina *f* angina; **angina de pecho** angina pectoris
angloparlante *adj* English-speaking || *mf* speaker of English
anglosa•jón -jona *adj & mf* Anglo-Saxon
angos•to -ta *adj* narrow
anguila *f* eel; **anguilas** (*para botar un barco al agua*) ways; **escurrirse como una anguila** to be as slippery as an eel
angular *adj* angular
ángulo *m* angle; corner
angulo•so -sa *adj* (*facciones*) angular
angustia *f* anguish, distress, grief
angustia•do -da *adj* distressed, grieved
angustiar *tr* to distress, afflict, grieve
angustio•so -sa *adj* distressed, grieved; worrisome
anhelar *tr* to crave, to want badly || *intr* to pant; to yearn; **anhelar por** to long for
anhélito *m* hard breathing
anhelo *m* craving; yearning, longing
anhelo•so -sa *adj* eager, yearning; breathless, panting
anhi•dro -dra *adj* anhydrous
Aníbal *m* Hannibal
anidar *tr* to harbor, to shelter || *intr & ref* to nestle, make a nest; to live
anilina *f* aniline
anilla *f* curtain ring; (*en la gimnasia*) ring; hoop
anillo *m* ring; cigar band; **anillo de compromiso** or **de pedida** engagement ring; **anillo sigilar** signet ring
ánima *f* soul; (*de arma de fuego*) bore
animación *f* animation; liveliness; bustle, movement
anima•do -da *adj* animated, lively
animador *m* (*de un café-cantante*) master of ceremonies
animal *adj & m* animal
animar *tr* to enliven; to encourage; to strengthen; to drive || *ref* to take heart, feel encouraged
ánimo *m* mind, spirit; courage, valor, energy; attention, thought
animosidad *f* animosity, ill will
animo•so -sa *adj* brave, courageous; spirited; ready, disposed
aniña•do -da *adj* babyish, childish
anión *m* anion
aniquilar *tr* to annihilate, destroy || *ref* to be annihilated; to decline, waste away; to be humbled
anís *m* anise; anise-flavored brandy
aniversa•rio -ria *adj & m* anniversary
anoche *adv* last night
anochecer *m* nightfall, dusk || *v* §22 *intr* to grow dark; to arrive or happen at nightfall; to end the day; to go to sleep || *ref* to get dark; to get cloudy; (coll) to slip away
anochecida *f* nightfall, dusk
anodi•no -na *adj* innocuous, ineffective, harmless
ánodo *m* anode
anomalía *f* anomaly
anóma•lo -la *adj* anomalous
anonadar *tr* to annihilate, destroy; to overwhelm; to humble
anóni•mo -ma *adj* anonymous || *m* anonymity; **guardar** or **conservar el anónimo** to preserve one's anonymity
anormal *adj* abnormal
anotar *tr* to annotate; to note, jot down; to point out
anquilosa•do -da *adj* stiff-jointed; old-fashioned
ánsar *m* goose; wild goose
ansia *f* anxiety, anguish; eagerness; **ansias** (Ven) nausea
ansiar §77 & **regular** *tr* to long for, yearn for || *intr* to be madly in love
ansiedad *f* anxiety, worry; pain
ansio•so -sa *adj* anxious; anguished; longing; covetous
ant. *abbr* **anticuado**
anta *f* elk
antagonismo *m* antagonism
antaño *adv* last year; of yore, long ago
antárti•co -ca *adj* antarctic
ante *prep* before, in the presence of; in front of; at, with || *m* elk; buff
antea•do -da *adj* buff; (Mex) damaged, shopworn
anteanoche *adv* the night before last
anteayer *adv* the day before yesterday
antebrazo *m* forearm
antecámara *f* antechamber, anteroom
antecedente *adj* antecedent || *m* antecedent; **antecedentes** antecedents
anteceder *tr* to precede, to go before
antece•sor -sora *mf* predecessor; ancestor
antedatar *tr* to antedate
antedi•cho -cha *adj* aforesaid, above-mentioned
antelación *f* previousness, anticipation
antemano — de antemano in advance, beforehand

antena *f* (ent) antenna; (rad) antenna, aerial; **en antena** on the air; **llevar a las antenas** to put on the air
antenombre *m* title, honorific
anteojera *f* spectacle case; blinker, blinder
anteojo *m* eyeglass; spyglass; **anteojos** eyeglasses, spectacles; binoculars; blinkers
antepasa•do -da *adj* before last ‖ **antepasados** *mpl* ancestors
antepecho *m* railing, guardrail; parapet; window sill
antepenúltima *f* antepenult
anteponer **§54** *tr* to place in front; to prefer
anteportada *f* half title, bastard title
anteportal *m* porch, vestibule
antepuerta *f* portière
antepuerto *m* entrance to a mountain pass; (naut) outer harbor
anterior *adj* front; previous; earlier
antes *adv* before; sooner, soonest; rather; previously; **antes bien** rather; on the contrary; **antes de** before; **antes (de) que** before; **cuanto antes** as soon as possible
antesala *f* antechamber; (*p.ej., de médico*) waiting room; **hacer antesala** to dance attendance
antiaére•o -a *adj* anti-aircraft
antiartísti•co -ca *adj* inartistic
antibéli•co -ca *adj* antiwar
anticartel *adj* antitrust
anticientífi•co -ca *adj* unscientific
anticipación *f* preparation, anticipation; **con anticipación** in advance
anticipa•do -da *adj* future; advance; **por anticipado** in advance
anticipar *tr* to anticipate, hasten; to move ahead ‖ *ref* to happen early; **anticiparse a** to anticipate, to get ahead of
anticipo *m* anticipation; advance payment, down payment; retaining fee
anticoncepti•vo -va *adj & m* contraceptive
anticongelante *m* antifreeze
anticonstitucional *adj* unconstitutional
anticua•do -da *adj* antiquated; old-fashioned; obsolete
anticua•rio -ria *adj* antiquarian ‖ *mf* antiquarian, antiquary; antique dealer
anticuerpo *m* antibody
antideporti•vo -va *adj* unsportsmanlike
antiderrapante *adj* nonskid
antideslizante *adj* nonskid
antideslumbrante *adj* antiglare
antidetonante *adj & m* antiknock
antídoto *m* antidote
antieconómi•co -ca *adj* uneconomic(al)
antier *adv* (coll) the day before yesterday
antiesclavista *adj* antislavery ‖ *mf* abolitionist
anti•faz *m* (*pl* **-faces**) veil, mask
antífona *f* anthem
antigás *adj invar* gas (*e.g., mask, shelter*)
antigramatical *adj* ungrammatical
antigualla *f* antique; (coll) relic, antique; (coll) has-been
antiguar **§10** *intr & ref* to attain seniority
antigüedad *f* antiquity; seniority; (*mueble u otro objeto de arte antiguos*) antique; **antigüedades** antiquities; antiques
anti•guo -gua *adj* old; ancient; antique; former ‖ *mf* veteran; senior
antihigiéni•co -ca *adj* unsanitary
antílope *m* antelope
antilla•no -na *adj & mf* West Indian
Antillas *fpl* Antilles
antimonio *m* antimony
antiobre•ro -ra *adj* antilabor
antiparras *spl* (coll) spectacles
antipatía *f* dislike, antipathy
antipáti•co -ca *adj* disagreeable, uncongenial
antipatrióti•co -ca *adj* unpatriotic
antiproyectil *adj* antimissile
antirresbaladi•zo -za *adj* nonskid
antisemíti•co -ca *adj* anti-Semitic
antisépti•co -ca *adj & m* antiseptic
antisono•ro -ra *adj* soundproof
antisoviéti•co -ca *adj* anti-Soviet
antitanque *adj* antitank
antíte•sis *f* (*pl* **-sis**) antithesis
antitoxina *f* antitoxin
antojadi•zo -za *adj* capricious, whimsical
antojar *ref* to seem; to fancy; to seem likely; to have a notion to + *inf;* to take a fancy to + *inf*
antojo *m* caprice, fancy, whim; snap judgment; birthmark; **antojos** moles, warts; **a su antojo** as one pleases
antología *f* anthology
antónimo *m* antonym
antorcha *f* torch; **antorcha a soplete** blowtorch
antracita *f* anthracite
ántrax *m* anthrax
antro *m* cave, cavern; (fig) den
antropología *f* anthropology
antruejo *m* carnival
anual *adj* annual
anualidad *f* annuity; year's pay; annual occurrence
anuario *m* yearbook; directory; bulletin, catalogue; **anuario telefónico** telephone directory
anublar *tr* to cloud; to dim, darken; to blight, to wither ‖ *ref* to become cloudy; to be withered; (*las esperanzas de uno*) to fade away
anudar *tr* to tie, fasten, knot; to unite; to resume ‖ *ref* to get knotted; to be united; to fade away, to wilt, to fail
anuente *adj* consenting
anular *tr* to annul; to nullify; to remove, to discharge ‖ *ref* to be passed over
anunciar *tr* to announce; to advertise ‖ *intr* to advertise
anunciante *mf* advertiser
anuncio *m* announcement; advertisement
anverso *m* obverse
anzuelo *m* fishhook; **picar en el anzuelo** or **tragar el anzuelo** to swallow the bait, swallow the hook

añadi•do -da *adj* additional || *m* false hair, switch
añadidura *f* addition; extra weight, extra measure; **de añadidura** extra, in the bargain; **por añadidura** besides
añadir *tr* to add; to increase
añafil *m* straight Moorish trumpet
añagaza *f* bird call; decoy, lure; trap, trick
añe•jo -ja *adj* aged; stale; musty, rancid
añicos *mpl* bits, pieces; **hacer añicos** to tear to pieces, to break to pieces; **hacerse añicos** (coll) to wear oneself out
añil *m* indigo; bluing
añilar *tr* to dye with indigo; (*la ropa blanca*) to blue
año *m* year; **año bisiesto** leap year; **año económico** fiscal year; **año lectivo** school year; **año luz** (*pl* **años luz**) light-year; **años** birthday; **cumplir . . . años** to be . . . years old
añoranza *f* longing, sorrow
añorar *tr* to long for, to sorrow for; to grieve over || *intr* to yearn; to sorrow, to grieve
año•so -sa *adj* aged, old
aojada *f* (Col) skylight; (Col) transom
aojar *tr* to cast the evil eye on, to jinx
aojo *m* evil eye, jinx
aovar *intr* to lay eggs
ap. *abbr* **aparte, apóstol**
apabilar *tr* to trim
apabullar *tr* (coll) to mash, crush; (coll) to squelch
apacentar **§2** *tr & ref* to pasture, to graze; to feed
apacible *adj* gentle, mild; calm
apaciguamiento *m* pacification, appeasement
apaciguar **§10** *tr* to pacify, to appease || *ref* to calm down
apachurrar *tr* to crush, squash, mash
apadrinar *tr* to sponsor; to act as godfather for; to back, support; to second
apagabron•cas *m* (*pl* **-cas**) bouncer
apagador *m* extinguisher; (*de piano*) damper
apagaincen•dios *m* (*pl* **-dios**) fire extinguisher
apagar **§44** *tr* to extinguish, to put out; (*la luz, la radio*) to turn off; (*la cal*) to slake; (*el sonido*) to damp, to muffle; (*el fuego del enemigo*) to silence; (*la sed*) to quench; (*el dolor*) to deaden || *ref* to go out; to subside, calm down, fade away
apagón *m* blackout
apalabrar *tr* to bespeak; to consider || *ref* to agree
apalancar **§73** *tr* to raise with a lever or crowbar
apalear *tr* to shovel; to beat; to pile up
apandar *tr* (coll) to steal
apantallar *tr* (elec) to shield, to screen; (Am) to dazzle, amaze
apañar *tr* to grasp; to pick up; to steal; to repair, to mend; (coll) to wrap up || *ref* (coll) to be handy
apañuscar **§73** *tr* (coll) to crumple, to rumple; (coll) to steal; (CAm, Col, Ven) to jam, to crowd
aparador *m* sideboard, buffet; showcase; workshop
aparar *tr* to prepare; to adorn; to block; (*las manos, la falda, el pañuelo, la capa*) to hold out
aparato *m* apparatus; ostentation, show; exaggeration; radio set; television set; telephone; airplane; camera; bandage, application; (theat) scenery, properties; **aparato auditivo** hearing aid; **aparato de relojería** clockwork; **aparatos sanitarios** bathroom fixtures; **ponerse al aparato** to go or to come to the phone
aparato•so -sa *adj* showy, pompous, ostentatious
aparcamiento *m* parking; parking space
aparcar **§44** *tr & intr* to park
aparcería *f* partnership, sharecropping
aparce•ro -ra *mf* partner, sharecropper; (Arg) customer
aparear *tr* to pair, to match; to mate || *ref* to pair; to mate
aparecer **§22** *intr & ref* to appear; to show up
aparecido *m* ghost, specter
aparejador *m* builder
aparejar *tr* to prepare; to prime, to size; to harness
aparejo *m* preparation; harness; set, kit; priming, sizing; (mas) bond; **aparejos** tools, implements, equipment
aparentar *tr* to feign, pretend; to look, to look to be
aparente *adj* apparent, seeming; evident; right, proper
aparición *f* apparition
apariencia *f* appearance, aspect; sign, indication; **salvar las apariencias** to save face
aparqueamiento *m* parking
aparquear *tr & intr* to park
aparqueo *m* parking
aparragar **§44** *ref* (Am) to crouch, to squat; (CAm) to loll, to sprawl
apartadero *m* siding, side track; turnout
aparta•do -da *adj* distant, remote; aloof; (*camino*) side, back; different || *m* side room; post-office box; vocabulary entry; section
apartamento *m* apartment, apartment house
apartar *tr* to take aside; to separate; to push away; to shunt; (*el ganado*) to sort || *ref* to separate; to move away, keep away, stand aside; to withdraw; to get divorced; to give up
aparte *adv* apart, aside; **aparte de** apart from || *prep* apart from || *m* (theat) aside
apasiona•do -da *adj* passionate; devoted, tender, loving; sore
apasionar *tr* to impassion, appeal deeply to; to afflict || *ref* to become impassioned; to be stirred up; to fall madly in love
apatía *f* apathy

apáti•co -ca *adj* apathetic
apatusco *m* (coll) ornament, finery
apdo. *abbr* **apartado**
apeadero *m* horse block; flag stop, wayside station; platform; temporary quarters
apear *tr* to help dismount, to help down; to bring down; to remove; to overcome; to prop up || *ref* to dismount, get off; to back down; to stop, to put up
apechugar **§44** *intr* to push with the chest; **apechugar con** (coll) to make the best of
apedazar **§60** *tr* to mend, to patch; to cut or tear to pieces
apedrear *tr* to stone; to stone to death; to pit; to speckle || *intr* to hail || *ref* to be damaged by hail; to be pitted
apegar **§44** *ref* to become attached, grow fond
apego *m* attachment, fondness
apelación *f* (coll) medical consultation; (coll) remedy, help; (law) appeal
apelar *intr* to appeal, make an appeal; to have recourse; to refer
apeldar *tr* — **apeldarlas** (coll) to flee, run away
apelmazar **§60** *tr* to squeeze, compress || *ref* to cake
apelotonar *tr* to form into a ball || *ref* to form a ball; to curl up
apellidar *tr* to call, to name; to proclaim
apellido *m* name; surname, last name, family name; **apellido de soltera** maiden name
apenar *tr & ref* to grieve
apenas *adv* hardly, scarcely; **apenas si** hardly, scarcely || *conj* no sooner, as soon as
apéndice *m* appendage; (anat) appendix
apendicitis *f* appendicitis
apercancar **§73** *ref* (Chile) to get moldy, to mildew
apercibir *tr* to prepare; to provide; to warn; to perceive; (coll) to collect || *ref* to get ready; to be provided; **apercibirse de** to notice
apergaminar *ref* (coll) to dry up, to become yellow and wrinkled
aperitivo *m* appetizer
aperla•do -da *adj* pearly
apero *m* tools, equipment, outfit; (Am) riding gear
aperrear *tr* to set the dogs on; to harass, plague, pester
apersogar **§44** *tr* to tether
apersona•do -da *adj* — **bien apersonado** presentable; **mal apersonado** unpresentable
apersonar *ref* to appear in person; to have an interview
apertura *f* opening
apesadumbrar or **apesarar** *tr & ref* to grieve
apestar *tr* to infect with the plague; to corrupt; (coll) to sicken, to nauseate; to infest || *intr* to stink || *ref* to be infected with the plague
apesto•so -sa *adj* stinking, foul-smelling; pestilent; sickening
apetecer **§22** *tr* to hunger for, to thirst for, to crave
apetecible *adj* desirable, tempting
apetencia *f* hunger, appetite, craving
apetito *m* appetite
apetito•so -sa *adj* tasty; tempting; gourmand
ápex *m* apex
apiadar *tr* to move to pity; to take pity on || *ref* to have pity
ápice *m* apex; bit, whit; crux; **estar en los ápices de** (coll) to be up in
apilar *tr & ref* to pile, to pile up
apimpollar *ref* to sprout, to put forth shoots
apiñar *tr & ref* to crowd, to jam
apio *m* celery
apisonadora *f* road roller
apisonar *tr* to tamp; to roll
aplacar **§73** *tr* to placate, appease, pacify; (*la sed*) to quench
aplanar *tr* to smooth, make even; (coll) to astonish || *ref* to collapse; to become discouraged
aplanchar *tr* to iron
aplanetizar **§60** *intr* to land on another planet
aplastar *tr* to flatten, crush, smash; (coll) to dumbfound
aplaudir *tr & intr* to applaud
aplauso *m* applause; **aplausos** applause
aplazar **§60** *tr* to postpone; to convene; to summon
aplicación *f* appliance, application; diligence
aplica•do -da *adj* industrious, studious; applied
aplicar **§73** *tr* to apply; to attribute || *ref* to apply; to apply oneself
aplomar *tr* to plumb; to make straight or vertical || *intr* to be vertical || *ref* to collapse; (Chile) to be embarrassed; (Mex) to be slow, be backward
aplomo *m* aplomb, poise, self-possession; gravity
apoca•do -da *adj* diffident, timid, irresolute; humble, lowly
apocar **§73** *tr* to cramp, contract; to narrow; to humble, belittle
apodar *tr* to nickname; to make fun of
apodera•do -da *adj* empowered, authorized || *m* proxy; attorney
apoderar *tr* to empower, to authorize || *ref* — **apoderarse de** to seize, grasp; to take possession of
apodo *m* nickname
apofonía *f* ablaut
apogeo *m* apogee; (fig) height, apogee
apolilla•do -da *adj* moth-eaten, mothy
apolilladura *f* moth hole
apolillar *tr* (*la polilla, p.ej., las ropas*) to eat || *ref* to become moth-eaten
apología *f* eulogy
apoltronar *ref* to loaf around; to loll, to sprawl
apontizaje *m* deck-landing
apontizar **§60** *intr* to deck-land
apoplejía *f* apoplexy
apopléti•co -ca *adj & mf* apoplectic
aporcar **§73** *tr* (*las hortalizas*) to hill

aporrear *tr* to beat, to club, to cudgel; to annoy || *ref* to drudge, to slave
aportación *f* contribution; dowry
aportar *tr* to contribute; to bring; to lead; (*como dote*) to bring || *intr* to show up; to reach port
aporte *m* contribution
aposentar *tr* to put up, to lodge || *ref* to take lodging
aposento *m* lodging; room; inn
apostadero *m* stand, post; naval station
apostar *tr* to post, to station || **§61** *tr* to bet, to wager || *intr* to bet; to compete
apostilla *f* note, comment
apóstol *m* apostle
apóstrofe *m & f* apostrophe (*words addressed to absent person*)
apóstrofo *m* apostrophe (*written sign*)
apostura *f* neatness, spruceness; bearing, carriage
apoyabra•zos *m* (*pl* **-zos**) armrest
apoyali•bros *m* (*pl* **-bros**) book end
apoyar *tr* to support, hold up; to lean, rest; to abet, back || *intr & ref* to lean, rest, be supported
apoyatura *f* (mus) grace note
apoyo *m* support, prop; backing, approval
apreciable *adj* appreciable; estimable
apreciación *f* appraisal
apreciar *tr* to appreciate; to appraise; to esteem
aprecio *m* appreciation, esteem
aprehender *tr* to apprehend, catch; to think, conceive
aprehensión *f* apprehension
aprehensi•vo -va *adj* apprehensive
aprehensor *m* captor
apremiar *tr* to press, urge; to compel, force; to hurry; to harass; (*a un deudor*) to dun || *intr* to be urgent
apremio *m* pressure; urgency; compulsion; oppression; surtax for late payment; (*demanda de pago*) dun
aprender *tr & intr* to learn
apren•diz -diza *mf* apprentice; **aprendiz de imprenta** printer's devil
aprendizaje *m* apprenticeship; **pagar el aprendizaje** (coll) to pay for one's inexperience
aprensar *tr* to press; to oppress
aprensión *f* apprehension; misgiving, prejudice
aprensi•vo -va *adj* apprehensive
apresar *tr* to grasp, to seize; to capture
aprestador *m* primer
aprestar *tr* to prepare; (*tejidos*) to process; to prime; to size || *ref* to get ready
apresto *m* preparation; equipment; priming; sizing
apresurar *tr & ref* to hurry, to hasten
apretadera *f* strap, rope; **apretaderas** (coll) pressure
apreta•do -da *adj* compact, tight; close, intimate; dense, thick; difficult, dangerous; (coll) mean, stingy; **estar muy apretado** (coll) to be in a bad way
apretar §2 *tr* to tighten; to squeeze; to pinch; to hug; to harass, to importune; to afflict, to beset; (*un botón*) to press; (*los puños*) to clench; (*los dientes*) to grit; (*la mano*) to shake || *intr* to pinch; to insist; to get worse; to push hard, press forward; **apretar a correr** to start running; **apretar con** (coll) to close in on || *ref* to grieve, be distressed; to crowd
apretón *m* pressure, squeeze; struggle; dash, run; **apretón de manos** handshake
apretura *f* crush, jam; tightness; fix, trouble; need, want
aprietarropa *m* clothespin
aprieto *m* crush, jam; fix
aprisa *adv* fast, quickly
aprisco *m* sheepfold
aprisionar *tr* to imprison; to bind, tie; to shackle
aprobación *f* approbation, approval; pass, passing grade
aproba•do -da *adj* excellent || *m* pass
aprobar §61 *tr & intr* to approve; to pass
aprontar *tr* to hand over without delay; to expedite
apropia•do -da *adj* appropriate, fitting, proper
apropiar *tr* to hand over; to fit, adapt || *ref* to appropriate; to preëmpt
aprovechable *adj* available, usable
aprovecha•do -da *adj* thrifty; stingy; diligent; well-spent || *mf* opportunist
aprovechar *tr* to make good use of, take advantage of; (*una caída de agua*) to harness || *intr* to be useful; to progress, improve || *ref* — **aprovecharse de** to avail oneself of, to take advantage of
aprovisionar *tr* to provision, supply, furnish
aproxima•do -da *adj* approximate, rough
aproximar *tr* to bring near; to approximate || *ref* to come near; to approximate
aptitud *f* aptitude; suitability
ap•to -ta *adj* apt; suitable
apuesta *f* bet, wager
apues•to -ta *adj* neat, spruce, elegant || *f* see **apuesta**
apulgarar *ref* to become mildewed
apuntador *m* (theat) prompter
apuntalar *tr* to prop up, underpin
apuntar *tr* to point; to point at; to aim; to aim at; to take note of; to sharpen; to stitch, to darn, to patch; to correct; to prompt; to stake, to put up; (theat) to prompt || *intr* to begin to appear; to dawn || *ref* (*el vino*) to begin to turn sour; to register; (coll) to get tipsy
apunte *m* note; rough sketch; stake; (coll) rogue, rascal; (theat) cue
apuñalar *tr & intr* to stab
apuñear *tr* to punch
apura•do -da *adj* needy, hard up; difficult, dangerous; (coll) hurried, rushed
apurar *tr* to purify, refine; to clear up, verify; to finish; to drain, use up,

exhaust; to hurry, press; to annoy || *ref* to worry, grieve; to exert oneself, to strive
apuro *m* need, want; grief, sorrow; (Am) haste, urgency; **apuros** financial embarrassment
aquejar *tr* to grieve, afflict
aquel, aquella *adj dem* (*pl* **aquellos, aquellas**) that, that . . . yonder
aquél, aquélla *pron dem* (*pl* **aquéllos, aquéllas**) that; that one, that one yonder; the one; the former || *m* (coll) charm, appeal
aquelarre *m* witches' Sabbath
aquello *pron dem* that; that thing, that matter
aquende *adv* on this side || *prep* on this side of
aquerenciar *ref* to become fond or attached
aquí *adv* here; **aquí dentro** in here; **de aquí en adelante** from now on; **por aquí** this way
aquiescencia *f* acquiescence
aquietar *tr* to quiet, to calm
aquilatar *tr* to assay; to check; to refine
Aquiles *m* Achilles
aquilón *m* north wind
ara *f* altar; altar slab; **en aras de** for the sake of
árabe *adj* Arab, Arabian; (archit) Moresque || *mf* Arab, Arabian || *m* (*idioma*) Arabic
Arabia, la Arabia
arábi•go -ga *adj* Arabian, Arabic || *m* (*idioma*) Arabic; **estar en arábigo** (coll) to be Greek
aracanga *f* macaw
arado *m* plow
Aragón *m* Aragon
arago•nés -nesa *adj & mf* Aragonese
arancel *m* tariff
arancela•rio -ria *adj* tariff, customs
arándano *m* whortleberry; **arándano agrio** cranberry
arandela *f* bobèche; (mach) washer
araña *f* spider; chandelier
arañar *tr* to scratch; to scrape; (coll) to scrape together
arañazo *m* scratch
araño *m* scratching
aráquida *f* peanut
arar *tr* to plow
arbitraje *m* arbitration
arbitrar *tr & intr* to arbitrate; to referee; to umpire
arbitra•rio -ria *adj* arbitrary
arbitrio *m* free will; means, ways; **arbitrios** excise taxes
arbitrista *mf* wild-eyed dreamer
árbi•tro -tra *mf* arbiter; referee || *m* umpire
árbol *m* tree; axle, shaft; **árbol del caucho** rubber plant; **árbol de levas** camshaft; **árbol de mando** drive shaft; **árbol de Navidad** Christmas tree; **árbol motor** drive shaft
arbola•do -da *adj* wooded; (*mar*) high || *m* woodland
arboleda *f* grove
arbollón *m* sewer, drain
arbotante *m* flying buttress
arbusto *m* shrub
arca *f* chest, coffer; tank; ark; **arca de agua** water tower; **arca de la alianza** ark of the covenant; **arca de Noé** ark, Noah's ark
arcada *f* arcade; archway; stroke of bow; **arcadas** retching
arcai•co -ca *adj* archaic
arcaísmo *m* archaism
arcaizante *adj* obsolescent
arcángel *m* archangel
arca•no -na *adj & m* secret
arcar §73 *tr* to arch
arce *m* maple tree
arcilla *f* clay; **arcilla figulina** potter's clay
arco *m* arch; (*de cuna o mecedor*) rocker; (elec, geom) arc; (mus) bow; **arco iris** rainbow; **arco triunfal** triumphal arch; memorial arch
arcón *m* large chest; bin, bunker
archiduque *m* archduke
archienemigo *m* archenemy
archipiélago *m* archipelago; (coll) maze, entanglement || **Archipiélago** *m* Aegean Sea
archiva•dor -dora *mf* file clerk || *m* filing cabinet; letter file
archivar *tr* to file; to file away; (coll) to hide away
archivero *m* city clerk
archivo *m* archives; files; filing; (Col) office
ardentía *f* heartburn; (*en las olas de la mar*) phosphorescence
arder *tr* to burn || *intr* to burn; to blaze; **estar que arde** to be coming to a head || *ref* to burn up
ardid *m* artifice, trick, wile
ardi•do -da *adj* burnt-up; bold, intrepid; (Am) angry
ardiendo *adj invar* burning
ardiente *adj* ardent; fiery, passionate; burning, hot
ardilla *f* squirrel; **ardilla de tierra** gopher; **ardilla ladradora** prairie dog; **ardilla listada** chipmunk
ardillón *m* gopher
ardite *m* old Spanish coin of little value; **no me importa un ardite** (coll) I don't care a hang; **no valer un ardite** (coll) to be not worth a straw
ardor *m* ardor; eagerness, fervor, zeal; vehemence; courage, dash
ardoro•so -sa *adj* fiery, enthusiastic; balky, restive
ar•duo -dua *adj* arduous, difficult
área *f* area; small plot
arena *f* sand; grit; arena; **arena movediza** quicksand; **arenas** arena; (pathol) stones
arenal *m* sandy place; quicksand
arenga *f* harangue
arengar *tr & intr* to harangue
arenis•co -ca *adj* sandy, gritty; sand || *f* sandstone
areno•so -sa *adj* sandy
arenque *m* herring
areómetro *m* hydrometer
arepa *f* (Am) corn griddle cake
arete *m* eardrop, earring
arfada *f* (naut) pitching
arfar *intr* (naut) to pitch

argadijo or **argadillo** *m* bobbin, reel; (coll) restless fellow
argado *m* prank, trick, artifice
argamasa *f* mortar
argamasar *tr* to mortar, to plaster; (*los materiales de construcción*) to mix
árgana *f* (mach) crane; **árganas** panniers
Argel *f* Algiers
Argelia *f* Algeria
argeli•no -na *adj & mf* Algerian
argentar *tr* to silver
argenti•no -na *adj & mf* Argentine, Argentinean || **la Argentina** Argentina, the Argentine
argolla *f* large iron ring; (*que se pone en la nariz a un animal*) ring; (Am) engagement ring
argonauta *m* Argonaut
argucia *f* subtlety; trick
argüir §6 *tr* to argue, argue for; to prove; to accuse || *ref* to argue, to dispute
argumenta•dor -dora *adj* argumentative || *mf* arguer
argumentar *tr* to argue for; to prove || *intr & ref* to argue, dispute
argumento *m* argument
aria *f* (mus) aria
aridez *f* aridity, dryness
ári•do -da *adj* arid; (*aburrido, falto de interés*) dry
ariete *m* battering ram; **ariete hidráulico** hydraulic ram
arimez *m* projection
a•rio -ria *adj & mf* Aryan || *f* see **aria**
aris•co -ca *adj* churlish, surly, evasive; (*caballo*) vicious
arista *f* edge; (*intersección de dos planos*) ridge; (*del grano de trigo*) beard; **arista de encuentro** (archit) groin
aristocracia *f* aristocracy
aristócrata *mf* aristocrat
aristocráti•co -ca *adj* aristocratic
Aristóteles *m* Aristotle
aristotéli•co -ca *adj & mf* Aristotelian
aritméti•co -ca *adj* arithmetical || *mf* arithmetician || *f* arithmetic
arlequín *m* harlequin
arma *f* arm, weapon; **alzarse en armas** to rise up, rebel; **arma blanca** steel blade; **arma corta** pistol; **arma de fuego** firearm; **jugar a las armas** to fence; **sobre las armas** under arms
armada *f* fleet, armada; navy
armadía *f* raft, float
armadijo *m* trap, snare
arma•do -da *adj* armed; (*hormigón*) reinforced || *f* see **armada**
arma•dor -dora *mf* assembler || *m* recruiter of fishermen and whalers
armadura *f* armor; framework; skeleton; (elec) armature; (*de imán*) keeper
armamento *m* armament
armar *tr* to arm; (*un arma*) to load; (*una bayoneta*) to fix; to mount, assemble; to build; to equip; (*el hormigón*) to reinforce; (*una nave*) to fit out; (*caballero*) to dub; (coll) to start, stir up; **armarla** (coll) to start a row || *ref* to arm oneself; to get ready; (Am) to balk
armario *m* closet, wardrobe; **armario botiquín** medicine cabinet; **armario de luna** wardrobe with mirror; **armario frigorífico** refrigerator
armatoste *m* hulk
armazón *f* frame; assemblage; skeleton
armella *f* screw eye, eyebolt
arme•nio -nia *adj & mf* Armenian || **Armenia** *f* Armenia
armería *f* arms shop; arms museum; arms
armero *m* gunsmith; (*para las armas*) rack
armiño *m* ermine
armisticio *m* armistice
armonía *f* harmony
armóni•co -ca *adj & m* harmonic || *f* harmonica; **armónica de boca** mouth organ
armonio•so -sa *adj* harmonious
armonizar §60 *tr & intr* to harmonize
arnés *m* armor, coat of mail; harness; **arneses** harness, trappings; outfit, equipment; accessories
aro *m* hoop; rim; **aro de émbolo** piston ring
aroma *m* aroma, fragrance
aromáti•co -ca *adj* aromatic
arpa *f* harp
arpar *tr* to claw, scratch; to tear, rend
arpegio *m* arpeggio
arpeo *m* grappling iron
arpía *f* harpy; (coll) shrew, jade
arpillera *f* burlap, sackcloth
arpista *mf* harpist
arpón *m* harpoon
arponear *tr & intr* to harpoon
arqueada *f* (mus) bow
arquear *tr* to arch; (*la lana*) to beat; (*una nave*) to gauge; to audit || *intr* to retch || *ref* to bow
arqueología *f* archeology
arquería *f* arcade
arquero *m* archer, bowman
arquitecto *m* architect
arquitectóni•co -ca *adj* architectural
arquitectura *f* architecture
arrabal *m* suburb; **arrabales** outskirts
arracada *f* earring with pendant
arracimar *ref* to cluster, to bunch
arraiga•do -da *adj* deep-rooted; property-owning, landed
arraigar §44 *tr* to establish, to strengthen || *intr* to take root || *ref* to take root; to become settled
arraigo *m* taking root; stability; property, real estate
arramblar *tr* to cover with sand or gravel; to sweep away
arrancadero *m* starting point
arrancar §73 *tr* to root up, pull out, pull up; to snatch, to wrest; (*lágrimas*) to draw forth || *intr* to start; to set sail; (coll) to leave; to originate
arranque *m* pull; fit, impulse; jerk, sudden start; sally, outburst; (aut) start, starter; **arranque a mano** (aut) hand cranking; **arranque automático** (aut) self-starter

arrapiezo *m* rag, tatter; (coll) whippersnapper

arras *fpl* earnest money, pledge; dowry

arrasar *tr* to level; to wreck, to demolish; to fill to the brim || *intr* to clear up || *ref* to clear up; to fill up

arrastra•do -da *adj* (coll) mean, crooked || *mf* (coll) wretch, crook

arrastrar *tr* to drag, drag along; to drag down; to impel || *intr* to drag, to trail; to crawl, creep || *ref* to drag, to trail; to crawl, creep; to drag on; to cringe

arrastre *m* drag; crawl; washout; influence; haulage; (*influencia política y social*) (Cuba, Mex) drag

arrayán *m* myrtle

arre *interj* gee!, get up!

arreador *m* muleteer; (SAm) whip

arrear *tr* to drive || *intr* (coll) to hurry || *ref* to lose all one's money

arrebata•do -da *adj* rash, reckless; (*color del rostro*) flushed, ruddy

arrebatar *tr* to snatch; to carry away; to attract; to move, to stir || *ref* to be carried away, to be overcome

arrebatiña *f* scuffle, scramble; **andar a la arrebatiña** (coll) to scramble

arrebato *m* rage, fury; ecstasy, rapture

arrebol *m* (*de las nubes*) red; (*de las mejillas*) rosiness; (*afeite*) rouge; **arreboles** red clouds

arrebozar **§60** *tr* to muffle || *ref* to muffle one's face

arrebujar *tr* to jumble together; to wrap || *ref* to wrap oneself up

arreciar *intr & ref* to grow worse; to become more violent; to grow stronger

arrecife *m* stone-paved road; dike; reef; **arrecife de coral** coral reef

arredrar *tr* to drive back; to frighten || *ref* to draw back; to shrink; to be frightened

arregazar **§60** *tr* to tuck up

arreglar *tr* to adjust, regulate, settle; to arrange; to fix, repair || *ref* to adjust, settle; to arrange; to conform; **arreglárselas** (coll) to manage, to make out

arreglo *m* adjustment, regulation; settlement; arrangement; order, rule; agreement; **con arreglo a** in accordance with

arregostar *ref* (coll) to take a liking

arregosto *m* (coll) liking, taste

arrellanar *ref* to loll, to sprawl; to like one's work

arremangar *tr* (*las mangas*) to turn up; (*la ropa*) to tuck up || *ref* to turn up one's sleeves; to tuck up one's dress; (coll) to take a firm stand

arremeter *tr* to attack, assail; (*un caballo*) to spur || *intr* to attack; to be offensive to look at; **arremeter contra** to light into, sail into

arremetida *f* attack; (*de un caballo*) sudden start; push; short, wild run

arremolinar *ref* to crowd, mill around; to whirl

arrendajo *m* (orn) jay; (coll) mimic

arrendar **§2** *tr* to rent; (*una caballería*) to tie || *ref* to rent, be rented

arreo *m* adornment; (SAm) drove; **arreos** harness, trappings

arrepenti•do -da *adj* repentant || *mf* penitent

arrepentimiento *m* repentance

arrepentir **§68** *ref* to repent, be repentant; **arrepentirse de** (*p.ej., un pecado*) to repent

arrequives *mpl* finery; (coll) attendant circumstances

arresta•do -da *adj* bold, daring

arrestar *tr* to arrest || *ref* to rush boldly

arresto *m* arrest; boldness, daring; **bajo arresto** under arrest

arrezagar **§44** *tr* to tuck up

arriada *f* flood

arriar **§77** *tr* to flood; (naut) to lower, to strike; (naut) to slacken || *ref* to be flooded

arriba *adv* up, upward; above; upstairs; uptown; on top; **arriba de** up; **de arriba abajo** from top to bottom; from beginning to end; superciliously; **más arriba** farther up; **río arriba** upstream || *interj* up with . . .!

arribada *f* arrival (*by sea*); **de arribada** (naut) emergency

arribar *intr* to put into port; to arrive; (naut) to fall off to leeward; to recover, make a comeback

arribista *adj & mf* parvenu, upstart

arribo *m* arrival

arricete *m* shoal, bar

arriendo *m* rent, rental; lease

arriero *m* muleteer

arriesga•do -da *adj* dangerous, risky; bold, daring

arriesgar **§44** *tr* to risk, jeopardize || *ref* to take a risk

arrimadillo *m* wainscot

arrimar *tr* to bring close, move up; (*un golpe*) to give; to abandon, neglect; to give up; to get rid of || *ref* to come close, move up; to snuggle up; to lean; to depend

arrinconar *tr* to corner; to put aside; to abandon, neglect; to get rid of || *ref* to live in seclusion

arrisca•do -da *adj* enterprising; brisk, spirited; craggy

arriscar **§73** *tr* to risk || *ref* to take a risk; (*las reses*)' to plunge over a cliff

arrisco *m* risk

arrivista *adj & mf* parvenu, upstart

arrizar **§60** *tr* to reef

arroba *f* Spanish weight of about 25 pounds

arrobar *tr* to entrance, to enrapture || *ref* to be enraptured

arrobo *m* ecstasy, rapture

arroce•ro -ra *adj* rice || *mf* rice grower; rice merchant

arrocinar *tr* to bestialize || *ref* to become bestialized; to fall madly in love

arrodajar *ref* (CAm) to squat down with one's legs crossed

arrodillar *ref* to kneel, to kneel down

arrogancia *f* arrogance

arrogante *adj* arrogant
arrogar §44 *tr* to adopt || *ref* to arrogate to oneself
arrojadi•zo -za *adj* for throwing, projectile
arroja•do -da *adj* bold, fearless, rash
arrojalla•mas *m* (*pl* **-mas**) flame thrower
arrojar *tr* to throw, to hurl; to emit; to bring forth; to yield || *ref* to rush, rush forward
arrojo *m* boldness, fearlessness, rashness
arrollado *m* (elec) coil
arrolla•dor -dora *adj* sweeping, devastating
arrollamiento *m* winding
arrollar *tr* to roll; to roll up; to wind, to coil; (*al enemigo*) to rout; to dumbfound; (coll) to knock down, to run over
arropar *tr* to wrap, to wrap up || *ref* to bundle up
arrope *m* grape syrup; honey syrup
arropía *f* taffy
arrostrar *tr* to face; to like || *intr* — **arrostrar con** or **por** to face, to resist || *ref* to rush into the fight
arroyada *f* gully; flood, freshet
arroyo *m* stream, brook; gutter; street; (*de lágrimas, sangre, etc.*) stream
arroz *m* rice
arrufar *tr* to sic, to incite
arruga *f* wrinkle; crease, rumple
arrugar §44 *tr* to wrinkle; to crease, rumple; (*la frente*) to knit || *ref* to wrinkle; to crease, rumple; to shrink, shrivel
arruinar *tr* to ruin || *ref* to go to ruin
arrullar *tr* to sing to sleep, to lull to sleep; (coll) to court, to woo || *intr* to coo || *ref* to coo; (*las palomas*) to bill
arrullo *m* billing and cooing; lullaby
arrumaje *m* stowage; ballast
arrumar *tr* to stow || *ref* to become overcast
arrumbar *tr* to cast aside, to neglect; to silence; (*una costa*) to determine the lay of || *intr* (*naut*) to take bearings || *ref* to get seasick; (naut) to take bearings
arsenal *m* arsenal, armory; dockyard, shipyard
arsénico *m* arsenic
art. *abbr* **artículo**
arte *m* & *f* art; trick; knack; fishing gear; **artes y oficios** arts and crafts; **bellas artes** fine arts; **no tener arte ni parte en** to have nothing to do with
artefacto *m* artifact; appliance, device, contrivance; **artefactos de alumbrado** lighting fixtures; **artefactos sanitarios** bathroom fixtures
artemisa *f* sagebrush
arteria *f* artery
artería *f* craftiness, cunning
arte•ro -ra *adj* crafty, cunning, sly
artesa *f* trough; Indian canoe
artesanía *f* craftsmanship
artesa•no -na *mf* artisan, craftsman || *f* craftswoman
artesón *m* kitchen tub; coffer, caisson (*in ceiling*)
árti•co -ca *adj* arctic
articulación *f* articulation; (*de huesos*) joint; **articulación universal** universal joint
articular *tr* to articulate
articulista *mf* feature writer
artículo *m* article; item; joint; (*en un diccionario*) entry; **artículo de fondo** leader, editorial; **artículos de consumo** consumers' goods; **artículos de deporte** sporting goods; **artículos de primera necesidad** basic commodities; **artículos para caballeros** men's furnishings
artífice *mf* artificer; craftsman
artificial *adj* artificial
artificio *m* artifice; workmanship; appliance, device; cunning; trick, ruse
artificio•so -sa *adj* ingenious, skillful; cunning, scheming, deceptive
artilugio *m* (coll) contraption, jigger
artillería *f* artillery
artillero *m* artilleryman, gunner
artimaña *f* trap; (coll) trick, cunning
artista *mf* artist
artísti•co -ca *adj* artistic
artolas *fpl* mule chair, cacolet
artríti•co -ca *adj* & *mf* arthritic
artritis *f* arthritis
arúspice *m* diviner, soothsayer
arveja *f* vetch, tare; (Chile) pea
arzobispo *m* archbishop
arzón *m* saddletree; **arzón delantero** saddlebow; **arzón trasero** cantle
as *m* ace; **as de fútbol** football star; **as de la pantalla** movie star; **as del volante** speed king
asa *f* handle; juice; **en asas** with arms akimbo
asa•do -da *adj* roasted; **bien asado** well done; **poco asado** rare || *m* roast
asador *m* spit
asadura *f* entrails
asalaria•do -da *mf* wage earner
asaltar *tr* to assail, to assault, to storm; to overtake, overcome
asalto *m* assault, attack; (box) round; (mil) storm; **tomar por asalto** to take by storm
asamblea *f* assembly
asar *tr* to roast || *ref* to be burning up
asbesto *m* asbestos
ascendencia *f* ancestry
ascendente *adj* ascending; up
ascender §51 *tr* to promote || *intr* to ascend, go up; to be promoted; **ascender a** to amount to
ascendiente *adj* ascending; up || *mf* ancestor || *m* ascendancy, upper hand
ascensión *f* ascension, ascent
ascenso *m* ascent; promotion
ascensor *m* elevator; freight elevator
ascensorista *mf* elevator operator
asceta *mf* ascetic
ascéti•co -ca *adj* ascetic
asco *m* disgust, nausea, loathing; **dar asco** (coll) to turn the stomach; **estar hecho un asco** (coll) to be filthy; **hacer ascos de** (coll) to turn one's nose

up at; **ser un asco** (coll) to be contemptible; (coll) to be worthless

ascua *f* ember, live coal; **estar sobre ascuas** (coll) to be on needles and pins || **ascuas** *interj* (coll) ouch!

asea·do -da *adj* clean, neat, tidy

asear *tr & ref* to clean up, tidy up

asechamiento *m* or **asechanza** *f* snare, trap

asechar *tr* to set a trap for

asediar *tr* to besiege; to harass

asedio *m* siege

asegundar *tr* to repeat right away

aseguración *f* insurance policy

asegura·dor -dora *mf* insurer, underwriter

asegurar *tr* to fasten, secure; to assure; to assert; to seize; to imprison; (*garantizar por un precio contra determinado accidente o pérdida*) to insure || *ref* to make sure; to take out insurance

asemejar *tr* to make like; to compare; to resemble || *ref* to be similar

asenso *m* assent; **dar asenso a** to believe

asentada *f* sitting; **de una asentada** at one sitting

asentaderas *fpl* (coll) buttocks

asentadillas — **a asentadillas** sidesaddle

asenta·do -da *adj* sedate; stable || *f* see **asentada**

asentador *m* strap, razor strap

asentar §2 *tr* to seat; to place; to establish; to tamp down, to level; to hone, sharpen; to note down; (*un golpe*) to impart; (*en la mente de uno*) to impress; to affirm; to suppose || *intr* to be becoming || *ref* to sit down; to be established, to establish oneself; to settle

asentimiento *m* assent

asentir §68 *intr* to assent

aseo *m* cleanliness, neatness, tidiness; care; toilet

asépti·co -ca *adj* aseptic

aseptizar §60 *tr* to purify, make aseptic

asequible *adj* accessible, obtainable

aserción *f* assertion

aserradero *m* sawmill

aserra·dor -dora *mf* sawyer; (coll) fiddler || *f* power saw

aserraduras *fpl* sawdust

aserrar §2 *tr* to saw

aserrín *m* sawdust

aserto *m* assertion

asesinar *tr* to assassinate, to murder

asesinato *m* assassination, murder

asesi·no -na *adj* murderous || *mf* assassin, murderer

asesorar *tr* to advise || *ref* to seek advice; to get advice

asestar *tr* to aim; to shoot; (*un golpe*) to deal

aseveración *f* assertion, declaration

aseverar *tr* to assert, to declare

asfaltar *tr* to asphalt

asfalto *m* asphalt

asfixia *f* asphyxiation

asfixiar *tr* to asphyxiate

así *adv* so, thus; **así . . . como** both . . . and; **así como** as soon as; as well as; **así que** as soon as; with the result that; **así y todo** even so, anyhow; **por decirlo así** so to speak; **y así sucesivamente** and so on

Asia *f* Asia; **el Asia Menor** Asia Minor

asiáti·co -ca *adj & mf* Asian, Asiatic

asidero *m* handle; occasion, pretext

asi·duo -dua *adj* assiduous; frequent, persistent

asiento *m* seat; site; (*de un edificio*) settling; (*de una botella, una silla, etc.*) bottom; sediment; list, roll; wisdom, maturity; **asiento de rejilla** cane seat; **asiento lanzable** (aer) ejection seat; **asientos** buttocks; **planchar el asiento** (Am) to be a wallflower; **tome Vd. asiento** have a seat

asignación *f* assignment; salary; allowance

asignar *tr* to assign

asignatura *f* course, subject

asila·do -da *mf* inmate

asilar *tr* to shelter; to place in an asylum; to silo || *ref* to take refuge; to be placed in an asylum

asilo *m* asylum; shelter, refuge; (*para menesterosos*) home; **asilo de huérfanos** orphan asylum; **asilo de locos** insane asylum; **asilo de pobres** poorhouse

asilla *f* fastener; collarbone; **asillas** shoulder pole

asimetría *f* asymmetry

asimilar *tr* to compare; to take in || *intr* to be alike || *ref* to assimilate; **asimilarse a** to resemble

asimismo *adv* also, likewise

asir §7 *tr* to grasp, seize || *intr* to take root || *ref* to take hold; to fight, to grapple; **asirse a** or **de** to cling to

Asiria *f* Assyria

asi·rio -ria *adj & mf* Assyrian

asistencia *f* attendance; assistence; reward; audience, persons present; welfare, social work; (Mex) sitting room, parlor; **asistencias** allowance, support

asistenta *f* charwoman, cleaning woman

asistente *adj* attendant; present || *m* assistant, helper; bystander, spectator, person present; (mil) orderly

asistir *tr* to assist, help; to attend; to serve, wait on || *intr* to be present; **asistir a** to be present at, to attend

asma *f* asthma

asna *f* she-ass, jenny ass; **asnas** rafters

asnal *adj* donkey; (coll) brutish

asno *m* ass, donkey, jackass

asociación *f* association

asocia·do -da *adj* associated; associate || *mf* associate, partner

asociar *tr* to associate; to take as partner || *ref* to become associated; to become a partner; to become partners

asolamiento *m* razing, destruction

asolar *tr* to parch, burn || *ref* to become parched || §61 *tr* to raze, destroy

asolear *tr* to sun || *ref* to bask; to get sunburned

asomar *tr* (*p.ej., la cabeza*) to show, to stick out || *intr* to begin to show or appear; to show || *ref* to show, to appear; to stick out; to get tipsy
asombradi•zo -za *adj* timid, shy
asombrar *tr* to shade; (*un color*) to darken; to frighten; to astonish, amaze || *ref* to be frightened; to be astonished, be amazed
asombro *m* fright; astonishment
asombro•so -sa *adj* astonishing, amazing
asomo *m* mark, token, sign; appearance; **ni por asomo** nothing of the kind, not by a long shot
asordar *tr* to deafen
aspa *f* X-shaped figure; reel; (*de molino de viento*) wheel, vane; propeller blade
aspar *tr* to reel; to crucify; to annoy, harass || *ref* to writhe; to take great pains
aspaviento *m* fuss, excitement
aspecto *m* aspect
aspereza *f* harshness; roughness; bitterness, sourness; gruffness
asperjar *tr* to sprinkle; to sprinkle with holy water
áspe•ro -ra *adj* harsh; rough; bitter; gruff
áspid *m* asp
aspirador *m* vacuum cleaner; **aspirador de gasolina** (aut) vacuum tank
aspirante *m* applicant, candidate; **aspirante a cabo** private first class; **aspirante de marina** midshipman
aspirar *tr* to suck in, draw in; to inhale || *intr* to aspire; to inhale, to breathe in
aspirina *f* aspirin
asquear *tr* to loathe || *ref* to be nauseated
asquero•so -sa *adj* disgusting, loathsome; nauseating; squeamish
asta *f* spear; shaft; flagpole, staff, mast; antler; (*de toro*) horn; **a media asta** at half-mast; **dejar en las astas del toro** (coll) to leave high and dry
asta•do -da *adj* horned || *m* bull
ástato *m* astatine
aster *m* aster
asterisco *m* asterisk
astil *m* handle; shaft
astilla *f* chip, splinter
astillar *tr & ref* to chip, splinter
Astillejos *mpl* (astr) Castor and Pollux
astillero *m* dockyard, shipyard
astro *m* star, heavenly body; (fig) star, leading light
astrología *f* astrology
astronauta *m* astronaut
astronáuti•co -ca *adj* astronautic || *f* astronautics
astronave *f* spaceship; **astronave tripulada** manned spaceship
astronomía *f* astronomy
astronómi•co -ca *adj* astronomic(al)
astróno•mo -ma *mf* astronomer
astro•so -sa *adj* ill-fated; vile, contemptible; (coll) ragged, shabby
astucia *f* cunning, craftiness; trick
asturia•no -na *adj & mf* Asturian
astu•to -ta *adj* astute, cunning; tricky
asueto *m* day off; (coll) leisure
asumir *tr* to assume, take on
asunción *f* assumption
asunto *m* subject, matter; affair, business; theme; **asuntos internacionales** world affairs
asurar *tr* to burn; to parch; to harass, worry
asurcar **§73** *tr* to furrow, to plow
asustadi•zo -za *adj* scary, skittish
asustar *tr* to scare, frighten
atabal *m* kettledrum; timbrel
ataca•do -da *adj* irresolute, undecided; mean, stingy
atacar **§73** *tr* to attack; to attach, fasten; to pack, jam; (*un barreno*) to tamp; to corner, to contradict || *intr* to attack
ata•do -da *adj* timid, shy; weak, irresolute; insignificant; cramped || *m* pack, bundle, roll
ataguía *f* cofferdam
atajar *tr* to stop, intercept, interrupt; to partition off || *intr* to take a short cut || *ref* to be abashed
atajo *m* short cut; (*en un escrito*) cut
atalaya *m* guard, lookout || *f* watchtower; elevation
atalayar *tr* to watch from a watchtower; to spy on
atanquía *f* depilatory ointment
atañer **§70** *tr* to concern
ataque *m* attack
atar *tr* to tie, fasten
ataracea *f* marquetry, inlaid work
atarantar *tr* to stun, daze
atardecer *m* late afternoon || *v* **§22** *intr* to draw toward evening; to happen in the late afternoon
atarea•do -da *adj* busy
atarear *tr* to give an assignment to; to overload with work || *ref* to toil, to work hard, to keep busy
atarjea *f* sewer
atarugar **§44** *tr* to peg, to wedge; to plug; to stuff, to fill; (coll) to silence, shut up || *ref* (coll) to become confused
atasajar *tr* to slash, hack; (*carne*) to jerk
atascadero *m* mudhole; (fig) pitfall
atascar **§73** *tr* to stop, to stop up, clog, obstruct || *ref* to get stuck; to stuff oneself; to clog, get clogged
atasco *m* sticking, clogging; obstruction
ataúd *m* casket, coffin
ataujía *f* damascene work
ataujiar **§77** *tr* to damascene
ataviar **§77** *tr* to dress, adorn, deck out
atavío *m* dress, adornment; **atavíos** finery, frippery, chiffons
atediar *tr* to tire, bore
ateísmo *m* atheism
ateísta *mf* atheist
atelaje *m* harness
atemorizar **§60** *tr* to frighten
atemperar *tr* to soften, moderate, temper; to adjust, adapt
Atenas *f* Athens
atención *f* attention; **en atención a** in view of

atender **§51** *tr* to attend to; to heed, pay attention to; to take care of; (*a los parroquianos*) to wait on
atener **§71** *ref* — **atenerse a** to abide by, to rely on
ateniense *adj & mf* Athenian
atenta•do -da *adj* moderate, prudent; cautious || *m* attempt, assault
atentar *tr* to attempt, to try to commit || *intr* — **atentar a** or **contra** (*p.ej., la vida de una persona*) to attempt || **§2** *ref* to grope
aten•to -ta *adj* attentive; courteous, polite || *f* favor (*letter*)
atenuar **§21** *tr* to extenuate
ate•o -a *adj & mf* atheist
aterciopela•do -da *adj* velvety
ateri•do -da *adj* stiff, numb with cold
aterrada *f* landfall
aterrajar *tr* to thread, to tap
aterraje *m* landing
aterrar *tr* to terrify || **§2** *tr* to destroy, demolish; to cover with earth || *intr* to land || *ref* to stand inshore
aterrizaje *m* landing; **aterrizaje a ciegas** blind landing; **aterrizaje aplastado** or **en desplome** pancake landing; **aterrizaje forzoso** emergency landing
aterrizar **§60** *intr* to land
aterronar *tr* to make lumpy || *ref* to cake, to lump
aterrorizar **§60** *tr* to terrify
atesorar *tr* to treasure; to hoard; (*virtudes, perfecciones*) to possess
atesta•do -da *adj* stuffed, jammed; obstinate, stubborn || *m* certificate
atestar *tr* (law) to attest || **§2** & **regular** *tr* to jam, pack, stuff, cram; (coll) to stuff
atestiguar **§10** *tr* to attest, testify, depose
atezar **§60** *tr* to tan; to blacken || *ref* to become tanned, become sunburned
atiborrar *tr* to stuff || *ref* (coll) to stuff, stuff oneself
atiesar *tr* to stiffen; to tighten || *ref* to become stiff; to become tight
atildar *tr* to mark with a tilde, dash, or accent mark; to point out; to find fault with; to tidy up, to trim, to adorn
atina•do -da *adj* careful, keen, wise
atinar *tr* to find, come upon || *intr* to guess, guess right; to be right; to manage
atisbadero *m* peephole
atisbar *tr* to watch, spy on
atisbo *m* glimpse, look, peek
atizar **§60** *tr* to stir, to poke; to snuff; to rouse; (*p.ej., un puntapié*) to let go
Atlánti•co -ca *adj & m* Atlantic
at•las *m* (*pl* **-las**) atlas
atleta *mf* athlete
atleticismo *m* athletics
atléti•co -ca *adj* athletic || *f* athletics
atmósfera *f* atmosphere
atmosféri•co -ca *adj* atmospheric
atoar *tr* (naut) to tow
atocinar *tr* (*un cerdo*) to cut up; to make into bacon; (coll) to murder || *ref* to get angry; to fall madly in love
atocha *f* esparto
atolondra•do -da *adj* confused; scatterbrained
atolondrar *tr* to confuse, bewilder
atolladero *m* mudhole; obstacle, difficulty
atollar *intr & ref* to get stuck, to get stuck in the mud
atómi•co -ca *adj* atomic
átomo *m* atom
atóni•to -ta *adj* astounded, aghast
atontar *tr* to stun; to confuse, bewilder
atorar *tr* to clog, obstruct || *intr & ref* to stick, get stuck; to choke
atormentar *tr* to torment; to torture
atornillar *tr* to screw, screw on
atortolar *tr* to rattle, scare, intimidate
atosigar **§44** *tr* to poison; to harass || *ref* to be in a hurry
atrabanca•do -da *adj* overworked; (Mex) hasty, rash; (Ven) deep in debt
atrabancar **§73** *tr & intr* to rush through
atrabilia•rio -ria *adj* irascible, grouchy
atracador *m* hold-up man
atracar **§73** *tr* to hold up; to bring up; (naut) to bring alongside, to dock; (coll) to stuff || *intr* (naut) to come alongside, to dock || *ref* (coll) to stuff; (Am) to quarrel
atracción *f* attraction; amusement
atraco *m* holdup
atracón *m* (coll) stuffing, gluttony; (Am) fight; (Am) push, shove
atracti•vo -ca *adj* attractive || *m* attraction; attractiveness
atraer **§75** *tr* to attract
atragantar *tr* to choke down || *ref* to choke; **atragantarse con** to choke on
atraillar **§4** *tr* to leash; to master, subdue
atrampar *ref* to fall into a trap; to be stopped up; to stick; to get stuck
atrancar **§73** *tr* to bar; to obstruct || *intr* (coll) to stride; (coll) to read falteringly || *ref* to get stuck; (*una ventana*) to stick; (Mex) to stick to one's opinion
atrapamos•cas *m* (*pl* **-cas**) flytrap; (bot) Venus's-flytrap
atrapar *tr* (coll) to trap, to catch; to get, to land, to net
atrás *adv* back, backward; behind; before; previously; **atrás de** back of, behind; **hacerse atrás** to back up, move back; **hacia atrás** backwards; the other way
atrasa•do -da *adj* late; (*reloj*) slow; needy; back; retarded; in arrears; **atrasado de medios** short of funds; **atrasado de noticias** behind the times
atrasar *tr* to slow down; to retard; to set back, to turn back; to delay; to leave behind; to postdate || *intr* to be slow || *ref* to be slow; to lose time; to lag, to stay behind; to be late; to be in debt
atraso *m* delay, slowness; backwardness; lag; **atrasos** arrears, delinquency

atravesar §2 *tr* to cross, to go across; to pierce; to pass through, go through; to put crosswise; to stake, wager || *ref* to butt in; to fight, wrangle; to get stuck
atrayente *adj* attractive
atreguar §10 *tr* to give a truce to; to grant an extension to || *ref* to agree to a truce
atrever *ref* to dare; **atreverse con** or **contra** to be impudent toward
atrevi·do -da *adj* bold, daring; impudent
atrevimiento *m* boldness, daring; impudence
atribuir §20 *tr* to attribute, ascribe || *ref* to assume
atribular *tr & ref* to grieve
atributo *m* attribute
atril *m* lectern; music stand
atrincherar *tr* to entrench || *ref* to dig in
atrio *m* hall, vestibule; court, courtyard; parvis
atri·to - ta *adj* contrite
atrocidad *f* atrocity; (coll) enormity
atrofia *f* atrophy
atrofiar *tr & ref* to atrophy
atrojar *tr* (*granos*) to garner; (Mex) to befuddle
atrona·do -da *adj* reckless, thoughtless
atronar §61 *tr* to deafen; to stun || *intr* to thunder
atropella·do -da *adj* brusk, violent; hasty; tumultuous
atropellar *tr* to trample; to knock down; to run over; to disregard; to do hurriedly || *intr & ref* to act hastily or recklessly
atropello *m* trampling; knocking down; running over; abuse, insult; outrage
a·troz *adj* (*pl* **-troces**) atrocious; (coll) huge, enormous
atto. *abbr* **atento**
atufar *tr* to anger, irritate || *ref* to get angry; (*el vino*) to turn sour
atún *m* tuna
aturdi·do -da *adj* reckless, harebrained
aturdir *tr* to stun; to perplex, bewilder
atusar *tr* to trim; to smooth || *ref* to dress fancily; (*el bigote*) to twist
audacia *f* audacity
au·daz *adj* (*pl* **-daces**) audacious
audición *f* audition; hearing; concert; listening
audiencia *f* audience, hearing; audience chamber; royal tribunal; provincial high court
audífono *m* hearing aid; earphone
audiofrecuencia *f* audio frequency
audiómetro *m* audiometer
auditor *m* judge advocate; **auditor de guerra** judge advocate (*in army*); **auditor de marina** judge advocate (*in navy*)
auditorio *m* (*concurso de oyentes*) audience; (*local*) auditorium
auge *m* height, acme; boom; vogue; **estar en auge** to be booming
augur *m* augur
augurar *tr* to augur; (Am) to wish || *intr* to augur
augurio *m* augury; (Am) wish
augus·to -ta *adj* august
aula *f* classroom, lecture room; **aula magna** assembly hall
aulaga *f* gorse, furze
aullar §8 *intr* to howl
aullido *m* howl, howling
aúllo *m* howl
aumentar *tr* to augment, increase, enlarge; to promote; (coll) to exaggerate || *intr & ref* to augment, increase
aumento *m* augmentation, increase, enlargement; promotion; **ir en aumento** to be on the increase
aun *adv* even; **aun cuando** although
aún *adv* still, yet
aunar §8 *tr & ref* to join, unite; to combine, mix
aunque *conj* although, though
aúpa *interj* up!; **de aúpa** (coll) swanky; **los de aúpa** (taur) the picadors
aupar §8 *tr* (coll) to help up; (coll) to extol
aura *f* gentle breeze; breath; popularity; turkey vulture
áure·o -a *adj* gold, golden
aureola *f* halo, aureole
auricular *m* earpiece, receiver; **auricular de casco** headpiece
auriga *m* (poet) coachman, charioteer
aurora *f* aurora, dawn; roseate hue
ausencia *f* absence
ausentar *tr* to send away || *ref* to absent oneself
ausente *adj* absent; absent-minded || *mf* absentee
auspiciar *tr* (Am) to sponsor, foster, back
auspicio *m* auspice; **bajo los auspicios de** under the auspices of
auste·ro -ra *adj* austere; harsh; honest; penitent
Australia *f* Australia
australia·no -na *adj & mf* Australian
Austria *f* Austria
austría·co -ca *adj & mf* Austrian
austro *m* south wind
auténtica *f* certificate; certification
autenticar §73 *tr* to authenticate
auténti·co -ca *adj* authentic; real || *f* see **auténtica**
autillo *m* tawny owl
auto *m* edict; short Biblical play; miracle play; auto; **auto de prisión** commitment, warrant for arrest; **auto sacramental** play in honor of the Sacrament
autoamortizable *adj* self-liquidating
autobanco *m* drive-in bank
autobiografía *f* autobiography
autobombo *m* self-glorification
autobús *m* autobus, bus
autocamión *m* motor truck
autocráti·co -ca *adj* autocratic(al)
autócto·no -na *adj* native, indigenous
autodefensa *f* self-defense
autodeterminación *f* self-determination
autodidac·to -ta *adj* self-taught
autodisciplina *f* self-discipline
autódromo *m* automobile race track
auto-escuela *f* driving school
autógena *f* welding
autogobierno *m* self-government

autografiar §77 *tr* to autograph
autógra•fo -fa *adj & m* autograph
autoguia•do -da *adj* self-guided, homing
automación *f* automation
autómata *m* automaton
automáti•co -ca *adj* automatic
automatización *f* automation
automóvil *m* automobile
automovilista *mf* motorist
autonomía *f* autonomy; cruising radius
autóno•mo -ma *adj* autonomous, independent
autopiano *m* player piano
autopista *f* turnpike, automobile road
autopsia *f* autopsy
au•tor -tora *mf* author; (*de un crimen*) perpetrator || *f* authoress
autoridad *f* authority; pomp, display
autorita•rio -ria *adj & mf* authoritarian
autoriza•do -da *adj* authoritative
autorizar §60 *tr* to authorize; to legalize; to exalt
autorretrato *m* self-portrait
autoservicio *m* self-service
autostop *m* hitchhiking; **viajar en autostop** to hitchhike
autostopista *mf* hitchhiker
auto-teatro *m* drive-in movie theater
autovía *m* railway motor coach || *f* turnpike, automobile road
auxiliar *adj* auxiliary || *mf* auxiliary; aid, helper; substitute teacher || *v* §77 & **regular** *tr* to aid, help, assist; (*a un moribundo*) to attend
auxilio *m* aid, help, assistance; **acudir en auxilio a** or **de** to come to the aid of; **auxilio en carretera** road service; **primeros auxilios** first aid
avahar *tr* to steam; to breathe warmth on || *intr* to steam, give off vapor || *ref* to steam, give off vapor; to warm one's hands with one's breath
aval *m* indorsement; countersignature
avalancha *f* avalanche
avalorar *tr* to estimate; to encourage
avaluación *f* appraisal, valuation
avaluar §21 *tr* to appraise, to estimate
avalúo *m* appraisal, valuation
avance *m* advance; advance payment; (com) balance; (com) estimate; (mov) preview
avante *adv* (naut) fore
avanza•do -da *adj* advanced; **avanzado de edad** advanced in years || *f* outpost, advance guard
avanzar §60 *tr* to advance, extend; to propose || *intr & ref* to advance; to approach
avanzo *m* balance sheet; estimate
avaricia *f* avarice
avaricio•so -sa *adj* avaricious
avarien•to -ta *adj* avaricious || *mf* miser
ava•ro -ra *adj* miserly || *mf* miser
avasallar *tr* to subject, subjugate, enslave || *ref* to submit
ave *f* bird; fowl; **ave canora** songbird; **ave de corral** barnyard fowl; **ave de mal agüero** Jonah, jinx; **ave de paso** bird of passage; **ave de rapiña** bird of prey; **ave fría** lapwing; **ave zancuda** wading bird
avecinar *tr* to bring near || *ref* to approach; to take up residence
avecindar *tr* to domicile || *ref* to become a resident
avejentar *tr & ref* to age prematurely
avejigar §44 *tr, intr & ref* to blister
avellana *f* hazelnut
avellanar *tr* to countersink || *ref* to shrivel, shrivel up
avellano *m* hazel, hazel tree
avemaría *f* Hail Mary, Ave Maria; **al avemaría** at sunset; **en un avemaría** (coll) in a jiffy; **saber como el avemaría** (coll) to have a thorough knowledge of
avena *f* oats
avenar *tr* to drain
avenate *m* gruel, oatmeal gruel
avenencia *f* agreement; deal, bargain
avenida *f* avenue; allée; flood, freshet; gathering, assemblage
aveni•do -da *adj* — **bien avenido** in agreement; **mal avenido** in disagreement || *f* see **avenida**
avenimiento *m* agreement; reconciliation
avenir §79 *tr* to reconcile, bring together || *ref* to be reconciled, to agree; to compromise; to correspond
aventa•dor -dora *mf* winnower || *m* fan
aventaja•do -da *adj* excellent, outstanding; advantageous
aventajar *tr* to advance; to put ahead; to excel || *ref* to advance, win an advantage; to excel
aventar §2 *tr* to fan; to winnow; to scatter to the winds; to blow; (coll) to drive away || *ref* to swell up; (coll) to flee, run away
aventón *m* (Guat, Mex, Peru) push, shove; (*llevada gratuita*) (Mex) free ride; **pedir aventón** (Mex) to hitchhike
aventura *f* adventure; danger, risk
aventura•do -da *adj* hazardous, venturesome
aventurar *tr* to adventure, to venture, to hazard || *ref* to adventure, to take a risk; to venture, to risk
aventure•ro -ra *adj* adventuresome, adventurous || *m* adventurer, soldier of fortune || *f* adventuress
avergonzar §9 *tr* to shame; to embarrass || *ref* to be ashamed; to be embarrassed
avería *f* aviary; breakdown, failure; (com) damage; (naut) average
averiar §77 *tr* to damage || *ref* to suffer damage; to break down
averiguable *adj* ascertainable
averiguar §10 *tr* to ascertain, to find out
aversión *f* aversion, dislike; **cobrar aversión a** to take a dislike for
aves•truz *m* (*pl* **-truces**) ostrich
avezar §60 *tr* to accustom || *ref* to become accustomed
aviación *f* aviation
avia•dor -dora *mf* aviator, flyer || *m* aviator, airman; (mil) airman; **aviador postal** air-mail pilot || *f* aviatrix, airwoman
aviar §77 *tr* to make ready, prepare;

(coll) to equip, provide; **estar, encontrarse** or **quedar aviado** (coll) to be in a mess, be in a jam || *ref* to hurry; (aer) to take off
avia•triz (*pl* **-trices**) aviatrix
avidez *f* avidity, greediness
ávi•do -da *adj* avid, greedy, eager
aviejar *tr & ref* to age prematurely
aviento *m* winnowing fork, pitchfork
avie•so -sa *adj* crooked, distorted; evil-minded, perverse
avilantar *ref* to be insolent
avilantez *f* insolence; meanness
avillana•do -da *adj* rustic, boorish
avillanar *tr* to debase, make boorish || *ref* to become boorish
avinagra•do -da *adj* (coll) vinegarish, sour, crabbed
avinagrar *tr* to sour || *ref* to become sour; to turn into vinegar
avío *m* provision; arrangement; (Am) load; **¡al avío!** let's go!; **avíos** equipment, tools, outfit; **avíos de pescar** fishing tackle
avión *m* airplane; (orn) martin; **avión birreactor** twin-jet plane; **avión de caza** pursuit plane; **avión a chorro, avión de propulsión a chorro** or **a reacción** jet plane
avión-correo *m* mailplane
avioneta *f* small plane; **avioneta de alquiler** taxiplane
avisaco•ches *m* (*pl* **-ches**) car caller
avisa•do -da *adj* prudent, wise; **mal avisado** rash, thoughtless
avisa•dor -dora *adj* warning || *mf* informer; · adviser || *m* electric bell; **avisador de incendio** fire alarm
avisar *tr* to advise, inform; to warn; to report on
aviso *m* advice, information; warning; care, prudence; dispatch boat; (Am) advertisement; **sobre aviso** on the lookout
avispa *f* wasp
avispa•do -da *adj* (coll) brisk, wide-awake
avispar *tr* to spur; (coll) to stir up || *ref* to fret, worry
avispón *m* hornet
avistar *tr* to descry || *ref* to meet, have an interview
avituallar *tr* to supply, provision || *ref* to take in supplies
avivar *tr* to brighten, enlive, revive || *intr & ref* to brighten, revive
avizor *adj* watchful, alert || *m* watcher; **avizores** (slang) eyes
avizorar *tr* to watch, spy on || *ref* to hide and watch, to spy
ax *interj* ouch!, ow!
axioma *m* axiom
axiomáti•co -ca *adj* axiomatic
ay *interj* ay!, alas! **¡ay de mí!** woe is me! || *m* sigh
aya *f* nurse, governess
ayer *adj & m* yesterday
ayo *m* tutor
ayuda *m* valet; **ayuda de cámara** valet de chambre || *f* help, aid; enema
ayudanta *f* assistant; **ayudanta de cocina** kitchenmaid
ayudante *m* aid, assistant; adjutant; **ayudante de campo** aide-de-camp
ayudar *tr* to aid, help, assist
ayunar *intr* to fast
ayu•no -na *adj* fasting; uninformed; **en ayunas** or **en ayuno** fasting; before breakfast; uninformed; missing the point || *m* fast, fasting
ayuntamiento *m* town or city council; town or city hall; sexual intercourse
azabacha•do -da *adj* jet, jet-black
azabache *m* jet; **azabaches** jet trinkets
aza•cán -cana *adj* menial || *mf* drudge || *m* water carrier
azada *f* hoe
azadón *m* hoe; grub hoe; **azadón de peto** or **de pico** mattock
azadonar *tr* to hoe
azafata *f* air hostess, stewardess; lady of the queen's wardrobe
azafate *m* wicker tray
azafrán *m* saffron
azafrana•do -da *adj* saffron
azafranar *tr* to saffron
azahar *m* orange or lemon blossom
azar *m* chance, hazard; accident, misfortune; fate, destiny; losing card; losing throw; (*persona o cosa que traen mala suerte*) Jonah
azarar *ref* to go awry; to get rattled
azaro•so -sa *adj* hazardous, risky; unlucky
ázi•mo -ma *adj* unleavened
azófar *m* brass
azoga•do -da *adj* fidgety, restless || *m* quicksilver foil; **temblar como un azogado** (coll) to shake like a leaf
azogar §44 *tr* (*un espejo*) to silver || *ref* to have mercury poisoning; (coll) to shake, become agitated
azogue *m* quicksilver; market place; (coll) mirror
azor *m* goshawk
azorar *tr* to abash; to excite, stir up
Azores *fpl* Azores
azotar *tr* to whip, to scourge; to beat; to flail; to beat down upon
azote *m* whip; lash; (fig) scourge; **azotes y galeras** (coll) tiresome fare
azotea *f* flat roof, roof terrace
azteca *adj & mf* Aztec
azúcar *m* sugar; **azúcar de caña** cane sugar; **azúcar de remolacha** beet sugar
azucarar *tr* to sugar, to sugarcoat; (coll) to sugar over
azucare•ro -ra *adj* sugar || *m* sugar bowl
azucena *f* Madonna lily, white lily
azufrar *tr* to sulphur
azufre *m* sulfur; brimstone
azul *adj & m* blue; **azul marino** navy blue
azular *tr* to color blue, to dye blue
azulear *intr* to turn blue
azulejar *tr* to tile, to cover with tiles
azulejo *m* glazed colored tile; (orn) roller; (orn) indigo bunting; (orn) bee eater
azuzar §60 *tr* to sic; (coll) to tease, incite

B

B, b (be) *f* second letter of the Spanish alphabet
B. *abbr* **Beato, Bueno**
baba *f* drivel, spittle, slobber; (*de culebras, peces, etc.*) slime
babear *intr* to slobber, to drivel; to froth, foam
babel *m & f* (coll) bedlam, confusion; **estar en babel** (coll) to be daydreaming
babero *m* bib
Babia *f* — **estar en Babia** (coll) to be daydreaming
babieca *adj* (coll) silly, simple || *mf* (coll) simpleton
Babilonia *f* (*imperio*) Babylonia; (*ciudad*) Babylon
babilóni•co -ca *adj* Babylonian
babilo•nio -nia *adj & mf* Babylonian || *f* see **Babilonia**
bable *m* Asturian dialect; patois
babor *m* (naut) port
babosa *f* slug
babosear *tr* to slobber over || *intr* to slobber
babo•so -sa *adj* slobbery; (*con las damas*) (coll) mushy || *m* (CAm) scoundrel || *f* see **babosa**
babucha *f* slipper, mule
babuino *m* baboon
bacalao or **bacallao** *m* codfish
baceta *f* (cards) widow
bacía *f* basin, vessel; shaving dish
bacilo *m* bacillus
bacín *m* chamber pot
Baco *m* Bacchus
bacteria *f* bacterium
bacteria•no -na *adj* bacterial
bacteriología *f* bacteriology
bacteriólo•go -ga *mf* bacteriologist
báculo *m* staff; crook; (fig) staff, comfort; **báculo pastoral** crozier
bache *m* hole, rut; blip; **bache aéreo** air pocket
bachi•ller -llera *adj* garrulous || *mf* garrulous person || **bachiller** *mf* bachelor
bachillerar *tr* to confer the bachelor's degree on || *ref* to receive the bachelor's degree
bachillerato *m* baccalaureate, bachelor's degree
bachillerear *intr* (coll) to babble, prattle
bachillería *f* (coll) babble, prattle; (coll) gossip
badajo *m* clapper
badana *f* (dressed) sheepskin; **zurrarle a uno la badana** (coll) to tan someone's hide
badén *m* gully, gutter
badil *m* fire shovel
badulaque *m* (coll) nincompoop
bagaje *m* beast of burden; (mil) baggage
bagatela *f* trinket; triviality; (Chile, Peru) pinball
bagazo *m* waste pulp, bagasse
bagre *adj* (Bol, Col) showy, gaudy; (CAm) sly, slick; (SAm) coarse, ill-bred; (Mex) stupid || *m* catfish
bahía *f* bay
bahorrina *f* (coll) slop; (coll) riffraff
bailable *adj* for dancing || *m* ballet
bailadero *m* dance floor, dance hall
baila•dor -dora *mf* dancer
bailar *tr* (*p.ej., un vals*) to dance; (*un trompo*) to spin || *intr* to dance; to spin; to wobble
baila•rín -rina *mf* dancer || *f* ballerina; **bailarina ombliguista** (coll) belly dancer
baile *m* dance; ball; ballet; **baile de etiqueta** dress ball, formal dance; **baile de los globos** bubble dance; **baile de máscaras** masked ball, masquerade ball; **baile de San Vito** (pathol) Saint Vitus's dance; **baile de trajes** costume ball, fancy-dress ball
baja *f* (*de los precios*) fall, drop; (*en la guerra*) casualty; **dar baja** to go down, decline; **dar de baja** to drop; (mil) to mark absent; **darse de baja** to drop out; **jugar a la baja** to bear the market
bajaca *f* (Ecuad) hair ribbon
bajada *f* descent; slope; downspout; (rad) lead-in wire
bajagua *f* (Mex) cheap tobacco
bajamar *f* low tide
bajar *tr* to lower, take down; to bring down; (*la escalera*) to go down, descend; to humble || *intr* to come down, to go down; to get off || *ref* to bend down; to get off; to humble oneself
bajel *m* ship, vessel
bajeza *f* humbleness, lowliness; meanness, baseness
bajío *m* shoal, sandbank; pitfall; (Am) lowland
bajista *adj* bearish || *mf* (fig) bear
ba•jo -ja *adj* low, under, lower; short; mean, base; lowly, humble; (mus) bass || *m* shoal, sandbank; (mus) bass || *f* see **baja** || **bajo** *adv* down; low, in a low voice || **bajo** *prep* under
bajón *m* bassoon; (*en el caudal, la salud, etc.*) (coll) decline, loss
bajonista *mf* bassoon player
bajorrelieve *m* bas-relief
bala *f* bullet; bale; **bala fría** spent bullet; **bala perdida** stray bullet
balaca *f* (Am) boasting, show
balada *f* ballad; (mus) ballade
bala•dí *adj* (*pl* **-díes**) trivial, paltry
baladro *m* scream, shout, outcry
baladronada *f* boast, boasting
baladronear *intr* to boast, to brag
bálago *m* chaff
balance *m* balance, balance sheet; rocking, swinging; hesitation, doubt; (*de una nave*) rolling
balancear *tr* to balance || *intr & ref* to rock, to swing; to hesitate, to waver; (*la nave*) to roll
balancín *m* balance beam; singletree; rocker arm; seesaw

balandra *f* sloop
balandrán *m* cassock
balanza *f* scales, balance; comparison, judgment; **balanza de pagos** balance of payments
balar *intr* to bleat; (coll) to pine
balastar *tr* to ballast
balasto *m* ballast
balaustre *m* baluster, banister
balay *m* (Am) wicker basket
balazo *m* shot; bullet wound
balbucear *tr* to stammer || *intr* to stammer, stutter; to babble, to prattle
balbucir **§1** *tr & intr* var of **balbucear**
Balcanes, los the Balkans
balcarrotas *fpl* (SAm) sideburns; (Mex) locks falling over sides of face
balcón *m* balcony
baldar *tr* to cripple; to incapacitate; to inconvenience; to trump
balde *m* bucket, pail; **de balde** free, gratis; over, in excess; **en balde** in vain
baldear *tr* to wash with pails of water; (*una excavación*) to bail out
baldí•o -a *adj* uncultivated; idle, lazy; careless; useless, vain; unfounded || *m* untilled land
baldón *m* insult; blot, disgrace
baldonar *tr* to insult; to stain, disgrace
baldosa *f* floor tile, paving tile; flagstone
baldra•gas *m* (*pl* **-gas**) (coll) jellyfish
balduque *s* red tape, wrapping tape
balear *adj* Balearic || *tr* to shoot at, to shoot, to shoot to death
balido *m* bleat, bleating
balísti•co -ca *adj* ballistic
baliza *f* buoy, beacon; danger signal
balizaje *m* (aer) airway lighting; (naut) buoys
balizar **§60** *tr* to mark with buoys; to mark off
balnea•rio -ria *adj* bathing || *m* watering place, spa
balompié *m* football, soccer
balón *m* football; bale; balloon
baloncesto *m* basketball
balota *f* ballot
balotar *intr* to ballot
balsa *f* pool, puddle; raft; float; corkwood; **balsa salvavidas** life float
bálsamo *m* balsam, balm
balsear *tr* to cross by raft; to ferry across
balsero *m* ferryman
bálti•co -ca *adj* Baltic
baluarte *m* bulwark
ballena *f* whale; whalebone; (*de corsé*) stay
ballesta *f* crossbow; spring, auto spring
ba•llet *m* (*pl* **-llets**) ballet
bambalinas *fpl* (theat) flies, borders
bambolear *intr* to sway, reel, wobble
bambolla *f* (coll) hulk; (coll) show, sham; (coll) show-off
bam•bú *m* (*pl* **-búes**) bamboo
banana *f* banana; (rad) plug
banane•ro -ra *adj* banana || *m* banana tree
banano *m* banana tree
banas *fpl* (Mex) banns
banasta *f* hamper, large basket
banca *f* bench; banking; stand, fruit stand; (*en el juego*) bank; **banca de hielo** iceberg; **hacer saltar la banca** to break the bank
banca•rio -ria *adj* banking, bank
bancarrota *f* bankruptcy; **hacer bancarrota** to go bankrupt
bancarrote•ro -ra *adj & mf* bankrupt
banco *m* bench; bank; (*de peces*) school; **banco de ahorros** savings bank; **banco de hielo** iceberg; **banco de liquidación** clearing house
banda *f* band; ribbon; faction, party; flock; border, edge; bank, shore; (*de la mesa de billar*) cushion; **banda de rodamiento** (aut) tread; **banda de tambores** drum corps; **irse a la banda** (naut) to list
bandada *f* flock, covey; (*de gente*) (coll) flock
bandaje *m* tire
bandazo *m* swerving; (naut) lurch
bandear *tr* (Am) to go through, to pierce; (Am) to pursue; (Am) to make love to || *ref* to manage
bandeja *f* tray; (Am) dish, platter
bandera *f* flag, banner; **con banderas desplegadas** with flying colors
banderilla *f* (taur) banderilla; **poner una banderilla a** (coll) to taunt; (coll) to hit for a loan
banderín *m* (mil) color corporal; recruiting post
banderola *f* streamer, pennant; (Am) transom
bandido *m* bandit
bando *m* proclamation; faction, side
bandolera *f* bandoleer; female bandit; **en bandolera** across the shoulders
bandolero *m* highwayman, brigand
bandurria *f* Spanish lute
banquero *m* banker
banqueta stool, footstool; (Guat, Mex) sidewalk
banquete *m* banquet
banquetear *tr, intr & ref* to banquet
banquisa *f* floe, iceberg
bañadera *f* (Am) bathtub
bañado *m* chamber pot; (Am) marshland
baña•dor -dora *adj* bathing || *mf* bather || *m* bathing suit
bañar *tr* to bathe; to dip; to coat by dipping || *ref* to bathe
bañera *f* bathtub
bañista *mf* bather; frequenter of a spa or seaside resort
baño *m* bath; bathing; bathroom; bathtub; **baño de asiento** sitz bath; **baño de ducha** shower bath; **baños** bathing place; spa
bao *m* (naut) beam
baptista *adj & mf* Baptist
baptisterio *m* baptistery
baque *m* thud, thump; bump, bruise
baquelita *f* bakelite
ba•quet *m* (*pl* **-quets**) bucket seat
baqueta *f* ramrod; drumstick; **correr baquetas** or **pasar por baquetas** to run the gauntlet
baquía *f* (Am) knowledge of the road, paths, rivers, etc. of a region; (Am) manual skill

baquia·no -na *adj* (Am) skillful, expert || *mf* (Am) scout, pathfinder, guide
báqui·co -ca *adj* Bacchic
bar *m* bar; cocktail bar
barahunda *f* uproar, tumult
baraja *f* (*de naipes*) deck, pack; gang, mob; confusion, mix-up
barajadura *f* shuffling; dispute, quarrel
barajar *tr* (*naipes*) to shuffle; to jumble, to mix || *intr* to shuffle; to fight, quarrel || *ref* to get jumbled or mixed
baranda *f* railing; (*de la mesa de billar*) cushion
barandilla *f* balustrade, railing
barata *f* cheapness; barter; (Mex) bargain sale; (Chile, Peru) cockroach
baratija *f* trinket
baratillo *m* second-hand goods; second-hand shop; bargain counter
bara·to -ta *adj* cheap || *m* bargain sale; **dar de barato** (coll) to admit for the sake of argument; **de barato** gratis, free || *f* see **barata** || **barato** *adv* cheap
báratro *m* (poet) hell
baratura *f* cheapness
baraúnda *f* uproar, tumult
barba *f* (*parte de la cara*) chin; (*pelo en ella*) beard; (*del papel*) deckle edge; (*de ave*) gill, wattle; **barba española** Spanish moss; **barbas** whiskers; **hacer la barba a** to shave; to bore, annoy; (Mex) to fawn on; **llevar por la barba** to lead by the nose; **mentir por la barba** (coll) to tell fish stories || *m* (theat) old man
barbacoa *f* barbecue; (Col) kitchen cupboard; (Peru) attic
barbada *f* lower jaw of horse; bridle curb || **la Barbada** Barbados
barbar *intr* to grow a beard; to strike root
barbaridad *f* barbarism; outrage; piece of folly; (coll) large amount; **¡qué barbaridad!** how awful!, what nonsense!
barbarie *f* barbarity, barbarism
barbarismo *m* illiteracy; outrage; (gram) barbarism
bárba·ro -ra *adj* barbaric; barbarous || *mf* barbarian
barbear *tr* to reach with the chin; to be as high as || *intr* to reach the same height; **barbear con** to be as high as
barbechar *tr* to plow for seeding; to fallow
barbecho *m* fallow; **firmar como en un barbecho** (coll) to sign with one's eyes closed
barbería *f* barber shop
barberil *adj* barber
barbe·ro -ra *mf* barber; (Mex) flatterer
barbilampi·ño -ña *adj* smooth-faced, beardless; beginning, green
barbilla *f* tip of chin; (*de pluma*) barb; (*de pez*) wattle
bar·bón -bona *adj* bearded || *m* greybeard; solemn old fellow; billy goat
barboquejo *m* chin strap
barbotar *tr & intr* to mutter, to mumble
barbu·do -da *adj* bearded, long-bearded, heavy-bearded || *m* shoot, sucker
barbullar *tr & intr* to blabber
barca *f* small boat; bark
barcia *f* chaff
barco *m* boat, ship; **barco de carga** cargo boat; **barco náufrago** shipwreck
barchi·lón -lona *mf* (Ecuad, Peru) nurse, orderly; (Arg, Bol, Peru) quack
barda *f* thatch; bard, horse armor
bardana *f* burdock
bardar *tr* to thatch; (*un caballo*) to bard
bardo *m* bard
bargueño *m* carved inlaid secretary
bario *m* barium
barjuleta *f* haversack
barloventear *intr* to wander around; to turn to windward
barlovento *m* windward
bar·niz *m* (*pl* **-nices**) varnish; (*de la loza, la porcelana, etc.*) glaze; gloss, polish; (*conocimientos superficiales*) smattering; (aer) dope
barnizar **§60** *tr* to varnish
barómetro *m* barometer; **barómetro aneroide** aneroid barometer
barón *m* baron
baronesa *f* baroness
barquero *m* boatman
barquilla *f* (naut) log; (naut) log chip; (aer) nacelle
barquillero *m* waffle iron; harbor boatman
barquillo *m* cone; waffle
barquín *m* bellows
barra *f* bar; (*de dinamita*) stick; (*en el tribunal*) bar, railing; **barra colectora** (elec) bus bar; **barra de labios** or **para los labios** lipstick; **barra imantada** bar magnet; **barras paralelas** (sport) parallel bars
barrabasada *f* (coll) fiendish prank, mean trick
barraca *f* cabin, hut; cottage; (Am) storage shed
barracón *m* barracks; fair booth
barragana *f* concubine
barranca *f* gorge, ravine, gully
barranco *m* gorge, ravine, gully; difficulty, obstruction; (Am) cliff, precipice
barrar *tr* to daub, to smear
barrear *tr* to barricade; to bar shut
barredera *f* street sweeper
barre·dor -dora *mf* sweeper; **barredora de alfombras** carpet sweeper; **barredora de nieve** snowplow
barredura *f* sweeping; **barreduras** sweepings
barremi·nas *m* (*pl* **-nas**) mine sweeper
barrena *f* auger, drill, gimlet; (*espiga para taladrar*) bit; (aer) spin; **barrena picada** (aer) tail spin; **entrar en barrena** (aer) to go into a spin
barrenar *tr* to drill; (*un buque*) to scuttle; to blast; to upset, to frustrate; to violate
barrende·ro -ra *mf* sweeper
barreno *m* large drill; drill hole; blast

hole; pride, vanity; (Chile) mania, pet idea; **dar barreno a** (*un buque*) to scuttle
barreño *m* earthen dishpan
barrer *tr* to sweep, to sweep away; to graze || *intr* to sweep; **barrer hacia dentro** to look out for oneself
barrera *f* barrier; barricade; (mil) barrage; crockery cupboard; tollgate; (rr) crossing gate; (taur) fence around inside of ring; (taur) first row of seats; **barrera de arrecifes** barrier reef; **barrera de paso a nivel** (rr) crossing gate
barriada *f* district, quarter
barrica *f* cask, barrel
barriga *f* belly; (*de una vasija, una pared, etc.*) bulge
barri•gón -gona or **barrigu•do -da** *adj* big-bellied
barril *m* barrel
barrilero *m* cooper, barrel maker
barrio *m* ward, quarter; suburb; **barrio bajo** slums; **barrio comercial** shopping district, business district; **el otro barrio** the other world; **estar vestido de barrio** (coll) to be dressed in house clothes
barro *m* mud; clay; earthenware; pimple; (coll) money; (Arg, Urug) blunder
barro•co -ca *adj & m* baroque
barro•so -sa *adj* muddy; pimply
barrote *m* heavy bar; bolt; cross brace
barruntar *tr* to guess; to sense
barrunto *m* guess, conjecture; sign, token, foreboding
bartola *f* (coll) belly; **a la bartola** (coll) lazily
bartolina *f* (CAm, W-I) jail, dungeon
bártulos *mpl* household tools; **liar los bártulos** (coll) to pack up one's belongings
barullo *m* confusion, tumult
basar *tr* to base; to build || *ref* — **basarse en** to base one's judgment on, to rely on
basca *f* nausea, squeamishness; (coll) fit of temper, tantrum
basco•so -sa *adj* nauseated, squeamish
báscula *f* scales; platform scale
base *f* base; basis; **a base de** on the basis of
bási•co -ca *adj* basic
Basilea *f* Basle, Basel
basílica *f* basilica
basilisco *m* basilisk; **estar hecho un basilisco** (coll) to be in a rage
basquear *intr* to be nauseated
bastante *adj* enough || *adv* enough; fairly, rather || *m* enough
bastar *intr* to be enough, to suffice; to abound, be more than enough || *ref* to be self-sufficient
bastardilla *f* italics
bastar•do -da *adj & mf* bastard
bastidor *m* frame; stretcher; (theat) wing; **entre bastidores** behind the scenes
bástilla *f* hem
bastillar *tr* to hem
bas•to -ta *adj* coarse, rough; uncouth || *m* packsaddle; (*naipe*) club; **el basto** the ace of clubs
bastón *m* stick, staff; cane, walking stick; baton; **bastón de esquiar** ski pole or stick
bastoncillo *m* small stick; (*de la retina*) rod
bastonear *tr* to cane, to beat
basura *f* sweepings; rubbish, litter, refuse; horse manure
basurero *m* trash can; rubbish dump; rubbish collector
bata *f* smock; dressing gown, wrapper; **bata de baño** bathrobe
batacazo *m* thud, bump
bataclán *m* (Cuba) burlesque show
bataclana *f* (Cuba) showgirl, stripteaser
batahola *f* (coll) racket, hubbub
batalla *f* battle; (*de un vehículo*) wheel base; (*de la silla de montar*) seat; (paint) battle piece; **batalla campal** pitched battle; **librar batalla** to do battle
batallar *intr* to battle, to fight; to hesitate, to waver
bata•llón -llona *adj* (*cuestión*) controversial, moot || *m* battalion
batata *f* sweet potato; (Arg) timidity
bate *m* baseball bat
batea *f* tray; flat-bottomed boat; (rr) flatcar
bateador *m* batter
batear *tr & intr* to bat
batel *m* small boat
batelero *m* boatman
batería *f* battery; footlights; **batería de cocina** kitchen utensils
bati•do -da *adj* (*camino*) beaten; (*tejido*) moiré || *m* batter; milk shake; (rad) beat || *f* battue; combing, search
batidor *m* beater; scout, ranger; **batidor de huevos** egg beater; **batidor de oro** goldbeater
batidora *f* beater, mixer
batiente *m* jamb; (*hoja de puerta*) leaf, door; (*de piano*) damper; wash, place where surf breaks
batihoja *m* goldbeater; sheet-metal worker
batimiento *m* beating; (phys) beat
batín *m* smoking jacket
batintín *m* Chinese gong
batir *tr* to beat; to batter, beat down; (*las alas*) to flap; (*manos*) to clap; (*las olas*) to ply; **batir tiendas** (mil) to strike camp
bato *m* simpleton, rustic
batuque *m* (Arg) uproar, rumpus, jamboree; **armar un batuque** (Arg) to raise a rumpus
baturrillo *m* hodgepodge
batuta *f* (mus) baton; **llevar la batuta** (coll) to boss the show
baúl *m* trunk; **baúl mundo** large trunk; **baúl ropero** wardrobe trunk
bauprés *m* bowsprit
bautismo *m* baptism; **bautismo de aire** first flight
bautista *adj* Baptist || *mf* Baptist; baptizer; **el Bautista** John the Baptist
bautisterio *m* baptistery

bautizar §60 *tr* to baptize; (*el vino*) (coll) to water
bautizo *m* baptism; christening party
báva•ro -ra *adj & mf* Bavarian
Baviera *f* Bavaria
baya *f* berry
bayeta *f* baize
ba•yo -ya *adj* bay || *m* bay horse || *f* see **baya**
bayoneta *f* bayonet
bayonetear *tr* (Am) to bayonet
baza *f* trick; **meter baza en** (coll) to butt into
bazar *m* bazaar
ba•zo -za *adj* yellowish-brown || *m* yellowish brown; spleen || *f* see **baza**
bazofia *f* refuse, offal, garbage
bazuca *f* bazooka
bazucar §73 *tr* to stir, to shake; to tamper with
be *m* baa
beata *f* lay sister
beatería *f* cant, hypocrisy
beatificar §73 *tr* to beatify
beatísi•mo -ma *adj* most holy
bea•to -ta *adj* blessed; pious, devout; bigoted, prudish || *mf* beatified person; devout person; bigot; (coll) churchgoer || *f* see **beata**
bebé *m* baby; doll
bebede•ro -ra *adj* (archaic) drinkable || *m* watering place; (Col, Ecuad, Mex) watering trough
bebedi•zo -za *adj* drinkable || *m* potion, philter
bebe•dor -dora *adj* drinking || *mf* drinker; hard drinker
beber *m* drink, drinking || *tr & intr* to drink; **beber de** or **en** to drink out of || *ref* to drink, drink up; (*p.ej., un libro*) to drink in
bebestible *adj* drinkable || *m* drink
bebezón *f* (Col) drunk, spree
bebible *adj* drinkable
bebi•do -da *adj* tipsy, unsteady || *f* drink
bebistrajo *m* (coll) dose, mixture
beborrotear *intr* (coll) to tipple
beca *f* scholarship, fellowship; (*de los colegiales*) sash
becacín *m* snipe, whole snipe
becacina *f* snipe, great snipe
becada *f* woodcock
beca•rio -ria *mf* scholar, fellow
becerra *f* snapdragon
becerrillo *m* calfskin
bece•rro -rra *mf* yearling calf || *m* calfskin || *f* see **becerra**
becuadro *m* (mus) natural sign
bedel *m* beadle
befa *f* jeer, flout, scoff
befar *tr* to jeer at, to scoff at || *intr* (*un caballo*) to move the lips
be•fo -fa *adj* blobber-lipped; knock-kneed || *m* (*de animal*) lip || *f* see **befa**
béisbol *m* baseball
bejuco *m* cane, liana
beldad *f* beauty
beldar §2 *tr* to winnow
belén *m* crèche; (coll) bedlam, confusion; (coll) madhouse; (coll) gossip || **Belén** Bethlehem
bel•fo -fa *adj* (*labio*) blobber; blobber-lipped || *m* (*de animal*) lip; blobber lip
belga *adj & mf* Belgian
Bélgica *f* Belgium
bélgi•co -ca *adj* Belgian || *f* see **Bélgica**
belicista *mf* warmonger
béli•co -ca *adj* warlike
belico•so -sa *adj* bellicose
beligerante *adj & mf* belligerent
belitre *adj* low, mean || *m* scoundrel
bella•co -ca *adj* cunning, sly; wicked || *mf* scoundrel
bellaquear *intr* to cheat, be crooked; (SAm) to be stubborn; (SAm) to rear
bellaquería *f* cunning, slyness; wickedness
belleza *f* beauty; **belleza exótica** glamour girl
be•llo -lla *adj* beautiful, fair
bellota *f* acorn; carnation bud
bem•bo -ba *adj* (Am) thick-lipped; (Mex) simple, silly || *mf* (*persona*) (Am) thicklips
bemol *adj & m* (mus) flat; **tener bemoles** (coll) to be a tough job
bencina *f* benzine
bendecir §11 *tr* to bless; to consecrate; **bendecir la mesa** to say grace
bendición *f* benediction, blessing; godsend; (*en la mesa*) grace; **bendiciones** wedding ceremony; **echar la bendición a** (coll) to have nothing more to do with
bendi•to -ta *adj* blessed, saintly; simple, silly; happy; (*agua*) holy; **como el pan bendito** (coll) as easy as pie || *m* simple-minded soul
benedícite *m* grace; **rezar el benedícite** to say grace
benedicti•no -na *adj & mf* Benedictine || *m* benedictine
beneficencia *f* beneficence; charity, welfare; social service
beneficia•do -da *mf* person or charity receiving the proceeds of a benefit performance
beneficiar *tr* to benefit; (*la tierra*) to cultivate; (*una mina*) to work, to exploit; (*minerales*) to process, to reduce; (*una región del país*) to serve; to season; (Am) to slaughter || *ref* — **beneficiarse de** to take advantage of
beneficia•rio -ria *mf* beneficiary
beneficio *m* benefit; profit, gain, yield; (*de una mina*) exploitation; smelting, ore reduction; benefit performance; **a beneficio de** for the benefit of; on the strength of
beneficio•so -sa *adj* beneficial, profitable
benéfi•co -ca *adj* charitable, benevolent
beneméri•to -ta *adj & mf* worthy; **benemérito de la patria** national hero
beneplácito *m* approval, consent
benevolencia *f* benevolence
benévo•lo -la *adj* benevolent, kind-hearted
bengala *f* Bengal light; (aer) flare

benignidad *f* benignity, mildness, kindness; (*del tiempo*) mildness
benig•no -na *adj* benign, mild, kind; (*tiempo*) clement, mild
benjamín *m* baby (*the youngest child*)
beodez *f* drunkenness
beo•do -da *adj & mf* drunk
berbi•quí *m* (*pl* **-quíes**) brace; **berbiquí y barrena** brace and bit
berenjena *f* eggplant
berenjenal *m* eggplant patch; (coll) predicament, jam, fix
bergante *m* scoundrel, rascal
bergantín *m* (naut) brig; **bergantín goleta** (naut) brigantine
berilio *m* beryllium
berkelio *m* berkelium
berli•nés -nesa *adj* Berlin || *mf* Berliner
bermejear *intr* to turn bright red; to look bright red
berme•jo -ja *adj* vermilion, bright-red
berme•jón -jona *adj* red, reddish
bermellón *m* vermilion
berrear *intr* to bellow, to low; to bawl, yowl
berrenchín *m* (coll) rage, tantrum
berrido *m* bellow; scream, yowl
berrín *m* (coll) touchy person, cross child
berrinche *m* (coll) tantrum, conniption
berro *m* water cress
berza *f* cabbage
berzal *m* cabbage patch
besalamano *m* announcement, written in the third person and marked B.L.M. (*kisses your hand*)
besamanos *m* levee, reception at court; throwing kisses
besar *tr* to kiss; (coll) to graze || *ref* (coll) to bump heads together
beso *m* kiss; **beso sonado** buss
bestia *adj* stupid || *mf* dunce || *f* beast; **bestia de carga** beast of burden
bestial *adj* beastly; (coll) terrific
besucar §73 *tr & intr* (coll) to keep on kissing
besu•cón -cona *adj* (coll) kissing || *mf* (coll) kisser
besuquear *tr & intr* (coll) to keep on kissing
betabel *m* (Mex) beet
betún *m* bitumen, pitch; shoe polish
bezo *m* blubber lip; proud flesh
bezu•do -da *adj* thick-lipped
biberón *m* nursing bottle
Biblia *f* Bible
bíbli•co -ca *adj* Biblical
biblióﬁ•lo -la *mf* bibliophile
bibliografía *f* bibliography
bibliógra•fo -fa *mf* bibliographer
biblioteca *f* library; **biblioteca de consulta** reference library; **biblioteca de préstamo** lending library
biblioteca•rio -ria *mf* librarian
bibliotecnia *f* bookmaking
bicameral *adj* bicameral
bicarbonato *m* bicarbonate
bicicleta *f* bicycle
bichero *m* boat hook
bicho *m* bug, insect; vermin; animal; fighting bull; simpleton; brat; **bicho viviente** (coll) living soul; **mal bicho** scoundrel; ferocious bull
bidón *m* (*bote, lata*) can; (*tonel de metal*) drum
biela *f* connecting rod
bielda *f* winnowing rack; winnowing
bieldar *tr* to winnow
bieldo *m* winnowing pitch rake
bien *adv* well; readily; very; indeed; **ahora bien** now then; **bien como** just as; **bien que** although; **más bien** rather; somewhat; **no bien** as soon as; scarcely || *s* welfare; property; darling; **bienes** wealth, riches, possessions; **bienes de fortuna** worldly possessions; **bienes dotales** dower; **bienes inmuebles** real estate; **bienes muebles** personal property; **bienes raíces** real estate; **bienes relictos** estate; **bienes semovientes** livestock; **bien público** commonweal; **en bien de** for the sake of
bienal *adj* biennial
bienama•do -da *adj* dearly beloved
bienandanza *f* happiness, prosperity
bienaventura•do -da *adj* happy, blissful; blessed; simple
bienaventuranza *f* happiness, bliss; blessedness
bienestar *m* well-being, welfare
bienhabla•do -da *adj* well-spoken
bienhada•do -da *adj* fortunate, lucky
bienhe•chor -chora *adj* beneficent || *m* benefactor || *f* benefactress
bienintenciona•do -da *adj* well-meaning
bienio *m* biennium
bienquerencia *f* affection, fondness
bienquistar *tr* to bring together, reconcile
bienvenida *f* safe arrival; welcome; **dar la bienvenida a** to welcome
bienveni•do -da *adj* welcome || *f* see **bienvenida**
bienvivir *intr* to live in comfort; to live decently, properly
bif•tec *m* (*pl* **-tecs**) beefsteak
bifurcar §73 *ref* to branch, to fork
bigamia *f* bigamy
bíga•mo -ma *adj* bigamous || *mf* bigamist
bigornia *f* two-horn anvil
bigote *m* mustache; **bigotes** (*del gato*) whiskers; **tener bigotes** (coll) to have a mind of one's own
bilingüe *adj* bilingual
bilis *f* bile; **descargar la bilis** to vent one's spleen
billar *m* billiards; billiard table; billiard room; **billar romano** pinball
billete *m* ticket; note, bill; **billete de abono** season ticket; commutation ticket; **billete de banco** bank note; **billete de ida y vuelta** round-trip ticket; **billete kilométrico** mileage ticket; **medio billete** half fare
billetero *m* billfold; ticket agent
billón *m* (U.S.A.) trillion; (Brit) billion
bimotor *adj* twin-motor || *m* twin-motor plane
biofísi•co -ca *adj* biophysical || *f* biophysics

biografía *f* biography
biógra•fo -fa *mf* biographer
biología *f* biology
biólo•go -ga *mf* biologist
biombo *m* folding screen
bióxido *m* dioxide
bioquími•co -ca *adj* biochemical || *mf* biochemist || *f* biochemistry
bipartición *f* fission, splitting
biplano *m* biplane
biplaza *m* (aer) two-seater
birimbao *m* jews'-harp
birlar *tr* to knock down, to shoot down; (coll) to outwit; **birlar algo a alguien** (coll) to snitch something from someone
birlocha *f* kite
Birmania *f* Burma
birma•no -na *adj & mf* Burmese
birreta *f* biretta, red biretta
birrete *m* mortarboard, academic cap
bis *interj* encore! || *m* encore
bisabue•lo -la *mf* great-grandparent || *m* great-grandfather || *f* great-grandmother
bisagra *f* hinge
bisar *tr* to repeat
bisbisar *tr* (coll) to mutter, mumble
bisecar §73 *tr* to bisect
bisel *m* bevel edge
biselar *tr* to bevel
bisies•to -ta *adj* leap
bismuto *m* bismuth
bisnie•to -ta *mf* great-grandchild || *m* great-grandson || *f* great-granddaughter
biso•jo -ja *adj* squint-eyed, cross-eyed
bisonte *m* bison; buffalo
biso•ño -ña *adj* green, inexperienced || *mf* greenhorn, rookie
bisté *m* or **bistec** *m* beefsteak
bisun•to -ta *adj* dirty, greasy
bisutería *f* costume jewelry
bitácora *f* binnacle
bitoque *m* bung; (CAm) sewer; (Mex) spigot
Bizancio Byzantium
bizanti•no -na *adj & mf* Byzantine
bizarría *f* gallantry, bravery; magnanimity
biza•rro -rra *adj* gallant, brave; magnanimous
bizcar §73 *tr* to wink || *intr* to squint
biz•co -ca *adj* squint-eyed, cross-eyed
bizcocho *m* biscuit; cake, sponge cake; hardtack; bisque
bizma *f* poultice
bizmar *tr* to poultice
biznie•to -ta *mf* var of **bisnieto**
bizquear *intr* to squint
bizquera *f* squint
blanca *f* steel blade; **sin blanca** (coll) penniless
blanca•zo -za *adj* (coll) whitish
blan•co -ca *adj* white; (*tez*) fair; (*fuerza*) water; (*arma*) steel; (*cobarde*) (coll) yellow; blank || *mf* (*persona*) white; (coll) coward || *m* (*color*) white; blank; target; aim, object; interval; white heat; blank form; **dar en el blanco** to hit the mark; **en blanco** (*hoja*) blank; **hacer blanco** to hit the mark; **quedarse en blanco** to not get the point; to be disappointed || *f* see **blanca**
blancor *m* whiteness
blancura *f* whiteness; purity
blancuz•co -ca *adj* whitish; dirty-white
blandear *tr* to persuade; to brandish || *intr & ref* to yield, give in
blandengue *adj* (coll) soft, colorless
blandir §1 *tr, intr & ref* to brandish
blan•do -da *adj* bland, soft; indulgent; flabby; sensual; (coll) cowardly; (*ojos*) (coll) tender
blandón *m* wax candle; candlestick
blandura *f* blandness, softness; tolerance; flabbiness; sensuality; flattery; mild weather; (coll) cowardice
blanquear *tr* to whiten, bleach; to blanch; to whitewash; to tin || *intr* to turn white
blanqueci•no -na *adj* whitish
blanqui•llo -lla *adj* white, whitish || *m* (Guat, Mex) egg; (Chile, Peru) white peach
blanqueci•no -na *adj* whitish
blasfemar *intr* to blaspheme, to curse
blasfemia *f* blasphemy
blasfe•mo -ma *adj* blasphemous || *mf* blasphemer
blasón *m* (*ciencia de los escudos de armas; escudo de armas*) heraldry; (heral) charge; (fig) glory, honor
blasonar *tr* to emblazon; (fig) to emblazon, to extol || *intr* to boast; **blasonar de** to boast of being
bledo *m* straw; **no me importa un bledo** or **no se me da un bledo de ello** that doesn't matter a rap to me
blindaje *m* armor; (elec) shield
blindar *tr* to armor, armor-plate; (elec) to shield
b.l.m. *abbr* **besa la mano**
bloc *m* (*pl* **bloques**) pad
blon•do -da *adj* blond, fair, flaxen, light; (Arg) curly || *f* blond lace
bloque *m* block; (*de papel*) pad; **bloque de hormigón** concrete block
bloquear *tr* to blockade; (*un coche, un tren*) to brake; (*créditos*) to freeze
bloqueo *m* blockade; (*de crédito*) freezing; **bloqueo vertical** (telv) vertical hold
b.l.p. *abbr* **besa los pies**
blusa *f* blouse, smock; (*de mujer*) shirtwaist; (Col) jacket
boardilla *f* dormer window; garret
boato *m* show, pomp
bobada *f* folly, piece of folly
bobalías *mf* (coll) simpleton, dunce
bobali•cón -cona *adj* simple, silly || *mf* simpleton, nitwit
bobear *intr* to talk nonsense; to dawdle, loiter around
bobería *f* folly, nonsense
bóbilis: de bóbilis (coll) free, for nothing; (coll) without effort
bobina *f* bobbin; (elec) coil; **bobina de chispas** spark coil; **bobina de encendido** ignition coil, spark coil; **bobina de sintonía** tuning coil
bobinar *tr* to wind
bo•bo -ba *adj* simple, foolish, stupid || *mf* simpleton, fool || *m* (archaic) clown, jester

boca *f* mouth; speech; taste, flavor; (*del estómago*) pit; **a boca de jarro** immoderately; at close range; **boca de agua** hydrant; **boca de dragón** (bot) snapdragon; **boca de riego** hydrant; **buscarle a uno la boca** to draw someone out; **decir con la boca chica** (coll) to offer as a mere formality; **no decir esta boca es mía** (coll) to not say a word
bocacalle *f* street entrance
boca•caz *m* (*pl* **-caces**) spillway
bocadillo *m* tape, ribbon; snack, bite; farmer's snack in the field; sandwich
bocadito *m* little bit; (Cuba) cigarillo (*cigaret wrapped in tobacco*)
bocado *m* bite, morsel; bit; **bocado de Adán** Adam's apple; **no tener para un bocado** (coll) to not have a cent
bocal *m* narrow-mouthed pitcher; (*de un puerto*) narrows
bocallave *f* keyhole
bocamanga *f* cuff, wristband
bocanada *f* (*de líquido*) swallow; (*de humo*) puff; (*de viento*) gust; boasting
bocartear *tr* to crush, to stamp
bocera *f* smear on lips
boceto *m* sketch, outline; wax model, clay model
bocina *f* horn, trumpet; auto horn; phonograph horn; (Am) ear trumpet
bocio *m* goiter
bocoy *m* large barrel
bocha *f* bowling ball
boche *m* small hole in ground for boys' game; (Ven) slight, snub
bochinche *m* uproar, tumult, row
bochorno *m* sultry weather; blush, embarrassment, shame
bochorno•so -sa *adj* sultry, stuffy; embarrassing, shameful
boda *f* marriage, wedding; **bodas de Camacho** banquet, lavish feast
bodega *f* wine cellar; dock warehouse; granary; (*de nave*) hold; (coll) cellar; (*hombre que bebe mucho*) (coll) tank; (Am) grocery store
bodegón *m* hash house, beanery; saloon; still life
bodegue•ro -ra *mf* cellarer; (Am) grocer
bodijo *m* (coll) unequal match; (coll) simple wedding
bodoque *m* lump; (coll) dunce, dolt; (Mex) bump, lump
bodoquera *f* peashooter
bóer *mf* Boer
bofe *m* (coll) lung; (P-R) cinch, snap; **echar el bofe** or **los bofes** (coll) to drudge, to grind; **bofes** lights (*of sheep, etc.*)
bofetada *f* slap in the face
boga *mf* rower || *f* vogue, fashion; rowing
bogar **§44** *intr* to row
bogavante *m* lobster
bohardilla *f* dormer window; garret
bohe•mio -mia *adj & mf* Bohemian
bohío *m* (Am) hut, shack
boicotear *tr* to boycott
boicoteo *m* boycott, boycotting
boina *f* beret
boj *m* boxwood
boja *f* southernwood
bojar *tr* to measure the perimeter of; (*el cuero*) to scrape clean || *intr* to measure
bola *f* ball; marble; bowling; shoe polish; shoeshine; (cards) slam; lie, deceit; (Mex) brawl, riot; **bola de alcanfor** moth ball; **bola de cristal** crystal ball; **bola de nieve** snowball; **bola rompedora** wrecking ball; **bolas** Gaucho lasso tipped with balls; **dejar que ruede la bola** to let things take their course; **raspar la bola** (Chile) to clear out, beat it
bolada *f* (*de una bola*) throw; (Am) luck, opportunity; (Arg) billiard stroke; (Chile) dainty, tidbit; (Guat, Mex) lie, fib
bolazo *m* hit with a ball; **de bolazo** (coll) hurriedly, right away; (Mex) at random
bolchevique *adj & mf* Bolshevik
bolchevismo *m* Bolshevism
boleada *f* (Arg) hunting with bolas; (Mex) shoeshine; (Peru) flunking
bolear *tr* (coll) to throw; (Arg) to catch with bolas; (*zapatos*) (Mex) to shine; (SAm) to kick out, to flunk || *intr* to play for fun; to lie; to boast || *ref* (Arg, Urug) to rear and fall backwards; (Arg, Urug) to upset; (Arg, Urug) to blush
bole•ro -ra *mf* bolero dancer || *m* bolero (*dance; music; jacket*); (Mex) bootblack || *f* bowling alley; **bolera encespada** bowling green
boleta *f* pass, permit, admission ticket; (mil) billet; (Am) ballot
boletería *f* (Am) ticket office
boletín *m* bulletin; ticket; form; press release
boleto *m* (Am) ticket
boliche *m* bowling; bowling alley; (SAm) hash house
bólido *m* fireball, bolide
bolígrafo *m* ball-point pen
bolillo *m* bobbin for making lace; frame for stiffening lace cuffs
Bolivia *f* Bolivia
bolivia•no -na *adj & mf* Bolivian
bolo *m* ninepin, tenpin; dunce, blockhead; (*de escalera*) newel; (cards) slam; **bolos** bowling, ninepins, tenpins; **jugar a los bolos** to bowl
Bolonia *f* Bologna
bolsa *f* purse, pocketbook; pouch; stock exchange, stock market; (*en el vestido*) bag, pucker; grant, award; **bolsa de agua caliente** hot-water bottle; **bolsa de hielo** ice bag; **bolsa de trabajo** employment bureau; **hacer bolsa** (*un vestido*) to bag; **jugar a la bolsa** to play the market
bolsear *tr* (Arg, Bol, Urug) to jilt; (Am) to pick the pocket of; (Chile) to sponge on
bolsillo *m* pocket; purse, pocketbook
bolsista *m* broker, stockbroker; (CAm, Mex) pickpocket

bolso *m* purse, pocketbook; **bolso de mano** handbag

bollo *m* bun, roll; bump, lump; dent; (*en un vestido*) puff; (*en adorno de tapicería*) tuft; **bollo de crema** cream puff

bomba *f* pump; bomb; fire engine; lamp globe; high hat; firecracker; soap bubble; bombshell; **a prueba de bombas** bombproof; **bomba atómica** atomic bomb; **bomba cohete** rocket bomb; **bomba de hidrógeno** hydrogen bomb; **bomba de incendios** fire engine; **bomba de profundidad** depth bomb; **bomba de sentina** bilge pump; **bomba rompedora** blockbuster; **bomba volante** buzz bomb; **caer como una bomba** (coll) to fall like a bombshell; (coll) to burst in unexpectedly

bombachas *fpl* loose-fitting baggy trousers

bombardear *tr & intr* to bomb; to bombard; **bombardear en picado** to dive-bomb

bombardeo *m* bombing; bombarding; **bombardeo en picado** dive bombing

bombardero *m* bomber; bombardier

bomba-reloj *f* time bomb

bombazo *m* bomb explosion; bomb hit; bomb damage

bombear *tr* to bomb; to ballyhoo, to puff up; (Am) to pump; (SAm) to reconnoiter; (Col) to fire, dismiss ‖ *ref* to camber, bulge

bombero *m* fireman; pumpman

bombilla *f* bulb, light bulb; lamp chimney; (Am) tube for sucking up maté; **bombilla de destello** flash bulb

bombillo *m* trap, stench trap; (naut) pump

bombista *m* lamp maker; (*el que da bombos*) (coll) booster

bom•bo -ba *adj* (coll) astounded, stunned; (W-I) lukewarm ‖ *m* bass drum; ballyhoo; (naut) barge, lighter; **dar bombo a** (coll) to ballyhoo, puff up; **irse al bombo** (Arg) to fail ‖ *f* see **bomba**

bombón *m* bonbon, candy

bombona *f* carboy

bombonera *f* candy box

bona•chón -chona *adj* (coll) good-natured, kind, simple

bonancible *adj* (*tiempo*) fair; (*mar*) calm; (*viento*) moderate

bonanza *f* fair weather, calm seas; prosperity, boom; rich ore pocket

bona•zo -za *adj* (coll) kind-hearted

bondad *f* kindness; favor; **tener la bondad de** to have the kindness to

bondado•so -sa *adj* kind, generous

bonete *m* cap, hat; candy bowl

boniato *m* sweet potato

bonificar §73 *tr* to improve; to give a discount on

boni•to -ta *adj* pretty, nice; pretty good

bono *m* bond; food voucher

boñiga *f* manure, cow dung

boqueada *f* gasp of death

boquear *tr* to pronounce, utter ‖ *intr* to gasp

boquerel *m* nozzle

boquete *m* gap, breach, opening

boquiabier•to -ta *adj* open-mouthed

boquian•cho -cha *adj* wide-mouthed

boquiangos•to -ta *adj* narrow-mouthed

boquihundi•do -da *adj* hollow-mouthed

boquilla *f* (*de instrumento de viento*) mouthpiece; (*de pipa*) stem; (*de cigarro*) tip; (*de aparato de alumbrado*) burner; cigar holder, cigarette holder; (*de manguera*) nozzle; opening in irrigation canal; opening at bottom of trouser leg

boquirro•to -ta *adj* (coll) garrulous

boquiverde *adj* (coll) obscene, smutty

bórax *m* borax

borbollar or **borbollear** *intr* to bubble up

borbollón *m* bubbling; **a borbollones** impetuously

borborigmos *mpl* rumbling of the bowels

borbotar *intr* to bubble up, bubble over

borce•guí *m* (*pl* **-guíes**) high shoe

borda *f* hut; (naut) gunwale; **arrojar, echar** or **tirar por la borda** to throw overboard

bordada *f* (naut) tack; **dar bordadas** (naut) to tack; to pace to and fro

bordado *m* embroidery

bordadura *f* embroidery

bordar *tr* to embroider

borde *m* border, edge; fringe; rim; **borde de la acera** curb; **borde del mar** seaside

bordear *tr* to border ‖ *intr* to go on the edge; (naut) to tack

bordo *m* (naut) board; (naut) side; (naut) tack; (Guat, Mex) dam, dike; **a bordo** (naut) on board; **al bordo** (naut) alongside; **de alto bordo** seagoing; distinguished, important

bordón *m* (*de tambor*) snare; pilgrim's staff; pet word; burden, refrain

bordonear *intr* to grope along with a stick; to go around begging

borgoña *m* Burgundy (*wine*) ‖ **la Borgoña** Burgundy

borgo•ñón -ñona *adj & mf* Burgundian

boricua or **borinque•ño -ña** *adj & mf* Puerto Rican

borla *f* tassel; powder puff; **tomar la borla** to take a higher degree, to take the doctor's degree

borne *m* binding post; (*de la lanza*) tip

bornear *tr* to bend, to twist; (*sillares pesados*) to set in place ‖ *intr* to swing at anchor ‖ *ref* to warp

borra *f* fuzz, nap, lint

borrachera *f* drunkenness; spree, binge; great exaltation; (coll) piece of folly; **pegarse una borrachera** to go on a binge

borrachín *m* drunkard

borra•cho -cha *adj* drunk; (*habitualmente*) drinking ‖ *mf* drunkard

borrador *m* blotter, day book; rough draft; (Am) eraser

borradura *f* striking out, scratching out

borraj *m* borax

borrajear *tr & intr* to scribble; to doodle
borrar *tr* to scratch out, cross out; to erase, rub out; to darken, obscure; to blot, to smear
borrasca *f* storm, tempest; upset, setback
borrasco•so -sa *adj* stormy
borregos *mpl* (coll) fleecy clouds
borrica *f* she-ass; (coll) stupid woman
borrico *m* ass, donkey; sawhorse; (coll) stupid fellow, ass
borricón *m* or **borricote** *m* (coll) drudge
borrón *m* blot; rough draft; blemish; (fig) blot, stain
borronear *tr* to scribble
borro•so -sa *adj* blurred, smudgy, fuzzy; muddy, thick
boruca *f* noise, clamor, uproar
borujo *m* lump, clump
boscaje *m* woodland; (paint) woodland scene
bosque *m* forest, woodland; **bosque maderable** timberland
bosquejar *tr* to sketch, to outline; to make a rough model of
bosquejo *m* sketch, outline; rough model
bostezar **§60** *intr* to yawn, gape
bostezo *m* yawn, yawning
bota *f* shoe, boot; leather wine bag; liquid measure (*125 gallons or 516 liters*); **bota de agua** gum boot; **bota de montar** riding boot; **ponerse las botas** (coll) to hit the jack pot, come out on top
botador *m* boat pole; punch, nailset
botadura *f* launching
botafuego *m* (coll) hothead, firebrand
botalón *m* (naut) boom; **botalón de foque** (naut) jib boom
botáni•co -ca *adj* botanical || *mf* botanist || *f* botany
botanista *mf* botanist
botar *tr* to throw, hurl; to throw away, throw out; (*un buque*) to launch; (*el timón*) to shift; (Am) to fire, dismiss; (Am) to squander || *intr* to jump; to bounce || *ref* (*un caballo*) to buck
botarate *m* madcap, wild man; (Am) spendthrift
bote *m* boat, small boat; can, jar, pot; bounce; blow, thrust; (Mex) jug, jail; **bote de paso** ferryboat; **bote de porcelana** apothecary's jar; **bote de remos** rowboat; **bote de salvamento** or **bote salvavidas** lifeboat; **de bote en bote** (coll) crowded, jammed; **de bote y voleo** (coll) thoughtlessly
botella *f* bottle
botica *f* drug store; medicine
botica•rio -ria *mf* druggist, apothecary
botija *f* earthenware jug with short narrow neck; (CAm, Ven) hidden treasure; **decirle a uno botija verde** (Cuba) to let someone have it, to tell someone off; **estar hecho una botija** (*un niño*) (coll) to be cross and scream; (*una persona*) (coll) to be fat, be pudgy
botijo *m* earthenware jar with spout and handle
botín *m* booty, plunder, spoils; spat, legging; (Chile) sock
botina *f* shoe, high shoe
botiquín *m* medicine kit, first-aid kit; medicine chest; first-aid station; (Ven) saloon
bo•to -ta *adj* (*sin filo o punta*) blunt, dull; (fig) dull, slow || *m* leather bag || *f* see **bota**
botón *m* button; (*de mueble o puerta*) knob; (*de reloj de bolsillo*) stem; (bot) bud; (elec) push button; **botón de oro** buttercup; **botón de puerta** doorknob; **botones** *msg* bellboy, bellhop
bou *m* fishing with a dragnet between two boats
bóveda *f* dome, vault; crypt; (aut) cowl; **bóveda celeste** canopy of heaven
boxeador *m* boxer; (Mex) brass knuckles
boxear *intr* to box
boxeo *m* boxing
bóxer *m* brass knuckles
boxibalón *m* punching bag
boya *f* buoy; **boya salvavidas** life buoy
boyante *adj* buoyant; lucky, successful; (*que no cala lo que debe calar*) (naut) light
boyera or **boyeriza** *f* ox stable
boyerizo or **boyero** *m* ox driver
bozal *adj* simple, stupid; (*negro*) just brought in || *m* muzzle; head-harness bells; (Am) headstall
bozo *m* down on upper lip, lips, mouth; headstall
B.p. *abbr* **Bendición papal**
Br. *abbr* **bachiller**
bracear *intr* to swing the arms; to swim with overhead strokes; to struggle
brace•ro -ra *adj* arm, hand; thrown with the hand || *m* man who offers his arm to a lady; day laborer; **de bracero** arm in arm
bra•co -ca *adj* pug-nosed
braga *f* diaper, clout; hoisting rope; **bragas** panties, step-ins; breeches; **calzarse las bragas** (coll) to wear the pants
bragadura *f* crotch
braga•zas *m* (*pl* **-zas**) (coll) easy mark, henpecked fellow
braguero *m* (*para hernias*) truss; (*entrepiernas*) crotch
bragueta *f* fly
bragui•llas *m* (*pl* **-llas**) (coll) brat
brama *f* rut, mating, mating time
bramante *adj* bellowing, roaring || *m* packthread, twine
bramar *intr* to bellow, roar; (*el viento*) to howl; to rage, storm
bramido *m* bellow, roar; howling; raging
brasa *f* live coal, red-hot coal
brasero *m* brazier; (Col) bonfire; (Mex) hearth, fireplace
Brasil, el Brazil
brasile•ño -ña *adj & mf* Brazilian
bravata *f* bravado, bragging; **echar bravatas** to talk big

bravear *intr* to talk big, to four-flush
braveza *f* bravery; ferocity; (*de los elementos*) fury, violence
braví•o -a *adj* ferocious; wild, untamed, uncultivated; crude, unpolished; (*mar*) rough, wild; (*terreno*) rough, rugged
bra•vo -va *adj* (*valiente*) brave; fine, excellent; fierce, savage, wild; (*mar*) rough; magnificent; angry, mad; (*perro*) vicious; (*toro*) game; (coll) boasting; (*chili*) (coll) strong || *interj* bravo!
bravu•cón -cona *adj* (coll) four-flushing || *mf* (coll) fourflusher
bravura *f* bravery; fierceness; gameness; bravado, boasting
braza *f* fathom
brazada *f* stroke, pull (*with the arm*); **brazada de pecho** breast stroke
brazado *m* armful, armload
brazal *m* arm band; **brazal de luto** mourning band
brazalete *m* bracelet
brazo *m* arm; (*de animal*) foreleg; **a brazo partido** hand to hand (*i.e., without weapons*); **asidos del brazo** arm in arm; **brazo derecho** right-hand man; **brazos** hands, workmen; backers; **hecho un brazo de mar** dressed to kill
brea *f* tar, wood tar; calking substance; packing canvas; **brea seca** rosin
brear *tr* to annoy, mistreat, beat; to tar
brebaje *m* beverage, drink
brécol *m* or **brécoles** *mpl* broccoli
brecha *f* opening; (*en un muro*) breach; breakthrough
brega *f* fight, struggle, quarrel; trickery; drudgery
bregar §44 *intr* to strive, struggle, toil
breña *f*, **breñal** *m* or **breñar** *m* rocky thicket
bresca *f* honeycomb
Bretaña *f* Brittany; **la Gran Bretaña** Great Britain
brete *m* fetters, shackles; tight squeeze, fix
bretones *mpl* Brussels sprouts
breva *f* early fig; cinch, snap
breval *m* early-fig tree
breve *adj* brief, short; **en breve** shortly, soon
brevedad *f* brevity, shortness; **a la mayor brevedad** as soon as possible
brevete *m* note, mark
brezal *m* heath, moor
brezo *m* heath, heather
briba *f* loafing; **andar a la briba** to loaf around
bri•bón -bona *adj* loafing, crooked || *mf* loafer, crook
bribonada *f* loafing, crookedness
bribonear *intr* to loaf around, to be crooked
brida *f* bridle
brigada *f* brigade; gang, squad; warrant officer
brillante *adj* bright, brilliant, shining || *m* diamond, gem
brillantez *f* brilliance
brillar *intr* to shine; to sparkle
brillazón *f* (Arg, Bol, Urug) pampa mirage
brillo *m* brightness, brilliance; sparkle; **sacar brillo a** to shine
brillo•so -sa *adj* (*que brilla por el mucho uso*) shiny; (Am) shining, brilliant
brin *m* canvas
brincar §73 *tr* to bounce up and down; to skip, skip over || *intr* to jump, to leap; (coll) to be touchy, get angry easily
brinco *m* bounce; jump, leap; **en dos brincos** or **en un brinco** in an instant
brindador *m* toaster
brindar *tr* to invite; to offer; **brindar a uno con una cosa** to offer someone something || *intr* — **brindar a** or **por** to drink to, to toast || *ref* — **brindarse a** to offer to
brin•dis *m* (*pl* **-dis**) invitation, treat; toast
brío *m* spirit, enterprise; elegance; **cortar los bríos a** to cut the wings of
brio•so -sa *adj* spirited, lively, enterprising; elegant
brisa *f* breeze; residue of pressed grapes
brisera *f* or **brisero** *m* (Am) glass lamp shade (*for candles*)
británi•co -ca *adj* British, Britannic
brita•no -na *adj* British || *mf* Briton, Britisher
brizna *f* chip, particle; (Ven) drizzle
brl. *abbr* **barril**
broca *f* reel, spindle; drill, bit
brocado *m* brocade
brocal *m* (*de pozo*) curbstone; (*de bota*) mouthpiece; (*de banqueta*) (Mex) curb
brocamantón *m* diamond brooch
bróculi *m* broccoli
brocha *f* brush; loaded dice; **de brocha gorda** house (*painter*); (coll) crude, heavy-handed
brochada *f* stroke with a brush; rough sketch
brochazo *m* stroke with a brush
broche *m* clasp, clip, fastener; (*conjunto de dos piezas*) hook and eye; (Chile) paper clip; **broche de oro** punch line; **broche de presión** snap, catch; **broches** (Ecuad) cuff buttons
brocheta *f* skewer
broma *f* joke, jest; fun; shipworm; **bromas aparte** joking aside; **en broma** in fun, jokingly; **gastar una broma a** to play a joke on
bromear *intr & ref* to joke, jest; to have a good time
bromhídri•co -ca *adj* hydrobromic
bromista *adj* joking || *mf* joker
bromo *m* bromine
bromuro *m* bromide
bronca *f* (coll) row, quarrel; (coll) rough joke, poor joke; **armar una bronca** (coll) to start a row
bronce *m* bronze; **bronce de cañón** gun metal
broncea•do -da *adj* bronze; tanned, sunburned || *m* bronzing; bronze finish; tan, sunburn

broncear *tr, intr & ref* to bronze; to tan, sunburn
bron•co -ca *adj* coarse, rough; gruff, crude; (*voz*) harsh, hoarse || *f* see **bronca**
bronquitis *f* bronchitis
broquel *m* buckler, shield; (fig) shield
broqueta *f* skewer
brota *f* bud, shoot
brotadura *f* budding, sprouting; gushing; (*de la piel*) eruption, rash
brotar *tr* to bring forth, to produce || *intr* to bud, sprout; to gush; (*la piel*) to break out
brote *m* bud, shoot; outbreak; (*de petróleo*) gush, spurt
broza *f* (*maleza*) underbrush; (*hojas, ramas, cortezas*) brushwood; (*desperdicio*) trash, rubbish; printer's brush
bruces — **dar** or **caer de bruces** to fall on one's face
bruja *f* witch, sorceress; barn owl; (*mujer fea*) hag; (*mujer de mala vida*) prostitute; (W-I) spook
brujear *tr* (*bestias salvajes*) (Ven) to hunt || *intr* to practice witchcraft
brujería *f* witchcraft, sorcery, magic
brujo *m* sorcerer, wizard
brújula *f* (*flechilla*) magnetic needle; (*instrumento*) compass; (*agujero para la puntería*) sight; **perder la brújula** to lose one's touch
brujulear *tr* (*las cartas*) to uncover gradually; (coll) to suspect
brulote *m* fire ship; (Arg, Chile, Bol) vulgarity, insult
bruma *f* fog, mist
brumo•so -sa *adj* foggy, misty
bruñido *m* burnish, polish; burnishing
bruñir §12 *tr* to burnish, to polish; to put rouge on; (CAm) to annoy
brus•co -ca *adj* brusque, gruff; sudden; (*curva*) sharp
bruselas *fpl* tweezers || **Bruselas** Brussels
brusquedad *f* brusqueness, gruffness; suddenness; (*de una curva*) sharpness
brutal *adj* brutal; sudden; (coll) huge, terrific; (coll) stunning
brutalidad *f* brutality; stupidity; (coll) tremendous amount
bruteza *f* brutality; (archaic) roughness
bru•to -ta *adj* brute; rough, coarse; stupid; gross || *mf* (*persona*) brute; blockhead || *m* (*animal*) brute
bu *m* (*pl* **búes**) (coll) bugaboo; **hacer el bu a** (*coll*) to scare, frighten
bucear *intr* to dive, be a diver; to delve, search
buceo *m* diving
bucle *m* curl, lock
buche *m* (*de ave*) craw, crop, maw; (*de líquido*) mouthful; (*del vestido*) bag, pucker; (*para secretos*) bosom; (coll) belly; (Ecuad) high hat; (Guat, Mex) goiter; **sacar el buche a** (coll) to make (*someone*) open up
budín *m* pudding
buen *adj* var of **bueno,** used before masculine singular nouns
buenamente *adv* with ease; gladly, willingly; conveniently
buenaventura *f* fortune, good luck; (*adivinación*) fortune; **decirle a uno la buenaventura** to tell someone his fortune
bue•no -na *adj* good; kind; (*sano*) well; (*tiempo*) good, fine; **a buenas** willingly; **¡buena es ésa** (or **ésta**)! (coll) that's a good one; **de buenas a primeras** all of a sudden; from the start; **¿de dónde bueno?** (coll) where have you been?, what's new?
buey *m* ox, bullock, steer
búfa•lo -la *mf* buffalo
bufanda *f* muffler, scarf
bufar *intr* to snort
bufete *m* writing desk; law office; (*de un abogado*) clients; law practice; (Am) refreshment; (Col) bedpan; **abrir bufete** to open a law office
bufido *m* snort
bu•fo -fa *adj* comic; (Ven) spongy || *mf* buffoon
bu•fón -fona *adj* clownish || *m* clown, buffoon; jester; peddler
bufonada *f* buffoonery; sarcasm
bufonería *f* buffoonery; peddling
bufones•co -ca *adj* clownish; coarse, crude
bugui-bugui *m* boogie-woogie
buharda *f* dormer; dormer window; garret
buhardilla *f* dormer window; garret
buho *m* eagle owl; (coll) shy fellow
buhonería *f* peddler's kit; peddler's wares
buhonero *m* peddler, hawker
buitre *m* vulture
buje *m* axle box, bushing
bujería *f* gewgaw, trinket
bujía *f* candle; candlestick; candle power; (*de motor de explosión*) spark plug
bulbo *m* bulb
bulevar *m* boulevard
bulevardero *m* boulevardier, man about town
Bulgaria *f* Bulgaria
búlga•ro -ra *adj & mf* Bulgarian
bulto *m* bulk, volume; bust, statue; parcel, piece of baggage; bump, swelling; pillowcase; form, mass; **a bulto** broadly, by guess; **buscar el bulto a** (coll) to keep after; **de bulto** evident; **escurrir** or **huir el bulto** (coll) to duck
bulla *f* noise; crowd; loud argument
bullaje *m* crush, mob (*of people*)
bullanga *f* racket, disturbance
bullebulle *mf* (coll) busybody, bustler
bullicio *m* brawl, riot, uprising; (*rumor que hace mucha gente*) rumble
bullicio•so -sa *adj* brawling, riotous; rumbling || *mf* rioter
bullir §13 *tr* to move || *intr* to boil; to abound; to bustle, to hustle; to swarm; to move, to stir; (coll) to be restless || *ref* to move, to stir
buniato *m* sweet potato
buñuelo *m* cruller, fritter, bun; (coll) botch, bungle
buque *m* ship, vessel; (*de una nave*)

hull; (*de cualquier cosa*) capacity; (C-R) doorframe; **buque almirante** admiral; **buque cisterna** tanker; **buque de guerra** warship; **buque de vapor** steamer, steamship; **buque de vela** sailboat; **buque escucha** vedette; **buque escuela** training ship; **buque fanal** or **buque faro** lightship; **buque mercante** merchantman, merchant vessel; **buque portaminas** mine layer; **buque tanque** tanker; **buque velero** sailing vessel

burbuja *f* bubble

burbujear *intr* to bubble

burdégano *m* hinny

burdel *m* brothel, disorderly house

Burdeos Bordeaux

bur•do -da *adj* coarse, rough

burear *tr* (Col) to fool || *intr* to have fun

burga *f* hot springs

bur•gués -guesa *adj* middle-class, bourgeois; (*antiartístico*) bourgeois || *m* middle-class man || *f* middle-class woman

burguesía *f* middle class, bourgeoisie; **alta burguesía** upper middle class; **pequeña burguesía** lower middle class

burla *f* hoax, trick; joke; ridicule; **burlas aparte** joking aside; **de burlas** in fun, for fun

burladero *m* safety island, safety zone; (*en las plazas de toros*) covert; (*en los túneles*) safety niche; hiding place

burla•dor -dora *adj* joking; deceptive || *mf* wag, prankster, practical joker || *m* seducer, libertine

burlar *tr* to make fun of; to deceive; to disappoint; to outwit, frustrate; (*a una mujer*) to seduce || *intr* to scoff || *ref* to joke; **burlarse de** to make fun of

burlería *f* derision, mockery; deception, trick; scorn, derision; fish story

burles•co -ca *adj* (coll) funny, comic, burlesque

burlete *m* weather stripping

bur•lón -lona *adj* joking || *mf* joker || *m* mockingbird

bu•ró *m* (*pl* **-rós**) writing desk; (Mex) night table

burócrata *mf* jobholder, bureaucrat

burra *f* she-ass; stupid woman; drudge (*woman*)

burrajear *tr & intr* to scribble; to doodle

burra•jo -ja *adj* (Mex) coarse, stupid || *m* dung (*used as fuel*)

bu•rro -rra *adj* (coll) stupid, asinine || *m* donkey, jackass; sawbuck, sawhorse; (Mex) stepladder; **burro cargado de letras** (coll) learned jackass; **burro de carga** (coll) drudge || *f* see **burra**

bursátil *adj* stock-market

busca *f* search; **en busca de** in search of

buscani•guas *m* (*pl* **-guas**) (Col) snake

buscapié *m* (*para dar a entender algo*) hint; (*para averiguar algo*) feeler || **busca•piés** *m* (*pl* **-piés**) snake

buscaplei•tos *mf* (*pl* **-tos**) (Am) troublemaker

buscar §73 *tr* to seek, to hunt, to look for; (Mex) to provoke; **buscar tres pies al gato** to be looking for trouble || *ref* to take care of oneself; **buscársela** (coll) to manage to get along; (coll) to ask for it

buscareta *f* wren

buscarrui•dos *mf* (*pl* **-dos**) (coll) troublemaker

buscavi•das *mf* (*pl* **-das**) (coll) snoop, busybody; (coll) go-getter

bus•cón -cona *adj* searching; cheating || *mf* seeker; thief, cheat; (min) prospector || *f* loose woman

busi•lis *m* (*pl* **-lis**) (coll) trouble; **ahí está el busilis** (coll) that's the trouble; **dar en el busilis** (coll) to hit the nail on the head

búsqueda *f* search, hunt

busto *m* bust

butaca *f* armchair, easy chair; orchestra seat

butifarra *f* Catalonian sausage; (coll) loose sock, loose stocking; (Peru) ham and salad sandwich

bution•do -da *adj* lewd, lustful

buz *m* (*pl* **buces**) kiss of gratitude and reverence; lip; **hacer el buz** (archaic) to bow and scrape

buzo *m* diver

buzón *m* plug, stopper; mailbox, letter box; (*agujero para echar las cartas*) slot, letter drop; **buzón de alcance** special-delivery box; late-collection slot

C

C, c (ce) *f* third letter of the Spanish alphabet

c. *abbr* **capítulo, compañía, corriente, cuenta**

c *abbr* **caja, cargo, contra, corriente**

cabal *adj* exact; full, complete, perfect; **no estar en sus cabales** to be not in one's right mind || *adv* exactly; completely || *interj* right!

cábala *f* intrigue; divination

cabalgada *f* raid on horseback; gathering of riders

cabalgador *m* rider, horseman

cabalgadura *f* mount, horse; beast of burden

cabalgar §44 *intr* to go horseback riding

cabalgata *f* cavalcade

caballa *f* mackerel
caballada *f* drove of horses; (Am) nonsense, stupidity
caballaje *m* stud service
caballazo *m* (Am) collision of two horses, trampling by a horse; (Chile, Peru) bitter attack
caballerango *m* (Mex) stableman
caballeres•co -ca *adj* chivalric, knightly; gentlemanly
caballerete *m* (coll) dude
caballería *f* mount, horse, mule; cavalry; chivalry, knighthood; **andarse en caballerías** (coll) to fall all over oneself in compliments; **caballería andante** knight-errantry; **caballería mayor** horse, mule; **caballería menor** ass, donkey
caballeriza *f* stable; stable hands
caballerizo *m* groom, stableman
caballe•ro -ra *adj* riding, mounted; stubborn || *m* knight, nobleman; gentleman; mister; horseman, cavalier, rider; **armar caballero** to knight; **caballero andante** knight errant; **caballero de industria** crook, adventurer, sharper; **Caballero de la triste figura** Knight of the Rueful Countenance (*Don Quijote*); **ir caballero en** to ride
caballerosidad *f* chivalry, gentlemanliness
caballerote *m* boorish fellow, cad
caballete *m* (*bastidor para sostener un cuadro o pizarra*) easel; (*de tejado*) ridge, hip; (*lomo de tierra*) ridge; (*artificio usado como soporte*) trestle, sawbuck, horse; (*de la nariz*) bridge; chimney cap; (*del ave*) breastbone; little horse
caballista *m* horseman; mounted smuggler || *f* horsewoman
caballito *m* little horse; merry-go-round; **caballito del diablo** dragonfly
caballo *m* horse; (*en ajedrez*) knight; playing card (*figure on horseback equivalent to queen*); **a caballo** on horseback; **a caballo de** astride; **a caballo regalado no se le mira el diente** never look a gift horse in the mouth; **caballo blanco** (*persona que da dinero para una empresa dudosa*) angel; **caballo de batalla** battle horse; (*de una controversia*) gist, main point; (*aquello en que uno sobresale*) forte, strong point; **caballo de carreras** race horse; **caballo de fuerza** French horsepower, metric horsepower; **caballo de tiro** draft horse; **caballo de Troya** Trojan horse; **caballo de vapor** French horsepower, metric horsepower; **caballo de vapor inglés** horsepower; **caballo mecedor** rocking horse, hobbyhorse; **caballo padre** stallion; **caballo semental** stallion
caballu•no -na *adj* horse, horselike
cabaña *f* cabin, hut; drove, flock; livestock; pastoral scene; (Arg) cattle-breeding ranch
cabañuelas *fpl* (Arg, Bol) first summer rains; (Mex) winter rains
caba•ret *m* (*pl* **-rets**) cabaret
cabecear *tr* (*un libro*) to put a headband on; (*el vino*) to head; (*una media*) to put a new foot on || *intr* to nod; to bob the head; (*en señal de negación*) to shake the head; (*los caballos*) to toss the head; (*la caja de un carruaje*) to lurch; (*un buque*) to pitch
cabeceo *m* (*de la cabeza*) nod, bob, shake; (*de la caja del carruaje*) lurching; (*del buque*) pitch, pitching
cabecera *f* (*de cama, mesa, etc.*) head; bedside; headboard; headwaters; (*de una casa, un campo*) end; (*del capítulo de un libro*) heading; (*de periódico*) headline; capital, county seat; bolster, pillow; (typ) headpiece, vignette; **cabecera de cartel** top billing; **cabecera de puente** (mil) bridgehead
cabecilla *mf* (coll) scalawag || *m* ringleader || *f* **cabecilla de alfiler** pinhead
cabellar *intr* to grow hair; to put on false hair || *ref* to put on false hair
cabellera *f* head of hair; foliage; (*del cometa*) coma; (bot) mistletoe
cabello *m* hair; **cabello de Venus** maidenhair; **cabellos de ángel** cotton candy; **en cabello** with the hair down; **en cabellos** bareheaded; **traído por los cabellos** far-fetched
cabellu•do -da *adj* hairy
caber §14 *intr* to fit, to go; to have enough room; to be possible; to happen, to befall; **no cabe duda** there is no doubt; **no cabe más** that's the limit; **no caber de** to be bursting with; **no caber en sí** to be beside oneself; to be puffed up with pride; **todo cabe en** anything can be expected of
cabestrar *tr* to put a halter on
cabestrillo *m* sling
cabestro *m* halter; **llevar** or **traer del cabestro** (coll) to lead by the halter; (fig) to lead by the nose
cabeza *f* head; chief city, capital; **cabeza de chorlito** (coll) scatterbrains; (Arg) forgetful person; **cabeza de motín** ringleader; **cabeza de playa** beachhead; **cabeza de puente** bridgehead; **cabeza de turco** butt, scapegoat; **cabeza mayor** head of cattle; **cabeza menor** head of sheep, goats, etc.; **de cabeza** headfirst; on end; on one's own; by heart; **ir cabeza abajo** (coll) to go downhill; **irse de la cabeza** to go out of one's mind; **mala cabeza** headstrong person; **por su cabeza** on one's own; **romperse la cabeza** (coll) to rack one's brains
cabezada *f* butt with the head; blow on the head; (*de buque*) pitch, pitching; (*de bota*) instep; (*de libro*) headband; **dar cabezadas** to nod; (*un buque*) to pitch
cabezal *m* pillow, cushion; bolster
cabezo *m* hillock; summit, peak; reef
cabe•zón -zona *adj* big-headed; stubborn; (*licor*) (Chile) strong || *m* (*en la ropa*) hole for the head; tax register
cabezonada *f* (coll) stubbornness

cabezu•do -da *adj* big-headed; (coll) headstrong; (*vino*) heady
cabezuela *f* little head; (*harina gruesa del trigo*) middling; cornflower
cabida *f* room, space, capacity; influence, pull; **tener cabida en** to be included in
cabildear *intr* to lobby
cabildeo *m* lobbying
cabildero *m* lobbyist
cabildo *m* chapter (*of a cathedral*); chapter meeting; town hall
cabina *f* cabin; (*locutorio del teléfono*) booth; bathhouse, dressing room
cabio *m* rafter; joist
cabizba•jo -ja *adj* crestfallen, downcast
cable *m* cable; rope, hawser; **cable de remolque** towline; **cable de retén** guy wire
cablegrafiar **§77** *tr & intr* to cable
cablegráfi•co -ca *adj* cable
cablegrama *m* cablegram
cabo *m* end, tip; (*punta de tierra que penetra en el mar*) cape; (*mango*) handle; small bundle; small piece; boss, foreman; cord, rope, cable; (mil) corporal; **al cabo** finally, at last; **al cabo de** at the end of; **atar cabos** (coll) to put two and two together; **Cabo de Buena Esperanza** Cape of Good Hope; **Cabo de Hornos** Cape Horn; **cabos** (*de caballo*) paws, nose, and mane; eyes, eyebrows, and hair; clothing; **cabo suelto** (coll) loose end; **estar al cabo de** (coll) to be well informed about; **llevar a cabo** to carry out, to accomplish
cabotaje *m* coasting trade
cabra *f* goat; nanny goat; (Chile) light two-wheel carriage; (Chile) sawbuck; (Col, Cuba, Ven) trick, gyp, loaded dice; **cabras** light clouds
cabrahigo wild fig
cabrería *f* goat stable; goat-milk dairy
cabre•ro -ra *mf* goatherd
cabrestante *m* capstan
cabrilla *f* sawbuck, sawhorse; (ichth) grouper; **cabrillas** skipping stones; (*olas blancas en el mar*) whitecaps
cabrillear *intr* (*el mar*) to be covered with whitecaps; to shimmer
cabrio *m* rafter; joist
cabrí•o -a *adj* goat; goatish || *m* herd of goats
cabriola *f* caper; somersault; **dar cabriolas** to cut capers
cabriolear *intr* to caper, frisk, prance
cabritilla *f* kid, kidskin
cabrito *m* kid; **cabritos** (Chile) popcorn
cabrón *m* buck, billy goat; (coll) complaisant cuckold; (Chile) pimp
cabronada *f* (coll) shamelessness; (coll) shameless forbearance
cabru•no -na *adj* goat
cacahuate *adj* (Mex) pocked || *m* peanut
cacahuete *m* peanut
cacahuete•ro -ra *mf* peanut vendor
cacalote *m* (Mex) raven; (CAm, Mex) candied popcorn; (Cuba) break, blunder
cacao *m* chocolate tree; cocoa, chocolate; **pedir cacao** (Am) to call quits; **tener mucho cacao** (Guat) to have a lot of pep
cacaraña *f* pit, pock
cacarear *tr* (coll) to crow over, boast of || *intr* (*la gallina*) to cackle; (*el gallo*) to crow
cacareo *m* (*de la gallina*) cackling; (*del gallo*) crowing; (*de una persona*) (coll) crowing, boasting
cacatúa *f* cockatoo
cacea *f* trolling; **pescar a la cacea** to troll
cacear *tr* to stir with a dipper or ladle || *intr* to troll
cacería *f* hunting; hunting party; (*animales cobrados en la caza*) bag; hunting scene
cacerola *f* casserole, saucepan
cacique *m* Indian chief; bossy fellow; (*en asuntos políticos*) (coll) boss; (Chile) lazy lummox; **cacique veranero** Baltimore oriole, hangbird
caciquismo *m* bossism
caco *m* thief, pickpocket; (coll) coward
cacto *m* cactus
cacumen *m* summit; acumen, keen insight
cacha•co -ca *adj* (SAm) sporty || *m* (SAm) sport, dude
cachada *f* (Am) thrust or wound made with the horns
cachalote *m* sperm whale
cachar *tr* to break to pieces; (*la madera*) to slit, split; (Arg, Ecuad, Urug) to make fun of; (Am) to butt with the horns; (Chile) to grasp, understand
cacharpari *m* (Arg, Bol, Peru) send-off party
cacharro *m* crock, earthen pot; piece of crockery; piece of junk; (CAm, W-I) jail; (Col) trinket
cachaza *f* (coll) sloth, phlegm; rum; (Am) first froth on cane juice when boiled
cachazu•do -da *adj* (coll) slothful, phlegmatic || *mf* (coll) sluggard
cachear *tr* to frisk
cacheo *m* frisking
cachete *m* slap in the face; cheek, swollen cheek; dagger
cachetero *m* dagger; dagger man
cachetina *f* (coll) brawl, fistfight
cachicuer•no -na *adj* horn-handled
cachillada *f* brood, litter
cachimba *f* (*para fumar*) (Am) pipe; (Arg, Urug) well, spring; (Chile) revolver
cachimbo *m* (*para fumar*) (Am) pipe; (Cuba) sugar mill; **chupar cachimbo** (Ven) to smoke a pipe; (*un niño*) (Ven) to suck its finger
cachiporra *f* billy, bludgeon
cachivache *m* good-for-nothing; **cachivaches** broken pottery; pots and pans; junk, trash
cacho *m* slice, piece; (*mercadería que no se vende*) (Chile) drug on the market

cachón *m* (*ola de agua*) breaker; splash of water; **cachones** surf
cachon•do -da *adj* (*perra*) in rut; sexy
cacho•rro -rra *mf* cub, whelp, pup || *m* little pistol
cachucha *f* rowboat; cap; Andalusian dance
cachuela *f* gizzard; fricassee of pork
cachu•pín -pina *mf* (CAm, Mex) Spanish settler in Latin America
cada *adj* each; every; **cada vez más** more and more; **cada vez que** whenever
cadalso *m* stand, platform; (*para la ejecución de un reo*) scaffold
cadarzo *m* floss, floss silk
cadáver *m* corpse, cadaver
cadavéri•co -ca *adj* cadaverous
cadena *f* chain; **cadena de presidiarios** chain gang; **cadena perpetua** life imprisonment
cadencia *f* cadence, rhythm
cadencio•so -sa *adj* rhythmical
cadenero *m* (surv) lineman
cadera *f* hip
cadete *m* (mil) cadet; (Arg, Bol) apprentice (*without pay*), errand boy
cadillo *m* burdock
cadmio *m* cadmium
caducar **§73** *intr* to be in one's dotage; to be worn out; to lapse, expire
caedi•zo -za *adj* tottery, ready to fall over || *m* (Am) lean-to
caer **§15** *intr* to fall; to droop; to fall due; to be, be found; to fade; (*el sol, el día, el viento*) to decline; to happen; **caer a** to face, overlook; **caer bien** to fit; to be becoming; (coll) to make a hit; **caer de plano** to fall flat; **caer en** (*cierto día*) to come on, fall on, happen on; (*cierta página*) to be found on; **caer en cama** to fall ill; **caer en favor** to be in favor; **caer en la cuenta** to catch on, get the point; **caer en que** to realize that; **caer mal** to fit badly; to be unbecoming; (coll) to fall flat; **no caigo** (coll) I don't get it || *ref* to fall, fall down; to be, be found; **caerse de su peso, caerse de suyo** to be self-evident; **caerse muerto de** (*p.ej., alegría, miedo, risa*) to be overcome with
café *adj* (Am) tan || *m* coffee; coffee tree; coffee house; café; (Arg) reprimand; (Mex) tantrum; **café cantante** night club; **café de maquinilla** drip coffee; **café solo** black coffee
cafetal *m* coffee plantation
cafetera *f* coffee pot; (Arg) jalopy; **cafetera eléctrica** electric percolator
cafetería *f* cafeteria
cafete•ro -ra *adj* coffee || *mf* coffee dealer; coffee-bean picker || *f* see **cafetera**
cafeto *m* coffee tree
cagar **§44** *tr* (coll) to spot, stain, spoil || *intr* to defecate || *ref* to defecate; to be scared
cagatin•ta *m* or **cagatin•tas** *m* (*pl* **-tas**) office drudge, penpusher
ca•gón -gona *adj* (coll) cowardly || *mf* (coll) coward
caída *f* fall; spill, tumble; drop; failure; blunder, slip; (*de una cortina*) hang; **a la caída de la noche** at nightfall; **a la caída del sol** at sunset; **caída de agua** waterfall; **caída radiactiva** fallout; **caídas** coarse wool; (coll) witticisms
caí•do -da *adj* fallen; (*cuello*) turndown; (*párpado, hombro*) drooping; dejected, crestfallen; **caído en desuso** obsolete || **caídos** *mpl* interest due; **los caídos** (*en la guerra*) the fallen || *f* see **caída**
caimán *m* alligator; (coll) schemer
Caín *m* Cain; **pasar las de Caín** (coll) to have a frightful time
Cairo, El Cairo
caja *f* box; case, chest, coffer; (*de caudales*) safe, strongbox; (*para dinero contante*) cashbox; (*dinero contante*) cash; (*ataúd*) casket, coffin; (*de reloj de bolsillo*) case; (*donde se pagan las cuentas en los hoteles*) desk; cashier's desk; (*del aparato de radio o televisión*) cabinet; (*de coche*) body; (*tambor*) drum; (*de fusil*) stock; (*de ascensor, de escalera*) shaft, well; (mach) housing; (typ) case; **caja alta** upper case; **caja baja** lower case; **caja clara** snare drum; **caja de ahorros** savings bank; **caja de cambio de marchas** transmission-gear box; **caja de caudales** safe; **caja de cigüeñal** crankcase; **caja de colores** paintbox; **caja de embalaje** packing box or case; **caja de enchufe** (elec) outlet; **caja de engranajes** gear case; **caja de fuego** firebox; **caja de fusibles** fuse box; **caja de ingletes** miter box; **caja de menores** petty cash; **caja de registro** manhole; **caja de reloj** watchcase; **caja de seguridad** safe; safe-deposit box; **caja de sorpresa** jack-in-the-box; **caja de velocidades** transmission-gear box; **caja fuerte** safe, bank vault; **caja postal de ahorros** postal savings bank; **caja registradora** cash register; **despedir** or **echar con cajas destempladas** (coll) to send packing, to give the gate
caje•ro -ra *mf* boxmaker; (*en un banco*) cashier, teller; (*en un hotel*) desk clerk
cajeta *f* little box; tobacco box; **de cajeta** (CAm, Mex) fine
cajetilla *f* pack (*of cigarettes*)
cajetín *m* rubber stamp; (typ) box
cajista *mf* compositor
cajón *m* large box, bin; (*caja movible de un mueble*) drawer; (*que se cierra con llave*) locker; (*que sirve de tienda*) booth, stall; (Chile) long gully; (Mex) dry-goods store; (SAm) coffin; **cajón de aire comprimido** caisson; **cajón de sastre** (coll) odds and ends; (coll) muddlehead; **ser de cajón** (coll) to be in vogue, be the thing
cal *f* lime; **cal apagada** slaked lime; **cal viva** quicklime; **de cal y canto** (coll) strong, tough
cala *f* calla lily; cove, inlet; (*de fruta*)

sample slice; (*de buque*) hold; suppository
calabacear *tr* (*a un alumno*) (coll) to flunk; (*una mujer a un pretendiente*) (coll) to jilt
calabacera *f* calabash, pumpkin, squash
calabaza *f* calabash, gourd, pumpkin, squash; (coll) dolt; **dar calabaza** a (*un alumno*) (coll) to flunk; (*un pretendiente*) (coll) to jilt
calabo•bos *m* (*pl* **-bos**) (coll) steady drizzle
calabocero *m* jailer, warden
calabozo *m* dungeon; cell, prison cell
calada *f* soaking; (*del ave de rapiña*) swoop; (coll) scolding
calado *m* openwork, drawn work; fretwork; (*del agua*) depth; (naut) draught
calafatear *tr* to calk
calafateo *m* calking
calamar *m* squid
calambre *m* cramp
calamidad *f* calamity
calamita *f* magnetic needle
calamito•so -sa *adj* calamitous
cálamo *m* reed, stalk; (poet) pen; (poet) flute, reed
calamoca•no -na *adj* (*algo embriagado*) (coll) tipsy; (*chocho*) (coll) doddering
calaña *f* nature, kind; pattern; fan
calar *tr* to pierce; to soak; to wedge; to cut open work in; (*un melón*) to cut a plug in; (*la bayoneta*) to fix; (*un puente levadizo*) to lower; (*las redes de pesca*) to lower in the water; (*un buque cierta profundidad*) to draw; (*a una persona o las intenciones de una persona*) to size up, to see through; (Arg) to stare at || *ref* to get soaked, get drenched; (*introducirse*) to slip in; (*el ave de rapiña*) to swoop down; to miss fire; (*el sombrero*) to pull down tight; (*las gafas*) to stick on; **calarse hasta los huesos** to get soaked to the skin
cala•to -ta *adj* (Peru) naked; (Peru) penniless
calavera *m* daredevil; libertine || *f* skull; (*imitación de la calavera*) death's-head; (Mex) tail light
calaverada *f* recklessness, daredeviltry; (Am) escapade
calaverear *tr* to spoil, make ugly || *intr* (coll) to act recklessly; (Am) to go on a spree
calcado *m* tracing
calcañal *m* or **calcañar** *m* heel
calcar §73 *tr* to trace; to copy, imitate; to tread on
calce *m* wedge; iron tire; iron tip; (*de un documento*) (CAm, Mex, P-R) bottom, foot
calceta *f* stocking; fetter, shackle; **hacer calceta** to knit
calcetería *f* hosiery; hosiery shop
calcete•ro -ra *mf* hosier; stocking mender
calcetín *m* sock
calcificar §73 *tr & ref* to calcify
calcio *m* calcium
calco *m* tracing; copy, imitation
calcula•dor -dora *adj* calculating; (*egoísta, interesado*) (fig) calculating || *mf* calculator || *f* calculating machine
calcular *tr & intr* to calculate; (*suponer*) (fig) to calculate
cálculo *m* calculation; (math, pathol) calculus; **cálculo biliar** gallstone; **cálculo renal** kidney stone
calchona *f* (Chile) goblin, bogey; (Chile) witch, old hag
calda *f* heating, warming; **caldas** hot springs
caldeamiento *m* heating
caldear *tr* to heat; to weld || *ref* to get hot; to get overheated
caldeo *m* heating; welding
caldera *f* boiler; pot, kettle; (Arg) coffee pot, teapot
calderero *m* boilermaker
calderilla *f* holy-water vessel; copper coin; small change; mountain currant
caldero *m* kettle, pot; (*reloj de bolsillo*) (Arg) turnip
calderón *m* caldron; (*signo*) (mus) pause, hold
caldo *m* broth; sauce, gravy, dressing; salad dressing; (Mex) syrup; (Mex) sugar-cane juice; **caldo de la reina** eggnog; **caldos** wet goods
calefacción *f* heating; **calefacción por agua caliente** hot-water heat; **calefacción por aire caliente** hot-air heat
calefactor *m* heater man; (electron) heater, heater element
calefón *m* (Arg) hot-water heater
calendar *tr* to date
calendario *m* calendar; **hacer calendarios** (coll) to meditate; (coll) to make wild predictions
calenta•dor -dora *adj* heating || *m* heater; warming pan; (*reloj de bolsillo*) (coll) turnip; **calentador a gas** gas heater; **calentador de agua** water heater
calentamiento *m* heating
calentar §2 *tr* to heat; to warm; to beat; (Chile) to bore, annoy; **calentar la silla** (*detenerse demasiado*) to warm a chair || *ref* to heat up, run hot; to warm oneself; to warm up; (*estar en celo las bestias*) to be in heat; (Chile, Ven) to become annoyed, get angry
calentón *m* (coll) warm-up; **darse un calentón** (coll) to stop and warm up
calentura *f* fever, temperature
calenturien•to -ta *adj* feverish; exalted; (Chile) consumptive
calenturón *m* high fever
calenturo•so -sa *adj* feverish
calera *f* limekiln; limestone quarry
calesa *f* chaise
caleta *f* cove, inlet
caletre *m* (coll) judgment, acumen
calibrador *m* calipers; **calibrador de alambre** wire gauge
calibrar *tr* to calibrate; to gauge
calibre *m* caliber; gauge; bore, diameter
calicanto *m* rubble masonry

cali•có *m* (*pl* **-cós**) calico
calidad *f* quality; condition, term; rank, nobility; importance; **a calidad de que** provided that; **en calidad de** in the capacity of
cáli•do -da *adj* warm, hot
calidoscopio *m* kaleidoscope
calientaca•mas *m* (*pl* **-mas**) bed warmer
calienta•piés *m* (*pl* **-piés**) foot warmer
caliente *adj* hot; fiery, vehement; (*en celo*) hot; **caliente de cascos** hotheaded; **en caliente** while hot; at once
califa *m* caliph
califato *m* caliphate
calificación *f* qualification; (*nota en un examen*) grade, mark; rating, standing
calificar **§73** *tr* to qualify; to certify; to ennoble; (*un examen*) to mark; (*en los registros electorales*) (Chile) to register || *ref* (archaic) to prove one's noble birth; (*en los registros electorales*) (Chile) to register
calificati•vo -va *adj* qualifying || *m* (*nota en la escuela*) grade, mark; (*en un diccionario*) usage label
California *f* California; **la Baja California** Lower California
caligrafía *f* penmanship
calina *f* haze
calino•so -sa *adj* hazy
Calíope *f* Calliope
calipso *m* calypso || **Calipso** *f* Calypso
calistenia *f* calisthenics
calisténi•co -ca *adj* calisthenic
cá•liz *m* (*pl* **-lices**) chalice; **cáliz de dolor** cup of sorrow
cali•zo -za *adj* lime, limestone || *f* limestone
calma *f* calm; calm weather; quiet, tranquillity; slowness; (*cesación*) letup, suspension; **calma chicha** dead calm; **calmas ecuatoriales** doldrums; **en calma** in suspension; (*mercado*) steady; (*mar*) calm, smooth
calmante *adj* soothing; pain-relieving || *m* sedative
calmar *tr* to calm, sooth || *intr* to grow calm; to abate || *ref* to calm down
calmazo *m* dead calm
cal•mo -ma *adj* barren, treeless; fallow, uncultivated || *f* see **calma**
calmo•so -sa *adj* calm; (coll) slow, lazy
calmu•do -da *adj* calm; (*viento*) (naut) light; (*tiempo*) (naut) mild
caló *m* gypsy slang, underworld slang
calofriar **§77** *ref* to become chilled
calofrío *m* chill
calor *m* heat; warmth; (fig) warmth, enthusiasm; **hace calor** it is hot, it is warm; **tener calor** (*una persona*) to be hot, be warm
calorífe•ro -ra *adj* heat || *m* heater, furnace; heating system; foot warmer
caloríf•go -ga *adj* heatproof; fireproof
caloro•so -sa *adj* warm, hot; (fig) warm, enthusiastic, hearty
calotear *tr* (Arg) to gyp, cheat
calpul *m* (Guat) gathering, meeting; (Hond) Indian mound
caluma *f* (Peru) gorge in the Andes; (Peru) Indian hamlet
calumnia *f* calumny, slander
calumniar *tr* to slander
calumnio•so -sa *adj* slanderous
caluro•so -sa *adj* warm, hot; (fig) warm, enthusiastic, hearty
calva *f* bald spot; bare spot, clearing; (*en un tejido*) worn spot
calvario *m* (*sufrimiento moral*) cross; (coll) series of misfortunes; (coll) string of debts || **Calvario** *m* Calvary; Stations of the Cross
calvero *m* clearing; clay pit
calvez *f* or **calvicie** *f* baldness
cal•vo -va *adj* bald; barren, bare || *f* see **calva**
calza *f* wedge; (coll) stocking; **calzas** hose, breeches, tights; **en calzas prietas** (coll) in a tight fix
calzada *f* highway, causeway; (S-D) sidewalk
calzado *m* footwear, shoes
calzador *m* shoehorn
calzar **§60** *tr* to shoe, put shoes on; to provide with shoes; (*cierto tamaño de zapatos, guantes, etc.*) to wear, to take; (*un zapato a una persona*) to fit; to wedge; (*una rueda*) to block, scotch; (*la pata de una mesa*) to block up; to tip or trim with iron; (*plantas*) (hort) to hill || *intr* (Arg) to get the place sought; **calzar bien** to wear good footwear; **calzar mal** to wear poor footwear || *ref* to get; (*zapatos, guantes*) to put on, to wear; to put one's shoes on; (*a una persona*) (coll) to dominate, to manage
calzo *m* wedge; chock, skid
calzón *m* trousers, pants; **calzones** trousers, breeches; **calzarse los calzones** to wear the pants
calzonarias *fpl* (Col) suspenders
calzona•zos *m* (*pl* **-zos**) (coll) jellyfish; (coll) henpecked husband
calzoncillos *mpl* underdrawers
callada *f* (naut) abatement, lull; **a las calladas** or **de callada** (coll) on the quiet; **dar la callada por respuesta** to give no answer
calla•do -da *adj* silent; mysterious, secret || *f* see **callada**
callampa *f* (Chile) felt hat; (Chile) large ear; (Chile) mushroom
callana *f* (SAm) Indian baking bowl; (*reloj de bolsillo*) (Chile) turnip; (Chile) behind; (Chile, Peru) flowerpot
callao *m* pebble
callar *tr* to silence; to not mention; (*un secreto*) to keep; to calm, quiet || *intr & ref* to become silent, keep silent; to keep quiet, keep still; **callarse la boca** (coll) to shut up, to clam up
calle *f* street; **calle de travesía** cross street; **calle mayor** main street; **dejar en la calle** (coll) to deprive of one's livelihood
calleja *f* side street, alley; (coll) subterfuge, pretext
callejear *intr* to walk around the streets, to ramble around
calleje•ro -ra *adj* street; gadabout || *m*

street guide; list of addresses of newspaper subscribers
callejón *m* alley, lane; **callejón sin salida** blind alley
callejuela *f* side street, alley; (coll) subterfuge, pretext
callicida *m* corn cure
callo *m* callus; (*en el pie*) corn; **callos** tripe
callo•so -sa *adj* callous
cama *f* bed; (*para las bestias*) bedding, litter; **cama imperial** four-poster; **cama turca** day bed; **guardar cama** to be sick in bed
camachuelo *m* (orn) bullfinch
camada *f* brood, litter; layer, stratum; (*de ladrones*) den
camafeo *m* cameo
camaleón *m* chameleon
cámara *f* chamber; hall; (*cuerpo legislador*) house, chamber; (*aparato fotográfico*) camera; (*tubo de goma del neumático*) inner tube; (*del arma de fuego*) chamber, breech; (*para cartuchos*) magazine; board, council; (*mueble donde se conservan los alimentos*) icebox; (*evacuación*) bowels; (aer) cockpit; **cámara agrícola** grange; **cámara ardiente** funeral chamber; **cámara de compensación** clearing house; **cámara de fuelle** folding camera; **cámara de las máquinas** (naut) engine room; **Cámara de los Comunes** House of Commons; **Cámara de los Lores** House of Lords; **cámara de oxígeno** oxygen tent; **Cámara de Representantes** House of Representatives; **cámara frigorífica** cold-storage room; **cámara indiscreta** candid camera; **cámaras** loose bowels
camarada *m* comrade
camarera *f* waitress; chambermaid, maid; (*en los barcos*) stewardess; (*que sirve a una reina o princesa*) lady in waiting
camarero *m* waiter; valet; (*en un barco o avión*) steward
camarilla *f* clique, coterie, cabal; palace coterie
camarín *m* boudoir; (theat) dressing room
cámaro *m* var of **camarón**
camarógrafo *m* cameraman
camarón *m* shrimp, prawn; (CAm, Col) tip, gratuity; (Ven) nap; **ponerse como un camarón** (Am) to blush
camarote *m* stateroom, cabin
camasquin•ce *mf* (*pl* **-ce**) (coll) meddlesome person, kibitzer
cambalachar *tr* & *intr* var of **cambalachear**
cambalache *m* exchange, swap; (Arg) second-hand shop
cambalachear *tr* to swap, exchange, trade off || *intr* to swap, exchange
cambiadis•cos *m* (*pl* **-cos**) record changer
cambiante *adj* changing; fickle; iridescent || **cambiantes** *mpl* iridescence
cambiar *tr* to change; to exchange || *intr* to change; **cambiar de** (*p.ej.*, *sombreros, ropa, trenes*) to change; **cambiar de marcha** to shift gears || *ref* to change
cambiavía *m* (Am) switch; (Am) switchman
cambio *m* change; exchange; rate of exchange; (aut) shift; (rr) switch; **cambio de marchas, cambio de velocidades** gearshift; **en cambio** on the other hand
cambista *mf* moneychanger; banker || *m* (Arg) switchman
cambullón *m* (Mex, Col, Ven) barter, exchange; (Chile) subversion; (Peru) scheming, trickery
camelar *tr* (coll) to flirt with; (coll) to cajole, to tease
camelo *m* (coll) flirtation; (coll) joke; (coll) false rumor
camellero *m* camel driver
camello *m* camel
camellón *m* drinking trough; flower bed
came•ro -ra *adj* bed || *mf* maker of bedding || *m* (Col) highway
camilla *f* stretcher; couch; round table with heater underneath; (Mex) clothing store
camillero *m* stretcher-bearer
caminante *mf* walker; traveler on foot || *m* groom attending his master's horse
caminar *tr* (*cierta distancia*) to walk || *intr* to walk; to go; to travel, to journey; to behave
caminata *f* (coll) long walk, hike; (coll) outing, jaunt
camine•ro -ra *adj* road, highway
camino *m* road, way; (*viaje*) journey; (*tira larga que se pone en mesas o pisos*) (SAm) runner; **a medio camino (entre)** halfway (between); **camino de** on the way to; **camino de herradura** bridle path; **camino de hierro** railway; **camino de ruedas** wagon road; **Camino de Santiago** Way of St. James (*Milky Way*); **camino de sirga** towpath; **camino de tierra** dirt road; **camino real** highroad; **camino trillado** beaten path; **echar camino adelante** to strike out
camión *m* truck, motor truck; (Mex) bus; **camión volquete** dump truck
camionaje *m* trucking
camione•ro -ra *adj* truck || *m* trucker, teamster
camioneta *f* light truck
camión-grúa *m* tow truck
camionista *m* trucker, teamster
camisa *f* (*de hombre*) shirt; (*de mujer*) chemise; (*de la culebra*) slough; (*de un libro*) jacket; (*para papeles*) folder; (*de una pieza mecánica*) jacket, casing; (*de un horno de fundición*) lining; **camisa de agua** water jacket; **camisa de dormir** nightshirt; **camisa de fuerza** strait jacket; **cambiarse la camisa** to become a turncoat
camisería *f* haberdashery; shirt factory
camise•ro -ra *mf* haberdasher; shirt maker

camiseta *f* undershirt; (*de traje de baño*) top
camisola *f* stiff shirt
camisolín *m* dickey, shirt front
camón *m* bay window; **camón de vidrios** glass partition
camorra *f* (coll) quarrel, row; **armar camorra** (coll) to raise Cain, to raise a row; **buscar camorra** (coll) to be looking for trouble
camorrista *adj* (coll) quarrelsome || *mf* (coll) quarrelsome person
camote *m* (Mex) sweet potato; (Am) onion; (Chile) lie, fib; (Chile, Peru) sweetheart; (Arg, Ecuad) blockhead; (Mex) churl; (El Salv) black-and-blue mark; **tomar un camote** (Am) to become infatuated
camotear *tr* (Arg) to filch, to snitch; (Guat) to bother || *intr* (Mex) to wander around aimlessly
campal *adj* pitched (*battle*)
campamento *m* camp; encampment
campana *f* bell; (*para la protección de plantas*) bell glass, bell jar; (*de las guarniciones de alumbrado eléctrico*) canopy; **campana de buzo** diving bell; **por campana de vacante** (Mex) rarely, seldom
campanada *f* stroke of a bell, ring of a bell; scandal
campanario *m* belfry, steeple
campanear *tr* (*las campanas*) to ring || *intr* to ring the bells || *ref* (coll) to strut
campanero *m* bell ringer; bell founder
campanil *adj* bell || *m* belfry, bell tower
campanilla *f* hand bell; door bell; bubble; (anat) uvula; **de (muchas) campanillas** (coll) of great importance
campano *m* cowbell
campante *adj* (coll) proud, satisfied; (coll) outstanding
campanu•do -da *adj* bell-shaped; pompous, high-sounding
campaña *f* campaign; cruise; countryside
campar *intr* to camp; to excel, stand out
campear *intr* to go to pasture; (*las sementeras*) to turn green; to stand out, excel; to reconnoiter; (Am) to ride through the fields to check the cattle
campecha•no -na *adj* (coll) frank, good-natured, cheerful || *f* (Mex) mixed drink; (Ven) hammock
campeche *m* logwood
campeón *m* champion; **campeón de venta** best seller
campeona *f* championess
campeonato *m* championship
campe•ro -ra *adj* unsheltered, in the open
campesi•no -na *adj* country, rural, peasant || *mf* peasant, farmer || *m* countryman || *f* countrywoman
campestre *adj* country, rural
campiña *f* countryside, open country
campo *m* (*terreno sembradío; sitio o foco de varias actividades*) field; (*en oposición a la ciudad*) country; ground, background; (*campamento*) (mil) camp; **a campo traviesa** across country; **campo de batalla** battlefield; **campo de juego** playground; **campo de tiro** range, shooting range; **campo santo** cemetery; **levantar el campo** (mil) to break camp; **quedar en el campo** to fall in battle
camposanto *m* cemetery
camuesa *f* pippin (*apple*)
camueso *m* pippin (*tree*)
camuflaje *m* camouflage
camuflar *tr* to camouflage
can *m* dog; (*de arma de fuego*) trigger
cana *f* grey hair; **echar una cana al aire** (coll) to cut loose, to step out; **peinar canas** (coll) to be getting old
Canadá, el Canada
canadiense *adj & mf* Canadian
canal *m* (*cauce artificial*) canal; (*estrecho en el mar*) channel; (anat) duct, canal; (telv) channel; **Canal de la Mancha** English Channel; **Canal de Panamá** Panama Canal; **Canal de Suez** Suez Canal; **canal alimenticio** alimentary canal || *f* channel; (*conducto del tejado*) gutter; (*estría*) flute, groove; pipe; (*de un libro*) fore edge
canalización *f* (*de agua o gas*) mains, pipes; ductwork; (elec) wiring; **canalización de consumo** (elec) house current
canalizar §60 to channel; to pipe; (elec) to wire
canalizo *m* (naut) waterway, fairway
canalón *m* rain-water spout; shovel hat; **canalones** ravioli
canalla *m* (coll) churl, scoundrel || *f* (coll) riffraff, canaille
canallada *f* (coll) dirty trick, meanness
canana *f* cartridge belt
canapé *m* sofa, couch
Canarias *fpl* Canaries
cana•rio -ria *adj & mf* Canarian || *m* canary, canary bird || *fpl* see **Canarias**
canasta *f* basket, hamper
canastilla *f* basket; (*ropa para el niño que ha de nacer*) layette; (*equipo de novia*) (dial) trousseau
canastillo *m* basket-weave tray
canasto *m* hamper || **canastos** *interj* confound it!
cáncamo *m* eyebolt; **cáncamo de argolla** ringbolt
cancanear *intr* (coll) to loaf around; (Am) to stammer
cancel *m* storm door; (Am) folding screen
cancela *f* door of ironwork
cancelar *tr* to cancel; (*una deuda*) to pay off
cáncer *m* cancer
cancero•so -sa *adj* cancerous
cancilla *f* lattice gate
canciller *m* chancellor
cancillería *f* chancellery
canción *f* song; poem, lyric poem; **canción de amor** love song; **canción de cuna** cradlesong, lullaby; **canción típica** folk song; **volver a la misma canción** to sing the same old song
cancionero *m* songbook; anthology

cancionista *mf* popular singer
canco *m* (Chile) flowerpot; (Chile) earthen jug; (Chile) chamber pot; (Bol) buttock; **cancos** (Chile) woman's broad hips
cancón *m* (coll) bugaboo; **hacer un cancón a** (Mex) to try to bluff
cancha *f* field, ground; race track; golf links; tennis court; cockpit; (Urug) path, way; **estar en su cancha** (Arg, Chile, Urug) to be in one's element; **tener cancha** (Arg) to have pull || *interj* gangway!
canche *adj* (Col) tasteless, poorly seasoned; (CAm) blond
candado *m* padlock
candar *tr* to lock, to padlock
candela *f* candle; candlestick; fire, light; **con la candela en la mano** at death's door
candelabro *m* candelabrum
candelecho *m* elevated hut for watching the vineyard
candelero *m* candlestick; brass olive-oil lamp; fishing torch
candelilla *f* catkin; (Arg, Chile) will-o'-the-wisp; (Am) glowworm
candida•to -ta *mf* candidate
candidatura *f* candidacy; list of candidates; voting paper
candidez *f* whiteness; innocence
cándi•do -da white; simple, innocent
candil *m* open olive-oil lamp
candilejas *fpl* footlights
candon•go -ga *adj* fawning, slick; loafing, shirking || *mf* fawner, flatterer; loafer, shirker || *f* fawning; teasing
candonguear *tr* (coll) to kid, tease || *intr* (coll) to scheme to get out of work
candor *m* innocence, ingenuousness
caneca *f* glazed earthen bottle
cane•co -ca *adj* (Arg, Bol) tipsy || *f* see **caneca**
canela *f* cinnamon; (*cosa fina*) (coll) peach
canela•do -da *adj* cinnamon-colored
cane•lo -la *adj* cinnamon || *m* (*árbol*) cinnamon || *f* see **canela**
canelón *m* rain-water spout; large icicle; cinnamon candy
cane•sú *m* (*pl* **-súes**) (*prenda*) guimpe; (*pieza de una prenda*) yoke
cangilón *m* jug, jar, bucket; (*de draga*) bucket, scoop; (Am) rut, track
cangrejo *m* crab
cangrena *f* gangrene
cangrenar *ref* to have gangrene
canguro *m* kangaroo
caníbal *adj* & *mf* cannibal
canica *f* (*bolita*) marble; (*juego*) marbles
canicie *f* whiteness (*of hair*)
canícula *f* dog days || **Canícula** *f* Dog Star
caniculares *mpl* dog days
cani•jo -ja *adj* (coll) weak, sickly || *mf* (coll) weakling
canilla *f* shank (*of leg*); (*espita, grifo*) tap; bobbin, spool; (Mex) strength
cani•no -na *adj* canine || *m* canine, canine tooth || *f* excrement of dogs
canje *m* exchange
canjear *tr* to exchange
ca•no -na *adj* gray; gray-haired; hoary, old || *f* see **cana**
canoa *f* canoe; launch
canoe•ro -ra *mf* canoeist
canon *m* canon
canóni•co -ca *adj* canonical || *f* rules of canonical life
canóniga *f* (coll) nap before eating; (coll) drunk
canónigo *m* canon
canonizar §60 *tr* to canonize; to approve
canonjía *f* (coll) sinecure
cano•ro -ra *adj* (*voz*) melodious; (*ave*) song, sweet-singing
cano•so -sa *adj* gray-haired
canotié *m* straw hat, skimmer
cansa•do -da *adj* tired, weary; exhausted, worn-out; tiresome
cansancio *m* tiredness, fatigue
cansar *tr* to tire, weary; to bore || *intr* be tiresome || *ref* to tire, get tired
cantable *adj* tuneful, singable || *m* (*del libreto de una zarzuela*) lyric; (*de una zarzuela*) musical passage
canta•dor -dora *mf* singer of popular songs
cantaletear *tr* (Am) to say over and over again; (Am) to make fun of
cantalupo *m* cantaloupe
cantante *adj* singing || *mf* singer
cantar *m* song, singing; chant; **Cantar de los Cantares** Song of Songs || *tr* to sing; to chant; to sing of; **cantarlas claras** (coll) to speak out|| *intr* to sing; to chant; (coll) to creak, squeak; (coll) to squeal, to peach; **cantar de plano** (coll) to make a full confession
cántara *f* jug, pitcher
cantárida *f* Spanish fly
canta•rín -rina *adj* (*voz*) melodious; (coll) fond of singing || *mf* singer || *m* professional singer
cántaro *m* jug, pitcher; jugful; ballot box; **llover a cántaros** to rain pitchforks
canta•triz *f* (*pl* **-trices**) singer
cantera *f* quarry; talent, genius
cántico *m* canticle
cantidad *f* quantity; amount; sum; **cantidad de movimiento** (mech) momentum
cantiga *f* poem of the troubadours
cantilena *f* ballad, song; **salir con la misma cantilena** (coll) to sing the same old song
cantimplora *f* siphon; carafe, decanter; (*frasco para llevar bebida*) canteen; (Col) powder flask; (Guat) mumps
cantina *f* cantine; lunchroom, station restaurant; (Am) barroom
cantinera *f* camp follower
cantinero *m* bartender
canto *m* song; singing; (*división del poema épico*) canto; (*de notas iguales y uniformes*) chant; (*extremidad*) edge; (*esquina*) corner; (*de cuchillo*) back; (*de pan*) crust; stone, pebble; **canto de corte** cutting edge; **canto del cisne** swan song
cantonera *f* corner reinforcement; corner table, corner shelf; streetwalker

cantonero *m* corner loafer
can·tor -tora *adj* singing; (*pájaro*) song || *mf* singer || *m* chanter; minstrel; poet, bard
canto·so -sa *adj* rocky, stony
canturrear *tr & intr* to hum
canturreo *m* hum, humming
canzonetista *mf* popular singer
caña *f* cane; reed; stalk, stem; (*del brazo o la pierna*) long bone; (*de bota o media*) leg; wineglass; **caña de azúcar** sugar cane; **caña de pescar** fishing rod
cañada *f* glen, ravine, gully; cattle path; (Am) brook
cañamazo *m* canvas, burlap; embroidered canvas
cañamiel *f* sugar cane
cáñamo *m* hemp
cañamones *mpl* birdseed
cañaveral *m* canebrake; sugar-cane plantation
cañería *f* pipe; pipe line; piping; **cañería maestra** gas main, water main
cañero *m* pipe fitter, plumber; (Am) sugar-cane dealer; (SAm) cheat; (SAm) bluffer
cañista *m* pipe fitter, plumber
caño *m* pipe, tube; gutter, sewer; ditch; (*chorro*) spurt, jet; (*canal angosto*) channel; organ pipe; (*río pequeño*) (Col) stream
cañón *m* (*pieza de artillería*) cannon; (*valle estrecho*) canyon; (*de arma de fuego; de pluma*) barrel; (*pluma de ave*) quill; (*de escalera*) well; (*de columna; de ascensor*) shaft; organ pipe; (Col) trunk of tree; **cañón de campaña** fieldpiece; **cañón de chimenea** flue, chimney flue; **cañón obús** howitzer
cañonear *tr* to cannonade, to shell
cañutazo *m* (coll) gossip
caoba *f* mahogany
caos *m* chaos
caóti·co -ca *adj* chaotic
cap. *abbr* **capitán, capítulo**
capa *f* cloak, cape, mantle; (*de pintura*) coat; (*lo que cubre*) bed, layer; (*apariencia, pretexto*) (fig) cloak, mask; **capa del cielo** canopy of heaven; **andar de capa caída** to be on the decline, be in a bad way; (*comedia*) **de capa y espada** cloak-and-sword; (*intriga, espionaje*) **de capa y espada** cloak-and-dagger; **so capa de** under the guise of
capacidad *f* capacity
capacitar *tr* to enable, qualify; to empower || *ref* to become qualified
capacha *f* fruit basket; (SAm) jail
capacho *m* fruit basket; hamper; (*de albañil*) hod
capar *tr* to geld, castrate; to curtail
caparazón *m* caparison; horse blanket; nose bag; (*de crustáceo*) shell
caparrosa *f* vitriol
capa·taz *m* (*pl* **-taces**) overseer, foreman, boss
ca·paz *adj* (*pl* **-paces**) (*grande*) capacious, spacious; (*que tiene cierta aptitud; diestro, instruído*) capable; **capaz de** capable of; with a capacity of; **capaz para** competent in; qualified for; with room for
capcio·so -sa *adj* crafty, deceptive
capea *f* amateur free-for-all bullfight
capear *tr* (*al toro*) to challenge; (*el mal tiempo*) to weather; (coll) to deceive, take in || *intr* (naut) to lay to; (Guat) to play hooky
capellán *m* chaplain
capeo *m* capework (*of bullfighter*)
caperucita *f* little pointed hood; **Caperucita Roja** Little Red Ridinghood
caperuza *f* pointed hood; chimney cap
capilla *f* (*parte de una iglesia con altar*) chapel; (*de los reos de muerte*) death house; (*pliego suelto*) proof sheet; cowl, hood, cape; **estar en capilla** to be in the death house; (coll) to be on pins and needles; **estar expuesto en capilla ardiente** to be on view, to lie in state
capiller *m* churchwarden, sexton
capillo *m* baby cap; baptismal cap; hood; cocoon; (*del cigarro*) filler
capirotazo *m* fillip
capirote *m* hood; doctor's cap and hood; cardboard or paper cone (*worn on head*); fillip
capitación *f* poll tax
capital *adj* capital; main, principal; paramount; (*enemigo*) mortal || *m* (*dinero que produce renta*) capital; (*dinero que se presta para producir renta*) principal || *f* capital
capitalismo *m* capitalism
capitalista *adj* capitalistic || *mf* capitalist; shareholder, investor
capitalizar §60 *tr* to capitalize; (*los intereses devengados*) to compound
capitán *m* captain; leader; **capitán de bandera** flag captain; **capitán de corbeta** (nav) lieutenant commander; **capitán del puerto** harbor master
capitana *f* flagship
capitanear *tr* to captain; to lead, to command
capitanía *f* captaincy; (mil) company
capitel *m* (*de una iglesia*) spire; (*de una columna*) capital
capitolio *m* capitol
capítula *f* chapter (*of Scriptures*)
capitular *tr* to accuse; to agree on || *intr* to capitulate
capitulear *intr* (Arg, Chile, Peru) to lobby
capituleo *m* (Arg, Chile, Peru) lobbying
capitulero *m* (Arg, Chile, Peru) political henchman, lobbyist
capítulo *m* chapter; chapter house; subject, matter; errand; main point; **ganar capítulo** (coll) to win one's point; **llamar a capítulo** to take to task, call to account; **perder capítulo** (coll) to lose one's point
ca·pó *m* (*pl* **-pós**) hood (*of auto*)
capolar *tr* to cut to pieces, chop up
ca·pón -pona *adj* castrated || *m* eunuch; (*pollo*) capon; bundle of firewood; (*golpe*) (coll) fillip || *f* shoulder strap
caponera *f* coop for fattening capons; place of welcome; (*cárcel*) (coll) coop, jail

caporal *m* chief, leader; (Am) foreman (*on cattle ranch*)
capota *f* bonnet; (aer) cowling; (aut) top
capotaje *m* (aer) nosing over
capotar *intr* to upset; (aer) to nose over
capote *m* cape, cloak; (coll) frown, scowl; (Chile, Mex) beating; **capote de monte** poncho; **de capote** (Mex) on the sly; **dar capote a** (coll) to flabbergast; (*un rezagado*) (coll) to leave hungry; **decir para su capote** to say to oneself; **echar un capote** (coll) to turn the conversation
capotear *tr* (*al toro*) to challenge; (*dificultades*) to evade, duck; (coll) to beguile, take in; (*una obra teatral*) to cut, make cuts in
Capricornio *m* Capricorn
capricho *m* caprice, whim, fancy
capricho•so -sa *adj* capricious, whimsical; willful
caprichu•do -da *adj* (coll) capricious, whimsical
cápsula *f* capsule; (*de botella*) cap
capsular *tr* to cap
captación *f* capture; (*de las aguas de un río*) harnessing; (rad) tuning in, picking up
captar *tr* to catch; (*la confianza de una persona*) to win; (*las aguas de un río*) to harness; (*las ondas radiofónicas*) to tune in, to pick up; (*lo que uno dice*) to get, grasp || *ref* to attract, win
captura *f* capture, catch
capturar *tr* to capture, catch
capucha *f* cowl, hood; circumflex accent
capuchina *f* garden nasturtium, Indian cress; Capuchin nun; confection of egg yolks
capucho *m* cowl, hood
capuchón *m* lady's cloak and hood; (*de una plumafuente*) cap; (aut) valve cap
capullo *m* cocoon; coarse spun silk; bud; **capullo de rosa** rosebud
capuzar **§60** *tr* to throw in headfirst; (*un buque*) to overload at the bow
caqui *adj* khaki || *m* khaki; Japanese persimmon
caquinos *mpl* (Mex) guffaw, outburst of laughter
cara *f* face; look, countenance; façade, front; (*de disco de fonógrafo*) side; **a cara descubierta** openly; **a cara o cruz** heads or tails; **cara a** facing; **cara al público** with an audience; **cara de acelga** (coll) sallow face; **cara de ajo** (coll) vinegar face; **cara de hereje** (*persona de feo aspecto*) (coll) fright, baboon; **cara de vinagre** (coll) vinegar face; **dar la cara** to take the consequences; **de cara** in the face; facing; **echar a cara o cruz** to flip a coin; **hacer cara a** to stand up to; **tener buena cara** to look well, to look good; **tener mala cara** to look ill, to look bad
cárabe *m* amber
carabina *f* carbine; (coll) chaperon
caracol *m* snail; snail shell; (*de pelo*) curl; (*trazado en espiral*) spiral; (*del oído*) cochlea
carácter *m* (*pl* **caracteres**) character; (*marca que se pone a las reses*) brand
característi•co -ca *adj* characteristic || *m* (theat) old man || *f* characteristic; (theat) old woman
caracteriza•do -da *adj* distinguished
caracterizar **§60** *tr* to characterize; to confer a distinction on; (*un personaje en la escena*) to interpret || *ref* to dress and make up for a role
caramba *interj* confound it!; upon my word!
carámbano *m* icicle
carambola *f* carom; (coll) double shot; (coll) trick, cheating
carambolear *intr* to carom || *ref* (coll) to get tipsy
caramelo *m* caramel; drop, lozenge
carantamaula *f* (coll) ugly false face; (*persona*) (coll) ugly mug
carantoña *f* (coll) ugly false face; **carantoñas** (coll) adulation, fawning
carátula *f* mask; (*profesión de actor*) stage, theater; (Am) title page; (*de reloj*) (Mex, Guat) face
caravana *f* caravan; (*casa rodante*) trailer
caravanera *f* caravansary
caray *m* var of **carey**
carbohielo *m* dry ice
carbóli•co -ca *adj* carbolic
carbón *m* (*de leña*) charcoal; (*de piedra*) coal; (*electrodo de carbono de la lámpara de arco o la pila*) carbon; black crayon; (*honguillo parásito*) smut; **carbón de bujía** cannel coal, jet coal; **carbón tal como sale** run-of-mine coal
carboncillo *m* charcoal, charcoal pencil
carbonera *f* bunker, coal bunker; coalbin; (Col) coal mine
carbonería *f* coalyard
carbone•ro -ra *adj* coal, charcoal; coaling || *mf* coaldealer; charcoal burner || *f* see **carbonera**
carbonilla *f* fine coal; (*en los cilindros*) carbon
carbonizar **§60** *tr* to char
carbono *m* carbon
carbunclo *m* (*piedra*) carbuncle; (pathol) carbuncle
carbunco *m* (pathol) carbuncle
carbúnculo *m* (*piedra*) carbuncle
carburador *m* carburetor
carburo *m* carbide
carcacha *f* (Mex) jalopy
carcaj *m* quiver
carcajada *f* outburst of laughter
cárcel *f* jail, prison; (*para oprimir dos piezas de madera encoladas*) clamp
carcele•ro -ra *adj* jail || *m* jailer, warden
carcoma *f* woodworm, borer; anxiety, worry; spendthrift
carcomer *tr* to bore, gnaw away at; to undermine, to harass || *ref* to become worm-eaten
cardán *m* universal joint
cardenal *m* cardinal; cardinal bird; black-and-blue mark

cardenillo *m* verdigris
cárde•no -na *adj* purple; dapple-gray; (*agua*) opaline
cardía•co -ca *adj* cardiac || *mf* (*persona que padece del corazón*) cardiac || *m* (*remedio*) cardiac
cardinal *adj* cardinal
cardo *m* thistle
cardume *m* school (*of fish*)
carear *tr* to bring face to face; to compare || *intr* — **carear a** to overlook || *ref* to meet face to face
carecer **§22** *intr* — **carecer de** to lack, need, be in want of
carecimiento *m* lack, need, want
carencia *f* lack, need, want
carente *adj* — **carente de** lacking
careo *m* meeting; confrontation
care•ro -ra *adj* (coll) dear, expensive
carestía *f* scarcity, want, dearth; high prices; **carestía de la vida** high cost of living
careta *f* mask; **careta antigás** gas mask
carey *m* hawksbill turtle; tortoise shell
carga *f* load, loading; (*mercancías que se transportan*) freight, cargo; (*peso u obligación que pesan sobre una persona*) burden; (*de substancia explosiva, de electricidad, de soldados contra el enemigo*) charge; charge, responsibility, obligation; **carga de familia** dependent; **carga de punta** (elec) peak load; **carga útil** pay load; **echar la carga a** to put the blame on; **volver a la carga** to keep at it
cargaderas *fpl* (Col) suspenders
cargadero *m* loading platform; freight station
carga•do -da *adj* loaded; (*cielo*) overcast, cloudy; (*atmósfera, tiempo*) close, sultry; (*alambre eléctrico*) hot, charged; (*café, té*) strong; (*rato, hora*) busy; **cargado de años** along in years; **cargado de espaldas** round-shouldered, stoop-shouldered
cargador *m* loader, stevedore; carrier, porter; (*de acumulador*) charger
cargamento *m* load; (naut) loading; (naut) cargo, shipment
cargante *adj* (coll) boring, annoying, tiresome
cargar **§44** *tr* (*un peso, mercancías; un carro, un mulo, un barco; un horno; un arma de fuego; a una persona*) to load; (*a una persona con un peso u obligación*) to burden; (*un acumulador; al enemigo*) to charge; (*a una persona*) to charge with; to entrust with; (coll) to annoy, bore, weary; **cargar en cuenta a** (*una persona*) to charge to the account of; **cargar** (*a una persona*) **de** to charge with; to burden with || *intr* to load; (*el viento*) to turn; to crowd; to incline, tip; (*el acento*) to fall; (coll) to eat too much, drink too much; **cargar con** to pick up; to walk away with; (*un fusil*) to shoulder; to take on; **cargar sobre** to rest on; to bother, pester; to devolve on || *ref* (*el cielo*) to become overcast; (*el viento*) to turn; (coll) to become annoyed, be bored; **cargarse de** to have a lot of; (*lágrimas*) to be bathed in
cargaréme *m* receipt, voucher
cargazón *f* loading; (*en el estómago, la cabeza, etc.*) heaviness; mass of heavy clouds; (Arg) clumsy job; (Chile) good crop
cargo *m* job, position; duty, responsibility; burden, weight; management; (*falta que se atribuye a uno; cantidad que uno debe y la acción de anotarla*) charge; **a cargo de** in charge of; **cargo de conciencia** sense of guilt; **girar a cargo de** to draw on; **hacerse cargo de** to take charge of; to realize, become aware of; to look into; **librar a cargo de** to draw on; **vestir el cargo** to look the part
cargosear *tr* (Arg, Chile) to pester
cargo•so -sa *adj* annoying, bothersome; onerous, costly
carguero *m* (naut) freighter; (Arg, Urug) beast of burden
cariaconteci•do -da *adj* (coll) downcast, woebegone
cariar **§77** *tr & intr* to decay
cariátide *f* caryatid
Caribdis *f* Charybdis
caribe *adj* Caribbean || *m* savage, brute
caricatura *f* (*descripción o figura grotescas; retrato festivo*) caricature; (*retrato festivo*) cartoon
caricaturista *mf* caricaturist; cartoonist
caricaturizar **§60** *tr* to caricature; to cartoon
caricia *f* caress; endearment
caridad *f* charity; **la caridad bien ordenada empieza por uno mismo** charity begins at home
caries *f* decay, tooth decay; caries
carilla *f* (*de colmenero*) mask; (*de libro*) page
carille•no -na *adj* full-faced
carillón *m* carillon
carine•gro -gra *adj* swarthy
cariño *m* love, affection; loved one; (Chile) gift, present; **cariños** caresses, endearments; (Arg) greetings
cariño•so -sa *adj* loving, affectionate
caripare•jo -ja *adj* (coll) stone-faced, impassive
carirraí•do -da *adj* brazen-faced, shameless
carita *f* little face; **dar** or **hacer carita** (*una mujer coqueta*) (Mex) to smile back
caritati•vo -va *adj* charitable
cariz *m* (*de la atmósfera, el tiempo*) appearance, look; (*de un asunto*) (coll) look, outlook; (*de la cara de uno*) (coll) look; **mal cariz** black look, scowl
carlinga *f* (aer) cockpit
Carlomagno *m* Charlemagne
Carlos *m* Charles
carlota *f* pudding; **carlota rusa** charlotte russe || **Carlota** *f* Charlotte
carmen *m* song, poem; house and garden (*in Granada*)
carmesí (*pl* **-síes**) *adj & m* crimson
carnada *f* bait; (coll) bait, trap
carnal *adj* carnal; (*hermano*) full; (*primo*) first

carne *f* (*parte blanda del cuerpo humano y del animal*) flesh; (*la comestible del animal*) meat; **carne de cañón** cannon fodder; **carne de cerdo asada** roast pork; **carne de cordero** lamb; **carne de gallina** goose flesh; **carne de horca** gallows bird; **carne de res** beef; **carne de ternera** veal; **carne de vaca asada** roast of beef; **carne de venado** venison; **carne fiambre** cold meat; **carne sin hueso** (coll) cinch, snap; **carne y sangre** flesh and blood; **cobrar carnes** (coll) to put on flesh; **en carnes** naked; **en vivas carnes** stark-naked

carnear *tr* (Arg, Chile, Urug) to butcher, slaughter; (Arg, Urug) to stab; (Chile) to take in, swindle

carnero *m* sheep; (*carne de este animal*) mutton; (*osario*) charnel house; family vault; (*persona que no tiene voluntad propia*) (Arg, Chile) sheep; **cantar para el carnero** (Arg, Bol, Urug) to die; **no hay tales carneros** there's no truth to it

car•net *m* (*pl* **-nets**) notebook; membership card; (Arg) dance card; **carnet de chófer** driver's license; **carnet de identidad** identification card

carnicería *f* butcher shop, meat market; (fig) carnage, massacre

carnice•ro -ra *adj* carnivorous; bloodthirsty || *mf* butcher

carnosidad *f* fleshiness, corpulence; (*excrecencia carnosa anormal*) proud flesh

carno•so -sa *adj* fleshy; meaty, fat

ca•ro -ra *adj* (*de subido precio; amado, querido*) dear || *f* see **cara** || **caro** *adv* dear

carpa *f* carp; (Am) awning, tent; (Am) stand at a fair; **carpa dorada** goldfish

carpanta *f* (coll) raging hunger

carpeta *f* (*cubierta para mesas*) table cover; (*par de cubiertas para documentos*) letter file, portfolio; (*factura*) invoice; (Col) accounting department; (Peru) writing desk

carpintería *f* carpentry; carpenter shop; **carpintería de taller** millwork

carpintero *m* carpenter; woodpecker; **carpintero de carreta** wheelwright

carra•co -ca *adj* (coll) old, decrepit || *f* (*barco viejo*) tub, hulk; (*instrumento de madera para producir un ruido desapacible*) rattle; (*berbiquí*) ratchet drill || **la Carraca** Cádiz navy yard

carraspear *intr* to be hoarse

carraspera *f* hoarseness

carrera *f* (*paso del que corre*) run; (*lucha de velocidad*) race; (*sitio para correr*) race track; (*espacio recorrido corriendo*) course, stretch; (*curso de la vida, profesión*) career; (*calle*) avenue, boulevard; (*raya, crencha*) part (*in hair*); (*en las medias*) run; (*hilera*) row, line; (*viga*) rafter, girder; (*movimiento del émbolo del motor*) stroke; **a carrera abierta** at full speed; **carrera a pie** foot race; **carrera ascendente** upstroke; **carrera de baquetas** gantlet; **carrera de caballos** horse race; **carrera de campanario** steeplechase; **carrera de obstáculos** obstacle race; steeplechase; **carrera de relevos** relay race; **carrera descendente** downstroke; **carrera de vallas** hurdle race; **carreras** horse racing, turf

carrerista *adj* horsy || *mf* racegoer; auto racer; bicycle racer || *m* outrider || *f* (slang) streetwalker

carreta *f* cart; **carreta de bueyes** oxcart

carrete *m* reel, spool; fishing reel; (elec) coil

carretear *tr* to cart, haul; (*un carro, una carreta*) to drive; (aer) to taxi || *intr* (aer) to taxi

carretera *f* highway, road; **carretera de peaje** turnpike; **carretera de vía libre** expressway, limited-access highway

carretería *f* carts; wagon work; carting business; wagon shop

carrete•ro -ra *adj* wagon, carriage || *m* wheelwright; teamster; charioteer; **jurar como un carretero** (coll) to swear like a trooper || *f* see **carretera**

carretilla *f* wheelbarrow; baggage truck; (*para enseñar a los niños a andar*) gocart; (*buscapiés*) snake, serpent; (Arg, Chile, Urug) jaw; **carretilla de mano** handcart; **carretilla elevadora** lift truck; **de carretilla** (coll) offhand

carretón *m* cart, wagon, dray; gocart; (rr) truck; (Am) covered wagon

carricoche *m* covered wagon

carricuba *f* street sprinkler

carril *m* (*barra de acero en el ferrocarril*) rail, track; (*huella*) track, rut; (*hecho por el arado*) furrow; lane, path; (Chile) train; (Chile, P-R) railroad; **carril de toma** third rail

carrilera *f* track, rut

carrilero *m* (Peru) railroader

carrillera *f* jaw; chin strap

carrillo *m* cheek, jowl; pulley; **comer a dos carrillos** (coll) to eat like a glutton; (coll) to have two sources of income; (coll) to play both sides

carrizo *m* ditch reed

carro *m* cart, wagon; (mach) carriage; (Am) car, auto; **carro alegórico** float; **carro blindado** armored car; **carro correo** mail car; **carro de asalto** tank; **carro de combate** combat car, tank; **carro de equipajes** baggage car; **carro de mudanza** moving van; **carro de riego** street sprinkler; **carro frigorífero** refrigerator car; **carro fúnebre** hearse; **Carro mayor** Big Dipper; **Carro menor** Little Dipper; **carro romano** chariot; **pare Vd. el carro** hold your horses

ca•rró *m* (*pl* **-rrós**) diamond

carrocería *f* (*de automóvil*) body

carrocha *f* eggs (*of insect*)

carromato *m* covered wagon

carro•ño -ña *adj* & *f* carrion

carroza *f* coach, carriage; **carroza alegórica** float; **carroza fúnebre** hearse

carruaje *m* carriage

carta *f* (*comunicación escrita*) letter; (*constitución escrita de un país*) charter; (*naipe*) card, playing card; map; **carta aérea** air-mail letter; **carta blanca** carte blanche; **carta certificada** registered letter; **carta de marear** (naut) chart; **carta de naturaleza** naturalization papers; **carta general** form letter; **carta por avión** air-mail letter; **poner las cartas boca arriba** to put one's cards on the table

cartabón *m* carpenter's square

cartagi·nés -nesa *adj & mf* Carthaginian

Cartago *f* Carthage

cartapacio *m* notebook; schoolboy's satchel; writing book; (*papeles contenidos en una carpeta*) file, dossier

cartear *intr* to play low cards (*in order to see how the game stands*) || *ref* to write to each other

cartel *m* show bill, poster, placard; cartel, trust; (*pasquín*) lampoon; (*de toreros*) bill, line-up; (*del torero*) fame, reputation; **cartel de teatro** bill, show bill; **dar cartel a** (coll) to headline; **se prohibe fijar carteles** post no bills; **tener cartel** (coll) to be the rage

cartela *f* card; bracket

cartelera *f* billboard; (*en los periódicos*) amusement page, theater section

cartelero *m* billposter

cartelón *m* show bill

carteo *m* finessing; exchange of letters

cárter *m* (mach) housing; **cárter de engranajes** gearcase; **cárter del cigüeñal** crankcase

cartera *f* portfolio; pocket flap; **cartera de bolsillo** billfold, wallet

cartería *f* sorting room

carterista *m* pickpocket, purse snatcher

cartero *m* letter carrier, postman

cartilagino·so -sa *adj* gristly

cartílago *m* gristle

cartilla *f* primer, speller, reader; notebook; (*de la caja de ahorros*) deposit book; **cartilla de racionamiento** ration book

cartivana *f* (bb) hinge, joint

cartón *m* cardboard, pasteboard; cardboard box; **cartón de yeso y fieltro** plasterboard; **cartón picado** stencil; **cartón tabla** wallboard

cartoné — **en cartoné** (bb) in boards, bound in boards

cartucho *m* cartridge

cartulina *f* fine cardboard

casa *f* (*edificio para habitar*) house; (*hogar, domicilio*) home; (*establecimiento comercial o industrial*) firm, concern; (*familia*) household; (*escaque*) square; **a casa** home, homeward; **casa consistorial** town hall, city hall; **casa de azotea** penthouse; **casa de campo** country house; **casa de caridad** poorhouse; **casa de citas** house of assignation; **casa de correos** post office; **casa de empeños** pawnshop; **casa de expósitos** foundling home; **casa de fieras** menagerie; **casa de huéspedes** boarding house; **casa de juego** gambling house; **casa de locos** madhouse; **casa de modas** dress shop; **casa de moneda** mint; **casa de préstamos** pawnshop; **casa de salud** private hospital; **casa de socorro** first-aid station; **casa de vecindad** or **de vecinos** apartment house, tenement house; **casa editorial** publishing house; **casa matriz** main office; **casa pública** brothel; **casa real** royal palace; royal family; **casas baratas** low-cost housing; **casa solar** or **solariega** ancestral mansion, manor house; **casa y comida** board and lodging; **¡convida la casa!** the drinks are on the house!; **en casa** home, at home; **ir a buscar casa** to go house hunting; **poner casa** to set up housekeeping

casaca *f* dress coat; (coll) marriage contract; (Guat, Hond) lively whispered conversation; **volver la casaca** (coll) to become a turncoat

casade·ro -ra *adj* marriageable

casa·do -da *adj* married || *mf* married person

casal *m* country place; (Arg) pair, couple

casamente·ro -ra *adj* matchmaking || *mf* matchmaker

casamiento *m* marriage; wedding

casapuerta *f* entrance hall, vestibule

casaquilla *f* jacket

casar *tr* to marry; to marry off; to match; to harmonize; (law) to annul, repeal || *intr* to marry, get married || *ref* to marry, get married; **no casarse con nadie** (coll) to get tied up with nobody

casatienda *f* store and home combined

cascabel *m* sleigh bell, jingle bell; rattlesnake; **ponerle cascabel al gato** (coll) to bell the cat

cascabelear *intr* to jingle; (coll) to act tactlessly

cascabeleo *m* jingle

cascabele·ro -ra *adj* (coll) tactless, thoughtless || *mf* (coll) featherbrain || *m* baby's rattle

cascabillo *m* jingle bell; chaff, husk; cup of acorn

cascada *f* cascade, waterfall

cascajo *m* pebble; gravel, rubble; (coll) broken jar; (coll) piece of junk; **estar hecho un cascajo** (coll) to be old and worn-out, to be a wreck

cascanue·ces *m* (*pl* **-ces**) nutcracker

cascar §73 *tr* to crack, break, split; (coll) to beat, strike, hit || *ref* to crack, break, split

cáscara *f* hull, peel, rind, shell; bark, crust; **cáscara rueda** (Arg) ring-around-a-rosy; **ser de la cáscara amarga** (coll) to be wild and flighty; (coll) to hold advanced views; (Mex) to be determined

cascarón *m* eggshell

cascarra·bias *mf* (*pl* **-bias**) (coll) crab, grouch

casco *m* (*pieza que sirve para proteger la cabeza del soldado, el bombero, etc.*) helmet; (*uña de las caba-*

llerías) hoof; (*pedazo de vasija rota*) potsherd; (*capa de la cebolla*) coat, shell; (*del sombrero*) crown; (*cuerpo de la nave*) hull; (*de un barco inservible*) hulk; (*barril, pipa*) barrel, tank, cask, vat; (*pieza del teléfono*) headset, headpiece; bottle; (mach) shell, casing; (*gajo de la naranja*) (Arg, Col, Chile) slice; (Peru) chest, breast; **casco de población** or **casco urbano** city limits; **romperse los cascos** (coll) to rack one's brain

casera *f* landlady; housekeeper

casería *f* country place; (Am) customers

caserío *m* country house; small settlement, hamlet

case•ro -ra *adj* homemade; homeloving; (*remedio*) household; house, home; (*sencillo*) homely || *mf* owner, proprietor; renter; caretaker; janitor; (Am) huckster; (Am) vendor || *m* landlord || *f* see **casera**

caseta *f* (*casa sin piso alto*) cottage; (*de una feria*) stall, booth; bathhouse

casi *adv* almost, nearly; **casi nada** next to nothing; **casi nunca** hardly ever

casilla *f* hut, shack, shed; cabin, lodge; stall, booth; (*escaque*) square; (*compartimiento en un mueble*) pigeonhole; (*división del papel rayado*) column, square; (*taquilla*) ticket office; (*de locomotora o camión*) cab; (Bol, Chile, Peru, Urug) post-office box; (Ecuad) water closet; (Cuba) bird trap; **sacarle a uno de sus casillas** (coll) to jolt someone out of his old habits; (coll) to drive someone crazy

casille•ro -ra *mf* (rr) crossing guard || *m* filing cabinet, set of pigeonholes

casino *m* casino; club; clubhouse

caso *m* case; chance; event; **caso de conformidad** in case you agree; **caso que** in case; **de caso pensado** deliberately, on purpose; **en todo caso** at all events; **hacer al caso** (coll) to be to the purpose; **hacer caso de** (coll) to take into account, pay attention to; **hacer caso omiso de** to pass over in silence, not mention; **no venir al caso** to be beside the point; **poner por caso** to take as an example; **venir al caso** to be just the thing

casorio *m* (coll) hasty marriage, unwise marriage

caspa *f* dandruff, scurf

cáspita *interj* well, well!, upon my word!

caspo•so -sa *adj* full of dandruff

casquete *m* (*cubierta que se ajusta al casco de la cabeza*) skullcap; skull, cranium; (*pieza de la armadura que cubre el casco de la cabeza*) helmet; (*pieza del teléfono*) headset

casquillo *m* butt, cap, tip; bushing, sleeve; ferrule; (Am) horseshoe

casquiva•no -na *adj* (coll) scatterbrained

casta *f* caste; kind, quality; breed, race

castaña *f* chestnut; (*moño*) knot, chignon; demijohn; **castaña de Indias** horse chestnut; **castaña de Pará** Brazil nut

castañeta *f* castanet; snapping of the fingers

castañetear *tr* (*los dedos*) to snap, to click; (*p.ej., una seguidilla*) to click off with the castanets || *intr* to click; (*los dientes*) to chatter

casta•ño -ña *adj* chestnut, chestnut-colored; (*p.ej., pelo*) brown; (*p.ej., ojos*) hazel || *m* chestnut tree; **castaño de Indias** horse chestnut || *f* see **castaña**

castañuela *f* castanet; **estar como unas castañuelas** (coll) to be bubbling over with joy

castella•no -na *adj & mf* Castilian || *m* Castilian, Spanish (*language*) || *f* chatelaine

casticidad *f* purity, correctness (*in language*)

casticismo *m* purism

castidad *f* chastity

castiga•dor -dora *mf* punisher || *m* (coll) seducer, Don Juan

castigar §44 *tr* to punish, chastise; (*la carne*) to mortify; (*los gastos*) to cut down, curtail; (*obras, escritos*) to correct, emend; (*un tornillo*) (Mex) to tighten

castigo *m* punishment, chastisement

Castilla *f* Castile; **Castilla la Nueva** New Castile; **Castilla la Vieja** Old Castile

castillo *m* castle; (*montura sobre un elefante*) howdah; **castillo en el aire** castle in Spain, castle in the air; **castillo de naipes** house of cards; **castillo de proa** forecastle

casti•zo -za *adj* chaste, pure, correct; pure-blooded; real, regular

cas•to -ta *adj* chaste, pure || *f* see **casta**

castor *m* beaver

castrar *tr* to castrate; (*una planta*) to prune, cut back; to weaken

casual *adj* casual, accidental, chance

casualidad *f* accident, chance; chance event; **por casualidad** by chance

casuca or **casucha** *f* shack, shanty

casulla *f* chasuble

cata *f* tasting; taste, sample

catacal•dos *mf* (*pl* **-dos**) (coll) rolling stone; (coll) busybody

catacumba *f* catacomb

cata•lán -lana *adj & mf* Catalan, Catalonian

catalejo *m* spyglass

catalogar §44 *tr* to catalogue

catálogo *m* catalogue

Cataluña *f* Catalonia

cataplasma *f* poultice; **cataplasma de mostaza** mustard plaster

catapulta *f* catapult

catapultar *tr* to catapult

catar *tr* to taste, sample; to check, examine; to be on the look out for

catarata *f* cataract, waterfall; (pathol) cataract

catarro *m* (*inflamación de las membranas mucosas*) catarrh; (*resfriado*) head cold

catástrofe *f* catastrophe

catavino *m* cup for tasting wine
catavi•nos *m* (*pl* **-nos**) winetaster; (*borracho*) (coll) rounder
catear *tr* to hunt, look for; (*a un alumno*) to flunk; (Am) to explore; (*una casa*) (Am) to search
catecismo *m* catechism
cátedra *f* chair, professorship; academic subject; teacher's desk; classroom; **poner cátedra** to hold forth
catedral *f* cathedral
catedrático *m* university professor
categoría *f* category; status, standing; class, kind; condition, quality; **de categoría** prominent
caterva *f* throng, crowd
catéter *m* catheter
cateterizar **§60** *tr* to catheterize
cátodo *m* cathode
católi•co -ca *adj* catholic; Catholic; **no estar muy católico** (coll) to be under the weather || *mf* Catholic; **católico romano** Roman Catholic
catorce *adj & pron* fourteen || *m* fourteen; (*en las fechas*) fourteenth
catorcea•vo -va *adj & m* fourteenth
catorza•vo -va *adj & m* fourteenth
catre *m* cot; **catre de tijera** folding cot
catrecillo *m* campstool, folding canvas chair
ca•trín -trina *adj* (CAm, Mex) sporty, swell || *mf* (CAm, Mex) sport, dude
caucasia•no -na or **caucási•co -ca** *adj & mf* Caucasian
Cáucaso *m* Caucasus
cauce *m* river bed; channel, ditch, trench
caución *f* precaution; (law) bail, security
caucionar *tr* to guard against; (law) to give bail for
cauchal *m* rubber plantation
caucho *m* rubber; rubber plant; (Col) rubber raincoat; **caucho esponjoso** foam rubber; **cauchos** (*chanclos*) (Am) rubbers
caudal *adj* of great volume || *m* (*de agua*) volume; abundance; wealth
caudalo•so -sa *adj* of great volume; abundant; rich, wealthy
caudillo *m* chief, leader; military leader; caudillo, head of state
causa *f* cause; (law) suit, trial; (Chile) bite, snack; (Peru) potato salad; **a** or **por causa de** on account of, because of
causa•dor -dora *adj* causing || *mf* (*persona*) cause
causante *mf* (*persona*) cause; (law) principal, constituent; (Mex) taxpayer
causar *tr* to cause
causear *tr* (Chile) to get the best of || *intr* (Chile) to have a bite
causeo *m* (Chile) bite, snack
cáusti•co -ca *adj* caustic
cautela *f* caution
cautelo•so -sa *adj* cautious, guarded
cauterizar **§60** *tr* to cauterize
cautín *m* soldering iron
cautivar *tr* to take prisoner; to attract, win over; (*encantar*) to captivate
cautiverio *m* or **cautividad** *f* captivity
cauti•vo -va *adj & mf* captive
cau•to -ta *adj* cautious
cavar *tr* to dig, dig up || *intr* (*una herida*) to go deep; (*el caballo*) to paw; **cavar en** to study thoroughly, to delve into
caverna *f* cavern, cave
cavidad *f* cavity
cavilar *tr* to brood over || *intr* to worry, fret
cavilo•so -sa *adj* suspicious, mistrustful; (CAm) gossipy; (Col) touchy
cayado *m* (*de pastor*) crook; (*de obispo*) crozier
cayo *m* key, reef; **Cayo Hueso** Key West; **Cayos de la Florida** Florida Keys
caz *m* (*pl* **caces**) flume, millrace
caza *m* pursuit plane, fighter; **caza de reacción** jet fighter || *f* chase, hunt; hunting; (*animales que se cazan*) game; **a caza de** on the hunt for; **caza al hombre** man hunt; **caza de grillos** fool's errand, wild-goose chase; **ir de caza** to go hunting
cazaautógra•fos *mf* (*pl* **-fos**) autograph seeker
caza•dor -dora *adj* hunting || *m* hunter; huntsman; **cazador de alforja** trapper; **cazador de cabezas** head-hunter; **cazador de dotes** fortune hunter; **cazador furtivo** poacher || *f* huntress; hunting jacket; jacket
cazanoti•cias (*pl* **-cias**) *m* newshawk || *f* newshen
cazar **§60** *tr* to chase; to hunt; to catch; (*en un descuido o error*) (coll) to catch up; (*un descuido o error*) (coll) to catch; (*adquirir con maña*) (coll) to wangle; (*con halagos o engaños*) to take in || *intr* to hunt
cazarreactor *m* jet fighter
cazcalear *intr* (coll) to buzz around
cazo *m* dipper, ladle; glue pot; (*de cuchillo*) back
cazuela *f* earthen casserole; stew; (archaic) gallery for women; (SAm) chicken stew
cazu•rro -rra *adj* (coll) sullen, surly
cazuz *m* ivy
C. de J. *abbr* **Compañía de Jesús**
cebada *f* barley
cebadera *f* nose bag
cebador *m* (mach) primer
cebar *tr* (*a un animal*) to fatten; (*un horno*) to feed; (*un arma de fuego, una bomba, un carburador*) to prime; (*una pasión, la esperanza*) to nourish; (*atraer*) to lure; (*un clavo, un tornillo*) to make catch, make take hold; (*un anzuelo*) to bait || *intr* (*un clavo, un tornillo*) to catch, take hold || *ref* (*una enfermedad, una epidemia*) to rage; **cebarse en** to be absorbed in; to vent one's fury on
cebo *m* fattening; feed; bait; lure; (*carga de un arma de fuego*) primer; priming
cebolla *f* onion; bulb; (*del velón*) oil receptacle
cebra *f* zebra
ce•bú *m* (*pl* **-búes**) zebu

ceca *f* mint; **de Ceca en Meca** or **de la Ceca a la Meca** hither and thither, from pillar to post
cecear *intr* to lisp
ceceo *m* lisp, lisping
cecina *f* dried beef
cedazo *m* sieve
ceder *tr* to yield, cede, give up || *intr* to yield, give way, give in; to slacken, relax; to go down, decline
cedro *m* cedar; **cedro de Virginia** juniper, red cedar
cédula *f* (*de papel*) slip; form, blank; rent sign; certificate, document; **cédula de vecindad** or **cédula personal** identification papers
cedulón *m* proclamation, public notice; (*pasquín*) lampoon
céfiro *m* zephyr
cegar §66 *tr* to blind; (*un agujero*) to plug, stop up; (*una puerta, una ventana*) to wall up || *intr* to go blind; to be blinded || *ref* to be blinded
ciega·to -ta *adj* (coll) dim-sighted, weak-eyed
ceguedad *f* blindness
ceguera *f* blindness
Ceilán Ceylon
ceila·nés -nesa *adj & mf* Ceylonese
ceja *f* (*pelo sobre la cuenca del ojo*) eyebrow; edge, rim; cloud cap; (Am) clearing for a road; **arquear las cejas** to raise one's eyebrows; **fruncir las cejas** to knit one's brow; **quemarse las cejas** to burn the midnight oil
cejar *intr* to back up; to turn back; to slacken
cejijun·to -ta or **ceju·do -da** *adj* beetle-browed; (coll) scowling
celada *f* ambush; trap, trick
celador *m* guard (*e.g., in a museum*); (elec) lineman; (Urug) policeman
celaje *m* cloud effect; skylight, transom; (Am) ghost
celar *tr* to see to; to watch over, to keep an eye on; to hide; to carve
celda *f* cell; **celda de castigo** solitary confinement
celdilla *f* cell; niche
celebración *f* celebration; applause; (*de una reunión*) holding
celebrante *m* (*sacerdote*) celebrant
celebrar *tr* to celebrate; (*una reunión*) to hold; (*aprobar*) to welcome; (*un matrimonio*) to perform; (*misa*) to say || *intr* (*decir misa*) to celebrate; to be glad || *ref* to take place, be held; to be celebrated
célebre *adj* celebrated, famous; (coll) funny, witty; (Am) pretty
celebridad *f* (*fama; persona*) celebrity
celeridad *f* speed, swiftness
celeste *adj* celestial; sky-blue
celestial *adj* celestial, heavenly; (coll) stupid, silly
celestina *f* procuress, bawd
celestinaje *m* procuring, pandering
celibato *m* celibacy; (coll) bachelor
célibe *adj* celibate, single, unmarried || *mf* celibate, single person || *m* bachelor || *f* spinster
celinda *f* mock orange
celo *m* zeal; envy; (*impulso reproductivo en las bestias*) heat, rut; **celos** jealousy
celofán *m* or **celofana** *f* cellophane
celosía *f* (*celotipia*) jealousy; (*enrejado de listoncillos*) lattice window, jalousie
celo·so -sa *adj* (*que tiene celo*) zealous; (*que tiene celos*) jealous; fearful, distrustful; (naut) unsteady
celotipia *f* jealousy
celta *adj* Celtic || *mf* Celt || *m* (*idioma*) Celtic
célti·co -ca *adj* Celtic
célula *f* cell
celuloide *m* celluloid; **llevar al celuloide** to put on the screen
cellisca *f* sleet, sleet storm
cellisquear *intr* to sleet
cementerio *m* cemetery
cemento *m* cement; concrete; **cemento armado** reinforced concrete
cena *f* supper; dinner || **la Cena** the Last Supper
cena·dor -dora *mf* diner-out || *m* arbor, bower, summerhouse
cenaduría *f* (Mex) supper club
cenagal *m* quagmire
cenago·so -sa *adj* muddy, miry
cenaoscu·ras *mf* (*pl* **-ras**) (coll) recluse; (coll) skinflint
cenar *tr* to have for supper, have for dinner || *intr* to have supper, have dinner
cencerrada *f* tin-pan serenade
cencerrear *intr* to keep jingling; to rattle, jangle; (coll) to play out of tune
cencerro *m* cowbell; **a cencerros tapados** (coll) cautiously
cendal *m* gauze, sendal
cenefa *f* edging, trimming, border
cenicero *m* ash tray
cenicien·to -ta *adj* ashen, ash-gray || **la Cenicienta** Cinderella
cenit *m* zenith
ceniza *f* ash; ashes; **cenizas** ashes; **huir de las cenizas y caer en las brasas** to jump from the frying pan into the fire
ceni·zo -za *adj* ashen, ash-gray || *f* see **ceniza**
cenojil *m* garter
cenote *m* (Mex) deep underground water reservoir
censo *m* census; **levantar el censo** to take the census
censor *m* censor; **censor jurado de cuentas** certified public accountant
censura *f* censure; censoring; gossip; **censura de cuentas** auditing
censurar *tr* (*criticar, reprobar*) to censure; (*formar juicio de*) to censor
centauro *m* centaur
centa·vo -va *adj* hundredth || *m* hundredth; cent
centella *f* flash of lightning; flash of light; spark; (*de ingenio, de ira*) (fig) spark, flash
centellar or **centellear** *intr* to flash, to spark; to glimmer, gleam, twinkle
centenar *m* hundred; **a centenares** by the hundreds

centena•rio -ria *adj* centennial || *mf* centenarian || *m* centennial
cente•no -na *adj* hundredth || *m* rye
centési•mo -ma *adj* & *m* hundredth
centígra•do -da *adj* centigrade
centímetro *m* centimeter
cénti•mo -ma *adj* hundredth || *m* hundredth; centime
centinela *mf* (*persona*) watch, guard || *m* & *f* (*soldado*) sentinel, sentry; **hacer de centinela** to stand sentinel
centípedo *m* centipede
central *adj* central || *m* sugar mill, sugar refinery || *f* headquarters, main office; powerhouse; (telp) exchange, central; **central de correos** main post office; **central de teléfonos** telephone exchange
centralizar **§60** *tr* & *ref* to centralize
centrar *tr* to center
céntri•co -ca *adj* center, central; (*próximo al centro de la ciudad*) downtown
centro *m* center; middle; business district, downtown; club; object, goal, purpose; **centro de mesa** centerpiece; **centro docente** educational institution; **pegar centro** (CAm) to hit the bull's-eye
Centro América *f* Central America
centroamerica•no -na *adj* & *mf* Central American
cénts. *abbr* **céntimos**
ceñi•do -da *adj* tight, tight-fitting; lithe, svelte; thrifty
ceñidor *m* belt, girdle, sash
ceñir **§72** *tr* to gird; to girdle; to fasten around the waist; to fasten, to tie; to abridge, shorten; to surround; (*la espada*) to gird on; (mil) to besiege || *ref* (*reducirse en los gastos*) to tighten one's belt; (*a pocas palabras*) to restrict oneself; to adapt oneself; **ceñirse a** (*p.ej., un muro*) to hug, keep close to
ceño *m* frown; (*del cielo, las nubes, el mar*) threatening look; (*cerco, aro*) hoop, ring, band; **arrugar el ceño** to knit one's brow; **mirar con ceño** to frown at
ceño•so -sa or **ceñu•do -da** *adj* beetle-browed; frowning, grim, gruff
cepa *f* (*de árbol*) stump; (*de la cola del animal*) stub; (*de la vid*) vinestalk; (*de una famila o linaje*) strain; **de buena cepa** of well-known quality
cepillar *tr* to plane; to brush; to smooth
cepillo *m* (*instrumento para alisar la madera*) plane; (*utensilio para limpieza*) brush; (*cepo para limosnas*) charity box, poor box; (CAm, Mex) flatterer; **cepillo de cabeza** hairbrush; **cepillo de dientes** toothbrush; **cepillo de ropa** clothesbrush; **cepillo de uñas** nail brush
cepo *m* (*de limosnas*) poor box; (*rama de árbol*) bough, branch; (*trampa*) snare, trap; (*del yunque*) stock; (*para devanar la seda*) reel; clamp, vise; (*para asegurar a un reo*) stocks, pillory; **¡cepos quedos!** (coll) quiet!, stop it!
cera *f* wax; **cera de abejas** beeswax; **cera de los oídos** earwax; **cera de lustrar** polishing wax; **cera de pisos** floor wax; **ceras** honeycomb; **ser como una cera** to be wax in one's hands
cerámi•co -ca *adj* ceramic
cerbatana *f* peashooter; ear trumpet; (coll) spokesman, go-between
cerca *m* (coll) close-up; **tener buen cerca** (coll) to look good at close quarters || *f* fence, wall; **cerca viva** hedge || *adv* near; **cerca de** near, close to; about; to, at the court of; **de cerca** closely; at close range
cercado *m* fence, wall; walled-in garden or field
cercanía *f* nearness, proximity; **cercanías** neighborhood, vicinity
cerca•no -na *adj* close, near; adjoining, neighboring; (*que debe acontecer en breve*) early
cercar **§73** *tr* to fence in, wall in; to encircle, surround; to crowd around; (mil) to besiege
cercenar *tr* to clip, trim; to curtail; to cut out
cerciorar *tr* to inform, assure || *ref* to find out; **cerciorarse de** to ascertain, find out about
cerco *m* (*aro, anillo*) hoop, ring; (*marco de puerta o ventana*) casing, frame; (*círculo que aparece alrededor del sol o la luna*) halo; (*reunión de personas*) circle, group; fence, wall; (mil) siege; **poner cerco a** (mil) to lay siege to
cerda *f* bristle, horsehair; (*hembra del cerdo*) sow
cerdear *intr* to be weak in the forelegs; (*las cuerdas de un instrumento*) to rasp, to grate; (coll) to hold back, look for excuses
Cerdeña *f* Sardinia
cerdo *m* hog; (*persona sucia*) (coll) pig, swine; (*hombre sin cortesía*) (coll) cad, ill-bred fellow; **cerdo de muerte** pig to be slaughtered; **cerdo de vida** pig not old enough to be slaughtered; **cerdo marino** porpoise
cerdo•so -sa *adj* bristly
cereal *adj* & *m* cereal
cerebro *m* brain; (*seso, inteligencia*) brain, brains
ceremonia *f* ceremony; formality; **de ceremonia** formal; **hacer ceremonias** to stand on ceremony; **por ceremonia** as a matter of form
ceremonio•so -sa *adj* ceremonious, punctilious; (*que gusta de ceremonias*) formal
cereza *f* cherry
cerezo *m* cherry tree
cerilla *f* wax taper; wax match
cerillera *f* or **cerillero** *m* match box
cerneja *f* fetlock
cerner **§51** *tr* to sift; (*el horizonte*) to scan || *intr* to bud, blossom; to drizzle || *ref* to waddle; (*el ave*) to soar, to hover; (*un mal*) to threaten; **cernerse sobre** (*amenazar*) to hang over
cernícalo *m* (orn) sparrow hawk; (coll) ignoramus; (coll) jag, drunk

cernir §28 *tr* to sift
cero *m* zero; **ser un cero a la izquierda** (coll) to not count, to be a nobody
cerote *m* shoemaker's wax; (coll) fear
cerotear *tr* (*el hilo*) to wax || *intr* (Chile) to drip
cerra•do -da *adj* closed; close; incomprehensible; (*cielo*) cloudy, overcast; (*barba*) thick; (*curva*) sharp; (coll) quiet, reserved, secretive; (coll) dense, stupid
cerradura *f* lock; closing, locking; **cerradura embutida** mortise lock
cerrajería *f* locksmith business; hardware; hardware store
cerrajero *m* locksmith; hardware dealer; (*el que trabaja el hierro frío*) ironworker
cerrar §2 *tr* to close, shut; to lock; to bolt; (*el puño*) to clench; to enclose; (*la radio*) to turn off; **cerrar con llave** to lock || *intr* to close, to shut; (*la noche*) to fall; **cerrar con** (*el enemigo*) to close in on; **cerrar en falso** (*una puerta, cerradura, etc.*) to not catch || *ref* to close, to shut; to lock; **cerrarse en falso** to not heal right
cerrazón *f* gathering storm clouds; (Arg) heavy fog
cerre•ro -ra *adj* free, loose; untamed; haughty; (Mex) rough, unpolished; (*café*) (Ven) bitter
cerril *adj* rough, uneven; wild, untamed; (coll) boorish, rough
cerrillar *tr* to knurl, to mill
cerro *m* hill, hillock; (*entre dos surcos*) ridge; (*espinazo*) backbone; (*del animal*) neck; **en cerro** bareback; **echar por los cerros de Úbeda** (coll) to talk nonsense; **por los cerros de Úbeda** (coll) off the beaten path
cerrojo *m* bolt; **cerrojo dormido** dead bolt
certamen *m* literary competition; contest, match
certe•ro -ra *adj* certain, sure, accurate; well-informed; (*tiro*) well-aimed; (*tirador*) good, crack
certeza *f* certainty
certidumbre *f* certainty; sureness
certificación *f* certification; certificate
certifica•do -da *adj* registered || *m* registered letter, registered package; certificate; **certificado de estudios** transcript
certificar §73 *tr* to certify; (*una carta*) to register
certitud *f* certainty
cerval *adj* deer; (*miedo*) intense
cervato *m* fawn
cervecería *f* brewery; beer saloon
cervece•ro -ra *adj* beer || *mf* brewer
cerveza *f* beer; **cerveza a presión** draught beer; **cerveza de marzo** bock beer
cer•viz *f* (*pl* **-vices**) cervix; nape of the neck; **bajar** or **doblar la cerviz** to humble oneself; **levantar la cerviz** to raise one's head, become proud; **ser de dura cerviz** to be ungovernable
cesación *f* cessation, suspension
cesante *adj* retired, out of office || *mf* pensioner
cesantía *f* retirement; dismissal (*of a public official*)
cesar *intr* to stop, cease
César *m* Caesar
cese *m* ceasing; notice of retirement; **cese de alarma** all-clear; **cese de fuego** ceasefire
césped *m* lawn, sward; sod, turf
cesta *f* basket; (*para jugar a la pelota*) wicker scoop; **cesta de costura** sewing basket; **cesta para compras** market basket
cesto *m* basket; washbasket; **cesto de la colada** clothesbasket, washbasket; **estar hecho un cesto** (coll) to be overcome with sleep; **ser un cesto** (coll) to be crude and ignorant
cetrería *f* falconry
cetrero *m* falconer
cetri•no -na *adj* (*tez*) sallow; jaundiced, melancholy
cetro *m* scepter; (*para aves*) perch, roost; (eccl) verge; **cetro de bufón** bauble; **cetro de locura** fool's scepter; **empuñar el cetro** to ascend the throne
cf. *abbr* **confesor**
cg. *abbr* **centigramo**
C.I. *abbr* **cociente intelectual**
cía. *abbr* **compañía**
cía *f* hipbone
cianamida *f* cyanamide
cianuro *m* cyanide
ciar §77 *intr* to back up; to back water; to ease up
ciborio *m* ciborium
cicatear *intr* (coll) to be stingy
cicate•ro -ra *adj* (coll) stingy || *mf* (coll) miser, niggard
cica•triz *f* (*pl* **-trices**) scar
cicatrizar §60 *tr* to heal; (*una impresión dolorosa*) (Arg) to heal || *ref* to heal; to scar
Cicerón *m* Cicero
ciclamor *m* Judas tree; **ciclamor del Canadá** redbud
cícli•co -ca *adj* cyclic(al)
ciclismo *m* bicycle racing
ciclista *mf* bicyclist; bicycle racer
ciclo *m* cycle; series (of lectures); (*en las escuelas*) (Arg, Urug) term
ciclón *m* cyclone
cicuta *f* hemlock
cidra *f* citron (*fruit*)
cidrada *f* citron (*candied rind*)
cidro *m* citron (*tree or shrub*)
cie•go -ga *adj* blind; blocked, stopped up; **más ciego que un topo** blind as a bat || *mf* blind person || *m* blind man || *f* blind woman; **a ciegas** blindly; thoughtlessly; without looking
cielo *m* sky, heavens; (*clima, tiempo*) skies, climate, weather; (*de una cama*) canopy; (*mansión de los bienaventurados*) Heaven; **a cielo abierto** in the open air, outdoors; **a cielo descubierto** openly; **a cielo raso** in the open air, outdoors; in the country; **cielo de la boca** roof of the mouth; **cielo máximo** (aer) ceiling;

cielo raso ceiling; **llovido del cielo** heaven-sent, manna from heaven
cielorraso *m* ceiling
ciem·piés *m* (*pl* **-piés**) centipede
cien *adj* hundred, a hundred, one hundred
ciénaga *f* swamp, marsh, mudhole
ciencia *f* science; knowledge; learning; **a ciencia cierta** with certainty
cieno *m* mud, mire, silt
cieno·so -sa *adj* muddy, miry, silty
ciento *adj & m* hundred, a hundred, one hundred; **por ciento** per cent
cierne *m* budding, blossoming; **en cierne** in blossom; only beginning
cierrarrenglón *m* marginal stop
cierre *m* closing; shutting; snap, clasp, fastener; latch, lock; (*de una tienda, de la Bolsa*) close; (*paro de trabajo*) shutdown; **cierre cremallera** zipper; **cierre de portada** metal shutter (*of store front*); **cierre de puerta** door check; **cierre hermético** weather stripping; **cierre relámpago** zipper
cierro *m* closing; shutting; (Chile) fence, wall; (Chile) envelope
cier·to -ta *adj* certain; a certain; (*acertado, verdadero*) true; (*seguro*) sure; **por cierto** for sure || **cierto** *adv* surely, certainly
cierva *f* hind
ciervo *m* deer, stag, hart
cierzo *m* cold north wind
cifra *f* (*número*) cipher; (*escritura secreta*) code; (*enlace de dos o más letras empleado en sellos*) device, monogram, emblem; abbreviation; amount, sum; **en cifra** in code; in brief; mysteriously
cifrar *tr* to cipher, to code; to abridge; to calculate; **cifrar la dicha en** to base one's happiness in; **cifrar la esperanza en** to place one's hope in || *ref* to be abridged; **cifrarse en** to be based on
cifrario *m* (com) code
cigarra *f* harvest fly, locust
cigarrera *f* cigar case; cigar girl
cigarrería *f* cigar store, tobacco store
cigarre·ro -ra *mf* cigar maker; cigar dealer || *f* see **cigarrera**
cigarrillo *m* cigarette; **cigarrillo con filtro** filter cigarette
cigarro *m* cigar; **cigarro de papel** cigarette; **cigarro puro** cigar
cigoñal *m* well sweep; (*del motor de explosión*) crankshaft
cigüeña *f* stork; crank, winch
cigüeñal *m* var of **cigoñal**
cilicio *m* haircloth, hair shirt
cilindrada *f* piston displacement
cilindrar *tr* to roll
cilíndri·co -ca *adj* cylindrical
cilindro *m* cylinder; roll, roller; (Mex) barrel organ, hand organ
cima *f* (*de árbol*) top; (*de montaña*) top, summit; **dar cima a** to complete, to carry out; **por cima** (coll) at the very top
cimarra *f* — **hacer cimarra** (Arg, Chile) to play hooky
cima·rrón -rrona *adj* (*animal*) (Am) wild, untamed; (*planta*) (Am) wild; (*esclavo*) (Am) fugitive; (*marinero*) (Am) lazy; (*mate*) (Arg, Urug) black, bitter
cimarronear *intr* (Arg, Urug) to drink black maté || *ref* (*el esclavo*) (Am) to flee, run away
címbalo *m* cymbal
cimbel *m* decoy pigeon, stool pigeon
cimborio or **cimborrio** *m* dome
cimbrar or **cimbrear** *tr* to brandish; to swing, sway; to bend; (coll) to thrash, beat || *ref* to swing, sway; to shake
cimbre·ño -ña *adj* flexible, pliant; lithe, willowy
cimentar §2 *tr* to found, establish; to lay the foundations of
cime·ro -ra *adj* top, uppermost
cimiento *m* foundation, groundwork; basis, source
cimitarra *f* scimitar
cinabrio *m* cinnabar
cinanquia *f* quinsy
cinc *m* (*pl* **cinces**) zinc
cincel *m* chisel, graver
cincelar *tr* to chisel, engrave
cinco *adj & pron* five; **las cinco** five o'clock || *m* five; (*en las fechas*) fifth; **¡choque Vd. esos cinco!** or **¡vengan esos cinco!** put it here!, shake!; **decirle a uno cuántas son cinco** (coll) to tell someone what's what
cincograbado *m* zinc etching
cincuenta *adj, pron & m* fifty
cincuenta·vo -va *adj & m* fiftieth
cincha *f* cinch; **a revienta cinchas** at breakneck speed; (Am) reluctantly
cinchar *tr* to cinch; to band, to hoop
cincho *m* girdle, sash; iron hoop; iron tire
cine *m* movie; **cine en colores** color movies; **cine hablado** talkie; **cine mudo** silent movie; **cine parlante** talkie; **cine sonoro** sound movie
cineasta *mf* motion-picture producer; movie fan || *m* movie actor || *f* movie actress
cinedrama *m* screenplay
cinelandia *f* (coll) movieland
cinema *m* var of **cine**
cinematografiar §77 *tr & intr* to cinematograph, to film
cinematógrafo *m* cinematograph; motion picture; motion-picture projector; motion-picture theater
cinematurgo *m* scriptwriter
cinescopio (telv) *m* kinescope
cineteatro *m* movie house
cinéti·co -ca *adj* kinetic || *f* kinetics
cínga·ro -ra *adj & mf* gypsy
cíni·co -ca *adj* cynical; impudent; slovenly, untidy || *mf* cynic || *m* Cynic
cinismo *m* cynicism; impudence
cinta *f* ribbon; (*tira de papel, celuloide, etc.*) tape; film; measuring tape; (*borde de la acera*) curb; fillet, scroll; **cinta aislante** electric tape, friction tape; **cinta de medir** tape measure; **cinta de teleimpresor** ticker tape; **cinta grabada de televisión** video tape; **cinta perforada** punched tape

cintillo *m* hatband; fancy hat cord; ring set with a gem; (*borde de la acera*) (P-R) curb; (Am) hair ribbon
cinto *m* belt, girdle; waist
cintura *f* (*parte estrecha del cuerpo humano sobre las caderas*) waist; waistline; (*de una chimenea*) throat; **meter en cintura** (coll) to bring to reason
cinturón *m* belt, sash; sword belt; **cinturón de asiento** seat belt; **cinturón salvavidas** (naut) safety belt
cipo *m* milestone; signpost; memorial pillar
cipote *adj* (Col, Ven) stupid; (Guat) chubby || *mf* (Hond, El Salv, Ven) brat
ciprés *m* cypress
circo *m* circus
circón *m* zircon
circonio *m* zirconium
circuito *m* circuit; (*de carreteras, ferrocarriles, etc.*) network; race track; **corto circuito** (elec) short circuit
circulación *f* circulation; traffic; **circulación rodada** vehicular traffic
circular *adj* circular || *f* circular, circular letter || *tr & intr* to circulate
círculo *m* circle; club; clubhouse
circuncidar *tr* to circumcise; to clip, curtail
circundante *adj* surrounding
circundar *tr* to surround, go around
circunferencia *f* circumference
circunfle•jo -ja *adj* circumflex
circunlocución *f* or **circunloquio** *m* circumlocution
circunnavegación *f* circumnavigation
circunnavegar §44 *tr* to circumnavigate
circunscribir §83 *tr* to circumscribe || *ref* to hold oneself down; to be held down
circunscripción *f* circumscription; district, subdivision
circunspec•to -ta *adj* circumspect
circunstancia *f* circumstance
circunstancia•do -da *adj* circumstantial, detailed
circunstancial *adj* circumstantial
circunstanciar *tr* to circumstantiate, to describe in detail
circunstante *adj* surrounding; present || *mf* bystander, onlooker
circunveci•no -na *adj* neighboring
circunvolar §61 *tr* to fly around
cirial *m* (eccl) processional candlestick
ciriga•llo -lla *mf* gadabout
ciríli•co -ca *adj* Cyrillic
cirio *m* wax candle
Ciro *m* Cyrus
ciruela *f* plum; **ciruela claudia** greengage; **ciruela pasa** prune
ciruelo *m* plum, plum tree; (coll) stupid fellow
cirugía *f* surgery; **cirugía cosmética, decorativa** or **estética** face lifting
ciruja•no -na *mf* surgeon
ciscar §73 *tr* (coll) to soil, dirty || *ref* (coll) to soil one's clothes, to have an accident
cisco *m* culm; (coll) row, disturbance
cisma *m* schism; discord, disagreement; (Arg) worry, concern; (Col) gossip; (Col) fastidiousness
cismáti•co -ca *adj* schismatic; dissident; (Col) gossipy; (Col) fastidious || *mf* schismatic; dissident
cisne *m* swan; (Arg) powder puff
cisterna *f* cistern; reservoir
cita *f* date, appointment, engagement; (*mención, pasaje textual*) citation, quotation; **cita a ciegas** blind date; **cita previa** by appointment; **darse cita** to make a date
citación *f* citation, quotation; (*ante un juez*) citation, summons
citar *tr* to make a date with, have an appointment with; to cite, to quote; (*ante un juez*) to cite, to summon; (*al toro*) to incite, provoke || *ref* to make a date, have an appointment
cítara *f* (mus) zither
ciudad *f* city; city council; **la ciudad Condal** Barcelona; **la ciudad del Apóstol** Santiago de Compostela; **la ciudad del Betis** Seville; **la ciudad del Cabo** Capetown or Cape Town; **la ciudad de los Califas** Cordova; **la ciudad de los Reyes** Lima, Peru; **la ciudad de María Santísima** Seville; **la ciudad Imperial** or **Imperial ciudad** Toledo
ciudadanía *f* citizenship
ciudada•no -na *adj* city; citizen; civic || *mf* citizen; urbanite
ciudadela *f* citadel; (Cuba) tenement house
cívi•co -ca *adj* civic; city; domestic; public-spirited
civil *adj* civil; civilian || *mf* civilian || *m* guard, policeman
civilidad *f* civility
civilista *adj* civil-law || *mf* authority on civil law; (Chile) antimilitarist
civilización *f* civilization
civilizar §60 *tr* to civilize
civismo *m* good citizenship
cizalla *f* shears; metal shaving, metal clipping; **cizalla de guillotina** gate shears, guillotine shears; **cizallas** shears
cizallar *tr* to shear
cizaña *f* darnel; contamination, corruption; discord; **sembrar cizaña** to sow discord
clac *m* (*pl* **claques**) opera hat, claque, crush hat; (*sombrero de tres picos*) cocked hat
clamar *tr* to cry out for || *intr* to cry out; **clamar contra** to cry out against; **clamar por** to cry out for
clamor *m* clamor, outcry; (*toque de difuntos*) knell, toll; fame
clamorear *tr* to clamor for || *intr* to clamor; (*tocar a muerto*) to toll
clamoreo *m* clamoring; tolling
clamoro•so -sa *adj* clamorous; loud, noisy
clan *m* clan
clandestinista *mf* (Guat) bootlegger
clandesti•no -na *adj* clandestine
claque *f* claque, hired clappers
clara *f* white of egg; bald spot; (*de un trozo de tela*) thin spot; (*en el tiempo lluvioso*) break, let-up

claraboya *f* (*ventana en el techo*) skylight; (*en la parte alta de la pared*) transom; (*esp. en las iglesias la parte superior de la nave que tiene una serie de ventanas*) clerestory
clarear *tr* to brighten, light up || *intr* (*empezar a amanecer*) to get light, to dawn; (*el mal tiempo*) to clear up || *ref* (*una tela*) to show through; (coll) to show one's hand
clarecer §22 *ref* to dawn
clarete *m* claret
claridad *f* clarity; clearness; brightness; fame, glory; blunt remark; **claridades** plain language
clarido·so -sa *adj* (CAm, Mex) blunt, rude, plain-spoken
clarificar §73 *tr* to clarify; to brighten, light up; (*lo que estaba turbio*) to clear
clarín *m* clarion; fine cambric; (Chile) sweet pea
clarinada *f* clarion call; (coll) uncalled-for remark
clarinete *m* clarinet
clarión *m* chalk
clarividencia *f* clairvoyance; clear-sightedness
clarividente *adj* clairvoyant; clear-sighted || *mf* clairvoyant
cla·ro -ra *adj* clear; (*de color*) light; (*pelo*) thin, sparse; (*té*) weak; famous, illustrious; (*cerveza*) light; **a las claras** publicly, openly, frankly || *m* gap; (*en el bosque*) glade, clearing; space, interval; (*ventana u otra abertura*) light; (*claraboya*) skylight; (*en las nubes*) break; **claro de luna** brief moonlight; **de claro en claro** evidently; from one end to the other; **pasar la noche de claro en claro** to not sleep all night; **poner** or **sacar en claro** to explain, clear up; (*un borrador*) to copy || *f* see **clara** || **claro** *adv* clearly || **claro** *interj* sure!, of course!; **¡claro está!, ¡claro que sí!** sure!, of course!
claror *m* brightness; **claror de luna** moonlight, moonglow
claru·cho -cha *adj* (coll) watery, thin
clase *f* class; classroom; **clase alta** upper class; **clase baja** lower class; **clase media** middle class; **clase obrera** working class; **clases** noncommissioned officers, warrant officers; **clases pasivas** pensioners
clasicista *mf* classicist
clási·co -ca *adj* classical || *mf* classicist || *m* classic
clasificador *m* filing cabinet
clasificar §73 *tr* to classify; to class; to sort; to file || *ref* to class
clasismo *m* segregation
clasista *mf* segregationist
claudicar §73 *intr* (*cojear*) to limp; (*obrar defectuosamente*) to bungle; (coll) to back down
claustral *adj* cloistral
claustro *m* cloister; (*junta de la universidad*) faculty
cláusula *f* (*de un contrato u otro documento*) clause; (gram) sentence
clausula·do -da *adj* (*estilo*) choppy || *m* series of clauses
clausular *tr* to close, finish, conclude
clausura *f* confinement; seclusion; enclosure; adjournment
clausurar *tr* (*una asamblea, un tribunal, etc.*) to close, to adjourn; (*un comercio por orden gubernativa*) to suspend, to close up
clava *f* club
clavadista *mf* (Mex) diver
clava·do -da *adj* studded with nails; exact, precise; (*reloj*) stopped; sharp, e.g., **a las siete clavadas** at seven o'clock sharp || *m* (Mex) dive
clavar *tr* to nail; (*un clavo*) to drive; (*una daga, un punzón*) to stick; (*una piedra preciosa*) to set; (*los ojos, la atención*) to fix; (*a un caballo al herrarlo*) to prick; (coll) to cheat || *ref* to prick oneself; (coll) to get cheated; (Mex) to dive; **clavárselas** (CAm) to get drunk
clave *m* harpsichord || *f* (*de un enigma, código, etc.*) key; (*piedra con que se cierra el arco*) (archit) keystone; (mus) clef
clavel *m* carnation, pink; **clavel de ramillete** sweet william; **clavel reventón** double-flowered carnation
clavelón *m* marigold
clavellina *f* carnation, pink
clave·ro -ra *mf* keeper of the keys || *m* clove tree || *f* nail hole
claveta *f* peg, wooden peg
clavetear *tr* to stud; to tip, put a tip on; to wind up, settle
clavicordio *m* clavichord
clavícula *f* clavicle, collarbone
clavija *f* pin, peg, dowel; (elec) plug; (mus) peg; **apretarle a uno las clavijas** (coll) to put the screws on someone
clavillo or **clavito** *m* brad, tack; (*que sujeta las hojas de unas tijeras*) pin, rivet; clove
clavo *m* nail; (*capullo seco de la flor del clavero*) clove; migraine; keen sorrow; (*artículo que no se vende*) (Arg, Bol, Chile) drug on the market; (Col) bad deal; (Hond, Mex) rich vein of ore; (Ven) heartburn; **clavo de alambre** wire nail; **clavo de especia** (*flor*) clove; **clavo de herrar** horseshoe nail; **dar en el clavo** (coll) to hit the nail on the head
clemátide *f* clematis
clemencia *f* clemency
clemente *adj* clement, merciful
cleptóma·no -na *mf* kleptomaniac
clerecía *f* clergy
clerical *adj & m* clerical
clericato *m* or **clericatura** *f* priesthood
clerigalla *f* (contemptuous) priests
clérigo *m* cleric, priest; **clérigo de misa y olla** (coll) priestlet
clerizonte *m* shabby-looking priest; fake priest
clero *m* clergy
clerófo·bo -ba *adj* priest-hating || *mf* priest hater
cliché *m* (*lugar común*) cliché
cliente *mf* (*parroquiano de una tienda*)

customer; (*de un abogado*) client; (*de un médico*) patient; (*de un hotel*) guest
clientela *f* customers; clientele; patronage, protection; practice
clima *m* climate; country, region; **clima artificial** air conditioning
climatizar **§60** *tr* to air-condition
clíni•co -ca *adj* clinical || *mf* clinician || *f* clinic; private hospital; **clínica de reposo** nursing home, convalescent home
cliqueteo *m* clicking
clisar *tr* (typ) to plate
clisé *m* (*plancha clisada*) cliché, plate; (phot) plate; (*lugar común*) cliché
clo *m* cluck; **decir clo** (Chile) to kick the bucket; **hacer clo clo** (*la gallina clueca*) to cluck
cloaca *f* sewer
clocar **§81** *intr* to cluck
cloquear *intr* to cluck
cloqueo *m* cluck, clucking
clorhídri•co -ca *adj* hydrochloric
cloro *m* chlorine
clorofila *f* chlorophyll
cloroformizar **§60** *tr* to chloroform
cloroformo *m* chloroform
cloruro *m* chloride
club *m* (*pl* **clubs**) club; **club náutico** yacht club
clubista *mf* club member
clue•co -ca *adj* broody; (coll) decrepit
c.m.b., C.M.B. *abbr* **cuyas manos beso**
coa *f* (Mex) hoe; (Chile) thieves' jargon
coacción *f* coercion, compulsion
coaccionar *tr* to coerce, compel
coacervar *tr* to pile up
coactar *tr* to coerce, compel
coadunar *tr* & *ref* to mix together
coadyuvar *tr* & *intr* to help, aid, assist
coagular *tr* & *ref* (*la sangre*) to coagulate; (*la leche*) to curdle
coágulo *m* clot
coalición *f* coalition
coalla *f* woodcock
coartada *f* alibi
coartar *tr* to limit, restrict
coba *f* (coll) hoax; (coll) flattery
cobalto *m* cobalt
cobarde *adj* cowardly; timid; (*vista*) dim, weak || *mf* coward
cobardear *intr* to act cowardly; to be timid
cobardía *f* cowardice; timidity
cobayo *m* guinea pig
cobertera *f* lid; bawd, procuress
cobertizo *m* shed; (*tejado saledizo*) covered balcony, penthouse
cobertor *m* bedcover, bedspread; lid
cobertura *f* cover; covering; (*garantía metálica*) coverage
cobija *f* curved tile; top, lid; short mantilla; (W-I) guano roof; **cobijas** (Am) bedclothes
cobijar *tr* to cover; to shelter, protect
cobijo *m* covering; shelter, protection; (*hospedaje sin manutención*) lodging
cobra *f* team of mares used in threshing; (hunt) retrieval
cobra•dor -dora *adj* (*perro*) retrieving || *mf* collector; trolley conductor
cobranza *f* collecting; (hunt) retrieval
cobrar *tr* (*lo perdido*) to recover; (*lo que otro le debe*) to collect; (*un cheque*) to cash; (*cierto precio*) to charge; to acquire, get; (*una cuerda*) to pull in; (hunt) to retrieve; (*pedir, reclamar*) (Am) to dun; **cobrar afición a** to take a liking for; **cobrar al número llamado** (telp) to reverse the charges; **cobrar ánimo** to take courage; **cobrar carnes** to put on flesh; **cobrar fuerzas** to gain strength || *intr* to get hit || *ref* to recover, to come to
cobre *m* copper; copper or brass kitchen utensils; **batir el cobre** (coll) to hustle, to work with a will; **cobres** (mus) brasses
cobre•ño -ña *adj* copper
cobrero *m* coppersmith
cobri•zo -za *adj* coppery
cobro *m* collection; recovery; **cobro contra entrega** collect on delivery; **en cobro** in a safe place
coca *f* (*en una cuerda*) kink; (coll) head; **de coca** (Mex) free; (Mex) in vain
cocaína *f* cocaine
cocción *f* cooking, baking; (*de objetos cerámicos*) baking, burning
cocear *intr* to kick; (*resistir*) (coll) to balk, rebel
cocer **§16** *tr* to cook; to boil; (*pan; ladrillos*) to bake; to digest || *intr* to cook; to boil; to ferment || *ref* to suffer a long time
coci•do -da *adj* cooked || *m* Spanish stew
cociente *m* quotient; **cociente intelectual** intelligence quotient
cocina *f* (*pieza*) kitchen; (*arte*) cooking, cuisine; (*aparato*) stove; **cocina de presión** pressure cooker; **cocina económica** kitchen range
cocinar *tr* to cook || *intr* to meddle
cocine•ro -ra *mf* cook
cocinilla *m* (coll) meddler || *f* kitchenette; chafing dish; **cocinilla sin fuego** fireless cooker
coco *m* cocoanut; (*moño*) topknot, chignon; (*duende*) (coll) bogeyman; (*gesto, mueca*) (coll) face, grimace; (*sombrero hongo*) (Col, Ecuad) derby hat; **hacer cocos** (coll) to make a face; (*los enamorados*) (coll) to make eyes
cocodrilo *m* crocodile
cócora *adj* (coll) boring, tiresome || *mf* (coll) bore, pest
coco•so -sa *adj* worm-eaten
cocotero *m* cocoanut palm or tree
coctel *m* or **cóctel** *m* cocktail; cocktail party
coctelera *f* cocktail shaker
cocuma *f* (Peru) roast corn on the cob
cochambre *m* (coll) dirty, stinking thing, pigsty
cochambro•so -sa *adj* (coll) dirty, stinking
coche *m* carriage; coach; car; taxi; (*puerco*) hog; **caminar en el coche de San Francisco** to go or to ride on shank's mare; **coche bar** (rr) club

car; **coche bomba** fire engine; **coche celular** Black Maria, prison van; **coche de alquiler** cab, hack; **coche de carreras** racing car; **coche de correos** mail car; **coche de plaza** or **de punto** cab, hack; **coche de serie** (aut) stock car; **coche fúnebre** hearse
coche-cama *m* (*pl* **coches-camas**) sleeping car
cochecillo *m* baby carriage; **cochecillo para inválidos** wheelchair; **cochecillo para niños** baby carriage
coche-comedor *m* (*pl* **coches-comedores**) (rr) diner, dining car
coche-correo *m* (*pl* **coches-correo**) (rr) mail car
coche-fumador *m* (*pl* **coches-fumadores**) (rr) smoker, smoking car
coche-habitación *m* (*pl* **coches-habitación**) trailer
cochera *f* coach house; livery stable; carbarn; garage
cochería *f* (Arg, Chile) livery stable
coche•ro -ra *adj* easy to cook || *m* coachman, driver; **cochero de punto** cabby, hackman || *f* see **cochera**
cocherón *m* coach house; (*depósito de locomotoras*) roundhouse
coche-salón *m* (*pl* **coches-salón**) (rr) parlor car
cochevira *f* lard
cochina *f* sow; (*mujer sucia y desaliñada*) trollop
cochinada *f* (coll) piggishness, filthiness; (coll) dirty trick
cochinillo *m* sucking pig
cochi•no -na *adj* (coll) piggish, filthy; (*tacaño*) (coll) stingy; (Ven) cowardly || *mf* hog; (*persona muy sucia*) (coll) pig, dirty person || *f* see **cochina**
cochite hervite *adj, adv* & *m* (coll) helter-skelter
cochitril *m* pigsty; (coll) den, hovel
cochura *f* batch of dough
codadura *f* (hort) layer
codal *adj* elbow || *m* prop, shoring
codazo *m* poke, nudge; **dar codazo a** (Mex) to tip off
codear *tr* (SAm) to sponge on || *intr* to elbow, elbow one's way || *ref* to hobnob, to rub elbows
codelincuencia *f* complicity
codelincuente *mf* accomplice
codera *f* elbow patch; elbow itch
códice *m* codex
codicia *f* covetousness, greed, cupidity
codiciar *tr* to covet
codicilo *m* codicil
codicio•so -sa *adj* covetous, greedy; (*laborioso*) hard-working
codificar **§73** *tr* to codify
código *m* code; **código penal** criminal code
codillo *m* (*de animal*) knee; (*estribo*) stirrup; (*de un tubo*) elbow; (*de la rama cortada*) stump
codo *m* elbow; **dar de codo a** to nudge; (coll) to spurn; **empinar el codo** (coll) to crook the elbow; **hablar por los codos** (coll) to talk too much
codor•niz *f* (*pl* **-nices**) quail
coeducación *f* coeducation
coeficiente *adj* & *m* coefficient
coetáne•o -a *adj* & *mf* contemporary
coexistencia *f* coexistence
coexistir *intr* to coexist
cofa *f* (naut) top; **cofa de vigía** (naut) crow's-nest
cofrade *mf* member, fellow member || *m* brother || *f* sister
cofradía *f* brotherhood, sisterhood; association, fraternity
cofre *m* coffer, chest, trunk
cogedor *m* dustpan; coal shovel, ash shovel
coger **§17** *tr* to catch, seize, take hold of: to collect, gather, pick; to overtake; to surprise; to hold || *intr* to be, be located; to fit || *ref* to get caught; to cling; to get involved
cogida *f* (coll) collecting, gathering, picking; (taur) hook
cogollo *m* (*de la lechuga*) heart; (*de la berza*) head; (*de una planta*) shoot; (*del árbol*) top; (*lo mejor*) cream, pick
cogote *m* back of the neck
cogotera *f* havelock
cogotu•do -da *adj* thick-necked; (coll) proud, stiff-necked; (SAm) moneyed
cogulla *f* cowl, frock; **cogulla de fraile** (bot) monkshood
cohabitar *intr* to live together; (*el hombre y la mujer*) to cohabit
cohechar *tr* to bribe; to plow just before sowing || *intr* to take a bribe
cohecho *m* bribe
coherede•ro -ra *mf* coheir || *f* coheiress
coherente *adj* coherent
cohesión *f* cohesion
cohete *m* (*fuego artificial*) rocket, skyrocket; (*motor a reacción*) rocket; (coll) fidgety person; **cohete de señales** (aer) flare; **cohete lanzador** booster rocket
cohibente *adj* (elec) nonconducting
cohibi•do -da *adj* timid, self-conscious
cohibir *tr* to check, restrain, inhibit; (Mex) to oblige
cohombro *m* cucumber
cohonestar *tr* to gloss over, to rationalize
coima *f* rake-off paid to operator of a gambling table; concubine; (SAm) bribe
coincidencia *f* coincidence
coincidir *intr* to coincide; to happen at the same time; to be at the same time (*at a given place*); to agree
coito *m* coition, coitus
coja *f* lame woman; (coll) lewd woman
cojear *intr* to limp; (*una mesa, una silla*) to wobble; (*adolecer de algún vicio*) to slip, lapse, have a weakness
cojera *f* (*anormalidad del que cojea*) lameness; (*movimiento del que cojea*) limp
cojijo *m* bug, insect; (coll) peeve
cojijo•so -sa *adj* peevish
cojín *m* cushion
cojincillo *m* pad
cojinete *m* cushion; sewing cushion; (mach) bearing; **cojinete de bolas** ball bearing; **cojinete de rodillos** roller bearing

co•jo -ja *adj* lame, crippled; (*mesa, silla*) wobbly; (*pierna*) game || *mf* lame person, cripple || *f* see **coja**
cojón *m* testicle
cok *m* var of **coque**
col. *abbr* **colonia, columna**
col *f* cabbage; **col de Bruselas** Brussels sprouts
cola *f* (*de animal, de ave, de cometa*) tail; (*de un vestido*) train, trail; (*de personas que esperan turno*) queue; (*extremidad posterior*) tail end, rear end; (*de una clase de alumnos*) bottom; (*pasta fuerte*) glue; **cola del pan** bread line; **cola de milano** or **de pato** dovetail; **cola de pescado** isinglass; **cola de retazo** size, sizing; **hacer cola** to queue, to stand in line
colaboración *f* collaboration; (*en un periódico, coloquio, etc.*) contribution
colaboracionista *mf* collaborationist
colabora•dor -dora *adj* collaborating || *mf* collaborator; contributor
colaborar *intr* to collaborate; (*en un periódico, coloquio, etc.*) to contribute
colación *f* (*cotejo; refacción ligera*) collation; (*de un grado de universidad*) conferring; parish land; **sacar a colación** to mention, bring up; **traer a colación** to bring up; to adduce as proof; to bring up irrelevantly
colacionar *tr* to collate; to compare; (*un beneficio*) to confer
colactánea *f* foster sister
colactáneo *m* foster brother
colada *f* washing powder; wash; (*garganta entre montañas*) gulch; cattle run; **todo saldrá en la colada** (coll) it will all come out in the wash; (coll) the day of reckoning will come
coladera *f* strainer; (Mex) sewer
coladero *m* strainer; cattle run; narrow pass
colador *m* strainer, colander
colapez *f* or **colapiscis** *f* isinglass
colapso *m* breakdown, collapse; **colapso nervioso** nervous breakdown
colar *tr* (*un grado universitario*) to confer || **§61** *tr* (*un líquido*) to strain; to bleach in hot lye, to buck; (*metales*) to cast; (*una moneda falsa*) (coll) to pass off; **colar el hueso por** (coll) to squeeze through || *intr* to run, to ooze; to squeeze through; to come in, slip in; (coll) to drink wine; **colar a fondo** to sink; **no colar** (*una cosa*) (coll) to not be believed || *ref* to seep, seep through; to slip in, slip through; to make a slip; to lie; **colarse de gorra** (coll) to crash the gate
colateral *adj* collateral || *mf* (*pariente*) collateral || *m* (com) collateral
colcrén *m* cold cream
colcha *f* quilt, counterpane, bedspread
colchón *m* mattress; **colchón de aire** air mattress; **colchón de muelles** bedspring, spring mattress; **colchón de plumas** feather bed
coleada *f* wag (*of the tail*); (Mex, Ven) throwing the bull by twisting its tail
colear *tr* (taur) to grab by the tail; (*la res*) (Mex, Ven) to throw by twisting the tail; (Col, Ven) to nag, harass; (Guat) to trail after; (*reprobar en un examen*) (Chile) to flunk || *intr* to wag the tail; (aer) to fishtail; (coll) to stay alive, to keep going; (*los últimos vagones de un tren*) (Am) to sway; **colear en** (*cierta edad*) (CAm, W-I) to border on, be close to; **todavía colea** (coll) it's not over yet
colección *f* collection
coleccionar *tr* to collect
coleccionista *mf* collector
colecta *f* collection for charity; (eccl) collect
colectar *tr* to collect; (*obras antes sueltas*) to collect in one volume
colecti•cio -cia *adj* new, untrained, green; (*tomo*) omnibus
colecti•vo -va *adj* collective
colector *m* collector; catch basin; (elec) commutator; (aut) manifold
colega *mf* colleague || *m* confrere
colegial *m* schoolboy
colegiala *f* schoolgirl
colegiatura *f* scholarship; (Mex) tuition
colegio *m* school, academy; (*sociedad de hombres de una misma profesión*) college (*e.g., of cardinals, electors*)
colegir §57 *tr* to gather, collect; to conclude, infer
cólera *m* cholera || *f* anger, wrath; (*bilis*) bile; **montar en cólera** to fly into a rage
coléri•co -ca *adj* choleric, irascible
colesterol *m* cholesterol
coleta *f* pigtail; (*del torero*) cue, queue; (coll) postscript; **cortarse la coleta** to quit the bull ring; to quit, retire; **tener** or **traer coleta** to have serious consequences
coletero *m* wren
coleto *m* buff jacket; (coll) body, one's body, oneself; **decir para su coleto** (coll) to say to oneself; **echarse al coleto** (coll) to eat up, drink up; (coll) to read from cover to cover
colgadero *m* hanger, hook; clothes rack
colgadizo *m* lean-to, penthouse; projection over a door, canopy
colga•do -da *adj* pending, unsettled; **dejar colgado** (coll) to disappoint, frustrate; **quedarse colgado** (coll) to be disappointed, frustrated
colgador *m* clothes hanger, coat hanger
colgajo *m* rag, tatter
colgante *adj* hanging, dangling; (*puente*) suspension || *m* drop, pendant; (archit) festoon; (P-R) watch fob
colgar §63 *tr* to hang; to impute, attribute; (*a un alumno*) to flunk; (*a un reo*) (coll) to hang || *intr* to hang, hang down, dangle; to droop; (telp) to hang up; **colgar de** to hang from, hang on; to depend on
coli•brí *m* (*pl* **-bríes**) humming bird
cóli•co -ca *adj & m* colic || *f* upset stomach
coliche *m* (coll) at-home, open house
coliflor *f* cauliflower

coligar §44 *ref* to join forces, make common cause
colilla *f* butt, stump, stub
co•lín -lina *adj* (*caballo o yegua*) bobtailed || *m* bobwhite; **colín de Virginia** bobwhite || *f* see **colina**
colina *f* hill, knoll
colindante *adj* adjacent, contiguous
colindar *intr* to be adjacent
colino•so -sa *adj* hilly
colirio *m* eyewash
coliseo *m* coliseum
colisión *f* collision; bruise, bump
colista *mf* (coll) person standing in line
colma•do -da *adj* abundant, plentiful || *m* food store, grocery store; seafood restaurant
colmar *tr* to fill up; (*las esperanzas de uno*) to fulfill; to overwhelm; **colmar de** to shower with, overwhelm with
colmena *f* beehive
colmenar *m* apiary
colmene•ro -ra *mf* beekeeper
colmillo *m* eyetooth, canine tooth; (*del elefante*) tusk; **tener el colmillo retorcido** (coll) to cut one's eyeteeth
col•mo -ma *adj* brimful, overflowing || *m* overflow; thatch, thatch roof; (*de un sorbete*) topping; **eso es el colmo** (coll) that's the limit; **para colmo de** to top off
colocación *f* (*acción de poner una persona o cosa en un lugar*) location; (*disposición de una cosa respecto del lugar que ocupa*) placement; (*inversión de dinero*) investment; (*empleo*) position, employment, job
colocar §73 *tr* to place, put; (*una trampa*) to set || *ref* to get placed, find a job; (*venderse*) to sell
colodra *f* milk bucket; drinking horn; (*bebedor de vino*) (coll) toper
colofón *m* colophon
colofonia *f* rosin
coloide *adj & m* coloid
colon *m* colon; (gram) main clause
Colón *m* Columbus
colonia *f* colony; cologne; silk ribbon; housing development; (W-I) sugar plantation || **Colonia** *f* Cologne; **la Colonia del Cabo** Cape Colony
colonial *adj* colonial; overseas || **coloniales** *mpl* imported foods
colonizar §60 *tr & intr* to colonize
colono *m* colonist, settler; tenant farmer; (W-I) owner of sugar plantation
coloquial *adj* colloquial
coloquialismo *m* colloquialism
coloquio *m* colloquy, talk, conference
color *m* color; (*substancia para pintar*) paint; (*para pintarse el rostro*) rouge; **colores** (*bandera*) colors; (*persona*) **de color** colored; (*zapatos*) tan; **sacar los colores a** to make blush; **so color de** under color of, under pretext of; **verlo todo de color de rosa** to see everything through rose-colored glasses
colora•do -da *adj* red, reddish; (*libre, obsceno*) off-color; (*aparentemente justo y razonable*) specious; **ponerse colorado** to blush
colorado•te -ta *adj* (coll) ruddy, sanguine
colorante *adj & m* coloring
colorar *tr* to color; to dye; to stain
colorear *tr* to color; (fig) to color, excuse, palliate || *ref* (*la cereza, el tomate, etc.*) to redden, turn red
colorete *m* rouge; **ponerse colorete** to put on rouge
colorir §1 *tr* to color; (fig) to color, to palliate || *intr* to take on color
colosal *adj* colossal
coloso *m* colossus
columbrar *tr* to discern, descry, glimpse; to guess
columna *f* column; **quinta columna** fifth column
columnata *f* colonnade
columnista *mf* columnist
columpiar *tr* to swing || *ref* to swing; to seesaw; (coll) to swing, swagger
columpio *m* swing; **columpio de tabla** seesaw
colusión *f* collusion
collada *f* mountain pass; (naut) steady blow
collado *m* hill, height
collar *m* necklace; dog collar, horse collar; (*aro de hierro asegurado al cuello del malhechor*) collar, band; (*plumas del cuello de ciertas aves*) frill, ring; (*cadena que rodea el cuello como insignia*) cord, chain; (mach) collar
collera *f* horse collar; chain gang; **colleras** (Arg, Chile) cuff links
co•llón -llona *adj* (coll) cowardly || *mf* (coll) coward
coma *m* (pathol) coma || *f* comma; (*en inglés se emplea el punto en aritmética para separar los enteros de las fracciones decimales*) decimal point
comadre *f* mother or godmother (*with respect to each other*); gossip (*woman*); friend, neighbor (*woman*)
comadrear *intr* (coll) to gossip, go around gossiping
comadreja *f* weasel
comadrería *f* (coll) gossip, idle gossip
comadre•ro -ra *adj* (coll) gossipy || *mf* (coll) gossip
comadrón *m* accoucheur
comadrona *f* midwife
comandancia *f* command; commander's headquarters; (mil) majority
comandante *m* commander, commandant; (mil) major
comandar *tr* (mil, nav) to command
comando *m* (mil) command; **comando a distancia** remote control
comarca *f* district, region, country
comarcar §73 *tr* to plant in a line at regular intervals || *intr* to border, be contiguous
comato•so -sa *adj* comatose
comba *f* bend, curve; warp, bulge; skipping rope; **saltar a la comba** to jump rope, to skip rope
combar *tr* to bend, curve || *ref* to bend, curve; to warp, bulge; to sag
combate *m* combat, fight; **combate revancha** (box) return bout; **fuera de**

combate hors de combat; (box) knockout
combatiente *adj & m* combatant
combatir *tr* to combat, fight; to beat, beat upon || *intr & ref* to combat, fight, struggle
combinación *f* combination; (*de trenes*) connection
combinar *tr & ref* to combine
com•bo -ba *adj* bent, curved, crooked; warped || *m* trunk or rock to stand wine casks on || *f* see **comba**
combustible *adj* combustible || *m* (*substancia que arde con facilidad*) combustible; (*substancia que sirve para calentar, cocinar, etc.*) fuel
combustión *f* combustion
comede•ro -ra *adj* eatable || *m* manger, feed trough; (Mex) haunt, hangout; **limpiarle a uno el comedero** (coll) to deprive someone of his bread and butter
comedia *f* drama, play; theater; comedy; (fig) farce; **comedia cómica** (*drama de desenlace festivo*) comedy; **hacer la comedia** (coll) to pretend, make believe
comedian•te -ta *mf* (coll) hypocrite || *m* actor, comedian || *f* actress, comedienne
comedi•do -da *adj* courteous, polite; moderate; (Am) obliging, accommodating
comedimiento *m* courtesy, politeness; moderation
comediógra•fo -fa *mf* playwright
comedir §50 *ref* to be courteous; to restrain oneself, be moderate; (Am) to be obliging; **comedirse a** (Am) to offer to, to volunteer to
comedón *m* blackhead
come•dor -dora *adj* heavy-eating || *m* dining room; restaurant, eating place; dining-room suite; **comedor de beneficencia** soup kitchen
comején *m* termite
comendador *m* prelate, prior; knight commander; (*de una orden militar*) commander
comensal *mf* dependent, servant; table companion
comentar *tr* to comment on || *intr* to comment; (coll) to gossip
comentario *m* comment, commentary; **commentarios** (coll) talk, gossip
comentarista *mf* commentator
comento *m* comment, commentary; deceit, falsehood
comenzar §18 *tr & intr* to commence, begin, start
comer *m* eating, food || *tr* to eat; to feed on; to gnaw away; to consume; (*alguna renta*) to enjoy; to itch; (*una pieza en el juego de damas*) to take; **comer vivo** (coll) to have it in for; **sin comerlo ni beberlo** (coll) without having anything to do with it; **tener qué comer** (coll) to have enough to live on || *intr* to eat; to dine, to have dinner; to itch || *ref* to eat up; (*las uñas*) to bite; (*el dinero*) (coll) to consume, eat up; (*omitir*) to skip, skip over; **comerse unos a otros** (coll) to be at loggerheads
comerciable *adj* marketable; sociable
comercial *adj* commercial, business
comerciante *mf* merchant, trader, dealer; **comerciante al por mayor** wholesaler; **comerciante al por menor** retailer
comerciar *intr* to trade, to deal
comercio *m* commerce, trade, business; store, shop; business center; commerce, intercourse; **comercio de artículos de regalo** gift shop; **comercio exterior** foreign trade
comestible *adj* eatable || *m* food, foodstuff
cometa *m* comet || *f* kite
cometer *tr* (*un crimen, una falta*) to commit; (*un negocio a una persona*) to commit, to entrust; (*figuras retóricas*) to employ
cometido *m* assignment, duty; commitment
comezón *f* itch
comicastro *m* ham, ham actor
comicios *mpl* polls; **acudir a los comicios** to go to the polls
cómi•co -ca *adj* comic, comical; dramatic || *mf* actor; comedian; **cómico de la legua** strolling player, barnstormer || *f* actress; comedienne
comida *f* (*alimento*) food; (*el que se toma a horas señaladas*) meal; (*el principal de cada día*) dinner; **comida corrida** (Mex) table d'hôte
comidilla *f* (coll) hobby; **la comidilla del pueblo** (coll) the talk of the town
comienzo *m* beginning, start; **a comienzos de** around the beginning of
comilitona *f* (coll) spread, feast
comi•lón -lona *adj* (coll) heavy-eating || *mf* (coll) hearty eater || *f* (coll) hearty meal, spread
comillas *fpl* quotation marks
cominear *intr* (*el hombre*) (coll) to fuss around like a woman
comiquear *intr* to put on amateur plays
comiquillo *m* ham, ham actor
comisar *tr* to seize, confiscate
comisario *m* commissary; commissioner; **comisario de a bordo** purser
comisión *f* commission; committee; (*recado*) errand
comisiona•do -da *mf* commissioner || *m* committeeman
comisionar *tr* to commission
comiso *m* seizure, confiscation; confiscated goods
comisura *f* corner (*e.g., of lips*)
comité *m* committee
comitente *mf* constituent
comitiva *f* retinue, suite; procession
como *adv* as, like; so to speak, as it were || *conj* as; when; if; so that; as soon as; as long as; inasmuch as; **así como** as soon as; **como no** unless; **como que** because, inasmuch as; **como quien dice** so to speak; **tan luego como** as soon as
cómo *adv* how; why; what; **¿a cómo es . . .?** how much is . . .?; **¿cómo no?** why not?
cómoda *f* bureau, commode, chest

comodidad *f* comfort; convenience; advantage, interest
comodín *m* joker, wild card; gadget, jigger; excuse, alibi
cómo•do -da *adj* handy, convenient; comfortable || *f* see **cómoda**
como•dón -dona *adj* (coll) comfort-loving, self-indulgent, easy-going
compac•to -ta *adj* compact
compadecer §22 *tr* to pity, feel sorry for || *ref* to harmonize; **compadecerse con** to harmonize with; **compadecerse de** to pity, feel sorry for
compadraje *m* clique, cabal
compadrar *intr* to become a godfather; to become friends
compadre *m* father or godfather (*with respect to each other*); friend, companion
compadrear *intr* (coll) to be close friends; (Arg, Urug) to brag, show off
compadrería *f* close companionship
compadrito *m* (Arg) bully
compaginar *tr* to arrange, put in order || *ref* to fit, agree; to blend
companage *m* snacks, cold cuts
compañerismo *m* companionship
compañe•ro -ra *mf* companion; partner; mate; **compañero de cama** bedfellow; **compañero de cuarto** roommate; **compañero de juego** playmate; **compañero de viaje** fellow traveler || *f* (*esposa*) helpmeet
compañía *f* company; society; **compañía de desembarco** (nav) landing force; **hacerle compañía a una persona** to keep someone company
compañón *m* testicle; **compañón de perro** orchid
comparación *f* comparison
comparar *tr* to compare
comparati•vo -va *adj* comparative
comparecencia *f* (law) appearance
comparecer §22 *intr* (law) to appear
comparendo *m* (law) summons
comparsa *mf* (theat) supernummerary, extra || *f* supernummeraries, extras
compartimiento *m* distribution, division; compartment
compartir *tr* to distribute, divide; to share
compás *m* (*brújula*) compass; (*instrumento para trazar curvas*) compass or compasses; rule, measure; (mus) time, measure; (mus) bar, measure; (mus) beat; **a compás** (mus) in time; **compás de calibres** calipers; **compás de división** dividers; **llevar el compás** (mus) to keep time
compasible *adj* compassionate; pitiful
compasión *f* compassion; **¡por compasión!** for pity's sake!
compasi•vo -va *adj* compassionate
compatri•cio -cia or **compatriota** *mf* fellow countryman, compatriot
compeler *tr* to compel
compendiar *tr* to condense, to summarize
compendio *m* compendium; **en compendio** in a word
compendio•so -sa *adj* compendious
compensación *f* compensation; (com) clearing, clearance
compensar *tr* to compensate; to compensate for || *intr* to compensate || *ref* to be compensated for
competencia *f* (*aptitud*) competence; (*rivalidad*) competition; dispute; area, field; **de la competencia de** in the domain of; **sin competencia** unmatched (*prices*)
competente *adj* competent; reliable
competer *intr* to be incumbent
competición *f* competition
competi•dor -dora *adj* competing || *mf* competitor
competir §50 *intr* to compete
compilación *f* compilation
compilar *tr* to compile
compinche *mf* (coll) chum, crony, pal
complacencia *f* complacency
complacer §22 *tr* to please, to humor || *ref* to be pleased, take pleasure
complaciente *adj* obliging; indulgent
comple•jo -ja *adj* & *m* complex; **complejo de inferioridad** inferiority complex
complementar *tr* to complement
complemento *m* complement; completion; perfection; accessory; **complemento directo** (gram) direct object
completar *tr* to complete; to perfect
comple•to -ta *adj* complete; (*autobús, tranvía*) full
complexión *f* constitution
complexiona•do -da *adj* — **bien complexionado** strong, robust; **mal complexionado** weak, frail
comple•xo -xa *adj* complex
complica•do -da *adj* complicated, complex
complicar §73 *tr* to complicate; to involve || *ref* to become complicated; to become involved
cómplice *mf* accomplice, accessory
complicidad *f* complicity
com•plot *m* (*pl* **-plots**) plot, intrigue
compone•dor -dora *mf* composer, compositor; typesetter; arbitrator; repairer || *m* stick, composing stick; **amigable componedor** mediator, umpire
componenda *f* compromise, settlement, reconciliation
componente *adj* component, constituent || *m* component, constituent; member || *f* (mech) component
componer §54 *tr* to compose; to compound; to mend, repair; to pacify, reconcile; to arrange, put in order; (coll) to restore, strengthen; (*huesos dislocados*) (Am) to set; (Col) to bewitch || *ref* to compose oneself; to get dressed; to make up, become friends again; (*pintarse el rostro*) to make up; **componérselas** (coll) to make out, to manage
comportable *adj* bearable, tolerable
comportamiento *m* behavior, conduct
comportar *tr* to support; (Am) to bring about, entail || *ref* to act, behave
comporte *m* behavior; carriage, bearing
composición *f* composition; agreement; (*circunspección*) composure, restraint; **hacer una composición de lugar** to carefully lay one's plans

compositi·vo -va *adj* (gram) combining
composi·tor -tora *mf* composer || *m* (Arg, Urug) horse trainer, trainer of fighting cocks
compostura *f* composition; agreement; (*circunspección*) composure, restraint; repair, repairing, mending; (*aseo*) neatness; adulteration; (Arg, Urug) training
compota *f* compote, preserves; **compota de frutas** stewed fruit; **compota de manzanas** applesauce
compotera *f* (*vasija*) compote
compra *f* purchase, buy; shopping; **compra al contado** cash purchase; **compra a plazos** installment buying; **hacer compras, ir de compras** to go shopping
compra·dor -dora *mf* purchaser, buyer; shopper
comprar *tr* to purchase, to buy; (*sobornar*) to buy off || *intr* to shop
compraventa *f* dealing, business, bargain, trading; resale
comprender *tr* (*entender*) to understand; (*entender; abrazar*) to comprehend; (*contener, incluir*) to comprise
comprensible *adj* comprehensible, understandable
comprensión *f* understanding, comprehension; inclusion
comprensi·vo -va *adj* understanding; comprehensive; **comprensivo de** inclusive of
compresa *f* (med) compress; **compresa higiénica** sanitary napkin
compresión *f* compression
comprimido *m* tablet
comprimir *tr* to compress; to restrain, repress; to flatten
comprobación *f* checking, verification; proof
comprobante *adj* proving || *m* certificate, voucher, warrant; proof; claim check
comprobar §61 *tr* to check, verify; to prove
comprometer *tr* to compromise, endanger, jeopardize; to force, to oblige; (*un negocio a un tercero*) to entrust || *ref* to promise; to commit oneself; to become engaged
comprometi·do -da *adj* awkward, embarrassing; engaged to be married
comprometimiento *m* commitment, promise; predicament, awkward situation; compromise
compromiso *m* commitment, promise; appointment, engagement; predicament, awkward situation; betrothal
compuerta *f* hatch, half door; floodgate, sluice
compues·to -ta *adj* & *m* composite, compound
compulsar *tr* to collate; to make an authentic copy of
compungi·do -da *adj* remorseful
compungir §27 *tr* to make remorseful || *ref* to feel remorse
compurgar §44 *tr* (*el reo la pena*) (Mex) to finish serving
computador *m* computer
computar *tr* & *intr* to compute
cómputo *m* computation, calculation
comulgante *mf* (eccl) communicant
comulgar §44 *tr* to administer communion to || *intr* to take communion
comulgatorio *m* communion rail, altar rail
común *adj* common || *m* community; water closet; toilet; **el común de las gentes** the general run of people; **por lo común** commonly
comunal *adj* common; community || *m* community
comune·ro -ra *adj* popular || *m* shareholder
comunicación *f* communication; connection
comunicado *m* communiqué; letter to the editor; official announcement
comunica·dor -dora *adj* communicating
comunicante *mf* communicant, informant
comunicar §73 *tr* to communicate; to notify, inform; to connect, put into communication || *intr* to communicate || *ref* to communicate; to communicate with each other
comunicati·vo -va *adj* communicative
comunidad *f* community
comunión *f* communion; political party; sect
comunismo *m* communism
comunista *mf* communist
comunistizar §60 *tr* to convert to communism || *ref* to become communistic
comunizar §60 *tr* to communize
con *prep* with; to, towards; in spite of; **con que** and so; whereupon; **con tal (de) que** provided that; **con todo** however, nevertheless
conato *m* effort, endeavor; (*delito que no llegó a consumarse*) attempt
cónca·vo -va *adj* concave
concebible *adj* conceivable
concebir §50 *tr* & *intr* to conceive
conceder *tr* to concede, admit; to grant
concejal *m* alderman, councilman; **concejales** city fathers
concejo *m* town council; town hall; council meeting; (*expósito*) foundling
concentrar *tr* & *ref* to concentrate
concéntri·co -ca *adj* concentric
concepción *f* conception
concepto *m* concept; opinion, judgment; (*dicho ingenioso*) conceit, witticism; point of view; **en concepto de** under the head of; **tener buen concepto de** or **tener en buen concepto** to have a high opinion of, to hold in high esteem
conceptuar §21 *tr* to deem, to judge, to regard
conceptuo·so -sa *adj* witty, epigrammatic
concerniente *adj* relative
concernir §28 *tr* to concern
concertar §2 *tr* to concert; to mend, repair; (*un casamiento; la paz*) to arrange; (*huesos dislocados*) to set; (*poner de acuerdo*) to reconcile; (*un pacto*) to conclude; to harmonize || *intr* to concert; to agree || *ref* to

come to terms, become reconciled; to agree
concertino *m* concertmaster
concertista *mf* (mus) manager; (mus) performer, soloist
concesión *f* concession, admission; grant
concesionario *m* licensee; (*comerciante*) dealer
concesi•vo -va *adj* concessive
conciencia *f* (*conocimiento que uno tiene de su propia existencia*) consciousness; (*sentimiento del bien y del mal*) conscience; (*conocimiento*) awareness; **cobrar conciencia de** to become aware of; **en conciencia** in all conscience
concienzu•do -da *adj* conscientious; thorough
concierto *m* concert, harmony; (*función de música*) concert; (*composición de música*) concerto
concilia•dor -dora *adj* conciliatory
conciliar *tr* to conciliate, to reconcile || *ref* (*el respeto, la estima, etc.*) to conciliate, to win
concilio *m* (eccl) council
conci•so -sa *adj* concise
concitar *tr* to stir up, incite, agitate
conciudada•no -na *mf* fellow citizen
concluir §20 *tr* to conclude; to convince || *intr & ref* to conclude, to end
conclusión *f* conclusion
concluyente *adj* conclusive, convincing
concomitar *tr* to accompany, go with
concordancia *f* concordance; (gram, mus) concord
concordar §61 *tr* to harmonize; to reconcile; to make agree || *intr* to agree
concordia *f* concord; **de concordia** by common consent
concre•to -ta *adj* concrete
concubina *f* concubine
concubio *m* (archaic) bedtime
concuñada *f* sister-in-law
concuñado *m* brother-in-law
concurrencia *f* (*acaecimiento de varios sucesos en un mismo tiempo*) concurrence; (*competencia comercial*) competition; (*ayuda*) assistance; crowd, gathering, attendance
concurrente *adj* concurrent; competing || *mf* competitor, contender, entrant
concurri•do -da *adj* crowded, full of people; well-attended
concurrir *intr* to concur; to gather, meet, come together; to compete, contend; to coincide; **concurrir con** (*p.ej., dinero*) to contribute
concursante *mf* contender
concursar *tr* to declare insolvent || *intr* to contend, to compete
concurso *m* contest, competition; (*de gente*) concourse, crowd, throng; backing, coöperation; show, exhibition; **concurso de acreedores** meeting of creditors; **concurso de belleza** beauty contest; **concurso hípico** horse show
concusión *f* concussion; extortion, shakedown
concha *f* (*de molusco o crustáceo*) shell; (*cada una de las dos partes del caparazón de los moluscos bivalvos*) half shell; (*en que se sirve el pescado*) scallop; (*carey*) tortoise shell; oyster; shellfish; horseshoe bay; (theat) prompter's box; **concha de peregrino** scallop shell; (zool) scallop; (*ostras*) **en su concha** on the half shell; **tener muchas conchas** (coll) to be sly, cunning
conchabanza *f* comfort; (coll) collusion, cabal
conchabar *tr* to join, unite; (Am) to hire || *ref* (coll) to gang up; (Am) to hire out
conchabero *m* (Col) pieceworker
condado *m* county; earldom
conde *m* count, earl; gypsy chief
condecoración *f* decoration
condecorar *tr* to decorate
condena *f* sentence; penalty, jail term; **condena judicial** conviction
condenación *f* condemnation; (*la eterna*) damnation
condena•do -da *adj* condemned; damned; (Chile) shrewd, clever || *mf* sentenced person; **los condenados** the damned
condenar *tr* to condemn; to convict; (*a la pena eterna*) to damn; (*p.ej., una ventana*) to shut off, to block up; (*una habitación*) to padlock || *ref* to condemn oneself, confess one's guilt; (*a la pena eterna*) to be damned
condensar *tr* to condense || *ref* to condense, be condensed
condesa *f* countess
condescendencia *f* acquiescence, compliance
condescender §51 *intr* to acquiesce, comply; **condescender a** to accede to
condescendiente *adj* acquiescent, obliging
condición *f* condition, state; position, situation; standing; nature, character, temperament; **a condición (de) que** on condition that; **en buenas condiciones** in good condition, in good shape; **tener condición** to have a bad temper
condicional *adj* conditional
condimentar *tr* to season
condimento *m* condiment, seasoning
condiscípulo *m* fellow student
condolencia *f* condolence
condoler §47 *ref* to condole; **condolerse de** to sympathize with, feel sorry for, commiserate with
condonar *tr* to condone, overlook
conducción *f* conveyance, transportation; guiding. leading; (aut) drive, driving; **conducción a la derecha** right-hand drive; **conducción a la izquierda** left-hand drive; **conducción interior** closed car
conducente *adj* conducive
conducir §19 *tr* to conduct; to manage, direct; to guide, lead; to convey, transport; to drive; to employ, hire || *intr* to lead; to conduce || *ref* to conduct oneself, behave
conducta *f* conduct; management, direction; guidance; conveyance; conduct, behavior

conducto *m* pipe; conduit; (anat) duct, canal; agency, intermediary, channel; **por conducto de** through
conduc·tor -tora *adj* conducting ‖ *mf* driver, motorist; (*cobrador en un vehículo público*) (Am) conductor ‖ *m & f* (elec & phys) conductor; **buen conductor, buena conductora** good conductor; **mal conductor, mala conductora** bad or poor conductor ‖ *m* (rr) engineman, engine driver
conectar *tr* to connect
conejera *f* burrow, warren; (coll) joint, dive
conejillo *m* young rabbit; **conejillo de Indias** guinea pig
conejo *m* rabbit
conexión *f* connection
conexionar *tr* to connect; to put in touch ‖ *ref* to connect; to make contacts
confabulación *f* collusion, connivance
confabular *ref* to connive, scheme, plot
confección *f* making, preparation, confection; tailoring; ready-made suit; **confección a medida** suit made to order; **de confección** ready-made
confeccionar *tr* (*ropa*) to make; (*una receta*) to make up, concoct
confeccionista *mf* ready-made clothier
confederación *f* confederacy; alliance
confedera·do -da *adj & mf* confederate
confederar *tr & ref* to confederate
conferencia *f* (*reunión para tratar asuntos internacionales, etc.*) conference; (*plática para tratar de algún negocio*) interview; (*disertación en público o en la universidad*) lecture; **conferencia telefónica** (telp) long-distance call
conferenciante *mf* conferee; lecturer
conferenciar *intr* to confer, hold an interview
conferencista *mf* (Arg) lecturer
conferir §68 *tr* to confer, award, bestow; to discuss; to compare ‖ *intr* to confer
confesante *mf* confessor
confesar §2 *tr, intr & ref* to confess
confesión *f* confession; denomination, faith, religion
confe·so -sa *adj* confessed; (*judío*) converted ‖ *mf* converted Jew ‖ *m* lay brother
confesonario *m* confessional
confesor *m* confessor
confiable *adj* reliable, dependable
confia·do -da *adj* unsuspecting; haughty, self-confident
confianza *f* confidence; self-confidence, self-assurance; familiarity; secret deal; **de confianza** reliable
confianzu·do -da *adj* (coll) overconfident; (Am) overfamiliar
confiar §77 *tr* to confide, entrust; to strengthen the confidence of ‖ *intr & ref* to confide, trust; **confiar** or **confiarse de** or **en** to confide in, trust in; to rely on
confidencia *f* confidence; secret
confidencial *adj* confidential
confiden·te -ta *adj* trustworthy, faithful ‖ *mf* confident ‖ *m* spy; informer; secret agent; love seat
configurar *tr* to shape, form
confín *m* confine, border, boundary; **los confines** the confines
confina·do -da *adj* exiled ‖ *m* prisoner
confinamiento *m* confinement; abutment
confinar *tr* to exile; to confine ‖ *intr* to border
confirmar *tr* to confirm
confiscar §73 *tr* to confiscate
confita·do -da *adj* hopeful, confident; (*bañado de azúcar*) candied
confitar *tr* (*frutas*) to candy; (*en almíbar*) to preserve; (*endulzar*) to sweeten
confite *m* candy, bonbon, confection; **confites** confectionery
confitera *f* candy box; candy jar
confitería *f* confectionery; confectionery store
confite·ro -ra *mf* confectioner ‖ *f* see **confitera**
confitura *f* preserves, confiture; **confituras** confectionery
conflagración *f* conflagration
conflagrar *tr* to set fire to
conflicto *m* conflict; (*apuro*) fix, jam
confluencia *f* confluence
confluir §20 *intr* to flow together; to crowd, gather
conformador *m* hat block
conformar *tr* to shape; (*un sombrero*) to block ‖ *intr & ref* to conform, to comply, to yield, to agree
conforme *adj* in agreement ‖ *adv* depending on circumstances; fine, O.K.; **conforme a** according to ‖ *conj* as, in proportion as; as soon as ‖ *m* approval
conformidad *f* conformance, conformity; resignation
confort *m* comfort
confortable *adj* comfortable; comforting
confortante *adj* comforting; tonic ‖ *mf* comforter ‖ *m* tonic
confr. *abbr* **confesor**
confricar *tr* to rub
confrontar *tr* (*poner en presencia; cotejar*) to confront ‖ *intr* to border; to agree ‖ *ref* to get along, to agree; **confrontarse con** (*hacer frente a*) to confront
confundir *tr* to confuse; (*turbar, dejar desarmado*) to confound ‖ *ref* to become confused; (*en la muchedumbre*) to get lost
confusión *f* confusion
confutar *tr* to confute
congelador *m* freezer
congelar *tr* to congeal, freeze; (*créditos*) (fig) to freeze ‖ *ref* to congeal, freeze
congenial *adj* congenial (*having the same nature*)
congeniar *intr* to be congenial, to get along well
congéni·to -ta *adj* congenital
congestión *f* congestion
congestionar *tr* to congest ‖ *ref* to congest, become congested

conglobar *tr* to lump together
congoja *f* anguish, grief
congojo•so -sa *adj* distressing; distressed
congosto *m* narrow mountain pass
congraciar *tr* to win over || *ref* to ingratiate oneself; **congraciarse con** to get into the good graces of
congratulación *f* congratulation
congratular *tr* to congratulate || *ref* to congratulate oneself, to rejoice
congregación *f* congregation; **la Congregación de los fieles** the Roman Catholic Church
congregar §44 *tr* to bring together || *ref* to congregate, to come together
congresal *m* (Arg, Chile) congressman
congresista *mf* delegate; member of congress || *m* congressman
congreso *m* (*asamblea legislativa*) congress; (*reunión para deliberar sobre intereses comunes*) meeting, convention
congrio *m* conger eel
cóni•co -ca *adj* conical
conjetura *f* conjecture, guess
conjeturar *tr* & *intr* to conjecture, guess
conjugación *f* conjugation
conjugar §44 *tr* to conjugate; to combine
conjunción *f* conjunction; combination
conjuntamente *adv* together
conjuntista *m* chorus man || *f* chorus girl
conjunti•vo -va *adj* conjunctive; subjunctive
conjun•to -ta *adj* joined, combined, united || *m* whole, entirety, ensemble; unit; group; (theat) chorus; **de conjunto** general; **en conjunto** as a whole; **en su conjunto** in its entirety
conjura or **conjuración** *f* conspiracy, plot
conjuramentar *tr* to swear in || *ref* to take an oath
conjurar *tr* to swear in; to conjure, entreat; to conjure away, to exorcise || *intr* to conspire, plot || *ref* to conspire, join in a conspiracy
conjuro *m* (*invocación supersticiosa*) conjuration; adjuration, entreaty
conllevar *tr* (*los trabajos*) to share in bearing; (*a una persona*) to tolerate, stand for; (*las adversidades*) to suffer
conmemorar *tr* to commemorate, memorialize
conmigo *pron* with me, with myself
conmilitón *m* fellow soldier
conminar *tr* to threaten
conmoción *f* commotion; concussion, shock
conmove•dor -dora *adj* touching, moving, stirring
conmover §47 *tr* to touch, move, affect; to stir, stir up; to shake, upset || *ref* to be touched, be moved
conmutación *f* commutation
conmutador *m* (elec) change-over switch
conmutar *tr* to commute
connivencia *f* connivance; **estar en connivencia** to connive
cono *m* cone; **cono de proa** nose cone; **cono de viento** (aer) wind cone, wind sock
conoce•dor -dora *adj* knowledgeable || *mf* expert, connoisseur
conocer §22 *tr* to know; to meet, get to know; to tell, to distinguish; (law) to try || *intr* to know; **conocer de** or **en** to know, have knowledge of || *ref* to know oneself; to know each other; to meet, meet each other
conoci•do -da *adj* known, well-known, familiar; distinguished, prominent || *mf* acquaintance
conocimiento *m* knowledge; understanding; acquaintance; consciousness; (com) bill of lading; **con conocimiento de causa** knowingly, with full knowledge; **conocimiento de embarque** (com) bill of lading; **conocimientos** knowledge; **hablar con pleno conocimiento de causa** to know what one is talking about; **perder el conocimiento** to lose consciousness; **por su real conocimiento** (Arg) for real money; **recobrar el conocimiento** to regain consciousness; **venir en conocimiento de** to come to know
conque *adv* and so || *m* (coll) condition, terms
conquista *f* conquest
conquista•dor -dora *adj* conquering || *m* conqueror; (*ladrón de corazones*) lady-killer
conquistar *tr* to conquer; (*ganar la voluntad de*) to win over
consabi•do -da *adj* well-known; abovementioned
consagrar *tr* to consecrate; to devote; to dedicate; (*una nueva palabra*) to authorize || *ref* to devote oneself; to make a name for oneself
consciente *adj* conscious
conscripción *f* conscription
conscripto *m* conscript, draftee
consecución *f* obtaining, getting
consecuencia *f* (*correspondencia lógica entre sus elementos*) consistency; (*acontecimiento que resulta necesariamente de otro*) consequence; **en consecuencia** accordingly; **guardar consecuencia** to remain consistent; **traer a consecuencia** to bring in
consecuente *adj* (*que tiene proporción consigo mismo*) consistent; (*que sigue en orden a otra cosa*) consecutive
consecuti•vo -va *adj* consecutive
conseguir §67 *tr* to get, obtain; **conseguir** + *inf* to succeed in + *ger*
conseja *f* story, fairy tale; cabal
conseje•ro -ra *adj* advisory || *mf* advisor, counselor; councilor
consejo *m* advice, counsel; board; council; **consejos** advice; **un consejo** a piece of advice
consenso *m* consensus
consenti•do -da *adj* spoiled, pampered; (*marido*) indulgent
consenti•dor -dora *adj* acquiescent; pampering || *mf* acquiescent person; (*de niños*) pamperer || *m* cuckold

consentimiento *m* consent
consentir **§68** *tr* to allow; to admit; to pamper, to spoil || *intr* to consent; to come loose; **consentir** + *inf* to think that + *ind;* **consentir con** to be indulgent toward; **consentir en** to consent to || *ref* to begin to crack up; (Arg) to be proud
conserje *m* janitor, concierge
conserva *f* preserves; preserved food; pickles; (naut) convoy; **conservas alimenticias** canned goods; **llevar en su conserva** (naut) to convoy; **navegar en (la) conserva** (naut) to sail in a convoy
conservación *f* conservation; preservation; self-preservation; maintenance, upkeep
conserva·dor -dora *adj* preservative; (pol) conservative || *mf* conservative || *m* curator
conservar *tr* to conserve, keep, maintain; to preserve || *ref* to take good care of oneself; to keep
conservati·vo -va *adj* conservative, preservative
conservatorio *m* (*p.ej., de música*) conservatory; (Arg) private school; (Chile) hothouse, greenhouse
conservera *f* cannery; (Mex) preserve dish
conservería *f* canning
conserve·ro -ra *adj* canning || *mf* canner || *f* see **conservera**
considerable *adj* considerable; large, great, important
consideración *f* consideration; **ser de consideración** to be of importance, be of concern; **someter a consideración** to take under advisement
considera·do -da *adj* (*que guarda consideración a los demás*) considerate; (*digno de respeto*) respected, esteemed; (*que obra con reflexión*) cautious, prudent
considerando *conj & m* whereas
considerar *tr* to consider; to treat with consideration
consigna *f* slogan; watchword; (mil) orders; (rr) checkroom
consignación *f* consignment
consignar *tr* to consign; to assign; to state in writing, to set forth
consignatario *m* consignee
consigo *pron* with him, with her, with them, with you; with himself, with herself, with themselves, with yourself or yourselves
consiguiente *adj* consequential; **ir** or **proceder consiguiente** to act consistently || *m* consequence; **por consiguiente** consequently, therefore
consilia·rio -ria *mf* advisor, counselor
consistencia *f* consistence, consistency
consistente *adj* consistent
consistir *intr* to consist; **consistir en** (*estar compuesto de*) to consist of; (*residir en*) to consist in
consistorio *m* consistory; town council; town hall
conso·cio -cia *mf* copartner; companion, fellow member
consola *f* console, console table; bracket
consolación *f* consolation
consolar **§61** *tr* to console
consolidar *tr* to fund, refund; to strengthen; to repair
consommé *m* consommé
consonancia *f* consonance; rhyme
consonante *adj* consonantal; rhyming || *m* rhyme || *f* consonant
consonar **§61** *intr* to be in harmony; to rhyme
cónsone *adj* harmonious || *m* (mus) chord
consorcio *m* consortium; partnership; fellowship
consorte *mf* consort, mate, spouse; partner, companion; **consortes** (law) colitigants; (law) accomplices
conspi·cuo -cua *adj* outstanding, prominent
conspiración *f* conspiracy
conspirar *intr* to conspire
constancia *f* constancy; certainty, proof
constante *adj* constant; steady, regular; sure, certain || *f* constant
constar *intr* to be clear, be certain; to be on record; to have the right rhythm; **constar de** to consist of; **hacer constar** to state, make known; **y para que conste** in witness whereof
constatación *f* proof
constatar *tr* to prove, establish, show
constelación *f* constellation; climate, weather; epidemic
consternar *tr* to depress, dismay
constipación *f* or **constipado** *m* cold, cold in the head
constipar *tr* (*los poros*) to stop up || *ref* to catch cold
constitución *f* constitution
constituir **§20** *tr* to constitute; to establish, found; **constituir en** to force into || *ref* — **constituirse en** to set oneself up as
constituti·vo -va *adj & m* constituent
constituyente *adj* (*para dictar o reformar la constitución*) constituent
constreñir **§72** *tr* to constrain, force, compel; to constrict, compress
construcción *f* construction; building, structure; **construcción de buques** shipbuilding
construc·tor -tora *adj* construction || *mf* builder, constructor; **constructor de buques** shipbuilder
construir **§20** *tr* to build, to construct
consuegro *m* fellow father-in-law (*with respect to the father of one's son-in-law or daughter-in-law*), father-in-law of one's child
consuelda *f* comfrey; **consuelda real** field larkspur; **consuelda sarracena** goldenrod
consuelo *m* consolation; joy, delight; **sin consuelo** inconsolably; (coll) to excess
consueta *m* (theat) prompter
consuetudina·rio -ria *adj* customary, usual
cónsul *m* consul
consulado *m* consulate, consulship; (*casa u oficina*) consulate

consular *adj* consular
consulta *f* consultation; opinion; reference
consultación *f* consultation
consultar *tr* to consult; to take up, discuss; to advise || *intr* to consult, confer
consulti·vo -va *adj* advisory
consul·tor -tora *mf* consultant
consultorio *m* doctor's office
consuma·do -da *adj* consummate || *m* consommé
consumar *tr* to consummate; to fulfill, carry out
consumición *f* consumption; drink (*in bar or restaurant*)
consumi·do -da *adj* (coll) thin, weak, emaciated; (coll) fretful
consumi·dor -dora *mf* consumer; customer (*in bar or restaurant*)
consumir *tr* to consume; to exhaust; (coll) to harass, wear down || *ref* to consume, waste away; to long, yearn
consumo *m* consumption; drink (*in bar or restaurant*); customers; **consumos** octroi
consunción *f* consumption; (pathol) consumption
consuno *adv* — **de consuno** together, in accord
consunti·vo -va *adj* consumptive; (*crédito*) consumer
contabilidad *f* accounting, bookkeeping
contabilista *mf* accountant, bookkeeper
contabilizadora *f* computer
contabilizar **§60** *tr* to enter in the ledger
contable *adj* countable || *mf* accountant, bookkeeper
contactar *intr* to contact, be in contact
contacto *m* contact; **ponerse en contacto con** to get in touch with
conta·do -da *adj* scarce, rare; **al contado** cash, for cash; **contados** a few; **de contado** right away; **por de contado** of course
contador *m* counter; accountant; (*que mide el agua, gas, electricidad*) meter; (law) receiver; **contador de abonado** house meter; **contador kilométrico** speedometer; **contador público titulado** certified public accountant
contaduría *f* accountancy; accountant's office; box office for advanced sales
contagiar *tr* to infect; to corrupt
contagio *m* contagion
contagio·so -sa *adj* contagious
contaminación *f* contamination
contaminar *tr* to contaminate; (*un texto*) to corrupt; (*la ley de Dios*) to break
contante *adj* (*dinero*) ready
contar **§61** *tr* to count; to regard, consider; to tell, relate; **contar . . . años** to be . . . years old; **dejarse contar diez** (box) to take the count; **tiene sus horas contadas** his days are numbered || *intr* to count; **a contar desde** beginning with; **contar con** to count on, rely on; to reckon with; to expect to
contemplación *f* contemplation; leniency, condescension
contemplar *tr* to contemplate; to be lenient to || *intr* to contemplate
contemporáne·o -a *adj* contemporaneous, contemporary || *mf* contemporary
contemporizar **§60** *intr* to temporize
contención *f* containment; contention, strife; (law) suit, litigation
contencio·so -sa *adj* contentious
contender **§51** *intr* to contend
contendiente *mf* contender, contestant
contener **§71** *tr* to contain || *ref* to contain oneself
conteni·do -da *adj* moderate, restrained || *m* content, contents
contenta *f* gift or treat; indorsement; (mil) certificate of good conduct; (law) release
contentadi·zo -za *adj* easy to please
contentamiento *m* contentment
contentar *tr* to content; (com) to indorse; (Am) to reconcile
conten·to -ta *adj* content, contented, glad || *m* content, contentment; **a contento** to one's satisfaction; **no caber de contento** (coll) to be beside oneself with joy || *f* see **contenta**
contera *f* tip, metal tip
contesta *f* (Am) answer; (Mex) chat
contestación *f* answer; argument, debate; **mala contestación** (coll) back talk
contestar *tr* to answer || *intr* to answer; to agree
contexto *m* interweaving; context
conticinio *m* dead of night
contienda *f* contest, dispute, fight
contigo *pron* with thee, with you
conti·guo -gua *adj* contiguous, adjoining
continencia *f* continence
continental *adj* continental
continente *adj* continent || *m* (*cosa que contiene en sí a otra*) container; (*aire del semblante, compostura del cuerpo*) mien, bearing; (*gran extensión de tierra rodeada por los océanos*) continent
contingencia *f* contingency
contingente *adj* contingent || *m* contingent; share, quota
continuar **§21** *tr* & *intr* to continue; **continuará** to be continued
continuidad *f* continuity
conti·nuo -nua *adj* continuous, continual; (mach) endless || **continuo** *adv* continuously
contonear *ref* to strut, swagger
contoneo *m* strut, swagger
contorcer **§74** *ref* to writhe
contorno *m* contour, outline; **contornos** environs, neighborhood
contorsión *f* contorsion
contra *prep* against; toward, facing || *m* (*concepto opuesto*) con || *f* trouble, inconvenience; (*al comprador*) (Cuba) gift, extra; (Chile) antidote; **llevar la contra a** (coll) to disagree with
contraalmirante *m* rear admiral
contraatacar **§73** *tr* & *intr* to counterattack
contraataque *m* counterattack

contrabajo *m* contrabass, double bass
contrabajón *m* double bassoon
contrabalancear *tr* to counterbalance
contrabalanza *f* counterbalance
contrabandear *intr* to smuggle
contrabandista *adj* smuggling; contraband || *mf* smuggler, contrabandist
contrabando *m* smuggling, contraband; **meter de contrabando** to smuggle, smuggle in
contrabarrera *f* second row of seats (*in bull ring*)
contracalle *f* parallel side street
contracarril *m* (rr) guardrail
contracción *f* contraction; (*reducción del ritmo normal de los negocios*) recession; (*al estudio*) (Chile, Peru) concentration
contracepti•vo -va *adj & m* contraceptive
contracorriente *f* countercurrent, crosscurrent; (*entre aguas*) undertow
contrachapado *m* plywood
contradecir **§24** *tr* to contradict
contradicción *f* contradiction
contradic•tor -tora *adj* contradictory || *mf* contradicter
contradicto•rio -ria *adj* contradictory
contraer **§75** *tr* to contract; (*deudas*) to incur; (*el discurso o idea*) to condense || *ref* to contract; to shrink; (Chile, Peru) to concentrate, apply oneself
contraescalón *m* riser (*of stairway*)
contraespía *mf* counterspy
contraespionaje *m* counterespionage
contrafallar *tr & intr* to overtrump
contrafallo *m* overtrump
contrafigura *f* counterpart
contrafuero *m* infringement, violation
contrafuerte *m* abutment, buttress
contragolpe *m* counterstroke; kickback; (box) counter
contrahace•dor -dora *adj* counterfeiting; fake || *mf* counterfeiter; fake; impersonator
contrahacer **§39** *tr* to counterfeit, copy, imitate; to fake; to impersonate; (*un libro*) to pirate || *ref* to pretend to be
contra•haz *f* (*pl* **-haces**) wrong side
contrahe•cho -cha *adj* counterfeit, fake; deformed
contrahechura *f* counterfeit, fake
contrahuella *f* riser (*of stairway*)
contralor *m* comptroller
contralto *mf* contralto (*person*) || *m* contralto (*voice*)
contraluz *f* view against the light; **a contraluz** against the light
contramaestre *m* foreman; (naut) boatswain; **segundo contramaestre** boatswain's mate
contramandar *tr* to countermand
contramandato *m* countermand
contramano *adv* — **a contramano** in the wrong direction, the wrong way
contramarcha *f* countermarch; reverse
contramarchar *intr* to countermarch; to go in reverse
contraofensiva *f* counteroffensive
contraorden *f* cancellation
contraparte *f* counterpart
contrapasar *intr* to go over to the other side
contrapelo *adv* — **a contrapelo** against the hair, against the grain; the wrong way; **a contrapelo de** against, counter to
contrapesar *tr* to offset, counterbalance
contrapeso *m* counterweight; counterbalance; (*para completar el peso de carne, etc.*) makeweight
contraponer **§54** *tr* to set opposite; to oppose; to compare
contraproducente *adj* self-defeating, unproductive
contraprueba *f* second proof
contrapuerta *f* storm door; vestibule door
contrapuntear *tr* to sing in counterpoint; to taunt, be sarcastic to || *ref* to taunt each other
contrapunto *m* counterpoint
contrapunzón *m* nailset, punch
contrariar **§77** *tr* to counteract, to oppose; to annoy, provoke
contrariedad *f* opposition; interference; annoyance, bother
contra•rio -ria *adj* opposite, contrary; harmful || *mf* enemy, opponent, rival || *m* opposite, contrary; **al contrario** on the contrary; **de lo contrario** otherwise
contrarreferencia *f* cross reference
Contrarreforma *f* Counter Reformation
contrarregistro *m* (*para comprobar si algún género ha pasado por la frontera*) double check; (*de una experiencia científica*) control
contrarréplica *f* (law) rejoinder
contrarrestar *tr* to resist, counteract; (*la pelota*) to return
contrarrevolución *f* counterrevolution
contrasentido *m* misinterpretation; mistranslation; nonsense
contraseña *f* countersign; baggage check; **contraseña de salida** (mov, theat) check
contrastar *tr* to resist; (*las pesas y medidas*) to check || *intr* to resist; to contrast
contraste *m* resistance; contrast; assayer; assayer's office; (naut) sudden shift in the wind
contratar *tr* to contract for; to hire, engage
contratiempo *m* misfortune, disappointment, setback
contratista *mf* contractor
contrato *m* contract
contratreta *f* counterplot
contratuerca *f* lock nut, jam nut
contraveneno *m* counterpoison, antidote
contravenir **§79** *intr* to act contrary; **contravenir a** to contravene, act counter to
contraventana *f* window shutter
contravidriera *f* storm sash
contrayente *mf* contracting party (*to a marriage*)
contribución *f* contribution; tax; **contribución de sangre** military service;

contribución industrial excise tax; **contribución territorial** land tax
contribui•dor -dora *mf* contributor; taxpayer
contribuir §20 *tr & intr* to contribute
contribuyente *mf* contributor; taxpayer
contrición *f* contrition
contrincante *m* competitor, rival; fellow candidate
contristar *tr* to sadden
contri•to -ta *adj* contrite
control *m* control, check
controlar *tr* to control, check
controversia *f* controversy
controvertible *adj* controversial, controvertible
controvertir §68 *tr* to controvert
contubernio *m* cohabitation; evil alliance
contumacia *f* contumacy; (law) contempt
contu•maz *adj* (*pl* **-maces**) contumacious; germ-bearing; (law) guilty of contempt of court
contumelia *f* contumely
contundente *adj* bruising; impressive, convincing
contundir *tr* to bruise
conturbar *tr* to trouble, worry, upset
contusión *f* contusion
contusionar *tr* (Chile) to bruise
convalecencia *f* convalescence
convalecer §22 *intr* to convalesce, recover
convaleciente *adj & mf* convalescent
convalidar *tr* to confirm
conveci•no -na *adj* neighboring || *mf* neighbor
convencer §78 *tr* to convince
convencimiento *m* conviction
convención *f* (*acuerdo; conformidad; asamblea*) convention; (Am) political convention
convencional *adj* conventional
convenible *adj* docile, compliant; (*precio*) fair, reasonable
conveniencia *f* (*comodidad*) convenience; (*acuerdo, convenio*) agreement; fitness, suitability; (*formas sociales*) propriety; domestic employment; **conveniencias** income, property
conveniencie•ro -ra *adj* (coll) comfort-loving
conveniente *adj* (*cómodo*) convenient; fit, suitable; advantageous; proper
convenio *m* pact, covenant, treaty
convenir §79 *intr* to agree; (*concurrir, juntarse*) to convene; to be suitable, be becoming; to be important, to be necessary; **conviene a saber** to wit, namely || *ref* to agree, come to an agreement
conventillo *m* (SAm) tenement house
convento *m* convent, monastery; **convento de religiosas** convent
converger §17 or **convergir** §27 *intr* to converge; to concur
conversa *f* (coll) chat, conversation
conversación *f* conversation
conversacional *adj* conversational
conversar *intr* to converse; to live, dwell
conversión *f* conversion
conver•so -sa *adj* converted || *mf* convert || *m* lay brother || *f* see **conversa**
convertible *adj* convertible || *m* (aut) convertible
convertir §68 *tr* to convert; to turn || *ref* to convert; to be converted; **convertirse en** to turn into, become
conve•xo -xa *adj* convex
convic•to -ta *adj* convicted, found guilty
convida•do -da *mf* guest || *f* (coll) treat
convidar *tr* to invite; to treat; to move, incite; **convidarle a uno con alguna cosa** to treat someone to something || *ref* to offer one's services
convincente *adj* convincing
convite *m* invitation; treat, banquet, party; **convite a escote** Dutch treat
convivir *intr* to live together
convocar §73 *tr* to convoke, call together; (*p.ej., una huelga*) to call; to acclaim
convoy *m* convoy; escort; cruet stand; (rr) train
convoyar *tr* to convoy
convulsionar *tr* to convulse
conyugal *adj* conjugal
cónyuge *mf* spouse, consort || **cónyuges** *mpl* couple, husband and wife
co•ñac *m* (*pl* **-ñacs** or **-ñaques**) cognac
cooperación *f* coöperation
cooperar *intr* to coöperate
cooperati•vo -va *adj* coöperative
coordena•do -da *adj* coördinate || *f* (math) coördinate
coordinante *adj* (gram) coördinating
coordinar *tr & intr* to coördinate
copa *f* goblet, wineglass; (*del sombrero*) crown; brazier; vase; drink; sundae; playing card, representing a bowl, equivalent to heart; (*del dolor*) (fig) cup; (sport) cup
copar *tr* (*la puesta equivalente a todo el dinero de la banca*) to cover; (*todos los puestos en una elección*) to sweep; (mil) to cut off and capture
copartícipe *mf* copartner, joint partner
copear *intr* to sell wine or liquor by the glass; (coll) to tipple
copero *m* cabinet for wineglasses
copete *m* (*cabello levantado sobre la frente*) pompadour; (*de plumas; de una montaña*) crest; (*de un caballo*) forelock; (*de lana, cabello, plumas, etc.*) tuft; (*de un mueble*) top, finial; (*de un sorbete*) topping; **de alto copete** aristocratic, important; **tener mucho copete** to be high-hat
copetu•do -da *adj* tufted; high, lofty; (coll) high-hat
copia *f* plenty, abundance; copy; **copia al carbón** carbon copy; **copia fiel** true copy
copiador *m* copier, copying machine
copiante *mf* copier, copyist
copiar *tr* to copy, copy down
copiloto *m* copilot
copio•so -sa *adj* copious, abundant

copista *mf* copier, copyist
copla *f* couplet; ballad, popular song; **coplas** (coll) verse, poetry; **coplas de ciego** (coll) doggerel
cople•ro -ra *mf* vendor of ballads; poetaster
coplista *mf* poetaster
copo *m* bundle of cotton, flax, hemp, etc. to be spun; **copo de nieve** snowflake; **copos de jabón** soap flakes
copón *m* ciborium, pyx
copo•so -sa *adj* bushy; flaky, woolly
copu•do -da *adj* bushy, thick
copular *ref* to copulate
coque *m* coke
coqueluche *f* whooping cough
coqueta *adj* coquettish || *f* coquette, flirt; (W-I) dressing table
coquetear *intr* to coquette, to flirt; to try to please everybody
coquetería *f* coquetry, flirting; affectation
coque•tón -tona *adj* (coll) coquettish, kittenish || *m* (coll) flirt, lady-killer
coracha *f* leather bag
coraje *m* anger; mettle, spirit
coraju•do -da *adj* (coll) ill-tempered; (Arg) brave, courageous
coral *adj* (mus) choral || *m* (mus) chorale; (*zoófito; esqueleto calizo del zoófito; color*) coral; **corales** coral beads
corambre *f* hides, skins
Corán *m* Koran
coranvo•bis *m* (*pl* **-bis**) (coll) fat solemn look
coraza *f* armor; cuirass; (sport) guard
corazón *m* heart; (*centro de una cosa*) core; **de corazón** heartily; **hacer de tripas corazón** to pluck up courage
corazonada *f* impulsiveness; hunch, presentiment; (coll) entrails
corbata *f* necktie, cravat; scarf; **corbata de mariposa, corbata de lazo** bow tie; **corbata de nudo corredizo** four-in-hand tie
corbatín *m* bow tie
corbeta *f* corvette
Córcega *f* Corsica
corcel *m* steed, charger
corcova *f* hump, hunch
corcova•do -da *adj* humpbacked, hunchbacked || *mf* humpback, hunchback
corcovar *tr* to bend
corcovear *intr* to buck; (Am) to grumble; (Mex) to be afraid
corcha *f* cork bark; cork bucket (*for cooling wine*)
corchea *f* (mus) quaver, eighth note
corche•ro -ra *adj* cork || *f* cork bucket (*for cooling wine*)
corcheta *f* eye (*of hook and eye*)
corchete *m* snap; hook and eye; hook (*of hook and eye*); (*signo*) bracket; **corchete de presión** snap fastener
corcho *m* cork; cork, cork stopper; cork wine cooler; cork box; cork mat; **corcho bornizo, corcho virgen** virgin cork
cordada *f* (mountaineering) party of two or three men roped together
cordaje *m* cordage; (naut) rigging
cordal *adj* wisdom (*tooth*) || *m* (mus) tailpiece
cordel *m* cord, string; (distance of) five steps; cattle run; **a cordel** in a straight line
cordelejo *m* string; **dar cordelejo a** to make fun of; (Mex) to keep putting off
cordera *f* ewe lamb; (*mujer dócil y humilde*) (fig) lamb
cordería *f* cordage
corderillo *m* lambskin
corderi•no -na *adj* lamb || *f* lambskin
cordero *m* lamb; lambskin; (*hombre dócil y humilde*) (fig) lamb
corderuna *f* lambskin
cordial *adj* cordial; (*dedo*) middle || *m* cordial
cordialidad *f* cordiality
cordillera *f* chain of mountains
cordobana *f* — **andar a la cordobana** (coll) to go naked
cordón *m* lace; (*de cuerda o alambre*) strand; cordon; milled edge of coin; (*de monje*) rope belt; **cordón umbilical** umbilical cord
cordoncillo *m* rib, ridge; braid; (*de monedas*) milling
cordura *f* prudence, wisdom
Corea *f* Korea; **la Corea del Norte** North Korea; **la Corea del Sur** South Korea
corea•no -na *adj & mf* Korean
corear *tr* to compose for a chorus; to accompany with a chorus; to join in singing; to agree obsequiously with
coreografía *f* choreography
coriáce•o -a *adj* leathery
Corinto *f* Corinth
corista *m* choir priest; (theat) chorus man || *f* chorus girl, chorine
cori•to -ta *adj* naked; bashful, timid
cormorán *m* cormorant
cor•nac *m* (*pl* **-nacs**) or **cornaca** *m* mahout
cornada *f* hook with horns; goring; (*en la esgrima*) upward thrust
cornadura or **cornamenta** *f* (*del toro, la vaca, etc.*) horns; (*del ciervo*) antlers
cornamusa *f* bagpipe
córnea *f* cornea
cornear *tr* to butt; to gore
corneja *f* daw, crow
cornejo *m* dogwood
córne•o -a *adj* horn, horny || *f* see **córnea**
corneta *f* bugle; swineherd's horn; **corneta acústica** ear trumpet; **corneta de llaves** cornet, cornet-à-pistons; **corneta de monte** hunting-horn
cornisa *f* cornice
cornisamento *m* (archit) entablature
corno *m* horn; dogwood; **corno inglés** (mus) English horn
Cornualles Cornwall
cornucopia *f* cornucopia; sconce with mirror
cornu•do -da *adj* horned, antlered; cuckold || *m* cuckold
coro *m* chorus; choir; choir loft; **a**

coros alternately; **de coro** by heart; **hacer coro a** to echo
corolario *m* corollary
corona *f* (*cerco de metal; moneda; dignidad real; parte visible de una muela*) crown; (*cerco de flores*) garland, wreath; (*aureola*) halo; (*de eclesiástico*) tonsure; (*la que corresponde a un título nobiliario*) coronet; **corona nupcial** bridal wreath
coronación *f* coronation
coronamento or **coronamiento** *m* coronation; completion, termination; (archit) coping; (naut) taffrail
coronar *tr* to crown; to complete, finish; to top, surmount; (checkers) to crown
coronel *m* colonel
coronelía *f* colonelcy
coronilla *f* (*de la cabeza*) crown; **andar** or **bailar de coronilla** (coll) to be hard at it; **estar hasta la coronilla** (coll) to be fed up
corpiño *m* bodice, waist; (Arg) brassière
corporación *f* corporation
corporal *adj* corporal, bodily
corpu·do -da *adj* corpulent
corpulen·to -ta *adj* corpulent
corpúsculo *m* corpuscle; particle
corral *m* corral, stockyard; barnyard; fishpound; theater; **corral de madera** lumberyard; **corral de vacas** (coll) pigpen; **hacer corrales** (coll) to play hooky
correa *f* strap, thong; (aer, mach) belt; **besar la correa** (coll) to eat humble pie; **correa de seguridad** (aer, aut) safety belt
corrección *f* (*acción de corregir; reprensión*) correction; (*calidad de correcto*) correctness
correcti·vo -va *adj & m* corrective
correc·to -ta *adj* correct
correc·tor -tora *mf* corrector; **corrector de pruebas** proofreader
corredera *f* track, slide; slide valve; (*del trombón*) slide; (naut) log; (naut) log line; (*puerta*) **de corredera** sliding
corredi·zo -za *adj* slide; sliding; (*nudo*) slip
corre·dor -dora *adj* running || *mf* runner || *m* corridor; porch, gallery; (*el que interviene en compras y ventas de efectos comerciales, etc.*) broker; (mil) scout; **corredor de apuestas** bookmaker
corregidor *m* Spanish magistrate; chief magistrate of Spanish town
corregir §57 *tr* to correct; to temper, moderate || *intr* (W-I) to have a bowel movement || *ref* to mend one's ways
correlación *f* correlation
correlacionar *tr & intr* to correlate
correlati·vo -va *adj & m* correlative
correncia *f* bashfulness; (coll) looseness of the bowels
correntí·o -a *adj* running; (coll) free, easy || *f* (coll) looseness of the bowels
corren·tón -tona *adj* jolly, full of fun
corrento·so -sa *adj* (Am) swift, rapid
correo *m* mail; post office; mail train; postman; courier; **correo aéreo** air mail; **correo urgente** special delivery; **echar al correo** to mail, to post
correo·so -sa *adj* leathery, tough
correr *tr* (*un caballo*) to run, to race; (*un riesgo*) to run; to travel over; to overrun; (*una cortina*) to draw; (*un toro*) to fight; to chase, pursue; to auction; to confuse; (Am) to throw out; **correrla** (coll) to run around all night || *intr* to run; to race; to pass, elapse; to circulate, be common talk; to be current; **a todo correr** at full speed; **correr a** to sell for; **correr a cargo de** or **por cuenta de** to be the business of; **correr con** to be on good terms with; to be in charge of; (*mes*) **que corre** current || *ref* (*a derecha o a izquierda*) to turn; to be confused; to be embarrassed, be ashamed; to slide, glide; (*una bujía, un color*) to run; to go too far
correría *f* short trip, excursion; foray, raid
correspondencia *f* correspondence; contact, communication; agreement, harmony; (*en el metro*) connection; (*en una carretera*) interchange
corresponder *intr* to correspond; (*dos habitaciones*) to communicate; **corresponder a** (*un beneficio, el afecto de una persona*) to return, reciprocate; to concern; to be up to || *ref* (*comunicarse por escrito*) to correspond; (*dos cosas*) to correspond with each other; to be in agreement; to be attached to each other
correspondiente *adj* corresponding; correspondent; respective || *mf* correspondent
corresponsal *mf* correspondent
corretaje *m* brokerage
corretear *tr* (Am) to harass, pursue; (CAm) to drive away; (Chile) to speed up || *intr* (coll) to race around
correveidi·le *mf* (*pl* **-le**) (coll) gossip; (coll) go-between
corrida *f* run; bullfight; (*carrera de entrenamiento de un caballo*) (Am) trial run; **corrida de banco** (Am) run on the bank; **corrida de toros** bullfight
corri·do -da *adj* (*peso, medida*) in excess; (*letra*) cursive; continued, unbroken; abashed, ashamed; (coll) worldly-wise, sophisticated || *m* overhang; (Am) street ballad || *f* see **corrida**
corriente *adj* (*agua*) running; (*actual*) current; common, ordinary; regular; well-known; fluent || *adv* all right, O.K. || *m* current month; **al corriente** on time; informed, aware, posted || *f* current, stream; (elec) current; **corriente de aire** draft; **Corriente del Golfo** Gulf Stream; **ir contra la corriente** to go against the tide
corrillo *m* circle, clique
corrimiento *m* running; sliding; watery

discharge; embarrassment, shyness; landslide; (Am) rheumatism
corro *m* (*cerco de gente; espacio circular*) ring; (*juego de niñas*) ring-around-a-rosy; **corro de brujas** fairy ring; **hacer corro** to make room
corroborar *tr* to corroborate; to strengthen
corroer §62 *tr & ref* to corrode
corromper *tr* to corrupt; to spoil; to rot; to seduce; to bribe; (coll) to annoy || *intr* to smell bad || *ref* to become corrupted; to spoil; to rot
corrosión *f* corrosion
corrosi•vo -va *adj & m* corrosive
corrugar §44 *tr* to shrink; to wrinkle
corrupción *f* corruption; seduction; bribery; stench
corruptela *f* corruption
corruptible *adj* corruptible; (*p.ej., frutas*) perishable
corrusco *m* (coll) crust of bread
corsa *f* (naut) day's run
corsario *m* corsair
corsé *m* corset
cor•so -sa *adj & mf* Corsican || *m* (naut) privateering; (SAm) drive, promenade || *f* see **corsa**
corta *f* clearing, cutting, felling
cortaalam•bres *m* (*pl* **-bres**) wire cutter
cortabol•sas *m* (*pl* **-sas**) (coll) pickpocket
cortacésped *m* lawn mower
cortaciga•rros *m* (*pl* **-rros**) cigar cutter
cortacircui•tos *m* (*pl* **-tos**) (elec) fuse
cortacorriente *m* (elec) change-over switch
cortada *f* (Am) cut, cutting
cortadillo *m* drinking cup
corta•do -da *adj* (*estilo*) choppy; (SAm) hard up || *f* see **cortada**
corta•dor -dora *adj* cutting || *mf* cutter || *m* butcher || *f* cutting machine
cortafrío *m* cold chisel
cortafuego *s* fire wall
cortahie•los *m* (*pl* **-los**) icebreaker
cortalápi•ces *m* (*pl* **-ces**) pencil sharpener
cortante *adj* cutting, sharp || *m* butcher; butcher knife
cortapape•les *m* (*pl* **-les**) paper cutter
cortapi•cos *m* (*pl* **-cos**) (ent) earwig; **cortapicos y callares** (coll) little children should be seen and not heard
cortaplu•mas *m* (*pl* **-mas**) penknife
cortapu•ros *m* (*pl* **-ros**) cigar cutter
cortar *tr* to cut; to trim; to chop; to cut off; to cut out, omit; to cut short; to cut up; to carve; (*la corriente; la ignición*) to cut off || *intr* to cut; (*el viento, el frío*) to be cutting; **cortar de vestir** to cut cloth; (coll) to gossip || *ref* to become speechless; (*la leche*) to curdle, turn sour; (*la piel*) to chap, to crack
cortarrenglón *m* marginal stop
cortaú•ñas *m* (*pl* **-ñas**) nail clipper
cortavi•drios *m* (*pl* **-drios**) glass cutter
cortaviento *m* windshield
corte *m* cut; cutting; (*filo de un arma, cuchillo, etc.; borde de un libro*) edge; cross section; (*de un vestido*) cut, fit; piece of material; **corte de pelo** haircut; **corte de pelo a cepillo** crew cut; **corte de traje** suiting || *f* (*de un rey*) court; (*corral*) yard; stable, fold; (*tribunal de justicia*) (Am) court; **Cortes** Parliament; **darse cortes** (SAm) to put on airs; **hacer la corte a** to pay court to; **la Corte** the Capital (*Madrid*)
cortedad *f* shortness; smallness; lack; bashfulness
cortejar *tr* to escort, attend, court; to court, to woo
cortejo *m* courting; courtship; (*séquito*) cortege; gift, treat; (coll) beau
cortera *f* (Chile) streetwalker
cortero *m* (Chile) day laborer
cortés *adj* courteous, polite, courtly
cortesana *f* courtesan
cortesana•zo -za *adj* overpolite, obsequious
cortesanía *f* courtliness
cortesa•no -na *adj* courtly, courteous || *m* courtier || *f* see **cortesana**
cortesía *f* courtesy, politeness, courtliness; gift, favor; (*inclinación de la cabeza o el cuerpo en señal de respeto*) curtsy; (*de una carta*) conclusion; **hacer una cortesía** to make a bow; to curtsy
corteza *f* bark; peel, rind, skin; (*de pan*) crust; coarseness; (*envoltura exterior de un órgano*) cortex; **corteza cerebral** cortex
cortijo *m* farm, farmhouse
cortil *m* barnyard
cortina *f* curtain; **correr la cortina** to pull the curtain aside; **cortina de hierro** iron curtain; **cortina de humo** smoke screen
cortinal *m* fenced-in field
cortinilla *f* shade, window shade
cortisona *f* cortisone
cor•to -ta *adj* short; dull; bashful, shy; speechless; **a la corta o a la larga** sooner or later; **desde muy corta edad** from earliest childhood || *f* see **corta**
cortocircuitar *tr & ref* (elec) to short-circuit
cortocircuito *m* (elec) short circuit
cortometraje *m* (mov) short
corva *f* ham, back of knee; (vet) curb
corvejón *m* gambrel, hock; (orn) cormorant
cor•vo -va *adj* arched, bent, curved || *m* hook || *f* see **corva**
cor•zo -za *mf* roe deer
cosa *f* thing; **cosa de** a matter of; **cosa de cajón** a matter of course; **cosa de mieles** (coll) something fine; **cosa de nunca acabar** endless bore; **cosa de oír** something worth hearing; **cosa de risa** something to laugh at; **cosa de ver** something worth seeing; **cosa nunca vista** (coll) something unheard-of; **cosa que** (Am coll) so that; **cosa rara** strange to say; **como si tal cosa** (coll) as if nothing had happened; **en cosa de** in a matter of; **no . . . gran cosa** not much; **no haber**

tal cosa to be not so; **otra cosa** something else; **¿qué cosa?** what's new?
cosa•co -ca *adj & mf* Cossack || *m* Cossack (*horseman*)
coscolina *f* (Mex) loose woman
cos•cón -cona *adj* sly, crafty
cosecha *f* crop, harvest; harvest time; **cosecha de vino** vintage; **de su cosecha** (coll) out of one's own head
cosechar *tr* to harvest, reap || *intr* to harvest
coseche•ro -ra *mf* harvester, reaper; vintner
cose-pape•les *m* (*pl* **-les**) stapler
coser *tr* to sew; to join, unite closely; **coser a preguntas** to riddle with questions; **coser a puñaladas** to cut to pieces || *intr* to sew; **ser coser y cantar** (coll) to be a cinch || *ref* — **coserse con** or **contra** to be closely attached to
cosméti•co -ca *adj & m* cosmetic
cósmi•co -ca *adj* cosmic
cosmonauta *mf* cosmonaut
cosmopolita *adj & mf* cosmopolitan
cosmos *m* cosmos; (bot) cosmos
coso *m* enclosure for bullfighting
cosquillas *fpl* tickling, ticklishness; **buscarle a uno las cosquillas** (coll) to try to irritate a person; **no sufrir cosquillas** or **tener malas cosquillas** (coll) to be touchy
cosquillear *tr* to tickle; to tease, taunt; to stir up the curiosity of; to scare || *intr* to tickle || *ref* to be curious; to enjoy oneself
cosquilleo *m* tickling, tickling sensation
cosquillo•so -sa *adj* ticklish; (*que se ofende fácilmente*) touchy
costa *f* coast, shore; cost, price; **a toda costa** at all costs; **Costa Brava** Mediterranean coast in province of Gerona, Spain; **Costa Firme** Spanish Main; **costa marítima** seacoast; **costas** (law) costs
costado *m* side; (*del ejército*) flank; (Mex) station platform; **costados** ancestors, stock
costal *m* bag, sack; **costal de los pecados** human body (*full of sin*); **estar hecho un costal de huesos** (coll) to be nothing but skin and bones
costanera *f* slope; **costaneras** rafters
costane•ro -ra *adj* sloping; coastal || *f* see **costanera**
costanilla *f* short steep street
costar §61 *intr* to cost; **cueste lo que cueste** cost what it may
costarricense or **costarrique•ño -ña** *adj & mf* Costa Rican
coste *m* cost; **a coste y costas** at cost
costear *tr* to pay for, to defray the cost of; to sail along the coast of || *intr* to sail along the coast || *ref* to pay; to pay one's way
coste•ño -ña *adj* sloping; coastal
coste•ro -ra *adj* coastal
costilla *f* rib; (coll) wealth; **costillas** back, shoulders
costillu•do -da *adj* heavy-set, broad-shouldered
costo *m* cost; **costo de la vida** cost of living; **costo, seguro y flete** cost, insurance, and freight
costo•so -sa *adj* costly, expensive; grievous
costra *f* scab, scale; (*moco de una vela*) snuff
costro•so -sa *adj* scabby, scaly
costumbre *f* custom, habit; **de costumbre** usual; usually; **tener por costumbre** to be in the habit of
costumbrista *mf* critic of manners and customs
costura *f* sewing, needlework; dressmaking; (*unión de dos piezas cosidas*) seam; **alta costura** fashion designing, haute couture
costurera *f* seamstress, dressmaker
costurero *m* sewing table
cota *f* coat of arms; coat of mail
cotarrera *f* (coll) gossipy woman
cotarro *m* night shelter (*for beggars and tramps*); **alborotar el cotarro** (coll) to raise a row
cotejar *tr* to compare, collate
cotejo *m* comparison, collation
cotidia•no -na *adj* daily, everyday
cotilla *f* (coll) gossip, tattletale
cotín *m* (sport) backstroke
cotización *f* quotation; dues
cotizante *adj* dues-paying
cotizar §60 *tr* to quote; to prorate || *intr* to collect dues; to pay dues
coto *m* price; fixed price; term, limit
cotón *m* printed cotton
cotona *f* (Am) work shirt
cotonía *f* dimity
cotorra *f* parrot; parakeet; magpie; (coll) chatterbox; (Mex) night shelter
cotorrear *intr* (coll) to gossip, gabble
cotufa *f* Jerusalem artichoke; delicacy, tidbit; **hacer cotufas** (Bol) to be fastidious; **pedir cotufas en el golfo** (coll) to ask for the moon
coturno *m* buskin
covacha *f* cave; (Am) cubbyhole; (Am) shanty; (Am) doghouse
covachuelista *m* (coll) clerk, government clerk
coxcojita *f* hopscotch; **a coxcojita** hippety-hop
coy *m* (naut) hammock
coyunda *f* strap for yoking oxen; sandal string; marriage; tyranny
coyuntura *f* joint, articulation; (*sazón, oportunidad*) juncture
coz *f* (*pl* **coces**) kick; big end; ebb; (coll) insult; **dar coces contra el aguijón** to kick against the pricks
c.p.b., C.P.B. *abbr* **cuyos pies beso**
cps. *abbr* **compañeros**
crabrón *m* hornet
crac *m* (*ruido seco*) crack; crash; **hacer crac** to crash, to fail
cráneo *m* cranium, skull
crápula *f* drunkenness, debauchery; riffraff
crapulo•so -sa *adj* drunken; vicious, evil
crascitar *intr* to crow, croak

cra•so -sa *adj* fat, greasy, thick; (*ignorancia*) crass, gross
cráter *m* crater
creación *f* creation
crea•dor -dora *adj* creative || *mf* creator
crear *tr* to create; to appoint; to found || *ref* to make for oneself, to build up; to trump up
creati•vo -va *adj* creative
crecede•ro -ra *adj* growth; large enough to allow for growth
crecepelo *m* hair restorer
crecer §22 *intr* to grow; to increase; (*el río*) to rise, swell; (*la luna*) to wax || *ref* to grow; to take on more authority; to get bolder
creces *fpl* growth, increase; excess, extra; **con creces** amply, in abundance
crecida *f* freshet, flood
creciente *adj* growing, increasing || *f* — **creciente de la luna** waxing of the moon, crescent; **creciente del mar** high tide, flood tide
crecimiento *m* growth, increase
credenciales *fpl* credentials
crédito *m* credit
credo *m* creed; credo; **con el credo en la boca** (coll) with one's heart in one's mouth; **en un credo** (coll) in a trice
crédu•lo -la *adj* credulous
creederas *fpl* — **tener buenas creederas** (coll) to be gullible
creencia *f* belief; (*crédito que se presta a un hecho*) credence; (*secta*) creed
creer §43 *tr & intr* to believe; **¡ya lo creo!** (coll) I should say so! || *ref* to believe; to believe oneself to be
creíble *adj* believable, credible
crema *f* cream; cold cream; shoe polish; (gram) diaeresis; **crema de menta** crème de menthe; **crema desvanecedora** vanishing cream
cremación *f* cremation
cremallera *f* rack; zipper
cremato•rio -ria *adj & m* crematory
crémor *m* cream of tartar
cremo•so -sa *adj* creamy
crencha *f* part (*in hair*); hair on each side of part
crepitar *intr* to crackle
crepuscular *adj* twilight
crepúsculo *m* twilight
cresa *f* maggot
crespar *tr & ref* to curl
cres•po -pa *adj* curly; curled; angry, irritated; stylish, conceited; (*estilo*) turgid || *m* (Am) curl
crespón *m* crape; **crespón fúnebre** crape; mourning band
cresta *f* crest; **cresta de gallo** cockscomb; (bot) cockscomb
creta *f* chalk || **Creta** *f* Crete
cretense *adj & mf* Cretan
cretona *f* cretonne
creyente *adj* believing || *mf* believer
creyón *m* crayon
cría *f* brood, litter; breeding; raising, rearing; nursing
criada *f* female servant, maid; **criada de casa, criada de servir** housemaid
criadero *m* nursery, tree nursery; fish hatchery; oyster bed
criadilla *f* testicle; potato
cria•do -da *adj* — **bien criado** well-bred; **mal criado** ill-bred || *mf* servant || *f* see **criada**
cria•dor -dora *mf* breeder || *f* wet nurse
criamiento *m* care, upkeep
crianza *f* raising, rearing; nursing; (*urbanidad*) breeding, manners; **buena crianza** good breeding; **mala crianza** bad breeding
criar §77 *tr* to raise, rear, bring up; to breed; to grow; to nurse, nourish; to fatten; to create; to foster
criatura *f* (*toda cosa creada; persona que debe su cargo o situación a otra*) creature; little child, little creature
criba *f* screen, sieve
cribar *tr* to screen, sieve
cribo *m* screen, sieve
cric *m* (*pl* **crics**) jack
crimen *m* crime; **crimen de lesa majestad** lese majesty
criminal *adj & mf* criminal
criminar *tr* to accuse, incriminate
crimino•so -sa *adj & mf* criminal
crines *fpl* mane
crío *m* (coll) baby, infant
crio•llo -lla *adj & mf* Creole
cripta *f* crypt
crisálida *f* chrysalis
crisantemo *m* chrysanthemum
cri•sis *f* (*pl* **-sis**) crisis; (*pánico económico*) depression, slump; mature judgment; **crisis del servicio doméstico** servant problem; **crisis de llanto** crying fit; **crisis de vivienda** housing shortage; **crisis ministerial** cabinet crisis; **crisis nerviosa** fit of nerves
crisma *f* (coll) head, bean
crisol *m* crucible
crispar *tr* to cause to twitch || *ref* to twitch
crispatura *f* twitch, twitching
crispir *tr* to grain, to marble
cristal *m* crystal; glass; pane of glass; mirror, looking glass; **cristal cilindrado** plate glass; **cristal de reloj** watch crystal; **cristal de roca** rock crystal; **cristal hilado** glass wool, spun glass; **cristal tallado** cut glass
cristalera *f* China closet; sideboard; glass door
cristalería *f* glassworks, glass store; glassware; glass cabinet
cristali•no -na *adj* crystalline || *m* lens, crystalline lens
cristalizer §60 *tr & ref* to crystallize
cristianar *tr* (coll) to baptize, christen
cristiandad *f* Christendom
cristianismo *m* Christianity
cristianizar §60 *tr* to Christianize
cristia•no -na *adj & mf* Christian || *m* soul, person; Spanish; (coll) watered wine
Cristo *m* Christ; crucifix; **donde Cristo dió las tres voces** (coll) in the middle of nowhere
Cristóbal *m* Christopher
criterio *m* criterion
crítica *f* (*jucio sobre una obra literaria, etc.; censura de la conducta de al-*

guno) criticism; (*arte de juzgar una obra literaria, etc.*) critique; gossip
criticar §73 *tr & intr* to criticize
críti•co -ca *adj* critical; (*criticón*) (Am) critical (*faultfinding*) || *mf* critic || *f* see **crítica**
criti•cón -cona *adj* (coll) critical, faultfinding || *mf* (coll) critic, faultfinder
critiquizar §60 *tr* to overcriticize
crizneja *f* braid of hair
croar *intr* to croak
croata *adj & mf* Croatian
crocante *m* almond brittle, peanut brittle
crocitar *intr* to crow, croak
croco *m* crocus
croché *m* crochet
crochet *m* (box) hook
croma•do -da *adj* chrome || *m* chromium plating
cromar *tr* to chrome
cromo *m* chromium
cromosoma *m* chromosome
crónica *f* chronicle; news chronicle, feature story
cróni•co -ca *adj* chronic; longstanding; (*vicio*) inveterate || *f* see **crónica**
cronista *mf* chronicler; reporter, feature writer; **cronista de radio** newscaster
cronología *f* chronology
cronometra•dor -dora *mf* (sport) timekeeper
cronometraje *m* (sport) clocking, timing
cronómetro *m* chronometer; stop watch
croqueta *f* croquette
cro•quis *m* (*pl* **-quis**) sketch
croscitar *intr* to crow, croak
crótalo *m* rattlesnake; castanet
cruce *m* crossing; crossroads, intersection; exchange (*e.g., of letters*); (*avería*) (elec) crossed wires, short circuit; **cruce a nivel** grade crossing; **cruce en trébol** cloverleaf intersection
crucero *m* crossroads; railroad crossing; (archit) transept; (aer, naut) cruise, cruising; (nav) cruiser; **crucero a nivel** grade crossing
crucial *adj* crucial
crucificar §73 *tr* to crucify
crucifijo *m* crucifix
crucifixión *f* crucifixion
crucigrama *m* crossword puzzle
cruda *f* (Mex) hangover
crudeza *f* crudeness, rawness; (*del agua*) hardness; harshness, roughness; (coll) blustering; **crudezas** undigested food
cru•do -da *adj* crude, raw; (*agua*) hard; harsh, rough; (*tiempo*) raw; (*lienzo*) unbleached; **estar crudo** (P-R) to be rusty; (Mex) to have a hangover || *f* see **cruda**
cruel *adj* cruel
crueldad *f* cruelty
cruen•to -ta *adj* bloody
crujía *f* corridor, hall; hospital ward; block of houses; (naut) midship gangway; **crujía de piezas** suite of rooms; **sufrir una crujía** (coll) to have a hard time of it
crujido *m* creak; crackle; clatter; chatter; rustle
crujir *intr* to creak; to crackle; to clatter; to chatter; to rustle; to crunch
crup *m* croup
crustáce•o -a *adj* crustaceous || *m* crustacean
cruz *f* (*pl* **cruces**) cross; (*de una moneda*) tails; (typ) dagger; **Cruz del Sur** Southern Cross; **¡cruz y raya!** (coll) that's enough!; **de la cruz a la fecha** from beginning to end
cruzada *f* (*expedición contra los infieles; propaganda contra un vicio*) crusade; crossroads, intersection
cruza•do -da *adj* crossed; (*de raza mixta*) cross; double-breasted || *m* (*el que toma parte en una cruzada*) crusader; (*caballero de una orden militar*) knight; twill || *f* see **cruzada**
cruzar §60 *tr* to cross; (*la tela*) to twill; (*cartas*) to exchange; to crossbreed; (naut) to cruise, cruise over || *intr* to cross; to cruise || *ref* to cross each other, to cross one's another's path; (*alistarse para una cruzada*) to take the cross; **cruzarse con** (*otro automóvil*) to pass; **cruzarse de brazos** (*estar ocioso*) to cross one's arms
cs. *abbr* **céntimos, cuartos**
cte. *abbr* **corriente**
c/u *abbr* **cada uno**
cuad. *abbr* **cuadrado**
cuaderna *f* (naut) frame
cuaderno *m* notebook; folder; **cuaderno de bitácora** (naut) logbook; **cuaderno de hojas cambiables** or **sueltas** loose-leaf notebook
cuadra *f* hall, large room; stable; dormitory, ward; croup, rump; (Am) block
cuadra•do -da *adj* square; square-shouldered; perfect || *m* square; (*regla*) ruler; (*en las medias*) clock; **de cuadrado** perfectly; (*que se mira frente a frente*) full-faced
cuadragési•mo -ma *adj & m* fortieth
cuadrangular *adj* quadrangular || *m* home run
cuadrángu•lo -la *adj* quadrangular || *m* quadrangle
cuadrante *m* quadrant; (*de reloj*) face, dial; **cuadrante solar** sundial
cuadrar *tr* to square; to please; (*al toro*) (taur) to square off, to line up || *ref* to square; to stand at attention; (coll) to take on a serious air
cuadrilla *f* group, party; crew, gang
cuadrillazo *m* (SAm) surprise attack
cuadrillo *m* (*saeta*) bolt (*arrow*)
cuadrimotor *m* four-motor plane
cua•dro -dra *adj* square || *m* square; (*lienzo, pintura*) painting, picture; (*marco de pintura, ventana, etc.*) frame; (*de jardín*) patch, flower bed; staff, personnel; (mil) cadre; (sport) team; (theat) scene; (coll) sight, mess; **a cuadros** checked; **cuadro de costumbres** sketch of manners and customs; **cuadro de distribución** switchboard; **cuadro indicador** score

board; **cuadro vivo** tableau; **en cuadro** square, e.g., **ocho pulgadas en cuadro** eight inches square; (coll) topsy-turvy; **quedarse en cuadro** to be all alone in the world; (mil) to be skeletonized || *f* see **cuadra**

cuadrúpe·do -da *adj & m* quadruped

cuádruple *adj & m* quadruple

cuadruplicar §73 *tr & ref* to quadruple

cuajada *f* curd

cuajado *m* mincemeat

cuajar *tr* to curd, curdle, thicken, jelly; (coll) to please, to suit || *intr* (coll) to take hold, catch on, jell, take shape; (Mex) to chatter, prattle || *ref* to curd, curdle, thicken, jelly; to sleep sound; (coll) to become crowded

cuajo *m* curd; (Mex) chatter, prattle; (*en la escuela*) (Mex) recess

cual *adj rel & pron rel* such as; **el cual** which; who; **lo cual** which; **por lo cual** for which reason || *adv* as || *prep* like

cuál *adj interr & pron interr* which, what; which one

cualidad *f* quality, characteristic, trait

cualquier *adj indef* (*pl* **cualesquier**) apocopated form of **cualquiera**, used only before masculine nouns and adjectives

cualquiera (*pl* **cualesquiera**) *pron indef* anyone; **cualquiera que** whichever; whoever || *adj indef* any || *adj rel* whichever || *m* (*persona poco importante*) nobody

cuan *adv* as

cuán *adv* how, how much

cuando *conj* when; although; in case; since; **aun cuando** even if, even though; **cuando más** at most; **cuando menos** at least; **cuando mucho** at most; **cuando quiera** whenever; **de cuando en cuando** from time to time || *prep* (coll) at the time of

cuándo *adv* when; **cuándo . . . cuándo** sometimes . . . sometimes; **¿de cuándo acá?** since when?; how come?

cuantía *f* quantity; importance; **delito de mayor cuantía** felony; **delito de menor cuantía** misdemeanor; **de mayor cuantía** first-rate; **de menor cuantía** second-rate, of little importance

cuantiar §77 *tr* to estimate, appraise

cuánti·co -ca *adj* quantum

cuantio·so -sa *adj* large, substantial

cuan·to -ta *adj rel & pron rel* as much as, whatever, all that which; **cuantos** as many as, all those who, everybody who; **unos cuantos** some few || **cuanto** *adv* as soon as; as long as; **cuanto antes** as soon as possible; **cuanto más . . . tanto más** the more . . . the more; **cuanto más que** all the more because; **en cuanto** as soon as; while; insofar as; **en cuanto a** as to, as for; **por cuanto** inasmuch as; **por cuanto . . . por tanto** inasmuch as . . . therefore || **cuan·to** *m* (*pl* **-ta**) quantum

cuán·to -ta *adj interr & pron interr* how much; **cuántos** how many || **cuánto** *adv* how, how much; how long; how long ago; **cada cuánto** how often

cuáque·ro -ra *adj & mf* Quaker

cuarenta *adj, pron & m* forty

cuarenta·vo -va *adj & m* fortieth

cuarentena *f* forty; quarantine; forty days, forty months, forty years; **poner en cuarentena** to quarantine; to withhold one's credence in

cuaresma *f* Lent

cuaresmal *adj* Lenten

cuarta *f* fourth, fourth part; (*de la mano*) span; (CAm, W-I) horse whip

cuartago *m* nag, pony

cuartear *tr* to divide in four parts; to divide; (*la aguja*) (naut) to box; (CAm, W-I) to whip || *ref* to crack, split; (taur) to step aside, dodge

cuartel *m* quarter; (*de una ciudad*) section, ward; (*terreno*) lot; flower bed; (mil) barracks; (*buen trato*) (mil) quarter; (*armazón de tablas para cerrar la escotilla*) (naut) hatch; (coll) house, home; **cuartel de bomberos** engine house, firehouse; **cuarteles** (mil) quarters; **cuartel general** (mil) headquarters

cuartelada *f* mutiny, military uprising

cuarte·rón -rona *mf* quadroon || *m* quarter; (*de puerta*) panel; (*de ventana*) shutter

cuarteto *m* quartet

cuartilla *f* sheet of paper

cuar·to -ta *adj* fourth; quarter || *m* fourth; quarter; room, bedroom; quarter-hour; **cuarto creciente** (*de la luna*) first quarter; **cuarto de aseo** lavatory; **cuarto de baño** bathroom; **cuarto de dormir** bedroom; **cuarto de estar** living room; **cuarto delantero** (*de la res*) forequarter; **cuarto de los niños** nursery; **cuarto de luna** quarter; **cuarto menguante** (*de la luna*) last quarter; **cuarto obscuro** (phot) darkroom; **cuartos** (coll) money, cash; **cuarto trasero** (*p.ej., de vaca*) rump || *f* see **cuarta**

cuarzo *m* quartz

cuate *adj* (Mex) twin; (Mex) like || *mf* (Mex) twin; (Mex) pal

cuatrilli·zo -za *mf* quadruplet

cuatrinca *f* foursome

cuatro *adj & pron* four; **las cuatro** four o'clock || *m* four; (*en las fechas*) fourth; (*de voces*) quartet; **más de cuatro** (coll) quite a number

cuatrocien·tos -tas *adj & pron* four hundred || **cuatrocientos** *m* four hundred

cuba *f* cask, barrel; tub, vat; (*persona de mucho vientre*) (coll) tub; (*persona que bebe mucho*) (coll) toper; **cuba de riego** street sprinkler

cuba·no -na *adj & mf* Cuban

cubeta *f* keg, cask; pail; bowl, toilet bowl; (*del termómetro*) cup; (chem, phot) tray; (Mex) high hat

cubicaje *m* piston displacement, cylinder capacity

cubicar *tr* (*elevar al cubo*) to cube; to measure the volume of; to have a piston displacement of

cúbi•co -ca *adj* cubic; (*raíz*) cube
cubierta *f* cover; envelope; roof; (*de un libro*) paper cover; (*de un neumático*) casing, shoe; (*del motor de un coche*) hood; (naut) deck; **bajo cubierta separada** under separate cover; **cubierta de aterrizaje** (nav) flight deck; **cubierta de cama** bedcover; **cubierta de mesa** table cover; **cubierta de paseo** (naut) promenade deck; **cubierta de vuelo** (nav) flight deck; **cubierta principal** (naut) main deck; **entre cubiertas** (naut) between decks
cubiertamente *adv* secretly
cubier•to -ta *adj* covered; (*cielo*) overcast || *m* cover, roof, shelter; (*servicio de mesa para una persona*) cover; knife, fork, and spoon; table d'hôte, prix fixe; **a cubierto de** under cover of; protected from; **bajo cubierto** under cover, indoors || *f* see **cubierta**
cubil *m* (*de fieras*) lair, den; (*de arroyo*) bed
cubilete *m* (*de cocinero*) copper mold; dicebox; mince pie; (Am) high hat; (SAm) scheming, wirepulling
cubo *m* bucket; (*de rueda*) hub; (*de un candelero; de una llave de caja*) socket; cube; (mach) barrel, drum; (math) cube; (Arg) finger bowl
cubreasiento *m* seat cover
cubrecama *f* counterpane, bedcover
cubrecorsé *m* corset cover
cubrefuego *m* curfew
cubrelibro *m* jacket
cubrenuca *f* havelock
cubrerrueda *f* mudguard
cubresexo *m* G-string
cubretablero *m* (aut) cowl
cubretetera *f* cozy, tea cozy
cubrir §83 *tr* to cover, cover over, cover up || *ref* to cover oneself; to be covered; to put one's hat on; (*el cielo*) to become overcast; (*satisfacer una deuda*) to cover
cucaña *f* greased pole to be climbed as a game; (coll) cinch
cucañe•ro -ra *mf* (coll) loafer, parasite
cucar §73 *tr* to wink; to make fun of; (*la caza*) to sight; (Am) to incite, stir up || *intr* (*el ganado*) to go off on a run (*when bitten by flies*)
cucaracha *f* roach, cockroach
cucarache•ro -ra *adj* (W-I) sly, tricky; (W-I) amorous, lecherous
cucarda *f* cockade
cuclillas — **en cuclillas** squatting, crouching
cuclillo *m* cuckoo; (coll) cuckold
cu•co -ca *adj* sly, tricky; (coll) cute || *mf* (coll) sly person || *m* bogeyman; cuckoo
cu•cú *m* (*pl* **-cúes**) cuckoo (*call*)
cuculla *f* cowl, hood
cucurucho *m* paper cone, ice-cream cone; **hacer cucurucho a** (Chile) to deceive, take in
cuchara *f* spoon; (*cazo*) dipper, ladle; (*para áridos; para achicar el agua en los botes*) scoop; (*de albañil*) trowel; (Mex) pickpocket; **cuchara de sopa** tablespoon; **media cuchara** (coll) ordinary fellow; (Am) fellow with heavy accent; (Mex) mason's helper; **meter su cuchara** to butt in
cucharada *f* spoonful; ladleful; scoop
cucharear *tr* to spoon, ladle out
cucharetear *intr* (coll) to stir the pot, stir with a spoon; (coll) to meddle
cucharilla *f* teaspoon; (*de soldador*) ladle
cucharón *m* large spoon; soup ladle, dipper; scoop; **despacharse con el cucharón** (coll) to look out for number one
cuchichear *intr* to whisper
cuchilla *f* knife; (*hoja de arma blanca de corte*) blade; (*de patín de hielo*) runner; (*cerro escarpado*) hogback; (*de interruptor*) (elec) blade; (poet) sword; **cuchilla de carnicero** butcher knife, cleaver
cuchillada *f* slash, gash, hack; **cuchilladas** fight, quarrel; **dar cuchillada** (*un actor o un teatro*) (coll) to be the hit of the town
cuchillería *f* cutlery; cutler's shop
cuchillero *m* cutler
cuchillo *m* knife; (*en un vestido*) gore; (naut) triangular sail; **cuchillo de trinchar** carving knife; **cuchillo de vidriero** putty knife; **pasar a cuchillo** to put to the sword
cuchitril *m* hovel, den
cuchufleta *f* (coll) joke, fun, wisecrack
cuchufletear *intr* (coll) to joke, make fun, wisecrack
cuelga *f* fruit hung up for keeping; (coll) birthday present
cuelgaca•pas *m* (*pl* **-pas**) cloak hanger
cuello *m* (*del cuerpo*) neck; (*de una prenda*) collar; shirt collar; **cuello almidonado** stiff collar; **cuello de camisa** shirtband; **cuello de cisne** gooseneck; **cuello de pajarita** or **doblado** wing collar; **levantar el cuello** (coll) to get back on one's feet again
cuenca *f* wooden bowl; (*del ojo*) socket; basin, river basin; **cuenca de polvo** dust bowl
cuenco *m* earthen bowl; hollow
cuenta *f* count, calculation; account; (*factura*) bill; (*en un restaurante*) check; (*del rosario*) bead; **abonar en cuenta a** to credit to the account of; **a cuenta** or **a buena cuenta** on account; **adeudar en cuenta a** to charge to the account of; **a fin de cuentas** after all; **caer en la cuenta** (coll) to get the point; **cargar en cuenta a** to charge to the account of; **correr por cuenta de** to be the responsibility of, to be under the administration of; **cuenta corriente** current account; **cuenta de gastos** expense account; **cuenta de la vieja** (coll) counting on one's fingers; **cuentas del gran capitán** overdrawn account; **cuentas galanas** (coll) illusions; **darse cuenta de** to realize, become aware of; **de cuenta** of importance; **más de la cuenta** too long; too much; **pedir cuentas a** to bring to account; **por la cuenta** apparently;

por mi cuenta to my way of thinking; **tomar por su cuenta** to take upon oneself; **vamos a cuentas** (coll) let's settle this

cuentacorrentista *mf* depositor

cuentago•tas *m* (*pl* **-tas**) dropper, medicine dropper

cuentakilóme•tros *m* (*pl* **-tros**) odometer

cuente•ro -ra *adj* (coll) gossipy || *mf* (coll) gossip

cuentista *adj* (coll) gossipy || *mf* story teller; short-story writer; (coll) gossip

cuento *m* story, tale; short story; prop, support; tip, point; (*cómputo*) count; (coll) gossip, evil talk; (coll) disagreement; **cuento de hadas** fairy tale; **cuento del tío** (SAm) gyp, swindle; **cuento de nunca acabar** (coll) endless affair; **cuento de penas** (coll) hard-luck story; **cuento de viejas** old wives' tale; **Cuentos de Calleja** collection of nursery stories; **dejarse de cuentos** (coll) to come to the point; **estar en el cuento** to be well-informed; **¡puro cuento!** pure fiction!; **sin cuento** countless; **traer a cuento** to bring up; **venir a cuento** (coll) to be opportune; **vivir del cuento** to live by one's wits

cuerda *f* cord, rope; watch spring; winding a watch or clock; (*acción de ahorcar*) hanging; fishing line; (aer, anat, geom) chord; (mus) string; **acabarse la cuerda** to run down, e.g., **se acabó la cuerda** the watch ran down; **bajo cuerda** secretly, underhandedly; **cuerda de presos** chain gang; **cuerda de remolcar** tow rope; **cuerda de tripa** (mus) catgut; **cuerda tirante** tight rope; **dar cuerda a** to give free rein to; (*un reloj*) to wind; **sin cuerda** unwound, run-down

cuer•do -da *adj* wise, prudent; sane || *f* see **cuerda**

cuerna *f* antler; horns

cuerno *m* horn; (mus) horn; **cuerno de caza** huntinghorn; **cuerno inglés** (mus) English horn

cuero *m* (*pellejo de buey*) hide; (*después de curtido*) leather; wineskin; **cuero cabelludo** scalp; **cuero en verde** rawhide; **en cueros** stark-naked

cuerpear *intr* (Arg) to duck, dodge

cuerpo *m* body; (*parte del vestido hasta la cintura*) waist; (*talle, aspecto*) build; (*de escritos, leyes, etc.*) corpus; corps, staff; (mil) corps; **cuerpo a cuerpo** hand to hand; **cuerpo celeste** heavenly body; **cuerpo compuesto** (chem) compound; **cuerpo de aviación** air corps; **cuerpo de baile** corps de ballet; **cuerpo de bomberos** fire brigade, fire company; **cuerpo de ejército** army corps; **cuerpo de redacción** editorial staff; **cuerpo simple** (chem) simple substance; **dar con el cuerpo en tierra** (coll) to fall flat on the ground; **de cuerpo entero** full-length; **de medio cuerpo** half-length; **descubrir el cuerpo** to drop one's guard; **en cuerpo** or **en cuerpo de camisa** in shirt sleeves; **estar de cuerpo presente** to be on view, to lie in state; **hacer del cuerpo** (coll) to have a movement of the bowels

cueru•do -da *adj* (Am) thick-skinned; (Am) annoying, boring; (Am) bold, shameless

cuervo *m* raven; **cuervo marino** cormorant; **cuervo merendero** rook

cuesco *m* (*de la fruta*) stone; (*del molino de aceite*) millstone; (coll) windiness

cuesta *f* hill, slope, grade; charity drive; **cuesta abajo** downhill; **cuesta arriba** uphill; **llevar a cuestas** (coll) to be burdened with

cuestión *f* question; dispute, quarrel; matter; **cuestión batallona** much-debated question; **cuestión palpitante** burning question; **en cuestión de** in a matter of

cuestionable *adj* questionable

cuestionar *tr* to question || *intr* (Arg) to argue

cuestionario *m* questionnaire

cuestua•rio -ria or **cuestuo•so -sa** *adj* profitable, lucrative

cuetear *ref* (Col) to blow up, explode; (Col) to die, kick the bucket; (Mex) to get drunk

cueva *f* cave; cellar; (*de ladrones, fieras, etc.*) den

cufi•fo -fa *adj* (Chile) tipsy

cugulla *f* cowl

cui•co -ca *adj* (Am) foreign, outside || *m* (Mex) cop, policeman

cuidado *m* care, concern, worry; **¡cuidado con . . .!** beware of . . .!, look out for!; **de cuidado** dangerously; **estar de cuidado** (coll) to be dangerously ill; **pierda Vd. cuidado** don't worry; **salir de su cuidado** (*una mujer*) to be delivered; **tener cuidado** to beware, be careful

cuidadora *f* (Mex) governess, chaperon

cuidado•so -sa *adj* careful, concerned, worried; watchful

cuidar *tr* to take care of, to watch over || *intr* — **cuidar de** to take care of, to care for; to care to || *ref* to take care of oneself; **cuidarse de** to care about; to be careful to

cuita *f* trouble, worry; longing, yearning

cuja *f* bedstead

culata *f* buttock, haunch; (*de la escopeta*) butt; (*de imán*) keeper, yoke; **culata de cilindro** cylinder head

culatazo *m* kick, recoil

culebra *f* snake; (*del alambique*) coil; **culebra de anteojos** cobra; **culebra de cascabel** rattlesnake; **saber más que las culebras** (coll) to be foxy

culebrear *intr* to wriggle; to wind, meander; to zigzag

culebrón *m* (coll) foxy fellow; (Mex) poor farce

cule•co -ca *adj* (Am) self-satisfied; (Am) madly in love

cu•lí *m* (*pl* **-líes**) coolie

culina•rio -ria *adj* culinary
culipandear *intr & ref* (CAm, W-I) to welsh, be evasive
culminar *intr* to culminate
culo *m* seat, behind, backside; (*de animal*) buttocks; (*de un vaso*) bottom; **culo de mal asiento** (coll) fidgety person; **volver el culo** (coll) to run away
culote *m* base
culpa *f* blame, guilt, fault; **echar la culpa a** to put the blame on; **tener la culpa** to be wrong, to be to blame
culpable *adj* blamable, guilty, culpable
culpa•do -da *adj* guilty || *mf* culprit
culpar *tr* to blame, censure, accuse || *ref* to take the blame
cultedad *f* fustian, affectation
culteranismo *m* euphuism, Gongorism
cultiparlar *intr* to speak in a euphuistic manner
cultismo *m* learned word; cultism, Gongorism
cultivar *tr* to cultivate; to till
cultivo *m* cultivation; **cultivo de secano** dry farming
cul•to -ta *adj* cultivated, cultured; (*vocablo*) learned || *m* worship; cult; **culto a la personalidad** personality cult
cultura *f* culture, cultivation
culturar *tr* to cultivate, to till
cumbre *adj* top, greatest || *f* summit; acme, pinnacle
cúmel *m* kümmel
cumiche *m* (CAm) baby (*youngest member of family*)
cúmplase *m* approval, O.K.
cumplea-ños *m* (*pl* **-ños**) birthday
cumpli•do -da *adj* full; perfect; (*en muestras de urbanidad*) correct || *m* correctness; courtesy; present
cumplimentar *tr* to compliment; to pay a complimentary visit to; to carry out, execute; (*un cuestionario*) to fill out
cumplimente•ro -ra *adj* (coll) effusive, obsequious
cumplimiento *m* (*muestra de urbanidad*) compliment; (*conducta decorosa*) correctness; fulfillment; perfection; **por cumplimiento** as a matter of pure formality
cumplir *tr* to fulfill, perform, execute; **cumplir años** to have a birthday; **cumplir . . . años** to be . . . years old || *intr* to fall due; to expire; to keep one's promise; to finish one's service in the army; **cumplir con** to fulfill; to fulfill one's obligation to; **cumplir por** to act on behalf of; to pay the respects of || *ref* to be fulfilled, to come true; to fall due; **cúmplase** approved
cumquibus *m* (coll) wherewithal
cúmulo *m* heap, pile, lot
cuna *f* cradle
cundido *m* olive, vinegar, and salt for shepherds; olive oil, cheese. and honey to make children eat
cundir *intr* to spread; to swell, puff up; to increase
cunear *tr* to cradle, rock in a cradle || *intr* (coll) to rock, swing, sway
cune•co -ca *mf* (Ven) baby (*youngest member of family*)
cuneta *f* gutter, ditch
cuña *f* wedge; (typ) quoin; **ser buena cuña** (coll) to take up a lot of room
cuñada *f* sister-in-law
cuñado *m* brother-in-law
cuñete *m* keg
cuño *m* die; stamp; mark
cuota *f* quota, share; fee, dues; tuition fee
cupé *m* coupé
cupo *m* quota, share; (Mex) capacity
cupón *m* coupon
cúpula *f* cupola; dome
cuquillo *m* cuckoo
cura *m* curate; (coll) priest; **este cura** (*yo*) (coll) yours truly (*I*) || *f* **cure**; care, treatment; **cura de aguas** water cure; **cura de almas** care of souls; **cura de hambre** starvation diet; **cura de reposo** rest cure; **cura de urgencia** first aid; **no tener cura** (coll) to be hopeless, be incorrigible
curaca *m* (SAm) boss, chief || *f* (Bol, Peru) priest's housekeeper
curación *f* cure, treatment
curade•ro -ra *mf* caretaker || *m* (law) guardian
curande•ro -ra *mf* quack, healer
curar *tr* (*a un enfermo*) to treat; (*sanar*) to cure, to heal; (*curtir*) to cure; (*la madera*) to season; (*una herida*) to dress || *intr* to cure; to recover; **curar de** to take care of; to recover from; to mind, pay attention to || *ref* to cure; to cure oneself; to get well, to recover; (Am) to get drunk; **curarse de** to recover from, get over; **curarse en salud** to be forewarned
curati•vo -va *adj & f* curative
curda *f* (coll) jag, drunk
cureña *f* gun carriage
curia *f* (hist) curia; (*de rey*) court; (*conjunto de abogados*) bar
curiales•co -ca *adj* hairsplitting, legalistic
curiosear *tr* (coll) to pry into || *intr* (coll) to snoop; (coll) to browse around
curiosidad *f* curiosity; (*objeto de arte raro y curioso*) curio; neatness, tidiness; care, carefulness
curio•so -sa *adj* curious; neat, tidy; careful || *mf* busybody || *m* (Ven) healer, medical man
currinche *m* (coll) cub reporter; (coll) hit playwright
cu•rro -rra *adj* (coll) flashy, sporty || *m* (coll) sport, dandy
curruca *f* (orn) whitethroat; **curruca de cabeza negra** blackcap, warbler
curruta•co -ca *adj* (coll) dudish, sporty; (Am) chubby || *m* (coll) dude, sport || *f* (coll) chic dame
cursa•do -da *adj* skilled, experienced; (*asignatura*) taken
cursante *mf* student
cursar *tr* (*una materia, estudios*) to take, to study; (*conferencias*) to attend; (*una carta*) to forward; (*un*

paraje) to frequent, to haunt || *intr* to study; to be current
cursería *f* cheapness, flashiness, vulgarity; flashy lot of people
cursi *adj* cheap, flashy, vulgar, loud || *m* sporty guy || *f* flashy dame
cursien•to -ta *adj* (Am) diarrheic
cursilería *f* cheapness, flashiness, vulgarity; flashy lot of people
cursillo *m* refresher course; short course of lectures
cursi•vo -va *adj* cursive; italic || *f* cursive; italics
curso *m* course; academic year, school year; price, quotation, current rate; **curso académico** academic year; **curso legal** legal tender; **cursos** loose bowels; **dar curso a** to give way to; to forward
cursor *m* slide; sliding contact; **cursor de procesiones** marshal
curtiduría *f* tannery
curtiembre *f* (Am) tannery
curtir *tr* (*las pieles*) to tan; (*el cutis de una persona*) to tan, sunburn; to harden, to inure; **estar curtido en** to be skilled in, be expert in || *ref* to become tanned, sunburned; to become hardened; to be weather-beaten
curva *f* curve; bend
curvadura *f* painful exhaustion
cur•vo -va *adj* curved, bent || *f* see **curva**
cusca *f* (Col) jag, drunk; (Mex) prostitute, slut
cúspide *f* (*de montaña*) peak; (*de diente*) cusp; apex, tip, top
custodia *f* custody, care; (*de un preso*) guard; (eccl) monstrance
custodiar *tr* to guard, watch over
custodio *m* custodian; guard
cususa *f* (CAm) rum
cu•tí *m* (*pl* **-tíes**) bedtick, ticking
cutícula *f* cuticle
cutio *m* work, labor
cu•tis *m* (*& f*) (*pl* **-tis**) skin, complexion; **cutis anserina** goose flesh
cu•yo -ya *adj rel* whose
c/v *abbr* **cuenta de venta**

Ch

Ch, ch (che) *f* fourth letter of the Spanish alphabet
chabacanada or **chabacanería** *f* crudeness, coarseness, vulgarity
chabaca•no -na *adj* crude, coarse, vulgar || *m* (Mex) apricot tree
chabola *f* shack, shanty; (mil) foxhole
chacal *m* jackal
chacanear *tr* (Chile) to spur, goad on; (Chile) to annoy, bother
chacare•ro -ra *mf* (SAm) farm laborer, field worker; (Col) quack doctor; (Urug) gossip
chacarrachaca *f* (coll) row, racket
chacolotear *intr* to clatter
chacota *f* laughter, racket; **hacer chacota de** (coll) to make fun of
chacotear *intr* to laugh and make a racket
chacra *f* (Am) farm house; (Am) small farm; (Am) sown field
chacua•co -ca *adj* (Am) ugly, crude, boorish || *m* (CAm) cigar butt; (CAm) cheap cigar
cháchara *f* (coll) chatter, idle talk; **cháchars** (coll) trinkets, junk
chacharear *intr* (coll) to chatter
chafallar *tr* (coll) to botch
chafandín *m* conceited ass
chafar *tr* to rumple, muss; to flatten; (coll) to cut short; (Chile) to dismiss, send off
chafarrinar *tr* to blot, stain
chafarrinón *m* blot, stain; **echar un chafarrinón a** (coll) to insult, throw mud at
chaflán *m* chamfer
chaflanar *tr* to chamfer
chal *m* shawl
cha•lán -lana *adj* horse-dealing || *mf* horse dealer; horse trader || *m* (Am) broncobuster, horsebreaker || *f* scow, flatboat
chalanear *tr* (*un negocio*) to pull off shrewdly; (*un caballo*) (Am) to break; (Arg) to take advantage of || *intr* to horse-trade
chalanería *f* horse trading
chalanes•co -ca *adj* horse-trading
chaleco *m* vest, waistcoat
chalupa *f* small two-master; launch, lifeboat; (Mex) corncake
chama•co -ca *mf* (Mex) youngster, urchin
chamago•so -sa *adj* (Mex) dirty, filthy; (Mex) botched
chamarasca *f* brushwood; brush fire
chamarille•ro -ra *mf* junk dealer, second-hand dealer || *m* gambler
chamari•llón -llona *mf* poor card player
chamarra *f* sheepskin jacket
chamarreta *f* loose jacket; (Am) square poncho
chamba *f* fluke, scratch
chambelán *m* chamberlain; (Mex) atomizer, spray
chambergo *m* (orn) bobolink; (Arg) soft hat
chambe•rí *adj* (*pl* **-ríes**) (Peru) showy, flashy
cham•bón -bona *adj* (coll) awkward, clumsy; (coll) lucky
chambonada *f* (coll) awkwardness, clumsiness; (coll) stroke of luck
chambonear *intr* to foozle
chambra *f* blouse; (Ven) din, uproar
chambrana *f* trim (*around a door*)
chamburgo *m* (Col) stagnant water, puddle

chamico *m* jimson weed; **dar chamico a** (SAm) to bewitch
chamorrar *tr* (coll) to shear
champán *m* sampan; (coll) champagne
champaña *m* champagne
cham•pú *m* (*pl* **-púes**) shampoo
chamuscar §73 *tr* to singe, scorch; (Mex) to undersell
chamusco *m* singe, scorch
chamusquina *f* singeing; (coll) fight, row, quarrel; **oler a chamusquina** (coll) to look like a fight; (coll) to smack of heresy
chancar §73 *tr* (Am) to crush; (Am) to beat, beat up; (Am) to botch
chancear *intr* & *ref* to joke, jest
chance•ro -ra *adj* joking, jesting
canciller *m* chancellor
chancla *f* old shoe; house slipper
chancleta *mf* (coll) good-for-nothing || *f* slipper; (Ven) accelerator
chanclo *m* overshoe, rubber
chancha *f* cheat, lie; (Chile) slut; **hacer la chancha** (Bol, Col, Chile) to play hooky
chanche•ro -ra *mf* (Arg, Chile) pork butcher
chan•cho -cha *adj* (Am) dirty, filthy || *m* (Am) pig || *f* see **chancha**
chanchulle•ro -ra *mf* (coll) crook
changador *m* (SAm) errand boy
changarro *m* (Mex) small shop
chan•go -ga *adj* (Chile) dull, stupid; (Mex) sly, crafty || *mf* (Mex) monkey || *m* (Arg) house boy
chan•guí *m* (*pl* **-guíes**) (coll) trick, deception
chantaje *m* blackmail
chantajista *mf* blackmailer
chantar *tr* to put on; (SAm) to throw hard; (Urug) to keep waiting || *ref* (*p.ej., el sombrero*) to clap on
chantre *m* cantor, precentor
chanza *f* joke, jest
chapa *f* sheet, plate; (*hoja fina de madera*) veneer; (*en las mejillas*) flush; (coll) good sense, judgment; (Chile) lock, bolt; **chapa de circulación** (aut) license plate; **chapas** flipping coins
chapa•do -da *adj* plated; veneered; **chapado a la antigua** old-fashioned
chapalear *intr* (*el agua; las manos y los pies en el agua*) to splash; (*la herradura floja*) to clatter
chapar *tr* to cover or line with sheets of metal; to veneer
chaparrear *intr* to pour
chapa•rro -rra *mf* (Mex) child, little one; (Mex) runt || *m* scrub oak
chaparrón *m* downpour
chapea•do -da *adj* lined with sheets of metal; veneered || *m* plywood; veneer
chapear *tr* to cover or line with sheets of metal; to veneer
chapista *m* tinsmith, tinman
chapitel *m* (*remate de torre*) spire; (*capitel de columna*) capital
chapodar *tr* to trim, clear of branches; to curtail
chapotear *tr* to sponge, moisten || *intr* to splash
chapucear *tr* & *intr* to botch, bungle
chapuce•ro -ra *adj* crude, rough; clumsy, bungling || *mf* bungler; amateur || *m* blacksmith; junk dealer
chapurrar *tr* & *intr* to jabber
chapurreo *m* jabber
cha•puz *m* (*pl* **-puces**) duck, ducking
chapuzar §60 *tr, intr* & *ref* to duck
chaqué *m* cutaway coat, morning coat
chaqueta *f* jacket
chaquetilla *f* short jacket; (Ecuad) lady's vest
chaquetón *m* reefer, pea jacket
charamusca *f* (Am) brushwood, firewood; (Mex) candy twist
charanga *f* (mil) brass band
charangue•ro -ra *adj* crude, rough; bungling, clumsy || *mf* bungler
charca *f* pool
charco *m* puddle
charla *f* (coll) talk, chat; (coll) talk, lecture; (coll) chatter, prattle
charla•dor -dora *adj* (coll) garrulous; (coll) gossipy || *mf* (coll) chatterbox; (coll) gossip
charlar *intr* (coll) to talk, chat; (coll) to chatter, prattle
charla•tán -tana *adj* garrulous; gossipy || *mf* chatterbox; gossip; charlatan
charlatanería *f* garrulity, loquacity
charlatanismo *m* charlatanism; garrulity, loquacity
charnela *f* (*de puerta; de molusco*) hinge; (mach) knuckle
charol *m* varnish; patent leather; (Am) lacquered tray; **calzarse las de charol** (Arg, Urug) to hit the jackpot; **darse charol** (coll) to blow one's own horn
charola•do -da *adj* shiny
charolar *tr* to varnish, to lacquer
charpa *f* pistol belt; (*cabestrillo*) sling
charquear *tr* (*carne de vaca*) (Am) to jerk; (Am) to slash, cut to pieces
charqui *m* (Am) jerked beef
charrada *f* country dance; boorishness; (coll) tawdry ornamentation
charretera *f* epaulet; garter; (*del aguador*) (coll) shoulder pad
charriada *f* (Mex) rodeo
cha•rro -rra *adj* coarse, ill-bred; flashy, loud, showy; Salamanca || *mf* peasant; Salamanca peasant || *m* broad-brimmed hat; Mexican cowboy
chasca *f* brushwood
chascar §73 *tr* (*la lengua*) to click; (*algún manjar*) to crunch; (*engullir*) to swallow || *intr* to crack, crackle
chascarrillo *m* (coll) funny story
chas•co -ca *adj* (Arg, Bol) crinkly, crinkly-haired || *m* joke, trick; disappointment; **dar un chasco a** to play a trick on; **llevar** or **llevarse (un) chasco** to be disappointed
chas•cón -cona *adj* (Bol, Chile) disheveled; (Bol, Chile) bushy-haired; (Bol, Chile) clumsy, unskilled
cha•sis *m* (*pl* **-sis**) chassis
chasquear *tr* (*un látigo*) to crack; to play a trick on; to disappoint || *intr* to crack || *ref* to be disappointed
chasqui *m* (SAm) messenger, courier
chasquido *m* crack; crackle
chata *f* barge, scow; flatcar; bedpan
chatarra *f* iron slag; junk, scrap iron

chatarrería *f* junk yard
chatarre•ro -ra *mf* junk dealer, scrap-iron dealer
cha•to -ta *adj* flat; flat-nosed; blunt; (Am) commonplace; (Am) disappointed || *m* (coll) wineglass || *f* see **chata**
chatre *adj* (Chile, Ecuad) all dressed up
cha•val -vala *adj* (coll) young || *m* (coll) lad || *f* (coll) lass
chaveta *f* cotter pin; **perder la chaveta** (coll) to go out of one's head
chayote *m* (Am) chayote, vegetable pear; (Am) dunce, fool
chazar **§60** *tr* (*la pelota*) to stop; (*el sitio donde paró la pelota*) to mark
che *interj* (SAm) say!, hey!
che•co -ca *adj & mf* Czech
checoeslova•co -ca *adj & mf* Czecho-Slovak
Checoeslovaquia *f* Czecho-Slovakia
checoslova•co -ca *adj & mf* Czecho-Slovak
Checoslovaquia *f* Czecho-Slovakia
chechén *m* (Mex) poison ivy
chécheres *mpl* (Am) trinkets, junk
chelín *m* shilling
cheque *m* check; **cheque de viajeros** traveler's check
chica *f* lass, little girl; girl; (coll) my dear; **chica de cita** call girl; **chica de la vida alegre** party girl
chicalote *m* Mexican poppy
chicle *m* (Am) chewing gum
chiclear *intr* (Mex) to chew gum
chi•co -ca *adj* small, little; young || *mf* child, youngster || *m* lad, little boy; (coll) young fellow; (coll) old man; (Am) hand, turn || *f* see **chica**
chicolear *intr* to pay compliments, to flirt || *ref* (Arg, Peru) to enjoy oneself
chico•te -ta *mf* husky youngster || *m* (coll) cigar; (Am) cigar stub; (Am) whip
chicue•lo -la *adj* small, little || *m* little boy || *f* little girl
chicha *f* corn liquor; **no ser ni chicha ni limonada** (coll) to be good for nothing
chícharo *m* (Am) pea; (Col) poor cigar; (Mex) apprentice
chicharra *f* harvest fly; (coll) chatterbox; **cantar la chicharra** (coll) to be hot and sultry
chicharrón *m* residue of hog's fat; burnt meat; (coll) sunburned person; (Am) wrinkled person
chichear *tr & intr* to hiss
chi•chón -chona *adj* (CAm) easy; (SAm) joking; (Guat) large-breasted || *m* lump, bump on the head
chifla *f* hissing, whistling; paring knife; **estar de chifla** (Mex) to be in a bad humor
chifla•do -da *adj* (coll) daffy, nutty || *mf* (coll) crackbrain, nut
chifladura *f* (coll) daffiness, nuttiness; (coll) whim, wild idea
chiflar *tr* (*a un actor*) to hiss; (*vino o licor*) to gulp down; (*el cuero*) to pare || *intr* to whistle; (*las aves*) (Guat, Mex) to sing || *ref* to go crazy
chifle *m* whistle; (*para cazar aves*) bird call; powder flask
chiflido *m* whistle, hiss
chiflón *m* (SAm) cold blast of air; (Am) rapids; (Am) slide of loose stone
chilaba *f* jelab, jellaba
Chile *m* Chile
chile•no -na *adj & mf* Chilean
chilla *f* fox call, hare call; clapboard; (Chile) small fox; (Mex) top gallery
chillar *intr* to shriek; to squeak; to hiss, sizzle; (*los colores*) to scream || *ref* (Am) to take offense
chillido *m* shriek, scream
chi•llón -llona *adj* shrill, high-pitched; (coll) screaming; (*color*) loud
chimenea *f* chimney, smokestack; fireplace, hearth; stovepipe hat; (naut) funnel
chimpancé *m* chimpanzee
china *f* Chinese woman; china, porcelain; pebble; (Am) nursemaid; (Col) spinning top || **China** *f* China
chinche *mf* (coll) bore, tiresome person || *m* (*clavito de cabeza chata*) thumbtack || *f* (*insecto*) bedbug; **caer** or **morir como chinches** to die like flies
chinchorre•ro -ra *adj* (coll) gossipy, mischievous
chincho•so -sa *adj* (coll) boring, tiresome
chinero *m* china closet
chines•co -ca *adj* Chinese || **chinescos** *mpl* (mus) bell tree
chingar **§44** *tr* (coll) to tipple; (CAm) to bob, dock; (CAm, Mex) to bother, annoy || *ref* (coll) to tipple; (Am) to fail
chin•go -ga *adj* (CAm) short; (CAm) dull, blunt; (CAm) naked
chinguirito *m* (Am) cheap rum; (Am) swig of liquor
chi•no -na *adj & mf* Chinese || *m* (*idioma*) Chinese; (Col) boy, newsboy; (Mex) curl || *f* see **china**
chipichipi *m* (Am) drizzle, mist
Chipre *f* Cyprus
chiquero *m* pigsty; bull pen
chiquillada *f* childish prank
chiqui•to -ta *adj* small, little || *mf* little one || *m* (*de vino*) snifter; (Arg) moment, instant || *f* five cents; **no andarse con** or **en chiquitas** (coll) to talk right off the shoulder
chiribita *f* spark; daisy; **chiribitas** (coll) spots before the eyes
chiribitil *m* garret; cubbyhole
chirimbolos *mpl* (coll) utensils, vessels
chirimía *f* hornpipe
chiripa *f* (billiards) fluke, scratch; (coll) stroke of luck
chirivía *f* parsnip
chirle *adj* (coll) insipid, tasteless
chirlo *m* slash or scar on the face
chirlota *f* (Mex) meadow lark
chirona *f* (coll) jail, jug
chirriar **§77** *intr* to creak, squeak; to shriek; to hiss, sizzle; to sing or play out of tune || *ref* (Col) to go on a spree; (Col) to shiver

chirrido *m* creak, squeak; shriek; hiss, sizzle
chis *interj* sh-sh!; **¡chis, chis!** pst!
chischás *m* clash of swords
chisguete *m* (coll) swig of wine; (coll) squirt
chisme *m* piece of gossip; (coll) trinket; **chisme de vecindad** (coll) idle talker; **chismes** gossip; articles; **chismes de aseo** toilet articles
chismear *intr* to gossip
chismo•so -sa *adj* gossipy, catty || *mf* gossip
chispa *f* spark; (*pequeña cantidad*) drop; lightning; (fig) sparkle, wit; (coll) drunk, spree; (Col) rumor; **coger una chispa** (coll) to go on a drunk; **chispa de entrehierro** (elec) jump spark; **chispas** sprinkle (*of rain*); **dar chispa** (Guat, Mex) to work, to click; **echar chispas** (coll) to blow up, hit the ceiling
chispeante *adj* sparkling
chispear *intr* to spark; to sparkle; to drizzle, to sprinkle
chis•po -pa *adj* (coll) tipsy || *m* (coll) swallow, drink || *f* see **chispa**
chisporrotear *intr* (coll) to spark, to sputter
chispo•so -sa *adj* sputtering, sparking
chisquero *m* pocket lighter
chistar *intr* to speak, say something; **no chistar** to not say a word
chiste *m* joke; witticism; **caer en el chiste** (coll) to get the point; **dar en el chiste** (coll) to hit the nail on the head
chistera *f* fish basket; (coll) top hat
chisto•so -sa *adj* funny; witty || *mf* funny person; wit
chita *f* anklebone; quoits; **a la chita callando** (coll) quietly, secretly; **dar en la chita** (coll) to hit the nail on the head
chiticalla *mf* (*persona que no revela lo que sabe*) (coll) clam || *f* (coll) secret
chito *interj* hush!, sh-sh!
chivato *m* kid, young goat; (*soplón*) (coll) squealer; (Bol) apprentice, helper; (Chile) cheap rum
chi•vo -va *mf* kid || *m* billy goat || *f* nanny goat
chocante *adj* shocking; coarse, crude; (Col) annoying; (Mex) disagreeable
chocar §73 *tr* to shock, annoy, irritate; to surprise; (*vasos*) to clink; (coll) to please; **¡choque Vd. esos cinco!** (coll) shake! || *intr* to shock; to collide; to clash, fight
chocarre•ro -ra *adj* coarse, crude || *mf* crude joker
choclo *m* wooden overshoe; (Mex) low shoe; (SAm) tender ear of corn
chocolate *m* chocolate
chocha *f* woodcock
chochear *intr* to be in one's dotage; (coll) to dote, be infatuated
chochera *f* dotage; (Arg, Peru) favorite
cho•chez *f* (*pl* **-checes**) dotage; doting act or remark
cho•cho -cha *adj* doting; doddering || *m* stick of cinnamon candy; **chochos** candy to quiet a child || *f* see **chocha**
chófer *m* chauffeur
chofeta *f* fire pan (*for lighting cigars*)
cho•lo -la *adj* (Am) half-breed (*Indian and white*); (Am) half-civilized (*Indian*) || *mf* (Am) Indian; (Am) half-breed; (Am) half-civilized Indian; (Chile) coward; (SAm) darling
cholla *f* (coll) noodle, head; (coll) ability, brains
chomite *m* (Mex) coarse wool; (Mex) woolen skirt
chopo *m* black poplar; (coll) gun, rifle; **chopo de Italia** Lombardy poplar; **chopo del Canadá** or **de Virginia** cottonwood; **chopo lombardo** Lombardy poplar
choque *m* shock; collision, impact; clash, conflict, skirmish; (elec) choke, choke coil
choricería *f* sausage shop
chorizo *m* smoked pork sausage
chorlito *m* plover, golden plover; (coll) scatterbrains
chorrear *intr* to gush, spurt, spout; to drip; to trickle
chorrera *f* spout, channel; cut, gulley; rapids; lace front, jabot; (Arg) string, stream
chorrillo *m* constant stream; **irse por el chorrillo** (coll) to follow the current; **tomar el chorrillo de** (coll) to get the habit of
chorro *m* jet, spurt; stream, flow; **a chorros** in abundance; **chorro de arena** sandblast
chotaca•bras *m* (*pl* **-bras**) goatsucker
chotear *tr* (Am) to make fun of; (Guat) to keep an eye on
choteo *m* (Am) jeering, mocking
choza *f* hut, cabin, lodge
chubasco *m* squall, shower; (fig) temporary setback; **chubasco de agua** rainstorm; **chubasco de nieve** blizzard
chubasco•so -sa *adj* stormy, threatening
chucruta *f* sauerkraut
chucha *f* (coll) female dog, bitch; (coll) drunk, jag; (Col) opossum; (Col) body odor
chuchaque *m* (Ecuad) hangover
chuchear *tr* (*caza menor*) to trap || *intr* to whisper
chuchería *f* knickknack, trinket; delicacy, tidbit
chu•cho -cha *adj* (CAm) mean, stingy; (*fruto*) (Col) watery; (Col) wrinkled || *m* (coll) dog || *f* see **chucha**
chue•co -ca *adj* (Mex) twisted, bent; (SAm) bow-legged; (Mex) crippled || *m* (Mex) dealing in stolen goods || *f* stump; hockey; hockey ball
chufa *f* groundnut
chufletear *intr* (coll) to joke, jest
chula *f* flashy dame (*in lower classes of Madrid*)
chulada *f* light-hearted remark; vulgarity
chul•co -ca *mf* (Bol) baby (*youngest child*)
chulear *tr* to tease; (Mex) to flirt with
chuleta *f* chop, cutlet; (coll) slap, smack; (*de los estudiantes*) (coll) crib, pony; **chuleta de cerdo** pork

chop; **chuleta de ternera** veal chop; **chuletas** sideburns, side whiskers
chu•lo -la *adj* flashy, sporty; foxy, slick; (Guat, Mex) pretty, cute || *m* sporty fellow (*in lower classes of Madrid*); pimp, procurer; gigolo; butcher's helper; (taur) attendant on foot || *f* see **chula**
chumbera *f* prickly pear
chunga *f* (coll) jest, fun
chunguear *ref* (coll) to jest, joke
chupa *f* frock, coat; (Arg) drunk, jag; (Arg) tobacco pouch
chupa•do -da *adj* (coll) thin, skinny; (Am) drunk; (*falda*) (Am) tight || *f* suck; pull (*on a cigar*)
chupador *m* teething ring, pacifier
chupaflor *m* (Mex, Ven) hummingbird
chupamirto *m* (Mex) hummingbird
chupar *tr* to suck; (*la hacienda ajena*) to milk, sap; (coll) to absorb || *intr* to suck || *ref* to get thin, lose strength; (*los labios*) to smack
chupatin•tas *mf* (*pl* **-tas**) (coll) office drudge
chupete *m* (*para un niño*) pacifier; (Am) lollipop; **de chupete** (coll) fine, splendid
chu•pón -pona *mf* (coll) swindler || *m* (bot) sucker, shoot; (mach) plunger
chupópte•ro -ra *mf* (coll) sponger
chuquisa *f* (Chile, Peru) prostitute
churrasco *m* (Am) barbecue
churrasquear *tr* (Am) to barbecue
churre *m* (coll) filth, dirt, grease
churrete *m* dirty spot (*on hands or face*)
churrigueres•co -ca *adj* churrigueresque; loud, flashy, tawdry
chu•rro -rra *adj* (*lana*) coarse; (*carnero*) coarse-wooled || *m* coarse-wooled sheep; fritter; (coll) botch
churrulle•ro -ra *adj* gossipy, loquacious || *mf* gossip, chatterbox
churrusco *m* burnt piece of bread
churumbela *f* hornpipe, flageolet; (Am) maté cup; (Col) worry, anxiety; (Col, Ecuad) pipe
churumo *m* (coll) substance (*money, brains, etc.*)
chus *interj* here! (*to call a dog*); **no decir chus ni mus** (coll) to not say boo
chus•co -ca *adj* droll, funny; (Peru) ill-mannered; (*perro*) (Peru) mongrel
chusma *f* galley slaves; mob, rabble
chuza *f* (Mex) strike (*in bowling*)

D

D, d (de) *f* fifth letter of the Spanish alphabet
D. *abbr* **don**
D.ª *abbr* **doña**
daca give me, hand over; **andar al daca y toma** (coll) to be at cross purposes
dactilógra•fo -fa *mf* typist, typewriter || *m* typewriter
dactilograma *m* fingerprint
dádiva *f* gift, present
dadivo•so -sa *adj* liberal, generous
da•do -da *adj* given; **dado que** provided, as long as || *m* die; **cargar los dados** to load the dice; **dados** dice; **el dado está tirado** the die is cast
daga *f* dagger
dalia *f* dahlia
dama *f* lady, dame; maid-in-waiting; (*en el juego de damas*) king; (*en el ajedrez y los naipes*) queen; (theat) leading lady; concubine, mistress; **dama joven** (theat) young lead; **damas** checkers; **señalar dama** (*en el juego de damas*) to crown a man
damajuana *f* demijohn
damasquina•do -da *adj & m* damascene
damasquinar *tr* to damascene
damasqui•no -na *adj* damascene
damero *m* checkerboard
damisela *f* young lady; courtesan
damnación *f* damnation
damnificar §73 *tr* to damage, hurt
da•nés -nesa *adj* Danish || *mf* Dane || *m* (*idioma*) Danish
dáni•co -ca *adj* Danish
Danubio *m* Danube
danza *f* dance; dancing; dance team; **danza de cintas** Maypole dance; **danza de figuras** square dance; **meter en la danza** (coll) to drag in, involve
danza•dor -dora *mf* dancer
danzar §60 *tr* to dance || *intr* to dance; (coll) to butt in
danza•rín -rina *mf* dancer; (coll) meddler, scatterbrain
dañable *adj* harmful; reprehensible
daña•do -da *adj* bad, wicked; spoiled
dañar *tr* to hurt, damage, injure; to spoil || *ref* to be damaged; to spoil
dañi•no -na *adj* harmful, destructive, noxious; wicked
daño *m* damage, harm; (Arg) witchcraft; **a daño de** on the responsibility of; **daños y perjuicios** (law) damages; **en daño de** to the detriment of; **hacer daño** to be harmful; **hacer daño a** to hurt; **hacerse daño** to hurt oneself; to get hurt
daño•so -sa *adj* harmful, injurious
dar §23 *tr* to give; to cause; to hit, strike; (*el reloj la hora*) to strike; (*cartas*) to deal; (*un paseo*) to take; (*los buenos días*) to wish; (*un film*) to show; (*una capa de pintura*) to put on, apply; **dar a conocer** to make known; **dar a luz** to bring out, publish; **dar cuerda a** (*un reloj*) to wind; **dar curso a** to circulate; **dar de beber a** to give something to drink to; **dar de comer a** to give

something to eat to; **dar la razón a** to admit that (*someone*) is right; **dar prestado** to lend; **dar palmadas** to clap the hands; **dar por** to consider as; **dar que hablar** to cause talk; to stir up criticism; **dar que hacer** to cause annoyance or trouble; **dar que pensar** to give food for thought; to give rise to suspicion || *intr* to take place; to hit, strike; (*el reloj; dos, tres, etc. horas*) to strike; to tell, intimate; **dar a** to overlook; **dar con** to run into; **dar contra** to run against, strike against; **dar de sí** to stretch, to give; **dar en** to overlook; to hit; to run into; to fall into; to be bent on; (*un chiste*) to catch on to; **dar sobre** to overlook; **dar tras** to pursue hotly || *ref* to give oneself up; to give in, yield; to occur, be found; **darse a** to devote oneself to; **darse a conocer** to make a name for oneself, make oneself known; to get to know each other; **darse cuenta de** to realize, become aware of; **darse la mano** to shake hands; **dárselas de** to pose as; **darse por aludido** to take the hint; **darse por entendido** to show an understanding; to show appreciation; **darse por ofendido** to take offense; **darse por vencido** to give up, to acknowledge defeat

dardo *m* dart; cutting remark

dares y tomares *mpl* (coll) quarrels, disputes

dársena *f* basin, dock, inner harbor

data *f* date; (*en una cuenta*) item; **de larga data** of long standing; **estar de mala data** (coll) to be in a bad humor

datar *tr & intr* to date; **datar de** to date from

dátil *m* date

datilera *f* date, date palm

dati•vo -va *adj & m* dative

dato *m* datum; basis, foundation

de *prep* of; from; about; **acompañado de** accompanied by; **cubierto de** covered with; **de noche** in the nighttime; **de no llegar nosotros a la hora** if we do not arrive on time; **más de** more than; **tratar de** to try to

deán *m* (eccl) dean

debajo *adv* below, underneath; **debajo de** below, under

debate *m* debate; altercation, argument

debatir *tr & intr* to debate; to fight, argue || *ref* to struggle

debe *m* debit

debelar *tr* to conquer, vanquish

deber *m* duty; (*deuda*) debt; homework, school work; **últimos deberes** last rites || *tr* to owe || *v aux* to have to, ought to, must, should; **deber de** must, most likely || *ref* to be committed; **deberse a** to be due to

debidamente *adv* duly

debi•do -da *adj* due, owed; proper, right; **debido a** due to

débil *adj* weak

debilidad *f* weakness, debility

debilitar *tr & ref* to weaken

débito *m* debt, debit; responsibility

debutar *intr* to make one's start, appear for the first time

decadencia *f* decadence

decadente *adj & mf* decadent

decaer **§15** *intr* to decay, decline, fail, weaken; (naut) to drift from the course

decampar *intr* (mil) to decamp

decanato *m* deanship

decano *m* dean

decanta•do -da *adj* puffed-up, overrated

decapitar *tr* to decapitate

decelerar *tr, intr, & ref* to decelerate

decencia *f* decency

decenio *m* decade

dece•no -na *adj & m* tenth

decentar **§2** *tr* to cut the first slice of; to begin to damage || *ref* to get bedsores

decente *adj* decent, proper; decent-looking

decepción *f* disappointment

decepcionar *tr* to disappoint

decidi•do -da *adj* decided, determined

decidir *tr* to decide; to persuade || *intr & ref* to decide

deci•dor -dora *adj* facile, fluent, witty

decimal *adj & m* decimal

déci•mo -ma *adj & m* tenth

decimocta•vo -va *adj* eighteenth

decimocuar•to -ta *adj* fourteenth

decimono•no -na *adj* nineteenth

decimonove•no -na *adj* nineteenth

decimoquin•to -ta *adj* fifteenth

decimosépti•mo -ma *adj* seventeenth

decimosex•to -ta *adj* sixteenth

decimoterce•ro -ra *adj* thirteenth

decimoter•cio -cia *adj* thirteenth

decir *m* say-so; **al decir de** according to || **§24** *tr* to say; to tell; (*disparates*) to talk; **como si dijéramos** so to speak, in a manner of speaking; **decir entre sí** to say to oneself; **decirle a uno cuántas son cinco** (coll) to tell a person what's what; **decir para sí** to say to oneself; **decir por decir** to talk for talk's sake; **decir que no** to say no; **decir que sí** to say yes; **decírselo a una persona deletreado** (coll) to spell it out to a person; **es decir** that is to say; **mejor dicho** rather; **¡por algo te lo dije!** I told you so!; **por decirlo así** so to speak || *intr* to suit, fit; **¡diga!** (*al contestar el teléfono*) hello! || *ref* to be said; to be called; **se dice** it is said, they say

decisión *f* decision

decisi•vo -va *adj* decisive

declamar *tr & intr* to declaim

declaración *f* declaration; (*en bridge*) bid

declarante *mf* declarant, deponent; (*en el juego de bridge*) bidder

declarar *tr* to declare; (*en bridge*) to bid; (law) to depose || *ref* to declare oneself; to break out, take place

declarati•vo -va *adj* declarative

declinación *f* declination; fall, drop; decline; (gram) declension

declinar *tr & intr* to decline

declive *m* descent, declivity, slope

declividad *f* declivity
decollaje *m* (aer) take-off
decollar *intr* (aer) to take off
decomisar *tr* to seize, confiscate
decomiso *m* seizure, confiscation
decoración *f* decoration; memorizing; (theat) set, scenery; **decoraciones** (theat) scenery; **decoración interior** interior decoration
decorado *m* decoration; (theat) décor, scenery; memorizing
decora•dor -dora *mf* decorator
decorar *tr* to decorate; to memorize
decoro *m* decorum; honor, respect; decency, propriety
decoro•so -sa *adj* decorous; respectful; decent
decrecer §22 *intr* to decrease, grow smaller, grow shorter
decrepitar *intr* to crackle
decrépi•to -ta *adj* decrepit
decretar *tr* to decree
decreto *m* decree
decurso *m* course; **en el decurso de** in the course of
dechado *m* sample, model, example; (*labor de las niñas*) sampler
dedada *f* touch, spot; **dar una dedada de miel a** (coll) to feed the hopes of
dedal *m* thimble
dedalera *f* foxglove
dedeo *m* (mus) finger dexterity
dedicación *f* dedication
dedicar §73 *tr* to dedicate; to devote; to autograph || *ref* to devote oneself
dedicatoria *f* dedication
dedil *m* fingerstall
dedillo *m* little finger; **saber** or **tener al dedillo** (coll) to have at one's finger tips, to have a thorough knowledge of
dedo *m* finger; toe; (coll) bit; **alzar el dedo** (*en señal de dar palabra*) (coll) to raise one's hand; **cogerse los dedos** (coll) to burn one's fingers; **dedo auricular** little finger; **dedo cordial, de en medio,** or **del corazón** middle finger; **dedo gordo** thumb; big toe; **dedo índice** index finger, forefinger; **dedo meñique** little finger; **dedo mostrador** forefinger; **dedo pulgar** thumb; big toe; **estar a dos dedos de** (coll) to be within an ace of; **irse de entre los dedos** (coll) to slip between the fingers; **tener en la punta de los dedos** (coll) to have at one's finger tips
deducción *f* deduction; drawing off
deducir §19 *tr* (*concluir*) to deduce; (*rebajar*) to deduct; (law) to allege
defecar §73 *intr* to defecate
defección *f* defection
defeccionar *intr & ref* (Chile) to defect
defecti•vo -va *adj* defective
defecto *m* defect; shortage, lack; **en defecto de** for lack of
defectuo•so -sa *adj* defective; lacking
defender §51 *tr* to defend; to protect; to delay, interfere with
defensa *f* defense; fender, guard; (*del toro*) horn; (*del elefante*) tusk; (*del automóvil*) (Am) bumper; **defensa marítima** (Arg) sea wall; **defensa propia** self-defense
defensi•vo -va *adj & f* defensive
defen•sor -sora *adj* defending || *mf* defender; (law) counsel for the defense
deferencia *f* deference
deferente *adj* deferential
deferir §68 *tr to* delegate || *intr* to defer
deficiencia *f* deficiency
deficiente *adj* deficient
défi•cit *m* (*pl* **-cits**) deficit
deficita•rio -ria *adj* deficit
definición *f* definition; decision, verdict
defini•do -da *adj* definite; sharp, defined
definir *tr* to define; to settle, determine
definiti•vo -va *adj* definitive; **en definitiva** after all, in short
deflación *f* deflation
deflector *m* baffle
deformación *f* deformation; (rad) distortion
deformar *tr* to deform; to disfigure; to distort
deforme *adj* deformed
deformidad *f* deformity; gross error
defraudar *tr* to defraud, to cheat; (*las esperanzas de una persona*) to defeat; (*la claridad del día*) to cut off
defuera *adv* outside; **por defuera** on the outside
defunción *f* decease, demise
degeneración *f* (*acción y efecto de degenerar*) degeneration; (*estado de degenerado; depravación*) degeneracy
degenera•do -da *adj & mf* degenerate
degenerar *intr* to degenerate
deglutir *tr & intr* to swallow
degollar §3 *tr* to cut the throat of; to kill, massacre; (*un vestido*) to cut low in the neck; (*el actor una obra dramática*) to butcher, to murder; (coll) to become obnoxious to
degradante *adj* degrading
degradar *tr* to degrade; (mil) to break
degüello *m* throat-cutting; massacre; (*de un arma*) neck; **tirar a degüello** (coll) to try to harm
degustar *tr* (*probar*) to taste; (*percibir con deleite el sabor de*) to savor
dehesa *f* pasture land, meadow; (taur) range
deidad *f* deity
deificar §73 *tr* to deify
dejación *f* abandonment; (CAm, Chile, Col) negligence
dejadez *f* laziness; negligence; slovenliness; low spirits
deja•do -da *adj* lazy; negligent; slovenly; dejected
dejamiento *m* laziness; negligence; indolence, languor, indifference
dejar *tr* to leave; to abandon; to let, allow, permit; **dejar caer** to drop, let fall; **dejar feo** (coll) to slight; **dejar fresco** (coll) to leave in the lurch; **dejar por** + *inf* or **que** + *inf* to leave (*something*) to be + *pp,* e.g., **hemos dejado dos manuscritos por corregir** or **que corregir** we left two manuscripts to be corrected || *intr* to stop; **dejar de** to stop, to cease; to fail to || *ref* to be slovenly, to neglect oneself; (*una barba*) to grow; **dejarse de**

(*disparates*) to cut out; (*preguntas*) to stop asking; (*dudas*) to put aside; **dejarse ver** to show up; to be evident
dejillo *m* (*gusto que deja alguna comida*) aftertaste; (*acento regional*) local accent
dejo *m* (*gusto que deja alguna comida*) aftertaste; abandonment; slovenliness, neglect; local accent; (*placer o disgusto que queda después de hecha una cosa*) (fig) aftertaste
delación *f* accusation, denunciation
delantal *m* apron
delante *adv* before, ahead, in front; **delante de** before, ahead of, in front of
delantera *f* front; front row; advantage, lead; cowcatcher; **coger** or **tomar la delantera a** to get ahead of; to get a start on; **delanteras** overalls
delante•ro -ra *adj* front, foremost, first || *f* see **delantera**
delatar *tr* to accuse, denounce
delega•do -da *mf* delegate
delegar §44 *tr* to delegate
deleitable *adj* delectable, enjoyable
deleitar *tr & ref* to delight
deleite *m* delight
deleito•so -sa *adj* delightful
deletrear *tr & intr* to spell; to decipher
deletreo *m* spelling
deleznable *adj* (*poco durable*) perishable; (*que se rompe fácilmente*) crumbly, fragile; (*que se desliza con facilidad*) slippery
delfín *m* (*primogénito del rey de Francia*) dauphin; (*mamífero cetáceo*) dolphin
delgadez *f* thinness, leanness; delicateness, lightness; perspicacity
delga•do -da *adj* thin, lean; delicate, light; sharp, perspicacious; (*terreno*) poor, exhausted || *adv* — **hilar delgado** (coll) to hew close to the line; (coll) to split hairs
deliberar *tr & intr* to deliberate
delicadeza *f* delicacy, delicateness; scrupulousness
delica•do -da *adj* delicate; scrupulous
delicia *f* delight
delicio•so -sa *adj* delicious, delightful
delincuencia *f* guilt, criminality
delincuente *adj* guilty, criminal || *mf* criminal
delineante *mf* designer || *m* draughtsman
delinquir §25 *intr* to transgress, be guilty
deliquio *m* faint, swoon; weakening
delirante *adj* delirious
delirar *intr* to be delirious, rant, rave; to talk nonsense
delirio *m* delirium; nonsense
delito *m* crime; **delito de incendio** arson; **delito de lesa majestad** lese majesty; **delito de mayor cuantía** (law) felony; **delito de menor cuantía** (law) misdemeanor
deludir *tr* to delude
demacra•do -da *adj* emaciated, wasted, thin
demago•go -ga *mf* demagogue
demanda *f* demand, petition; charity box; lawsuit; undertaking; (*del Santo Grial*) quest; **en demanda de** in search of; **tener demanda** to be in demand
demanda•do -da *mf* (law) defendant
demandante *mf* (law) complainant, plaintiff
demandar *tr* to ask for, request; (law) to sue || *intr* (law) to sue, bring suit
demarcar §73 *tr* to demarcate
demás *adj* — **el demás . . .** the other . . . , the rest of the . . .; **estar demás** to be useless, to be in the way; **lo demás** the rest; **por lo demás** furthermore, besides || *pron* others; **los demás** the others, the rest || *adv* besides; **por demás** in vain; too, too much
demasía *f* excess, surplus; daring, boldness; evil, guilt, wrong; insolence; **en demasía** excessively, too much
demasia•do -da *adj & pron* too much; **demasia•dos -das** too many || **demasiado** *adv* too, too much, too hard
demasiar §77 *intr* (coll) to go too far
demediar *tr* to divide in half; to use up half of; to reach the middle of || *intr* to be divided in half
demente *adj* insane || *mf* lunatic
democracia *f* democracy
demócrata *mf* democrat
democráti•co -ca *adj* democratic
demoler §47 *tr* to demolish
demolición *f* demolition
demonía•co -ca *adj* demoniacal
demonio *m* demon, devil; **estudiar con el demonio** (coll) to be full of devilishness
demora *f* delay
demorar *tr & ref* to delay
demostración *f* demonstration
demostra•dor -dora *mf* demonstrator || *m* hand (*of clock*)
demostrar §61 *tr* to demonstrate
demostrati•vo -va *adj* demonstrative
demudar *tr* to change, alter; to disguise, cloak || *ref* to change countenance, to color
denegación *f* denial, refusal
denegar §66 *tr* to deny, to refuse
denegrecer §22 *tr* to blacken || *ref* to turn black
dengo•so -sa *adj* affected, finicky, overnice; (Col) strutting
dengue *m* affectation, finickiness, overniceness; (Col) strut, swagger
denguear *ref* (Col) to strut, swagger
denigrar *tr* to defame, revile; to insult
denominación *f* denomination
denoda•do -da *adj* bold, daring
denostar §61 *tr* to abuse, insult, mistreat
denotar *tr* to denote
densidad *f* density; darkness, confusion
den•so -sa *adj* dense; dark, confused; crowded, thick, close
denta•do -da *adj* toothed; (*sello de correo*) perforated || *m* gear; teeth
dentadura *f* set of teeth; **dentadura artificial** or **postiza** denture
dental *adj & f* dental
dentellada *f* bite; tooth mark
dentellar *intr* (*los dientes*) to chatter
dentellear *tr* to nibble, nibble at
dentera *f* (coll) envy; (coll) eagerness;

dar **dentera** to set the teeth on edge; to make the mouth water
dentición *f* teething
dentífri·co -ca *adj* (*pasta, polvos*) tooth || *m* dentifrice
dentista *mf* dentist
dentistería *f* dentistry
dentística *f* (Chile) dentistry
dentro *adv* inside, within; **dentro de** inside, within; **dentro de poco** shortly; **por dentro** on the inside
denuedo *m* bravery, courage, daring
denuesto *m* abuse, insult, mistreatment
denuncia *f* denunciation; report; proclamation
denunciar *tr* to denounce; to report; (*la guerra*) to proclaim
deparar *tr* to furnish, provide; to offer, present
departamento *m* department; (rr) compartment; (*piso*) (Am) apartment; naval district (*in Spain*)
departir *intr* to chat, converse
depauperación *f* impoverishment; exhaustion, weakening
depauperar *tr* to impoverish; to exhaust, weaken
dependencia *f* dependence, dependency; branch, branch office; relationship, friendship; accessory; personnel
depender *intr* to depend; **depender de** to depend on; to be attached to, to belong to
dependienta *f* female employee, clerk
dependiente *adj* dependent; branch || *mf* employee, clerk
deplorable *adj* deplorable
deplorar *tr* to deplore
deponer §54 *tr* to depose; to set aside, remove; (*las armas*) to lay down || *intr* to depose; (*evacuar el vientre*) to have a movement; (CAm, Mex) to vomit
deportación *f* deportation
deporta·do -da *mf* deportee
deportar *tr* to deport
deporte *m* sport; outdoor recreation
deportista *mf* sport fan || *m* sportsman || *f* sportswoman
deporti·vo -va *adj* sport, sports
depositante *mf* depositor
depositar *tr* to deposit; (*la esperanza, la confianza*) to put, place; (*el equipaje*) to check; (*a una persona en seguro*) to commit; to store || *ref* to deposit, settle
deposita·rio -ria *mf* trustee; (*de un secreto*) repository || *m* public treasurer
depósito *m* deposit; depot, warehouse; tank, reservoir; (*de libros en una biblioteca*) stack; (mil) depot; **depósito comercial** bonded warehouse; **depósito de agua** reservoir; **depósito de cadáveres** morgue; **depósito de cereales** grain elevator; **depósito de equipajes** (rr) checkroom; **depósito de gasolina** (aut) gas tank; **depósito de locomotoras** roundhouse; **depósito de municiones** munition dump
depravación *f* depravity, depravation
deprava·do -da *adj* depraved
depravar *tr* to deprave || *ref* to become depraved
deprecar §73 *tr* to entreat, implore
depreciación *f* depreciation
depreciar *tr & ref* to depreciate
depresión *f* depression; drop, dip; (*en un muro*) recess
deprimir *tr* to depress; to press down; to push in; to belittle; to humiliate || *ref* to be depressed; (*la frente de una persona*) to recede
depurar *tr* to purify, cleanse; to purge
derecha *f* right hand; right-hand side; (pol) right; **a la derecha** on the right, to the right
derechamente *adv* rightly; straight, direct; properly; wisely
derechazo *m* blow with the right; (box) right
dereche·ro -ra *adj* right, just
derechista *adj* rightist || *mf* rightist, right-winger
dere·cho -cha *adj* right; right-hand; right-handed; straight; upright, standing || *m* right; law; exemption, privilege; road, path; (*de tela, papel, tabla*) right side; **derecho consuetudinario** common law; **derecho de gentes** law of nations, international law; **derecho de subscripción** (*a una nueva emisión de acciones*) (com) right; **derecho de tránsito** or **paso** right of way; **derecho internacional** international law; **derecho penal** criminal law; **derechos** dues, fees, taxes; (*de aduana*) duties; **derechos de almacenaje** storage, cost of storage; **derechos de autor** royalty; **derechos del hombre** rights of man; **derechos de propiedad literaria** or **derechos reservados** copyright; **según derecho** by right, by rights || *f* see **derecha** || **derecho** *adv* straight, direct; rightly
deriva (aer, naut) drift; **ir a la deriva** (naut) to drift, to be adrift
derivado *m* by-product
derivar *tr* to derive || *intr & ref* to derive, be derived; (aer, naut) to drift
derogar §44 *tr* to abolish, destroy, repeal
derrabar *tr* to dock, cut off the tail of
derrama·do -da *adj* extravagant, lavish
derramamiento *m* pouring, spilling; shedding; spreading; lavishing, wasting
derramar *tr* to pour, to spill; (*sangre*) to shed; to spread, publish abroad; (*dinero*) to lavish, waste || *ref* to run over, overflow; to spread, scatter; (*una corriente, un río*) to open, empty; (*la plumafuente*) to leak
derrame *m* pouring, spilling; (*de sangre*) shed, shedding; spread, scattering; lavishing, wasting; overflow; leakage; slope; chamfering; (pathol) discharge, effusion
derredor *m* circumference; **al** or **en derredor** around, round about
derrelicto *m* (naut) derelict
derrelinquir §25 *tr* to abandon, forsake
derrenga·do -da *adj* crooked, out of shape; crippled, lame
derrengar §44 or §66 *tr* to bend, make crooked; to cripple

derreniego *m* (coll) curse
derreti•do -da *adj* madly in love; (*mantequilla*) drawn || *m* concrete
derretimiento *m* thawing, melting; intense love, passion
derretir §50 *tr* to thaw, melt; (*la mantequilla*) to draw; (*la hacienda*) to squander || *ref* to thaw, melt; to fall madly in love; to be quite susceptible; (coll) to be worried, be impatient
derribar *tr* to destroy, tear down, knock down; to wreck; (*un árbol*) to fell; to bring down, shoot down; to overthrow; to humiliate || *ref* to fall down, tumble down; to throw oneself on the ground
derribo *m* demolition, wrecking; (*de un árbol*) felling; overthrow; (*de un avión enemigo*) bringing down; **derribos** debris, rubble
derrocadero *m* rocky precipice
derrocar §73 or §81 *tr* to throw or hurl from a height; to ruin, wreck, tear down; to bring down, humble, overthrow
derrocha•dor -dora *mf* wastrel, squanderer
derrochar *tr* to waste, squander
derroche *m* wasting, squandering, extravagance
derrota *f* defeat, rout; road, route, way; (*de embarcación*) course
derrotadamente *adv* shabbily, poorly
derrotar *tr* to rout, put to flight; to wear out; to ruin || *ref* (naut) to drift from the course
derrotero *m* course, route; ship's course
derrotismo *m* defeatism
derrotista *adj & mf* defeatist
derrubiar *tr & ref* to wash away, wear away
derrubio *m* washout
derruir §20 *tr* to tear down, demolish
derrumbadero *m* crag, precipice; hazard, risky business
derrumbamiento *m* headlong plunge; cave-in, collapse; **derrumbamiento de tierra** landslide
derrumbar *tr* to throw headlong || *ref* to plunge headlong; to collapse, cave in, crumble
derrumbe *m* precipice; landslide; cave-in
derviche *m* dervish
desabonar *ref* to drop one's subscription
desabono *m* cancellation of subscription; discredit, disparagement
desabor *m* insipidity, tastelessness
desabotonar *tr* to unbutton || *intr* to blossom, bloom
desabri•do -da *adj* insipid, tasteless; gruff, surly; (*tiempo*) unsettled
desabrigar §44 *tr* to uncover, bare || *ref* to bare oneself; to undress
desabrir *tr* to give a bad taste to; to displease, to embitter
desabrochar *tr* to unclasp, unbutton, unfasten || *ref* (coll) to unbosom oneself
desacalorar *ref* to cool off
desacatamiento *m* incivility, disrespect
desacatar *tr* to treat disrespectfully
desacato *m* incivility, disrespect, contempt; (*para con las cosas sagradas*) profanation
desacelerar *tr & ref* to decelerate
desacerta•do -da *adj* mistaken, wrong
desacertar §2 *intr* to be mistaken, be wrong
desacierto *m* error, mistake, blunder
desacomoda•do -da *adj* inconvenient; out of work; in straightened circumstances
desacomodar *tr* to inconvenience; to discharge, dismiss
desacomodo *m* discharge, dismissal
desaconseja•do -da *adj* ill-advised
desaconsejar *tr* to dissuade
desacordar §61 *tr* to put out of tune || *ref* to get out of tune; to become forgetful
desacorde *adj* out of tune; incongruous
desacostumbra•do -da *adj* unusual
desacostumbrar *tr* to break of a habit
desacreditar *tr* to discredit; to disparage
desacuerdo *m* discord, disagreement; error, mistake; unconsciousness; forgetfulness
desadaptación *f* maladjustment
desadeudar *tr* to free of debt || *ref* to get out of debt
desadormecer §22 *tr* to awaken; to free of numbness || *ref* to get awake; to shake off the numbness
desadorna•do -da *adj* unadorned, plain; bare, uncovered
desadverti•do -da *adj* unnoticed; inattentive
desadvertimiento *m* inadvertence
desafección *f* dislike
desafec•to -ta *adj* adverse, hostile; opposed || *m* dislike
desaferrar *tr* to unfasten, loosen; to make (*a person*) change his mind; (*las áncoras*) to weigh
desafiar §77 *tr* to challenge, defy, dare; to rival, compete with
desafición *f* dislike
desaficionar *tr* to cause to dislike
desafilar *tr* to make dull || *ref* to become dull
desafina•do -da *adj* flat, out of tune
desafío *m* challenge, dare; rivalry, competition
desafora•do -da *adj* colossal, huge; disorderly, outrageous
desafortuna•do -da *adj* unfortunate
desafuero *m* excess, outrage
desagracia•do -da *adj* ungraceful, graceless
desagradable *adj* disagreeable
desagradar *tr & intr* to displease || *ref* to be displeased
desagradeci•do -da *adj* ungrateful
desagradecimiento *m* ungratefulness
desagrado *m* displeasure
desagraviar *tr* to make amends to, to indemnify
desagravio *m* amends, indemnification
desagregación *f* disintegration
desagregar §44 *ref* to disintegrate
desaguadero *m* drain, outlet; (*ocasión de continuo gasto*) (fig) drain
desaguar §10 *tr* to drain, empty; to

squander, waste || *intr* to flow, empty || *ref* to drain, be drained
desagüe *m* drainage, sewerage; drain, outlet
desaguisa•do -da *adj* illegal || *m* offense, outrage, wrong
desahijar *tr* (*las crías del ganado*) to wean || *ref* (*las abejas*) to swarm
desahogadamente *adv* freely; comfortably, easily; impudently
desahoga•do -da *adj* brazen, forward; roomy; in comfortable circumstances
desahogar §44 *tr* to relieve, comfort; (*deseos, pasiones*) to give free rein to || *ref* to take it easy, get comfortable; to unbosom oneself, open up one's heart; to get out of debt; **desahogarse en** (*denuestos*) to burst forth in
desahogo *m* brazenness; ample room; comfort; outlet, relief; comfortable circumstances
desahuciar *tr* to deprive of hope; to evict, oust, dispossess || *ref* to lose all hope
desahucio *m* eviction, ousting, dispossession
desaira•do -da *adj* unattractive, unprepossessing; unsuccessful
desairar *tr* to slight, snub, disregard
desaire *m* slight, snub, disregard; unattractiveness, lack of charm
desajustar *tr* to put out of order || *ref* to get out of order; to disagree
desalabanza *f* belittling, disparagement
desalabar *tr* to belittle, disparage
desala•do -da *adj* eager, in a hurry
desalar *tr* to desalt; to clip the wings of || *ref* to hasten, rush; **desalarse por** to be eager to
desalentar §2 *tr* to put out of breath; to discourage || *ref* to become discouraged
desalforjar *ref* to loosen one's clothing
desaliento *m* discouragement
desalinización *f* desalinization
desaliña•do -da *adj* slovenly, untidy; careless, slipshod
desaliño *m* slovenliness, untidiness; carelessness, neglect
desalma•do -da *adj* cruel, inhuman
desalojar *tr* to oust, evict; (*al enemigo*) to dislodge; (*el camino*) to clear || *intr* to leave, move away, move out
desalquila•do -da *adj* vacant, unrented
desalterar *tr* to calm, quiet
desalumbra•do -da *adj* dazzled, blinded; confused, unsure of oneself
desamable *adj* unlikeable, unlovable
desamar *tr* to dislike, hate, detest
desamarrar *tr* to untie, unfasten; (naut) to unmoor
desamistar *ref* to fall out, become estranged
desamor *m* dislike, coldness; hatred
desamorrar *tr* to make (*a person*) talk
desamparar *tr* to abandon, forsake; to give up
desamparo *m* abandonment, desertion; helplessness
desamuebla•do -da *adj* unfurnished
desandar §5 *tr* to retrace, go back over
desandraja•do -da *adj* ragged, in tatters
desangrar *tr* to bleed; to drain; (fig) to bleed, impoverish || *ref* to lose a lot of blood
desanimación *f* discouragement, downheartedness
desanima•do -da *adj* discouraged, downhearted; (*reunión*) lifeless, dull
desanimar *tr* to discourage, dishearten || *ref* to become discouraged
desánimo *m* discouragement
desanublar *tr & ref* to clear up, brighten up
desanudar *tr* to untie; to disentangle
desapacible *adj* unpleasant, disagreeable
desapadrinar *tr* to disavow; to disapprove
desaparecer §22 *intr & ref* to disappear
desapareci•do -da *adj* missing; extinct || **desaparecidos** *mpl* missing persons
desaparecimiento *m* disappearance
desaparejar *tr* to unharness, unhitch; (naut) to unrig
desaparición *f* disappearance; (Ven) death
desapasiona•do -da *adj* dispassionate, impartial
desapego *m* dislike, coolness, indifference
desapercibi•do -da *adj* unprepared; wanting; unnoticed
desapiada•do -da *adj* merciless, pitiless
desaplica•do -da *adj* idle, lazy
desapodera•do -da *adj* headlong, impetuous; violent, wild; excessive
desapoderar *tr* to dispossess; to deprive of power || *ref* — **desapoderarse de** to lose possession of, give up possession of
desapolillar *tr* to free of moths || *ref* (coll) to expose oneself to the weather
desapreciar *tr* to depreciate
desaprecio *m* depreciation
desaprender *tr* to unlearn
desaprensión *f* composure, nonchalance
desapretar §2 *tr* to slacken, loosen; (typ) to unlock
desaprobación *f* disapproval
desaprobar §61 *tr & intr* to disapprove
desapropiar *tr* to divest || *ref* — **desapropiarse de** to divest oneself of
desaprovecha•do -da *adj* unproductive; indifferent, lackadaisical
desaprovechar *tr* to not take advantage of || *intr* to slip back
desarmable *adj* dismountable
desarmador *m* hammer (*of gun*); (Mex) screwdriver
desarmar *tr* to disarm; to dismount, dismantle, take apart; (*la cólera*) to temper, calm || *intr & ref* to disarm
desarme *m* disarmament; dismantling, dismounting
desarraigar §44 *tr* to uproot, dig up; to expel, drive out
desarregla•do -da *adj* out of order; slovenly, disorderly; intemperate
desarrollar *tr & intr* to develop; to unroll, unfold || *ref* to develop; to unroll, unfold; to take place
desarrollo *m* development; unrolling, unfolding
desarropar *tr & ref* to undress
desarrugar §44 *tr & ref* to unwrinkle

desarzonar *tr* to unsaddle, unhorse
desasea•do -da *adj* dirty, unclean, slovenly
desasentar §2 *tr* to remove; to displease || *ref* to stand up
desaseo *m* dirtiness, uncleanliness, slovenliness
desasir §7 *tr* to let go, let go of || *ref* to come loose; to let go; **desasirse de** to let go of; to give up, get free of
desasosegar §66 *tr* to disquiet, worry, disturb
desasosiego *m* disquiet, worry
desastra•do -da *adj* disastrous; unfortunate, wretched; ragged, shabby
desastre *m* disaster; **ir al desastre** to go to rack and ruin
desastro•so -sa *adj* disastrous
desatacar §73 *tr* to unbuckle, untie
desatar *tr* to untie, undo, unfasten; to solve, unravel || *ref* to come loose; to free oneself; (*la tempestad*) to break loose; to forget oneself, go too far; **desatarse en** (*denuestos*) to burst forth in
desatascar §73 *tr* to pull out of the mud; (*un conducto obstruído*) to unclog; (*a una persona de un apuro*) to extricate
desataviar §77 *tr* to disarray, undress
desatavío *m* disarray, undress, slovenliness
desate *m* (*de palabras*) flood; **desate del vientre** loose bowels
desatención *f* inattention; discourtesy, disrespect
desatender §51 *tr* to slight, disregard, pay no attention to
desatenta•do -da *adj* wild, disorderly, extreme
desaten•to -ta *adj* inattentive; discourteous, disrespectful
desatina•do -da *adj* wild, disorderly; foolish, nonsensical || *mf* fool
desatinar *tr* to bewilder, confuse || *intr* to talk nonsense, to act foolishly; to lose one's bearings
desatino *m* folly, nonsense; awkwardness, loss of touch
desatolondrar *tr* to bring to || *ref* to come to one's senses
desatollar *tr* to pull out of the mud
desatornillar *tr* to unscrew
desatraillar §4 *tr* to unleash
desatrampar *tr* to unclog
desatrancar §73 *tr* to unbar, unbolt; to unclog
desatufar *ref* to get out of the close air; to cool off, quiet down
desautoriza•do -da *adj* unauthorized
desavenencia *f* disagreement, discord
desavenir §79 *tr* to cause disagreement among || *ref* to disagree; **desavenirse con** to differ with, disagree with
desaventura *f* misfortune
desaviar §77 *tr* to mislead, lead astray
desayuna•do -da *adj* — **estar desayunado** to have had breakfast
desayunar *intr* to breakfast || *ref* to breakfast; **desayunarse con** to have breakfast on; **desayunarse de** to get the first news of
desayuno *m* breakfast
desazón *f* insipidity, tastelessness; annoyance, displeasure; discomfort
desazonar *tr* to make tasteless; to annoy, displease || *ref* to feel ill
desbancar §73 *tr* to win the bank from; to cut out, to supplant
desbandada *f* — **a la desbandada** helter-skelter, in confusion
desbandar *ref* to run away; to disband; to desert
desbarajustar *tr* to put out of order || *ref* to get out of order, break down
desbarata•do -da *adj* (coll) debauched, corrupt || *mf* (coll) libertine
desbaratar *tr* to destroy, spoil, ruin; to squander, waste; (mil) to rout, throw into confusion || *intr* to talk nonsense || *ref* to be unbalanced
desbarrancadero *m* (Am) precipice
desbastar *tr* to smooth off; to waste, weaken; (*a una persona inculta*) to polish || *ref* to become polished
desbautizar §60 *ref* (coll) to lose one's temper
desbeber *intr* (coll) to urinate
desbloquear *tr* to relieve the blockade of; (*crédito*) to unfreeze
desboca•do -da *adj* (*pieza de artillería*) wide-mouthed; (*herramienta*) nicked; (*caballo*) runaway; (*persona*) (coll) foul-mouthed
desbocar §73 *tr* to break the mouth of, break the spout of || *intr* (*un río*) to empty; (*una calle*) to run, open, end || *ref* (*un caballo*) to run away, to break loose; to curse, swear
desbordamiento *m* overflow
desbordar *tr* to overwhelm || *intr & ref* to overflow
desbozalar *tr* to unmuzzle
desbravar *tr* to tame, break in || *intr & ref* to abate, moderate; to cool off, calm down
desbrozar §60 *tr* to clear of underbrush, to clear of rubbish
desbulla *f* oyster shell
desbulla•dor -dora *mf* oyster opener || *m* oyster fork
desbullar *tr* (*la ostra*) to open
descabal *adj* incomplete, imperfect
descabalgar §44 *intr* to dismount, alight from a horse
descabella•do -da *adj* disheveled; rash, wild
descabellar *tr* to muss, dishevel
descabeza•do -da *adj* crazy, rash, wild
descabezar §60 *tr* to behead; (*un árbol*) to top; (*una dificultad*) (coll) to get the best off; **descabezar el sueño** to doze, snooze || *intr* to border || *ref* to rack one's brains
descabullir §13 *ref* to sneak out, slip away; to refuse to face the facts
descacharra•do -da *adj* (CAm) dirty, slovenly, ragged
descaecer §22 *intr* to decline, lose ground
descaecimiento *m* weakness; depression, despondency
descalabazar §60 *ref* (coll) to rack one's brain
descalabra•do -da *adj* banged on the

head; **salir descalabrado** to come out the loser, to be worsted

descalabrar *tr* to bang on the head; to knock down || *ref* to bang one's head

descalabro *m* misfortune, setback, loss

descalificar **§73** *tr* to disqualify

descalzar **§60** *tr* (*las botas, los guantes*) to take off; (*a una persona*) to take the shoes or stockings off; to undermine || *ref* to take one's shoes or stockings off; to take one's gloves off; (*las botas, los guantes*) to take off; (*el caballo*) to lose a shoe

descal•zo -za *adj* barefooted; seedy, down at the heel

descamar *ref* to scale, scale off

descaminadamente *adv* off the road, on the wrong track

descaminar *tr* to mislead, lead astray || *ref* to get lost; to run off the road

descamino *m* going astray; leading astray; nonsense; contraband, smuggled goods

descamisa•do -da *adj* shirtless, ragged || *m* wretch, ragamuffin

descampa•do -da *adj* free, open || *m* open country

descansadero *m* resting place, stopping place

descansa•do -da *adj* rested, refreshed; calm, restful

descansar *tr* to rest, relieve; (*la cabeza, el brazo*) to rest, lean || *intr* to rest; to lean; to not worry; (*yacer en el sepulcro*) to rest; **descansar en** to trust in

descanso *m* rest; peace, quiet; (*de la escalera*) landing; (theat) intermission; (Chile) toilet

descantillar *tr* to chip off; to deduct

descañonar *tr* to pluck; to shave against the grain; (coll) to gyp

descapiruzar **§60** *tr* (Col) to muss, rumple, crumple

descapotable *adj & m* (aut) convertible

descara•do -da *adj* barefaced, brazen, saucy

descarar *ref* to be impudent; **descararse a** to have the nerve to

descarga *f* unloading; (*de un arma de fuego*) discharge; (com) discount; (elec) discharge; **descarga de aduana** customhouse clearance

descargar **§44** *tr* to unload; (*de una deuda u obligación*) to free; (*un arma de fuego*) to discharge; (*un golpe*) to strike, to deal; (elec) to discharge || *intr* to unload; (*un río*) to empty; (*una calle, paseo*) to open; (*una nube en lluvia*) to burst || *ref* to unburden oneself; to resign; **descargarse con** or **en uno de algo** to unload something on someone; **descargarse de** to get rid of; to resign from; (*una imputación, un cargo*) to clear oneself of

descargo *m* unloading; (*de una obligación*) discharge; (*del cargo que se hace a uno*) release, acquittal; receipt

descargue *m* unloading

descariño *m* coolness, indifference

descarnadamente *adv* right off the shoulder, bluntly

descarnar *tr* to remove the flesh from; to chip; to wear away; to detach from earthly matters || *ref* to lose flesh

descaro *m* brazenness, effrontery

descarriar **§77** *tr* to mislead, to lead astray || *ref* to go wrong, to go astray

descarrilamiento *m* derailment

descarrilar *intr* to jump the track; (coll) to wander from the point || *ref* to jump the track

descartable *adj* disposable

descartar *tr* to cast aside, reject; to discard || *ref* to shirk, evade; **descartarse de** (*un compromiso*) to shirk, evade

descarte *m* casting aside, rejection; discarding; (*cartas desechadas*) discard; shirking, evasion

descasar *tr* to divorce; to disturb, disarrange

descascar **§73** *tr* to husk, shell, peel || *ref* to break to pieces; to jabber, talk too much

descascarar *tr* to shell, peel || *ref* to shell off, peel off

descascarillar *tr & ref* to shell, peel

descasta•do -da *adj* ungrateful, ungrateful to one's family

descaudala•do -da *adj* ruined, penniless

descendencia *f* descent

descendente *adj* descendent, descending; (*tren*) down

descender **§51** *tr* to bring down, lower; (*la escalera*) to descend, to go down || *intr* to descend, go down; to flow, run; to decline

descendiente *mf* descendant

descenso *m* descent; (*de temperatura*) drop; decline

descentralizar **§60** *tr* to decentralize

desceñi•do -da *adj* loose-fitting, loose

descepar *tr* to pull up by the roots; to extirpate, exterminate

descerebrar *tr* to brain

descerraja•do -da *adj* (coll) corrupt, evil, wicked

descifrar *tr* to decipher, to decode, to figure out

desclasificar **§73** *tr* to disqualify

descocer **§16** *tr* to digest

descoco *m* (coll) impudence, insolence

descocholla•do -da *adj* (Chile) ragged

descolar *tr* to dock, crop; (*a un empleado*) (CAm) to discharge, fire; (Mex) to slight, snub

descolgar **§63** *tr* to unhook; to take down, lower; (*el auricular*) to pick up || *ref* to come down, come off; to show up suddenly; **descolgarse con** (coll) to blurt out

descolón *m* (Mex) slight, snub

descolorar *tr & ref* to discolor, to fade

descolori•do -da *adj* faded, off color

descollante *adj* prominent, outstanding; chief, main

descollar **§61** *intr* to tower, stand out; (fig) to excel, stand out

descomedi•do -da *adj* immoderate, excessive; rude, discourteous

descomedir **§50** *ref* to be rude, be discourteous

descomer *intr* to have a bowel movement

descómo•do -da *adj* inconvenient
descompasa•do -da *adj* extreme, excessive
descompletar *tr* to break (*a set or series*)
descomponer **§54** *tr* to decompose; to disturb, disorganize; to put out of order; to set at odds || *ref* to decompose; (*una persona, la salud de una persona*) to fall to pieces; (*el tiempo*) to change for the worse; (*el rostro*) to become distorted; (*un aparato*) to get out of order; to lose one's temper; **descomponerse con** to get angry with
descomposición *f* decomposition; disorder, disorganization; discord
descompostura *f* decomposition; disorder, untidiness; brazenness
descompresión *f* decompression
descompues•to -ta *adj* out of order; brazen, discourteous; irritated; (Am) drunk
descomulgar **§44** *tr* to excommunicate
descomunal *adj* huge, colossal, enormous, extraordinary
desconcerta•do -da *adj* out of order; disconcerted, baffled, bewildered; slovenly; unbridled
desconcertar **§2** *tr* to put out of order; to disturb, upset; (*un hueso*) to dislocate; to disconcert, bewilder
desconcierto *m* disrepair; disorder; mismanagement; confusion; discomfiture; disagreement; lack of restraint; loose bowels
desconchabar *tr* (Am) to dislocate || *ref* (Am) to become dislocated; (Am) to disagree, fall out
desconchado *m* scaly part of wall; (*en la porcelana*) chip
desconchar *tr & ref* to chip, chip off; to scale off
desconectar *tr* to detach; to disconnect
desconfia•do -da *adj* distrustful, suspicious
desconfianza *f* distrust
desconfiar **§77** *intr* to lose confidence; **desconfiar de** to lose confidence in, to distrust
desconformar *intr* to dissent, disagree || *ref* to not go well together
descongelar *tr* to melt; to defrost; (com) to unfreeze
desconocer **§22** *tr* to not know; to disavow, disown; to not recognize; to slight, ignore; to not see || *ref* to be unknown; to be quite changed, be unrecognizable
desconocidamente *adv* unknowingly
desconoci•do -da *adj* unknown; strange, unfamiliar; ungrateful || *mf* unknown, unknown person
desconsentir **§68** *tr* to not consent to
desconsidera•do -da *adj* ill-considered; inconsiderate
desconsola•do -da *adj* disconsolate, downhearted; (*estómago*) weak
desconsuelo *m* disconsolateness, grief; upset stomach
descontaminación *f* decontamination
descontar **§61** *tr* to discount; to deduct; to take for granted; **dar por descontado que** to take for granted that
descontentadi•zo -za *adj* hard to please
desconten•to -ta *adj & m* discontent
descontinuar **§21** *tr* to discontinue
desconvenir **§79** *intr* to disagree; to not go together, to not match; to not be suitable || *ref* to disagree
desconvidar *tr* to cancel an invitation to; (*lo prometido*) to take back
descopar *tr* to top (*a tree*)
descorazonar *tr* to discourage
descorchar *tr* to remove the bark from; (*una botella*) to uncork; to break into
descornar **§61** *tr* to dehorn || *ref* (coll) to rack one's brains
descorrer *tr* to run back over; (*una cortina, un cerrojo*) to draw || *intr & ref* to flow, run off
descortés *adj* discourteous, impolite
descortesía *f* discourtesy, impoliteness
descortezar **§60** *tr* to strip the bark from; to take the crust off; (coll) to polish || *ref* (coll) to become polished
descoser *tr* to unstitch, to rip || *ref* to loose one's tongue; (coll) to break wind
descosi•do -da *adj* disorderly, wild; indiscreet; desultory || *m* wild man; rip, open seam
descote *m* low neck
descoyuntar *tr* to dislocate; to bore, annoy || *ref* (*p.ej., el brazo*) to throw out of joint
descrédito *m* discredit
descreer **§43** *tr* to disbelieve; to discredit || *intr* to disbelieve
descreí•do -da *adj* disbelieving, unbelieving || *mf* disbeliever, unbeliever
descriar **§77** *ref* to spoil; to waste away
describir **§83** *tr* to describe
descripción *f* description
descripti•vo -va *adj* descriptive
descto. *abbr* **descuento**
descuadrar *intr* to disagree; **descuadrar con** (Mex) to displease
descuajar *tr* to liquefy, dissolve; to uproot; to discourage || *ref* to liquefy; to drudge
descuartizar **§60** *tr* to tear to pieces; to quarter
descubierta *f* open pie; inspection; reconnoitering; (naut) scanning the horizon; **a la descubierta** openly; in the open; reconnoitering
descubiertamente *adv* clearly, openly
descubier•to -ta *adj* bareheaded; (*campo*) bare, barren; (*expuesto a reconvenciones*) under fire || *m* deficiency, shortage; exposition of the Holy Sacrament; **al descubierto** in the open; unprotected; (*sin tener disponibles las acciones que se venden*) short, e.g., **vender al descubierto** to sell short || *f* see **descubierta**
descubri•dor -dora *mf* discoverer || *m* (mil) scout
descubrimiento *m* discovery
descubrir **§83** *tr* to discover; to uncover, lay open, reveal; to invent; (*p.ej., una estatua*) to unveil || *ref* to take off one's hat, uncover; to be discovered; to open one's heart

descuello *m* excellence, superiority; great height; haughtiness
descuento *m* discount; deduction, rebate
descuerar *tr* (Chile) to skin, flay; (Chile) to discredit, flay
descuerno *m* (coll) slight, snub
descuida·do -da *adj* careless, negligent; slovenly, dirty; off guard
descuidar *tr* to overlook, neglect; to divert, distract, relieve || *ref* to be careless, not bother; to be diverted
descuide·ro -ra *mf* sneak thief
descuido *m* carelessness, negligence, neglect; slip, mistake, blunder; oversight; **al descuido** with studied carelessness; **en un descuido** (Am) when least expected
descuita·do -da *adj* carefree
desde *prep* since, from; after; **desde ahora** from now on; **desde entonces** since then, ever since; **desde hace** for, e.g., **estoy aquí desde hace cinco días** I've been here for five days; **desde luego** at once; of course; **desde que** since
desdecir §24 *intr* to slip back; to be out of harmony || *ref* — **desdecirse de** to take back, retract
desdén *m* scorn, disdain; **al desdén** with studied neglect
desdenta·do -da *adj* toothless
desdeñar *tr* to scorn, disdain || *ref* to be disdainful; **desdeñarse de** to loathe, despise; to not deign to
desdeño·so -sa *adj* scornful, disdainful
desdicha *f* misfortune; indigence
desdicha·do -da *adj* unfortunate, unlucky; poor, wretched; (coll) backward, timid
desdinerar *tr* to impoverish
desdoblar *tr & intr* to unfold, spread open; to split, divide
desdorar *tr* to remove the gold or gilt from; to tarnish, sully; to disparage
desdoro *m* tarnish, blemish, blot; disparagement
deseable *adj* desirable
desear *tr* to desire, wish
desecar §73 *tr & ref* to dry; to drain
desechable *adj* disposable
desechar *tr* to discard, to throw out, to cast aside; to underrate; to blame, censure; (*la llave de una puerta*) to turn
desecho *m* remainder; offal, rubbish; castoff; scorn, contempt; (Am) short cut; **desecho de hierro** scrap iron
desegregación *f* desegregation
desellar *tr* to unseal
desembalaje *m* unpacking
desembalar *tr* to unpack
desembarazar §60 *tr* to free, clear, empty, open || *ref* to free oneself; to be cleared, be emptied; **desembarazarse de** to get rid of
desembarazo *m* naturalness, lack of restraint; (Am) delivery, childbirth; **con desembarazo** naturally, readily
desembarcadero *m* wharf, pier, landing
desembarcar §73 *tr* to unload, debark, disembark || *intr* to land, debark, disembark; (*de un carruaje*) to get out, alight; (*la escalera al plano bajo*) to end || *ref* to land, debark, disembark
desembarco *m* landing, debarkation, disembarkation; (*de la escalera*) landing
desembarque *m* unloading, debarkation, disembarkation
desembocadura *f* (*de una calle*) opening, outlet; (*de un río*) mouth
desembocar §73 *intr* (*una calle*) open, to end; (*un río*) to flow, empty
desembolsar *tr* to disburse, pay out
desembolso *m* disbursement, payment
desembragar §44 *tr* (*el motor*) to disengage || *intr* to throw the clutch out
desembrague *m* disengagement, clutch release
desembravecer §22 *tr* to tame; to calm, quiet, pacify
desembriagar §44 *tr & ref* to sober up
desembrollar *tr* to untangle, unravel
desemejante *adj* — **desemejante de** dissimilar from or to, unlike; **desemejantes** dissimilar, unlike
desemejar *tr* to change, disfigure || *intr* to be different, not look alike
desempacar §73 *tr* to unpack, unwrap || *ref* to cool off, calm down
desempalagar §44 *tr* to rid of nausea || *ref* to get rid of nausea
desempañar *tr* (*el vidrio*) to wipe the steam or smear from; to take the diaper off
desempapelar *tr* to unwrap; (*una pared, una habitación*) to scrape the wallpaper from
desempaquetar *tr* to unpack; to unwrap
desempatar *tr* to break the tie between; (*los votos*) to break the tie in
desempate *m* breaking a tie
desempedrar §2 *tr* to remove the paving stones from; (*un sitio empedrado*) (coll) to pound; **ir desempedrando la calle** (coll) to dash down the street
desempeñar *tr* (*un papel*) to play (*a rôle*); (*un cargo*) to fill, perform; (*a uno de un empeño*) to disengage; (*un deber*) to discharge; to free of debt; to take out of hock || *ref* to get out of a jam; to get out of debt
desempeño *m* acting, performance; disengagement; (*de un deber*) discharge; payment of a debt; taking out of hock
desempernar *tr* to unbolt
desemplea·do -da *adj & mf* unemployed
desempleo *m* unemployment
desempolvar *tr* to dust; to renew, take up again || *ref* to brush up
desempolvorar *tr* to dust, dust off
desencadenar *tr* to unchain, unleash || *ref* to break loose
desencajar *tr* to dislocate; to disconnect || *ref* to get out of joint; (*el rostro*) to be contorted
desencaminar *tr* to lead astray, mislead
desencantamiento *m* disenchantment, disillusion
desencantar *tr* to disenchant, disillusion
desencantarar *tr* (*nombres o números*) to draw; (*un nombre o nombres*) to exclude from balloting

desencanto *m* disenchantment, disillusion
desencarecer §22 *tr* to lower the price of || *intr & ref* to come down in price
desencerrar §2 *tr* to release, set free; to disclose, reveal
desencoger §17 *tr* to unfold, spread out || *ref* to relax, shake off one's timidity
desencolar *tr* to unglue || *ref* to become unglued
desenconar *tr* to take the soreness out of; to calm down
desenchufar *tr* to unplug, to disconnect
desendiosar *tr* to bring down a peg
desenfadaderas *fpl* — **tener buenas desenfadaderas** (coll) to be resourceful
desenfada•do -da *adj* free, easy, unconstrained
desenfado *m* ease, naturalness; relaxation, calmness
desenfoca•do -da *adj* out of focus
desenfrena•do -da *adj* unbridled, wanton, licentious
desenfrenar *tr* to unbridle || *ref* to yield to temptation; to fly into a passion; (*la tempestad, el viento*) to break loose
desenfreno *m* unruliness, wantonness, licentiousness
desenfundar *tr* to take out of its sheath, bag, pillowcase, etc.
desenganchar *tr* to unhook, uncouple, unfasten, disengage; to unhitch
desenganche *m* unhooking, disengaging; unhitching
desengañar *tr* to disabuse, undeceive; to disillusion; to disappoint
desengaño *m* disabusing; disillusionment; disappointment; plain fact, plain truth
desengrana•do -da *adj* out of gear
desengranar *tr* to unmesh; to disengage, throw out of gear
desengraso *m* (Chile) dessert
desenlace *m* outcome, result; (*de un drama, novela, etc.*) dénouement
desenlazar §60 *tr* to untie; to solve; (*el nudo de un drama*) to unravel
desenmarañar *tr* to disentangle; (*una cosa obscura*) to unravel
desenmascarar *tr* to unmask || *ref* to take one's mask off
desenojar *tr* to appease, to free of anger || *ref* to calm down; to be amused
desenredar *tr* to disentangle; to clear up || *ref* to extricate oneself
desenredo *m* disentanglement; (*de un drama, novela, etc.*) dénouement
desenrollar *tr* to unroll, unwind, unreel
desensartar *tr* to unstring, unthread
desensillar *tr* to unsaddle (*a horse*)
desentablar *tr* to disrupt; to break off (*a bargain, friendship, etc.*)
desentender §51 *ref* — **desentenderse de** to take no part in, to not participate in; to affect ignorance of, pretend to be unaware of
desenterrar §2 *tr* to dig up; to disinter; (fig) to unearth, dig up; (fig) to recall to mind
desentona•do -da *adj* out of tune, flat
desentonar *tr* to humble, bring down a peg || *intr* to be out of tune; to be out of harmony || *ref* to talk loud and disrespectfully
desentono *m* dissonance, false note; loud tone of voice
desentornillar *tr* to unscrew
desentrampar *ref* (coll) to get out of debt
desentrañar *tr* to disembowel; to figure out, unravel || *ref* to give away all that one has
desentrena•do -da *adj* out of training
desentronizar §60 *tr* to dethrone; to strip of influence
desentumecer §22 *tr* to relieve of numbness || *ref* to be relieved of numbness
desenvainar *tr* to unsheathe; (*las uñas el animal*) to show, stretch out; (coll) to bare, uncover, show
desenvoltura *f* naturalness, ease of manner, offhandedness; fluency; lewdness, boldness (*chiefly in women*)
desenvolver §47 & §83 *tr* to unfold, unroll, unwrap; to unwind; to unravel, clear up; to develop || *ref* to unroll; to unwind; to develop, evolve; to extricate oneself; to be forward
desenvuel•to -ta *adj* free and easy, offhand; fluent; brazen, bold, lewd
deseo *m* desire, wish
deseo•so -sa *adj* desirous, anxious
desequilibra•do -da *adj* unbalanced
desequilibrar *tr* to unbalance || *ref* to become unbalanced
desequilibrio *m* disequilibrium, imbalance; derangement, mental instability
deserción *f* desertion
desertar *tr & intr* to desert
desertor *m* deserter
deservicio *m* disservice
desesperación *f* despair; **ser una desesperación** to be unbearable
desespera•do -da *adj* despairing, desperate || *mf* desperate person
desesperanza *f* hopelessness
desesperanza•do -da *adj* hopeless
desesperanzar §60 *tr* to discourage || *ref* to lose hope
desesperar *tr* to drive to despair; (coll) to exasperate || *intr* to lose hope; (coll) to be exasperated || *ref* to be desperate, lose all hope
desestancar §73 *tr* to open up, to unclog; to make free of duty; to open the market to
desestimar *tr* to hold in low regard; to refuse, reject
deséxito *m* failure
desfachata•do -da *adj* (coll) brazen, impudent
desfachatez *f* (coll) brazenness, impudence
desfalcar §73 *tr & intr* to embezzle
desfalco *m* embezzlement
desfallecer §22 *tr* to weaken || *intr* to grow weak; to faint, faint away; to lose courage
desfalleci•do -da *adj* weak; faint
desfallecimiento *m* weakness; fainting; discouragement
desfavorable *adj* unfavorable
desfigurar *tr* to disfigure; to distort,

misrepresent; to disguise; to change, alter || *ref* to look different
desfiladero *m* defile, pass
desfilar *intr* to defile, parade, file by
desfile *m* review, parade
desflorar *tr* to deflower; to mention in passing
desfogar §44 *tr* (*un horno*) to vent; (*la cal*) to slake; (*una pasión*) to give free rein to || *intr* (*una tempestad*) to break into rain and wind || *ref* to give vent to one's anger
desfondar *tr* to stave in; (*una nave*) to bilge; (agr) to trench-plow
desforestar *tr* to deforest
desgaire *m* slovenliness; disdain, scorn; **al desgaire** scornfully; carelessly, with affected carelessness
desgajar *tr* to tear off; to split off || *ref* to come off, to come loose; to arise, originate; to separate, break away
desgana *f* lack of appetite; indifference; boredom; **a desgana** unwillingly, reluctantly
desgarba·do -da *adj* ungainly, uncouth
desgarrar *tr* to tear, rend; (*la flema*) to cough up || *ref* to tear oneself away
desgarro *m* tear, rent; brazenness, effrontery; boasting, bragging; (Chile, Col) phlegm, mucus
desgastar *tr* to wear away, wear down; to weaken, spoil || *ref* to wear away; to grow weak, decline
desgaste *m* wear, wearing away
desgoberna·do -da *adj* ungovernable, uncontrollable
desgobernar §2 *tr* to misgovern; (*un hueso*) to dislocate || *intr* (naut) to steer poorly || *ref* to twist and turn in dancing
desgobierno *m* misgovernment; dislocation
desgonzar §60 *tr* to unhinge; to disconnect
desgracia *f* misfortune; (*acontecimiento adverso*) mishap; (*pérdida de favor*) disfavor, disgrace; (*aspereza en el trato*) gruffness; (*falta de gracia*) lack of charm; **correr con desgracia** to have no luck; **por desgracia** unfortunately
desgracia·do -da *adj* unfortunate; unattractive, unpleasant; disagreeable || *mf* wretch, unfortunate
desgraciar *tr* to displease; to spoil || *ref* to spoil; to fail; to fall out, to disagree
desgranar *tr* (*el maíz*) to shell; (*un racimo*) to pick the grapes from || *ref* (*piezas ensartadas*) to come loose
desgreñar *tr* to dishevel || *ref* to get disheveled; to pull each other's hair
deshabita·do -da *adj* unoccupied
deshabituar §21 *tr* to break of a habit
deshacer §39 *tr* to undo; to untie; to take apart; to wear away, consume, destroy; to melt; to put to flight, to rout; (*un tratado o negocio*) to violate || *ref* to get out of order; to vanish, disappear; **deshacerse de** to get rid of; **deshacerse en** (*cumplidos*) to lavish; (*lágrimas*) to burst into; **deshacerse por** to strive hard to
desharrapa·do -da *adj* ragged, in rags
deshebillar *tr* to unbuckle
deshebrar *tr* to unravel, unthread
deshecha *f* sham, pretense; dismissal; **hacer la deshecha** to feign, pretend; (Mex) to pretend lack of interest
deshelar §2 *tr* to thaw, melt; to defrost; (aer) to deice || *intr* to thaw, melt
deshereda·do -da *adj* disinherited; underprivileged
desheredar *tr* to disinherit || *ref* to be a disgrace to one's family
desherrar §2 *tr* to unchain, unshackle; (*a una caballería*) to unshoe
desherrumbrar *tr* to remove the rust from
deshidratar *tr* to dehydrate
deshielo *m* thaw, melting; defrosting
deshilachar *ref* to fray
deshila·do -da *adj* in a file; **a la deshilada** in single file; secretly || *m* openwork, drawn work
deshilar *tr* to unweave; (*reducir a hilos*) to shred || *ref* to fray; to get thin
deshilvana·do -da *adj* disconnected, desultory
deshincar §73 *tr* to pull up, to pull out
deshinchar *tr* to deflate; (*la cólera*) to give vent to || *ref* (*un tumor*) to go down; (*una persona orgullosa*) (coll) to become deflated
deshojar *tr* to strip of leaves; to tear the pages out of || *ref* to lose the leaves
deshollejar *tr* (*la uva*) to peel, skin; (*las habichuelas*) to shell
deshollina·dor -dora *mf* chimney sweep; (coll) curious observer || *m* long-handled brush or broom
deshones·to -ta *adj* immodest, indecent; improper
deshonor *m* dishonor; disgrace
deshonorar *tr* to dishonor; to degrade; to disfigure
deshonra *f* dishonor; disrespect; **tener a deshonra** to consider improper
deshonrabue·nos *mf* (*pl* **-nos**) (coll) slanderer; (coll) black sheep
deshonrar *tr* to disgrace; (*a una mujer*) to seduce; to insult
deshonro·so -sa *adj* disgraceful, improper, discreditable
deshora *f* wrong time; **a deshora** at the wrong time, inopportunely; suddenly, unexpectedly
deshuesar *tr* (*la carne de un animal*) to bone; (*la fruta*) to stone, to take the pits out of
deshumedecer §22 *tr* to dehumidify
desidia *f* laziness, indolence
desidio·so -sa *adj* lazy, indolent || *mf* lazy person
desier·to -ta *adj* desert; deserted || *m* desert; wilderness
designar *tr* to designate; (*un trabajo*) to plan
designio *m* design, plan, scheme
desigual *adj* unequal; unlike; rough, uneven; difficult; inconstant
desigualar *tr* to make unequal || *ref* to become unequal; (*aventajarse*) to get ahead

desigualdad *f* inequality; roughness, unevenness
desilusión *f* disillusionment; disappointment
desilusionar *tr* to disillusion; to disappoint || *ref* to become disillusioned; to be disappointed
desimanar or **desimantar** *tr* to demagnetize
desimpresionar *tr* to undeceive
desinclina•do -da *adj* disinclined
desinencia *f* (gram) termination, ending
desinfectante *adj & m* disinfectant
desinfectar or **desinficionar** *tr* to disinfect
desinflación *f* deflation
desinflamar *tr* to take the soreness out of
desinflar *tr* to deflate; to let the air out of; (*a una persona*) (coll) to deflate
desintegración *f* disintegration
desintegrar *tr & ref* to disintegrate
desinterés *m* disinterestedness
desinteresa•do -da *adj* (*imparcial*) disinterested; (*poco interesado*) uninterested
desinteresar *ref* to lose interest
desintonizar **§60** *tr* (rad) to tune out; (rad) to put out of tune
desistir *intr* to desist
desjarretar *tr* to hamstring; (coll) to bleed to excess
desjuicia•do -da *adj* lacking judgment, senseless
desjuntar *tr* to disjoin, separate
deslabonar *tr* to unlink; to disconnect || *ref* to come loose; to withdraw
deslastrar *tr* to unballast
deslava•do -da *adj* faded, colorless; barefaced || *mf* barefaced person
deslavar *tr* to wash superficially; to fade, to take the life out of
desleal *adj* disloyal; unfair
deslealtad *f* disloyalty
deslechar *tr* (Col) to milk
desleír **§58** *tr* to dissolve; to dilute; (*los colores, la pintura*) to thin; (*sus pensamientos*) to express too diffusely || *ref* to dissolve; to become diluted
deslengua•do -da *adj* foul-mouthed, shameless
desliar **§77** *tr* to untie, undo; to unravel || *ref* to come untied
desligar **§44** *tr* to untie, unbind; to disentangle; to excuse || *ref* to come untied, come loose
deslindar *tr* to mark the boundaries of; to distinguish; to define, explain
des•liz *m* (*pl* **-lices**) sliding; (*superficie lisa*) slide; slip, blunder; peccadillo, indiscretion
deslizade•ro -ra *adj* slippery || *m* slippery place; launching way
deslizadi•zo -za *adj* slippery
deslizador *m* (aer) glider
deslizar **§60** *tr* to slide; (*decir por descuido*) to let slip || *intr* to slide; to slip; to glide || *ref* to slide; to slip; to glide; to slip away, sneak away; (*un reparo*) to slip out; (*caer en una flaqueza*) to slide back, to backslide
deslomar *tr* to break or strain the back of || *ref* to break or strain one's back; **no deslomarse** (coll) to not strain oneself
desluci•do -da *adj* quiet, lackluster; dull, undistinguished
deslucir **§45** *tr* to tarnish; to deprive of charm, deprive of distinction; to discredit
deslumbramiento *m* dazzle, glare; bewilderment, confusion
deslumbrante *adj* dazzling; bewildering, confusing
deslumbrar *tr* to dazzle; to bewilder, confuse
deslustra•do -da *adj* dull, flat, dingy; (*vidrio*) ground, frosted
deslustrar *tr* to tarnish; to dull, dim; (*el vidrio*) to frost; to discredit || *ref* to tarnish
deslustre *m* tarnishing; dulling, dimming; discredit; (*del vidrio*) frosting
deslustro•so -sa *adj* ugly, unbecoming
desmadejar *tr* to enervate, weaken
desmagnetizar **§60** *tr* to demagnetize
desmán *m* excess, misconduct; misfortune, mishap
desmanchar *tr* (Chile) to clean of spots
desmanda•do -da *adj* disobedient, unruly
desmandar *tr* to cancel, countermand || *ref* to misbehave; to go away, keep apart; to get out of control
desmanear *tr* to unfetter, unshackle
desmantela•do -da *adj* dilapidated
desmantelar *tr* to dismantle; (naut) to unmast; (naut) to unrig
desmaña *f* awkwardness, clumsiness
desmaña•do -da *adj* awkward, clumsy
desmaya•do -da *adj* faint, languid, weak; unconscious; (*color*) dull
desmayar *tr* to depress, discourage || *intr* to lose heart, be discouraged; to falter || *ref* to faint
desmayo *m* depression, discouragement; faint, fainting fit; weeping willow
desmedi•do -da *adj* excessive; boundless, limitless
desmedir **§50** *ref* to go too far, be impudent
desmedra•do -da *adj* weak, run-down
desmedrar *tr* to impair || *intr & ref* to decline, deteriorate
desmejorar *tr* to impair, spoil || *intr & ref* to decline, go into a decline
desmelenar *tr* to muss, dishevel, rumple
desmembrar **§2** *tr* to dismember
desmemoria *f* forgetfulness
desmemoria•do -da *adj* forgetful
desmemoriar *ref* to become forgetful
desmentida *f* contradiction; **dar una desmentida a** to give the lie to
desmentir **§68** *tr* to belie, give the lie to; to conceal || *intr* to be out of line || *ref* to contradict oneself
desmenudear *tr & intr* (Col) to sell at retail
desmenuzar **§60** *tr* to crumble; to chop up; to examine in detail; to criticize harshly || *ref* to crumb, crumble
desmerece•dor -dora *adj* unworthy
desmerecer **§22** *tr* to be unworthy of || *intr* to decline in value; **desmerecer de** to compare unfavorably with
desmesura *f* excess, lack of restraint

desmesura•do -da *adj* excessive, disproportionate; insolent || *mf* insolent person
desmigajar *tr & ref* to crumble, break up
desmigar **§44** *tr & ref* to crumble, crumb
desmilitarizar **§60** *tr* to demilitarize
desmirria•do -da *adj* (coll) exhausted, emaciated, run-down
desmochar *tr* (*un árbol*) to top; (*al toro*) to dehorn; (*una obra artística*) to cut
desmodular *tr* to demodulate
desmola•do -da *adj* toothless
desmontable *adj* demountable
desmontar *tr* (*un terreno*) to level; (*un bosque*) to clear; to dismantle, dismount, take apart, knock down; (*las piezas de artillería del enemigo*) to knock out; (*al jinete el caballo*) to unhorse, to throw; (*un arma de fuego*) to uncock || *ref* to dismount, alight
desmoralizar **§60** *tr* to demoralize
desmoronadi•zo -za *adj* crumbly
desmoronar *tr* to wear away || *ref* to wear away; to crumble, decline
desmotadera *f* burler; **desmotadera de algodón** cotton gin
desmotar *tr* (*la lana*) to burl; (*el algodón*) to gin
desmovilizar **§60** *tr* to demobilize
desmurador *m* mouser
desnatadora *f* cream separator
desnatar *tr* to skim; to remove the slag from; to take the choicest part of
desnaturalizar **§60** *tr* to denaturalize; (*el alcohol*) to denature; to alter, pervert
desnivel *m* unevenness; difference of level
desnivelar *tr* to make uneven || *ref* to become uneven
desnudar *tr* to undress; to strip, lay bare; (*la espada*) to draw || *ref* to undress, get undressed; to become evident; **desnudarse de** to get rid of
desnudez *f* nakedness; bareness
desnu•do -da *adj* naked, nude; bare; destitute, penniless || **el desnudo** the nude
desnutrición *f* undernourishment, malnutrition
desnutri•do -da *adj* undernourished
desobedecer *tr & intr* to disobey
desobediencia *f* disobedience
desobediente *adj* disobedient
desocupación *f* unemployment; idleness, leisure
desocupa•do -da *adj* unemployed; idle; free, unoccupied, vacant, empty || *mf* unemployed person
desocupar *tr* to empty, vacate || *intr* (*una mujer*) (coll) to be delivered || *ref* to become empty, vacated; to become unemployed, become idle
desodorante *adj & m* deodorant
desodorizar **§60** *tr* to deodorize
desoír **§48** *tr* to not hear, to pretend not to hear
desolación *f* desolation
desola•do -da *adj* desolate, disconsolate
desolar **§61** *tr* to desolate, lay waste || *ref* to be desolate, be disconsolate
desoldar **§61** *tr* to unsolder || *ref* to come unsoldered
desolla•do -da *adj* (coll) brazen, impudent
desollar **§61** *tr* to skin, flay; to harm, hurt; **desollar vivo** (*hacer pagar mucho más de lo justo*) (coll) to fleece, to skin alive; (*murmurar acerbamente de*) (coll) to flay
desopilar *ref* to roar with laughter
desopinar *tr* to defame, discredit
desorbita•do -da *adj* (Am) popeyed; (Am) crazy
desorbitar *ref* to pop wide-open
desorden *m* disorder
desordena•do -da *adj* disorderly, unruly
desordenar *tr* to put out of order || *ref* to get out of order; to be unruly; to go too far
desoreja•do -da *adj* (coll) infamous, degraded; (*que canta mal*) (Peru) off tune; (Cuba) shameless; (Cuba) spendthrift, prodigal; (Guat) stupid; (Chile) without handles
desorganizar **§60** *tr* to disorganize
desorientar *tr* to lead astray; to confuse
desovar *intr* to spawn
desove *m* spawning; spawning season
desovillar *tr* to unravel, disentangle; to encourage
desoxidar *tr* to deoxidize; to clean of rust
despabiladeras *fpl* snuffers
despabila•do -da *adj* wide-awake
despabilar *tr* (*una candela*) to snuff, to trim; (*la hacienda*) to dissipate; (*una comida*) to dispatch; (*robar*) to snitch; (*matar*) to dispatch || *ref* to brighten up; to wake up; (Am) to leave, disappear
despacio *adv* slow, slowly; at leisure; (Arg, Chile) in a low voice
despacio•so -sa *adj* slow, easy-going
despachaderas *fpl* (coll) surly reply; (coll) resourcefulness
despacha•do -da *adj* (coll) brazen, impudent; (coll) quick, resourceful
despachante *m* (Arg) clerk; **despachante de aduana** (Arg) customhouse broker
despachar *tr* to send, to ship; to dispatch, expedite; to discharge, dismiss; to decide, settle; to sell; (*a los parroquianos*) to wait on; (*la correspondencia*) to attend to; to hurry; (*matar*) (coll) to dispatch, to kill || *intr* to hurry; to make up one's mind; to work, be employed || *ref* to hurry; (*una mujer*) to be delivered; to speak out
despacho *m* shipping; dispatch, expedition; discharge, dismissal; (*tienda*) store, shop; (*aposento para el estudio*) study; (*aposento para los negocios*) office; (*comunicación por telégrafo o teléfono*) dispatch; (Chile) attic; **despacho de billetes** ticket office; **despacho de localidades** box office; **estar al despacho** to be pending; **tener buen despacho** to be expeditious

despachurrar *tr* to crush, smash, squash; (*dejar sin tener que replicar*) (coll) to squelch; (*lo que uno trata de decir*) (coll) to butcher, murder
despampanante *adj* (coll) stunning, terrific
despampanar *tr* (*las vides*) to prune, to trim; (coll) to astound || *intr* (coll) to give vent to one's feelings || *ref* to fall and hurt oneself
despancar §73 *tr* to husk (*corn*)
desparejar *tr* (*dos cosas que forman pareja*) to break, separate (*a pair*)
desparpajar *tr* to tear apart || *intr* (coll) to rant, rave || *ref* (coll) to rant, rave; (CAm, Mex, W-I) to wake up
desparramar *tr* to scatter, spread; (*el agua*) to spill; (*la hacienda*) to squander || *ref* to scatter, spread; to make merry
despartir *tr* to divide, part, separate; to reconcile
despatarrada *f* (coll) split (*in dancing*); **hacer la despatarrada** (coll) to stretch out on the floor pretending to be ill or injured
despatarrar *tr* to dumbfound || *ref* (coll) to open one's legs wide, to fall down with legs outspread; (coll) to lie motionless; to be dumbfounded
despavori·do -da *adj* terrified
despea·do -da *adj* footsore
despear *ref* to get sore feet
despecti·vo -va *adj* contemptuous; (gram) pejorative
despecha·do -da *adj* spiteful, enraged
despechar *tr* to spite, enrage; (*destetar*) (coll) to wean || *ref* to be enraged; to despair, lose hope
despecho *m* spite; despair; (Am) weaning; **a despecho de** despite, in spite of; **por despecho** out of spite
despechugar §44 *tr* to carve the breast of || *ref* (coll) to go with bare breast, to bare one's breast
despedazar §60 *tr* to break to pieces; (*la honra de uno*) to ruin; (*el alma de una persona*) to break || *ref* to break to pieces; **despedazarse de risa** (coll) to split one's sides laughing
despedida *f* farewell, leave-taking; (*de una carta*) close, conclusion; (*copla final*) envoi
despedir §50 *tr* to throw; to emit, send forth; to discharge, dismiss; (*al que sale de la casa*) to see off; (*un mal pensamiento*) to banish; **despedir en la puerta** to see to the door || *ref* to take leave, say good-by; to give up one's job; **despedirse a la francesa** to take French leave; **despedirse de** to take leave of, say good-by to
despega·do -da *adj* (coll) gruff, surly
despegar §44 *tr* to loosen, unglue, unseal; to open; to separate, detach || *intr* (aer) to take off || *ref* to come off; **despegarse con** to be unbecoming to
despego *m* dislike, indifference
despegue *m* (aer) take-off
despeina·do -da *adj* unkempt
despeja·do -da *adj* (*frente*) wide; (*día, cielo*) clear, cloudless; bright, sprightly; (*en el trato*) unconstrained
despejar *tr* to clarify, explain; to free; (*una incógnita*) (math) to find || *ref* to brighten up, cheer up; (*el cielo, el tiempo; una situación dificultosa*) to clear up; (*un borracho*) to sober up
despejo *m* ease, naturalness; talent, intelligence, understanding
despeluzar §60 *tr* to muss the hair of; to make the hair of (*a person*) stand on end || *ref* (*el pelo*) to stand on end
despeluznante *adj* hair-raising, horrifying
despellejar *tr* to skin, flay; (coll) to slander, malign
despenar *tr* to console; (coll) to kill; (Chile) to deprive of hope
despender *tr* to spend, squander; (*el tiempo*) to waste
despensa *f* pantry; food supplies; day's marketing; stewardship; (naut) storeroom
despensero *m* butler, steward; (naut) storekeeper
despeñade·ro -ra *adj* precipitous || *m* precipice; danger, risk
despeñadi·zo -za *adj* precipitous
despeñar *tr* to hurl, throw, push || *ref* to hurl oneself, jump; to fall headlong; (*en vicios, pecados, pasiones*) to plunge downward
despeño *m* plunge; headlong fall; ruin, failure, collapse; (coll) loose bowels
despepitar *tr* to seed, remove the seeds from || *ref* to rush around madly, to go around screaming; **despepitarse por** (coll) to be mad about
desperdicia·do -da *adj* wasteful, prodigal || *mf* spendthrift, prodigal
desperdiciar *tr* to waste, squander; (*la ocasión de aprovechar una cosa*) to miss, to lose
desperdicio *m* waste, squandering; **desperdicios** waste; waste products; byproducts; rubbish; **no tener desperdicio** (coll) to be excellent, be useful
desperdigar §44 *tr* to separate, scatter
desperecer §22 *ref* to long eagerly
desperezar §60 *ref* to stretch, to stretch one's arms and legs
desperfecto *m* blemish, flaw, imperfection
desperna·do -da *adj* footsore, weary
desperta·dor -dora *mf* awakener || *m* alarm clock; warning
despertar §2 *tr* to awaken; to arouse, stir || *intr & ref* to awaken, wake up
despestañar *tr* to pluck the eyelashes of || *ref* to look hard, strain one's eyes
despiada·do -da *adj* cruel, pitiless
despichar *tr* to squeeze dry; (Col, Chile) to crush, flatten || *intr* (coll) to croak, die
despidiente *m* stick placed between a hanging scaffold and wall; **despidiente de agua** flashing
despido *m* layoff, discharge
despier·to -ta *adj* wide-awake, alert; **soñar despierto** to daydream
despilfarra·do -da *adj* wasteful; ragged || *mf* prodigal; raggedy person

despilfarrar *tr* to squander, waste || *ref* (coll) to spend recklessly
despilfarro *m* squandering, waste, extravagance; slovenliness
despintar *tr* to remove the paint from; to disfigure, distort, spoil; **no despintarle a uno los ojos** to not take one's eyes from a person || *intr* to decline, slip back; **despintar de** to be unworthy of || *ref* to fade, wash off; **no despintársele a uno** (coll) to not fade from one's memory
despiojar *tr* to delouse; (coll) to free from poverty
despique *m* revenge
despistar *tr* to outwit, to throw off the track || *ref* to run off the track, run off the road
desplacer *m* displeasure || §22 *tr* to displease
desplantar *tr* to uproot; to throw out of plumb || *ref* to get out of plumb; to lose one's upright posture
desplaya·do -da *adj* broad, open, wide || *m* (Arg) wide sandy beach
desplayar *tr* to widen, spread out || *ref* (*el mar*) to recede from the beach
desplaza·do -da *adj* displaced || *mf* displaced person
desplazar §60 *tr* (*cierto peso de agua*) to displace; to move, to transport || *ref* to move
desplegar §66 *tr* to unfold, spread; to display; to explain; (mil) to deploy || *ref* to unfold, spread out; (mil) to deploy
despliegue *m* unfolding, spreading out; display; (mil) deployment
desplomar *tr* to throw out of plumb || *ref* to get out of plumb; to collapse, tumble; to fall down in a faint; (*un trono*) to crumble; (aer) to pancake
desplome *m* leaning; collapse, tumbling; falling in a faint; downfall; (aer) pancaking
desplumar *tr* to pluck; (*dejar sin dinero*) (coll) to fleece || *ref* to molt
despoblado *m* wilderness, deserted spot
despoblar §61 *tr* to depopulate; to lay waste; to clear, lay bare
despojar *tr* to strip, despoil, divest; to dispossess || *ref* to undress; **despojarse de** to divest oneself of; (*ropa*) to take off
despojo *m* dispoilment; dispossession; booty, plunder, spoils; prey, victim; **despojos** scraps, leavings; mortal remains; second-hand building materials
despolarizar §60 *tr* to depolarize
despolvar *tr* to dust
despolvorear *tr* to dust, dust off; to scatter
desportillar *tr* to chip, nick || *ref* to chip, chip off
desposa·do -da *adj* handcuffed; newly married || *mf* newlywed
desposar *tr* to marry || *ref* to be betrothed, get engaged; to get married
desposeer §43 *tr* to dispossess || *ref* — **desposeerse de** to divest oneself of
desposorios *mpl* betrothal, engagement; marriage, nuptials
déspota *m* despot
despóti·co -ca *adj* despotic
despotismo *m* despotism
despotricar §73 *intr & ref* to rave, rant
despreciable *adj* contemptible, despicable
despreciar *tr* to scorn, despise; to slight, snub; to overlook, forgive; to reject || *ref* — **despreciarse de** to not deign to
despreciati·vo -va *adj* contemptuous, scornful
desprecio *m* scorn, contempt; slight, snub
desprender *tr* to loosen, unfasten, detach; to emit, give off; (chem) to liberate || *ref* to come loose, to come off; to issue, come forth; **desprenderse de** to give up, part with; to be deduced from
desprendi·do -da *adj* generous, disinterested
desprendimiento *m* loosening, detachment; emission, liberation; generosity, disinterestedness; landslide; (chem) liberation
despreocupación *f* relaxation; impartiality
despreocupa·do -da *adj* relaxed, unconcerned; impartial; indifferent
despreocupante *adj* relaxing
despreocupar *ref* to relax; **despreocuparse de** to forget about, be unconcerned about
desprestigiar *tr* to disparage, run down || *ref* to lose caste, lose one's standing, to lose face
desprestigio *m* disparagement; loss of standing, discredit
despreveni·do -da *adj* off one's guard; **coger a uno desprevenido** to catch someone unawares
desproporciona·do -da *adj* disproportionate
despropósito *m* absurdity, nonsense
desproveer §43 & §83 *tr* to deprive
desprovis·to -ta *adj* destitute; **desprovisto de** lacking, devoid of
después *adv* after, afterwards; **después de** after; **después (de) que** after
despuli·do -da *adj* ground (*glass*)
despumar *tr* to skim
despuntar *tr* to dull, blunt; (*un cabo o punta*) (naut) to double, round || *intr* to begin to sprout; (*empezar a amanecer*) to dawn; to stand out || *ref* to get dull
desquiciar *tr* to unhinge; to shake loose, upset; to unsettle, perturb; to overthrow, undermine
desquitar *tr* to recover, retrieve; to compensate || *ref* to retrieve a loss; to get revenge, get even
desquite *m* recovery, retrieval; retaliation, revenge; (sport) return match
desrazonable *adj* unreasonable
desrielar *intr* (Am) to jump the track
destaca·do -da *adj* outstanding, distinguished
destacamiento *m* (mil) detachment; (mil) detail
destacar §73 *tr* to highlight, point up; to emphasize; to make stand out;

(mil) to detach; (mil) to detail || *intr* to stand out, be conspicuous || *ref* to stand out, to project; (fig) to stand out

destajar *tr* to arrange for, establish the terms for; (*la baraja*) to cut; (Am) to carve up

destaje·ro -ra or **destajista** *mf* pieceworker, jobber; free lance

destajo *m* piecework; job, contract; **a destajo** by the piece, by the job; freelancing; **hablar a destajo** (coll) to talk too much

destapar *tr* to open, uncover, take the lid off; to uncock, unplug; to reveal || *ref* to get uncovered; to throw off the covers; to unbosom oneself

destaponar *tr* to uncock, unplug; (*una botella; las fosas nasales*) to unstop

destartala·do -da *adj* tumble-down, ramshackle

destazar §60 *tr* to carve up

destechar *tr* to unroof

destejar *tr* to remove the tiles from; to leave unprotected

destejer *tr* to unbraid, unknit, unweave; to upset, disturb

destellar *tr & intr* to flash

destello *m* flash, beam, sparkle

destempla·do -da *adj* disagreeable, unpleasant; inharmonious, out of tune; indisposed; (*clima; pulso*) irregular

destemplanza *f* unpleasantness; discord; indisposition; (*del pulso*) irregularity; (*del tiempo*) inclemency; excess

destemple *m* dissonance; indisposition; disorder, disturbance

desteñir §72 *tr* to discolor || *intr & ref* to fade

desternillante *adj* sidesplitting

desternillar *ref* — **desternillarse de risa** to split one's sides with laughter

desterra·do -da *adj* exiled || *mf* exile

desterrar §2 *tr* to exile, to banish; (fig) to banish

destetar *tr* to wean || *ref* — **destetarse con** to have known since childhood

destete *m* weaning

destiempo *m* — **a destiempo** untimely

destiento *m* surprise, shock

destierro *m* exile; backwoods

destilación *f* distillation

destiladera *f* still; scheme, stratagem

destilar *tr* to distill; to filter; to exude || *intr* to drip

destilatorio *m* distillery; (*alambique*) still

destilería *f* distillery

destinación *f* destination

destinar *tr* to destine; to assign, designate

destinata·rio -ria *mf* addressee; consignee; (*de homenaje, aplausos*) recipient

destino *m* (*lugar a donde va una persona o una remesa*) destination; (*suerte, encadenamiento fatal de los sucesos*) fate, destiny; employment; place of employment; **con destino a** bound for

destituir §20 *tr* to deprive; to dismiss, discharge

destorcer §74 *tr* to untwist, straighten || *ref* to become untwisted; (naut) to drift

destornilla·do -da *adj* rash, reckless, out of one's head

destornillador *m* screwdriver

destornillar *tr* to unscrew || *ref* to lose one's head, go berserk

destoser *ref* to cough (*artificially, to attract attention*)

destrabar *tr* to loosen, untie, detach

destraillar §4 *tr* to unleash

destral *m* hatchet

destreza *f* skill, dexterity

destripacuen·tos *m* (*pl* **-tos**) (coll) butter-in

destripar *tr* to disembowel, to gut; to crush, mangle; (coll) to spoil (*a story by telling its outcome*)

destripaterro·nes *m* (*pl* **-nes**) (coll) clodhopper

destriunfar *tr* to force to play trump

destrocar §81 *tr* to swap back again

destronar *tr* to dethrone; to overthrow

destroncar §73 *tr* to chop down; to chop off; to ruin; to exhaust, wear out

destrozar §60 *tr* to shatter, break to pieces; to destroy; to squander; (*al ejército enemigo*) to wipe out

destrozo *m* havoc, destruction; rout, annihilation, defeat

destrucción *f* destruction

destructi·vo -va *adj* destructive

destructor *m* (nav) destroyer

destruir §20 *tr* to destroy || *ref* (alg) to cancel each other

desuellaca·ras *m* (*pl* **-ras**) (coll) sloppy barber; (coll) scoundrel

desuello *m* skinning, flaying; shamelessness; (*precio excesivo*) (coll) highway robbery

desuncir §36 *tr* to unyoke

desunir *tr* to disunite; to take apart || *ref* to disunite; to come apart

desusa·do -da *adj* obsolete, out of use; uncommon, unusual; **estar desusado** (*perder la práctica*) to be rusty

desuso *m* disuse; **caído en desuso** obsolete

desvaí·do -da *adj* lank, ungainly; (*color*) dull

desvainar *tr* to shell

desvali·do -da *adj* helpless, destitute

desvalijar *tr* (*una valija, baúl, etc.*) to rifle; to rob, wipe out

desvalorar *tr* to devalue

desvalorizar §60 *tr* to devalue

desván *m* garret, loft

desvanecedor *m* (phot) mask

desvanecer §22 *tr* to dispel, dissipate; (*una conspiración*) to break up; (*la sospecha*) to banish; (phot) to mask || *ref* to disappear, vanish, evanesce; to evaporate; to faint, faint away, swoon; (rad) to fade

desvanecimiento *m* disappearance, evanescence; dissipation; pride, vanity; faintness, fainting spell; (phot) masking; (rad) fading, fadeout

desvaria·do -da *adj* delirious, raving

desvariar §77 *intr* to be delirious, to rave, to rant

desvarío *m* delirium, raving; absurdity,

nonsense, extravagance; whim, caprice; inconstancy
desvela•do -da *adj* wakeful, sleepless; watchful, vigilant; anxious, worried
desvelar *tr* to keep awake, not let sleep || *ref* to keep awake, go without sleep; to be watchful, be vigilant; **desvelarse por** to be anxious about, be worried about
desvelo *m* wakefulness, sleeplessness; watchfulness, vigilance; anxiety, worry, concern
desvenar *tr* to strip (*tobacco*)
desvencija•do -da *adj* rickety, ramshackle
desvencijar *tr* to break, tear apart || *ref* to go to rack and ruin
desvendar *tr* to unbandage, to undress
desventaja *f* disadvantage
desventajo•so -sa *adj* disadvantageous
desventura *f* misfortune
desventura•do -da *adj* unfortunate; faint-hearted; stingy
desvergonza•do -da *adj* shameless, impudent
desvergüenza *f* shamelessness, impudence
desvestir §50 *tr & ref* to undress
desviación *f* deviation, deflection; detour; (rad, telv) drift
desviacionismo *m* deviationism
desviacionista *mf* deviationist
desviadero *m* (rr) siding, turnout
desvia•do -da *adj* devious
desviar §77 *tr* to deviate, deflect; to turn aside; to dissuade; to parry, ward off; (rr) to switch || *ref* to deviate, deflect; to turn aside; to branch off; to be dissuaded
desvío *m* deviation, deflection; coldness, indifference; detour; (rr) siding, sidetrack
desvirgar §44 *tr* to deflower, ravish
desvirtuar §21 *tr* to weaken, spoil, impair
desvivir *ref* — **desvivirse por** to be crazy about; **desvivirse por** + *inf* to be eager to + *inf*, to do one's best to + *inf*
desvolvedor *m* wrench
desvolver §47 & §83 *tr* to alter, change; (*la tierra*) to turn up; (*una tuerca o tornillo*) to loosen, unscrew
detall *m* — **al detall** at retail
detalladamente *adv* in detail
detallar *tr* to detail, tell in detail; to retail, sell at retail
detalle *m* detail; (Am) retail; **ahí está el detalle** that's the point
detallista *mf* retailer; person fond of details
detección *f* detection
detectar *tr* to detect
detective *m* detective
detector *m* detector; **detector de mentiras** lie detector
detención *f* detention, detainment; delay; care, thoroughness
detener §71 *tr* to detain; to stop; to arrest; to keep, retain; (*el aliento*) to hold || *ref* to stop; to linger, tarry
detenidamente *adv* carefully, thoroughly
deteni•do -da *adj* careful, thorough; hesitant, timid; stingy, mean || *mf* person held in custody
detenimiento *m* var of **detención**
detergente *adj & m* detergent
deteriorar *tr & ref* to deteriorate
deterioro *m* deterioration
determinación *f* determination; decision
determina•do -da *adj* determined, resolute; (*artículo*) (gram) definite
determinar *tr* to determine; to cause, to bring about || *ref* to decide
detestar *tr* to detest; to curse; **detestar** + *inf* to hate to + *inf*
detonar *intr* to detonate
detraer §75 *tr* to withdraw, take away, detract; to defame, vilify
detrás *adv* behind; **detrás de** behind, back of; **por detrás** behind; behind one's back; **por detrás de** behind the back of
detrimento *m* harm, detriment
deuda *f* debt; indebtedness
deu•do -da *mf* relative || *m* kinship || *f* see **deuda**
deu•dor -dora *adj* indebted || *mf* debtor; **deudor hipotecario** mortgagor; **deudor moroso** delinquent (*in payment*)
devalar *intr* (naut) to drift from the course
devaluación *f* devaluation
devanar *tr* to wind, to roll; (*un cuento*) to unfold || *ref* (CAm, Mex, W-I) to roll with laughter; (CAm, Mex, W-I) to writhe in pain
devanear *intr* to talk nonsense; to loaf around
devaneo *m* nonsense; loafing; flirtation
devastación *f* devastation
devastar *tr* to devastate
develar *tr* to reveal; (*p.ej., una estatua*) to unveil
devengar §44 *tr* (*salarios*) to earn; (*intereses*) to draw, to earn
devoción *f* devotion
devolución *f* return, restitution
devolver §47 & §83 *tr* to return, give back, send back; to pay back; (coll) to vomit || *ref* (Am) to return, come back
devorar *tr* to devour
devo•to -ta *adj* devout; devoted; devotional || *mf* devotee; devout person || *m* object of worship
D.F. *abbr* **Distrito Federal**
d/f *abbr* **días fecha**
dho. *abbr* **dicho**
día *m* day; daytime; daylight; **al día** per day; up to date; **al otro día** on the following day; **buenos días** good morning; **dar los días a** to wish (*someone*) many happy returns of the day; **de día** in the daytime, in the daylight; **día de años** birthday; **día de ayuno** fast day; **día de carne** meat day; **día de engañabobos** December 28th, day when practical jokes are played on unsuspecting people; **día de inauguración** (fa) private view; **día de la raza** Columbus Day; **día del juicio** judgment day; **día de los caídos** Memorial Day; **día de los difuntos**

All Souls' Day; **día de ramos** Palm Sunday; **día de Reyes** Epiphany; **día de todos los santos** All Saints' Day; **día de trabajo** workday; weekday; **día de vigilia** fast day; **día festivo** holiday; **día laborable** workday, weekday; **día lectivo** school day; **día puente** day off between two holidays; **el día de Año Nuevo** New Year's Day; **el día menos pensado** (coll) when least expected; **el mejor día** some fine day; **en cuatro días** in a few days; **en pleno día** in broad daylight; **en su día** in due time; **ocho días** a week; **poner al día** to bring up to date; **quince días** two weeks, a fortnight; **tener sus días** to be up in years; **un día sí y otro no** every other day; **vivir al día** to live from hand to mouth

diabetes *f* diabetes

diabéti•co -ca *adj & mf* diabetic

diablillo *m* imp

diablo *m* devil; (Chile) ox-drawn log drag; **ahí será el diablo** (coll) there will be the devil to pay; **diablo cojuelo** tricky devil; **diablos azules** (Am) delirium tremens

diablura *f* devilment, deviltry, mischief

diabóli•co -ca *adj* devilish, diabolical

diaconisa *f* deaconess

diácono *m* deacon

diacríti•co -ca *adj* diacritical

diadema *f* diadem; (*adorno femenino*) tiara

diáfa•no -na *adj* diaphanous

diafragma *m* diaphragm

diagno•sis *f* (*pl* **-sis**) diagnosis

diagnosticar §73 *tr* to diagnose

diagonal *adj* diagonal || *f* diagonal, bias

diagrama *m* diagram

dialecto *m* dialect

diálogo *m* dialogue

diamante *m* diamond

diametral or **diamétri•co -ca** *adj* diametrical

diámetro *m* diameter

diana *f* bull's-eye; (mil) reveille; **hacer diana** to hit the bull's-eye

diantre *m* (coll) devil || *interj* (coll) the devil!, the deuce!

diapasón *m* tuning fork; pitch pipe; (*p.ej., del violín*) finger board; **bajar el diapasón** (coll) to lower one's voice, to change one's tune

diapositiva *f* slide, lantern slide

dia•rio -ria *adj* daily || *m* diary; daily, daily paper; **diario hablado** newscast

diarismo *m* (Am) journalism

diarrea *f* diarrhea

diástole *f* diastole

diatermia *f* diathermy

dibujante *mf* sketcher, illustrator || *m* draftsman

dibujar *tr* to draw, sketch, design; to outline || *ref* to be outlined; to appear, show

dibujo *m* drawing, sketch, design; outline; **dibujo al carbón** charcoal drawing; **dibujo animado** animated cartoon; **no meterse en dibujos** (coll) to attend to one's business

di•caz *adj* (*pl* **-caces**) sarcastic, witty

dicción *f* diction; word

diccionario *m* dictionary

diciembre *m* December

dicloruro *m* dichloride

dicotomía *f* dichotomy; (*entre médicos*) split fee

dictado *m* dictation; **escribir al dictado** to take dictation; (*lo que otro dicta*) to take down

dictador *m* dictator

dictadura *f* dictatorship

dictáfono *m* dictaphone

dictamen *m* dictum, judgment, opinion

dictar *tr* to dictate; (*una ley*) to promulgate; to inspire, suggest; (*una conferencia*) (Am) to give, deliver (*a lecture*)

dicterio *m* taunt, insult

dicha *f* happiness; luck; **por dicha** by chance

dicharache•ro -ra *adj* (coll) obscene, vulgar

dicharacho *m* (coll) obscenity, vulgarity; (coll) wisecrack

di•cho -cha *adj* said; **dicho y hecho** no sooner said than done; **mejor dicho** rather; **tener por dicho** to consider settled || *m* saying; promise of marriage, one's word; witticism; (coll) insult; **dicho de las gentes** (coll) talk, hearsay, gossip || *f* see **dicha**

dicho•so -sa *adj* happy; lucky, fortunate; annoying, tiresome

didácti•co -ca *adj* didactic

diecinueve *adj & pron* nineteen || *m* nineteen; (*en las fechas*) nineteenth

diecinuevea•vo -va *adj & m* nineteenth

dieciocha•vo -va *adj & m* eighteenth

dieciocho *adj & pron* eighteen || *m* eighteen; (*en las fechas*) eighteenth

dieciséis *adj & pron* sixteen || *m* sixteen; (*en las fechas*) sixteenth

dieciseisa•vo -va *adj & m* sixteenth

diecisiete *adj & pron* seventeen || *m* seventeen; (*en las fechas*) seventeenth

diecisietea•vo -va *adj & m* seventeenth

diente *m* tooth; (*de elefante y otros animales*) tusk, fang; (*de peine, sierra, rastrillo*) tooth; (*de rueda dentada*) cog; **dar diente con diente** (coll) to shake all over; **decir entre dientes** (coll) to mutter, to mumble; **diente canino** eyetooth, canine tooth; **diente de león** dandelion; **estar a diente** (coll) to be famished; **tener buen diente** (coll) to be a hearty eater; **traer entre dientes** (coll) to have a grudge against; (coll) to talk about

diére•sis *f* (*pl* **-sis**) diaeresis; (*señal que indica la metafonía*) umlaut

dies•tro -tra *adj* right; handy, skillful; shrewd, sly; favorable; **a diestro y siniestro** wildly, right and left || *m* expert fencer; bullfighter on foot; matador; halter, bridle || *f* right hand; **juntar diestra con diestra** to join forces

dieta *f* diet; **dietas** per diem; **estar a dieta** to diet, be on a diet

dietario *m* family budget

dietista *mf* dietitian

diez *adj & pron* ten; **las diez** ten o'clock || *m* ten; (*en las fechas*) tenth
diezmar *tr* (*causar gran mortandad en*) to decimate; (*pagar el diezmo de*) to tithe
diezmo *m* tithe
difamación *f* defamation, vilification
difamar *tr* to defame, to vilify
diferencia *f* difference; **a diferencia de** unlike; **partir la diferencia** to split the difference
diferenciar *tr* to differentiate || *intr* (*discordar*) to differ, dissent || *ref* (*distinguirse una cosa de otra*) to differ, be different
diferente *adj* different
diferir §68 *tr* to defer, postpone, put off || *intr* to differ, be different
difícil *adj* difficult, hard; hard to please
difícilmente *adv* with difficulty
dificultad *f* difficulty; (*reparo que se opone a una opinión*) objection
dificultar *tr* to make difficult; to consider difficult || *intr* to raise objections || *ref* to become difficult
dificulto·so -sa *adj* difficult, troublesome; objecting; (coll) ugly, homely
difidencia *f* distrust
difidente *adj* distrustful
difteria *f* diphtheria
difundir *tr* to diffuse; to spread, disseminate; to divulge, publish; to broadcast || *ref* to diffuse; to spread
difun·to -ta *adj & mf* deceased; **difunto de taberna** dead-drunk || *m* corpse
difu·so -sa *adj* diffuse; extended; wordy
digerible *adj* digestible
digerir §68 *tr* to digest; **no digerir** to not bear, to not stand || *intr* to digest
digestible *adj* digestible
digestión *f* digestion
digesti·vo -va *adj & m* digestive
digesto *m* (law) digest
dígito *m* digit
dignación *f* condescension
dignar *ref* to deign, to condescend
dignatario *m* dignitary, official
dignidad *f* dignity; bishop, archbishop
dignificar §73 *tr* to dignify
dig·no -na *adj* worthy; fitting, suitable; (*grave, decoroso*) dignified
digresión *f* digression
dije *m* amulet, charm, trinket; (*persona de excelentes cualidades*) (coll) jewel; (coll) person all dressed-up; (coll) handy person
dilacerar *tr* to tear to pieces; (*la honra, el orgullo*) to damage
dilación *f* delay
dilapidar *tr* to squander
dilatación *f* expansion; serenity
dilatar *tr* to dilate, expand; to defer, postpone; (*p.ej., la fama*) to spread || *ref* to dilate, expand; to spread; to be wordy; (Am) to delay
dilección *f* true love
dilec·to -ta *adj* dearly beloved
dilema *m* dilemma
diletante *adj & mf* dilettante
diligencia *f* diligence; step, démarche; errand; dispatch, speed; stagecoach; **hacer una diligencia** to do an errand; (coll) to have a bowel movement
diligente *adj* diligent; quick, ready
dilucidar *tr* to elucidate, explain
dilución *f* dilution
diluí·do -da *adj* dilute
diluir §20 *tr* to dilute; to thin || *ref* to dilute; to melt; to dissolve
diluviar *intr* to rain hard, to pour
diluvio *m* deluge
dimanar *intr* to spring up; **dimanar de** to spring from, originate in
dimensión *f* dimension
dimes *mpl* — **andar en dimes y diretes con** (coll) to bicker with
diminuti·vo -va *adj & m* (gram) diminutive
diminu·to -ta *adj* tiny, diminutive; defective
dimisión *f* resignation
dimisorias *fpl* — **dar dimisorias a** (coll) to discharge, to fire
dimitir *tr* to resign, resign from || *intr* to resign
din *m* (coll) dough, money
Dinamarca *f* Denmark
dinamar·qués -quesa *adj* Danish || *mf* Dane || *m* Danish (*language*)
dinámi·co -ca *adj* dynamic
dinamita *f* dynamite
dinamitar *tr* to dynamite
dínamo *f* dynamo
dinasta *m* dynast
dinastía *f* dynasty
dindán *m* ding-dong
dinerada *f* or **dineral** *m* large sum of money
dinero *m* money; currency; wealth; **dinero contante** cash; **dinero contante y sonante** ready cash, spot cash; **dinero de bolsillo** pocket money
dinero·so -sa *adj* moneyed, wealthy
dintel *m* lintel, doorhead
dióce·si *f* or **dióce·sis** *f* (*pl* **-sis**) diocese
diodo *m* diode
dios *m* god; **Dios mediante** God willing; **¡por Dios!** goodness!, for heaven's sake; **¡válgame Dios!** bless me!; **¡vaya con Dios!** off with you!
diosa *f* goddess
diploma *m* diploma
diplomacia *f* diplomacy
diploma·do -da *adj & mf* graduate
diplomar *tr & ref* (Am) to graduate
diplomáti·co -ca *adj* diplomatic || *mf* diplomat
diptongar §44 *tr & ref* to diphthongize
diptongo *m* diphthong
diputación *f* congress; commission
diputa·do -da *mf* deputy, representative
diputar *tr* to commission, delegate; to designate
dique *m* dike, jetty; dry dock; check, stop; **dique seco** dry dock
dirección *f* direction; (*señas en una carta*) address; administration, management; directorship; (aut) steering; **de dirección única** one-way; **dirección a la derecha** right-hand drive; **dirección a la izquierda** left-hand drive; **perder la dirección** to lose control of the car
directi·vo -va *adj* managing || *mf* director, manager || *f* management
direc·to -ta *adj* direct; straight

direc•tor -tora *adj* directing, guiding; managing, governing || *mf* director, manager; (*de un periódico*) editor; (*de una escuela*) principal; (*de una orquesta*) conductor; **director de escena** stage manager; **director de funeraria** funeral director; **director gerente** managing director
directorio *m* directorship; directory
dirigente *mf* leader, head, executive
dirigible *adj* & *m* dirigible
dirigir §27 *tr* to direct; to manage; (*un automóvil*) to steer; (*una carta; la palabra*) to address; (*una obra*) to dedicate || *ref* to go, to betake oneself; to turn; **dirigirse a** to address; to apply to
dirimir *tr* to dissolve, annul; (*una dificultad*) to solve; (*una controversia*) to settle, mediate
discar §73 *tr* & *intr* to dial
disceptar *intr* to discuss, debate
discerniente *adj* discerning
discernir §28 *tr* to discern; to distinguish
disciplina *f* discipline; **disciplinas** scourge, whip
disciplina•do -da *adj* disciplined; (*flores*) many-colored
disciplinar *tr* to discipline; to teach; to scourge, whip
disciplinazo *m* lash
discípu•lo -la *mf* disciple; pupil
disco *m* disk; (*del gramófono*) record, disk; (sport) discus; **disco de cola** (rr) taillight; **disco de goma** (*para un grifo*) washer (*for a spigot*); **disco de identificación** identification tag; **disco de larga duración** long-playing record; **disco de señales** (rr) semaphore; **disco selector** (telp) dial; **siempre el mismo disco** (coll) the same old song
discóbolo *m* discus thrower
discófi•lo -la *mf* record lover, discophile
dísco•lo -la *adj* ungovernable, wayward
disconforme *adj* disagreeing
discontinuar §21 *tr* to discontinue
discordancia *f* discordance
discordar §61 *intr* to be out of tune; to disagree
discorde *adj* discordant, disagreeing; (mus) discordant, out of tune
discordia *f* discord
discoteca *f* record cabinet; record library
discreción *f* discretion; wit; witticism; **a discreción** at discretion; (mil) unconditionally
discrepancia *f* discrepancy; dissent
discrepar *intr* to differ, to disagree
discretear *intr* to try to be clever, to try to sparkle
discre•to -ta *adj* (*juicioso*) discreet; (*discontinuo*) discrete; witty
discrimen *m* risk, hazard; difference
discriminación *f* discrimination
discriminar *tr* to discriminate against || *intr* to discriminate
discriminato•rio -ria *adj* discriminatory
disculpa *f* excuse, apology
disculpar *tr* to excuse; (coll) to pardon, overlook || *ref* to apologize; **disculparse con** to apologize to; **disculparse de** to apologize for
discurrir *tr* to contrive, invent; to guess, conjecture || *intr* to ramble, roam; to occur, take place; to discourse; to reason; to pass, elapse
discursi•vo -va *adj* meditative
discurso *m* discourse, speech; (*paso del tiempo*) course; **discurso de sobremesa** after-dinner speech
discusión *f* discussion
discutible *adj* debatable
discutir *tr* to discuss || *intr* to discuss; to argue
disecar §73 *tr* to dissect; (*un animal muerto*) to stuff; (*una planta*) to mount
diseminar *tr* to disseminate; to scatter || *ref* to scatter
disensión *f* (*oposición*) dissent; (*contienda*) dissension
disentería *f* dysentery
disentir §68 *intr* to dissent
diseñar *tr* to draw, sketch; to design, outline
diseño *m* drawing, sketch; design, outline
disertar *intr* to discourse, discuss
diser•to -ta *adj* fluent, eloquent
disfavor *m* disfavor
disforme *adj* formless; monstrous, ugly
disforzar §35 *ref* (Peru) to be prudish, be finical
dis•fraz *m* (*pl* **-fraces**) disguise; (*traje de máscara*) costume, fancy dress
disfrazar §60 *tr* to disguise || *ref* to disguise oneself; to wear fancy dress, to masquerade, to dress in costume
disfrutar *tr* to enjoy, to use || *intr* — **disfrutar de** to enjoy, to use; **disfrutar con** to enjoy, take enjoyment in
disfrute *m* enjoyment, use
disgregar §44 *tr* & *intr* to disintegrate, break up
disgusta•do -da *adj* tasteless, insipid; sad, sorrowful; disagreeable; (Mex) hard to please
disgustar *tr* to displease || *ref* to be displeased; to fall out, become estranged
disgusto *m* displeasure; annoyance, unpleasantness; grief, sorrow; difference, quarrel; **a disgusto** against one's will
disidencia *f* dissidence; (*de una doctrina*) dissent
disidente *adj* dissident || *mf* dissident, dissenter
disidir *intr* to dissent
disíla•bo -ba *adj* dissyllabic || *m* dissyllable
disímil *adj* dissimilar
disimilar *tr* & *ref* to dissimilate
disimula•do -da *adj* sly, underhanded; **a lo disimulado** or **a la disimulada** underhandedly; **hacer la disimulada** (coll) to feign ignorance
disimular *tr* to dissemble, dissimulate, hide, conceal; to overlook, pardon || *intr* to dissemble, dissimulate
disimulo *m* dissembling, dissimulation; indulgence

disipación *f* dissipation
disipa•do -da *adj* dissipated; spendthrift || *mf* debauchee; spendthrift
disipar *tr* to dissipate || *ref* to be dissipated; to disappear, evanesce
dislate *m* nonsense
dislocar §73 *tr* to dislocate || *ref* to dislocate; to be dislocated
disloque *m* (coll) tops, top notch
disminuir §20 *tr, intr & ref* to diminish
disociar *tr* to dissociate
disolución *f* dissolution; disbandment; (*relajación de costumbres*) dissoluteness, dissipation
disolu•to -ta *adj* dissolute || *mf* debauchee
disolver §47 & §83 *tr* to dissolve; to disband; to destroy, ruin || *intr & ref* to dissolve
disonancia *f* dissonance
disonar §61 *intr* to be dissonant, lack harmony, disagree; to cause surprise; to sound bad
dispar *adj* unlike, different; (*que no hace juego*) odd
disparada *f* (Am) sudden flight; **a la disparada** (Am) like a shot, in mad haste; **de una disparada** (Arg) right away; **tomar la disparada** (Arg) to take to one's heels
disparadero *m* trigger
disparador *m* trigger; (*de reloj*) escapement; **poner en el disparador** (coll) to drive mad
disparar *tr* to throw, hurl; to shoot, to fire || *intr* to rant, talk nonsense || *ref* to dash away, rush away; (*un caballo*) to run away; (*una escopeta*) to go off; to be beside oneself
disparata•do -da *adj* absurd, nonsensical; frightful
disparatar *intr* to talk nonsense; to act foolishly
disparate *m* folly, nonsense; blunder, mistake; (coll) outrage
dispare•jo -ja *adj* unequal, different, uneven, disparate; rough, broken
disparidad *f* disparity
disparo *m* shot, discharge; nonsense; (mach) release, trip; **cambiar disparos** to exchange shots
dispendio *m* waste, extravagance
dispendio•so -sa *adj* expensive
dispensar *tr* to excuse, to pardon; to exempt; to dispense; to dispense with
dispensario *m* dispensary; **dispensario de alimentos** soup kitchen
dispepsia *f* dyspepsia
dispersar *tr & ref* to disperse
displicente *adj* disagreeable; cross, fretful, peevish
disponer §54 *tr* to dispose, arrange; to direct, order || *intr* to dispose; **disponer de** to dispose of, have at one's disposal || *ref* to prepare, get ready; to get ready to die, make one's will
disponible *adj* available, disposable
disposición *f* disposition, arrangement, layout; inclination; preparation; disposal; predisposition; state of health; elegance; **estar a la disposición de** to be at the disposal of, be at the service of; **última disposición** last will and testament
dispositivo *m* appliance, device
dispues•to -ta *adj* ready, prepared; comely, graceful; clever, skillful; **bien dispuesto** well-disposed; well, in good health; **mal dispuesto** ill-disposed, unfavorable; ill, indisposed
disputa *f* dispute; fight, struggle; **sin disputa** beyond dispute
disputar *tr* to dispute, to question; to argue over; to fight for || *intr* to dispute; to debate, to argue; to fight
disque•ro -ra *mf* record dealer
distancia *f* distance; **a distancia** at a distance; **a larga distancia** long-distance; **tomar distancia** to stand aside, to stand off
distante *adj* distant
distar *intr* to be distant, be far; to be different
distender §51 *tr* to distend; (*p.ej., las piernas*) to stretch || *ref* to distend; to relax; (*un reloj*) to run down
distensión *f* distension; relaxation of tension
distinción *f* (*honor, prerrogativa*) distinction; (*diferencia*) distinctness; **a distinción de** unlike
distingui•do -da *adj* distinguished; refined, urbane, smooth
distinguir §29 *tr* to distinguish; to give distinction to; to make out
distinti•vo -va *adj* distinctive || *m* badge, insignia; distinction; distinctive mark
distin•to -ta *adj* distinct; different; **distintos** various, several
distorsión *f* distortion
distracción *f* distraction; (*licencia en las costumbres*) dissipation; (*substracción de fondos*) embezzlement
distraer §75 *tr* to distract; to amuse, divert, entertain; to seduce; to embezzle
distraí•do -da *adj* absent-minded, distracted; licentious, dissolute; (Chile, Mex) untidy, careless
distribución *f* distribution; electric supply system; timing gears, valve gears
distribui•dor -dora *adj* distributing || *mf* distributor || *m* (aut) distributor; slide valve; **distribuidor automático** vending machine
distribuir §20 *tr* to distribute
distrito *m* district; (rr) section; **distrito electoral** precinct; **distrito postal** zone, postal zone
disturbar *tr* to disturb
disturbio *m* disturbance
disuadir *tr* to dissuade
disyunti•vo -va *adj* disjunctive || *f* dilemma
disyuntor *m* circuit breaker
dita *f* bond, surety
diuca *m* (Arg, Chile) teacher's pet || *f* (Arg, Chile) finch (*Fringilla diuca*)
diur•no -na *adj* day, daytime
diva *f* goddess; (mus) diva
divagación *f* digression; wandering
divagar §44 *intr* to digress; to ramble, wander
diván *m* divan

divergir §27 *intr* to diverge
diversidad *f* diversity; abundance
diversificación *f* diversification
diversificar §73 *tr & ref* to diversify
diversión *f* diversion
diver•so -sa *adj* diverse, different; **diversos** several, various, divers
diverti•do -da *adj* amusing, funny; (Am) tipsy
divertimiento *m* diversion, amusement
divertir §68 *tr* to divert; to amuse ‖ *ref* to enjoy oneself, have a good time
dividendo *m* dividend
dividir *tr* to divide ‖ *ref* to divide, be divided; to separate
divieso *m* boil
divinidad *f* divinity; (*persona dotada de gran belleza*) beauty
divinizar §60 *tr* to deify; to exalt, extol
divi•no -na *adj* divine
divisa *f* badge; emblem; motto; goal, ideal; currency, foreign exchange
divisar *tr* to descry, espy
división *f* division
divisor *m* (math) divisor; **máximo común divisor** greatest common divisor; **divisor de voltaje** (rad) voltage divider
divisoria *f* dividing line; (geog) divide
di•vo -va *adj* godlike, divine ‖ *m* god; (mus) opera star ‖ *f* see **diva**
divorciar *tr* to divorce ‖ *ref* to divorce, get divorced
divorcio *m* divorce; divergency (*in opinion*); (Col) jail for women
divulgación *f* divulging, disclosure; popularization
divulgar §44 *tr* to divulge, disclose; to popularize
D.ⁿ *abbr* **don**
dobladillar *tr* to hem
dobladillo *m* hem
dobla•do -da *adj* rough, uneven; stocky, thickset; double-dealing ‖ *m* (mov) dubbing
doblaje *m* (mov) dubbing
doblar *tr* to double; to fold, to crease; to bend; (*una esquina*) to turn, to round; (*un promontorio*) to double; (*una película, generalmente en otro idioma*) to dub; (bridge) to double; (Mex) to shoot down ‖ *intr* to turn; (*tocar a muerto*) to toll; (mov, theat) to double, stand in; (bridge) to double ‖ *ref* to double; to fold, to crease; to bend; to bow, to stoop; to give in, yield
doble *adj* double; heavy, thick; stocky, thickset; deceitful, two-faced ‖ *adv* double, doubly ‖ *mf* (mov, theat) double, stand-in ‖ *m* double; fold, crease; (*toque de difuntos*) toll, knell; (*suma que se paga por la prórroga de una operación a plazos en la bolsa*) margin; **al doble** doubly
doblegar §44 *tr* to fold; to bend; (*una espada*) to brandish, flourish; to sway, dominate ‖ *ref* to fold; to bend; to give in, to yield
doblete *adj* medium ‖ *m* (*piedra falsa; cada una de dos palabras que poseen un mismo origen*) doublet; (bridge) doubleton
do•blez *m* (*pl* **-bleces**) fold, crease; (*del pantalón*) cuff; duplicity, double-dealing
doce *adj & pron* twelve; **las doce** twelve o'clock ‖ *m* twelve; (*en las fechas*) twelfth
docea•vo -va *adj & m* twelfth
docena *f* dozen; **docena del fraile** baker's dozen
docencia *f* (Arg) teaching; (Arg) teaching staff
docente *adj* educational, teaching
dócil *adj* docile; soft, ductile
doc•to -ta *adj* learned ‖ *mf* scholar
doc•tor -tora *mf* doctor ‖ *f* (coll) bluestocking
doctorado *m* doctorate
doctoran•do -da *mf* candidate for the doctor's degree
doctorar *tr* to grant the doctor's degree to ‖ *ref* to get the doctor's degree
doctrina *f* doctrine; teaching, instruction; learning; catechism; preaching the Gospel
doctrinar *tr* to teach, instruct
doctrino *m* orphan (*in orphanage*); **parecer un doctrino** (coll) to look scared
documentación *f* documentation; **documentación del buque** ship's papers
documental *adj* documentary ‖ *m* (mov) documentary
documentar *tr* to document
documento *m* document; **documento de prueba** (law) exhibit
dogal *m* (*para atar las caballerías*) halter; (*para ahorcar a un reo*) noose, halter, hangman's rope; **estar con el dogal a la garganta** or **al cuello** (coll) to be in a tight spot
dogmáti•co -ca *adj* dogmatic
do•go -ga *mf* bulldog
dolamas *fpl* or **dolames** *mpl* hidden defects of a horse; (Am) complaints, aches and pains
dolar §61 *tr* to hew
dólar *m* dollar
dolencia *f* ailment, complaint
doler §47 *tr* to ache, to pain; to grieve, distress; **dolerle a uno el dinero** (coll) to hate to spend money ‖ *intr* to ache, to hurt, to pain ‖ *ref* to complain; to feel sorry; to repent
doliente *adj* sick, ill; aching, suffering; sad, sorrowful ‖ *mf* sufferer, patient ‖ *m* mourner
dolo *m* deceit, fraud, guile
dolor *m* ache, pain; grief, sorrow; regret, repentance; **dolor de cabeza** headache; **dolor de muelas** toothache; **dolor de oído** earache; **dolor de yegua** (CAm) lumbago; **estar con dolores** to be in labor
dolori•do -da *adj* sore, painful; grieving, disconsolate
doloro•so -sa *adj* painful; sorrowful, sad
dolo•so -sa *adj* deceitful, guileful
domador *m* horsebreaker; animal tamer
domar *tr* to tame, to break; to master
domeñar *tr* to master, subdue
domesticar §73 *tr* to domesticate; to tame

domésti•co -ca *adj* domestic, household || *mf* domestic, servant
domiciliar *tr* to domicile, settle; (*una carta*) (Mex) to address || *ref* to be domiciled, to take up one's residence
domicilio *m* domicile, home; dwelling, house; **domicilio social** home office, company office
dominación *f* domination; (mil) eminence, high ground
dominante *adj* dominant; (*mandón*) domineering || *f* (mus) dominant
dominar *tr* to dominate; to check, restrain, subdue; (*una ciencia, un idioma*) to master || *intr* to dominate; (*mandar imperiosamente*) to domineer || *ref* to restrain oneself
dómine *m* (coll) schoolmaster, Latin teacher; (coll) pedant
domingo *m* Sunday; **domingo de ramos** Palm Sunday; **domingo de resurrección** Easter Sunday; **guardar el domingo** to keep the Sabbath
dominguillo *m* tumbler
dominica•no -na *adj & mf* Dominican
dominio *m* dominion; domain; (*de una ciencia, de un idioma*) mastery; (*del aire*) supremacy
domi•nó *m* (*pl* **-nós**) (*traje*) domino; (*juego*) dominoes; (*fichas*) set of dominoes
dom.° *abbr* **domingo**
domo *m* dome
dompedro *m* four-o'clock
don *m* gift, present; talent, natural gift; Don (*Spanish title used before masculine Christian names*); **don de acierto** knack for doing the right thing; **don de errar** knack for doing the wrong thing; **don de gentes** charm, social grace; **don de lenguas** linguistic facility; **don de mando** ability to lead, generalship
dona *f* gift, present; **donas** wedding presents from the bridegroom to the bride
donación *f* gift, bequest; endowment
donada *f* lay sister
donado *m* lay brother
dona•dor -dora *mf* donor
donaire *m* charm, grace; witticism; cleverness
donairo•so -sa *adj* charming, graceful; witty; clever
donar *tr* to donate, to give
doncel *adj* mild, mellow || *m* (*joven noble aun no armado caballero*) bachelor; (*hombre virgen*) virgin
doncella *f* maiden, virgin; housemaid; lady's maid; maid of honor; (Col, Ven) felon, whitlow
doncellez *f* maidenhood, virginity
doncellona or **doncellueca** *f* spinster, maiden lady
donde *conj* where; wherever; in which; **donde no** otherwise; **por donde quiera** anywhere, everywhere || *prep* (Am) at or to the house, office, or store of
dónde *adv* where; **a dónde** where, whither; **de dónde** from where, whence; **por dónde** which way; for what cause, for what reason
dondequiera *adv* anywhere; **dondequiera que** wherever
dondiego *m* four-o'clock; **dondiego de día** morning-glory; **dondiego de noche** four-o'clock
donillero *m* sharper, smoothy
donjuán *m* four-o'clock
donosidad *f* charm, grace, wit
dono•so -sa *adj* charming, graceful, witty
donostiarra *adj* San Sebastian || *mf* native or inhabitant of San Sebastian
donosura *f* charm, grace, wit
doña *f* Doña (*Spanish title used before feminine Christian names*)
doñear *intr* (coll) to hang around women
doquier or **doquiera** *conj* wherever; **por doquier** everywhere
dorada *f* (ichth) gilthead
doradillo *m* fine brass wire
dora•do -da *adj* golden; gilt || *m* gilt, gilding; **dorados** bronze trimmings (*on furniture*) || *f* see **dorada**
dorar *tr* to gold-plate; to gild; (*tostar ligeramente*) to brown; (*paliar*) to sugar-coat || *ref* to turn golden; to turn brown
dormi•lón -lona *adj* (coll) sleepy || *mf* (coll) sleepyhead || *f* reclining armchair; (Mex) headrest; (Ven) sleeping gown; (Am) mimosa; **dormilonas** pearl earrings
dormir §30 *tr* to put to sleep; (*p.ej., una borrachera*) to sleep off || *intr* to sleep; to spend the night || *ref* to sleep; to fall asleep; (*entorpecerse, p.ej., el pie*) to go to sleep
dormirlas *m* hide-and-seek
dormitar *intr* to doze, nap
dormitorio *m* bedroom; (*muebles propios de esta habitación*) bedroom suit
dorsal *m* (sport) number (*worn on shirt*)
dorso *m* back
dos *adj & pron* two; **las dos** two o'clock || *m* two; (*en las fechas*) second
dosal•bo -ba *adj* (*horse*) with two white feet
doscien•tos -tas *adj & pron* two hundred || **doscientos** *m* two hundred
dosel *m* canopy, dais
doselera *f* valance, drapery
dosificación *f* dosage
dosificar §73 *tr* (*un medicamento*) to dose, to give in doses
do•sis *f* (*pl* **-sis**) dose
dos-pie•zas *m* (*pl* **-zas**) two-piece bathing suit
dotación *f* (*de una mujer; de una fundación*) endowment; (nav) complement; (aer) crew; (*de remeros*) (sport) crew; staff, personnel
dotar *tr* to give a dowry to; to endow; (*un buque*) to man; (*una oficina*) to staff; to equip; to fix the wages for
dote *m & f* dowry, marriage portion || *m* (*en el juego de naipes*) stack of chips || *f* endowment, talent, gift; **dotes de mando** leadership
dovela *f* voussoir
doza•vo -va *adj & m* twelfth
d/p *abbr* **días plazo**

dracma *f* (*moneda griega*) drachma; (*peso farmacéutico*) dram
draga *f* dredge; (*barco*) dredger
dragado *m* dredging
dragami•nas *m* (*pl* **-nas**) mine sweeper
dragar §44 *tr* to dredge
dragón *m* dragon; (*planta*) snapdragon; (*soldado*) dragoon
dragonear *intr* (Am) to flirt; (Am) to boast; **dragonear de** (Am) to boast of being; (Am) to pretend to be, to pass oneself off as
drama *m* drama
dramáti•co -ca *adj* dramatic || *mf* (*autor*) dramatist; actor || *f* (*arte y género*) drama
dramatizar §60 *tr* to dramatize
dramaturgo *m* dramatist
drásti•co -ca *adj* drastic
dren *m* drain
drenaje *m* drainage
drenar *tr* to drain
driblar *tr & intr* to dribble
dril *m* drill; duck; **dril de algodón** denim
driza *f* (naut) halyard
dro. *abbr* **derecho**
droga *f* drug; annoyance, bother; deceit, trick; (Chile, Mex, Peru) bad debt; (Cuba) drug on the market; **drogas milagrosas** wonder drugs
drogado *m* doping
drogar §44 *tr* to dope
droguería *f* drug store; drug business; (*comercio de substancias usadas en química, industria, medicina, bellas artes*) drysaltery (Brit)
drogue•ro -ra *mf* druggist; drysalter (Brit)
droguista *mf* druggist; (coll) crook, cheat; (Arg) toper, drunk
droláti•co -ca *adj* droll, snappy
dromedario *m* dromedary; big heavy animal; (coll) brute (*person*)
druida *m* druid
dúa *f* (min) gang of workmen
dual *adj & m* dual
dualidad *f* duality; (Chile) tie vote
ducado *m* duchy, dukedom; (*moneda antigua*) ducat; **gran ducado** grand duchy
dúctil *adj* ductile; easy to handle
ducha *f* (*chorro de agua en una cavidad del cuerpo*) douche; (*chorro de agua sobre el cuerpo entero*) shower bath; (*lista en los tejidos*) stripe; **ducha en alfileres** needle bath
duchar *tr* to douche; to give a shower bath to || *ref* to douche; to take a shower bath
du•cho -cha *adj* experienced, expert, skillful || *f* see **ducha**
duda *f* doubt; **sin duda** doubtless, no doubt, without doubt
dudable *adj* doubtful
dudar *tr* to doubt; to question || *intr* to hesitate; **dudar de** to doubt
dudo•so -sa *adj* doubtful; dubious
duela *f* stave (*of barrel*)
duelista *m* duelist
duelo *m* (*combate entre dos*) duel; grief, sorrow; bereavement, mourning; (*los que asisten a los funerales*) mourners; **batirse en duelo** to duel, to fight a duel; **duelos** hardships; **sin duelo** in abundance
duende *m* elf, goblin; gold cloth, silver cloth; (coll) restless daemon; **tener duende** (coll) to be burning within
due•ño -ña *mf* owner, proprietor; **dueño de sí mismo** one's own master; **ser dueño de** to be master of; to be at liberty to, be free to || *m* master, landlord || *f* mistress, landlady, housekeeper; duenna; matron; **dueña de casa** housewife
duermevela *f* (coll) doze, light sleep; (*sueño fatigoso e interrumpido*) fitful sleep
dula *f* common pasture land; land irrigated from common ditch
dulce *adj* sweet; (*agua*) fresh; (*metal*) soft, ductile; gentle, mild, pleasant; (*manjar*) tasteless, insipid || *m* candy; piece of candy; preserves; **dulce de almíbar** preserved fruit; **dulces** candy
dulcera *f* candy dish, preserve dish
dulcería *f* candy store, confectionery store
dulce•ro -ra *adj* (coll) sweet-toothed || *mf* confectioner || *f* see **dulcera**
dulcificar §73 *tr* to sweeten; to appease, mollify || *ref* to sweeten, turn sweet
dulcinea *f* (coll) sweetheart; (coll) ideal
dulzaina *f* flageolet
dulza•rrón -rrona *adj* (coll) cloying, sickening
dulzura *f* sweetness; pleasantness, kindliness; (*del clima*) mildness; endearment, sweet word
duna *f* dune
dun•do -da *adj* (CAm, Col) simple, stupid || *mf* (CAm, Col) simpleton
dúo *m* duet, duo
duodéci•mo -ma *adj & m* twelfth
duodeno *m* duodenum
duplica•do -da *adj & m* duplicate; **por duplicado** in duplicate
duplicar §73 *tr* to duplicate; to double; to repeat
duplicata *f* duplicate
duplicidad *f* (*falsedad*) duplicity; (*calidad de doble*) doubleness
du•plo -pla *adj & m* double
duque *m* duke; **gran duque** grand duke
duquesa *f* duchess; **gran duquesa** grand duchess
dura *f* (coll) durability; **de dura** or **de mucha dura** (coll) strong, durable
durable *adj* durable, lasting
duración *f* duration, endurance; (*espacio de tiempo del uso de una cosa*) life
durade•ro -ra *adj* durable, lasting
durante *prep* during, for
durar *intr* to last; to remain; (*la ropa*) to last, to wear, to wear well
durazno *m* peach; peach tree
dureza *f* hardness; harshness, roughness; **dureza de corazón** hardheartedness; **dureza de oído** hardness of hearing; **dureza de vientre** constipation
durmiente *adj* sleeping || *mf* sleeper || *m* girder, sleeper, stringer; (Am) tie, railroad tie; (Ven) steel bar

du•ro -ra *adj* hard; (*huevo*) hard-boiled; harsh, rough; cruel; stubborn, obstinate; unbearable; strong, tough; stingy; (*tiempo*) stormy; **duro de corazón** hard-hearted; **duro de oído** hard of hearing; **estar muy duro con** to be hard on; **ser duro de pelar** (coll) to be hard to put across; (coll) to be hard to deal with || *m* dollar (*Spanish coin worth five pesetas*) || *f* see **dura** || **duro** *adv* hard
dux *m* (*pl* **dux**) doge
d/v *abbr* **días vista**

E

E, e (e) *f* sixth letter of the Spanish alphabet
e *conj* (used before words beginning with *i* or *hi* not followed by a vowel) and
ea *interj* hey!
ebanista *m* cabinetmaker, woodworker
ebanistería *f* cabinetmaking, woodwork; cabinetmaker's shop
ébano *m* ebony
ebriedad *f* drunkenness
e•brio -bria *adj* drunk; (*p.ej., de ira*) blind || *mf* drunk
ebrio•so -sa *adj* drinking || *mf* drinker
ebullición *f* boiling
eccema *m & f* eczema
ecléctí•co -ca *adj & mf* eclectic
eclesiásti•co -ca *adj & m* ecclesiastic
eclipsar *tr* to eclipse; (fig) to outshine || *ref* to be in eclipse; (fig) to disappear
eclipse *m* eclipse
eclip•sis *f* (*pl* **-sis**) var of **elipsis**
eclisa *f* (rr) fishplate
eco *m* echo; (*del tambor*) rumbling; **hacer eco** to echo; to attract attention; **tener eco** to be well received, to catch on
economato *m* stewardship; commissary, company store, coöperative store
economía *f* economy; want, poverty; **economía política** economics; **economías** savings
económi•co -ca *adj* economic; (*que gasta poco; poco costoso*) economical; cheap; miserly, niggardly
economista *mf* economist
economizar **§60** *tr* to economize, to save; to avoid || *intr* to economize, save; to skimp
ecónomo *m* steward, trustee; supply priest
ecuación *f* equation
ecuador *m* equator || **el Ecuador** Ecuador
ecuánime *adj* calm, composed; impartial
ecuanimidad *f* equanimity; impartiality
ecuatoria•no -na *adj & mf* Ecuadoran, Ecuadorian
ecuestre *adj* equestrian
ecuméni•co -ca *adj* ecumenic(al)
eczema *m & f* eczema
echacan•tos *m* (*pl* **-tos**) (coll) good-for-nothing
echacuer•vos *m* (*pl* **-vos**) (coll) pimp, procurer; (coll) cheat
echada *f* cast, throw; man's length; (Arg, Mex) boast, hoax
echadero *m* place to stretch out
echadi•zo -za *adj* discarded, waste; spying || *mf* foundling || *m* spy
echa•do -da *adj* stretched out; (C-R) lazy, indolent || *f* see **echada**
echar *tr* to throw, throw away, throw out; to issue, emit; to publish; to discharge, dismiss; to swallow; (*p.ej., agua*) to pour; (*p.ej., un cigarrillo*) to smoke; (*la baraja*) to deal; (*una partida de cartas*) to play; (*una llave*) to turn; (*un discurso*) to deliver; (*un drama*) to put on; (*maldiciones*) to utter; (*pelo, dientes, renuevos*) to grow, put forth; (*impuestos*) to impose, to levy; (*la buenaventura*) to tell; (*precio, distancia, edad, etc.*) to ascribe, attribute; (*una mirada*) to cast; (*sangre*) to shed; (*la culpa*) to lay; (*una mano*) to lend; **echar abajo** to demolish, destroy; to overthrow; **echar a pasear** (coll) to dismiss unceremoniously; **echar a perder** to spoil, to ruin; **echar a pique** to sink; **echar de menos** to miss; **echarla de** (coll) to claim to be, boast of being; **echarlo todo a rodar** (coll) to upset everything; (coll) to hit the ceiling || *intr* — **echar a** to begin to; to burst out (*e.g., crying*); **echar a perder** to spoil, to ruin; **echar de ver** to notice, to happen to see; **echar por** (*un empleo, un oficio*) to go into, take up; (*la derecha, la izquierda*) to turn toward; (*un camino*) to go down || *ref* to throw oneself; to lie down, stretch out; (*el viento*) to fall; (*un abrigo*) to throw on; (*una gallina*) to set; **echarse a** to begin to; **echarse a morir** (coll) to give up in despair; **echarse a perder** to spoil, to be ruined; **echarse atrás** to back out; **echarse de ver** to be easy to see; **echárselas de** to claim to be, to boast of being; **echarse sobre** to rush at, fall upon
echazón *f* jettison, jetsam
echiquier *m* Exchequer
edad *f* age; **edad crítica** change of life; **edad de quintas** draft age; **edad escolar** school age; **Edad Media** Middle Ages; **edad viril** prime of life; **mayor edad** majority; **menor edad** minority
edecán *m* aide-de-camp
edición *f* edition; publication; **la segun-**

da edición de (coll) the spit and image of
edicto *m* edict
edificación *f* construction, building; buildings; (*inspiración con el buen ejemplo*) edification, uplift
edificante *adj* edifying
edificar **§73** *tr* to construct, build; (*dar buen ejemplo a*) to edify, to uplift
edificio *m* edifice, building
editar *tr* to publish
edi•tor -tora *adj* publishing || *mf* publisher
editorial *adj* publishing; editorial || *m* editorial || *f* publishing house
editorialista *mf* (Am) editorial writer
editorializar **§60** *intr* (Urug) to editorialize
edredón *m* eider down
educación *f* education
educacional *adj* educational
educa•dor -dora *mf* educator
educan•do -da *mf* pupil, student
educar **§73** *tr* to educate; (*los sentidos*) to train; (*al niño o el adolescente*) to rear, to bring up
educati•vo -va *adj* educational
EE.UU. *abbr* **Estados Unidos**
efectismo *m* sensationalism
efectista *adj* sensational, theatrical || *mf* sensationalist
efectivamente *adv* actually, really; as a matter of fact
efecti•vo -va *adj* actual, real; (*empleo, cargo*) regular, permanent; (*vigente*) effective; **hacer efectivo** to carry out; (*un cheque*) to cash; **hacerse efectivo** to become effective || *m* cash; **efectivo en caja** cash on hand
efecto *m* effect; end, purpose; article; (*en el juego de billar*) English; **a ese efecto** for that purpose; **al efecto** for the purpose; **con efecto** or **en efecto** indeed, as a matter of fact; **efecto útil** efficiency, output; **llevar a efecto** or **poner en efecto** to put into effect, to carry out; **surtir efecto** to work, to have the desired effect
efectuar **§21** *tr* to carry out, to effect, to effectuate || *ref* to take place
efervescencia *f* effervescence
efervescente *adj* effervescent
eficacia *f* efficacy
efi•caz *adj* (*pl* **-caces**) efficacious, effectual; efficient
eficiencia *f* efficiency
eficiente *adj* efficient
efigie *f* effigy
efíme•ro -ra *adj* ephemeral
efugio *m* evasion, subterfuge
efusión *f* effusion; (*manifestación de afectos muy viva*) warmth, effusiveness; **efusión de sangre** bloodshed
efusi•vo -va *adj* effusive
égida *f* aegis
egip•cio -cia *adj & mf* Egyptian
Egipto *m* Egypt
eglantina *f* sweetbriar
eglefino *m* haddock
égloga *f* eclogue
egoísmo *m* egoism
egoísta *adj* egoistic || *mf* egoist
egotismo *m* egotism
egotista *adj* egotistic(al) || *mf* egotist
egre•gio -gia *adj* distinguished, eminent
egresar *intr* (Am) to graduate
egreso *m* departure; (Am) graduation
eje *m* (*pieza alrededor de la cual gira un cuerpo*) axle, shaft; (*línea que divide en dos mitades; línea recta alrededor de la cual se supone que gira un cuerpo*) axis; (fig) core, crux; **eje de balancín** rocker, rockershaft; **eje de carretón** axletree; **eje motor** drive shaft
ejecución *f* execution
ejecutante *mf* performer
ejecutar *tr* to execute; to perform
ejecutivamente *adv* expeditiously
ejecuti•vo -va *adj* urgent, pressing; insistent; executive || *m* (Am) executive
ejecu•tor -tora *adj* executive || *mf* executor; **ejecutor de la justicia** executioner; **ejecutor testamentario** executor (*of a will*) || *f* — **ejecutora testamentaria** executrix
ejemplar *adj* exemplary || *m* pattern, model; (*de una obra impresa*) copy; precedent; (*caso que sirve de escarmiento*) example; **ejemplar de cortesía** complimentary copy; **ejemplar muestra** sample copy; **sin ejemplar** unprecedented; as a special case
ejemplarizar **§60** *tr* (Am) to set an example to; (Am) to exemplify
ejemplificar **§73** *tr* to exemplify
ejemplo *m* example, instance; **por ejemplo** for example, for instance; **sin ejemplo** unexampled
ejercer **§78** *tr* (*la medicina*) to practice; (*la caridad*) to show, exercise; (*una fuerza*) to exert || *intr* to practice; **ejercer de** to practice as, to work as
ejercicio *m* exercise; drill, practice; (*de un cargo u oficio*) tenure; (*uso constante*) exertion; (*año económico*) fiscal year; **hacer ejercicio** to take exercise; (mil) to drill
ejercitar *tr* to exercise; to practice; to drill, to train || *ref* to exercise; to practice
ejército *m* army; **ejército permanente** standing army; **los tres ejércitos** the three arms of the service
ejido *m* commons
ejote *m* (CAm, Mex) string bean
el, la (*pl* **los, las**) *art def* the || *pron dem* that, the one; **el que** who, which, that; he who, the one that
él *pron pers masc* he, it; him, it
elabora•do -da *adj* elaborate; finished
elaborar *tr* to elaborate; (*una teoría*) to work out; (*el metal, la madera*) to fashion, to work
elación *f* magnanimity, nobility; (*de estilo y lenguaje*) pomposity
elástica *f* knit undershirt; **elásticas** (Ven) suspenders
elasticidad *f* elasticity
elásti•co -ca *adj* elastic || *m* elastic; (Am) bedspring || *f* see **elástica**
eléboro *m* hellebore
elección *f* election; choice
electi•vo -va *adj* elective
elec•to -ta *adj* elect
electorado *m* electorate

electorero *m* henchman, heeler
electricidad *f* electricity
electricista *mf* electrician
eléctrico -ca *adj* electric(al)
electrificar §73 *tr* to electrify
electrizar §60 *tr* to electrify
electro *m* electromagnet
electroafeitadora *f* electric shaver
electrocutar *tr* to electrocute
electrodo *m* electrode
electrodomésti·co -ca *adj* electric-household
electróge·no -na *adj* generating electricity || *m* electric generator
electroimán *m* electromagnet
electrólisis *f* electrolysis
electrólito *m* electrolyte
electromagnéti·co -ca *adj* electromagnetic
electromo·tor -tora or **-triz** *adj* (*pl* **-tores -toras -trices**) electromotive
electrón *m* electron
electróni·co -ca *adj* electronic || *f* electronics
electrostáti·co -ca *adj* electrostatic
electrotecnia *f* electrical engineering
electrotipar *tr* to electrotype
electrotipo *m* electrotype
elefante *m* elephant; **elefante blanco** (fig) (SAm) white elephant
elegancia *f* elegance; style, stylishness
elegante *adj* elegant; stylish || *mf* fashion plate
elegía *f* elegy
elegía·co -ca *adj* elegiac
elegible *adj* eligible
elegir §57 *tr* to elect; to choose, select
elemental *adj* (*primordial; simple, no compuesto*) elemental; (*que se refiere a los principios de una ciencia o arte; de fácil comprensión*) elementary
elemento *m* element; (*de una pila o batería*) cell; **elemento de compuestos** (gram) combining form; **estar en su elemento** to be in one's element
elenco *m* catalogue, list, table; (theat) (Am) cast
elevación *f* elevation; **elevación a potencias** (math) involution
eleva·do -da *adj* elevated, high; lofty, sublime
elevador *m* (Am) elevator; **elevador de granos** (Am) grain elevator
elevar *tr* to elevate, to lift; (math) to raise || *ref* to ascend, rise; to be exalted; to become conceited
elfo *m* elf
elidir *tr* to eliminate; (*una vocal*) to elide
eliminar *tr* to eliminate; to strike out
elipse *f* (geom) ellipse
elip·sis *f* (*pl* **-sis**) (gram) ellipsis
elípti·co -ca *adj* (geom & gram) elliptic(al)
elisión *f* elision
elocución *f* public speaking, elocution
elocuencia *f* eloquence
elocuente *adj* eloquent
elogiable *adj* praiseworthy
elogiar *tr* to praise, eulogize
elogio *m* praise, eulogy
elogio·so -sa *adj* (Am) laudatory, glowing
elote *m* (Mex, Guat) ear of corn; **coger asando elotes** (CAm) to catch in the act; **pagar los elotes** (CAm) to be the goat
elucidar *tr* to elucidate
eludir *tr* to elude, evade, avoid
ella *pron pers fem* she, it; her, it; (coll) the trouble
ello *pron pers neut* it; (coll) the trouble; **ello es que** the fact is that || *m* (psychoanalysis) id
E.M. *abbr* **Estado Mayor**
emancipar *tr* to emancipate
embadurnamiento *m* daub, daubing
embadurnar *tr* to daub
embaír §1 *tr* to deceive, take in, hoax
embajada *f* embassy; ambassadorship; (iron) fine proposition
embajador *m* ambassador; **embajadores** ambassador and wife
embajadora *f* ambassadress
embalaje *m* packing; package; (sport) sprint
embalar *tr* to pack || *intr* (sport) to sprint || *ref* (*el motor*) to race; (sport) to sprint
embaldosado *m* tile paving
embaldosar *tr* to pave with tile
embalsamar *tr* to embalm; to perfume
embalsar *tr* to dam, to dam up
embalse *m* dam; damming; backwater
embanastar *tr* to put in a basket; to pack, jam, overcrowd
embanquetar *tr* (Mex) to line with sidewalks
embarazada *adj fem* pregnant || *f* pregnant woman
embarazar §60 *tr* (*estorbar*) to embarrass; to obstruct; to make pregnant || *ref* to be embarrassed, be encumbered; to become pregnant
embarazo *m* embarrassment; obstruction; awkwardness; pregnancy
embarazo·so -sa *adj* embarrassing, troublesome
embarbillar *tr* to rabbet
embarcación *f* boat, ship; embarkation (*of passengers*)
embarcadero *m* pier, wharf; (rr) (Am) platform; **embarcadero de ganado** (Arg) loading chute; **embarcadero flotante** landing stage
embarcador *m* shipper
embarcar §73 *tr* to ship || *intr* to entrain || *ref* to embark, to ship; to get involved
embarco *m* embarkation (*of passengers*)
embargar §44 *tr* to embargo; to paralyze; (law) to seize, attach
embargo *m* embargo; indigestion; (law) seizure, attachment; **sin embargo** however, nevertheless
embarnizar §60 *tr* to varnish
embarque *m* shipment, embarkation (*of freight*)
embarrada *f* (Am) blunder
embarrancar §73 *tr, intr & ref* to run into a ditch; (*una nave*) to run aground
embarrar *tr* to splash with mud; to

smear, stain; (CAm, Mex) to involve in a shady deal; **embarrarla** (Arg) to spoil the whole thing
embarrilar *tr* to barrel, put in barrels
embarullar *tr* (coll) to muddle, make a mess of; (coll) to bungle, botch
embastar *tr* to baste, to stitch
embate *m* blow, attack; (*del mar*) beating, dashing; (*de viento*) gust; **embates de la fortuna** hard knocks
embaucar §73 *tr* to trick, bamboozle, swindle
embaula·do -da *adj* crowded, packed, jammed
embaular §8 *tr* to put in a trunk; (coll) to jam, pack in
embayar *ref* (Ecuad) to fly into a rage
embazar §60 *tr* to dye brown; to hinder, obstruct; to astound, dumbfound || *ref* to get bored; to be upset, get sick at the stomach
embebecer §22 *tr* to entertain, amuse, fascinate, enchant
embeber *tr* to absorb, soak up; to soak; to contain, include; to embed; to contract, shrink || *intr* to contract, shrink || *ref* to be enchanted, be enraptured; to become absorbed or immersed; to become well versed
embebi·do -da *adj* (*vocal*) elided; (*columna*) engaged
embelecar §73 *tr* to cheat, dupe, bamboozle
embeleco *m* cheating, fraud; (coll) bore; **embelecos** cuteness
embeleñar *tr* to dope, stupefy; to enchant, bewitch
embelesar *tr* to charm, enrapture, fascinate
embeleso *m* charm, fascination, delight
embellece·dor -dora *adj* embellishing, beautifying || *m* (aut) hubcap || *f* beautician
embellecer §22 *tr* to embellish, beautify
embellecimiento *m* embellishment, beautification
embermejecer §22 *tr* to dye red; to make blush || *ref* to blush
emberrinchar *ref* (coll) to fly into a rage
embestida *f* attack, assault; (*detención intempestiva*) (coll) buttonholing
embesti·dor -dora *mf* (coll) beat, sponger
embestir §50 *tr* to attack, assail; to strike; (coll) to buttonhole, waylay || *intr* to attack, to charge, to rush
embetunar *tr* to blacken; to cover with tar
embicar §73 *tr* (Mex) to turn upside down, to tilt || *intr* (Arg, Chile) to run aground
emblandecer §22 *tr* to soften; to placate, mollify || *ref* to soften, to yield
emblanquecer §22 *tr* to whiten; to bleach || *ref* to turn white
emblema *m* emblem
emblemáti·co -ca *adj* emblematic(al)
embobar *tr* to amaze, fascinate || *ref* to stand gaping
embocadero *m* mouth, outlet
embocadura *f* nozzle; (*de río*) mouth; (*del freno; de instrumento de viento*) mouthpiece; (*de cigarrillo*) tip; (*del vino*) taste; stage entrance
embocar §73 *tr* to catch in the mouth; to put in the mouth; to take on, undertake; (coll) to gulp down; (coll) to try to put over || *intr & ref* to enter, pass
embolada *f* stroke
embolado *m* bull with wooden balls on horns; (theat) minor role; (coll) trick, hoax
embolar *tr* (*los cuernos del toro*) to put wooden balls on; (*el calzado*) to shine
embolia *f* embolism
émbolo *m* (mach) piston; **émbolo buzo** (mach) plunger
embolsar *tr* to pocket, take in
embonar *tr* (Am) to fertilize; (Am) to suit, be becoming to
emboquillar *tr* (*los cigarrillos*) to put tips on; (*una galería o túnel*) to cut an entrance in; (*las junturas entre los ladrillos*) (Chile) to point, to chink
emborrachar *tr* to intoxicate || *ref* to get drunk; (*los colores de una tela*) to run
emborrar *tr* to stuff, pad, wad; (coll) to gulp down
emborrascar §73 *tr* to stir up, irritate || *ref* to get stormy; (*un negocio*) to fail; (*la veta de una mina*) (Arg, CAm, Mex) to peter out
emborronar *tr* to blot; to scribble
emboscada *f* ambush, ambuscade
emboscado *m* draft dodger
emboscar §73 *tr* (*tropas para sorprender al enemigo*) to ambush || *ref* to ambush, lie in ambush; to shirk, take an easy way out
embota·do -da *adj* blunt, dull; (Chile) black-pawed
embotadura *f* bluntness, dullness
embotar *tr* to blunt, to dull; to dull, weaken; (*el tabaco*) to put in a jar
embotella·do -da *adj* (*discurso*) prepared || *m* bottling; (*del tráfico*) bottleneck
embotellamiento *m* bottling; traffic jam
embotellar *tr* to bottle; (*un negocio*) to tie up; (nav) to bottle up
embotijar *tr* (*un suelo*) to underlay with jugs || *ref* (coll) to swell up with anger
embovedar *tr* to vault, vault over; to put in a vault
emboza·do -da *adj* muffled up || *mf* person muffled up to eyes
embozar §60 *tr* to muffle up to the eyes; (*p.ej., a un perro*) to muzzle; to disguise || *ref* to muffle oneself up to the eyes
embozo *m* muffler, cloak held over the face; fold back (*of bed sheet*); cunning, dissimulation; **quitarse el embozo** (coll) to drop one's mask
embragar §44 *tr* (*el motor*) to engage || *intr* to throw the clutch in
embrague *m* clutch; engagement
embravecer §22 *tr* to enrage, make angry || *ref* to get angry; (*el mar*) to get rough

embraveci•do -da *adj* angry; rough, wild
embrear *tr* to tar, cover with tar; to calk with tar
embregar **§44** *ref* to wrangle
embriagar **§44** *tr* to intoxicate, make drunk; to enrapture || *ref* to get drunk
embriaguez *f* drunkenness; rapture
embridar *tr* to bridle; to check, restrain
embriología *f* embriology
embrión *m* embryo
embroca *f* poultice
embrocar **§73** *tr* to empty; (*el toro al torero*) to catch between the horns || *ref* (C-R) to fall on one's face; (Mex) to put on over the head
embrollar *tr* to tangle, muddle, embroil
embrollo *m* entanglement, muddle, embroilment; deception, trick
embromar *tr* to joke with, play jokes on; (Am) to bore, annoy || *ref* (Am) to be bored, be annoyed
embrujar *tr* to bewitch
embrutecer **§22** *tr* to brutify, stupefy
embuchado *m* pork sausage; subterfuge; (*de la urna electoral*) stuffing (of ballot box)
embudar *tr* to put a funnel in; to trick, trap
embudista *adj* tricky, scheming || *mf* schemer
embudo *m* funnel; trick; (mil) shell hole; **embudo de bomba** (mil) bomb crater
embullar *tr* to stir up, excite, key up || *ref* to become excited, keyed up
emburujar *tr* to jumble, pile up || *ref* (Am) to wrap oneself up
embuste *m* lie, falsehood, trick; **embustes** baubles, trinkets; (*del niño*) cuteness
embuste•ro -ra *adj* lying, false, tricky || *mf* liar, cheat
embuti•do -da *adj* inlaid, flush || *m* inlay, marquetry; pork sausage; (Am) lace insertion
embutir *tr* to stuff, pack tight; to insert; to inlay; to set flush; (*una hoja de metal*) to fashion, to hammer into shape || *ref* to squeeze in; (coll) to stuff oneself
emergencia *f* emergence; incident
emerger **§17** *intr* to emerge; (*un submarino*) to surface
emersión *f* emersion; (*de un submarino*) surfacing
eméti•co -ca *adj & m* emetic
emigración *f* emigration; migration
emigra•do -da *mf* émigré
emigrante *adj & mf* emigrant
emigrar *intr* to emigrate; to migrate
eminencia *f* eminence
eminente *adj* eminent
emisa•rio -ria *mf* emissary || *m* outlet
emisión *f* (*acción de exhalar; acción de lanzar ondas luminosas, etc.*) emission; (*títulos creados de una vez*) (com) issue; (*acción de emitir títulos nuevos*) (com) issuance; (rad) broadcast; **emisión seriada** (rad) serial
emi•sor -sora *adj* emitting; broadcasting || *m* (rad) transmitter || *f* broadcasting station
emitir *tr* to emit, send forth; to issue, give out; (*p.ej., opiniones*) to utter, express; (com) to issue; (rad) to broadcast
emoción *f* emotion
emocional *adj* emotional
emocionante *adj* moving, touching; thrilling, exciting
emocionar *tr* to move, stir; to thrill
emoti•vo -va *adj* emotional
empacadi•zo -za *adj* (Arg) touchy
empaca•do -da *adj* (Arg) gruff, grim
empacar **§73** *tr* to pack, to crate || *ref* to be stubborn; (*un animal*) (Am) to balk, get balky
empa•cón -cona *adj* (Am) stubborn; (Am) balky
empacha•do -da *adj* backward, fumbling
empachar *tr* to hinder, embarrass; to disguise; to surfeit, upset the stomach of || *ref* to blush, be embarrassed; to be upset, have indigestion
empacho *m* hindrance; embarrassment, bashfulness; indigestion
empacho•so -sa *adj* sickening; shameful
empadronar *tr* to register, to take the census of || *ref* to register, be registered in the census
empalagar **§44** *tr* to cloy, pall, surfeit; to bore, to weary
empalago•so -sa *adj* cloying, sickening, mawkish; boring, annoying; fawning
empalar *tr* impale
empalizada *f* palisade, stockade, fence
empalizar **§60** *tr* to fence in
empalmar *tr* to splice, connect, join, couple; to combine || *intr* to connect, make connections; **empalmar con** to connect with; to follow, succeed
empalme *m* splice, connection, joint, coupling; combination; (elec) joint; (rr) connection, junction
empanada *f* pie; fraud
empanadilla *f* pie
empana•do -da *adj* unlighted, unventilated || *f* see **empanada**
empanar *tr* to crumb, to bread; (*las tierras*) to sow with wheat
empantanar *tr* to flood; to obstruct
empaña•do -da *adj* dim, misty; blurred, fogged; (*voz*) flat
empañar *tr* (*a las criaturas*) to swaddle; to blur, fog, dim, dull; to tarnish, sully || *ref* to blur, fog, dim, dull
empañetar *tr* (Am) to plaster
empapar *tr* to soak; to soak up, absorb; to drench || *ref* to soak; to be soaked; to become imbued; (coll) to be surfeited
empapelado *m* papering, paper hanging; wallpaper; paper lining
empapela•dor -dora *mf* paper hanger
empapelar *tr* to wrap in paper; to paper, line with paper; to wallpaper; (coll) to bring a criminal charge against
empaque *m* packing; (coll) look, appearance, mien; stiffness, stuffiness; (Am) brazenness
empaquetadura *f* gasket

empaquetar *tr* to pack; to jam, stuff || *ref* to pack; to pack in; (coll) to dress up
empareda·do -da *mf* recluse || *m* sandwich
emparedar *tr* to wall in, to confine
emparejar *tr* to pair, to match; to smooth, make level; to even, make even; (*una puerta*) to close flush || *intr* to come up, come abreast; **emparejar con** to catch up with || *ref* to pair, to match
emparentar §2 *intr* to become related by marriage; **emparentar con** (*buena gente*) to marry into the family of; (*una familia rica*) to marry into
emparrado *m* arbor, bower
emparrillar *tr* to grill
empasta·dor -dora *mf* (Am) bookbinder
empastadura *f* (Am) binding
empastar *tr* (*un diente*) to fill; (*un libro*) to bind with stiff covers; (Am) to convert into pasture land || *ref* (Chile) to be overgrown with weeds
empaste *m* (*de diente*) filling; stiff binding
empastelar *tr* (typ) to pie
empatar *tr* (*en la votación y los juegos*) to tie; (Am) to join, connect; (Am) to tie, fasten || *intr* to tie || *ref* to tie; **empatársela a una persona** to be a match for someone; **empatárselo a una persona** (Guat, Hond) to put it over on someone
empate *m* tie, draw; (Col) penholder; (Ven) waste of time
empavar *tr* (Ecuad) to annoy; (Peru) to kid, to razz
empavesado *m* (naut) dressing, bunting
empavesar *tr* to bedeck with flags and bunting; (*un buque*) to dress; (*un monumento*) to veil || *ref* to become overcast
empavonar *tr* to blue; (Am) to grease, spread grease over || *ref* (CAm) to dress up
empecina·do -da *adj* (Am) stubborn
empederni·do -da *adj* hardened, inveterate; hard-hearted
empedra·do -da *adj* cloud-flecked; pock-marked; (*caballo*) dark-spotted || *m* stone paving
empedrar §2 *tr* to pave with stones; to bespatter
empegado *m* tarpaulin
empegar §44 *tr* to coat with pitch, to dip in pitch; (*el ganado lanar*) to mark with pitch
empeine *m* instep; (*de la bota*) vamp; (*enfermedad cutánea*) tetter; (*región central del hipogastrio*) pubes
empelotar *ref* (coll) to get all tangled up; (coll) to get into a row; (Am) to take all one's clothes off; (Mex, W-I) to fall madly in love
empella *f* vamp
empellar *tr* to push, shove
empeller §31 *tr* to push, shove
empellón *m* push, shove; **a empellones** pushing, roughly
empenachar *tr* to adorn with plumes
empeña·do -da *adj* (*disputa*) bitter, heated; **no empeñado** noncommitted
empeñar *tr* (*dar en prenda*) to pawn; (*una lucha*) to launch, begin; (*prendar, hipotecar*) to pledge; (*la palabra*) to pledge; to force, compel || *ref* to commit oneself, bind oneself; to go into debt; (*una lucha, una disputa*) to begin, to start; **empeñarse en** to engage in; to persist in, insist on
empeñe·ro -ra *mf* (Mex) pawnbroker
empeño *m* pledge, engagement, commitment; (*prenda*) pawn; pawnshop; persistence, insistence; eagerness, perseverance; effort, endeavor; pledge, backer, patron; favor, protection; **con empeño** eagerly
empeño·so -sa *adj* (Am) eager, persistent
empeorar *tr* to impair, make worse || *intr & ref* to get worse, deteriorate
empequeñecer §22 *tr* (*hacer más pequeño*) to make smaller, to dwarf; (*amenguar la importancia de*) to belittle || *ref* to get smaller, to dwarf
emperador *m* emperor; **los emperadores** the emperor and empress
empera·triz *f* (*pl* **-trices**) empress
emperchar *tr* to hang on a clothes rack
emperejilar *tr & ref* (coll) to dress up, to spruce up
emperezar §60 *tr* to delay, put off || *intr & ref* to get lazy
empericar §73 *ref* (Col, Ecuad) to get drunk; (Mex) to blush
emperifollar *tr & ref* to dress up gaudily
empernar *tr* to bolt
empero *conj* but, however, yet
emperrar *ref* (coll) to get stubborn
empezar §18 *tr & intr* to begin
empicar §73 *ref* to become infatuated
empicotar *tr* to pillory
empiema *m* empyema
empina·do -da *adj* high, lofty; steep; stiff, stuck-up || *f* (aer) zoom, zooming; **irse a la empinada** (*un caballo*) to rear
empinar *tr* to raise, lift; to tip over; (aer) to zoom; (*el codo*) (coll) to crook || *intr* to be a toper || *ref* to stand on tiptoe; (*un caballo*) to rear; to tower, rise high; (aer) to zoom
empingorota·do -da *adj* influential; (coll) proud, haughty
empingorotar *tr* (coll) to put on top || *ref* (coll) to climb up, get up; (coll) to be stuck-up
empíre·o -a *adj & m* empyrean
empíri·co -ca *adj* empiric(al) || *mf* empiricist
empizarrado *m* slate roof
empizarrar *tr* to roof with slate
emplastar *tr* to put a plaster on; to put make-up on; (*un negocio*) to tie up, obstruct || *ref* to put make-up on; to smear oneself up
emplásti·co -ca *adj* sticky
emplasto *m* plaster, poultice
emplazamiento *m* emplacement, location; (law) summons
emplazar §60 *tr* to place, locate; to summon, to summons
emplea·do -da *mf* employee; (*de ofi-*

cina, de tienda) clerk; **empleado público** civil servant

emplear *tr* to employ; to use; (*el dinero*) to invest; **estarle a uno bien empleado** (coll) to serve someone right || *ref* to be employed; to busy oneself; **empleárselo mal** (coll) to act up, to misbehave

empleo *m* employ, employment; use; job, position, occupation

empleomanía *f* (coll) eagerness to hold public office

empleóma•no -na *mf* (Am) public officeholder, bureaucrat

emplomar *tr* to lead; to line with lead; (*un techo*) to cover with lead; to put a lead seal on; (*un diente*) (Arg) to fill

emplumar *tr* to put a feather on; to adorn with feathers; to tar and feather; (Hond) to thrash; **emplumarlas** (Col) to beat it || *intr* to fledge, grow feathers

emplumecer **§22** *intr* to fledge, grow feathers

empobrecer **§22** *tr* to impoverish || *intr & ref* to become poor

empodrecer **§22** *intr & ref* to rot

empolva•do -da *adj* (Mex) rusty

empolvar *tr* to cover with dust; (*el rostro*) to powder || *ref* to get dusty; (*el rostro*) to powder; (Mex) to get rusty

empolla•do -da *adj* primed for an examination

empollar *tr* (*huevos*) to brood, hatch; (*estudiar con mucha detención*) (coll) to bone up on || *intr* (coll) to grind, be a grind; **empollar sobre** (coll) to bone up on || *ref* to hatch; to bone up cn

empo•llón -llona *mf* (coll) grind

emponcha•do -da *adj* (SAm) poncho-wearing; (SAm) crafty, hypocritical; (SAm) suspicious-looking

emponzoñar *tr* to poison; to corrupt

emporcar **§81** *tr* to soil, to dirty

empotra•do -da *adj* built-in; recessed

empotrar *tr* to embed, recess, fasten in a wall || *intr & ref* to fit, interlock

emprende•dor -dora *adj* enterprising

emprender *tr* to undertake; **emprenderla con** (coll) to squabble with, have it out with; **emprenderla para** (coll) to set out for

empreñar *tr* to make pregnant || *ref* to become pregnant

empresa *f* enterprise, undertaking; company, concern, firm; device, motto; (*la parte patronal*) management; **empresa anunciadora** advertising agency; **empresa de tranvías** traction company; **pequeña empresa** small business

empresarial *adj* managerial

empresa•rio -ria *mf* contractor; business leader, industrialist; manager; promoter; theatrical manager; **empresario de circo** showman; **empresario de pompas fúnebres** undertaker; **empresario de publicidad** advertising man; **empresario de teatro** impresario, theater manager

emprestar *tr* to borrow

empréstito *m* loan, government loan

empujar *tr* to push, to shove; to replace || *intr* to push, to shove

empujatierra *f* bulldozer

empuje *m* push; (*fuerza o presión ejercidas por una cosa sobre otra*) thrust; (*espíritu emprendedor*) enterprise, push

empujón *m* hard push, shove; **tratar a empujones** (coll) to push around

empuñadura *f* (*de la espada*) hilt; (coll) first words of a story; (*de bastón o paraguas*) (Am) handle

empuñar *tr* to seize, grasp, clutch; (*un empleo o puesto*) to obtain; (*la mano*) (Chile) to clench; (Bol) to punch; **empuñar el bastón** (fig) to seize the reins

emular *tr & intr* to emulate; **emular con** to emulate, vie with

ému•lo -la *adj* emulous || *mf* rival

emulsión *f* emulsion

emulsionar *tr* to emulsify

en *prep* at; in; into; by; on; of, e.g., **pensar en** to think of

enaceitar *tr* to oil || *ref* to get oily, get rancid

enagua *f* petticoat; (Am) skirt; **enaguas** petticoat

enagüillas *fpl* kilt, short skirt

enajenación *f* alienation; estrangement; rapture; (*distracción*) absent-mindedness; **enajenación mental** mental derangement

enajenar *tr* (*la propiedad, el dominio; a un amigo*) to alienate, estrange; to enrapture, to transport || *ref* to be enraptured, be transported; **enajenarse de** to dispossess oneself of; (*un amigo*) to become alienated from

enaltecer **§22** *tr* to exalt, extol

enamoradi•zo -za *adj* susceptible

enamora•do -da *adj* lovesick; (*propenso a enamorarse*) susceptible || *mf* sweetheart || *m* lover

enamorar *tr* to make love to; to enamor, captivate || *ref* to fall in love

enamoricar **§73** *ref* (coll) to trifle in love

enangostar *tr & ref* to narrow

ena•no -na *adj* dwarfish || *mf* dwarf

enarbolar *tr* to hoist, hang out; (*una espada*) to brandish || *ref* to get angry; (*el caballo*) to rear

enarcar **§73** *tr* to arch; (*los toneles*) to hoop || *ref* to become confused, be bashful; (*el caballo*) (Mex) to rear

enardecer **§22** *tr* to inflame, excite || *ref* to get excited; (*una parte del cuerpo*) to become inflamed, get sore

enarenar *tr* to throw sand on || *ref* (naut) to run aground

enastar *tr* (*una herramienta*) to put a handle on; (*una bandera*) to put a shaft on

encabalgamiento *m* gun carriage; trestlework; (*en el verso*) enjambment

encabalgar **§44** *tr* to provide with horses || *intr* to lean, to rest

encaballar *tr* to overlap; (typ) to pie

encabezamiento *m* heading; (*fórmula con que comienza un documento*)

opening words; tax list; tax rate; **encabezamiento de factura** billhead
encabezar **§60** *tr* (*un escrito*) to put a heading or title on; to head; to register; (*vinos*) to fortify
encabritar *ref* (*un caballo*) to rear; (*un buque*) to shoot up, pitch up; (*un avión*) to nose up
encadenar *tr* to chain, put in chains; to brace, buttress; to bind, tie together; to tie down
encajar *tr* to fit, fit in, make fit; to insert, put in; (*un golpe*) to give, let go; (*dinero*) to put away; (*un chiste*) to tell at the wrong time; to palm off; to throw, hurl; **encajar una cosa a uno** to foist something on someone, to palm something off on someone || *intr* to fit; (*una puerta*) to close right || *ref* to squeeze one's way; (*una prenda de vestir*) to put on; (coll) to butt in, to intrude
encaje *m* (*tejido de mallas*) lace; (*labor de taracea*) inlay, mosaic; recess, groove; fitting, matching; insertion; appearance, look
encaje·ro -ra *mf* lacemaker; lace dealer
encajonado *m* cofferdam
encajonar *tr* to box, crate, case; to squeeze in || *ref* (*un río*) to narrow, narrow down; to squeeze in, squeeze through
encalambrar *ref* (Am) to get cramps
encalar *tr* (*espolvorear con cal*) to lime, sprinkle with lime; (*blanquear con cal*) to whitewash
encalma·do -da *adj* (*mercado de valores*) dull, quiet; (*mar, viento*) becalmed
encalvecer **§22** *intr* to get bald
encalladero *m* sand bank, shoal
encallar *intr* to run aground; to fail, get stuck
encallecer **§22** *intr* (*la piel*) to become callous || *ref* to become callous; (fig) to become callous, become hardened
encamar *tr* to spread out on the ground || *ref* (coll) to take to bed; (*el grano*) to droop, bend over
encaminar *tr* to direct, show the way to; (*sus esfuerzos, su atención*) to direct || *ref* to set out
encanalar *tr* to channel, to pipe
encandecer **§22** *tr* to make white-hot
encandila·do -da *adj* (*sombrero*) cocked; (coll) stiff, erect
encandilar *tr* to daze, befuddle; (*un fuego*) to stir || *ref* (*los ojos*) to flash
encanecer **§22** *intr* & *ref* to turn gray; to get old; to become moldy
encanta·do -da *adj* (coll) absent-minded, distracted; (*casa*) (coll) rambling
encanta·dor -dora *adj* charming, enchanting || *mf* charmer || *f* enchantress
encantamiento *m* charm, enchantment
encantar *tr* to charm, enchant, bewitch
encante *m* auction sale; auction house
encanto *m* charm, enchantment, spell
encantusar *tr* (coll) to coax, wheedle
encañada *f* gorge, ravine
encañar *tr* (*el agua*) to pipe; (*las tierras*) to drain; (*las plantas*) to prop up; to wind on a spool
encañizada *f* reed fence; weir
encañonar *tr* to pipe; to wind on a spool; (*un pliego*) (typ) to tip in
encaperuzar **§60** *tr* to put a hood on || *ref* to put on one's hood
encapotar *tr* to cloak || *ref* to frown; to cloud over, become overcast
encaprichar *ref* to insist on getting one's way; to become infatuated
encaracolado *m* spiral ornament, spiral work
encara·do -da *adj* — **bien encarado** well-featured; **mal encarado** ill-featured
encaramar *tr* to raise up, lift up; to praise, extol; (coll) to elevate, exalt || *ref* to climb, get on top; to rise, to tower; (Am) to blush
encarar *tr* to aim, point; (*una dificultad*) to face || *intr* & *ref* to come face to face
encarcelar *tr* to incarcerate, imprison, jail; (*piezas de madera recién encoladas*) to clamp; to plaster in || *ref* to stay indoors
encarecer **§22** *tr* (*el precio*) to raise; to raise the price of; to extol; to urge; to overrate || *intr* & *ref* to rise, to rise in price
encarecidamente *adv* earnestly, insistently, eagerly
encarga·do -da *mf* agent, representative; **encargado de negocios** chargé d'affaires
encargar **§44** *tr* (*mercancías*) to order; (*confiar*) to entrust; to urge, to warn || *ref* to take charge, be in charge
encargo *m* assignment, job, charge; (*pedido*) order; warning; **como de encargo** or **ni de encargo** (coll) just the thing, as if made to order
encariñar *tr* to awaken love in || *ref* — **encariñarse con** to become fond of, become attached to
encarnación *f* incarnation, embodiment
encarna·do -da *adj* red; flesh-colored; (*de forma humana*) incarnate
encarnar *tr* to incarnate, to embody; (*el anzuelo*) to bait || *intr* to become incarnate; (*una herida*) to heal over
encarnecer **§22** *intr* to put on flesh
encarniza·do -da *adj* bloodshot; bloody, fierce, bitter, hard-fought
encarnizar **§60** *tr* to anger, provoke || *ref* to get angry; to become fierce; **encarnizarse con** or **en** to be merciless to
encaro *m* aim; stare; blunderbuss
encarrilar *tr* to put back on the rails; to set right, to put on the right track; to guide, direct
encarruja·do -da *adj* wrinkled; (*pelo*) kinky; (*terreno*) (Mex) rough
encartar *tr* to enroll, register; to outlaw; (*un naipe*) to slip in || *ref* to be unable to discard
encartonar *tr* to cover with cardboard; (*libros*) to bind in boards
encasar *tr* (*un hueso dislocado*) to set (*a broken bone*)
encasillado *m* set of pigeonholes; (*lista*

de candidatos apoyados por el gobierno) government slate; (SAm) checkerwork
encasillar *tr* to pigeonhole; to sort out, classify; (*el gobierno a un candidato*) to slate
encasquetar *tr* (*un sombrero*) to stick on the head; (*una idea*) to drive in; to force on
encasquillar *tr* to put a tip on; (*un caballo*) (Am) to shoe || *ref* to stick, get stuck
encastilla·do -da *adj* haughty, proud
encastillar *tr* to fortify with castles; to pile up || *ref* to stick, get stuck; to take to the hills; to stick to one's opinion
encastrar *tr* to engage, to mesh
encastre *m* engaging, meshing; groove, socket; insert
encauchar *tr* to cover with rubber, line with rubber
encausar *tr* to prosecute, to sue, to bring to trial
encausticar §73 *tr* to wax
encáustico *m* floor wax, furniture polish
encauzar §60 *tr* (*una corriente*) to channel; to guide, direct
encavar *ref* to hide, burrow
encebollado *m* beef stew with onions
encelar *tr* to make jealous || *ref* to get jealous; to be in rut
encella *f* cheese mold
encenagar §44 *ref* to get covered with mud; to wallow in vice
encencerrar *tr* (*al ganado*) to put a bell on
encendajas *fpl* kindling, brush
encendedor *m* lighter; **encendedor de bolsillo** pocket lighter
encender §51 *tr* to light, kindle; to ignite, set fire to; (*la luz, la radio*) to turn on; (*la lengua*) to burn; to stir up, excite || *ref* to catch fire, to ignite; to become excited; to blush
encendi·do -da *adj* bright, high-colored; red, flushed; keen, enthusiastic || *m* ignition
encenizar §60 *tr* to cover with ashes || *ref* to get covered with ashes
encepar *tr* to put in the stocks || *intr* & *ref* to take deep root
encera·do -da *adj* wax, wax-colored; (*huevo*) boiled || *m* oilcloth; tarpaulin; (*pizarra*) blackboard
encerar *tr* to wax || *intr* & *ref* (*el grano*) to ripen, turn yellow
encerotar *tr* (*el hilo*) to wax
encerradero *m* sheepfold; (taur) bull pen
encerrar §2 *tr* to shut in; to lock in, lock up; to contain, include; to encircle; to imply || *ref* to lock oneself in; to go into seclusion; **encerrarse con** to be closeted with
encespedar *tr* to sod
encía *f* gum
encíclica *f* encyclical
enciclopedia *f* encyclopedia
enciclopédi·co -ca *adj* encyclopedic
encierro *m* locking up, confinement; inclusion: encirclement; lockup, prison; solitary confinement; retirement, retreat; (taur) bull pen
encima *adv* above, overhead, on top; at hand, here now; besides, in addition; **de encima** (Chile) in the bargain; **echarse encima** to take upon oneself; **encima de** on, upon; above, over; **por encima** hastily, superficially; **por encima de** above, over; in spite of; **quitarse de encima** to get rid of, to shake off
encina *f* holm oak, evergreen oak
encinta *adj* pregnant
encintado *m* curb
encintar *tr* to trim with ribbons; to provide with curbs
enclaustrar *tr* to cloister; to hide away
enclavar *tr* to nail; to pierce, transfix; (*el pie del caballo*) to prick; (coll) to cheat
enclave *m* enclave
enclavijar *tr* to dowel; (*un instrumento*) to peg
enclenque *adj* sickly, feeble
enclíti·co -ca *adj* & *m* enclitic
enclocar §81 *intr* & *ref* to brood
encofrado *m* planking, timbering; (*para el hormigón*) form
encoger §17 *tr* to shrink, shrivel; to discourage; to draw in || *intr* to shrink, shrivel || *ref* to shrink, shrivel; to be discouraged; to be bashful; (*humillarse*) to cringe; (*en la cama*) to curl up; **encogerse de hombros** to shrug one's shoulders
encogi·do -da *adj* bashful, timid
encogimiento *m* shrinkage; crouch; bashfulness, timidity; **encogimiento de hombros** shrug
encojar *tr* to cripple, to lame || *ref* to become lame; (coll) to feign illness
encolar *tr* to glue; (*la superficie que ha de pintarse*) to size; (*el vino*) to clarify; (*p.ej., una pelota*) to throw out of reach
encolerizar §60 *tr* to anger || *ref* to get angry
encomendar §2 *tr* to commend, entrust, commit; to knight || *ref* to commend oneself; to send regards
encomiar *tr* to praise, extol
encomienda *f* charge, commission; commendation, praise; favor, protection; knight's cross; royal land grant (*with Indian inhabitants*); (Am) parcel post; (Mex) fruit stand
encomio *m* encomium
enconamiento *m* soreness; **rancor, ill** will
enconar *tr* to make sore, inflame; to aggravate, irritate || *ref* to get sore, become inflamed; (*una herida; el ánimo de uno*) to rankle, to fester
enconchar *ref* (Am) to draw back into one's shell, keep aloof
encono *m* rancor, ill will; (Col, Chile, Mex, W-I) soreness
encono·so -sa *adj* sore, sensitive; harmful; rancorous
encontra·do -da *adj* opposite, facing; contrary; hostile; **estar encontrados** to be at odds
encontrar *tr* to encounter, to meet; (*ha-*

llar) to find || *intr* to meet; to collide || *ref* to meet, meet each other; to be, be situated; to find oneself; **encontrarse con** to meet, run into
encontrón *m* bump, jolt, collision
encopeta•do -da *adj* aristocratic, of noble descent; conceited, boastful
encorajar *tr* to encourage || *ref* to fly into a rage
encorajinar *ref* (coll) to fly into a rage; (Chile) to break up, go to ruin
encorchar *tr* (*botellas*) to cork; (*abejas*) to hive
encordar **§61** *tr* (*un violín, una raqueta*) to string; to wrap, wind up with rope
encordelar *tr* to string; to tie with strings
encornudar *tr* to cuckold, make a cuckold of || *intr* to grow horns
encorralar *tr* to corral
encortinar *tr* to curtain
encorvada *f* stoop, bending over; **hacer la encorvada** (coll) to malinger
encorvar *tr* to bend over || *ref* to stoop, bend over; to be partial, be biased
encovar **§61** *tr & ref* to hide away
encrespar *tr* to curl; (*el pelo*) to make stand on end; (*plumas*) to ruffle; (*las olas*) to stir up; to irritate, anger || *ref* to curl; to bristle, stand on end; (*el mar, las olas*) to get rough; to get involved; to bristle, get angry
encresta•do -da *adj* proud, haughty
encrucijada *f* crossroads, street intersection; ambush, snare, trap
encrudecer **§22** *tr* to make raw; to aggravate
encuadernación *f* bookbinding; (*taller*) bindery; **encuadernación a la holandesa** half binding
encuaderna•dor -dora *mf* bookbinder
encuadernar *tr* to bind; **sin encuadernar** unbound
encuadrar *tr* (*encerrar en un marco o cuadro*) to frame; (*incluir dentro de sí*) to encompass; (*encajar*) to insert, fit in; (Arg) to summarize
encuadre *m* film adaptation; (mov & telv) frame
encubar *tr* to put in a cask or vat; (min) to shore up
encubierta *f* fraud, deception
encubrimiento *m* concealment; (law) complicity
encubrir **§83** *tr* to hide, conceal || *ref* to hide; to disguise oneself
encuentro *m* encounter, meeting; clash, collision; (*hallazgo*) find; (sport) game, match; **encuentro fronterizo** border clash; **llevarse de encuentro** (CAm, Mex, W-I) to knock down, run over; (CAm, Mex, W-I) to drag down to ruin; **mal encuentro** foul play; **salir al encuentro a** to go to meet; to get ahead of; to take a stand against
encuerar *tr* (Am) to strip of clothes; (Am) to fleece || *ref* (Am) to strip, get undressed
encuesta *f* inquiry; (*cuestionario para conocer la opinión pública*) poll, survey
encuitar *ref* to grieve
encumbra•do -da *adj* high, lofty; sublime; influential
encumbramiento *m* height, elevation; exaltation
encumbrar *tr* to raise, elevate; to exalt || *ref* to rise; to be exalted; to be proud; to be flowery, use flowery speech; (*subir una cosa a mucha altura*) to tower
encunar *tr* to cradle; to catch between the horns
encurtido *m* pickle
encurtir *tr* to pickle
enchapado *m* veneer
enchapar *tr* to veneer
encharcar **§73** *tr* to make a puddle of; (*el estómago*) to upset || *ref* to turn into a puddle; to wallow in vice
enchavetar *tr* to key
enchilada *f* (Guat, Mex) corn cake with tomato sauce seasoned with chili
enchilado *m* (Cuba, Mex) shellfish stew with chili sauce
enchinar *tr* to pave with pebbles; (Mex) to curl || *ref* (Mex) to get goose flesh
enchispar *tr* (Am) to make drunk || *ref* (Am) to get drunk
enchivar *ref* (Col, Ecuad, CAm) to fly into a rage
enchufar *tr* (*un tubo o caño*) to fit; (*dos tubos o caños*) to connect, connect together; (*dos negocios*) to merge; (elec) to connect, plug in || *intr* to fit || *ref* to merge
enchufe *m* fitting; (*de tubo o caño*) male end; (*de dos tubos*) joint; (elec) connector; (elec) plug; (elec) receptacle; (coll) sinecure, easy job; **tener enchufe** (coll) to have pull, to have a drag
enchufismo *m* (coll) spoils system
enchufista *m* (coll) spoilsman
ende *adv* — **por ende** therefore
endeble *adj* feeble, weak; worthless
endecha *f* dirge
endechadera *f* hired mourner
endemia *f* endemic
endémi•co -ca *adj* endemic
endemonia•do -da *adj* possessed of the devil; furious, wild; (coll) devilish
endentar **§2** *tr & intr* to mesh
endentecer **§22** *intr* to teethe
enderezar **§60** *tr* to stand up; to straighten; to direct; to put in order; to regulate || *intr* to go straight || *ref* to stand up, straighten up; to head, make one's way; to go straight; (aer) to flatten out, to level off
endeuda•do -da *adj* indebted
endeudar *ref* to run into debt; to acknowledge one's indebtedness
endevota•do -da *adj* pious, devout; fond, devoted
endiabla•do -da *adj* devilish; deformed, ugly; mean, wicked; (Arg) difficult, complicated
endilgar **§44** *tr* (coll) to send, direct; (coll) to spring, unload
endiosar *tr* to deify || *ref* to get stuck-up; to get absorbed
endominga•do -da *adj* Sunday; all dressed up

endomingar **§44** *ref* to get dressed in one's Sunday best
endosante *mf* endorser
endosar *tr* (*un documento de crédito*) to endorse; (*una cosa poco grata*) to unload
endosata•rio -ria *mf* endorsee
endoso *m* endorsement
endriago *m* fabulous monster
endri•no -na *adj* sloe-colored || *m* (*arbusto*) sloe, blackthorn || *f* (*fruto*) sloe
endrogar **§44** *ref* (Am) to run into debt
endulzar **§60** *tr* to sweeten; to make bearable
endura•dor -dora *adj* saving, stingy
endurar *tr* to harden; to delay, put off; (*tolerar*) to endure; to save, spare || *ref* to get hard
endurecer **§22** *tr* to harden; (*robustecer, acostumbrar*) to inure
endureci•do -da *adj* hard, strong; inured; hard-hearted; tenacious, obstinate
enebrina *f* juniper berry
enebro *m* juniper
enecha•do -da *adj & mf* foundling
eneldo *m* dill
enema *f* enema
enemiga *f* enmity, hatred
enemi•go -ga *adj* enemy; hostile || *mf* enemy, foe; **el enemigo malo** the Evil One || *f* see **enemiga**
enemistad *f* enmity
enemistar *tr* to make an enemy of; to make enemies of || *ref* to become enemies
energía *f* energy; power
enérgi•co -ca *adj* energetic
energúme•no -na *adj* fiendish || *mf* crazy person, wild person
enero *m* January
enervar *tr* to enervate; to weaken
enési•mo -ma *adj* nth
enfadadi•zo -za *adj* peevish, irritable
enfadar *tr* to annoy, bother; to anger
enfado *m* annoyance, bother; anger
enfado•so -sa *adj* annoying, disagreeable
enfaldar *ref* to tuck up one's skirt
enfardar *tr* to bale, to pack
énfa•sis *m* (*pl* **-sis**) emphasis; bombast, affected speech
enfasizar **§60** *tr* to emphasize
enfáti•co -ca *adj* emphatic; affected
enfermar *tr* to make sick || *intr* to get sick
enfermedad *f* sickness, illness, disease
enfermera *f* nurse; **enfermera ambulante** visiting nurse
enfermería *f* infirmary
enfermero *m* male nurse
enfermi•zo -za *adj* sickly; (*clima*) unhealthy
enfer•mo -ma *adj* sick, ill; (*enfermizo*) sickly; **enfermo de amor** lovesick || *mf* patient
enfermo•so -sa *adj* (Am) sickly
enfiestar *ref* (Am) to have a good time
enfilar *tr* to line up; (*p.ej., perlas*) to string; to aim; to go down, to go up; (mil) to enfilade || *intr* to bear
enfisema *m* emphysema
enflaquecer **§22** *tr* to make thin; to weaken || *intr* to get thin; to flag, slacken || *ref* to get thin, lose weight
enflauta•do -da adj (coll) pompous, inflated
enflautar *tr* to blow up, inflate; (coll) to cheat
enfocar **§73** *tr* to focus; (fig) to size up
enfoque *m* focus, focusing; (fig) approach (*to a problem*)
enfoscar **§73** *tr* to trim with mortar; to patch with mortar; to darken, make dark || *ref* to become sullen, become grouchy; to become absorbed in business; to become overcast
enfrailar *tr* to make a friar or monk of || *ref* to become a friar or monk
enfranque *m* shank
enfrascar **§73** *tr* to bottle || *ref* to become involved, intangled; to be sunk in work; to have a good time
enfrenar *tr* (*un caballo*) to bridle; (*un tren*) to brake; to check
enfrentar *tr* to put face to face; (*p.ej., al enemigo*) to face || *intr* to be facing || *ref* to meet face to face; **enfrentarse con** to stand up to; to cope with
enfrente *adv* opposite, in front; **enfrente de** opposite, in front of; opposed to
enfriadera *f* bottle cooler, ice pail
enfriar **§77** *tr* to cool, to chill; (Am) to kill || *intr & ref* to cool off
enfundar *tr* to sheathe, to put in a case; to stuff; (*un tambor*) to muffle
enfurecer **§22** *tr* to infuriate, anger || *ref* to rage
enfurruñar *ref* (coll) to sulk
engalanar *tr* to adorn, deck out, dress
engalla•do -da *adj* straight, erect; haughty
engallador *m* checkrein
enganchar *tr* to hook; (*un caballo*) to hitch; (*un coche de ferrocarril*) to couple; to recruit; to inveigle || *intr* to get caught || *ref* to get caught; (mil) to enlist
enganche *m* hook; hooking; hitching; coupling; inveigling; recruiting; enlisting; (rr) coupler
engañabo•bos *mf* (*pl* **-bos**) (coll) bamboozler
engaña•dor -dora *adj* deceptive; (*simpático*) winsome
engañar *tr* to deceive, cheat, fool; (*el tiempo*) to while away; (*el sueño, el hambre*) to ward off; to wheedle || *ref* to be mistaken
engañifa *f* (coll) deception, trick
engaño *m* deception, deceit, fraud; mistake; falsehood; **llamarse a engaño** to back out because of fraud
engaño•so -sa *adj* deceptive
engargantar *tr* (*un ave*) to stuff the throat of || *intr & ref* to mesh, to engage
engarzar **§60** *tr* to link, string, wire; to curl; to enchase; (Col) to hook
engastar *tr* to enchase, mount, set
engaste *m* enchasing, mounting, setting
engatusar *tr* (coll) to coax, wheedle; to inveigle

engendrar *tr* to beget, engender; (geom) to generate
engendro *m* foetus; botch, bungle; (*criatura informe*) runt, stunt; **mal engendro** (coll) young tough
engolfar *intr* to go far out in the ocean || *ref* to go far out in the ocean; to become deeply involved; to be lost in thought
engoma·do -da *adj* (Chile) all dressed up || *m* (CAm) hangover
engomar *tr* to gum || *ref* (Am) to have a hangover
engorda *f* (Am) fattening; (Am) animals being fattened
engordar *tr* to fatten || *intr* to get fat; (coll) to get fat, get rich
engorro *m* bother, nuisance, obstacle
engorro·so -sa *adj* annoying
engoznar *tr* to hinge, to hang on a hinge
engranaje *m* gear, gears, teeth; (fig) link, connection; **engranaje de distribución** (aut) timing gears; **engranaje de tornillo sin fin** worm gear
engranar *tr* to gear, to mesh; to throw into gear || *intr* to gear, to mesh
engrandecer **§22** *tr* to amplify, enlarge, magnify; to exalt, extol; to enhance
engrane *m* gear; mesh
engranerar *tr* (*el grano*) to store
engrapar *tr* to clamp, to cramp
engrasador *m* grease cup; **engrasador de pistón** grease gun
engrasar *tr* to grease; to smear with grease
engrase *m* greasing; grease
engravar *tr* to spread gravel over
engredar *tr* to chalk, to clay
engreí·do -da *adj* conceited, vain
engreimiento *m* conceit, vanity
engreír **§58** *tr* to make conceited; (Am) to spoil, pamper || *ref* to become conceited
engreña·do -da *adj* disheveled
engrescar **§73** *tr* to incite to fight; to incite to merriment || *ref* to pick a fight; to join in the fun
engrifar *tr* to curl, to crisp || *ref* to curl up; to stand on end; (*un caballo*) to rear
engrillar *tr* to shackle, fetter || *ref* (*las patatas*) to sprout
engringar **§44** *ref* to act like a foreigner
engrosar **§61** *tr* to broaden; to enlarge || *intr* to get fat || *ref* to broaden; to swell, get bigger
engrudar *tr* to paste
engrudo *m* paste
engualdrapar *tr* to caparison
enguapear *ref* (Mex) to get drunk
enguirnaldar *tr* to garland, to wreathe; to trim, bedeck
engullir **§13** *tr* to gulp down
engurrio *m* sadness, melancholy
enhebrar *tr* (*una aguja*) to thread; (*perlas*) to string; (*mentiras*) (coll) to rattle off
enhestar **§2** *tr* to stand upright, to erect; to hoist, lift up
enhies·to -ta *adj* upright, straight, erect
enhilar *tr* to thread; to direct; to line up; (*ideas*) to marshal || *intr* to set out
enhorabuena *adv* safely, luckily; **enhorabuena que** thank heavens that || *f* congratulations; **dar la enhorabuena a** to congratulate
enhoramala *adv* unluckily, under an unlucky star; **nacer enhoramala** to be born under an unlucky star; **vete enhoramala** go to the devil
enhornar *tr* to put into the oven
enigma *m* enigma, riddle, puzzle
enigmáti·co -ca *adj* enigmatic(al)
enjabonar *tr* to soap, to lather; (*adular*) (coll) to soft-soap; (*reprender*) (coll) to upbraid
enjaezar **§60** *tr* to harness, put trappings on
enjalbegado *m* whitewashing
enjalbegar **§44** *tr* to whitewash; (*el rostro*) to paint || *ref* to paint the face
enjambrar *intr* (*las abejas*) to swarm; to multiply in great numbers
enjambre *m* swarm
enjaretado *m* grating, lattice work
enjarrar *ref* (C-R, Mex) to stand with arms akimbo
enjaular *tr* to cage; (coll) to jail, lock up
enjergar **§44** *tr* (coll) to launch, get started, to start on a shoestring
enjoyar *tr* to adorn with jewels; to set with precious stones; to adorn
enjuagadien·tes *m* (*pl* **-tes**) mouthwash
enjuagar **§44** *tr* to rinse, rinse out
enjuague *m* rinse; rinsing water; mouthwash; rinsing cup; (coll) plot
enjugador *m* drier; clotheshorse
enjugama·nos *m* (*pl* **-nos**) towel, hand towel
enjugaparabri·sas *m* (*pl* **-sas**) windshield wiper
enjugar **§44** *tr* (*secar*) to dry; (*el sudor*) to wipe, wipe off; (*lágrimas*) to wipe away; (*deudas, un déficit*) to wipe out || *ref* to lose weight
enjuiciamiento *m* procedure; prosecution, suit; trial; judgment, sentence
enjuiciar *tr* to prosecute, to sue; to try; to judge
enjundio·so -sa *adj* fatty, greasy; solid, substantial
enju·to -ta *adj* (*tiempo, clima; ojos*) dry; lean, skinny; quiet, stolid || **enjutos** *mpl* brushwood; (*para excitar la gana de beber*) tidbits
enlabiar *tr* to entice, take in; to press one's lips against
enlace *m* connection, linking; relationship; betrothal, engagement; marriage; (mil, phonet) liaison; (rr) connection, junction
enlaciar *tr, intr & ref* to wither, wilt, shrivel; to rumple
enladrillado *m* brickwork; bricklaying; brick paving
enladrillar *tr* to pave with bricks
enlajado *m* (Ven) flagstone
enlajar *tr* (Ven) to pave with flagstones
enlardar *tr* to baste
enlatado *m* canning
enlatar *tr* to can; (Am) to roof with tin, to line with tin
enlazar **§60** *tr* to connect, to link; to lace; (*un animal con el lazo*) to lasso

|| *intr* (*p.ej., dos trenes*) to connect || *ref* to be connected, to be linked; to connect; to get married; to become related by marriage
enlechar *tr* to grout
enlistonado *m* lathing, lath
enlistonar *tr* to lath
enlodar *tr* to muddy, smear with mud; to plaster with mud; to seal with mud; (fig) to sling mud at
enloquecer **§22** *tr* to drive crazy || *intr* to go crazy
enloquecimiento *m* insanity, madness
enlosado *m* flagstone paving
enlosar *tr* to pave with flagstone
enlozar **§60** *tr* (Am) to enamel
enlozado *m* (Am) enamelware
enlucido *m* plaster, coat (*of plaster*)
enlucir **§45** *tr* (*una pared*) to plaster; (*la plata*) to polish
enlutar *tr* to put in mourning, to hang with crape; to darken, sadden || *ref* to dress in mourning
enmaderar *tr* to cover with boards; to build the framework for
enmagrecer **§22** *tr* to make thin || *intr* & *ref* to get thin
enmalecer **§22** *tr* to spoil || *ref* to get full of weeds, to be overgrown with weeds
enmarañar *tr* to entangle; to confuse || *ref* to become entangled; to become overcast, get cloudy
enmarcar **§73** *tr* to frame
enmarchitar *tr* & *ref* to wither
enmaridar *intr* & *ref* to take a husband
enmarillecer **§22** *ref* to turn yellow, to turn pale
enmasar *tr* (*tropas*) to mass
enmascarar *tr* to mask; to camouflage || *ref* to put on a mask; to masquerade
enmasillar *tr* to putty
enmendación *f* emendation
enmendar **§2** *tr* (*corregir*) to emend; (*reformar*) to amend; (*resarcir*) to make amends for || *ref* to amend, to mend one's ways, to go straight
enmienda *f* (*corrección*) emendation; (*propuesta de variante*) amendment; (*satisfacción del daño hecho*) amends
enmohecer **§22** *tr* to make moldy; to rust; to neglect || *ref* to get moldy; to rust; (*la memoria*) to get rusty; to fade away
enmontar *ref* (CAm, Mex, Col, Ven) to become overgrown with brush
enmudecer **§22** *tr* to hush, to silence || *intr* to hush up, keep quiet; to become dumb, lose one's voice
enmuescar **§73** *tr* to notch; (carp) to mortise
ennegrecer **§22** *tr* to blacken, dye black || *ref* to turn black; (*el porvenir*) to be black
ennoblecer **§22** *tr* to ennoble; to glorify, enhance
ennoblecimiento *m* ennoblement; glory, splendor; (*grandeza de alma*) nobility
enodio *m* fawn, young deer
enojada *f* (Mex) fit of anger
enojadi•zo -za *adj* irritable, ill-tempered
enojar *tr* to anger; to annoy, vex || *ref* to get angry; **enojarse con** or **contra** to get angry with (*a person*); **enojarse de** to get angry at (*a thing*)
enojo *m* anger; annoyance, bother
eno•jón -jona *adj* (Chile, Ecuad, Mex) irritable, ill-tempered
enojo•so -sa *adj* annoying, bothersome
enorgullecer **§22** *tr* to fill with pride, make proud || *ref* to be proud; **enorgullecerse de** to pride oneself on
enorme *adj* enormous, huge
enquiciar *tr* (*una puerta, una ventana*) to hang; to fasten, make firm
enrabiar *tr* to enrage || *intr* to have rabies || *ref* to become enraged
enramar *tr* (*ramos*) to intertwine; to adorn with branches || *intr* to sprout branches || *ref* to hide in the branches
enranciar *tr* to make rancid || *ref* to get rancid
enrarecer **§22** *tr* to rarefy; to make scarce || *intr* to become scarce || *ref* to rarefy; to become scarce
enrarecimiento *m* (*p.ej., del aire*) thinness; scarceness, scarcity
enrasar *tr* to make flush; to grade, to level || *intr* to be flush
enratonar *ref* (coll) to get sick from eating mice; (Ven) to have a hangover
enredadera *adj* (*planta*) climbing || *f* climbing plant, vine
enreda•dor -dora *mf* (coll) gossip, busybody
enredar *tr* to catch in a net; (*redes, una trampa*) to set; to tangle up; to involve, to entangle; (*una pelea*) to start; to intertwine, interweave; to endanger, compromise || *intr* to romp around, be frisky || *ref* to get tangled up; to get involved, become entangled; (coll) to have an affair
enredijo *m* entanglement
enredo *m* tangle; involvement, entanglement, complication; restlessness; friskiness; mischievous lie; (*de una novela, un drama*) plot; (*trato ilícito de hombre y mujer*) liaison
enre•dón -dona *adj* scheming || *mf* schemer
enredo•so -sa *adj* entangled, complicated, difficult
enrejado *m* grating, trellis, latticework; iron railing; grill; openwork embroidery
enrejar *tr* to grate, lattice; (*una ventana*) to put a grate on; to fence with an iron grating; (*ladrillos, tablas*) to pile alternately crosswise; (Mex) to darn
enrielar *tr* to make into ingots; (Am) to lay rails on; (Am) to put on the tracks; (Am) to put on the right track
enriquecer **§22** *tr* to enrich || *intr* & *ref* to get rich
enrisca•do -da *adj* craggy, full of cliffs
enrizar **§60** *tr* & *ref* to curl
enrocar **§73** *tr* & *intr* (chess) to castle
enrodrigar **§44** *tr* to prop, prop up
enrojar *tr* to redden, make red; (*el*

horno) to heat up || *ref* to redden, turn red
enrojecer §22 *tr* to make red; to make red-hot; to make blush || *intr* to blush || *ref* to turn red; to get red-hot; to flush; to get sore, get inflamed
enromar *tr* to make dull, make blunt
enronquecer §22 *tr* to make hoarse || *intr & ref* to get hoarse
enronquecimiento *m* hoarseness
enroque *m* (chess) castling
enroscar §73 *tr* to coil, twist; to screw in || *ref* to coil, twist
enrubiar *tr* to bleach, make blond || *ref* to turn blond
enrubio *m* bleaching; bleaching lotion
enrular *tr & ref* (Arg) to curl
ensacar §73 *tr* to bag, put in a bag
ensaimada *f* twisted coffee cake
ensalada *f* salad; hodgepodge; fiasco, flop
ensaladera *f* salad bowl
ensalmar *tr* (*un hueso*) to set; to treat or heal by incantation
ensalmo *m* incantation, spell; **como por ensalmo** as if by magic
ensalzar §60 *tr* to exalt, elevate, extol
ensamblar *tr* to assemble, join, fit together; **ensamblar a cola de milano** or **a cola de pato** to dovetail
ensanchador *m* glove stretcher
ensanchar *tr* to widen, to enlarge; (*una prenda ajustada*) to ease, let out; (*el corazón*) to unburden || *intr & ref* to be proud and haughty
ensanche *m* widening, extension; (*de una calle*) extension; suburban development; allowance (*for enlargement of garment*)
ensandecer §22 *intr* to go crazy
ensangrenta•do -da *adj* bloody, gory
ensangrentar §2 *tr* to bathe in blood; to stain with blood || *ref* to rage, to go wild; (*p.ej., las manos*) to bloody, make bloody
ensañar *tr* to anger, enrage || *ref* to be cruel, be merciless; (*una enfermedad*) to rage
ensartar *tr* (*una aguja*) to thread; (*cuentas*) to string; to stick; (coll) to rattle off || *ref* to squeeze in
ensayar *tr* to try, try on, try out; (*un espectáculo*) to rehearse; (*minerales*) to assay; to teach, train; to test || *ref* to practice
ensaye *m* assay
ensayista *mf* essayist; (Chile) assayer
ensayo *m* trying, trial; testing, test; (*género literario*) essay; (*de minerales*) assay; exercise, practice; (theat) rehearsal; **ensayo general** dress rehearsal
ensenada *f* inlet, cove
enseña *f* standard, ensign
enseña•do -da *adj* trained, informed; (*perro de caza*) trained
enseñanza *f* teaching; education, instruction; (*ejemplo que sirve de experiencia*) lesson; **enseñanza superior** higher education
enseñar *tr* to teach; to train; to show, point out || *intr* to teach
enseñorear *ref* to control oneself; **enseñorearse de** to take possession of
enseres *mpl* utensils, equipment, household goods
enseriar *ref* (Am) to become serious
ensillar *tr* to saddle
ensimismamiento *m* absorption in thought, deep thought
ensimismar *ref* to become absorbed in thought; (Chile, Ecuad, Peru) to be proud, be boastful
ensoberbecer §22 *tr* to make proud || *ref* to become proud; (*el mar, las olas*) to swell, get rough
ensoberbecimiento *m* haughtiness
ensombrecer §22 *tr* to darken || *ref* to get dark; to become sad and gloomy
ensoña•dor -dora *adj* dreamy || *mf* dreamer
ensopar *tr* to dip, to dunk; (Am) to soak, to drench
ensordece•dor -dora *adj* deafening
ensordecer §22 *tr* to deafen; (*una consonante sonora*) to unvoice || *intr* to become deaf; to play deaf, to not answer || *ref* to unvoice
ensortijar *tr* to curl, make curly; (*la nariz de un animal*) to ring, put a ring in || *ref* to curl
ensuciar *tr* to dirty, soil; to stain, smear; to defile, sully || *ref* to soil oneself; to take bribes
ensueño *m* dream; daydream
entablado *m* flooring; wooden framework
entablar *tr* to board, board up; (*un hueso roto*) to splint; (*una conversación*) to start; (*p.ej., una batalla*) to launch; (*un pleito*) to bring; (*las piezas del ajedrez y de las damas*) to set up || *ref* (*el viento*) to settle
entable *m* boarding; (*en los juegos de ajedrez y damas*) position of men; (Col) business, undertaking
entablillar *tr* (*un hueso roto*) to splint
enta•blón -blona *adj* (Peru) blustering, bragging || *mf* (Peru) bully
entalegar §44 *tr* to bag, put in a bag; (*dinero*) to hoard
entalladura *f* carving, sculpture; engraving; slot, groove, mortise; cut, incision (*in a tree*)
entallar *tr* to carve, to sculpture; to engrave; to notch; to groove, mortise; (*un traje*) to fit, to tailor || *intr* to take shape; (*el vestido*) to fit; (coll) to go well, be fitting
entallecer §22 *intr & ref* to shoot, to sprout
entapizar §60 *tr* to tapestry, to hang with tapestry; to cover with a fabric; to overgrow, to spread over
entarimado *m* parquet, inlaid floor, hardwood floor
entarimar *tr* to parquet, to put an inlaid floor on || *ref* (coll) to put on airs
entarugar §44 *tr* to pave with wooden blocks || *ref* (*el sombrero*) (Ven) to stick on
ente *m* being; (coll) guy, queer duck
enteca•do -da or **ente•co -ca** *adj* sickly, frail

enteleri·do -da *adj* shaking with cold, shaking with fright; (Am) sickly, frail
entena *f* lateen yard
entenado -da *mf* stepchild || *m* stepson || *f* stepdaughter
entendederas *fpl* (coll) brains; **tener malas entendederas** (coll) to have no brains
entende·dor -dora *adj* understanding, intelligent || *mf* understanding person; **al buen entendedor, pocas palabras** a word to the wise is enough
entender *m* understanding, opinion || §51 *tr* to understand; to intend, mean || *intr* — **entender de** to be a judge of; to be experienced as; **entender de razón** to listen to reason; **entender en** to be familiar with, to deal with || *ref* to be understood; to be meant; to have a secret understanding; **entenderse con** to get along with; to concern; (*una mujer*) to have an affair with
entendi·do -da *adj* expert, skilled; informed; **no darse por entendido** to take no notice, to pretend not to understand; **los entendidos** informed sources; **un entendido en** a well-informed person in
entendimiento *m* understanding
entenebrecer §22 *tr* to darken; to confuse || *ref* to get dark; to become confused
entera·do -da *adj* informed, posted; (Chile) conceited; (Chile) intrusive, meddlesome || *mf* insider
enterar *tr* to inform, acquaint; (Am) to pay; (Arg, Chile) to complete || *intr* (Chile) to get better; (Chile) to drift along || *ref* to find out; (Am) to recover; **enterarse de** to find out about, to become aware of
entereza *f* entirety, completeness; wholeness; perfection; fairness; constancy, fortitude; strictness
enteri·zo -za *adj* in one piece
enternece·dor -dora *adj* moving, touching
enternecer §22 *tr* to move, to touch || *ref* to be moved to pity
enternecimiento *m* pity, compassion
ente·ro -ra *adj* entire, whole, complete; honest, upright; firm, energetic; sound, vigorous; (*tela*) strong, heavy || *m* (arith) integer; (Am) payment; (Chile) balance; **por entero** entirely, wholly, completely
enterrador *m* gravedigger
enterramiento *m* burial, interment; (*hoyo*) grave; (*monumento*) tomb
enterrar §2 *tr* to bury, inter; to outlive, survive || *ref* to hide away
entesar §2 *tr* to stretch, make taut
entibar *tr* to prop up, shore up || *intr* to rest, lean
entibiar *tr* to cool off; to temper, moderate || *ref* to cool off, cool down
entidad *f* entity; importance, consequence, moment; body, organization
entierro *m* burial, interment; (*hoyo*) grave; (*monumento*) tomb; funeral; funeral cortege; buried treasure
entintar *tr* to ink; to ink in; to stain with ink; to dye
entoldar *tr* to cover with awnings; to adorn with hangings || *ref* to get cloudy, become overcast; to swell with pride
entomología *f* entomology
entonación *f* intonation; blowing of bellows
entona·do -da *adj* arrogant; haughty; harmonious, in tune
entonar *tr* to intone; to sing in tune; (*el órgano*) to blow; (*colores*) to harmonize; to tone, tone up; (*alabanzas*) to sound || *intr* to sing in tune || *ref* to be puffed up with pride
entonces *adv* then || *m* — **por aquel entonces** at that time
entonelar *tr* to put in barrels, put in casks
entongar §44 *tr* (Mex, W-I) to pile up, pile in rows; (Col) to drive crazy
entono *m* intoning; arrogance, haughtiness
entontecer §22 *tr* to make foolish, make stupid || *intr & ref* to become foolish, become stupid
entorchado *m* bullion; **ganar los entorchados** to win one's stripes
entorna·do -da *adj* ajar, half-closed
entornar *tr* to half-close; (*los ojos*) to squint; (*una puerta*) to leave ajar; (*volcar*) to upset || *ref* to upset
entornillar *tr* to twist, to screw up
entorpecer §22 *tr* to stupefy; to obstruct, delay; to benumb; (*una cerradura, una ventana*) to make stick || *ref* to stick, get stuck
entortar §61 *tr* to bend, make crooked; to knock out the eye of || *ref* to bend, get crooked
entrada *f* entrance, entry; admission; arrival; income, receipts; admission ticket; entrance hall; (*número de personas que asisten a un espectáculo*) house; (*producto de cada función*) gate; (*amistad en alguna casa*) entree; (*naipes que guarda un jugador*) hand; (*de una comida*) entree; (*visita breve*) (coll) short call; (Col) down payment; (Mex) attack, onslaught; (elec) input; **dar entrada a** to admit; to give an opening to; (*un buque*) to give the right of entry to; **entrada de taquilla** gate; **entrada general** top gallery; **entrada llena** full house; **mucha entrada** good house, good turnout; **se prohibe la entrada** no admittance
entra·do -da *adj* (Chile) officious, self-assertive; **entrado en años** advanced in years || *f* see **entrada**
entra·dor -dora *adj* (Mex) lively, energetic; (*enamoradizo*) (Am) susceptible; (Chile) officious, self-assertive
entrama·do -da *adj* half-timbered || *m* timber framework
entram·bos -bas *adj & pron indef* both; **entrambos a dos** both
entrampar *tr* to ensnare, trap; to trick, deceive; (coll) to overload with debt || *ref* to get trapped; to be tricked; (coll) to run into debt

entrante *adj* entering; (*p.ej., tren*) inbound, incoming; (*próximo, que viene*) next || *mf* entrant; **entrantes y salientes** (coll) hangers-on
entraña *f* internal organ; (fig) heart, center; **entrañas** entrails; (fig) heart, feeling; (fig) disposition, temper
entrañable *adj* close, intimate
entrañar *tr* to put away deep, bury deep; to involve; (*malos pensamientos*) to harbor || *ref* to go deep into; to be buried deep; to be close, be intimate
entrapajar *tr* to wrap up, to bandage
entrar *tr* to bring in; to overrun, invade; to influence || *intr* to enter, go in, come in; (*un río*) to empty; (*el viento, la marea*) to rise; to attack; to begin; **entrar a matar** (taur) to go in for the kill; **entrar en** to enter, enter into, go into; to fit into; to adopt, take up; **que entra** next
entre *prep* (*en medio de*) between; (*en el número de*) among; (*en el intervalo de*) in the course of; **entre manos** at hand; **entre mí** to myself; **entre que** while; **entre tanto** meanwhile; **entre Vd. y yo** between you and me
entreabier•to -ta *adj* half-open; (*puerta*) ajar
entreabrir **§83** *tr* to half-open; to leave ajar
entreacto *m* entr'acte
entreca•no -na *adj* graying, grayish
entrecarril *m* (Ven) gauge
entrecejo *m* space between the eyebrows; frown; **fruncir el entrecejo** to frown; **mirar con entrecejo** to frown at
entrecoger **§17** *tr* to catch, seize; to press hard, to hold down
entrecoro *m* chancel
entrecorta•do -da *adj* broken, intermittent
entrecortar *tr* to break in on, keep interrupting
entre•cruz *m* (*pl* **-cruces**) interweaving
entrecruzar **§60** *tr & ref* to intercross; to interweave, interlace; to interbreed
entrecubiertas *fpl* between-decks
entrechocar **§73** *ref* to collide, to clash
entredicho *m* interdiction, prohibition; (law) injunction; (Bol) alarm bell; **poner en entredicho** to cast doubt upon
entredós *m* (*tira de encaje*) insertion; (typ) long primer
entrefilete *m* short feature, special item
entrefi•no -na *adj* medium
entrega *f* delivery; (*p.ej., de una plaza fuerte*) surrender; (*cuaderno de un libro que se vende suelto*) fascicle; (*de una revista*) issue, number; **por entregas** in instalments
entregar **§44** *tr* to deliver; to hand over, surrender; to fit in, insert; **entregarla** (coll) to die || *ref* to give in, surrender; to abandon oneself; to devote oneself; **entregarse de** to take possession of, take charge of
entrehierro *m* (elec) spark gap; (phys) air gap
entrelazar **§60** *tr* to interlace, interweave
entremediar *tr* to put between
entremedias *adv* in between; in the meantime; **entremedias de** between; among
entremés *m* hors d'œuvre, side dish; short farce (*inserted in an auto or performed between two acts of a comedia*)
entremesear *tr* (*una conversación*) to enliven
entremeter *tr* to put in, to insert || *ref* to meddle, intrude, butt in
entremeti•do -da *adj* meddling, meddlesome || *mf* meddler, intruder, busybody
entremezclar *tr & ref* to intermingle, intermix
entremorir **§30 & §83** *intr* to flicker, die out
entrenador *m* (sport) coach, trainer, handler
entrenamiento *m* (sport) coaching, training
entrenar *tr & ref* (sport) to coach, to train
entrepaño *m* (*de una puerta*) panel; (*espacio entre dos columnas, etc.*) pier; shelf
entreparecer **§60** *ref* to show through
entrepiernas *fpl* crotch; patches in the crotch of trousers; (Chile) bathing trunks
entrepuentes *mpl* between-decks; (naut) steerage
entrerrenglonar *tr* to write between the lines
entrerriel *m* gauge
entrerrisa *f* giggle
entrerrosca *f* (mach) nipple
entresacar **§73** *tr* to pick, pick out, select; to cull, sift; (*árboles; el pelo*) to thin out
entresijo *m* secret; mystery; **tener muchos entresijos** to be mysterious, to be hard to figure out
entresuelo *m* mezzanine, entresol
entretallar *tr* to carve, to engrave; to carve in bas-relief; to do openwork in; to intercept
entretanto *adv* meantime, meanwhile || *m* meanwhile; **en el entretanto** in the meantime
entretecho *m* (Arg, Chile, Urug) attic, garret
entretejer *tr* to interweave
entretela *f* interlining
entretelar *tr* to interline
entretención *f* (Am) amusement, entertainment
entretener **§71** *tr* to amuse, entertain; (*el tiempo*) to while away; to maintain, keep up; to put off, delay; (*el dolor*) to allay; (*el hambre*) to stave off (*by taking a bite before mealtime*); to try to get one's mind off || *ref* to amuse oneself, to be amused
entreteni•do -da *adj* amusing, entertaining; (rad) continuous, undamped || *f* kept woman; **dar la entretenida a** or **dar con la entretenida a** to stall off by constant talk

entretenimiento *m* amusement, entertainment; upkeep, maintenance
entretiempo *m* in-between season; **de entretiempo** spring-and-fall (*coat*)
entreventana *f* pier
entrever §80 *tr* to glimpse, descry, catch a glimpse of; to guess, suspect
entreverar *tr* to mix || *ref* (Arg) to get all mixed together; (*dos grupos de caballería*) (Arg) to clash in hand-to-hand combat
entrevía *f* gauge
entrevista *f* interview
entrevistar *ref* to have an interview
entristecer §22 *tr* to sadden, make sad || *ref* to sadden, become sad
entrojar *tr* to store in a granary
entrometer *tr & ref* var of **entremeter**
entrometi•do -da *adj & mf* var of **entremetido**
entronar *tr* to enthrone
entroncamiento *m* connection, relationship; (*de caminos, ferrocarriles*) (Am) junction
entroncar §73 *tr* to prove relationship between || *intr* to be related; (*dos caminos, ferrocarriles, etc.*) (Am) to connect
entronerar *tr* (*una bola de billar*) to pocket
entronizar §60 *tr* to enthrone; to exalt; to popularize || *ref* to be puffed up with pride
entronque *m* connection, relationship; (*de caminos, ferrocarriles*) (Am) junction
entruchar *tr* (coll) to decoy, to trick
entru•chón -chona *adj* (coll) tricky || *mf* (coll) trickster
entuerto *m* wrong, harm, injustice
entumecer §22 *tr* to make numb || *ref* (*un miembro*) to get numb, go to sleep; (*el mar*) to swell, get rough
entupir *tr* to stop up, clog; to pack tight || *ref* to get stopped up, get clogged
enturbiar *tr* to stir up, make muddy; to confuse, upset
entusiasmar *tr* to enthuse, make enthusiastic || *ref* to enthuse, become enthusiastic
entusiasmo *m* enthusiasm; inspiration
entusiasta *adj* enthusiastic || *mf* enthusiast
entusiásti•co -ca *adj* enthusiastic
enumerar *tr* to enumerate
enunciar *tr* to enunciate, to enounce
enunciati•vo -va *adj* (gram) declarative
envainar *tr* to sheathe
envalentonar *tr* to embolden, make bold || *ref* to pluck up, take courage
envanecer §22 *tr* to make vain || *ref* to become vain, get conceited
envanecimiento *m* vanity, conceit
envarar *tr* to make numb, to stiffen
envasar *tr* (*p.ej., trigo*) to pack, to sack; (*p.ej., vino*) to bottle; (*p.ej., pescado*) to can; (*una espada*) to thrust, poke; (*mucho vino*) to put away || *intr* to tipple
envase *m* container; bottle, jar; can; packing; bottling; canning; **envase de hojalata** tin can
envedijar *ref* to get tangled; (coll) to come to blows
envejecer §22 *tr* to age, make old || *intr & ref* to age, grow old; to get out of date
envejeci•do -da *adj* old, aged; experienced, tried
envenenar *tr* to poison; (*llenar de amargura*) to envenom, embitter; (*las palabras o conducta de una persona*) to put an evil interpretation on || *ref* to take poison
enverdecer §22 *intr* to turn green
envergadura *f* (*de las alas abiertas del ave*) spread; (*ancho de una vela*) breadth; (aer) span, wingspread; (fig) compass, spread, reach
envés *m* wrong side; (*del cuerpo humano*) back
enviado *m* envoy
enviar §77 *tr* to send; (*mercancías*) to ship; **enviar a buscar** to send for; **enviar a paseo** (coll) to send on his way, to dismiss without ceremony; **enviar por** to send for
enviciar *tr* to corrupt, vitiate; (*mimar*) to spoil || *intr* to have many leaves and little fruit || *ref* to become addicted; **enviciarse con** or **en** to addict oneself to, become addicted to
envidar *tr* to bid against, to bet against || *intr* to bid, to bet
envidia *f* envy; desire
envidiable *adj* enviable
envidiar *tr* to envy, to begrudge; to desire, want
envidio•so -sa *adj* envious; greedy, covetous || *mf* envious person
envilecer §22 *tr* to debase, vilify, revile || *ref* to degrade oneself
envío *m* sending; (*de mercancías*) shipment; (*de dinero*) remittance; (*en una obra*) autograph, inscription
envirota•do -da *adj* stiff, stuck-up
envite *m* bet; bid, offer, invitation; push, shove; (*apuesta adicional a un lance o suerte*) side bet; **al primer envite** right off, at the start
enviudar *intr* (*una mujer*) to become a widow; (*un hombre*) to become a widower
envoltorio *m* bundle; (*defecto en el paño*) knot
envoltura *f* cover, wrapper, envelope; swaddling clothes
envolver §47 & §83 *tr* to wrap, wrap up; (*hilo, cinta*) to wind, roll up; (*al niño*) to swaddle; to imply, mean; to involve; to envelop; (*dejar cortado y sin salida en la disputa*) to floor; (mil) to encircle || *ref* to become involved; to have an affair
enyerbar *tr* (Col, Chile, Mex) to bewitch || *ref* (Am) to be covered with grass; (Mex) to fall madly in love; (Mex) to take poison
enyesar *tr* to plaster; to put in a plaster cast; (*la tierra, el vino*) to gypsum
enyugar §44 *tr* to yoke
enzima *f* cnzyme
enzolvar *tr* (Mex) to clog, stop up
epazote *m* (CAm, Mex) Mexican tea
E.P.D. *abbr* **en paz descanse**

epénte•sis *f* (*pl* **-sis**) epenthesis
eperlano *m* smelt
épica *f* epic poetry
epice•no -na *adj* (gram) epicene, common
épi•co -ca *adj* epic || *m* epic poet || *f* see **épica**
epicúre•o -a *adj* epicurean || *mf* epicurean, epicure
epidemia *f* epidemic
epidémi•co -ca *adj* epidemic
epidemiología *f* epidemiology
epidermis *f* epidermis; **tener la epidermis fina** or **sensible** (coll) to be touchy
Epifanía *f* Epiphany, Twelfth-day
epígrafe *m* epigraph; inscription; headline, title; device, motto
epigrama *m* epigram
epilepsia *f* epilepsy
epilépti•co -ca *adj & mf* epileptic
epilogar §44 *tr* to sum up, summarize
episcopalista *adj & mf* Episcopalian
episodio *m* episode
epistemología *f* epistemology
epístola *f* epistle
epitafio *m* epitaph
epíteto *m* epithet
epitomar *tr* to epitomize
epítome *m* epitome
E.P.M. *abbr* **en propia mano**
época *f* epoch; **hacer época** to be epoch-making
epopeya *f* epic, epic poem
equidad *f* equity; (*templanza habitual*) equableness; (*moderación en el precio*) reasonableness
equiláte•ro -ra *adj* equilateral
equilibrar *tr* to balance, equilibrate; (*el presupuesto*) to balance || *ref* to balance, equilibrate
equilibrio *m* equilibrium, balance, equipoise; (*del presupuesto*) balancing; **equilibrio político** balance of power
equilibrista *mf* balancer, ropedancer
equinoccial *adj* equinoctial
equinoccio *m* equinox
equipaje *m* baggage; piece of baggage; equipment; (naut) crew; **equipaje de mano** hand baggage
equipar *tr* to equip
equiparar *tr* to compare
equi•pier *m* (*pl* **-piers**) teammate
equipo *m* equipment, outfit; crew, gang; (sport) team; **equipo de novia** trousseau; **equipo de urgencia** first-aid kit
equitación *f* horsemanship, riding
equitati•vo -va *adj* fair, equitable; (*tranquilo*) equable
equivalente *adj & m* equivalent
equivaler §76 *intr* to be equal, be equivalent
equivocación *f* mistake; mistakenness
equivoca•do -da *adj* mistaken, wrong
equivocar §73 *tr* (*una cosa por otra*) to mistake, to mix || *ref* to be mistaken, to make a mistake; to be wrong; **equivocarse con** to be mistaken for; **equivocarse de** to be wrong in, take the wrong . . .
equívo•co -ca *adj* equivocal, ambiguous || *m* equivocation, ambiguity; pun
equivoquista *mf* equivocator; punster
era *f* era, age; threshing floor; vegetable patch, garden bed
eral *m* two-year-old bull
erario *m* state treasury
erección *f* erection; foundation, establishment
eremita *m* hermit
ergástulo *m* dungeon, slave prison
ergio *m* erg
erguir §33 *tr* to raise; to straighten up || *ref* to straighten up; to swell with pride
erial *adj* unplowed, uncultivated || *m* unplowed land, uncultivated land
erigir §27 *tr* to erect, build; to found, establish; (*a nueva condición*) to elevate || *ref* — **erigirse en** to be elevated to; to set oneself up as
eriza•do -da *adj* bristling, bristly, spiny
erizar §60 *tr* to make stand on end, cause to bristle || *ref* to stand on end, to bristle
erizo *m* (*mamífero*) hedgehog; (*zurrón espinoso de la castaña*) bur, thistle; (*púas de hierro que coronan lo alto de una muralla*) cheval-de-frise; (*persona de carácter áspero*) (coll) curmudgeon; **erizo de mar** (zool) sea urchin
ermita *f* hermitage
ermita•ño -ña *mf* hermit
erogación *f* (*de bienes o caudales*) distribution; (Am) expenditure; (Peru, Ven) gift, charity; (Mex) outlay
erogar §44 *tr* to distribute; (Ecuad) to contribute; (Mex) to cause
erosión *f* erosion
erosionar *tr & ref* to erode
erradicar §73 *tr* to eradicate
erra•do -da *adj* mistaken, wrong
errar §34 *tr* to miss || *intr* to err, to be mistaken, to be wrong; to wander || *ref* to be mistaken, to be wrong
errata *f* erratum; printer's error
erróne•o -a *adj* erroneous
error *m* error, mistake; **error de pluma** clerical error; **salvo error u omisión** barring error or omission
eructar *intr* to belch; (coll) to brag
eructo *m* belch, belching
erudición *f* erudition, learning
erudi•to -ta *adj* erudite, learned || *mf* scholar, savant; **erudito a la violeta** egghead, highbrow
erugino•so -sa *adj* rusty
erumpir *intr* (*un volcán*) to erupt
erupción *f* eruption
esbel•to -ta *adj* slender, lithe, willowy
esbirro *m* bailiff, constable; (*el que ejecuta órdenes injustas*) myrmidon, henchman
esbozar §60 *tr* to sketch, outline
esbozo *m* sketch, outline
escabechar *tr* to pickle; (*el pelo, la barba*) to dye; (*reprobar en un examen*) (coll) to flunk; (coll) to stab to death || *ref* to dye one's hair; (*el pelo, la barba*) to dye
escabeche *m* pickle; pickled fish; hair dye

escabel *m* stool; footstool; (*para medrar*) stepping stone
escabio•so -sa *adj* mangy
escabro•so -sa *adj* scabrous, risqué; scabrous, uneven, rough, harsh
escabuche *m* weeding hoe
escabullir §13 *ref* to slip away, sneak away; to slip out, wiggle out
escafandra *f* diving suit; **escafandra espacial** space suit
escafandrista *mf* diver
escala *f* (*escalera de mano*) ladder, stepladder; (*línea graduada de instrumento*) scale; (*de buque*) call; (*de avión*) stop; (*puerto donde toca una embarcación*) port of call; (*serie de las notas musicales*) scale; **en escala de** on a scale of; **en grande escala** on a large scale; **escala móvil** (*de salarios*) sliding scale; **hacer escala** (naut) to call
escalada *f* scaling, climbing; breaking in; escalation
escalador *m* climber; (*ladrón*) burglar, housebreaker
escalación *f* escalation
escalafón *m* roster, roll, register
escalar *tr* (*subir, trepar*) to scale; to break in, to burglarize; (*la compuerta de la acequia*) to open || *intr* to climb; (naut) to call || *ref* to escalate
escalato•rres *m* (*pl* **-rres**) steeplejack, human fly
escalda•do -da *adj* (coll) cautious, scared, wary; (*mujer*) (coll) lewd, loose
escaldar *tr* to scald; to make red hot || *ref* to get scalded; to chafe
escalera *f* stairs, stairway; (*la portátil*) ladder; (*de naipes*) sequence; (*en el póker*) straight; **de escalera abajo** from below stairs, from the servants; **escalera de caracol** winding stairway; **escalera de escape** fire escape; **escalera de husillo** winding stairway; **escalera de incendios** fire escape; **escalera de mano** ladder; **escalera de salvamento** fire escape; **escalera de tijera** or **escalera doble** ladder; **escalera excusada** or **falsa** private stairs; **escalera extensible** extension ladder; **escalera hurtada** secret stairway; **escalera mecánica, móvil** or **rodante** escalator, moving stairway
escalerilla *f* low step; car step; (*en las medias*) runner; (*de naipes*) sequence; thumb index
escalfar *tr* (*huevos*) to poach; (*el pan*) to bake brown
escalinata *f* stone steps, front steps
escalo *m* burglary, breaking in
escalofria•do -da *adj* chilly
escalofrío *m* chill
escalón *m* step, rung; (*grada de la escalera*) tread; (fig) step, echelon, grade; (*paso con que uno adelanta sus pretensiones*) (fig) stepping stone; (mil) echelon; (rad) stage
escalonar *tr* to space out, spread out; (*las horas de trabajo*) to stagger; (mil) to echelon
escalope *m* (*loncha delgada de carne*) scallop (*thin slice of meat*)
escalpar *tr* to scalp
escalpelo *m* scalpel
escama *f* scale; fear, suspicion
escamar *tr* (*los peces*) to scale; (coll) to frighten || *ref* to be frightened
escamondar *tr* to trim, to prune
escamo•so -sa *adj* scaly
escamotea•dor -dora *mf* prestidigitator; swindler
escamotear *tr* to whisk out of sight, cause to vanish; (*una carta*) to palm; to swipe, to snitch
escampada *f* (coll) clear spell, break in rain
escampar *tr* to clear out || *intr* to stop raining; to ease up; **¡ya escampa!** (coll) there you go again! || *ref* — **escamparse del agua** (Am) to get in out of the rain
escampavía *f* (naut) cutter, revenue cutter
escamujar *tr* (*un árbol, esp. un olivo*) to prune; (*ramas*) to clear out
escanciar *tr* (*vino*) to pour, to serve, to drink || *intr* to drink wine
escandalizar §60 *tr* to scandalize || *ref* to be scandalized; to be outraged, be exasperated
escándalo *m* scandal; **causar escándalo** to make a scene
escandalo•so -sa *adj* scandalous; noisy, riotous; (Am) loud, flashy
escandallo *m* (naut) sounding lead; (*del contenido de varios envases*) testing, sampling; cost accounting
escandina•vo -va *adj & mf* Scandinavian
escandir *tr* (*versos*) to scan
escansión *f* scansion; (telv) scanning
escaño *m* settle, bench with a back; (*en las Cortes*) seat; (Am) park bench; (Guat) nag
escañuelo *m* footstool
escapada *f* escape, flight; short trip, quick trip
escapar *tr* to free, to save; (*un caballo*) to drive hard || *intr* to escape; to flee, run away; **escapar en una tabla** to have a narrow escape || *ref* to escape; to flee, run away; (*el gas, el agua*) to leak; **escapársele a uno** to let slip; to not notice
escaparate *m* show window; (*armario con cristales*) cabinet; (Am) wardrobe, clothes closet
escaparatista *mf* window dresser
escapatoria *f* escape, getaway; (*de atenciones, deberes, etc.*) (fig) escape; (*efugio, pretexto*) (coll) evasion, subterfuge
escape *m* escape; flight; (*de gas, agua*) leak; (*de reloj*) escapement; (aut) exhaust valve; (aut) exhaust, exhaust pipe; **a escape** at full speed, on the run; **escape de rejilla** (rad) grid leak; **escape libre** (aut) cutout
escápula *f* shoulder blade, scapula
escaque *m* square; **escaques** chess
escarabajear *tr* (coll) to bother, worry, harass || *intr* to swarm, crawl; to scrawl, scribble
escarabajo *m* black beetle; (*imperfec-*

ción en los tejidos) flaw; (*persona pequeña*) (coll) runt
escaramuza *f* skirmish
escaramuzar §60 *intr* to skirmish
escarapela *f* (*divisa en forma de lazo*) cockade; dispute ending in hair pulling
escarapelar *intr* & *ref* to quarrel, to wrangle
escarbadien•tes *m* (*pl* **-tes**) toothpick
escarbar *tr* (*el suelo*) to scratch, scratch up; (*la lumbre*) to poke; (*los dientes, los oídos*) to pick; to pry into
escarcha *f* frost, hoarfrost
escarchar *tr* (*confituras*) to frost, put frosting on; (*la tierra del alfarero*) to dilute with water; to spangle || *intr* — **escarcha** there is frost
escardar or **escardillar** *tr* to weed, weed out
escardillo *m* weeding hoe
escariar *tr* to ream
escarlata *adj* scarlet || *f* scarlet fever
escarlatina *f* scarlet fever
escarmentar §2 *tr* to make an example of || *intr* to learn one's lesson
escarmiento *m* example, lesson, warning; caution, wisdom; punishment
escarnecer §22 *tr* to scoff at, make fun of
escarnio *m* scoff, scoffing
escarola *f* endive
escarpa *f* scarp, escarpment; (Mex) sidewalk
escarpa•do -da *adj* steep; abrupt, craggy
escarpia *f* hooked spike
escarpín *m* pump
escasear *tr* to give sparingly; to cut down on, to avoid; to bevel || *intr* to be scarce
escase•ro -ra *adj* sparing; saving, frugal; stingy || *mf* skinflint
escasez *f* (*falta de una cosa*) scarcity; (*pobreza*) need, want; (*mezquindad*) stinginess
esca•so -sa *adj* (*poco abundante*) scarce; (*no cabal*) scant; (*muy económico*) parsimonious, frugal; (*tacaño*) stingy; (*oportunidad*) dim, slim, slight; **estar escaso de** to be short of
escatimar *tr* & *intr* to scrimp
escena *f* (*parte del teatro donde se representan las obras*) stage; (*subdivisión de un acto*) scene; incident, episode; **poner en escena** to stage
escenario *m* stage; (*disposición de la representación*) setting; (*guión de un cine*) scenario; (*antecedentes de una persona o cosa*) background
escenarista *mf* scenarist
escéni•co -ca *adj* scenic
escenificar §73 *tr* to adapt for the stage
escépti•co -ca *adj* sceptic(al) || *mf* sceptic
Escila *f* Scylla; **entre Escila y Caribdis** between Scylla and Charybdis
Escipión *m* Scipio
escisión *f* (biol) fission; (surg) excision
esclarecer §22 *tr* to light up, brighten; to explain, elucidate; to ennoble || *intr* to dawn
esclareci•do -da *adj* noble, illustrious
esclavitud *f* slavery
esclavización *f* enslavement
esclavizar §60 *tr* to enslave
escla•vo -va *adj* & *mf* slave
escla•vón -vona *adj* & *mf* Slav
esclusa *f* lock; floodgate; **esclusa de aire** caisson
esclusero *m* lock tender
escoba *f* broom
escobada *f* sweep; sweeping
escobar *tr* to sweep with a broom
escobazar §60 *tr* to sprinkle with a wet broom
escobén *m* (naut) hawse
escobilla *f* brush, whisk; gold and silver sweepings; (elec) brush
escocer §16 *intr* to smart, sting || *ref* to hurt; to chafe, become chafed
esco•cés -cesa *adj* Scotch, Scottish || *mf* Scot || *m* Scotchman; (*whisky; dialecto*) Scotch; **los escoceces** the Scotch, the Scottish
Escocia *f* Scotland; **la Nueva Escocia** Nova Scotia
escofina *f* rasp
escofinar *tr* to rasp
escoger §17 *tr* to choose, pick out
escogi•do -da *adj* choice, select
escolar *adj* school || *m* pupil
escolaridad *f* schooling, school attendance; curriculum
escolimo•so -sa *adj* (coll) impatient, gruff, restless
escolta *f* escort
escoltar *tr* to escort
escollar *intr* (Arg) to run aground on a reef; (Arg, Chile) to fail
escollera *f* jetty, breakwater
escollo *m* (*peñasco a flor de agua*) reef, rock; (*peligro*) pitfall; (*obstáculo*) stumbling block
escombrar *tr* to clear out
escombro *m* (*pez*) mackerel; **escombros** debris, rubble, rubbish
esconder *tr* to hide, conceal; to harbor, contain || *ref* to hide; to lurk
escondi•do -da *adj* hidden; **a escondidas** secretly; **a escondidas de** without the knowledge of
escondite *m* hiding place; (*juego de muchachos*) hide-and-seek; **jugar al escondite** to play hide-and-seek
escondrijo *m* hiding place
escopeta *f* shotgun; **escopeta blanca** gentleman hunter; **escopeta de caza** fowling piece; **escopeta de viento** air rifle; **escopeta negra** professional hunter
escopetazo *m* gunshot; gunshot wound; bad news, blow
escoplear *tr* to chisel
escoplo *m* chisel
escorbuto *m* scurvy
escoria *f* dross, scoria, slag; (fig) dross, dregs
escorial *m* cinder bank, slag dump
escorpión *m* scorpion
escorzar §60 *tr* to foreshorten
escorzo *m* foreshortening
escota *f* (naut) sheet
escota•do -da *adj* low-neck || *m* low neck
escotadura *f* low neck, low cut in neck
escotar *tr* to cut to fit; to draw water

from, to drain; to cut low in the neck || *intr* to go Dutch
escote *m* low neck; (*encajes en el cuello de una vestidura*) tucker; **ir a escote** or **pagar a escote** to go Dutch
escotilla *f* (naut) hatchway, scuttle
escotillón *m* hatch, trap door, scuttle; (theat) trap door
escozor *m* burning, smarting, stinging; grief, sorrow
escriba *m* scribe
escribanía *f* court clerkship; desk; writing materials
escribano *m* court clerk; lawyer's clerk
escribiente *mf* clerk, office clerk; **escribiente a máquina** typist
escribir §83 *tr & intr* to write || *ref* to enroll, enlist; to write to each other; **no escribirse** to be impossible to describe
escriño *m* casket, jewel case; straw basket
escri•to -ta *adj* streaked || *m* writing; (law) brief, writ; **poner por escrito** to write down, put in writing
escri•tor -tora *mf* writer
escritorio *m* writing desk; office; **escritorio ministro** kneehole desk, office desk; **escritorio norteamericano** rolltop desk
escritura *f* writing; script, handwriting, longhand; (law) deed, indenture; (law) sworn statement; **escritura al tacto** touch typewriting || **Escritura** *f* Scripture; **Sagrada Escritura** Holy Scripture, Holy Writ
escriturar *tr* to notarize; (*p.ej., a un actor*) to book || *ref* (taur) to sign up for a fight
escrnía. *abbr* **escribanía**
escrno. *abbr* **escribano**
escrófula *f* scrofula
escrúpulo *m* scruple
escrupulo•so -sa *adj* scrupulous; exact
escrutar *tr* to scrutinize; (*los votos*) to count
escrutinio *m* scrutiny; counting of votes
escuadra *f* (*pequeño número de personas o de soldados*) squad; (*pieza de metal para asegurar las ensambladuras*) angle iron; (*de carpintero*) square; (*de dibujante*) triangle; (nav) squadron
escuadrar *tr* (carp) to square
escuadrilla *f* (aer) squadron
escuadrón *m* (mil) squadron
escualidez *f* squalor
escuáli•do -da *adj* squalid
escualor *m* squalor
escucha *mf* listener || *m* (mil) scout, vedette || *f* listening; (*en un convento*) chaperon; **estar de escucha** (coll) to eavesdrop
escuchar *tr* to listen to; (*atender a*) to heed; (*radiotransmisiones*) to monitor || *intr* to listen || *ref* to like the sound of one's own voice
escudar *tr* to shield
escudero *m* esquire; nobleman; lady's page
escudete *m* escutcheon; (*refuerzo en la ropa*) gusset; (*planchuela delante de la cerradura*) escutcheon, escutcheon plate
escudilla *f* bowl
escudo *m* shield; buckler; (*delante de la cerradura*) escutcheon plate; **escudo de armas** coat of arms; **escudo térmico** (*de una cápsula espacial*) heat shield
escudriñar *tr* to scrutinize
escuela *f* school; **escuela de artes y oficios** trade school; **escuela de párvulos** kindergarten; **escuela de verano** summer school; **escuela dominical** Sunday school; **Escuela Naval Militar** Naval Academy; **hacer escuela** to be the leader of a school (*of thought*)
escuelante *mf* (Mex) schoolteacher || *m* (Mex) schoolboy || *f* (Mex) schoolgirl
escuerzo *m* toad
escue•to -ta *adj* free, unencumbered; bare, unadorned
escuintle *adj* (Mex) sickly || *m* (*perro*) (Mex) mutt; (Mex) brat
esculcar §73 *tr* (dial & Am) to frisk
esculpir *tr & intr* to sculpture, to carve; to engrave
escultismo *m* outdoor activities
escultista *m* outdoorsman
escultor *m* sculptor
escultora *f* sculptress
escultura *f* sculpture
escultural *adj* sculptural; statuesque
escupidera *f* cuspidor; (Am) chamber pot
escupidura *f* spit; fever blister
escupir *tr & intr* to spit
escurrepla•tos *m* (*pl* **-tos**) dish rack
escurridero *m* drainpipe; drainboard; slippery spot
escurridi•zo -za *adj* slippery
escurri•do -da *adj* narrow-hipped; (Am) abashed, confused
escurridor *m* colander
escurriduras *fpl* dregs, lees
escurrir *tr* (*una vasija; un líquido; la vajilla*) to drain; to wring, wring out; **escurrir el bulto** (coll) to duck || *intr* to drip, ooze, trickle; to slide, to slip || *ref* to drip, ooze, trickle; to slide, to slip; to slip away; (*un reparo*) to slip out
esdrúju•lo -la *adj* accented on the antepenult || *m* word or verse accented on the antepenult
ese, esa *adj dem* (*pl* **esos, esas**) that (*near you*) || **ese** *f* sound hole (*of violin*); **hacer eses** to reel, stagger
ése, ésa *pron dem* (*pl* **ésos, ésas**) that (*near you*); **ésa** your city
esencia *f* essence; **esencia de pera** banana oil; **quinta esencia** quintessence
esencial *adj & m* essential
esfera *f* sphere; (*del reloj*) dial
esféri•co -ca *adj* spherical || *m* football
esfinge *f* sphinx; spiteful woman
esforza•do -da *adj* brave, vigorous, enterprising
esforzar §35 *tr* to strengthen, to invigorate; to encourage || *ref* to exert oneself; to strive
esfuerzo *m* effort, exertion, endeavor; courage, vigor, spirit

esfumar *tr* to stump || *ref* to disappear, fade away
esgarrar *tr* (*la flema*) to try to cough up || *intr* to clear the throat
esgrima *f* fencing
esgrimidura *f* fencing
esgrimir *tr* to wield, to brandish; (*un argumento*) to swing || *intr* to fence
esgrimista *mf* (Arg, Chile, Peru) fencer; (Chile) swindler, panhandler
esguazar **§60** *tr* to ford
esguazo *m* fording; ford
esguince *m* dodge, duck; (*gesto de disgusto*) frown; twist, sprain, wrench
eslabón *m* (*de cadena*) link; (*hierro acerado para sacar fuego de un pedernal; cilindro de acero para afilar cuchillos*) steel
eslabonar *tr* to link; to link together, to string together || *intr* to link
eslálom *m* slalom
esla•vo -va *adj* Slav, Slavic || *mf* Slav || *m* (*idioma*) Slavic
esla•vón -vona *adj* & *mf* Slav
eslogan *m* (*consigna usada en fórmulas publicitarias*) slogan
eslora *f* (naut) length
eslova•co -ca *adj* & *mf* Slovak
esmaltar *tr* to enamel; to embellish
esmalte *m* enamel; **esmalte para las uñas** nail polish
esmera•do -da *adj* careful, painstaking
esmeralda *f* emerald
esmerar *tr* to polish, to shine; to examine, to check || *ref* to take pains, to do one's best
esmeril *s* emery
esmeriladora *f* emery wheel
esmerilar *tr* to grind or polish with emery
esmero *m* care, neatness
esmoladera *f* grindstone
esmoquin *m* tuxedo, dinner coat
esnob *adj* snobbish || *mf* (*pl* **esnobs**) snob
esnobismo *m* snobbery, snobbishness
esnobista *adj* snobbish
eso *pron dem* that; **a eso de** about; **eso es** that's it; that is; **por eso** for that reason; therefore
esófago *m* esophagus
espaciador *m* space bar
espacial *adj* space, spatial
espaciar **§77** (Arg, Chile) & **regular** *tr* to space; to spread, scatter || *ref* to expatiate; to amuse oneself, to relax
espacio *m* space; **espacio de chispa** spark gap; **espacio exterior** outer space; **espacio libre** (*entre dos cosas*) clearance; **espacio muerto** (*en el cilindro de un motor*) clearance; **por espacio de** in the space of
espacio•so -sa *adj* spacious, roomy; slow, deliberate
espada *m* swordsman; (taur) matador || *f* sword; playing card (*representing a sword*) equivalent to spade; **entre la espada y la pared** between the devil and the deep blue sea
espadachín *m* swordsman; (*amigo de pendencias*) bully
espadaña *f* cattail, bulrush, reed mace; (*campanario*) bell gable
espadilla *f* (*remo que se usa como timón*) scull; (*aguja para sujetar el pelo*) bodkin; red insignia of Order of Santiago
espadín *m* rapier
espadón *m* (coll) brass hat
espalar *tr* to shovel
espalda *f* back; **a espaldas de uno** behind one's back; **de espaldas a** with one's back to; **tener buenas espaldas** to have broad shoulders; **volver las espaldas a** to turn a cold shoulder to
espaldar *m* (*de silla*) back; (*enrejado para plantas*) trellis, espalier
espaldarazo *m* slap on the back; (*ceremonia para armar caballero*) accolade; **dar el espaldarazo a** to accept, approve
espalera *f* trellis, espalier
espantada *f* (*de un animal*) sudden flight; (*desistimiento ocasionado por el miedo*) cold feet
espantadi•zo -za *adj* shy, skittish, scary
espantajo *m* scarecrow; (*persona fea*) fright
espantamos•cas *m* (*pl* **-cas**) (*para poner a los caballos*) fly net; (*aparato para asustar y alejar las moscas*) fly chaser
espantapája•ros *m* (*pl* **-ros**) scarecrow
espantar *tr* to scare, frighten; to scare away || *ref* to get scared; to be surprised, to marvel
espanto *m* fright, terror; (*amenaza*) threat; (Am) ghost
espanto•so -sa *adj* frightening, terrifying
España *f* Spain; **la Nueva España** New Spain (*Mexico in the early days*)
espa•ñol -ñola *adj* Spanish; **a la española** in the Spanish manner || *mf* Spaniard || *m* (*idioma*) Spanish; **los españoles** the Spanish || *f* Spanish woman
españolizar **§60** *tr* to make Spanish, to Hispanicize; to translate into Spanish || *ref* to become Spanish
esparadrapo *m* sticking plaster
esparaván *m* spavin
esparavel *m* mortarboard
esparcimiento *m* spreading, scattering, dissemination; diversion, relaxation; frankness, openness
esparcir **§36** *tr* to spread, scatter; to divert, relax || *ref* to spread, scatter; to disperse; to take it easy, to relax
espárrago *m* asparagus; (*perno*) stud bolt; awning pole
esparrancar **§73** *ref* to spread one's legs wide apart
esparta•no -na *adj* & *mf* Spartan
esparto *m* esparto grass
espasmo *m* spasm
espasmódi•co -ca *adj* spasmodic
espásti•co -ca *adj* spastic
espato *m* spar; **espato flúor** fluor spar
espátula *f* spatula; putty knife
especia *f* spice
especia•do -da *adj* spicy
especial *adj* especial, special
especialidad *f* speciality; (*ramo a que se consagra una persona o negocio*) specialty
especialista *mf* specialist

especializar **§60** *tr, intr & ref* to specialize
especiar *tr* to spice
especie *f* (*categoría de la clasificación biológica*) species; (*clase, género*) sort, kind; (*caso, asunto*) matter; (*chisme, cuento*) news, rumor; appearance, pretext, show; remark; **en especie** in kind; **soltar una especie** to try to draw someone out
especie•ro -ra *mf* spice dealer || *m* spice box
especificar **§73** *tr* to specify; to itemize
específi•co -ca *adj* specific || *m* specific; patent medicine
espécimen *m* (*pl* **especímenes**) specimen
especio•so -sa *adj* (*engañoso*) specious; nice, neat, perfect
especiota *f* (coll) hoax, wild idea
espectáculo *m* spectacle; **dar un espectáculo** to make a scene; **espectáculo de atracciones** side show
especta•dor -dora *mf* witness; spectator
espectral *adj* ghostly
espectro *m* specter, phantom, ghost; (phys) spectrum
especular *tr* to check, examine; to contemplate || *intr* to speculate
espejear *intr* to sparkle
espejismo *m* mirage
espejo *m* mirror, looking glass; model; **espejo de cuerpo entero** full-length mirror, pier glass; **espejo de retrovisión** rear-view mirror; **espejo de vestir** full-length mirror, pier glass; **espejo retrovisor** rear-view mirror
espelunca *f* cave, cavern
espeluznante *adj* hair-raising
espera *f* wait, waiting; (*puesto para cazar*) blind, hunter's blind; composure, patience, respite; delay; (law) stay; **no tener espera** to be of the greatest urgency
esperanza *f* hope; **tener puesta su esperanza en** to pin one's faith on
esperanza•do -da *adj* hopeful (*having hope*)
esperanza•dor -dora hopeful (*giving hope*)
esperanzar **§60** *tr* to give hope to
esperanzo•so -sa *adj* hopeful, full of hope
esperar *tr* (*aguardar*) to wait for, to await; (*tener esperanza de conseguir*) to expect, to hope for; **ir a esperar** to go to meet || *intr* to wait; to hope; **esperar** + *inf* to hope to + *inf;* **esperar a que** to wait until; **esperar desesperando** to hope against hope; **esperar en** to put one's hope in; **esperar que** to hope that; **esperar sentado** to have a good wait
esperinque *m* smelt
esperma *f* sperm
espesar *m* depth, thickness (*of woods*) || *tr* to thicken; (*un tejido*) to weave tighter || *ref* to thicken, to get thick or thicker
espe•so -sa *adj* thick; dirty, greasy
espesor *m* thickness; (*de un flúido, gas, masa*) density
espesura *f* thickness; (*matorral*) thicket; (*cabellera muy espesa*) shock of hair; dirtiness, greasiness
espetar *tr* to skewer; to pierce, pierce through; **espetar algo a** to spring something on || *ref* to be solemn, be pompous; (coll) to settle down
espetón *m* (*hurgón*) poker; (*asador*) skewer, spit; jab, poke
espía *mf* spy; (coll) squealer || *f* (naut) warping; (*cuerda*) (naut) warp
espiar **§77** *tr* to spy on || *intr* to spy; (naut) to warp
espichar *tr* to prick; (*dinero*) (Chile) to cough up; (Chile, Peru) to tap || *intr* (coll) to die || *ref* (Mex, W-I) to get thin
espiche *m* (*arma o instrumento puntiagudo*) prick; (naut) peg, bung
espichón *m* stab, prick
espiga *f* (bot) ear, spike; peg, pin, tenon; (*clavo sin cabeza*) brad; (*badajo*) clapper; (*de una llave*) stem
espigar **§44** *tr* to glean; to tenon, to dowel || *intr* (*los cereales*) to form ears || *ref* to grow tall, to shoot up
espigón *m* sharp point, spur; (*mazorca*) ear of corn; (*cerro puntiagudo*) peak; breakwater
espina *f* thorn, spine; (*de los peces*) fishbone; doubt, uncertainty; sorrow; (anat) spine; **dar mala espina a** (coll) to worry; **espina de pescado** herringbone; **espina de pez** fishbone; **espina dorsal** spinal column; **estar en espinas** (coll) to be on pins and needles
espinaca *f* spinach; **espinacas** spinach
espinal *adj* spinal
espinapez *m* herringbone; thorny matter, difficulty
espinar *m* thorny spot; (fig) thorny matter || *tr* to prick; (*árboles*) to protect with thornbushes; to hurt, offend
espinazo *m* backbone; (*de un arco*) keystone
espinel *m* trawl, trawl line
espineta *f* spinet
espinilla *f* (*de la pierna*) shin, shinbone; (*granillo en la piel*) blackhead
espino *m* hawthorn; **espino artificial** barbed wire; **espino negro** blackthorn
espinochar *tr* (*el maíz*) to husk
espino•so -sa *adj* thorny; (*pez*) bony; (*difícil*) (fig) thorny, knotty
espiocha *f* pickaxe
espión *m* spy
espionaje *m* spying, espionage
espira *f* turn
espiración *f* breathing; exhalation
espiral *adj* spiral || *f* (*línea curva que da vueltas alrededor de un punto*) spiral; (*del reloj*) hairspring; (*de humo*) curl, wreath
espirar *tr* to breath; to encourage || *intr* to breathe; to exhale, expire; (*el viento*) (poet) to blow gently
espiritismo *m* espiritualism
espirito•so -sa *adj* spirited, lively; (*licor*) spirituous
espíritu *m* spirit; (*mente*) mind; (*aparecido, fantasma*) ghost, spirit; **espíritu de equipo** teamwork; **Espíritu Santo** Holy Ghost, Holy Spirit; **dar, despe-**

dir, exhalar or **rendir el espíritu** to give up the ghost
espiritual *adj* spiritual; sharp, witty
espiritualismo *m* spiritualism
espita *f* tap, cock; (coll) tippler
espitar *tr* to tap
esplendidez *f* splendor, magnificence
espléndi•do -da *adj* splendid, magnificent; generous, open-handed; (poet) brilliant, radiant
esplendor *m* splendor
esplendoro•so -sa *adj* resplendent
espliego *m* lavender
esplín *m* melancholy
espolada *f* prick with spur; **espolada de vino** (coll) shot of wine
espolear *tr* to spur, to spur on
espoleta *f* fuse; (*hueso*) wishbone
espolón *m* (*del gallo, una montaña, un buque de guerra*) spur; dike, jetty, mole, cutwater; (*prominencia córnea de las caballerías*) fetlock; (*sabañón*) chilblain
espolvorear *tr* (*quitar el polvo de; esparcir el polvo sobre*) to dust; (*el azúcar*) to sprinkle
esponja *f* sponge; (*sablista*) (coll) sponge, sponger; **beber como una esponja** (coll) to drink like a fish; **tirar la esponja** (coll) to throw in (or up) the sponge
esponja•do -da *adj* proud, puffed-up; (coll) fresh, healthy
esponjar *tr* to puff up, make fluffy || *ref* to puff up, become fluffy; (coll) to be puffed up, be conceited; (coll) to look fresh and healthy
esponjo•so -sa *adj* spongy
esponsales *mpl* betrothal, engagement
espontanear *ref* to make a clean breast of it; to open one's heart
espontáne•o -a *adj* spontaneous || *m* (taur) spectator who jumps into the ring to take on the bull
espora *f* spore
esporádi•co -ca *adj* sporadic
esposa *f* wife; **esposas** handcuffs, manacles
esposar *tr* to handcuff, to manacle
espo•so -sa *mf* spouse || *m* husband || *f* see **esposa**
espuela *f* spur; **echar la espuela** (coll) to take a nightcap; **espuela de caballero** delphinium, rocket larkspur; **espuela de galán** nasturtium
espuerta *f* two-handled esparto basket
espulgar §44 *tr* to delouse; to scrutinize
espuma *f* foam; (*en un vaso de cerveza; saliva parecida a la espuma*) froth; (*película de impurezas en la superficie de un líquido*) scum; **crecer como espuma** (coll) to grow like weeds; (coll) to have a meteoric rise; **espuma de caucho** foam rubber; **espuma de jabón** lather; **espuma de mar** meerschaum
espumadera *f* skimmer
espumajear *intr* to froth at the mouth
espumajo•so -sa *adj* foamy, frothy
espumante *adj* foaming; (*vino*) sparkling
espumar *tr* to skim || *intr* to foam, to froth; (*el jabón*) to lather; (*el vino*) to sparkle; to increase rapidly
espumarajo *m* froth, frothing at the mouth
espumilla *f* voile; (CAm, Ecuad) meringue
espumo•so -sa *adj* foamy, frothy; (*cubierto de una película*) scummy; (*jabonoso*) lathery; (*vino*) sparkling
espu•rio -ria *adj* spurious
espurrear or **espurriar** *tr* to squirt with water from the mouth
esputar *tr & intr* to spit
esputo *m* spit, saliva
esq. *abbr* **esquina**
esqueje *m* cutting, slip
esquela *f* note; announcement; death notice; **esquela amorosa** billet-doux
esqueléti•co -ca *adj* skeleton; skeletal, thin, wasted
esqueleto *m* skeleton; (CAm, Mex) blank form; (Chile) sketch, outline
esquema *m* scheme, diagram
es•quí *m* (*pl* **-quís**) ski; skiing; **esquí acuático** water ski; water skiing; **esquí remolcado** skijoring
esquia•dor -dora *adj* ski || *mf* skier
esquiar §77 *intr* to ski
esquiciar *tr* to sketch
esquicio *m* sketch
esquifar *tr* (naut) to fit out, to man
esquife *m* skiff
esquiismo *m* skiing
esquila *f* sheepshearing; hand bell
esquilar *tr* to shear, to fleece
esquilimo•so -sa *adj* (coll) fastidious, squeamish
esquilmar *tr* to harvest; (*las plantas el jugo de la tierra*) to drain, exhaust; (*una fuente de riqueza*) to drain, squander, use up; to carry away, steal
esquilmo *m* harvest, farm produce; (Mex) farm scrapings
esquilmo•so -sa *adj* (coll) fastidious
esquimal *adj & mf* Eskimo
esquina *f* corner; (SAm) corner store; **a la vuelta de la esquina** around the corner; **doblar la esquina** to turn the corner; **hacer esquina** (*un edificio*) to be on the corner; **las cuatro esquinas** puss in the corner
esquina•do -da *adj* sharp-cornered; difficult, unsociable
esquinar *tr* to be on the corner of; to put in the corner; to alienate || *intr* — **esquinar con** to be on the corner of || *ref* — **esquinarse con** to fall out with
esquinazo *m* (coll) corner; (Arg, Chile) serenade; **dar esquinazo a** (coll) to give the slip to, to shake off
esquinencia *f* quinsy
esquinera *f* (Am) corner piece (*of furniture*)
esquirla *f* splinter
esquirol *m* scab, strikebreaker
esquisto *m* schist
esquite *m* (CAm, Mex) popcorn
esquivar *tr* to avoid, evade, shun; to dodge || *ref* to withdraw; to dodge
esquivez *f* aloofness, gruffness
esqui•vo -va *adj* aloof, gruff

estable *adj* stable, permanent; full-time || *mf* regular guest, permanent guest
establecer §**22** *tr* to establish, to institute || *ref* to settle, take up residence; to start a business, to open an office
establecimiento *m* establishment; place of business; decree, ordinance, statute
establo *m* stable
estaca *f* stake, picket, pale; cudgel, club; (*clavo largo*) spike; (hort) cutting
estacada *f* stockade, palisade; dueling ground; **dejar en la estacada** to leave in the lurch; **quedarse en la estacada** to succumb on the field of battle, to fall in a duel; to fail; to lose out
estacar §**73** *tr* to stake, to stake off; to tie to a stake || *ref* to stand stiff
estación *f* (*cada una de las cuatro divisiones del año*) season; (*sitio en que paran los trenes; radioemisora*) station; (*lugar en que se hace alto en un paseo, etc.*) stop; **estación balnearia** bathing resort; **estación de cabeza** (rr) terminal; **estación de carga** freight station; **estación de empalme** junction; **estación de gasolina** gas station, filling station; **estación de la seca** dry season; **estación de paso** (rr) way station; **estación de radiodifusión** broadcasting station; **estación de seguimiento** tracking station; **estación de servicio** service station; **estación difusora** or **emisora** broadcasting station; **estación gasolinera** gas station, filling station; **estación telefónica** telephone exchange
estacional *adj* seasonal
estacionamiento *m* stationing; parking; parking lot
estacionar *tr* to station; to stand, to park || *intr* to stand, to park || *ref* to station oneself; to be stationary; to stand, to park; **se prohibe estacionarse** no standing, no parking
estaciona•rio -ria *adj* stationary
estada *f* stay, stop
estadía *f* (*ante un pintor*) sitting; (com) demurrage; (Am) stop, stay
estadio *m* stadium; phase, stage; (*longitud*) furlong
estadista *mf* (*perito en estadística*) statistician || *m* statesman
estadística *f* statistics
estadísti•co -ca *adj* statistical || *m* (Am) statistician || *f* see **estadística**
estadiunense *adj* American, United States || *mf* American
estadi•zo -za *adj* (*aire*) heavy, stifling; (*agua*) stagnant
estado *m* state; state, condition, status; statement, report; **en estado de buena esperanza** or **en estado interesante** in the family way; **estado civil** marital status; **estado de ánimo** state of mind; **estado de cuentas** (com) statement; **estado libre asociado** commonwealth; **estado llano** commons, common people; **estado mayor** (mil) staff; **estado mayor conjunto** joint chiefs of staff; **estado mayor general** general staff; **Estados Unidos** *msg* the United States; **estado tapón** buffer state; **estar en estado de guerra** to be under martial law; **los Estados Unidos** *mpl* the United States; **tomar estado** to take a wife; to go into the church
estado-policía *m* (*pl* **estados-policías**) police state
estadounidense or **estadunidense** *adj* American, United States || *mf* American
estafa *f* swindle, trick; (*estribo*) stirrup
estafar *tr* to swindle, trick; to overcharge
estafeta *f* post, courier; post office; diplomatic mail
estallar *intr* to burst; to explode; (*un incendio, una revolución; la guerra*) to break out; (*la ira*) to break forth
estallido *m* report, crash, explosion; crack; (*p.ej., de la guerra*) outbreak; **dar un estallido** to crash, explode
estambre *m* (*hebras de lana e hilo formado de ellas*) worsted; (bot) stamen; **estambre de la vida** course or thread of life
estampa *f* stamp, print, engraving; press, printing; footstep, track; aspect, appearance; **dar a la estampa** to publish, bring out; **parecer la estampa de la herejía** (coll) to be a sight, be a mess; **la propia estampa de** the very image of
estampado *m* printing, stamping; printed fabric, cotton print
estampar *tr* to stamp, to print, to engrave; (*en el ánimo*) to fix, engrave; (*p.ej., el pie*) to leave a mark of; (bb) to tool; (*arrojar con fuerza*) (coll) to dash, to slam
estampida *f* report, crash, explosion; (Am) stampede
estampido *m* report, crash, explosion; **estampido sónico** (aer) sonic boom
estampilla *f* (*sello con letrero para estampar*) stamp; (*sello con una firma en facsímile*) rubber stamp; (*sello de correos o fiscal*) (Am) stamp
estampillar *tr* to stamp; to rubber-stamp
estanca•do -da *adj* stagnant; (fig) stagnant, dead
estancar §**73** *tr* to stanch; to stem, check; (*un negocio*) to suspend, hold up; to corner; to monopolize || *ref* to become stagnant, to become choked up
estancia *f* stay, sojourn; (*aposento*) living room; day in hospital; cost of day in hospital; (*estrofa*) stanza; (mil) bivouac; (Arg, Urug, Chile) cattle ranch; (Col) small country place; (Ven) truck farm
estanciero *m* (Am) rancher, cattle raiser
estan•co -ca *adj* stanch, watertight || *m* government monopoly; cigar store, government store (*for sale of tobacco, matches, postage stamps, etc.*); archives; (Ecuad) liquor store
estándar *m* standard
estandardizar §**60** or **estandarizar** §**60** *tr* to standardize
estandarte *m* banner, standard

estandartizar §60 *tr* to standardize
estanque *m* basin, reservoir; pond, pool
estanque·ro -ra *mf* storekeeper, tobacconist; (Ecuad) saloonkeeper || *m* reservoir tender
estanquillo *m* cigar store, government store (*for sale of tobacco, matches, postage stamps, etc.*); (Col, Ecuad) bar, saloon; (Mex) booth, stand
estante *adj* located, being; settled, permanent || *m* shelf; shelving; bookcase, open bookcase
estantería *f* shelves, shelving; book stack
estañar *tr* to tin; to tin-plate; to solder; (Ven) to hurt, injure; (Ven) to fire
estaño *m* tin
estaquilla *f* peg, dowel, pin; (*clavo pequeño sin cabeza*) brad; (*clavo largo*) spike
estaquillar *tr* to peg, dowel; to nail
estar §37 *v aux* (*to form progressive form*) to be, e.g., **están aprendiendo el español** they are learning Spanish || *intr* to be; to be in, be home; to be ready; **¿a cuántos estamos?** what day of the month is it?; **¡está bien!** O.K.!, all right!; **estar a** to cost, sell at; **estar bien** to be well; **estar bien con** to be on good terms with; **estar de** to be (*on a temporary basis*); **estar de más** (coll) to be in the way; (coll) to be unnecessary; (coll) to be idle; **estar de viaje** to be on a trip; **estar mal** to be sick, be ill; **estar mal con** to be on bad terms with; **estar para** to be about to; **estar por** to be for, be in favor of; to be about to; to have a mind to; to remain to be + *pp;* **estar sobre sí** to be wary, be on one's guard || *ref* (*p.ej., en casa*) to stay; (*p.ej., quieto*) to keep
estarcido *m* stencil
estarcir §36 *tr* to stencil
estatal *adj* state
estáti·co -ca *adj* static; dumbfounded, speechless
estatificar §73 *tr* to nationalize
estatizar §60 *tr* (Am) to nationalize
estatua *f* statue; **quedarse hecho una estatua** (coll) to stand aghast
estatuir §20 *tr* to order, decree; to establish, prove
estatura *f* stature
estatuta·rio -ria *adj* statutory
estatuto *m* statute
estay *m* (naut) stay; **estay mayor** (naut) mainstay
este, esta *adj dem* (*pl* **estos, estas**) this || *m* east; east wind
éste, ésta *pron dem* (*pl* **éstos, éstas**) this one, this one here; the latter; **ésta** this city
estela *f* (*de un buque*) wake; (*de cohete, humo, cuerpo celeste, etc.*) trail
estepa *f* steppe
estera *f* mat; matting; **cargado de esteras** (coll) out of patience
esterar *tr* to cover with matting || *intr* (coll) to bundle up for the cold
estercolar *m* dunghill || §61 *tr* to dung, to manure
estercolero *m* manure pile, dunghill; manure collector
estereofóni·co -ca *adj* stereophonic, stereo
estereoscópi·co -ca *adj* stereoscopic, stereo
estereotipa·do -da *adj* stereotyped
estéril *adj* (*que no produce nada*) sterile; (*inútil, vano*) futile
esterilizar §60 *tr* to sterilize || *ref* to become sterile
esterlina *adj fem* (*libra*) sterling (*pound*)
esternón *m* breastbone
estero *m* tideland; estuary; (Arg) swamp, marsh; (Chile) stream; (Col, Ven) pool, puddle
esterto *m* death rattle; (*ruido en ciertas enfermedades, perceptible por la auscultación*) stertor, râle; **estertor agónico** death rattle
esteta *mf* aesthete || *f* beautician
estéti·co -ca *adj* aesthetic || *f* aesthetics
estetoscopio *m* stethoscope
estiaje *m* low water
estiba *f* (naut) stowage
estibador *m* stevedore, longshoreman
estibar *tr* to pack, to stuff; (naut) to stow
estiércol *m* dung, manure
esti·gio -gia *adj* Stygian || **Estigia** *f* Styx
estigma *m* stigma
estigmatizar §60 *tr* to stigmatize
estilar *tr* (*una escritura*) to draw up in proper form; to be given to || *intr & ref* to be in fashion
estilete *m* (*puñal*) stiletto
estilo *m* style; **por el estilo** like that, of the kind; **por el estilo de** like; **estilo directo** (gram) direct discourse; **estilo indirecto** (gram) indirect discourse
estilográfica *f* fountain pen
estima *f* esteem; (naut) dead reckoning
estimable *adj* estimable; considerable; appreciable, computable; esteemed
estimación *f* esteem, estimation; estimate, evaluation
estimar *tr* (*tener en buen concepto*) to esteem; (*apreciar, valuar*) to estimate; to think, believe; to appreciate, thank; to be fond of, to like; **estimar en poco** to hold in low esteem
estimativa *f* judgment; instinct
estimulante *adj & m* stimulant
estimular *tr* to stimulate
estímulo *m* stimulus
estío *m* summer
estipendio *m* stipend; wages
estípti·co -ca *adj* styptic; constipated; mean, stingy
estipular *tr* to stipulate
estiradamente *adv* scarcely, hardly; violently
estira·do -da *adj* conceited, stuck-up; prim, neat; tight, closefisted
estirar *tr* to stretch; (*alambre, metal*) to draw; (*planchar ligeramente*) to iron lightly; (*un escrito, discurso, cargo, etc.*) (fig) to stretch out; (*el dinero*) (fig) to stretch || *ref* to stretch; to put on airs

estirón *m* jerk, tug; **dar un estirón** (coll) to grow up in no time
estirpe *f* race, stock, lineage; (*linaje*) strain, pedigree
estival *adj* summer
esto *pron dem* that; **en esto** at this point; **por esto** for this reason
estocada *f* thrust, stab, lunge; (*herida*) stab, stab wound; (*cosa que ocasiona dolor*) blow
Estocolmo *f* Stockholm
estofa *f* brocade; quality, kind
estofado *m* stew
estoi·co -ca *adj & mf* stoic
estóli·do -da *adj* stupid, imbecile
estómago *m* stomach; **estómago de avestruz** iron digestion; **tener buen estómago** or **mucho estómago** (coll) to be thick-skinned; (coll) to have an easy conscience
estopa *f* (*de lino o cáñamo*) tow; (*de calafatear*) (naut) oakum; **estopa de acero** steel wool; **estopa de algodón** cotton waste
estopilla *f* (*tela muy sutil*) lawn; (*tela ordinaria de algodón*) cheesecloth
estoque *m* rapier; sword lily, gladiola
estoquear *tr* to stab with a rapier
estor *m* blind, shade, window shade
estorbar *tr* to hinder, obstruct; to inconvenience, bother, annoy || *intr* (coll) to be in the way
estorbo *m* hindrance, obstruction; inconvenience, bother, annoyance
estorbo·so -sa *adj* hindering; bothersome, annoying
estornino *m* starling; **estornino de los pastores** grackle, myna
estornudar *intr* to sneeze
estornudo *m* sneeze, sneezing
estrado *m* (*tarima del trono*) dais; lecture platform; (archaic) lady's drawing room; **estrados** courtrooms, law courts; **citar para estrados** to subpoena
estrafala·rio -ria *adj* (coll) queer, eccentric, odd; (coll) sloppy, sloppily dressed || *mf* (coll) screwball
estragar §44 *tr* to spoil, damage, vitiate
estrago *m* damage, ruin, havoc
estrambote *m* tail (*of sonnet*)
estrambóti·co -ca *adj* (coll) odd, queer
estrangul *m* (mus) reed, mouthpiece
estrangular *tr & ref* to strangle, to choke
estraperlear *intr* to deal in the black market
estraperlista *adj* black-market || *mf* black-market dealer
estraperlo *m* black market
estrapontín *m* folding seat, jump seat
estratagema *f* stratagem; craftiness
estratega *m* strategist
estrategia *f* strategy; **alta estrategia** grand strategy
estratégi·co -ca *adj* strategic(al) || *m* strategist
estratificar §73 *tr & ref* to stratify
estrato *m* stratum, layer
estratosfera *f* stratosphere
estraza *f* rag; brown paper
estrechar *tr* (*reducir a menor ancho*) to narrow; (*apretar*) to tighten; to press, pursue; to force, compel; to hug, embrace; to squeeze; **estrechar la mano a** to shake hands with || *ref* to narrow down; to contract; to hug, embrace; (*reducir los gastos*) to retrench; **estrecharse en** to squeeze in; **estrecharse la mano** (*dos personas*) to shake hands
estrechez *f* narrowness; rightness; (*amistad íntima*) closeness, intimacy; austerity, strictness; poverty, want, need; trouble, jam; **estrechez de miras** narrow outlook, narrow-mindedness; **hallarse en gran estrechez** to be in dire straits
estre·cho -cha *adj* narrow; tight; close, intimate; austere, strict; stingy, tight; poor, needy; mean || *m* (*paso angosto en el mar*) strait; fix, predicament
estrechura *f* narrowness; tightness; closeness, intimacy; austerity, strictness; trouble, predicament
estregar §66 *tr* to rub hard; to scour
estregón *m* hard rub
estrella *f* star; (typ) asterisk, star; (mov & theat) star; (*hado, destino*) (fig) star; **estrella de los Alpes** edelweiss; **estrella de mar** starfish; **estrella de rabo** comet; **estrella filante** or **fugaz** shooting star; **estrella fulgurante** (astr) flare star; **estrella polar** polestar; **estrella vespertina** evening star; **ver las estrellas** (coll) to see stars
estrella·do -da *adj* (*cielo*) starry; star-spangled; star-shaped; (*huevos*) fried
estrellamar *m* starfish
estrellar *adj* star || *tr* to star, to spangle with stars; (*huevos*) to fry; to shatter, dash to pieces || *ref* to be spangled with stars; to crash; **estrellarse con** to clash with
estrellón *m* large star; (*fuego artificial*) star; (Am) smash-up
estremecer §22 *tr* to shake; (*el aire*) to rend; (fig) to shake, upset || *ref* to shake, tremble, shiver, shudder
estrena *f* (*regalo que se da en señal de agradecimiento*) handsel; first use
estrenar *tr* to use for the first time, to wear for the first time; (*un drama*) to perform for the first time; (*un cine*) to show for the first time; to try out for the first time || *ref* to make the day's first transaction; to appear for the first time; (*un drama, un cine*) to open
estrenista *mf* first-nighter
estreno *m* beginning, debut; première, first performance; first use
estre·nuo -nua *adj* strenuous, vigorous, enterprising
estreñimiento *m* constipation
estreñir §72 *tr* to constipate
estrépito *m* racket, crash; fuss, show
estrepito·so -sa *adj* loud, noisy, boisterous; notorious; shocking
estría *f* flute, groove
estriar §77 *tr* to flute, groove
estribar *intr* to lean, rest; to be based, to depend
estriberón *m* stepping stone
estribillo *m* (*de un poema*) burden, refrain; pet word, pet phrase

estribo *m* (*de coche*) step; (*de automóvil*) running board; (*apoyo para el pie*) footboard; (*para el pie del jinete*) stirrup; abutment, buttress; (fig) foundation, support; **perder los estribos** to fly off the handle; to lose one's head
estribor *m* starboard
estricnina *f* strychnine
estricote *m* (Ven) riotous living; **al estricote** hither and thither
estric·to -ta *adj* strict, severe, rigorous; proper, punctual; (*sentido de una palabra*) narrow
estrictura *f* (pathol) stricture
estrige *f* barn owl; (*Athene noctua*) little owl
estro *m* poetic inspiration; (*de animal*) rut, heat
estrofa *f* strophe
estroncio *m* strontium
estropajo *m* mop; dishcloth; **servir de estropajo** (coll) to be forced to do the dirty work; (coll) to be treated with indifference
estropajo·so -sa *adj* (coll) raggedy, slovenly; (*carne*) (coll) tough, leathery; (coll) spluttering
estropear *tr* to spoil, ruin, damage; to abuse, mistreat; to cripple, maim || *ref* to spoil, go to ruin; to fail
estropicio *m* (coll) breakage; (coll) havoc, ruin; (coll) fracas, rumpus
estructura *f* structure
estruendo *m* noise, crash, boom; confusion, uproar; pomp, show; fame
estruendo·so -sa *adj* noisy, booming
estrujar *tr* to squeeze; to press, crush, mash; to bruise; to rumple; (coll) to drain, exhaust
estuante *adj* hot, burning
estuario *m* estuary; tideland
estucar §73 *tr* to stucco
estuco *m* stucco; **estuco de París** plaster of Paris
estuche *m* case, box; (*caja y utensilios que se guardan en ella*) kit; casket, jewel case; (*para tijeras*) sheath; **estuche de afeites** compact, vanity case; **ser un estuche** (coll) to be a handy fellow
estudia·do -da *adj* affected, studied
estudiantado *m* student body
estudiante *mf* student
estudiantil *adj* student
estudiar *tr* to study; (*la lección a una persona*) to hear (*someone's lesson*) || *intr* to study; **estudiar para . . .** to study to become . . .
estudio *m* study; (*aposento*) studio; (mus) étude; **altos estudios** advanced studies
estudio·so -sa *adj* studious || *m* student, scholar
estufa *f* stove; steam cabinet, steam room; foot stove; (*invernáculo*) hothouse
estul·to -ta *adj* stupid, silly, foolish
estupefac·to -ta *adj* stupefied, dumbfounded
estupen·do -da *adj* stupendous; (coll) famous, distinguished
estúpi·do -da *adj* stupid || *mf* dolt
estupor *m* stupor; surprise, amazement
estuprar *tr* to rape, violate
estupro *m* rape, violation
estuque *m* stucco
esturión *m* sturgeon
etapa *f* stage; **a etapas pequeñas** by easy stages
éter *m* ether
etére·o -a *adj* ethereal
eternidad *f* eternity
eternizar §60 *tr* to prolong endlessly || *ref* to be endless, be interminable
eter·no -na *adj* eternal
éti·co -ca *adj* ethical || *f* ethics
etileno *m* ethylene
etilo *m* ethyl
étimo *m* etymon
etimología *f* etymology
etíope *adj* & *mf* Ethiopian
etiópi·co -ca *adj* & *m* Ethiopic
etiqueta *f* (*marbete*) tag, label; (*ceremonial que se debe observar*) etiquette; (*ceremonia en la manera de tratarse*) formality; **de etiqueta** formal, full-dress; **de etiqueta menor** semiformal; **estar de etiqueta** to have become cool toward each other
etiquetar *tr* to tag, to label
etiquete·ro -ra *adj* formal, ceremonious; full of compliments
etiquez *f* (pathol) consumption
étni·co -ca *adj* ethnic(al); (gram) gentilic
etnografía *f* ethnography
etnología *f* ethnology
E.U.A *abbr* **Estados Unidos de América**
eucalipto *m* eucalyptus
Eucaristía *f* Eucharist
eufemismo *m* euphemism
eufemísti·co -ca *adj* euphemistic
eufonía *f* euphony
eufóni·co -ca *adj* euphonic, euphonious
euforia *f* euphoria; endurance, fortitude
eufuísmo *m* euphuism
eufuísti·co -ca *adj* euphuistic
eugenesia *f* eugenics
eunuco *m* eunuch
euritmia *f* regular pulse
euro *m* east wind
Europa *f* Europe
europe·o -a *adj* & *mf* European
eutanasia *f* euthanasia
eutrapelia *f* moderation; lightheartedness; simple pastime
evacuación *f* evacuation; **evacuación de basuras** garbage disposal
evacuar §21 & **regular** *tr* to evacuate; (*un trámite*) to transact; (*una visita*) to pay; (*un encargo, un asunto*) to do, carry out; **evacuar el vientre** to have a movement of the bowels || *intr* to evacuate; to have a movement of the bowels
evadi·do -da *adj* escaped || *mf* escapee
evadir *tr* to avoid, evade, elude || *ref* to evade; to escape, to flee
evaluar §21 *tr* to evaluate; to value
evangéli·co -ca *adj* evangelic(al)
evangelio *m* (coll) gospel, gospel truth || **Evangelio** *m* Gospel, Evangel
evangelista *m* Gospel singer or chanter;

(Mex) public writer, penman || **Evangelista** *m* Evangelist
evaporar *tr & ref* to evaporate
evaporizar **§60** *tr, intr & ref* to vaporize
evasión *f* (*efugio, evasiva*) evasion; (*fuga*) escape
evasi•vo -va *adj* evasive || *f* loophole, pretext, excuse
evento *m* chance, happening, contingency; (Col) sports event; **a todo evento** in any event
eventual *adj* contingent; (*emolumentos; gastos*) incidental
eventualidad *f* eventuality, contingency; uncertainty
evidencia *f* evidence, obviousness; (*prueba judicial*) (Am) evidence; **evidencia moral** moral certainty
evidenciar *tr* to show, make evident
evidente *adj* evident, obvious
evitable *adj* avoidable
evitación *f* avoidance; prevention
evitar *tr* to avoid, shun; (*p.ej., el polvo*) to keep off; to prevent; **evitar** + *inf* to avoid + *ger;* to save from + *ger,* e.g., **la luz de la luna nos evitó tener que encender los faroles** the light of the moon saved us from having to light the lights
evo *m* (poet) age, aeon; (theol) eternity
evocar **§73** *tr* to evoke; (*p.ej., los demonios*) to invoke
evolución *f* evolution; change, development (*of one's point of view, plans, conduct, etc.*)
evolucionar *intr* to evolve; to change, develop; (mil & nav) to maneuver
ex *adj* ex- (*former*), e.g., **el ex presidente** the ex-president
ex abrupto *adv* brashly || *m* brash remark
exacción *f* (*de impuestos, deudas, multas, etc.*) exaction, levy; (*cobro injusto*) extortion
exacerbar *tr* to exacerbate, aggravate
exactitud *f* exactness; punctuality
exac•to -ta *adj* exact; punctual, faithful || **exacto** *interj* right!
exactor *m* tax collector
exagerar *tr* to exaggerate
exalta•do -da *adj* exalted; extreme, hotheaded; wrought-up; radical
exaltar *tr* to exalt; to extol || *ref* to be wrought-up, get excited
examen *m* examination; **examen de ingreso** entrance examination; **sufrir un examen** to take an examination
examinar *tr* to examine; to inspect || *ref* to take an examination; **examinarse de ingreso** to take entrance examinations
exangüe *adj* bloodless; (coll) weak, exhausted; (coll) dead
exánime *adj* (*sin vida*) lifeless; (*desmayado*) faint, in a faint, lifeless
exasperar *tr* to exasperate
Exc.ª *abbr* **Excelencia**
excandecer **§22** *tr* to incense, enrage
excarcelación *f* release
excarcelar *tr* (*a un preso*) to release
excavadora *f* power shovel
excavar *tr* to excavate; to loosen soil around
excedente *adj* excess; excessive; on leave || *m* excess, surplus
exceder *tr* (*ser mayor que*) to exceed; (*aventajar*) to excel || *ref* to go too far, go to extremes; **excederse a sí mismo** to outdo oneself
excelencia *f* excellence, excellency; **por excelencia** par excellence; **Su Excelencia** Your Excellency
excelente *adj* excellent
excel•so -sa *adj* lofty, sublime || **el Excelso** the Most High
excéntrica *f* eccentric
excentricidad *f* eccentricity
excéntri•co -ca *adj* eccentric; (*barrio*) outlying || *mf* eccentric || *f* see **excéntrica**
excepción *f* exception; **a excepción de** with the exception of
excepcional *adj* exceptional
excepto *prep* except
exceptuar **§21** *tr* to except; (*eximir*) to exempt
excerpta or **excerta** *f* excerpt
excesi•vo -va *adj* excessive; excess
exceso *m* excess; **exceso de equipaje** excess baggage; **exceso de peso** excess weight; **exceso de velocidad** speeding
excitable *adj* excitable
excitación *f* excitement; excitation
excitante *adj & m* stimulant
excitar *tr* to excite, stir up, stimulate || *ref* to become excited
exclamación *f* exclamation
exclamar *tr & intr* to exclaim
exclaustrar *tr* (*a un religioso*) to secularize
excluir **§20** *tr* to exclude
exclusión *f* exclusion; **con exclusión de** to the exclusion of
exclusiva *f* rejection, turndown; sole right, monopoly; (*anticipación de una noticia por un periódico*) news beat
exclusive *adv* exclusively || *prep* exclusive of, not counting
exclusivista *adj* exclusive, clannish || *mf* snob
exclusi•vo -va *adj* exclusive || *f* see **exclusiva**
Exc.^{mo} *abbr* **Excelentísimo**
ex combatiente *m* ex-serviceman
excomulgar **§44** *tr* to excommunicate; (coll) to ostracize, banish
excomunión *f* excommunication
excoriar *tr* to skin || *ref* to skin oneself; (*p.ej., el codo*) to skin
excrementar *intr* to have a bowel movement
excremento *m* excrement
exculpar *tr* to exculpate, exonerate
excursión *f* excursion, outing
excursionista *mf* excursionist, tourist
excusa *f* excuse; **a excusa** secretly; **excusa es decir** it is unnecessary to say
excusabaraja *f* basket with lid
excusable *adj* excusable; avoidable
excusadamente *adv* unnecessarily
excusa•do -da *adj* exempt; unnecessary; private, set apart; (*puerta*) side || *m* toilet
excusa•lí *m* (*pl* **-líes**) small apron

excusar *tr* to excuse; to exempt; to avoid; to prevent; to make unnecessary; **excusar** + *inf* to not have to + *inf* || *ref* to excuse oneself; to apologize; **excusarse de** + *inf* to decline to + *inf*
exención *f* exemption
exencionar *tr* to exempt
exentamente *adv* freely; frankly, simply
exentar *tr* to exempt
exen•to -ta *adj* exempt; open, unobstructed; free, disengaged
exequias *fpl* obsequies
exfolia•dor -dora *adj* (Am) tear-off
exhalación *f* exhalation; flash of lightning; shooting star; fume, vapor; **como una exhalación** (coll) like a flash of lightning
exhalar *tr* to exhale, emit; (*suspiros, quejas*) to breathe forth; **exhalar el último suspiro** to breathe one's last || *ref* to exhale; (*con el ejercicio violento del cuerpo*) to breathe hard; to hurry; to crave
exhausti•vo -va *adj* exhaustive
exhaus•to -ta *adj* exhausted; (coll) wasted away
exheredar *tr* to disinherit
exhibición *f* exhibition; exhibit
exhibir *tr* to exhibit; (Mex) to pay || *ref* (coll) to make oneself evident
exhilarante *adj* exhilarating; (*gas*) laughing
exhortar *tr* to exhort
exhumar *tr* to exhume
exigencia *f* exigency, requirement
exigente *adj* exigent, demanding
exigir §27 *tr* to exact, require, demand
exi•guo -gua *adj* meager, scanty
exila•do -da *adj & mf* (Am) exile
exi•mio -mia *adj* choice, select, superior; distinguished
eximir *tr* to exempt
existencia *f* existence; **en existencia** in stock; **existencias** (com) stock
existente *adj* existing, extant; in stock
existir *intr* to exist
exitazo *m* smash hit
exitista *adj* (Arg) me-too || *mf* (Arg) me-tooer
éxito *m* (*resultado feliz*) success; (*canción, cine, etc. que ha tenido mucho éxito*) hit; (*resultado de un negocio*) outcome, result; **éxito de librería** best seller; **éxito de taquilla** box-office hit, good box office; **éxito de venta** best seller; **éxito rotundo** smash hit
exito•so -sa *adj* (Arg) successful
ex li•bris *m* (*pl* **-bris**) bookplate
éxodo *m* exodus; **éxodo de técnicos** brain drain
exonerar *tr* to exonerate, to relieve; to discharge, dismiss; **exonerar el vientre** to have a movement of the bowels
exorar *tr* to beg, entreat
exorbitante *adj* exorbitant
exorcizar §60 *tr* to exorcise
exornar *tr* to adorn, embellish
exóti•co -ca *adj* exotic; striking, stunning, glamorous
expandir *tr & ref* (Arg, Chile) to expand, extend, spread
expansión *f* expansion; (*manifestación efusiva*) expansiveness; (*difusión de una opinión*) spread; rest, recreation
expansionar *ref* to expand; to open one's heart; to relax, take it easy
expansi•vo -va *adj* expansive
expatria•do -da *adj & mf* expatriate
expectación *f* expectancy
expectativa *f* expectation; **estar en la expectativa de** to be expecting, to be on the lookout for
expectorar *tr & intr* to expectorate
expedición *f* (*excursión para realizar una empresa*) expedition; (*remesa*) shipment; (*de un certificado, títulos, etc.*) issuance; (*agilidad, facilidad*) expedition
expedi•dor -dora *mf* sender, shipper
expediente *m* expedient; makeshift, apology; (*agilidad, facilidad*) expedition; (*todos los papeles correspondientes a un asunto*) dossier; (law) action, proceedings; **expediente académico** (educ) record
expedienteo *m* red tape
expedir §50 *tr* to send, ship, remit; (*títulos*) to issue; (*despachar, cursar*) to expedite
expeditar *tr* (Am) to expedite
expediti•vo -va *adj* expeditious
expedi•to -ta *adj* ready; clear, open, unencumbered
expeler *tr* to expel, eject
expende•dor -dora *mf* dealer, retailer; ticket agent; **expendedor de moneda falsa** distributor of counterfeit money
expendeduría *f* cigar store (*for sale of state-monopolized articles*)
expender *tr* to spend; to dispense; to sell at retail; (*moneda falsa*) to circulate
expendio *m* (Am) shop, store; (Am) retail; (Mex) cigar store
expensar *tr* (Chile, Guat, Mex) to pay the cost of
expensas *fpl* expenses
experiencia *f* (*enseñanza que se adquiere con la práctica o con el vivir; suceso en que uno ha participado, cosa que uno ha experimentado*) experience; (*ensayo, experimento*) experiment
experimenta•do -da *adj* experienced
experimentar *tr* to experience, undergo, feel; to test, try, try out || *intr* to experiment
experimento *m* experiment
exper•to -ta *adj & m* expert
expiación *f* expiation, atonement; purification
expiar §77 *tr* to expiate, atone for; to purify
expirar *intr* to expire
explanación *f* grading, leveling; explanation
explanada *f* esplanade
explanar *tr* to grade, to level; to explain
explayar *tr* to enlarge, extend || *ref* to spread out, extend; to go for an outing; to expatiate, talk at length; **explayarse con** to unbosom oneself to
explicación *f* explanation

explicar **§73** *tr* to explain; (*exponer*) to expound; (*exculpar*) to explain away; (*una clase*) to teach || *intr* to explain || *ref* to explain oneself; to understand, make out
explicati•vo -va *adj* explanatory
explíci•to -ta *adj* explicit
exploración *f* exploration; (mil) scouting; (telv) scanning
explora•dor -dora *mf* explorer || *m* boy scout; (mil) scout
explorar *tr* to explore; (mil) to scout; (telv) to scan
explosión *f* explosion; (*de gases en un motor*) combustion
explosi•vo -va *adj & m* explosive || *f* (phonet) explosive
explotación *f* operation, running; exploitation
explotar *tr* to operate, to run; (*una mina*) to work; to exploit || *intr* to explode
exponente *m* exponent
exponer **§54** *tr* to expose; (*explicar*) to expound; (*a un niño recién nacido*) to abandon || *intr* to display, show, exhibit; (eccl) to expose the Host || *ref* to expose oneself; to be on view
exportación *f* exportation, export; (*mercaderías que se exportan*) exports
exporta•dor -dora *mf* exporter
exportar *tr & intr* to export
exposición *f* exposition; (*a un peligro; con relación a los puntos cardinales*) exposure; (phot) exposure; (rhet) exposition; **exposición universal** world's fair
exposímetro *m* light meter
expósi•to -ta *mf* foundling
exposi•tor -tora *mf* exhibitor
exprés *m* express train; (Mex) express company
expresa•do -da *adj* above-mentioned
expresamente *adv* express, expressly
expresar *tr* to express || *ref* to express oneself
expresión *f* expression; (*acción de exprimir*) squeezing; (*zumo exprimido*) juice; **expresiones** regards
expresi•vo -va *adj* expressive; kind, affectionate
expre•so -sa *adj* express || *m* (*tren muy rápido; correo extraordinario*) express; (Am) express company
exprimidera *f* squeezer; **exprimidera de naranjas** orange squeezer
exprimi•do -da *adj* lean, skinny; stiff, stuck-up; affected, prim, prudish
exprimidor *m* wringer; squeezer; **exprimidor de ropa** clothes wringer
exprimir *tr* to squeeze, press; (*p.ej., la ropa blanca*) to wring, wring out; (*extraer apretando*) to express
ex profeso *adv* on purpose
expropiar *tr* to expropriate
expues•to -ta *adj* dangerous, hazardous
expugnar *tr* to take by storm
expulsanie•ves *m* (*pl* **-ves**) snowplow
expulsar *tr* to expel
expulsión *f* expulsion
expurgar **§44** *tr* to expurgate
exquisi•to -ta *adj* exquisite
extasiar **§77** & **regular** *ref* to go into ecstasy
éxta•sis *m* (*pl* **-sis**) ecstasy
extáti•co -ca *adj* ecstatic
extemporal *adj* unseasonable
extemporáne•o -a *adj* unseasonable; untimely, inopportune
extender **§51** *tr* to extend, to stretch out, to spread out; to spread; (*un documento*) to draw up || *ref* to extend, to stretch out; to spread; **extenderse a** or **hasta** to amount to
extendidamente *adv* at length, in detail
extensión *f* extension; (*vasta superficie p.ej., del océano*) expanse; (*alcance importancia*) extent; extending
extensi•vo -va *adj* extensive; **hacer extensivos a** to extend (*e.g., good wishes*) to
exten•so -sa *adj* extensive, extended, vast; **por extenso** at length, in detail
extenuar **§21** *tr* to weaken, emaciate
exterior *adj* exterior, outer, outside; foreign || *m* exterior, outside; appearance, bearing; **al exterior** or **a lo exterior** on the outside; outwardly; **del exterior** from abroad; **en el exterior** on the outside; abroad; **en exteriores** (mov) on location
exterioridad *f* externals, outward appearance; **exterioridades** pomp, show
exteriorista *adj* outgoing, outgiving || *mf* extrovert
exteriorizar **§60** *tr* to reveal || *ref* to unbosom one's heart
exterminar *tr* to exterminate
exterminio *m* extermination
exter•no -na *adj* external || *mf* day pupil
extinción *f* extinction; cancellation, elimination
extinguir **§29** *tr* to extinguish, put out; to wipe out, put an end to; to fulfil, carry out; (*un plazo, un tiempo*) to spend, to serve || *ref* to be extinguished, go out; to come to an end
extin•to -ta *adj* (*volcán*) extinct; (Am) deceased || *mf* (Am) deceased
extintor *m* fire extinguisher; **extintor de espuma** foam extinguisher; **extintor de granada** fire grenade
extirpar *tr* to extirpate, to eradicate
extorno *m* premium adjustment (*based on change in policy*)
extorsión *f* extortion; harm, damage
extorsionar *tr* to harm, damage; (Am) to extort
extra *adj* extra; **extra de** (coll) in addition to, besides || *mf* (theat) extra || *m* (*de un periódico*) extra; (coll) extra, bonus
extracción *f* extraction; (*en la lotería*) drawing numbers; **extracción de raíces** (math) evolution
extractar *tr* (*un escrito*) to abstract
extracto *m* (*de un escrito*) abstract; (pharm) extract
extracurricular *adj* extracurricular
extradición *f* extradition
extraer **§75** *tr* to extract; to pull; (*la raíz*) (math) to extract
extrafuerte *adj* heavy-duty
extralimitar *ref* to go too far
extramural *adj* extramural

extranjerismo *m* borrowing
extranje•ro -ra *adj* foreign, alien || *mf* foreigner, alien; **extranjero enemigo** enemy alien || *m* foreign country; **al extranjero** abroad; **del extranjero** from abroad; **en el extranjero** abroad
extrañar *tr* to banish, expatriate; to surprise; to find strange; (Am) to miss || *ref* to be surprised; to refuse
extrañeza *f* strangeness, peculiarity; (*desavenencia*) estrangement; wonder, surprise
extra•ño -ña *adj* foreign; (*raro, singular*) strange; extraneous; **extraño a** unconnected with || *mf* foreigner
extraoficial *adj* unofficial
extraordina•rio -ria *adj* extraordinary; extra, special || *m* extra dish; special mail; (*de un periódico*) extra
extrapla•no -na *adj* extra-flat
extrapolar *tr & intr* to extrapolate
extrarradio *m* outer edge of town
extrasensorial *adj* extrasensory
extravagancia *f* (*singularidad, ridiculez*) extravagance, wildness, folly
extravagante *adj* (*singular, ridículo*) extravagant, wild, foolish; (*correspondencia en la casa de correos*) in transit
extravia•do -da *adj* lost, misplaced; astray, gone astray; (*lugar*) out-of-the-way
extraviar §77 *tr* to lead astray, mislead; to mislay, misplace || *ref* to get lost, go astray; to go wrong; to get out of line
extravío *m* going astray; loss; misleading; misconduct; misplacement
extrema *f* (*escasez grande*) (coll) extremity; (*de la vida*) (coll) end, last moment
extremar *tr* to carry far, carry to the limit || *ref* to strive hard
extremaunción *f* extreme unction
extreme•ño -ña *adj* frontier
extremidad *f* extremity; end, tip; **extremidades** (*pies y manos*) extremities; **la última extremidad** one's last moment
extremista *mf* extremist
extre•mo -ma *adj* extreme; utmost; critical, desperate || *m* extremity; (*de la calle*) end; (*del dedo*) tip; (*punto último*) extreme; great care; (*de una conversación, una carta*) point; winter pasture; **al extremo de** to the point of; **de extremo a extremo** from one end to the other; **hacer extremos** to be demonstrative, to gush || *f* see **extrema**
extremo•so -sa *adj* extreme, forthright; effusive, gushy, demonstrative
extrínse•co -ca *adj* extrinsic
extroverti•do -da *mf* extrovert
exuberante *adj* exuberant; luxuriant
exudar *tr & intr* to exude
exultante *adj* exultant
exultar *intr* to exult
exvoto *m* votive offering
eyacular *tr & intr* to ejaculate

F

F, f (efe) *f* seventh letter of the Spanish alphabet
f.a.b. *abbr* **franco a bordo**
fabada *f* pork-and-bean stew (*in Asturias*)
fábrica *f* factory, plant; building, masonry; (eccl) vestry
fabricación *f* manufacture; **fabricación en serie** mass production
fabricante *mf* manufacturer
fabricar §73 *tr* to manufacture; to devise, invent; to fabricate
fabril *adj* factory
fabriquero *m* manufacturer; charcoal burner; churchwarden
fábula *f* fable; (*p.ej., de un drama*) plot, story; rumor, gossip; (*mentira*) story, lie; (*objeto de murmuración*) talk of the town
fabulario *m* book of fables
fabulo•so -sa *adj* fabulous
facción *f* faction; feature; battle; **estar de facción** (mil) to be on duty; **facciones** features
facciona•rio -ria *adj* factional
faceta *f* facet
facetada *f* (Mex) flat joke
face•to -ta *adj* (Mex) affected; (Mex) finicky || *f* see **faceta**
facial *adj* facial
fácil *adj* easy; pliant, yielding; likely; loose, wanton
facilidad *f* facility, ease, easiness; **facilidades de pago** easy payments
facilitar *tr* to facilitate, to expedite; to furnish, supply
facili•tón -tona *adj* (coll) bumbling, brash || *mf* (coll) bumbler
facinero•so -sa *adj* wicked || *mf* villain
facistol *m* choir desk
facón *m* (Arg, Urug) gaucho knife
facsímile *m* facsimile
factible *adj* feasible
factor *m* factor; commission merchant; baggageman; freight agent
factoría *f* trading post; (Ecuad, Peru) foundry; (Mex) factory
factura *f* invoice, bill; workmanship; **factura simulada** pro forma invoice; **según factura** as per invoice
facturación *f* invoicing, billing; (*del equipaje*) checking
facturar *tr* to invoice, to bill; (*el equipaje*) to check
facultad *f* faculty; (*de la universidad*) school; knowledge, skill; power; **facultad de altos estudios** graduate school

facultar *tr* to empower, to authorize
facultati•vo -va *adj* faculty; optional || *m* doctor, physician
facundia *f* eloquence, fluency
facun•do -da *adj* eloquent, fluent
facha *mf* (*adefesio*) (coll) sight || *f* look, appearance; **facha a facha** face to face
fachada *f* façade; (*de un libro*) title page; (coll) look, build, bearing; **hacer fachada con** to overlook, to look out on
facha•do -da *adj* — **bien fachado** good-looking || *f* see **fachada**
fachenda *m* (coll) boaster, show-off || *f* (coll) boasting
fachendear *intr* (coll) to boast, to show off
fachendista, fachen•dón -dona, fachendo•so -sa *adj* (coll) boastful || *mf* (coll) boaster, show-off
fachinal *m* (Arg) marshland
fada *f* fairy, witch
faena *f* work; toil; chore, task, job; (taur) windup; (taur) stunt, trick; (mil) fatigue, fatigue duty; (Guat, Mex, W-I) extra work, overtime; (Ecuad) morning work in the field; (Chile) gang of farm hands
faenero *m* (Chile) farm hand
Faetón *m* Phaëthon
fagot *m* bassoon
faisán *m* pheasant
faja *f* sash, girdle; bandage; band, strip; newspaper wrapper; (*de carretera*) lane; (*de tierra*) strip; **faja central** or **divisoria** median strip; **faja medical** supporter
fajar *tr* to wrap; to bandage; to swaddle; (*un periódico o revista*) to put a wrapper on; (Am) to beat, thrash; (Am) to attack || *ref* to put on a sash
fajardo *m* meat pie
fajín *m* sash
fajina *f* fagot; fire wood; (mil) call to quarters
fajo *m* bundle; (*de papel moneda*) roll; (Am) swig; (Mex) blow; (Mex) leather belt; **fajos** swaddling clothes
falacia *f* deception; deceitfulness
falange *f* phalanx
falangia *f* daddy-longlegs
fa•laz *adj* (*pl* **-laces**) deceitful; deceptive
falba•lá *m* (*pl* **-laes**) gore; flounce, ruffle
falce *m* sickle; falchion
falda *f* skirt, dress; (*regazo*) lap; flap, fold; (*del sombrero*) brim; foothill; (*mujer*) (coll) skirt; **cosido a las faldas de** tied to the apron strings of
falde•ro -ra *adj* skirt; (*perro*) lap; lady-loving || *m* lap dog
faldillas *fpl* skirts, coattails
faldón *m* coattail; shirttail; saddle flap
falible *adj* fallible
falsada *f* swoop (*of bird of prey*)
falsa•rio -ria *adj* lying || *mf* falsifier, crook; liar
falsear *tr* to falsify; to counterfeit; to forge; (*la verdad*) to distort; (*una cerradura*) to pick; to bevel || *intr* to sag, to buckle; to give, give way
falsedad *f* falsity; (*mentira*) falsehood
falsete *m* falsetto; plug, tap; door (*between rooms*)
falsetista *f* falsetto
falsía *f* falsity, treachery; unsteadiness
falsificación *f* falsification; fake; counterfeit; forgery
falsificar **§73** *tr* to falsify; to fake; to counterfeit; to forge
falsilla *f* guide lines
fal•so -sa *adj* false; counterfeit; (*caballo*) vicious || *m* patch; **coger en falso** (Mex) to catch in a lie; **envidar en falso** to bluff
falta *f* fault; lack, want; misdeed; absence; (*ausencia de la clase*) cut; (sport) fault; **a falta de** for want of; **echar en falta** to miss; **falta de ortografía** misspelling; **hacer falta** to be needed; to be lacking; **hacerle falta a uno** to need, e.g., **le hacen falta a Juan estos libros** John needs these books; to miss, e.g., **Vd. me hace mucha falta** I miss you very much; **sin falta** without fail
faltar *intr* to be missing, be lacking, be wanting; to fall short; to run out; to be absent; to fail; to die; to lack, to need, e.g., **me falta dinero** I lack money, I need money; **faltar a la clase** to cut class; **faltar a la verdad** to fail to tell the truth; **faltar a una cita** to fail to keep an appointment; **faltar . . . para** to be . . . to, e.g., **faltan cinco minutos para las dos** it is five minutes to two; **faltar poco para** to come near; **faltar por** to remain to be, e.g., **faltan por escribir dos cartas** two letters remain to be written
fal•to -ta *adj* short, lacking; (*peso o medida*) short; (Arg) dull, stupid; (Col) proud, vain; **falto de** short of || *f* see **falta**
fal•tón -tona *adj* (coll) dilatory, remiss; (Arg) simple-minded
falto•so -sa *adj* (coll) addlebrained; (Col) quarrelsome; (CAm, Mex) disrespectful
faltriquera *f* pocket; handbag; **faltriquera de reloj** watch fob; **rascarse la faltriquera** (coll) to cough up
falúa *f* barge, tender
falucho *m* felucca
falla *f* failure, breakdown; defect; (geol) fault; (Mex) baby's bonnet
fallar *tr* to trump; to judge, pass judgment on || *intr* to fail, to miss; to misfire; to sag, weaken; to break down; to judge, pass judgment
falleba *f* espagnolette
fallecer **§22** *intr* to die; to fail, expire
falleci•do -da *adj* deceased, late
falli•do -da *adj* unsuccessful; bankrupt; (*deuda*) uncollectible
fallir **§13** *intr* to fail; (Ven) to go bankrupt
fa•llo -lla *adj* (Chile) silly, simple; **estar fallo a** to be out of (*cards of a suit*) || *m* short suit; decision; judgment, verdict; **tener fallo a** or **de** to be out of || *f* see **falla**
fama *f* fame; reputation; rumor; (Chile) bull's-eye; **correr fama** to be ru-

mored; **es fama** it is said, it is rumored

faméli•co -ca *adj* famished, starving

familia *f* family

familiar *adj* familiar; family; (*sin ceremonia*) informal; (*lenguaje, estilo*) colloquial || *m* member of the family; member of the household; acquaintance; **familiar dependiente** dependent

familiaridad *f* familiarity

familiarizar §60 *tr* to familiarize || *ref* to become familiar; to become too familiar; to familiarize oneself

famo•so -sa *adj* famous; (*excelente*) (coll) famous; (*formidable*) (coll) some, e.g., **famoso sujeto** some guy

fámu•lo -la *mf* (coll) servant

fanal *m* beacon, lighthouse; lantern; bell glass, bell jar; lamp shade

fanáti•co -ca *adj* fanatic(al) || *mf* fanatic; (sport) fan

fanatismo *m* fanaticism

fanega *f* 1.58 bu.; **fanega de tierra** 1.59 acres

fanfarria *f* fanfare; (coll) blustering

fanfa•rrón -rrona *adj* (coll) blustering, bragging; (coll) flashy || *mf* (coll) blusterer, braggart

fanfarronada *f* (coll) bluster, bravado

fanfarronnear *intr* (coll) to bluster, to brag

fanfarronería *f* (coll) blustering, bragging, sword rattling

fanfurriña *f* (coll) pet, peeve

fango *m* mud, mire; **llenar de fango** (fig) to sling mud at

fango-so -sa *adj* muddy; sticky, gooey

fantasear *tr* to dream of || *intr* to fancy, to daydream; **fantasear de** to boast of being

fantasía *f* fantasy; fancy; conceit, vanity; imagery; **con fantasía** (Arg) hard; **de fantasía** fancy, imitation; **tocar por fantasía** (Ven) to play by ear

fantasio•so -sa *adj* (coll) vain, conceited

fantasma *m* phantom, ghost; stuffed shirt; (telv) ghost; **fantasma magnético** magnetic curves || *f* scarecrow, hobgoblin

fantas•món -mona *adj* (coll) conceited || *mf* (coll) conceited person || *m* (coll) stuffed shirt; (coll) scarecrow

fantásti•co -ca *adj* fantastic; fancy; conceited

fantoche *m* puppet, marionette; (coll) nincompoop, whippersnapper

faquín *m* street porter, errand boy

fara•lá *m* (*pl* **-laes**) ruffle, flounce; (coll) frill

faramalla *mf* (coll) cheat, swindler || *f* (coll) jabber, claptrap; (coll) bluff, fake; (Chile) bragging

faramalle•ro -ra or **farama•llón -llona** *adj* (coll) scheming, swindling || *mf* (coll) schemer, swindler

farándula *f* (*baile*) farandole; (coll) gossip, scheming; (coll) theater people; (*de gente*) (Arg) crush, milling

farandulear *intr* (coll) to boast, to show off

Faraón *m* Pharaoh

faraute *m* herald, messenger; interpreter; (*actor*) prologue; (coll) busybody

fardel *m* bag, bundle; (coll) sloppy person

fardo *m* bundle, package

farfa•lá *m* (*pl* **-laes**) ruffle, flounce

farfullar *tr* (*p.ej., una lección*) (coll) to sputter through; (*p.ej., una tarea*) (coll) to stumble through || *intr* (coll) to sputter

faringe *f* pharynx

fariseo *m* pharisee; Pharisee; (coll) lanky good-for-nothing

farmacéuti•co -ca *adj* pharmaceutical || *mf* pharmacist

farmacia *f* pharmacy, drug store; **farmacia de guardia** drug store open all night

fármaco *m* drug, medicine

faro *m* lighthouse, beacon; floodlight; (aut) headlight; (fig) beacon; **faro piloto** (aut) spotlight; **faros de carretera** (aut) bright lights; **faros de cruce** (aut) dimmers; **faros de población** or **de situación** (aut) parking lights

farol *m* lamp, light; lantern; street light; (rr) headlight; (coll) conceited fellow; (Bol) bay window; **farol de tope** (naut) headlight

farola *f* lighthouse; street lamp, lamppost

farolear *intr* (coll) to boast, brag

farole•ro -ra *adj* (coll) boasting || *mf* (coll) boaster || *m* lamplighter

farolillo *m* heartseed; Canterbury bell; **farolillo veneciano** Chinese lantern, Japanese lantern

farota *f* (coll) minx, vixen

farotear *intr* (Col) to romp around, make a racket

faro•tón -tona *adj* (coll) brazen, cheeky || *mf* (coll) cheeky person

farra *f* salmon trout; (SAm) revelry

fárrago *m* hodgepodge

farro *m* grits

farru•co -ca *adj* (coll) bold, fearless; (coll) ill-humored || *mf* (coll) Galician abroad, Asturian abroad

farru•to -ta *adj* (Arg, Bol, Chile) sickly

farsa *f* farce; humbug

farsante *adj* & *mf* (coll) fake, fraud, humbug

fas — **por fas o por nefas** rightly or wrongly, in any event

fascinante *adj* fascinating

fascinar *tr* to fascinate, to bewitch; to cast a spell on, cast the evil eye on

fascismo *m* fascism

fascista *adj* & *mf* fascist

fase *f* phase

fastidiar *tr* to bore, annoy; to cloy, sicken; to disappoint || *ref* to get bored; to suffer, be a victim

fastidio *m* boredom, annoyance; distaste, nausea

fastidio•so -sa *adj* boring, annoying; cloying, sickening; annoyed, displeased

fas•to -ta *adj* happy, blessed || *m* pomp, show

fastuo·so -sa *adj* vain, pompous; magnificent
fatal *adj* fatal; bad, evil; (law) unextendible
fatalidad *f* fatality; misfortune
fatalismo *m* fatalism
fatalista *mf* fatalist
fatalmente *adv* fatally; inevitably; unfortunately; badly, poorly
fatídi·co -ca *adj* ominous, fateful
fatiga *f* fatigue; hard breathing; **fatigas** hardship
fatigar §44 *tr* to fatigue, tire, weary; to annoy, bother || *ref* to get tired
fatigo·so -sa *adj* fatiguing, tiring; (coll) trying, tedious
fa·tuo -tua *adj* fatuous; conceited || *mf* simpleton
fauces *fpl* (anat) fauces; (fig) jaws, mouth
fauna *f* fauna
fauno *m* faun
faus·to -ta *adj* happy, fortunate || *m* pomp, magnificence
fausto·so -sa *adj* magnificent
fau·tor -tora *mf* abettor; accomplice
favor *m* favor; **a favor de** under cover of; by means of; in favor of; **hágame Vd. el favor de** do me the favor to; **por favor** please; **vender favores** to peddle influence
favorable *adj* favorable
favorecer §22 *tr* to favor; to flatter
favoritismo *m* favoritism
favori·to -ta *adj & mf* favorite
fayanca *f* unstable posture
faz *f* (*pl* **faces**) face; aspect, look; (*de monedas o medallas*) obverse; **faces** cheeks; **faz a faz** face to face
F.C. *abbr* **ferrocarril**
fe *f* faith; testimony, witness; certificate; **¡a fe mía!** upon my faith!; **dar fe de** to certify; **en fe de lo cual** in witness whereof; **fe de erratas** list of errata; **hacer fe** to be valid; **la fe del carbonero** simple faith
fealdad *f* ugliness
Febe *f* Phoebe
feble *adj* weak, sickly; (*moneda, aleación*) lacking in weight or fineness
Febo *m* Phoebus
febrero *m* February
febril *adj* feverish
fécula *f* starch
feculen·to -ta *adj* starchy; fecal
fecundar *tr* to fecundate, to fertilize
fecun·do -da *adj* fecund, fertile
fecha *f* date; **con fecha de** under date of; **de larga fecha** of long standing; **hasta la fecha** to date
fechador *m* (Chile, Mex) canceler, postmark
fechar *tr* to date
fechoría *f* misdeed, villainy
federación *f* federation
federal *adj & mf* federal
federar *tr & ref* to federate
Federico *m* Frederick
feéri·co -ca *adj* fairy
fehaciente *adj* authentic
feldespato *m* feldspar
felicidad *f* felicity, happiness; luck
felicitar *tr* to felicitate, congratulate, wish happiness to
feli·grés -gresa *mf* parishioner, church member
feligresía *f* parish; congregation
Felipe *m* Philip
fe·liz *adj* (*pl* **-lices**) happy; lucky; (*oportuno*) felicitous
fe·lón -lona *adj* perfidious, treacherous || *mf* wicked person
felonía *f* perfidy, treachery
felpa *f* plush; (coll) drubbing; (coll) severe reprimand
felpu·do -da *adj* plushy, downy || *m* mat, door mat
femenil *adj* feminine, womanly
femeni·no -na *adj* feminine; (*sexo*) female || *m* feminine
fementi·do -da *adj* false, treacherous
feminismo *m* feminism
fenecer §22 *tr* to finish, to close || *intr* to come to an end; to die
Fenicia *f* Phoenicia
feni·cio -cia *adj & mf* Phoenician || *f* see **Fenicia**
fé·nix *m* (*pl* **-nix** or **-nices**) phoenix
fenobarbital *m* phenobarbital
fenomenal *adj* phenomenal
fenómeno *m* phenomenon; (coll) monster, freak
fe·o -a *adj* ugly || *m* (coll) slight; **hacer un feo a** (coll) to slight || **feo** *adv* (Arg, Col, Mex) bad, e.g., **oler feo** to smell bad
feo·te -ta *adj* ugly, hideous
feral *adj* cruel, bloody
fe·raz *adj* (*pl* **-races**) fertile
féretro *m* bier
feria *f* weekday; market; fair; day off; (Mex) change; (CAm) extra; **revolver la feria** (coll) to upset the applecart
ferial *adj* week (*day*); market (*day*) || *m* market; fair
feriante *adj* fair-going || *mf* fairgoer
feriar *tr* to buy, to sell; to give, present; (Mex) to give change for
feri·no -na *adj* wild, savage; (*tos*) whooping (*cough*)
fermentación *f* ferment; fermentation
fermentar *tr & intr* to ferment
fermento *m* ferment
ferocidad *f* ferocity, fierceness
ferósti·co -ca *adj* (coll) irritable; (coll) hideous
fe·roz *adj* (*pl* **-roces**) ferocious, fierce
férre·o -a *adj* iron
ferrería *f* ironworks, foundry
ferretear *tr* to trim with iron; to work in iron
ferretería *f* ironworks; hardware; hardware store
ferrete·ro -ra *mf* hardware dealer
ferrocarril *m* railroad, railway; **ferrocarril de cremallera** rack railway, mountain railroad
ferrocarrile·ro -ra *adj* (Am) railroad, rail || *m* (Am) railroader
ferrotipo *m* tintype
ferrovia·rio -ria *adj* railroad, rail || *m* railroader
fértil *adj* fertile
fertilizar §60 *tr* to fertilize

férula *f* flexible splint; ferule; **estar bajo la férula de** to be under the thumb of
férvi·do -da *adj* fervid; (*fiebre; sed*) burning
ferviente *adj* fervent
fervor *m* fervor, zeal
fervoro·so -sa *adj* ardent, zealous
festejar *tr* to fete, honor, entertain; to celebrate; to court, to woo; (Mex) to beat, thrash
festejo *m* feast, entertainment; celebration; courting, wooing; (Peru) revelry; **festejos** public festivities
festín *m* feast, banquet
festinar *tr* (Am) to hurry through; (CAm) to entertain
festival *m* festival, music festival
festividad *f* festivity; feast day; witticism
festi·vo -va *adj* festive, gay; witty; (*digno de celebrarse*) solemn
festón *m* festoon
festonear *tr* to festoon
fetiche *m* fetish
féti·do -da *adj* fetid, foul
feto *m* fetus
feú·co -ca or **feú·cho -cha** *adj* hideous, repulsive
feudal *adj* feudal
feudalismo *m* feudalism
feudo *m* fief; **feudo franco** freehold
fiable *adj* trustworthy
fiado *m* — **al fiado** on credit; **en fiado** on bail
fia·dor -dora *mf* bail; **salir fiador por** to go bail for || *m* fastener; catch, pawl; (Chile, Ecuad) chin strap
fiambre *adj* cold, cold-served; (*noticias*) old, stale || *m* cold lunch, cold food; stale news; (Arg) dull party; **fiambres** cold cuts
fiambrera *f* dinner pail, lunch basket
fiambrería *f* (Arg) delicatessen store
fianza *f* guarantee, surety; bond; bail; **fianza carcelera** bail
fiar §77 *tr* to entrust, confide; to guarantee; to give credit to; to sell on credit || *intr & ref* to trust
fiasco *m* fiasco
fibra *f* fiber; (fig) fiber, strength, vigor; **fibras del corazón** heartstrings
fibro·so -sa *adj* fibrous
ficción *f* fiction
ficciona·rio -ria *adj* fictional
fice *m* (ichth) hake
ficti·cio -cia *adj* fictitious
ficha *f* chip; counter; domino; filing card; police record; (elec) plug; **ficha catalográfica** index card; **llevar ficha** to have a police record; **ser una buena ficha** (Am) to be a sly fox
ficha·dor -dora *mf* file clerk
fichar *tr* to file; to play, to move; (coll) to black-list; (Cuba) to cheat || *intr* (Col) to die
fichero *m* card index, filing cabinet
fidedig·no -na *adj* reliable, trustworthy
fideicomisa·rio -ria *mf* trustee
fideicomiso *m* trusteeship
fidelería *f* (Arg, Ecuad, Peru) vermicelli factory, noodle factory
fidelidad *f* fidelity; punctiliousness; **alta fidelidad** (rad) high fidelity
fideo *m* (coll) skinny person; (Arg) joke; (Arg) confusion, disorder; **fideos** vermicelli
Fidias *m* Phidias
fiducia·rio -ria *adj & mf* fiduciary
fiebre *f* fever; **fiebre del heno** hay fever; **fibre tifoidea** typhoid fever
fiel *adj* faithful; exact; punctilious; honest, trustworthy || *m* inspector of weights and measures; (*en las balanzas*) pointer; (*de las tijeras*) pin; **fiel de romana** inspector of weights in a slaughterhouse; **los fieles** the faithful
fielato *m* inspector's office; octroi
fieltro *m* felt; felt hat; felt rug
fiera *f* wild animal; (*persona*) fiend; (taur) bull; **ser una fiera para** (coll) to be a fiend for
fierabrás *m* (coll) spitfire, little terror
fierecilla *f* shrew
fiereza *f* fierceness; cruelty; deformity
fie·ro -ra *adj* fierce, wild; cruel; deformed, ugly; huge, tremendous; **echar** or **hacer fieros** to bluster || *f* see **fiera**
fiesta *f* feast, holy day; holiday; celebration, festivity; **estar de fiesta** (coll) to be in a holiday mood; **fiesta de la hispanidad** or **fiesta de la raza** Columbus Day; **fiesta de todos los santos** All Saints' Day; **fiesta onomástica** saint's day, birthday; **fiestas** holiday, vacation; **hacer fiesta** to take off (*from work*); **hacer fiestas a** to act up to, to fawn on; **la fiesta brava** bullfighting; **no estar para fiestas** (coll) to be in no mood for joking; **por fin de fiestas** to top it off; **se acabó la fiesta** (coll) let's drop it
fieste·ro -ra *adj* merry, gay || *mf* merrymaker, party-goer
figón *m* cheap restaurant
figura *f* figure; face, countenance; (*naipe*) face card; (mus) note; (theat) character; **figura retórica** figure of speech; **hacer figura** to cut a figure
figuración *f* representation; (Arg) status, social standing
figura·do -da *adj* figurative
figurar *tr* to depict, trace, represent; to feign || *intr* to figure, to be in the limelight || *ref* to figure, to imagine
figurati·vo -va *adj* figurative, representative
figurería *f* face, grimace
figurilla *mf* (coll) silly little runt || *f* figurine
figurín *m* dummy, model; fashion plate
figurina *f* figurine
figurita *mf* (coll) silly little runt
figurón *m* (coll) stuffed shirt; **figurón de proa** (naut) figurehead
fija *f* hinge; trowel; (*caballo*) (Peru) sure bet; **la fija** (coll) sure thing
fijacarte·les *m* (*pl* **-les**) billposter
fijación *f* fixing, fastening; posting; **fijación de precios** price fixing
fijado *m* (phot) fixing
fija·dor -dora *adj* fixing || *m* carpenter who installs doors and windows; fixing bath; sprayer; (mas) pointer; hair set, hair spray
fijamárge·nes *m* (*pl* **-nes**) margin stop

fijapeina•dos *m* (*pl* **-dos**) hair set, hair spray
fijar *tr* to fix; to fasten; (*carteles*) to post; (*una fecha; los cabellos; una imagen fotográfica; los precios; la atención; una hora, una cita*) to fix; (*residencia*) to establish; to paste, glue || *ref* to settle; to notice; **fijarse en** to notice; to pay attention to; to be intent on
fijeza *f* firmness, stability; steadfastness; **mirar con fijeza** to stare at
fi•jo -ja *adj* fixed; firm, solid, secure, fast; sure, determined; **de fijo** surely || *f* see **fija**
fil *m* — **estar en fil** or **en un fil** to be alike; **fil derecho** leapfrog
fila *f* row, line; file; (*línea que los soldados forman de frente*) rank; (coll) dislike, hatred; **cerrar las filas** (mil) to close ranks; **en fila** in single file; **en filas** (mil) in active service; **fila india** single file, Indian file; **llamar a filas** (mil) to call to the colors; **pasarse a las filas de** to go over to; **romper filas** (mil) to break ranks
filamento *m* filament
filantropía *f* philanthropy
filántro•po -pa *mf* philanthropist
filar *tr* (naut) to pay out slowly
filarmóni•co -ca *adj* philharmonic
filatelia *f* philately
filatelista *mf* philatelist
filatería *f* fast talking; wordiness
filate•ro -ra *adj* fast-talking; wordy || *mf* fast talker; great talker
file•no -na *adj* (coll) cute, tiny
filete *m* (*de carne o pescado*) filet or fillet; (*asador*) spit; edge, rim; narrow hem; (*de tornillo*) thread; snaffle bit; (archit, bb) fillet; (typ) rule, fancy rule
filetear *tr* to fillet; (*un tornillo*) to thread; (bb) to tool
filiación *f* filiation; description, characteristics; (mil) regimental register
filial *adj* filial || *f* affiliate, branch
filiar **§77** *tr* to register || *ref* to enroll
filibustero *m* filibuster, buccaneer
filigrana *f* filigree; (*en el papel*) watermark
filipi•no -na *adj* Filipine, Filipino || *mf* Filipino || **Filipinas** *fpl* Philippines
Filipo *m* Philip (*of Macedonia*)
Filis *f* Phyllis
filiste•o -a *adj* & *mf* Philistine || *m* tall, fat fellow
film *m* (*pl* **films** or **filmes**) film
filmar *tr* to film
filo *m* edge; ridge; dividing line; (CAm, Mex) hunger; **al filo de** at, at about; **dar filo a** to sharpen; **filo del viento** direction of the wind; **pasar al filo de la espada** to put to the sword; **por filo** exactly
filobús *m* trolley bus, trackless trolley
filocomunista *adj* & *mf* procommunist
filología *f* philology
filólo•go -ga *mf* philologist
filón *m* seam, vein; (fig) gold mine
filo•so -sa *adj* (Am) sharp
filosofía *f* philosophy
filosófi•co -ca *adj* philosophic(al)
filóso•fo -fa *mf* philosopher
filote *m* (Col) corn silk; (Col) ear of green corn
filtración *f* filtering; leak; (fig) leak, loss
filtrado *m* filtrate
filtrar *tr* to filter || *intr* to leak; to ooze || *ref* to filter; (*el dinero*) to leak away, to disappear
filtro *m* filter; (*brebaje para conciliar el amor*) philter, love potion
filu•do -da *adj* (SAm) sharp-edged
filván *m* featheredge
fimo *m* dung, manure
fin *m* end; aim, purpose, end; **a fin de** to, in order to; **a fin de que** in order that, so that; **a fines de** toward the end of, late in; **al fin** finally; **al fin del mundo** far, far away; **al fin y a la postre** or **al fin y al cabo** after all, in the end; **dar fin a** to put an end to; **fin de semana** weekend; **por fin** finally, in short; **sin fin** endless; endlessly; **un sin fin de** no end of
fina•do -da *adj* deceased, late || *mf* deceased
final *adj* final || *m* end; (mus) finale; **por final** finally || *f* (sport) finals; **final de partido** windup
finalidad *f* end, purpose
finalista *mf* finalist
finalizar **§60** *tr* to end, terminate; (*una escritura*) (law) to execute || *intr* to end, terminate
financiación *f* financing
financiar *tr* to finance
financie•ro -ra *adj* financial || *mf* financier
finanzas *fpl* finances
finar *intr* to die || *ref* to yearn
finca *f* property, piece of real estate; farm, ranch; **buena finca** (coll) sly fellow
fincar **§73** *tr* (P-R) to cultivate, to farm || *intr* to buy up real estate; (Col) to reside, rest, be based || *ref* to buy up real estate
fincha•do -da *adj* (coll) vain, conceited
fi•nés -nesa *adj* Finnic; Finnish || *mf* Finn || *m* (*idioma uraliano*) Finnic; (*idioma de Finlandia*) Finnish
fineza *f* fineness; kindness, courtesy; token of affection, favor
fingi•do -da *adj* fake, sham; false, deceitful
fingir **§27** *tr* & *intr* to feign, pretend, fake || *ref* to pretend to be
finiquitar *tr* (*una cuenta*) to settle, to close; (coll) to finish, wind up
finiquito *m* settlement, closing; **dar finiquito a** to settle, close; (coll) to finish, wind up
finíti•mo -ma *adj* bordering, neighboring
fini•to -ta *adj* finite
finlan•dés -desa *adj* Finnish || *mf* Finn, Finlander || *m* Finnish
Finlandia *f* Finland
fi•no -na *adj* fine; (*ligero, casi transparente*) sheer; (*esbelto*) thin, slender; (*paño, papel, etc.*) thin; (*agua*)

pure; polite, courteous; shrewd, cunning
finta *f* feint
finura *f* fineness, excellence; politeness, courtesy
finústi•co -ca *adj* (coll) overobsequious
firma *f* signature; signing; firm; firm name; mail to be signed; **con mi firma** under my hand; **firma en blanco** blank check
firmamento *m* firmament
firmante *adj* signatory || *mf* signer, signatory
firmar *tr & intr* to sign
firme *adj* firm, steady; solid, hard; staunch, unswerving || *adv* firmly, steadily || *m* roadbed; **de firme** hard, e.g., **llover de firme** to rain hard
firmeza *f* firmness; constancy, fortitude
firmón *m* shyster who signs anything
fiscal *adj* fiscal, treasury || *m* treasurer; district attorney; busybody
fiscalizar §60 *tr* to control, inspect; to prosecute; to pry into
fisco *m* state treasury, exchequer
fisga *f* fish spear; prying, snooping; banter, raillery
fisgar §44 *tr* to harpoon, fish with a spear; to pry into || *intr* to pry, to snoop; to mock, to jeer || *ref* to mock, to jeer
fis•gón -gona *mf* (coll) mocker, jester; (coll) snooper, busybody
físi•co -ca *adj* physical; (Mex, W-I) finicky, prudish || *mf* physicist || *m* physique || *f* physics
fisiología *f* physiology
fisiológi•co -ca *adj* physiological
fisión *f* fission
fisionable *adj* fissionable
fisonomía *f* physiognomy
fistol *m* sly fellow; (Mex) necktie pin
fisura *f* (anat, min) fissure; **fisura del paladar** cleft palate
fla•co -ca *adj* thin, skinny; feeble, weak, frail; insecure, unstable || *m* weak spot
flacu•cho -cha *adj* (coll) skinny
flagrante *adj* occurring, actual; **en flagrante** in the act
flamante *adj* bright, flaming; brand-new, spick-and-span
flameante *adj* flamboyant
flamear *intr* to flame; to flare up (*with anger*); to flutter, to wave
flamen•co -ca *adj* Flemish; buxom; Andalusian gypsy; (coll) flashy, snappy, gypsyish || *mf* Fleming || *m* (*idioma*) Flemish; Andalusian gypsy dance, song, or music; (orn) flamingo
flámе•o -a *adj* flamelike
flamíge•ro -ra *adj* (poet) flaming; (archit) flamboyant
flan *m* custard
flanco *m* side, flank; **coger por el flanco** to catch off guard
Flandes *f* Flanders
flanquear *tr* to flank
flaquear *intr* to weaken, flag; to become faint; to become discouraged
flaqueza *f* thinness, skinniness; weakness; instability
flato *m* gas; (Am) gloominess, melancholy
flato•so -sa *adj* flatulent, windy; (Am) gloomy, melancholy
flauta *f* flute
flautín *m* piccolo
flautista *mf* flautist, flutist
flebitis *f* phlebitis
fleco *m* fringe; ragged edge; **flecos** bangs
flecha *f* arrow; (aer) sweepback
flechar *tr* (*el arco*) to draw; (*a una persona*) to wound with an arrow, to kill with an arrow; (coll) to infatuate
flechero *m* archer, bowman
fleje *m* iron strap, iron hoop
flema *f* phlegm
flemáti•co -ca *adj* phlegmatic(al)
flemón *m* gumboil
flequillo *m* bangs
Flesinga *f* Flushing
fletante *m* shipowner; (Arg, Chile, Ecuad) conveyancer
fletar *tr* (*una nave*) to charter; (*ganado*) to load; (*bestias de carga, carros, etc.*) (Arg, Chile, Ecuad, Mex) to hire || *ref* (Arg) to sneak in, slip in; (Cuba, Mex) to beat it, clear out
flete *m* (naut) freight, cargo; (Arg, Bol, Col, Urug) race horse; **salir sin flete** (Col, Ven) to beat it
flexible *adj* flexible; (*sombrero*) soft || *m* soft hat; (elec) flexible cord
flexo *m* gooseneck lamp
flinflanear *intr* to tinkle
flirt *m* flirting
flirtear *intr* to flirt
flojear *intr* to ease up, to idle; to flag, weaken
flojedad *f* slackness, looseness; limpness; laziness; weakness
flojel *m* fluff, nap; down, soft feathers
flo•jo -ja *adj* slack, loose; limp; languid, lazy; weak; (*precios*) sagging; (*viento*) light; lax, careless
flor *f* flower; (*de árbol frutal*) blossom; (*del cuero*) grain; (fig) compliment, bouquet; **a flor de** even with, flush with; **a flor de agua** at water level; **decir flores a** to flatter; to flirt with; **flor de la edad** bloom of youth; **flor de la vida** prime of life; **flor del campo** wild flower; **flor de lis** (*escudo de armas de Francia*) lily, fleur-de-lis; **flor de mano** paper flower, artificial flower; **la flor de la canela** the tops; **la flor y nata de** the cream of
flora *f* flora
floral *adj* floral
florcita *f* (Am) little flower; **andar de florcita** (Arg, Bol, Chile, Urug) to stroll around with a flower in one's buttonhole, to take it easy
florear *tr* to flower, decorate with flowers; (*los naipes*) to stack; (*harina*) to bolt || *intr* (*la punta de la espada*) to quiver; to twang away on a guitar; (coll) to throw bouquets
florecer §22 *intr* to flower, to blossom, to bloom; (*prosperar*) to flourish || *ref* to become moldy
floreciente *adj* flowering, florescent; flourishing

florenti•no -na *adj & mf* Florentine
floreo *m* idle talk; bright remark; (*de la punta de la espada*) quivering; (*de la guitarra*) twanging; (mus) flourish; **andarse con floreos** (coll) to beat about the bush
florera *f* flower girl
florería *f* (Am) flower shop
flore•ro -ra *adj* flattering, jesting || *mf* flatterer, jester; florist || *m* (*vaso para flores*) vase; (*maceta con flores*) flowerpot; flower stand, jardiniere; (*cuadro, pintura*) flower piece || *f* see **florera**
florescencia *f* florescence
floresta *f* woods, woodland; grove; rural setting; anthology
florete *m* (*esgrima*) fencing; (*espadín*) foil
floretear *tr* to decorate with flowers || *intr* to fence
flori•do -da *adj* flowery, full of flowers; choice, select
florilegio *m* anthology
floripondio *m* (SAm) angel's-trumpet
florista *mf* florist
floristería *f* flower shop
florón *m* large flower; finial; rosette; (typ) tailpiece, vignette
flota *f* fleet
flotación *f* buoyancy
flotador *m* float
flotaje *m* log driving
flotante *adj* floating; (*barba*) flowing || *m* (Col) braggart
flotar *intr* to float; (*una bandera*) to wave
flote *m* floating; **a flote** afloat
fluctuar §21 *intr* to fluctuate; to bob up and down; to wave; to waver; to be in danger
fluente *adj* fluent, flowing; (*hemorroides*) bleeding
fluidez *f* fluidity
flúi•do -da *adj* fluid; (*estilo, lenguaje*) fluent || *m* fluid
fluir §20 *intr* to flow
flujo *m* flow, flux; (*acceso de la marea*) floodtide; **flujo de risa** fit of noisy laughter; **flujo de vientre** loose bowels; **flujo y reflujo** ebb and flow
flúor *m* fluorine
fluorescencia *f* fluorescence
fluorescente *adj* fluorescent
fluorhídri•co -ca *adj* hydrofluoric
fluorización *f* fluoridation
fluorizar §60 *tr* to fluoridate
fluoroscopio *m* fluoroscope
fluoruro *m* fluoride
flux *m* (*en el póker*) flush; (Am) suit of clothes; **estar en flux** (Am) to be penniless; **hacer flux** (coll) to blow in everything without settling accounts; **tener flux** (Am) to be lucky
fluxión *f* (*acumulación morbosa de humores*) congestion; (*enrojecimiento de la cara y el cuello*) flush; (*constipado de narices*) cold in the head; **fluxión de muelas** swollen cheek; **fluxión de pecho** pneumonia
foca *f* seal
focal *adj* focal
foco *m* focus; (*de vicios*) center; (*de un absceso*) core; electric light
fodo•lí *adj* (*pl* **-líes**) meddlesome
fodon•go -ga *adj* (Mex) dirty, slovenly
fo•fo -fa *adj* soft, fluffy, spongy
fogaje *m* (*contribución*) hearth money; (Arg) fire, blaze; (Arg, Mex) rash, eruption; (Am) blush, flush
fogata *f* blaze, bonfire
fogón *m* cooking stove; (*de máquina de vapor*) firebox
fogonazo *m* powder flash
fogonero *m* fireman, stoker
fogosidad *f* fire, spirit, dash
fogo•so -sa *adj* fiery, spirited
fol. *abbr* **folio**
folgo *m* foot muff
foliar *tr* to folio
folio *m* folio; **al primer folio** right off; **de a folio** (coll) enormous; **en folio** folio
folklore *m* folklore
follaje *m* foliage; gaudy ornament; (*palabrería*) fustian
follar *tr* to shape like a leaf || §61 *tr* to blow with bellows
folletín *m* newspaper serial (*printed at bottom of page*); pamphlet
folleto *m* brochure, pamphlet, tract
fo•llón -llona *adj* careless, indolent, lazy; arrogant, cowardly || *mf* lazy loafer, knave || *m* noiseless rocket
fomentar *tr* to foment; to foster, encourage, promote; to warm
fonda *f* inn, restaurant; (Chile) refreshment stand
fondeadero *m* anchorage
fondea•do -da *adj* (Am) well-heeled
fondear *tr* (*un buque*) to search; to scrutinize, examine closely || *intr* to cast anchor || *ref* (Am) to save up for a rainy day
fondillos *mpl* seat (*of trousers*)
fondista *mf* innkeeper
fondo *m* bottom; (*de un cuarto, una tienda*) back, rear; (*del mar, de una piscina, etc.*) floor; (*de un cilindro, barril, etc.*) head; background; (*de una casa*) depth; (*de un paño*) ground; (*caudal*) fund; (*lo esencial*) bottom; **a fondo** thoroughly; **bajos fondos sociales** underworld, scum of the earth; **colar a fondo** to sink; **dar fondo** to cast anchor; **echar a fondo** to sink; **en el fondo** at bottom; **estar en fondos** to have funds available; **fondo de amortización** sinking fund; **fondos** (*caudales, dinero*) funds; **irse a fondo** to go to the bottom; (*un negocio*) to fail; **tener buen fondo** to be good-natured
fonducho *m* cheap eating house
fonéti•co -ca *adj* phonetic
fono *m* (Chile) earphone
fonocaptor *s* pickup
fonógrafo *m* phonograph
fonología *f* phonology
fontanería *f* plumbing; water-supply system
fontane•ro -ra *adj* fountain || *m* plumber, tinsmith
foque *m* (naut) jib; (coll) piccadilly collar

foraji·do -da *adj* fugitive || *mf* fugitive, outlaw, bandit
foráne·o -a *adj* foreign, strange; offshore
foraste·ro -ra *adj* outside, strange; foreign || *mf* outsider, stranger
forbante *m* freebooter
forcejar or **forcejear** *intr* to struggle, resist, contend
forceju·do -da *adj* strong, husky, robust
fór·ceps *m* (*pl* **-ceps**) forceps
forestal *adj* forest
forja *f* forge; forging; silversmith's forge; foundry, ironworks; mortar
forjar *tr* to forge; to build with stone and mortar; to roughcast; (*mentiras*) to forge || *ref* to forge; to hatch, think up
forma *f* form, shape; way; (*de un libro*) format; **de forma que** so that, with the result that; **tener buenas formas** to have a good figure
formación *f* formation; **formación de palabras** word formation
formal *adj* formal, ceremonious; express, definite; reliable; sedate; serious
formalidad *f* formality; reliability; seriousness
formar *tr* to form; to shape, to fashion; to train, educate || *intr* to form; to form a line, to stand in line || *ref* to form; to form a line, to stand in line; to take form, to grow, to develop
formato *m* format
formidable *adj* formidable
formidolo·so -sa *adj* scared, frightened; frightful, horrible
fórmula *f* formula; prescription; **por fórmula** as a matter of form
formular *tr* to formulate
formulario *m* form, blank; **formulario de pedido** order blank
forni·do -da *adj* husky, sturdy, robust
foro *m* forum; (*abogacía*) bar; (*del escenario*) back, rear
forraje *m* forage, fodder
forrajear *tr & intr* to forage
forrar *tr* to line; (*un vestido*) to face; (*un libro, un paraguas*) to cover; (*un lienzo*) to stretch || *ref* (Guat, Mex) to stuff oneself
forro *m* lining; cover, covering; (naut) sheathing, planking; **forro de freno** brake lining; **ni por el forro** (coll) not by a long shot
fortalecer §22 *tr* to fortify, strengthen
fortaleza *f* fortitude; strength, vigor; fortress, stronghold
fortificación *f* fortification
fortificante *m* tonic
fortificar §73 *tr* to fortify
fortín *m* small fort; bunker
fortui·to -ta *adj* fortuitous
fortuna *f* fortune; **correr fortuna** (naut) to ride the storm; **de fortuna** makeshift; **por fortuna** fortunately; **probar fortuna** to try one's luck
fortunón *m* (coll) windfall
forza·do -da *adj* forced; (*p.ej., entrada*) forcible; (*sonrisa*) (fig) forced; (*trabajos*) hard || *m* galley slave
forzar §35 *tr* to force
forzo·so -sa *adj* unavoidable; strong, husky; (*trabajos*) hard; (*aterrizaje; marcha*) forced || *f* — **hacer la forzosa a** (coll) to put the squeeze on
forzu·do -da *adj* strong, husky, robust
fosa *f* grave; (aut) pit; **fosa de los leones** (Bib) lions' den
fosar *tr* to dig a ditch around
fos·co -ca *adj* dark; cross, sullen; (*tiempo*) threatening
fosfato *m* phosphate
fosforera *f* matchbox
fosforescente *adj* phosphorescent
fósforo *m* (*cuerpo simple*) phosphorus; match; **fósforo de seguridad** safety match
fósil *adj & m* fossil
foso *m* hole, pit; (*que rodea un castillo o fortaleza*) moat; (theat & aut) pit
fotingo *m* (Am) jalopy, jitney
foto *f* (coll) photo; **foto fija** (phot) still
fotodrama *m* photoplay
fotofija *m* photo-finish camera
fotogéni·co -ca *adj* photogenic
fotograbado *m* photoengraving
fotografía *f* (*arte*) photography; (*imagen, retrato*) photograph; photograph gallery
fotografiar §77 *tr & intr* to photograph
fotógra·fo -fa *mf* photographer
fotómetro *m* light meter
fotoperiodismo *m* photojournalism
fotopila *f* solar battery
fotostatar *tr & intr* to photostat
fotóstato *m* photostat
fototubo *m* phototube
fra. *abbr* **factura**
frac *m* (*pl* **fraques**) full-dress coat, tails, swallow-tailed coat
fracasar *intr* to fail; to break to pieces
fracaso *m* failure; breakdown, crash
fracción *f* fraction
fraccionar *tr* to divide up; to break up
fracciona·rio -ria *adj* fractional
fractura *f* fracture; breaking open, breaking in
fracturar *tr* to fracture; to break open, break in || *ref* (*p.ej., un brazo*) to fracture
fragancia *f* fragrance; good reputation
fragante *adj* fragrant; **en fragante** (archaic) in the act
fragata *f* frigate; **fragata ligera** corvette
frágil *adj* fragile; (*quebradizo; que cae fácilmente en el pecado*) frail; (Mex) poor, needy
fragmento *m* fragment
fragor *m* crash, roar, thunder
fragoro·so -sa *adj* noisy, thundering
fragosidad *f* roughness, unevenness; (*de un bosque*) thickness, denseness; rough road
frago·so -sa *adj* rough, uneven; thick, dense; noisy, thundering
fragua *f* forge
fraguar §10 *tr* to forge; to hatch, scheme; (*mentiras*) to forge || *intr* to forge; (*la cal, el cemento*) to set
fraile *m* friar, monk; **fraile de misa y olla** (coll) friarling; **fraile rezador** praying mantis
frambesia *f* (pathol) yaws

frambuesa *f* raspberry
frambueso *m* raspberry bush
francachela *f* (coll) feast, spread; (coll) carousal, high time; (Arg) excessive familiarity
francalete *m* strap with buckle
fran•cés -cesa *adj* French; **despedirse a la francesa** (coll) to take French leave || *m* Frenchman; (*idioma*) French || *f* Frenchwoman
francesada *f* French remark; French invasion of Spain in 1808
francesilla *f* French roll; (bot) turban buttercup
Francia *f* France
Francisca *f* Frances
francisca•no -na *adj & mf* Franciscan
Francisco *m* Francis
francmasón *m* Freemason
francmasonería *f* Freemasonry
fran•co -ca *adj* generous, liberal; outspoken, candid, frank; (*camino*) free, open; (*suelo*) loamy; free, gratis; Frankish; **franco a bordo** free on board; **franco de porte** postpaid || *mf* Frank || *m* franc; (*idioma*) Frankish
francolín *m* black partridge
franco•te -ta *adj* (coll) frank, wholehearted
francotirador *m* sniper
franela *f* flannel
frangente *m* accident, mishap
frangir §27 *tr* to break up, break to pieces
frangollar *tr* (coll) to bungle, to botch
frangollo *m* porridge; mash for cattle; (coll) bungle, botch
franja *f* fringe; strip, band; (opt) fringe
franjar *tr* to fringe
franquear *tr* to exempt; to cross, go over; to grant; to free, enfranchise; (*un camino*) to open, to clear; (*una carta*) to frank, pay the postage for; **a franquear en destino** postage will be paid by addressee || *ref* to yield; **franquearse con** to open one's heart to
franqueo *m* freeing, liberation; postage; **franqueo concertado** postage permit
franqueza *f* generosity; candidness, frankness; freedom
franquía *f* (naut) sea room; **en franquía** (naut & fig) in the open
franquicia *f* franchise; exemption, tax exemption; **franquicia postal** franking privilege
franquista *mf* Francoist
frasca *f* leaves, twigs, brush; (Guat, Mex) high jinks
frasco *m* flask; (*p.ej., de aceitunas*) jar
frase *f* phrase; (*oración cabal*) sentence; idiom; **frase hecha** saying, proverb; cliché; **gastar frases** (coll) to talk all around the subject
frasear *tr* to phrase || *intr* (coll) to talk all around the subject
frasquera *f* bottle frame, liquor case
fratás *m* plastering trowel
fraternal *adj* brotherly, fraternal
fraternidad *f* fraternity, brotherhood
fraternizar §60 *intr* to fraternize
frater•no -na *adj* brotherly, fraternal
fraude *m* fraud
fraudulen•to -ta *adj* fraudulent
fray *m* Fra
frecuencia *f* frequency; **alta frecuencia** high frequency; **baja frecuencia** low frequency; **con frecuencia** frequently
frecuentar *tr* (*ir con frecuencia a*) to frequent; to keep up, repeat
frecuente *adj* frequent; (*usual*) common
fregadero *m* sink, kitchen sink
frega•do -da *adj* (Am) annoying, bothersome; (SAm) stubborn; (Am) cunning; (P-R) brazen || *m* scrubbing; mopping; (coll) mess
frega•dor -dora *mf* dishwasher
fregar §66 *tr* (*restregar*) to rub; (*restregar para limpiar*) to scrub, to scour; (*el pavimento*) to mop; (*los platos*) to wash; (Am) to annoy, bother
fregasue•los *m* (*pl* **-los**) mop, floor mop
frega•triz *f* (*pl* **-trices**) var of **fregona**
fre•gón -gona *adj* (Am) annoying, bothersome; (Am) brazen || *f* (*criada que friega el pavimento*) scrub woman; (*criada que lava la vajilla*) dishwasher, scullery maid
freiduría *f* fried-fish shop
freír §58 & §83 *tr* to fry; (coll) to bore to death || *intr* to fry; **dejarle a uno freír en su aceite** (coll) to let someone stew in his own juice || *ref* to fry; (coll) to be bored to death; **freírsele a** to try to fool, to scheme to deceive
fréjol *m* kidney bean
frenar *tr* to bridle, to check, hold back; (*un automóvil, tren*) to brake
frene•sí *m* (*pl* **-síes**) frenzy
frenéti•co -ca *adj* frantic; mad, furious; wild
frenillo *m* muzzle; **no tener frenillo en la lengua** (coll) to not mince one's words
freno *m* (*parte de la brida*) bit; (*aparato para parar el movimiento de los vehículos*) brake; (fig) brake, check, curb; **freno de contrapedal** coaster brake; **morder el freno** to champ the bit
frenología *f* phrenology
frentazo *m* (Mex) rebuff
frente *m & f* (*de un edificio*) front || *m* (mil) front, front line; **al frente de** at the head of, in charge of || *f* brow, forehead; face, front; head; **a frente** straight ahead; **arrugar la frente** to knit the brow; **de frente** straight ahead; abreast; **en frente de** in front of; against, opposed to; **frente a** in front of; compared with
freo *m* channel, strait
fresa *f* strawberry; (*de fresadora*) cutter
fresado *m* milling, millwork
fresadora *f* milling machine
fresal *m* strawberry patch
fresar *tr* to mill
fresca *f* fresh air; cool part of the day; (coll) blunt remark, piece of one's mind
fresca•chón -chona *adj* bouncing, buxom; (*viento*) brisk
fresca•les *mf* (*pl* **-les**) (coll) forward sort of person

frescamente *adv* recently; cheekily, brazenly

fres•co -ca *adj* (*acabado de hacer o suceder*) fresh; (*moderadamente frío*) cool; (*pintura*) fresh, wet; (*tela, vestido*) light; calm, unruffled; buxom, ruddy; (coll) cheeky, fresh; **estar fresco** (coll) to be in a fine pinch; **quedarse tan fresco** (coll) to show no offense, to be indifferent or unconcerned || *m* coolness; fresh air; fresh bacon; (fa) fresco; (Am) cool drink; **al fresco** in the open air; in the night air; **hace fresco** it is cool; **tomar el fresco** to go out for some fresh air || *f* see **fresca**

frescor *m* freshness; cool, coolness

fresco•te -ta *adj* (coll) plump and rosy

frescura *f* freshness; cool, coolness; unconcern, offhand manner; sharp reply; (coll) cheek, impudence

fresno *m* ash tree; (*madera*) ash

fresquera *f* meat closet, food cabinet, icebox

fresquería *f* (Am) ice-cream parlor, soft-drink store

fresque•ro -ra *mf* fish dealer; (Peru) soft-drink vendor || *f* see **fresquera**

freudismo *m* Freudianism

freza *f* dung; spawning; hole made by game

frialdad *f* coldness; carelessness, laxity; stupidity; (pathol) frigidity; (pathol) impotence; (fig) coolness, coldness

friáti•co -ca *adj* chilly; awkward, stupid; (*ropa*) cold

fricar §73 *tr* to rub

fricasé *m* fricassee

fricción *f* rubbing; massage; (pharm) rubbing liniment; (phys) friction

friccionar *tr* to rub; to massage

friega *f* rubbing, massage; (Am) annoyance, bother; (Am) flogging, whipping

frigidez *f* frigidity; coldness

frígi•do -da *adj* frigid; cold

frigorífero *m* freezing chamber

frigorífi•co -ca *adj* refrigerating; cold-storage || *m* refrigerator; (Arg, Urug) packing house, cold-storage plant

fríjol *m* bean, kidney bean; **fríjol de media luna** Lima bean; **¡fríjoles!** (W-I) absolutely no!

frijolear *tr* (Guat) to annoy, molest

frijolizar §60 *tr* (Peru) to bewitch

frí•o -a *adj* cold; dull, weak, colorless; (fig) cold, cool || *m* cold; **fríos** (Am) chills and fever; **coger frío** to catch cold; **hace frío** it is cold; **tener frío** (*una persona*) to be cold; **tomar frío** to catch cold

friole•ro -ra *adj* chilly || *f* trifle, trinket; snack, bite

frisar *tr* to rub; to fit, fasten; (naut) to calk || *intr* to agree, get along; **frisar con** or **en** to border on

friso *m* dado, wainscot; (archit) frieze

fri•són -sona *adj & mf* Frisian

fritada *f* fry

fri•to -ta *adj* fried; (coll) bored to death || *m* fry; (Ven) daily bread

fritura *f* fry

frívo•lo -la *adj* frivolous; trifling

fronda *f* leaf; (*del helecho*) frond; sling-shaped bandage; **frondas** frondage, foliage

frondo•so -sa *adj* leafy; woodsy

frontalera *f* yoke pad

frontera *f* frontier, border; front, façade

fronteri•zo -za *adj* frontier, border; facing, opposite

fronte•ro -ra *adj* frontier, border; facing, opposite; front || *f* see **frontera**

frontín *m* (Mex) flip, fillip

fron•tis *m* (*pl* **-tis**) front, façade

frontispicio *m* frontispiece; (coll) face

frontón *m* (*encima de puertas o ventanas*) gable, pediment; pelota court; pelota wall; handball court

frotamiento *m* rubbing; (phys) friction

frotar *tr* to rub; to chafe || *ref* to rub

fro•tis *m* (*pl* **-tis**) (bact) smear

fructuo•so -sa *adj* fruitful

frugal *adj* (*en comer y beber*) temperate; (*no muy abundante*) frugal

fruición *f* enjoyment, satisfaction; (*del mal ajeno*) evil satisfaction

fruiti•vo -va *adj* enjoyable

frunce *m* shirr, shirring, gathering

frunci•do -da *adj* grim, gruff, stern; (Chile) temperate; (Chile) sad, gloomy || *m* shirr, shirring, gathering

fruncir §36 *tr* to wrinkle, pucker, pleat; (*la frente*) to knit; (*los labios*) to curl, to purse; (*la verdad*) to twist, disguise; to shirr, to gather || *ref* to affect modesty, to be shocked

fruslería *f* trifle, trinket; (coll) futility, triviality

frusle•ro -ra *adj* futile, trivial, trifling || *m* rolling pin

frustrar *tr* to frustrate, to thwart

fruta *f* fruit; **fruta del tiempo** fruit in season; **fruta de sartén** fritter, pancake; **frutas** fruit; **frutas agrias** citrus fruit

frutal *adj* fruit || *m* fruit tree

frutería *f* fruit store

frute•ro -ra *adj* fruit || *mf* fruit dealer || *m* fruit dish; tray of imitation fruit

frutilla *f* (*del rosario*) bead; Chilean strawberry; gumdrop

fruto *m* (bot & fig) fruit; **fruto de bendición** legitimate offspring; **frutos** produce; **sacar fruto de** to derive benefit from

fu *interj* faugh!, fie!; (*del gato*) spit!; **ni fu ni fa** (coll) neither this nor that

fucilazo *m* heat lightning, sheet lightning

fuego *m* fire; (*para encender un cigarrillo*) light; (*de arma de fuego*) firing; lighthouse, beacon; hearth, home; rash, eruption; sore, fever blister; **abrir fuego** to open fire; **echar fuego** (coll) to blow up, hit the ceiling; **¡fuego!** fire!; **fuego fatuo** will-o'-the-wisp; **fuego graneado** or **nutrido** drumfire; **fuegos artificiales** fireworks; **hacer fuego** to fire, to shoot; **marcar a fuego** to brand; **pegar fuego a** to set fire to, to set on fire; **poner a fuego y sangre** to lay waste; **prenderse fuego** to catch on fire; **romper fuego** to open fire; to

stir up a row; **tocar a fuego** to sound the fire alarm
fuelle *m* fold, pucker, wrinkle; (*instrumento para soplar*) bellows; (*cubierta de coche*) folding carriage top; wind clouds; (*persona soplona*) (coll) gossip, talebearer
fuente *f* fountain, spring; public hydrant; font, baptismal font; platter, tray; (fig) source; **beber en buenas fuentes** (coll) to have good sources of information; **fuente de gasolina** gasoline pump; **fuente de sodas** soda fountain; **fuente para beber** drinking fountain; **fuentes termales** hot springs
fuer *m* — **a fuer de** as a, by way of
fuera *adv* out, outside; away, out of town; **desde fuera** from the outside; **fuera de** outside of; away from; out of; aside from; in addition to; **fuera de que** aside from the fact that; **fuera de sí** beside oneself; **por fuera** on the outside
fuere•ño -ña *mf* (Mex) hick, stranger
fuero *m* law, statute; code of laws; jurisdiction; exemption, privilege; **fuero interior** conscience, inmost heart; **fueros** (coll) pride, arrogance
fuerte *adj* strong; hard; loud; heavy; **hacerse fuerte** to stick to one's guns; (mil) to hole up, to dig in || *adv* hard; loud || *m* fort, fortress; forte, strong point
fuerza *f* force, strength, power; (*de un ejército*) main body; literal meaning; (phys) force; **a fuerza de** by dint of, by force of; **a la fuerza** forcibly, by force; **a viva fuerza** by main strength; **fuerza aérea** air force; **fuerza de agua** water power; **fuerza de sangre** animal power; **fuerza mayor** (law) force majeure, act of God; **fuerza motriz** motive power; **fuerza pública** police; **fuerza viva** kinetic energy; **hacer fuerza** to strain, struggle; to carry weight; **por fuerza** perforce, necessarily; **ser fuerza** + *inf* to be necessary to + *inf*
fuete *m* (Am) whip
fufar *intr* (*el gato*) to spit
fuga *f* flight; (*salida de un gas o líquido*) leak; ardor, vigor; (mus) fugue; **darse a la fuga** to take flight, to run away; **poner en fuga** to put to flight
fugar **§44** *ref* to flee, escape, run away
fu•gaz *adj* (*pl* **-gaces**) fleeting, passing; (*estrella*) shooting
fugiti•vo -va *adj & mf* fugitive
fugui•llas *m* (*pl* **-llas**) (coll) hustler
fula•no -na *mf* so-and-so
fulcro *m* fulcrum
fulgor *m* brilliance, radiance
fulgurar *intr* to flash
fulmicotón *m* guncotton
fulminar *tr* to strike with lightning; to strike dead; (*censuras, amenazas, etc.*) to thunder; (*balas o bombas*) to hurl
fullería *f* trickery, cheating
fulle•ro -ra *adj* crooked, cheating || *mf* crook, cheat; **fullero de naipes** cardsharp
fumada *f* puff, whiff
fumadero *m* smoking room; **fumadero de opio** opium den
fuma•dor -dora *adj* smoking || *mf* smoker
fumar *tr* to smoke || *intr* to smoke; **fumar en pipa** to smoke a pipe; **se prohibe fumar** no smoking || *ref* (coll) to squander; (coll) to stay away from; (*la clase*) (coll) to cut
fumarada *f* (*de humo*) puff; (*de tabaco*) pipeful
fumigación *f* fumigation; **fumigación aérea** crop dusting
fumigar **§44** *tr* to fumigate
fumista *m* stove or heater repairman; stove or heater dealer
fumistería *f* stove or heater shop
fumo•so -sa *adj* smoky
funámbu•lo -la *mf* ropewalker
función *f* function; duty, office, function; (*espectáculo teatral*) show, performance; **entrar en funciones** to take office, take up one's duties; **función benéfica** charitable performance; **función de aficionados** amateur performance; **función de títeres** puppet show; **función secundaria** side show
funcional *adj* functional
funcionario *m* functionary, public official, civil servant
funcione•ro -ra *adj* (coll) officious, fussy
fund. *abbr* **fundador**
funda *f* case, sheath, envelope, slip; (*para una espada*) scabbard; (*para proteger los muebles*) slip cover; **funda de almohada** pillowcase; **funda de asientos** seat cover; **funda de gafas** spectacle case
fundación *f* foundation
fundadamente *adv* with good reason; on good authority
funda•dor -dora *adj* founding || *mf* founder
fundamental *adj* fundamental
fundamentar *tr* to lay the foundations of
fundamento *m* foundation; (*razón, motivo*) grounds, reason; basis; reliability, sense; (Col) skirt
fundar *tr* to found, to base || *ref* — **fundarse en** to be based on; to base one's opinion on
fundente *adj* molten || *m* flux
fundería *f* foundry
fundible *adj* fusible
fundición *f* (*acción de fundir*) founding; (*fábrica*) foundry; (*herrería*) forge; (*hierro colado*) cast iron; (typ) font
fundidor *m* founder, foundryman
fundir *tr* (*p.ej., metales*) to found; (*campanas, estatuas*) to cast; (*derretir para purificar*) to smelt; (*colores*) to mix; (*un filamento eléctrico*) to burn out || *intr* to smelt || *ref* to melt; to fuse; (*un filamento eléctrico*) to burn out; (fig) to fuse, merge; (Am) to fail, founder
fúnebre *adj* (*marcha, procesión*) funeral; (*triste*) funereal
funeral *adj* funeral; (*triste, lúgubre*)

funereal || *m* funeral; **funerales** funeral
funerala — a la funerala (mil) with arms inverted (*as a token of mourning*)
funera•rio -ria *adj* funeral || *m* mortician, funeral director || *f* (*empresa*) undertaking establishment; (*local*) funeral home, funeral parlor
funes•to -ta *adj* ill-fated; sad, sorrowful; (*p.ej., influencia*) baneful
fungir **§27** *intr* (CAm, Mex) to act, function
fungo *m* (pathol) fungus
fungo•so -sa *adj* fungous
funicular *adj & m* funicular
fuñique *adj* awkward; dull, tiresome
furgón *m* wagon, truck; (rr) freight car, boxcar; (rr) caboose
furgoneta *f* light truck, delivery truck
furia *f* fury
furibun•do -da *adj* furious, frenzied
furio•so -sa *adj* furious; (*muy grande*) terrific, tremendous
furor *m* rage, furor; **hacer furor** to be all the rage
furti•vo -va *adj* furtive; sneaky; poaching
furúnculo *m* boil
fusa *f* (mus) demisemiquaver
fus•co -ca *adj* dark
fusela•do -da *adj* streamlined
fuselaje *m* fuselage
fusible *adj* fusible || *m* (elec) fuse
fusil *m* gun, rifle
fusilar *tr* to shoot, execute; (coll) to plagiarize
fusilazo *m* (*tiro de fusil*) gunshot, rifle shot; (*relámpago sin ruido*) heat lightning, sheet lightning
fusilería *f* rifle corps; rifles, guns; (*descarga*) fusillade
fusión *f* fusion; melting; **fusión de empresas** (com) merger
fusionar *tr & ref* to fuse, to merge
fusta *f* brushwood, twigs; teamster's whip
fustán *m* fustian; (Am) cotton petticoat; (Ven) skirt
fuste *m* wood, timber; shaft, stem; (fig) importance, substance
fustigar **§44** *tr* to whip, lash; to rebuke harshly
fútbol *m* football; soccer; **fútbol asociación** soccer
fútil *adj* futile, trifling, inconsequential
futilidad *f* futility
futre *m* (SAm) dandy, dude
futu•ro -ra *adj* future || *m* future; (gram) future; (coll) fiancé; **futuros** (com) futures || *f* fiancée

G

G, g (ge) *f* eighth letter of the Spanish alphabet
G. *abbr* **gracia**
gaba•cho -cha *adj & mf* Pyrenean; (coll) Frenchy || *m* (coll) Frenchified Spanish (*language*)
gabán *m* overcoat
gabardina *f* gabardine; raincoat with belt
gabarra *f* barge, lighter
gabarro *m* (*en una piedra*) nodule; (*en un tejido*) flaw, defect; mistake
gabinete *m* cabinet; (*de médico, abogado, etc.*) office; studio, study; laboratory; (Col) glassed-in balcony; **de gabinete** armchair, theoretical; **gabinete de aseo** washroom; **gabinete de lectura** reading room
gablete *m* gable
gacela *f* gazelle
gaceta *f* government journal; (Am) newspaper; **mentir más que la gaceta** to lie like a trooper
gacetilla *f* town talk, gossip column; short item
gacetillero *m* gossip columnist
gacetista *mf* newspaper reader; newsmonger
gacha *f* watery mass; (Col, Ven) earthenware bowl; **gachas** mush, pap; porridge; (coll) mud; **gachas de avena** oatmeal; **hacerse unas gachas** to be mushy
ga•cho -cha *adj* turned down; flopping; (*sombrero*) slouch; **a gachas** on all fours || *f* see **gacha**
gachumbo *m* (SAm) hard fruit shell
gachu•pín -pina *mf* (CAm, Mex) Spanish settler in Latin America
gaéli•co -ca *adj* Gaelic || *mf* Gael || *m* Gaelic (*language*)
gafa *f* clamp; (*enganche de los anteojos*) temple; **gafas** glasses; **gafas de sol** or **gafas para sol** sunglasses
gafe *m* (coll) jinx, hoodoo
ga•fo -fa *adj* claw-handed; (Am) footsore || *f* see **gafa**
gaguear *intr* (Am) to stutter
gaita *f* hornpipe; hurdy-gurdy; (coll) chore, hard task; (coll) neck; **gaita gallega** bagpipe
gaite•ro -ra *adj* (coll) flashy, gaudy || *m* piper, bagpipe player
gajes *mpl* wages, salary; **gajes del oficio** cares of office, occupational annoyances
gajo *m* broken branch; (*de un racimo de uvas*) small stem; (*división interior de ciertas frutas*) slice; (*de horca*) tine, prong; (*ramal de montes*) spur; (Am) curl
gala *f* fine clothes; (*lo más selecto*) choice, cream; (Am) tip, fee; **de gala** full-dress; **hacer gala de** to glory in; **llevarse la gala** to win approval
galafate *m* slick thief
galai•co -ca *adj* Galician
galán *m* good-looking fellow; lover,

gallant, ladies' man; (*el que sirve de escolta a una dama*) escort, cavalier; (theat) leading man; **galán joven** (theat) juvenile; **primer galán** (theat) leading man
galancete *m* (theat) juvenile
gala·no -na *adj* elegant, graceful; spruce, smartly dressed; rich, tasteful
galante *adj* (*con las damas*) gallant; (*con los caballeros*) flirtatious; (*mujer*) wanton, loose
galantear *tr* to court, woo, make love to; to sue, entreat
galantería *f* gallantry; charm, elegance; generosity
galanura *f* charm, elegance
galápago *m* pond tortoise; (*del arado*) moldboard; light saddle; ingot
galardón *m* reward, recompense
galardonar *tr* to reward, recompense
galaxia *f* galaxy
galeón *m* (naut) galleon
galeote *m* galley slave
galera *f* covered wagon; women's jail; (*de hospital*) ward; (naut & typ) galley
galerada *f* wagonload; (typ) galley; (typ) galley proof
galería *f* gallery; **galería de tiro** shooting gallery; **galerías** department store; **hablar para la galería** (coll) to play to the gallery
galerna *f* stormy wind from the northwest (*on the northern coast of Spain*)
Gales *f* Wales; **el país de Gales** Wales; **la Nueva Gales del Sur** New South Wales
ga·lés -lesa *adj* Welsh || *m* Welshman; Welsh (*language*) || *f* Welsh woman
gal·go -ga *adj* (Col) sweet-toothed || *m* greyhound || *f* greyhound bitch; rolling stone; mange, rash
Galia, la Gaul
gálibo *m* template, pattern; (rr) gabarit
galicismo *m* Gallicism
gáli·co -ca *adj* Gallic || *m* syphilis; syphilitic
galillo *m* uvula; (coll) gullet
galimatí·as *m* (*pl* **-as**) (coll) gibberish, nonsense; (coll) confusion
galiparla *f* Frenchified Spanish
ga·lo -la *adj* Gaulish || *mf* Gaul || *m* Gaulish (*language*)
galocha *f* clog, wooden shoe
galón *m* braid, galloon; (*medida para líquidos*) gallon; (mil) chevron, stripe
galopar *intr* to gallop
galope *m* gallop; **a galope** at a gallop; in great haste; **a galope tendido** on the run
galopea·do -da *adj* (coll) hasty, sketchy || *m* (coll) beating, punching
galopear *intr* to gallop
galopillo *m* scullion, kitchen boy
galopín *m* ragamuffin; (*hombre taimado*) wise guy; (naut) cabin boy
galpón *m* (SAm) iron shed; (Col) tile works
galvanizar **§60** *tr* to electroplate; to galvanize
galvanoplastia *f* electroplating
galladura *f* tread (*of egg*)
gallardete *m* streamer, pennant
gallardía *f* gallantry; elegance; nobility; generosity
gallar·do -da *adj* gallant; elegant; noble; generous; (*temporal*) fierce
gallear *intr* to stand out, excel; (coll) to shout, yell, threaten
galle·go -ga *adj & mf* Galician
gallera *f* cockpit
galleta *f* hardtack, ship biscuit; cracker; little pitcher; (coll) slap
gallina *adj* chicken-hearted || *mf* chicken-hearted person || *f* hen; **estar como gallina en corral ajeno** (coll) to be like a fish out of water; **gallina ciega** blindman's buff; **gallina de Guinea** guinea fowl
gallinería *f* poultry shop; cowardice
galline·ro -ra *mf* poultry dealer || *m* hencoop, henhouse; poultry basket; top gallery; babel, madhouse
gallipavo *m* turkey; (coll) sour note
gallito *m* (*el que figura sobre los demás*) somebody; **gallito del lugar** cock of the walk
gallo *m* cock, rooster; (coll) false note, sour note; (coll) boss; frog in the throat; **gallo de bosque** wood grouse; **gallo de pelea** gamecock; **tener mucho gallo** (coll) to be cocky
gallofa *f* vegetables; French roll; talk, gossip
gallofear *intr* to beg, bum, loaf around
gallofe·ro -ra *adj* begging, loafing || *mf* beggar, loafer
gama *f* doe, female fallow deer; (mus & fig) gamut
gamberrismo *m* gangsterism, rowdyism
gambe·rro -rra *adj & mf* libertine || *m* hoodlum, tough, rowdy
gambeta *f* crosscaper; caper, prance
gambito *m* gambit
gamo *m* buck, male fallow deer
gamón *m* asphodel
gamonal *m* field of asphodel; (Am) boss
gamuza *f* chamois
gana *f* desire; will; **darle a uno la gana de** to feel like, e.g., **le da la gana de trabajar** he feels like working; **de buena gana** willingly; **de gana** in earnest; willingly; **de mala gana** unwillingly; **tener ganas de** to feel like, to have a mind to
ganadería *f* cattle, livestock; brand, stock; cattle raising; cattle ranch
ganade·ro -ra *adj* cattle, livestock || *mf* cattle breeder; cattle dealer || *m* cattleman
ganado *m* cattle, livestock; **ganado caballar** horses; **ganado cabrío** goats; **ganado lanar** sheep; **ganado mayor** large farm animals (*cows, bulls, horses, and mules*); **ganado menor** small farm animals (*sheep, goats, pigs*); **ganado menudo** young cattle; **ganado moreno** swine; **ganado ovejuno** sheep; **ganado porcino** swine; **ganado vacuno** cattle
gana·dor -dora *adj* winning; earning; (coll) hard-working || *mf* winner; earner
ganancia *f* gain, profit; (Guat, Mex)

extra, bonus; **ganancias y pérdidas** profit and loss
ganancial *adj* profit
ganancio•so -sa *adj* gainful, profitable; earning || *mf* earner
ganapán *m* errand boy; (coll) boor
ganapierde *m & f* giveaway
ganar *tr* (*dinero trabajando*) to earn; (*la victoria luchando*) to win; (*beneficios en los negocios*) to gain; (*a una persona en una contienda*) to beat, defeat; (*aventajar*) to excel; (*la voluntad de una persona*) to win over; (*alcanzar*) to reach; **ganar algo a alguien** to win something from someone; **ganar de comer** to earn a living || *intr* to earn; (*mejorar*) to improve || *ref* to win over; **ganarse la vida** to earn a livelihood
ganchero *m* log driver; (Chile) oddjobber; (Ecuad) gentle mount
ganchillo *m* crochet needle; crochet, crochet work; **hacer ganchillo** to crochet
gancho *m* hook; shepherd's crook; coaxer; procurer, pimp; (Am) hairpin; (Col, Ecuad) lady's saddle; **gancho de botalones** (naut) gooseneck; **echar el gancho a** (coll) to hook in, to land; **tener gancho** (*una mujer*) (coll) to have a way with the men
gandaya *f* (coll) bumming, loafing
gandujar *tr* to pleat, shirr
gan•dul -dula *adj* (coll) loafing, idling || *mf* (coll) loafer, idler
gandulear *intr* (coll) to loaf, idle
ganfo•rro -rra *mf* (coll) scoundrel
ganga *f* bargain
ganglio *m* ganglion
gangocho *m* (Am) burlap
gango•so -sa *adj* snuffling, nasal
gangrena *f* gangrene
gangrenar *tr & ref* to gangrene
ganguear *intr* to snuffle, talk through the nose
gangue•ro -ra *adj* (coll) bargain-hunting; (coll) self-seeking || *mf* (coll) bargain hunter
gano•so -sa *adj* desirous; (*caballo*) (Chile) spirited, fiery
gan•so -sa *mf* (coll) dope, dullard || *m* goose; gander; **ganso bravo** wild goose || *f* female goose
Gante Ghent
ganzúa *f* (*garfio*) picklock, lock pick; (*persona*) picklock; (coll) pumper (*of secrets*)
gañán *m* farm hand; rough, husky fellow
gañido *m* yelp; croak
gañir §12 *intr* (*el perro*) to yelp; (*p.ej., el cuervo*) to croak
garabatear *tr* to scribble || *intr* to hook; to beat about the bush; to scribble
garabato *m* hook; pothook; scribbling; weeding hoe; (*bozal*) muzzle; (*de una mujer*) (coll) winsomeness; **garabato de carnicero** meathook; **garabatos** wiggling of hands and fingers
garabato•so -sa *adj* full of scrawls; (coll) winsome
garage *m* or **garaje** *m* garage
garagista *m* garage man
garambaina *f* gaudy trimming; **garambainas** simpering, smirking; (coll) scribble
garante *adj* responsible || *mf* guarantor, voucher
garantía *f* guarantee, guaranty
garantir §1 *tr* to guarantee
garantizar §60 *tr* to guarantee
garañón *m* stud jackass; stud camel; (Am) stallion
garapiña *f* icing, sugar-coating; (Am) iced pineapple drink
garapiñar *tr* to ice, to sugar-coat; to candy
garapiñera *f* ice-cream freezer
garbanzo *m* chickpea; **garbanzo negro** (fig) black sheep
garbillar *tr* to sieve, screen, riddle
garbillo *s* sieve, screen; riddled ore
garbo *m* jauntiness, grace, fine bearing; generosity
garbo•so -sa *adj* jaunty, graceful, spruce, sprightly; generous
gardu•ño -ña *mf* (archaic) sneak thief || *f* stone marten, beech marten
garete *m* — **al garete** (naut) adrift
garfa *f* claw
garfio *m* hook, gaff
gargajear *intr* to cough up phlegm, to hawk
gargajo *m* phlegm
garganta *f* throat; (*de un río, una vasija, etc.*) neck, throat; (*del pie*) instep; (*entre montañas*) ravine, gorge; (*del arado*) sheath; (*de una polea*) groove; (archit) shaft; **tener buena garganta** to have a good voice
gargantear *intr* to warble
gargantilla *f* necklace
gárgara *f* gargling; **gárgaras** (*líquido*) (Am) gargle; **hacer gárgaras** to gargle
gargarear *intr* (Am) to gargle
gargarismo *m* gargling; (*líquido*) gargle
gargarizar §60 *intr* to gargle
gárgola *f* gargoyle
garguero *m* gullet; (*caña del pulmón*) windpipe
garita *f* sentry box; porter's lodge; (*de una fortificación*) watchtower; railroad-crossing box; privy (*with one seat*); **garita de centinela** sentry box; **garita de señales** (rr) signal tower
garito *m* gambling den
garlito *m* fish trap; (coll) trap, snare
garlopa *f* jack plane, trying plane
garra *f* claw, talon; catch, hook; **caer en las garras de** (coll) to fall into the clutches of
garrafa *f* carafe, decanter; **garrafa corchera** demijohn
garrafal *adj* awful, terrible
garrafiñar *tr* (coll) to snatch
garrafón *m* carboy, demijohn
garramar *tr* (coll) to snitch
garranchuelo *m* crab grass
garrapata *f* cattle tick, sheep tick; (mil) disabled horse; (Chile) little runt; (Mex) slut
garrapatear *intr* to scrawl, scribble
garrapato *m* pothook, scrawl; **garrapatos** scrawl
garri•do -da *adj* handsome, elegant
garroba *f* carob bean

garrocha *f* goad; (sport) pole
garrotazo *m* blow with a club
garrote *m* club, cudgel; garrote (*method of execution; iron collar used for such execution*); (Mex) brake; **dar garrote a** to garrote
garrote·ro -ra *adj* (Chile) stingy ‖ *m* (Mex) brakeman
garrotillo *m* croup
garrucha *f* pulley, sheave
gárru·lo -la *adj* chirping; (*hablador*) garrulous; (*arroyo*) babbling; (*viento*) rustling
garúa *f* (Am) drizzle
garuar §21 *intr* (Am) to drizzle
garulla *f* (coll) mob, rabble
garza *f* heron; **garza real** gray heron
gar·zo -za *adj* blue ‖ *f* see **garza**
garzón *m* boy, youth; suitor; woman chaser
gas *m* gas; **gas de alumbrado** illuminating gas; **gas exhilarante** or **hilarante** laughing gas; **gas lacrimógeno** tear gas
gasa *f* gauze, chiffon; (*tira de gasa negra con que se rodea el sombrero en señal de luto*) hatband
Gascuña *f* Gascony
gasear *tr* to gas
gaseo·so -sa *adj* gaseous ‖ *f* soda water, carbonated water
gasificar §73 *tr* to gasify; to exalt, elate ‖ *ref* to gasify
gasista *m* gas fitter; (Chile) gasworker
gasoducto *m* gas pipe line
gasógeno *m* gas generator, gas producer; mixture of benzine and alcohol used for lighting and cleaning
gas-oil *m* diesel oil
gasolina *f* gasoline
gasolinera *f* motor boat; gas station, filling station
gasómetro *m* gasholder, gas tank
gastadero *m* waste
gasta·do -da *adj* worn-out; used up; spent; (*chiste*) (coll) crummy, corny
gasta·dor -dora *adj & mf* spendthrift ‖ *m* convict; (mil) sapper, pioneer
gastadura *f* worn spot
gastar *tr* (*dinero, tiempo*) to spend; (*en cosas inútiles*) to waste; (*echar a perder con el uso*) to wear out; (*consumir*) to use up; (*p.ej., una barba*) to wear; (*un coche*) to keep; **gastarlas** (coll) to act, behave ‖ *intr* to spend ‖ *ref* to wear; to wear out; to become used up; to waste away
gasto *m* cost, expense; wear; **gastos de conservación** or **de entretenimiento** upkeep; **gastos de explotación** operating expenses; **gastos menudos** petty expenses; **hacer el gasto** (coll) to do most of the talking; (coll) to be the subject of conversation; **hacer frente a los gastos** to meet expenses; **meterse en gastos con** to go to the expense of
gasto·so -sa *adj* wasteful, extravagant
gástri·co -ca *adj* gastric
gastronomía *f* gastronomy
gastróno·mo -ma *mf* gourmet
gata *f* she-cat; low-hanging cloud; (coll) Madrid woman; (Mex) maid, servant girl; **a gatas** on all fours, on hands and knees
gatada *f* catty act
gatatumba *f* (coll) faked attention, fake emotion, faked pain
gatazo *m* (coll) gyp
gatea·do -da *adj* catlike; grained, striped ‖ *m* crawling, climbing; (coll) scratching, clawing
gatear *tr* (coll) to scratch, claw; (coll) to snitch ‖ *intr* to crawl, to climb
gatera *f* cathole; (naut) hawsehole
gatería *f* (coll) cats; (coll) gang of toughs; (coll) fake humility
gate·ro -ra *adj* full of cats ‖ *mf* cat lover ‖ *f* see **gatera**
gates·co -ca *adj* (coll) catlike, feline
gatillo *m* (*de arma de fuego*) trigger; (coll) little pickpocket
gato *m* cat; tomcat; (*instrumento para levantar pesos*) jack, lifting jack; (coll) sly fellow; (coll) sneak thief; (coll) native of Madrid; **gato montés** wildcat; **gato rodante** dolly; **vender gato por liebre** (coll) to gyp, cheat
gauchada *f* (SAm) sly trick; (SAm) good turn
gauchaje *m* (SAm) gathering of Gauchos
gauches·co -ca *adj* Gaucho
gau·cho -cha *adj* (SAm) Gaucho; (Arg, Chile) sly, crafty ‖ *m* (SAm) Gaucho; (SAm) good horseman ‖ *f* (Arg) mannish woman; (Arg) loose woman
gaulteria *f* wintergreen
gaveta *f* drawer, till
gavia *f* ditch, drain; (*ave*) gull; (min) gang of basket passers; (naut) topsail
gavilán *m* sparrow hawk; (*de la pluma*) nib; (*en la escritura*) hair stroke; (Am) ingrowing nail
gavilla *f* sheaf, bundle; gang
gaviota *f* sea gull
gavota *f* gavotte
gaya *f* colored stripe; (*ave*) magpie
gayar *tr* to trim with colored stripes
ga·yo -ya *adj* gay, bright, showy ‖ *m* (orn) jay ‖ *f* see **gaya**
gayola *f* cage; (coll) jail
gayomba *f* Spanish broom
gazapa *f* (coll) lie
gazapatón *m* (coll) blunder, slip
gazapera *f* rabbit warren; (coll) gang, gang of thugs; (coll) brawl, row
gazapo *m* young rabbit; sly fellow; slip, boner, blunder; (*de actor*) fluff
gazmiar *tr* (*oliendo*) to sniff; (*comiendo*) to nibble ‖ *ref* (coll) to complain
gazmoñada or **gazmoñería** *f* prudishness, priggishness
gazmoñe·ro -ra or **gazmo·ño -ña** *adj* prudish, priggish, strait-laced, demure ‖ *mf* prude, prig
gaznápiro *m* gawk, boob, bumpkin
gaznate *m* gullet; (Mex) fritter
gazpacho *m* cold vegetable soup; (Hond) leftovers
gazuza *f* (coll) hunger
Gedeón *m* Gideon
gehena *m* Gehenna
géiser *m* geyser
gel *m* gel

gelatina *f* gelatine
gema *f* gem; (bot) bud
geme•lo -la *adj & mf* twin; **gemelos** twins; binoculars; cuff links; **gemelos de campo** field glasses; **gemelos de teatro** opera glasses || **Gemelos** *mpl* (astr) Gemini
gemido *m* moan, groan; wail, whine; howl, roar
Géminis *m* (astr) Gemini
gemiquear *intr* (Chile) to whine
gemir §50 *intr* to moan, groan; to wail, whine; to howl, roar
gen *m* gene
genciana *f* gentian
gendarme *m* (Am) policeman
genealogía *f* genealogy
generación *f* generation
genera•dor -dora *adj* generating || *m* generator
general *adj* general; common, usual; **en general** or **por lo general** in general || *m* general; **general de brigada** brigadier, brigadier general; **general de división** major general || **generales** *fpl* general information, personal data
generala *f* general's wife; call to arms
generalato *m* generalship
generalidad *f* generality; majority; **la generalidad de** the general run of
generalísimo *m* generalissimo
generalizar §60 *tr & intr* to generalize || *ref* to become generalized
generar *tr* to generate
genéri•co -ca *adj* generic; (*artículo*) indefinite; (*nombre*) common; showing gender
género *m* kind, sort; way, manner; cloth, material; (biol, log) genus; (gram) gender; **de género** genre; **género chico** one-act play, one-act operetta; **género de punto** knit goods, knitwear; **género humano** humankind; **género ínfimo** light vaudeville; **género novelístico** fiction; **género picaresco** burlesque; **géneros** goods, merchandise, material; **géneros de pieza** yard goods; **géneros para vestidos** dress goods
genero•so -sa *adj* generous; highborn; noble, magnanimous; (*vino*) rich, full
géne•sis *f* (*pl* **-sis**) genesis || **el Génesis** (Bib) Genesis
genéti•co -ca *adj* genetic || *f* genetics
genial *adj* inspired, genius-like; pleasant, agreeable; temperamental
geniazo *m* (coll) fiery temper
genio *m* (*índole, carácter*) temperament, disposition; (*don altísimo de invención; persona que lo posee; espíritu tutelar, deidad pagana*) genius; fire, spirit
genital *adj* genital || **genitales** *mpl* genitals
geniti•vo -va *adj & m* genitive
genocida *adj* genocidal || *mf* genocide
genocidio *m* genocide
Génova *f* Genoa
geno•vés -vesa *adj & mf* Genoese
gente *f* people; (*parentela, familia*) folks; race, nation; troops; **gente baja** lower classes, rabble; **gente bien** nice people; **gente de bien** decent people; **gente de capa parda** country people; **gente de coleta** (coll) bullfighters; **gente de color** colored people; **gente de la cuchilla** (coll) butchers; **gente de la vida airada** bullies; underworld; **gente del bronce** bright, lively people; **gente del rey** convicts; **gente de mal vivir** toughs, underworld; **gente de mar** seafaring people; **gente de paz** (*palabras con las cuales se contesta al que pregunta ¿quién?*) friend; **gente de pluma** (coll) clerks; **gente de su majestad** convicts; **gente de trato** tradespeople; **gente forzada** convicts; **gente menuda** (coll) small fry; (coll) common people
gentecilla *f* (coll) mob, rabble
gentil *adj* heathen, gentile; elegant, genteel; noble || *mf* heathen, pagan
gentileza *f* elegance, gentility, courtesy; gallantry; show, splendor; (*hidalguía*) nobility
gentilhombre *m* (*pl* **gentileshombres**) gentleman; messenger to the king; my good man; **gentilhombre de cámara** gentleman in waiting
gentili•cio -cia *adj* national; family; (gram) gentile
gentilidad *f* heathendom
gentío *m* crowd, mob
gentualla or **gentuza** *f* (coll) rabble, riffraff
genui•no -na *adj* genuine
geofísi•co -ca *adj* geophysical || *mf* geophysicist || *f* geophysics
geografía *f* geography
geográfi•co -ca *adj* geographic(al)
geógra•fo -fa *mf* geographer
geología *f* geology
geológi•co -ca *adj* geologic(al)
geólo•go -ga *mf* geologist
geómetra *mf* geometrician
geometría *f* geometry; **geometría del espacio** solid geometry
geométri•co -ca *adj* geometric(al)
geopolíti•co -ca *adj* geopolitical || *f* geopolitics
geranio *m* geranium
gerencia *f* management; manager's office
gerente *m* manager, director; **gerente de publicidad** advertising manager; **gerente de ventas** sales manager
geriatría *f* geriatry
geriatra *adj* geriatrical || *mf* geriatrician
geriátri•co -ca *adj* geriatrical
germanía *f* gypsy slang, cant of thieves
germanizar §60 *tr* to Germanize
germen *m* germ; **germen plasma** germ plasm
germicida *adj* germicidal || *m* germicide
germinal *adj* germ; germinal
germinar *intr* to germinate
gerontología *f* gerontology
gerundio *m* gerund; present participle; bombastic writer or speaker
gestación *f* gestation
gestear *intr* to make faces
gesticular *intr* to make a face, to make faces; (*hacer ademanes*) to gesticulate

gestión *f* step, measure; management; action, proceeding, negotiation
gestionar *tr* to promote, pursue; to manage; to negotiate
gesto *m* face; wry face, grimace; look, appearance; (*movimiento, ademán*) gesture
ges•tor -tora *adj* managing || *m* manager
gestu•do -da *adj* (coll) cross-looking
ghetto *m* ghetto
giba *f* hump; (coll) annoyance
giga *f* jig
giganta *f* giantess
gigante *adj* giant || *m* giant; (*en las procesiones*) giant figure
gigantes•co -ca *adj* gigantic
gigantez *f* giant size
gigantilla *f* large-headed masked figure; little fat woman
gigan•tón -tona *mf* huge giant || *m* giant figure
gigote *m* chopped-meat stew; **hacer gigote** (coll) to chop up
gimnasia *f* gymnastics; **gimnasia sueca** Swedish movements, setting-up exercises
gimnasio *m* gymnasium; secondary school, academy
gimnasta *mf* gymnast
gimnásti•co -ca *adj* gymnastic || *f* gymnastics
gimotear *intr* (coll) to whine
gimoteo *m* (coll) whining
ginebra *f* gin; (*de voces*) buzz, din; confusion, disorder || **Ginebra** *f* Geneva
ginebri•no -na *adj & mf* Genevan
ginecología *f* gynecology
ginecólo•go -ga *mf* gynecologist
ginesta *f* Spanish broom
gira *f* var of **jira**
gira•do -da *mf* drawee
gira•dor -dora *mf* drawer
giralda *f* weathercock (*in the form of person or animal*)
girándula *f* girandole
girar *tr* (*una visita*) to pay; (com) to draw || *intr* to turn; to rotate, gyrate; to trade; (com) to draw
girasol *m* sunflower; sycophant
girato•rio -ria *adj* revolving || *f* revolving bookcase
gi•ro -ra *adj* (Guat) drunk; (Mex) cocky || *m* turn; rotation; revolution; course, trend, turn; turn of phrase; boast, threat; gash, slash; line of business; trade; (com) draft; **giro a la vista** sight draft; **giro postal** money order || *f* see **gira**
giroflé *m* clove
giroscopio *m* gyroscope
gis *m* (Col) slate pencil
gitana *f* gypsy woman, gypsy girl
gitanada *f* gypsy trick; fawning, flattery
gitanería *f* band of gypsies; gypsy life; fawning, flattery
gitanes•co -ca *adj* gypsyish
gita•no -na *adj* gypsy; flattering; sly, tricky || *mf* gypsy || *m* Gypsy (*language*) || *f* see **gitana**
glacial *adj* glacial; (*zona*) frigid; (fig) cold, indifferent
glaciar *m* glacier
glándula *f* gland; **glándula cerrada** ductless gland
glasé *m* glacé silk
glasea•do -da *adj* glossy, shiny
glicerina *f* glycerin
global *adj* total; global, world-wide
globo *m* globe; (*aparato que, lleno de un gas, se eleva en el aire*) balloon; (*bomba de lámpara*) globe, lamp shade; **globo del ojo** eyeball; **globo sonda** trial balloon; **lanzar un globo sonda** (fig) to send up a trial balloon
glóbulo *m* globule; (physiol) corpuscle; **glóbulo rojo** red cell
gloria *f* glory; **ganar la gloria** to go to glory; **oler a gloria** (coll) to smell heavenly; **saber a gloria** (coll) to taste heavenly
gloriar §77 *tr* to glorify || *intr* to recite the rosary || *ref* to glory
glorieta *f* arbor, bower, summerhouse; public square; traffic circle
glorificar §73 *tr* to glorify || *ref* to glory
glorio•so -sa *adj* glorious; boastful
glosa *f* gloss
glosa•dor -dora *adj* commenting || *mf* commentator
glosar *tr* to gloss; to audit; (Col) to scold || *intr* to find fault
glosario *m* glossary
glóti•co -ca *adj* glottal
glo•tón -tona *adj* gluttonous || *mf* glutton
glotonería *f* gluttony
glucosa *f* glucose
gluglú *m* (*del agua*) gurgle, glug; (*del pavo*) gobble; **hacer gluglú** to gurgle, to glug
gluglutear *intr* to gobble
gnomo *m* gnome
gob. *abbr* **gobierno**
gobernación *f* governing; government; department of the interior; (Arg) territory
goberna•dor -dora *adj* governing || *m* governor
gobernalle *m* rudder, helm
gobernante *adj* governing || *mf* ruler || *m* (coll) self-appointed head
gobernar §2 *tr* to govern; to guide, direct; to control, rule; (*un buque*) to steer || *intr* to govern; to steer
goberno•so -sa *adj* (coll) orderly
gobierno *m* government; governor's office, governorship; management; control, rule; guidance; (*de un buque*) navigability; **de buen gobierno** (*buque*) navigable; **gobierno de monigotes** puppet government; **gobierno doméstico** housekeeping; **gobierno exilado** government in exile; **para su gobierno** for your guidance; **servir de gobierno** (coll) to serve as a guide
goce *m* enjoyment
go•do -da *adj* Gothic || *mf* Goth; Spanish noble; (Arg, Chile) Spaniard
gofio *m* (Am) roasted corn meal
gol *m* goal
gola *f* gullet
goldre *m* quiver
goleta *f* schooner
golf *m* golf

golfán *m* white water lily
golfista *mf* golfer
gol•fo -fa *mf* ragamuffin || *m* gulf; open sea; **golfo de Méjico** Gulf of Mexico; **golfo de Vizcaya** Bay of Biscay
Gólgota, el (Bib) Golgotha
golilla *f* gorget, ruff; magistrate's collar; pipe flange; (*de los caños de barro*) collar, sleeve; (*del gallo*) (Am) erectile bristles
golondrina *f* swallow
golosina *f* delicacy, tidbit; eagerness, appetite; trifle
golosinear *intr* to go around eating candy
golo•so -sa *adj* sweet-toothed; (*glotón*) gluttonous; (*apetitoso*) tasty
golpe *m* blow, stroke, hit; bump, bruise; heartbeat; crowd, throng, flock; (*del bolsillo*) flap; (*pestillo*) bolt, latch; (*de licor*) shot; surprise, wonder; (*infortunio*) blow; witticism; **dar golpe** to make a hit; **de golpe** all at once, suddenly; **de golpe y porrazo** slambang; **de un golpe** at one stroke; **golpe de ariete** water hammer; **golpe de estado** coup d'état; **golpe de fortuna** stroke of fortune; **golpe de gracia** coup de grâce; **golpe de mano** surprise attack; **golpe de mar** surge; **golpe de ojo** glance; **golpe de teatro** dramatic turn of events; **golpe de tos** fit of coughing; **golpe de vista,** glance, look; view; **golpe en vago** miss, flop; **golpe mortal** deathblow; **no dar golpe** to not raise a hand, not do a stroke of work
golpear *tr* to strike, hit, beat; to bump, bruise || *intr* to beat, strike; (*el reloj*) to tick; (*el motor de combustión interna*) to knock
golpete *m* door catch, window catch
golpetear *tr & intr* to beat; to rattle
golpismo *m* government by coup d'état
gollería *f* delicacy, dainty; **pedir gollerías** (coll) to ask for too much
gollete *m* throat, neck; (*de botella*) neck
goma *f* gum, rubber; (*tira de goma elástica*) rubber band; (*neumático*) tire; **goma arábiga** gum arabic; **goma de borrar** eraser, rubber; **goma de mascar** chewing gum; **goma espumosa** foam rubber; **goma laca** shellac
gomecillo *m* (coll) blind man's guide
gomia *f* bugaboo; (coll) waster; (coll) glutton
gomo•so -sa *adj* gum; gummy || *m* dude, dandy
góndola *f* gondola
gondolero *m* gondolier
gongo *m* gong
gonorrea *f* gonorrhea
gordal *adj* large-size
gordia•no -na *adj* Gordian
gordi•flón -flona or **gordin•flón -flona** *adj* (coll) chubby, pudgy, fatty || *mf* (coll) fatty
gor•do -da *adj* fat, plump; fatty, greasy; coarse; big, large; whopping big; (*agua*) hard || *m* fat, suet; (coll) first prize (*in lottery*) || **gordo** *adv* — **hablar gordo** (coll) to talk big
gordura *f* fatness, plumpness, stoutness, corpulence; fat, grease
gorgojo *m* grub, weevil; (coll) dwarf, runt; **gorgojo del algodón** boll weevil
gorgojo•so -sa *adj* grubby
gorgón *m* (Col) concrete
gorgonear *intr* (*el pavo*) to gobble
gorgoritear *intr* (coll) to trill
gorgorito *m* (coll) trill
gorgotear *intr* to burble, gurgle
gorgotero *m* peddler, hawker
gorigori *m* (coll) lugubrious funeral chant
gorila *f* gorilla
gorjear *intr* to warble, trill || *ref* (*el niño*) to gurgle
gorra *f* cap; bumming, sponging; **andar de gorra** to sponge; **colarse de gorra** (coll) to crash the gate; **gorra de visera** cap; **vivir de gorra** to live on other people
gorrada *f* tipping the hat
gorrear *intr* (Ecuad) to sponge
gorretada *f* tipping the hat
gorrión *m* sparrow; **gorrión triguero** bunting
gorrista *adj* sponging || *mf* sponger
gorro *m* cap, bonnet; baby's bonnet; **gorro de dormir** nightcap
go•rrón -rrona *adj* sponging || *mf* sponger || *m* pivot; journal, gudgeon
gota *f* drop; (pathol) gout; **gotas** touch of rum or brandy in coffee; **sudar la gota gorda** (coll) to work one's head off
gotear *intr* to drip, dribble; (*llover a gotas espaciadas*) to sprinkle
gotera *f* drip, dripping; mark left by dripping; (*en el techo*) leak; (*adorno de una cama*) valance; **estar lleno de goteras** (coll) to be full of aches and pains; **es una gotera** (coll) it's a constant drain; **goteras** (coll) aches, pains; (Col) environs, outskirts
góti•co -ca *adj* Gothic; noble, illustrious || *m* Gothic
goto•so -sa *adj* gouty || *mf* gout sufferer
gozar §60 *tr* (*poseer*) to enjoy || *intr* to enjoy oneself; **gozar de** (*poseer*) to enjoy || *ref* to enjoy oneself; to rejoice
gozne *m* hinge
gozo *m* joy, enjoyment; **no caber en sí de gozo** (coll) to be beside oneself with joy; **saltar de gozo** to leap with joy
gozo•so -sa *adj* joyful; **gozoso con** or **de** joyful over
gozque *m* or **gozquejo** *m* little yapping dog
grabación *f* (*de disco*) recording; **grabación sobre cinta** tape recording
grabado *m* engraving; print, cut, picture; (*de disco*) recording; **grabado en madera** wood engraving, woodcut; **grabado fuera de texto** inset, insert
graba•dor -dora *adj* recording || *mf* engraver || *f* recorder; **grabadora de cinta** tape recorder
grabadura *f* engraving
grabar *tr* to engrave; (*un sonido, una canción, un disco, etc.*) to record;

grabar en or **sobre cinta** to tape-record || *ref* to become engraved
gracejada *f* (CAm, Mex) cheap comedy, clownishness
gracejar *intr* to be engaging, be witty; to joke
gracejo *m* lightness, winsome manner, charm; (CAm, Mex) clown
gracia *f* witticism, witty remark, joke; grace; gracefulness; favor; pardon; (*de un chiste*) point; (coll) name; **caer en gracia a** to be pleasing to; **de gracia** gratis; **decir dos gracias a** (coll) to tell someone a thing or two; **en gracia a** because of; **gracia de Dios** daily bread; air and sunshine; **gracias** thanks; **¡gracias!** thanks!; **gracias a** thanks to; **¡gracias a Dios!** thank heavens!; **hacer gracia** to be pleasing; **hacer gracia de algo a uno** to exempt or free someone from something; **hacerle a uno gracia** to strike someone as funny; **¡linda gracia!** nonsense!; **tener gracia** to be funny, be surprising
graciable *adj* kind, gracious; easy to grant
grácil *adj* thin, small, slender
gracio·so -sa *adj* (*que tiene donaire, gracia*) graceful; (*afable, fino*) gracious; (*agudo, chistoso*) funny, witty; (*que se da de balde*) free, gratis || *mf* comic || *m* gracioso (*gay, comic character in Spanish comedy*)
grada *f* step, stair; row of seats; grandstand; altar step; (agr) harrow; (*plano inclinado sobre el cual se construyen los barcos*) slip; **gradas** stone steps; (Chile, Peru) atrium; **gradas al aire libre** bleachers
gradar *tr* (agr) to harrow
gradería *f* stone steps; row of seats; bleachers; **gradería cubierta** grandstand
gradiente *m* (phys) gradient || *f* (Am) slope, gradient
grado *m* step; grade; degree; (*título que se da en las universidades*) degree; (*sección en las escuelas*) grade, form, class; (mil) rank; **de buen grado** willingly; **de grado en grado** by degrees; **de grado o por fuerza** willy-nilly; **de mal grado** unwillingly; **en sumo grado** to a great extent; **mal de mi grado** unwillingly, against my wishes
graduación *f* graduation; (*de las bebidas espirituosas*) strength; (mil) rank
gradual *adj* gradual
graduan·do -da *mf* (*persona próxima a graduarse en la universidad*) graduate (*candidate for a degree*)
graduar **§21** *tr* to graduate, to grade; (*un grifo, una válvula, etc.*) to regulate; to appraise, estimate || *ref* to graduate
grafía *f* graph
gráfi·co -ca *adj* graphic(al); printing; illustrated; picture, camera || *m* diagram || *f* graph
grafito *m* graphite
grafospasmo *m* writer's cramp
gragea *f* colored candy; sugar-coated pill
grajear *intr* (*los cuervos*) to caw; (*los niños*) to gurgle
grajien·to -ta *adj* (Am) foul-smelling
gra·jo -ja *mf* rook, crow; (coll) chatterbox || *m* (Am) body odor
gral. *abbr* **general**
gramática *f* grammar; **gramática parda** (coll) shrewdness, mother wit
gramatical *adj* grammatical
gramáti·co -ca *adj* grammatical || *mf* grammarian || *f* see **gramática**
gramil *m* marking gauge, gauge
gramo *m* gram
gramófono *m* gramophone
gramola *f* console phonograph; portable phonograph
gran *adj* apocopated form of **grande,** used only before nouns of both genders in the singular
grana *f* seed; seeding; seeding time; red; **dar en grana** to go to seed
granada *f* pomegranate; (*proyectil explosivo*) grenade; **granada de mano** hand grenade; **granada de metralla** shrapnel; **granada extintora** fire extinguisher, fire grenade
granadero *m* grenadier
granadilla *f* passionflower
granadina *f* grenadine
grana·do -da *adj* choice, select; mature, expert || *m* pomegranate; **granado blanco** rose of Sharon || *f* see **granada**
granalla *f* filings
granangular *adj* wide-angle
granate *m adj invar & m* garnet
Gran Bretaña, la Great Britain
grande *adj* big, large; great || *m* grandee
grandeza *f* bigness, largeness; greatness; (*tamaño*) size; (*magnificencia*) grandeur; grandees; grandeeship
grandi·llón -llona *adj* (coll) oversize, overgrown
grandio·so -sa *adj* grandiose, grand
grandor *m* size
granea·do -da *adj* spattered; (*fuego*) heavy and continuous
granear *tr* to sow; (*la pólvora; una piedra litográfica*) to grain; to stipple
granel — a granel in bulk, loose; at random; lavishly
granelar *tr* (*el cuero*) to grain
granero *m* granary
granete *m* center punch
granífu·go -ga *adj* hail-dispersing
granito *m* granite
granizada *f* hailstorm; (Arg, Chile) iced drink
granizar **§60** *tr* (*p.ej., golpes*) to hail; to sprinkle || *intr* to hail
granizo *m* hail
granja *f* farm, grange; dairy; country place
granjear *tr* to earn, gain; to win, win over || *ref* to win, win over
granjería *f* husbandry; gain, profit
granje·ro -ra *mf* farmer; merchant, trader
grano *m* grain; (*baya*) berry; (*baya de la uva*) grape; (*tumorcillo en la piel*)

pimple; (*peso*) grain; **grano de belleza** beauty spot; **grano de café** coffee bean; **granos** (*fruto de los cereales*) grain; **ir al grano** (coll) to come to the point
granuja *m* scoundrel; (*muchacho vagabundo*) (coll) waif || *f* loose grape; grapeseed
granujo *m* (coll) pimple
granular *adj* granular; pimply || *tr & ref* to granulate
gránulo *m* granule
grapa *f* clamp, clip, staple
grasa *f* fat, grease; (*polvo*) pounce; (Mex) shoe polish; **grasa de ballena** blubber; **grasas** slag
grasien•to -ta *adj* greasy
grasilla *f* pounce
gra•so -sa *adj* fatty, greasy || *m* fattiness, greasiness || *f* see **grasa**
grasones *mpl* wheat porridge
graso•so -sa *adj* greasy; (pathol) fatty
grata *f* wire brush; (*carta*) favor
gratificar **§73** *tr* to gratify; to reward, recompense; to tip, to fee
gratín *m* — **al gratín** au gratin
gratis *adv* gratis
gratisda•to -ta *adj* free, gratis
gratitud *f* gratitude
gra•to -ta *adj* pleasing; free; (Bol, Chile) grateful || *f* see **grata**
gratui•to -ta *adj* gratuitous; free, gratis
grava *f* gravel; crushed stone
gravamen *m* burden, obligation; encumbrance, lien; assessment
gravar *tr* to burden, encumber; to assess
grave *adj* grave, serious, solemn; hard, difficult; (*que pesa*) heavy; (*sonido*) grave, deep, low; (*música*) majestic, noble; (*negocio*) important; (*enfermedad*) serious; (*acento*) grave; paroxytone
gravedad *f* gravity; seriousness; **de gravedad** seriously; gravely; **gravedad nula** weightlessness, zero gravity
gravedo•so -sa *adj* heavy, pompous
gravidez *f* pregnancy
grávi•do -da *adj* pregnant
gravitación *f* gravitation
gravitar *intr* to gravitate; **gravitar sobre** to weigh down on
gravo•so -sa *adj* burdensome, onerous, costly; boring, tiresome
graznar *intr* to caw, to croak; to cackle; (*al cantar*) (fig) to cackle
graznido *m* caw, croak; cackle; (*canto que disuena mucho*) (fig) cackle
Grecia *f* Greece
grecia•no -na *adj* Grecian
gre•co -ca *adj & mf* Greek
greda *f* clay, fuller's earth
grega•rio -ria *adj* (*que vive confundido con otros*) gregarious; slavish, servile
gregoria•no -na *adj* Gregorian
gremial *adj* guild; trade-union, union || *m* guildsman; union member
gremio *m* guild, corporation; trade union, union; association, society
greña *f* confusion, entanglement; (*de cabello*) shock, tangled mop; **andar a la greña** (coll) to get into a hot argument; (*dos mujeres*) (coll) to pull each other's hair
greñu•do -da *adj* bushy-headed, shock-headed
gres *m* sandstone; stoneware
gresca *f* tumult, uproar; row, quarrel
grey *f* (*de ganado menor*) flock; group, party; nation, people; (*de fieles*) flock, congregation
grie•go -ga *adj* Greek || *mf* Greek || *m* (*idioma*) Greek; **hablar en griego** (coll) to not make sense
grieta *f* crack, crevice, chink; (*en la piel*) chap
grieta•do -da *adj* crackled || *m* crackleware
grietar *ref* to crack, split; (*la piel*) to become chapped
gri•fo -fa *adj* (*pelo*) kinky, tangled; (*letra*) script; (W-I) colored; (Mex) drunk; (Col) conceited || *mf* (W-I) colored person; (Mex) drunk || *m* faucet, spigot, tap, cock; (myth) griffin; (Peru) gas station
grilla *f* female cricket; (rad) grid; (Col) fight, quarrel; (SAm) annoyance, bother; **¡ésa es grilla!** (coll) you expect me to believe that!
grillar *intr* (*el grillo*) to chirp || *ref* (*las semillas, bulbos, etc.*) to sprout
grillete *m* fetter, shackle
grillo *m* (*insecto*) cricket; (*brote tierno*) sprout, shoot; **grillos** fetters, shackles
grima *f* fright, horror; **dar grima** to grate on the nerves
grin•go -ga *mf* (disparaging) foreigner; (*anglosajón*) (Am) gringo || *m* (coll) gibberish
griñón *m* (*toca de monja*) wimple; (*melocotón*) nectarine
gripe *f* grippe
gris *adj* gray; dull, gloomy || *m* gray; **hacer gris** (*el tiempo*) (coll) to be sharp, be brisk
grisáce•o -a *adj* grayish
gri•sú *m* (*pl* **-súes**) firedamp
grita *f* shouting; hubbub, uproar; **dar grita a** (coll) to hoot at
gritar *intr* to shout, cry out
gritería *f* shouting, outcry, uproar
grito *m* cry, shout; scream, shriek; **el último grito** (coll) the latest thing, all the rage; **poner el grito en el cielo** (coll) to raise the roof, to scream wildly
gro. *abbr* **género**
Groenlandia *f* Greenland
grosella *f* currant; **grosella silvestre** gooseberry
grosellero *m* currant bush; **grosellero silvestre** gooseberry bush
grosería *f* grossness, coarseness; churlishness, rudeness; stupidity; vulgarity
grose•ro -ra *adj* gross, coarse; churlish, rude; stupid; vulgar || *mf* churl, boor
grosor *m* thickness, bulk
grosura *f* fat, suet, tallow; meat diet; coarseness, vulgarity
grotes•co -ca *adj* grotesque
grúa *f* crane, derrick; **grúa de bote** (naut) davit; **grúa de auxilio** wrecking crane; **grúa de caballete** gantry crane

grúa-remolque *m* tow truck
grue•so -sa *adj* big, thick, bulky, heavy; coarse, ordinary; stout, fat; (*mar*) rough, heavy; **en grueso** in gross, in bulk || *f* (*doce docenas*) gross
grulla *f* (orn) crane
grumete *m* ship's boy, cabin boy
grumo *m* clot, curd; bunch, cluster
grumo•so -sa *adj* clotty, curdly
gruñido *m* (*de cerdo*) grunt; (*de perro cuando amenaza*) growl; (*de persona*) grumble; (*de puerta*) creak; (coll) grumble, scolding
gruñir §12 *intr* (*el cerdo*) to grunt; (*el perro*) to growl; (*una persona*) to grumble; (*una puerta*) to creak
gru•ñón -ñona *adj* (coll) grumpy, grumbly || *mf* (coll) crosspatch
grupa *f* croup, rump
grupada *f* squall
grupal *adj* group
grupo *m* group; (mach & elec) unit
gruta *f* grotto
grutes•co -ca *adj* & *m* (fa) grotesque
Gruyère *m* Swiss cheese
gte. *abbr* **gerente**
guaca *f* (Bol, Peru) Indian tomb; (Am) hidden treasure
guacal *m* (Am) crate
guacama•yo -ya *adj* (P-R) flashy, sporty || *m* (Am) macaw
guachapear *tr* to splash with the feet; to bungle, botch || *intr* to clank, clatter
guachinan•go -ga *adj* (Am) flattering, sly || *mf* (disparaging term used by Cubans) Mexican
gua•cho -cha *adj* (SAm) homeless, orphan; (SAm) odd, unmatched
guadal *m* (Am) bog, swamp; (Am) sand hill, dune
Guadalupe *f* Guadeloupe
guadama•cí *m* (*pl* **-cíes**) embossed leather
guadaña *f* scythe
guadañadora *f* mowing machine
guadañar *tr* to cut with a scythe
guadarnés *m* harness room; harness man
guagua *f* trifle; (SAm) baby; (W-I) bus; (Col) paca
guajada *f* (Mex) nonsense, folly
guaje *adj* (Hond, Mex) foolish, stupid || *m* (Hond, Mex) calabash, gourd; (CAm) piece of junk
guaji•ro -ra *mf* (W-I) peasant, yokel
guajolote *m* (Am) turkey; (Mex) simpleton
gualda *f* (bot) weld, dyer's rocket
gual•do -da *adj* yellow || *f* see **gualda**
gualdrapa *f* housing, trappings; (coll) dirty rag hanging from clothes
gualdrapear *tr* to line up head to tail || *intr* (*las velas*) to flap
Gualterio *m* Walter
guanaco *m* (SAm) dope, simpleton; (SAm) tall lanky fellow; (zool) guanaco
guanajo *m* (W-I) boob, dunce; (Am) turkey
guano *m* (Am) palm tree; (Am) bird manure
guante *m* glove; **arrojar el guante** to throw down the gauntlet; **echar un guante** to pass the hat; **guantes** tip, fee; **recoger el guante** to take up the gauntlet; **salvo el guante** (coll) excuse my glove
guantelete *m* gauntlet
guantería *f* glove shop
guapear *intr* (coll) to bluster, to swagger; (coll) to dress to kill
guape•tón -tona *adj* (coll) handsome; (coll) flashy, sporty; (coll) bold, fearless || *m* (coll) bully, tough
guapeza *f* (coll) good looks; (coll) flashiness, sportiness; (coll) boldness, daring; (coll) bravado
gua•po -pa *adj* (coll) handsome, good-looking; (coll) flashy, sporty; (coll) bold, daring || *m* (*hombre pendenciero*) bully; gallant, lady's man
guapura *f* (coll) good looks
guarache *m* (Mex) leather sandal; (Mex) tire patch
guarapo *m* sugar-cane juice; (Am) fermented juice of sugar cane
guarda *mf* guard, custodian || *m* (Arg) trolley-car conductor; **guarda de la aduana** customhouse officer; **guarda forestal** forest ranger || *f* guard, custody; (*de la ley*) observance; (*de la espada*) guard; (*de la cerradura*) ward; (bb) flyleaf
guardabarrera *mf* (rr) gatekeeper
guardaba•rros *m* (*pl* **-rros**) fender, mudguard, dashboard
guardabosque *m* gamekeeper; forest ranger; (Am) shortstop
guardabrisa *m* windshield; (naut) glass candle shade
guardacantón *m* spur stone
guardacarril *m* (rr) railguard
guardacar•tas *m* (*pl* **-tas**) letter file
guardaco•ches *m* (*pl* **-ches**) car watcher
guardacos•tas *m* (*pl* **-tas**) revenue cutter, coast guard cutter; **guardacostas** *mpl* (*servicio*) coast guard
guarda•dor -dora *adj* guarding, protecting; mindful, observant; stingy || *m* guardian, keeper; observer
guardaespal•das *m* (*pl* **-das**) bodyguard
guardafango *m* fender, mudguard
guardafre•nos *m* (*pl* **-nos**) (rr) brakeman, flagman
guardafuego *m* fender, fireguard
guardagu•jas *m* (*pl* **-jas**) (rr) switchman
guardajo•yas *m* (*pl* **-yas**) jewel case
guardalado *m* railing, parapet
guardalmacén *m* warehouseman; (Cuba) country station master
guardamalleta *f* valance
guardameta *m* goalkeeper
guardamue•bles *m* (*pl* **-bles**) warehouse, furniture warehouse
guardanieve *m* snowshed
guardapelo *m* locket
guardapolvo *m* (*sobretodo ligero*) duster; (*resguardo para preservar del polvo*) cover, cloth; (*del reloj*) inner lid; (*sobre una puerta o ventana*) hood
guardapuerta *f* storm door
guardar *tr* to guard; to watch over; to protect; to put away; to show, observe; to save, e.g., **¡Dios guarde a**

la Reina God save the Queen || *intr* to keep, to save; **¡guarda!** look out!, watch out! || *ref* to be on one's guard; **guardarse de** to look out for, watch out for, guard against

guardarraya *f* (CAm, W-I) boundary line, property line

guardarropa *mf* keeper of the wardrobe || *m* (*armario donde se guarda la ropa*) wardrobe; (*local destinado a la custodia de ropa en establecimientos públicos*) checkroom, cloakroom; check boy || *f* check girl, hat girl

guardarropía *f* (theat) wardrobe

guardasilla *f* chair rail

guardaventana *f* storm window

guardavía *m* (rr) trackwalker, lineman

guardavida *m* lifeguard

guardavien•tos *m* (*pl* **-tos**) (*abrigo contra los vientos*) windbreak; (*mitra de chimenea*) chimney pot

guardavivo *m* bead, corner bead

guardería *f* guard, guardship; **guardería infantil** day nursery

guardesa *f* woman guard

guardia *m* guard, guardsman; **guardia civil** rural policeman; **guardia marina** midshipman, middy; **guardia urbano** policeman || *f* (*cuerpo de hombres armados; manera de defenderse en la esgrima*) guard; (naut) watch; **de guardia** on duty; on guard; **guardia civil** rural police; **guardia de asalto** shock troops; **guardia de corps** (mil) bodyguard; **guardia de cuartillo** (naut) dogwatch; **guardia suiza** Swiss Guards

guar•dián -diana *mf* guardian || *m* watchman

guardilla *f* attic; attic room

guardo•so -sa *adj* careful, neat, tidy; (*que ahorra mucho*) thrifty; (*mezquino*) stingy

guarecer §22 *tr* to take in, give shelter to; to keep, preserve; (*a un enfermo*) to treat || *ref* to take refuge, take shelter

guarida *f* den, lair; shelter; haunt, hangout, hide-out

guarismo *m* cipher, figure

guarnecer §22 *tr* to trim, adorn; to equip, provide; to bind, to edge; (*joyas*) to set; to stucco, to plaster; (*frenos*) to line; (*un cojinete*) to bush; (*una plaza fuerte*) to man, garrison; (culin) to garnish

guarnición *f* trimming; equipping; binding, edging; (*de joyas*) setting; stuccoing, plastering; (*de la espada*) guard; (*de frenos*) lining; (*del émbolo*) packing; (*tropa que guarnece un lugar*) garrison; (culin) garnish; **guarniciones** fixtures, fittings; (*de la caballería*) harness

guarnicionar *tr* to garrison

guarnicionero *m* harness maker

gua•rro -rra *mf* hog

guasa *f* (coll) heaviness, churlishness; (coll) joking, kidding

guasca *f* (Am) rawhide; (Am) whip; **dar guasca a** (Am) to whip, thrash

guasería *f* (SAm) coarseness, crudity; (Chile) timidity

gua•so -sa *adj* (SAm) coarse, crude, uncouth || *mf* (Chile) peasant || *f* see **guasa**

gua•són -sona *adj* (coll) heavy, churlish; (coll) funny, comical || *mf* (coll) dullard, churl; (coll) joker, kidder

guata *f* wadding, padding; (Arg, Chile, Peru) belly, paunch; (*de una pared*) (Chile) bulging, warping; (Ecuad) boon companion; **echar guata** (Chile) to prosper

guatemalte•co -ca *adj & mf* Guatemalan

guáter *m* (coll) toilet, water closet

guau *m* (*ladrido del perro*) bowwow; (bot) woodbine, Virginia creeper; **guau guau** (*perro*) bowwow || *interj* bowwow!

guay *interj* — **¡guay de mí!** (poet) woe is me!

guayaba *f* guava, guava apple

guayabo *m* guava tree; (Am) lie, trick

guayaco *m* lignum vitae

Guayana *f* Guiana

gubernamental *adj* governmental; (*defensor*) strong-government

gubernati•vo -va *adj* governmental

gubia *f* gouge

guedeja *f* shock of hair; lion's mane

guerra *f* war, warfare; billiards; **Gran guerra** Great War; **guerra a muerte** war to the death; **guerra bacteriana** germ warfare; **guerra de guerrillas** guerrilla warfare; **guerra de las dos Rosas** War of the Roses; **guerra de los Cien Años** Hundred Years' War; **guerra del Transvaal** Boer War; **guerra de ondas** radio jamming; **guerra de Troya** Trojan War; **guerra fría** cold war; **Guerra Mundial** World War; **guerra relámpago** blitzkrieg; **hacer la guerra** to wage war

guerrea•dor -dora *adj* warring || *mf* warrior

guerrear *intr* to war, wage war, fight; to struggle, resist

guerre•ro -ra *adj* war, warlike; warring; (coll) mischievous || *mf* fighter || *m* warrior, soldier, fighting man || *f* tight-fitting military jacket

guerrilla *f* band of skirmishers; guerrilla band; guerrilla warfare

guerrillear *intr* to skirmish; to wage guerrilla warfare

guerrillero *m* guerrilla

guía *mf* guide, leader; adviser || *m* (mil) guide || *f* guide; guidance; directory; (*del viajero*) guidebook; (*caballo*) leader; (*de la bicicleta*) handle bar; (*del bigote*) turned-up end; (*de la sierra*) fence; marker; shoot, sprout; (mach) guide; (rr) timetable; **guías** reins; **guía sonora** sound track; **guía telefónica** telephone directory

guiadera *f* (mach) guide

guiar §77 *tr* to guide, to lead; (*un automóvil*) to steer, to drive; to pilot; (*una planta, una vid*) to train || *intr* to shoot, to sprout || *ref* — **guiarse por** to be guided by, to go by

guija *f* pebble; grass pea

guijarro *m* cobble, cobblestone

guije•ño -ña *adj* pebbly; hard-hearted

guijo *m* gravel
guijo•so -sa *adj* gravelly; pebbly
guillame *m* rabbet plane
Guillermo *m* William
guillotina *f* guillotine; paper cutter
guillotinar *tr* to guillotine
guimbalete *m* pump handle
guinda *f* sour cherry
guindal *m* sour cherry tree
guindaleza *f* (naut) hawser
guindar *tr* to hoist, raise; (coll) to win; (*ahorcar*) (coll) to hang, to string up
guindilla *m* (coll) policeman, cop; Guinea pepper
guindo *m* sour cherry tree
guindola *f* (naut) boatswain's chair; (naut) life buoy
guinea *f* (*moneda*) guinea
guineo *m* small banana
guinga *f* gingham
guiña *f* (Col, Ven) bad luck
guiñada *f* wink; (naut) yaw
guiñapo *m* rag, tatter; ragamuffin
guiñar *tr* (*el ojo*) to wink || *intr* to wink; (naut) to yaw || *ref* to wink at each other
guiño *m* wink; **hacer guiños a** to make eyes at; **hacerse guiños** to make faces at each other
guión *m* banner, standard; cross (*carried before prelate in procession*); (*signo ortográfico*) hyphen; (*signo ortográfico largo*) dash; (mil) guidon; (mov & theat) scenario; (rad & telv) script; (mus) repeat sign; **guión de montaje** (mov) cutter's script; **guión de rodaje** (mov) shooting script
guionista *mf* (mov) scenarist; (mov) scriptwriter; (mov) subtitle writer
guirigay *m* (coll) gibberish; (coll) confusion, hubbub
guirindola *f* frill, jabot
guirlache *m* almond brittle, peanut brittle
guirnalda *f* garland, wreath
guisa *f* way, manner, wise; **a guisa de** in the manner of, like
guisado *m* stew, meat stew
guisante *m* pea; **guisante de olor** sweet pea
guisar *tr* to cook; to stew; to arrange, prepare || *intr* to cook
guiso *m* dish
guisote *m* hash
guita *f* twine; (coll) dough, money
guitarra *f* guitar
guitarrista *mf* guitarist
gui•tón -tona *mf* tramp, bum
gula *f* gluttony; gorging, guzzling
gulo•so -sa *adj* gluttonous; guzzling
gumía *f* Moorish poniard
gurrumi•no -na *adj* weak, puny || *m* henpecked husband || *f* uxoriousness
gusanear *intr* to swarm
gusanera *f* nest of worms; (coll) ruling passion
gusanien•to -ta *adj* wormy, grubby
gusanillo *m* small worm; twist stitch; (*de la barrena*) spur; **matar el gusanillo** (coll) to take a shot of liquor before breakfast
gusano *m* worm; **gusano de luz** glowworm; **gusano de seda** silk worm; **gusano de tierra** earthworm
gusano•so -sa *adj* wormy, grubby
gusarapo *m* waterworm, vinegar worm
gustación *f* tasting; taste
gustar *tr* to taste; to try, sample; to please, be pleasing to; to like, e.g., **me gustan estas peras** I like these pears || *intr* to like, e.g., **como Vd. guste** as you like; **gustar de** to like; to like to
gustillo *m* slight taste, touch
gusto *m* taste; flavor; liking; caprice, whim; pleasure; **a gusto** as you like it; **con mucho gusto** with pleasure, gladly; **encontrarse a gusto** or **estar a gusto** to like it (*e.g., in the country*); **tanto gusto** so glad to meet you
gusto•so -sa *adj* tasty; agreeable, pleasant; ready, willing, glad
gutapercha *f* gutta-percha
gutural *adj* guttural

H

H, h (hache) *f* ninth letter of the Spanish alphabet
haba *f* bean, broad bean; (*simiente del café y el cacao*) bean; **ser habas contadas** (coll) to be a sure thing
Habana, La Havana
haber *m* salary, wages; credit, credit side; **haberes** property, wealth || *v* **§38** *tr* to have; to get, get hold of || *v aux* to have, e.g., **lo he visto a menudo** I have seen it often; **haber de** + *inf* to be to + *inf*, e.g., **ha de llegar a mediodía** he is to arrive at noon || *v impers* there to be, e.g., **ha habido tres personas allí** there were three people there; **haber que** + *inf* to be necessary to + *inf;* **no hay de qué** you're welcome, don't mention it || *ref* to behave oneself; **habérselas con** to deal with; to have it out with
habichuela *f* kidney bean; **habichuela verde** string bean
hábil *adj* skillful, capable; (*día*) work
habilidad *f* skill, ability, capability; (*lo que se ejecuta con gracia*) feat; (*enredo, embuste*) scheme, trick
habilido•so -sa *adj* skillful
habilitación *f* qualification; backing, financing; equipping, outfitting; **habilitaciones** fixtures
habilitar *tr* to qualify; to back, finance; to equip, fit out; (*en un examen*) to pass
habitable *adj* inhabitable

habitación *f* habitation; (*edificio donde se habita*) house, home, dwelling; (*aposento de la casa o el hotel*) room; (*donde vive una especie vegetal o animal*) habitat
habitante *mf* (*de una casa*) dweller, occupant; (*de una población*) inhabitant
habitar *tr* to inhabit, live in; (*una casa, un piso*) to occupy || *intr* to live
hábito *m* garment, dress; habit, custom; **ahorcar los hábitos** (coll) to doff the cassock, to leave the priesthood; (coll) to change jobs; **el hábito no hace al monje** clothes don't make the man
habitua·do -da *mf* habitué
habitual *adj* habitual; regular, usual
habituar **§21** *tr* to accustom || *ref* to become accustomed
habitud *f* relationship, connection; custom, habit
habla *f* speech; **al habla** speaking
habla·dor -dora *adj* talkative; gossipy || *mf* talker, chatterbox; gossip
habladuría *f* cut, sarcasm; **andar con habladurías** to go around gossiping
hablante *adj* speaking || *mf* speaker
hablar *tr* (*una lengua*) to speak, to talk; (*disparates*) to talk || *intr* to speak, to talk; **es hablar por demás** it's wasted talk; **estar hablando** (*una pintura, una estatua*) to be almost alive; **hablar claro** to talk straight from the shoulder
hablilla *f* story, piece of gossip
hablista *mf* speaker, good speaker
hacede·ro -ra *adj* feasible, practicable
hacenda·do -da *adj* landed, property-owning || *mf* landholder, property owner; (Am) cattle rancher; (Am) plantation owner
hacendar **§2** *tr* (*el dominio de bienes raíces*) to pass on || *ref* to buy property in order to settle down
hacende·ro -ra *adj* thrifty
hacendista *m* economist, fiscal expert; man of independent means
hacendo·so -sa *adj* hard-working, thrifty
hacer **§39** *tr* (*crear, producir, formar*) to make; (*ejecutar, llevar a cabo*) to do; (*un baúl*) to pack; (*un papel*) to play; (*un mandato*) to give; (*un drama*) to act, perform; to pretend to be; (*una pregunta*) to ask; **hace** ago, e.g., **hace un mes** a month ago; **hacer** + *inf* to have + *inf,* e.g., **le hice tomar un libro en la biblioteca** I had him get a book at the library; to make + *inf,* e.g., **el médico me hizo guardar cama** the doctor made me stay in bed; to have + *pp,* e.g., **hará construir una casa** he will have a house built; **hacer . . . que** to be . . . since, e.g., **hace un año que yo estuve aquí** it is a year since I was here; to be for . . ., e.g., **hace un año que estoy aquí** I have been here for a year; for expressions like **hacer frío** to be cold, see the noun || *intr* to act; **hacer a** to fit; **hacer al caso** (coll) to be to the purpose; **hacer como que** + *ind* to pretend to + *inf;* **hacer de** to act as, to work as; **hacer por** to try to || *ref* to become, get to be, grow; **hacerse a** to become accustomed to; **hacerse a un lado** to step aside; **hacerse con** to make off with; **hacerse chiquito** (coll) to sing small; **hacérsele a uno difícil** to strike one as difficult; **hacerse viejo** to grow old; (coll) to kill time
hacia *prep* toward; (*cierta hora o época*) about, near; **hacia abajo** downward; **hacia adelante** forward; **hacia arriba** upward; **hacia atrás** backward; (coll) the wrong way; **hacia dentro** inward; **hacia fuera** outward
hacienda *f* farmstead, landed estate, country property; property, possessions; (Arg) cattle, livestock; (Am) ranch; **hacienda pública** public finance, federal income; **haciendas** household chores
hacina *f* pile, heap; shock, stack
hacinar *tr* to pile, heap, stack
hacha *f* axe; (*hacha pequeña*) hatchet; torch, firebrand; four-wick wax candle; **hacha de armas** battleaxe
hachazo *m* blow with an axe
hachear *tr & intr* to hew, hack, or chop with an axe
hachero *m* torchbearer; (*candelero*) torch stand; (*leñador*) woodcutter
hachich *m* or **hachís** *m* hashish
hacho *m* torch; (*sitio elevado cerca de la costa*) beacon, beacon hill
hada *f* fairy; (*mujer que encanta por su belleza, gracia, etc.*) charmer; **hada madrina** fairy godmother
hadar *tr* (*determinar el hado*) to predestine, foreordain; (*pronosticar*) to foretell; (*encantar*) to charm, cast a spell on
hado *m* fate, destiny
haiga *m* (slang) flashy auto; (slang) sport
halagar **§44** *tr* (*lisonjear*) to flatter; (*demostrar cariño a*) to cajole, fawn on; (*agradar*) to gratify, please
halago *m* flattery; cajolery; gratification; **halagos** flattery, blandishments
halagüe·ño -ña *adj* flattering; fawning; gratifying, pleasing; bright, rosy, promising
halar *tr* (naut) to haul, to pull
halcón *m* falcon
halconear *intr* (*la mujer*) to chase after men
halconería *f* falconry
halconero *m* falconer
halda *f* skirt; **poner haldas en cinta** (coll) to pull up one's skirts to run; (coll) to roll up one's sleeves
halieto *m* fish hawk, osprey
hálito *m* breath; vapor; (poet) gentle breeze
halitosis *f* halitosis
halo *m* halo
halógeno *m* halogen
halterio *m* dumbbell
haluro *m* halide
hallar *tr* to find; (*averiguar*) to find out, discover || *ref* to find oneself; to be; **hallarse bien con** to be satisfied with; **hallárselo todo hecho** to never

have to turn a hand; **no hallarse** to feel uncomfortable, to not like it

hallazgo *m* (*cosa hallada*) find; (*acción de hallar*) finding, discovery; (*premio al que ha hallado una cosa perdida*) reward, finder's reward, e.g., **diez dólares de hallazgo** ten dollars reward

hallulla *f* bread baked on embers or hot stones; (Chile) fine bread

hamaca *f* hammock

hamamelina *f* witch hazel

hambre *f* hunger; (*escasez general de comestibles*) famine; **matar de hambre** to starve to death; **morir de hambre** to starve to death, die of starvation; **pasar hambre** to go hungry; **tener hambre** to be hungry

hambrear *tr & intr* to starve, to famish

hambrien•to -ta *adj* hungry, starving

hambruna *f* (SAm) mad hunger; (Ecuad) starvation

hamburguesa *f* hamburger sandwich

hamo *m* fishhook

hampa *f* underworld life; denizens of the underworld

hampes•co -ca *adj* underworld

hampón *m* bully, tough

hangar *m* (aer) hangar

hara•gán -gana *adj* idling, loafing, lazy || *mf* idler, loafer

haraganear *intr* to idle, to loaf, to hang around

harapien•to -ta *adj* ragged, tattered

harapo *m* rag, tatter; **andar** or **estar hecho un harapo** (coll) to go around in rags

harapo•so -sa *adj* ragged, tattered

harén *m* harem

harina *f* (*especialmente del trigo*) flour; (*de cualquier grano*) meal; **estar metido en harina** (coll) to be deeply absorbed; (coll) to be fat and heavy; **harina de avena** oatmeal; **harina de maíz** corn meal; **ser harina de otro costal** (coll) to be a horse of another color

harine•ro -ra *adj* flour || *m* flour dealer; flour bin

harino•so -sa *adj* floury, mealy

harnear *tr* (Col, Chile) to sift

harnero *m* sieve

ha•rón -rona *adj* lazy || *mf* lazy loafer

harpillera *f* burlap, sackcloth

hartar *tr* to stuff, to cram; to satisfy, to satiate; to tire, to bore; to overwhelm, deluge || *intr* to have one's fill || *ref* to stuff; to be satiated; to tire, be bored

hartazgo or **hartazón** *m* fill, bellyful; **darse un hartazgo** (coll) to eat one's fill; **darse un hartazgo de** (coll) to have or to get one's fill of

har•to -ta *adj* full, fed up; very much; **harto de** full of, fed up with, sick of || **harto** *adv* enough; very, quite

hartura *f* fill, satiety; full satisfaction; abundance

hasta *adv* even || *prep* until, till; to, as far as; down to, up to; as much as; **hasta ahora** up till now; **hasta aquí** so far; **hasta después** (coll) so long, good-by; **hasta la vista** or **hasta luego** so long, good-by; **hasta mañana** see you tomorrow; **hasta más no poder** to the utmost; **hasta no más** to the utmost; **hasta que** until, till

hastial *m* gable end; (*hombrón rústico*) bumpkin

hastiar **§77** *tr* to surfeit, sicken, cloy; (*fastidiar*) to bother, annoy, bore

hastío *m* surfeit, loathing, disgust; bother, annoyance, boredom

hataca *f* large wooden ladle; (*cilindro para extender la masa*) rolling pin

hatajo *m* small herd, small flock; (*p.ej., de disparates*) (coll) lot, flock

hato *m* (*de ganado vacuno*) herd; (*de ovejas*) flock; (*de ropa*) pack, bundle; (*de gente*) clique, ring; (*de gente malvada*) gang; everyday outfit; (*de disparates*) flock, lot; (Am) cattle ranch; **liar el hato** (coll) to pack up, pack one's baggage; **revolver el hato** (coll) to stir up trouble

haya *f* beech tree; (*madera*) beech || **La Haya** The Hague

hayaca *f* (Ven) mince pie

hayo *m* (Col) coca; (Col) coca leaves (*mixed for chewing*)

hayuco *m* beechnut, mast

haz *m* (*pl* **haces**) bunch, bundle; (*de leña*) fagot; (*de mieses*) sheaf; (*de rayos*) beam, pencil; (*de soldados*) file || *f* (*pl* **haces**) face; (*de la tierra*) surface; (*de paño o tela*) right side; (*de un edificio*) façade, front; **a sobre haz** on the surface; **ser de dos haces** to be two-faced

hazaña *f* feat, exploit, deed

hazañería *f* fuss

hazañe•ro -ra *adj* fussy

hazaño•so -sa *adj* gallant, courageous

hazmerreír *m* (coll) laughingstock, butt

he *adv* behold, lo and behold; **he aquí** here is, here are; **he allí** there is, there are

hebilla *f* buckle

hebra *f* thread; fiber; (*en la madera*) grain; (*del discurso*) (fig) thread; **de una hebra** (Chile) all at once; **pegar la hebra** (coll) to strike up a conversation; (coll) to keep on talking

hebre•o -a *adj & mf* Hebrew || *m* (*idioma*) Hebrew; (coll) usurer

hebro•so -sa *adj* fibrous, stringy

hecatombe *f* hecatomb

hechicera *f* witch, sorceress; (*mujer que por su belleza cautiva*) enchantress

hechicería *f* witchcraft, sorcery, wizardry; (fig) fascination, charm

hechice•ro -ra *adj* bewitching, charming, enchanting; magic || *mf* sorcerer, magician; charmer, enchanter || *m* wizard, sorcerer || *f* see **hechicera**

hechizar **§60** *tr* to bewitch, cast a spell on; (fig) to bewitch, charm, enchant || *intr* to practice sorcery; (fig) to be charming, to enchant

hechi•zo -za *adj* fake, artificial; (*de quita y pon*) detachable; made, manufactured; (*producto*) (Am) local, home || *m* spell, charm; magic, sorcery; (fig) magic, sorcery, glamour; (fig) charmer; **hechizos** (*de una mujer*) charms

he•cho -cha *adj* accustomed; finished; turned into; (*traje*) ready-made; (*llegado a la edad adulta*) full-grown || *m* act, deed; fact; event; (*hazaña*) feat; **de hecho** in fact; **en hecho de verdad** as a matter of fact; **estar en el hecho de** to catch on to; **hecho consumado** fait accompli || **hecho** *interj* all right!, OK!

hechura *f* form, shape, cut, build; creation, creature; workmanship; (Chile) drink, treat; **hechuras** cost of making; **no tener hechura** to be impracticable

heder §51 *tr* to bore, annoy, tire || *intr* to stink, to reek

hediondez *f* stench, stink

hedion•do -da *adj* stinking, smelly; annoying, boring; obscene, filthy, dirty || *m* bean trefoil; skunk

hedor *m* stench, stink

helada *f* freezing; (*escarcha*) frost; **helada blanca** hoarfrost

heladera *f* refrigerator; (Chile) ice-cream tray

heladería *f* (Am) ice-cream parlor

hela•do -da *adj* cold, icy; (*pasmado por el miedo, la sorpresa, etc.*) frozen; (*esquivo, indiferente*) cold, chilly; (*cubierto de azúcar*) (Ven) iced || *m* cold drink; (*manjar*) water ice; (*sorbete*) ice cream; **helado al corte** brick ice cream || *f* see **helada**

hela•dor -dora *adj* freezing || *f* ice-cream freezer

helar §2 *tr* to freeze; to harden, congeal; to dumbfound; to discourage || *intr* to freeze || *ref* to freeze; to harden, congeal, set; (*cubrirse de hielo*) to ice

helecho *m* fern

helénl•co -ca *adj* Hellenic

hele•no -na *adj* Hellenic || *mf* Hellene

helero *m* glacier

hélice *f* helix; (*de un buque*) screw, propeller; (*de un avión*) propeller

helicóptero *m* helicopter

helio *m* helium

heliotropo *m* heliotrope

helipuerto *m* heliport

hematíe *m* red cell

hembra *adj invar* (*animal, planta, herramienta*) female; weak, thin, delicate || *f* female; (*del corchete*) eye; (*tuerca*) nut; **hembra de terraja** (mach) die

hembraje *m* (SAm) females of a flock or herd

hembrilla *f* (mach) female part or piece; (*armella*) eyebolt

hemeroteca *f* periodical library

hemiciclo *m* (*semicírculo*) hemicycle; (*gradería semicircular*) amphitheater; (*espacio central del salón de sesiones de las Cortes*) floor

hemisferio *m* hemisphere

hemistiquio *m* hemistich

hemofilia *f* hemophilia

hemoglobina *f* hemoglobin

hemorragia *f* hemorrhage

hemorroides *fpl* hemorrhoids

hemóstato *m* hemostat

henal *m* hayloft

henar *m* hayfield

henchir §50 *tr* to fill; (*un colchón*) to stuff; (*a una persona, p.ej., de favores*) to heap, to shower || *ref* to be filled; to stuff, to stuff oneself

hendedura *f* crack, split, cleft

hender §51 *tr* to crack, split, cleave; (*el aire, las ondas*) to cleave; to make one's way through || *ref* to crack, to split

hendidura *f* crack, split, cleft

henil *m* hayloft, haymow

henna *f* henna

heno *m* hay

heñir §72 *tr* to knead; **hay mucho que heñir** (coll) there's still a lot of work to do

heraldía *f* heraldry

heráldi•co -ca *adj* heraldic || *f* heraldry

heraldo *m* herald

herbáce•o -a *adj* herbaceous

herbajar *tr & intr* to graze

herbaje *m* herbage

herba•rio -ria *adj* herbal || *m* (*libro*) herbal; (*colección*) herbarium

herbicida *m* weed killer

herbo•so -sa *adj* grassy

hercúle•o -a *adj* herculean

heredad *f* country estate

heredar *tr & intr* to inherit; **heredar a** to inherit from

herede•ro -ra *mf* heir, inheritor; owner of an estate; **heredero forzoso** heir apparent || *m* heir || *f* heiress

heredita•rio -ria *adj* hereditary

hereje *mf* heretic

herejía *f* heresy; insult, outrage; (coll) outrageous price

herencia *f* heritage, inheritance; (*transmisión de caracteres biológicos*) heredity; (*patrimonio de un difunto*) estate

heréti•co -ca *adj* heretic(al)

herida *f* injury, wound; insult, outrage; **renovar la herida** to open an old sore; **tocar en la herida** to sting to the quick

heri•do -da *adj* hurt, wounded; (*ofendido*) hurt || *mf* injured person, wounded person; **los heridos** the injured, the wounded || *f* see **herida**

herir §68 *tr* to injure, hurt, wound; (*ofender*) (fig) to hurt; (*golpear*) to strike; (*el sol sobre*) to beat down upon; (*un instrumento de cuerda*) to play; (*la cuerda de un instrumento*) to pluck; to touch, to move

hermana *f* sister; **hermana de leche** foster sister; **hermana política** sister-in-law; **media hermana** half sister

hermanar *tr* to match, to mate; to combine, join; to harmonize || *ref* to match; to become attached as brothers or sisters or brother and sister

hermanastra *f* stepsister

hermanastro *m* stepbrother

hermandad *f* brotherhood; sisterhood; close friendship; close relationship

herma•no -na *adj* (*p.ej., idioma*) sister || *mf* companion, mate || *m* brother; **hermano de leche** foster brother; **hermano político** brother-in-law; **hermanos** brother and sister; brothers and sisters; **hermanos siameses** Siamese twins; **medio hermano** half brother; **primo hermano** first cousin || *f* see **hermana**

herméti•co -ca *adj* hermetic(al); airtight; impenetrable; tight-lipped

hermosear *tr* to beautify, to embellish

hermo•so -sa *adj* beautiful; (*caballero*) handsome

hermosura *f* beauty; (*mujer hermosa*) belle, beauty

hernia *f* hernia

héroe *m* hero

heroi•co -ca *adj* heroic; (*remedio*) desperate

heroína *f* heroine; (pharm) heroin

heroísmo *m* heroism

herrada *f* wooden bucket

herrador *m* horseshoer

herradura *f* horseshoe; **mostrar las herraduras** (*un caballo*) to kick, be vicious; (coll) to show one's heels

herraje *m* hardware, ironwork

herramental *adj* tool || *m* toolbox, tool bag

herramienta *f* tool; set of tools; (coll) teeth; (coll) horns

herrar §2 *tr* (*guarnecer con hierro*) to fit with hardware; (*un caballo*) to shoe; (*marcar con hierro candente*) to brand; (*un barril*) to hoop

herrería *f* forge, blacksmith shop; blacksmithing; ironworks; rumpus

herrero *m* blacksmith; **herrero de grueso** ironworker; **herrero de obra** steelworker

herrete *m* tip, metal tip

herretear *tr* to tip, put a metal tip on

herrín *m* rust

herrón *m* (*tejo de hierro horadado*) quoit; (*arandela*) washer

herrumbre *f* rust; (*honguillo parásito*) rust, plant rot

herrumbro•so -sa *adj* rusty

herventar §2 *tr* to boil

hervidero *m* boiling; bubbling spring; (*en el pecho*) rattle; (*de gente*) swarm

hervidor *m* boiler, cooker

hervir §68 *intr* to boil; (*el mar; una persona encolerizada*) to boil, to seethe; to swarm, to teem

hervor *m* boil, boiling; (*de la juventud*) fire, restlessness; **alzar el hervor** to begin to boil

hervoro•so -sa *adj* ardent, fiery, impetuous

heterócli•to -ta *adj* irregular; unconventional

heterodinar *tr* to heterodyne

heterodi•no -na *adj* heterodyne

heterodo•xo -xa *adj* heterodox

heterogeneidad *f* heterogeneity

heterogéne•o -a *adj* heterogeneous

hexámetro *m* hexameter

hez *f* (*pl* **heces**) (fig) scum, dregs; **heces** lees, dregs; feces, excrement

hiato *m* hiatus

hibisco *m* hibiscus

hibridación *f* hybridization

hibridar *tr & intr* to hybridize

híbri•do -da *adj & m* hybrid

hidal•go -ga *adj* noble, illustrious || *m* nobleman || *f* noblewoman

hidalguez *f* or **hidalguía** *f* nobility

hidra *f* hydra

hidratar *tr & ref* to hydrate

hidrato *m* hydrate

hidráuli•co -ca *adj* hydraulic || *f* hydraulics

hidroala *m* (*vehículo mixto de buque y avión*) hydrofoil

hidroaleta *f* (*miembro alar del hidroala*) hydrofoil

hidroavión *m* hydroplane

hidrocarburo *m* hydrocarbon

hidroeléctri•co -ca *adj* hydroelectric

hidrófi•lo -la *adj* (*algodón*) absorbent (*cotton*)

hidrofobia *f* hydrophobia

hidrófu•go -ga *adj* waterproof

hidrógeno *m* hydrogen

hidropesía *f* dropsy

hidróxido *m* hydroxide

hiedra *f* ivy

hiel *f* bile, gall; (fig) gall, bitterness, sorrow; **echar la hiel** (coll) to strain, to overwork

hielo *m* ice; (fig) coldness, coolness; **hielo flotante** drift ice, ice pack; **hielo seco** dry ice; **romper el hielo** (*quebrantar la reserva*) to break the ice

hiena *f* hyena

hienda *f* dung

hierba *f* grass; (*especialmente la que tiene propiedades medicinales*) herb; **hierba de la plata** honesty; **hierba del asno** evening primrose; **hierba de París** truelove; **hierba gatera** catnip; **hierba pastel** woad; **hierbas** grass, pasture; herb poison; (coll) years of age (*said of animals*); **mala hierba** weed; (coll) wayward young fellow

hierbabuena *f* mint

hierro *m* iron; (*marca candente que se pone a los ganados*) brand; **hierro colado** cast iron; **hierro colado en barras** pig iron; **hierro de desecho** scrap iron; **hierro de marcar** branding iron; **hierro dulce** wrought iron; **hierro fundido** cast iron; **hierro galvanizado** galvanized iron; **hierro ondulado** corrugated iron; **hierros** irons, fetters; **llevar hierro a Vizcaya** to carry coals to Newcastle

higa *f* baby's fist-shaped amulet; (coll) scorn, contempt; **dar higa** to miss fire; **no dar dos higas por** (coll) to not give a rap for

hígado *m* liver; **echar los hígados** (coll) to strain, to overwork; **hígados** (coll) guts, courage; **malos hígados** (coll) hatred, grudge

higiene *f* hygiene

higiéni•co -ca *adj* hygienic

higo *m* fig; **higo chumbo** prickly pear; **higo paso** dried fig; **no valer un higo** (coll) to be not worth a continental

higuera *f* fig tree; **higuera chumba** prickly pear

hija *f* daughter; **hija política** daughter-in-law

hijas•tro -tra *mf* stepchild || *m* stepson || *f* stepdaughter

hi•jo -ja *mf* child; (*de un animal*) young; **hijo de bendición** legitimate child; good child; **hijo de la cuna**

foundling; **hijo del amor** love child; **hijo de leche** foster child || *m* son; **cada hijo de vecino** (coll) every man Jack, every mother's son; **hijo del agua** good sailor; good swimmer; **hijo de su padre** (coll) chip off the old block; **hijo de sus propias obras** self-made man; **hijo político** son-in-law; **hijos** children; descendants || *f* see **hija**

hijodalgo *m* (*pl* **hijosdalgo**) nobleman

hijuela *f* little girl, little daughter; (*tira de tela*) gore; branch drain; side path

hijuelero *m* rural postman

hijuelo *m* shoot, sucker

hila *f* row, line; (*acción de hilar*) spinning; **a la hila** in single file; **hilas** (*hebras para curar heridas*) lint

hilacha *f* shred, fraying; **hilacha de acero** steel wool; **hilacha de algodón** cotton waste; **hilacha de vidrio** spun glass; **hilachas** lint; **mostrar la hilacha** (Arg) to show one's worst side

hilachos *mpl* (Mex) rags, tatters

hilacho•so -sa *adj* frayed, raggedy

hilada *f* row, line; (mas) course

hilado *m* spinning; (*hilo*) yarn, thread

hila•dor -dora *adj* spinning || *mf* spinner || *f* spinning machine

hilandería *f* spinning; spinning mill

hilande•ro -ra *adj* spinning || *m* spinning mill

hilar *tr* & *intr* to spin; **hilar delgado** to hew close to the line; **hilar largo** to drag on

hilarante *adj* laughable; (*gas*) laughing

hilaza *f* yarn, thread; lint; **descubrir la hilaza** (coll) to show one's true nature

hilera *f* row, line; fine thread, fine yarn; (*parhilera*) ridgepole; (mil) file

hilo *m* thread; (*hebras retorcidas*) yarn; (*alambre*) wire; (*de perlas*) string; (*de agua*) thin stream; (*de luz*) beam; linen, linen fabric; (*de un discurso, de la vida*) (fig) thread; **hilo bramante** twine; **hilo de la muerte** end of life; **hilo de masa** (aut) ground wire; **hilo de medianoche** midnight sharp; **hilo dental** dental floss; **hilo de tierra** (elec) ground wire; **irse al hilo** or **tras el hilo de la gente** to follow the crowd; **manejar los hilos** to pull strings; **perder el hilo de** to lose the thread of

hilván *m* basting, tacking; basting stitch; (Chile) basting thread; (Ven) hem; **hablar de hilván** (coll) to jabber along

hilvanar *tr* to baste, to tack; to sketch, outline; (*hacer con precipitación*) (coll) to hurry; (Ven) to hem || *intr* to baste, to tack

himnario *m* hymnal, hymn book

himno *m* hymn; **himno nacional** national anthem

hin *m* neigh, whinny

hincadura *f* driving, thrusting, sticking

hincapié *m* stamping the foot; **hacer hincapié en** (coll) to lay great stress on, to emphasize

hincar **§73** *tr* to drive, thrust, stick, sink; (*la rodilla*) to go down on, to fall on || *ref* to kneel, kneel down; **hincarse de rodillas** to go down on one's knees

hincha *mf* (sport) fan, rooter || *f* (coll) grudge, ill will

hinchable *adj* inflatable; (*goma de mascar*) bubble

hincha•do -da *adj* swollen; swollen with pride; (*estilo, lenguaje*) pompous, high-flown || *m* (*de un neumático*) inflation || *f* (sport) fans, rooters

hinchar *tr* to swell; to inflate; (*un neumático*) to pump up; to exaggerate, embroider || *ref* to swell; to swell up, become puffed up (*with pride*)

hinchazón *f* swelling; vanity, conceit; (*del estilo, lenguaje*) bombast

hinchismo *m* (sport) fans, rooters

hin•dú -dúa (*pl* **-dúes -dúas**) *adj* & *mf* Hindoo, Hindu

hiniesta *f* Spanish broom

hinojo *m* fennel; **de hinojos** on one's knees

hipar *intr* to hiccup; (*los perros cuando siguen la caza*) to pant, to snuffle; (*gimotear*) to wimper; to be worn out; **hipar por** to long for; to long to

hiperacidez *f* hyperacidity

hipérbola *f* (geom) hyperbola

hipérbole *f* (rhet) hyperbole

hiperbóli•co -ca *adj* (geom & rhet) hyperbolic

hipersensible *adj* (*alérgico*) hypersensitive

hipertensión *f* hypertension, high blood pressure

hípi•co -ca *adj* horse, equine

hipnosis *f* hypnosis

hipnóti•co -ca *adj* hypnotic || *mf* hypnotic || *m* (*medicamento que provoca el sueño*) hypnotic

hipnotismo *m* hypnotism

hipnotista *mf* hypnotist

hipnotizar **§60** *tr* to hypnotize

hipo *m* hiccup; longing, desire; **tener hipo contra** to have a grudge against; **tener hipo por** to desire eagerly

hipocondría•co -ca *adj* & *mf* hypochondriac

hipocresía *f* hypocrisy

hipócrita *adj* hypocritical || *mf* hypocrite

hipodérmi•co -ca *adj* hypodermic

hipódromo *m* hippodrome, race track

hipopótamo *m* hippopotamus

hiposulfito *m* hyposulfite

hipoteca *f* mortgage; **¡buena hipoteca!** (coll) you may believe it, if you want to!

hipotecar **§73** *tr* to mortgage

hipoteca•rio -ria *adj* mortgage

hipotenusa *f* hypotenuse

hipóte•sis *f* (*pl* **-sis**) hypothesis

hipotéti•co -ca *adj* hypothetic(al)

hiriente *adj* cutting, stinging

hirsu•to -ta *adj* hairy, bristly; (fig) brusque, gruff

hirviente *adj* boiling

hisopear *tr* to sprinkle with holy water

hisopo *m* (bot) hyssop; aspergillum, sprinkler of holy water; (Am) paint brush, shaving brush

hispalense *adj* & *mf* Sevillian

hispáni•co -ca *adj* Hispanic
hispanista *mf* Hispanist
hispa•no -na *adj* Spanish; Spanish American || *mf* Spaniard; Spanish American
hispanohablante *adj* Spanish-speaking || *mf* speaker of Spanish
híspi•do -da *adj* bristly, spiny
histéri•co -ca *adj* hysteric(al)
histerismo *m* hysteria
histología *f* histology
historia *f* history; story, tale; **de historia** (coll) notorious, infamous; **dejarse de historias** (coll) to come to the point; **historia de lagrimitas** (coll) sob story; **historias** (coll) gossip, meddling; **pasar a la historia** to become a thing of the past; **picar en historia** to turn out to be serious
historia•do -da *adj* richly adorned; overadorned; (*cuadro, dibujo*) storied
historial *adj* historical || *m* record, dossier
historiar §77 & regular *tr* to tell the history of; to tell the story of; (*un suceso histórico*) (fa) to depict
históri•co -ca *adj* historic(al)
historieta *f* anecdote, brief story; **historieta gráfica** comic strip
histrión *m* actor; juggler, buffoon
histrióni•co -ca *adj* histrionic
hita *f* brad; landmark, milestone
hi•to -ta *adj* fixed, firm; (*casa, calle*) next; (*caballo*) black || *m* (*clavo fijado en la tierra*) peg, hob; (*juego*) quoits; (*blanco*) target; (*mojón*) landmark, milestone; **dar en el hito** to hit the nail on the head; **mirar de hito en hito** to eye up and down || *f* see **hita**
Hno. *abbr* **Hermano**
hoba•chón -chona *adj* (coll) lumpish
hocicar §73 *tr* to nuzzle, to root; (coll) to keep on kissing || *intr* to nuzzle, to root; to run into a snag; (*la proa*) (naut) to dip
hocico *m* snout; (*de una persona*) (coll) snout; sour face; **caer de hocicos** (coll) to fall on one's face; **meter el hocico en todo** (coll) to poke one's nose into everything; **poner hocico** (coll) to make a face
hogaño *adv* (coll) this year; (coll) at the present time
hogar *m* fireplace, hearth; furnace; home; family life; (*hoguera*) bonfire
hogare•ño -ña *adj* home-loving || *mf* homebody, stay-at-home
hogaza *f* large loaf of bread
hoguera *f* bonfire
hoja *f* (*de planta, libro, mesa, muelle, puerta plegadiza, etc.; pétalo de flor*) leaf; (*de planta acuática*) pad; (*de papel*) sheet; blank sheet; (*de cuchillo, sierra, espada, etc.*) blade; (*hojuela de metal*) foil; (*de persiana*) slat; (*del patín*) runner; **doblar la hoja** (coll) to change the subject; **hoja clínica** clinical chart; **hoja de afeitar** razor blade; **hoja de embalaje** packing slip; **hoja de encuadernador** (bb) end paper; **hoja de estaño** tin foil; **hoja de estudios** transcript; **hoja de guarda** (bb) flyleaf; **hoja del anunciante** tear sheet; **hoja de lata** tin, tin plate; **hoja de nenúfar** lily pad; **hoja de paga** pay roll; **hoja de parra** fig leaf; **hoja de pedidos** order blank; **hoja de rodaje** (mov) shooting record; **hoja de ruta** waybill; **hoja de servicios** service record; **hoja de trébol** cloverleaf (*intersection*); **hoja maestra** master blade (*of spring*); **hojas del autor** (typ) advance sheets; **hoja suelta** leaflet, handbill; (bb) flyleaf; **hoja volante** leaflet, handbill
hojalata *f* tin, tin plate
hojalatería *f* tinsmith's shop; tinwork
hojalatero *m* tinsmith, tinner
hojaldre *m & f* puff paste
hojarasca *f* dead leaves; trash, rubbish; bluff, vain show
hojear *tr* to leaf through || *intr* to scale off; (*las hojas de los árboles*) to flutter
hojita *f* leaflet; **hojita de afeitar** razor blade
hojo•so -sa *adj* leafy
hojuela *f* (*hoja de otra compuesta*) leaflet; (*fruta de sartén*) pancake; (*hoja muy delgada de metal*) foil; **hojuela de estaño** tin foil
hola *interj* hey!, hello!
Holanda *f* Holland
holan•dés -desa *adj* Dutch; **a la holandesa** (*bb*) half-bound || *mf* Hollander || *m* Dutchman; (*idioma*) Dutch || *f* Dutch woman
holga•chón -chona *adj* (coll) lazy, idle || *mf* (coll) loafer, idler
holgadero *m* hangout
holga•do -da *adj* idle, unoccupied; (*vestido*) loose, full, roomy; (*que vive con bienestar*) fairly well-off
holganza *f* idleness, leisure; pleasure, enjoyment
holgar §63 *intr* to idle, be idle; to take it easy, to rest up; to not fit, be too loose; to be unnecessary, be of no use; to be glad || *ref* to be glad; to be amused
holga•zán -zana *adj* idle, lazy || *mf* idler, loafer
holgazanear *intr* to idle, loaf, bum around
hol•gón -gona *adj* pleasure-loving || *mf* loafer, lizard
holgorio *m* (coll) fun, merriment
holgura *f* looseness, fulness; enjoyment, merriment; comfort, easy circumstances; (mach) play
holocausto *m* holocaust
hollar §61 *tr* to tread on, to trample on
hollejo *m* hull, peel, skin
hollín *m* soot
hollinar *tr* (Chile) to cover with soot
hollinien•to -ta *adj* sooty
hombracho *m* big husky fellow
hombrada *f* manly act
hombradía *f* manliness, courage
hombre *m* man; (coll) husband, man; (coll) my boy, old chap; **buen hombre** good-natured fellow; **¡hombre al agua!** or **¡hombre a la mar!** man overboard!; **hombre bueno** arbiter,

referee; **hombre de bien** honorable man; **hombre de buenas prendas** man of parts; **hombre de dinero** man of means; **hombre de estado** statesman; **hombre de letras** man of letters; **hombre de mundo** man of the world; **hombre de suposición** man of straw; **hombre hecho** grown man || *interj* man alive!, upon my word!

hombre-anuncio *m* sandwich man

hombrear *tr* (Arg) to carry on the shoulders; (Mex) to aid, back || *intr* to try to be somebody; (*una mujer*) to be mannish; **hombrear con** to try to equal

hombrecillo *m* little man; (*lúpulo*) hop

hombrera *f* (*del vestido*) shoulder; shoulder pad; epaulet

hombre-rana *m* (*pl* **hombres-ranas**) frogman

hombría *f* manliness; **hombría de bien** honor, probity

hombrillo *m* (*de la camisa*) yoke; shoulder piece

hombro *m* shoulder; **arrimar el hombro** to lend a hand, put one's shoulder to the wheel; **encoger los hombros** to let one's shoulders droop; **encogerse de hombros** to shrug one's shoulders; to crouch, to shrink with fear; to not answer; **mirar por encima del hombro** to look down upon; **salir en hombros** to be carried off on the shoulders of the crowd

hombru•no -na *adj* (coll) mannish

homenaje *m* homage; (feud) homage; (Chile) gift, favor; **homenaje de boca** lip service; **rendir homenaje a** to swear allegiance to

homeópata *mf* homeopath

homeopatía *f* homeopathy

homicida *adj* homicidal || *mf* homicide

homicidio *m* homicide

homilía *f* homily

homogeneidad *f* homogeniety

homogeneizar §60 *tr* to homogenize

homogéne•o -a *adj* homogeneous

homologación *f* confirmation, ratification; (sport) validation

homologar §44 *tr* to confirm, ratify; (*un récord*) (sport) to validate

homóni•mo -ma *adj* homonymous; of the same name || *mf* namesake || *m* homonym

homosexual *adj & mf* homosexual

homúnculo *m* (coll) guy, little runt

honda *f* sling

hondazo *m* blow with a sling

hondear *tr* (naut) to sound

hondillos *mpl* patches in the crotch of pants

hon•do -da *adj* deep; (*terreno*) low || *m* bottom || *f* see **honda** || **hondo** *adv* deep

hondón *m* (*de la aguja*) eye; (*de un vaso*) bottom; lowland

hondonada *f* lowland, ravine

hondura *f* depth, profundity; **meterse en honduras** (coll) to go beyond one's depth

hondure•ño -ña *adj & mf* Honduran

honestidad *f* decency; chastity; modesty; honesty, probity; fairness, reasonableness

hones•to -ta *adj* decent; chaste, pure; modest; honest, upright; (*precio*) fair, reasonable

hongo *m* fungus, mushroom; (*sombrero*) bowler, derby

honor *m* honor; **en honor a la verdad** as a matter of fact, to tell the truth; **hacer honor a** to do honor to; (*la firma*) to honor

honorable *adj* honorable

honora•rio -ria *adj* honorary || *s* fee, honorarium

honorífi•co -ca *adj* honorific

honra *f* honor; **tener a mucha honra** to be proud of

honradez *f* honesty, integrity

honra•do -da *adj* honorable

honrar *tr* to honor || *ref* to feel honored

honrilla *f* — **por la negra honrilla** out of concern for what people will say

honro•so -sa *adj* honorable

hopo *m* tuft, shock (*of hair*); bushy tail; **seguir el hopo a** (coll) to keep right after

hora *f* hour; (*momento determinado para algo*) time; **a la hora** on time; **a la hora de ahora** right now; **a la hora en punto** on the hour; **a las pocas horas** within a few hours; **dar hora** to fix a time; **dar la hora** (*el reloj*) to strike; **de última hora** up-to-date; most up-to-date; (*noticias*) late; **en buen hora** or **en hora buena** safely, luckily; all right; **en mal hora** or **en hora mala** unluckily, in an evil hour; **fuera de horas** after hours; **hasta altas horas** until late into the night; **hora de acostarse** bedtime; **hora de aglomeración** rush hour; **hora de comer** mealtime; **hora deshorada** fatal hour; **hora de verano** daylight-saving time; **hora de verdad** (taur) kill; **hora legal** or **oficial** standard time; **hora punta** peak hour; rush hour; **horas de consulta** office hours (*of a doctor*); **horas de ocio** leisure hours; **horas de punta** rush hour; **horas extraordinarias de trabajo** overtime

horadar *tr* to drill, bore, pierce

hora•rio -ria *adj* hour || *m* hour hand; clock; (*de ferrocarriles*) timetable; **horario escolar** roster

horca *f* (*para levantar la paja*) pitchfork; (*para ahorcar a un condenado*) gallows, gibbet; (*de ajos, cebollas, etc.*) string

horcajadas — **a horcajadas** astride, astraddle

horcajadillas — **a horcajadillas** astride, astraddle

horcajadura *f* crotch

horcajo *m* (*confluencia de dos ríos*) fork; (*para mulas*) yoke

horcón *m* pitchfork; forked prop (*for fruit trees*); (Am) upright, prop

horchata *f* orgeat

horda *f* horde

horizontal *adj & f* horizontal

horizonte *m* horizon

horma *f* form, mold; shoe tree; hat block; **hallar la horma de su zapato** (coll) to meet one's match
hormiga *f* ant; (*enfermedad que causa comezón*) itch
hormigón *m* concrete; **hormigón armado** reinforced concrete
hormigonera *f* concrete mixer
hormigo·so -sa *adj* ant; full of ants; ant-eaten; (*picante*) itchy
hormiguear *intr* (*ponerse en movimiento gente o animales*) to swarm; (*experimentar una sensación de hormigas corriendo por el cuerpo*) to crawl, to creep; to abound, to teem
hormiguero *m* anthill; (*de gente*) swarm, mob
hormillón *m* hat block
hormón *m* or **hormona** *f* hormone
hornacina *f* niche
hornada *f* (*cantidad que se cuece de una vez en un horno*) batch, bake; (*conjunto de individuos de una misma promoción*) crop
hornazo *m* Easter cake filled with hard-boiled eggs; Easter gift to Lenten preacher
horne·ro -ra *mf* baker
hornilla *f* kitchen grate; pigeonhole
hornillo *m* kitchen stove; hot plate; (*de la pipa de fumar*) bowl
horno *m* oven, furnace; (*para cocer ladrillos*) kiln; **alto horno** blast furnace; **horno de cal** limekiln; **horno de fundición** smelting furnace; **horno de ladrillero** brickkiln
horóscopo *m* horoscope; **sacar un horóscopo** to cast a horoscope
horqueta *f* pitchfork; fork, prop; (*ángulo agudo en un río*) (Arg) bend
horquilla *f* pitchfork; (*de bicicleta*) fork; (*de microteléfono*) cradle; (*alfiler para sujetar el pelo*) hairpin
hórreo *m* granary; (in Asturias and Galicia) crib or granary raised on pillars (*to protect grain from mice and dampness*)
horrible *adj* horrible
horripilante *adj* hair-raising, blood-curdling
horror *m* horror; **tener horror a** to have a horror of
horrorizar **§60** *tr* to horrify
horroro·so -sa *adj* horrid; (coll) hideous, ugly
hortaliza *f* vegetable
hortela·no -na *adj* garden ‖ *mf* gardener
hortera *m* (coll) clerk, helper ‖ *f* wooden bowl
hortícola *adj* horticultural
horticul·tor -tora *mf* horticulturist
horticultura *f* horticulture
hos·co -ca *adj* dark, dark-skinned; sullen, grim, gloomy
hospedaje *m* lodging
hospedar *tr* to lodge ‖ *ref* to lodge, stop, put up
hospedería *f* hospice; inn, hostelry
hospede·ro -ra *mf* innkeeper
hospicio *m* hospice; poorhouse; orphan asylum
hospital *m* hospital; **estar hecho un hospital** (*una persona*) (coll) to be full of aches and pains; (*una casa*) (coll) to be turned into a hospital; **hospital de la sangre** poor relations; **hospital de primera sangre** (mil) field hospital; **hospital robado** (coll) bare house
hospitala·rio -ria *adj* hospitable
hospitalidad *f* hospitality; (*estancia del enfermo en el hospital*) hospitalization
hospitalizar **§60** *tr* to hospitalize
hosquedad *f* darkness; sullenness, grimness, gloominess
hostería *f* inn, hostelry
hostia *f* sacrificial victim; wafer; (eccl) wafer, Host
hostigar **§44** *tr* to scourge; to harass; to pester; (Am) to cloy, surfeit
hostigo·so -sa *adj* (Am) cloying, sickening
hostil *adj* hostile
hostilidad *f* hostility
hostilizar **§60** *tr* to antagonize; (*al enemigo*) to harry, harass
hotel *m* (*establecimiento donde se da comida y alojamiento por dinero*) hotel; (*casa particular lujosa*) mansion
hotele·ro -ra *adj* hotel ‖ *mf* hotelkeeper
hoy *adv & s* today; **de hoy a mañana** any time now; **de hoy en adelante** from now on; **hoy día** nowadays
hoya *f* hole, pit, ditch; (*sepultura*) grave; valley; (*almáciga*) seedbed; (Am) river basin
hoyanca *f* potter's field
hoyo *m* hole; grave; pockmark
hoyo·so -sa *adj* full of holes
hoyuelo *m* dimple; (*juego de muchachos*) pitching pennies
hoz *f* (*pl* **hoces**) sickle; narrow pass, defile; **de hoz y de coz** (coll) headlong, recklessly
hozar **§60** *tr & intr* to nuzzle, to root
hta. *abbr* **hasta**
huacal *m* var of **guacal**
huachinango *m* (Mex) red snapper
hucha *f* workingman's chest; (*alcancía*) toy bank; (*dinero ahorrado*) savings, nest egg
huchear *intr* to cry, shout
hue·co -ca *adj* hollow; (*mullido*) soft, fluffy, spongy; (*voz*) deep, resounding; vain, conceited; (*estilo, lenguaje*) affected, pompous ‖ *m* hollow; interval; (*en un muro, una hilera de coches, etc.*) opening; (*empleo sin proveer*) (coll) opening; **hueco de la axila** armpit; **hueco de escalera** stair well
huélfago *m* (vet) heaves
huelga *f* (*ocio*) rest, leisure, idleness; recreation; pleasant spot; (*cesación del trabajo en señal de protesta*) strike; (mach) play; **huelga de brazos caídos** sit-down strike; **huelga de hambre** hunger strike; **huelga patronal** lockout; **huelga sentada** sit-down strike; **ir a la huelga** or **ponerse en huelga** to go on strike
huelguista *mf* striker
huella *f* track, footprint; trace, mark; rut; (*acción de hollar*) tread, tread-

ing; (*peldaño en que se asienta el pie*) tread; **huella dactilar** or **digital** fingerprint; **huella de sonido** sound track; **seguir las huellas de** to follow in the footsteps of

huérfa·no -na *adj* orphan; orphaned; alone, deserted || *mf* orphan; (Chile, Peru) foundling

hue·ro -ra *adj* rotten; (fig) empty, hollow; (Guat, Mex) blond; **salir huero** (coll) to flop, to turn out bad || *mf* (Guat, Mex) blond

huerta *f* vegetable garden; fruit garden; irrigated region

huerte·ro -ra *mf* (Arg, Peru) gardener

huerto *m* (*de árboles frutales*) orchard; (*de verduras*) kitchen garden

huesa *f* grave

huesillo *m* (Chile, Peru) sun-dried peach

hueso *m* bone; (*de ciertas frutas*) stone, pit; drudgery; **a otro perro con ese hueso** (coll) tell that to the marines; **calarse hasta los huesos** to get soaked to the skin; **hueso de la alegría** crazy bone, funny bone; **hueso de la suerte** wishbone; **hueso duro de roer** (coll) a hard nut to crack; **la sin hueso** (coll) the tongue; **no dejarle a uno un hueso sano** (coll) to beat someone up; (coll) to pick someone to pieces; **no poder con sus huesos** (coll) to be all in; **soltar la sin hueso** (coll) to talk too much; (coll) to pour forth insults; **tener los huesos molidos** (coll) to be all fagged out

hueso·so -sa *adj* bony

hués·ped -peda *mf* (*persona alojada en casa ajena*) guest; (*persona que hospeda a otra en su casa*) host; (*mesonero*) innkeeper, host

hueste *f* followers; (*ejército*) army, host

huesu·do -da *adj* bony, big-boned

hueva *f* roe, fish roe

hueve·ro -ra *mf* egg dealer || *f* eggcup; oviduct

huevo *m* egg; **huevo a la plancha** fried egg; **huevo al plato** shirred egg; **huevo del té** tea ball; **huevo de zurcir** darning egg or gourd; **huevo duro** hard-boiled egg; **huevo escalfado** poached egg; **huevo estrellado** or **frito** fried egg; **huevo pasado por agua** soft-boiled egg; **huevos revueltos** scrambled eggs

huída *f* flight; (*de un líquido*) leak; (*ensanche en un agujero*) flare, splay; (*de caballo*) shying

huidi·zo -za *adj* fugitive; evasive

huincha *f* (SAm) tape; (SAm) tape measure

huipil *m* (Mex) colorful poncho worn by Indian women

huir §20 *tr* to flee, avoid, shun; (*el cuerpo*) to duck || *intr* to flee; (*el tiempo*) to fly; (*de la memoria*) to slip || *ref* to flee

hule *m* (*tela impermeable*) oilcloth; rubber; (taur) blood, goring

hulear *intr* (CAm) to gather rubber

hulla *f* coal; **hulla azul** tide power; wind power; **hulla blanca** white power, water power

hullera *f* colliery, coal mine

humanidad *f* humanity; (coll) fatness

humanista *adj & mf* humanist

humanita·rio -ria *adj & mf* humanitarian

huma·no -na *adj* (*perteneciente al hombre*) human; (*compasivo, misericordioso; civilizador*) humane

humareda *f* cloud of smoke

humeante *adj* smoking, smoky; steamy, reeking

humear *tr* (SAm) to fumigate || *intr* to smoke; to steam, to reek; to put on airs; (*reliquias de un alboroto, enemistad, etc.*) to last, persist

humectador *m* humidifier

humedad *f* humidity, dampness, moisture

humedecer §22 *tr* to humidify, dampen, moisten, wet

húme·do -da *adj* humid, damp, moist

humero *m* smokestack, chimney

húmero *m* humerus

humildad *f* humility

humilde *adj* humble

humilladero *m* calvary, road shrine; prie-dieu

humillante *adj* humiliating

humillar *tr* (*abatir el orgullo de*) to humble; (*avergonzar*) to humiliate; (*la cabeza*) to bow; (*el cuerpo, las rodillas*) to bend || *ref* to humble oneself; to cringe, grovel

humo *m* smoke; steam, fume; **a humo de pajas** (coll) lightly, thoughtlessly; **bajar los humos a** (coll) to humble, take down a peg; **echar más humo que una chimenea** to smoke like a chimney; **humos** airs, conceit; hearths, homes; **irse todo en humo** to go up in smoke; **tragar el humo** to inhale; **vender humos** to peddle influence

humor *m* humor; **de mal humor** out of humor; **estar de humor para** to be in the humor for; **seguir el humor a** to humor

humorismo *m* humor, humorousness

humorista *mf* humorist

humorísti·co -ca *adj* humorous

humo·so -sa *adj* smoky

hundible *adj* sinkable

hundir *tr* to sink; to plunge; (*abrumar*) to overwhelm; to confound, confute; to destroy, ruin || *ref* to sink; to collapse; to settle, cave in; to come to ruin; (coll) to disappear, vanish

húnga·ro -ra *adj & mf* Hungarian || *m* (*idioma*) Hungarian

Hungría *f* Hungary

hupe *m* punk

huracán *m* hurricane

hurañía *f* shyness, unsociability

hura·ño -ña *adj* shy, unsociable

hurgar §44 *tr* to poke; (fig) to stir up, incite; **peor es hurgallo** (i.e., **hurgarlo**) better keep hands off || *intr* to poke || *ref* (*la nariz*) to pick

hurgón *m* poker; (coll) thrust, stab

hurgonazo *m* (*con hurgón*) poke; (coll) jab, stab, thrust

hurgonear *tr* to poke; (coll) to jab, to stab at
hurgonero *m* poker
hu•rón -rona *adj* (coll) shy, diffident || *mf* (coll) prier, snooper; (coll) shy person, diffident person || *m* ferret
huronear *tr* to ferret, hunt with a ferret; (coll) to ferret out
huronera *f* ferret hole; (coll) lair, hiding place
hurtadillas — a hurtadillas by stealth, on the sly; **a hurtadillas de** unbeknown to
hurtar *tr* to steal; (*en pesos y medidas*) to cheat; (*el suelo*) to wear away; to plagiarize; **hurtar el cuerpo** to dodge, to duck || *ref* to withdraw, to hide
hurto *m* thieving; theft; **a hurto** stealthily, on the sly; **coger con el hurto en las manos** to catch with the goods
husma *f* snooping; **andar a la husma** to go around snooping
husmear *tr* to scent, to smell out; (coll) to pry into || *intr* (*la carne*) to smell bad, to become gamy
husmo *m* gaminess, high odor; **estar al husmo** (coll) to wait for a chance
huso *m* (*para hilar*) spindle; (*para devanar*) bobbin; (*cilindro del torno*) drum; **huso horario** time zone; **ser más derecho que un huso** (coll) to be as straight as a ramrod
huta *f* hunter's blind
huy *interj* ouch!
huyente *adj* (*frente*) receding; (*ojeada*) shifty

I

I, i (i) *f* tenth letter of the Spanish alphabet
ib. *abbr* **ibídem**
ibéri•co -ca *adj* Iberian
ibe•ro -ra *adj & mf* Iberian
íbice *m* ibex
ice•berg *m* (*pl* **-bergs**) iceberg
iconoclasia *f* or **iconoclasmo** *m* iconoclasm
iconoclasta *mf* iconoclast
iconoscopio *m* (telv) iconoscope
ictericia *f* jaundice
ictericia•do -da *adj* jaundiced
ictiología *f* ichthyology
ida *f* going; departure; rashness; sally; trail; **de ida y vuelta** round-trip; **idas y venidas** comings and goings
idea *f* idea; **mudar de idea** to change one's mind
ideal *adj & m* ideal
idealista *adj & mf* idealist
idealizar §60 *tr* to idealize
idear *tr* to think up, to devise
idemista *adj* yes-saying || *mf* yes sayer
idénti•co -ca *adj* identic(al); (*muy parecido*) very similar
identidad *f* identity, sameness
identificación *f* identification
identificar §73 *tr* to identify
ideología *f* ideology
idíli•co -ca *adj* idyllic
idilio *m* idyll
idioma *m* language; (*modo particular de hablar*) idiom, speech
idiomáti•co -ca *adj* idiomatic; language, linguistic
idiosincrasia *f* idiosyncrasy
idiota *adj* idiotic || *mf* idiot
idiotez *f* idiocy
idiotismo *m* ignorance; (*idiotez*) idiocy; (gram) idiom
i•do -da *adj* wild, scatterbrained; (Am) drunk || **los idos** the dead || *f* see **ida**
idolatrar *tr* to idolize
idolatría *f* idolotry; (*amor excesivo a una persona*) idolization
ídolo *m* idol
idoneidad *f* fitness, suitability
idóne•o -a fit, suitable
idus *mpl* ides
iglesia *f* church; **entrar en la iglesia** to go into the church; **llevar a la iglesia** to lead to the altar
iglesie•ro -ra *adj* (Arg) church-going || *mf* (Arg) church goer
igna•ro -ra *adj* ignorant
ignominio•so -sa *adj* ignominious
ignorancia *f* ignorance
ignorante *adj* ignorant || *mf* ignoramus
ignorar *tr* to not know, be ignorant of
igno•to -ta *adj* unknown
igual *adj* equal; (*liso, llano*) smooth, even, level; (*no variable*) firm, constant, equable; indifferent; **me es igual** it makes no difference to me || *m* equal; equal sign; **al igual de** like, after the fashion of; **al igual que** as; while, whereas; **en igual de** instead of
iguala *f* equalization; agreement
igualización *f* equalization; agreement
igualar *tr* to equal; (*alisar, allanar*) to smooth, to even, to level; to make equal, to match; to deem equal || *intr & ref* to be equal
igualdad *f* equality; smoothness, evenness; **igualdad de ánimo** equanimity
igualmente *adv* likewise; **igualmente que** the same as
ijada *f* (*de animal*) flank; (*del cuerpo humano*) loin; (*dolor en estas partes*) stitch; **tener su ijada** to have its weak side or point
ijadear *intr* to pant
ijar *m* flank; loin
ilegal *adj* illegal
ilegible *adj* illegible
ilegíti•mo -ma *adj* illegitimate
ile•so -sa *adj* unscathed, unharmed
iletra•do -da *adj* unlettered, uncultured
ilíci•to -ta *adj* illicit, unlawful
ilimita•do -da *adj* limitless
ilitera•to -ta *adj* illiterate
ilógi•co -ca *adj* illogical
iludir *tr* to elude, evade

iluminación *f* illumination
iluminar *tr* to illuminate, light, light up || *ref* to light up, brighten
ilusión *f* illusion; (*esperanza infundada*) delusion; enthusiasm, zeal; dream; **forjarse** or **hacerse ilusiones** to kid oneself, to indulge in wishful thinking
ilusionar *tr* to delude || *ref* to have illusions, to indulge in wishful thinking; to be enraptured, be beguiled
ilusionista *mf* prestidigitator, magician
ilusi•vo -va *adj* illusive
ilu•so -sa *adj* deluded, misguided; (*propenso a ilusionarse*) visionary
iluso•rio -ria *adj* illusory
ilustración *f* illustration; enlightenment; illustrated magazine
ilustra•do -da *adj* illustrated; learned, informed; enlightened
ilustrar *tr* (*adornar con grabados alusivos al texto*) to illustrate; to make illustrious, make famous; to explain, elucidate; to enlighten || *ref* to become famous; to be enlightened
ilustre *adj* illustrious
imagen *f* image; picture
imaginación *f* imagination
imaginar *tr, intr & ref* to imagine
imagina•rio -ria *adj* imaginary
imaginati•vo -va *adj* imaginative || *f* imagination; understanding
imaginería *f* fancy colored embroidery; carving or painting of religious images
imán *m* magnet; (fig) loadstone; **imán de herradura** horseshoe magnet; **imán inductor** (elec) field magnet
imanar or **imantar** *tr* to magnetize
imbatible *adj* unbeatable
imbécil *adj & mf* imbecile
imbecilidad *f* imbecility
imberbe *adj* beardless
imbornal *m* drain hole
imborrable *adj* indelible; ineffaceable; unforgettable
imbuir §20 *tr* to imbue
imitación *adj invar* imitation || *f* imitation; **a imitación de** in imitation of; **de imitación** imitation, fake
imita•do -da *adj* imitated; mock, sham; imitation
imitar *tr* to imitate
impaciencia *f* impatience
impacientar *tr* to make impatient || *ref* to get impatient
impaciente *adj* impatient
impacto *m* impact, hit; (*señal que deja el proyectil*) mark; **impacto directo** direct hit
impar *adj* odd, uneven; (*que no tiene igual*) unmatched || *m* odd number
imparcial *adj* impartial; (*que no entra en ningún partido*) nonpartisan
impartir *tr* to distribute, impart
impás *m* finesse
impasible *adj* impassible, impassive
impávi•do -da *adj* dauntless, fearless, intrepid
impecable *adj* impeccable
impedancia *f* impedance
impedi•do -da *adj* disabled, crippled, paralytic
impedimento *m* impediment, obstacle, hindrance
impedir §50 *tr* to hinder, prevent
impeler *tr* to impel; to spur, incite
impenetrable *adj* impenetrable
impenitente *adj & mf* impenitent
impensable *adj* unthinkable
impensa•do -da *adj* unexpected
imperar *intr* to rule, reign, command
imperati•vo -va *adj & m* imperative
imperceptible *adj* imperceptible
imperdible *m* safety pin
imperdonable *adj* unpardonable, unforgivable
imperecede•ro -ra *adj* imperishable, undying
imperfección *f* imperfection
imperfec•to -ta *adj & m* imperfect
imperial *adj* imperial || *f* imperial, roof (*of a coach or bus*)
imperialista *adj & mf* imperialist
impericia *f* unskillfulness, inexpertness
imperio *m* empire; dominion, sway
imperio•so -sa *adj* (*que manda con imperio*) imperious; (*indispensable*) imperative
imperi•to -ta *adj* unskilled, inexpert
impermeable *adj* impermeable; waterproof || *m* raincoat
impersonal *adj* impersonal
impertérri•to -ta *adj* dauntless, intrepid
impertinencia *f* impertinence; irrelevance; fussiness
impertinente *adj* impertinent; (*que no viene al caso*) irrelevant; (*nimiamente susceptible*) fussy || **impertinentes** *mpl* lorgnette
impetrar *tr* to beg, beg for; to obtain by entreaty
ímpetu *m* impetus; force; haste
impetuo•so -sa *adj* impetuous
impiedad *f* (*falta de religión*) impiety; (*falta de compasión*) pitilessness
impí•o -a *adj* (*irreligioso*) impious; (*falto de compasión*) pitiless
impla *f* wimple
implacable *adj* relentless
implantar *tr* to implant; to introduce
implicar §73 *tr* (*envolver*) to implicate; (*incluir en esencia*) to imply || *intr* to stand in the way
implíci•to -ta *adj* implicit, implied
implorar *tr* to implore
implume *adj* featherless
imponente *adj* imposing || *mf* depositor, investor
imponer §54 *tr* (*la voluntad de uno, silencio, tributos*) to impose; (*dinero a rédito*) to invest; (*dinero en depósito*) to deposit; to instruct; to impute falsely || *intr* to dominate, command respect || *ref* (*responsabilidades*) to assume; to command attention, command respect; **imponerse a** to dominate, command the respect of; **imponerse de** to learn, to find out
imponible *adj* taxable
impopular *adj* unpopular
impopularidad *f* unpopularity
importación *f* importation; import; imports
importa•dor -dora *mf* importer
importancia *f* importance; (*extensión,*

tamaño) size; **ser de la importancia de** to be the concern of
importante *adj* important; large
importar *tr* (*introducir en un país*) to import; to amount to; to involve, imply; to concern || *intr* to import; to be important; to matter
importe *m* amount
importunar *tr* to importune
importu·no -na *adj* (*molesto*) importunate; (*fuera de sazón*) inopportune
imposibilita·do -da *adj* paralyzed, disabled
imposibilitar *tr* to make impossible || *ref* to become paralyzed, become disabled
imposible *adj* impossible
imposición *f* (*de la voluntad de uno*) imposition; burden; imposture; (*de dinero*) deposit; (typ) make-up
impos·tor -tora *mf* impostor; slanderer
impostura *f* imposture
impotable *adj* undrinkable
impotencia *f* impotence
impotente *adj* impotent
impracticable *adj* impracticable, impassable; impractical
impregnar *tr* to impregnate, to saturate
impremedita·do -da *adj* unpremeditated
imprenta *f* printing; printing shop; (*lo que se publica impreso*) printed matter; (*máquina para imprimir o prensar; conjunto de periódicos o periodistas*) press
imprentar *tr* (*la ropa*) (Chile) to press, to iron; (Ecuad) to mark
imprescindible *adj* indispensable, essential
impresentable *adj* unpresentable
impresión *f* (*efecto producido en el ánimo; señal que una cosa deja en otra por presión*) impression; (*acción de imprimir*) printing; (*los ejemplares de una edición*) edition, issue; (phot) print; **impresión dactilar** or **digital** fingerprint
impresionable *adj* impressionable
impresionante *adj* impressive
impresionar *tr* to impress; (*un disco fonográfico*) to record; (phot) to expose || *intr* to make an impression || *ref* to be impressed
impreso *m* printed paper or book; **impresos** printed matter
impre·sor -sora *mf* printer
imprevisible *adj* unforeseeable
imprevisión *f* improvidence, lack of foresight
imprevi·sor -sora *adj* improvident
imprevis·to -ta *adj* unforeseen, unexpected || **imprevistos** *mpl* emergencies, unforeseen expenses
imprimar *tr* to prime
imprimir *tr* (*respeto, miedo; movimiento*) to impart || §83 *tr* to stamp, imprint, impress; (*un disco fonográfico*) to press; (typ) to print
improbable *adj* improbable
improbar §61 *tr* to disapprove
improbidad *f* dishonesty; hardness, arduousness
ímpro·bo -ba *adj* dishonest; (*trabajo*) arduous
improcedente *adj* wrong; unfit, untimely
improducti·vo -va *adj* unproductive; unemployed
impronunciable *adj* unpronounceable
improperar *tr* to insult, revile
improperio *m* insult, affront
impropi·cio -cia *adj* unpropitious
impro·pio -pia *adj* improper; (*ajeno*) foreign
impróspe·ro -ra *adj* unsuccessful
impróvi·do -da *adj* unprepared
improvisación *f* improvisation; meteoric rise; (mus) impromptu
improvisadamente *adv* suddenly, unexpectedly; extempore
improvisar *tr & intr* to improvise
improvi·so -sa *adj* unforeseen, unexpected
imprudencia *f* imprudence; **imprudencia temeraria** criminal negligence
imprudente *adj* imprudent
impudicia *f* immodesty
impúdi·co -ca *adj* immodest
impues·to -ta *adj* informed || *m* tax; **impuesto sobre la renta** income tax
impugnar *tr* to impugn, to contest
impulsar *tr* to impel; to drive
impulsión *f* impulse, drive
impulsi·vo -va *adj* impulsive
impulso *m* impulse
impune *adj* unpunished
impunidad *f* impunity
impureza *f* impurity
impu·ro -ra *adj* impure
imputar *tr* to impute; to credit on account
inabordable *adj* unapproachable
inacabable *adj* endless, interminable
inaccesible *adj* inaccessible
inacción *f* inaction
inacentua·do -da *adj* unaccented
inactividad *f* inactivity
inacti·vo -va *adj* inactive
inadecua·do -da *adj* inadequate; unsuited
inadvertencia *f* inadvertence, oversight
inadverti·do -da *adj* inadvertent, unwitting; careless, thoughtless; unseen, unnoticed
inagotable *adj* inexhaustible
inaguantable *adj* unbearable
inalámbri·co -ca *adj* wireless
inalcanzable *adj* unattainable
inamisto·so -sa *adj* unfriendly
inamovible *adj* irremovable; undetachable; (*incorporado*) built-in
inamovilidad *f* irremovability; tenure, permanent tenure
inane *adj* inane
inanición *f* starvation
inanima·do -da *adj* inanimate, lifeless
inapelable *adj* unappealable; unavoidable
inapetencia *f* loss of appetite
inapreciable *adj* inappreciable; imperceptible
inarmóni·co -ca *adj* unharmonious
inarrugable *adj* wrinkle-free
inarticula·do -da *adj* inarticulate
inartísti·co -ca *adj* inartistic
inasequible *adj* unattainable; unobtainable

inastillable *adj* nonshatterable, shatterproof
inatacable *adj* unattackable; **inatacable por** resistant to
inaudi•to -ta *adj* unheard-of; outrageous
inauguración *f* inauguration; (*de una estatua*) unveiling
inaugural *adj* inaugural
inaugurar *tr* to inaugurate; (*p.ej., una estatua*) to unveil
inaveriguable *adj* unascertainable
inca *mf* Inca
incai•co -ca *adj* Inca, Incan
incalificable *adj* unqualifiable; (*infame, atroz*) unspeakable
incambiable *adj* unchangeable
incandescent *adj* incandescent
incansable *adj* untiring, indefatigable
incapacitar *tr* to incapacitate; (law) to declare incompetent
inca•paz *adj* (*pl* **-paces**) incapable, unable; not large enough; stupid; (law) incompetent; (coll) frightful, unbearable
incasable *adj* unmarriageable; opposed to marriage; (*por su fealdad*) unable to find a husband
incautar *ref* — **incautarse de** to hold until claimed; (law) to seize, to attach
incau•to -ta *adj* unwary, heedless
incendajas *fpl* kindling
incendiar *tr* to set on fire || *ref* to catch fire
incendia•rio -ria *adj* incendiary || *mf* incendiary, firebug
incendio *m* fire; (fig) fire, passion
incensar §2 *tr* to incense, to burn incense before; (fig) to flatter
incensario *m* censer, incense burner
incenti•vo -va *adj & m* incentive
inceremonio•so -sa *adj* unceremonious
incertidumbre *f* uncertainty, incertitude
incesante *adj* unceasing
incesto *m* incest
incestuo•so -sa *adj* incestuous
incidencia *f* incidence; **por incidencia** by chance
incidente *adj* incident; incidental || *m* incident
incidir *tr* to make an incision in || *intr* — **incidir en culpa** to fall into guilt; **incidir en** or **sobre** to strike, to impinge on
incienso *m* incense; (*olíbano*) frankincense
incier•to -ta *adj* uncertain
incineración *f* incineration; (*de cadáveres*) cremation
incinerar *tr* to incinerate; (*cadáveres*) to cremate
incipiente *adj* incipient
incisión *f* incision; (*mordacidad en el lenguaje*) incisiveness, sarcasm
incisi•vo -va *adj* incisive; biting, sarcastic
inci•so -sa *adj* (*estilo del escritor*) choppy || *m* comma; clause; sentence
incitar *tr* to incite
incivil *adj* rude, impolite
inciviliza•do -da *adj* uncivilized
inclemencia *f* inclemency; **a la inclemencia** in the open, without shelter
inclemente *adj* inclement
inclinación *f* inclination; bent, leaning, propensity; nod, bow
inclinar *tr, intr & ref* to incline; to bend, to bow
ínclito -ta *adj* illustrious, renowned
incluir §20 *tr* to include; (*en una carta*) to inclose
inclusa *f* foundling home
incluse•ro -ra *mf* (coll) foundling
inclusión *f* inclusion; friendship
inclusive *adv* inclusive, inclusively || *prep* including
inclusi•vo -va *adj* inclusive
inclu•so -sa *adj* inclosed || *f* see **inclusa** || **incluso** *adv* inclusively; (*hasta, aun*) even || **incluso** *prep* including
incobrable *adj* uncollectible; irrecoverable
incógni•to -ta *adj* (*no conocido*) unknown; (*que no se da a conocer*) incognito || *mf* (*persona*) incognito || *m* (*condición de no ser conocido*) incognito; **de incógnito** (*sin ser conocido*) incognito || *f* (math & fig) unknown quantity
incoherente *adj* incoherent
íncola *m* inhabitant
incolo•ro -ra *adj* colorless
incólume *adj* unharmed, safe
incombustible *adj* incombustible, fireproof; cold, indifferent
incomerciable *adj* unmarketable
incomible *adj* uneatable, inedible
incomodar *tr* to inconvenience, to disturb
incomodidad *f* inconvenience; annoyance, discomfort
incómo•do -da *adj* inconvenient; annoying, uncomfortable || *m* inconvenience; discomfort
incomparable *adj* incomparable
incompartible *adj* unsharable
incompasi•vo -va *adj* pitiless, unsympathetic
incompatible *adj* incompatible; (*acontecimientos, citas, horas de clase, etc.*) conflicting
incompetente *adj* incompetent
incompetible *adj* unmatchable
incomple•to -ta *adj* incomplete
incomponible *adj* unmendable, beyond repair
incomprable *adj* unpurchasable
incomprensible *adj* incomprehensible
incomunicación *f* isolation, solitary confinement
inconcebible *adj* inconceivable
inconclu•so -sa *adj* unfinished
inconcluyente *adj* inconclusive
inconcu•so -sa *adj* undeniable
incondicional *adj* unconditional
incone•xo -xa *adj* unconnected; (*inaplicable*) irrelevant
inconfidente *adj* distrustful
inconfundible *adj* unmistakable
incon•gruo -grua *adj* incongruous
inconocible *adj* unknowable
inconquistable *adj* unconquerable; (*que no se deja vencer con ruegos y dádivas*) unbending, unyielding
inconsciencia *f* unconsciousness; unawareness

inconsciente *adj* unconscious; unaware; **lo inconsciente** the unconscious
inconsecuencia *f* (*falta de consecuencia o correspondencia en dichos y hechos*) inconsistency
inconsecuente *adj* inconsistent; (*que no se deduce de otra cosa*) inconsequential
inconsidera·do -da *adj* inconsiderate
inconsiguiente *adj* inconsequential, illogical
inconsistencia *f* (*falta de cohesión*) inconsistency
inconsistente *adj* inconsistent
inconsolable *adj* inconsolable
inconstante *adj* inconstant
inconstitucional *adj* unconstitutional
inconsútil *adj* seamless
incontable *adj* countless, innumerable
incontenible *adj* irrepressible
incontestable *adj* incontestable
incontinente *adj* incontinent || *adv* at once, instantly
incontrastable *adj* invincible; inconvincible; (*argumento*) unanswerable
incontrovertible *adj* incontrovertible
inconveniencia *f* inconvenience; unsuitability; impoliteness; impropriety
inconveniente *adj* inconvenient; unsuitable; impolite; improper || *m* drawback, disadvantage; objection
incordio *m* (coll) bore, nuisance
incorporación *f* incorporation, embodiment
incorpora·do -da *adj* (*el que estaba echado*) sitting up; (*montado en la construcción*) built-in
incorporar *tr* to incorporate, embody || *ref* to incorporate; (*el que estaba echado*) to sit up; **incorporarse a** to join
incorrec·to -ta *adj* incorrect
incrédu·lo -la *adj* incredulous || *mf* disbeliever, doubter
increíble *adj* incredible
incremento *m* increment, increase
increpar *tr* to chide, to rebuke
incriminar *tr* to incriminate; (*un delito, falta, defecto*) to exaggerate the gravity of
incruen·to -ta *adj* bloodless
incrustar *tr* to incrust; (*embutir por adorno*) to inlay
incubadora *f* incubator
incubar *tr & intr* to incubate || *ref* (fig) to be brewing
incuestionable *adj* unquestionable
inculcar §73 *tr* to inculcate || *ref* to become obstinate
inculpable *adj* blameless, guiltless
inculpar *tr* to accuse, to blame
incultivable *adj* untillable
incul·to -ta *adj* uncultivated, untilled; uncultured; (*estilo*) coarse, sloppy
incumbencia *f* incumbency, duty, obligation, province
incumbir *intr* — **incumbir a** to be incumbent on
incumplimiento *m* nonfulfillment
incunable *m* incunabulum
incurable *adj & mf* incurable
incuria *f* carelessness, negligence
incurio·so -sa *adj* careless, negligent
incurrir *intr* — **incurrir en** to incur
incursión *f* incursion, inroad, raid
indagación *f* investigation, research
indagar §44 *tr* to investigate
indebidamente *adv* unduly
indebi·do -da *adj* undue; wrong
indecencia *f* indecency
indecente *adj* indecent
indecible *adj* unspeakable, unutterable
indeci·so -sa *adj* undecided, indecisive; (*contorno, forma*) vague, obscure
indeclinable *adj* unavoidable; (gram) indeclinable
indecoro·so -sa *adj* improper
indefectible *adj* unfailing
indefendible *adj* indefensible
indefen·so -sa *adj* defenceless, undefended
indefinible *adj* indefinable
indefini·do -da *adj* indefinite; limitless; vague
indeleble *adj* indelible
indelibera·do -da *adj* unpremeditated
indelica·do -da *adj* indelicate
indemne *adj* unharmed, undamaged
indemnidad *f* (*seguridad contra un daño*) indemnity
indemnización *f* (*compensación*) indemnity, indemnification; **indemnización por despido** severance pay
indemnizar §60 *tr* to indemnify
independencia *f* independence
independiente *adj & mf* independent
independizar §60 *tr* to free, to emancipate || *ref* to become independent
indescriptible *adj* indescribable
indeseable *adj & mf* undesirable
indesea·do -da *adj* unwanted
indesmallable *adj* runproof
indestructible *adj* indestructible
indetermina·do -da *adj* indeterminate; (gram) indefinite
indevo·to -ta *adj* impious; not fond, not devoted
india *f* wealth, riches; **Indias Occidentales** West Indies; **la India** India
indiana *f* printed calico
india·no -na *adj & mf* Spanish American; East Indian; West Indian || *m* man back from America with great wealth; **indiano de hilo negro** (coll) skinflint || *f* see **indiana**
indicación *f* indication; **por indicación de** at the direction of
indica·do -da *adj* appropriate, advisable; **muy indicado** just the thing, just the person
indica·dor -dora *adj* indicating, pointing || *m* indicator; gauge; (*de tránsito*) traffic signal
indicar §73 *tr* to indicate
indicati·vo -va *adj & m* indicative
índice *m* index; **índice de libros prohibidos** (eccl) Index; **índice de materias** table of contents; **índice en el corte** thumb index
indiciar *tr* to betoken, indicate; to surmise, suspect
indicio *m* sign, token, indication; **indicios vehementes** circumstantial evidence
indiferente *adj* indifferent; (*que no importa*) immaterial

indígena *adj* indigenous || *mf* native
indigente *adj* indigent
indigestar *ref* to be indigestible; (coll) to be disliked, to be unbearable
indigestible *adj* indigestible
indigestión *f* indigestion
indignación *f* indignation
indigna·do -da *adj* indignant
indignar *tr* to anger, to provoke || *ref* to become indignant
indignidad *f* (*falta de mérito*) unworthiness; (*acción reprobable*) indignity
indig·no -na *adj* unworthy
índigo *m* indigo
in·dio -dia *adj & mf* Indian || *f* see **india**
indirec·to -ta *adj* indirect || *f* hint, innuendo; **indirecta del padre Cobos** broad hint
indiscernible *adj* indiscernible
indiscre·to -ta *adj* indiscreet
indisculpable *adj* inexcusable
indiscutible *adj* undeniable
indisoluble *adj* indissoluble
indispensable *adj* unpardonable; indispensable
indisponer **§54** *tr* (*alterar la salud de*) to indispose, upset; to disturb, to upset; **indisponer a uno con** to set someone against, to prejudice someone against || *ref* to become indisposed; **indisponerse con** to fall out with
indisponible *adj* unavailable
indispues·to -ta *adj* indisposed
indistintamente *adv* indistinctly; indiscriminately, without distinction
indistin·to -ta *adj* indistinct
individual *adj* individual; (*habitación en un hotel; partido de tenis*) single
individualidad *f* individuality
indivi·duo -dua *adj* individual; indivisible || *mf* (*persona indeterminada*) (coll) individual || *m* (*cada persona*) individual; (*miembro de una corporación*) member, fellow
indócil *adj* unteachable; headstrong, unruly
indocumenta·do -da *adj* unidentified; unqualified || *mf* nobody (*person of no account*)
indochi·no -na *adj & mf* Indo-Chinese || **la Indochina** Indochina
indoeurope·o -a *adj & m* Indo-European
índole *f* kind, class; nature, disposition, temper
indolente *adj* stolid, impassive; (*perezoso*) indolent
indolo·ro -ra *adj* painless
indoma·do -da *adj* untamed
indone·sio -sia *adj & mf* Indonesian || **la Indonesia** Indonesia
inducción *f* induction
inducido *m* (*de dínamo o motor*) (elec) armature
inducir **§19** *tr* to induce
inductor *m* (*de dínamo o motor*) (elec) field
indudable *adj* doubtless
indulgente *adj* indulgent
indultar *tr* to pardon; to free, exempt
indulto *m* pardon; exemption
indumentaria *f* clothing, dress; historical study of clothing
indumento *m* clothing, dress
industria *f* industry; **de industria** on purpose
industrial *adj* industrial || *m* industrialist
industrializar **§60** *tr* to industrialize
industriar *tr* to teach, instruct, train || *ref* to get along, to manage
industrio·so -sa *adj* industrious
inédi·to -ta *adj* unpublished; new, novel, unknown
inefable *adj* ineffable
ineficacia *f* inefficacy
inefi·caz *adj* (*pl* **-caces**) inefficacious, ineffectual
inelegible *adj* ineligible
ineludible *adj* inescapable
inenarrable *adj* indescribable
inencogible *adj* unshrinkable
inencontrable *adj* unobtainable
inequidad *f* inequity
inequívo·co -ca *adj* unmistakable
inercia *f* inertia
inerme *adj* unarmed
inerte *adj* inert; slow, sluggish
inescrupulo·so -sa *adj* unscrupulous
inescrutable or **inescudriñable** *adj* inscrutable
inespera·do -da *adj* unexpected, unforeseen; unhoped-for
inestable *adj* unstable
inevitable *adj* unavoidable, inevitable
inexactitud *f* inaccuracy, inexactness
inexac·to -ta *adj* inaccurate, inexact
inexcusable *adj* inexcusable, unpardonable; unavoidable; indispensable
inexorable *adj* inexorable
inexperiencia *f* inexperience
inexplicable *adj* inexplicable, unexplainable
inexplica·do -da *adj* unexplained, unaccounted-for
inexplora·do -da *adj* unexplored; (*mar*) uncharted
inexpresable *adj* inexpressible
inexpues·to -ta *adj* (phot) unexposed
inexpugnable *adj* impregnable; firm, unshakable
inextinguible *adj* unextinguishable; perpetual, lasting; (*sed*) unquenchable; (*risa*) uncontrollable
inextirpable *adj* ineradicable
infalible *adj* infallible
infamación *f* defamation
infamar *tr* to defame, discredit
infame *adj* infamous; (coll) vile, frightful || *mf* scoundrel
infamia *f* infamy
infancia *f* infancy
infan·do -da *adj* odious, unmentionable
infanta *f* female child; infanta (*any daughter of a king of Spain; wife of an infante*)
infante *m* male child; infante (*any son of a king of Spain who is not heir to the throne*); (mil) infantryman; **infante de coro** choirboy
infantería *f* infantry; **infantería de marina** marines, marine corps
infantil *adj* infant, infantile, childlike; innocent

infatigable *adj* indefatigable
infatuar §21 *tr* to make vain || *ref* to become vain
infaus•to -ta *adj* fatal, unlucky
infección *f* infection
infeccionar *tr* to infect
infeccio•so -sa *adj* infectious
infectar *tr* to infect
infec•to -ta *adj* foul, corrupt; infected; fetid
infecun•do -da *adj* sterile, barren
infe•liz (*pl* **-lices**) *adj* unhappy; (coll) simple, good-hearted || *m* wretch, poor soul
inferior *adj* inferior; lower; **inferior a** inferior to; lower than; less than; smaller than || *m* inferior
inferioridad *f* inferiority
inferir §68 *tr* to infer; to lead to, to entail; (*una herida*) to inflict; (*una ofensa*) to cause, offer
infernáculo *m* hopscotch
infernal *adj* infernal
infernar §2 *tr* to damn; to irritate, annoy
infernillo *m* chafing dish
infestar *tr* infest || *ref* to become infested
inficionar *tr* to infect || *ref* to become infected
infidelidad *f* infidelity; (*conjunto de infieles*) unbelievers
infidente *adj* faithless, disloyal
infiel *adj* (*falto de fidelidad*) unfaithful; (*no exacto*) inaccurate, inexact; (*no cristiano*) infidel || *mf* infidel
infierno *m* hell; **en el quinto infierno** or **en los quintos infiernos** (coll) far, far away
infijo *m* (gram) infix
infiltrar *tr* & *ref* to infiltrate
ínfi•mo -ma *adj* lowest; humblest, most abject; meanest, vilest
infinidad *f* infinity
infiniti•vo -va *adj* & *m* infinitive
infini•to -ta *adj* infinite || *m* infinite; (math) infinity || **infinito** *adv* greatly, very much
infirme *adj* infirm
inflación *f* inflation; (*vanidad*) conceit
inflado *m* inflation (*of a tire*)
inflamable *adj* inflammable, flammable
inflamación *f* ignition, inflammation; ardor, enthusiasm; (pathol) inflammation
inflamar *tr* to set on fire; to inflame || *ref* to catch fire; to become inflamed
inflar *tr* to inflate; to exaggerate; to puff up with pride || *ref* to inflate; to be puffed up with pride
inflexible *adj* inflexible; unyielding, unbending
inflexión *f* inflection; **inflexión vocálica** (*metafonía*) umlaut
inflexionar *tr* to umlaut
infligir §27 *tr* to inflict
influencia *f* influence
influenciar *tr* to influence
influenza *f* influenza
influir §20 *intr* to have influence; to have great weight; **influir en** or **sobre** to influence
influjo *m* influence; rising tide
influyente *adj* influential
información *f* information; (law) judicial inquiry, investigation; **informaciones** testimonial
informal *adj* (*que no se ajusta a las reglas debidas*) informal; unreliable
informar *tr* & *intr* to inform || *ref* to inquire, find out
informati•vo -va *adj* informational; (*sección de un periódico*) news
informe *adj* shapeless, formless; misshapen || *m* piece of information; report; **informes** information; **informes confidenciales** inside information
infortuna•do -da *adj* unfortunate, unlucky
infortunio *m* misfortune; (*acaecimiento desgraciado*) mishap
infracción *f* infraction, infringement
infraconsumo *m* underconsumption
infrac•to -ta *adj* unperturbable
infraestructura *f* substructure; (rr) roadbed
inframundo *m* underworld
infrarro•jo -ja *adj* & *m* infrared
infrascri•to -ta *adj* undersigned; hereinafter mentioned
infrecuente *adj* infrequent
infringir §27 *tr* to infringe, to break, to violate
infructuo•so -sa *adj* fruitless, unfruitful
ínfulas *fpl* conceit, airs; **darse ínfulas** to put on airs
infunda•do -da *adj* unfounded, groundless, baseless
infundio *m* (coll) lie, fib
infundir *tr* to infuse, to instill
infusión *f* infusion; (*acción de echar agua sobre el que se bautiza*) sprinkling; **estar en infusión para** (coll) to be all set for
ingeniar *tr* to think up || *ref* to manage; **ingeniarse a** or **para** to manage to; **ingeniarse para ir viviendo** to manage to get along
ingeniería *f* engineering
ingeniero *m* engineer; **ingeniero de caminos, canales y puertos** government civil engineer
ingenio *m* talent, creative faculty; talented person; cleverness, skill, wit; (*artificio mecánico*) apparatus, device; (*del encuadernador*) paper cutter; engine of war; **afilar** or **aguzar el ingenio** to sharpen one's wits; **ingenio de azúcar** sugar refinery
ingeniosidad *f* ingenuity; wittiness
ingenio•so -sa *adj* (*dotado de ingenio; hecho con ingenio*) ingenious; (*agudo, sutil*) witty
ingéni•to -ta *adj* innate, inborn
ingente *adj* huge, enormous
ingenuidad *f* ingenuousness
inge•nuo -nua *adj* ingenuous
ingerir §68 *tr* & *ref* var of **injerir**
Inglaterra *f* England; **la Nueva Inglaterra** New England
ingle *f* groin
in•glés -glesa *adj* English; **a la inglesa** in the English manner || *m* Englishman; (*idioma*) English; **el inglés medio** Middle English; **los ingleses** the English || *f* Englishwoman

ingramatical *adj* ungrammatical
ingratitud *f* ingratitude, ungratefulness
ingra•to -ta *adj* (*desagradecido*) ungrateful; (*desagradecido; desagradable, áspero; improductivo*) thankless || *mf* ingrate
ingravidez *f* lightness, tenuousness; (*gravedad nula*) weightlessness
ingrávi•do -da *adj* light, tenuous; weightless
ingrediente *m* ingredient
ingresa•do -da *mf* new student
ingresar *tr* to deposit || *intr* to enter, become a member; (*beneficios*) to come in || *ref* (Mex) to enlist
ingreso *m* entrance; admission; **ingresos** income, revenue
íngri•mo -ma *adj* (Am) solitary, alone
inhábil *adj* unable; unskillful; unfit, unqualified
inhabilidad *f* inability; unskillfulness; unfitness
inhabilitar *tr* to disable, to disqualify, to incapacitate
inhabita•do -da *adj* uninhabited
inhabitua•do -da *adj* unaccustomed
inherente *adj* inherent
inhibir *tr* to inhibit
inhospitala•rio -ria *adj* inhospitable
inhóspi•to -ta *adj* inhospitable
inhumanidad *f* inhumanity
inhuma•no -na *adj* inhuman, inhumane; (Chile) filthy
iniciación *f* initiation
inicial *adj & f* initial
iniciar *tr* to initiate || *ref* to be initiated
iniciativa *f* initiative
ini•cuo -cua *adj* wicked, iniquitous
iniguala•do -da *adj* unequaled
ininteligente *adj* unintelligent
ininteligible *adj* unintelligible
ininterrumpi•do -da *adj* uninterrupted
iniquidad *f* iniquity
injerencia *f* interference, meddling
injerir **§68** *tr* to insert, introduce; (hort) to graft; (*alimentos*) (Am) to take in || *ref* to interfere, meddle, intrude
injertar *tr* (hort & surg) to graft
injerto *m* (hort & surg) graft
injuria *f* offense, insult; abuse, wrong; damage, harm
injuriar *tr* to offend, insult; to abuse, to wrong; to harm, damage
injurio•so -sa *adj* offensive, insulting; abusive; harmful; (*lenguaje*) profane
injusticia *f* injustice
injustifica•do -da *adj* unjustified
injus•to -ta *adj* unjust
inmacula•do -da *adj* immaculate
inmanejable *adj* unmanageable; unhandy
inmarcesible *adj* unfading
inmaterial *adj* immaterial
inmaturo -ra *adj* immature
inmediación *f* immediacy; proximity, nearness; **inmediaciones** neighborhood, outskirts
inmediatamente *adv* immediately; **inmediatamente que** as soon as
inmedia•to -ta *adj* immediate; close, adjoining, next; next above; next below; (*pago*) prompt; **venir a las inmediatas** (coll) to get into the thick of the fight
inmejorable *adj* superb, unsurpassable
inmemorial *adj* immemorial
inmen•so -sa *adj* immense
inmensurable *adj* immesurable
inmereci•do -da *adj* undeserved
inmergir **§27** *tr* to immerse
inmersión *f* immersion
inmigración *f* immigration
inmigrante *mf* immigrant
inmigrar *intr* to immigrate
inminente *adj* imminent
inmiscuir **§20 & regular** *tr* to mix || *ref* to meddle, to interfere
inmobila•rio -ria *adj* real-estate
inmoble *adj* motionless; firm, constant
inmodera•do -da *adj* immoderate
inmodes•to -ta *adj* immodest
inmódi•co -ca *adj* excessive
inmoral *adj* immoral
inmortal *adj* immortal, deathless || *mf* immortal
inmortalizar **§60** *tr* to immortalize
inmovilizar **§60** *tr* to immobilize; (*un caudal*) to tie up
inmueble *m* property, piece of real estate; **inmuebles** real estate
inmun•do -da *adj* dirty, filthy
inmune *adj* immune
inmunizar **§60** *tr* to immunize
inmutar *tr* to change, alter; to disturb, upset || *ref* to change, alter; to change countenance; **sin inmutarse** without batting an eye
inna•to -ta *adj* innate, inborn; natural
innatural *adj* unnatural
innavegable *adj* (*río*) unnavigable; (*embarcación*) unseaworthy
innecesa•rio -ria *adj* unnecessary
innegable *adj* undeniable
innoble *adj* ignoble
inno•cuo -cua *adj* harmless
innovación *f* innovation
innovar *tr* to innovate
innumerable *adj* innumerable
inocencia *f* innocence
inocentada *f* (coll) simpleness; (coll) blunder; (Ecuad) April Fools' joke
inocente *adj & mf* innocent; **coger por inocente** to make an April fool of
inocen•tón -tona *adj* (coll) simple, gullible || *mf* (coll) gull, dupe
inoculación *f* inoculation
inocular *tr* to inoculate; to contaminate, to pervert
inodo•ro -ra *adj* odorless || *m* deodorizer; (*excusado que funciona con agua corriente*) toilet
inofensi•vo -va *adj* inoffensive
inolvidable *adj* unforgettable
inope *adj* impecunious
inopia *f* indigence
inoportu•no -na *adj* inopportune, untimely
inorgáni•co -ca *adj* inorganic
inortodo•xo -xa *adj* unorthodox
inoxidable *adj* (*acero*) stainless; inoxidizable
inquietante *adj* disquieting, upsetting
inquietar *tr* to disquiet, to worry; to stir up, excite
inquie•to -ta *adj* anxious, worried

inquietud *f* disquiet, worry, concern
inquili•no -na *mf* tenant, renter
inquina *f* aversion, dislike, ill will
inquirir §40 *tr* to inquire, inquire into
inquisición *f* inquiry; inquisition
insabible *adj* unknowable
insaciable *adj* insatiable
insania *f* insanity
insa•no -na *adj* insane; imprudent
insatisfe•cho -cha *adj* unsatisfied
inscribir §83 *tr* to inscribe; (law) to record || *ref* to enroll, register
inscripción *f* inscription; enrollment, registration
insecticida *adj & m* insecticide
insecto *m* insect
insegu•ro -ra *adj* insecure, unsafe; uncertain
insensa•to -ta *adj* foolish, stupid
insensible *adj* callous, hard-hearted, unfeeling; imperceptible
inseparable *adj* inseparable; undetachable || *mf* inseparable || *m* lovebird
insepul•to -ta *adj* unburied
inserción *f* insertion
inserir §68 *tr* to insert; (*injertar*) to graft, engraft
insertar *tr* to insert
inservible *adj* useless
insidia *f* snare, ambush; plotting
insidiar *tr* to ambush, to waylay; to trap, to trick
insidio•so -sa *adj* insidious
insigne *adj* noted, famous, renowned
insignia *f* badge, decoration, insignia; banner, standard
insignificante *adj* insignificant
insince•ro -ra *adj* insincere
insinuación *f* insinuation, hint
insinuante *adj* engaging, slick, crafty
insinuar §21 *tr* to insinuate; to suggest, to hint at || *ref* to creep in, to slip in; to ingratiate oneself; to flow, to run; **insinuarse en** to work one's way in
insípi•do -da *adj* insipid, vapid
insistir *intr* to insist
ínsi•to -ta *adj* inbred, innate
insociable *adj* unsociable
insolencia *f* insolence
insolentar *tr* to make insolent || *ref* to become insolent
insolente *adj* insolent
insóli•to -ta *adj* unusual
insoluble *adj* insoluble
insolvencia *f* insolvency
insomne *adj* sleepless
insomnio *m* insomnia
insondable *adj* fathomless; inscrutable
insonorizar §60 *tr* to soundproof
insono•ro -ra *adj* soundproof
insospecha•do -da *adj* unsuspected
insostenible *adj* untenable
inspección *f* inspection; inspectorship
inspeccionar *tr* to inspect
inspiración *f* inspiration; inhalation
inspirante *adj* inspiring
inspirar *tr & intr* to inspire; (*atraer a los pulmones*) to inhale, to breathe in || *ref* to be inspired
instalación *f* plant, factory; outfit, equipment; arrangements, fittings; installment; **instalación sanitaria** plumbing
instalar *tr* to install || *ref* to settle
instantáne•o -a *adj* instantaneous || *f* snapshot
instante *m* instant, moment; **al instante** right away, immediately; **por instantes** uninterruptedly; any time
instantemente *adv* insistently, urgently
instar *tr* to press, to urge || *intr* to be pressing, to be urgent
instaurar *tr* to restore; to reëstablish
instigar §44 *tr* to instigate
instilar *tr* to instill
instinti•vo -va *adj* instinctive
instinto *m* instinct
institución *f* institution; **instituciones** (*de un Estado*) constitution; (*de una ciencia, arte, etc.*) principles
instituir §20 *tr* to institute, found
instituto *m* institute; (*de una orden religiosa*) rule, constitution; **instituto de segunda enseñanza** or **de enseñanza media** high school
institu•triz *f* (*pl* **-trices**) governess
instrucción *f* instruction; education
instructi•vo -va *adj* instructive
instruc•tor -tora *mf* teacher, instructor || *m* (mil) drillmaster || *f* instructress
instruí•do -da *adj* well-educated; well-posted
instruir §20 *tr* to instruct; (*un proceso o expediente*) to draw up
instrumentar *tr* to instrument
instrumentista *mf* instrumentalist
instrumento *m* instrument; (*persona que se emplea para alcanzar un resultado*) tool; **instrumento de cuerda** (mus) stringed instrument; **instrumento de viento** (mus) wind instrument
insubordina•do -da *adj* insubordinate
insubstituíble *adj* irreplaceable
insudar *intr* to drudge
insuficiente *adj* insufficient
insufrible *adj* insufferable
ínsula *f* island; one-horse town
insular *adj* insular || *mf* islander
insulina *f* insulin
insulsez *f* tastelessness; dullness, heaviness
insul•so -sa *adj* tasteless; dull, heavy
insultar *tr* to insult || *ref* to faint, swoon
insulto *m* insult; fainting spell
insume *adj* expensive
insumergible *adj* unsinkable
insuperable *adj* insurmountable
insurgente *adj & mf* insurgent
insurrección *f* insurrection
intac•to -ta *adj* intact, untouched
intachable *adj* blameless, irreproachable
integración *f* integration
integridad *f* integrity; virginity
ínte•gro -gra *adj* integral, whole; honest
intelecto *m* intellect
intelectual *adj & mf* intellectual
intelectualidad *f* intellectuality; (*conjunto de los intelectuales de un país o región*) intelligentsia
inteligencia *f* intelligence; **estar en inteligencia con** to be in collusion with
inteligente *adj* intelligent; trained, skilled
inteligible *adj* intelligible

intemperancia *f* intemperance
intemperante *adj* intemperate
intemperie *f* inclement weather; **a la intemperie** in the open, unsheltered
intempesti•vo -va *adj* unseasonable, inopportune, untimely
intención *f* intention; (*cautelosa advertencia*) caution; (*instinto dañino de un animal*) viciousness; **con intención** deliberately, knowingly; **de intención** on purpose
intendencia *f* intendance; (SAm) mayoralty
intendente *m* intendant; quartermaster general; (SAm) mayor
intensar *tr & ref* to intensify
intensidad *f* intensity
intensificar **§73** *tr & ref* to intensify
intensión *f* intensity
intensi•vo -va *adj* intensive
inten•so -sa *adj* intense
intentar *tr* to try, to attempt; to intend; to try out
intento *m* intent, purpose; **de intento** on purpose
intentona *f* (coll) rash attempt (*e.g., to rob, escape, etc.*)
interacción *f* interaction
interamerica•no -na *adj* inter-American
intercalar *tr* to intercalate, to insert
intercambiar *tr & ref* to interchange
intercambio *m* interchange, exchange
interceder *intr* to intercede
interceptar *tr* to intercept
intercep•tor -tora *mf* interceptor || *m* trap; separator; (aer) interceptor
interdecir **§24** *tr* to interdict, forbid
interés *m* interest; **intereses creados** vested interests; **poner a interés** to put out at interest
interesa•do -da *adj* interested || *mf* interested party
interesante *adj* interesting
interesar *tr* to interest; to involve || *intr* to be interesting || *ref* — **interesarse en** or **por** to be interested in, take an interest in
interescolar *adj* interscholastic, intercollegiate
interfec•to -ta *adj* murdered || *mf* victim of murder
interferencia *f* interference
interferir **§68** *tr* to interfere with || *intr* to interfere
interfono *m* intercom
ínterin *adv* meanwhile || *conj* (coll) while, as long as || *s* (*pl* **intérines**) temporary incumbency
interinar *tr* to fill temporarily, to fill in an acting capacity
interi•no -na *adj* temporary, acting, interim
interior *adj* interior, inner, inside; home, domestic || *m* interior, inside; mind, soul; **interiores** entrails, insides
interioridad *f* inside; **interioridades** inside story, private matters
interjección *f* interjection
interlinear *tr* to interline; (typ) to space, to lead
interlocu•tor -tora *mf* speaker, party; interviewer
intermedia•rio -ria *adj & mf* intermediary || *m* (com) middleman
interme•dio -dia *adj* intermediate || *m* interval, interim; (mus) intermezzo; (theat) intermission, entr'acte
intermitente *adj* intermittent
internacional *adj* international
internacionalizar **§60** *tr* to internationalize
interna•do -da *mf* (mil) internee || *m* boarding school
internamiento *m* internment
internar *tr* to send inland; to intern || *intr* to move inland || *ref* to move inland; to take refuge, to hide; to insinuate oneself; **internarse en** to go deeply into
internista *mf* internist
inter•no -na *adj* internal; inside || *mf* boarding-school student; **interno de hospital** intern
interpelar *tr* to seek the protection or aid of; to interrogate; to interpellate
interpolar *tr* to interpolate; to interpose; to interrupt briefly
interponer **§54** *tr* to interpose; to appoint as mediator || *ref* to intervene, intercede
interprender *tr* to take by surprise
interpresa *f* surprise action; surprise seizure
interpretar *tr* to interpret
intérprete *mf* interpreter
interrogación *f* interrogation; question mark
interrogar **§44** *tr & intr* to question, interrogate
interrumpir *tr* to interrupt
interruptor *m* (elec) switch; **interruptor automático** (elec) circuit breaker; **interruptor del encendido** (aut) ignition switch; **interruptor de resorte** (elec) snap switch
intersección *f* (geom) intersection
intersticio *m* interstice; interval
intervalo *m* interval
intervención *f* intervention; inspection; (*de cuentas*) audit, auditing; (surg) operation; **intervención de los precios** price control; **no intervención** nonintervention
intervenir **§79** *tr* to take up, work on; to inspect, supervise; (*cuentas*) to audit; (*un teléfono*) to tap; (surg) to operate on || *intr* to mediate, intervene, intercede; to participate; to happen
interventor *m* election supervisor; (com) auditor
inter•viev *m* (*pl* **-vievs**) interview
intervievar *tr* to interview
intesta•do -da *adj & mf* intestate
intesti•no -na *adj* internal; domestic || *m* intestine; **intestino delgado** small intestine; **intestino grueso** large intestine
intimación *f* announcement, notification
intimar *tr* to announce || *intr & ref* to become well-acquainted, to become intimate
intimidad *f* intimacy; (*parte íntima o personal*) privacy
intimidar *tr* intimidate

ínti•mo -ma *adj* intimate; (*más interno*) innermost
intitular *tr* to entitle || *ref* to use a title; to be called
intocable *mf* untouchable
intolerante *adj & mf* intolerant
inton•so -sa *adj* unshorn; ignorant; (*libro o revista*) uncut || *mf* ignoramus
intoxicar §73 *tr* to poison, intoxicate
intracruzamiento *m* inbreeding
intraquilidad *f* uneasiness, worry
intraquilizar §60 *tr* to make uneasy, worry
intranqui•lo -la *adj* uneasy, worried
intransigente *adj & mf* intransigent, diehard
intransiti•vo -va *adj* intransitive
intratable *adj* unmanageable; impassable; unsociable
intrepidez *f* intrepidity
intrépi•do -da *adj* intrepid
intriga *f* intrigue
intrigar §44 *tr* (*excitar la curiosidad de*) to intrigue || *intr* to intrigue || *ref* to be intrigued
intrinca•do -da *adj* intricate
intrincar §73 *tr* to complicate; to confuse, bewilder
intríngu•lis *m* (*pl* **-lis**) (coll) hidden motive, mystery
intrínse•co -ca *adj* intrinsic(al)
introducción *f* introduction
introducir §19 *tr* to introduce; to insert, put in || *ref* to gain access; to meddle, interfere, intrude
introito *m* (*de un escrito o una oración*) introduction; (*de un poema dramático*) prologue; (eccl) introit
introspecti•vo -va *adj* introspective
introverti•do -da *mf* introvert
intruso -sa *adj* intrusive || *mf* intruder, interloper
intuición *f* intuition
intuir §20 *tr* to guess, to sense
intuito *m* view, glance, look; **por intuito de** in view of
inundación *f* flood, inundation
inundar *tr* to flood, to inundate
inurba•no -na *adj* discourteous, unmannerly
inusita•do -da *adj* (*no ordinario*) unusual; obsolete, out of use
inusual *adj* unusual
inútil *adj* useless
invadir *tr* to invade
invalidar *tr* to invalidate
invalidez *f* invalidity
inváli•do -da *adj & mf* invalid
invariable *adj* invariable
invasión *f* invasion
inva•sor -sora *mf* invader
invectiva *f* invective
invectivar *tr* to inveigh against
invencible *adj* invincible
invención *f* invention; finding, discovery; deception
invendible *adj* unsalable
inventar *tr* to invent
inventariar §77 & **regular** *tr* to inventory
inventario *m* inventory
inventi•vo -va *adj* inventive || *f* inventiveness
invento *m* invention
inven•tor -tora *adj* inventive || *mf* inventor
inverecun•do -da *adj* shameless, brazen
inverisímil *adj* improbable, unlikely
invernáculo *m* greenhouse, hothouse, conservatory
invernada *f* wintertime; (SAm) pasture land; (Ven) torrential rain
invernadero *m* greenhouse, hothouse; winter resort; winter pasture
invernal *adj* winter || *m* cattle shed (*in winter-pasture land*)
invernar §2 *intr* to winter; to be winter
inverni•zo -za *adj* winter; wintery
inverosímil *adj* improbable, unlikely
inversión *f* inversion; (*de dinero*) investment; (gram) inverted order
inversionista *adj* investment || *mf* investor
inver•so -sa *adj* inverse, opposite; **a** or **por la inversa** on the contrary
invertebra•do -da *adj & m* invertebrate
inverti•do -da *adj* inverted || *mf* invert
invertir §68 *tr* to invert; (*dinero*) to invest; (*tiempo*) to spend; to reverse
investidura *f* investment, investiture; station, standing
investigación *f* investigation, research
investigar §44 *tr* to investigate || *intr* to research
investir §50 *tr* — **investir con** or **de** (*poner en posesión de*) to invest with
invetera•do -da *adj* inveterate confirmed
invic•to -ta *adj* unconquered
invidencia *f* blindness
invidente *adj* blind || *mf* blind person
invierno *m* winter; (Am) rainy season
invisible *adj* invisible || *m* (Mex) hair net; **en un invisible** in an instant
invitación *f* invitation
invita•do -da *mf* guest
invitar *tr* to invite
invocar §73 *tr* to invoke
involunta•rio -ra *adj* involuntary
invulnerable *adj* invulnerable
inyección *f* injection
inyecta•do -da *adj* bloodshot, inflamed
inyectar *tr* to inject || *ref* to become congested; to become inflamed
ionizar §60 *tr* to ionize || *ref* to be ionized
ir §41 *intr* to go; to be becoming, to fit, to suit; to be at stake; **ir a** + *inf* to be going to + *inf* (*to express futurity*); **ir a buscar** to go get, to go for; **ir a parar en** to end up in; **ir con cuidado** to be careful; **ir con miedo** to be afraid; **ir con tiento** to watch one's step; **ir de caza** to go hunting; **ir de pesca** to go fishing; **lo que va de** so far (as); **¡qué va!** of course not!; **¡vaya!** the deuce!; what a . . .! || *ref* to go away; to leak; to wear away; to get old; to break to pieces
ira *f* anger, wrath, ire
iracun•do -da *adj* angry, wrathful, irate
Irak, el Irak or Iraq
Irán, el Iran

ira•nés -nesa or **ira•nio -nia** *adj & mf* Iranian
ira•qués -quesa or **iraquiano -na** *adj & mf* Iraqui
iris *m* (*pl* **iris**) (*del ojo*) iris; rainbow
Irlanda *f* Ireland
irlan•dés -desa *adj* Irish || *m* Irishman; (*idioma*) Irish; **los irlandeses** the Irish || *f* Irishwoman
ironía *f* irony
iróni•co -ca *adj* ironic(al)
ironizar **§60** *tr* to ridicule
irracional *adj* irrational
irradiar *tr* to radiate, to irradiate; (*difundir*) to broadcast || *intr* to radiate
irrazonable *adj* unreasonable
irreal *adj* unreal
irrealidad *f* unreality
irrebatible *adj* irrefutable
irreconocible *adj* unrecognizable
irrecuperable *adj* irretrievable
irrecusable *adj* unimpeachable
irredimible *adj* irredeemable
irreemplazable *adj* irreplaceable
irreflexión *f* rashness, thoughtlessness
irreflexi•vo -va *adj* rash, thoughtless
irregular *adj* irregular || *m* (mil) irregular
irregularidad *f* irregularity; embezzlement
irreligio•so -sa *adj* irreligious
irrellenable *adj* nonrefillable
irremediable *adj* irremediable
irremisible *adj* unpardonable
irreparable *adj* irreparable
irreprimible *adj* irrepressible
irreprochable *adj* irreproachable
irresistible *adj* irresistible
irresoluble *adj* unworkable, unsolvable
irrespetuo•so -sa *adj* disrespectful
irresponsable *adj* irresponsible
irresuel•to -ta *adj* hesitant, wavering
irreverente *adj* irreverent
irrigación *f* irrigation
irrigar **§44** *tr* to irrigate
irrisible *adj* laughable, absurd
irrisión *f* derision, ridicule; (coll) laughingstock
irritante *adj & m* irritant
irritar *tr* to irritate || *ref* to become exasperated
irrompible *adj* unbreakable
irrumpir *intr* to burst in; **irrumpir en** to burst into
irrupción *f* sudden attack; invasion
isi•dro -dra *mf* (coll) hick, jake, yokel
isla *f* island; (*manzana de casas*) block; **isla de seguridad** safety island, safety zone; **islas Baleares** Balearic Islands; **islas Canarias** Canary Islands; **islas de Barlovento** Windward Islands; **islas de Sotavento** Leeward Islands; **Islas Filipinas** Philippine Islands
Islam, el Islam
islan•dés -desa *adj* Icelandic || *mf* Icelander || *m* (*idioma*) Icelandic
Islandia *f* Iceland
isle•ño -ña *adj* island || *mf* islander; (Cuba) Canarian
isleta *f* isle
isósce•les *adj* (*pl* **-les**) isosceles
isótopo *m* isotope
israe•lí (*pl* **-líes**) *adj & mf* Israeli
israelita *adj & mf* Israelite
istmo *m* isthmus
Italia *f* Italy
italia•no -na *adj & mf* Italian
itáli•co -ca *adj* Italic; (typ) italic || *f* (typ) italics
itinera•rio -ria *adj & m* itinerary
izar **§60** *tr* (naut) to hoist, to haul up
izquierda *f* left hand; left-hand side; (pol) left; **a la izquierda** left, on the left, to the left
izquierdear *intr* to go wild, to go astray, to go awry
izquierdista *adj* leftist || *mf* leftist, left-winger
izquierdizante *adj* leftish
izquier•do -da *adj* left; left-hand; left-handed; crooked; **levantarse del izquierdo** to get out of bed on the wrong side || *f* see **izquierda**

J

J, j (jota) *f* eleventh letter of the Spanish alphabet
jabalcón *m* strut, brace
jaba•lí *m* (*pl* **-líes**) wild boar
jabalina *f* javelin; wild sow
jabardillo *m* (*de insectos*) noisy swarm; (coll) noisy throng
jabeque *m* (naut) xebec; (coll) gash in the face
jabón *m* soap; cake of soap; **dar jabón a** (coll) to softsoap; **dar un jabón a** (coll) to upbraid, to reprimand; **jabón de afeitar** shaving soap; **jabón de Castilla** Castile soap; **jabón de tocador** or **de olor** toilet soap; **jabón de sastre** soapstone, French chalk; **jabón en polvo** soap powder
jabonado *m* soaping; (*ropa lavada o por lavar*) wash
jabonadura *f* soaping; **dar una jabonadura a** (coll) to lambaste, to upbraid; **jabonaduras** soapy water; soapsuds
jabonar *tr* to soap; (coll) to reprimand
jaboncillo *m* cake of toilet soap; **jaboncillo de sastre** soapstone, French chalk
jabone•ro -ra *adj* soap; (*toro*) yellowish, dirty-white || *mf* soapmaker; soap dealer || *f* soap dish
jabonete *m* cake of toilet soap
jabono•so -sa *adj* soapy, lathery
jaca *f* pony, jennet
jacal *m* (Guat, Mex, Ven) hut, shack
jácara *f* merry ballad; gay song and

dance; night revelers; (coll) story, argument; (coll) fake, hoax, lie; (coll) annoyance, bother

jacarear *intr* (coll) to go serenading, to go singing in the street; (coll) to be disagreeable

jáca•ro -ra *adj & m* braggart || *f* see **jácara**

jacinto *m* hyacinth

jaco *m* nag, jade; gray parrot

jactancia *f* boasting, bragging

jactancio•so -sa *adj* boastful, bragging

jactar *ref* to boast, to brag; **jactarse de** to boast of

jade *m* jade

jadeante *adj* panting

jadear *intr* to pant

jadeo *m* panting

ja•ez *m* (*pl* **-eces**) harness, piece of harness; ilk, stripe, kind; **jaeces** trappings

jaguar *m* jaguar

jagüel *m* (Arg) reservoir

jaharrar *tr* to plaster

jalar *tr* (coll) to pull; (Am) to flirt with || *intr* (Am) to get out, to beat it || *ref* (Am) to get drunk

jalbegar **§44** *tr* to whitewash; (*el rostro*) to paint || *ref* to paint the face

jalbegue *m* whitewash; whitewashing; paint, make-up

jalda•do -da *adj* bright-yellow

jalea *f* jelly; **hacerse una jalea** (coll) to be madly in love

jalear *tr* (*a los que bailan y cantan*) to animate with clapping and shouting; (*a los perros*) to incite, urge on; (*Chile*) to tease, pester || *intr* to dance the jaleo || *ref* to have a noisy time; to swing and sway

jaleo *m* cheering, shouting; jamboree; jaleo (*vivacious Spanish solo dance*)

jalis•co -ca *adj* (Guat, Mex) drunk || *m* (Mex) straw hat

jalma *f* small packsaddle

jalón *m* surveying rod, range pole; (Guat, Mex) swig of liquor; (CAm) beau; **jalón de mira** leveling rod

jalonar *tr* to stake out, mark out

jalonear *tr* (Mex) to pull, to jerk

jalonero *m* (surv) rodman

jamaica *m* Jamaica rum || *f* (Mex) charity fair

jamaica•no -na *adj & mf* Jamaican

jamaiqui•no -na *adj & mf* (Am) Jamaican

jamar *tr* (coll) to eat

jamás *adv* never; ever

jamba *f* jamb

jambaje *m* doorframe, window frame

jamelgo *m* (coll) jade, nag

jamete *m* samite

jamón *m* ham

jamona *f* (coll) fat middle-aged woman

jamugas *fpl* mule chair

jánda•lo -la *adj & mf* Andalusian

Jantipa or **Jantipe** *f* Xanthippe

Japón, el Japan

japo•nés -nesa *adj & mf* Japanese || *m* (*idioma*) Japanese

jaque *m* (*lance del ajedrez*) check; (coll) bully; **dar jaque a** to check; **dar jaque mate a** to checkmate; **en jaque** in check; **estar muy jaque** (coll) to be full of pep; **jaque mate** checkmate; **tener en jaque** to hold a threat over the head of || *interj* check!

jaquear *tr* to check; (*al enemigo*) to harass

jaqueca *f* sick headache; **dar una jaqueca a** (coll) to bore to death

jaqueco•so -sa *adj* boring, tiresome

jaquemar *m* jack (*figure which strikes a clock bell*)

jarabe *m* syrup; sweet drink; **jarabe de pico** (coll) lip service, idle promise

jarana *f* (coll) merrymaking; (coll) rumpus; (coll) carousal, spree; (coll) trick, deceit; (Am) jest, joke; (Am) small guitar; **ir de jarana** (coll) to go on a spree

jaranear *tr* (CAm, Col) to swindle, cheat || *intr* (coll) to go on a spree; (coll) to raise a rumpus; (Am) to joke

jarane•ro -ra *adj* merrymaking; gay, merry || *mf* merrymaker, reveler

jarano *m* sombrero

jarcia *f* fishing tackle; (coll) jumble, mess; **jarcias** tackle, rigging; **jarcia trozada** junk (*old cable*)

jardín *m* garden, flower garden; (baseball) field, outfield; (naut) privy, latrine; **jardín central** (baseball) center field; **jardín de la infancia** kindergarten; **jardín derecho** (baseball) right field; **jardín izquierdo** (baseball) left field

jardinera *f* jardiniere, flower stand; basket carriage; summer trolley car, open trolley car

jardinería *f* gardening

jardine•ro -ra *mf* gardener; **jardinero adornista** landscape gardener || *m* (baseball) fielder, outfielder || *f* see **jardinera**

jardinista *mf* landscape gardener

jarea *f* (Mex) hunger

jarear *intr* (Bol) to stop for a rest || *ref* (Mex) to flee, run away; (Mex) to swing, to sway; (Mex) to die of starvation

jareta *f* (sew) casing

jari•fo -fa *adj* showy, spruce, natty

jaro•cho -cha *adj* brusk, bluff || *m* insulting fellow; Veracruz peasant

jarope *m* syrup; (coll) nasty potion

jarra *f* jug, jar, water pitcher; **de jarras** or **en jarras** with arms akimbo

jarrete *m* hock, gambrel

jarretera *f* garter

jarro *m* pitcher; **echar un jarro de agua (fría) a** to pour cold water on

jarrón *m* (*vaso para adornar chimeneas, consolas, etc.*) vase; (*sobre un pedestal*) urn

jaspe *m* jasper

jaspea•do -da *adj* marbled, speckled || *m* marbling, speckling

jaspear *tr* to marble, speckle

jateo *m* foxhound

ja•to -ta *mf* calf

Jauja *f* Cockaigne; **¿estamos aquí o en Jauja?** (coll) where do you think you are?; **vivir en Jauja** (coll) to live in the lap of luxury

jaula *f* cage; (*embalaje de listones de madera*) crate; (Mex) open freight car; (Cuba, P-R) police wagon; **jaula de locos** insane asylum, madhouse
jauría *f* pack (*of hounds*)
java·nés -nesa *adj & mf* Javanese || *m* (*idioma*) Javanese
Javier *m* Xavier
jazmín *m* jasmine; **jazmín de la India** gardenia
jazz *m* jazz
J.C. *abbr* **Jesucristo**
jebe *m* alum; (SAm) rubber
jedive *m* khedive
jefa *f* female head or leader; **jefa de ruta** hostess (*on a bus*)
jefatura *f* headship, leadership; (*de policía*) headquarters
jefe *m* chief, head, leader; (*de una tribu*) chieftain; **jefe de cocina** chef; **jefe de coro** choirmaster; **jefe de equipajes** (rr) baggage master; **jefe de estación** stationmaster; **jefe del estado** chief of state; **jefe del gobierno** chief executive; **jefe de redacción** editor in chief; **jefe de ruta** guide; **jefe de tren** (rr) conductor; **quedar jefe** (Chile) to gamble away everything
jején *m* gnat, sandfly
jenabe *m* or **jenable** *m* mustard
jengibre *m* ginger
Jenofonte *m* Xenophon
jeque *m* sheik
jerarca *m* hierarch, head
jerarquía *f* hierarchy; **de jerarquía** important
jeremiada *f* jeremiad
jerez *m* sherry
jerga *f* coarse cloth; straw mattress; (*lenguaje especial de ciertos oficios; lenguaje difícil de entender*) jargon
jergón *m* straw mattress; (coll) ill-fitting clothes; (*persona torpe y estúpida*) (coll) lummox
Jericó Jericho
jerife *m* shereef
jerigonza *f* (*lenguaje especial de ciertos oficios; lenguaje difícil de entender*) jargon; (*lenguaje vulgar, caló*) slang; (coll) piece of folly
jeringa *f* syringe; (*para inyectar materias blandas en una máquina*) gun; (coll) annoyance, plague; **jeringa de engrase** or **grasa** grease gun
jeringar §44 *tr* to syringe; to inject; to give an enema to; (coll) to plague
jeringazo *m* injection, shot; squirt
jeringuilla *f* (*jeringa pequeña*) syringe; (bot) mock orange
Jerjes *m* Xerxes
jeroglífi·co -ca *adj & m* hieroglyphic
Jerónimo *m* Jerome
jer·sey *m* (*pl* **-seis**) jersey, sweater
Jerusalén Jerusalem
Jesucristo *m* Jesus Christ
jesuíta *adj & m* Jesuit
jesuíti·co -ca *adj* Jesuitic(al)
Jesús *m* Jesus; (*imagen del niño Jesús*) bambino; **en un decir Jesús** in an instant; **¡Jesús, María y José!** my gracious!
jeta *f* hog's snout, pig face; (*rostro de una persona*) (coll) phiz, mug; **estar con tanta jeta** (coll) to make a long face; **poner jeta** (coll) to pucker one's lips
jetu·do -da *adj* thick-lipped; (coll) grim, gruff
Jhs. *abbr* **Jesús**
jíba·ro -ra *mf* (W-I) white peasant
jibia *f* cuttlefish
jícara *f* chocolate cup; (CAm, Mex, W-I) calabash cup
jifia *f* swordfish
jilguero *m* linnet, goldfinch
jineta *f* (zool) genet
jinete *m* rider, horseman
jinetear *tr* (*caballos cerriles*) (Am) to break in || *intr* to show off one's horsemanship
jinglar *intr* to swing, to rock
jingoísmo *m* jingoism
jingoísta *adj & mf* jingo
jipa·to -ta *adj* (Am) pale, wan; (Am) insipid, tasteless; (Guat) drunk
jipijapa *m* Panama hat || *f* jipijapa; strip of jipijapa straw
jira *f* strip of cloth; outing, picnic; trip, tour; swing, political trip
jirón *m* rag, tatter, shred; (*de una falda*) facing; pennant; bit, drop, shred; **hacer jirones** to tear to shreds
jitomate *m* (Mex) tomato
joco·so -sa *adj* jocose, jocular
jocotal *m* (CAm, Mex) Spanish plum (*tree*)
jocote *m* (CAm, Mex) Spanish plum (*fruit*)
jocoyote *m* (Mex) baby (*youngest child*)
jofaina *f* washbowl, basin
jolgorio *m* (coll) fun, merriment
jonrón *m* (baseball) home run
Jordán *m* Jordan (*river*); **ir al Jordán** (coll) to be born again
Jordania *f* Jordan (*country*)
jorda·no -na *adj & mf* Jordanian
jorguín *m* sorcerer, wizard
jorguina *f* sorceress, witch
jorguinería *f* sorcery, witchcraft
jornada *f* journey, trip, stage; day's journey; (*horas del trabajo diario del obrero*) workday; (*tiempo que dura la vida de un hombre*) lifetime; battle; (*muerte*) passing; summer residence of diplomat or diplomatic corps; event, occasion; undertaking; (mil) expedition; (*de un drama*) (archaic) act; **a grandes** or **largas jornadas** by forced marches; **al fin de la jornada** in the end; **caminar por sus jornadas** to proceed with circumspection; **hacer mala jornada** to get nowhere; **jornada ordinaria** full time
jornal *m* day's work; day's pay; **a jornal** by the day; **jornal mínimo** minimum wage
jornalero *m* day laborer
joroba *f* hump; (coll) annoyance, bother
joroba·do -da *adj* humpbacked, hunchbacked; (coll) annoyed, bothered || *mf* humpback, hunchback
jorobar *tr* (coll) to annoy, pester
jorongo *m* (Mex) poncho; (Mex) woolen blanket

jota *f* (*letra del alfabeto*) J; jota (*Spanish folk dance and music*); jot, iota, tittle; vegetable soup; **sin faltar una jota** (coll) with not a whit left out

joven *adj* young; **ser joven de esperanzas** (coll) to have a bright future || *mf* youth, young person; **de joven** as a youth, as a young man, as a young woman

jovial *adj* jovial

joya *f* jewel; (*brocamantón*) diamond brooch; (*agasajo*) gift, present; (*persona o cosa de mucha valía*) (fig) jewel, gem; **joya de familia** heirloom; **joyas** jewelry; trousseau; **joyas de fantasía** costume jewelry

joyante *adj* glossy

joyelero *m* jewel case, casket

joyería *f* (*conjunto de joyas*) jewelry; jewelry shop; jewelry trade

joye·ro -ra *mf* jeweler || *m* jewel case, casket

Juan *m* John; **Buen Juan** (coll) sap, easy mark; **Juan Español** the Spanish people, the typical Spaniard; **San Juan Bautista** John the Baptist

Juana *f* Jane, Jean, Joan; **Juana de Arco** Joan of Arc, Jeanne d'Arc; **juanas** glove stretcher

juanete *m* bunion; high cheekbone

jubilación *f* retirement; (*renta de la persona jubilada*) pension, retirement annuity

jubila·do -da *adj* retired || *mf* retired person, pensioner

jubilar *tr* to retire, to pension; (coll) to throw out || *intr* to rejoice; to retire, be pensioned || *ref* to rejoice; to retire, be pensioned; (Col) to decline, go to pieces; (CAm, Ven) to play hooky; (Cuba, Mex) to become a past master

jubileo *m* (coll) much coming and going, great doings; (eccl) jubilee; **por jubileo** (coll) once in a long time

júbilo *m* jubilation

jubilo·so -sa *adj* jubilant, joyful

jubón *m* jerkin

judaísmo *m* Judaism

judería *f* (*raza judaica*) Jewry; (*barrio de los judíos*) ghetto

judía *f* Jewess; kidney bean, string bean; **judía de careta** black-eyed bean; **judía de la peladilla** Lima bean

judicatura *f* judicature; (*cargo de juez*) judgeship

judicial *adj* judicial, judiciary

judí·o -a *adj* Jewish || *mf* Jew || *f* see **judía**

juego *m* (*acción de jugar*) play, playing; (*ejercicio recreativo en el cual se gana o se pierde*) game; (*vicio de jugar*) gambling; (*lugar donde se ejecutan ciertos juegos*): (bowling) alley; (tennis) court; (baseball) field; (*tantos necesarios para ganar la partida*) game; (*de muebles*) suit, suite; (*de café*) service; (*de vajilla*) set; (*de luces, colores, aguas*) play; (mach) play; (*p.ej., de diplomacia*) (fig) game; **a juego** to match, e.g., **una silla a juego** a chair to match; **conocer el juego de** to see through, to have the number of; **en juego** at hand; **hacer juego** to match; **hacer juego con** to match, to go with; **juego de alcoba** bedroom suit; **juego de azar** game of chance; **juego de bolas** (mach) ball bearing; **juego de campanas** chimes; **juego de comedor** dining-room suit; **juego de envite** gambling game, game played for money; **juego de escritorio** desk set; **juego de la cuna** cat's cradle; **juego de la pulga** tiddlywinks; **juego del corro** ring-around-a-rosy; **juego del salto** leapfrog; **juego del tres en raya** tick-tack-toe played with movable counters or pebbles; **juego de manos** legerdemain, sleight of hand; (coll) roughhousing; **juego de niños** (*cosa muy fácil*) child's play; **juego de palabras** play on words, pun; **juego de pelota;** ball game; pelota; **juego de piernas** footwork; **juego de por ver** (Chile) game played for fun; **juego de prendas** game of forfeits, forfeits; **juego de suerte** game of chance; **juego de tejo** shuffleboard; **juego de timbres** glockenspiel; **juego de vocablos** or **voces** play on words, pun; **juego limpio** fair play; **juego público** gambling house; **juegos de sociedad** parlor games; **juegos malabares** juggling; flimflam; **juego sucio** foul play; **no ser cosa de juego** to be no laughing matter; **por juego** in fun, for fun; **verle a uno el juego** to be on to someone

juerga *f* (coll) carousal, spree; **juerga de borrachera** (coll) drinking bout, binge; **ir de juerga** (coll) to go on a spree

juerguista *mf* (coll) carouser, reveler

jue·ves *m* (*pl* **-ves**) Thursday; **Jueves Santo** Maundy Thursday

juez *m* (*pl* **jueces**) judge; **juez de guardia** coroner; **juez de instrucción** examining magistrate; **juez de paz** justice of the peace; **juez de salida** (sport) starter; **juez de tiempo** (sport) timekeeper

jugada *f* (*lance*) play, throw, stroke, move; **mala jugada** dirty trick

juga·dor -dora *mf* player; gambler; **jugador de manos** prestidigitator; **jugador de ventaja** sharper

jugar §42 *tr* (*p.ej., un naipe, una partida de juego*) to play; (*una espada*) to wield; (*arriesgar*) to stake, to risk; (*las manos, los dedos*) to move; **jugarle a uno las bebidas** to match someone for the drinks || *intr* to play; to gamble; (*hacer juego dos cosas*) to match; (*intervenir*) to figure, participate; **jugar a** (*p.ej., los naipes, el tenis*) to play; **jugar con** (*un contrario*) to play; (*una persona; los sentimientos de una persona*) to toy with; to match; **jugar en** to have a hand in || *ref* (*p.ej., la vida*) to risk; to be at stake; **jugarse el todo por el todo** to stake all, to shoot the works

jugarreta *f* (coll) bad play, poor play; (coll) mean trick, dirty trick

juglar *m* minstrel, jongleur; (*bufón*) (archaic) juggler
juglaría *f* minstrelsy
jugo *m* (*p.ej., de la naranja*) juice; (*de la carne*) gravy; (*líquido orgánico*) juice; (fig) gist, essence, substance; **en su jugo** (culin) au jus; **jugo de muñeca** (coll) elbow grease
jugo•so -sa *adj* juicy; substantial, important
juguete *m* toy, plaything; (*burla*) joke, jest; (theat) skit; **de juguete** toy, e.g., **soldado de juguete** toy soldier; **juguete de movimiento** mechanical toy; **por juguete** for fun, in fun
juguetear *intr* to frolic, romp, sport
juguete•ro -ra *adj* toy || *mf* toy dealer || *m* whatnot, étagère
juguete-sorpresa *m* (*pl* **juguetes-sorpresa**) jack-in-the-box
jugue•tón -tona *adj* playful, frolicsome, frisky
juicio *m* judgment; (law) trial; **estar en su cabal juicio** to be in one's right mind; **estar fuera de juicio** to be out of one's mind; **juicio de Dios** (hist) ordeal; **pedir en juicio** (law) to sue
juicio•so -sa *adj* judicious, wise
julepe *m* julep; (coll) scolding; (Am) scare, fright
julepear *tr* (coll) to scold; (coll) to whip; (SAm) to scare, frighten; (Mex) to weary, tire out
julio *m* July
julo *m* lead cow, lead mule
jumen•to -ta *mf* ass, donkey
juncal *adj* willowy, rushy; (fig) willowy, lissome
juncia *f* sedge; **vender juncia** (coll) to boast, brag
junco *m* (*embarcación china*) junk; (bot) rush, bulrush; **junco de Indias** (bot) rattan; **junco de laguna** (bot) rush, bulrush
junco•so -sa *adj* rushy, full of rushes
jungla *f* jungle
junio *m* June
junípero *m* juniper
junquera *f* rush, bulrush
junquillo *m* jonquil
junta *f* meeting, conference; board, council; junction, union; joint, seam; (*empaquetadura*) gasket; (*arandela*) washer; **junta de comercio** board of trade; **junta de charnela** (mach) knuckle; **junta de sanidad** board of health; **junta universal** (mach) universal joint
juntamente *adv* together; at the same time
juntar *tr* to join, unite; to gather, gather together; (*una puerta*) to half-close || *ref* to gather together; to go along; to copulate
jun•to -ta *adj* joined, united; **jun•tos -tas** together || *f* see **junta** || **junto** *adv* together; at the same time; **junto a** near, close to; **junto con** along with, together with; **todo junto** at the same time, all at once
juntura *f* junction; (*p.ej., de una cañería; de un hueso*) joint; connection, coupling
jura *f* oath
jura•do -da *adj* (*enemigo*) sworn || *m* (*conjunto de ciudadanos encargados de determinar la culpabilidad del acusado; conjunto de examinadores de un certamen*) jury; (*cada uno de los expresados individuos*) juror, juryman
juramentar *tr* to swear in || *ref* to take an oath, to be sworn in
juramento *m* oath; (*voto, reniego*) curse, swearword; **prestar juramento a** to swear to; **tomar juramento a** to swear in
jurar *tr* to swear; (*la verdad de una cosa*) to swear to; to swear allegiance to || *intr* (*pronunciar un juramento*) to swear, take an oath; (*echar votos o reniegos*) to swear, to curse; **jurar** + *inf* to swear to + *inf* || *ref* to swear; **jurársela** or **jurárselas a uno** (coll) to have it in for someone, to swear to get even with someone
jure•ro -ra *mf* (SAm) false witness
jurídi•co -ca *adj* juridical
jurisconsulto *m* (*el que escribe sobre el derecho*) jurist; (*jurisperito*) legal expert
jurisdicción *f* jurisdiction
jurisperito *m* jurist, legal expert
jurisprudencia *f* jurisprudence
jurista *mf* jurist
juro *m* right of perpetual ownership; **de juro** inevitably, for sure
justa *f* joust, tournament
justamente *adv* just, just at that time; justly; (*ajustadamente*) tightly
justar *intr* to joust, to tilt
justicia *f* justice; (*castigo de muerte*) execution; **de justicia** justly, deservedly; **hacer justicia a** to do justice to; **ir por justicia** to go to court, to bring suit
justicie•ro -ra *adj* just, fair; stern, righteous
justificable *adj* justifiable
justifica•do -da *adj* (*hecho*) just, right; (*persona*) just, upright
justificante *m* voucher, proof
justificar **§73** *tr* to justify; (typ) to justify
justillo *m* jerkin, waist
justipreciar *tr* to estimate, appraise
jus•to -ta *adj* just; right, exact; (*apretado*) tight || *mf* just person || *f* see **justa** || **justo** *adv* just; right, in tune; tight; (*con estrechez*) in straitened circumstances
Jutlandia *f* Jutland
ju•to -ta *mf* Jute
juvenil *adj* juvenile, youthful
juventud *f* youth; young people
juzgado *m* court of law; courtroom; court of one judge
juzgar **§44** *tr* & *intr* to judge; **a juzgar por** judging by; **juzgar de** to judge, pass judgment on

K

K, k (ka) *f* twelfth letter of the Spanish alphabet
kermesse *f* var of **quermés**
keroseno *m* kerosene, coal oil
kg. *abbr* **kilogramo**
kilate *m* var of **quilate**
kilo *m* kilo, kilogram
kilociclo *m* kilocycle
kilogramo *m* kilogram
kilometraje *m* kilometrage, distance in kilometers
kilométri•co -ca *adj* kilometric; (coll) interminable, long-drawn-out
kilómetro *m* kilometer
kilovatio *m* kilowatt
kilovatio-hora *m* (*pl* **kilovatios-hora**) kilowatt-hour
kimono *m* var of **quimono**
kinescopio *m* (telv) kinescope
kiosco *m* var of **quiosco**
kirieleisón *m* (coll) dirge; **cantar el kirieleisón** (coll) to beg mercy
km. *abbr* **kilómetro**
kph. *abbr* **kilómetros por hora**
kv. *abbr* **kilovatio**
kv-h *abbr* **kilovatio-hora**

L

L, l (ele) *f* thirteenth letter of the Spanish alphabet
la *art def fem* of **el** || *pron pers fem* her, it; you || *pron dem* that, the one; **la que** who, which, that; she who, the one that
laberinto *m* labyrinth, maze
labia *f* (coll) fluency, smoothness
labial *adj & f* labial
labio *m* lip; (fig) edge, lip; **chuparse los labios** to smack one's lips; **labio leporino** harelip; **leer en los labios** to lip-read
labiolectura *f* lip reading
labio•so -sa *adj* (Am) fluent, smooth
labor *f* labor, work; (*cultivo de los campos*) farming, tilling; (*obra de coser, bordar, etc.*) needlework, fancywork, embroidery; **hacer labor** to match; **labor blanca** linen work, linen embroidery; **labor de ganchillo** crocheting
laborable *adj* workable; arable, tillable; (*día*) work
laborante *m* journeyman; political henchman
laborar *tr* to work || *intr* to scheme
laboratorio *m* laboratory
laborio•so -sa *adj* (*trabajador*) laborious, industrious; (*trabajoso*) laborious, arduous
laborismo *m* British Labour Party
laborista *adj* Labour || *mf* Labourite
labra *f* carving
labrada *f* fallow ground (*to be sown the following year*)
labrade•ro -ra *adj* arable, tillable
labra•do -da *adj* wrought, fashioned; carved; figured, embroidered || *m* carving; **labrado de madera** wood carving || *f* see **labrada**
labra•dor -dora *adj* work; farm || *mf* farmer; (*campesino*) peasant || *m* plowman; **el Labrador** Labrador
labrantí•o -a *adj* farm || *m* farmland
labranza *f* farming; farm, farmland
labrar *tr* to work, to fashion; (*la piedra, la madera*) to carve; (*arar*) to plow; (*construir o mandar construir*) to build; to till, to cultivate; to cause, bring about || *intr* to make a lasting impression
labrie•go -ga *mf* peasant
laca *f* lacquer; shellac; **laca de uñas** nail polish; **lacas** lacquer ware
lacayo *m* lackey, footman
lacear *tr* to tie with a bow; to adorn with bows; (*la caza*) to drive within shot; (*la caza menor*) to trap, to snare
laceria *f* poverty, want; trouble, bother; leprosy
lacerio•so -sa *adj* poor, needy
lacero *m* lassoer; poacher; dogcatcher
la•cio -cia *adj* faded, withered; languid; (*cabello*) lank, straight
lacóni•co -ca *adj* laconic
lacra *f* fault, defect; (*señal dejada por una enfermedad*) mark, remains; (Am) sore; (Am) scab
lacrimóge•no -na *adj* tear, tear-producing
lacrimo•so -sa *adj* lachrymose, tearful
lactar *tr* to suckle
lácte•o -a *adj* milky
lacustre *adj* lake
ladear *tr* to tip, to tilt; to bend, to lean; (*un avión*) to bank || *intr* to tip, to tilt; to bend, to lean; to turn away, turn off; (*la aguja de brújula*) to deviate || *ref* to tip, to tilt; to bend, to lean; to be equal, be even; (Chile) to fall in love; **ladearse a** (*un dictamen, un partido*) to lean to or toward
ladeo *m* tipping, tilting; bending, leaning; inclination, bent
lade•ro -ra *adj* side, lateral || *f* hillside
ladilla *f* crab louse; **pegarse como ladilla** (coll) to stick like a leech
ladi•no -na *adj* crafty, sly, cunning; polyglot
lado *m* side; direction; (*del hilo telefónico*) end; **al lado** nearby; **dejar a un lado** to leave aside; **de lado** square, e.g., **diez centímetros de lado** ten centimeters square; **de otro lado**

on the other hand; **de un lado** on the one hand; **echar a un lado** to cast aside; to finish up; **hacer lado** to make room; **hacerse a un lado** to step aside; **lados** backers, advisers; **mirar de lado** or **de medio lado** to look askance at; to sneak a look at; **ponerse al lado de** to take sides with; **por el lado de** in the direction of; **tirar por su lado** to pull for oneself

ladrar *tr* (*p.ej., injurias*) to bark ‖ *intr* to bark

ladrido *m* bark, barking; (coll) slander, blame

ladrillador *m* bricklayer

ladrillal *m* brickyard

ladrillo *m* brick; (*azulejo*) tile; (*p.ej., de chocolate*) cake; **ladrillo de fuego** or **ladrillo refractario** firebrick

la•drón -drona *adj* thievish, thieving ‖ *mf* thief ‖ *m* sluice gate; **ladrón de corazones** heartbreaker, lady-killer

ladronera *f* den of thieves; thievery; (*alcancía*) child's bank

ladronerío *m* (Arg) gang of thieves; (Arg) wave of thieving

ladronzue•lo -la *mf* petty thief

lagaña *f* var of **legaña**

lagar *m* wine press; olive press; (*establecimiento*) winery

lagarta *f* female lizard; (ent) gypsy moth; (coll) sly woman

lagartija *f* green lizard; wall lizard

lagarto *m* lizard; (coll) sly fellow; **lagarto de Indias** alligator

lago *m* lake

lagotear *tr & intr* to flatter, to wheedle

lágrima *f* tear; (*de cualquier licor*) drop; **beberse las lágrimas** (coll) to hold back one's tears; **deshacerse en lágrimas** to weep one's eyes out; **lágrimas de cocodrilo** crocodile tears; **llorar a lágrima viva** to shed bitter tears

lagrimear *intr* to weep easily, to be tearful; (*los ojos*) to fill

lagrimo•so -sa *adj* tearful; (*ojos*) watery

laguna *f* (*lago pequeño*) lagoon; (*hueco, omisión*) lacuna, gap

laical *adj* lay

laicismo *m* secularism

laja *f* slab, flagstone

lama *f* mud, ooze, slime; pond scum

lambrija *f* earthworm; (coll) skinny person

lamedero *m* salt lick

lame•dor -dora *adj* licking ‖ *mf* licker ‖ *m* syrup; **dar lamedor** (coll) to lose at first in order to take in one's opponent

lamedura *f* lick, licking

lamentable *adj* lamentable

lamentación *f* lamentation

lamentar *tr, intr & ref* to lament, to mourn

lamento *m* lament

lamento•so -sa *adj* lamentable; plaintive

lamer *tr* to lick; to lap, lap against; (*las llamas un tejado*) to lick ‖ *ref* (*p.ej., los dedos*) to lick

lame•rón -rona *adj* (coll) sweet-toothed

lametada *f* lap, lick

lámina *f* sheet, plate, strip; (*plancha grabada*) engraving; (*pintura en cobre*) copper plate; (*figura estampada*) cut, picture, illustration

laminador *m* rolling mill

laminar *tr* to laminate; (*el hierro, el acero*) to roll

lampadario *m* floor lamp

lámpara *f* lamp, light; (*mancha en la ropa*) grease spot, oil spot; (rad) vacuum tube; **atizar la lámpara** (coll) to fill up the glasses again; **lámpara de alcohol** spirit lamp; **lámpara de arco** arc lamp, arc light; **lámpara de bolsillo** flashlight; **lámpara de carretera** (aut) bright light; **lámpara de cruce** (aut) dimmer; **lámpara de pie** floor lamp; **lámpara de sobremesa** table lamp; **lámpara de socorro** trouble light; **lámpara de soldar** blowtorch; **lámpara de techo** ceiling light; (aut) dome light; **lámpara inundante** floodlight; **lámpara testigo** pilot light

lamparilla *f* rushlight; aspen

lampi•ño -ña *adj* beardless; hairless

lampista *mf* lamplighter ‖ *m* tinsmith, plumber, glazier, electrician

lana *f* wool; **lana de acero** steel wool; **lana de ceiba** kapoc; **lana de escorias** mineral wool, rock wool; **lana de vidrio** glass wool

lance *m* cast, throw; (*en la red*) catch, haul; (*accidente en el juego*) play, move, stroke; (*ocasión crítica*) chance, pass, juncture; incident, event; (*riña*) row, quarrel; (taur) capework; **de lance** cheap; secondhand; **echar buen lance** (coll) to have a break; **lance de honor** affair of honor, duel; **tener pocos lances** (coll) to be dull and uninteresting

lancero *m* lancer, spearman, pikeman

lanceta *f* (surg) lancet

lancinante *adj* piercing

lancha *f* barge, lighter; flagstone, slab; (naut) longboat; (nav) launch; (Ecuad) mist, fog; (Ecuad) frost; **lancha automóvil** launch, motor launch; **lancha de auxilio** lifeboat (*stationed on shore*); **lancha de carreras** speedboat; **lancha de desembarco** (nav) landing craft; **lancha salvavidas** lifeboat (*on shipboard*)

lanchar *intr* (Ecuad) to get foggy; (Ecuad) to freeze

lan•dó *m* (*pl* **-dós**) landau

landre *f* swollen gland; hidden pocket

lanería *f* wool shop; **lanerías** woolens, woolen goods

langosta *f* (*insecto*) locust; (*crustáceo*) lobster, spiny lobster

langostera *f* lobster pot

langostín *m* or **langostino** *m* prawn (*Peneus*)

langostón *m* green grasshopper

languidecer **§22** *intr* to languish

languidez *f* languor

lángui•do -da *adj* languid, languorous

lano•so -sa *adj* woolly

lanu•do -da *adj* woolly; (Ecuad, Ven) coarse, ill-bred

lanza *f* lance, pike; (*de la manguera*) nozzle; (*palo de coche*) wagon pole

lanzabom•bas *m* (*pl* **-bas**) (aer) bomb release; (mil) trench mortar
lanzacohe•tes *m* (*pl* **-tes**) rocket launcher
lanzadera *f* shuttle; **parecer una lanzadera** (coll) to buzz around
lanza•do -da *adj* sloping; (*salida de una carrera*) (sport) running (*start*)
lanza•dor -dora *mf* thrower; **lanzador de lodo** (fig) mudslinger || *m* launcher; (aer) jettison gear; (baseball) pitcher
lanzaespu•mas *m* (*pl* **-mas**) foam extinguisher
lanzalla•mas *m* (*pl* **-mas**) flame thrower
lanzamiento *m* throw, hurl, fling, launch; (*de un buque*) launching; (*de un cohete*) shot, launch; (*p.ej., de víveres*) (aer) airdrop; (*de bombas*) (aer) release; (*de paracaidistas*) (aer) jump; (law) dispossession; (naut) steeve
lanzami•nas *m* (*pl* **-nas**) (nav) mine layer
lanzapla•tos *m* (*pl* **-tos**) trap
lanzar §60 *tr* to throw, hurl, fling; (*un proyecto, un cohete, maldiciones, una ofensiva, un producto nuevo, un buque*) to launch; (*una mirada*) to cast; to vomit, to throw up; (*flores, hojas una planta*) to put forth; (*una advertencia*) to toss, toss out; (aer) to airdrop; (*bombas*) (aer) to release; (law) to dispossess || *ref* to launch, launch forth; to throw oneself; to dash, to rush; (aer) to jump; (sport) to sprint
lanzatorpe•dos *m* (*pl* **-dos**) (nav) torpedo tube
laña *f* clamp; rivet
lañar *tr* to clamp; (*objetos de porcelana*) to rivet
lapicero *m* pencil holder; mechanical pencil
lápida *f* tablet, stone; **lápida sepulcral** gravestone
lapidar *tr* to stone to death
lá•piz *m* (*pl* **-pices**) (*grafito*) black lead; (*barrita que sirve para escribir*) pencil, lead pencil; **lápiz de labios** lipstick; **lápiz de pizarra** slate pencil; **lápiz de plomo** graphite; **lápiz estíptico** styptic pencil; **lápiz labial** lipstick
lapizar §60 *tr* to mark or line with a pencil
la•pón -pona *adj* Lapp || *mf* Lapp, Laplander || *m* (*idioma*) Lapp
Laponia *f* Lapland
lapso *m* lapse
laquear *tr* to lacquer
lardo•so -sa *adj* greasy, fatty
larga *f* long billiard cue; **dar largas a** to postpone, to put off
largamente *adv* at length, extensively; in comfort; generously; long, for a long time
largar §44 *tr* to get go, release; to ease, slack; (naut) to unfurl; (coll) to utter; (*un golpe*) (coll) to deal, strike, give; (Col) to give || *ref* to move away; to get away, sneak away, beat it; to take to sea; (*el ancla*) to come loose
lar•go -ga *adj* long; abundant; liberal, generous; quick, ready; (coll) shrewd, cunning; (naut) loose, slack; **a la larga** in the long run, in the end; **a lo largo** lengthwise; at great length; far away; **a lo largo de** along; along with; throughout; in the course of; (*el mar*) far out in; **a lo más largo** at most; **hacerse a lo largo** to get out in the open sea; **largo de lengua** loose-tongued; **largo de uñas** light-fingered; **pasar de largo** to pass without stopping; to take a quick look; to miss; **ponerse de largo** to come out, make one's debut; **vestir de largo** to wear long clothes || *m* length || *f* see **larga** || **largo** *adv* at length, at great length; abundantly || **largo** *interj* get out of here!
largometraje *m* full-featured film, full-length movie
largor *m* length
larguero *m* (*palo, madero*) stringer; (*almohada larga*) bolster; (aer) longeron
largueza *f* length; liberality, generosity
larguiru•cho -cha *adj* (coll) gangling, lanky
largura *f* length
lárice *m* larch tree
laringe *f* larynx
laringe•o -a *adj* laryngeal
laringitis *f* laryngitis
laringoscopio *m* laryngoscope
larva *f* larva; mask; (*duende*) hobgoblin
lascar §73 *tr* (naut) to pay out, to slacken; (Mex) to scratch, to bruise; (*un objeto de porcelana*) (Mex) to chip
lascivia *f* lasciviousness
lasci•vo -va *adj* lascivious; playful
la•so -sa *adj* tired, exhausted; weak, wan
lástima *f* pity; (*quejido*) complaint; **contar lástimas** to tell a hard-luck story; **dar lástima** to be pitiful; **es lástima (que)** it is a pity (that); **estar hecho una lástima** to be a sorry sight; **hacer lástima** to be pitiful; **llorar lástimas** (coll) to put on a show of tears; **poner lástima** to be pitiful; **¡qué lástima!** what a pity!, what a shame!; **¡qué lástima de saliva!** (coll) what a waste of breath!
lastimar *tr* to hurt, injure; to hurt, offend; to bruise || *ref* to hurt oneself; to bruise oneself; to complain
lastime•ro -ra *adj* hurtful, injurious; pitiful, sad, doleful
lastimo•so -sa *adj* pitiful
lastra *f* slab, flagstone
lastrar *tr* (aer & naut) to ballast
lastre *m* (aer & naut) ballast; (fig) wisdom, maturity; (coll) food; (rr) (Chile) ballast
lat. *abbr* **latín, latitud**
lata *f* (*hojalata*) tin, tin plate; (*envase*) tin, tin can; (*madero sin pulir*) log; (*tabla delgada*) lath; (coll) annoyance, bore; **dar la lata a** (coll) to pester; **estar en la lata** (Col) to be penniless
latebra *f* hiding place

latebro·so -sa *adj* furtive, secretive
latente *adj* latent
lateral *adj* lateral
latido *m* (*del perro*) yelp; (*del corazón*) beat, throb; (*dolor*) pang, twinge
latifundio *m* large neglected landed estate
latigazo *m* lash; crack of whip; (*reprensión áspera*) lashing
látigo *m* whip, horsewhip; cinch strap
latiguear *tr* (Am) to lash, to whip || *intr* to crack a whip
latiguillo *m* small whip; (*del actor u orador*) claptrap
latín *m* Latin; **latín de cocina** dog Latin, hog Latin; **latín rústico** or **vulgar** Vulgar Latin; **saber latín** or **mucho latín** (coll) to be very shrewd
latinajo *m* (coll) dog Latin, hog Latin; (coll) Latin word or phrase (*slipped into the vernacular*)
latinar or **latinear** *intr* to use Latin
lati·no -na *adj* Latin; (naut) lateen || *mf* Latin
Latinoamérica *f* Latin America
latinoamerica·no -na *adj* Latin-American || *mf* Latin American
latir *tr* (Ven) to annoy, bore, molest || *intr* (*el perro*) to bark, yelp; (*el corazón*) to beat, throb; **me late que** (Mex) I have a hunch that
latitud *f* latitude
la·to -ta *adj* broad || *f* see **lata**
latón *m* brass; (Cuba) garbage pail
lato·so -sa *adj* annoying, boring || *mf* bore
latrocinio *m* thievery; thievishness
laucha *f* (Arg, Chile) mouse
laúd *m* (mus) lute; (zool) leatherback turtle
laudable *adj* laudable
láudano *m* laudanum
laudato·rio -ria *adj* laudatory
laudo *m* (law) finding, decision
láurea *f* laurel wreath
laurea·do -da *adj* & *mf* laureate
laurean·do -da *mf* graduate, candidate for a degree
laurear *tr* to trim or adorn with laurel; to crown with laurel; to decorate, honor, reward
laurel *m* laurel; (*de la victoria*) laurels; **dormirse sobre sus laureles** to rest or sleep on one's laurels
láure·o -a *adj* laurel || *f* see **láurea**
lauréola *f* crown of laurel, laurel wreath; (*aureola*) halo
lava *f* lava; (min) washing
lavable *adj* washable
lavabo *m* washstand; washroom, lavatory
lavaca·ras *mf* (*pl* **-ras**) (coll) fawner, flatterer, bootlicker
lavaco·ches *m* (*pl* **-ches**) car washer
lavade·dos *m* (*pl* **-dos**) finger bowl
lavadero *m* laundry; (*tabla de lavar*) washboard; (*a orillas de un río*) washing place; (Guat, Mex, SAm) placer
lava·do -da *adj* (coll) brazen, fresh, impudent || *m* wash, washing; **lavado a seco** dry cleaning; **lavado cerebral** or **de cerebro** brain-washing; **lavado químico** dry cleaning
lava·dor -dora *mf* washer || *m* (phot) washer || *f* washing machine; **lavadora de platos** or **de vajilla** dishwasher
lavadura *f* washing; (*agua sucia; rozadura de una cuerda*) washings
lavafru·tas *m* (*pl* **-tas**) fruit bowl, finger bowl
lavama·nos *m* (*pl* **-nos**) (*pila con caño y llave*) washstand; (*jofaina*) washbowl
lavanda *f* lavender
lavandera *f* laundress, laundrywoman, washerwoman; (orn) sandpiper
lavandero *m* launderer, laundryman
lavándula *f* lavender
lavao·jos *m* (*pl* **-jos**) eyecup
lavaparabri·sas *m* (*pl* **-sas**) windshield washer
lavapla·tos (*pl* **-tos**) *mf* (*persona*) dishwasher || *m* (*aparato*) dishwasher; (Chile) kitchen sink
lavar *tr* & *ref* to wash
lavativa *f* enema; (coll) annoyance, bore
lavatorio *m* washing; washstand; toilet; (*ceremonia de lavar los pies*) maundy; (med) wash, lotion; (Am) washroom
lavazas *fpl* dirty water, wash water
laxante *adj* & *m* laxative
laxar *tr* to ease, to slack; (*el vientre*) to loosen
la·xo -xa *adj* lax, slack; (fig) lax, loose
laya *f* spade; kind, quality
layar *tr* to spade, dig with a spade
lazada *f* bowknot
lazar **§60** *tr* to lasso
lazarillo *m* blind man's guide
lazari·no -na *adj* leprous || *mf* leper
lázaro *m* raggedy beggar; **estar hecho un lázaro** to be full of sores
lazo *m* bow, knot, tie; lasso, lariat; snare, trap; bond, tie; **armar lazo a** (coll) to set a trap for; **caer en el lazo** (coll) to fall into the trap; **lazo de amor** truelove knot; **lazo de unión** (fig) tie, bond
Ldo. *abbr* **Licenciado**
le *pron pers* to him, to her, to it; to you; him; you
leal *adj* loyal, faithful; reliable, trustworthy || *m* loyalist
lealtad *f* loyalty; reliability, trustworthiness
le·brel -brela *mf* whippet, small greyhound
lebrillo *m* earthen washtub
lebrón *m* large hare; (coll) coward; (Mex) slicker
lección *f* lesson; (*interpretación de un pasaje*) reading; **dar la lección** to recite one's lesson; **echar** or **señalar lección** to assign the lesson; **tomar una lección a** to hear the lesson of
leccionista *mf* private tutor
lecti·vo -va *adj* school (*e.g., day*)
lec·tor -tora *adj* reading || *mf* reader || *m* foreign-language teacher; (*empleado que anota el consumo registrado por el contador de agua, gas o*

electricidad) meter reader; **lector mental** mind reader
lectura *f* reading; broad culture; public lecture; college subject; (*interpretación de un pasaje*) reading; (elec) playback; (typ) pica; **lectura de la mente** mind reading
lechada *f* grout; whitewash; (*para hacer papel*) pulp; (CAm, Mex, W-I) whitewash
lechar *tr* (Am) to milk; (CAm, Mex, W-I) to whitewash
leche *f* milk; **estar con la leche en los labios** to lack experience, to be young and inexperienced; **leche de manteca** buttermilk; **leche desnatada** skim milk; **leche en polvo** milk powder
lechecillas *fpl* sweetbread
lechera *f* milkmaid, dairymaid; (*vasija para guardar la leche*) milk can; (*vasija para servir la leche*) milk pitcher
lechería *f* dairy, creamery
leche•ro -ra *adj* (*que da leche*) milch; (*perteneciente a la leche*) milk; (*cicatero*) (coll) stingy || *m* milkman, dairyman || *f* see **lechera**
lecho *m* bed; (*especie de sofá*) couch; (*cauce de río*) bed; layer, stratum; **abandonar el lecho** to get up (*from illness*); **lecho de plumas** (fig) feather bed
le•chón -chona *adj* (coll) filthy, sloppy || *mf* suckling pig; (*persona sucia, desaseada*) (coll) pig || *m* pig || *f* sow
lecho•so -sa *adj* milky || *m* papaya (*tree*) || *f* papaya (*fruit*)
lechuga *f* lettuce; head of lettuce; (*fuelle formado en la tela*) frill; **lechuga romana** romaine lettuce
lechugui•no -na *adj* stylish, sporty || *m* dandy || *f* stylish young lady
lechuza *f* barn owl, screech owl; (coll) owllike woman
lechu•zo -za *adj* owlish; (*muleto*) yearling || *m* bill collector; summons server; (coll) owllike fellow || *f* see **lechuza**
leer §43 *tr* to read || *intr* to read; to lecture; **leer en** to read (*someone's thoughts*) || *ref* to read, e.g., **este libro se lee con facilidad** this book reads easily
leg. *abbr* **legal, legislatura**
lega *f* lay sister
legación *f* legation
legado *m* (*don que se hace por testamento*) legacy; (*enviado diplomático*) legate
legajo *m* file, docket, dossier
legal *adj* legal; faithful, prompt, right
legalidad *f* legality; faithfulness, promptness
legalizar §60 *tr* to legalize; to authenticate
légamo *m* slime, ooze
legamo•so -sa *adj* slimy, oozy
legaña *f* gum (*on edge of eyelids*)
legaño•so -sa *adj* gummy
legar §44 *tr* to bequeath, to will
legata•rio -ria *mf* legatee
legenda•rio -ria *adj* legendary
legible *adj* legible
legión *f* legion
legislación *f* legislation
legisla•dor -dora *adj* legislating || *mf* legislator
legislar *intr* to legislate
legislati•vo -va *adj* legislative
legislatura *f* session of a legislature; (Am) legislature
legista *m* law professor; law student
legitimar *tr* to legitimate; to legitimize
legitimidad *f* legitimacy
legíti•mo -ma *adj* legitimate
le•go -ga *adj* lay; uninformed || *m* layman; lay brother || *f* see **lega**
legua *f* league; **a leguas** far, far away
leguleyo *m* pettifogger
legumbre *f* (*hortaliza*) vegetable; (bot) legume; (Chile) vegetable stew
leíble *adj* legible, readable
leída *f* reading
leí•do -da *adj* well-read; **leído y escribido** (coll) posing as learned || *f* see **leída**
lejanía *f* distance, remoteness
leja•no -na *adj* distant, remote; (*pariente*) distant
lejía *f* lye; wash water; (coll) severe rebuke
lejiadora *f* washing machine
lejos *adv* far; **a lo lejos** in the distance; **de lejos** or **desde lejos** from a distance || *m* glimpse; look from afar; **tener buen lejos** to look good at a distance
le•lo -la *adj* stupid, inane
lema *m* motto, slogan; theme
len *adj* soft, flossy
lena *f* spirit, vigor; breathing
lencería *f* linen goods, dry goods; linen closet; dry-goods store
lence•ro -ra *mf* linen dealer, dry-goods dealer
lendrera *f* fine-toothed comb
lendro•so -sa *adj* nitty, lousy
lene *adj* (*suave al tacto*) soft; (*ligero*) light; kind, agreeable
lengua *f* (anat) tongue; (*idioma*) language, tongue; (*de tierra, de fuego, de zapato; badajo de campana; lengua de un animal usada como alimento*) tongue; **buscar la lengua a** (coll) to pick a fight with; **dar la lengua** (coll) to chew the rag; **hacerse lenguas de** (coll) to rave about; **írsele a** (*uno*) **la lengua** (coll) to blab; **lengua madre** or **matriz** mother tongue (*language from which another is derived*); **lengua materna** mother tongue (*language acquired by reason of nationality*); **morderse la lengua** to hold one's tongue; **tener en la lengua** (coll) to have on the tip of one's tongue; **tener la lengua gorda** (coll) to talk thick; (coll) to be drunk; **tener mala lengua** (coll) to be blasphemous; (coll) to have an evil tongue; **tener mucha lengua** (coll) to be a great talker; **tirar de la lengua a** (coll) to draw out; **tomar en lenguas** (coll) to gossip about; **tomar lengua** or **lenguas** to pick up news
lenguado *m* sole
lenguaje *m* language

lengua•raz (*pl* **-races**) *adj* foul-mouthed, scurrilous; polyglot || *mf* linguist
len•guaz *adj* (*pl* **-guaces**) garrulous
lengüeta *f* (*de la balanza*) pointer, needle; (*del zapato*) tongue; (anat) epiglottis; (carp) tongue; (*de un instrumento de viento*) (mus) reed; (Chile) paper cutter; (Mex) petticoat fringe; (SAm) chatterbox
lengüetada *f* licking, lapping
lengüetear *intr* to stick the tongue out; to flicker, to flutter; (Am) to jabber, to rant
lengüilar•go -ga *adj* (coll) foul-mouthed, scurrilous
lengüisu•cio -cia *adj* (Mex, P-R) foul-mouthed, scurrilous
lenidad *f* lenience
lenocinio *m* pandering, procuring
lente *m* & *f* lens; **lente de aumento** magnifying glass; **lente de contacto** or **lente invisible** contact lens; **lentes** *mpl* nose glasses; **lentes de nariz** or **de pinzas** pince-nez
lenteja *f* lentil; (*del reloj*) bob, pendulum bob
lentejuela *f* sequin, spangle
lentitud *f* slowness
len•to -ta *adj* slow; sticky; (*fuego*) low
leña *f* firewood, kindling wood; **cargar de leña** (coll) to give a drubbing to; **llevar leña al monte** to carry coals to Newcastle
leña•dor -dora *mf* woodcutter || *m* woodsman
leñame *m* lumber, timber; stock of firewood
leñero *m* wood merchant; wood purchaser; (*sitio donde se guarda la leña*) woodshed
leño *m* (*madera*) wood; (*tronco de árbol, limpio de ramas*) log; (coll) sap, blockhead; (poet) ship, vessel; **dormir como un leño** to sleep like a log
leño•so -sa *adj* woody
león *m* lion
leona *f* lioness
leona•do -da *adj* tawny, fulvous
leonera *f* lion cage, den of lions; (coll) dive, gambling joint; (coll) junk room, lumber room
leonero *m* lion keeper; (coll) keeper of a gambling joint
leontina *f* watch chain
leopardo *m* leopard
leopoldina *f* watch fob; (mil) Spanish shako
leotardo *m* leotard
lepe *m* (Ven) flip in the ear; **saber más que Lepe** to be wide-awake
leperada *f* (CAm, Mex) coarseness, vulgarity
lepisma *f* (ent) silver fish, fish moth
lepori•no -na *adj* hare, harelike
lepra *f* leprosy
leprosería *f* leper house
lepro•so -sa *adj* leprous || *mf* leper
ler•do -da *adj* slow, dull; coarse, crude
lesbianismo *m* lesbianism
les•bio -bia *adj* & *mf* Lesbian || *f* (*mujer homosexual*) Lesbian, lesbian
lesión *f* harm, hurt; (pathol) lesion
lesionar *tr* to harm, hurt, injure
lesi•vo -va *adj* harmful, injurious
lesna *f* awl
le•so -sa *adj* hurt, harmed, injured; wounded; offended; perverted; (SAm) simple, foolish
leste *m* (naut) east
letal *adj* lethal, deadly
letame *m* manure
letanía *f* litany; (*enumeración seguida*) (coll) litany
letárgi•co -ca *adj* lethargic
letargo *m* lethargy
letargo•so -sa *adj* lethargic
le•tón -tona *adj* Lettish || *mf* Lett || *m* (*idioma*) Lettish, Lett
Letonia *f* Latvia
letra *f* (*del alfabeto*) letter; (*modo de escribir propio de una persona*) hand, handwriting; (*de una canción*) words, lyric; (com) draft; (typ) type; (*sentido material*) (fig) letter; **a la letra** (*al pie de la letra*) to the letter; **a letra vista** (com) at sight; **bellas letras** belles lettres; **cuatro letras** or **dos letras** (*esquela, cartita*) a line; **en letras de molde** in print; **escribir en letra de molde** to print; **las letras y las armas** the pen and the sword; **letra a la vista** (com) sight draft; **letra de cambio** (com) bill of exchange; **letra de imprenta** (typ) type; **letra de mano** handwriting; **letra de molde** printed letter; **letra menuda** fine print; (fig) cunning; **letra muerta** dead letter; **letra negrilla** (typ) boldface; **letra redonda** or **redondilla** (typ) roman; **letras** (*literatura*) letters; (coll) a few words, a line; **primeras letras** elementary education, three R's
letra•do -da *adj* learned, lettered; (coll) pedantic || *m* lawyer
letrero *m* sign, notice; (*p.ej., en una botella*) label
letrina *f* privy, latrine; (*cloaca*) sewer; (*cosa sucia*) (fig) cesspool
letrista *mf* lyricist, writer of lyrics (*for songs*); calligrapher, engrosser
leucemia *f* leukemia
leucorrea *f* leucorrhea
leudar *tr* to leaven, to ferment with yeast || *ref* (*la masa con la levadura*) to rise
leu•do -da *adj* leavened, fermented
leva *f* weighing anchor; (mach) cam; (mil) levy
levada *f* (*de la espada, el florete, etc.*) flourish; (*de los astros*) rise; (*del émbolo*) stroke
levadi•zo -za *adj* (*puente*) lift
levadura *f* leaven; leavening; yeast; (*tabla*) board; **levadura comprimida** yeast cake; **levadura de cerveza** brewer's yeast; **levadura en polvo** baking powder
levantaco•ches *m* (*pl* **-ches**) auto jack
levantada *f* rising, getting up (*from bed or from sickbed*)
levantamiento *m* rise, elevation; insurrection, revolt, uprising; **levantamiento del cadáver** inquest; **levantamiento del censo** census taking; **le-**

vantamiento de planos surveying
levantar *tr* to raise, to lift, to elevate; to agitate, rouse, stir up; (*una sesión*) to adjourn; (*la mesa*) to clear; (*la voz*) to raise; (*el campo*) to break; (*gente para el ejército; un sitio; fondos*) to raise; (*el ancla*) to weigh; to straighten up; to build, construct, erect; to establish, found; **levantar casa** to break up housekeeping; **levantar planos** to make a survey || *ref* to rise; (*de la cama*) to get up; (*de una silla*) to stand up; to straighten up; (*sublevarse*) to rise up, rebel
levantaválvu•las *m* (*pl* **-las**) valve lifter
levantaventana *m* sash lift
levante *m* east; (*viento*) levanter || **Levante** *m* (*países de la parte oriental del Mediterráneo*) Levant; northeastern Mediterranean shores of Spain, especially around Valencia, Alicante, and Murcia
levanti•no -na *adj* Levantine; of the northeastern Mediterranean shores of Spain || *mf* Levantine; native or inhabitant of the northeastern Mediterranean shores of Spain
levar *tr* (*el ancla*) to weigh || *ref* to set sail
leve *adj* (*de poco peso*) light; slight, trivial, trifling
levedad *f* lightness; trivialness
leviatán *m* (Bib & fig) leviathan
levita *m* deacon || *f* coat, frock coat
levitón *m* heavy frock coat
léxi•co -ca *adj* lexical || *m* lexicon; (*caudal de voces de un autor*) vocabulary; (*conjunto de vocablos de una lengua o dialecto*) wordstock
lexicografía *f* lexicography
lexicográfi•co -ca *adj* lexicographic(al)
lexicógra•fo -fa *mf* lexicographer
lexicología *f* lexicology
lexicón *m* lexicon
ley *f* law; loyalty, devotion; norm, standard; (*de un metal*) fineness; **a ley de caballero** on the word of a gentleman; **de buena ley** sterling, genuine; **ley de la selva** law of the jungle; **ley del menor esfuerzo** line of least resistance; **ley marcial** martial law; **ley seca** dry law; **tener** or **tomar ley a** to become devoted to; **venir contra una ley** to break a law
leyenda *f* legend
leyente *adj* reading || *mf* reader
lezna *f* awl
lía *f* plaited esparto rope; **lías** lees, dregs
lianza *f* (Chile) account, credit (*in a store*)
liar §77 *tr* to tie, bind; to tie up, wrap up; (*un cigarrillo*) to roll; (coll) to embroil, to involve; **liarlas** (coll) to beat it; (coll) to kick the bucket || *ref* to join together, to be associated; to have a liaison; (coll) to become embroiled, become involved; **liárselos** (coll) to roll one's own (*i.e., cigarettes*)
libación *f* libation; (*acción de beber vino u otro licor*) libation
liba•nés -nesa *adj & mf* Lebanese
Líbano, el Lebanon
libar *tr* to suck; to taste, to sip || *intr* to pour out a libation; to imbibe
libelo *m* lampoon, libel; (law) petition
libélula *f* dragonfly
liberación *f* liberation; (*cancelación de la carga que grava un inmueble*) redemption; (*de una cuenta*) settlement, closing; quittance
liberal *adj* liberal; (*expedito*) quick, ready; (pol) liberal; (*de amplias miras*) (Arg) liberal-minded || *mf* (pol) liberal
liberalidad *f* liberality
liberar *tr* to free
libertad *f* liberty, freedom; **libertad de cátedra** academic freedom; **libertad de cultos** freedom of worship; **libertad de empresa** free enterprise; **libertad de enseñanza** academic freedom; **libertad de imprenta** freedom of the press; **libertad de los mares** freedom of the seas; **libertad de palabra** freedom of speech, free speech; **libertad de reunión** freedom of assembly; **libertad vigilada** probation; **plena libertad** free hand; **tomarse la libertad de** to take the liberty to
liberta•do -da *adj* bold, daring; free, brash, unrestrained
liberta•dor -dora *mf* liberator
libertar *tr* to liberate, to set free; (*de un peligro, la muerte, etc.*) to save
liberta•rio -ria *adj* anarchistic
libertinaje *m* licentiousness, profligacy; impiety, ungodliness
liberti•no -na *adj & mf* libertine
liber•to -ta *mf* (law) probationer || *m* freedman || *m* freedwoman
libídine *f* lewdness, lust; (*impulso a las actividades sexuales*) libido
libidino•so -sa *adj* libidinous
libido *f* libido
libra *f* pound; **libra esterlina** pound sterling
libraco or **libracho** *m* (coll) trashy book
libra•do -da *mf* (com) drawee
libra•dor -dora *mf* (com) drawer
libranza *f* (com) draft; **libranza postal** money order
librar *tr* to free; to save, to spare; (*la esperanza*) to place; (*batalla*) to give, to join; (com) to draw || *intr* to be delivered, to give birth; (*una religiosa*) to receive a visitor in the locutory; (com) to draw; **librar bien** to come off well, to succeed; **librar mal** to come off badly, to fail || *ref* to free oneself; to escape
libre *adj* free; free, brash, outspoken; free, unmarried; free, loose, licentious; innocent, guiltless; **libre de porte** postage prepaid
librea *f* livery
librecambio *m* free trade
librecambista *mf* freetrader
librepensa•dor -dora *adj* freethinking || *mf* freethinker
librería *f* bookstore, bookshop; book business; (*mueble*) bookshelf; **librería de viejo** second-hand bookshop
libreril *adj* book

librero *m* bookseller; (*encuadernador*) bookbinder; (Cuba, Mex) bookshelf
libres·co -ca *adj* bookish
libreta *f* notebook; **libreta de banco** bankbook
libreto *m* (mus) libretto
librillo *m* earthen washtub; (*de papel de fumar, de sellos, etc.*) book
libro *m* book; **ahorcar los libros** (coll) to become a dropout; **a libro abierto** at sight; **hacer libro nuevo** (coll) to turn over a new leaf; **libro a la rústica** paperbound book; **libro de caballerías** romance of chivalry; **libro de cocina** cookbook; **libro de cheques** checkbook; **libro de chistes** joke book; **libro de lance** second-hand book; **libro de mayor venta** best seller; **libro de memoria** memo book; **libro de oro** guest book; **libro de recuerdos** scrapbook; **libro de teléfonos** telephone book; **libro de texto** textbook; **libro diario** day book; **libro en rústica** paperbound book; **libro mayor** (com) ledger; **libro talonario** checkbook, stub book
libro-registro *m* (com) book
licencia *f* license; leave of absence; (mil) furlough; **licencia absoluta** (mil) discharge; **licencia por enfermedad** sick leave
licencia·do -da *adj* pedantic || *mf* licenciate || *m* lawyer; (mil) discharged soldier; (coll) university student (*wearing the long student gown*)
licenciar *tr* to license; to allow, permit; to confer the degree of licenciate or master on; (mil) to discharge || *ref* to receive the degree of licenciate or master; to become dissolute; (mil) to be discharged
licenciatura *f* licenciate, master's degree; graduation with a licenciate or master's degree; work leading to a licenciate or master's degree
licencio·so -sa *adj* licentious
liceo *m* (*sociedad literaria, establecimiento de enseñanza popular*) lyceum; (*instituto de segunda enseñanza*) (Chile) lycée; (Mex) primary school
licitación *f* bidding
licita·dor -dora *mf* bidder
licitar *tr* to bid on; (Arg) to buy at auction, to sell at auction || *intr* to bid
líci·to -ta *adj* fair, just; licit, legal
licor *m* (*bebida espiritosa; cuerpo líquido*) liquor; (*bebida espiritosa preparada por mezcla de azúcar y substancias aromáticas*) liqueur
licorera *f* cellaret
licorista *mf* distiller; liquor dealer
licoro·so -sa *adj* spirituous, alcoholic; (*vino*) rich, generous
licuar §21 & regular *tr* to liquefy
lid *f* fight, combat; dispute, argument; **en buena lid** by fair means
líder *m* leader
lidia *f* fight; bullfight
lidiadera *f* (Ecuad) quarreling, bickering
lidia·dor -dora *mf* fighter || *m* bullfighter
lidiar *tr* (*un toro*) to fight || *intr* to fight; **lidiar con** to fight with; to have to put up with
liebre *f* hare; (*hombre cobarde*) (coll) coward
liendre *f* nit
lien·to -ta *adj* damp, dank
lienza *f* strip of cloth
lienzo *m* linen, linen cloth; linen handkerchief; (*de edificio o pared*) face, front; (*pintura sobre lienzo*) canvas; **lienzo de la Verónica** veronica (*representing face of Christ*)
liga *f* (*cinta elástica para asegurar las medias*) garter; (*aleación*) alloy; (*materia pegajosa para cazar pájaros*) birdlime; (*confederación, alianza*) league; (*muérdago*) mistletoe; band; **liga de goma** rubber band
ligado *m* (mus & typ) ligature
ligadura *f* tie, bond; (mus) ligature, glide; (surg) ligature
ligamento *m* ligament
ligar §44 *tr* to tie, bind; to join, combine; to alloy; (*bebidas*) to mix; (surg) to ligate || *ref* to league together; to be committed; to be bound or attached (*e.g., in friendship*)
ligereza *f* lightness; speed, rapidity; fickleness, inconstancy; tactlessness
lige·ro -ra *adj* light; (*té*) weak; (*tejido*) light, thin; quick; slight; **a la ligera** lightly; quickly; unceremoniously; **de ligero** thoughtlessly, rashly; **ligero de cascos** light-headed, scatterbrained; **ligero de lengua** loose-tongued; **ligero de pies** light-footed; **ligero de ropa** scantily clad || **ligero** *adv* (Am) fast, rapidly
lignito *m* lignite
ligustro *m* privet
lija *f* (*pez*) dogfish; (*papel que sirve para pulir*) sandpaper; **darse lija** (W-I) to boast, brag, pat oneself on the back
lijar *tr* to sand, to sandpaper
lila *adj* (coll) silly, simple || *m* lilac (*color*) || *f* lilac (*plant and flower*)
li·lac *f* (*pl* **-laques**) lilac
liliputiense *adj & mf* Lilliputian
lima *f* (*herramienta*) file; sweet lime; sweet-lime tree; (*del tejado*) hip; hip rafter; correcting, polishing; **lima de uñas** nail file; **lima hoya** valley (*of roof*)
limadura *f* filing; (*partecillas*) filings
limalla *f* filings
limar *tr* to file; to file down; to polish, touch up; to smooth, smooth over; (*cercenar*) to curtail
limaza *f* (*babosa*) slug; (Ven) large file
limazo *m* slime, sliminess
limbo *m* (*borde*) edge; (theol) limbo; **estar en el limbo** (coll) to be quite distraught
limen *m* (physiol, psychol & fig) threshold
limenso *m* (Chile) honeydew melon
lime·ño -ña *adj & mf* Limean
limero *m* sweet-lime tree
limita·do -da *adj* limited; dull-witted

limitador *m* — **limitador de corriente** clock meter; slot meter
limitar *tr* to limit; to cut down, reduce || *intr* — **limitar con** to border on
límite *m* limit; boundary, border
limítrofe *adj* bordering
limo *m* slime, mud
limón *m* lemon; lemon tree; (*de un coche o carro*) shaft
limonada *f* lemonade
limoncillo *m* citronella
limonera *f* shaft
limonero *m* lemon tree
limosna *f* alms
limosnear *intr* to beg
limosne•ro -ra *adj* almsgiving, charitable || *mf* almsgiver; (Am) beggar || *m* alms box
limo•so -sa *adj* slimy, muddy
limpia *f* cleaning
limpiaba•rros *m* (*pl* **-rros**) scraper, foot scraper
limpiabo•tas *m* (*pl* **-tas**) bootblack
limpiacrista•les *m* (*pl* **-les**) windshield washer
limpiachimene•as *m* (*pl* **-as**) chimney sweep
limpiadien•tes *m* (*pl* **-tes**) toothpick
limpia•dor -dora *adj* cleaning || *mf* cleaner
limpiadura *f* cleaning; **limpiaduras** cleanings, dirt
limpiama•nos *m* (*pl* **-nos**) (Guat, Hond) towel
limpiamente *adv* in a clean manner; with ease, skillfully; simply, sincerely; unselfishly
limpiameta•les *m* (*pl* **-les**) metal polish
limpianieve *m* snowplow
limpiaparabri•sas *m* (*pl* **-sas**) windshield wiper
limpia•piés *m* (*pl* **-piés**) (Mex) door mat
limpiapi•pas *m* (*pl* **-pas**) pipe cleaner
limpiaplu•mas *m* (*pl* **-mas**) penwiper
limpiar *tr* to clean; (*purificar*) to cleanse; (*de culpas*) to exonerate; (*un árbol*) to clean out, to prune; (*zapatos*) to shine; (*hurtar*) (coll) to snitch; (*a una persona en el juego*) (coll) to clean out; (*dinero en el juego*) (coll) to clean up; (mil) to mop up; **limpiarle a uno de** to clean someone out of || *ref* to clean, to clean oneself
limpiaú•ñas *m* (*pl* **-ñas**) nail cleaner, orange stick
limpiaví•as *m* (*pl* **-as**) track cleaner
limpieza *f* (*acción de limpiar*) cleaning; (*calidad de limpio*) cleanness; (*hábito del aseo*) cleanliness; neatness, tidiness; honesty; chastity; ease, skill; (*observancia de las reglas en los juegos*) fair play; **limpieza de bolsa** (coll) emptiness of the pocketbook; **limpieza de la casa** house cleaning; **limpieza en seco** dry cleaning
lim•pio -pia *adj* clean; (*que tiene el hábito del aseo*) cleanly; neat, tidy; honest; chaste; clear, free; **dejar limpio** (coll) to clean out; **en limpio** (com) net; **limpio de polvo y paja** (coll) free, for nothing; (coll) net, after deducting expenses; **poner en limpio** to make a clear or fair copy of; **quedar limpio** (coll) to be cleaned out; **sacar en limpio** to make a clear or clean copy of; to deduce, to understand || *f* see **limpia** || **limpio** *adv* fair; cleanly; **jugar limpio** to play fair
limpión *m* (*limpiadura ligera*) lick; (coll) cleaner; (Col) scolding; (Col, Ven) dustcloth; (Ecuad) dishcloth
limusina *f* limousine
lín. *abbr* **línea**
lina *f* (Chile) coarse wool
linaje *m* lineage; class, description; **linaje humano** mankind
linaju•do -da *adj* highborn || *mf* highborn person
linaza *f* flaxseed, linseed
lince *adj* keen, shrewd, discerning; (*ojos*) keen || *m* lynx; (fig) keen person
lincear *tr* (coll) to see into
linchamiento *m* lynching
linchar *tr* to lynch
lindante *adj* bordering, adjoining
lindar *intr* to border, be contiguous; **lindar con** to border on
linde *m* & *f* limit, boundary
linde•ro -ra *adj* bordering, adjoining || *m* edge; (Am) boundary stone, landmark || *f* limit, boundary; (bot) spicebush
lindeza *f* prettiness, niceness; elegance; witticism, funny remark; (coll) flirting; **lindezas** (coll) insults
lin•do -da *adj* pretty, nice; fine, perfect; **de lo lindo** (coll) a lot, a great deal; wonderfully || *m* (coll) dude, sissy
lindura *f* prettiness, niceness
línea *f* line; (*contorno de una figura, un vestido*) lines; figure, waistline; **conservar la línea** to keep one's figure; **leer entre líneas** to read between the lines; **línea de agua** water line; **línea de batalla** line of battle; **línea de empalme** (rr) branch line; **línea de flotación** water line; **línea de fuego** firing line; **línea de fuerza** (elec) power line; (phys) line of force; **línea del partido** party line; **línea de mira** line of sight; **línea de montaje** assembly line; **línea de puntos** dotted line; **línea de tiro** (mil) line of fire; **línea férrea** railway; **línea internacional de cambio de fecha** international date line; **línea suplementaria** (mus) added line, ledger line
lineal *adj* linear
lineamentos *mpl* lineaments
linfa *f* lymph; (poet) water
linfáti•co -ca *adj* lymphatic
lingote *m* ingot, slug; (naut) ballast bar
lingual *adj* & *f* lingual
lingüista *mf* linguist
lingüísti•co -ca *adj* linguistic || *f* linguistics
linimento *m* liniment
lino *m* flax; (*tela*) linen; (poet) sail
linóleo *m* linoleum
linón *m* lawn
linotipia *f* linotype

linotípi•co -ca *adj* linotype
linotipista *mf* linotype operator
linotipo *m* linotype
linterna *f* lantern; **linterna eléctrica** flashlight
lío *m* bundle; (*de papeles*) batch; (coll) muddle, mess; (coll) liaison, affair; **armar un lío** (coll) to raise a row; **hacerse un lío** (coll) to get into a jam
lionesa — **a la lionesa** (culin) lyonnaise
liorna *f* (coll) hubbub, uproar || **Liorna** *f* Leghorn
lio•so -sa *adj* (coll) trouble-making; (coll) knotty, troublesome
liq.ⁿ *abbr* **liquidación**
líq.° *abbr* **líquido**
liquen *m* lichen
liquidar *tr* to liquefy; (com) to liquidate || *intr* (com) to liquidate || *ref* to liquefy
liquidez *f* liquidity
líqui•do -da *adj* & *m* liquid; (com) net || *f* (phonet) liquid
lira *f* (mus) lyre; (*numen de un poeta*) inspiration; poems, poetry
lírica *f* lyric poetry
líri•co -ca *adj* lyric(al); (*músico, operístico*) lyric; (Am) fantastic, utopian || *m* lyric poet; (Arg, Ven) visionary || *f* see **lírica**
lirio *m* (bot) iris; **lirio blanco** (*azucena*) Madonna lily; **lirio de agua** (bot) calla, calla lily; **lirio de los valles** (bot) lily of the valley
lirismo *m* lyricism; spellbinding; (Am) fancy, illusion
lirón *m* (bot) water plantain; (zool) dormouse; (coll) sleepyhead
lis *m* (bot) lily || *f* (bot) iris; (heral) fleur-de-lis
Lisboa *f* Lisbon
lisia•do -da *adj* hurt, injured; crippled; (*muy deseoso*) eager || *mf* cripple
lisiar *tr* to hurt, injure; to cripple || *ref* to become crippled
lisimaquia *f* loosestrife
li•so -sa *adj* even, smooth; (*vestido*) plain, unadorned; (*franco, sincero*) simple, plain-dealing; (Am) brash, insolent; **liso y llano** (coll) simple, easy
lisonja *f* flattery
lisonjear *tr* to flatter; to please || *intr* to flatter
lisonje•ro -ra *adj* flattering; pleasing || *mf* flatterer
lista *f* list; (*tira*) strip; (*en un tejido*) colored stripe; (*recuento en alta voz de las personas que deben estar en un lugar*) roll call; **lista de bajas** casualty list; **lista de comidas** bill of fare; **lista de correos** general delivery; **lista de espera** waiting list; **lista de frecuencia** frequency list; **lista de pagos** pay roll; **pasar lista** to call the roll
listar *tr* to list
listero *m* roll keeper, timekeeper
lis•to -ta *adj* ready; quick, prompt; alert, wide-awake; **estar listo** to be ready; to be finished; **listo de manos** (coll) light-fingered; **pasarse de listo** to be shrewd, to be clever || *f* see **lista**
listón *m* (*cinta*) ribbon, tape; (*pedazo de tabla angosta*) lath, strip of wood
listonado *m* lath, lathing
lisura *f* evenness, smoothness; plainness; simpleness, candor; (Am) brashness, insolence
lit. *abbr* **literalmente**
lite *f* lawsuit
litera *f* (*vehículo llevado por hombres o por animales*) litter; (*cama fija en los camarotes*) berth; **litera alta** upper berth; **litera baja** lower berth
literal *adj* literal
litera•rio -ria *adj* literary
litera•to -ta *adj* literary || *mf* literary person; **literatos** literati
literatura *f* literature; **literatura de escape** or **de evasión** escape literature
litigación *s* litigation
litigante *adj* & *mf* litigant
litigar §44 *tr* & *intr* to litigate
litigio *m* litigation, lawsuit; argument, dispute
litigio•so -sa *adj* litigious
litina *s* (chem) lithia
litio *m* (chem) lithium
litisexpensas *fpl* (law) costs
litografía *f* (*arte de grabar en piedra para la reproducción en estampa*) lithography; (*estampa*) lithograph
litografiar §77 *tr* to lithograph
litógra•fo -fa *mf* lithographer
litoral *adj* coastal, littoral || *m* coast, shore
litro *m* liter
liturgia *f* liturgy
litúrgi•co -ca *adj* liturgic(al)
liviandad *f* lightness; inconstancy, fickleness; lewdness
livia•no -na *adj* light; inconstant, fickle; lewd || *m* leading donkey; **livianos** lights, lungs
lívi•do -da *adj* livid
liza *f* combat, fight; (*campo para lidiar*) lists; **entrar en liza** to enter the lists
lo *art def neut* (used with *masc sg* form of *adj*) the, e.g., **lo bueno** the good; what is, e.g., **lo útil** what is useful; **lo mío** what is mine; (used with *adv* or inflected *adj*) the + noun, e.g., **lo aprisa que habla** the speed with which he speaks; **lo tacaños que son** the stinginess of them; how, e.g., **Vd., no sabe lo felices que son** you do not know how happy they are; **lo más** as . . . as, e.g., **lo más temprano posible** as early as possible || *pron pers masc* him, it; you; (with **estar, ser, parecer,** and the like, it stands for an adjective or noun understood and is either not translated or is translated by 'so'), e.g., **Vd. está preparado pero ella no lo está** you are ready but she is not || *pron dem* that; **de lo que** + *verb* than + *verb,* e.g., **ese libro ha costado más dinero de lo que vale** that book cost more money than it is worth; **lo de** the matter of, the question of, e.g., **lo de sus deudas** the matter of your debts; **lo de que** the fact that, the statement that; **lo de siempre** the same old story; **lo que** what, that which; **todo lo que** all

(that), e.g., **me dió todo lo que tenía** he gave me all he had
loa *f* praise; (*del teatro antiguo*) prologue; short dramatic poem
loable *adj* laudable, praiseworthy
loar *tr* to praise
loba *f* she-wolf; ridge
lobagante *m* lobster (*Homarus*)
lobanillo *m* wen, cyst
lobato *m* wolf cub
lo•bo -ba *adj & mf* (Mex) half-breed || *m* wolf; **coger** or **pillar un lobo** (coll) to go on a jag; **desollar** or **dormir un lobo** (coll) to sleep off a drunk; **lobo de mar** (ichth) sea wolf; (coll) old salt, sea dog; **lobo solitario** (fig) lone wolf || *f* see **loba**
lóbre•go -ga *adj* dark, dismal; gloomy
lobreguez *f* darkness; gloominess
lobu•no -na *adj* wolf, wolfish
locación *f* lease
local *adj* local || *m* quarters, place
localidad *f* (*lugar, sitio*) location, locality; (*plaza en un tren*) accommodations; (theat) seat
localización *f* localization; location; **localización de averías** trouble shooting
localizar §60 *tr* (*limitar a un punto determinado*) to localize; (*determinar el lugar de*) to locate
locería *f* (Am) pottery
loción *f* wash; (pharm) lotion
lo•co -ca *adj* crazy, insane, mad; terrific, wonderful; **estar loco por** (coll) to be crazy about, to be mad about; **loco de amor** madly in love; **loco de atar** (coll) raving mad; **loco perenne** insane, demented; (coll) full of fun; **loco rematado** (coll) stark-mad; **volver loco** to drive crazy || *mf* crazy person, lunatic || *m* (*bufón*) fool
locomotora *f* engine, locomotive; **locomotora de maniobras** shifting engine
locro *m* (SAm) meat and vegetable stew
lo•cuaz *adj* (*pl* **-cuaces**) loquacious
locución *f* expression, locution; idiomatic phrase, idiom
locuela *f* speech, way of speaking
locue•lo -la *adj* (coll) wild, frisky || *f* see **locuela**
locura *f* insanity, madness; folly, madness
locu•tor -tora *mf* announcer, commentator
locutorio *m* (*en un convento de monjas*) parlor, locutory; telephone booth
lodazal *m* mudhole
lodo *m* mud, mire; (*substancia que sirve para cerrar junturas, tapar grietas, etc.*) (chem) lute
lodo•so -sa *adj* muddy
logaritmo *m* logarithm
logia *f* (*p.ej., de francmasones*) lodge; (archit) loggia
lógi•co -ca *adj* logical || *mf* logician || *f* logic
logísti•co -ca *adj* logistic(al) || *f* logistics
logrado -da *adj* successful
lograr *tr* to get, to obtain; to achieve, attain; **lograr** + *inf* to succeed in + *ger* || *ref* to be successful
logrear *intr* to be a moneylender; to profiteer
logre•ro -ra *adj* moneylending; profiteering || *mf* moneylender; profiteer; (Chile) sponger
logro *m* attainment, success; gain, profit; usury; **dar** or **prestar a logro** to lend at usurious rates
loma *f* low hill, elevation
Lombardía *f* Lombardy
lombar•do -da *adj & mf* Lombard
lombriguera *f* wormhole in the ground; (bot) tansy
lom•briz *f* (*pl* **-brices**) worm, earthworm; (pathol) worm; (*persona muy alta y delgada*) (coll) beanpole; **lombriz de tierra** earthworm; **lombriz solitaria** tapeworm
lomera *f* (*de la guarnición*) backstrap; (*del tejado*) ridgepole; (bb) backing
lominhies•to -ta *adj* high-backed; (coll) conceited
lomo *m* (*de animal, libro, cuchillo*) back; (*tierra que levanta el arado*) ridge; (*carne de lomo del animal*) loin; (*pliegue del tejido*) crease; (bb) spine; **lomos** ribs
lona *f* canvas; sailcloth; (Mex) burlap
loncha *f* slab, flagstone; slice, strip
londinense *adj* London || *mf* Londoner
Londres *m* London; **el Gran Londres** Greater London
longáni•mo -ma *adj* long-suffering
longaniza *f* pork sausage
longevidad *f* longevity
longe•vo -va *adj* long-lived
longitud *f* length; (astr & geog) longitud
lonja *f* exchange, commodity exchange; grocery store; wool warehouse; (*de carne*) slice; (*de cuero*) strip; (*a la entrada de un edificio*) elevated parvis; (Arg) rawhide
lonjeta *f* bower, summerhouse
lonjista *mf* grocer
lontananza *f* (*de una pintura*) background; **en lontananza** in the distance, on the horizon
loor *m* praise
loquear *intr* to talk nonsense, to play the fool; to carry on, to have a high time
loquería *f* (Chile) madhouse, insane asylum
loque•ro -ra *mf* guard in a mental hospital || *m* (Arg) confusion, pandemonium; (Arg) insane asylum
loques•co -ca *adj* crazy; funny, jolly
lord *m* (*pl* **-lores**) lord
lo•ro -ra *adj* dark-brown || *m* parrot; cherry laurel; (Chile) spy; (Chile) glass bedpan; (Chile) third degree
losa *f* slab, flagstone; tomb
losange *m* lozenge; (baseball) diamond
lote *m* lot, share, portion; lottery prize; (Cuba, Mex) remnant; (Arg) dunce, simpleton; (Col) swallow, swig; (*de terreno*) (Cuba, Mex) lot
lotear *tr* (Chile) to divide up, divide into lots
lotería *f* lottery; (*juego casero*) lotto; (*cosa insegura, riesgo*) gamble
lote•ro -ra *mf* vendor of lottery tickets
lotizar §60 *tr* (Peru) to divide into lots

loto *m* lotus
loza *f* (*barro cocido y barnizado*) porcelain; crockery, earthenware; **loza fina** china, chinaware
lozanear *intr* to be luxuriant; to be full of life || *ref* (*deleitarse*) to luxuriate
lozanía *f* luxuriance, verdure; exuberance, vigor; pride, haughtiness
loza•no -na *adj* luxuriant, verdant; exuberant, vigorous; proud, haughty
lubricante *adj & m* lubricant
lubricar §73 *tr* to lubricate
lúbri•co -ca *adj* (*resbaladizo; lascivo*) lubricous (*slippery; lewd*)
lubrificar §73 *tr* to lubricate
lucera *f* skylight
lucerna *f* large chandelier; (*abertura, tronera*) loophole
lucero *m* bright star; (*planeta*) Venus; (*ventanillo en un muro*) light; **lucero del alba** or **de la mañana** morning star; **lucero de la tarde** evening star; **luceros** (poet) eyes
luci•do -da *adj* generous, magnificent; brilliant, successful; sumptuous; (Arg) striking, dashing
lúci•do -da *adj* lucid
luciente *adj* bright, shining
luciérnaga *f* glowworm, firefly
lucifer *m* overbearing fellow || **Lucifer** *m* Lucifer
lucífe•ro -ra *adj* (poet) bright, dazzling || *m* morning star; (Col) match
lucimiento *m* brilliance, luster; show, dash; success; **quedar** or **salir con lucimiento** to come off with flying colors
lu•cio -cia *adj* shiny || *m* salt pool; (*pez*) pike, luce
lucir §45 *tr* to light, light up; to show, display; (*p.ej., un traje nuevo*) to sport; to help; to plaster || *intr* to shine || *ref* to dress up; to come off with great success; (*sobresalir, distinguirse*) to shine; (coll) to flop, e.g., **lucido me quedé** I was a flop
lucrar *tr* to get, obtain || *intr & ref* to profit, make money
lucrati•vo -va *adj* lucrative
lucro *m* gain, profit; **lucros y daños** profit and loss
lucro•so -sa *adj* lucrative
luctuo•so -sa *adj* sad, mournful, gloomy
lucha *f* fight; (*disputa*) quarrel; (*actividad forzada*) struggle; (*combate cuerpo a cuerpo*) wrestling; **lucha de la cuerda** (sport) tug of war; **lucha por la vida** struggle for existence
lucha•dor -dora *mf* fighter; wrestler
luchar *intr* (*combatir*) to fight; (*disputar*) to quarrel; (*esforzarse*) to struggle; (*pelear cuerpo a cuerpo*) to wrestle
ludibrio *m* derision, mockery, scorn
ludir *tr, intr & ref* to rub, rub together
luego *adv* next, then; therefore; soon; **desde luego** right away; of course; **hasta luego** good-bye, so long; **luego como** as soon as; **luego de** after, right after; **luego que** as soon as
luen•go -ga *adj* long
lúes *f* pestilence; **lúes canina** distemper; **lúes venérea** syphilis
lugano *m* (orn) siskin
lugar *m* place; site, spot; job, position; (*espacio*) room, space; (*asiento*) seat; village, hamlet; (geom) locus; **dar lugar** to make room; **dar lugar a** to give cause for; to give rise to; **en lugar de** instead of, in place of; **hacer lugar** to make room; **lugar común** (*expresión trivial*) commonplace; (*retrete*) toilet, water closet; **lugar de cita** tryst; **lugares estrechos** close quarters; **lugar geométrico** locus; **lugar religioso** place of burial
lugarejo *m* hamlet
lugare•ño -ña *adj* village || *mf* villager
lugarteniente *m* lieutenant
luge *m* sled
lúgubre *adj* dismal, gloomy, lugubrious
luir §20 *tr* (naut) to gall, to wear; (Chile) to muss, to rumple; (*vasijas de barro*) (Chile) to polish || *ref* (Chile) to rub, wear away
luisa *f* (bot) lemon verbena
lujo *m* luxury; **de lujo** de luxe; **gastar mucho lujo** to live in high style; **lujo de** abundance of, excess of
lujo•so -sa *adj* luxurious
lujuria *f* lust, lechery
lujuriante *adj* (*lozano*) luxuriant, lush; (*libidinoso*) lustful
lujuriar *intr* to lust, be lustful; (*los animales*) to copulate
lujurio•so -sa *adj* lustful, lecherous || *mf* lecher
lu•lo -la *adj* (Chile) lank, slender || *m* (Chile) bundle
lu•lú *m* (*pl* **-lúes**) spitz dog
lumbago *m* lumbago
lumbre *f* light; fire; (*para encender el cigarrillo*) light; (*hueco en un muro por donde entra la luz*) light; brightness, brilliance; knowledge, learning; **echar lumbre** (coll) to blow one's top; **lumbre del agua** surface of the water; **lumbres** tinderbox; **ni por lumbre** (coll) not for love or money; **ser la lumbre de los ojos de** to be the light of the eyes of
lumbrera *f* light, source of light; light, lamp; (*abertura por donde entran el aire y la luz*) louver; sky light; dormer window; air duct, ventilating shaft; (*persona insigne*) light, luminary; (mach) port; **lumbreras** eyes
luminar *m* luminary
luminiscente *adj* luminescent
lumino•so -sa *adj* luminous; (*idea*) bright
luminotecnia *f* lighting engineering
lun. *abbr* **lunes**
luna *f* moon; moonlight; (*tabla de cristal*) plate glass; (*espejo*) mirror; (*de los anteojos*) lens, glass; (coll) caprice, whim; **estar de buena luna** to be in a good mood; **estar de mala luna** to be in a bad mood; **luna de miel** honeymoon; **luna llena** full moon; **luna menguante** waning moon; **luna nueva** new moon; **media luna** half moon; (*figura de cuarto de luna creciente o menguante*) crescent; **quedarse a la luna de Valencia** (coll) to be disappointed

lunar *adj* lunar || *m* (*mancha de la piel*) mole; (*punto en un diseño de puntos*) polka dot; (fig) stain, blot, stigma; **lunar postizo** beauty spot
lunáti•co -ca *adj & mf* lunatic
lu•nes *m* (*pl* **-nes**) Monday; **hacer San Lunes** (Am) to knock off on Monday
luneta *f* (*de los anteojos*) lens, glass; orchestra seat; (aut) rear window
lunfardo *m* (Arg) thief; (Am) underworld slang
lupa *m* magnifying glass
lupanar *m* brothel, bawdyhouse
lupia *mf* (Hond) quack, healer || *f* wen, cyst; **lupias** (Col) small amount of money, small change
lúpulo *m* (*vid*) hop; (*flores desecadas de la vid*) hops
luquete *m* slice of orange or lemon used to flavor wine; (Chile) bald spot; (*en la ropa*) (Chile) spot, hole
lu•rio -ria *adj* (Mex) mad, crazy
lusitanismo *m* Lusitanism
lusitano -na *adj & mf* Lusitanian, Portuguese
lustrabo•tas *m* (*pl* **-tas**) (Am) bootblack
lustrar *tr* to shine, to polish || *intr* to wander, roam
lustre *m* shine, polish; luster, gloss; (*fama, gloria*) (fig) luster
lustrina *f* (Chile) shoe polish
lustro *m* five years; chandelier
lustro•so -sa *adj* shining, bright, lustrous
lutera•no -na *adj & mf* Lutheran
luto *m* (*señal exterior de duelo*) mourning; (*duelo, aflicción*) sorrow, bereavement; **estar de luto** to be in mourning; **lutos** crape; **luto riguroso** deep mourning
lutocar *m* (Chile) trash cart
luz *f* (*pl* **luces**) light; window, light; guiding light; (*dinero*) (coll) money, cash; **a primera luz** at dawn; **a toda luz** or **a todas luces** everywhere; by all means; **dar a luz** to have a child; to give birth to; to bring out, to publish; **entre dos luces** at twilight; (coll) half-seas over; **luces de carretera** (aut) bright lights; **luces de cruce** (aut) dimmers; **luz de balizaje** (aer) marker light; **luz de magnesio** magnesium light; (phot) flash bulb, flashlight; **luz de matrícula** license-plate light; **luz de parada** stop light; **luz trasera** tail light; **sacar a luz** to bring to light; **salir a luz** to come to light; to come out, be published; to take place; **ver la luz** to see the light, see the light of day
Luzbel *m* Lucifer

Ll

Ll, ll (elle) *f* fourteenth letter of the Spanish alphabet
llaga *f* sore, ulcer; sorrow, grief; (*entre dos ladrillos*) (mas) seam, joint; (fig) ulcer
llagar **§44** *tr* to make sore; to hurt
llama *f* flame, blaze; marsh, swamp; (zool) llama; (fig) fire, passion; **saltar de las llamas y caer en las brasas** to jump out of the frying pan into the fire
llamada *f* call; (*movimiento con que se llama la atención de uno*) sign, signal; knock, ring; reference, reference mark; (mil) call, call to arms; **batir** or **tocar a llamada** (mil) to sound the call to arms; **llamada a filas** (mil) call to the colors; **llamada a quintas** draft call
llamadera *f* goad
llama•do -da *adj* so-called || *f* see **llamada**
llama•dor -dora *mf* caller || *m* messenger; door knocker; push button
llamamiento *m* call; calling, vocation
llamar *tr* to call; (*dar nombre a*) to name, to call; to summon; to invoke, call upon; (*la atención*) to attract || *intr* to call; (*golpear en la puerta*) to knock; (*hacer sonar la campanilla*) to ring; (*el viento*) (naut) to veer || *ref* to be called, to be named; **se llama Juan** his name is John
llamarada *f* blaze, flare-up; (*encendimiento repentino del rostro*) flush; (fig) flare-up, outburst
llamarón *m* (Am) flare-up
llamati•vo -va *adj* showy, loud, flashy, gaudy; (*manjar*) thirst-raising
llamazar *m* swamp, marsh
llame *m* (Chile) bird net, bird trap
llamear *intr* to blaze, flame, flash
llampo *m* (Chile) ore
llana *f* trowel, float; plain; **dar de llana** to smooth with the trowel
llanada *f* plain
llanero *m* (Am) ranger, plainsman
llaneza *f* plainness, simplicity; familiarity; sincerity
lla•no -na *adj* even, level, smooth; (*parecido a un plano geométrico*) plane; (*sencillo*) plain, simple; clear, evident; (*palabras*) frank; accented on the next to last syllable || *m* plain; (*de la escalera*) landing || *f* see **llana**
llanque *m* (Peru) rawhide sandal
llanta *f* (*cerco exterior de la rueda*) tire (*of iron or rubber*); (*borde exterior de la rueda*) rim; (*pieza de hierro más ancha que gruesa*) iron flat; **llanta de goma** rubber tire; **llanta de oruga** (*de un tractor de oruga*) track
llanto *m* weeping, crying; **en llanto** in tears
llanura *f* evenness, level, smoothness; (*terreno extenso y llano*) plain
llapan•go -ga *adj* (Ecuad) barefooted
llares *m* pothanger

llave *adj* key || *f* (*pieza para abrir y cerrar las cerraduras*) key; (*herramienta*) wrench; (*grifo*) faucet, spigot, cock; (*de arma de fuego*) cock; (elec) switch; (*de un instrumento de viento*) (mus) key; (*de un enigma, secreto, traducción, cifra; lugar estratégico más propicio*) key; **bajo llave** under lock and key; **echar la llave a** to lock; **llave de caja** socket wrench; **llave de caño** pipe wrench; **llave de cubo** socket wrench; **llave de chispa** flintlock; **llave de estufa** damper; **llave de mandíbulas dentadas** alligator wrench; **llave de paso** stopcock; passkey; **llave de purga** drain cock; **llave espacial** space key; **llave inglesa** monkey wrench; **llave maestra** master key, skeleton key; **llave para tubos** pipe wrench

llave•ro -ra *mf* keeper of the keys; (*carcelero*) turnkey || *m* key ring

llavín *m* latchkey

llegada *f* arrival

llegar §44 *tr* to bring up, bring close || *intr* to arrive; to happen; **llegar a** to arrive at; to reach; to amount to; to be equal to; **llegar a** + *inf* to come to + *inf;* to succeed in + *ger;* **llegar a ser** to become || *ref* to come close

llena *f* flood

llenado *m* filling

llena•dor -dora *adj* (*alimento*) (Chile) filling

llenar *tr* to fill; (*un formulario*) to fill out; (*ciertas condiciones*) to fulfill; to satisfy; (*colmar*) to overwhelm || *intr* (*la luna*) to be full || *ref* to fill, fill up; (coll) to stuff oneself; **llenarse a rebosar** to be filled to overflowing

llene *m* filling; full tank

lle•no -na *adj* full; **lleno a rebosar** full to overflowing; **lleno de goteras** (coll) full of aches and pains || *m* fill, plenty; fulness, full enjoyment; completeness; full moon; (*en el teatro*) full house || *f* see **llena**

lleva or **llevada** *f* carrying, conveying; ride; **lleva gratuita** free ride

llevade•ro -ra *adj* bearable, tolerable

llevar *tr* (*transportar*) to carry; (*traer consigo*) to take; (*conducir*) to lead; to carry away, to take away; (*cuentas, libros; la anotación en los naipes*) to keep; (*la correspondencia con una persona*) to carry on; (*un drama a la pantalla*) to put on; (*buena o mala vida*) to lead; (*aguantar*) to bear, to stand for; (*castigo*) to suffer; to get, obtain; to win; (*cierto precio*) to charge; (*traje, vestido*) to wear; (*armas*) to bear; (*cierto tiempo*) to have been, e.g., **llevo ocho días en cama** I have been in bed for a week; (*ropa*) **a todo llevar** for all kinds of wear; **llevar** (*cierto tiempo*) **a** (*uno*) to be older than (*someone*) by (*a certain age*); (*cierta distancia*) **a** (*uno*) to be ahead of (*someone*) by (*a certain distance*); (*cierto peso*) **a** (*uno*) to be heavier than (*someone*) by (*a certain weight*); **llevarla hecha** (coll) to have it all figured out; **llevar puesto** to wear, to have on; **llevar** + *pp* to have + *pp,* e.g., **lleva conseguidas muchas victorias** he has won many victories || *ref* to carry away; to take, take away; to carry off; to win; to get along; **llevarse algo a alguien** to take something away from someone

lloradue•los *mf* (*pl* **-los**) crybaby, sniveler

lloralásti•mas *mf* (*pl* **-mas**) (coll) poverty-crying skinflint

llorar *tr* to weep over; to mourn, lament || *intr* to weep, to cry; (*los ojos*) to water, to run

lloriquear *intr* to whine, to whimper

lloriqueo *m* whining, whimpering

lloro *m* weeping, crying; tears

llo•rón -rona *adj* weeping, crying || *mf* weeper, crybaby || *m* weeping willow; pendulous plume || *f* hired mourner

lloro•so -sa *adj* weepy; sad, tearful

llovedi•zo -za *adj* (*agua*) rain; (*techo*) leaky

llover §47 *tr* (*enviar como lluvia*) to rain || *intr* to rain; **como llovido** unexpectedly; **llueva o no** rain or shine; **llueve** it is raining || *ref* (*el techo*) to leak

llovido *m* stowaway

llovizna *f* drizzle

lloviznar *intr* to drizzle

llovizno•so -sa *adj* moist, damp (*from drizzle*); (Am) drizzly

lluvia *f* rain; rain water; (*copia, muchedumbre*) (fig) shower, downpour; **lluvia radiactiva** fallout, radioactive fallout

lluvio•so -sa *adj* rainy

M

M, m (eme) *f* fifteenth letter of the Spanish alphabet

m. *abbr* **mañana, masculino, meridiano, metro, minuto, muerto**

maca *f* flaw, blemish; bruise (*on fruit*); spot, stain; hammock

maca•co -ca *adj* (Am) ugly, misshapen || *m* — **macaco de la India** rhesus

macadamizar §60 *tr* to macadamize

macadán *m* macadam

macana *f* cudgel, club; drug on the market; (Am) nonsense; (Arg) botch; (Arg) lie, trick

macanu•do -da *adj* terrific, swell, grand; (Col, Ecuad) strong, husky

macarrón *m* macaroon; **macarrones** macaroni

macear *tr* to mace, hammer || *intr* to pester, to bore

macelo *m* slaughterhouse

macero *m* macebearer
maceta *f* stone hammer; flowerpot; flower vase; (*de herramienta*) handle; (*de cantero*) hammer; (Mex) head
macfarlán *m* inverness cape
macilen•to -ta *adj* pale, wan, gaunt
macillo *m* hammer (*of piano*)
macis *m* mace (*spice*)
macizar **§60** *tr* to fill in, fill up
maci•zo -za *adj* solid; massive || *m* solid; flower bed; bulk, mass; massif; wall space
macu•co -ca *adj* (Chile) sly, cunning; (Arg, Chile, Ven) important, notable; (Ecuad) old, worthless; (Arg, Chile, Peru) strong, husky || *m* (Arg, Bol, Col) overgrown boy
mácula *f* spot; stain; blemish; (coll) trick, deception
macha *f* (Bol) drunkenness; (Arg) joke; (Bol) mannish woman
machaca *mf* (coll) pest, bore || *f* crusher
machacar **§73** *tr* to crush, mash, pound || *intr* to pester, bore
macha•cón -cona *adj* boring, tiresome, importunate || *mf* bore
machada *f* flock of billy goats; (coll) stupidity
machado *m* hatchet
machamartillo — **a machamartillo** (coll) solidly, firmly, lastingly
machaque•ro -ra *adj* (coll) tiresome, boring || *mf* (coll) bore
machar *tr* to crush, grind, pound || *ref* (Bol, Ecuad) to get drunk
machete *m* machete, cane knife
machi *mf* (Chile) quack, healer
machihembrar *tr* (*ensamblar a ranura y lengüeta*) to feather; (*ensamblar a caja y espiga*) to mortise
machina *f* derrick, crane; pile driver; (P-R) merry-go-round
macho *adj invar* (*animal, planta, herramienta*) male; strong, robust; dull, stupid || *m* sledge hammer; abutment, pillar; male; he-mule; dullard; (*del corchete*) hook; (mach) male piece; (coll) he-man; (C-R) blond foreigner; **macho cabrío** he-goat, billy goat; **macho de aterrajar** or **macho de terraja** (mach) tap, screw tap
machona *f* (Arg, Bol, Ecuad, Guat) mannish woman
macho•rro -rra *adj* barren, sterile || *f* barren woman; (Mex) mannish woman
machucar **§73** *tr* to beat, pound, bruise
machu•cho -cha *adj* sedate, judicious; elderly
madamita *m* (coll) sissy
madeja *f* hank, skein; tangle of hair; (*hombre flojo*) (coll) jellyfish; **madeja sin cuenda** (coll) hopeless tangle
madera *m* Madeira wine || *f* wood; piece of wood; (coll) knack, flair; (coll) makings; **madera aserradiza** lumber; **madera contrachapada** plywood; **madera de sierra** lumber; **madera laminada** plywood
maderada *f* raft, float
maderaje *m* or **maderamen** *m* woodwork
maderería *f* lumberyard
madere•ro -ra *adj* lumber || *m* lumberman; carpenter; log driver
madero *m* log, beam; ship, vessel; (coll) blockhead
madrastra *f* stepmother; bother
madraza *f* (coll) doting mother
madre *adj* mother || *f* mother; matron; womb; main sewer; river bed; dregs, sediment; **madre adoptiva** foster mother; **madre de leche** wet nurse; **madre patria** mother country, old country; **madre política** mother-in-law; stepmother; **sacar de madre** (coll) to annoy, to upset
madreperla *f* (*molusco*) pearl oyster; (*nácar*) mother-of-pearl
madreselva *f* honeysuckle
madriga•do -da *adj* twice-married; (*toro*) that has sired; (coll) worldly-wise
madriguera *f* burrow, lair, den
madrile•ño -ña *adj* Madrid || *mf* native or inhabitant of Madrid
madrina *f* godmother; patroness, protectress; prop, shore, brace; joke; leading mare; **madrina de boda** bridesmaid; **madrina de guerra** war mother
madrugada *f* early morning, dawn; early rising
madruga•dor -dora *adj* early-rising || *mf* early riser
madrugar **§44** *intr* to get up early; to be out in front
madurar *tr* to ripen; to mature; to think out || *intr* to ripen; to mature
madurez *f* ripeness; maturity
madu•ro -ra ripe; mature
maestra *f* teacher; elementary girls' school; **maestra de escuela** schoolmistress
maestranza *f* arsenal, armory; navy yard; order of equestrian knights
maestría *f* mastery; mastership
maes•tro -tra *adj* master; masterly; chief, main; (*perro*) trained || *m* master; teacher; (*en la música y la pintura*) maestro; **maestro de capilla** choirmaster; **maestro de ceremonias** master of ceremonies; **maestro de equitación** riding master; **maestro de escuela** elementary schoolteacher; **maestro de esgrima** fencing master; **maestro de obras** master builder || *f* see **maestra**
Magallanes *m* Magellan
magancear *intr* (Col, Chile) to loaf around
magan•to -ta *adj* dull, spiritless
magia *f* magic
magiar *adj* & *mf* Magyar
mági•co -ca *adj* magic || *mf* magician, wizard || *f* magic
magín *m* (coll) fancy, imagination
magisterio *m* teaching; teachers
magistrado *m* magistrate
magistral *adj* masterly
magnáni•mo -ma *adj* magnanimous
magnesio *m* magnesium; (phot) flashlight
magnetismo *m* magnetism
magnetizar **§60** *tr* magnetize
magneto *m* & *f* magneto

magnetofón *m* or **magnetófono** *m* tape recorder, wire recorder
magnificar §73 *tr* to magnify; to exalt
magnífi•co -ca *adj* magnificent
magnitud *f* magnitude
mag•no -na *adj* great, e.g., **Alejandro Magno** Alexander the Great
mago *m* magician; soothsayer; (fig) wizard, expert; **Magos de Oriente** Wise Men of the East
ma•gro -gra *adj* lean, thin || *m* (coll) loin of pork || *f* slice of ham
maguar §10 *ref* (Ven, W-I) to be disappointed
magüeta *f* heifer
magüeto *m* young bull
maguey *m* century plant
magullar *tr* to bruise || *ref* to get bruised
mahometa•no -na *adj & mf* Mohammedan
mahometismo *m* Mohammedanism
mahonesa *f* mayonnaise
maído *m* meow
maitines *mpl* matins
maíz *m* maize, Indian corn; **maíz en la mazorca** corn on the cob
maizal *m* cornfield
maja *f* flashy dame
majada *f* sheepfold; dung, manure
majadería *f* piece of folly, nonsensical remark
majade•ro -ra *adj* pestiferous, stupid || *mf* bore, dunce || *m* pestle
majar *tr* to crush, mash, grind, pound; (coll) to annoy, bother
majestad *f* majesty
majestuo•so -sa *adj* majestic
ma•jo -ja *adj* sporty; handsome, dashing; pretty, nice; (coll) all dressed up || *mf* sport || *m* bully || *f* see **maja**
mal *adj* apocopated form of **malo,** used only before nouns in masculine singular || *adv* badly, poorly; wrong; hardly, scarcely; **mal de** short of; **mal que le pese** in spite of him || *m* evil; damage, harm; wrong; sickness; misfortune; **mal de altura** mountain sickness; **mal de la tierra** homesickness; **mal de mar** seasickness; **mal de piedra** (pathol) stone; **mal de rayos** radiation sickness; **mal de vuelo** airsickness; **por mal de mis pecados** to my sorrow; **tener a mal** to object to; **¡mal haya . . .!** curses on . . .!
mala *f* mail; mailbag; mailboat
malabarista *mf* juggler; (Am) sneak thief
malacate *m* whim; (*hoisting machine*) (Mex, Hond) spindle
malaconseja•do -da *adj* ill-advised
malagradeci•do -da *adj* (Am) ungrateful
malandante *adj* unlucky, unfortunate
malandanza *f* bad luck, misfortune
malan•drín -drina *adj* evil, wicked || *mf* scoundrel, rascal
malaria *f* malaria
malaventura *f* misfortune
mala•yo -ya *adj & mf* Malay
malbaratar *tr* to undersell; to squander
malcasa•do -da *adj* mismated; undutiful
malcasar *tr* to mismate || *intr & ref* to be mismated
malcaso *m* treachery
malconten•to -ta *adj & mf* malcontent
malcria•do -da *adj* ill-bred
malcriar §77 *tr* to spoil, pamper
maldad *f* evil, wickedness
maldecir §11 *tr* to curse || *intr* to curse, to damn; **maldecir de** to slander, to vilify
maldición *f* malediction, curse; (coll) oath, curse
maldispues•to -ta *adj* ill, indisposed; unwilling, ill-disposed
maldi•to -ta *adj* damned, accursed; wicked; (Mex) coarse, crude, indecent; **no saber maldita la cosa de** (coll) to not know a single thing about || **el Maldito** the Evil One || *f* (coll) tongue; **soltar la maldita** (coll) to talk too much
maleante *adj* wicked, evil || *mf* crook, hoodlum, rowdy
malear *tr* to spoil; to corrupt || *ref* to spoil, get spoiled; to be corrupted
malecón *m* levee, dike, mole, jetty
maledicencia *f* calumny, slander
maleficiar *tr* to damage, harm; to curse, bewitch, cast a spell on
maleficio *m* curse, spell; witchcraft
malentender §51 *tr* to misunderstand
malentendido *m* misunderstanding, misapprehension
malestar *m* malaise, indisposition
maleta *m* (coll) bungler; (coll) ham bullfighter || *f* valise; **hacer la maleta** to pack up
maletín *m* satchel
malevolencia *f* malice, malevolence
malévo•lo -la *adj* malevolent
maleza *f* thicket, underbrush; weeds
malgasta•do -da *adj* ill-spent
malgastar *tr* to waste, squander
malgenio•so -sa *adj* (Am) ill-tempered, irritable
malhabla•do -da *adj* foul-mouthed
malhada•do -da *adj* ill-starred
malhe•cho -cha *adj* deformed || *m* misdeed
malhe•chor -chora *mf* malefactor || *f* malefactress
malherir §68 *tr* to injure badly
malhumora•do -da *adj* ill-humored
malicia *f* (*maldad*) evil; (*bellaquería, malevolencia*) malice; insidiousness, trickiness; (coll) suspicion
malicio•so -sa *adj* evil; malicious; insidious, tricky
malignar *tr* to corrupt, vitiate; to spoil
malignidad *f* malignity
malig•no -na *adj* (*malévolo; pernicioso*) malign; (*malicioso; perjudicial*) malignant; (pathol) malignant
malintenciona•do -da *adj* ill-disposed, evil-minded
malmaridada *f* (coll) faithless wife
malmeter *tr* to lead astray, misguide; to alienate, estrange
ma•lo -la *adj* bad, poor, evil; (*travieso*) naughty, mischievous; (*enfermo*) sick, ill; (*que no es como debiera ser*) wrong; (*inflamado, dolorido*) sore; **estar de malas** to be out of luck; **lo malo es que** the trouble is that; **malo con** or **para con** mean to; **por malas o por buenas** willingly or unwillingly;

ser **malo de engañar** to be hard to trick || **el Malo** the Evil One || *f* see **mala**
malogra•do -da *adj* late, ill-fated
malograr *tr* to miss || *ref* to fail; to come to an untimely end
malogro *m* failure; disappointment
maloliente *adj* malodorous, foul-smelling
malón *m* mean trick; (SAm) Indian incursion; (Chile) surprise party
malpara•do -da *adj* hurt; **salir malparado (de)** to fail (in), to come out worsted (in)
malparar *tr* to mistreat
malparir *intr* to miscarry, have a miscarriage
malparto *m* miscarriage
malquerencia *f* dislike
malquerer §55 *tr* to dislike
malquistar *tr* to alienate, estrange || *ref* to become alienated
malquis•to -ta *adj* disliked, unpopular
malrotar *tr* to squander
malsa•no -na *adj* unhealthy
malsín *m* mischief-maker
malsonante *adj* obnoxious, odious
malsufri•do -da *adj* impatient
malta *m* malt || *f* asphalt, tar; (Am) dark beer; (Chile) premium beer
maltraer §75 *tr* to abuse, ill-treat; to call down, scold
maltratar *tr* to abuse, ill-treat, maltreat; to damage, spoil
maltre•cho -cha *adj* battered, damaged
malu•co -ca or **malu•cho -cha** *adj* (coll) sickish, upset
malva *f* mallow; **malva arbórea** hollyhock, rose mallow; **ser como una malva** (coll) to be meek and mild
malvado -da *adj* evil, wicked || *mf* evildoer
malvarrosa *f* hollyhock, rose mallow
malvavisco *m* marsh mallow
malvender *tr* to sell at a loss
malversación *f* graft, embezzlement, misappropriation
malversar *tr & intr* to graft, embezzle
malvezar §60 *tr* to give bad habits to || *ref* to acquire bad habits
malla *f* mesh, meshing; (*de la armadura*) mail; (*traje*) tights; bathing suit
mallete *m* mallet
Mallorca *f* Majorca
mallor•quín -quina *adj & mf* Majorcan
mama *f* mamma
ma•má *f* (*pl* **-más**) mamma
mamada *f* suck; sucking; (Am) cinch
mama•lón -lona *adj* (Ven, W-I) loafing || *mf* (Cuba) sponger
mamama *f* (Hond) granny
mamamama *f* (Peru) granny
mamar *tr* to suck; to learn as a child; (coll) to swallow; (coll) to wangle; **mamóla** (coll) he was taken in || *intr* to suck || *ref* (coll) to swallow; (*obtener sin mérito*) (coll) to wangle; (SAm) to get drunk; **mamarse a uno** (coll) to get the best of someone; (coll) to take someone in; (Col, Chile, Peru) to do away with someone
mamarracho *m* (coll) mess, sight; (*hombre ridículo*) milksop
mamelón *m* knoll, mound
mamífe•ro -ra *adj* mammalian || *m* mammal, mammalian
mamola *f* chuck (*under the chin*); **hacer la mamola a** to chuck under the chin; (coll) to take in, make a fool of
ma•món -mona *adj* sucking; fond of sucking || *mf* suckling || *m* shoot, sucker; (Guat, Hond) club; (Mex) soft cake || *f* chuck (*under chin*)
mamonear *tr* (Guat, Hond) to beat, cudgel; (S-D) to put off, delay; (*el tiempo*) (S-D) to waste
mamotreto *m* memo book; (coll) batch of papers; (coll) hulk, bulk
mampara *f* screen; folding screen; (Peru) glass door
mamparo *m* bulkhead
mampostería *f* rubble, rubblework; masonry, stone masonry
ma•mut *m* (*pl* **-muts**) mammoth
manada *f* (*de ganado vacuno*) herd, drove; (*de ganado lanar*) flock; (*de lobos*) pack; (*de gente*) gang, troop; (*de hierba, trigo, etc.*) handful
manade•ro -ra *adj* flowing || *m* spring, source; shepherd
manantial *adj* flowing, running || *m* spring, source; (fig) source
manar *tr* to run with || *intr* to pour forth, to run; to abound
manaza *f* big hand
mancar §73 *tr* to maim, cripple || *intr* (*el viento*) (naut) to abate, subside
manca•rrón -rrona *adj* (*caballería*) skinny, worn-out; (Chile) tired out, exhausted || *m* old nag; (Chile, Peru) dam, dike
manceba *f* mistress, concubine
mancebía *f* bawdyhouse, brothel; wild oats; youth
mance•bo -ba *adj* youthful || *m* youngster; youth, young man; (*en una farmacia, barbería, etc.*) helper || *f* see **manceba**
mancerina *f* saucer with hook to hold chocolate cup
mancilla *f* spot, blemish
mancillar *tr* to spot, blemish
man•co -ca *adj* armless, one-armed; one-handed; defective, faulty || *mf* cripple || *m* (Chile) old nag
mancomún — **de mancomún** jointly, in common
mancomunar *tr* to unite, combine; (*fuerzas, caudales, etc.*) to pool || *ref* to unite, combine
mancomunidad *f* association, union; (*asociación de provincias*) commonwealth
mancornar §61 *tr* (*un novillo*) to throw and hold on the ground; (*una res vacuna*) to tie a horn and front leg of; (*dos reses*) to tie together by the horns; (coll) to join, bring together
mancuernas *fpl* (Mex) cuff links
mancuernillas *fpl* (Guat, Hond) cuff links
mancha *f* spot, stain; (*de vegetación*) patch; speckle; (fig) stain, blot; **mancha solar** sunspot
manchar *tr* to spot, stain; to speckle;

(fig) to stain, disgrace || *intr* to spot; **¡mancha!** wet paint!
manda *f* gift, offer; bequest, legacy
mandade•ro -ra *mf* messenger || *m* errand boy
mandado *m* order, command; errand; **hacer un mandado** to run an errand
manda•más *m* (*pl* **-mases**) (slang) big shot; (*jefe político*) (slang) boss
mandamiento *m* order, command; (Bib) commandment; (law) writ; **los cinco mandamientos** (coll) the five fingers of the hand
mandar *tr* to order, command; (*legar*) to bequeath; (*enviar*) to send; **mandar** + *inf* to have + *inf*, e.g., **la mandé leer en voz alta** I had her read aloud || *intr* to be in command, be the boss; **mandar llamar** to send for; **mandar por** to send for; **mande Vd.** I beg your pardon || *ref* (*un enfermo*) to manage to get around; (*dos piezas*) to be communicating; **mandarse con** (*otra pieza*) to communicate with; (Am) to be rude to
mandarina *f* tangerine
mandatario *m* agent, proxy; (Am) chief executive
mandato *m* mandate; (Am) term (*of office*)
mandíbula *f* jaw, jawbone; **reír a mandíbula batiente** (coll) to roar with laughter
mandil *m* apron
mando *m* command; control, drive; **alto mando** (mil) high command; **mando a distancia** remote control; **mando a punta de dedo** finger-tip control; **mando de las válvulas** timing gears; **mando por botón** push-button control; **tener el mando y el palo** (coll) to be the boss, rule the roost
mandolina *f* mandolin
man•dón -dona *adj* bossy || *mf* domineering person || *m* (*en las minas*) (Am) boss, foreman; (*en las carreras de caballos*) (Chile) starter
mandrágora *f* mandrake
mandril *m* (mach) chuck
mandrilar *tr* to bore
manea *f* hobble
manear *tr* to hobble
manecilla *f* (*de reloj*) hand; clasp, book clasp; (bot) tendril; (typ) fist, index
manejable *adj* manageable
manejar *tr* to manage; to handle, wield; (*un automóvil*) (Am) to drive || *ref* to behave; to get around, move about
manejo *m* management; handling; intrigue, scheming; horsemanship; (Am) driving; **manejo a distancia** remote control; **manejo doméstico** housekeeping
manera *f* manner, way; **a la manera de** in the manner of; like; **de manera que** so that; **en gran manera** to a great extent; extremely; **sobre manera** exceedingly
manga *f* (*parte del vestido*) sleeve; (*tubo de caucho*) hose; waterspout; (bridge) game; **en mangas de camisa** in shirt sleeves; **ir de manga** (coll) to be in cahoots; **manga de agua** waterspout; cloudburst; **manga de camisa** shirt sleeve; **manga de riego** watering hose; **manga de viento** whirlwind; **manga marina** waterspout; **mangas** extras, profits
mangana *f* lasso
manganear *tr* to lasso; (Peru) to annoy, bother
manganeso *m* manganese
mango *m* handle; **mango de escoba** broomstick; (aer) stick, control stick
mangonear *tr* (Am) to plunder || *intr* (coll) to loaf around; (coll) to meddle; (coll) to dabble
mangosta *f* mongoose
mangote *m* sleeve protector
manguera *f* hose; (*tubo de ventilación*) funnel
mangueta *f* fountain syringe; door jamb
manguitero *m* furrier
manguito *m* muff; sleeve guard; coffee cake; (mach) sleeve
ma•ní *m* (*pl* **-níes** or **-nises**) peanut
manía *f* mania; craze, whim; (coll) grudge; **tener manía a** (coll) to dislike
maniabier•to -ta *adj* open-handed
manía•co -ca *adj* maniac(al) || *mf* maniac
maniatar *tr* to tie the hands of
maniáti•co -ca *adj* stubborn; queer, eccentric; (*entusiasta*) crazy || *mf* crank, eccentric
manicomio *m* madhouse, insane asylum
manicor•to -ta *adj* closefisted, tight
manicu•ro -ra *mf* manicure, manicurist || *f* manicure, manicuring
mani•do -da *adj* shabby, worn; hackneyed; (culin) high || *f* haunt, hangout
manifestación *f* manifestation; (*reunión pública para dar a conocer un sentimiento u opinión*) demonstration
manifestante *mf* demonstrator
manifestar **§2** *tr* to manifest; (*el Santísimo Sacramento*) to expose || *intr* to demonstrate || *ref* to become manifest
manifies•to -ta *adj* manifest || *m* manifesto; (eccl) exposition of the Host; (naut) manifest
manigua *f* (Mex, W-I) thicket, jungle; **irse a la manigua** (W-I) to revolt
manija *f* handle; clamp; crank
manilar•go -ga *adj* ready-fisted; generous
manilla *f* bracelet; handcuff, manacle
manillar *m* handle bar
maniobra *f* handling; lever; maneuver; (naut) gear, tackle
maniobrar *intr* to work with the hands; to maneuver; (rr) to shift
maniota *f* hobble
manipula•dor -dora *mf* manipulator || *m* (telg) key
manipular *tr* to manipulate
mani•quí (*pl* **-quíes**) *m* manikin, mannequin; (*para exponer prendas de ropa*) dress form; (*de pintores y escultores*) lay figure; (fig) puppet; **ir hecho un maniquí** to be a fashion plate || *f* (*mujer joven que luce los trajes de última moda*) mannequin, model
manirro•to -ta *adj* lavish, prodigal

manivací·o -a *adj* empty-handed
manivela *f* crank; **manivela de arranque** starting crank
manjar *m* dish, food, tidbit, delicacy; lift, recreation
mano *m* first to play, e.g., **soy mano** I'm first || *f* hand; (*de cuadrúpedo*) forefoot; (*de pintura*) coat; (*de papel*) quire; (*saetilla de reloj u otro instrumento*) hand; (*lance en un juego*) round, hand; (*del elefante*) trunk; pestle, masher; **a la mano** at hand, on hand; within reach; understandable; **a mano airada** violently; **asidos de la mano** hand in hand; **bajo mano** underhandedly; **caer en manos de** to fall into the hands of; **¡dame esa mano!** put it here!; **dar la mano** to lend a hand; **darse las manos** to join hands; to shake hands; **de las manos** hand in hand; **de primera mano** at first hand; first-hand; **de segunda mano** second-hand; **echar mano de** to resort to; **echar una mano** to lend a hand; to play a game; **en buena mano está** (coll) after you, you drink first; **escribir a la mano** to take dictation; **escribir a manos de** to write in care of; **estrecharse la mano** to shake hands; **ganarle a uno por la mano** to steal a march on someone; **lavarse las manos de** to wash one's hands of; **llegar a las manos** to come to blows; **malas manos** awkwardness; **mano de gato** cat's-paw; master hand, master touch; **mano de obra** labor; **mano derecha** right-hand man; **mano de santo** (coll) sure cure; **¡manos a la obra!** let's get to work!; **manos libres** outside work; **manos limpias** extras, perquisites; (coll) clean hands; **manos puercas** (coll) graft; **probar la mano** to try one's hand; **tener mano con** to have a pull with; **tener mano izquierda** (coll) to be on one's toes; **untar la mano a** (coll) to grease the palm of; **venir a las manos** to come to blows; **vivir de la mano a la boca** to live from hand to mouth
manojo *m* bunch, bundle, handful; **a manojos** in abundance
manopla *f* gauntlet; postilion's whip; (Chile) knuckles, brass knuckles
manosear *tr* to finger, to paw; to muss, to rumple; to fiddle with; (Am) to pet || *ref* (Am) to spoon, to neck
manotada *f* slap
manotear *tr* to slap, to smack || *intr* to gesticulate
manquedad *f* lack of one or both hands or arms; disability; deficiency
mansalva — **a mansalva** without risk; without warning; **a mansalva de** safe from
mansarda *f* mansard, mansard roof
mansedumbre *f* gentleness, mildness, meekness; tameness
mansión *f* stay, sojourn; abode, dwelling; **hacer mansión** to stop, stay
man·so -sa *adj* gentle, mild, meek; tame || *m* bellwether; farm
manta *f* blanket; heavy shawl; (coll) beating, thrashing; (Chile, Ecuad) poncho; (Col, Mex, Ven) coarse cotton cloth; **a manta de Dios** copiously; **dar una manta a** to toss in a blanket; **manta de coche** lap robe; **manta de viaje** steamer rug; **tirar de la manta** (coll) to let the cat out of the bag
mantear *tr* to toss in a blanket; (Am) to abuse, mistreat
manteca *f* (*grasa de los animales, esp. la del cerdo*) lard; butter; pomade; (*dinero*) (slang) dough; **como manteca** smooth as butter; **manteca de puerco** lard; **manteca de vaca** butter
mantecado *m* custard ice cream, French ice cream
mantecón *m* (coll) mollycoddle, milksop
mantel *m* tablecloth; altar cloth
mantelería *f* table linen
mantelillo *m* embroidered centerpiece
mantelito *m* lunch cloth
mantener §71 *tr* to maintain; to keep; to keep up; to sustain, defend || *ref* to keep, remain, continue
mantenida *f* (Am) kept woman
mantenido *m* (*hombre que vive a expensas de su mujer*) (Guat, Mex, W-I) gigolo; (Guat, Mex, W-I) sponger
mantenimiento *m* maintenance; food, support, living
manteo *m* mantle, cloak
mantequera *f* churn, butter churn; butter dish
mantequería *f* creamery; delicatessen
mantequilla *f* butter; **mantequilla azucarada** hard sauce; **mantequilla derretida** drawn butter
mantilla *f* mantilla (*silk or lace head scarf*); **mantillas** swaddling clothes
mantillo *m* humus, mold
manto *m* mantle, cloak; (*de chimenea*) mantel; (*ropa talar de algunos religiosos, catedráticos, alumnos*) robe, gown; (fig) cloak
mantón *m* shawl, kerchief
manuable *adj* handy
manual *adj* (*que se hace con las manos*) hand; (*fácil de manejar*) handy; easy; easy to understand; easy-going; manual || *m* manual, handbook; notebook
manubrio *m* handle; crank, winch
manuela *f* open hack (*in Madrid*)
manufactura *f* (*fábrica*) factory; (*obra fabricada*) manufacture
manufacturar *tr* to manufacture
manuscribir §83 *tr* to write by hand
manuscri·to -ta *adj & m* manuscript
manutención *f* maintenance; care, upkeep; shelter, protection
manutener §71 *tr* (law) to maintain, support
manzana *f* apple; (*conjunto aislado de varias casas contiguas*) block, city block; (*remate en un mueble*) knob, finial; **manzana de Adán** (Chile) Adam's apple
manzanar *m* apple orchard
manzanilla *f* camomile; (*aceituna pequeña; vino blanco*) manzanilla (*small olive; white wine*); (*remate en un mueble*) knob, finial

manzano *m* apple tree
maña *f* skill, dexterity; cunning, craftiness; bad habit, vice; (*de lino, cáñamo, etc.*) bunch; (Am) sister; **darse maña** to manage, contrive; **hacer maña** (Col) to fool around
mañana *adv* tomorrow; **¡hasta mañana!** see you tomorrow!; **pasado mañana** the day after tomorrow || *m* tomorrow; (*tiempo venidero*) morrow || *f* morning; **de mañana** in the morning; **muy de mañana** very early in the morning; **por la mañana** in the morning; **tomar la mañana** to get up early; (coll) to have a shot of liquor before breakfast
mañanear *intr* to be in the habit of getting up early
mañane•ro -ra *adj* morning; early-rising
mañanica *f* early morning, break of day
mañanita *f* woman's bed jacket
mañear *tr* to manage craftily || *intr* to act with cunning
mañerear *intr* (Arg) to dawdle, dilly-dally
mañería *f* sterility
mañe•ro -ra *adj* clever, shrewd; simple, easy; (Am) skittish
ma•ño -ña *mf* (coll) Aragonese || *m* (Am) brother || *f* see **maña**
maño•so -sa *adj* skillful, clever; crafty, tricky; vicious
mañuela *f* craftiness, trickiness
mañue•las *mf* (*pl* **-las**) (coll) tricky person
mapa *m* map; **mapa itinerario** road map || *f* — **llevarse la mapa** (coll) to take the prize
mapache *m* coon, raccoon
mapamundi *m* map of the world; (coll) buttocks, behind
mapurite *m* (CAm) skunk
maque *m* lacquer
maquear *tr* to lacquer; (Mex) to varnish
maqueta *f* (*en tamaño reducido*) maquette; (*en tamaño natural*) mock-up; (*de un libro*) dummy
maquillador *m* (theat) make-up man
maquillaje *m* (theat) make-up
maquillar *tr & ref* to make up
máquina *f* machine; (*motor*) engine; locomotive; plan, project; (fig) machinery; (coll) heap, pile, lot; (Cuba) auto; (Chile) ganging up; **escribir a máquina** to typewrite; **máquina de afeitar** safety razor; **máquina de apostar** gambling machine; **máquina de componer** typesetter; **máquina de coser** sewing machine; **máquina de escribir** typewriter; **máquina de lavar** washing machine; **máquina de sumar** adding machine; **máquina de volar** flying machine; **máquina fotográfica** camera; **máquina parlante** talking machine; **máquina sacaperras** slot machine
maquinación *f* machination, scheming
máquina-herramienta *f* (*pl* **máquinas-herramientas**) machine tool
maquinal *adj* mechanical
maquinar *tr* to plot, to scheme
maquinaria *f* machinery; applied mechanics
maquinilla *f* windlass, winch; clippers; **maquinilla cortapelos** clippers, hair clippers; **maquinilla de afeitar** safety razor; **maquinilla de rizar** curling iron
maquinista *mf* (*persona que fabrica máquinas*) machinist; (*persona que dirige una máquina o locomotora*) engineer; **segundo maquinista** (naut) machinist
mar *m & f* sea; tide, flood; **alta mar** high seas; **a mares** abundantly, copiously; **arrojarse a la mar** to plunge, take great risks; **baja mar** low tide; **correr los mares** to follow the sea; **hablar de la mar** (coll) to talk wildly, to talk on and on; **hacerse a la mar** to put to sea; **la mar de** (fig) oceans of, large numbers of; **mar alta** rough sea; **mar ancha** high seas; **mar bonanza** calm sea; **mar Caribe** Caribbean Sea, Caribbean; **mar de las Antillas** Caribbean Sea; **mar de las Indias** Indian Ocean; **mar de nubes** cloud bank; **mar Latino** Mediterranean Sea; **mar llena** high tide; **meter la mar en un pozo** to attempt the impossible; **meterse mar adentro** (fig) to go beyond one's depth
maraña *f* undergrowth, thicket; silk waste; (*de hilo, pelo, etc.*) tangle; trick, scheme; puzzle
marañón *m* cashew
maraño•so -sa *adj* scheming || *mf* schemer
maravilla *f* wonder, marvel; (bot) marigold, calendula; **a las maravillas** or **a las mil maravillas** magnificently; **a maravilla** wonderfully well; **por maravilla** rarely, occasionally
maravillar *tr* to astonish || *ref* to wonder, to marvel; **maravillarse con** or **de** to marvel at, to wonder at
maravillo•so -sa *adj* wonderful, marvelous
marbete *m* label, tag; baggage check; edge, border; **marbete engomado** sticker
marca *f* mark; (*tipo de producto*) make, brand; (*de tamaño*) standard; score; record; height-measuring device; **de marca** outstanding; **marca de agua** watermark; **marca de fábrica** trademark; **marca de reconocimiento** (naut) landmark, seamark; **marca de taquilla** box-office record; **marca registrada** registered trademark
marca•do -da *adj* marked, pronounced
marcaje *m* (sport) scoring; (sport) interfering; (telp) dialing
marcapaso *m* pacemaker
marcar **§73** *tr* to mark; to brand; to embroider; (*p.ej., un pañuelo*) to initial; (*la hora un reloj*) to show; (*un tanto*) to make, to score; (*el número telefónico*) to dial || *ref* (*un buque*) to take bearings
marcear *tr* to shear || *ref* to be March-like
marcial *adj* martial; gallant, noble

marco *m* frame; framework; (*de pesas y medidas*) standard
marcha *f* march; (*funcionamiento*) running, operation; (*p.ej., de los astros*) course, path; (*desenvolvimiento de un asunto*) course, march, progress; (*grado de velocidad*) rate of speed; (*de los engranajes*) (aut) speed; **cambiar de marcha** to shift gears; **en marcha** on the march; underway; in motion; **marcha atrás** reverse; **marcha del hambre** hunger march; **marcha directa** high gear; **marcha forzada** (mil) forced march
marchamo *m* customhouse mark; (Arg, Bol) tax on slaughtered cattle
marchante *adj* commercial || *m* dealer, merchant; (Am) customer
marchapié *m* running board
marchar *intr* to march; to run, work, go; to leave, go away; to come along, proceed; **marchar en vacío** to idle || *ref* to leave, go away
marchitar *tr* to wilt, wither || *ref* to wilt, wither; to languish
marchi•to -ta *adj* withered, faded; (fig) languid
marea *f* tide; tideland; gentle sea breeze; dew; drizzle; **marea alta** high tide; **marea baja** low tide; **marea creciente** or **entrante** flood tide; **marea menguante** ebb tide; **marea muerta** neap tide; **marea viva** spring tide; **rendir la marea** to stem the tide
marea•do -da *adj* nauseated, sick, lightheaded; seasick
mareaje *m* navigation, seamanship; (*de un buque*) course
marear *tr* to sail; (coll) to annoy, pester || *intr* (coll) to be annoying || *ref* to get sick, to get giddy; to get seasick; to be damaged at sea; (Am) to fade
marejada *f* heavy sea; (*de desorden*) stirring, undercurrent; **marejada de fondo** ground swell
maremagno or **maremágnum** *m* (coll) big mess
mareo *m* nausea, dizziness, sickness; seasickness; (coll) annoyance
marfil *m* ivory
marfile•ño -ña *adj* ivory
mar•fuz -fuza *adj* (*pl* **-fuces -fuzas**) cast aside, rejected; deceptive
marga *f* marl
margar **§44** *tr* to marl
margarita *f* pearl; (bot) daisy; **margarita de los prados** English daisy
margen *m & f* margin; border, edge; marginal note; **al margen de** aloof from; outside of; independent of; aside from; **dar margen para** to give occasion for; **dejar al margen** to leave out; **quedar al margen de** to be left out of
marginal *adj* marginal
mariache *m* Mexican band and singers
marica *m* (coll) sissy, milksop || *f* magpie
maricón *m* (coll) sissy
maridable *adj* marital
maridaje *m* married life; (fig) union
maridar *tr* to combine, unite || *intr* to get married; to live as man and wife
marido *m* husband
mariguana *f* marihuana
mariguanza *f* (Chile) hocus-pocus; (Chile) pirouette; **mariguanzas** (Chile) clowning; (Chile) powwowing
marimacho *m* (coll) mannish woman
marimandona *f* (coll) queen bee, bossy woman
marimarica *m* (coll) sissy
marimorena *f* (coll) fight, row
marina *f* navy; (*conjunto de buques*) marine, fleet; (*cuadro o pintura*) seascape; shore, seaside; sailing, navigation; **marina de guerra** navy; **marina mercante** merchant marine
marinar *tr* to marinate, to salt; (*un buque*) to man || *intr* to be a sailor
marinera *f* sailor blouse; (*blusa de niño*) middy, middy blouse
marinería *f* sailoring; sailors
marine•ro -ra *adj* sea, marine; seaworthy; seafaring || *m* mariner, seaman, sailor; **marinero de agua dulce** (*el que ha navegado poco*) landlubber (*person unacquainted with the sea*); **marinero matalote** (*hombre de mar, rudo y torpe*) landlubber (*awkward and unskilled seaman*) || *f* see **marinera**
marines•co -ca *adj* sailor; sailorly
mari•no -na *adj* marine, sea || *m* mariner, seaman, sailor || *f* see **marina**
marioneta *f* marionette
mariposa *f* butterfly; butterfly valve; wing nut; rushlight; (Col) blindman's buff; **mariposa nocturna** moth
mariposear *intr* to flit about; to be fickle
mariposón *m* (Cuba, Guat, Mex) fickle flirt
mariquita *m* (coll) sissy, milksop, popinjay || *f* (ent) ladybird
marisabidilla *f* (coll) bluestocking
mariscal *m* blacksmith; (mil) marshal; **mariscal de campo** (mil) field marshal
marisco *m* shellfish; **mariscos** seafood
marisma *f* swamp, marsh, salt marsh
marisquería *f* seafood store, seafood restaurant
maríti•mo -ma *adj* maritime; marine, sea
maritor•nes *f* (*pl* **-nes**) (coll) mannish maidservant, wench
marmita *f* pot, boiler, kettle
marmitón *m* kitchen scullion
mármol *m* marble
marmóre•o -a *adj* marble
marmosete *m* vignette
marmota *f* marmot; sleepyhead; worsted cap; **marmota de Alemania** hamster; **marmota de América** ground hog, woodchuck
maroma *f* hemp rope, esparto rope; (Am) acrobatic stunt
maromear *intr* (Am) to perform acrobatic stunts, to walk the tight rope; (Am) to wobble, to sway from side to side (*e.g., in politics*); (Am) to hesitate
marome•ro -ra *mf* (Am) acrobat, tightrope walker; (Am) weaseler

marqués *m* marquis; **los marqueses** the marquis and marchioness
marquesa *f* marchioness, marquise; (*sobre la puerta de un hotel*) marquee
marquesina *f* cover over field tent; (*sobre la puerta de un hotel*) marquee; locomotive cab
marquetería *f* cabinetwork, woodwork; (*taracea*) marquetry
marra·jo -ja *adj* sly, tricky; (*toro*) vicious
marrana *f* sow; (coll) slattern, slut
marranada *f* (coll) piggishness, filth
marranalla *f* (coll) rabble, riffraff
marra·no -na *adj* base, vile; (coll) dirty, sloppy || *mf* hog || *m* male hog, boar; filthy person, hog; cad, cur || *f* see **marrana**
marrar *intr* to miss, fail; to go astray
marras *adv* (coll) long ago; **hacer marras que** (Bol, Ecuad) to be a long time since
marro *m* game resembling quoits and played with a stone; (*juego de muchachos*) tag; (*ladeo*) dodge, duck; slip, miss
marrón *adj invar* maroon (*dark-red*); tan (*shoes*) || *m* maroon; candied chestnut; stone (*used as a sort of quoit*)
marro·quí (*pl* **-quíes**) *adj & mf* Moroccan || *m* morocco, morocco leather
marro·quín -quina *adj & mf* var of **marroquí**
marrubio *m* horehound
marrue·co -ca *adj & mf* Moroccan
Marruecos *m* Morocco
marrulle·ro -ra *adj* cajoling, wheedling || *mf* cajoler, wheedler
Marsella *f* Marseille
marsopa or **marsopla** *f* porpoise
mart. *abbr* **martes**
marta *f* pine marten; **marta cebellina** sable, Siberian sable; **marta del Canadá** fisher
Marte *m* Mars
mar·tes *m* (*pl* **-tes**) Tuesday; **martes de carnaval** or **carnestolendas** Shrove Tuesday
martillar *tr* to hammer; to pester, worry || *intr* to hammer
martillazo *m* blow with a hammer
martillear *tr & intr* var of **martillar**
martillero *m* (Chile) auctioneer
martillo *m* hammer; auction house; (*persona*) scourge; (mus) tuning hammer; (*de arma de fuego*) cock
martín *m* — **martín pescador** (*pl* **martín pescadores**) kingfisher
martinete *m* drop hammer; pile driver; (*del piano*) hammer
martinico *m* (coll) ghost, goblin
mártir *mf* martyr
martirio *m* martyrdom
márts. *abbr* **mártires**
marullo *m* surge, swell
marxista *adj & mf* Marxist or Marxian
marzo *m* March
mas *conj* but
más *adv* more; most; **a lo más** at most, at the most; **a más de** besides, in addition to; **como el que más** as the next one, as well as anybody; **cuando más** at the most; **de más** extra; too much, too many; **estar de más** to be in the way; to be unnecessary; to be superfluous; **los más de** most of, the majority of; **más bien** rather; **más de** + *número* more than; **más de lo que** + *verbo* more than; **más que** more than; better than; **no . . . más** no longer; **no . . . más nada** nothing more; **no . . . más que** only || *prep* plus || *m* more; (*signo de adición*) plus
masa *f* mass; (*pasta que se forma con agua y harina*) dough; (*masa aplastada*) mash; nature, disposition; (Chile, Ecuad) puff paste; (*p.ej., de un automóvil*) (elec) ground; **las masas** the masses
masada *f* farm
masadero *m* farmer
masaje *m* massage; **masaje facial** facial
masajear *tr* to massage
masajista *m* masseur || *f* masseuse
masar *tr* to knead; to massage
mascar §73 *tr* to chew; (coll) to mumble, mutter || *ref* (*un cabo*) (naut) to gall
máscara *mf* (*persona*) mask, mummer || *f* mask; (*traje, disfraz*) masquerade; **máscara antigás** gas mask
mascarada *f* masquerade
mascarilla *f* half mask; false face; death mask
mascarón *m* false face; (*persona fea*) fright; (archit) mask; **mascarón de proa** (naut) figurehead
mascota *f* mascot
mascujar *tr & intr* (coll) to chew with difficulty; (coll) to mumble
masculi·no -na *adj* masculine; (*sexo*) male; (*traje*) men's || *m* masculine
mascullar *tr & intr* (coll) to mumble, mutter; (coll) to chew with difficulty
masera *f* kneading trough
masilla *f* putty
masita *f* (mil) money withheld for clothing; (Arg, Bol) cake
masón *m* Mason
masonería *f* Masonry
mastelero *m* (naut) topmast
masticar §73 *tr* to chew, masticate; to meditate on; to mumble
mástil *m* (*de una embarcación*) mast; (*de un violín o guitarra*) neck; stalk; (*de pluma*) shaft, stem; upright
mas·tín -tina *mf* mastiff; **mastín danés** Great Dane
mastodonte *m* mastodon
mastuerzo *m* (bot) cress; (coll) dolt
masturbar *ref* to masturbate
mat. *abbr* **matématica**
mata *f* bush, shrub; blade, sprig; brush, underbrush; **mata de pelo** crop of hair, head of hair; **mata parda** chaparro (*oak*); **saltar de la mata** (coll) to come out of hiding
mataca·bras *m* (*pl* **-bras**) cold blast from the north
matacán *m* dog poison
matacande·las *m* (*pl* **-las**) candle snuffer
matadero *m* abattoir, slaughterhouse; (coll) drudgery

mata•dor -dora *mf* killer || *m* matador; **matador de mujeres** lady-killer
matadura *f* sore, gall
matafue•gos *m* (*pl* **-gos**) fire extinguisher; (*oficial*) fireman
matalo•bos *m* (*pl* **-bos**) wolf's-bane
mata•lón -lona *mf* (coll) skinny old nag
matalotaje *m* (naut) ship stores; (coll) mess, hodgepodge
matamale•zas *m* (*pl* **-zas**) weed killer
matamari•dos *f* (*pl* **-dos**) (coll) many times a widow
matamo•ros *m* (*pl* **-ros**) (coll) bully
matamos•cas *m* (*pl* **-cas**) fly swatter; flypaper
matanza *f* slaughter, massacre; butchering; pork products; (CAm) butcher shop; (Ven) slaughterhouse
matape•rros *m* (*pl* **-rros**) (coll) harum-scarum, street urchin
matar *tr* to kill; to butcher; (*el fuego, la luz*) to put out; (*la cal*) to slack; (*el metal*) to mat; (*un color*) to tone down; (*un naipe*) to spot; to play a card higher than; (*a un caballo*) to gall; to bore to death; (*el tiempo, el hambre, etc.*) (fig) to kill || *intr* to kill || *ref* to kill oneself; to drudge, overwork; to be disappointed; **matarse con** to quarrel with; **matarse por** to struggle for; to struggle to
matarratas *m* rat poison; (*aguardiente de mala calidad*) (coll) rotgut
matarro•tos *m* (*pl* **-tos**) (Chile) pawnshop
matasa•nos *m* (*pl* **-nos**) quack doctor
matasellar *tr* to cancel, to postmark
matase•llos *m* (*pl* **-llos**) postmark
matasie•te *m* (*pl* **-te**) (coll) bully, swashbuckler
matatí•as *m* (*pl* **-as**) (coll) moneylender, pawnbroker
matazar•zas *m* (*pl* **-zas**) weed killer
mate *adj* dull, flat || *m* checkmate; (SAm) maté; (SAm) maté gourd; **dar mate a** to checkmate; to make fun of; **dar mate ahogado a** to stalemate; **mate ahogado** stalemate
matear *tr* to plant at regular intervals; to make dull; (Chile) to checkmate || *ref* (*el trigo*) to sprout; (*un perro de caza*) to hunt through the bushes
matemáti•co -ca *adj* mathematical || *mf* mathematician || *f* mathematics; **matemáticas** mathematics
materia *f* matter; material, stuff; **materia colorante** dyestuff; **materia prima** or **primera materia** raw material
material *adj* material; (*grosero*) crude || *m* material; (*conjunto de objetos necesario para un servicio*) matériel; (typ) matter, copy; **material de guerra** matériel; **material fijo** (rr) permanent way; **material móvil** or **rodante** (rr) rolling stock; **ser material** (coll) to be immaterial
materialismo *m* materialism
materializar **§60** *tr* (*beneficios*) to realize
maternal *adj* maternal, mother; (*afectos, cuidados, etc.*) motherly
maternidad *f* maternity; motherhood
mater•no -na *adj* maternal, mother
matinal *adj* morning
matinée *f* matinée; dressing gown, wrapper
ma•tiz *m* (*pl* **-tices**) shade, hue, nuance
matizar **§60** *tr* (*diversos colores*) to blend; (*un color, un sonido*) to shade; (*en cuanto al color*) to match
matón *m* (coll) bully, browbeater
matorral *m* thicket, underbrush
matraca *f* rattle, noisemaker; taunting, bantering; bore, pest; **dar matraca a** (coll) to taunt, to tease
matraquear *intr* (coll) to make a racket; (coll) to taunt, to tease
ma•traz *m* (*pl* **-traces**) flask
matre•ro -ra *adj* cunning, shrewd || *m* (SAm) cheat, swindler
matriarca *f* matriarch
matricida *adj* matricidal || *mf* matricide
matricidio *m* matricide
matrícula *f* register, roster, roll; licence; registry
matricular *tr & ref* to matriculate
matrimonialmente *adv* as husband and wife
matrimoniar *intr* to marry, get married
matrimonio *m* marriage, matrimony; (*marido y mujer*) (coll) married couple; **matrimonio consensual** common-law marriage
ma•triz (*pl* **-trices**) *adj* main, first, mother || *f* matrix; (*del libro talonario*) stub; screw nut; first draft
matrona *f* matron; (coll) matronly lady
matronal *adj* matronly
matun•go -ga *adj* (Am) skinny, full of sores || *m* (Am) old nag
maturran•go -ga *adj* (SAm) poor, clumsy || *m* (SAm) stranger; (SAm) old nag || *f* (coll) trickery
Matusalén *m* Methuselah; **vivir más años que Matusalén** to be as old as Methuselah
matute *m* smuggling; smuggled goods; gambling den
matutear *intr* to smuggle
matute•ro -ra *mf* smuggler
matutinal or **matuti•no -na** *adj* morning
maula *mf* (coll) lazy loafer; (coll) poor pay; (coll) tricky person, cheat || *f* junk, trash; remnant; trickery
maulería *f* remnant shop; trickiness
maullar **§8** *intr* to meow
maullido or **maúllo** *m* meow
mausoleo *m* mausoleum
máxima *f* maxim; principle
máxime *adv* chiefly, mainly, especially
máxi•mo -ma *adj* maximum; top; superlative || *m* maximum || *f* see **máxima**
may. *abbr* **mayúscula**
maya *f* May queen; English daisy
mayal *m* flail
mayear *intr* to be Maylike
mayestáti•co -ca *adj* royal
mayido *m* meow
mayo *m* May; Maypole
mayonesa *f* mayonnaise
mayor *adj* greater; larger; older, elder; greatest; largest; oldest, eldest; major; elderly; (*calle*) main; (*altar; misa*) high; **hacerse mayor de edad**

to come of age; **ser mayor de edad** to be of age || *m* chief, head, superior; **al por mayor** wholesale; **mayor de edad** (*persona de edad legal*) major; **mayores** elders; ancestors, forefathers; **mayor general** staff officer
mayoral *m* boss, foreman; head shepherd; stagecoach driver; (Arg) streetcar conductor
mayorazgo *m* primogeniture; entailed estate descending by primogeniture; first-born son
mayordoma *f* stewardess, housekeeper
mayordomo *m* steward, butler, majordomo
mayoreo *m* (Am) wholesale
mayoría *f* (*mayor edad; el mayor número, la mayor parte*) majority; superiority; **alcanzar su mayoría de edad** to come of age; **mayoría de edad** majority
mayoridad *f* majority
mayorista *adj* (Arg, Chile) wholesale || *mf* (Arg, Chile) wholesaler
mayorita•rio -ria *adj* majority
mayormente *adv* chiefly, mainly, mostly
mayúscu•lo -la *adj* (*letra*) capital; (coll) awful, tremendous || *f* capital, capital letter
maza *f* mace; heavy drumstick; (coll) bore, pedant; **la maza y la mona** constant companions; **maza de gimnasia** Indian club
mazacote *m* barilla; concrete, cement; botched job; (coll) tough, doughy food; (coll) bore
mazar **§60** *tr* to churn
mazmorra *f* dungeon
mazo *m* mallet, maul; bunch; (*de la campana*) clapper; (*hombre fastidioso*) bore, pest
mazonería *f* stone masonry; (*obra de relieve*) relief; gold or silver embroidery
mazorca *f* ear of corn; cocoa bean; (*husada*) spindleful; (*de un balustre*) spindle; **comer maíz de** or **en la mazorca** to eat corn on the cob
mazorral *adj* coarse, crude
m/c *abbr* **mi cargo, mi cuenta, moneda corriente**
m/cta *abbr* **mi cuenta**
m/cte *abbr* **moneda corriente**
me (used as object of verb) *pron pers* me, to me || *pron reflex* myself, to myself
meada *f* urination, water; urine stain
meadero *m* urinal
meados *mpl* urine
meaja *f* crumb; **meaja de huevo** tread
meandro *m* meander; wandering speech, wandering writing
mear *tr* to urinate on || *intr & ref* to urinate
Meca, La Mecca
mecáni•co -ca *adj* mechanical; (coll) low, mean || *m* (*obrero perito en el arreglo de las máquinas*) mechanic; (*obrero que fabrica y compone máquinas*) machinist; workman, repairman; driver, chauffeur || *f* mechanics; (*aparato que da movimiento a un artefacto*) machinery, works; (coll) meanness; **mecánicas** (coll) household chores
mecanismo *m* mechanism, machinery
mecanizar **§60** *tr* to mechanize; to motorize
mecanografía *f* typewriting; **mecanografía al tacto** touch typewriting
mecanografiar **§77** *tr & intr* to typewrite
mecanógra•fo -fa *mf* typist, typewriter
mecapale•ro -ra *m* (Mex) messenger, porter
mece•dor -dora *adj* swinging, rocking || *m* stirrer; (*columpio*) swing || *f* rocker, rocking chair
mecer **§46** *tr* (*un líquido*) to stir; (*la cuna*) to rock || *ref* to rock, swing
mecha *f* (*de vela o bujía*) wick; (*tubo de pólvora*) fuse; lock of hair; (*para mechar carne*) slice of bacon; bundle of thread; (Col, Ecuad, Ven) joke
mechar *tr* (*la carne*) to lard, interlard
mechera *f* (coll) shoplifter
mechero *m* (*p.ej., de cigarrillos*) lighter, pocket lighter; (*de aparato de alumbrado*) burner; (*de candelero*) socket; **mechero encendedor** pilot, pilot light
mechón *m* cowlick; (Guat) torch
medalla *f* medal; medallion
medallón *m* medallion; (*joya en que se colocan retratos, etc.*) locket
médano *m* dune, sandbank
media *f* stocking; (math) mean; **media corta** (Arg) sock; **media media** (Arg, Ecuad, Ven) sock; **y media** half past, e.g., **las dos y media** half past two
mediación *f* mediation
media•do -da *adj* half over; half-full; **a mediados de** about the middle of; **mediada la tarde** in the middle of the afternoon
media•dor -dora *mf* mediator
mediana *f* long billiard cue
medianería *f* party wall; party fence
mediane•ro -ra *adj* middle; mediating || *mf* mediator; partner; owner of a row house
medianía *f* average; (*persona que carece de dotes relevantes*) mediocrity
media•no -na *adj* middling, medium; average, fair; (coll) mediocre || *f* see **mediana**
medianoche *f* midnight; small meat pie
mediante *adj* interceding || *prep* by means of, by virtue of
mediar *intr* to be half over; to be in the middle; to intercede, mediate; to elapse; to take place
mediatinta *f* half-tone
medible *adj* measurable
medical *adj* medical
medicamento *m* medicine
medicamento•so -sa *adj* medicinal
medicastro *m* quack
medicina *f* medicine
medicinar *tr* to treat || *ref* to take medicine
medición *f* measurement; metering
médi•co -ca *adj* medical || *mf* doctor, physician; **médico de cabecera** family physician
medida *f* measurement; measure; caution, moderation; **a medida de** in pro-

portion to; according to; **a medida que** in proportion as; **en la medida que** to the extent that; **hecho a la medida** custom-made; **medida para áridos** dry measure; **medida para líquidos** liquid measure; **tomarle a uno las medidas** to take someone's measure, to size up someone

medidamente *adv* with moderation

medidor *m* measurer; (Mex, SAm) meter

medie•ro -ra *mf* hosier; partner

medieval *adj* medieval

medievalista *mf* medievalist

medievo *m* Middle Ages

me•dio -dia *adj* middle; medium; medieval; half; a half, e.g., **media libra** a half pound; half a, e.g., **media naranja** half an orange; average, mean; mid, in the middle of, e.g., **a media tarde** in mid afternoon, in the middle of the afternoon; **a medias** half; half-and-half; **ir a medias (con)** to go halves (with), to go fifty-fifty (with) || *m* middle; medium, environment; step, measure; means; (*en el espiritismo*) medium; (baseball) shortstop; (arith) half; (*del ruedo*) (taur) center; **a medio** half; **en medio de** in the middle of; in the midst of; **justo medio** happy medium, golden mean; **por medio de** by means of; **quitarse de en medio** (coll) to get out of the way || *f* see **media** || **medio** *adv* half

mediocre *adj* mediocre

mediocridad *f* mediocrity

mediodía *m* noon, midday; south; **en pleno mediodía** at high noon; **hacer mediodía** to stop for the noon meal

mediquillo *m* quack

medir **§50** *tr* to measure || *intr* to measure || *ref* to act with moderation

meditabun•do -da *adj* meditative

meditar *tr* to meditate; to plan, contemplate || *intr* to meditate

mediterráne•o -na *adj* inland || **Mediterráne•o -na** *adj & m* Mediterranean

mé•dium *m* (*pl* **-dium** or **-diums**) medium

medra *f* growth, prosperity

medrana *f* fear

medrar *intr* to thrive, prosper, improve

medro *m* growth, prosperity; **medros** progress

medro•so -sa *adj* fearful, scared; frightful, terrible

médula or **medula** *f* marrow, medulla; (bot) pith; (fig) pith, gist, essence; **médula espinal** spinal cord

medular *adj* pithy

medusa *f* jellyfish

mefistoféli•co -ca *adj* Mephistophelian

megaciclo *m* megacycle

megáfono *m* megaphone

me•go -ga *adj* meek, gentle, mild

megohmio *m* megohm

Méj. *abbr* **Méjico**

mejica•no -na *adj & mf* Mexican

Méjico *m* Mexico; **Nuevo Méjico** New Mexico

meji•do -da *adj* beaten with sugar and milk

mejilla *f* cheek

mejor *adj* better; best; (*licitador*) highest; **a lo mejor** (coll) unexpectedly; (coll) worse luck; (coll) perhaps, maybe; **el mejor día** some fine day || *adv* better; best; **mejor dicho** rather

mejora *f* growth, improvement; higher bid; alteration

mejoramiento *m* improvement

mejorana *f* sweet marjoram

mejorar *tr* to improve; (*los licitadores el precio de una cosa*) to raise; **mejorando lo presente** present company excepted || *intr & ref* to improve, get better, recover; to make progress; (*el tiempo*) to clear up

mejoría *f* improvement; (*en una enfermedad*) betterment, recovery

mejunje *m* brew, potion, mixture

mela•do -da *adj* honey-colored || *m* (Am) thick cane syrup

melancolía *f* (*tristeza vaga*) melancholy; (*depresión moral*) melancholia

melancóli•co -ca *adj* melancholy

melaza *f* molasses

melcocha *f* taffy, molasses candy

melchor *m* German silver

melena *f* hair falling over the eyes; long hair, loose hair; (*del león*) mane; (*del caballo*) forelock; **andar a la melena** (coll) to pull each other's hair; (coll) to get into a fight; **estar en melena** (coll) to have one's hair down

melga *f* (Am) ridge made by plow; (Col, Chile) plot of ground to be sown; (Hond) small piece of work to be finished

melindre *m* honey fritter; (*dulce de pasta de mazapán*) ladyfinger; narrow ribbon; prudery, finickiness

melindrear *intr* to be prudish, be finicky

melindro•so -sa *adj* prudish, finicky

melocotón *m* peach tree; peach

melocotonero *m* peach tree

melodía *f* melody

melodio•so -sa *adj* melodious

melodramáti•co -ca *adj* melodramatic

melón *m* melon; (*Cucumis melo*) muskmelon; (coll) blockhead; (coll) bald head; **melón de agua** watermelon

melo•so -sa *adj* sweet, honeyed; gentle, mild, mellow

mella *f* dent, nick, notch; gap, hollow; harm, injury; **hacer mella a** to have an effect on; **hacer mella en** to harm

mellar *tr* to dent, nick, notch; to harm

melli•zo -za *adj & mf* twin

membrana *f* membrane; (*del teléfono, micrófono*) diaphragm

membrete *m* note, memo; letterhead; heading; written invitation

membrillero *m* quince tree

membrillo *m* quince; quince tree

membru•do -da *adj* brawny, burly

memeches — **a memeches** (CAm) on horseback

memela *f* (CAm, Mex) cornmeal pancake

me•mo -ma *adj* foolish, simple || *mf* fool, simpleton

memorán•dum *m* (*pl* **-dum**) memorandum book, notebook; (*sección en los*

periódicos) professional services; (*papel con membrete*) letterhead
memorar *tr & ref* to remember
memoria *f* memory; (*exposición de ciertos hechos*) memoir; account, record; **de memoria** by heart; **encomendar a la memoria** to commit to memory; **hablar de memoria** (coll) to say the first thing that comes to one's mind; **hacer memoria de** to bring up; **memorias** memoirs; regards
memorial *m* memorandum book; memorial, petition; (law) brief
memorizar §60 *tr* to memorize
mena *f* ore
menaje *m* household furniture; school supplies
mención *f* mention
mencionar *tr* to mention
men•daz (*pl* **-daces**) *adj* mendacious ‖ *mf* liar
mendicante *adj & mf* mendicant
mendigante *adj* begging, mendicant ‖ *mf* beggar, mendicant
mendigar §44 *tr* to beg for ‖ *intr* to beg, go begging
mendi•go -ga *mf* beggar
mendiguez *f* begging
mendo•so -sa *adj* false, wrong
mendrugo *m* crumb, crust
menear *tr* to stir, to shake; to wiggle; (*la cola*) to wag; (*un negocio*) to manage; **peor es meneallo** (i.e., **menearlo**) better keep hands off ‖ *ref* to shake; to wiggle; to wag; (coll) to hustle, bestir oneself
meneo *m* stirring, shaking; wagging; hustling; (coll) drubbing, thrashing
menester *m* need; want, lack; job, occupation; **haber menester** to be necessary, to be need for; **menesteres** bodily needs; property; (coll) implements, tools; **ser menester** to be necessary
menestero•so -sa *adj* needy ‖ *mf* needy person
menestra *f* vegetable soup
menes•tral -trala *mf* mechanic
meng. *abbr* **menguante**
mengua *f* want, lack; poverty; decline; decrease, diminution; **en mengua de** to the discredit of
mengua•do -da *adj* timid, cowardly; simple, silly; mean, stingy; wretched, miserable; poor, needy; fatal
menguante *adj* decreasing; declining; waning ‖ *f* decrease; decline; low water; ebb tide; **menguante de la luna** wane, waning of the moon
menguar §10 *tr* to diminish, lessen; to discredit ‖ *intr* to diminish, lessen; to decline; to decrease; (*la luna*) to wane; (*la marea*) to fall
mengue *m* (coll) devil
menina *f* young lady in waiting
menino *m* noble page of the royal family
menor *adj* less, lesser; smaller; younger; least; smallest; youngest; slightest; minor ‖ *m* minor; **al por menor** retail; **menor de edad** minor; **por menor** retail; in detail, minutely ‖ *f* minor premise
Menorca *f* Minorca
menoría *f* inferiority, subordination; (*tiempo de menor edad*) minority
menorista *adj* (Arg, Chile) retail ‖ *mf* (Arg, Chile) retailer
menor•quín -quina *adj & mf* Minorcan
menos *adv* less; fewer; least; fewest; **al menos** at least; **a lo menos** at least; **a menos que** unless; **echar de menos** to miss; **¡menos mal!** lucky break!; **menos mal que** it is a good thing that; **no poder menos de** + *inf* to not be able to help + *ger;* **por lo menos** at least; **tener en menos** to think little of; **venir a menos** to decline; to become poor ‖ *prep* less, minus; (*al decir la hora*) of, to, e.g., **las tres menos diez** ten minutes of (or to) three ‖ *m* less; (*signo de resta o sustracción*) minus, minus sign
menoscabar *tr* to lessen, diminish, reduce; to damage; to discredit
menoscabo *m* lessening, reduction; damage; discredit; **con menoscabo de** to the detriment of
menoscuenta *f* part payment
menospreciable *adj* despicable, contemptible
menospreciar *tr* to underestimate, underrate; to scorn, despise
menosprecio *m* underestimation; scorn
mensaje *m* message
mensajería *f* public conveyance; **mensajerías** transportation company; shipping line
mensaje•ro -ra *mf* messenger ‖ *m* harbinger
men•so -sa *adj* (Mex) foolish, stupid
menstruar §21 *intr* to menstruate
menstruo *m* menses
mensual *adj* monthly
mensualidad *f* monthly pay, monthly instalment
ménsula *f* bracket; elbow rest
mensurar *tr* to measure
menta *f* mint; **menta piperita** peppermint; **menta romana** or **verde** spearmint
menta•do -da *adj* famous, renowned
mentar §2 *tr* to mention
mente *f* mind
mentecatería or **mentecatez** *f* simpleness, folly
menteca•to -ta *adj* simple, foolish ‖ *mf* simpleton, fool
mentidero *m* (coll) hangout; (coll) gossip column
mentir §68 *tr* to disappoint ‖ *intr* to lie; to be misleading; (*un color*) to clash; **¡miento!** my mistake!
mentira *f* lie; error, mistake; **mentira inocente** or **oficiosa** white lie; **parece mentira** it's hard to believe
mentirilla *f* fib, white lie; **de mentirillas** for fun
mentirón *m* whopper
mentiro•so -sa *adj* lying; false, deceptive; full of errors ‖ *mf* liar
men•tís *m* (*pl* **-tís**) insulting contradiction; **dar un mentís a** to give the lie to
mentón *m* chin
me•nú *m* (*pl* **-nús**) menu

menudamente *adv* in detail; at retail
menudear *tr* to make frequently; to tell in detail; (Col) to sell at retail || *intr* to happen frequently, to be frequent; to go into detail; (Arg) to grow, increase
menudencia *f* smallness; trifle; meticulousness; **menudencias** pork products; (Col, Mex) giblets
menudeo *m* constant repetition; detailed accounting; **al menudeo** at retail
menudillos *mpl* giblets
menu•do -da *adj* small, slight, minute; futile, worthless; meticulous; common, vulgar; petty || *m* innards (*of fowl and other animals*); rice coal; **al menudo** at retail; **a menudo** often; **menudos** small change; **por menudo** in detail; at retail
meñique *adj* little, tiny; (*dedo*) little || *m* little finger
meollo *m* marrow; pith; (*seso*) brain; brains, intelligence; gist, marrow, essence
me•ón -ona *adj* (*niño*) piddling; (*niebla*) dripping
mequetrefe *m* (coll) whippersnapper, jackanapes
mercachifle *m* peddler; small dealer
mercadear *intr* to deal, to trade
merca•der -dera *mf* merchant; **mercader de grueso** wholesale merchant
mercadería *f* merchandise, commodity; **mercaderías** goods, merchandise
mercado *m* market; **lanzar al mercado** to put on the market; **mercado de valores** stock market; **mercado negro** black market
mercaduría *f* commodity
mercancía *f* trade, commerce; merchandise; piece of merchandise; **mercancías** goods, merchandise || **mercancías** *msg* (*pl* **-as**) freight train
mercante *adj & m* merchant
mercantil *adj* mercantile
mercar **§73** *tr* to buy || *intr* to trade, deal
merced *f* pay, wages; favor, grace; **a merced de** at the mercy of; **merced a** thanks to; **merced de agua** distribution of irrigating water; **vuestra merced** your grace
mercena•rio -ria *adj* mercenary || *m* mercenary; day laborer, hireling
mercería *f* haberdashery, notions store; (Am) dry-goods store; (Chile) hardware store
mercología *f* marketing
mercurio *m* mercury
merecer **§22** *tr* to deserve, merit; (*lo que se desea*) to attain; (*alabanza*) to win; (*cierta suma*) to be worth; **merecer la pena** to be worth while || *intr* to be deserving; **merecer bien de** to deserve the gratitude of
mereci•do -da *adj* deserved || *m* just deserts; **llevar su merecido** to get what's coming to one
mereciente *adj* deserving
merecimiento *m* desert, merit
merendar **§2** *tr* to lunch on, have for lunch; to keep an eye on, to peep at || *intr* to lunch || *ref* to manage to get; (*en el juego*) (Chile) to clean out
merendero *m* lunchroom; picnic grounds
merendona *f* fine spread
merengar **§44** *tr* to whip (*cream*)
merengue *m* meringue
mere•triz *f* (*pl* **-trices**) harlot
meridiana *f* lounge, couch; afternoon nap; meridian line; **a la meridiana** at noon
meridia•no -na *adj* meridian; bright, dazzling || *m* meridian || *f* see **meridiana**
meridional *adj* southern || *mf* southerner
merienda *f* lunch, snack; (coll) hunchback
meri•no -na *adj* merino; (*cabello*) thick and curly || *mf* merino || *m* merino shepherd; merino wool
mérito *m* merit, desert; value, worth; **hacer mérito de** to make mention of; **hacer méritos** to try to please, to put one's best foot forward
merito•rio -ria *adj* meritorious || *m* volunteer worker; unpaid learner, apprentice
merluza *f* (*pez*) hake; (coll) drunk, spree
merma *f* decrease, reduction; leakage, shrinkage
mermar *tr* to decrease, reduce || *intr* to decrease, shrink, dwindle
mermelada *f* marmalade
me•ro -ra *adj* mere, pure; (Col, Ven) alone || *m* grouper, jewfish || **mero** *adv* (CAm) almost, soon
merodea•dor -dora *adj* marauding || *m* marauder
merodear *intr* to maraud
mes *m* month; monthly pay; menses; **caer en el mes del obispo** (coll) to come at the right time
mesa *f* table; (*mostrador*) counter; (*escritorio*) desk; (*de arma blanca o herramienta*) flat side; (*de escalera*) landing; (*comida*) fare, food; (*conjunto de dirigentes*) board; **alzar la mesa** to clear the table; **hacer mesa limpia** to clean up (*in gambling*); **levantar la mesa** to clear the table; **mesa de batalla** sorting table; **mesa de extensión** extension table; **mesa de juego** gambling table; **mesa de milanos** (coll) scanty fare; **mesa de trucos** pool table; **mesa perezosa** drop table; **poner la mesa** to set or lay the table; **tener a mesa y mantel** to feed, to support; **tener mesa** to keep open house
mesana *f* (naut) mizzen
mesar *tr* (*los cabellos*) to tear, pull out || *ref* — **mesarse los cabellos** to pull out one's hair; to pull out each other's hair
mescolanza *f* (coll) jumble, hodgepodge, medley
meseguería *f* harvest watch
mesera *f* (Am) waitress
mesero *m* journeyman on monthly pay; (Am) waiter
meseta *f* plateau, tableland; (*de escalera*) landing

Mesías *m* Messiah
mesilla *f* mantel, mantelpiece; (*de escalera*) landing; window sill
mesita *f* stand, small table; **mesita portateléfono** telephone table
mesnada *f* armed retinue; band, company
mesón *m* inn, tavern; (Chile) bar; (Chile) counter
mesone•ro -ra *adj* inn, tavern || *mf* innkeeper, tavern keeper
mester *m* (archaic) craft, trade; (archaic) literary genre; **mester de clerecía** clerical verse of the Middle Ages; **mester de juglaría** popular minstrelsy of the Middle Ages
mesti•zo -za *adj & mf* half-breed; (*perro*) mongrel
mesura *f* dignity, gravity; calm, restraint; courtesy, civility
mesura•do -da *adj* dignified, sedate; calm, restrained; polite; moderate, temperate
mesurar *tr* to temper, moderate || *ref* to act with restraint
meta *f* goal
metafonía *f* umlaut
metáfora *f* metaphore
metafóri•co -ca *adj* metaphorical
metal *m* metal; money; (*de la voz*) timbre; condition, quality; (mus) brass; **el vil metal** (coll) filthy lucre; **metal blanco** nickel silver; **metal de imprenta** type metal
metale•ro -ra *adj* (Bol, Chile, Peru) metal || *m* (Bol, Chile, Peru) metalworker
metáli•co -ca *adj* metallic || *m* metalworker; cash, coin
metalistería *f* metalwork
metalizar **§60** *tr* to make metallic; to put a metal coating on; to turn into cash || *ref* to become mercenary
metaloide *m* nonmetal
metalurgia *f* metallurgy
metamorfo•sis *f* (*pl* **-sis**) metamorphosis
metano *m* methane
metate *m* (CAm, Mex) flat stone on which corn is ground
metáte•sis *f* (*pl* **-sis**) metathesis
mete•dor -dora *mf* smuggler
meteduría *f* smuggling
metemuer•tos *m* (*pl* **-tos**) stagehand; busybody, meddler
meteo *f* weather bureau, weather report
meteóri•co -ca *adj* meteoric
meteoro or **metéoro** *m* meteor; atmospheric phenomenon
meteorología *f* meteorology
meter *tr* to put, to place; to insert; (*un ruido*) to make; (*miedo*) to cause; (*mentiras*) to tell; (*chismes, enredos*) to start; (*dinero en el juego*) to stake; to smuggle; (*un golpe*) (Am) to strike || *ref* to project; to meddle, butt in; **meterse a** to set oneself up as; to take it upon oneself to; **meterse con** to pick a quarrel with; **meterse en** to get into; to plunge into; to empty into
meticulo•so -sa *adj* meticulous; shy, timid
meti•do -da *adj* close, tight; rich, abundant; (Am) meddlesome; **muy metido con** on close terms with; **muy metido en** deeply involved in || *m* push; punch; strong lye; loose leaf; (*tela sobrante en las costuras de una prenda*) seam
metódi•co -ca *adj* methodic(al)
metodista *adj & mf* Methodist
método *m* method
metraje *m* distance or length in meters; (*cine*) **de corto metraje** short; (*cine*) **de largo metraje** full-length
metralla *f* scrap iron; grapeshot; shrapnel
métri•co -ca *adj* metric(al) || *f* prosody
metro *m* meter; ruler; tape measure; subway; **metro plegadizo** folding rule
metrónomo *m* metronome
metrópoli *f* metropolis; mother country
metropolita•no -na *adj* metropolitan || *m* subway; (eccl) metropolitan
Méx. *abbr* **México**
mexica•no -na *adj & mf* (Am) Mexican
México *m* (Am) Mexico; **Nuevo México** New Mexico
mezcla *f* mixture; (*argamasa*) mortar; (*tejido*) tweed
mezclar *tr* to mix; to blend || *ref* to mix; (*introducirse uno entre otros*) to mingle; to intermarry; to meddle
mezclilla *f* light tweed
mezcolanza *f* jumble, hodgepodge, medley
mezquinar *tr* (Am) to be stingy with || *intr* (Am) to be stingy
mezquindad *f* meanness, stinginess; need, poverty; smallness, tininess; wretchedness
mezqui•no -na *adj* mean, stingy; needy, poor; small, tiny; wretched
mezquita *f* mosque
mi *adj poss* my
mí (used as object of a preposition) *pron pers* me || *pron reflex* myself
miar **§77** *intr* to meow
miau *m* meow
mica *f* mica; (Guat) flirt; **ponerse una mica** (CAm) to go on a jag
mico *m* long-tailed monkey; libertine; (coll) hoodlum; **dar mico** (coll) to not keep a date
microbio *m* microbe
microbiología *f* microbiology
microbús *m* (Chile) jitney
microfaradio *m* microfarad
microficha *f* microcard
micro•film *m* (*pl* **-films** o **-filmes**) microfilm
microfilmar *tr* to microfilm
micrófono *m* microphone
microonda *f* microwave
micropelícula *f* microfilm
microscópi•co -ca *adj* microscopic
microscopio *m* microscope
microsurco *adj invar* microgroove || *m* microgroove
microteléfono *m* handset, French telephone
mi•cho -cha *mf* (coll) pussy cat
miedo *m* fear, dread; **miedo cerval**

great fear; **por miedo de** for fear of; **por miedo (de) que** for fear that; **tener miedo (a)** to be afraid (of); **tener miedo de** to be in fear of, be afraid of; to be afraid to
miedo•so -sa *adj* (coll) fearful, afraid
miel *f* honey; (*jarabe saturado*) molasses; **dejar con la miel en los labios** to spoil the fun for; **hacerse de miel** to be peaches and cream
mielga *f* lucerne
miembro *m* member; (*extremidad del hombre y los animales*) member, limb
mientes *fpl* mind, thought; wish, desire; **caer en las mientes** or **en mientes** to come to mind; **parar** or **poner mientes en** to reflect on; **venírsele a uno a las mientes** to come to one's mind
mientras *conj* while; whereas; **mientras que** while; whereas; **mientras tanto** meanwhile
miérco•les *m* (*pl* **-les**) Wednesday; **miércoles de ceniza** Ash Wednesday
mies *f* cereal, grain; harvest time; **mieses** grain fields
miga *f* (*porción pequeña*) bit; (*parte más blanda del pan*) crumb; (fig) substance; **hacer buenas migas con** to get along well with; **migas** fried crumbs
migaja *f* bit, piece; (*de inteligencia*) smattering; **migajas** crumbs; leavings
migajón *m* crumb; (coll) substance
migar §44 *tr* (*el pan*) to crumb; (*p.ej., la leche*) to put crumbs in
migrato•rio -ria *adj* migratory
miguelear *tr* (CAm) to make love to
miguele•ño -ña *adj* (Hond) impolite, discourteous
mijo *m* millet
mil *adj & m* thousand, a thousand, one thousand; **a las mil quinientas** (coll) at an unearthly hour
milagre•ro -ra *adj* superstitious; miracle-working
milagro *m* (*hecho sobrenatural*) miracle; (*cosa rara*) wonder; votive offering; **colgar el milagro a** (coll) to put the blame on; **vivir de milagro** to have a hard time getting along; to have had a narrow escape
milagrón *m* (coll) fuss, excitement
milagro•so -sa *adj* miraculous; marvelous, wonderful
milano *m* burr, down; (orn) kite
mil•deu *m* (*pl* **-deues**) mildew
milena•rio -ria *adj* millennial || *m* millennium
milenio *m* millennium
milenrama *f* yarrow
milési•mo -ma *adj & m* thousandth
miliamperio *m* milliampere
milicia *f* militia; soldiery; warfare; military service
milicia•no -na *adj* military || *m* militiaman
miligramo *m* milligram
milímetro *m* millimeter
militante *adj* militant
militar *adj* military; army || *m* soldier, military man || *intr* to fight, go to war; to struggle; to serve in the army; (*surtir efecto*) to militate
militarismo *m* militarism
militarista *adj & mf* militarist
militarizar §60 *tr* to militarize
mílite *m* soldier
milpa *f* (CAm, Mex) cornfield
milla *f* mile
millar *m* thousand
millarada *f* about a thousand; **echar millaradas** to boast about one's wealth
millo *m* millet
millón *m* million
millona•rio -ria *adj* of a million or more inhabitants || *mf* millionaire
mimar *tr* to fondle, to pet; to pamper, indulge, spoil
mimbre *m & f* (bot) osier; osier, wicker, withe
mimbrear *intr & ref* to sway
mimbre•ño -ña *adj* willowy
mimbrera *f* (bot) osier, osier willow
mimbro•so -sa *adj* osier; (*hecho de mimbre*) wicker
mimeografiar §77 *tr* to mimeograph
mimeógrafo *m* mimeograph
mímica *f* mimicry; sign language
mimo *m* (*entre los griegos y romanos*) mime; fondling, petting; pampering
mimo•so -sa *adj* delicate, tender; finicky, fussy
mina *f* mine; (*de lápiz*) lead; (fig) mine, gold mine, storehouse; underground passage; (SAm) moll; **beneficiar una mina** to work a mine; **mina de carbón** or **mina hullera** coal mine; **voló la mina** the truth is out
minado *m* mine work; (nav) mining
mina•dor -dora *adj* (nav) mine-laying || *m* (mil) miner; (nav) mine layer
minar *tr* to mine; to undermine; to consume; to plug away at || *intr* to mine
minarete *m* minaret
mineraje *m* mining; **mineraje a tajo abierto** strip mining
mineral *adj & m* mineral
mineralogía *f* mineralogy
minería *f* mining; mine operators
mine•ro -ra *adj* mining || *m* miner; mine operator; (fig) source, origin
mingitorio *m* street urinal
min•gón -gona *adj* (Ven) spoiled, pampered
miniar *tr* to paint in miniature; (*un manuscrito*) to illuminate
miniatura *f* miniature
miniaturización *f* miniaturization
míni•mo -ma *adj* minimum; tiny, small, minute; least, smallest || *m* minimum || *f* tiny bit
mini•no -na *mf* (coll) kitty, pussy
ministerial *adj* ministerial
ministerio *m* ministry, cabinet, government; **formar ministerio** to form a government; **ministerio de Hacienda** Treasury Department (U.S.A.); Treasury (Brit); **ministerio de la Gobernación** Department of the Interior (U.S.A.); Home Office (Brit); **ministerio del Ejército** Department of the Army (U.S.A.); War Office (Brit); **ministerio de Marina** Department of

the Navy (U.S.A.); Board of Admiralty (Brit)
ministrar *tr* to administer; to furnish
ministro *m* minister; bailiff, constable; **ministro de asuntos exteriores** foreign minister; **ministro de Gobernación** Home Secretary (Brit); **ministro de Hacienda** Secretary of the Treasury (U.S.A.); Chancellor of the Exchequer (Brit); **ministro de Justicia** Attorney General (U.S.A.); **primer ministro** prime minister, premier
minorar *tr* to diminish, reduce; to weaken
minorati•vo -va *adj & m* laxative
minoría *f* minority
minoridad *f* minority
minorita•rio -ria *adj* minority
minucia *f* trifle; **minucias** minutiae
minucio•so -sa *adj* minute, meticulous
minué *m* or **minuete** *m* minuet
minúscu•lo -la *adj* (*letra*) small; (coll) small, tiny || *f* small letter
minuta *f* first draft, rough draft; memorandum; menu, bill of fare; roll, list
minutero *m* minute hand
minu•to -ta *adj* minute || *m* minute || *f* see **minuta**
mí•o -a *adj poss* mine; of mine, e.g., **un amigo mío** a friend of mine || *pron poss* mine
miope *adj* near-sighted || *mf* near-sighted person
miopía *f* near-sightedness
mira *f* (*de arma de fuego, telescopio, etc.*) sight; aim, object, purpose; target; watchtower; **estar a la mira** to be on the lookout; **poner la mira en** to have designs on
mirada *f* glance, look; **apuñalar con la mirada** to look daggers at; **mirada de soslayo** side glance
miradero *m* (*lugar desde donde se mira*) lookout; (*persona o cosa que es objeto de la atención pública*) cynosure
mira•do -da *adj* cautious, circumspect; **bien mirado** highly regarded || *f* see **mirada**
mirador *m* belvedere; bay window, oriel
miramiento *m* considerateness, courtesy, regard; look; **miramientos** (coll) fuss, bother
miranda *f* eminence, vantage point
mirar *tr* to look at, to watch; to consider, contemplate; **mirar bien** to look with favor on; **mirar por encima** to glance at || *intr* to look, to glance; **¡mira!** look out!; **mirar a** to look at, glance at; to face, overlook; to aim at; to aim to; **mirar por** to look after || *ref* to look at oneself; to look at each other; **mirarse en ello** to watch one's step; **mirarse en una persona** to be all wrapped up in a person
mirasol *m* sunflower
miríada *f* myriad
mirilla *f* peephole; (*para dirigir visuales*) target; (phot) finder
miriñaque *m* hoop skirt, crinoline; bauble, trinket; (Arg) cowcatcher
mirística *f* nutmeg tree
mirlar *ref* (coll) to try to look important
mirlo *m* blackbird; (coll) solemn look; **mirlo blanco** (coll) rare bird; **soltar el mirlo** (coll) to start to jabber
mirmidón *m* tiny fellow, nincompoop
mi•rón -rona *adj* onlooking; nosy || *mf* onlooker; (*de una partida de juego*) kibitzer; busybody
mirra *f* myrrh
mirto *m* myrtle
misa *f* mass; **cantar misa** to say mass; **como en misa** in dead silence; **misa cantada** High Mass; **misa de prima** early mass; **misa mayor** High Mass; **misa rezada** Low Mass
misal *m* missal
misantropía *f* misanthropy
misántropo *m* misanthrope
misar *intr* (coll) to say mass; (coll) to hear mass
misario *m* acolyte
misceláne•o -na *adj* miscellaneous || *f* miscellany
miserable *adj* miserable, wretched; mean, stingy; despicable, vile || *mf* cur, cad; wretch; miser
miseran•do -da *adj* pitiful
miserear *intr* (coll) to be stingy
miseria *f* misery, wretchedness; poverty; stinginess; (coll) trifle, pittance; **comerse de miseria** (coll) to live in great poverty
misericordia *f* compassion, mercy, pity
misericordio•so -sa *adj* merciful
míse•ro -ra *adj* miserable, wretched || *mf* wretch
misión *f* mission; ration for harvesters; **ir a misiones** to go away as a missionary
misional *adj* missionary
misionario *m* missionary; envoy, messenger
misionero *m* missionary
misi•vo -va *adj & f* missive
mismísi•mo -ma *adj* very same, self-same
mis•mo -ma *adj & pron indef* same; own, very; -self, e.g., **ella misma** herself; myself, e.g., **yo mismo** I myself; yourself, himself, herself, itself; **así mismo** likewise, also; **casi lo mismo** much the same; **lo mismo** just the same; **lo mismo me da** (coll) it's all the same to me; **mismo . . . que** same . . . as; **por lo mismo** for that very reason || **mismo** *adv* right, e.g., **ahora mismo** right now; **aquí mismo** right here
mistela *f* flavored brandy; needled must, spiked must
misterio *m* mystery; **hablar de misterio** to talk mysteriously
misterio•so -sa *adj* mysterious
misticismo *m* mysticism
místi•co -ca *adj* mystic(al) || *mf* mystic
mistificación *f* hoax, mystification
mistificar **§73** *tr* to hoax, to mystify
mistifori *m* (coll) hodgepodge
misturera *f* (Peru) flower girl
mita *f* mite, cheese mite; (SAm) Indian slave labor; (*turno en el trabajo*) (Arg, Chile) shift, turn

mitad *f* half; middle; **a (la) mitad de** halfway through; **cara mitad** (coll) better half; **en la mitad de** in the middle of; **la mitad de** half the; **mitad y mitad** half-and-half; **por la mitad** in half, in the middle
míti•co -ca *adj* mythical
mitigar **§44** *tr* to mitigate, appease, allay
mitin *m* (*pl* **mitins** or **mítines**) meeting, rally
mito *m* myth
mitología *f* mythology
mitológi•co -ca *adj* mythological
mitón *m* mitten
mitra *f* chimney pot; (eccl) miter
mixtificación *f* hoax, mystification
mixtificar **§73** *tr* to hoax, to mystify
mixtifori *m* (coll) hodgepodge
mixtión *f* mixture
mix•to -ta *adj* mixed || *m* compound number; sulphur match; explosive compound
mixtura *f* mixture
mixturar *tr* to mix
mixturera *f* (Peru) flower girl
miz *interj* here, pussy!, here, kitty!
mízcalo *m* edible milk mushroom
m/l *abbr* **mi letra**
m/n *abbr* **moneda nacional**
mobilia•rio -ria *adj* personal (*property*) || *m* furniture, suit of furniture
moblaje *m* furniture, suit of furniture
moblar **§61** *tr* to furnish
moca *m* Mocha coffee || *f* (Ecuad) mudhole; (Mex) wineglass
mocador *m* handkerchief
mocar **§73** *tr* to blow the nose of || *ref* to blow one's nose
mocarro *m* (coll) snot
mocasín *m* moccasin
mocear *intr* to act young; to sow one's wild oats
mocedad *f* youth; wild oats
mocerío *m* young people
mocero *adj masc* woman-crazy
mocetón *m* strapping young fellow
mocetona *f* buxom young woman
mocil *adj* youthful
moción *f* motion, movement; (*en junta deliberante*) motion; **hacer** or **presentar una moción** to make a motion
mocionante *mf* (Am) mover
mocionar *tr & intr* (Am) to move
moci•to -ta *adj* young || *mf* youngster
moco *m* (*humor segregado por una membrana mucosa*) mucus; (*mocarro*) snot; (*extremo del pabilo de una vela*) snuff; **a moco de candil** by candle light; **llorar a moco tendido** (coll) to cry like a baby; **moco de pavo** crest of a turkey; (bot) cockscomb; (col) trifle
moco•so -sa *adj* snotty, snively; rude, ill-bred; flip, saucy; mean, worthless || *mf* brat
mochar *tr* to butt; (Arg) to rob; (Am) to chop off; (Col) to fire
mochil *m* errand boy for farmers in the field
mochila *f* knapsack, haversack; tool bag; (mil) ration
mochín *m* (slang) executioner
mo•cho -cha *adj* blunt, stub, flat; (*árbol*) topped; stub-horned || *m* butt end
mochuelo *m* (orn) little owl; (*de una o más palabras*) omission; **cargar con el mochuelo** or **tocarle a** (*uno*) **el mochuelo** (coll) to get the worst of a deal
moda *f* fashion, mode, style; **a la moda de** after the fashion of, in the style of; **alta moda** haute couture; **de moda** in fashion; **fuera de moda** out of fashion; **pasar de moda** to go out of fashion
modales *mpl* manners
modalidad *f* manner, way, nature, kind
modelar *tr* to model; to form, shape; to mold || *ref* to model; **modelarse sobre** to pattern oneself after
modelo *adj invar* model, e.g., **ciudad modelo** model city || *mf* model, mannequin, fashion model || *m* model, pattern; form, blank; equal, peer; style
modera•do -da *adj* moderate
moderador *m* regulator; (*para retardar el efecto de los neutrones*) moderator
moderar *tr* to moderate, control, restrain || *ref* to moderate, control oneself, restrain oneself
modernizar **§60** *tr* to modernize
moder•no -na *adj* modern
modestia *f* modesty
modes•to -ta *adj* modest
modicidad *f* moderateness, reasonableness
módi•co -ca *adj* moderate, reasonable
modificante *adj* modifying || *m* (gram) modifier
modificar **§73** *tr* to modify
modismo *m* idiom
modista *f* dressmaker; **modista de sombreros** milliner
modistería *f* dressmaking; (Am) ladies' dress shop
modistilla *f* (coll) dressmaker's helper; (coll) unskilled dressmaker
modisto *m* ladies' tailor
modo *m* manner, mode, way; (gram) mood, mode; **al** or **a modo de** like, on the order of; **de buen modo** politely; **de ese modo** at that rate; **de tal modo que** with the result that; **de modo que** so that; and so; **de ningún modo** by no means; **de todos modos** anyhow, at any rate; **en cierto modo** after a fashion; **modo de ser** nature, disposition; **por modo de** as, by way of; **sobre modo** extremely; **uno a modo de** a sort of, a kind of
modorra *f* drowsiness, heaviness
modorrar *tr* to make drowsy || *ref* to get drowsy, fall asleep; (*la fruta*) to get squashy
modo•rro -rra *adj* drowsy, heavy; dull, stupid; (*fruta*) squashy || *f* see **modorra**
modo•so -sa *adj* quiet, well-behaved
modrego *m* (coll) boor, awkward fellow
modulación *f* modulation; **modulación de altura** or **de amplitud** amplitude

modulation; **modulación de frecuencia** frequency modulation
modular *tr & intr* to modulate
modulo•so -sa *adj* harmonious
mofa *f* jeering, scoffing, mockery
mofeta *f* skunk; (*gas pernicioso que se desprende de las minas*) blackdamp, firedamp
moflete *m* (coll) fat cheek, jowl
mofletu•do -da *adj* fat-cheeked
mo•gol -gola *adj & mf* Mongol, Mongolian
mogollón *m* — **comer de mogollón** (coll) to sponge
mo•gón -gona *adj* one-horned, broken-horned
mogote *m* knoll, hillock; stack of sheaves; budding antler
mohatra *f* fake sale; cheating
mohien•to -ta *adj* moldy, musty; (*hierro*) rusty
mohín *m* face, grimace
mohina *f* annoyance, displeasure
mohi•no -na *adj* sad, melancholy, moody; (*caballo, buey, vaca*) black, black-nosed || *mf* hinny || *m* blue magpie || *f* see **mohina**
moho *m* mold, must; (*del hierro*) rust; sloth, laziness; **no dejar criar moho** (coll) to keep in constant use, to use up quickly
moho•so -sa *adj* moldy, musty; (*hierro*) rusty; (*chiste*) stale
Moisés *m* Moses
moja•do -da *adj* wet; (*p.ej., por la lluvia*) drenched, soaked; (*húmedo*) moist; (phonet) liquid || *m* (Mex) wetback
mojar *tr* to wet; (*la lluvia a una persona*) to drench, soak; (*humedecer*) to dampen, to moisten; (*ensopar*) to dunk; (coll) to stab || *intr* — **mojar en** to get mixed up in || *ref* to get wet; to get drenched, get soaked
mojarrilla *mf* (coll) jolly person
moje *m* sauce, gravy
mojicón *m* muffin, bun; (coll) slap in the face
mojiganga *f* masquerade, mummery; clowning
mojigatería or **mojigatez** *f* hypocrisy; prudery, sanctimoniousness
mojiga•to -ta *adj* hypocritical; prudish, sanctimonious || *mf* hypocrite; prude, sanctimonious person
mojinete *m* (*de un muro*) coping; (*de un tejado*) ridge; (Arg) gable; (Chile) gable end
mojón *m* boundary stone, landmark; (*montón sin orden*) pile, heap; (*guía en desplobado*) road mark; (*porción de excremento humano*) turd
moldar *tr* to mold; to put molding on
molde *m* mold; pattern; cast, stamp, matrix; (*persona*) model, ideal; (*letra*) **de molde** printed; **venir de molde** to be just right
moldear *tr* to mold; (*vaciar*) to cast; to put molding on
moldura *f* molding
moldurar *tr* to put molding on
mole *adj* soft || *m* (Mex) stew seasoned with chili sauce || *f* bulk, mass
molécula *f* molecule
molende•ro -ra *mf* miller, grinder || *m* chocolate grinder; (CAm) grinding table
moler §47 *tr* (*granos*) to grind, to mill; to annoy, harass, weary; to tire out, fatigue; (coll) to chew; **moler a palos** (coll) to beat up
molesquina *f* moleskin
molestar *tr* to disturb, molest; to bother, annoy; to tire, weary || *ref* to bother; to be annoyed; **molestarse en** to take the trouble to
molestia *f* disturbance, discomfort; annoyance, bother, nuisance
moles•to -ta *adj* bothersome, troublesome; boring, tedious; bored, tired
molesto•so -sa *adj* (Am) bothersome
moleteado *m* knurl
moletear *tr* to knurl
molibdeno *m* molybdenum
molicie *f* softness; effeminacy, voluptuous living
moli•do -da *adj* exhausted, worn out
molienda *f* grinding, milling; (*cantidad que se muele de una vez*) grist; (*molino*) mill; (coll) bore, annoyance; (coll) fatigue, weariness
molimiento *m* grinding; weariness
moline•ro -ra *adj* mill || *m* miller || *f* miller's wife
molinete *m* little mill; ventilating fan; (*juguete de papel*) windmill; (*movimiento que se hace con el bastón*) twirl; (*con la espada*) flourish; (naut) windlass; (*rueda de cohetes*) (Mex) pinwheel
molinillo *m* hand mill; **molinillo de café** coffee grinder
molino *m* mill; **luchar con los molinos de viento** to tilt at windmills; **molino de sangre** animal-driven mill; **molino de viento** windmill; **molino harinero** gristmill, flour mill
moloc *m* (Ecuad) mashed potatoes
molondrón *m* (coll) lazy bum; (Ven) large inheritance, large amount of money
molusco *m* mollusk
mollar *adj* soft, tender; mushy, squashy; (*carne*) lean; profitable; (coll) gullible, easily taken in
mollear *intr* to give, to yield; to bend
molleja *f* gizzard; **criar molleja** (coll) to get lazy; **mollejas** sweetbread
mollejón *m* grindstone; (coll) big fat loafer; (coll) good-natured fellow
mollera *f* crown (*of the head*); (coll) brains, sense; **cerrado de mollera** (coll) stupid; **duro de mollera** (coll) stubborn
mollete *m* muffin
molli•no -na *adj* drizzly || *f* drizzle
mollizna *f* drizzle
momentáne•o -a *adj* momentary
momento *m* moment; **al momento** at once; **de un momento a otro** at any moment
momería *f* clowning
mome•ro -ra *adj* clowning || *mf* clown
momia *f* mummy
momificar §73 *tr* to mummify

mo•mio -mia *adj* lean, skinny || *m* extra; (*ganga*) bargain; sinecure || *f* see **momia**
momo *m* face, grimace; (coll) caress
mona *f* female monkey; Barbary ape; (coll) ape, copycat; (coll) drunkenness; (*persona*) (coll) drunk; (taur) guard for right leg; **dormir la mona** (coll) to sleep off a drunk; **pillar una mona** (coll) to go on a jag; **pintar la mona** (coll) to put on airs
monacal *adj* monachal
monacato *m* monkhood
monacillo *m* altar boy, acolyte
monada *f* monkeyshine; (*gesto*) face, grimace, monkey face; darling; cuteness; flattery; folly, childishness
monaguillo *m* altar boy, acolyte
monaquismo *m* monasticism
monarca *m* monarch
monarquía *f* monarchy
monárqui•co -ca *adj* monarchic(al) || *mf* monarchist
monasterio *m* monastery
monásti•co -ca *adj* monastic
monda *f* pruning, trimming; parings, peelings; (Am) beating, whipping
mondadien•tes *m* (*pl* **-tes**) toothpick
mondadura *f* pruning, trimming; **mondaduras** peelings
mondar *tr* to clean; to prune, to trim; to peel, pare, hull, husk; (*quitar con engaño los bienes a*) to fleece; (Am) to beat, whip
mon•do -da *adj* clean; pure; **mondo y lirondo** (coll) pure, unadulterated || *f* see **monda**
mondonga *f* (coll) kitchen wench
mondongo *m* intestines, insides; (*del hombre*) (coll) guts
monear *intr* (coll) to act like a monkey; (Am) to boast || *ref* (Hond) to plug away; (Hond) to punch each other
moneda *f* coin; (coll) money; **la Moneda** the government of Chile; **moneda corriente** currency; (coll) common knowledge; **moneda falsa** counterfeit; **moneda menuda** change; **moneda metálica** or **sonante** specie; **moneda suelta** change; **pagar en la misma moneda** to pay back in one's own coin
monedar *tr* to coin, to mint
monedero *m* moneybag; **monedero falso** counterfeiter
monería *f* monkeyshine; cuteness; childishness
mones•co -ca *adj* (coll) apish
moneta•rio -ria *adj* monetary
mon•gol -gola *adj & mf* Mongol, Mongolian
monigote *m* lay brother; rag figure, stuffed form; botched painting, botched statue; (coll) sap, boob
monipodio *m* (coll) collusion, deal, plot
monís *m* trinket; **monises** (coll) money, dough
mónita *f* (coll) cunning, smoothness, slickness
monitor *m* monitor
monja *f* nun; **monjas** lingering sparks in burning paper
monje *m* monk
monjía *f* monkhood
monjil *adj* nunnish || *m* nun's dress
mono -na *adj* (coll) cute, nice; (Am) blond; (*cabello*) (Am) red || *m* monkey, ape; (*traje de faena*) coveralls; whippersnapper, squirt; (taur) attendant of picador; (Chile) pyramid of fruit or vegetables; **estar de monos** (coll) to be on the outs; **mono de Gibraltar** Barbary ape || *f* see **mona**
monóculo *m* monocle
monogamia *f* monogamy
monografía *f* monograph
monograma *m* monogram
monolíti•co -ca *adj* monolithic
monologar §44 *intr* to soliloquize
monólogo *m* monologue
monomanía *f* monomania
monomio *m* monomial
mono•no -na *adj* (coll) cute, sweet
monopatín *m* scooter
monoplano *m* monoplane
monopolio *m* monopoly
monopolizar §60 *tr* to monopolize
monorriel *m* monorail
monosabio *m* (taur) attendant of picador
monosílabo *m* monosyllable
monoteísta *adj* monotheistic || *mf* monotheist
monotipia *f* monotype
monotipista *mf* monotype operator
monotipo *m* monotype
monotonía *f* monotony
monóto•no -na *adj* monotonous
monóxido *m* monoxide
monseñor *m* monseigneur; (eccl) monsignor
monserga *f* (coll) gibberish
monstruo *m* monster
monstruosidad *f* monstrosity
monstruo•so -sa *adj* monstruous
monta *f* sum, total; **de poca monta** of little account
montacar•gas *m* (*pl* **-gas**) hoist, freight elevator
montadero *m* horse block
montadura *f* mounting; (*de una caballería de silla*) harness; (*engaste*) setting, mount
montaje *m* montage; setting up; (mach) assembly; (rad) hookup
montanero *m* forest ranger
montante *m* post, upright; (*suma*) amount; (*hueco cuadrilongo sobre una puerta*) transom; (*espadón*) broadsword || *f* flood tide
montaña *f* mountain; mountain country; **la Montaña** the Province of Santander, Spain; **montaña de hielo** iceberg; **montaña rusa** roller coaster
monta•ñés -ñesa *adj* mountain || *mf* mountaineer, highlander
montaño•so -sa *adj* mountainous
montapla•tos *m* (*pl* **-tos**) dumbwaiter
montar *tr* to mount, to get on; (*un caballo, una bicicleta, los hombros de una persona*) to ride; (*un servicio*) to set up, establish; (*un fusil*) to cock; (*una piedra preciosa*) to set, to mount; (*el caballo a la yegua*) to cover; (*un reloj*) to wind; (elec) to hook up; (mach) to assemble, to

mount; (*la guardia*) (mil) to mount; (*un cabo*) (naut) to round; (*un buque*) (naut) to command; (*importar*) to amount to || *intr* to mount; to get on top; to weigh, to be important; **tanto monta** it's all the same || *ref* to mount; to get on top; **montarse en cólera** to fly into a rage

monta•raz (*pl* **-races**) *adj* backwoods; wild, untamed || *m* forester, warden

monte *m* mountain, mount; woods, woodland; obstruction, interference; backwoods, wilds; bank, kitty; (coll) dirty head of hair; **andar al monte** (coll) to take to the woods; **monte alto** forest; **monte bajo** thicket, brushwood; **monte de piedad** pawnshop; **monte pío** pension fund for widows and orphans; mutual benefit society; **monte tallar** tree farm

montear *tr* to hunt, to track down; to make a working drawing of; to arch, to vault

montecillo *m* mound, hillock

montepío *m* pension fund for widows and orphans; mutual benefit society

montera *f* cloth cap; glass roof; wife of hunter; bullfighter's black bicorne; (Hond) drunk, jag

montería *f* hunting, big-game hunting; hunting party; (Bol, Ecuad) canoe to shoot the rapids; (Mex) lumbermen's camp

monterilla *f* (naut) moonsail

montero *m* hunter, huntsman

montés or **montesi•no -na** *adj* wild (*e.g., goat*)

montículo *m* mound, hillock

montilla *f* montilla (*a pale dry sherry*)

monto *m* sum, total

montón *m* pile, heap; (*de gente*) crowd; (coll) lot, great deal, great many; **a, de,** or **en montón** (coll) taken together; **a montones** (coll) in abundance; **ser del montón** (coll) to be quite ordinary

montonera *f* (Am) heap, pile; (Am) band of mounted rebels

montu•no -na *adj* wooded; (Am) wild, untamed, rustic

montuo•so -sa *adj* wooded, woody; rugged, hilly

montura *f* (*cabalgadura*) mount; (*de una cabalgadura*) harness; seat, saddle; (*de una piedra preciosa, de un instrumento astronómico*) mounting; (*de gafas*) frame

monumento *m* monument

monzón *m* monsoon

moña *f* doll; mannequin; ribbon, hair ribbon; (coll) drunk, jag

moño *m* topknot; crest, top; (Col) caprice, whim; (*de caballo*) (Chile) forelock; **moños** frippery

moquear *intr* to snivel

moqueo *m* snivel, sniveling

moquero *m* handkerchief

moquete *m* punch in the nose

moquillo *m* runny nose; (vet) distemper

moquita *f* mucus, snivel

mor *m* — **por mor de** for love of; because of

mora *f* black mulberry; blackberry, brambleberry; white mulberry

morada *f* dwelling; stay, sojourn

mora•do -da *adj* purple, mulberry || *f* see **morada**

moral *adj* moral || *m* black mulberry tree || *f* (*ciencia de la conducta; conducta*) morals; (*espíritu, confianza*) morale; (*p.ej., de una fábula*) (coll) moral

moraleja *f* moral

moralidad *f* morality; (*de una fábula*) moral

morar *intr* to live, dwell

moratoria *f* moratorium

mórbi•do -da *adj* (*perteneciente a la enfermedad*) morbid; soft, delicate, mellow

morbo *m* sickness, illness; **morbo gálico** syphilis; **morbo regio** jaundice

morbo•so -sa *adj* morbid, diseased

morcilla *f* blood pudding, black pudding; (*añadidura que mete un actor en su papel*) gag

mor•daz *adj* (*pl* **-daces**) mordant, mordacious, sharp, caustic

mordaza *f* (*pañuelo o instrumento que se pone en la boca para impedir el hablar*) gag; (*aparato que sirve para apretar*) clamp, jaw; pipe vise; **poner la mordaza a** to gag

mordedura *f* bite

morder **§47** *tr* to bite; to nibble at; to wear away; to gossip about, ridicule; (Mex, Ven, W-I) to cheat || *intr* to bite; to take hold

mordicar **§73** *tr & intr* to bite, sting

mordida *f* (Am) bite; (*para eludir una multa*) (Mex) payoff

mordiente *m* mordant

mordiscar **§73** *tr* to nibble at || *intr* to nibble, gnaw away; to champ

mordisco *m* nibble, bite; champ

more•no -na *adj* brown, dark-brown; dark, dark-complexioned; (*de la raza negra*) (coll) colored; (Am) mulato || *mf* (coll) colored person; (Am) mulato || *m* brunet || *f* brunette; loaf of brown bread; rick of new-mown hay

morería *f* Moorish quarter; Moorish land

moretón *m* (coll) black-and-blue mark

morfina *f* morphine

morfinomanía *f* morphine habit, drug habit

morfinóma•no -na *adj* addicted to morphine, addicted to drugs || *mf* morphine addict, drug addict

morfología *f* morphology

moribun•do -da *adj* moribund, dying || *mf* dying person

morillo *m* andiron, firedog

morir **§30** & **§83** *intr* to die; (*el fuego, la luz, etc.*) to die away; **morir ahogado** to drown; **morir de risa** to die laughing; **morir de viejo** to die of old age; **morir helado** to freeze to death; **morir quemado** to burn to death; **morir vestido** (coll) to die a violent death || *ref* to die; to be dying; to die away, die out; (*una pierna, un brazo*) to go to sleep; **morirse por** to be crazy about; to be dying to

moris•co -ca *adj* Morisco, Moorish || *mf* Moor converted to Christianity (*after the Reconquest*); (*descendiente de mulato y española o de mulata y español*) (Mex) Morisco
mo•ro -ra *adj* Moorish; (*vino*) (coll) unwatered || *mf* Moor; **hay moros en la costa** (coll) there's trouble brewing; **moro de paz** man of peace || *f* see **mora**
moro•cho -cha *adj* (Am) strong, robust; (SAm) dark
morón *m* mound, knoll; moron
moron•do -da *adj* bare, stripped
moro•so -sa *adj* slow, tardy; (*retrasado en el pago de deudas*) delinquent
morra *f* (*de la cabeza*) top, crown; (*de gato*) purr; **andar a la morra** to come to blows
morrada *f* slap, punch; (*golpe dado con la cabeza*) butt
morral *m* nose bag; (*saco de cazador*) game bag; (*de soldado, viandante, etc.*) knapsack; (coll) boor, lout
morralla *f* small fish; (*gente de escaso valor*) rabble, trash; (*mezcla de cosas inútiles*) junk, trash; (Mex) change, small change
morriña *f* (coll) blues, melancholy; **morriña de la tierra** (coll) homesickness
morriño•so -sa *adj* sickly; (coll) blue, melancholy
morrión *m* helmet; (mil) bearskin
morro *m* (*cosa redonda*) knob; (*monte redondo*) knoll; (*guijarro*) pebble; (*saliente que forman los labios*) snout; **beber a morro** (slang) to drink out of the bottle; **estar de morro** or **de morros** (coll) to be on the outs; **poner morro** to make a snout
morrocotu•do -da *adj* (coll) strong, thick, heavy; (*asunto, negocio*) (coll) weighty; (Am) big, enormous; (Col) rich, wealthy; (Chile) graceless, monotonous
morsa *f* walrus
mortaja *f* shroud, winding sheet; (carp) mortise; (Am) cigarette paper
mortal *adj* mortal; deadly; mortally ill; deathly pale; sure, conclusive || *m* mortal
mortalidad *f* mortality; death rate
mortandad *f* massacre, mortality, butchery
morteci•no -na *adj* dead; dying; failing, weak; **hacer la mortecina** (coll) to play dead, to play possum
mortero *m* (*vaso que sirve para machacar; argamasa*) mortar; (*en los molinos de aceite*) nether stone; (arti) mortar
mortífe•ro -ra *adj* deadly
mortificar §73 *tr* to vex, annoy, bother; to mortify || *ref* (Mex) to be mortified, be embarrassed
mortuo•rio -ria *adj* mortuary, funeral; (*casa*) of the deceased || *m* (archaic) funeral
morueco *m* ram
moru•no -na *adj* Moorish
mosai•co -ca *adj* Mosaic || *m* tile, paving tile; mosaic; **mosaico de madera** marquetry
mosca *f* fly; (*barba*) imperial; (coll) cash, dough; (coll) disappointment; (coll) bore, nuisance; **aflojar la mosca** (coll) to shell out, to fork out; **mosca borriquera** horsefly; **mosca de las frutas** fruit fly; **mosca del vinagre** fruit fly; **mosca muerta** (coll) hypocrite; **moscas** sparks; **moscas volantes** spots before the eyes; **papar moscas** (coll) to gape, gawk
moscareta *f* (orn) flycatcher
moscona *f* hussy, brazen woman
Moscú Moscow
mosquear *tr* (*moscas*) to shoo; to beat, to whip; to answer sharply || *intr* (Mex) to sneak a ride || *ref* to shake off annoyances; to take offense
mosquero *m* flytrap; fly swatter
mosquete *m* musket
mosquetear *intr* (Arg, Bol) to snoop
mosquete•ro -ra *adj* idle || *mf* (Arg, Bol) bystander, snooper || *m* musketeer || *f* wallflower
mosquetón *m* snap hook
mosquitera *f* or **mosquitero** *m* mosquito net; fly net
mosquito *m* (*Culex pungens*) mosquito; (*insecto parecido al anterior*) gnat; (coll) tippler
mostacera *f* mustard jar
mostacho *m* mustache; (coll) spot on the face
mostachón *m* macaroon
mostaza *f* mustard; (*semilla; munición*) mustard seed; **subírsele a** (*uno*) **la mostaza a las narices** (coll) to fly into a rage
mosto *m* must; **mosto de cerveza** wort
mostrador *m* (*en las tiendas*) counter; (*en las tabernas*) bar; (*de reloj*) dial
mostrar §61 *tr* to show || *ref* to show; to show oneself to be
mostrear *tr* to spot, to splash
mostren•co -ca *adj* ownerless, unclaimed; (*que no tiene casa ni hogar*) (coll) homeless; (*animal*) (coll) stray; (coll) slow, dull; (coll) fat, heavy || *mf* (coll) dolt, dullard
mota *f* mote, speck; (*en el paño*) burl, knot; hill, rise; defect, fault; (Mex, W-I) powder puff
mote *m* device, emblem, riddle; (*apodo*) nickname; (Chile) mistake; (SAm) stewed corn
motear *tr* to speck, speckle; to dapple, mottle || *intr* (Peru) to eat stewed corn
motejar *tr* to call names; to scoff at, make fun of; **motejar de** to brand as
motín *m* mutiny, riot
motinista *mf* (Peru) rioter
motivar *tr* to explain, account for; to rationalize
moti•vo -va *adj* motive || *m* motive, reason; (mus) motif; **con motivo de** because of; on the occasion of; **de su motivo propio** on his own accord; **motivo conductor** (mus) leitmotif; **motivos** grounds, reasons; (Chile) finickiness, prudery

moto *m* guidepost, landmark || *f* (coll) motorcycle
motobomba *f* fire truck, fire engine
motocarro *m* three-wheel delivery truck
motocicleta *f* motorcycle
motogrúa *f* truck crane
motoli•to -ta *adj* simple, stupid; **vivir de motolito** to be a sponger, to live on other people || *f* (orn) wagtail; (Ven) decent woman
motón *m* (naut) block, pulley
motonáuti•co -ca *adj* motorboat || *f* motorboating
motonautismo *m* (sport) motorboating
motonave *f* motor launch; motor ship
motoneta *f* motor scooter; light three-wheel delivery truck
mo•tor -tora *adj* motor, motive || *m* motor, engine; **motor a chorro** jet engine; **motor de arranque** (aut) starter, starting motor; **motor de cuatro tiempos** four-cycle engine; **motor de dos tiempos** two-cycle engine; **motor de explosión** internal-combustion engine; **motor fuera de borda** outboard motor; **motor térmico** heat engine || *f* small motor boat
motorista *mf* motorist; motorcyclist; motorcycle racer || *m* motorcycle policeman; (Am) motorman
motorizar **§60** *tr* to motorize
motosegadora *f* power mower
motovelero *m* (naut) motor sailer
motriz *adj fem* (*fuerza*) motive
movedi•zo -za *adj* shaky, unsteady; fickle, inconstant; (*arena*) quick, shifting
mover **§47** *tr* to move; (*la cola el perro*) to wag; (*discordia*) to stir up || *intr* to move; to abort, miscarry; to bud, sprout || *ref* to move; to be moved
movible *adj* movable; fickle, inconstant, changeable
móvil *adj* movable, mobile; fickle, changeable; moving || *m* moving body; cause, motive
movilizar **§60** *tr* to mobilize
movimiento *m* movement, motion
moza *f* girl, lass; mistress, concubine; maid, kitchen maid; (*en algunos juegos de naipes*) last hand; wash bat; **buena moza** or **real moza** good-looking girl or woman; **moza de fortuna** or **del partido** prostitute; **moza de taberna** barmaid
mozalbete *m* lad, young fellow
mozárabe *adj* Mozarabic || *mf* Mozarab
mo•zo -za *adj* young, youthful; single, unmarried || *m* youth, lad; (*camarero*) waiter; (*criado*) servant; porter; (*cuelgacapas*) cloak hanger; **buen mozo** or **real mozo** handsome fellow; **mozo de caballerías** hostler, stable boy; **mozo de café** waiter; **mozo de cámara** (naut) cabin boy; **mozo de ciego** blind man's guide; **mozo de cordel** street porter, public errand boy; **mozo de cuadra** stable boy; **mozo de cuerda** public errand boy; **mozo de espuelas** groom who walks in front of master's horse; **mozo de esquina** street porter, public errand boy; **mozo de estación** station porter; **mozo de estoques** (taur) sword handler; **mozo de hotel** bellboy, bellhop; **mozo de paja y cebada** hostler (*at an inn*); **mozo de restaurante** waiter || *f* see **moza**
mozue•lo -la *mf* youngster || *m* lad, young fellow || *f* lass, young girl
m/p *abbr* **mi pagaré**
m/r *abbr* **mi remesa**
Mro. *abbr* **Maestro**
M.S. *abbr* **manuscrito**
mtd. *abbr* **mitad**
mu *m* moo || *f* bye-bye; **ir a la mu** to go bye-bye
muaré *adj invar & m* moiré
muca•mo -ma *mf* (Arg, Urug) house servant || *f* (Arg, Chile, Urug) servant girl
muceta *f* (*de los doctores en los actos universitarios*) hood; (eccl) mozzetta
muco•so -sa *adj* mucous || *f* mucous membrane
múcura *f* (Bol, Col, Ven, W-I) water pitcher; (Col) thickhead
muchacha *f* girl; maid, servant girl
muchachada *f* youthful prank
muchachez *f* boyishness, girlishness
mucha•cho -cha *adj* young, youthful || *mf* youth, young person; servant || *m* boy || *f* see **muchacha**
muchedumbre *f* crowd, multitude, flock
mu•cho -cha *adj* much, a lot of, a great deal of; (*tiempo*) a long || *pron* much, a lot, a great deal || **mu•chos -chas** *adj & pron* many || **mucho** *adv* much; (*más de lo regular*) hard; often; a long time; **con mucho** by far; **ni con mucho** or **ni mucho menos** not by a long shot; **por mucho que** however much; **sentir mucho** to be very sorry; **tener mucho de** to take after
muda *f* change; change of voice; change of clothes; (*cambio de plumas o de piel*) molt, molting; molting season; **estar de muda** to be changing one's voice; **estar en muda** (coll) to keep too quiet; **hacer la muda** to molt; **muda de ropa** change of clothing
mudable *adj* fickle, inconstant
mudada *f* (Am) change of clothing; (Am) move, change of residence
mudadi•zo -za *adj* fickle, inconstant
mudanza *f* change; (*cambio de domicilio*) moving; fickleness, inconstancy; (*en el baile*) figure
mudar *tr* to change || *intr* to change; **mudar de** to change || *ref* to change; to change clothing; to move; to move away; to have a movement of the bowels; **mudarse de** to change
mudez *f* muteness, dumbness; continued silence
mu•do -da *adj* dumb, mute; (phonet) voiceless, surd || *mf* mute || *f* see **muda**
mueblaje *m* furniture, suit of furniture
mueble *adj* movable || *m* piece of furniture; (*p.ej., de un aparato de radio*) cabinet; **muebles** furniture
mueblería *f* furniture shop
mueblista *mf* furniture dealer
mueca *f* face, grimace

muela *f* grindstone; knoll, mound; back tooth, grinder; **muela cordal** wisdom tooth; **muela de esmeril** emery wheel; **muela del juicio** wisdom tooth; **muela de molino** millstone
muellaje *m* dockage, wharfage
muelle *adj* soft; voluptuous || *m* (*pieza elástica de metal*) spring; (*obra en la orilla del mar o de un río*) dock, wharf, pier; (rr) freight platform; **muelle real** mainspring
muérdago *m* mistletoe
muérgano *m* (Col, Ven) piece of junk, drug on the market; (Col, Ecuad, Ven) boor, nobody
muermo *m* (vet) glanders
muerte *f* death; **cada muerte de obispo** once in a blue moon; **dar la muerte a** to put to death; **de mala muerte** (coll) crummy, not much of a; **estar a la muerte** to be at death's door; **muerte chiquita** (coll) nervous shudder
muer•to -ta *adj* dead; (*apagado, marchito*) flat, dull; (*cal, yeso*) slaked; **muerto de** dying of; **muerto por** crazy about || *mf* corpse, dead person || *m* (*en los naipes*) dummy; **hacerse el muerto** to play possum; to play deaf; **tocar a muerto** to toll
muesca *f* nick, notch; (carp) mortise
muestra *f* (*porción de un producto que sirve para conocer su calidad*) sample; model, specimen; (*rótulo sobre una tienda u hotel*) sign; show, exhibition, indication; (*esfera de reloj*) dial, face; (*parada del perro para levantar la caza*) set; (*ademán, porte*) bearing; **dar muestras de** to show signs of
mugido *m* moo, low; bellow, roar
mugir §27 *intr* (*la res vacuna*) to moo, to low; (*con ira*) to bellow; (*el viento, el mar*) to roar
mugre *f* dirt, filth, grime
mugrien•to -ta *adj* dirty, filthy, grimy
muguete *m* lily of the valley
mujer *f* woman; (*esposa*) wife; **mujer de gobierno** housekeeper; **mujer de su casa** good manager; **mujer fatal** vamp; **ser mujer** to be a grown woman
mujeren•go -ga *adj* (Arg, Urug, CAm) effeminate
mujerie•go -ga *adj* feminine, womanly; effeminate, womanish; fond of women; **a mujeriegas** sidesaddle || *m* flock of women
mujeril *adj* womanly; womanish
mújol *m* mullet, striped mullet
mula *f* mule, she-mule; junk, trash; (Arg) ingrate, traitor; (Arg) hoax; (C-R) jag, drunk; (Guat, Hond) anger, rage; (Mex) drug on the market; (Ven) flask; **devolver la mula** (CAm) to pay back in one's own coin; **echar la mula a** (Mex) to rake over the coals; **en mula de San Francisco** on shank's mare
mulada *f* drove of mules
muladar *m* dungheap, dunghill; dump, trash heap; filth
mula•to -ta *adj* & *mf* mulatto
muleta *f* (*palo para apoyarse al andar*) crutch; muleta (*cloth attached to a stick, used by matador*); support, prop; snack
muletilla *f* cross-handle cane; pet word, pet phrase; (taur) muleta
mulo *m* mule
multa *f* fine
multar *tr* to fine
multicopista *m* duplicating machine, copying machine
multigrafiar §77 *tr* to multigraph
multígrafo *m* multigraph
multilateral *adj* multilateral
multiláte•ro -ra *adj* multilateral
múltiple *adj* multiple, manifold || *m* manifold; **múltiple de admisión** intake manifold; **múltiple de escape** exhaust manifold
multiplicar §73 *tr, intr,* & *ref* to multiply
multiplicidad *f* multiplicity
múlti•plo -pla *adj* multiple, manifold || *m* (math) multiple
multitud *f* multitude
mulli•do -da *adj* soft, fluffy || *m* stuffing (*for cushions, pillows, etc.*) || *f* bedding, litter (*for animals*)
mullir §13 *tr* to soften, fluff up; (*la cama*) to beat up, shake up; (*la tierra*) to loosen around a stalk || *ref* to get fluffy
munda•no -na *adj* mundane, worldly; (*mujer*) loose
mundial *adj* world-wide, world
mundillo *m* arched clotheshorse; cushion for making lace; warming pan; guelder-rose, cranberry tree; world (*of artists, scholars, etc.*)
mundo *m* world; **así va el mundo** so it goes; **desde que el mundo es mundo** (coll) since the world began; **echar al mundo** to bring into the world; to bring forth; **el otro mundo** the other world; **gran mundo** high society; **medio mundo** (*mucha gente*) (coll) half the world; **tener mucho mundo** (coll) to know one's way around; **todo el mundo** everybody; **ver mundo** to see the world, to travel
mundonuevo *m* peep show
munición *f* munition, ammunition; **de munición** (mil) government issue; (coll) done hurriedly
municionar *tr* to supply with munition
municipal *adj* municipal || *m* policeman
munícipe *m* citizen
municipio *m* municipality; town council
munidad *f* susceptibility to infection
munífi•co -ca *adj* munificent
muñeca *f* (*figurilla infantil con que juegan las niñas*) doll; (*parte del cuerpo humano en donde se articula la mano con el brazo*) wrist; manikin, dress form; tea bag; (*mujer linda; mozuela frívola*) (coll) doll; **muñeca de trapo** rag doll, rag baby; **muñeca parlante** talking doll
muñeco *m* doll (*representing a male child or animal*); dummy, manikin; fop, effeminate fellow; (fig) puppet; (coll) lad, little fellow

muñequera *f* strap for wrist watch
muñequilla *f* (mach) chuck; (Arg, Chile) young ear of corn
muñidor *m* heeler, henchman
muñir **§12** *tr* to convoke, summon; (pol) to fix, to rig
muñón *m* (*p.ej., de un brazo cortado*) stump; (mach) journal, gudgeon; **muñón de cola** dock
mural *adj* mural
muralla *f* wall, rampart
murar *tr* to surround with a wall
murciélago *m* bat
murga *f* (coll) tin-pan band
muriente *adj* dying, faint
murmujear *tr & intr* (coll) to mumble
murmullar *intr* to murmur
murmullo *m* murmur; whisper; (*de aguas corrientes*) ripple; (*del viento*) rustle
murmurar *tr* to murmur, to mutter; to murmur at || *intr* to murmur, to mutter; to whisper; (*las aguas corrientes*) to ripple, to purl; (*el viento*) to rustle; (coll) to gossip
muro *m* wall
murria *f* (coll) blues, dejection
musa *f* muse; **las Musas** the Muses; **soplarle a uno la musa** (coll) to be inspired to write poetry; (coll) to be lucky at games of chance
musaraña *f* shrew, shrewmouse; bug, worm; **mirar a las musarañas** (coll) to stare vacantly
músculo *m* muscle
musculo•so -sa *adj* muscular
muselina *f* muslin
museo *m* museum; **museo de cera** waxworks
muserola *f* noseband
mus•go -ga *adj* dark-brown || *m* moss
musgo•so -sa *adj* mossy, moss-covered
música *f* music; (*músicos que tocan juntos*) band; (coll) noise, racket; **con la música a otra parte** (coll) don't bother me, get out; **música celestial** (coll) nonsense, piffle; **música de fondo** background music; **poner en música** to set to music
musical *adj* musical
musicalidad *f* musicianship
music-hall *s* vaudeville theater, burlesque show
músi•co -ca *adj* musical || *mf* musician; **músico mayor** bandmaster || *f* see **música**
musicología *f* musicology
musicólo•go -ga *mf* musicologist
musiquero *m* music cabinet
musitar *tr & intr* to mutter, mumble
muslime *adj & mf* Moslem
muslo *m* thigh; (*de ave cocida*) (coll) leg, drumstick
mustiar *ref* to wither
mus•tio -tia *adj* sad, gloomy; (*marchito*) withered; (Mex) hypocritical; (Mex) stand-offish
musul•mán -mana *adj & mf* Mussulman
mutación *f* mutation; unsettled weather, change of weather; (biol) mutation, sport; (theat) change of scene
mutila•do -da *adj* crippled || *mf* cripple
mutilar *tr* to mutilate; to cripple
múti•lo -la *adj* mutilated; crippled
mutis *m* (theat) exit; **hacer mutis** (theat) to exit; to keep quiet
mutual *adj* mutual
mutualidad *f* mutuality; mutual benefit; mutual benefit association
mutualista *mf* member of a mutual benefit association
mu•tuo -tua *adj* mutual, reciprocal
muy *adv* very; very much; too, e.g., **es muy tarde para dar un paseo tan largo** it is too late to take such a long walk; **muy de noche** late at night; **Muy señor mío** Dear Sir

N

N, n (ene) *f* sixteenth letter of the Spanish alphabet
n/ *abbr* **nuestro**
N. *abbr* **Norte**
nabo *m* turnip; (naut) mast
Nabucodonosor *m* Nebuchadnezzar
nácar *m* mother-of-pearl
nacara•do -da *adj* mother-of-pearl
nacatamal *m* (CAm, Mex) meat-filled tamale
nacela *f* nacelle
nacencia *f* birth; growth, tumor
nacer **§22** *intr* to be born; to bud, take rise, originate, appear; to dawn || *ref* to bud, to shoot, to sprout; (*abrirse la ropa por las costuras*) to split
naci•do -da *adj* natural, innate; apt, proper, fit; **nacida** née or nee || *m* human being; growth, boil
naciente *adj* incipient; resurgent; (*sol*) rising || *m* east
nacimiento *m* birth; origin, beginning, fountainhead; descent, lineage; (*de agua*) spring, fountainhead; crèche
nación *f* nation
nacional *adj* national; domestic || *mf* national || *m* militiaman
nacionalidad *f* nationality
nacionalismo *m* nationalism
nacionalista *adj & mf* nationalist
nacionalizar **§60** *tr* to nationalize || *ref* to be naturalized; to become a citizen
nacista *adj & mf* Nazi
naco *m* (Arg, Bol, Urug) black rolled leaf of chewing tobacco; (Arg) fear, scare; (Col) stewed corn; (Col) mashed potatoes
nada *pron indef* nothing, not . . . anything; **de nada** don't mention it, you're welcome || *adv* not at all
nadaderas *fpl* water wings
nada•dor -dora *adj* swimming, floating

|| *mf* swimmer || *m* (Chile) fishnet float
nadar *intr* to swim; to float; to fit loosely or too loosely; **nadar en** (*riqueza*) to be rolling in; (*suspiros*) to be full of; (*sangre*) to be bathed in
nadear *tr* to destroy, wipe out
nadería *f* trifle
nadie *pron indef* nobody, not . . . anybody; **nadie más** nobody else; **nadie más que** nobody but || *m* nobody; **un don nadie** a nonentity
nado — a nado swimming, floating; **echarse a nado** to dive in; **pasar a nado** to swim across
nafta *f* naphtha
nagual *m* (Guat, Hond) (*dícese de un animal*) inseparable companion; (Mex) sorcerer, wizard; (Mex) lie
nagualear *intr* (Mex) to lie; (Mex) to be out looking for trouble all night
naguas *fpl* petticoat
naipe *m* playing card; deck of cards; **naipe de figura** face card; **tener buen naipe** to be lucky
naire *m* mahout
nalgada *f* shoulder, ham; blow on or with the buttocks
nalgas *fpl* buttocks, rump
nana *f* grandma; lullaby, cradlesong; (CAm, Mex, W-I) child's nurse; (Arg, Chile, Urug) child's complaint
nao *f* ship, vessel
napoleóni·co -ca *adj* Napoleonic
Napoles *f* Naples
napolita·no -na *adj & mf* Neapolitan
naranja *f* orange; **media naranja** (coll) sidekick, better half; **naranja cajel** Seville orange, sour orange; **¡naranjas!** nonsense!
naranjada *f* orangeade; orange juice; orange marmalade
naranjal *m* orange grove
naranjo *m* orange tree; (coll) boob, simpleton
narciso *m* narcissus; fop, dandy; **narciso trompón** daffodil || **Narciso** *m* Narcissus
narcóti·co -ca *adj & m* narcotic
narcotizar **§60** *tr* to dope, to drug
narguile *m* hookah
narigada *f* (SAm) pinch of snuff
nari·gón -gona *adj* big-nosed || *m* big nose
narigu·do -da *adj* big-nosed; nose-shaped
nariguera *f* nose ring
na·riz (*pl* **-rices**) *f* nose; nostril; sense of smell; (*del vino*) bouquet; **nariz de pico de loro** hooknose; **sonarse las narices** to blow one's nose; **tabicarse las narices** to hold one's nose; **tener agarrado por las narices** to lead by the nose
narración *f* narration
narra·dor -dora *adj* narrating || *mf* narrator
narrar *tr* to narrate
narrati·vo -va *adj* narrative || *f* (*relato; habilidad en narrar*) narrative
narria *f* sled, sledge, drag
nasal *adj & f* nasal
nasalizar **§60** *tr* to nasalize
nata *f* cream; whipped cream; élite, choice; skim, scum
natación *f* swimming
natal *adj* natal; native || *m* birth; birthday
natali·cio -cia *adj* birth || *m* birthday
natalidad *f* birth rate
naterón *m* cottage cheese
natillas *fpl* custard
natividad *f* birth; Christmas; (*día; festividad; pintura*) Nativity
nati·vo -va *adj* native; natural; natural-born; innate
na·to -ta *adj* born, e.g., **criminal nato** born criminal || *f* see **nata**
natural *adj* natural; native; (mus) natural || *mf* native || *m* temper, disposition, nature; **al natural** au naturel; rough, unfinished; live; **del natural** from life, from nature
naturaleza *f* nature; disposition, temperament; nationality; **naturaleza muerta** still life
naturalidad *f* naturalness; nationality
naturalismo *m* naturalism
naturalista *mf* naturalist
naturalización *f* naturalization
naturalizar **§60** *tr* to naturalize; to acclimatize || *ref* to become naturalized; to go native
naturalmente *adv* naturally; easily, readily
naufragar **§44** *intr* to be shipwrecked; to fail
naufragio *m* shipwreck; failure, ruin
náufra·go -ga *adj* shipwrecked || *mf* shipwrecked person || *m* shark
náusea *f* nausea; **dar náuseas a** to nauseate; to sicken, disgust; **tener náuseas** to be nauseated, to be sick at one's stomach
nauseabun·do -da *adj* nauseating, nauseous, loathsome, sickening
nauta *m* mariner, sailor
náuti·co -ca *adj* nautical || *f* sailing, navigation
nava *f* hollow plain between mountains
navaja *f* folding knife; razor; penknife; tusk of wild boar; razor clam; (coll) evil tongue; **navaja barbera** straight razor
navajada *f* or **navajazo** *m* slash, gash
navajero *m* razor case; razor cloth
naval *adj* naval; nautical; **naval militar** naval
nava·rro -rra *adj & mf* Navarrese || **Navarra** *f* Navarre
navazo *m* garden in sandy marshland
nave *f* ship, vessel; (*de un taller, fábrica, tienda, iglesia, etc.*) aisle; commercial ground floor; hall, shed, bay, building; **nave central** or **principal** (archit) nave; **nave lateral** (archit) aisle
navegable *adj* navigable
navegación *f* navigation; sailing; sea voyage; **navegación a vela** sailing
navega·dor -dora or **navegante** *adj* navigating || *mf* navigator
navegar **§44** *tr* to sail || *intr* to navigate, to sail; to move around
navel *f* (*pl* **-vels**) navel orange
Navidad *f* Christmas; Christmas time;

¡Felices Navidades! Merry Christmas!; **contar** or **tener muchas Navidades** to be pretty old
navidal *m* Christmas card
navide·ño -ña *adj* Christmas
navie·ro -ra *adj* ship, shipping || *m* shipowner; outfitter
navío *m* ship, vessel; **navío de guerra** warship
náyade *f* naiad
nazare·no -na *adj & mf* Nazarene || *m* penitent in Passion Week procession || **nazarenas** *fpl* (SAm) large gaucho spurs
nazi *adj & mf* Nazi
N.B. *abbr* **nota bene (Lat) note well**
nébeda *f* catnip
neblina *f* fog, mist
neblino·so -sa *adj* foggy, misty
nebulo·so -sa *adj* nebulous, cloudy, misty, hazy, vague; gloomy, sullen || *f* nebula
necedad *f* foolishness, stupidity, nonsense
necesa·rio -ria *adj* necessary || *f* water closet, privy
neceser *m* toilet case; sewing kit; **neceser de belleza** vanity case; **neceser de costura** workbasket
necesidad *f* necessity; need, want; starvation; **de necesidad** from weakness; of necessity; **necesidad mayor** bowel movement; **necesidad menor** urination
necesita·do -da *adj* necessitous, poor, needy; **estar necesitado de** to be in need of || *mf* needy person
necesitar *tr* to necessitate; to need; **necesitar** + *inf* to have to, to need to + *inf* || *intr* to be in need; **necesitar de** to be in need of, to need || *ref* to be needed, to be necessary
ne·cio -cia *adj* foolish, stupid; imprudent; stubborn; (Am) touchy || *mf* fool
necrología *f* necrology
necromancia *f* necromancy
néctar *m* nectar
neerlan·dés -desa *adj* Netherlandish, Dutch || *mf* Netherlander || *m* Dutchman; (*idioma*) Netherlandish or Dutch || *f* Dutchwoman
nefalista *mf* teetotaler
nefan·do -da *adj* base, infamous
nefas·to -ta *adj* ominous, fatal, tragic
negable *adj* deniable
negación *f* negation; denial; refusal
nega·do -da *adj* unfit, incompetent; dull, indifferent
negar §66 *tr* to deny; to refuse; to prohibit; to disown; to conceal || *intr* to deny || *ref* to avoid; to refuse; to deny oneself to callers; **negarse a** to refuse; **negarse a** + *inf* to refuse to + *inf*
negati·vo -va *adj* negative || *f* negative; denial; refusal
negligencia *f* negligence
negligente *adj* negligent
negociable *adj* negotiable
negociación *f* negotiation; deal, matter
negociado *m* department, bureau; affair, business; (SAm) illegal dealing; (Chile) store
negociante *m* dealer, trader
negociar *tr* to negotiate || *intr* to negotiate; to deal, to trade
negocio *m* business; affair, deal, transaction; profit; (SAm) store
negocio·so -sa *adj* businesslike
negrear *intr* to turn black; to look black
negre·ro -ra *adj* slave-trading; (fig) slave-driving || *mf* slave trader; (fig) slave driver
negrilla *f* (typ) boldface
ne·gro -gra *adj* black; dark; gloomy, dismal; fatal, evil, wicked; Negro; (coll) broke || *mf* Negro; (Am) dear, darling || *m* black; **negro de humo** lampblack
negror *m* or **negrura** *f* blackness
negruz·co -ca *adj* blackish
néme·sis *f* (*pl* **-sis**) (*justo castigo; castigador*) nemesis || **Némesis** *f* Nemesis
nemoro·so -sa *adj* (poet) woody, sylvan
ne·ne -na *mf* baby; dear, darling || *m* rascal, villain
nenúfar *m* white water lily
neo *m* neon
neocelan·dés -desa *adj* New Zealand || *mf* New Zealander
neoesco·cés -cesa *adj & mf* Nova Scotian
neófi·to -ta *mf* neophyte
neologismo *m* neologism
neomejica·no -na *adj & mf* New Mexican
neomicina *f* neomycin
neón *m* neon
neoyorki·no -na *adj* New York || *mf* New Yorker
Nepal, el Nepal
nepa·lés -lesa *adj & mf* Nepalese
nepente *m* nepenthe
nepote *m* relative and favorite of the Pope || **Nepote** *m* Nepos
neptunio *m* neptunium
Neptuno *m* Neptune
nereida *f* Nereid
Nerón *m* Nero
nervio *m* nerve; (*del ala del insecto*) rib; strength, vigor
nerviosidad *f* nervousness
nervio·so -sa *adj* nervous; energetic, vigorous, sinewy; (*célula; centro; tónico*) nerve; (*sistema; enfermedad; postración, colapso*) nervous
nervosidad *f* nervosity; ductility, flexibility; (*de un argumento*) force, cogency
nervo·so -sa *adj* var of **nervioso**
nervu·do -da *adj* vigorous, sinewy
nervura *f* backbone (*of book*)
nesga *f* gore
nesgar §44 *tr* to gore
ne·to -ta *adj* net
neumáti·co -ca *adj* pneumatic; air || *m* tire
neumonía *f* pneumonia
neuralgia *f* neuralgia
neurología *f* neurology
neuro·sis *f* (*pl* **-sis**) neurosis; **neurosis de guerra** shell shock
neuróti·co -ca *adj & mf* neurotic
neutral *adj & mf* neutral
neutralidad *f* neutrality
neutralismo *m* neutralism

neutralista *adj & mf* neutralist
neutralizar §60 *tr* to neutralize
neu•tro -tra *adj* neuter; (*que no es de un color ni de otro*) neutral; (bot, chem, elec, phonet, zool) neutral; (*verbo*) intransitive
neutrón *m* neutron
neva•do -da *adj* snow-covered; snow-white || *f* snowfall
nevar §2 *tr* to make snow-white || *intr* to snow
nevasca *f* snowfall; snowstorm, blizzard
nevazón *f* (SAm) snowfall
nevera *f* icebox, refrigerator; icehouse; (P-R) jail
nevería *f* ice-cream parlor
neve•ro -ra *mf* ice-cream dealer || *m* place of perpetual snow; perpetual snow || *f* see **nevera**
nevisca *f* snow flurry
neviscar §73 *intr* to snow lightly
nevo *m* mole; **nevo materno** birth mark
nevo•so -sa *adj* snowy
ni *conj* neither, nor; **ni . . . ni** neither . . . nor; **ni . . . siquiera** not even
niacina *f* niacin
nicaragüense or **nicaragüe•ño -ña** *adj & mf* Nicaraguan
Nicolás *m* Nicholas
nicotina *f* nicotine
nicho *m* niche
nidada *f* (*huevos en el nido*) nestful of eggs; (*pajarillos en el nido*) nest, brood, hatch
nidal *m* (*donde la gallina pone sus huevos*) nest; nest egg; haunt; source; basis, foundation
nido *m* nest; haunt; home; source; (*de ladrones*) nest, den
niebla *f* fog, mist, haze; mildew; fog, confusion; **hay niebla** it is foggy; **niebla artificial** smoke screen
nie•to -ta *mf* grandchild || *m* grandson; **nietos** grandchildren || *f* granddaughter
nieve *f* snow; (Am) water ice
nigromancia *f* necromancy
nihilismo *m* nihilism
nihilista *mf* nihilist
Nilo *m* Nile; **Nilo Azul** Blue Nile
nilón *m* nylon
nimbo *m* nimbus; halo
nimiedad *f* excess; fussiness, fastidiousness; (coll) timidity
ni•mio -mia *adj* excessive; fussy, fastidious; (Am) tiny
ninfa *f* nymph; **ninfa marina** mermaid
ninfea *f* white water lily
ningún *adj indef* apocopated form of **ninguno,** used only before masculine singular nouns and adjectives
ningu•no -na *adj indef* no, not any || *pron indef* none, not any; neither, neither one; **ninguno de los dos** neither one || **ninguno** *pron indef* nobody, no one
niña *f* child, girl; (*del ojo*) pupil; **niña del ojo** (coll) apple of one's eye; **niña exploradora** girl scout
niñada *f* childishness
niñera *f* nursemaid
niñería *f* childishness; trifle
niñero -ra *adj* fond of children || *f* see **niñera**
niñez *f* childhood; childishness; (fig) infancy
ni•ño -ña *adj* childlike, childish; young, inexperienced || *mf* child; (*persona joven e inexperta*) babe; **desde niño** from childhood; **niño expósito** foundling; **niño travieso** imp || *m* child, boy; **niño bonito** playboy; **niño de coro** choirboy; **niño de la bola** child Jesus; (coll) lucky fellow; **niño explorador** boy scout; **niño gótico** playboy || *f* see **niña**
ni•pón -pona *adj & mf* Nipponese
níquel *m* nickel
niquelar *tr* to nickel-plate
nirvana, el nirvana
níspero *m* medlar (*tree and fruit*)
níspola *f* medlar (*fruit*)
nitidez *f* brightness, clearness; sharpness
níti•do -da *adj* bright, clear; sharp
nitrato *m* nitrate
nítri•co -ca *adj* nitric
nitro *m* niter; **nitro de Chile** saltpeter
nitrógeno *m* nitrogen
nitro•so -sa *adj* nitrous
nitruro *m* nitride
nivel *m* level; **nivel de burbuja** spirit level; **nivel de vida** standard of living
nivelar *tr* to level; to even, make even; to grade; to survey
no *adv* not; no; **¿cómo no?** why not?; of course, certainly; **creer que no** to think not, to believe not; **¿no?** is it not so?; **no bien** no sooner; **no más que** not more than; only; **no sea que** lest; **no . . . sino** only; **ya no** no longer
nobabia *f* (aer) dope
noble *adj* noble || *m* noble, nobleman
nobleza *f* nobility
noción *f* notion, idea; rudiment
noci•vo -va *adj* noxious, harmful
noctur•no -na *adj* nocturnal; lonely, sad, melancholy; night, nighttime
noche *f* night, nighttime; darkness; **buenas noches** good evening; good night; **de la noche a la mañana** overnight; unexpectedly, suddenly; **de noche** at night, in the nighttime; **esta noche** tonight; **hacer noche en** to spend the night in; **hacerse de noche** to grow dark; **muy de noche** late at night; **por la noche** at night, in the nighttime; **noche buena** Christmas Eve; **noche de estreno** (theat) first night; **noche de uvas** New Year's Eve; **noche vieja** New Year's Eve; watch night
nochebuena *f* Christmas Eve
nochebueno *m* Christmas cake; Yule log
nodo *m* (astr, med, phys) node
No-Do *m* (acronym for **Noticiario y Documentales**) newsreel; newsreel theater
nodriza *f* wet nurse; vacuum tank
Noé *m* Noah
nogal *m* walnut; **nogal de la brujería** witch hazel
nómada or **nómade** *adj & mf* nomad

nomádi·co -ca *adj* nomadic
nombradía *f* fame, renown, reputation
nombra·do -da *adj* famous
nombramiento *m* naming; appointment
nombrar *tr* to name; to appoint
nombre *m* name; fame, reputation; nickname; watchword; noun; **del mismo nombre** (elec) like; **de nombres contrarios** (elec) unlike; **nombre comercial** firm name; **nombre de lugar** place name; **nombre de pila** first name, Christian name; **nombre de soltera** maiden name; **nombre substantivo** noun; **nombre supuesto** alias
nomeolvi·des *f* (*pl* **-des**) forget-me-not; German madwort
nómina *f* list, roll; pay roll
nominal *adj* nominal; noun
nominar *tr* to name; to appoint
nominati·vo -va *adj & m* nominative
non *adj* odd, uneven || *m* odd number
nonada *f* trifle, nothing
no·na -na *adj & m* ninth
nopal *m* prickly pear
norcorea·no -na *adj & mf* North Korean
nordestada *f* or **nordeste** *m* (*viento*) northeaster (*wind*)
noria *f* chain pump; (*pozo*) draw well; Ferris wheel; (coll) treadmill, drudgery
norma *f* norm, standard; rule, method; (carp) square
normal *adj* normal; standard; perpendicular
Normandía *f* Normandy
norman·do -da *adj & mf* Norman || *m* Norseman
norte *m* north; north wind; (*guía*) (fig) polestar, lodestar
Norteamérica *f* North America; America, the United States
norteamerica·no -na *adj & mf* North American; (*estadunidense*) American
norte·ño -ña *adj* northern
norue·go -ga *adj & mf* Norwegian || **Noruega** *f* Norway
nos (used as object of verb) *pron pers* us; to us || *pron reflex* ourselves, to ourselves; each other, to each other
noso·tros -tras *pron pers* we; us; ourselves
nostalgia *f* nostalgia
nota *f* note; (*en la escuela*) mark, grade; (*en el restaurante*) check; (mus) note; **nota de adorno** grace note; **nota tónica** keynote
notar *tr* to note; to dictate; to annotate; to criticize; to discredit
notario *m* notary, notary public
noticia *f* news; notice, information; notion, rudiment; knowledge; **noticias de actualidad** news of the day; **noticias de última hora** late news; **una noticia** a piece of news, a news item
noticiar *tr* to notify; to give notice of
noticia·rio -ria *adj* news || *m* up-to-the-minute news; newsreel; newscast; **noticiario gráfico** picture page; **noticiario teatral** theater page
noticie·ro -ra *adj* news || *m* newsman, reporter; late news
noticio·so -sa *adj* informed; learned; well-informed; (Am) newsy || *m* (Am) news item
notificar **§73** *tr* to notify; to report on
no·to -ta *adj* known, well-known || *m* south wind || *f* see **nota**
notoriedad *f* general knowledge; fame
noto·rio -ria *adj* manifest, well-known
nov. *abbr* **noviembre**
novatada *f* hazing; beginner's blunder
nova·to -ta *adj* beginning || *mf* beginner; freshman
novecien·tos -tas *adj & pron* nine hundred || **novecientos** *m* nine hundred
novedad *f* newness, novelty; news; fashion; happening; change; failing health; **sin novedad** as usual; safe; well; without anything happening
novel *adj* new, inexperienced, beginning || *m* beginner
novela *f* novel; story, lie; **novela caballista** novel of western life; **novela policíaca** or **policial** detective story; **novela por entregas** serial
novele·ro -ra *adj* fond of novelty; fond of fiction; gossipy; fickle
noveles·co -ca *adj* novelistic, fictional; romantic, fantastic
novelista *mf* novelist
novelísti·co -ca *adj* fictional || *f* fiction
novelizar **§60** *tr* to fictionalize
nove·no -na *adj & m* ninth
noventa *adj, pron & m* ninety
noventa·vo -va *adj & m* ninetieth
novia *f* fiancée; bride; **novia de guerra** war bride
noviazgo *m* engagement, courtship
novi·cio -cia *adj & mf* novice
noviembre *m* November
novilunio *m* new moon
novilla *f* heifer
novillada *f* drove of young bulls; (taur) fight with young bulls by aspiring bullfighters
novillero *m* herdsman of young cattle; (taur) aspiring fighter, untrained fighter; (coll) truant
novillo *m* young bull; (coll) cuckold; **hacer novillos** (coll) to play truant
novio *m* suitor; fiancé; bridegroom; **novios** engaged couple; bride and groom, newlyweds
novocaína *f* novocaine
nro. *abbr* **nuestro**
N.S. *abbr* **Nuestro Señor**
ntro. *abbr* **nuestro**
nubada *f* local shower; abundance
nubarrón *m* storm cloud
nube *f* cloud; **andar** (*los precios*) **por las nubes** to be sky-high; **bajar de las nubes** to come back to or down to earth; **poner en** or **sobre las nubes** to praise to the skies
nube-hongo *f* mushroom cloud
nubla·do -da *adj* cloudy || *m* storm cloud; impending danger; abundance; **aguantar el nublado** to suffer resignedly
nublar *tr* to cloud, cloud over || *ref* to become cloudy
nu·blo -bla *adj* cloudy || *m* storm cloud
nublo·so -sa *adj* cloudy; adverse, unfortunate

nubo•so -sa *adj* cloudy
nuca *f* nape
nuclear *adj* nuclear
núcleo *m* nucleus; core; (*de nuez*) kernel; (*de la fruta*) stone; (*de un electroimán*) core
nudillo *m* knuckle; stocking stitch; plug (*in wall*)
nudo *m* knot; bond, tie, union; crux; tangle, plot; difficulty; (*en el drama*) crisis; center, juncture; (bot) node; (naut) knot; **cortar el nudo gordiano** to cut the Gordian knot; **hacérsele a** (*uno*) **un nudo en la garganta** to get a lump in one's throat
nudo•so -sa *adj* knotted, knotty
nuera *f* daughter-in-law
nues•tro -tra *adj poss* our || *pron poss* ours
nueva *f* news; piece of news; **nuevas** *fpl* news
Nueva York *m & f* New York; **el Gran Nueva York** Greater New York
Nueva Zelanda New Zealand
nueve *adj & pron* nine; **las nueve** nine o'clock || *m* nine; (*en las fechas*) ninth
nue•vo -va *adj* new; **de nuevo** again, anew; **nuevo flamante** brand-new; **¿qué hay de nuevo?** what's new? || *mf* novice; freshman || *f* see **nueva**
nuevomejica•no -na *adj & mf* New Mexican
Nuevo Méjico *m* New Mexico
nuez *f* (*pl* **nueces**) nut; walnut; Adam's apple; **nuez dura** (*árbol*) hickory; hickory nut; **nuez moscada** nutmeg
nulidad *f* nullity; incapacity; (coll) nobody
nu•lo -la *adj* null, void, worthless
núm. *abbr* **número**
numen *m* deity; inspiration
numeral *adj* numeral
numerar *tr* to number; to count; to numerate
numerario *m* cash, coin, specie
numéri•co -ca *adj* numerical
número *m* number; (*de un periódico*) copy, issue; (*de zapatos*) size; lottery ticket; **cargar** or **cobrar al número llamado** (telp) to reverse the charges; **de número** (*dícese de los individuos de una sociedad*) regular; **mirar por el número uno** to look out for number one; **número de serie** series number; **número equivocado** (telp) wrong number
numero•so -sa *adj* numerous
nunca *adv* never; **no . . . nunca** not . . . ever, never **nunca jamás** never more
nupcial *adj* nuptial
nupcialidad *f* marriage rate
nupcias *fpl* nuptials, marriage; **casarse en segundas nupcias** to marry the second time
nutria *f* otter
nutrición *f* nutrition
nutri•do -da *adj* great, intense, robust, vigorous, steady; full, abounding, rich, heavy; (*carácter, letra*) thick; (*cañoneo*) heavy, sustained
nutrimento or **nutrimiento** *m* nourishment, nutriment
nutrir *tr* to nourish, to feed; to supply, to stock; to support, back up; to fill to overflowing
nu•triz *f* (*pl* **-trices**) wet nurse

Ñ

Ñ, ñ (eñe) *f* seventeenth letter of the Spanish alphabet
ñadi *m* (Chile) broad, shallow swamp
ñajú *m* (Am) okra, gumbo
ñámbar *m* Jamaica rosewood
ñame *m* yam; (W-I) blockhead, dunce
ñan•dú *m* (*pl* **-dúes**) nandu, American ostrich
ña•ño -ña *adj* (Am) close, intimate; (Am) spoiled, overindulged || *m* (Am) elder brother || *f* (Am) elder sister; (Am) nursemaid; (Am) dear
ñapa *f* (Am) something thrown in; **de ñapa** (Am) in the bargain
ñaque *m* junk, pile of junk
ña•to -ta *adj* (Am) pug-nosed; (Arg) ugly, deformed
ñeque *adj* (Am) strong, vigorous; (*dícese de los ojos*) (Am) drooping || *m* (Am) slap, blow; (Am) pep
ñiqueñaque *m* (coll) trash
ñisca *f* (Am) bit, fragment; (Am) excrement
ñoclo *m* macaroon
ñolombre *m* (Am) old peasant; **¡viene ñolombre!** (Am) here comes the bogeyman
ñon•go -ga *adj* (Am) slow, lazy; (Am) foolish, stupid; (Am) tricky; (Am) suspicious
ñoñería or **ñoñez** *f* timidity; inanity; dotage
ño•ño -ña *adj* timid; inane; doting

O

O, o (o) *f* eighteenth letter of the Spanish alphabet
o *conj* or; **o . . . o** either . . . or
oa•sis *m* (*pl* **-sis**) oasis
ob. *abbr* **obispo**
obduración *f* obduracy
obedecer §22 *tr* (with personal **a**) to obey || *intr* to obey; **obedecer a** to yield to, be due to, be in keeping with, arise from

obediencia *f* obedience
obediente *adj* obedient
obelisco *m* obelisk; (typ) dagger
obertura *f* (mus) overture
obesidad *f* obesity
obe•so -sa *adj* obese
obispo *m* bishop
óbito *m* decease, demise
obituario *m* (Am) obituary
objeción *f* objection
objetable *adj* objectionable (*open to objection*)
objetar *tr* to object; (*dudas*) to raise; (*una razón contraria*) to set up, offer, present; to object to
objeti•vo -va *adj* & *m* objective
objeto *m* object; subject matter; **objetos de cotillón** favors
oblea *f* wafer; pill, tablet; **hecho una oblea** (coll) nothing but skin and bones
obli•cuo -cua *adj* oblique
obligación *f* obligation, duty; bond, debenture; **obligaciones** *fpl* family responsibilities
obligacionista *mf* bondholder
obliga•do -da *adj* obliged, grateful; submissive; (mus) obbligato || *m* (mus) obbligato
obligar **§44** *tr* to obligate; to oblige
obliterar *tr* to cancel
oblon•go -ga *adj* oblong
oboe *m* oboe; oboist
oboísta *mf* oboist
óbolo *m* mite
obra *f* work; **obra de** a matter of; **obra de consulta** reference work; **obra maestra** masterpiece; **obra pía** charity; (coll) useful effort; **obra prima** shoemaking; **obras** construction, repairs, alterations; **obra segunda** shoe repairing; **poner por obra** to undertake, set to work on
obra•dor -dora *mf* worker || *m* workman; shop, workshop || *f* workingwoman
obrajero *m* foreman; (Arg) lumberman; (Bol) artisan
obrar *tr* to build; to perform; to work || *intr* to work; to act, operate, proceed; to have a movement of the bowels; **obra en mi poder** I have at hand, I have in my possession
obrera *f* workingwoman
obrerismo *m* labor; labor movement
obre•ro -ra *adj* working; labor || *m* workman; **los obreros** labor || *f* see **obrera**
obrero-patronal *adj* labor-management
obscenidad *f* obscenity
obsce•no -na *adj* obscene
obscurecer **§22** *tr* to darken; to dim; to discredit; to cloud, confuse || *intr* to grow dark || *ref* to cloud over; to become dimmed; (coll) to fade away
obscuridad *f* obscurity; darkness
obscu•ro -ra *adj* obscure; dark; gloomy; uncertain, dangerous; **a obscuras** in the dark || *m* dark; (paint) shading
obsequia•do -da *mf* recipient; guest of honor
obsequiar *tr* to fawn over, flatter; to present, to give; to court, to woo
obsequio *m* flattery; gift; attention, courtesy; **en obsequio de** in honor of
obsequio•so -sa *adj* obsequious; obliging, courteous
observación *f* observation
observa•dor -dora *adj* observant || *mf* observer
observancia *f* observance; deference, respectfulness
observar *tr* to observe
observatorio *m* observatory
obsesión *f* obsession
obsesionar *tr* to obsess
obstaculizar **§60** *tr* to prevent; to obstruct
obstáculo *m* obstacle
obstante *adj* standing in the way; **no obstante** however, nevertheless; in spite of
obstar *intr* to stand in the way; **obstar a** or **para** to hinder, check, oppose
obstetricia *f* obstetrics
obstétri•co -ca *adj* obstetrical || *mf* obstetrician
obstinación *f* obstinacy
obstina•do -da *adj* obstinate
obstinar *ref* to be obstinate
obstrucción *f* obstruction
obstruir **§20** *tr* to obstruct; to block; to stop up
obtención *f* obtaining
obtener **§71** *tr* to obtain; to keep
obtenible *adj* obtainable
obturador *m* stopper, plug; (aut) choke; (aut) throttle; (phot) shutter; **obturador de guillotina** drop shutter
obtu•so -sa *adj* obtuse
obús *m* howitzer; shell; (*de válvula de neumático*) plunger
obvención *f* extra, bonus, incidental
obvencional *adj* incidental
obviar **§77 & regular** *tr* to obviate, prevent || *intr* to stand in the way
ob•vio -via *adj* obvious; unnecessary
oca *f* goose
ocasión *f* occasion; opportunity, chance; danger, risk; **aprovechar la ocasión** to improve the occasion; **aprovechar la ocasión de** to avail oneself of the opportunity to; **asir la ocasión por la melena** to take time by the forelock; **de ocasión** secondhand
ocasiona•do -da *adj* dangerous, risky; exposed, subject, liable; annoying
ocasionar *tr* to occasion, to cause; to stir up; to endanger
ocasional *adj* occasional; causal; causing; (*causa*) responsible; accidental
ocaso *m* west; (*de un cuerpo celeste*) setting; sunset; decline; end, death
occidental *adj* western; occidental
occidente *m* occident
oceáni•co -ca *adj* oceanic
océano *m* ocean
ocio *m* idleness, leisure; distraction, pastime; spare time
ocio•so -sa *adj* idle; useless, needless
oclusión *f* occlusion
oclusi•vo -va *adj* & *f* occlusive
ocote *m* (Mex) torch pine
octava *f* octave
octavilla *f* handbill; eight-syllable verse

octavín *m* piccolo
octa•vo -va *adj* eighth || *mf* octoroon || *m* eighth || *f* see **octava**
oct.e *abbr* **octubre**
octogési•mo -ma *adj & m* eightieth
octubre *m* October
ocular *adj* ocular, eye || *m* eyepiece, eyeglass, ocular
oculista *mf* oculist; (Am) fawner, flatterer
ocultar *tr & ref* to hide
ocul•to -ta *adj* hidden, concealed; (*misterioso, sobrenatural*) occult
ocupación *f* occupation; occupancy; employment
ocupa•do -da *adj* busy; occupied; **ocupada** pregnant
ocupante *adj* occupying || *mf* occupant || **ocupantes** *mpl* occupying forces
ocupar *tr* to occupy; to busy, keep busy; to employ; to bother, annoy; to attract the attention of || *ref* to be occupied; to be busy; to be preoccupied; to bother
ocurrencia *f* occurrence; witticism; bright idea
ocurrente *adj* witty
ocurrir *intr* to occur, happen; to come; (*venir a la mente*) to occur
ocha•vo -va *adj* eighth; octagonal || *m* eighth; octagon
ochenta *adj, pron & m* eighty
ochenta•vo -va *adj & m* eightieth
ocho *adj & pron* eight; **las ocho** eight o'clock || *m* eight; (*en las fechas*) eighth
ochocien•tos -tas *adj & pron* eight hundred || **ochocientos** *m* eight hundred
oda *f* ode
odiar *tr* to hate
odio *m* hate, hatred
odio•so -sa *adj* odious, hateful
Odisea *f* Odyssey
Odiseo *m* Odysseus
odontología *f* odontology, dentistry
odontólo•go -ga *mf* odontologist, dentist
odre *m* goatskin wine bag; (coll) toper
OEA *f* OAS
oeste *m* west; west wind
ofender *tr & intr* to offend || *ref* to take offense
ofensa *f* offense
ofensi•vo -va *adj & f* offensive
ofen•sor -sora *adj* offending || *mf* offender
oferta *f* offer; gift, present; **oferta y demanda** supply and demand
oficial *adj* official || *m* official, officer; skilled workman; clerk, office worker; journeyman; commissioned officer; **oficial de derrota** navigator
oficiar *tr* to announce officially in writing; (*la misa*) to celebrate; to officiate at || *intr* to officiate; **oficiar de** (coll) to act as
oficina *f* office; shop; pharmacist's laboratory; **oficina de objetos perdidos** lost-and-found department
oficines•co -ca *adj* office, clerical; bureaucratic
oficinista *mf* clerk, office worker
oficio *m* office, occupation; function, rôle; craft, trade; memo, official note; (eccl) office, service; **de oficio** officially; professionally; **hacer oficios de** to function as; **tomar por oficio** (coll) to take to, to keep at
oficio•so -sa *adj* diligent; obliging; officious, meddlesome; profitable; unofficial
ofrecer *tr & intr* to offer; (*una recepción*) to give || *ref* to offer; to offer oneself; to happen
ofrecimiento *m* offer, offering; **ofrecimiento de presentación** introductory offer
ofrenda *f* offering; gift
ofrendar *tr* to make offerings of; to contribute
oftalmología *f* ophthalmology
oftalmólo•go -ga *mf* ophthalmologist
ofuscar §73 *tr* to obfuscate; to dazzle
ogro *m* ogre
Oh *interj* O!, Oh!
ohmio *m* ohm
oíble *adj* audible
oída *f* hearing; **de** or **por oídas** by hearsay
oído *m* hearing; ear; **abrir tanto oído** to be all ears; **al oído** by listening; confidentially; **decir al oído** to whisper; **hacer** or **tener oídos de mercader** to turn a deaf ear
oír §48 *tr* to hear; to listen to; (*una conferencia*) to attend; **oír** + *inf* to hear + *inf*, e.g., **oí entrar a mi hermano** I heard my brother come in; to hear + *ger*, e.g., **oí cantar a la muchacha** I heard the girl singing; to hear + *pp*, e.g., **oí tocar la campana** I heard the bell rung; **oír decir que** to hear that; **oír hablar de** to hear about || *intr* to hear; to listen; **¡oiga!** say!, listen!; the idea!, the very idea!
ojada *f* (Col) skylight
ojal *m* buttonhole; eyelet; grommet
ojalá *interj* God grant . . . !, would to God . . . !; **¡ojalá que . . . !** would that . . . !, I hope that . . . !
ojeada *f* glimpse, glance; **buena ojeada** eyeful
ojear *tr* to eye, stare at; to hoodoo, to cast the evil eye on; (*la caza*) to start, to rouse; to frighten, to startle
ojera *f* eyecup, eyeglass; **ojeras** (*bajo los párpados inferiores*) rings, circles
ojeriza *f* grudge, ill will
ojero•so -sa *adj* with rings or circles under the eyes
ojete *m* eyelet, eyehole
ojienju•to -ta *adj* dry-eyed, tearless
ojituer•to -ta *adj* cross-eyed
ojiva *f* ogive, pointed arch
ojo *m* eye; (*de la escalera*) opening, well; (*del puente*) bay, span; (*de agua*) spring; **a ojos vistas** visibly, openly; **costar un ojo de la cara** to cost a mint, to cost a fortune; **dar los ojos de la cara por** to give one's eyeteeth for; **hasta los ojos** up to one's ears; **mirar con ojos de carnero degollado** to make sheep's eyes at; **no pegar el ojo** to not sleep a wink; **ojo de buey** (archit, meteor, naut) bull's-eye; (bot) oxeye; **ojo de la cerradura**

keyhole; **poner los ojos en blanco** to roll one's eyes; **saltar a los ojos** to be self-evident; **valer un ojo de la cara** to be worth a mint || *interj* beware!; look out!; attention!; **¡mucho ojo!** be careful!, watch out!; **¡ojo con . . . !** look out for . . . !; **¡ojo, mancha!** fresh paint!
ojota *f* (SAm) sandal; (SAm) tanned llama hide
ola *f* wave; (*de gente apiñada*) surge
ole *m* or **olé** *m* bravo || *interj* bravo!
oleada *f* big wave; (*de gente apiñada*) surge, swell
oleaje *m* surge, rush of waves
óleo *m* oil; holy oil; oil painting; **los santos óleos** extreme unction
oleoducto *m* pipe line
oler §49 *tr* to smell; to pry into; to sniff out || *intr* to smell, to smell fragrant, to smell bad; **no oler bien** (coll) to look suspicious; **oler a** to smell of, to smell like; to smack of
olfatear *tr* to smell, scent, sniff; (coll) (*p.ej., un buen negocio*) to scent, to sniff out
olfato *m* smell, sense of smell; scent; keen insight
olíbano *m* frankincense
oliente *adj* smelling, odorous
oligarquía *f* oligarchy
Olimpíada *f* Olympiad
olímpi•co -ca *adj* Olympian; Olympic; haughty
oliscar §73 *tr* to smell, scent, sniff; to investigate || *intr* to smell bad
oliva *f* olive; olive tree; barn owl; olive branch, peace
olivar *m* olive grove
olivillo *m* mock privet
olivo *m* olive tree; **tomar el olivo** (taur) to duck behind the barrier; (coll) to beat it
olmeda *f* or **olmedo** *m* elm grove
olmo *m* elm tree
olor *m* odor; promise, hope; trace, suspicion; **olores** (Chile, Mex) spice, condiment
oloro•so -sa *adj* odorous, fragrant
olote *m* (CAm & Mex) cob, corncob
olvidadi•zo -za *adj* forgetful; ungrateful
olvida•do -da *adj* forgetful; ungrateful
olvidar *tr* & *intr* to forget; **olvidar** + *inf* to forget to + *inf* || *ref* to forget oneself; **olvidarse de** to forget; **olvidarse de** + *inf* to forget to + *inf*; **olvidársele a uno** to forget, e.g., **se me olvidó mi pasaporte** I forgot my passport; **olvidársele a uno** + *inf* to forget to + *inf*, e.g., **se me olvidó cerrar la ventana** I forgot to close the window
olvido *m* forgetfulness; oblivion
olla *f* pot, kettle; stew; eddy, whirlpool; **olla a** or **de presión** pressure cooker
ombligo *m* navel; (*centro, punto medio*) (fig) navel
omino•so -sa *adj* ominous
omisión *f* omission; oversight, neglect
omi•so -sa *adj* neglectful, remiss
omitir *tr* to omit; to overlook, neglect
ómni•bus *adj* (*tren*) accommodation || *m* (*pl* **-bus**) bus, omnibus; **ómnibus de dos pisos** double-decker
omnímo•do -da *adj* all-inclusive
omnipotente *adj* omnipotent
omnisciente or **omnis•cio -cia** *adj* omniscient
omnívo•ro -ra *adj* omnivorous
omóplato *m* shoulder blade
once *adj* & *pron* eleven; **las once** eleven o'clock || *m* eleven; (*en las fechas*) eleventh
oncea•vo -va *adj* & *m* eleventh
once•no -na *adj* & *m* eleventh
onda *f* wave; flicker; (*en el pelo*) wave; **onda portadora** (rad) carrier wave; **ondas entretenidas** (rad) continuous waves
ondear *tr* (*el pelo*) to wave || *intr* to wave; to ripple; to flow; to flicker; to be wavy || *ref* to wave, sway, swing
ondo•so -sa *adj* wavy
ondulación *f* undulation; wave; wave motion
ondula•do -da *adj* wavy, ripply; rolling; corrugated || *m* (*en el pelo*) wave
ondular *tr* (*el pelo*) to wave || *intr* to undulate; (*una bandera*) to wave, flutter; (*las ondas del mar*) to billow; (*una culebra*) to wriggle
onero•so -sa *adj* onerous, burdensome
ónice *m*, **ónique** *m* or **ónix** *m* onyx
onomásti•co -ca *adj* of proper names || *m* name day || *f* study of proper names
ONU *f* UN
onza *f* ounce; (zool) snow leopard
onza•vo -va *adj* & *m* eleventh
opa•co -ca *adj* opaque; sad, gloomy
ópalo *m* opal
opción *f* option, choice
ópera *f* opera; **ópera semiseria** light opera; **ópera seria** grand opera
operación *f* operation; transaction
operar *tr* to operate on || *intr* to operate; to work || *ref* to occur, come about; to be operated on
opera•rio -ria *mf* worker || *m* workman || *f* working woman
opereta *f* operetta
operista *mf* opera singer
operísti•co -ca *adj* operatic
opia•to -ta *adj, m* & *f* opiate
opinable *adj* moot
opinar *intr* to opine; to think; to pass judgment
opinión *f* opinion, view; reputation, public image
opio *m* opium
opípa•ro -ra *adj* sumptuous, lavish
oponer §54 *tr* to oppose; (*resistencia*) to offer, put up || *ref* to oppose each other; to face each other; **oponerse a** to oppose, be opposed to; to be against, to resist; to compete for
oporto *m* port, port wine
oportunidad *f* opportunity; opportuneness; **oportunidades** *fpl* witticisms
oportunista *adj* opportunistic || *mf* opportunist
oportu•no -na *adj* opportune, timely; proper; witty

oposición *f* opposition; competitive examination
oposi•tor -tora *adj* rivaling, competing || *mf* opponent; competitor
opresión *f* oppression
opresi•vo -va *adj* oppressive
opre•sor -sora *adj* oppressive || *mf* oppressor
oprimir *tr* to oppress; to squeeze, to press
oprobiar *tr* to defame, to revile
oprobio *m* opprobrium
oprobio•so -sa *adj* opprobrious
optar *tr* to choose, to select; *intr* — **optar entre** to choose between; **optar por** to choose to
ópti•co -ca *adj* optical || *mf* optician || *f* optics
óptimamente *adv* to perfection
optimismo *m* optimism
optimista *adj* optimistic || *mf* optimist
ópti•mo -ma *adj* fine, excellent
optometrista *mf* optometrist
opues•to -ta *adj* opposite, contrary
opugnar *tr* to attack; to lay siege to; to contradict
opulen•to -ta *adj* oppulent
opúsculo *m* short work, opuscule
oquedad *f* hollow; hollowness
ora *conj* — **ora . . . ora** now . . . now, now . . . then
oración *f* oration, speech; prayer; sentence; **oración dominical** Lord's prayer; **ponerse en oración** to get down on one's knees
oráculo *m* oracle
ora•dor -dora *mf* orator, speaker; **orador de plazuela** soapbox orator; **orador de sobremesa** after-dinner speaker
oraje *m* rough weather, storm
oral *adj* oral
orangután *m* orang-outang
orar *intr* to pray; to make a speech
orato•rio -ria *adj* oratorical || *m* oratorio; (*capilla privada*) oratory || *f* (*arte de la elocuencia*) oratory
orbe *m* orb; world
órbita *f* orbit
orca *f* killer whale
Órcadas *fpl* Orkney Islands
órdago — **de órdago** (coll) swell, real
orden *m & f* order; **hasta nueva orden** until further notice; **orden** *f* **de allanamiento** search warrant; **orden** *m* **de colocación** word order
ordenancista *adj* strict, severe || *mf* taskmaster, disciplinarian, martinet
ordenanza *m* errand boy; (mil) orderly || *f* ordinance; order, system; command; **ser de ordenanza** (coll) to be the rule
ordenar *tr* to order; to put in order; to ordain || *ref* to be ordained, to take orders
ordeñadero *m* milk pail
ordeñar *tr* to milk
ordeño *m* milking
ordinal *adj* orderly; ordinal || *m* ordinal
ordinariez *f* (coll) coarseness, crudeness
ordina•rio -ria *adj* ordinary || *m* daily household expenses; delivery man
orear *tr* to air || *ref* to be aired; to dry in the air; to take an airing
orégano *m* pot or wild marjoram, winter sweet
oreja *f* ear; (*del zapato*) flap; (*de martillo*) claw; lug, flange, ear; **aguzar las orejas** to prick up one's ears; **con las orejas caídas** crestfallen; **con las orejas tan largas** all ears; **descubrir** or **enseñar las orejas** (coll) to give oneself away
oreja•no -na *adj* (*res*) unbranded; (*animal*) (Am) skittish; (Am) shy; (Am) cautious
orejera *f* earflap, earmuff
orejeta *f* lug
ore•jón -jona *adj* (Am) coarse, uncouth; (Mex) skinny || *m* strip of dried peach; pull on the ear; (*de la hoja de un libro*) dog's-ear
oreju•do -da *adj* big-eared
oreo *m* breeze
orfanato *m* orphanage
orfandad *f* orphanage, orphanhood
orfebre *m* goldsmith; silversmith
Orfeo *m* Orpheus
orfeón *m* glee club, choral society
organ•dí *m* (*pl* **-díes**) organdy
orgáni•co -ca *adj* organic
organillero -ra *mf* organ-grinder
organillo *m* barrel organ, hand organ, hurdy-gurdy
organismo *m* organism; organization
organista *mf* organist
organizar **§60** *tr* to organize
órgano *m* organ; (*de una máquina*) part; (*medio, conducto*) organ; (mus) organ
orgía *f* orgy
orgullo *m* haughtiness; pride
orgullo•so -sa *adj* haughty; proud
oriental *adj* eastern; oriental
orientar *tr* to orient; to guide, direct; (*una vela*) to trim || *ref* to orient oneself; to find one's bearings
oriente *m* east; source, origin; east wind; youth || **Oriente** *m* Orient; **el Cercano Oriente** the Near East; **el Extremo Oriente** the Far East; **el Lejano Oriente** the Far East; **el Oriente Medio** the Middle East; **el Próximo Oriente** the Near East; **gran oriente** (*logia masónica central*) grand lodge
orificar **§73** *tr* to fill with gold
orífice *m* goldsmith
orificio *m* orifice, aperture, hole
origen *m* origin; source
original *adj* original; queer, odd, quaint || *m* original; character, queer duck; **de buen original** on good authority; **original de imprenta** copy
originar *tr & ref* to originate, to start
orilla *f* border, edge; margin; bank, shore; sidewalk; breeze; **orillas** (Arg, Mex) outskirts; **salir a la orilla** to manage to get through
orillar *tr* to put a border or edge on; to trim || *intr* to come up to the shore
orillo *m* selvage, list
orín *m* rust; **orines** urine; **tomarse de orines** to get rusty
orina *f* urine
orinal *m* chamber pot

orinar *tr* to pass, to urinate || *intr & ref* to urinate
oriun•do -da *adj & mf* native; **ser oriundo de** to come from, to hail from
orla *f* border, edge; trimming, fringe
orlar *tr* to border, to put an edge on; to trim, to trim with a fringe
orn. *abbr* **orden**
ornamentar *tr* to ornament, adorn
ornamento *m* ornament, adornment
ornar *tr* to adorn
ornato *m* adornment, show
oro *m* gold; playing card (*representing a gold coin*) equivalent to diamond; **de oro y azul** (coll) all dressed up; **oro batido** gold leaf; **oro de ley** standard gold; **poner de oro y azul** (coll) to rake over the coals; **ponerle colores al oro** to gild the lily
oron•do -da *adj* big-bellied; (coll) hollow, spongy, puffed up; (coll) pompous, self-satisfied
oropel *m* tinsel; **gastar mucho oropel** (coll) to put up a big front
oropéndola *f* golden oriole
orozuz *m* licorice
orquesta *f* orchestra; **orquesta típica** regional orchestra
orquestar *tr* to orchestrate
órquide *f* or **orquídea** *f* orchid
ortiga *f* nettle; **ser como unas ortigas** (coll) to be a grouch
orto *m* rise (*of sun or star*)
ortodo•xo -xa *adj* orthodox
ortografía *f* orthography; spelling
ortografiar §77 *tr & intr* to spell
oruga *f* caterpillar
orujo *m* bagasse of grapes or olives
orzuelo *m* sty
os *pron pers & reflex* (used as object of verb and corresponding to **vos** and **vosotros**) you, to you; yourself, to yourself; yourselves, to yourselves; each other, to each other
osa *f* she-bear; **Osa mayor** Great Bear; **Osa menor** Little Bear
osadía *f* boldness, daring
osa•do -da *adj* bold, daring
osamenta *f* skeleton; bones
osar *intr* to dare
osario *m* ossuary, charnel house
oscilar *intr* to oscillate; to fluctuate; to waver, hesitate
ósculo *m* kiss
oscurecer §22 *tr, intr & ref* var of **obscurecer**
oscuridad *f* var of **obscuridad**
oscu•ro -ra *adj & m* var of **obscuro**
osera *f* bear's den
osificar §73 *tr & ref* to ossify
oso *m* bear; **hacer el oso** (coll) to make a fool of oneself; (coll) to make love in the open; **oso blanco** polar bear; **oso hormiguero** ant bear, anteater; **oso lavador** raccoon
ostensorio *m* (eccl) monstrance
ostentar *tr* to show; to make a show of || *ref* to show off; to boast
ostentati•vo -va *adj* ostentatious
ostento *m* portent, prodigy
ostento•so -sa *adj* magnificent, showy
osteópata *mf* osteopath
osteopatía *f* osteopathy
ostión *m* large oyster
ostra *f* oyster; **ostras en su concha** oyster cocktail, oysters on the half shell
ostracismo *m* ostracism
ostral *m* oyster bed, oyster farm
ostrería *f* oysterhouse
ostre•ro -ra *adj* oyster || *m* oysterman; oyster bed, oyster farm
osu•do -da *adj* bony
osu•no -na *adj* bearish, bearlike
O.T.A.N., la Nato
O.T.A.S.E., la Seato
otate *m* Mexican giant grass (*Guadua amplexifolia*); otate stick
otero *m* hillock, knoll
otomán *m* ottoman
otoma•no -na *adj & mf* Ottoman || *f* ottoman
otoñal *adj* autumnal
otoño *m* autumn, fall
otorgar §44 *tr* to agree to; to grant, to confer; (law) to execute
o•tro -tra *adj indef* other, another || *pron indef* other one, another one; **como dijo el otro** as someone said
ovación *f* ovation
ovacionar *tr* to give an ovation to
oval *adj* oval
óvalo *m* oval
ovante *adj* victorious, triumphant
ovario *m* ovary
oveja *f* ewe, female sheep; **oveja negra** (fig) black sheep; **oveja perdida** (fig) lost sheep
oveje•ro -ra *adj* sheep || *mf* sheep raiser
oveju•no -na *adj* sheep, of sheep
ove•ro -ra *adj* blossom-colored; egg-colored
Ovidio *m* Ovid
ovillar *tr* to wind up; to sum up || *intr* to form into a ball || *ref* to curl up into a ball
ovillo *m* ball of yarn; ball, heap; tangled ball; **hacerse un ovillo** (coll) to cower, to recoil; (*hablando*) (coll) to get all tangled up
oxear *tr & intr* to shoo
oxiacanta *f* hawthorn
oxidar *tr* to oxidize || *ref* to oxidize; to get rusty
óxido *m* oxide; **óxido de carbono** carbon monoxide; **óxido de mercurio** mercuric oxide
oxígeno *m* oxygen
oxíto•no -na *adj* oxytone
oxte *interj* get out!, beat it!; **sin decir oxte ni moxte** (coll) without opening one's mouth
oyente *mf* hearer; (*a la radio*) listener; (*en la escuela*) auditor
ozono *m* ozone

P

P, p (pe) *f* nineteenth letter of the Spanish alphabet
P. *abbr* **Padre, Papa, Pregunta**
pabellón *m* pavilion; bell tent; flag, banner; (*de fusiles*) stack; canopy; summerhouse; (*de instrumento de viento*) bell
pabilo *or* **pábilo** *m* wick
Pablo *m* Paul
pábulo *m* food; support, encouragement, fuel
pacana *f* pecan
paca•to -ta *adj* mild, gentle
pacer **§22** *tr* to pasture, graze; to gnaw, eat away || *intr* to pasture, graze
paciencia *f* patience
paciente *adj* & *mf* patient
pacienzu•do -da *adj* long-suffering
pacificar **§73** *tr* to pacify || *intr* to sue for peace || *ref* to calm down
pacífi•co -ca *adj* pacific
pacifismo *m* pacifism
pacifista *adj* & *mf* pacifist
pa•co -ca *adj* (Chile) bay, reddish || *m* paco, alpaca; Moorish sniper; sniper || **Paco** *m* Frank
pacotilla *f* trash, junk; (Chile) rabble, mob; **hacer su pacotilla** (coll) to make a cleanup; **ser de pacotilla** to be shoddy, to be poorly made
pacotille•ro -ra *mf* (Chile, Ven) peddler
pactar *tr* to agree upon || *intr* to come to an agreement
pacto *m* pact, covenant
pacha•cho -cha *adj* (Chile) short-legged; (Chile) lax, lazy; (Chile) chubby
pa•chón -chona *adj* (CAm) shaggy, hairy, wooly || *m* (*perro*) pointer; (*hombre flemático*) (coll) sluggard
pachorra *f* (coll) sluggishness, indolence
padecer **§22** *tr* to suffer; to be victim of || *intr* to suffer
padrastro *m* stepfather; hangnail
padre *adj* (Am) huge; (Peru) terrific || *m* father; stallion, sire; **padres** parents; ancestors; **tener el padre alcalde** to have pull, to have a friend at court
padrina *f* godmother
padrinazgo *m* godfathership; sponsorship, patronage
padrino *m* godfather; sponsor; (*en un desafío*) second; **padrino de boda** best man; **padrinos** godparents
padrón *m* poll, census; pattern, model; memorial column; (coll) indulgent father; (Am) stallion; (Col) stock bull
padrote *m* (Am) stock animal; (Mex) pimp, procurer
paella *f* saffron-flavored stew of chicken, seafood, and rice with vegetables
paf *interj* bang!
pág. *abbr* **página**
paga *f* pay, payment; wages; fine
paga-alquiler *f* rent, rent money
pagadero -ra *adj* payable
paga•do -da *adj* pleased, cheerful; **estamos pagados** we are quits; **pagado de sí mismo** self-satisfied, conceited
paga•dor -dora *adj* paying || *mf* payer || *m* paymaster
paganismo *m* paganism
paga•no -na *adj* & *mf* pagan || *m* (coll) easy mark
pagar **§44** *tr* to pay; to pay for; (*una bondad, una visita*) to return || *intr* to pay || *ref* to become fond; to be flattered; to boast; to be satisfied
pagaré *m* promissory note, I.O.U.
página *f* page
paginar *tr* to page
pago *m* payment; (*de viñas u olivares*) district, region
pagote *m* (coll) easy mark
paila *f* large pan
pairar *intr* (naut) to lie to
país *m* country, land; landscape; **el país de Gales** Wales; **los Países Bajos** (*Bélgica, Holanda y Luxemburgo*) the Low Countries; (*Holanda*) The Netherlands
paisaje *m* landscape
paisajista *mf* landscape painter
paisa•no -na *adj* of the same country || *mf* peasant; civilian; (Mex) Spaniard || *m* fellow countryman; **de paisano** in civies
paja *f* straw; chaff; trash, rubbish; **no dormirse en las pajas** to not let the grass grow under one's feet; **no levantar paja del suelo** to not lift a hand, to not do a stroke of work
pájara *f* paper kite; paper rooster; bird; crafty female
pajarera *f* aviary; large bird cage
pajarería *f* flock of birds; bird store; pet shop
pajare•ro -ra *adj* (coll) bright, cheerful; (coll) bright-colored, gaudy || *m* bird dealer; bird fancier || *f* see **pajarera**
pajarita *f* paper kite; bow tie; wing collar, piccadilly
pájaro *m* bird; crafty fellow; expert; **pájaro bobo** penguin; (Am) motmot; **pájaro carpintero** woodpecker; **pájaro de cuenta** (coll) big shot; **pájaro mosca** hummingbird
pajarota or **pajarotada** *f* hoax, canard
paje *m* page; valet; dressing table; (naut) cabin boy
pajilla *f* cornhusk cigarette; **pajilla de madera** excelsior
paji•zo -za *adj* straw; straw-colored; straw-thatched
pajuela *f* short straw; sulfur match or fuse; (Am) toothpick; (Bol) match
Pakistán, el var of **Paquistán**
pakista•ní (*pl* **-níes**) *adj* & *mf* var of **paquistaní**
pala *f* shovel; (*de remo, de la azada, etc.*) blade; (*del panadero*) peel; scoop; racket; (*del calzado*) upper; (*de excavadora*) bucket; shoulder strap; (coll) cunning, craftiness
palabra *f* word; speech; (*de una canción*) words; (*derecho para hablar en asambleas*) floor; **palabras mayores**

words, angry words; **remojar la palabra** (coll) to wet one's whistle; **usar de la palabra** to speak, make a speech
palabre·ro -ra *adj* wordy, windy || *mf* windbag
palabrota *f* vulgarity, obscenity
palacie·go -ga *adj* palace, court || *m* courtier
palacio *m* palace; mansion; **palacio municipal** city hall
palada *f* shovelful; (*de remo*) stroke
paladar *m* palate; taste; gourmet
paladear *tr* to taste, to relish
paladín *m* champion, hero
palafrén *m* palfrey
palanca *f* lever; pole; crowbar; **palanca de mando** (aer) control stick; **palanca de mayúsculas** shift key
palancada *f* leverage
palangana *f* washbowl, basin
palanganero *m* washstand
palangre *m* trawl, trawl line
palanqueta *f* jimmy; **palanquetas** (Arg) dumbbell
palatal *adj* & *f* palatal
palco *m* (theat) box
palear *tr* to beat, to pound; (Am) to shovel
palenque *m* paling, palisade; (SAm) hitching post; (C-R) Indian ranch; (Chile) pandemonium
paleta *f* palette; small shovel; trowel; (*de una rueda*) paddle; blade, bucket, vane; shoulder blade; (*dulce con un palito que sirve de mango*) lollipop
paletilla *f* shoulder blade
paleto *m* fallow deer; rustic, yokel
palia *f* altar cloth; (eccl) pall
paliacate *m* (Mex) bandanna
paliar §77 & regular *tr* to palliate
palidecer §22 *intr* to pale, to turn pale
palidez *f* paleness, pallor
páli·do -da *adj* pale, pallid
palillo *m* toothpick; drumstick; bobbin; **palillos** chopsticks; castanets; (coll) rudiments; (coll) trifles
palinodia *f* backdown; **cantar la palinodia** to eat crow, eat humble pie
palique *m* (coll) chit-chat, small talk
paliquear *intr* (coll) to chat, to gossip
paliza *f* beating, thrashing
palizada *f* fenced-in enclosure; stockade; embankment
palma *f* (*de la mano*) palm; (*árbol y hoja*) palm; **batir palmas** to clap, to applaud; **llevarse la palma** to carry off the palm
palmada *f* slap; hand, applause, clapping; **dar palmadas** to clap hands
palma·rio -ria *adj* clear, evident
palmatoria *f* candlestick
palmera *f* date palm
palmito *m* palmetto; (coll) woman's face; (coll) slender figure
palmo *m* span, palm; **dejar con un palmo de narices** (coll) to disappoint
palmotear *tr* to pat; to clap, applaud || *intr* to clap, applaud
palo *m* stick; pole; staff; handle; (*golpe*) whack; (*madera*) wood; (*grupo de naipes de la baraja*) suit; (naut) mast; (Am) tree; **dar palos de ciego** to lay about, to swing wildly; **de tal palo tal astilla** like father like son; **palo de escoba** broomstick; **palo en alto** (fig) big stick; **palo mayor** (naut) mainmast; **servir del palo** to follow suit
paloma *f* pigeon, dove; prostitute; (fig) dove, meek person; **paloma mensajera** carrier pigeon; **palomas** whitecaps
palomar *m* pigeon house, dovecot
palomilla *f* doveling; small butterfly; white horse; (*del caballo*) back; pillow block, journal bearing; **palomillas** whitecaps
palomita *f* doveling; (baseball) fly; **palomitas** (Am) popcorn
palpable *adj* palpable
palpar *tr* to touch, to feel; to grope through || *intr* to grope
palpitante *adj* throbbing; thrilling; (*cuestión*) burning
palpitar *intr* to palpitate, to throb; (*un afecto*) to flash, break forth
pálpito *m* (SAm) hunch
palta *f* (SAm) alligator pear, avocado (*fruit*)
palto *m* (SAm) alligator pear, avocado (*tree*)
palúdi·co -ca *adj* marshy; malarial
paludismo *m* malaria
palur·do -da *adj* rustic, boorish || *mf* rustic, boor
pallador *m* (SAm) Gaucho minstrel
pampa *f* pampa; **La Pampa** the Pampas
pámpana *f* vine leaf
pámpano *m* tendril; vine leaf
pan *m* bread; loaf; loaf of bread; wheat; food; livelihood; pie dough; (*de jabón, cera, etc.*) cake; gold foil or leaf; silver foil or leaf; **como el pan bendito** (coll) as easy as pie; **de pan llevar** arable, tillable; **llamar al pan pan y al vino vino** to call a spade a spade; **panes** grain, breadstuff; **venderse como pan bendito** to sell like hot cakes || **Pan** *m* Pan
pana *f* corduroy; (aut) breakdown
panacea *f* panacea
panadería *f* bakery; baking business
panade·ro -ra *mf* baker; (Chile) flatterer
panadizo *m* felon; (coll) sickly person
panal *m* honeycomb
pana·má *m* (*pl* **-maes**) Panama hat
paname·ño -ña *adj* & *mf* Panamanian
panamerica·no -na *adj* Pan-American
pancarta *f* placard, poster
pancista *adj* weaseling || *mf* weaseler
páncre·as *m* (*pl* **-as**) pancreas
pancho *m* (coll) paunch, belly
pandear *intr* & *ref* to warp, to bulge, to buckle, to sag, to bend
pandereta *f* tambourine
pandilla *f* party, faction; gang, band; picnic, excursion
pan·do -da *adj* bulging; slow-moving; slow, deliberate
pandorga *f* kite; (coll) fat, lazy woman
panecillo *m* roll, crescent
panfleto *m* pamphlet
paniaguado *m* servant, minion; protégé, favorite

páni•co -ca *adj* panic, panicky || *m* panic
panizo *m* Italian millet; (Chile) gangue; (Chile) abundance
panocha *f* ear of grain; ear of corn; (Am) pancake made of corn and cheese; (Mex) panocha (*brown sugar*)
panoja *f* ear of grain; ear of corn
panorama *m* panorama
pano•so -sa *adj* mealy
panqué *m* or **panqueque** *m* pancake
pantalán *m* pier, wooden pier
pantalón *m* trousers; **calzarse los pantalones** to wear the pants; **pantalones** trousers, pants
pantalla *f* lamp shade; fire screen; motion-picture screen; television screen; (*persona que encubre a otra*) blind; (*cine, arte del cine*) screen; (Am) fan; **llevar a la pantalla** to put on the screen; **pantalla de plata** silver screen; **servir de pantalla a** to be a blind for
pantano *m* bog, marsh, swamp; dam, reservoir; trouble, obstacle
pantano•so -sa *adj* marshy, swampy; muddy; knotty, difficult
panteísmo *m* pantheism
panteón *m* pantheon; cemetery
pantera *f* panther
pantomima *f* pantomime
pantoque *m* (naut) bilge
pantorrilla *f* calf (*of leg*)
pantufla *f* or **pantuflo** *m* house slipper
panza *f* paunch, belly
panzu•do -da *adj* paunchy, big-bellied
pañal *m* diaper; shirttail; **pañales** swaddling clothes; infancy; early stages
pañe•ro -ra *adj* dry-goods, cloth || *mf* dry-goods dealer, clothier
paño *m* cloth; rag; (*de agujas*) paper; (*ancho de la tela*) breadth; (*mancha en el rostro*) spot; (*en, p.ej., un espejo*) blur; sailcloth, canvas; **al paño** off-stage; **conocer el paño** (coll) to know one's business, to know the ropes; **paño de adorno** doily; **paño de cocina** washrag, dishcloth; **paño de lágrimas** helping hand, stand-by; **paño de mesa** tablecloth; **paño de tumba** crape; **paño mortuorio** pall; **paños menores** underclothing
pañuelo *m* handkerchief; shawl; **pañuelo de hierbas** bandanna
papa *m* pope || *f* potato; (coll) fake, hoax; (coll) food, grub; (Am) snap, cinch; **ni papa** (Am) nothing
pa•pá *m* (*pl* **-pás**) papa, daddy
papada *f* double chin; (*de animal*) dewlap; (Guat) stupidity
papado *m* papacy
papagayo *m* parrot
papalina *f* sunbonnet; (coll) drunk
papana•tas *m* (*pl* **-tas**) (coll) simpleton, gawk
paparrucha *f* (coll) hoax; (coll) trifle
papel *m* paper; piece of paper; rôle, part; character, figure; **desempeñar** or **hacer un papel** to play a rôle; **papel alquitranado** tar paper; **papel cebolla** onionskin; **papel de empapelar** wallpaper; **papel de esmeril** emery paper; **papel de estaño** tin foil; **papel de excusado** toilet paper; **papel de fumar** cigarette paper; **papel de lija** sandpaper; **papel de oficio** foolscap; **papel de seda** tissue paper; **papel de segundón** (fig) second fiddle; **papel de tornasol** litmus paper; **papel filtrante** filter paper; **papel higiénico** toilet paper; **papel moneda** paper money; **papel pintado** wallpaper; **papel secante** blotting paper; **papel viejo** waste paper; **papel volante** handbill, printed leaflet
papeleo *m* red tape
papelera *f* paper case; writing desk; wastebasket; paper factory
papelería *f* stationery store; mess of papers, litter
papele•ro -ra *adj* paper; boastful, showy || *mf* stationer; paper manufacturer; (Mex) paperboy || *f* see **papelera**
papeleta *f* slip of paper; card, file card; ticket; **papeleta de empeño** pawn ticket
papelista *m* paper maker, paper manufacturer; stationer; paper hanger
pape•lón -lona *adj* (coll) bluffing, four-flushing || *mf* (coll) bluffer, four-flusher || *m* thin cardboard
papelonear *intr* (coll) to bluff, to four-flush
papelote *m* worthless piece of paper; (Am) paper kite
papel-prensa *m* newsprint
papera *f* goiter; mumps
papilla *f* pap; guile, deceit
papiro *m* papyrus
papirote *m* fillip, flick; (coll) nincompoop
paq. *abbr* **paquete**
paquear *tr* to snipe at || *intr* to snipe
paque•te -ta *adj* (Arg) chic, dolled-up; (Am) self-important, pompous || *m* package, parcel, bundle, bale; (coll) sport, dandy; **darse paquete** (Guat, Mex) to put on airs; **en paquete aparte** under separate cover, in a separate package; **paquetes postales** parcel post
Paquistán, el Pakistan
paquista•ní (*pl* **-níes**) or **paquistano -na** *adj & mf* Pakistani
Paquita *f* Fanny
par *adj* like, similar, equal; (math) even || *m* pair, couple; peer; (elec, mech) couple; (math) even number; **a pares** in twos; **de par en par** wide-open; completely; overtly; **¿pares o nones?** odd or even? || *f* par; **a la par** equally; jointly; at the same time; at par; **bajo la par** below par, under par; **sobre la par** above par
para *prep* to, for; towards; compared to; (*antes de*) by; **para** + *inf* in order to + *inf;* about to + *inf;* **para con** towards; **para que** in order that, so that
parabién *m* congratulation
parábola *f* parable
parabri•sa *m* or **parabri•sas** *m* (*pl* **-sas**) windshield
paracaí•das *m* (*pl* **-das**) parachute; **lanzarse en paracaídas** to parachute; **sal-**

varse en paracaídas to parachute to safety
paracaidismo *m* parachute jumping; (sport) sky diving
paracaidista *mf* parachutist || *m* paratrooper
parachis•pas *m* (*pl* **-pas**) spark arrester
paracho•ques *m* (*pl* **-ques**) bumper
parada *f* stop; end; stay; shutdown; (*en el juego*) stake; dam; (*para el ganado*) stall; stud farm; (*en la esgrima*) parry; (*tiro de caballerías de reemplazo*) relay; (mil) parade, dress parade, review; **parada de taxi** taxi stand
paradero *m* end; whereabouts; stopping place; (Am) wayside station
para•do -da *adj* slow, spiritless, witless; idle, unemployed; closed; (Am) proud, stiff || *f* see **parada**
paradoja *f* paradox
paradóji•co -ca *adj* paradoxical
parador *m* inn, wayside inn; motel
parafina *f* paraffin
paragol•pes *m* (*pl* **-pes**) buffer, bumper
para•guas *m* (*pl* **-guas**) umbrella
Paraguay, el Paraguay
paraguaya•no -na or **paragua•yo -ya** *adj & mf* Paraguayan
paragüero *m* umbrella man; umbrella stand
paraíso *m* paradise
paraje *m* place, spot; state, condition
paralela *f* parallel, parallel line; **paralelas** parallel bars
paralelizar **§60** *tr* to parallel, compare
parale•lo -la *adj* parallel || *m* (geog) parallel || *f* see **paralela**
paráli•sis *f* (*pl* **-sis**) paralysis
paralíti•co -ca *adj & mf* paralytic
paralizar **§60** *tr* to paralyze || *ref* to become paralyzed
páramo *m* high barren plain; bleak windy spot; (Bol, Col, Ecuad) cold drizzle
paranie•ves *m* (*pl* **-ves**) snow fence
paraninfo *m* assembly hall, auditorium
paranoi•co -ca *adj & mf* paranoiac
parapeto *m* parapet
parar *tr* to stop; to check; to change; to prepare; to put up, to stake; to parry; to order; to get, acquire; (*la atención*) to fix; (*la caza*) to point; (typ) to set || *intr* to stop; (*en un hotel*) to put up; **parar en** to become; to run to, to run as far as || *ref* to stop; to stop work; to turn, to become; (*el perro de muestra*) to point; (*el pelo*) to stand on end; (Am) to stand; **pararse en** to pay attention to
pararra•yo or **pararra•yos** *m* (*pl* **-yos**) (*barra metálica que sirve para preservar los edificios del rayo*) lightning rod; (*dispositivo que sirve para preservar una instalación eléctrica de la electricidad atmosférica o de las chispas que produce*) lightning arrester
parasíti•co -ca *adj* parasitic
parási•to -ta *adj* parasitic; (elec) stray || *m* parasite; **parásitos atmosféricos** atmospherics, static
parasol *m* parasol
parato•pes *m* (*pl* **-pes**) bumper
Parcas *fpl* Fates
parcela *f* particle; plot of ground
parcelar *tr* to parcel, to divide into lots
parcial *adj* partial; partisan || *mf* partisan
par•co -ca *adj* frugal, sparing; moderate
parchar *tr* (Am) to mend, patch
parche *m* plaster, sticking plaster; patch; drum; drumhead; daub, botch, splotch; **parche poroso** porous plaster
pardal *m* linnet; (coll) sly fellow
pardiez *interj* (coll) by Jove!
pardillo *m* linnet
par•do -da *adj* brown, drab; dark; cloudy; (*voz*) dull, flat; (*cerveza*) dark; (Am) mulatto || *mf* (Am) mulatto || *m* brown, drab; leopard
pardus•co -ca *adj* dark-brown, drabbish
parea•do -da *adj* rhymed || *m* couplet
parear *tr* to pair; to match || *ref* to pair off
parecer *m* opinion; look, mien, countenance || *v* **§22** *intr* to appear; to show up; to look, to seem; **me parece que . . .** I think that . . . || *ref* to look alike, to resemble each other; **parecerse a** to look like
pareci•do -da *adj* like, similar; **bien parecido** good-looking; **parecido a** like, e.g., **esta casa es parecida a la otra** this house is like the other one; **parecidos** alike, e.g., **estas casas son parecidas** these houses are alike || *m* similarity, resemblance, likeness; **tener un gran parecido** to be a good likeness
pared *f* wall; **dejar pegado a la pared** to nonplus; **paredes** house
pareja *f* pair, couple; dancing partner; **correr parejas** or **a las parejas** to be abreast, arrive together; to go together, match, be equal; **correr parejas con** to keep up with, to keep abreast of; **parejas** (*de naipes*) pair
pareje•ro -ra *adj* even, equal; (Am) servile, fawning; (Am) forward, overfamiliar || *m* (Am) race horse
pare•jo -ja *adj* equal, like; even, smooth || *m* (CAm) dancing partner || *f* see **pareja**
parentela *f* kinsfolk, relations
parentesco *m* relationship; bond, tie
parénte•sis *m* (*pl* **-sis**) parenthesis; break, interval
parhilera *f* ridgepole
paria *mf* pariah, outcast
paridad *f* par, parity; comparison
parien•te -ta *adj* related || *mf* relative; (coll) spouse
parihuela *f* handbarrow; (*camilla*) stretcher
parir *tr* to bear, give birth to, bring forth || *intr* to give birth; to come forth, to come to light; to talk well
parisiense *adj & mf* Parisian
parlamentar *intr* to talk, chat; to parley
parlamento *m* parliament; parley; speech; (theat) speech
parlan•chín -china *adj* (coll) jabbering || *mf* (coll) chatterbox
parlar *intr* to speak with facility; to

chatter, talk too much; (*el loro*) to talk

parle•ro -ra *adj* loquacious, garrulous; gossipy; (*ave*) singing, song; (*ojos*) expressive; (*arroyo, fuente*) babbling

parlotear *intr* (coll) to prattle, jabber, chin

parloteo *m* (coll) jabber, prattle

parnaso *m* (*colección de poesías*) Parnassus; **el Parnaso** Parnassus, Mount Parnassus

paro *m* shutdown, work stoppage; lockout; titmouse; (*de dados*) (SAm) throw; **paro forzoso** layoff

parodia *f* parody, travesty

parodiar *tr* to parody, to travesty, to burlesque

paroxíto•no -na *adj & m* paroxytone

parpadear *intr* to blink, wink; to flicker

parpadeo *m* blinking, winking; flicker

párpado *m* eyelid

parque *m* park; parking; parking lot; **parque de atracciones** amusement park

parqué *m* floor, inlaid floor

parqueadero *m* (Col) parking lot

parquear *tr* to park

parquímetro *m* parking meter

parra *f* grapevine; earthen jug

párrafo *m* paragraph; (coll) chat

parral *m* grape arbor

parranda *f* (coll) spree, party; (Col) large number; **andar de parranda** (coll) to go out on a spree, go out to celebrate

parricida *mf* patricide, parricide

parricidio *m* patricide, parricide

parrilla *f* grill, gridiron, broiler; grate, grating; grillroom, grill; **asar a la parrilla** to broil

párroco *m* parish priest

parroquia *f* parish; parish church; customers, clientele

parroquial *adj* parochial

parroquia•no -na *mf* parishioner; customer

parte *m* dispatch, communiqué; **parte meteorológico** weather report || *f* part; share; party; side; direction; (*papel de un actor*) role; (law) party; **de un mes a esta parte** for about a month past; **en ninguna otra parte** nowhere else; **en ninguna parte** nowhere; **ir a la parte** to go shares; **la mayor parte** most, the majority; **parte del león** lion's share; **parte de por medio** (theat) bit part, walk-on; **partes** parts, gifts, talent; faction; parts, genitals; **por otra parte** in another direction; elsewhere; on the other hand; **por todas partes** everywhere; **salva sea la parte** excuse me for not mentioning where

partea•guas *m* (*pl* **-guas**) divide, ridge

partear *tr* to deliver

parte•luz *m* (*pl* **-luces**) mullion, sash bar

Partenón *m* Parthenon

partera *f* midwife

partición *f* partition, division

participar *tr* to notify, to inform; to give notice of || *intr* to participate; to partake

participio *m* participle

partícula *f* particle

particular *adj* particular; peculiar; private, personal || *m* particular; matter, subject; individual

particulizar §60 *tr* to itemize || *ref* to stand out; to specialize

partida *f* departure; entry, item; certificate; party, group, band; band of guerrillas; game; (*de cartas*) hand; (*de tenis*) set; lot, shipment; (coll) behavior; **mala partida** (coll) mean trick; **partida de campo** picnic; **partida doble** (com) double entry; **partida sencilla** (com) single entry

partida•rio -ria or **partidista** *adj & mf* partisan

parti•do -da *adj* generous, open-handed || *m* (pol) party; decision; profit; advantage; step, measure; deal, agreement; protection, support; (*casamiento que elegir*) match; district, county; (sport) team; (sport) game, match; **partido de desempate** play-off; **tomar partido** to take a stand, to take sides || *f* see **partida**

partir *tr* to divide; to distribute; to share; to split, split open; to break, crack; (coll) to upset, disconcert || *intr* to start, depart, leave, set out; **a partir de** beginning with || *ref* to become divided; to crack, to split

partisa•no -na *mf* (mil) partisan

partitura *f* (mus) score

parto *m* childbirth, confinement; newborn child; offspring; **estar de parto** to be in labor, to be confined; **parto del ingenio** brain child

parva *f* light breakfast (*on fast days*); heap of unthreshed grain; heap, pile

parvulista *mf* kindergarten teacher

párvu•lo -la *adj* small, tiny; simple, innocent; humble || *mf* child, tot; (*niño*) kindergartner

pasa *f* raisin; (*del pelo de los negros*) kink; **pasa de Corinto** currant

pasada *f* passage; passing; **de pasada** in passing, hastily; **mala pasada** (coll) mean trick

pasade•ro -ra *adj* passable || *f* stepping stone; walkway, catwalk

pasadizo *m* passage, corridor, hallway, alley; catwalk

pasa•do -da *adj* past; gone by; overripe, spoiled; overdone; stale; burned out; antiquated; faded || *m* past; **pasados** ancestors || *f* see **pasada**

pasa•dor -dora *mf* smuggler || *m* door bolt; bolt, pin; hatpin; brooch; stickpin; safety pin; strainer

pasaje *m* passage; fare; fares; passengers; **cobrar el pasaje** to collect fares

pasaje•ro -ra *adj* passing, fleeting; (*camino, calle*) common, traveled || *mf* passenger; **pasajero colgado** straphanger; **pasajero no presentado** no-show

pasamano *m* lace trimming; (*baranda*) handrail; (naut) gangway

pasamonta•ña *m* or **pasamonta•ñas** *m* (*pl* **-ñas**) ski mask, storm hood

pasaporte *m* passport

pasar *m* livelihood || *tr* to pass; to

cross; to take across; to send, transfer, transmit; (*contrabando*) to slip in; to spend; to swallow; to excel; to overlook, stand for; to undergo, suffer; (*un libro*) to go through; (*una película*) to show; to dry in the sun; to tutor; to study with or under; **pasarlo** to get along; to live; (*dícese de la salud*) to be; **pasar por alto** to disregard; to omit, leave out, skip || *intr* to pass; to go; to pass away; to pass over; to happen; to last; to spread; to get along; to yield; to come in, e.g., **pase Vd.** come in; **pasar de** to go beyond, to exceed; to go above; to be more than; **pasar por** to pass by, down, through, over, etc.; to pass as, pass for; to stop or call at; **pasar sin** to do without || *ref* to pass; to go; to excel; to pass over; to get along; to pass away; to take an examination; to leak; to go too far; to become overripe, become overcooked; to rot; to melt; to burn out; (*una llave, un tornillo*) to not fit, to be loose; to forget; **pasarse por** to stop or call at; **pasarse sin** to do without

pasarela *f* footbridge; catwalk, gangplank

pasatiempo *m* pastime

pascua *f* Passover; Easter; Twelfthnight; Pentecost; Christmas; **dar las pascuas** to wish a Happy New Year; **estar como una pascua** or **unas pascuas** (coll) to be bubbling over with joy; **¡Felices Pascuas!** Merry Christmas!; **Pascua de flores** Easter; **Pascua del Espíritu Santo** Pentecost; **Pascua de Navidad** Christmas; **Pascua de Resurrección** or **Pascua florida** Easter; **Pascuas navideñas** Christmas

pase *m* (*permiso; billete gratuito; movimiento de las manos del mesmerista, el torero*) pass; (*en la esgrima*) feint; **pase de cortesía** complimentary ticket

paseante *adj* strolling || *mf* stroller

pasear *tr* to walk; to promenade, show off || *intr* to take a walk; to go for a ride || *ref* to take a walk; to go for a ride; to wander, ramble; to take it easy

paseíllo *m* processional entrance of bullfighters

paseo *m* walk, stroll, promenade; ride; drive; avenue; **dar un paseo** to take a walk; to take a ride; **enviar a paseo** (coll) to send on his way, to dismiss without ceremony; **paseo de caballos** bridle path; **paseo de la cuadrilla** processional entrance of the bullfighters

pasillo *m* short step; passage, corridor; (theat) short piece, sketch

pasión *f* passion

pasi•vo -va *adj* passive; (*pensión*) retirement || *m* liabilities; debit side

pasmar *tr* to chill; to frostbite; to stun, benumb; to dumbfound, astound || *ref* to chill; to become frostbitten; to be astounded; to get lockjaw; (*los colores*) to become dull or flat

pasmo *m* cold; lockjaw, tetanus; astonishment; wonder, prodigy

pasmo•so -sa *adj* astounding; awesome

paso *m* step; pace; (*de la escalera*) step; gait; walk; passing; passage; step, measure, démarche; pass, permit; strait; footstep, footprint; incident, happening; (*de hélice, tornillo*) pitch; (elec) pitch; (rad) stage; (theat) short piece, sketch, skit; **al paso** in passing, on the way; **al paso que** at the rate that; (*a la vez que, mientras*) while, whereas; **ceder el paso** to make way; to keep clear; **de paso** in passing; at the same time; **paso a nivel** grade crossing; **paso de ganado** cattle crossing; **paso de ganso** goose step

paspa *f* (SAm) crack in the lips

pasquín *m* lampoon

pasquinar *tr* to lampoon

pasta *f* paste, dough, pie crust, soup paste; mash; (*para hacer papel*) pulp; cardboard; board binding; (*de un diente*) filling; (*dinero*) (coll) dough; **pasta dentrífica** tooth paste; **pasta española** marbled leather binding, tree calf; **pastas** noodles, macaroni, spaghetti, etc.; **pasta seca** cookie

pastar *tr & intr* to graze

pastel *m* pie; pastry roll; pastel; settlement, pacification; cheat, trick; (typ) pi; (typ) smear; (coll) plot, deal; **pastel de cumpleaños** birthday cake

pastelería *f* pastry; pastry shop

pastele•ro -ra *mf* pastry cook

pastelillo *m* tart, cake; (*de mantequilla*) pat

pasterizar **§60** *tr* to pasteurize

pastilla *f* tablet, lozenge, drop; (*pequeña masa pastosa*) dab; (*de jabón, chocolate, etc.*) cake

pasto *m* pasture; grass; food, nourishment; **a pasto** to excess; in abundance; **a todo pasto** freely, without restriction; **de pasto** ordinary, everyday

pastor *m* shepherd; pastor

pastora *f* shepherdess

pastoral *adj & f* pastoral

pastorear *tr* (*a las ovejas o los fieles*) to shepherd; (Am) to lie in ambush for; (Am) to spoil, pamper; (Arg, Urug) to court

pasto•so -sa *adj* pasty, doughy; (*voz*) mellow; (Arg, Chile) grassy

pastura *f* pasture; fodder

pasu•do -da *adj* (Am) kinky

pata *f* paw, foot, leg; (*de un mueble*) leg; duck; **a cuatro patas** (coll) on all fours; **estirar la pata** (coll) to kick the bucket; **meter la pata** (coll) to butt in, to put one's foot in it; **pata de gallo** crow's-foot; (coll) blunder; (coll) piece of nonsense; **pata de palo** peg leg, wooden leg; **pata galana** (coll) game leg; (coll) lame person; **patas arriba** (coll) on one's back, upside down; (coll) topsy-turvy

patada *f* kick; stamp, stamping; (coll) step; (coll) footstep, track; **en dos patadas** (Am) in a jiffy

patalear *intr* to kick; to stamp the feet

pataleta *f* (coll) fit; (coll) feigned fit or convulsion; (dial) tantrum
patán *m* (coll) churl, boor, lout; (coll) peasant
pataplún *interj* kerplunk!
patata *f* potato
patear *tr* (coll) to kick; (coll) to trample on || *intr* (coll) to stamp one's foot; (coll) to bustle around; (Am) to kick
patentar *tr* to patent
patente *adj* patent, clear, evident || *f* grant, privilege, warrant; patent; **de patente** (Chile) excellent, first-class; **patente de circulación** owner's license; **patente de invención** patent; **patente de sanidad** bill of health
paternal *adj* paternal, fatherly
paternidad *f* paternity, fatherhood; **paternidad literaria** authorship
pater•no -na *adj* paternal
pateta *m* (coll) the devil; (coll) cripple
patéti•co -ca *adj* pathetic
patetismo *m* pathos
patibula•rio -ria *adj* hair-raising
patíbulo *m* scaffold
patiesteva•do -da *adj* bowlegged
patilla *f* small paw or foot; pocket flap; (naut) compass; (Am) watermelon; **patillas** sideburns, side whiskers
patín *m* small patio; skate; skid, slide, runner; (*ave marina*) petrel; **patín de cuchilla** or **de hielo** ice skate; **patín de ruedas** roller skate
patinadero *m* skating rink
patina•dor -dora *mf* skater
patinaje *m* skating; skidding; **patinaje artístico** figure skating; **patinaje de fantasía** fancy skating; **patinaje de figura** figure skating
patinar *intr* to skate; to skid; to slip
patinazo *m* skid; slip; (coll) slip, blunder
patinete *m* scooter
patio *m* patio, court, yard; campus; (rr) yard, switchyard; **patio de recreo** playground
patituer•to -ta *adj* crooked-legged; (coll) crooked, lopsided
patizam•bo -ba *adj* knock-kneed
pato *m* duck, drake; **pagar el pato** (coll) to be the goat; **pato de flojel** eider duck
patochada *f* (coll) blunder, stupidity
patología *f* pathology
patota *f* (Arg, Urug) teen-age gang
patraña *f* fake, humbug, hoax
patria *f* country; mother country, fatherland, native land; birthplace; (*p.ej., de las artes*) home; **patria chica** native heath
patriarca *m* patriarch
patri•cio -cia *adj* & *mf* patrician
patrimonio *m* patrimony
pa•trio -tria *adj* native, home; paternal || *f* see **patria**
patriota *mf* patriot
patrióti•co -ca *adj* patriotic
patriotismo *m* patriotism
patrocinar *tr* to sponsor, patronize
patrocinio *m* sponsorship
patrón *m* sponsor, protector; patron saint; patron; landlord; owner, master; boss, foreman, host; (*de un barco*) skipper; pattern; standard; **patrón oro** gold standard; **patrón picado** stencil
patrona *f* patroness; landlady; owner, mistress; hostess
patronal *adj* management, employers'
patronato *m* employers' association; foundation; board of trustees; patronage
patronear *tr* to skipper
patro•no -na *mf* sponsor, protector; employer || *m* patron; landlord; boss, foreman; lord of the manor; **los patronos** the management || *f* see **patrona**
patrulla *f* patrol; gang, band
patrullar *tr* & *intr* to patrol
paulati•no -na *adj* slow, gradual
Paulo *m* Paul
pausa *f* pause; slowness, delay; (mus) rest
pausa•do -da *adj* slow, calm, deliberate || **pausado** *adv* slowly, calmly
pausar *tr* & *intr* to slow down
pauta *f* ruler; guide lines; guideline, rule, guide, standard, model
pava *f* turkey hen; **pelar la pava** (coll) to make love at a window
pavesa *f* ember, cinder, spark
pavimentar *tr* to pave
pavimento *m* pavement
pavo *m* turkey; turkey cock; **comer pavo** (coll) to be a wallflower; **pavo real** peacock
pavón *m* bluing; peacock
pavonar *tr* to blue
pavonear *intr* & *ref* to strut, swagger
pavor *m* fear, terror, dread
pavoro•so -sa *adj* frightful, dreadful
payador *m* (SAm) gaucho minstrel
payasada *f* clownishness, clownish remark
payaso *m* clown; laughingstock
paz *f* (*pl* **paces**) peace; peacefulness; **dejar en paz** to leave alone, stop pestering; **estar en paz** to be even; to be quits; **hacer las paces con** to make peace with, to come to terms with; **salir en paz** to break even
pazgua•to -ta *adj* simple, doltish || *mf* simpleton, dolt
pazpuerca *f* (coll) slut, slattern
P.D. *abbr* **posdata**
peaje *m* toll
peatón *m* pedestrian; rural postman
pebete *m* punk, joss stick; fuse; (*cosa hedionda*) (coll) stinker
peca *f* freckle
pecado *m* sin
peca•dor -dora *adj* sinning, sinful || *mf* sinner
pecamino•so -sa *adj* sinful
pecar §73 *intr* to sin; **pecar de** to be too, e.g., **pecar de confiado** to be too trusting
pecera *f* fish globe, fish bowl
pecino•so -sa *adj* slimy
pecio *m* flotsam
pecíolo *m* leafstalk
pécora *f* head of sheep; **buena pécora** or **mala pécora** (coll) schemer, scheming woman

peco•so -sa *adj* freckly, freckle-faced
peculado *m* embezzlement, peculation
peculiar *adj* peculiar
pecunia•rio -ria *adj* pecuniary
pechada *f* (Am) bump or push with the chest; (Am) tossing an animal (*with a bump of horse's chest*); (Am) bumping contest between two horsemen
pechar *tr* to pay as a tax; to fulfill; to take on; (Am) to drive one's horse against; (Am) to bump with the chest; (Am) to strike for a loan || *ref* (*dos jinetes*) (Am) to vie in a bumping contest
pechera *f* shirt front, shirt bosom; chest protector; (*del delantal*) bib; breast strap; (coll) bosom; **pechera postiza** dickey
pecho *m* chest; breast, bosom; heart, courage; **dar el pecho** to nurse, to suckle; (coll) to face it out; **de dos pechos** double-breasted; **de un solo pecho** single-breasted; **echar el pecho al agua** (coll) to put one's shoulder to the wheel; (coll) to speak out; **en pechos de camisa** (Am) in shirt sleeves; **tomar a pecho** to take to heart; **¡pecho al agua!** take heart!, put your shoulder to the wheel!
pechuga *f* (*del ave*) breast; (coll) breast, bosom; (coll) slope, hill; (Am) brass, cheek; (Am) treachery, perfidy
pechu•gón -gona *adj* (coll) big-chested; (Am) brazen || *mf* (Am) sponger || *m* slap or blow on the chest; fall on the chest
pedagogía *f* pedagogy
pedal *m* pedal, treadle
pedalear *intr* to pedal
pedante *adj* pedantic || *mf* pedant
pedantería *f* pedantry
pedantes•co -ca *adj* pedantic
pedantismo *m* pedantry
pedazo *m* piece; **hacer pedazos** (coll) to break to pieces; **hacerse pedazos** (coll) to fall to pieces; (coll) to strain, to wear oneself out; **pedazo de alcornoque, de animal** or **de bruto** (coll) dolt, imbecile, good-for-nothing; **pedazo del alma, de las entrañas** or **del corazón** (*niño*) (coll) darling, apple of one's eye; **pedazo de pan** (*pequeña cantidad*) crumb; (*precio bajo*) (coll) song
pedernal *m* flint; flintiness; flint-hearted person
pedestal *m* pedestal
pedestre *adj* pedestrian
pedestrismo *m* pedestrianism; walking; foot racing; cross-country racing
pediatría *f* pediatrics
pedido *m* request; (*encargo de mercancías*) order
pedigüe•ño -ña *adj* insistent, demanding, bothersome
pedir **§50** *tr* to ask, to ask for; to request; to demand, require; to need; to ask for the hand of; (*mercancías*) to order; (gram) to govern; **pedir prestado a** to borrow from || *intr* to ask; to beg; to bring suit; **a pedir de boca** opportunely; as desired
pedorre•ro -ra *adj* flatulent || *f* flatulence; (orn) tody; **pedorreras** tights
pedrada *f* stoning; hit or blow with a stone; (coll) hint, taunt
pedregal *m* rocky ground; pile of rocks
pedrego•so -sa *adj* stony, rocky; suffering from gallstones || *mf* sufferer from gallstones
pedrejón *m* boulder
pedrera *f* quarry, stone quarry
pedrería *f* precious stones, jewelry
Pedro *m* Peter
pedrusco *m* boulder
pedúnculo *m* stem, stalk
peer **§43** *intr & ref* to break wind
pega *f* sticking; pitch varnish; drubbing; (*en un examen*) catch question; (coll) trick, joke; (W-I) work, jobs; **de pega** (coll) fake
pegadi•zo -za *adj* sticky; catching, contagious; sponging; fake, imitation
pegajo•so -sa *adj* sticky; contagious; tempting; (coll) soft, gentle; (coll) mushy
pegar **§44** *tr* to stick, to paste; to fasten, attach, tie; (*carteles*) to post; (*fuego*) to set; (*una enfermedad*) to transmit; (*un botón*) to sew on; (*un grito*) to let out; (*un salto*) to take; (*un golpe, una bofetada*) to let go; to beat; **no pegar el ojo** to not sleep a wink || *intr* to stick, to catch; to take root, take hold; to cling; to join; to fit, to match; to be fitting; to pass, be accepted; to beat; to knock || *ref* to stick, to catch; to take root, take hold; to hang on, stick around; (*una enfermedad*) to be catching; **pegársela a uno** (coll) to make a fool of someone
pegotear *intr* (coll) to hang around, to sponge
peina•do -da *adj* groomed; effeminate || *m* hairdo, coiffure; (*manera de componer el pelo*) hairstyle; **peinado al agua** finger wave
peina•dor -dora *mf* hairdresser || *m* wrapper, dressing gown
peinar *tr* to comb || *ref* to comb oneself, comb one's hair
peine *m* comb; (coll) sly fellow
peineta *f* back comb
pelada *f* pelt, sheepskin
peladilla *f* sugar almond; small pebble
peladillo *m* clingstone peach
pela•do -da *adj* bare; bald; barren; penniless; (*decena, centena, etc.*) even || *m* raggedy fellow; (W-I) haircut || *f* see **pelada**
pelafus•tán -tana *mf* (coll) derelict, good-for-nothing
pelaga•tos *m* (*pl* **-tos**) (coll) wretch, ragamuffin
pelaje *m* coat, fur; (*especie, calidad*) (coll) sort, stripe
pelar *tr* (*pelo*) to cut; (*pelo, plumas*) to pluck, pull out; to peel, skin, husk, hull, shell; (*los dientes*) to show; (*en el juego*) (coll) to clean out; (Am) to beat, thrash || *ref* to peel off; to lose one's hair; to get a haircut; (Am) to clear out, make a getaway; **pelárselas por** (coll) to crave; (coll) to crave to

peldaño *m* step
pelea *f* fight; quarrel; struggle; **pelea de gallos** cockfight
pelear *intr* to fight; to quarrel; to struggle || *ref* to fight, fight each other
pele•ón -ona *adj* (coll) pugnacious, quarrelsome; (*vino*) (coll) cheap, ordinary || *mf* (coll) quarrelsome person || *m* (coll) cheap wine || *f* row, scuffle, fracas
peletería *f* furriery; fur shop; (Cuba) shoe store
pelete•ro -ra *mf* furrier; (Cuba) shoe dealer
peliagu•do -da *adj* furry, long-haired; (coll) arduous, ticklish
película *f* film; motion picture; **película de dibujos** animated cartoon; **película del Oeste** western; **película sonora** sound film
pelicule•ro -ra *adj* moving-picture || *mf* scenario writer || *m* movie actor || *f* movie actress
peligrar *intr* to be in danger
peligro *m* danger, peril, risk; **ponerse en peligro de paz** to be alerted for war
peligro•so -sa *adj* dangerous
pelillo *m* (coll) trifle; **echar pelillos a la mar** (coll) to bury the hatchet; **no pararse en pelillos** (coll) to not bother about trifles, to pay no attention to small matters; **no tener pelillos en la lengua** (coll) to speak right out
pelirro•jo -ja *adj* red-haired, redheaded || *mf* redhead
pelo *m* hair; (*en las frutas y el cuerpo humano*) down; (*del paño*) nap; (*de la madera*) grain; (*de un animal*) coat; (*en las piedras preciosas*) flaw; (*del caballo*) color; (*en el billar*) kiss; (*del reloj*) hairspring; hair trigger; fiber, filament; raw silk; **al pelo** with the hair, with the nap; (coll) perfectly, to the point; **con todos sus pelos y señales** chapter and verse; **en pelo** bareback; **escapar por un pelo** to escape by a hairbreadth, to have a narrow escape; **no tener pelos en la lengua** (coll) to be outspoken, to not mince words; **ponerle a uno los pelos de punta** to make one's hair stand on end; **tomar el pelo a** (coll) to make fun of, make a fool of; **venir a pelo** to come in handy
pe•lón -lona *adj* bald, hairless; (coll) dull, stupid; (coll) penniless
Pélope *m* Pelops
peloponense *adj & mf* Peloponnesian
Peloponeso *m* Pelóponnesus
pelo•so -sa *adj* hairy
pelota *f* ball; ball game; handball; **en pelota** stripped; stark-naked; **pelota acuática** water polo; **pelota rodada** (baseball) grounder; **pelota vasca** pelota, jai alai
pelotari *mf* pelota player
pelotear *intr* to knock a ball around; to wrangle, to argue
pelotera *f* (coll) row, brawl
pelotón *m* large ball; gang, crowd; platoon; **pelotón de fusilamiento** firing squad; **pelotón de los torpes** awkward squad
peltre *m* pewter
peluca *f* wig
pelu•do -da *adj* hairy, furry; bushy
peluquería *f* hairdresser's, barbershop
peluque•ro -ra *mf* hairdresser, barber; wigmaker
pelusa *f* down; lint, fuzz; nap; (coll) jealousy, envy
pellejo *m* skin; pelt, rawhide; peel, rind; wineskin; (*la vida de uno*) (coll) hide, skin; (coll) sot, drunkard; **dar, dejar** or **perder el pellejo** (coll) to die
pellizcar §73 to pinch; to nip; to take a pinch of || *ref* (coll) to long, to pine
pellizco *m* pinch; nip; bit, pinch
pena *f* punishment; penalty; pain, hardship, toil; sorrow, grief; effort, trouble; **a duras penas** hardly, with great difficulty; **de pena** of a broken heart; **¡qué pena!** what a pity!; **so pena de** on pain of, under penalty of; **valer la pena** to be worth while (to)
penacho *m* crest; tuft, plume; arrogance; (bot) tassel
pena•do -da *adj* afflicted, grieved; difficult || *mf* convict
penalidad *f* trouble, hardship; (law) penalty
penar *tr* to penalize; to punish || *intr* to suffer; to linger; **penar por** to pine for, long for || *ref* to grieve
penca *f* pulpy leaf; cowhide; **coger una penca** (Am) to get a jag on
penco *m* nag, jade; (Am) boor
pendejo *m* pubes; (coll) coward
pendencia *f* dispute, quarrel, fight; pending litigation
pendencie•ro -ra *adj* quarrelsome || *mf* wrangler
pender *intr* to hang, dangle; to depend; to be pending
pendiente *adj* pendent, hanging, dangling; pending; under way; expecting; **estar pendiente de** (*las palabras de una persona*) to hang on; to depend on; to be in the process of || *m* earring, pendant; watch chain || *f* slope, grade; dip, pitch
péndola *f* feather; pendulum; clock; pen, quill; queen post
pendolón *m* king post
pendón *m* banner, standard, pennon
péndulo *m* pendulum; clock
penetrar *tr* to penetrate; to pierce; to grasp, fathom || *intr* to penetrate || *ref* to grasp, fathom; to realize; to become convinced
penicilina *f* penicilin
península *f* peninsula
peninsular *adj & mf* peninsular; (*ibero*) Peninsular
penique *m* penny
penitencia *f* penitence; penance; **hacer penitencia** to do penance; to eat sparingly; to take potluck
penitente *adj & mf* penitent
penol *m* (naut) yardarm
peno•so -sa *adj* arduous, difficult; suffering; (coll) conceited; (Am) shy

pensa•dor -dora *adj* thinking || *mf* thinker
pensamiento *m* thought; (*planta y flor*) pansy
pensar **§2** *tr* to think; to think over; (*un naipe, un número, etc.*) to think of; to intend to; **pensar de** to think of, e.g., **¿qué piensa Vd. de este libro?** what do you think of this book? || *intr* to think; **pensar en** (*dirigir sus pensamientos a*) to think of (*to turn one's thoughts to*)
pensati•vo -va *adj* pensive, thoughtful
pensión *f* pension; annuity; allowance; boardinghouse; (*para ampliar estudios*) fellowship; **pensión completa** board and lodging
pensionar *tr* to pension
pensionista *mf* pensioner; boarder; boarding-school pupil; **medio pensionista** day boarder
pentagrama *m* staff, musical staff
Pentecostés, el Pentecost
penúlti•mo -ma *adj* penultimate; next to last || *f* penult
penumbra *f* penumbra; semidarkness, half-light
penuria *f* shortage
peña *f* rock, boulder; cliff; club, group, circle
peñasco *m* pinnacle; crag
peñasco•so -sa *adj* rocky, craggy
peñón *m* rock, spire; **peñón de Gibraltar** rock of Gibraltar
peón *m* laborer; pedestrian; foot soldier; (*en el ajedrez*) pawn; (*en las damas*) man; top, peg top; spindle, axle; (taur) attendant; (Am) farm hand; **peón de albañil** or **de mano** hod carrier
peor *adj & adv* worse; worst
pepa *f* (*de la manzana*) (Col) seed; (*del durazno*) (Arg) stone; (*canica*) (Arg) marble; (Col) lie, cheat, trick
Pepe *m* Joe
pepinillo *m* gherkin
pepino *m* cucumber
pepita *f* seed, pip; nugget; (vet) pip
peque *m* tot
pequén *m* (Chile) burrowing owl
pequeñez *f* (*pl* **-ñeces**) smallness; infancy; trifle
peque•ño -ña *adj* little, small; young; low, humble
Pequín *m* Peking
pequi•nés -nesa *adj & mf* Pekinese
pera *f* pear; goatee; cinch, sinecure; pear-shaped bulb; pear-shaped switch
peral *m* pear tree
perca *f* (ichth) perch
percance *m* mischance, misfortune; **percances** perquisites
percatar *ref* — **percatarse de** to be aware of; to beware of, guard against
percebe *m* barnacle; (coll) fool, sap
percepción *f* perception; collection
percibir *tr* to perceive; to collect
percudir *tr* to tarnish, to dull; to spread through
percha *f* perch, pole, roost; clothes tree; coat hanger; coat hook; barber pole
perchero *m* rack, clothes rack, clothes hanger
perde•dor -dora *adj* losing || *mf* loser
perder **§51** *tr* to lose; to waste, squander; (*un tren, una ocasión*) to miss; (*una asignatura*) to flunk; to ruin; to spoil || *intr* to lose; to fade || *ref* to get lost; to miscarry; to sink; to become ruined; to spoil; to go to the dogs
perdición *f* perdition; loss; outrage; ruination
pérdida *f* loss; waste; ruination; **no tener pérdida** (coll) to be easy to find
perdi•do -da *adj* (*bala*) stray, wild; (*manga*) wide, loose; fruitless; (*horas*) off, spare, idle; distracted; inveterate; madly in love || *m* profligate, rake
perdido•so -sa *adj* unlucky; easily lost
perdigón *m* young partridge; (coll) profligate; (coll) heavy loser; (*alumno*) (coll) failure; **perdigones** (*granos de plomo*) shot; **perdigón zorrero** buckshot
per•diz *f* (*pl* **-dices**) partridge
perdón *m* pardon, forgiveness; **con perdón** by your leave
perdonable *adj* pardonable
perdonar *tr* to pardon, forgive, excuse; **no perdonar** to not miss, to not omit
perdula•rio -ria *adj* careless, sloppy; incorrigible, vicious || *mf* good-for-nothing, profligate
perdurable *adj* long-lasting; everlasting
perdurar *intr* to last, last a long time, survive
perecede•ro -ra *adj* perishable; mortal || *m* (coll) extreme want
perecer **§22** *intr* to perish; to suffer; to be in great want || *ref* to pine; **perecerse por** to be dying for; (*una mujer*) to be mad about
peregrinación *f* peregrination; pilgrimage
peregri•no -na *adj* wandering, traveling; foreign; rare, strange; beautiful; mortal; (*ave*) migratory || *mf* pilgrim
perejil *m* parsley; (coll) frippery
perenne *adj* perennial
pereza *f* laziness; slowness
perezo•so -sa *adj* lazy; slow, dull, heavy || *mf* lazybones; sleepyhead || *m* (zool) sloth
perfección *f* perfection
perfeccionar *tr* to perfect, to improve
perfec•to -ta *adj & m* perfect
perfidia *f* perfidy
pérfi•do -da *adj* perfidious
perfil *m* profile; side view; cross section; thin stroke; outline, sketch; **perfil aerodinámico** streamlining; **perfiles** finishing touches; courtesies
perfila•do -da *adj* (*cara*) long and thin; (*nariz*) well-formed; (*facciones*) delicate; streamlined
perfilar *tr* to profile, outline; to perfect, polish, finish || *ref* to be outlined; to show one's profile, to stand sidewise; to stand out; (coll) to dress up
perfora•dor -dora *adj* perforating; drilling || *f* pneumatic drill, rock drill

perforar *tr* to perforate; to drill, to bore; to puncture; (*una tarjeta*) to punch
perfumar *tr* to perfume
perfume *m* perfume
pergamino *m* parchment
pericia *f* skill, expertness
periclitar *intr* to be in jeopardy, to be shaky
perico *m* (*pelo postizo*) periwig; parakeet; (slang) chamber pot; **perico entre ellas** (coll) lady's man
periferia *f* periphery; surroundings
perifollos *mpl* finery, frippery, chiffons
perilla *f* pear-shaped ornament; goatee; knob, doorknob; (*del arzón*) pommel; (*de la oreja*) lobe; **de perilla** (coll) apropos, to the point
periodísti•co -ca *adj* newspaper, journalistic
periódi•co -ca *adj* periodic || *m* newspaper; periodical
periodismo *m* journalism
periodista *mf* journalist || *m* newspaperman || *f* newspaperwoman
período *m* period; compound sentence; (phys) cycle; **período lectivo** (*en la escuela*) term
peripues•to -ta *adj* (coll) dudish, all spruced up, sporty
periquete *m* (coll) jiffy; **en un periquete** (coll) in a jiffy
periquito *m* parakeet; **periquito de Australia** budgerigar
periscopio *m* periscope
peri•to -ta *adj* skilled, skillful; expert || *m* expert
perjudicar **§73** *tr* to damage, impair, hurt, prejudice
perjudicial *adj* harmful, injurious, detrimental, prejudicial
perjuicio *m* harm, injury, damage, prejudice; **en perjuicio de** to the detriment of
perjurar *intr* to commit perjury; to swear, be profane || *ref* to commit perjury; to perjure oneself
perjurio *m* perjury
perla *f* pearl; **de perlas** perfectly
perlesía *f* palsy
permanecer **§22** *intr* to stay, to remain
permanencia *f* permanence; stay, sojourn
permanente *adj* permanent || *f* permanent wave
permiso *m* permission; permit; time off; (*en el monedaje*) tolerance; leave; **con permiso** excuse me; **permiso de circulación** owner's license; **permiso de conducir** driver's license
permitir *tr* to permit, to allow || *ref* to be permitted; **no se permite fumar** no smoking
permutar *tr* to interchange; to barter; to permute
pernear *intr* to kick; (coll) to hustle; (coll) to fuss, fret
pernera *f* trouser leg
pernicio•so -sa *adj* pernicious
pernil *m* trouser leg; (*anca y muslo*) ham
perno *m* bolt; **perno con anillo** ringbolt; **perno roscado** screw bolt
pernoctar *intr* to spend the night
pero *conj* but, yet || *m* (coll) but; (coll) fault, defect; **poner pero a** (coll) to find fault with
perogrullada *f* (coll) platitude, inanity
peroración *f* peroration; (coll) harangue
perorar *intr* to perorate; (coll) to orate
peróxido *m* peroxide; **peróxido de hidrógeno** hydrogen peroxide
perpendicular *adj & f* perpendicular
perpetrar *tr* to perpetrate
perpetuar **§21** *tr* to perpetuate
perpe•tuo -tua *adj* perpetual; life
perplejidad *f* perplexity; worry, anxiety
perple•jo -ja *adj* perplexed; worried, anxious; baffling, perplexing
perra *f* bitch; tantrum; drunkenness
perrada *f* pack of dogs; (coll) dirty trick
perrera *f* kennel, doghouse; tantrum; toil, drudgery
perro *m* dog; **el perro del hortelano** dog in the manger; **perro caliente** (slang) hot dog; **perro cobrador** retriever; **perro de aguas** spaniel; **perro de lanas** poodle; **perro de muestra** pointer; **perro faldero** lap dog; **perro marino** dogfish, shark; **perro raposero** foxhound; **perro viejo** (coll) wise old owl
perro-lazarillo *m* (*pl* **perros-lazarillos**) Seeing Eye dog
persa *adj & mf* Persian
persecución *f* persecution; pursuit; annoyance, harassment
perseguir **§67** *tr* to persecute; to pursue; to annoy, harass
perseverar *intr* to persevere
persiana *f* slatted shutter; flowered silk; louver; Venetian blind; **persiana del radiador** (aut) louver
persistir *intr* to persist
persona *f* person; personage; **persona desplazada** displaced person; **personas** people; **por persona** per capita
personaje *m* personage; (theat) character; person of importance
personal *adj* personal || *m* personnel, staff, force
personalidad *f* personality
personificar **§73** *tr* to personify
perspectiva *f* perspective; outlook, prospect; appearance
perspi•caz *adj* (*pl* **-caces**) perspicacious, discerning; keen-sighted
persuadir *tr* to persuade
persuasión *f* persuasion
pertenecer **§22** *intr* to belong; to pertain || *ref* to be independent, be free
perteneciente *adj* pertaining
pértiga *f* pole, rod, staff
perti•naz *adj* (*pl* **-naces**) pertinacious; (*dolor de cabeza*) persistent
pertinente *adj* pertinent, relevant
pertrechos *mpl* supplies, provisions, equipment; tools; **pertrechos de guerra** ordnance
perturbar *tr* to perturb; to disturb; to upset, disconcert; to confuse, interrupt
Perú, el Peru
perua•no -na *adj & mf* Peruvian
perversidad *f* perversity

perversión *f* perversion
perver•so -sa *adj* perverse; wicked, depraved || *mf* profligate
perverti•do -da *mf* pervert
pervertir §68 *tr* to pervert || *ref* to become perverted; to go to the bad
pesa *f* weight
pesacar•tas *m* (*pl* **-tas**) letter scales
pesadez *f* heaviness; slowness; tiresomeness; harshness; (phys) gravity
pesadilla *f* nightmare
pesa•do -da *adj* heavy; slow; tiresome; harsh; boring
pesadumbre *f* sorrow, grief; trouble; weight, heaviness
pesaje *m* weighing; (sport) weigh-in
pésame *m* condolence; **dar el pésame a** to extend one's sympathy to
pesantez *f* (phys) gravity
pesar *m* sorrow, regret; **a pesar de** in spite of || *tr* to weigh; to make sorry || *intr* to weigh; to be heavy; to cause regret, cause sorrow
pesaro•so -sa *adj* sorrowful, regretful
pesca *f* fishing; catch; **ir de pesca** to go fishing; **pesca de bajura** off-shore fishing; **pesca de gran altura** deep-sea fishing
pescadería *f* fish market; fish store; fish stand
pescade•ro -ra *mf* fish dealer, fishmonger
pescado *m* fish (*that has been caught*)
pesca•dor -dora *adj* fishing || *m* fisherman || *f* fisherwoman, fishwife
pescante *m* coach box; (*de una grúa*) jib; (aut) front seat; (naut) davit; (theat) trap door
pescar §73 *tr* to fish; to fish for; to fish out; (*peces*) to catch; (coll) to manage to get || *intr* to fish
pescozón *m* slap on the neck or head
pescuezo *m* neck
pesebre *m* crib, rack, manger; (Am) crèche
pesimismo *m* pessimism
pesimista *adj* pessimistic || *mf* pessimist
pési•mo -ma *adj* very bad, abominable
peso *m* weight; scale, balance; burden, load; judgment, good sense; (*unidad monetaria*) (Am) peso; **caerse de su peso** to be self-evident; **llevar el peso de la batalla** to bear the brunt of the battle
pespuntar *tr & intr* to backstitch
pespunte *m* backstitch
pesquera *f* fishery; fishing grounds; (*presa para detener los peces*) weir
pesquería *f* fishing; fishery
pesque•ro -ra *adj* fishing || *m* fishing boat || *f* see **pesquera**
pesquis *m* acumen, keenness
pesquisa *m* (Arg) detective || *f* inquiry, investigation
pesquisar *tr* to investigate, inquire into
pestaña *f* eyelash; flange; fringe, edging; index tab
pestañear *intr* to wink, blink; **sin pestañear** without batting an eye
peste *f* pest, plague; epidemic; stink, stench; (coll) abundance; (Col, Peru) head cold; (Chile) smallpox; **pestes** (coll) insults
pesticida *m* pesticide
pestífe•ro -ra *adj* pestiferous; stinking
pestilencia *f* pestilence
pestillo *m* bolt; doorlatch
petaca *f* cigar case; cigarette case; tobacco pouch; leather-covered hamper
pétalo *m* petal
petardear *tr* to swindle || *intr* (aut) to backfire
petardeo *m* swindling; (aut) backfire
petardo *m* petard; bomb; swindle, cheat
petate *m* sleeping bag; bedding; (coll) luggage; (coll) cheat; (coll) poor soul; **liar el petate** (coll) to pack up and get out; (coll) to kick the bucket
petición *f* petition; request; plea; (law) claim, bill; **a petición de** at the request of; **petición de mano** formal betrothal
petimetre *m* dude, sport, dandy
petirrojo *m* redbreast, robin
Petrarca *m* Petrarch
petrificar §73 *tr & ref* to petrify
petróleo *m* petroleum; **petróleo combustible** fuel oil
petrole•ro -ra *adj* oil, petroleum || *mf* oil dealer || *m* oil tanker
petulancia *f* flippancy, pertness
petulante *adj* flippant, pert
pez *m* (*pl* **peces**) fish; (coll) reward, just desert; **como un pez en el agua** (coll) snug as bug in a rug; **pez de plata** (ent) silverfish **salga pez o salga rana** (coll) blindly, hit or miss || *f* pitch, tar
pezón *m* stem; nipple, teat
pezonera *f* linchpin
pezuña *f* hoof
piado•so -sa *adj* merciful; pitiful; pious
piafar *intr* (*el caballo*) to paw, to stamp
piano *m* piano; **piano de cola** grand piano; **piano de media cola** baby grand
piar §77 *intr* to peep, to chirp
pica *f* pike; pikeman; picador's goad; (Col) pique, resentment
picada *f* peck; bite; (Bol) knock at the door; (Arg, Bol, Urug) narrow ford; (SAm) path, trail
picadillo *m* (*carne, verduras, ajos, etc. reducidos a pequeños trozos*) hash; (*carne picada*) mincemeat
pica•do -da *adj* perforated; pitted; (*tabaco*) cut; (*hielo*) cracked; (*mar*) choppy; piqued || *m* mincemeat; (aer) dive; **picado con motor** (aer) power dive || *f* see **picada**
picador *m* horsebreaker; (*torero de a caballo*) picador (*mounted bullfighter*); chopping block
picadura *f* bite, prick, sting; nick; puncture; cut tobacco; (*en un diente*) cavity
picaflor *m* hummingbird
picahie•los *m* (*pl* **-los**) ice pick
picamade•ros *m* (*pl* **-ros**) green woodpecker
picante *adj* biting, pricking, stinging; piquant, juicy, racy; (SAm) highly seasoned || *m* mordancy; piquancy
picapedrero *m* stonecutter
picaplei•tos *m* (*pl* **-tos**) (coll) troublemaker; (coll) shyster, pettifogger

picaporte *m* latch; latchkey; door knocker
picar §73 *tr* to prick, pierce, puncture; to sting; to bite; to burn; to peck; to nibble; to pit, to pock; to mince, chop up, cut up; to stick, poke; to spur; to goad; to perforate; (*hielo*) to crack; to harass, pursue; to tame; to pique, annoy || *intr* to itch; (*el sol*) to burn; to nibble; to have a smattering; to be catching; (*los negocios*) to pick up; (aer) to dive; (*caer en el lazo*) (coll) to bite; **picar en** to nibble at; to dabble in; **picar muy alto** (coll) to aim high, expect too much || *ref* to rot; (*la ropa*) to be moth-eaten; (*el vino*) to turn sour; (*un diente*) to be decayed; (*el mar*) to get rough; to be offended; (Am) to get drunk; **picarse de** to boast of being
picardía *f* roguishness, knavery; crudeness, coarseness; mischief
picares•co -ca *adj* roguish, rascally; picaresque; rough, coarse, crude; (coll) witty, humorous, gay
píca•ro -ra *adj* roguish; scheming, tricky; low, vile; mischievous || *mf* rogue; schemer
picaza *f* magpie
picazón *f* itch, itching; (coll) annoyance
pícea *f* spruce tree
pick-up *m* pickup; phonograph
pico *m* beak, bill; (*de jarra*) spout; (*del yunque*) beak; (*del pañuelo*) corner; nib, tip; (*de la pluma de escribir*) point; peak; (*herramienta*) pick; (*de dinero*) pile, lot; talkativeness; (elec) peak; (naut) bow, prow; **callar el pico** (coll) to shut up; **darse el pico** (*las palomas*) to bill; **pico de oro** silver-tongue; **tener mucho pico** (coll) to talk too much; **y pico** odd, e.g., **trescientos y pico** three hundred odd; a little after, e.g., **a las tres y pico** a little after three o'clock
picor *m* (*del paladar*) smarting; itch, itching, burning
pico•so -sa *adj* pock-marked
picota *f* pillory; peak, point, spire
picotazo *m* peck
picotear *tr* to peck || *intr* (*el caballo*) to toss the head; (coll) to chatter, jabber, gab; (*las mujeres*) (coll) to wrangle
pichel *m* pewter tankard
pi•chón -chona *mf* (coll) darling || *m* young pigeon; **pichón de barro** clay pigeon
pie *m* foot; footing; foothold; base, stand; (*de copa*) stem; (*de la cama*) footboard; cause, origin, reason; (*de la página*) foot, bottom; (theat) cue; (Chile) down payment; **a cuatro pies** on all fours; **al pie de fábrica** (coll) at the factory; **al pie de la letra** literally; **al pie de la obra** (com) delivered; **a pie** on foot, walking; **buscar cinco** (or **tres**) **pies al gato** (coll) to be looking for trouble; **de pie** standing; up and about; firm, steady; firmly, steadily; **en pie de guerra** on a war footing; **ir a pie** to go on foot, to walk; **morir al pie del cañón** to die in the harness, to die with one's boots on; **nacer de pie** or **de pies** to be born with a silver spoon in one's mouth; **pie de atleta** athlete's foot; **pie de cabra** crowbar; **pie de imprenta** imprint, printer's mark; **pie derecho** upright, stanchion; **pie marino** sea legs; **pie quebrado** (*de verso*) short line; **vestirse por los pies** (coll) to be a man
piedad *f* (*devoción a las cosas santas*) piety; (*misericordia*) pity, mercy
piedra *f* stone; rock; (*pedernal*) flint; heavy hailstone; (pathol) stone; **piedra angular** cornerstone; (fig) cornerstone, keystone; **piedra arenisca** sandstone; **piedra azul** (chem) bluestone; **piedra de albardilla** copestone; **piedra de amolar** grindstone; **piedra de chispa** flint; **piedra de pipas** meerschaum; **piedra imán** loadstone; **piedra miliar** or **miliaria** milestone; **piedra movediza** rolling stone; **piedra pómez** pumice, pumice stone
piel *f* skin; hide, pelt; fur; leather; (*de las frutas*) peel, skin; **piel de cabra** goatskin; **piel de foca** sealskin; **piel de gallina** goose flesh; **piel roja** *m* (*pl* **pieles rojas**) (*indio norteamericano*) redskin
pienso *m* feed, feeding; **ni por pienso** by no means, don't think of it
pierna *f* leg; post, upright; **dormir a pierna suelta** or **tendida** (coll) to sleep like a log; **estirar la pierna** (coll) to lie down on the job; (coll) to kick the bucket; **estirar** or **extender las piernas** (coll) to stretch one's legs, go for a walk; **ser buena pierna** (Arg, Urug) to be a good-natured fellow
pieza *f* (*órgano de una máquina o artefacto; obra dramática; composición suelta de música; cañón; figura que sirve para jugar a las damas, al ajedrez, etc.; moneda*) piece; (*objeto; mueble; porción de tela*) piece or article; (*habitación, cuarto*) room; **buena pieza** hussy; sly fox; **pieza de recambio** or **de repuesto** spare part; **quedarse en una pieza** or **hecho una pieza** to be dumbfounded, to stand motionless
pífano *m* fife; fifer
pifia *f* (billiards) miscue; (coll) miscue, slip
pifiar *intr* to miscue
pigmentar *tr & ref* to pigment
pigmento *m* pigment
pigme•o -a *adj & mf* pygmy
pijama *f* pajamas
pila *f* basin; trough; sink; font; pile, heap; (elec) battery, cell; (elec & phys) pile; **pila de linterna** flashlight battery
pilar *m* (*de una fuente*) basin, bowl; pillar; stone post, milestone; (*persona*) (fig) pillar || *tr* (*el grano*) to crush, to pound
Pilatos *m* Pilate
píldora *f* pill; (coll) bad news; **píldora para dormir** sleeping pill
pileta *f* sink; basin, bowl; font; swimming pool

pilón *m* pylon; drinking trough; loaf of sugar; counterpoise; drop hammer
pilotar *tr* to pilot
pilote *m* pile
piloto *m* pilot; first mate; (Chile) hail fellow well met
pillar *tr* to pillage, plunder; to catch
pi·llo -lla *adj* (coll) roguish, rascally; (coll) sly, crafty || *m* (coll) rogue, rascal; (coll) crafty fellow
pilluelo *m* (coll) scamp, little scamp
pimentero *m* pepper, black pepper; pepperbox
pimentón *m* cayenne pepper, red pepper; (*condimento preparado moliendo pimientos encarnados secos*) paprika
pimienta *f* pepper, black pepper; allspice, pimento; allspice tree
pimiento *m* (*planta*) pepper, black pepper; Guinea pepper
pimpante *adj* smart, spruce
pimpollo *m* sucker, shoot, sprout; rosebud; (*árbol nuevo*) sapling; (coll) handsome child; (coll) handsome young person
pina *f* felloe
pinacoteca *f* picture gallery
pináculo *m* pinnacle
pincel *m* brush; painter; painting; (*de luz*) pencil, beam
pincelada *f* brush stroke; touch, finish, flourish
pincelar *tr* to paint; to picture; (med) to pencil
pincia·no na *adj* Vallladolid || *mf* native or inhabitant of Valladolid
pincha *f* kitchenmaid
pinchar *tr* to prick, jab, pierce, puncture; to stir up, prod, provoke || *intr* to have a puncture; **no pinchar ni cortar** to have no say
pinchazo *m* prick, jab, puncture; provocation; **a prueba de pinchazos** puncture-proof
pinche *m* scullion, kitchen boy; helper
pincho *m* thorn, prick; snack; spike
Píndaro *m* Pindar
pingajo *m* (coll) rag, tatter
pingo *m* (coll) rag, tatter; (coll) ragamuffin; (coll) horse; **andar** or **ir de pingo** (*una mujer*) (coll) to gad about
pingüe *adj* oily, greasy, fat; abundant, rich; fertile; profitable
pingüino *m* penguin
pinito *m* first step, little step; **hacer pinitos** to begin to walk; (fig) to take the first steps
pino *m* pine tree; first step; **hacer pinos** to begin to walk; (fig) to take the first steps
pinocha *f* pine needle
pinta *m* (coll) scoundrel || *f* spot, mark, sign; dot; pint
pintacilgo *m* goldfinch
pintada *f* Guinea hen
pinta·do -da *adj* spotted, mottled; tipsy; accented; **el más pintado** (coll) the aptest one; (coll) the shrewdest one; (coll) the best one; **venir como pintado** to be just the thing || *m* (*acto de pintar*) painting || *f* see **pintada**
pintar *tr* to paint; (*una letra, un acento, etc.*) to draw; to picture, depict; to put an accent mark on; **pintarla** (coll) to put it on, to put on airs || *intr* to paint; to begin to turn red, begin to ripen; (coll) to show, to turn out || *ref* to paint, put on make-up; to begin to turn red, begin to ripen
pintarrajear *tr* to daub, to smear
pin·to -ta *adj* (Am) speckled, spotted || *f* see **pinta**
pin·tor -tora *mf* painter; **pintor de brocha gorda** painter, house painter; (coll) dauber
pintores·co -ca *adj* picturesque
pintura *f* (*color preparado para pintar*) paint; (*arte; obra pintada*) painting; **hacer pinturas** (coll) to prance; **no poder ver ni en pintura** to not be able to stand the sight of
pinture·ro -ra *adj* (coll) showy, conceited || *mf* (coll) show-off
pinza *f* clothespin; (*de langosta, cangrejo, etc.*) claw; **pinzas** pliers; pincers; tweezers; forceps
pinzón *m* pump handle; (orn) finch
piña *f* fir cone, pine cone; knob; plug; cluster, knot; pineapple
piñonear *intr* (*un arma de fuego*) to click; (coll) to reach the age of puberty; (coll) to be an old goat
piñoneo *m* click (*of a firearm*)
pí·o -a *adj* pious; merciful, compassionate; (*caballo*) pied, dappled || *m* peeping, chirping; (coll) keen desire
piocha *f* jeweled head adornment; artificial flower made of feathers; pick
piojo *m* louse
piojo·so -sa *adj* lousy; mean, stingy
pione·ro -ra *adj* & *mf* pioneer
pipa *f* (*para fumar tabaco*) pipe; (*medida para vinos*) butt; wine cask; (*simiente*) pip; (mus) pipe, reed; **pipa de espuma de mar** meerschaum pipe; **pipa de riego** watering cart; **pipa de tierra** clay pipe
pique *m* pique, resentment; eagerness; (*insecto*) chigger; (*naipe*) spade; **a pique** steep; **a pique de** in danger of; on the verge of; **echar a pique** to sink; to ruin; **irse a pique** to sink; to go to ruin, be ruined
piquera *f* bung, bunghole; (Mex) dive, joint
piquete *m* sharp jab; small hole; stake, picket; (*de soldados, de huelguistas*) picket; **piquete de ejecución** firing squad; **piquete de salvas** firing squad
pira *f* pyre
piragua *f* pirogue; (sport) single shell
piragüista *m* (sport) crewman
pirámide *f* pyramid
pirata *m* pirate
piratear *intr* to pirate, be a pirate
pirca *f* (SAm) dry stone wall
pirco *m* (Chile) succotash
Pireo, el Piraeus
pirine·o -a *adj* Pyrenean || **Pirineos** *mpl* Pyrenees
pirita *f* pyrites
pirófa·go -ga *adj* fire-eating || *mf* fire-eater
piropear *tr* (coll) to flatter, flirt with

piropo *m* garnet, carbuncle; (coll) flattery, compliment, flirtatious remark
piróscafo *m* steamship
pirotecnia *f* pyrotechnics
pirotécni•co -ca *adj* pyrotechnical ‖ *m* powder maker, fireworks manufacturer
pirueta *f* pirouette; somersault; caper
piruetear *intr* to pirouette
pisada *f* tread; footstep; footprint; trampling
pisapape•les *m* (*pl* **-les**) paperweight
pisar *tr* to trample, tread on, step on; to tamp, pack down; (*p.ej., uvas*) to tread; to cover part of; to ram; (*una tecla*) to strike; (mus) to pluck; (coll) to abuse, tread all over; **pisar algo a alguien** (coll) to snitch something from someone ‖ *intr* to be right above; to step ‖ *ref* (Arg) to guess wrong, come out wrong
pisaverde *m* (coll) fop, dandy
piscina *f* swimming pool; fishpond
pisco *m* Peruvian brandy
pisicorre *f* (W-I) station wagon
piso *m* tread; floor; flooring; (*de una carretera*) surface; flat, apartment; **buscar piso** to be looking for a place to live; **piso alto** top floor; **piso bajo** street floor, ground floor; **piso principal** main floor, second floor
pisón *m* ram, tamper
pisotear *tr* to trample, to tread on, to tread under foot; (coll) to abuse, tread all over
pisotón *m* stamp, tread
pista *f* track; trace, trail; clew; race track; (*de bolera*) alley; (*de cabaret*) floor; (aer) runway; **pista de esquí** ski run; **pista de patinar** skating rink
pisto *m* (*para los enfermos*) chicken broth; vegetable cutlet; jumbled speech or writing; mess
pistola *f* pistol; sprayer; rock drill; **pistola de arzón** horse pistol; **pistola engrasadora** grease gun
pistolera *f* holster
pistolerismo *m* gangsterism
pistolero *m* gangster, gunman
pistón *m* piston
pistonear *intr* to knock
pistoneo *m* knock
pistonu•do -da *adj* (coll) stunning, swank
pita *f* century plant; hiss, hissing; glass marble
pitar *tr* to pay, pay off; (*a un torero*) to whistle disapproval of ‖ *intr* to blow a whistle, to whistle; to blow the horn, to honk; (coll) to talk nonsense; **no pitar** (coll) to not be popular; **salir pitando** to run away, dash away
pitazo *m* blast, toot, honk
pitillera *f* cigarette maker; cigarette case
pitillo *m* cigarette
pito *m* whistle; horn; fife; fifer; cigarette; jackstone; (*insecto*) tick; woodpecker; (coll) continental, straw, tinker's dam
pitón *m* lump, sprig; tenderling; (*del cuerno*) tip; nozzle, spout; python
pitonisa *f* witch, siren; pythoness
pitu•so -sa *adj* tiny, cute ‖ *mf* tot
piular *intr* to peep, to chirp
pivotar *intr* to pivot
pivote *m* pivot; **pivote de dirección** (aut) kingpin
píxide *f* pyx
pizarra *f* slate; blackboard
pizarrero *m* roofer, slater
pizarrín *m* slate pencil
pizca *f* (coll) mite, whit, jot
placa *f* plaque, tablet; badge; plate; slab, sheet; (anat, elec, electron, phot, zool) plate; (Am) scab; **placa de matrícula** license plate; **placa giratoria** (*de ferrocarril; de gramófono*) turntable
placaminero *m* persimmon
placebo *m* placebo
pláceme *m* congratulation
placente•ro -ra *adj* pleasant, agreeable
placer *m* pleasure; sandbank, reef; **a placer** at one's convenience ‖ *v* **§52** *tr* to please
place•ro -ra *adj* public ‖ *mf* market vendor; loafer, town gossip
pláci•do -da *adj* placid; pleasing
plaga *f* plague; pest; scourge; abundance; sore; clime, region
plagar §44 *tr* to plague, infest; (*de minas*) to sow
plagiar *tr* to plagiarize
plagio *m* plagiarism; (Am) abduction, kidnaping
plan *m* plan; level, height; **plan de estudios** or **plan escolar** curriculum
plana *f* plain, flat country; trowel; cooper's plane; page
plancha *f* plate, sheet; iron, flatiron; gangplank; (coll) blunder; **a la plancha** grilled; (*huevo*) fried; **plancha de blindaje** armor plate
planchado *m* ironing; pressing
planchar *tr* (*la ropa interior blanca*) to iron; (*un traje de hombre*) to press ‖ *intr* (Am) to be a wallflower
planchear *tr* to plate
planear *tr* to plan, to outline; (*una tabla*) to plane ‖ *intr* to hover; (aer) to volplane, to glide
planeta *m* planet
planicie *f* plain
planificar §73 *tr* to plan
planilla *f* (Am) list, roll, schedule; (*de candidatos para un puesto público*) (Mex) panel; (Mex) ballot; (Mex) commutation ticket
pla•no -na *adj* plane; level, smooth, even; flat ‖ *m* plan; map; (*superficie*) plane; (aer) plane; **de plano** clearly, plainly, flatly; flat; **levantar un plano** to make a survey; **primer plano** foreground ‖ *f* see **plana**
planta *f* (*del pie*) sole; foot; plan; project; floor plan; (*del personal de una oficina*) roster; plant, factory; (bot) plant; (sport) stance; **de planta** from the ground up; **echar plantas** to swagger, to bully; **planta baja** ground floor; **planta del sortilegio** (bot) witch hazel; **tener buena planta** (coll) to make a fine appearance
plantar *tr* to plant; to establish, to

found; (*un golpe*) (coll) to plant; (coll) to jilt; (*en la calle, en la cárcel*) (coll) to throw || *ref* to take a stand; to gang together; (*un animal*) (coll) to balk; (coll) to land, to arrive

plantear *tr* to plan, to outline; to establish, execute, carry out; to state, set up, expound, pose

plantel *m* nursery garden; educational establishment

plantificar **§73** *tr* to plan, to outline; (*un golpe*) (coll) to plant; (*en la calle, la cárcel*) (coll) to throw || *ref* (coll) to land, to arrive

plantilla *f* plantlet, young plant; insole; reinforced sole; model, pattern, template; (*de empleados*) staff; (*del personal de una oficina*) roster; plan, design; (*bizcocho*) (Am) ladyfinger

plantío *m* planting; garden patch; tree nursery

plantón *m* (*que ha de ser transplantado*) shoot; graft; guard, watchman; waiting, standing around

plañide•ro -ra *adj* mournful, plaintive || *f* hired mourner

plañir **§12** *tr* to lament, grieve over || *intr* to lament, grieve, bewail

plasmar *tr* to mold, shape

plasta *f* paste, soft mass; flattened object; (coll) poor job, bungle

plástica *f* (*arte de plasmar*) plastic; plastic arts

plásti•co -ca *adj* plastic || *m* (*substancia*) plastic || *f* see **plástica**

plata *f* silver; (*moneda o monedas*) silver; wealth; money; **en plata** (coll) briefly, to the point; (coll) plainly; **plata de ley** sterling silver

plataforma *f* platform; platform car; (*del ferrocarril*) roadbed; (*programa político*) platform; (*de lanzamiento de cohete*) pad; **plataforma giratoria** (rr) turntable

platanal *m* or **platanar** *m* banana plantation

plátano *m* banana; banana tree; plane tree; **plátano de occidente** buttonwood tree

platea *f* (theat) orchestra, parquet

platear *tr* to silver, coat or plate with silver

platero *m* silversmith; jeweler

plática *f* talk, chat; talk, informal lecture; sermon

platicar **§73** *tr* to talk over, to discuss || *intr* to talk, to chat; to discuss; to preach

platillo *m* plate; saucer; (*de la balanza*) pan; (mus) cymbal; **platillo volador** or **volante** flying saucer

platino *m* platinum

plato *m* dish; plate; (*de una comida*) course; daily fare; **plato fuerte** main course; **plato giratorio** (*del gramófono*) turntable

pla•tó *m* (*pl* **-tós**) (mov) set

Platón *m* Plato

plausible *adj* praiseworthy; acceptable

playa *f* beach, shore, strand; **playa infantil** sand pile

playera *f* fishwoman; beach shoe

plaza *f* plaza, square; market place; town, city; fortified town; space, room; yard; office, employment; character, reputation; seat; **sentar plaza** to enlist; **plaza de armas** parade ground; (Am) public square; **plaza de gallos** cockpit; **plaza de toros** bullring; **plaza mayor** main square

plazo *m* term; time; time limit; date of payment; instalment; **a plazo** on credit, on time; **en plazos** in instalments

pleamar *f* high tide, high water

plebe *f* common people

plebe•yo -ya *adj & mf* plebeian

plegadi•zo -za *adj* folding; pliable

plegar **§66** *tr* to fold; to crease; to pleat || *ref* to yield, to give in

plegaria *f* prayer; noon call to prayer

pleito *m* litigation, lawsuit; dispute, quarrel; fight; **pleito de acreedores** bankruptcy proceedings; **pleito homenaje** (feud) homage; **pleito viciado** mistrial

plenilunio *m* full moon

plenitud *f* fullness, abundance

ple•no -na *adj* full; **en plena marcha** in full swing; **en pleno rostro** right in the face

pleuresía *f* pleurisy

pliego *m* (*de papel*) sheet; folder; cover, envelope; bid, specification; sealed letter; printer's proof

pliegue *m* fold, crease, pleat; **pliegue de tabla** box pleat

plisar *tr* to pleat

plomada *f* carpenter's lead pencil; plummet; plumb bob; sinker, sinkers; scourge tipped with lead balls

plomar *tr* to seal with lead

plomazo *m* (Guat, Mex, W-I) gunshot

plomería *f* lead roofing; leadwork, plumbing

plomero *m* lead worker; plumber

plomi•zo -za *adj* lead, leaden

plomo *m* lead; (*pedazo de plomo; bala*) lead; (elec) fuse; (coll) bore; **a plomo** plumb, perpendicularly; straight down; (coll) just right

pluma *f* feather; quill; plume; pen; (Am) faucet; (CAm) hoax; (Chile) crane, derrick; **pluma esferográfica** (Am) ball-point pen; **pluma estilográfica** or **pluma fuente** fountain pen

plumaje *m* plumage

plúmbe•o -a *adj* lead

plumero *m* (*caja o vaso para las plumas*) penholder; feather duster

plumífe•ro -ra *adj* (*escritor*) (coll) hack, second-rate; (poet) feathered || *m* padded or quilted jacket, ski jacket; (coll) hack writer; (coll) newshound

plumilla *f* small feather; (*de la pluma fuente*) point, tip

plumón *m* down; feather bed

plumo•so -sa *adj* downy, feathery

plural *adj & m* plural

pluriempleo *m* moonlighting

plus *m* extra, bonus

plusmarca *f* (sport) record

plusmarquista *mf* (sport) record breaker

plusvalía *f* appreciation (*in value*)
Plutarco *m* Plutarch
plutonio *m* plutonium
población *f* population; village, town, city
poblada *f* (SAm) riot, mob
pobla·do -da *adj* thick, bushy || *m* town, community || *f* see **poblada**
poblar **§61** *tr* to people, to populate; to found, settle, colonize; (*un estanque, una colmena*) to stock; (*con árboles*) to plant || *intr* to settle, colonize; to multiply, be prolific || *ref* to become full, covered, or crowded
pobre *adj* poor || *mf* pauper; beggar
pobreza *f* poverty, want; poorness
pocilga *f* pigpen
poción *f* potion, dose
po·co -ca *adj* & *pron* (*comp* & *super* **menos**) little; few, e.g., **poca gente** few people; **pocos** few; **unos pocos** a few || **poco** *adv* little; **a poco** shortly afterwards; **a poco de** shortly after; **dentro de poco** shortly; **por poco** almost, nearly; **tener en poco** to hold in low esteem, to think little of; **un poco (de)** a little
po·cho -cha *adj* faded, discolored; overripe; rotten; (Chile) chubby
podar *tr* to prune, to trim
podenco *m* hound
poder *m* power; power of attorney, proxy; **el cuarto poder** the fourth estate; **obra en mi poder** I have at hand, I have in my possession; **poder adquisitivo** purchasing power || *v* **§53** *intr* to be possible; to be able, to have power or strength; **a más no poder** as hard as possible; **no poder con** to not be able to stand, to not be able to manage; **no poder más** to be exhausted, to be all in; **no poder menos de** to not be able to keep from, to not be able to help || *v aux* to be able to, may, can, might, could; **no poder ver** to not be able to stand
poderhabiente *mf* attorney, proxy
poderío *m* power, might; wealth, riches; sway, dominion
podero·so -sa *adj* powerful, mighty; wealthy, rich
podre *f* pus
podredumbre *f* corruption, putrefaction; pus; deep grief
poema *m* poem
poesía *f* poetry; poem; **bella poesía** (fig) fairy tale
poeta *m* poet
poéti·co -ca *adj* poetic(al) || *f* poetics
poetisa *f* poetess
pola·co -ca *adj* Polish || *mf* Pole || *m* (*idioma*) Polish
polaina *f* legging
polar *adj* pole; polar || *f* polestar
polarizar **§60** *tr* to polarize
polea *f* pulley
poleame *m* (naut) tackle
polen *m* pollen
policía *m* policeman || *f* police; policing; politeness; cleanliness, neatness; **policía urbana** street cleaning
policía·co -ca or **policial** *adj* police; (*novela*) detective
polifacéti·co -ca *adj* many-sided
políga·mo -ma *adj* polygamous || *mf* polygamist
poliglo·to -ta *adj* polyglot || *mf* polyglot, linguist
polígono *m* polygon
polígrafo *m* prolific writer; copying machine; ball-point pen; lie detector
polilla *f* moth
Polimnia *f* Polyhymnia
polinizar **§60** *tr* to pollinate
polinomio *m* polynomial
polio *f* (path) polio
pólipo *m* polyp
polisón *m* bustle
polista *mf* poloist, polo player
politeísta *adj* polytheistic || *mf* polytheist
política *f* politics; policy; manners, politeness, courtesy; **política de café** parlor politics; **política del buen vecino** Good Neighbor Policy
políti·co -ca *adj* political; politic, tactful; polite, courteous; -in-law, e.g., **padre político** father-in-law || *mf* politician || *f* see **política**
póliza *f* policy, contract; draft, check; customhouse permit; **póliza de seguro** insurance policy
polizón *m* bum, tramp; stowaway
polizonte *m* (coll) cop, policeman
polo *m* pole; popsicle; (*juego*) polo; **polo de agua** water polo; **polo de atracción popular** drawing card
Polonia *f* Poland
pol·trón -trona *adj* idle, lazy, comfort-loving || *f* easy chair
polvareda *f* cloud of dust; rumpus
polvera *f* compact, powder case
polvo *m* dust; powder; pinch of snuff; **polvo dentífrico** tooth powder; **polvos** dust; powder; **polvos de la madre Celestina** (coll) hocus-pocus; **polvos de talco** talcum powder
pólvora *f* powder, gunpowder; fireworks; (*persona avispada*) (coll) live wire; **correr como pólvora en reguero** to spread like wildfire
polvorear *tr* to dust, sprinkle with dust or powder
polvorien·to -ta *adj* dusty; powdery
polvorín *m* powder magazine; powder flask; (*insecto*) (Am) tick; (Chile) spitfire
polvoro·so -sa *adj* dusty; **poner pies en polvorosa** (coll) to take to one's heels
polla *f* pullet; (*puesta en juegos de naipes*) stake, kitty; (coll) lassie
pollera *f* poultry woman; chicken coop; poultry yard; gocart; (Arg, Chile) skirt
pollero *m* poulterer; poultry yard
polli·no -na *mf* donkey, ass
polli·to -ta *mf* chick; (*persona joven*) (coll) chick, chicken
pollo *m* chicken; (*persona joven*) chicken
pomada *f* pomade
pómez *f* pumice stone
pomo *m* pome; (*de la guarnición de la espada*) pommel; (*bola aromática*) pomander; (*frasco para perfume*) flacon; **pomo de puerta** doorknob

pompa *f* pomp; soap bubble; swell, bulge; (*de la ropa*) billowing, ballooning; (*de las alas del pavo real*) spread; (naut) pump; **pompa fúnebre** funeral
pompo•so -sa *adj* pompous; high-flown, highfalutin
pómulo *m* cheekbone
ponche *m* (*bebida*) punch; **ponche de huevo** eggnog
ponchera *f* punch bowl
pon•cho -cha *adj* lazy, careless, easy-going; (Col) chubby || *m* poncho; greatcoat
ponderar *tr* to weigh; to ponder, ponder over; to exaggerate; to praise to the skies; to balance; to weight
ponencia *f* paper, report
poner §54 *tr* to put, place, lay, set; to arrange, dispose; (*una observación*) to put in; (*una pieza dramática*) to put on; (*la mesa*) to set; to assume, suppose; (*una ley, un impuesto*) to impose; to wager, to stake; (*huevos*) to lay; (*por escrito*) to set down, put down; (*tiempo*) to take; (*p.ej., miedo*) to cause; to make, to turn; (*la luz, la radio*) to turn on; (*marcha directa*) (aut) to go in; **poner en limpio** to make a clean copy of; **poner por encima** to prefer, to put ahead || *ref* to put or place oneself; to become, to get, to turn; (*el sol, los astros*) to set; (*sombrero, saco, etc.*) to put on; to dress, dress up; to get spotted; to get, reach, arrive; **ponerse a** to set out to, to begin to; **ponerse tan alto** to take offense, to become hoity-toity
poniente *m* west; west wind
ponqué *m* (Am) poundcake
pontífice *m* pontiff
pontón *m* pontoon; pontoon bridge; (*buque viejo*) hulk
ponzoña *f* poison
ponzoño•so -sa *adj* poisonous
popa *f* poop, stern
popote *m* (Mex) straw for brooms; (*para tomar refrescos*) (Mex) straw
populache•ro -ra *adj* popular; cheap, vulgar; rabble-rousing || *mf* rabble rouser
populacho *m* populace, mob, rabble
popular *adj* popular
popularizar §60 *tr* to popularize
populo•so -sa *adj* populous
popu•rrí *m* (*pl* **-rríes**) medley
poquedad *f* paucity, scantiness; scarcity; timidity; trifle
poqui•to -ta *adj* very little; (Am) timid, shy, backward
por *prep* by; through, over; via, by way of; in, e.g., **por la mañana** in the morning; for; because of; for the sake of; on account of; in exchange for; in order to; as; about, e.g., **por Navidad** about Christmastime; out of, e.g., **por ignorancia** out of ignorance; times, e.g., **tres por cuatro** four times three; **estar por** to be on the point of, to be ready to; to be still to be, e.g., **la carta está por escribir** the letter is still to be written; **ir por** to go for, to go after; to follow; **por ciento** per cent; **por entre** among, between; **por que** because; in order that; **por qué** why; **por** + *adj* or *adv* + **que** however
porcelana *f* porcelain, chinaware; (*usado por los plateros*) enamel; (Mex) washbowl
porcentaje *m* percentage
porción *f* portion
porche *m* porch, portico
pordiosear *intr* to beg, to go begging
pordiose•ro -ra *mf* beggar
porfía *f* persistence, stubbornness, obstinacy; **a porfía** in emulation; insistently
porfia•do -da *adj* persistent, stubborn, obstinate; opinionated
porfiar §77 *intr* to persist; to argue stubbornly
pórfido *m* porphyry
pormenor *m* detail, particular
pormenorizar §60 *tr* to detail, tell in detail; to itemize
poro *m* pore
poro•so -sa *adj* porous
poroto *m* (SAm) bean, string bean; (Chile) little runt
porque *conj* because; in order that
porqué *m* (coll) why; (coll) quantity, share; (coll) wherewithal, money
porquería *f* (coll) dirt, filth; (coll) trifle; (coll) crudity; (*alimento dañoso a la salud*) (coll) junk
porra *f* club, bludgeon; (coll) bore, nuisance; (coll) boasting; (*pelos enredados*) (Arg, Bol) knot, tangle; (Mex) claque
porrazo *m* clubbing; blow, bump, thump
porta *f* porthole
portaavio•nes *m* (*pl* **-nes**) aircraft carrier, flattop
portacandado *m* hasp
portada *f* front, façade; portal; title page; (*de una revista*) cover; **falsa portada** half title
portadis•cos *m* (*pl* **-cos**) turntable
porta•dor -dora *adj* (*onda*) (rad) carrier || *mf* bearer; carrier || *m* waiter's tray
portaequipaje *m* (aut) trunk
portaequipa•jes *m* (*pl* **-jes**) baggage rack
portaguan•tes *m* (*pl* **-tes**) (aut) glove compartment
portal *m* vestibule, entrance hall; porch, portico; arcade; city gate; (*de un túnel*) portal *m*; (Am) crèche
portalámpa•ras *m* (*pl* **-ras**) (elec) socket
portalón *m* gate, portal; (*en el costado del buque*) gangway
portamira *m* (surv) rodman
portamone•das *m* (*pl* **-das**) pocketbook
portanue•vas *mf* (*pl* **-vas**) newsmonger
portañuela *f* (*de los pantalones*) fly; (Col, Mex) carriage door
portapape•les *m* (*pl* **-les**) brief case
portaplu•mas *m* (*pl* **-mas**) penholder
portar *tr* (Am) to carry, to bear; (hunt) to retrieve || *ref* to behave, conduct oneself
portase•nos *m* (*pl* **-nos**) brassière
portátil *adj* portable

portatinte•ro *m* inkstand
portavian•das *m* (*pl* **-das**) dinner pail
porta•voz *m* (*pl* **-voces**) megaphone; mouthpiece, spokesman
portazgo *m* toll, road toll
portazo *m* bang, slam
porte *m* portage; carrying charge, freight; postage; behavior, conduct; dress, bearing; size, capacity; (Chile) birthday present; **porte concertado** mailing permit; **porte pagado** postage prepaid, freight prepaid
portear *tr* to carry, transport || *intr* to slam || *ref* (*las aves*) to migrate
portento *m* prodigy, wonder
portento•so -sa *adj* portentous, extraordinary
porte•ño -ña *adj* Buenos Aires; Valparaiso; pertaining to any large South American city with a port || *mf* native or inhabitant of Buenos Aires, Valparaiso or any large South American city with a port
porte•ro -ra *mf* doorkeeper; gatekeeper; (sport) goalkeeper || *m* porter, janitor; doorman || *f* portress, janitress
portezuela *f* small door; (*de un coche o automóvil*) door; pocket flap
pórtico *m* portico, porch; little gate
portilla *f* porthole; private cart road, private cattle pass
portillo *m* gap, opening; nick, notch; (*puerta chica en otra mayor*) wicket; gate; narrow pass; side entrance
portorrique•ño -ña *adj & mf* Puerto Rican
portua•rio -ria *adj* port, harbor, dock || *m* dock hand, dock worker
Portugal *m* Portugal
portu•gués -guesa *adj & mf* Portuguese
porvenir *m* future
pos — **en pos de** after, behind; in pursuit of
posa *f* knell, toll
posada *f* inn, wayside inn; lodging; boarding house; home, dwelling; camp; **posadas** (Mex) pre-Christmas celebration
posadero -ra *mf* innkeeper; **posaderas** buttocks
posar *tr* to put down || *intr* to put up, lodge; to alight, to perch; to pose || *ref* to alight, to perch; to settle; to rest
posbéli•co -ca *adj* postwar
posdata *f* postscript
pose *f* pose; (phot) exposure
poseer **§43** *tr* to own, possess, hold; to have a mastery of || *ref* to control oneself
posesión *f* possession; **tomar posesión de** (*un cargo*) to take up
posesionar *tr* to give possession to || *ref* to take possession
posfecha *f* postdate
posguerra *f* postwar period
posible *adj* possible; **hacer todo lo posible** to do one's best || **posibles** *mpl* means, income, property
posición *f* position; standing
positi•vo -va *adj* positive || *f* (phot) print, positive

poso *m* sediment, dregs; grounds; rest, quiet; **poso del café** coffee grounds
posponer **§54** *tr* to subordinate; to think less of
posta *f* (*de caballos*) relay; posthouse; stage; stake, wager; slice; **a posta** (coll) on purpose; **por la posta** (coll) posthaste; **postas** buckshot
postal *adj* postal || *f* post card; **postal ilustrada** picture post card
poste *m* post, pilar, pole; **poste de alumbrado** or **de farol** lamppost; **poste de telégrafo** telegraph pole; (*persona muy alta y delgada*) beanpole; **poste indicador** road sign
postergar **§44** *tr* to delay, postpone; to pass over
posteridad *f* posterity; posthumous fame
posterior *adj* back, rear; later, subsequent
postigo *m* (*puerta chica en otra mayor*) wicket; (*puertecilla en una ventana*) peep window; (*puerta excusada*) postern; shutter
posti•zo -za *adj* false, artificial; (*cuello*) detachable || *m* switch, false hair, rat
postóni•co -ca *adj* posttonic
postor *m* bidder; **el mejor postor** the highest bidder
postración *f* prostration
postrar *tr* to prostrate; to weaken, exhaust || *ref* to collapse, be prostrated; to prostrate oneself
postre *adj* last, final; **a la postre** at last; afterwards || *m* dessert; **postres** dessert
postulación *f* postulation; nomination
postulante *mf* applicant, candidate
póstu•mo -ma *adj* posthumous
postura *f* posture; attitude, stand; stake, wager; agreement, pact; egg, eggs; (*de huevos*) laying; **postura del sol** sunset
potabilizar **§60** *tr* to make drinkable
potable *adj* drinkable
potaje *m* pottage; jumble; (*bebida*) mixture; (Am) scheme; **potajes** vegetables
potasa *f* potash
potasio *m* potassium
pote *m* pot, jug; flowerpot; **a pote** (coll) in abundance
potencia *f* potency; power; **potencia de choque** striking power
potenciación *f* (math) involution
potencial *adj & m* potential
potenciar *tr* (*las aguas de un río; el entusiasmo de una persona*) to harness; (*elevar a una potencia*) (math) to raise
potentado *m* potentate
potente *adj* powerful; (coll) big, huge
potestad *f* power
potista *mf* (coll) toper, soak
potosí *m* great wealth, gold mine
potra *f* filly; (coll) hernia, rupture
potranca *f* young mare
potro *m* colt; pest, annoyance
pozal *m* bucket, pail
pozo *m* well; pit; whirlpool; (min) shaft; (naut) hold; (Chile, Col) pool, puddle; (Ecuad) spring, fountain;

pozo de ciencia fountain of knowledge; **pozo de lanzamiento** launching silo; **pozo de lobo** (mil) foxhole; **pozo negro** cesspool
P.P. *abbr* **porte pagado, por poder**
p.p.do *abbr* **próximo pasado**
práctica *f* practice; method; skill; **prácticas** studies, training
prácticamente *adv* through practice, by experience
practicar §73 *tr* to practice; to bring about; (*un agujero*) to make, to cut
prácti•co -ca *adj* practical; skillful, practiced; practicing || *m* medical practitioner; (naut) pilot || *f* see **práctica**
pradera *f* meadowland; prairie
prado *m* meadow, pasture; promenade
Praga *f* Prague
pral. *abbr* **principal**
pralte. *abbr* **principalmente**
prángana — estar en la prángana (Mex, W-I) to be broke; (P-R) to be naked
preámbulo *m* preamble; evasion; **no andarse en preámbulos** (coll) to come to the point
prebéli•co -ca *adj* prewar
prebenda *f* prebend; (coll) sinecure
preca•rio -ria *adj* precarious
precaución *f* precaution
precaver *tr* to stave off, head off || *intr & ref* to be on one's guard; **precaverse contra** or **de** to guard against
precavido -da *adj* cautious
precedente *adj* preceding || *m* precedent
preceder *tr & intr* to precede
precepto *m* precept; order, injunction; **los preceptos** the Ten Commandments
preces *fpl* devotions; supplications
precia•do -da *adj* esteemed, valued; precious, valuable; boastful, proud
preciar *tr* to appraise, estimate || *ref* to boast
precintar *tr* to bind, strap; to seal
precio *m* price; value, worth; esteem, credit; **a precio de quemazón** (coll) at a giveaway price; **precios de cierre** closing prices; **precio tope** ceiling price
preciosidad *f* preciousness; beauty, gem, jewel
precio•so -sa *adj* precious; valuable; witty; (coll) beautiful
precipicio *m* precipice; destruction
precipitación *f* precipitation; **precipitación acuosa** rainfall; **precipitación radiactiva** fallout
precipitar *tr* to precipitate; to rush, hurl, throw headlong || *ref* to rush, throw oneself headlong
precipito•so -sa *adj* precipitous, rash, reckless; risky, dangerous
precisar *tr* to state precisely, to specify; to fix; to need; to oblige, to force || *intr* to be necessary; to be important; to be urgent; **precisar de** to need
precisión *f* precision; necessity, obligation; (Chile) haste; **precisiones** data
preci•so -sa *adj* necessary; precise; (Ven) haughty
precita•do -da *adj* above-mentioned
precla•ro -ra *adj* illustrious, famous
preconizar §60 *tr* to proclaim, commend publicly
pre•coz *adj* (*pl* **-coces**) precocious
predato•rio -ria *adj* predatory
predecir §24 *tr* to predict, foretell
prédica *f* protestant sermon; harangue
predicar §73 *tr* to preach; to praise to the skies; to scold, preach to
predicción *f* prediction; **predicción del tiempo** weather forecasting
predilec•to -ta *adj* favorite, preferred
predio *m* property, estate
predisponer §54 *tr* to predispose
predominante *adj* predominant
preeminente *adj* preëminent
preestreno *m* (mov) preview
prefabricar §73 *tr* to prefabricate
prefacio *m* preface
preferencia *f* preference; **de preferencia** preferably
preferente *adj* preferable; favored; (*acciones*) preferred
preferible *adj* preferable
preferir §68 *tr* to prefer
prefigurar *tr* to foreshadow
prefijar *tr* to prefix; to prearrange
prefijo *m* prefix
pregón *m* proclamation, public announcement (*by town crier*)
pregonar *tr* to proclaim, announce publicly; to hawk; to reveal; to outlaw; to praise openly
pregonero *m* auctioneer; town crier
preguerra *f* prewar period
pregunta *f* question; **hacer una pregunta** to ask a question
preguntar *tr* to ask; to question || *intr* to ask, to inquire; **preguntar por** to ask after or for || *ref* to ask oneself; to wonder
pregun•tón -tona *adj* (coll) inquisitive || *mf* (coll) inquisitive person
prejudicio or **prejuicio** *m* prejudgment; prejudice
prelado *m* prelate
preliminar *adj & m* preliminary; **preliminares** (*de un libro*) front matter
preludio *m* prelude
premeditar *tr* to premeditate
premiar *tr* to reward; to give an award to
premio *m* reward, prize; premium; **a premio** at a premium; **premio de enganche** (mil) bounty; **premio gordo** first prize
premio•so -sa *adj* tight, close; bothersome; strict, rigid; slow, dull
premisa *f* premise; mark, token, clue
premura *f* pressure, haste, urgency
premuro•so -sa *adj* pressing, urgent
prenda *f* pledge; security; pawn; jewel, household article; garment, article of clothing; gift, talent; darling, loved one; **en prenda** in pawn; **en prenda de** as a pledge of; **prenda perdida** forfeit; **prendas** (*juego*) forfeits
prendar *tr* to pawn; to pledge; to charm, captivate || *ref* — **prendarse de** to take a liking for, fall in love with
prendedero *m* fillet, brooch; stickpin
prender *tr* to seize, grasp; to catch; to imprison; to dress up; to pin; to

fasten || *intr* to catch; to catch fire; to take root; to turn out well || *ref* to dress up; to be fastened; to catch hold

prendería *f* second-hand shop

prende•ro -ra *mf* second-hand dealer

prensa *f* press; printing press; vise; press, newspapers; press, frame; **entrar en prensa** to go to press; **meter en prensa** (coll) to put the squeeze on; **prensa taladradora** drill press

prensado *m* pressing; (*lustre de los tejidos prensados*) sheen

prensar *tr* to press; to squeeze

preña•do -da *adj* pregnant; sagging, bulging; full, charged

preñez *f* pregnancy; fullness; impending danger; inherent confusion

preocupación *f* (*posesión anticipada; cuidado, desvelo*) preoccupation; (*posesión anticipada*) preoccupancy; bias, prejudice

preocupar *tr* to preoccupy, to worry || *ref* to become preoccupied, to be worried

preparación *f* preparation

prepara•do -da *adj* ready, prepared || *m* (pharm) preparation

preparar *tr* to prepare || *ref* to prepare, to get ready

preparati•vo -va *adj* preparatory || *m* preparation, readiness

preponderante *adj* preponderant

preposición *f* preposition

prepóste•ro -ra *adj* reversed, upset, out of order, inopportune

prerrogativa *f* prerogative

presa *f* capture, seizure; catch, prey; booty, spoils; dam; trench, ditch, flume; bit, morsel; fang, tusk, claw; fishweir; (sport) hold; **hacer presa** to seize; **ser presa de** to be a victim of; to be prey to

presagiar *tr* to presage, forebode

presagio *m* presage, omen, token

présbita or **présbite** *adj* far-sighted || *mf* presbyte

presbiteria•no -na *adj & mf* Presbyterian

prescindir *intr* — **prescindir de** to leave aside, leave out, disregard; to do without, dispense with; to avoid

prescribir **§83** *tr & intr* to prescribe

presencia *f* presence; show, display; **presencia de ánimo** presence of mind

presenciar *tr* to witness, be present at

presentación *f* presentation; (*de una persona en el trato de otra u otras*) introduction; (*de un nuevo automóvil, libro, etc.*) appearance

presentar *tr* to present; to introduce || *ref* to present oneself; to appear, show up; to introduce oneself

presente *adj* present; **hacer presente** to notify of, to remind of; **tener presente** to bear or keep in mind || *interj* here!, present! || *m* present, gift; person present

presentimiento *m* presentiment, premonition

presentir **§68** *tr* to have a presentiment of

preservar *tr* to preserve, protect

preservati•vo -va *adj & m* preventive; preservative

presidencia *f* presidency; chairmanship

presidente *m* president; chairman; presiding judge

presidiario *m* convict

presidio *m* garrison; fortress; citadel; penitentiary; imprisonment; hard labor; aid, help

presidir *tr* to preside over; to dominate || *intr* to preside

presilla *f* loop, fastener; clip; shoulder strap

presión *f* pressure; (*cerveza*) **a presión** on draught; **presión de inflado** tire pressure

presionar *tr* to press; to put pressure on || *intr* to press; **presionar sobre** to put pressure on

pre•so -sa *adj* seized; imprisoned || *mf* prisoner; convict; *f* see **presa**

presta•do -da *adj* lent, loaned; **dar prestado** to lend; **pedir** or **tomar prestado** to borrow

prestamista *mf* moneylender; pawnbroker

préstamo *m* loan; **préstamo lingüístico** loan word, borrowing

prestar *tr* to lend, to loan; (*oído; ayuda; noticias*) to give; (*atención*) to pay; (*un favor*) to do; (*un servicio*) to render; (*juramento*) to take; (*silencio*) to keep; (*paciencia*) to show || *intr* (*un paño, la ropa*) to give, to yield; to be useful || *ref* to lend oneself, to lend itself

prestatar•rio -ria *mf* borrower

presteza *f* speed, promptness, readiness

prestidigitación *f* sleight of hand

prestidigita•dor -dora *adj* captivating || *mf* magician; faker, impostor

prestigio *m* prestige; good standing; spell; illusion

prestigio•so -sa *adj* captivating, spellbinding; famous, renowned; illusory

pres•to -ta *adj* quick, prompt, ready; nimble || **presto** *adv* right away

presumi•do -da *adj* conceited, vain || *mf* would-be

presumir *tr* to presume || *intr* to boast, be conceited

presunción *f* presumption; conceit

presuntuo•so -sa *adj* conceited, vain

presuponer **§54** *tr* to presuppose; to budget

presupuestar *tr* to budget; (*el coste de una obra*) to estimate

presupuesto *m* budget; reason, motive; supposition; estimate

presuro•so -sa *adj* speedy, quick, hasty; zealous, persistent

pretencio•so -sa *adj* pretentious, showy; conceited, vain

pretender *tr* to claim, to pretend to; to try for, to try to do; to be a suitor for || *intr* to insist; **pretender** + *inf* to try to + *inf*

pretendiente *mf* pretender, claimant; office seeker || *m* suitor

pretensión *f* pretension; claim; pretense; presumption; effort, pursuit

pretéri•to -ta *adj & m* past

pretil *m* parapet, railing; walk along a parapet
pretina *f* girdle, belt; waistband
pretóni•co -ca *adj* pretonic
prevalecer §22 *intr* to prevail; to take root; to thrive
prevaler §76 *ref* — **prevalerse de** to avail oneself of, take advantage of
prevaricar §73 *intr* to collude, connive; to play false; to transgress; (coll) to rave, be delirious
prevención *f* preparation; prevention; foresight; warning; prejudice; stock, supply; jail, lockup; guardhouse; **a** or **de prevención** spare, emergency
preveni•do -da *adj* prepared, ready; foresighted, forewarned; stocked, full
prevenir §79 *tr* to prepare, make ready; to forestall, prevent, anticipate; to overcome; to warn; to prejudice || *intr* (*una tempestad*) to come up || *ref* to get ready; to come to mind
prever §80 *tr* to foresee
pre•vio -via *adj* previous; preliminary; after, with previous, subject to, e.g., **previo acuerdo** subject to agreement
previsión *f* prevision, foresight; foresightedness; forecast; **previsión del tiempo** weather forecasting
prie•to -ta *adj* dark, blackish; stingy, mean; tight, compact; (Am) dark-complexioned || *mf* (W-I) darling
prima *f* early morning; bonus, bounty; (ins) premium; (mil) first quarter of the night; (*cuerda*) (mus) treble
pri•mal -mala *adj & mf* yearling
prima•rio -ria *adj* primary || *m* (elec) primary
primavera *f* spring, springtime; cowslip, primrose; robin
primer *adj* apocopated form of **primero,** used only before masculine singular nouns and adjectives
prime•ro -ra *adj* first; former; early; primary; prime; (*materia*) raw || *m* first; **a primeros de** around the beginning of || **primero** *adv* first
primicia *f* first fruits
primige•nio -nia *adj* original, primitive
primiti•vo -va *adj* primitive
pri•mo -ma *adj* first; prime, excellent; skillful; (*materia*) raw || *mf* cousin; (coll) sucker, dupe; **primo carnal** or **primo hermano** first cousin, cousin-german || *f* see **prima** || **primo** *adv* in the first place
primogéni•to -ta *adj & mf* first-born
primor *m* care, skill, elegance; beauty
primoro•so -sa *adj* careful, skillful, elegant; fine, exquisite
princesa *f* princess; **princesa viuda** dowager princess
principal *adj* principal, main, chief; first, foremost; essential, important; famous, illustrious; (*piso*) second || *m* principal, head, chief
príncipe *m* prince; **portarse como un príncipe** to live like a prince; **príncipe de Asturias** heir apparent of the King of Spain; **príncipe de Gales** prince of Wales; **príncipes** prince and princess
principiante *adj* beginning || *mf* beginner, apprentice, novice
principiar *tr, intr & ref* to begin
principio *m* start, beginning; principle; origin, source; (culin) entree; **a principios de** around the beginning of; **en un principio** at the beginning; **principio de admiración** inverted exclamation point; **principio de interrogación** inverted question mark
pringar §44 *tr* to dip or soak in grease or fat; to spot or stain with grease; (coll) to make bleed; (coll) to slander, run down; (Am) to splash || *intr* (coll) to meddle; (CAm, Mex) to drizzle || *ref* to peculate
pringo•so -sa *adj* greasy, fatty
prioridad *f* priority; **de máxima prioridad** of the highest priority
prisa *f* hurry, haste; urgency; crush, crowd; **darse prisa** to hurry, make haste; **estar de prisa** or **tener prisa** to be in a hurry
prisión *f* seizure, capture; imprisonment; prison; **prisión celular** cell house; **prisiones** shackles, fetters
prisione•ro -ra *mf* prisoner; (*cautivo de una pasión o afecto*) captive || *m* setscrew; studbolt
prisma *m* prism
prismáticos *mpl* binoculars
priva•do -da *adj* private || *m* (*de un alto personaje*) favorite || *f* cesspool
privar *tr* to deprive; to forbid, prohibit || *intr* to be in vogue; to prevail; to be in favor || *ref* to deprive oneself; **privarse de** to give up
privilegiar *tr* to grant a privilege to
privilegio *m* privilege
pro *m & f* profit, advantage; **¡buena pro!** good appetite!; **de pro** of note, of worth; **el pro y el contra** the pros and the cons; **en pro de** on behalf of
proa *f* (aer) nose; (naut) prow
probable *adj* probable, likely
probar §61 *tr* to prove; to test; to try; (*clothing*) to try on; to try out; to sample; to fit; to suit; (*vino*) to touch || *intr* to taste; **probar de** to take a taste of || *ref* to try on
probidad *f* probity, integrity, honesty
problema *m* problem
pro•caz *adj* (*pl* **-caces**) impudent, insolent, bold
procedencia *f* origin, source; point of departure
procedente *adj* coming, originating; proper
proceder *m* conduct, behavior || *intr* to proceed; to originate; to behave; to be proper
procedimiento *m* procedure; proceeding; process
procelo•so -sa *adj* tempestuous, stormy
prócer *adj* high, lofty || *m* hero, leader
procesar *tr* to sue, prosecute; to indict; to try
procesión *f* procession; origin, emergence
proceso *m* process; progress; suit, lawsuit; **proceso verbal** (Am) minutes
proclama *f* proclamation; marriage banns

proclamar *tr* to proclaim; to acclaim
proclíti•co -ca *adj & m* proclitic
procurador *m* attorney, solicitor; proxy
procurar *tr* to strive for; to manage as attorney; to yield, produce; to try to
prodigar §44 *tr* to lavish; to squander; to waste || *ref* to be a show-off
prodigio *m* prodigy
prodigio•so -sa *adj* prodigious, marvelous; fine, excellent
pródigo -ga *adj* prodigal; lavish || *mf* prodigal
producción *f* production; crop, yield, produce; **producción en masa** or **en serie** mass production
producir §19 *tr* to produce; to yield, to bear; to cause, bring about || *ref* to explain oneself; to come about; to take place
producto *m* product; produce; proceeds
proeza *f* prowess; feat, stunt
prof. *abbr* **profeta**
profanar *tr* to profane
profa•no -na *adj* profane; indecent, immodest; worldly; lay || *mf* profane; worldly person; layman
profecía *f* prophecy || **las Profecías** (Bib) the Prophets
proferir §68 *tr* to utter
profesar *tr & intr* to profess
profesión *f* profession; **profesión de fe** confession of faith
profe•sor -sora *mf* teacher; professor
profeta *m* prophet
profetisa *f* prophetess
profetizar §60 *tr* to prophesy
profilácti•co -ca *adj & m* prophylactic; preventive || *f* hygiene
prófu•go -ga *adj & mf* fugitive || *m* slacker, draft dodger
profundidad *f* profundity; depth
profundizar §60 *tr* to deepen; to fathom, get to the bottom of
profun•do -da *adj* profound; deep
progenie *f* descent, lineage, parentage
progno•sis *f* (*pl* **-sis**) prognosis; (*del tiempo*) forecast
programa *m* program; **programa continuo** (mov) continuous showing; **programa de estudios** curriculum
programar *tr* to program
progresar *intr* to progress
progresista *adj & mf* (pol) progressive
progreso *m* progress; **hacer progresos** to make progress
prohibir *tr* to prohibit, forbid || *ref* **se prohibe fijar carteles** post no bills
prohijar *tr* to adopt
prohombre *m* (*en los gremios de los artesanos*) master; leader, head; (coll) big shot
prójimo *m* fellow man, fellow creature, neighbor; (coll) fellow
pról. *abbr* **prólogo**
prole *f* progeny, offspring
proletariado *m* proletariat
proleta•rio -ria *adj & m* proletarian
proliferar *intr* to proliferate
prolífi•co -ca *adj* prolific
proli•jo -ja *adj* tedious, too long; fussy, fastidious; long-winded; tiresome
prologar §44 *tr* to preface, write a preface for
prólogo *m* prologue; preface
prolongar §44 *tr* to prolong, extend; (geom) to produce
promediar *tr* to divide into two equal parts; to average || *intr* to mediate; to be half over
promedio *m* average, mean; middle
promesa *f* promise
promete•dor -dora *adj* promising
prometer *tr & intr* to promise || *ref* to become engaged
prometi•do -da *adj* engaged, betrothed || *m* promise; fiancé || *f* fiancée
prominente *adj* prominent
promiso•rio -ria *adj* promissory
promoción *f* promotion; advancement; (*conjunto de individuos que obtienen un grado en un mismo año*) class, year, crop
promontorio *m* promontory, headland; unwieldy thing
promover §47 *tr* to promote; to advance, to further
promulgar §44 *tr* to promulgate
pronombre *m* pronoun
pronosticar §73 *tr* to prognosticate, to foretell
pronóstico *m* prognostic, forecast; almanac; (med) prognosis
pron•to -ta *adj* quick, speedy; prompt; ready || *m* jerk; (coll) sudden impulse, fit of anger || **pronto** *adv* right away, soon; early; promptly; **lo más pronto posible** as soon as possible; **tan pronto como** as soon as
pronunciación *f* pronunciation
pronuncia•do -da *adj* marked; (*curva*) sharp; (*pendiente*) steep; bulky
pronunciamiento *m* insurrection, uprising; (*golpe de estado militar*) pronunciamento; (law) decree
pronunciar *tr* to pronounce; to utter; (*un discurso*) to make, to deliver; to decide on || *ref* to rebel; to declare oneself
propaganda *f* propaganda; advertising
propagar §44 *tr* to propagate; to spread; to broadcast
propalar *tr* to divulge, to spread
proparoxíto•no -na *adj & m* proparoxytone
propasar *ref* to go too far, to take undue liberty
propender *intr* to tend, to incline, to be inclined
propensión *f* propensity; predisposition
propen•so -sa *adj* inclined, disposed, prone
propiciar *tr* to propitiate; (Am) to support, favor, sponsor
propi•cio -cia *adj* propitious, favorable
propiedad *f* property; ownership; naturalness, likeness; **es propiedad** copyrighted; **propiedad horizontal** one-floor ownership in an apartment house; **propiedad literaria** copyright
propieta•rio -ria *mf* owner || *m* proprietor || *f* proprietress
propina *f* tip, fee, gratuity
propinar *tr* (*algo a beber*) to offer; (*medicamentos*) to prescribe or ad-

minister; (*palos, golpes, etc.*) (coll) to give || *ref* (*una bebida*) to treat oneself to
propin•cuo -cua *adj* near, close at hand
pro•pio -pia *adj* proper, suitable; peculiar, characteristic; natural; same; himself, herself, etc.; own || *m* messenger; native; **propios** public lands
proponer §54 *tr* to propose; to propound; (*a una persona para un empleo*) to name, to present || *ref* to plan; to propose
proporción *f* proportion; opportunity
proporciona•do -da *adj* proportionate; fit, suitable
proporcionar *tr* to furnish, provide, supply, give; to proportion; to adapt, adjust
proposición *f* proposition; **proposición dominante** main clause
propósito *m* aim, purpose, intention; subject matter; **a propósito** by the way; apropos, fitting; in place; **a propósito de** apropos of; **de propósito** on purpose; **fuera de propósito** irrelevant, beside the point
propuesta *f* proposal, proposition
propulsar *tr* to propel, to drive
propulsión *f* propulsion; **propulsión a chorro** jet propulsion; **propulsión a cohete** rocket propulsion
pror. *abbr* **procurador**
prorratear *tr* to prorate
prórroga *f* extension, renewal
prorrogar §44 *tr* to defer, postpone, extend
prorrumpir *intr* to spurt, shoot forth; to break forth, burst out
prosa *f* prose; (coll) chatter, idle talk
prosai•co -ca *adj* prose; prosaic, dull
proscribir §83 *tr* to outlaw, to proscribe
proscrip•to -ta *mf* exile, outlaw
prosecución *f* continuation, prosecution; pursuit
proseguir §67 *tr* to continue, carry on || *intr* to continue
prosélito *m* proselyte
prosista *mf* prose writer; (coll) chatterbox
prosódi•co -ca *adj* (*acento*) stress
prospectar *tr* & *intr* to prospect
prosperar *tr* to make prosper || *intr* to prosper, to thrive
prosperidad prosperity
próspe•ro -ra *adj* prosperous, thriving, successful
prosternar *ref* to prostrate oneself
prostituir §20 *tr* to prostitute || *ref* to prostitute oneself; to become a prostitute
prostituta *f* prostitute
prosu•do -da *adj* (Chile, Ecuad, Peru) pompous, solemn
protagonista *mf* protagonist
protagonizar §60 *tr* to play the leading rôle of
protección *f* protection; **protección aduanera** protective tariff; **protección a la infancia** child welfare
proteger §17 *tr* to protect
protegida *f* protégée
protegido *m* protégé
proteína *f* protein
proter•vo -va *adj* perverse
protesta *f* protest; pledge, promise
protestante *adj* & *mf* protestant; Protestant
protestar *tr* to protest, asseverate; (*la fe*) to profess || *intr* to protest; **protestar de** (*aseverar con ahinco*) to protest (*to state positively*); **protestar contra** (*negar la validez de*) to protest (*to deny forcibly*)
protocolo *m* protocol
protoplasma *m* protoplasm
prototipo *m* prototype
protozoario or **protozoo** *m* protozoön
provec•to -ta *adj* old, ripe
provecho *m* advantage, benefit; profit, gain; advance, progress; **¡buen provecho!** good luck!; good appetite!; **de provecho** useful; **provechos** perquisites
provecho•so -sa *adj* advantageous, beneficial; profitable; useful
proveedor -dora *mf* supplier, provider, purveyor; steward
proveer §43 & §83 *tr* to provide, furnish; to supply; to resolve, settle || *intr* to provide; **proveer a** to provide for || *ref* to supply oneself; to have a movement of the bowels
provenir §79 *intr* to come, arise
Provenza, la Provence
provenzal *adj* & *mf* Provençal
proverbio *m* proverb
providencia *f* providence, foresight; step, measure
providencial *adj* providential
provincia *f* province
provisión *f* provision; supply, stock; **provisiones de boca** foodstuffs
proviso•rio -ria *adj* provisory, provisional
provocar §73 *tr* to provoke; to promote, bring about; to incite, to tempt, to move || *intr* to provoke; (coll) to vomit
proxeneta *mf* go-between
proximidad *f* proximity; **proximidades** neighborhood
próxi•mo -ma *adj* next; near; neighboring, close; early; **próximo pasado** last
proyección *f* projection; influence
proyectar *tr* to project; to cast; to design || *ref* to project, stick out; (*una sombra*) to be projected, to fall
proyectil *m* projectile; **proyectil buscador del blanco** homing missile; **proyectil dirigido** or **teleguiado** guided missile
proyecto *m* project; **proyecto de ley** bill
proyector *m* projector, searchlight; projection machine
prudencia *f* prudence
prudente *adj* prudent
prueba *f* proof; trial, test; examination; (*de un traje*) fitting; (*de un alimento o una bebida*) sample, sampling; evidence; (sport) event; (Am) acrobatics; (Am) sleight of hand; **a prueba** on approval, on trial; **a prueba de** proof against, -proof, e.g., **a prueba de escaladores** burglarproof;

pruebas de planas page proof; **pruebas de primeras** first proof (*for proofreader*); **pruebas de segundas** galley proof (*for author*)
pruebista *mf* (Am) acrobat
prurito *m* itching; eagerness, itch
psicoanálisis *m* psychoanalysis
psicoanalizar §60 *tr* to psychoanalyze
psicología *f* psychology
psicológi•co -ca *adj* psychologic(al)
psicólo•go -ga *mf* psychologist
psicópata *mf* psychopath
psico•sis *f* (*pl* **-sis**) psychosis; **psicosis de guerra** war psychosis, war scare
psicóti•co -ca *adj & mf* psychotic
psique *f* cheval glass || **Psique** *f* Psyche
psiquiatra *mf* psychiatrist
psiquiatría *f* psychiatry
psíqui•co -ca *adj* psychic
P.S.M. *abbr* **por su mandato**
pte. *abbr* **parte, presente**
púa *f* point; prick, barb; tine, prong; (*del fonógrafo*) needle; (*del peine*) tooth; thorn; (*del puerco espín*) spine, quill; sting; graft; plectrum; (coll) tricky person
pubertad *f* puberty
publicación *f* publication
publicar §73 *tr* to publish; to publicize
publicidad *f* publicity; advertising; **publicidad de lanzamiento** advance publicity
publicita•rio -ria *adj* publicity; advertising
públi•co -ca *adj & m* public
pucha *f* (W-I) small bouquet; (Mex) crescent roll
puchero *m* pot, kettle; stew; (coll) daily bread; (coll) pouting; **hacer pucheros** to pout, screw up one's face
pucho *m* (Am) fag end, remnant; (*de cigarro*) (Am) stump; (Am) trifle, trinket; (*el hijo menor*) (Am) baby
puden•do -da *adj* ugly, shameful; obscene; (*partes*) private
pudiente *adj* powerful; well-off, well-to-do
pudín *m* pudding
pudor *m* modesty, shyness; chastity
pudoro•so -sa *adj* modest, shy; chaste
pudrición *f* rot, rotting
pudrir §83 *tr* to rot; to worry || *intr* to be dead and buried || *ref* to rot; to be worried; (*en la cárcel*) to languish
pueblo *m* people; common people; town, village; **pueblo de Dios** or **de Israel** children of Israel
puente *m* bridge; (dent, mus) bridge; (aut) axle, rear axle; **hacer puente** to take the intervening day off; **puente aéreo** airlift, air bridge; **puente colgante** suspension bridge; **puente de engrase** grease lift; **puente levadizo** drawbridge, lift bridge
puer•co -ca *adj* piggish, hoggish; dirty, filthy; slovenly; coarse, mean; lewd || *m* hog; **puerco espín** or **espino** porcupine || *f* sow; slattern, slut
puericia *f* childhood
pueril *adj* puerile, childish
puerilidad *f* puerility, childishness
puerro *m* leek
puerta *f* door, doorway; gate, gateway; **a puerta cerrada** or **a puertas cerradas** behind closed doors
puerto *m* harbor, port; haven; mountain pass; **puerto aéreo** airport; **puerto brigantino** Corunna; **puerto de arribada** port of call; **puerto de mar** seaport; **puerto franco** free port; **puerto marítimo** dock, port; **puerto seco** frontier customhouse
puertorrique•ño -ña *adj & mf* Puerto Rican
pues *adv* then, well; yes, certainly; why; anyhow; **pues bien** well then; **pues que** since || *conj* for, since, because, inasmuch as || *interj* well!, then!
puesta *f* setting; laying; putting; (*dinero apostado*) stake; **a puesta del sol** or **a puestas del sol** at sunset; **puesta a punto** adjustment; carrying out, completion; **puesta a tierra** (elec) grounding; **puesta de largo** coming out, social debut
pues•to -ta *adj* dressed; **puesto que** since, inasmuch as || *m* place; booth, stand; office; station; barracks; (*para cazadores*) blind; **puesto de socorros** first-aid station || *f* see **puesta**
púgil *m* pugilist
pugilato *m* boxing; fist fight
pugilismo *m* pugilism
pugna *f* fight, battle; struggle, conflict; **en pugna** at issue; **en pugna con** at odds with
pugnar *intr* to fight; to struggle; to strive, persist
pug•naz *adj* (*pl* **-naces**) pugnacious
pujante *adj* powerful, mighty, vigorous
pujar *tr* (*un proyecto*) to push; (*un precio*) to raise, bid up || *intr* to struggle, strain; to falter; (*por decir una cosa*) to grope; (coll) to snivel; **pujar para adentro** (CAm, W-I) to keep silent, say nothing
pul•cro -cra *adj* neat, tidy, trim; circumspect
pulga *f* flea; **de malas pulgas** peppery, hot-tempered; **hacer de una pulga un camello** or **un elefante** (coll) to make a mountain out of a molehill; **no aguantar pulgas** (coll) to stand for no nonsense
pulgada *f* inch
pulgar *m* thumb
puli•do -da *adj* pretty; neat; polished; clean, spotless
pulimentar *tr* to polish
pulimento *m* polish
pulir *tr* to polish; to finish; to give a polish to
pulmón *m* lung; **pulmón de acero** or **de hierro** iron lung
pulmonía *f* pneumonia
púlpito *m* pulpit
pulpo *m* octopus
pulsación *f* pulsation, throb, beat; strike, striking; (*del pianista, el mecanógrafo*) touch
pulsar *tr* (*un botón*) to push; (*un piano, arpa, guitarra*) to play; (*una tecla*) to strike; to feel or take the pulse

of; to sound out, examine || *intr* to pulsate, throb, beat
pulsear *intr* to hand-wrestle
pulsera *f* bracelet; wristlet, watch strap; **pulsera de pedida** engagement bracelet
pulso *m* pulse; steadiness, steady hand; tact, care, caution; (Am) bracelet; (Am) wrist watch; **a pulso** with hand and wrist; by main strength; (*dibujo*) freehand; **sacar a pulso** (coll) to carry out against odds; **tomar el pulso a** to feel or take the pulse of
pulular *intr* to swarm; to bud, to sprout
pulverizar §60 *tr* to pulverize; to atomize; to spray
pulla *f* dig, cutting remark; filthy remark; witticism
pum *interj* bang!
puma *m* cougar
puna *f* (SAm) bleak tableland in the Andes; (SAm) mountain sickness
pundonor *m* point of honor; face
pundonoro·so -sa *adj* punctilious, scrupulous; haughty, dignified
pungir §27 *tr* to prick; to sting
punta *f* (*extremo agudo*) point; tip, end; (*del cigarro*) butt; nail; point, cape, headland; (*del toro*) horn; (*del asta del ciervo*) tine, prong; style, graver; touch, tinge, trace; (*del vino*) souring; (elec) point; **de punta** on end; on tiptoe; **de punta en blanco** in full armor; (coll) in full regalia; **estar de punta (con)** to be at odds (with); **punta de combate** (*del torpedo*) warhead; **punta de lanza** spearhead; **punta de París** wire nail; **sacar punta a** to put a point on, to sharpen; **tener en la punta de la lengua** (coll) to have on the tip of one's tongue
puntada *f* hint; (sew) stitch; (*dolor agudo*) (Am) stitch, sharp pain
puntal *m* prop, support; stay, stanchion; (naut) depth of hold; backing, support; (Am) bite, snack
puntapié *m* kick; **echar a puntapiés** (coll) to kick out
puntear *tr* to dot, mark with dots; (*guitarra*) to pluck; to stipple; to stitch || *intr* (naut) to tack
puntera *f* toe, toe patch; leather tip; (coll) kick
puntería *f* aim, aiming; marksmanship
puntero *m* pointer; (*del reloj*) hand; stonecutter's chisel; punch; (Am) leading animal
puntiagu·do -da *adj* sharp-pointed
puntilla *f* brad; narrow lace edging; (*de la pluma fuente*) point; (carp) tracing point; dagger; **de puntillas** on tiptoe; **puntilla francesa** finishing nail
puntillero *m* bullfighter who delivers coup de grace with dagger
puntillo·so -sa *adj* punctilious
punto *m* (*señal de dimensiones poco perceptibles*) point, dot; stitch, loop; mesh; (*rotura en un tejido de punto*) break; jot; cabstand, hackstand; (gram) period; (math, typ, sport, fig) point; **a buen punto** opportunely; **al punto** at once; **a punto de** on the point of; **a punto fijo** for certain; **de punto** knitted; **dos puntos** (gram) colon; **en punto** sharp, on the dot; **poner punto final a** to wind up, to bring to an end; **punto de admiración** exclamation mark or point; **punto de aguja** knitting; **punto de Hungría** herringbone; **punto de media** knitwork; **punto de mira** aim; center of attraction; **¡punto en boca!** mum's the word!; **punto interrogante** question mark; **punto menos** almost; **puntos y rayas** dots and dashes; **punto y coma** *msg* semicolon
puntuación *f* punctuation; mark, grade; scoring
puntual *adj* punctual; certain, sure; exact, accurate
puntualizar §60 *tr* to fix in the memory; to give a detailed account of; to finish; to draw up
puntuar §21 *tr & intr* to punctuate; to score
puntura *f* puncture, prick
punzada *f* prick; shooting pain; (*del remordimiento*) pang
punzante *adj* sharp, pricking; barbed, biting, caustic
punzar §60 *tr* to prick, puncture, punch; to sting; to grieve || *intr* to sting
punzón *m* punch; pick; burin, graver; budding horn, tenderling; **punzón de marcar** center punch
puñada *f* punch
puñado *m* handful, bunch
puñal *m* dagger, poniard
puñalada *f* stab; blow, sudden sorrow; **puñalada de misericordia** coup de grâce; **puñalada trapera** stab in the back
puñetazo *m* punch; bang with the fist
puño *m* fist; cuff; wristband; grasp; fistful, handful; hilt; (*p.ej., del paraguas*) handle; (*del bastón*) head; punch; **como un puño** (coll) whopping big; (coll) tiny, microscopic; (coll) close-fisted; **de su propio puño** or **de su puño y letra** in his own hand, in his own writing
pupa *f* pimple; fever blister
pupila *f* (*del ojo*) pupil
pupi·lo -la *mf* boarder; orphan, ward; pupil || *f* see **pupila**
pupitre *m* writing desk
puquio *m* (SAm) spring or pool of fresh, clear water
puré *m* purée; **puré de patatas** mashed potatoes; **puré de tomates** stewed tomatoes
pureza *f* purity
purga *f* purge; purgative; drain valve
purgante *adj & m* purgative
purgar §44 *tr* to purge; to physic; to drain; to purify, refine; to expiate; (*pasiones*) to control, to check; (*sospechas*) to clear away || *ref* to take a physic; to unburden oneself
puridad *f* purity
purificar §73 *tr* to purify

purita•no -na *adj & mf* puritan; Puritan
pu•ro -ra *adj* pure; sheer; (*cielo*) clear; out-and-out, outright; **de puro** completely, totally; because of being || *m* cigar
púrpura *f* purple
purpura•do -da *adj* purple || *m* (eccl) cardinal
purpúre•o -a *adj* purple
pusilánime *adj* pusillanimous
pústula *f* pustule
puta *f* whore
putañear or **putear** *intr* (coll) to whore around, to chase after lewd women
putati•vo -va *adj* spurious
putrefac•to -ta *adj* rotten, putrid
pútri•do -da *adj* putrid, rotten
puya *f* steel point; (*del gallo*) spur

Q

Q, q (cu) *f* twentieth letter of the Spanish alphabet
q.b.s.m. *abbr* **que besa su mano**
q.b.s.p. *abbr* **que besa sus pies**
q.e.p.d. *abbr* **que en paz descanse**
q.e.s.m. *abbr* **que estrecha su mano**
quántum *m* (*pl* **quanta**) quantum
que *pron rel* that, which; who, whom; **el que** he who; which, the one which; who, the one who || *adv* than || *conj* that; for, because; let, e.g., **que entre** let him come in; **a que** (coll) I'll bet that
qué *adj & pron interr* what, which; **¿qué tal?** how?; hello, how's everything? || *interj* what!; what a!; how!
quebrada *f* gorge, ravine, gap; failure, bankruptcy; (Am) brook
quebradi•zo -za *adj* brittle, fragile; frail
quebra•do -da *adj* weakened; bankrupt; ruptured; rough; winding; fractional || *m* (math) fraction; (Am) tobacco leaf full of holes || *f* see **quebrada**
quebrantable *adj* breakable
quebrantar *tr* to break; to break open; to break out of; to grind, crush; to soften, mollify; (*un contrato; la ley; un hábito; un testamento; el corazón de una persona*) to break || *ref* to break; to become broken
quebrantaterro•nes *m* (*pl* **-nes**) (coll) clodhopper
quebranto *m* break, breaking; heavy loss; great sorrow; discouragement
quebrar §2 *tr* to break; to bend, twist; to crush; to overcome; to temper, soften || *intr* to break; to fail; to weaken, give in || *ref* to break; to weaken; to become ruptured
queda *f* curfew
quedar *intr* to remain; to stay; to be left; to be left over; to stop, leave off; to turn out; to be; to be found, be located; **quedar en** to agree on; to agree to; **quedar por** + *inf* or **sin** + *inf* to remain to be + *pp* || *ref* to remain; to stay; to stop; to be; to be left; to put up; **quedarse con** to keep, to take; **quedarse tan fresco** (coll) to show no offense
que•do -da *adj* quiet, still; gentle || *f* see **queda** || **quedo** *adv* softly, in a low voice; gropingly
quehacer *m* work, task, chore
queja *f* complaint, lament; whine, moan
quejar *ref* to complain, lament; to whine, moan
quejido *m* complaint, whine, moan
quejumbre *f* complaining, whine, moan
quejumbro•so -sa *adj* complaining; whining, whiny
quema *f* fire; burning; **a quema ropa** point-blank; **de quema** distilled; **hacer quema** (Arg, Bol) to hit the mark
quemada *f* burnt brush; (Mex) fire
quemadero *m* incinerator; (*poste destinado para quemar a los condenados a la pena de fuego*) stake
quema•do -da *adj* burned; burnt out; (Am) angry || *m* burnt brush; **oler a quemado** (coll) to smell of fire; **saber a quemado** (coll) to taste burned || *f* see **quemada**
quema•dor -dora *adj* burning; incendiary || *m* burner
quemadura *f* burn; (agr) smut
quemar *tr* to burn; to scald; to set on fire; to scorch; to frostbite; to sell too cheap || *intr* to burn, be hot || *ref* to burn; to be burning up; (coll) to fret; (*estar cercano a lo que se busca*) (coll) to be warm, to be hot; **quemarse las cejas** (coll) to burn the midnight oil
quemarropa — a quemarropa point-blank
quemazón *f* burn; burning; intense heat; (*de un fusible*) blowout; (coll) itch; (coll) cutting remark; (coll) pique, anger; (hum) bargain sale; (Arg, Bol, Chile) mirage on the pampas
que•pis *m* (*pl* **-pis**) kepi
querella *f* complaint; dispute, quarrel
querellar *ref* to complain; to whine
querencia *f* liking, affection; attraction; love of home; (*de animales*) haunt; favorite spot
querencio•so -sa *adj* homing; (*sitio*) favorite
querer *m* love, affection; liking, fondness || *v* §55 *tr* to wish, want, desire; to like; to love; **como quiera** anyhow; anyway; **como quiera que** whereas; inasmuch as; no matter how; **cuando quiera** any time; **donde quiera** anywhere; **querer bien** to love; **sin querer** unwillingly; unintentionally || *v aux* to wish to, to want to, to desire to; will; to be about to, to be trying to,

e.g., **quiere llover** it is trying to rain; **querer decir** to mean; **querer más** to prefer to, would rather
queri•do -da *adj* dear || *mf* lover; paramour; (coll) dearie || *f* mistress
quermés *f* or **quermese** *f* bazaar; village or country fair
queroseno *m* var of **keroseno**
querubín *m* cherub
quesadilla *f* cheesecake; sweet pastry
quese•ro -ra *adj* cheesy || *mf* cheesemonger; cheesemaker || *f* cheese board; cheese mold; cheese dish
queso *m* cheese; **queso de cerdo** headcheese; **queso helado** brick ice cream
quevedos *mpl* nose glasses
quiá *interj* oh, no!
quicio *m* pivot hole (*of hinge*); **fuera de quicio** out of order; **sacar de quicio** to put out of order; to unhinge
quiebra *f* crack; damage, loss; bankruptcy
quien *pron rel* who, whom; he who, she who; someone who, anyone who
quién *pron interr* who, whom
quienquiera *pron indef* anyone, anybody; **quienquiera que** whoever; **a quienquiera que** whomever
quie•to -ta *adj* quiet, calm; virtuous
quietud *f* quiet, calm, stillness
quijada *f* jaw, jawbone
quijotes•co -ca *adj* quixotic
quilate *m* carat
quilo *m* kilogram; **sudar el quilo** (coll) to slave, be a drudge
quilla *f* keel; (*de ave*) breastbone; **dar de quilla** (naut) to keel over
quimera *f* chimera; dispute, quarrel
química *f* chemistry
quími•co -ca *adj* chemical || *mf* chemist || *f* see **química**
quimicultura *f* tank farming
quimono *m* kimono
quina *f* cinchona, Peruvian bark
quincalla *f* hardware
quincallería *f* hardware store; hardware business; hardware factory
quincalle•ro -ra *mf* hardware merchant
quince *adj & pron* fifteen || *m* fifteen; (*en las fechas*) fifteenth
quincea•vo -va *adj & m* fifteenth
quince•no -na *adj & m* fifteenth || *f* fortnight, two weeks; two weeks' pay
quincuagési•mo -ma *adj & m* fiftieth
quiniela *f* pelota game of five; soccer lottery; daily double; (Arg, Urug) numbers game
quinien•tos -tas *adj & pron* five hundred || **quinientos** *m* five hundred
quinina *f* quinine
quinqué *m* student lamp, oil lamp
quinquenal *adj* five-year
quinta *f* villa, country house; draft, induction; **ir a quintas** to be drafted; **redimirse de las quintas** to be exempted from the draft
quintacolumnista *mf* fifth columnist
quintal *m* quintal, hundredweight
quintar *tr* to draft
quinteto *m* quintet
quintilla *f* five-line stanza of eight syllables and two rhymes; any five-line stanza with two rhymes
quintilli•zo -za *mf* quint, quintuplet
Quintín — armar la de San Quintín to raise a rumpus, raise a row
quin•to -ta *adj* fifth || *m* fifth; lot; pasture; draftee || *f* see **quinta**
quinza•vo -va *adj & m* fifteenth
quiosco *m* kiosk, summerhouse; stand; **quiosco de música** bandstand; **quiosco de necesidad** comfort station; **quiosco de periódicos** newsstand
quiquiri•quí *m* (*pl* **-quíes**) cock-a-doodle-doo; (coll) cock of the walk
quirófano *m* operating room
quiromancia or **quiromancía** *f* palmistry
quiropodista *mf* chiropodist
quiroprácti•co -ca *adj* chiropractic || *mf* chiropractor
quirúrgi•co -ca *adj* surgical
quirurgo *m* surgeon
quiscal *m* grackle
quisicosa *f* puzzler
quisqui•do -da *adj* (Arg) constipated
quisquilla *f* trifle, triviality; **pararse en quisquillas** to bicker, to make a fuss over trifles; **quisquillas** hairsplitting, quibbling
quisquillo•so -sa *adj* trifling; touchy; fastidious; hairsplitting
quiste *m* cyst
quis•to -ta *adj* — **bien quisto** well-liked, welcome; **mal quisto** disliked, unwelcome
quitaesmalte *m* nail-polish remover
quitaman•chas (*pl* **-chas**) *mf* (*persona*) clothes cleaner, spot remover || *m* (*substancia*) clothes cleaner, spot remover
quitamo•tas *mf* (*pl* **-tas**) (coll) bootlicker, apple polisher
quitanie•ve *m* or **quitanie•ves** *m* (*pl* **-ves**) snowplow
quitapie•dras *m* (*pl* **-dras**) cowcatcher
quitapintura *m* paint remover
quitapón *m* pompon for draft mules; **de quitapón** detachable, removable
quitar *tr* to remove; to take away; (*la mesa*) to clear; (*esfuerzo, trabajo*) to save; (*tiempo*) to take; to free; to parry; **quitar algo a algo** to take something off something, to remove something from something; **quitar algo a uno** to remove something from someone; to take something away from someone || *intr* — **de quita y pon** detachable, removable || *ref* (*el sombrero, una prenda de vestir*) to take off; (*el sombrero en señal de cortesía*) to tip; (*una mancha*) to come out, to come off; (*un vicio*) to give up; to withdraw
quitasol *m* parasol
quite *m* removal; hindrance; dodge; (*en la esgrima*) parry; (taur) passes made with the cape to draw the bull away from the man in danger
quizá or **quizás** *adv* maybe, perhaps
quó•rum *m* (*pl* **-rum**) quorum

R

R, r (ere) *f* twenty-first letter of the Spanish alphabet
R. *abbr* **respuesta, Reverencia, Reverendo**
rabada *f* hind quarter, rump
rabadilla *f* base of the spine
rábano *m* radish; **rábano picante** or **rusticano** horseradish; **tomar el rábano por las hojas** (coll) to be on the wrong track
ra•bí *m* (*pl* **-bíes**) rabbi
rabia *f* anger, rage; (*hidrofobia*) rabies; **tener rabia a** (coll) to have a grudge against
rabiar *intr* to rage, to rave; to get mad; to go mad, to have rabies; **que rabia** like the deuce; **rabiar por** to be dying for; to be dying to
rabieta *f* (coll) tantrum
rabillo *m* leafstalk; flower stalk; (*en los cereales*) mildew spot; (*del ojo*) corner
rabio•so -sa *adj* mad, rabid
rabo *m* tail; (*del ojo*) corner; (fig) tail, train; **rabo verde** (CAm) old rake
ra•bón -bona *adj* bobtail; (Chile) bare, naked; (Mex) mean, wretched ‖ *f* (Am) camp follower; **hacer rabona** (coll) to play hooky
rabotada *f* swish of the tail; (coll) coarse remark
rabu•do -da *adj* long-tailed
racial *adj* racial
racimar *ref* to cluster, to gather together
racimo *m* bunch; cluster; (*de perlas*) string
raciocinio *m* reasoning
ración *f* ration; allowance; **ración de hambre** starvation wages
racional *adj* rational
racionar *tr* to ration
racha *f* split, crack; chip; squall, gust of wind; streak of luck
rada *f* (naut) road, roadstead
radar *m* radar
radiación *f* radiation
radiacti•vo -va *adj* radioactive
radia•dor -dora *adj* radiating ‖ *m* radiator
radiante *adj* radiant; (*alegre, sonriente*) radiant
radiar *tr* to radiate; to radio; to broadcast; to cross out, erase ‖ *intr* to radiate
radicación *f* taking root; (math) evolution
radical *adj & m* radical
radicar §73 *intr* to take root; to be located ‖ *ref* to take root; to settle; (*un negocio*) to be based
radio *m* edge, outskirts; (*de una rueda*) spoke, rung; (*de acción*) radius; (chem) radium; (math) radius ‖ *m & f* radio
radioaficiona•do -da *mf* radio amateur, radio fan
radiodifundir *tr & intr* to broadcast
radiodifusión *f* broadcasting
radioemisora *f* broadcasting station
radioescucha *mf* radio listener; radio monitor
radiofrecuencia *f* radio frequency
radiografiar §77 *tr* to X-ray; to radio, to wireless
radiograma *m* X ray (*photograph*)
radioperturbación *f* jamming
radioyente *mf* radio listener
raer §56 *tr* to scrape, scrape off; to smooth, to level; to wipe ‖ *ref* to become frayed, to wear away
ráfaga *f* gust, puff; gust of wind; flash of light; (*de ametralladora*) burst
raí•do -da *adj* threadbare; barefaced
ra•íz *f* (*pl* **-íces**) root; **a raíz de** close to the root of; even with; right after, hard upon; **de raíz** by the root; completely; **echar raíces** to take root
raja *f* crack, split; splinter, chip; slice
rajar *tr* to crack, to split; to splinter, chip; to slice ‖ *intr* (coll) to boast; (coll) to chatter ‖ *ref* to crack, to split; to splinter, chip; (Mex, CAm, W-I) to back down, to break one's promise
rajatabla — a rajatabla (coll) desperately, ruthlessly
ralea *f* kind, quality; breed, ilk
ralear *intr* to thin out; to be true to form
ra•lo -la *adj* sparse, thin
rallador *m* grater
rallar *tr* to grate; (coll) to grate on, annoy
rallo *m* grater; scraper; rasp; (*de la regadera*) spout, nozzle; unglazed porous jug (*for cooling water by evaporation*)
rama *f* branch, bough; **andarse por las ramas** (coll) to beat about the bush; **en rama** raw; unbound, in sheets; in the grain
ramaje *m* branches, foliage
ramal *m* (*de una cuerda*) strand; halter; branch; (rr) branch line
ramalazo *m* lash; (*señal en el cutis por un golpe o enfermedad*) spot, pock; sharp pain; blow, sudden sorrow
rambla *f* dry ravine; avenue, boulevard
ramera *f* whore, harlot
ramificar §73 *tr & ref* to ramify
ramillete *m* bouquet; centerpiece, epergne; (bot) cluster
ramo *m* branch, limb; bouquet, cluster; (*de géneros, negocios, etc.*) line; (*p.ej., de una ciencia*) branch; (*de una enfermedad*) touch, slight attack
ramojo *m* brushwood, dead wood
ramonear *intr* to trim twigs; to browse
rampa *f* ramp; cramp; (aer) apron; (Bol) litter, stretcher
ram•plón -plona *adj* (*zapato*) heavy, coarse; common, vulgar
ramplonería *f* coarseness, vulgarity
rana *f* frog; **no ser rana** (coll) to be a past master; **rana toro** bullfrog
ran•cio -cia *adj* rank, rancid, stale;

(*vino*) old; old, ancient; old, old-fashioned
ranchar *ref* (Col, Ven) to balk
ranchear *tr* (Am) to sack, pillage || *intr & ref* to build huts, form a settlement
ranchero *m* messman; (Am) rancher, ranchman
rancho *m* mess; meeting, gathering; camp; thatched hut; (naut) stock of provisions; (Am) ranch; (Arg) straw hat; **hacer rancho** (coll) to make room; **hacer rancho aparte** (coll) to be a lone wolf, to go one's own way
randa *m* (coll) pickpocket || *f* lace trimming
rango *m* rank; class, nature; (Am) pomp, splendor; (*elevada condición social*) (Am) status, standing
ranura *f* groove; slot
rapagón *m* stripling
rapar *tr* to shave; to crop; to scrape; (coll) to snatch, filch || *ref* to shave; (*una vida regalada*) to lead
ra·paz (*pl* **-paces**) *adj* thievish; rapacious || *m* young boy, lad
rapaza *f* young girl, lass
rapé *m* snuff
rápi·do -da *adj* rapid || *m* (rr) express; **rápidos** (*de un río*) rapids
raposa *f* fox; female fox; (*persona*) (coll) fox
raposo *m* male fox; (coll) foxy fellow; (coll) slipshod fellow
raptar *tr* to abduct; to kidnap
rapto *m* abduction; kidnaping; rapture; faint, swoon
raque *m* beachcombing; **andar al raque** to go beachcombing
raquear *intr* to beachcomb
raquero *m* pirate; beachcomber
raqueta *f* racket; battledore; badminton; snowshoe; **raqueta y volante** battledore and shuttlecock
raquíti·co -ca *adj* (*que padece raquitis*) rickety; flimsy, weak, miserable
raquitis *f* rickets
raramente *adv* rarely, seldom; oddly
rareza *f* rareness; rarity; oddness, strangeness; peculiarity
ra·ro -ra *adj* rare; odd, strange; thin, sparse
ras *m* evenness; **a ras** close, even, flush; **a ras de** even with, flush with; **ras con ras** flush, at the same level; grazing
rasar *tr* to graze, to skim || *ref* to clear up
rascacie·los *m* (*pl* **-los**) skyscraper
rascamoño *m* fancy hairpin; (bot) zinnia
rascar §73 *tr* to scrape; to scuff; to scratch; to scrape clean || *ref* (*una cicatriz, un grano*) to pick; (Am) to get drunk
rasete *m* satinet
rasga·do -da *adj* (*boca; ventana*) wide-open; (*ojos*) large; (Am) outspoken; (Col) generous || *m* tear, rip, rent
rasgar §44 *tr* to tear, to rip || *ref* to become torn
rasgo *m* (*de una pluma de escribir*) flourish, stroke; trait, characteristic; feat, deed; flash of wit, bright remark; **a grandes rasgos** in bold strokes; **rasgos** (*de la cara*) features
rasguear *tr* to thrum on || *intr* to make a flourish
rasgón *m* tear, rip, rent
rasguñar *tr* to scratch; to sketch, outline
rasguño *m* scratch; sketch, outline
ra·so -sa *adj* smooth, flat, level, even; common, plain; clear, cloudless; (coll) brazen, shameless || *m* flat country; satin; **al raso** in the open
raspa *f* stalk, stem; (*de mazorca de maíz*) beard; (*de pez*) spine, backbone; shell, rind
raspadura *f* scraping; erasure; (Am) pan sugar
raspar *tr* to scrape, scrape off; to scratch, scratch out; to graze; (*el vino*) to bite; to take, to steal; (W-I) to dismiss, fire; (W-I) to scold || *intr* (Ven) to go away; (Ven) to die
raspear *tr* (SAm) to scold || *intr* (*una pluma*) to scratch
rastra *f* rake; harrow; drag; track, trail; (*p.ej., de cebollas*) string; (naut) drag; **pescar a la rastra** to trawl
rastracuero *m* (Am) show-off; (Am) upstart; (Am) sharper, adventurer
rastreador *m* dredge; (nav) mine sweeper
rastrear *tr* to trail, track, trace; to drag; to dredge; to check into || *intr* to rake; to skim the ground, fly low
rastre·ro -ra *adj* dragging, trailing; creeping; low-flying; groveling, cringing; low, vile
rastrillar *tr* to rake; (*cáñamo, lino*) to hatchel, to comb; (Arg, Col) to shoot, to fire; (*un fósforo*) (Arg, Col) to strike (*a match*)
rastrillo *m* rake; hackle, hatchel, flax comb; (*de cerradura o llave*) ward; grating, iron grate; (rr) cowcatcher
rastro *m* rake; harrow; track, trail; scent; trace, vestige; slaughterhouse; wholesale meat market; rag fair; **rastro de condensación** (aer) contrail
rastrojo *m* stubble
rasura *f* shaving; scraping
rasurar *tr & ref* to shave
rata *f* rat; female rat; **rata del trigo** hamster
ratear *tr* to apportion; to snitch
ratería *f* baseness, meanness, vileness; petty thievery; petty theft
rate·ro -ra *adj* thievish; trailing, dragging; base, vile || *mf* sneak thief
ratificar §73 *tr* to ratify
rato *m* time, while, little while; **a ratos** from time to time; **a ratos perdidos** in spare time, in one's leisure hours; **buen rato** pleasant time; (coll) large amount; **pasar el rato** (coll) to waste one's time; **un rato** awhile
ratón *m* mouse; (Ven) hangover; **ratón de biblioteca** (coll) bookworm
ratonera *f* (*trampa*) mousetrap; (*agujero*) mousehole; nest of mice; (Am) hut, shop
raudal *m* stream, torrent; abundance
rau·do -da *adj* rapid, swift, impetuous

raya *f* stripe; (*línea fina; pez*) ray; (*en la imprenta, la escritura y la telegrafía*) dash; (*de los pantalones*) crease; (*en los cabellos*) part; boundary line, limit; (*para impedir la comunicación del incendio en los campos*) firebreak; (*del espectro*) (phys) line; (Mex) pay, wages; **a rayas** striped; **hacerse la raya** to part one's hair; **pasar de la raya** to go too far; **tener a raya** to keep within bounds
raya•no -na *adj* bordering; borderline
rayar *tr* (*papel*) to rule, to line; to stripe; to scratch, score, mark; to cross out; to underscore || *intr* to border; to stand out; (*el alba, el día, la luz, el sol*) to begin, arise, come forth; **rayar en** to verge on, to border on || *ref* (Col) to get rich
rayo *m* (*de luz*) ray; (*de rueda*) spoke; lightning, flash of lightning, stroke of lightning, thunderbolt; (*persona*) (fig) live wire; **echar rayos** (coll) to blow up, hit the ceiling; **rayo mortífero** death ray; **rayos X** X rays
rayón *m* rayon
raza *f* race; breed, stock; crack, slit; quality; ray of light (*coming through a crack*)
razón *f* reason; right, justice; account, story; (*cantidad o grado medidos por otra cosa tomada como unidad*) rate; (math) ratio; **a razón de** at the rate of; **con razón o sin ella** right or wrong; **hacer la razón** to return a toast; to join at table; **meterse en razón** to listen to reason; **no tener razón** to be wrong; **razón social** firm name, trade name; **tener razón** to be right; to be in the right
razonable *adj* reasonable
razonar *tr* to reason, reason out; to itemize || *intr* to reason
reabrir **§83** *tr & ref* to reopen
reacción *f* reaction; **reacción en cadena** chain reaction
reaccionar *intr* to react
reacciona•rio -ria *adj & mf* reactionary
rea•cio -cia *adj* stubborn, obstinate
reactivo *m* reagent
real *adj* real; royal; fine, splendid || *m* army camp; fairground; real (*old Spanish coin; Spanish money of account equal to a quarter of a peseta*)
realce *m* embossment, raised work; enhancement, lustre; emphasis; **bordar de realce** to embroider in relief; (fig) to embroider, to exaggerate
realeza *f* royalty
realidad *f* reality; truth; **hecho realidad** come true, e.g., **un sueño hecho realidad** a dream come true
realismo *m* realism
realista *mf* (*persona que tiende a ver las cosas como son*) realist; (*partidario de la monarquía*) royalist
realización *f* realization, fulfillment; achievement; sale; **realización de beneficios** profit taking
realizar **§60** *tr* to fulfill; to carry out; to turn into cash || *ref* to become fulfilled; to be carried out
realquilar *tr* to sublet
realzar **§60** *tr* to raise, elevate; to emboss; to enhance, set off; to emphasize
reanimar *tr* to revive, restore; to cheer, encourage || *ref* to revive, recover one's spirits
reanudar *tr* to renew, to resume
reaparecer **§22** *intr* to reappear
reata *f* rope to keep animals in single file; single file; **de reata** in single file; (coll) in blind submission; (coll) next, following
rebaba *f* burr, fin
rebaja *f* rebate; diminution
rebajar *tr* to lower; to diminish, reduce; to rebate; (*precios*) to mark down; (*a una persona*) to deflate; (carp) to rabbet || *ref* to stoop; to humble oneself
rebajo *m* rabbet, groove; offset, recess
rebalsar *tr* to dam || *ref* to become dammed up; to be checked; to pile up, accumulate
rebanada *f* slice
rebanar *tr* to slice; to cut through
rebañadera *f* grapnel
rebaño *m* flock
rebarbati•vo -va *adj* crabbed, surly
rebasar *tr* to exceed; to overflow; to sail past
rebatiña *f* grabbing, scramble; **andar a la rebatiña** (coll) to scramble
rebatir *tr* to repel, drive back; to check; to resist; to strengthen; to rebut, refute; to deduct, rebate; to beat hard
rebato *m* alarm, call to arms; alarm, excitement; (mil) surprise attack
rebeca *f* cardigan
rebelar *ref* to revolt, rebel; to resist; to break away
rebelde *adj* rebellious; stubborn || *mf* rebel
rebeldía *f* rebelliousness; defiance, stubbornness
rebelión *f* rebellion, revolt
rebe•lón -lona *adj* balky, restive
reborde *m* flange, rim, collar
rebosar *tr* to cause to overflow || *intr* to overflow, run over; to be in abundance; **rebosar de** or **en** to overflow with, to burst with; to be rich in; to have an abundance of || *ref* to overflow, run over
rebotar *tr* to bend back; to repel; (coll) to annoy, worry || *intr* to bounce; to bounce back, rebound || *ref* (coll) to become annoyed, become worried
rebote *m* bounce; rebound
rebozar **§60** *tr* (*la cara*) to muffle up; to cover with batter || *ref* to muffle up, to muffle oneself up
rebozo *m* muffling; muffler; shawl; **de rebozo** secretly; **sin rebozo** frankly, openly
rebulta•do -da *adj* bulky, massive
rebullicio *m* hubbub, loud uproar
rebullir **§13** *intr* to stir, begin to move; to give signs of life || *ref* to stir, begin to move
rebusca *f* seeking, searching; gleaning; leavings, refuse

rebusca•do -da *adj* affected, unnatural, recherché
rebuscar §73 *tr* to seek after; to search into; to glean
rebuznar *intr* to bray; (coll) to talk nonsense
rebuzno *m* braying; (coll) nonsense
recade•ro -ra *mf* messenger || *m* errand boy
recado *m* errand; message; gift, present; daily marketing; compliments, regards; safety, security; equipment, outfit; **mandar recado** to send word; **recado de escribir** writing materials
recaer §15 *intr* to fall again; to fall back; to relapse; to backslide; **recaer en** to fall to; **recaer sobre** to fall upon, devolve upon
recaída *f* relapse; backsliding
recalar *tr* to soak, saturate || *intr* to sight land
recalcar §73 *tr* to press, squeeze; to cram, pack, stuff; (*sus palabras*) to stress || *intr* (naut) to list, to heel; **recalcar en** to lay stress on || *ref* (coll) to harp on the same string; (coll) to sprawl; (*p.ej., la muñeca*) (coll) to sprain
recalentar §2 *tr* to overheat; (*la comida*) to warm over
recalmón *m* (naut) lull
recamado *m* embroidery
recamar *tr* to embroider
recámara *f* dressing room; (*de un arma de fuego*) breech, chamber; (coll) reserve, caution; (Mex) bedroom
recamarera *f* (Mex) chambermaid
recambio *m* spare part; (*parte, rueda, etc.*) **de recambio** spare
recapacitar *tr* to run over in one's mind || *intr* to refresh one's memory; to reflect
recargar §44 *tr* to reload; to overload; to recharge; to overcharge; to overadorn; (*una cuota de impuesto*) to increase; (elec) to recharge || *ref* to become more feverish
recargo *m* new burden; extra charge; new charge; (*que paga el contribuyente moroso*) penalty; (pathol) rise in temperature; **recargo de tarifa** extra fare
recata•do -da *adj* cautious, circumspect; modest; shy
recatar *tr* to hide, conceal || *ref* to hide; to be afraid to take a stand
recato *m* caution, reserve; modesty
recauchutaje *m* recapping, retreading
recauchutar *tr* to recap, to retread
recaudar *tr* (*impuestos, tributos*) to gather, collect; to guard, watch over
recaudo *m* tax collecting; care, precaution; bail, surety; **a buen recaudo** under guard, in safety
recelar *tr* to fear, distrust || *intr & ref* to fear, be afraid
recelo *m* fear, distrust
recelo•so -sa *adj* fearful, distrustful
recensión *f* review, book review
recepción *f* reception; reception desk
recepcionista *m* room clerk || *f* receptionist
receptáculo *m* receptacle; shelter, refuge
receptar *tr* to receive, welcome; (*delincuentes*) to hide, conceal; (*cosas robadas*) to receive
recepti•vo -va *adj* receptive; susceptible
receptor *m* receiver; **receptor de cabeza** headpiece; **receptor telefónico** receiver
receta *f* recipe; (pharm) prescription
recetar *tr* (*un medicamento*) to prescribe; (coll) to request
recibí *m* receipt; received payment
recibi•dor -dora *mf* receiver; receiving teller; ticket collector || *m* reception room
recibimiento *m* reception; welcome; reception room; (*visita en que una persona recibe a sus amistades*) athome
recibir *tr* to receive; (*visitas*) to entertain || *intr* to receive; to entertain || *ref* to be received, be admitted; **recibirse de** to be admitted to practice as; to be graduated as
recibo *m* reception; receipt; hall; parlor; at-home; **acusar recibo de** to acknowledge receipt of; **estar de recibo** to be at home; **ser de recibo** to be acceptable
recién *adv* (used before past participles) recently, just, newly, e.g., **recién llegado** newly arrived; (Am) just now, recently
reciente *adv* recently
recinto *m* area, inclosure, place
re•cio -cia *adj* strong; thick, coarse, heavy; harsh; hard, bitter, arduous; (*tiempo*) severe; swift, impetuous || **recio** *adv* strongly; swiftly; hard; loud
reciprocidad *f* reciprocity
recípro•co -ca *adj* reciprocal
recital *m* (*de música o poesía*) recital
recitar *tr* to recite; (*un discurso*) to deliver
reclamación *f* claim, demand; objection; protest, complaint
reclamar *tr* to claim, demand; (*un ave*) to decoy, lure || *intr* to cry out, protest, complain
reclamo *m* bird call; decoy bird; (*para aves*) lure; allurement, attraction; advertisement; blurb, puff; reference; (typ) catchword
reclinar *tr* (*p.ej., la cabeza*) to lean, to bend || *ref* to recline
reclinatorio *m* prie-dieu; couch, lounge
recluir §20 *tr* to seclude, shut in; to imprison || *ref* to go into seclusion
reclusión *f* seclusion; imprisonment
reclu•so -sa *adj* secluded; imprisoned || *mf* prisoner; inmate
recluta *m* recruit || *f* recruiting; (*del ganado disperso*) (Arg) roundup
reclutar *tr* to recruit; (Arg) to round up
recobrar *tr* to recover || *ref* to recover; to come to
recobro *m* recovery; (*de un motor*) pickup
recodar *intr* to lean; to bend, twist, turn, wind
recodo *m* bend, twist, turn
recoger §17 *tr* to pick up; to gather,

collect; to harvest; to shorten, draw in; to keep; to welcome; to lock up || *ref* to take shelter, take refuge; to withdraw; (*echarse en la cama*) to retire; to go home; to cut down expenses

recogida *f* collection; withdrawal; suspension

recogimiento *m* gathering, collecting; harvesting; seclusion, retreat; concentration; self-communion

recolectar *tr* to gather, gather in; (*el algodón*) to pick

recomendable *adj* commendable

recomendar **§2** *tr* to recommend; to commend

recompensa *f* recompense, reward

recompensar *tr* to recompense, reward

recomprar *tr* to buy back, to repurchase

reconcentrar *tr* to bring together; (*un sentimiento o afecto*) to conceal, disguise || *ref* to come together; to be absorbed in thought

reconciliar *tr* to reconcile || *ref* to become reconciled

recóndi•to -ta *adj* hidden, concealed

reconfortar *tr* to comfort, to cheer

reconocer **§22** *tr* to recognize; to admit, to acknowledge; to examine; (mil) to reconnoiter || *intr* (mil) to reconnoiter || *ref* to be clear

reconoci•do -da *adj* grateful

reconocimiento *m* recognition; admission, acknowledgment; gratitude; reconnaissance; **reconocimiento médico** inquest

reconquista *f* reconquest

reconsiderar *tr* to reconsider

reconstruir **§20** *tr* to reconstruct, to rebuild, to recast

recontar **§61** *tr* (*volver a contar; narrar*) to recount (*to count again; to narrate*)

reconvenir **§79** *tr* to expostulate with, to remonstrate with

reconversión *f* reconversion

recopilar *tr* to compile

re•cord *m* (*pl* **-cords**) (sport) record; **batir un record** to break a record; **establecer un record** to make a record

recordar **§61** *tr* to remember; to remind || *intr* to remember; to get awake; to come to; **si mal no recuerdo** (coll) if I remember correctly

recordati•vo -va *adj* reminding, reminiscent || *m* reminder

recordatorio *m* reminder; memento

record•man (*pl* **-men**) record holder

recorrer *tr* to go over, to go through; to look over, look through; (*un libro*) to run through; to overhaul

recorrido *m* trip, run, route; (*del émbolo*) stroke; repair

recortado *m* cutout

recortar *tr* to trim, to cut off; (*figuras en una tela, en un papel*) to cut out; to outline || *ref* to stand out

recorte *m* cutting; (*de un periódico*) clipping; dodge, duck; **recortes** cuttings, trimmings

recostar **§61** *tr* to lean || *ref* to lean, lean back, sit back

recova *f* poultry business; poultry stand; (Arg) portico; (SAm) food market

recoveco *m* bend, turn, twist; subterfuge, trick

recreación *f* recreation

recreo *m* recreation; place of amusement

recrudecer **§22** *intr & ref* to flare up, get worse

rectángu•lo -la *adj* right-angled || *m* rectangle

rectificar **§73** *tr* to rectify; (*un cilindro de motor*) to rebore

rec•to -ta *adj* straight; (*ángulo*) right; right, just, righteous || *m* rectum

rec•tor -tora *adj* governing, managing || *mf* principal, superior || *m* rector; (*de una universidad*) rector, president

recua *f* drove; (*de personas o cosas*) (coll) string, line

recuadro *m* panel, square; (*sección de un impreso encerrada dentro de un marco*) box

recubrir **§83** *tr* to cover, cap, coat

recuento *m* count; recount; inventory

recuerdo *m* memory, remembrance; keepsake, souvenir

recuero *m* muleteer

recular *intr* to back up; (*un arma de fuego*) to recoil; (coll) to back down

reculón *m* (Am) backing; **a reculones** (coll) backing away, recoiling

recuperar *tr & ref* to recuperate, to recover

recurrir *intr* to resort, have recourse; to revert

recurso *m* recourse; resource; resort; appeal, petition

recusar *tr* to refuse, reject; (law) to challenge

rechazar **§60** *tr* to refuse, to reject; to repel, drive back

rechazo *m* rejection; rebound, recoil

rechifla *f* catcall

rechiflar *tr & intr* to catcall, to hiss || *ref* to make fun

rechinar *intr* to creak, grate, squeak; to act with bad grace

rechon•cho -cha *adj* (coll) chubby, tubby, plump

rechupete — **de rechupete** (coll) fine, wonderful

red *f* net; netting; network, system; baggage netting; (fig) net, snare, trap; **a red barredera** with a clean sweep; **red barredera** dragnet

redacción *f* writing; editing; editorial staff; newspaper office, city room

redactar *tr* to write up; to edit

redac•tor -tora *mf* writer; editor, newspaper editor; **redactor publicitario** copy writer

redada *f* (*de peces*) catch, netful; (*p.ej., de criminales*) (coll) haul, roundup

redecilla *f* hair net

rededor *m* surroundings; **al rededor (de)** around

redención *f* redemption; help, recourse

reden•tor -tora *mf* redeemer

redición *f* constant repetition

redi•cho -cha *adj* (coll) overprecise

redil *m* sheepfold

redimir *tr* to redeem; to ransom; to buy back
rédito *m* income, revenue, yield
redituar §21 *tr* to yield, produce
redobla·do -da *adj* stocky, heavy-built; heavy, strong; (mil) double-quick
redoblar *tr* to double; to clinch; to repeat || *intr* (*un tambor*) to roll
redoble *m* doubling; clinching; repeating; roll of a drum
redoma *f* phial, flask
redoma·do -da *adj* sly, crafty
redonda *f* district, neighborhood; (mus) semibreve; **a la redonda** around, roundabout
redondear *tr* to round, make round; to round off; to round out || *ref* to be well-off; to be out of debt
redondel *m* circle; round cloak; (*espacio destinado a la lidia*) (taur) ring
redondilla *f* eight-syllable quatrain with rhyme abba or abab
redon·do -da *adj* round; straightforward; (*terreno*) pasture; (Am) honest; (Am) stupid || *m* ring, circle; (coll) cash || *f* see **redonda**
redopelo *m* (coll) row, scuffle; **al redopelo** against the grain, the wrong way; (coll) roughly, violently
reducir §19 *tr & ref* to reduce; **reducirse a** to come to, to amount to; to be obliged to
reducto *m* (fort) redoubt
redundante *adj* redundant
redundar *intr* to redound; to overflow; **redundar en** to redound to
reelección *f* reëlection
reembarcar §73 *tr, intr & ref* to reship, to reëmbark
reembarco *m* reshipment (*of persons*), reëmbarkation
reembarque *m* reshipment (*of goods*)
reembolsar *tr* to reimburse; to refund || *ref* to collect a debt, to be reimbursed
reembolso *m* reimbursement; refund; **contra reembolso** collect on delivery; cash on delivery
reemplazar §60 *tr* to replace
reemplazo *m* replacement; (mil) replacements; (*hombre que sirve en lugar de otro*) (mil) replacement
reencuadernar *tr* (bb) to rebind
reencuentro *m* collision; (*de tropas*) clash
reenganchar *tr & ref* to reënlist
reentrada *f* reëntry
reestrenar *tr* (theat) to revive
reestreno *m* (theat) revival
reexamen *m* or **reexaminación** *f* reëxamination
reexpedición *f* forwarding, reshipment
reexpedir §50 *tr* to forward, reship
refacción *f* refreshment; allowance; repair, repairs; (coll) extra, bonus; (Am) spare part
refajo *m* underskirt, slip
referencia *f* reference; account, report
referi·do -da *adj* above-mentioned
referir §68 *tr* to refer; to tell, report || *ref* to refer
refinamiento *m* refinement
refinar *tr* to refine; to polish, perfect
refinería *f* refinery
reflejar *tr* to reflect; to reflect on; to show, reveal || *intr* to reflect
reflejo *m* glare; reflection; reflex; **reflejo patelar** or **rotuliano** knee jerk
reflexión *f* reflection
reflexionar *tr* to reflect on or upon || *intr* to reflect
reflujo *m* ebb
refocilar *tr* to cheer; to strengthen || *intr* (Arg, Urug) to lighten || *ref* to be cheered; to take it easy
reforma *f* reform; reformation; alteration, renovation || **la Reforma** the Reformation
reformación *f* reformation
reformar *tr* to reform; to mend, repair; to alter, renovate; to revise; to reorganize || *ref* to reform; to hold oneself in check
reforzar §35 *tr* to reinforce; to strengthen; to encourage
refracción *f* refraction
refracta·rio -ria *adj* rebellious, unruly, stubborn
refrán *m* proverb, saying
refregar §66 *tr* to rub; (coll) to upbraid
refrenar *tr* to curb, to rein; to check, restrain
refrendar *tr* to countersign; to authenticate; to visé; (coll) to repeat
refrescar §73 *tr* to refresh; to cool, to refrigerate || *intr & ref* to refresh; to refresh oneself; to cool off; to go out for fresh air; (*el viento*) (naut) to blow up
refresco *m* refreshment; cold drink, soft drink
refriega *f* fray, scuffle
refrigerador *m* refrigerator; ice bucket
refrigerio *m* coolness; relief; pick-me-up, light lunch
refuerzo *m* reinforcement
refugia·do -da *mf* refugee
refugiar *tr* to shelter || *ref* to take refuge
refugio *m* refuge; hospice; shelter; haunt; (*para peatones en medio de la calle*) safety zone; **refugio antiaéreo** air-raid shelter; **refugio antiatómico** fallout shelter
refundición *f* recast; revision; (*de una pieza dramática*) adaptation
refundir *tr* to recast; to revise; (*una pieza dramática*) to adapt || *intr* to redound
refunfuñar *intr* to grumble, to growl
refutar *tr* to refute
regadera *f* watering can; street sprinkler
regadí·o -a or **regadi·zo -za** *adj* irrigable || *m* irrigated land
regala *f* gunwale
regala·do -da *adj* dainty, delicate; pleasing, pleasant; (*vida*) of ease
regalar *tr* to give; to regale, entertain; to treat; to caress, fondle; to indulge
regalía *f* privilege, perquisite; bonus; (Arg, Chile) muff; (Am) royalty
regaliz *m* licorice
regalo *m* gift, present; treat; joy, pleasure; **regalos de fiesta** favors
rega·lón -lona *adj* (coll) comfort-loving, pampered; (*vida*) (coll) soft, easy
regañar *tr* (coll) to scold || *intr* to

growl, snarl; to grumble; to quarrel; (coll) to scold
regaño *m* (coll) scolding; growl, snarl; grumble
regar **§66** *tr* to water, sprinkle; to irrigate; to spread, sprinkle, strew
regate *m* dodge, duck; (fig) dodge, subterfuge
regatear *tr* to haggle over; to sell at retail; (coll) to avoid, to shun || *intr* to haggle, to bargain; (naut) to race; (coll) to duck, to dodge
regazo *m* lap
regenerar *tr & ref* to regenerate
regente *m* director, manager; registered pharmacist; (typ) foreman
regicida *mf* regicide
regicidio *m* regicide
regi•dor -dora *adj* ruling, governing || *m* alderman, councilman
régimen *m* (*pl* **regímenes**) regime; diet; rate; management; (gram) government; **régimen de hambre** starvation diet; **régimen de justicia** rule of law
regimental *adj* regimental
regimentar **§2** *tr* to regiment
regimiento *m* regiment; rule, government; city council
re•gio -gia *adj* regal, royal; magnificent
región *f* region
regir **§57** *tr* to rule, govern; to control, manage; to guide, steer; (gram) to govern || *intr* to prevail, be in force
registra•dor -dora *adj* registering; recording || *m* registrar, recorder; inspector || *f* cash register
registrar *tr* to register; to record; to examine, inspect || *ref* to register; to be recorded; to take place
registro *m* registration, registry; recording; examination, inspection; entry, record; bookmark; manhole; (*de chimenea*) damper; (*de reloj*) regulator; (*de órgano*) (mus) stop; (*de piano*) (mus) pedal
regla *f* rule; (*para trazar líneas*) ruler; measure, moderation; order; menstruation; **regla de cálculo** slide rule; **reglas** monthlies, menses
reglamenta•rio -ria *adj* prescribed, statutory
reglamento *m* rules, regulations
reglar *tr* to regulate; (*papel*) to rule || *ref* to guide oneself, be guided
regleta *f* (typ) lead
regletear *tr* (typ) to lead, to space
regocijar *tr* to cheer, delight || *ref* to rejoice
regocijo *m* cheer, delight, rejoicing
regoldar **§3** *intr* to belch
regolfar *intr & ref* to surge back, flow back, back up
regorde•te -ta *adj* dumpy, plump
regresar *intr* to return
regreso *m* return; **estar de regreso** to be back
regüeldo *m* belch, belching
reguero *m* drip, trickle; (*señal que deja una cosa que se va vertiendo*) track; irrigating ditch; **ser un reguero de pólvora** to spread like wildfire
regulador *m* regulator; (*de locomotora*) throttle; (mach) governor
regular *adj* regular; fair, moderate, medium; **por lo regular** as a rule || *tr* to regulate; to put in order; to throttle
rehacer **§39** *tr* to remake, make over, do over; to mend, repair, renovate || *ref* to recover, to rally
rehén *m* hostage; **llevarse en rehenes** to carry off as a hostage
rehilandera *f* pinwheel
rehilar *intr* to quiver; to whiz by
rehilete *m* shuttlecock; (*que se lanza por diversión*) dart; dig, cutting remark; (taur) banderilla
rehuir **§20** *tr* to avoid, shun; to shrink from; to refuse; to dislike || *intr & ref* to flee
rehusar *tr* to refuse, turn down
reimpresión *f* reprint
reimprimir **§83** *tr* to reprint
reina *f* queen; **reina Margarita** aster, China aster; **reina viuda** queen dowager
reinado *m* reign
reinar *intr* to reign; to prevail
reincidir *intr* to backslide; to repeat an offense
reingreso *m* reëntry
reino *m* kingdom; **Reino Unido** United Kingdom
reinstalar *tr* to reinstate, reinstall
reintegrar *tr* to refund, pay back
reintegro *m* refund, payment
reír **§58** *tr* to laugh at || *intr & ref* to laugh; **reír de** or **reírse de** to laugh at
reja *f* grate, grating, grille; plowshare, colter; **entre rejas** behind bars
rejilla *f* screen; grating; lattice, latticework; cane, cane upholstery; foot brasier; fire grate; (electron) grid; (*de acumulador*) (elec) grid; (rr) baggage rack
rejón *m* spear; dagger; (taur) lance
rejonear *tr* (*el jinete al toro*) (taur) to jab with a lance made to break off in the bull's neck
rejuvenecimiento *m* rejuvenation
relación *f* relation; account; list; (*en un drama*) speech; **relación de ciego** blind man's ballad; **relaciones** betrothal, engagement
relacionar *tr* to relate || *ref* to be related
relai *m* or **relais** *m* (elec) relay
relajación *f* or **relajamiento** *m* relaxation; slackening; laxity; rupture, hernia
relajar *tr* to relax; to slacken; to debauch || *intr* to relax || *ref* to relax, become relaxed; to become debauched; to be ruptured
relamer *ref* to lick one's lips; to gloat; to relish; to boast; to slick oneself up
relami•do -da *adj* prim, overnice
relámpago *m* flash of lightning; flash of wit; **relámpago fotogénico** flash bulb, flashlight; **relámpagos** lightning
relampaguear *intr* to lighten; to flash
relatar *tr* to relate, report
relati•vo -va *adj* relative
relato *m* story; statement, report
relé *m* (elec) relay
releer **§43** *tr* to reread

relegar §44 *tr* to relegate; to banish, exile; to shelve, lay aside
relente *m* night dew, light drizzle
relevador *m* (elec) relay
relevante *adj* outstanding
relevar *tr* to emboss; to make stand out; to relieve; to release; to absolve; to replace || *intr* to stand out in relief
relevo *m* (elec) relay; (mil) relief; **relevos** (sport) relay race
relicario *m* shrine; (*medallón*) (Am) locket
relieve *m* relief; merit, distinction; **en relieve** in relief; **poner de relieve** to point out; to make stand out; **relieves** scraps, leftovers
religión *f* religion
religio•so -sa *adj* religious
relinchar *intr* to neigh
relincho *m* neigh, neighing; cry of joy
reliquia *f* relic; trace, vestige; **reliquia de familia** heirloom
reloj *m* watch; clock; meter; **como un reloj** like clockwork; **conocer el reloj** to know how to tell time; **reloj de caja** grandfather's clock; **reloj de carillón** chime clock; **reloj de cuclillo** cuckoo clock; **reloj de ocho días cuerda** eight-day clock; **reloj de pulsera** wrist watch; **reloj de sol** sundial; **reloj despertador** alarm clock; **reloj registrador** time clock; **reloj registrador de tarjetas** punch clock
relojera *f* watch case; watch pocket
relojería *f* watchmaking, clockmaking; watchmaker's shop
reloje•ro -ra *mf* watchmaker, clockmaker || *f* see **relojera**
reluciente *adj* shining, brilliant, flashing
relucir §45 *intr* to shine
relumbrar *intr* to shine, dazzle, glare
relumbre *m* beam, sparkle; flash; dazzle, glare
relumbrón *m* flash, glare; tinsel; **de relumbrón** showy, tawdry
rellano *m* (*en la pendiente de un terreno*) level stretch; (*de escalera*) landing
rellenar *tr* to refill; to fill up; to stuff; to pad; to fill out; (coll) to cram, to stuff || *ref* to fill up; (coll) to cram, stuff oneself
relle•no -na *adj* full, packed; stuffed || *m* refill; filling, stuffing; padding, wadding; (*en un escrito*) filler
remachar *tr* (*un clavo ya clavado*) to clinch; (*un roblón*) to rivet; to stress, emphasize || *ref* (Col) to maintain strict silence
remache *m* clinching; riveting; rivet
remanso *m* dead water, backwater
remar *intr* to row; to toil, struggle
remata•do -da *adj* hopeless; **loco rematado** (coll) raving mad
rematar *tr* to finish, put an end to; to finish off, kill off; (*en una subasta*) to knock down || *intr* to end || *ref* to come to ruin
remate *m* end; crest, top, finial; closing; highest bid; (*en una subasta*) sale; **de remate** hopelessly
remecer §46 *tr & ref* to shake, swing, rock
remedar *tr* to copy, imitate; to ape, mimic; to mock
remediar *tr* to remedy; to help; to prevent; (*del peligro*) to free, to save
remediava•gos *m* (*pl* **-gos**) short cut
remedio *m* remedy; help; recourse; **no hay remedio** or **no hay más remedio** it can't be helped; **no tener remedio** to be unavoidable
remedión *m* (theat) substitute performance
remedo *m* copy, imitation; poor imitation
remendar §2 *tr* to patch, mend, repair; to darn; to emend, correct; to touch up
remen•dón -dona *mf* mender, repairer; shoe mender; tailor (*who does mending*)
reme•ro -ra *mf* rower || *m* oarsman
remesa *f* remittance; shipment
remesar *tr* to remit; to ship
remezón *m* (Am) hard shake; (Am) tremor
remiendo *m* patch; mending, repair; retouching; emendation, correction; job printing, job work; **a remiendos** (coll) piecemeal
remilga•do -da *adj* prim and finicky; affected, smirking
remilgar §44 *intr* to be prim and finicky, to smirk
remilgo *m* primness, affectation
remira•do -da *adj* circumspect, discreet
remisión *f* remission; reference
remitente *mf* sender, shipper
remitido *m* (*noticia de un particular a un periódico*) personal; letter to the editor
remitir *tr* to remit; to forward, send, ship; to refer; to defer, postpone; to pardon, forgive || *intr* to remit, let up; to refer || *ref* to remit, let up; to defer, yield
remo *m* oar; leg, arm, wing; toil, labor; (sport) rowing; **aguantar los remos** to lie or rest on one's oars
remoción *f* discharge, dismissal; removal
remojar *tr* to soak, to steep, to dip; to celebrate with a drink; **remojar la palabra** (coll) to wet one's whistle
remojo *m* soaking, steeping; **poner en remojo** (coll) to put off to a more suitable time
remolacha *f* beet; **remolacha azucarera** sugar beet
remolcador *m* tug, tugboat; towboat; tow car
remolcar §73 *tr* to tow; to take in tow
remoler §47 *tr* to grind up; (coll) to bore
remolinear *tr, intr & ref* to eddy, whirl about
remolino *m* eddy, whirlpool; swirl, whirl; disturbance, commotion; throng, crowd; cowlick
remo•lón -lona *adj* lazy, indolent || *mf* shirker, quitter
remolonear *intr* to refuse to budge
remolque *m* tow; towing; trailer; **a remolque** in tow
remontar *tr* to mend, repair; to frighten

away; to elevate, raise up; (*p.ej., un río*) to go up || *intr* (*en el tiempo*) to go back || *ref* to rise, rise up; to soar; (*en el tiempo*) to go back
remontuar *m* stem-winder
remoquete *m* punch; nickname; sarcasm; (coll) flirting
rémora *f* hindrance, obstacle
remordimiento *m* remorse
remo•to -ta *adj* remote; unlikely; **estar remoto** to be rusty
remover §47 *tr* to remove; to shake; to stir; to disturb, upset; to dismiss, to discharge || *ref* to move away
remozar §60 *tr* to rejuvenate || *ref* to become rejuvenated
rempujar *tr* (coll) to push, jostle
rempujón *m* (coll) push, jostle
remuda *f* change, replacement; change of clothes
remudar *tr* to change, replace; to move around
remuneración *f* remuneration; **remuneración por rendimiento** piece wage
renacer §22 *intr* to be reborn, to be born again; to recover
renacimiento *m* rebirth; renaissance
renacuajo *m* tadpole; (coll) shrimp, little squirt
Renania *f* Rhineland
ren•co -ca *adj* lame
rencor *m* rancor; **guardar rencor** to bear malice
rendición *f* surrender; submission; fatigue, exhaustion; yield
rendi•do -da *adj* tired, worn-out; submissive
rendija *f* crack, split, slit
rendimiento *m* submission; exhaustion; yield; output; (mech) efficiency
rendir §50 *tr* to conquer; to subdue; to surrender; to exhaust, wear out; to return, give back; to yield, produce; (*gracias, obsequios, homenaje*) to render || *intr* to yield || *ref* to surrender; to yield, give in; to be exhausted, to be worn out
renegar §66 *tr* to deny vigorously; to abhor, detest || *intr* to curse; (coll) to be insulting; **renegar de** to deny; to curse; to abhor, detest
renegociación *f* renegotiation
Renfe, la acronym for **la Red Nacional de los Ferrocarriles Españoles** the Spanish National Railroad System
renglón *m* line; **a renglón seguido** right below; **leer entre renglones** to read between the lines
reniego *m* curse
reno *m* reindeer
renombra•do -da *adj* renowned, famous
renombre *m* renown, fame
renovar §61 *tr* to renew; to renovate; to transform, restore; to remodel
renquear *intr* to limp
renta *f* income; private income; annuity; public debt; rent; **renta nacional** gross national product
rentar *tr* to produce, yield
rentista *mf* bondholder; financier; person of independent means
renuente *adj* reluctant, unwilling
renuevo *m* sprout, shoot; renewal
renuncia *f* renunciation; resignation; (law) waiver
renunciar *tr* to renounce; to resign || *intr* to renounce; (*no servir al palo que se juega*) to renege; **renunciar a** to give up, to renounce, to waive
renuncio *m* slip, mistake; (*en juegos de naipes*) renege; (coll) lie
reñi•do -da *adj* on bad terms; bitter, hard-fought
reñir §72 *tr* (*regañar*) to scold; (*una batalla, un desafío*) to fight || *intr* to fight; to be at odds, to fall out
re•o -a *adj* guilty, criminal || **reo** *mf* offender, criminal; (law) defendant
reojo — de reojo askance, out of the corner of one's eye; hostilely
reorganizar §60 *tr & ref* to reorganize
reóstato *m* rheostat
repanchigar or **repantigar §44** *ref* to sprawl, to loll
reparar *tr* to repair, to mend; to make amends for; to notice, observe; (*un golpe*) to parry || *intr* to stop; **reparar en** to notice, pay attention to || *ref* to stop; to refrain
reparo *m* repairing, repairs; notice, observation; doubt, objection; shelter; bashfulness
repa•rón -rona *adj* (coll) faultfinding || *mf* (coll) faultfinder
repartir *tr* to distribute; (*naipes*) to deal
reparto *m* distribution; (*de naipes*) deal; (theat) cast; **reparto de acciones gratis** stock dividend
repasar *tr* to repass; to retrace; to review; to revise; (*la ropa*) to mend
repasata *f* (coll) scolding, reprimand
repaso *m* revision; (*de una lección*) review; mending; (coll) reprimand
repatriar §77 *tr* to repatriate; to send home || *intr & ref* to be repatriated; to go or come home
repeler *tr* to repel, to repulse
repente *m* start, sudden movement; **de repente** suddenly
repenti•no -na *adj* sudden, unexpected
repentista *mf* (mus) improviser; (mus) sight reader
repentizar §60 *intr* to improvise; (mus) to sight-read, perform at sight
repercutir *intr* to rebound; to reëcho, reverberate
repertorio *m* repertory
repetición *f* repetition; (mus) repeat
repetir §50 *tr & intr* to repeat
repicar §73 *tr* to mince, to chop up; to ring, to sound; to sting again || *intr* to peal, ring out, resound || *ref* to boast, be conceited
repique *m* chopping, mincing; peal, ringing; (coll) squabble, quarrel
repiqueteo *m* pealing, ringing; beating, rapping
repisa *f* shelf, ledge; bracket; **repisa de chimenea** mantelpiece; **repisa de ventana** window sill
replantear *tr* to lay out again; to reaffirm, to reimplement
replegar §66 *tr* to fold over and over || *ref* to fold, fold up; (mil) to fall back
reple•to -ta *adj* replete, full, loaded; fat, chubby

réplica *f* answer, retort; replica
replicar **§73** *tr* to argue against || *intr* to answer back, retort
repli·cón -cona *adj* (coll) saucy, flip
repliegue *m* fold, crease; (mil) falling back
repollo *m* cabbage; (*p.ej., de lechuga, col*) head
reponer **§54** *tr* to replace, put back; to restore; (*una pieza dramática*) to revive; **repuso** he replied || *ref* to recover; to calm down
reportaje *m* reporting; news coverage; report
reportar *tr* to check, restrain; to get, obtain; to bring, carry; to report || *ref* to restrain or control oneself
reporte *m* report, news report; gossip
repórter *m* reporter
reporte·ro -ra *mf* reporter
reposar *intr & ref* to rest, repose; to take a nap; (*en la sepultura*) to lie, be at rest; (*poso, sedimento*) to settle
reposición *f* replacement; (*de la salud*) recovery; (theat) revival
reposo *m* rest, repose
repostar *tr, intr & ref* to stock up; to refuel
repostería *f* pastry shop, confectionery; pantry
reposte·ro -ra *mf* pastry cook, confectioner
repregunta *f* (law) cross-examination
repreguntar *tr* (law) to cross-examine
reprender *tr* to reprehend, to scold
represa *f* dam; damming; repression, check; (*de un buque*) recapture
represalia *f* reprisal; retaliation
represar *tr* to dam; to repress, to check; (*un buque*) to recapture
representación *f* representation; dignity, standing; performance; **en representación de** representing
representante *adj* representing || *mf* representative; actor, player; (com) agent, representative
representar *tr* to represent; to show, express; to state, declare; to act, perform, play; (*determinada edad*) to appear to be || *ref* to imagine
representati·vo -va *adj* representative
reprimenda *f* reprimand
reprimir *tr* to repress
reprobación *f* reproof; flunk, failure
reprobar **§61** *tr* to reprove; to flunk, to fail
reprochar *tr* to reproach
reproche *m* reproach
reproducción *f* reproduction; breeding
reproducir **§19** *tr & ref* to reproduce
repro·pio -pia *adj* balky
reptar *intr* to crawl; to cringe
reptil *m* reptile
república *f* republic
republica·no -na *adj & mf* republican || *m* patriot
repudiar *tr* to repudiate, to disown, to disavow
repues·to -ta *adj* secluded; spare, extra || *m* stock, supply; serving table; pantry; **de repuesto** spare, extra
repugnante *adj* repugnant, disgusting
repugnar *tr* to conflict with; to contradict; to object to, to avoid; to revolt, be repugnant to || *intr* to be repugnant
repujar *tr* to emboss
repulgar **§44** *tr* to hem, to border
repulgo *m* hem, border
repuli·do -da *adj* highly polished; all dolled up
repulsar *tr* to reject, refuse
repulsi·vo -va *adj* repulsive
repuntar *tr* (*animales dispersos*) (Arg, Chile, Urug) to round up || *intr* to begin to appear; (naut) to begin to rise; (naut) to begin to ebb || *ref* to begin to turn sour; (coll) to fall out
repuso see **reponer**
reputación *f* reputation, repute
reputar *tr* to repute; to esteem
requebra·dor -dora *adj* flirtatious || *mf* flirt
requebrar **§2** *tr* to break into smaller pieces; to flatter, to flirt with
requemar *tr* to burn again; to parch; to overcook; to inflame; to bite, sting || *ref* to become tanned or sunburned; to smolder, burn within
requerir **§68** *tr* to notify; to summon; to request; to urge; to check, examine; to require; to seek, look for; to reach for; to court, make love to
requesón *m* cottage cheese
requiebro *m* fine crushing; flattery, flattering remarks, flirtation
requisi·to -ta *adj* requisite || *m* requisite, requirement; accomplishment; **requisito previo** prerequisite
res *f* head of cattle; beast; **reses** cattle
resabio *m* unpleasant aftertaste; bad habit, vice
resabio·so -sa *adj* (Am) sly, crafty; (*caballo*) (Am) vicious
resaca *f* surge, surf; undertow; (com) redraft; (slang) hangover
resalir **§65** *intr* to jut out, project
resaltar *tr* to emphasize || *intr* to bounce, rebound; to jut out, project; to stand out
resanar *tr* to retouch, patch, repair
resarcir **§36** *tr* to indemnify, to make amends to; (*un daño, un agravio*) to repay; (*una pérdida*) to make good; to mend, repair || *ref* — **resarcirse de** to make up for
resbaladi·zo -za *adj* slippery; skiddy; risky; (*memoria*) shaky
resbalar *intr* to slide; to skid; to slip || *ref* to slide; to slip; (fig) to slip, to misstep
rescatar *tr* to ransom, redeem; to rescue; (*el tiempo perdido*) to make up for; to relieve; to atone for
rescate *m* ransom, redemption; rescue; salvage; ransom money
rescindir *tr* to rescind
rescoldera *f* heartburn
rescoldo *m* embers; smoldering; doubt, scruple; **arder en rescoldo** to smolder
resenti·do -da *adj* resentful
resentimiento *m* resentment; sorrow, disappointment
resentir **§68** *ref* to be resentful; **resentirse de** to feel the bad effects of; to resent; to suffer from

reseña *f* outline; book review; newspaper account; (mil) review
reseñar *tr* to outline; (*un libro*) to review; (mil) to review
reserva *f* reserve; reservation; **con** or **bajo la mayor reserva** in strictest confidence; **reserva de caza** game preserve
reservar *tr* to reserve; to put aside; to postpone; to exempt; to keep secret || *ref* to save oneself, to bide one's time; to beware, be distrustful
resfriado *m* cold
resfriar §77 *tr* to cool, chill || *intr* to turn cold || *ref* to catch cold; to cool off, grow cold
resguardar *tr* to defend; to protect, shield || *ref* to take shelter; to protect oneself
resguardo *m* defense; protection; check, voucher; collateral; (naut) wide berth, sea room
residencia *f* residence; impeachment
residenciar *tr* to call to account; to impeach
residir *intr* to reside
residuo *m* residue, remains; remainder
resignación *f* resignation
resignar *tr* to resign || *ref* to resign, become resigned; **resignarse con** (*p.ej., su suerte*) to be resigned to
resina *f* resin
resistencia *f* resistance; strength; **resistencia de rejilla** (electron) grid leak
resistente *adj* resistant; strong; (hort) hardy
resistir *tr* to bear, to stand; (*la tentación*) to resist || *intr* to resist; to hold out; **resistir a** (*la violencia; la risa*) to resist; to refuse to || *ref* to resist; to struggle; **resistirse a** to refuse to
resma *f* ream
resobrina *f* grandniece, greatniece
resobrino *m* grandnephew, greatnephew
resolución *f* resolution; **en resolución** in brief, in a word
resolver §47 & §83 *tr* to resolve; to solve; to decide on; to dissolve; || *ref* to resolve; to make up one's mind
resollar §61 *intr* to breathe; to breathe hard, pant; to stop for a rest
resonar §61 *intr* to resound, to echo
resoplar *intr* to puff; to snort
resoplido *m* puffing; snort
resorte *m* spring; springiness; means; province, scope; (Am) rubber band; **resorte espiral** coil spring; **tocar resortes** to pull wires, to pull strings
respailar *intr* — **ir respailando** (coll) to scurry along
respaldar *m* back || *tr* to back; to indorse || *ref* to lean back; to sprawl
respaldo *m* back; backing; indorsement
respectar *tr* (with personal **a**) to concern; **por lo que respecta a . . .** as far as . . . is concerned
respecti•vo -va *adj* respective
respecto *m* respect, reference, relation; **al respecto** in the matter; **respecto a** or **de** with respect to, in or with regard to
respetable *adj* respectable
respetar *tr* to respect
respeto *m* respect; consideration; **campar por sus respetos** (coll) to be inconsiderate, to go one's (his, her, etc.) own way; **de respeto** spare, extra
respetuo•so -sa *adj* respectful; awesome, impressive; humble, obedient
respigón *m* hangnail
respingar §44 *intr* to balk, to shy; (*elevarse el borde, p.ej., de la falda*) to curl up; (coll) to give in unwillingly
respin•gón -gona *adj* (*nariz*) snubby, upturned; (Am) surly, churlish
respirar *tr* to breathe || *intr* to breathe; to breath freely; to breathe a sigh of relief; to catch one's breath, to stop for a rest; **no respirar** (coll) to not breathe a word; **sin respirar** without respite, without letup
respiro *m* breathing; respite, breather, breathing spell; (*para el pago de una deuda*) extension of time
resplandecer §22 *intr* to shine; to flash, glitter
resplandeciente *adj* brilliant; resplendent
resplandor *m* brilliance, radiance; resplendence; glare
responder *tr* to answer || *intr* to answer, respond; to correspond; to answer back; **responder de** (*una cosa*) to answer for; **responder por** (*una persona*) to answer for
respon•dón -dona *adj* (coll) saucy
responsable *adj* responsible; **responsable de** responsible for
respuesta *f* answer, response
resquebrajar *tr & ref* to crack, to split
resquemar *tr & intr* to bite, to sting || *ref* to be parched; (*resentirse sin manifestarlo*) to smolder
resquemo *m* bite, sting
resquicio *m* crack, chink; chance, opportunity
restablecer §22 *tr* to reëstablish, to restore || *ref* to recover
restañar *tr* to retin; (*sangre*) to stanch, stop the flow of
restar *tr* to deduct; to reduce; to take away; (*una pelota*) to return; to subtract || *intr* to remain, be left
restaurante *m* restaurant; **restaurante automático** automat
restaurar *tr* to restore; to recover
restitución *f* restitution, return
restituir §20 *tr* to return, give back; to restore || *ref* to return, come back
resto *m* rest, remainder, residue; (*en juegos de naipes*) stakes; (*de una pelota*) return; **a resto abierto** (coll) without limit; **echar el resto** to stake all, to shoot the works; **restos** remains, mortal remains; **restos de serie** remnants
restregar §66 *tr* to rub hard; to scrub hard
restringir §27 *tr* to restrict; to constrict, to contract
resucitar *tr & intr* to resuscitate; to resurrect; (coll) to revive
resuel•to -ta *adj* resolute, resolved, determined; prompt, quick

resuello *m* breathing; hard breathing, panting
resulta *f* result; outcome; vacancy; **de resultas de** as a result of
resultado *m* result
resultar *intr* to result; to prove to be, to turn out to be; to be, to become
resumen *m* summary, résumé; **en resumen** in brief, in a word
resumir *tr* to summarize, to sum up || *ref* to be reduced, be transformed
resurrección *f* resurrection
retaguardia *f* rearguard
retal *m* piece, remnant
retama *f* Spanish broom; **retama de escoba** furze
retar *tr* to challenge, to dare; (coll) to blame, find fault with
retardar *tr* to retard, slow down
retardo *m* retard, delay
retazo *m* piece, remnant; scrap, fragment
retén *m* store, stock, reserve; catch, pawl; (mil) reserve
retener **§71** *tr* to retain, keep, withhold; to detain, arrest; (*el pago de un haber*) to stop
reticente *adj* deceptive, misleading; noncommittal
retintín *m* jingle, tinkling; (*en el oído*) ringing; (coll) tone of reproach, sarcasm, mockery
retiñir **§12** *intr* to jingle, to tinkle; (*los oídos*) to ring
retirada *f* retirement, withdrawal; place of refuge; (mil) retreat, retirement; (*toque*) (mil) retreat; **batirse en retirada** to beat a retreat
retirar *tr* to retire, to withdraw; to take away; to pull back || *ref* to retire, to withdraw; (mil) to retire
reto *m* challenge, dare; threat
retocar **§73** *tr* to retouch; to touch up; (*un disco de fonógrafo*) to play back
retoño *m* sprout, shoot, sucker
retorcer **§74** *tr* to twist; to twist together; (*las manos*) to wring; (fig) to twist, misconstrue || *ref* to twist; to writhe
retóri•co -ca *adj* rhetorical || *f* rhetoric
retornar *tr* to return, give back; to back, back up || *intr & ref* to return, go back
retorno *m* return; barter, exchange; reward, requital; **retorno terrestre** (elec) ground
retorta *f* (chem) retort
retozar **§60** *intr* to frolic, gambol, romp
retozo *m* frolic, gambol, romping; **retozo de la risa** giggle, titter
reto•zón -zona *adj* frolicsome, frisky
retractar *tr & ref* to retract
retraer **§75** *tr* to bring again, to bring back; to dissuade || *ref* to withdraw, retire; to take refuge
retraí•do -da *adj* solitary; reserved, shy
retransmisión *f* rebroadcasting
retransmitir *tr* to rebroadcast
retrasar *tr* to delay, retard; to put off; (*un reloj*) to set or turn back || *intr* to be too slow; (*en los estudios*) to be or fall behind || *ref* to delay, be late, be slow, be behind time; (*un reloj*) to go or be slow
retraso *m* delay; **tener retraso** to be late
retratar *tr* to portray; to photograph; to imitate || *ref* to sit for a portrait; to have one's picture taken
retrato *m* portrait; photograph; copy, imitation; description; **el vivo retrato de** the living image of
retrepar *ref* to lean back, to lean back in the chair
retreta *f* (mil) retreat, tattoo; (Am) outdoor band concert
retrete *m* toilet, lavatory
retribuir **§20** *tr* to repay, to pay back
retroacti•vo -va *adj* retroactive
retroceder *intr* to retrogress; to back away; to back down, back out
retroceso *m* retrogression; (*de un arma de fuego*) recoil; (*de una enfermedad*) flare-up
retrocohete *m* retrorocket
retrodisparo *m* retrofiring
retropropulsión *f* (aer) jet propulsion
retrospecti•vo -va *adj* retrospective || *f* (mov) flashback
retrovisor *m* rear-view mirror
retrucar **§73** *intr* to answer, reply; (billiards) to kiss
retruco *m* (billiards) kiss
retruécano *m* pun
retumbar *intr* to resound, to rumble
retumbo *m* resounding, rumble, echo
reumáti•co -ca *adj & mf* rheumatic
reumatismo *m* rheumatism
reunificación *f* reunification
reunión *f* reunion, gathering, meeting; assemblage
reunir **§59** *tr* to join, unite; to assemble, gather together, bring together; to reunite; (*dinero*) to raise || *ref* to unite; to assemble, gather together, come together, meet; to reunite
reválida *f* final examination (*for a higher degree*)
revejecer **§22** *intr & ref* to grow old before one's time
revelación *f* revelation
revelado *m* (phot) development
revelador *m* (phot) developer
revelar *tr* to reveal; (phot) to develop
revender *tr* to resell; to retail
reventa *f* resale
reventar **§2** *tr* to smash, crush; to burst, blow out, explode; to ruin; to annoy, bore; (*a una persona*) to work to death; (*a un caballo*) to run to death || *intr* to burst, blow out, explode; (*las olas*) to break; (*morir*) (coll) to croak; (*de ira*) (coll) to blow up, hit the ceiling; **reventar por** to be dying to || *ref* to burst, blow out, explode; to be worked to death; (*un caballo*) to be run to death
reventón *m* burst; (aut) blowout
rever **§80** *tr* to revise, to review; (*un caso legal*) to retry
reverberar *intr* to reverberate
reverbero *m* reflector; street lamp; (Am) chafing dish
reverencia *f* reverence; bow, curtsy
reverenciar *tr* to revere, to reverence || *intr* to bow, to curtsy

reveren•do -da *adj & m* reverend
reverso *m* back; wrong side; reverse
revertir **§68** *intr* to revert
revés *m* back, reverse; wrong side; backhand; (*desgracia, contratiempo*) reverse, setback; **al revés** wrong side out; inside out; upside down; backwards
revestir **§50** *tr* to put on, to don; to cover, coat, face, line, surface; to assume, take on; to disguise; (*un cuento*) to adorn; to invest || *ref* to put on vestments; to be haughty; to gird oneself
revirar *tr* to turn, twist; to turn over
revisar *tr* to revise, review, check; to audit
revisión *f* revision, review, check
revisionismo *m* revisionism
revisionista *adj & mf* revisionist
revisor *m* inspector, examiner; (rr) conductor, ticket collector
revista *f* review; (mil) review; (theat) review, revue; (law) new trial
revistar *tr* (mil) to review
revivir *tr & intr* to revive
revocar **§73** *tr* to revoke; to dissuade; to drive back, drive away; to plaster, to stucco
revolar **§61** *intr & ref* to flutter, to flutter around
revolcar **§81** *tr* to knock down; (*a un adversario*) (coll) to floor; (*a un alumno en un examen*) (coll) to flunk, to fail || *ref* to wallow, roll around; to be stubborn
revolotear *tr* to fling up || *intr* to flutter, flutter around, flit
revoltijo or **revoltillo** *m* mess, jumble; (Am) stew
revolto•so -sa *adj* rebellious, riotous; (*niño*) unruly, mischievous; complicated; winding || *mf* troublemaker, rioter
revolución *f* revolution
revoluciona•rio -ria *adj & mf* revolutionary
revolver **§47** & **§83** *tr* to shake; to stir; to turn around; to turn upside down; to wrap up; to mess up; to disturb; (*sus pasos*) to retrace; to alienate, estrange || *intr* to retrace one's steps || *ref* to retrace one's steps; to turn around; to toss and turn; (*un astro en su órbita*) to revolve; (*el mar*) to get rough
revólver *m* revolver
revuelco *m* upset, tumble; wallowing
revuelo *m* whirl, flying around; stir, commotion
revuelta *f* revolution, revolt; disturbance; turning point; fight, row
rey *m* king; (coll) swineherd; **los Reyes Católicos** Ferdinand and Isabella; **los Reyes Magos** the Three Wise Men; **ni rey ni roque** (coll) nobody; **rey de zarza** wren; **reyes** king and queen; **Reyes** Twelfth-night
reyerta *f* quarrel, wrangle
reyezuelo *m* (orn) kinglet; **reyezuelo moñudo** goldcrest
rezaga•do -da *mf* straggler, laggard
rezagar **§44** *tr* to outstrip, leave behind; to postpone || *ref* to fall behind
rezar **§60** *tr* (*una oración*) to pray; (*una oración; la misa*) to say; (coll) to say, to read; (*anunciar*) (coll) to call for || *intr* to pray; (coll) to grumble; (coll) to say, to read; **rezar con** (coll) to concern
rezo *m* prayer; devotions
rezón *m* grapnel
rezongar **§44** *tr* (CAm) to scold || *intr* to grumble, growl
rezumar *intr* to ooze, seep || *ref* to ooze, seep; to leak; (*una especie*) (coll) to leak out
ría *f* estuary, fiord
riachuelo *m* rivulet, streamlet
riada *f* flood, freshet
ribazo *m* slope, embarkment
ribera *f* bank, shore; riverside
ribere•ño -ña *adj* riverside
ribero *m* levee, dike
ribete *m* edge, trimming, border; (*a un cuento*) embellishment
ribetear *tr* to edge, trim, border, bind
ri•co -ca *adj* rich; dear, darling
ridiculizar **§60** *tr* to ridicule
ridícu•lo -la *adj* ridiculous; touchy || *m* ridiculous situation; **poner en ridículo** to ridicule, to expose to ridicule
riego *m* irrigation; watering
riel *m* ingot; curtain rod; rail
rielar *intr* to shimmer, gleam; (poet) to twinkle
rienda *f* rein; **a rienda suelta** swiftly, violently; with free rein
riente *adj* laughing; bright, cheerful
riesgo *m* risk, danger; **correr riesgo** to run or take a risk
rifa *f* raffle; fight, quarrel
rifar *tr* to raffle, to raffle off || *intr* to raffle; to fight, quarrel
rígi•do -da *adj* rigid, stiff; strict, severe
riguro•so -sa *adj* rigorous; severe
rima *f* rhyme; **rimas** poems, poetry
rimar *tr & intr* to rhyme
rimbombante *adj* resounding; flashy
rimero *m* heap, pile
Rin *m* Rhine
rincón *m* corner; nook; piece of land; (coll) home
rinconera *f* corner piece of furniture; corner table; corner cupboard
ringla *f*, **ringle** *m* or **ringlera** *f* row, tier
ringorrango *m* (coll) curlicue; (coll) frill, frippery
rinoceronte *m* rhinoceros
riña *f* fight, scuffle
riñón *m* kidney; (fig) heart, center, interior; **tener bien cubierto el riñón** (coll) to be well-heeled
río *m* river; **pescar en río revuelto** to fish in troubled waters
riostra *f* brace, stay; guy wire
riostrar *tr* to brace, stay
ripia *f* shingle
ripio *m* debris; rubble; (*palabras inútiles empleadas para completar el verso*) padding; **no perder ripio** (coll) to not miss a trick
riqueza *f* riches, wealth; richness
risa *f* laugh, laughter
risco *m* cliff, crag; honey fritter

risible *adj* laughable
risotada *f* guffaw, horse laugh
ristra *f* string of onions, string of garlic; (coll) string, row, file
ristre *m* lance rest
risue•ño -ña *adj* smiling
rítmi•co -ca *adj* rhythmic(al)
ritmo *m* rhythm; **a gran ritmo** at great speed
rito *m* rite
rival *mf* rival
rivalidad *f* rivalry; enmity
rivalizar §60 *intr* to vie, compete; **rivalizar con** to rival
riza•do -da *adj* curly; ripply || *m* curl, curling; rippling
rizador *m* curling iron, hair curler
rizar §60 *tr & ref* to curl; (*la superficie del agua*) to ripple
ri•zo -za *adj* curly || *m* curl, ringlet; ripple; (aer) loop; **rizar el rizo** (aer) to loop the loop
ro *interj* — **¡ro ro!** hushaby!, bye-bye!
roba•dor -dora *mf* robber, thief
róbalo or **robalo** *m* (*Labrax lupus*) bass; (*Centropomus undecimalis*) snook
robar *tr* to rob, steal; (*un naipe o ficha de dominó*) to draw || *intr & ref* to steal
robinete *m* faucet, spigot, cock
roblar *tr* to clinch, to rivet
roble *m* oak; (*Quercus robur*) British oak tree; (coll) husky fellow
roblón *m* rivet
robo *m* robbery, theft; (*naipe tomado del monte*) draw; **robo con escalamiento** burglary
ro•bot *m* (*pl* **-bots**) robot
robus•to -ta *adj* robust
roca *f* rock
rocalla *f* pebbles; stone chips; large glass bead
rocallo•so -sa *adj* stony, pebbly
roce *m* rubbing; close contact
rociada *f* sprinkling; dew; (*de balas, piedras, etc.*) shower; (*de invectivas*) volley
rociadera *f* sprinkling can
rociar §77 *tr* to sprinkle; to spray; to bedew; to scatter || *intr* to drizzle; **rocía** there is dew
rocín *m* hack, nag; work horse, draft horse; (coll) rough fellow; (Am) riding horse
rocío *m* dew; drizzle; sprinkling
roco•so -sa *adj* rocky
rodada *f* rut, track
roda•do -da *adj* (*fácil, flúido*) rounded, fluent; (*tránsito*) vehicular || *f* see **rodada**
rodadura *f* rolling; rut; (*de neumático*) tread
rodaja *f* disk, caster; round slice
rodaje *m* wheels; (*de una película cinematográfica*) shooting, filming; **en rodaje** (aut) being run in; (mov) being filmed
rodamiento *m* bearing; (*de un neumático*) tread; **rodamientos** running gear
Ródano *m* Rhone
rodante *adj* rolling; on wheels; (Chile) wandering
rodapié *m* baseboard, washboard
rodar §61 *tr* to roll; (*una película cinematográfica*) to shoot, to film, to take; to screen, to project; to drag along; (*una llave*) to turn; (*la escalera*) to roll down; (*un nuevo coche*) to run in; (*válvulas de un motor*) to grind || *intr* to roll, roll along; to roll down; to rotate, revolve; to tumble; to roam, wander about; (*por medio de ruedas*) to run; to prowl
Rodas *f* Rhodes
rodear *tr* to surround; (Am) to round up || *intr* to go around; to go by a roundabout way; to beat about the bush || *ref* to turn, twist, toss about
rodela *f* buckler, target; padded ring
rodeo *m* detour, roundabout way; dodge, duck; rodeo, roundup; **andar con rodeos** to beat about the bush; **dar un rodeo** to go a roundabout way
rodilla *f* knee; floor rag, mop; padded ring; **de rodillas** kneeling, on one's knees
rodillera *f* kneepad; baggy knee; (*de prenda de vestir*) knee; (*del órgano*) (mus) knee swell
rodillo *m* roller; rolling pin; road roller; inking roller; (*de la máquina de escribir*) platen
rodrigar §44 *tr* to prop, prop up, stake
rodrigón *m* prop, stake
roer §62 *tr* to gnaw, to gnaw away at; (*un hueso*) to pick; to wear down
rogar §63 *tr & intr* to beg; to pray; **hacerse de rogar** to like to be coaxed
roí•do -da *adj* (coll) miserly, stingy
ro•jo -ja *adj* red; ruddy; red-haired; Red || *mf* (*comunista*) Red || *m* red; **al rojo** to a red heat
rollar *tr* to roll, roll up
rolli•zo -za *adj* round, cylindrical; plump, stocky || *m* round log
rollo *m* roll, coil; roller, rolling pin; round log; yoke pad; rôle; (*de tela*) bolt
romadizo *m* cold in the head
romance *adj* (*neolatino*) Romance || *m* Romance language; Spanish language; romance of chivalry; octosyllabic verse with alternate lines in assonance; narrative poem in octosyllabic verse; ballad; **romance heroico** hendecasyllabic verse with alternate lines in assonance
romancero *m* collection of Old Spanish romances
romancillo *m* verse of less than eight syllables with alternate lines in assonance
románi•co -ca *adj* (*neolatino*) Romance, Romanic; (*arquitectura*) Romanesque || *m* Romanesque
roma•no -na *adj & mf* Roman
romanticismo *m* romanticism
románti•co -ca *adj* romantic
romanza *f* (mus) romance, romanza
romería *f* pilgrimage; crowd, gathering
rome•ro -ra *mf* pilgrim || *m* rosemary
ro•mo -ma *adj* blunt, dull; flat-nosed
rompeáto•mos *m* (*pl* **-mos**) atom smasher
rompecabe•zas *m* (*pl* **-zas**) riddle, puz-

zle; (*figura que ha sido cortada en trozos menudos y que hay que recomponer*) jigsaw puzzle
rompehie•los *m* (*pl* **-los**) iceboat, icebreaker
rompehuel•gas *m* (*pl* **-gas**) strikebreaker
rompeo•las *m* (*pl* **-las**) mole, breakwater
romper §83 *tr* to break; to break through; to break up; to tear || *intr* to break; (*las flores*) to break open, to burst open; to break down; **romper a** to start to, to burst out
rompiente *m* reef, shoal; (*oleaje que choca contra las rocas*) breaker
rompope *m* (Am) eggnog
ron *m* rum; **ron de laurel** or **de malagueta** bay rum
ronca *f* (*época del celo*) rut; cry of buck in rutting season; (coll) bullying
roncar §73 *intr* to snore; (*el viento, el mar*) to roar; to cry in rutting season; (coll) to bully
ronce•ro -ra *adj* slow, poky; grouchy
ron•co -ca *adj* hoarse; harsh || *f* see **ronca**
roncha *f* weal, welt; black-and-blue mark
ronchar *tr* to crunch
ronda *f* (*de un policía; de visitas; de cigarros o bebidas*) round; (*juego del corro*) (Chile) ring-around-a-rosy
rondar *tr* to go around; to fly around; to patrol; (coll) to hang around; (coll) to court || *intr* to patrol by night; to gad about at nighttime; to go serenading; to prowl; (mil) to make the rounds
ronquedad *f* hoarseness; harshness
ronquera *f* hoarseness
ronquido *m* snore; rasping sound
ronronear *intr* to purr
ronroneo *m* purr, purring
ronzal *m* halter
ronzar §60 *tr* to crunch, to munch
roña *f* scab, mange; sticky dirt; pine bark; stinginess; (Col) malingering; (Am) spite, ill will; **jugar a roña** (Peru) to play for fun
roño•so -sa *adj* scabby, mangy; dirty, filthy; stingy; (Am) spiteful
ropa *f* clothing, clothes; dry goods; **a quema ropa** point-blank; **ropa blanca** linen; **ropa de cama** bed linen; bedclothes; **ropa dominguera** Sunday best; **ropa hecha** ready-made clothes; **ropa interior** underwear; **ropa sucia** laundry
ropaje *m* clothes, clothing; gown, robe; drapery
ropaveje•ro -ra *mf* old-clothes dealer
rope•ro -ra *mf* ready-made clothier; wardrobe keeper || *m* wardrobe, clothes closet
roque *m* rook, castle
roque•ño -ña *adj* rocky; hard, flinty
rorro *m* baby; (Mex) doll
rosa *f* rose; **rosa de los vientos** or **rosa náutica** (naut) compass card; **rosas** popcorn; **verlo todo de color de rosa** to see everything through rose-colored glasses
rosa•do -da *adj* rose-colored, rosy; pink; flushed || *f* frost
rosaleda or **rosalera** *f* rose garden
rosario *m* rosary; (*de sucesos*) string; chain pump
ros•bif *m* (*pl* **-bifs**) roast beef
rosca *f* coil, spiral; (*de una espiral*) turn; twisted roll; (*de un tornillo*) thread; (Chile) padded ring
roscar §73 *tr* to thread
roseta *f* sprinkling spout or nozzle; red spot on cheek; **rosetas** popcorn
rosetón *m* rose window
rosita *f* little rose; (Chile) earring; **rositas** popcorn
rosquilla *f* coffeecake, doughnut, cruller
rostro *m* face; snout; beak; (*retrato*) **de rostro entero** full-faced
rostropáli•do -da *mf* paleface
rota *f* rout, defeat; (naut) route, course
rotograbado *m* rotogravure
rótula *f* lozenge; kneecap; knuckle
rotular *tr* to label, title, letter
rótulo *m* label, title; poster, show bill
rotun•do -da *adj* round; rotund, sonorous, full; peremptory
rotura *f* break, breaking; breach, opening; tear, tearing
roya *f* (agr) blight, rust
rozamiento *m* rubbing; friction; (*desavenencia*) (fig) friction
rozar §60 *tr* to graze; to scrape; to border on; to grub, to stub; (*las tierras*) to clear; (*la hierba*) to nibble; (*leña menuda*) to cut and gather || *intr* to graze by || *ref* to be on close terms, to rub elbows, to hobnob; to falter, stammer; to be alike
roznar *tr* to crunch || *intr* to bray
roznido *m* crunch, crunching noise; bray, braying
Rte. *abbr* **Remite**
ru•bí *m* (*pl* **-bíes**) ruby; (*de un reloj*) ruby, jewel
rubia *f* blonde; station wagon; (coll) peseta; **rubia oxigenada** peroxide blonde; **rubia platino** platinum blonde
rubia•les *mf* (*pl* **-les**) (coll) goldilocks
ru•bio -bia *adj* blond, fair; golden || *m* blond || *f* see **rubia**
rubor *m* bright red; blush, flush; bashfulness
ruborizar §60 *tr* to make blush || *ref* to blush
rúbrica *f* title, heading; (*rasgo después de la firma de uno*) flourish
ru•bro -bra *adj* red || *m* (Am) title, heading; (Chile) (com) entry
rudimento *m* rudiment
ru•do -da *adj* coarse, rough; rude, crude; dull, stupid; hard, severe
rueca *f* distaff
rueda *f* wheel; caster, roller; (*de gente*) ring, circle; round slice; pinwheel; (*de la cola del pavo*) spread; sunfish; **hacer la rueda** (*el pavo*) to spread its tail; **hacer la rueda a** (coll) to play up to; **rueda de andar** treadmill; **rueda de cadena** sprocket, sprocket wheel; **rueda de escape** escapement wheel; **rueda de fuego** pinwheel; **rueda dentada** gearwheel; **rueda de paletas** paddle wheel; **rueda de pre-**

sos line-up; **rueda de recambio** spare wheel; **rueda de tornillo sin fin** worm wheel; **rueda motriz** drive wheel
ruedo *m* turn, rotation; round mat; selvage; hemline; (taur) ring; **a todo ruedo** at all events
ruego *m* request, entreaty; prayer
ru•fián -fiana *mf* bawd, go-between || *m* cur, cad
ru•fo -fa *adj* sandy, sandy-haired; curly-haired
rugido *m* roar; (*de las tripas*) rumble
rugir §27 *intr* to roar; to rumble
rugo•so -sa *adj* rugged, wrinkled
ruibarbo *m* rhubarb
ruido *m* noise; rumor; row, rumpus
ruido•so -sa *adj* noisy; loud; sensational
ruin *adj* base, mean, vile; stingy; (*animal*) vicious
ruina *f* ruin
ruindad *f* baseness, meanness, vileness; stinginess; viciousness
ruino•so -sa *adj* tottery, run-down
ruiseñor *m* nightingale
ruleta *f* roulette; (CAm, Arg) tape measure
ruletero *m* (Mex) cruising taxi driver (*in search of fares*)
ruma•no -na *adj & mf* Rumanian
rumbo *m* bearing, course, direction; (coll) pomp, show; (coll) generosity; **por aquellos rumbos** in those parts; **rumbo a** bound for
rumbo•so -sa *adj* pompous, magnificent; (coll) generous
rumiar *tr & intr* to ruminate
rumor *m* rumor; (*de voces*) murmur, buzz; rumble
rumorear *tr* to rumor, to circulate by a rumor || *intr* to murmur, buzz, rumble || *ref* to be rumored; **se rumorea que** it is rumored that
rumoro•so -sa *adj* noisy, loud, rumbling
runfla or **runflada** *f* (coll) string, row; (*en los naipes*) (coll) sequence
ruptor *m* (elec) contact breaker
ruptura *f* rupture, break; crack, split; (*cesación de relaciones*) rupture
Rusia *f* Russia; **la Rusia Soviética** Soviet Russia
ru•so -sa *adj & mf* Russian
rúst. *abbr* **rústica**
rústi•co -ca *adj* rustic; coarse, crude, clumsy; (*latín*) Vulgar; **en rústica** paper-bound || *m* rustic, peasant
ruta *f* route; **ruta aérea** air lane
rutilante *adj* shining, sparkling
rutina *f* routine
rutina•rio -ria *adj* routine

S

S, s (ese) *f* twenty-second letter of the Spanish alphabet
S. *abbr* **San, Santo, sobresaliente, sur**
sábado *m* (*de los cristianos*) Saturday; (*de los judíos*) Sabbath
sábalo *m* shad
sabana *f* (Am) savanna, pampa; **ponerse en la sabana** (Ven) to get rich overnight
sábana *f* sheet; altar cloth
sabandija *f* insect, bug, worm; (*persona*) vermin; **sabandijas** (*animales o personas*) vermin
sabanilla *f* kerchief; altar cloth
sabañón *m* chilblain
sabe•dor -dora *adj* aware, informed
sabelotodo *m* (*pl* **sabelotodo**) know-it-all, wise guy
saber *m* knowledge, learning || *v* §64 *tr & intr* to know; to find out; to taste; **a saber** namely, to wit; **no saber dónde meterse** to not know which way to turn; **que yo sepa** as far as I know; **saber a** to taste of; to smack of; **saber a poco** to be just a taste, to taste like more; **saber de** to be aware of; to hear from || *ref* to know; to be or become known
sabidi•llo -lla *adj & mf* (coll) know-it-all
sabi•do -da *adj* well-informed; learned; **de sabido** certainly, surely
sabiduría *f* wisdom; knowledge, learning
sabiendas — a sabiendas knowingly, consciously; **a sabiendas de que** knowing that, aware that
sabihon•do -da *adj & mf* (coll) know-it-all
sa•bio -bia *adj* wise; learned; (*animal*) trained || *mf* wise person, scholar, scientist || *m* wise man, sage
sablazo *m* stroke with a saber, wound made by a saber; (coll) sponging; **dar un sablazo a** (coll) to hit for a loan
sable *m* saber, cutlass; (coll) sponging
sablear *tr* (coll) to hit for a loan, to sponge on || *intr* (coll) to go around sponging
sablista *mf* (coll) sponger
sabor *m* taste, flavor
saborcillo *m* slight taste, touch
saborear *tr* to flavor; to taste; to savor; to entice || *ref* to smack one's lips; **saborearse de** to taste; to savor
sabotaje *m* sabotage
sabotear *tr & intr* to sabotage
sabro•so -sa *adj* tasty, savory, delicious
sabueso *m* bloodhound; sleuth
saburro•so -sa *adj* (*boca*) foul; (*lengua*) coated
sacaboca•do or **sacaboca•dos** *m* (*pl* **-dos**) ticket punch; (coll) sure thing
sacabotas *m* (*pl* **-tas**) bootjack
sacacor•chos *m* (*pl* **-chos**) corkscrew
sacaman•chas *mf* (*pl* **-chas**) clothes cleaner, spot remover; dry cleaner; dyer

sacamue·las *mf* (*pl* **-las**) (coll) tooth puller; (coll) quack, cheat
sacamuer·tos *m* (*pl* **-tos**) stagehand
sacapintura *m* paint remover
sacapun·tas *m* (*pl* **-tas**) pencil sharpener
sacar §73 *tr* (*un clavo, una espada, agua, una conclusión*) to draw; to pull out; to pull up; to take out; to extract, remove; to show; to bring out, publish; to find out, to solve; (*un secreto*) to elicit, draw out; to copy; (*una fotografía*) to take; to except, exclude; to get, obtain; to produce, invent, imitate; (*un premio*) to win; (*una pelota*) to serve; (*el pecho*) to stick out; **sacar a bailar** (coll) to drag in; **sacar a relucir** (coll) to bring up unexpectedly; **sacar en claro** or **en limpio** to recopy clearly; to deduce, to clear up
sacarina *f* saccharin
sacasi·llas *m* (*pl* **-llas**) stagehand
sacerdocio *m* priesthood
sacerdote *m* priest
saciar *tr* to satiate
saco *m* bag, sack; coat, jacket; sack, plunder, pillage; (*de mentiras*) pack; **saco de dormir** sleeping bag; **saco de noche** overnight bag
sacramento *m* sacrament
sacrificar §73 *tr* to sacrifice; to slaughter || *intr* to sacrifice || *ref* to sacrifice; to sacrifice onself
sacrificio *m* sacrifice; **sacrificio del altar** Sacrifice of the Mass
sacrilegio *m* sacrilege
sacríle·go -ga *adj* sacrilegious
sacristán *m* sacristan; sexton; **sacristán de amén** yes man
sacristía *f* sacristy, vestry
sa·cro -cra *adj* sacred
sacudida *f* shake, jar, jolt, jerk, bump; (elec) shock
sacudi·do -da *adj* intractable; determined || *f* see **sacudida**
sacudir *tr* to shake; to beat; to jar, jolt; to rock; to shake off || *ref* to shake, to shake oneself; to rock; **sacudirse bien** (coll) to wangle one's way out
sádi·co -ca *adj* sadistic || *mf* sadist
saeta *f* arrow, dart; (*del reloj*) hand; magnetic needle
saetilla *f* small arrow; (*del reloj*) hand; magnetic needle; (bot) arrowhead
saetín *m* flume, millrace
sa·gaz *adj* (*pl* **-gaces**) sagacious; keen-scented
sagra·do -da *adj* sacred || *m* asylum, haven, sanctuary; **acogerse a sagrado** to take sanctuary
sagrario *m* sanctuary, shrine; ciborium
sahariana *f* tight-fitting military jacket
sahornar *ref* to skin oneself
sahumar *tr* to perfume with smoke or incense; (Chile) to gold-plate, to silver-plate
sainete *m* one-act farce; flavor, relish, spice, zest; sauce, seasoning; tidbit
sa·jón -jona *adj & mf* Saxon
sal *f* salt; grace, charm; wit; (CAm) misfortune; **sal de sosa** washing soda; **sales aromáticas** smelling salts; **sal gema** rock salt
sala *f* hall; drawing room, living room, sitting room; **sala de batalla** sorting room; **sala de calderas** boiler room; **sala de enfermos** infirmary; **sala de espera** waiting room; **sala de estar** living room, sitting room; **sala de fiestas** night club; **sala del cine** moving-picture house; **sala de máquinas** engine room
saladillo *m* salted peanut
Salamina *f* Salamis
salar *tr* to salt; (Am) to spoil, ruin; (Am) to bring bad luck to
salario *m* wages, pay; **salario de hambre** starvation wages
salcochar *tr* to boil in salt water
salcocho *m* (Am) food boiled in salt water
salchicha *f* sausage
salchiche·ro -ra *mf* pork butcher
saldar *tr* to settle, liquidate; to sell out
saldo *m* settlement; balance; remnant; bargain; **saldo de mercancías** job lot; **saldo deudor** debit balance
salero *m* saltshaker, saltcellar; salt lick; (coll) grace, charm, wit
salero·so -sa *adj* (coll) charming, winsome, lively; (coll) salty, witty
salgar §44 *tr* (*el ganado*) to salt
salida *f* start; departure; exit; outcome, result; subterfuge; pretext; outlay, expenditure; projection; outlying fields; (elec) output; (sport) start; (mil) sally, sortie; (coll) witticism, sally; **salida de baño** bathrobe; **salida del sol** sunrise; **salida de teatro** evening wrap; **salida de teatros** after-theater party; **salida de tono** (coll) irrelevancy, impropriety; **salida lanzada** (sport) running start; **tener salida** to sell well; (*una muchacha*) to be popular with the boys
saliente *adj* projecting; (*p.ej., tren*) outbound; (*sol*) rising || *m* east || *f* projection; (*de la carretera*) shoulder
salir §65 *intr* to go out, come out; to leave, go away, depart; to sail; to run out, come to an end; to appear, show up; (*una mancha*) to come out, come off; (*p.ej., el sol*) to rise; to shoot, spring, come up; to project, stick out; to make the first move; to result, turn out; to be elected; **salga lo que saliere** (coll) come what may; **salir a** to amount to; to open into; to resemble, look like; **salir al encuentro a** to go to meet; to take a stand against; to get ahead of; **salir bien en un examen** to pass an examination; **salir con bien** to be successful; **salir de** to depart from; to cease being; to get rid of; (*p.ej., su juicio, sentido*) to lose; **salir disparado** to start like a shot; **salir pitando** (coll) to start off on a mad run; (coll) to blow up, hit the ceiling; **salir reprobado** (*en un examen*) to fail || *ref* to slip out, escape; to slip off, run off; to leak; to boil over; **salirse con la suya** to have one's own way; to carry one's point
salitre *m* saltpeter

saliva *f* saliva; **gastar saliva** (coll) to rattle along; (coll) to waste one's breath
salmo *m* psalm
salmón *m* salmon
salmuera *f* brine, pickle; salty food or drink
salobre *adj* brackish, saltish
salón *m* salon, drawing room; (*de un buque*) saloon; meeting room; **salón de actos** auditorium; **salón de baile** ballroom; **salón de belleza** beauty parlor; **salón del automóvil** automobile show; **salón de refrescos** ice-cream parlor; **salón de tertulia** or **salón social** lounge
saloncillo *m* (*p.ej., de un teatro*) rest room
salpicar **§73** *tr* to splash; to sprinkle
salpimentar **§2** *tr* to salt and pepper, season with salt and pepper; (fig) to sweeten
salpullido *m* rash, eruption
salpullir **§13** *tr* to cause a rash in; to splotch || *ref* to break out
salsa *f* sauce, dressing, gravy; **salsa de ají** chili sauce; **salsa de tomate** catsup, ketchup; **salsa inglesa** Worcestershire sauce
salsera *f* gravy dish; small saucer (*to mix paints*)
saltaban•co or **saltaban•cos** *m* (*pl* **-cos**) quack, mountebank; prestidigitator; (coll) nuisance
saltamon•tes *m* (*pl* **-tes**) grasshopper
saltar *tr* to jump, jump over; to skip, skip over || *intr* to jump, leap, hop, skip; to bounce; to shoot up, spurt; to come loose, come off; to crack, break, burst; to chip; to project, stick out; **saltar a la vista** or **los ojos** to be self-evident; **saltar por** to jump over, to jump out of || *ref* to skip; to come off
saltatum•bas *m* (*pl* **-bas**) (coll) burying parson
salteador *m* highwayman, holdup man
saltear *tr* to attack, hold up, waylay; to take by surprise
saltimbanco *m* var of **saltabanco**
salto *m* jump, leap, bound; skip; dive; fall, waterfall; leapfrog; **salto de altura** high jump; **salto de ángel** swan dive; **salto de cama** morning wrap, dressing gown; **salto de carpa** jackknife; **salto de esquí** ski jump; **salto de viento** (naut) sudden shift in the wind; **salto mortal** somersault; **salto ornamental** fancy dive
salubre *adj* healthful, salubrious
salud *f* health; welfare; salvation; greeting; **gastar, vender** or **verter salud** (coll) to radiate health || *interj* greetings!; **¡salud y pesetas!** health and wealth!
saludar *tr* to greet, salute, hail, bow to; to give regards to || *intr* to salute; to bow
saludo *m* greeting, salute, bow; salutation; **saludo final** conclusion
salutación *f* salutation, greeting, bow
salva *f* greeting, welcome; salvo; oath; tray; (*de aplausos; de una batería de artillería*) round
salvado *m* bran
salva•dor -dora *mf* savior, saver, rescuer || **el Salvador** the Saviour; (*país de la América Central*) El Salvador
salvadore•ño -ña *adj & mf* Salvadoran
salvaguardar *tr* to safeguard
salvaguardia *m* bodyguard, escort || *f* safeguard, safe-conduct; protection, shelter
salvaje *adj* wild, uncultivated; savage; stupid || *mf* savage; dolt
salvaji•no -na *adj* wild; (*de la carne de los animales monteses*) gamy || *f* wild animal; wild animals
salvamante•les *m* (*pl* **-les**) coaster
salvamento *m* salvation; lifesaving; rescue; salvage; place of safety
salvar *tr* to save, rescue; to salvage; (*una dificultad*) to avoid, overcome; (*un obstáculo*) to clear, get around; (*una distancia*) to cover, get over; to rise above; to jump over; to make an exception of; **salvar apariencias** to save face || *ref* to save onself, escape danger; to be saved; **sálvese el que pueda** every man for himself
salvavi•das *m* (*pl* **-das**) life preserver; lifeboat; (*empleado de una estación de salvamento*) lifeguard
salvedad *f* reservation, exception
salvia *f* (bot) sage
sal•vo -va *adj* safe; omitted; **a salvo** safe, out of danger; **a salvo de** safe from || **salvo** *prep* save, except for; **salvo error u omisión** barring error or omission; **salvo que** unless || *f* see **salva**
salvoconducto *m* safe-conduct
sámara *f* (bot) key, key fruit
san *adj* apocopated and unstressed form of **santo**
sanaloto•do *m* (*pl* **-do**) cure-all
sanar *tr* to cure, heal || *intr* to heal; to recover
sanción *f* (*aprobación*) sanction; (*castigo, pena*) penalty
sancionar *tr* (*aprobar*) to sanction; (*imponer pena a*) to penalize
sancochar *tr* to parboil
sandalla *f* sandal
sándalo *m* (yellow) sandalwood
san•dez *f* (*pl* **-deces**) folly, nonsense; piece of folly
sandía *f* watermelon
san•dio -dia *adj* foolish, nonsensical
saneamiento *m* sanitation, drainage; guarantee
sanear *tr* to guarantee; to indemnify; to make sanitary, to drain, dry up
sangrar *tr* to bleed; to drain; to tap; (typ) to indent; (coll) to rob || *intr* to bleed; **estar sangrando** to be new or recent; to be plain or obvious || *ref* to have oneself bled; (*los colores*) to run
sangre *f* blood; **a sangre** by horsepower; **a sangre fría** in cold blood; **pura sangre** *m* thoroughbred; **sangre torera** bullfighting in the blood
sangría *f* bleeding; outlet, draining;

ditch, trench; (*bebida*) sangaree; tap; tapping; (typ) indentation
sangrien•to -ta *adj* bloody; bleeding; cruel, sanguinary
sangüesa *f* raspberry
sangüeso *m* raspberry bush
sanguijuela *f* leech
sanguina•rio -ria *adj* sanguinary, bloodthirsty
sanidad *f* healthiness; healthfulness; health; sanitation; **sanidad pública** health department
sanita•rio -ria *adj* sanitary
sa•no -na *adj* hale, healthy; healthful; sound; sane; earnest, sincere; safe, sure; (coll) whole, untouched, unharmed; **sano y salvo** safe and sound
santiague•ro -ra *adj* Santiago de Cuba || *mf* native or inhabitant of Santiago de Cuba
santia•gués -guesa *adj* Santiago de Compostela || *mf* native or inhabitant of Santiago de Compostela
santiagui•no -na *adj* Santiago de Chile || *mf* native or inhabitant of Santiago de Chile
santiamén *m* (coll) jiffy; **en un santiamén** (coll) in the twinkling of an eye
santidad *f* holiness, sanctity, saintliness; **su Santidad** his Holiness
santificar **§73** *tr* to sanctify, to hallow, to consecrate; (*las fiestas*) to keep; (coll) to excuse, justify
santiguar **§10** *tr* to bless, make the sign of the cross over; (coll) to punish, slap, abuse || *ref* to cross oneself, make the sign of the cross
san•to -ta *adj* holy, saintly, blessed; (*día*) live-long; (coll) artless, simple; **santo y bueno** well and good || *mf* saint || *m* name day; image of a saint; **a santo de** because of; **desnudar a un santo para vestir a otro** to rob Peter to pay Paul; **írsele a uno el santo al cielo** (coll) to forget what one was up to; **santo y seña** password, watchword
Santo Domingo Hispaniola
santuario *m* sanctuary, shrine; (Col) buried treasure; (Col, Ven) Indian idol
santu•rrón -rrona *adj* sanctimonious || *mf* sanctimonious person
saña *f* fury, rage; cruelty
sañu•do -da *adj* furious, enraged; cruel
sapiente *adj* wise, intelligent
sapo *m* toad; (coll) stuffed shirt; (Chile) little runt
saque *m* (*en el tenis*) serve, service; server; service line; (Col) distillery; **tener buen saque** (coll) to be a heavy eater and drinker
saquear *tr* to sack, plunder, pillage, loot
sarampión *m* measles
sarao *m* soirée, evening party
sarape *m* (Guat, Mex) bright-colored woolen poncho
sarcásti•co -ca *adj* sarcastic
sardina *f* sardine; **como sardinas en banasta** or **en lata** (coll) packed in like sardines
sar•do -da *adj & mf* Sardinian
sarga *f* serge
sargento *m* sergeant
sarmiento *m* vine shoot, running stem
sarna *f* itch, mange
sarno•so -sa *adj* itchy, mangy
sarrace•no -na *adj & mf* Saracen
sarracina *f* scuffle, free fight; bloody brawl
sarro *m* crust; (*p.ej., en la lengua*) fur; (*en los dientes*) tartar
sarta *f* string; line, file, series
sartén *f* frying pan; **saltar de la sartén y dar en las brasas** (coll) to jump from the frying pan into the fire
sastre *m* tailor
satélite *m* satellite
satelizar **§60** *tr* to put into orbit; (pol) to make a satellite of || *ref* to go into orbit
satén *m* sateen
satíri•co -ca *adj* satiric(al) || *mf* satirist
satirizar **§60** *tr & intr* to satirize
satisfacción *f* satisfaction
satisfacer **§39** *tr & intr* to satisfy || *ref* to satisfy oneself, be satisfied, take satisfaction
satisfacto•rio -ria *adj* satisfactory
saturar *tr* to saturate; to satiate
sauce *m* willow tree; **sauce de Babilonia** or **sauce llorón** weeping willow
saúco *m* elder, elderberry
savia *f* sap
saxofón *m* or **saxófono** *m* saxophone
saya *f* skirt; petticoat
sayo *m* smock frock, tunic; (coll) garment
sazón *f* ripeness; season; time, occasion; taste, seasoning; **a la sazón** at that time; **en sazón** in season, ripe; on time, opportunely
sazonar *tr* to ripen; to season || *ref* to ripen, mature
s/c *abbr* **su cuenta**
S.E. *abbr* **Su Excelencia**
se *pron reflex* himself, to himself; herself, to herself; itself, to itself; themselves, to themselves; yourself, to yourself; yourselves, to yourselves; oneself, to oneself; each other, to each other || *pron pers* (used before the pronouns **lo, la, le,** etc.) **to him,** to her, to it, to them, to you
sebo *m* tallow; fat, suet
seca *f* drought; dry season
secador *m* drier, hair drier
secadora *f* clothes dryer
secafir•mas *m* (*pl* **-mas**) blotter
secano *m* dry land, unwatered land
secansa *f* sequence
secante *m* blotting paper
secar **§73** *tr* to dry, wipe dry; to annoy, bore || *ref* to dry, get dry; to dry oneself; to wither; to be dry, be thirsty; (*un pozo*) to run dry
secarropa *f* clothes dryer; **secarropa de travesaños** clotheshorse
sección *f* section; cross section; **sección de fondo** editorial section
secesión *f* secession
se•co -ca *adj* dry; dried up, withered; lank, lean; harsh, sharp; (*bebida*) straight; indifferent; plain, unadorned || *f* see **seca**

secreta•rio -ria *adj* confidential, trusted || *mf* secretary

secreter *m* secretary (*writing desk*)

secre•to -ta *adj* secret || *m* secret; secrecy; hiding place, secret drawer; (*mecanismo oculto para abrir una cerradura*) key; **en el secreto de las cosas** on the inside

secta *f* sect

secta•rio -ria *adj & mf* sectarian

sector *m* sector; **sector de distribución** house current, power line

se•cuaz (*pl* **-cuaces**) *adj* partisan || *mf* partisan, follower

secuela *f* sequel, result

secuencia *f* sequence

secuestrar *tr* to kidnap; (law) to sequester

secular *adj* secular

secundar *tr* to second, to back

secunda•rio -ria *adj* secondary || *m* (elec) secondary

sed *f* thirst; drought; **tener sed** to be thirsty

seda *f* silk; **como una seda** smooth as silk; easy as pie; sweet-natured; **seda encerada** dental floss

sedal *m* fish line

sedán *m* sedan; **sedán de reparto** delivery truck

sede *f* (*p.ej., del gobierno*) seat; (eccl) see; **Santa Sede** Holy See

sedenta•rio -ria *adj* sedentary

sede•ño -ña *adj* silk, silken

sedición *f* sedition

sedicio•so -sa *adj* seditious

sedien•to -ta *adj* thirsty; (*terreno*) dry; anxious, eager

sedimento *m* sediment

sedo•so -sa *adj* silky

seducción *f* seduction; charm, captivation

seducir §19 *tr* to seduce; to tempt, lead astray; to charm, captivate

seducti•vo -va *adj* seductive; tempting; charming, captivating

seduc•tor -tora *adj* seductive; tempting; charming || *mf* seducer; tempter; charmer

sefar•dí (*pl* **-fíes**) *adj* Sephardic || *mf* Sephardi

sega•dor -dora *adj* harvesting || *m* harvestman || *f* harvester; mowing machine; **segadora de césped** lawn mower; **segadora trilladora** combine

segar §66 *tr* to reap, harvest, mow; to mow down || *intr* to reap, harvest, mow

segazón *f* harvest; harvest time

seglar *adj* secular, lay || *m* layman || *f* laywoman

segmento *m* segment; **segmento de émbolo** piston ring

segregacionista *mf* segregationist

segregar §44 *tr* to segregate

seguida *f* series, succession; **de seguida** without interruption, continuously; at once; in a row; **en seguida** at once, immediately

seguidilla *f* Spanish stanza made up of a quatrain and a tercet; **seguidillas** seguidilla (*Spanish dance and music*)

segui•do -da *adj* continued, successive; straight, direct; running, in a row; **todo seguido** straight ahead || *f* see **seguida**

seguimiento *m* chase, hunt, pursuit; continuation; (*de vehículos espaciales*) tracking

seguir §67 *tr* to follow; to pursue; to continue; to dog, to hound || *intr* to go on, to continue; to still be, to be now; to keep + *ger* || *ref* to follow, ensue; to issue, to spring

según *prep* according to, as per; **según que** according as || *conj* as, according as

segunda *f* double meaning; (aut & mus) second

segundero *m* second hand; **segundero central** sweep-second, center-second

segun•do -da *adj* second || *m* second; **ser sin segundo** to be second to none || *f* see **segunda**

segur *f* axe; sickle

segurador *s* security, bondsman

seguridad *f* security; safety; surety; certainty; assurance; confidence

segu•ro -ra *adj* sure, certain; secure, safe; reliable; constant; steady, unfailing || *m* assurance, certainty; safety; confidence; insurance; **a buen seguro** surely, truly; **seguro contra accidentes** accident insurance; **seguro de desempleo** or **desocupación** unemployment insurance; **seguro de enfermedad** health insurance; **seguro de incendios** fire insurance; **seguro sobre la vida** life insurance; **sobre seguro** without risk || **seguro** *adv* surely

seis *adj & pron* six; **las seis** six o'clock || *m* six; (*en las fechas*) sixth

seiscien•tos -tas *adj & pron* six hundred || **seiscientos** *m* six hundred

selección *f* selection

seleccionar *tr* to select, to choose

selec•to -ta *adj* select, choice

selva *f* forest, woods; jungle

selváti•co -ca *adj* woodsy; rustic, wild

sellar *tr* to seal; to stamp; to close; to finish up

sello *m* seal; stamp; signet; wafer; **sello aéreo** air-mail stamp; **sello de correo** postage stamp; **sello de urgencia** special-delivery stamp; **sello fiscal** revenue stamp

semáforo *m* semaphore; traffic light

semana *f* week; week's pay; **semana inglesa** working week of five and a half days

semanal *adj* weekly

semanalmente *adv* weekly

semana•rio -ria *adj & m* weekly

semánti•co -ca *adj* semantic || *f* semantics

semblante *m* face, mien, countenance; appearance, expression, look

semblanza *f* biographical sketch, portrait

sembrado *m* sown ground, grain field

sembrar §2 *tr* to seed, to sow; to scatter, to spread; to sprinkle

semejante *adj* like, similar; such; **semejante a** like; **semejantes** alike, e.g., **estas sillas son semejantes** these

chairs are alike || *m* resemblance, likeness; fellow, fellow man
semejanza *f* similarity, resemblance; simile; **a semejanza de** like
semejar *tr* to resemble, to be like || *intr & ref* to be alike; **semejar a** or **semejarse a** to resemble, to be like
semen *m* semen
semental *adj* (*animal*) stud, breeding || *m* sire; stallion; stock bull
semestral *adj* semester
semestre *m* semester
semibola *f* little slam
semibreve *f* (mus) whole note
semiconductor *m* semiconductor
semiconsciente *adj* semiconscious
semicul•to -ta *adj* semilearned
semidifun•to -ta *adj* half-dead
semidormi•do -da *adj* half-asleep
semifinal *adj & f* (sport) semifinal
semilla *f* seed; **semilla de césped** grass seed
semillero *m* seedbed
seminario *m* seminary; seminar; nursery
semi-remolque *m* semitrailer
semita *mf* Semite || *m* (*idioma*) Semitic
semíti•co -ca *adj* Semitic
semivi•vo -va *adj* half-alive
semovientes *mpl* stock, livestock
sempiter•no -na *adj* everlasting
Sena *m* Seine
senado *m* senate
senador *m* senator
senaduría *f* senatorship
sencillez *f* simplicity, plainness, candor
senci•llo -lla *adj* simple, plain, candid; single || *m* change, loose change
senda *f* path, footpath
sendero *m* path, footpath, byway
sen•dos -das *adj pl* one each, one to each, e.g., **les dio sendos libros** he gave one book to each of them, he gave each of them a book
senectud *f* age, old age
senil *adj* senile
senilidad *f* senility
senilismo *m* (pathol) senility
seno *m* bosom, breast; lap; heart; womb; bay, gulf; cavity, hollow, recess; asylum, refuge
sensación *f* sensation
sensatez *f* good sense
sensa•to -ta *adj* sensible
sensibilizar **§60** *tr* to sensitize
sensible *adj* appreciable, perceptible, noticeable, sensible; considerable; sensitive; deplorable, regrettable
sensiblería *f* mawkishness
sensible•ro -ra *adj* mawkish
sensiti•vo -va *adj* (*de los sentidos*) sense, sensitive; sentient; stimulating
senso•rio -ria *adj* sensory
sensual *adj* sensual, sensuous
sentada *f* sitting; **de una sentada** at one sitting
senta•do -da *adj* seated; settled; stable, permanent; sedate; **dar por sentado** to take for granted || *f* see **sentada**
sentar **§2** *tr* to seat; to settle; to fit, to suit; to agree with || *ref* to sit, to sit down; to settle, settle down
sentencia *f* maxim; (law) sentence
sentenciar *tr* to sentence; (*una cuestión*) to decide; (*p.ej., un libro a la hoguera*) (coll) to consign
senti•do -da *adj* felt; deep-felt; sensitive; eloquent; **darse por sentido** to take offense || *m* sense, meaning; direction; consciousness; **sentido común** common sense
sentimiento *m* sentiment; feeling; sorrow, regret
sentir *m* feeling; opinion; judgment || **§68** *tr* to feel; to hear; to be or feel sorry for; to sense || *intr* to feel; to be sorry, to feel sorry || *ref* to feel; to feel oneself to be; to be resentful; to crack, be cracked; **sentirse de** to feel; to have a pain in; to resent
seña *f* sign, mark, token; password, watchword; **por las señas** (coll) to all appearances; **por más señas** or **por señas** (coll) as a greater proof; **señas** address; description
señal *f* sign, mark, token; landmark; bookmark; trace, vestige; scar; signal; traffic light; representation; reminder; pledge; brand; down payment; **señal de ocupado** (telp) busy signal; **señal de tramo** (rr) block signal; **señal de vídeo** video signal; **señal digital** fingerprint; **señal para marcar** (telp) dial tone
señala *f* (Chile) earmark (*on livestock*)
señala•do -da *adj* noted, distinguished
señalar *tr* to mark; to show, indicate; to point at, point out; to signal; to brand; to determine, fix; to appoint; to sign and seal; to scar; to threaten || *ref* to distinguish oneself, to excel
señalizar **§60** *tr* to signal
señor *m* sir, mister; lord, master, owner; **muy señor mío** Dear Sir; **señores** Mr. and Mrs.; ladies and gentlemen
señora *f* madam, missus; mistress, owner; wife; **muy señora mía** Dear Madam; **Nuestra Señora** our Lady; **señora de compañía** chaperon
señorear *tr* to dominate, to rule; to master, to control; to seize, take control of; to tower over; to excel || *intr* to strut, to swagger || *ref* to strut, to swagger; to control oneself; **señorearse de** to seize, take control of
señoría *f* lordship; ladyship; rule, sway
señoril *adj* lordly; haughty; majestic
señorío *m* dominion, sway, rule; mastery; arrogance, lordliness, majesty; gentry, nobility
señorita *f* young lady; miss
señorito *m* master; young gentleman; (coll) playboy
señuelo *m* decoy, lure; bait; enticement
separa•do -da *adj* separate; separated; apart; **por separado** separately; under separate cover
separar *tr* to separate; to dismiss, discharge || *ref* to separate; to resign
separata *f* reprint, offprint
sept.[e] *abbr* **septiembre**
septeto *m* septet
sépti•co -ca *adj* septic
septiembre *m* September
sépti•mo -ma *adj & m* seventh

sepulcro *m* sepulcher, tomb, grave; **santo sepulcro** Holy Sepulcher
sepultar *tr* to bury; to hide away
sepultura *f* burial; grave; **estar con un pie en la sepultura** to have one foot in the grave
sepulturero *m* gravedigger
sequedad *f* dryness, drought; gruffness, surliness
sequía *f* drought
séquito *m* retinue, suite; following, popularity
ser *m* being; essence; life || *v* §69 *v aux* (to form passive voice) to be, e.g., **el discurso fue aplaudido por todos** the speech was applauded by everybody || *intr* to be; **a no ser por** if it were not for; **a no ser que** unless; **érase que se era** (coll) once upon a time there was; **es decir** that is to say; **sea lo que fuere** be that as it may; **ser de** to belong to; to become of; to be, e.g., **el reloj es de oro** the watch is gold; **ser de ver** to be worth seeing; **soy yo** it is I
serafín *m* seraph; great beauty (*person*)
serena *f* night love song; (coll) night dew, night air
serenar *tr* to calm; to pacify; to cool; to settle
serenata *f* serenade
serenidad *f* serenity; **serenidad del espíritu** peace of mind
sere•no -na *adj* serene, calm; clear, cloudless || *m* night watchman; night dew, night air || *f* see **serena**
serial *adj* serial || *m* (rad) serial; **serial lacrimógeno** soap opera; **serial radiado** (rad) serial
serie *f* series; **de serie** stock, e.g., **coche de serie** stock car; **en serie** mass; **fuera de serie** custom-built, special; outsize
seriedad *f* seriousness; reliability; sternness, severity; solemnity
se•rio -ria *adj* serious; reliable; stern; solemn
sermón *m* sermon
sermonear *tr & intr* to sermonize
serpear or **serpentear** *intr* to wind, meander; to wriggle, squirm
serpentín *m* coil
serpiente *f* serpent, snake; **serpiente de cascabel** rattlesnake
serranía *f* range of mountains, mountainous country
serra•no -na *adj* highland, mountain || *mf* highlander, mountaineer
serrar §2 *tr* to saw
serrería *f* sawmill
serrín *m* sawdust
serrucho *m* handsaw
Servia *f* Serbia
servicial *adj* accommodating, obliging
servicio *m* service; (tennis) service, serve; (Am) toilet; **libre servicio** self-service; **servicio de grúa** (aut) towing service
servi•dor -dora *mf* servant; humble servant; (tennis) server; **servidor de Vd.** your servant, at your service || *m* waiter; suitor || *f* waitress
servidumbre *f* servitude; servants, help; compulsion; (law) easement; **servidumbre de la gleba** serfdom; **servidumbre de paso** (law) right of way; **servidumbre de vía** (rr) right of way
servil *adj* servile
servilleta *f* napkin
servilletero *m* napkin ring
ser•vio -via *adj & mf* Serbian || *f* see **Servia**
servir §50 *tr* to serve; to help, wait on; (*un pedido*) to fill; (tennis) to serve; **para servir a Vd.** at your service || *intr* to serve; (*en los naipes*) to follow suit; **servir de** to serve as; to be used as; **servir para** to be good for, to be used for || *ref* to help oneself, to serve oneself; to have the kindness to, to deign to; **servirse de** to use, to make use of; **sírvase** please
serv.° *abbr* **servicio**
servocroata *adj & mf* Serbo-Croatian
servodirección *f* (aut) power steering
servoembrague *m* (aut) automatic clutch
sésamo *m* sesame; **sésamo ábrete** open sesame
sesenta *adj, pron & m* sixty
sesenta•vo -va *adj & m* sixtieth
sesgar §44 *tr* (*el paño*) to cut on the bias; to bevel, slant, slope
ses•go -ga *adj* beveled, slanting, sloped; oblique; stern; calm || *m* bevel; bias; slant, slope; turn; compromise; **al sesgo** obliquely; on the bias
sesión *f* session; sitting; meeting; (*cada representación de un drama o película*) show; **sesión continua** (mov) continuous showing; **sesión de espiritistas** séance, spiritualistic séance
sesionar *intr* to be in session
seso *m* brain; brains, intelligence; **calentarse** or **devanarse los sesos** to rack one's brain
sestear *intr* to take a siesta; (*el ganado*) to rest in the shade
sesu•do -da *adj* brainy; (Chile) stubborn
seta *f* bristle; toadstool
setecien•tos -tas *adj & pron* seven hundred || **setecientos** *m* seven hundred
setenta *adj, pron & m* seventy
setenta•vo -va *adj & m* seventieth
seto *m* fence; **seto vivo** hedge, quickset
seudónimo *m* pseudonym, pen name
s.e.u.o. *abbr* **salvo error u omisión**
seve•ro -ra *adj* severe; stern; strict
sevicia *f* ferocity, cruelty
sexo *m* sex; **el bello sexo** the fair sex; **el sexo feo** the sterner sex
sextante *m* sextant
sex•to -ta *adj & m* sixth
sexual *adj* sexual, sex
si *conj* if; whether; I wonder if; **por si acaso** just in case; **si acaso** if by chance; **si no** otherwise
sí *adv* yes; indeed; (gives emphasis to verb and is often equivalent to English auxiliary verb) **él sí habla español** he does speak Spanish || *pron reflex* himself, herself, itself, themselves; yourself, yourselves; oneself; each other || *m* (*pl* **síes**) yes; **dar el sí** to say yes

sia•més -mesa *adj & mf* Siamese
siberia•no -na *adj & mf* Siberian
sibila *f* sibyl
sicalipsis *f* spiciness, suggestiveness
sicalípti•co -ca *adj* spicy, suggestive, sexy
Sicilia *f* Sicily
sicilia•no -na *adj & mf* Sicilian
sicoanálisis *m* var of **psicoanálisis**
sicoanalizar §60 *tr* var of **psicoanalizar**
sicología *f* var of **psicología**
sicológi•co -ca *adj* var of **psicológico**
sicólo•go -ga *mf* var of **psicólogo**
sicópata *mf* var of **psicópata**
sico•sis *f* (*pl* **-sis**) psychosis; (*afección de la piel*) sycosis
sicóti•co -ca *adj* var of **psicótico**
sideral or **sidére•o -a** *adj* sidereal
siderurgia *f* iron and steel industry
sidra *f* cider; **sidra achampañada** hard cider
siega *f* reaping, mowing; harvest; crop
siembra *f* sowing; seeding; seedtime; sown field
siempre *adv* always; **de siempre** usual; **para siempre** or **por siempre** forever; **por siempre jamás** forever and ever; **siempre que** whenever; provided
siempreviva *f* everlasting flower
sien *f* temple
sierpe *f* serpent, snake
sierra *f* saw; sierra, mountain range; **sierra circular** buzz saw; **sierra continua** band saw; **sierra de armero** hacksaw; **sierra de bastidor** bucksaw; **sierra de hilar** ripsaw; **sierra de vaivén** jig saw; **sierra sin fin** band saw
sier•vo -va *mf* slave; servant; **siervo de la gleba** serf
siesta *f* siesta; hot time of day; **siesta del carnero** nap before lunch
siete *adj & pron* seven; **las siete** seven o'clock || *m* seven; (*en las fechas*) seventh; (coll) V-shaped tear or rip
sífilis *f* syphilis
sifón *m* siphon; siphon bottle; (*tubo doblemente acodado*) trap
sig.[e] *abbr* **siguiente**
sigilar *tr* to seal, to stamp; to conceal, keep silent
sigilo *m* seal; concealment, reserve; **sigilo sacramental** inviolable secrecy of the confessional
sigilo•so -sa *adj* tight-lipped; reserved
sigla *f* initial; abbreviation, symbol
siglo *m* (*cien años*) century; (*comercio de los hombres*) world; (*largo tiempo*) age; **siglo de la ilustración** or **de las luces** Age of Enlightenment
signar *tr* to mark; to sign; to make the sign of the cross over
signatura *f* library number; (mus & typ) signature
significado *m* meaning
significar §73 *tr* to signify, to mean; to point out, make known || *intr* to be important
signo *m* sign; mark; sign of the cross; fate, destiny; **signo de admiración** exclamation mark; **signo de interrogación** question mark
siguiente *adj* following; next
sílaba *f* syllable; **última sílaba** ultima
silbar *tr* (*p.ej., una canción*) to whistle; (*un silbato*) to blow; (*a un actor*) to hiss || *intr* to whistle; (*ir zumbando por el aire*) to whiz, to whiz by
silbato *m* whistle
silbido *m* whistle, whistling, hiss; (rad) howling, squealing; **silbido de oídos** ringing in the ears
silbo *m* whistle, hiss
silenciador *m* silencer; (aut) muffler
silencio *m* silence; (*toque que manda que cada cual se acueste*) (mil) taps; (mus) rest
silencio•so -sa *adj* silent, noiseless; quiet, still || *m* (aut) muffler
sílfide *f* sylph
silo *m* silo; cave, dark place
silogismo *m* syllogism
silueta *f* silhouette
siluetear *tr* to silhouette
silva *f* (*materias escritas sin orden*) miscellany; verse of iambic hendecasyllables intermingled with seven-syllable lines
silvestre *adj* wild; rustic, uncultivated
silvicultura *f* forestry
silla *f* chair; **silla alta** high chair; **silla de balanza** (Am) rocking chair; **silla de cubierta** deck chair; **silla de junco** rush-bottomed chair; **silla de manos** sedan chair; **silla de montar** saddle, riding saddle; **silla de ruedas** wheel chair; **silla de tijera** folding chair; **silla giratoria** swivel chair; **silla hamaca** (Arg) rocking chair; **silla plegadiza** folding chair; **silla poltrona** armchair, easy chair
sillar *m* ashlar
silleta *f* bedpan
sillico *m* chamber pot, commode
sillín *m* saddle (*of bicycle*)
sillón *m* armchair, easy chair; **sillón de orejas** wing chair
sima *f* chasm, abyss
simbóli•co -ca *adj* symbolic(al)
simbolizar §60 *tr* to symbolize
símbolo *m* symbol; **Símbolo de la fe** or **de los Apóstoles** Apostles' Creed
simetría *f* symmetry
simétri•co -ca *adj* symmetric(al)
simiente *f* seed
símil *adj* like, similar || *m* similarity; (rhet) simile
similar *adj* similar
similigrabado *m* (typ) half-tone
similor *m* ormolu, similor; **de similor** fake, sham
simón *m* cab, hack (*in old Madrid*); hackman
simpatía *f* affection, attachment, fondness, liking; friendliness; congeniality; **tomar simpatía a** to take a liking for
simpáti•co -ca *adj* agreeable, pleasant, likeable, congenial
simpatizar §60 *intr* to be congenial, to get on well together; **simpatizar con** to get on well with
simple *adj* simple; single || *mf* simpleton || *m* (*planta medicinal*) simple
simpleza *f* simpleness; stupidity
simulacro *m* phantom, vision; idol,

image; semblance, show; pretense; sham battle; **simulacro de ataque aéreo** air-raid drill; **simulacro de combate** sham battle
simula•do -da *adj* fake; (com) pro forma
simular *tr* to simulate, feign, fake || *intr* to malinger; to pretend
simultáne•o -a *adj* simultaneous
simún *m* simoon
sin *prep* without; **sin embargo** nevertheless, however; **sin que** + *subj* without + *ger*
sinagoga *f* synagogue
sinapismo *m* mustard plaster; (coll) bore, nuisance
sincerar *tr* to vindicate, justify
sinceridad *f* sincerity
since•ro -ra *adj* sincere
síncopa *f* (phonet) syncope
síncope *m* fainting spell
sincróni•co -ca *adj* synchronous
sincronizar **§60** *tr & intr* to synchronize
sindicar **§73** *tr & ref* to syndicate
sindicato *m* syndicate; labor union
síndico *m* trustee; (*en una quiebra*) receiver
sin•diós (*pl* **-diós**) *adj* godless || *mf* atheist
sinecura *f* sinecure
sinfín *m* endless amount, number
sinfonía *f* symphony
sinfóni•co -ca *adj* symphonic
singladura *f* (naut) day's run; (*de mediodía a mediodía*) (naut) day
singular *adj* singular; special; single || *m* singular; **en singular** in particular
singularizar **§60** *tr* to distinguish, to single out || *ref* to distinguish oneself, to stand out
sinhueso *f* (coll) tongue
sinies•tro -tra *adj* evil, perverse; calamitous, disastrous || *m* calamity, disaster || *f* left hand, left-hand side
sinnúmero *m* great amount, great number
sino *conj* but, except; **no . . . sino** only; **no . . . sino que** only; **no solo . . . sino que** not only . . . but also || *m* fate, destiny
sinóni•mo -ma *adj* synonymous || *m* synonym
sinop•sis *f* (*pl* **-sis**) synopsis
sinrazón *f* wrong, injustice
sinsabor *m* displeasure; anxiety, trouble, worry
sinsonte *m* mockingbird
sintaxis *f* syntax
sínte•sis *f* (*pl* **-sis**) synthesis
sintéti•co -ca *adj* synthetic(al)
sintetizar **§60** *tr* to synthesize
síntoma *m* symptom
sintonía *f* (rad) tuning; (rad) theme song
sintonizar **§60** *tr* (*el aparato receptor*) to tune; (*la estación emisora*) to tune in
sinuo•so -sa *adj* sinuous, winding; wavy; evasive
sinvergüenza *adj* (coll) brazen, shameless || *mf* (coll) scoundrel, rascal
sionismo *m* Zionism
siquiatra *mf* var of **psiquiatra**
siquiatría *f* var of **psiquiatría**
síqui•co -ca *adj* var of **psíquico**
siquiera *adv* even; at least || *conj* although, even though
sirena *f* siren; mermaid; **sirena de la playa** bathing beauty; **sirena de niebla** foghorn
sirga *f* towrope, towline
sirgar **§44** *tr* to tow
Siria *f* Syria
si•rio -ria *adj & mf* Syrian || **Sirio** *m* (astr) Sirius || *f* see **Siria**
sirvienta *f* maid, servant girl
sirviente *m* servant; waiter
sisa *f* petty theft; (*para fijar los panes de oro*) sizing
sisar *tr* to filch, to snitch; (*lo que se ha de dorar*) to size
sisear *tr* to hiss || *intr* to hiss; to sizzle
siseo *m* hiss, hissing; sizzle, sizzling
Sísifo *m* Sisyphus
sismógrafo *m* seismograph
sismología *f* seismology
sistema *m* system
sistematizar **§60** *tr* to systematize
sístole *f* systole
sitiar *tr* to surround, hem in; to siege, besiege
sitio *m* place, spot, room; location, site; country place; seat; (mil) siege; (Am) cattle ranch; (Am) taxi stand
si•to -ta *adj* situated, located
situación *f* situation, position; **pedir situación** (aer) to ask for bearings
situar **§21** *tr* to situate, locate, place; (*dinero*) to place, invest; (*un pedido*) to place || *ref* to take a position; to settle; (aer) to get one's bearings
s.l. *abbr* **sin lugar**
S.M. *abbr* **Su majestad**
smo•king *m* (*pl* **-kings**) tuxedo, dinner coat
so *prep* under, e.g., **so pena de** under penalty of || *interj* whoa!; (coll) you . . . !, e.g., **¡so animal!** you beast!
sobaco *m* armpit
sobajar *tr* to crush, to rumple; (Am) to humiliate
sobaquera *f* (*en el vestido*) armhole; (*para resguardar del sudor la parte del vestido correspondiente al sobaco*) shield
sobar *tr* to knead; to massage; to beat, slap; to paw, pet, feel; to annoy, be fresh to; (Am) to flatter; (*un hueso dislocado*) (CAm) to set; (*la cabalgadura*) (Arg) to tire out; (Col) to flay, to skin; (P-R) to bribe
sobarba *f* noseband
soberanía *f* sovereignty
sobera•no -na *adj* sovereign; superb || *mf* sovereign || *m* (*moneda*) sovereign
sober•bio -bia *adj* proud, haughty; arrogant; magnificent, superb || *f* pride, haughtiness; arrogance; magnificence
so•bón -bona *adj* (coll) malingering; (coll) fresh, mushy, spoony
sobornar *tr* to bribe
soborno *m* bribery; (SAm) extra load; **de soborno** (Bol) in addition; **soborno de testigo** (law) subornation of perjury

sobra *f* extra, surplus; **sobras** leftovers, leavings; trash
sobradillo *m* penthouse
sobra•do -da *adj* excessive, superfluous; bold, daring; rich, wealthy || *m* attic, garret || **sobrado** *adv* too
sobrante *adj* remaining, leftover, surplus || *m* leftover, surplus
sobrar *tr* to exceed, surpass || *intr* to be more than enough; to be in the way; to be left, to remain
sobre *prep* on, upon; over; above; about; near; after; in addition to; out of, e.g., **en nueve casos sobre diez** in nine out of ten cases || *m* envelope; **sobre de ventanilla** window envelope
sobrealimentar *tr* to overfeed; to supercharge
sobrecama *f* bedspread
sobrecarga *f* overload, extra load; overcharge; surcharge
sobrecargar **§44** *tr* to overload, to overburden; to overcharge; to surcharge
sobrecargo *m* (naut) supercargo; (Am) purser || *f* (Am) air hostess, stewardess
sobrecejo *m* frown
sobreceño *m* frown
sobrecoger **§17** *tr* to surprise, catch; to scare, terrify || *ref* to be surprised; to be scared; **sobrecogerse de** to be seized with
sobrecubierta *f* extra cover; (*de un libro*) jacket, dust jacket
sobredi•cho -cha *adj* above-mentioned
sobreexcitar *tr* to overexcite || *ref* to become overexcited
sobreexponer **§54** *tr* to overexpose
sobreexposición *f* overexposure
sobregirar *tr & intr* to overdraw
sobregiro *m* overdraft
sobrehombre *m* superman
sobrehuma•no -na *adj* superhuman
sobrellevar *tr* to bear, carry; (*la carga de otra persona*) to ease; (*los trabajos o molestias de la vida*) to share; (*molestias*) to suffer with patience
sobremanera *adv* exceedingly, beyond measure
sobremesa *f* tablecloth, table cover; **de sobremesa** desk, e.g., **reloj de sobremesa** desk clock; after-dinner, e.g., **discurso de sobremesa** after-dinner speech
sobremodo *adv* var of **sobremanera**
sobrenadar *intr* to float
sobrenatural *adj* supernatural
sobrenombrar *tr* to surname; to nickname
sobrenombre *m* surname; nickname
sobrentender **§51** *tr* to understand || *ref* to be understood, be implied
sobrepasar *tr* to excel, surpass, outdo; to exceed; to overtake || *ref* to outdo each other; to go too far
sobrepe•lliz *f* (*pl* **-llices**) surplice
sobreponer **§54** *tr* to superpose, put on top; to superimpose || *ref* to control oneself; to triumph over adversity; **sobreponerse a** to overcome
sobreprecio *m* extra charge, surcharge
sobreproducción *f* overproduction
sobrepujar *tr* to excel, surpass
sobresaliente *adj* projecting; conspicuous, outstanding; (*en un examen*) distinguished || *mf* substitute; understudy
sobresalir **§65** *intr* to project, jut out; to stand out, excel
sobresaltar *tr* to assail, to rush upon; to startle, frighten || *intr* to stand out clearly || *ref* to be startled, be frightened; to start, to wince
sobresalto *m* fright, scare; start, shock, wince; **de sobresalto** suddenly, unexpectedly
sobrescribir **§83** *tr* to address
sobrescrito *m* address
sobrestante *m* boss, foreman
sobresueldo *m* extra wages, extra pay
sobretiro *m* offprint
sobretodo *adv* especially || *m* overcoat, topcoat
sobrevenir **§79** *intr* to happen, take place; to supervene, to set in; **sobrevenir a** to overtake
sobrevidriera *f* window screen; window grill; storm window
sobrevivencia *f* (Ecuad) survival
sobreviviente *adj* surviving || *mf* survivor
sobrevivir *intr* to survive; **sobrevivir a** to survive, to outlive
sobrevolar **§61** *tr* to overfly
sobriedad *f* sobriety, moderation
sobrina *f* niece
sobrino *m* nephew
so•brio -bria *adj* sober, moderate, temperate
socaire *m* (naut) lee; **al socaire de** (naut) under the lee of; (coll) under the shelter of; **estar al socaire** (coll) to shirk
socapa *f* subterfuge; **a socapa** clandestinely
socarrén *m* eaves
socarrar *tr* to singe, scorch
soca•rrón -rrona *adj* crafty, cunning, sly; sneering; roguish
socavar *tr* to undermine, to dig under
socavón *m* cave-in; cave; (min) gallery
sociable *adj* sociable
social *adj* social; company, e.g., **edificio social** company building
socialismo *m* socialism
socialista *mf* socialist
sociedad *f* society; company, firm; **buena sociedad** (*mundo elegante*) society; **sociedad anónima** stock company; **sociedad de control** holding company; **Sociedad de las Naciones** League of Nations
so•cio -cia *mf* partner; companion; member || *m* fellow; (scornful) fellow, guy
sociología *f* sociology
socorrer *tr* to aid, help, succor
socorri•do -da *adj* ready; handy, useful; hackneyed, trite, worn; well stocked
socorro *m* aid, help, succor
socoyote *m* (Mex) baby, youngest son
soda *f* soda; soda water
sodio *m* sodium
so•ez *adj* (*pl* **-eces**) base, mean, vile
so•fá *m* (*pl* **-fás**) sofa; **sofá cama** day bed

soflama *f* glow, flicker; blush; deceit, cheating

soflamar *tr* to flimflam; to make blush || *ref* to become scorched

sofocar **§73** *tr* to choke, suffocate, stifle, smother; to quench, extinguish; to make blush; (coll) to bother, harass || *ref* to choke, suffocate; to blush; to get excited; to get out of breath

sofoco *m* blush, embarrassment

sofrenar *tr* (*un caballo*) to check suddenly; (*una pasión*) to control; to chide, reprimand

soga *m* sly fellow || *f* rope, cord; **dar soga a** (coll) to make fun of; **hacer soga** (coll) to lag behind

soja *f* soy, soy bean

sojuzgar **§44** *tr* to subjugate, subdue

sol *m* sun; sunlight; sunny side; **de sol a sol** from sunrise to sunset; **hacer sol** to be sunny; **soles** (poet) eyes

solamente *adv* only

solana *f* sunny spot; sun porch

solapa *f* lapel; pretext, pretense; flap

solapa•do -da *adj* overlapping; cunning, underhanded, sneaky

solapar *tr* to put lapels on; to overlap; to conceal, cover up || *intr* to overlap

solapo *m* lapel; flap; (coll) chuck under chin

solar *adj* solar; ancestral || *m* ground, plot; manor house, ancestral mansion; noble lineage; (Cuba) tenement || *v* **§61** *tr* to pave, to floor; (*zapatos*) to sole

solarie•go -ga *adj* ancestral; manorial

so•laz *m* (*pl* **-laces**) solace, consolation; recreation; **a solaz** with pleasure

soldada *f* wages, pay

soldadera *f* (Mex) camp follower

soldadesca *f* soldiery; undisciplined troops

soldado *m* soldier; **soldado de a pie** foot soldier; **soldado de juguete** toy soldier; **soldado de marina** marine; **soldado de plomo** tin soldier; **soldado de primera** private first class; **soldado raso** buck private

soldadura *f* solder; soldering; weld; welding; **soldadura al arco** arc welding; **soldadura autógena** welding; **soldadura a tope** butt welding; **soldadura por puntos** spot welding

soldar **§61** *tr* to solder; (*sin materia extraña*) to weld || *ref* (*los huesos*) to knit

solear *tr* to sun || *ref* to sun, sun oneself

soledad *f* solitude, loneliness; longing, grieving; lonely spot

soledo•so -sa *adj* solitary, lonely; longing, grieving

solemne *adj* solemn; (*error, mentira, etc.*) (coll) downright

soler **§47** *intr* to be accustomed to

solera *f* crossbeam; lumber, timber; mother liquor, mother of the wine; blend of sherry; old vintage sherry; tradition, standing; (Chile) curb; (Mex) brick, tile, stone; **de solera** or **de rancia solera** of the good old school, of the good old times

solevantar *tr* to raise up; to rouse, stir up, incite || *ref* to rise up; to revolt

solevar *tr* to raise up; to incite to rebellion || *ref* to rise up; to revolt

solicitante *mf* petitioner; applicant

solicitar *tr* to solicit, ask for; to apply for; to woo, to court; to drive, to pull; (*la atención*) to attract; (phys) to attract

solíci•to -ta *adj* solicitous; careful, diligent; obliging; (coll) fond, affectionate

solicitud *f* solicitude; petition, request; application

solidar *tr* to harden; to establish, to prove

solida•rio -ria *adj* jointly liable; jointly binding; **solidario con** or **de** integral with

solidez *f* solidity; strength, soundness; constancy

sóli•do -da *adj* solid; strong, sound || *m* solid

soliloquio *m* soliloquy

solista *adj* (*p.ej., instrumento*) (mus) solo || *mf* (mus) soloist

solita•rio -ria *adj* solitary; lonely || *mf* hermit, recluse, solitary || *m* (*juego y diamante*) solitaire || *f* tapeworm

sóli•to -ta *adj* accustomed, customary

soliviantar *tr* to rouse, stir up, incite

soliviar *tr* to lift, lift up

so•lo -la *adj* only, sole; alone; lonely; (*p.ej., whisky*) straight; (*café*) black; **a mis solas** alone, all by myself; **a solas** alone, unaided || *pron* only one || *m* (mus) solo

sólo *adv* only, solely

solomillo *m* sirloin

solomo *m* sirloin; loin of pork

solsticio *m* solstice

soltador *m* release; **soltador del margen** margin release

soltar **§61** *tr* to untie, unfasten, loosen; to let go; to let go of; (*una observación*) to drop, to let slip; (*el agua*) to turn on || *ref* to get loose or free; to come loose, come off; to loosen up; to burst out; to thaw out, let oneself go

solte•ro -ra *adj* single, unmarried || *m* bachelor || *f* spinster, maiden lady

solterona *f* (coll) old maid

soltura *f* looseness; agility, ease, freedom; fluency; dissoluteness; release

solución *f* solution

solucionar *tr* to solve, to resolve

solventar *tr* (*lo que uno debe*) to settle, to pay up; (*una dificultad*) to solve

solvente *adj & m* solvent

sollastre *m* scullion

sollozar **§60** *intr* to sob

sollozo *m* sob

sombra *f* (*falta de luz brillante*) shade; (*imagen obscura que proyecta un cuerpo opaco*) shadow; shady side; darkness; parasol; ignorance; ghost, spirit; grace, charm, wit; favor, protection; (coll) luck; **a la sombra** in the shade; (coll) in jail; **a sombra de tejado** (coll) stealthily, sneakingly; **ni por sombra** by no means; without any notice; **no ser su sombra** to be but a shadow of one's former self; **tener buena sombra** (coll) to be likeable; (coll) to bring good luck

sombrear *tr* to shade; (*un dibujo*) to hatch
sombrerera *f* bandbox, hatbox
sombrerería *f* hat store, hat factory; millinery shop
sombrere·ro -ra *mf* hatter, hat maker ‖ *f* see **sombrerera**
sombrero *m* hat; **sombrero de copa** high hat, top hat; **sombrero de muelles** opera hat; **sombrero de paja** straw hat; **sombrero de pelo** (Am) high hat; **sombrero de tres picos** three-cornered hat; **sombrero gacho** slouch hat; **sombrero hongo** derby; **sombrero jarano** (Am) sombrero
sombrilla *f* parasol, sunshade; **sombrilla de playa** beach umbrella; **sombrilla protectora** (mil) umbrella
sombrí·o -a *adj* shady; somber; gloomy
sombro·so -sa *adj* shadowy, full of shadows; shady
some·ro -ra *adj* brief, summary; slight; superficial, shallow
someter *tr* to subdue, to subject; (*razones, reflexiones; un negocio*) to submit ‖ *ref* to yield, submit, surrender
someti·do -da *adj* humble, submissive
sometimiento *m* subjection
somier *m* bedspring, spring mattress
somorgujar *tr* to plunge, to submerge ‖ *intr* to dive ‖ *ref* to plunge
son *m* sound; news, rumor; pretext, motive; manner, mode; **en son de** in the manner of, by way of; as
sona·do -da *adj* talked-about; famous, noted
sonaja *f* jingle
sonajero *m* rattle, child's rattle
sonámbu·lo -la *mf* sleepwalker, somnambulist
sonar §61 *tr* to sound, to ring; (*un instrumento de viento, un silbato*) to blow; (*un instrumento de viento*) to play ‖ *intr* to sound, to ring; (*un reloj*) to strike; to seem; (coll) to sound familiar; **sonar a** to sound like, have the appearance of ‖ *ref* to be rumored; (*las narices*) to blow
sonda *f* sounding; plummet, lead; drill; (surg) probe, sound
sondar or **sondear** *tr & intr* to sound, to probe
sonetizar §60 *intr* to sonneteer
soneto *m* sonnet
sóni·co -ca *adj* sonic
sonido *m* sound; report, rumor
sonoridad *f* sonority
sonorizar §60 *tr* (*una película cinematográfica*) to record sound effects on; (*una consonante sorda*) to voice ‖ *ref* to voice
sono·ro -ra *adj* sound; clear, loud, resounding
sonreír §58 *intr & ref* to smile
sonriente *adj* smiling
sonrisa *f* smile
sonrojar or **sonrojear** *tr* to make blush ‖ *ref* to blush
sonrojo *m* blush; word that causes blushing
sonrosar or **sonrosear** *tr* to rose-color; to make blush ‖ *ref* to become rose-colored; to blush
sonsacar §73 *tr* to pilfer; to entice away; to elicit, draw out
sonsonete *m* rhythmical tapping; singsong
soña·dor -dora *adj* dreamy ‖ *mf* dreamer
soñar §61 *tr* to dream; **ni soñarlo** (coll) not even in a dream, by no means ‖ *intr* to dream; **soñar con** to dream of; **soñar despierto** to daydream
soñolien·to -ta *adj* sleepy, dozy, drowsy, somnolent; lazy
sopa *f* (*pan u otra cosa empapada en un líquido*) sop; soup; **hecho una sopa** (coll) soaked to the skin, sopping wet; **sopa de pastas** noodle soup
sopapo *m* chuck under the chin; (coll) blow, slap
sopetear *tr* to dip, to dunk; to abuse
sopetón *m* slap, box; **de sopetón** suddenly
sopista *mf* beggar
soplar *tr* to blow; to blow away; to blow up, inflate; to snitch, swipe; to inspire; to prompt; to tip off; (*la dama a un rival*) to cut out; (coll) to squeal on ‖ *intr* to blow; (coll) to squeal ‖ *ref* to be puffed up, be conceited; (coll) to swill, gulp, gobble
soplete *m* blowpipe
soplillo *m* blower, fan; chiffon, silk gauze; light sponge cake
soplo *m* blowing, blast; breath; gust of wind; instant, moment; (*informe dado en secreto*) tip; (coll) squealing; (coll) squealer
so·plón -plona *adj* (coll) tattletale ‖ *mf* (coll) tattletale, squealer
sopor *m* sleepiness, drowsiness; stupor
soportal *m* porch, portico, arcade
soportar *tr* to support, hold up, bear; to endure, suffer
soporte *m* support, bearing, rest, standard; base, stand
soprano *mf* (*persona*) soprano ‖ *m* (*voz*) soprano
sor *f* (used before names of nuns) Sister
sorber *tr* to sip; to absorb, soak up
sorbete *m* sherbet, water ice
sorbetera *f* ice-cream freezer; (coll) high hat
sorbo *m* sip; gulp
sordera *f* deafness
sórdi·do -da *adj* sordid
sordina *f* silencer; (mus) mute; (mus) damper; **a la sordina** silently, on the quiet
sor·do -da *adj* deaf; silent, mute; muffled, dull; (*dolor, ruido*) dull ‖ *mf* deaf person; **hacerse el sordo** to pretend to be deaf; to turn a deaf ear
sordomu·do -da *adj* deaf and dumb ‖ *mf* deaf-mute
sorgo *m* sorghum, broomcorn
sorna *f* slowness; sluggishness; cunning
sorochar *ref* (SAm) to become mountain-sick; (Am) to blush
soroche *m* (SAm) mountain sickness; (Am) flush, blush; (Bol, Chile) silver-bearing galena
sorprendente *adj* surprising
sorprender *tr* to surprise; to catch; (*un secreto*) to discover

sorpresa *f* surprise; surprise package
sortear *tr* to draw or cast lots for; to choose by lot; to dodge; to duck through || *intr* to draw or cast lots
sorteo *m* drawing, casting of lots; choosing by lot; dodging; (taur) workout, performance
sortija *f* ring; curl; hoop; **sortija de sello** signet ring
sortilegio *m* sorcery, witchery
sortíle•go -ga *mf* fortuneteller || *m* sorcerer || *f* sorceress
sosa *f* soda
sosega•do -da *adj* calm, quiet, peaceful
sosegar **§66** *tr* to calm, quiet, allay || *intr* to become calm, to rest || *ref* to calm down, to quiet down
sosiega *f* nightcap
sosiego *m* calm, quiet, serenity
sosla•yo -ya *adj* slanting, oblique; **al soslayo** or **de soslayo** slantingly; askance
so•so -sa *adj* insipid; tasteless; dull, inane || *f* see **sosa**
sospecha *f* suspicion
sospechar *tr* to suspect
sospecho•so -sa *adj* suspicious; suspect || *m* suspect
sostén *m* support; (*de un buque*) steadiness; brassière
sostener **§71** *tr* to support, hold up; to sustain; to maintain; to bear, to stand || *ref* to remain
sosteni•do -da *adj* & *m* (mus) sharp
sota *m* (Chile) boss, foreman || *f* (*en los naipes*) jack; jade, hussy
sotana *f* soutane, cassock
sótano *m* basement, cellar
sotavento *m* (naut) leeward
soterrar **§2** *tr* to bury; to hide away
soto *m* grove; brush, thicket, copse
so•viet *m* (*pl* **-viets**) soviet
soviéti•co -ca *adj* soviet, sovietic
sovietizar **§60** *tr* to sovietize
sovoz — a sovoz sotto voce, in a low tone
Sr. *abbr* **Señor**
Sra. *abbr* **Señora**
Srta. *abbr* **Señorita**
S.S.S. *abbr* **su seguro servidor**
ss. ss. *abbr* **seguros servidores**
su *adj poss* his, her, its, their, your, one's
suave *adj* suave, smooth, soft; gentle, mild, meek
suavizador *m* razor strop
suavizar **§60** *tr* to smooth, ease, sweeten, soften, mollify; (*una navaja de afeitar*) to strop
subalter•no -na *adj* & *mf* subaltern, subordinate
subasta *f* auction, auction sale; **sacar a pública subasta** to sell at auction
subastar *tr* to auction, sell at auction
subcampe•ón -ona *mf* (sport) runner-up
subcentral *f* (elec) substation
subconsciencia *f* subconscious, subconsciousness
subconsciente *adj* subconscious
subdesarrolla•do -da *adj* underdeveloped
súbdi•to -ta *adj* & *mf* subject
subentender **§51** *tr* to understand || *ref* to be understood, be implied
subestimar *tr* to underestimate
subfusil *m* submachine gun
subi•do -da *adj* high, fine, superior; strong, intense; (*color*) bright; high, high-priced || *f* rise; ascent; (*p.ej., al trono*) accession
subir *tr* to raise; to lift; to carry up; (*p.ej., una escalera*) to go up; (mus) to raise the pitch of || *intr* to go up, to come up; to rise; to get worse; to spread; **subir a** to climb; to climb on; to get in or into; to get on, to mount || *ref* to rise
súbi•to -ta *adj* sudden, unexpected; hurried; hasty, impetuous || **súbito** *adv* suddenly
subjeti•vo -va *adj* subjective
subjunti•vo -va *adj* & *m* subjunctive
sublevación *f* uprising, revolt
sublevado *m* rebel, insurrectionist
sublevar *tr* to incite to rebellion || *ref* to revolt
submarinista *mf* (sport) skin diver || *m* (nav) submariner
submari•no -na *adj* & *m* submarine
suboficial *m* sergeant major; noncommissioned officer
subordina•do -da *adj* & *mf* subordinate
subordinar *tr* to subordinate
subproducto *m* by-product
subrayar *tr* to underline; to emphasize
subrepti•cio -cia *adj* surreptitious
subsanar *tr* to excuse, overlook; to correct, repair
subscribir **§83** *tr* to subscribe; to subscribe to, to endorse; to subscribe to or for; to sign; to sign up || *ref* to subscribe
subseguir **§67** *intr* & *ref* to follow next
subsidiar *tr* to subsidize
subsidio *m* subsidy; aid, help
subsiguiente *adj* subsequent
subsistencia *f* subsistence, sustenance
subsistir *intr* to subsist
substancia *f* substance
substanciar *tr* to abstract, to abridge
substanti•vo -va *adj* & *m* substantive
substitución *f* replacement; (chem, law, math) substitution
substitui•dor -dora *adj* & *mf* substitute
substituir **§20** *tr* to replace; to substitute for, take the place of || *intr* to take someone's place || *ref* to be replaced; to relieve each other
substituti•vo -va *adj* & *m* substitute
substitu•to -ta *mf* substitute
substraer **§75** *tr* to remove; to deduct; to rob, steal; to subtract || *ref* to withdraw; **substraerse a** to evade, avoid, slip away from
subte *m* (Arg, Urug) subway
subteniente *m* second lieutenant
subterráne•o -a *adj* subterranean, underground || *m* subterranean; (Arg) subway
subtitular *tr* to subtitle
subtítulo *m* subtitle, subheading
suburbio *m* suburb; outlying slum
subvención *f* subvention, subsidy
subvencionar *tr* to subvention, to subsidize

subvenir §79 *intr* to provide; **subvenir a** to provide for; (*gastos*) to defray
subvertir §68 *tr* to subvert
subyugar §44 *tr* to subjugate, to subdue
sucedáne·o -a *adj & m* substitute
suceder *tr* to succeed, follow || *intr* to happen; **suceder a** (*p.ej., el trono*) to succeed to || *ref* to follow one another
sucesi·vo -va *adj* successive; **en lo sucesivo** in the future
suceso *m* event, happening; issue, outcome; **sucesos de actualidad** current events
suciedad *f* dirt, filth; dirtiness, filthiness
su·cio -cia *adj* dirty, filthy; base, low; tainted; blurred; (sport) foul || **sucio** *adv* (sport) foully, unfairly
sucumbir *intr* to succumb
sucursal *f* branch, branch office
Sudamérica *f* South America
sudamerica·no -na *adj & mf* South American
sudar *tr* to sweat; (coll) to cough up || *intr* to sweat; (*trabajar mucho*) (coll) to sweat
sudario *m* shroud, winding sheet
sudcorea·no -na *adj & mf* South Korean
sudor *m* sweat; (fig) sweat, toil; **chorrear de sudor** to swelter
sudoro·so -sa *adj* sweaty
Suecia *f* Sweden
sue·co -ca *adj* Swedish || *mf* Swede || *m* (*idioma*) Swedish
suegra *f* mother-in-law
suegro *m* father-in-law
suela *f* sole; sole leather; (*fish*) sole
sueldacostilla *f* grape hyacinth
sueldo *m* salary, pay
suelo *m* ground, soil, land; floor, flooring; pavement; (*p.ej., de una botella*) bottom; **no pisar en el suelo** to walk on air; **suelo franco** loam; **suelo natal** home country
suel·to -ta *adj* loose; free; easy; swift, agile, nimble; fluent; bold, daring; (*ejemplar*) single; (*verso*) blank; odd, separate; spare; bulk; **suelto de lengua** loose-tongued || *m* small change; news item
sueñecillo *m* nap; **descabezar un sueñecillo** to take a nap
sueño *m* sleep; dream; (*cosa de gran belleza*) (fig) dream; **conciliar el sueño** to manage to go to sleep; **ni por sueños** by no means; **no dormir sueño** to not sleep a wink; **tener sueño** to be sleepy; **último sueño** (*muerte*) last sleep; **sueño hecho realidad** dream come true; **sueños dorados** daydreams
suero *m* serum
suerte *f* fortune, luck; piece of luck; fate, lot; kind, sort; way, manner; feat, trick; (taur) play, suerte; (Peru) lottery ticket; **de esta suerte** in this way; **de suerte que** so that, with the result that; **la suerte está echada** the die is cast; **suerte de capa** (taur) capework
suerte·ro -ra *adj* (Am) fortunate, lucky
sué·ter *m* (*pl* **-ters**) sweater
suficiente *adj* sufficient; adequate; fit, competent
sufijo *m* suffix
sufragar §44 *tr* to help, support, favor; to defray || *intr* (SAm) to vote
sufragio *m* help, succor; benefit; (*voto*) suffrage
sufragismo *m* woman suffrage
sufragista *mf* woman-suffragist || *f* suffragette
sufri·do -da *adj* long-suffering; (*color*) serviceable; (*marido*) complaisant
sufrir *tr* to suffer; to undergo, experience; to support, hold up; to tolerate; (*un examen*) to take || *intr* to suffer
sugerencia *f* suggestion
sugerir §68 *tr* to suggest
sugestión *f* suggestion
sugestionar *tr* to influence by suggestion
sugesti·vo -va *adj* suggestive; stimulating, striking, conspicuous
suicida *adj* suicidal || *mf* suicide
suicidar *ref* to commit suicide
suicidio *m* suicide
Suiza *f* Switzerland
sui·zo -za *adj & mf* Swiss || *f* see **Suiza**
sujeción *f* subjection; surrender; fastening; fastener
sujetahilo *m* (elec) binding post
sujetapape·les *m* (*pl* **-les**) paper clip
sujetar *tr* to subject; to subdue; to fasten, tighten || *ref* to subject oneself, to submit; to stick, adhere
suje·to -ta *adj* subject, liable; (Am) able, capable || *m* subject; fellow, individual; **buen sujeto** good egg
sulfato *m* sulfate
sulfito *m* sulfite
sulfúri·co -ca *adj* sulfuric
sulfuro *m* sulfide; **sulfuro de hidrógeno** hydrogen sulfide
sulfuro·so -sa *adj* sulfurous
sultán *m* sultan; (*galanteador*) (coll) sheik
suma *f* sum, addition; summary; sum and substance; **en suma** in short, in a word
sumadora *f* adding machine
sumamente *adv* extremely, exceedingly
sumar *tr* to add; to sum up; to amount to || *intr* to add; to amount; **suma y sigue** add and carry || *ref* to add up; to adhere
suma·rio -ria *adj & m* summary
sumergir §27 *tr* to submerge || *ref* to submerge; (*un submarino*) to dive
sumersión *f* submersion; (*de un submarino*) dive
sumidad *f* top, apex, summit
sumidero *m* drain, sewer; sink
suministrar *tr* to provide, to supply
suministro *m* provision, supply; **suministros** supplies
sumir *tr* to sink; to press down; to overwhelm || *ref* to sink; (*p.ej., los carrillos, el pecho*) to be sunken; (Am) to shrink, to shrivel; (Am) to cower; (*p.ej., el sombrero*) (Am) to pull down
sumisión *f* submission; (*sometimiento*) subjection
sumi·so -sa *adj* submissive
su·mo -ma *adj* high, great, extreme;

supreme; **a lo sumo** at most, at the most || *f* see **suma**
suncho *m* hoop
suntuo•so -sa *adj* sumptuous
supeditar *tr* to hold down, oppress
superar *tr* to surpass, excel; to conquer
superávit *m* (com) surplus
supercarburante *m* high-test fuel
supercherería *f* fraud, deceit
superficial *adj* superficial; surface
superficie *f* surface; exterior, outside; area; **superficie de sustentación** (aer) airfoil
super•fluo -flua *adj* superfluous
superhombre *m* superman
superintendente *mf* superintendent, supervisor; **superintendente de patio** (rr) yardmaster
superior *adj* superior; upper; higher; **superior a** superior to; higher than; more than; larger than || *m* superior
superiora *f* mother superior
superioridad *f* superiority; authorities
superlati•vo -va *adj & m* superlative
supermercado *m* supermarket
super•no -na *adj* highest, supreme
superpoblar **§61** *tr* to overpopulate
superponer **§54** *tr* to superpose
superproducción *f* overproduction
supersóni•co -ca *adj* supersonic || *f* supersonics
superstición *f* superstition
supersticio•so -sa *adj* superstitious
supervisar *tr* to supervise
supervivencia *f* survival; (law) survivorship
súpi•to -ta *adj* sudden; (coll) impatient; (Col) dumbfounded
suplantar *tr* to supplant by treachery; (*un documento*) to alter fraudulently
suplefal•tas *mf* (*pl* **-tas**) substitute, fill-in
suplemento *m* supplement; excess fare
súplica *f* entreaty, supplication; request
suplicante *adj & mf* suppliant
suplicar **§73** *tr & intr* to entreat, implore; (law) to petition
suplicio *m* torture; punishment, execution; anguish
suplir *tr* to supplement, make up for; to replace, take the place of; (*un defecto de otra persona*) to cover up; (gram) to understand
suponer **§54** *tr* to suppose; to presuppose, imply; to entail || *intr* to have weight, have authority
suposición *f* supposition; distinction; falsehood, imposture
supositorio *m* suppository
supradi•cho -cha *adj* above-mentioned
supre•mo -ma *adj* supreme
supresión *f* suppression, elimination, omission; cancellation; deletion
suprimir *tr* to suppress, eliminate, do away with; to cancel; to delete
supues•to -ta *adj* supposed, assumed, hypothetical; **supuesto que** since, inasmuch as || *m* assumption, hypothesis; **dar por supuesto** to take for granted; **por supuesto** of course, naturally
supurar *intr* suppurate, discharge pus
sur *m* south; south wind
Suramérica *f* South America
surcar **§73** *tr* to furrow; to plough; to cut through; to streak through
surco *m* furrow; wrinkle, rut, cut; (*del disco gramofónico*) groove; **echarse en el surco** (coll) to lie down on the job
surcorea•no -na *adj & mf* South Korean
sure•ño -ña *adj* (Am) southern || *mf* (Am) southerner
surestada *f* (Arg) southeaster
surgir **§27** *intr* to spout, spurt; to come forth, spring up; to arise, appear
suripanta *f* (hum) chorine; (scornful) slut, jade
surti•do -da *adj* assorted || *m* assortment; supply, stock
surtidor *m* jet, spout, fountain; **surtidor de gasolina** gasoline pump
surtir *tr* to furnish, provide, supply || *intr* to spout, spurt, shoot up
susceptible *adj* susceptible; touchy
suscitar *tr* to stir up, provoke; (*dudas, una cuestión*) to raise
susodi•cho -cha *adj* above-mentioned
suspender *tr* to hang; to suspend; to astonish; to postpone; to fail, to flunk || *ref* to be suspended
suspensión *f* suspension; astonishment; **suspensión de fuegos** cease fire
suspen•so -sa *adj* suspended, hanging; baffled, bewildered; (theat) closed || *m* flunk, condition
suspensores *mpl* (Am) suspenders
suspensorio *m* jockstrap, supporter
suspi•caz *adj* (*pl* **-caces**) suspicious, distrustful
suspirar *intr* to sigh
suspiro *m* sigh; ladyfinger; (mus) quarter rest
sustentación *f* support, prop; (aer) lift
sustentar *tr* to sustain, support, feed; to maintain; (*una tesis*) to defend
sustento *m* sustenance, support, food; maintenance
susto *m* scare, fright
susurrar *tr* to whisper || *intr* to whisper; to murmur, rustle, purl, hum; to be bruited about || *ref* to be bruited about
susurro *m* whisper; murmur, rustle, purling, hum
susu•rrón -rrona *adj* (coll) whispering || *mf* (coll) whisperer
sutil *adj* subtle; keen, observant; thin, delicate
su•yo -ya *adj poss* of his, of hers, of yours, of theirs, e.g., **un amigo suyo** a friend of his; *pron poss* his, hers, yours, theirs, its, one's; **hacer de las suyas** (coll) to be up to one's old tricks; **salirse con la suya** to have one's way; to carry one's point

T

T, t (te) *f* twenty-third letter of the Spanish alphabet
t. *abbr* **tarde**
taba *f* anklebone; (*del carnero*) knucklebone; (*juego*) knucklebones
tabaco *m* tobacco; cigar; snuff; (Cuba, CAm, Mex) punch; **tabaco en rama** leaf tobacco
tabalada *f* (coll) bump, thump, heavy fall; (coll) slap
tabalear *tr* to rock, to sway || *intr* to drum with the fingers
tabanazo *m* (coll) slap; (coll) slap in the face
tabanco *m* stand, stall, booth
tábano *m* horsefly, gadfly
tabanque *m* treadle wheel
tabaola *f* noise, hubbub
tabaquera *f* snuffbox; (*de la pipa de fumar*) bowl; (Arg, Chile) tobacco pouch
tabaquería *f* tobacco store, cigar store
tabaque·ro -ra *adj* tobacco || *mf* tobacconist; cigar maker || *m* (Bol) pocket handkerchief || *f* see **tabaquera**
tabardete *m* or **tabardillo** *m* (coll) sunstroke; (coll) harum-scarum
tabarra *f* (coll) bore, tiresome talk
taberna *f* tavern, saloon, barroom, pub
tabernáculo *m* tabernacle
tabernera *f* barmaid
tabernero *m* tavern keeper; bartender
tabica *f* (*para cubrir un hueco*) board; (*del frente de un escalón*) riser
tabicar **§73** *tr* to close up, to shut up; to wall up
tabique *m* thin wall; partition wall, partition
tabla *f* (*de madera*) board; (*de metal*) sheet; (*de piedra*) slab; (*de tierra*) strip; (*cuadro pintado en una tabla*) panel; (*lista, catálogo; índice de materias*) table; **escapar** or **salvarse en una tabla** to have a narrow escape; **tabla de lavar** washboard; **tabla de planchar** ironing board; **tabla de salvación** lifesaver, helping hand; **tablas** draw, tie; (*escenario del teatro*) stage; (*de la plaza de toros*) barrier; **tener tablas** to have stage presence
tablado *m* flooring; scaffold; (*escenario del teatro*) stage
tablear *tr* to cut into boards; to divide into plots or patches; to level, to grade
tablero *m* boarding; timber; table top; gambling table; cutting board; checkerboard, chessboard; counter; blackboard; **poner al tablero** to risk; **tablero de instrumentos** (aer) control panel; (aut) dashboard
tableta *f* small board; (*taco de papel; comprimido, pastilla*) tablet
tabletear *intr* to rattle
tablilla *f* tablet; splint; bulletin board
tablón *m* plank; beam
tabloncillo *m* (taur) seat in last row
ta·bú *m* (*pl* **-búes**) taboo
tabuco *m* hovel
tabulador *m* tabulator
tabular *tr* to tabulate
taburete *m* stool
tac *m* tick
tacada *f* stroke (*of a billiard cue*)
taca·ño -ña *adj* stingy
táci·to -ta *adj* tacit; silent
tacitur·no -na *adj* taciturn; melancholy
taco *m* bung, plug; wad, wadding; billiard cue; pad, tablet; drumstick; (coll) snack, bite; (coll) drink; (coll) oath, curse; (Am) heel; (Am) muddle, mess
tacón *m* heel
taconear *tr* (Chile) to fill, to stuff || *intr* to click the heels; to strut
taconeo *m* click, clicking (*of heels*)
tácti·co -ca *adj* tactical || *m* tactician || *f* tactics
tacto *m* (sense of) touch; (*del dactilógrafo, el pianista, el instrumento*) touch; skill; tact
tacha *f* defect, fault, flaw
tachar *tr* to erase; to strike out; to blame, find fault with
tacho *m* (Arg) garbage can; (Arg) watch; (Arg, Chile) boiler; (Cuba) sugar pan; (Am) tin sheet
tachón *m* scratch, erasure; ornamental tack or nail; trimming
tachonar *tr* to adorn with ornamental tacks; to trim with ribbon; to spangle, to stud
tachuela *f* tack; hobnail; (Chile, Mex) runt, half pint; (SAm) drinking cup
Tadeo *m* Thaddeus
tafetán *m* taffeta; **tafetanes** flags, colors; (coll) finery; **tafetán inglés** court plaster
tafilete *m* morocco leather; (Am) sweatband
tagarote *m* sparrow hawk; scrivener; (coll) lout; (coll) gentleman sponger
tagua *f* (Chile) mud hen; (*arbusto*) (SAm) ivory palm; (*fruto*) (SAm) ivory nut
taha·lí *m* (*pl* **-líes**) baldric
tahona *f* horse-driven flour mill; bakery
ta·hur -hura *adj* gambling; cheating || *mf* gambler; cheat; cardsharp
tailan·dés -desa *adj* & *mf* Thai
Tailandia *f* Thailand
taima·do -da *adj* sly, crafty; (Arg, Ecuad) lazy; (Chile) gruff, sullen
tajada *f* cut; slice; (coll) hoarseness, (coll) drunk
tajadero *m* chopping block
tajalá·piz *m* (*pl* **-pices**) pencil sharpener
tajamar *m* cutwater; (Am) dike, dam
tajar *tr* to cut; to slice; (*un lápiz*) to sharpen
tajo *m* cut; cutting edge; chopping block; execution block; steep cliff || **Tajo** *m* Tagus
tal *adj indef* such; such a || *pron indef* so-and-so; such a thing; someone || *adv* so; in such a way; **con tal (de) que** provided (that); **¿qué tal?** how?; hello!, how's everything?

talabarte *m* sword belt
talabartero *m* saddler, harness maker
talache *m* or **talacho** *m* (Mex) mattock
taladrar *tr* to bore, drill, pierce, perforate; (*un billete*) to punch; (*un problema*) to get to the bottom of
taladro *m* drill; auger; drill hole; drill press
tálamo *m* bridal bed
talán *m* ding-dong
talante *m* countenance, mien; desire, will, pleasure; way, manner
talar *adj* (*traje, vestidura*) long || *tr* (*árboles*) to fell; to destroy, lay waste
talco *m* tinsel; talc; **talco en polvo** talcum powder
talega *f* bag, sack; **talegas** (coll) money, wealth
talego *m* big bag, sack; (coll) slob; **tener talego** (coll) to have money tucked away
taleguilla *f* small bag; bullfighter's breeches
talento *m* talent
talento•so -sa *adj* talented
Tales *m* Thales
Talía *f* Thalia
talismán *m* talisman
talón *m* heel; (aut) lug, flange; check, voucher, coupon; (*de un cheque*) stub
talona•rio -ria *adj* stub || *m* stub book, checkbook
talonear *intr* (coll) to dash along
talud *m* slope
talla *f* cut; carving; height, stature; size; ransom; reward; (Arg) chatting, prattle; (CAm) fraud, lie; (Col) beating, thrashing
tallar *tr* to carve; (*una piedra preciosa*) to cut; (*naipes*) to deal; to appraise; to engrave; to grind; to size up; (Col) to beat, to thrash || *intr* (Arg) to chat, converse; (Chile) to make love
tallarín *m* noodle
talle *m* shape, figure, stature; waist; fit; appearance, outline; (Am) bodice
taller *m* shop, workshop; factory, mill; atelier, studio; laboratory; **taller agremiado** closed shop; **taller franco** open shop; **taller penitenciario** workhouse
tallo *m* stem, stalk; shoot, sprout; (Col) cabbage
tamal *m* (CAm, Mex) tamale; (Am) intrigue; (Chile) bundle
tamañi•to -ta *adj* so small; very small; confused, disconcerted
tama•ño -ña *adj* so big; such a big; very big, very large; so small; **abrir tamaños ojos** to open one's eyes wide || *m* size
tambaleante *adj* staggering
tambalear *intr & ref* to stagger, reel, totter
también *adv* also, too
tambo *m* (Arg, Chile) brothel; (SAm) roadside inn; (Arg, Urug) dairy
tambor *m* drum; (*persona que toca el tambor*) drummer; sieve, screen; eardrum; coffee roaster; **a tambor batiente** with drums beating; in triumph; **tambor mayor** drum major
tamborilear *tr* to praise to the skies || *intr* to drum
Támesis *m* Thames
ta•miz *m* (*pl* **-mices**) sieve
tamizar **§60** *tr* to sift, to sieve
tamo *m* fuzz, fluff
tampoco *adv* neither, not either; **ni yo tampoco** nor I either
tampón *m* stamp pad
tan *adv* so; **tan . . . como** or **cuan** as . . . as; **tan siquiera** at least; **un tan** + *adj* such a + *adj* || *m* boom (*of a drum*)
tanda *f* turn; shift, relay; task; coat, layer; game, match; flock, lot, pack; (Am) show; (Am) habit, bad habit
tangente *adj & f* tangent; **escaparse, irse** or **salir por la tangente** (coll) to evade the issue
Tánger *f* Tangier
tanguista *f* hostess (*in a night club*)
ta•no -na *adj & mf* (Arg) Neapolitan, Italian
tanque *m* tank; (dial) dipper, drinking cup
tantán *m* tom-tom; clanging; boom
tantear *tr* to compare; to size up; to probe, test, feel out; to sketch, outline; to keep the score of || *intr* to keep score; (Am) to grope; **¡tantee Vd.!** (Am) just imagine!, fancy that!
tanteo *m* comparison; careful consideration; test, probe, trial; trial and error; score
tan•to -ta *adj & pron indef* so much; as much; **tanto . . . como** as much . . . as; both . . . and; **tan•tos -tas** so many; as many; **tantos . . . como** as many . . . as; **y tantos** odd, or more, e.g., **veinte y tantos** twenty odd, twenty or more || *m* copy; counter, chip; point; (Am) portion, part; **apuntar los tantos** to keep score; **entre tanto** in the meantime; **estar al tanto de** to be aware of, to be or keep informed about; **poner al tanto de** to make aware of, to keep informed of; **por lo tanto** or **por tanto** therefore || **tanto** *adv* so much; so hard; so often; so long; as much
tañer **§70** *tr* (*un instrumento músico*) to play; (*una campana*) to ring || *intr* to drum with the fingers
tañido *m* sound, tone; twang; ring, tang
tapa *f* lid, cover, top, cap; (*de un cilindro, un barril*) head; (*de una compuerta*) gate; (*de un libro*) board cover; shirt front; (aut) valve cap; **levantarse** or **saltarse la tapa de los sesos** to blow one's brains out; **tapas** appetizer, free lunch
tapabalazo *m* (Am) fly (*of trousers*)
tapabarro *m* (Chile) mudguard
tapaboca *f* slap in the mouth; muffler; (coll) squelch, squelcher
tapacu•bo or **tapacu•bos** *m* (*pl* **-bos**) (aut) hubcap
tapadera *f* lid, cover, cap
tapagote•ras *m* (*pl* **-ras**) (Arg) roofing cement; (Col) roofer
tapaguje•ros *m* (*pl* **-ros**) (coll) bungling mason; (coll) substitute, replacement
tapar *tr* to cover; to cover up, to hide;

to plug, stop, stop up; to conceal; to obstruct; to wrap up; (*un diente*) (Chile) to fill
tapara *f* (Ven) gourd; **vaciarse como una tapara** (Ven) to spill all one knows
taparrabo *m* loincloth; bathing trunks
tapera *f* (SAm) ruins; (SAm) shack
tapete *m* rug; runner; table scarf; **estar sobre el tapete** to be on the carpet, be under discussion; **tapete verde** card table, gambling table
tapia *f* mud wall, adobe wall
tapiar *tr* to wall up, wall in; to close up
tapicería *f* tapestries; upholstery; tapestry shop; upholstery shop
tapicero *m* tapestry maker; upholsterer; carpet maker; carpet layer
ta•piz *m* (*pl* **-pices**) tapestry
tapizar §60 *tr* to tapestry; to upholster; to carpet; to cover
tapón *m* stopper, cork; cap; bottle cap; bung, plug; (elec) fuse; (surg) tampon; **tapón de algodón** (surg) swab; **tapón de cubo** (aut) hubcap; **tapón de desagüe** drain plug; **tapón de tráfico** traffic jam; **tapón de vaciado** (aut) drain plug
taponar *tr* to plug, stop up; (surg) to tampon
taponazo *m* pop
taque *m* click; knock, rap
taqué *m* (aut) tappet
taquigrafía *f* shorthand, stenography
taquigrafiar §77 *tr* to take down in shorthand || *intr* to take shorthand
taquígra•fo -fa *mf* stenographer
taquilla *f* ticket rack; ticket window; ticket office; box office; gate, take; file; (C-R) inn, tavern
taquille•ro -ra *adj* box-office || *mf* ticket agent
taquimeca *mf* (coll) shorthand-typist
taquimecanógra•fo -fa *mf* shorthand-typist
tarabilla *f* millclapper; catch; turnbuckle; (*de la hebilla de la correa*) tongue; (coll) chatterbox; (coll) jabber; **soltar la tarabilla** (coll) to talk a blue streak
tarabita *f* (*clavillo de la hebilla*) tongue; (SAm) rope of rope bridge
taracea *f* marquetry, inlaid work
tarambana *adj & mf* (coll) crackpot
tararear *tr & intr* to hum
tarasca *f* dragon (*in Corpus Christi procession*); (*mujer fea*) (coll) hag
tarascada *f* bite; (coll) tart reply
tardanza *f* slowness, delay, tardiness
tardar *intr* to be long, to be slow; to be late; **a más tardar** at the latest; **tardar en** + *inf* to be late in + *ger* || *ref* to be long, to be slow; to be late
tarde *adv* late; too late; **hacerse tarde** to grow late; **tarde o temprano** sooner or later || *f* afternoon; evening; **de la tarde a la mañana** overnight; suddenly, in no time; unexpectedly
tardecer §22 *intr* to grow dark, to grow late
tardí•o -a *adj* late, delayed; dilatory, tardy; slow
tar•do -da *adj* slow; late; slow, dull, dense
tar•dón -dona *mf* (coll) poke, slow poke
tarea *f* task, job; care, worry
tarifa *f* tariff; price list; rate; fare; (telp) toll; **tarifa recargada** extra fare
tarima *f* platform; stand; stool; low bench; (*entablado para dormir*) bunk
tarjeta *f* card; **tarjeta de buen deseo** or **de felicitación** greeting card; **tarjeta de visita** calling card, visiting card; **tarjeta navideña** Christmas card; **tarjeta perforada** punch card; **tarjeta postal** post card, postal card
tarjetero *m* card case; card index
tarquín *m* mire, slime, mud
tarro *m* jar; milk pail; (Am) horn; (SAm) top hat
tarta *f* tart, cake; pan
tartajear *intr* to stutter
tartalear *intr* (coll) to stagger, to sway; (coll) to be speechless
tartamudear *intr* to stutter, to stammer
tartamudeo *m* stuttering, stammering
tartamu•do -da *mf* stutterer, stammerer
tartán *m* Scotch plaid
tartana *f* tartana (*two-wheeled round-top carriage of Valencia*)
tarugo *m* wooden plug; wooden paving block; (Guat, Mex) dolt, blockhead
tasa *f* appraisal; measure, standard; rate; ceiling price
tasación *f* appraisal; regulation
tasajo *m* jerked beef
tasar *tr* to appraise; to regulate; to hold down, keep within bounds; to grudge
tasca *f* dive, joint; tavern; (Peru) surf, breakers
tata *m* (coll) daddy || *f* (coll) nursemaid; (Am) little sister
tato *m* (Am) little brother
tatuaje *m* tattoo, tattooing
tatuar §21 *tr & ref* to tattoo
tauri•no -na *adj* bullfighting
taurófi•lo -la *mf* bullfight fan
tauromaquia *f* bullfighting
taxear *intr* (aer) to taxi
taxi *m* taxi, taxicab || *f* taxi dancer
taxista *mf* taxi driver
taza *f* cup; (*de la fuente*) basin; (*del inodoro*) bowl
te *pron pers & reflex* thee, to thee; you, to you; thyself, to thyself; yourself, to yourself
té *m* tea; **té bailable** tea dance
tea *f* torch, firebrand
teatral *adj* theatrical
teatre•ro -ra *mf* (Am) theater-goer
teatro *m* theater; **dar teatro a** to ballyhoo; **teatro de estreno** first-run house; **teatro de repertorio** stock company
teatrólo•go -ga *mf* theater critic || *m* actor || *f* actress
Tebas *f* Thebes
tebe•o -a *adj & mf* Theban || *m* comic book, funny paper
teca *f* teak
tecla *f* (*de piano, máquina de escribir, etc.*) key; touchy subject; **dar en la tecla** (coll) to get the knack of it; **tecla de cambio** shift key; **tecla de escape** margin release; **tecla de espa-**

cios space bar; **tecla de retroceso** backspacer
teclado *m* keyboard; **teclado manual** (mus) manual
teclear *tr* (coll) to feel out || *intr* to run over the keys; to drum, to thrum; (Chile) to be at death's door; (*un jugador*) (Chile) to be losing one's last cent
tecleo *m* fingering; touch; (*de la máquina de escribir*) click
técni·co -ca *adj* technical || *m* technician; expert || *f* technique; technics
tecolote *m* eagle owl (*of Central America*); (Mex) night policeman
techado *m* roof; **bajo techado** indoors
techar *tr* to roof
techo *m* ceiling; roof; (*sombrero*) (coll) hat; **techo de paja** thatched roof
techumbre *f* ceiling; roof
tedio *m* ennui, boredom
tedio·so -sa *adj* tedious, boresome
teja *f* roofing tile; shovel hat; yew tree; linden tree; **a toca teja** (coll) for cash; **teja de madera** shingle
tejadillo *m* cover, top; (*de coche*) roof
tejado *m* tile roof; roof; **tejado de vidrio** (fig) glass house
tejama·ní *m* (*pl* **-níes**) (Am) shake (*long shingle*)
tejar *m* tile works || *tr* to tile, roof with tiles
teja·roz *m* (*pl* **-roces**) eaves
teje·dor -dora *adj* weaving; (coll) scheming || *mf* weaver; (coll) schemer
tejer *tr & intr* to weave
tejido *m* weave, texture; web; fabric, textile; tissue; (biol & fig) tissue; **tejido adhesivo** friction tape; **tejido de saco** (Mex) burlap; **tejido de punto** knitted fabric, jersey
tejo *m* disk; quoit; yew tree
tejón *m* badger
tela *f* cloth, fabric; (*de cebolla*) skin; (*del insecto*) web; film; (bb) cloth; (paint) canvas; (*dinero*) (slang) dough; **poner en tela de juicio** to question, to doubt; **tela de alambre** wire screen; **tela de araña** spider web, cobweb; **tela emplástica** court plaster; **tela metálica** chicken wire; wire screen
telar *m* loom; frame; embroidery frame; (bb) sewing press
telaraña *f* spider web, cobweb
telecontrol *m* remote control
teledifundir *tr & intr* to telecast
teledifusión *f* telecasting; telecast
telefonar *tr & intr* (Am) to telephone
telefonazo *m* (coll) telephone call
telefonear *tr & intr* to telephone
telefonema *m* telephone message
telefonista *mf* telephone operator
teléfono *m* telephone; **teléfono automático** dial telephone; **teléfono público** pay station
teleg. *abbr* **telégrafo, telegrama**
telegrafiar §77 *tr & intr* to telegraph
telegrafista *mf* telegrapher
telégrafo *m* telegraph; **telégrafo de banderas** wigwagging; **telégrafo de máquinas** (naut) engine-room telegraph; **telégrafo sin hilos** wireless telegraph
telegrama *m* telegram
teleimpresor *m* teletype, teleprinter
Telémaco *m* Telemachus
telemando *m* remote control
telemetrar *tr* to telemeter
telemetría *f* telemetry
telémetro *m* telemeter; (mil) range finder
telen·do -da *adj* sprightly, lively
telerreceptor *m* television set
telescopar *tr & ref* to telescope
telescopio *m* telescope
telesilla *f* chair lift
telespecta·dor -dora *mf* viewer, televiewer
telesquí *m* ski lift, ski tow
teleta *f* blotter, blotting paper
teletipo *m* teletype
teletubo *m* (telv) picture tube
televidente *mf* viewer, televiewer
televisar *tr* to televise
televisión *f* television; **televisión en circuito cerrado** closed-circuit television; **televisión en colores** color television
televi·sor -sora *adj* televising; television || *m* television set || *f* television transmitter
telón *m* drop curtain; **telón de acero** (fig) iron curtain; **telón de boca** (theat) front curtain; **telón de fondo** or **foro** (theat) backdrop
tema *m* theme, subject; exercise; (gram) stem; (mus) theme || *f* fixed idea; persistence; grudge; **a tema** in emulation
temario *m* agenda
temblar §2 *intr* to tremble, shake, quiver, shiver; **estar temblando** to teeter
tem·blón -blona *adj* (coll) shaking, tremulous || *m* aspen tree
temblor *m* tremor, shaking, trembling; **temblor de tierra** earthquake
tembloro·so -sa *adj* trembling, shaking, tremulous
tem·bo -ba *adj* (Col) silly, stupid
temer *tr & intr* to fear
temera·rio -ria *adj* rash, reckless, foolhardy
temeridad *f* rashness, recklessness, foolhardiness, temerity
temero·so -sa *adj* frightful, dread; timid; fearful
temible *adj* dreadful, terrible, fearful
temor *m* fear, dread
témpano *m* small drum; drumhead; (*de barril*) head; (*de tocino*) flitch; (*de hielo*) iceberg, floe; (archit) tympan; (mus) kettledrum
temperamental *adj* temperamental
temperamento *m* temperament; conciliation, compromise; weather
temperar *tr* to temper, soften, moderate, calm; to tune || *intr* (Am) to go to a warmer climate
temperatura *f* temperature; weather
temperie *f* weather, state of the weather
tempestad *f* storm, tempest; **tempestad de arena** sandstorm; **tempestades de risas** gales of laughter

tempesti•vo -va *adj* opportune, timely
tempestuo•so -sa *adj* stormy, tempestuous
templa•do -da *adj* temperate; moderate; lukewarm, medium; (coll) brave, courageous; (SAm) in love; (Am) drunk, tipsy; (CAm, Mex) clever
templanza *f* temperance; mildness
templar *tr* to temper; to soften; to ease; to dilute; (*colores*) to blend; (*velas*) to trim || *intr* (*el tiempo*) to warm up || *ref* to temper; to moderate; (Am) to fall in love; (Am) to die
temple *m* weather, state of the weather; temper, disposition; humor; average; dash, boldness; (*del acero, el vidrio, etc.*) temper
templo *m* temple
témpora *f* Ember days
temporada *f* season; period; (*p.ej., de buen tiempo*) spell; **de temporada** temporarily; vacationing
temporal *adj* temporal; temporary || *m* weather; storm, tempest; spell of rainy weather
temporáne•o -a or **tempora•rio -ria** *adj* temporary
temporizar **§60** *intr* to temporize; to putter around
temprane•ro -ra *adj* early
tempra•no -na *adj* early || **temprano** *adv* early
tenacidad *f* tenacity; persistence
tenacillas *fpl* sugar tongs; hair curler; tweezers; snuffers
te•naz *adj* (*pl* **-naces**) tenacious; persistent
tenazas *fpl* pincers, pliers; tongs
tenazón — a or **de tenazón** without taking aim; offhand
tenazuelas *fpl* tweezers
tendedera *f* (Am) clothesline; (Am) litter
tendedero *m* drier, frame for drying clothes; drying ground
tendencia *f* tendency
tender **§51** *tr* to spread; to stretch out; to extend; to reach out; to offer, to tender; (*la ropa*) to hang out; (*con una capa de cal o yeso*) to coat; (*un puente*) to throw, build; (*una trampa*) to set; (*conductores eléctricos, vías de ferrocarril, cañerías*) to lay; (*la cama*) (Am) to make; (*un cadáver*) (Am) to lay out || *intr* to tend || *ref* to stretch out; to throw one's cards on the table; to run at full gallop
ténder *m* tender
tenderete *m* stand, booth
tende•ro -ra *mf* shopkeeper, storekeeper || *m* tent maker
tendido *m* (*p.ej., de un cable*) laying; (*de una cortina de humo*) spreading; (*de alambres*) hanging, stretching; wires; (*trecho de ferrocarril*) stretch; (*ropa que tiende la lavandera*) wash; (*de cal o yeso*) coat; (*del tejado*) slope; (*de panes*) batch; (taur) uncovered stand; (Col) bedclothes
tendón *m* tendon
tenducha *f* or **tenducho** *m* miserable old store
tenebro•so -sa *adj* dark, gloomy; (*negocio*) dark, shady; (*estilo*) obscure
tenedor *m* holder, bearer; fork, table fork; **tenedor de acciones** stockholder; **tenedor de bonos** bondholder; **tenedor de libros** bookkeeper
teneduría *f* bookkeeping
tenencia *f* tenure, tenancy; (mil & nav) lieutenancy
tener **§71** *tr* to have; to hold; to keep; to own, possess; to consider; (*recibir*) to get; to esteem; to stop; **no tenerlas todas consigo** (coll) to be alarmed, dismayed; **no tener nada que ver con** to have nothing to do with; **no tener sobre qué caerse muerto** (coll) to not have a cent to one's name; **tener que** to have to; for expressions like **tener hambre** to be hungry, see the noun || *ref* to stop; to catch oneself, to keep from falling; to consider oneself; to fit, to go
tenería *f* tannery
tenida *f* (Am) meeting, session
teniente *adj* holding, owning; unripe; mean, miserly; (coll) hard of hearing || *m* lieutenant; **teniente coronel** lieutenant colonel; **teniente de navío** (nav) lieutenant
tenis *m* tennis
tenista *mf* tennis player
tenor *m* tenor, character, import, drift; (mus) tenor; **a tenor de** in accordance with
tenorio *m* lady-killer
tensión *f* tension, stress; (elec) tension, voltage; (mech) stress; **tensión arterial** or **sanguínea** blood pressure
ten•so -sa *adj* tense, tight, taut
tentación *f* temptation
tentáculo *m* tentacle, feeler
tenta•dor -dora *adj* tempting || *m* tempter
tentar **§2** *tr* to touch; (*el camino*) to feel; to try, to attempt; to examine; to try out, to test; to tempt; to probe
tentati•vo -va *adj* tentative || *f* attempt; trial, feeler
tentempié *m* (coll) snack, bite, pick-me-up; (*juguete*) (coll) tumbler
tenue *adj* tenuous; light, soft; faint, subdued; (*estilo*) simple
teñir **§72** *tr* to dye; to stain; to tinge, shade, color
teología *f* theology; **no meterse en teologías** (coll) to keep out of deep water
teorema *m* theorem
teoría *f* theory
tepe *m* turf, sod
tequila *m* (Mex) tequila (*distilled liquor*)
terapéuti•co -ca *adj* therapeutic(al) || *f* therapeutics
terapia *f* therapy
tercena *f* government tobacco warehouse; (Ecuad) butcher shop
terce•ro -ra *adj* third || *mf* third; mediator; go-between || *m* procurer, bawd; referee, umpire
terceto *m* tercet; trio
terciar *tr* to place diagonally; to divide into three parts; (*p.ej., la capa, el*

fusil) to swing over one's shoulder; (*licor*) (Am) to water || *intr* to intercede, mediate || *ref* to happen; to be opportune
tercia·rio -ria *adj* tertiary
ter·cio -cia *adj* third || *m* third; (mil) corps; **hacer buen tercio a** to do a good turn
terciopelo *m* velvet
ter·co -ca *adj* stubborn; hard, resistant
Teresa *f* Theresa
tergiversar *tr* to slant, to twist, to distort
terliz *m* ticking
termal *adj* thermal; steam
termas *fpl* hot baths
térmi·co -ca *adj* temperature; steam; steam-generated
terminación *f* termination
terminal *adj* terminal || *m* (elec) terminal
terminante *adj* final, definitive, peremptory
terminar *tr* to end, terminate; to finish || *intr* to end, terminate
término *m* end, limit; boundary; bearing, manner; term; **medio término** subterfuge, evasion; compromise; **primer término** foreground; (mov) close-up; **segundo término** middle distance; **término medio** average; **último término** background
termistor *m* (elec) thermistor
termite *m* termite
termodinámi·co -ca *adj* thermodynamic || *f* thermodynamics
termómetro *m* thermometer; **termómetro clínico** clinical thermometer
termonuclear *adj* thermonuclear
termopar *m* (elec) thermocouple
Termópilas, las Thermopylae
ter·mos *m* (*pl* **-mos**) thermos bottle; hot-water heater; **termos de acumulación** (elec) off-peak heater
termosifón *m* hot-water boiler
termóstato *m* thermostat
terna *f* trio
terne·jo -ja *adj* (Ecuad, Peru) peppy, energetic
ternera *f* calf; (*carne*) veal
terneza *f* tenderness; fondness, love; **ternezas** flirting, flirtation
ternilla *f* gristle
terno *m* suit of clothes; oath, curse; trio; (coll) piece of luck; (Col) cup and saucer; (W-I) set of jewelry
ternura *f* tenderness; fondness, love
terquedad *f* stubbornness; hardness, resistance
terraja *f* diestock
terral *adj* (*viento*) land || *m* land breeze
Terranova *m* (*perro*) Newfoundland (*dog*) || *f* (*isla y provincia*) Newfoundland (*island and province*)
terraplén *m* fill; embankment; terrace, platform; earthwork, rampart
terrateniente *mf* landholder, landowner
terraza *f* terrace; veranda; flat roof; (*de jardín*) border, edge; sidewalk cafe; glazed jar with two handles
terremoto *m* earthquake
terrenal *adj* earthly, mundane, worldly
terre·no -na *adj* terrestrial; mundane, worldly || *m* land, ground, terrain; lot, plot; (sport) field; (fig) field, sphere; **sobre el terreno** on the spot; with data in hand; **terreno echadizo** refuse dump
terre·ro -ra *adj* earthly; of earth; humble || *m* pile, heap; mark, target; terrace; public square; (min) dump
terrestre *adj* terrestrial; ground, land
terrible *adj* terrible; gruff, surly, ill-tempered
territorio *m* territory
terromontero *m* hill, butte
terrón *m* clod; lump, cake
terror *m* terror
terrorismo *m* terrorism, frightfulness
terro·so -sa *adj* earthly; dirty
terruño *m* piece of ground; soil; country, native soil
ter·so -sa *adj* smooth, glossy, polished; smooth, limpid, flowing
tertulia *f* party, social gathering; literary gathering; game room; **estar de tertulia** to sit around and talk
tertulia·no -na *mf* party-goer; regular member
Tesalia, la Thessaly
te·sis *f* (*pl* **-sis**) thesis
te·so -sa *adj* taut, tight, tense || *m* top of hill; (*en superficie lisa*) rough spot
tesón *m* grit, pluck, tenacity
tesone·ro -ra *adj* (Am) obstinate, stubborn, tenacious
tesorería *f* treasury
tesore·ro -ra *mf* treasurer
tesoro *m* treasure; treasury; treasure house; thesaurus
Tespis *m* Thespis
testa *f* head; front; (coll) head, brains; **testa coronada** crowned head
testaferro *m* (coll) dummy, figurehead, straw man
testamento *m* testament, will; **Antiguo Testamento** Old Testament; **Nuevo Testamento** New Testament; **Viejo Testamento** Old Testament
testar *tr* (Ecuad) to cross out || *intr* to make a will
testaru·do -da *adj* stubborn, pig-headed
testera *f* front; (*de animal*) forehead; (*de coche*) back seat
testículo *m* testicle
testificar **§73** *tr & intr* to testify
testigo *mf* witness; **testigo de vista, testigo ocular,** or **testigo presencial** eyewitness || *m* (*evidencia*) witness; (*en un experimento*) control
testimoniar *tr* to attest, to testify to, to bear witness to
testimonio *m* testimony; affidavit; false witness
tes·tuz *m* (*pl* **-tuces**) (*p.ej., de caballo*) face; nape
teta *f* teat; breast
tetera *f* teapot, teakettle
tetilla *f* nipple
tétri·co -ca *adj* dark, gloomy; sad, sullen, gloomy
textil *adj & m* textile
texto *m* text; **fuera de texto tipped-in**
textura *f* texture
tez *f* complexion
ti *pron pers* thee; you

tía *f* aunt; old lady, old woman; (coll) bawd; **no hay tu tía** (coll) there's no chance; **tía abuela** grandaunt
tiara *f* tiara
tibante *adj* (Col) haughty, proud
tibia *f* shinbone; pipe, flute
ti·bio -bia *adj* tepid, lukewarm; (SAm) angry || *f* see **tibia**
tibor *m* large porcelain vase; (Am) chamber pot
tiburón *m* shark
Ticiano, El Titian
tictac *m* tick-tock
tiemblo *m* aspen tree
tiempo *m* time; weather; (gram) tense; (*de un motor de combustión interna*) cycle; (*de una sinfonía*) (mus) movement; (mus) tempo; **darse buen tiempo** to have a good time; **de cuatro tiempos** (mach) four-cycle; **de dos tiempos** (mach) two-cycle; **de un tiempo a esta parte** for some time now; **el Tiempo** Father Time; **fuera de tiempo** untimely, at the wrong time; **hacer buen tiempo** to be clear; **mucho tiempo** a long time; **tomarse tiempo** to bide one's time
tienda *f* store, shop; tent; **ir de tiendas** to go shopping; **tienda de campaña** army tent; camping tent; **tienda de modas** ladies' dress shop; **tienda de objetos de regalo** gift shop; **tienda de raya** (Mex) company store
tienta *f* cleverness; probe; (taur) testing the mettle of a young bull; **andar a tientas** to grope in the dark; to feel one's way
tiento *m* touch; blind man's stick; ropewalker's pole; steady hand; care, caution; mahlstick; (coll) blow, hit; (coll) swig; **andarse con tiento** to watch one's step; **perder el tiento** to lose one's touch
tier·no -na *adj* tender; loving; tearful; soft
tierra *f* earth; ground; land; dirt; (elec) ground; **dar en tierra con** to upset, overthrow, ruin; **echar tierra a** to hush up; **en tierra, mar y aire** on land, on sea, and in the air; **irse a tierra** to topple, to collapse; **la tierra de nadie** (mil) no man's land; **tierra adentro** inland; **tierra de pan llevar** wheat land, cereal-growing land; **tierra firme** mainland; land, terra firma; **Tierra Firme** Spanish Main; **Tierra Santa** Holy Land; **tomar tierra** to land; to find one's way around; **venir** or **venirse a tierra** to topple, to collapse; **ver tierras** to see the world, to go traveling
tierral *m* (Am) cloud of dust
tie·so -sa *adj* stiff; tight, taut, tense; stubborn; bold, enterprising; strong, well; stiff, stuck-up; **tenérselas tiesas a** or **con** to stand up to || **tieso** *adv* hard
ties·to -ta *adj* stiff; tight, taut, tense; stubborn || *m* flowerpot; (*pedazo roto*) potsherd || **tiesto** *adv* hard
tiesura *f* stiffness
ti·fo -fa *adj* (coll) full, satiated || *m* typhus; **tifo de América** yellow fever; **tifo de Oriente** bubonic plague
tifón *m* waterspout; typhoon
tigra *f* tigress; (Am) female jaguar
tigre *m* tiger; (Am) jaguar
tijera *f* scissors, shears; sawbuck; **buena tijera** (coll) good cutter; (coll) good eater; (coll) gossip; **tijeras** scissors, shears
tijeretear *tr* to snip, clip, cut; (coll) to meddle with || *intr* (Am) to gossip
tila *f* linden tree; linden-blossom tea
tildar *tr* to put a tilde or dash over; to erase, strike out; **tildar de** to brand as
tilde *m & f* tilde; accent mark; superior dash; blemish, flaw; censure || *f* jot, tittle
tiliche *m* (CAm, Mex) trinket
tiliche·ro -ra *mf* (CAm) peddler
tilín *m* ting-a-ling
tilo *m* linden tree; (Am) linden-blossom tea
tilo·so -sa *adj* (CAm) dirty, filthy
timar *tr* to snitch; to swindle || *ref* (coll) to make eyes at each other
timba *f* (coll) game of chance; (coll) gambling den; (CAm, Mex) belly
timbal *m* kettledrum; (*pastel relleno*) casserole
timbrar *tr* to stamp
timbre *m* stamp, seal; tax stamp; stamp tax; deed of glory; (phonet & phys) timbre; **timbre nasal** twang; **timbres** glockenspiel
tími·do -da *adj* timid, bashful
timo *m* (coll) theft, swindle; (coll) lie; (coll) catch phrase
timón *m* (*del arado*) beam; rudder; (fig) helm; **timón de dirección** (aer) vertical rudder; **timón de profundidad** (aer) elevator
timonel *m* helmsman, steersman
timonera *f* (naut) pilot house, wheelhouse
timora·to -ta *adj* God-fearing; chicken-hearted
tímpano *m* eardrum; kettledrum
tina *f* large earthen jar; wooden vat; bathtub
tinaja *f* large earthen jar
tincazo *m* (Arg, Ecuad) fillip
tinglado *m* shed; intrigue, trick; (zool) leatherback
tinieblas *fpl* darkness
tino *m* feel (*for things*); good aim; knack; insight, wisdom; **coger el tino** to get the knack of it
tinta *f* ink; tint, hue; dyeing; **de buena tinta** (coll) on good authority; **tinta china** India ink; **tinta simpática** invisible ink
tinte *m* dye; dyeing; dyer's shop; (fig) coloring, false appearance
tinterillo *m* (coll) clerk, lawyer's clerk; (Am) pettifogger
tintero *m* inkstand, inkwell
tintín *m* clink; jingle
tintinear *intr* to clink; to jingle
tin·to -ta *adj* red || *m* red table wine || *f* see **tinta**
tintorería *f* dyeing; dyeing establishment; dry-cleaning establishment
tintore·ro -ra *mf* dyer; dry cleaner

tintura *f* dye; dyeing; rouge; tincture; (fig) smattering; **tintura de tornasol** litmus, litmus solution; **tintura de yodo** iodine
tiña *f* ringworm; (coll) stinginess
tiño·so -sa *adj* scabby, mangy; (coll) stingy
tío *m* uncle; old man; (coll) guy, fellow; **tío abuelo** granduncle; **tíos** uncle and aunt
tiovivo *m* merry-go-round, carrousel
tipiadora *f* (*máquina*) typewriter; (*mujer*) typist
tipiar *tr & intr* to type, to typewrite
tipicista *adj* regional, local
típi·co -ca *adj* typical; regional; quaint
tipismo *m* quaintness
tipista *mf* typist, typewriter
tiple *mf* soprano (*person*); treble-guitar player || *m* soprano (*voice*); treble guitar
tipo *m* type; (*de descuento, de interés, de cambio*) rate; shape, figure, build; (coll) fellow, guy, specimen; **tener buen tipo** to have a good figure; **tipo de ensayo** or **prueba** eye-test chart; **tipo de impuesto** tax rate; **tipo de letra** typeface; **tipo menudo** small print
tipografía *f* typography
típula *f* (ent) daddy-longlegs
tira *m* (Arg, Chile, Col) detective || *f* strip; **hecho tiras** (Chile) in rags; **tira emplástica** (Arg) court plaster; **tira proyectable** film strip; **tiras cómicas** comics, funnies
tirabala *f* popgun
tirabuzón *m* corkscrew; corkscrew curl
tirada *f* throw; distance, stretch; time, period; printing; edition, issue; shooting party, hunting party; tirade; **de** or **en una tirada** at one stroke; **tirada aparte** reprint
tira·do -da *adj* dirt-cheap; (*letra*) cursive || *f* see **tirada**
tira·dor -dora *mf* shot, good shot || *m* knob; doorknob; pull chain; **tirador certero** sharpshooter; **tirador emboscado** sniper
tirafondo *m* wood screw
tiraje *m* draft; printing, edition
tiramira *f* long, narrow mountain range; (*de personas o cosas*) string; distance, stretch
tiranía *f* tyranny
tiráni·co -ca *adj* tyrannic(al)
tira·no -na *adj* tyrannous || *mf* tyrant
tirante *adj* tense, taut, tight; (fig) tense, strained || *m* (*de los arreos de una caballería*) trace; **tirantes** suspenders
tirantez *f* tenseness, tautness, tightness; strain
tirar *tr* to throw, cast, fling; to throw away; to shoot, fire; (*alambre*) to draw, pull, stretch; (*una línea*) to draw; (*una coz, un pellizco*) to give; to print; to attract; to tear down, knock down; (phot) to print || *intr* to pull; to last; to appeal, have an appeal; (*una chimenea*) to draw; (*a la derecha, a la izquierda*) to bear, to turn; **ir tirando** (coll) to get along; **tirar a** to shoot at; (*la espada*) to handle; to shade into; to tend to; to aspire to; **tirar de** to pull, pull on; (*una espada*) to draw; to attract; to boast of being; **tira y afloja** (coll) give and take; (coll) hot and cold || *ref* to rush, throw oneself; to give oneself over; to lie down
tirilla *f* neckband; **tirilla de bota** bootstrap; **tirilla de camisa** collarband
tiritar *intr* to shiver
tiro *m* throw; shot; charge, load; (*estampido*) report; rifle range; (*p.ej., de chimenea*) draft; (*de caballos*) team; (*de escalera*) flight; (*de las guarniciones*) trace; (*de un paño*) length; pull cord, pull chain; reach; hurt, damage; trick; theft; (min) shaft; (sport) drive, shot; (*alusión desfavorable*) shot; (fig) shot, marksman; **a tiro de fusil** within gunshot; **a tiro de piedra** within a stone's throw; **matar a tiros** to shoot to death; **ni a tiros** not for love nor money; **poner el tiro muy alto** to hitch one's wagon to a star; **tiro al blanco** target practice; **tiro al vuelo** trapshooting; **tiro de la pesa** (sport) shot-put
tirón *m* tyro, novice; jerk; tug, pull; **de un tirón** all at once; at a stretch
tirotear *tr* to snipe at, to blaze away at || *ref* to fire at each other; to bicker
tirria *f* (coll) dislike, grudge; **tener tirria a** (coll) to have it in for
tisana *f* tea, infusion
tisis *f* consumption, tuberculosis
titanio *m* titanium
tít. *abbr* **título**
títere *m* marionette, puppet; fixed idea; (coll) whipper-snapper, nincompoop; **no dejar títere con cabeza** or **cara** (coll) to upset the applecart; **títeres** puppet show
titilar *tr* to titillate || *intr* to flutter, quiver; to twinkle
titubear *intr* to stagger, totter; to stammer, stutter; to waver, hesitate
titular *m* bearer, holder; incumbent; headline || *f* capital letter || *tr* to title, entitle || *intr* to receive a title || *ref* to be called; to call oneself
titulillo *m* running head
título *m* title; titled person; regulation; bond; certificate; degree; diploma; headline; **a título de** as a, by way of, on the score of; **títulos** credentials
tiza *f* chalk
tiznar *tr* to soil with soot; to spot, stain; to defame || *ref* to become soiled; to get spotted or stained; (Arg, Chile, CAm) to get drunk
tizne *m & f* soot || *m* firebrand
tiznón *m* smudge, spot of soot
tizón *m* brand, firebrand; wheat smut; brand, dishonor
tizonear *intr* to stir up the fire
tlapalería *f* (Mex) paint store
toalla *f* towel; **toalla rusa** Turkish towel; **toalla sin fin** roller towel
toallero *m* towel rack
toar *tr* (naut) to tow
tobar *tr* (Col) to tow
tobillera *f* anklet; (sport) ankle support; (coll) subdeb; (coll) flapper

tobillo *m* ankle
tobo *m* (Ven) bucket
tobogán *m* toboggan; chute, slide
toca *f* toque; headdress
tocadis•cos *m* (*pl* **-cos**) record player; **tocadiscos automático** record changer
toca•do -da *adj* (*echado a perder; medio loco*) touched; **tocado de la cabeza** (coll) touched in the head || *m* hairdo, coiffure; headdress
toca•dor -dora *mf* performer, player || *m* boudoir; dressing table; dressing case, toilet case
tocante *adj* touching; **tocante a** concerning, with reference to
tocar §73 *tr* to touch; to touch on; to feel; to ring; to toll; to strike; to come to know, to suffer, to feel; (*el cabello*) to do; (*un tambor*) to beat; (mus) to play; (paint) to touch up || *intr* to touch; **tocar a** to knock at; to pertain to, to concern; to fall to the lot of; to be the turn of; (*el fin*) to approach; **tocar en** (*un puerto*) to touch at; (*tierra*) to touch; to touch on; to approach, border on || *ref* to put one's hat on, to cover one's head; to touch each other; to be related; to make one's toilet; to become mentally unbalanced; (*el sombrero*) to tip; **tocárselas** (coll) to beat it
toca•yo -ya *mf* namesake
tocino *m* bacon; salt pork
tocón *m* stump
tocuyo *m* (SAm) coarse cotton cloth
tochimbo *m* (Peru) smelting furnace
to•cho -cha *adj* rough, coarse, crude
todavía *adv* still, yet; **todavía no** not yet
to•do -da *adj* all, whole, every; any || *m* whole; everything; **con todo** still, however; **del todo** wholly, entirely; **jugar el todo por el todo** to stake everything, to shoot the works; **sobre todo** above all, especially; **todo el que** everybody who; **todo lo que** all that; **todos** all, everybody; **todos cuantos** all those who
todopodero•so -sa *adj* all-powerful, almighty
toga *f* (academic) gown
toldilla *f* poop, poop deck
toldería *f* (SAm) Indian camp, Indian village
toldo *m* awning; pride, haughtiness; (SAm) Indian hut
tole *m* hubbub, uproar; **tole tole** gossip, talk; **tomar el tole** (coll) to run away
tolerancia *f* tolerance; **por tolerancia** on sufferance
tolerar *tr* to tolerate
tolete *m* (Am) club, cudgel; (Am) raft; (Cuba) dunce
toletole *m* (Col) persistence, obstinacy; (Ven) merry life of a wanderer
tolon•dro -dra *adj* scatterbrained || *mf* scatterbrain || *m* bump, lump
tolva *f* hopper; chute
tolvanera *f* dust storm
tolla *f* quagmire; (Cuba) watering trough
tom. *abbr* **tomo**
toma *f* taking; seizure, capture; tap; intake, inlet; (elec) tap, outlet; (elec) plug; (elec) terminal; (*de rapé*) pinch; **toma de posesión** installation, induction; inauguration; **toma de tierra** (aer) landing; (rad) ground connection; **toma directa** high gear
toma-corrien•te *m* or **toma-corrien•tes** *m* (*pl* **-tes**) (elec) current collector; (elec) tap, outlet; (elec) plug
tomadero *m* handle; intake, inlet
toma•dor -dora *mf* (com) drawee; (coll) thief; (Am) drinker, toper
tomar *tr* to take; to get; to seize; to take on; (*un resfriado*) to catch; (*p.ej., el desayuno*) to have, to eat; (*el café, un trago*) to take, to drink; **tomar a bien** to take in the right spirit; **tomar a mal** to take offense at; **tomarla con** to pick a quarrel with; to have a grudge against; **tomar prestado** to borrow; **tomar sobre sí** to take upon oneself || *intr* to take, to turn || *ref* to take; (*p.ej., el desayuno*) to have, to eat; (*el café*) to take, to drink; to get rusty
tomate *m* tomato; (*en medias, calcetines, etc.*) (coll) tear, run
tomavis•tas *m* (*pl* **-tas**) motion-picture camera; cameraman
tómbola *f* raffle, charity raffle
tomillo *m* thyme
tomo *m* volume; bulk; importance, consequence; **de tomo y lomo** of consequence; (coll) bulky and heavy
ton. *abbr* **tonelada**
ton *m* — **sin ton ni son** without rhyme or reason
tonada *f* air, melody, song; (Cuba) hoax; (*pronunciación particular*) (Arg, Chile) accent; (Am) singsong
tonel *m* cask, barrel
tonelada *f* (*unidad de peso; unidad de volumen; unidad de desplazamiento*) ton; (*medida de capacidad para el vino*) tun
tonelaje *m* tonnage
tonele•ro -ra *mf* barrelmaker, cooper
tonga *f* coat, layer; (Arg, Col) task; (Col) sleep; (Cuba) heap, pile
tongonear *ref* (Am) to strut, swagger
tóni•co -ca *adj* & *m* tonic || *f* (mus) keynote
tonillo *m* singsong; (*pronunciación particular*) accent
tono *m* tone; tune; (mus) pitch; (mus) key; (*de un instrumento de bronce*) (mus) slide; **dar el tono** to set the standard; **darse tono** (coll) to put on airs; **de buen tono** stylish, elegant; **estar a tono** (coll) to be in style; **poner a tono** (*un motor de automóvil*) to tune up; **tono mayor** (mus) major key; **tono menor** (mus) minor key
tonsila *f* tonsil
tonsilitis *f* tonsilitis
tonsurar *tr* to shear, to clip
tontear *intr* to talk nonsense, to act foolishly
tontería *f* foolishness, nonsense
ton•to -ta *adj* foolish, stupid, silly; **a tontas y a locas** wildly, recklessly; in disorder, haphazardly || *mf* fool,

dolt; **tonto de capirote** (coll) blatant fool

tonu•do -da *adj* (Arg) magnificent, showy, conceited

topacio *m* topaz

topar *tr* to butt; to bump; to run into, encounter || *intr* to butt; to succeed; to lie, be found; **topar con** or **en** to run into, encounter

tope *adj* (*precio*) top; (*fecha*) last || *m* butt; bumper; bump, collision; rub, difficulty; scuffle; masthead; **al tope** or **a tope** end to end; flush; **estar hasta el tope** or **los topes** to be loaded to the gunwales; (coll) to be fed up; **tope de puerta** doorstop

topera *f* molehill

topetada *f* butt

topetar *tr* to butt || *intr* to butt; **topetar con** (coll) to bump, bump into; (coll) to run across

topetón *m* butt; bump, collision

tópi•co -ca *adj* local || *m* topic; (med) external application

topinera *f* molehill; **beber como una topinera** to drink like a fish

topo *m* mole; (coll) blunderer; (coll) stumbler, awkward person

topografía *f* topography

toque *m* touch; (*de una campana*) ringing; (*del tambor*) beat; sound; knock; stroke; check, test; (*punto esencial*) gist; (paint) touch; (coll) blow; **dar un toque a** (coll) to put to the test; (coll) to feel out, to sound out; **toque a muerto** knell, toll; **toque de diana** reveille; **toque de queda** curfew; **toque de retreta** (mil) tattoo; **toque de tambor** drumbeat

torada *f* drove of bulls

tó•rax *m* (*pl* **-rax**) thorax

torbellino *m* whirlwind; (*persona bulliciosa*) (coll) harum-scarum

torcecuello *m* (orn) wryneck

torcedura *f* twist; sprain; dislocation

torcer §74 *tr* to twist; to bend; to turn; to sprain; (*la cara*) to screw up; (*el tobillo*) to wrench; to turn; (*interpretar mal*) to distort, to misconstrue || *intr* to turn || *ref* to twist; to bend; to sprain, dislocate; to turn sour; to go crooked; to fail

torci•do -da *adj* twisted; crooked; bent; (*ojos*) cross; (*persona o conducta*) crooked; (Guat) unlucky || *f* wick, lampwick; curlpaper

tor•do -da *adj* dapple-gray || *mf* dapple-gray horse || *m* thrush; (Am) starling

torear *tr* (*toros*) to fight; to banter, tease, string along || *intr* to fight bulls, be a bullfighter

toreo *m* bullfighting; (taur) performance

tore•ro -ra *adj* (coll) bullfighting || *mf* bullfighter

toril *m* (taur) bull pen

tormenta *f* storm; adversity, misfortune

tormento *m* torment, torture; anguish

tormento•so -sa *adj* stormy; (*barco*) storm-ridden

torna *f* return; dam; tap; **se han vuelto las tornas** the luck has changed; **volver las tornas** to give tit for tat

tornar *tr* to return, give back; to turn, to make || *intr* to return; to turn; **tornar a** + *inf* verb + again, e.g., **tornó a abrir la puerta** he opened the door again || *ref* to turn, to become

tornasol *m* sunflower; litmus; iridescence

tornasola•do -da *adj* changeable, iridescent

tornavía *m* (rr) turntable

torna•voz *m* (*pl* **-voces**) sounding board; **hacer tornavoz** to cup one's hands to one's mouth

tornear *tr* to turn, turn up || *intr* to go around; to tourney; to muse, meditate

torneo *m* tourney; match, tournament; **torneo radiofónico** quiz program

tornillo *m* (*cilindro que entra en la tuerca*) screw; (*clavo con resalto helicoidal*) bolt; (*instrumento con dos mandíbulas*) vise; (mil) desertion; (CAm, Ven) screw tree; **apretar los tornillos a** (coll) to put the screws on; **tener flojos los tornillos** (coll) to have a screw loose; **tornillo de mariposa** or **de orejas** thumbscrew; **tornillo de presión** setscrew; **tornillo para metales** machine screw

torniquete *m* (*para contener hemorragias*) tourniquet; (*torno para cerrar un paso*) turnstile; **dar torniquete a** to twist the meaning of

torno *m* turn, revolution; (*máquina simple que consiste en un cilindro que gira sobre su eje*) winch, windlass; (*de alfarero*) potter's wheel; (*instrumento con dos mandíbulas*) vise; (*máquina herramienta que sirve para labrar metal o madera*) lathe; (*de coche*) brake; (*de un río*) bend, turn; revolving server; **en torno a** or **de** around; **torno de alfarero** potter's wheel; **torno de banco** bench vise; **torno de hilar** spinning wheel

toro *m* bull; **toro corrido** (coll) smart fellow; **toros** bullfight

torón *m* strand

toronja *f* grapefruit

toronjo *m* grapefruit (*tree*)

torpe *adj* slow, heavy; clumsy, awkward; stupid; lewd; crude, ugly

torpedear *tr* to torpedo

torpedo *m* torpedo; touring car

torpeza *f* torpidity, slowness; clumsiness, awkwardness; stupidity; lewdness; turpitude; crudeness, ugliness

torrar *tr* to toast

torre *f* tower; watchtower; (*en el ajedrez*) castle, rook; **torre del homenaje** donjon, keep; **torre de lanzamiento** launching tower; **torre de marfil** (fig) ivory tower; **torre de vigía** (naut) crow's-nest; **torre maestra** donjon, keep; **torre reloj** clock tower

torreja *f* (dial, Am) French toast

torrentada *f* flash flood

torrente *m* torrent

torreón *m* (archit) turret

torreta *f* (nav) turret

tórri•do -da *adj* torrid

torrija *f* French toast

torta *f* cake; (typ) font; (coll) slap; **ser tortas y pan pintado** (coll) to be a cinch; **torta a la plancha** hot cake, griddle cake

torticolis *m* or **tortícolis** *m* wryneck, stiff neck

tortilla *f* omelet; (CAm, Mex) tortilla (*corn-meal cake*); **tortilla a la española** potato omelet; **tortilla a la francesa** plain omelet; **tortilla de tomate** Spanish omelet

tórtola *f* turtledove

tortuga *f* tortoise, turtle

tortuo•so -sa *adj* winding; (fig) devious

tortura *f* torture

torturar *tr* to torture

tor•vo -va *adj* grim, stern

tos *f* cough; **tos ferina** whooping cough

tosca•no -na *adj* Tuscan ‖ **la Toscana** Tuscany

tos•co -ca *adj* coarse, rough; uncouth

toser *intr* to cough

tósigo *m* poison; sorrow

tosiguero *m* poison ivy

tosquedad *f* coarseness, roughness; uncouthness

tostada *f* piece of toast; toast; **dar** or **pegar la tostada** or **una tostada a** (coll) to cheat, to trick; **tostadas** toast

tosta•do -da *adj* brown; tan, sunburned ‖ *m* toasting; roasting ‖ *f* see **tostada**

tostador *m* toaster, roaster

tostar §61 *tr & ref* to toast; to roast; to tan, to burn

tostón *m* roasted chickpea; toast dipped in olive oil; roast pig; scorched food

total *adj & m* total ‖ *adv* (coll) in a word

totalidad *f* totality; entirety; **en su totalidad** in its entirety

tóxi•co -ca *adj & m* toxic

toxicomanía *f* drug addiction

toxicóma•no -na *adj* drug-addicted ‖ *mf* drug addict

tozu•do -da *adj* stubborn

tpo. *abbr* **tiempo**

traba *f* bond, tie; clasp, lock; hobble, clog; obstacle, hindrance

traba•do -da *adj* tied, fastened; joined, connected; robust, sinewy; (*sílaba*) checked; (Am) tongue-tied; (*ojos*) (Col) cross

trabaja•do -da *adj* overworked, worn-out; strained, forced, labored; busy

trabaja•dor -dora *adj* working; industrious, hard-working ‖ *mf* worker, toiler ‖ *m* workman, workingman ‖ *f* workingwoman

trabajar *tr* to work; to till; to bother, disturb; (*a una persona*) to work, to drive ‖ *intr* to work; to strain; to warp; **trabajar en** or **por** to strive to ‖ *ref* to strive, to exert oneself

trabajo *m* work; trouble; (*en contraposición de capital*) labor; **costar trabajo + *inf*** to be hard to + *inf;* **trabajo a destajo** piecework; **trabajo a domicilio** homework; **trabajo a jornal** timework; **trabajo de menores** child labor; **trabajo de oficina** clerical work; **trabajo de taller** shopwork; **trabajos** hardships, tribulations; **trabajos forzados** or **forzosos** hard labor, penal labor

trabajo•so -sa *adj* arduous, laborious; (*maganto*) wan, languid; (*falto de espontaneidad*) labored; (Am) unpleasant, annoying

trabalen•guas *m* (*pl* **-guas**) tongue twister, jawbreaker

trabar *tr* to join, unite; to catch, seize; to fasten; to fetter; to lock; to begin; (*una batalla*) to join; (*una conversación, amistad*) to strike up ‖ *intr* to take hold ‖ *ref* to become entangled; to jam; to foul; **trabársele a uno la lengua** to become tongue-tied

trabe *f* beam

trabilla *f* gaiter strap; belt loop; **end** stitch, loose stitch

trabuco *m* blunderbuss; popgun

trac *m* stage fright

tracale•ro -ra *adj* (CAm, Mex, W-I) cheating, tricky ‖ *mf* (CAm, Mex, W-I) cheat, trickster

tracción *f* traction; **tracción delantera** front drive; **tracción trasera** rear drive

tractor *m* tractor; **tractor de oruga** caterpillar tractor

tradición *f* tradition

tradicionista *mf* folklorist

traducción *f* translation; **traducción automática** machine translation

traducir §19 *tr* to translate; to change

traduc•tor -tora *mf* translator

traer §75 *tr* to bring; to bring on; to draw, pull; to make, keep; to wear; to have, carry; **traer a mal traer** (coll) to abuse, mistreat ‖ *intr* — **traer y llevar** to gossip ‖ *ref* to dress; to behave; **traérselas** (coll) to get worse and worse, to cause a lot of trouble

tráfago *m* traffic, trade; toil, drudgery

trafa•gón -gona *adj* (coll) hustling, lively; (coll) slick, tricky ‖ *mf* hustler, live wire

traficante *mf* dealer, merchant

traficar §73 *intr* to deal, trade, traffic; to travel about

tráfico *m* trade; traffic

tragaderas *fpl* (coll) gullibility; (coll) tolerance; **tener buenas tragaderas** (coll) to be too gullible

tragalda•bas *mf* (*pl* **-bas**) (coll) glutton; (coll) easy mark

tragale•guas *mf* (*pl* **-guas**) (coll) great walker

traga•luz *m* (*pl* **-luces**) skylight, bull's-eye; cellar window

tragamone•das *m* (*pl* **-das**) or **tragape•rras** *m* (*pl* **-rras**) (coll) slot machine

tragar §44 *tr* to swallow; to swallow up; to gulp down; (*creer fácilmente*) to swallow; to overlook; **no poder tragar** (coll) to not be able to stomach ‖ *intr & ref* to swallow

tragasable *m* sword swallower

tragavenado *f* (SAm) anaconda

tragaviro•tes *m* (*pl* **-tes**) (coll) stuffed shirt

tragedia *f* tragedy

trági•co -ca *adj* tragic(al) ‖ *m* tragedian

trago *m* swallow; swig; (coll) misfortune; **a tragos** (coll) slowly

tra•gón -gona *adj* (coll) gluttonous ‖ *mf* (coll) glutton

traición *f* treachery, betrayal; (*delito contra la patria*) treason; treacherous act; **alta traición** high treason; **a traición** treacherously; **hacer traición a** to betray
traicionar *tr* to betray
traicione•ro -ra *adj* treacherous; treasonable || *mf* traitor
traída *f* conveyance, transfer; (Guat) sweetheart; **traída de aguas** water supply
traí•do -da *adj* worn, threadbare || *f* see **traída**
trai•dor -dora *adj* treacherous; treasonable || *mf* traitor; betrayer || *m* villain || *f* traitress
traílla *f* leash; road scraper
traje *m* suit; clothes; dress; gown; **cortar un traje a** (coll) to gossip about; **traje a la medida** suit made to order; **traje de baño** bathing suit; **traje de calle** street clothes; **traje de ceremonia** or **de etiqueta** dress suit; full dress; evening clothes; **traje de faena** (mil) fatigue clothes; **traje de luces** bullfighter's costume; **traje de malla** tights; **traje de montar** riding habit; **traje de paisano** civilian clothes; **traje hecho** ready-made suit; **traje sastre** lady's tailor-made suit; **traje serio** formal dress; **vestir su primer traje largo** to come out, to make one's debut
trajear *tr* to dress, clothe
trajín *m* carrying, transfer, conveyance; going and coming; bustle, commotion
trajinar *tr* to carry, convey; (Arg, Chile) to poke into; (Arg, Chile) to deceive; (Pan) to annoy || *intr* to bustle around
tralla *f* lash, whiplash, whipcord
trama *f* weft, woof; plot, scheme, machination; (*de un drama o novela*) plot
tramar *tr* to weave; to plot, to scheme; (*un enredo*) to hatch (*a plot*)
trambucar **§73** *intr* (Col, Ven) to be shipwrecked; (Col, Ven) to go out of one's mind
tramitación *f* transaction, negotiation; procedure, steps; **tramitación automática de datos** data processing
tramitar *tr* to transact, to negotiate
trámite *m* step, procedure; proceeding; transaction
tramo *m* tract; stretch; (*de una escalera*) flight; (*de un puente*) span; (*de un canal entre dos esclusas*) level
tramontana *f* north; north wind; pride, haughtiness
tramoya *f* stage machinery; scheme
tramoyista *adj* scheming, tricky || *mf* schemer, impostor || *m* stagehand
trampa *f* trap; trap door; (*de un mostrador*) flap; (*de los pantalones*) fly; **armar una trampa a** (coll) to lay a trap for; **trampa explosiva** (mil) booby trap
trampear *tr* (coll) to trick, to swindle || *intr* (coll) to cheat; (coll) to manage to get along
trampilla *f* peephole in the floor; (*de los pantalones*) fly; (*de un secreter*) top, lid; (*de una mesa*) leaf, hinged leaf
trampolín *m* diving board; springboard; ski jump
trampo•so -sa *adj* tricky, crooked || *mf* cheat, swindler
tranca *f* beam, pole; crossbar; (Arg, Chile) drunk, spree; (P-R) dollar; **a trancas y barrancas** (coll) through fire and water
trancar **§73** *tr* to bar || *intr* (coll) to stride along
trance *m* crisis; peril; trance; **a todo trance** at any cost; **último trance** (*de la vida*) last stage, end
tranco *m* long stride; threshold
tranquera *f* palisade, fence
tranquilidad *f* tranquillity
tranquilizante *m* tranquilizer
tranquilizar **§60** *tr, intr & ref* to tranquilize, to calm down
tranqui•lo -la *adj* tranquil, calm
tranquilla *f* feeler
tranquillo *m* knack
transacción *f* settlement, compromise; transaction
transaéreo *m* air liner
transar *tr* (Am) to settle || *intr* (Am) to yield, give in, compromise
transatlánti•co -ca *adj & m* transatlantic
transbordador *m* ferry
transbordar *tr* to transship; to transfer || *intr* to transfer, to change trains
transbordo *m* transshipment; transfer
transcribir **§83** *tr* to transcribe
transcripción *f* transcription
transcurrir *intr* to pass, elapse
transcurso *m* course (*of time*)
transepto *m* transept
transeúnte *adj* transient || *mf* transient; passer-by
transferencia *f* transfer
transferir **§68** *tr* to transfer; to postpone
transformador *m* transformer
transformar *tr* to transform || *ref* to transform, be transformed
tránsfuga *mf* turncoat; fugitive
transfusión *f* transfusion; **transfusión de sangre** transfusion, blood transfusion
transgredir **§1** *tr* to transgress
transgresión *f* transgression
transi•do -da *adj* overcome, paralyzed; mean, cheap, stingy
transigencia *f* compromise; compromising
transigente *adj* compromising
transigir **§27** *tr* to settle, to compromise || *intr* to settle, to compromise; to agree
transistor *m* transistor
transitable *adj* passable, practicable
transitar *intr* to go, walk; to travel
transiti•vo -va *adj* transitive
tránsito *m* transit; traffic; stop; passage; transfer
transito•rio -ria *adj* transitory
translúci•do -da *adj* translucent
transmisión *f* transmission; **transmisión del pensamiento** thought transference
transmisor *m* transmitter; **transmisor de órdenes** (naut) engine-room telegraph
transmitir *tr & intr* to transmit
transmudar *tr* to transfer; to persuade, convince
transmutar *tr, intr & ref* to transmute

transparecer §22 *intr* to show through
transparencia *f* transparency; slide
transparentar *ref* to show through
transparente *adj* transparent || *m* curtain, window curtain; **transparente de resorte** window blind or shade
transpirar *intr* to transpire; (*dejarse conocer una cosa secreta*) to transpire
transplantar *tr* to transplant
transponer §54 *tr* to transpose; to disappear behind || *ref* (*ocultarse detrás del horizonte*) to set; to get sleepy
transportar *tr* to transport; (mus) to transpose
transporte *m* transport; transportation; (aer & naut) transport
transportista *mf* transport worker
tranvía *m* trolley, trolley car, streetcar; **tranvía de sangre** horsecar
tranzar §60 *tr* to cut off, rip off; to plait, braid
trapacear *tr* to cheat, swindle
trapacería *f* cheating, swindling
trapace•ro -ra *adj* cheating, swindling || *mf* cheat, swindler
trapajo *m* rag, tatter
trápala *adj* (coll) chattering; (coll) cheating || *mf* (coll) chatterbox; (coll) cheat || *m* loquacity || *f* noise, uproar; (*del trote de un caballo*) clatter; (coll) cheating
trapear *tr* (Am) to mop
trapecio *m* (geom) trapezoid; (sport) trapeze
trapecista *mf* trapeze performer
trape•ro -ra *mf* ragpicker; junk dealer
trapiche *m* sugar mill; olive press; ore crusher
trapien•to -ta *adj* raggedy, in rags
trapío *m* (coll) flipness, pertness; (*del toro de lidia*) spirit
trapisonda *f* (coll) brawl, row; (coll) scheming
trapisondista *mf* (coll) schemer
trapo *m* rag; (naut) canvas, sails; bullfighter's bright-colored cape; (*de la muleta*) cloth; **a todo trapo** full sail; **poner como un trapo** (coll) to rake over the coals; **sacar los trapos a la colada, a relucir** or **al sol** (coll) to wash one's dirty linen in public; **soltar el trapo** (coll) to burst out crying, to burst out laughing; **trapos** (coll) rags, duds; **trapos de cristianar** (coll) Sunday best
trapo•so -sa *adj* (Am) raggedy, in rags
tráquea *f* trachea, windpipe
traquea•do -da *adj* (*sendero*) (Arg) beaten
traquear *tr* to shake, to rattle; (coll) to fool with || *intr* to crackle; to rattle, to chatter
traqueo *m* shake, rattle, chatter
traquetear *tr & intr* to rattle; to jerk
tras *prep* after; behind; **tras de** behind; in addition to
trasatlánti•co -ca *adj & m* var of **transatlántico**
trasbordador *m* var of **transbordador**
trasbordar *tr & intr* var of **trasbordar**
trasbordo *m* var of **transbordo**
trascendencia *f* penetration, keenness; importance
trascendente *adj* penetrating; important
trascender §51 *tr* to go into, dig up || *intr* to smell; to come to be known, to leak out
trascendi•do -da *adj* keen, perspicacious
trascocina *f* scullery
trascorral *m* back yard; (coll) backside
trascribir §83 *tr* var of **transcribir**
trascripción *f* var of **transcripción**
trascuarto *m* back room
trascurrir *intr* var of **transcurrir**
trascurso *m* var of **transcurso**
trasegar §66 *tr* to upset, turn topsy-turvy; to decant, to draw off
trase•ro -ra *adj* back, rear || *m* buttock rump
trasferir §68 *tr* var of **transferir**
trasformador *m* var of **transformador**
trasformar *tr & intr* var of **transformar**
trásfuga *mf* var of **tránsfuga**
trasfusión *f* var of **transfusión**
trasgo *m* goblin, hobgoblin; imp
trashojar *tr* to leaf through
trasiego *m* upset, disorder; decantation
trasladar *tr* to transfer; to postpone; to copy, transcribe; to transmit; to move || *intr* to go; to move
traslado *m* transfer; copy, transcript; moving
traslapar *tr, intr & ref* to overlap
traslapo *m* lap, overlap
traslúci•do -da *adj* var of **translúcido**
traslucir §45 *tr* to guess || *intr* to leak out || *ref* to be translucent; to leak out
traslumbrar *tr* to dazzle || *ref* to be dazzled; to vanish
trasluz *m* diffused light; glint, gleam; **al trasluz** against the light
trasmisión *f* var of **transmisión**
trasmisor *m* var of **transmisor**
trasmitir *tr & intr* var of **transmitir**
trasmóvil *m* (Col) mobile unit, radio pickup
trasmudar *tr* var of **transmudar**
trasmundo *m* afterlife, future life
trasmutar *tr, intr & ref* var of **transmutar**
trasnocha•do -da *adj* stale; haggard, run-down; hackneyed || *f* last night; sleepless night; (mil) night attack
trasnocha•dor -dora *mf* night owl
trasnochar *tr* (*un problema*) to sleep over || *intr* to spend the night; to spend a sleepless night; to stay up late
trasoír §48 *tr* to hear wrong
traspapelar *tr* to mislay || *ref* to become mislaid
trasparecer §22 *intr* var of **transparecer**
trasparencia *f* var of **transparencia**
trasparente *adj & m* var of **transparente**
traspasar *tr* to cross, cross over; to send; to transfer; to move; to pierce, to transfix; to pain, grieve || *ref* to go too far
traspié *m* slip, stumble; trip
traspirar *intr* var of **transpirar**
trasplantar *tr* var of **transplantar**
trasponer §54 *tr & ref* var of **transponer**
trasportar *tr* var of **transportar**
trasporte *m* var of **transporte**
trasportista *mf* var of **transportista**

traspunte *m* (theat) callboy
traspuntín *m* flap seat, folding seat, jump seat
trasquilar *tr* to crop, to lop; (*las ovejas*) to shear; (coll) to curtail
trastazo *m* (coll) whack, blow
traste *m* fret; **dar al traste con** to throw away, ruin, spoil
trastera *f* attic, junk room
trastienda *f* back room
trasto *m* piece of furniture; piece of junk; (coll) good-for-nothing; **trastos** tools, implements, utensils; arms, weapons; junk; muleta and sword
trastornar *tr* to upset, overturn; to disturb; to perplex; to daze, to make dizzy; to persuade
trastorno *m* upset; disturbance
trastrocar **§81** *tr* to turn around, to reverse, to change
trasudor *m* cold sweat
trasueño *m* blurred dream, vague recollection
trasuntar *tr* to copy; to abstract, to sum up
trasunto *m* copy; record; likeness
trasverter **§51** *intr* to run over, to overflow
trasvolar **§61** *tr* to fly over
trata *f* traffic, trade, slave trade; **trata de blancas** white slavery; **trata de esclavos** slave trade
tratado *m* (*escrito, libro*) treatise; (*convenio entre gobiernos*) treaty; agreement
tratamiento *m* treatment; title; **apear el tratamiento** to leave off the title
tratante *mf* dealer, retailer
tratar *tr* to handle; to deal with; to treat; **tratar a uno de** to address someone as; to charge someone with being || *intr* to deal; to treat; to try; **tratar de** to deal with; to treat of; to come in contact with; to try to || *ref* to deal; to behave; (*bien o mal*) to live; **tratarse de** to deal with; to be a question of
trate•ro -ra *mf* (Chile) pieceworker
trato *m* treatment; deal, agreement; manner; business; title; friendly relations; **tener buen trato** to be very nice, to be very pleasant; **trato colectivo** collective bargaining; **trato doble** double-dealing; **¡trato hecho!** it's a deal!
través *m* bend, bias, turn; reverse, misfortune; (naut) beam; **al** or **a través de** through, across; **dar al través con** to do away with; **mirar de través** to squint; to look at out of the corner of one's eye
travesaño *m* crosspiece; (*de cama*) bolster; (*p.ej., de una silla*) rung
travesear *intr* to romp, carry on; to sparkle, be witty; to lead a wild life
travesía *f* crossing, voyage; crossroad; distance, passage; cross wind; (Arg, Bol) wasteland; (Chile) west wind
travesura *f* prank, antic, caper; mischief; sparkle, wit; slick trick
traviesa *f* crossing, voyage; rafter; side bet; (rr) tie
travie•so -sa *adj* cross; keen, shrewd; restless, fidgety; naughty, mischievous; debauched || *f* see **traviesa**
trayecto *m* journey, passage, course; stretch, run
trayectoria *f* trajectory; path
traza *f* plan, design; scheme; means; appearance; mark, trace; footprint; streak, trait; **tener trazas de** to show signs of; to look like
trazar **§60** *tr* to plan, design; to outline; to trace; (*una línea*) to draw; to lay out, to plot
trazo *m* line, stroke; trace; outline
trebejo *m* implement; chessman
trébol *m* clover; (*naipe que corresponde al basto*) club
trece *adj & pron* thirteen || *m* thirteen; (*en las fechas*) thirteenth; **estarse, mantenerse** or **seguir en sus trece** (coll) to stand firm
trecea•vo -va *adj & m* thirteenth
trecho *m* stretch; while; **a trechos** at intervals
tregua *f* truce; respite, letup
treinta *adj & pron* thirty || *m* thirty; (*en las fechas*) thirtieth
treinta•vo -va *adj & m* thirtieth
tremar *intr* to tremble, to shake
tremen•do -da *adj* frightful, terrible, tremendous; (*muy grande*) (coll) tremendous
trementina *f* turpentine
tremer *intr* to tremble, shake
tremolar *tr & intr* to wave
tren *m* (*de coches o vagones; de ondas*) train; outfit, equipment; following, retinue; show, pomp; (*de la vida*) way; **tren aerodinámico de lujo** (rr) streamliner; **tren ascendente** (rr) up train; **tren correo** (rr) mail train; **tren de aterrizaje** (aer) landing gear; **tren de laminadores** rolling mill; **tren de lavado** (Am) laundry; **tren de mercancías** freight train; **tren de mudadas** (Am) moving company; **tren descendente** (rr) down train; **tren de viajeros** passenger train; **tren ómnibus** (rr) accommodation train; **tren rápido** (rr) flyer
treno *m* dirge
trenza *f* braid, plait; tress; (*p.ej., de ajos*) (Am) string; **en trenzas** with her hair down
trenzar **§60** *tr* to braid, plait || *intr* to caper; to prance
trepa•dor -dora *adj* climbing || *mf* climber || *f* (bot) climber
trepar *tr* to climb; to drill, bore || *intr* to climb; **trepar por** to climb up || *ref* to lean back
trepidar *intr* to shake, vibrate; (Chile) to hesitate, waver
tres *adj & pron* three; **las tres** three o'clock || *m* three; (*en las fechas*) third
trescien•tos -tas *adj & pron* three hundred || **trescientos** *m* three hundred
tresillo *m* ombre; three-piece living-room suit; (mus) triplet
tresnal *m* (agr) shock
treta *f* trick, scheme; (*del esgrimidor*) feint
treza•vo -va *adj & m* thirteenth

triángulo *m* triangle
triar §77 *tr* to sort
tribu *f* tribe
tribuna *f* tribune, rostrum, platform; grandstand; (*en la iglesia*) gallery; **tribuna de la prensa** press box; **tribuna del órgano** (mus) organ loft; **tribuna de los acusados** (law) dock
tribunal *m* tribunal, court; **tribunal tutelar de menores** juvenile court
tributar *tr* (*contribuciones, impuestos, etc.*) to pay; (*admiración, gratitud, etc.*) to render
tributa•rio -ria *adj* tributary; tax; **ser tributario de** to be indebted to || *m* tributary
tributo *m* tribute; tax
tricornio *m* tricorn, three-cornered hat
trifocal *adj* trifocal
trifulca *f* (coll) wrangle, squabble
trigési•mo -ma *adj & m* thirtieth
trigo *m* wheat; (slang) dough, money; **trigo sarraceno** buckwheat
trigonometría *f* trigonometry
trigue•ño -ña *adj* swarthy, olive-skinned
trilogía *f* trilogy
trilla *f* threshing
trilla•do -da *adj* (*sendero*) beaten; trite, commonplace
trilladora *f* threshing machine
trillar *tr* to thresh; to mistreat; (coll) to frequent
trilli•zo -za *mf* triplet
trillón *m* British trillion; quintillion (*in U.S.A.*)
trimestral *adj* quarterly
trimestre *m* quarter
trinado *m* trill, warble
trinar *intr* to trill, warble, quaver; (coll) to get angry
trinca *f* trinity
trincar §73 *tr* to bind, to lash, to tie fast; to crush; (slang) to kill || *intr* to take a drink
trinchar *tr* to carve, to slice
trinchera *f* cut; trench; trench coat
trineo *m* sleigh, sled
Trinidad *f* Trinity
trino *m* trill
trinquete *m* pawl, ratchet; (naut) foresail
trin•quis *m* (*pl* **-quis**) drink, swig
trío *m* sorting; trio; (mus) trio
tripa *f* gut, intestine; belly; (*del cigarro*) filler; **hacer de tripas corazón** (coll) to pluck up courage
triple *adj & m* triple
triplica•do -da *adj & m* triplicate; **por triplicado** in triplicate
triplicar §73 *tr* to triplicate || *intr* to treble
trípode *m* tripod
tríptico *m* triptych
tripu•do -da *adj* big-bellied, potbellied
tripulación *f* crew
tripulante *m* crew member
tripular *tr* to man; to fit out, equip
trique *m* crack, swish; **a cada trique** (coll) at every turn; **triques** (Mex) tools, implements
triquiñuela *f* (coll) chicanery, subterfuge
triquitraque *m* clatter; firecracker
tris *m* crackle; (coll) shave, inch; (coll) trice
trisar *tr* (Chile) to crack, to chip || *intr* to chirp
triscar §73 *tr* to mix; (*una sierra*) to set || *intr* to stamp the feet; to romp, frisk around; (Col) to gossip
trismo *m* lockjaw
triste *adj* sad; dismal, gloomy; (*despreciable, ridículo*) sorry
tristeza *f* sadness; gloominess
tris•tón -tona *adj* wistful, melancholy
tritón *m* eft, newt, triton; (*hombre experto en la natación*) merman
trituradora *f* crushing machine
triturar *tr* to grind, crush; to abuse
triunfal *adj* triumphal
triunfante *adj* triumphant
triunfar *intr* to triumph; to trump; **triunfar de** to triumph over; to trump
triunfo *m* triumph; trump; **sin triunfo** no trump
trivial *adj* trivial; trite, commonplace; (*sendero*) beaten
trivialidad *f* triviality; triteness
triza *f* shred; **hacer trizas** to tear to pieces
trizar §60 *tr* to tear to pieces
trocar §81 *tr* to exchange, to swap; to barter; to confuse, to twist, to distort || *intr* to swap || *ref* to change; to change seats
trocha *f* trail, narrow path; (Am) gauge
trofeo *m* trophy; victory
troj *f* or **troje** *f* granary; olive bin
trole *m* trolley pole
trolebús *m* trolley bus, trackless trolley
tromba *f* (*de polvo, agua, etc.*) whirl, column; **tromba marina** waterspout; **tromba terrestre** tornado
trombón *m* trombone
trompa *f* (*del elefante*) trunk; waterspout; top; nozzle; (anat) duct, tube; (mus) horn; (Col, Chile) cowcatcher; **trompa de armonía** French horn; **trompa de Eustaquio** Eustachian tube
trompada *f* (coll) bump, collision; (coll) punch
trompar *intr* to spin a top
trompeta *f* trumpet; bugle, clarion; (coll) good-for-nothing; (Am) drunkenness
trompetear *intr* (coll) to trumpet, to sound the trumpet
trompetilla *f* ear trumpet; (Am) Bronx cheer
trompicar §44 *tr* to trip, make stumble || *intr* to stumble
trompicón *m* stumble
trompiza *f* (Am) fist fight
trompo *m* (*juguete*) top; (*en el ajedrez*) man; (*buque malo y pesado*) tub
tronada *f* thunderstorm
tronar §61 *tr* (Mex) to shoot || *intr* to thunder; (coll) to fail, collapse; **por lo que pueda tronar** (coll) just in case
troncar §44 *tr* to cut off the head of; (*un escrito*) to cut, shorten
tronco *m* (*del cuerpo, del árbol, de una familia, del ferrocarril*) trunk; (*leño*) log; (*de caballerías*) team; (coll) sap, fathead; **estar hecho un tronco** (coll)

to be knocked out; (coll) to be sound asleep
troncha *f* (Am) slice; (Am) cinch
tronchar *tr* to smash, split; to chop off
tronera *m* madcap, roisterer || *f* embrasure, loophole; louver; (*de la mesa de billar*) pocket
tronido *m* thunderclap
trono *m* throne
tronquista *m* driver, teamster
tronzar §60 *tr* to shatter, break to pieces; to pleat; to wear out
tropa *f* troop; (Am) herd, drove; **en tropa** straggling, without formation; **tropas de asalto** shock troops, storm troops
tropel *m* crowd, throng; rush, hurry; jumble; **de** or **en tropel** in a mad rush
tropelía *f* mad rush; outrage
tropero *m* (Arg) cowboy
tropezar §18 *tr* to strike || *intr* to stumble; to slip, to blunder; **tropezar con** or **en** to stumble over, to trip over; to run into; to come upon
trope·zón -zona *adj* stumbly || *m* stumble; stumbling place; **a tropezones** by fits and starts; falteringly; **dar un tropezón** to stumble, to trip
tropical *adj* tropic(al)
trópico *m* tropic
tropiezo *m* stumble; stumbling block; slip, blunder, fault; obstacle; quarrel
tropilla *f* (Arg, Urug) drove of horses following a leading mare
troposfera *f* troposphere
troquel *m* die
trotaconven·tos *f* (*pl* **-tos**) (coll) procuress, bawd
trotamun·dos *m* (*pl* **-dos**) globetrotter
trotar *intr* to trot; (coll) to hustle
trote *m* trot; (coll) chore; **al trote** (coll) right away; **para todo trote** (coll) for everyday wear; **trote de perro** jog trot
trotona *f* chaperone
trovador *m* troubadour
trovadores·co -ca *adj* troubadour
trovero *m* trouvère
Troya *f* Troy; **ahí fué Troya** (coll) it's a shambles; **¡arda Troya!** (coll) come what may!
troya·no -na *adj* & *mf* Trojan
troza *f* log
trozar §60 *tr* to break to pieces; (*un tronco*) to cut into logs
trozo *m* piece, fragment; block; excerpt, selection
truco *m* contrivance, device; trick; pocketing of ball; **truco de naipes** card trick; **trucos** pool
truculen·to -ta *adj* truculent
trucha *f* trout
trueno *m* thunder, thunderclap; shot, report; (coll) rake, roué; **trueno gordo** finale (*of fireworks*); big scandal; **truenos** (Ven) heavy shoes
trueque *m* barter; exchange, swap; trade-in; **a trueque de** in exchange for; **trueques** (Col) change
trufa *f* truffle; fib, lie
tru·hán -hana *adj* crooked; clownish || *mf* crook; clown
trujal *m* wine press; oil press
trulla *f* noise, bustle; crowd; trowel
truncar §73 *tr* to cut off the head of; (*palabras o frases*) to cut, slash; to cut off, interrupt
trusas *fpl* trunk hose; (Am) trunks
tu *adj poss* thy, your
tú *pron pers* thou, you
tubérculo *m* (*rizoma engrosado, p.ej., de la patata*) tuber; (*protuberancia*) tubercle
tuberculosis *f* tuberculosis
tubería *f* tubing; piping
tubo *m* tube; pipe; **tubo de desagüe** drainpipe; **tubo de ensayo** test tube; **tubo de humo** flue; **tubo de imagen** picture tube; **tubo de vacío** vacuum tube; **tubo digestivo** alimentary canal; **tubo sonoro** chime
tuerca *f* nut; **tuerca de aletas** wing nut
tuer·to -ta *adj* crooked, bent; one-eyed; **a tuertas** upside down; crosswise; **a tuertas o a derechas** rightly or wrongly; thoughtlessly || *mf* one-eyed person || *m* wrong, harm, injustice; **tuertos** afterpains
tuétano *m* marrow; pith; **hasta los tuétanos** (coll) through and through; (coll) head over heels
tufi·llas *mf* (*pl* **-llas**) (coll) touchy person
tufillo *m* whiff, smell
tufo *m* fume, vapor; sidelock; foul odor, foul breath; **tufos** (coll) airs, conceit
tugurio *m* shepherd's hut; hovel
tuición *f* protection, custody
tulipán *m* tulip
tullecer §22 *tr* to abuse, mistreat || *intr* to be crippled
tulli·do -da *adj* paralyzed, crippled || *mf* paralytic, cripple
tullir §13 *tr* to cripple, to paralyze; to abuse, mistreat || *ref* to become crippled or paralyzed
tumba *f* grave, tomb; tombstone; arched top; (Am) felling of trees
tumbacuarti·llos *mf* (*pl* **-llos**) (coll) old toper, rounder
tumbar *tr* to knock down; to catch, to trick; (coll) to stun || *intr* to tumble; to capsize || *ref* (coll) to lie down
tumbo *m* fall, tumble; boom, rumble; crisis; rise and fall of sea; rough surf
tumbona *f* hammock
tumor *m* tumor
túmulo *m* catafalque
tumulto *m* tumult
tuna *f* loafing, bumming
tunante *adj* bumming, loafing; crooked, tricky || *mf* bum, loafer; crook
tundidora *f* lawn mower
tuneci·no -na *adj* & *mf* Tunisian
túnel *m* tunnel
tunes *mpl* (Col) little steps, first steps
Túnez (*ciudad*) Tunis; (*país*) Tunisia
tungsteno *m* tungsten
túnica *f* tunic
tu·no -na *adj* crooked, tricky || *mf* crook || *f* see **tuna**
tupé *m* toupee; (coll) nerve, cheek, brass
tupi·do -da *adj* thick, dense, compact; dull, stupid; (Am) clogged up

tupir *tr* to pack tight || *ref* to stuff, stuff oneself
turba *f* crowd, mob; peat
turbamulta *f* (coll) mob, rabble
turbar *tr* to disturb, trouble; to stir up || *ref* to be confused
turbiedad *f* muddiness; confusion
turbina *f* turbine
tur•bio -bia *adj* turbid, muddy, cloudy; confused; obscure
turbión *m* squall, thunderstorm; (*p.ej., de balas*) (fig) hail
turbopropulsor *m* turboprop (*engine*)
turborreactor *m* turbojet (*engine*)
turbulen•to -ta *adj* turbulent
tur•co -ca *adj* Turkish || *mf* Turk || *m* (*idioma*) Turkish
turfista *adj* horsy || *m* turfman
turismo *m* touring; touring car
turista *mf* tourist
turísti•co -ca *adj* tourist; touring
turnar *intr* to alternate, take turns
tur•nio -nia *adj* (*ojos*) cross; cross-eyed; (*que mira con ceño*) cross-looking
turno *m* turn, shift; **aguardar turno** to wait one's turn; **por turno** in turn; **turno diurno** day shift
turón *m* polecat
turquesa *s* turquoise
Turquía *s* Turkey
turrón *m* nougat; (coll) plum
tusa *f* (Am) corncob; (Am) corn silk; (Chile) mane; (Col) pockmark; (CAm, W-I) trollop
tusar *tr* to shear, clip, cut
tutear *tr* to thou, to address familiarly || *ref* to thou each other, to address each other familiarly
tutela *f* guardianship; protection
tutelar *adj* guardian; protecting || *tr* to protect, shelter, guide
tu•tor -tora or **-triz** (*pl* **-trices**) *mf* guardian, tutor
tu•yo -ya *adj poss* of thee || *pron poss* thine, yours
tuza *f* gopher

U

U, u (u) *f* twenty-fourth letter of the Spanish alphabet
u *conj* (used before words beginning with *o* or *ho*) or
U. *abbr* **usted**
ubicar §73 *tr* (Am) to locate, place || *intr & ref* to be situated
ubi•cuo -cua *adj* ubiquitous
ubre *f* udder
Ucrania *f* Ukraine
ucrania•no -na *adj & mf* Ukrainian
ucra•nio -nia *adj & mf* Ukrainian || *f* see **Ucrania**
Ud. *abbr* **usted**
Uds. *abbr* **ustedes**
ufanar *ref* — **ufanarse con** or **de** to boast of, be proud of
ufanía *f* pride, conceit; cheer, satisfaction; ease, smoothness
ufa•no -na *adj* proud, conceited; cheerful, satisfied; easy, smooth
ujier *m* doorman, usher
úlcera *f* ulcer, fester, sore; **úlcera de decúbito** bedsore
ulcerar *tr & ref* to ulcerate, to fester
ulterior *adj* ulterior; subsequent
ulteriormente *adv* subsequently, later
últimamente *adv* finally; lately, recently
ultimar *tr* to finish, end, conclude, wind up; (Am) to kill, finish off
ultimátum *m* (*pl* **-tums**) ultimatum; (coll) definite decision
últi•mo -ma *adj* last, latest; final; excellent, superior; (*precio*) lowest, final; most remote; (*piso*) top; (*hora*) late; **a la última** in the latest fashion; **a última hora** at the eleventh hour; **a últimos de** toward the end of, in the latter part of; **de última hora** last-minute; **estar a lo último** or **en las últimas** to be up to date, to be well-informed; to be on one's last legs; **por último** at last, finally; **último suplicio** capital punishment
ultraatmosféri•co -ca *adj* outer (*space*)
ultraeleva•do -da *adj* (rad) ultrahigh
ultrajar *tr* to outrage, to offend
ultraje *m* outrage, offense
ultrajo•so -sa *adj* outrageous, offensive
ultramar *m* country overseas
ultramari•no -na *adj* overseas || **ultramarinos** *mpl* groceries, delicatessen
ultranza — **a ultranza** to the death; unflinchingly
ultrarro•jo -ja *adj & m* infrared
ultratumba *adv* beyond the grave
ultraviola•do -da or **ultravioleta** *adj & m* ultraviolet
ululación *f* howl; whoop; (*del buho*) hoot; (*del disco del fonógrafo*) wow
ulular *intr* to howl; to whoop; (*el buho*) to hoot
ululato *m* howl; (*del buho*) hoot
umbilical *adj* umbilical
umbral *m* threshold, doorsill; (*madero que sostiene el muro encima de un vano*) lintel; (physiol, psychol & fig) threshold; **atravesar** or **pisar los umbrales** to cross the threshold; **estar en los umbrales de** to be on the threshold of
umbralada *f* (Col) threshold
umbrí•o -a *adj* shady || *f* shady side
umbro•so -sa *adj* shady
un, una (the apocopated form **un** is used before masculine singular nouns and adjectives and before feminine singular nouns beginning with stressed *a* or *ha*) *art indef* a || *adj* one
unánime *adj* unanimous
unanimidad *f* unanimity
unción *f* unction

uncir §36 *tr* (*bueyes*) to yoke, to hitch
undéci•mo -ma *adj* & *m* eleventh
undo•so -sa *adj* wavy
ungir §27 *tr* to smear with ointment or with oil; to anoint
ungüento *m* unguent, ointment, salve
únicamente *adv* only, solely
úni•co -ca *adj* only, sole; (*sin otro de su especie*) unique; one, e.g., **precio único** one price
unicornio *m* unicorn
unidad *f* (*concepto de una sola cosa o persona; cantidad que se toma como medida común de todas las demás de su clase; el número entero más pequeño*) unit; (*indivisión; armonía de conjunto; el número uno*) unity
uni•do -da *adj* united; smooth, even; close-knit
unificar §73 *tr* to unify
uniformar *tr* to make uniform; to provide with a uniform
uniforme *adj* uniform || *m* uniform; **uniforme de gala** (mil) full dress
uniformidad *f* uniformity
unilateral *adj* unilateral
unión *f* union; double ring
unir *tr* & *ref* to unite
unisonancia *f* (mus) unison; (*de un orador*) monotony
unísono — al unísono in unison; unanimously; **al unísono de** in unison with
unita•rio -ria *adj* unit
universal *adj* universal; (*teclado de máquina de escribir*) standard
universidad *f* university
universita•rio -ria *adj* university || *mf* (Am) university student, college student || *m* university professor
universo *m* universe
u•no -na *pron* one, someone; **a una** of one accord; **la una** one o'clock; **somos uno** we are one; **uno a otro, unos a otros** each other, one another; **uno que otro** one or more, a few; **u•nos -nas** some; a pair of, e.g., **unas gafas** a pair of glasses; **unas tijeras** a pair of scissors; **unos cuantos** some; **uno y otro** both || *pron indef* one, e.g., **uno no sabe qué hacer aquí** one does not know what to do here || *m* (*unidad y signo que la representa*) one
untar *tr* to smear, to grease; to anoint; (coll) to bribe || *ref* to get smeared; to grease oneself; (coll) to peculate
unto *m* grease; (*gordura del cuerpo del animal*) fat; (Chile) shoe polish; **unto de Méjico** or **de rana** (coll) bribe money
untuo•so -sa *adj* unctuous, greasy, sticky
uña *f* nail, fingernail, toenail; (*pezuña*) hoof; (*del ancla*) fluke, bill; (mach) claw, gripper; **enseñar** or **mostrar las uñas** to show one's teeth; **ser largo de uñas** to have long fingers; **ser uña y carne** (coll) to be hand in glove; **tener en la uña** to have on the tip of one's fingers
uñada *f* scratch, nail scratch; (*impulso dado con la uña*) flip
uñero *m* ingrowing nail; (*inflamación del dedo en la raíz de la uña*) whitlow
ural *adj* Ural || **Urales** *mpl* Urals
uranio *m* uranium
urbanidad *f* urbanity
urbanismo *m* city planning
urbanista *mf* city planner
urbanísti•co -ca *adj* city-planning || *f* city planning
urbanizar §60 *tr* (*convertir en poblado*) to urbanize; to refine, polish
urba•no -na *adj* urban, city; (*atento, cortés*) urbane || *m* policeman
urbe *f* metropolis
urdema•las *mf* (*pl* **-las**) (coll) schemer
urdimbre *f* warp; scheme, scheming; **estar en la urdimbre** (Chile) to be thin, be emaciated
urdir *tr* (*los hilos*) to beam; (*una conspiración*) to hatch
urente *adj* burning, smarting
uretra *f* urethra
urgencia *f* urgency; **de urgencia** special-delivery
urgente *adj* urgent; (*correo*) special-delivery
urgir §27 *intr* to be urgent
urina•rio -ria *adj* urinary || *m* urinal
urna *f* glass case; ballot box; (*para guardar las cenizas de los cadáveres*) urn; **acudir** or **ir a las urnas** to go to the polls
urología *f* urology
urraca *f* magpie
U.R.S.S. *abbr* **Unión de Repúblicas Socialistas Soviéticas**
urticaria *f* hives
Uruguay, el Uruguay
urugua•yo -ya *adj* & *mf* Uruguayan
usa•do -da *adj* (*empleado; gastado por el uso; acostumbrado*) used; skilled, experienced; (*vocablo*) **poco usado** rare
usanza *f* use, usage, custom
usar *tr* to use, make use of; (*un cargo, un oficio*) to follow || *intr* — **usar** + *inf* to be accustomed to + *inf;* **usar de** to use, to have recourse to; **usar de la palabra** to speak, make a speech || *ref* to be the custom
usina *f* (Am) factory, plant; (Am) powerhouse; (*estación de tranvía*) (Arg) carbarn
uso *m* use; custom, usage; wear, wear and tear; habit, practice; **al uso** according to custom; **en buen uso** (coll) in good condition; **hacer uso de la palabra** to speak, make a speech
usted *pron pers* you
usual *adj* (*de uso común*) usual; (*que se usa con facilidad*) usable; sociable
usualmente *adv* usually
usua•rio -ria *mf* user
usufructo *m* use, enjoyment
usufructuar §21 *tr* to enjoy the use of
usura *f* usury; profit; **pagar con usura** to pay back a thousandfold
usurero *m* loan shark; profiteer
usurpar *tr* to usurp
utensilio *m* utensil
útero *m* uterus, womb
útil *adj* useful || **útiles** *mpl* utensils, tools, equipment

utilería *f* (Arg) properties, stage equipment
utilero *m* (Arg) property man
utilidad *f* utility, usefulness; profit, earnings
utilita•rio -ra *adj* utilitarian
utilizable *adj* usable
utilizar §60 *tr* to utilize, to use || *ref* — **utilizarse con, de** or **en** to make use of; **utilizarse para** to be good for
utopía *f* utopia
utopista *adj & mf* utopian
UU. *abbr* **ustedes**
uva *f* grape; wart on eyelid; (*baya*) berry; **estar hecho una uva** (coll) to have a load on; **uva crespa** gooseberry; **uva de Corinto** currant; **uva de raposa** nightshade; **uva espín** or **espina** gooseberry; **uva pasa** raisin; **uvas verdes** (*de la fábula de Esopo*) sour grapes
uve *f* (*letra del alfabeto*) V
uxoricida *m* uxoricide (*husband*)
uxoricidio *m* uxoricide (*act*)
uxo•rio -ria *adj* uxorious

V

V, v (ve *or* uve) *f* twenty-fifth letter of the Spanish alphabet
V. *abbr* **usted, véase, venerable**
V.A. *abbr* **Vuestra Alteza**
vaca *f* cow; (*cuero*) cowhide; (*carne de vaca o de buey*) beef; gambling pool; **hacer vaca** (Peru) to play truant; **vaca de la boda** (coll) goat, laughingstock; (coll) friend in need; **vaca de leche** milch cow; **vaca de San Antón** (ent) ladybird
vacación *f* (*cargo que está sin proveer*) vacancy; **de vacaciones** on vacation; **vacaciones** vacation; **vacaciones retribuídas** vacation with pay
vacacionista *mf* vacationist
vacancia *f* vacancy
vacante *adj* vacant || *f* vacancy
vacar §73 *intr* (*un empleo, un cargo*) to be vacant, be unfilled; to take off, take a vacation; **vacar a** to attend to; **vacar de** to lack, be devoid of
vacia•do -da *adj* hollow-ground || *m* cast, casting; plaster cast
vaciante *f* ebb tide
vaciar §77 & regular *tr* to empty, to drain; to cast, to mold; (*formar un hueco en*) to hollow out; to sharpen on a grindstone; to copy, transcribe; to explain in detail || *intr* to empty; to flow; (*el agua en el río*) to fall, go down || *ref* (coll) to blab
vacilación *f* vacillation; flickering; hesitancy, hesitation
vacilada *f* (Mex) spree, high time; (Mex) drunk
vacilante *adj* vacillating; (*luz*) flickering; (*irresoluto*) hesitant
vacilar *intr* to vacillate; (*la luz*) to flicker; to shake, wobble; (*estar irresoluto*) to hesitate, to waver
vací•o -a *adj* empty; (*hueco*) hollow; idle; useless, unsuccessful; (*vaca*) barren; presumptuous || *m* emptiness; (*laguna, abertura; vacante*) vacancy; (*espacio que no contiene ninguna materia*) void; (*espacio de que se ha extraído el aire*) vacuum; (*ijada*) side, flank; **de vacío** light, unloaded; **hacer el vacío a** to isolate
vacuidad *f* vacuity, emptiness
vacuna *f* (*enfermedad de las vacas*) cowpox; (*virus cuya inoculación preserva de una enfermedad determinada*) vaccine
vacunación *f* vaccination
vacunar *tr* to vaccinate
vacu•no -na *adj* bovine; cowhide || *f* see **vacuna**
va•cuo -cua *adj* vacant || *m* cavity, hollow
vadear *tr* (*un río*) to ford; to wade through; to overcome; to sound out || *ref* to behave; to manage
vado *m* ford; expedient, resource; **al vado o a la puente** (coll) one way or another; **no hallar vado** to see no way out; **tentar el vado** to feel one's way
vagabundaje *m* vagrancy
vagabundear *intr* to wander, to roam; to loaf around
vagabun•do -da *adj* vagabond || *mf* vagabond, tramp; wanderer
vagancia *f* loafing, vagrancy
vagar *m* leisure; **con vagar** slowly; **estar de vagar** to have nothing to do || **§44** *intr* to wander, to roam; to be idle; to have plenty of leisure; (*una cosa*) to lie around; (*p.ej., una sonrisa por los labios*) to play
vagido *m* cry of a newborn baby
vagneria•no -na *adj & mf* Wagnerian
va•go -ga *adj* wandering, roaming; idle, loafing; lax, loose; hesitating, wavering; (*indefinido, indeciso*) vague; (*mirada*) blank || *m* vagabond; idler, loafer; **en vago** shakily; in vain; **in the air**; **poner en vago** to tilt
vagón *m* car, railroad car; **vagón cama** sleeping car; **vagón carbonero** coal car; **vagón cerrado** boxcar; **vagón cisterna** tank car; **vagón de carga** freight car; **vagón de cola** caboose; **vagón de mercancías** freight car; **vagón de plataforma** flatcar; **vagón frigorífico** refrigerator car; **vagón salón** chair car; **vagón tolva** hopper-bottom car; **vagón volquete** dump car
vagoneta *f* tip car; station wagon
vaguear *intr* to wander around
vaguedad *f* vagueness; vague remark
vaguido *m* faintness, fainting spell
vaharada *f* breath, exhalation

vahear *intr* to emit odors, to give forth an aroma
vahido *f* faintness, fainting spell
vaho *m* odor, aroma, vapor, fume
vaina *f* sheath; scabbard; knife case; (*de ciertas semillas*) pod, husk; (Am) annoyance, bother; (Col) luck, stroke of luck
vainica *f* hemstitch
vainilla *f* vanilla
vainita *f* (Ven) string bean
vaivén *m* swing, seesaw, backward and forward motion; unsteadiness, inconstancy; risk, chance
vajilla *f* dishes, set of dishes; **lavar la vajilla** to wash the dishes; **vajilla de oro** gold plate; **vajilla de plata** silver plate, silverware; **vajilla de porcelana** chinaware
vale *m* promissory note; voucher; farewell; (Ven) chum, pal; **vale respuesta** reply coupon
valede•ro -ra *adj* valid, effective
vale•dor -dora *mf* defender, protector; (Mex) friend, companion
valedura *f* (Mex) favor, protection
valencia *f* (chem) valence
valentía *f* bravery, valor; feat, exploit; dash, boldness; boast; **pisar de valentía** to strut, swagger
valen•tón -tona *adj* arrogant, boastful || *mf* braggart, boaster || *f* bragging
valer *m* worth, merit, value || **§76** *tr* to defend, protect; to favor, patronize; to avail; to yield; to be worth, be valued at; to be equal to; to suit; **valer la pena** to be worth while (to); **valerle a uno** + *inf* to help someone to + *inf*, to get someone to + *inf;* **valer lo que pesa** (coll) to be worth its (his, her, etc.) weight in gold; **valga lo que valiere** come what may; **¡válgame Dios!** bless my soul!, so help me God! || *intr* to have worth; to be worthy; to be valuable; to be valid; to prevail; to hold, to count; to have influence; **hacer valer** (*sus derechos*) to assert; to make felt; to make good; to turn to account; **más vale** it is better (to); **vale** O.K.; **valer para** to be useful for; **valer por** to be equal to || *ref* to help oneself, to defend oneself; **valerse de** to make use of, to avail oneself of
valero•so -sa *adj* valorous, brave; strong, active, effective
va•let *m* (*pl* **-lets**) (cards) jack
valía *f* value, worth; favor, influence; **mayor valía** or **plus valía** appreciation, increased value; unearned increment
validación *f* validation
validar *tr* to validate
validez *f* validity; strength, vigor
vali•do -da *adj* highly esteemed, influential || *m* court favorite; prime minister
váli•do -da *adj* valid; strong, robust
valiente *adj* valiant; strong, robust; fine, excellent; (*grande y excesivo*) terrific || *m* brave fellow; bully
valija *f* satchel, brief case; mailbag, mailpouch; mail; **valija diplomática** diplomatic pouch
valimiento *m* favor, protection; favor at court, favoritism
valio•so -sa *adj* valuable; influential; wealthy
va•lón -lona *adj & mf* Walloon
valor *m* value, worth; valor, courage; meaning, import; efficacy; equivalence; (*rédito*) income, return; effrontery; (*persona, cosa o cualidad dignas de ser poseídas*) (fig) asset; **¿cómo va ese valor?** (coll) how are you?; **valor de rescate** (ins) surrender value; **valores** securities
valoración *f* valuation, appraisal
valorar or **valorear** *tr* (*poner precio a*) to value, to appraise; to enhance the value of
valorizar §60 *tr* to value; to enhance the value of; (Am) to sell off (*for quick realization*)
vals *m* waltz
valsar *intr* to waltz
valuación *f* valuation, appraisal
valuar §21 *tr* to estimate
válvula *f* valve; **válvula corrediza** slide valve; **válvula de admisión** intake valve; **válvula de escape** exhaust valve; **válvula de escape libre** cutout; **válvula de seguridad** safety valve; **válvula en cabeza** valve in the head, overhead valve
valla *f* fence, railing; barricade; hindrance, obstacle; (sport) hurdle; (W-I) cockpit; **valla paranieves** snow fence
vallado *m* barricade, stockade
valle *m* valley; river bed; valley dwellings; **valle de lágrimas** vale of tears
vampiresa *f* vampire
vampíri•co -ca *adj* vampire; ghoulish
vampiro *m* vampire; (*persona que se deleita con cosas horribles*) ghoul
vanadio *m* vanadium
vanagloriar §77 & regular *ref* to boast
vanaglorio•so -sa *adj* vainglorious, conceited, boastful
vanamente *adv* vainly
vandalismo *m* vandalism
vánda•lo -la *adj & mf* Vandal; (fig) vandal
vanguardia *f* (mil & fig) vanguard, van; **a vanguardia** in the vanguard
vanguardismo *m* avant-garde
vanguardista *adj* avant-garde || *mf* avant-gardist
vanidad *f* vanity; (*fausto*) pomp, show; **ajar la vanidad de** (coll) to take down a peg; **hacer vanidad de** to boast of
vanido•so -sa *adj* vain, conceited
va•no -na *adj* vain; hollow, empty; **en vano** in vain || *m* opening in a wall
vapor *m* steam; (*el visible: exhalación, vaho, niebla, etc.*) vapor; steamer, steamboat; **al vapor** at full speed; **vapores** gas (*belched*); blues; **vapor volandero** tramp steamer
vaporar *tr & ref* to evaporate
vaporizador *m* atomizer, sprayer
vaporizar §60 *tr* to vaporize; to spray || *ref* to vaporize
vaporo•so -sa *adj* vaporous

vapular or **vapulear** *tr* whip, to flog
vaquería *f* drove of cattle; dairy; (Mex) party
vaqueri•zo -za *adj* cattle || *f* winter stable for cattle
vaque•ro -ra *adj* cattle || *mf* cattle tender; (Peru) truant || *m* cow hand; cowboy
vaqueta *f* leather; (P-R) strop; **zurrarle a uno la vaqueta** (Am) to tan someone's hide
vaquillona *f* (Arg, Chile) heifer
vara *f* pole, rod, staff; (*de carruaje*) shaft; (*bastón de mando*) wand; measuring stick; (taur) thrust with goad; **tener vara alta** to have the upper hand; **vara alcándara** shaft; **vara alta** upper hand; **vara buscadora** divining rod (*ostensibly to discover water or metals*); **vara de adivinar** divining rod; **vara de oro** goldenrod; **vara de pescar** fishing rod; **vara de San José** goldenrod
vara-alta *m* (coll) boss
varada *f* beaching; running aground
varadero *m* repair dock
varapalo *m* long pole; (coll) setback, disappointment, reverse
varar *tr* (*una embarcación*) to beach || *intr* to run aground; (*un negocio*) to come to a standstill
varear *tr* (*los frutos de los árboles*) to beat down, knock down; to beat, strike; (taur) to goad; (*los caballos de carreras*) (SAm) to exercise, to train || *ref* to lose weight, get thin
varec *m* (bot) wrack
varenga *f* (naut) floor, floor timber
vareta *f* twig, stick; lime twig for catching birds; colored stripe; (coll) cutting remark; (coll) hint; **irse de vareta** (coll) to have diarrhea
variable *adj & f* variable
variación *f* variation
varia•do -da *adj* varied; variegated
variante *adj & f* variant
variar §77 to vary, to change || *intr* to vary, to change; to be different; **variar de or en opinión to** change one's mind
varice *f* or **várice** *f* varicose veins
varicela *f* chicken pox
varico•so -sa *adj* varicose
variedad *f* variety; **variedades** variety show, vaudeville
varilla *f* rod, stem, twig; (*bastón de mando*) wand; (*de paraguas, abanico, etc.*) rib; (*del corsé*) stay; (*de rueda*) wire spoke; (coll) jawbone; (Mex) peddler's wares; **varilla de nivel** dipstick; **varilla de virtudes** wand, magician's wand
varillaje *m* ribs, ribbing; (*de máquina de escribir*) type bars
varille•ro -ra *adj* (*caballo*) (Ven) race || *m* (Mex) peddler
va•rio -ria *adj* (*de diversos colores; que tiene variedad*) various, varied; fickle, inconstant; **varios** various; several
varón *adj* male, e.g., **hijo varón** male child || *m* man, male; grown man, adult male; man of standing; **santo varón** (coll) plain artless fellow
varonía *f* male issue
varonil *adj* manly, virile; courageous
Varsovia *f* Warsaw
vasa•llo -lla *adj & mf* vassal
vas•co -ca *adj & mf* Basque (*of Spain and France*) || *m* Basque (*language*)
vas•cón -cona *adj & mf* Basque (*of old Spain*)
vasconga•do -da *adj & mf* Basque (*of Spain*) || *m* Basque (*language*) || **las Vascongadas** the Basque Provinces
vascuence *adj & m* Basque (*language*) || *m* (coll) gibberish
vaselina *f* vaseline
vasera *f* kitchen shelf; bottle rack, tumbler rack
vasija *f* container, vessel
vaso *m* tumbler, glass; vase, flower jar; (anat) duct, vessel; **vaso de engrase** (mach) grease cup; **vaso de noche** pot, chamber pot; **vaso graduado** measuring glass; **vaso sanguíneo** blood vessel
vástago *m* shoot, sapling; scion, offspring; rod, stem; **vástago de émbolo** piston rod; **vástago de válvula** valve stem
vastedad *f* vastness
vas•to -ta *adj* vast
vate *m* bard, seer, poet
váter *m* (coll) toilet, water closet
vatiaje *m* wattage
vaticinar *tr* to prophesy, predict
vaticinio *m* prophecy, prediction
vatídi•co -ca *adj* prophetical || *mf* prophet
vatímetro *m* wattmeter
vatio *m* watt
vatio-hora *m* (*pl* **vatios-hora**) watt-hour
vaya *f* jest, jeer
Vd. *abbr* **usted**
Vds. *abbr* **ustedes**
V.E. *abbr* **Vuestra Excelencia**
vece•ro -ra *adj* alternating; yielding in alternate years || *mf* person waiting his turn
vecinamente *adv* nearby
vecindad *f* neighborhood, vicinity; residency; residents; **hacer mala vecindad** to be a bad neighbor
vecindario *m* neighborhood, community; people, population
veci•no -na *adj* neighboring; like, similar || *mf* neighbor; resident, citizen
veda *f* prohibition; (*de la caza y la pesca*) closed season
vedado *m* game preserve
vedar *tr* to forbid, prohibit; to hinder, stop; to veto
vedija *f* fleece, tuft of wool; mat of hair; matted hair
vee•dor -dora *adj* curious, spying || *mf* busybody || *m* supervisor, overseer
vega *f* fertile plain; (Cuba) tobacco plantation
vegetación *f* vegetation; **vegetaciones adenoideas** adenoids
vegetal *adj & m* vegetable
vegetaria•no -na *adj & mf* vegetarian
vego•so -sa *adj* (Chile) damp, wet
vehemencia *f* vehemence
vehemente *adj* vehement

vehículo *m* vehicle; **vehículo espacial** space vehicle
veinta·vo -va *adj & m* twentieth
veinte *adj & pron* twenty; **a las veinte** (coll) late, untimely || *m* twenty; (*en las fechas*) twentieth
veintena *f* score, twenty
veintiún *adj* this apocopated form of **veintiuno** is used before masculine singular nouns and adjectives
veintiu·no -na *adj & pron* twenty-one || *m* twenty-one; (*en las fechas*) twenty-first || *f* (*juego de naipes*) twenty-one
vejación *f* vexation, annoyance
vejamen *m* vexation, annoyance; bantering, taunting
vejar *tr* to vex, annoy; to taunt
vejestorio *m* (coll) old dodo
vejete *m* (coll) little old fellow
vejez *f* old age; oldness; dotage; platitude, old story; **a la vejez, viruelas** there's no fool like an old fool
vejiga *f* (*órgano que recibe la orina de los riñones*) bladder; (*ampolla*) blister; (*saco hecho de piel, goma, etc.*) bag, pouch, bladder; **vejiga de la bilis** or **de la hiel** gall bladder
vela *f* wakefulness; pilgrimage; evening; work in the evening; sail; sailboat; (*cilindro con una torcida que sirve para alumbrar*) candle; vigil (*before Eucharist*); awning; (Mex) scolding; **a toda vela** full sail; **a vela** under sail; **a vela llena** under full sail; **en vela** awake; **estar entre dos velas** to be half-seas over, to have a sheet in the wind; **hacerse a la vela** to set sail; **vela latina** lateen sail; **vela mayor** mainsail; **vela romana** Roman candle
velada *f* evening party, soirée; vigil, watch
vela·do -da *adj* veiled, hidden; (phot) light-struck || *f* see **velada**
velador *m* pedestal table, gueridon; wooden candlestick; watchman; (SAm) night table; (Mex) lamp globe
velaje *m* or **velamen** *m* (naut) canvas, sails
velar *adj & f* velar || *tr* to watch over; to guard; (*la guardia*) to keep; to hold a wake over; (*cubrir con un velo*) to veil; (phot) to fog; (fig) to veil, hide, conceal || *intr* to stay awake; to stay awake working; to keep vigil; (*el viento*) to keep up all night; (*un escollo, un peñasco*) to stick up out of the water; **velar por** or **sobre** to watch over || *ref* (phot) to fog, to be light-struck
velatorio *m* wake
veleidad *f* whim, caprice; fickleness, flightiness
veleido·so -sa *adj* whimsical, capricious; fickle, flighty
vele·ro -ra *adj* swift-sailing || *m* sailboat
veleta *mf* (*persona inconstante*) (coll) weathercock || *f* vane, weathervane, weathercock; (*de un molino*) rudder vane; (*de la caña de pescar*) bob; streamer, pennant; **veleta de manga** (aer) air sleeve, air sock
velís *m* (Mex) valise
velita *f* little candle
velo *m* veil; taking the veil; confusion, perplexity; (*disfraz*) veil; (*de lágrimas*) mist; (phot) fog; **correr el velo** to pull aside the curtain, to dispel the mystery; **tomar el velo** to take the veil; **velo del paladar** soft palate
velocidad *f* (*rapidez*) speed, velocity; (mech) velocity; **en gran velocidad** (rr) by express; **en pequeña velocidad** (rr) by freight; **primera velocidad** (aut) low gear; **segunda velocidad** (aut) second; **tercera velocidad** (aut) high gear; **velocidad con respecto al suelo** (aer) ground speed; **velocidad permitida** speed limit
velocímetro *m* speedometer
velón *m* brass olive-oil lamp
velorio *m* evening party or bee; wake; wake for a dead child; (Am) dull party; (Am) come-on
ve·loz *adj* (*pl* **-loces**) swift, speedy; agile, quick
vello *m* down, fuzz
vellocino *m* fleece; **vellocino de oro** Golden Fleece
vellón *m* fleece; unsheared sheepskin; lock of wool; copper coin; copper-silver alloy
vello·so -sa *adj* downy, hairy, fuzzy
velludillo *m* velveteen
vellu·do -da *adj* shaggy, hairy, fuzzy || *m* (*felpa*) plush; (*terciopelo*) velvet
vena *f* vein; (*en piedras*) grain; (fig) poetical inspiration; **estar en vena** (coll) to be all set, to be inspired; (coll) to sparkle with wit; **vena de loco** fickle disposition
venablo *m* dart, javelin; **echar venablos** to burst forth in anger
venado *m* deer, stag; **pintar el venado** (Mex) to play hooky
venáti·co -ca *adj* (coll) fickle, unsteady; (coll) daffy, nutty
vence·dor -dora *adj* conquering, victorious || *mf* conqueror, victor
vencejo *m* band, string; (orn) European swift, black martin
vencer §78 *tr* to vanquish, conquer; to excel, outdo; to overcome, to surmount || *intr* to conquer, be victorious; (*un plazo*) to be up; (*un contrato*) to expire; (*una letra*) to mature, fall due || *ref* to control oneself; (*un camino*) to bend, turn; (Chile) to wear out, become useless
vencetósigo *m* milkweed, tame poison
venci·do -da *adj* conquered; (com) due, mature, payable
vencimiento *m* (*acción de vencer*) victory; (*hecho de ser vencido*) defeat; (com) expiration, maturity
venda *f* (*para ligar un miembro herido*) bandage; (*para tapar los ojos*) blindfold
vendaje *m* bandage, dressing; **vendaje enyesado** plaster cast
vendar *tr* (*un miembro, una herida*) to bandage; (*los ojos*) to blindfold; (*cegar*) (fig) to blind; (*engañar*) (fig) to hoodwink
vendaval *m* strong southeasterly wind from the sea; strong wind, gale
vendedera *f* saleswoman, saleslady

vende•dor -dora *adj* selling || *m* salesman || *f* saleslady, sales girl
vendehu•mos *mf* (*pl* **-mos**) (coll) influence peddler
vendeja *f* public sale
vender *tr* to sell; to betray, sell out; **vender salud** to be the picture of health || *intr* to sell; **¡vendo, vendo, vendí!** going, going, gone! || *ref* to sell oneself; to sell, be for sale; to betray oneself, to give oneself away; **venderse caro** to be hard to see; to be quite a stranger; **venderse en** (*p.ej., cien pesetas*) to sell for; **venderse por** to pass oneself off as
ven•dí *m* (*pl* **-díes**) certificate of sale
vendible *adj* salable, marketable
vendimia *f* vintage; (fig) big profit
vendimia•dor -dora *mf* vintager
vendimiar *tr* (*la uva*) to gather, to harvest; (*las viñas*) to gather the grapes of; to make off with; (coll) to kill
venduta *f* (Am) public sale; (W-I) greengrocery
Venecia *f* (*ciudad*) Venice; (*provincia*) Venetia
venecia•no -na *adj & mf* Venetian
veneno *m* poison, venom
veneno•so -sa *adj* poisonous, venomous
venera *f* scallop shell; (*manantial de agua*) spring; **empeñar la venera** (coll) to go all out, spare no expense
venerable *adj* venerable
venerar *tr* to venerate, revere; to worship
venére•o -a *adj* venereal || *m* venereal disease
venero *m* (*de agua*) spring; (*filón de mineral*) lode, vein; (fig) source
venezola•no -na *adj & mf* Venezuelan
Venezuela *f* Venezuela
venga•dor -dora *adj* avenging || *mf* avenger
venganza *f* vengeance, revenge
vengar **§44** *tr* to avenge || *ref* to take revenge; **vengarse de** to take revenge on
vengati•vo -va *adj* vengeful, vindictive
venia *f* forgiveness, pardon; leave, permission; bow, greeting
venida *f* coming; return; flood, freshet
venide•ro -ra *adj* coming, future || **venideros** *mpl* successors, posterity
venir **§79** *intr* to come; **que viene** coming, next; **venga lo que viniere** come what may; **venir** + *ger* to be + *ger;* **venir a** + *inf* to come to + *inf;* to amount to + *ger;* to happen to + *inf;* to finally + *inf,* e.g., **después de una larga enfermedad, vino a morir** after a long illness he finally died; **venir a ser** to turn out to be || *ref* to ferment; **venirse abajo** to collapse
veno•so -sa *adj* venous
venta *f* sale; roadside inn; (Chile) refreshment stand; (S-D) grocery store; **de venta** or **en venta** on sale, for sale; **ser una venta** (coll) to be an expensive place; **venta al descubierto** short sale
ventaja *f* advantage; (*en juegos o apuestas*) odds; extra pay
ventajo•so -sa *adj* advantageous
ventalla *f* valve
ventana *f* window; (*de la nariz*) nostril; **echar la casa por la ventana** (coll) to go to a lot of expense; **ventana batiente** casement; **ventana de guillotina** sash window; **ventana salediza** bay window
ventanal *m* church window; picture window
ventanear *intr* (coll) to be at the window all the time
ventanilla *f* (*de coche, de banco, de sobre*) window; ticket window; (*de la nariz*) nostril
ventanillo *m* (*postigo de puerta o ventana*) wicket; (*mirilla*) peephole
ventar **§2** *tr* to sniff || *impers* — **vienta** it is windy
ventarrón *m* gale, windstorm
ventear *tr* to sniff; to dry in the wind; to snoop into || *intr* to snoop, pry around || *impers* — **ventea** it is windy || *ref* (*henderse*) to split; (coll) to break wind; (Am) to spend a lot of time in the open
vente•ro -ra *mf* innkeeper
ventilador *m* ventilator; fan; (naut) funnel; **ventilador aspirador** exhaust fan
ventilar *tr* to ventilate; (fig) to air, ventilate
ventisca *f* drift, snowdrift; (*borrasca*) blizzard
ventiscar **§73** *intr* to snow and blow; (*la nieve*) to drift
ventisquero *m* snowdrift; blizzard; snow-capped mountain; glacier
ventolera *f* blast of wind; (*molinete*) pinwheel; vanity, pride; (coll) wild idea; (Mex) wind
ventosa *f* vent, air hole; **pegar una ventosa a** (coll) to swindle
ventosear *intr* to break wind
vento•so -sa *adj* windy || *f* see **ventosa**
ventregada *f* brood, litter; outpouring, abundance
ventrículo *m* ventricle
ventrílo•cuo -cua *mf* ventriloquist
ventriloquia *f* or **ventriloquismo** *m* ventriloquism
ventura *f* happiness; luck, chance; danger, risk; **a la ventura** at random; at a risk; **por ventura** perhaps, perchance; **probar ventura** to try one's luck
venture•ro -ra *adj* adventurous; fortunate, lucky || *mf* adventurer
ventu•ro -ra *adj* future, coming || *f* see **ventura**
venturón *m* stroke of luck
venturo•so -sa *adj* fortunate, lucky
Venus *m* (astr) Venus || *f* (myth) Venus; (*mujer de gran belleza*) Venus
venus•to -ta *adj* beautiful, graceful
venza *f* goldbeater's skin
ver *m* (*vista*) sight; (*apariencia*) appearance; opinion; **a mi ver** in my opinion || **§80** *tr* to see; to look at; (law) to hear, to try; **no poder ver** to not be able to bear; **no tener nada que ver con** to have nothing to do with; **ver** + *inf* to see + *inf,* e.g., **ví entrar a mi hermano** I saw my

brother come in; to see + *ger,* e.g., **ví bailar a la muchacha** I saw the girl dancing; to see + *pp,* e.g., **ví ahorcar al criminal** I saw the criminal hanged; **ver venir a uno** to see what someone is up to || *intr* to see; **a más ver** so long; **a ver** let's see; **hasta más ver** good-bye, so long; **ver de** to try to; **ver y creer** seeing is believing || *ref* to be seen; to be obvious; to see oneself; to see each other; to meet; (*encontrarse*) to be, to find oneself; **verse con** to see, have a talk with; **ya se ve** of course, certainly

vera *f* edge, border; **a la vera de** near, beside; **de veras** in truth; **jugar de veras** to play for keeps; **veras** truth, reality; earnestness

veracidad *f* veracity, truthfulness

veranda *f* verandah; bay window, closed porch

veraneante *mf* summer vacationist, summer resident

veranear *intr* to summer

veranie•go -ga *adj* summer; unimportant, insignificant

veranillo *m* Indian summer; **veranillo de San Martín** Indian summer

ve•raz *adj* (*pl* **-races**) veracious, truthful

verbena *f* fair, country fair, night festival; (bot) verbena

verbigracia *adv* for example

verbo *m* verb || **Verbo** *m* (theol) Word

verbo•so -sa *adj* verbose, wordy

verdacho *m* green earth

verdad *f* truth; **a la verdad** in truth, as a matter of fact; **de verdad** really; **la verdad desnuda** the plain truth; **¿no es verdad?** or **¿verdad?** isn't that so? La traducción al inglés de esta pregunta depende generalmente de la aseveración que la precede. Si la aseveración es afirmativa, la pregunta es negativa, p.ej., **Vd. vivió aquí. ¿No es verdad?** You lived here. Did you not?; Si la aseveración es negativa, la pregunta es afirmativa, p.ej., **Vd. no vivió aquí. ¿No es verdad?** You did not live here? Did you? Si el sujeto de la aseveración es un nombre sustantivo, va representado en la pregunta con un pronombre personal, p.ej., **Juan no estuvo aquí anoche. ¿No es verdad?** John was not here last evening. Was he?; **ser verdad** to be true; **verdad trillada** truism

verdade•ro -ra *adj* true; real; (*que dice siempre la verdad*) truthful

verde *adj* green; young, youthful; (*viuda*) merry; (*viejo*) gay; (*cuento*) shady, off-color; **están verdes** (coll) they're hard to reach || *m* green; foliage, verdure

verdear *intr* to turn green, to look green

verdecer **§22** *intr* to turn green, to grow green again

verdecillo *m* (orn) greenfinch

verdemar *m* sea green

verdete *m* verdigris

verdín *m* fresh green; (*capa verde de aguas estancadas*) mold, pond scum; (*cardenillo*) verdigris

verdise•co -ca *adj* half-dry

verdor *m* verdure; youth

verdo•so -sa *adj* greenish

verdugado *m* hoop skirt

verdugo *m* shoot, sucker; (*estoque*) rapier; (*azote*) scourge; (*roncha*) welt; executioner, hangman; torment; butcher bird, shrike

verdugón *m* wale, weal

verdulería *f* greengrocery

verdule•ro -ra *mf* greengrocer || *f* fishwife

verdura *f* greenness; (*color verde de las plantas*) verdure; (*obscenidad*) smuttiness; **verduras** vegetables, greens

verecundia *f* bashfulness, shyness

verecun•do -da *adj* bashful, shy

vereda *f* path, lane; (Am) sidewalk

veredicto *m* verdict

verga *f* (naut) yard

vergel *m* flower and fruit garden

vergonzo•so -sa *adj* (*que causa vergüenza*) shameful; (*que tiene vergüenza*) ashamed; (*que se avergüenza con facilidad*) bashful, shy; (*que causa humillación*) embarrassing; shabby, wretched || *mf* bashful person || *m* armadillo

vergüenza *f* (*arrepentimiento*) shame; (*oprobio*) shamefulness; (*pudor, timidez*) bashfulness, shyness; (*desconcierto, humillación*) embarrassment; (*pundonor*) dignity, face; public punishment; **¡qué vergüenza!** shame on you!; **tener vergüenza** to be ashamed; **vergüenzas** privates, genitals

vericueto *m* rough, rocky ground

verídi•co -ca *adj* truthful

verificación *f* verification; checking, testing, inspection

verifica•dor -dora *adj* verifying || *m* meter inspector

verificar **§73** *tr* to verify, to check; (*llevar a cabo*) to carry out; (*los contadores de agua, gas y electricidad*) to inspect || *ref* to prove true; to take place

verja *f* iron gate, iron fence, grating

ver•mú *m* (*pl* **-mús**) vermouth; (Am) matinée

vernácu•lo -la *adj* vernacular

verónica *f* (bot) veronica; (taur) veronica (*graceful pass in which the bullfighter waits for the bull with open cape*)

veroniquear *intr* (taur) to perform veronicas

verosímil *adj* likely, probable

verraco *m* male hog, boar

verraquear *intr* (coll) to grunt, grumble; (coll) to cry hard

verruga *f* wart; (coll) bore, nuisance

verrugo *m* (coll) miser

versal *adj* & *f* capital

versalilla or **versalita** *f* small capital

Versalles Versailles

versar *intr* — **versar acerca de** or **sobre** to deal with, to treat of || *ref* — **versarse en** to be or become versed in

versátil *adj* fickle

versículo *m* verse (*in the Bible*)
versificación *f* versification
versificar §73 *tr & intr* to versify
versión *f* version; translation
verso *m* verse; (typ) verso; **versos pareados** rhymed couplet
vertebra·do -da *adj & m* vertebrate
vertedero *m* dump; weir, spillway
verter §51 *tr* (*un líquido, un polvo*) to pour; (*un recipiente*) to empty; (*lágrimas; luz; sangre*) to shed; (*descargar*) to dump; to translate || *intr* to flow || *ref* to run, to empty
vertical *adj & f* vertical
vértice *m* vertex
vertiente *m & f* (*declive*) slope; (*colina por donde corre el agua*) shed || *f* (Arg, Col, Chile) spring, fountain
vertigino·so -sa *adj* dizzy
vértigo *m* vertigo, dizziness; fit of insanity
vesícula *f* vesicle; **vesícula biliar** gall bladder
veso *m* polecat
Véspero *m* Vesper
vesperti·no -na *adj* evening || *m* evening sermon
vestíbulo *m* vestibule; (theat) foyer, lobby
vestido *m* clothing, dress; (*de mujer*) gown, dress; (*de hombre*) suit; costume; **vestido de ceremonia** dress suit; **vestido de etiqueta** evening clothes; **vestido de etiqueta de mujer** or **vestido de noche** evening gown; **vestido de gala** (mil) full dress; **vestido de serio** evening clothes; **vestido de tarde-noche** cocktail dress
vestidura *f* clothing; (*del sacerdote*) vestment
vestigio *m* vestige, trace; track, footprint
vestir §50 *tr* to dress, to clothe; to adorn; to cover up; to disguise; (*tal o cual vestido*) to wear; to put on; **vestir el cargo** to look the part || *intr* to dress; (*una prenda o la materia*) to be dressy; **vestir de** (*p.ej., blanco*) to dress in; **vestir de etiqueta** to dress in evening clothes; **vestir de paisano** to dress in civilian clothes || *ref* to dress, to get dressed; to dress oneself; (*de una enfermedad*) to be up, to be about; **vestirse de** (*nubes, flores, hierba, etc.*) to be covered with; (*importancia, humildad, etc.*) to assume
vestuario *m* (*las prendas de uno*) wardrobe; dressing room; bathhouse; checkroom, cloakroom; (mil) uniform; (theat) dressing room
Vesubio, el Vesuvius
veta *f* vein; streak, stripe; **descubrir la veta de** (coll) to be on to
vetar *tr* to veto
vetea·do -da *adj* veined, striped || *m* graining || *f* (Ecuad) whipping
vetear *tr* to grain, to stripe; (Ecuad) to whip, to flog
veteranía *f* experience, know-how
vetera·no -na *adj & mf* veteran
veterina·rio -ria *adj* veterinary || *mf* veterinarian || *f* veterinary medicine
vetus·to -ta *adj* old, ancient
vez *f* (*pl* **veces**) time; (*tiempo de hacer una cosa por turno*) turn; **a la vez** at the same time; **a la vez que** while; **alguna vez** sometimes; ever; **a su vez** in turn; on his part; **a veces** at times, sometimes; **cada vez** every time; **cada vez más** more and more; **cuántas veces** how often; **de una vez** at one time; once and for all; **de vez en cuando** once in a while; **dos veces** twice; **en vez de** instead of; **esperar vez** to wait one's turn; **hacer las veces de** to take the place of; **las más veces** most of the time; **muchas veces** often; **otra vez** again; **raras veces** or **rara vez** seldom, rarely; **repetidas veces** over and over again; **tal vez** perhaps; **tomar la vez a** (coll) to get ahead of; **una que otra vez** once in a while; **una vez** once
veza *f* vetch, spring vetch
v.g. or **v.gr.** *abbr* **verbigracia**
vía *f* road, route, way; (*par de rieles y el suelo en que se asientan*) (rr) track; (*el mismo carril*) (rr) rail, track; (anat) passage, tract; (fig) way; **por la vía de** via; **por vía aérea** by air; **por vía bucal** by mouth; **vía aérea** airway; **vía ancha** (rr) broad gauge; **vía de agua** waterway; (naut) leak; **vía estrecha** (rr) narrow gauge; **vía férrea** railway; **vía fluvial** waterway; **Vía Láctea** Milky Way; **vía muerta** (rr) siding; **vía normal** (rr) standard gauge; **vía pública** thoroughfare; **vías de hecho** (law) assault and battery || *prep* via
viable *adj* feasible
viaducto *m* viaduct
viajante *adj* traveling || *mf* traveler || *m* drummer, traveling salesman
viajar *tr* to sell on the road; (*ciertas comarcas*) to cover as salesman || *intr* to travel, to journey
viaje *m* trip, journey; travel book; water supply; **¡buen viaje!** bon voyage!; **viaje de ida y vuelta** or **viaje redondo** round trip
viaje·ro -ra *adj* traveling || *mf* traveler; passenger
vial *adj* road, highway || *m* tree-lined road
vianda *f* food, viand; meal
viandante *mf* traveler; itinerant
viático *m* travel allowance; (eccl) viaticum
víbora *f* viper
vibración *f* vibration
vibrar *tr* to vibrate; (*la voz; la r*) to roll; (*una lanza*) to hurl || *intr* to vibrate || *ref* to be thrilled
vicaría *f* vicarage
vicario *m* vicar
vicealmirante *m* vice-admiral
vicepresiden·te -ta *mf* vice-president
viceversa *adv* vice versa
viciar *tr* to vitiate; (*una proposición*) to slant || *ref* to become vitiated; to give oneself up to vice; to become addicted; (*una tabla*) to warp
vicio *m* vice; pampering, spoiling; luxuriance, overgrowth; **hablar de**

vicio (coll) to talk all the time, to talk too much; **quejarse de vicio** (coll) to be a chronic complainer
vicio·so -sa *adj* vicious; faulty, defective; strong, robust; luxuriant, overgrown; dissolute; (*niño*) (coll) spoiled
víctima *f* victim, **víctima propiciatoria** scapegoat
victimar *tr* (Am) to kill, murder
victoria *f* victory
victorio·so -sa *adj* victorious
vid *f* vine, grapevine
vida *f* life; living, livelihood; **darse buena vida** to live high; to live in comfort; **de por vida** for life; **en mi vida** never; **escapar con vida** to have a narrow escape; **ganar** or **ganarse la vida** to earn one's livelihood, to make a living; **hacer por la vida** (coll) to get a bite to eat; **mudar de vida** to mend one's ways; **¡por vida mía!** upon my soul!; **vida airada** licentious living; **vida ancha** loose living; **vida de familia** or **de hogar** home life; **vida mía** my darling
vidalita *f* (Arg, Chile, Urug) mournful love song
vidente *mf* clairvoyant ‖ *m* prophet, seer ‖ *f* seeress
videograbación *f* video-tape recording
videoseñal *f* picture signal
vidria·do -da *adj* glazed; brittle ‖ *m* glaze, glazing; glazed pottery; dishes
vidriar §77 & **regular** *tr* to glaze ‖ *ref* (*los ojos*) to become glassy
vidriera *f* glass window, glass door; (Am) shopwindow, store window; **vidriera de colores** or **vidriera pintada** stained-glass window
vidriería *f* glassworks; glass store
vidriero *m* glass blower, glassworker; glazier; glass dealer
vidrio *m* glass; piece of glass; windowpane; **pagar los vidrios rotos** (coll) to take the blame, to be the goat; **vidrio cilindrado** plate glass; **vidrio de aumento** magnifying glass; **vidrio de color** stained glass; **vidrio deslustrado** ground glass; **vidrio tallado** cut glass
vidrio·so -sa *adj* glassy, vitreous; (*quebradizo*) brittle; (*resbaladizo*) slippery; (*que se resiente fácilmente*) (coll) touchy; (*mirada, ojos*) (fig) glassy
vie·jo -ja *adj* old ‖ *m* old man; **viejo verde** old goat, old rake ‖ *f* old woman
vie·nés -nesa *adj & mf* Viennese
viento *m* wind; course, direction; (*cuerda que mantiene una cosa derecha*) guy; (*gases intestinales*) (coll) wind; **ceñir el viento** (naut) to sail close to the wind; **viento de cola** (aer) tail wind; **viento en popa** (naut) tail wind; **vientos alisios** trade winds
vientre *m* belly; (*parte de la ondulación entre dos nodos*) (phys) loop; **evacuar** or **exonerar el vientre** to have a bowel movement; **vientre flojo** loose bowels
vier·nes *m* (*pl* **-nes**) Friday; **Viernes santo** Good Friday
viertea·guas *m* (*pl* **-guas**) *m* flashing
vietna·més -mesa *adj & mf* Vietnamese
viga *f* beam, girder, rafter; **estar contando las vigas** (coll) to gaze blankly at the ceiling; **viga de celosía** lattice girder
vigencia *f* force, operation; (*de una póliza de seguro*) life; **en vigencia** in force, in effect
vigente *adj* effective, in force
vigési·mo -ma *adj & m* twentieth
vigía *m* lookout, watch; **vigía de incendios** firewarden ‖ *f* watch; watchtower; (naut) rock, reef
vigiar §77 *tr* to watch over
vigilancia *f* vigilance, watchfulness; **bajo vigilancia médica** under the care of a physician
vigilante *adj* vigilant, watchful ‖ *m* guard, watchman; **vigilante nocturno** night watchman
vigilar *tr* to watch over; to look out for ‖ *intr* to watch, keep guard
vigilia *f* vigil; wakefulness; night work, night study; (*víspera*) eve; (mil) guard, watch; **comer de vigilia** to fast, to abstain from meat
vigor *m* vigor; **en vigor** in force; into effect
vigoriza·dor -dora *adj* invigorating ‖ *m* tonic; **vigorizador del cabello** hair tonic
vigorizante *adj* invigorating
vigorizar §60 *tr* to invigorate; to encourage
vigoro·so -sa *adj* vigorous
vigueta *f* small beam, small girder
vihuela *f* Spanish lute
vil *adj* vile, base, mean ‖ *mf* scoundrel
vilano *m* bur, down
vileza *f* vileness, baseness
vilipendiar *tr* to scorn, despise
vilipendio·so -sa *adj* contemptible
vilo — **en vilo** in the air; (fig) up in the air
vilorta *f* reed hoop; (*arandela*) washer
villa *f* town; (*casa de recreo en el campo*) villa; **la Villa** the city (*Madrid*)
villancico *m* carol, Christmas carol
villanes·co -ca *adj* boorish, crude, rustic
villanía *f* humbleness, humble birth; vileness, meanness; foul remark
villa·no -na *adj* base, vile; rude, impolite ‖ *mf* peasant; knave, scoundrel
villorrio *m* small country town
vinagre *m* vinegar; (*persona de genio áspero*) (coll) grouch
vinagrera *f* vinaigrette; (bot) sorrel; (SAm) heartburn; **vinagreras** cruet stand
vinagreta *f* French dressing, vinaigrette sauce
vinagro·so -sa *adj* vinegary
vinariego *m* vineyardist
vinatería *f* wine business; wine shop
vinate·ro -ra *adj* wine ‖ *m* wine dealer, vintner
vincular *tr* to bind, to tie, to unite; to continue, to perpetuate; (*esperanzas*) to found, to base; (law) entail
vínculo *m* bond, tie; (law) entail
vindicar §73 *tr* (*vengar*) to avenge; (*exculpar*) to vindicate
vindicta *f* revenge

vinicul·tor -tora *mf* winegrower
vinicultura *f* winegrowing
vinilo *m* vinyl
vino *m* wine; sherry reception, wine party; **tener mal vino** to be a quarrelsome drunk; **vino cubierto** dark-red wine; **vino de Jerez** sherry; **vino del terruño** local wine; **vino de mesa** table wine; **vino de Oporto** port wine; **vino de pasto** table wine; **vino de postre** after-dinner wine; **vino de segunda** second-run wine; **vino de solera** solera sherry; **vino tinto** red table wine
vinolen·to -ta *adj* too fond of wine
viña *f* vineyard; **ser una viña** (coll) to be a mine; **tener una viña** (coll) to have a sinecure
viña·dor -dora *mf* vineyardist, vine-dresser || *m* guard of a vineyard
viñedo *m* vineyard
viñeta *f* vignette, headpiece
viola·do -da *adj* & *m* violet (*color*)
violar *m* bed of violets || *tr* to violate; to ravish, rape; to profane, desecrate; to tamper with
violencia *f* violence
violentar *tr* to do violence to; (*p.ej., una casa*) to break into || *ref* to force oneself
violen·to -ta *adj* violent
violeta *m* (*color; colorante*) violet || *f* (bot) violet
violín *m* violin; (billiards) bridge, cue rest; **embolsar el violín** (Arg, Ven) to cower, to slink away
violinista *mf* violinist
violón *m* (mus) bass viol; **tocar el violón** (coll) to talk nonsense
violoncelista *mf* cellist, violoncellist
violoncelo *m* (mus) cello, violoncello
violonchelista *mf* cellist, violoncellist
violonchelo *m* (mus) cello, violoncello
vira *f* welt; (*saetilla*) dart
virada *f* turn, change of direction; (naut) tack
virago *f* mannish woman
viraje *m* turn, swerve; (phot) toning
virar *tr* (naut) to wind; (naut) to tack, to veer; (phot) to tone || *intr* to turn, to swerve; (naut) to tack, to veer
virgen *adj* virgin || *f* virgin, maiden
virginidad *f* virginity
vírgula *f* rod; thin line, light dash
virgulilla *f* fine line; diacritic mark
virilidad *f* virility
virin·go -ga *adj* (Col) naked
virolen·to -ta *adj* pock-marked; having smallpox
virología *f* virology
virote *m* (*saeta*) bolt; (coll) sporty young fellow; (coll) stuffed shirt
virrey *m* viceroy
virtual *adj* virtual
virtud *f* virtue
virtuosismo *m* virtuosity
virtuo·so -sa *adj* virtuous || *m* virtuoso
viruela *f* smallpox; pock mark; **viruelas locas** chicken pox
virulencia *f* virulence
virulen·to -ta *adj* virulent
vi·rus *m* (*pl* **-rus**) virus
viruta *f* shaving
virutilla *f* thin shaving; **virutillas de acero** steel wool
visado *m* visa
visaje *m* face, grimace
visar *tr* to visa; to O.K.; (arti & surv) to sight
vísceras *fpl* viscera
visco *m* birdlime
viscosa *f* viscose
viscosilla *f* rayon thread
visco·so -sa *adj* viscous || *f* see **viscosa**
visera *f* (*del yelmo, de las gorras, del parabrisas del automóvil, etc.*) visor; (*pequeña pantalla que se pone en la frente para resguardar la vista*) eye-shade; (W-I) blinder, blinker
visible *adj* visible; (*manifiesto*) evident; (*que llama la atención*) conspicuous
visigo·do -da *adj* Visigothic || *mf* Visigoth
visillo *m* window curtain, window shade
visión *f* vision; view; (*persona fea y ridícula*) (coll) sight, scarecrow; **ver visiones** (coll) to be seeing things; **visión negra** (*del aviador*) blackout
visionar *tr* to contemplate, to look at
visiona·rio -ria *adj* & *mf* visionary
visir *m* vizier; **gran visir** grand vizier
visita *f* visit; visitor, caller; inspection; **ir de visitas** to go calling; **pagar la visita a** to return the call of; **tener visita** to have callers; **visita de cumplido** formal call; **visita de médico** (coll) short call
visita·dor -dora *mf* frequent caller || *m* inspector || *f* (Hond, Ven) enema
visitante *adj* visiting || *mf* visitor
visitar *tr* to visit; to inspect
visite·ro -ra *adj* (coll) visiting; (*médico*) (coll) fond of making calls || *mf* (coll) visitor
vislumbrar *tr* to descry, to glimpse; to surmise, suspect || *ref* (*verse confusamente por la distancia*) to glimmer; (*aparecer en la distancia*) to loom
vislumbre *f* glimpse, glimmer; **vislumbres** inkling, notion
viso *m* sheen, gleam; (*de ciertas telas*) luster; streak, strain; appearance, thin veneer; elevation, height; colored material worn under transparent outer garment; **a dos visos** with a double purpose; **de viso** conspicuous; **hacer visos** to be iridescent
visón *m* mink
visor *m* (aer) bombsight; (phot) finder
víspera *f* eve, day before; **en vísperas de** on the eve of; **víspera de año nuevo** New Year's Eve; **víspera de Navidad** Christmas Eve; **vísperas** (eccl) vespers, evensong
vista *m* custom-house inspector || *f* (*sentido del ver*) vision, sight; (*paisaje que se ve desde un punto; estampa que representa un lugar*) view; (*panorama, perspectiva*) vista; comparison; purpose, design; (*ojeada*) glance, look; interview; eye; eyes; (law) hearing, trial; **a la vista** (com) at sight; **a vista de** in view of; compared with; **con vistas a** with a view to; **de vista** by sight; **doble vista** second sight; **hacer la vista gorda**

ante to shut one's eyes to; **hasta la vista** good-bye, so long; **medir con la vista** to size up; **saltar a la vista** to be self-evident; **tener a la vista** to keep one's eyes on; (*p.ej., una carta*) to have at hand; **torcer la vista** to squint; **vista a ojo de pájaro** bird's-eye view; **vistas** (*aberturas de un edificio*) lights, openings; view, outlook; visible parts, parts that show
vistazo *m* look, glance
vistillas *fpl* eminence, height; **irse a las vistillas** (coll) to try to get a look at one's opponent's cards
vis•to -ta *adj* evident, obvious; in view of; **bien visto** looked upon with approval; **mal visto** looked upon with disapproval; **no visto** or **nunca visto** unheard-of; **por lo visto** apparently, judging from the facts; **visto bueno** approved, O.K.; **visto que** whereas, inasmuch as || *m* whereas || *f* see **vista**
visto•so -sa *adj* showy, flashy, loud
visual *adj* visual || *f* line of sight
vital *adj* vital
vitali•cio -cia *adj* life, lifetime || *m* life-insurance policy; life annuity
vitalidad *f* vitality
vitalizar **§60** *tr* to vitalize
vitamina *f* vitamin
vitan•do -da *adj* hateful, odious; to be shunned
vitela *f* vellum
viticul•tor -tora *mf* grape grower, vineyardist
viticultura *f* grape growing
vitola *f* cigar size; mien, appearance; (Cuba) cigar band
vítor *interj* hurray! || *m* panegyric tablet; triumphal pageant
vitorear *tr* to cheer, to acclaim
vitral *m* stained-glass window
vítre•o -a *adj* vitreous, glassy
vitrina *f* showcase, glass cabinet; (Am) shopwindow
vitrióli•co -ca *adj* (chem) vitriolic
vituallas *fpl* victuals
vituperable *adj* vituperable
vituperar *tr* to vituperate
viuda *f* widow; **viuda de marido vivo** or **viuda de paja** grass widow
viudedad *f* widowhood; dower, widow's pension
viudez *f* (*estado de viuda*) widowhood; (*estado de viudo*) widowerhood
viu•do -da *adj* left a widow; left a widower || *m* widower || *f* see **viuda**
viva *interj* viva!, long live! || *m* viva
vivacidad *f* longevity; vivacity, liveliness; brightness, brilliance
vivande•ro -ra *mf* (mil) sutler, camp follower
vivaque *m* bivouac; guardhouse; (Am) police headquarters; **estar al vivaque** to bivouac
vivaquear *intr* to bivouac
vivar *m* warren, burrow; aquarium || *tr* (Am) to cheer, acclaim
vivara•cho -cha *adj* (coll) vivacious, lively
vi•vaz *adj* (*pl* **-vaces**) long-lived; vivacious, lively; keen, perceptive; (bot) perennial
víveres *mpl* food, provisions, victuals
vivero *m* tree nursery; fishpond; (*origen de cosas perjudiciales*) (fig) hotbed
viveza *f* agility, briskness; ardor, vehemence; sharpness, keenness; perception; brightness, brilliance; witticism; (*de los ojos*) sparkle; (*acción o palabra poco consideradas*) thoughtlessness
vivide•ro -ra *adj* livable
víví•do -da *adj* quick, perceptive; lively
vivienda *f* dwelling; life, way of life
viviente *adj* living, alive
vivificar **§73** *tr* to vivify, to enliven
vivir *m* life, living || *tr* (*una experiencia o ventura*) to live; (*toda la vida; la vejez*) to live out; (*habitar*) to live in || *intr* to live; **¿quién vive?** (mil) who goes there?; **vivir de** (*p.ej., carne*) to live on; **vivir para ver** to live and learn; **vivir y dejar vivir** to live and let live
vivisección *f* vivisection
vi•vo -va *adj* living, alive, live; (*lleno de vida; intenso*) live; (*sutil, agudo*) sharp, keen; (*dolor*) acute; (*carne*) raw; active, effective; (*luz*) bright, intense; (*pronto y ágil*) quick; (*idioma*) living, modern; **de viva voz** viva voce, by word of mouth; **herir en lo vivo** to cut or to sting to the quick || *mf* living person; **los vivos y los muertos** the quick and the dead || *m* edging, border; (vet) mange
Vizcaya *f* Biscay; **llevar hierro a Vizcaya** to carry coals to Newcastle
vizconde *m* viscount
vizcondesa *f* viscountess
V.M. *abbr* **Vuestra Majestad**
V.°B.° *abbr* **visto bueno**
vocablista *mf* punster
vocablo *m* word; **jugar del vocablo** to pun
vocabulario *m* vocabulary
vocación *f* vocation, calling
vocal *adj* vocal || *mf* director || *f* vowel
vocalista *mf* singer, vocalist
vocativo *m* vocative
voceador *m* town crier; (Col, Ecuad) paper boy
vocear *tr* to cry, shout; to cheer, acclaim; to call, to page; (coll) to boast about publicly || *intr* to shout
vocería *f* shouting, outcry; spokesmanship
vocerío *m* shouting, outcry
vocero *m* spokesman, mouthpiece
vociferar *tr* (*injurias*) to shout; to boast loudly about || *intr* to vociferate, to shout
vocingle•ro -ra *adj* loudmouthed; loud, talkative
vo•dú *m* (*pl* **-dúes**) voodoo
voduísta *adj* & *mf* voodoo
vol. *abbr* **volumen, voluntad**
volada *f* short flight; (*del jugador de billar*) (Arg) stroke; (Col, Ecuad) trick; (*noticia inventada*) (Mex) hoax
voladi•zo -za *adj* projecting || *m* projection

vola•do -da *adj* (typ) superior || *f* see **volada**

vola•dor -dora *adj* flying; hanging, dangling; swift, fast || *m* rocket; flying fish

voladura *f* blast, explosion

volandas — en volandas in the air; fast

volante *adj* flying; unsettled || *m* shuttlecock; battledore and shuttlecock; (*rueda que regula el movimiento de una máquina*) flywheel; (*rueda de mano para la dirección del automóvil*) steering wheel; (*pieza del reloj movida por la espiral*) balance wheel; flunkey, lackey; (*criado que iba a pie delante del coche o caballo*) outrunner; (*de papel*) slip, leaflet; (sew) flounce, ruffle; **un buen volante** a good driver

volan•tín -tina *adj* unsettled || *m* fish line; (Am) kite

volantista *m* (coll) driver, man at the wheel

volan•tón -tona *mf* fledgling || *f* (Ven) loose woman

volapié *m* (taur) stroke in which the matador moves in for the kill; **a volapié** half running, half flying; half walking, half swimming

volar §61 *tr* (*llevar en un aparato de aviación*) to fly; to blow up, to explode; to irritate; (*una letra, tipo o signo*) (typ) to raise || *intr* to fly; to fly away; to disappear; to jut out, project; (*una especie*) to spread rapidly; (*p.ej., una torre*) to rise in the air; **volar sin motor** (aer) to glide || *ref* to fly away; (Am) to fly off the handle

volatería *f* fowling with decoys; **de volatería** offhand

volátil *adj* volatile

volatilizar *tr & ref* to volatilize

volatín *m* ropewalker, acrobat, tumbler

volatine•ro -ra *mf* ropewalker, acrobat, tumbler

volcán *m* volcano

volcar §81 *tr* to upset, overturn, dump; to tip, to tilt; (*a una persona un olor fuerte*) to make dizzy; to change the mind of; to irritate, tease || *intr* to upset || *ref* to turn upside down

volear *tr* (tennis) to volley

voleo *m* (tennis) volley; reeling punch; **del primer voleo** or **de un voleo** (coll) with a smash, all at once; **sembrar al voleo** to sow broadcast

volframio *m* wolfram

volibol *m* volleyball

volquete *m* dumpcart, dump truck

voltai•co -ca *adj* voltaic

voltaje *m* voltage

volta•rio -ria *adj* fickle, inconstant; (Chile) willful; (Chile) sporty

voltea•do -da *mf* (Col) turncoat, deserter

voltear *tr* to upset, turn over; to turn around; to move, to transform || *intr* to roll over, to tumble

volteo *m* upset, overturning; tumbling; (P-R) scolding

voltereta *f* tumble; turning up card to determine trump

voltímetro *m* voltmeter

voltio *m* volt

volti•zo -za *adj* curled, twisted; fickle

voluble *adj* easily turned; fickle, inconstant

volumen *m* volume; **volumen sonoro** volume; (geom) volume

volumino•so -sa *adj* voluminous

voluntad *f* will; (*amor, cariño*) fondness, love; **a voluntad** at will; **buena voluntad** willingness; **de buena voluntad** willingly; **de mala voluntad** unwillingly; **de su propia voluntad** of one's own volition; **última voluntad** last will and testament; last wish; **voluntad de hierro** iron will

voluntariedad *f* willfulness

volunta•rio -ria *adj* (*que se hace por espontánea voluntad*) voluntary; (*que tiene voluntad obstinada*) willful; (*que se presta voluntariamente a hacer algo*) volunteer || *mf* volunteer

voluntario•so -sa *adj* willful

voluptuo•so -sa *adj* (*que inspira complacencia en los placeres sensuales*) voluptuous; (*dado a los placeres sensuales*) voluptuary || *mf* voluptuary

voluta *f* (archit) scroll, volute; (*p.ej., de humo*) ring

volvedor *m* screwdriver; (Col) extra, something thrown in; **volvedor de machos** tap wrench

volver §47 & §83 *tr* to turn; to turn upside down; to turn inside out; to return, send back, give back; (*una puerta*) to push to, to pull to; to translate; to vomit || *intr* to turn; to return, come back; **volver a** + *inf* verb + again, e.g., **volvió a abrir la puerta** he opened the door again; **volver en sí** to come to; **volver por** to defend, to stand up for || *ref* to become; to turn around; to return, come back; to change one's mind; to turn, turn sour; **volverse atrás** to back out; **volverse contra** to turn on

vomitar *tr* to vomit, throw up; (*fuego los cañones*) to belch forth; (*maldiciones*) to utter; (*un secreto*) to let out; (*lo que uno retiene indebidamente*) (coll) to cough up || *intr* to vomit, throw up; (coll) to come across, disgorge

vómito *m* vomit, vomiting; **provocar a vómito** (coll) to nauseate; **vómitos del embarazo** morning sickness

voracidad *f* voracity

vorágine *f* whirlpool, vortex

vo•raz *adj* (*pl* **-races**) voracious

vormela *f* polecat

vórtice *m* vortex

vos *pron pers* (subject of verb and object of preposition; takes plural form of verb but is singular in meaning; used in addressing the Deity, the Virgin, etc., and distinguished persons; in Spanish America is much used instead of **tú**) you

voso•tros -tras *pron pers* (plural of **tú**) you

votación *f* vote, voting

votante *adj* voting || *mf* voter

votar *tr* to vote for; (*sí, no*) to vote; (*p.ej., un cirio a la Virgen*) to vow || *intr* to vote; to vow; to swear, curse

voti•vo -va *adj* votive

voto *m* (*sufragio; derecho de votar; persona que da su voto*) vote; (*promesa solemne*) vow; (*exvoto*) votive offering; (*blasfemia*) oath, curse; wish, desire; **echar votos** to swear, to curse; **regular los votos** to tally the votes; **voto de amén** (coll) vote of a yes man; (coll) yes man; **voto de calidad** casting vote; **voto informativo** straw vote; **votos** good wishes; **¡voto va!** come now!

voz *f* (*pl* **voces**) voice; (*vocablo*) word; **aclarar la voz** to clear one's throat; **a una voz** with one voice; **a voces** shouting; **a voz en cuello** or **en grito** at the top of one's voice; **correr la voz que** to be rumored that; **dar voces** to shout, to cry out; **de viva voz** viva voce, by word of mouth; **en alta voz** aloud, in a loud voice; **en voz baja** in a low voice; **llevar la voz cantante** (coll) to have the say, to be the boss; **voces** outcry

vro. *abbr* **vuestro**

V.S. *abbr* **Vueseñoría**

vuelco *m* upset, overturn; **darle a uno un vuelco el corazón** (coll) to have a presentiment

vuelo *m* flight; flying; (*de una falda*) flare, fullness; projection; lace cuff trimming; **al vuelo** at once; on the wing; scattered at random; (chess) en passant; **alzar el vuelo** to take flight; (coll) to dash away; **echar a vuelo las campanas** to ring a full peal; **tirar al vuelo** to shoot on the wing; **tocar a vuelo las campanas** to ring a full peal; **vuelo a ciegas** (aer) blind flying; **vuelo de distancia** (aer) long-distance flight; **vuelo de ensayo** or **de prueba** (aer) test flight; **vuelo espacial tripulado** manned space flight; **vuelo planeado** (aer) volplane; **vuelo rasante** (aer) hedgehopping; **vuelo sin escala** (aer) nonstop flight; **vuelo sin motor** (aer) glide, gliding

vuelta *f* turn; (*regreso; devolución*) return; (*dinero sobrante de un pago*) change; (*de un camino*) bend, turn; (*del pantalón*) cuff; cuff trimming; (*paseo corto*) stroll; (*revés*) other side; (*paliza*) beating, whipping; (*en un cabo*) loop; (*en la media*) clock; (*mudanza*) change; **a la vuelta** on returning; please turn the page; **a la vuelta de** at the end of; at the turn of; (*la esquina*) around; **a vuelta de** about; **a vuelta de correo** by return mail; **dar cien vueltas a** to run rings around, be away ahead of; **dar la vuelta de campana** to turn somersault; **darse una vuelta a la redonda** (coll) to tend to one's own business; **dar una vuelta** to take a stroll, take a walk; to take a look; to change one's ways; **dar vuelta** to turn around; (*el vino*) to turn sour; **dar vuelta a** to reverse, to turn around; **estar de vuelta** to be back; **quedarse con la vuelta** to keep the change; **vuelta de campana** somersault; **vuelta del mundo** trip around the world

vuelto *m* (Am) change

vues•tro -tra (corresponds to **vos** and **vosotros**) *adj poss* your || *pron poss* yours

vulcanizar §60 *tr* to vulcanize

vulgacho *m* (coll) populace, mob

vulgar *adj* vulgar, popular, common, vernacular

vulgarismo *m* popular expression; (philol) popular word, popular form

vulgarizar §60 *tr* to popularize; to translate into the vernacular || *ref* to associate with the people

Vulgata *f* Vulgate

vulgo *adv* commonly || *m* common people; (*personas que en una materia sólo conocen la parte superficial*) laity

vulnerable *adj* vulnerable

vulnerar *tr* to hurt, injure; (*la reputación de una persona*) to damage; (*una ley, un precepto*) to break

vulpeja *f* she-fox, vixen

V.V. or **VV** *abbr* **ustedes**

X

X, x (equis) *f* twenty-sixth letter of the Spanish alphabet

xenia *f* xenia

xenofobia *f* xenophobia

xenófo•bo -ba *mf* xenophobe

xenón *m* xenon

xilófono *m* (mus) xylophone

xilografía *f* (*arte*) xylography; (*grabado*) xylograph

xpiano *abbr* **cristiano**

Xpo *abbr* **Cristo**

xptiano *abbr* **cristiano**

Xpto *abbr* **Cristo**

xunde *m* (Mex) reed basket, palm basket

Y

Y, y (ye) *f* twenty-seventh letter of the Spanish alphabet

y *conj* and

ya *adv* already; right away; now; **no ya** not only; **ya no** no longer; **ya que** since, inasmuch as

yac *m* (*bandera de proa*) (naut) jack; (*bóvido del Tibet*) yak

yacer §82 *intr* to lie
yacija *f* bed, couch; (*sepultura*) grave
yacimiento *m* bed, field, deposit
yámbi•co -ca *adj* iambic
yambo *m* iamb, iambus
yanqui *adj & mf* Yankee
Yanquilandia *f* Yankeedom
yapa *f* (Am) bonus, extra, allowance; **de yapa** (Am) in the bargain, extra
yarda *f* yard; yardstick
yate *m* yacht
yedra *f* ivy
yegua *f* mare; (CAm) cigar butt
yeguada *f* stud
yelmo *m* helmet
yema *f* (*de huevo*) yolk; candied yolk; (*del invierno*) dead; (*renuevo*) bud; (fig) cream; **dar en la yema** (coll) to put one's finger on the spot; **yema del dedo** finger tip; **yema mejida** eggnog
yente — yentes y vinientes *mpl* habitués, frequenters
yerba *f* var of **hierba**
yer•mo -ma *adj* deserted, uninhabited; (*suelo*) unsown; (*mujer*) not pregnant || *m* desert, wilderness
yerno *m* son-in-law
yerro *m* error, mistake; **yerro de cuenta** miscalculation; **yerro de imprenta** printer's error
yer•to -ta *adj* stiff, rigid
yesca *f* punk, tinder; (*cosa que excita una pasión*) fuel; **echar una yesca** to strike a light
yeso *m* gypsum; plaster cast
yo *pron pers* I; **soy yo** it is I
yodhídri•co -ca *adj* hydriodic
yodo *m* iodine
yoduro *m* iodide
yola *f* (sport) shell
yugo *m* yoke; **sacudir el yugo** to throw off the yoke
Yugoeslavia *f* Yugoslavia
yugoesla•vo -va *adj & mf* Yugoslav
yugular *adj & f* jugular || *tr* to cut off, to nip in the bud
yunque *m* anvil; (fig) drudge, work horse
yunta *f* yoke, team
yute *m* jute
yuxtaponer §54 *tr* to juxtapose
yuyo *m* (Arg, Chile) weed; **yuyos** (Col, Ecuad, Peru) greens

Z

Z, z (zeda or zeta) *f* twenty-eighth letter of the Spanish alphabet
zabordar *intr* (naut) to run aground
zabullir §13 *tr* (*p.ej., a un perro*) to duck, give a ducking to; (coll) to throw, to hurl || *ref* (*meterse debajo del agua con ímpetu*) to dive; (*esconderse rápidamente*) to duck
zacapela or **zacapella** *f* row, rumpus
zacate *m* (CAm, Mex) hay, fodder; **zacate de empaque** (Am) excelsior
zacateca *m* (Cuba) undertaker, gravedigger
zacatín *m* old-clothes market
zacear *tr* (*al perro*) to chase away || *intr* to lisp
zafaduría *f* (Arg) brazenness, effrontery
zafar *tr* to adorn, bedeck; to loosen, untie; to clear, to free; (*un buque*) to lighten || *ref* to slip away; to slip off, come off; **zafarse de** to get out of
zafarrancho *m* (naut) clearing the decks; (coll) havoc, ravage; (coll) scuffle, row; **zafarrancho de combate** (naut) clearing the deck for action
za•fio -fia *adj* rough, uncouth, boorish
zafiro *m* sapphire
za•fo -fa *adj* unhurt, intact; (naut) free, clear || **zafo** *prep* (Col) except
zafra *f* olive-oil can; drip jar; sugar crop; sugar making; sugar-making season; (min) rubbish, muck
zaga *f* rear; load carried in the rear; (mil) rearguard; **a la zaga, a zaga** or **en zaga** behind, in the rear; **no ir en zaga a** (coll) to not be behind, to be as good as
zagal *m* young fellow; strapping young fellow; shepherd boy; footboy
zagala *f* lass, maiden; young shepherdess
zaguán *m* vestibule, hall, entry
zague•ro -ra *adj* back, rear || *m* (sport) back, backstop
zaherir §68 *tr* to upbraid, reproach; to scold shamefully
zahones *mpl* chaps, hunting breeches
zaho•rí *m* (*pl* **-ríes**) keen observer; seer, clairvoyant
zahurda *f* pigpen
zai•no -na *adj* treacherous, false; (*caballo*) vicious; (*caballo*) dark-chestnut; **mirar a lo zaino** or **de zaino** to look askance at
za•lá *f* (*pl* **-laes**) Mohammedan prayer; **hacer la zalá a** (coll) to fawn on
zalagarda *f* ambush; skirmish; (*trampa para cazar animales*) trap; (coll) trick; (coll) row, rumpus; (coll) mock fight
zalamería *f* flattery, cajolery
zalame•ro -ra *adj* flattering, fawning || *mf* flatterer, fawner
zalea *f* unsheared sheepskin
zalear *tr* to drag around, to shake; (*al perro*) to chase away
zalema *f* salaam
zamacuco *m* (coll) blockhead; (coll) sullen fellow; (coll) drunkenness
zamacueca *f* cueca (*Chilean courtship dance*)
zamarra *f* undressed sheepskin; sheepskin jacket
zam•bo -ba *adj* knock-kneed
zambra *f* merrymaking, celebration; Moorish boat
zambucar §73 *tr* (coll) to slip away, hide away

zambullida *f* dive, plunge; (fencing) thrust to the breast
zambulli•dor -dora *adj* diving, plunging || *mf* diver, plunger || *m* (orn) diver, loon
zambullir **§13** *tr* (*p.ej., a un perro*) to duck, to give a ducking to; (coll) to throw, to hurl || *ref* (*meterse debajo del agua con ímpetu*) to dive; (*esconderse rápidamente*) to duck
zampa *f* pile, bearing pile
zampacuarti•llos *mf* (*pl* **-llos**) (coll) toper, soak
zampalimos•nas *mf* (*pl* **-nas**) (coll) bum, ordinary bum
zampar *tr* to slip away, hide away; to gobble down || *ref* to slip away, hide away
zampator•tas *mf* (*pl* **-tas**) (coll) glutton; (coll) boor
zampear *tr* (*el terreno*) to strengthen with piles and rubble
zampoña *f* shepherd's pipe, rustic flute; (coll) nonsense, folly
zampuzar **§60** *tr* to duck, give a ducking to; (coll) to slip away, hide away
zanahoria *f* carrot
zanca *f* long leg; (*de la escalera*) horse
zancada *f* long stride; **en dos zancadas** (coll) in a flash, in a jiffy
zancadilla *f* (coll) booby trap; **echar la zancadilla a** to stick out one's foot and trip
zancajo *m* heel; **no llegar a los zancajos a** (coll) to not come up to, to not be equal to
zancajo•so -sa *adj* duck-toed; down-at-the-heel
zancarrón *m* (coll) dirty old fellow
zanco *m* stilt; **en zancos** (coll) from a vantage point
zancu•do -da *adj* long-legged; (orn) wading || *m* mosquito || *f* wading bird
zanfonía *f* hurdy-gurdy
zangala *f* buckram
zangamanga *f* (coll) trick
zanganada *f* (coll) impertinence, impudence
zanganear *intr* (coll) to loaf around
zángano *m* (ent) drone; (fig) drone, loafer; (CAm) scoundrel
zangarrear *intr* (coll) to thrum a guitar
zangolotear *tr* (coll) to jiggle || *intr* (coll) to fuss around || *ref* (coll) to jiggle, to flop around, to rattle
zangoloteo *m* (coll) jiggle, jiggling, rattle; (coll) fuss, bother
zanguanga *f* (coll) malingering; (coll) flattery; **hacer la zanguanga** (coll) to malinger
zanguan•go -ga *adj* (coll) slow, lazy || *mf* (coll) loafer || *f* see **zanguanga**
zanja *f* ditch, trench; (SAm) gully; **abrir las zanjas** to lay the foundations
zanquear *intr* to waddle; to rush around
zanquilar•go -ga *adj* leggy, long-legged
zanquituer•to -ta *adj* bandy-legged
zapa *f* spade; sharkskin, shagreen; (mil) sap
zapapico *m* mattock, pickax
zapar *tr* (mil) to sap, mine, excavate
zaparrastrar *intr* — **ir zaparrastrando** (coll) to go along trailing one's clothes on the ground
zapateado *m* clog dance, tap dance
zapatear *tr* to hit with the shoe; to tap with the feet; (coll) to abuse, ill-treat || *intr* to tap-dance; (*las velas*) to flap || *ref* — **zapatearse con** to hold out against
zapatería *f* shoemaking; shoemaker's shop; (*tienda*) shoe store
zapate•ro -ra *adj* poorly cooked || *mf* shoemaker; shoe dealer; **quedarse zapatero** (coll) to not take a trick; **¡zapatero, a tus zapatos!** stick to your last!; **zapatero de viejo** or **zapatero remendón** cobbler, shoemaker
zapatilla *f* slipper; (*escarpín*) pump; (*del grifo*) washer; (*del florete*) leather tip or button; cloven hoof
zapato *m* shoe, low shoe; **andar con zapatos de fieltro** to gumshoe; **como tres en un zapato** (coll) hard up; (coll) like sardines; **zapato de goma** overshoe; **zapato inglés** low shoe
zapatón *m* (Guat, SAm) overshoe
zapear *tr* (*al gato*) to scare away, chase away
zaque *m* wineskin; (coll) tippler, drunk
zaquiza•mí *m* (*pl* **-míes**) attic, garret; hovel, pigpen
zar *m* czar
zarabanda *f* (mus) saraband; (coll) noise, confusion, uproar; (Mex) beating, thrashing
zaragata *f* (coll) scuffle, row; **zaragatas** (W-I) flattery
Zaragoza *f* Saragossa
zaranda *f* sieve, screen; colander; (Ven) horn; (Ven) top
zarandajas *fpl* (coll) odds and ends, trinkets
zarandar *tr* to sift, to screen; to winnow, pick out, select; (coll) to jiggle || *ref* (coll) to jiggle; (Am) to swagger, strut
zaraza *f* chintz, printed cotton
zarcillo *m* eardrop; (bot) tendril
zarigüeya *f* opossum
zarina *f* czarina
zarpa *f* claw, paw; (naut) weighing anchor
zarpar *tr* (*el ancla*) (naut) to weigh (*anchor*) || *intr* (naut) to weigh anchor, to set sail
zarpo•so -sa *adj* mud-splashed
zarracatería *f* (coll) cajolery, insincere flattery
zarracatín *m* (coll) sharp trader
zarramplín *m* (coll) botcher, bungler
zarrien•to -ta *adj* mud-splashed
zarza *f* blackberry, bramble (*bush*)
zarzamora *f* blackberry (*fruit*)
zarzaparrilla *f* sarsaparilla
zarzo *m* hurdle, wattle
zarzo•so -sa *adj* brambly
zarzuela *f* small bramble; (theat) zarzuela (*Spanish musical comedy*); **zarzuela grande** three-act zarzuela
zas *interj* bang!; **¡zas, zas!** bing, bang!
zascandilear *intr* (coll) to meddle, to scheme
zepelín *m* zeppelin
Zeus *m* Zeus

zigzag *m* zigzag
zigzaguear *intr* to zigzag
zinc *m* (*pl* **zinces**) zinc
zipizape *m* (coll) scuffle, row, rumpus
ziszás *m* zigzag
zoca *f* public square
zócalo *m* (archit) socle; (*de una pared*) dado; (rad) socket; (Mex) public square, center square
zoca·to -ta *adj* (*fruto*) corky, pithy; (coll) left; (coll) left-handed ‖ *mf* (coll) left-handed person
zoclo *m* clog, wooden shoe
zo·co -ca *adj* (coll) left; (coll) left-handed ‖ *mf* (coll) left-handed person ‖ *m* clog, wooden shoe; Moroccan market place; (archit) socle; **andar de zocos en colodros** (coll) to jump from the frying pan into the fire ‖ *f* see **zoca**
zodíaco *m* zodiac
zofra *f* Moorish carpet, Moorish rug
zolo·cho -cha *adj* (coll) stupid, simple ‖ *mf* (coll) simpleton
zollipar *intr* (coll) to sob
zollipo *m* (coll) sob
zona *m* (pathol) shingles ‖ *f* zone; (*banda, faja*) belt, girdle; **zona a batir** target area
zon·zo -za *adj* tasteless, insipid; dull, inane ‖ *mf* dolt, dimwit
zoófito *m* zoöphyte
zoología *f* zoölogy
zoológi·co -ca *adj* zoölogic(al)
zoólo·go -ga *mf* zoölogist
zopen·co -ca *adj* (coll) dull, stupid ‖ *mf* (coll) dullard, blockhead
zopilote *m* (Mex, CAm) turkey buzzard, turkey vulture
zo·po -pa *adj* crippled; awkward, gauche ‖ *mf* cripple
zoquete *m* (*de madera*) block, chunk, end; (*de pan*) bit, crust; (coll) chump, lout
zoquetu·do -da *adj* coarse, crude
zorra *f* fox; female fox; (coll) foxy person; (coll) prostitute; (coll) drunkenness; dray, truck; **pillar una zorra** (coll) to get drunk
zorrera *f* (*cueva de zorros*) foxhole; smoke-filled room; (coll) worry, confusion
zorrería *f* (coll) foxiness
zorre·ro -ra *adj* (coll) sly, foxy; (coll) slow, heavy, tardy ‖ *f* see **zorrera**
zorrillo *m* (Am) skunk
zorro *m* male fox; (*piel*) fox; (*hombre taimado*) (coll) fox; **estar hecho un zorro** (coll) to be overwhelmed with sleep; (coll) to be dull and sullen; **zorros** duster
zorzal *m* (orn) fieldfare; sly fellow; (Chile) simpleton
zozobra *f* capsizing, sinking; anxiety
zozobrar *tr* (*un buque*) to sink; (*un negocio*) to wreck ‖ *intr* to capsize, sink; (*la embarcación en la tempestad*) to wallow; (*un negocio*) to be in great danger; to be greatly worried ‖ *ref* to capsize, sink
zueco *m* clog, wooden shoe, sabot
zulacar §73 *tr* to waterproof
zulaque *m* waterproofing
zulú (*pl* **-lús** o **-lúes**) *adj* & *mf* Zulu
zullar *ref* (coll) to have a movement of the bowels; (coll) to break wind
zullen·co -ca *adj* (coll) windy, flatulent
zumaque *m* sumach; (coll) wine
zumaya *f* (*autillo*) tawny owl; (*chotacabras*) goatsucker
zumba *f* bell worn by leading mule; (Mex) drunkenness; **hacer zumba a** to make fun of; **sin zumba** (Mex) in a rush, in a hurry
zumbador *m* buzzer; (Mex) pauraque; (Mex, CAm, W-I) hummingbird
zumbar *tr* to make fun of; (*un golpe, una bofetada*) to let have ‖ *intr* to buzz; to zoom; (*los oídos*) to ring; **zumbar a** (*frisar con*) to be close to, to border on ‖ *ref* (Cuba) to go too far, to forget oneself; (P-R) to rush ahead; **zumbarse de** to make fun of
zumbido *m* buzz; zoom; (coll) blow, smack; **zumbido de ocupación** (telp) busy signal; **zumbido de oídos** ringing in the ears
zum·bón -bona *adj* waggish, playful ‖ *mf* wag, jester
zumien·to -ta *adj* juicy
zumo *m* juice; advantage, profit; **zumo de cepas** or **de parras** (coll) fruit of the vine
zumo·so -sa *adj* juicy
zunchar *tr* to band, to hoop
zuncho *m* band, hoop
zupia *f* (*del vino*) dregs; slop, wine full of dregs; (fig) junk, trash
zurcido *m* darning; darn; invisible mending
zurcir §36 *tr* to darn; (*una mentira*) (coll) to hatch, concoct; (*unas mentiras*) (coll) to weave (*a tissue of lies*)
zurdazo *m* (box) left, blow with the left
zur·do -da *adj* left; left-handed; **a zurdas** with the left hand; the wrong way ‖ *mf* left-handed person
zurear *intr* to coo
zuro *m* stripped corncob
zurra *f* dressing, currying; scuffle, quarrel; drubbing, thrashing; (*trabajo o estudio continuados*) grind
zurrapa *f* thread, filament; (coll) trash, rubbish; **con zurrapas** (coll) in a sloppy manner
zurrar *tr* (*el cuero*) to dress, to curry; to get the best of; (*censurar con dureza*) to dress down; (*castigar con azotes*) to drub, to thrash ‖ *ref* (*hacer sus necesidades involuntariamente*) to have an accident; (coll) to be scared to death; (Arg) to break wind noiselessly
zurriagar §44 *tr* to whip, to horsewhip
zurriago *m* whip, lash
zurribanda *f* (coll) rain of blows; (coll) rumpus, scuffle
zurrir *intr* to buzz, to grate
zurrón *m* shepherd's leather bag; leather bag; (*cáscara*) husk
zurrona *f* (coll) loose, evil woman
zurullo *m* (coll) soft roll; (coll) turd
zurupeto *m* (coll) unregistered broker; (coll) shyster notary
zuta·no -na *mf* (coll) so-and-so

Model Verbs

ORDER OF TENSES

(a) gerund
(b) past participle
(c) imperative
(d) present indicative
(e) present subjunctive
(f) imperfect indicative
(g) future indicative
(h) preterit indicative

All simple tenses are shown in these tables if they contain one irregular form or more, except the conditional (which can always be derived from the stem of the future indicative) and the imperfect and future subjunctive (which can always be derived from the third plural preterit indicative minus the last syllable **-ron**). The tenses are identified with the letters (a) to (h) as shown above.

§1 **abolir:** defective verb used only in forms whose endings contain the vowel **i**

§2 **acertar**
(c) **acierta,** acertad
(d) **acierto, aciertas, acierta,** acertamos, acertáis, **aciertan**
(e) **acierte, aciertes, acierte,** acertemos, acertéis, **acierten**

§3 **agorar:** like **§61** but with diaeresis on the **u** of **ue**
(c) **agüera,** agorad
(d) **agüero, agüeras, agüera,** agoramos, agoráis, **agüeran**
(e) **agüere, agüeres, agüere,** agoremos, agoréis, **agüeren**

§4 **airar**
(c) **aíra,** airad
(d) **aíro, aíras, aíra,** airamos, airáis, **aíran**
(e) **aíre, aíres, aíre,** airemos, airéis, **aíren**

§5 **andar**
(h) **anduve, anduviste, anduvo, anduvimos, anduvisteis, anduvieron**

§6 **argüir:** like **§20** but with diaeresis on **u** in forms with accented **i** in the ending
(a) **arguyendo**
(b) **argüído**
(c) **arguye,** argüid
(d) **arguyo, arguyes, arguye,** argüimos, argüís, **arguyen**
(e) **arguya, arguyas, arguya, arguyamos, arguyáis, arguyan**
(h) argüí, argüiste, **arguyó,** argüimos, argüisteis, **arguyeron**

§7 **asir**
(d) **asgo,** ases, ase, asimos, asís, asen
(e) **asga, asgas, asga, asgamos, asgáis, asgan**

§8 **aunar**
(c) **aúna,** aunad
(d) **aúno, aúnas, aúna,** aunamos, aunáis, **aúnan**
(e) **aúne, aúnes, aúne,** aunemos, aunéis, **aúnen**

§9 **avergonzar:** combination of **§3** and **§60**
(c) **avergüenza,** avergonzad

(d) **avergüenzo, avergüenzas, avergüenza,** avergonzamos, avergonzáis, **avergüenzan**
(e) **avergüence, avergüences, avergüence, avergoncemos, avergoncéis, avergüencen**
(h) **avergoncé,** avergonzaste, avergonzó, avergonzamos, avergonzasteis, avergonzaron

§10 **averiguar**
(e) **averigüe, averigües, averigüe, averigüemos, averigüéis, averigüen**
(h) **averigüé,** averiguaste, averiguó, averiguamos, averiguasteis, averiguaron

§11 **bendecir**
(a) **bendiciendo**
(c) **bendice,** bendecid
(d) **bendigo, bendices, bendice,** bendecimos, bendecís, **bendicen**
(e) **bendiga, bendigas, bendiga, bendigamos, bendigáis, bendigan**
(h) **bendije, bendijiste, bendijo, bendijimos, bendijisteis, bendijeron**

§12 **bruñir**
(a) **bruñendo**
(h) bruñí, bruñiste, **bruñó,** bruñimos, bruñisteis, **bruñeron**

§13 **bullir**
(a) **bullendo**
(h) bullí, bulliste, **bulló,** bullimos, bullisteis, **bulleron**

§14 **caber**
(d) **quepo,** cabes, cabe, cabemos, cabéis, caben
(e) **quepa, quepas, quepa, quepamos, quepáis, quepan**
(g) **cabré, cabrás, cabrá, cabremos, cabréis, cabrán**
(h) **cupe, cupiste, cupo, cupimos, cupisteis, cupieron**

§15 **caer**
(a) **cayendo**
(b) **caído**
(d) **caigo,** caes, cae, caemos, caéis, caen
(e) **caiga, caigas, caiga, caigamos, caigáis, caigan**
(h) caí, **caíste, cayó, caímos, caísteis, cayeron**

§16 **cocer:** combination of §47 and §78
(c) **cuece,** coced
(d) **cuezo, cueces, cuece,** cocemos, cocéis, **cuecen**
(e) **cueza, cuezas, cueza, cozamos, cozáis, cuezan**

§17 **coger**
(d) **cojo,** coges, coge, cogemos, cogéis, cogen
(e) **coja, cojas, coja, cojamos, cojáis, cojan**

§18 **comenzar:** combination of §2 and §60
(c) **comienza,** comenzad
(d) **comienzo, comienzas, comienza,** comenzamos, comenzáis, **comienzan**
(e) **comience, comiences, comience, comencemos, comencéis, comiencen**
(h) **comencé,** comenzaste, comenzó, comenzamos, comenzasteis, comenzaron

§19 **conducir**
(d) **conduzco,** conduces, conduce, conducimos, conducís, conducen
(e) **conduzca, conduzcas, conduzca, conduzcamos, conduzcáis, conduzcan**
(h) **conduje, condujiste, condujo, condujimos, condujisteis, condujeron**

§20 **construir**
(a) **construyendo**
(b) **construído**
(c) **construye,** construid
(d) **construyo, construyes, construye,** construimos, construís, **construyen**
(e) **construya, construyas, construya, construyamos, construyáis, construyan**
(h) construí, construiste, **construyó,** construimos, construisteis, **construyeron**

§21 **continuar**
(c) **continúa,** continuad
(d) **continúo, continúas, continúa,** continuamos, continuáis, **continúan**
(e) **continúe, continúes, continúe,** continuemos, continuéis, **continúen**

§22 **crecer**
(d) **crezco,** creces, crece, crecemos, crecéis, crecen
(e) **crezca, crezcas, crezca, crezcamos, crezcáis, crezcan**

§23 **dar**
(d) **doy,** das, da, damos, dais, dan
(e) **dé,** des, **dé,** demos, deis, den
(h) **dí, diste, dio, dimos, disteis, dieron**

§24 **decir**
(a) **diciendo**
(b) **dicho**
(c) **di,** decid
(d) **digo, dices, dice,** decimos, decís, **dicen**
(e) **diga, digas, diga, digamos, digáis, digan**
(g) **diré, dirás, dirá, diremos, diréis, dirán**
(h) **dije, dijiste, dijo, dijimos, dijisteis, dijeron**

§25 **delinquir**
(d) **delinco,** delinques, delinque, delinquimos, delinquís, delinquen
(e) **delinca, delincas, delinca, delincamos, delincáis, delincan**

§26 **desosar:** like §**61** but with **h** before **ue**
(c) **deshuesa,** desosad
(d) **deshueso, deshuesas, deshuesa,** desosamos, desosáis, **deshuesan**
(e) **deshuese, deshueses, deshuese,** desosemos, desoséis, **deshuesen**

§27 **dirigir**
(d) **dirijo,** diriges, dirige, dirigimos, dirigís, dirigen
(e) **dirija, dirijas, dirija, dirijamos, dirijáis, dirijan**

§28 discernir
(c) **discierne,** discernid
(d) **discierno, disciernes, discierne,** discernimos, discernís, **disciernen**
(e) **discierna, disciernas, discierna,** discernamos, discernáis, **disciernan**

§29 distinguir
(d) **distingo,** distingues, distingue, distinguimos, distinguís, distinguen
(e) **distinga, distingas, distinga, distingamos, distingáis, distingan**

§30 dormir
(a) **durmiendo**
(c) **duerme,** dormid
(d) **duermo, duermes, duerme,** dormimos, dormís, **duermen**
(e) **duerma, duermas, duerma, durmamos, durmáis, duerman**
(h) dormí, dormiste, **durmió,** dormimos, dormisteis, **durmieron**

§31 empeller
(a) **empellendo**
(h) empellí, empelliste, **empelló,** empellimos, empellisteis, **empelleron**

§32 enraizar: combination of **§4** and **§60**
(c) **enraíza,** enraizad
(d) **enraízo, enraízas, enraíza,** enraizamos, enraizáis, **enraízan**
(e) **enraíce, enraíces, enraíce, enraicemos, enraicéis, enraícen**
(h) **enraicé,** enraizaste, enraizó, enraizamos, enraizasteis, enraizaron

§33 erguir: combination of **§29** and **§50** or **§68**
(a) **irguiendo**
(c) **irgue** or **yergue,** erguid
(d) **irgo, irgues, irgue,** / **yergo, yergues, yergue,** } erguimos, erguís, { **irguen** / **yerguen**
(e) **irga, irgas, irga,** / **yerga, yergas, yerga,** } **irgamos, irgáis,** { **irgan** / **yergan**
(h) erguí, erguiste, **irguió,** erguimos, erguisteis, **irguieron**

§34 errar: like **§2** but with initial **ye** for **ie**
(c) **yerra,** errad
(d) **yerro, yerras, yerra,** erramos, erráis, **yerran**
(e) **yerre, yerres, yerre,** erremos, erréis, **yerren**

§35 esforzar: combination of **§60** and **§61**
(c) **esfuerza,** esforzad
(d) **esfuerzo, esfuerzas, esfuerza,** esforzamos, esforzáis, **esfuerzan**
(e) **esfuerce, esfuerces, esfuerce, esforcemos, esforcéis, esfuercen**
(h) **esforcé,** esforzaste, esforzó, esforzamos, esforzasteis, esforzaron

§36 esparcir
(d) **esparzo,** esparces, esparce, esparcimos, esparcís, esparcen
(e) **esparza, esparzas, esparza, esparzamos, esparzáis, esparzan**

§37 estar
(c) **está**, estad
(d) **estoy, estás, está**, estamos, estáis, **están**
(e) **esté, estés, esté**, estemos, estéis, **estén**
(h) **estuve, estuviste, estuvo, estuvimos, estuvisteis, estuvieron**

§38 haber
(c) **hé**, habed
(d) **he, has, ha, hemos**, habéis, **han** (*v impers*) **hay**
(e) **haya, hayas, haya, hayamos, hayáis, hayan**
(g) **habré, habrás, habrá, habremos, habréis, habrán**
(h) **hube, hubiste, hubo, hubimos, hubisteis, hubieron**

§39 hacer
(b) **hecho**
(c) **haz**, haced
(d) **hago**, haces, hace, hacemos, hacéis, hacen
(e) **haga, hagas, haga, hagamos, hagáis, hagan**
(g) **haré, harás, hará, haremos, haréis, harán**
(h) **hice, hiciste, hizo, hicimos, hicisteis, hicieron**

§40 inquirir
(c) **inquiere**, inquirid
(d) **inquiero, inquieres, inquiere**, inquirimos, inquirís, **inquieren**
(e) **inquiera, inquieras, inquiera**, inquiramos, inquiráis, **inquieran**

§41 ir
(a) **yendo**
(c) **vé, vamos**, id
(d) **voy, vas, va, vamos, vais, van**
(e) **vaya, vayas, vaya, vayamos, vayáis, vayan**
(f) **iba, ibas, iba, íbamos, ibais, iban**
(h) **fui, fuiste, fue, fuimos, fuisteis, fueron**

§42 jugar: like **§63** but with radical **u**
(c) **juega**, jugad
(d) **juego, juegas, juega**, jugamos, jugáis, **juegan**
(e) **juegue, juegues, juegue, juguemos, juguéis, jueguen**
(h) **jugué**, jugaste, jugó, jugamos, jugasteis, jugaron

§43 leer
(a) **leyendo**
(b) **leído**
(h) leí, **leíste, leyó, leímos, leísteis, leyeron**

§44 ligar
(e) **ligue, ligues, ligue, liguemos, liguéis, liguen**
(h) **ligué**, ligaste, ligó, ligamos, ligasteis, ligaron

§45 lucir
(d) **luzco**, luces, luce, lucimos, lucís, lucen
(e) **luzca, luzcas, luzca, luzcamos, luzcáis, luzcan**

§46 mecer
(d) **mezo**, meces, mece, mecemos, mecéis, mecen
(e) **meza, mezas, meza, mezamos, mezáis, mezan**

§47 mover
(c) **mueve,** moved
(d) **muevo, mueves, mueve,** movemos, movéis, **mueven**
(e) **mueva, muevas, mueva,** movamos, mováis, **muevan**

§48 oír
(a) **oyendo**
(b) **oído**
(c) **oye, oíd**
(d) **oigo, oyes, oye, oímos,** oís, **oyen**
(e) **oiga, oigas, oiga, oigamos, oigáis, oigan**
(h) oí, **oíste, oyó, oímos, oísteis, oyeron**

§49 oler: like §47 but with **h** before **ue**
(c) **huele,** oled
(d) **huelo, hueles, huele,** olemos, oléis, **huelen**
(e) **huela, huelas, huela,** olamos, oláis, **huelan**

§50 pedir
(a) **pidiendo**
(c) **pide,** pedid
(d) **pido, pides, pide,** pedimos, pedís, **piden**
(e) **pida, pidas, pida, pidamos, pidáis, pidan**
(h) pedí, pediste, **pidió,** pedimos, pedisteis, **pidieron**

§51 perder
(c) **pierde,** perded
(d) **pierdo, pierdes, pierde,** perdemos, perdéis, **pierden**
(e) **pierda, pierdas, pierda,** perdamos, perdáis, **pierdan**

§52 placer
(d) **plazco,** places, place, placemos, placéis, placen
(e) **plazca, plazcas, plazca, plazcamos, plazcáis, plazcan**
(h) plací, placiste, plació (or **plugo**), placimos, placisteis, placieron

§53 poder
(a) **pudiendo**
(c) (**puede,** poded)
(d) **puedo, puedes, puede,** podemos, podéis, **pueden**
(e) **pueda, puedas, pueda,** podamos, podáis, **puedan**
(g) **podré, podrás, podrá, podremos, podréis, podrán**
(h) **pude, pudiste, pudo, pudimos, pudisteis, pudieron**

§54 poner
(b) **puesto**
(c) **pon,** poned
(d) **pongo,** pones, pone, ponemos, ponéis, ponen
(e) **ponga, pongas, ponga, pongamos, pongáis, pongan**
(g) **pondré, pondrás, pondrá, pondremos, pondréis, pondrán**
(h) **puse, pusiste, puso, pusimos, pusisteis, pusieron**

§55 querer
(c) **quiere,** quered
(d) **quiero, quieres, quiere,** queremos, queréis, **quieren**
(e) **quiera, quieras, quiera,** queramos, queráis, **quieran**
(g) **querré, querrás, querrá, querremos, querréis, querrán**
(h) **quise, quisiste, quiso, quisimos, quisisteis, quisieron**

§56 raer
(a) **rayendo**
(b) **raído**
(d) **raigo** (or **rayo**), raes, rae, raemos, raéis, raen
(e) **raiga** (or **raya**), **raigas, raiga, raigamos, raigáis, raigan**
(h) raí, **raíste, rayó, raímos, raísteis, rayeron**

§57 regir: combination of **§27** and **§50**
(a) **rigiendo**
(c) **rige,** regid
(d) **rijo, riges, rige,** regimos, regís, **rigen**
(e) **rija, rijas, rija, rijamos, rijáis, rijan**
(h) regí, registe, **rigió,** regimos, registeis, **rigieron**

§58 reír
(a) **riendo**
(b) **reído**
(c) **ríe, reíd**
(d) **río, ríes, ríe, reímos,** reís, **ríen**
(e) **ría, rías, ría, riamos, riáis, rían**
(h) reí, **reíste, rió, reímos, reísteis, rieron**

§59 reunir
(c) **reúne,** reunid
(d) **reúno, reúnes, reúne,** reunimos, reunís, **reúnen**
(e) **reúna, reúnas, reúna,** reunamos, reunáis, **reúnan**

§60 rezar
(e) **rece, reces, rece, recemos, recéis, recen**
(h) **recé,** rezaste, rezó, rezamos, rezasteis, rezaron

§61 rodar
(c) **rueda,** rodad
(d) **ruedo, ruedas, rueda,** rodamos, rodáis, **ruedan**
(e) **ruede, ruedes, ruede,** rodemos, rodéis, **rueden**

§62 roer
(a) **royendo**
(b) **roído**
(d) roo (**roigo,** or **royo**), roes, roe, roemos, roéis, roen
(e) roa (**roiga,** or **roya**), roas, roa, roamos, roáis, roan
(h) roí, **roíste, royó, roímos, roísteis, royeron**

§63 rogar: combination of **§44** and **§61**
(c) **ruega,** rogad
(d) **ruego, ruegas, ruega,** rogamos, rogáis, **ruegan**
(e) **ruegue, ruegues, ruegue, roguemos, roguéis, rueguen**
(h) **rogué,** rogaste, rogó, rogamos, rogasteis, rogaron

§64 saber
(d) **sé,** sabes, sabe, sabemos, sabéis, saben
(e) **sepa, sepas, sepa, sepamos, sepáis, sepan**
(g) **sabré, sabrás, sabrá, sabremos, sabréis, sabrán**
(h) **supe, supiste, supo, supimos, supisteis, supieron**

§65 salir
(c) **sal,** salid
(d) **salgo,** sales, sale, salimos, salís, salen
(e) **salga, salgas, salga, salgamos, salgáis, salgan**
(g) **saldré, saldrás, saldrá, saldremos, saldréis, saldrán**

§66 segar: combination of **§2** and **§44**
(c) **siega,** segad
(d) **siego, siegas, siega,** segamos, segáis, **siegan**
(e) **siegue, siegues, siegue, seguemos, seguéis, sieguen**
(h) **segué,** segaste, segó, segamos, segasteis, segaron

§67 seguir: combination of **§29** and **§50**
(a) **siguiendo**
(c) **sigue,** seguid
(d) **sigo, sigues, sigue,** seguimos, seguís, **siguen**
(e) **siga, sigas, siga, sigamos, sigáis, sigan**
(h) seguí, seguiste, **siguió,** seguimos, seguisteis, **siguieron**

§68 sentir
(a) **sintiendo**
(c) **siente,** sentid
(d) **siento, sientes, siente,** sentimos, sentís, **sienten**
(e) **sienta, sientas, sienta, sintamos, sintáis, sientan**
(h) sentí, sentiste, **sintió,** sentimos, sentisteis, **sintieron**

§69 ser
(c) **sé,** sed
(d) **soy, eres, es, somos, sois, son**
(e) **sea, seas, sea, seamos, seáis, sean**
(f) **era, eras, era, éramos, erais, eran**
(h) **fui, fuiste, fue, fuimos, fuisteis, fueron**

§70 tañer
(a) **tañendo**
(h) tañí, tañiste, **tañó,** tañimos, tañisteis, **tañeron**

§71 tener
(c) **ten,** tened
(d) **tengo, tienes, tiene,** tenemos, tenéis, **tienen**
(e) **tenga, tengas, tenga, tengamos, tengáis, tengan**
(g) **tendré, tendrás, tendrá, tendremos, tendréis, tendrán**
(h) **tuve, tuviste, tuvo, tuvimos, tuvisteis, tuvieron**

§72 teñir: combination of **§12** and **§50**
(a) **tiñendo**
(c) **tiñe,** teñid
(d) **tiño, tiñes, tiñe,** teñimos, teñís, **tiñen**
(e) **tiña, tiñas, tiña, tiñamos, tiñáis, tiñan**
(h) teñí, teñiste, **tiñó,** teñimos, teñisteis, **tiñeron**

§73 tocar
(e) **toque, toques, toque, toquemos, toquéis, toquen**
(h) **toqué,** tocaste, tocó, tocamos, tocasteis, tocaron

§74 torcer: combination of **§47** and **§78**
(c) **tuerce,** torced
(d) **tuerzo, tuerces, tuerce,** torcemos, torcéis, **tuercen**
(e) **tuerza, tuerzas, tuerza, torzamos, torzáis, tuerzan**

§75 traer
(a) **trayendo**
(b) **traído**
(d) **traigo,** traes, trae, traemos, traéis, traen
(e) **traiga, traigas, traiga, traigamos, traigáis, traigan**
(h) **traje, trajiste, trajo, trajimos, trajisteis, trajeron**

§76 **valer**

(d) **valgo,** vales, vale, valemos, valéis, valen
(e) **valga, valgas, valga, valgamos, valgáis, valgan**
(g) **valdré, valdrás, valdrá, valdremos, valdréis, valdrán**

§77 **variar**

(c) **varía,** variad
(d) **varío, varías, varía,** variamos, variáis, **varían**
(e) **varíe, varíes, varíe,** variemos, variéis, **varíen**

§78 **vencer**

(d) **venzo,** vences, vence, vencemos, vencéis, vencen
(e) **venza, venzas, venza, venzamos, venzáis, venzan**

§79 **venir**

(a) **viniendo**
(c) **ven,** venid
(d) **vengo, vienes, viene,** venimos, venís, **vienen**
(e) **venga, vengas, venga, vengamos, vengáis, vengan**
(g) **vendré, vendrás, vendrá, vendremos, vendréis, vendrán**
(h) **vine, viniste, vino, vinimos, vinisteis, vinieron**

§80 **ver**

(b) **visto**
(d) **veo,** ves, ve, vemos, veis, ven
(e) **vea, veas, vea, veamos, veáis, vean**
(f) **veía, veías, veía, veíamos, veíais, veían**

§81 **volcar:** combination of **§61** and **§73**

(c) **vuelca,** volcad
(d) **vuelco, vuelcas, vuelca,** volcamos, volcáis, **vuelcan**
(c) **vuelque, vuelques, vuelque, volquemos, volquéis, vuelquen**
(h) **volqué,** volcaste, volcó, volcamos, volcasteis, volcaron

§82 **yacer**

(c) **yaz** (or yace), yaced
(d) **yazco (yazgo,** or **yago),** yaces, yace, yacemos, yacéis, yacen
(e) **yazca (yazga,** or **yaga), yazcas, yazca, yazcamos, yazcáis, yazcan**

§83 The following verbs, some of which are included in the foregoing table, and their compounds have irregular past participles:

abrir	**abierto**	**morir**	**muerto**
cubrir	**cubierto**	**poner**	**puesto**
decir	**dicho**	**proveer**	**provisto**
escribir	**escrito**	**pudrir**	**podrido**
freír	**frito**	**romper**	**roto**
hacer	**hecho**	**solver**	**suelto**
imprimir	**impreso**	**ver**	**visto**
		volver	**vuelto**

PART TWO

Inglés-Español

La pronunciación del inglés

Los símbolos siguientes representan aproximadamente todos los sonidos del idioma inglés.

VOCALES

SÍMBOLO	SONIDO	EJEMPLO
[æ]	Más cerrado que la **a** de **caro.**	**hat** [hæt]
[ɑ]	Como la **a** de **bajo.**	**father** [ˈfɑðər] **proper** [ˈprɑpər]
[ɛ]	Como la **e** de **perro.**	**met** [mɛt]
[e]	Más cerrado que la **e** de **canté.** Suena como si fuese seguido de [ɪ].	**fate** [fet] **they** [ðe]
[ə]	Como la **e** de la palabra francesa **le.**	**heaven** [ˈhɛvən] **pardon** [ˈpɑrdən]
[i]	Como la **i** de **nido.**	**she** [ʃi] **machine** [məˈʃin]
[ɪ]	Como la **i** de **tilde.**	**fit** [fɪt] **beer** [bɪr]
[o]	Más cerrado que la **o** de **habló.** Suena como si fuese seguido de [ʊ].	**nose** [noz] **road** [rod]
[ɔ]	Menos cerrado que la **o** de **torre.**	**bought** [bɔt] **law** [lɔ]
[ʌ]	Más o menos como **eu** en la palabra francesa **peur.**	**cup** [kʌp] **come** [kʌm] **mother** [ˈmʌðər]
[ʊ]	Menos cerrado que la **u** de **bulto.**	**pull** [pʊl] **book** [bʊk] **wolf** [wʊlf]
[u]	Como la **u** de **agudo.**	**rude** [rud] **move** [muv] **tomb** [tum]

DIPTONGOS

SÍMBOLO	SONIDO	EJEMPLO
[aɪ]	Como **ai** de **amáis.**	**night** [naɪt] **eye** [aɪ]
[aʊ]	Como **au** de **causa.**	**found** [faʊnd] **cow** [kaʊ]
[ɔɪ]	Como **oy** de **estoy.**	**voice** [vɔɪs] **oil** [ɔɪl]

CONSONANTES

SÍMBOLO	SONIDO	EJEMPLO
[b]	Como la **b** de **hombre.** Sonido bilabial oclusivo sonoro.	**bed** [bɛd] **robber** [ˈrɑbər]
[d]	Como la **d** de **conde.** Sonido dental oclusivo sonoro.	**dead** [dɛd] **add** [æd]
[dʒ]	Como la **y** de **cónyuge.** Sonido palatal africado sonoro.	**gem** [dʒɛm] **jail** [dʒel]
[ð]	Como la **d** de **nada.** Sonido interdental fricativo sonoro.	**this** [ðɪs] **father** [ˈfɑðər]
[f]	Como la **f** de **fecha.** Sonido labiodental sordo.	**face** [fes] **phone** [fon]
[g]	Como la **g** de **gato.** Sonido velar oclusivo sonoro.	**go** [go] **get** [gɛt]

SÍMBOLO	SONIDO	EJEMPLO
[h]	Sonido más aspirado pero menos áspero que el sonido velar fricativo sordo de la **j** de **junto.**	**hot** [hɑt] **alcohol** [ˈælkə ˌhɔl]
[j]	Como la **y** de **cuyo.** Sonido palatal semiconsonantal sonoro.	**yes** [jɛs] **unit** [ˈjunɪt]
[k]	Como la **c** de **cama.** Sonido velar oclusivo sordo.	**cat** [kæt] **chord** [kɔrd] **kill** [kɪl]
[l]	Como la **l** de **lado.** Sonido alveolar fricativo lateral sonoro.	**late** [let] **allow** [əˈlaʊ]
[m]	Como la **m** de **madre.** Sonido bilabial nasal sonoro.	**more** [mor] **command** [kəˈmænd]
[n]	Como la **n** de **carne.** Sonido alveolar nasal sonoro.	**nest** [nɛst] **manner** [ˈmænər]
[ŋ]	Como la **n** de **banco.** Sonido velar nasal sonoro.	**king** [kiŋ] **conquer** [ˈkɑŋkər]
[p]	Como la **p** de **tapar.** Sonido bilabial oclusivo sordo.	**pen** [pɛn] **cap** [kæp]
[r]	La **r** más común en muchas partes de Inglaterra y en la mayor parte de los Estados Unidos y el Canadá es un sonido semivocal que se articula con la punta de la lengua elevada más hacia el paladar duro que en la **r** fricativa española y aun doblada hacia atrás. Intervocálica y al final de sílaba, es muy débil y casi no se puede oír.	**run** [rʌn] **far** [fɑr] **art** [ɑrt] **carry** [ˈkæri]
	La **r,** precedida de los sonidos [ʌ] o [ə], da colorido propio a estos sonidos y desaparece completamente como sonido consonantal.	**burn** [bʌrn] **learn** [lʌrn] **weather** [ˈwɛðər]
[s]	Como la s de **clase.** Sonido alveolar fricativo sordo.	**send** [sɛnd] **cellar** [ˈsɛlər]
[ʃ]	Como **ch** de la palabra francesa **chose.** Sonido palatal fricativo sordo.	**shall** [ʃæl] **machine** [məˈʃin] **nation** [ˈneʃən]
[t]	Como la **t de arte.** Sonido dental oclusivo sordo.	**ten** [tɛn] **dropped** [drɑpt]
[tʃ]	Como la **ch** de **mucho.** Sonido palatal africado sordo.	**child** [tʃaɪld] **much** [mʌtʃ] **nature** [ˈnetʃər]
[θ]	Como la **z** de **zapato** en la pronunciación de Castilla. Sonido interdental fricativo sordo.	**think** [θɪŋk] **truth** [truθ]
[v]	Como la **v** de la palabra francesa **avant.** Sonido labiodental fricativo sonoro.	**vest** [vɛst] **over** [ˈovər] **of** [ɑv]
[w]	Como la **u** de **hueso.** Sonido labiovelar fricativo sonoro.	**work** [wʌrk] **tweed** [twid] **queen** [kwin]
[z]	Como la **s** de **mismo.** Sonido alveolar fricativo sonoro.	**zeal** [zil] **busy** [ˈbɪzi] **his** [hɪz]
[ʒ]	Como la **j** de la palabra francesa **jardin.** Sonido palatal fricativo sonoro.	**azure** [ˈeʒər] **measure** [ˈmɛʒər]

A

A, a [e] primera letra del alfabeto inglés

a [e] *art indef* un

aback [əˈbæk] *adv* atrás; **to be taken aback** quedar desconcertado; **to take aback** desconcertar

abaft [əˈbæft] o [əˈbɑft] *adv* a popa, en popa; *prep* detrás de

abandon [əˈbændən] *s* abandono ‖ *tr* abandonar

abase [əˈbes] *tr* degradar, humillar

abash [əˈbæʃ] *tr* avergonzar

abate [əˈbet] *tr* disminuir, reducir; deducir ‖ *intr* disminuir, moderarse

aba·tis [ˈæbətɪs] *s* (*pl* **-tis**) abatida

abattoir [ˈæbəˌtwɑr] *s* matadero

abba·cy [ˈæbəsi] *s* (*pl* **-cies**) abadía

abbess [ˈæbɪs] *s* abadesa

abbey [ˈæbi] *s* abadía

abbot [ˈæbət] *s* abad *m*

abbreviate [əˈbrivɪˌet] *tr* abreviar

abbreviation [əˌbrivɪˈeʃən] *s* (*shortening*) abreviación; (*shortened form*) abreviatura

A B C [ˌeˌbiˈsi] *s* abecé *m;* **A B C's** abecedario

abdicate [ˈæbdɪˌket] *tr & intr* abdicar

abdomen [ˈæbdəmən] o [æbˈdomən] *s* abdomen *m*

abduct [æbˈdʌkt] *tr* raptar, secuestrar

abed [əˈbɛd] *adv* en cama, acostado

abet [əˈbɛt] *v* (*pret & pp* **abetted;** *ger* **abetting**) *tr* incitar (*a una persona, esp. al mal*); fomentar (*el crimen*)

abeyance [əˈbe·əns] *s* suspensión; **in abeyance** en suspenso

ab·hor [æbˈhɔr] *v* (*pret & pp* **-horred;** *ger* **-horring**) *tr* aborrecer, detestar

abhorrent [æbˈhɑrənt] o [æbˈhɔrənt] *adj* aborrecible, detestable

abide [əˈbaɪd] *v* (*pret & pp* **abode** o **abided**) *tr* esperar; tolerar ‖ *intr* permanecer; **to abide by** cumplir con; atenerse a

abili·ty [əˈbɪlɪti] *s* (*pl* **-ties**) habilidad, capacidad; talento

abject [æbˈdʒɛkt] *adj* abyecto, servil

ablative [ˈæblətɪv] *s* ablativo

ablaut [ˈæblaʊt] *s* apofonía

ablaze [əˈblez] *adj* brillante; ardiente; encolerizado ‖ *adv* en llamas, ardiendo

able [ˈebəl] *adj* hábil, capaz; **to be able to** poder

able-bodied [ˈebəlˈbɑdid] *adj* sano; fornido; experto

abloom [əˈblum] *adj* floreciente ‖ *adv* en flor

abnormal [æbˈnɔrməl] *adj* anormal

aboard [əˈbord] *adv* a bordo; al bordo; **all aboard!** ¡señores viajeros al tren!; **to go aboard** ir a bordo; **to take aboard** embarcar ‖ *prep* a bordo de; (*a train*) en

abode [əˈbod] *s* domicilio, residencia

abolish [əˈbɑlɪʃ] *tr* eliminar, suprimir

A-bomb [ˈeˌbɑm] *s* bomba atómica

abomination [əˌbɑmɪˈneʃən] *s* abominación

aborigines [ˌæbəˈrɪdʒɪˌniz] *spl* aborígenes *mf*

abort [əˈbɔrt] *tr & intr* abortar

abortion [əˈbɔrʃən] *s* aborto

abound [əˈbaʊnd] *intr* abundar

about [əˈbaʊt] *adv* casi; aquí; **to be about to** estar a punto de, estar para ‖ *prep* acerca de; con respecto a; cerca de; hacia, a eso de; **to be about** tratar de

above [əˈbʌv] *adj* antedicho ‖ *adv* arriba, encima ‖ *prep* sobre, encima de, más alto que; superior a; **above all** sobre todo

above-mentioned [əˈbʌvˈmɛnʃənd] *adj* sobredicho, antedicho, susodicho

abrasive [əˈbresɪv] o [əˈbreziv] *adj & s* abrasivo

abreast [əˈbrɛst] *adj & adv* de frente; **to be abreast of** correr parejas con; estar al corriente de

abridge [əˈbrɪdʒ] *tr* abreviar; disminuir; condensar, resumir

abroad [əˈbrɔd] *adv* al extranjero; en el extranjero; fuera de casa

abrupt [əˈbrʌpt] *adj* brusco; repentino; áspero; abrupto, escarpado

abscess [ˈæbsɛs] *s* absceso

abscond [æbˈskɑnd] *intr* irse a hurtadillas; **to abscond with** alzarse con

absence [ˈæbsəns] *s* ausencia

absent [ˈæbsənt] *adj* ausente ‖ [æbˈsɛnt] *tr*—**to absent oneself** ausentarse

absentee [ˌæbsənˈti] *s* ausente *mf*

absent-minded [ˈæbsəntˈmaɪndɪd] *adj* distraído, absorto

absinth [ˈæbsɪnθ] *s* (*plant*) absintio, ajenjo; (*drink*) absenta, ajenjo

absolute [ˈæbsəˌlut] *adj & s* absoluto

absolutely [ˈæbsəˌlutli] *adv* absolutamente ‖ [ˌæbsəˈlutli] *adv* (coll) positivamente

absolve [æbˈsɑlv] *tr* absolver

absorb [æbˈsɔrb] *tr* absorber; **to be** o **become absorbed** ensimismarse

absorbent [æbˈsɔrbənt] *adj* absorbente; (*cotton*) hidrófilo

absorbing [æbˈsɔrbɪŋ] *adj* absorbente

abstain [æbˈsten] *intr* abstenerse

abstemious [æbˈstimɪ·əs] *adj* abstemio, sobrio

abstinent [ˈæbstɪnənt] *adj* abstinente

abstract ['æbstrækt] *adj* abstracto || *s* resumen *m,* sumario, extracto || *tr* resumir, compendiar, extractar || [æb'strækt] *tr* abstraer; quitar
abstruse [æb'strus] *adj* abstruso
absurd [æb'sʌrd] o [æb'zʌrd] *adj* absurdo
absurdi•ty [æb'sʌrdɪti] o [æb'zʌrdɪti] *s* (*pl* **-ties**) absurdidad, absurdo
abundant [ə'bʌndənt] *adj* abundante
abuse [ə'bjus] *s* maltrato; injuria, insulto; (*bad practice; injustice*) abuso || [ə'bjuz] *tr* maltratar; injuriar, insultar; (*to misapply, take unfair advantage of*) abusar de
abusive [ə'bjusɪv] *adj* injurioso, insultante; abusivo
abut [ə'bʌt] *v* (*pret & pp* **abutted;** *ger* **abutting**) *intr*—**to abut on** confinar con, terminar en
abutment [ə'bʌtmənt] *s* confinamiento; estribo, contrafuerte *m*
abyss [ə'bɪs] *s* abismo
academic [,ækə'dɛmɪk] *adj* académico
academic costume *s* toga, traje *m* de catedrático
academic freedom *s* libertad de cátedra, libertad de enseñanza
academician [ə,kædə'mɪʃən] *s* académico
academic subjects *spl* materias no profesionales
academic year *s* año escolar
acade•my [ə'kædəmi] *s* (*pl* **-mies**) academia
accede [æk'sid] *intr* acceder; **to accede to** acceder a, condescender a; (*e.g., the throne*) ascender a, subir a
accelerate [æk'sɛlə,ret] *tr* acelerar || *intr* acelerarse
accelerator [æk'sɛlə,retər] *s* acelerador *m*
accent ['æksɛnt] *s* acento || ['æksɛnt] o [æk'sɛnt] *tr* acentuar
accent mark *s* acento ortográfico
accentuate [æk'sɛntʃʊ,et] *tr* acentuar
accept [æk'sɛpt] *tr* aceptar
acceptable [æk'sɛptəbəl] *adj* aceptable
acceptance [æk'sɛptəns] *s* aceptación
access ['æksɛs] *s* acceso
accessible [æk'sɛsɪbəl] *adj* accesible
accession [æk'sɛʃən] *s* accesión; (*to a dignity*) ascenso; (*of books in a library*) adquisición
accesso•ry [æk'sɛsəri] *adj* accesorio || *s* (*pl* **-ries**) accesorio; (*to a crime*) cómplice *mf*
accident ['æksɪdənt] *s* accidente *m;* **by accident** por casualidad
accidental [,æksɪ'dɛntəl] *adj* accidental
acclaim [ə'klem] *s* aclamación || *tr & intr* aclamar
acclimate ['æklɪ,met] *tr* aclimatar || *intr* aclimatarse
accolade [,ækə'led] *s* acolada; elogio, premio
accommodate [ə'kɑmə,det] *tr* acomodar; alojar
accommodating [ə'kɑmə,detɪŋ] *adj* acomodadizo, servicial
accommodation [ə,kɑmə'deʃən] *s* acomodación; **accommodations** facilidades, comodidades; (*in a train*) localidad; (*in a hotel*) alojamiento
accommodation train *s* tren *m* omnibus
accompaniment [ə'kʌmpənɪmənt] *s* acompañamiento
accompanist [ə'kʌmpənɪst] *s* acompañante *m*
accompa•ny [ə'kʌmpəni] *v* (*pret & pp* **-nied**) *tr* acompañar
accomplice [ə'kɑmplɪs] *s* cómplice *mf,* codelincuente *mf*
accomplish [ə'kɑmplɪʃ] *tr* realizar, llevar a cabo
accomplished [ə'kɑmplɪʃt] *adj* realizado; culto, talentoso; (*fact*) consumado
accomplishment [ə'kɑmplɪʃmənt] *s* realización; **accomplishments** prendas, talentos
accord [ə'kɔrd] *s* acuerdo; **in accord with** de acuerdo con: **of one's own accord** de buen grado, voluntariamente; **with one accord** de común acuerdo || *tr* conceder, otorgar || *intr* concordar, avenirse
accordance [ə'kɔrdəns] *s* conformidad; **in accordance with** de acuerdo con
according [ə'kɔrdɪŋ] *adj* — **according as** según que; **according to** según
accordingly [ə'kɔrdɪŋli] *adv* en conformidad; por consiguiente
accordion [ə'kɔrdɪ·ən] *s* acordeón *m*
accost [ə'kɔst] o [ə'kɑst] *tr* abordar, acercarse a
accouchement [ə'kuʃmənt] *s* alumbramiento, parto
account [ə'kaʊnt] *s* informe *m,* relato; cuenta; estado de cuenta; importancia; **by all accounts** según el decir general; **of no account** de poca importancia; **on account of** a causa de; **to bring to account** pedir cuentas a; **to buy on account** comprar a plazos; **to turn to account** sacar provecho de, hacer valer || *intr*—**to account for** explicar; responder de
accountable [ə'kaʊntəbəl] *adj* responsable; explicable
accountant [ə'kaʊntənt] *s* contador *m,* contable *m*
accounting [ə'kaʊntɪŋ] *s* arreglo de cuentas; contabilidad
accouterments [ə'kutərmənts] *spl* equipo, avíos
accredit [ə'krɛdɪt] *tr* acreditar
accrue [ə'kru] *intr* acumularse; resultar
acct. *abbr* **account**
accumulate [ə'kjumjə,let] *tr* acumular || *intr* acumularse
accuracy ['ækjərəsi] *s* exactitud, precisión
accurate ['ækjərɪt] *adj* exacto
accusation [,ækjə'zeʃən] *s* acusación
accusative [ə'kjuzətɪv] *adj & s* acusativo
accuse [ə'kjuz] *tr* acusar
accustom [ə'kʌstəm] *tr* acostumbrar
ace [es] *s* as *m;* **to be within an ace of** estar a dos dedos de

acetate [ˈæsɪ͵tet] *s* acetato
acetic acid [əˈsitɪk] *s* ácido acético
aceti·fy [əˈsɛtɪ͵faɪ] *v* (*pret & pp* **-fied**) *tr* acetificar || *intr* acetificarse
acetone [ˈæsɪ͵ton] *s* acetona
acetylene [əˈsɛtɪ͵lin] *s* acetileno
acetylene torch *s* soplete oxiacetilénico
ache [ek] *s* achaque *m,* dolor *m* || *intr* doler
achieve [əˈtʃiv] *tr* llevar a cabo; alcanzar, ganar, lograr
achievement [əˈtʃivmənt] *s* realización; (*feat*) hazaña
Achilles' heel [əˈkɪliz] *s* talón *m* de Aquiles
acid [ˈæsɪd] *adj* ácido; agrio, mordaz || *s* ácido
acidi·fy [əˈsɪdɪ͵faɪ] *v* (*pret & pp* **-fied**) *tr* acidificar || *intr* acidificarse
acidi·ty [əˈsɪdɪti] *s* (*pl* **-ties**) acidez *f*
acid test *s* prueba decisiva
ack-ack [ˈækˈæk] *s* (slang) artillería antiaérea; (slang) fuego antiaéreo
acknowledge [ækˈnɑlɪdʒ] *tr* reconocer; acusar (*recibo de una carta*); agradecer (*p. ej., un favor*)
acknowledgment [ækˈnɑlɪdʒmənt] *s* reconocimiento; (*of receipt of a letter*) acuse *m;* (*of a favor*) agradecimiento
acme [ˈækmi] *s* auge *m,* colmo
acolyte [ˈækə͵laɪt] *s* acólito
acorn [ˈekɔrn] o [ˈekərn] *s* bellota
acoustic [əˈkustɪk] *adj* acústico || **acoustics** *ssg* acústica
acquaint [əˈkwent] *tr* informar, poner al corriente; **to be acquainted** conocerse; **to be acquainted with** conocer; estar al corriente de
acquaintance [əˈkwentəns] *s* conocimiento; (*person*) conocido
acquiesce [͵ækwɪˈɛs] *intr* consentir, condescender, asentir
acquiescence [͵ækwɪˈɛsəns] *s* consentimiento, condescendencia, aquiescencia
acquire [əˈkwaɪr] *tr* adquirir
acquisition [͵ækwɪˈzɪʃən] *s* adquisición
acquit [əˈkwɪt] *v* (*pret & pp* **acquitted;** *ger* **acquitting**) *tr* absolver, exculpar; **to acquit oneself** conducirse, portarse
acquittal [əˈkwɪtəl] *s* absolución, exculpación
acrid [ˈækrɪd] *adj* acre, acrimonioso
acrobat [ˈækrə͵bæt] *s* acróbata *mf*
acrobatic [͵ækrəˈbætɪk] *adj* acrobático || **acrobatics** *ssg* (*profession*) acrobatismo; *spl* (*stunts*) acrobacia
acronym [ˈækrənɪm] *s* acrónimo
acropolis [əˈkrɑpəlɪs] *s* acrópolis *f*
across [əˈkrɔs] o [əˈkrɑs] *prep* al través de; al otro lado de; **to come across** encontrarse con; **to go across** atravesar
across'-the-board' *adj* comprensivo, general
acrostic [əˈkrɔstɪk] o [əˈkrɑstɪk] *s* acróstico
act [ækt] *s* acto; (law) decreto; **in the act** en flagrante || *tr* representar; desempeñar (*un papel*); **to act the fool** hacer el bufón; **to act the part of** hacer o desempeñar el papel de || *intr* actuar; funcionar, obrar; conducirse; **to act as if** hacer como que; **to act for** representar; **to act up** travesear; **to act up to** hacer fiestas a
acting [ˈæktɪŋ] *adj* interino || *s* actuación
action [ˈækʃən] *s* acción; **to take action** tomar medidas
activate [ˈæktɪ͵vet] *tr* activar
active [ˈæktɪv] *adj* activo
activi·ty [ækˈtɪvɪti] *s* (*pl* **-ties**) actividad
act of God *s* fuerza mayor
actor [ˈæktər] *s* actor *m*
actress [ˈæktrɪs] *s* actriz *f*
actual [ˈæktʃʊ·əl] *adj* real, efectivo
actually [ˈæktʃʊ·əli] *adv* en realidad
actuar·y [ˈæktʃʊ͵ɛri] *s* (*pl* **-ies**) actuario (de seguros)
actuate [ˈæktʃʊ͵et] *tr* actuar; estimular, mover
acuity [əˈkju·ɪti] *s* agudeza
acumen [əˈkjumən] *s* cacumen *m,* perspicacia
acute [əˈkjut] *adj* agudo
A.D. *abbr* **anno Domini** (Lat) **in the year of our Lord**
ad [æd] *s* (coll) anuncio
adage [ˈædɪdʒ] *s* adagio, refrán *m*
Adam [ˈædəm] *s* Adán *m;* **the old Adam** la inclinación al pecado
adamant [ˈædəmənt] *adj* firme, inexorable
Adam's apple *s* nuez *f*
adapt [əˈdæpt] *tr* adaptar; refundir (*un drama*)
adaptation [͵ædæpˈteʃən] *s* adaptación; (*of a play*) refundición
add [æd] *tr* agregar, añadir; sumar || *intr* sumar; **to add up to** subir a; (coll) querer decir
added line *s* (mus) línea suplementaria
adder [ˈædər] *s* víbora; serpiente *f*
addict [ˈædɪkt] *s* enviciado; adicto, partidario || [əˈdɪkt] *tr* enviciar; entregar; **to addict oneself to** enviciarse con o en; entregarse a
addiction [əˈdɪkʃən] *s* enviciamiento; adhesividad
adding machine *s* sumadora, máquina de sumar
addition [əˈdɪʃən] *s* adición; **in addition to** además de
additive [ˈædɪtɪv] *adj & s* aditivo
address [əˈdrɛs] o [ˈædrɛs] *s* dirección; consignación || [əˈdrɛs] *s* alocución, discurso; **to deliver an address** hacer uso de la palabra || *tr* dirigirse a; dirigir (*p. ej., una alocución, una carta*); consignar
addressee [͵ædrɛˈsi] *s* destinatario; (com) consignatario
addressing machine *s* máquina para dirigir sobres
adduce [əˈdjus] o [əˈdus] *tr* aducir
adenoids [ˈædə͵nɔɪdz] *spl* vegetaciones adenoides
adept [əˈdɛpt) *adj & s* experto, perito
adequate [ˈædɪkwɪt] *adj* suficiente

adhere [æd'hɪr] *intr* adherir, adherirse; conformarse
adherence [æd'hɪrəns] *s* adhesión
adherent [æd'hɪrənt] *adj & s* adherente *m*
adhesion [æd'hiʒən] *s* (*sticking*) adherencia; (*support, loyalty*) adhesión; (pathol) adherencia; (phys) adherencia o adhesión
adhesive [æd'hisɪv] o [æd'hizɪv] *adj* adhesivo
adhesive tape *s* tafetán adhesivo
adieu [ə'dju] o [ə'du] *interj* ¡adiós! || *s* (*pl* **adieus** o **adieux**) adiós *m;* **to bid adieu to** despedirse de
adjacent [ə'dʒesənt] *adj* adyacente
adjective ['ædʒɪktɪv] *adj & s* adjetivo
adjoin [ə'dʒɔɪn] *tr* lindar con || *intr* colindar
adjoining [ə'dʒɔɪnɪŋ] *adj* colindante, contiguo
adjourn [ə'dʒʌrn] *tr* prorrogar, suspender || *intr* prorrogarse, suspenderse; (coll) ir
adjournment [ə'dʒʌrnmənt] *s* prorrogación, suspensión
adjust [ə'dʒʌst] *tr* ajustar, arreglar; corregir, verificar; (ins) liquidar
adjustable [ə'dʒʌstəbəl] *adj* ajustable, arreglable
adjustment [ə'dʒʌstmənt] *s* ajuste *m,* arreglo; (ins) liquidación de la avería
adjutant ['ædʒətənt] *s* ayudante *m*
ad·lib [,æd'lɪb] *v* (*pret & pp* **-libbed;** *ger* **-libbing**) *tr & intr* improvisar
Adm. *abbr* **Admiral**
administer [æd'mɪnɪstər] *tr* administrar; **to administer an oath** tomar juramento || *intr* — **to administer to** cuidar de
administrator [æd'mɪnɪs,tretər] *s* administrador *m*
admiral ['ædmɪrəl] *s* almirante *m;* buque *m* almirante
admiral·ty ['ædmɪrəlti] *s* (*pl.* **-ties**) almirantazgo
admire [æd'maɪr] *tr* admirar
admirer [æd'maɪrər] *s* admirador *m;* enamorado
admissible [æd'mɪsɪbəl] *adj* admisible
admission [æd'mɪʃən] *s* admisión; (*in a school*) ingreso; precio de entrada; **to gain admission** lograr entrar
ad·mit [æd'mɪt] *v* (*pret & pp* **-mitted;** *ger* **-mitting**) *tr* admitir || *intr* dar entrada; **to admit of** admitir, permitir
admittance [æd'mɪtəns] *s* admisión; derecho de entrar; **no admittance** acceso prohibido, se prohibe la entrada
admonish [æd'mɑnɪʃ] *tr* amonestar
ado [ə'du] *s* bulla, excitación
adobe [ə'dobi] *s* adobe *m;* casa de adobe
adolescence [,ædə'lɛsəns] *s* adolescencia
adolescent [,ædə'lɛsənt] *adj & s* adolescente *mf*
adopt [ə'dɑpt] *tr* adoptar
adoption [ə'dɑpʃən] *s* adopción
adorable [ə'dorəbəl] *adj* adorable
adore [ə'dor] *tr* adorar
adorn [ə'dɔrn] *tr* adornar
adornment [ə'dɔrnmənt] *s* adorno
adrenal gland [æd'rinəl] *s* glándula suprarrenal
Adriatic [,edrɪ'ætɪk] o [,ædrɪ'ætɪk] *adj & s* Adriático
adrift [ə'drɪft] *adj & adv* al garete, a la deriva
adroit [ə'drɔɪt] *adj* diestro
adult [ə'dʌlt] o ['ædʌlt] *adj & s* adulto
adulterate [ə'dʌltə,ret] *tr* adulterar
adulterer [ə'dʌltərər] *s* adúltero
adulteress [ə'dʌltərɪs] *s* adúltera
adulter·y [ə'dʌltəri] *s* (*pl* **-ies**) adulterio
advance [æd'væns] o [æd'vɑns] *adj* adelantado; anticipado || *s* adelanto, avance *m;* aumento, subida; **advances** propuestas; requerimiento amoroso; propuesta indecente; préstamo; **in advance** de antemano, por anticipado || *tr* adelantar || *intr* adelantar; adelantarse
advanced [æd'vænst] o [æd'vɑnst] *adj* avanzado; **advanced in years** avanzado de edad, entrado en años
advanced standing *s* traspaso de matrículas, traspaso de crédito académico
advanced studies *spl* altos estudios
advancement [æd'vænsmənt] o [æd'vɑnsmənt] *s* adelanto, avance *m;* subida; promoción
advance publicity *s* publicidad de lanzamiento
advantage [æd'væntɪdʒ] o [æd'vɑntɪdʒ] *s* ventaja; **to take advantage of** aprovecharse de; abusar de, engañar
advantageous [,ædvən'tedʒəs] *adj* ventajoso
advent ['ædvɛnt] *s* advenimiento || **Advent** *s* (eccl) Adviento
adventure [æd'vɛntʃər] *s* aventura || *tr* aventurar || *intr* aventurarse
adventurer [æd'vɛntʃərər] *s* aventurero
adventuresome [æd'vɛntʃərsəm] *adj* aventurero
adventuress [æd'vɛntʃərɪs] *s* aventurera
adventurous [æd'vɛntʃərəs] *adj* aventurero
adverb ['ædvʌrb] *s* adverbio
adversar·y ['ædvər,sɛri] *s* (*pl* **-ies**) adversario
adversi·ty [æd'vʌrsɪti] *s* (*pl* **-ties**) adversidad
advertise ['ædvər,taiz] o [,ædvər'taɪz] *tr & intr* anunciar
advertisement [,ædvər'taɪzmənt] o [æd'vʌrtɪzmənt] *s* anuncio
advertiser ['ædvər,taɪzər] o [,ædvər'taɪzər] *s* anunciante *mf*
advertising ['ædvər,taɪzɪŋ] *s* propaganda, publicidad, anuncios
advertising agency *s* empresa anunciadora
advertising campaign *s* campaña de publicidad
advertising man *s* empresario de publicidad
advertising manager *s* gerente *m* de publicidad

advice [æd'vaɪs] *s* consejo; aviso, noticia; **a piece of advice** un consejo
advisable [æd'vaɪzəbəl] *adj* aconsejable
advise [æd'vaɪz] *tr* aconsejar, asesorar; advertir, avisar
advisement [æd'vaɪzmənt] *s* consideración; **to take under advisement** someter a consideración
advisory [æd'vaɪʒəri] *adj* consultivo
advocate ['ædvə,ket] *s* defensor *m;* abogado || *tr* abogar por
Aegean Sea [ɪ'dʒi·ən] *s* Archipiélago; (*of the ancients*) mar Egeo
aegis ['idʒɪs] *s* égida
aerate ['ɛret] o ['e·ə,ret] *tr* airear
aerial ['ɛrɪ·əl] *adj* aéreo || *s* antena
aerialist ['ɛrɪ·əlɪst] *s* volatinero
aerodrome ['ɛrə,drom] *s* aeródromo
aerodynamic [,ɛrodaɪ'næmɪk] *adj* aerodinámico || **aerodynamics** *ssg* aerodinámica
aeronaut ['ɛrə,nɔt] *s* aeronauta *mf*
aeronautic [,ɛrə'nɔtɪk] *adj* aeronáutico || **aeronautics** *ssg* aeronáutica
aerosol ['ɛrə,sol] *s* aerosol *m*
aerospace ['ɛro,spes] *adj* aeroespacial
aesthete ['ɛsθit] *s* esteta *mf*
aesthetic [ɛs'θɛtɪk] *adj* estético || **aesthetics** *ssg* estética
afar [ə'fɑr] *adv* lejos
affable ['æfəbəl] *adj* afable
affair [ə'fɛr] *s* asunto, negocio; lance *m;* amorío; encuentro, combate *m;* **affairs** negocios
affect [ə'fɛkt] *tr* influir en; impresionar, enternecer; (*to assume; to pretend*) afectar; aficionarse a
affectation [,æfɛk'teʃən] *s* afectación
affected [ə'fɛktɪd] *adj* afectado
affection [ə'fɛkʃən] *s* afecto, cariño, afección; (pathol) afección
affectionate [ə'fɛkʃənɪt] *adj* afectuoso, cariñoso
affidavit [,æfɪ'devɪt] *s* declaración jurada, acta notarial
affiliate [ə'fɪlɪ,et] *adj* afiliado || *s* afiliado; filial *f* || *tr* afiliar || *intr* afiliarse
affini·ty [ə'fɪnɪti] *s* (*pl* **-ties**) afinidad
affirm [ə'fʌrm] *tr & intr* afirmar
affirmative [ə'fʌrmətɪv] *adj* afirmativo || *s* afirmativa
affix ['æfɪks] *s* añadidura; (gram) afijo || [ə'fɪks] *tr* añadir; atribuir (*p.ej., culpa*); poner (*una firma, sello, etc.*)
afflict [ə'flɪkt] *tr* afligir; **to be afflicted with** sufrir de, adolecer de
affliction [ə'flɪkʃən] *s* aflicción, desgracia; achaque *m*
affluence ['æflu·əns] *s* (*abundance*) afluencia; (*wealth*) opulencia
afford [ə'fɔrd] *tr* proporcionar; **to be able to afford (to)** poder darse el lujo de, poder permitirse
affray [ə'fre] *s* pendencia, riña
affront [ə'frʌnt] *s* afrenta || *tr* afrentar
Afghan ['æfgən] o ['æfgæn] *adj & s* afgano
Afghanistan [æf'gænɪ,stæn] *s* el Afganistán
afire [ə'faɪr] *adj & adv* ardiendo
aflame [ə'flem] *adj & adv* en llamas
afloat [ə'flot] *adj & adv* a flote; a bordo; inundado; sin rumbo; (*rumor*) en circulación
afoot [ə'fʊt] *adj & adv* a pie; en marcha
afoul [ə'faʊl] *adj & adv* enredado; en colisión; **to run afoul of** enredarse con
afraid [ə'fred] *adj* asustado; **to be afraid** tener miedo
Africa ['æfrɪkə] *s* África
African ['æfrɪkən] *adj & s* africano
aft [æft] o [ɑft] *adj & adv* en popa
after ['æftər] o ['ɑftər] *adj* siguiente || *adv* después || *prep* después de; según; **after all** al fin y al cabo || *conj* después de que
af'ter-din'ner speaker *s* orador *m* de sobremesa
after-dinner speech *s* discurso de sobremesa
af'ter·hours' *adv* después del trabajo
af'ter·life' *s* vida venidera; resto de la vida
aftermath ['æftər,mæθ] o ['ɑftər,mæθ] *s* segunda siega; consecuencias, consecuencias desastrosas
af'ter·noon' *s* tarde *f*
af'ter·taste' *s* dejo, gustillo, resabio
af'ter·thought' *s* idea tardía, expediente tardío
afterward ['æftərwərd] o ['ɑftərwərd] *adv* después, luego
af'ter·while' *adv* dentro de poco
again [ə'gɛn] *adv* otra vez, de nuevo; además; **to** + *inf* + **again** volver a + *inf*, p.ej., **he will come again** volverá a venir
against [ə'gɛnst] *prep* contra; cerca de; en contraste con; por; para
agape [ə'gep] *adj* abierto de par en par || *adv* con la boca abierta
age [edʒ] *s* edad; (*old age*) vejez *f;* (*one hundred years; a long time*) siglo; edad mental; **of age** mayor de edad; **to come of age** alcanzar su mayoría de edad, llegar a mayor edad; **under age** menor de edad || *tr* envejecer || *intr* envejecer, envejecerse
aged [edʒd] *adj* de la edad de || ['edʒɪd] *adj* anciano, viejo
ageless ['edʒlɪs] *adj* eternamente joven
agen·cy ['edʒənsi] *s* (*pl* **-cies**) agencia; mediación
agenda [ə'dʒɛndə] *s* agenda, temario
agent ['edʒənt] *s* agente *m*
Age of Enlightenment *s* siglo de las luces
agglomeration [ə,glɑmə'reʃən] *s* aglomeración
aggrandizement [ə'grændɪzmənt] *s* engrandecimiento
aggravate ['ægrə,vet] *tr* agravar; (coll) exasperar, irritar
aggregate ['ægrɪ,get] *adj & s* agregado || *tr* agregar, juntar; ascender a
aggression [ə'grɛʃən] *s* agresión

aggressive [ə'grɛsɪv] *adj* agresivo
aggressor [ə'grɛsər] *s* agresor *m*
aghast [ə'gæst] o [ə'gɑst] *adj* horrorizado
agile ['ædʒɪl] *adj* ágil
agitate ['ædʒɪ,tet] *tr & intr* agitar
aglow [ə'glo] *adj & adv* fulgurante
agnostic [æg'nɑstɪk] *adj & s* agnóstico
ago [ə'go] *adv* hace, p.ej., **two days ago** hace dos días
ago·ny ['ægəni] *s* (*pl* **-nies**) angustia, congoja; (*anguish; death struggle*) agonía
agrarian [ə'grɛrɪ·ən] *adj* agrario || *s* agrariense *mf*
agree [ə'gri] *intr* estar de acuerdo, ponerse de acuerdo; sentar bien; (gram) concordar
agreeable [ə'gri·əbəl] *adj* (*to one's liking*) agradable; (*willing to consent*) acorde, conforme
agreement [ə'grimənt] *s* acuerdo, convenio; concordancia; **in agreement** de acuerdo
agric. *abbr* **agriculture**
agriculture ['ægrɪ,kʌltʃər] *s* agricultura
agronomy [ə'grɑnəmi] *s* agronomía
aground [ə'graʊnd] *adv* encallado, varado; **to run aground** encallar, varar
agt. *abbr* **agent**
ague ['egju] *s* escalofrío; fiebre *f* intermitente
ahead [ə'hɛd] *adj & adv* delante, al frente; **ahead of** antes de; delante de; al frente de; **to get ahead (of)** adelantarse (a)
ahoy [ə'hɔɪ] *interj* — **ship ahoy!** ¡ah del barco!
aid [ed] *s* ayuda, auxilio; (mil) ayudante *m* || *tr* ayudar, auxiliar; **to aid and abet** auxiliar e incitar, ser cómplice de || *intr* ayudar
aide-de-camp ['eddə'kæmp] *s* (*pl* **aides-de-camp**) ayudante *m* de campo, edecán *m*
ail [el] *tr* inquietar; **what ails you?** ¿qué tiene Vd.? || *intr* sufrir, estar enfermo
aileron ['elə,rɑn] *s* alerón *m*
ailing ['elɪŋ] *adj* enfermo, achacoso
ailment ['elmənt] *s* enfermedad, achaque *m*
aim [em] *s* puntería; intento; punto de mira || *tr* apuntar, encarar; dirigir (*p.ej., una observación*) || *intr* apuntar
air [ɛr] *s* aire *m;* **by air** por vía aérea; **in the open air** al aire libre; **on the air** en antena, en la radio; **to let the air out of** desinflar; **to put on airs** darse aires; **to put on the air** llevar a las antenas; **to walk on air** no pisar en el suelo || *tr* airear, ventilar; radiodifundir; (fig) ventilar
air'-a·tom'ic *adj* aeroatómico
air'-borne' *adj* aerotransportado
air brake *s* freno de aire comprimido
air castle *s* castillo en el aire
air'-condi'tion *tr* climatizar
air conditioner *s* acondicionador *m* de aire
air conditioning *s* acondicionamiento del aire, clima *m* artificial
air corps *s* cuerpo de aviación
air'craft' *ssg* máquina de volar; *spl* máquinas de volar
aircraft carrier *s* portaaviones *m*
airdrome ['ɛr,drom] *s* aeródromo
air'drop' *s* lanzamiento || *tr* lanzar
air field *s* campo de aviación
air'foil' *s* superficie *f* de sustentación
air force *s* fuerza aérea, ejército del aire
air gap *s* (phys) entrehierro
air'-ground' *adj* aeroterrestre
air hostess *s* aeromoza, azafata
air lane *s* ruta aérea
air'lift' *s* puente aéreo
air liner *s* transaéreo, avión *m* de travesía
air mail *s* correo aéreo, aeroposta
air'-mail' letter *s* carta aérea, carta por avión
air-mail pilot *s* aviador *m* postal
air-mail stamp *s* sello aéreo
air·man ['ɛrmən] o ['ɛr,mæn] *s* (*pl* **-men** [mən] o [,mɛn]) aviador *m*
air'plane' *s* avión *m*
airplane carrier *s* portaaviones *m*
air pocket *s* bache aéreo
air pollution *s* contaminación atmosférica
air'port' *s* aeropuerto
air raid *s* ataque aéreo
air'-raid' drill *s* simulacro de ataque aéreo
air-raid shelter *s* abrigo antiaéreo
air-raid warning *s* alarma aérea
air rifle *s* escopeta de viento, escopeta de aire comprimido
air'ship' *s* aeronave *f*
air'sick' *adj* mareado en el aire
air sleeve o **sock** *s* veleta de manga
air'strip' *s* pista de despegue, pista de aterrizaje
air'tight' *adj* herméticamente cerrado, estanco al aire
air'waves' *spl* ondas de radio
air'way' *s* aerovía, vía aérea
airway lighting *s* balizaje *m*
air·y ['ɛri] *adj* (*comp* **-ier;** *super* **-iest**) airoso; aireado; alegre; impertinente; (coll) afectado
aisle [aɪl] *s* (*in theater, movie, etc.*) pasillo; (*in a store, factory, etc.*) nave *f;* (archit) nave *f* lateral; (*any of the long passageways of a church*) (archit) nave *f*
ajar [ə'dʒɑr] *adj* entreabierto, entornado
akimbo [ə'kɪmbo] *adj & adv* — **with arms akimbo** en jarras
akin [ə'kɪn] *adj* emparentado; semejante
alabaster ['ælə,bæstər] o ['ælə,bɑstər] *s* alabastro
alarm [ə'lɑrm] *s* alarma || *tr* alarmar
alarm clock *s* reloj *m* despertador
alarmist [ə'lɑrmɪst] *s* alarmista *mf*
alas [ə'læs] o [ə'lɑs] *interj* ¡ay!, ¡ay de mí!
Albanian [æl'benɪ·ən] *adj & s* albanés *m*

albatross ['ælbəˌtrɔs] o ['ælbəˌtrɑs] *s* albatros *m*
album ['ælbəm] *s* álbum *m*
albumen [æl'bjumən] *s* albumen *m;* albúmina
alchemy ['ælkɪmi] *s* alquimia
alcohol ['ælkəˌhɔl] o ['ælkəˌhɑl] *s* alcohol *m*
alcoholic [ˌælkə'hɔlɪk] o [ˌælkə'hɑlɪk] *adj & s* alcohólico
alcove ['ælkov] *s* gabinete *m,* rincón *m;* (*in a bedroom*) trasalcoba; (*in a garden*) cenador *m*
alder ['ɔldər] *s* aliso
alder•man ['ɔldərmən] *s* (*pl* **-men** [mən]) concejal *m*
ale [el] *s* ale *f* (*cerveza inglesa, obscura, espesa y amarga*)
alembic [ə'lɛmbɪk] *s* alambique *m*
alert [ə'lʌrt] *adj* listo, vivo; vigilante ‖ *s* (aer) alarma; (mil) alerta *m;* **to be on the alert** estar sobre aviso, estar alerta ‖ *tr* alertar
Aleutian Islands [ə'luʃən] *spl* islas Aleutas, islas Aleutianas
Alexandrine [ˌælɪg'zændrɪn] *adj & s* alejandrino
alg. *abbr* **algebra**
algae ['ældʒi] *spl* algas
algebra ['ældʒɪbrə] *s* álgebra
algebraic [ˌældʒɪ'bre•ɪk] *adj* algebraico
Algeria [æl'dʒɪrɪ•ə] *s* Argelia
Algerian [æl'dʒɪrɪ•ən] *adj & s* argelino
Algiers [æl'dʒɪrz] *s* Argel *f*
alias ['elɪ•əs] *adv* alias ‖ *s* alias *m,* nombre supuesto
ali•bi ['ælɪˌbaɪ] *s* (*pl* **-bis**) coartada; (coll) excusa
alien ['eljən] o ['elɪ•ən] *adj & s* extranjero
alienate ['eljəˌnet] o ['elɪ•əˌnet] *tr* enajenar, alienar
alight [ə'laɪt] *v* (*pret & pp* **alighted** o **alit** [ə'lɪt]) *intr* bajar, apearse; posarse (*un ave*)
align [ə'laɪn] *tr* alinear ‖ *intr* alinearse
alike [ə'laɪk] *adj* semejantes; **to look alike** parecerse ‖ *adv* igualmente
alimentary canal [ˌælɪ'mɛntəri] *s* canal alimenticio, tubo digestivo
alimony ['ælɪˌmoni] *s* alimentos
alive [ə'laɪv] *adj* vivo, viviente; animado; **alive to** despierto para, sensible a; **alive with** hormigueante en
alka•li ['ælkəˌlaɪ] *s* (*pl* **-lis** o **-lies**) álcali *m*
alkaline ['ælkəˌlaɪn] o ['ælkəlɪn] *adj* alcalino
all [ɔl] *adj indef* todo, todos; todo el, todos los ‖ *pron indef* todo; todos, todo el mundo; **after all** sin embargo; **all of** todo el, todos los; **all that** todo lo que, todos los que; **for all I know** que yo sepa; a lo mejor; **not at all** nada; no hay de qué ‖ *adv* enteramente; **all along** desde el principio; a lo largo de; **all at once** de golpe; **all right** bueno, corriente; **all too** excesivamente
Allah ['ælə] *s* Alá *m*
allay [ə'le] *tr* aliviar, calmar
all-clear ['ɔl'klɪr] *s* cese *m* de alarma
allege [ə'lɛdʒ] *tr* alegar
allegiance [ə'lidʒəns] *s* fidelidad, lealtad; homenaje *m;* **to swear allegiance to** jurar fidelidad a; rendir homenaje a
allegoric(al) [ˌælɪ'gɑrɪk(əl)] o [ˌælɪ'gɔrɪk(əl)] *adj* alegórico
allego•ry ['ælɪˌgori] *s* (*pl* **-ries**) alegoría
aller•gy ['ælərdʒi] *s* (*pl* **-gies**) alergia
alleviate [ə'livɪˌet] *tr* aliviar
alley ['æli] *s* callejuela; paseo arbolado, paseo de jardín; (bowling) pista; (tennis) espacio lateral
All Fools' Day *s* var of **April Fools' Day**
Allhallows [ˌɔl'hæloz] *s* día *m* de todos los santos
alliance [ə'laɪ•əns] *s* alianza
alligator ['ælɪˌgetər] *s* caimán *m*
alligator pear *s* aguacate *m*
alligator wrench *s* llave *f* de mandíbulas dentadas
alliteration [əˌlɪtə'reʃən] *s* aliteración
all-knowing ['ɔl'no•ɪŋ] *adj* omnisciente
allocate ['æləˌket] *tr* asignar, distribuir
allot [ə'lɑt] *v* (*pret & pp* **allotted;** *ger* **allotting**) *tr* asignar, distribuir
all'-out' *adj* acérrimo
allow [ə'laʊ] *tr* dejar, permitir; admitir; conceder ‖ *intr* — **to allow for** tener en cuenta; **to allow of** permitir; admitir
allowance [ə'laʊ•əns] *s* permiso; concesión; ración; descuento, rebaja; tolerancia; **to make allowance for** tener en cuenta
alloy ['ælɔɪ] o [ə'lɔɪ] *s* aleación, liga ‖ [ə'lɔɪ] *tr* alear, ligar
all-powerful ['ɔl'paʊ•ərfəl] *adj* todopoderoso
All Saints' Day *s* día *m* de todos los santos
All Souls' Day *s* día *m* de los difuntos
allspice ['ɔlˌspaɪs] *s* pimienta inglesa
all'-star' game *s* (sport) juego de estrellas
allude [ə'lud] *intr* aludir
allure [ə'lʊr] *s* tentación, encanto, fascinación ‖ *tr* tentar, encantar
alluring [ə'lʊrɪŋ] *adj* tentador, encantador, fascinante
allusion [ə'luʒən] *s* alusión
al•ly ['ælaɪ] o [ə'laɪ] *s* (*pl* **-lies**) aliado ‖ [ə'laɪ] *v* (*pret & pp* **-lied**) *tr* aliar ‖ *intr* aliarse
almanac ['ɔlməˌnæk] *s* almanaque *m*
almighty [ɔl'maɪti] *adj* todopoderoso, omnipotente
almond ['ɑmənd] o ['æmənd] *s* almendra
almond brittle *s* crocante *m*
almond tree *s* almendro
almost ['ɔlmost] o [ɔl'most] *adv* casi
alms [ɑmz] *s* limosna
alms'house' *s* casa de beneficencia
aloe ['ælo] *s* áloe *m*
aloft [ə'lɔft] o [ə'lɑft] *adv* arriba; (aer) en vuelo; (naut) en la arboladura
alone [ə'lon] *adj* solo; **let alone** sin

mencionar; y mucho menos; **to let alone** no molestar; no mezclarse en || *adv* solamente
along [ə'lɔŋ] o [ə'lɑŋ] *adv* conmigo, consigo, etc.; **all along** desde el principio; **along with** junto con || *prep* a lo largo de
along'side' *adv* a lo largo; (naut) al costado; **to bring alongside** acostar || *prep* a lo largo de; (naut) al costado de
aloof [ə'luf] *adj* apartado; reservado || *adv* lejos, a distancia
aloud [ə'laʊd] *adv* alto, en voz alta
alphabet ['ælfə,bɛt] *s* alfabeto
alpine ['ælpaɪn] *adj* alpestre, alpino
Alps [ælps] *spl* Alpes *mpl*
already [ɔl'rɛdi] *adv* ya
Alsace [æl'ses] o ['ælsæs] *s* Alsacia
Alsatian [æl'seʃən] *adj & s* alsaciano
also ['ɔlso] *adv* también
alt. *abbr* **alternate, altitude**
altar ['ɔltər] *s* altar *m;* **to lead to the altar** conducir al altar
altar boy *s* acólito, monaguillo
altar cloth *s* sabanilla, palia
al'tar·piece' *s* retablo
altar rail *s* comulgatorio
alter ['ɔltər] *tr* alterar || *intr* alterarse
alteration [,ɔltə'reʃən] *s* alteración; (*in a building*) reforma; (*in clothing*) arreglo
alternate ['ɔltərnɪt] o ['æltərnɪt] *adj* alterno || ['ɔltər,net] o ['æltər,net] *tr & intr* alternar
alternating current *s* corriente alterna o alternativa
although [ɔl'ðo] *conj* aunque
altimetry [æl'tɪmɪtri] *s* altimetría
altitude ['æltɪ,tjud] o ['æltɪ,tud] *s* altitud, altura
al·to ['ælto] *s* (*pl* **-tos**) contralto
altogether [,ɔltə'gɛðər] *adv* enteramente; en conjunto
altruist ['æltrʊ·ɪst] *s* altruísta *mf*
altruistic [,æltrʊ'ɪstɪk] *adj* altruísta
alum ['æləm] *s* alumbre *m*
aluminum [ə'lumɪnəm] *s* aluminio
alum·na [ə'lʌmnə] *s* (*pl* **-nae** [ni]) graduada
alum·nus [ə'lʌmnəs] *s* (*pl* **-ni** [naɪ]) graduado
alveo·lus [æl'vi·ələs] *s* (*pl* **-li** [,laɪ]) alvéolo
always ['ɔlwɪz] o ['ɔlwez] *adv* siempre
A.M. *abbr* **ante meridiem,** i.e., **before noon; amplitude modulation**
Am. *abbr* **America, American**
amalgam [ə'mælgəm] *s* amalgama *f*
amalgamate [ə'mælgə,met] *tr* amalgamar || *intr* amalgamarse
amass [ə'mæs] *tr* amontonar; amasar (*dinero*)
amateur ['æmətʃər] *adj & s* chapucero, principiante *mf;* aficionado
amateur performance *s* función de aficionados
amaze [ə'mez] *tr* asombrar, maravillar
amazing [ə'mezɪŋ] *adj* asombroso, maravilloso
Amazon ['æmə,zɑn] o ['æməzən] *s* Amazonas *m*
ambassador [æm'bæsədər] *s* embajador *m*
ambassadress [æm'bæsədrɪs] *s* embajadora
amber ['æmbər] *adj* ambarino || *s* ámbar *m*
ambigui·ty [,æmbɪ'gju·ɪti] *s* (*pl* **-ties**) ambigüidad
ambiguous [æm'bɪgju·əs] *adj* ambiguo
ambition [æm'bɪʃən] *s* ambición
ambitious [æm'bɪʃəs] *adj* ambicioso
amble ['æmbəl] *s* ambladura || *intr* amblar
ambulance ['æmbjələns] *s* ambulancia
ambush ['æmbʊʃ] *s* emboscada; **to lie in ambush** estar emboscado || *tr* (*to station in ambush*) emboscar; (*to lie in wait for and attack*) insidiar || *intr* emboscarse
amelioration [ə,miljə'reʃən] *s* mejoramiento
amen ['e'mɛn] o ['ɑ'mɛn] *interj* ¡amén! || *s* amén *m*
amenable [ə'minəbəl] o [ə'mɛnəbəl] *adj* dócil; responsable
amend [ə'mɛnd] *tr* enmendar || *intr* enmendarse || **amends** *spl* enmienda; **to make amends for** enmendar
amendment [ə'mɛndmənt] *s* enmienda
ameni·ty [ə'minɪti] o [ə'mɛnɪti] *s* (*pl* **-ties**) amenidad
America [ə'mɛrɪkə] *s* América
American [ə'mɛrɪkən] *adj & s* americano; norteamericano, estadounidense
Americanize [ə'mɛrɪkə,naɪz] *tr* americanizar
amethyst ['æmɪθɪst] *s* amatista
amiable ['emɪ·əbəl] *adj* amable, bonachón
amicable ['æmɪkəbəl] *adj* amigable
amid [ə'mɪd] *prep* en medio de
amidship [ə'mɪdʃɪp] *adv* en medio del navío
amiss [ə'mɪs] *adj* inoportuno; malo || *adv* inoportunamente; mal; **to take amiss** llevar a mal, tomar en mala parte
ami·ty ['æmɪti] *s* (*pl* **-ties**) amistad
ammeter ['æm,mitər] *s* anmetro, amperímetro
ammonia [ə'monɪ·ə] *s* amoníaco; agua amoniacal
ammunition [,æmjə'nɪʃən] *s* munición
amnes·ty ['æmnɪsti] *s* (*pl* **-ties**) amnistía || *v* (*pret & pp* **-tied**) *tr* amnistiar
amoeba [ə'mibə] *s* amiba
among [ə'mʌŋ] *prep* entre, en medio de, en el número de
amorous ['æmərəs] *adj* amoroso; erótico, sensual, voluptuoso
amortize ['æmər,taɪz] *tr* amortizar
amount [ə'maʊnt] *s* cantidad, importe *m* || *intr* — **to amount to** ascender a; significar
amp. *abbr* **ampere, amperage**
ampere ['æmpɪr] *s* amperio
am'pere-hour' *s* amperio-hora *m*
amphibious [æm'fɪbɪ·əs] *adj* anfibio
amphitheater ['æmfɪ,θi·ətər] *s* anfiteatro
ample ['æmpəl] amplio; bastante, suficiente; abundante

amplifier ['æmplɪ,faɪ·ər] *s* amplificador *m*
ampli•fy ['æmplɪ,faɪ] *v* (*pret & pp* **-fied**) *tr* amplificar || *intr* espaciarse
amplitude ['æmplɪ,tjud] o ['æmplɪ,tud] *s* amplitud
amplitude modulation *s* modulación de amplitud
amputate ['æmpjə,tet] *tr* amputar
amt. *abbr* **amount**
amuck [ə'mʌk] *adv* frenéticamente; **to run amuck** atacar a ciegas
amulet ['æmjəlɪt] *s* amuleto
amuse [ə'mjuz] *tr* divertir, entretener
amusement [ə'mjuzmənt] *s* diversión, entretenimiento; pasatiempo, recreación; (*in a park or circus*) atracción
amusement park *s* parque *m* de atracciones
amusing [ə'mjuzɪŋ] *adj* divertido, gracioso
an [æn] o [ən] *art indef* (antes de sonido vocal) un
anachronism [ə'nækrə,nɪzəm] *s* anacronismo
anaemia [ə'nimɪ·ə] *s* anemia
anaemic [ə'nimɪk] *adj* anémico
anaesthesia [,ænɪs'θiʒə] *s* anestesia
anaesthetic [,ænɪs'θɛtɪk] *adj & s* anestésico
anaesthetize [æ'nɛsθɪ,taɪz] *tr* anestesiar
analogous [ə'næləgəs] *adj* análogo
analo•gy [ə'nælədʒi] *s* (*pl* **-gies**) analogía
analyse ['ænə,laɪz] *tr* analizar
analy•sis [ə'nælɪsɪs] *s* (*pl* **-ses** [,siz]) análisis *m & f*
analyst ['ænəlɪst] *s* analista *mf*
analytic(al) [,ænə'lɪtɪk(əl)] *adj* analítico
analyze ['ænə,laɪz] *tr* analizar
anarchist ['ænərkɪst] *s* anarquista *mf*
anarchy ['ænərki] *s* anarquía
anathema [ə'næθɪmə] *s* anatema *m & f*
anatomic(al) [,ænə'tɑmɪk(əl)] *adj* anatómico
anato•my [ə'nætəmi] *s* (*pl* **-mies**) anatomía
ancestor ['ænsɛstər] *s* antecesor *m*, antepasado
ances•try ['ænsɛstri] *s* (*pl* **-tries**) abolengo, alcurnia
anchor ['æŋkər] *s* ancla, áncora; (fig) áncora; **to cast anchor** echar anclas; **to weigh anchor** levar anclas || *tr* sujetar con el ancla || *intr* anclar, ancorar
ancho•vy ['æntʃovi] *s* (*pl* **-vies**) anchoa
ancient ['enʃənt] *adj* antiguo
and [ænd] o [ənd] *conj* y; **and so forth** y así sucesivamente
Andalusia [,ændə'luʒə] *s* Andalucía
Andalusian [,ændə'luʒən] *adj & s* andaluz *m*
Andean [æn'di·ən] o ['ændɪ·ən] *adj & s* andino
Andes ['ændiz] *spl* Andes *mpl*
andirons ['ænd,aɪ·ərnz] *spl* morillos
anecdote ['ænɪk,dot] *s* anécdota
anemia [ə'nimɪ·ə] *s* anemia
anemic [ə'nimɪk] *adj* anémico
aneroid barometer ['ænə,rɔɪd] *s* barómetro aneroide
anesthesia [,ænɪs'θiʒə] *s* anestesia
anesthetic [,ænɪs'θɛtɪk] *adj & s* anestésico
anesthetize [æ'nɛsθɪ,taɪz] *tr* anestesiar
aneurysm ['ænjə,rɪzəm] *s* aneurisma *m*
anew [ə'nju] o [ə'nu] *adv* de nuevo, nuevamente
angel ['endʒəl] *s* ángel *m*; (*financial backer*) caballo blanco
angelic(al) [æn'dʒɛlɪk(əl)] *adj* angélico, angelical
anger ['æŋgər] *s* cólera, ira || *tr* encolerizar, airar
angina pectoris [æn'dʒaɪnə 'pɛktərɪs] *s* angina de pecho
angle ['æŋgəl] *s* ángulo; punto de vista || *intr* pescar con caña; intrigar
angle iron *s* ángulo de hierro, hierro angular
angler ['æŋglər] *s* pescador *m* de caña; intrigante *mf*
Anglo-Saxon [,æŋglo'sæksən] *adj & s* anglosajón *m*
an•gry ['æŋgri] *adj* (*comp* **-grier**; *super* **-griest**) encolerizado, airado; (pathol) inflamado, irritado; **to become angry at** enojarse de; **to become angry with** enojarse con o contra
anguish ['æŋgwɪʃ] *s* angustia, congoja
angular ['æŋgjələr] *adj* angular; (*features*) anguloso
anhydrous [æn'haɪdrəs] *adj* anhidro
aniline dyes ['ænɪlɪn] o ['ænɪ,laɪn] *s* colores *mpl* de anilina
animal ['ænɪməl] *adj & s* animal *m*
animal spirits *spl* ardor *m*, vigor *m*, vivacidad
animated cartoon ['ænɪ,metɪd] *s* película de dibujos, dibujo animado
animation [,ænɪ'meʃən] *s* animación
animosi•ty [,ænɪ'mɑsɪti] *s* (*pl* **-ties**) animosidad
anion ['æn,aɪ·ən] *s* anión *m*
anise ['ænɪs] *s* anís *m*
aniseed ['ænɪ,sid] *s* grano de anís
anisette [,ænɪ'zɛt] *s* anisete *m*
ankle ['æŋkəl] *s* tobillo
an'kle•bone' *s* hueso del tobillo
ankle support *s* tobillera
anklet ['æŋklɪt] *s* ajorca; (*sock*) tobillera
annals ['ænəlz] *spl* anales *mpl*
anneal [ə'nil] *tr* recocer
annex ['ænɛks] *s* anexo; (*of a building*) pabellón *m* || [ə'nɛks] *tr* anexar
annihilate [ə'naɪ·ɪ,let] *tr* aniquilar
anniversa•ry [,ænɪ'vʌrsəri] *adj* aniversario || *s* (*pl* **-ries**) aniversario
annotate ['ænə,tet] *tr* anotar
announce [ə'nauns] *tr* anunciar
announcement [ə'naunsmənt] *s* anuncio
announcer [ə'naunsər] *s* anunciador *m*; (rad) locutor *m*
annoy [ə'nɔɪ] *tr* fastidiar, molestar
annoyance [ə'nɔɪ·əns] *s* fastidio, molestia
annoying [ə'nɔɪ·ɪŋ] *adj* fastidioso, molesto
annual ['ænju·əl] *adj* anual || *s* publicación anual; planta anual

annui·ty [ə'nju·ɪti] o [ə'nu·ɪti] *s* (*pl* **-ties**) anualidad; renta vitalicia
an·nul [ə'nʌl] *v* (*pret & pp* **-nulled;** *ger* **-nulling**) *tr* anular, invalidar
anode ['ænod] *s* ánodo
anoint [ə'nɔɪnt] *tr* ungir, untar
anomalous [ə'nɑmələs] *adj* anómalo
anoma·ly [ə'nɑməli] *s* (*pl* **-lies**) anomalía
anon. *abbr* **anonymous**
anonymity [ˌænə'nɪmɪti] *s* anónimo; **to preserve one's anonymity** guardar o conservar el anónimo
anonymous [ə'nɑnɪməs] *adj* anónimo
another [ə'nʌðər] *adj & pron indef* otro
ans. *abbr* **answer**
answer ['ænsər] o ['ɑnsər] *s* contestación, respuesta; (*to a problem or puzzle*) solución || *tr* contestar, responder; resolver (*un problema o un enigma*) || *intr* contestar, responder; **to answer for** responder de (*una cosa*); responder por (*una persona*)
ant [ænt] *s* hormiga
antagonism [æn'tægəˌnɪzəm] *s* antagonismo
antagonize [æn'tægəˌnaɪz] *tr* oponerse a; enemistar, enajenar
antarctic [ænt'ɑrktɪk] *adj* antártico || **the Antarctic** las Tierras Antárticas
antecedent [ˌæntɪ'sidənt] *adj* antecedente || *s* antecedente *m;* **antecedents** antecedentes *mpl;* antepasados
antechamber ['æntɪˌtʃembər] *s* antecámara
antedate ['æntɪˌdet] *tr* antedatar; preceder
antelope ['æntɪˌlop] *s* antílope *m*
anten·na [æn'tɛnə] *s* (*pl* **-nae** [ni]) (ent) antena || *s* (*pl* **-nas**) (rad) antena
antepenult [ˌæntɪ'pinʌlt] *s* antepenúltima
anteroom ['æntɪˌrum] o ['æntɪˌrum] *s* antecámara
anthem ['ænθəm] *s* himno; antífona
ant'hill' *s* hormiguero
antholo·gy [æn'θɑlədʒi] *s* (*pl* **-gies**) antología
anthracite ['ænθrəˌsaɪt] *s* antracita
anthrax ['ænθræks] *s* ántrax *m*
anthropology [ˌænθrə'pɑlədʒi] *s* antropología
anti-aircraft [ˌæntɪ'ɛrˌkræft] o [ˌæntɪ'ɛrˌkrɑft] *adj* antiaéreo
antibiotic [ˌæntɪbaɪ'ɑtɪk] *adj & s* antibiótico
antibod·y ['æntɪˌbɑdi] *s* (*pl* **-ies**) anticuerpo
anticipate [æn'tɪsɪˌpet] *tr* esperar, prever; anticipar; (*to get ahead of*) anticiparse a; impedir; prometerse (*p. ej., un placer*); temerse (*algo desagradable*)
antics ['æntɪks] *spl* cabriolas, gracias, travesuras
antidote ['æntɪˌdot] *s* antídoto
antifreeze [ˌæntɪ'friz] *s* anticongelante *m*
antiglare [ˌæntɪ'glɛr] *adj* antideslumbrante
antiknock [ˌæntɪ'nɑk] *adj & s* antidetonante *m*
antilabor [ˌæntɪ'lebər] *adj* antiobrero
Antilles [æn'tɪliz] *spl* Antillas
antimissile [ˌæntɪ'mɪsɪl] *adj* antiproyectil
antimony ['æntɪˌmoni] *s* antimonio
antipas·to [ˌɑntɪ'pɑsto] *s* (*pl* **-tos**) aperitivo, entremés *m*
antipa·thy [æn'tɪpəθi] *s* (*pl* **-thies**) antipatía
antiquar·y ['æntɪˌkwɛri] *s* (*pl* **-ies**) anticuario
antiquated ['æntɪˌkwetɪd] *adj* anticuado
antique [æn'tik] *adj* antiguo || *s* antigüedad
antique dealer *s* anticuario
antique store *s* tienda de antigüedades
antiqui·ty [æn'tɪkwɪti] *s* (*pl* **-ties**) antigüedad
anti-Semitic [ˌæntɪsɪ'mɪtɪk] *adj* antisemítico
antiseptic [ˌæntɪ'sɛptɪk] *adj & s* antiséptico
antislavery [ˌæntɪ'slevəri] *adj* antiesclavista
anti-Soviet [ˌæntɪ'sovɪˌɛt] *adj* antisoviético
antitank [ˌæntɪ'tæŋk] *adj* antitanque
antithe·sis [æn'tɪθɪsɪs] *s* (*pl* **-ses** [ˌsiz]) antítesis *f*
antitoxin [ˌæntɪ'tɑksɪn] *s* antitoxina
antitrust [ˌæntɪ'trʌst] *adj* anticartel
antiwar [ˌæntɪ'wɔr] *adj* antibélico
antler ['æntlər] *s* cuerna
antonym ['æntənɪm] *s* antónimo
Antwerp ['æntwərp] *s* Amberes *f*
anvil ['ænvɪl] *s* yunque *m*
anxie·ty [æŋ'zaɪ·əti] *s* (*pl* **-ties**) ansiedad, inquietud; ansia, anhelo
anxious ['æŋkʃəs] *adj* ansioso, inquieto; anhelante; **to be anxious to** tener ganas de
any ['ɛni] *adj indef* algún, cualquier; todo; **any place** dondequiera; **any time** cuando quiera; alguna vez || *pron indef* alguno, cualquiera || *adv* algo
an'y·bod'y *pron indef* alguno, alguien, cualquiera, quienquiera; todo el mundo; **not anybody** nadie
an'y·how' *adv* de cualquier modo; de todos modos; sin embargo
an'y·one' *pron indef* alguno, alguien, cualquiera
an'y·thing' *pron indef* algo, alguna cosa; cualquier cosa; todo cuanto; **anything at all** cualquier cosa que sea; **anything else** cualquier otra cosa; **anything else?** ¿algo más?; **not anything** nada
an'y·way' *adv* de cualquier modo; de todos modos; sin embargo; sin esmero, sin orden ni concierto
an'y·where' *adv* dondequiera; adondequiera; **not anywhere** en ninguna parte
apace [ə'pes] *adv* aprisa
apart [ə'pɑrt] *adv* aparte; en pedazos; **to fall apart** caerse a pedazos; desunirse; ir al desastre; **to live apart**

vivir separados; vivir aislado; **to stand apart** mantenerse apartado; **to take apart** descomponer, desarmar, desmontar; **to tell apart** distinguir
apartment [ə'pɑrtmənt] *s* apartamento
apartment house *s* casa de pisos
apathetic [,æpə'θɛtɪk] *adj* apático
apa·thy ['æpəθi] *s* (*pl* **-ties**) apatía
ape [ep] *s* mono || *tr* imitar, remedar
aperture ['æpərtʃər] *s* abertura, orificio
apex ['epɛks] *s* (*pl* **apexes** o **apices** ['æpɪ,siz]) ápex *m*, ápice *m*
aphorism ['æfə,rɪzəm] *s* aforismo
aphrodisiac [,æfrə'dɪzɪ,æk] *adj* & *s* afrodisíaco
apiar·y ['epɪ,ɛri] *s* (*pl* **-ies**) abejar *m*, colmenar *m*
apiece [ə'pis] *adv* cada uno; por persona
apish ['epɪʃ] *adj* monesco; tonto
aplomb [ə'plɑm] *s* aplomo, sangre fría
apogee ['æpə,dʒi] *s* apogeo
apologetic [ə,pɑlə'dʒɛtɪk] *adj* lleno de excusas
apologize [ə'pɑlə,dʒaɪz] *intr* excusarse, disculparse; **to apologize for** disculparse de; **to apologize to** disculparse con
apolo·gy [ə'pɑlədʒi] *s* (*pl* **-gies**) excusa; (*makeshift*) expediente *m*
apoplectic [,æpə'plɛktɪk] *adj* & *s* apoplético
apoplexy ['æpə,plɛksi] *s* apoplejía
apostle [ə'pɑsəl] *s* apóstol *m*
apostrophe [ə'pɑstrəfi] *s* (*written sign*) apóstrofo; (*words addressed to absent person*) apóstrofe *m* & *f*
apothecar·y [ə'pɑθɪ,kɛri] *s* (*pl* **-ies**) boticario
apothecary's jar *s* bote *m* de porcelana
apothecary's shop *s* botica
appall [ə'pɔl] *tr* espantar, pasmar
appalling [ə'pɔlɪŋ] *adj* aterrador, espantoso, pasmoso
appara·tus [,æpə'retəs] o [,æpə'rætəs] *s* (*pl* **-tus** o **-tuses**) aparato
apparel [ə'pærəl] *s* indumentaria, vestido
apparent [ə'pærənt] o [ə'pɛrənt] *adj* aparente
apparition [,æpə'rɪʃən] *s* aparición
appeal [ə'pil] *s* súplica, instancia, solicitud; atracción, interés *m;* (law) apelación || *intr* ser atrayente; **to appeal to** (*to make an entreaty to*) suplicar; (*to be attractive to*) atraer, interesar; (law) apelar a
appear [ə'pɪr] *intr* (*to come into sight; to be in sight; to be published*) aparecer; (*to come into sight; to be in sight; to look; to seem*) parecer; (*to come before the public*) presentarse; (*to come before a court*) comparecer
appearance [ə'pɪrəns] *s* (*act of appearing*) aparición; (*outward look*) apariencia, aspecto; (law) comparecencia
appease [ə'piz] *tr* apaciguar
appeasement [ə'pizmənt] *s* apaciguamiento
appendage [ə'pɛndɪdʒ] *s* apéndice *m*
appendicitis [ə,pɛndɪ'saɪtɪs] *s* apendicitis *f*
appen·dix [ə'pɛndɪks] *s* (*pl* **-dixes** o **-dices** [dɪ,siz]) apéndice *m*
appertain [,æpər'ten] *intr* relacionarse
appetite ['æpɪ,taɪt] *s* apetito
appetizer ['æpɪ,taɪzər] *s* aperitivo, apetite *m*
appetizing ['æpɪ,taɪzɪŋ] *adj* apetitoso
applaud [ə'plɔd] *tr* & *intr* aplaudir
applause [ə'plɔz] *s* aplauso, aplausos
apple ['æpəl] *s* manzana
ap'ple·jack' *s* aguardiente *m* de manzana
apple of the eye *s* niña del ojo
apple pie *s* pastel *m* de manzana
apple polisher *s* (slang) quitamotas *mf*
ap'ple·sauce' *s* compota de manzanas; (slang) música celestial
apple tree *s* manzano
appliance [ə'plaɪ·əns] *s* artificio, dispositivo, aparato; aplicación
applicant ['æplɪkənt] *s* aspirante *mf*, pretendiente *mf*, solicitante *mf*
ap·ply [ə'plaɪ] *v* (*pret* & *pp* **-plied**) *tr* aplicar || *intr* aplicarse; dirigirse; **to apply for** pedir, solicitar
appoint [ə'pɔɪnt] *tr* designar, nombrar; señalar; amueblar
appointment [ə'pɔɪntmənt] *s* designación, nombramiento; empleo, puesto; cita; **appointments** instalación, accesorios, adornos; **by appointment** cita previa
apportion [ə'porʃən] *tr* prorratear
appraisal [ə'prezəl] *s* tasación, valoración, apreciación
appraise [ə'prez] *tr* tasar, valorar, apreciar
appreciable [ə'priʃɪ·əbəl] *adj* apreciable; sensible
appreciate [ə'priʃɪ,et] *tr* apreciar; aprobar; comprender; estar agradecido por || *intr* subir de valor
appreciation [ə,priʃɪ'eʃən] *s* aprecio; agradecimiento; plusvalía, aumento de valor
appreciative [ə'priʃɪ,etɪv] *adj* apreciador; agradecido
apprehend [,æprɪ'hɛnd] *tr* aprehender, prender; comprender; temer
apprehension [,æprɪ'hɛnʃən] *s* aprehensión; (*fear, worry*) aprensión; comprensión
apprehensive [,æprɪ'hɛnsɪv] *adj* (*fearful, worried*) aprehensivo, aprensivo
apprentice [ə'prɛntɪs] *s* aprendiz *m*, meritorio || *tr* poner de aprendiz
apprenticeship [ə'prɛntɪs,ʃɪp] *s* aprendizaje *m*
apprise o **apprize** [ə'praɪz] *tr* informar; apreciar, tasar
approach [ə'protʃ] *s* acercamiento; vía de entrada; proposición; (*to a problem*) enfoque *m* || *tr* abordar, acercarse a; (*to bring closer*) acercar || *intr* acercarse, aproximarse
approbation [,æprə'beʃən] *s* aprobación
appropriate [ə'proprɪ·ɪt] *adj* apropiado, a propósito || [ə'proprɪ,et] *tr*

apropiarse; asignar, destinar (*el parlamento determinada suma a un determinado fin*)
approval [ə'pruvəl] *s* aprobación; **on approval** a prueba
approve [ə'pruv] *tr & intr* aprobar
approximate [ə'prɑksɪmɪt] *adj* aproximado || [ə'prɑksɪ,met] *tr* aproximar || *intr* aproximarse
apricot ['eprɪ,kɑt] o ['æprɪ,kɑt] *s* albaricoque *m*
apricot tree *s* albaricoquero
April ['eprɪl] *s* abril *m*
April fool *s* — **to make an April fool of** coger por inocente
April Fools' Day *s* día *m* de engañabobos, primer día de abril, en que se coge por inocente a la gente
apron ['eprən] *s* delantal *m;* (*of a workman*) mandil *m;* **tied to the apron strings of** cosido a las faldas de
apropos [,æprə'po] *adj* oportuno || *adv* a propósito; **apropos of** a propósito de
apse [æps] *s* ábside *m*
apt [æpt] *adj* apto; a propósito; dispuesto, inclinado
aptitude ['æptɪ,tjud] o ['æptɪ,tud] *s* aptitud
aquamarine [,ækwəmə'rin] *s* aguamarina
aquaplane ['ækwə,plen] *s* acuaplano || *intr* correr en acuaplano
aquari•um [ə'kwɛrɪ•əm] *s* (*pl* **-ums** o **-a** [ə]) acuario
aquatic [ə'kwætɪk] o [ə'kwɑtɪk] *adj* acuático || **aquatics** *spl* deportes acuáticos
aqueduct ['ækwə,dʌkt] *s* acueducto
aquiline nose ['ækwɪ,laɪn] *s* nariz aguileña
Arab ['ærəb] *adj* árabe || *s* árabe *mf;* caballo árabe
Arabia [ə'rebɪ•ə] *s* la Arabia
Arabian [ə'rebɪ•ən] *adj* árabe; arábigo || *s* árabe *mf*
Arabic ['ærəbɪk] *adj* arábigo || *s* árabe *m,* arábigo
Aragon ['ærə,gɑn] *s* Aragón *m*
Arago•nese [,ærəgə'niz] *adj* aragonés || *s* (*pl* **-nese**) aragonés *m*
arbiter ['ɑrbɪtər] *s* árbitro
arbitrary ['ɑrbɪ,trɛri] *adj* arbitrario
arbitrate ['ɑrbɪ,tret] *tr & intr* arbritrar
arbitration [,ɑrbɪ'treʃən] *s* arbitraje *m*
arbor ['ɑrbər] *s* emparrado, glorieta
arbore•tum [,ɑrbə'ritəm] *s* (*pl* **-tums** o **-ta** [tə]) jardín botánico de árboles
arbor vitae ['ɑrbər 'vaɪti] *s* árbol *m* de la vida
arbutus [ɑr'bjutəs] *s* madroño
arc [ɑrk] *s* arco
arcade [ɑr'ked] *s* arcada, galería
arch. *abbr* **archaic, archaism, archipelago, architect**
arch [ɑrtʃ] *adj* astuto; travieso; principal || *s* arco || *tr* arquear, enarcar; atravesar
archaeology [,ɑrkɪ'ɑlədʒi] *s* arqueología
archaic [ɑr'ke•ɪk] *adj* arcaico
archaism ['ɑrke,ɪzəm] o ['ɑrki,ɪzəm] *s* arcaísmo
archangel ['ɑrk,endʒəl] *s* arcángel *m*
archbishop ['ɑrtʃ'bɪʃəp] *s* arzobispo
archduke ['ɑrtʃ'djuk] o ['ɑrtʃ'duk] *s* archiduque *m*
archene•my ['ɑrtʃ,ɛnɪmi] *s* (*pl* **-mies**) archienemigo
archeology [,ɑrkɪ'ɑlədʒi] *s* arqueología
archer ['ɑrtʃər] *s* arquero, flechero
archery ['ɑrtʃəri] *s* tiro de flechas
archipela•go [,ɑrkɪ'pɛləgo] *s* (*pl* **-gos** o **-goes**) archipiélago
architect ['ɑrkɪ,tɛkt] *s* arquitecto
architectural [,ɑrkɪ'tɛktʃərəl] *adj* arquitectónico, arquitectural
architecture ['ɑrkɪ,tɛktʃər] *s* arquitectura
archives ['ɑrkaɪvz] *spl* archivo
arch'way' *s* arcada
arc lamp *s* lámpara de arco
arctic ['ɑrktɪk] *adj* ártico || **the Arctic** las Tierras Árticas
arc welding *s* soldadura de arco
ardent ['ɑrdənt] *adj* ardiente
ardor ['ɑrdər] *s* ardor *m*
arduous ['ɑrdʒʊ•əs] o ['ɑrdjʊ•əs] *adj* arduo, difícil; enérgico; (*steep*) escarpado
area ['ɛrɪ•ə] *s* área, superficie *f;* comarca, región; zona; patio
ar'ea•way' *s* entrada baja de un sótano
Argentina [,ɑrdʒən'tinə] *s* la Argentina
Argentine ['ɑrdʒən,tin] o ['ɑrdʒən,taɪn] *adj & s* argentino || **the Argentine** la Argentina
Argentinean [,ɑrdʒən'tɪnɪ•ən] *adj & s* argentino
Argonaut ['ɑrgə,nɔt] *s* argonauta *m*
argue ['ɑrgju] *tr* argüir; **to argue into** persuadir a + *inf;* **to argue out of** disuadir de + *inf* || *intr* argüir
argument ['ɑrgjəmənt] *s* argumento; disputa
argumentative [,ɑrgjə'mɛntətɪv] *adj* argumentador
aria ['ɑrɪ•ə] o ['ɛrɪ•ə] *s* (mus) aria
arid ['ærɪd] *adj* árido
aridity [ə'rɪdɪti] *s* aridez *f*
aright [ə'raɪt] *adv* acertadamente; **to set aright** rectificar
arise [ə'raɪz] *v* (*pret* **arose** [ə'roz]; *pp* **arisen** [ə'rɪzən]) *intr* levantarse; subir; aparecer; **to arise from** provenir de
aristocra•cy [,ærɪs'tɑkrəsi] *s* (*pl* **-cies**) aristocracia
aristocrat [ə'rɪstə,kræt] *s* aristócrata *mf*
aristocratic [ə,rɪstə'krætɪk] *adj* aristocrático
Aristotelian [,ærɪstə'tilɪ•ən] *adj & s* aristotélico
Aristotle ['ærɪ,tɑtəl] *s* Aristóteles *m*
arith. *abbr* **arithmetic**
arithmetic [ə'rɪθmətɪk] *s* aritmética
arithmetical [,ærɪθ'mɛtɪkəl] *adj* aritmético
arithmetician [ə,rɪθmə'tɪʃən] *s* aritmético
ark [ɑrk] *s* arca de Noé

ark of the covenant *s* arca de la alianza
arm [ɑrm] *s* brazo; (*weapon*) arma; **arm in arm** de bracero, asidos del brazo; **in arms** de pecho, de teta; **the three arms of the service** los tres ejércitos; **to be up in arms** estar en armas; **to keep at arm's length** mantener a distancia; mantenerse a distancia; **to lay down one's arms** rendir las armas; **to rise up in arms** alzarse en armas; **under arms** sobre las armas || *tr* armar || *intr* armarse
armament ['ɑrməmənt] *s* armamento
armature ['ɑrmə ˌtʃər] *s* armadura; (*of a dynamo or motor*) (elec) inducido
arm'chair' *adj* de gabinete || *s* butaca, sillón *m*, silla de brazos
Armenian [ɑr'minɪ·ən] *adj* & *s* armenio
armful ['ɑrm ˌfʊl] *s* brazado
arm'hole' *s* (*in clothing*) sobaquera
armistice ['ɑrmɪstɪs] *s* armisticio
armor ['ɑrmər] *s* armadura; coraza, blindaje *m* || *tr* acorazar, blindar
armored car *s* carro blindado
armorial bearings [ɑr'morɪ·əl] *spl* blasón *m*, escudo de armas
armor plate *s* plancha de blindaje
ar'mor-plate' *tr* acorazar, blindar
armor·y ['ɑrməri] *s* (*pl* **-ies**) arsenal *m*; (*arms factory*) armería
arm'pit' *s* sobaco, hueco de la axila
arm'rest' *s* apoyabrazos *m*
ar·my ['ɑrmi] *adj* militar, castrense || *s* (*pl* **-mies**) ejército
army corps *s* cuerpo de ejército
aroma [ə'romə] *s* aroma *m*, fragancia
aromatic [ˌærə'mætɪk] *adj* aromático
around [ə'raʊnd] *adv* alrededor, a la redonda; en la dirección opuesta || *prep* alrededor de, en torno a o de; cerca de; (*the corner*) a la vuelta de
arouse [ə'raʊz] *tr* despertar; excitar, incitar
arpeg·gio [ɑr'pɛdʒo] *s* (*pl* **-gios**) arpegio
arraign [ə'ren] *tr* acusar; presentar al tribunal
arrange [ə'rendʒ] *tr* arreglar, disponer; (mus) adaptar, refundir
array [ə're] *s* orden *m*; orden *m* de batalla; adorno, atavío || *tr* poner en orden; poner en orden de batalla; adornar, ataviar
arrears [ə'rɪrz] *spl* atrasos; **in arrears** atrasado en pagos
arrest [ə'rɛst] *s* arresto, prisión; detención; **under arrest** bajo arresto || *tr* arrestar; detener; atraer (*la atención*)
arresting [ə'rɛstɪŋ] *adj* impresionante
arrival [ə'raɪvəl] *s* llegada; (*person*) llegado
arrive [ə'raɪv] *intr* llegar; tener éxito
arrogance ['ærəgəns] *s* arrogancia
arrogant ['ærəgənt] *adj* arrogante
arrogate ['ærə ˌget] *tr* — **to arrogate to oneself** arrogarse
arrow ['æro] *s* flecha
ar'row·head' *s* punta de flecha; (bot) saetilla
arsenal ['ɑrsənəl] *s* arsenal *m*
arsenic ['ɑrsɪnɪk] *s* arsénico
arson ['ɑrsən] *s* incendio premeditado, delito de incendio
art [ɑrt] *s* arte *m* & *f*
arter·y ['ɑrtəri] *s* (*pl* **-ies**) arteria
artful ['ɑrtfəl] *adj* astuto, mañoso; diestro, ingenioso
arthritic [ɑr'θrɪtɪk] *adj* & *s* artrítico
arthritis [ɑr'θraɪtɪs] *s* artritis *f*
artichoke ['ɑrtɪ ˌtʃok] *s* alcachofa
article ['ɑrtɪkəl] *s* artículo; **an article of clothing** una prenda de vestir
articulate [ɑr'tɪkjəlɪt] *adj* claro, distinto; capaz de hablar || [ɑr'tɪkjə-ˌlet] *tr* articular
artifact ['ɑrtɪ ˌfækt] *s* artefacto
artifice ['ɑrtɪfɪs] *s* artificio
artificial [ˌɑrtɪ'fɪʃəl] *adj* artificial
artillery [ɑr'tɪləri] *s* artillería
artillery·man [ɑr'tɪlərimən] *s* (*pl* **-men** [mən]) artillero
artisan ['ɑrtɪzən] *s* artesano
artist ['ɑrtɪst] *s* artista *mf*
artistic [ɑr'tɪstɪk] *adj* artístico
artistry ['ɑrtɪstri] *s* habilidad artística
artless ['ɑrtlɪs] *adj* sencillo, natural; ingenuo, inocente; (*crude, clumsy*) chabacano
arts and crafts *spl* artes y oficios
art·y ['ɑrti] *adj* (*comp* **-ier**; *super* **-iest**) (coll) ostentosamente artístico
Aryan ['ɛrɪ·ən] o ['ɑrjən] *adj* & *s* ario
as [æz] o [əz] *pron rel* que; **the same as** el mismo que || *adv* tan; **as . . . as** tan . . . como; **as for** en cuanto a; **as long as** mientras que; ya que; **as many as** tantos como; **as much as** tanto como; **as regards** en cuanto a; **as soon as** tan pronto como; **as soon as possible** cuanto antes, lo más pronto posible; **as though** como si; **as to** en cuanto a; **as well** también; **as yet** hasta ahora || *conj* como; que; ya que; a medida que; **as it seems** por lo visto, según parece || *prep* por, como; **as a rule** por regla general
asbestos [æs'bɛstəs] *s* asbesto, amianto
ascend [ə'sɛnd] *tr* subir a (*p.ej., el trono*) || *intr* ascender
ascendancy [ə'sɛndənsi] *s* ascendiente *m*
ascension [ə'sɛnʃən] *s* ascensión
Ascension Day *s* fiesta de la Ascensión
ascent [ə'sɛnt] *s* ascensión, subida; ascenso, promoción
ascertain [ˌæsər'ten] *tr* averiguar
ascertainable [ˌæsər'tenəbəl] *adj* averiguable
ascetic [ə'sɛtɪk] *adj* ascético || *s* asceta *mf*
ascorbic acid [ə'skɔrbɪk] *s* ácido ascórbico
ascribe [ə'skraɪb] *tr* atribuir
aseptic [ə'sɛptɪk] o [e'sɛptɪk] *adj* aséptico
ash [æʃ] *s* ceniza; (*tree; wood*) fresno; **ashes** ceniza, cenizas; (*mortal remains*) cenizas
ashamed [ə'ʃemd] *adj* avergonzado; **to be ashamed** tener vergüenza
ashlar ['æʃlər] *s* sillar *m*
ashore [ə'ʃor] *adv* en tierra, a tierra

ash tray *s* cenicero
Ash Wednesday *s* miércoles *m* de ceniza
Asia ['eʒə] o ['eʃə] *s* Asia
Asia Minor *s* el Asia Menor
Asian ['eʒən] o ['eʃən] o **Asiatic** [,eʒɪ'ætɪk] o [,eʃɪ'ætɪk] *adj* & *s* asiático
aside [ə'saɪd] *adv* aparte; **aside from** además de; **to step aside** hacerse a un lado || *s* (theat) aparte *m*
asinine ['æsɪ,naɪn] *adj* tonto, necio
ask [æsk] o [ɑsk] *tr* (*to request*) pedir; (*to inquire of*) preguntar; hacer (*una pregunta*); invitar; **to ask in** invitar a entrar || *intr* — **to ask about, after,** or **for** preguntar por; **to ask for** pedir
askance [ə'skæns] *adv* al sesgo, de soslayo; con desdén, sospechosamente
asleep [ə'slip] *adj* dormido; **to fall asleep** dormirse
asp [æsp] *s* áspid *m*
asparagus [ə'spærəgəs] *s* espárrago
aspect ['æspɛkt] *s* aspecto
aspen ['æspən] *s* tiemblo, álamo temblón
aspersion [ə'spʌrʒən] o [ə'spʌrʃən] *s* calumnia, difamación
asphalt ['æsfɔlt] o ['æsfælt] *s* asfalto || *tr* asfaltar
asphyxiate [æs'fɪksɪ,et] *tr* asfixiar
aspirant [ə'spaɪrənt] o ['æspɪrənt] *s* pretendiente *mf,* candidato
aspire [ə'spaɪr] *intr* aspirar
aspirin ['æspɪrɪn] *s* aspirina
ass [æs] *s* asno
assail [ə'sel] *tr* asaltar, acometer
assassin [ə'sæsɪn] *s* asesino
assassinate [ə'sæsɪ,net] *tr* asesinar
assassination [ə,sæsɪ'neʃən] *s* asesinato
assault [ə'sɔlt] *s* asalto || *tr* asaltar
assault and battery *s* vías de hecho, violencias
assay [ə'se] o ['æse] *s* ensaye *m;* muestra de ensaye || [ə'se] *tr* ensayar; apreciar
assemble [ə'sɛmbəl] *tr* reunir; (mach) armar, montar || *intr* reunirse
assem·bly [ə'sɛmbli] *s* (*pl* **-blies**) asamblea; reunión; (mach) armadura, montaje *m*
assembly hall *s* aula magna, paraninfo; salón *m* de sesiones
assembly line *s* línea de montaje
assembly plant *s* fábrica de montaje
assembly room *s* sala de reunión; (mach) taller *m* de montaje
assent [ə'sɛnt] *s* asentimiento, asenso || *intr* asentir
assert [ə'sʌrt] *tr* afirmar, aseverar, declarar; **to assert oneself** imponerse, hacer valer sus derechos
assertion [ə'sʌrʃən] *s* aserción, aseveración
assess [ə'sɛs] *tr* amillarar, gravar; fijar (*daños y perjuicios*); apreciar, estimar
assessment [ə'sɛsmənt] *s* amillaramiento, gravamen *m;* fijación; apreciación, estimación
asset ['æsɛt] *s* posesión, ventaja; (*person, thing, or quality worth having*) (fig) valor *m;* **assets** (com) activo
assiduous [ə'sɪdʒu·əs] o [ə'sɪdju·əs] *adj* asiduo
assign [ə'saɪn] *tr* asignar
assignment [ə'saɪnmənt] *s* asignación, cometido; lección
assimilate [ə'sɪmɪ,let] *tr* asimilarse (*los alimentos, el conocimiento*) || *intr* asimilarse
assist [ə'sɪst] *tr* ayudar, asistir, auxiliar
assistant [ə'sɪstənt] *adj* & *s* auxiliar *mf,* ayudante *mf*
assn. *abbr* **association**
associate [ə'soʃɪ·ɪt] o [ə'soʃɪ,et] *adj* asociado || *s* asociado, socio || [ə'soʃɪ,et] *tr* asociar || *intr* asociarse
association [ə,soʃɪ'eʃən] *s* asociación
assort [ə'sɔrt] *tr* clasificar, ordenar
assortment [ə'sɔrtment] *s* surtido; clase *f,* grupo
asst. *abbr* **assistant**
assume [ə'sum] o [ə'sjum] *tr* asumir (*p.ej., responsabilidades*); arrogarse; suponer, dar por sentado
assumption [ə'sʌmpʃən] *s* asunción; suposición
assurance [ə'ʃurəns] *s* aseguramiento; seguridad, confianza; (com) seguro
assure [ə'ʃur] *tr* asegurar; (com) asegurar
Assyria [ə'sɪrɪ·ə] *s* Asiria
Assyrian [ə'sɪrɪ·ən] *adj* & *s* asirio
astatine ['æstə,tin] *s* ástato
aster ['æstər] *s* (bot) aster *m;* (*China aster*) reina Margarita
asterisk ['æstə,rɪsk] *s* asterisco
astern [ə'stʌrn] *adv* por la popa
asthma ['æzmə] *o* ['æsmə] *s* asma *f*
astonish [ə'stɑnɪʃ] *tr* asombrar
astonishing [ə'stɑnɪʃɪŋ] *adj* asombroso
astound [ə'staund] *tr* pasmar
astounding [ə'staundɪŋ] *adj* pasmoso
astraddle [ə'strædəl] *adv* a horcajadas
astray [ə'stre] *adv* por mal camino; **to go astray** extraviarse; **to lead astray** extraviar
astride [ə'straɪd] *adv* a horcajadas || *prep* a horcajadas de
astrology [ə'strɑlədʒi] *s* astrología
astronaut ['æstrə,nɔt] *s* astronauta *m*
astronautic [,æstrə'nɔtɪk] *adj* astronáutico || **astronautics** *s* astronáutica
astronomer [ə'strɔnəmər] *s* astrónomo
astronomic(al) [,æstrə'nɑmɪk(əl)] *adj* astronómico
astronomy [ə'strɑnəmi] *s* astronomía
Asturian [ə'sturɪ·ən] *adj* & *s* asturiano
astute [ə'stjut] o [ə'stut] *adj* astuto, sagaz
asunder [ə'sʌndər] *adv* a pedazos, en dos
asylum [ə'saɪləm] *s* asilo
asymmetry [ə'sɪmɪtri] *s* asimetría
at [æt] o [ət] *prep* en, p.ej., **I saw her at the library** la ví en la biblioteca; a, p.ej., **at five o'clock** a las cinco; de, p.ej., **to be surprised at** estar sorprendido de; **to laugh at** reírse de; en casa de, p.ej., **at John's** en casa de Juan

atheism [ˈeθi,ɪzəm] *s* ateísmo
atheist [ˈeθi·ɪst] *s* ateísta *mf,* ateo
Athenian [əˈθinɪ·ən] *adj & s* ateniense *mf*
Athens [ˈæθɪnz] *s* Atenas *f*
athirst [əˈθʌrst] *adj* sediento
athlete [ˈæθlit] *s* atleta *mf*
athlete's foot *s* pie *m* de atleta
athletic [æθˈlɛtɪk] *adj* atlético || **athletics** *s* atletismo
Atlantic [ætˈlæntɪk] *adj & s* Atlántico
atlas [ˈætləs] *s* atlas *m*
atmosphere [ˈætməs,fɪr] *s* atmósfera
atmospheric [,ætməsˈfɛrɪk] *adj* atmosférico || **atmospherics** *spl* parásitos atmosféricos
atom [ˈætəm] *s* átomo
atom bomb *s* bomba atómica
atomic [əˈtɑmɪk] *adj* atómico
atomic bomb *s* bomba atómica
atomize [ˈætə,maɪz] *tr* atomizar
atomizer [ˈætə,maɪzər] *s* pulverizador *m,* vaporizador *m*
atom smasher *s* rompeátomos *m*
atone [əˈton] *intr* dar reparación; **to atone for** dar reparación por, expiar
atonement [əˈtonmənt] *s* reparación, expiación
atop [əˈtɑp] *adv* encima || *prep* encima de
atrocious [əˈtroʃəs] *adj* atroz; (coll) abominable, muy malo
atroci·ty [əˈtrɑsɪti] *s pl* **-ties)** atrocidad
atro·phy [ˈætrəfi] *s* atrofia || *v* (*pret & pp* **-phied)** *tr* atrofiar || *intr* atrofiarse
attach [əˈtætʃ] *tr* atar, ligar; atribuir (*p.ej., importancia*); (law) embargar; **to be attached to** aficionarse a; (*to be officially associated with*) depender de
attaché [,ætəˈʃe] o [əˈtæʃe] *s* agregado
attachment [əˈtætʃmənt] *s* atadura, enlace *m;* atribución; apego, cariño; accesorio; (law) embargo
attack [əˈtæk] *s* ataque *m* || *tr & intr* atacar
attain [əˈten] *tr* alcanzar, lograr
attainment [əˈtenmənt] *s* consecución, logro; **attainments** dotes *fpl,* prendas
attempt [əˈtɛmpt] *s* tentativa; (*assault*) atentado, conato || *tr* procurar, intentar; (*e.g., the life of a person*) atentar a o contra
attend [əˈtɛnd] *tr* atender, asistir; asistir a (*p.ej., la escuela*); auxiliar (*a un moribundo*) || *intr* atender; **to attend to** atender a
attendance [əˈtɛndəns] *s* asistencia, concurrencia; **to dance attendance** hacer antesala
attendant [əˈtɛndənt] *adj & s* asistente *mf;* concomitante *m*
attention [əˈtɛnʃən] *s* atención; **to attract attention** llamar la atención; **to call attention to** hacer presente; **to pay attention to** hacer caso de
attentive [əˈtɛntɪv] *adj* atento
attenuate [əˈtɛnjʊ,et] *tr* adelgazar; debilitar || *intr* debilitarse; desaparecer
attest [əˈtɛst] *tr* atestiguar; juramentar || *intr* dar fe; **to attest to** dar fe de
attic [ˈætɪk] *s* buharda, guardilla, desván *m*
attire [əˈtaɪr] *s* atavío, traje *m* || *tr* ataviar, vestir
attitude [ˈætɪ,tjud] o [ˈætɪ,tud] *s* actitud, ademán *m*
attorney [əˈtʌrni] *s* abogado; procurador *m*
attract [əˈtrækt] *tr* atraer; llamar (*la atención*)
attraction [əˈtrækʃən] *s* atracción; (*personal charm*) atractivo
attractive [əˈtræktɪv] *adj* atractivo; (*agreeable, interesting*) atrayente
attribute [ˈætrɪ,bjut] *s* atributo || [əˈtrɪbjʊt] *tr* atribuir
atty. *abbr* **attorney**
auburn [ˈɔbərn] *adj & s* castaño rojizo
auction [ˈɔkʃən] *s* almoneda, remate *m,* subasta || *tr* rematar, subastar
auctioneer [,ɔkʃənˈɪr] *s* subastador *m* || *tr & intr* rematar, subastar
auction house *s* martillo
audacious [ɔˈdeʃəs] *adj* audaz
audaci·ty [ɔˈdæsɪti] *s* (*pl* **-ties)** audacia
audience [ˈɔdɪ·əns] *s* (*hearing; formal interview*) audiencia; público, auditorio
audio frequency [ˈɔdɪ,o] *s* audiofrecuencia
audiometer [,ɔdɪˈɑmɪtər] *s* audiómetro
audit [ˈɔdɪt] *s* intervención || *tr* intervenir
audition [ɔˈdɪʃən] *s* audición || *tr* dar audición a
auditor [ˈɔdɪtər] *s* oyente *mf;* (com) interventor *m*
auditorium [,ɔdɪˈtorɪ·əm] *s* auditorio, anfiteatro, paraninfo
auger [ˈɔgər] *s* barrena
augment [ɔgˈmɛnt] *tr & intr* aumentar
augur [ˈɔgər] *s* augur *m* || *tr & intr* augurar; **to augur well** ser de buen agüero
augu·ry [ˈɔgəri] *s* (*pl* **-ries)** augurio
august [ɔˈgʌst] *adj* augusto || **August** [ˈɔgəst] *s* agosto
aunt [ænt] o [ɑnt] *s* tía
aurora [əˈrorə] *s* aurora
auspice [ˈɔspɪs] *s* auspicio; **under the auspices of** bajo los auspicios de
austere [ɔsˈtɪr] *adj* austero
Australia [ɔˈstreljə] *s* Australia
Australian [ɔˈstreljən] *adj & s* australiano
Austria [ˈɔstrɪ·ə] *s* Austria
Austrian [ˈɔstrɪ·ən] *adj & s* austríaco
authentic [ɔˈθɛntɪk] *adj* auténtico
authenticate [ɔˈθɛntɪ,ket] *tr* autenticar
author [ˈɔθər] *s* autor *m*
authoress [ˈɔθərɪs] *s* autora
authoritarian [ɑ,θɑrɪˈtɛrɪ·ən] o [ɔ,θɔrɪˈtɛrɪ·ən] *adj & s* autoritario
authoritative [ɔˈθɑrɪ,tetɪv] o [ɔˈθɔrɪ,tetɪv] *adj* autorizado; (*dictatorial*) autoritario
authori·ty [ɔˈθɑrɪti] o [ɔˈθɔrɪti] *s* (*pl* **-ties)** autoridad; **on good authority** de buena tinta, de fuente fidedigna
authorize [ˈɔθə,raɪz] *tr* autorizar

authorship ['ɔθər,ʃɪp] *s* paternidad literaria
au•to ['ɔto] *s* (*pl* **-tos**) (coll) auto, coche *m*
autobiogra•phy [,ɔtobaɪ'ɑgrəfi] u [,ɔtobɪ'ɑgrəfi] *s* (*pl* **-phies**) autobiografía
autobus ['ɔto,bʌs] *s* autobús *m*
autocratic(al) [,ɔtə'krætɪk(əl)] *adj* autocrático
autograph ['ɔtə,græf] u ['ɔtə,grɑf] *adj & s* autógrafo || *tr* autografiar
autograph seeker *s* cazaautógrafos *m*
automat ['ɔtə,mæt] *s* restaurante automático
automatic [,ɔtə'mætɪk] *adj* automático
automatic clutch *s* servoembrague *m*
automation [,ɔtə'meʃən] *s* automación, automatización
automa•ton [ɔ'tɑmə,tɑn] *s* (*pl* **-tons** o **-ta** [tə]) autómata
automobile [,ɔtəmo'bil] u [,ɔtə'mobil] *s* automóvil *m*
automobile show *s* salón *m* del automóvil
autonomous [ɔ'tɑnəməs] *adj* autónomo
autonomy [ɔ'tɑnəmi] *s* autonomía
autop•sy ['ɔtɑpsi] *s* (*pl* **-sies**) autopsia
autumn ['ɔtəm] *s* otoño
autumnal [ə'tʌmnəl] *adj* otoñal
auxilia•ry [ɔg'zɪljəri] *adj* auxiliar || *s* (*pl* **-ries**) auxiliar *mf;* **auxiliaries** tropas auxiliares
av. *abbr* **avenue, average, avoirdupois**
avail [ə'vel] *s* provecho, utilidad || *tr* beneficiar; **to avail oneself of** aprovecharse de, valerse de || *intr* aprovechar
available [ə'veləbəl] *adj* disponible; **to make available to** poner a la disposición de
avalanche ['ævə,læntʃ] o ['ævə,lɑntʃ] *s* alud *m,* avalancha
avant-garde [avɑ̃'gard] *adj* vanguardista || *s* vanguardismo
avant-guardist [avɑ̃'gardɪst] *s* vanguardista *mf*
avarice ['ævərɪs] *s* avaricia
avaricious [,ævə'rɪʃəs] *adj* avaricioso, avariento
Ave. *abbr* **Avenue**
avenge [ə'vɛndʒ] *tr* vengar; **to avenge oneself on** vengarse en
avenue ['ævə,nju] o ['ævə,nu] *s* avenida
aver [ə'vʌr] *v* (*pret & pp* **averred;** *ger* **averring**) *tr* afirmar, declarar
average ['ævərɪdʒ] *adj* común, mediano, ordinario || *s* promedio, término medio; (naut) avería || *tr* calcular el término medio de; prorratear; ser de un promedio de
averse [ə'vʌrs] *adj* renuente, contrario
aversion [ə'vʌrʒən] *s* aversión, antipatía; cosa aborrecida
avert [ə'vʌrt] *tr* apartar, desviar; impedir
aviar•y ['evɪ,ɛri] *s* (*pl* **-ies**) avería, pajarera
aviation [,evɪ'eʃən] *s* aviación
aviation medicine *s* aeromedicina
aviator ['evɪ,etər] *s* aviador *m*
avid ['ævɪd] *adj* ávido
avidity [ə'vɪdɪti] *s* avidez *f*
avocation [,ævə'keʃən] *s* distracción, diversión
avoid [ə'vɔid] *tr* evitar
avoidable [ə'vɔɪdəbəl] *adj* evitable
avoidance [ə'vɔɪdəns] *s* evitación
avow [ə'vaʊ] *tr* admitir, confesar
avowal [ə'vaʊ·əl] *s* admisión, confesión
await [ə'wet] *tr* aguardar, esperar
awake [ə'wek] *adj* despierto || *v* (*pret & pp* **awoke** [ə'wok] o **awaked**) *tr & intr* despertar
awaken [ə'wekən] *tr & intr* despertar
awakening [ə'wekənɪŋ] *s* despertamiento; desilusión
award [ə'wɔrd] *s* premio; condecoración; adjudicación || *tr* conceder; adjudicar
aware [ə'wɛr] *adj* enterado; **to become aware of** enterarse de, darse cuenta de
awareness [ə'wɛrnɪs] *s* conciencia
away [ə'we] *adj* ausente; distante || *adv* lejos; a lo lejos; **away from** lejos de; **to do away with** deshacerse de; **to get away** escapar; **to go away** irse; **to make away with** robar, hurtar; **to run away** fugarse; **to send away** enviar; despedir; **to take away** llevarse; quitar
awe [ɔ] *s* temor *m* reverencial || *tr* infundir temor reverencial a
awesome ['ɔsəm] *adj* imponente
awestruck ['ɔ,strʌk] *adj* espantado
awful ['ɔfəl] *adj* atroz, horrible; impresionante; (coll) muy malo, muy feo, enorme
awfully ['ɔfəli] *adv* atrozmente, horriblemente; (coll) muy, excesivamente
awhile [ə'hwaɪl] *adv* un rato, algún tiempo
awkward ['ɔkwərd] *adj* desmañado, torpe, lerdo; embarazoso, delicado
awkward squad *s* pelotón *m* de los torpes
awl [ɔl] *s* alesna, lezna
awning ['ɔnɪŋ] *s* toldo
ax [æks] *s* hacha
axiom ['æksɪ·əm] *s* axioma *m*
axiomatic [,æksɪ·ə'mætɪk] *adj* axiomático
axis ['æksɪs] *s* (*pl* **axes** ['æksiz]) *s* eje *m*
axle ['æksəl] *s* eje *m,* árbol *m*
ax'le•tree' *s* eje *m* de carretón
ay [aɪ] *adv & s* sí || [e] *adv* siempre; **for ay** por siempre || [e] *interj* ¡ay!
aye [aɪ] *adv & s* sí || [e] *adv* siempre; **for aye** por siempre
azimuth ['æzɪməθ] *s* acimut *m*
Azores [ə'zorz] o ['ezorz] *spl* Azores *fpl*
Aztec ['æztɛk] *adj & s* azteca *mf*
azure ['æʒər] o ['eʒər] *adj & s* azul *m*

B

B, b [bi] segunda letra del alfabeto inglés
b. *abbr* **bass, bay, born, brother**
baa [bɑ] *s* be *m,* balido || *intr* balar
babble [ˈbæbəl] *s* barboteo; charla; (*of a brook*) murmullo || *tr* barbotar; decir indiscretamente || *intr* barbotar; murmurar (*un arroyo*)
babe [beb] *s* rorro, criatura; (*innocent, gullible person*) niño; (slang) chica, chica hermosa
baboon [bæˈbun] *s* babuíno
ba•by [ˈbebi] *s* (*pl* **-bies**) rorro, criatura, bebé *m;* (*the youngest child*) benjamín *m* || *v* (*pret & pp* **-bied**) *tr* mimar; tratar como niño
baby carriage *s* cochecillo para niños
baby grand *s* piano de media cola
babyhood [ˈbebi ˌhʊd] *s* primera infancia, niñez *f*
babyish [ˈbebi•ɪʃ] *adj* aniñado, infantil
Babylon [ˈbæbɪlən] o [ˈbæbɪˌlɑn] *s* Babilonia (*ciudad*)
Babylonia [ˌbæbɪˈlonɪ•ə] *s* Babilonia (*imperio*)
Babylonian [ˌbæbɪˈlonɪ•ən] *adj & s* babilonio
baby sitter *s* niñera tomada por horas
baccalaureate [ˌbækəˈlərɪ•ɪt] *s* bachillerato
bachelor [ˈbætʃələr] *s* (*unmarried man*) soltero; (*holder of bachelor's degree*) bachiller *mf;* (*apprentice knight*) doncel *m*
bachelorhood [ˈbætʃələrˌhʊd] *s* celibato, soltería (*del hombre*)
bacil•lus [bəˈsɪləs] *s* (*pl* **-li** [laɪ]) bacilo
back [bæk] *adj* trasero, posterior; atrasado || *adv* atrás, detrás; de vuelta; (*ago*) hace; **back of** detrás de; **to go back to** remontarse a; **to send back** devolver || *s* espalda; dorso; (*of a coin*) reverso; (*of a chair*) espaldar *m,* respaldo; (*of an animal, of a book*) lomo; (*of a hall, a room*) fondo; (*of a writing, a book*) final *m;* **behind one's back** a espaldas de uno; **on one's back** postrado, en cama; a cuestas || *tr* mover hacia atrás; apoyar, respaldar || *intr* moverse hacia atrás; **to back down** u **out** volverse atrás, echarse atrás; **to back up** retroceder; regolfar (*el agua*)
back'ache' *s* dolor *m* de espalda
back'bone' *s* espinazo; (*of a book*) nervura; firmeza, resistencia
back'break'ing *adj* deslomador
back'down' *s* palinodia, retractación
back'drop' *s* telón *m* de fondo o de foro
backer [ˈbækər] *s* sostenedor *m,* defensor *m;* (*of a business venture*) impulsador *m*
back'fire' *s* (aut) petardeo || *intr* (aut) petardear
back'ground' *s* fondo; antecedentes *mpl;* conocimientos, educación; (*of a painting*) lontananza
background music *s* música de fondo
backing [ˈbækɪŋ] *s* apoyo, sostén *m;* garantía, respaldo; (bb) lomera
back'lash' *s* (mach) contragolpe *m;* (mach) juego; (fig) reacción violenta
back'log' *s* (com) reserva de pedidos pendientes; (*e.g., of work*) acumulación
back number *s* número atrasado; (coll) persona anticuada
back pay *s* sueldo retrasado
back seat *s* puesto secundario; **to take a back seat** perder influencia
back'side' *s* espalda; trasero
back'slide' *v* (*pret & pp* **-slid** [ˌslɪd]) *intr* reincidir
backspacer [ˈbæk ˌspesər] *s* tecla de retroceso
back'stage' *adv* detrás del telón; entre bastidores
back'stairs' *adj* indirecto, secreto
back stairs *spl* escalera trasera; medios indirectos
back'stitch' *s* pespunte *m* || *tr & intr* pespuntar
back'stop' *s* reja o red *f* para detener la pelota
back'swept' wing *s* (aer) ala en flecha
back talk *s* respuesta insolente
backward [ˈbækwərd] *adj* atrasado, tardío; tímido || *adv* de atrás; de espaldas; al revés; cada vez peor; para atrás, hacia atrás
back'wa'ter *s* remanso; (fig) atraso, yermo
back'woods' *spl* monte *m,* región alejada de los centros de población
back yard *s* patio trasero, corral trasero
bacon [ˈbekən] *s* tocino
bacteria [bækˈtɪrɪ•ə] *pl de* **bacterium**
bacterial [bækˈtɪrɪ•əl] *adj* bacteriano
bacteriologist [bæk ˌtɪrɪˈɑlədʒɪst] *s* bacteriólogo
bacteriology [bæk ˌtɪrɪˈɑlədʒi] *s* bacteriología
bacteri•um [bækˈtɪrɪ•əm] *s* (*pl* **-a** [ə]) bacteria
bad [bæd] *adj* (*comp* **worse** [wʌrs]; *super* **worst** [wʌrst]) malo; (*money*) falso; (*debt*) incobrable; **from bad to worse** de mal en peor; **to be in bad** (coll) caer en desgracia; **to be too bad** ser lástima; **to go to the bad** (coll) ir por mal camino; (coll) arruinarse; **to look bad** tener mala cara
bad breath *s* mal aliento
badge [bædʒ] *s* divisa, insignia
badger [ˈbædʒər] *s* tejón *m*
badly [ˈbædli] *adv* mal; con urgencia; gravemente
badly off *adj* malparado; muy enfermo
badminton [ˈbædmɪntən] *s* juego del volante
baffle [ˈbæfəl] *s* deflector *m;* (rad)

pantalla acústica || *tr* confundir; burlar, frustrar
baffling [ˈbæflɪŋ] *adj* perplejo, desconcertador
bag [bæg] *s* saco; saquito de mano; (*in clothing*) bolsa; (*purse*) bolso; (*take of game*) caza; **to be in the bag** (slang) ser cosa segura || *v* (*pret & pp* **bagged;** *ger* **bagging**) *tr* ensacar; coger, cazar || *intr* hacer bolsa (*un vestido*)
baggage [ˈbægɪdʒ] *s* equipaje *m;* (mil) bagaje *m*
baggage car *s* furgón *m* de equipajes
baggage check *s* contraseña de equipajes
baggage rack *s* red *f* de equipajes
baggage room *s* sala de equipajes
bag'pipe' *s* gaita, cornamusa
bag'pi'per *s* gaitero
bail [bel] *s* caución, fianza; **to go bail for** salir fiador por || *tr* caucionar, afianzar; achicar (*la embarcación; el agua*); **to bail out** salir fiador por; achicar || *intr* achicar; **to bail out** lanzarse en paracaídas
bailiff [ˈbelɪf] *s* algualcil *m,* corchete *m*
bailiwick [ˈbelɪwɪk] *s* alguacilazgo; **to be in the bailiwick of** ser de la pertenencia de
bait [bet] *s* carnada, cebo; señuelo; **to swallow the bait** tragar el anzuelo || *tr* cebar, encarnar (*el anzuelo*); tentar, seducir; (*to pester*) hostigar
baize [bez] *s* bayeta
bake [bek] *tr* cocer al horno; cocer (*loza, gres, etc.*)
bakelite [ˈbekəˌlaɪt] *s* baquelita
baker [ˈbekər] *s* panadero, hornero
baker's dozen *s* docena del fraile
baker·y [ˈbekəri] *s* (*pl* **-ies**) panadería
baking powder [ˈbekɪŋ] *s* levadura en polvo
baking soda *s* bicarbonato de sosa
bal. *abbr* **balance**
balance [ˈbæləns] *s* (*instrument for weighing*) balanza; (*state of equilibrium*) equilibrio; (*amount left over*) resto; (*amount still owed*) saldo; (*statement of debits and credits*) balance *m;* **to lose one's balance** perder el equilibrio; **to strike a balance** hacer o pasar balance || *tr* balancear; equilibrar; equilibrar, nivelar (*el presupuesto*) || *intr* equilibrarse; (*to waver*) balancear
balance of payments *s* balanza de pagos
balance of power *s* equilibrio político
balance sheet *s* balance *m,* avanzo
balco·ny [ˈbælkəni] *s* (*pl* **-nies**) balcón *m;* (*in a theater*) galería, paraíso
bald [bɔld] *adj* calvo; franco, directo
baldness [ˈbɔldnɪs] *s* calvicie *f*
baldric [ˈbɔldrɪk] *s* tahalí *m*
bale [bel] *s* bala || *tr* embalar
Balearic [ˌbælɪˈærɪk] *adj* balear
Balearic Islands *spl* islas Baleares
baleful [ˈbelfəl] *adj* funesto, maligno
balk [bɔk] *tr* burlar, frustrar || *intr* emperrarse, resistirse
Balkan [ˈbɔlkən] *adj* balcánico || **the Balkans** los Balcanes
balk·y [ˈbɔki] *adj* (*comp* **-ier;** *super* **-iest**) rebelón, repropio
ball [bɔl] *s* bola, pelota; esfera, globo; (*of wool, yarn*) ovillo; (*of finger*) yema; (*projectile*) bala; (*dance*) baile *m*
ballad [ˈbæləd] *s* balada
ballade [bəˈlɑd] *s* (mus) balada
ballast [ˈbæləst] *s* (aer, naut) lastre *m;* (rr) balasto || *tr* lastrar; balastar
ball bearing *s* cojinete *m* de bolas
ballerina [ˌbæləˈrinə] *s* bailarina
ballet [ˈbæle] *s* ballet *m,* baile *m*
ballistic [bəˈlɪstɪk] *adj* balístico
balloon [bəˈlun] *s* globo
ballot [ˈbælət] *s* balota; sufragio || *intr* balotar
ballot box *s* urna electoral
ball'play'er *s* pelotari *m;* beisbolero
ball'-point' pen *s* polígrafo, bolígrafo, pluma esferográfica
ball'room' *s* salón *m* de baile
ballyhoo [ˈbælɪˌhu] *s* alharaca, bombo || *tr* dar teatro a, dar bombo a
balm [bɑm] *s* bálsamo
balm·y [ˈbɑmi] *adj* (*comp* **-ier;** *super* **-iest**) bonancible, suave
balsam [ˈbɔlsəm] *s* bálsamo
Baltic [ˈbɔltɪk] *adj* báltico
Baltimore oriole [ˈbɔltɪˌmor] *s* cacique veranero
baluster [ˈbæləstər] *s* balaustre *m*
bamboo [bæmˈbu] *s* bambú *m*
bamboozle [bæmˈbuzəl] *tr* (coll) embaucar, engañar
bamboozler [bæmˈbuzlər] *s* (coll) embaucador *m,* engañabobos *mf*
ban [bæn] *s* prohibición; excomunión, entredicho; (*of marriage*) amonestación || *v* (*pret & pp* **banned;** *ger* **banning**) *tr* prohibir; excomulgar
banana [bəˈnænə] *s* banana, plátano; (*tree*) banano, bananero, plátano
banana oil *s* esencia de pera
band [bænd] *s* banda; (*of people*) cuadrilla; (*of a hat*) cintillo; (*of a cigar*) anillo; liga de goma; (mus) banda, música, charanga || *intr* abanderizarse
bandage [ˈbændɪdʒ] *s* venda || *tr* vendar
bandanna [bænˈdænə] *s* pañuelo de hierbas
band'box' *s* sombrerera
bandit [ˈbændɪt] *s* bandido
band'mas'ter *s* músico mayor
bandoleer [ˌbændəˈlɪr] *s* bandolera
band saw *s* sierra continua, sierra sin fin
band'stand' *s* quiosco de música
baneful [ˈbenfəl] *adj* nocivo, venenoso; (*e.g., influence*) funesto
bang [bæŋ] *adv* de golpe || *interj* ¡pum! || *s* golpazo; (*of a door*) portazo; **bangs** flequillo || *tr* golpear con ruido; cerrar (*p.ej., una puerta*) de golpe || *intr* hacer estrépito
banish [ˈbænɪʃ] *tr* desterrar; despedir (*p.ej., miedo*)
banishment [ˈbænɪʃmənt] *s* destierro
banister [ˈbænɪstər] *s* balaustre *m*
bank [bæŋk] *s* banco; (*in certain games*) banca; (*small container for*

coins) alcancía; (*of a river*) ribera, orilla; (*of earth, snow, clouds*) montón *m* || *tr* depositar o guardar (*dinero*) en un banco; amontonar; cubrir (*un fuego*) con cenizas || *intr* depositar dinero; **to bank on** (coll) contar con
bank account *s* cuenta de banco
bank'book' *s* libreta de banco
banker ['bæŋkər] *s* banquero
banking ['bæŋkɪŋ] *adj* bancario || *s* banca
bank note *s* billete *m* de banco
bank roll *s* lío de papel moneda
bankrupt ['bæŋkrʌpt] *adj* & *s* bancarrotero; **to go bankrupt** hacer bancarrota || *tr* hacer quebrar; arruinar
bankrupt·cy ['bæŋkrʌptsi] *s* (*pl* **-cies**) bancarrota
banner ['bænər] *s* bandera, estandarte *m*
banner cry *s* grito de combate
banquet ['bæŋkwɪt] *s* banquete *m* || *tr* & *intr* banquetear
banter ['bæntər] *s* burla, chanza || *intr* burlar, chancear
baptism ['bæptɪzəm] *s* bautismo, bautizo; (fig) bautismo
Baptist ['bæptɪst] *adj* & *s* baptista *mf*, bautista *mf*
baptister·y ['bæptɪstəri] *s* (*pl* **-ies**) baptisterio, bautisterio
baptize [bæp'taɪz] o ['bæptaɪz] *tr* bautizar
bar. *abbr* **barometer, barrel, barrister**
bar [bɑr] *s* barra; (*of door or window*) tranca; (*of jail*) reja; barrera; (*legal profession*) abogacía; (*members of legal profession*) curia; (*of public opinion*) tribunal *m;* (mus) barra; (*unit between two bars*) (mus) compás *m;* **behind bars** entre rejas || *prep* salvo; **bar none** sin excepción || *v* (*pret* & *pp* **barred;** *ger* **barring**) *tr* barrear, atrancar; impedir; prohibir; excluir
bar association *s* colegio de abogados
barb [bɑrb] *s* púa, lengüeta; (*of a pen*) barbilla
Barbados [bɑr'bedoz] *s* la Barbada
barbarian [bɑr'bɛrɪ·ən] *s* bárbaro
barbaric [bɑr'bærɪk] *adj* bárbaro
barbarism ['bɑrbə,rɪzəm] *s* barbaridad *f;* (gram) barbarismo
barbari·ty [bɑr'bærɪti] *s* (*pl* **-ties**) barbarie *f*
barbarous ['bɑrbərəs] *adj* bárbaro
Barbary ape ['bɑrbəri] *s* mono de Gibraltar
barbed [bɑrbd] *adj* armado de púas; mordaz, punzante
barbed wire *s* alambre *m* de espino, alambre de púas
barber ['bɑrbər] *adj* barberil || *s* barbero, peluquero
barber pole *s* percha de barbero
bar'ber·shop' *s* barbería, peluquería
bard [bɑrd] *s* bardo; (*horse armor*) barda || *tr* bardar
bare [bɛr] *adj* desnudo; (*head*) descubierto; (*unfurnished*) desamueblado; (*wire*) sin aislar; mero, sencillo, puro || *tr* desnudar; descubrir
bare'back' *adj* & *adv* en pelo, sin silla
barefaced ['bɛr,fest] *adj* desvergonzado
bare'foot' *adj* descalzo || *adv* con los pies desnudos
bareheaded ['bɛr,hɛdɪd] *adj* descubierto || *adv* con la cabeza descubierta
barelegged ['bɛr,lɛgɪd] o ['bɛr,lɛgd] *adj* con las piernas desnudas
barely ['bɛrli] *adv* apenas
bargain ['bɑrgɪn] *s* (*deal*) convenio, trato; (*cheap purchase*) ganga; **in the bargain** de añadidura || *tr* — **to bargain away** vender regalado || *intr* negociar; (*to haggle*) regatear
bargain counter *s* baratillo
bargain sale *s* venta de saldos
barge [bɑrdʒ] *s* gabarra, lanchón *m* || *intr* moverse pesadamente; **to barge in** entrar sin pedir permiso, entrar sin llamar a la puerta
barium ['bɛrɪ·əm] *s* bario
bark [bɑrk] *s* (*of tree*) corteza; (*of dog*) ladrido; (*boat*) barca || *tr* ladrar (*p.ej., injurias*) || *intr* ladrar
barley ['bɑrli] *s* cebada
barley water *s* hordiate *m*
bar magnet *s* barra imantada
bar'maid' *s* moza de taberna
barn [bɑrn] *s* granero, troje *m;* caballeriza, establo; cochera
barnacle ['bɑrnəkəl] *s* cirrópodo
barn owl *s* lechuza, oliva
barn'yard' *s* corral *m*
barnyard fowl *spl* aves *fpl* de corral
barometer [bə'rɑmɪtər] *s* barómetro
baron ['bærən] *s* barón *m*
baroness ['bærənɪs] *s* baronesa
baroque [bə'rok] *adj* & *s* barroco
barracks ['bærəks] *spl* cuartel *m*
barrage [bə'rɑʒ] *s* (*dam*) presa; (mil) barrera de fuego
barrel ['bærəl] *s* barril *m*, tonel *m;* (*of a gun, pen, etc.*) cañón *m*
barrel organ *s* organillo
barren ['bærən] *adj* árido, estéril
barricade [,bærɪ'ked] *s* barrera || *tr* barrear
barrier ['bærɪ·ər] *s* barrera
barrier reef *s* barrera de arrecifes
barrister ['bærɪstər] *s* (Brit) abogado
bar'room' *s* bar *m*, cantina
bar'tend'er *s* cantinero, tabernero
barter ['bɑrtər] *s* trueque *m* || *tr* trocar
base [bes] *adj* bajo, humilde; infame, vil; (*metal*) bajo de ley || *s* base *f;* (*of electric light or vacuum tube; of projectile*) culote *m;* (mus) bajo || *tr* basar
base'ball' *s* béisbol *m;* pelota de béisbol
base'board' *s* rodapié *m*
Basel ['bɑzəl] *s* Basilea
baseless ['beslɪs] *adj* infundado
basement ['besmənt] *s* sótano
bashful ['bæʃfəl] *adj* encogido, tímido
basic ['besɪk] *adj* básico
basic commodities *spl* artículos de primera necesidad
basilica [bə'sɪlɪkə] *s* basílica
basin ['besɪn] *s* jofaina, palangana;

(*of a fountain*) tazón *m;* (*of a river*) cuenca; (*of a harbor*) dársena
ba•sis ['besɪs] *s* (*pl* **-ses** [siz]) base *f;* **on the basis of** a base de
bask [bæsk] o [bɑsk] *intr* asolearse, calentarse
basket ['bæskɪt] o ['bɑskɪt] *s* cesta; (*large basket*) cesto; (*with two handles*) canasta; (*with lid*) excusabaraja; (*sport*) cesto, red *f*
bas'ket•ball' *s* baloncesto, basquetbol *m*
Basle [bɑl] *s* Basilea
Basque [bæsk] *adj & s* (*of Spain*) vascongado; (*of Spain and France*) vasco; (*of old Spain*) vascón *m*
bas-relief [,bɑrɪ'lif] o [,bærɪ'lif] *s* bajo relieve
bass [bes] *adj & s* (mus) bajo ‖ [bæs] *s* (ichth) róbalo; (ichth) micróptero
bass drum *s* bombo
bass horn *s* tuba
bas•so ['bæso] o ['bɑso] *s* (*pl* **-sos** o **-si** [si]) (mus) bajo
bassoon [bə'sun] *s* bajón *m*
bass viol ['vaɪ•əl] *s* violón *m,* contrabajo
bastard ['bæstərd] *adj & s* bastardo
bastard title *s* anteportada
baste [best] *tr* (*to sew slightly*) hilvanar; (*to moisten with drippings while roasting*) enlardar; (*to thrash*) azotar; (*to scold*) regañar
bat. *abbr* **battalion, battery**
bat [bæt] *s* palo; (coll) golpe *m;* (zool) murciélago ‖ *v* (*pret & pp* **batted;** *ger* **batting**) *tr* golpear; batear (*una pelota*)*;* **without batting an eye** sin inmutarse, sin pestañear ‖ *intr* golpear
batch [bætʃ] *s* (*of bread*) hornada; (*of papers*) lío
bath [bæθ] o [bɑθ] *s* baño
bathe [beð] *tr* bañar ‖ *intr* bañarse; **to go bathing** ir a bañarse
bather ['beðər] *s* bañista *mf*
bath'house' *s* casa de baños; caseta de baños
bathing beach *s* playa de baños
bathing beauty *s* sirena de la playa
bathing resort *s* estación balnearia
bathing suit *s* traje *m* de baño, bañador *m*
bathing trunks *spl* taparrabo
bath'robe' *s* albornoz *m,* bata de baño; bata, peinador *m*
bath'room' *s* baño, cuarto de baño
bathroom fixtures *spl* aparatos sanitarios
bath'tub' *s* bañera, baño
baton [bæ'tɑn] o ['bætən] *s* bastón *m;* (mus) batuta
battalion [bə'tæljən] *s* batallón *m*
batter ['bætər] *s* pasta, batido; (baseball) bateador *m* ‖ *tr* magullar, estropear
battering ram *s* ariete *m*
batter•y ['bætəri] *s* (*pl* **-ies**) batería; (*primary*) (elec) pila; (*secondary*) (elec) acumulador *m;* (law) violencia
battle ['bætəl] *s* batalla; **to do battle** librar batalla ‖ *tr* batallar
battle array *s* orden *m* de batalla
battle cry *s* grito de combate
battledore ['bætəl,dor] *s* raqueta; **battledore and shuttlecock** raqueta y volante
bat'tlefield' *s* campo de batalla
battle front *s* frente *m* de combate
battlement ['bætəlmənt] *s* almenaje *m*
battle piece *s* (paint) batalla
bat'tle•ship' *s* acorazado
battue [bæ'tu] o [bæ'tju] *s* batida
bauble ['bɔbəl] *s* chuchería; cetro de bufón
Bavaria [bə'vɛrɪ•ə] *s* Baviera
Bavarian [bə'vɛrɪ•ən] *adj & mf* bávaro
bawd [bɔd] *s* alcahuete *m,* alcahueta
bawd•y ['bɔdi] *adj* (*comp* **-ier;** *super* **-iest**) indecente, obsceno
bawd'y•house' *s* mancebía, lupanar *m*
bawl [bɔl] *s* voces *fpl,* gritos ‖ *tr* — **to bawl out** (slang) regañar ‖ *intr* vocear, gritar; llorar ruidosamente
bay [be] *adj* bayo ‖ *s* bahía; aullido, ladrido; caballo bayo; (bot) laurel *m;* **to keep at bay** tener a raya ‖ *intr* aullar, ladrar
Bay of Biscay *s* golfo de Vizcaya
bayonet ['be•ənɪt] *s* bayoneta ‖ *tr* herir o matar con bayoneta
bay rum *s* ron *m* de laurel, ron de malagueta
bay window *s* ventana salediza, mirador *m*
bazooka [bə'zukə] *s* bazuca
bbl. *abbr* **barrel, barrels**
B.C. *abbr* **before Christ**
bd. *abbr* **board**
be [bi] *v* (*pres* **am** [æm], **is** [ɪz], **are** [ɑr]; *pret* **was** [wɑz] o [wʌz], **were** [wʌr]; *pp* **been** [bɪn]) *intr* estar; ser; tener, p.ej., **to be cold** tener frío; **to be wrong** no tener razón; tener la culpa; **here is** o **here are** aquí tiene Vd.; **there is** o **there are** hay ‖ *v aux* estar, p.ej., **he is studying** está estudiando; ser, p.ej., **she was hit by a car** fué atropellada por un coche; deber, p.ej., **what am I to do?** ¿qué debo hacer? ‖ *v impers* ser, p.ej., **it is necessary to get up early** es necesario levantarse temprano; haber, p.ej., **it is sunny** hay sol; hacer, p.ej., **it is cold** hace frío
beach [bitʃ] *s* playa
beach'comb' *intr* raquear; **to go beachcombing** andar al raque
beach'comb'er *s* raquero; vago de playa
beach'head' *s* cabeza de playa
beach robe *s* albornoz *m*
beach shoe *s* playera
beach umbrella *s* sombrilla de playa
beach wagon *s* rubia, coche *m* rural
beacon ['bikən] *s* señal luminosa; (*lighthouse*) faro; (*hill overlooking sea*) hacho; radiofaro; (*guide*) faro ‖ *tr* iluminar, guiar ‖ *intr* brillar
bead [bid] *s* cuenta; (*of glass*) abalorio; (*of sweat*) gota; (*moulding on corner of wall*) guardavivo; **to say** o **tell one's beads** rezar el rosario
beadle ['bidəl] *s* bedel *m*
beagle ['bigəl] *s* sabueso
beak [bik] *s* pico; cabo, promontorio

beam [bim] *s* (*of wood*) viga; (*of light, heat, etc.*) rayo; (naut) bao; (*direction perpendicular to the keel*) (naut) través *m;* (*of hope*) (fig) rayo; **on the beam** siguiendo el haz del radiofaro; (coll) siguiendo el buen camino || *tr* emitir (*luz, ondas*) || *intr* brillar; sonreír alegremente

bean [bin] *s* haba (*Vicia faba*); alubia, judía (*Phaseolus vulgaris*); (*of coffee, cocoa*) haba; (slang) cabeza

bean′pole′ *s* rodrigón *m* para frijoles; (*tall, skinny person*) (coll) poste *m* de telégrafo

bear [bɛr] *s* oso; (*in stock market*) bajista *mf* || *v* (*pret* **bore** [bor]; *pp* **borne** [born]) *tr* cargar; traer; llevar (*armas*); apoyar; aguantar; sentir, experimentar; producir, rendir (*frutos; interés*); (*to give birth to*) parir; tener (*amor, odio*); **to bear out** confirmar || *intr* dirigirse, volver; **to bear on** referirse a; **to bear up** no perder la esperanza; **to bear with** ser indulgente para con

beard [bɪrd] *s* barba; (*of wheat*) arista

beardless [ˈbɪrdlɪs] *adj* imberbe

bearer [ˈbɛrər] *s* portador *m*

bearing [ˈbɛrɪŋ] *s* porte *m,* presencia; referencia, relación; (mach) cojinete *m;* **bearings** orientación; **to lose one's bearings** desorientarse

bearish [ˈbɛrɪʃ] *adj* bajista

bear′skin′ *s* piel *f* de oso; (*military cap*) morrión *m*

beast [bist] *s* bestia

beast·ly [ˈbistli] *adj* (*comp* **-lier;** *super* **-liest**) bestial; (coll) muy malo || *adv* (coll) muy mal

beast of burden *s* bestia de carga, acémila

beat [bit] *s* golpe *m;* (*of heart*) latido; (*of rhythm*) compás *m;* marca del compás; (mus) tiempo; (phys) batimiento; (rad) batido; (*of a policeman*) ronda; (*sponger*) (slang) embestidor *m* || *v* (*pret* **beat;** *pp* **beat** o **beaten**) *tr* azotar, pegar; batir; sacudir (*una alfombra*); aventajar; llevar (*el compás*); tocar (*un tambor*); (*a una persona en una contienda*) ganar; **to beat it** (slang) largarse; **to beat up** batir (*p.ej., huevos*); (slang) aporrear || *intr* batir; latir (*el corazón*); **to beat against** azotar

beaten path [ˈbitən] *s* camino trillado

beater [ˈbitər] *s* batidor *m;* (*mixer*) batidora

beati·fy [bɪˈætɪˌfaɪ] *v* (*pret & pp* **-fied**) *tr* beatificar

beating [ˈbitɪŋ] *s* golpeo; (*of wings*) aleteo; (*with a whip*) paliza; (*defeat*) derrota

beau [bo] *s* (*pl* **beaus** o **beaux** [boz]) galán *m,* cortejo; novio; elegante *m*

beautician [bjuˈtɪʃən] *s* embellecedora, esteta *mf,* esteticista *mf*

beautiful [ˈbjutɪfəl] *adj* bello, hermoso

beauti·fy [ˈbjutɪˌfaɪ] *v* (*pret & pp* **-fied**) *tr* hermosear, embellecer

beau·ty [ˈbjuti] *s* (*pl* **-ties**) beldad *f,* belleza

beauty contest *s* concurso de belleza

beauty parlor *s* salón *m* de belleza

beauty queen *s* reina de la belleza

beauty sleep *s* primer sueño (*antes de medianoche*)

beauty spot *s* lunar postizo; sitio pintoresco

beaver [ˈbivər] *s* castor *m;* piel *f* de castor

becalm [bɪˈkɑm] *tr* calmar, serenar

because [bɪˈkɔz] *conj* porque; **because of** por, por causa de

beck [bɛk] *s* seña (*con la cabeza o la mano*); **at the beck and call of** a la disposición de

beckon [ˈbɛkən] *s* seña (*con la cabeza o la mano*) || *tr* llamar por señas; atraer, tentar || *intr* hacer señas

be·come [bɪˈkʌm] *v* (*pret* **-came;** *pp* **-come**) *tr* convenir, sentar bien || *intr* hacerse; llegar a ser; ponerse, volverse; convertirse en; **to become of** ser de, p.ej., **what will become of the soldier?** ¿qué será del soldado; hacerse, p.ej., **what became of his pencil?** ¿qué se ha hecho su lápiz?

becoming [bɪˈkʌmɪŋ] *adj* conveniente, decente; que sienta bien

bed [bɛd] *s* cama; (*of a river*) cauce *m;* (*of flower garden*) macizo; **to go to bed** acostarse; **to take to bed** encamarse

bed and board *s* pensión completa, casa y comida

bed′bug′ *s* chinche *f*

bed′cham′ber *s* alcoba, cuarto de dormir

bed′clothes′ *spl* ropa de cama

bed′cov′er *s* cubrecama, cobertor *m*

bedding [ˈbɛdɪŋ] *s* ropa de cama; (*for animals*) cama

bedev·il [bɪˈdɛvəl] *v* (*pret & pp* **-iled** o **-illed;** *ger* **-iling** o **-illing**) *tr* atormentar, confundir

bed′fast′ *adj* postrado en cama

bed′fel′low *s* compañero o compañera de cama

bedlam [ˈbɛdləm] *s* confusión, desorden *m,* tumulto

bed linen *s* ropa de cama

bed′pan′ *s* silleta

bed′post′ *s* pilar *m* de cama

bedridden [ˈbɛdˌrɪdən] *adj* postrado en cama

bed′room′ *s* alcoba, cuarto de dormir

bed′side′ *s* cabecera

bed′sore′ *s* úlcera de decúbito; **to get bedsores** decentarse

bed′spread′ *s* sobrecama, cobertor *m*

bed′spring′ *s* colchón *m* de muelles, somier *m*

bed′stead′ *s* cuja

bed′straw′ *s* paja de jergón

bed′tick′ *s* cutí *m*

bed′time′ *s* hora de acostarse

bed warmer *s* calientacamas *m*

bee [bi] *s* abeja

beech [bitʃ] *s* haya

beech′nut′ *s* hayuco

beef [bif] *s* carne *f* de vaca; ganado vacuno de engorde; (coll) fuerza muscular; (slang) queja || *tr* — **to**

beef up (coll) reforzar || *intr* (slang) quejarse; (slang) soplar
beef cattle *s* ganado vacuno de engorde
beef'steak' *s* biftec *m*
bee'hive' *s* colmena
bee'line' *s* — **to make a beeline for** ir en línea recta hacia, ir derecho a
beer [bɪr] *s* cerveza; **dark beer** cerveza parda, cerveza negra; **light beer** cerveza clara
beeswax ['biz,wæks] *s* cera de abejas || *tr* encerar
beet [bit] s remolacha
beetle ['bitəl] *s* escarabajo
beetle-browed ['bitəl,braud] *adj* cejijunto; (*sullen*) ceñudo
beet sugar *s* azúcar *m* de remolacha
be·fall [bɪ'fɔl] *v* (*pret* **-fell** ['fɛl]; *pp* **-fallen** ['fɔlən]) *tr* acontecer a || *intr* acontecer
befitting [bɪ'fɪtɪŋ] *adj* conveniente; decoroso
before [bɪ'for] *adv* antes; delante, enfrente || *prep* (*in time*) antes de; (*in place*) delante de; (*in the presence of*) ante || *conj* antes (de) que
before'hand' *adv* de antemano, con anticipación
befriend [bɪ'frɛnd] *tr* ofrecer amistad a, amparar, proteger
befuddle [bɪ'fʌdəl] *tr* aturdir, confundir
beg [bɛg] *v* (*pret & pp* **begged;** *ger* **begging**) *tr* pedir, rogar, solicitar; mendigar || *intr* mendigar; **to beg off** excusarse
be·get [bɪ'gɛt] *v* (*pret* **-got** ['gɑt]; *pp* **-gotten** o **-got;** *ger* **-getting**) *tr* engendrar
beggar ['bɛgər] *s* mendigo; pobre *mf;* pícaro, bribón *m;* sujeto, tipo
be·gin [bɪ'gɪn] *v* (*pret* **-gan** ['gæn]; *pp* **-gun** ['gʌn]; *ger* **-ginning**) *tr & intr* comenzar, empezar; **beginning with** a partir de
beginner [bɪ'gɪnər] *s* principiante *mf;* iniciador *m*
beginning [bɪ'gɪnɪŋ] *s* comienzo, principio
begrudge [bɪ'grʌdʒ] *tr* dar de mala gana; envidiar
beguile [bɪ'gaɪl] *tr* engañar; divertir, entretener; engañar (*el tiempo*)
behalf [bɪ'hæf] o [bɪ'hɑf] *s* — **on behalf of** en nombre de; a favor de
behave [bɪ'hev] *intr* conducirse, comportarse; portarse bien; funcionar
behavior [bɪ'hevjər] *s* conducta, comportamiento; funcionamiento
behead [bɪ'hɛd] *tr* decapitar, descabezar
behind [bɪ'haɪnd] *adv* detrás; hacia atrás; con retraso; **to stay behind** quedarse atrás || *prep* detrás de; **behind the back of** a espaldas de; **behind the times** atrasado de noticias; **behind time** tarde || *s* (slang) trasero
behold [bɪ'hold] *v* (*pret & pp* **-held** ['hɛld]) *tr* contemplar || *interj* ¡he aquí!
behoove [bɪ'huv] *tr* convenir, tocar
being ['bi·ɪŋ] *adj* existente; **for the time being** por ahora, por el momento || *s* ser, ente *m*
belch [bɛltʃ] *s* eructo, regüeldo || *tr* vomitar (*p.ej., llamas, injurias*) || *intr* eructar, regoldar
beleaguer [bɪ'ligər] *tr* sitiar, cercar
bel·fry ['bɛlfri] *s* (*pl* **-fries**) campanario
Belgian ['bɛldʒən] *adj & s* belga *mf*
Belgium ['bɛldʒəm] *s* Bélgica
be·lie [bɪ'laɪ] *v* (*pret & pp* **-lied** ['laɪd]; *ger* **-lying** ['laɪ·ɪŋ]) *tr* desmentir
belief [bɪ'lif] *s* creencia
believable [bɪ'livəbəl] *adj* creíble
believe [bɪ'liv] *tr & intr* creer
believer [bɪ'livər] *s* creyente *mf*
belittle [bɪ'lɪtəl] *tr* empequeñecer, despreciar
bell [bɛl] *s* campana; (*electric bell*) timbre *m,* campanilla; (*ring of bell*) campanada || *intr* bramar, berrear
bell'boy' *s* botones *m*
belle [bɛl] *s* beldad *f,* belleza
belles-lettres [,bɛl'lɛtrə] *spl* bellas letras
bell gable *s* espadaña
bell glass *s* fanal *m*
bell'hop' *s* (slang) botones *m*
bellicose ['bɛlɪ,kos] *adj* belicoso
belligerent [bə'lɪdʒərənt] *adj & s* beligerante *mf*
bellow ['bɛlo] *s* bramido; **bellows** fuelle *m,* barquín *m* || *tr* gritar || *intr* bramar
bell ringer *s* campanero
bellwether ['bɛl,wɛðər] *s* manso
bel·ly ['bɛli] *s* (*pl* **-lies**) barriga, vientre *m;* estómago || *v* (*pret & pp* **-lied**) *intr* hacer barriga; hacer bolso (*las velas*)
bel'ly·ache' *s* (slang) dolor *m* de barriga || *intr* (slang) quejarse
belly button *s* (coll) ombligo
belly dance *s* (coll) danza del vientre
bellyful ['bɛlɪ,ful] *s* (slang) panzada
bel'ly-land' *intr* (aer) aterrizar de panza
belong [bɪ'lɔŋ] o [bɪ'lɑŋ] *intr* pertenecer; deber estar
belongings [bɪ'lɔŋɪŋz] o [bɪ'lɑŋɪŋz] *spl* pertenencias, efectos
beloved [bɪ'lʌvɪd] o [bɪ'lʌvd] *adj & s* querido, amado
below [bɪ'lo] *adv* abajo; (*in a text*) más abajo; bajo cero, p.ej., **ten below** diez grados bajo cero || *prep* debajo de; inferior a
belt [bɛlt] *s* cinturón *m;* (aer, mach) correa; (geog) faja, zona; **to tighten one's belt** ceñirse
bemoan [bɪ'mon] *tr* deplorar, lamentar
bench [bɛntʃ] *s* banco; (law) tribunal *m*
bend [bɛnd] *s* curva; (*in a road, river, etc.*) recodo, vuelta || *v* (*pret & pp* **bent** [bɛnt]) *tr* encorvar; doblar (*un tubo; la rodilla*); inclinar (*la cabeza*); dirigir (*sus esfuerzos*) || *intr* encorvarse; doblarse; inclinarse
beneath [bɪ'niθ] *adv* abajo || *prep* debajo de; inferior a

benediction [ˌbɛnɪˈdɪkʃən] *s* bendición *f*
benefaction [ˌbɛnɪˈfækʃən] *s* beneficio
benefactor [ˈbɛnɪˌfæktər] o [ˌbɛnɪˈfæktər] *s* bienhechor *m*
benefactress [ˈbɛnɪˌfæktrɪs] o [ˌbɛnɪˈfæktrɪs] *s* bienhechora
beneficence [bɪˈnɛfɪsəns] *s* beneficencia
beneficent [bɪˈnɛfɪsənt] *adj* bienhechor
beneficial [ˌbɛnɪˈfɪʃəl] *adj* beneficioso
beneficiar•y [ˌbɛnɪˈfɪʃɪˌɛri] *s* (*pl* **-ies**) beneficiario
benefit [ˈbɛnɪfɪt] *s* beneficio; **for the benefit of** a beneficio de || *tr* beneficiar
benefit performance *s* beneficio
benevolence [bɪˈnɛvələns] *s* benevolencia
benevolent [bɪˈnɛvələnt] *adj* benévolo; (*e.g., institution*) benéfico
benign [bɪˈnaɪn] *adj* benigno
benigni•ty [bɪˈnɪgnɪti] *s* (*pl* **-ties**) benignidad
bent [bɛnt] *adj* encorvado, doblado, torcido; **bent on** resuelto a, empeñado en; **bent over** cargado de espaldas || *s* encorvadura; inclinación *f*, propensión *f*
benzine [bɛnˈzin] *s* bencina
bequeath [bɪˈkwið] o [bɪˈkwiθ] *tr* legar
bequest [bɪˈkwɛst] *s* manda, legado
berate [bɪˈret] *tr* regañar, reñir
be•reave [bɪˈriv] *v* (*pret & pp* **-reaved** o **-reft** [ˈrɛft]) *tr* despojar, privar; desconsolar
bereavement [bɪˈrivmənt] *s* despojo, privación *f*; desconsuelo
berkelium [bərˈkilɪ•əm] *s* berkelio
Berliner [bərˈlɪnər] *s* berlinés *m*
ber•ry [ˈbɛri] *s* (*pl* **-ries**) baya; (*of coffee plant*) grano, haba
berserk [ˈbʌrsʌrk] *adj* frenético || *adv* frenéticamente
berth [bʌrθ] *s* (*bed*) litera; (*room*) camarote *m*; (*for a ship*) amarradero; (coll) empleo, puesto
beryllium [bəˈrɪlɪ•əm] *s* berilio
be•seech [bɪˈsitʃ] *v* (*pret & pp* **-sought** [ˈsɔt] o **-seeched**) *tr* suplicar
be•set [bɪˈsɛt] *v* (*pret & pp* **-set**; *ger* **-setting**) *tr* acometer, acosar; cercar, sitiar
beside [bɪˈsaɪd] *adv* además, también || *prep* cerca de, junto a; en comparación de; excepto; **beside oneself** fuera de sí; **beside the point** incongruente
besiege [bɪˈsidʒ] *tr* asediar, sitiar
besmirch [bɪˈsmʌrtʃ] *tr* ensuciar, manchar
bespatter [bɪˈspætər] *tr* salpicar
be•speak [bɪˈspik] *v* (*pret* **-spoke** [ˈspok]; *pp* **-spoken**) *tr* apalabrar, pedir de antemano
best [bɛst] *adj super* mejor; óptimo || *adv super* mejor; **had best** debería || *s* (lo) mejor; (lo) más; **at best** a lo más; **to do one's best** hacer lo mejor posible; **to get the best of** aventajar, sobresalir; **to make the best of** sacar el mejor partido de
best girl *s* (coll) amiga preferida, novia
be•stir [bɪˈstʌr] *v* (*pret & pp* **-stirred**; *ger* **-stirring**) *tr* excitar, incitar; **to bestir oneself** esforzarse, afanarse
best man *s* padrino de boda
bestow [bɪˈsto] *tr* otorgar, conferir; dedicar
best seller *s* éxito de venta, campeón *m* de venta; éxito de librería
bet. *abbr* **between**
bet [bɛt] *s* apuesta || *v* (*pret & pp* **bet** o **betted**; *ger* **betting**) *tr & intr* apostar; **I bet** a que, apuesto a que; **to bet on** apostar por; **you bet** (slang) ya lo creo
be•take [bɪˈtek] *v* (*pret* **-took** [ˈtʊk]; *pp* **-taken**) *tr* — **to betake oneself** dirigirse; darse, entregarse
be•think [bɪˈθɪŋk] *v* (*pret & pp* **-thought** [ˈθɔt]) *tr* — **to bethink oneself of** considerar, acordarse de
Bethlehem [ˈbɛθlɪ•əm] o [ˈbɛθlɪˌhɛm] *s* Belén *m*
betide [bɪˈtaɪd] *tr* presagiar; acontecer a || *intr* acontecer
betoken [bɪˈtokən] *tr* anunciar, indicar, presagiar
betray [bɪˈtre] *tr* traicionar; descubrir, revelar
betrayal [bɪˈtre•əl] *s* traición; descubrimiento, revelación
betroth [bɪˈtroð] o [bɪˈtrɔθ] *tr* prometer en matrimonio; **to become betrothed** desposarse
betrothal [bɪˈtroðəl] o [bɪˈtrɔθəl] *s* desposorios, esponsales *mpl*
betrothed [bɪˈtroðd] o [bɪˈtrɔθt] *s* prometido, novio
better [ˈbɛtər] *adj comp* mejor; **it is better to** más vale; **to grow better** mejorarse; **to make better** mejorar || *adv comp* mejor; más; **had better** debería; **to like better** preferir || *s* superior; ventaja; **to get the better of** llevar la ventaja a || *tr* aventajar; mejorar; **to better oneself** mejorar su posición
better half *s* (coll) cara mitad
betterment [ˈbɛtərmənt] *s* mejoramiento; (*in an illness*) mejoría
between [bɪˈtwin] *adv* en medio, entremedias || *prep* entre; **between you and me** entre Vd. y yo; acá para los dos
be•tween′-decks′ *s* entrecubiertas, entrepuentes *mpl*
between decks *adv* entrecubiertas
bev•el [ˈbɛvəl] *adj* biselado || *s* (*instrument*) cartabón *m*; (*sloping part*) bisel *m* || *v* (*pret & pp* **-eled** o **-elled**; *ger* **-eling** o **-elling**) *tr* biselar
beverage [ˈbɛvərɪdʒ] *s* bebida
bev•y [ˈbɛvi] *s* (*pl* **-ies**) (*of birds*) bandada; (*of girls*) grupo
bewail [bɪˈwel] *tr & intr* lamentar
beware [bɪˈwɛr] *tr* guardarse de || *intr* tener cuidado; **beware of . . . !** ¡ojo con . . . !, ¡cuidado con . . . !; **to beware of** guardarse de

bewilder [bɪ'wɪldər] *tr* aturdir, dejar perplejo, desatinar
bewilderment [bɪ'wɪldərmənt] *s* aturdimiento, perplejidad
beyond [bɪ'jɑnd] *adv* más allá, más lejos || *prep* más allá de; además de; no capaz de; **beyond a doubt** fuera de duda; **beyond the reach of** fuera del alcance de || *s* — **the great beyond** el más allá, el otro mundo
bg. *abbr* **bag**
bias ['baɪ·əs] *s* sesgo, diagonal *f;* prejuicio; (electron) polarización de rejilla || *tr* predisponer, prevenir
Bib. *abbr* **Bible, Biblical**
bib [bɪb] *s* babero; (*of apron*) pechera
Bible ['baɪbəl] *s* Biblia
Biblical ['bɪblɪkəl] *adj* bíblico
bibliographer [,bɪblɪ'ɑgrəfər] *s* bibliógrafo
bibliogra·phy [,bɪblɪ'ɑgrəfi] *s* (*pl* **-phies**) bibliografía
bibliophile ['bɪblɪ·ə,faɪl] *s* bibliófilo
bicameral [baɪ'kæmərəl] *adj* bicameral
bicarbonate [baɪ'kɑrbə,net] *s* bicarbonato
bicker ['bɪkər] *s* discusión ociosa || *intr* discutir ociosamente
bicycle ['baɪsɪkəl] *s* bicicleta
bid [bɪd] *s* oferta, postura; (*in bridge*) declaración || *v* (*pret* **bade** [bæd] o **bid;** *ger* **bidden** ['bɪdən]) *tr & intr* ofrecer, pujar, licitar; (*in bridge*) declarar
bidder ['bɪdər] *s* postor *m;* (*in bridge*) declarante *mf;* **the highest bidder** el mejor postor
bidding ['bɪdɪŋ] *s* mandato, orden *f;* postura; (*in bridge*) declaración
bide [baɪd] *tr* — **to bide one's time** esperar la hora propicia
biennial [baɪ'ɛnɪ·əl] *adj* bienal
bier [bɪr] *s* féretro, andas
bifocal [baɪ'fokəl] *adj* bifocal || **bifocals** *spl* anteojos bifocales
big [bɪg] *adj* (*comp* **bigger;** *super* **biggest**) grande; (*considerable*) importante; (*grown-up*) adulto; **big with child** preñada || *adv* (coll) con jactancia; **to talk big** (coll) hablar gordo
bigamist ['bɪgəmɪst] *s* bígamo
bigamous ['bɪgəməs] *adj* bígamo
bigamy ['bɪgəmi] *s* bigamia
big-bellied ['bɪg ,bɛlɪd] *adj* panzudo
Big Dipper *s* Carro mayor
big game *s* caza mayor
big-hearted ['bɪg ,hɑrtɪd] *adj* magnánimo, generoso
bigot ['bɪgət] *s* intolerante *mf,* fanático
bigoted ['bɪgətɪd] *adj* intolerante, fanático
bigot·ry ['bɪgətri] *s* (*pl* **-ries**) intolerancia, fanatismo
big shot *s* (slang) pájaro de cuenta, señorón *m*
big stick *s* palo en alto
big toe *s* dedo gordo o grande (*del pie*)
bile [baɪl] *s* bilis *f*
bilge [bɪldʒ] *s* pantoque *m* || *tr* desfondar
bilge pump *s* bomba de sentina
bilge water *s* agua de pantoque
bilge ways *spl* anguilas
bilingual [baɪ'lɪŋgwəl] *adj* bilingüe
bilious ['bɪljəs] *adj* bilioso
bilk [bɪlk] *tr* estafar, trampear
bill [bɪl] *s* (*statement of charges for goods or service*) cuenta, factura; (*paper money*) billete *m;* (*poster*) cartel *m,* aviso; cartel de teatro; (*draft of law*) proyecto de ley; (*handbill*) hoja suelta; (*of bird*) pico; (com) giro, letra de cambio || *tr* facturar; cargar en cuenta a; anunciar por carteles || *intr* darse el pico (*las palomas*); acariciarse (*los enamorados*); **to bill and coo** acariciarse y arrullarse
bill'board' *s* cartelera
billet ['bɪlɪt] *s* (mil) boleta; (mil) alojamiento || *tr* (mil) alojar
billet-doux ['bɪle'du] *s* (*pl* **billets-doux** ['bɪle'duz]) esquela amorosa
bill'fold' *s* cartera de bolsillo, billetero
bill'head' *s* encabezamiento de factura
billiards ['bɪljərdz] *s* billar *m*
billion ['bɪljən] *s* (U.S.A.) mil millones; (Brit) billón *m*
bill of exchange *s* letra de cambio
bill of fare *s* lista de comidas, menú *m*
bill of lading *s* conocimiento de embarque
bill of sale *s* escritura de venta
billow ['bɪlo] *s* oleada, ondulación || *intr* ondular, hincharse
bill'post'er *s* fijacarteles *m,* fijador *m* de carteles
bil·ly ['bɪli] *s* (*pl* **-lies**) cachiporra
billy goat *s* macho cabrío
bin [bɪn] *s* arcón *m,* hucha
bind [baɪnd] *v* (*pret & pp* **bound** [baʊnd]) *tr* ligar, atar; juntar, unir; (*with a garland*) enguirlandar; ribetear (*la orilla del vestido*); agavillar (*las mieses*); vendar (*una herida*); encuadernar (*un libro*); estreñir (*el vientre*)
binder·y ['baɪndəri] *s* (*pl* **-ies**) taller *m* de encuadernación
binding ['baɪndɪŋ] *s* atadura; (*of a book*) encuadernación
binding post *s* borne *m,* sujetahilo
binge [bɪndʒ] *s* (slang) borrachera; **to go on a binge** (slang) pegarse una mona
binnacle ['bɪnəkəl] *s* bitácora
binoculars [bɪ'nɑkjələrz] o [baɪ'nɑkjələrz] *spl* gemelos, prismáticos
biochemical [,baɪ·ə'kɛmɪkəl] *adj* bioquímico
biochemist [,baɪ·ə'kɛmɪst] *s* bioquímico
biochemistry [,baɪ·ə'kɛmɪstri] *s* bioquímica
biog. *abbr* **biographical, biography**
biographer [baɪ'ɑgrəfər] *s* biógrafo
biographic(al) [,baɪ·ə'græfɪk(əl)] *adj* biográfico
biogra·phy [baɪ'ɑgrəfi] *s* (*pl* **-phies**) biografía

biologist [baɪ'ɑlədʒɪst] *s* biólogo
biology [baɪ'ɑlədʒi] *s* biología
biophysical [ˌbaɪ·ə'fɪzɪkəl] *adj* biofísico
biophysics [ˌbaɪ·ə'fɪzɪks] *s* biofísica
birch [bʌrtʃ] *s* abedul *m* || *tr* azotar, varear
bird [bʌrd] *s* ave *f*, pájaro
bird cage *s* jaula
bird call *s* reclamo
bird'lime' *s* liga
bird of passage *s* ave *f* de paso
bird of prey *s* ave *f* de rapiña
bird'seed' *s* alpiste *m*, cañamones *mpl*
bird's'-eye' view *s* vista a ojo de pájaro
bird shot *s* perdigones *mpl*
birth [bʌrθ] *s* nacimiento; (*childbirth*) parto; origen *m*
birth certificate *s* partida de nacimiento
birth control *s* limitación de la natalidad
birth'day' *s* cumpleaños *m*, natal *m*; (*of any event*) aniversario; **to have a birthday** cumplir años
birthday cake *s* pastel *m* de cumpleaños
birthday present *s* regalo de cumpleaños
birth'mark' *s* antojo, nevo materno
birth'place' *s* suelo natal, patria, lugar *m* de nacimiento
birth rate *s* natalidad
birth'right' *s* derechos de nacimiento; primogenitura
Biscay ['bɪske] *s* Vizcaya
biscuit ['bɪskɪt] *s* panecillo redondo; bizcocho
bisect [baɪ'sɛkt] *tr* bisecar || *intr* empalmar (*dos caminos*)
bishop ['bɪʃəp] *s* obispo; (*in chess*) alfil *m*
bismuth ['bɪzməθ] *s* bismuto
bison ['baɪsən] o ['baɪzən] *s* bisonte *m*
bit [bɪt] *s* poquito, pedacito; (*of food*) bocado; (*of time*) ratito; (*part of bridle*) bocado, freno; (*for drilling*) barrena; **a good bit** una buena cantidad
bitch [bɪtʃ] *s* (*dog*) perra; (*fox*) zorra; (*wolf*) loba; (vulg) mujer *f* de mal genio
bite [baɪt] *s* mordedura; (*of bird or insect*) picadura; (*burning sensation on tongue*) resquemo; (*of food*) bocado; (*snack*) (coll) tentempié *m*, refrigerio || *v* (*pret* **bit** [bɪt]; *pp* **bit** o **bitten** ['bɪtən]) *tr* morder; picar (*los peces, los insectos*); resquemar (*la lengua los alimentos*); comerse (*las uñas*) || *intr* morder; picar; resquemar; (*to be caught by a trick*) (slang) picar
biting ['baɪtɪŋ] *adj* penetrante; mordaz, picante
bitter ['bɪtər] *adj* amargo; (*e.g., struggle*) encarnizado; **to the bitter end** hasta el extremo; hasta la muerte
bitter almond *s* almendra amarga
bitterness ['bɪtərnɪs] *s* amargura
bitumen [bɪ'tjumən] o [bɪ'tumən] *s* betún *m*
bivou·ac ['bɪvʊ·æk] o ['bɪvwæk] *s* vivaque *m* || *v* (*pret & pp* **-acked**; *ger* **-acking**) *intr* vivaquear
bizarre [bɪ'zɑr] *adj* original, raro
bk. *abbr* **bank, block, book**
bkg. *abbr* **banking**
bl. *abbr* **barrel**
b.l. *abbr* **bill of lading**
blabber ['blæbər] *tr & intr* barbullar
black [blæk] *adj* negro || *s* negro; luto; **to wear black** ir de luto
black'-and-blue' *adj* encardenalado, amoratado
black'-and-white' *adj* en blanco y negro
black'ber'ry *s* (*pl* **-ries**) (*bush*) zarza; (*fruit*) zarzamora
black'bird' *s* mirlo
black'board' *s* encerado, pizarra
black'damp' *s* mofeta
blacken ['blækən] *tr* ennegrecer; (*to defame*) desacreditar, denigrar
blackguard ['blægɑrd] *s* bribón *m*, canalla *m* || *tr* injuriar, vilipendiar
black'head' *s* espinilla, comedón *m*
blackish ['blækɪʃ] *adj* negruzco
black'jack' *s* (*club*) cachiporra; (*flag*) bandera negra (*de pirata*) || *tr* aporrear
black'mail' *s* chantaje *m* || *tr* amenazar con chantaje
blackmailer ['blækˌmelər] *s* chantajista *mf*
Black Maria [mə'raɪ·ə] *s* (coll) coche *m* celular
black market *s* estraperlo, mercado negro
blackness ['blæknɪs] *s* negror *m*, negrura
black'out' *s* (*in wartime*) apagón *m*; (*in theater*) apagamiento de luces; (*of aviators*) visión negra; pérdida de la memoria
black sheep *s* (fig) oveja negra, garbanzo negro
black'smith' *s* (*man who works with iron*) herrero; (*man who shoes horses*) herrador *m*
black'thorn' *s* espino negro, endrino
black tie corbata de smoking; smoking *m*
bladder ['blædər] *s* vejiga
blade [bled] *s* (*of a knife, sword*) hoja; (*of a propeller*) aleta; (*of a fan*) paleta; (*of an oar*) pala; (*of an electric switch*) cuchilla; (*sword*) espada; tallo de hierba; (coll) gallardo joven
blame [blem] *s* culpa || *tr* culpar
blameless ['blemlɪs] *adj* inculpable, irreprochable
blanch [blæntʃ] o [blɑntʃ] *tr* blanquear || *intr* palidecer
bland [blænd] *adj* apacible; suave; (*character; weather*) blando
blandish ['blændɪʃ] *tr* engatusar, lisonjear
blank [blæŋk] *adj* en blanco; blanco, vacío; (*stare, look*) vago || *s* blanco; papel blanco; formulario
blank check *s* firma en blanco; (fig) carta blanca

blanket ['blæŋkɪt] *adj* general, comprensivo || *s* manta, frazada; (fig) capa, manto || *tr* cubrir con manta; cubrir, obscurecer
blasé [bla'ze] *adj* hastiado
blaspheme [blæs'fim] *tr* blasfemar contra || *intr* blasfemar
blasphemous ['blæsfɪməs] *adj* blasfemo
blasphe·my ['blæsfɪmi] *s* (*pl* **-mies**) blasfemia
blast [blæst] o [blɑst] *s* (*of wind*) ráfaga; (*of air, sand, water*) chorro; (*of bellows*) soplo; (*of a horn*) toque *m;* carga de pólvora; voladura, explosión; **full blast** en plena marcha || *tr* (*to blow up*) volar; arruinar; infamar, maldecir
blast furnace *s* alto horno
blast'off' *s* lanzamiento de cohete
blatant ['bletənt] *adj* ruidoso; vocinglero; intruso; chillón, cursi
blaze [blez] *s* llamarada; (*fire*) incendio; (*bonfire*) hoguera; luz *f* brillante || *tr* encender, inflamar; **to blaze a trail** abrir una senda || *intr* encenderse; resplandecer
bldg. *abbr* **building**
bleach [blitʃ] *s* blanqueo || *tr* blanquear; colar (*la ropa*)
bleachers ['blitʃərz] *spl* gradas al aire libre
bleak [blik] *adj* desierto, yermo, frío, triste
bleat [blit] *s* balido || *intr* balar
bleed [blid] *v* (*pret & pp* **bled** [blɛd]) *tr & intr* sangrar
blemish ['blɛmɪʃ] *s* mancha || *tr* manchar
blend [blɛnd] *s* mezcla; armonía || *v* (*pret & pp* **blended** o **blent** [blɛnt]) *tr* mezclar; armonizar; fusionar || *intr* mezclarse; armonizar; fusionarse
bless [blɛs] *tr* bendecir; **to be blessed with** estar dotado de
blessed ['blɛsɪd] *adj* bendito, santo
blessedness ['blɛsɪdnɪs] *s* bienaventuranza
blessing ['blɛsɪŋ] *s* bendición
blight [blaɪt] *s* niebla, roya; ruina || *tr* anublar; arruinar
blimp [blɪmp] *s* dirigible pequeño
blind [blaɪnd] *adj* ciego || *s* (*window shade*) estor *m,* transparente *m* de resorte; (*Venetian blind*) persiana; pretexto, subterfugio || *tr* cegar; (*to dazzle*) deslumbrar; (*to deceive*) cegar, vendar
blind alley *s* callejón *m* sin salida
blind date *s* cita a ciegas
blinder ['blaɪndər] *s* anteojera
blind flying *s* (aer) vuelo a ciegas
blind'fold' *adj* vendado de ojos || *s* venda || *tr* vendar los ojos a
blind landing *s* aterrizaje *m* a ciegas
blind man *s* ciego
blind'man's' buff *s* gallina ciega
blindness ['blaɪndnɪs] *s* ceguedad
blink [blɪŋk] *s* guiñada, parpadeo || *tr* guiñar (*el ojo*) || *intr* guiñar, parpardear, pestañear; oscilar (*la luz*)
blip [blɪp] *s* bache *m*
bliss [blɪs] *s* bienaventuranza, felicidad
blissful ['blɪsfəl] *adj* bienaventurado, feliz
blister ['blɪstər] *s* ampolla, vejiga || *tr* ampollar || *intr* ampollarse
blithe [blaɪð] *adj* alegre, animado
blitzkrieg ['blɪts,krig] *s* guerra relámpago
blizzard ['blɪzərd] *s* ventisca, chubasco de nieve
bloat [blot] *tr* hinchar || *intr* hincharse, abotagarse
block [blɑk] *s* bloque *m;* (*of hatter*) horma; (*of houses*) manzana; (*for chopping meat*) tajo; estorbo, obstáculo || *tr* cerrar, obstruir; conformar (*un sombrero*)
blockade [blɑ'ked] *s* bloqueo || *tr* bloquear
blockade runner *s* forzador *m* de bloqueo
block and tackle *s* aparejo de poleas
block'bust'er *s* (coll) bomba rompedora
block'head' *s* tonto, zoquete *m*
block signal *s* (rr) señal *f* de tramo
blond [blɑnd] *adj* rubio, blondo || *s* rubio (*hombre rubio*)
blonde [blɑnd] *s* rubia (*mujer rubia*)
blood [blʌd] *s* sangre *f;* **in cold blood** a sangre fría
bloodcurdling ['blʌd,kʌrdlɪŋ] *adj* horripilante
blood'hound' *s* sabueso
blood poisoning *s* envenenamiento de la sangre
blood pressure *s* presión arterial
blood pudding *s* morcilla
blood relation *s* pariente consanguíneo
blood'shed' *s* efusión de sangre
blood'shot' *adj* inyectado en sangre, encarnizado
blood test *s* análisis *m* de sangre
blood'thirst'y *adj* sanguinario
blood transfusion *s* transfusión de sangre
blood vessel *s* vaso sanguíneo
blood·y ['blʌdi] *adj* (*comp* **-ier;** *super* **-iest**) sangriento || *v* (*pret & pp* **-ied**) *tr* ensangrentar
bloom [blum] *s* florecimiento; flor *f* || *intr* florecer
blossom ['blɑsəm] *s* brote *m,* flor *f;* **in blossom** en cierne || *intr* cerner, florecer
blot [blɑt] *s* borrón *m* || *v* (*pret & pp* **blotted;** *ger* **blotting**) *tr* (*to smear*) borrar; secar con papel secante; **to blot out** borrar || *intr* borrarse; echar borrones (*una pluma*)
blotch [blɑtʃ] *s* manchón *m;* (*in the skin*) erupción
blotter ['blɑtər] *s* teleta, secafirmas *m*
blotting paper *s* papel *m* secante
blouse [blaʊs] *s* blusa
blow [blo] *s* (*hit, stroke*) golpe; (*blast of air*) soplo, soplido; (*blast of wind*) ventarrón *m;* (*of horn*) toque *m,* trompetazo; (*sudden sorrow*) estocada, ramalazo; (*boaster*) (slang) fanfarrón *m;* **to come to blows** venir a las manos || *v* (*pret* **blew** [blu]; *pp*

blown) || *tr* soplar; sonar, tocar (*un instrumento de viento*); silbar (*un silbato*); sonarse (*las narices*); quemar (*un fusible*); (slang) malgastar (*dinero*); **to blow out** apagar soplando; quemar (*un fusible*); **to blow up** (*with air*) inflar; (*e.g., with dynamite*) volar, hacer saltar; ampliar (*una foto*) || *intr* soplar; (*to pant*) jadear, resoplar; fundirse (*un fusible*); (slang) fanfarronear; **to blow out** apagarse con el aire; quemarse, fundirse (*un fusible*); reventar (*un neumático*); **to blow up** volarse; (*to fail*) fracasar; (*with anger*) (slang) estallar, reventar

blow′out′ *s* (aut) reventón *m;* (*of a fuse*) quemazón *f;* (slang) tertulia concurrida, festín *m*

blowout patch *s* parche *m* para neumático

blow′pipe′ *s* (*torch*) soplete *m;* (*peashooter*) cerbatana

blow′torch′ *s* antorcha a soplete, lámpara de soldar

blubber [ˈblʌbər] *s* grasa de ballena; lloro ruidoso || *intr* llorar ruidosamente

bludgeon [ˈblʌdʒən] *s* cachiporra || *tr* aporrear; intimidar

blue [blu] *adj* azul; abatido, triste || *s* azul *m;* **the blues** la murria, la morriña || *tr* azular; añilar (*la ropa blanca*) || *intr* azularse

blue′ber′ry *s* (*pl* **-ries**) mirtilo

blue chip *s* valor *m* de primera fila

blue′jay′ *s* cianocita

blue moon *s* cosa muy rara; **once in a blue moon** cada muerte de obispo, de Pascuas a Ramos

Blue Nile *s* Nilo Azul

blue′-pen′cil *tr* marcar o corregir con lápiz azul

blue′print′ *s* cianotipo || *tr* copiar a la cianotipia

blue′stock′ing *s* (coll) marisabidilla

blue streak *s* (coll) rayo; **to talk a blue streak** (coll) soltar la tarabilla

bluff [blʌf] *adj* escarpado || *s* risco, peñasco escarpado; (*deception*) farol *m;* **to call someone's bluff** cogerle la palabra a uno || *intr* farolear, papelonear

blunder [ˈblʌndər] *s* disparate *m,* desatino || *intr* disparatar, desatinar

blunt [blʌnt] *adj* despuntado, embotado; brusco, franco, directo || *tr* despuntar, embotar

bluntness [ˈblʌntnɪs] *s* embotadura; brusquedad, franqueza

blur [blʌr] *s* borrón *m,* mancha || *v* (*pret & pp* **blurred;** *ger* **blurring**) *tr* empañar; obscurecer (*la vista*) || *intr* empañarse

blurb [blʌrb] *s* anuncio efusivo

blurt [blʌrt] *tr* — **to blurt out** soltar abrupta e impulsivamente

blush [blʌʃ] *s* rubor *m,* sonrojo || *intr* ruborizarse, sonrojarse

bluster [ˈblʌstər] *s* tumulto, gritos; jactancia || *intr* soplar con furia (*el viento*); bravear, fanfarronear

blustery [ˈblʌstəri] *adj* tempestuoso; (*wind*) violento; (*swaggering*) fanfarrón

blvd. *abbr* **boulevard**

boar [bor] *s* (*male swine*) verraco; (*wild hog*) jabalí *m*

board [bord] *s* tabla; (*to post announcements*) tablillo; (*table with meal*) mesa; (*daily meals*) pensión; (*organized group*) junta, consejo; (naut) bordo; **in boards** (bb) en cartoné; **on board** en el tren; (naut) a bordo || *tr* entablar; subir a (*un tren*); embarcarse en (*un buque*) || *intr* hospedarse; estar de pupilo

board and lodging *s* mesa y habitación, pensión completa

boarder [ˈbordər] *s* pensionista *mf,* pupilo

boarding house *s* pensión, casa de huéspedes

boarding school *s* escuela de internos

board of health *s* junta de sanidad

board of trade *s* junta de comercio

board of trustees *s* consejo de administración

board′walk′ *s* paseo entablado a la orilla del mar

boast [bost] *s* jactancia, baladronada || *intr* jactarse, baladronear

boastful [ˈbostfəl] *adj* jactancioso

boat [bot] *s* barco, buque *m,* nave *f;* (*small boat*) bote *m;* **to be in the same boat** correr el mismo riesgo

boat hook *s* bichero

boat′house′ *s* casilla para botes

boating [ˈbotɪŋ] *s* paseo en barco

boat•man [ˈbotmən] *s* (*pl* **-men** [mən]) barquero, lanchero

boat race *s* regata

boatswain *s* [ˈbosən] o [ˈbot ˌswən] *s* contramaestre *m*

boatswain's chair *s* guindola

boatswain's mate *s* segundo contramaestre

bob [bɑb] *s* (*of pendulum of clock*) lenteja; (*of plumb line*) plomo; (*of a fishing line*) corcho; (*of a horse*) cola cortada; (*of a girl*) pelo cortado corto; (*jerky motion*) sacudida || *v* (*pret & pp* **bobbed;** *ger* **bobbing**) *tr* cortar corto || *intr* agitarse, menearse; **to bob up and down** subir y bajar con sacudidas cortas

bobbin [ˈbɑbɪn] *s* broca, canilla, bobina

bobby pin [ˈbɑbi] *s* horquillita para el pelo

bob′by•socks′ *spl* (coll) tobilleras (*de jovencita*)

bobbysoxer [ˈbɑbɪ ˌsɑksər] *s* (coll) tobillera

bobolink [ˈbɑbə ˌlɪŋk] *s* chambergo

bob′sled′ *s* doble trineo articulado

bob′tail′ *s* animal *m* rabón; cola corta; cola cortada

bob′white′ *s* colín *m* de Virginia

bock beer [bɑk] *s* cerveza de marzo

bode [bod] *tr & intr* anunciar, presagiar; **to bode ill** ser un mal presagio; **to bode well** ser un buen presagio

bodice [ˈbɑdɪs] *s* jubón *m,* corpiño
bodily [ˈbɑdɪli] *adj* corporal, corpóreo || *adv* en persona; en conjunto
bodkin [ˈbɑdkɪn] *s* (*needle*) aguja roma; (*for lady's hair*) espadilla; (*to make holes in cloth*) punzón *m*
bod·y [ˈbɑdi] *s* (*pl* **-ies**) cuerpo; (*of a carriage or auto*) caja, carrocería
bod'y·guard' *s* (mil) guardia de corps; guardaespaldas *m*
Boer [bor] o [bʊr] *s* bóer *mf*
Boer War *s* guerra del Transvaal
bog [bɑg] *s* pantano || *v* (*pret & pp* **bogged;** *ger* **bogging**) *intr* — **to bog down** atascarse, hundirse
bogey [ˈbogi] *s* duende *m,* coco
bo'gey·man' *s* (*pl* **-men** [ˌmɛn]) duende *m,* espantajo
bogus [ˈbogəs] *adj* (coll) fingido, falso
bo·gy [ˈbogi] *s* (*pl* **-gies**) duende *m,* demonio, coco
Bohemian [boˈhimɪ·ən] *adj & s* bohemio
boil [bɔɪl] *s* hervor *m,* ebullición; (pathol) divieso, furúnculo || *tr* hacer hervir, herventar || *intr* hervir, bullir; **to boil over** salirse (*un líquido*) al hervir
boiler [ˈbɔɪlər] *s* caldera; (*for cooking*) marmita, olla
boil'er·mak'er *s* calderero
boiler room *s* sala de calderas
boiling [ˈbɔɪlɪŋ] *adj* hirviente, hirviendo || *s* hervor *m,* ebullición
boiling point *s* punto de ebullición
boisterous [ˈbɔɪstərəs] *adj* bullicioso, ruidoso, estrepitoso
bold [bold] *adj* audaz, arrojado, osado; descarado, impudente; temerario
bold'face' *s* negrilla
boldness [ˈboldnɪs] *s* audacia, arrojo, osadía; descaro, impudencia; temeridad
Bolivia [boˈlɪvɪ·ə] *s* Bolivia
Bolivian [boˈlɪvɪ·ən] *adj & s* boliviano
boll weevil [bol] *s* gorgojo del algodón
Bologna [bəˈlonjə] *s* Bolonia
Bolshevik [ˈbɑlʃəvɪk] o [ˈbolʃəvɪk] *adj & s* bolchevique *mf*
Bolshevism [ˈbɑlʃəˌvɪzəm] o [ˈbolʃəˌvɪzəm] *s* bolchevismo
bolster [ˈbolstər] *s* (*of bed*) larguero, travesaño; refuerzo, soporte *m* || *tr* apoyar, sostener; animar, alentar
bolt [bolt] *s* perno; (*to fasten a door*) cerrojo, pasador *m;* (*arrow*) cuadrillo; (*of lightning*) rayo; (*of cloth or paper*) rollo || *tr* empernar; acerrojar; deglutir de una vez; cribar, tamizar; disidir de (*un partido político*) || *intr* salir de repente; disidir; desbocarse (*un caballo*)
bolter [ˈboltər] *s* disidente *mf;* (*sieve*) criba, tamiz *m*
bolt from the blue *s* rayo en cielo sin nubes; suceso inesperado
bomb [bɑm] *s* bomba || *tr* bombear, bombardear
bombard [bɑmˈbɑrd] *tr* bombardear; (*e.g., with questions*) asediar
bombardment [bɑmˈbɑrdmənt] *s* bombardeo
bombast [ˈbɑmbæst] *s* ampulosidad
bombastic [bɑmˈbæstɪk] *adj* ampuloso
bomb crater *s* (mil) embudo de bomba
bomber [ˈbɑmər] *s* bombardero
bomb'proof' *adj* a prueba de bombas
bomb release *s* lanzabombas *m*
bomb'shell' *s* bomba; **to fall like a bombshell** caer como una bomba
bomb shelter *s* refugio antiaéreo
bomb'sight' *s* mira de bombardeo, visor *m*
bona fide [ˈbonə ˌfaɪdə] *adj & adv* de buena fe
bonbon [ˈbɑn ˌbɑn] *s* bombón *m,* confite *m*
bond [bɑnd] *s* (*tie, union*) enlace *m,* vínculo, lazo de unión; (*interest-bearing certificate*) bono, obligación; (*surety*) fianza; (mas) aparejo; **bonds** cadenas, grillos; **in bond** en depósito bajo fianza
bondage [ˈbɑndɪdʒ] *s* cautiverio, servidumbre
bonded warehouse *s* depósito comercial
bond'hold'er *s* obligacionista *mf,* tenedor *m* de bonos
bonds·man [ˈbɑndzmən] *s* (*pl* **-men** [mən]) fiador *m*
bone [bon] *s* hueso; (*of fish*) espina; **bones** esqueleto; (*mortal remains*) huesos; castañuelas; (*dice*) (coll) dados; **to have a bone to pick with** tener una queja con; **to make no bones about** no andarse con rodeos en || *tr* desosar; quitar la espina a; emballenar (*un corsé*) || *intr* — **to bone up on** (coll) empollar, estudiar con ahinco
bone'head' *s* (coll) mentecato, zopenco
boneless [ˈbonlɪs] *adj* mollar, desosado; (*fish*) sin espinas
boner [ˈbonər] *s* (coll) patochada, plancha, gazapo
bonfire [ˈbɑn ˌfaɪr] *s* hoguera
bonnet [ˈbɑnɪt] *s* gorra; (*sunbonnet*) papalina; (*of auto*) cubierta, capó *m*
bonus [ˈbonəs] *s* prima, plus *m;* dividendo extraordinario
bon·y [ˈboni] *adj* (*comp* **-ier;** *super* **-iest**) osudo; descarnado; (*fish*) espinoso
boo [bu] *s* rechifla; **not to say boo** no decir ni chus ni mus || *tr & intr* abuchear, rechiflar
boo·by [ˈbubi] *s* (*pl* **-bies**) bobalicón *m,* zopenco; el peor jugador
booby prize *s* premio al peor jugador
booby trap *s* (*mine*) trampa explosiva; (*trick*) zancadilla
boogie-woogie [ˈbʊgiˈwʊgi] *s* bugui-bugui *m*
book [bʊk] *s* libro; (*bankbook*) libreta; (*book containing records of business transactions*) libro-registro; (*of cigaret paper, stamps, etc.*) librillo; **to keep books** llevar libros || *tr* reservar (*un pasaje*); escriturar (*a un actor*)
bookbinder [ˈbʊk ˌbaɪndər] *s* encuadernador *m*

book'bind'er•y *s* (*pl* **-ies**) encuadernación (*taller*)
book'bind'ing *s* encuadernación (*acción, arte*)
book'case' *s* armario para libros, estante *m* para libros
book end *s* apoyalibros *m*
bookie ['bʊki] *s* (coll) corredor *m* de apuestas
booking ['bʊkɪŋ] *s* (*of passage*) reservación; (*of an actor*) escritura
booking clerk *s* taquillero (*que despacha pasajes o localidades*)
bookish ['bʊkɪʃ] *adj* libresco
book'keep'er *s* tenedor *m* de libros
book'keep'ing *s* teneduría de libros, contabilidad
book'mak'er *s* corredor *m* de apuestas
book'mark' *s* registro
book'plate' *s* ex libris *m*
book review *s* reseña
book'sell'er *s* librero
book'shelf' *s* (*pl* **-shelves** [,ʃɛlvz]) estante *m* para libros
book'stand' *s* (*rack*) atril *m;* mostrador *m* para libros; puesto de venta para libros
book'store' *s* librería
book'worm' *s* polilla que roe los libros; (fig) ratón *m* de biblioteca
boom [bum] *s* (*sudden prosperity*) auge *m;* (*noise*) estampido, trueno; (*of a crane*) aguilón *m;* (naut) botalón *m* || *intr* hacer estampido, tronar; estar en auge
boomerang ['bumə,ræŋ] *s* bumerán *m*
boom town *s* pueblo en bonanza
boon [bun] *s* bendición, dicha
boon companion *s* buen compañero
boor [bʊr] *s* patán *m,* rústico
boorish ['bʊrɪʃ] *adj* rústico, zafio
boost [bust] *s* empujón *m* hacia arriba; (*in price*) alza; alabanza; ayuda || *tr* empujar hacia arriba; alzar (*el precio*); alabar; ayudar
booster ['bustər] *s* cohete *m* lanzador; primera etapa de un cohete lanzador; (*enthusiastic backer*) bombista *mf;* (med) inyección secundaria
boot [but] *s* bota; **to boot** de añadidura, además; **to die with one's boots on** morir al pie del cañón || *tr* dar un puntapié a; **to boot out** (slang) poner en la calle
boot'black' *s* limpiabotas *m*
booth [buθ] *s* casilla, quiosco; (*to telephone, to vote, etc.*) cabina; (*at a fair or market*) puesto
boot'jack' *s* sacabotas *m*
boot'leg' *adj* contrabandista; de contrabando || *s* contrabando de licores || *v* (*pret & pp* **-legged;** *ger* **-legging**) *tr* pasar de contrabando || *intr* contrabandear en bebidas alcohólicas
bootlegger ['but,lɛgər] *s* destilador *m* clandestino, contrabandista *m*
boot'leg'ging *s* contrabando en bebidas alcohólicas
bootlicker ['but,lɪkər] *s* (slang) quitamotas *mf,* lavacaras *mf*
boot'strap' *s* tirilla de bota

boo•ty ['buti] *s* (*pl* **-ties**) botín *m,* presa
booze [buz] *s* (coll) bebida alcohólica || *intr* borrachear
bor. *abbr* **borough**
borax ['boræks] *s* bórax *m*
Bordeaux [bɔr'do] *s* Burdeos
border ['bɔrdər] *adj* frontero, fronterizo || *s* borde *m,* margen *m & f;* frontera; **borders** bambalinas || *tr* bordear; deslindar || *intr* confinar
border clash *s* encuentro fronterizo
bor'der•line' *adj* incierto, indefinido || *s* frontera
bore [bor] *s* (*drill hole*) barreno; (*size of hole*) calibre *m;* (*of firearm*) alma, ánima; (*of cylinder*) alesaje *m;* (*wearisome person*) latoso, machaca *mf;* fastidio || *tr* aburrir, fastidiar; barrenar, hacer (*un agujero*)
boredom ['bordəm] *s* aburrimiento, fastidio
boring ['borɪŋ] *adj* aburrido, pesado
born [bɔrn] *adj* nacido; (*natural, by birth*) nato, innato; **to be born** nacer
borough ['bʌro] *s* (*town*) villa; distrito electoral de municipio
borrow ['bɑro] o ['bɔro] *tr* pedir o tomar prestado; apropiarse (*p.ej., una idea*); incorporar (*un elemento lingüístico extranjero*); **to borrow trouble** tomarse una molestia sin motivo alguno
borrower ['bɑro•ər] o ['bɔro•ər] *s* prestatario
borrowing ['bɑro•ɪŋ] o ['bɔro•ɪŋ] *s* préstamo; préstamo lingüístico, extranjerismo
bosom ['bʊzəm] *s* seno; (*of shirt*) pechera; corazón *m,* pecho
bosom friend *s* amigo de la mayor confianza
Bosporus ['bɑspərəs] *s* Bósforo
boss [bɔs] o [bɑs] *s* (coll) amo, capataz *m,* mandamás, *m,* jefe *m;* (*in politics*) (coll) cacique *m;* protuberancia || *tr* (coll) mandar, dominar
boss•y ['bɔsi] o ['bɑsi] *adj* (*comp* **-ier;** *super* **-iest**) mandón
botanical [bə'tænɪkəl] *adj* botánico
botanist ['bɑtənɪst] *s* botánico
botany ['bɑtəni] *s* botánica
botch [bɑtʃ] *s* remiendo chapucero || *tr* remendar chapuceramente
both [boθ] *adj & pron* ambos || *adv* igualmente || *conj* a la vez; **both . . . and** tanto . . . como, así . . . como
bother ['bɑðər] *s* incomodidad, molestia || *tr* incomodar, molestar || *intr* molestarse
bothersome ['bɑðərsəm] *adj* incómodo, molesto, fastidioso
bottle ['bɑtəl] *s* botella, frasco || *tr* embotellar; **to bottle up** (nav) embotellar
bot'tle•neck' *s* gollete *m;* (*in traffic*) embotellado
bottle opener ['opənər] *s* abrebotellas *m*
bottom ['bɑtəm] *adj* (*price*) (el) más bajo; (*e.g., dollar*) último || *s* fondo; (*of a chair*) asiento; (*of jar*) culo;

(coll) trasero; **at bottom** en el fondo; **to go to the bottom** irse a pique
bottomless ['bɑtəmlɪs] *adj* sin fondo, insondable
boudoir [bu'dwɑr] *s* tocador *m*
bough [baʊ] *s* rama
bouillon ['buljɑn] *s* caldo
boulder ['boldər] *s* pedrejón *m*
boulevard ['bʊlə,vɑrd] *s* bulevar *m*
bounce [baʊns] *s* rebote *m* || *tr* hacer botar; (slang) despedir || *intr* botar, rebotar; saltar; **to bounce along** dar saltos al andar
bouncer ['baʊnsər] *s* cosa grande; (slang) apagabroncas *m*
bouncing ['baʊnsɪŋ] *adj* frescachón, vigoroso; (*baby*) gordinflón
bound [baʊnd] *adj* atado, ligado; (*book*) encuadernado; dispuesto, propenso; puesto en aprendizaje; **bound for** con destino a, con rumbo a; **bound in boards** (bb) encartonado, en cartoné; **bound up in** entregado a, muy adicto a; absorto en || *s* salto; (*of a ball*) bote *m;* límite *m,* confín *m;* **bounds** región, comarca; **out of bounds** fuera de los límites; **within bounds** a raya
bounda•ry ['baʊndəri] *s* (*pl* **-ries**) límite *m,* frontera
boundary stone *s* mojón *m*
bounder ['baʊndər] *s* persona vulgar y malcriada
boundless ['baʊndlɪs] *adj* ilimitado, inmenso, infinito
bountiful ['baʊntɪfəl] *adj* generoso, liberal; abundante
boun•ty ['baʊnti] *s* (*pl* **-ties**) generosidad, liberalidad; don *m,* favor *m;* galardón *m,* premio; (*bonus*) prima; (mil) premio de enganche
bouquet [bu'ke] o [bo'ke] *s* ramillete *m;* (*aroma of a wine*) nariz *f*
bourgeois ['burʒwɑ] *adj* & *s* burgués *m*
bourgeoisie [,burʒwɑ'zi] *s* burguesía
bout [baʊt] *s* encuentro; rato; (*of an illness*) ataque *m*
bow [baʊ] *s* inclinación, reverencia; (*of a ship*) proa || *tr* inclinar (*la cabeza*) || *intr* inclinarse; **to bow and scrape** hacer reverencias obsequiosas; **to bow to** saludar, inclinarse delante || [bo] *s* (*for shooting an arrow*) arco; lazo, nudo; (mus) arco; (*stroke of bow*) (mus) arqueada || *tr* (mus) tocar con arco || *intr* arquearse
bowdlerize ['baʊdlə,raɪz] *tr* expurgar
bowel ['baʊ·əl] *s* intestino; **bowels** intestinos; (*inner part*) entrañas
bowel movement *s* evacuación del vientre; **to have a bowel movement** evacuar el vientre
bower ['baʊ·ər] *s* emparrado, glorieta
bower•y ['baʊ·əri] *adj* frondoso, sombreado || *s* (*pl* **-ies**) finca, granja
bowknot ['bo,nɑt] *s* lazada
bowl [bol] *s* (*for soup or broth*) escudilla, cuenco; (*for washing hands*) jofaina, palangana; (*of toilet*) cubeta, taza; (*of fountain*) tazón *m;* (*of spoon*) paleta; (*of pipe*) hornillo; (*hollow place*) concavidad, cuenco || *tr* — **to bowl over** tumbar || *intr* jugar a los bolos; **to bowl along** rodar
bowlegged ['bo,lɛgd] o ['bo,lɛgɪd] *adj* patiestevado
bowler ['bolər] *s* jugador *m* de bolos; (Brit) sombrero hongo
bowling ['bolɪŋ] *s* juego de bolos, boliche *m*
bowling alley *s* bolera, boliche *m*
bowling green *s* bolera encespada
bowshot ['bo,ʃɑt] *s* tiro de flecha
bowsprit ['baʊsprɪt] o ['bosprɪt] *s* bauprés *m*
bow tie [bo] *s* corbata de mariposa, pajarita
bowwow ['baʊ,waʊ] *interj* ¡guau! || *s* guau guau *m*
box [bɑks] *s* caja; (*slap*) bofetada; (*plant*) boj *m;* (*in newspaper*) recuadro; (theat) palco || *tr* encajonar; (*to slap*) abofetear; (naut) cuartear (*la aguja*) || *intr* boxear
box'car' *s* vagón *m* de carga cerrado
boxer ['bɑksər] *s* embalador *m;* (sport) boxeador *m*
boxing ['bɑksɪŋ] *s* embalaje *m;* (sport) boxeo
boxing gloves *spl* guantes *mpl* de boxeo
box office *s* taquilla, despacho de localidades; boletería (Am)
box'-of'fice hit *s* éxito de taquilla
box-office record *s* marca de taquilla
box-office sale *s* venta de localidades en taquilla
box pleat *s* pliegue *m* de tabla
box seat *s* asiento de palco
box'wood' *s* boj *m*
boy [bɔɪ] *s* muchacho; (*servant*) mozo; (coll) compadre *m*
boycott ['bɔɪkɑt] *s* boicoteo || *tr* boicotear
boyhood ['bɔɪhʊd] *s* muchachez *f;* muchachería
boyish ['bɔɪ·ɪʃ] *adj* amuchachado, muchachil
boy scout *s* niño explorador
Bp. *abbr* **bishop**
b.p. *abbr* **bills payable, boiling point**
br. *abbr* **brand, brother**
b.r. *abbr* **bills receivable**
bra [brɑ] *s* (coll) portasenos *m,* sostén *m*
brace [bres] *s* riostra; berbiquí *m;* **braces** (Brit) tirantes *mpl* || *tr* arriostrar; asegurar, vigorizar; **to brace oneself** (coll) cobrar ánimo || *intr* — **to brace up** (coll) cobrar ánimo
brace and bit *s* berbiquí y barrena
bracelet ['breslɪt] *s* brazalete *m,* pulsera
bracer ['bresər] *s* (coll) trago de licor
bracing ['bresɪŋ] *adj* fortificante, tónico
bracket ['brækɪt] *s* puntal *m,* soporte *m;* ménsula, repisa; (*mark used in printing*) corchete *m;* clase *f,* categoría || *tr* acorchetar; agrupar
brackish ['brækɪʃ] *adj* salobre
brad [bræd] *s* clavito, estaquilla
brag [bræg] *s* jactancia || *v* (*pret* & *pp* **bragged;** *ger* **bragging**) *intr* jactarse

braggart ['brægərt] *s* fanfarrón *m*
braid [bred] *s* (*flat strip of cotton, silk, etc.*) cinta, galón *m;* (*something braided*) trenza || *tr* encintar, galonear; trenzar
brain [bren] *s* cerebro; **brains** cerebro, inteligencia; **to rack one's brains** devanarse los sesos || *tr* descerebrar
brain child *s* parto del ingenio
brain drain *s* (coll) éxodo de técnicos
brainless ['brenlɪs] *adj* tonto, sin seso
brain power *s* capacidad mental
brain'storm' *s* acceso de locura; (coll) confusión mental; (coll) buena idea, hallazgo
brain trust *s* grupo de peritos
brain'wash'ing *s* lavado cerebral
brain wave *s* onda encefálica; (coll) buena idea, hallazgo
brain'work' *s* trabajo intelectual
brain•y ['breni] *adj* (*comp* **-ier;** *super* **-iest**) (coll) inteligente, sesudo
braise [brez] *tr* soasar y cocer (*la carne*) a fuego lento en vasija bien tapada
brake [brek] *s* freno; (*for dressing flax*) agramadera; (*thicket*) matorral *m;* (*fern*) helecho común || *tr* frenar; agramar (*el lino o el cáñamo*)
brake band *s* cinta de freno
brake drum *s* tambor *m* de freno
brake lining *s* forro o cinta de freno
brake•man ['brekmən] *s* (*pl* **-men** [mən]) guardafrenos *m*
brake shoe *s* zapata de freno
bramble ['bræmbəl] *s* frambueso, zarza
bram•bly ['bræmbli] *adj* (*comp* **-blier;** *super* **-bliest**) zarzoso
bran [bræn] *s* afrecho, salvado
branch [bræntʃ] *s* (*of tree*) rama; (*smaller branch; branch cut from tree; of a science, etc.*) ramo; (*of vine*) sarmiento; (*of road, railroad*) ramal *m;* (*of candlestick, river, etc.*) brazo; (*of a store, bank*) sucursal *f* || *intr* ramificarse; **to branch out** extender sus actividades
branch line *s* ramal *m,* línea de empalme
branch office *s* sucursal *f*
brand [brænd] *s* (*kind, make*) marca; (*trademark*) marca de fábrica; (*branding iron*) hierro de marcar; (*mark stamped with hot iron*) hierro; (*dishonor*) tizón *m* || *tr* poner marca de fábrica en; herrar con hierro candente; tiznar (*la reputación de una persona*); **to brand as** tildar de
brandied ['brændid] *adj* macerado en aguardiente
branding iron *s* hierro de marcar
brandish ['brændɪʃ] *tr* blandear
brand'-new' *adj* nuevecito, flamante
bran•dy ['brændi] *s* (*pl* **-dies**) aguardiente *m*
brash [bræʃ] *adj* atrevido, impetuoso; descarado, respondón || *s* acceso, ataque *m*
brass [bræs] o [brɑs] *s* latón *m;* (*in army and navy*) (slang) los mandamases; (coll) descaro; **brasses** (mus) cobres *mpl*
brass band *s* banda, charanga
brass hat *s* (slang) espadón *m,* mandamás *m*
brassière [brə'zɪr] *s* portasenos *m,* sostén *m*
brass knuckles *s* llave inglesa, bóxer *m*
brass tack *s* clavito dorado de tapicería; **to get down to brass tacks** (coll) entrar en materia
brass winds *spl* (mus) cobres *mpl,* instrumentos músicos de metal
brass•y ['bræsi] o ['brɑsi] *adj* (*comp* **-ier;** *super* **-iest**) hecho de latón; metálico; descarado
brat [bræt] *s* rapaz *m,* mocoso, braguillas *m*
brava•do [brə'vɑdo] *s* (*pl* **-does** o **-dos**) bravata
brave [brev] *adj* bravo, valiente || *s* valiente *m;* guerrero indio norteamericano || *tr* hacer frente a, arrostrar; desafiar, retar
bravery ['brevəri] *s* bravura, valor *m*
bra•vo ['brɑvo] *interj* ¡bravo! || *s* (*pl* **-vos**) bravo
brawl [brɔl] *s* pendencia, reyerta; alboroto || *intr* armar pendencia; alborotar
brawler ['brɔlər] *s* pendenciero; alborotador *m*
brawn [brɔn] *s* fuerza musculosa
brawn•y ['brɔni] *adj* (*comp* **-ier;** *super* **-iest**) fornido, musculoso
bray [bre] *s* rebuzno || *intr* rebuznar
braze [brez] *s* soldadura de latón || *tr* soldar con latón; cubrir de latón; adornar con latón
brazen ['brezən] *adj* de latón; descarado || *tr* — **to brazen through** llevar a cabo descaradamente
brazier ['breʒər] *s* brasero
Brazil [brə'zɪl] *s* el Brasil
Brazilian [brə'zɪljən] *adj & s* brasileño
Brazil nut *s* castaña de Pará
breach [britʃ] *s* (*opening*) abertura; (*in a wall*) brecha; abuso, violación || *tr* abrir brecha en
breach of faith *s* falta de fidelidad
breach of peace *s* perturbación del orden público
breach of promise *s* incumplimiento de la palabra de matrimonio
breach of trust *s* abuso de confianza
bread [brɛd] *s* pan *m* || *tr* empanar
bread and butter *s* pan *m* con mantequilla; (coll) pan de cada día
bread crumbs *spl* pan rallado
breaded ['brɛdɪd] *adj* empanado
bread line *s* cola del pan
breadth [brɛdθ] *s* anchura; alcance *m,* extensión; (*e.g., of judgment*) amplitud *f*
bread'win'ner *s* sostén *m* de la familia
break [brek] *s* rompimiento; interrupción; intervalo, pausa; (*split*) hendidura, grieta; (*in prices*) baja; (*in clouds*) claro; (*from jail*) evasión, huída; (*among friends*) ruptura; (*luck, good or bad*) (slang) suerte *f;* (slang) disparate *m;* **to give someone a break** abrirle a uno la puerta || *v* (*pret* **broke** [brok]; *pp* **broken**) *tr*

romper, quebrar; cambiar (*un billete*); comunicar (*una mala noticia*); suspender (*relaciones*); faltar a (*la palabra*); batir (*un récord*); cortar (*un circuito*); quebrantar (*un testamento; un hábito*); romper (*una ley*); levantar (*el campo*); (mil) degradar; **to break in** forzar (*una puerta*); **to break open** abrir por la fuerza || *intr* romperse, quebrarse; reventar; aclarar (*el tiempo*); bajar (*los precios*); quebrantarse (*la salud*); **to break down** perder la salud; prorrumpir en llanto; **to break even** salir sin ganar ni perder; **to break in** entrar por fuerza; irrumpir en; **to break loose** desprenderse; escaparse; desbocarse (*un caballo*); desencadenarse (*una tempestad*); **to break out** estallar, declararse; (*in laughter, weeping*) romper; (*on the skin*) brotar granos; **to break through** abrirse paso; abrir paso por entre; **to break up** desmenuzarse; levantarse (*una reunión*); **to break with** romper con

breakable [ˈbrekəbəl] *adj* rompible

breakage [ˈbrekɪdʒ] *s* estropicio; indemnización por objetos rotos

break′down′ *s* mal éxito; avería, pana; (*in health*) colapso; (*in negotiations*) ruptura; análisis *m*

breaker [ˈbrekər] *s* cachón *m*, rompiente *m*

breakfast [ˈbrɛkfəst] *s* desayuno || *intr* desayunar

breakfast food *s* cereal *m* para el desayuno

break′neck′ *adj* vertiginoso; **at breakneck speed** a mata caballo

break of day *s* alba, amanecer *m*

break′through′ *s* (mil) brecha, ruptura; (fig) descubrimiento sensacional

break′up′ *s* disolución, dispersión; desplome *m*; (*in health*) postración

break′wa′ter *s* rompeolas *m*, escollera

breast [brɛst] *s* pecho, seno; (*of fowl*) pechuga; (*of garment*) pechera; **to make a clean breast of it** confesarlo todo

breast′bone′ *s* esternón *m*; (*of fowl*) quilla

breast drill *s* berbiquí *m* de pecho

breast′pin′ *s* alfiler *m* de pecho

breast stroke *s* brazada de pecho

breath [brɛθ] *s* aliento, respiración; **out of breath** sin aliento; **short of breath** corto de resuello; **to gasp for breath** respirar anhelosamente; **under one's breath** por lo bajo, en voz baja

breathe [brið] *tr* respirar; **to breathe one's last** dar el último suspiro || *intr* respirar; **to breathe freely** cobrar aliento; **to breathe in** aspirar; **to breathe out** espirar

breathing spell *s* respiro, rato de descanso

breathless [ˈbrɛθlɪs] *adj* falto de aliento, jadeante; intenso, vivo; sin aliento

breath′tak′ing *adj* conmovedor, imponente

breech [britʃ] *s* culata, recámara; **breeches** [ˈbrɪtʃɪz] calzones *mpl*; (coll) pantalones *mpl*; **to wear the breeches** (coll) calzarse los pantalones

breed [brid] *s* casta, raza; clase *f*, especie *f* || *v* (*pret & pp* **bred** [brɛd]) *tr* criar || *intr* criar; criarse

breeder [ˈbridər] *s* (*of animals*) criador *m*; (*animal*) reproductor *m*

breeding [ˈbridɪŋ] *s* cría; crianza, modales *mpl*; **bad breeding** mala crianza; **good breeding** buena crianza

breeze [briz] *s* brisa

breez·y [ˈbrizi] *adj* (*comp* **-ier**; *super* **-iest**) airoso; animado, vivo; (coll) desenvuelto, vivaracho

brevi·ty [ˈbrɛvɪti] *s* (*pl* **-ties**) brevedad

brew [bru] *s* calderada de cerveza; mezcla || *tr* fabricar (*cerveza*); preparar (*té*); (fig) tramar, urdir || *intr* amenazar (*una tormenta*)

brewer [ˈbru·ər] *s* cervecero

brewer's yeast *s* levadura de cerveza

brewer·y [ˈbru·əri] *s* (*pl* **-ies**) cervecería, fábrica de cerveza

bribe [braɪb] *s* soborno || *tr* sobornar

briber·y [ˈbraɪbəri] *s* (*pl* **-ies**) soborno

bric-a-brac [ˈbrɪkə,bræk] *s* chucherías, curiosidades *fpl*

brick [brɪk] *s* ladrillo; (coll) buen sujeto || *tr* enladrillar

brick′bat′ *s* pedazo de ladrillo; (coll) palabra hiriente

brick ice cream *s* queso helado, helado al corte

brickkiln [ˈbrɪk,kɪl] *s* horno de ladrillero

bricklayer [ˈbrɪk,le·ər] *s* ladrillador *m*

brick′yard′ *s* ladrillal *m*

bridal [ˈbraɪdəl] *adj* nupcial; de novia

bridal wreath *s* corona nupcial

bride [braɪd] *s* desposada, novia

bride′groom′ *s* desposado, novio

bridesmaid [ˈbraɪdz,med] *s* madrina de boda

bridge [brɪdʒ] *s* puente *m*; (*of nose*) caballete *m*; (*card game*) bridge *m* || *tr* tender un puente sobre; salvar (*un obstáculo*); colmar, llenar (*un vacío*)

bridge′head′ *s* (mil) cabeza de puente

bridle [ˈbraɪdəl] *s* brida || *tr* embridar || *intr* engallarse, erguirse

bridle path *s* camino de herradura

brief [brif] *adj* breve, corto, conciso || *s* resumen *m*; (law) escrito; **in brief** en resumen || *tr* resumir; dar consejos anticipados a; dar informes a

brief case *s* cartera

brier [ˈbraɪ·ər] *s* zarza; brezo blanco

brig [brɪg] *s* (naut) bergantín *m*; prisión en buque de guerra

brigade [brɪˈged] *s* brigada

brigadier [,brɪgəˈdɪr] *s* general *m* de brigada

brigand [ˈbrɪgənd] *s* bandolero

brigantine [ˈbrɪgən,tin] o [ˈbrɪgən,taɪn] *s* (naut) bergantín *m* goleta

bright [braɪt] *adj* brillante; (*e.g., day*) claro; (*color*) subido; listo, inteligente, despierto; (*idea, thought*) luminoso; (*disposition*) alegre, vivo

brighten ['braɪtən] *tr* abrillantar; alegrar, avivar || *intr* avivarse; alegrarse; despejarse (*el cielo*)
bright lights *spl* luces *fpl* brillantes; (aut) faros o luces de carretera
brilliance ['brɪljəns] o **brilliancy** ['brɪljənsi] *s* brillantez *f*, brillo
brilliant ['brɪljənt] *adj* brillante
brim [brɪm] *s* borde *m;* (*of hat*) ala
brim'stone' *s* azufre *m*
brine [braɪn] *s* salmuera, agua salobre
bring [brɪŋ] *v* (*pret & pp* **brought** [brɔt]) *tr* traer; llevar; **to bring about** efectuar; **to bring back** devolver; **to bring down** abatir; **to bring forth** sacar a luz; **to bring in** traer a colación; servir (*una comida*); introducir, presentar; **to bring into play** poner en juego; **to bring on** causar, producir; **to bring out** sacar; presentar al público; **to bring suit** poner pleito; **to bring to** sacar de un desmayo; **to bring together** reunir; confrontar; reconciliar; **to bring to pass** efectuar, llevar a cabo; **to bring up** arrimar (*p.ej., una silla*); educar, criar; traer a colación; **to bring upon oneself** atraerse (*un infortunio*)
bringing-up ['brɪŋɪŋ'ʌp] *s* educación, crianza
brink [brɪŋk] *s* borde *m,* margen *m;* **on the brink of** al borde de
brisk [brɪsk] *adj* animado, vivo, vivaz
bristle ['brɪsəl] *s* cerda || *intr* erizarse, encresparse; (*to be visibly annoyed*) encresparse
bris•tly ['brɪsli] *adj* (*comp* **-tlier;** *super* **-tliest**) cerdoso, erizado
Britannic [brɪ'tænɪk] *adj* británico
British ['brɪtɪʃ] *adj* británico || **the British** los britanos
Britisher ['brɪtɪʃər] *s* britano
Briton ['brɪtən] *s* britano
Brittany ['brɪtəni] *s* Bretaña
brittle ['brɪtəl] *adj* quebradizo, frágil
bro. *abbr* **brother**
broach [brotʃ] *s* (*skewer*) asador *m,* espetón *m;* (*ornamental pin*) broche *m,* prendedero || *tr* sacar a colación
broad [brɔd] *adj* ancho; liberal, tolerante; (*day, noon, etc.*) pleno
broad'cast' *s* radiodifusión; audición, programa radiotelefónico || *v* (*pret & pp* **-cast**) *tr* difundir, esparcir || (*pret & pp* **-cast** o **-casted**) *tr* radiodifundir, radiar, emitir
broadcasting station *s* emisora, estación de radiodifusión
broad'cloth' *s* paño fino
broaden ['brɔdən] *tr* ensanchar || *intr* ensancharse
broad'loom' *adj* tejido en telar ancho y en color sólido
broad-minded ['brɔd'maɪndɪd] *adj* tolerante, de amplias miras
broad-shouldered ['brɔd'ʃoldərd] *adj* ancho de espaldas
broad'side' *s* (naut) costado; (naut) andanada; (coll) torrente *m* de injurias
broad'sword' *s* espada ancha
brocade [bro'ked] *s* brocado
broccoli ['brɑkəli] *s* brécol *m,* brécoles *mpl*
brochure [bro'ʃʊr] *s* folleto
brogue [brog] *s* acento irlandés
broil [brɔɪl] *tr* asar a la parrilla || *intr* asarse
broiler ['brɔɪlər] *s* parrilla; pollo para asar a la parrilla
broken ['brokən] *adj* roto, quebrado; agotado; amansado; (*accent*) chapurrado; suelto
bro'ken-down' *adj* abatido; descompuesto; destartalado
broken-hearted ['brokən'hɑrtɪd] *adj* abrumado por el dolor
broker ['brokər] *s* corredor *m*
brokerage ['brokərɪdʒ] *s* corretaje *m*
bromide ['bromaɪd] *s* bromuro; (slang) trivialidad
bromine ['bromin] *s* bromo
bronchitis [brɑŋ'kaɪtɪs] *s* bronquitis *f*
bron•co ['brɑŋko] *s* (*pl* **-cos**) potro cerril
bron'co•bust'er *s* domador *m* de potros; vaquero
bronze [brɑnz] *adj* bronceado || *s* bronce *m* || *tr* broncear || *intr* broncearse
brooch [brotʃ] o [brutʃ] *s* alfiler *m* de pecho, prendedero, pasador *m*
brood [brud] *s* cría; nidada; casta, raza || *tr* empollar || *intr* enclocar; **to brood on** meditar con preocupación
brook [brʊk] *s* arroyo || *tr* — **to brook no** no tolerar, no aguantar
broom [brum] o [brʊm] *s* escoba; (bot) hiniesta
broom'corn' *s* sorgo
broom'stick' *s* palo de escoba
bros. *abbr* **brothers**
broth [brɔθ] o [brɑθ] *s* caldo
brothel ['brɑθəl] o ['brɑðəl] *s* burdel *m*
brother ['brʌðər] *s* hermano
brotherhood ['brʌðər,hʊd] *s* hermandad
broth'er-in-law' *s* (*pl* **brothers-in-law**) cuñado, hermano político; (*husband of one's wife's or husband's sister*) concuñado
brotherly ['brʌðərli] *adj* fraternal
brow [braʊ] *s* (*forehead*) frente *f;* (*eyebrow*) ceja; **to knit one's brow** fruncir las cejas
brow'beat' *v* (*pret* **-beat;** *pp* **beaten**) *tr* intimidar con mirada ceñuda
brown [braʊn] *adj* pardo, castaño, moreno; (*race*) cobrizo; tostado del sol || *s* castaño, moreno || *tr* poner moreno; tostar, quemar, broncear; (culin) dorar
brownish ['braʊnɪʃ] *adj* que tira a moreno
brown study *s* absorción, pensamiento profundo, ensimismamlento
brown sugar *s* azúcar terciado
browse [braʊz] *intr* (*to nibble at twigs*) ramonear; (*to graze*) pacer; hojear un libro ociosamente; **to browse about** o **around** curiosear
bruise [bruz] *s* contusión, magulladura

|| *tr* contundir, magullar || *intr* contundirse, magullarse
brunet [bru'nɛt] *adj* moreno || *s* moreno (*hombre moreno*)
brunette [bru'nɛt] *s* morena (*mujer morena*)
brunt [brʌnt] *s* fuerza, choque *m*, empuje *m;* (*e.g., of a battle*) peso, (lo) más reñido
brush [brʌʃ] *s* brocha, cepillo, escobilla; (*stroke*) brochada; (*light touch*) roce *m;* (*brief encounter*) encuentro, escaramuza; (*growth of bushes*) maleza; (elec) escobilla || *tr* acepillar; (*to graze*) rozar; **to brush aside** echar a un lado || *intr* pasar ligeramente; **to brush up on** repasar
brush'-off' *s* (slang) desaire *m;* **to give the brush-off to** (slang) despedir noramala
brush'wood' *s* broza, ramojo
brusque [brʌsk] *adj* brusco, rudo
brusqueness ['brʌsknɪs] *s* brusquedad
Brussels ['brʌsəlz] *s* Bruselas
Brussels sprouts *spl* bretones *mpl*, col *f* de Bruselas
brutal ['brutəl] *adj* brutal, bestial
brutali·ty [bru'tælɪti] *s* (*pl* **-ties**) brutalidad, crueldad
brute [brut] *adj* bruto; (*force*) inconsciente, ciego || *s* bruto
brutish ['brutɪʃ] *adj* abrutado, estúpido
bu. *abbr* **bushel**
bubble ['bʌbəl] *s* burbuja; ampolla; ilusión, quimera || *intr* burbujear; **to bubble over** desbordar, rebosar
buck [bʌk] *s* (*goat*) cabrón *m;* (*deer*) gamo; (*rabbit*) conejo; (*of a horse*) corveta, encorvada; (*youth*) pisaverde *m;* (slang) dólar *m;* **to pass the buck** (coll) echar la carga a otro || *tr* hacer frente a, resistir a; (*to butt*) acornear, topetar; colar (*la ropa*); **to buck up** (coll) alentar, animar || *intr* botarse, encorvarse; **to buck against** embestir contra
bucket ['bʌkɪt] *s* balde *m*, cubo; (*of a well*) pozal *m;* **to kick the bucket** (slang) estirar la pata, liar el petate
bucket seat *s* baquet *m*
buckle ['bʌkəl] *s* hebilla; (*bend, bulge*) alabeo, pandeo || *tr* abrochar con hebilla || *intr* (*to bend, bulge*) alabearse, pandear; **to buckle down to** (coll) dedicarse con empeño a
buck private *s* (slang) soldado raso
buckram ['bʌkrəm] *s* zangala; (bb) bocací *m*, bucarán *m*
buck'saw' *s* sierra de bastidor
buck'shot' *s* postas
buck'tooth' *s* (*pl* **-teeth**) diente *m* saliente
buck'wheat' *s* alforfón *m*, trigo sarraceno
bud [bʌd] *s* botón *m*, brote *m;* **to nip in the bud** cortar de raíz || *v* (*pret & pp* **budded;** *ger* **budding**) *intr* abotonar, brotar
bud·dy ['bʌdi] *s* (*pl* **-dies**) (coll) camarada *m;* (coll) muchachito
budge [bʌdʒ] *tr* mover || *intr* moverse
budget ['bʌdʒɪt] *s* presupuesto || *tr* presuponer, presupuestar
budgetary ['bʌdʒɪ,tɛri] *adj* presupuestario
buff [bʌf] *adj* de ante || *s* (*leather*) ante *m;* color *m* de ante; chaqueta de ante; rueda pulidora; (coll) piel desnuda; aficionado || *tr* dar color de ante a; pulimentar
buffa·lo ['bʌfə,lo] *s* (*pl* **-loes** o **-los**) búfalo || *tr* (slang) intimidar
buffer ['bʌfər] *s* amortiguador *m* de choques; tope *m*, paragolpes *m;* pulidor *m*
buffer state *s* estado tapón
buffet [bʊ'fe] *s* (*piece of furniture*) aparador *m;* restaurante *m* de estación || ['bʌfɪt] *tr* abofetear, golpear, pegar
buffet car [bʊ'fe] *s* coche *m* bar
buffet lunch [bʊ'fe] *s* servicio de bufet
buffet supper [bʊ'fe] *s* ambigú *m*, bufet *m*
buffoon [bə'fun] *s* bufón *m*, payaso
buffoner·y [bə'funəri] *s* (*pl* **-ies**) bufonada, chocarrería
bug [bʌg] *s* insecto, bicho, sabandija; microbio; (*bedbug*) (Brit) chinche *f;* (coll) defecto; (slang) micrófono escondido; (slang) loco; (slang) entusiasta *mf* || *v* (*pret & pp* **bugged;** *ger* **bugging**) *tr* (slang) esconder un micrófono en
bug'bear' *s* espantajo; aversión
bug·gy ['bʌgi] *adj* (*comp* **-gier;** *super* **-giest**) infestado de bichos; (slang) loco || *s* (*pl* **-gies**) calesa
bug'house' *adj* (slang) loco || *s* (slang) manicomio, casa de locos
bugle ['bjugəl] *s* corneta
bugle call *s* toque *m* de corneta
bugler ['bjuglər] *s* corneta *m*
build [bɪld] *s* forma, hechura, figura; (*of human being*) talle *m* || *v* (*pret & pp* **built** [bɪlt]) *tr* construir, edificar; componer; establecer, fundar; crearse (*p.ej., una clientela*)
builder ['bɪldər] *s* constructor *m;* aparejador *m*, maestro de obras
building ['bɪldɪŋ] *s* construcción; edificio; (*one of several in a group*) pabellón *m*
building and loan association *s* sociedad *f* de crédito para la construcción
building lot *s* solar *m*
building site *s* terreno para construir
building trades *spl* oficios de edificación
build'-up' *s* acumulación, formación; (coll) propaganda anticipada
built'in' *adj* integrante, incorporado, empotrado
built'-up' *adj* armado, montado; (*land*) aglomerado
bulb [bʌlb] *s* (*of plant*) bulbo; (*of thermometer*) bola, cubeta; (*of syringe*) pera; (*of electric light*) ampolla, bombilla
Bulgaria [bʌl'gɛrɪ·ə] *s* Bulgaria
Bulgarian [bʌl'gɛrɪ·ən] *adj & s* búlgaro
bulge [bʌldʒ] *s* protuberancia, bulto, bombeo; **to get the bulge on** (coll)

llevar la ventaja a || *intr* hacer bulto, bombearse
bulk [bʌlk] *s* bulto, volumen *m;* (*main mass*) grueso; **in bulk** a granel || *intr* abultar, hacer bulto; tener importancia
bulk'head' *s* mamparo; tabique hermético
bulk·y ['bʌlki] *adj* (*comp* **-ier;** *super* **-iest**) abultado, voluminoso, grueso
bull [bʊl] *s* toro; (*in stockmarket*) alcista *m;* (*papal document*) bula; disparate *m;* **to take the bull by the horns** asir al toro por las astas || *tr* — **to bull the market** jugar al alza
bull'dog' *s* dogo
bulldoze ['bʊl,doz] *tr* coaccionar, intimidar con amenazas
bulldozer ['bʊl,dozər] *s* explanadora de empuje, empujatierra
bullet ['bʊlɪt] *s* bala
bulletin ['bʊlətɪn] *s* boletín *m;* comunicado; (*of a school*) anuario
bulletin board *s* tablilla
bul'let·proof' *adj* a prueba de balas, blindado
bull'fight' *s* corrida de toros
bull'fight'er *s* torero
bull'fight'ing *adj* torero || *s* toreo
bull'finch' *s* (orn) camachuelo
bull'frog' *s* rana toro
bull-headed ['bʊl,hɛdɪd] *adj* obstinado, terco
bullion ['bʊljən] *s* oro en barras, plata en barras; (*twisted fringe*) entorchado
bullish ['bʊlɪʃ] *adj* obstinado; (*market*) en alza; (*speculator*) alcista; optimista
bullock ['bʊlək] *s* buey *m*
bull'pen' *s* (taur) toril *m;* (*jail*) (coll) prevención
bull'ring' *s* plaza de toros
bull's-eye ['bʊlz,aɪ] *s* (*of a target*) diana; (archit, meteor, naut) ojo de buey; **to hit the bull's-eye** hacer diana
bul·ly ['bʊli] *adj* (coll) excelente, magnífico || *s* (*pl* **-lies**) matón *m,* valentón *m* || *v* (*pret & pp* **-lied**) *tr* intimidar, maltratar
bulrush ['bʊl,rʌʃ] *s* junco; junco de laguna; (*Typha*) anea, espadaña; (Bib) papiro
bulwark ['bʊlwərk] *s* baluarte *m* || *tr* abaluartar; defender, proteger
bum [bʌm] *s* (slang) holgazán *m;* (slang) vagabundo; (slang) mendigo || *v* (*pret & pp* **bummed;** *ger* **bumming**) *tr* (slang) mendigar || *intr* holgazanear; (slang) vagabundear; (slang) mendigar
bumblebee ['bʌmbəl,bi] *s* abejorro
bump [bʌmp] *s* (*collision*) topetón *m;* (*shake*) sacudida; (*on falling*) batacazo; (*of plane in rough air*) rebote *m;* (*swelling*) hinchazón *f,* chichón *m;* protuberancia || *tr* dar contra, topar; (*to bruise*) abollar || *intr* chocar; dar sacudidas; **to bump into** tropezar con; encontrarse con
bumper ['bʌmpər] *adj* (coll) abundante, grande || *s* tope *m,* paratopes *m;* (aut) amortiguador *m,* parachoques *m;* vaso lleno
bumpkin ['bʌmpkɪn] *s* patán *m,* palurdo
bumptious ['bʌmpʃəs] *adj* engreído, presuntuoso
bump·y ['bʌmpi] *adj* (*comp* **-ier;** *super* **-iest**) (*ground*) desigual, áspero; (*air*) agitado
bun [bʌn] *s* buñuelo, bollo; (*of hair*) castaña
bunch [bʌntʃ] *s* manojo, puñado; (*of grapes, bananas, etc.*) racimo; (*of flowers*) ramillete *m;* (*of people*) grupo || *tr* agrupar, juntar || *intr* agruparse; arracimarse
bundle ['bʌndəl] *s* atado, bulto, lío, paquete *m;* (*of papers*) legajo; (*of wood*) haz *m* || *tr* atar, liar, empaquetar, envolver; **to bundle off** despedir precipitadamente; **to bundle up** arropar || *intr* — **to bundle up** arroparse
bung [bʌŋ] *s* bitoque *m,* tapón *m*
bungalow ['bʌŋgə,lo] *s* bungalow *m,* casa de una sola planta
bung'hole' *s* piquera, boca de tonel
bungle ['bʌŋgəl] *s* chapucería || *tr & intr* chapucear
bungler ['bʌŋglər] *s* chapucero
bungling ['bʌŋglɪŋ] *adj* chapucero || *s* chapucería
bunion ['bʌnjən] *s* juanete *m*
bunk [bʌŋk] *s* tarima; (slang) palabrería vana, música celestial
bunker ['bʌŋkər] *s* carbonera; (mil) fortín *m*
bun·ny ['bʌni] *s* (*pl* **-nies**) conejito
bunting ['bʌntɪŋ] *s* banderas colgadas como adorno; (*of a ship*) empavesado; (orn) gorrión triguero
buoy [bɔɪ] o ['bu·i] *s* boya; boya salvavidas, guindola || *tr* — **to buoy up** mantener a flote; animar, alentar
buoyancy ['bɔɪ·ənsi] o ['bujənsi] *s* flotación; alegría, animación
buoyant ['bɔɪ·ənt] o ['bujənt] *adj* boyante; alegre, animado
bur [bʌr] *s* erizo, vilano
burble ['bʌrbəl] *s* burbujeo || *intr* burbujear
burden ['bʌrdən] *s* carga; (*of a speech*) tema *m;* (*of a poem*) estribillo || *tr* cargar; agobiar, gravar
burden of proof *s* peso de la prueba
burdensome ['bʌrdənsəm] *adj* gravoso, oneroso
burdock ['bʌrdɑk] *s* bardana, cadillo
bureau ['bjʊro] *s* cómoda; despacho, oficina; departamento, negociado
bureaucra·cy [bjʊ'rɑkrəsi] *s* (*pl* **-cies**) burocracia
bureaucrat ['bjʊrə,kræt] *s* burócrata *mf*
bureaucratic [,bjʊrə'krætɪk] *adj* burocrático
burgess ['bʌrdʒɪs] *s* burgués *m,* ciudadano; alcalde *m* de un pueblo o villa
burglar ['bʌrglər] *s* escalador *m*
burglar alarm *s* alarma de ladrones

bur'glar·proof' *adj* a prueba de escaladores
burglar·y ['bʌrgləri] *s* (*pl* **-ies**) robo con escalamiento
Burgundian [bər'gʌndɪ·ən] *adj* & *s* borgoñón *m*
Burgundy ['bʌrgəndi] *s* la Borgoña; (*wine*) borgoña *m*
burial ['bɛrɪ·əl] *s* entierro
burial ground *s* cementerio
burlap ['bʌrlæp] *s* arpillera
burlesque [bər'lɛsk] *adj* burlesco, festivo || *s* parodia || *tr* parodiar
burlesque show *s* espectáculo de bailes y cantos groseros, music-hall *m*
bur·ly ['bʌrli] *adj* (*comp* **-lier;** *super* **-liest**) fornido, corpulento, membrudo
Burma ['bʌrmə] *s* Birmania
Bur·mese [bər'miz] *adj* birmano || *s* (*pl* **-mese**) birmano
burn [bʌrn] *s* quemadura, quemazón *f* || *v* (*pret* & *pp* **burned** o **burnt** [bʌrnt]) *tr* quemar || *intr* quemar, quemarse; estar encendido (*p.ej., un faro*); **to burn out** quemarse (*un fusible*); fundirse (*una bombilla*); **to burn within** requemarse
burner ['bʌrnər] *s* (*of furnace*) quemador *m;* (*of gas fixture or lamp*) mechero
burning ['bʌrnɪŋ] *adj* ardiente || *s* quema, incendio
burning question *s* cuestión palpitante
burnish ['bʌrnɪʃ] *s* bruñido || *tr* bruñir || *intr* bruñirse
burnoose [bər'nus] *s* albornoz *m*
burnt almond [bʌrnt] *s* almendra tostada
burr [bʌr] *s* (*of plant*) erizo; (*of cut in metal*) rebaba
burrow ['bʌro] *s* madriguera, conejera || *tr* hacer madrigueras en; socavar || *intr* amadrigarse; esconderse
bursar ['bʌrsər] *s* tesorero universitario
burst [bʌrst] *s* explosión, reventón *m,* estallido; (*of machine gun*) ráfaga; salida brusca || *v* (*pret* & *pp* **burst**) *tr* reventar || *intr* reventar, reventarse; partirse (*el corazón*); **to burst into** irrumpir en (*un cuarto*); desatarse en (*amenazas*); prorrumpir en (*lágrimas*); **to burst out crying** deshacerse en lágrimas; **to burst with laughter** reventar de risa
bur·y ['bɛri] *v* (*pret* & *pp* **-ied**) *tr* enterrar; **to be buried in thought** estar absorto en meditación; **to bury the hatchet** hacer la paz, echar pelillos a la mar
burying ground *s* cementerio
bus. *abbr* **business**
bus [bʌs] *s* (*pl* **busses** o **buses**) autobús *m* || *tr* llevar en un autobús
bus boy *s* ayudante *m* de camarero
bus·by ['bʌzbi] *s* (*pl* **-bies**) morrión *m* de húsar, colbac *m*
bush [bʊʃ] *s* arbusto; (*scrubby growth*) matorral *m,* monte *m;* **to beat about the bush** andar con rodeos
bushel ['bʊʃəl] *s* medida para áridos (*35,23 litros en E.U.A. y 36,35 litros en Inglaterra*)
bushing ['bʊʃɪŋ] *s* buje *m,* forro
bush·y ['bʊʃi] *adj* (*comp* **-ier;** *super* **-iest**) arbustivo; peludo, lanudo; espeso
business ['bɪznɪs] *adj* comercial, de negocios || *s* negocio, comercio; (*company, concern*) empresa; (*job, employment*) empleo, oficio; (*matter*) asunto, cuestión; (*duty*) obligación; (*right*) derecho; **on business** por negocios; **to have no business to** no tener derecho a; **to make it one's business to** proponerse; **to mean business** (coll) obrar en serio, hablar en serio; **to mind one's own business** no meterse en lo que no le importa a uno; **to send about one's business** mandar a paseo
business district *s* barrio comercial
businesslike ['bɪznɪs,laɪk] *adj* práctico, sistemático, serio
business·man ['bɪznɪs,mæn] *s* (*pl* **-men** [,mɛn]) comerciante *m,* hombre *m* de negocios
business suit *s* traje *m* de calle
bus·man ['bʌsmən] *s* (*pl* **-men** [mən]) conductor *m* de autobús
buss [bʌs] *s* (coll) beso sonado || *tr* (coll) dar besos sonados a || *intr* (coll) dar besos sonados; (coll) darse besos sonados
bust [bʌst] *s* busto; (*of woman*) pecho; (slang) fracaso; (slang) borrachera || *tr* (slang) reventar, romper; (slang) arruinar; (slang) golpear, pegar || *intr* (slang) reventar; (slang) fracasar
buster ['bʌstər] *s* muchachito
bustle ['bʌsəl] *s* (*of woman's dress*) polisón *m;* alboroto, bullicio || *intr* ajetrearse, menearse
bus·y ['bɪzi] *adj* (*comp* **-ier;** *super* **-iest**) ocupado; (*e.g., street*) concurrido; (*meddling*) intruso, entremetido || *v* (*pret* & *pp* **-ied**) *tr* ocupar; **to busy oneself with** ocuparse de
busybod·y ['bɪzɪ,badi] *s* (*pl* **-ies**) entremetido, fisgón *m*
busy signal *s* (telp) señal *f* de ocupado
but [bʌt] *adv* sólo, solamente, no . . . más que; **but for** a no ser por; **but little** muy poco || *prep* excepto, salvo; **all but** casi || *conj* pero; sino, p.ej., **nobody came but John** no vino sino Juan
butcher ['bʊtʃər] *s* carnicero || *tr* matar (*reses para el consumo*); dar muerte a; (*to bungle*) chapucear
butcher knife *s* cuchilla de carnicero
butcher shop *s* carnicería
butcher·y ['bʊtʃəri] *s* (*pl* **-ies**) (*slaughterhouse*) matadero; (*wanton slaughter*) matanza, carnicería
butler ['bʌtlər] *s* despensero, mayordomo
butt [bʌt] *s* (*of gun*) culata; (*of cigaret*) colilla, punta; (*of horned animal*) cabezada, topetada, topetón *m;* (*target*) blanco; hazmerreír *m;* (*large*

cask) pipa || *tr* topar, topetar; acornear || *intr* dar cabezadas; **to butt against** confinar con; **to butt in** (slang) entremeterse
butter [ˈbʌtər] *s* mantequilla || *tr* untar con mantequilla; **to butter up** (coll) adular, lisonjear
but′ter•cup′ *s* botón *m* de oro
butter dish *s* mantequillera
but′ter•fly′ *s* (*pl* **-flies**) mariposa
butter knife *s* cuchillo mantequillero
but′ter•milk′ *s* leche *f* de manteca
butter sauce *s* mantequilla fundida
but′ter•scotch′ *s* bombón *m* escocés, bombón hecho con azúcar terciado y mantequilla
buttocks [ˈbʌtəks] *spl* nalgas
button [ˈbʌtən] *s* botón *m* || *tr* abotonar, abrocharse
but′ton•hole′ *s* ojal *m* || *tr* detener con conversación
but′ton•hook′ *s* abotonador *m*
but′ton•wood′ tree *s* plátano de occidente
buttress [ˈbʌtrɪs] *s* contrafuerte *m;* (fig) apoyo, sostén *m* || *tr* estribar; (fig) apoyar, sostener
butt weld *s* soldadura a tope
buxom [ˈbʌksəm] *adj* rolliza, frescachona
buy [baɪ] *s* (coll) compra; (*bargain*) (coll) ganga || *v* (*pret & pp* **bought** [bɔt]) *tr* comprar; **to buy back** recomprar; **to buy off** comprar, sobornar; **to buy out** comprar la parte de (*un socio*); **to buy up** acaparar
buyer [ˈbaɪ•ər] *s* comprador *m*
buzz [bʌz] *s* zumbido || *intr* zumbar; **to buzz about** ajetrearse, cazcalear
buzzard [ˈbʌzərd] *s* alfaneque *m*
buzz bomb *s* bomba volante
buzzer [ˈbʌzər] *s* zumbador *m*
buzz saw *s* sierra circular
bx. *abbr* **box**
by [baɪ] *adv* cerca; a un lado; **by and by** luego || *prep* por; cerca de, al lado de; (*not later than*) para; **by far** con mucho; **by the way** de paso; a propósito
by-and-by [ˈbaɪ•əndˈbaɪ] *s* porvenir *m*
bye-bye [ˈbaɪˈbaɪ] *s* mu *f;* **to go bye-bye** ir a la mu || *interj* (coll) ¡adiosito!; (*to a child*) ¡ro ro!
bygone [ˈbaɪˌgɔn] o [ˈbaɪˌgɑn] *adj* pasado || *s* pasado; **let bygones be bygones** olvidemos lo pasado
bylaw [ˈbaɪˌlɔ] *s* reglamento, estatuto
bypass [ˈbaɪˌpæs] o [ˈbaɪˌpɑs] *s* desviación; tubo de paso || *tr* desviar; (*a difficulty*) eludir
by′-prod′uct *s* subproducto, derivado
bystander [ˈbaɪˌstændər] *s* asistente *mf,* circunstante *mf*
byway [ˈbaɪˌwe] *s* camino apartado
byword [ˈbaɪˌwʌrd] *s* objeto de oprobio; refrán *m,* muletilla; apodo
Byzantine [ˈbɪzənˌtin] o [bɪˈzæntin] *adj & s* bizantino
Byzantium [bɪˈzænʃɪ•əm] o [bɪˈzæntɪ•əm] *s* Bizancio

C

C, c [si] tercera letra del alfabeto inglés
c. *abbr* **cent, center, centimeter**
C. *abbr* **centigrade, Congress, Court**
cab [kæb] *s* coche *m* de plaza o de punto; taxi *m;* (*of a truck*) casilla
cabaret [ˌkæbəˈre] *s* cabaret *m*
cabbage [ˈkæbɪdʒ] *s* col *f,* berza
cab driver *s* cochero de plaza; taxista *mf*
cabin [ˈkæbɪn] *s* (*hut, cottage*) cabaña; (aer) cabina; (naut) camarote *m*
cabin boy *s* mozo de cámara
cabinet [ˈkæbɪnɪt] *s* (*piece of furniture for displaying objects*) escaparate *m,* vitrina; (*for a radio*) caja, mueble *m;* (*closet*) armario; (*private room; ministry of a government*) gabinete *m*
cab′inet•ma′ker *s* ebanista *m*
cab′inet•ma′king *s* ebanistería
cable [ˈkebəl] *adj* cablegráfico || *s* cable *m;* cablegrama *m* || *tr & intr* cablegrafiar
cable address *s* dirección cablegráfica
cable car *s* tranvía *m* de tracción por cable
cablegram [ˈkebəlˌgræm] *s* cablegrama *m*
caboose [kəˈbus] *s* (rr) furgón de cola
cab′stand′ *s* punto de coches, punto de taxis
cache [kæʃ] *s* escondrijo; víveres escondidos || *tr* depositar en un escondrijo; ocultar
cachet [kæˈʃe] *s* sello
cackle [ˈkækəl] *s* (*of a hen*) cacareo; (*idle talk*) charla || *intr* cacarear; charlar
cac•tus [ˈkæktəs] *s* (*pl* **-tuses** o **-ti** [taɪ]) cacto
cad [kæd] *s* sinvergüenza *mf*
cadaver [kəˈdævər] *s* cadáver *m*
cadaverous [kəˈdævərəs] *adj* cadavérico
caddie [ˈkædi] *s* caddie *m* (*muchacho que lleva los utensilios en el juego de golf*) || *intr* servir de caddie
cadence [ˈkedəns] *s* cadencia
cadet [kəˈdɛt] *s* hermano menor, hijo menor; (*student at military school*) cadete *m*
cadmium [ˈkædmɪ•əm] *s* cadmio
cadre [ˈkædri] *s* (mil) cuadro
Caesar [ˈsizər] *s* César *m*

café [kæ'fe] *s* bar *m,* cabaret *m;* restaurante *m*
café society *s* gente *f* del mundo elegante que frecuenta los cabarets de moda
cafeteria [ˌkæfə'tɪrɪ·ə] *s* cafetería
cage [kedʒ] *s* jaula || *tr* enjaular
cageling ['kedʒlɪŋ] *s* pájaro enjaulado
ca·gey ['kedʒi] *adj* (*comp* **-gier;** *super* **-giest**) (coll) astuto
cahoots [kə'huts] *s* — **to be in cahoots** (slang) confabularse (*dos o más personas*); **to go cahoots** (slang) entrar por partes iguales
Cain [ken] *s* Caín *m;* **to raise Cain** (slang) armar camorra
Cairo ['kaɪro] *s* El Cairo
caisson ['kesən] *s* cajón *m* de aire comprimido, esclusa de aire
cajole [kə'dʒol] *tr* adular, lisonjear, halagar
cajoler·y [kə'dʒoləri] *s* (*pl* **-ies**) adulación, lisonja, halago
cake [kek] *s* pastel *m,* bollo; (*small cake*) pastelillo; (*sponge cake*) bizcocho; (*of fish*) fritada; (*of earth*) terrón *m;* (*of soap*) pan *m,* pastilla; (*of ice*) témpano; **to take the cake** (coll) ser el colmo || *intr* apelmazarse, aterronarse
calabash ['kæləˌbæʃ] *s* calabacera; (*fruit*) calabaza
calamitous [kə'læmɪtəs] *adj* calamitoso
calami·ty [kə'læmɪti] *s* (*pl* **-ties**) calamidad
calci·fy ['kælsɪˌfaɪ] *v* (*pret & pp* **-fied**) calcificar || *intr* calcificarse
calcium ['kælsɪ·əm] *s* calcio
calculate ['kælkjəˌlet] *tr* calcular; (*to reckon*) (coll) calcular || *intr* calcular; **to calculate on** contar con
calculating ['kælkjəˌletɪŋ] *adj* de calcular; astuto, intrigante
calculating machine *s* calculadora, máquina de calcular
calcu·lus ['kælkjələs] *s* (*pl* **-luses** o **-li** [ˌlaɪ]) (math, pathol) cálculo
caldron ['kɔldrən] *s* calderón *m*
calendar ['kæləndər] *s* calendario, almanaque *m*
calf [kæf] o [kɑf] *s* (*pl* **calves** [kævz] o [kɑvz]) ternero; (*of the leg*) pantorrilla
calf'skin' *s* becerro, becerrillo
caliber ['kælɪbər] *s* calibre *m*
calibrate ['kælɪˌbret] *tr* calibrar
cali·co ['kælɪˌko] *s* (*pl* **-coes** o **-cos**) calicó *m,* indiana
California [ˌkælɪ'fɔrnɪ·ə] *s* California
calipers ['kælɪpərz] *spl* calibrador *m,* compás *m* de calibres
caliph ['kelɪf] o ['kælɪf] *s* califa *m*
caliphate ['kælɪˌfet] *s* califato
calisthenic [ˌkælɪs'θɛnɪk] *adj* calisténico || **calisthenics** *spl* calistenia
calk [kɔk] *tr* calafatear
calking ['kɔkɪŋ] *s* calafateo
call [kɔl] *s* llamada; visita; (*of a boat or airplane*) escala; vocación; **within call** al alcance de la voz || *tr* llamar; convocar (*p.ej., una huelga*); **to call back** mandar volver; **to call down** (coll) reprender, regañar; **to call in** hacer entrar; (*from circulation*) retirar; **to call off** aplazar, suspender; **to call out** llamar (*a uno*) que salga; **to call together** convocar, reunir; **to call up** llamar por teléfono; evocar, recordar || *intr* llamar, gritar; hacer una visita; (naut) hacer escala; **to call on** acudir a; visitar; **to call out** gritar; **to go calling** ir de visitas
calla lily ['kælə] *s* cala, lirio de agua
call bell *s* timbre *m* de llamada
call'boy' *s* (*in a hotel*) botones *m;* (theat) traspunte *m*
caller ['kɔlər] *s* visitante *mf*
call girl *s* chica de cita
calling ['kɔlɪŋ] *s* profesión, vocación
calling card *s* tarjeta de visita
calliope [kə'laɪ·əpi] o ['kælɪ·op] *s* (mus) órgano de vapor || **Calliope** [kə'laɪ·əpi] *s* Calíope *f*
call number *s* número de teléfono; (*of a book*) número de clasificación
callous ['kæləs] *adj* calloso; (fig) duro, insensible
call to arms *s* — **to sound the call to arms** (mil) batir o tocar a llamada
call to the colors *s* (mil) llamada a filas
callus ['kæləs] *s* callo
calm [kɑm] *adj* tranquilo, quieto; (*sea*) bonancible || *s* tranquilidad, calma || *tr* tranquilizar, calmar || *intr* — **to calm down** tranquilizarse, calmarse; abonanzar, calmar (*el viento, el tiempo*)
calmness ['kɑmnɪs] *s* tranquilidad, calma
calorie ['kæləri] *s* caloría
calum·ny ['kæləmni] *s* (*pl* **-nies**) calumnia
calva·ry ['kælvəri] *s* (*pl* **-ries**) (*at the entrance to a town*) humilladero || **Calvary** *s* Calvario
calyp·so [kə'lɪpso] *s* (*pl* **-sos**) calipso || **Calypso** *s* Calipso *f*
cam [kæm] *s* leva
cambric ['kembrɪk] *s* batista
camel ['kæməl] *s* camello
came·o ['kæmɪ·o] *s* (*pl* **-os**) camafeo
camera ['kæmərə] *s* cámara fotográfica, máquina fotográfica
camera·man ['kæmərəˌmæn] *s* (*pl* **-men** [ˌmɛn]) camarógrafo, tomavistas *m*
camomile ['kæməˌmaɪl] *s* manzanilla
camouflage ['kæməˌflɑʒ] *s* camuflaje *m* || *tr* camuflar
camp [kæmp] *s* campamento || *intr* acampar
campaign [kæm'pen] *s* campaña || *intr* hacer campaña
campaigner [kæm'penər] *s* propagandista *mf;* veterano
camp'fire' *s* hoguera de campamento
camphor ['kæmfər] *s* alcanfor *m*
camp'stool' *s* silla de tijera, catrecillo
campus ['kæmpəs] *s* terrenos, recinto (*de la universidad*)
cam'shaft' *s* árbol *m* de levas
can [kæn] *s* bote *m,* envase *m,* lata || *v* (*pret & pp* **canned;** *ger* **canning**) *tr* envasar, enlatar || *v* (*pret & cond*

could) *v aux* **he can come tomorrow** puede venir mañana; **can you swim?** ¿sabe Vd. nadar?
Canada [ˈkænədə] *s* el Canadá
Canadian [kəˈnedɪ·ən] *adj & s* canadiense
canal [kəˈnæl] *s* canal *m*
canar•y [kəˈnɛri] *s* (*pl* **-ies**) canario ‖ **Canaries** *spl* Canarias
can•cel [ˈkænsəl] (*pret & pp* **-celed** o **-celled;** *ger* **-celing** o **-celling**) *tr* cancelar, eliminar, suprimir; matasellar, obliterar (*sellos de correo*)
canceler [ˈkænsələr] *s* matasellos *m*
cancellation [ˌkænsəˈleʃən] *s* cancelación, eliminación, supresión; (*of stamps*) obliteración
cancer [ˈkænsər] *s* cáncer *m*
cancerous [ˈkænsərəs] *adj* canceroso
candela•brum [ˌkændəˈlebrəm] *s* (*pl* **-bra** [brə] o **-brums**) candelabro
candid [ˈkændɪd] *adj* franco, sincero; imparcial
candida•cy [ˈkændɪdəsi] *s* (*pl* **-cies**) candidatura
candidate [ˈkændɪˌdet] *s* candidato; (*for a degree*) graduando
candid camera *s* cámara indiscreta
candle [ˈkændəl] *s* bujía, candela, vela
can′dle•hold′er *s* candelero
can′dle•light′ *s* luz *f* de vela; crepúsculo
candle power *s* bujía
can′dle•stick′ *s* palmatoria
candor [ˈkændər] *s* franqueza, sinceridad; imparcialidad
can•dy [ˈkændi] *s* (*pl* **-dies**) bombón *m,* confite *m,* dulce *m;* dulces *mpl* ‖ *v* (*pret & pp* **-died**) *tr* almibarar, confitar, garapiñar ‖ *intr* almibararse
candy box *s* bombonera, confitera
candy store *s* confitería, dulcería
cane [ken] *s* (*plant; stem*) caña; (*walking stick*) bastón *m;* (*for chair seats*) junco, mimbre *m,* rejilla
cane seat *s* asiento de rejilla
cane sugar *s* azúcar *m* de caña
canine [ˈkenaɪn] *adj* canino ‖ *s* (*tooth*) canino; perro
canned goods *spl* conservas alimenticias
canner•y [ˈkænəri] *s* (*pl* **-ies**) conservera, fábrica de conservas
cannibal [ˈkænɪbəl] *adj & s* caníbal *mf*
canning [ˈkænɪŋ] *adj* conservero ‖ *s* conservería
cannon [ˈkænən] *s* cañón *m;* cañones
cannonade [ˌkænəˈned] *s* cañoneo ‖ *tr* cañonear
cannon ball *s* bala de cañón
cannon fodder *s* carne *f* de cañón
can•ny [ˈkæni] *adj* (*comp* **-nier;** *super* **-niest**) cauteloso, cuerdo; astuto
canoe [kəˈnu] *s* canoa
canoeist [kəˈnu·ɪst] *s* canoero
canon [ˈkænən] *s* canon *m;* (*priest*) canónigo
canonical [kəˈnɑnɪkəl] *adj* canónico; aceptado, auténtico, establecido ‖
canonicals *spl* vestiduras sacerdotales
canonize [ˈkænəˌnaɪz] *tr* canonizar
canon law *s* cánones *mpl,* derecho canónico
canon•ry [ˈkænənri] *s* (*pl* **-ries**) canonjía
can opener [ˈopənər] *s* abrelatas *m*
cano•py [ˈkænəpi] *s* (*pl* **-pies**) dosel *m,* pabellón *m;* (*over an entrance*) marquesina; (*for electrical fixtures*) campana
canopy of heaven *s* bóveda celeste
cant [kænt] *s* hipocresía; jerga, jerigonza
cantaloupe [ˈkæntəˌlop] *s* cantalupo
cantankerous [kænˈtæŋkərəs] *adj* de mal genio, pendenciero
canteen [kænˈtin] *s* (*shop*) cantina; (*water flask*) cantimplora; (mil) centro de recreo
canter [ˈkæntər] *s* medio galope ‖ *intr* ir a medio galope
canticle [ˈkæntɪkəl] *s* cántico
cantilever [ˈkæntɪˌlivər] *adj* voladizo ‖ *s* viga voladiza
cantle [ˈkæntəl] *s* arzón trasero
canton [kænˈtɑn] *tr* acantonar
cantonment [kænˈtɑnmənt] *s* acantonamiento
cantor [ˈkæntər] o [ˈkæntɔr] *s* chantre *m;* (*in a synagogue*) cantor *m* principal
canvas [ˈkænvəs] *s* cañamazo, lona; (naut) vela, lona; (*painting*) lienzo; **under canvas** (mil) en tiendas; (naut) con las velas izadas
canvass [ˈkænvəs] *s* pesquisa, escrutinio; (*of votes*) solicitación ‖ *tr* escrutar, solicitar; discutir detenidamente
canyon [ˈkænjən] *s* cañón *m*
cap. *abbr* **capital, capitalize**
cap [kæp] *s* gorra, gorra de visera; (*of academic costume*) birrete *m;* (*of bottle*) cápsula; (*e.g., of a fountain pen*) capuchón *m* ‖ *v* (*pret & pp* **capped;** *ger* **capping**) *tr* cubrir con gorra; capsular (*una botella*); **to cap the climax** ser el colmo
capabili•ty [ˌkepəˈbɪlɪti] *s* (*pl* **-ties**) habilidad, capacidad
capable [ˈkepəbəl] *adj* hábil, capaz
capacious [kəˈpeʃəs] *adj* espacioso, capaz
capaci•ty [kəˈpæsɪti] *s* (*pl* **-ties**) (*room, space; ability, aptitude*) capacidad; (*status, function*) calidad; **in the capacity of** en calidad de
cap and bells *spl* caperuza de bufón; cetro de la locura
cap and gown *s* birrete y toga
caparison [kəˈpærɪsən] *s* caparazón *m* ‖ *tr* engualdrapar
cape [kep] *s* cabo, promontorio; (*garment*) capa, esclavina
Cape Colony *s* la Colonia del Cabo
Cape Horn *s* el Cabo de Hornos
Cape of Good Hope *s* Cabo de Buena Esperanza
caper [ˈkepər] *s* (*gay jump*) cabriola; (*prank*) travesura; **to cut capers** dar

cabriolas; hacer travesuras || *intr* cabriolear; retozar
Cape'town' o **Cape Town** *s* El Cabo, la Ciudad del Cabo
cape'work' *s* (taur) suerte *f* de capa, lance *m*
capital ['kæpɪtəl] *adj* capital || *s* (*money*) capital *m;* (*city*) capital *f;* (*top of a column*) capitel *m;* **to make capital out of** sacar beneficio de
capitalism ['kæpɪtə,lɪzəm] *s* capitalismo
capitalize ['kæpɪtə,laɪz] *tr* escribir con mayúscula; capitalizar || *intr* — **to capitalize on** aprovecharse de
capital letter *s* letra mayúscula
capitol ['kæpɪtəl] *s* capitolio
capitulate [kə'pɪtʃə,let] *intr* capitular
capon ['kepɑn] *s* capón *m*
caprice [kə'pris] *s* capricho, antojo; veleidad
capricious [kə'prɪʃəs] *adj* caprichoso, antojadizo
Capricorn ['kæprɪ,kɔrn] *s* Capricornio
capsize ['kæpsaɪz] *tr* volcar || *intr* volcar; tumbar, zozobrar (*un barco*)
capstan ['kæpstən] *s* cabrestante *m*
cap'stone' *s* coronamiento
capsule ['kæpsəl] *s* cápsula
Capt. *abbr* **Captain**
captain ['kæptən] *s* capitán *m* || *tr* capitanear
captain·cy ['kæptənsi] *s* (*pl* **-cies**) capitanía
caption ['kæpʃən] *s* título; (*in a movie*) subtítulo
captivate ['kæptɪ,vet] *tr* cautivar, encantar
captive ['kæptɪv] *adj & s* cautivo
captivi·ty [kæp'tɪvɪti] *s* (*pl* **-ties**) cautividad, cautiverio
captor ['kæptər] *s* aprenhensor *m*
capture ['kæptʃər] *s* apresamiento, captura; (*of a stronghold*) toma || *tr* apresar, capturar; tomar (*una plaza*); captar (*p.ej., la atención de una persona*)
Capuchin nun ['kæpjʊtʃɪn] o ['kæpjʊʃɪn] *s* capuchina
car [kɑr] *s* coche *m;* (*of an elevator*) caja, carro
carafe [kə'ræf] *s* garrafa
caramel ['kærəməl] o ['kɑrməl] *s* (*burnt sugar*) caramelo; bombón *m* de caramelo
carat ['kærət] *s* quilate *m*
caravan ['kærə,væn] *s* caravana
caravansa·ry [,kærə'vænsəri] *s* (*pl* **-ries**) caravanera
caraway ['kærə,we] *s* alcaravea
car'barn' *s* cochera de tranvías
carbide ['kɑrbaɪd] *s* carburo
carbine ['kɑrbaɪn] *s* carabina
carbolic acid [kɑr'bɑlɪk] *s* ácido carbólico
carbon ['kɑrbən] *s* (*chemical element*) carbono; (*pole of arc light or battery*) carbón *m;* papel *m* carbón; (*in auto cylinders*) carbonilla
carbon copy *s* copia al carbón
carbon dioxide *s* dióxido de carbono
carbon monoxide *s* óxido de carbono, monóxido de carbono
carbon paper *s* papel *m* carbón
car'boy' *s* bombona, garrafón *m*
carbuncle ['kɑrbʌŋkəl] *s* (*stone*) carbunclo, carbúnculo; (pathol) carbunclo, carbunco
carburetor ['kɑrbə,retər] o ['kɑrbjə,retər] *s* carburador *m*
car caller *s* avisacoches *m*
carcass ['kɑrkəs] *s* res muerta, cadáver *m*
card [kɑrd] *s* tarjeta; (*for playing games*) naipe *m,* carta; (*for filing*) ficha; (*person*) (coll) sujeto, tipo
card'board' *s* cartón *m*
cardboard binding *s* encuadernación en pasta
card case *s* tarjetero
card catalogue *s* catálogo de fichas
cardiac ['kɑrdɪ,æk] *adj* cardíaco || *s* (*medicine; sufferer*) cardíaco
cardigan ['kɑrdɪgən] *s* albornoz *m,* rebeca
cardinal ['kɑrdɪnəl] *adj* cardinal; purpurado || *s* (*prelate; bird*) cardenal *m;* número cardinal
card index *s* fichero, tarjetero
card party *s* tertulia de baraja
card'sharp' *s* fullero, tahur *m*
card trick *s* truco de naipes
care [kɛr] *s* (*worry*) inquietud, ansiedad; (*watchful attention*) esmero; (*charge*) cargo, custodia; **care of** suplicada en casa de; **to take care of oneself** cuidarse || *intr* inquietarse, preocuparse; **to care for** cuidar de; amar, querer; **to care to** tener ganas de
careen [kə'rin] *intr* inclinarse; mecerse precipitadamente
career [kə'rɪr] *adj* de carrera || *s* carrera
care'free' *adj* despreocupado, libre de cuidados
careful ['kɛrfəl] *adj* (*acting with care*) cuidadoso; (*done with care*) esmerado; **to be careful to** cuidarse de
careless ['kɛrlɪs] *adj* descuidado, negligente
carelessness ['kɛrlɪsnɪs] *s* descuido, negligencia
caress [kə'rɛs] *s* caricia || *tr* acariciar || *intr* acariciarse
caretaker ['kɛr,tekər] *s* curador *m,* guardián *m,* custodio
care'worn' *adj* fatigado, rendido
car'fare' *s* pasaje *m* de tranvía o autobús
car·go ['kɑrgo] *s* (*pl* **-goes** o **-gos**) carga, cargamento
cargo boat *s* barco de carga
Caribbean [,kærɪ'bi·ən] o [kə'rɪbɪ·ən] *adj* caribe || *s* mar *m* Caribe
caricature ['kærɪkətʃər] *s* caricatura || *tr* caricaturizar
caricaturist ['kærɪkətʃərɪst] *s* caricaturista *mf*
carillon ['kærɪ,lɑn] o [kə'rɪljən] *s* carillón *m*
car'load' *s* furgonada, vagonada

carnage ['kɑrnɪdʒ] *s* carnicería, matanza
carnation [kɑr'neʃən] *adj* encarnado || *s* clavel *m,* clavel reventón
carnival ['kɑrnɪvəl] *adj* carnavalesco || *s* (*period before Lent*) carnaval *m;* verbena, espectáculo de atracciones
car·ol ['kærəl] *s* canción alegre, villancico || *v* (*pret & pp* **-oled** o **-olled;** *ger* **-oling** o **-olling**); *tr* celebrar con villancicos || *intr* cantar con alegría
carom ['kærəm] *s* carambola || *intr* carambolear
carousal [kə'raʊzəl] *s* juerga, borrachera, jarana
carouse [kə'raʊz] *intr* emborracharse, jaranear
carp [kɑrp] *s* carpa || *intr* quejarse
carpenter ['kɑrpəntər] *s* carpintero
carpentry ['kɑrpəntri] *s* carpintería
carpet ['kɑrpɪt] *s* alfombra; **to be on the carpet** estar sobre el tapete || *tr* alfombrar
carpet sweeper *s* barredora de alfombras
car'-rent'al service *s* alquiler *m* de coches
carriage ['kærɪdʒ] *s* carruaje *m;* (*cost of carrying*) porte *m,* transporte *m;* (*bearing*) porte *m,* continente *m;* (mach) carro
carrier ['kærɪ·ər] *s* portador *m,* transportador *m;* portador de gérmenes; empresa de transportes; (*mailman*) cartero; vendedor *m* de periódicos; portaaviones *m;* (rad) onda portadora
carrier pigeon *s* paloma mensajera
carrier wave *s* (rad) onda portadora
carrion ['kærɪ·ən] *adj* carroño; inmundo || *s* carroña; inmundicia
carrot ['kærət] *s* zanahoria
carrousel [,kærə'zɛl] *s* caballitos, tiovivo
car·ry ['kæri] *v* (*pret & pp* **-ried**) *tr* llevar, portar, traer; transportar; sostener (*una carga*); **to carry away** llevarse; encantar, entusiasmar; **to carry into effect** llevar a cabo; **to carry one's point** salirse con la suya; **to carry out** llevar a cabo; **to carry the day** quedar victorioso, ganar la palma; **to carry weight** ser de peso || *intr* tener alcance; **to carry on** continuar, perseverar; (coll) travesear; (coll) comportarse de un modo escandaloso; (coll) hacer locuras
cart [kɑrt] *s* carreta, carro || *tr* carretear
carte blanche ['kɑrt'blɑnʃ] *s* carta blanca
cartel [kɑr'tɛl] *s* cartel *m*
Carthage ['kɑrθɪdʒ] *s* Cartago
Carthaginian [,kɑrθə'dʒɪnɪ·ən] *adj & s* cartaginés *m*
cart horse *s* caballo de tiro
cartilage ['kɑrtɪlɪdʒ] *s* cartílago
cartoon [kɑr'tun] *s* caricatura; (*comic strip*) tira cómica; (*film*) película de dibujos || *tr* caricaturizar
cartoonist [kɑr'tunɪst] *s* caricaturista *mf*
cartridge ['kɑrtrɪdʒ] *s* cartucho
cartridge belt *s* canana
carve [kɑrv] *tr* trinchar (*carne*); esculpir, tallar
carving knife ['kɑrvɪŋ] *s* cuchillo de trinchar
car washer *s* lavacoches *m*
caryatid [,kærɪ'ætɪd] *s* cariátide *f*
cascade [kæs'ked] *s* cascada
case [kes] *s* (*instance; form of a word*) caso; (*box*) caja; (*small container*) estuche *m;* (*for cigarettes*) pitillera; (*sheath*) vaina, funda; (law) causa, pleito; **in case** caso que; **in no case** de ninguna manera || *tr* encajonar, enfundar
casement ['kesmənt] *s* ventana batiente; bastidor *m* (*de la ventana*)
cash [kæʃ] *s* dinero contante; pago al contado; **cash on delivery** contra reembolso, pago contra entrega; **to pay cash** pagar al contado || *tr* cobrar (*un cheque el portador*); abonar, pagar (*un cheque el banco*) || *intr* — **to cash in on** (coll) sacar provecho de
cash and carry *s* pago al contado con transporte a cargo del comprador
cash'box' *s* caja
cashew ['kæʃu] *s* anacardo, marañón *m*
cashew nut *s* anacardo, nuez *f* de marañón
cashier [kæ'ʃɪr] *s* cajero || *tr* destruir; (*in the army*) degradar
cashier's check *s* cheque *m* de caja
cashier's desk *s* caja
cashmere ['kæʃmɪr] *s* casimir *m,* cachemir *m*
cash on hand *s* efectivo en caja
cash payment *s* pago al contado
cash purchase *s* compra al contado
cash register *s* caja registradora
casing ['kesɪŋ] *s* caja, cubierta, envoltura; (*of door or window*) marco, cerco; (*of tire*) cubierta; (sew) jareta
cask [kæsk] o [kɑsk] *s* casco, pipa, tonel *m*
casket ['kæskɪt] o ['kɑskɪt] *s* (*box for valuables*) cajita, joyero; (*coffin*) caja, ataúd *m*
casserole ['kæsə,rol] *s* cacerola; (*dish cooked in a casserole*) timbal *m*
cassock ['kæsək] *s* balandrán *m,* sotana
cast [kæst] o [kɑst] *s* echada, tiro; forma, molde *m;* aire *m,* semblante *m;* matiz *m,* tinte *m;* (*of actors*) reparto || *v* (*pret & pp* **cast**) *tr* echar, tirar; volver (*los ojos*); proyectar (*una sombra*); colar, fundir (*metales*); depositar (*votos*); echar (*suertes*); (theat) repartir (*papeles*); **to cast aside** desechar; **to cast loose** soltar; **to cast out** arrojar, echar fuera; despedir, desterrar || *intr* echar los dados; arrojar el sedal o el anzuelo; **to cast about** revolver proyectos; **to cast off** (naut) soltar las amarras

castanet [ˌkæstəˈnɛt] *s* castañuela, castañeta
cast′a·way′ *adj & s* proscrito, réprobo; náufrago
caste [kæst] o [kɑst] *s* casta; **to lose caste** desprestigiarse
caster [ˈkæstər] o [ˈkɑstər] *s* ruedecilla de mueble; (*cruet stand*) angarillas, vinagreras; frasco
Castile [kæsˈtil] *s* Castilla
Castile soap *s* jabón *m* de Castilla
Castilian [kæsˈtɪljən] *adj & s* castellano
casting [ˈkæstɪŋ] o [ˈkɑstɪŋ] *s* fundición, pieza fundida; (theat) reparto
casting vote *s* voto de calidad
cast iron *s* hierro colado, hierro fundido
cast′-i′ron *adj* de hierro colado; fuerte, endurecido; duro, inflexible
castle [ˈkæsəl] o [ˈkɑsəl] *s* castillo; (chess) roque *m,* torre *f* ‖ *tr & intr* (chess) enrocar
castle in Spain, castle in the air *s* castillo en el aire
cast′off′ *adj* abandonado, desechado; (*clothing*) de desecho ‖ *s* desecho
castor oil [ˈkæstər] o [kɑstər] *s* aceite *m* de ricino
castrate [ˈkæstret] *tr* capar, castrar
casual [ˈkæʒʊ·əl] *adj* casual, fortuito; descuidado, indiferente
casual·ty [ˈkæʒʊ·əlti] *s* (*pl* **-ties**) desgracia, accidente *m;* accidentado, víctima; (*in war*) baja
casualty list *s* lista de bajas
cat. *abbr* **catalogue, catechism**
cat [kæt] *s* gato; mujer maligna; **to bell the cat** ponerle cascabel al gato; **to let the cat out of the bag** revelar el secreto
catacomb [ˈkætəˌkom] *s* catacumba
Catalan [ˈkætəˌlæn] *adj & s* catalán *m*
catalogue [ˈkætəˌlɔg] o [ˈkætəˌlɑg] *s* catálogo ‖ *tr* catalogar
Catalonia [ˌkætəˈlonɪ·ə] *s* Cataluña
Catalonian [ˌkætəˈlonɪ·ən] *adj & s* catalán *m*
catapult [ˈkætəˌpʌlt] *s* catapulta ‖ *tr* catapultar
cataract [ˈkætəˌrækt] *s* catarata; (pathol) catarata
catarrh [kəˈtɑr] *s* catarro
catastrophe [kəˈtæstrəfi] *s* catástrofe *f*
cat′call′ *s* rechifla ‖ *tr & intr* rechiflar
catch [kætʃ] *s* (*of a ball*) cogida; (*of fish*) pesca; (*of a lock*) cerradera, pestillo; (*booty*) botín *m,* presa; (*fastener*) broche *m;* (*good match*) buen partido ‖ *v* (*pret & pp* **caught** [kɔt]) *tr* asir, coger, atrapar; llegar a oír; coger (*un resfriado*); (*to come upon suddenly*) sorprender; comprender; capturar (*al delincuente*); **to catch fire** encenderse; **to catch hold of** agarrar, coger; apoderarse de; **to catch it** (coll) merecerse un regaño; **to catch oneself** contenerse; recobrar el equilibrio; **to catch sight of** alcanzar a ver; **to catch up** arrebatar; coger al vuelo; (*in a mistake*) cazar ‖ *intr* pegarse (*una enfermedad*); enredarse; encenderse; **to catch at** agarrarse a, tratar de asir; **to catch on** prender en (*p.ej., un gancho*); comprender, coger el tino; **to catch up** salir del atraso; (*in one's debts*) ponerse al día; **to catch up with** emparejar con
catcher [ˈkætʃər] *s* (baseball) receptor, parador *m*
catching [ˈkætʃɪŋ] *adj* pegajoso, contagioso; atrayente, cautivador
catch question *s* pega
catchup [ˈkætʃəp] o [ˈkɛtʃəp] *s* salsa de tomate condimentada
catch′word′ *s* lema *m,* palabra de efecto; (*actor's cue*) pie *m;* (typ) reclamo
catch·y [ˈkætʃi] *adj* (*comp* **-ier;** *super* **-iest**) (*tune*) animado, vivo; (*title of a book*) impresionante, llamativo; (*question*) intrincado; (*breathing*) espasmódico
catechism [ˈkætɪˌkɪzəm] *s* catecismo
catego·ry [ˈkætɪˌgori] *s* (*pl* **-ries**) categoría
cater [ˈketər] *tr & intr* abastecer, proveer; **to cater to** proveer a
cater-cornered [ˈkætərˌkɔrnərd] *adj* diagonal ‖ *adv* diagonalmente
caterer [ˈketərər] *s* abastecedor *m,* proveedor *m* de alimentos (*esp. para fiestas caseras*)
caterpillar [ˈkætərˌpɪlər] *s* oruga
caterpillar tractor *s* tractor *m* de oruga
cat′fish′ *s* bagre *m*
cat′gut′ *s* (mus) cuerda de tripa; (surg) catgut *m*
Cath. *abbr* **Catholic**
cathartic [kəˈθɑrtɪk] *adj & s* catártico
cathedral [kəˈθidrəl] *s* catedral *f*
catheter [ˈkæθɪtər] *s* catéter *m*
catheterize [ˈkæθɪtəˌraɪz] *tr* cateterizar
cathode [ˈkæθod] *s* cátodo
catholic [ˈkæθəlɪk] *adj* católico ‖ **Catholic** *adj & s* católico
catkin [ˈkætkɪn] *s* candelilla, amento
cat nap *s* sueñecito
catnip [ˈkætnɪp] *s* hierba gatera, nébeda
cat-o'-nine-tails [ˌkætəˈnaɪnˌtelz] *s* azote *m* con nueve ramales
cat's cradle *s* juego de la cuna
cat's-paw o **catspaw** [ˈkætsˌpɔ] *s* mano *f* de gato, instrumento
catsup [ˈkætsəp] o [kɛtʃəp] *s* salsa de tomate condimentada
cat′tail′ *s* anea, espadaña; amento
cattle [ˈkætəl] *s* ganado vacuno
cattle crossing *s* paso de ganado
cattle·man [ˈkætəlmən] *s* (*pl* **-men** [mən]) *s* ganadero
cattle raising *s* ganadería
cattle ranch *s* hacienda de ganado
cat·ty [ˈkæti] *adj* (*comp* **-tier;** *super* **-tiest**) (*like a cat*) felino, gatuno; (*spiteful*) malicioso; (*gossipy*) chismoso
cat′walk′ *s* pasadero, pasarela

Caucasian [kɔ'keʒən] o [kɔ'keʃən] *adj* & *s* caucasiano, caucásico
Caucasus ['kɔkəsəs] *s* Cáucaso
caucus ['kɔkəs] *s* junta de políticos
cauliflower ['kɔlɪ,flaʊ·ər] *s* coliflor *f*
cause [kɔz] *s* causa; (*person*) causante *mf* || *tr* causar
cause'way' *s* (*highway*) calzada; calzada elevada
caustic ['kɔstɪk] *adj* cáustico
cauterize ['kɔtə,raɪz] *tr* cauterizar
caution ['kɔʃən] *s* (*carefulness*) cautela; (*warning*) advertencia, amonestación || *tr* advertir, amonestar
cautious ['kɔʃəs] *adj* cauteloso, cauto
Cav. *abbr* **Cavalry**
cavalcade [,kævəl'ked] o ['kævəl,ked] *s* cabalgata
cavalier [,kævə'lɪr] *adj* (*haughty*) altivo, desdeñoso; (*offhand*) alegre, desenvuelto, inceremonioso || *s* (*horseman*) caballero; (*lady's escort*) galán *m*
caval·ry ['kævəlri] *s* (*pl* **-ries**) caballería
cavalry·man ['kævəlrimən] *s* (*pl* **-men** [mən]) soldado de caballería
cave [kev] *s* cueva, caverna || *intr* — **to cave in** hundirse; (*to give in, yield*) (coll) ceder, rendirse
cave'-in' *s* hundimiento, derrumbe *m*, socavón *m*
cave man *s* hombre grosero
cavern ['kævərn] *s* caverna
cav·il ['kævɪl] *v* (*pret* & *pp* **-iled** o **-illed;** *ger* **-iling** o **-illing**) *intr* buscar quisquillas
cavi·ty ['kævɪti] *s* (*pl* **-ties**) cavidad; (*in a tooth*) picadura
cavort [kə'vɔrt] *intr* (coll) cabriolar
caw [kɔ] *s* graznido || *intr* graznar
cc. *abbr* **cubic centimeter**
cease [sis] *tr* parar, suspender || *intr* cesar; cesar de, dejar de + *inf*
cease'fire' *s* cese *m* de fuego || *intr* suspender hostilidades
ceaseless ['sislɪs] *adj* incesante, continuo
cedar ['sidər] *s* cedro
cede [sid] *tr* ceder, traspasar
ceiling ['silɪŋ] *s* techo, cielo raso; (aer) techo, cielo máximo
ceiling price *s* precio tope
celebrant ['sɛlɪbrənt] *s* celebrante *m*
celebrate ['sɛlɪ,bret] *tr* celebrar || *intr* (*to say mass*) celebrar; divertirse, festejarse
celebrated ['sɛlɪ,bretɪd] *adj* célebre, renombrado
celebration [,sɛlɪ'breʃən] *s* celebración; diversión, festividad
celebri·ty [sɪ'lɛbrɪti] *s* (*pl* **-ties**) (*fame; famous person*) celebridad
celery ['sɛləri] *s* apio
celestial [sɪ'lɛstʃəl] *adj* celeste, celestial
celiba·cy ['sɛlɪbəsi] *s* (*pl* **-cies**) celibato
celibate ['sɛli,bet] o ['sɛlɪbɪt] *adj* & *s* célibe *mf*
cell [sɛl] *s* (*of convent or jail*) celda; (*of honeycomb*) celdilla; (*of electric battery*) elemento; (*of plant or animal; of photoelectric device; of political group*) célula
cellar ['sɛlər] *s* sótano; (*for wine*) bodega
cellaret [,sɛlə'rɛt] *s* licorera
cell house *s* prisión celular
cellist o **'cellist** ['tʃɛlɪst] *s* violoncelista *mf*
cel·lo o **'cel·lo** ['tʃɛlo] *s* (*pl* **-los**) violoncelo
cellophane ['sɛlə,fen] *s* celofán *m*
celluloid ['sɛljə,lɔɪd] *s* celuloide *m*
Celt [sɛlt] o [kɛlt] *s* celta *mf*
Celtic ['sɛltɪk] o ['kɛltɪk] *adj* céltico || *s* (*language*) celta *m*
cement [sɪ'mɛnt] *s* cemento || *tr* revestir con cemento; (*la amistad*) consolidar
cemeter·y ['sɛmɪ,tɛri] *s* (*pl* **-ies**) cementerio
cen. *abbr* **central**
censer ['sɛnsər] *s* incensario
censor ['sɛnsər] *s* censor *m* || *tr* censurar
censure ['sɛnʃər] *s* censura || *tr* censurar
census ['sɛnsəs] *s* censo; **to take the census** levantar el censo
cent. *abbr* **centigrade, central, century**
cent [sɛnt] *s* centavo
centaur ['sɛntɔr] *s* centauro
centennial [sɛn'tɛnɪ·əl] *adj* & *s* centenario
center ['sɛntər] *adj* centrista || *s* centro || *tr* centrar
cen'ter·piece' *s* centro de mesa
center punch *s* granete *m*, punzón *m* de marcar
centigrade ['sɛntɪ,gred] *adj* centígrado
centimeter ['sɛntɪ,mitər] *s* centímetro
centipede ['sɛntɪ,pid] *s* ciempiés *m*
central ['sɛntrəl] *adj* central || *s* (telp) central *f*, central de teléfonos; (*operator*) telefonista *mf*
Central America *s* Centro América, la América Central
Central American *adj* & *mf* centroamericano
centralize ['sɛntrə,laɪz] *tr* centralizar || *intr* centralizarse
centu·ry ['sɛntʃəri] *s* (*pl* **-ries**) siglo
century plant *s* pita, maguey *m*
ceramic [sɪ'ræmɪk] *adj* cerámico
cereal ['sɪrɪ·əl] *adj* & *s* cereal *m*
ceremonious [,sɛrɪ'monɪ·əs] *adj* ceremonioso, etiquetero
ceremo·ny ['sɛrɪ,moni] *s* (*pl* **-nies**) ceremonia; **to stand on ceremony** hacer ceremonias, ser etiquetero
certain ['sʌrtən] *adj* cierto; **a certain** cierto; **for certain** por cierto
certainly ['sɛrtənli] *adj* ciertamente; (*gladly*) con mucho gusto
certain·ty ['sʌrtənti] *s* (*pl* **-ties**) certeza; **with certainty** a ciencia cierta
certificate [sər'tɪfɪkɪt] *s* certificación, certificado; (*of birth, death, etc.*) partida, fe *f*; (*document representing financial assets*) título || [sər'tɪfɪ,ket] *tr* certificar

certified public accountant ['sʌrtɪ,faɪd] *s* censor jurado de cuentas
certi·fy ['sʌrtɪ,faɪ] *v* (*pret & pp* **-fied**) *tr* certificar
cervix ['sʌrvɪks] *s* (*pl* **cervices** [sər'vaɪsiz]) cerviz *f*
cessation [sɛ'seʃən] *s* cesación
cessation of hostilities *s* suspensión de hostilidades
cesspool ['sɛs,pul] *s* pozo negro; (fig) sitio inmundo
Ceylon [sɪ'lɑn] *s* Ceilán
Ceylo·nese [,silə'niz] *adj* ceilanés || *s* (*pl* **-nese**) ceilanés *m*
cf. *abbr* **confer,** i.e., **compare**
C.F.I., c.f.i. *abbr* **cost, freight, and insurance**
cg. *abbr* **centigram**
ch. *abbr* **chapter, church**
chafe [tʃef] *s* fricción, roce *m;* desgaste *m;* irritación || *tr* (*to rub*) frotar; (*to rub and make sore*) escocer; (*to wear*) desgastar; irritar || *intr* escocerse; desgastarse; irritarse
chaff [tʃæf] o [tʃɑf] *s* barcia; paja menuda; broza, desperdicio
chafing dish ['tʃefɪŋ] *s* cocinilla, infernillo
chagrin [ʃə'grɪn] *s* desazón *f,* disgusto || *tr* desazonar, disgustar
chain [tʃen] *s* cadena || *tr* encadenar
chain gang *s* cadena de presidiarios, collera, cuerda de presos
chain reaction *s* reacción en cadena
chain'smoke' *intr* fumar un pitillo tras otro
chain store *s* empresa con una cadena de tiendas; tienda de una cadena de tiendas
chair [tʃɛr] *s* silla; (*de catedrático*) cátedra; presidencia; **to take the chair** presidir la reunión; abrir la sesión || *tr* presidir (*una reunión*)
chair lift *s* telesilla
chair·man ['tʃɛrmən] *s* (*pl* **-men** [mən]) presidente *m*
chairmanship ['tʃɛrmən,ʃɪp] *s* presidencia
chair rail *s* guardasilla
chalice ['tʃælɪs] *s* cáliz *m*
chalk [tʃɔk] *s* (*soft white limestone*) creta; (*piece used for writing*) tiza || *tr* marcar o escribir con tiza; **to chalk up** apuntar; marcar (*un tanto*)
challenge ['tʃælɪndʒ] *s* desafío; (law) recusación || *tr* desafiar; (law) recusar
chamber ['tʃembər] *s* cámara; (*of a gun*) recámara; dormitorio; **chambers** oficina de juez
chamberlain ['tʃembərlɪn] s chambelán *m*
cham'ber·maid' *s* camarera
chamber pot *s* orinal *m*
chameleon [kə'milɪ·ən] *s* camaleón *m*
chamfer ['tʃæmfər] *s* chaflán *m* || *tr* chaflanar
cham·ois ['ʃæmi] *s* (*pl* **-ois**) gamuza
champ [tʃæmp] *s* mordisco; (slang) campeón *m* || *tr & intr* mordiscar; (*el freno*) morder
champagne [ʃæm'pen] *s* champaña *m*
champion ['tʃæmpɪ·ən] *s* campeón *m* || *tr* defender
championess ['tʃæmpɪ·ənɪs] *s* campeona
championship ['tʃæmpɪ·ən,ʃɪp] *s* campeonato
chance [tʃæns] o [tʃɑns] *adj* casual, imprevisto || *s* oportunidad, ocasión; casualidad, suerte *f;* probabilidad; peligro, riesgo; **by chance** por casualidad; **to not stand a chance** no tener probabilidad de éxito; **to take a chance** probar fortuna; comprar un billete de lotería; **to take chances** probar fortuna; **to wait for a chance** esperar la oportunidad || *intr* acontecer; **to chance on** o **upon** tropezar con; **to chance to** acertar a
chancel ['tʃænsəl] o ['tʃɑnsəl] *s* entrecoro
chanceller·y ['tʃænsələri] o ['tʃɑnsələrɪ] *s* (*pl* **-ies**) cancillería
chancellor ['tʃænsələr] o ['tʃɑnsələr] *s* canciller *m*
chandelier [,ʃændə'lɪr] *s* araña de luces
change [tʃendʒ] *s* cambio, mudanza; suelto, moneda suelta; (*surplus money returned with a purchase*) vuelta; (*of clothing*) muda; **for a change** por variedad; **to keep the change** quedarse con la vuelta; || *tr* cambiar, mudar; cambiar de, mudar de; reemplazar; **to change clothes** cambiar de ropa; **to change gears** cambiar de velocidades; **to change hands** cambiar de dueño; **to change money** cambiar moneda; **to change one's mind** cambiar de parecer; **to change trains** cambiar de tren, transbordar || *intr* cambiar, mudar; corregirse
changeable ['tʃendʒəbəl] *adj* cambiable; inconstante, cambiante, mudable
change of clothing *s* muda de ropa
change of heart *s* arrepentimiento, conversión
change of life *s* cesación natural de las reglas
change of voice *s* muda
chan·nel ['tʃænəl] *s* (*body of water joining two others*) canal *m;* (*bed of river*) álveo, cauce *m;* (*means of communication*) vía; (*passage*) conducto; (*groove*) ranura, surco; (telv) canal *m;* **the Channel** el Canal de la Mancha || *v* (*pret & pp* **-neled** o **-nelled;** *ger* **-neling** o **-nelling**) *tr* acanalar; canalizar (*esfuerzos, dinero, etc.*)
chant [tʃænt] o [tʃɑnt] *s* (*song*) canción; (*song sung in a monotone*) canto || *tr & intr* cantar
chanter ['tʃæntər] o ['tʃɑntər] *s* cantor *m;* (*priest*) chantre *m*
chanticleer ['tʃæntɪ,klɪr] *s* el gallo
chaos ['ke·ɑs] *s* caos *m*
chaotic [ke'ɑtɪk] *adj* caótico
chap. *abbr* **chaplain, chapter**
chap [tʃæp] *s* (*jaw*) mandíbula; (*cheek*) mejilla; (*crack in the skin*)

grieta; chico, tipo; **chaps** zahones *mpl* || *v* (*pret & pp* **chapped;** *ger* **chapping**) *tr* agrietar, rajar || *intr* agrietarse, rajarse

chapel [ˈtʃæpəl] *s* capilla

chaperon o **chaperone** [ˈʃæpəˌron] *s* carabina, señora de compañía || *tr* acompañar (*una señora a una o más señoritas*)

chaplain [ˈtʃæplɪn] *s* capellán *m*

chaplet [ˈtʃæplɪt] *s* (*wreath for head*) guirnalda; rosario

chapter [ˈtʃæptər] *s* capítulo; (*of the Scriptures*) capítula; (*of a cathedral*) cabildo

chapter and verse *adv* con todos sus pelos y señales

char [tʃɑr] *v* (*pret & pp* **charred;** *ger* **charring**) *tr* carbonizar; (*to scorch*) socarrar

character [ˈkærɪktər] *s* carácter *m;* (*conspicuous person; person in a play or novel*) personaje *m;* (*part or role in a play*) papel *m;* (*fellow*) (coll) tipo, sujeto

characteristic [ˌkærɪktəˈrɪstɪk] *adj* característico || *s* característica

characterize [ˈkærɪktəˌraɪz] *tr* caracterizar

char'coal' *s* carbón *m* de leña; (*for sketching*) carboncillo; (*sketch*) dibujo al carbón

charcoal burner *s* (*person*) carbonero; horno para hacer carbón de leña

charge [tʃɑrdʒ] *s* (*of an explosive, of electricity, of soldiers against the enemy; responsibility*) carga; (*accusation; amount owed; recording of amount owed*) cargo; (heral) blasón *m;* (*attack*) embestida; **in charge of** a cargo de; **to reverse the charges** (telp) cargar al número llamado; **to take charge of** hacerse cargo de || *tr* cargar; cobrar (*cierto precio*); (*to order*) encargar, mandar; cargar (*un acumulador; al enemigo*); **to charge to the account of someone** cargarle a uno en cuenta; **to charge with** cargar de || *intr* embestir

charge account *s* cuenta corriente

chargé d'affaires [ʃɑrˈʒe dəˈfɛr] *s* (*pl* **chargés d'affaires**) encargado de negocios

charger [ˈtʃɑrdʒər] *s* caballo de guerra; (*of a battery*) cargador *m*

chariot [ˈtʃærɪ·ət] *s* carro romano

charioteer [ˌtʃærɪ·əˈtɪr] *s* carretero, auriga *m*

charitable [ˈtʃærɪtəbəl] *adj* caritativo

chari•ty [ˈtʃærɪti] *s* (*pl* **-ties**) caridad; asociación de beneficencia, obra pía; **charity begins at home** la caridad bien ordenada empieza por uno mismo

charity performance *s* función benéfica

charlatan [ˈʃɑrlətən] *s* charlatán *m*

charlatanism [ˈʃɑrlətənˌɪzəm] *s* charlatanismo

Charlemagne [ˈʃɑrləˌmen] *s* Carlomagno

Charles [tʃɑrlz] *s* Carlos *m*

charlotte [ˈʃɑrlət] *s* carlota || **Charlotte** *s* Carlota

charlotte russe [ˈʃɑrlət ˈrus] *s* carlota rusa

charm [tʃɑrm] *s* encanto, hechizo; (*trinket*) amuleto, dije *m* || *tr* encantar, hechizar

charming [ˈtʃɑrmɪŋ] *adj* encantador

charnel [ˈtʃɑrnəl] *adj* cadavérico, horrible || *s* carnero, osario

charnel house *s* carnero, osario

chart [tʃɑrt] *s* mapa geográfico; (naut) carta de marear; cuadro, diagrama *m* || *tr* bosquejar; **to chart a course** trazar una ruta

charter [ˈtʃɑrtər] *s* carta (de privilegio) || *tr* alquilar (*un autobús*); fletar (*un barco*)

charter member *s* socio fundador

char•woman [ˈtʃɑrˌwʊmən] *s* (*pl* **-women** [ˌwɪmɪn]) alquilona, asistenta

Charybdis [kəˈrɪbdɪs] *s* Caribdis *f*

chase [tʃes] *s* caza, persecución || *tr* cazar, perseguir; **to chase away** ahuyentar

chasm [ˈkæzəm] *s* abismo

chas•sis [ˈtʃæsi] *s* (*pl* **-sis** [siz]) chasis *m*

chaste [tʃest] *adj* casto; (*style*) castizo

chasten [ˈtʃesən] *tr* castigar, corregir

chastise [tʃæsˈtaɪz] *tr* castigar

chastity [ˈtʃæstɪti] *s* castidad

chasuble [ˈtʃæzjəbəl] *s* casulla

chat [tʃæt] *s* charla, plática || *v* (*pret & pp* **chatted;** *ger* **chatting**) *intr* charlar, platicar

chatelaine [ˈʃætəˌlen] *s* castellana

chattels [ˈtʃætəlz] *spl* bienes *mpl* muebles, enseres *mpl*

chatter [ˈtʃætər] *s* (*talk*) cháchara; (*rattling*) traqueo; (*of teeth*) castañeteo; (*of birds*) chirrido || *intr* chacharear; traquear; castañetear, dentellar (*los dientes*)

chat'ter•box' *s* charlador *m,* tarabilla

chauffeur [ˈʃofər] o [ʃoˈfʌr] *s* chófer *m*

cheap [tʃip] *adj* barato; (*charging low prices*) no carero, baratero; (*flashy*) cursi; **to feel cheap** sentirse avergonzado || *adv* barato

cheapen [ˈtʃipən] *tr* abaratar

cheapness [ˈtʃipnɪs] *s* baratura; (*flashiness*) cursilería

cheat [tʃit] *s* trampa, fraude *m;* (*person*) trampista *mf,* defraudador *m* || *tr* trampear, defraudar

check [tʃɛk] *s* (*of bank*) cheque *m;* (*for baggage*) talón *m,* contraseña; (*in a restaurant*) cuenta; (*in theater or movie*) contraseña, billete *m* de salida; (*restraint*) freno; (*to hold a door*) amortiguador *m;* (*in chess*) jaque *m;* inspección; comprobación, verificación; (*cloth*) paño a cuadros; **in check** en jaque; **to hold in check** contener, refrenar || *interj* ¡jaque! || *tr* parar súbitamente; contener, refrenar; amortiguar; facturar (*equipajes*); inspeccionar; comprobar, verificar; marcar, señalar; (*in chess*)

jaquear, dar jaque a; **to check up** comprobar, verificar || *intr* pararse súbitamente; corresponder punto por punto; **to check in** (*at a hotel*) llegar e inscribirse; **to check out** pagar la cuenta y despedirse; (slang) morir
check'book' *s* talonario (de cheques)
checker ['tʃɛkər] *s* inspector *m;* cuadro; dibujo a cuadros; (*in game of checkers*) ficha, pieza; **checkers** damas, juego de damas || *tr* marcar con cuadros; diversificar, variar
check'er·board' *s* damero, tablero
check girl *s* moza de guardarropa
checking account *s* cuenta corriente
check'mate' *s* mate *m,* jaque *m* mate || *tr* dar mate a, dar jaque mate a; (fig) derrotar completamente
check'out' *s* (*from a hotel*) salida; hora de salida; (*in a self-service retail store*) revisión y pago
checkout counter *s* mostrador *m* de revisión
check'point' *s* punto de inspección
check'rein' *s* engallador *m*
check'room' *s* guardarropa *m;* (rr) consigna, depósito de equipajes
check'up' *s* verificación rigurosa; (*of an automobile*) revisión; (med) reconocimiento general
cheek [tʃik] *s* mejilla, carrillo; (coll) descaro, frescura
cheek'bone' *s* pómulo
cheek by jowl *adv* cara a cara, en estrecha intimidad
cheek·y ['tʃiki] *adj* (*comp* **-ier;** *super* **-iest**) (coll) descarado, fresco
cheer [tʃɪr] *s* alegría, regocijo; (*shout*) viva *m,* aplauso; **what cheer?** ¿qué tal? || *tr* alegrar, animar; aplaudir, vitorear; dar la bienvenida a, con vivas y aplausos || *intr* alegrarse, animarse; **cheer up!** ¡ánimo!
cheerful ['tʃɪrfəl] *adj* alegre
cheerio ['tʃɪrɪ,o] *interj* (coll) ¡hola!, ¡qué tal!; (coll) ¡adiós!, ¡hasta la vista!
cheerless ['tʃɪrlɪs] *adj* sombrío, triste
cheese [tʃiz] *s* queso
cheese'cloth' *s* estopilla
chef [ʃɛf] *s* primer cocinero, jefe *m* de cocina
chem. *abbr* **chemical, chemist, chemistry**
chemical ['kɛmɪkəl] *adj* químico || *s* producto químico, substancia química
chemise [ʃə'miz] *s* camisa (de mujer)
chemist ['kɛmɪst] *s* químico
chemistry ['kɛmɪstri] *s* química
cherish ['tʃɛrɪʃ] *tr* acariciar; (*a hope*) abrigar, acariciar
cher·ry ['tʃɛri] *s* (*pl* **-ries**) (*fruit; color*) cereza; (*tree*) cerezo
cher·ub ['tʃɛrəb] *s* (*pl* **-ubim** [əbɪm]) querubín *m* || *s* (*pl* **-ubs**) niño angelical
chess [tʃɛs] *s* ajedrez *m*
chess'board' *s* tablero de ajedrez
chess·man ['tʃɛs,mæn] *s* (*pl* **-men** [,mɛn]) pieza de ajedrez, trebejo
chess player *s* ajedrecista *mf*
chess set *s* ajedrez *m*
chest [tʃɛst] *s* (*part of body*) pecho; (*receptacle*) cajón *m,* cofre *m;* (*piece of furniture*) cómoda
chestnut ['tʃɛsnət] *s* (*tree, wood, color*) castaño; (*fruit*) castaña
chest of drawers *s* cómoda
cheval glass [ʃə'væl] *s* psique *f*
chevalier [,ʃɛvə'lɪr] *s* caballero
chevron ['ʃɛvrən] *s* galón *m* en forma de V invertida
chew [tʃu] *s* mascadura || *tr* mascar; **to chew the rag** (slang) dar la lengua || *intr* mascar
chewing gum *s* goma de mascar, chicle *m*
chg. *abbr* **charge**
chic [ʃik] *adj* & *s* chic *m*
chicaner·y [ʃɪ'kenəri] *s* (*pl* **-ies**) triquiñuela
chick [tʃɪk] *s* pollito; (slang) polla
chicken ['tʃɪkən] *s* pollo; (*young person*) pollo; (*young girl*) polla
chicken coop *s* pollera
chicken feed *s* (coll) calderilla
chickenhearted ['tʃɪkən,hɑrtɪd] *adj* gallina
chicken pox *s* viruelas locas
chicken wire *s* alambrada, tela metálica
chick'pea' *s* garbanzo
chico·ry ['tʃɪkəri] *s* (*pl* **-ries**) achicoria
chide [tʃaɪd] *v* (*pret* **chided** o **chid** [tʃɪd]; *pp* **chided, chid** o **chidden** ['tʃɪdən]) *tr* reprender, regañar
chief [tʃif] *adj* principal || *s* jefe *m;* (*of American Indians*) cacique *m*
chief executive *s* jefe *m* del gobierno
chief justice *s* presidente *m* de sala; presidente del tribunal supremo
chiefly ['tʃifli] *adv* principalmente, mayormente
chief of staff *s* jefe *m* de estado mayor
chief of state *s* jefe *m* del estado
chieftain ['tʃiftən] *s* (*of a clan or tribe*) jefe *m;* adalid *m,* caudillo
chiffon [ʃɪ'fɑn] *s* gasa, soplillo; **chiffons** atavíos, perifollos
chiffonier [,ʃɪfə'nɪr] *s* cómoda alta
chignon ['ʃinjɑn] *s* castaña, moño
chilblain ['tʃɪl,blen] *s* sabañón *m*
child [tʃaɪld] *s* (*pl* **children** ['tʃɪldrən]) *s* (*infant, youngster*) niño; (*one's offspring*) hijo; descendiente *mf;* **with child** encinta, embarazada
child'birth' *s* alumbramiento, parto
childhood ['tʃaɪldhud] *s* niñez *f,* puericia; **from childhood** desde niño
childish ['tʃaɪldɪʃ] *adj* aniñado, pueril
childishness ['tʃaɪldɪʃnɪs] *s* puerilidad
child labor *s* trabajo de menores
childless ['tʃaɪldlɪs] *adj* sin hijos
child'like' *adj* aniñado
child's play *s* juego de niños
child welfare *s* protección a la infancia
Chile ['tʃɪli] *s* Chile *m*
Chilean ['tʃɪlɪ·ən] *adj* & *s* chileno
chili sauce ['tʃɪli] *s* ají *m,* salsa de ají
chill [tʃɪl] *adj* frío || *s* frío desapaci-

ble; (*sensation of cold*) escalofrío; (*lack of cordiality*) frialdad || *tr* enfriar || *intr* calofriarse

chill·y ['tʃɪli] *adj* (*comp* **-ier;** *super* **-iest**) (*causing shivering*) frío; (*sensitive to cold*) escalofriado, friolero; (*indifferent*) (fig) frío

chime [tʃaɪm] *s* campaneo, repique *m;* tubo sonoro; **chimes** juego de campanas || *tr & intr* campanear, repicar

chime clock *s* reloj *m* de carillón

chimera [kaɪ'mɪrə] o [kɪ'mɪrə] *s* quimera

chimney ['tʃɪmni] *s* chimenea; (*for a lamp*) tubo

chimney cap *s* caperuza

chimney flue *s* cañón *m* de chimenea

chimney pot *s* mitra, guardavientos *m*

chimney sweep *s* limpiachimeneas *m,* deshollinador *m*

chimpanzee [tʃɪm'pænzi] o [ˌtʃɪmpæn'zi] *s* chimpancé *m*

chin [tʃɪn] *s* barba, mentón *m;* **to keep one's chin up** (coll) no desanimarse || *v* (*pret & pp* **chinned;** *ger* **chinning**) *intr* (coll) charlar

china ['tʃaɪnə] *s* china, porcelana || **China** *s* China

china closet *s* chinero

China·man ['tʃaɪnəmən] *s* (*pl* **-men** [mən]) (offensive) chino

chi'na·ware' *s* porcelana, vajilla de porcelana

Chi·nese [tʃaɪ'niz] *adj* chino || *s* (*pl* **-nese**) chino

Chinese gong *s* batintín *m*

Chinese lantern *s* farolillo veneciano

Chinese puzzle *s* problema embrollado

chink [tʃɪŋk] *s* grieta, hendidura; sonido metálico

chin strap *s* barboquejo, carrillera

chintz [tʃɪnts] *s* zaraza

chip [tʃɪp] *s* astilla, brizna; (*in china*) desconchado; (*in poker*) ficha; **chip off the old block** hijo de su padre || *v* (*pret & pp* **chipped;** *ger* **chipping**) *tr* astillar (*la madera*); desconchar (*la porcelana*); **to chip in** contribuir con su cuota || *intr* astillarse; desconcharse

chipmunk ['tʃɪpˌmʌŋk] *s* ardilla listada

chipper ['tʃɪpər] *adj* (coll) alegre, jovial, vivo

chiropodist [kaɪ'rɑpədɪst] o [kɪ'rɑpədɪst] *s* quiropodista *mf*

chiropractor ['kaɪrəˌpræktər] *s* quiropráctico

chirp [tʃʌrp] *s* chirrido, gorjeo || *intr* chirriar, gorjear; hablar alegremente

chis·el ['tʃɪzəl] *s* (*for wood*) escoplo, formón *m;* (*for stone and metal*) cincel *m* || *v* (*pret & pp* **-eled** o **-elled;** *ger* **-eling** o **-elling**) *tr* escoplear; cincelar; (slang) estafar

chit-chat ['tʃɪtˌtʃæt] *s* charla, palique *m;* hablilla, chismes *mpl*

chivalric ['ʃɪvəlrɪk] o [ʃɪ'vælrɪk] *adj* caballeresco

chivalrous ['ʃɪvəlrəs] *adj* caballeroso

chivalry ['ʃɪvəlri] *s* (*knighthood*) caballería; (*gallantry, gentlemanliness*) caballerosidad

chloride ['kloraɪd] *s* cloruro

chlorine ['klorin] *s* cloro

chloroform ['kloroˌfɔrm] *s* cloroformo || *tr* cloroformizar

chlorophyll ['klorəfɪl] *s* clorofila

chock-full ['tʃɑk'fʊl] *adj* de bote en bote, colmado

chocolate ['tʃɔkəlɪt] o ['tʃɑkəlɪt] *s* chocolate *m*

choice [tʃɔɪs] *adj* escogido, selecto, superior || *s* elección, selección; lo más escogido; **to have no choice** no tener alternativa

choir [kwaɪr] *s* coro

choir'boy' *s* niño de coro, infante *m* de coro

choir desk *s* facistol *m*

choir loft *s* coro

choir'mas'ter *s* jefe *m* de coro, maestro de capilla

choke [tʃok] *s* estrangulación; (*of carburetor*) cierre *m,* obturador *m;* (elec) choque *m* || *tr* ahogar, sofocar, estrangular; obstruir, tapar; (aut) obturar; **to choke down** atragantar || *intr* sofocarse; atragantarse; **to choke on** atragantarse con

choke coil *s* (elec) bobina de reacción, choque *m*

cholera ['kɑlərə] *s* cólera *m*

choleric ['kɑlərɪk] *adj* colérico

cholesterol [kə'lɛstəˌrol] o [kə'lɛstəˌrɑl] *s* colesterol *m*

choose [tʃuz] *v* (*pret* **chose** [tʃoz]; *pp* **chosen** ['tʃozən]) *tr* escoger, elegir || *intr* — **to choose between** optar entre; **to choose to** optar por

chop [tʃɑp] *s* golpe *m* cortante; (*of meat*) chuleta; **chops** boca, labios || *v* (*pret & pp* **chopped;** *ger* **chopping**) *tr* cortar, tajar; picar (*la carne*); **to chop off** tronchar; **to chop up** desmenuzar

chop'house' *s* restaurante *m,* figón *m,* colmado

chopper ['tʃɑpər] *s* (*person*) tajador *m;* (*tool*) hacha; (*of butcher*) cortante *m;* (slang) helicóptero

chopping block *s* tajo

chop·py ['tʃɑpi] *adj* (*comp* **-pier;** *super* **-piest**) (*sea*) agitado, picado; (*wind*) variable; (*style*) cortado, inciso

chop'sticks' *spl* palillos

choral ['korəl] *adj* coral

chorale [ko'rɑl] *s* coral *m*

choral society *s* orfeón *m*

chord [kɔrd] *s* (*harmonious combination of tones*) (mus) acorde *m;* (aer, anat, geom) cuerda

chore [tʃor] *s* tarea, quehacer *m*

choreography [ˌkorɪ'ɑgrəfi] *s* coreografía

chorine [ko'rin] *s* (slang) corista, suripanta

chorus ['korəs] *s* coro; (*refrain of a song*) estribillo

chorus girl *s* corista, conjuntista

chorus man *s* corista *m,* conjuntista *m*

chowder ['tʃaʊdər] *s* estofado de almejas o pescado
Chr. *abbr* **Christian**
Christ [kraɪst] *s* Cristo
christen ['krɪsən] *tr* bautizar
Christendom ['krɪsəndəm] *s* cristiandad
christening ['krɪsənɪŋ] *s* bautismo, bautizo
Christian ['krɪstʃən] *adj* & *s* cristiano
Christianity [,krɪstʃɪ'ænɪti] *s* cristianismo
Christianize ['krɪstʃə,naɪz] *tr* cristianizar
Christian name *s* nombre *m* de pila
Christmas ['krɪsməs] *adj* navideño || *s* Navidad, Pascua de Navidad
Christmas card *s* aleluya navideña
Christmas carol *s* villancico
Christmas Eve *s* nochebuena
Christmas gift *s* aguinaldo, regalo de Navidad
Christmas tree *s* árbol *m* de Navidad
Christopher ['krɪstəfər] *s* Cristóbal *m*
chrome [krom] *adj* cromado || *s* cromo || *tr* cromar
chromium ['kromɪ·ən] *s* cromo
chro·mo ['kromo] *s* (*pl* **-mos**) (*colored picture*) cromo; (*piece of junk*) (slang) trasto
chromosome ['kromə,som] *s* cromosoma *m*
chron. *abbr* **chronological, chronology**
chronic ['krɑnɪk] *adj* crónico
chronicle ['krɑnɪkəl] *s* crónica || *tr* narrar en una crónica; narrar, contar
chronicler ['krɑnɪklər] *s* cronista *mf*
chronolo·gy [krə'nɑlədʒi] *s* (*pl* **-gies**) cronología
chronometer [krə'nɑmɪtər] *s* cronómetro
chrysanthemum [krɪ'sænθɪməm] *s* crisantemo
chub·by ['tʃʌbi] *adj* (*comp* **-bier;** *super* **-biest**) rechoncho, regordete
chuck [tʃʌk] *s* (*throw*) echada, tirada; (*under the chin*) mamola; (*of a lathe*) mandril *m* || *tr* arrojar; **to chuck under the chin** hacer la mamola a
chuckle ['tʃʌkəl] *s* risa ahogada || *intr* reírse con risa ahogada
chug [tʃʌg] *s* ruido explosivo sordo; (*of a locomotive*) resoplido || *v* (*pret* & *pp* **chugged;** *ger* **chugging**) *intr* hacer ruidos explosivos sordos, moverse con ruidos explosivos sordos
chum [tʃʌm] *s* (coll) compinche *mf;* compañero de cuarto || *v* (*pret* & *pp* **chummed;** *ger* **chumming**) *intr* (coll) ser compinche, ser compinches; (coll) compartir un cuarto
chum·my ['tʃʌmi] *adj* (*comp* **-mier;** *super* **-miest**) muy amigable, íntimo
chump [tʃʌmp] *s* tarugo, zoquete *m;* (coll) estúpido, tonto
chunk [tʃʌŋk] *s* trozo, pedazo grueso
church [tʃʌrtʃ] *s* iglesia
churchgoer ['tʃʌrtʃ,go·ər] *s* persona que frecuenta la iglesia
church·man ['tʃʌrtʃmən] *s* (*pl* **-men** [mən]) sacerdote *m,* eclesiástico; feligrés *m*
church member *s* feligrés *m*
Church of England *s* Iglesia Anglicana
church'ward'en *s* capiller *m*
church'yard' *s* patio de iglesia; cementerio
churl [tʃʌrl] *s* palurdo, patán *m*
churlish ['tʃʌrlɪʃ] *adj* palurdo, insolente
churn [tʃʌrn] *s* mantequera || *tr* mazar (*leche*); hacer (*mantequilla*) en una mantequera; agitar, revolver || *intr* revolverse
chute [ʃut] *s* cascada, salto de agua; rápidos; conducto inclinado; (*e.g., into a swimming pool*) tobogán *m;* (*e.g., for grain*) tolva; paracaídas *m*
cibori·um [sɪ'borɪ·əm] *s* (*pl* **-a** [ə]) (*canopy*) ciborio, baldaquín *m;* (*cup*) copón *m*
Cicero ['sɪsə,ro] *s* Cicerón *m*
cider ['saɪdər] *s* sidra
C.I.F., c.i.f. *abbr* **cost, insurance, and freight**
cigar [sɪ'gɑr] *s* cigarro, puro
cigar band *s* anillo de cigarro
cigar case *s* cigarrera, petaca
cigar cutter *s* cortacigarros *m*
cigaret o **cigarette** [,sɪgə'rɛt] *s* cigarrillo, pitillo
cigarette case *s* pitillera
cigarette holder *s* boquilla
cigarette lighter *s* mechero, encendedor *m* de bolsillo
cigarette paper *s* papel *m* de fumar
cigar holder *s* boquilla
cigar store *s* estanco, tabaquería
cinch [sɪntʃ] *s* (*of saddle*) cincha; (*sure grip*) (coll) agarro; (*something easy*) (slang) breva || *tr* cinchar; (coll) agarrar
cinder ['sɪndər] *s* ceniza; (*coal burning without flame*) pavesa
cinder bank *s* escorial *m*
Cinderella [,sɪndə'rɛlə] *s* la Cenicienta
cinder track *s* pista de cenizas
cinema ['sɪnəmə] *s* cine *m*
cinematograph [,sɪnə'mætə,græf] o [,sɪnə'mætə,grɑf] *s* cinematógrafo || *tr* & *intr* cinematografiar
cinnabar ['sɪnə,bɑr] *s* cinabrio
cinnamon ['sɪnəmən] *s* canela
cipher ['saɪfər] *s* cifra; cero; (*nonentity*) cero a la izquierda; (*key to a cipher*) clave *f* || *tr* cifrar; calcular
circle ['sʌrkəl] *s* círculo || *tr* circundar; dar la vuelta a; girar alrededor de
circuit ['sʌrkɪt] *s* circuito
circuit breaker *s* disyuntor *m*
circuitous [sər'kju·ɪtəs] *adj* indirecto, tortuoso
circular ['sʌrkjələr] *adj* tortuoso || *s* circular *f,* carta circular
circularize ['sʌrkjələ,raɪz] *tr* anunciar por circular; enviar circulares a
circulate ['sʌrkjə,let] *tr* & *intr* circular
circumcise ['sʌrkəm,saɪz] *tr* circuncidar

circumference [sər'kʌmfərəns] *s* circunferencia
circumflex ['sʌrkəm,flɛks] *adj* circunflejo
circumlocution [,sʌrkəmlo'kjuʃən] *s* circunlocución, circunloquio
circumnavigate [,sʌrkəm'nævɪ,get] *tr* circunnavegar
circumnavigation [,sʌrkəm,nævɪ'geʃən] *s* circunnavegación
circumscribe [,sʌrkəm'skraɪb] *tr* circunscribir
circumspect ['sʌrkəm,spɛkt] *adj* circunspecto
circumstance ['sʌrkəm,stæns] *s* circunstancia; ceremonia, ostentación; **in easy circumstances** acomodado; **under no circumstances** de ninguna manera
circumstantial [,sʌrkəm'stænʃəl] *adj* (*derived from circumstances*) circunstancial; (*detailed*) circunstanciado
circumstantial evidence *s* (law) indicios vehementes
circumstantiate [,sʌrkəm'stænʃɪ,et] *tr* apoyar con pruebas y detalles; (*to describe in detail*) circunstanciar
circumvent [,sʌrkəm'vɛnt] *tr* (*to catch by a trick*) entrampar, embaucar; (*to outwit*) burlar; (*to keep away from, get around*) evitar
circus ['sʌrkəs] *s* circo
cistern ['sɪstərn] *s* cisterna, aljibe *m*
citadel ['sɪtədəl] *s* ciudadela
citation [saɪ'teʃən] *s* (*of a text*) cita; (*before a court of law*) citación; (*for gallantry*) mención
cite [saɪt] *tr* (*to quote; to summon*) citar; (*for gallantry*) mencionar
citizen ['sɪtɪzən] *s* ciudadano; (*civilian*) paisano
citizen·ry ['sɪtɪzənri] *s* (*pl* **-ries**) conjunto de ciudadanos
citizenship ['sɪtɪzən,ʃɪp] *s* ciudadanía
citron ['sɪtrən] *s* (*fruit*) cidra; (*tree*) cidro; (*candied rind*) cidrada
citronella [,sɪtrə'nɛlə] *s* limoncillo (*Andropogon nardus*); aceite *m* de limoncillo
citrus fruit ['sɪtrəs] *s* agrios, frutas cítricas
cit·y ['sɪti] *s* (*pl* **-ies**) ciudad
city clerk *s* archivero
city council *s* ayuntamiento
city editor *s* redactor de periódico encargado de noticias locales
city fathers *spl* concejales *mpl*
city hall *s* casa consistorial
city plan *s* plano de la ciudad
city planner *s* urbanista *mf*
city planning *s* urbanismo
city room *s* redacción
cit'y-state' *s* ciudad-estado *f*
civic ['sɪvɪk] *adj* cívico || **civics** *s* estudio de los deberes y derechos del ciudadano
civies ['sɪviz] *spl* (coll) traje *m* de paisano; **in civies** (coll) de paisano
civil ['sɪvɪl] *adj* civil
civilian [sɪ'vɪljən] *adj* civil || *s* civil *mf*, paisano
civilian clothes *spl* traje *m* de paisano
civili·ty [sɪ'vɪlɪti] *s* (*pl* **-ties**) civilidad
civilization [,sɪvɪlɪ'zeʃən] *s* civilización
civilize ['sɪvɪ,laɪz] *tr* civilizar
civil servant *s* funcionario del estado
claim [klem] *s* demanda, pretensión, reclamación || *tr* demandar, pretender, reclamar; afirmar, declarar; **to claim to** + *inf* pretender + *inf*
claim check *s* comprobante *m*
clairvoyance [klɛr'vɔɪ·əns] *s* clarividencia
clairvoyant [klɛr'vɔɪ·ənt] *adj* & *s* clarividente *mf*
clam [klæm] *s* almeja; (*tight-lipped person*) (coll) chiticalla *m* || *intr* — **to clam up** (coll) callarse la boca
clamber ['klæmər] *intr* — **to clamber up** subir gateando
clamor ['klæmər] *s* clamor *m*, clamoreo || *intr* clamorear
clamorous ['klæmərəs] *adj* clamoroso
clamp [klæmp] *s* abrazadera, grapa; (*vise-like device*) mordaza || *tr* agrapar, afianzar con abrazadera; sujetar en una mordaza || *intr* — **to clamp down on** (coll) apretar los tornillos a
clan [klæn] *s* clan *m*
clandestine [klæn'dɛstɪn] *adj* clandestino
clang [klæŋ] *s* tantán *m*, sonido metálico resonante || *tr* hacer sonar fuertemente || *intr* sonar fuertemente
clank [klæŋk] *s* sonido metálico seco || *tr* hacer sonar secamente || *intr* sonar secamente
clannish ['klænɪʃ] *adj* exclusivista
clap [klæp] *s* golpe seco; (*of the hands*) palmada; (*of thunder*) estampido || *v* (*pret* & *pp* **clapped**; *ger* **clapping**) *tr* batir (*palmas*); palmotear, aplaudir; **to clap shut** cerrar de golpe || *intr* palmotear, dar palmadas
clap of thunder *s* estampido de trueno
clapper ['klæpər] *s* palmoteador *m*; (*of a bell*) badajo; (*to cause grain to slide*) tarabilla
clap'trap' *s* faramalla; (*of an actor*) latiguillo
claque [klæk] *s* (*paid clappers*) claque *f*; (*crush hat*) clac *m*
claret ['klærɪt] *s* clarete *m*
clari·fy ['klærɪ,faɪ] *v* (*pret* & *pp* **-fied**) *tr* clarificar; encolar (*el vino*)
clarinet [,klærɪ'nɛt] *s* clarinete *m*
clarion ['klærɪ·ən] *adj* claro, brillante || *s* clarín *m*
clarity ['klærɪti] *s* claridad
clash [klæʃ] *s* choque *m*, encontrón *m*; estruendo, ruido || *intr* chocar, entrechocarse
clasp [klæsp] o [klɑsp] *s* (*fastener*) abrazadera, cierre *m*; (*for, e.g., a necktie*) broche *m*; (*buckle*) hebilla; (*embrace*) abrazo; (*grip*) agarro || *tr*

abrochar; abrazar; agarrar, apretar (*la mano*); apretarse (*la mano*)
class. *abbr* **classical**
class [klæs] o [klɑs] *s* clase *f;* (slang) elegancia, buen tono || *tr* clasificar || *intr* clasificarse
class consciousness *s* sentimiento de clase
classic [ˈklæsɪk] *adj* & *s* clásico; **the classics** las obras clásicas
classical [ˈklæsɪkəl] *adj* clásico
classical scholar *s* erudito en las lenguas clásicas
classicist [ˈklæsɪsɪst] *s* clasicista *mf*
classified [ˈklæsɪˌfaɪd] *adj* clasificado; clasificado como secreto
classified ads *spl* anuncios clasificados en secciones
classi•fy [ˈklæsɪˌfaɪ] *v* (*pret* & *pp* **-fied**) *tr* clasificar
class'mate' *s* compañero de clase
class'room' *s* aula, sala de clase
class struggle *s* lucha de clases
class•y [ˈklæsi] *adj* (*comp* **-ier;** *super* **-iest**) (slang) elegante
clatter [ˈklætər] *s* estruendo confuso; algazara, gresca; (*of hoofs*) trápala || *intr* caer o moverse con estruendo confuso; hablar rápida y ruidosamente; **to clatter down the stairs** bajar la escalera ruidosamente
clause [klɔz] *s* (*article in a legal document*) cláusula; (gram) oración dependiente
clavichord [ˈklævɪˌkɔrd] *s* clavicordio
clavicle [ˈklævɪkəl] *s* clavícula
clavier [ˈklævɪ·ər] o [kləˈvɪr] *s* teclado || [kləˈvɪr] *s* instrumento musical con teclado
claw [klɔ] *s* garra, uña; (*of lobster, crab, etc.*) pinza; (*of hammer, wrench, etc.*) oreja; (coll) dedos, mano *f* || *tr* (*to clutch*) agarrar; (*to scratch*) arañar; (*to tear*) desgarrar
clay [kle] *adj* arcilloso || *s* arcilla
clay pigeon *s* pichón *m* de barro
clay pipe *s* pipa de tierra
clean [klin] *adj* limpio; distinto, neto, nítido; completo || *adv* completamente; **to come clean** (slang) confesarlo todo || *tr* limpiar; (*to tidy up*) asear; **to be cleaned out** (*of money*) (slang) quedar limpio; **to clean out** limpiar; (slang) dejar limpio || *intr* limpiarse; asearse; **to clean up** limpiarse; (coll) llevárselo todo; (*in gambling*) (slang) hacer mesa limpia; **to clean up after someone** limpiar lo que alguno ha ensuciado
clean bill of health *s* patente limpia de sanidad
cleaner [ˈklinər] *s* limpiador *m;* (*dry cleaner*) tintorero; (*preparation*) quitamanchas *m;* **to send to the cleaners** (slang) dejar limpio
cleaning [ˈklinɪŋ] *s* limpieza
cleaning fluid *s* quitamanchas *m*
cleaning woman *s* criada que hace la limpieza, alquilona
cleanliness [ˈklɛnlɪnɪs] *s* limpieza
clean•ly [ˈklɛnli] *adj* (*comp* **-lier;** *super* **-liest**) limpio (*que tiene el hábito del aseo*)
cleanse [klɛnz] *tr* limpiar, lavar, depurar
clean-shaven [ˈklinˈʃevən] *adj* lisamente afeitado
clean'up' *s* limpieza general; **to make a cleanup** (slang) hacer su pacotilla
clear [klɪr] *adj* claro; (*cloudless*) despejado; (*of guilt, debts, annoyances*) libre || *adv* claro, claramente; **clear through** de parte a parte || *tr* despejar (*un bosque*); clarificar (*lo que estaba turbio*); (*to make less dark*) aclarar; saltar por encima de; (*to prove the innocence of*) absolver; sacar (*una ganancia neta*); abonar, acreditar; liquidar (*una cuenta*); (*in the customhouse*) despachar; salvar (*un obstáculo*); levantar (*la mesa*); desmontar (*un terreno*); **to clear the way** abrir camino || *intr* clarificarse; aclararse; **to clear away** (coll) irse, desaparecer; **to clear up** abonanzarse (*el tiempo*); despejarse (*el cielo, el tiempo*)
clearance [ˈklɪrəns] *s* aclaración; abono, acreditación; (*between two objects*) espacio libre; (*in a cylinder*) espacio muerto; (com) compensación
clearance sale *s* venta de liquidación
clearing [ˈklɪrɪŋ] *s* (*in a woods*) claro; (com) compensación
clearing house *s* cámara de compensación
clear-sighted [ˈklɪrˈsaɪtɪd] *adj* clarividente, perspicaz
clear'sto'ry *s* (*pl* **-ries**) var of **clerestory**
cleat [klit] *s* abrazadera, listón *m*
cleavage [ˈklivɪdʒ] *s* división, hendidura; (fig) desunión
cleave [kliv] *v* (*pret* & *pp* **cleft** [klɛft] o **cleaved**) *tr* rajar, partir; hender (*las aguas un buque, los aires una flecha*) || *intr* adherirse, pegarse; apegarse, ser fiel
cleaver [ˈklivər] *s* cortante *m,* cuchilla de carnicero
clef [klɛf] *s* (mus) clave *f*
cleft palate [klɛft] *s* fisura del paladar
clematis [ˈklɛmətɪs] *s* clemátide *f*
clemen•cy [ˈklɛmənsi] *s* (*pl* **-cies**) clemencia; (*of the weather*) benignidad
clement [ˈklɛmənt] *adj* clemente; (*weather*) benigno
clench [klɛntʃ] *s* agarro || *tr* agarrar; apretar, cerrar (*el puño, los dientes*)
cleresto•ry [ˈklɪrˌstori] *s* (*pl* **-ries**) claraboya
cler•gy [ˈklɛrdʒi] *s* (*pl* **-gies**) clerecía, clero
clergy•man [ˈklɛrdʒimən] *s* (*pl* **-men** [mən]) clérigo, pastor *m*
cleric [ˈklɛrɪk] *s* clérigo
clerical [ˈklɛrɪkəl] *adj* (*of clergy*) clerical; (*of office work*) oficinesco || *s* clérigo, eclesiático; (*supporter of power of clergy*) clerical *m;* **clericals** (coll) hábitos clericales
clerical error *s* error *m* de pluma
clerical work *s* trabajo de oficina

clerk [klʌrk] *s* (*in a store*) dependiente *mf;* (*in an office*) oficinista *mf;* (*in a city hall*) archivero; (*in a church*) lego, seglar *m;* (*in law office, in court*) escribano
clever ['klɛvər] *adj* hábil, diestro, mañoso; inteligente
cleverness ['klɛvərnɪs] *s* habilidad, destreza, maña; inteligencia
clew [klu] *s* indicio, pista
cliché [kli'ʃe] *s* (*printing plate*) clisé *m;* (*trite expression*) cliché *m*
click [klɪk] *s* golpecito; (*of typewriter*) tecleo; (*of firearm*) piñoneo; (*of heels*) taconeo; (*of tongue*) claqueo, chasquido ‖ *tr* hacer sonar con un golpecito seco; chascar (*la lengua*); **to click the heels** taconear; cuadrarse (*un soldado*) ‖ *intr* sonar con un golpecito seco; piñonear (*el gatillo de un arma de fuego*); claquear (*la lengua*)
client ['klaɪ·ənt] *s* cliente *mf;* cliente de abogado
clientele [,klaɪ·ən'tɛl] *s* clientela
cliff [klɪf] *s* acantilado, escarpa, risco
climate ['klaɪmɪt] *s* clima *m*
climax ['klaɪmæks] *s* colmo; **to cap the climax** ser el colmo
climb [klaɪm] *s* subida, trepa ‖ *tr & intr* escalar, subir, trepar
climber ['klaɪmər] *s* trepador *m;* ambicioso de figurar; (bot) enredadera, trepadora
clinch [klɪntʃ] *s* agarro, abrazo; (*of a nail*) remache *m* ‖ *tr* afianzar, sujetar; agarrar, abrazar; apretar (*el puño*); remachar (*un clavo ya clavado*); resolver decisivamente
cling [klɪŋ] *v* (*pret & pp* **clung** [klʌŋ]) *intr* adherirse, pegarse; **to cling to** agarrarse a, asirse de
cling'stone' peach *s* albérchigo, peladillo
clinic ['klɪnɪk] *s* clínica
clinical ['klɪnɪkəl] *adj* clínico
clinical chart *s* hoja clínica
clinician [klɪ'nɪʃən] *s* clínico
clink [kliŋk] *s* tintín *m* ‖ *tr* hacer tintinear; chocar (*vasos, copas*) ‖ *intr* tintinear
clinker ['klɪŋkər] *s* escoria de hulla
clip [klɪp] *s* tijereteo, esquileo; grapa, pinza; (*to fasten papers*) sujetapapeles *m,* presilla de alambre; **at a good clip** a buen paso ‖ *v* (*pret & pp* **clipped;** *ger* **clipping**) *tr* tijeretear, esquilar; (*to fasten with a clip*) afianzar, sujetar; recortar (*p.ej., un cupón*) ‖ *intr* moverse con rapidez
clipper ['klɪpər] *s* tijera, cizalla; **clippers** maquinilla cortapelos; tijeras podadoras
clipping ['klɪpɪŋ] *s* tijereteo, esquileo; (*from a newspaper*) recorte *m*
clique [klik] *s* pandilla, corrillo ‖ *intr* — **to clique together** apandillarse
cliquish ['klikɪʃ] *adj* exclusivista
clk. *abbr* **clerk, clock**
cloak [klok] *s* capote *m;* (*disguise, excuse*) capa ‖ *tr* encapotar; disimular, encubrir
cloak-and-dagger ['klokən'dægər] *adj* de capa y espada (*dícese de duelos, espionaje, etc.*)
cloak-and-sword ['klokən'sord] *adj* de capa y espada (*dícese, p.ej., de las costumbres caballerescas*)
cloak hanger *s* cuelgacapas *m*
cloak'room' *s* guardarropa *m;* (Brit) excusado
clock [klɑk] *s* reloj *m* (de pared o de mesa); (*in a stocking*) cuadrado ‖ *tr* registrar; (sport) cronometrar
clock'mak'er *s* relojero
clock tower *s* torre *f* reloj
clock'wise' *adj & adv* en el sentido de las agujas del reloj
clock'work' *s* mecanismo de relojería; **like clockwork** como un reloj
clod [klɑd] *s* terrón *m*
clod'hop'per *s* destripaterrones *m,* quebrantaterrones *m;* **clodhoppers** zapatos fuertes de trabajo
clog [klɑg] *s* estorbo, obstáculo; (*wooden shoe*) zueco; (*dance*) zapateado; (*hobble on animal*) traba ‖ *v* (*pret & pp* **clogged;** *ger* **clogging**) *tr* atascar ‖ *intr* atascarse; bailar el zapateado
clog dance *s* zapateado
cloister ['klɔɪstər] *s* claustro ‖ *tr* enclaustrar
cloistral ['klɔɪstrəl] *adj* claustral
close [klos] *adj* cercano, próximo; casi igual; (*translation*) fiel, exacto; (*fabric*) compacto; (*weather, atmosphere*) pesado, sofocante; (*stingy*) tacaño; (*battle, race, election*) reñido; (*friend*) íntimo; (*shut in, enclosed*) cerrado; (*narrow*) estrecho ‖ *adv* cerca; **close to** cerca de ‖ [kloz] *s* fin *m,* terminación; (*of business, of stock market*) cierre *m;* **at the close of day** a la caída de la tarde; **to bring to a close** poner término a; **to come to a close** tocar a su fin ‖ *tr* cerrar; (*to cover*) tapar; (*to finish*) concluir; saldar (*una cuenta*); cerrar (*un trato*); **to close in** cerrar, encerrar; **to close ranks** cerrar las filas ‖ *intr* cerrar, cerrarse; **to close in on** cerrar con (*el enemigo*)
close call [klos] *s* (coll) escape *m* por un pelo
closed car [klozd] *s* coche cerrado, conducción interior
closed chapter *s* asunto concluído
closed season *s* veda
closed shop *s* taller agremiado
closefisted ['klos'fɪstɪd] *adj* cicatero, tacaño, manicorto
close-fitting ['klos'fɪtɪŋ] *adj* ajustado, ceñido al cuerpo
close-lipped ['klos'lɪpt] *adj* callado, reservado
closely ['klosli] *adv* de cerca; estrechamente; fielmente; atentamente
close quarters [klos] *spl* lugar muy estrecho, lugares estrechos
close shave [klos] *s* afeitado a ras; (coll) escape *m* por un pelo
closet ['klɑsɪt] *s* alacena; (*wardrobe*) armario; (*small private room*) apo-

sento, gabinete *m;* (*for keeping clothing*) guardarropa *m;* (*toilet*) retrete *m* || *tr* — **to be closeted with** encerrarse con

close-up [ˈklos ˌʌp] *s* (*moving picture*) vista de cerca; fotografía de cerca

closing [ˈklozɪŋ] *s* cerradura, cierre *m*

closing prices *spl* precios de cierre

clot [klɑt] *s* grumo, coágulo || *v* (*pret & pp* **clotted;** *ger* **clotting**) *intr* engrumecerse, coagularse

cloth [klɔθ] o [klɑθ] *s* paño, tela; ropa clerical; (*canvas, sails*) lona, trapo, vela; (*for binding books*) tela; **the cloth** la clerecía

clothe [kloð] *v* (*pret & pp* **clothed** o **clad** [klæd]) *tr* trajear, vestir; cubrir; (*e.g., with authority*) investir

clothes [kloz] o [kloθz] *spl* ropa, vestidos; ropa de cama

clothes'bas'ket *s* cesto de la ropa, cesto de la colada

clothes'brush' *s* cepillo de ropa

clothes closet *s* ropero

clothes dryer *s* secadora de ropa, secarropa

clothes hanger *s* colgador *m,* perchero

clothes'horse' *s* enjugador *m,* secarropa de travesaños

clothes'line' *s* cordel *m* para tender la ropa, tendedera

clothes'pin' *s* pinza, alfiler *m* de madera

clothes tree *s* percha

clothes wringer *s* exprimidor *m* de ropa

clothier [ˈkloðjər] *s* (*person who sells ready-made clothes*) ropero; (*dealer in cloth*) pañero

clothing [ˈkloðɪŋ] *s* ropa, vestidos, ropaje *m*

cloud [klaʊd] *s* nube *f* || *tr* anublar || *intr* — **to cloud over** anublarse

cloud bank *s* mar *m* de nubes

cloud'burst' *s* aguacero, chaparrón *m*

cloud-capped [ˈklaʊdˌkæpt] *adj* coronado de nubes

cloudless [ˈklaʊdlɪs] *adj* despejado, sin nubes

cloud of dust *s* polvareda, nube *f* de polvo

cloud•y [ˈklaʊdi] *adj* (*comp* **-ier;** *super* **-iest**) nuboso, nublado; (*muddy, turbid*) turbio; confuso, obscuro; melancólico, sombrío

clove [klov] *s* (*flower*) clavo de especia; (*spice*) clavo

clover [ˈklovər] *s* trébol *m;* **to be in clover** vivir en el lujo

clo'ver•leaf' *s* (*pl* **-leaves** [ˌlivz]) *s* cruce *m* en trébol

clove tree *s* clavero

clown [klaʊn] *s* bufón *m,* payaso; (*rustic*) patán *m* || *intr* hacer el payaso

clownish [ˈklaʊnɪʃ] *adj* bufonesco; rústico

cloy [klɔɪ] *tr* hastiar, empalagar

club [klʌb] *s* porra, clava; (*playing card*) basto, trébol *m;* club *m,* casino || *v* (*pret & pp* **clubbed;** *ger* **clubbing**) *tr* aporrear || *intr* — **to club together** unirse; formar club

club car *s* coche *m* club, coche bar

club'house' *s* casino, club *m*

club•man [ˈklʌbmən] *s* (*pl* **-men** [mən]) clubista *m*

club•woman [ˈklʌbˌwʊmən] *s* (*pl* **-women** [ˌwɪmɪn]) clubista *f*

cluck [klʌk] *s* cloqueo, clo clo || *intr* cloquear, hacer clo clo

clue [klu] *s* indicio, pista

clump [klʌmp] *s* (*of earth*) terrón *m;* (*of trees or shrubs*) grupo; pisada fuerte || *intr* — **to clump along** andar pesadamente

clum•sy [ˈklʌmzi] *adj* (*comp* **-sier;** *super* **-siest**) (*worker*) chapucero, desmañado, torpe; (*work*) chapucero, tosco, grosero

cluster [ˈklʌstər] *s* grupo; (*of grapes or other things growing or joined together*) racimo || *intr* arracimarse; **to cluster around** reunirse en torno a; **to cluster together** agruparse

clutch [klʌtʃ] *s* (*grasp, grip*) agarro, apretón *m* fuerte; (aut) embrague *m;* (aut) pedal *m* de embrague; **to fall into the clutches of** caer en las garras de; **to throw the clutch in** embragar; **to throw the clutch out** desembragar || *tr* agarrar, empuñar

clutter [ˈklʌtər] *tr* — **to clutter up** cubrir o llenar desordenadamente

cm. *abbr* **centimeter**

cml. *abbr* **commercial**

Co. *abbr* **Company, County**

coach [kotʃ] *s* coche *m,* diligencia; (aut) coche cerrado; (rr) coche de viajeros, coche ordinario *m;* (sport) entrenador *m* || *tr* aleccionar; (sport) entrenar || *intr* entrenarse

coach house *s* cochera

coaching [ˈkotʃɪŋ] *s* lecciones *fpl* particulares; (sport) entrenamiento

coach•man [ˈkotʃmən] *s* (*pl* **-men** [mən]) *s* cochero

coagulate [koˈægjəˌlet] *tr* coagular || *intr* coagularse

coal [kol] *s* carbón *m,* hulla || *tr* proveer de carbón || *intr* proveerse de carbón

coal'bin' *s* carbonera

coal bunker *s* carbonera

coal car *s* vagón carbonero

coal'deal'er *s* carbonero

coaling [ˈkolɪŋ] *adj* carbonero || *s* toma de carbón

coalition [ˌko•əˈlɪʃən] *s* unión; (*alliance between states or factions*) coalición

coal mine *s* mina de carbón

coal oil *s* aceite *m* mineral

coal scuttle *s* cubo para carbón

coal tar *s* alquitrán *m* de hulla

coal'yard' *s* carbonería

coarse [kors] *adj* (*of inferior quality*) basto, burdo; (*composed of large particles*) grueso; (*crude in manners*) grosero, rudo, vulgar

coast [kost] *s* costa; **the coast is clear** ya no hay peligro || *tr* costear || *intr*

deslizarse cuesta abajo; **to coast along** avanzar sin esfuerzo
coastal ['kostəl] *adj* costero
coaster ['kostər] *s* salvamanteles *m*
coaster brake *s* freno de contrapedal
coast guard *s* guardacostas *mpl;* guardia *m* de los guardacostas
coast guard cutter *s* escampavía de los guardacostas
coasting trade *s* cabotaje *m*
coast'land' *s* litoral *m*
coast'line' *s* línea de la costa
coast'wise' *adj* costanero ‖ *adv* a lo largo de la costa
coat [kot] *s* (*jacket*) americana, saco; (*topcoat*) abrigo, sobretodo; (*of an animal*) lana, pelo; (*of paint*) capa, mano *f* ‖ *tr* cubrir, revestir; dar una capa de pintura a
coated ['kotɪd] *adj* revestido; (*tongue*) saburroso
coat hanger *s* colgador *m*
coating ['kotɪŋ] *s* revestimiento; (*of paint*) capa; (*of plaster*) enlucido
coat of arms *s* escudo de armas
coat'room' *s* guardarropa *m*
coat'tail' *s* faldón *m*
coax [koks] *tr* engatusar
cob [kɑb] *s* zuro; **to eat corn on the cob** comer maíz en la mazorca
cobalt ['kobɔlt] *s* cobalto
cobbler ['kɑblər] *s* remendón *m*, zapatero de viejo
cob'ble·stone' *s* guijarro
cob'web' *s* telaraña
cocaine [ko'ken] *s* cocaína
cock [kɑk] *s* (*rooster*) gallo; (*faucet, valve*) espita, grifo; (*of firearm*) martillo; (*weathervane*) veleta; caudillo, jefe *m* ‖ *tr* amartillar (*un arma de fuego*); ladear (*la cabeza*); enderezar, levantar
cockade [kɑ'ked] *s* cucarda, escarapela
cock-a-doodle-doo ['kɑkə,dudəl'du] *s* quiquiriquí *m*
cock-and-bull story ['kɑkənd'bʊl] *s* cuento absurdo, cuento increíble
cocked hat [kɑkt] *s* sombrero de candil, sombrero de tres picos; **to knock into a cocked hat** (slang) apabullar
cockeyed ['kɑk,aɪd] *adj* bisojo, bizco; (coll) encorvado, torcido; (slang) disparatado, extravagante
cock'fight' *s* pelea de gallos
cockney ['kɑkni] *s* londinense *mf* de la clase pobre que habla un dialecto característico; dialecto de la clase pobre de Londres
cock of the walk *s* quiquiriquí *m*, gallito del lugar
cock'pit' *s* gallera; (aer) carlinga
cock'roach' *s* cucaracha
cockscomb ['kɑks,kom] *s* cresta de gallo; gorro de bufón; (bot) cresta de gallo, moco de pavo
cock'sure' *adj* muy seguro de sí mismo
cock'tail' *s* coctel *m;* (*of fruit, oysters, etc.*) aperitivo
cocktail party *s* coctel *m*
cocktail shaker ['ʃekər] *s* coctelera
cock·y ['kɑki] *adj* (*comp* **-ier;** *super* **-iest**) (coll) arrogante, hinchado; **to be cocky** (coll) tener mucho gallo
cocoa ['koko] *s* cacao; (*drink*) chocolate *m*
cocoanut o **coconut** ['kokə,nʌt] *s* coco
cocoanut palm o **tree** *s* cocotero
cocoon [kə'kun] *s* capullo
C.O.D., c.o.d. *abbr* **collect on delivery;** (Brit) **cash on delivery**
cod [kɑd] *s* abadejo, bacalao
coddle ['kɑdəl] *tr* consentir, mimar
code [kod] *s* (*of laws; of manners; of signals*) código; (*of telegraphy*) alfabeto; (*secret system of writing*) cifra, clave *f;* (com) cifrario; **in code** en cifra ‖ *tr* (*to put in code*) cifrar
code word *s* clave telegráfica
codex ['kodɛks] *s* (*pl* **codices** ['kodɪ,siz] o ['kɑdɪ,siz] *s* códice *m*
cod'fish' *s* abadejo, bacalao
codger ['kɑdʒər] *s* — **old codger** (coll) anciano, tío
codicil ['kɑdɪsɪl] *s* codicilo; apéndice *m*
codi·fy ['kɑdɪ,faɪ] o ['kodɪ,faɪ] *v* (*pret & pp* **-fied**) *tr* codificar
cod'-liv'er oil *s* aceite *m* de hígado de bacalao
coed o **co-ed** ['ko,ɛd] *s* alumna de una escuela coeducativa
coeducation [,ko,ɛdʒə'keʃən] *s* coeducación
coefficient [,ko·ɪ'fɪʃənt] *adj & s* coeficiente *m*
coerce [ko'ʌrs] *tr* forzar, coactar
coercion [ko'ʌrʃən] *s* compulsión, coacción
coeval [ko'ivəl] *adj & s* coetáneo
coexist [,ko·ɪg'zɪst] *intr* coexistir
coexistence [,ko·ɪg'zɪstəns] *s* coexistencia
coffee ['kɔfi] o ['kɑfi] *s* café *m;* (*plant*) cafeto; **black coffee** café solo
coffee bean *s* grano de café
cof'fee·cake' *s* rosquilla (que se come con el café)
coffee grinder *s* molinillo de café
coffee grounds *spl* poso del café
coffee mill *s* molinillo de café
coffee plantation *s* cafetal *m*
coffee pot *s* cafetera
coffee tree *s* cafeto
coffer ['kɔfər] o ['kɑfər] *s* arca, cofre *m;* **coffers** tesoro, fondos
cof'fer·dam' *s* ataguía, encajonado
coffin ['kɔfɪn] o ['kɑfɪn] *s* ataúd *m*
C. of S. *abbr* **Chief of Staff**
cog [kɑg] *s* diente *m* (*de rueda dentada*); rueda dentada; **to slip a cog** equivocarse
cogency ['kodʒənsi] *s* fuerza (*de un argumento*)
cogent ['kodʒənt] *adj* fuerte, convincente
cogitate ['kɑdʒɪ,tet] *tr & intr* cogitar, meditar
cognac ['konjæk] o ['kɑnjæk] *s* coñac *m*
cognizance ['kɑgnɪzəns] o ['kɑnɪzəns]

s conocimiento; **to take cognizance of** enterarse de
cognizant ['kɑgnɪzənt] o ['kɑnɪzənt] *adj* sabedor, enterado
cog'wheel' *s* rueda dentada
cohabit [ko'hæbɪt] *intr* cohabitar
coheir [ko'ɛr] *s* coheredero
cohere [ko'hɪr] *intr* adherirse, pegarse; conformarse, corresponder
coherent [ko'hɪrənt] *adj* coherente
cohesion [ko'hiʒən] *s* cohesión
coiffeur [kwɑ'fʌr] *s* peluquero
coiffure [kwɑ'fjʊr] *s* peinado, tocado
coil [kɔɪl] *s* (*something wound in a spiral*) rollo; (*single turn of spiral*) vuelta; (*of a still*) serpentín *m;* (*of hair*) rizo; (*of a spring*) espiral *f;* (elec) carrete *m* || *tr* arrollar, enrollar; (naut) adujar || *intr* arrollarse, enrollarse; (*like a snake*) serpentear
coil spring *s* resorte *m* espiral
coin [kɔɪn] *s* moneda; (*wedge*) cuña; **to pay back in one's own coin** pagar en la misma moneda; **to toss a coin** echar a cara o cruz || *tr* acuñar; forjar, inventar (*palabras o frases*); **to coin money** (coll) ganar mucho dinero
coincide [,ko·ɪn'saɪd] *intr* coincidir
coincidence [ko'ɪnsɪdəns] *s* coincidencia
coition [ko'ɪʃən] o **coitus** ['ko·ɪtəs] *s* coito
coke [kok] *s* coque *m,* cok *m*
col. *abbr* **colored, colony, column**
colander ['kʌləndər] o ['kɑləndər] *s* colador *m,* escurridor *m*
cold [kold] *adj* frío; **to be cold** (*said of a person*) tener frío; (*said of the weather*) hacer frío || *s* frío; (*indisposition*) resfriado; **to catch cold** resfriarse, coger un resfriado
cold blood *s* — **in cold blood** a sangre fría
cold chisel *s* cortafrío
cold comfort *s* poca consolación
cold cream *s* colcrén *m*
cold cuts *spl* fiambres *mpl*
cold feet *spl* (coll) desánimo, miedo
cold'heart'ed *adj* duro, insensible
cold meat *s* carne *f* fiambre
coldness ['koldnɪs] *s* frialdad
cold shoulder *s* — **to turn a cold shoulder on** (coll) tratar con suma frialdad
cold snap *s* corto rato de frío agudo
cold storage *s* conservación en cámara frigorífica
cold war *s* guerra fría
coleslaw ['kol,slɔ] *s* ensalada de col
colic ['kɑlɪk] *adj & s* cólico
coliseum [,kɑlɪ'si·əm] *s* coliseo
coll. *abbr* **colleague, collection, college, colloquial**
collaborate [kə'læbə,ret] *intr* colaborar
collaborationist [kə,læbə'reʃənɪst] *s* colaboracionista *mf*
collaborator [kə'læbə,retər] *s* colaborador *m*
collapse [kə'læps] *s* desplome *m;* (*in business*) fracaso; (pathol) colapso || *intr* desplomarse; fracasar; postrarse, sufrir colapso
collapsible [kə'læpsɪbəl] *adj* abatible, plegable, desmontable
collar ['kɑlər] *s* cuello; (*of dog, horse*) collar *m;* (mach) collar
col'lar·band' *s* tirilla de camisa
col'lar·bone' *s* clavícula
collate [kə'let] o ['kɑlet] *tr* colacionar, cotejar
collateral [kə'lætərəl] *adj* colateral || *s* (*relative*) colateral *mf;* (com) colateral *m*
collation [kə'leʃən] *s* (*act of comparing; light meal*) colación
colleague ['kɑlig] *s* colega *mf*
collect ['kɑlɛkt] *s* (eccl) colecta || [kə'lɛkt] *tr* acumular, reunir; colectar, recaudar (*impuestos*); coleccionar (*sellos de correo, antiguallas*); recolectar (*cosechas*); cobrar (*pasajes*); recoger (*billetes; el correo*); **to collect onself** reponerse || *intr* acumularse; **collect on delivery** contra reembolso, cobro contra entrega
collected [kə'lɛktɪd] *adj* sosegado, dueño de sí mismo
collection [kə'lɛkʃən] *s* colección; (*of taxes*) recaudación; (*of mail*) recogida
collection agency *s* agencia de cobros de cuentas
collective [kə'lɛktɪv] *adj* colectivo
collector [kə'lɛktər] *s* (*of stamps, antiques*) coleccionista *mf;* (*of taxes*) recaudador *m;* (*of tickets*) cobrador *m*
college ['kɑlɪdʒ] *s* colegio universitario; (*of cardinals, electors, etc.*) colegio
collide [kə'laɪd] *intr* chocar; **to collide with** chocar con
collie ['kɑli] *s* perro pastoril escocés
collier ['kɑljər] *s* barco carbonero; minero de carbón
collier·y ['kɑljəri] *s* (*pl* **-ies**) mina de carbón
collision [kə'lɪʒən] *s* colisión
colloid ['kɑlɔɪd] *adj & s* coloide *m*
colloquial [kə'lokwɪ·əl] *adj* coloquial, familiar
colloquialism [kə'lokwɪ·ə,lɪzəm] *s* coloquialismo
collo·quy ['kɑləkwi] *s* (*pl* **-quies**) coloquio
collusion [kə'luʒən] *s* colusión, confabulación; **to be in collusion with** estar en inteligencia con
cologne [kə'lon] *s* agua de colonia, colonia || **Cologne** *s* Colonia
colon ['kolən] *s* (anat) colon *m;* (gram) dos puntos
colonel ['kʌrnəl] *s* coronel *m*
colonel·cy ['kʌrnəlsi] *s* (*pl* **-cies**) coronelía
colonial [kə'lonɪ·əl] *adj* colonial || *s* colono
colonize ['kɑlə,naɪz] *tr & intr* colonizar
colonnade [,kɑlə'ned] *s* columnata
colo·ny ['kɑləni] *s* (*pl* **-nies**) colonia
colophon ['kɑlə,fɑn] *s* colofón *m*

color ['kʌlər] *s* color; **the colors** los colores, la bandera; **to call to the colors** llamar a filas; **to give** o **to lend color to** dar visos de probabilidad a; **under color of** so color de, bajo pretexto de; **with flying colors** con banderas desplegadas || *tr* colorar, colorear; (*to excuse, palliate*) colorear; (*to dye*) teñir || *intr* sonrojarse, ponerse colorado, demudarse
col'or-blind' *adj* ciego para los colores
colored ['kʌlərd] *adj* de color; (*specious*) colorado
colorful ['kʌlərfəl] *adj* colorido; pintoresco
coloring ['kʌlərɪŋ] *adj & s* colorante *m*
colorless ['kʌlərlɪs] *adj* incoloro; (fig) insulso
color photography *s* fotografía en colores
color salute *s* (mil) saludo con la bandera
color sargent *s* sargento abanderado
color screen *s* (phot) pantalla de color
color television *s* telivisión en colores
colossal [kə'lɑsəl] *adj* colosal
colossus [kə'lɑsəs] *s* coloso
colt [kolt] *s* potro
Columbus [kə'lʌmbəs] *s* Colón *m*
Columbus Day *s* día *m* de la raza, fiesta de la hispanidad
column ['kɑləm] *s* columna
columnist ['kɑləmɪst] *s* columnista *mf*
com. *abbr* **comedy, commerce, common**
Com. *abbr* **Commander, Commissioner, Committee**
coma ['komə] *s* (pathol) coma *m*
comb [kom] *s* peine *m;* (*currycomb*) almohaza; (*of rooster*) cresta; cresta de ola || *tr* peinar; explorar con minuciosidad
com•bat ['kɑmbæt] *s* combate *m* || ['kɑmbæt] o [kəm'bæt] *v* (*pret & pp* **-bated** o **-batted;** *ger* **-bating** o **-batting**) *tr & intr* combatir
combatant ['kɑmkətənt] *adj & s* combatiente *m*
combat duty *s* servicio de frente
combination [,kɑmbɪ'neʃən] *s* combinación
combine ['kɑmbaɪn] *s* monopolio; segadora trilladora; (coll) combinación || [kəm'baɪn] *tr* combinar || *intr* combinarse
combining form *s* (gram) elemento de compuestos
combustible [kəm'bʌstɪbəl] *adj* combustible; (fig) ardiente, impetuoso || *s* combustible *m*
combustion [kəm'bʌstʃən] *s* combustión
come [kʌm] *v* (*pret* **came** [kem]; *pp* **come**) *intr* venir; **to come about** suceder; **to come across** encontrarse con; **to come after** venir detrás de; venir después de; venir por, venir en busca de; **to come again** volver; **to come apart** desunirse, desprenderse; **to come around** restablecerse; volver en sí; rendirse; ponerse de acuerdo; cambiar de dirección; **to come at** alcanzar; **to come back** volver; (coll) rehabilitarse; **to come before** anteponerse; **to come between** interponerse; desunir, separar; **to come by** conseguir; **to come down** bajar; (*in social position, financial status, etc.*) descender; (*from one person to another*) ser transmitido; **to come downstairs** bajar (*de un piso a otro*); **to come down with** enfermarse de; **to come for** venir por, venir en busca de; **to come forth** salir; aparecer; **to come forward** avanzar; presentarse; **to come from** venir de; provenir de; **to come in** entrar; entrar en; empezar; ponerse en uso; **to come in for** conseguir, recibir; **to come into one's own** ser reconocido; **to come off** desprenderse; acontecer; **to come out** salir; salir a luz; ponerse de largo (*una joven*); divulgarse (*una noticia*); **to come out for** anunciar su apoyo de; **to come out with** descolgarse con; **to come over** dejarse persuadir; pasar, p.ej., **what's come over him?** ¿qué le ha pasado?; **to come through** salir bien, tener éxito; ganar; **to come to** volver en sí; **to come together** juntarse, reunirse; **to come true** hacerse realidad; **to come up** subir; presentarse; **to come upstairs** subir (*de un piso a otro*); **to come up to** acercarse a; subir a; estar a la altura de; **to come up with** proponer
come'back' *s* (coll) rehabilitación; (slang) respuesta aguda; **to stage a comeback** (coll) rehabilitarse
comedian [kə'midɪ•ən] *s* cómico, comediante *m;* autor *m* de comedias
comedienne [kə,midɪ'ɛn] *s* cómica, comedianta
come'down' *s* (coll) humillación, revés *m*
come•dy ['kɑmədi] *s* (*pl* **-dies**) comedia cómica; (*comicalness*) comicidad
come•ly ['kʌmli] *adj* (*comp* **-lier;** *super* **-liest**) (*attractive*) donairoso, gracioso; (*decorous*) conveniente, decente
comet ['kɑmɪt] *s* cometa *m*
comfort ['kʌmfərt] *s* comodidad, confort *m;* (*encouragement, consolation*) confortación; (*person*) confortador *m;* (*bed cover*) colcha, cobertor *m* || *tr* confortar
comfortable ['kʌmfərtəbəl] *adj* cómodo, confortable; (*fairly well off*) holgado; (*salary*) (coll) suficiente || *s* colcha, cobertor *m*
comforter ['kʌmfərtər] *s* confortador *m,* consolador *m;* colcha, cobertor *m;* bufanda de lana
comforting ['kʌmfərtɪŋ] *adj* confortante
comfort station *s* quiosco de necesidad
comfrey ['kʌmfri] *s* consuelda
comic ['kɑmɪk] *adj* cómico || *s* cómi-

co; (coll) periódico cómico; **comics** (coll) tiras cómicas
comical ['kamɪkəl] *adj* cómico
comic book *s* tebeo
comic opera *s* ópera cómica
comic strip *s* tira cómica
coming ['kʌmɪŋ] *adj* que viene, venidero; (coll) prometedor || *s* venida
coming out *s* (*of stocks, bonds, etc.*) emisión; (*of a young girl*) puesta de largo, entrada en sociedad
comma ['kamə] *s* coma
command [kə'mænd] o [kə'mand] *s* (*commanding*) dominio, mando; (*order, direction*) mandato, orden *f;* (*e.g., of a foreign language*) dominio; (mil) comando; **to be in command of** estar al mando de; **to take command** tomar el mando || *tr* mandar, ordenar; dominar (*un idioma extranjero*); merecer (*p.ej., respeto*); (mil) comandar || *intr* mandar
commandant [,kamən'dænt] o [,kamən'dant] *s* comandante *m*
commandeer [,kamən'dɪr] *tr* reclutar forzosamente; expropiar; (coll) apoderarse de
commander [kə'mændər] o [kə'mandər] *s* comandante *m;* (*of a military order*) comendador *m*
commandment [kə'mændmənt] o [kə'mandmənt] *s* (Bib) mandamiento
commemorate [kə'mɛmə,ret] *tr* conmemorar
commence [kə'mɛns] *tr & intr* comenzar, empezar
commencement [kə'mɛnsmənt] *s* comienzo, principio; día *m* de graduación; ceremonia de graduación
commend [kə'mɛnd] *tr* (*to entrust*) encargar, encomendar; (*to recommend*) recomendar; (*to praise*) alabar, elogiar
commendable [kə'mɛndəbəl] *adj* recomendable
commendation [,kamən'deʃən] *s* encargo, encomienda; recomendación; alabanza, elogio
comment ['kamɛnt] *s* comentario, comento || *intr* comentar; **to comment on** comentar
commentar•y ['kamən,tɛri] *s* (*pl* **-ies**) comentario
commentator ['kamən,tetər] *s* comentarista *mf*
commerce ['kamərs] *s* comercio
commercial [kə'mʌrʃəl] *adj* comercial || *s* anuncio publicitario radiofónico o televisivo; (rad & telv) programa publicitario
commercial traveler *s* agente viajero
commiserate [kə'mɪzə,ret] *intr* — **to commiserate with** condolerse de
commiseration [kə,mɪzə'reʃən] *s* conmiseración
commissar [,kamɪ'sar] *s* comisario (*en Rusia*)
commissar•y ['kamɪ,sɛri] *s* (*pl* **-ies**) (*deputy*) comisario; (*store*) economato
commission [kə'mɪʃən] *s* comisión; (mil) nombramiento; **to put in commission** poner en uso; poner (*un buque*) en servicio activo; **to put out of commission** inutilizar, descomponer; retirar (*un buque*) del servicio activo || *tr* comisionar; poner en uso; poner (*un buque*) en servicio activo; (mil) nombrar
commissioned officer *s* oficial *m*
commissioner [kə'mɪʃənər] *s* comisario; (*person authorized by a commission*) comisionado
com•mit [kə'mɪt] *v* (*pret & pp* **-mitted;** *ger* **-mitting**) *tr* cometer (*un crimen, una falta; un negocio a una persona*); (*to hand over*) confiar, entregar; dar, empeñar (*la palabra*); (*to bind, pledge*) comprometer; internar (*a un demente*); (*to memory*) encomendar; **to commit oneself** comprometerse, empeñarse; **to commit to writing** poner por escrito
commitment [kə'mɪtmənt] *s* (*act of committing*) comisión; (*to an asylum*) internación; (*written order*) auto de prisión; compromiso, cometido, empeño
committee [kə'mɪti] *s* comité *m,* comisión
commode [kə'mod] *s* (*chest of drawers*) cómoda; (*washstand*) lavabo; (*chamber pot*) sillico
commodious [kə'modɪ•əs] *adj* espacioso, holgado
commodi•ty [kə'madɪti] *s* (*pl* **-ties**) artículo de consumo, mercancía
commodity exchange *s* lonja, bolsa mercantil
common ['kamən] *adj* común || *s* campo común, ejido; **commons** estado llano; (*of a school*) refectorio; **the Commons** (Brit) los Comunes
common carrier *s* empresa de transportes públicos
commoner ['kamənər] *s* plebeyo; (Brit) miembro de la Cámara de los Comunes
common law *s* derecho consuetudinario
com'mon-law' marriage *s* matrimonio consensual
com'mon•place' *adj* común, trivial, ordinario || *s* lugar *m* común, trivialidad
common sense *s* sentido común
com'mon-sense' *adj* cuerdo, razonable
common stock *s* acción ordinaria; acciones ordinarias
commonweal ['kamən,wil] *s* bien público
com'mon•wealth' *s* estado, nación; república; (*state of U.S.A.*) estado; (*self-governing associated country*) estado libre asociado; (*association of states*) mancomunidad
commotion [kə'moʃən] *s* conmoción
commune [kə'mjun] *intr* conversar; (eccl) comulgar
communicant [kə'mjunɪkənt] *s* comunicante *mf;* (eccl) comulgante *mf*

communicate [kə'mjunɪ,ket] *tr* comunicar || *intr* comunicarse
communicating [kə'mjunɪ,ketɪŋ] *adj* comunicador
communicative [kə'mjunɪ,ketɪv] *adj* comunicativo
communion [kə'mjunjən] *s* comunión; **to take communion** comulgar
communion rail *s* comulgatorio
communiqué [kə,mjunɪ'ke] o [kə'mjunɪ,ke] *s* comunicado, parte *m*
communism ['kɑmjə,nɪzəm] *s* comunismo
communist ['kɑmjənɪst] *s* comunista *mf*
communi·ty [kə'mjunɪti] *s* (*pl* **-ties**) vecindario; (*group of people living together*) comunidad
communize ['kɑmjə,naɪz] *tr* comunizar
commutation ticket [,kɑmjə'teʃən] *s* billete *m* de abono
commutator ['kɑmjə,tetər] *s* (elec) colector *m*
commute [kə'mjut] *tr* conmutar || *intr* viajar con billete de abono
commuter [kə'mjutər] *s* abonado al ferrocarril
comp. *abbr* **compare, comparative, composer, composition, compound**
compact [kəm'pækt] *adj* compacto; breve, preciso || ['kɑmpækt] *s* convenio, pacto; estuche *m* de afeites
companion [kəm'pænjən] *s* compañero
companionable [kəm'pænjənəbəl] *adj* afable, sociable, simpático
companionship [kəm'pænjən,ʃɪp] *s* compañerismo
companionway [kəm'pænjən,we] *s* (naut) escalera de cámara
compa·ny ['kʌmpəni] *s* (*pl* **-nies**) compañía; visita, visitas, invitado, invitados; (naut) tripulación; **to be good company** ser compañero alegre; **to keep company** ir juntos (*un hombre y una mujer*); **to keep someone company** hacerle compañía a una persona; **to part company** separarse; enemistarse
company building *s* edificio social
company office *s* domicilio social
comparative [kəm'pærətɪv] *adj* & *s* comparativo
compare [kəm'pɛr] *s* — **beyond compare** sin comparación, sin par || *tr* comparar
comparison [kəm'pærɪsən] *s* comparación
compartment [kəm'pɑrtmənt] *s* compartimiento; (rr) departamento
compass ['kʌmpəs] *s* brújula, compás *m;* ámbito, recinto; alcance *m,* extensión; **compass** o **compasses** (*for drawing circles*) compás *m*
compass card *s* (naut) rosa náutica, rosa de los vientos
compassion [kəm'pæʃən] *s* compasión
compassionate [kəm'pæʃənɪt] *adj* compasivo
com·pel [kəm'pɛl] *v* (*pret* & *pp* **-pelled;** *ger* **-pelling**) *tr* forzar, obligar, compeler; imponer (*respeto, silencio*)
compendious [kəm'pɛndɪ·əs] *adj* compendioso
compendi·um [kəm'pɛndɪ·əm] *s* (*pl* **-ums** o **-a** [ə]) compendio
compensate ['kɑmpən,set] *tr* & *intr* compensar; **to compensate for** compensar
compensation [,kɑmpən'seʃən] *s* compensación
compete [kəm'pit] *intr* competir
competence ['kɑmpɪtens] o **competency** ['kɑmpɪtənsi] *s* (*aptitude; legal capacity*) competencia; (*sufficient means to live comfortably*) buen pasar *m*
competent ['kɑmpɪtənt] *adj* competente
competition [,kɑmpɪ'tɪʃən] *s* (*rivalry*) competencia; (*in a match, examination, etc.*) certamen *m,* concurso; (*in business*) concurrencia
competitive examination [kəm'pɛtɪtɪv] *s* oposición
competitive prices *spl* precios de competencia
competitor [kəm'pɛtɪtər] *s* competidor *m*
compilation [,kɑmpɪ'leʃən] *s* compilación, recopilación
compile [kəm'paɪl] *tr* compilar, recopilar
complacence [kəm'plesəns] o **complacency** [kəm'plesənsi] *s* (*quiet satisfaction*) complacencia; satisfacción de sí mismo
complacent [kəm'plesənt] *adj* (*willing to please*) complaciente; satisfecho de sí mismo
complain [kəm'plen] *intr* quejarse
complainant [kəm'plenənt] *s* (law) demandante *mf*
complaint [kəm'plent] *s* queja; (*grievance*) agravio; (*illness*) enfermedad, mal *m;* (law) demanda, querella
complaisance [kəm'plezəns] o ['kɑmplɪ,zæns] *s* amabilidad, cortesía
complaisant [kəm'plezənt] o ['kɑmplɪ,zænt] *adj* amable, cortés
complement ['kɑmplɪmənt] *s* complemento; (nav) dotación || ['kɑmplɪ,mɛnt] *tr* complementar
complete [kəm'plit] *adj* completo || *tr* completar, terminar, realizar
completion [kəm'pliʃən] *s* terminación, realización
complex [kəm'plɛks] o ['kɑmplɛks] *adj* (*not simple*) complexo; (*composite*) complejo; (*intricate*) complicado || ['kɑmplɛks] *s* complejo; (psychol) complejo; (coll) obsesión
complexion [kəm'plɛkʃən] *s* (*constitution*) complexión; (*texture of skin, esp. of face*) tez *f;* aspecto general, índole *f*
compliance [kəm'plaɪ·əns] *s* condescendencia; sumisión, rendimiento; **in compliance with** de acuerdo con, en conformidad con
complicate ['kɑmplɪ,ket] *tr* complicar

complicated ['kamplɪ,ketɪd] *adj* complicado

complici·ty [kəm'plɪsɪti] *s* (*pl* **-ties**) complicidad, codelincuencia

compliment ['kamplɪmənt] *s* (*show of courtesy*) cumplimiento; (*praise*) alabanza, halago; **compliments** saludos, recuerdos || ['kamplɪ,mɛnt] *tr* cumplimentar; alabar, halagar

complimentary copy [,kamplɪ'mɛntəri] *s* ejemplar *m* de cortesía

complimentary ticket *s* billete *m* de regalo, pase *m* de cortesía

com·ply [kəm'plaɪ] *v* (*pret & pp* **-plied**) *intr* conformarse; **to comply with** conformarse con, obrar de acuerdo con

component [kəm'ponənt] *adj* componente || *m* componente *m;* (mech) componente *f*

compose [kəm'poz] *tr* componer; **to be composed of** estar compuesto de

composed [kəm'pozd] *adj* sosegado, tranquilo

composer [kəm'pozer] *s* componedor *m;* (mus) compositor *m;* autor *m*

composing stick *s* componedor *m*

composite [kəm'pazɪt] *adj & s* compuesto

composition [,kampə'zɪʃən] *s* composición

compositor [kəm'pazɪtər] *s* cajista *mf,* componedor *m*

composure [kəm'poʒər] *s* serenidad, sosiego

compote ['kampot] *s* (*stewed fruit*) compota; (*dish*) compotera

compound ['kampaund] *adj* compuesto || *s* compuesto; (gram) vocablo compuesto || [kam'paund] *tr* componer, combinar; (*interest*) capitalizar

comprehend [,kamprɪ'hɛnd] *tr* comprender

comprehensible [,kamprɪ'hɛnsɪbəl] *adj* comprensible

comprehension [,kamprɪ'hɛnʃən] *s* comprensión

comprehensive [,kamprɪ'hɛnsɪv] *adj* comprensivo, inclusivo, completo

compress ['kamprɛs] *s* (med) compresa || [kəm'prɛs] *tr* comprimir

compression [kəm'prɛʃən] *s* compresión

comprise o **comprize** [kəm'praɪz] *tr* abarcar, comprender, incluir

compromise ['kamprə,maɪz] *s* (*adjustment*) componenda, transigencia, transacción; (*endangering*) comprometimiento || *tr* (*by mutual concessions*) componer, transigir; (*to endanger*) comprometer, exponer || *intr* transigir, avenirse

comptroller [kən'trolər] *s* contralor *m,* interventor *m*

compulsory [kəm'pʌlsəri] *adj* obligatorio

compute [kəm'pjut] *tr & intr* computar, calcular

computer [kəm'pjutər] *s* computador *m*

comrade ['kamræd] o ['kamrɪd] *s* camarada *m*

con. *abbr* **conclusion, consolidated, contra**

con [kan] *s* (*opposite opinion*) contra *m* || *v* (*pret & pp* **conned;** *ger* **conning**) *tr* leer con atención, aprender de memoria

concave ['kankev] o [kan'kev] *adj* cóncavo

conceal [kən'sil] *tr* encubrir, ocultar

concealment [kən'silmənt] *s* encubrimiento, ocultación; (*place*) escondite *m*

concede [kən'sid] *tr* conceder

conceit [kən'sit] *s* (*vanity*) orgullo, engreimiento; (*witty expression*) concepto, dicho ingenioso

conceited [kən'sitɪd] *adj* orgulloso, engreído

conceivable [kən'sivəbəl] *adj* concebible

conceive [kən'siv] *tr & intr* concebir

concentrate ['kansən,tret] *tr* concentrar || *intr* concentrarse; **to concentrate on** o **upon** reconcentrarse en

concentric [kən'sɛntrɪk] *adj* concéntrico

concept ['kansɛpt] *s* concepto

conception [kən'sɛpʃən] *s* concepción

concern [kən'sʌrn] *s* (*business establishment*) empresa, casa comercial, razón *f* social; (*worry*) inquietud, preocupación; (*relation, reference*) concernencia; (*matter*) asunto, negocio || *tr* atañer, concernir; interesar; **as concerns** respecto de; **to whom it may concern** a quien pueda interesar, a quien corresponda

concerning [kən'sʌrnɪŋ] *prep* respecto de, tocante a

concert ['kansərt] *s* concierto || [kən'sʌrt] *tr & intr* concertar

con'cert·mas'ter *s* concertino

concer·to [kən'tʃɛrto] *s* (*pl* **-tos** o **-ti** [ti]) concierto

concession [kən'sɛʃən] *s* concesión

concessive [kən'sɛsɪv] *adj* concesivo

concierge [,kansɪ'ʌrʒ] *s* conserje *m*

conciliate [kən'sɪlɪ,et] *tr* conciliar; conciliarse (*el respeto, la estima*)

conciliatory [kən'sɪlɪ·ə,tori] *adj* conciliador

concise [kən'saɪs] *adj* conciso

conclude [kən'klud] *tr & intr* concluir

conclusion [kən'kluʒən] *s* conclusión; (*of a letter*) despedida

conclusive [kən'klusɪv] *adj* concluyente

concoct [kən'kakt] *tr* confeccionar; (*a story*) forjar, inventar

concomitant [kən'kamɪtənt] *adj & s* concomitante *m*

concord ['kaŋkərd] *s* concordia; (gram, mus) concordancia

concordance [kən'kərdəns] *s* concordancia

concourse ['kaŋkors] *s* (*of people*) concurso; (*of streams*) confluencia; bulevar *m,* gran vía; (*of railroad station*) gran salón *m*

concrete ['kɑnkrit] o [kɑn'krit] *adj* concreto; de hormigón || *s* hormigón *m*
concrete block *s* bloque *m* de hormigón
concrete mixer *s* hormigonera, mezcladora de hormigón
concubine ['kɑŋkjə,baɪn] *s* concubina
con•cur [kən'kʌr] *v* (*pret & pp* **-curred**; *ger* **-curring**) *intr* concurrir
concurrence [kən'kʌrəns] *s* (*happening together*) concurrencia; (*agreement*) acuerdo
concussion [kən'kʌʃən] *s* concusión
condemn [kən'dɛm] *tr* condenar
condemnation [,kɑndɛm'neʃən] *s* condenación
condense [kən'dɛns] *tr* condensar || *intr* condensarse
condescend [,kɑndɪ'sɛnd] *intr* dignarse
condescending [,kɑndɪ'sɛndɪŋ] *adj* condescendiente con inferiores
condescension [,kɑndɪ'sɛnʃən] *s* dignación, aire *m* protector
condiment ['kɑndɪmənt] *s* condimento
condition [kən'dɪʃən] *s* condición; **on condition that** a condición (de) que || *tr* acondicionar
conditional [kən'dɪʃənəl] *adj* condicional
condole [kən'dol] *intr* condolerse
condolence [kən'doləns] *s* condolencia
condone [kən'don] *tr* condonar
conduce [kən'djus] o [kən'dus] *intr* conducir
conducive [kən'djusiv] o [kən'dusɪv] *adj* conducente, contribuyente
conduct ['kɑndʌkt] *s* conducta || [kən'dʌkt] *tr* conducir; **to conduct oneself** conducirse, comportarse
conductor [kən'dʌktər] *s* conductor *m*, guía *mf;* (elec & phys) conductor *m*, conductora *f;* (rr) revisor *m;* (*on trolley or bus*) cobrador *m*
conduit ['kɑndɪt] o ['kɑndʊ·ɪt] *s* canal *f* para alambres o cables
cone [kon] *s* cono; (*of pastry*) barquillo; (*of paper*) cucurucho
confectioner•y [kən'fɛkʃə,nɛri] *s* (*pl* **-ies**) (*shop*) confitería; (*sweetmeats*) dulces *mpl*, confites *mpl*, confituras
confedera•cy [kən'fɛdərəsi] (*pl* **-cies**) confederación; (*for unlawful purpose*) conjuración
confederate [kən'fɛdərɪt] *s* confederado; cómplice *mf* || [kən'fɛdə,ret] *tr* confederar || *intr* confederarse
con•fer [kən'fʌr] *v* (*pret & pp* **-ferred**; *ger* **-ferring**) *tr* conferir || *intr* conferenciar, consultar
conference ['kɑnfərəns] *s* conferencia, coloquio
confess [kən'fɛs] *tr* confesar || *intr* confesar, confesarse
confession [kən'fɛʃən] *s* confesión
confessional [kən'fɛʃənəl] *s* confesonario
confession of faith *s* profesión de fe
confessor [kən'fɛsər] *s* (*person who confesses*) confesante *mf;* (*Christian, esp. in spite of persecution; priest*) confesor *m*
confide [kən'faɪd] *tr* confiar || *intr* confiar, confiarse; **to confide in** confiarse en
confidence ['kɑnfɪdəns] *s* confianza; (*secret*) confidencia; **in strictest confidence** bajo la mayor reserva
confident ['kɑnfɪdənt] *adj* seguro || *s* confidente *m*, confidenta
confidential [,kɑnfɪ'dɛnʃəl] *adj* confidencial
confine ['kɑnfaɪn] *s* confín *m;* **the confines** los confines || [kən'faɪn] *tr* (*to keep within limits*) limitar, restringir; (*to keep shut in*) encerrar; **to be confined** estar de parto; **to be confined to bed** tener que guardar cama
confinement [kən'faɪnmənt] *s* limitación; encierro; parto, sobreparto
confirm [kən'fʌrm] *tr* confirmar
confirmed [kən'fʌrmd] *adj* confirmado; empedernido, inveterado
confiscate ['kɑnfɪs,ket] *tr* confiscar
conflagration [,kɑnflə'greʃən] *s* conflagración
conflict ['kɑnflɪkt] *s* conflicto; (*of interests, class hours, etc.*) incompatibilidad || [kən'flɪkt] *intr* chocar, desavenirse
conflicting [kən'flɪktɪŋ] *adj* contradictorio; (*events, appointments, class hours, etc.*) incompatible
confluence ['kɑnflu·əns] *s* confluencia
conform [kən'fɔrm] *intr* conformar, conformarse
conformance [kən'fɔrməns] *s* conformidad
conformi•ty [kən'fɔrmɪti] *s* (*pl* **-ties**) conformidad
confound [kɑn'faʊnd] *tr* confundir || ['kɑn'faʊnd] *tr* maldecir; **confound it!** ¡maldito sea!
confounded [kɑn'faʊndɪd] o ['kɑn'faʊndɪd] *adj* confundido; aborrecible; maldito
confrere ['kɑnfrɛr] *s* colega *m*
confront [kən'frʌnt] *tr* (*to face boldly*) confrontarse con, hacer frente a; (*to meet face to face*) encontrar cara a cara; (*to bring face to face; to compare*) confrontar
confuse [kən'fjuz] *tr* confundir
confusion [kən'fuʒən] *s* confusión
confute [kən'fjut] *tr* confutar
Cong. *abbr* **Congregation, Congressional**
congeal [kən'dʒil] *tr* congelar || *intr* congelarse
congenial [kən'dʒinjəl] *adj* simpático; agradable; compatible; (*having the same nature*) congenial
congenital [kən'dʒɛnɪtəl] *adj* congénito
conger eel ['kɑŋgər] *s* congrio
congest [kən'dʒɛst] *tr* congestionar || *intr* congestionarse
congestion [kən'dʒɛstʃən] *s* congestión
congratulate [kən'grætʃə,let] *tr* congratular, felicitar

congratulation [kən ˌgrætʃə'leʃən] *s* congratulación, felicitación
congregate ['kaŋgrɪ ˌget] *intr* congregarse
congregation [ˌkaŋgrɪ'geʃən] *s* congregación; feligresía, fieles *mf* (*de una iglesia*)
congress ['kaŋgrɪs] *s* congreso
congress•man ['kaŋgrɪsmən] *s* (*pl* **-men** [mən]) congresista *m*
conical ['kanɪkəl] *adj* cónico
conj. *abbr* **conjugation, conjunction**
conjecture [kən'dʒɛktʃər] *s* conjetura || *tr & intr* conjeturar
conjugal ['kandʒəgəl] *adj* conyugal
conjugate ['kandʒə ˌget] *tr* conjugar
conjugation [ˌkandʒə'geʃən] *s* conjugación
conjunction [kən'dʒʌŋkʃən] *s* conjunción
conjuration [ˌkandʒə'reʃən] *s* (*superstitious invocation*) conjuro; (*magic spell*) hechizo
conjure [kən'dʒur] *tr* (*to appeal to solemnly*) conjurar || ['kʌndʒər] o ['kandʒər] *tr* (*to exorcise, drive away*) conjurar; **to conjure away** conjurar; **to conjure up** evocar; crear, suscitar (*dificultades*)
connect [kə'nɛkt] *tr* conectar; asociar, relacionar || *intr* enlazarse; asociarse, relacionarse; empalmar, enlazar (*dos trenes*)
connecting rod *s* biela
connection [kə'nɛkʃən] *s* conexión; (*relative*) pariente *mf;* (*of trains*) combinación, enlace *m,* empalme *m;* (*in subway*) correspondencia; **in connection with** con respecto a; juntamente con
conning tower ['kanɪŋ] *s* torreta de mando
conniption [kə'nɪpʃən] *s* pataleta, berrinche *m*
connive [kə'naɪv] *intr* confabularse, estar en connivencia
conquer ['kaŋkər] *tr* vencer; (*by force of arms*) conquistar || *intr* triunfar
conqueror ['kaŋkərər] *s* conquistador *m,* vencedor *m*
conquest ['kaŋkwɛst] *s* conquista
conscience ['kanʃəns] *s* conciencia; **in all conscience** en conciencia
conscientious [ˌkanʃɪ'ɛnʃəs] *adj* concienzudo
conscientious objector [ab'dʒɛktər] *s* objetante *m* de conciencia
conscious ['kanʃəs] *adj* (*aware of one's own existence*) consciente; (*deliberate*) intencional; (*self-conscious*) encogido, tímido; **to become conscious** volver en sí
consciousness ['kanʃəsnɪs] *s* conciencia, conocimiento
conscript ['kanskrɪpt] *s* conscripto || [kən'skrɪpt] *tr* reclutar
conscription [kən'skrɪpʃən] *s* conscripción
consecrate ['kansɪ ˌkret] *tr* consagrar
consecutive [kən'sɛkjətɪv] *adj* (*successive*) consecutivo; (*continuous*) consecuente
consensus [kən'sɛnsəs] *s* consenso; **the consensus of opinion** la opinión general
consent [kən'sɛnt] *s* consentimiento; **by common consent** de común acuerdo || *intr* consentir; **to consent to** consentir en
consequence ['kansɪ ˌkwɛns] *s* consecuencia; aires *mpl* de importancia
consequential [ˌkansɪ'kwɛnʃəl] *adj* consiguiente; importante; altivo, pomposo
consequently ['kansɪ ˌkwɛntli] *adv* por consiguiente
conservation [ˌkansər'veʃən] *s* conservación
conservatism [kən'sʌrvə ˌtɪzəm] *s* conservadurismo
conservative [kən'sʌrvətɪv] *adj* (*preservative*) conservativo; (*disposed to maintain existing views and institutions*) conservador; cauteloso, moderado || *s* preservativo; conservador *m*
conservato•ry [kən'sʌrvə ˌtori] *s* (*pl* **-ries**) (*school of music*) conservatorio; (*greenhouse*) invernadero
consider [kən'sɪdər] *tr* considerar
considerable [kən'sɪdərəbəl] *adj* considerable
considerate [kən'sɪdərɪt] *adj* considerado
consideration [kən ˌsɪdə'reʃən] *s* consideración; **for a consideration** por un precio; **in consideration of** en consideración de; en cambio de; **on no consideration** bajo ningún concepto; **out of consideration for** por respeto a; **without due consideration** sin reflexión
considering [kən'sɪdərɪŋ] *adv* (coll) teniendo en cuentas las circunstancias || *prep* en vista de, en razón de || *conj* en vista de que
consign [kən'saɪn] *tr* consignar
consignee [ˌkansaɪ'ni] *s* consignatario
consignment [kən'saɪnmənt] *s* consignación
consist [kən'sɪst] *intr* — **to consist in** consistir en; **to consist of** consistir en, constar de
consisten•cy [kən'sɪstənsi] *s* (*pl* **-cies**) (*firmness, amount of firmness*) consistencia; (*logical connection*) consecuencia
consistent [kən'sɪstənt] *adj* (*holding firmly together*) consistente; (*agreeing with itself or oneself*) consecuente; **consistent with** (*in accord with*) compatible con
consisto•ry [kən'sɪstəri] *s* (*pl* **-ries**) consistorio
consolation [ˌkansə'leʃən] *s* consolación, consuelo
console ['kansol] *s* consola; mesa de consola || [kən'sol] *tr* consolar
consommé [ˌkansə'me] *s* consumado, consommé *m*
consonant ['kansənənt] *adj & s* consonante *f*
consort ['kansɔrt] *s* consorte *mf;* embarcación que acompaña a otra ||

[kən'sɔrt] *tr* asociar || *intr* asociarse; armonizar, concordar
consorti·um [kən'sɔrʃɪ·əm] *s* (*pl* **-a** [ə]) consorcio
conspicuous [kən'spɪkjʊ·əs] *adj* manifiesto, claro, evidente; llamativo, vistoso, sugestivo; conspicuo, notable
conspira·cy [kən'spɪrəsi] *s* (*pl* **-cies**) conspiración, conjuración
conspire [kən'spaɪr] *intr* conspirar, conjurar
constable ['kɑnstəbəl] o ['kʌnstəbəl] *s* policía *m*, guardia *m*, alguacil *m*
constancy ['kɑnstənsi] *s* constancia; fidelidad
constant ['kɑnstənt] *adj* constante; incesante; fiel || *s* constante *f*
constellation [,kɑnstə'leʃən] *s* constelación
constipate ['kɑnstɪ,pet] *tr* estreñir
constipation [,kɑnstɪ'peʃən] *s* estreñimiento
constituen·cy [kən'stɪtʃʊ·ənsi] *s* (*pl* **-cies**) votantes *mpl;* clientela; comitentes *mpl;* distrito electoral
constituent [kən'stɪtʃʊ·ənt] *adj* constitutivo, componente; (*having power to create or revise a constitution*) constituyente || *s* constitutivo, componente *m;* (*person who appoints another to act for him*) comitente *m*
constitute ['kɑnstɪ,tjut] o ['kɑnstɪ,tut] *tr* constituir
constitution [,kɑnstɪ'tjuʃən] o [,kɑnstɪ'tuʃən] *s* constitución
constrain [kən'stren] *tr* constreñir; detener, encerrar; restringir
construct [kən'strʌkt] *tr* construir
construction [kən'strʌkʃən] *s* construcción; interpretación
construe [kən'stru] *tr* interpretar; deducir, inferir; traducir; (*to combine syntactically*) construir; (*to explain the syntax of*) analizar
consul ['kɑnsəl] *s* cónsul *m*
consular ['kɑnsələr] o ['kɑnsjələr] *adj* consular
consulate ['kɑnsəlɪt] o ['kɑnsjəlɪt] *s* consulado
consulship ['kɑnsəl,ʃɪp] *s* consulado
consult [kən'sʌlt] *tr & intr* consultar
consultant [kən'sʌltənt] *s* consultor *m*
consultation [,kɑnsəl'teʃən] *s* (*consulting*) consulta; (*meeting*) consulta, consultación
consume [kən'sum] o [kən'sjum] *tr* consumir; (*to absorb the interest of*) preocupar; || *intr* consumirse
consumer [kən'sumər] o [kən'sjumər] *s* consumidor *m;* (*of gas, electricity, etc.*) abonado
consumer credit *s* crédito consuntivo
consumer goods *spl* bienes *mpl* de consumo
consummate [kən'sʌmɪt] *adj* consumado || ['kɑnsə,met] *tr* consumar
consumption [kən'sʌmpʃən] *s* consunción, consumo; (pathol) consunción, tisis *f*
consumptive [kən'sʌmptɪv] *adj* consuntivo; (path) tísico || *s* tísico
cont. *abbr* **contents, continental, continued**
contact ['kɑntækt] *s* contacto; (elec) contacto; (elec) toma de corriente || *tr* (coll) ponerse en contacto con || *intr* contactar
contact breaker *s* (elec) ruptor *m*
contact lens *s* lente *m* de contacto, lente invisible
contagion [kən'tedʒən] *s* contagio
contagious [kən'tedʒəs] *adj* contagioso
contain [kən'ten] *tr* contener; **to contain oneself** contenerse, refrenarse
container [kən'tenər] *s* continente *m*, recipiente *m*, vaso, caja, envase *m*
containment [kən'tenmənt] *s* contención, refrenamiento
contaminate [kən'tæmɪ,net] *tr* contaminar
contamination [kən,tæmɪ'neʃən] *s* contaminación
contd. *abbr* **continued**
contemplate ['kɑntəm,plet] *tr & intr* contemplar; pensar, proyectar
contemplation [,kɑntəm'pleʃən] *s* contemplación; intención, propósito
contemporaneous [kən,tɛmpə'renɪ·əs] *adj* contemporáneo
contemporar·y [kən'tɛmpə,rɛri] *adj* contemporáneo, coetáneo || *s* (*pl* **-ies**) contemporáneo, coetáneo
contempt [kən'tɛmpt] *s* desprecio; (law) contumacia
contemptible [kən'tɛmptɪbəl] *adj* despreciable
contemptuous [kən'tɛmptʃʊ·əs] *adj* despreciativo, desdeñoso
contend [kən'tɛnd] *tr* sostener, mantener || *intr* contender
contender [kən'tɛndər] *s* contendiente *mf*, concurrente *mf*
content [kən'tɛnt] *adj & s* contento || ['kɑntɛnt] *s* contenido; **contents** contenido || [kən'tɛnt] *tr* contentar
contented [kən'tɛntɪd] *adj* contento, satisfecho
contentedness [kən'tɛndɪdnɪs] *s* contentamiento, satisfacción
contention [kən'tɛnʃən] *s* (*strife; dispute*) contención; (*point argued for*) argumento
contentious [kən'tɛnʃəs] *adj* contencioso
contentment [kən'tɛntmənt] *s* contentamiento, contento
contest ['kɑntɛst] *s* (*struggle, fight*) contienda; (*competition*) competencia, concurso || [kən'tɛst] *tr* disputar; tratar de conseguir || *intr* contender
contestant [kən'tɛstənt] *s* contendiente *mf*
context ['kɑntɛkst] *s* contexto
contiguous [kən'tɪgjʊ·əs] *adj* contiguo
continence ['kɑntɪnəns] *s* continencia
continent ['kɑntɪnənt] *adj & s* continente *m;* **the Continent** la Europa continental
continental [,kɑntɪ'nɛntəl] *adj* continental || **Continental** *s* habitante *mf* del continente europeo

contingen·cy [kən'tɪndʒənsi] *s* (*pl* **-cies**) contingencia
contingent [kən'tɪndʒənt] *adj & s* contingente *m*
continual [kən'tɪnjʊ·əl] *adj* continuo
continue [kən'tɪnjʊ] *tr & intr* continuar; **to be continued** continuará
continui·ty [ˌkɑntɪ'nju·ɪti] o [ˌkɑntɪ'nu·ɪti] *s* (*pl* **-ties**) continuidad; (mov, rad, telv) guión *m;* (rad, telv) comentarios o anuncios entre las partes de un programa
continuous [kən'tɪnjʊ·əs] *adj* continuo
continuous showing *s* (mov) sesión continua
continuous waves *spl* (rad) ondas entretenidas
contortion [kən'tɔrʃən] *s* contorsión
contour ['kɑntʊr] *s* contorno
contr. *abbr* **contracted, contraction**
contraband ['kɑntrəˌbænd] *adj* contrabandista || *s* contrabando
contrabass ['kɑntrəˌbes] *s* contrabajo
contraceptive [ˌkɑntrə'sɛptɪv] *adj & s* anticonceptivo, contraceptivo
contract ['kɑntrækt] *s* contrato || ['kɑntrækt] o [kən'trækt] *tr* contraer (*p.ej., matrimonio*) || *intr* (*to shrink*) contraerse; (*to enter into an agreement*) comprometerse; **to contract for** contratar
contraction [kən'trækʃən] *s* contracción
contractor [kən'træktər] *s* contratista *mf*
contradict [ˌkɑntrə'dɪkt] *tr* contradecir
contradiction [ˌkɑntrə'dɪkʃən] *s* contradicción
contradictory [ˌkɑntrə'dɪktəri] *adj* (*involving contradiction*) contradictorio; (*inclined to contradict*) contradictor
contrail ['kɑnˌtrel] *s* (aer) estela de vapor, rastro de condensación
contral·to [kən'trælto] *s* (*pl* **-tos**) (*person*) contralto *mf;* (*voice*) contralto *m*
contraption [kən'træpʃən] *s* (coll) artilugio, dispositivo
contra·ry ['kɑntrɛri] *adv* contrariamente || *adj* contrario || [kən'trɛri] *adj* obstinado, terco || ['kɑntrɛri] *s* (*pl* **-ries**) contrario; **on the contrary** al contrario
contrast ['kɑntræst] *s* contraste *m* || [kən'træst] *tr* comparar; poner en contraste || *intr* contrastar
contravene [ˌkɑntrə'vin] *tr* contradecir; contravenir a (*una ley*)
contribute [kən'trɪbjʊt] *tr* contribuir || *intr* contribuir; (*to a newspaper, conference, etc.*) colaborar
contribution [ˌkɑntrɪ'bjuʃən] *s* contribución; (*to a newspaper, conference, etc.*) colaboración
contributor [kən'trɪbjʊtər] *s* contribuidor *m,* contribuyente *mf;* colaborador *m*
contrite [kən'traɪt] *adj* contrito
contrition [kən'trɪʃən] *s* contrición
contrivance [kən'traɪvəns] *s* aparato, dispositivio; idea, plan *m,* designio
contrive [kən'traɪv] *tr* (*to devise*) idear, inventar; (*to scheme up*) maquinar, tramar; (*to bring about*) efectuar || *intr* maquinar; **to contrive to** + *inf* ingeniarse a + *inf*
con·trol [kən'trol] *s* gobierno, mando; (*of a scientific experiment*) contrarregistro, control *m;* **controls** mandos; **to get under control** conseguir dominar (*un incendio*) || *v* (*pret & pp* **-trolled;** *ger* **-trolling**) *tr* gobernar, mandar; comprobar, controlar; **to control oneself** dominarse
controlling interest *s* (el) mayor porcentaje de acciones
control panel *s* (aer) tablero de instrumentos
control stick *s* (aer) mango de escoba, palanca de mando
controversial [ˌkɑntrə'vʌrʃəl] *adj* controvertible, disputable; disputador
controver·sy ['kɑntrəˌvʌrsi] *s* (*pl* **-sies**) controversia, polémica
controvert ['kɑntrəˌvʌrt] o [ˌkɑntrə'vʌrt] *tr* (*to argue against*) contradecir; (*to argue about*) controvertir
contumacious [ˌkɑntjʊ'meʃəs] o [ˌkɑntʊ'meʃəs] *adj* contumaz
contuma·cy ['kɑntjʊməsi] o ['kɑntʊməsi] *s* (*pl* **-cies**) contumacia
contume·ly ['kɑntjʊmɪli] o ['kɑntʊmɪli] *s* (*pl* **-lies**) contumelia
contusion [kən'tjuʒən] o [kən'tuʒən] *s* contusión
conundrum [kə'nʌndrəm] *s* acertijo, adivinanza; problema complicado
convalesce [ˌkɑnvə'lɛs] *intr* convalecer
convalescence [ˌkɑnvə'lɛsəns] *s* convalecencia
convalescent [ˌkɑnvə'lɛsənt] *adj & s* convaleciente *mf*
convalescent home *s* clínica de reposo
convene [kən'vin] *tr* convocar || *intr* convenir, reunirse
convenience [kən'vinjəns] *s* comodidad, conveniencia; **at your earliest convenience** a la primera oportunidad que Vd. tenga
convenient [kən'vinjənt] *adj* cómodo, conveniente; próximo
convent ['kɑnvɛnt] *s* convento; convento de religiosas
convention [kən'vɛnʃən] *s* (*agreement*) convención, conveniencia; (*accepted usage*) costumbre *f,* conveniencia social, convención; (*meeting*) congreso, convención
conventional [kən'vɛnʃənəl] *adj* convencional
conventionali·ty [kənˌvɛnʃə'nælɪti] *s* (*pl* **-ties**) precedente *m* convencional
converge [kən'vʌrd] *intr* convergir
conversant [kən'vʌrsənt] *adj* familiarizado, versado
conversation [ˌkɑnvər'seʃən] *s* conversación
conversational [ˌkɑnvər'seʃənəl] *adj* conversacional
converse ['kɑnvʌrs] *adj & s* contrario || [kən'vʌrs] *intr* conversar
conversion [kən'vʌrʒən] *s* conversión;

(*unlawful appropriation*) malversación
convert ['kɑnvʌrt] *s* convertido, converso || [kən'vʌrt] *tr* convertir || *intr* convertirse
convertible [kən'vʌrtɪbəl] *adj* convertible || *s* (aut) convertible *m,* descapotable *m*
convex ['kɑnvɛks] o [kɑn'vɛks] *adj* convexo
convey [kən've] *tr* llevar, transportar; comunicar, participar (*informes*); transferir, traspasar (*bienes de una persona a otra*)
conveyance [kən've·əns] *s* transporte *m;* comunicación, participación; vehículo; (*transfer of property*) traspaso; escritura de traspaso
convict ['kɑnvɪkt] *s* reo convicto, presidiario || [kən'vɪkt] *tr* probar la culpabilidad de; declarar convicto (*a un acusado*)
conviction [kən'vɪkʃən] *s* convencimiento; condena, fallo de culpabilidad
convince [kən'vɪns] *tr* convencer
convincing [kən'vɪnsɪŋ] *adj* convincente
convivial [kən'vɪvɪ·əl] *adj* jovial
convocation [,kɑnvə'keʃən] *s* asamblea
convoke [kən'vok] *tr* convocar
convoy ['kɑnvɔɪ] *s* convoy *m,* conserva || *tr* convoyar
convulse [kən'vʌls] *tr* convulsionar; agitar; **to convulse with laughter** mover a risas convulsivas
coo [ku] *intr* arrullar
cook [kʊk] *s* cocinero || *tr* cocer, cocinar, guisar; **to cook up** (coll) falsificar; (coll) maquinar, tramar || *intr* cocer, cocinar
cook'book' *s* libro de cocina
cookie ['kʊki] *s* var de **cooky**
cooking ['kʊkɪŋ] *s* cocina, arte *m* de cocinar
cook'stove' *s* cocina económica
cook·y ['kʊki] *s* (*pl* **-ies**) pasta seca, pastelito dulce
cool [kul] *adj* fresco; frío, indiferente || *s* fresco || *tr* refrescar; moderar || *intr* refrescarse; moderarse; **to cool off** refrescarse; serenarse
cooler ['kulər] *s* heladera, refrigerador *m;* refrigerante *m;* (coll) cárcel *f*
cool'-head'ed *adj* sereno, tranquilo, juicioso
coolie ['kuli] *s* culí *m*
coolish ['kulɪʃ] *adj* fresquito
coolness ['kulnɪs] *s* fresco, frescura; (fig) frialdad
coon [kun] *s* mapache *m,* oso lavandero
coop [kup] *s* gallinero; (*for fattening capons*) caponera; jaula, redil *m;* (*jail*) (slang) caponera; **to fly the coop** (slang) escabullirse || *tr* encerrar en un gallinero; enjaular; **to coop up** emparedar
coöp. *abbr* **cooperative**
cooper ['kupər] *s* barrilero, tonelero
coöperate [ko'ɑpə,ret] *intr* cooperar
coöperation [ko,ɑpə'reʃən] *s* cooperación
coöperative [ko'ɑpə,retɪv] *adj* cooperativo
coördinate [ko'ɔrdɪnɪt] *adj* coordenado; (gram) coordinante || *s* (math) coordenada || [ko'ɔrdɪ,net] *tr & intr* coordinar
cootie ['kuti] *s* (slang) piojo
cop [kɑp] *s* (slang) polizonte *m* || *v* (*pret & pp* **copped;** *ger* **copping**) *tr* (slang) hurtar
copartner [ko'pɑrtnər] *s* consocio, copartícipe *mf*
cope [kop] *intr* — **to cope with** hacer frente a, enfrentarse con
cope'stone' *s* piedra de albardilla
copier ['kɑpɪ·ər] *s* (*person who copies*) copiante *mf,* copista *mf;* imitador *m;* (*apparatus*) copiador *m*
copilot ['ko,paɪlət] *s* copiloto
coping ['kopɪŋ] *s* albardilla
copious ['kopɪ·əs] *adj* copioso
copper ['kɑpər] *adj* cobreño; (*in color*) cobrizo || *s* cobre *m;* (*coin*) calderilla, vellón *m;* (slang) polizonte *m*
cop'per·head' *s* víbora de cabeza de cobre
cop'per·smith' *s* cobrero
coppery ['kɑpəri] *adj* cobreño; (*in color*) cobrizo
coppice ['kɑpɪs] o **copse** [kɑps] *s* soto, monte bajo
copulate ['kɑpjə,let] *intr* copularse
cop·y ['kɑpi] *s* (*pl* **-ies**) copia; (*of a book*) ejemplar *m;* (*of a magazine*) número; (*document to be reproduced in print*) original *m,* manuscrito || *v* (*pret & pp* **-ied**) *tr* copiar
cop'y·book' *s* cuaderno de escritura
copyist ['kɑpɪ·ɪst] *s* copiante *mf,* copista *mf;* imitador *m*
cop'y·right' *s* (derechos de) propiedad literaria || *tr* registrar en el registro de la propiedad literaria
copy writer *s* escritor publicitario
co·quet [ko'kɛt] *v* (*pret & pp* **-quetted;** *ger* **-quetting**) *intr* coquetear; burlarse
coquet·ry ['kokətri] o [ko'kɛtri] *s* (*pl* **-ries**) coquetería; burla
coquette [ko'kɛt] *s* coqueta
coquettish [ko'kɛtɪʃ] *adj* coqueta
cor. *abbr* **corner, coroner, correction, corresponding**
coral ['kɑrəl] o ['kɔrəl] *adj* coralino || *s* coral *m*
coral reef *s* arrecife *m* de coral
cord [kɔrd] *s* cordón *m* || *tr* acordonar
cordial ['kɔrdʒəl] *adj* cordial || *s* licor tónico; (*stimulating medicine*) cordial *m*
cordiali·ty [kɔr'dʒælɪti] *s* (*pl* **-ties**) cordialidad
corduroy ['kɔrdə,rɔɪ] *s* pana; **corduroys** pantalones *mpl* de pana
core [kor] *s* corazón *m;* (*of an electromagnet*) núcleo
corespondent [,korɪs'pɑndənt] *s* cóm-

plice *mf* del demandado en juicio de divorcio

Corinth ['kɑrɪnθ] o ['kɔrɪnθ] *s* Corinto *f*

cork [kɔrk] *s* corcho; corcho, tapón *m* de corcho; tapón (*de cualquier materia*) || *tr* encorchar, tapar con corcho

corking ['kɔrkɪŋ] *adj* (slang) brutal, extraordinario

cork oak *s* alcornoque *m*

cork'screw' *s* sacacorchos *m*, tirabuzón *m*

cormorant ['kɔrmərənt] *s* cormorán *m*, cuervo marino

corn [kɔrn] *s* (*in U.S.A.*) maíz *m;* (*in England*) trigo; (*in Scotland*) avena; grano (*de maíz, trigo*); (*on the foot*) callo; (coll) aguardiente *m;* (slang) trivialidad

corn bread *s* pan *m* de maíz

corn'cake' *s* tortilla de maíz

corn'cob' *s* mazorca de maíz, carozo

corncob pipe *s* pipa de fumar hecha de una mazorca de maíz

corn'crib' *s* granero para maíz

corn cure *s* callicida *m*

cornea ['kɔrnɪ·ə] *s* córnea

corner ['kɔrnər] *s* ángulo; (*esp. where two streets meet*) esquina; (*inside angle formed by two or more surfaces; secluded place; region, quarter*) rincón *m;* (*of eye*) comisura, rabillo; (*of lips*) comisura; (*awkward position*) apuro, aprieto; monopolio; **around the corner** a la vuelta de la esquina; **to turn the corner** doblar la esquina; pasar el punto más peligroso || *tr* arrinconar; monopolizar

corner cupboard *s* rinconera

corner room *s* habitación de esquina

cor'ner•stone' *s* piedra angular; (*of a new building*) primera piedra

cornet [kɔr'nɛt] *s* corneta

corn exchange *s* bolsa de granos

corn'field' *s* (*in U.S.A.*) maizal *m;* (*in England*) trigal *m;* (*in Scotland*) avenal *m*

corn flour *s* harina de maíz

corn'flow'er *s* cabezuela

corn'husk' *s* perfolla

cornice ['kɔrnɪs] *s* cornisa

Cornish ['kɔrnɪʃ] *adj & s* córnico

corn liquor *s* chicha

corn meal *s* harina de maíz

corn on the cob *s* maíz *m* en la mazorca

corn plaster *s* emplasto para los callos

corn silk *s* cabellos, barbas del maíz

corn'stalk' *s* tallo de maíz

corn'starch' *s* almidón *m* de maíz

cornucopia [ˌkɔrnə'kopɪ·ə] *s* cornucopia

Cornwall ['kɔrnˌwɔl] o ['kɔrnwəl] *s* Cornualles

corn•y ['kɔrni] *adj* (*comp* **-ier;** *super* **-iest**) de maíz; (coll) gastado, trivial, pesado

corollar•y ['kɑrəˌlɛri] o ['kɔrəˌlɛri] *s* (*pl* **-ies**) corolario

coronation [ˌkɑrə'neʃən] o [ˌkɔrə'neʃən] *s* coronación

coroner ['kɑrənər] o ['kɔrənər] *s* juez *m* de guardia

coroner's inquest *s* pesquisa dirigida por el juez de guardia

coronet ['kɑrəˌnɛt] o ['kɔrəˌnɛt] *s* (*worn by members of nobility*) corona; (*ornamental band of jewels worn on head*) diadema *f*

Corp. *abbr* **Corporation**

corporal ['kɔrpərəl] *adj* corporal || *s* (mil) cabo

corporation [ˌkɔrpə'reʃən] *s* (*provincial, municipal, or service entity*) corporación; sociedad anónima por acciones

corps [kor] *s* (*pl* **corps** [korz]) cuerpo; (mil) cuerpo

corps de ballet [kɔr də bæ'lɛ] *s* cuerpo de baile

corpse [kɔrps] *s* cadáver *m*

corpulent ['kɔrpjələnt] *adj* corpulento

corpuscle ['kɔrpəsəl] *s* corpúsculo, partícula; (physiol) glóbulo

corr. *abbr* **correspondence, corresponding**

cor•ral [kə'ræl] *s* corral *m* || *v* (*pret & pp* **-ralled;** *ger* **-ralling**) *tr* acorralar

correct [kə'rɛkt] *adj* correcto; (*proper*) cumplido || *tr* corregir

correction [kə'rɛkʃən] *s* corrección

corrective [kə'rɛktɪv] *adj & s* correctivo

correctness [kə'rɛktnɪs] *s* corrección; cumplimiento, cumplido

correlate ['kɑrəˌlet] o ['kɔrəˌlet] *tr* correlacionar || *intr* correlacionarse

correlation [ˌkɑrə'leʃən] o [ˌkɔrə'leʃən] *s* correlación

correlative [kə'rɛlətɪv] *adj & s* correlativo

correspond [ˌkɑrɪ'spɑnd] o [ˌkɔrɪ'spɑnd] *intr* corresponder; (*to communicate by writing*) corresponderse

correspondence [ˌkɑrɪ'spɑndəns] o [ˌkɔrɪ'spɑndəns] *s* correspondencia

correspondence school *s* escuela por correspondencia

correspondent [ˌkɑrɪ'spɑndənt] o [ˌkɔrɪ'spɑndənt] *adj* correspondiente || *s* correspondiente *mf;* (*for a newspaper*) corresponsal *mf*

corresponding [ˌkɑrɪ'spɑndɪŋ] o [ˌkɔrɪ'spɑndɪŋ] *adj* correspondiente

corridor ['kɑrɪdər] o ['kɔrɪdər] *s* corredor *m*, pasillo

corroborate [kə'rɑbəˌret] *tr* corroborar

corrode [kə'rod] *tr* corroer || *intr* corroerse

corrosion [kə'roʒən] *s* corrosión

corrosive [kə'rosɪv] *adj & s* corrosivo

corrugated ['kɑrəˌgetɪd] o ['kɔrəˌgetɪd] *adj* acanalado, ondulado

corrupt [kə'rʌpt] *adj* corrompido || *tr* corromper || *intr* corromperse

corruption [kə'rʌpʃən] *s* corrupción

corsage [kɔr'sɑʒ] *s* (*bodice*) corpiño, jubón *m;* (*bouquet*) ramillete *m* que se lleva en el pecho o la cintura

corsair ['kɔrˌsɛr] *s* corsario

corset ['kɔrsɪt] *s* corsé *m*

corset cover *s* cubrecorsé *m*

Corsica ['kɔrsɪkə] *s* Córcega
Corsican ['kɔrsɪkən] *adj & s* corso
cortege [kɔr'teʒ] *s* procesión; (*retinue*) cortejo, séquito
cor•tex ['kɔr ˌtɛks] *s* (*pl* **-tices** [tɪ ˌsiz]) corteza; corteza cerebral
cortisone ['kɔrtɪ ˌson] *s* cortisona
corvette [kɔr'vɛt] *s* corbeta
cosmetic [kɑz'mɛtɪk] *adj & s* cosmético
cosmic ['kɑzmɪk] *adj* cósmico
cosmonaut ['kɑzmə ˌnɔt] *s* cosmonauta *mf*
cosmopolitan [ˌkɑzmə'pɑlɪtən] *adj & s* cosmopolita *mf*
cosmos ['kɑzməs] *s* cosmos *m;* (bot) cosmos
Cossack ['kɑˌsæk] *adj & s* cosaco
cost [kɔst] o [kɑst] *s* coste *m,* costo; **at cost** a coste y costas; **at all costs** a toda costa; **costs** (law) costas || *v* (*pret & pp* **cost**) *intr* costar; **cost what it may** cueste lo que cueste
cost accounting *s* escandallo
Costa Rican ['kɑstə 'rikən] o ['kɔste 'rikən] *adj & s* costarricense *mf,* costarriqueño
cost, insurance, and freight costo, seguro y flete
cost•ly ['kɔstli] o ['kɑstli] *adj* (*comp* **-lier;** *super* **-liest**) costoso, dispendioso; (*lavish*) pródigo; (*magnificent*) suntuoso
cost of living *s* costo de la vida, carestía de la vida
costume ['kɑstjum] o ['kɑstum] *s* traje *m;* (*garb worn on stage, at balls, etc.*) disfraz *m,* traje de época
costume ball *s* baile *m* de trajes
costume jewelry *s* joyas de fantasía, bisutería
cot [kɑt] *s* catre *m*
coterie ['kotəri] *s* círculo, grupo; (*clique*) corrillo
cottage ['kɑtɪdʒ] *s* cabaña; casita de campo
cottage cheese *s* naterón *m,* requesón *m*
cotter pin ['kɑtər] *s* chaveta
cotton ['kɑtən] *s* algodón *m* || *intr* — **to cotton up to** (coll) aficionarse a
cotton field *s* algodonal *m*
cotton gin *s* desmotadera de algodón
cotton picker ['pɪkər] *s* recogedor *m* de algodón; máquina para recolectar el algodón
cot'ton•seed' *s* semilla de algodón
cottonseed oil *s* aceite *m* de algodón
cotton waste *s* hilacha de algodón, estopa de algodón
cot'ton•wood' *s* chopo del Canadá, chopo de Virginia
cottony ['kɑtəni] *adj* algodonoso
couch [kaʊtʃ] *s* canapé *m,* sofá *m* || *tr* expresar
cougar ['kugər] *s* puma *m*
cough [kɔf] o [kɑf] *s* tos *f* || *tr* — **to cough up** arrojar por la boca; (slang) sudar, entregar || *intr* toser; (*artificially, to attract attention*) destoserse
cough drop *s* pastilla para la tos
cough syrup *s* jarabe *m* para la tos
could [kʊd] *v aux* pude, podía; podría
council ['kaʊnsəl] *s* (*deliberative or legislative assembly*) consejo; (*of a municipality*) concejo; (eccl) concilio
council•man ['kaʊnsəlmən] *s* (*pl* **-men** [mən]) concejal *m*
councilor ['kaʊnsələr] *s* consejero
coun•sel ['kaʊnsəl] *s* consejo; (*advisor*) consejero; (*consultant*) consultor *m;* (*lawyer*) abogado consultor; **to keep one's own counsel** no revelar sus intenciones || *v* (*pret & pp* **-seled** o **-selled;** *ger* **-seling** o **-selling**) *tr* aconsejar || *intr* aconsejarse
counselor ['kaʊnsələr] *s* consejero; abogado
count [kaʊnt] *s* (*act of counting*) cuenta, recuento; (*result of counting*) suma, total *m;* (*nobleman*) conde *m;* (*charge*) (law) cargo; **to take the count** (box) dejarse contar diez || *tr* contar; **to count off** separar contando; **to count out** no incluir; (sport) declarar vencido || *intr* contar; (*to be worth consideration*) valer; **to count for** valer; **to count on** contar con
countable ['kaʊntəbəl] *adj* contable
count'-down' *s* cuenta a cero
countenance ['kaʊntɪnəns] *s* cara, rostro, semblante *m;* (*composure*) compostura, serenidad; **to keep one's countenance** contenerse; **to lose countenance** conturbarse; **to put out of countenance** avergonzar, confundir || *tr* aprobar, apoyar, favorecer
counter ['kaʊntər] *adj* contrario || *adv* en el sentido opuesto; **counter to** a contrapelo de || *s* contador *m;* (*piece of wood or metal for keeping score*) ficha; (*board in shop over which business is transacted*) mostrador *m;* (box) contragolpe *m* || *tr* oponerse a; contradecir || *intr* (box) dar un contragolpe; **to counter with** replicar con
coun'ter•act' *tr* contrarrestar, contrariar
coun'ter•attack' *s* contraataque *m* || **coun'ter•attack'** *tr & intr* contraatacar
coun'ter•bal'ance *s* contrabalanza, contrapeso || **coun'ter•bal'ance** *tr* contrabalancear, contrapesar
coun'ter•clock'wise' *adj & adv* en el sentido contrario al de las agujas del reloj
coun'ter•es'pionage *s* contraespionaje *m*
counterfeit ['kaʊntərfɪt] *adj* contrahecho, falsificado || *s* contrahechura, falsificación; moneda falsa || *tr* contrahacer, falsificar
counterfeiter ['kaʊntər ˌfɪtər] *s* contrahacedor *m,* falsificador *m;* monedero falso
counterfeit money *s* moneda falsa
countermand ['kaʊndər ˌmænd] o ['kaʊntər ˌmɑnd] *s* contramandato || *tr* contramandar; hacer volver

coun'ter·march' *s* contramarcha || *intr* contramarchar
coun'ter·offen'sive *s* contraofensiva
coun'ter·pane' *s* cubrecama
coun'ter·part' *s* contraparte *f;* copia, duplicado
coun'ter·plot' *s* contratreta || *v* (*pret & pp* **-plotted;** *ger* **-plotting**) *tr* complotar contra (*la treta de otro u otros*)
coun'ter·point' *s* contrapunto
Counter Reformation *s* Contrarreforma
coun'ter·rev'olu'sion *s* contrarrevolución
coun'ter·sign' *s* contraseña || *tr* refrendar
coun'ter·sink' *v* (*pret & pp* **-sunk**) *tr* avellanar
coun'ter·spy' *s* (*pl* **-spies**) contraespía *mf*
coun'ter·stroke' *s* contragolpe *m*
coun'ter·weight' *s* contrapeso
countess ['kaʊntɪs] *s* condesa
countless ['kaʊntlɪs] *adj* incontable, innumerable
countrified ['kʌntrɪ,faɪd] *adj* campesino, rústico
coun·try ['kʌntri] *s* (*pl* **-tries**) (*territory of a nation*) país *m;* (*land of one's birth*) patria; (*not the city*) campo
country club *s* club *m* campestre
country cousin *s* isidro
country estate *s* heredad, hacienda de campo
coun'try·folk' *s* gente *f* del campo, campesinos
country gentleman *s* propietario acomodado de finca rural
country house *s* casa de campo, quinta
country jake [dʒek] *s* (coll) patán *m*
country life *s* vida rural
country·man ['kʌntrimən] *s* (*pl* **-men** [mən]) compatriota *m;* campesino
country people *s* gente *f* del campo, gente de capa parda
coun'try·side' *s* campiña
coun'try·wide' *adj* nacional
country·woman ['kʌntrɪ,wʊmən] *s* (*pl* **-women** [,wɪmɪn]) compatriota *f:* campesina
coun·ty ['kaʊnti] *s* (*pl* **-ties**) (*small political unit*) partido; (*domain of a count*) condado
county seat *s* cabeza de partido
coup [ku] *s* golpe *m*
coup de grâce [ku də 'grɑs] *s* puñalada de misericordia, golpe *m* de gracia
coup d'état [ku de'tɑ] *s* golpe *m* de estado
coupé [ku'pe] *s* cupé *m*
couple ['kʌpəl] *s* par *m;* (*man and wife*) matrimonio; (*two people dancing together*) pareja; (elec, mech) par *m;* (*two more or less*) (coll) par *m* || *tr* acoplar, juntar, unir || *intr* juntarse, unirse
coupler ['kʌplər] *s* (rr) enganche *m*
couplet ['kʌplɪt] *s* copla, pareado
coupon [ku'pɑn] o [kju'pɑn] *s* (*of a bond*) cupón *m;* (*piece detached from larger piece*) talón *m*
courage ['kʌrɪdʒ] *s* valor *m,* ánimo; firmeza, resolución; **to have the courage of one's convictions** ajustarse abiertamente con su conciencia; **to pluck up courage** hacer de tripas corazón
courageous [kə'redʒəs] *adj* valiente, animoso
courier ['kʌrɪ·ər] o ['kʊrɪ·ər] *s* estafeta, mensajero; guía *m*
course [kors] *s* (*onward movement*) curso; (*of a ship*) derrota, rumbo; (*of time*) transcurso; (*of events*) marcha; (*in school*) asignatura, curso; (*of a meal*) plato; campo de golf; (mas) hilada; **in the course of** en el decurso de; **of course** por supuesto, naturalmente
court [kort] *s* (*of justice*) tribunal *m;* (*of a king*) corte *f;* (*open space enclosed by a building*) atrio, patio; (*for tennis*) cancha, pista; **to pay court to** hacer la corte a || *tr* cortejar; buscar, solicitar
courteous ['kʌrtɪ·əs] *adj* cortés
courtesan ['kʌrtɪzən] o ['kortɪzən] *s* cortesana
courte·sy ['kʌrtɪsi] *s* (*pl* **-sies**) cortesía
court'house' *s* palacio de justicia
courtier ['kortɪ·ər] *s* cortesano, palaciego
court jester *s* bufón *m*
court·ly ['kortli] *adj* (*comp* **-lier;** *super* **-liest**) cortés, cortesano; (*pertaining to the court*) cortesano
court'-mar'tial *s* (*pl* **courts-martial**) consejo de guerra || *v* (*pret & pp* **-tialed** o **-tialled;** *ger* **-tialing** o **-tialling**) *tr* someter a consejo de guerra
court plaster *s* tafetán *m* inglés
court'room' *s* sala de justicia, tribunal *m*
courtship ['kort∫ɪp] *s* cortejo, galanteo; noviazgo
court'yard' *s* atrio, patio
cousin ['kʌzɪn] *s* primo
cove [kov] *s* cala, ensenada
covenant ['kʌvənənt] *s* convenio, pacto; contrato; (Bib) alianza || *tr & intr* pactar
cover ['kʌvər] *s* cubierta; (*of a magazine*) portada; (*place for one person at table*) cubierto; (*for a bed*) cobertor *m;* **to take cover** ocultarse; **under cover** bajo cubierto, bajo techado; oculto; disfrazado; **under cover of** (*e.g., the night*) a cubierto de; so capa de; **under separate cover** bajo cubierta separada, por separado || *tr* cubrir; (*to line, to coat*) recubrir, revestir; recorrer (*cierta distancia*); cubrirse (*la cabeza*); tapar (*una olla*) || *intr* cubrirse
coverage ['kʌvərɪdʒ] *s* (*amount or space covered*) alcance *m;* (*of news*) reportaje *m;* (*funds to meet liabilities*) cobertura
coveralls ['cʌvər,ɔlz] *s* mono

cover charge *s* precio del cubierto
covered ['kʌvərd] *adj* cubierto; (*wire*) forrado; (*bridge*) cubierto
covered wagon *s* carromato
cover girl *s* (coll) muchacha hermosa en la portada de una revista
covering ['kʌvərɪŋ] *s* cubierta, envoltura
covert ['kʌvərt] *adj* disimulado, secreto
cov'er·up' *s* efugio, subterfugio
covet ['kʌvɪt] *tr* codiciar
covetous ['kʌvɪtəs] *adj* codicioso
covetousness ['kʌvɪtəsnɪs] *s* codicia
covey ['kʌvi] *s* (*brood*) nidada; (*in flight*) bandada; corro, grupo
cow [kaʊ] *s* vaca || *tr* acobardar, intimidar
coward ['kaʊ·ərd] *s* cobarde *mf*
cowardice ['kaʊ·ərdɪs] *s* cobardía
cowardly ['kaʊ·ərdli] *adj* cobarde || *adv* cobardemente
cow'bell' *s* cencerro
cow'boy' *s* vaquero; gaucho (Arg)
cowcatcher ['kaʊ,kætʃər] *s* quitapiedras *m,* rastrillo; trompa (Col, Chile)
cower ['kaʊ·ər] *intr* agacharse
cow'herd' *s* vaquero, pastor *m* de ganado vacuno
cow'hide' *s* cuero; (*whip*) zurriago || *tr* zurriagar
cowl [kaʊl] *s* capucha, cogulla; (aer) cubierta del motor; (aut) cubretablero, bóveda
cow'lick' *s* mechón *m,* remolino (*pelos que se levantan sobre la frente*)
cowpox ['kaʊ,pɑks] *s* vacuna
coxcomb ['kɑks,kom] *s* petimetre *m,* mequetrefe *m*
coxswain ['kɑksən] o ['kɑk,swen] *s* timonel *m;* contramaestre *m*
coy [kɔɪ] *adj* recatado, modesto; coquetón
co·zy ['kozi] *adj* (*comp* **-zier;** *super* **-ziest**) cómodo || *s* (*pl* **-zies**) cubretetera
cp. *abbr* **compare**
c.p. *abbr* **candle power**
C.P.A. *abbr* **certified public accountant**
cpd. *abbr* **compound**
cr. *abbr* **credit, creditor**
crab [kræb] *s* cangrejo; (*grouch*) cascarrabias *mf*
crab apple *s* manzana silvestre
crabbed ['kræbɪd] *adj* avinagrado, ceñudo
crab grass *s* garranchuelo
crab louse *s* ladilla
crack [kræk] *adj* (coll) de primera clase; (*shot*) (coll) certero || *s* grieta, hendidura; (*noise*) crujido, estallido; (coll) instante *m,* momento; (*joke*) (slang) chiste *m;* **at the crack of dawn** al romper el alba || *tr* agrietar, hender; chasquear (*un látigo*); abrir (*una caja fuerte*) por la fuerza; cascar (*nueces*); descifrar (*un código*); (slang) decir (*un chiste*); (slang) descubrir (*un secreto*); **to crack a smile** (slang) sonreír; **to crack up** (coll) alabar, elogiar || *intr* agrietarse; crujir; cascarse (*la voz de una persona*); enloquecerse; ceder, someterse; **to crack up** fracasar; perder la salud; estrellarse (*un avión*)
cracked [krækt] *adj* agrietado; (*ice*) picado; (coll) mentecato, loco
cracker ['krækər] *s* galleta
crack'le·ware' *s* grietado
crack'pot' *adj* & *s* (slang) excéntrico, tarambana *mf*
crack'-up' *s* fracaso; colisión; derrota; (aer) aterrizaje violento; (coll) colapso
cradle ['kredəl] *s* cuna; (*of handset*) horquilla || *tr* acunar
cra'dle·song' *s* canción de cuna, arrullo
craft [kræft] o [krɑft] *s* arte *m,* arte manual; astucia, maña; nave *f* || *spl* naves
craftiness ['kræftɪnɪs] o ['krɑftɪnɪs] *s* astucia
crafts·man ['kræftsmən] o ['krɑftsmən] *s* (*pl* **-men** [mən]) artesano; artista *m*
craftsmanship ['kræftsmən,ʃɪp] o ['krɑftsmən,ʃɪp] *s* artesanía
craft·y ['kræfti] o ['krɑfti] *adj* (*comp* **-ier;** *super* **-iest**) astuto, mañoso
crag [kræg] *s* peñasco, despeñadero
cram [kræm] *v* (*pret* & *pp* **crammed;** *ger* **cramming**) *tr* atascar, atracar, embutir; (coll) aprender apresuradamente || *intr* atracarse; (*to study hard*) (coll) empollar
cramp [kræmp] *s* (*metal bar*) grapa, laña; (*clamp*) abrazadera; (*painful contraction of muscle*) calambre *m;* **cramps** retortijón *m* de tripas || *tr* engrapar, lañar; apretar; dar calambre a
cranber·ry ['kræn,bɛri] *s* (*pl* **-ries**) arándano agrio
crane [kren] *s* (*bird*) grulla; (*derrick*) grúa || *tr* estirar (*el cuello*) || *intr* estirar el cuello
crani·um ['krenɪ·əm] *s* (*pl* **-a** [ə]) cráneo
crank [kræŋk] *s* manivela, manubrio; (coll) estrafalario || *tr* hacer girar (*el motor*) con la manivela
crank'case' *s* caja de cigüeñal, cárter *m* del cigüeñal
crank'shaft' *s* cigüeñal *m*
crank·y ['kræŋki] *adj* (*comp* **-ier;** *super* **-iest**) malhumorado; (*queer*) estrafalario
cran·ny ['kræni] *s* (*pl* **-nies**) hendidura, grieta, rendija
crape [krep] *s* crespón *m;* crespón fúnebre, crespón negro
crape'hang'er *s* (slang) aguafiestas *mf*
craps [kræps] *s* juego de dados; **to shoot craps** jugar a los dados
crash [kræʃ] *s* caída, desplome *m;* colisión, choque *m;* estallido, estrépito; fracaso; crac financiero; lienzo grueso; (aer) aterrizaje violento || *tr* romper con estrépito, estrellar; **to crash a party** (slang) asistir a una fiesta sin invitación; **to crash the gate**

(slang) colarse de gorra || *intr* caer, desplomarse; romperse con estrépito, estallar; (*in business*) quebrar; aterrizar violentamente, estrellarse (*un avión*); **to crash into** chocar con
crash dive *s* sumersión instantánea (*de submarino*)
crash landing *s* aterrizaje violento
crash program *s* programa intensivo
crass [kræs] *adj* espeso, tosco; (*ignorance, mistake*) craso
crate [kret] *s* (*box made of slats*) jaula; (*basket*) banasta, cuévano || *tr* embalar en jaula, embalar con listones
crater ['kretər] *s* cráter *m*
cravat [krə'væt] *s* corbata
crave [krev] *tr* anhelar, ansiar; pedir (*indulgencia*) || *intr* — **to crave for** anhelar, ansiar; pedir con insistencia
craven ['krevən] *adj* & *s* cobarde *mf*
craving ['krevɪŋ] *s* anhelo, ansia, deseo ardiente
craw [krɔ] *s* buche *m*
crawl [krɔl] *s* arrastre *m;* gateado || *intr* reptar, arrastrarse, gatear; (*to have a feeling of insects on skin*) hormiguear; **to crawl along** andar paso a paso; **to crawl up** trepar
crayon ['kre·ən] *s* creyón *m*
craze [krez] *s* boga, moda; locura, manía || *tr* enloquecer
cra·zy ['krezi] *adj* (*comp* **-zier;** *super* **-ziest**) loco; (*rickety*) desvencijado; achacoso, débil; **crazy as a bedbug** (slang) loco de atar; **to be crazy about** (coll) estar loco por; **to drive crazy** volver loco
crazy bone *s* hueso de la alegría
creak [krik] *s* crujido, rechinamiento || *intr* crujir, rechinar
creak·y ['kriki] *adj* (*comp* **-ier;** *super* **-iest**) crujidero, rechinador
cream [krim] *s* crema; (*e.g., of society*) crema, nata y flor || *tr* desnatar (*la leche*)
creamer·y ['kriməri] *s* (*pl* **-ies**) mantequería, quesería, lechería
cream puff *s* bollo de crema
cream separator *s* desnatadora
cream·y ['krimi] *adj* (*comp* **-ier;** *super* **-iest**) cremoso
crease [kris] *s* arruga, pliegue *m;* (*in trousers*) raya || *tr* arrugar, plegar
create [kri'et] *tr* crear
creation [kri'eʃən] *s* creación
creative [kri'etɪv] *adj* creativo
creator [kri'etər] *s* creador *m*
creature ['kritʃər] *s* criatura; (*being, strange being*) ente *m;* animal *m*
credence ['kridəns] *s* creencia; **to give credence to** dar fe a
credentials [krɪ'dɛnʃəlz] *spl* credenciales *fpl*
credible ['krɛdɪbəl] *adj* creíble
credit ['krɛdɪt] *s* crédito; **to take credit for** atribuirse el mérito de || *tr* acreditar; **to credit a person with** atribuirle a una persona el mérito de
creditable ['krɛdɪtəbəl] *adj* honorable, estimable
credit card *s* tarjeta de crédito
creditor ['krɛdɪtər] *s* acreedor *m*
cre·do ['krido] o ['kredo] *s* (*pl* **-dos**) credo
credulous ['krɛdʒələs] *adj* crédulo
creed [krid] *s* credo
creek [krik] *s* arroyo, riachuelo
creep [krip] *v* (*pret* & *pp* **crept** [krɛpt]) *intr* arrastrarse; (*on all fours*) gatear; (*to climb*) trepar; (*with a sensation of insects*) hormiguear; **to creep up on** acercarse insensiblemente a
creeper ['kripər] *s* planta rastrera, planta trepadora
creeping ['kripɪŋ] *adj* lento, progresivo; (*plant*) rastrero || *s* arrastramiento
cremate ['krimet] *tr* incinerar
cremation [krɪ'meʃən] *s* cremación, incineración
cremato·ry ['krimə,tori] *adj* crematorio || *s* (*pl* **-ries**) crematorio
crème de menthe [krɛm də 'mɑ̃t] *s* crema de menta
Creole ['kri·ol] *adj* & *s* criollo
crescent ['krɛsənt] *s* (*moon in first or last quarter*) creciente *f* de la luna; (*shape of moon in either of these phases*) media luna; panecillo (*en forma de media luna*)
cress [krɛs] *s* mastuerzo
crest [krɛst] *s* cresta
crestfallen ['krɛst,fɔlən] *adj* cabizbajo
Cretan ['kritən] *adj* & *s* cretense *mf*
Crete [krit] *s* Creta
cretonne [krɪ'tɑn] *s* cretona
crevice ['krɛvɪs] *s* grieta
crew [kru] *s* equipo; (*of a ship*) dotación, tripulación; (*group, esp. of armed men*) banda, cuadrilla
crew cut *s* corte *m* de pelo a cepillo
crib [krɪb] *s* pesebre *m;* camita de niño; (coll) plagio; (*student's pony*) (coll) chuleta || *v* (*pret* & *pp* **cribbed;** *ger* **cribbing**) *tr* & *intr* (coll) hurtar
cricket ['krɪkɪt] *s* (ent) grillo; (sport) cricquet *m;* (coll) juego limpio
crier ['kraɪ·ər] *s* pregonero
crime [kraɪm] *s* crimen *m,* delito
criminal ['krɪmɪnəl] *adj* & *s* criminal *mf*
criminal code *s* código penal
criminal law *s* derecho penal
criminal negligence *s* imprudencia temeraria
crimp [krɪmp] *s* rizado, rizo; **to put a crimp in** (coll) estorbar, impedir || *tr* rizar
crimple ['krɪmpəl] *tr* arrugar, rizar || *intr* arrugarse, rizarse
crimson ['krɪmzən] *adj* & *s* carmesí *m* || *intr* enrojecerse
cringe [krɪndʒ] *intr* arrastrarse, reptar, encogerse
crinkle ['krɪŋkəl] *s* arruga, pliegue *m;* (*in the water*) rizo u onda || *tr* arrugar, plegar || *intr* arrugarse
cripple ['krɪpəl] *s* zopo, lisiado || *tr* lisiar, estropear; dañar, perjudicar
cri·sis ['kraɪsɪs] *s* (*pl* **-ses** [siz]) crisis *f*

crisp [krɪsp] *adj* frágil, quebradizo; (*air, weather*) refrescante; decisivo
criteri•on [kraɪˈtɪrɪ•ən] *s* (*pl* **-a** [ə]) u **-ons**) criterio
critic [ˈkrɪtɪk] *s* crítico; (*faultfinder*) criticón *m*
critical [ˈkrɪtɪkəl] *adj* crítico; (*faultfinding*) criticón
criticism [ˈkrɪtɪˌsɪzəm] *s* crítica
criticize [ˈkrɪtɪˌsaɪz] *tr & intr* criticar
critique [krɪˈtik] *s* (*art of criticism*) crítica; ensayo crítico
croak [krok] *s* (*of raven*) graznido; canto de ranas ‖ *intr* graznar (*el cuervo*); croar (*la rana*); (*morir*) (slang) reventar
Croat [krot] *s* (*native or inhabitant*) croata *mf;* (*language*) croata *m*
Croatian [kroˈeʃən] *adj & mf* croata *mf*
cro•chet [kroˈʃe] *s* croché *m* ‖ *v* (*pret & pp* **-cheted** [ˈʃed]); *ger* **-cheting** [ˈʃe•ɪŋ]) *tr* trabajar con aguja de gancho ‖ *intr* hacer croché
crocheting [kroˈʃe•ɪŋ] *s* labor *f* de ganchillo
crochet needle *s* aguja de gancho
crock [krɑk] *s* cacharro, vasija de barro cocido
crockery [ˈkrɑkəri] *s* loza
crocodile [ˈkrɑkəˌdaɪl] *s* cocodrilo
crocodile tears *spl* lágrimas de cocodrilo
crocus [ˈkrokəs] *s* azafrán *m,* croco
crone [kron] *s* vieja acartonada, vieja arrugada
cro•ny [ˈkroni] *s* (*pl* **-nies**) compinche *mf*
crook [krʊk] *s* gancho, garfio; curva; (*of shepherd*) cayado; (coll) fullero, ladrón *m* ‖ *tr* encorvar; (slang) empinar (*el codo*) ‖ *intr* encorvarse
crooked [ˈkrʊkɪd] *adj* encorvado, torcido; (*person or his conduct*) torcido; **to go crooked** (coll) torcerse
croon [krun] *intr* cantar con voz suave, cantar con melancolía exagerada
crooner [ˈkrunər] *s* cantor de voz suave, cantor melancólico
crop [krɑp] *s* cosecha; (*head of hair*) cabellera; cabello corto; (*of a bird*) buche *m;* (*whip*) látigo; (*of appointments, promotions, heroes, etc.*) hornada ‖ *v* (*pret & pp* **cropped;** *ger* **cropping**) *tr* desmochar (*un árbol*); desorejar (*a un animal*); esquilar, trasquilar ‖ *intr* — **to crop out** o **up** aflorar; asomar, dejarse ver, manifestarse inesperadamente
crop dusting *s* aerofumigación, fumigación aérea
croquet [kroˈke] *s* crocquet *m*
croquette [kroˈkɛt] *s* croqueta
crosier [ˈkroʒər] *s* báculo pastoral, cayado
cross [krɔs] o [krɑs] *adj* transversal, travieso; (*breed*) cruzado; malhumorado, enfadado ‖ *s* cruz *f;* (*of races; of two roads*) cruce *m;* **to take the cross** (*to join a crusade*) cruzarse ‖ *tr* cruzar; (*to oppose*) contrariar, frustrar; **to cross off** u **out** borrar; **to cross oneself** hacerse la señal de la cruz; **to cross one's mind** ocurrírsele a uno; **to cross one's t's** poner travesaño a las tes, poner el palo a las tes ‖ *intr* cruzar; cruzarse; **to cross over** atravesar de un lado a otro
cross'bones' *spl* huesos cruzados (*símbolo de la muerte*)
cross'bow' *s* ballesta
cross'breed' *v* (*pret & pp* **-bred** [ˌbrɛd]) *tr* cruzar (*animales o plantas*)
cross'coun'try *adj* a campo traviesa; a través del país
cross'cur'rent *s* contracorriente *f;* (fig) tendencia encontrada
cross'-exam'i•na'tion *s* interrogatorio riguroso; (law) repregunta
cross'-ex•am'ine *tr* interrogar rigurosamente; (law) repreguntar
cross-eyed [ˈkrɔsˌaɪd] o [ˈkrɑsˌaɪd] *adj* bisojo, bizco, ojituerto
crossing [ˈkrɔsɪŋ] o [ˈkrɑsɪŋ] *s* (*of lines, streets, etc.*) cruce *m;* (*of the ocean*) travesía; (*of a river*) vado; (rr) crucero, paso a nivel
crossing gate *s* barrera, barrera de paso a nivel
crossing point *s* punto de cruce
cross'patch' *s* (coll) gruñón *m*
cross'piece' *s* travesaño
cross reference *s* contrarreferencia, remisión
cross'road' *s* vía transversal; **crossroads** encrucijada, cruce *m;* **at the crossroads** en el momento crítico
cross section *s* corte *m* transversal; (fig) sección representativa
cross street *s* calle traviesa, calle de travesía
cross'word' puzzle *s* crucigrama *m*
crotch [krɑtʃ] *s* (*forked piece*) horcajadura, bifurcación; (*between legs*) entrepierna, bragadura, horcajadura
crotchety [ˈkrɑtʃɪti] *adj* caprichoso, estrambótico, de mal genio
crouch [kraʊtʃ] *s* posición agachada ‖ *intr* agacharse, acuclillarse
croup [krup] *s* garrotillo, crup *m;* (*of horse*) anca, grupa
croupier [ˈkrupɪ•ər] *s* crupié *m*
crouton [ˈkrutɑn] *s* corteza de pan
crow [kro] *s* corneja, grajo, chova; (*cry of the cock*) quiquiriquí *m;* (*crowbar*) alzaprima; **as the crow flies** a vuelo de pájaro; **to eat crow** (coll) cantar la palinodia; **to have a crow to pick with** (coll) tener que habérselas con ‖ *intr* cantar (*el gallo*); jactarse; **to crow over** jactarse de
crow'bar' *s* alzaprima, pie *m* de cabra
crowd [kraʊd] *s* gentío, multitud; (*flock of people*) caterva, tropel *m;* (*mob, common people*) populacho, vulgo; (*clique, set*) corrillo, grupo ‖ *tr* apiñar, apretar, atestar; (*to push*) empujar ‖ *intr* apiñarse, apretarse, atestarse; (*to mill around*) arremolinarse

crowded ['kraʊdɪd] *adj* atestado, concurrido
crown [kraʊn] *s* corona; (*of hat*) copa || *tr* coronar; (checkers) coronar; (slang) golpear en la cabeza
crowned head *s* testa coronada
crown prince *s* príncipe heredero
crown princess *s* princesa heredera
crow's'-foot' *s* (*pl* **-feet'**) pata de gallo
crow's'-nest' *s* (naut) cofa de vigía, torre *f* de vigía
crucial ['kruʃəl] *adj* crucial; difícil, penoso
crucible ['krusɪbəl] *s* crisol *m*
crucifix ['krusɪfɪks] *s* crucifijo
crucifixion [,krusɪ'fɪkʃən] *s* crucifixión
cruci•fy ['krusɪ,faɪ] *v* (*pret & pp* **-fied**) *tr* crucificar
crude [krud] *adj* (*raw, unrefined*) crudo; (*lacking culture*) grosero, tosco; (*unfinished*) basto, sin labrar
crudi•ty ['krudɪti] *s* (*pl* **-ties**) crudeza; grosería, tosquedad; bastedad
cruel ['kru·əl] *adj* cruel
cruel•ty ['kru·əlti] *s* (*pl* **-ties**) crueldad
cruet ['kru·ɪt] *s* ampolleta
cruet stand *s* angarillas, vinagreras
cruise [kruz] *s* viaje *m* por mar; (aer, naut) crucero || *tr* (naut) cruzar || *intr* cruzar; (coll) andar de un lado a otro
cruiser ['kruzər] *s* (nav) crucero
cruising ['kruzɪŋ] *adj* de crucero || *s* (aer, naut) crucero
cruising radius *s* autonomía
cruller ['krʌlər] *s* buñuelo
crumb [krʌm] *s* migaja; (*soft part of bread*) miga; (*given to a beggar*) mendrugo || *tr* desmigar (*el pan*); (culin) empanar, cubrir con pan rallado; limpiar (*la mesa*) de migajas || *intr* desmigarse, desmenuzarse
crumble ['krʌmbəl] *tr* desmenuzar || *intr* desmenuzarse; (*to fall to pieces gradually*) desmoronarse
crum•my ['krʌmi] *adj* (*comp* **-mier;** *super* **-miest**) (slang) desaseado, sucio; (slang) de mal gusto, de mala muerte
crumple ['krʌmpəl] *tr* arrugar, ajar, chafar || *intr* arrugarse, ajarse
crunch [krʌntʃ] *tr* ronchar, ronzar || *intr* crujir
crusade [kru'sed] *s* cruzada || *intr* hacer una cruzada
crusader [kru'sedər] *s* cruzado
crush [krʌʃ] *s* aplastamiento; (*of people*) aglomeración, bullaje *m;* **to have a crush on** (slang) estar perdido por || *tr* aplastar, machacar, magullar; (*to grind*) moler; bocartear (*el mineral*); (*to oppress, grieve*) abrumar
crush hat *s* clac *m*
crust [krʌst] *s* corteza; corteza de pan; (*scab*) costra
crustacean [krʌs'teʃən] *s* crustáceo
crustaceous [krʌs'teʃəs] *adj* crustáceo
crust•y ['krʌsti] *adj* (*comp* **-ier;** *super* **-iest**) (*scabby*) costroso; áspero, grosero, rudo
crutch [krʌtʃ] *s* muleta
crux [krʌks] *s* punto capital; enigma *m*
cry [kraɪ] *s* (*pl* **cries**) grito; (*weeping*) lloro; (*of peddler*) pregón *m;* (*of wolf*) aullido; (*of bull*) bramido; **in full cry** en plena persecución; **to have a good cry** desahogarse en lágrimas abundantes || *v* (*pret & pp* **cried**) *tr* decir a gritos; (*to announce publicly*) pregonar; **to cry one's eyes** o **heart out** llorar amargamente; **to cry out** decir a gritos; pregonar || *intr* gritar; (*to weep*) llorar; aullar (*el lobo*); bramar (*el toro*); **to cry for** clamar por; **to cry for joy** llorar de alegría; **to cry out** clamar; **to cry out against** clamar contra; **to cry out for** clamar, clamar por
cry'ba'by *s* (*pl* **-bies**) llorón *m,* llorona, lloraduelos *mf*
crypt [krɪpt] *s* cripta
cryptic(al) ['krɪptɪk(əl)] *adj* enigmático, misterioso
crystal ['krɪstəl] *s* cristal *m*
crystal ball *s* bola de cristal
crystalline ['krɪstəlɪn] o ['krɪstə,laɪn] *adj* cristalino
crystallize ['krɪstə,laɪz] *tr* cristalizar || *intr* cristalizarse
C.S. *abbr* **Christian Science, Civil Service**
ct. *abbr* **cent**
cu. *abbr* **cubic**
cub [kʌb] *s* cachorro
Cuban ['kjubən] *adj & s* cubano
cubbyhole ['kʌbɪ,hol] *s* chiribitil *m*
cube [kjub] *adj* (*root*) cúbico || *s* cubo; (*of ice*) cubito || *tr* cubicar
cubic ['kjubɪk] *adj* cúbico
cub reporter *s* (coll) reportero novato
cuckold ['kʌkəld] *adj & s* cornudo || *tr* encornudar
cuckoo ['kʊku] *adj* (slang) mentecato, loco || *s* cuclillo, cuco; (*call of cuckoo*) cucú *m*
cuckoo clock *s* reloj *m* de cuclillo
cucumber ['kjukəmbər] *s* pepino
cud [kʌd] *s* bolo alimenticio; **to chew the cud** rumiar
cuddle ['kʌdəl] *s* abrazo cariñoso || *tr* abrazar con cariño || *intr* estar abrazados, arrimarse cariñosamente
cudg•el ['kʌdʒəl] *s* garrote *m,* porra; **to take up the cudgels for** salir a la defensa de || *v* (*pret & pp* **-eled** o **-elled;** *ger* **-eling** o **-elling**) *tr* apalear, aporrear
cue [kju] *s* señal *f,* indicación; (*hint*) indirecta; (*rôle*) papel *m;* (*rod used in billiards*) taco; (*of hair*) coleta; (*of people in line*) cola; (theat) apunte *m*
cuff [kʌf] *s* (*of shirt*) puño; (*of trousers*) doblez *f,* vuelta; (*blow*) bofetada || *tr* abofetear
cuff links *spl* gemelos
cuirass [kwɪ'ræs] *s* coraza
cuisine [kwɪ'zin] *s* cocina (*arte culinario*)
culinary ['kjulɪ,neri] *adj* culinario
cull [kʌl] *tr* (*to choose, pick*) entresa-

car, escoger; (*to gather, pluck*) coger, recoger
culm [kʌlm] *s* (*coal dust*) cisco; (*stalk of grasses*) caña, tallo
culminate ['kʌlmɪ,net] *intr* culminar; **to culminate in** conducir a, terminar en
culpable ['kʌlpəbəl] *adj* culpable
culprit ['kʌlprɪt] *s* acusado; reo
cult [kʌlt] *s* culto; secta
cultivate ['kʌltɪ,vet] *tr* cultivar
cultivated ['kʌltɪ,vetɪd] *adj* culto, cultivado
cultivation [,kʌltɪ'veʃən] *s* (*of the land, the arts, one's memory, etc.*) cultivo; (*refinement*) cultura
culture ['kʌltʃər] *s* cultura
cultured ['kʌltʃərd] *adj* culto
culvert ['kʌlvərt] *s* alcantarilla
cumbersome ['kʌmbərsəm] *adj* incómodo, molesto; (*clumsy*) pesado, inmanejable
cunning ['kʌnɪŋ] *adj* (*sly*) astuto; (*clever*) hábil; (*attractive*) gracioso, mono || *s* astucia; habilidad, destreza
cup [kʌp] *s* taza; (*of thermometer*) cubeta; (mach) vaso de engrase; (sport) copa; (*of sorrow*) (fig) copa; **in one's cups** borracho || *v* (*pret & pp* **cupped**; *ger* **cupping**) *tr* ahuecar dando forma de taza o copa a; poner ventosa a
cupboard ['kʌbərd] *s* alacena, aparador *m*, armario
cupidity [kjʊ'pɪdɪti] *s* codicia
cupola ['kjupələ] *s* cúpula
cur [kʌr] *s* perro mestizo, perro de mala raza; (*despicable fellow*) canalla *m*
curate ['kjʊrɪt] *s* cura *m*
curative ['kjʊrətɪv] *adj* curativo || *s* curativa
curator [kjʊ'retər] *s* conservador *m*
curb [kʌrb] *s* (*of sidewalk*) encintado; (*of well*) brocal *m*; (*of bit*) barbada; (*market*) bolsín *m*; (*check, restraint*) freno; (vet) corva || *tr* contener, refrenar
curb'stone' *s* piedra de encintado; brocal *m* de pozo
curd [kʌrd] *s* cuajada || *tr* cuajar || *intr* cuajarse
curdle ['kʌrdəl] *tr* cuajar; **to curdle the blood** horrorizar || *intr* cuajar
cure [kjʊr] *s* cura, curación || *tr* curar || *intr* curar; curarse
cure'-all' *s* sanalotodo
curfew ['kʌrfju] *s* queda, cubrefuego; toque *m* de queda
curi·o ['kjʊrɪ,o] *s* (*pl* **-os**) curiosidad
curiosi·ty [,kjʊrɪ'ɑsɪti] *s* (*pl* **-ties**) curiosidad
curious ['kjʊrɪ·əs] *adj* curioso
curl [kʌrl] *s* bucle *m*, rizo; (*spiral-shaped curl*) tirabuzón *m*; (*of smoke*) espiral *f*; (*curling*) rizado || *tr* encrespar, ensortijar, rizar; (*to coil, to roll up*) arrollar; fruncir (*los labios*) || *intr* encresparse, ensortijarse, rizarse; arrollarse; **to curl up** arrollarse; (*in bed*) encogerse; (*to break up, collapse*) (coll) desplomarse
curlicue ['kʌrlɪ,kju] *s* ringorrango
curling iron *s* rizador *m*, maquinilla de rizar
curl'pa'per *s* torcida, papelito para rizar el pelo
curl·y ['kʌrli] *adj* (*comp* **-ier**; *super* **-iest**) crespo, rizo
curmudgeon [kər'mʌdʒən] *s* cicatero, tacaño, erizo
currant ['kʌrənt] *s* pasa de Corinto; (*Ribes alpinum*) calderilla
curren·cy ['kʌrənsi] *s* (*pl* **-cies**) moneda corriente, dinero en circulación; uso corriente
current ['kʌrənt] *adj* corriente || *s* corriente *f*; (elec) corriente *f*
current account *s* cuenta corriente
current events *spl* actualidades, sucesos de actualidad
curricu·lum [kə'rɪkjələm] *s* (*pl* **-lums** o **-la** [lə]) plan *m* de estudios
cur·ry ['kʌri] *s* (*pl* **-ries**) cari *m* || *v* (*pret & pp* **-ried**) *tr* curtir (*las pieles*); almohazar (*el caballo*); **to curry favor** procurar complacer
cur'ry·comb' *s* almohaza || *tr* almohazar
curse [kʌrs] *s* maldición; (*profane oath*) reniego, voto; (*evil, misfortune*) calamidad || *tr* maldecir || *intr* jurar, echar votos
cursed ['kʌrsɪd] o [kʌrst] *adj* maldito; aborrecible
cursive ['kʌrsɪv] *adj* cursivo || *s* cursiva
cursory ['kʌrsəri] *adj* apresurado, rápido, superficial, de paso
curt [kʌrt] *adj* áspero, brusco; corto, conciso
curtail [kər'tel] *tr* acortar, abreviar, cercenar
curtain ['kʌrtən] *s* cortina; (theat) telón *m*; **to draw the curtain** correr la cortina; **to drop the curtain** (theat) bajar el telón || *tr* encortinar; separar con cortina; cubrir, ocultar
curtain call *s* llamada a la escena para recibir aplausos
curtain raiser ['rezər] *s* (theat) pieza preliminar
curtain ring *s* anilla
curtain rod *s* riel *m*
curt·sy ['kʌrtsi] *s* (*pl* **-sies**) cortesía, reverencia || *v* (*pret & pp* **-sied**) *intr* hacer una cortesía
curve [kʌrv] *s* curva || *tr* encorvar || *intr* encorvarse; volver, virar
curved [kʌrvd] *adj* curvo, encorvado; (*crooked*) combo
cushion ['kʊʃən] *s* cojín *m*, almohada; (*of billiard table*) baranda || *tr* amortiguar
cusp [kʌsp] *s* cúspide *f*
cuspidor ['kʌspɪ,dɔr] *s* escupidera
custard ['kʌstərd] *s* flan *m*, natillas
custodian [kəs'todɪ·ən] *s* custodio; (*of a house or building*) casero
custo·dy ['kʌstədi] *s* (*pl* **-dies**) custodia; **in custody** en prisión; **to take into custody** prender
custom ['kʌstəm] *s* costumbre; (*cus-*

tomers) parroquia, clientela; **customs** aduana; derechos de aduana
customary [ˈkʌstəˌmɛri] *adj* acostumbrado, de costumbre
cus'tom-built' *adj* hecho por encargo, fuera de serie
customer [ˈkʌstəmər] *s* parroquiano, cliente *mf;* (*of a café or restaurant*) consumidor *m;* (coll) individuo, sujeto, tipo
cus'tom·house' *adj* aduanero ‖ *s* aduana
cus'tom-made' *adj* hecho a la medida
customs clearance *s* despacho de aduana
customs officer *s* aduanero
custom tailor *s* sastre *m* a la medida
custom work *s* trabajo hecho a la medida
cut [kʌt] *s* corte *m;* (*piece cut off*) tajada; (*wound*) cuchillada; (*for a canal, highway, etc.*) desmonte *m;* (*shortest way*) atajo; (*in prices, wages, etc.*) reducción; (*of a garment*) corte *m,* hechura; (*in winnings, earnings, etc.*) parte *f;* (typ) estampa, grabado; (tennis) golpe *m* cortante; (*absence from school*) (coll) falta de asistencia; (*snub*) (coll) desaire *m;* (coll) palabra hiriente ‖ *v* (*pret & pp* **cut;** *ger* **cutting**) *tr* cortar; practicar (*un agujero*); reducir (*gastos*); capar, castrar; desleír, diluir; (coll) ausentarse de, faltar a (*la clase*); (coll) desairar; (coll) herir; **to cut down** cortar; derribar cortando; castigar (*gastos*); **to cut off** cortar; desheredar; amputar (*una pierna*); (elec) cortar (*la corriente, la ignición*); cerrar (*el carburador*); **to cut open** abrir cortando; **to cut out** cortar; sacar cortando; labrar; suprimir, omitir; (*to take the place of*) desbancar; soplar (*la dama a un rival*); (slang) dejarse de (*disparates*); **to cut short** terminar de repente; interrumpir, chafar; **to cut teeth** endentecer; **to cut up** desmenuzar, despedazar; criticar severamente; (coll) afligir ‖ *intr* cortar; cortarse; salir (*los dientes*); (coll) fumarse la clase; **to cut in** entrar de repente; interrumpir; (*in a dance*) cortar o separar la pareja; **to cut under** vender a menor precio que; **to cut up** (slang) travesear, hacer travesuras; (slang) jaranear
cut-and-dried [ˈkʌtənˈdraɪd] *adj* dispuesto de antemano; monótono, poco interesante
cutaway coat [ˈkʌtəˌwe] *s* chaqué *m*
cut'back' *s* reducción; discontinuación, incumplimiento; (mov) retorno a una época anterior
cute [kjut] *adj* (coll) mono, monono; (coll) astuto, listo
cut glass *s* cristal tallado
cuticle [ˈkjutɪkəl] *s* cutícula
cutlass [ˈkʌtləs] *s* alfanje *m*
cutler [ˈkʌtlər] *s* cuchillero
cutlery [ˈkʌtləri] *s* cuchillería; (*knives, forks, and spoons*) cubierto
cutlet [ˈkʌtlɪt] *s* chuleta; croqueta
cut'out' *s* (*design to be cut out*) recortado; (aut) escape *m* libre, válvula de escape libre
cut'-rate' *adj* de precio reducido
cutter [ˈkʌtər] *s* cortador *m;* (*machine*) cortadora; (naut) escampavía
cut'throat' *adj* asesino; implacable ‖ *s* asesino
cutting [ˈkʌtɪŋ] *adj* cortante; hiriente, mordaz ‖ *s* corte *m;* (*from a newspaper*) recorte *m;* (hort) esqueje *m*
cutting edge *s* canto de corte
cuttlefish [ˈkʌtəlˌfɪʃ] *s* jibia
cut'wa'ter *s* espolón *m,* tajamar *m*
cwt. *abbr* **hundredweight**
cyanamide [saɪˈænəˌmaɪd] *s* cianamida; cianamida de calcio
cyanide [ˈsaɪ·əˌnaɪd] *s* cianuro
cycle [ˈsaɪkəl] *s* ciclo; bicicleta; (*of an internal-combustion engine*) tiempo; (phys) período ‖ *intr* montar en bicicleta
cyclic(al) [ˈsaɪklɪk(əl)] o [ˈsɪklɪk(əl)] *adj* cíclico
cyclone [ˈsaɪklon] *s* ciclón *m*
cyl. *abbr* **cylinder, cylindrical**
cylinder [ˈsɪlɪndər] *s* cilindro
cylinder block *s* bloque *m* de cilindros
cylinder bore *s* alesaje *m*
cylinder head *s* (*of steam engine*) tapa del cilindro; (*of gas engine*) culata del cilindro
cylindric(al) [sɪˈlɪndrɪk(əl)] *adj* cilíndrico
cymbal [ˈsɪmbəl] *s* címbalo, platillo
cynic [ˈsɪnɪk] *adj & s* cínico
cynical [ˈsɪnɪkəl] *adj* cínico
cynicism [ˈsɪnɪˌsɪzəm] *s* cinismo
cynosure [ˈsaɪnəˌʃur] o [ˈsɪnəˌʃur] *s* blanco de las miradas; guía, norte *m*
cypress [ˈsaɪprəs] *s* ciprés *m*
Cyprus [ˈsaɪprəs] *s* Chipre *f*
Cyrillic [sɪˈrɪlɪk] *adj* cirílico
Cyrus [ˈsaɪrəs] *s* Ciro
cyst [sɪst] *s* quiste *m*
czar [zɑr] *s* zar *m;* (fig) autócrata *m*
czarina [zɑˈrinə] *s* zarina
Czech [tʃɛk] *adj & s* checo
Czecho-Slovak [ˈtʃɛkoˈslovæk] *adj & s* checoeslovaco o checoslovaco
Czecho-Slovakia [ˌtʃɛkosloˈvækɪ·ə] *s* Checoeslovaquia o Checoslovaquia

D

D, d [di] cuarta letra del alfabeto inglés
d. *abbr* **date, day, dead, degree, delete, diameter, died, dollar, denarius (penny)**
D. *abbr* **December, Democrat, Duchess, Duke, Dutch**
D.A. *abbr* **District Attorney**
dab [dæb] *s* toque ligero; masa pastosa || *v* (*pret & pp* **dabbed;** *ger* **dabbing**) *tr* tocar ligeramente, frotar suavemente
dabble ['dæbəl] *tr* salpicar || *intr* chapotear; **to dabble in** meterse en; jugar a (*la Bolsa*); especular en (*granos*)
dad [dæd] *s* (coll) papá *m*
dad·dy ['dædi] *s* (*pl* **-dies**) (coll) papá *m*
daffodil ['dæfədɪl] *s* narciso trompón
daff·y ['dæfi] *adj* (*comp* **-ier;** *super* **-iest**) (coll) chiflado
dagger ['dægər] *s* daga, puñal *m;* (typ) cruz *f,* obelisco; **to look daggers at** apuñalar con la mirada
dahlia ['dæljə] *s* dalia
dai·ly ['deli] *adj* cotidiano, diario || *adv* diariamente || *s* (*pl* **-lies**) diario
dain·ty ['denti] *adj* (*comp* **-tier;** *super* **-tiest**) delicado || *s* (*pl* **-ties**) golosina
dair·y ['dɛri] *s* (*pl* **-ies**) lechería, vaquería
dais ['de·ɪs] *s* estrado
dai·sy ['dezi] *s* (*pl* **-sies**) margarita
dal·ly ['dæli] *v* (*pret & pp* **-lied**) *intr* juguetear, retozar; tardar, malgastar el tiempo
dam [dæm] *s* represa, embalse *m;* (*female quadruped*) madre *f;* (dent) dique *m* || *v* (*pret & pp* **dammed;** *ger* **damming**) *tr* represar, embalsar; cerrar, tapar, obstruir
damage ['dæmɪdʒ] *s* daño, perjuicio; (*to one's reputation*) desdoro; (com) avería; **damages** daños y perjuicios || *tr* dañar, perjudicar; averiar
damascene ['dæmə,sin] o [,dæmə'sin] *adj* damasquino || *s* ataujía, damasquinado || *tr* ataujiar, damasquinar
dame [dem] *s* dama, señora; (coll) mujer *f*
damn [dæm] *s* terno; **I don't give a damn** (slang) maldito lo que me importa; **that's not worth a damn** (slang) eso no vale un pito || *tr* condenar (a pena eterna); condenar; maldecir || *intr* maldecir, echar ternos
damnation [dæm'neʃən] *s* damnación; (theol) condenación
damned [dæmd] *adj* condenado (a pena eterna); abominable, detestable || **the damned** los malditos, los condenados (a pena eterna)
damp [dæmp] *adj* húmedo, mojado || *s* humedad; (*firedamp*) grisú *m* || *tr* humedecer, mojar; (*to deaden, muffle*) amortecer, amortiguar; (*to discourage*) abatir, desalentar; (elec) amortiguar (*ondas electromagnéticas*)
dampen ['dæmpən] *tr* humedecer, mojar; amortecer, amortiguar; abatir, desalentar
damper ['dæmpər] *s* (*of chimney*) registro; (*of piano*) apagador *m,* sordina
damsel ['dæmzəl] *s* señorita, muchacha
dance [dæns] o [dɑns] *s* baile *m,* danza || *tr & intr* bailar, danzar
dance band *s* orquesta de jazz
dance floor *s* pista de baile
dance hall *s* salón *m* de baile
dancer ['dænsər] o ['dɑnsər] *s* bailador *m,* danzador *m;* (*professional*) bailarín *m*
dancing partner *s* pareja (de baile)
dandelion ['dændɪ,laɪ·ən] *s* diente *m* de león
dandruff ['dændrəf] *s* caspa
dan·dy ['dændi] *adj* (*comp* **-dier;** *super* **-diest**) (coll) excelente, magnífico || *s* (*pl* **-dies**) currutaco, petimetre *m*
Dane [den] *s* danés *m,* dinamarqués *m*
danger ['dendʒər] *s* peligro
dangerous ['dendʒərəs] *adj* peligroso
dangle ['dæŋgəl] *tr & intr* colgar flojamente, colgar en el aire
Danish ['denɪʃ] *adj & s* danés *m,* dinamarqués *m*
dank [dæŋk] *adj* húmedo, liento
Danube ['dænjub] *s* Danubio
dapper ['dæpər] *adj* aseado, apuesto
dapple ['dæpəl] *adj* habado, rodado || *tr* motear
dare [dɛr] *s* desafío, reto || *tr* retar; **to dare to** (*to challenge to*) desafiar a || *intr* osar, atreverse; **I dare say** talvez; **to dare to** (*to have the courage to*) atreverse a
dare'dev'il *s* calavera *m,* temerario
daring ['dɛrɪŋ] *adj* atrevido, osado || *s* atrevimiento, osadía
dark [dɑrk] *adj* obscuro; (*in complexion*) moreno; secreto, oculto; (*gloomy*) lóbrego; (*beer*) pardo || *s* obscuridad, tinieblas; noche *f;* **in the dark** a obscuras
Dark Ages *spl* edad media; principios de la edad media
dark-complexioned ['dɑrkkəm'plɛkʃənd] *adj* moreno
darken ['dɑrkən] *tr* obscurecer; entristecer; cegar || *intr* obscurecerse
dark horse *s* caballo desconocido; candidato nombrado inesperadamente
darkly ['dɑrkli] *adv* obscuramente; secretamente, misteriosamente
dark meat *s* carne *f* del ave que no es la pechuga
darkness ['dɑrknɪs] *s* obscuridad
dark'room' *s* (phot) cuarto obscuro
darling ['dɑrlɪŋ] *adj & s* querido, amado; predilecto
darn [dɑrn] *tr & intr* zurcir; (coll) maldecir

darnel ['dɑrnəl] *s* cizaña
darning ['dɑrnɪŋ] *s* zurcido
darning needle *s* aguja de zurcir
dart [dɑrt] *s* dardo; (*small missile used in a game*) rehilete *m* || *intr* lanzarse, precipitarse; volar como dardo
dash [dæʃ] *s* arranque *m;* (*splash*) rociada; carrera corta; (*spirit*) brío; pequeña cantidad; (*in printing, writing, telegraphy*) raya || *tr* lanzar; estrellar, romper; frustrar (*las esperanzas de uno*); rociar, salpicar; **to dash off** escribir de prisa; **to dash to pieces** hacer añicos || *intr* estrellarse (*las olas del mar*); lanzarse, precipitarse; **to dash by** pasar corriendo; **to dash in** entrar como un rayo
dash'board' *s* tablero de instrumentos; (*on front or side of vehicle*) guardabarros *m*
dashing ['dæʃɪŋ] *adj* brioso; ostentoso, vistoso || *s* (*of waves*) embate *m*
dastard ['dæstərd] *adj & s* vil *mf,* miserable *mf,* cobarde *mf*
data processing ['detə] *s* tramitación automática de datos
date [det] *s* (*time*) fecha, data; (*palm*) datilera; (*fruit*) dátil *m;* (*appointment*) (coll) cita; **out of date** anticuado, fuera de moda; **to date** hasta la fecha; **under date of** con fecha de || *tr* fechar, datar; (coll) tener cita con || *intr* — **to date from** datar de
date line *s* línea de cambio de fecha
date palm *s* palmera (datilera)
dative ['detɪv] *adj & s* dativo
datum ['detəm] o ['dætəm] *s* (*pl* **data** ['detə] o ['dætə]) dato
dau. *abbr* **daughter**
daub [dɔb] *s* embadurnamiento || *tr* embadurnar
daughter ['dɔtər] *s* hija
daughter-in-law ['dɔtərɪn ˌlɔ] *s* (*pl* **daughters-in-law**) nuera, hija política
daunt [dɔnt] *tr* asustar, espantar; desanimar, acobardar
dauntless ['dɔntlɪs] *adj* atrevido, intrépido, impávido
dauphin ['dɔfɪn] *s* delfín *m*
davenport ['dævən ˌport] *s* sofá *m* cama
davit ['dævɪt] *s* (naut) pescante *m,* grúa de bote
daw [dɔ] *s* corneja
dawdle ['dɔdəl] *intr* malgastar el tiempo, haronear
dawn [dɔn] *s* amanecer *m,* alba || *intr* amanecer; despuntar (*el día, la mañana*); empezar a mostrarse; **to dawn on** empezar a hacerse patente a
day [de] *adj* diurno || *s* día *m;* (*of travel, work, worry, etc.*) jornada; (*from noon to noon*) (naut) singladura; **any day now** de un día para otro; **by day** de día; **the day after** el día siguiente; **the day after tomorrow** pasado mañana; **the day before** la víspera; la víspera de; **the day before yesterday** anteayer; **to call it a day** (coll) dejar de trabajar; **to win the day** ganar la jornada
day bed *s* sofá *m* cama
day'break' *s* amanecer *m*
day coach *s* (rr) coche *m* de viajeros
day'dream' *s* ensueño || *intr* soñar despierto
day laborer *s* jornalero
day'light' *s* luz *f* del día; amanecer *m;* **in broad daylight** en pleno día; **to see daylight** comprender; ver el fin de una tarea difícil
day'light'-sav'ing time *s* hora de verano
day nursery *s* guardería infantil
day off *s* asueto
day of reckoning *s* día *m* de ajustar cuentas
day shift *s* turno diurno
day'time' *adj* diurno || día *m*
daze [dez] *s* aturdimiento; **in a daze** aturdido || *tr* aturdir
dazzle ['dæzəl] *s* deslumbramiento || *tr* deslumbrar
dazzling ['dæzlɪŋ] *adj* deslumbrante
deacon ['dikən] *s* diácono
deaconess ['dikənɪs] *s* diaconisa
dead [dɛd] *adj* muerto; (coll) cansado || *adv* (coll) completamente, muy || *s* — **in the dead of night** en plena noche; **the dead** los muertos; **the dead of winter** lo más frío del invierno
dead beat *s* (slang) gorrón *m;* (slang) holgazán *m*
dead bolt *s* cerrojo dormido
dead calm *s* calma chicha, calmazo
dead center *s* punto muerto
dead'drunk' *adj* difunto de taberna
deaden ['dɛdən] *tr* amortiguar, amortecer
dead end *s* callejón *m* sin salida
dead'latch' *s* aldaba dormida
dead'-let'ter office *s* departamento de cartas no reclamadas
dead'line' *s* línea vedada; fin *m* del plazo
dead'lock' *s* cerradura dormida; desacuerdo insuperable || *tr* estancar
dead·ly ['dɛdli] *adj* (*comp* **-lier;** *super* **-liest**) mortal; (*sin*) capital; abrumador
dead pan *s* (slang) semblante *m* sin expresión
dead reckoning *s* (naut) estima
dead ringer ['rɪŋər] *s* segunda edición
dead'wood' *s* leña seca; cosa inútil, gente *f* inútil
deaf [dɛf] *adj* sordo; **to turn a deaf ear** hacerse el sordo, hacer oídos de mercader
deaf and dumb *adj* sordomudo
deafen ['dɛfən] *tr* asordar, ensordecer
deafening ['dɛfənɪŋ] *adj* ensordecedor
deaf'-mute' *s* sordomudo
deafness ['dɛfnɪs] *s* sordera
deal [dil] *s* negocio, trato; (*of cards*) mano *f;* turno de dar; (*share*) parte *f,* porción; (coll) convenio secreto; **a good deal (of)** o **a great deal (of)** mucho; **to make a great deal of** hacer fiestas a || *v* (*pret & pp* **dealt** [dɛlt]) *tr* asestar (*un golpe*); repartir (*la baraja*) || *intr* negociar, comerciar; intervenir; (*in card games*) ser

mano; **to deal with** entender en; tratar de; tratar con
dealer ['dilər] *s* comerciante *mf*, concesionario; (*of cards*) repartidor *m*
dean [din] *s* decano; (eccl) deán *m*
deanship ['dinʃɪp] *s* decanato
dear [dɪr] *adj* (*beloved*) caro; (*expensive*) caro; (*charging high prices*) carero; **dear me!** ¡Dios mío! || *s* querido
dearie ['dɪri] *s* (coll) queridito
dearth [dʌrθ] *s* carestía
death [dɛθ] *s* muerte *f;* **to bleed to death** morir desangrado; **to bore to death** matar de aburrimiento; **to burn to death** morir quemado; **to choke to death** morir atragantado; **to die a violent death** morir vestido; **to freeze to death** morir helado; **to put to death** dar la muerte a; **to shoot to death** matar a tiros; **to stab to death** escabechar; **to starve to death** matar de hambre; morir de hambre
death'bed' *s* lecho de muerte
death'blow' *s* golpe *m* mortal
death certificate *s* fe *f* de óbito, partida de defunción
death house *s* capilla (*de los reos de muerte*)
deathless ['dɛθlɪs] *adj* inmortal, eterno
deathly ['dɛθli] *adj* mortal, de muerte || *adv* mortalmente; excesivamente
death penalty *s* pena de muerte
death rate *s* mortalidad
death rattle *s* estertor agónico
death ray *s* rayo mortífero
death warrant *s* sentencia de muerte; fin *m* de toda esperanza
death'watch' *s* vela de un difunto; guardia de un reo de muerte
debacle [de'bɑkəl] *s* desastre *m*, ruina, derrota; (*in a river*) deshielo
de•bar [dɪ'bɑr] *v* (*pret & pp* **-barred;** *ger* **-barring**) *tr* excluir; prohibir
debark [dɪ'bɑrk] *tr & intr* desembarcar
debarkation [ˌdibɑr'keʃən] *s* (*of passengers*) desembarco; (*of freight*) desembarque *m*
debase [dɪ'bes] *tr* degradar; falsificar
debatable [dɪ'betəbəl] *adj* disputable
debate [dɪ'bet] *s* debate *m* || *tr* debatir || *intr* debatir; deliberar
debauchee [ˌdɛbɔ'ʃi] o [ˌdɛbɔ'tʃi] *s* libertino, disoluto
debaucher•y [dɪ'bɔtʃəri] *s* (*pl* **-ies**) libertinaje *m*, crápula
debenture [dɪ'bɛntʃər] *s* (*bond*) obligación; (*voucher*) vale *m*
debilitate [dɪ'bɪlɪˌtet] *tr* debilitar
debili•ty [dɪ'bɪlɪti] *s* (*pl* **-ties**) debilidad
debit ['dɛbɪt] *s* debe *m;* (*entry on debit side*) cargo || *tr* adeudar, cargar
debit balance *s* saldo deudor
debonair [ˌdɛbə'nɛr] *adj* alegre; cortés
debris [de'bri] *s* despojos, ruinas
debt [dɛt] *s* deuda; **to run into debt** endeudarse, entramparse
debtor ['dɛtər] *s* deudor *m*
debut [de'bju] o ['debju] *s* estreno, debut *m;* **to make one's debut** estrenarse, debutar; ponerse de largo, entrar en sociedad (*una joven*)
debutante [ˌdɛbju'tɑnt] o ['dɛbjəˌtænt] *s* joven *f* que se pone de largo
dec. *abbr* **deceased**
decade ['dɛked] *s* decenio
decadence [dɪ'kedəns] *s* decadencia
decadent [dɪ'kedənt] *adj & s* decadente *mf*
decanter [dɪ'kæntər] *s* garrafa
decapitate [dɪ'kæpɪˌtet] *tr* decapitar
decay [dɪ'ke] *s* (*decline*) decaimiento, descaecimiento; (*rotting*) podredumbre; (*of teeth*) caries *f* || *tr* pudrir || *intr* pudrirse; decaer; cariarse (*los dientes*)
decease [dɪ'sis] *s* fallecimiento || *intr* fallecer
deceased [dɪ'sist] *adj & s* difunto
deceit [dɪ'sit] *s* engaño, fraude *m*
deceitful [dɪ'sitfəl] *adj* engañoso, fraudulento
deceive [dɪ'siv] *tr & intr* engañar
decelerate [dɪ'sɛləˌret] *tr* desacelerar || *intr* desacelerarse
December [dɪ'sɛmbər] *s* diciembre *m*
decen•cy ['disənsi] *s* (*pl* **-cies**) decencia, honestidad; (*propriety*) conveniencia
decent ['disənt] *adj* decente, honesto; (*proper*) conveniente
decentralize [dɪ'sɛntrəˌlaɪz] *tr* descentralizar
deception [dɪ'sɛpʃən] *s* engaño
deceptive [dɪ'sɛptɪv] *adj* engañoso
decide [dɪ'saɪd] *tr & intr* decidir
decimal ['dɛsɪməl] *adj & s* decimal *m*
decimal point *s* (*in Spanish the comma is used to separate the decimal fraction from the integer*) coma
decimate ['dɛsɪˌmet] *tr* diezmar
decipher [dɪ'saɪfər] *tr* descifrar
decision [dɪ'sɪʒən] *s* decisión
decisive [dɪ'saɪsɪv] *adj* decisivo; determinado, resuelto
deck [dɛk] *s* (*of cards*) baraja; (*of ship*) cubierta; **between decks** (naut) entre cubiertas || *tr* — **to deck out** adornar, engalanar
deck chair *s* silla de cubierta
deck hand *s* marinero de cubierta
deck'-land' *intr* apontizar
deck'-land'ing *s* apontizaje *m*
deckle edge ['dɛkəl] *s* barba
declaim [dɪ'klem] *tr & intr* declamar
declaration [ˌdɛklə'reʃən] *s* declaración
declarative [dɪ'klærətɪv] *adj* declarativo; (gram) enunciativo
declare [dɪ'klɛr] *tr & intr* declarar
declension [dɪ'klɛnʃən] *s* declinación
declination [ˌdɛklɪ'neʃən] *s* declinación
decline [dɪ'klaɪn] *s* bajada, declinación; (*in prices*) baja; (*in health, wealth, etc.*) bajón *m;* (*of sun*) ocaso || *tr & intr* declinar; rehusar
declivi•ty [dɪ'klɪvɪti] *s* (*pl* **-ties**) declividad, declive *m*
decode [di'kod] *tr* descifrar
décolleté [ˌdekɑl'te] *adj* escotado

decompose [ˌdikəm'poz] *tr* descomponer || *intr* descomponerse
decomposition [ˌdikɑmpə'zɪʃən] *s* descomposición
decompression [ˌdikəm'prɛʃən] *s* descompresión
decontamination [ˌdikəmˌtæmɪ'neʃən] *s* descontaminación
décor [de'kɔr] *s* decoración; (theat) decorado
decorate ['dɛkəˌret] *tr* decorar; (*with medal, badge*) condecorar
decoration [ˌdɛkə'reʃən] *s* decoración; (*medal, badge*) condecoración
decorator ['dɛkəˌretər] *s* decorador *m;* (*of interiors*) adornista *mf*
decorous ['dɛkərəs] o [dɪ'korəs] *adj* decoroso
decorum [dɪ'korəm] *s* decoro
decoy [dɪ'kɔɪ] o ['dikɔɪ] *s* añagaza, señuelo; (*person*) entruchón *m* || [dɪ'kɔɪ] *tr* atraer con señuelo; entruchar
decoy pigeon *s* cimbel *m*
decrease ['dikris] o [dɪ'kris] *s* disminución || [dɪ'kris] *tr* disminuir || *intr* disminuir, disminuirse
decree [dɪ'kri] *s* decreto || *tr* decretar
decrepit [dɪ'krɛpɪt] *adj* decrépito
de·cry [dɪ'kraɪ] *v* (*pret & pp* **-cried**) *tr* censurar, denigrar
dedicate ['dɛdɪˌket] *tr* dedicar
dedication [ˌdɛdɪ'keʃən] *s* dedicación; (*inscription in a book*) dedicatoria
deduce [dɪ'djus] o [dɪ'dus] *tr* deducir (*inferir, concluir; derivar*)
deduct [dɪ'dʌkt] *tr* deducir (*rebajar, substraer*)
deduction [dɪ'dʌkʃən] *s* deducción
deed [did] *s* acto, hecho; (*feat, exploit*) hazaña; (law) escritura || *tr* traspasar por escritura
deem [dim] *tr & intr* creer, juzgar
deep [dip] *adj* profundo; (*sound*) grave; (*color*) subido; de hondo, p.ej., **two meters deep** dos metros de hondo; **deep in debt** cargado de deudas; **deep in thought** absorto en la meditación || *adv* hondo; **deep into the night** muy entrada la noche
deepen ['dipən] *tr* profundizar || *intr* profundizarse
deep-laid ['dipˌled] *adj* concebido con astucia
deep mourning *s* luto riguroso
deep-rooted ['dipˌrutɪd] *adj* profundamente arraigado
deep'-sea' fishing *s* pesca de gran altura
deep-seated ['dipˌsitɪd] *adj* profundamente arraigado
deer [dɪr] *s* ciervo, venado
deer'skin' *s* piel *f* de ciervo
def. *abbr* **defendant, deferred, definite**
deface [dɪ'fes] *tr* desfigurar
de facto [di'fækto] *adv* de hecho
defamation [ˌdɛfə'meʃən] o [ˌdifə'meʃən] *s* difamación
defame [dɪ'fem] *tr* difamar
default [dɪ'fɔlt] *s* falta, incumplimiento; **by default** (sport) por no presentarse; **in default of** por falta de || *tr* dejar de cumplir; no pagar || *intr* faltar; (sport) perder por no presentarse
defeat [dɪ'fit] *s* derrota || *tr* derrotar, vencer
defeatism [dɪ'fitɪzəm] *s* derrotismo
defeatist [dɪ'fitɪst] *adj & s* derrotista *mf*
defecate ['dɛfɪˌket] *intr* defecar
defect [dɪ'fɛkt] o ['difɛkt] *s* defecto, imperfección || [dɪ'fɛkt] *intr* desertar
defection [dɪ'fɛkʃən] *s* defección; (*lack, failure*) falta
defective [dɪ'fɛktɪv] *adj* defectivo, defectuoso
defend [dɪ'fɛnd] *tr* defender
defendant [dɪ'fɛndənt] *s* (law) demandado, acusado
defender [dɪ'fɛndər] *s* defensor *m*
defense [dɪ'fɛns] *s* defensa
defenseless [dɪ'fɛnslɪs] *adj* indefenso
defensive [dɪ'fɛnsɪv] *adj* defensivo || *s* defensiva
de·fer [dɪ'fʌr] *v* (*pret & pp* **-ferred;** *ger* **-ferring**) *tr* aplazar, diferir || *intr* deferir
deference ['dɛfərəns] *s* deferencia
deferential [ˌdɛfə'rɛnʃəl] *adj* deferente
deferment [dɪ'fʌrmənt] *s* aplazamiento, dilación
defiance [dɪ'faɪ·əns] *s* oposición; desafío, provocación; **in defiance of** sin mirar a, a despecho de
defiant [dɪ'faɪ·ənt] *adj* provocante, hostil
deficien·cy [dɪ'fɪʃənsi] *s* (*pl* **-cies**) carencia, deficiencia; (com) descubierto
deficient [dɪ'fɪʃənt] *adj* deficiente, defectuoso
deficit ['dɛfɪsɪt] *adj* deficitario || *s* déficit *m*
defile [dɪ'faɪl] o ['difaɪl] *s* desfiladero || [dɪ'fail] *tr* corromper, manchar || *intr* desfilar
define [dɪ'faɪn] *tr* definir
definite ['dɛfɪnɪt] *adj* definido
definition [ˌdɛfɪ'nɪʃən] *s* definición
definitive [dɪ'fɪnɪtɪv] *adj* definitivo
deflate [dɪ'flet] *tr* desinflar
deflation [dɪ'fleʃən] *s* desinflación; (*of prices*) deflación
deflect [dɪ'flɛkt] *tr* desviar || *intr* desviarse
deflower [di'flaʊ·ər] *tr* desflorar
deforest [di'fɑrɛst] o [di'fɔrɛst] *tr* desforestar, despoblar
deform [dɪ'fɔrm] *tr* deformar
deformed [dɪ'fɔrmd] *adj* deforme
deformi·ty [dɪ'fɔrmɪti] *s* (*pl* **-ties**) deformidad
defraud [dɪ'frɔd] *tr* defraudar
defray [dɪ'fre] *tr* sufragar, subvenir a
defrost [di'frɔst] o [di'frɑst] *tr* descongelar, deshelar
deft [dɛft] *adj* diestro, hábil
defunct [dɪ'fʌŋkt] *adj* difunto
de·fy [dɪ'faɪ] *v* (*pret & pp* **-fied**) *tr* desafiar, provocar
deg. *abbr* **degree**

degeneracy [dɪˈdʒɛnərəsi] *s* degeneración
degenerate [dɪˈdʒɛnərɪt] *adj & s* degenerado ‖ [dɪˈdʒɛnəˌret] *intr* degenerar
degrade [dɪˈgred] *tr* degradar
degrading [dɪˈgredɪŋ] *adj* degradante
degree [dɪˈgri] *s* grado; **by degrees** de grado en grado; **to take a degree** graduarse, recibir un grado o título
dehumidifier [ˌdihjuˈmɪdɪˌfaɪ·ər] *s* deshumedecedor *m*
dehydrate [diˈhaɪdret] *tr* deshidratar
deice [diˈaɪs] *tr* deshelar
dei·fy [ˈdi·ɪˌfaɪ] *v* (*pret & pp* **-fied**) *tr* deificar
deign [den] *intr* dignarse
dei·ty [ˈdi·ɪti] *s* (*pl* **-ties**) deidad; **the Deity** Dios *m*
dejected [dɪˈdʒɛktɪd] *adj* abatido
dejection [dɪˈdʒɛkʃən] *s* abatimiento
del. *abbr* **delegate, delete**
delay [dɪˈle] *s* retraso, tardanza ‖ *tr* retrasar ‖ *intr* demorarse
delectable [dɪˈlɛktəbəl] *adj* deleitable
delegate [ˈdɛlɪˌget] o [ˈdɛlɪgɪt] *s* diputado, delegado; (*to a convention*) congresista *mf* ‖ [ˈdɛlɪˌget] *tr* delegar
delete [dɪˈlit] *tr* borrar, suprimir
deletion [dɪˈliʃən] *s* supresión
deliberate [dɪˈlɪbərɪt] *adj* pensado, reflexionado; (*slow in deciding*) cauto, circunspecto; (*slow in moving*) espacioso, lento ‖ [dɪˈlɪbəˌret] *tr & intr* deliberar
delica·cy [ˈdɛlɪkəsi] *s* (*pl* **-cies**) delicadeza; (*choice food*) golosina
delicatessen [ˌdɛlɪkəˈtɛsən] *s* colmado, tienda de ultramarinos ‖ *spl* ultramarinos
delicious [dɪˈlɪʃəs] *adj* delicioso, sabroso
delight [dɪˈlaɪt] *s* deleite *m*, delicia ‖ *tr* deleitar ‖ *intr* deleitarse
delightful [dɪˈlaɪtfəl] *adj* deleitoso, ameno, exquisito
delinquen·cy [dɪˈlɪŋkwənsi] *s* (*pl* **-cies**) culpa; (*in payment of debt*) morosidad; (*debt in arrears*) atrasos
delinquent [dɪˈlɪŋkwənt] *adj* culpado; (*in payment*) moroso, atrasado; no pagado ‖ *s* culpado; deudor moroso
delirious [dɪˈlɪrɪ·əs] *adj* delirante
deliri·um [dɪˈlɪrɪ·əm] *s* (*pl* **-ums** o **-a** [ə]) delirio
deliver [dɪˈlɪvər] *tr* entregar; asestar (*un golpe*); pronunciar, recitar (*un discurso*); transmitir, rendir (*energía*); partear (*a la mujer que está de parto*)
deliver·y [dɪˈlɪvəri] *s* (*pl* **-ies**) entrega; (*of mail*) distribución, reparto; (*of a speech*) declamación; (*childbirth*) alumbramiento, parto
delivery·man [dɪˈlɪvərimən] *s* (*pl* **-men** [mən]) mozo de reparto
delivery room *s* sala de alumbramiento
delivery truck *s* sedán *m* de reparto
dell [dɛl] *s* vallecito
delouse [diˈlaʊs] o [diˈlaʊz] *tr* despiojar
delphinium [dɛlˈfɪnɪ·əm] *s* (*Delphinium ajacis*) espuela de caballero; (*Delphinium consolida*) consuelda real
delude [dɪˈlud] *tr* deludir, engañar
deluge [ˈdɛljudʒ] *s* diluvio ‖ *tr* inundar
delusion [dɪˈluʃən] *s* engaño, decepción
de luxe [dɪˈlʊks] o [dɪˈlʌks] *adj & adv* de lujo
delve [dɛlv] *intr* cavar; **to delve into** cavar en
demagnetize [diˈmægnɪˌtaɪz] *tr* desimantar
demagogue [ˈdɛməˌgɑg] *s* demagogo
demand [dɪˈmænd] o [dɪˈmɑnd] *s* demanda; **to be in demand** tener demanda ‖ *tr* demandar perentoriamente
demanding [dɪˈmændɪŋ] o [dɪˈmɑndɪŋ] *adj* exigente
demarcate [dɪˈmɑrket] o [ˈdimɑrˌket] *tr* demarcar
démarche [deˈmɑrʃ] *s* diligencia, gestión, paso
demeanor [dɪˈminər] *s* conducta, porte *m*
demented [dɪˈmɛntɪd] *adj* demente
demigod [ˈdɛmɪˌgɑd] *s* semidiós *m*
demijohn [ˈdɛmɪˌdʒɑn] *s* damajuana
demilitarize [diˈmɪlɪtəˌraɪz] *tr* desmilitarizar
demimonde [ˈdɛmɪˌmɑnd] *s* mujeres de vida alegre
demise [dɪˈmaɪz] *s* fallecimiento
demisemiquaver [ˌdɛmɪˈsɛmɪˌkwevər] *s* (mus) fusa
demitasse [ˈdɛmɪˌtæs] o [ˈdɛmɪˌtɑs] *s* taza pequeña
demobilize [diˈmobɪˌlaɪz] *tr* desmovilizar
democra·cy [dɪˈmɑkrəsi] *s* (*pl* **-cies**) democracia
democrat [ˈdɛməˌkræt] *s* demócrata *mf*
democratic [ˌdɛməˈkrætɪk] *adj* democrático
demodulate [diˈmɑdjəˌlet] *tr* desmodular
demolish [dɪˈmɑlɪʃ] *tr* demoler
demolition [ˌdɛməˈlɪʃən] o [ˌdiməˈlɪʃən] *s* demolición
demon [ˈdimən] *s* demonio
demoniacal [ˌdiməˈnaɪ·əkəl] *adj* demoníaco
demonstrate [ˈdɛmənˌstret] *tr* demostrar ‖ *intr* demostrar; (*to show feelings in public gatherings*) manifestar
demonstration [ˌdɛmənˈstreʃən] *s* demostración; (*public show of feeling*) manifestación
demonstrative [dɪˈmɑnstrətɪv] *adj* demostrativo; (*giving open exhibition of emotion*) extremoso
demonstrator [ˈdɛmənˌstretər] *s* demostrador *m*; manifestante *mf*
demoralize [dɪˈmɑrəˌlaɪz] o [dɪˈmɔrəˌlaɪz] *tr* desmoralizar

demote [dɪ'mot] *tr* degradar
demotion [dɪ'moʃən] *s* degradación
de·mur [dɪ'mʌr] *v* (*pret & pp* **-murred;** *ger* **-murring**) *intr* poner reparos
demure [dɪ'mjʊr] *adj* modesto, recatado; grave, serio
demurrage [dɪ'mʌrɪdʒ] *s* (com) estadía
den [dɛn] *s* (*of animals, thieves*) madriguera; (*dirty little room*) cuchitril *m;* lugar *m* de retiro; cuarto de estudio; (*of lions*) (Bib) fosa
denaturalize [di'nætjərə,laɪz] *tr* desnaturalizar
denatured alcohol [di'netʃərd] *s* alcohol desnaturalizado
denial [dɪ'naɪ·əl] *s* denegación; negación, desmentida
denim ['dɛnɪm] *s* dril *m* de algodón
denizen ['dɛnɪzən] *s* habitante *mf,* vecino
Denmark ['dɛnmɑrk] *s* Dinamarca
denomination [dɪ,nɑmɪ'neʃən] *s* denominación; categoría, clase *f;* secta, confesión, comunión
denote [dɪ'not] *tr* denotar
dénoument [denu'mɑ̃] *s* desenlace *m*
denounce [dɪ'naʊns] *tr* denunciar
dense [dɛns] *adj* denso; estúpido
densi·ty ['dɛnsɪti] *s* (*pl* **-ties**) densidad
dent [dɛnt] *s* abolladura, mella || *tr* abollar, mellar || *intr* abollarse, mellarse
dental ['dɛntəl] *adj & s* dental *f*
dental floss *s* hilo dental, seda encerada
dentifrice ['dɛntɪfrɪs] *s* dentífrico
dentist ['dɛntɪst] *s* dentista *mf*
dentistry ['dɛntɪstri] *s* odontología
denture ['dɛntʃər] *s* dentadura artificial
denunciation [dɪ,nʌnsɪ'eʃən] o [dɪ,nʌnʃɪ'eʃən] *s* denuncia
de·ny [dɪ'naɪ] *v* (*pret & pp* **-nied**) *tr* (*to declare not to be true*) negar; (*to refuse*) denegar; **to deny oneself to callers** negarse || *intr* negar; denegar
deodorant [di'odərənt] *adj & s* desodorante *m*
deodorize [di'odə,raɪz] *tr* desodorizar
deoxidize [di'ɑksɪ,daɪz] *tr* desoxidar
dep. *abbr* **department, departs, deputy**
depart [dɪ'pɑrt] *intr* partir, salir, irse; desviarse
department [dɪ'pɑrtmənt] *s* departamento; (*of government*) ministerio
department store *s* grandes almacenes *mpl*
departure [dɪ'pɑrtʃər] *s* partida, salida; desviación
depend [dɪ'pɛnd] *intr* depender; **to depend on** depender de
dependable [dɪ'pɛndəbəl] *adj* confiable, fidedigno
dependence [dɪ'pɛndəns] *s* dependencia
dependen·cy [dɪ'pɛndənsi] *s* (*pl* **-cies**) dependencia; (*country, territory*) posesión
dependent [dɪ'pɛndənt] *adj* dependiente || *s* carga de familia, familiar *m* dependiente
depict [dɪ'pɪkt] *tr* describir, representar, pintar
deplete [dɪ'plit] *tr* agotar, depauperar
deplorable [dɪ'plorəbəl] *adj* deplorable
deplore [dɪ'plor] *tr* deplorar
deploy [dɪ'plɔɪ] *tr* (mil) desplegar || *intr* (mil) desplegarse
deployment [dɪ'plɔɪmənt] *s* (mil) despliegue *m*
depolarize [di'polə,raɪz] *tr* despolarizar
depopulate [di'pɑpjə,let] *tr* despoblar
deport [dɪ'port] *tr* deportar; **to deport oneself** conducirse, portarse
deportation [,dipor'teʃən] *s* deportación
deportee [,dipor'ti] *s* deportado
deportment [dɪ'portmənt] *s* conducta, comportamiento
depose [dɪ'poz] *tr & intr* deponer
deposit [dɪ'pɑzɪt] *s* depósito; (*down payment*) señal *f,* pago anticipado; (min) yacimiento || *tr* depositar || *intr* depositarse
deposit account *s* cuenta corriente
depositor [dɪ'pɑzɪtər] *s* cuentacorrentista *mf,* imponente *mf*
depot ['dipo] o ['dɛpo] *s* almacén *m,* depósito; (mil) depósito; (rr) estación
depraved [dɪ'prevd] *adj* depravado
depravi·ty [dɪ'prævɪti] *s* (*pl* **-ties**) depravación
deprecate ['dɛprɪ,ket] *tr* desaprobar
depreciate [dɪ'priʃɪ,et] *tr* (*to lower value or price of*) depreciar; (*to disparage*) desapreciar || *intr* depreciarse
depreciation [dɪ,priʃɪ'eʃən] *s* (*drop in value*) depreciación; (*disparagement*) desaprecio
depress [dɪ'prɛs] *tr* deprimir; desanimar, desalentar; bajar (*los precios*)
depression [dɪ'prɛʃən] *s* depresión; desaliento; (*slump*) crisis *f*
deprive [dɪ'praɪv] *tr* privar
dept. *abbr* **department**
depth [dɛpθ] *s* profundidad; (*of a house, of a room*) fondo; **in the depth of night** en mitad de la noche; **in the depth of winter** en pleno invierno; **to go beyond one's depth** meterse en agua demasiado profunda; (fig) meterse en honduras
depth of hold *s* (naut) puntal *m*
depu·ty ['dɛpjəti] *s* (*pl* **-ties**) diputado
derail [dɪ'rel] *tr* hacer descarrilar || *intr* descarrilar
derailment [dɪ'relmənt] *s* descarrilamiento
derange [dɪ'rendʒ] *tr* desarreglar, descomponer; trastornar el juicio a
derangement [dɪ'rendʒmənt] *s* desarreglo, descompostura; locura
der·by ['dʌrbi] *s* (*pl* **-bies**) sombrero hongo
derelict ['dɛrɪlɪkt] *adj* abandonado; negligente || *s* pelafustán *m;* (naut) derrelicto
deride [dɪ'raɪd] *tr* burlarse de, ridiculizar

derision [dɪ'rɪʒən] *s* burla, irrisión
derive [dɪ'raɪv] *tr & intr* derivar
derogatory [dɪ'rɑgə,tori] *adj* despreciativo
derrick ['dɛrɪk] *s* grúa
dervish ['dʌrvɪʃ] *s* derviche *m*
desalinization [dɪ,selɪnɪ'zeʃən] *s* desalinización
desalt [di'sɔlt] *tr* desalar
descend [dɪ'sɛnd] *tr* bajar, descender (*la escalera*) || *intr* bajar, descender; **to descend on** caer sobre, invadir
descendant [dɪ'sɛndənt] *adj* descendente || *s* descendiente *mf*
descendent [dɪ'sɛndənt] *adj* descendente
descent [dɪ'sɛnt] *s* (*passing from higher to lower state*) descenso; (*extraction; lineage*) descendencia; cuesta, bajada; invasión
describe [dɪ'skraɪb] *tr* describir
description [dɪ'skrɪpʃən] *s* descripción
descriptive [dɪ'skrɪptɪv] *adj* descriptivo
de•scry [dɪ'skraɪ] *v* (*pret & pp* **-scried**) *tr* avistar, divisar; descubrir
desecrate ['dɛsɪ,kret] *tr* profanar
desegregation [di,sɛgrɪ'geʃən] *s* desegregación
desert ['dɛzərt] *adj & s* desierto, yermo || [dɪ'zʌrt] *s* mérito; **he received his just deserts** llevó su merecido || *tr* desertar de || *intr* desertar
deserter [dɪ'zʌrtər] *s* desertor *m*
desertion [dɪ'zʌrʃən] *s* deserción; abandono de cónyuge
deserve [dɪ'zʌrv] *tr & intr* merecer
deservedly [dɪ'zʌrvɪdli] *adv* merecidamente
design [dɪ'zaɪn] *s* diseño; (*combination of details; art of designing*) dibujo; (*plan, scheme*) designio; **to have designs on** poner la mira en || *tr* diseñar, dibujar; idear, proyectar || *intr* diseñar, dibujar
designate ['dɛzɪg,net] *tr* designar
designing [dɪ'zaɪnɪŋ] *adj* intrigante, maquinador
desirable [dɪ'zaɪrəbəl] *adj* deseable
desire [dɪ'zaɪr] *s* deseo || *tr* desear
desirous [dɪ'zaɪrəs] *adj* deseoso
desist [dɪ'zɪst] *intr* desistir
desk [dɛsk] *s* bufete *m*, escritorio; (*lectern*) atril *m*; (*clerk's counter in a hotel*) caja
desk clerk *s* cajero, recepcionista *m*
desk set *s* juego de escritorio
desolate ['dɛsəlɪt] *adj* (*hopeless*) desolado; despoblado, yermo, desierto; solitario; (*dismal*) lúgubre || ['dɛsə,let] *tr* desconsolar; (*to lay waste*) desolar, devastar; despoblar
desolation [,dɛsə'leʃən] *s* (*devastation; great affliction*) desolación; (*dreariness*) lobreguez *f*
despair [dɪ'spɛr] *s* desesperación || *intr* desesperar, desesperarse
despairing [dɪ'spɛrɪŋ] *adj* desesperado
despera•do [,dɛspə'redo] o [,dɛspə'rɑdo] *s* (*pl* **-does** o **-dos**) criminal dispuesto a todo
desperate ['dɛspərɪt] *adj* dispuesto a todo; (*bitter, excessive*) encarnizado; (*hopeless*) desesperado; (*remedy*) heroico
despicable ['dɛspɪkəbəl] *adj* despreciable, ruin
despise [dɪ'spaɪz] *tr* despreciar, desdeñar
despite [dɪ'spaɪt] *prep* a despecho de
desponden•cy [dɪ'spɑndənsi] *s* (*pl* **-cies**) abatimiento, desaliento
despondent [dɪ'spɑndənt] *adj* abatido, desalentado
despot ['dɛspɑt] *s* déspota *m*
despotic [dɛs'pɑtɪk] *adj* despótico
despotism ['dɛspə,tɪzəm] *s* despotismo
dessert [dɪ'zʌrt] *s* postre *m*
destination [,dɛstɪ'neʃən] *s* (*end of a journey or shipment*) destino; (*purpose*) destinación
destine ['dɛstɪn] *tr* destinar
desti•ny ['dɛstɪni] *s* (*pl* **-nies**) destino
destitute ['dɛstɪ,tjut] o ['dɛstɪ,tut] *adj* (*being in complete poverty*) indigente; (*lacking, deprived*) desprovisto
destitution [,dɛstɪ'tjuʃən] o [,dɛstɪ'tuʃən] *s* indigencia
destroy [dɪ'strɔɪ] *tr* destruir
destroyer [dɪ'strɔɪ•ər] *s* (nav) destructor *m*
destruction [dɪ'strʌkʃən] *s* destrucción
destructive [dɪ'strʌktɪv] *adj* destructivo
desultory ['dɛsəl,tori] *adj* deshilvanado, descosido
detach [dɪ'tætʃ] *tr* desprender, separar; (mil) destacar
detachable [dɪ'tætʃəbəl] *adj* desprendible, separable; (*collar*) postizo
detached [dɪ'tætʃt] *adj* separado, suelto; imparcial, desinteresado
detachment [dɪ'tætʃmənt] *s* desprendimiento, separación; imparcialidad, desinterés *m*; (mil) destacamento
detail [dɪ'tel] o ['ditel] *s* detalle *m*, pormenor *m*; (mil) destacamento || [dɪ'tel] *tr* detallar; (mil) destacar
detain [dɪ'ten] *tr* detener; tener preso
detect [dɪ'tɛkt] *tr* detectar
detection [dɪ'tɛkʃən] *s* detección
detective [dɪ'tɛktɪv] *s* detective *m*
detective story *s* novela policíaca o policial
detector [dɪ'tɛktər] *s* detector *m*
detention [dɪ'tɛnʃən] *s* detención
de•ter [dɪ'tʌr] *v* (*pret & pp* **-terred**; *ger* **-terring**) *tr* impedir, refrenar
detergent [dɪ'tʌrdʒənt] *adj & s* detergente *m*
deteriorate [dɪ'tɪrɪ•ə,ret] *tr* deteriorar || *intr* deteriorarse
determine [dɪ'tʌrmɪn] *tr* determinar
deterrent [dɪ'tʌrənt] *s* impedimento, refrenamiento
detest [dɪ'tɛst] *tr* detestar, aborrecer
dethrone [dɪ'θron] *tr* destronar
detonate ['dɛtə,net] o ['ditə,net] *tr* hacer estallar || *intr* detonar
detour ['ditʊr] o [dɪ'tʊr] *s* desvío;

rodeo, vuelta; manera indirecta || *tr* desviar (*el tráfico*) || *intr* desviarse
detract [dɪˈtrækt] *tr* detraer || *intr* — **to detract from** disminuir, rebajar
detriment [ˈdɛtrɪmənt] *s* perjuicio, detrimento; **to the detriment of** en perjuicio de
detrimental [ˌdɛtrɪˈmɛntəl] *adj* perjudicial
deuce [djus] o [dus] *s* (*in cards*) dos *m;* **the deuce!** ¡demonio!
devaluation [diˌvæljuˈeʃən] *s* desvalorización, devaluación
devastate [ˈdɛvəsˌtet] *tr* devastar
devastation [ˌdɛvəsˈteʃən] *s* devastación
develop [dɪˈvɛləp] *tr* desarrollar, desenvolver; (phot) revelar; explotar (*una mina*) || *intr* desarrollarse, desenvolverse; evolucionar, manifestarse
developer [dɪˈvɛləpər] *s* fomentador *m;* (phot) revelador *m*
development [dɪˈvɛləpmənt] *s* desarrollo, desenvolvimiento; (phot) revelado; (*of a mine*) explotación; acontecimiento nuevo
deviate [ˈdivɪˌet] *tr* desviar || *intr* desviarse
deviation [ˌdivɪˈeʃən] *s* desviación
deviationism [ˌdivɪˈeʃəˌnɪzəm] *s* desviacionismo
deviationist [ˌdivɪˈeʃənɪst] *s* desviacionista *mf*
device [dɪˈvaɪs] *s* dispositivo, aparato; (*trick*) ardid *m,* treta; (*motto*) lema *m,* divisa; **to leave someone to his own devices** dejarle a uno que haga lo que se le antoje
dev·il [ˈdɛvəl] *s* diablo; **between the devil and the deep blue sea** entre la espada y la pared; **to raise the devil** (slang) armar un alboroto || *v* (*pret & pp* **-iled** o **-illed;** *ger* **-iling** o **-illing**) *tr* condimentar con picantes; (coll) acosar, molestar
devilish [ˈdɛvəlɪʃ] *adj* diabólico
devilment [ˈdɛvəlmənt] *s* (*mischief*) diablura; (*evil*) maldad
devil·try [ˈdɛvəltri] *s* (*pl* **-tries**) maldad, crueldad; (*mischief*) diablura
devious [ˈdivɪ·əs] *adj* (*straying*) desviado, extraviado; (*roundabout; shifty*) tortuoso
devise [dɪˈvaɪz] *tr* idear, inventar; (law) legar
devoid [dɪˈvɔɪd] *adj* desprovisto
devote [dɪˈvot] *tr* dedicar
devoted [dɪˈvotɪd] *adj* (*zealous, ardent*) devoto; dedicado
devotee [ˌdɛvəˈti] *s* devoto
devotion [dɪˈvoʃən] *s* devoción; (*to study, work, etc.*) dedicación; **devotions** oraciones, preces *fpl*
devour [dɪˈvaʊr] *tr* devorar
devout [dɪˈvaʊt] *adj* devoto; cordial, sincero
dew [dju] o [du] *s* rocío
dew'drop' *s* gota de rocío
dew'lap' *s* papada
dew·y [ˈdju·i] o [ˈdu·i] *adj* rociado
dexterity [dɛksˈtɛrɪti] *s* destreza
D.F. *abbr* **Defender of the Faith**
diabetes [ˌdaɪ·əˈbitɪs] o [ˌdaɪ·əˈbitiz] *s* diabetes *f*
diabetic [ˌdaɪ·əˈbɛtɪk] o [ˌdaɪ·əˈbitɪk] *adj & s* diabético
diabolic(al) [ˌdaɪ·əˈbɑlɪk(əl)] *adj* diabólico
diacritical [ˌdaɪ·əˈkrɪtɪkəl] *adj* diacrítico
diadem [ˈdaɪ·əˌdɛm] *s* diadema *f*
diaere·sis [daɪˈɛrɪsɪs] *s* (*pl* **-ses** [ˌsiz]) diéresis *f*
diagnose [ˌdaɪ·əgˈnos] o [ˌdaɪ·əgˈnoz] *tr* diagnosticar
diagno·sis [ˌdaɪ·əgˈnosɪs] *s* (*pl* **-ses** [siz]) diagnosis *f,* diagnóstico
diagonal [daɪˈægənəl] *adj & s* diagonal *f*
diagram [ˈdaɪ·əˌgræm] *s* diagrama *m*
dial. *abbr* **dialect**
dial [ˈdaɪ·əl] *s* (*of radio*) cuadrante *m;* (*of watch*) cuadrante *m,* esfera, muestra; (*of telephone*) disco selector || *tr* sintonizar (*el radiorreceptor*); marcar (*el número telefónico*); llamar (*a una persona*) por teléfono automático || *intr* (telp) marcar
dialect [ˈdaɪ·əˌlɛkt] *s* dialecto
dialing [ˈdaɪ·əlɪŋ] *s* (telp) marcaje *m*
dialogue [ˈdaɪ·əˌlɔg] o [ˈdaɪ·əˌlɑg] *s* diálogo
dial telephone *s* teléfono automático
dial tone *s* (telp) señal *f* para marcar
diam. *abbr* **diameter**
diameter [daɪˈæmɪtər] *s* diámetro
diametric(al) [ˌdaɪ·əˈmɛtrɪk(əl)] *adj* diamétrico
diamond [ˈdaɪmənd] *s* diamante *m;* (*figure of a rhombus*) losange *m;* (*playing card*) carró *m,* diamante *m;* (baseball) losange *m*
diaper [ˈdaɪ·pər] *s* pañal *m*
diaphanous [daɪˈæfənəs] *adj* diáfano
diaphragm [ˈdaɪ·əˌfræm] *s* diafragma *m*
diarrhea [ˌdaɪ·əˈri·ə] *s* diarrea
dia·ry [ˈdaɪ·əri] *s* (*pl* **-ries**) diario
diastole [daɪˈæstəli] *s* diástole *f*
diathermy [ˈdaɪ·əˌθʌrmi] *s* diatermia
dice [daɪs] *spl* dados; (*small cubes*) cubitos; **to load the dice** cargar los dados || *tr* cortar en cubos
dice'box' *s* cubilete *m*
dichloride [daɪˈkloraɪd] *s* dicloruro
dichoto·my [daɪˈkɑtəmi] *s* (*pl* **-mies**) dicotomía
dickey [ˈdɪki] *s* camisolín *m,* pechera postiza; babero de niño
dict. *abbr* **dictionary**
dictaphone [ˈdɪktəˌfon] *s* dictáfono
dictate [ˈdɪktet] *s* mandato || [ˈdɪktet] o [dɪkˈtet] *tr* dictar; mandar
dictation [dɪkˈteʃən] *s* dictado; (*orders; giving orders*) mandato; **to take dictation** escribir al dictado
dictator [ˈdɪktetər] o [dɪkˈtetər] *s* dictador *m*
dictatorship [ˈdɪktetərˌʃɪp] o [dɪkˈtetərʃɪp] *s* dictadura
diction [ˈdɪkʃən] *s* dicción
dictionar·y [ˈdɪkʃənˌɛri] *s* (*pl* **-ies**) diccionario

dic·tum ['dɪktəm] *s* (*pl* **-ta** [tə]) dictamen *m;* aforismo, sentencia
didactic(al) [daɪ'dæktɪk(əl)] o [dɪ'dæktɪk(əl)] *adj* didáctico
die [daɪ] *s* (*pl* **dice** [daɪs]) dado; **the die is cast** la suerte está echada || *s* (*pl* **dies**) (*for stamping coins, medals, etc.*) troquel *m;* (*for cutting threads*) hembra de terraja || *v* (*pret & pp* **died;** *ger* **dying**) *intr* morir; **to be dying** estar agonizando; **to die laughing** morir de risa
die'-hard' *adj & s* intransigente *mf*
diesel oil ['dizəl] *s* gas-oil *m*
die'stock' *s* terraja
diet ['daɪ·ət] *s* dieta, régimen alimenticio || *intr* estar a dieta
dietitian [,daɪ·ə'tɪʃən] *s* dietista *mf*
diff. *abbr* **difference, different**
differ ['dɪfər] *intr* (*to be different*) diferir, diferenciarse; (*to dissent*) diferenciar; **to differ with** desavenirse con
difference ['dɪfərəns] *s* diferencia; **to make no difference** no importar; **to split the difference** partir la diferencia
different ['dɪfərənt] *adj* diferente
differentiate [,dɪfə'rɛnʃɪ,et] *tr* diferenciar || *intr* diferenciarse
difficult ['dɪfɪ,kʌlt] *adj* difícil
difficul·ty ['dɪfɪ,kʌlti] *s* (*pl* **-ties**) dificultad
diffident ['dɪfɪdənt] *adj* apocado, tímido
diffuse [dɪ'fjus] *adj* difuso || [dɪ'fjuz] *tr* difundir || *intr* difundirse
dig [dɪg] *s* (*poke*) empuje *m;* (*jibe*) pulla, palabra hiriente || *v* (*pret & pp* **dug** [dʌg] o **digged;** *ger* **digging**) *tr* cavar, excavar; **to dig up** desenterrar || *intr* cavar, excavar; **to dig in** (coll) poner manos a la obra; (mil) atrincherarse; **to dig under** socavar
digest ['daɪdʒɛst] *s* compendio, resumen *m;* (law) digesto || [dɪ'dʒɛst] o [daɪ'dʒɛst] *tr & intr* digerir
digestible [dɪ'dʒɛstɪbəl] o [daɪ'dʒɛstɪbəl] *adj* digerible, digestible
digestion [dɪ'dʒɛstʃən] o [daɪ'dʒɛstʃən] *s* digestión
digestive [dɪ'dʒɛstɪv] o [daɪ'dʒɛstɪv] *adj & s* digestivo
digit ['dɪdʒɪt] *s* dígito
dignified ['dɪgnɪ,faɪd] *adj* digno, grave, decoroso
digni·fy ['dɪgnɪ,faɪ] *v* (*pret & pp* **-fied**) *tr* dignificar; engrandecer el mérito de
dignitar·y ['dɪgnɪ,tɛri] *s* (*pl* **-ies**) dignatario
digni·ty ['dɪgnɪti] *s* (*pl* **-ties**) dignidad; **to stand upon one's dignity** ponerse tan alto
digress [dɪ'grɛs] o [daɪ'grɛs] *intr* divagar
digression [dɪ'grɛʃən] o [daɪ'grɛʃən] *s* digresión, divagación
dike [daɪk] *s* dique *m;* (*bank of earth thrown up in digging*) montón *m;* (*causeway*) arrecife *m,* malecón *m*
dilapidated [dɪ'læpɪ,detɪd] *adj* destartalado, desvencijado
dilate [daɪ'let] *tr* dilatar || *intr* dilatarse
dilatory ['dɪlə,tori] *adj* tardío
dilemma [dɪ'lɛmə] *s* dilema *m,* disyuntiva
dilettan·te [,dɪlə'tænti] *adj* diletante || *s* (*pl* **-tes** o **-ti** [ti]) diletante *mf*
diligence ['dɪlɪdʒəns] *s* diligencia
diligent ['dɪlɪdʒənt] *adj* diligente
dill [dɪl] *s* eneldo
dillydal·ly ['dɪlɪ,dæli] *v* (*pret & pp* **-lied**) *intr* malgastar el tiempo, haraganear
dilute [dɪ'lut] o [daɪ'lut] *adj* diluído || [dɪ'lut] *tr* diluir || *intr* diluirse
dilution [dɪ'luʃən] *s* dilución
dim. *abbr* **diminutive**
dim [dɪm] *adj* (*comp* **dimmer;** *super* **dimmest**) débil, indistinto, confuso; obscuro, poco claro; (*chance*) escaso; (*not clearly understanding*) torpe, lerdo; **to take a dim view of** mirar escépticamente || *v* (*pret & pp* **dimmed;** *ger* **dimming**) *tr* amortiguar (*la luz*)*;* poner (*un faro*) a media luz; disminuir || *intr* obscurecerse
dime [daɪm] *s* moneda de diez centavos
dimension [dɪ'mɛnʃən] *s* dimensión
diminish [dɪ'mɪnɪʃ] *tr* disminuir || *intr* disminuir, disminuirse
diminutive [dɪ'mɪnjətɪv] *adj* (*tiny*) diminuto; (gram) diminutivo || *s* diminutivo
dimi·ty ['dɪmɪti] *s* (*pl* **-ties**) cotonía
dimly ['dɪmli] *adv* indistintamente
dimmer ['dɪmər] *s* amortiguador *m* de luz; (aut) lámpara de cruce, luz *f* de cruce
dimple ['dɪmpəl] *s* hoyuelo
dimwit ['dɪm,wɪt] *s* (slang) mentecato, bobo
dim-witted ['dɪm,wɪtɪd] *adj* (slang) mentecato, bobo
din [dɪn] *s* estruendo, ruido ensordecedor || *v* (*pret & pp* **dinned;** *ger* **dinning**) *tr* ensordecer con mucho ruido; repetir insistentemente; impresionar con repetición ruidosa || *intr* sonar estrepitosamente
dine [daɪn] *tr* dar de comer a; obsequiar con una cena o comida || *intr* cenar, comer; **to dine out** cenar fuera de casa
diner ['daɪnər] *s* invitado a una cena, convidado a una comida; coche-comedor *m*
ding-dong ['dɪŋ,dɔŋ] o ['dɪŋ,dɑŋ] *s* dindán *m*
din·gy ['dɪndʒi] *adj* (*comp* **-gier;** *super* **-giest**) deslustrado, sucio
dining car *s* coche-comedor *m*
dining room *s* comedor *m*
din'ing-room' suit *s* juego de comedor
dinner ['dɪnər] *s* cena, comida; (*formal meal*) banquete *m*
dinner coat o **jacket** *s* smoking *m*
dinner pail *s* fiambrera, portaviandas *m*
dinner set *s* vajilla
dinner time *s* hora de la cena o comida

dint [dɪnt] *s* abolladura; **by dint of** a fuerza de || *tr* abollar
diocese ['daɪ·ə,sis] o ['daɪ·əsɪs] *s* diócesi *f* o diócesis *f*
diode ['daɪ·od] *s* diodo
dioxide [daɪ'ɑksaɪd] *s* dióxido
dip [dɪp] *s* zambullida, inmersión; baño corto; (*in a road*) depresión; (*of magnetic needle*) inclinación || *v* (*pret & pp* **dipped;** *ger* **dipping**) *tr* sumergir; sacar con cuchara; (*bread*) sopetear; **to dip the colors** saludar con la bandera || *intr* sumergirse; inclinarse hacia abajo; desaparecer súbitamente; **to dip into** hojear (*un libro*); meterse en (*un comercio*); **to dip into one's purse** gastar dinero
diphtheria [dɪf'θɪrɪ·ə] *s* difteria
diphthong ['dɪfθɔŋ] o ['dɪfθɑŋ] *s* diptongo
diphthongize ['dɪfθɔŋ,gaɪz] o ['dɪfθɑŋ,gaɪz] *tr* diptongar || *intr* diptongarse
diploma [dɪ'plomə] *s* diploma *m*
diploma·cy [dɪ'ploməsi] *s* (*pl* **-cies**) diplomacia
diplomat ['dɪplə,mæt] *s* diplomático
diplomatic [,dɪplə'mætɪk] *adj* diplomático
diplomatic pouch *s* valija diplomática
dipper ['dɪpər] *s* cazo, cucharón *m*
dip'stick' *s* varilla de nivel
dire [daɪr] *adj* horrendo, espantoso
direct [dɪ'rɛkt] o [daɪ'rɛkt] *adj* directo; franco, sincero || *tr* dirigir; mandar, ordenar
direct current *s* corriente continua
direct discourse *s* (gram) estilo directo
direct hit *s* blanco directo, impacto directo
direction [dɪ'rɛkʃən] o [daɪ'rɛkʃən] *s* dirección; instrucción
direct object *s* (gram) complemento directo
director [dɪ'rɛktər] o [daɪ'rɛktər] *s* director *m*, administrador *m;* (*member of a governing body*) vocal *m*
directorship [dɪ'rɛktər,ʃɪp] o [daɪ'rɛktər,ʃɪp] *s* dirección, directorio
directo·ry [dɪ'rɛktəri] o [daɪ'rɛktəri] *s* (*pl* **-ries**) (*list of names and addresses; board of directors*) directorio; anuario telefónico, guía telefónica
dirge [dʌrdʒ] *s* endecha, canto fúnebre, treno; (eccl) misa de réquiem
dirigible ['dɪrɪdʒɪbəl] *adj & s* dirigible *m*
dirt [dʌrt] *s* (*soil*) tierra, suelo; (*dust*) polvo; (*mud*) barro, lodo; excremento; (*accumulation of dirt*) suciedad; (*moral filth*) suciedad, porquería, obscenidad; (*gossip*) chismes *mpl*
dirt'cheap' *adj* tirado, muy barato
dirt road *s* camino de tierra
dirt·y ['dʌrti] *adj* (*comp* **-ier;** *super* **-iest**) puerco, sucio; barroso, enlodado; polvoriento; (*obscene*) hediondo; bajo, vil || *v* (*pret & pp* **-tied**) *tr* ensuciar
dirty linen *s* ropa sucia; **to air one's dirty linen in public** sacar los trapos sucios a relucir
dirty trick *s* (slang) perrada, mala partida
disabili·ty [,dɪsə'bɪlɪti] *s* (*pl* **-ties**) incapacidad, inhabilidad
disable [dɪs'ebəl] *tr* incapacitar, inhabilitar, lisiar; (law) descalificar
disabuse [,dɪsə'bjuz] *tr* desengañar
disadvantage [,dɪsəd'væntɪdʒ] o [,dɪsəd'vɑntɪdʒ] *s* desventaja
disadvantageous [dɪs,ædvən'tdʒəs] *adj* desventajoso
disagree [,dɪsə'gri] *intr* desavenirse, desconvenirse; (*to quarrel*) altercar, contender; **to disagree with** no estar de acuerdo con; no sentar bien
disagreeable [,dɪsə'gri·əbəl] *adj* desagradable
disagreement [,dɪsə'grimənt] *s* desavenencia, desacuerdo; disensión
disappear [,dɪsə'pɪr] *intr* desaparecer, desaparecerse
disappearance [,dɪsə'pɪrəns] *s* desaparecimiento, desaparición
disappoint [,dɪsə'pɔɪnt] *tr* decepcionar, desilusionar, chasquear; **to be disappointed** chasquearse, llevarse chasco
disappointment [,dɪsə'pɔɪntmənt] *s* decepción, desilusión, chasco
disapproval [,dɪsə'pruvəl] *s* desaprobación
disapprove [,dɪsə'pruv] *tr & intr* desaprobar
disarm [dɪs'ɑrm] *tr* desarmar || *intr* desarmar, desarmarse
disarmament [dɪs'ɑrməmənt] *s* desarme *m*
disarming [dɪs'ɑrmɪŋ] *adj* congraciador, simpático
disarray [,dɪsə're] *s* desorden *m;* (*in apparel*) desatavío || *tr* desordenar; desataviar
disaster [dɪ'zæstər] o [dɪ'zɑstər] *s* desastre *m*, siniestro
disastrous [dɪ'zæstrəs] o [dɪ'zɑstrəs] *adj* desastroso, desastrado
disavow [,dɪsə'vaʊ] *tr* desconocer, negar, repudiar
disband [dɪs'bænd] *tr* disolver (*una asamblea*); licenciar (*tropas*) || *intr* desbandarse
dis·bar [dɪs'bɑr] *v* (*pret & pp* **-barred;** *ger* **-barring**) *tr* (law) expulsar del foro
disbelief [,dɪsbɪ'lif] *s* incredulidad
disbelieve [,dɪsbɪ'liv] *tr & intr* descreer
disburse [dɪs'bʌrs] *tr* desembolsar
disbursement [dɪs'bʌrsmənt] *s* desembolso
disc. *abbr* **discount, discoverer**
disc [dɪsk] *s* disco
discard [dɪs'kɑrd] *s* descarte *m;* **to put into the discard** desechar || *tr* descartar; desechar
discern [dɪ'zʌrn] o [dɪ'sʌrn] *tr* discernir, percibir
discerning [dɪ'zʌrnɪŋ] o [dɪ'sʌrnɪŋ] *adj* discerniente, perspicaz
discharge [dɪs'tʃɑrdʒ] *s* (*of a gun, of*

a battery) descarga; (*of a prisoner*) liberación; (*of a duty*) desempeño; (*of a debt, of an obligation*) descargo; (*from a job*) despedida, remoción; (mil) certificado de licencia; (pathol) derrame *m* || *tr* descargar; desempeñar (*un deber*); libertar (*a un preso*); despedir, remover (*a un empleado*); (*from the hospital*) dar de alta; (mil) licenciar || *intr* descargar (*un tubo, río, etc.*); descargarse (*un arma de fuego*)
disciple [dɪ'saɪpəl] *s* discípulo
disciplinarian [,dɪsɪplɪ'nɛrɪ·ən] *s* ordenancista *mf*
discipline ['dɪsɪplɪn] *s* disciplina; castigo || *tr* disciplinar; castigar
disclaim [dɪs'klem] *tr* desconocer, negar
disclose [dɪs'kloz] *tr* divulgar, revelar; descubrir
disclosure [dɪs'kloʒər] *s* divulgación, revelación; descubrimiento
discolor [dɪs'kʌlər] *tr* descolorar || *intr* descolorarse
discomfiture [dɪs'kʌmfɪtʃər] *s* desconcierto; frustración
discomfort [dɪs'kʌmfərt] *s* incomodidad || *tr* incomodar
disconcert [,dɪskən'sʌrt] *tr* desconcertar, confundir
disconnect [,dɪskə'nɛkt] *tr* desunir, separar; desconectar
disconsolate [dɪs'kɑnsəlɪt] *adj* desconsolado, desolado
discontent [,dɪskən'tɛnt] *adj & s* descontento || *tr* descontentar
discontented [,dɪskən'tɛntɪd] *adj* descontento
discontinue [,dɪskən'tɪnjʊ] *tr* descontinuar
discord ['dɪskɔrd] *s* desacuerdo, discordia; discordancia
discordance [dɪs'kɔrdəns] *s* discordancia
discotheque [,dɪsko'tɛk] *s* discoteca
discount ['dɪskaʊnt] *s* descuento || ['dɪskaʊnt] o [dɪs'kaʊnt] *tr* descontar; descontar por exagerado
discount rate *s* tipo de descuento; tipo de redescuento
discourage [dɪs'kʌrɪdʒ] *tr* desalentar, desanimar; desaprobar; disuadir
discouragement [dɪs'kʌrɪdʒmənt] *s* desaliento; desaprobación; disuasión
discourse ['dɪskors] o [dɪs'kors] *s* discurso || [dɪs'kors] *intr* discurrir
discourteous [dɪs'kʌrtɪ·əs] *adj* descortés
discourte·sy [dɪs'kʌrtəsi] *s* (*pl* **-sies**) descortesía
discover [dɪs'kʌvər] *tr* descubrir
discover·y [dɪs'kʌvəri] *s* (*pl* **-ies**) descubrimiento
discredit [dɪs'krɛdɪt] *s* descrédito || *tr* desacreditar
discreditable [dɪs'krɛdɪtəbəl] *adj* deshonroso
discreet [dɪs'krit] *adj* discreto
discrepan·cy [dɪs'krɛpənsi] *s* (*pl* **-cies**) discrepancia
discrete [dɪs'krit] *adj* discreto
discretion [dɪs'krɛʃən] *s* discreción; **at discretion** a discreción
discriminate [dɪs'krɪmɪ,net] *intr* discriminar; **to discriminate against** discriminar
discrimination [dɪs,krɪmɪ'neʃən] *s* discriminación
discriminatory [dɪs'krɪmɪnə,tori] *adj* discriminatorio
discus ['dɪskəs] *s* (sport) disco
discuss [dɪs'kʌs] *tr & intr* discutir
discussion [dɪs'kʌʃən] *s* discusión
discus thrower ['θro·ər] *s* discóbolo
disdain [dɪs'den] *s* desdén *m* || *tr* desdeñar
disdainful [dɪs'denfəl] *adj* desdeñoso
disease [dɪ'ziz] *s* enfermedad
diseased [dɪ'zizd] *adj* morboso
disembark [,dɪsɛm'bɑrk] *tr & intr* desembarcar
disembarkation [dɪs,ɛmbɑr'keʃən] *s* (*of passengers*) desembarco; (*of freight*) desembarque *m*
disembowel [,dɪsɛm'baʊ·əl] *tr* desentrañar
disenchant [,dɪsɛn'tʃænt] o [,dɪsɛn'tʃɑnt] *tr* desencantar
disenchantment [,dɪsɛn'tʃæntmənt] o [,dɪsɛn'tʃɑntmənt] *s* desencanto
disengage [,dɪsɛn'gedʒ] *tr* (*from a pledge*) desempeñar; (*to disconnect*) desenganchar; desembragar (*el motor*)
disengagement [,dɪsɛn'gedʒmənt] *s* desempeño; desenganche *m;* desembrague *m*
disentangle [,dɪsɛn'tæŋgəl] *tr* desenredar
disentanglement [,dɪsɛn'tæŋgəlmənt] *s* desenredo
disestablish [,dɪsɛs'tæblɪʃ] *tr* separar (*la Iglesia*) del Estado
disfavor [dɪs'fevər] *s* disfavor *m*
disfigure [dɪs'fɪgjər] *tr* desfigurar
disfranchise [dɪs'fræntʃaiz] *tr* privar de los derechos de ciudadanía
disgorge [dɪs'gɔrdʒ] *tr & intr* vomitar
disgrace [dɪs'gres] *s* deshonra, vergüenza; disfavor *m* || *tr* deshonrar, avergonzar; despedir con ignominia
disgraceful [dɪs'gresfəl] *adj* deshonroso, vergonzoso
disgruntle [dɪs·grʌntəl] *tr* disgustar, enfadar
disguise [dɪs'gaɪz] *s* disfraz *m* || *tr* disfrazar
disgust [dɪs'gʌst] *s* asco, repugnancia || *tr* dar asco a, repugnar
disgusting [dɪs'gʌstɪŋ] *adj* asqueroso, repugnante
dish [dɪʃ] *s* (*any container used at table*) vasija; (*shallow, circular dish; its contents*) plato; **to wash the dishes** lavar la vajilla || *tr* servir en un plato; (slang) arruinar
dish'cloth' *s* albero
dishearten [dɪs'hɑrtən] *tr* descorazonar, desalentar, desanimar
dishev·el [dɪ'ʃɛvəl] *v* (*pret & pp* **-eled** o **-elled;** *ger* **-eling** o **-elling**) desgreñar, desmelenar

dishonest [dɪs'ɑnɪst] *adj* no honrado, ímprobo
dishones·ty [dɪs'ɑnɪsti] *s* (*pl* **-ties**) falta de honradez, improbidad
dishonor [dɪs'ɑnər] *s* deshonra, deshonor *m* ‖ *tr* deshonrar, deshonorar; (com) no aceptar, no pagar
dishonorable [dɪs'ɑnərəbəl] *adj* ignominioso, deshonroso
dish'pan' *s* paila de lavar la vajilla
dish rack *s* escurreplatos *m*
dish'rag' *s* albero
dish'tow'el *s* paño para secar platos
dish'wash'er *s* (*person*) fregona; (*machine*) lavaplatos *m*
dish'wa'ter *s* agua de lavar platos, agua sucia
disillusion [ˌdɪsɪ'luʒən] *s* desilusión ‖ *tr* desilusionar
disillusionment [ˌdɪsɪ'luʒənmənt] *s* desilusión
disinclination [dɪsˌɪnklɪ'neʃən] *s* aversión, desafición
disinclined [ˌdɪsɪn'klaɪnd] *adj* desinclinado
disinfect [ˌdɪsɪn'fɛkt] *tr* desinfectar, desinficionar
disinfectant [ˌdɪsɪn'fɛktənt] *adj* & *s* desinfectante *m*
disingenuous [ˌdɪsɪn'dʒɛnju·əs] *adj* insincero, poco ingenuo
disinherit [ˌdɪsɪn'hɛrɪt] *tr* desheredar
disintegrate [dɪs'ɪntɪˌgret] *tr* desagregar, desintegrar ‖ *intr* desagregarse, desintegrarse
disintegration [dɪsˌɪntɪ'greʃən] *s* desagregación, desintegración
disin·ter [ˌdɪsɪn'tʌr] *v* (*pret* & *pp* **-terred**; *ger* **-terring**) *tr* desenterrar
disinterested [dɪs'ɪntəˌrɛstɪd] o [dɪs'ɪntrɪstɪd] *adj* desinteresado
disinterestedness [dɪs'ɪntəˌrɛstɪdnɪs] o [dɪs'ɪntrɪstɪdnɪs] *s* desinterés *m*
disjunctive [dɪs'dʒʌŋktɪv] *adj* disyuntivo
disk [dɪsk] *s* disco
disk jockey *s* (rad) locutor *m* de un programa de discos
dislike [dɪs'laɪk] *s* aversión, antipatía; **to take a dislike for** cobrar aversión a ‖ *tr* desamar
dislocate ['dɪsloˌket] *tr* dislocar, dislocarse (*un hueso*)
dislodge [dɪs'lɑdʒ] *tr* desalojar
disloyal [dɪs'lɔɪ·əl] *adj* desleal
disloyal·ty [dɪs'lɔɪ·əlti] *s* (*pl* **-ties**) deslealtad
dismal ['dɪzməl] *adj* lúgubre, tenebroso; terrible, espantoso
dismantle [dɪs'mæntəl] *tr* desarmar, desmontar
dismay [dɪs'me] *s* consternación ‖ *tr* consternar
dismember [dɪs'mɛmbər] *tr* desmembrar
dismiss [dɪs'mɪs] *tr* despedir, destituir; desechar; alejar del pensamiento, echar en olvido
dismissal [dɪs'mɪsəl] *s* despedida, destitución
dismount [dɪs'maʊnt] *tr* desmontar ‖ *intr* desmontarse
disobedience [ˌdɪsə'bidɪ·əns] *s* desobediencia
disobedient [ˌdɪsə'bidɪ·ənt] *adj* desobediente
disobey [ˌdɪsə'be] *tr* & *intr* desobedecer
disorder [dɪs'ɔrdər] *s* desorden *m* ‖ *tr* desordenar
disorderly [dɪs'ɔrdərli] *adj* desordenado; alborotador, revoltoso
disorderly conduct *s* conducta contra el orden público
disorderly house *s* burdel *m*, lupanar *m*
disorganize [dɪs'ɔrgəˌnaɪz] *tr* desorganizar
disown [dɪs'on] *tr* desconocer, repudiar
disparage [dɪs'pærɪdʒ] *tr* desacreditar, desdorar
disparagement [dɪs'pærɪdʒmənt] *s* descrédito, desdoro
disparate ['dɪspərɪt] *adj* disparejo
dispari·ty [dɪs'pærɪti] *s* (*pl* **-ties**) disparidad
dispassionate [dɪs'pæʃənɪt] *adj* desapasionado
dispatch [dɪs'pætʃ] *s* despacho ‖ *tr* despachar; (coll) despabilar (*una comida*)
dis·pel [dɪs'pɛl] *v* (*pret* & *pp* **-pelled**; *ger* **-pelling**) *tr* desvanecer, disipar
dispensa·ry [dɪs'pɛnsəri] *s* (*pl* **-ries**) dispensario
dispense [dɪs'pɛns] *tr* dispensar (*medicamentos*); administrar (*justicia*); expender (*p.ej., gasolina*); (*to exempt*) eximir ‖ *intr* — **to dispense with** deshacerse de; pasar sin, prescindir de
disperse [dɪs'pʌrs] *tr* dispersar ‖ *intr* dispersarse
displace [dɪs'ples] *tr* remover, trasladar; despedir, deponer; reemplazar; desplazar (*un volumen de agua*)
displaced person *s* persona desplazada
display [dɪs'ple] *s* despliegue *m;* exhibición, exposición; ostentación ‖ *tr* (*to unfold; to reveal*) desplegar; (*to exhibit, show*) exhibir, exponer; (*to show ostentatiously*) ostentar
display cabinet *s* vitrina, escaparate *m*
display window *s* escaparate *m* de tienda
displease [dɪs'pliz] *tr* desagradar, disgustar, desplacer
displeasing [dɪs'plizɪŋ] *adj* desagradable
displeasure [dɪs'plɛʒər] *s* desagrado, disgusto, desplacer *m*
disposable [dɪs'pozəbəl] *adj* (*available for any use*) disponible; (*made to be thrown away after serving its purpose*) desechable, descartable
disposal [dɪs'pozəl] *s* disposición; donación, liquidación, venta; **at the disposal of** a la disposición de; **to have at one's disposal** disponer de
dispose [dɪs'poz] *tr* disponer; inducir, mover ‖ *intr* disponer; **to dispose of** disponer de; deshacerse de; dar, vender; acabar con

disposition [ˌdɪspəˈzɪʃən] *s* disposición; índole *f*, genio, natural *m;* ajuste *m*, arreglo; venta
dispossess [ˌdɪspəˈzɛs] *tr* desposeer; (*to evict, oust*) desahuciar
disproof [dɪsˈpruf] *s* confutación, refutación
disproportionate [ˌdɪsprəˈporʃənɪt] *adj* desproporcionado
disprove [dɪsˈpruv] *tr* confutar, refutar
dispute [dɪsˈpjut] *s* disputa; **beyond dispute** sin disputa; **in dispute** disputado || *tr & intr* disputar
disquali·fy [dɪsˈkwɑlɪˌfaɪ] *v* (*pret & pp* **-fied**) *tr* descalificar, desclasificar
disquiet [dɪsˈkwaɪ·ət] *s* desasosiego, inquietud || *tr* desasosegar, inquietar
disregard [ˌdɪsrɪˈgɑrd] *s* desatención, desaire *m* || *tr* desatender, desairar, pasar por alto
disrepair [ˌdɪsrɪˈpɛr] *s* desconcierto, descompostura
disreputable [dɪsˈrɛpjətəbəl] *adj* desacreditado, de mala fama; raído, usado, desaliñado
disrepute [ˌdɪsrɪˈpjut] *s* descrédito, mala fama; **to bring into disrepute** desacreditar, dar mala fama a
disrespect [ˌdɪsrɪˈspɛkt] *s* desacato || *tr* desacatar
disrespectful [ˌdɪsrɪˈspɛktfəl] *adj* irrespetuoso
disrobe [dɪsˈrob] *tr* desnudar || *intr* desnudarse
disrupt [dɪsˈrʌpt] *tr* romper; (*to throw into disorder*) desbaratar
dissatisfaction [ˌdɪssætɪsˈfækʃən] *s* desagrado, descontento
dissatisfied [dɪsˈsætɪsˌfaɪd] *adj* descontento
dissatis·fy [dɪsˈsætɪsˌfaɪ] *v* (*pret & pp* **-fied**) *tr* descontentar
dissect [dɪˈsɛkt] *tr* disecar
dissemble [dɪˈsɛmbəl] *tr* disimular || *intr* disimular; obrar hipócritamente
disseminate [dɪˈsɛmɪˌnet] *tr* diseminar, difundir
dissension [dɪˈsɛnʃən] *s* disensión
dissent [dɪˈsɛnt] *s* disensión; (*nonconformity*) disidencia || *intr* disentir; (*from doctrine or authority*) disidir
dissenter [dɪˈsɛntər] *s* disidente *mf*
disservice [dɪˈsʌrvɪs] *s* deservicio
dissidence [ˈdɪsɪdəns] *s* disidencia
dissident [ˈdɪsɪdənt] *adj & s* disidente *mf*
dissimilar [dɪˈsɪmɪlər] *adj* disímil, desemejante
dissimilate [dɪˈsɪmɪˌlet] *tr* disimilar || *intr* disimilarse
dissimulate [dɪˈsɪmjəˌlet] *tr & intr* disimular
dissipate [ˈdɪsɪˌpet] *tr* disipar || *intr* disiparse; entregarse a la disipación
dissipated [ˈdɪsɪˌpetɪd] *adj* disipado, disoluto
dissipation [ˌdɪsɪˈpeʃən] *s* disipación
dissociate [dɪˈsoʃɪˌet] *tr* disociar
dissolute [ˈdɪsəˌlut] *adj* disoluto
dissolution [ˌdɪsəˈluʃən] *s* disolución
dissolve [dɪˈzɑlv] *tr* disolver || *intr* (*to have the power of dissolving*) disolver; (*to pass into a liquid*) disolverse
dissonance [ˈdɪsənəns] *s* disonancia
dissuade [dɪˈswed] *tr* disuadir
dissyllabic [ˌdɪssɪˈlæbɪk] *adj* disílabo, disilábico
dissyllable [dɪˈsɪləbəl] *s* disílabo
dist. *abbr* **distance, distinguish, district**
distaff [ˈdɪstæf] o [ˈdɪstɑf] *s* rueca
distaff side *s* rama femenina de la familia
distance [ˈdɪstəns] *s* distancia; **at a distance** a distancia; **in the distance** a lo lejos; **to keep at a distance** no permitir familiaridades; **to keep one's distance** mantenerse a distancia
distant [ˈdɪstənt] *adj* distante; (*relative*) lejano; (*not familiar*) frío, indiferente
distaste [dɪsˈtest] *s* aversión, repugnancia
distasteful [dɪsˈtestfəl] *adj* desagradable, repugnante
distemper [dɪsˈtɛmpər] *s* enfermedad; (*of dogs*) moquillo
distend [dɪsˈtɛnd] *tr* ensanchar, distender || *intr* ensancharse, distender
distension [dɪsˈtɛnʃən] *s* ensanche *m*, distensión
distill [dɪsˈtɪl] *tr* destilar
distillation [ˌdɪstɪˈleʃən] *s* destilación
distiller·y [dɪsˈtɪləri] *s* (*pl* **-ies**) destilería, destilatorio
distinct [dɪsˈtɪŋkt] *adj* distinto; cierto, indudable; (*not blurred*) nítido, bien definido
distinction [dɪsˈtɪŋkʃən] *s* distinción; (*distinguishing characteristic*) distintivo
distinctive [dɪsˈtɪŋktɪv] *adj* distintivo
distinguish [dɪsˈtɪŋgwɪʃ] *tr* distinguir
distinguished [dɪsˈtɪŋgwɪʃt] *adj* distinguido
distort [dɪsˈtɔrt] *tr* deformar, torcer; (*the truth*) falsear
distortion [dɪsˈtɔrʃən] *s* deformación, torcimiento; (*of the truth*) falseamiento; (rad) deformación, distorsión
distract [dɪsˈtrækt] *tr* distraer
distraction [dɪsˈtrækʃən] *s* distracción
distraught [dɪsˈtrɔt] *adj* trastornado, perplejo, aturdido
distress [dɪsˈtrɛs] *s* pena, aflicción, angustia; infortunio, peligro || *tr* apenar, afligir, angustiar
distressing [dɪsˈtrɛsɪŋ] *adj* penoso, angustioso
distress signal *s* señal *f* de socorro
distribute [dɪsˈtrɪbjut] *tr* distribuir, repartir
distribution [ˌdɪstrɪˈbjuʃən] *s* distribución, repartimiento
distributor [dɪsˈtrɪbjətər] *s* distribuidor *m;* (aut) distribuidor
district [ˈdɪstrɪkt] *s* comarca, región; (*of a city*) barrio; (*administrative division*) distrito || *tr* dividir en distritos
district attorney *s* fiscal *m*

distrust [dɪsˈtrʌst] *s* desconfianza ‖ *tr* desconfiar de
distrustful [dɪsˈtrʌstfəl] *adj* desconfiado
disturb [dɪsˈtʌrb] *tr* disturbar, incomodar, molestar; desordenar, revolver; inquietar, dejar perplejo; perturbar (*el orden público*)
disturbance [dɪsˈtʌrbəns] *s* disturbio, molestia; desorden *m;* inquietud; tumulto, trastorno
disuse [dɪsˈjus] *s* desuso
ditch [dɪtʃ] *s* zanja ‖ *tr* zanjar; echar en una zanja; (slang) deshacerse de ‖ *intr* amarar forzosamente
ditch reed *s* carrizo
dither [ˈdɪðər] *s* agitación, temblor; **to be in a dither** (coll) estar muy agitado
dit·to [ˈdɪto] *s* (*pl* **-tos**) ídem *m;* (*ditto symbol*) íd.; copia, duplicado ‖ *tr* copiar, duplicar
ditto mark *s* la sigla " (*es decir:* íd.)
dit·ty [ˈdɪti] *s* (*pl* **-ties**) cancioneta
div. *abbr* **dividend, division**
diva [ˈdivɑ] *s* (mus) diva
divan [ˈdaɪvæn] o [dɪˈvæn] *s* diván *m*
dive [daɪv] *s* zambullida; (*of a submarine*) sumersión; (acr) picado; (coll) leonera, tasca ‖ *v* (*pret & pp* **dived** o **dove** [dov]) *intr* zambullirse; (*to work as a diver*) bucear; sumergirse (*un submarino*); (aer) picar
dive′-bomb′ *tr & intr* bombardear en picado
dive bombing *s* bombardeo en picado
diver [ˈdaɪvər] *s* zambullidor *m;* (*person who works under water*) escafandrista *mf,* buzo; (orn) zambullidor *m*
diverge [dɪˈvʌrdʒ] o [daɪˈvʌrdʒ] *intr* divergir
divers [ˈdaɪvərz] *adj* diversos, varios
diverse [dɪˈvʌrs], [daɪˈvʌrs] o [ˈdaɪvʌrs] *adj* (*different*) diverso; (*of various kinds*) variado
diversification [dɪˌvʌrsɪfɪˈkeʃən] o [daɪˌvʌrsɪfɪˈkeʃən] *s* diversificación
diversi·fy [dɪˈvʌrsɪˌfaɪ] o [daɪˈvʌrsɪˌfaɪ] *v* (*pret & pp* **-fied**) *tr* diversificar ‖ *intr* diversificarse
diversion [dɪˈvʌrʒən] o [daɪˈvʌrʒən] *s* diversión
diversi·ty [dɪˈvʌrsɪti] o [daɪˈvʌrsɪti] *s* (*pl* **-ties**) diversidad
divert [dɪˈvʌrt] o [daɪˈvʌrt] *tr* apartar, divertir; (*to entertain*) divertir, entretener; (mil) divertir
diverting [dɪˈvʌrtɪŋ] o [daɪˈvʌrtɪŋ] *adj* divertido
divest [dɪˈvɛst] o [daɪˈvɛst] *tr* desnudar; despojar, desposeer; **to divest oneself of** desposeerse de
divide [dɪˈvaɪd] *s* (geog) divisoria ‖ *tr* dividir ‖ *intr* dividirse
dividend [ˈdɪvɪˌdɛnd] *s* dividendo
dividers [dɪˈvaɪdərz] *spl* compás *m* de división
divination [ˌdɪvɪˈneʃən] *s* adivinación
divine [dɪˈvaɪn] *adj* divino ‖ *s* sacerdote *m,* clérigo ‖ *tr* adivinar
diving [ˈdaɪvɪŋ] *s* zambullida; buceo
diving bell *s* campana de buzo
diving board *s* trampolín *m*
diving suit *s* escafandra
divining rod [dɪˈvaɪnɪŋ] *s* vara de adivinar; (*ostensibly to discover water or metals*) vara buscadora
divini·ty [dɪˈvɪnɪti] *s* (*pl* **-ties**) divinidad; teología; **the Divinity** Dios *m*
division [dɪˈvɪʒən] *s* división
divisor [dɪˈvaɪzər] *s* (math) divisor *m*
divorce [diˈvors] *s* divorcio; **to get a divorce** divorciarse ‖ *tr* divorciar (*los cónyuges*); divorciarse de (*la mujer o el marido*) ‖ *intr* divorciarse
divorcee [dɪvorˈsi] *s* persona divorciada; mujer divorciada
divulge [dɪˈvʌldʒ] *tr* divulgar, revelar
dizziness [ˈdɪzɪnɪs] *s* vértigo; confusión, perplejidad
diz·zy [ˈdɪzi] *adj* (*comp* **-zier;** *super* **-ziest**) (*suffering or causing dizziness*) vertiginoso; confuso, perplejo; aturdido, incauto; (coll) tonto
do. *abbr* **ditto**
do [du] *v* (*tercera persona* **does** [dʌz]; *pret* **did** [dɪd]; *pp* **done** [dʌn]) *tr* hacer; resolver (*un problema*); recorrer (*cierta distancia*); cumplir con (*un deber*); aprender (*una lección*); componer (*la cama*); tocar (*el cabello*); rendir (*homenaje*); **to do one's best** hacer todo lo posible; **to do over** volver a hacer; repetir; renovar; **to do right by** tratar bien; **to do someone out of something** (coll) defraudar algo a alguien; **to do to death** despachar, matar; **to do up** empaquetar; poner en orden; almidonar y planchar (*una camisa*) ‖ *intr* actuar, obrar; conducirse; servir, ser suficiente; estar, hallarse; **how do you do?** ¿cómo está Vd.?; **that will do** eso sirve, eso es bastante; no digas más; **to have done** haber terminado; **to have done with** no tener más que ver con; **to have nothing to do with** no tener nada que ver con; **to have to do with** tratar de; **to do away with** suprimir; matar; **to do for** servir para; **to do well** salir bien; **to do without** pasar sin ‖ *v aux* úsase 1) en oraciones interrogativas: **Do you speak Spanish?** ¿Habla Vd. español?; 2) en oraciones negativas: **I do not speak Spanish** No hablo español; 3) para substituir a otro verbo en oraciones elípticas: **Did you go to church this morning? Yes, I did** ¿Fué Vd. a la iglesia esta mañana? Sí, fuí; 4) para dar más energía a la oración: **I do believe what you told me** Yo sí creo lo que me dijo Vd.; 5) en inversiones después de ciertos adverbios: **Seldom does he come to see me** él rara vez viene a verme; 6) en tono suplicante con el imperativo: **Do come in** pase Vd., por favor
docile [ˈdɑsɪl] *adj* dócil
dock [dɑk] *s* (*wharf*) muelle *m;* (*wa-*

terway between two piers) dársena; (*area including piers and waterways*) puerto de mar; muñón *m* de cola; (law) tribuna de los acusados || *tr* (naut) atracar en el muelle; derrabar, descolar (*a un animal*); reducir o suprimir (*el salario*) || *intr* (naut) atracar
dockage ['dakɪdʒ] *s* entrada en un puerto; (*charges*) muellaje *m*
docket ['dakɪt] *s* actas, orden *m* del día; lista de causas pendientes; **on the docket** (coll) pendiente, entre manos
dock hand *s* portuario
dock'yard' *s* arsenal *m*, astillero
doctor ['daktər] *s* doctor *m*; (*physician*) médico || *tr* medicinar; (coll) componer, reparar || *intr* (coll) ejercer la medicina; (coll) tomar medicinas
doctorate ['daktərɪt] *s* doctorado
doctrine ['daktrɪn] *s* doctrina
document ['dakjəmənt] *s* documento || ['dakjə,mɛnt] *tr* documentar
documenta·ry [,dakjə'mɛntəri] *adj* documental || *s* (*pl* **-ries**) documental *m*
documentation [,dakəmɛn'teʃən] *s* documentación
doddering ['dadərɪŋ] *adj* chocho, temblón
dodge [dadʒ] *s* esguince *m*, regate *m*; (fig) regate || *tr* evitar (*un golpe*); (fig) evitar mañosamente || *intr* regatear, hurtar el cuerpo; **to dodge around the corner** voltear la esquina
do·do ['dodo] *s* (*pl* **-dos** o **-does**) (coll) inocente *m* de ideas anticuadas
doe [do] *s* cierva, gama, coneja
doeskin ['do,skɪn] *s* ante *m*, piel *f* de ante; tejido fino de lana
doff [daf] o [dɔf] *tr* quitarse (*el sombrero, la ropa*)
dog [dɔg] o [dag] *s* perro; **to go to the dogs** darse al abandono; **to put on the dog** (coll) darse ínfulas || *v* (*pret & pp* **dogged**; *ger* **dogging**) *tr* acosar, perseguir
dog'catch'er *s* lacero
dog days *spl* canícula, caniculares *mpl*
doge [dodʒ] dux *m*
dogged ['dɔgɪd] o ['dagɪd] *adj* tenaz, terco
doggerel ['dɔgərəl] o ['dagərəl] *s* coplas de ciego
dog·gy ['dɔgi] o ['dagi] *adj* (*comp* **-gier**; *super* **-giest**) emperejilado || *s* (*pl* **-gies**) perrito
dog'house' *s* perrera
dog in the manger *s* el perro del hortelano
dog Latin *s* latinajo, latín *m* de cocina
dogmatic [dɔg'mætɪk] o [dag'mætɪk] *adj* dogmático
dog racing *s* carreras de galgos
dog's-ear ['dɔgz,ɪr] o ['dagz,ɪr] *s* orejón *m*
dog show *s* exposición canina
dog's life *s* vida miserable
Dog Star *s* Canícula
dog'-tired' *adj* cansadísimo
dog'tooth' *s* (*pl* **-teeth** [,tiθ]) colmillo
dog track *s* galgódromo
dog'watch' *s* (naut) guardia de cuartillo
dog'wood' *s* cornejo
doi·ly ['dɔɪli] *s* (*pl* **-lies**) pañito de adorno
doings ['du·ɪŋz] *spl* acciones, obras, actividad
doldrums ['daldrəmz] *spl* (naut) calmas ecuatoriales; desanimación, inactividad
dole [dol] *s* limosna; subsidio a los desocupados || *tr* — **to dole out** distribuir en pequeñas porciones
doleful ['dolfəl] *adj* triste, lúgubre
doll [dal] *s* muñeca || *intr* — **to doll up** (slang) emperejilarse
dollar ['dalər] *s* dólar *m*
dollar mark *s* signo del dólar
dol·ly ['dali] *s* (*pl* **-lies**) muñequita; (*low, wheeled frame for moving heavy loads*) gato rodante
dolphin ['dalfɪn] *s* delfín *m*
dolt [dolt] *s* bobalicón *m*
doltish ['doltɪʃ] *adj* bobalicón
dom. *abbr* **domestic, dominion**
domain [do'men] *s* dominio; heredad, propiedad; (*of learning*) campo
dome [dom] *s* cúpula, domo
dome light *s* (aut) lámpara de techo
domestic [də'mɛstɪk] *adj & s* doméstico
domesticate [də'mɛstɪ,ket] *tr* domesticar
domicile ['damɪsɪl] o ['damɪ,saɪl] *s* domicilio || *tr* domiciliar
dominance ['damɪnəns] *s* dominación
dominant ['damɪnənt] *adj & s* dominante *f*
dominate ['damɪ,net] *tr & intr* dominar
domination [,damɪ'neʃən] *s* dominación
domineer [,damɪ'nɪr] *intr* dominar
domineering [,damɪ'nɪrɪŋ] *adj* dominante, mandón
Dominican [də'mɪnɪkən] *adj & s* dominicano
dominion [də'mɪnjən] *s* dominio
domi·no ['damɪ,no] *s* (*pl* **-noes** o **-nos**) (*costume*) dominó *m*; antifaz *m*; persona que lleva dominó; ficha (*del juego de dominó*); **dominoes** *ssg* dominó (*juego*)
don [dan] *s* caballero, señor *m*, personaje *m* de alta categoría; (coll) preceptor *m*, socio de uno de los colegios de las Universidades de Oxford y Cambridge || *v* (*pret & pp* **donned**; *ger* **donning**) *tr* ponerse (*el sombrero, la ropa*)
donate ['donet] *tr* dar, donar
donation [do'neʃən] *s* donación
done [dʌn] *adj* hecho, terminado; cansado, rendido; bien asado
done for *adj* (coll) cansado, rendido, agotado; (coll) arruinado, destruído; (coll) fuera de combate; (coll) muerto
donjon ['dʌndʒən] o ['dandʒən] *s* torre *f* del homenaje

donkey ['daŋki] *s* asno, burro
donnish ['danɪʃ] *adj* magistral, pedantesco
donor ['donər] *s* donador *m*
doodle ['dudəl] *tr & intr* borrajear
doom [dum] *s* ruina, perdición, muerte *f;* condena, juicio; juicio final; hado, destino || *tr* condenar; sentenciar a muerte; predestinar a la ruina, a la muerte
doomsday ['dumz,de] *s* día *m* del juicio final; día del juicio
door [dor] *s* puerta; (*of a carriage or automobile*) portezuela; (*one part of a double door*) hoja, batiente *m;* **behind closed doors** a puertas cerradas; **to see to the door** acompañar a la puerta
door'bell' *s* campanilla de puerta, timbre *m* de puerta
door check *s* amortiguador *m,* cierre *m* de puerta
door'frame' *s* bastidor *m* de puerta, marco de puerta
door'head' *s* dintel *m*
door'jamb' *s* jamba de puerta
door'knob' *s* botón *m* de puerta, pomo de puerta
door knocker *s* aldaba
door latch *s* pestillo
door·man ['dormən] *s* (*pl* **-men** [mən]) portero; (*one who helps people in and out of cars*) abrecoches *m*
door'mat' *s* felpudo de puerta
door'nail' *s* clavo de adorno para puertas; **dead as a doornail** (coll) muerto sin duda alguna
door'post' *s* jamba de puerta
door scraper *s* limpiabarros *m*
door'sill' *s* umbral *m*
door'step' *s* escalón *m* delante de la puerta; escalera exterior
door'stop' *s* tope *m* de puerta
door'way' *s* puerta, portal *m*
dope [dop] *s* grasa lubricante; (aer) barniz *m,* nobabia; (slang) bobo, tonto; (slang) informes *mpl;* (slang) narcótico || *tr* (slang) narcotizar, drogar; **to dope out** (slang) descifrar
dope fiend *s* (slang) toxicómano
dope sheet *s* (slang) hoja confidencial sobre los caballos de carreras
dormant ['dɔrmənt] *adj* durmiente, latente
dormer window ['dɔrmər] *s* buharda, buhardilla
dormito·ry ['dɔrmɪ,tori] *s* (*pl* **-ries**) dormitorio común
dor·mouse ['dɔr,maʊs] *s* (*pl* **-mice** [,maɪs]) lirón *m*
dosage ['dosɪdʒ] *s* dosificación
dose [dos] *s* dosis *f;* (coll) mal trago || *tr* medicinar; dosificar (*un medicamento*)
dossier ['dasɪ,e] *s* expediente *m*
dot [dat] *s* punto; **on the dot** (coll) en punto || *v* (*pret & pp* **dotted;** *ger* **dotting**) *tr* (*to make with dots*) puntear; poner punto a; **to dot one's i's** poner los puntos sobre las íes
dotage ['dotɪdʒ] *s* chochera, chochez *f;* **to be in one's dotage** chochear
dotard ['dotərd] *s* viejo chocho
dote [dot] *intr* chochear; **to dote on** estar chocho por
doting ['dotɪŋ] *adj* chocho
dots and dashes *spl* (telg) puntos y rayas
dotted line ['datɪd] *s* línea de puntos; **to sign on the dotted line** firmar ciegamente
double ['dʌbəl] *adj* doble || *adv* doble; dos juntos || *s* doble *m,* duplo; (mov, theat) doble *mf;* **doubles** (tennis) juego de dobles || *tr* doblar; ser el doble de; (bridge) doblar || *intr* doblarse; (mov, theat, bridge) doblar; **to double up** doblarse en dos; ocupar una misma habitación, dormir en una misma cama (*dos personas*)
double-barreled ['dʌbəl'bærəld] *adj* de dos cañones; (fig) para dos fines
double bass [bes] *s* contrabajo
double bassoon *s* contrabajón *m*
double bed *s* cama de matrimonio
double-breasted ['dʌbəl'brɛstɪd] *adj* cruzado, de dos pechos
double chin *s* papada
dou'ble-cross' *tr* traicionar (*a un cómplice*)
double date *s* cita de dos parejas
doub'le-deal'er *s* persona doble
double-edged ['dʌbəl'ɛdʒd] *adj* de dos filos
double entry *s* (com) partida doble
double feature *s* (mov) programa *m* doble, programa de dos películas de largo metraje
double-header ['dʌbəl'hɛdər] *s* tren *m* con dos locomotoras; (baseball) dos partidos jugados sucesivamente
double-jointed ['dʌbəl'dʒɔɪntɪd] *adj* de articulaciones dobles
dou'ble-park' *tr & intr* aparcar en doble fila
dou'ble-quick' *adj & adv* a paso ligero || *s* paso ligero || *intr* marchar a paso ligero
doublet ['dʌblɪt] *s* (*close-fitting jacket*) jubón *m;* (*counterfeit stone; each of two words having the same origin*) doblete *m*
double talk *s* (coll) galimatías *m;* (coll) habla ambigua para engañar
double time *s* pago doble por horas extraordinarias de trabajo; (mil) paso redoblado
doubleton ['dʌbəltən] *s* doblete *m*
double track *s* doble vía
doubt [daʊt] *s* duda; **beyond doubt** sin duda; **if in doubt** en caso de duda; **no doubt** sin duda || *tr* dudar, dudar de || *intr* dudar
doubter ['daʊtər] *s* incrédulo
doubtful ['daʊtfəl] *adj* dudoso
doubtless ['daʊtlɪs] *adj* indudable || *adv* sin duda; probablemente
douche [duʃ] *s* ducha; (*instrument*) jeringa || *tr* duchar || *intr* ducharse
dough [do] *s* masa, pasta; (*money*) (slang) pasta
dough'boy' *s* (coll) soldado norteamericano de infantería

dough′nut′ *s* rosquilla, buñuelo
dough•ty [ˈdauti] *adj* (*comp* **-tier;** *super* **-tiest**) (hum) fuerte, valiente
dough•y [ˈdo·i] *adj* (*comp* **-ier;** *super* **-iest**) pastoso
dour [daʊr] o [dʊr] *adj* triste, melancólico, austero
douse [daʊs] *tr* empapar, mojar, salpicar; (slang) apagar (*la luz*)
dove [dʌv] *s* paloma
dovecote [ˈdʌv ˌkot] *s* palomar *m*
dove′tail′ *s* cola de milano, cola de pato || *tr* ensamblar a cola de milano, ensamblar a cola de pato; (*to make fit*) encajar || *intr* (*to fit*) encajar; concordar, corresponder
dowager [ˈdaʊ·ədʒər] *s* viuda con título o bienes que proceden del marido, p.ej., **dowager duchess** duquesa viuda; (coll) matrona, señora anciana respetable
dow•dy [ˈdaʊdi] *adj* (*comp* **-dier;** *super* **-diest**) desaliñado
dow•el [ˈdaʊ·əl] *s* clavija || *v* (*pret & pp* **-eled** o **-elled;** *ger* **-eling** o **-elling**) *tr* enclavijar
dower [ˈdaʊ·ər] *s* (*widow's portion*) viudedad; (*marriage portion*) dote *m & f;* (*natural gift*) prenda || *tr* señalar viudedad a; dotar
down [daʊn] *adj* descendente; abatido, triste; enfermo, malo; acostado, echado; (*money, payment*) anticipado; (*storage battery*) agotado || *adv* abajo; hacia abajo; en tierra; al sur; por escrito; al contado; **down and out** arruinado; sin blanca; **down from** desde; **down on one's knees** de rodillas; **down to** hasta; **down under** entre los antípodas; **down with . . . !** ¡abajo . . . !; **to get down to work** aplicarse resueltamente al trabajo; **to go down** bajar; **to lie down** acostarse; **to sit down** sentarse || *prep* bajando; **down the river** río abajo; **down the street** calle abajo || *s* (*of fruit and human body*) vello; (*of birds*) plumón *m;* descenso; revés *m* de fortuna; (*sand hill*) duna || *tr* derribar; (coll) tragar
down′cast′ *adj* cariacontecido
down′fall′ *s* caída, ruina; chaparrón *m;* nevazo
down′grade′ *adj* (coll) pendiente, en declive || *adv* (coll) cuesta abajo || *s* bajada, declive *m;* **to be on the downgrade** decaer, declinar || *tr* disminuir la categoría de
downhearted [ˈdaʊn ˌhɑrtɪd] *adj* abatido, desanimado
down′hill′ *adj* pendiente || *adv* cuesta abajo; **to go downhill** ir cabeza abajo
down′pour′ *s* aguacero, chaparrón *m*
down′right′ *adj* absoluto, categórico; franco; claro || *adv* absolutamente
down′stairs′ *adj* de abajo || *adv* abajo || *s* piso inferior, pisos inferiores; (*the help*) la servidumbre
down′stream′ *adv* aguas abajo, río abajo
down′stroke′ *s* carrera descendente
down′town′ *adj* céntrico || *adv* al centro de la ciudad, en el centro de la ciudad || *s* barrios céntricos, calles céntricas
down train *s* tren *m* descendente
down′trend′ *s* tendencia a la baja
downtrodden [ˈdaʊn ˌtrɑdən] *adj* pisoteado, oprimido
downward [ˈdaʊnwərd] *adj* descendente || *adv* hacia abajo; hacia una época posterior
down•y [ˈdaʊni] *adj* (*comp* **-ier;** *super* **-iest**) plumoso, felpudo, velloso; suave, blando
dow•ry [ˈdaʊri] *s* (*pl* **-ries**) dote *m & f*
doz. *abbr* **dozen**
doze [doz] *s* duermevela, sueño ligero || *intr* dormitar
dozen [ˈdʌzən] *s* docena
dozy [ˈdozi] *adj* soñoliento
D.P. *abbr* **displaced person**
dpt. *abbr* **department**
dr. *abbr* **debtor, drawer, dram**
Dr. *abbr* **debtor, Doctor**
drab [dræb] *adj* (*comp* **drabber;** *super* **drabbest**) gris amarillento; monótono || *s* gris amarillento; ramera; mujer desaliñada
drach•ma [ˈdrækmə] *s* (*pl* **-mas** o **-mae** [mi]) dracma
draft [dræft] o [drɑft] *s* corriente *f* de aire; (*pulling; current of air in a chimney*) tiro; (*sketch, outline*) bosquejo; (*first form of a writing*) borrador *m;* (*drink*) bebida, trago; (com) giro, letra de cambio, libranza; aire inspirado; (naut) calado; (mil) conscripción, quinta; **drafts** damas, juego de damas; **on draft** a presión; **to be exempted from the draft** redimirse de las quintas || *tr* dibujar; bosquejar; hacer un borrador de; redactar (*un documento*); (mil) quintar; **to be drafted** (mil) ir a quintas
draft age *s* edad *f* de quintas
draft beer *s* cerveza a presión
draft board *s* (mil) junta de reclutamiento
draft call *s* llamada a quintas
draft dodger [ˈdɑdʒər] *s* emboscado
draftee [ˌdræfˈti] o [ˌdrɑfˈti] *s* conscripto, quinto
draft horse *s* caballo de tiro
drafting room *s* sala de dibujo
drafts•man [ˈdræftsmən] o [ˈdrɑftsmən] *s* (*pl* **-men** [mən]) dibujante *m;* (*man who draws up documents*) redactor *m;* (*in checkers*) peón *m*
draft treaty *s* proyecto de convenio
draft•y [ˈdræfti] o [ˈdrɑfti] *adj* (*comp* **-ier;** *super* **-iest**) airoso, con corrientes de aire
drag [dræg] *s* (*sledge for conveying heavy bodies*) narria; (*on a cigarette*) chupada; fumada; (naut) rastra; (aer) resistencia al avance; (fig) estorbo, impedimento; **to have a drag** (slang) tener buenas aldabas, tener enchufe || *v* (*pret & pp* **dragged;** *ger* **dragging**) *tr* arrastrar; (naut) rastrear || *intr* arrastrarse por el suelo; avanzar muy lentamente; decaer (*el*

interés); **to drag on** ser interminable, prolongarse interminablemente
drag'net' *s* red barredera
dragon ['drægən] *s* dragón *m*
drag'on·fly' *s* (*pl* **-flies**) caballito del diablo, libélula
dragoon [drə'gun] *s* (*soldier*) dragón *m* || *tr* tiranizar; forzar, constreñir
drain [dren] *s* dren *m*, desaguadero, desagüe *m*; (surg) dren *m*; (*source of continual expense*) (fig) desaguadero || *tr* drenar, desaguar; avenar (*terrenos húmedos*); escurrir (*una vasija; un líquido*) || *intr* desaguarse; escurrirse
drainage ['drenɪdʒ] *s* drenaje *m*, desagüe *m*
drain'board' *s* escurridero
drain cock *s* llave *f* de purga
drain'pipe' *s* tubo de desagüe, escurridero
drain plug *s* tapón *m* de desagüe; (aut) tapón de vaciado
drake [drek] *s* pato
dram [dræm] *s* dracma; trago de aguardiente
drama ['drɑmə] o ['dræmə] *s* drama *m*; (*art and genre*) dramática
dramatic [drə'mætɪk] *adj* dramático || **dramatics** *ssg* representación de aficionados; *spl* obras representadas por aficionados
dramatist ['dræmətɪst] *s* dramático
dramatize ['dræmə,taɪz] *tr* dramatizar
dram'shop' *s* bar *m*, taberna
drape [drep] *s* cortina, colgadura; (*hang of a curtain, skirt, etc.*) caída || *tr* cubrir con colgaduras; adornar con colgaduras; disponer los pliegues de (*una colgadura, una prenda de vestir*)
draper·y ['drepəri] *s* (*pl* **-ies**) colgaduras, ropaje *m*
drastic ['dræstɪk] *adj* drástico
draught [dræft] o [drɑft] *s* & *tr* var de **draft**
draught beer *s* cerveza a presión
draw [drɔ] *s* (*in a game or other contest*) empate *m*; (*in chess or checkers*) tablas; (*in a lottery*) sorteo; (*card drawn from the bank*) robo; (*of a drawbridge*) compuerta; (*of a chimney*) tiro || *v* (*pret* **drew** [dru]; *pp* **drawn** [drɔn]) *tr* tirar (*una línea; alambre*); (*to attract*) tirar; (*to pull*) tirar de; derretir (*la mantequilla*); sacar (*un clavo, una espada, agua, una conclusión*); atraerse (*aplausos*); atraer (*a la gente*); aspirar (*el aire*); llamar (*la atención*); dar (*un suspiro*); correr (*una cortina*); cobrar (*un salario*); sacarse (*un premio*); empatar (*una partida*); robar (*fichas, naipes*); levantar (*un puente levadizo*); calar (*un buque cierta profundidad*); hacer (*una comparación*); consumir (*amperios*); (*to sketch in lines*) dibujar; (*to sketch in words*) redactar; (com) girar, librar; (com) devengar (*interés*); **to draw forth** hacer salir; **to draw off** sacar, extraer; trasegar (*un líquido*); **to draw on** ocasionar, provocar; ponerse (*p.ej., los zapatos*); (com) girar a cargo de; **to draw oneself up** enderezarse con dignidad; **to draw out** (*to persuade to talk*) sonsacar, tirar de la lengua a; **to draw up** redactar (*un documento*); (mil) ordenar para el combate || *intr* tirar, tirar bien (*una chimenea*); empatar; echar suertes; atraer mucha gente; dibujar; **to draw aside** apartarse; **to draw back** retroceder, retirarse; **to draw near** acercarse; acercarse a; **to draw to a close** estar para terminar; **to draw together** juntarse, unirse
draw'back' *s* desventaja, inconveniente *m*
draw'bridge' *s* puente levadizo
drawee [,drɔ'i] *s* girado, librado
drawer ['drɔ·ər] *s* dibujante *mf*; (com) girador *m*, librador *m* || [drɔr] *s* cajón *m*, gaveta; **drawers** calzoncillos
drawing ['drɔ·ɪŋ] *s* dibujo; (*in a lottery*) sorteo
drawing board *s* tablero de dibujo
drawing card *s* polo de atracción popular
drawing room *s* sala, salón *m*
draw'knife' *s* (*pl* **-knives** [,naɪvz]) cuchilla de dos mangos
drawl [drɔl] *s* habla lenta y prolongada || *tr* decir lenta y prolongadamente || *intr* hablar lenta y prolongadamente
drawn butter [drɔn] *s* mantequilla derretida
drawn work *s* calado, deshilado
dray [dre] *s* carro fuerte, camión *m*; (*sledge*) narria
drayage ['dre·ɪdʒ] *s* acarreo
dread [drɛd] *adj* espantoso, terrible || *s* pavor *m*, terror *m* || *tr* & *intr* temer
dreadful ['drɛdfəl] *adj* espantoso, terrible; (coll) feo, desagradable
dread'naught' *s* (nav) gran buque acorazado
dream [drim] *s* sueño, ensueño; (*thing of great beauty*) sueño; (*fancy, illusion*) ensueño; **dream come true** sueño hecho realidad || *v* (*pret* & *pp* **dreamed** o **dreamt** [drɛmt]) *tr* soñar; **to dream up** (coll) imaginar, inventar; || *intr* soñar; **to dream of** soñar con
dreamer ['drimər] *s* soñador *m*
dream'land' *s* reino del ensueño
dream world *s* tierra de la fantasía
dream·y ['drimi] *adj* (*comp* **-ier**; *super* **-iest**) soñador; visionario; vago
drear·y ['drɪri] *adj* (*comp* **-ier**; *super* **-iest**) sombrío, triste; monótono, pesado
dredge [drɛdʒ] *s* draga || *tr* dragar, rastrear; (culin) enharinar
dredger ['drɛdʒər] *s* draga (*barco*)
dredging ['drɛdʒɪŋ] *s* dragado
dregs [drɛgz] *spl* heces *fpl*; (*of society*) hez *f*
drench [drɛntʃ] *tr* mojar, empapar
dress [drɛs] *s* ropa, vestidos; vestido de mujer; (*skirt*) falda; traje *m* de

etiqueta; (*of a bird*) plumaje *m* || *tr* vestir; (*to provide with clothing*) trajear; peinar (*el pelo*); curar (*una herida*); zurrar (*el cuero*); empavesar (*un barco*); adornar, ataviar; aderezar, aliñar (*los manjares*); **to dress down** (coll) reprender; **to get dressed** vestirse || *intr* (*to put one's clothing on*) vestirse; (*to wear clothes*) vestir; (mil) alinearse; **to dress up** vestirse de etiqueta; ponerse de veinticinco alfileres; disfrazarse

dress ball *s* baile *m* de etiqueta

dress coat *s* frac *m*

dresser ['drɛsər] *s* tocador *m;* cómoda con espejo; (*sideboard*) aparador *m;* **to be a good dresser** vestir con elegancia

dress form *s* maniquí *m*

dress goods *spl* géneros para vestidos

dressing ['drɛsɪŋ] *s* adorno; (*for food*) aliño, salsa; (*stuffing for fowl*) relleno; (*fertilizer*) abono; (*for a wound*) vendaje *m*

dress'ing-down' *s* (coll) repasata, regaño

dressing gown *s* bata, peinador *m*

dressing room *s* cuarto de vestir; (theat) camarín *m*

dressing station *s* (mil) puesto de socorro

dressing table *s* tocador *m*

dress'mak'er *s* costurera, modista

dress'mak'ing *s* costura, modistería

dress rehearsal *s* ensayo general

dress shirt *s* camisa de pechera almidonada, camisa de pechera de encaje

dress shop *s* casa de modas

dress suit *s* traje *m* de etiqueta

dress tie *s* corbata de smoking, corbata de frac

dress•y ['drɛsi] *adj* (*comp* **-ier;** *super* **-iest**) (coll) elegante; (*showy*) acicalado, vistoso, peripuesto

dribble ['drɪbəl] *s* goteo; (coll) llovizna || *tr* (sport) driblar || *intr* gotear; (*at the mouth*) babear; (sport) driblar

driblet ['drɪblɪt] *s* gotita; pedacito

dried beef [draɪd] *s* cecina

dried fig *s* higo paso

dried peach *s* orejón *m*

drier ['draɪ•ər] *s* enjugador *m;* (*for hair*) secador *m;* (*for clothes*) secadora; (*rack for drying clothes*) tendedero (de ropa)

drift [drɪft] *s* movimiento; (*of sand, snow*) montón *m;* (*movement of snow*) ventisca; tendencia, dirección; intención, sentido; (aer, naut) deriva; (rad, telv) desviación || *intr* flotar a la deriva; amontonarse (*la nieve*); ventiscar; (aer, naut) derivar, ir a la deriva; (fig) vivir sin rumbo

drift ice *s* hielo flotante

drift'wood' *s* madera flotante; madera llevada por el agua; madera arrojada a la playa por el agua; (*people*) vagos

drill [drɪl] *s* taladro; instrucción; (*fabric*) dril *m;* (mil) ejercicio || *tr* taladrar; instruir; (mil) enseñar el ejercicio a || *intr* adiestrarse; (mil) hacer el ejercicio

drill'mas'ter *s* amaestrador *m;* (mil) instructor *m*

drill press *s* prensa taladradora

drink [drɪŋk] *s* bebida; **the drinks are on the house!** ¡convida la casa! || *v* (*pret* **drank** [dræŋk]; *pp* **drunk** [drʌŋk]) *tr* beber; beberse (*su sueldo*); **to drink down** beber de una vez; **to drink in** beber (*las palabras de una persona*); beberse (*un libro*); aspirar (*el aire*) || *intr* beber; **to drink out of** beber de o en; **to drink to the health of** beber a o por la salud de

drinkable ['drɪŋkəbəl] *adj* bebedizo, potable

drinker ['drɪŋkər] *s* bebedor *m*

drinking ['drɪnkɪŋ] *s* (el) beber

drinking cup *s* taza para beber

drinking fountain *s* fuente *f* para beber

drinking song *s* canción báquica, canción de taberna

drinking trough *s* abrevadero

drinking water *s* agua para beber

drip [drɪp] *s* goteo; gotas || *v* (*pret & pp* **dripped;** *ger* **dripping**) *intr* caer gota a gota, gotear

drip coffee *s* café *m* de maquinilla

drip'-dry' *adj* de lava y pon

drip pan *s* colector *m* de aceite

drive [draɪv] *s* paseo en coche; calzada; fuerza, vigor *m;* urgencia; campaña vigorosa; venta a bajo precio; (aut) tracción (*delantera o trasera*); (mach) transmisión, mando || *v* (*pret* **drove** [drov]; *ger* **driven** ['drɪvən]) *tr* conducir, guiar, manejar (*un automóvil*); clavar, hincar (*un clavo*); arrear (*a las bestias*); (*in a carriage or auto*) llevar (*a una persona*); empujar, impeler; estimular; forzar, compeler; obligar a trabajar mucho; (sport) golpear con gran fuerza; **to drive away** ahuyentar; **to drive back** rechazar; **to drive mad** volver loco || *intr* ir en coche; **to drive at** aspirar a; querer decir; **to drive hard** trabajar mucho; **to drive in** entrar en coche; entrar en (*un sitio*) en coche; **to drive on the right** circular por la derecha; **to drive out** salir en coche; **to drive up** llegar en coche

drive-in movie theater ['draɪv ,ɪn] *s* auto-teatro

drive-in restaurant *s* restaurante *m* donde los clientes no necesitan dejar sus coches

driv•el ['drɪvəl] *s* (*slobber*) baba; (*nonsense*) bobería || *v* (*pret* **-eled** o **-elled;** *ger* **-eling** o **-elling**) *intr* babear; (*to talk nonsense*) bobear

driver ['draɪvər] *s* conductor *m;* (*of a carriage*) cochero; (*of a locomotive*) maquinista *m;* (*of pack animals*) arriero

driver's license *s* carnet *m* de chófer, permiso de conducir

drive shaft *s* árbol *m* de mando, eje *m* motor

drive'way' *s* calzada; camino de entrada para coches
drive wheel *s* rueda motriz
drive'-your·self' service *s* alquiler *m* sin chófer
driving school *s* auto-escuela
drizzle ['drɪzəl] *s* llovizna || *intr* lloviznar
droll [drol] *adj* chusco, gracioso
dromedar·y ['drɑmə,deri] *s* (*pl* **-ies**) dromedario
drone [dron] *s* zángano; (*buzz, hum*) zumbido; (*of bagpipe*) bordón *m*, roncón *m;* avión radiodirigido || *tr* decir monótonamente || *intr* hablar monótonamente; (*to live in idleness*) zanganear; (*to buzz, hum*) zumbar
drool [drul] *s* (*slobber*) baba; (slang) bobería || *intr* babear; (slang) bobear
droop [drup] *s* inclinación || *intr* caer, colgar; inclinarse; marchitarse; abatirse; encamarse (*el grano*)
drooping ['drupɪŋ] *adj* (*eyelid, shoulder*) caído
drop [drɑp] *s* gota; (*slope*) pendiente *f;* (*earring*) pendiente *m;* (*in temperature*) descenso; (*of supplies from an airplane*) lanzamiento; (*trap door*) escotillón *m;* (*gallows*) horca; (*lozenge*) pastilla; (*small amount*) chispa; (*slit for letters*) buzón *m;* (*curtain*) telón *m;* **a drop in the bucket** una gota en el mar || *v* (*pret & pp* **dropped;** *ger* **dropping**) *tr* dejar caer; echar (*una carta*) al buzón; bajar (*una cortina*); soltar (*una indirecta*); escribir (*una esquela*); omitir, suprimir; abandonar, dejar; echar (*el ancla*); borrar de la lista (*a un alumno*); lanzar (*bombas o suministros de un avión*) || *intr* caer; bajar; cesar, terminar; **to drop dead** caer muerto; **to drop in** entrar al pasar, visitar de paso; **to drop off** desaparecer; quedarse dormido; morir de repente; **to drop out** desaparecer; retirarse; darse de baja
drop curtain *s* telón *m*
drop hammer *s* martinete *m*
drop'-leaf' table *s* mesa de hoja plegadiza
drop'light' *s* lámpara colgante
drop'out' *s* fracasado, desertor *m* escolar; **to become a dropout** ahorcar los libros
dropper ['drɑpər] *s* cuentagotas *m*
drop shutter *s* obturador *m* de guillotina
dropsical ['drɑpsɪkəl] *adj* hidrópico
dropsy ['drɑpsi] *s* hidropesía
drop table *s* mesa perezosa
dross [drɔs] o [drɑs] *s* (*of metals*) escoria; (fig) escoria, hez *f*
drought [draut] *s* (*long period of dry weather*) sequía; (*dryness*) sequedad
drove [drov] *s* manada, rebaño, hato; gentío, multitud
drover ['drovər] *s* ganadero
drown [draun] *tr* anegar, ahogar || *intr* anegarse, ahogarse
drowse [drauz] *intr* adormecerse, amodorrarse
drow·sy ['drauzi] *adj* (*comp* **-sier;** *super* **-siest**) soñoliento, modorro
drub [drʌb] *v* (*pret & pp* **drubbed;** *ger* **-drubbing**) *tr* apalear, pegar, tundir; derrotar completamente
drudge [drʌdʒ] *s* yunque *m*, esclavo del trabajo || *intr* afanarse
drudger·y ['drʌdʒəri] *s* (*pl* **-ies**) trabajo penoso
drug [drʌg] *s* droga, medicamento; narcótico; **drug on the market** macana, artículo invendible || *v* (*pret & pp* **drugged;** *ger* **drugging**) *tr* narcotizar; mezclar con drogas
drug addict *s* toxicómano
drug addiction *s* toxicomanía
druggist ['drʌgɪst] *s* boticario, farmacéutico; (*dealer in drugs, chemicals, dyes, etc.*) droguero
drug habit *s* vicio de los narcóticos
drug store *s* farmacia, botica, droguería
drug traffic *s* contrabando de narcóticos
druid ['dru·ɪd] *s* druida *m*
drum [drʌm] *s* (*cylinder; instrument of percussion*) tambor *m;* (*container for oil, gasoline, etc.*) bidón *m* || *v* (*pret & pp* **drummed;** *ger* **drumming**) *tr* reunir a toque de tambor; **to drum up trade** fomentar ventas || *intr* tocar el tambor; (*with the fingers*) teclear
drum'beat' *s* toque *m* de tambor
drum corps *s* banda de tambores
drum'fire' *s* fuego graneado, fuego nutrido
drum'head' *s* parche *m* de tambor
drum major *s* tambor *m* mayor
drummer ['drʌmər] *s* tambor *m*, tamborilero; agente viajero
drum'stick' *s* baqueta, palillo; (coll) muslo (*de ave cocida*)
drunk [drʌŋk] *adj* borracho; **to get drunk** emborracharse || *s* (coll) borracho; (*spree*) (coll) borrachera
drunkard ['drʌŋkərd] *s* borrachín *m*
drunken ['drʌŋkən] *adj* borracho
drunken driving *s* — **to be arrested for drunken driving** ser arrestado por conducir en estado de embriaguez
drunkenness ['drʌŋkənnɪs] *s* embriaguez *f*
dry [draɪ] *adj* (*comp* **drier;** *super* **driest**) seco; (*thirsty*) sediento; (*dull, boring*) árido || *s* (*pl* **drys**) (*prohibitionist*) (coll) seco || *v* (*pret & pp* **dried**) *tr* secar; (*to wipe dry*) enjugar || *intr* secarse; **to dry up** secarse completamente; (slang) callar, dejar de hablar
dry battery *s* pila seca; (*group of dry cells*) batería seca
dry cell *s* pila seca
dry'-clean' *tr* lavar en seco, limpiar en seco
dry cleaner *s* tintorero
dry cleaning *s* lavado a seco, limpieza en seco
dry'-clean'ing establishment *s* tintorería
dry dock *s* dique seco
dryer ['draɪ·ər] *s* var de **drier**

dry'-eyed' *adj* ojienjuto
dry farming *s* cultivo de secano
dry goods *spl* mercancías generales (*tejidos, lencería, pañería, sedería*)
dry ice *s* carbohielo, hielo seco
dry law *s* ley seca
dry measure *s* medida para áridos
dryness ['draɪnɪs] *s* sequedad; (*e.g., of a speaker*) aridez *f*
dry nurse *s* ama seca
dry season *s* estación de la seca
dry wash *s* ropa lavada y secada pero no planchada
d.s. *abbr* **days after sight, daylight saving**
D.S.T. *abbr* **Daylight Saving Time**
dual ['dju·əl] o ['du·əl] *adj & s* dual *m*
duali·ty [dju'ælɪti] o [du'ælɪti] *s* (*pl* **-ties**) dualidad
dub [dʌb] *s* (slang) jugador *m* torpe ‖ *v* (*pret & pp* **dubbed;** *ger* **dubbing**) *tr* apellidar; armar caballero; (mov) doblar
dubbing ['dʌbɪŋ] *s* doblado, doblaje *m*
dubious ['djubɪ·əs] o ['dubɪ·əs] *adj* dudoso
ducat ['dʌkət] *s* ducado
duchess ['dʌtʃɪs] *s* duquesa
duch·y ['dʌtʃi] *s* (*pl* **-ies**) ducado
duck [dʌk] *s* pato; (*female*) pata; agachada rápida; (*in the water*) zambullida; **ducks** (coll) pantalones *mpl* de dril ‖ *tr* bajar rápidamente (*la cabeza*); (*in water*) chapuzar; (coll) esquivar, evitar (*un golpe*) ‖ *intr* chapuzar; **to duck out** (coll) escabullirse
duck'-toed' *adj* zancajoso
duct [dʌkt] *s* conducto, canal *m*
ductile ['dʌktɪl] *adj* dúctil
ductless gland ['dʌktlɪs] *s* glándula cerrada
duct'work' *s* canalización
dud [dʌd] *s* (slang) bomba que no estalla; (slang) fracaso; **duds** (coll) trapos, prendas de vestir
dude [djud] o [dud] *s* caballerete *m*
due [dju] o [du] *adj* debido; aguardado, esperado; pagadero; **due to** debido a; **to fall due** vencer; **when is the train due?** ¿a qué hora debe llegar el tren? ‖ *adv* directamente, derecho ‖ *s* deuda; **dues** derechos; (*of a member*) cuota; **to get one's due** llevar su merecido; **to give the devil his due** ser justo hasta con el diablo
duel ['dju·əl] o ['du·əl] *s* duelo; **to fight a duel** batirse en duelo ‖ *v* (*pret & pp* **dueled** o **duelled;** *ger* **dueling** o **duelling**) *intr* batirse en duelo
duelist o **duellist** ['dju·əlɪst] o ['du·əlɪst] *s* duelista *m*
dues-paying ['djuz,pe·ɪŋ] o ['duz,pe·ɪŋ] *adj* cotizante
duet [dju'ɛt] o [du'ɛt] *s* dúo
duke [djuk] o [duk] *s* duque *m*
dukedom ['djukdəm] o ['dukdəm] *s* ducado
dull [dʌl] *adj* (*not sharp*) embotado, romo; (*color*) apagado; (*sound; pain*) sordo; (*stupid*) lerdo, torpe; (*business*) inactivo, muerto; (*boring*) aburrido, tedioso; (*flat*) deslucido, deslustrado ‖ *tr* embotar, enromar; deslucir, deslustrar; enfriar (*el entusiasmo*) ‖ *intr* embotarse, enromarse; deslucirse, deslustrarse
dullard ['dʌlərd] *s* estúpido
duly ['djuli] o ['duli] *adv* debidamente
dumb [dʌm] *adj* (*lacking the power to speak*) mudo; (coll) estúpido, torpe
dumb'bell' *s* halterio; (slang) estúpido, tonto
dumb creature *s* animal *m*, bruto
dumb show *s* pantomima
dumb'wait'er *s* montaplatos *m*
dumfound [,dʌm'faund] *tr* pasmar, dejar sin habla
dum·my ['dʌmi] *adj* falso, fingido, simulado ‖ *s* (*pl* **-mies**) (*dress form*) maniquí *m;* cabeza para pelucas; (*in card games*) muerto; cartas del muerto; (*figurehead, straw man*) testaferro; (*skeleton copy of a book*) maqueta; imitación, copia; (slang) estúpido
dump [dʌmp] *s* basurero, vertedero; montón *m* de basuras; (mil) depósito de municiones; (min) terrero; **to be down in the dumps** (coll) tener murria ‖ *tr* descargar, verter; vaciar de golpe; vender en grandes cantidades y a precios inferiores a los corrientes
dumping ['dʌmpɪŋ] *s* descarga; venta en grandes cantidades y a precios inferiores a los corrientes
dumpling ['dʌmplɪŋ] *s* bola de pasta rellena de fruta o carne
dump truck *s* camión *m* volquete
dump·y ['dʌmpi] *adj* (*comp* **-ier;** *super* **-iest**) regordete, rollizo
dun [dʌn] *adj* bruno, pardo, castaño ‖ *s* acreedor importuno; (*demand for payment*) apremio ‖ *v* (*pret & pp* **dunned;** *ger* **dunning**) *tr* importunar para el pago, apremiar (*a un deudor*)
dunce [dʌns] *s* zopenco, bodoque *m*
dunce cap *s* capirote *m* que se le pone al alumno torpe
dune [djun] o [dun] *s* duna, médano
dung [dʌŋ] *s* estiércol *m* ‖ *tr* estercolar
dungarees [,dʌŋgə'riz] *spl* pantalones *mpl* de trabajo de tela basta de algodón
dungeon ['dʌndʒən] *s* calabozo, mazmorra; (*fortified tower of medieval castle*) torre *f* del homenaje
dung'hill' *s* estercolar *m;* lugar inmundo
dunk [dʌŋk] *tr* sopetear, ensopar
duo ['dju·o] o ['du·o] *s* dúo
duode·num [,dju·ə'dinəm] o [,du·ə'dinəm] *s* (*pl* **-na** [nə]) duodeno
dupe [djup] o [dup] *s* víctima, primo, inocentón *m* ‖ *tr* embaucar, engañar
duplex house ['djuplɛks] o ['duplɛks] *s* casa para dos familias
duplicate ['djuplɪkɪt] o ['duplɪkɪt] *adj & s* duplicado; **in duplicate** por

duplicado || ['djuplɪ,ket] o ['duplɪ,ket] *tr* duplicar
duplici·ty [dju'plɪsɪti] o [du'plɪsɪti] *s* (*pl* **-ties**) duplicidad
durable ['djʊrəbəl] o ['dʊrəbəl] *adj* durable, duradero
durable goods *spl* artículos duraderos
duration [djʊ'reʃən] o [dʊ'reʃən] *s* duración
during ['djʊrɪŋ] o ['dʊrɪŋ] *prep* durante
dusk [dʌsk] *s* crepúsculo
dust [dʌst] *s* polvo || *tr* (*to free of dust*) desempolvar; (*to sprinkle with dust*) polvorear; **to dust off** desempolvar
dust bowl *s* cuenca de polvo
dust'cloth' *s* trapo para quitar el polvo
dust cloud *s* nube *f* de polvo, polvareda
duster ['dʌstər] *s* paño, plumero; (*light overgarment*) guardapolvo
dust jacket *s* sobrecubierta
dust'pan' *s* pala para recoger la basura
dust rag *s* trapo para quitar el polvo
dust storm *s* tolvanera
dust·y ['dʌsti] *adj* (*comp* **-ier**; *super* **-iest**) polvoriento; (*grayish*) grisáceo
Dutch [dʌtʃ] *adj* holandés; (slang) alemán || *s* (*language*) holandés *m;* (*language*) (slang) alemán *m;* **in Dutch** (slang) en la desgracia; (slang) en un apuro; **the Dutch** los holandeses; (slang) los alemanes; **to go Dutch** (coll) pagar a escote
Dutch·man ['dʌtʃmən] *s* (*pl* **-men** [mən]) holandés *m;* (slang) alemán *m*
Dutch treat *s* (coll) convite *m* a escote
dutiable ['djutɪ·əbəl] o ['dutɪ·əbəl] *adj* sujeto a derechos de aduana
dutiful ['djutɪfəl] o ['dutɪfəl] *adj* obediente, sumiso, solícito
du·ty ['djuti] o ['duti] *s* (*pl* **-ties**) deber *m;* (*task*) faena, quehacer *m;* derechos de aduana; **off duty** libre; **on duty** de servicio, de guardia; **to do one's duty** cumplir con su deber; **to take up one's duties** entrar en funciones
du'ty-free' *adj* libre de derechos
D.V. *abbr* **Deo volente, i.e., God willing**
dwarf [dwɔrf] *adj* & *s* enano || *tr* achicar, empequeñecer || *intr* achicarse, empequeñecerse
dwarfish ['dwɔrfɪʃ] *adj* enano, diminuto
dwell [dwɛl] *v* (*pret* & *pp* **dwelled** o **dwelt** [dwɛlt]) *intr* vivir, morar; **to dwell on** o **upon** hacer hincapié en
dwelling ['dwɛlɪŋ] *s* morada, vivienda
dwelling house *s* casa, domicilio
dwindle ['dwɪndəl] *intr* disminuir; decaer, consumirse
dwt. *abbr* **pennyweight**
dye [daɪ] *s* tinte *m,* tintura, color *m* || *v* (*pret* & *pp* **dyed;** *ger* **dyeing**) *tr* teñir
dyed-in-the-wool ['daɪdɪnðə,wʊl] *adj* intransigente
dyeing ['daɪ·ɪŋ] *s* tinte *m,* tintura
dyer ['daɪ·ər] *s* tintorero
dye'stuff' *s* materia colorante
dying ['daɪ·ɪŋ] *adj* moribundo
dynamic [daɪ'næmɪk] o [dɪ'næmɪk] *adj* dinámico
dynamite ['daɪnə,maɪt] *s* dinamita || *tr* dinamitar
dyna·mo ['daɪnə,mo] *s* (*pl* **-mos**) dínamo *f*
dynast ['daɪnæst] *s* dinasta *m*
dynas·ty ['daɪnəsti] *s* (*pl* **-ties**) dinastía
dysentery ['dɪsən,tɛri] *s* disentería
dyspepsia [dɪs'pɛpsɪ·ə] o [dɪs'pɛpʃə] *s* dispepsia
dz. *abbr* **dozen**

E

E, e [i] quinta letra del alfabeto inglés
ea. *abbr* **each**
each [itʃ] *adj indef* cada || *pron indef* cada uno; **each other** nos, se; uno a otro, unos a otros || *adv* cada uno; por persona
eager ['igər] *adj* (*enthusiastic*) ardiente, celoso; **eager for** muy deseoso de; **eager to** + *inf* muy deseoso de + *inf*
eagerness ['igərnɪs] *s* ardor *m,* celo; deseo ardiente, empeño
eagle ['igəl] *s* águila
eagle owl *s* buho
ear [ɪr] *s* (*organ and sense of hearing*) oído; (*external part*) oreja; (*of corn*) mazorca; (*of wheat*) espiga; **all ears** con las orejas tan largas; **to be all ears** ser todo oídos, abrir tanto oído; **to prick up one's ears** aguzar las orejas; **to turn a deaf ear** hacer o tener oídos de mercader
ear'ache' *s* dolor *m* de oído
ear'drop' *s* arete *m*
ear'drum' *s* tímpano
ear'flap' *s* orejera
earl [ʌrl] *s* conde *m*
earldom ['ʌrldəm] *s* condado
ear·ly ['ʌrli] (*comp* **-lier;** *super* **-liest**) *adj* (*occurring before customary time*) temprano; (*first in a series*) primero; (*far back in time*) primero, remoto, antiguo; (*occurring in near future*) cercano, próximo || *adv* temprano; al principio; en los primeros tiempos; **as early as** (*a certain time of day*) ya a; (*a certain time or date*) ya en; **as early as possible** lo más pronto posible; **early in** (*e.g., the month of December*) ya en; **early in**

the morning muy de mañana; **early in the year** a principios del año; **to rise early** madrugar
early bird *s* (coll) madrugador *m*
early mass *s* misa de prima
early riser *s* madrugador *m*
ear'mark' *s* señal *f*, distintivo ‖ *tr* destinar, poner aparte (*para un fin determinado*)
ear'muff' *s* orejera
earn [ʌrn] *tr* ganar, ganarse; (*to get as one's due*) merecerse; (com) devengar (*intereses*) ‖ *intr* ganar; rendir
earnest ['ʌrnɪst] *adj* serio, grave; **in earnest** en serio, de buena fe ‖ *s* arras
earnest money *s* arras
earnings ['ʌrnɪŋz] *s* ganancia; salario
ear'phone' *s* audífono
ear'piece' *s* auricular *m*
ear'ring' *s* arete *m*
ear'shot' *s* alcance *m* del oído; **within earshot** al alcance del oído
ear'split'ting *adj* ensordecedor
earth [ʌrθ] *s* tierra; **to come back to** o **down to earth** bajar de las nubes
earthen ['ʌrθən] *adj* de tierra; de barro
ear'then•ware' *s* loza, vasijas de barro
earthly ['ʌrθli] *adj* terrenal; concebible, posible; **to be of no earthly use** no servir para nada
earth'quake' *s* terremoto, temblor *m* de tierra
earth'work' *s* terraplén *m*
earth'worm' *s* lombriz *f* de tierra
earth•y ['ʌrθi] *adj* (*comp* **-ier**; *super* **-iest**) terroso; (*worldly*) mundanal; (*unrefined*) grosero; franco, sincero
ear trumpet *s* trompetilla
ear'wax' *s* cera de los oídos
ease [iz] *s* facilidad; (*readiness, naturalness*) desenvoltura, soltura; (*comfort, wellbeing*) comodidad, bienestar *m*; **with ease** con facilidad ‖ *tr* facilitar; aligerar (*un peso*); (*to let up on*) aflojar, soltar; aliviar, mitigar ‖ *intr* aliviarse, mitigarse, disminuir; moderar la marcha
easel ['izəl] *s* caballete *m*
easement ['izmənt] *s* alivio; (law) servidumbre
easily ['izɪli] *adj* fácilmente; suavemente; sin duda; probablemente
easiness ['izɪnɪs] *s* facilidad; desenvoltura, soltura; (*e.g., of motion of a machine*) suavidad; indiferencia
east [ist] *adj* oriental, del este ‖ *adv* al este, hacia el este ‖ *s* este *m*
Easter ['istər] *s* Pascua de flores, Pascua de Resurrección, Pascua florida
Easter egg *s* huevo duro decorado o huevo de imitación que se da como regalo en el día de Pascua de Resurrección
Easter Monday *s* lunes *m* de Pascua de Resurrección
eastern ['istərn] *adj* oriental
East'er•tide' *s* aleluya *m*, tiempo de Pascua
eastward ['istwərd] *adv* hacia el este
eas•y ['izi] *adj* (*comp* **-ier**; *super* **-iest**) fácil; (*conducive to ease*) cómodo; (*not tight*) holgado; (*amenable*) manejable; (*not forced or hurried*) lento, pausado, moderado ‖ *adv* (coll) fácilmente; (coll) despacio; **to take it easy** (coll) descansar, holgar; (coll) ir despacio
easy chair *s* poltrona, silla poltrona
eas'y•go'ing *adj* despacioso, comodón
easy mark *s* (coll) víctima, inocentón *m*
easy money *s* dinero ganado sin pena; (com) dinero abundante
easy payments *spl* facilidades de pago
eat [it] *v* (*pret* **ate** [et]; *pp* **eaten** ['itən]) *tr* comer; **to eat away** corroer; **to eat up** comerse ‖ *intr* comer
eatable ['itəbəl] *adj* comestible ‖ **eatables** *spl* comestibles *mpl*
eaves [ivz] *spl* alero, socarrén *m*, tejaroz *m*
eaves'drop' *v* (*pret & pp* **-dropped**; *ger* **-dropping**) *intr* escuchar a escondidas, estar de escucha
ebb [ɛb] *s* reflujo; decadencia ‖ *intr* bajar (*la marea*); decaer
ebb and flow *s* flujo y reflujo
ebb tide *s* marea menguante
ebon•y ['ɛbəni] *s* (*pl* **-ies**) ébano
ebullient [ɪ'bʌljənt] *adj* hirviente; entusiasta
eccentric [ɛk'sɛntrɪk] *adj* excéntrico ‖ *m* (*odd person*) excéntrico; (*device*) excéntrica
eccentrici•ty [,ɛksɛn'trɪsɪti] *s* (*pl* **-ties**) excentricidad
ecclesiastic [ɪ,klizɪ'æstɪk] *adj & s* eclesiástico
echelon ['ɛʃə,lɑn] *s* escalón *m*; (mil) escalón ‖ *tr* (mil) escalonar
ech•o ['ɛko] *s* (*pl* **-oes**) eco ‖ *tr* repetir (*un sonido*); imitar ‖ *intr* hacer eco
éclair [e'klɛr] *s* bollo de crema
eclectic [ɛk'lɛktɪk] *adj & s* ecléctico
eclipse [ɪ'klɪps] *s* eclipse *m* ‖ *tr* eclipsar
eclogue ['ɛklɔg] o ['ɛklɑg] *s* égloga
economic [,ikə'nɑmɪk] o [,ɛkə'nɑmɪk] *adj* económico (*perteneciente a la economía*)
economical [,ikə'nɑmɪkəl] o [,ɛkə'nɑmɪkəl] *adj* económico (*ahorrador; poco costoso*)
economics [,ikə'nɑmɪks] o [,ɛkə'nɑmɪks] *s* economía política
economist [ɪ'kɑnəmɪst] *s* economista *mf*
economize [ɪ'kɑnə,maɪz] *tr & intr* economizar
econo•my [ɪ'kɑnəmi] *s* (*pl* **-mies**) economía
ecsta•sy ['ɛkstəsi] *s* (*pl* **-sies**) éxtasis *m*
ecstatic [ɛk'stætɪk] *adj* extático
Ecuador ['ɛkwə,dɔr] *s* el Ecuador
Ecuadoran [,ɛkwə'dorən] o **Ecuadorian** [,ɛkwə'dorɪ•ən] *adj & s* ecuatoriano
ecumenic(al) [,ɛkjə'mɛnɪk(əl)] *adj* ecuménico
eczema ['ɛksɪmə] o [ɛg'zimə] *s* eczema *m & f*, eccema *m & f*
ed. *abbr* **edited, edition, editor**

ed·dy ['ɛdi] *s* (*pl* **-dies**) remolino || *v* (*pret & pp* **-died**) *tr & intr* remolinear
edelweiss ['edəl,vaɪs] *s* estrella de los Alpes
edge [ɛdʒ] *s* (*of a knife, sword, etc.*) filo, corte *m;* (*of a cup, glass, piece of paper, piece of cloth, an abyss, etc.*) borde *m;* (*of a piece of cloth; of a body of water*) orilla; (*of a table*) canto; (*of a book*) corte *m;* (*of clothing*) ribete *m;* (slang) ventaja; **on edge** de canto; (fig) nervioso; **to have the edge on** (coll) llevar ventaja a; **to set the teeth on edge** dar dentera || *tr* afilar, aguzar; bordear; ribetear (*un vestido*) || *intr* avanzar de lado; **to edge in** lograr entrar
edgeways ['ɛdʒ,wez] *adv* de filo, de canto; **to not let a person get a word in edgeways** no dejarle a una persona decir ni una palabra
edging ['ɛdʒɪŋ] *s* orla, pestaña
edgy ['ɛdʒi] *adj* agudo, angular; nervioso, irritable
edible ['ɛdɪbəl] *adj & s* comestible *m*
edict ['idɪkt] *s* edicto
edification [,ɛdɪfɪ'keʃən] *s* edificación
edifice ['ɛdɪfɪs] *s* edificio
edi·fy ['ɛdɪ,faɪ] *v* (*pret & pp* **-fied**) *tr* edificar
edifying ['ɛdɪ,faɪ·ɪŋ] *adj* edificante
edit. *abbr* **edited, edition, editor**
edit ['ɛdɪt] *tr* preparar para la publicación; dirigir, redactar (*un periódico*)
edition [ɪ'dɪʃən] *s* edición
editor ['ɛdɪtər] *s* (*of a newspaper or magazine*) director *m,* redactor *m;* (*of a manuscript*) revisor *m;* (*of an editorial*) cronista *mf*
editorial [,ɛdɪ'torɪ·əl] *adj* editorial || editorial *m,* artículo de fondo
editorial staff *s* redacción, cuerpo de redacción
editor in chief *s* jefe *m* de redacción
educate ['ɛdʒʊ,ket] *tr* educar, instruír
education [,ɛdʒʊ'keʃən] *s* educación, instrucción
educational [,ɛdʒʊ'keʃənəl] *adj* educativo, educacional
educational institution *s* centro docente
educator ['ɛdʒʊ,ketər] *s* educador *m*
eel [il] *s* anguila; **to be as slippery as an eel** escurrirse como una anguila
ee·rie o **ee·ry** ['ɪri] *adj* (*comp* **-rier;** *super* **-riest**) espectral, misterioso
efface [ɪ'fes] *tr* destruir; borrar; **to efface oneself** retirarse, no dejarse ver
effect [ɪ'fɛkt] *s* efecto; **in effect** vigente; en efecto, en realidad; **to feel the effects of** resentirse de; **to go into effect** o **to take effect** hacerse vigente, entrar en vigor; **to put into effect** poner en vigor || *tr* efectuar
effective [ɪ'fɛktɪv] *adj* eficaz; (*actually in effect*) efectivo; (*striking*) impresionante; **to become effective** hacerse efectivo, entrar en vigencia
effectual [ɪ'fɛktʃʊ·əl] *adj* eficaz
effectuate [ɪ'fɛktʃʊ,et] *tr* efectuar
effeminacy [ɪ'fɛmɪnəsi] *s* afeminación
effeminate [ɪ'fɛmɪnɪt] *adj* afeminado
effervesce [,ɛfər'vɛs] *intr* estar en efervescencia
effervescence [,ɛfər'vɛsəns] *s* efervescencia
effervescent [,ɛfər'vɛsənt] *adj* efervescente
effete [ɪ'fit] *adj* estéril, infructuoso
efficacious [,ɛfɪ'keʃəs] *adj* eficaz
effica·cy ['ɛfɪkəsi] *s* (*pl* **-cies**) eficacia
efficien·cy [ɪ'fɪʃənsi] *s* (*pl* **-cies**) eficiencia; (mech) rendimiento, efecto útil
efficient [ɪ'fɪʃənt] *adj* eficiente, eficaz; (*person*) competente; (mech) de buen rendimiento
effi·gy ['ɛfɪdʒi] *s* (*pl* **-gies**) efigie *f*
effort ['ɛfərt] *s* esfuerzo, empeño
effronter·y [ɪ'frʌntəri] *s* (*pl* **-ies**) desfachatez *f,* descaro
effusion [ɪ'fjuʒən] *s* efusión
effusive [ɪ'fjusɪv] *adj* efusivo, expansivo
e.g. *abbr* **exempli gratia, i.e., for example**
egg [ɛg] *s* huevo; (slang) buen sujeto || *tr* — **to egg on** incitar, instigar
egg beater *s* batidor *m* de huevos
egg'cup' *s* huevera
egg'head' *s* intelectual *mf,* erudito
eggnog ['ɛg,nɑg] *s* caldo de la reina, yema mejida
egg'plant' *s* berenjena
egg'shell' *s* cascarón *m,* cáscara de huevo
egoism ['ɛgo,ɪzəm] o ['igo,ɪzəm] *s* egoísmo
egoist ['ɛgo·ɪst] o ['igo·ɪst] *s* egoísta *mf*
egotism ['ɛgo,tɪzəm] o ['igo,tɪzəm] *s* egotismo
egotist ['ɛgotɪst] o ['igotɪst] *s* egotista *mf*
egregious [ɪ'gridʒəs] *adj* enorme, escandaloso
egress ['igrɛs] *s* salida
Egypt ['idʒɪpt] *s* Egipto
Egyptian [ɪ'dʒɪpʃən] *adj & s* egipcio
eider ['aɪdər] *s* pato de flojel
eider down *s* edredón *m*
eight [et] *adj & pron* ocho || *s* ocho; **eight o'clock** las ocho
eight'-day' clock *s* reloj *m* de ocho días cuerda
eighteen ['et'tin] *adj, pron & s* dieciocho, diez y ocho
eighteenth ['et'tinθ] *adj & s* (*in a series*) decimoctavo; (*part*) dieciochavo || *s* (*in dates*) dieciocho, diez y ocho
eighth [etθ] *adj & s* octavo, ochavo || *s* (*in dates*) ocho
eight hundred *adj & pron* ochocientos || *s* ochocientos *m*
eightieth ['etɪ·ɪθ] *adj & s* (*in a series*) octogésimo; (*part*) ochentavo
eigh·ty ['eti] *adj & pron* ochenta || *s* (*pl* **-ties**) ochenta *m*
either ['iðər] o ['aɪðər] *adj* uno u otro, cada . . . (de los dos), cual-

quier . . . de los dos; ambos || *pron* uno u otro, cualquiera de los dos || *adv* — **not either** tampoco, no . . . tampoco || *conj* — **either . . . or** o . . . o
ejaculate [ɪ'dʒækjə,let] *tr & intr* exclamar; (physiol) eyacular
eject [ɪ'dʒɛkt] *tr* arrojar, expulsar, echar; (*to evict*) desahuciar
ejection [ɪ'dʒɛkʃən] *s* expulsión; (*of a tenant*) desahucio
ejection seat *s* (aer) asiento lanzable
eke [ik] *tr* — **to eke out** ganarse (*la vida*) con dificultad
elaborate [ɪ'læbərɪt] *adj* (*done with great care*) elaborado; (*detailed, ornate*) primoroso, recargado || [ɪ'læbə,ret] *tr* elaborar || *intr* — **to elaborate on** o **upon** explicar con más detalles
elapse [ɪ'læps] *intr* pasar, transcurrir
elastic [ɪ'læstɪk] *adj & s* elástico
elasticity [ɪ,læs'tɪsɪti] o [,ilæs'tɪsɪti] *s* elasticidad
elated [ɪ'letɪd] *adj* alborozado, regocijado
elation [ɪ'leʃən] *s* alborozo, regocijo
elbow ['ɛlbo] *s* codo; (*in a river*) recodo; (*of a chair*) brazo; **at one's elbow** a la mano; **out at the elbows** andrajoso, enseñando los codos; **to crook the elbow** empinar el codo; **to rub elbows** codearse, rozarse; **up to the elbows** hasta los codos || *tr* — **to elbow one's way** abrirse paso a codazos || *intr* codear
elbow grease *s* (coll) muñeca, jugo de muñeca
elbow patch *s* codera
elbow rest *s* ménsula
el'bow·room' *s* espacio suficiente; libertad de acción
elder ['ɛldər] *adj* mayor, más antiguo || *s* mayor, señor *m* mayor; (eccl) anciano; (*plant*) saúco
el'der·ber'ry *s* (*pl* **-ries**) saúco; baya del saúco
elderly ['ɛldərli] *adj* viejo, anciano
elder statesman *s* veterano de la política
eldest ['ɛldɪst] *adj* (el) mayor, (el) más antiguo
elec. *abbr* **electrical, electricity**
elect [ɪ'lɛkt] *adj* (*chosen*) escogido; (*selected but not yet installed*) electo || *s* elegido; **the elect** los elegidos || *tr* elegir
election [ɪ'lɛkʃən] *s* elección
electioneer [ɪ,lɛkʃə'nɪr] *intr* solicitar votos
elective [ɪ'lɛktɪv] *adj* electivo || *s* asignatura electiva
electorate [ɪ'lɛktərɪt] *s* electorado
electric(al) [ɪ'lɛktrɪk(əl)] *adj* eléctrico
electric fan *s* ventilador eléctrico
electrician [ɪ,lɛk'trɪʃən] o [,ɛlɛk'trɪʃən] *s* electricista *mf*
electricity [ɪ,lɛk'trɪsɪti] o [,ɛlɛk'trɪsɪti] *s* electricidad
electric percolator *s* cafetera eléctrica
electric shaver *s* electroafeitadora
electric tape *s* cinta aislante
electri·fy [ɪ'lɛktrɪ,faɪ] *v* (*pret & pp* **-fied**) *tr* (*to provide with electric power*) electrificar; (*to communicate electricity to; to thrill*) electrizar
electrocute [ɪ'lɛktrə,kjut] *tr* electrocutar
electrode [ɪ'lɛktrod] *s* electrodo
electrolysis [ɪ,lɛk'trɑlɪsɪs] o [,ɛlɛk'trɑlɪsɪs] *s* electrolisis *f*
electrolyte [ɪ'lɛktrə,laɪt] *s* electrólito
electromagnet [ɪ,lɛktrə'mægnɪt] *s* electro, electroimán *m*
electromagnetic [ɪ,lɛktrəmæg'nɛtɪk] *adj* electromagnético
electromotive [ɪ,lɛktrə'motɪv] *adj* electromotor
electron [ɪ'lɛktrɑn] *s* electrón *m*
electronic [ɪ,lɛk'trɑnɪk] o [,ɛlɛk'trɑnɪk] *adj* electrónico || **electronics** *s* electrónica
electroplating [ɪ'lɛktrə,pletɪŋ] *s* galvanoplastia
electrostatic [ɪ,lɛktrə'stætɪk] *adj* electrostático
electrotype [ɪ'lɛktrə,taɪp] *s* electrotipo || *tr* electrotipar
eleemosynary [,ɛlɪ'mɑsɪ,nɛri] *adj* limosnero
elegance ['ɛlɪgəns] *s* elegancia
elegant ['ɛlɪgənt] *adj* elegante
elegiac [,ɛlɪ'dʒaɪ·æk] o [ɪ'lidʒɪ,æk] *adj* elegíaco
ele·gy ['ɛlɪdʒi] *s* (*pl* **-gies**) elegía
element ['ɛlɪmənt] *s* elemento; **to be in one's element** estar en su elemento
elementary [,ɛlɪ'mɛntəri] *adj* elemental
elephant ['ɛlɪfənt] *s* elefante *m*
elevate ['ɛlɪ,vet] *tr* elevar
elevated ['ɛlɪ,vetɪd] *adj* elevado || *s* (coll) ferrocarril aéreo o elevado
elevation [,ɛlɪ'veʃən] *s* elevación
elevator ['ɛlɪ,vetər] *s* ascensor *m;* elevador *m* (Am); (*for freight*) montacargas *m;* (*for hoisting grain*) elevador de granos; (*warehouse for storing grain*) depósito de cereales; (aer) timón *m* de profundidad
eleven [ɪ'lɛvən] *adj & pron* once || *s* once *m;* **eleven o'clock** las once
eleventh [ɪ'lɛvənθ] *adj & s* (*in a series*) undécimo, onceno; (*part*) onzavo || *s* (*in dates*) once *m*
eleventh hour *s* último momento
elf [ɛlf] *s* (*pl* **elves** [ɛlvz]) elfo, trasgo; enano
elicit [ɪ'lɪsɪt] *tr* sacar, sonsacar
elide [ɪ'laɪd] *tr* elidir
eligible ['ɛlɪdʒɪbəl] *adj* elegible; deseable, aceptable
eliminate [ɪ'lɪmɪ,net] *tr* eliminar
elision [ɪ'lɪʒən] *s* elisión
elite [e'lit] *adj* selecto || *s* — **the elite** la élite
elk [ɛlk] *s* alce *m*
ellipse [ɪ'lɪps] *s* (geom) elipse *f*
ellip·sis [ɪ'lɪpsɪs] *s* (*pl* **-ses** [siz]) (gram) elipsis *f*
elliptic(al) [ɪ'lɪptɪk(əl)] *adj* (geom & gram) elíptico
elm tree [ɛlm] *s* olmo

elope [ɪ'lop] *intr* fugarse con un amante
elopement [ɪ'lopmənt] *s* fuga con un amante
eloquence ['ɛləkwəns] *s* elocuencia
eloquent ['ɛləkwənt] *adj* elocuente
else [ɛls] *adj* — **nobody else** ningún otro, nadie más; **nothing else** nada más; **somebody else** algún otro, otra persona; **something else** otra cosa; **what else** qué más, qué otra cosa; **who else** quién más; **whose else** de qué otra persona || *adv* de otro modo; **how else** de qué otro modo; **or else** si no, o bien; **when else** en qué otro tiempo; a qué otra hora; **where else** en qué otra parte
else'where' *adv* en otra parte, a otra parte
elucidate [ɪ'lusɪ,det] *tr* elucidar
elude [ɪ'lud] *tr* eludir
elusive [ɪ'lusɪv] *adj* fugaz, efímero; evasivo; (*baffling*) deslumbrador
emaciated [ɪ'meʃɪ,etɪd] *adj* enflaquecido, macilento
emancipate [ɪ'mænsɪ,pet] *tr* emancipar
embalm [ɛm'bɑm] *tr* embalsamar
embankment [ɛm'bæŋkmənt] *s* terraplén *m*
embar•go [ɛm'bɑrgo] *s* (*pl* **-goes**) embargo || *tr* embargar
embark [ɛm'bɑrk] *intr* embarcarse
embarkation [,ɛmbɑr'keʃən] *s* (*of passengers*) embarco; (*of freight*) embarque *m*
embarrass [ɛm'bærəs] *tr* (*to make feel self-conscious*) avergonzar; (*to put obstacles in the way of*) embarazar; poner en apuros de dinero
embarrassing [ɛm'bærəsɪŋ] *adj* desconcertante, vergonzoso; embarazoso
embarrassment [ɛm'bærəsmənt] *s* desconcierto, vergüenza; (*interference; perplexity*) embarazo; (*financial difficulties*) apuros
embas•sy ['ɛmbəsi] *s* (*pl* **-sies**) embajada
em•bed [ɛm'bɛd] *s* (*pret & pp* **-bedded;** *ger* **-bedding**) *tr* empotrar, encajar
embellish [ɛm'bɛlɪʃ] *tr* embellecer
embellishment [ɛm'bɛlɪʃmənt] *s* embellecimiento
ember ['ɛmbər] *s* ascua, pavesa; **embers** rescoldo
Ember days *spl* témpora
embezzle [ɛm'bɛzəl] *tr & intr* desfalcar, malversar
embezzlement [ɛm'bɛzəlmənt] *s* desfalco, malversación
embezzler [ɛm'bɛzlər] *s* malversador *m*
embitter [ɛm'bɪtər] *tr* amargar
emblazon [ɛm'blezən] *tr* blasonar; (fig) blasonar
emblem ['ɛmbləm] *s* emblema *m*
emblematic(al) [,ɛmblə'mætɪk(əl)] *adj* emblemático
embodiment [ɛm'bɑdɪmənt] *s* incorporación; personificación, encarnación
embod•y [ɛm'bɑdi] *v* (*pret & pp* **-ied**) *tr* incorporar; personificar, encarnar
embolden [ɛm'boldən] *tr* envalentonar
embolism ['ɛmbə,lɪzəm] *s* embolia
emboss [ɛm'bɔs] o [ɛm'bɑs] *tr* (*to raise in relief*) realzar; abollonar (*metal*); repujar (*cuero*)
embrace [ɛm'bres] *s* abrazo || *tr* abrazar || *intr* abrazarse
embrasure [ɛm'breʒər] *s* alféizar *m*
embroider [ɛm'brɔɪdər] *tr* bordar, recamar
embroider•y [ɛm'brɔɪdəri] *s* (*pl* **-ies**) bordado, recamado
embroil [ɛm'brɔɪl] *tr* embrollar; (*to involve in contention*) envolver
embroilment [ɛm'brɔɪlmənt] *s* embrollo; (*in contention*) envolvimiento
embry•o ['ɛmbrɪ,o] *s* (*pl* **-os**) embrión *m*
embryology [,ɛmbrɪ'ɑlədʒi] *s* embriología
emend [ɪ'mɛnd] *tr* enmendar
emendation [,imɛn'deʃən] *s* enmienda
emerald ['ɛmərəld] *s* esmeralda
emerge [ɪ'mʌrdʒ] *intr* emerger
emergence [ɪ'mʌrdʒəns] *s* emergencia (*acción de emerger*)
emergen•cy [ɪ'mʌrdʒənsi] *s* (*pl* **-cies**) emergencia (*caso urgente*)
emergency exit *s* salida de auxilio
emergency landing *s* aterrizaje forzoso
emergency landing field *s* aeródromo de urgencia
emersion [ɪ'mʌrʒən] o [ɪ'mʌrʃən] *s* emersión
emery ['ɛməri] *s* esmeril *m*
emery cloth *s* tela de esmeril
emery wheel *s* esmeriladora, rueda de esmeril, muela de esmeril
emetic [ɪ'mɛtɪk] *adj & s* emético
emigrant ['ɛmɪgrənt] *adj & s* emigrante *mf*
emigrate ['ɛmɪ,gret] *intr* emigrar
émigré [emi'gre] o ['ɛmɪ,gre] *s* emigrado
eminence ['ɛmɪnəns] *s* eminencia
eminent ['ɛmɪnənt] *adj* eminente
emissar•y ['ɛmɪ,sɛri] *s* (*pl* **-ies**) emisario
emission [ɪ'mɪʃən] *s* emisión
emit [ɪ'mɪt] *v* (*pret & pp* **emitted;** *ger* **emitting**) *tr* emitir
emotion [ɪ'moʃən] *s* emoción
emotional [ɪ'moʃənəl] *adj* emocional, emotivo
emperor ['ɛmpərər] *s* emperador *m*
empha•sis ['ɛmfəsɪs] *s* (*pl* **-ses** [,siz]) énfasis *m*
emphasize ['ɛmfə,saɪz] *tr* acentuar, hacer hincapié en
emphatic [ɛm'fætɪk] *adj* enfático
emphysema [,ɛmfɪ'simə] *s* enfisema *m*
empire ['ɛmpaɪr] *s* imperio
empiric(al) [ɛm'pɪrɪk(əl)] *adj* empírico
empiricist [ɛm'pɪrɪsɪst] *s* empírico
emplacement [ɛm'plesmənt] *s* emplazamiento
employ [ɛm'plɔɪ] *s* empleo || *tr* emplear
employee [ɛm'plɔɪ·i] o [,ɛmplɔɪ'i] *s* empleado
employer [ɛm'plɔɪ·ər] *s* patrono

employment [ɛm'plɔɪmənt] *s* empleo, colocación
employment agency *s* agencia de colocaciones
empower [ɛm'paʊ·ər] *tr* autorizar, facultar; habilitar, permitir
empress ['ɛmprɪs] *s* emperatriz *f*
emptiness ['ɛmptɪnɪs] *s* vaciedad, vacuidad
emp·ty ['ɛmpti] *adj* (*comp* **-tier;** *super* **-tiest**) vacío; (coll) hambriento || *v* (*pret & pp* **-tied**) *tr & intr* vaciar
empty-handed ['ɛmpti'hændɪd] *adj* manivacío
empty-headed ['ɛmpti'hɛdɪd] *adj* tonto, ignorante
empye·ma [,ɛmpɪ'imə] *s* (*pl* **-mata** [mətə]) empiema *m*
empyrean [,ɛmpɪ'ri·ən] *adj & s* empíreo
emulate ['ɛmjə,let] *tr & intr* emular
emulator ['ɛmjə,letər] *s* émulo
emulous ['ɛmjələs] *adj* émulo
emulsi·fy [ɪ'mʌlsɪ,faɪ] *v* (*pret & pp* **-fied**) *tr* emulsionar
emulsion [ɪ'mʌlʃən] *s* emulsión
enable [ɛn'ebəl] *tr* habilitar, facilitar
enact [ɛn'ækt] *tr* decretar, promulgar; hacer el papel de
enactment [ɛn'æktmənt] *s* ley *f;* (*of a law*) promulgación; (*of a play*) representación
enam·el [ɛn'æməl] *s* esmalte *m* || *v* (*pret & pp* **-eled** o **-elled;** *ger* **-eling** o **-elling**) *tr* esmaltar
enam'el·ware' *s* utensilios de cocina de hierro esmaltado
enamor [ɛn'æmər] *tr* enamorar
encamp [ɛn'kæmp] *tr* acampar || *intr* acampar, acamparse
encampment [ɛn'kæmpmənt] *s* acampamiento
enchant [ɛn'tʃænt] o [ɛn'tʃɑnt] *tr* encantar
enchanting [ɛn'tʃæntɪŋ] o [ɛn'tʃɑntɪŋ] *adj* encantador
enchantment [ɛn'tʃæntmənt] o [ɛn'tʃɑntmənt] *s* encanto
enchantress [ɛn'tʃæntrɪs] o [ɛn'tʃɑntrɪs] *s* encantadora
enchase [ɛn'tʃes] *tr* engastar
encircle [ɛn'sʌrkəl] *tr* encerrar, rodear; (mil) envolver
enclitic [ɛn'klɪtɪk] *adj & s* enclítico
enclose [ɛn'kloz] *tr* encerrar; (*in a letter*) adjuntar, incluir; **to enclose herewith** remitir adjunto
enclosure [ɛn'kloʒər] *s* recinto; cosa inclusa, carta inclusa
encomi·um [ɛn'komɪ·əm] *s* (*pl* **-ums** o **-a** [ə]) encomio
encompass [ɛn'kʌmpəs] *tr* encuadrar, abarcar
encore ['ɑnkor] *s* bis *m* || *interj* ¡bis!, ¡que se repita! || *tr* pedir la repetición de (*p.ej., de una pieza o canción*); pedir la repetición a (*un actor*)
encounter [ɛn'kaʊntər] *s* encuentro || *tr* encontrar, encontrarse con || *intr* batirse, combatirse
encourage [ɛn'kʌrɪdʒ] *tr* animar, alentar; (*to foster*) fomentar
encouragement [ɛn'kʌrɪdʒmənt] *s* ánimo, aliento; fomento
encroach [ɛn'krotʃ] *intr* — **to encroach on** o **upon** pasar los límites de; abusar de; invadir, entremeterse en
encumber [ɛn'kʌmbər] *tr* embarazar, estorbar, impedir; (*to load with debts, etc.*) gravar
encumbrance [ɛn'kʌmbrəns] *s* embarazo; estorbo; gravamen *m*
ency. o **encyc.** *abbr* **encyclopedia**
encyclical [ɛn'sɪklɪkəl] o [ɛn'saɪklɪkəl] *s* encíclica
encyclopedia [ɛn,saɪklə'pidɪ·ə] *s* enciclopedia
encyclopedic [ɛn,saɪklə'pidɪk] *adj* enciclopédico
end [ɛnd] *s* (*in time*) fin *m;* (*in space*) extremo, remate *m;* (*e.g., of the month*) fines *mpl;* (*small piece*) cabo, pieza, fragmento; (*purpose*) intento, objeto, fin, mira; **at the end of** al cabo de; a fines de; **in the end** al fin; **no end of** (coll) un sin fin de; **to make both ends meet** pasar con lo que se tiene; **to no end** sin efecto; **to stand on end** poner de punta; ponerse de punta; erizarse, encresparse (*el pelo*); **to the end that** a fin de que || *tr* acabar, terminar || *intr* acabar, terminar; desembocar (*p.ej., una calle*); **to end up** acabar, morir; **to end up as** acabar siendo, parar en (*p.ej., ladrón*)
endanger [ɛn'dendʒər] *tr* poner en peligro
endear [ɛn'dɪr] *tr* hacer querer; **to endear oneself to** hacerse querer por
endeavor [ɛn'dɛvər] *s* esfuerzo, empeño || *intr* esforzarse, empeñarse
endemic [ɛn'dɛmɪk] *adj* endémico || *s* endemia
ending ['ɛndɪŋ] *s* fin *m,* terminación; (gram) desinencia, terminación
endive ['ɛndaɪv] *s* escarola
endless ['ɛndlɪs] *adj* interminable; (*chain, screw, etc.*) sin fin
end'most' *adj* último, extremo
endorse [ɛn'dɔrs] *tr* endosar; (fig) apoyar, aprobar
endorsee [,ɛndɔr'si] *s* endosatario
endorsement [ɛn'dɔrsmənt] *s* endoso; (fig) apoyo, aprobación
endorser [ɛn'dɔrsər] *s* endosante *mf*
endow [ɛn'daʊ] *tr* dotar
endowment [ɛn'daʊmənt] *adj* dotal || *s* (*of an institution*) dotación; (*gift, talent*) dote *f,* prenda
endurance [ɛn'djurəns] o [ɛn'durəns] *s* aguante *m,* paciencia; (*ability to hold out*) resistencia, fortaleza; (*lasting time*) duración
endure [ɛn'djur] o [ɛn'dur] *tr* aguantar, tolerar, sufrir || *intr* durar; sufrir con paciencia
enduring [ɛn'djurɪŋ] o [ɛn'durɪŋ] *adj* duradero, permanente, resistente
enema ['ɛnəmə] *s* enema, ayuda; (*liquid and apparatus*) lavativa
ene·my ['ɛnəmi] *adj* enemigo || *s* (*pl* **-mies**) enemigo

enemy alien *s* extranjero enemigo
energetic [ˌɛnərˈdʒɛtɪk] *adj* enérgico, vigoroso
ener·gy [ˈɛnərdʒi] *s* (*pl* **-gies**) energía
enervate [ˈɛnərˌvet] *tr* enervar
enfeeble [ɛnˈfibəl] *tr* debilitar
enfold [ɛnˈfold] *tr* arrollar, envolver
enforce [ɛnˈfors] *tr* hacer cumplir, poner en vigor; obtener por fuerza; (*e.g., obedience*) imponer; (*an argument*) hacer valer
enforcement [ɛnˈforsmənt] *s* compulsión; (*e.g., of a law*) ejecución
enfranchise [ɛnˈfræntʃaɪz] *tr* franquear, libertar; conceder el derecho de sufragio a
eng. *abbr* **engineer, engraving**
engage [ɛnˈgedʒ] *tr* ocupar, emplear; alquilar, reservar; atraer (*p.ej., la atención de una persona*); engranar con; trabar batalla con; **to be engaged, to be engaged to be married** estar prometido, estar comprometido para casarse; **to engage someone in conversation** entablar conversación con una persona ‖ *intr* empeñarse, comprometerse; empotrar, encajar; engranar; **to engage in** ocuparse en
engaged [ɛnˈgedʒd] *adj* comprometido, prometido; (*column*) embebido, entregado
engagement [ɛnˈgedʒmənt] *s* ajuste *m,* contrato, empeño; esponsales *mpl,* palabra de casamiento; (*duration of betrothal*) noviazgo; (*appointment*) cita; (mil) acción, batalla
engagement ring *s* anillo de compromiso, anillo de pedida
engaging [ɛnˈgedʒɪŋ] *adj* agraciado, simpático
engender [ɛnˈdʒɛndər] *tr* engendrar
engine [ˈɛndʒɪn] *s* máquina; (*of automobile*) motor *m;* (rr) máquina, locomotora
engine driver *s* maquinista *m*
engineer [ˌɛndʒəˈnɪr] *s* ingeniero; (*engine driver*) maquinista *m* ‖ *tr* dirigir o construir como ingeniero; llevar a cabo con acierto
engineering [ˌɛndʒəˈnɪrɪŋ] *s* ingeniería
engine house *s* cuartel *m* de bomberos
engine·man [ˈɛndʒɪnmən] *s* (*pl* **-men** [mən]) maquinista *m,* conductor *m* de locomotora
engine room *s* sala de máquinas; (naut) cámara de las máquinas
en'gine-room' telegraph *s* (naut) transmisor *m* de órdenes, telégrafo de máquinas
England [ˈɪŋglənd] *s* Inglaterra
Englander [ˈɪŋgləndər] *s* natural *m* inglés
English [ˈɪŋglɪʃ] *adj* inglés ‖ *s* inglés *m;* (*in billiards*) efecto; **the English** los ingleses
English Channel *s* Canal *m* de la Mancha
English daisy *s* margarita de los prados
English horn *s* (mus) corno inglés, cuerno inglés
English·man [ˈɪŋglɪʃmən] *s* (*pl* **-men** [mən]) inglés *m*
Eng'lish-speak'ing *adj* de habla inglesa
Eng'lish·wom'an *s* (*pl* **-wom'en**) inglesa
engraft [ɛnˈgræft] o [ɛnˈgrɑft] *tr* (hort & surg) injertar; (fig) implantar
engrave [ɛnˈgrev] *tr* grabar; (*in the memory*) grabar
engraver [ɛnˈgrevər] *s* grabador *m*
engraving [ɛnˈgrevɪŋ] *s* grabado
engross [ɛnˈgros] *tr* absorber; poner en limpio; copiar caligráficamente
engrossing [ɛnˈgrosɪŋ] *adj* acaparador, absorbente
engulf [ɛnˈgʌlf] *tr* hundir, inundar
enhance [ɛnˈhæns] o [ɛnˈhɑns] *tr* realzar
enhancement [ɛnˈhænsmənt] o [ɛnˈhɑnsmənt] *s* realce *m*
enigma [ɪˈnɪgmə] *s* enigma *m*
enigmatic(al) [ˌɪnɪgˈmætɪk(əl)] *adj* enigmático
enjambment [ɛnˈdʒæmmənt] o [ɛnˈdʒæmbmənt] *s* encabalgamiento
enjoin [ɛnˈdʒɔɪn] *tr* encargar, ordenar
enjoy [ɛnˈdʒɔɪ] *tr* gozar; **to enjoy** + *ger* gozarse en + *inf;* **to enjoy oneself** divertirse
enjoyable [ɛnˈdʒɔɪ·əbəl] *adj* agradable, deleitable
enjoyment [ɛnˈdʒɔɪmənt] *s* (*pleasure*) placer *m;* (*pleasurable use*) goce *m*
enkindle [ɛnˈkɪndəl] *tr* encender
enlarge [ɛnˈlɑrdʒ] *tr* agrandar, aumentar; (phot) ampliar ‖ *intr* agrandarse, aumentar; (*to talk at length*) explayarse; exagerar; **to enlarge on** o **upon** tratar con más extensión; exagerar
enlargement [ɛnˈlɑrdʒmənt] *s* agrandamiento, aumento; (phot) ampliación
enlighten [ɛnˈlaɪtən] *tr* ilustrar, instruir
enlightenment [ɛnˈlaɪtənmənt] *s* ilustración, instrucción
enlist [ɛnˈlɪst] *tr* alistar; ganar (*a una persona; el favor, los servicios de una persona*) ‖ *intr* alistarse; **to enlist in** (*a cause*) poner empeño en
enliven [ɛnˈlaɪvən] *tr* avivar, animar
enmesh [ɛnˈmɛʃ] *tr* enredar
enmi·ty [ˈɛnmɪti] *s* (*pl* **-ties**) enemistad
ennoble [ɛnˈnobəl] *tr* ennoblecer
ennui [ˈɑnwi] *s* aburrimiento, tedio
enormous [ɪˈnɔrməs] *adj* enorme
enough [ɪˈnʌf] *adj, adv & s* bastante *m* ‖ *interj* ¡basta!, ¡no más!
enounce [ɪˈnaʊns] *tr* enunciar; pronunciar
en passant [ˌɑn pæˈsɑnt] *adv* (chess) al vuelo
enrage [ɛnˈredʒ] *tr* enrabiar, encolerizar
enrapture [ɛnˈræptʃər] *tr* embelesar, transportar, arrebatar
enrich [ɛnˈrɪtʃ] *tr* enriquecer
enroll [ɛnˈrol] *tr* alistar, inscribir; (*to wrap up*) envolver, enrollar ‖ *intr* alistarse, inscribirse
en route [ɑn ˈrut) *adv* en camino; **en route to** camino de, rumbo a
ensconce [ɛnˈskɑns] *tr* esconder, abrigar; **to ensconce oneself** instalarse cómodamente
ensemble [ɑnˈsɑmbəl] *s* conjunto;

grupo de músicos que tocan o cantan juntos; traje armonioso
ensign ['ɛnsaɪn] *s* (*standard*) enseña, bandera; (*badge*) divisa, insignia || ['ɛnsən] o ['ɛnsaɪn] *s* (nav) alférez *m* de fragata
enslave [ɛn'slev] *tr* esclavizar
enslavement [ɛn'slevmənt] *s* esclavización
ensnare [ɛn'snɛr] *tr* entrampar
ensue [ɛn'su] o [ɛn'sju] *intr* seguirse; resultar
ensuing [ɛn'su·ɪŋ] o [ɛn'sju·ɪŋ] *adj* siguiente; resultante
ensure [ɛn'ʃur] *tr* asegurar, garantizar
entail [ɛn'tel] *s* (law) vínculo || *tr* acarrear, ocasionar; (law) vincular
entangle [ɛn'tæŋgəl] *tr* enmarañar, enredar
entanglement [ɛn'tæŋgəlmənt] *s* enmarañamiento, enredo
enter ['ɛntər] *tr* entrar en (*una habitación*); entrar por (*una puerta*); (*in the customhouse*) declarar; (*to make a record of*) registrar, asentar; matricular (*a un alumno*); matricularse en; hacer miembro a; hacerse miembro de; (*to undertake*) emprender; asentar (*un pedido*); **to enter one's head** metérsele a uno en la cabeza || *intr* entrar; (theat) entrar en escena, salir; **to enter into** entrar en; celebrar (*p.ej., un contrato*); **to enter on o upon** emprender
enterprise ['ɛntər,praɪz] *s* (*undertaking*) empresa; (*spirit, push*) empuje *m*
enterprising ['ɛntər,praɪzɪŋ] *adj* emprendedor
entertain [,ɛntər'ten] *tr* entretener, divertir; (*to show hospitality to*) recibir; considerar, abrigar (*esperanzas, ideas, etc.*) || *intr* recibir
entertainer [,ɛntər'tenər] *s* (*host*) anfitrión *m*; (*in public*) actor *m*, bailador *m*, músico, vocalista *mf* (*esp. en un café cantante*)
entertaining [,ɛntər'tenɪŋ] *adj* entretenido
entertainment [,ɛntər'tenmənt] *s* entretenimiento, diversión; atracción, espectáculo; buen recibimiento; (*of hopes, ideas, etc.*) consideración, abrigo
enthrall [ɛn'θrɔl] *tr* cautivar, encantar; esclavizar, sojuzgar
enthrone [ɛn'θron] *tr* entronizar
enthuse [ɛn'θuz] o [ɛn'θjuz] *tr* (coll) entusiasmar || *intr* (coll) entusiasmarse
enthusiasm [ɛn'θuzɪ,æzəm] o [ɛn'θjuzɪ,æzəm] *s* entusiasmo
enthusiast [ɛn'θuzɪ,æst] o [ɛn'θjuzi,æst] *s* entusiasta *mf*
enthusiastic [ɛn,θuzɪ'æstɪk] o [ɛn,θjuzɪ'æstɪk] *adj* entusiástico
entice [ɛn'taɪs] *tr* atraer, tentar; inducir al mal, extraviar
enticement [ɛn'taɪsmənt] *s* atracción, tentación; extravío
entire [ɛn'taɪr] *adj* entero
entirely [ɛn'taɪrli] *adv* enteramente; (*exclusively*) solamente
entire·ty [ɛn'taɪrti] *s* (*pl* **-ties**) entereza; conjunto, totalidad
entitle [ɛn'taɪtəl] *tr* dar derecho a; (*to give a name to; to honor with a title*) intitular
enti·ty ['ɛntɪti] *s* (*pl* **-ties**) entidad
entomb [ɛn'tum] *tr* sepultar
entombment [ɛn'tummənt] *s* sepultura
entomology [,ɛntə'mɑlədʒi] *s* entomología
entourage [,ɑntu'rɑʒ] *s* cortejo, séquito
entrails ['ɛntrelz] o ['ɛntrəlz] *spl* entrañas
entrain [ɛn'tren] *tr* despachar en el tren || *intr* embarcar, salir en el tren
entrance ['ɛntrəns] *s* entrada, ingreso; (theat) entrada en escena || [ɛn'træns] o [ɛn'trɑns] *tr* arrebatar, encantar
entrance examination *s* examen *m* de ingreso; **to take entrance examinations** examinarse de ingreso
entrancing [ɛn'trænsɪŋ] o [ɛn'trɑnsɪŋ] *adj* arrebatador, encantador
entrant ['ɛntrənt] *s* entrante *mf*; (sport) concurrente *mf*
en·trap [ɛn'træp] *v* (*pret & pp* **-trapped**; *ger* **-trapping**] *tr* entrampar
entreat [ɛn'trit] *tr* rogar, suplicar
entreat·y [ɛn'triti] *s* (*pl* **-ies**) ruego, súplica
entree ['ɑntre] *s* entrada, ingreso; (culin) entrada, principio
entrench [ɛn'trɛntʃ] *tr* atrincherar || *intr* — **to entrench on o upon** infringir, violar
entrust [ɛn'trʌst] *tr* confiar
en·try ['ɛntri] *s* (*pl* **-tries**) entrada; (*item*) partida, entrada; (*in a dictionary*) artículo; (sport) concurrente *mf*
entwine [ɛn'twaɪn] *tr* entretejer, entrelazar
enumerate [ɪ'njumə,ret] o [ɪ'numə,ret] *tr* enumerar
enunciate [ɪ'nʌnsɪ,et] o [ɪ'nʌnʃɪ,et] *tr* enunciar; pronunciar
envelop [ɛn'vɛləp] *tr* envolver
envelope ['ɛnvə,lop] o ['ɑnvə,lop] *s* (*for a letter*) sobre *m*; (*wrapper*) envoltura
envenom [ɛn'vɛnəm] *tr* envenenar
enviable ['ɛnvɪ·əbəl] *adj* envidiable
envious ['ɛnvɪ·əs] *adj* envidioso
environment [ɛn'vaɪrənmənt] *s* medio ambiente; (*surroundings*) inmediaciones
environs [ɛn'vaɪrəns] *spl* inmediaciones, alrededores *mf*
envisage [ɛn'vɪzɪdʒ] *tr* (*to look in the face of*) encarar; considerar, representarse
envoi ['ɛnvɔɪ] *s* despedida (*copla al fin de una composición poética*)
envoy ['ɛnvɔɪ] *s* (*diplomatic agent*) enviado; (*short concluding stanza*) despedida
en·vy ['ɛnvi] *s* (*pl* **-vies**) envidia || *v* (*pret & pp* **-vied**) *tr* envidiar
enzyme ['ɛnzaɪm] o ['ɛnzɪm] *s* enzima *f*

epaulet o **epaulette** ['ɛpə,lɛt] *s* charretera
epenthe·sis [ɛ'pɛnθɪsɪs] *s* (*pl* **-ses** [,siz]) epéntesis *f*
epergne [ɪ'pʌrn] o [e'pɛrn] *s* ramillete *m,* centro de mesa
ephemeral [ɪ'fɛmərəl] *adj* efímero
epic ['ɛpɪk] *adj* épico || *s* epopeya
epicure ['ɛpɪ,kjʊr] *s* epicúreo
epicurean [,ɛpɪkjʊ'ri·ən] *adj & s* epicúreo
epidemic [,ɛpɪ'dɛmɪk] *adj* epidémico || *s* epidemia
epidemiology [,ɛpɪ,dimɪ'ɑlədʒi] *s* epidemiología
epidermis [,ɛpɪ'dʌrmɪs] *s* epidermis *f*
epigram ['ɛpɪ,græm] *s* epigrama *m*
epilepsy ['ɛpɪ,lɛpsi] *s* epilepsia
epileptic [,ɛpɪ'lɛptɪk] *adj & s* epiléptico
Epiphany [ɪ'pɪfəni] *s* Epifanía
Episcopalian [ɪ,pɪskə'pelɪ·ən] *adj & s* episcopalista *mf*
episode ['ɛpɪ,sod] *s* episodio
epistemology [ɪ,pɪstɪ'mɑlədʒi] *s* epistemología
epistle [ɪ'pɪsəl] *s* epístola
epitaph ['ɛpɪ,tæf] *s* epitafio
epithet ['ɛpɪ,θɛt] *s* epíteto
epitome [ɪ'pɪtəmi] *s* epítome *m;* (fig) esencia, personificación
epitomize [ɪ'pɪtə,maɪz] *tr* epitomar; (fig) encarnar, personificar
epoch ['ɛpək] o ['ipɑk] *s* época
epochal ['ɛpəkəl] *adj* memorable, trascendental
ep'och-mak'ing *adj* que hace época
equable ['ɛkwəbəl] o ['ikwəbəl] *adj* constante, uniforme; sereno
equal ['ikwəl] *adj* igual; **equal to** a la altura de || *s* igual *mf* || *v* (*pret & pp* **equaled** o **equalled;** *ger* **equaling** o **equalling**) *tr* (*to be equal to*) igualarse a o con; (*to make equal*) igualar
equali·ty [ɪ'kwɑlɪti] *s* (*pl* **-ties**) igualdad
equalize ['ikwə,laɪz] *tr* igualar; (*to make uniform*) equilibrar
equally ['ikwəli] *adv* igualmente
equanimity [,ikwə'nɪmɪti] *s* ecuanimidad, igualdad de ánimo
equate [i'kwet] *tr* poner en ecuación; considerar equivalente(s)
equation [i'kweʒən] o [i'kweʃən] *s* ecuación
equator [i'kwetər] *s* ecuador *m*
equer·ry ['ɛkwəri] o [ɪ'kwɛri] *s* (*pl* **-ries**) caballerizo
equestrian [ɪ'kwɛstrɪ·ən] *adj* ecuestre || *m* jinete *m,* caballista *m*
equilateral [,ikwɪ'lætərəl] *adj* equilátero
equilibrium [,ikwɪ'lɪbrɪ·əm] *s* equilibrio
equinoctial [,ikwɪ'nɑkʃəl] *adj* equinoccial
equinox ['ikwɪ,nɑks] *s* equinoccio
equip [ɪ'kwɪp] *v* (*pret & pp* **equipped;** *ger* **equipping**) *tr* equipar
equipment [ɪ'kwɪpmənt] *s* equipo, avíos, pertrechos; aptitud, capacidad
equipoise ['ikwɪ,pɔɪz] o ['ɛkwɪ,pɔɪz] *s* equilibrio; contrapeso || *tr* equilibrar; equipesar
equitable ['ɛkwɪtəbəl] *adj* equitativo
equi·ty ['ɛkwɪti] *s* (*pl* **-ties**) (*fairness*) equidad; valor líquido
equivalent [ɪ'kwɪvələnt] *adj & s* equivalente *m*
equivocal [ɪ'kwɪvəkəl] *adj* equívoco
equivocate [ɪ'kwɪvə,ket] *intr* usar de equívocos para engañar, mentir
equivocation [ɪ,kwɪvə'keʃən] *s* equívoco
era ['ɪrə] o ['irə] *s* era
eradicate [ɪ'rædɪ,ket] *tr* erradicar
erase [ɪ'res] *tr* borrar
eraser [ɪ'resər] *s* goma de borrar; (*for blackboard*) cepillo
erasure [ɪ'reʃər] o [ɪ'reʒər] *s* borradura, tachón *m*
ere [ɛr] *prep* antes de || *conj* antes de que; más bien que
erect [ɪ'rɛkt] *adj* derecho, enhiesto, erguido; (*hair*) erizado || *tr* (*to set in upright position*) erguir, enhestar; erigir (*un edificio*); armar, montar (*una máquina*)
erection [ɪ'rɛkʃən] *s* erección
erg [ʌrg] *s* ergio
ermine ['ʌrmɪn] *s* armiño; (fig) toga, judicatura
erode [ɪ'rod] *tr* erosionar || *intr* erosionarse
erosion [ɪ'roʒən] *s* erosión
err [ʌr] *intr* errar, equivocarse, marrar; pecar, marrar
errand ['ɛrənd] *s* mandado, recado, comisión; **to run an errand** hacer un mandado
errand boy *s* recadero, mandadero
erratic [ɪ'rætɪk] *adj* irregular, inconstante, variable; excéntrico
erra·tum [ɪ'retəm] o [ɪ'rɑtəm] *s* (*pl* **-ta** [tə]) errata
erroneous [ɪ'ronɪ·əs] *adj* erróneo
error ['ɛrər] *s* error *m*
erudite ['ɛrʊ,daɪt] o ['ɛrjʊ,daɪt] *adj* erudito
erudition [,ɛrʊ'dɪʃən] o [,ɛrjʊ'dɪʃən] *s* erudición
erupt [ɪ'rʌpt] *intr* hacer erupción (*la piel, los dientes de un niño*); erumpir (*un volcán*)
eruption [ɪ'rʌpʃən] *s* erupción
escalate ['ɛskə,let] *intr* escalarse
escalation [,ɛskə'leʃən] *s* escalada, escalación
escalator ['ɛskə,letər] *s* escalera mecánica, móvil o rodante
escallop [ɛs'kæləp] *s* concha de peregrino; (*on edge of cloth*) festón *m* || *tr* hornear a la crema y con migajas de pan; cocer (*p.ej., ostras*) en su concha; festonear
escapade [,ɛskə'ped] *s* calaverada, aventura atolondrada; (*flight*) escapada
escape [ɛs'kep] *s* (*getaway*) escape *m,* escapatoria; (*from responsibilities, duties, etc.*) escapatoria || *tr* evitar, eludir; **to escape someone** escapársele a uno; olvidársele a uno || *intr* escapar, escaparse; **to escape from**

escaparse a (*una persona*); escaparse de (*la cárcel*)
escapee [ˌɛskəˈpi] *s* evadido
escape literature *s* literatura de escape o de evasión
escapement [ɛsˈkepmənt] *s* escape *m*
escapement wheel *s* rueda de escape
escarpment [ɛsˈkɑrpmənt] *s* escarpa
eschew [ɛsˈtʃu] *tr* evitar, rehuir
escort [ˈɛskɔrt] *s* escolta; (*man or boy who accompanies a woman or girl in public*) acompañante *m*, caballero, galán *m* || [ɛsˈkɔrt] *tr* escoltar
escutcheon [ɛsˈkʌtʃən] *s* escudo de armas; (*plate in front of lock on door*) escudo, escudete *m*
Eski·mo [ˈɛskɪˌmo] *adj* esquimal || *s* (*pl* **-mos** o **-mo**) esquimal *mf*
esopha·gus [iˈsɑfəgəs] *s* (*pl* **-gi** [ˌdʒaɪ]) esófago
esp. *abbr* **especially**
espalier [ɛsˈpæljər] *s* espaldar *m*, espalera
especial [ɛsˈpɛʃəl] *adj* especial
espionage [ˈɛspɪ·ənɪdʒ] o [ˌɛspɪ·əˈnɑʒ] *s* espionaje *m*
esplanade [ˌɛspləˈned] o [ˌɛspləˈnɑd] *s* explanada
espousal [ɛsˈpaʊzəl] *s* desposorios; (*of a cause*) adhesión
espouse [ɛsˈpaʊz] *tr* casarse con; (*to advocate, adopt*) abogar por, adherirse a
Esq. *abbr* **Esquire**
esquire [ɛsˈkwaɪr] o [ˈɛskwaɪr] *s* escudero || **Esquire** *s* título de cortesía que se escribe después del apellido y que se usa en vez de **Mr.**
essay [ˈɛse] *s* ensayo
essayist [ˈɛse·ɪst] *s* ensayista *mf*
essence [ˈɛsəns] *s* esencia
essential [ɛˈsɛnʃəl] *adj* & *s* esencial *m*
est. *abbr* **established, estate, estimated**
establish [ɛsˈtæblɪʃ] *tr* establecer
establishment [ɛsˈtæblɪʃmənt] *s* establecimiento
estate [ɛsˈtet] *s* estado; situación social; (*landed property*) finca, hacienda, heredad; (*a person's possessions*) bienes *mpl*, propiedad; (*left by a decedent*) herencia, bienes relictos
esteem [ɛsˈtim] *s* estima || *tr* estimar
esthete [ˈɛsθit] *s* esteta *mf*
esthetic [ɛsˈθɛtɪk] *adj* estético || **esthetics** *ssg* estética
estimable [ˈɛstɪməbəl] *adj* estimable
estimate [ˈɛstɪˌmet] o [ˈɛstɪmɪt] *s* (*calculation of value, judgment of worth*) estimación; (*statement of cost of work to be done*) presupuesto || [ˈɛstɪˌmet] *tr* (*to judge, deem*) estimar; presupuestar (*el coste de una obra*)
estimation [ˌɛstɪˈmeʃən] *s* estimación
estrangement [ɛsˈtrendʒmənt] *s* extrañeza
estuar·y [ˈɛstʃʊˌɛri] *s* (*pl* **-ies**) estero
etc. *abbr* **et cetera**
etch [ɛtʃ] *tr* & *intr* grabar al agua fuerte
etcher [ˈɛtʃər] *s* aguafortista *mf*
etching [ˈɛtʃɪŋ] *s* aguafuerte *f*
eternal [ɪˈtʌrnəl] *adj* eterno
eterni·ty [ɪˈtʌrnɪti] *s* (*pl* **-ties**) eternidad
ether [ˈiθər] *s* éter *m*
ethereal [ɪˈθɪrɪ·əl] *adj* etéreo
ethical [ˈɛθɪkəl] *adj* ético
ethics [ˈɛθɪks] *ssg* ética
Ethiopian [ˌiθɪˈopɪ·ən] *adj* & *s* etíope *mf*
Ethiopic [ˌiθɪˈopɪk] *adj* & *s* etiópico
ethnic(al) [ˈɛθnɪk(əl)] *adj* étnico
ethnography [ɛθˈnɑgrəfi] *s* etnografía
ethnology [ɛθˈnɑlədʒi] *s* etnología
ethyl [ˈɛθɪl] *s* etilo
ethylene [ˈɛθɪˌlin] *s* etileno
etiquette [ˈɛtɪˌkɛt] *s* etiqueta
et seq. *abbr* **et sequens, et sequentes, et sequentia** (Lat) **and the following**
étude [eˈtjud] *s* (mus) estudio
etymology [ˌɛtɪˈmɑlədʒi] *s* etimología
ety·mon [ˈɛtɪˌmɑn] *s* (*pl* **-mons** o **-ma** [mə]) étimo
eucalyp·tus [ˌjukəˈlɪptəs] *s* (*pl* **-tuses** o **-ti** [taɪ]) eucalipto
Eucharist [ˈjukərɪst] *s* Eucaristía
euchre [ˈjukər] *s* juego de naipes || *tr* (coll) ser más listo que
eugenics [jʊˈdʒɛnɪks] *s* eugenesia
eulogistic [ˌjuləˈdʒɪstɪk] *adj* elogiador
eulogize [ˈjuləˌdʒaɪz] *tr* elogiar
eulo·gy [ˈjulədʒi] *s* (*pl* **-gies**) elogio
eunuch [ˈjunək] *s* eunuco
euphemism [ˈjufɪˌmɪzəm] *s* eufemismo
euphemistic [ˌjufɪˈmɪstɪk] *adj* eufemístico
euphonic [juˈfɑnɪk] *adj* eufónico
eupho·ny [ˈjufəni] *s* (*pl* **-nies**) eufonía
euphoria [juˈforɪ·ə] *s* euforia
euphuism [ˈjufjuˌɪzəm] *s* eufuísmo
euphuistic [ˌjufjuˈɪstɪk] *adj* eufuístico
Europe [ˈjʊrəp] *s* Europa
European [ˌjʊrəˈpi·ən] *adj* & *s* europeo
euthanasia [ˌjuθəˈneʒə] *s* eutanasia
evacuate [ɪˈvækjʊˌet] *tr* & *intr* evacuar
evacuation [ɪˌvækjʊˈeʃən] *s* evacuación
evade [ɪˈved] *tr* evadir || *intr* evadirse
evaluate [ɪˈvæljʊˌet] *tr* evaluar
Evangel [ɪˈvændʒəl] *s* Evangelio
evangelic(al) [ˌivænˈdʒɛlɪk(əl)] o [ˌɛvənˈdʒɛlɪk(əl)] *adj* evangélico
Evangelist [ɪˈvændʒəlɪst] *s* Evangelista *m*
evaporate [ɪˈvæpəˌret] *tr* evaporar || *intr* evaporarse
evasion [ɪˈveʒən] *s* evasión, evasiva
evasive [ɪˈvesɪv] *adj* evasivo
eve [iv] *s* víspera; **on the eve of** en vísperas de
even [ˈivən] *adj* (*smooth*) parejo, llano, liso; (*number*) par; constante, uniforme, invariable; (*temperament*) apacible, sereno; exacto, igual; **even with** al nivel de; **to be even** estar en paz; no deber nada a nadie; **to get even** desquitarse || *adv* aun, hasta; sin embargo; también; exactamente, igualmente; **even as** así como; **even if** aunque, aun cuando; **even so** aun así; **even though** aunque, aun cuando; **even when** aun cuando; **not even** ni . . . siquiera; **to break even** salir

sin ganar ni perder; (*in gambling*) salir en paz || *tr* allanar, igualar
evening [ˈivnɪŋ] *adj* vespertino || *s* tarde *f*
evening clothes *spl* traje *m* de etiqueta
evening gown *s* vestido de noche (*de mujer*)
evening primrose *s* hierba del asno
evening star *s* estrella vespertina, lucero de la tarde
evening wrap *s* salida de teatro
e'ven•song' *s* canción de la tarde; (eccl) vísperas
event [ɪˈvɛnt] *s* acontecimiento, suceso; (*outcome*) resultado; (*public function*) acto; (sport) prueba; **at all events** o **in any event** en todo caso; **in the event that** en caso que
eventful [ɪˈvɛntfəl] *adj* lleno de acontecimientos; importante, memorable
eventual [ɪˈvɛntʃʊ·əl] *adj* final
eventuali•ty [ɪˌvɛntʃʊˈælɪti] *s* (*pl* **-ties**) eventualidad
eventually [ɪˈvɛntʃʊ·əli] *adv* finalmente, con el tiempo
eventuate [ɪˈvɛntʃʊˌet] *intr* concluir, resultar
ever [ˈɛvər] *adv* (*at all times*) siempre; (*at any time*) jamás, nunca, alguna vez; **as ever** como siempre; **as much as ever** tanto como antes; **ever since** (*since that time*) desde entonces; después de que; **ever so** muy; **ever so much** muchísimo; **hardly ever** o **scarcely ever** casi nunca; **not . . . ever** no . . . nunca
ev'er•glade' *s* tierra pantanosa cubierta de hierbas altas
ev'er•green' *adj* siempre verde || *s* planta siempre verde; **evergreens** ramas colgadas como adorno
ev'er•last'ing *adj* sempiterno; (*lasting indefinitely*) duradero; (*wearisome*) aburrido, cansado || *s* eternidad; (bot) siempreviva
ev'er•more' *adv* eternamente; **for evermore** para siempre jamás
every [ˈɛvri] *adj* todos los; (*each*) cada, todo; (*being each in a series*) cada, p.ej., **every three days** cada tres días; **every bit** (coll) todo, p.ej., **every bit a man** todo un hombre; **every now and then** de vez en cuando; **every once in a while** una que otra vez; **every other day** cada dos días, un día sí y otro no; **every which way** (coll) por todas partes; (coll) en desarreglo
ev'ery•bod'y *pron indef* todo el mundo
ev'ery•day' *adj* de todos los días; cotidiano, diario; común, ordinario
every man Jack o **every mother's son** *s* cada hijo de vecino
ev'ery•one' o **every one** *pron indef* cada uno, todos, todo el mundo
ev'ery•thing' *pron indef* todo
ev'ery•where' *adv* en o por todas partes; a todas partes
evict [ɪˈvɪkt] *tr* desahuciar
eviction [ɪˈvɪkʃən] *s* desahucio
evidence [ˈɛvɪdəns] *s* evidencia; (law) prueba
evident [ˈɛvɪdənt] *adj* evidente
evil [ˈivəl] *adj* malo, malvado || *s* mal *m,* maldad
e'vil•do'er *s* malhechor *m,* malvado
e'vil•do'ing *s* malhecho, maldad
evil eye *s* mal *m* de ojo
evil-minded [ˈivəlˈmaɪndɪd] *adj* mal pensado, malintencionado
Evil One, the el enemigo malo
evince [ɪˈvɪns] *tr* manifestar, mostrar
evoke [ɪˈvok] *tr* evocar
evolution [ˌɛvəˈluʃən] *s* evolución; (math) extracción de raíces, radicación
evolve [ɪˈvɑlv] *tr* desarrollar; desprender (*olores, gases, calor*) || *intr* evolucionar
ewe [ju] *s* oveja
ewer [ˈju·ər] *s* aguamaril *m*
ex. *abbr* **examination, example, except, exchange, executive**
ex [ɛks] *prep* sin incluir, sin participación en
exact [ɛgˈzækt] *adj* exacto || *tr* exigir
exacting [ɛgˈzæktɪŋ] *adj* exigente
exaction [ɛgˈzækʃən] *s* exacción
exactly [ɛgˈzæktli] *adv* exactamente; (*sharp, on the dot*) en punto
exactness [ɛgˈzæktnɪs] *s* exactitud
exaggerate [ɛgˈzædʒəˌret] *tr* exagerar
exalt [ɛgˈzɔlt] *tr* exaltar, ensalzar
exam [ɛgˈzæm] *s* (coll) examen *m*
examination [ɛgˌzæmɪˈneʃən] *s* examen *m;* **to take an examination** sufrir un examen, examinarse
examine [ɛgˈzæmɪn] *tr* examinar
example [ɛgˈzæmpəl] o [ɛgˈzɑmpəl] *s* ejemplo; (*case serving as a warning to others*) ejemplar *m;* (*of mathematics*) problema *m;* **for example** por ejemplo
exasperate [ɛgˈzæspəˌret] *tr* exasperar
excavate [ˈɛkskəˌvet] *tr* excavar
exceed [ɛkˈsid] *tr* exceder; sobrepasar (*p.ej., el límite de velocidad*)
exceedingly [ɛkˈsidɪŋli] *adv* sumamente, sobremanera
ex•cel [ɛkˈsɛl] *v* (*pret & pp* **-celled;** *ger* **-celling**) *tr* aventajar || *intr* sobresalir
excellence [ˈɛksələns] *s* excelencia
excellen•cy [ˈɛksələnsi] *s* (*pl* **-cies**) excelencia; **Your Excellency** Su Excelencia
excelsior [ɛkˈsɛlsɪ·ər] *s* pajilla de madera, virutas de madera
except [ɛkˈsɛpt] *prep* excepto; **except for** sin; **except that** a menos que || *tr* exceptuar
exception [ɛkˈsɛpʃən] *s* excepción; **to take exception** poner reparos, objetar; ofenderse; **with the exception of** a excepción de
exceptional [ɛkˈsɛpʃənəl] *adj* excepcional
excerpt [ˈɛksʌrpt] o [ɛkˈsʌrpt] *s* excerta, selección || [ɛkˈsʌrpt] *tr* escoger
excess [ˈɛksɛs] o [ɛkˈsɛs] *adj* excedente, sobrante || [ɛkˈsɛs] *s* (*amount or degree by which one thing exceeds another*) exceso, excedente *m;* (*excessive amount; immoderate indulgence, unlawful conduct*) exceso; **in excess of** más que, superior a

excess baggage *s* exceso de equipaje
excess fare *s* suplemento
excessive [ɛk'sɛsɪv] *adj* excesivo
ex'cess-prof'its tax *s* impuesto sobre beneficios extraordinarios
excess weight *s* exceso de peso
exchange [ɛks'tʃendʒ] *s* (*of greetings, compliments, blows, etc.*) cambio; (*of prisoners, merchandise, newspapers, credentials, etc.*) canje *m;* periódico de canje; (*place for buying and selling*) bolsa, lonja; estación telefónica, central *f* de teléfonos; **in exchange for** en cambio de, a trueque de ‖ *tr* cambiar; canjear (*prisioneros, mercancías, etc.*); darse, hacerse (*cortesías*); **to exchange greetings** saludarse; **to exchange shots** cambiar disparos
exchequer [ɛks'tʃɛkər] o ['ɛkstʃɛkər] *s* tesorería; fondos nacionales
excise tax [ɛk'saɪz] o ['ɛksaɪz] *m* impuesto sobre ciertas mercancías de comercio interior
excitable [ɛk'saɪtəbəl] *adj* excitable
excite [ɛk'saɪt] *tr* excitar
excitement [ɛk'saɪtmənt] *s* excitación
exciting [ɛk'saɪtɪŋ] *adj* emocionante, conmovedor; (*stimulating*) excitante
exclaim [ɛks'klem] *tr & intr* exclamar
exclamation [ˌɛksklə'meʃən] *s* exclamación
exclamation mark o **point** *s* punto de admiración
exclude [ɛks'klud] *tr* excluir
exclusion [ɛks'kluʒən] *s* exclusión; **to the exclusion of** con exclusión de
exclusive [ɛks'klusɪv] *adj* exclusivo; (*clannish*) exclusivista; (*expensive*) (coll) carero; (*fashionable*) (coll) muy de moda; **exclusive of** con exclusión de
excommunicate [ˌɛkskə'mjunɪˌket] *tr* excomulgar
excommunication [ˌɛkskəˌmjunɪ'keʃən] *s* excomunión
excoriate [ɛks'korɪˌet] *tr* (fig) desollar, vituperar
excrement ['ɛkskrəmənt] *s* excremento
excruciating [ɛks'kruʃɪˌetɪŋ] *adj* atroz, agudísimo, vivísimo
exculpate ['ɛkskʌlˌpet] o [ɛks'kʌlpet] *tr* exculpar
excursion [ɛks'kʌrʒən] o [ɛks'kʌrʃən] *s* excursión
excursionist [ɛks'kʌrʒənɪst] o [ɛks'kʌrʃənɪst] *s* excursionista *mf*
excusable [ɛks'kjusəbəl] *adj* excusable
excuse [ɛks'kjus] *s* excusa ‖ [ɛks'kjuz] *tr* excusar, disculpar; dispensar, perdonar
execute ['ɛksɪˌkjut] *tr* ejecutar; (law) celebrar, finalizar (*una escritura*)
execution [ˌɛksɪ'kjuʃən] *s* ejecución
executioner [ˌɛksɪ'kjuʃənər] *s* ejecutor *m* de la justicia, verdugo
executive [ɛg'zɛkjətɪv] *adj* ejecutivo ‖ *m* poder ejecutivo; (*of a school, business, etc.*) dirigente *mf*
Executive Mansion *s* (U.S.A.) palacio presidencial
executor [ɛg'zɛkjətər] *s* albacea *m,* ejecutor testamentario
executrix [ɛg'zɛkjətrɪks] *s* albacea *f,* ejecutora testamentaria
exemplary [ɛg'zɛmpləri] o ['ɛgzəmˌplɛri] *adj* ejemplar
exempli·fy [ɛg'zɛmplɪˌfaɪ] *v* (*pret & pp* **-fied**) *tr* ejemplificar
exempt [ɛg'zɛmpt] *adj* exento ‖ *tr* eximir, exentar
exemption [ɛg'zɛmpʃən] *s* exención
exercise ['ɛksərˌsaɪz] *s* ejercicio; ceremonia; **to take exercise** hacer ejercicio ‖ *tr* ejercer (*p.ej., caridad, influencia*); ejercitar (*un arte, profesión, etc.; adiestrar con el ejercicio*); inquietar, preocupar; poner (*cuidado*) ‖ *ref* ejercitarse
exert [ɛg'zʌrt] *tr* ejercer (*una fuerza*); **to exert oneself** esforzarse
exertion [ɛg'zʌrʃən] *s* esfuerzo, empeño; (*active use*) ejercicio
exhalation [ˌɛks·hə'leʃən] *s* (*of gas, vapors, etc.*) exhalación; (*of air from lungs*) espiración
exhale [ɛks'hel] o [ɛg'zel] *tr* exhalar (*gases, vapores*); espirar (*el aire aspirado*) ‖ *intr* exhalarse; espirar
exhaust [ɛg'zɔst] *s* escape *m;* tubo de escape ‖ *tr* (*to wear out, fatigue; to use up*) agotar; hacer el vacío en; apurar (*todos los medios*)
exhaust fan *s* ventilador *m* aspirador
exhaustion [ɛg'zɔstʃən] *s* agotamiento
exhaustive [ɛg'zɔstɪv] *adj* exhaustivo; comprensivo
exhaust manifold *s* múltiple *m* de escape
exhaust pipe *s* tubo de escape
exhaust valve *s* válvula de escape
exhibit [ɛg'zɪbɪt] *s* exhibición; (law) documento de prueba ‖ *tr* exhibir
exhibition [ˌɛksɪ'bɪʃən] *s* exhibición
exhibitor [ɛg'zɪbɪtər] *s* expositor *m*
exhilarating [ɛg'zɪləˌretɪŋ] *adj* alegrador, regocijador, alborozador
exhort [ɛg'zɔrt] *tr* exhortar
exhume [ɛks'hjum] o [ɛg'zjum] *tr* exhumar
exigen·cy ['ɛksɪdʒənsi] *s* (*pl* **-cies**) exigencia
exigent ['ɛksɪdʒənt] *adj* exigente
exile ['ɛgzaɪl] o ['ɛksaɪl] *s* destierro; (*person*) desterrado ‖ *tr* desterrar
exist [ɛg'zɪst] *intr* existir
existence [ɛg'zɪstəns] *s* existencia
existing [ɛg'zɪstɪŋ] *adj* existente
exit ['ɛgzɪt] o ['ɛksɪt] *s* salida ‖ *intr* salir
exodus ['ɛksədəs] *s* éxodo
exonerate [ɛg'zɑnəˌret] *tr* (*to free from blame*) exculpar; (*to free from an obligation*) exonerar
exorbitant [ɛg'zɔrbɪtənt] *adj* exorbitante
exorcise ['ɛksɔrˌsaɪz] *tr* exorcizar
exotic [ɛg'zɑtɪk] *adj* exótico
exp. *abbr* **expenses, expired, export, express**
expand [ɛks'pænd] *tr* dilatar (*un gas, el metal*); (*to enlarge, develop*) ampliar, ensanchar; (*to unfold, stretch out*) desplegar, extender; (math) desarrollar (*una ecuación*) ‖ *intr*

dilatarse; ampliarse, **ensancharse;** desplegarse, extenderse
expanse [ɛks'pæns] *s* extensión
expansion [ɛks'pænʃən] *s* expansión
expansive [ɛks'pænsɪv] *adj* expansivo
expatiate [ɛks'peʃɪ,et] *intr* espaciarse, explayarse
expatriate [ɛks'petrɪ·ɪt] *adj & s* expatriado
expect [ɛks'pɛkt] *tr* esperar; (coll) creer, suponer
expectan·cy [ɛks'pɛktənsi] *s* (*pl* **-cies**) expectación
expectant mother [ɛks'pɛktənt] *s* futura madre
expectation [,ɛkspɛk'teʃən] *s* expectativa
expectorate [ɛks'pɛktə,ret] *tr & intr* expectorar
expedien·cy [ɛks'pidɪ·ənsi] *s* (*pl* **-cies**) conveniencia, oportunidad; ventaja personal
expedient [ɛks'pidɪ·ənt] *adj* conveniente, oportuno; egoísta, ventajoso; (*acting with self-interest*) ventajista || *s* expediente *m*
expedite ['ɛkspɪ,daɪt] *tr* apresurar, despachar; dar curso a (*un documento*)
expedition [,ɛkspɪ'dɪʃən] *s* expedición
expeditious [,ɛkspɪ'dɪʃəs] *adj* expeditivo
expeditiously [,ɛkspɪ'dɪʃəsli] *adv* ejecutivamente
ex·pel [ɛks'pɛl] *v* (*pret & pp* **-pelled;** *ger* **-pelling**) *tr* expeler, expulsar
expend [ɛks'pɛnd] *tr* gastar, consumir
expendable [ɛks'pɛndəbəl] *adj* gastable; (*to be thrown away after use*) desechable; (*soldier*) sacrificable
expenditure [ɛks'pɛndɪtʃər] *s* gasto, consumo
expense [ɛks'pɛns] *s* gasto; **expenses** gastos, expensas; **to go to the expense of** meterse en gastos con; **to meet expenses** hacer frente a los gastos
expense account *s* cuenta de gastos
expensive [ɛks'pɛnsɪv] *adj* caro, costoso, dispendioso; (*charging high prices*) carero
experience [ɛks'pɪrɪ·əns] *s* experiencia || *tr* experimentar
experienced [ɛks'pɪrɪ·ənst] *adj* experimentado
experiment [ɛks'pɛrɪmənt] *s* experiencia, experimento || [ɛks'perɪ,mɛnt] *intr* experimentar
expert ['ɛkspərt] *adj & s* experto
expiate ['ɛkspɪ,et] *tr* expiar
expiation [,ɛkspɪ'eʃən] *s* expiación
expire [ɛks'paɪr] *tr* expeler (*el aire de los pulmones*) || *intr* expirar (*expeler el aire de los pulmones; acabarse, p.ej., un plazo; fallecer*)
explain [ɛks'plen] *tr* explicar; **to explain away** descartar con explicaciones; (*to make excuse for*) explicar || *intr* explicar, explicarse
explanation [,ɛksplə'neʃən] *s* explicación
explanatory [ɛks'plænə,tori] *adj* explicativo
explicit [ɛks'plɪsɪt] *adj* explícito
explode [ɛks'plod] *tr* volar, hacer saltar; desacreditar (*una teoría*) || *intr* explotar, estallar, reventar
exploit [ɛks'plɔɪt] o ['ɛksplɔɪt] *s* hazaña, proeza || [ɛks'plɔɪt] *tr* explotar
exploitation [,ɛksplɔɪ'teʃən] *s* explotación
exploration [,ɛksplə'reʃən] *s* exploración
explore [ɛks'plor] *tr* explorar
explorer [ɛks'plorər] *s* explorador *m*
explosion [ɛks'ploʒən] *s* explosión; (*of a theory*) refutación
explosive [ɛks'plosɪv] *adj* explosivo || *s* explosivo; (phonet) explosiva
exponent [ɛks'ponənt] *s* exponente *m,* expositor *m;* (math) exponente *m*
export ['ɛksport] *adj* de exportación || *s* exportación; **exports** (*articles exported*) exportación || [ɛks'port] o ['ɛksport] *tr & intr* exportar
exportation [,ɛkspor'teʃən] *s* exportación
exporter ['ɛksportər] o [ɛks'portər] *s* exportador *m*
expose [ɛks'poz] *tr* exponer; (*to unmask*) desenmascarar; (*the Host*) manifestar, exponer; (phot) impresionar
exposé [,ɛkspo'ze] *s* desenmascaramiento
exposition [,ɛkspə'zɪʃən] *s* exposición; (rhet) exposición
expostulate [ɛks'pɑstʃə,let] *intr* protestar; **to expostulate with** reconvenir
exposure [ɛks'poʒər] *s* (*to a danger; position with respect to points of compass*) exposición; (*unmasking*) desenmascaramiento; (phot) exposición
expound [ɛks'paʊnd] *tr* exponer
express [ɛks'prɛs] *adj* expreso || *adv* (*for a special purpose*) expresamente; por expreso || *s* expreso; **by express** (rr) en gran velocidad || *tr* expresar; (*to squeeze out*) exprimir; enviar por expreso; **to express oneself** expresarse
express company *s* compañía de transportes rápidos
expression [ɛks'prɛʃən] *s* expresión
expressive [ɛks'prɛsɪv] *adj* expresivo
expressly [ɛks'prɛsli] *adv* expresamente
express·man [ɛks'prɛsmən] *s* (*pl* **-men** [mən]) (U.S.A.) empleado del servicio de transportes rápidos
express train *s* tren expreso
express'way' *s* carretera de vía libre
expropriate [ɛks'proprɪ,et] *tr* expropiar
expulsion [ɛks'pʌlʃən] *s* expulsión
expunge [ɛks'pʌndʒ] *tr* borrar, cancelar, arrasar
expurgate ['ɛkspər,get] *tr* expurgar
exquisite ['ɛkskwɪzɪt] o [ɛks'kwɪzɪt] *adj* exquisito; agudo, vivo; sensible
ex-service·man [,ɛks'sʌrvɪs,mæn] *s* (*pl* **-men** [,mɛn]) ex militar *m,* **ex** combatiente *m*

extant ['ɛkstənt] o [ɛks'tænt] *adj* existente
extemporaneous [ɛks,tɛmpə'renɪ·əs] *adj* sin preparación; (*made for the occasion*) provisional
extempore [ɛks'tɛmpəri] *adj* improvisado || *adv* improvisadamente
extemporize [ɛks'tɛmpə,raɪz] *tr & intr* improvisar
extend [ɛks'tɛnd] *tr* extender; dar, ofrecer; hacer extensivos (*p.ej., vivos deseos*); prorrogar (*un plazo*) || *intr* extenderse
extended [ɛks'tɛndɪd] *adj* extenso; prolongado
extension [ɛks'tɛnʃən] *s* extensión; prolongación
extension ladder *s* escalera extensible
extension table *s* mesa de extensión
extensive [ɛks'tɛnsɪv] *adj* (*having great extent*) extenso; (*characterized by extension*) extensivo
extent [ɛks'tɛnt] *s* extensión; **to a certain extent** hasta cierto punto; **to a great extent** en sumo grado; **to the full extent** en toda su extensión
extenuate [ɛks'tɛnjʊ,et] *tr* (*to make seem less serious*) atenuar; (*to underrate*) menospreciar, no dar importancia a
exterior [ɛks'tɪrɪ·ər] *adj & s* exterior *m*
exterminate [ɛks'tʌrmɪ,net] *tr* exterminar
external [ɛks'tʌrnəl] *adj* externo || **externals** *spl* exterioridad
extinct [ɛks'tɪŋkt] *adj* desaparecido; (*volcano*) extinto
extinguish [ɛks'tɪŋgwɪʃ] *tr* extinguir
extinguisher [ɛks'tɪŋgwɪʃər] *s* apagador *m*, extintor *m*
extirpate ['ɛkstər,pet] o [ɛks'tʌrpet] *tr* extirpar
ex·tol [ɛks'tol] o [ɛks'tɑl] *v* (*pret & pp* **-tolled**; *ger* **-tolling**) *tr* ensalzar
extort [ɛks'tɔrt] *tr* obtener por amenazas, fuerza o engaño
extortion [ɛks'tɔrʃən] *s* extorción
extra ['ɛkstrə] *adj* extra; (*spare*) de repuesto || *adv* extraordinariamente || *s* (*of a newspaper*) extra *m;* pieza de repuesto; (*something additional*) extra *m;* (theat) extra *mf*
extract ['ɛkstrækt] *s* selección; (pharm) extracto || [ɛks'trækt] *tr* (*to pull out, remove*) extraer; seleccionar (*pasajes de un libro*); (math) extraer
extraction [ɛks'trækʃən] *s* extracción
extracurricular [,ɛkstrəkə'rɪkjələr] *adj* extracurricular
extradition [,ɛkstrə'dɪʃən] *s* extradición
extra fare *s* recargo de tarifa, tarifa recargada
ex'tra-flat' *adj* extraplano
extramural [,ɛkstrə'mjurəl] *adj* extramural
extraneous [ɛks'trenɪ·əs] *adj* ajeno, extraño
extraordinary [,ɛkstrə'ɔrdɪ,nɛri] o [ɛks'trɔrdɪ,nɛri] *adj* extraordinario
extrapolate [ɛks'træpə,let] *tr & intr* extrapolar
extrasensory [,ɛkstrə'sɛnsəri] *adj* extrasensorio
extravagance [ɛks'trævəgəns] *s* derroche *m*, prodigalidad, gasto excesivo; (*wildness, folly*) extravagancia
extravagant [ɛks'trævəgənt] *adj* derrochador, pródigo, gastador; (*wild, foolish*) extravagante
extreme [ɛks'trim] *adj & s* extremo; **in the extreme** en sumo grado; **to go to extremes** excederse, propasarse
extremely [ɛks'trimli] *adv* extremadamente, sumamente
extreme unction *s* extremaunción
extremi·ty [ɛks'trɛmɪti] *s* (*pl* **-ties**) extremidad; (*great want*) extrema necesidad; **extremities** medidas extremas; (*hands and feet*) extremidades
extricate ['ɛkstrɪ,ket] *tr* desembarazar, desenredar
extrinsic [ɛks'trɪnsɪk] *adj* extrínseco
extrovert ['ɛkstrə,vʌrt] *s* extrovertido
extrude [ɛks'trud] *intr* resaltar, sobresalir
exuberant [ɛg'zubərənt] o [ɛg'zjubərənt] *adj* exuberante
exude [ɛg'zud] o [ɛk'sud] *tr & intr* exudar
exult [ɛg'zʌlt] *intr* exultar, gloriarse
exultant [ɛg'zʌltənt] *adj* exultante
eye [aɪ] *s* ojo; (*of hook and eye*) hembra, corcheta; **to catch one's eye** llamar la atención a uno; **to feast one's eyes on** deleitar la vista en; **to lay eyes on** alcanzar a ver; **to make eyes at** hacer guiños a; **to roll one's eyes** poner los ojos en blanco; **to see eye to eye** estar completamente de acuerdo; **to shut one's eyes to** hacer la vista gorda ante; **without batting an eye** sin pestañear, sin inmutarse || *v* (*pret & pp* **eyed**; *ger* **eying** o **eyeing**) *tr* ojear; **to eye up and down** mirar de hito en hito
eye'ball' *s* globo del ojo
eye'bolt' *s* armella, cáncamo
eye'brow' *s* ceja; **to raise one's eyebrows** arquear las cejas
eye'cup' *s* ojera, lavaojos *m*
eyeful ['aɪful] *s* (coll) buena ojeada
eye'glass' *s* (*of optical instrument*) ocular *m;* (*eyecup*) ojera, lavaojos *m;* **eyeglasses** gafas, anteojos
eye'lash' *s* pestaña
eyelet ['aɪlɪt] *s* ojete *m*, ojal *m;* (*hole to look through*) mirilla
eye'lid' *s* párpado
eye of the morning *s* sol *m*
eye opener ['opənər] *s* noticia asombrosa o inesperada; (coll) trago de licor
eye'piece' *s* ocular *m*
eye'-shade' *s* visera
eye shadow *s* crema para los párpados
eye'shot' *s* alcance *m* de la vista
eye'sight' *s* vista; (*range*) alcance *m* de la vista
eye socket *s* cuenca del ojo
eye'sore' *s* cosa que ofende la vista
eye'strain' *s* vista fatigada
eye'-test' chart *s* escala tipográfica oftalmométrica, tipo de ensayo, tipo de prueba

eye'tooth' *s* (*pl* **teeth'**) colmillo, diente canino; **to cut one's eyeteeth** (coll) tener el colmillo retorcido; **to give one's eyeteeth for** (coll) dar los ojos de la cara por

eye'wash' *s* colirio; (slang) halago para engañar

eye'wit'ness *s* testigo ocular, testigo presencial

ey·rie o **ey·ry** ['ɛri] *s* (*pl* **-ries**) nido de águilas, nido de aves de rapiña; (fig) altura, morada elevada

F

F, f [ɛf] sexta letra del alfabeto inglés

f. *abbr* **feminine, folio**

F. *abbr* **Fahrenheit, Friday**

fable ['febəl] *s* fábula

fabric ['fæbrɪk] *s* tejido; textura; (*structure*) fábrica

fabricate ['fæbrɪ,ket] *tr* fabricar

fabrication [,fæbrɪ'keʃən] *s* fabricación; mentira

fabulous ['fæbjələs] *adj* fabuloso

façade [fə'sɑd] *s* fachada

face [fes] *s* cara, rostro; (*of cloth*) haz *f;* (*of earth*) faz *f;* (*grimace*) mueca; (*of watch*) esfera, muestra; (*impudence*) descaro; **in the face of** en presencia de; **to keep a straight face** contener la risa; **to lose face** desprestigiarse; **to save face** salvar las apariencias; **to show one's face** dejarse ver || *tr* volver la cara hacia; arrostrar; revestir (*un muro*); forrar (*un vestido*); **facing** cara a || *intr* — **to face about** volver la mirada; dar media vuelta; cambiar de opinión; **to face on** dar a o sobre; **to face up to** encararse con

face card *s* figura, naipe *m* de figura

face lifting *s* cirugía estética

face powder *s* polvos de tocador

facet ['fæsɪt] *s* faceta

facial ['feʃəl] *adj* facial || *s* masaje *m* facial

facilitate [fə'sɪlɪ,tet] *tr* facilitar

facili·ty [fə'sɪlɪti] *s* (*pl* **-ties**) facilidad

facing ['fesɪŋ] *s* revestimiento, paramento

facsimile [fæk'sɪmɪli] *s* facsímile *m*

fact [fækt] *s* hecho; **in fact** en realidad; **the fact is that** ello es que

faction ['fækʃən] *s* facción; discordia

factional ['fækʃənəl] *adj* faccionario

factionalism ['fækʃənə,lɪzəm] *s* parcialidad, partidismo

factor ['fæktər] *s* factor *m* || *tr* descomponer en factores

facto·ry ['fæktəri] *s* (*pl* **-ries**) fábrica

factual ['fæktʃʊ·əl] *adj* verdadero, objetivo

facul·ty ['fækəlti] *s* (*pl* **-ties**) facultad

fad [fæd] *s* afición pasajera, moda pasajera

fade [fed] *tr* desteñir || *intr* desteñir, desteñirse; apagarse (*un sonido*); (rad) desvanecerse

fade'out' *s* desaparición gradual; (rad) desvanecimiento

fag [fæg] *s* (*drudge*) yunque *m;* (coll) cigarrillo || *tr* — **to fag out** cansar

fagot ['fægət] *s* haz *m* de leña

fail [fel] *s* — **without fail** sin falta || *tr* faltar a; reprobar, suspender (*a un alumno*); salir mal en (*un examen*) || *intr* malograrse, fracasar; salir mal (*un alumno*); fallar (*un motor*); (com) quebrar, hacer bancarrota; **to fail to** dejar de

failure ['feljər] *s* malogro, fracaso, mal éxito; (*student*) perdigón *m;* (com) quiebra

faint [fent] *adj* débil; **to feel faint** sentirse desfallecido || *s* desmayo || *intr* desmayarse

faint-hearted ['fent'hɑrtɪd] *adj* cobarde, tímido, apocado

fair [fɛr] *adj* justo, imparcial; regular, ordinario; favorable, propicio; (*hair*) rubio; (*complexion*) blanco; (*sky*) despejado; (*weather*) bueno, bonancible || *adv* imparcialmente; **to play fair** jugar limpio || *s* (*exhibition*) feria; (*carnival*) quermese *m,* verbena

fair'ground' *s* real *m,* campo de una feria

fairly ['fɛrli] *adv* justamente; bastante

fair-minded ['fɛr'maɪndɪd] *adj* justo, imparcial

fairness ['fɛrnɪs] *s* justicia, imparcialidad; (*of weather*) serenidad; (*of complexion*) blancura

fair play *s* juego limpio, limpieza

fair sex *s* bello sexo

fair to middling *adj* bastante bueno, mediano

fair'weath'er *adj* — **a fair-weather friend** amigo del buen viento

fair·y ['fɛri] *adj* feérico || *s* (*pl* **-ies**) hada

fairy godmother *s* hada madrina

fair'y·land' *s* tierra de las hadas

fairy ring *s* corro de brujas

fairy tale *s* cuento de hadas; (fig) bella poesía

faith [feθ] *s* fe *f;* **to break faith with** faltar a la palabra dada a; **to keep faith with** cumplir la palabra dada a; **to pin one's faith on** tener puesta su esperanza en; **upon my faith!** ¡a fe mía!

faithful ['feθfəl] *adj* fiel, leal || **the faithful** los fieles

faithless ['feθlɪs] *adj* infiel, desleal

fake [fek] *adj* (coll) falso, fingido || *s* impostura, patraña; (*person*) farsante *mf* || *tr & intr* falsificar, fingir

faker ['fekər] *s* (coll) impostor *m,* patrañero; (*peddler*) (coll) buhonero

falcon ['fɔkən] o ['fɔlkən] *s* halcón *m*

falconer ['fɔkənər] o ['fɔlkənər] *s* cetrero, halconero
falconry ['fɔkənri] o ['fɔlkənri] *s* cetrería, halconería
fall [fɔl] *adj* otoñal || *s* caída; (*of water*) catarata, salto de agua; (*of prices*) baja; (*autumn*) otoño; **falls** catarata, caída de agua || *v* (*pret* **fell** [fɛl]; *pp* **fallen** ['fɔlən]) *intr* caer, caerse; **to fall apart** caerse a pedazos; **to fall back** (mil) replegarse; **to fall behind** quedarse atrás; **to fall down** caerse; **to fall due** vencer (*una letra*); **to fall flat** caer tendido; no tener éxito; **to fall for** (slang) ser engañado por; (slang) enamorarse de; **to fall in** desplomarse (*un techo*); ponerse de acuerdo; **to fall in with** trabar amistades con; ponerse de acuerdo con; **to fall off** caer de; disminuir; **to fall out** desavenirse; **to fall out of** caerse de; **to fall out with** esquinarse con; **to fall over** caerse; (coll) adular, halagar; **to fall through** fracasar, malograrse; **to fall to** recaer (*la herencia, la elección*) en; **to fall under** estar comprendido en
fallacious [fə'leʃəs] *adj* erróneo, engañoso
falla·cy ['fæləsi] *s* (*pl* **-cies**) error *m*, equivocación
fall guy *s* (slang) cabeza de turco
fallible ['fælɪbəl] *adj* falible
falling star *s* estrella fugaz
fall'out' *s* caída radiactiva, precipitación radiactiva
fallout shelter *s* refugio antiatómico
fallow ['fælo] *adj* barbechado; **to lie fallow** estar en barbecho (*tierra labrantía*); (fig) quedar sin emplear, quedar sin ejecutar (*una cosa provechosa*) || *s* barbecho || *tr* barbechar
false [fɔls] *adj* falso; (*hair, teeth, etc.*) postizo || *adv* falsamente; **to play false** traicionar
false colors *spl* pretextos falsos
false face *s* mascarilla; (*ugly false face*) carantamaula
false-hearted ['fɔls'hɑrtɪd] *adj* pérfido
falsehood ['fɔls·hʊd] *s* falsedad
false pretenses *spl* impostura, falsas apariencias
false return *s* declaración falsa
falset·to [fɔl'sɛto] *s* (*pl* **-tos**) (*voice*) falsete *m;* (*person*) falsetista *m*
falsi·fy ['fɔlsɪ,faɪ] *v* (*pret & pp* **-fied**) *tr* falsificar; (*to disprove*) refutar || *intr* falsificar; mentir
falsi·ty ['fɔlsɪti] *s* (*pl* **-ties**) falsedad
falter ['fɔltər] *s* vacilación; (*in speech*) balbuceo || *intr* vacilar; balbucear
fame [fem] *s* fama
famed [femd] *adj* afamado
familiar [fə'mɪljər] *adj* familiar; conocido; común; **familiar with** familiarizado con
familiari·ty [fə,mɪlɪ'ærɪti] *s* (*pl* **-ties**) familiaridad; conocimiento
familiarize [fə'mɪljə,raɪz] *tr* familiarizar
fami·ly ['fæmɪli] *adj* familiar; **in the family way** (coll) en estado de buena esperanza || *s* (*pl* **-lies**) familia
family man *s* padre *m* de familia; hombre casero
family name *s* apellido
family physician *s* médico de cabecera
family tree *s* árbol genealógico
famish ['fæmɪʃ] *tr & intr* hambrear
famished ['fæmɪʃt] *adj* famélico
famous ['feməs] *adj* famoso; (*notable, excellent*) (coll) famoso
fan [fæn] *s* abanico; ventilador *m;* (slang) hincha *mf,* aficionado || *v* (*pret & pp* **fanned;** *ger* **fanning**) *tr* abanicar; (*to winnow*) aventar; ahuyentar con abanico; avivar (*el fuego*); excitar (*las pasiones*); (slang) azotar || *intr* abanicarse; **to fan out** salir (*un camino*) en todas direcciones
fanatic [fə'nætɪk] *adj & s* fanático
fanatical [fə'nætɪkəl] *adj* fanático
fanaticism [fə'nætɪ,sɪzəm] *s* fanatismo
fancied ['fænsid] *adj* imaginario
fancier ['fænsɪ·ər] *s* aficionado; visionario; (*of animals*) criador aficionado
fanciful ['fænsɪfəl] *adj* fantástico, extravagante; imaginativo
fan·cy ['fænsi] *adj* (*comp* **-cier;** *super* **-ciest**) de fantasía, de imitación; fino, de lujo, precioso; ornamental; primoroso; fantástico, extravagante || *s* (*pl* **-cies**) fantasía; afición, gusto; **to take a fancy to** aficionarse a, prendarse de || *v* (*pret & pp* **-cied**) *tr* imaginar
fancy ball *s* baile *m* de trajes
fancy dive *s* salto ornamental
fancy dress *s* traje *m* de fantasía
fancy foods *spl* comestibles *mpl* de lujo
fan'cy-free' *adj* libre del poder del amor
fancy jewelry *s* joyas de fantasía
fancy skating *s* patinaje *m* de fantasía
fan'cy·work' *s* (sew) labor *f*
fanfare ['fænfɛr] *s* fanfarria
fang [fæŋ] *s* colmillo; (*of reptile*) diente *m*
fan'light' *s* abanico
fantastic(al) [fæn'tæstɪk(əl)] *adj* fantástico
fanta·sy ['fæntəzi] o ['fæntəsi] *s* (*pl* **-sies**) fantasía
far [fɑr] *adj* lejano; **on the far side of** del otro lado de || *adv* lejos; **as far as** hasta; en cuanto; **as far as I am concerned** por lo que a mí me toca; **as far as I know** que yo sepa; **by far** con mucho; **far and near** por todas partes; **far away** muy lejos; **far be it from me** no lo permita Dios; **far better** mucho mejor; **far different** muy diferente; **far from** lejos de; **far from it** ni con mucho; **far into** hasta muy adentro de; hasta muy tarde de; **far more** mucho más; **far off** a gran distancia; **how far** cuán lejos; **how far is it?** ¿cuánto hay de aquí?; **in so far as** en cuanto; **thus far** hasta ahora; **thus far this year** en lo que va del año; **to go far towards** contribuir mucho a
faraway ['fɑrə,we] *adj* lejano, distante; abstraído, preocupado

farce [fɑrs] *s* farsa
farcical ['fɑrsɪkəl] *adj* ridículo
fare [fɛr] *s* pasaje *m;* pasajero; alimento; comida; **to collect fares** cobrar el pasaje || *intr* pasarlo, p.ej., **how did you fare?** ¿cómo lo pasó Vd.?
Far East *s* Extremo Oriente, Lejano Oriente
fare'well' *s* despedida; **to bid farewell to** o **to take farewell of** despedirse de || *interj* ¡adiós!
far-fetched ['fɑr'fɛtʃt] *adj* traído por los pelos
far-flung ['fɑr'flʌŋ] *adj* de gran alcance, vasto
farm [fɑrm] *adj* agrícola; agropecuario || *s* granja; terreno agrícola || *tr* cultivar, labrar (*la tierra*) || *intr* cultivar la tierra y criar animales
farmer ['fɑrmər] *s* granjero; agricultor *m,* labrador *m*
farm hand *s* peón *m,* mozo de granja
farm'house' *s* alquería, cortijo
farming ['fɑrmɪŋ] *s* agricultura, labranza
farm'yard' *s* corral *m* de granja
far'-off' *adj* lejano, distante
far-reaching ['fɑr'ritʃɪŋ] *adj* de mucho alcance
far-sighted ['fɑr'saɪtɪd] *adj* longividente; precavido; présbita
farther ['fɑrðər] *adj* más lejano; adicional || *adv* más lejos, más allá; además, también; **farther on** más adelante
farthest ['fɑrðɪst] *adj* (el) más lejano; último || *adv* más lejos; más
farthing ['fɑrðɪŋ] *s* (Brit) cuarto de penique
Far West *s* (U.S.A.) Lejano Oeste
fascinate ['fæsɪ,net] *tr* fascinar
fascinating ['fæsɪ,netɪŋ] *adj* fascinante, cautivador
fascism ['fæsɪzəm] *s* fascismo
fascist ['fæsɪst] *adj & s* fascista *mf*
fashion ['fæʃən] *s* moda, boga; estilo, manera; alta sociedad; **after a fashion** en cierto modo; **in fashion** de moda; **out of fashion** fuera de moda; **to go out of fashion** pasar de moda || *tr* labrar, forjar
fashion designing *s* alta costura
fashion plate *s* figurín *m;* (*person*) (coll) figurín *m,* elegante *mf;* **to be a fashion plate** (coll) ir hecho un maniquí
fashion show *s* desfile *m* de modas
fast [fæst] o [fɑst] *adj* rápido, veloz; (*clock*) adelantado; fijado; disipado; (*friend*) fiel || *adv* aprisa, rápidamente; firmemente; (*asleep*) profundamente; **to hold fast** mantenerse firme; **to live fast** vivir de una manera disipada || *s* ayuno; **to break one's fast** romper el ayuno || *intr* ayunar
fast day *s* día *m* de ayuno
fasten ['fæsən] o ['fɑsən] *tr* fijar; atar; abrochar; cerrar con llave; (*one's belt*) ajustarse; (*blame*) aplicar || *intr* fijarse
fastener ['fæsənər] o ['fɑsənər] *s* asilla; (*snap, clasp*) cierre *m;* (*for papers*) sujetapapeles *m*
fastidious [fæs'tɪdɪ·əs] *adj* esquilmoso, quisquilloso, descontentadizo
fasting ['fæstɪŋ] o ['fɑstɪŋ] *s* ayuno
fat [fæt] *adj* (*comp* **fatter;** *super* **fattest**) gordo; poderoso; opulento; (*profitable*) pingüe; (*spark*) caliente; **to get fat** engordar || *s* grasa; (*suet*) gordo, sebo
fatal ['fetəl] *adj* fatal
fatalism ['fetə,lɪzəm] *s* fatalismo
fatalist ['fetəlɪst] *s* fatalista *mf*
fatali·ty [fə'tælɪti] *s* (*pl* **-ties**) fatalidad; (*in accidents, war, etc.*) muerte *f*
fate [fet] *s* sino, hado; **the Fates** las Parcas || *tr* condenar, predestinar
fated ['fetɪd] *adj* hadado, predestinado
fateful ['fetfəl] *adj* fatídico; fatal
fat'head' *s* (coll) tronco, estúpido
father ['fɑðər] *s* padre *m;* (*an elderly man*) (coll) tío || *tr* servir de padre a; engendrar; inventar
fatherhood ['fɑðər,hʊd] *s* paternidad
fa'ther-in-law' *s* (*pl* **fathers-in-law**) suegro
fa'ther·land' *s* patria
fatherless ['fɑðərlɪs] *adj* huérfano de padre, sin padre
fatherly ['fɑðərli] *adj* paternal
Father's Day *s* día *m* del padre
Father Time *s* el Tiempo
fathom ['fæðəm] *s* braza || *tr* sondear; profundizar
fathomless ['fæðəmlɪs] *adj* insondable
fatigue [fə'tig] *s* fatiga; (mil) faena || *tr* fatigar, cansar
fatigue clothes *spl* (mil) traje *m* de faena
fatigue duty *s* faena
fatten ['fætən] *tr & intr* engordar
fat·ty ['fæti] *adj* (*comp* **-tier;** *super* **-tiest**) graso; (pathol) grasoso; (*chubby*) (coll) gordiflón || *s* (*pl* **-ties**) (coll) gordiflón *m*
fatuous ['fætʃʊ·əs] *adj* fatuo; irreal, ilusivo
faucet ['fɔsɪt] *s* grifo
fault [fɔlt] *s* (*misdeed, blame*) culpa; (*defect*) falta; (geol) falla; (sport) falta; **it's your fault** Vd. tiene la culpa; **to a fault** excesivamente; **to find fault with** culpar, echar la culpa a; hallar defecto en
fault'find'er *s* criticón *m,* reparón *m*
fault'find'ing *adj* criticón, reparón || *s* manía de criticar
faultless ['fɔltlɪs] *adj* perfecto, impecable
fault·y ['fɔlti] *adj* (*comp* **-ier;** *super* **-iest**) defectuoso, imperfecto
faun [fɔn] *s* fauno
fauna ['fɔnə] *s* fauna
favor ['fevər] *s* favor *m;* (*letter*) atenta, grata; **do me the favor to** hágame Vd. el favor de; **by your favor** con permiso de Vd.; **favors** regalos de fiesta, objetos de cotillón; **to be in favor with** disfrutar del favor de; **to be out of favor** caer en desgracia || *tr* favorecer; (coll) parecerse a

favorable ['fevərəbəl] *adj* favorable
favorite ['fevərɪt] *adj & s* favorito
favoritism ['fevərɪ,tɪzəm] *s* favoritismo
fawn [fɔn] *s* cervato || *intr* — **to fawn on** adular servilmente; hacer fiestas a
faze [fez] *tr* (coll) molestar, desanimar
FBI [,ɛf,bi'aɪ] *s* (letterword) **Federal Bureau of Investigation**
fear [fɪr] *s* miedo; **for fear of** por miedo de, por temor de; **for fear that** por miedo (de) que; **no fear** no hay peligro; **to be in fear of** tener miedo de || *tr & intr* temer
fearful ['fɪrfəl] *adj* medroso; (coll) enorme, muy malo
fearless ['fɪrlɪs] *adj* arrojado, intrépido
feasible [fisɪbəl] *adj* factible, viable
feast [fist] *s* fiesta; (*sumptuous meal*) festín *m*, banquete *m* || *tr & intr* banquetear; **to feast on** regalarse con
feat [fit] *s* hazaña, proeza
feather ['fɛðər] *s* pluma; (*plume; arrogance*) penacho; clase *f*, género; **in fine feather** de buen humor; en buena salud || *tr* emplumar; (carp) machihembrar; **to feather one's nest** hacer todo para enriquecerse
feather bed *s* colchón *m* de plumas; (*comfortable situation*) lecho de plumas
feath'er•bed'ding *s* empleo de más obreros de lo necesario (*exigido por los sindicatos*)
feath'er•brain' *s* cascabelero
feath'er•edge' *s* (*of board*) bisel *m;* (*of sharpened tool*) filván *m*
feathery ['fɛðəri] *adj* plumoso
feature ['fitʃər] *s* facción; característica, rasgo distintivo; película principal; artículo principal; **features** facciones || *tr* delinear; ofrecer como cosa principal; (coll) destacar, hacer resaltar
feature writer *s* articulista *mf*
February ['fɛbru,ɛri] *s* febrero
feces ['fisiz] *spl* heces *fpl*
feckless ['fɛklɪs] *adj* abatido, sin valor; débil
federal ['fɛdərəl] *adj & s* federal *mf*
federate ['fɛdə,ret] *adj* federado || *tr* federar || *intr* federarse
federation [,fɛdə'reʃən] *s* federación
fedora [fɪ'dorə] *s* sombrero de fieltro suave con ala vuelta
fed up [fɛd] *adj* harto
fee [fi] *s* honorarios; (*for admission, tuition, etc.*) cuota, precio; (*tip*) propina || *tr* pagar; dar propina a
feeble ['fibəl] *adj* débil
feeble-minded ['fibəl'maɪndɪd] *adj* imbécil; irresoluto, vacilante
feed [fid] *s* alimento, comida; (mach) dispositivo de alimentación || *v* (*pret & pp* **fed** [fɛd]) *tr* alimentar || *intr* alimentarse
feed'back' *s* regeneración, realimentación
feed bag *s* cebadera, morral *m*
feed pump *s* bomba de alimentación
feed trough *s* comedero
feed wire *s* (elec) conductor *m* de alimentación
feel [fil] *s* sensación; (*sense of what is right*) tino || *v* (*pret & pp* **felt** [fɛlt]) *tr* sentir; (*e.g., with the hands*) palpar, tentar; tomar (*el pulso*); tantear (*el camino*) || *intr* (*sick, tired, etc.*) sentirse; palpar; **to feel bad** sentirse mal; condolerse; **to feel cheap** avergonzarse; **to feel comfortable** sentirse a gusto; **to feel for** buscar tentando; condolerse de; **to feel like** tener ganas de; **to feel safe** sentirse a salvo; **to feel sorry** sentir; arrepentirse; **to feel sorry for** compadecer; arrepentirse de
feeler ['filər] *s* (*something said to draw someone out*) buscapié *m*, tranquilla; **feelers** (*of insect*) anténulas, palpos; (*of mollusk*) tentáculos
feeling ['filɪŋ] *s* (*with senses*) sensación; (*impression, emotion*) sentimiento; presentimiento; parecer *m*
feign [fen] *tr* aparentar, fingir || *intr* fingir; **to feign to be** fingirse
feint [fent] *s* (*threat*) finta; (*of fencer*) pase *m*, treta || *intr* hacer una finta
feldspar ['fɛld,spɑr] *s* feldespato
felicitate [fə'lɪsɪ,tet] *tr* felicitar
felicitous [fə'lɪsɪtəs] *adj* (*opportune*) feliz; elocuente
fell [fɛl] *adj* cruel, feroz, mortal || *tr* talar (*árboles*)
felloe ['fɛlo] *s* aro de la rueda; (*part of this*) pina
fellow ['fɛlo] *s* (coll) mozo, tipo, sujeto; (coll) pretendiente *m;* prójimo; (*of a society*) socio, miembro; (*holder of fellowship*) pensionista *mf*
fellow being *s* prójimo
fellow citizen *s* conciudadano
fellow countryman *s* compatriota *mf*
fellow man *s* prójimo
fellow member *s* consocio
fellowship ['fɛlo,ʃɪp] *s* compañerismo; (*for study*) pensión
fellow traveler *s* compañero de viaje
felon ['fɛlən] *s* delincuente *mf* de mayor cuantía; (pathol) panadizo
felo•ny ['fɛləni] *s* (*pl* **-nies**) delito de mayor cuantía; **to compound a felony** aceptar dinero para no procesar
felt [fɛlt] *s* fieltro
female ['fimel] *adj* (*sex*) femenino; (*animal, plant, piece of a device*) hembra || *s* hembra
feminine ['fɛmɪnɪn] *adj & s* femenino
feminism ['fɛmɪ,nɪzəm] *s* feminismo
fen [fɛn] *s* pantano
fence [fɛns] *s* cerca, cercado; (*for stolen goods*) alcahuete *m;* (*of a saw*) guía; **on the fence** (coll) indeciso || *tr* cercar || *intr* esgrimir
fencing ['fɛnsɪŋ] *s* (*art*) esgrima; (*act*) esgrimidura
fencing academy *s* escuela de esgrima
fend [fɛnd] *tr* — **to fend off** apartar, resguardarse de || *intr* — **to fend for oneself** (coll) tirar por su lado
fender ['fɛndər] *s* (*mudguard*) guardafango, guardabarros *m;* (*of locomotive*) quitapiedras *m;* (*of trolley car*)

salvavidas *m;* (*of fireplace*) guardafuego
fennel [ˈfɛnəl] *s* hinojo
ferment [ˈfʌrmɛnt] *s* fermento; fermentación || [fərˈmɛnt] *tr & intr* fermentar
fern [fʌrn] *s* helecho
ferocious [fəˈroʃəs] *adj* feroz
feroci·ty [fəˈrɑsɪti] *s* (*pl* **-ties**) ferocidad
ferret [ˈfɛrɪt] *s* hurón *m* || *tr* — **to ferret out** huronear || *intr* huronear
Ferris wheel [ˈfɛrɪs] *s* rueda de feria, noria
fer·ry [ˈfɛri] *s* (*pl* **-ries**) bote *m* de paso, ferry-boat *m* || *v* (*pret & pp* **-ried**) *tr* pasar (*viajeros, mercancías*) a través del río || *intr* cruzar el río en barco
fer'ry·boat' *s* bote *m* de paso, ferry-boat *m*
fertile [ˈfʌrtɪl] *adj* fértil
fertilize [ˈfʌrtɪˌlaɪz] *tr* abonar, fertilizar; (*to impregnate*) fecundar
fervid [ˈfʌrvɪd] *adj* férvido, vehemente
fervor [ˈfʌrvər] *s* fervor *m*
fervent [ˈfʌrvənt] *adj* ferviente, fervoroso
fester [ˈfɛstər] *s* úlcera || *tr* enconar || *intr* enconarse (*una herida; el ánimo de uno*)
festival [ˈfɛstɪvəl] *adj* festivo || *s* fiesta; (*of music*) festival *m*
festive [ˈfɛstɪv] *adj* festivo
festivi·ty [fɛsˈtɪvɪti] *s* (*pl* **-ties**) festividad
festoon [fɛsˈtun] *s* festón *m* || *tr* festonear
fetch [fɛtʃ] *tr* ir por, hacer venir, traer; venderse a, venderse por
fetching [ˈfɛtʃɪŋ] *adj* (coll) encantador, atractivo
fete [fet] *s* fiesta || *tr* festejar
fetid [ˈfɛtɪd] o [ˈfitɪd] *adj* fétido
fetish [ˈfitɪʃ] o [ˈfɛtɪʃ] *s* fetiche *m*
fetlock [ˈfɛtlɑk] *s* espolón *m;* (*tuft of hair*) cerneja
fetter [ˈfɛtər] *s* grillete *m*, grillo || *tr* engrillar; impedir
fettle [ˈfɛtəl] *s* estado, condición; **in fine fettle** en buena condición
fetus [ˈfitəs] *s* feto
feud [fjud] *s* odio hereditario, enemistad de larga duración
feudal [ˈfjudəl] *adj* feudal
feudalism [ˈfjudəˌlɪzəm] *s* feudalismo
fever [ˈfivər] *s* fiebre *f*, calentura
fever blister *s* escupidura, fuegos en los labios
feverish [ˈfivərɪʃ] *adj* febril, calenturiento
few [fju] *adj & pron* pocos, no muchos; **a few** unos pocos, unos cuantos; **quite a few** muchos
fiancé [ˌfi·ɑnˈse] *s* novio, prometido
fiancée [ˌfi·ɑnˈse] *s* novia, prometida
fias·co [fɪˈæsko] *s* (*pl* **-cos** o **-coes**) fiasco
fib [fɪb] *s* mentirilla || *v* (*pret & pp* **fibbed;** *ger* **fibbing**) *intr* decir mentirillas
fiber [ˈfaɪbər] *s* fibra; carácter *m*, índole *f*
fibrous [ˈfaɪbrəs] *adj* fibroso
fickle [ˈfɪkəl] *adj* inconstante, veleidoso
fiction [ˈfɪkʃən] *s* (*invention*) ficción; (*branch of literature*) novelística; **pure fiction!** ¡puro cuento!
fictional [ˈfɪkʃənəl] *adj* novelesco
fictionalize [ˈfɪkʃənəˌlaɪz] *tr* novelizar
fictitious [fɪkˈtɪʃəs] *adj* ficticio
fiddle [ˈfɪdəl] *s* violín *m* || *tr* tocar (*un aire*) con el violín; **to fiddle away** (coll) malgastar || *intr* tocar el violín; **to fiddle with** manosear
fiddler [ˈfɪdlər] *s* (coll) violinista *mf*
fiddling [ˈfɪdlɪŋ] *adj* (coll) despreciable, insignificante
fideli·ty [faɪˈdɛlɪti] o [fɪˈdɛlɪti] *s* (*pl* **-ties**) fidelidad
fidget [ˈfɪdʒɪt] *intr* agitarse, menearse; **to fidget with** manosear
fidgety [ˈfɪdʒɪti] *adj* inquieto, nervioso
fiduciar·y [fɪˈdjuʃɪˌɛri] o [fɪˈduʃɪˌɛri] *adj* fiduciario || *s* (*pl* **-ies**) fiduciario
fie [faɪ] *interj* ¡qué vergüenza!
fief [fif] *s* feudo
field [fild] *adj* (mil) de campaña || *s* campo; (*sown with grain*) sembrado; (baseball) jardín *m;* (elec) campo magnético; (*of motor or dynamo*) (elec) inductor *m*
fielder [ˈfildər] *s* (baseball) jardinero
field glasses *spl* gemelos de campo
field hockey *s* hockey *m* sobre hierba
field magnet *s* imán *m* inductor
field marshal *s* (mil) mariscal *m* de campo
field'piece' *s* cañón *m* de campaña
fiend [find] *s* diablo; (*person*) fiera; **to be a fiend for** ser una fiera para
fiendish [ˈfindɪʃ] *adj* diabólico
fierce [fɪrs] *adj* feroz, fiero; (*wind*) furioso; (coll) muy malo
fierceness [ˈfɪrsnɪs] *s* ferocidad, fiereza; furia
fier·y [ˈfaɪri] o [ˈfaɪ·əri] *adj* (*comp* **-ier;** *super* **-iest**) ardiente, caliente; brioso
fife [faɪf] *s* pífano
fifteen [ˈfɪfˈtin] *adj, pron & s* quince *m*
fifteenth [ˈfɪfˈtinθ] *adj & s* (*in a series*) decimoquinto; (*part*) quinzavo || *s* (*in dates*) quince *m*
fifth [fɪfθ] *adj & s* quinto || *s* (*in dates*) cinco
fifth column *s* quinta columna
fifth columnist *s* quintacolumnista *mf*
fiftieth [ˈfɪftɪ·ɪθ] *adj & s* (*in a series*) quincuagésimo; (*part*) cincuentavo
fif·ty [ˈfɪfti] *adj & pron* cincuenta || *s* (*pl* **-ties**) cincuenta *m*
fif'ty-fif'ty *adv* — **to go fifty-fifty** (coll) ir a medias
fig. *abbr* **figure, figuratively**
fig [fɪg] *s* higo, breva; (*tree*) higuera; (*merest trifle*) bledo
fight [faɪt] *s* lucha, pelea; ánimo, brío; **to pick a fight with** meterse con, buscar la lengua a || *tr* luchar con; dar (*batalla*); lidiar (*al toro*) || *intr* luchar, pelear; **to fight shy of** tratar de evitar

fighter ['faɪtər] *s* luchador *m,* peleador *m;* (*warrior*) combatiente *m;* (*game person*) porfiador *m;* (aer) avión *m* de combate, caza *m*
fig leaf *s* hoja de higuera; (*on statues*) hoja de parra
figment ['fɪgmənt] *s* ficción, invención
figurative ['fɪgjərətɪv] *adj* figurado; (*representing by a likeness*) figurativo
figure ['fɪgjər] *s* figura; (*bodily form*) talle *m;* precio; **to be good at figures** ser listo en aritmética; **to cut a figure** hacer figura; **to have a good figure** tener buen tipo; **to keep one's figure** conservar la línea || *tr* adornar con figuras; figurarse, imaginar; suponer, calcular; **to figure out** descifrar || *intr* figurar; **to figure on** contar con
fig'ure·head' *s* (naut) figurón *m* de proa, mascarón *m* de proa; (*straw man*) testaferro
figure of speech *s* figura retórica
figure skating *s* patinaje artístico
figurine [ˌfɪgjə'rin] *s* figurilla, figurina
filament ['fɪləmənt] *s* filamento
filch [fɪltʃ] *tr* birlar, ratear
file [faɪl] *s* fila, hilera; (*tool*) lima; (*collection of papers*) archivo; (*cabinet*) archivador *m,* fichero || *tr* poner en fila; limar; archivar, clasificar; anotar || *intr* desfilar; **to file for** solicitar
file case *s* fichero
file clerk *s* fichador *m*
filet [fɪ'le] o ['fɪle] *s* filete *m* || *tr* cortar en filetes
filial ['fɪlɪ·əl] o ['fɪljəl] *adj* filial
filiation [ˌfɪlɪ'eʃən] *s* filiación
filibuster ['fɪlɪˌbʌstər] *s* obstrucción (*de la aprobación de una ley*); obstruccionista *mf;* (*buccaneer*) filibustero || *tr* obstruir (*la aprobación de una ley*)
filigree ['fɪlɪˌgri] *adj* afiligranado || *s* filigrana || *tr* afiligranar
filing ['faɪlɪŋ] *s* (*of documents*) clasificación; limadura; **filings** limadura, limalla
filing cabinet *s* archivador *m,* clasificador *m*
filing card *s* ficha
Filipi·no [ˌfɪlɪ'pino] *adj* filipino || *s* (*pl* **-nos**) filipino
fill [fɪl] *s* (*sufficiency*) hartazgo; (*place filled with earth*) terraplén *m;* **to have** o **get one's fill of** darse un hartazgo de || *tr* llenar; rellenar; despachar (*un pedido*); tapar (*un agujero*); empastar (*un diente*); inflar (*un neumático*); llenar, ocupar (*un puesto*); colmar (*lagunas*); **to fill out** llenar (*un formulario*) || *intr* llenarse; rellenarse; **to fill in** hacer de suplente; **to fill up** ahogarse de emoción
filler ['fɪlər] *s* relleno; (*of cigar*) tripa; (*sizing*) aparejo; (*in a writing*) relleno
fillet ['fɪlɪt] *s* cinta, tira; (*for hair*) prendedero; (archit, bb) filete *m* || *tr* filetear || ['fɪle] o ['fɪlɪt] *s* (*of meat or fish*) filete *m* || *tr* cortar en filetes
filling ['fɪlɪŋ] *s* (*of a tooth*) empaste *m;* (*e.g., of a turkey*) relleno; (*of cigar*) tripa
filling station *s* estación gasolinera
fillip ['fɪlɪp] *s* aguijón *m,* estímulo; (*with finger*) capirotazo
fil·ly ['fɪli] *s* (*pl* **-lies**) potra; (coll) muchacha retozona
film [fɪlm] *s* película; (mov) película, film *m;* (phot) película || *tr* filmar
film star *s* estrella de la pantalla
film strip *s* tira proyectable
film·y ['fɪlmi] *adj* (*comp* **-ier;** *super* **-iest**) delgadísimo, diáfano, sutil
filter ['fɪltər] *s* filtro || *tr* filtrar || *intr* filtrarse
filtering ['fɪltərɪŋ] *s* filtración
filter paper *s* papel *m* filtrante
filter tip *s* embocadura de filtro
filth [fɪlθ] *s* suciedad, porquería
filth·y ['fɪlθi] *adj* (*comp* **-ier;** *super* **-iest**) sucio, puerco
filthy lucre ['lukər] *s* (coll) el vil metal (*dinero, raíz de muchos males*)
filtrate ['fɪltret] *s* filtrado || *tr* filtrar || *intr* filtrarse
fin. *abbr* **finance**
fin [fɪn] *s* aleta
final ['faɪnəl] *adj* final; (*last in a series*) último; decisivo, terminante || *s* examen *m* final; **finals** (sport) final *f*
finale [fɪ'nɑli] *s* (mus) final *m*
finalist ['faɪnəlɪst] *s* finalista *mf*
finally ['faɪnəli] *adv* finalmente, por último
finance [fɪ'næns] o ['faɪnæns] *s* financiación; **finances** finanzas || *tr* financiar
financial [fɪ'nænʃəl] o [faɪ'nænʃəl] *adj* financiero
financier [ˌfɪnən'sɪr] o [ˌfaɪnən'sɪr] *s* financiero
financing [fɪ'nænsɪŋ] o ['faɪnænsɪŋ] *s* financiación
finch [fɪntʃ] *s* pinzón *m*
find [faɪnd] *s* hallazgo || *v* (*pret & pp* **found** [faʊnd]) *tr* hallar, encontrar; **to find out** averiguar, darse cuenta de || *intr* (*law*) pronunciar fallo; **to find out about** informarse de
finder ['faɪndər] *s* (*of camera*) visor *m;* (*of microscope*) portaobjeto cuadriculado
finding ['faɪndɪŋ] *s* descubrimiento; (law) laudo, fallo
fine [faɪn] *adj* fino; (*weather*) bueno; divertido || *adv* (coll) muy bien; **to feel fine** (coll) sentirse muy bien de salud || *s* multa || *tr* multar
fine arts *spl* bellas artes
fineness *s* fineza; (*of metal*) ley *f*
fine print *s* letra menuda, tipo menudo
finer·y ['faɪnəri] *s* (*pl* **-ies**) adorno, galas, atavíos
fine-spun ['faɪnˌspʌn] *adj* estirado en hilo finísimo; (fig) alambicado
finesse [fɪ'nɛs] *s* sutileza; (*in bridge*) impás *m* || *tr* hacer el impás con || *intr* hacer un impás
fine-toothed comb ['faɪnˌtuθt] *s* len-

drera, peine *m* de púas finas; **to go over with a fine-toothed comb** escudriñar minuciosamente
finger ['fɪŋgər] *s* dedo; **to burn one's fingers** cogerse los dedos; **to put one's finger on the spot** poner el dedo en la llaga; **to slip between the fingers** irse de entre los dedos; **to snap one's fingers at** tratar con desprecio; **to twist around one's little finger** manejar a su gusto || *tr* manosear; (slang) acechar, espiar; (slang) identificar
finger board *s* (*of guitar*) diapasón *m;* (*of piano*) teclado
finger bowl *s* lavadedos *m,* lavafrutas *m*
finger dexterity *s* (mus) dedeo
fingering ['fɪŋgərɪŋ] *s* manoseo; (mus) digitación
fin'ger•nail' *s* uña
fingernail polish *s* esmalte *m* para las uñas
fin'ger•print' *s* huella digital, dactilograma *m* || *tr* tomar las huellas digitales de
finger tip *s* punta del dedo; **to have at one's finger tips** tener en la punta de los dedos, saber al dedillo
finial ['fɪnɪ•əl] *s* florón *m*
finical ['fɪnɪkəl] o **finicky** ['fɪnɪki] *adj* delicado, melindroso
finish ['fɪnɪʃ] *s* acabado; fin *m,* conclusión || *tr* acabar; **to be finished** estar listo || *intr* acabar; **to finish** + *ger* acabar de + *inf;* **to finish by** + *ger* acabar por + *inf*
finishing nail *s* puntilla francesa
finishing school *s* escuela particular de educación social para señoritas
finishing touch *s* toque *m* final, última mano
finite ['faɪnaɪt] *adj* finito
finite verb *s* forma verbal flexional
Finland ['fɪnlənd] *s* Finlandia
Finlander ['fɪnləndər] *s* finlandés *m*
Finn [fɪn] *s* (*member of a Finnish-speaking group of people*) finés *m;* (*native or inhabitant of Finland*) finlandés *m*
Finnish ['fɪnɪʃ] *adj* finlandés || *s* (*language*) finlandés *m*
fir [fʌr] *s* abeto
fire [faɪr] *s* fuego; (*destructive burning*) incendio; **through fire and water** a trancos y barrancos; **to be on fire** estar ardiendo; **to be under enemy fire** estar expuesto al fuego del enemigo; **to catch fire** encenderse; **to hang fire** estar en suspensión; **to open fire** abrir fuego, romper el fuego; **to set on fire, to set fire to** pegar fuego a; **under fire** bajo el fuego del enemigo; acusado, inculpado || *interj* (mil) ¡fuego! || *tr* encender; calentar (*el horno*); cocer (*ladrillos*); disparar (*un arma de fuego*); pegar (*un tiro*); excitar (*la imaginación*); (coll) despedir (*a un empleado*) || *intr* encenderse; **to fire on** hacer fuego sobre; **to fire up** cargar el horno; calentar el horno
fire alarm *s* alarma de incendios, avisador *m* de incendios; **to sound the fire alarm** tocar a fuego
fire'arm' *s* arma de fuego
fire'ball' *s* bola de fuego; (*lightning*) rayo en bola
fire'bird' *s* cacique veranero
fire'boat' *s* buque *m* con mangueras para incendios
fire'box' *s* caja de fuego, fogón *m*
fire'brand' *s* tizón *m;* (*hothead*) botafuego
fire'break' *s* raya
fire'brick' *s* ladrillo refractario
fire brigade *s* cuerpo de bomberos
fire'bug' *s* (coll) incendiario
fire company *s* cuerpo de bomberos; compañía de seguros
fire'crack'er *s* triquitraque *m*
fire'damp' *s* grisú *m,* mofeta
fire department *s* servicio de bomberos
fire'dog' *s* morillo
fire drill *s* ejercicio para caso de incendio
fire engine *s* coche *m* bomba, bomba de incendios, motobomba
fire escape *s* escalera de salvamento
fire extinguisher *s* extintor *m,* apagafuegos *m*
fire'fly' *s* (*pl* **-flies**) luciérnaga
fire'guard' *s* guardafuego
fire hose *s* manguera para incendios
fire'house' *s* cuartel *m* de bomberos, estación de incendios
fire hydrant *s* boca de incendio
fire insurance *s* seguro contra incendios
fire irons *spl* badil *m* y tenazas
fireless cooker ['faɪrlɪs] *s* cocinilla sin fuego
fire•man ['faɪrmən] *s* (*pl* **-men** [mən]) (*man who stokes fires*) fogonero; (*man who extinguishes fires*) bombero
fire'place' *s* chimenea, chimenea francesa
fire plug *s* boca de agua
fire power *s* (mil) potencia de fuego
fire'proof' *adj* incombustible || *tr* hacer incombustible
fire sale *s* venta de mercancías averiadas en un incendio
fire screen *s* pantalla de chimenea
fire ship *s* brulote *m*
fire shovel *s* badil *m*
fire'side' *s* hogar *m*
fire'trap' *s* edificio sin medios adecuados de escape en caso de incendio
fire wall *s* cortafuego
fire'ward'en *s* vigía *m* de incendios
fire'wa'ter *s* aguardiente *m*
fire'wood' *s* leña
fire'works' *spl* fuegos artificiales
firing ['faɪrɪŋ] *s* encendimiento; (*of bricks*) cocción; (*of a gun*) disparo; (*of soldiers*) tiroteo; (*of an internal-combustion engine*) encendido; (*of an employee*) (coll) despedida
firing line *s* línea de fuego, frente *m* de batalla
firing order *s* (aut) orden *m* del encendido
firing squad *s* (*for saluting at a burial*)

piquete *m* de salvas; (*for executing*) pelotón *m* de fusilamiento, piquete *m* de ejecución
firm [fʌrm] *adj* firme || *s* empresa, casa comercial
firmament [ˈfʌrməmənt] *s* firmamento
firm name *s* razón *f* social
firmness [ˈfʌrmnɪs] *s* firmeza
first [fʌrst] *adj* primero || *adv* primero; **first of all** ante todo || *s* primero; (aut) primera (velocidad); (mus) voz *f* principal; **at first** al principio; en primer lugar; **from the first** desde el principio
first aid *s* cura de urgencia, primeros auxilios
first′-aid′ kit *s* botiquín *m*, equipo de urgencia
first-aid station *s* puesto de socorro, puesto de primera intención
first′-born′ *adj* & *s* primogénito
first′-class′ *adj* de primera, de primera clase || *adv* en primera clase
first cousin *s* primo hermano
first draft *s* borrador *m*
first finger *s* dedo índice, dedo mostrador
first floor *s* piso bajo
first fruits *spl* primicia
first lieutenant *s* teniente
firstly [ˈfʌrstli] *adv* en primer lugar
first mate *s* (naut) piloto
first name *s* nombre *m* de pila
first night *s* (theat) noche *f* de estreno
first′-night′er *s* (theat) estrenista *mf*
first officer *s* (naut) piloto
first quarter *s* cuarto creciente (*de la luna*)
first′-rate′ *adj* de primer orden; (coll) excelente || *adv* (coll) muy bien
first′-run′ house *s* teatro de estreno
fiscal [ˈfɪskəl] *adj* (*pertaining to public treasury*) fiscal; económico || *s* (*public prosecutor*) fiscal *m*
fiscal year *s* año económico, ejercicio
fish [fɪʃ] *s* pez *m;* (*that has been caught, that is ready to eat*) pescado; **to be like a fish out of water** estar como gallina en corral ajeno; **to be neither fish nor fowl** no ser carne ni pescado; **to drink like a fish** beber como una topinera, beber como una esponja || *tr* pescar || *intr* pescar; **to fish for compliments** buscar alabanzas; **to go fishing** ir de pesca; **to take fishing** llevar de pesca
fish′bone′ *s* espina de pez
fish bowl *s* pecera
fisher [ˈfɪʃər] *s* pescador *m;* embarcación de pesca; (zool) marta del Canadá
fisher•man [ˈfɪʃərmən] *s* (*pl* **-men** [mən]) pescador *m;* barco pesquero
fisher•y [ˈfɪʃəri] *s* (*pl* **-ies**) (*activity*) pesca; (*business*) pesquería; (*grounds*) pesquera
fish glue *s* cola de pescado
fish hawk *s* halieto
fish′hook′ *s* anzuelo
fishing [ˈfɪʃɪŋ] *adj* pesquero || *s* pesca
fishing ground *s* pesquería, pesquera
fishing reel *s* carrete *m*
fishing rod *s* caña de pescar
fishing tackle *s* aparejo de pescar, avíos de pescar
fishing torch *s* candelero
fish line *s* sedal *m*
fish market *s* pescadería
fish′plate′ *s* (rr) eclisa
fish′pool′ *s* piscina
fish spear *s* fisga
fish story *s* (coll) andaluzada, patraña; **to tell fish stories** (coll) mentir por la barba
fish′tail′ *s* (aer) coleadura || *intr* (aer) colear
fish′wife′ *s* (*pl* **-wives** [ˌwaɪvz]) pescadera; (*foul-mouthed woman*) verdulera
fish′worm′ *s* lombriz *f* de tierra (*cebo para pescar*)
fish•y [ˈfɪʃi] *adj* (*comp* **-ier;** *super* **-iest**) que huele o sabe a pescado; (coll) dudoso, inverosímil
fission [ˈfɪʃən] *s* (biol) escisión; (phys) fisión
fissionable [ˈfɪʃənəbəl] *adj* fisionable
fissure [ˈfɪʃər] *s* hendidura, grieta; (anat, min) fisura
fist [fɪst] *s* puño; (typ) manecilla; **to shake one's fist at** amenazar con el puño
fist fight *s* pelea con los puños
fisticuff [ˈfɪstɪˌkʌf] *s* puñetazo; **fisticuffs** pelea a puñetazos
fit [fɪt] *adj* (*comp* **-fitter;** *super* **-fittest**) apropiado, conveniente; apto; sano; **fit to be tied** (coll) impaciente, encolerizado; **fit to eat** bueno de comer; **to feel fit** gozar de buena salud; **to see fit** juzgar conveniente || *s* ajuste *m*, talle *m;* (*of one piece with another*) encaje *m;* (*of coughing*) acceso, ataque *m;* (*of anger*) arranque *m;* **by fits and starts** intermitentemente || *v* (*pret* & *pp* **-fitted;** *ger* **fitting**) *tr* ajustar, entallar; cuadrar, sentar; encajar; cuadrar con (*p.ej., las señas de una persona*); equipar, preparar; servir para; estar de acuerdo con (*p.ej., los hechos*); **to fit out** o **up** pertrechar || *intr* ajustar; encajar; sentar; **to fit in** caber en; encajar en
fitful [ˈfɪtfəl] *adj* caprichoso; intermitente, vacilante
fitness [ˈfɪtnɪs] *s* conveniencia; aptitud; tempestividad; buena salud
fitter [ˈfɪtər] *s* ajustador *m;* (*of machinery*) montador *m;* (*of clothing*) probador *m*
fitting [ˈfɪtɪŋ] *adj* apropiado, conveniente, justo || *s* ajuste *m;* encaje *m;* (*of a garment*) prueba; tubo de ajuste; **fittings** accesorios, avíos; (*iron trimmings*) herraje *m*
five [faɪv] *adj* & *pron* cinco || *s* cinco; **five o'clock** las cinco
five hundred *adj* & *pron* quinientos || *s* quinientos *m*
five′-year′ plan *s* plan *m* quinquenal
fix [fɪks] *s* — **in a tight fix** (coll) en calzas prietas; **to be in a fix** (coll) hallarse en un aprieto || *tr* arreglar, componer, reparar; fijar (*una fecha;*

los cabellos; una imagen fotográfica; los precios; la atención; una hora, una cita); calar (*la bayoneta*); (coll) desquitarse con; (pol) muñir || *intr* fijarse; **to fix on** decidir, escoger
fixed [fɪkst] *adj* fijo
fixing ['fɪksɪŋ] *adj* fijador || *s* (*fastening*) fijación; (phot) fijado
fixing bath *s* fijador *m*
fixture ['fɪkstʃər] *s* accesorio, artefacto; (*of a lamp*) guarnición; **fixtures** (*e.g., of a store*) instalaciones
fizz [fɪz] *s* ruido sibilante; bebida gaseosa; (Brit) champaña || *intr* hacer un ruido sibilante
fizzle ['fɪzəl] *s* (coll) fracaso || *intr* chisporrotear débilmente; (coll) fracasar
fl. *abbr* **flourished, fluid**
flabbergast ['flæbər,gæst] *tr* (coll) dejar sin habla, dejar estupefacto
flab•by ['flæbi] *adj* (*comp* **-bier;** *super* **-biest**) flojo, lacio
flag [flæg] *s* bandera || *v* (*pret & pp* **flagged;** *ger* **flagging**) *tr* hacer señal a (*una persona*) con una bandera; hacer señal de parada a (*un tren*) || *intr* aflojar, flaquear
flag captain *s* (nav) capitán *m* de bandera
flageolet [,flædʒə'lɛt] *s* chirimía, dulzaina
flag•man ['flægmən] *s* (*pl* **-men** [mən]) (rr) guardafrenos *m;* (rr) guardavía *m*
flag of truce *s* bandera de parlamento
flag'pole' *s* asta de bandera; (surv) jalón *m*
flagrant ['flegrənt] *adj* enorme, escandaloso
flag'ship' *s* (nav) capitana
flag'staff' *s* asta de bandera
flag'stone' *s* losa
flag stop *s* (rr) apeadero
flail [flel] *s* mayal *m* || *tr* golpear con mayal; golpear, azotar
flair [flɛr] *s* instinto, perspicacia
flak [flæk] *s* fuego antiaéreo
flake [flek] *s* (*thin piece*) hojuela; (*of snow*) copo || *intr* desprenderse en hojuelas; caer en copos pequeños
flak•y ['fleki] *adj* (*comp* **-ier;** *super* **-iest**) escamoso, laminoso
flamboyant [flæm'bɔɪ•ənt] *adj* flameante; llamativo; rimbombante; (archit) flameante, flamígero
flame [flem] *s* llama || *tr* (*to sterilize with a flame*) llamear || *intr* flamear
flame thrower ['θro•ər] *s* lanzallamas *m*
flaming ['flemɪŋ] *adj* llameante; flamante, resplandeciente; apasionado
flamin•go [flə'mɪŋgo] *s* (*pl* **-gos** o **-goes**) flamenco
flammable ['flæməbəl] *adj* inflamable
Flanders ['flændərz] *s* Flandes *f*
flange [flændʒ] *s* pestaña
flank [flæŋk] *s* flanco; *tr* flanquear
flannel ['flænəl] *s* franela
flap [flæp] *s* (*fold in clothing; of a hat*) falda; (*of a pocket*) cartera; (*of a table*) hoja plegadiza; (*of shoe*) oreja; (*of an envelope*) tapa; (*of wings*) aletazo; (*of the counter in a store*) trampa || *v* (*pret & pp* **flapped;** *ger* **flapping**) *tr* golpear con ruido seco; batir, sacudir (*las alas*) || *intr* aletear; flamear con ruido
flare [flɛr] *s* llamarada, destello; cohete *m* de señales; (aer) bengala; (*outward curvature*) abocinamiento; (*of a dress*) vuelo || *tr* abocinar || *intr* arder con gran llamarada, destellar; (*to spread outward*) abocinarse; **to flare up** inflamarse; recrudecer (*una enfermedad*); encolerizarse
flare star *s* (astr) estrella fulgurante
flare'-up' *s* llamarada; (*of an illness*) retroceso; (coll) llamarada, arrebato de cólera
flash [flæʃ] *s* (*of light*) relumbrón *m,* ráfaga; (*of lightning*) relámpago; (*of hope*) rayo; (*of joy*) acceso; (*of insight*) rasgo; mensaje *m* urgente || *tr* quemar (*pólvora*); enviar (*un mensaje*) como un rayo || *intr* destellar, centellear; relampaguear (*los ojos*); **to flash by** pasar como un rayo
flash'back' *s* (mov) retrospectiva
flash bulb *s* luz *f* de magnesio; bombilla de destello
flash flood *s* torrentada, avenida repentina
flashing ['flæʃɪŋ] *s* despidiente *m* de agua, vierteaguas *m*
flash'light' *s* linterna eléctrica, lámpara eléctrica de bolsillo; (*of a lighthouse*) luz *f* intermitente, fanal *m* de destellos; (*for taking photographs*) flash *m,* relámpago
flashlight battery *s* pila de linterna
flashlight bulb *s* bombilla de linterna
flashlight photography *s* fotografía instantánea de relámpago
flash sign *s* anuncio intermitente
flash•y ['flæʃi] *adj* (*comp* **-ier;** *super* **-iest**) chillón, llamativo
flask [flæsk] o [flɑsk] *s* frasco; frasco de bolsillo; (*for laboratory use*) matraz *m,* redoma
flat [flæt] *adj* (*comp* **flatter;** *super* **flattest**) plano; (*nose; boat*) chato; (*surface*) mate, deslustrado; (*beer*) muerto; (*tire*) desinflado; (*e.g., denial*) terminante; (mus) bemol || *adv* — **to fall flat** caer de plano; (fig) no surtir efecto, no tener éxito || *s* banco, bajío; (*apartment*) piso; (mus) bemol *m;* (coll) neumático desinflado
flat'boat' *s* chalana
flat'car' *s* vagón *m* de plataforma
flat-footed ['flæt,fʊtɪd] *adj* de pies planos; (coll) inflexible
flat'head' *s* (*of a bolt*) cabeza chata; clavo, tornillo o perno de cabeza chata; (coll) tonto, mentecato
flat'i'ron *s* plancha
flatten ['flætən] *tr* allanar, aplanar; chafar, aplastar; achatar || *intr* allanarse, aplanarse; aplastarse; achatarse; **to flatten out** ponerse horizontal, enderezarse
flatter ['flætər] *tr* lisonjear; (*to make more attractive than is*) favorecer || *intr* lisonjear

flatterer ['flætərər] *s* lisonjero
flattering ['flætərɪŋ] *adj* lisonjero
flatter·y ['flætəri] *s* (*pl* **-ies**) lisonja
flat'top' *s* portaaviones *m*
flatulence ['flætʃələns] *s* flatulencia
flat'ware' *s* vajilla de plata; vajilla de porcelana
flaunt [flɔnt] o [flɑnt] *tr* ostentar, hacer gala de
flautist ['flɔtɪst] *s* flautista *mf*
flavor ['flevər] *s* sabor *m*, gusto; condimento, sazón *f*; (*of ice cream*) clase *f* || *tr* saborear; condimentar, sazonar; aromatizar, perfumar
flavoring ['flevərɪŋ] *s* condimento, sainete *m*
flaw [flɔ] *s* defecto, imperfección; (*crack*) grieta
flawless ['flɔlɪs] *adj* perfecto, entero
flax [flæks] *s* lino
flaxen ['flæksən] *adj* blondo, rubio
flax'seed' *s* linaza
flay [fle] *tr* desollar
flea [fli] *s* pulga
flea'bite' *s* picadura de pulga; molestia insignificante
fleck [flɛk] *s* pinta, punto; partícula, pizca || *tr* puntear
fledgling ['flɛdʒlɪŋ] *s* pajarito, volantón *m*; (fig) novato, novel *m*
flee [fli] *v* (*pret & pp* **fled** [flɛd]) *tr & intr* huir
fleece [flis] *s* (*coat of wool*) lana; (*wool shorn at one time; tuft of wool or hair*) vellón *m* || *tr* esquilar; (*to strip of money*) desplumar
fleec·y ['flisi] *adj* (*comp* **-ier**; *super* **-iest**) lanudo; (*clouds*) aborregado
fleet [flit] *adj* veloz || *s* armada; (*of merchant vessels, airplanes, automobiles*) flota
fleeting ['flitɪŋ] *adj* fugaz, efímero; transitorio
Fleming ['flɛmɪŋ] *s* flamenco
Flemish ['flɛmɪʃ] *adj & s* flamenco
flesh [flɛʃ] *s* carne *f*; **in the flesh** en persona; **to lose flesh** perder carnes; **to put on flesh** cobrar carnes
flesh and blood *s* (*relatives*) carne y sangre; el cuerpo humano
flesh-colored ['flɛʃ,kʌlərd] *adj* encarnado, de color de carne
fleshiness ['flɛʃɪnɪs] *s* carnosidad
fleshless ['flɛʃlɪs] *adj* descarnado
flesh'pot' *s* olla, marmita; **fleshpots** vida regalona; suntuosos nidos de vicios
flesh wound *s* herida superficial
flesh·y ['flɛʃi] *adj* (*comp* **-ier**; *super* **-iest**) carnoso
flex [flɛks] *tr* doblar || *intr* doblarse
flexible ['flɛksɪbəl] *adj* flexible
flexible cord *s* (elec) flexible *m*
flick [flɪk] *s* (*with finger*) papirote *m*; (*with whip*) latigazo; ruido seco || *tr* golpear rápida y ligeramente
flicker ['flɪkər] *s* llama trémula; (*of eyelids*) parpadeo; (*of emotion*) temblor momentáneo || *intr* flamear con llama trémula; aletear
flier ['flaɪ·ər] *s* aviador *m*; tren rápido; (coll) negocio arriesgado; (coll) hoja volante
flight [flaɪt] *s* fuga, huída; (*of an airplane*) vuelo; (*of birds*) bandada; (*of stairs*) tramo; (*of fancy*) arranque *m*; **to put to flight** poner en fuga; **to take flight** darse a la fuga
flight deck *s* (nav) cubierta de vuelo
flight·y ['flaɪti] *adj* (*comp* **-ier**; *super* **-iest**) veleidoso; casquivano
flim·flam ['flɪm,flæm] *s* (coll) engaño, trampa; (coll) tontería || *v* (*pret & pp* **-flammed**; *ger* **-flamming**) *tr* (coll) engañar, trampear
flim·sy ['flɪmzi] *adj* (*comp* **-sier**; *super* **-siest**] débil, endeble, flojo
flinch [flɪntʃ] *intr* encogerse de miedo
fling [flɪŋ] *s* echada, tiro; baile escocés muy vivo; **to go on a fling** echar una cana al aire; **to have a fling at** ensayar, probar; **to have one's fling** correrla, mocear || *v* (*pret & pp* **flung** [flʌŋ]) *tr* arrojar; (*e.g., on the floor, out the window, in jail*) echar; **to fling open** abrir de golpe; **to fling shut** cerrar de golpe
flint [flɪnt] *s* pedernal *m*
flint'lock' *s* llave *f* de chispa; trabuco de chispa
flint·y ['flɪnti] *adj* (*comp* **-ier**; *super* **-iest**) pedernalino; (fig) empedernido
flip [flɪp] *adj* (*comp* **flipper**; *super* **flippest**) (coll) petulante || *s* capirotazo || *v* (*pret & pp* **flipped**; *ger* **flipping**) *tr* echar de un capirotazo, mover de un tirón; **to flip a coin** echar a cara o cruz; **to flip shut** cerrar de golpe (*p.ej., un abanico*)
flippancy ['flɪpənsi] *s* petulancia
flippant ['flɪpənt] *adj* petulante
flirt [flʌrt] *s* (*woman*) coqueta; (*man*) galanteador *m* || *intr* coquetear (*una mujer*); galantear (*un hombre*); **to flirt with** flirtear con; acariciar (*una idea*); jugar con (*la muerte*)
flit [flɪt] *v* (*pret & pp* **flitted**; *ger* **flitting**) *intr* revolotear, volar; pasar rápidamente
flitch [flɪtʃ] *s* hoja de tocino
float [flot] *s* (*raft*) balsa; (*of fishing line*) flotador *m*; (*of mason*) llana; carroza alegórica, carro alegórico || *tr* poner a flote; lanzar (*una empresa*); emitir (*acciones, bonos, etc.*) || *intr* flotar
floating ['flotɪŋ] *adj* flotante
flock [flɑk] *s* (*of birds*) bandada; (*of sheep*) grey *f*, rebaño, manada; (*of people*) muchedumbre; (*e.g., of nonsense*) hatajo; (*of faithful*) grey *f*, rebaño || *intr* congregarse, reunirse; llegar en tropel
floe [flo] *s* banquisa, témpano
flog [flɑg] *v* (*pret & pp* **flogged**; *ger* **flogging**) *tr* azotar, fustigar
flood [flʌd] *s* inundación; (*caused by heavy rain*) diluvio; (*sudden rise of river*) crecida; (*of tide*) pleamar *f*; (*of words, etc.*) diluvio, torrente *m* || *tr* inundar; (*to overwhelm*) abrumar || *intr* desbordar, rebosar; entrar a raudales
flood'gate' *s* (*of a dam*) compuerta; (*of a canal*) esclusa

flood'light' *s* faro de inundación ‖ *tr* iluminar con faro de inundación
flood tide *s* pleamar *f*, marea montante
floor [flor] *s* (*inside bottom surface of room*) piso, suelo; (*story of a building*) piso, alto; (*of the sea, a swimming pool, etc.*) fondo; (*of an assembly hall*) hemiciclo; (naut) varenga; **to ask for the floor** pedir la palabra; **to have the floor** tener la palabra; **to take the floor** tomar la palabra ‖ *tr* entarimar; derribar, echar al suelo; (coll) confundir, envolver, revolcar (*al adversario en controversia*); (coll) vencer
floor lamp *s* lámpara de pie
floor mop *s* fregasuelos *m*, estropajo
floor plan *s* planta
floor show *s* espectáculo de cabaret
floor timber *s* (naut) varenga
floor'walk'er *s* jefe *m* de sección
floor wax *s* cera de pisos
flop [flɑp] *s* (coll) fracaso, caída; **to take a flop** (coll) caerse ‖ *v* (*pret & pp* **flopped**; *ger* **flopping**) *intr* agitarse; caerse; venirse abajo; fracasar; **to flop over** volcarse; cambiar de partido
flora ['florə] *s* flora
floral ['florəl] *adj* floral
Florentine ['flɑrən,tin] o ['flɔrən,tin] *adj & s* florentino
florescence [flo'rɛsəns] *s* florescencia
florid ['flɑrɪd] o ['flɔrɪd] *adj* (*complexion*) encarnado; (*showy, ornate*) florido
Florida Keys ['flɑrɪdə] o ['flɔrɪdə] *s* Cayos de la Florida
florist ['florɪst] *s* florero, florista *mf*
floss [flɔs] o [flɑs] *s* cadarzo; (*of corn*) cabellos
floss silk *s* seda floja sin torcer
floss·y ['flɔsi] o ['flɑsi] *adj* (*comp* **-ier**; *super* **-iest**) ligero, velloso; (slang) cursi, vistoso
flotsam ['flɑtsəm] *s* pecio
flotsam and jetsam *s* pecios, despojos; (*trifles*) baratijas; gente *f* trashumante, gente perdida
flounce [flaʊns] *s* faralá *m*, volante *m* ‖ *tr* adornar con faralaes o volantes ‖ *intr* moverse airadamente
flounder ['flaʊndər] *s* platija ‖ *intr* forcejear, obrar torpemente, andar tropezando
flour [flaʊr] *adj* harinero ‖ *s* harina
flourish ['flʌrɪʃ] *s* (*with the sword*) molinete *m*; (*with the pen*) plumada, rasgo; (*as part of signature*) rúbrica; (mus) floreo ‖ *tr* blandir (*la espada*) ‖ *intr* florecer, prosperar
flourishing ['flʌrɪʃɪŋ] *adj* floreciente, próspero
flour mill *s* molino de harina
floury ['flaʊri] *adj* harinoso
flout [flaʊt] *tr* mofarse de, burlarse de ‖ *intr* mofarse, burlarse
flow [flo] *s* flujo ‖ *intr* fluir; subir (*la marea*); ondear (*el pelo en el aire*); **to flow into** desaguar en, desembocar en; **to flow over** rebosar; **to flow with** nadar en, abundar en
flower ['flaʊ·ər] *s* flor *f* ‖ *tr* florear ‖ *intr* florecer
flower bed *s* macizo, parterre *m*
flower garden *s* jardín *m*
flower girl *s* florera; (*at a wedding*) damita de honor
flower piece *s* ramillete *m*; (*painting*) florero
flow'er·pot' *s* tiesto, maceta
flower shop *s* floristería
flower show *s* exposición de flores
flower stand *s* florero
flowery ['flaʊ·əri] *adj* florido, cubierto de flores
flu [flu] *s* (coll) gripe *f*, influenza
fluctuate ['flʌktʃʊ,et] *intr* fluctuar
flue [flu] *s* cañón *m* de chimenea; tubo de humo
fluency ['flu·ənsi] *s* afluencia, facundia
fluent ['flu·ənt] *adj* (*flowing*) fluente; afluente, facundo, flúido
fluently ['flu·əntli] *adv* corrientemente
fluff [flʌf] *s* pelusa, tamo; vello, pelusilla; (*of an actor*) gazapo ‖ *tr* esponjar, mullir ‖ *intr* esponjarse
fluff·y ['flʌfi] *adj* (*comp* **-ier**; *super* **-iest**) fofo, esponjoso, mullido; velloso
fluid ['flu·ɪd] *adj & s* flúido
fluidity [flu'ɪdɪti] *s* fluidez *f*
fluke [fluk] *s* (*of anchor*) uña; (*in billiards*) chiripa
flume [flum] *s* caz *m*, saetín *m*
flunk [flʌŋk] *s* (coll) reprobación ‖ *tr* (coll) reprobar, dar calabazas a; perder (*un examen o asignatura*) ‖ *intr* (coll) fracasar, salir mal; **to flunk out** (coll) tener que abandonar los estudios por no poder aprobar
flunk·y ['flʌŋki] *s* (*pl* **-ies**) lacayo; adulador *m*
fluor ['flu·ɔr] *s* fluorita
fluorescence [,flu·ə'rɛsəns] *s* fluorescencia
fluorescent [,flu·ə'rɛsənt] *adj* fluorescente
fluoridate ['flu·ərɪ,det] *tr* fluorizar
fluoridation [,flu·ərɪ'deʃən] *s* fluorización
fluoride ['flu·ə,raɪd] *s* fluoruro
fluorine ['flu·ə,rin] *s* flúor *m*
fluorite ['flu·ə,raɪt] *s* fluorita
fluoroscope ['flu·ərə,skop] *s* fluoroscopio
fluor spar *s* espato flúor
flur·ry ['flʌri] *s* (*pl* **-ries**) agitación; (*of wind*) racha, ráfaga; (*of rain*) chaparrón *m*; (*of snow*) nevisca ‖ *v* (*pret & pp* **-ried**) *tr* agitar
flush [flʌʃ] *adj* rasante, nivelado; (*set in, in order to be flush*) embutido; abundante; robusto, vigoroso; próspero, bien provisto; coloradote; (*in printing*) justificado; **flush with** a ras de ‖ *adv* ras con ras, al mismo nivel ‖ *s* (*of water*) flujo repentino; (*in the cheeks*) rubor *m*; sonrojo; (*in the springtime*) floración repentina; (*of joy*) acceso; (*of youth*) vigor *m*; chorro del inodoro; (*in poker*) flux *m* ‖ *tr* (*to cause to blush*) abochornar; limpiar con un chorro de agua; hacer saltar (*una liebre*) ‖ *intr*

abochornarse, estar encendido (*el rostro*); (*to gush*) brotar
Flushing ['flʌʃɪŋ] *s* Flesinga
flush outlet *s* (elec) caja de enchufe embutida
flush switch *s* (elec) llave embutida
flush tank *s* depósito de limpia
flush toilet *s* inodoro con chorro de agua
fluster ['flʌstər] *s* confusión, aturdimiento || *tr* confundir, aturdir
flute [flut] *s* (*of a column*) estría; (mus) flauta || *tr* estriar, acanalar
flutist ['flutɪst] *s* flautista *mf*
flutter ['flʌtər] *s* aleteo, revoloteo; confusión, turbación || *intr* aletear, revolotear; flamear, ondear; agitarse; alterarse (*el pulso*); palpitar (*el corazón*)
flux [flʌks] *s* (*flow; flowing of tide*) flujo; (*for fusing metals*) flujo, fundente *m*
fly [flaɪ] *s* (*pl* **flies**) mosca; (*of trousers*) portañuela, bragueta; (*for fishing*) mosca artificial; **flies** (theat) bambalinas; **to die like flies** morir como chinches || *v* (*pret* **flew** [flu]; *pp* **flown** [flon]) *tr* hacer volar (*una cometa*); dirigir (*un avión*); (*to carry in an airship*) volar; atravesar en avión; desplegar, llevar (*una bandera*) || *intr* volar; huir; ondear (*una bandera*); **to fly off** salir volando; desprenderse; **to fly open** abrirse de repente; **to fly over** trasvolar; **to fly shut** cerrarse de repente
fly ball *s* (baseball) palomita
fly'blow' *s* cresa
fly'-by-night' *adj* indigno de confianza
fly'catch'er *s* moscareta, papamoscas *m*
fly chaser *s* espantamoscas *m*
flyer ['flaɪ·ər] *s* var de **flier**
fly'-fish' *tr* & *intr* pescar con moscas artificiales
flying ['flaɪ·ɪŋ] *adj* volante; rápido, veloz || *s* aviación
flying boat *s* hidroavión *m*
flying buttress *s* arbotante *m*
flying colors *spl* gran éxito
flying field *s* campo de aviación
flying saucer *s* platillo volante
flying sickness *s* mal *m* de altura
flying time *s* horas de vuelo
fly in the ointment *s* mosca muerta que malea el perfume
fly'leaf' *s* (*pl* **-leaves'**) guarda, hoja de guarda
fly net *s* (*for a bed*) mosquitero; (*for a horse*) espantamoscas *m*
fly'pa'per *s* papel *m* matamoscas
fly'speck' *s* mancha de mosca
fly swatter ['swɑtər] *s* matamoscas *m*
fly'trap' *s* atrapamoscas *m*
fly'wheel' *s* volante *m*
fm. *abbr* **fathom**
F.M. *abbr* **frequency modulation**
foal [fol] *s* potro || *intr* parir (*la yegua*)
foam [fom] *s* espuma || *intr* espumar
foam extinguisher *s* lanzaespumas *m*, extintor *m* de espuma
foam rubber *s* caucho esponjoso, espuma de caucho
foam·y ['fomi] *adj* (*comp* **-ier**; *super* **-iest**) espumoso, espumajoso
fob [fɑb] *s* faltriquera de reloj; (*chain*) leopoldina; (*ornament*) dije *m*
F.O.B. *abbr* **free on board**
focal ['fokəl] *adj* focal
fo·cus ['fokəs] *s* (*pl* **-cuses** o **-ci** [saɪ]) foco; **in focus** enfocado; **out of focus** desenfocado || *v* (*pret* & *pp* **-cused** o **-cussed**; *ger* **-cusing** o **-cussing**) *tr* enfocar; fijar (*la atención*) || *intr* enfocarse
fodder ['fɑdər] *s* forraje *m*
foe [fo] *s* enemigo
fog [fɑg] o [fɔg] *s* niebla; (phot) velo || *v* (*pret* & *pp* **fogged**; *ger* **fogging**) *tr* envolver en niebla; (*to blur*) empañar; (phot) velar || *intr* empañarse; (phot) velarse
fog bank *s* banco de nieblas
fog bell *s* campana de nieblas
fog'bound' *adj* atascado en la niebla, envuelto en la niebla
fog·gy ['fɑgi] o ['fɔgi] *adj* (*comp* **-gier**; *super* **-giest**) neblinoso, brumoso; confuso; (phot) velado; **it is foggy** hay neblina
fog'horn' *s* sirena de niebla
foible ['fɔɪbəl] *s* flaqueza, lado flaco
foil [fɔɪl] *s* (*thin sheet of metal*) hojuela, laminilla; (*of mirror*) azogado, plateado; contraste *m*, realce *m*; (*sword*) florete *m* || *tr* frustrar; azogar, platear (*un espejo*)
foist [fɔɪst] *tr* — **to foist something on someone** encajar una cosa a uno
fol. *abbr* **folio, following**
fold [fold] *s* pliegue *m*, doblez *m*; arruga; (*for sheep*) aprisco, redil *m*; (*of the faithful*) rebaño || *tr* plegar, doblar; cruzar (*los brazos*); **to fold up** doblar (*p.ej., un mapa*) || *intr* plegarse, doblarse
folder ['foldər] *s* (*covers for holding papers*) carpeta; (*pamphlet*) folleto
folderol ['fɑldə,rɑl] *s* tontería, necedad; bagatela
folding ['foldɪŋ] *adj* plegadizo, plegable; plegador
folding camera *s* cámara de fuelle
folding chair *s* silla de tijera, silla plegadiza; (*of canvas*) catrecillo
folding cot *s* catre m de tijera
folding door *s* puerta plegadiza
folding rule *s* metro plegadizo
foliage ['folɪ·ɪdʒ] *s* follaje *m*
foli·o ['folɪ·o] *adj* en folio || *s* (*pl* **-os**) (*sheet*) folio; infolio, libro en folio || *tr* foliar
folk [fok] *adj* popular, tradicional, del pueblo || *s* (*pl* **folk** o **folks**) gente *f*; **folks** (coll) gente (*familia*)
folk'lore' *s* folklore *m*
folk music *s* música folklórica
folk song *s* canción típica, canción tradicional
folk·sy ['foksi] *adj* (*comp* **-sier**; *super* **-siest**) (coll) sociable, tratable; (*like common people*) (coll) plebeyo
folk'way' *s* costumbre tradicional
follicle ['fɑlɪkəl] *s* folículo
follow ['fɑlo] *tr* seguir; seguir el hilo de; interesarse en (*las noticias del*

día) || *intr* seguir; resultar; **as follows** como sigue; **it follows** síguese
follower ['fɑlo·ər] *s* seguidor *m;* secuaz *mf,* partidario; imitador *m;* discípulo
following ['fɑlo·ɪŋ] *adj* siguiente || *s* séquito; partidarios
fol'low-up' *adj* consecutivo; recordativo || *s* carta recordativa, circular recordativa
fol·ly ['fɑli] *s* (*pl* **-lies**) desatino, locura; empresa temeraria; **follies** revista teatral
foment [fo'mɛnt] *tr* fomentar
fond [fɑnd] *adj* afectuoso, cariñoso; **to become fond of** encariñarse con, aficionarse a o de
fondle ['fɑndəl] *tr* acariciar, mimar
fondness ['fɑndnɪs] *s* afición, cariño
font [fɑnt] *s* (*source; source of water*) fuente *f;* (*for holy water*) pila; (*of type*) fundición
food [fud] *adj* alimenticio || *s* comida, alimento; **food for thought** cosa en qué pensar
food store *s* tienda de comestibles, colmado
food'stuffs' *spl* comestibles *mpl,* víveres *mpl*
fool [ful] *s* tonto, necio; (*jester*) bufón *m;* (*person imposed on*) inocente *mf,* víctima; **to make a fool of** poner en ridículo; **to play the fool** hacer el tonto || *tr* embaucar, engañar; **to fool away** malgastar (*tiempo, dinero*) || *intr* tontear; **to fool around** (coll) malgastar el tiempo; **to fool with** (coll) ajar, manosear
fooler·y ['fuləri] *s* (*pl* **-ies**) locura, tontería
fool'har'dy *adj* (*comp* **-dier;** *super* **-diest**) temerario
fooling ['fulɪŋ] *s* broma; engaño; **no fooling** hablando en serio
foolish ['fulɪʃ] *adj* tonto; ridículo
fool'proof' *adj* (coll) a prueba de mal trato; (coll) infalible
fools'cap' *s* gorro de bufón; papel *m* de oficio
fool's errand *s* caza de grillos
fool's scepter *s* cetro de locura
foot [fut] *s* (*pl* **feet** [fit]) pie *m;* **to drag one's feet** ir a paso de caracol; **to have one foot in the grave** estar con un pie en la sepultura; **to put one's best foot forward** (coll) hacer méritos; **to put one's foot in it** (coll) meter la pata; (coll) tirarse una plancha; **to stand on one's own feet** volar con sus propias alas; **to tread under foot** hollar || *tr* pagar (*la cuenta*); **to foot it** andar a pie; bailar
footage ['futɪdʒ] *s* distancia o largura en pies
foot'ball' *s* (*game*) balompié *m,* fútbol *m;* (*ball*) balón *m*
foot'board' *s* (*support for foot*) estribo; (*of bed*) pie *m*
foot'bridge' *s* pasarela, puente *m* para peatones
foot'fall' *s* paso
foot'hill' *s* colina al pie de una montaña
foot'hold' *s* arraigo, pie *m;* **to gain a foothold** ganar pie
footing ['futɪŋ] *s* pie *m,* p.ej., **he lost his footing** perdió el pie; **on a friendly footing** en relaciones amistosas; **on an equal footing** en pie de igualdad; **on a war footing** en pie de guerra
foot'lights' *spl* candilejas, batería; (fig) tablas, escena
foot'loose' *adj* libre, no comprometido
foot·man ['futmən] *s* (*pl* **-men** [mən]) lacayo, criado de librea
foot'mark' *s* huella
foot'note' *s* nota al pie de la página
foot'path' *s* senda para peatones
foot'print' *s* huella
foot race *s* carrera a pie
foot'rest' *s* apoyapié *m,* descansapié *m*
foot rule *s* regla de un pie
foot soldier *s* soldado de a pie
foot'sore' *adj* despeado
foot'step' *s* paso; **to follow in the footsteps of** seguir los pasos de
foot'stone' *s* lápida al pie de una sepultura
foot'stool' *s* escabel *m,* escañuelo
foot warmer *s* calientapiés *m*
foot'wear' *s* calzado
foot'work' *s* juego de piernas
foot'worn' *adj* (*road*) trillado; (*person*) despeado
foozle ['fuzəl] *s* chambonada; (coll) chambón *m,* torpe *m* || *tr* chafallar; errar (*un golpe*) de manera torpe || *intr* chambonear
fop [fɑp] *s* currutaco, petimetre *m*
for [fɔr] *prep* para; por; como, p.ej., **he uses his living room for an office** usa la sala como oficina; de, p.ej., **time for bed** hora de acostarse; desde hace, p.ej., **he has been here for a week** está aquí desde hace una semana; en honor de; a pesar de || *conj* pues, porque
for. *abbr* **foreign**
forage ['fɑrɪdʒ] o ['fɔrɪdʒ] *adj* forrajero || *s* forraje *m* || *tr & intr* forrajear; saquear
foray ['fɑre] o ['fɔre] *s* correría; saqueo || *intr* hacer correrías
for·bear [fɔr'bɛr] *v* (*pret* **-bore** ['bor]; *pp* **-borne** ['born]) *tr* abstenerse de || *intr* contenerse
forbearance [fɔr'bɛrəns] *s* abstención; paciencia
for·bid [fɔr'bɪd] *v* (*pret* **-bade** ['bæd] o **-bad** ['bæd]; *pp* **-bidden** ['bɪdən]; *ger* **-bidding**) *tr* prohibir
forbidding [fɔr'bɪdɪŋ] *adj* repugnante, repulsivo
force [fors] *s* fuerza; (*staff of workers*) personal *m;* (*of soldiers, police, etc.*) cuerpo; (phys) fuerza; **by force of** a fuerza de; **by main force** con todas sus fuerzas; **in force** vigente, en vigor; en gran número; **to join forces** juntar diestra con diestra || *tr* forzar; obligar; **to force back** hacer retroceder; **to force open** abrir por

fuerza; **to force through** llevar a cabo por fuerza
forced [forst] *adj* forzado
forced air *s* aire *m* a presión
forced landing *s* aterrizaje forzado o forzoso
forced march *s* marcha forzada
forceful ['forsfəl] *adj* enérgico, eficaz
for•ceps ['fɔrsəps] *s* (*pl* **-ceps** o **-cipes** [sɪ,piz]) (dent, surg) pinzas; (obstet) fórceps *m*
force pump *s* bomba impelente
forcible ['forsɪbəl] *adj* eficaz, convincente; forzado
ford [ford] *s* vado || *tr* vadear
fore [for] *adj* anterior; (naut) de proa || *adv* antes, anteriormente; delante; (naut) avante || *interj* ¡ojo!, ¡cuidado! || *s* delantera; **to the fore** destacado; a mano; vivo
fore and aft *adv* de popa a proa
fore'arm' *s* antebrazo || **fore•arm'** *tr* armar de antemano; prevenir
fore'bear' *s* antepasado
forebode [for'bod] *tr* (*to portend*) presagiar; (*to have a presentiment of*) presentir, prever
foreboding [for'bodɪŋ] *s* presagio; presentimiento
fore'cast' *s* pronóstico || *v* (*pret & pp* **-cast** o **-casted**) *tr* pronosticar
forecastle ['foksəl], ['for,kæsəl] o ['for,kɑsəl] *s* castillo de proa
fore•close' *tr* excluir; extinguir el derecho de redimir (*una hipoteca*); privar del derecho de redimir una hipoteca
fore•doom' *tr* condenar de antemano, predestinar al fracaso
fore edge *s* canal *f*
fore'fa'ther *s* antepasado
fore'fin'ger *s* dedo índice, dedo mostrador
fore'front' *s* puesto delantero; sitio de actividad más intensa; **in the forefront** a vanguardia
fore•go' *v* (*pret* **-went'**; *pp* **-gone'**) *tr & intr* preceder
foregoing ['for,go•ɪŋ] o [for'go•ɪŋ] *adj* anterior, precedente
fore'gone' conclusion *s* resultado inevitable; decisión adoptada de antemano
fore'ground' *s* primer plano, primer término
forehanded ['for,hændɪd] *adj* (*thrifty*) ahorrado; hecho de antemano
forehead ['fɑrɪd] o ['fɔrɪd] *s* frente *f*
foreign ['fɑrɪn] o ['fɔrɪn] *adj* extranjero, exterior; **foreign to** (*not belonging to or connected with*) ajeno a
foreign affairs *spl* asuntos exteriores
for'eign-born' *adj* nacido en el extranjero
foreigner ['fɑrɪnər] o ['fɔrɪnər] *s* extranjero
foreign exchange *s* cambio extranjero; (*currency*) divisa
foreign minister *s* ministro de asuntos exteriores
foreign office *s* ministerio de asuntos exteriores
foreign service *s* servicio diplomático y consular; servicio militar extranjero
foreign trade *s* comercio extranjero
fore'leg' *s* brazo, pata delantera
fore'lock' *s* mechón *m* de pelo sobre la frente; (*of a horse*) copete *m;* **to take time by the forelock** asir la ocasión por la melena
fore•man ['formən] *s* (*pl* **-men** [mən]) capataz *m,* mayoral *m,* sobrestante *m;* (*in a machine shop*) contramaestre *m;* presidente *m* de jurado
foremast ['formәst], ['for,mæst] o ['for,mɑst] *s* palo de trinquete
foremost ['for,most] *adj* primero, principal, más eminente
fore'noon' *adj* matinal || *s* mañana
fore'part' *s* parte delantera; primera parte
fore'paw' *s* pata delantera
fore'quar'ter *s* cuarto delantero
fore'run'ner *s* precursor *m;* predecesor *m;* antepasado; anuncio, presagio
fore•sail ['forsəl] o ['for,sel] *s* trinquete *m*
fore•see' *v* (*pret* **-saw'**; *pp* **-seen'**) *tr* prever
foreseeable [for'si•əbəl] *adj* previsible
fore•shad'ow *tr* presagiar, prefigurar
fore•short'en *tr* escorzar
fore•short'ening *s* escorzo
fore'sight' *s* previsión, presciencia
fore'sight'ed *adj* previsor, presciente
fore'skin' *s* prepucio
forest ['fɑrɪst] o ['fɔrɪst] *adj* forestal || *s* bosque *m*
fore•stall' *tr* impedir, prevenir; anticipar; acaparar
forest ranger ['rendʒər] *s* guarda *m* forestal, montanero
forestry ['fɑrɪstri] o ['fɔrɪstri] *s* silvicultura, ciencia forestal
fore'taste' *s* goce anticipado, conocimiento anticipado
fore•tell' *v* (*pret & pp* **-told'**) *tr* predecir; presagiar
fore'thought' *s* premeditación; providencia, previsión
forever [fɔr'ɛvər] *adv* por siempre; siempre
fore•warn' *tr* prevenir, poner sobre aviso
fore'word' *s* advertencia, prefacio
forfeit ['fɔrfɪt] *adj* perdido || *s* multa, pena; prenda perdida; **forfeits** (*game*) prendas || *tr* perder el derecho a
forfeiture ['fɔrfɪtʃər] *s* multa, pena; prenda perdida
forgather [fɔr'gæðər] *intr* reunirse; encontrarse; **to forgather with** asociarse con
forge [fordʒ] *s* fragua; (*blacksmith shop*) herrería; || *tr* fraguar, forjar; falsificar (*la firma de otra persona*); fraguar, forjar (*mentiras*) || *intr* fraguar, forjar; **to forge ahead** avanzar despacio y con esfuerzo
forger•y ['fordʒəri] *s* (*pl* **-ies**) falsificación
for•get [fɔr'gɛt] *v* (*pret* **-got** ['gɑt]; *pp* **-got** o **-gotten;** *ger* **-getting**) *tr* olvidar,

olvidarse de, olvidársele a uno, p.ej., **he forgot his overcoat** se le olvidó su abrigo; **forget it!** ¡no se preocupe!; **to forget oneself** no pensar en sí mismo; ser distraído; propasarse
forgetful [fɔr'gɛtfəl] *adj* olvidado, olvidadizo; descuidado
forgetfulness [fɔr'gɛtfəlnɪs] *s* olvido; descuido
for•get'-me-not' *s* nomeolvides *m*
forgivable [fɔr'gɪvəbəl] *adj* perdonable
for•give [fɔr'gɪv] *v* (*pret* **-gave'**; *pp* **-giv'en**) *tr* perdonar
forgiveness [fɔr'gɪvnɪs] *s* perdón *m;* misericordia
forgiving [fɔr'gɪvɪŋ] *adj* perdonador, misericordioso, clemente
for•go [fɔr'go] *v* (*pret* **-went'**; *pp* **-gone'**) *tr* privarse de
fork [fɔrk] *s* horca; (*of a gardener; of bicycle*) horquilla; (*of two rivers*) horcajo; (*of railroad*) ramal *m;* (*of a tree*) horqueta; (*for eating*) tenedor *m* ‖ *tr* ahorquillar; cargar con horquilla; (*in chess*) amenazar (*dos piezas*); **to fork out** (slang) entregar, sudar ‖ *intr* bifurcarse
forked [fɔrkt] *adj* ahorquillado
forked lightning *s* relámpago en zigzag
fork'lift' truck *s* carretilla elevadora de horquilla
forlorn [fɔr'lɔrn] *adj* desamparado; desesperado; miserable
forlorn hope *s* empresa desesperada
form [fɔrm] *s* forma; (*paper to be filled out*) formulario; (*construction to give shape to cement*) encofrado; (*type in a frame*) molde *m* ‖ *tr* formar ‖ *intr* formarse
formal ['fɔrməl] *adj* formal, ceremonioso; etiquetero
formal attire *s* vestido de etiqueta
formal call *s* visita de cumplido
formali•ty [fɔr'mælɪti] *s* (*pl* **-ties**) (*standard procedure*) formalidad; ceremonia, etiqueta
formal party *s* reunión de etiqueta
formal speech *s* discurso de aparato
format ['fɔrmæt] *s* formato
formation [fɔr'meʃən] *s* formación
former ['fɔrmər] *adj* (*preceding*) anterior; (*long past*) antiguo; primero (*de dos*); **the former** aquél
formerly ['fɔrmərli] *adv* antes, en tiempos pasados
form'-fit'ting *adj* ceñido al cuerpo
formidable ['fɔrmɪdəbəl] *adj* formidable
formless ['fɔrmlɪs] *adj* informe
form letter *s* carta general
formu•la ['fɔrmjələ] *s* (*pl* **-las** o **-lae** [ˌli]) formula
formulate ['fɔrmjəˌlet] *tr* formular
for•sake [fɔr'sek] *v* (*pret* **-sook** ['sʊk]; *pp* **-saken** ['sekən]) *tr* abandonar, desamparar; dejar
fort [fort] *s* fuerte *m,* fortaleza
forte [fort] *s* (*strong point*) fuerte *m,* caballo de batalla
forth [forθ] *adv* adelante; **and so forth** y así sucesivamente; **from this day forth** de hoy en adelante; **to go forth** salir
forth'com'ing *adj* próximo, venidero
forth'right' *adj* directo, franco, sincero ‖ *adv* derecho; sinceramente, francamente; en seguida
forth'with' *adv* inmediatamente
fortieth ['fɔrtɪ·ɪθ] *adj & s* (*in a series*) cuadragésimo; (*part*) cuarentavo
fortification [ˌfɔrtɪfɪ'keʃən] *s* fortificación
forti•fy ['fɔrtɪˌfaɪ] *v* (*pret & pp* **-fied**) *tr* fortificar; encabezar (*vinos*)
fortitude ['fɔrtɪˌtjud] o ['fɔrtɪˌtud] *s* fortaleza, firmeza
fortnight ['fɔrtnaɪt] o ['fɔrtnɪt] *s* quincena, dos semanas
fortress ['fɔrtrɪs] *s* fortaleza
fortuitous [fɔr'tju·ɪtəs] o [fɔr'tu·ɪtəs] *adj* fortuito
fortunate ['fɔrtʃənɪt] *adj* afortunado
fortune ['fɔrtjən] *s* fortuna; **to make a fortune** enriquecerse; **to tell someone his fortune** decirle a uno la buenaventura
fortune hunter *s* cazador *m* de dotes
for'tune•tel'ler *s* adivino, agorero
for•ty ['fɔrti] *adj & pron* cuarenta ‖ *s* (*pl* **-ties**) cuarenta *m*
fo•rum ['forəm] *s* (*pl* **-rums** o **-ra** [rə]) foro; (*e.g., of public opinion*) tribunal *m*
forward ['fɔrwərd] *adj* delantero; precoz; atrevido, impertinente ‖ *adv* hacia adelante; **to bring forward** pasar a cuenta nueva; **to come forward** adelantarse; **to look forward to** esperar con placer anticipado ‖ *tr* cursar, hacer seguir, reexpedir; fomentar, patrocinar
fossil ['fɑsɪl] *adj & s* fósil *m*
foster ['fɑstər] o ['fɔstər] *adj* adoptivo, de leche, de crianza ‖ *tr* fomentar
foster home *s* hogar *m* de adopción
foul [faʊl] *adj* sucio, puerco; (*air*) viciado; (*wind*) contrario; (*weather*) malo; obsceno; pérfido; (*breath*) fétido; (baseball) fuera del cuadro
foul-mouthed ['faʊl'maʊðd] o ['faʊl'maʊθt] *adj* deslenguado
foul play *s* mal encuentro; (sport) juego sucio
foul'spo'ken *adj* malhablado
found [faʊnd] *tr* fundar; (*to melt, to cast*) fundir
foundation [faʊn'deʃən] *s* fundación; (*endowment*) dotación; (*basis*) fundamento; (*masonry support*) cimiento
founder ['faʊndər] *s* fundador *m;* (*of metals*) fundidor *m* ‖ *intr* despearse (*un caballo*); hundirse, irse a pique (*un buque*); (*to fail*) fracasar
foundling ['faʊndlɪŋ] *s* niño expósito
foundling hospital *s* casa de expósitos
found•ry ['faʊndri] *s* (*pl* **-ries**) fundición
foundry•man ['faʊndrɪmən] *s* (*pl* **-men** [mən]) fundidor *m*
fount [faʊnt] *s* fuente *f*
fountain ['faʊntən] *s* fuente *f,* manantial *m*

foun′tain·head′ *s* nacimiento
fountain pen *s* pluma estilográfica, pluma fuente
fountain syringe *s* mangueta
four [for] *adj & pron* cuatro || *s* cuatro; **four o'clock** las cuatro; **on all fours** a gatas
four′-cy′cle *adj* (mach) de cuatro tiempos
four′-cyl′inder *adj* (mach) de cuatro cilindros
four′-flush′ *intr* (coll) bravear, papelonear
fourflusher [ˈfor ˌflʌʃər] *s* (coll) bravucón *m*
four-footed [ˈforˈfʊtɪd] *adj* cuadrúpedo
four hundred *adj & pron* cuatrocientos || *s* cuatrocientos *m;* **the four hundred** la alta sociedad
four′-in-hand′ *s* corbata de nudo corredizo; coche tirado por cuatro caballos
four′-lane′ *adj* cuadriviario
four′-leaf′ *adj* cuadrifoliado
four-legged [ˈforˈlɛgɪd] o [ˈforˈlɛgd] *adj* de cuatro patas; (*schooner*) de cuatro mástiles
four′-let′ter word *s* palabra impúdica de cuatro letras
four′-mo′tor plane *s* cuadrimotor *m*
four′-o'clock′ *s* dondiego
four′-post′er *s* cama imperial
four′score′ *adj* cuatro veintenas de
foursome [ˈforsəm] *s* cuatrinca; cuatro jugadores; juego de cuatro
fourteen [ˈforˈtin] *adj, pron & s* catorce *m*
fourteenth [ˈforˈtinθ] *adj & s* (*in a series*) decimocuarto; (*part*) catorzavo || *s* (*in dates*) catorce *m*
fourth [forθ] *adj & s* cuarto || *s* (*in dates*) cuatro
fourth estate *s* cuarto poder
four′-way′ *adj* de cuatro direcciones; (elec) de cuatro terminales
fowl [faʊl] *s* ave *f;* aves; gallina; gallo; carne *f* de ave
fowling piece *s* escopeta de caza
fox [fɑks] *s* zorra; (*fur*) zorro; (*cunning person*) (fig) zorro || *tr* (coll) engañar con astucia
fox′glove′ *s* dedalera
fox′hole′ *s* zorrera; (mil) pozo de lobo
fox′hound′ *s* perro raposero, perro zorrero
fox hunt *s* caza de zorras
fox terrier *s* fox-terrier *m* (*casta de perro de talla pequeña*)
fox trot *s* trote corto (*de caballo*); foxtrot *m* (*baile de compás cuaternario*)
fox·y [ˈfɑksi] *adj* (*comp* **-ier;** *super* **-iest**) zorrero, astuto, taimado
foyer [ˈfɔɪ·ər] *s* (*of a private house*) vestíbulo; (theat) salón *m* de entrada, vestíbulo
fr. *abbr* **fragment, franc, from**
Fr. *abbr* **Father, French, Friday**
Fra [frɑ] *s* fray *m*
fracas [ˈfrekəs] *s* alboroto, riña
fraction [ˈfrækʃən] *s* fracción; porción muy pequeña
fractional [ˈfrækʃənəl] *adj* fraccionario; insignificante
fractious [ˈfrækʃəs] *adj* reacio, rebelón; quisquilloso, regañón
fracture [ˈfræktʃər] *s* fractura || *tr* fracturar; (*e.g., an arm*) fracturarse; *intr* fracturarse
fragile [ˈfrædʒɪl] *adj* frágil
fragment [ˈfrægmənt] *s* fragmento
fragrance [ˈfregrəns] *s* fragancia
fragrant [ˈfregrənt] *adj* fragante
frail [frel] *adj* (*not robust*) débil; (*easily broken; morally weak*) frágil || *s* cesto de junco
frail·ty [ˈfrelti] *s* (*pl* **-ties**) debilidad; (*moral weakness*) fragilidad
frame [frem] *s* (*of a picture, mirror*) marco, (*of glasses*) montura, armadura; (*structure*) armazón *f*, esqueleto; (*for embroidering*) bastidor *m;* (*of government*) sistema *m;* (mov, telv) encuadre *m;* (naut) cuaderna || *tr* (*to put in a frame*) enmarcar; formar, forjar; construir; redactar, formular; (slang) incriminar (*a un inocente*)
frame house *s* casa de madera
frame of mind *s* manera de pensar
frame′-up′ *s* (slang) treta, trama para incriminar a un inocente
frame′work′ *s* armazón *f*, esqueleto, entramado
franc [fræŋk] *s* franco
France [fræns] o [frɑns] *s* Francia
Frances [ˈfrænsɪs] o [ˈfrɑnsɪs] *s* Francisca
franchise [ˈfræntʃaɪz] *s* franquicia, privilegio; (*right to vote*) sufragio
Francis [ˈfrænsɪs] o [ˈfrɑnsɪs] *s* Francisco
Franciscan [frænˈsɪskən] *adj & s* franciscano
frank [fræŋk] *adj* franco, sincero || *s* carta franca, envío franco; franquicia postal; sello de franquicia || *tr* franquear || **Frank** *s* (*member of a Frankish tribe*) franco; (*masculine name*) Paco
frankfurter [ˈfræŋkfərtər] *s* salchicha de carne de vaca y de cerdo
frankincense [ˈfræŋkɪn ˌsɛns] *s* olíbano
Frankish [ˈfræŋkɪʃ] *adj & s* franco
frankness [ˈfræŋknɪs] *s* franqueza, abertura, sinceridad
frantic [ˈfræntɪk] *adj* frenético
frappé [fræˈpe] *adj* helado || *s* refresco helado de zumo de frutas
frat [fræt] *s* (slang) club *m* de estudiantes
fraternal [frəˈtʌrnəl] *adj* fraternal
fraterni·ty [frəˈtʌrnɪti] *s* (*pl* **-ties**) (*brotherliness*) fraternidad; cofradía; asociación secreta; (U.S.A.) club *m* de estudiantes
fraternize [ˈfrætər ˌnaɪz] *intr* fraternizar
fraud [frɔd] *s* fraude *m;* (*person*) (coll) impostor *m*
fraudulent [ˈfrɔdjələnt] *adj* fraudulento
fraught [frɔt] *adj* — **fraught with** cargado de, lleno de

fray [fre] *s* combate *m*, riña, batalla || *intr* deshilacharse, raerse
freak [frik] *s* (*sudden fancy*) capricho, antojo; (*person, animal*) fenómeno
freakish ['frikɪʃ] *adj* caprichoso, antojadizo; raro, fantástico
freckle ['frɛkəl] *s* peca
freckle-faced ['frɛkəl,fest] *adj* pecoso
freckly ['frɛkli] *adj* pecoso
Frederick ['frɛdərɪk] *s* Federico
free [fri] *adj* (*comp* **freer** ['fri·ər]; *super* **freest** ['fri·ɪst]) libre; gratis, franco; liberal, generoso; **to be free with** dar abundantemente; **to set free** libertar || *adv* libremente; en libertad; de balde, gratis || *v* (*pret & pp* **freed** [frid]; *ger* **freeing** ['fri·ɪŋ]) *tr* libertar, poner en libertad; soltar; exentar, eximir
free and easy *adj* despreocupado
freebooter ['fri,butər] *s* forbante *m*, filibustero, pirata *m*
free'born' *adj* nacido libre; propio de un pueblo libre
freedom ['fridəm] *s* libertad
freedom of speech *s* libertad de palabra
freedom of the press *s* libertad de imprenta
freedom of the seas *s* libertad de los mares
freedom of worship *s* libertad de cultos
free enterprise *s* libertad de empresa
free fight *s* sarracina, riña tumultuaria
free'-for-all' *s* concurso abierto a todo el mundo; sarracina, riña tumultuaria
free hand *s* plena libertad, carta blanca
free'hand' drawing *s* dibujo a pulso
freehanded ['fri,hændɪd] *adj* dadivoso, generoso
free'hold' *s* (law) feudo franco
free lance *s* soldado mercenario; periodista *mf* sin empleo fijo; (*writer not on regular salary*) destajista *mf*
free lunch *s* tapas, enjutos
free·man ['frimən] *s* (*pl* **-men** [mən]) hombre *m* libre; ciudadano
Free'ma'son *s* francmasón *m*
Free'ma'sonry *s* francmasonería
free of charge *adj* gratis, de balde
free on board *adj* franco a bordo
free port *s* puerto franco
free ride *s* llevada gratuita
free service *s* servicio post-venta
free'-spo'ken *adj* franco, sin reserva
free'stone' *adj & s* abridero
free'think'er *s* librepensador *m*
free thought *s* librepensamiento
free trade *s* librecambio
free'trad'er *s* librecambista *mf*
free'way' *s* autopista
free will *s* libre albedrío
freeze [friz] *s* helada || *v* (*pret* **froze** [froz]; *pp* **frozen**) *tr* helar; congelar (*créditos, fondos, etc.*) || *intr* helarse; congelarse; helársele a uno la sangre (*p.ej., de miedo*)
freezer ['frizər] *s* heladora, sorbetera
freight [fret] *s* carga; (naut) flete *m*; **by freight** como carga; (rr) en pequeña velocidad || *tr* enviar por carga
freight car *s* vagón *m* de carga, vagón de mercancías
freighter ['fretər] *s* buque *m* de carga, carguero
freight platform *s* (rr) muelle *m*
freight station *s* (rr) estación de carga
freight train *s* mercancías *msg*, tren *m* de mercancías
freight yard *s* (rr) patio de carga
French [frɛntʃ] *adj & s* francés *m*; **the French** los franceses
French chalk *s* jaboncillo de sastre
French doors *spl* puertas vidrieras dobles
French dressing *s* salsa francesa, vinagreta
French fried potatoes *spl* patatas fritas en trocitos
French horn *s* (mus) trompa de armonía
French horsepower *s* caballo de fuerza, caballo de vapor
French leave *s* despedida a la francesa; **to take French leave** despedirse a la francesa
French·man ['frɛntʃmən] *s* (*pl* **-men** [mən]) francés *m*
French telephone *s* microteléfono
French toast *s* torrija
French window *s* puerta ventana
French'wom'an *s* (*pl* **-wom'en**) francesa
frenzied ['frɛnzid] *adj* frenético
fren·zy ['frɛnzi] *s* (*pl* **-zies**) frenesí *m*
frequen·cy ['frikwənsi] *s* (*pl* **-cies**) frecuencia
frequency list *s* lista de frecuencia
frequency modulation *s* modulación de frecuencia
frequent ['frikwənt] *adj* frecuente || [frɪ'kwɛnt] o ['frikwənt] *tr* frecuentar
frequently ['frikwəntli] *adv* con frecuencia, frecuentemente
fres·co ['frɛsko] *s* (*pl* **-coes** o **-cos**) fresco || *tr* pintar al fresco
fresh [frɛʃ] *adj* fresco; (*water*) dulce; (*wind*) fresquito; novicio, inexperto; (*cheeky*) (slang) fresco; (*toward women*) (slang) atrevido; **fresh paint!** ¡ojo mancha! || *adv* recientemente, recién; **fresh in** (coll) recién llegado, acabado de llegar; **fresh out** (coll) recién agotado
freshen ['frɛʃən] *tr* refrescar || *intr* refrescarse
freshet ['frɛʃɪt] *s* avenida, crecida
fresh·man ['frɛʃmən] *s* (*pl* **-men** [mən]) novato; estudiante *mf* de primer año
freshness ['frɛʃnɪs] *s* frescura; (*cheek*) (slang) frescura
fresh'-wa'ter *adj* de agua dulce; no acostumbrado a navegar; de poca monta
fret [frɛt] *s* (*interlaced design*) calado; (mus) ceja, traste *m*; queja || *v* (*pret & pp* **fretted**; *ger* **fretting**) *tr* adornar con calados || *intr* irritarse, quejarse, agitarse
fretful ['frɛtfəl] *adj* irritable, enojadizo, displicente
fret'work' *s* calado

Freudianism ['frɔɪdɪ·ə,nɪzəm] *s* freudismo
friar ['fraɪ·ər] *s* fraile *m*
friar·y ['fraɪ·əri] *s* (*pl* **-ies**) convento de frailes
fricassee [,frɪkə'si] *s* fricasé *m*
friction ['frɪkʃən] *s* fricción, rozamiento; (fig) desavenencia, rozamiento
friction tape *s* cinta aislante
Friday ['fraɪdi] *s* viernes *m*
fried [fraɪd] *adj* frito
fried egg *s* huevo a la plancha, huevo frito o estrellado
friend [frɛnd] *s* amigo; (*in answer to "Who is there?"*) gente *f* de paz; **to be friends with** ser amigo de; **to make friends** trabar amistades; **to make friends with** hacerse amigo de
friend·ly ['frɛndli] *adj* (*comp* **-lier;** *super* **-liest**) amigo, amistoso, amigable
friendship ['frɛndʃɪp] *s* amistad
frieze [friz] *s* (archit) friso
frigate ['frɪgɪt] *s* fragata
fright [fraɪt] *s* susto, espanto; (*grotesque or ridiculous person*) (coll) espantajo; **to take fright at** asustarse de
frighten ['fraɪtən] *tr* asustar, espantar; **to frighten away** espantar, ahuyentar || *intr* asustarse
frightful ['fraɪtfəl] *adj* espantoso, horroroso; (coll) feúcho, repugnante; (coll) enorme, tremendo
frightfulness ['fraɪtfəlnɪs] *s* espanto, horror *m;* terrorismo
frigid ['frɪdʒɪd] *adj* frío; (fig) frío; (*zone*) glacial
frigidity [frɪ'dʒɪdɪti] *s* frialdad; (pathol) frialdad; (fig) frialdad, frigidez *f*
frill [frɪl] *s* lechuga; (*of birds and other animals*) collarín *m;* (*frippery*) (coll) ringorrango; (*in dress, speech, etc.*) (coll) afectación
fringe [frɪndʒ] *s* franja, orla; (opt) franja || *tr* franjar, orlar
fringe benefits *spl* beneficios accesorios
fripper·y ['frɪpəri] *s* (*pl* **-ies**) (*flashiness*) cursilería; (*flashy clothes*) perejil *m,* perifollos
frisk [frɪsk] *tr* (slang) cachear; (slang) registrar y robar || *intr* retozar
frisk·y ['frɪski] *adj* (*comp* **-ier;** *super* **-iest**) juguetón, retozón; (*horse*) fogoso
fritter ['frɪtər] *s* fruta de sartén; fragmento || *tr* — **to fritter away** desperdiciar, malgastar poco a poco
frivolous ['frɪvələs] *adj* frívolo
friz [frɪz] *s* (*pl* **frizzes**) rizo, pelo rizado apretadamente || *v* (*pret & pp* **frizzed;** *ger* **frizzing**) *tr* rizar, rizar apretadamente
frizzle ['frɪzəl] *s* rizo apretado; chirrido, siseo || *tr* rizar apretadamente; asar o freír en parrilla || *intr* chirriar, sisear
friz·zly ['frɪzli] *adj* (*comp* **-zlier;** *super* **-zliest**) muy ensortijado
fro [fro] *adv* — **to and fro** de acá para allá; **to go to and fro** ir y venir
frock [frɑk] *s* vestido; bata, blusa; (*of priest*) vestido talar
frock coat *s* levita
frog [frɑg] o [frɔg] *s* rana; (*button and loop on a garment*) alamar *m;* (*in throat*) ronquera, gallo
frog'man' *s* (*pl* **-men'**) hombre-rana *m*
frol·ic ['frɑlɪk] *s* juego alegre, travesura; fiesta, holgorio || *v* (*pret & pp* **-icked;** *ger* **-icking**) *intr* juguetear, travesear, jaranear
frolicsome ['frɑlɪksəm] *adj* juguetón, travieso
from [frʌm], [frɑm] o [frəm] *prep* de; desde; de parte de; según; a, p.ej., **to take something away from someone** quitarle algo a alguien
front [frʌnt] *adj* delantero; anterior || *s* frente *m & f;* (*of a shirt*) pechera; (*of a book*) principio; apariencia falsa (*p.ej., de riqueza*); ademán estudiado; (mil) frente *m;* **in front of** delante de, frente a, en frente de; **to put on a front** (coll) gastar mucho oropel; **to put up a bold front** (coll) hacer de tripas corazón || *tr* (*to face*) dar a; (*to confront*) afrontar, arrostrar; (*to supply with a front*) poner frente o fachada a || *intr* — **to front on** dar a; **to front towards** mirar hacia
frontage ['frʌntɪdʒ] *s* fachada, frontera; terreno frontero
front door *s* puerta de entrada
front drive *s* (aut) tracción delantera
frontier [frʌn'tɪr] *adj* fronterizo || *s* frontera
•**frontiers·man** [frʌn'tɪrzmən] *s* (*pl* **-men** [mən]) hombre *m* de la frontera, explorador *m*
frontispiece ['frʌntɪs,pis] *s* (*of book*) portada; (archit) frontispicio
front matter *s* preliminares *mpl* (*de un libro*)
front page *s* primera plana
front porch *s* soportal *m*
front room *s* cuarto que da a la calle
front row *s* primera fila
front seat *s* asiento delantero
front steps *spl* escalones *mpl* de acceso a la puerta de entrada
front view *s* vista de frente
frost [frɔst] o [frɑst] *s* (*freezing*) helada; (*frozen dew*) escarcha; (slang) fracaso || *tr* cubrir de escarcha; escarchar (*confituras*); helar (*el frío las plantas*); deslustrar (*el vidrio*)
frost'bit'ten *adj* dañado por la helada; quemado por la helada o la escarcha
frosted glass *s* vidrio deslustrado
frosting ['frɔstɪŋ] o ['frɑstɪŋ] *s* garapiña; (*of glass*) deslustre *m*
frost·y ['frɔsti] o ['frɑsti] *adj* (*comp* **-ier;** *super* **-iest**) cubierto de escarcha; escarchado; frío, poco amistoso; canoso, gris
froth [frɔθ] o [frɑθ] *s* espuma; frivolidad, vanidad || *intr* espumar, echar espuma; (*at the mouth*) espumajear
froth·y ['frɔθi] o ['frɑθi] *adj* (*comp* **-ier;** *super* **-iest**) espumoso; frívolo, vano

froward [ˈfrowərd] *adj* díscolo, indócil

frown [fraʊn] *s* ceño, entrecejo || *intr* fruncir el entrecejo; **to frown at u on** mirar con ceño, desaprobar

frows•y o **frowz•y** [ˈfraʊzi] *adj* (*comp* **-ier;** *super* **-iest**) desaseado, desaliñado; maloliente; mal peinado

frozen foods [ˈfrozən] *spl* viandas congeladas

F.R.S. *abbr* **Fellow of the Royal Society**

frt. *abbr* **freight**

frugal [ˈfrugəl] *adj* (*moderate in the use of things*) parco; (*not very abundant*) frugal

fruit [frut] *adj* (*tree*) frutal; (*boat, dish*) frutero || *s* (*such as apple, pear, strawberry*) fruta; frutas, p.ej., **I like fruit** me gustan las frutas; (*part containing seed*) fruto; (*effect, result*) (fig) fruto

fruit cake *s* torta de frutas

fruit cup *s* compota de frutas picadas

fruit fly *s* mosca del vinagre; mosca de las frutas

fruitful [ˈfrutfəl] *adj* fructuoso

fruition [fruˈɪʃən] *s* buen resultado, cumplimiento; **to come to fruition** lograrse cumplidamente

fruit jar *s* tarro para frutas

fruit juice *s* jugo de frutas

fruitless [ˈfrutlɪs] *adj* infructuoso

fruit of the vine *s* zumo de cepas o de parras

fruit salad *s* ensalada de frutas, macedonia de frutas

fruit stand *s* puesto de frutas

fruit store *s* frutería

frumpish [ˈfrʌmpɪʃ] *adj* basto, desgarbado, desaliñado

frustrate [ˈfrʌstret] *tr* frustrar

fry [fraɪ] *s* (*pl* **fries**) fritada || *v* (*pret & pp* **fried**) *tr & intr* freír

frying pan [ˈfraɪ·ɪŋ] *s* sartén *f;* **to jump from the frying pan into the fire** saltar de la sartén y dar en las brasas

ft. *abbr* **foot, feet**

fudge [fʌdʒ] *s* dulce *m* de chocolate

fuel [ˈfju·əl] *s* combustible *m;* (fig) pábulo || *v* (*pret & pp* **fueled** o **fuelled;** *ger* **fueling** o **fuelling**) *tr* aprovisionar de combustible || *intr* aprovisionarse de combustible

fuel cell *s* cámara de combustible, célula electrógena

fuel oil *s* aceite *m* combustible

fuel tank *s* depósito de combustible

fugitive [ˈfjudʒɪtɪv] *adj & s* fugitivo

fugue [fjug] *s* (mus) fuga

ful•crum [ˈfʌlkrəm] *s* (*pl* **-crums** o **-cra** [krə]) fulcro

fulfill [fʊlˈfɪl] *tr* (*to carry out*) cumplir, realizar; cumplir con (*una obligación*); llenar (*una condición*)

fulfillment [fʊlˈfɪlmənt] *s* cumplimiento, realización

full [fʊl] *adj* lleno; (*dress, garment*) amplio, holgado; (*formal dress*) de etiqueta; (*voice*) sonoro, fuerte; (*of food*) harto; **full of aches and pains** lleno de goteras; **full of fun** muy divertido, muy chistoso; **full of play** muy juguetón; **full to overflowing** lleno a rebosar || *adv* completamente; **full many (a)** muchísimos; **full well** muy bien, perfectamente || *s* colmo; **in full** por completo; sin abreviar; **to the full** completamente || *tr* abatanar

full-blooded [ˈfʊlˈblʌdɪd] *adj* vigoroso; completo, pletórico; de raza

full-blown [ˈfʊlˈblon] *adj* (*flower, blossom*) abierto; desarrollado, maduro

full-bodied [ˈfʊlˈbɑdid] *adj* fuerte, espeso, consistente; aromático

full dress *s* traje *m* de etiqueta; (mil) uniforme *m* de gala

full′-dress′ coat *s* frac *m*

full-faced [ˈfʊlˈfest] *adj* carilleno; (*view*) de cuadrado; (*portrait*) de rostro entero

full-fledged [ˈfʊlˈflɛdʒd] *adj* hecho y derecho, nada menos que

full-grown [ˈfʊlˈgron] *adj* crecido, completamente desarrollado

full house *s* lleno, entrada llena; (poker) fulján *m*

full′-length′ mirror *s* espejo de cuerpo entero, espejo de vestir

full-length movie *s* largometraje *m*, cinta de largo metraje

full load *s* plena carga; (aer) peso total

full moon *s* luna llena, plenilunio

full name *s* nombre *m* y apellidos

full′-page′ *adj* a página entera

full powers *spl* plenos poderes, amplias facultades

full sail *adv* a todo trapo

full′-scale′ *adj* de tamaño natural; total, completo; pleno

full-sized [ˈfʊlˈsaɪzd] *adj* de tamaño natural

full speed *adv* a toda velocidad

full stop *s* parada completa; (gram) punto

full swing *s* plena actividad

full tilt *adv* a toda velocidad

full′-time′ *adj* a tiempo completo

full′-view′ *adj* de vista completa

full volume *s* (rad) máximo de volumen

fully [ˈfʊli] o [ˈfʊlli] *adv* completamente; cabalmente; por lo menos

fulsome [ˈfʊlsəm] o [ˈfʌlsəm] *adj* bajo, craso, de mal gusto

fumble [ˈfʌmbəl] *tr* no coger (*la pelota*), dejar caer (*la pelota*) desmañadamente; manosear desmañadamente || *intr* revolver papeles; titubear; andar a tientas; (*in one's pockets*) buscar con las manos

fume [fjum] *s* humo, vapor *m,* gas *m,* vaho || *tr* (*to treat with fumes*) ahumar || *intr* (*to give off fumes*) humear; (*to show anger*) echar pestes; **to fume at** echar pestes contra

fumigate [ˈfjumɪˌget] *tr* fumigar

fumigation [ˌfjumɪˈgeʃən] *s* fumigación

fun [fʌn] *s* divertimiento; broma, chacota; **to be fun** ser divertido; **to have fun** divertirse; **to make fun of** reírse de, burlarse de

function [ˈfʌŋkʃən] *s* función || *intr* funcionar
functional [ˈfʌŋkʃənəl] *adj* funcional
functionar·y [ˈfʌŋkʃəˌneri] *s* (*pl* **-ies**) funcionario
fund [fʌnd] *s* fondo; **funds** fondos || *tr* consolidar (*una deuda*)
fundamental [ˌfʌndəˈmentəl] *adj* fundamental || *s* fundamento
funeral [ˈfjunərəl] *adj* funeral; (*march, procession*) fúnebre; (*expense*) funerario || *s* funeral *m,* funerales *mpl,* pompa fúnebre (*de cuerpo presente*); **it's not my funeral** (slang) no corre a mi cuidado
funeral director *s* empresario de pompas fúnebres
funeral home o **parlor** *s* funeraria
funeral service *s* oficio de difuntos, misa de cuerpo presente
funereal [fjuˈnɪrɪ·əl] *adj* fúnebre
fungous [ˈfʌŋgəs] *adj* fungoso
fungus [ˈfʌŋgəs] *s* (*pl* **funguses** o **fungi** [ˈfʌndʒaɪ]) hongo; (pathol) fungo
funicular [fjuˈnɪkjələr] *adj* & *s* funicular *m*
funk [fʌŋk] *s* (coll) miedo, cobardía; (coll) cobarde *mf;* **in a funk** (coll) asustado
fun·nel [ˈfʌnəl] *s* embudo; (*smokestack*) chimenea; (*tube for ventilation*) manguera, ventilador *m* || *v* (*pret* & *pp* **-neled** o **-nelled;** *ger* **-neling** o **-nelling**) *tr* verter por medio de un embudo
funnies [ˈfʌniz] *spl* páginas cómicas, tiras cómicas, tebeo
fun·ny [ˈfʌni] *adj* (*comp* **-nier;** *super* **-niest**) cómico; divertido, chistoso; (coll) extraño, raro; **to strike someone as funny** hacerle a uno gracia
funny bone *s* hueso de la alegría
funny paper *s* páginas cómicas
fur. *abbr* **furlong, furnished**
fur [fʌr] *s* piel *f;* abrigo de pieles; (*on the tongue*) sarro
furbelow [ˈfʌrbəˌlo] *s* (*ruffle*) faralá *m;* (*frippery*) ringorrango
furbish [ˈfʌrbɪʃ] *tr* acicalar, limpiar; **to furbish up** renovar
furious [ˈfjʊrɪ·əs] *adj* furioso
furl [fʌrl] *tr* enrollar; (naut) aferrar
fur-lined [ˈfʌrˌlaɪnd] *adj* forrado con pieles
furlong [ˈfʌrlɔŋ] o [ˈfʌrlɑŋ] *s* estadio
furlough [ˈfʌrlo] *s* licencia || *tr* dar licencia a
furnace [ˈfʌrnɪs] *s* horno; (*to heat a house*) calorífero
furnish [ˈfʌrnɪʃ] *tr* amueblar; proporcionar, suministrar
furnishings [ˈfʌrnɪʃɪŋz] *spl* muebles *mpl;* (*things to wear*) artículos
furniture [ˈfʌrnɪtʃər] *s* muebles *mpl,* mobiliario; (naut) aparejo; **a piece of furniture** un mueble
furniture dealer *s* mueblista *mf*
furniture store *s* mueblería
furrier [ˈfʌrɪ·ər] *s* peletero
furrier·y [ˈfʌrɪ·əri] *s* (*pl* **-ies**) peletería
furrow [ˈfʌro] *s* surco || *tr* surcar
further [ˈfʌrðər] *adj* adicional; nuevo; más lejano || *adv* además; más lejos || *tr* adelantar, promover, fomentar
furtherance [ˈfʌrðərəns] *s* adelantamiento, promoción, fomento
furthermore [ˈfʌrðərˌmor] *adv* además
furthest [ˈfʌrðɪst] *adj* (el) más lejano || *adv* más lejos
furtive [ˈfʌrtɪv] *adj* furtivo
fu·ry [ˈfjʊri] *s* (*pl* **-ries**) furia
furze [fʌrz] *s* aulaga; retama de escoba
fuse [fjuz] *s* (*tube or wick filled with explosive material*) mecha; (*device for detonating an explosive charge*) espoleta; (elec) fusible *m,* cortacircuitos *m,* tapón *m;* **to burn out a fuse** quemar un fusible || *tr* fundir; (*to unite*) fusionar || *intr* fundirse; fusionarse
fuse box *s* caja de fusibles
fuselage [ˈfjuzəlɪdʒ] o [ˌfjuzəˈlɑʒ] *s* fuselaje *m*
fusible [ˈfjuzɪbəl] *adj* fundible, fusible
fusillade [ˌfjuzɪˈled] *s* fusilería; (*e.g., of questions*) andanada || atacar o matar con una descarga de fusilería, fusilar
fusion [ˈfjuʒən] *s* fusión
fuss [fʌs] *s* alharaca, hazañería; (coll) disputa por ligero motivo; **to make a fuss** hacer alharacas; **to make a fuss over** hacer fiestas a; disputar sobre || *tr* atolondrar, inquietar, confundir || *intr* hacer alharacas, inquietarse por bagatelas
fuss·y [ˈfʌsi] *adj* (*comp* **-ier;** *super* **-iest**) alharaquiento, alborotado; descontentadizo, quisquilloso, melindroso; funcionero, hazañero; muy adornado
fustian [ˈfʌstʃən] *s* (*coarse cloth*) fustán *m;* (*sort of velveteen*) pana; (*bombast*) cultedad, follaje *m*
fust·y [ˈfʌsti] *adj* (*comp* **-ier;** *super* **-iest**) mohoso, rancio; que huele a cerrado; pasado de moda
futile [ˈfjutɪl] *adj* (*unproductive*) estéril; (*unimportant*) fútil
futili·ty [fjuˈtɪlɪti] *s* (*pl* **-ties**) esterilidad; futilidad
future [ˈfjutʃər] *adj* futuro || *s* futuro, porvenir *m;* (gram) futuro; **futures** (com) futuros; **in the future** en el futuro; **in the near future** en un futuro próximo
fuze [fjuz] *s* (*tube or wick filled with explosive material*) mecha; (*device for detonating an explosive charge*) espoleta; (elec) fusible *m* || *tr* poner la espoleta a
fuzz [fʌz] *s* (*as on a peach*) pelusa, vello; (*in pockets and corners*) borra, tamo
fuzz·y [ˈfʌzi] *adj* (*comp* **-ier;** *super* **-iest**) cubierto de pelusa, velloso; polvoriento; (*indistinct*) borroso

G

G, g [dʒi] *s* séptima letra del alfabeto inglés
G. *abbr* **German, Gulf**
g. *abbr* **gender, genitive, gram**
gab [gæb] *s* (coll) cotorreo || (*pret & pp* **gabbed;** *ger* **gabbing**) *intr* (coll) cotorrear
gabardine ['gæbər,din] *s* gabardina
gabble ['gæbəl] *s* cotorreo, parloteo || *intr* cotorrear, parlotear
gable ['gebəl] *s* (*of roof*) aguilón *m;* (*over a door or window*) gablete *m,* frontón *m*
gable end *s* hastial *m*
gable roof *s* tejado de dos aguas
gad [gæd] *v* (*pret & pp* **gadded;** *ger* **gadding**) *intr* callejear, andar de acá para allá; **to gad about** pindonguear (*una mujer*)
gad'a·bout' *adj* callejero || *s* cirigallo; (*woman*) pindonga
gad'fly' *s* (*pl* **-flies**) tábano
gadget ['gædʒɪt] *s* adminículo, chisme *m,* artilugio
Gael [gel] *s* gaélico
Gaelic ['gelɪk] *adj & s* gaélico
gaff [gæf] *s* garfio, arpón *m;* **to stand the gaff** (slang) tener aguante
gag [gæg] *s* mordaza; (*interpolation by an actor*) morcilla; (*joke*) chiste *m,* payasada || *v* (*pret & pp* **gagged;** *ger* **gagging**) *tr* amordazar; dar bascas a || *intr* sentir bascas, arquear
gage [gedʒ] *s* (*pledge*) prenda; (*challenge*) desafío
gaie·ty ['ge·ɪti] *s* (*pl* **-ties**) alegría, algazara, diversión; (*of colors*) viveza
gaily ['geli] *adv* alegremente
gain [gen] *s* ganancia; (*increase*) aumento || *tr* ganar; (*to reach*) alcanzar || *intr* ganar terreno; mejorar (*un enfermo*); adelantarse (*un reloj*); **to gain on** ir alcanzando
gainful ['genfəl] *adj* ganancioso, provechoso
gain'say' *v* (*pret & pp* **-said** ['sed] o ['sɛd]) *tr* negar; contradecir; prohibir
gait [get] *s* paso, manera de andar
gaiter ['getər] *s* polaina corta
gal. *abbr* **gallon**
gala ['gælə] o ['gelə] *adj* de gala || *s* fiesta
galax·y ['gæləksi] *s* (*pl* **-ies**) galaxia
gale [gel] *s* ventarrón *m;* **gales of laughter** tempestades de risas; **to weather the gale** correr el temporal; (fig) ir tirando
Galician [gə'lɪʃən] *adj & s* gallego
gall [gɔl] *s* bilis *f,* hiel *f;* vejiga de la bilis; (*something bitter*) (fig) hiel *f;* rencor *m,* odio; (*gallnut*) agalla; (*audacity*) (coll) descaro || *tr* lastimar rozando; irritar || *intr* raerse; (naut) mascarse (*un cabo*)
gallant ['gælənt] o [gə'lænt] *adj* (*attentive to women*) galante; (*pertaining to love*) amoroso || ['gælənt] *adj* (*stately, grand*) gallardo; (*spirited, daring*) hazañoso; (*showy, gay*) vistoso, festivo || *s* hombre *m* valiente; (*man attentive to women*) galán *m*
gallant·ry ['gæləntri] *s* (*pl* **-ries**) galantería; gallardía
gall bladder *s* vejiga de la bilis, vesícula biliar
gall duct *s* conducto biliar
galleon ['gælɪ·ən] *s* (naut) galeón *m*
galler·y ['gæləri] *s* (*pl* **-ies**) galería; (*in church, theater, etc.*) tribuna; (*cheapest seats in theater*) gallinero; **to play to the gallery** (coll) hablar para la galería
galley ['gæli] *s* (naut & typ) galera; (naut) cocina
galley proof *s* (typ) galerada, pruebas de segundas
galley slave *s* galeote *m;* (*drudge*) esclavo del trabajo
Gallic ['gælɪk] *adj* gálico
galling ['gɔlɪŋ] *adj* irritante, ofensivo
gallivant ['gælɪ,vænt] *intr* andar a placer
gall'nut' *s* agalla
gallon ['gælən] *s* galón *m* (*medida*)
galloon [gə'lun] *s* galón *m* (*cinta*)
gallop ['gæləp] *s* galope *m;* **at a gallop** a galope || *tr* hacer galopar || *intr* galopar; **to gallop through** (fig) hacer muy aprisa
gal·lows ['gæloz] *s* (*pl* **-lows** o **-lowses**) horca
gallows bird *s* (coll) carne *f* de horca
gall'stone' *s* cálculo biliar
galore [gə'lor] *adv* en abundancia
galosh [gə'lɑʃ] *s* chanclo alto
galvanize ['gælvə,naɪz] *tr* galvanizar
galvanized iron *s* hierro galvanizado
gambit ['gæmbɪt] *s* gambito
gamble ['gæmbəl] *s* (coll) empresa arriesgada || *tr* aventurar en el juego; **to gamble away** perder en el juego || *intr* jugar; (*in the stock market*) especular, aventurarse
gambler ['gæmblər] *s* jugador *m;* especulador *m*
gambling ['gæmblɪŋ] *s* juego
gambling den *s* garito
gambling house *s* casa de juego, juego público
gambling table *s* mesa de juego
gam·bol ['gæmbəl] *s* cabriola, retozo, salto || *v* (*pret & pp* **-boled** o **-bolled;** *gen* **-boling** o **-bolling**) *intr* cabriolar, retozar, saltar
gambrel ['gæmbrəl] *s* corvejón *m*
gambrel roof *s* techo a la holandesa
game [gem] *adj* bravo, peleón; dispuesto, resuelto; (*leg*) cojo; de caza || *s* (*form of play*) juego; (*single contest*) partida; (*score*) tantos; (*in bridge*) manga; (*any sport*) deporte *m;* (*animal or bird hunted for sport or food*) caza; (*any pursuit*) actividad; (*pursuit of diplomacy*) juego;

the game is up estamos frescos; **to make game of** burlarse de; **to play the game** jugar limpio
game bag *s* morral *m*
game bird *s* ave *f* de caza
game′cock′ *s* gallo de pelea
game′keep′er *s* guardabosque *m*
game of chance *s* juego de azar
game preserve *s* vedado
game warden *s* guardabosque *m*
gamut [ˈgæmət] *s* (mus & fig) gama
gam•y [ˈgemi] *adj* (*comp* **-ier;** *super* **-iest**) (*having flavor of uncooked game*) salvajino; bravo, peleón
gander [ˈgændər] *s* ganso
gang [gæŋ] *adj* múltiple ‖ *s* (*of workmen*) brigada, cuadrilla; (*of thugs*) pandilla ‖ *intr* — **to gang up** acuadrillarse; **to gang up against** u **on** atacar juntos; conspirar contra
gangling [ˈgæŋglɪŋ] *adj* larguirucho
gangli•on [ˈgæŋglɪ•ən] *s* (*pl* **-ons** o **-a** [ə]) ganglio
gang′plank′ *s* plancha, pasarela
gangrene [ˈgæŋgrin] *s* gangrena ‖ *tr* gangrenar ‖ *intr* gangrenarse
gangster [ˈgæŋstər] *s* (coll) gángster *m,* pistolero
gang′way′ *s* (*passageway*) pasillo; (*gangplank*) plancha, pasarela; (*in ship's side*) portalón *m* ‖ *interj* ¡abran paso!, ¡paso libre!
gantlet [ˈgɑntlɪt] o [ˈgɔntlɪt] *s* (rr) vía traslapada
gan•try [ˈgæntri] *s* (*pl* **-tries**) caballete *m,* poíno; (rr) puente *m* transversal de señales
gantry crane *s* grúa de caballete
gap [gæp] *s* (*break, open space*) laguna; (*in a wall*) boquete *m;* (*between mountains*) garganta, quebrada; (*between two points of view*) sima
gape [gep] o [gæp] *s* abertura, brecha; (*yawn*) bostezo; mirada de asombro; **the gapes** ganas de bostezar ‖ *intr* estar abierto de par en par; bostezar; embobarse; **to gape at** mirar embobado; **to stand gaping** embobarse
G.A.R. *abbr* **Grand Army of the Republic**
garage [gəˈrɑz] *s* garage *m*
garb [gɑrb] *s* vestidura ‖ *tr* vestir
garbage [ˈgɑrbɪdʒ] *s* basuras, desperdicios, bazofia
garbage can *s* cubo para bazofia, latón *m* de la basura
garbage disposal *s* evacuación de basuras
garble [ˈgɑrbəl] *tr* mutilar (*un texto*)
garden [ˈgɑrdən] *s* (*of vegetables*) huerto; (*of flowers*) jardín *m*
gardener [ˈgɑrdənər] *s* (*of vegetables*) hortelano; (*of flowers*) jardinero
gardenia [gɑrˈdinɪ•ə] *s* gardenia, jazmín *m* de la India
gardening [ˈgɑrdənɪŋ] *s* horticultura; jardinería
garden party *s* fiesta que se da en un jardín o parque
gargle [ˈgɑrgəl] *s* gargarismo ‖ *intr* gargarizar
gargoyle [ˈgɑrgɔɪl] *s* gárgola
garish [ˈgɛrɪʃ] o [ˈgærɪʃ] *adj* charro, chillón, cursi
garland [ˈgɑrlənd] *s* guirnalda
garlic [ˈgɑrlɪk] *s* ajo
garment [ˈgɑrmənt] *s* prenda de vestir
garner [ˈgɑrnər] *tr* (*to gather, collect*) acopiar; adquirir; (*cereales*) entrojar
garnet [ˈgɑrnɪt] *adj* & *s* granate *m*
garnish [ˈgɑrnɪʃ] *s* adorno; (culin) aderezo, condimento de adorno ‖ *tr* adornar; (culin) aderezar; (law) embargar
garret [ˈgærɪt] *s* buhardilla, desván *m*
garrison [ˈgærɪsən] *s* plaza fuerte; (*troops*) guarnición ‖ *tr* guarnecer, guarnicionar (*una plaza fuerte*); guarnecer una plaza fuerte de (*tropas*)
garrote [gəˈrɑt] o [gəˈrot] *s* estrangulación para robar; (*method of execution; iron collar used for such execution*) garrote *m* ‖ *tr* estrangular; estrangular para robar; agarrotar, dar garrote a
garrulous [ˈgærələs] o [ˈgærjələs] *adj* gárrulo, locuaz
garter [ˈgɑrtər] *s* liga, jarretera
garth [gɑrθ] *s* patio de claustro
gas [gæs] *s* gas *m;* (coll) gasolina; (coll) palabrería ‖ *v* (*pret & pp* **gassed;** *ger* **gassing**) *tr* abastecer de gas; (*to attack, asphyxiate, or poison with gas*) gasear; (coll) abastecer de gasolina ‖ *intr* despedir gas; (slang) charlar
gas′bag′ *s* (aer) cámara de gas; (slang) charlatán *m*
gas burner *s* mechero de gas
Gascony [ˈgæskəni] *s* Gascuña
gas engine *s* motor *m* a gas
gaseous [ˈgæsɪ•əs] *adj* gaseoso
gas fitter *s* gasista *m*
gas generator *s* gasógeno
gash [gæʃ] *s* cuchillada, chirlo ‖ *tr* acuchillar
gas heat *s* calefacción por gas
gas′hold′er *s* gasómetro
gasi•fy [ˈgæsɪˌfaɪ] *v* (*pret & pp* **-fied**) *tr* gasificar ‖ *intr* gasificarse
gas jet *s* mechero de gas; llama de gas
gasket [ˈgæskɪt] *s* empaquetadura
gas′light′ *s* luz *f* de gas
gas main *s* cañería de gas
gas mask *s* careta antigás
gas meter *s* contador *m* de gas
gasoline [ˈgæsəˌlin] o [ˌgæsəˈlin] *s* gasolina
gasoline pump *s* poste *m* distribuidor *m* de gasolina, surtidor *m* de gasolina
gasp [gæsp] o [gɑsp] *s* respiración entrecortada; (*of death*) boqueada ‖ *tr* decir con voz entrecortada ‖ *intr* boquear
gas producer *s* gasógeno
gas range *s* cocina a gas
gas station *s* estación gasolinera
gas stove *s* cocina a gas
gas tank *s* gasómetro; (aut) depósito de gasolina
gastric [ˈgæstrɪk] *adj* gástrico

gastronomy [gæs'trɑnəmi] *s* gastronomía
gas'works' *s* fábrica de gas
gate [get] *s* puerta; (*in fence or wall; of bird cage*) portillo; (*of sluice or lock*) compuerta; (*number of people paying admission; amount they pay*) entrada, taquilla; (rr) barrera; (fig) entrada, camino; **to crash the gate** (coll) colarse de gorra
gate'keep'er *s* portero; (rr) guardabarrera *mf*
gate'post' *s* poste *m* de una puerta de cercado
gate'way' *s* entrada, paso, camino
gather ['gæðər] *tr* recoger, reunir; recolectar (*la cosecha*); coger (*leña, flores, etc.*); cubrirse de (*polvo*); recoger (*una persona sus pensamientos*); (bb) alzar; (sew) fruncir; (*to deduce*) (fig) calcular, deducir; **to gather oneself together** componerse || *intr* reunirse; amontonarse; saltar (*lágrimas*)
gathering ['gæðərɪŋ] *s* reunión; recolección; (bb) alzado; (sew) frunce *m*
gaud·y ['gɔdi] *adj* (*comp* **-ier;** *super* **-iest**) cursi, chillón, llamativo
gauge [gedʒ] *s* medida, norma; calibre *m;* (*of liquid in a container*) nivel *m;* (*of carpenter*) gramil *m;* (*of gasoline*) medidor *m;* (rr) ancho de vía, entrevía || *tr* medir; calibrar; graduar; aforar (*la cantidad de agua de una corriente*); arquear (*una nave*)
gauge glass *s* tubo indicador, vidrio de nivel
Gaul [gɔl] *s* la Galia; (*native*) galo
Gaulish ['gɔlɪʃ] *adj & s* galo
gaunt [gɔnt] o [gɑnt] *adj* desvaído, macilento; hosco, tétrico
gauntlet ['gɔntlɪt] o ['gɑntlɪt] *s* guantelete *m;* guante con puño abocinado; carrera de baquetas; (rr) vía traslapada; **to run the gauntlet** correr baquetas, pasar por baquetas; **to take up the gauntlet** recoger el guante; **to throw down the gauntlet** arrojar el guante
gauze [gɔz] *s* gasa, cendal *m*
gavel ['gævəl] *s* mazo, martillo
gavotte [gə'vɑt] *s* gavota
gawk [gɔk] *s* (coll) palurdo, papanatas *m* || *intr* (coll) mirar de modo impertinente; papar moscas, mirar embobado
gawk·y ['gɔki] *adj* (*comp* **-ier;** *super* **-iest**) desgarbado, torpe, bobo
gay [ge] *adj* alegre, festivo; (*brilliant*) vistoso; amigo de los placeres
gaye·ty ['ge·ɪti] *s* var de **gaiety**
gaze [gez] *s* mirada fija || *intr* mirar fijamente
gazelle [gə'zɛl] *s* gacela
gazette [gə'zɛt] *s* periódico; anuncio oficial
gazetteer [,gæzə'tɪr] *s* diccionario geográfico
gear [gɪr] *s* pertrechos, utensilios; (*of transmission, steering, etc.*) mecanismo, aparato; rueda dentada; (*two or more toothed wheels meshed together*) engranaje *m;* **out of gear** desengranado; (fig) descompuesto; **to throw into gear** engranar; **to throw out of gear** desengranar; (fig) descomponer || *tr & intr* engranar
gear'box' *s* caja de engranajes; (aut) caja de velocidades
gear case *s* caja de engranajes
gear'shift' *s* cambio de marchas, cambio de velocidades
gearshift lever *s* palanca de cambio de marchas
gear'wheel' *s* rueda dentada
gee [dʒi] *interj* ¡caramba!; **gee up!** (*get up!, said to a horse*) ¡arre!
Gehenna [gɪ'hɛnə] *s* gehena *m*
gel [dʒɛl] *s* gel *m* || *v* (*pret & pp* **gelled;** *ger* **gelling)** *intr* cuajarse en forma de gel
gelatine ['dʒɛlətɪn] *s* gelatina
geld [gɛld] *v* (*pret & pp* **gelded** o **gelt** [gɛlt]) *tr* castrar
gem [dʒɛm] *s* gema, piedra preciosa; (fig) joya, preciosidad
Gemini ['dʒɛmɪ,naɪ] *s* (*constellation*) Géminis *m* o Gemelos; (*sign of zodiac*) Géminis *m*
gen. *abbr* **gender, general, genitive, genus**
gender ['dʒɛndər] *s* (gram) género; (coll) sexo
genealo·gy [,dʒɛnɪ'ælədʒi] o [,dʒinɪ'ælədʒi] *s* (*pl* **-gies**) genealogía
general ['dʒɛnərəl] *adj & s* general *m;* **in general** en general o por lo general
general delivery *s* lista de correos
generalissi·mo [,dʒɛnərə'lɪsɪmo] *s* (*pl* **-mos**) generalísimo
generali·ty [,dʒɛnə'rælɪti] *s* (*pl* **-ties**) generalidad
generalize ['dʒɛnərə,laɪz] *tr & intr* generalizar
generally ['dʒɛnərəli] *adv* por lo general
general practitioner *s* médico general
generalship ['dʒɛnərəl,ʃɪp] *s* generalato; don *m* de mando
general staff *s* estado mayor general
generate ['dʒɛnə,ret] *tr* (*to beget*) engendrar; generar (*electricidad*); (geom) engendrar
generating station *s* central *f*
generation [,dʒɛnə'reʃən] *s* generación
generator ['dʒɛnə,retər] *s* generador *m*
generic [dʒɪ'nɛrɪk] *adj* genérico
generous ['dʒɛnərəs] *adj* generoso; abundante, grande
gene·sis ['dʒɛnɪsɪs] *s* (*pl* **-ses** [,siz]) génesis *f* || **Genesis** *s* (Bib) el Génesis
genetic [dʒɪ'nɛtɪk] *adj* genético || **genetics** *s* genética
Geneva [dʒɪ'nivə] *s* Ginebra
Genevan [dʒɪ'nivən] *adj & s* ginebrino
genial ['dʒinɪ·əl] *adj* afable, complaciente
genie ['dʒini] *s* genio
genital ['dʒɛnɪtəl] *adj* genital || **genitals** *spl* genitales *mpl,* órganos genitales
genitive ['dʒɛnɪtɪv] *adj & s* genitivo
genius ['dʒinjəs] o ['dʒinɪ·əs] *s* (*pl* **geniuses**) (*great inventive gift; person possessing it*) genio || *s* (*pl* **genii**

[ˈdʒinɪˌaɪ]) (*guardian spirit; pagan deity*) genio
Genoa [ˈdʒeno·ə] *s* Génova
genocidal [ˌdʒenəˈsaɪdəl] *adj* genocida
genocide [ˈdʒenəˌsaɪd] *s* (*act*) genocidio; (*person*) genocida *mf*
Geno·ese [ˌdʒenoˈiz] *adj* genovés ‖ *s* (*pl* **-ese**) genovés *m*
genre [ˈʒɑnrə] *adj* de género
gent. o **Gent.** *abbr* **gentleman, gentlemen**
genteel [dʒenˈtil] *adj* gentil, elegante; cortés, urbano
gentian [ˈdʒenʃən] *s* genciana
gentile [ˈdʒentɪl] o [ˈdʒentaɪl] *adj* gentilicio; (gram) gentilicio ‖ [ˈdʒentaɪl] *adj & s* no judío; cristiano; (*pagan*) gentil *mf*
gentili·ty [dʒenˈtɪlɪti] *s* (*pl* **-ties**) gentileza
gentle [ˈdʒentəl] *adj* apacible, benévolo; dulce, manso, suave; cortés, fino; (*e.g., tap on the shoulder*) ligero
gen′tle·folk′ *s* gente bien nacida
gentle·man [ˈdʒentəlmən] *s* (*pl* **-men** [mən]) *s* caballero; (*attendant to a person of high rank*) gentilhombre *m*
gentleman in waiting *s* gentilhombre *m* de cámara
gentlemanly [ˈdʒentəlmənli] *adj* caballeroso
gentleman of leisure *s* señor *m* que vive sin trabajar, caballero de vida holgada
gentleman of the road *s* salteador *m* de caminos
gentleman's agreement *s* acuerdo verbal
gentle sex *s* bello sexo, sexo débil
gentry [ˈdʒentri] *s* gente bien nacida
genuine [ˈdʒenjʊ·ɪn] *adj* genuino; sincero, franco
genus [ˈdʒinəs] *s* (*pl* **genera** [ˈdʒenərə] o **genuses**) (biol, log) género
geog. *abbr* **geography**
geographer [dʒɪˈɑgrəfər] *s* geógrafo
geographic(al) [ˌdʒi·əˈgræfɪk(əl)] *adj* geográfico
geogra·phy [dʒɪˈɑgrəfi] *s* (*pl* **-phies**) geografía
geol. *abbr* **geology**
geologic(al) [ˌdʒi·əˈlɑdʒɪk(əl)] *adj* geológico
geologist [dʒɪˈɑlədʒɪst] *s* geólogo
geolo·gy [dʒɪˈɑlədʒi] *s* (*pl* **-gies**) geología
geom. *abbr* **geometry**
geometric(al) [ˌdʒi·əˈmetrɪk(əl)] *adj* geométrico
geometrician [dʒɪˌɑmɪˈtrɪʃən] *s* geómetra *mf*
geome·try [dʒɪˈɑmɪtri] *s* (*pl* **-tries**) geometría
geophysics [ˌdʒi·əˈfɪzɪks] *s* geofísica
geopolitics [ˌdʒi·əˈpɑlɪtɪks] *s* geopolítica
George [dʒɔrdʒ] *s* Jorje *m*
geranium [dʒɪˈrenɪ·əm] *s* geranio
geriatrical [ˌdʒerɪˈætrɪkəl] *adj* geriátrico
geriatrician [ˌdʒerɪ·əˈtrɪʃən] *s* geriatra *mf*
geriatrics [ˌdʒerɪˈætrɪks] *s* geriatría
germ [dʒʌrm] *s* germen *m*
German [ˈdʒʌrmən] *adj & s* alemán *m*
germane [dʒərˈmen] *adj* pertinente, relacionado
Germanize [ˈdʒʌrməˌnaɪz] *tr* germanizar
German measles *s* rubéola
German silver *s* melchor *m*, alpaca
Germany [ˈdʒʌrməni] *s* Alemania
germ carrier *s* portador *m* de gérmenes
germ cell *s* célula germen
germicidal [ˌdʒʌrmɪˈsaɪdəl] *adj* germicida
germicide [ˈdʒʌrmɪˌsaɪd] *s* germicida *m*
germinate [ˈdʒʌrmɪˌnet] *intr* germinar
germ plasm *s* germen *m* plasma
germ theory *s* teoría germinal
germ warfare *s* guerra bacteriana
gerontology [ˌdʒerɑnˈtɑlədʒi] *s* gerontología
gerund [ˈdʒerənd] *s* gerundio
gerundive [dʒɪˈrʌndɪv] *s* gerundio adjetivo
gestation [dʒesˈteʃən] *s* gestación
gesticulate [dʒesˈtɪkjəˌlet] *intr* accionar, manotear
gesticulation [dʒesˌtɪkjəˈleʃən] *s* ademán *m*, manoteo
gesture [ˈdʒestʃər] *s* ademán *m*, gesto; demostración, muestra ‖ *intr* hacer ademanes, hacer gestos
get [get] *v* (*pret* **got** [gɑt]; *pp* **got** o **gotten** [ˈgɑtən]; *ger* **getting**) *tr* conseguir, obtener; recibir; ir por, buscar; tomar (*p.ej., un billete*); alcanzar; encontrar, hallar; hacer (*p.ej., la comida*); resolver (*un problema*); aprender de memoria; captar (*una estación emisora*); **to get across** hacer aceptar; hacer comprender; **to get back** recobrar; **to get down** descolgar; (*to swallow*) tragar; **to get off** quitar (*p.ej., una mancha*); **to get someone to** + *inf* lograr que alguien + *subj;* **to get** + *pp* hacer + *inf;* **to have got** (coll) tener; **to have got to** + *inf* (coll) tener que + *inf* ‖ *intr* (*to become*) hacerse, ponerse, volverse; (*to arrive*) llegar; **get up!** (*to an animal*) ¡arre!; **to get about** estar levantado (*un convaleciente*); **to get along** seguir andando; irse; ir tirando; tener éxito; llevarse bien; **to get along in years** ponerse viejo; **to get along with** congeniar con; **to get angry** enfadarse; **to get around** divulgarse; salir mucho, ir a todas partes; eludir; manejar (*a una persona*); **to get away** conseguir marcharse; evadirse; **to get away with** llevarse, escaparse con; (coll) hacer impunemente; **to get back** volver, regresar; **to get back at** (coll) desquitarse con; **to get behind** quedarse atrás; apoyar, abogar por; **to get by** lograr pasar; (*to manage to shift*) (coll) arreglárselas; **to get going** ponerse en marcha; **to get in** entrar; volver a casa; llegar (*un tren*); **to get in with**

llegar a ser amigo de; **to get married** casarse; **to get off** apearse; marcharse; **to get old** envejecer; **to get on** subir; llevarse bien; **to get out** salir, marcharse; divulgarse; **to get out of** bajar de (*un coche*); librarse de; perder (*la paciencia*); **to get out of the way** quitarse de en medio; **to get run over** ser atropellado; **to get through** pasar por entre; terminar; **to get to be** llegar a ser; **to get under way** ponerse en camino; **to get up** levantarse; **to not get over it** (coll) no volver de su asombro

get'a·way' *s* escapatoria, escape *m;* (*of an automobile*) arranque *m*

get'-to·geth'er *s* reunión, tertulia

get'-up' *s* (coll) disposición, presentación; (coll) atavío, traje *m*

gewgaw ['gjugɔ] *adj* cursi, charro, chillón || *s* fruslería, chuchería; adorno charro

geyser ['gaɪzər] *s* géiser *m* || ['gizər] *s* (Brit) calentador *m* de agua

ghast·ly ['gæstli] o ['gɑstli] *adj* (*comp* **-lier;** *super* **-liest**) cadavérico, espectral; espantoso, horrible

Ghent [gɛnt] *s* Gante

gherkin ['gʌrkɪn] *s* pepinillo

ghet·to ['gɛto] *s* (*pl* **-tos**) ghetto

ghost [gost] *s* espectro, fantasma *m;* (telv) fantasma *m;* **not a ghost of a** ni sombra de; **to give up the ghost** entregar el alma, rendir el alma

ghost·ly ['gostli] *adj* (*comp* **-lier;** *super* **-liest**) espectral

ghost story *s* cuento de fantasmas

ghost writer *s* colaborador anónimo, escritor anónimo de obras firmadas por otra persona

ghoul [gul] *s* demonio que se alimenta de cadáveres; ladrón *m* de tumbas; (*person who revels in horrible things*) vampiro

ghoulish ['gulɪʃ] *adj* vampírico, horrible

G.H.Q. *abbr* **General Headquarters**

GI ['dʒi'aɪ] *s* (*pl* **GI's**) (coll) soldado raso (*del ejército norteamericano*)

giant ['dʒaɪ·ənt] *adj* & *s* gigante *m*

giantess ['dʒaɪ·əntɪs] *s* giganta

gibberish ['dʒɪbərɪʃ] o ['gɪbərɪʃ] *s* guirigay *m*

gibbet ['dʒɪbɪt] *s* horca || *tr* ahorcar; poner a la vergüenza

gibe [dʒaɪb] *s* remoque *m,* mofa || *intr* mofarse; **to gibe at** mofarse de

giblets ['dʒɪblɪts] *spl* menudillos

giddiness ['gɪdɪnɪs] *s* vértigo, vahido; falta de juicio

gid·dy ['gɪdi] *adj* (*comp* **-dier;** *super* **-diest**) vertiginoso; mareado; casquivano, ligero de cascos

Gideon ['gɪdɪ·ən] *s* (Bib) Gedeón *m*

gift [gɪft] *s* regalo; (*natural ability*) don *m,* dote *f,* prenda

gifted ['gɪftɪd] *adj* talentoso; muy inteligente

gift horse *s* — **never look a gift horse in the mouth** a caballo regalado no se le mira el diente

gift of gab *s* (coll) facundia, labia

gift shop *s* comercio de objetos de regalo, tienda de regalos

gift'-wrap' *v* (*pret* & *pp* **-wrapped;** *ger* **wrapping)** *tr* envolver en paquete regalo

gigantic [dʒaɪ'gæntɪk] *adj* gigantesco

giggle ['gɪgəl] *s* risita, risa ahogada, retozo de la risa || *intr* reírse bobamente

gigo·lo ['dʒɪgə,lo] *s* (*pl* **-los**) acompañante *m* profesional de mujeres; (*man supported by a woman*) mantenido

gild [gɪld] *v* (*pret* & *pp* **gilded** o **gilt** [gɪlt]) *tr* dorar

gilding ['gɪldɪŋ] *s* dorado

gill [gɪl] *s* (*of fish*) agalla; (*of cock*) barba || [dʒɪl] *s* cuarta parte de una pinta

gillyflower ['dʒɪlɪ,flaʊ·ər] *s* alhelí *m*

gilt [gɪlt] *adj* & *s* dorado

gilt-edged ['gɪlt,ɛdʒd] *adj* de toda confianza, de lo mejor que hay

gilt'head' *s* dorada

gimcrack ['dʒɪm,kræk] *adj* de oropel || *s* chuchería

gimlet ['gɪmlɪt] *s* barrena de mano

gimmick ['gɪmɪk] *s* (slang) adminículo; (slang) adminículo mágico

gin [dʒɪn] *s* (*alcoholic liquor*) ginebra; desmotadera de algodón; trampa; (*fish trap*) garlito; torno de izar || *v* (*pret* & *pp* **ginned;** *ger* **ginning)** *tr* desmotar

gin fizz *s* ginebra con gaseosa

ginger ['dʒɪndʒər] *s* jenjibre *m;* (coll) energía, viveza

ginger ale *s* cerveza de jengibre gaseosa

gin'ger·bread' *s* pan *m* de jengibre; adorno charro

gingerly ['dʒɪndʒərli] *adj* cauteloso, cuidadoso || *adv* cautelosamente

gin'ger·snap' *s* galletita de jengibre

gingham ['gɪŋəm] *s* guinga

giraffe [dʒɪ'ræf] o [dʒɪ'rɑf] *s* jirafa

girandole ['dʒɪrən,dol] *s* girándula

gird [gʌrd] *v* (*pret* & *pp* **girt** [gʌrt] o **girded**) *tr* ceñir; (*to equip*) dotar; (*to prepare*) aprestar; (*to surround, hem in*) rodear, encerrar

girder ['gʌrdər] *s* viga, trabe *f*

girdle ['gʌrdəl] *s* faja; corsé pequeño || *tr* ceñir; circundar, rodear

girl [gʌrl] *s* muchacha, niña, chica; (*servant*) moza

girl friend *s* (coll) amiguita

girlhood ['gʌrlhʊd] *s* muchachez *f;* juventud femenina

girlish ['gʌrlɪʃ] *adj* de muchacha; juvenil

girl scout *s* niña exploradora

girth [gʌrθ] *s* (*band*) cincha; (*waistband*) pretina; circunferencia

gist [dʒɪst] *s* esencia

give [gɪv] *s* elasticidad || *v* (*pret* **gave** [gev]; *pp* **given** ['gɪvən]) *tr* dar; ocasionar (*molestia, trabajo, etc.*); representar (*una obra dramática*); pronunciar (*un discurso*); **to give away** dar de balde; revelar; llevar (*a la novia*); (coll) traicionar; **to give back** devolver; **to give forth** despedir (*p.ej., olores*); **to give oneself up**

entregarse; **to give up** abandonar, dejar (*un empleo*); renunciar ‖ *intr* dar; dar de sí; romperse (*p.ej., una cuerda*); **to give in** ceder, rendirse; **to give out** agotarse; no poder más; **to give up** darse por vencido

give'-and-take' *s* concesiones mutuas; conversación sazonada de burlas

give'a·way' *s* (coll) revelación involuntaria; (coll) traición; (*e.g., in checkers*) (coll) ganapierde *m* & *f*

given ['gɪvən] *adj* dado; (math) conocido; **given that** dado que, suponiendo que

given name *s* nombre *m* de pila

giver ['gɪvər] *s* dador *m*, donador *m*

gizzard ['gɪzərd] *s* molleja

glacial ['gleʃəl] *adj* glacial

glacier ['gleʃər] *s* glaciar *m*, helero

glad [glæd] *adj* (*comp* **gladder;** *super* **gladdest**) alegre, contento; **to be glad (to)** alegrarse (de)

gladden ['glædən] *tr* alegrar

glade [gled] *s* claro, claro herboso (*en un bosque*)

glad hand *s* (coll) acogida efusiva

gladiola [,glædɪ'olə] o [glə'daɪ·ələ] *s* estoque *m*

gladly ['glædli] *adv* alegremente; de buena gana, con mucho gusto

gladness ['glædnɪs] *s* alegría, regocijo

glad rags *spl* (slang) trapitos de cristianar; (slang) vestido de etiqueta

glamorous ['glæmərəs] *adj* fascinador, elegante

glamour ['glæmər] *s* fascinación, elegancia, hechizo

glamour girl *s* belleza exótica

glance [glæns] o [glɑns] *s* ojeada, vistazo, golpe *m* de vista; **at a glance** de un vistazo; **at first glance** a primera vista ‖ *intr* lanzar una mirada; **to glance at** lanzar una mirada a; examinar de paso; **to glance off** desviarse de soslayo; desviarse de, al chocar; **to glance over** mirar por encima

gland [glænd] *s* glándula

glanders ['glændərz] *spl* muermo

glare [glɛr] *s* fulgor *m* deslumbrante, luz intensa; mirada feroz, mirada de indignación ‖ *intr* relumbrar; lanzar miradas feroces; **to glare at** echar una mirada feroz a

glaring ['glɛrɪŋ] *adj* deslumbrante, relumbrante; (*look*) feroz, penetrante; manifiesto, que salta a la vista

glass [glæs] o [glɑs] *s* vidrio, cristal *m;* (*tumbler*) vaso, copa; (*mirror*) espejo; (*glassware*) vajilla de cristal; **glasses** anteojos

glass blower ['blo·ər] *s* soplador *m* de vidrio, vidriero

glass case *s* vitrina

glass cutter *s* cortavidrios *m*

glass door *s* puerta vidriera

glassful ['glæsfʊl] o ['glɑsfʊl] *s* vaso

glass'house' *s* invernadero; (fig) tejado de vidrio

glassine [glæ'sin] *s* papel *m* cristal

glass'ware' *s* cristalería, vajilla de vidrio

glass wool *s* cristal hilado

glass'works' *s* cristalería, vidriería

glass'work'er *s* vidriero

glass·y ['glæsi] o ['glɑsi] *adj* (*comp* **-ier;** *super* **-iest**) vidrioso

glaze [glez] *s* vidriado, esmalte *m;* (*of ice*) capa resbaladiza ‖ *tr* vidriar, esmaltar; garapiñar (*golosinas*)

glazier ['gleʒər] *s* vidriero

gleam [glim] *s* destello, rayo de luz; luz *f* tenue; (*of hope*) rayo ‖ *intr* destellar; brillar con luz tenue

glean [glin] *tr* espigar; (*to gather bit by bit, e.g., out of books*) espigar

glee [gli] *s* alegría, regocijo

glee club *s* orfeón *m*

glib [glɪb] *adj* (*comp* **glibber;** *super* **glibbest**) locuaz; (*tongue*) suelto; fácil e insincero

glide [glaɪd] *s* deslizamiento; (aer) vuelo sin motor, planeo; (mus) ligadura ‖ *intr* deslizarse; (aer) volar sin motor, planear; **to glide along** pasar suavemente

glider ['glaɪdər] *s* (aer) planeador *m*, deslizador *m*

glimmer ['glɪmər] *s* luz *f* tenue; (*faint perception*) vislumbre *f* ‖ *intr* brillar con luz tenue; (*to appear faintly*) vislumbrarse

glimmering ['glɪmərɪŋ] *adj* tenue, trémulo ‖ *s* luz *f* tenue; vislumbre *f*

glimpse [glɪmps] *s* vislumbre *f;* **to catch a glimpse of** entrever, vislumbrar ‖ *tr* vislumbrar

glint [glɪnt] *s* destello, rayo ‖ *intr* destellar

glisten ['glɪsən] *s* centelleo ‖ *intr* centellear

glitter ['glɪtər] *s* resplandor *m*, brillo ‖ *intr* resplandecer, brillar

gloaming ['glomɪŋ] *s* crepúsculo vespertino

gloat [glot] *intr* relamerse; **to gloat over** mirar con satisfacción maligna

globe [glob] *s* globo

globetrotter ['glob,trɑtər] *s* trotamundos *m*

globule ['glɑbjʊl] *s* glóbulo

glockenspiel ['glɑkən,spil] *s* juego de timbres, órgano de campanas

gloom [glum] *s* lobreguez *f*, tinieblas, obscuridad; abatimiento, tristeza; aspecto abatido

gloom·y ['glumi] *adj* (*comp* **-ier;** *super* **-iest**) (*dark; sad*) lóbrego; pesimista

glori·fy ['glorɪ,faɪ] *v* (*pret & pp* **-fied**) *tr* glorificar; (*to enhance*) realzar

glorious ['glorɪ·əs] *adj* glorioso; espléndido, magnífico; (coll) alegre

glo·ry ['glori] *s* (*pl* **-ries**) gloria; **to go to glory** ganar la gloria; (slang) fracasar ‖ *v* (*pret & pp* **-ried**) *intr* gloriarse

gloss [glɔs] o [glɑs] *s* brillo, lustre *m;* (*note, commentary*) glosa; glosario ‖ *tr* (*to annotate*) glosar; lustrar, satinar; **to gloss over** disculpar, paliar

glossa·ry ['glɑsəri] *s* (*pl* **-ries**) glosario

gloss·y ['glɔsi] o ['glɑsi] *adj* (*comp* **-ier;** *super* **-iest**) brillante, lustroso; (*silk*) joyante

glottal ['glɑtəl] *adj* glótico
glove [glʌv] *s* guante *m*
glove compartment *s* portaguantes *m*
glove stretcher *s* ensanchador *m*, juanas
glow [glo] *s* (*light of incandescence*) resplandor *m*; (*e.g., of sunset*) brillo, esplendor *m*; sensación de calor; color *m* en las mejillas || *intr* brillar sin llama; estar encendido (*el rostro, el cielo*); estar muy animado
glower ['glaʊ·ər] *s* ceño, mirada ceñuda || *intr* mirar con ceño
glowing ['glo·ɪŋ] *adj* ardiente, encendido; radiante; entusiasta, elogioso
glow'worm' *s* gusano de luz, luciérnaga
glucose ['glukos] *s* glucosa
glue [glu] *s* cola || *tr* encolar; pegar fuertemente
glue pot *s* cazo de cola
gluey ['glu·i] *adj* (*comp* **gluier**; *super* **gluiest**) pegajoso; (*smeared with glue*) encolado
glug [glʌg] *s* gluglú *m* || *v* (*pret & pp* **glugged**; *ger* **glugging**) *intr* hacer gluglú (*el agua*)
glum [glʌm] *adj* (*comp* **glummer**; *super* **glummest**) hosco
glut [glʌt] *s* abundancia, gran acopio; exceso; **to be a glut on the market** abarrotarse || *v* (*pret & pp* **glutted**; *ger* **glutting**) *tr* hartar, saciar; inundar (*el mercado*); obstruir
glutton ['glʌtən] *adj & s* glotón *m*
gluttonous ['glʌtənəs] *adj* glotón
glutton·y ['glʌtəni] *s* (*pl* **-ies**) glotonería, gula
glycerine ['glɪsərɪn] *s* glicerina
G.M. *abbr* **general manager, Grand Master**
G-man ['dʒi ˌmæn] *s* (*pl* **-men** [ˌmɛn]) (coll) agente *m* de la policía federal
G.M.T. *abbr* **Greenwich mean time**
gnarl [nɑrl] *s* nudo || *tr* torcer || *intr* gruñir
gnarled [nɑrld] *adj* nudoso, retorcido
gnash [næʃ] *tr* hacer rechinar (*los dientes*) || *intr* hacer rechinar los dientes
gnat [næt] *s* jején *m*
gnaw [nɔ] *tr* roer; practicar (*un agujero*) royendo
gnome [nom] *s* gnomo
go [go] *s* (*pl* **goes**) ida; (coll) energía, ímpetu *m*; (coll) boga; (coll) ensayo; (*for traffic*) paso libre; **it's a go** (coll) es un trato hecho; **it's all the go** (coll) hace furor; **it's no go** (coll) es imposible; **on the go** (coll) en continuo movimiento; **to make a go of** (coll) lograr éxito en || *v* (*pret* **went** [wɛnt]; *pp* **gone** [gɔn] o [gɑn]) *tr* (coll) soportar, tolerar; **to go it alone** obrar sin ayuda || *intr* ir; (*to work, operate*) funcionar, marchar; andar (*p.ej., desnudo*); volverse (*p.ej., loco*); **going, going, gone!** ¡vendo, vendo, vendí!; **so it goes** así va el mundo; **to be going to** + *inf* ir a + *inf*; **to be gone** haber ido; haberse agotado; haber dejado de ser; **to go against** ir en contra de; **to go ahead** seguir adelante; **to go away** irse, marcharse; **to go back** volver; **to go by** pasar por; guiarse por; atenerse a; **to go down** bajar; hundirse (*un buque*); **to go fishing** ir de pesca; **to go for** ir por; **to go get** ir por, ir a buscar; **to go house hunting** ir a buscar casa; **to go hunting** ir de caza; **to go in** entrar; entrar en; (*to fit in*) caber en; **to go in for** dedicarse a, interesarse por; **to go into** entrar en; investigar; (aut) poner (*p.ej., primera*); **to go in with** asociarse con; **to go off** irse, marcharse; llevarse a cabo; estallar (*p.ej., una bomba*); dispararse (*un fusil*); **to go on** seguir adelante; ir tirando; **to go on** + *ger* seguir + *ger*; **to go on with** continuar; **to go out** salir; pasar de moda; apagarse (*un fuego, una luz*); declararse en huelga; (*for entertainment, etc.*) salir; **to go over** tener éxito; releer; examinar, revisar; pasar por encima de; **to go over to** pasarse a las filas de; **to go through** pasar por; llegar al fin de; agotar (*una fortuna*); **to go with** ir con, acompañar; salir con (*una muchacha*); hacer juego con; **to go without** andarse sin, pasarse sin
goad [god] *s* aguijada, aguijón *m* || *tr* aguijonear
go'-a·head' *adj* (coll) emprendedor || *s* (coll) señal *f* para seguir adelante, luz *f* verde
goal [gol] *s* meta; (*in football*) gol *m*
goal'keep'er *s* guardameta *m*, portero
goal line *s* raya de la meta
goal post *s* poste *m* de la meta
goat [got] *s* cabra; (*male goat*) macho cabrío; (coll) víctima inocente; **to be the goat** (slang) pagar el pato; **to get the goat of** (slang) tomar el pelo a; **to ride the goat** (coll) ser iniciado en una sociedad secreta
goatee [go'ti] *s* perilla
goat'herd' *s* cabrero
goat'skin' *s* piel *f* de cabra
goat'suck'er *s* chotacabras *m*
gob [gɑb] *s* (coll) masa informe y pequeña; (coll) marinero de guerra
gobble ['gɑbəl] *s* gluglú *m* || *tr* engullir; **to gobble up** engullirse ávidamente; (coll) asir de repente, apoderarse ávidamente de || *intr* engullir; gluglutear, gorgonear (*el pavo*)
gobbledegook ['gɑbəldɪˌgʊk] *s* (coll) lenguaje obscuro e incomprensible, galimatías *m*
go'-be·tween' *s* (*intermediary*) medianero; (*in promoting marriages*) casamentero; (*in shady love affairs*) alcahuete *m*, alcahueta
goblet ['gɑblɪt] *s* copa
goblin ['gɑblɪn] *s* duende *m*, trasgo
go'-by' *s* (coll) desaire *m*; **to give someone the go-by** (coll) negarse al trato de alguien
go'cart' *s* andaderas; cochecito para niños; carruaje ligero
god [gɑd] *s* dios *m*; **God forbid** no lo quiera Dios; **God grant** permita Dios; **God willing** Dios mediante

god'child' *s* (*pl* **chil'dren**) ahijado, ahijada
god'daugh'ter *s* ahijada
goddess ['gɑdɪs] *s* diosa
god'fa'ther *s* padrino
God'-fear'ing *adj* timorato; devoto, pío
God'for•sak'en *adj* dejado de la mano de Dios; (coll) desolado, desierto
god'head' *s* divinidad || **Godhead** *s* Dios *m*
godless ['gɑdlɪs] *adj* infiel, impío; desalmado, malvado
god•ly ['gɑdli] *adj* (*comp* **-lier;** *super* **-liest**) devoto, pío
god'moth'er *s* madrina
God's acre *s* campo santo
god'send' *s* cosa llovida del cielo, bendición
god'son' *s* ahijado
God'speed' *s* bienandanza, buena suerte, buen viaje *m*
go'-get'ter *s* (slang) buscavidas *mf*, persona emprendedora
goggle ['gɑgəl] *intr* volver los ojos; abrir los ojos desmesuradamente
goggle-eyed ['gɑgəl,aɪd] *adj* de ojos saltones
goggles ['gɑgəlz] *spl* anteojos de camino, gafas contra el polvo
going ['go·ɪŋ] *adj* en marcha, funcionando; **going on** casi, p.ej., **it is going on nine o'clock** son casi las nueve || *s* ida, partida
going concern *s* empresa que marcha
goings on *spl* actividades; bulla, jarana
goiter ['gɔɪtər] *s* bocio
gold [gold] *adj* áureo, de oro; dorado || *s* oro
gold'beat'er *s* batidor *m* de oro, batihoja *m*
goldbeater's skin *s* venza
gold brick *s* — **to sell a gold brick** (coll) vender gato por liebre
gold'crest' *s* reyezuelo moñudo
gold digger ['dɪgər] *s* (slang) extractora de oro
golden ['goldən] *adj* áureo, de oro; (*gilt*) dorado; (*hair*) rubio; excelente, favorable, floreciente
golden age *s* edad de oro, siglo de oro
golden calf *s* becerro de oro
Golden Fleece *s* vellocino de oro
golden mean *s* justo medio
golden plover *s* chorlito
gold'en•rod' *s* vara de oro, vara de San José
golden rule *s* regla de la caridad cristiana
golden wedding *s* bodas de oro
gold-filled ['gold,fɪld] *adj* empastado en oro
gold'finch' *s* jilguero, pintacilgo
gold'fish' *s* carpa dorada, pez *m* de color
goldilocks ['goldɪ,lɑks] *s* rubiales *mf*
gold leaf *s* pan *m* de oro
gold mine *s* mina de oro; **to strike a gold mine** (fig) encontrar una mina
gold plate *s* vajilla de oro
gold'-plate' *tr* dorar
gold'smith' *s* orfebre *m*
gold standard *s* patrón *m* oro
golf [gɑlf] *s* golf *m* || *intr* jugar al golf
golf club *s* palo de golf; asociación de jugadores de golf
golfer ['gɑlfər] *s* golfista *mf*
golf links *spl* campo de golf
Golgotha ['gɑlgəθə] *s* el Gólgota
gondola ['gɑndələ] *s* góndola
gondolier [,gɑndə'lɪr] *s* gondolero
gone [gɔn] o [gɑn] *adj* agotado; arruinado; desaparecido; muerto; **gone on** (coll) enamorado de
gong [gɔŋ] o [gɑŋ] *s* batintín *m*
gonorrhea [,gɑnə'ri·ə] *s* gonorrea
goo [gu] *s* (slang) substancia pegajosa
good [gʊd] *adj* (*comp* **better;** *super* **best**) bueno; **good and . . .** (coll) muy, p.ej., **good and cheap** muy barato; **good for** bueno para; capaz de hacer; capaz de pagar; capaz de vivir (*cierto tiempo*); **to be good at** tener talento para; **to be no good** (coll) no servir para nada; (coll) ser un perdido; **to make good** tener éxito; cumplir (*sus promesas*); pagar (*una deuda*); responder de (*los daños*) || *s* bien *m*, provecho, utilidad; **for good** para siempre; **for good and all** de una vez para siempre; **goods** efectos; géneros, mercancías; **the good** lo bueno; los buenos; **to catch with the goods** (slang) coger en flagrante; **to deliver the goods** (slang) cumplir lo prometido; **to do good** hacer el bien; dar salud o fuerzas a; **to the good** de sobra, en el haber; **what is the good of . . . ?** ¿para qué sirve . . . ?
good afternoon *s* buenas tardes
good'-by' o **good'-bye'** *s* adiós *m* || *interj* ¡adiós!
good day *s* buenos días
good evening *s* buenas noches, buenas tardes
good fellow *s* (coll) buen chico, buen sujeto
good fellowship *s* compañerismo
good'-for-noth'ing *adj* inútil, sin valor || *s* pelafustán *m*, perdido
Good Friday *s* Viernes santo
good graces *spl* favor *m*, estimación
good-hearted ['gʊd'hɑrtɪd] *adj* de buen corazón
good-humored ['gʊd'hjumərd] o ['gʊd'jumərd] *adj* de buen humor; afable
good-looking ['gʊd'lʊkɪŋ] *adj* guapo, bien parecido
good looks *spl* hermosura, guapeza
good•ly ['gʊdli] *adj* (*comp* **-lier;** *super* **-liest**) considerable; bien parecido, hermoso; bueno, excelente
good morning *s* buenos días
good-natured ['gʊd'netʃərd] *adj* bonachón, afable
Good Neighbor Policy *s* política del buen vecino
goodness ['gʊdnɪs] *s* bondad; **for goodness' sake!** ¡por Dios!; **goodness knows!** ¡quién sabe! || *interj* ¡válgame Dios!
good night *s* buenas noches
good sense *s* buen sentido, sensatez *f*

good-sized ['gʊd'saɪzd] *adj* bastante grande, de buen tamaño
good speed *s* adiós *m* y buena suerte
good-tempered ['gʊd'tɛmpərd] *adj* de natural apacible
good time *s* rato agradable; **to have a good time** divertirse; **to make good time** ir a buen paso; llegar en poco tiempo
good turn *s* favor *m,* servicio
good way *s* buen trecho
good will *s* buena voluntad; (com) buen nombre *m,* clientela
good•y ['gʊdi] *adj* (coll) beatuco, santurrón || *s* (*pl* **-ies**) (coll) golosina || *interj* (coll) ¡qué bien!, ¡qué alegría!
gooey ['gu·i] *adj* (*comp* **gooier;** *super* **gooiest**) (slang) pegajoso, fangoso
goof [guf] *s* (slang) tonto || *tr & intr* (slang) chapucear
goof•y ['gufi] *adj* (*comp* **-ier;** *super* **-iest**) (slang) tonto, mentecato
goon [gun] *s* (*roughneck*) (coll) gamberro, canalla *m;* (coll) terrorista *m* de alquiler; (slang) estúpido
goose [gus] *s* (*pl* **geese** [gis]) *s* ánsar *m,* ganso, oca; **the goose hangs high** todo va a pedir de boca; **to cook one's goose** malbaratarle a uno los planes; **to kill the goose that lays the golden eggs** matar la gallina de los huevos de oro || *s* (*pl* **gooses**) plancha de sastre
goose'ber'ry *s* (*pl* **-ries**) (*plant*) grosellero silvestre; (*fruit*) grosella silvestre
goose egg *s* huevo de oca; (slang) cero
goose flesh *s* carne *f* de gallina
goose'neck' *s* cuello de cisne; (naut) gancho de botalones
goose pimples *spl* carne *f* de gallina
goose step *s* (mil) paso de ganso
G.O.P. *abbr* **Grand Old Party**
gopher ['gofər] *s* ardilla de tierra, ardillón *m;* (*Geomys*) tuza
Gordian knot ['gɔrdɪ·ən] *s* nudo gordiano; **to cut the Gordian knot** cortar el nudo gordiano
gore [gor] *s* sangre derramada, sangre cuajada; (*insert in a piece of cloth*) cuchillo, nesga || *tr* (*to pierce with a horn*) acornar; poner cuchillo o nesga a; nesgar
gorge [gɔrdʒ] *s* garganta, desfiladero; (*in a river*) atasco de hielo || *tr* atiborrar || *intr* atiborrarse
gorgeous ['gɔrdʒəs] *adj* primoroso, brillante, magnífico, suntuoso
gorilla [gə'rɪlə] *s* gorila
gorse [gɔrs] *s* aulaga
gor•y ['gori] *adj* (*comp* **-ier;** *super* **-iest**) ensangrentado, sangriento
gosh [gɑʃ] *interj* ¡caramba!
goshawk ['gɑs,hɔk] *s* azor *m*
gospel ['gɑspəl] *s* evangelio || **Gospel** *s* Evangelio
gospel truth *s* evangelio, pura verdad
gossamer ['gɑsəmər] *s* telaraña flotante; gasa sutilísima; tela impermeable muy delgada; impermeable *m* de tela muy delgada
gossip ['gɑsɪp] *s* chismes *m;* (*person*) chismoso; **piece of gossip** chisme *m* || *intr* chismear
gossip column *s* mentidero
gossip columnist *s* gacetillero, cronista *mf* social
gossipy ['gɑsɪpi] *adj* chismoso
Goth [gɑθ] *s* godo; (fig) bárbaro
Gothic ['gɑθɪk] *adj & s* gótico
gouge [gaʊdʒ] *s* gubia; (*cut made with a gouge*) muesca; (coll) estafa || *tr* excavar con gubia; (coll) estafar
goulash ['gulɑʃ] *s* puchero húngaro
gourd [gord] o [gʊrd] *s* calabaza
gourmand ['gʊrmənd] *s* gastrónomo; glotón *m,* goloso
gourmet ['gʊrme] *s* gastrónomo delicado
gout [gaʊt] *s* gota
gout•y ['gaʊti] *adj* (*comp* **-ier;** *super* **-iest**) gotoso
gov. *abbr* **governor, government**
govern ['gʌvərn] *tr* gobernar; (gram) regir || *intr* gobernar
governess ['gʌvərnɪs] *s* aya, institutriz *f*
government ['gʌvərnmənt] *s* gobierno; (gram) régimen *m*
governmental [,gʌvərn'mɛntəl] *adj* gubernamental, gubernativo
government in exile *s* gobierno exilado
governor ['gʌvərnər] *s* gobernador *m;* (*of a jail, castle, etc.*) alcaide *m;* (mach) regulador *m*
governorship ['gʌvərnər,ʃɪp] *s* gobierno
govt. *abbr* **government**
gown [gaʊn] *s* (*of a woman*) vestido; (*of a professor, judge, etc.*) toga; (*of a priest*) traje *m* talar; (*dressing gown*) bata, peinador *m;* (*nightgown*) camisa de dormir
G.P.O. *abbr* **General Post Office, Government Printing Office**
gr. *abbr* **gram, grams, grain, grains, gross**
grab [græb] *s* asimiento, presa; (coll) robo || *v* (*pret & pp* **grabbed;** *ger* **grabbing**) *tr* asir, agarrar; arrebatar || *intr* — **to grab at** tratar de asir
grace [gres] *s* (*charm; favor; pardon*) gracia; (*prayer at table*) benedícite *m;* (*extension of time*) demora; **to be in the good graces of** gozar del favor de; **to say grace** rezar el benedícite; **with good grace** de buen talante || *tr* adornar, engalanar; favorecer
graceful ['gresfəl] *adj* agraciado, gracioso
grace note *s* apoyatura, nota de adorno
gracious ['greʃəs] *adj* graciable, gracioso; misericordioso || *interj* ¡válgame Dios!
grackle ['grækəl] *s* (*myna*) estornino de los pastores; (*purple grackle*) quiscal *m*
grad. *abbr* **graduate**
gradation [gre'deʃən] *s* (*gradual change*) paso gradual; (*arrangement in grades*) graduación; (*step in a series*) paso, grado
grade [gred] *s* grado; (*slope*) pendiente *f;* (*mark for work in class*) calificación, nota; **to make the grade**

lograr subir la cuesta; vencer los obstáculos || *tr* graduar, calificar; dar nota a (*un alumno*); explanar, nivelar
grade crossing *s* (rr) paso a nivel, cruce *m* a nivel
grade school *s* escuela elemental
gradient ['gredɪ·ənt] *adj* pendiente || *s* pendiente *f;* (phys) gradiente *m*
gradual ['grædʒʊ·əl] *adj* paulatino
gradually ['grædʒʊ·əli] *adv* paulatinamente, gradualmente, poco a poco
graduate ['grædʒʊ·ɪt] *adj* graduado || *s* graduado; (*candidate for a degree*) graduando; vasija graduada || ['grædʒʊ,et] *tr* graduar || *intr* graduarse
graduate school *s* facultad de altos estudios
graduate student *s* estudiante graduado
graduate work *s* altos estudios
graduation [,grædʒʊ'eʃən] *s* graduación; ceremonia de graduación
graft [græft] o [grɑft] *s* (hort & surg) injerto; (coll) soborno político, ganancia ilegal || *tr & intr* (hort & surg) injertar; (coll) malversar
graham bread ['gre·əm] *s* pan *m* integral
graham flour *s* harina de trigo sin cerner
grain [gren] *s* (*small seed; tiny particle of sand, etc.; small unit of weight*) grano; (*cereal seeds*) granos; (*in stone*) vena; (*in wood*) fibra; **against the grain** a contrapelo || *tr* granear (*la pólvora; una piedra litográfica*); crispir, vetear (*la madera*); granular (*una piel*)
grain elevator *s* elevador *m* de granos; (*tall building where grain is stored*) depósito de cereales
grain'field' *s* sembrado
graining ['grenɪŋ] *s* veteado
gram [græm] *s* gramo
grammar ['græmər] *s* gramática
grammarian [grə'mɛrɪ·ən] *s* gramático
grammar school *s* escuela pública elemental
grammatical [grə'mætɪkəl] *adj* gramático
gramophone ['græmə,fon] *s* (trademark) gramófono
grana·ry ['grænəri] *s* (*pl* **-ries**) granero
grand [grænd] *adj* espléndido, grandioso; importante, principal
grand'aunt' *s* tía abuela
grand'child' *s* (*pl* **-chil'dren**) nieto, nieta
grand'daugh'ter *s* nieta
grand duchess *s* gran duquesa
grand duchy *s* gran ducado
grand duke *s* gran duque *m*
grandee [græn'di] *s* grande *m* de España
grandeur ['grændʒər] o ['grændʒʊr] *s* grandeza, magnificencia
grand'fa'ther *s* abuelo; (*forefather*) antepasado
grandfather's clock *s* reloj *m* de caja
grandiose ['grændɪ,os] *adj* grandioso; hinchado, pomposo
grand jury *s* jurado de acusación
grand larceny *s* hurto mayor
grand lodge *s* gran oriente *m*
grandma ['grænd,mɑ], ['græm,mɑ] o ['græmə] *s* (coll) abuela, abuelita
grand'moth'er *s* abuela
grand'neph'ew *s* resobrino
grand'niece *s* resobrina
grand opera *s* ópera seria
grandpa ['grænd,pɑ], ['græn,pɑ] o ['græmpə] *s* (coll) abuelo, abuelito
grand'par'ent *s* abuelo, abuela
grand piano *s* piano de cola
grand slam *s* bola
grand'son' *s* nieto
grand'stand' *s* gradería cubierta, tribuna
grand strategy *s* alta estrategia
grand total *s* gran total *m,* suma de totales
grand'un'cle *s* tío abuelo
grand vizier *s* gran visir *m*
grange [grendʒ] *s* (*farm with barns, etc.*) granja; (*organization of farmers*) cámara agrícola
granite ['grænɪt] *s* granito
grant [grænt] o [grɑnt] *s* concesión; donación, subvención; traspaso de propiedad || *tr* conceder; dar (*permiso, perdón*); transferir (*bienes inmuebles*); **to take for granted** dar por sentado; tratar con indiferencia
grantee [græn'ti] o [grɑn'ti] *s* cesionario
grant'-in-aid' *s* (*pl* **grants-in-aid**) subvención concedida por el gobierno para obras de utilidad pública; pensión para estimular conocimientos científicos, literarios, artísticos
grantor [græn'tɔr] o [grɑn'tɔr] *s* cesionista *mf,* otorgante *mf*
granular ['grænjələr] *adj* granular
granulate ['grænjə,let] *tr* granular || *intr* granularse
granule ['grænjul] *s* gránulo
grape [grep] *s* (*fruit*) uva; (*vine*) vid *f*
grape arbor *s* parral *m*
grape'fruit' *s* (*fruit*) toronja; (*tree*) toronjo
grape hyacinth *s* sueldacostilla
grape juice *s* zumo de uva
grape'shot' *s* metralla
grape'vine' *s* vid *f,* parra; **by the grapevine** por vías secretas, por vías misteriosas
graph [græf] o [grɑf] *s* (*diagram*) gráfica; (gram) grafía
graphic(al) ['græfɪk(əl)] *adj* gráfico
graphite ['græfaɪt] *s* grafito
graph paper *s* papel cuadriculado
grapnel ['græpnəl] *s* rebañadera; (*anchor*) rezón *m*
grapple ['græpəl] *s* asimiento, presa; lucha cuerpo a cuerpo || *tr* asir, agarrar || *intr* agarrarse; luchar a brazo partido; **to grapple with** luchar a brazo partido con; tratar de resolver
grappling iron *s* arpeo
grasp [græsp] o [grɑsp] *s* asimiento; (*power, reach*) poder *m,* alcance *m;* (fig) comprensión; **to have a good grasp of** saber a fondo; **within the grasp of** al alcance de || *tr* (*with hand*) empuñar; (*to get control of*)

apoderarse de; (fig) comprender || *intr* — **to grasp at** tratar de asir; aceptar con avidez
grasping ['græspɪŋ] o ['grɑspɪŋ] *adj* avaro, codicioso
grass [græs] o [grɑs] *s* hierba; (*pasture land*) pasto; (*lawn*) césped *m;* **to go to grass** ir a pacer; disfrutar de una temporada de descanso; gastarse, arruinarse; morir; **to not let the grass grow under one's feet** no dormirse en las pajas
grass court *s* cancha de césped
grass'hop'per *s* saltamontes *m*
grass pea *s* almorta, guija
grass'-roots' *adj* (coll) de la gente común
grass seed *s* semilla de césped
grass widow *s* viuda de paja, viuda de marido vivo
grass•y ['græsi] o ['grɑsi] *adj* (*comp* **-ier;** *super* **-iest**) herboso
grate [gret] *s* (*at a window*) reja; (*for cooking*) parrilla || *tr* (*to put a grate on*) enrejar; rallar (*p.ej., queso*) || *intr* crujir, rechinar; **to grate on** (fig) rallar
grateful ['gretfəl] *adj* agradecido; (*pleasing*) agradable
grater ['gretər] *s* rallador *m*
grati•fy ['grætɪ,faɪ] *v* (*pret & pp* **-fied**) *tr* complacer, gratificar
gratifying ['grætɪ,faɪ•ɪŋ] *adj* grato, satisfactorio
grating ['gretɪŋ] *adj* áspero, irritante; (*sound*) chirriante || *s* enrejado
gratis ['gretɪs] o ['grætɪs] *adj* gracioso, gratuito || *adv* gratis, de balde
gratitude ['grætɪ,tjud] o ['grætɪ,tud] *s* gratitud, reconocimiento
gratuitous [grə'tju•ɪtəs] o [grə'tu•ɪtəs] *adj* gratuito
gratui•ty [grə'tju•ɪti] o [grə'tu•ɪti] *s* (*pl* **-ties**) propina
grave [grev] *adj* (*serious, dangerous; important*) grave; solemne; (*sound; accent*) grave || *s* sepulcro, sepultura; **to have one foot in the grave** estar con un pie en la sepultura
gravedigger ['grev,dɪgər] *s* enterrador *m,* sepulturero
gravel ['grævəl] *s* grava, cascajo
graven image ['grevən] *s* ídolo
grave'stone' *s* lápida sepulcral
grave'yard' *s* camposanto
gravitate ['grævɪ,tet] *intr* gravitar; ser atraído
gravitation [,grævɪ'teʃən] *s* gravitación
gravi•ty ['grævɪti] *s* (*pl* **-ties**) gravedad
gravure [grə'vjur] o ['grevjur] *s* fotograbado
gra•vy ['grevi] *s* (*pl* **-vies**) (*juice from cooking meat*) jugo; (*sauce made with this juice*) salsa; (slang) ganga, breva
gravy dish *s* salsera
gray [gre] *adj* gris; (*gray-haired*) cano, canoso || *s* gris *m;* traje *m* gris || *intr* encanecer
gray'beard' *s* anciano, viejo
gray-haired ['gre,hɛrd] *adj* canoso
gray'hound' *s* galgo
grayish ['gre•ɪʃ] *adj* grisáceo; (*person; hair*) entrecano
gray matter *s* substancia gris; (*intelligence*) (coll) materia gris
graze [grez] *tr* (*to touch lightly*) rozar; (*to scratch lightly in passing*) raspar; pacer (*la hierba*); apacentar (*el ganado*); (*to lead to the pasture*) pastar || *intr* pacer, pastar
grease [gris] *s* grasa || [gris] o [griz] *tr* engrasar; (slang) sobornar
grease cup [gris] *s* vaso de engrase
grease gun [gris] *s* engrasador *m* de pistón, jeringa de engrase
grease lift [gris] *s* puente *m* de engrase
grease paint [gris] *s* maquillaje *m*
grease pit [gris] *s* fosa de engrase
grease spot [gris] *s* lámpara, mancha de grasa
greas•y ['grisi] o ['grizi] *adj* (*comp* **-ier;** *super* **-iest**) grasiento, pringoso
great [gret] *adj* grande; (coll) excelente || **the great** los grandes
great'-aunt' *s* tía abuela
Great Bear *s* Osa Mayor
Great Britain ['brɪtən] *s* la Gran Bretaña
great'coat' *s* gabán *m* de mucho abrigo
Great Dane *s* mastín *m* danés
Greater London *s* el Gran Londres
Greater New York *s* el Gran Nueva York
great'-grand'child' *s* (*pl* **-chil'dren**) bisnieto, bisnieta
great'-grand'daugh'ter *s* bisnieta
great'-grand'fa'ther *s* bisabuelo
great'-grand'moth'er *s* bisabuela
great'-grand'par'ent *s* bisabuelo, bisabuela
great'-grand'son' *s* bisnieto
greatly ['gretli] *adj* grandemente
great'-neph'ew *s* resobrino
greatness ['gretnɪs] *s* grandeza
great'-niece' *s* resobrina
great'-un'cle *s* tío abuelo
Great War *s* Gran guerra
Grecian ['griʃən] *adj & s* griego
Greece [gris] *s* Grecia
greed [grid] *s* codicia, avaricia; (*in eating and drinking*) glotonería
greed•y ['gridi] *adj* (*comp* **-ier;** *super* **-iest**) codicioso, avaro; glotón
Greek [grik] *adj & s* griego
green [grin] *adj* verde; inexperto || *s* verde *m;* (*lawn*) césped *m;* **greens** verduras
green'back' *s* (U.S.A.) billete *m* de banco (*de dorso verde*)
green corn *s* maíz tierno
green earth *s* verdacho
greener•y ['grinəri] *s* (*pl* **-ies**) (*foliage*) verdura; (*hothouse*) invernáculo
green-eyed ['grin,aɪd] *adj* de ojos verdes; celoso
green'gage' *s* ciruela claudia
green grasshopper *s* langostón *m*
green'gro'cer *s* verdulero
green'gro'cer•y *s* (*pl* **-ies**) verdulería
green'horn' *s* novato; (*dupe*) primo, inocentón *m;* (coll) papanatas *m,* isidro
green'house' *s* invernáculo

greenish ['grinɪʃ] *adj* verdoso
Greenland ['grinlənd] *s* Groenlandia
greenness ['grinnɪs] *s* verdura, verdor *m;* falta de experiencia
green'room' *s* saloncillo; chismería de teatro
greensward ['grin,swɔrd] *s* césped *m*
green thumb *s* pulgares *mpl* verdes (*don de criar plantas*)
green vegetables *spl* verduras
green'wood' *s* bosque *m* verde, bosque frondoso
greet [grit] *tr* saludar; acoger, recibir; presentarse a (*los ojos u los oídos de uno*)
greeting ['gritɪŋ] *s* saludo; acogida, recibimiento || **greetings** *interj* ¡salud!
greeting card *s* tarjeta de buen deseo
gregarious [grɪ'gɛrɪ·əs] *adj* (*living in the midst of others*) gregario; (*fond of the company of others*) sociable
Gregorian [grɪ'gorɪ·ən] *adj* gregoriano
grenade [grɪ'ned] *s* granada; (*to put out fires*) granada extintora
grenadier [,grɛnə'dɪr] *s* granadero
grenadine [,grɛnə'din] *s* granadina
grey [gre] *adj, s & intr* var de **gray**
grid [grɪd] *s* parrilla, rejilla; (electron) rejilla; (*of a storage battery*) (elec) rejilla
griddle ['grɪdəl] *s* plancha
grid'dle·cake' *s* tortada (de harina) a la plancha
grid'i'ron *s* parrilla; campo de fútbol
grid leak *s* (electron) resistencia de rejilla, escape *m* de rejilla
grief [grif] *s* aflicción, pesar *m;* (coll) desgracia, disgusto; **to come to grief** fracasar, arruinarse
grievance ['grivəns] *s* agravio, injusticia; despecho, disgusto; motivo de queja
grieve [griv] *tr* afligir, penar || *intr* afligirse, apenarse; **to grieve over** añorar
grievous ['grivəs] *adj* doloroso, penoso; atroz, cruel; (*deplorable*) lastimoso
griffin ['grɪfɪn] *s* (myth) grifo
grill [grɪl] *s* parrilla || *tr* emparrillar; someter (*a un acusado*) a un interrogatorio muy apremiante
grille [grɪl] *s* reja, verja; (*of an automobile*) parrilla, rejilla
grill'room' *s* parrilla
grim [grɪm] *adj* (*comp* **grimmer;** *super* **grimmest**) (*fierce*) cruel, feroz; (*repellent*) horrible, siniestro; (*unyielding*) formidable, implacable; (*stern-looking*) ceñudo
grimace ['grɪməs] o [grɪ'mes] *s* mueca, gesto || *intr* hacer muecas, gestear
grime [graɪm] *s* mugre *f;* (*soot*) tizne *m & f*
grim·y ['graɪmi] *adj* (*comp* **-ier;** *super* **-iest**) mugriento; tiznado
grin [grɪn] *s* sonrisa bonachona; mueca (*mostrando los dientes*) || *v* (*pret & pp* **grinned;** *ger* **grinning**) *intr* sonreírse bonachonamente; hacer una mueca (*mostrando los dientes*)
grind [graɪnd] *s* molienda; (*long hard work or study*) (coll) zurra; (*student*) (coll) empollón *m* || *v* (*pret & pp* **ground** [graʊnd]) *tr* moler; (*to sharpen*) afilar, amolar; tallar (*lentes*); pulverizar; picar (*carne*); rodar (*las válvulas de un motor*); dar vueltas a (*un manubrio*) || *intr* hacer molienda; molerse; rechinar; (coll) echar los bofes
grinder ['graɪndər] *s* (*to sharpen tools*) muela, esmoladera; (*to grind coffee, pepper, etc.*) molinillo; (*back tooth*) muela
grind'stone' *s* esmoladera, piedra de amolar; **to keep one's nose to the grindstone** trabajar con ahinco
grin·go ['grɪŋgo] *s* (*pl* **-gos**) (disparaging) gringo
grip [grɪp] *s* (*grasp*) asimiento; (*with hand*) apretón *m;* (*handle*) asidero; saco de mano; **to come to grips (with)** luchar cuerpo a cuerpo (con); arrostrarse (con) || *v* (*pret & pp* **gripped;** *ger* **gripping**) *tr* asir, agarrar; tener asido; absorber (*la atención*); absorber la atención a (*una persona*)
gripe [graɪp] *s* (coll) queja; **gripes** retortijón *m* de tripas || *intr* (coll) quejarse, refunfuñar
grippe [grɪp] *s* gripe *f*
gripping ['grɪpɪŋ] *adj* conmovedor, impresionante
gris·ly ['grɪzli] *adj* (*comp* **-lier;** *super* **-liest**) espantoso, espeluznante
grist [grɪst] *s* (*batch of grain for one grinding*) molienda; (*grain that has been ground*) harina; (coll) acopio, acervo; **to be grist to one's mill** (coll) serle a uno de mucho provecho
gristle ['grɪsəl] *s* cartílago, ternilla
gris·tly ['grɪsli] *adj* (*comp* **-tlier;** *super* **-tliest**) cartilaginoso, ternilloso
grist'mill' *s* molino harinero
grit [grɪt] *s* arena, guijo fino; (fig) ánimo, valentía; **grits** farro, sémola || *v* (*pret & pp* **gritted;** *ger* **gritting**) *tr* hacer rechinar (*los dientes*); cerrar fuertemente (*los dientes*)
grit·ty ['grɪti] *adj* (*comp* **-tier;** *super* **-tiest**) arenoso; (fig) valiente, resuelto
griz·zly ['grɪzli] *adj* (*comp* **-zlier;** *super* **-zliest**) grisáceo; canoso || *s* (*pl* **-zlies**) oso gris
grizzly bear *s* oso gris
groan [gron] *s* gemido, quejido || *intr* gemir, quejarse; estar muy cargado, crujir por exceso de peso
grocer ['grosər] *s* abacero, tendero de ultramarinos
grocer·y ['grosəri] *s* (*pl* **-ies**) abacería, tienda de ultramarinos, colmado; **groceries** víveres *mpl,* ultramarinos
grocery store *s* abacería, tienda de ultramarinos, colmado
grog [grɑg] *s* grog *m*
grog·gy ['grɑgi] *adj* (*comp* **-gier;** *super* **-giest**) (coll) inseguro, vacilante;

(*shaky, e.g., from a blow*) (coll) atontado; (coll) borracho
groin [grɔɪn] *s* (anat) ingle *f;* (archit) arista de encuentro
groom [grum] *s* (*bridegroom*) novio; mozo de caballos || *tr* asear, acicalar; almohazar (*caballos*); enseñar (*a un político*) para presentarse como candidato
grooms•man ['grumzmən] *s* (*pl* **-men** [mən]) padrino de boda
groove [gruv] *s* ranura; (*of a pulley*) garganta; (*of a phonograph record*) surco; (*mark left by a wheel*) rodada; (coll) rutina, hábito arraigado || *tr* ranurar, acanalar
grope [grop] *intr* andar a tientas; (*for words*) pujar; **to grope for** buscar a tientas, buscar tentando; **to grope through** palpar (*p.ej., la obscuridad*)
gropingly ['gropɪŋli] *adv* a tientas
grosbeak ['gros,bik] *s* pico duro
gross [gros] *adj* (*dense, thick*) denso, espeso; (*coarse; vulgar*) grosero; (*fat, burly*) grueso; (*with no deductions*) bruto || *s* conjunto, totalidad; (*twelve dozen*) gruesa; **in gross** en grueso || *tr* obtener un ingreso bruto de
grossly ['grosli] *adv* aproximadamente
gross national product *s* renta nacional
grotesque [gro'tɛsk] *adj* (*ridiculous, extravagant*) grotesco; (f.a.) grutesco || *s* (f.a.) grutesco
grot•to ['grɑto] *s* (*pl* **-toes** o **-tos**) gruta
grouch [grauʃ] *s* (coll) mal humor *m;* (*person*) (coll) cascarrabias *mf,* vinagre *m* || *intr* (coll) refunfuñar
grouch•y ['grauʃi] *adj* (*comp* **-ier;** *super* **-iest**) (coll) gruñón, malhumorado
ground [graund] *s* (*earth, soil, land*) tierra; (*piece of land*) terreno; (*basis, foundation*) causa, fundamento; motivo, razón *f;* (elec) tierra; (*body of automobile corresponding to ground*) (elec) masa; (elec) borne *m* de tierra; **ground for complaint** motivo de queja; **grounds** terreno; jardines *mpl;* causa, fundamento; (*of coffee*) posos; **on the ground of** con motivo de; **to break ground** empezar la excavación; **to fall to the ground** fracasar, abandonarse; **to gain ground** ganar terreno; **to give ground** ceder terreno; **to lose ground** perder terreno; **to stand one's ground** mantenerse firme; **to yield ground** ceder terreno || *tr* establecer, fundar; (elec) poner a tierra; **to be grounded** estar sin volar (*un avión*); **to be well grounded** ser muy versado || *intr* (naut) encallar, varar
ground connection *s* (rad) toma de tierra
ground crew *s* (aer) personal *m* de tierra
grounder ['graundər] *s* (baseball) pelota rodada
ground floor *s* piso bajo
ground glass *s* vidrio deslustrado
ground hog *s* marmota de América
ground lead [lid] *s* (elec) conductor *m* a tierra
groundless ['graundlɪs] *adj* infundado
ground plan *s* primer proyecto; (*of a building*) planta
ground speed *s* (aer) velocidad con respecto al suelo
ground swell *s* marejada de fondo
ground troops *spl* (mil) tropas terrestres
ground wire *s* (rad) alambre *m* de tierra; (aut) hilo de masa
ground'work' *s* infraestructura
group [grup] *adj* grupal; colectivo || *s* grupo || *tr* agrupar || *intr* agruparse
grouse [graus] *s* perdiz blanca, bonasa americana, gallo de bosque; (slang) refunfuño || *intr* (slang) refunfuñar
grout [graut] *s* lechada || *tr* enlechar
grove [grov] *s* arboleda, bosquecillo
grov•el ['grʌvəl] o ['grɑvəl] *v* (*pret & pp* **-eled** o **-elled;** *ger* **-eling** o **-elling**) *intr* arrastrarse servilmente; rebajarse servilmente; deleitarse en vilezas
grow [gro] *v* (*pret* **grew** [gru]; *pp* **grown** [gron]) *tr* cultivar (*plantas*); criar (*animales*); dejarse (*la barba*) || *intr* crecer; cultivarse; criarse; brotar, nacer; (*to become*) hacerse, ponerse, volverse; **to grow angry** enfadarse; **to grow old** envejecerse; **to grow out of** tener su origen en; perder (*p.ej., la costumbre*); **to grow together** adherirse el uno al otro; **to grow up** crecer, desarrollar
growing child ['gro•ɪŋ] *s* muchacho de creces
growl [graul] *s* gruñido; refunfuño || *intr* gruñir (*el perro*); refunfuñar
grown'-up' *adj* adulto; juicioso || *s* (*pl* **grown-ups**) adulto; **grown-ups** personas mayores
growth [groθ] *s* crecimiento; desarrollo; aumento; (*of trees, grass, etc.*) cobertura; (pathol) tumor *m*
growth stock *s* acción crecedera
grub [grʌb] *s* (*drudge*) esclavo del trabajo; (*larva*) gorgojo; (coll) comida, alimento || *v* (*pret & pp* **grubbed;** *ger* **grubbing**) *tr* arrancar (*tocones*); desmalezar (*un terreno*) || *intr* cavar; trabajar como esclavo
grub•by ['grʌbi] *adj* (*comp* **-bier;** *super* **-biest**) gorgojoso; sucio, roñoso
grudge [grʌdʒ] *s* rencor *m,* inquina; **to have a grudge against** guardar rencor a, tener inquina a || *tr* dar de mala gana; envidiar
grudgingly ['grʌdʒɪŋli] *adv* de mala gana
gru•el ['gru•əl] *s* avenate *m* || *v* (*pret & pp* **-eled** o **-elled;** *ger* **-eling** o **-elling**) *tr* agotar, castigar cruelmente
gruesome ['grusəm] *adj* espantoso, horripilante
gruff [grʌf] *adj* áspero, brusco, rudo; (*voice, tone*) ronco
grumble ['grʌmbəl] *s* gruñido, refunfuño; ruido sordo y prolongado || *intr* gruñir, refunfuñar; retumbar

grump•y ['grʌmpi] *adj* (*comp* **-ier;** *super* **-iest**) gruñón, malhumorado
grunt [grʌnt] *s* gruñido || *intr* gruñir
G-string ['dʒi ˌstrɪŋ] *s* (*loincloth*) taparrabo; (*worn by women entertainers*) cubresexo
gt. *abbr* **great; gutta** (Lat) **drop**
g.u. *abbr* **genitourinary**
Guadeloupe [ˌgwɑdə'lup] *s* Guadalupe *f*
guarantee [ˌgærən'ti] *s* garantía; (*guarantor*) garante *mf;* persona de quien otra sale fiadora || *tr* garantizar
guarantor ['gærən ˌtɔr] *s* garante *mf*
guaran•ty ['gærənti] *s* (*pl* **-ties**) garantía || *v* (*pret & pp* **-tied**) *tr* garantizar
guard [gɑrd] *s* (*act of guarding; part of handle of sword*) guarda; (*person who guards or takes care of something*) guarda *mf;* (*group of armed men; posture in fencing*) guardia; (*member of group of armed men*) guardia *m;* (*in front of trolley car*) salvavidas *m;* (sport) coraza; (rr) guardabarrera *mf;* (rr) guardafrenos *m;* **off guard** desprevenido; **on guard** alerta, prevenido; de centinela; **to mount guard** montar la guardia; **under guard** a buen recaudo || *tr* guardar || *intr* estar de centinela; **to guard against** guardarse de, precaverse contra o de
guard'house' *s* cuartel *m* de la guardia; prisión militar
guardian ['gɑrdɪ·ən] *adj* tutelar || *s* guardián *m;* (law) curador *m,* tutor *m*
guardian angel *s* ángel *m* custodio, ángel de la guarda
guardianship ['gɑrdɪ·ənˌʃɪp] *s* amparo, protección; (law) curaduría, tutela
guard'rail' *s* baranda; (naut) barandilla; (rr) contracarril *m*
guard'room' *s* cuarto de guardia; cárcel *f* militar
guards•man ['gɑrdzmən] *s* (*pl* **-men** [mən]) guardia *m,* soldado de guardia
Guatemalan [ˌgwɑtɪ'mɑlən] *adj & s* guatemalteco
guerrilla [gə'rɪlə] *s* guerrillero
guerrilla warfare *s* guerra de guerrillas
guess [gɛs] *s* conjetura, suposición; adivinación || *tr & intr* conjeturar, suponer; (*to judge correctly*) acertar, adivinar; (coll) creer, suponer; **I guess so** (coll) creo que sí, me parece que sí
guess'work' *s* conjetura; **by guesswork** por conjeturas
guest [gɛst] *s* convidado; (*lodger*) huésped *m;* (*of a boarding house*) pensionista *mf;* (*of a hotel*) cliente *mf;* (*caller*) visita
guest book *s* libro de oro
guest room *s* cuarto de reserva
guffaw [gə'fɔ] *s* risotada, carcajada || *intr* risotear, reír a carcajadas
Guiana [gɪ'ɑnə] o [gɪ'ænə] *s* Guayana
guidance ['gaɪdəns] *s* guía, gobierno, dirección; **for your guidance** para su gobierno
guide [gaɪd] *s* (*person*) guía *mf;* (*book*) guía; (*guidance*) guía; dirección; poste *m* indicador; (mach) guía, guiadera; (mil) guía *m* || *tr* guiar
guide'board' *s* señal *f* de carretera
guide'book' *s* guía *m,* guía del viajero
guided missile ['gaɪdɪd] *s* proyectil dirigido o teleguiado
guide dog *s* perro-lazarillo
guide'line' *s* cuerda de guía; norma, pauta, directorio
guide'post' *s* poste *m* indicador
guidon ['gaɪdən] *s* (mil) guión *m;* (mil) portaguión *m*
guild [gɪld] *s* (*medieval association of craftsmen*) gremio; asociación benéfica
guild'hall' *s* casa consistorial
guile [gaɪl] *s* astucia, dolo, maña
guileful ['gaɪlfəl] *adj* astuto, doloso, mañoso
guileless ['gaɪllɪs] *adj* cándido, inocente, sencillo
guillotine ['gɪlə ˌtin] *s* guillotina || [ˌgɪlə'tin] *tr* guillotinar
guilt [gɪlt] *s* culpa
guiltless ['gɪltlɪs] *adj* inocente, libre de culpa
guilt•y ['gɪlti] *adj* (*comp* **-ier;** *super* **-iest**) culpable; (*charged with guilt*) culpado; (*found guilty*) reo
guimpe [gɪmp] o [gæmp] *s* canesú *m*
guinea ['gɪni] *s* (*monetary unit*) guinea; gallina de Guinea
guinea fowl *s* pintada, gallina de Guinea
guinea hen *s* pintada, gallina de Guinea (*hembra*)
guinea pig *s* conejillo de Indias
guise [gaɪz] *s* traje *m;* aspecto, semejanza; **under the guise of** so capa de
guitar [gɪ'tɑr] *s* guitarra
guitarist [gɪ'tɑrɪst] *s* guitarrista *mf*
gulch [gʌltʃ] *s* barranco, quebrada
gulf [gʌlf] *s* golfo
Gulf of Mexico *s* golfo de Méjico
Gulf Stream *s* Corriente *f* del Golfo
gull [gʌl] *s* gaviota; (coll) bobo || *tr* estafar, engañar
gullet ['gʌlɪt] *s* gaznate *m,* garguero; esófago
gullible ['gʌlɪbəl] *adj* crédulo; **to be too gullible** tener buenas tragaderas
gul•ly ['gʌli] *s* (*pl* **-lies**) barranca, arroyada; (*channel made by rain water*) badén *m*
gulp [gʌlp] *s* trago || *tr* — **to gulp down** engullir; reprimir (*p.ej., sollozos*) || *intr* respirar entrecortadamente
gum [gʌm] *s* goma; chanclo de goma; (*firm flesh around base of teeth*) encía; (*mucous on edge of eyelid*) legaña || *v* (*pret & pp* **gummed;** *ger* **gumming**) *tr* engomar || *intr* exudar goma
gum arabic *s* goma arábiga
gum'boil' *s* flemón *m*
gum boot *s* bota de agua

gum'drop' *s* frutilla
gum·my ['gʌmi] *adj* (*comp* **-mier;** *super* **-miest**) gomoso; (*eyelid*) legañoso
gumption ['gʌmpʃən] *s* (coll) ánimo, iniciativa, empuje *m,* fuerza; (coll) juicio, seso
gum'shoe' *s* chanclo de goma; (coll) detective *m* || *v* (*pret & pp* **-shoed;** *ger* **-shoeing**) *intr* (slang) andar con zapatos de fieltro
gun [gʌn] *s* escopeta, fusil *m;* cañón *m;* (*for injections*) jeringa; (coll) revólver *m;* **to stick to one's guns** mantenerse en sus trece || *v* (*pret & pp* **gunned;** *ger* **gunning**) *tr* hacer fuego sobre; (slang) acelerar rápidamente (*un motor, un avión*) || *intr* andar a caza; disparar; **to gun for** ir en busca de; buscar para matar
gun'boat' *s* cañonero
gun carriage *s* cureña, encabalgamiento
gun'cot'ton *s* fulmicotón *m,* algodón *m* pólvora
gun'fire' *s* fuego (*de armas de fuego*); cañoneo
gun·man ['gʌnmən] *s* (*pl* **-men** [mən]) bandido armado, pistolero
gun metal *s* bronce *m* de cañón; metal pavonado
gunnel ['gʌnəl] *s* (naut) borda, regala
gunner ['gʌnər] *s* artillero; cazador *m*
gunnery ['gʌnəri] *s* artillería
gunny sack ['gʌni] *s* saco de yute
gun'pow'der *s* pólvora
gun'run'ner *s* contrabandista *m* de armas de fuego
gun'run'ning *s* contrabando de armas de fuego
gun'shot' *s* escopetazo, tiro de fusil; alcance *m* de un fusil; **within gunshot** a tiro de fusil
gunshot wound *s* escopetazo
gun'smith' *s* armero
gun'stock' *s* caja de fusil
gunwale ['gʌnəl] *s* (naut) borda, regala
gup·py ['gʌpi] *s* (*pl* **-pies**) lebistes *m*
gurgle ['gʌrgəl] *s* gorgoteo, gluglú *m;* (*of a child*) gorjeo || *intr* gorgotear, hacer gluglú; gorjearse (*el niño*)
gush [gʌʃ] *s* borbollón *m,* chorro || *intr* surgir, salir a borbollones; (coll) hacer extremos, ser extremoso
gusher ['gʌʃər] *s* pozo de chorro de petróleo; (coll) persona extremosa
gushing ['gʌʃɪŋ] *adj* surgente; (coll) extremoso || *s* borbollón *m,* chorro; (coll) efusión, extremos
gush·y ['gʌʃi] *adj* (*comp* **-ier;** *super* **-iest**) (coll) efusivo, extremoso
gusset ['gʌsɪt] *s* escudete *m*
gust [gʌst] *s* (*of wind*) ráfaga; (*of rain*) aguacero; (*of smoke*) bocanada; (*of noise*) explosión; (*of anger or enthusiasm*) arrebato
gusto ['gʌsto] *s* deleite *m,* entusiasmo; **with gusto** con sumo placer
gust·y ['gʌsti] *adj* (*comp* **-ier;** *super* **-iest**) tempestuoso, borrascoso
gut [gʌt] *s* tripa; cuerda de tripa; **guts** tripas; (slang) agallas || *v* (*pret & pp* **gutted;** *ger* **gutting**) *tr* destripar; destruir lo interior de
gutta-percha ['gʌtə'pʌrtʃə] *s* gutapercha
gutter ['gʌtər] *s* (*on side of road*) cuneta; (*in street*) arroyo; (*of roof*) canal *f;* (*ditch formed by rain water*) badén *m;* barrios bajos
gut'ter·snipe' *s* pilluelo, hijo de la miseria; gamberro
guttural ['gʌtərəl] *adj* gutural || *s* sonido gutural
guy [gaɪ] *s* viento, cable *m* de retén; (coll) tipo, tío, sujeto || *tr* (coll) burlarse de
guy wire *s* cable *m* de retén
guzzle ['gʌzəl] *tr & intr* beber con exceso
guzzler ['gʌzlər] *s* borrachín *m*
gym [dʒɪm] *s* (coll) gimnasio
gymnasi·um [dʒɪm'nezɪ·əm] *s* (*pl* **-ums** o **-a** [ə]) gimnasio
gymnast ['dʒɪmnæst] *s* gimnasta *mf*
gymnastic [dʒɪm'næstɪk] *adj* gimnástico || **gymnastics** *spl* gimnasia, gimnástica
gynecologist [,gaɪnə'kɑlədʒɪst], [,dʒaɪnə'kɑlədʒɪst] o [,dʒɪnə'kɑlədʒɪst] *s* ginecólogo
gynecology [,gaɪnə'kɑlədʒi], [,dʒaɪnə'kɑlədʒi] o [,dʒɪnə'kɑlədʒi] *s* ginecología
gyp [dʒɪp] *s* (slang) estafa, timo; (*person*) (slang) estafador *m,* timador *m* || *v* (*pret & pp* **gypped;** *ger* **gypping**) *tr* (slang) estafar, timar
gypsum ['dʒɪpsəm] *s* yeso, aljez *m*
gyp·sy ['dʒɪpsi] *adj* gitano || *s* (*pl* **-sies**) gitano || **Gypsy** *s* gitano (*idioma*)
gypsyish ['dʒɪpsɪ·ɪʃ] *adj* gitanesco
gypsy moth *s* lagarta
gyrate ['dʒaɪret] *intr* girar
gyroscope ['dʒaɪrə,skop] *s* giroscopio

H

H, h [etʃ] octava letra del alfabeto inglés
h. *abbr* **harbor, high, hour, husband**
haberdasher ['hæbər,dæʃər] *s* camisero; (*dealer in notions*) mercero
haberdasher·y ['hæbər,dæʃəri] *s* (*pl* **-ies**) camisería, tienda de artículos para hombres; artículos para hombres
habit ['hæbɪt] *s* costumbre *f,* hábito; (*costume*) traje *m;* **to be in the habit of** acostumbrar

habitat ['hæbɪ,tæt] *s* habitación
habitation [,hæbɪ'teʃən] *s* habitación
habit-forming ['hæbɪt,fɔrmɪŋ] *adj* enviciador
habitual [hə'bɪtʃʊ·əl] *adj* habitual
habitué [hə,bɪtʃʊ'e] *s* habituado
hack [hæk] *s* (*cut*) corte *m;* (*notch*) mella; (*cough*) tos seca; coche *m* de alquiler; caballo de alquiler; caballo de silla; (*old nag*) rocín *m;* escritor *m* a sueldo || *tr* cortar, machetear
hack•man ['hækmən] *s* (*pl* **-men** [mən]) cochero de punto
hackney ['hækni] *s* caballo de silla; coche *m* de alquiler; esclavo del trabajo
hackneyed ['hæknid] *adj* trillado, gastado
hack'saw' *s* sierra de armero, sierra de cortar metales
haddock ['hædək] *s* eglefino
haft [hæft] o [hɑft] *s* mango, puño
hag [hæg] *s* (*ugly old woman*) tarasca; (*witch*) bruja
haggard ['hægərd] *adj* ojeroso, macilento, trasnochado
haggle ['hægəl] *intr* regatear
Hague, The [heg] La Haya
hail [hel] *s* (*frozen rain*) granizo; (*greeting*) saludo; **within hail** al alcance de la voz || *interj* ¡salud!, ¡salve! || *tr* saludar; dar vivas a, acoger con vivas; aclamar; granizar (*p ej., golpes*) || *intr* granizar; **to hail from** venir de, ser oriundo de
hail'-fel'low well met *s* compañero muy afable y simpático
Hail Mary *s* avemaría
hail'stone' *s* piedra de granizo
hail'storm' *s* granizada
hair [hɛr] *s* pelo, cabellos; **to a hair** con la mayor exactitud; **to get in one's hair** (slang) enojarle a uno; **to have one's hair down** estar en melena; **to let one's hair down** (slang) hablar con mucha desenvoltura; **to make one's hair stand on end** ponerle a uno los pelos de punta; **to not turn a hair** no inmutarse; **to split hairs** pararse en quisquillas
hair'breadth' *s* (el) grueso de un pelo, casi nada; **to escape by a hairbreadth** escapar por un pelo
hair'brush' *s* cepillo de cabeza
hair'cloth' *s* tela de crin; (*worn as a penance*) cilicio
hair curler ['kʌrlər] *s* rizador *m,* tenacillas
hair'cut' *s* corte *m* de pelo; **to get a haircut** cortarse el pelo
hair'do' *s* (*pl* **-dos**) peinado, tocado
hair'dress'er *s* peinador *m,* peluquero
hair dryer *s* secador *m*
hair dye *s* tinte *m* para el pelo
hairless ['hɛrlɪs] *adj* pelón
hair net *s* redecilla
hair'pin' *s* horquilla
hair-raising ['hɛr,rezɪŋ] *adj* (coll) espeluznante, horripilante
hair restorer [rɪ'storər] *s* crecepelo
hair ribbon *s* cinta para el cabello
hair set *s* fijapeinados *m*
hair shirt *s* cilicio
hairsplitting ['hɛr,splɪtɪŋ] *adj* quisquilloso || *s* quisquillas
hair'spring' *s* espiral *f*
hair'style' *s* peinado
hair tonic *s* vigorizador *m* del cabello
hair•y ['hɛri] *adj* (*comp* **-ier;** *super* **-iest**) peludo, cabelludo
hake [hek] *s* merluza; (genus: *Urophycis*) fice *m*
halberd ['hælbərd] *s* alabarda
halberdier [,hælbər'dɪr] *s* alabardero
halcyon days ['hælsɪ·ən] *s* días tranquilos, época de paz
hale [hel] *adj* sano, robusto; **hale and hearty** sano y fuerte || *tr* llevar a la fuerza
half [hæf] o [hɑf] *adj* medio; **a half** o **half a** medio; **half the** la mitad de || *adv* medio, p.ej., **half asleep** medio dormido; a medio, p.ej., **half finished** a medio acabar; a medias, p.ej., **half owner** dueño a medias; **half past** y media, p.ej., **half past three** las tres y media; **half . . . half** medio . . . medio || *s* (*pl* **halves** [hævz] o [hɑvz]) mitad; (arith) medio; **in half** por la mitad; **to go halves** ir a medias
half'-and-half' *adj* mitad y mitad; indeterminado || *adv* a medias, en partes iguales || *s* mezcla de leche y crema; mezcla de dos cervezas inglesas
half'back' *s* (football) medio
half-baked ['hæf,bekt] o ['hɑf,bekt] *adj* a medio cocer; incompleto; poco juicioso, inexperto
half binding *s* (bb) encuadernación a la holandesa, media pasta
half'-blood' *s* mestizo; medio hermano
half boot *s* bota de media caña
half'-bound' *adj* (bb) a la holandesa
half'-breed' *s* mestizo
half brother *s* medio hermano
half-cocked ['hæf'kɑkt] o ['hɑf'kɑkt] *adv* (coll) con precipitación
half fare *s* medio billete
half'-full' *adj* mediado
half-hearted ['hæf,hartɪd] o ['hɑf,hartɪd] *adj* indiferente, frío
half holiday *s* mañana o tarde *f* de asueto
half hose *spl* calcetines *mpl*
half'-hour' *s* media hora; **on the half-hour** a la media en punto cada media hora
half leather *s* (bb) encuadernación a la holandesa, media pasta
half'-length' *adj* de medio cuerpo
half'-mast' *s* — **at half-mast** a media asta
half moon *s* media luna
half mourning *s* medio luto
half note *s* (mus) nota blanca
half pay *s* media paga; medio sueldo
halfpen•ny ['hepəni] o ['hepni] *s* (*pl* **-nies**) medio penique
half pint *s* media pinta; (*little runt*) (slang) gorgojo, mirmidón *m*
half'-seas' over *adj* — **to be half-seas over** (slang) estar entre dos velas, estar entre dos luces

half shell *s* (*either half of a bivalve*) concha; (*oysters*) **on the half shell** en su concha

half sister *s* media hermana

half sole *s* media suela

half′-sole′ *tr* poner media suela a

half′-staff′ *s* — **at half-staff** a media asta

half-timbered ['hæf,tɪmbərd] o ['hɑf-,tɪmbərd] *adj* entramado

half title *s* anteportada, falsa portada

half′-tone′ *s* (phot & paint) mediatinta; (typ) similigrabado

half′-track′ *s* media oruga, semitractor *m*

half′truth′ *s* verdad a medias

half′way′ *adj* a medio camino; incompleto, hecho a medias || *adv* a medio camino; **halfway through** a la mitad de; **to meet halfway** partir el camino con; partir la diferencia con; hacer concesiones mutuas (*dos personas*)

half-witted ['hæf,wɪtɪd] o ['hɑf-,wɪtɪd] *adj* imbécil; necio, tonto

halibut ['hælɪbət] *s* halibut *m*

halide ['hælaɪd] o ['helaɪd] *s* (chem) haluro

halitosis [,hælɪ'tosɪs] *s* halitosis *f*, aliento fétido

hall [hɔl] *s* (*passageway*) corredor *m;* (*entranceway*) vestíbulo, zaguán *m;* (*large meeting room*) sala, salón *m;* (*assembly room of a university*) paraninfo; (*building, e.g., of a university*) edificio

halleluiah o **hallelujah** [,hælɪ'lujə] *s* aleluya *m & f* || *interj* ¡aleluya!

hall′mark′ *s* marca de constraste; (*distinguishing feature*) (fig) sello

hal·lo [hə'lo] *s* (*pl* **-los**) grito || *interj* ¡hola!; (*to incite dogs in hunting*) ¡sus! || *intr* gritar

hallow ['hælo] *tr* santificar

hallowed ['hælod] *adj* santo, sagrado

Halloween o **Hallowe′en** [,hælo'in] *s* víspera de Todos los Santos

hallucination [hə,lusɪ'neʃən] *s* alucinación

hall′way′ *s* corredor *m;* vestíbulo, zaguán *m*

ha·lo ['helo] *s* (*pl* **-los** o **-loes**) halo

halogen ['hælədʒən] *s* halógeno

halt [hɔlt] *adj* cojo, renco || *s* alto, parada; **to call a halt** mandar hacer alto; **to come to a halt** pararse, detenerse, interrumpirse || *tr* parar, detener || *intr* hacer alto

halter ['hɔltər] *s* (*for leading or fastening horse*) cabestro, ronzal *m*, dogal *m;* (*noose*) dogal *m*, cuerda de ahorcar; muerte *f* en la horca

halting ['hɔltɪŋ] *adj* cojo, renco; vacilante

halve [hæv] o [hɑv] *tr* partir en dos, partir por la mitad

halyard ['hæljərd] *s* (naut) driza

ham [hæm] *s* (*part of leg behind knee*) corva; (*thigh and buttock*) pernil *m;* (*cured meat from hog's hind leg*) jamón *m;* (slang) comicastro; (slang) aficionado (*a la radio*); **hams** nalgas

ham and eggs *spl* huevos con jamón

hamburger ['hæm,bʌrgər] *s* hamburguesa

hamlet ['hæmlɪt] *s* aldehuela, caserío

hammer ['hæmər] *s* martillo; (*of piano*) macillo, martinete *m;* **to go under the hammer** venderse en pública subasta || *tr* martillar; **to hammer out** formar a martillazos; sacar en limpio a fuerza de mucho esfuerzo || *intr* martillar; **to hammer away** trabajar asiduamente

hammock ['hæmək] *s* hamaca

hamper ['hæmpər] *s* canasto, cesto grande con tapa || *tr* estorbar, impedir

hamster ['hæmstər] *s* marmota de Alemania, rata del trigo

ham·string ['hæm,strɪŋ] *v* (*pret & pp* **-strung**) *tr* desjarretar; (fig) estropear, incapacitar

hand [hænd] *adj* (*done or operated with the hands*) manual || *s* mano *f;* (*workman*) obrero, peón *m;* (*way of writing*) escritura, puño y letra; (*signature*) firma; (*clapping of hands*) salva de aplausos; (*of clock or watch*) mano *f*, manecilla; (*all the cards in one's hand*) juego; (*a round of play*) mano *f;* (*player*) jugador *m;* (*source, origin*) fuente *f;* (*skill*) destreza; **all hands** (naut) toda la tripulación; (coll) todos; **at first hand** de primera mano; directamente, de buena tinta; **at hand** disponible; **hand in glove** uña y carne; **hand in hand** asidos de la mano; juntos; **hands up!** ¡arriba las manos!; **hand to hand** cuerpo a cuerpo; **in hand** entre manos; **in his own hand** de su propio puño; **on hand** entre manos; disponible; **on hands and knees** (*crawling*) a gatas; (*beseeching*) de rodillas; **on the one hand** por una parte; **on the other hand** por otra parte; **out of hand** luego, en seguida; desmandado; **to be at hand** obrar en mi (nuestro) poder (*una carta*); **to change hands** mudar de manos; **to clap hands** batir palmas; **to eat out of one's hand** aceptar dócilmente la autoridad de uno; **to fall into the hands of** caer en manos de; **to have a hand in** tomar parte en; **to have one's hands full** estar ocupadísimo; **to hold hands** tomarse de las manos; **to hold up one's hands** (*as a sign of surrender*) alzar las manos; **to join hands** darse las manos; casarse; **to keep one's hands off** no tocar, no meterse en; **to lend a hand** echar una mano; **to live from hand to mouth** vivir al día, vivir de la mano a la boca; **to not lift a hand** no levantar paja del suelo; **to play into the hands of** hacer el caldo gordo a; **to raise one's hand** (*in taking an oath*) alzar el dedo; **to shake hands** estrecharse la mano; **to show one's hand** descubrir su juego; **to take in hand** hacerse cargo de; tratar, estudiar (*una cuestión*); **to throw up one's hands** darse por vencido; **to try one's hand** probar la mano; **to turn one's hand**

to dedicarse a, ocuparse en; **to wash one's hands of** lavarse las manos de; **under my hand** con mi firma, bajo mi firma, de mi puño y letra; **under the hand and seal of** firmado y sellado por || *tr* dar, entregar; **to hand in** entregar; **to hand on** transmitir; **to hand out** repartir

hand'bag' *s* saco de noche; bolso de señora

hand baggage *s* equipaje *m* de mano

hand'ball' *s* pelota; juego de pelota a mano

hand'bill' *s* hoja volante

hand'book' *s* manual *m;* guía de turistas; registro para apuestas

hand'breadth' *s* palmo menor

hand'car' *s* (rr) carrito de mano

hand'cart' *s* carretilla de mano

hand control *s* mando a mano

hand'cuff' *s* manilla; **handcuffs** manillas, esposas || *tr* poner esposas a

handful ['hænd,fʊl] *s* puñado, manojo

hand glass *s* espejo de mano; lupa

hand grenade *s* granada de mano

handi•cap ['hændɪ,kæp] *s* desventaja, obstáculo; (sport) handicap *m* || *v* (*pret & pp* **-capped;** *ger* **-capping**) *tr* poner trabas a; (sport) handicapar

handicraft ['hændɪ,kræft] o ['hændɪ,krɑft] *s* destreza manual; arte mecánica

handiwork ['hændɪ,wʌrk] *s* hechura, trabajo; obra manual

handkerchief ['hæŋkərtʃɪf] o ['hæŋkər,tʃif] *s* pañuelo

handle ['hændəl] *s* (*of a basket, crock, pitcher*) asa; (*of a shovel, rake, etc.*) mango; (*of an umbrella, sword*) puño; (*of a door, drawer*) tirador *m;* (*of a hand organ*) manubrio; (*of a water pump*) guimbalete *m;* (*opportunity, pretext*) asidero; **to fly off the handle** (slang) salirse de sus casillas || *tr* manosear, manipular; dirigir, manejar, gobernar; comerciar en || *intr* manejarse

handle bar *s* manillar *m,* guía

handler ['hændlər] *s* (sport) entrenador *m*

hand'made' *adj* hecho a mano

hand'maid' o **hand'maid'en** *s* criada, sirvienta

hand'-me-down' *s* (coll) prenda de vestir de segunda mano

hand organ *s* organillo

hand'out' *s* comida que se da de limosna; comunicado de prensa

hand-picked ['hænd,pɪkt] *adj* escogido a mano; escogido escrupulosamente; escogido con motivos ocultos

hand'rail' *s* barandilla, pasamano

hand'saw' *s* serrucho, sierra de mano

hand'set' *s* microteléfono

hand'shake' *s* apretón *m* de manos

handsome ['hænsəm] *adj* hermoso, elegante, guapo; considerable

hand'spring' *s* voltereta sobre las manos

hand'-to-hand' *adj* cuerpo a cuerpo

hand'-to-mouth' *adj* inseguro, precario; impróvido

hand'work' *s* trabajo a mano

hand'-wres'tle *intr* pulsear

hand'-writ'ing *s* escritura; (*writing by hand which characterizes a particular person*) letra

hand•y ['hændi] *adj* (*comp* **-ier;** *super* **-iest**) (*easy to handle*) manuable; (*within easy reach*) próximo, a la mano; (*skillful*) diestro, hábil; **to come in handy** venir a pelo

handy man *s* dije *m,* factótum *m*

hang [hæŋ] *s* (*of a dress, curtain, etc.*) caída; (*skill; insight*) tino; **I don't care a hang** (coll) no me importa un bledo; **to get the hang of it** (coll) coger el tino || *v* (*pret & pp* **hung** [hʌŋ]) *tr* colgar; tender (*la ropa mojada*); pegar (*el papel pintado*); fijar (*un cartel, un letrero*); enquiciar (*una puerta, una ventana*); bajar (*la cabeza*); **hang it!** (coll) ¡caramba!; **to hang up** colgar (*el sombrero*); impedir los progresos de || *intr* colgar, pender; estar agarrado; vacilar; **to hang around** esperar sin hacer nada; haraganear; rondar; **to hang on** colgar de; depender de; estar pendiente de (*las palabras de una persona*); estar sin acabar de morir; agarrarse; **to hang out** asomarse; (slang) recogerse, alojarse; **to hang over** (*to threaten*) cernerse sobre; **to hang together** mantenerse unidos; **to hang up** (telp) colgar || *v* (*pret* **hanged** o **hung**) *tr* ahorcar || *intr* ahorcarse

hangar ['hæŋər] o ['hæŋgɑr] *s* cobertizo; (aer) hangar *m*

hang'bird' *s* pájaro de nido colgante; (*Baltimore oriole*) cacique veranero

hanger ['hæŋər] *s* colgador *m,* suspensión; (*hook*) colgadero

hang'er•on' *s* (*pl* **hangers-on**) secuaz *mf;* parásito; (*sponger*) pegote *m*

hanging ['hæŋɪŋ] *adj* colgante, pendiente || *s* ahorcadura, muerte *f* en la horca; **hangings** colgaduras

hang•man ['hæŋmən] *s* (*pl* **-men** [mən]) verdugo

hang'nail' *s* padrastro, respigón *m*

hang'out' *s* guarida, querencia; (*place to loaf and gossip*) mentidero

hang'o'ver *s* (slang) resaca

hank [hæŋk] *s* madeja

hanker ['hæŋkər] *intr* sentir anhelo

Hannibal ['hænɪbəl] *s* Aníbal *m*

haphazard [,hæp'hæzərd] *adj* casual, fortuito, impensado || *adv* al acaso, a la ventura

hapless ['hæplɪs] *adj* desgraciado, desventurado

happen ['hæpən] *intr* acontecer, suceder; (*to turn out*) resultar; (*to be the case by chance*) dar la casualidad; **to happen in** entrar por casualidad; **to happen on** encontrarse con; **to happen to** hacerse de; **to happen to** + *inf* por casualidad + *ind,* p.ej., **I happened to see her at the theater** por casualidad la ví en el teatro

happening ['hæpənɪŋ] *s* acontecimiento, suceso

happily ['hæpɪli] *adv* felizmente

happiness ['hæpɪnɪs] *s* felicidad

hap•py ['hæpi] *adj* (*comp* **-pier;** *super* **-piest**) feliz; (*pleased*) contento; **to be happy to** alegrarse de, tener gusto en

hap'py-go-luck'y *adj* irresponsable, impróvido || *adv* a la buenaventura

happy medium *s* justo medio

Happy New Year *interj* ¡Feliz Año Nuevo!

harangue [hə'ræŋ] *s* arenga || *tr* & *intr* arengar

harass ['hærəs] o [hə'ræs] *tr* acosar, hostigar; molestar, vejar

harbinger ['hɑrbɪndʒər] *s* precursor *m;* anuncio, presagio || *tr* anunciar, presagiar

harbor ['hɑrbər] *adj* portuario || *s* puerto || *tr* albergar; alcahuetar, encubrir (*delincuentes u objetos robados*); guardar (*sentimientos de odio*)

harbor master *s* capitán *m* de puerto

hard [hɑrd] *adj* duro; (*difficult*) difícil; (*water*) crudo, duro; (*solder*) fuerte; (*work*) asiduo; (*drinker*) empedernido; espiritoso, fuertemente alcohólico; **to be hard on** (*to treat severely*) ser muy duro con; (*to wear out fast*) gastar, echar a perder || *adv* duro; fuerte; mucho; **hard upon** a raíz de; **to drink hard** beber de firme; **to rain hard** llover de firme

hard and fast *adj* inflexible, riguroso || *adv* firmemente

hard-bitten ['hɑrd'bɪtən] *adj* terco, tenaz, inflexible

hard-boiled ['hɑrd'bɔɪld] *adj* (*egg*) duro, muy cocido; (coll) duro, inflexible

hard candy *s* caramelos

hard cash *s* dinero contante y sonante

hard cider *s* sidra muy fermentada

hard coal *s* antracita

hard-earned ['hɑrd'ʌrnd] *adj* ganado a pulso

harden ['hɑrdən] *tr* endurecer || *intr* endurecerse

hardening ['hɑrdənɪŋ] *s* endurecimiento

hard facts *spl* realidades

hard-fought ['hɑrd'fɔt] *adj* reñido

hard-headed ['hɑrd'hɛdɪd] *adj* astuto, sagaz; terco, tozudo

hard-hearted ['hɑrd'hɑrtɪd] *adj* duro de corazón

hardihood ['hɑrdɪ,hʊd] *s* audacia, resolución; descaro, insolencia

hardiness ['hɑrdɪnɪs] *s* fuerza, robustez; audacia, resolución

hard labor *s* trabajos forzados

hard luck *s* mala suerte

hard'-luck' story *s* (coll) cuento de penas; **to tell a hard-luck story** (coll) contar lástimas

hardly ['hɑrdli] *adv* apenas; casi no; (*with great difficulty*) a duras penas; (*grievously*) penosamente; **hardly ever** casi nunca

hardness ['hɑrdnɪs] *s* dureza; (*of water*) crudeza

hard of hearing *adj* duro de oído, teniente

hard-pressed ['hɑrd'prɛst] *adj* acosado; (*for money*) apurado, alcanzado

hard rubber *s* vulcanita

hard sauce *s* mantequilla azucarada

hard'-shell' clam *s* almeja redonda

hard-shell crab *s* cangrejo de cáscara dura

hardship ['hɑrdʃɪp] *s* penalidad, infortunio, apuro

hard'tack' *s* galleta, sequete *m*

hard times *spl* período de miseria, apuros

hard to please *adj* difícil de contentar

hard up *adj* (coll) apurado, alcanzado

hard'ware' *s* ferretería, quincalla; (*metal trimmings*) herraje *m*

hardware•man ['hɑrd,wɛrmən] *s* (*pl* **-men** [mən]) ferretero, quincallero

hardware store *s* ferretería, quincallería

hard-won ['hɑrd,wʌn] *adj* ganado a pulso

hard'wood' *s* madera dura; árbol *m* de madera dura

hardwood floor *s* entarimado

har•dy ['hɑrdi] *adj* (*comp* **-dier;** *super* **-diest**) fuerte, robusto; audaz, resuelto; (*rash*) temerario; (hort) resistente

hare [hɛr] *s* liebre *f*

harebrained ['hɛr,brend] *adj* atolondrado

hare'lip' *s* labio leporino

harelipped ['hɛr,lɪpt] *adj* labiohendido

harem ['hɛrəm] *s* harén *m*

hark [hɑrk] *intr* escuchar; **to hark back** volver (*la jauría*) sobre la pista; **to hark back to** volver a, recordar

harken ['hɑrkən] *intr* escuchar, atender

harlequin ['hɑrləkwɪn] *s* arlequín *m*

harlot ['hɑrlət] *s* meretriz *f*

harm [hɑrm] *s* daño, perjuicio || *tr* dañar, perjudicar, hacer daño a

harmful ['hɑrmfəl] *adj* dañoso, perjudicial; (*e.g., pests*) dañino

harmless ['hɑrmlɪs] *adj* innocuo, inofensivo

harmonic [hɑr'mɑnɪk] *adj* & *s* armónico

harmonica [hɑr'mɑnɪkə] *s* armónica

harmonious [hɑr'monɪ·əs] *adj* armonioso

harmonize ['hɑrmə,naɪz] *tr* & *intr* armonizar

harmo•ny ['hɑrməni] *s* (*pl* **-nies**) armonía

harness ['hɑrnɪs] *s* arreos, guarniciones; **to get back in the harness** volver a la rutina; **to die in the harness** morir al pie del cañón || *tr* enjaezar, poner las guarniciones a; enganchar; captar (*las aguas de un río*)

harness maker *s* guarnicionero

harness race *s* carrera con sulky

harp [hɑrp] *s* arpa || *intr* — **to harp on** repetir porfiadamente

harpist ['hɑrpɪst] *s* arpista *mf*

harpoon [hɑr'pun] *s* arpón *m* || *tr* & *intr* arponear

harpsichord ['hɑrpsɪ,kɔrd] *s* clave *m*

har·py ['hɑrpi] *s* (*pl* **-pies**) arpía
harrow ['hæro] *s* (agr) grada || *tr* (agr) gradar; atormentar
harrowing ['hæro·ɪŋ] *adj* horripilante, espantoso
har·ry ['hæri] *v* (*pret & pp* **-ried**) *tr* acosar, hostilizar, hostigar; atormentar, molestar
harsh [hɑrʃ] *adj* (*to touch, taste, eyes, hearing*) áspero; duro, cruel
harshness ['hɑrʃnɪs] *s* aspereza; dureza, crueldad
hart [hɑrt] *s* ciervo
harum-scarum ['hɛrəm'skɛrəm] *adj* atolondrado || *adv* atolondradamente || *s* mataperros *m*
harvest ['hɑrvɪst] *s* cosecha || *tr & intr* cosechar
harvester ['hɑrvɪstər] *s* cosechero; (*helper*) agostero; (*machine*) segadora
harvest home *s* entrada de los frutos; fiesta de segadores; canción de segadores
harvest moon *s* luna de la cosecha
has-been ['hæz,bɪn] *s* (coll) antigualla
hash [hæʃ] *s* picadillo || *tr* picar
hash house *s* bodegón *m*
hashish ['hæʃiʃ] *s* hachich *m*
hasp [hæsp] o [hɑsp] *s* portacandado; (*of book covers*) broche *m*
hassle ['hæsəl] *s* (coll) riña, disputa
hassock ['hæsək] *s* cojín *m* (*para los pies o las rodillas*)
haste [hest] *s* prisa; **in haste** de prisa; **to make haste** darse prisa
hasten ['hesən] *tr* apresurar; apretar (*el paso*) || *intr* apresurarse
hast·y ['hesti] *adj* (*comp* **-ier;** *super* **-iest**) apresurado; inconsiderado, impulsivo, colérico
hat [hæt] *s* sombrero; **to keep under one's hat** (coll) callar, no divulgar; **to throw one's hat in the ring** (coll) decidirse a bajar a la arena
hat'band' *s* cintillo; (*worn to show mourning*) gasa
hat block *s* horma, conformador *m*
hat'box' *s* sombrerera
hatch [hætʃ] *s* (*brood*) cría, nidada; (*trap door*) escotillón *m;* (*lower half of door*) media puerta; (*opening in ship's deck*) escotilla; (*lid for opening in ship's deck*) cuartel *m* || *tr* empollar (*huevos*); sombrear (*un dibujo*); maquinar, tramar || *intr* empollarse; salir del huevo
hat'-check' girl *s* guardarropa
hatchet ['hætʃɪt] *s* destral *m,* hacha pequeña; **to bury the hatchet** envainar la espada
hatch'way' *s* (*trap door*) escotillón *m;* (*opening in ship's deck*) escotilla
hate [het] *s* odio, aborrecimiento || *tr & intr* odiar, aborrecer, detestar
hateful ['hetfəl] *adj* odioso, aborrecible
hat'pin' *s* aguja de sombrero, pasador *m*
hat'rack' *s* percha
hatred ['hetrɪd] *s* odio, aborrecimiento
hatter ['hætər] *s* sombrerero
haughtiness ['hɔtɪnɪs] *s* altanería, altivez *f*
haugh·ty ['hɔti] *adj* (*comp* **-tier;** *super* **-tiest**) altanero, altivo
haul [hɔl] *s* (*pull, tug*) tirón *m;* (*amount caught*) redada; (*distance transported*) trayecto, recorrido; (*roundup, e.g., of thieves*) redada || *tr* acarrear, transportar; (naut) halar
haunch [hɔntʃ] o [hɑntʃ] *s* (*hip*) cadera; (*hind quarter of an animal*) anca; (*leg of animal used for food*) pierna
haunt [hɔnt] o [hɑnt] *s* guarida, nidal *m,* querencia || *tr* andar por, vagar por; frecuentar; inquietar, molestar; perseguir (*las memorias a una persona*)
haunted house *s* casa de fantasmas
haute couture [ot ku'tyr] *s* alta moda
Havana [hə'vænə] *s* La Habana
have [hæv] *v* (*pret & pp* **had** [hæd]) *tr* tener; (*to get, to take*) tomar; **to have and to hold** (úsase sólo en el infinitivo) para ser poseído en propiedad; **to have got** (coll) tener, poseer; **to have got to** + *inf* (coll) tener que + *inf;* **to have it in for** (coll) tener tirria a; **to have it out with** (coll) habérselas con, emprenderla con; **to have on** llevar puesto; **to have** (*something*) **to do with** tener que ver con; **to have** + *inf* hacer, mandar + *inf,* p.ej., **I had him go out that door** le hice salir por esa puerta; **to have** + *pp* hacer, mandar + *inf,* p.ej., **I had my watch repaired** hice componer mi reloj || *intr* — **to have at** atacar, embestir; **to have to** + *inf* tener que + *inf;* **to have to do with** (*to be concerned with*) tratar de; (*to have connections with*) tener relaciones con || *v aux* haber, p.ej., **he has studied his lesson** ha estudiado su lección
havelock ['hævlɑk] *s* cogotera
haven ['hevən] *s* puerto; abrigo, asilo, buen puerto
have-not ['hæv,nɑt] *s* — **the haves and the have-nots** (coll) los ricos y los desposeídos
haversack ['hævər,sæk] *s* barjuleta; (*of soldier*) mochila
havoc ['hævək] *s* estrago, estragos; **to play havoc with** hacer grandes estragos en
haw [hɔ] *s* (*of hawthorn*) baya, simiente *f;* (*in speech*) vacilación || *interj* ¡a la izquierda! || *tr & intr* volver a la izquierda
haw'-haw' *s* carcajada
hawk [hɔk] *s* halcón *m,* gavilán *m,* cernícalo; (*mortarboard*) esparavel *m;* (*sharper*) (coll) fullero || *tr* pregonar; **to hawk up** arrojar tosiendo || *intr* carraspear, gargajear
hawker ['hɔkər] *s* buhonero
hawksbill turtle ['hɔks,bɪl] *s* carey *m*
hawse [hɔz] *s* (naut) muz *m;* (*hole*) (naut) escobén *m;* (naut) longitud de cadenas
hawse'hole' *s* (naut) escobén *m*

hawser ['hɔzər] *s* (naut) guindaleza
haw'thorn' *s* espino, oxiacanta
hay [he] *s* heno; **to hit the hay** (slang) acostarse; **to make hay while the sun shines** hacer su agosto
hay fever *s* fiebre *f* del heno
hay'field' *s* henar *m*
hay'fork' *s* horca; (*machine*) elevador *m* de heno
hay'loft' *s* henil *m*, henal *m*
hay'mak'er *s* (box) golpe *m* que pone fuera de combate
haymow ['he,maʊ] *s* henil *m;* acopio de heno
hay'rack' *s* pesebre *m*
hayrick ['he,rɪk] *s* almiar *m*
hay ride *s* paseo de placer en carro de heno
hay'seed' *s* simiente *f* de heno; (coll) patán *m*, campesino
hay'stack' *s* almiar *m*
hay'wire' *adj* (slang) descompuesto; (slang) destornillado, loco || *s* alambre *m* para embalar el heno
hazard ['hæzərd] *s* peligro, riesgo; (*chance*) acaso, azar *m;* (golf) obstáculo; **at all hazards** por grande que sea el riesgo || *tr* arriesgar; aventurar (*una opinión*)
hazardous ['hæzərdəs] *adj* peligroso, arriesgado
haze [hez] *s* calina, bruma; (fig) confusión, vaguedad || *tr* dar novatada a
hazel ['hezəl] *adj* castaño claro || *s* avellano
ha'zel·nut' *s* avellana
hazing ['hezɪŋ] *s* novatada
ha·zy ['hezi] *adj* (*comp* **-zier;** *super* **-ziest**) calinoso, brumoso; confuso, vago
H-bomb ['etʃ,bɑm] *s* bomba de hidrógeno
H.C. *abbr* **House of Commons**
hd. *abbr* **head**
hdqrs. *abbr* **headquarters**
H.E. *abbr* **His Eminence, His Excellency**
he [hi] *pron pers* (*pl* **they**) él || *s* (*pl* **hes**) macho, varón *m*
head [hɛd] *s* cabeza; (*of a bed*) cabecera; (*caption*) encabezamiento; (*of a boil*) centro; (*on a glass of beer*) espuma; (*of a drum*) parche *m;* (*of a cane*) puño; (*of a barrel, cylinder, etc.*) fondo, tapa; (*of cylinder of automobile engine*) culata; crisis *f*, punto decisivo; **at the head of** al frente de; **from head to foot** de pies a cabeza; **head over heels** en un salto mortal; hasta los tuétanos; precipitadamente; **heads** (*of a coin*) cara; **heads or tails** a cara o cruz; **over one's head** fuera del alcance de uno; (*going to a higher authority*) por encima de uno; **to be out of one's head** (coll) delirar; **to come into one's head** pasarle a uno por la cabeza; **to go to one's head** subírsele a uno a la cabeza; **to keep one's head** no perder la cabeza; **to keep one's head above water** no dejarse vencer; **to put heads together** consultarse entre sí; **to not make head or tail of** no ver pies ni cabeza a || *tr* acaudillar, dirigir, mandar; estar a la cabeza de (*p.ej., la clase*); venir primero en (*una lista*) || *intr* — **to head towards** dirigirse hacia
head'ache' *s* dolor *m* de cabeza
head'band' *s* cinta para la cabeza; (*of a book*) cabezada
head'board' *s* cabecera de cama
head'cheese' *s* queso de cerdo
head'dress' *s* (*style of hair*) tocado; prenda para la cabeza
header ['hɛdər] *s* — **to take a header** (coll) caerse de cabeza
head'first' *adv* de cabeza; precipitadamente
head'gear' *s* sombrero; (*for protection*) casco
head'hunt'er *s* cazador *m* de cabezas
heading ['hɛdɪŋ] *s* encabezamiento; (*of a letter*) membrete *m;* (*of a chapter of a book*) cabecera
headland ['hɛdlənd] *s* promontorio
headless ['hɛdlɪs] *adj* sin cabeza; sin jefe; estúpido
head'light' *s* (aut) faro; (naut) farol *m* de tope; (rr) farol *m*
head'line' *s* (*of newspaper*) cabecera; (*of a page of a book*) titulillo, título de página || *tr* poner cabecera a; (slang) destacar, dar cartel a (*un actor*)
head'lin'er *s* (slang) atracción principal
head'long' *adj* de cabeza; precipitado || *adv* de cabeza; precipitadamente
head·man ['hɛd,mæn] *s* (*pl* **-men** [,mɛn]) caudillo, jefe *m*
head'mas'ter *s* director *m* de un colegio
head'most' *adj* delantero, primero
head office *s* oficina central
head of hair *s* cabellera
head'-on' *adj & adv* de frente; **head-on collision** colisión de frente
head'phone' *s* auricular *m* de casco, receptor *m* de cabeza
head'piece' *s* (*any covering for head*) casco, yelmo, morrión *m;* (*brains, judgment*) cabeza, juicio; cabecera de cama; (*headset*) auricular *m* de casco, receptor *m* de cabeza; (typ) cabecera, viñeta
head'quar'ters *s* centro de dirección; (*of police*) jefatura; (mil) cuartel *m* general
head'rest' *s* apoyo para la cabeza
head'set' *s* auricular *m* de casco, receptor *m* de cabeza
head'ship' *s* jefatura, dirección
head'stone' *s* (*cornerstone*) piedra angular; (*on a grave*) lápida sepulcral
head'stream' *s* afluente *m* principal
head'strong' *adj* cabezudo, terco
head'wait'er *s* jefe *m* de camareros, encargado de comedor
head'wa'ters *spl* cabecera
head'way' *s* avance *m*, progreso; espacio libre; **to make headway** avanzar, progresar
head'wear' *s* prendas de cabeza
head wind *s* viento de frente, viento por la proa

head'work' *s* trabajo intelectual
head·y ['hɛdi] *adj* (*comp* **-ier;** *super* **-iest**) excitante, emocionante; impetuoso, violento; (*intoxicating*) cabezudo; (*clever*) sesudo
heal [hil] *tr* curar, sanar; cicatrizar; remediar (*un daño*) || *intr* curar, sanar; cicatrizarse; remediarse
healer ['hilər] *s* curador *m*, sanador *m*
health [hɛlθ] *s* salud *f;* **to be in good health** estar bien de salud; **to be in poor health** estar mal de salud; **to drink to the health of** beber a la salud de; **to radiate health** verter salud; **to your health!** ¡a su salud!
healthful ['hɛlθfəl] *adj* saludable; sano
health·y ['hɛlθi] *adj* (*comp* **-ier;** *super* **-iest**) sano; saludable
heap [hip] *s* montón *m* || *tr* amontonar, apilar; (*to supply with, e.g., favors*) colmar; (*to bestow in great quantity*) dar generosamente || *intr* amontonarse, apilarse
hear [hɪr] *v* (*pret & pp* **heard** [hʌrd]) *tr* oír; **to hear it said** oírlo decir || *intr* oír; **hear! hear!** ¡bravo!; **to hear about** oír hablar de; **to hear from** tener noticias de; **to hear of** oír hablar de; **to hear tell of** oír hablar de; **to hear that** oír decir que
hearer ['hɪrər] *s* oyente *mf*
hearing ['hɪrɪŋ] *s* (*sense*) oído; (*act*) oída; audiencia; **in the hearing of** en presencia de; **within hearing** al alcance del oído
hearing aid *s* aparato auditivo
hear'say' *s* rumor *m;* **by hearsay** de o por oídas
hearse [hʌrs] *s* coche *m* fúnebre, carroza fúnebre
heart [hɑrt] *s* corazón *m;* (*e.g., of lettuce*) cogollo; **after one's heart** enteramente del gusto de uno; **by heart** de memoria; **heart and soul** de todo corazón; **to break the heart of** partir el corazón de; **to die of a broken heart** morir de pena; **to eat one's heart out** sufrir en silencio; **to get to the heart of** llegar al fondo de; **to have one's heart in one's work** trabajar con entusiasmo; **to have one's heart in the right place** tener buenas intenciones; **to lose heart** descorazonarse; **to open one's heart to** descubrirse con; **to take heart** cobrar aliento; **to take to heart** tomar a pecho; **to wear one's heart on one's sleeve** llevar el corazón en la mano; **with all one's heart** con toda el alma de uno; **with one's heart in one's mouth** con el credo en la boca
heart'ache' *s* angustia, congoja
heart attack *s* ataque *m* de corazón, ataque cardíaco
heart'beat' *s* latido del corazón
heart'break' *s* angustia, dolor *m* abrumador
heart'break'er *s* ladrón *m* de corazones
heartbroken ['hɑrt ,brokən] *adj* transido de dolor, muerto de pena
heart'burn' *s* acedía, rescoldera; (*jealousy*) celos
heart disease *s* enfermedad del corazón
hearten ['hɑrtən] *tr* alentar, animar
heart failure *s* debilidad coronaria; (*death*) paro del corazón; (*faintness*) desfallecimiento, desmayo
heartfelt ['hɑrt ,fɛlt] *adj* cordial, sentido, sincero
hearth [hɑrθ] *s* hogar *m*
hearth'stone' *s* solera del hogar; (*home*) hogar *m*
heartily ['hɑrtɪli] *adv* cordialmente; con buen apetito; de buena gana; bien, mucho
heartless ['hɑrtlɪs] *adj* cruel, inhumano
heart-rending ['hɑrt ,rɛndɪŋ] *adj* angustioso, que parte el corazón
heart'seed' *s* farolillo
heart'sick' *adj* afligido, desconsolado
heart'strings' *spl* fibras del corazón, entretelas
heart'-to-heart' *adj* franco, sincero
heart trouble *s* — **to have heart trouble** enfermar del corazón
heart'wood' *s* madera de corazón
heart·y ['hɑrti] *adj* (*comp* **-ier;** *super* **-iest**) cordial, sincero; sano, fuerte; (*meal*) abundante; (*laugh*) bueno; (*eater*) grande
heat [hit] *adj* térmico || *s* calor *m;* (*warming of a room, house, etc.*) calefacción; (*rut of animals*) celo; (*in horse racing*) carrera de prueba; (fig) ardor *m*, ímpetu *m;* **in heat** en celo || *tr* calentar; calefaccionar (*p.ej., una casa*); (fig) acalorar, excitar || *intr* calentarse; (fig) acalorarse, excitarse
heated ['hitɪd] *adj* acalorado
heater ['hitər] *s* calentador *m;* (*for central heating*) calorífero; (electron) calefactor *m*
heater man *s* calefactor *m*
heath [hiθ] *s* (*shrub*) brezo; (*tract of land*) brezal *m*
hea·then ['hiðən] *adj* gentil, pagano; irreligioso || *s* (*pl* **-then** o **-thens**) gentil *mf*, pagano
heathendom ['hiðəndəm] *s* gentilidad
heather ['hɛðər] *s* brezo
heating ['hitɪŋ] *adj* calentador || *s* calefacción
heat lightning *s* fucilazo, relámpago de calor
heat shield *s* blindaje térmico, escudo térmico
heat'stroke' *s* insolación
heat wave *s* (phys) onda calorífica; (coll) ola de calor
heave [hiv] *s* esfuerzo para levantar; esfuerzo para levantarse; **heaves** (vet) huélfago || *v* (*pret & pp* **heaved** o **hov** [hov]) *tr* alzar, levantar; arrojar, lanzar; exhalar (*un suspiro*) || *intr* levantarse y bajar alternativamente; palpitar (*el pecho*); elevarse; hacer esfuerzos por vomitar
heaven ['hɛvən] *s* cielo; **for heaven's sake!** o **good heavens!** ¡válgame Dios!; **heavens** (*firmament*) cielo ||

Heaven *s* cielo (*mansión de los bienaventurados*)
heavenly ['hɛvənli] *adj* (*body*) celeste; (*life, home*) celestial; (fig) celestial
heavenly body *s* astro, cuerpo celeste
heav•y ['hɛvi] *adj* (*comp* **-ier;** *super* **-iest**) (*of great weight*) pesado; (*liquid*) espeso, denso; (*cloth, paper, sea, line*) grueso; (*traffic*) denso; (*crop, harvest*) abundante, copioso; (*expense*) fuerte; (*rain*) recio; (*features*) basto; (*eyes*) agravado; (*gunfire*) fragoroso; (*heart*) abatido, triste; (*drinker*) grande; (*stock market*) postrado; (*clothing*) de mucho abrigo ‖ *adv* pesadamente; **to hang heavy** pasar (*el tiempo*) con gran lentitud
heav'y•du'ty *adj* extrafuerte
heavy-hearted ['hɛvɪ'hɑrtɪd] *adj* afligido, acongojado
heav'y•set' *adj* costilludo, espaldudo
heav'y•weight' *s* (box) peso pesado
Hebrew ['hibru] *adj & s* hebreo
hecatomb ['hɛkə,tom] o ['hɛkə,tum] *s* hecatombe *f*
heckle ['hɛkəl] *tr* interrumpir (*a un orador*) con preguntas impertinentes
hectic ['hɛktɪk] *adj* (coll) agitado, turbulento
hedge [hɛdʒ] *s* cercado, vallado; (*of bushes*) seto vivo; apuesta compensatoria; (*in stock market*) operación compensatoria ‖ *tr* cercar con vallado; cercar con seto vivo; **to hedge in** encerrar, rodear ‖ *intr* no querer comprometerse; hacer apuestas compensatorias; hacer operaciones compensatorias
hedge'hog' *s* erizo; (*porcupine*) puerco espín *m*
hedge'hop' *v* (*pret & pp* **-hopped;** *ger* **-hopping**) *intr* (aer) volar rasando el suelo
hedgehopping ['hɛdʒ,hɑpɪŋ] *s* (aer) vuelo rasante
hedge'row' *s* cercado de arbustos, seto vivo
heed [hid] *s* atención, cuidado; **to take heed** ir con cuidado ‖ *tr* atender a, hacer caso de ‖ *intr* atender, hacer caso
heedless ['hidlɪs] *adj* desatento, descuidado
heehaw ['hi,hɔ] *s* (*of donkey*) rebuzno; risotada ‖ *intr* rebuznar; reír groseramente
heel [hil] *s* (*of foot*) calcañar *m,* talón *m;* (*of stocking or shoe*) talón *m;* (*raised part of shoe below heel*) tacón *m;* (slang) sinvergüenza *mf;* **down at the heel** desaliñado, mal vestido; **to cool one's heels** (coll) hacer antesala; **to kick up one's heels** (slang) mostrarse alegre; **to show a clean pair of heels** o **to take to one's heels** poner pies en polvorosa
heeler ['hilər] *s* (slang) muñidor *m*
heft•y ['hɛfti] *adj* (*comp* **-ier;** *super* **-iest**) (*heavy*) pesado; (*strong*) fuerte, fornido
hegemo•ny [hɪ'dʒɛməni] o ['hɛdʒɪ,moni] *s* (*pl* **-nies**) hegemonía
hegira [hɪ'dʒaɪrə] o ['hɛdʒɪrə] *s* fuga, huída
heifer ['hɛfər] *s* novilla, vaquilla
height [haɪt] *s* altura; (*e.g., of folly*) colmo
heighten ['haɪtən] *tr* hacer más alto; (*to increase the amount of*) aumentar; (*to set off, bring out*) realzar ‖ *intr* aumentarse
heinous ['henəs] *adj* atroz, nefando
heir [ɛr] *s* heredero
heir apparent *s* (*pl* **heirs apparent**) heredero forzoso
heirdom ['ɛrdəm] *s* herencia
heiress ['ɛrɪs] *s* heredera
heirloom ['ɛr,lum] *s* joya de familia, reliquia de familia
helicopter ['hɛlɪ,kɑptər] *s* helicóptero
heliotrope ['hilɪ·ə,trop] *s* heliotropo
heliport ['hɛlɪ,port] *s* helipuerto
helium ['hilɪ·əm] *s* helio
helix ['hilɪks] *s* (*pl* **helixes** o **helices** ['hɛlɪ,siz]) hélice *f*
hell [hɛl] *s* infierno
hell-bent ['hɛl'bɛnt] *adj* (slang) muy resuelto; **hell-bent on** (slang) empeñado en
hell'cat' *s* (*bad-tempered woman*) arpía, mujer perversa; (*witch*) bruja
hellebore ['hɛlɪ,bor] *s* eléboro
Hellene ['hɛlin] *s* heleno
Hellenic [hɛ'lɛnɪk] o [hɛ'linɪk] *adj* helénico
hell'fire' *s* fuego del infierno
hellish ['hɛlɪʃ] *adj* infernal
hel•lo [hɛ'lo] *s* saludo ‖ *interj* ¡qué tal!; (*on telephone*) ¡diga!
hello girl *s* (coll) chica telefonista
helm [hɛlm] *s* barra del timón; rueda del timón; (fig) timón *m* ‖ *tr* dirigir, gobernar
helmet ['hɛlmɪt] *s* casco; (*of ancient armor*) yelmo
helms•man ['hɛlmzmən] *s* (*pl* **-men** [mən]) timonel *m*
help [hɛlp] *s* ayuda, socorro; (*of food*) ración; (*relief*) remedio, p.ej., **there's no help for it** no hay remedio; criados; empleados; obreros; **to come to the help of** acudir en socorro de ‖ *interj* ¡socorro! ‖ *tr* ayudar, socorrer; aliviar, mitigar; (*to wait on*) servir; **it can't be helped** no hay remedio; **so help me God!** ¡así Dios me salve!; **to help down** ayudar a bajar; **to help a person with his coat** ayudarle a una persona a ponerse el abrigo; **to help oneself** valerse por sí mismo; servirse; **to help up** ayudar a subir; ayudar a levantarse; **to not be able to help** + *ger* no poder menos de + *inf,* p.ej., **he can't help laughing** no puede menos de reír ‖ *intr* ayudar
helper ['hɛlpər] *s* ayudante *mf;* (*in a drug store, barbershop, etc.*) mancebo
helpful ['hɛlpfəl] *adj* útil, provechoso; servicial
helping ['hɛlpɪŋ] *s* ración (*de alimento*)
helpless ['hɛlplɪs] *adj* (*weak*) débil; (*powerless*) impotente; (*penniless*)

desvalido; (*confused*) perplejo; (*situation*) irremediable
help'meet' *s* compañero; (*wife*) compañera
helter-skelter ['heltər'skeltər] *adj, adv & s* cochite hervite *m*
hem [hem] *s* tos fingida; (*of a garment*) bastilla, dobladillo || *interj* ¡ejem! || *v* (*pret & pp* **hemmed;** *ger* **hemming**) *tr* bastillar, dobladillar; **to hem in** encerrar, rodear || *intr* destoserse; vacilar; **to hem and haw** vacilar al hablar; ser evasivo
hemisphere ['hemɪ,sfɪr] *s* hemisferio
hemistich ['hemɪ,stɪk] *s* hemistiquio
hem'line' *s* ruedo de la falda, borde *m* de la falda
hem'lock' *s* (*Tsuga canadensis*) abeto del Canadá; (*herb and poison*) cicuta
hemoglobin [,hemə'globɪn] o [,himə'globɪn] *s* hemoglobina
hemophilia [,hemə'fɪlɪ·ə] o [,himə'fɪlɪ·ə] *s* hemofilia
hemorrhage ['hemərɪdʒ] *s* hemorragia
hemorrhoids ['hemə,rɔɪdz] *spl* hemorroides *fpl*
hemostat ['hemə,stæt] o ['himə,stæt] *s* hemóstato
hemp [hemp] *s* cáñamo
hemstitch ['hem,stɪtʃ] *s* vainica || *tr* hacer vainica en || *intr* hacer vainica
hen [hen] *s* gallina
hence [hens] *adv* de aquí; desde ahora; por lo tanto, por consiguiente; de aquí a, p.ej., **three weeks hence** de aquí a tres semanas
hence'forth' *adv* de aquí en adelante
hench·man ['hentʃmən] *s* (*pl* **-men** [mən]) secuaz *m,* servidor *m;* (*political schemer*) muñidor *m*
hen'coop' *s* gallinero
hen'house' *s* gallinero
henna ['henə] *s* alcana, alheña; (*dye*) henna *f* || *tr* alheñarse (*el pelo*)
hen'peck' *tr* dominar (*la mujer al marido*)
henpecked husband *s* calzonazos *m,* gurrumino
hep [hep] *adj* (slang) enterado; **to be hep to** (slang) estar al corriente de
her [hʌr] *adj poss* su; el . . . de ella || *pron pers* la; ella; **to her** le; a ella
herald ['herəld] *s* heraldo; anunciador *m* || *tr* anunciar; ser precursor de
heraldic [he'rældɪk] *adj* heráldico
herald·ry ['herəldri] *s* (*pl* **-ries**) (*office or duty of herald*) heraldía; (*science of armorial bearings*) blasón *m,* heráldica; (*heraldic device; coat of arms*) blasón; pompa heráldica
herb [ʌrb] o [hʌrb] *s* hierba; hierba aromática; hierba medicinal
herbaceous [hʌr'beʃəs] *adj* herbáceo
herbage ['ʌrbɪdʒ] o ['hʌrbɪdʒ] *s* herbaje *m*
herbal ['ʌrbəl] o ['hʌrbəl] *adj & s* herbario
herbalist ['hʌrbəlɪst] o ['ʌrbəlɪst] *s* herbolario
herbari·um [hʌr'berɪ·əm] *s* (*pl* **-ums** o **-a** [ə]) herbario
herb doctor *s* herbolario
herculean [hʌr'kjulɪ·ən] o [,hʌrkju'li·ən] *adj* (*hard to perform*) penoso, laborioso; (*strong, big*) hercúleo
herd [hʌrd] *s* manada, rebaño, hato; (*of people*) chusma, multitud || *tr* reunir en manada; reunir || *intr* reunirse en manada; reunirse, ir juntos
herds·man ['hʌrdzmən] *s* (*pl* **-men** [mən]) manadero; (*of sheep*) pastor *m;* (*of cattle*) vaquero
here [hɪr] *adj* presente || *adv* aquí; **here and there** acá y allá; **here is** o **here are** aquí tiene Vd.; **that's neither here nor there** eso no viene al caso || *s* — **the here and the hereafter** esta vida y la futura || *interj* ¡presente!
hereabouts ['hɪrə,bauts] *adv* por aquí, cerca de aquí
here·af'ter *adv* de aquí en adelante; en lo sucesivo; en la vida futura || **the hereafter** la otra vida, el más allá
here·by' *adv* por esto; por la presente
hereditary [hɪ'redɪ,teri] *adj* hereditario
heredi·ty [hɪ'redɪti] *s* (*pl* **-ties**) herencia
here·in' *adv* aquí dentro; en este asunto
here·of' *adv* de esto
here·on' *adv* en esto, sobre esto
here·sy ['herəsi] *s* (*pl* **-sies**) herejía
heretic ['herətɪk] *adj* herético || *s* hereje *mf*
heretical [hɪ'retɪkəl] *adj* herético
heretofore [,hɪrtu'for] *adv* antes, hasta ahora
here'u·pon' *adv* en esto, sobre esto; en seguida
here·with' *adv* adjunto, con la presente; de este modo
heritage ['herɪtɪdʒ] *s* herencia
hermetic(al) [hʌr'metɪk(əl)] *adj* hermético
hermit ['hʌrmɪt] *s* eremita *m,* ermitaño
hermitage ['hʌrmɪtɪdʒ] *s* ermita
herni·a ['hʌrnɪ·ə] *s* (*pl* **-as** o **-ae** [,i]) hernia
he·ro ['hɪro] *s* (*pl* **-roes**) héroe *m*
heroic [hɪ'ro·ɪk] *adj* heroico || **heroics** *spl* verso heroico; lenguaje rimbombante
heroin ['hero·ɪn] *s* heroína (*polvo cristalino*)
heroine ['hero·ɪn] *s* heroína (*mujer*)
heroism ['hero,ɪzəm] *s* heroísmo
heron ['herən] *s* garza; (*Ardea cinerea*) airón *m,* garza real
herring ['herɪŋ] *s* arenque *m*
her'ring·bone' *s* (*in fabrics*) espina de pescado; (*in hardwood floors*) espinapez *m,* punto de Hungría
hers [hʌrz] *pron poss* el suyo, el de ella; suyo
herself [hʌr'self] *pron pers* ella misma; sí, sí misma; se, p.ej., **she enjoyed herself** se divirtió; **with herself** consigo
hesitan·cy ['hezɪtənsi] *s* (*pl* **-cies**) vacilación
hesitant ['hezɪtənt] *adj* vacilante

hesitate ['hɛzɪ,tet] *intr* vacilar, titubear; (*to stutter*) titubear
hesitation [,hɛzɪ'teʃən] *s* vacilación
heterodox ['hɛtərə,dɑks] *adj* heterodoxo
heterodyne ['hɛtərə,daɪn] *adj* heterodino || *tr* heterodinar
heterogenei•ty [,hɛtərədʒɪ'ni·ɪti] *s* (*pl* **-ties**) heterogeneidad
heterogeneous [,hɛtərə'dʒinɪ·əs] *adj* heterogéneo
hew [hju] *v* (*pret* **hewed;** *pp* **hewed** o **hewn**) *tr* cortar, tajar; (*with an ax*) hachear; labrar (*madera*); picar (*piedra*); **to hew down** derribar a hachazos || *intr* — **to hew close to the line** (coll) hilar delgado
hex [hɛks] *s* (coll) bruja; (coll) hechizo || *tr* (coll) embrujar
hexameter [hɛks'æmɪtər] *s* hexámetro
hey [he] *interj* ¡oye!, ¡oiga!
hey'day' *s* época de mayor prosperidad
hf. *abbr* **half**
H.H. *abbr* **His Highness, Her Highness; His Holiness**
hia•tus [haɪ'etəs] *s* (*pl* **-tuses** o **-tus**) (*gap*) abertura, laguna; (*in a text; in verse*) hiato
hibernate ['haɪbər,net] *intr* invernar; estar inactivo
hibiscus [hɪ'bɪskəs] o [haɪ'bɪskəs] *s* hibisco
hiccough o **hiccup** ['hɪkəp] *s* hipo || *intr* hipar
hick [hɪk] *adj* & *s* (coll) campesino, palurdo
hicko•ry ['hɪkəri] *s* (*pl* **-ries**) nuez encarcelada, nuez dura (*árbol*)
hickory nut *s* nuez encarcelada, nuez dura (*fruto*)
hidden ['hɪdən] *adj* escondido, oculto; obscuro
hide [haɪd] *s* cuero, piel *f;* **hides** corambre *f;* **neither hide nor hair** ni un vestigio; **to tan someone's hide** (coll) zurrarle a uno la badana || *v* (*pret* **hid** [hɪd]; *pp* **hid** o **hidden** ['hɪdən]) *tr* esconder, ocultar || *intr* esconderse, ocultarse; **to hide out** (coll) recatarse
hide'-and-seek' *s* escondite *m;* **to play hide-and-seek** jugar al escondite
hide'bound' *adj* fanático, obstinado, dogmático
hideous ['hɪdɪ·əs] *adj* (*very ugly*) feote; (*heinous*) atroz, nefando; (*distressingly large*) brutal, enorme
hide'-out' *s* (coll) guarida, refugio, escondrijo
hiding ['haɪdɪŋ] *s* ocultación; (*place of concealment*) escondite *m,* escondrijo; **in hiding** escondido, oculto; (*in ambush*) emboscado
hiding place *s* escondite *m,* escondrijo
hie [haɪ] *v* (*pret* & *pp* **hied;** *ger* **hieing** o **hying**) *tr* — **hie thee home** apresúrate a volver a casa || *intr* apresurarse, ir volando
hierar•chy ['haɪ·ə,rɑrki] *s* (*pl* **-chies**) jerarquía
hieroglyphic [,haɪ·ərə'glɪfɪk] *adj* & *s* jeroglífico
hi•fi ['haɪ'faɪ] *adj* (coll) de alta fidelidad || *s* (coll) alta fidelidad
hi-fi fan *s* (coll) aficionado a la alta fidelidad
higgledy-piggledy ['hɪgəldi'pɪgəldi] *adj* confuso, revuelto || *adv* confusamente, revueltamente
high [haɪ] *adj* alto; (*river*) crecido; (*sound*) agudo; (*wind*] fuerte; (coll) borracho; (culin) manido; **high and dry** abandonado, desamparado; **high and mighty** (coll) muy arrogante || *adv* en sumo grado; a gran precio; **to aim high** poner el tiro muy alto; **to come high** venderse caro || *s* (aut) marcha directa; **on high** en el cielo
high altar *s* altar *m* mayor
high'ball' *s* highball *m*
high blood pressure *s* hipertensión arterial
high'born' *adj* linajudo, de ilustre cuna
high'boy' *s* cómoda alta con patas altas
high'brow' *adj* & *s* (slang) erudito
high chair *s* silla alta
high command *s* alto mando
high cost of living *s* carestía de la vida
higher education *s* enseñanza superior
higher-up [,haɪ·ər'ʌp] *s* (coll) superior jerárquico
high explosive *s* explosivo rompedor
highfalutin [,haɪfə'lutən] *adj* (coll) pomposo, presuntuoso
high fidelity *s* alta fidelidad
high'-fre'quency *adj* de alta frecuencia
high gear *s* marcha directa, toma directa
high'-grade' *adj* de calidad superior
high-handed ['haɪ'hændɪd] *adj* arbitrario
high hat *s* sombrero de copa
high'-hat' *adj* (coll) copetudo, esnob; **to be high-hat** (coll) tener mucho copete || **high'-hat'** *v* (*pret* & *pp* **-hatted;** *ger* **-hatting**) *tr* (coll) desairar
high-heeled shoe ['haɪ,hild] *s* zapato de tacón alto
high horse *s* ademán *m* arrogante
high'jack' *tr* var de **hijack**
high jinks [dʒɪŋks] *s* (slang) jarana, payasada
high jump *s* salto de altura
highland ['haɪlənd] *s* región montañosa; **highlands** montañas, tierras altas
high life *s* alta sociedad, gran mundo
high'light' *s* elemento sobresaliente || *tr* destacar
highly ['haɪli] *adv* altamente; en sumo grado; a gran precio; con aplauso general; **to speak highly of** decir mil bienes de
High Mass *s* misa cantada, misa mayor
high-minded ['haɪ'maɪndɪd] *adj* noble, magnánimo
highness ['haɪnɪs] *s* altura || **Highness** *s* Alteza
high noon *s* pleno mediodía
high-pitched ['haɪ'pɪtʃt] *adj* agudo; tenso, impresionable
high-powered ['haɪ'paʊ·ərd] *adj* de alta potencia
high'-pres'sure *adj* de alta presión;

(fig) emprendedor, enérgico || *tr* (coll) apremiar
high-priced ['haɪ'praɪst] *adj* de precio elevado
high priest *s* sumo sacerdote
high rise *s* edificio de muchos pisos
high'road' *s* camino real
high school *s* escuela de segunda enseñanza
high sea *s* mar gruesa; **high seas** alta mar
high society *s* alta sociedad, gran mundo
high'-speed' *adj* de alta velocidad
high-spirited ['haɪ'spɪrɪtɪd] *adj* animoso; vivaz; (*horse*) fogoso
high spirits *spl* alegría, buen humor *m*, animación
high-strung ['haɪ'strʌŋ] *adj* tenso, impresionable
high'-test' fuel *s* supercarburante *m*
high tide *s* pleamar *f*, marea alta; (fig) punto culminante
high time *s* hora, p.ej., **it is high time for you to go** ya es hora de que Vd. se marche; (slang) jarana, parranda
high treason *s* alta traición
high water *s* aguas altas; pleamar *f*, marea alta
high'way' *s* carretera
highway•man ['haɪ,wemən] *s* (*pl* **-men** [mən]) salteador *m* de caminos
hijack ['haɪ,dʒæk] *tr* (coll) robar (*a un contrabandista de licores*); (coll) robar (*el licor a un contrabandista*)
hike [haɪk] *s* caminata, marcha; (*increase, rise*) aumento || *tr* elevar de un tirón; aumentar || *intr* dar una caminata
hiker ['haɪkər] *s* caminador *m*, aficionado a las caminatas
hilarious [hɪ'lɛrɪ·əs] o [haɪ'lɛrɪ·əs] *adj* jubiloso, regocijado
hill [hɪl] *s* colina, collado || *tr* aporcar (*las hortalizas*)
hillbil•ly ['hɪl,bɪli] *s* (*pl* **-lies**) (coll) rústico montañés (*del sur de los EE.UU.*)
hillock ['hɪlək] *s* altozano, montecillo
hill'side' *s* ladera
hill'top' *s* cumbre *f*, cima
hill•y ['hɪli] *adj* (*comp* **-ier**; *super* **-iest**) colinoso; (*steep*) empinado
hilt [hɪlt] *s* empuñadura, puño; **up to the hilt** completamente
him [hɪm] *pron pers* le, lo; él; **to him** le; a él
himself [hɪm'sɛlf] *pron pers* él mismo; sí, sí mismo; se, p.ej., **he enjoyed himself** se divirtió; **with himself** consigo
hind [haɪnd] *adj* posterior, trasero || *s* cierva
hinder ['hɪndər] *tr* estorbar, impedir
hindmost ['haɪnd,most] *adj* postrero, último
Hindoo ['hɪndu] *adj* & *s* hindú *m*
hind'quar'ter *s* cuarto trasero
hindrance ['hɪndrəns] *s* estorbo, impedimento, obstáculo
hind'sight' *s* (*of a firearm*) mira posterior; percepción tardía, sabiduría tardía
Hindu ['hɪndu] *adj* & *s* hindú *m*
hinge [hɪndʒ] *s* (*of a door*) charnela, gozne *m*, bisagra; (*of a mollusk*) charnela; (bb) cartivana; punto capital || *tr* engoznar || *intr* — **to hinge on** depender de
hin•ny ['hɪni] *s* (*pl* **-nies**) burdégano, mohino
hint [hɪnt] *s* indirecta, insinuación; **to take the hint** darse por aludido || *tr* & *intr* insinuar; indicar; **to hint at** aludir indirectamente a
hinterland ['hɪntər,lænd] *s* región interior
hip [hɪp] *s* cadera; (*of a roof*) caballete *m*, lima
hip'bone' *s* cía, hueso de la cadera
hipped [hɪpt] *adj* (*livestock*) renco; (*roof*) a cuatro aguas; **hipped on** (coll) obsesionado por
hippety-hop ['hɪpɪtɪ'hɑp] *adv* (coll) a coxcojita
hip•po ['hɪpo] *s* (*pl* **-pos**) (coll) hipopótamo
hippodrome ['hɪpə,drom] *s* hipódromo
hippopota•mus [,hɪpə'pɑtəməs] *s* (*pl* **-muses** o **-mi** [,maɪ]) hipopótamo
hip roof *s* tejado a cuatro aguas
hire [haɪr] *s* alquiler *m;* precio; salario; **for hire** de alquiler || *tr* alquilar (*p.ej., un coche*); ajustar (*p.ej., a un criado*) || *intr* — **to hire out** ajustarse
hired girl *s* criada
hired man *s* (coll) mozo de campo
hireling ['haɪrlɪŋ] *adj* & *s* alquiladizo
his [hɪz] *adj poss* su; el . . . de él || *pron poss* el suyo, el de él; suyo
Hispanic [hɪs'pænɪk] *adj* hispánico
Hispaniola [,hɪspən'jolə] *s* Santo Domingo
hispanist ['hɪspənɪst] *s* hispanista *mf*
hiss [hɪs] *s* siseo, silbido || *tr* sisear, silbar (*p.ej., una escena, a un actor por malo*) || *intr* sisear, silbar
hist. *abbr* **historian, history**
histology [hɪs'tɑlədʒi] *s* histología
historian [hɪs'torɪ·ən] *s* historiador *m*
historic(al) [hɪs'tɑrɪk(əl)] o [hɪs'tɔrɪk(əl)] *adj* histórico
histo•ry ['hɪstəri] *s* (*pl* **-ries**) historia
histrionic [,hɪstrɪ'ɑnɪk] *adj* histriónico; teatral || **histrionics** *s* actitud teatral, modales *mpl* teatrales
hit [hɪt] *s* golpe *m;* (*of a bullet*) impacto; (*blow that hits its mark*) tiro certero; (*sarcastic remark*) censura acerba; (baseball) batazo; (coll) éxito; **to make a hit** (coll) dar golpe; **to make a hit with** caer en la gracia de (*una persona*) || *v* (*pret* & *pp* **hit**; *ger* **hitting**) *tr* golpear, pegar; dar con, dar contra, chocar con; dar en (*p.ej., el blanco*); censurar acerbamente; (*to run over in a car*) atropellar; afectar mucho (*un acontecimiento a una persona*) || *intr* chocar; **to hit against** dar contra; **to hit on** dar con (*lo que se busca*)
hit'-and-run' *adj* que atropella y se da a la huída
hitch [hɪtʃ] *s* (*jerk*) tirón *m;* dificultad; obstáculo; **without a hitch** a

pedir de boca, sin tropiezo || *tr* (*to tie*) atar, sujetar; enganchar (*un caballo*); uncir (*bueyes*); (slang) casar
hitch'hike' *intr* (coll) hacer autostop, viajar en autostop
hitch'hik'er *s* autostopista *mf*
hitching post *s* poste *m* para atar a las cabalgaduras
hither ['hɪðər] *adv* acá, hacia acá; **hither and thither** acá y allá
hith'er•to' *adv* hasta ahora, hasta aquí
hit'-or-miss' *adj* descuidado, casual
hit parade *s* (rad) canciones que gozan de más popularidad en la actualidad
hit record *s* (coll) disco de mucho éxito
hit'-run' *adj* que atropella y se da a la huída
hive [haɪv] *s* (*box for bees*) colmena; (*swarm*) enjambre *m;* **hives** urticaria || *tr* encorchar (*abejas*)
H.M. *abbr* **Her Majesty, His Majesty**
H.M.S. *abbr* **Her Majesty's Ship, His Majesty's Ship**
hoard [hord] *s* (*of money, provisions, etc.*) cúmulo; tesoro escondido || *tr* acumular secretamente; atesorar (*dinero*) || *intr* guardar víveres; atesorar dinero
hoarding ['hordɪŋ] *s* acumulación secreta; atesoramiento
hoar'frost' *s* helada blanca, escarcha
hoarse [hors] *adj* ronco
hoarseness ['horsnɪs] *s* ronquedad; (*from a cold*) ronquera
hoar•y ['hori] *adj* (*comp* **-ier;** *super* **-iest**) cano, canoso; (*old*) vetusto
hoax [hoks] *s* pajarota, mistificación || *tr* mistificar
hob [hɑb] *s* repisa interior del hogar; **to play hob with** (coll) trastornar
hobble ['hɑbəl] *s* (*limp*) cojera; (*rope used to tie legs of animal*) manea, traba || *tr* dejar cojo; manear, trabar; dificultar || *intr* cojear; tambalear
hobble skirt *s* falda de medio paso
hob•by ['hɑbi] *s* (*pl* **-bies**) comidilla, afición favorita, trabajo preferido; **to ride a hobby** entregarse demasiado al tema favorito
hob'by•horse' *s* (*stick with horse's head*) caballito; (*rocking horse*) caballo mecedor
hob'gob'lin *s* duende *m,* trasgo; (*bogy*) bu *m,* coco
hob'nail' *s* tachuela || *tr* clavetear con tachuelas; (fig) atropellar
hob•nob ['hɑb,nɑb] *v* (*pret & pp* **-nobbed;** *ger* **-nobbing**) *intr* codearse, rozarse; beber juntos
ho•bo ['hobo] *s* (*pl* **-bos** o **-boes**) vagabundo
Hobson's choice ['hɑbsənz] *s* alternativa entre la cosa ofrecida o ninguna
hock [hɑk] *s* jarrete *m,* corvejón *m* || *tr* (*to hamstring*) desjarretar; (coll) empeñar
hockey ['hɑki] *s* hockey *m,* chueca
hock'shop' *s* (slang) casa de empeños, monte *m* de piedad
hocus-pocus ['hokəs'pokəs] *s* (*meaningless formula*) abracadabra *m;* burla, engaño; juego de manos
hod [hɑd] *s* capacho, cuezo; cubo para carbón
hod carrier *s* peón *m* de albañil, peón de mano
hodgepodge ['hɑdʒ,pɑdʒ] *s* baturrillo
hoe [ho] *s* azada, azadón *m* || *tr & intr* azadonar
hog [hɑg] o [hɔg] *s* cerdo, puerco || *v* (*pret & pp* **hogged;** *ger* **hogging**) *tr* (slang) tragarse lo mejor de
hog'back' *s* cuchilla
hoggish ['hɑgɪʃ] o ['hɔgɪʃ] *adj* comilón; glotón; egoísta
hog Latin *s* latín *m* de cocina
hogs'head' *s* pipa de 63 galones o más; medida de capacidad de 63 galones
hog'wash' *s* bazofia
hoist [hɔɪst] *s* (*apparatus for lifting*) montacargas *m,* torno izador, grúa; empujón *m* hacia arriba || *tr* alzar, levantar; enarbolar (*p.ej., una bandera*); (naut) izar
hoity-toity ['hɔɪti'tɔɪti] *adj* frívolo, veleidoso; arrogante, altanero; **to be hoity-toity** ponerse tan alto
hokum ['hokəm] *s* (coll) música celestial, tonterías
hold [hold] *s* (*grip*) agarro; (*handle*) asa, mango; autoridad, dominio; (*in wrestling*) presa; (aer) cabina de carga; (mus) calderón *m;* (naut) bodega; **to take hold of** agarrar, coger; apoderarse de || *v* (*pret & pp* **held** [hɛld]) *tr* tener, retener; (*to hold up, support*) apoyar, sostener; (*e.g., with a pin*) sujetar; contener, tener cabida para; ocupar (*un cargo, puesto, etc.*); celebrar (*una reunión*); sostener (*una opinión*); (mus) sostener (*una nota*); **to hold back** detener; retener; contener; **to hold in** refrenar; **to hold one's own** mantenerse firme, no perder terreno; **to hold over** aplazar, diferir; **to hold up** apoyar, sostener; (*to rob*) (coll) atracar || *intr* ser valedero, seguir vigente; pegarse; **hold on!** ¡un momento!; **to hold back** refrenarse; **to hold forth** poner cátedra; **to hold off** esperar; mantenerse a distancia; **to hold on** agarrarse bien; **to hold on to** asirse de; **to hold out** no cejar; ir tirando; **to hold out for** insistir en
holder ['holdər] *s* tenedor *m,* posesor *m;* (*for a cigar or cigaret*) boquilla; (*to hold, e.g., a hot plate*) cojinillo; (*e.g., of a passport*) titular *m;* asa, mango
holding ['holdɪŋ] *s* tenencia, posesión; **holdings** valores habidos
holding company *s* sociedad de control, compañía tenedora
hold'up' *s* (*stop, delay*) detención; (coll) atraco, asalto; (coll) precio excesivo
holdup man *s* (coll) atracador *m,* salteador *m*
hole [hol] *s* agujero; (*in cheese, bread, etc.*) ojo; (*in a road*) bache *m;* (*den of animals; den of vice*) guarida; (*dirty, disorderly dwelling*) cochitril

m; **in the hole** adeudado, perdidoso; **to burn a hole in one's pocket** írsele a uno (*el dinero*) de entre las manos; **to pick holes in** (coll) poner reparos a || *intr* — **to hole up** encovarse; buscar un rincón cómodo
holiday ['halɪ,de] *s* día festivo; vacación
holiday attire *s* trapos de cristianar
holiness ['holɪnɪs] *s* santidad; **his Holiness** su Santidad
Holland ['halənd] *s* Holanda
Hollander ['haləndər] *s* holandés *m*
hollow ['halo] *adj* hueco; (*voice*) ahuecado, sepulcral; (*eyes, cheeks*) hundido; falso, engañoso || *adv* — **to beat all hollow** (coll) derrotar completamente || *s* hueco, cavidad; (*small valley*) vallecito || *tr* ahuecar, excavar
hol·ly ['hali] *s* (*pl* **-lies**) acebo
hol'ly·hock' *s* malva arbórea
holm oak [hom] *s* encina
holocaust ['halə,kɔst] *s* holocausto
holster ['holstər] *s* pistolera
ho·ly ['holi] *adj* (*comp* **-lier;** *super* **-liest**) santo; (*e.g., writing*) sagrado; (*e.g., water*) bendito
Holy Ghost *s* Espíritu Santo
holy orders *spl* órdenes sagradas; **to take holy orders** recibir las órdenes sagradas, ordenarse
holy rood [rud] *s* crucifijo || **Holy Rood** *s* Santa Cruz
Holy Scripture *s* Sagrada Escritura
Holy See *s* Santa Sede
Holy Sepulcher *s* santo sepulcro
holy water *s* agua bendita
Holy Writ *s* Sagrada Escritura
homage ['hamɪdʒ] o ['amɪdʒ] *s* homenaje *m;* (feud) homenaje, pleito homenaje
home [hom] *adj* casero, doméstico; nacional || *s* casa, domicilio, hogar *m;* (*native heath*) patria chica; (*of the arts, etc.*) patria; (*for the sick, poor, etc.*) asilo; (sport) meta; **at home** en casa; en su propio país; (*ready to receive callers*) de recibo; (*at ease, comfortable*) a gusto; (sport) en campo propio; **away from home** fuera de casa; **make yourself at home** está Vd. en su casa || *adv* en casa; a casa; **to see home** acompañar a casa; **to strike home** dar en lo vivo
home'bod'y *s* (*pl* **-ies**) hogareño
homebred ['hom,brɛd] *adj* doméstico; sencillo, inculto, tosco
home'-brew' *s* cerveza o vino caseros
home-coming ['hom,kʌmɪŋ] *s* regreso al hogar
home country *s* suelo natal
home delivery *s* distribución a domicilio
home front *s* frente doméstico
home'land' *s* tierra natal, patria
homeless ['homlɪs] *adj* sin casa, sin hogar
home life *s* vida de familia
home-loving ['hom,lʌvɪŋ] *adj* casero, hogareño
home·ly ['homli] *adj* (*comp* **-lier;** *super* **-liest**) (*not attractive or good-looking*) feo; (*plain, not elegant*) sencillo, llano
homemade ['hom'med] *adj* casero, hecho en casa
homemaker ['hom,mekər] *s* ama de casa
home office *s* domicilio social, oficina central || **Home Office** *s* (Brit) ministerio de la Gobernación
homeopath ['homɪ·ə,pæθ] o ['hamɪ·ə,pæθ] *s* homeópata *mf*
homeopathy [,homɪ'apəθi] o [,hamɪ'apəθi] *s* homeopatía
home plate *s* (baseball) puesto meta
home port *s* puerto de origen
home rule *s* autonomía, gobierno autónomo
home run *s* (baseball) jonrón *m,* cuadrangular *m*
home'sick' *adj* nostálgico; **to be homesick (for)** sentir nostalgia (de)
home'sick'ness *s* nostalgia, mal *m* de la tierra
homespun ['hom,spʌn] *adj* hilado en casa; sencillo, llano
home'stead' *s* casa y terrenos, heredad
home stretch *s* esfuerzo final, último trecho
home town *s* ciudad natal
homeward ['homwərd] *adj* de regreso || *adv* hacia casa; hacia su país
home'work' *s* trabajo a domicilio; (*of a student*) deber *m,* trabajo escolar
homey ['homi] *adj* (*comp* **homier;** *super* **homiest**) (coll) íntimo, cómodo
homicidal [,hamɪ'saɪdəl] *adj* homicida
homicide ['hamɪ,saɪd] *s* (*act*) homicidio; (*person*) homicida *mf*
homi·ly ['hamɪli] *s* (*pl* **-lies**) homilía
homing ['homɪŋ] *adj* (*animal*) querencioso; (*weapon*) buscador del blanco
homing pigeon *s* paloma mensajera
hominy ['hamɪni] *s* maíz molido
homogenei·ty [,homədʒɪ'ni·ɪti] o [,hamədʒɪ'ni·ɪti] *s* (*pl* **-ties**) homogeneidad
homogeneous [,homə'dʒinɪ·əs] o [,hamə'dʒinɪ·əs] *adj* homogéneo
homogenize [hə'madʒə,naɪz] *tr* homogeneizar
homonym ['hamənɪm] *s* homónimo
homonymous [hə'manɪməs] *adj* homónimo
homosexual [,homə'sɛkʃʊ·əl] *adj & s* homosexual *mf*
hon. *abbr* **honorary**
Hon. *abbr* **Honorable**
Honduran [han'durən] *adj & s* hondureño
hone [hon] *s* piedra de afilar || *tr* afilar, amolar, asentar
honest ['anɪst] *adj* honrado, probo, recto; (*money*) bien adquirido; sincero; genuino
honesty ['anɪsti] *s* honradez *f,* probidad, rectitud; (bot) hierba de la plata
hon·ey ['hʌni] *adj* meloso, dulce; (coll) querido || *s* miel *f;* (coll) vida mía; **it's a honey** (slang) es una preciosidad || *v* (*pret & pp* **-eyed o -ied**)

tr enmelar, endulzar con miel; adular, lisonjear
hon'ey•bee' *s* abeja doméstica, abeja de miel
hon'ey•comb' *s* panal *m* || *tr* (*to riddle*) acribillar; llenar, penetrar
hon'ey•dew' melon *s* melón muy dulce, blanco y terso
honeyed ['hʌnid] *adj* dulce, enmelado; melodioso; adulador
honey locust *s* acacia de tres espinas
hon'ey•moon' *s* luna de miel; viaje *m* de bodas || *intr* pasar la luna de miel
honeysuckle ['hʌni,sʌkəl] *s* madreselva
honk [haŋk] o [hɔŋk] *s* (*of wild goose*) graznido; (*of automobile horn*) bocinazo || *tr* tocar (*la bocina*) || *intr* graznar (*el ganso silvestre*); tocar la bocina
honkytonk ['haŋki,taŋk] o ['hɔŋki,tɔŋk] *s* (slang) sala de fiestas de mala muerte
honor ['anər] *s* (*distinction; award for distinction; integrity*) honor *m;* (*good reputation; chastity*) honor, honra || *tr* honrar; hacer honor a (*su firma*); aceptar y pagar (*una letra*)
honorable ['anərəbəl] *adj* (*behaving with honor; performed with honor*) honrado; (*bringing honor; associated with honor*) honroso; (*worthy, of honor*) honorable
honorary ['anə,rɛri] *adj* honorario
honorific [,anə'rɪfɪk] *adj* honorífico || *s* antenombre *m*
honor system *s* acatamiento voluntario del reglamento
hood [hʊd] *s* capilla; (*one with a point*) caperuza; (*one which covers the face*) capirote *m;* (*worn with academic gown*) muceta, capirote *m;* (*of a chimney*) sombrerete *m;* (aut) capó *m,* cubierta; (slang) gamberro || *tr* encapirotar; ocultar
hoodlum ['hudləm] *s* (coll) gamberro, maleante *m*
hoodoo ['hudu] *s* (*body of primitive rites*) vudú *m;* (coll) mala suerte || *tr* traer mala suerte a
hood'wink' *tr* burlar, engañar, vendar
hooey ['hu·i] *s* (slang) música celestial
hoof [huf] o [hʊf] *s* casco, pezuña; **on the hoof** (*cattle*) vivo, en pie || *tr* & *intr* (coll) caminar; **to hoof it** (coll) caminar, ir a pie; (coll) bailar
hoof'beat' *s* pisada, ruido de la pisada (*de animal ungulado*)
hook [hʊk] *s* gancho; (*for fishing*) anzuelo; (*to join two things*) enganche *m;* (*bend, curve*) ángulo, recodo; (box) crochet *m,* golpe *m* de gancho; (*of hook and eye*) corchete *m,* macho; **by hook or by crook** por fas o por nefas; **to swallow the hook** tragar el anzuelo || *tr* enganchar; (*to bend*) encorvar, doblar; coger, pescar (*un pez*); (*to wound with the horns*) acornar || *intr* engancharse; encorvarse, doblarse
hookah ['hʊkə] *s* narguile *m*
hook and eye *s* broche *m,* corchete *m* (*macho y hembra*)
hook and ladder *s* carro de escaleras de incendio
hooked rug *s* tapete *m* de crochet
hook'nose' *s* nariz *f* de pico de loro
hook'up' *s* montaje *m*
hook'worm' *s* anquilostoma *m*
hooky ['hʊki] *s* — **to play hooky** hacer novillos
hooligan ['hulɪgən] *s* gamberro
hooliganism ['hulɪgən,ɪzəm] *s* gamberrismo
hoop [hup] o [hʊp] *s* aro || *tr* herrar, enarcar, enzunchar
hoop skirt *s* miriñaque *m*
hoot [hut] *s* resoplido, ululato; grito || *tr* reprobar a gritos; echar a gritos (*p.ej., a un cómico*) || *intr* resoplar, ulular; **to hoot at** dar grita a
hoot owl *s* autillo, cárabo
hop [hap] *s* saltito; (coll) vuelo en avión; (coll) sarao; (coll) baile *m;* lúpulo, hombrecillo; **hops** (*dried flowers of hop vine*) lúpulo || *v* (*pret & pp* **hopped;** *ger* **hopping**) *tr* cruzar de un salto; (coll) atravesar (*p.ej., el mar*) en avión; (coll) subir a (*un tren, taxi, etc.*) || *intr* saltar, brincar; (*on one foot*) saltar a la pata coja
hope [hop] *s* esperanza || *tr* & *intr* esperar; **to hope for** esperar
hope chest *s* ajuar *m* de novia
hopeful ['hopfəl] *adj* (*feeling hope*) esperanzado; (*giving hope*) esperanzador
hopeless ['hoplɪs] *adj* desesperanzado; (*situation*) desesperado
hopper ['hapər] *s* (*funnel-shaped container*) tolva; (*of blast furnace*) tragante *m*
hopper car *s* (rr) vagón *m* tolva
hop'scotch' *s* infernáculo
horde [hord] *s* horda
horehound ['hor,haʊnd] *s* marrubio; extracto de marrubio
horizon [hə'raɪzən] *s* horizonte *m*
horizontal [,harɪ'zantəl] o [,hɔrɪ'zantəl] *adj* & *s* horizontal *f*
hormone ['hɔrmon] *s* hormón *m* u hormona
horn [hɔrn] *s* (*bony projection on head of certain animals*) cuerno; (*of bull*) asta, cuerno; (*of moon, anvil, etc.*) cuerno; (*of automobile*) bocina; (mus) cuerno; (*French horn*) (mus) trompa de armonía; **to blow one's own horn** cantar sus propias alabanzas; **to pull in one's horns** contenerse, volverse atrás || *intr* — **to horn in** (slang) entrometerse (en)
hornet ['hɔrnɪt] *s* crabrón *m,* avispón *m*
hornet's nest *s* panal *m* del avispón; **to stir up a hornet's nest** (coll) armar camorra, armar cisco
horn of plenty *s* cuerno de la abundancia
horn'pipe' *s* chirimía
horn-rimmed glasses ['hɔrn'rɪmd] *spl* anteojos de concha
horn•y ['hɔrni] *adj* (*comp* **-ier;** *super*

-iest) córneo; (*callous*) calloso; (*having hornlike projections*) cornudo
horoscope ['hɑrə,skop] o ['hɔrə,skop] *s* horóscopo; **to cast a horoscope** sacar un horóscopo
horrible ['hɑrɪbəl] o ['hɔrɪbəl] *adj* horrible; (coll) muy desagradable
horrid ['hɑrɪd] o ['hɔrɪd] *adj* horroroso; (coll) muy desagradable
horri•fy ['hɑrɪ,faɪ] o ['hɔrɪ,faɪ] *v* (*pret & pp* **-fied**) *tr* horrorizar
horror ['hɑrər] o ['hɔrər] *s* horror *m;* **to have a horror of** tener horror a
hors d'oeuvre [ɔr 'dʌrv] *s* (*pl* **hors d'oeuvres** [ɔr 'dʌrvz]) *s* entremés *m*
horse [hɔrs] *s* caballo; (*of carpenter*) caballete *m;* **hold your horses** (coll) pare Vd. el carro; **to back the wrong horse** (coll) jugar a la carta mala; **to be a horse of another color** (coll) ser harina de otro costal
horse'back' *s* — **on horseback** a caballo || *adv* — **to ride horseback** montar a caballo
horse blanket *s* manta para caballo
horse block *s* montadero
horse'break'er *s* domador *m* de caballos
horse'car' *s* tranvía *m* de sangre
horse chestnut *s* (*tree*) castaño de Indias; (*nut*) castaña de Indias
horse collar *s* collera
horse dealer *s* chalán *m*
horse doctor *s* veterinario
horse'fly' *s* (*pl* **-fies**) mosca borriquera, tábano
horse'hair' *s* crines *fpl* de caballo; (*fabric*) tela de crin
horse'hide' *s* cuero de caballo
horse laugh *s* risotada
horse•man ['hɔrsmən] *s* (*pl* **-men** [mən]) jinete *m,* caballista *m*
horsemanship ['hɔrsmən,ʃɪp] *s* equitación, manejo
horse meat *s* carne *f* de caballo
horse opera *s* (U.S.A.) melodrama *m* del Oeste
horse pistol *s* pistola de arzón
horse'play' *s* chanza pesada, payasada
horse'pow'er *s* caballo de vapor inglés
horse race *s* carrera de caballos
horse'rad'ish *s* (*plant*) rábano picante o rusticano; (*condiment*) mostaza de los alemanes
horse sense *s* (coll) sentido común
horse'shoe' *s* herradura
horseshoe magnet *s* imán *m* de herradura
horseshoe nail *s* clavo de herrar
horse show *s* concurso hípico
horse'tail' *s* cola de caballo
horse thief *s* abigeo, cuatrero
horse'-trade' *intr* chalanear
horse trading *s* chalanería
horse'-trad'ing *adj* chalanesco
horse'whip' *s* látigo || *v* (*pret & pp* **-whipped;** *ger* **-whipping**) *tr* dar latigazos a
horse•woman ['hɔrs,wʊmən] *s* (*pl* **-women** [,wɪmɪn]) amazona, caballista *f*
hors•y ['hɔrsi] *adj* (*comp* **-ier;** *super* **-iest**) caballar, hípico; (*interested in horses and horse racing*) carrerista, turfista; (coll) desmañado
horticultural [,hɔrtɪ'kʌltʃərəl] *adj* hortícola
horticulture ['hɔrtɪ,kʌltʃər] *s* horticultura
horticulturist [,hɔrtɪ'kʌltʃərɪst] *s* horticultor *m*
hose [hoz] *s* (*stocking*) media; (*sock*) calcetín *m;* (*flexible tube*) manguera || **hose** *spl* calzas
hosier ['hoʒər] *s* mediero, calcetero
hosiery ['hoʒəri] *s* calcetas; calcetería
hospice ['hɑspɪs] *s* hospicio
hospitable ['hɑspɪtəbəl] o [hɑs'pɪtəbəl] *adj* hospitalario
hospital ['hɑspɪtəl] *s* hospital *m*
hospitali•ty [,hɑspɪ'tælɪti] *s* (*pl* **-ties**) hospitalidad
hospitalize ['hɑspɪtə,laɪz] *tr* hospitalizar
host [host] *s* anfitrión *m;* (*at an inn*) huésped *m,* mesonero; (*army*) hueste *f;* multitud, sinnúmero || **Host** *s* (eccl) hostia
hostage ['hɑstɪdʒ] *s* rehén *m;* **to be held a hostage** quedar en rehenes
hostel•ry ['hɑstəlri] *s* (*pl* **-ries**) parador *m,* hostería
hostess ['hostɪs] *s* anfitriona; dueña, patrona; (*in a night club*) tanguista; (aer) azafata, aeromoza; (*e.g., on a bus*) jefa de ruta
hostile ['hɑstɪl] *adj* hostil
hostili•ty [hɑs'tɪlɪti] *s* (*pl* **-ties**) hostilidad
hostler ['hɑslər] o ['ɑslər] *s* mozo de cuadra, mozo de paja y cebada
hot [hɑt] *adj* (*comp* **hotter;** *super* **hottest**) (*water, air, coffee, etc.*) caliente; (*climate, country; taste*) cálido; (*fiery, excitable*) caluroso; (*pursuit*) enérgico; (*in rut*) caliente; (coll) muy radiactivo; **to be hot** (*said of a person*) tener calor; (*said of the weather*) hacer calor; **to make it hot for** (coll) hostilizar
hot air *s* (slang) palabrería, música celestial
hot'-air' furnace *s* calorífero de aire
hot and cold running water *s* circulación de agua fría y caliente
hot baths *spl* caldas, termas
hot'bed' *s* (hort) almajara; (*e.g., of vice*) sementera, semillero
hot-blooded ['hɑt'blʌdɪd] *adj* apasionado; temerario, irreflexivo
hot cake *s* torta a la plancha; **to sell like hot cakes** (coll) venderse como pan bendito
hot dog *s* (slang) perro caliente
hotel [ho'tɛl] *adj* hotelero || *s* hotel *m*
ho•tel'-keep'er *s* hotelero
hot'head' *s* botafuego
hot-headed ['hɑt'hɛdɪd] *adj* caliente de cascos
hot'house' *s* estufa, invernáculo
hot plate *s* hornillo, calientaplatos *m*
hot springs *spl* fuentes *fpl* termales

hot-tempered ['hɑt'tɛmpərd] *adj* irascible
hot water *s* — **to be in hot water** (coll) estar en calzas prietas
hot'-wa'ter boiler *s* termosifón *m*
hot-water bottle *s* bolsa de agua caliente
hot-water heater *s* calentador *m* de acumulación
hot-water heating *s* calefacción por agua caliente
hot-water tank *s* depósito de agua caliente
hound [haʊnd] *s* podenco, perro de caza; **to follow the hounds** o **to ride to hounds** cazar a caballo con jauría || *tr* acosar, hostigar
hour [aʊr] *s* hora; **by the hour** por horas; **in an evil hour** en hora mala; **on the hour** a la hora en punto cada hora; **to keep late hours** acostarse tarde; **to work long hours** trabajar muchas horas cada día
hour'glass' *s* reloj *m* de arena
hour hand *s* horario
hourly ['aʊrli] *adj* de cada hora; por hora || *adv* cada hora; muy a menudo
house [haʊs] *s* (*pl* **houses** ['haʊzɪz]) casa; (*legislative body*) cámara; teatro; (*size of audience*) entrada, p.ej., **a good house** mucha entrada; **to keep house** tener casa puesta; hacer los quehaceres domésticos; **to put one's house in order** arreglar sus asuntos || [haʊz] *tr* domiciliar, alojar, hospedar
house arrest *s* arresto domiciliario
house'boat' *s* barco vivienda
house'break'er *s* escalador *m*
housebreaking ['haʊs,brekɪŋ] *s* escalo, allanamiento de morada
housebroken ['haʊs,brokən] *adj* (*perro o gato*) enseñado (*a hábitos de limpieza*)
house cleaning *s* limpieza de la casa
house coat *s* bata
house current *s* sector *m* de distribución, canalización de consumo
house'fly' *s* (*pl* **-flies**) mosca doméstica
houseful ['haʊs,fʊl] *s* casa llena
house'fur'nishings *spl* menaje *m*, enseres domésticos
house'hold' *adj* casero, doméstico || *s* casa, familia
house'hold'er *s* dueño de la casa; jefe *m* de familia
house'-hunt' *intr* — **to go house-hunting** ir a buscar casa
house'keep'er *s* ama de llaves, mujer *f* de gobierno
house'keep'ing *s* manejo doméstico, gobierno doméstico; **to set up housekeeping** poner casa
housekeeping apartment *s* apartamento con cocina
house'maid' *s* criada de casa
house meter *s* contador *m* de abonado
house'moth'er *s* mujer encargada de una residencia de estudiantes
house of cards *s* castillo de naipes
house of ill fame *s* lupanar *m*, casa de prostitución
house painter *s* pintor *m* de brocha gorda
house physician *s* médico residente
house'top' *s* tejado; **to shout from the housetops** pregonar a los cuatro vientos
housewarming ['haʊs,wɔrmɪŋ] *s* fiesta para celebrar el estreno de una casa; **to have a housewarming** estrenar la casa
house'wife' *s* (*pl* **-wives**) ama de casa, madre *f* de familia
house'work' *s* quehaceres domésticos
housing ['haʊzɪŋ] *s* (*of a horse*) gualdrapa; (aut) cárter *m;* (mach) caja, bastidor *m*
housing shortage *s* crisis *f* de viviendas
hovel ['hʌvəl] o ['hɑvəl] *s* casucha, choza; (*shed for cattle, tools, etc.*) cobertizo
hover ['hʌvər] o ['hɑvər] *intr* cernerse (*un ave*); (*to hesitate; to be in danger*) fluctuar; asomar (*p.ej., una sonrisa en los labios de uno*)
how [haʊ] *adv* cómo; (*at what price*) a cómo; **how early** cuándo, a qué hora; **how else** de qué otra manera; **how far** hasta dónde; cuánto, p.ej., **how far is it to the airport?** ¿cuánto hay de aquí al aeropuerto?; **how long** cuánto tiempo; **how many** cuántos; **how much** cuánto; lo mucho que; **how often** cuántas veces; **how old are you?** ¿cuántos años tiene Vd.?; **how soon** cuándo, a qué hora; **how** + *adj* qué + *adj*, p.ej., **how beautiful she is!** ¡qué hermosa es!; lo + *adj*, p.ej., **you know how intelligent he is** Vd. sabe lo inteligente que es; **to know how to** + *inf* saber + *inf*
howdah ['haʊdə] *s* castillo
how·ev'er *adv* no obstante, sin embargo; por muy . . . que, por mucho . . . que
howitzer ['haʊ·ɪtsər] *s* cañón *m* obús
howl [haʊl] *s* aullido; chillido; risa muy aguda; (*of wind*) bramido || *tr* decir a gritos; **to howl down** imponerse a gritos a (*una persona*) || *intr* aullar; chillar; reír a más no poder; bramar (*el viento*)
howler ['haʊlər] *s* aullador *m;* (coll) plancha, desacierto
hoyden ['hɔɪdən] *s* muchacha traviesa, tunantuela
H.P. *abbr* **horsepower**
hr. *abbr* **hour**
H.R.H. *abbr* **Her** (o **His**) **Royal Highness**
ht. *abbr* **height**
hub [hʌb] *s* cubo; (fig) centro, eje *m*
hubbub ['hʌbəb] *s* gritería, alboroto
hub'cap' *s* tapacubo, embellecedor *m*
huckster ['hʌkstər] *s* (*peddler*) buhonero; vendedor *m* ambulante de hortalizas; vil traficante *m*, sujeto ruin
huddle ['hʌdəl] *s* (coll) reunión secreta; **to go into a huddle** (coll) conferenciar en secreto || *intr* acurrucarse, arrimarse
hue [hju] *s* matiz *m;* gritería; **hue and cry** vocería de indignación

huff [hʌf] *s* arrebato de cólera; **in a huff** encolerizado, ofendido
hug [hʌg] *s* abrazo ‖ *v* (*pret & pp* **hugged;** *ger* **hugging**) *tr* abrazar, apretar con los brazos; ahogar entre los brazos; navegar muy cerca de (*la costa*); ceñirse a (*p.ej., un muro*) ‖ *intr* abrazarse
huge [hjudʒ] *adj* enorme, descomunal
huh [hʌ] *interj* ¡eh!
hulk [hʌlk] *s* (*body of an old ship*) casco; (*clumsy old ship*) carcamán *m*, carraca; (*old ship tied up at a wharf and used as a warehouse, prison, etc.*) pontón *m;* (*shell of an old building, piece of furniture, machine, etc.; heavy, unwieldy person*) armatoste *m*
hulking [ˈhʌlkɪŋ] *adj* grueso, pesado
hull [hʌl] *s* (*of ship or hydroplane*) casco; (*of a dirigible*) armazón *f;* (*of certain vegetables*) hollejo, vaina ‖ *tr* deshollejar, desvainar; mondar, pelar
hullabaloo [ˈhʌləbəˌlu] o [ˌhʌləbəˈlu] *s* alboroto, gritería, tumulto
hum [hʌm] *s* canturreo, tarareo; (*of a bee, machine, etc.*) zumbido ‖ *interj* ¡ejem! ‖ *v* (*pret & pp* **hummed;** *ger* **humming**) *tr* canturrear, tararear ‖ *intr* canturrear, tararear; (*to buzz*) zumbar; (coll) estar muy activo
human [ˈhjumən] *adj* humano (*perteneciente al hombre*)
human being *s* ser humano
humane [hjuˈmen] *adj* humano (*compasivo*)
humanist [ˈhjumənɪst] *adj & s* humanista *mf*
humanitarian [hjuˌmænɪˈtɛrɪ·ən] *adj & s* humanitario
humani·ty [hjuˈmænɪti] *s* (*pl* **-ties**) humanidad
hu'man·kind' *s* género humano
humble [ˈhʌmbəl] o [ˈʌmbəl] *adj* humilde ‖ *tr* humillar
humble pie *s* — **to eat humble pie** cantar la palinodia
hum'bug' *s* patraña; (*person*) patrañero ‖ *v* (*pret & pp* **-bugged;** *ger* **-bugging**) *tr* embaucar, engaitar
hum'drum' *adj* monótono, tedioso
humer·us [ˈhjumərəs] *s* (*pl* **-i** [ˌaɪ]) húmero
humid [ˈhjumɪd] *adj* húmedo
humidifier [hjuˈmɪdɪˌfaɪ·ər] *s* humectador *m*
humidi·fy [hjuˈmɪdɪˌfaɪ] *v* (*pret & pp* **-fied**) *tr* humedecer
humidity [hjuˈmɪdɪti] *s* humedad
humiliate [hjuˈmɪlɪˌet] *tr* humillar
humiliating [hjuˈmɪlɪˌetɪŋ] *adj* humillante
humili·ty [hjuˈmɪlɪti] *s* (*pl* **-ties**) humildad
hummingbird [ˈhʌmɪŋˌbʌrd] *s* colibrí *m*, pájaro mosca
humor [ˈhjumər] o [ˈjumər] *s* humor *m;* **out of humor** de mal humor; **to be in the humor for** estar de humor para ‖ *tr* seguir el humor a; manejar con delicadeza
humorist [ˈhjumərɪst] o [ˈjumərɪst] *s* humorista *mf*
humorous [ˈhjumərəs] o [ˈjumərəs] *adj* humorístico
hump [hʌmp] *s* corcova, joroba; (*in the ground*) montecillo
hump'back' *s* corcova, joroba; (*person*) corcovado, jorobado
humus [ˈhjuməs] *s* mantillo
hunch [hʌntʃ] *s* corcova, joroba; (*premonition*) (coll) corazonada ‖ *tr* encorvar ‖ *intr* encorvarse
hunch'back' *s* corcova, joroba; (*person*) corcovado, jorobado
hundred [ˈhʌndrəd] *adj* cien ‖ *s* ciento, cien; **a hundred** u **one hundred** ciento, cien; **by the hundreds** a centenares
hundredth [ˈhʌndrədθ] *adj & s* centésimo
hun'dred·weight' *s* quintal *m*
Hundred Years' War *s* guerra de los Cien Años
Hungarian [hʌŋˈgɛrɪ·ən] *adj & s* húngaro
Hungary [ˈhʌŋgəri] *s* Hungría
hunger [ˈhʌŋgər] *s* hambre *f* ‖ *intr* hambrear; **to hunger for** tener hambre de
hunger march *s* marcha del hambre
hunger strike *s* huelga de hambre
hun·gry [ˈhʌŋgri] *adj* (*comp* **-grier;** *super* **-griest**) hambriento; **to be hungry** tener hambre; **to go hungry** pasar hambre
hunk [hʌŋk] *s* (coll) buen pedazo, pedazo grande
hunt [hʌnt] *s* (*act of hunting*) caza; (*hunting party*) cacería; (*a search*) busca; **on the hunt for** a caza de ‖ *tr* cazar; (*to seek, look for*) buscar ‖ *intr* cazar; buscar; **to go hunting** ir de caza; **to hunt for** buscar; **to take hunting** llevar de caza
hunter [ˈhʌntər] *s* cazador *m;* perro de caza
hunting [ˈhʌntiŋ] *adj* de caza ‖ *s* (*act*) caza; (*art*) cacería, montería
hunting dog *s* perro de caza
hunting ground *s* cazadero
hunt'ing·horn' *s* cuerno de caza
hunting jacket *s* cazadora
hunting lodge *s* casa de montería
hunting season *s* época de caza
huntress [ˈhʌntrɪs] *s* cazadora
hunts·man [ˈhʌntsmən] *s* (*pl* **-men** [mən]) cazador *m*, montero
hurdle [ˈhʌrdəl] *s* (*hedge over which horses must jump*) zarzo; (*wooden frame over which runners and horses must jump*) valla; (fig) obstáculo; **hurdles** carrera de vallas ‖ *tr* saltar por encima de
hurdle race *s* carrera de vallas
hurdy-gur·dy [ˈhʌrdiˈgʌrdi] *s* (*pl* **-dies**) organillo
hurl [hʌrl] *s* lanzamiento ‖ *tr* lanzar
hurrah [hʊˈrɑ] o **hurray** [hʊˈre] *s* viva *m* ‖ *interj* ¡viva!; **hurrah for . . . !** ¡viva . . . ! ‖ *tr* aplaudir, vitorear ‖ *intr* dar vivas
hurricane [ˈhʌrɪˌken] *s* huracán *m*

hurried [ˈhʌrid] *adj* apresurado; hecho de prisa
hur•ry [ˈhʌri] *s* (*pl* **-ries**) prisa; **to be in a hurry** tener prisa, estar de prisa || *v* (*pret & pp* **-ried**) *tr* apresurar, dar prisa a || *intr* apresurarse, darse prisa; **to hurry after** correr en pos de; **to hurry away** marcharse de prisa; **to hurry back** volver de prisa; **to hurry up** darse prisa
hurt [hʌrt] *adj* (*injured*) lastimado, herido; (*offended*) resentido, herido || *s* (*harm*) daño; (*injury*) herida; (*pain*) dolor *m* || *v* (*pret & pp* **hurt**) *tr* (*to harm*) dañar, perjudicar; (*to injure*) lastimar, herir; (*to offend*) ofender, herir; (*to pain*) doler || *intr* doler
hurtle [ˈhʌrtəl] *intr* lanzarse con violencia, pasar con gran estruendo
husband [ˈhʌzbənd] *s* marido, esposo || *tr* manejar con economía
husband•man [ˈhʌzbəndmən] *s* (*pl* **-men** [mən]) agricultor *m*, granjero
husbandry [ˈhʌzbəndri] *s* agricultura, labranza; buena dirección, buen gobierno (*de la hacienda de uno*)
hush [hʌʃ] *s* silencio || *interj* ¡chito! || *tr* callar; **to hush up** echar tierra a (*un escándalo*) || *intr* callarse
hushaby [ˈhʌʃəˌbaɪ] *interj* ¡ro ro!
hush'-hush' *adj* muy secreto
hush money *s* precio del silencio
husk [hʌsk] *s* cáscara, hollejo, vaina; (*of corn*) perfolla || *tr* descascarar, deshollejar, desvainar; espinochar (*el maíz*)
husk•y [ˈhʌski] *adj* (*comp* **-ier**; *super* **-iest**) fortachón, fornido; (*voice*) ronco
hus•sy [ˈhʌzi] o [ˈhʌsi] *s* (*pl* **-sies**) buena pieza, moza descarada; mujer desvergonzada
hustle [ˈhʌsəl] *s* (coll) energía, vigor *m* || *tr* apresurar; echar a empellones || *intr* apresurarse; (coll) menearse, trabajar con gran ahinco
hustler [ˈhʌslər] *s* trafagón *m*, buscavidas *mf*
hut [hʌt] *s* casucha, choza
hyacinth [ˈhaɪ·əsɪnθ] *s* jacinto
hybrid [ˈhaɪbrɪd] *adj & s* híbrido
hybridization [ˌhaɪbrɪdɪˈzeʃən] *s* hibridación
hybridize [ˈhaɪbrɪˌdaɪz] *tr & intr* hibridar
hy•dra [ˈhaɪdrə] *s* (*pl* **-dras** o **-drae** [dri]) hidra
hydrant [ˈhaɪdrənt] *s* boca de agua, boca de riego; (*water faucet*) grifo
hydrate [ˈhaɪdret] *s* hidrato || *tr* hidratar || *intr* hidratarse
hydraulic [haɪˈdrɔlɪk] *adj* hidráulico || **hydraulics** *s* hidráulica
hydraulic ram *s* ariete hidráulico
hydriodic [ˌhaɪdrɪˈɑdɪk] *adj* yodhídrico
hydrobromic [ˌhaɪdrəˈbromɪk] *adj* bromhídrico
hydrocarbon [ˌhaɪdrəˈkɑrbən] *s* hidrocarburo
hydrochloric [ˌhaɪdrəˈklorɪk] *adj* clorhídrico
hydroelectric [ˌhaɪdro·ɪˈlɛktrɪk] *adj* hidroeléctrico
hydrofluoric [ˌhaɪdrəfluˈɑrɪk] o [ˌhaɪdrəfluˈɔrɪk] *adj* fluorhídrico
hydrofoil [ˈhaɪdrəˌfɔɪl] *s* superficie hidrodinámica; (*wing designed to lift vessel*) hidroaleta; (*vessel*) hidroala *m*
hydrogen [ˈhaɪdrədʒən] *s* hidrógeno
hydrogen bomb *s* bomba de hidrógeno
hydrogen peroxide *s* peróxido de hidrógeno
hydrogen sulfide *s* sulfuro de hidrógeno
hydrometer [haɪˈdrɑmɪtər] *s* areómetro
hydrophobia [ˌhaɪdrəˈfobɪ·ə] *s* hidrofobia
hydroplane [ˈhaɪdrəˌplen] *s* hidroavión *m*
hydroxide [haɪˈdrɑksaɪd] *s* hidróxido
hyena [haɪˈinə] *s* hiena
hygiene [ˈhaɪdʒin] o [ˈhaɪdʒɪˌin] *s* higiene *f*
hygienic [ˌhaɪdʒɪˈɛnɪk] o [haɪˈdʒinɪk] *adj* higiénico
hymn [hɪm] *s* himno
hymnal [ˈhɪmnəl] *s* himnario
hyp. *abbr* **hypotenuse, hypothesis**
hyperacidity [ˌhaɪpərəˈsɪdɪti] *s* hiperacidez *f*
hyperbola [haɪˈpʌrbələ] *s* (geom) hipérbola
hyperbole [haɪˈpʌrbəli] *s* (rhet) hipérbole *f*
hyperbolic [ˌhaɪpərˈbɑlɪk] *adj* (geom & rhet) hiperbólico
hypersensitive [ˌhaɪpərˈsɛnsɪtɪv] *adj* extremadamente sensible; (*allergic*) hipersensible
hypertension [ˌhaɪpərˈtɛnʃən] *s* hipertensión
hyphen [ˈhaɪfən] *s* guión *m*
hyphenate [ˈhaɪfəˌnet] *tr* unir con guión; escribir con guión
hypno•sis [hɪpˈnosɪs] *s* (*pl* **-ses** [siz]) hipnosis *f*
hypnotic [hɪpˈnɑtɪk] *adj* hipnótico || *s* (*person; sedative*) hipnótico
hypnotism [ˈhɪpnəˌtɪzəm] *s* hipnotismo
hypnotist [ˈhɪpnətɪst] *s* hipnotista *mf*
hypnotize [ˈhɪpnəˌtaɪz] *tr* hipnotizar
hypochondriac [ˌhaɪpəˈkɑndrɪˌæk] o [ˌhɪpəˈkɑndrɪˌæk] *s* hipocondríaco
hypocri•sy [hɪˈpɑkrəsi] *s* (*pl* **-sies**) hipocresía
hypocrite [ˈhɪpəkrɪt] *s* hipócrita *mf*
hypocritical [ˌhɪpəˈkrɪtɪkəl] *adj* hipócrita
hypodermic [ˌhaɪpəˈdʌrmɪk] *adj* hipodérmico
hyposulfite [ˌhaɪpəˈsʌlfaɪt] *m* hiposulfito
hypotenuse [haɪˈpɑtɪˌnus] o [haɪˈpɑtɪˌnjus] *s* hipotenusa
hypothe•sis [haɪˈpɑθɪsɪs] *s* (*pl* **-ses** [ˌsiz]) hipótesis *f*
hypothetic(al) [ˌhaɪpəˈθɛtɪk(əl)] *adj* hipotético

hyssop ['hɪsəp] *s* (bot) hisopo
hysteria [hɪs'tɪrɪ·ə] *s* histerismo, histeria
hysteric [hɪs'terɪk] *adj* histérico || **hysterics** *s* paroxismo histérico
hysterical [hɪs'terɪkəl] *adj* histérico

I

I, i [aɪ] novena letra del alfabeto inglés
I. *abbr* **Island**
I [aɪ] *pron pers* (*pl* **we** [wi]) yo; **it is I** soy yo
iambic [aɪ'æmbɪk] *adj* yámbico
iam·bus [aɪ'æmbəs] *s* (*pl* **-bi** [baɪ]) yambo
ib. *abbr* **ibidem**
Iberian [aɪ'bɪrɪ·ən] *adj* ibérico || *s* ibero
ibex ['aɪbeks] *s* (*pl* **ibexes** o **ibices** ['ɪbɪ,siz]) íbice *m*, cabra montés
ibid. *abbr* **ibidem**
ice [aɪs] *s* hielo; **to break the ice** (*to overcome reserve*) romper el hielo; **to cut no ice** (coll) no importar nada; **to skate on thin ice** (coll) buscar el peligro || *tr* helar; enfriar con hielo; (*to cover with icing*) garapiñar || *intr* helarse
ice age *s* época glacial
ice bag *s* bolsa para hielo
iceberg ['aɪs,bʌrg] *s* banquisa, iceberg *m*
ice'boat' *s* cortahielos *m*, rompehielos *m;* trineo con vela para deslizarse sobre el hielo
ice'bound' *adj* rodeado de hielo; detenido por el hielo
ice'box' *s* nevera, fresquera
ice'break'er *s* cortahielos *m*, rompehielos *m*
ice'cap' *s* bolsa para hielo; manto de hielo
ice cream *s* helado
ice'-cream' cone *s* cucurucho de helado, barquillo de helado
ice-cream freezer *s* heladora, garapiñera
ice-cream parlor *s* salón *m* de refrescos, tienda de helados
ice-cream soda *s* agua gaseosa con helado
ice cube *s* cubito de hielo
ice hockey *s* hockey *m* sobre patines
Iceland ['aɪslənd] *s* Islandia
Icelander ['aɪs,lændər] o ['aɪsləndər] *s* islandés *m*
Icelandic [aɪs'lændɪk] *adj* islandés || *s* islandés *m* (*idioma*)
ice·man ['aɪs,mæn] *s* (*pl* **-men** [,men]) vendedor *m* de hielo, repartidor *m* de hielo
ice pack *s* hielo flotante; bolsa de hielo
ice pail *s* enfriadera
ice pick *s* picahielos *m*
ice skate *s* patín *m* de cuchilla, patín de hielo
ice tray *s* bandejita de hielo
ice water *s* agua helada
ichthyology [,ɪkθɪ'ɑlədʒi] *s* ictiología
icicle ['aɪsɪkəl] *s* carámbano
icing ['aɪsɪŋ] *s* garapiña, capa de azúcar; (aer) formación de hielo
iconoclasm [aɪ'kɑnə,klæzəm] *s* iconoclasia, iconoclasmo
iconoclast [aɪ'kɑnə,klæst] *s* iconoclasta *mf*
iconoscope [aɪ'kɑnə,skop] *s* (trademark) iconoscopio
icy ['aɪsi] *adj* (*comp* **icier;** *super* **iciest**) cubierto de hielo; (*slippery*) resbaladizo; (fig) frío
id. *abbr* **idem**
id [ɪd] *s* (psychoanalysis) ello
idea [aɪ'di·ə] *s* idea
ideal [aɪ'di·əl] *adj & s* ideal *m*
idealist [aɪ'di·əlɪst] *adj & s* idealista *mf*
idealize [aɪ'di·ə,laɪz] *tr* idealizar
identic(al) [aɪ'dentɪk(əl)] *adj* idéntico
identification [aɪ,dentɪfɪ'keʃən] *s* identificación
identification tag *s* disco de identificación
identify [aɪ'dentɪ,faɪ] *v* (*pret & pp* **-fied**) *tr* identificar
identi·ty [aɪ'dentɪti] *s* (*pl* **-ties**) identidad
ideolo·gy [,aɪdɪ'ɑlədʒi] o [,ɪdɪ'ɑlədʒi] *s* (*pl* **-gies**) ideología
ides [aɪdz] *spl* idus *mpl*
idio·cy ['ɪdɪ·əsi] *s* (*pl* **-cies**) idiotez *f*
idiom ['ɪdɪ·əm] *s* (*expression that is contrary to the usual patterns of the language*) modismo; (*style of language*) idioma *m*, lenguaje *m;* (*style of an author*) estilo; (*character of a language*) índole *f*
idiomatic [,ɪdɪ·ə'mætɪk] *adj* idiomático
idiosyncra·sy [,ɪdɪ·ə'sɪnkrəsi] *s* (*pl* **-sies**) idiosincrasia
idiot ['ɪdɪ·ət] *s* idiota *mf*
idiotic [,ɪdɪ·'ɑtɪk] *adj* idiota
idle ['aɪdəl] *adj* desocupado, ocioso; **at idle moments** a ratos perdidos; **to run idle** marchar en ralentí || *tr* — **to idle away** gastar ociosamente (*el tiempo*) || *intr* estar ocioso, holgar; marchar (*un motor*) en ralentí
idleness ['aɪdəlnɪs] *s* desocupación, ociosidad
idler ['aɪdlər] *s* haragán *m*, ocioso
idol ['aɪdəl] *s* ídolo
idola·try [aɪ'dɑlətri] *s* (*pl* **-tries**) idolatría
idolize ['aɪdə,laɪz] *tr* idolatrar
idyll ['aɪdəl] *s* idilio
idyllic [aɪ'dɪlɪk] *adj* idílico
if [ɪf] *conj* si; **as if** como si; **even if**

aunque; **if so** si es así; **if true** si es cierto
ignis fatuus [ˈɪgnɪsˈfætʃʊ·əs] *s* (*pl* **ignes fatui** [ˈɪgnizˈfætʃʊˌaɪ]) fuego fatuo
ignite [ɪgˈnaɪt] *tr* encender ‖ *intr* encenderse
ignition [ɪgˈnɪʃən] *s* inflamación; (aut) encendido
ignition switch *s* (aut) interruptor *m* de encendido
ignoble [ɪgˈnobəl] *adj* innoble
ignominious [ˌɪgnəˈmɪnɪ·əs] *adj* ignominioso
ignoramus [ˌɪgnəˈreməs] *s* ignorante *mf*
ignorance [ˈɪgnərəns] *s* ignorancia
ignorant [ˈɪgnərənt] *adj* ignorante
ignore [ɪgˈnor] *tr* no hacer caso de, pasar por alto
ilk [ɪlk] *s* especie *f*, jaez *m*
ill. *abbr* **illustrated, illustration**
ill [ɪl] *adj* (*comp* **worse** [wʌrs]; *super* **worst** [wʌrst]) enfermo, malo ‖ *adv* mal; **to take ill** tomar a mal; caer enfermo
ill-advised [ˈɪlədˈvaɪzd] *adj* desaconsejado, malaconsejado
ill at ease *adj* inquieto, incómodo
ill-bred [ˈɪlˈbrɛd] *adj* malcriado
ill-considered [ˈɪlkənˈsɪdərd] *adj* desconsiderado, mal considerado
ill-disposed [ˈɪldɪsˈpozd] *adj* malintencionado, maldispuesto
illegal [ɪˈligəl] *adj* ilegal
illegible [ɪˈlɛdʒɪbəl] *adj* ilegible
illegitimate [ˌɪlɪˈdʒɪtɪmɪt] *adj* ilegítimo
ill fame *s* mala fama, reputación de inmoral
ill-fated [ˈɪlˈfetɪd] *adj* aciago, funesto
ill-gotten [ˈɪlˈgɑtən] *adj* mal ganado
ill health *s* mala salud
ill-humored [ˈɪlˈhjumərd] *adj* malhumorado
illicit [ɪˈlɪsɪt] *adj* ilícito
illitera·cy [ɪˈlɪtərəsi] *s* (*pl* **-cies**) ignorancia; analfabetismo
illiterate [ɪˈlɪtərɪt] *adj* (*uneducated*) iliterato; (*unable to read or write*) analfabeto ‖ *s* analfabeto
ill-mannered [ˈɪlˈmænərd] *adj* de malos modales
illness [ˈɪlnɪs] *s* enfermedad
illogical [ɪˈlɑdʒɪkəl] *adj* ilógico
ill-spent [ˈɪlˈspɛnt] *adj* malgastado
ill-starred [ˈɪlˈstɑrd] *adj* malhadado
ill-tempered [ˈɪlˈtɛmpərd] *adj* de mal genio
ill-timed [ˈɪlˈtaɪmd] *adj* inoportuno, intempestivo
ill'-treat' *tr* maltratar
illuminate [ɪˈlumɪˌnet] *tr* alumbrar, iluminar; miniar (*un manuscrito*)
illuminating gas *s* gas *m* de alumbrado
illumination [ɪˌlumɪˈneʃən] *s* iluminación
illusion [ɪˈluʒən] *s* ilusión
illusive [ɪˈlusɪv] *adj* ilusivo
illusory [ɪˈlusəri] *adj* ilusorio
illustrate [ˈɪləsˌtret] o [ɪˈlʌstret] *tr* ilustrar
illustration [ˌɪləsˈtreʃən] *s* ilustración
illustrious [ɪˈlʌstrɪ·əs] *adj* ilustre
ill will *s* mala voluntad
image [ˈɪmɪdʒ] *s* imagen *f*; **the very image of** la propia estampa de
image·ry [ˈɪmɪdʒri] o [ˈɪmɪdʒəri] *s* (*pl* **-ries**) (*formation of mental images; product of the imagination*) fantasía; (*images collectively*) imágenes *fpl*
imaginary [ɪˈmædʒɪˌnɛri] *adj* imaginario
imagination [ɪˌmædʒɪˈneʃən] *s* imaginación
imagine [ɪˈmædʒɪn] *tr & intr* imaginar; (*to conjecture*) imaginarse
imbecile [ˈɪmbɪsɪl] *adj & s* imbécil *mf*
imbecili·ty [ˌɪmbɪˈsɪlɪti] *s* (*pl* **-ties**) imbecilidad
imbibe [ɪmˈbaɪb] *tr* (*to drink*) beber; (*to absorb*) embeber; (*to become absorbed in*) embeberse de o en ‖ *intr* beber, empinar el codo
imbue [ɪmˈbju] *tr* imbuir
imitate [ˈɪmɪˌtet] *tr* imitar
imitation [ˌɪmɪˈteʃən] *adj* (*e.g., jewelry*) imitado, imitación, de imitación ‖ *s* imitación; **in imitation of** a imitación de
immaculate [ɪˈmækjəlɪt] *adj* inmaculado
immaterial [ˌɪməˈtɪrɪ·əl] *adj* inmaterial; poco importante
immature [ˌɪməˈtjʊr] o [ˌɪməˈtʊr] *adj* inmaturo
immeasurable [ɪˈmɛʒərəbəl] *adj* inmensurable
immediacy [ɪˈmidɪ·əsi] *s* inmediación
immediate [ɪˈmidɪ·ɪt] *adj* inmediato
immediately [ɪˈmidɪ·ɪtli] *adv* inmediatamente
immemorial [ˌɪmɪˈmorɪ·əl] *adj* inmemorial
immense [ɪˈmɛns] *adj* inmenso; (coll) excelente
immerge [ɪˈmʌrdʒ] *intr* sumergirse
immerse [ɪˈmʌrs] *tr* sumergir, inmergir
immersion [ɪˈmʌrʃən] o [ɪˈmʌrʒən] *s* sumersión, inmersión
immigrant [ˈɪmɪgrənt] *adj & s* inmigrante *mf*
immigrate [ˈɪmɪˌgret] *intr* inmigrar
immigration [ˌɪmɪˈgreʃən] *s* inmigración
imminent [ˈɪmɪnənt] *adj* inminente
immobile [ɪˈmobɪl] o [ɪˈmobil] *adj* inmoble, inmóvil
immobilize [ɪˈmobɪˌlaɪz] *tr* inmovilizar
immoderate [ɪˈmɑdərɪt] *adj* inmoderado
immodest [ɪˈmɑdɪst] *adj* inmodesto
immoral [ɪˈmɑrəl] o [ɪˈmɔrəl] *adj* inmoral
immortal [ɪˈmɔrtəl] *adj & s* inmortal *mf*
immortalize [ɪˈmɔrtəˌlaɪz] *tr* inmortalizar
immune [ɪˈmjun] *adj* inmune
immunize [ˈɪmjəˌnaɪz] o [ɪˈmjunaɪz] *tr* inmunizar
imp [ɪmp] *s* diablillo; (*child*) niño travieso

impact ['ɪmpækt] *s* impacto
impair [ɪm'pɛr] *tr* empeorar, deteriorar
impan·el [ɪm'pænəl] *v* (*pret & pp* **-eled** o **-elled;** *ger* **-eling** o **-elling)** *tr* inscribir en la lista de los jurados; elegir (*un jurado*)
impart [ɪm'pɑrt] *tr* (*to make known*) dar a conocer, hacer saber; (*to transmit, communicate*) imprimir
impartial [ɪm'pɑrʃəl] *adj* imparcial
impassable [ɪm'pæsəbəl] o [ɪm'pɑsəbəl] *adj* intransitable, impracticable
impasse [ɪm'pæs] o ['ɪmpæs] *s* callejón *m* sin salida
impassible [ɪm'pæsɪbəl] *adj* impasible
impassioned [ɪm'pæʃənd] *adj* ardiente, vehemente
impassive [ɪm'pæsɪv] *adj* impasible
impatience [ɪm'peʃəns] *s* impaciencia
impatient [ɪm'peʃənt] *adj* impaciente
impeach [ɪm'pitʃ] *tr* residenciar
impeachment [ɪm'pitʃmənt] *s* residencia
impeccable [ɪm'pɛkəbəl] *adj* impecable
impecunious [,ɪmpɪ'kjunɪ·əs] *adj* inope
impedance [ɪm'pidəns] *s* impedancia
impede [ɪm'pid] *tr* estorbar, dificultar
impediment [ɪm'pɛdɪmənt] *s* impedimento; (*e.g., in speech*) defecto
im·pel [ɪm'pɛl] *v* (*pret & pp* **-pelled;** *ger* **-pelling)** *tr* impeler, impulsar
impending [ɪm'pɛndɪŋ] *adj* inminente
impenetrable [ɪm'pɛnətrəbəl] *adj* impenetrable
impenitent [ɪm'pɛnɪtənt] *adj & s* impenitente *mf*
imperative [ɪm'pɛrɪtɪv] *adj* (*commanding*) imperativo; (*urgent, absolutely necessary*) imperioso || *s* imperativo
imperceptible [,ɪmpər'sɛptɪbəl] *adj* imperceptible, inapreciable
imperfect [ɪm'pʌrfɪkt] *adj & s* imperfecto
imperfection [,ɪmpər'fɛkʃən] *s* imperfección
imperial [ɪm'pɪrɪ·əl] *adj* imperial; majestuoso || *s* (*goatee*) perilla; (*top of coach*) imperial *f*
imperialist [ɪm'pɪrɪ·əlɪst] *adj & s* imperialista *mf*
imper·il [ɪm'pɛrɪl] *v* (*pret & pp* **-iled** o **-illed;** *ger* **-iling** o **-illing)** *tr* poner en peligro
imperious [ɪm'pɪrɪ·əs] *adj* imperioso
imperishable [ɪm'pɛrɪʃəbəl] *adj* imperecedero
impersonal [ɪm'pʌrsənəl] *adj* impersonal
impersonate [ɪm'pʌrsə,net] *tr* personificar; hacer el papel de
impertinence [ɪm'pʌrtɪnəns] *s* impertinencia
impertinent [ɪm'pʌrtɪnənt] *adj & s* impertinente *mf*
impetuous [ɪm'pɛtʃʊ·əs] *adj* impetuoso
impetus ['ɪmpɪtəs] *s* ímpetu *m*
impie·ty [ɪm'paɪ·əti] *s* (*pl* **-ties)** impiedad
impinge [ɪm'pɪndʒ] *intr* — **to impinge on** o **upon** incidir en o sobre, herir; infringir, violar
impious ['ɪmpɪ·əs] *adj* impío
impish ['ɪmpɪʃ] *adj* endiablado, travieso
implant [ɪm'plænt] *tr* implantar
implement ['ɪmplɪmənt] *s* instrumento, utensilio, herramienta || ['ɪmplɪ,mɛnt] *tr* poner por obra, llevar a cabo; (*to provide with implements*) pertrechar
implicate ['ɪmplɪ,ket] *tr* implicar, comprometer, enredar
implicit [ɪm'plɪsɪt] *adj* implícito; (*unquestioning*) absoluto, ciego
implied [ɪm'plaɪd] *adj* implícito, sobrentendido
implore [ɪm'plor] *tr* implorar, suplicar
im·ply [ɪm'plaɪ] *v* (*pret & pp* **-plied)** *tr* dar a entender; implicar, incluir en esencia
impolite [,ɪmpə'laɪt] *s* descortés
import ['ɪmport] *s* importación; artículo importado; importancia, significación || [ɪm'port] o ['ɪmport] *tr* importar; significar || *intr* importar
importance [ɪm'pɔrtəns] *s* importancia
important [ɪm'pɔrtənt] *adj* importante
importation [,ɪmpor'teʃən] *s* importación
importer [ɪm'portər] *s* importador *m*
importunate [ɪm'pɔrtʃənɪt] *adj* importuno
importune [,ɪmpər'tjun] o [,ɪmpər'tun] *tr* importunar
impose [ɪm'poz] *tr* imponer || *intr* — **to impose on** o **upon** abusar de
imposing [ɪm'pozɪŋ] *adj* imponente
imposition [,ɪmpə'zɪʃən] *s* (*of someone's will*) imposición; abuso, engaño
impossible [ɪm'pɑsɪbəl] *adj* imposible
impostor [ɪm'pɑstər] *s* impostor *m*
imposture [ɪm'pɑstʃər] *s* impostura
impotence ['ɪmpətəns] *s* impotencia
impotent ['ɪmpətənt] *adj* impotente
impound [ɪm'paʊnd] *tr* acorralar, encerrar; rebalsar (*agua*); (law) embargar, secuestrar
impoverish [ɪm'pɑvərɪʃ] *tr* empobrecer
impracticable [ɪm'præktɪkəbəl] *adj* impracticable; (*intractable*) intratable
impractical [ɪm'præktɪkəl] *adj* impracticable; soñador, utópico
impregnable [ɪm'prɛgnəbəl] *adj* inexpugnable
impregnate [ɪm'prɛgnet] *tr* (*to make pregnant*) empreñar; (*to soak*) empapar; (*to fill the interstices of*) impregnar; (*to infuse, infect*) imbuir
impresari·o [,ɪmprɪ'sɑrɪ,o] *s* (*pl* **-os)** empresario, empresario de teatro
impress [ɪm'prɛs] *tr* (*to have an effect on the mind or emotions of*) impresionar; (*to mark by using pres-*

sure) imprimir; (*on the memory*) grabar; (mil) enganchar
impression [ɪm'prɛʃən] *s* impresión
impressionable [ɪm'prɛʃənəbəl] *adj* impresionable
impressive [ɪm'prɛsɪv] *adj* impresionante
imprint ['ɪmprɪnt] *s* impresión; (typ) pie *m* de imprenta ‖ [ɪm'prɪnt] *tr* imprimir
imprison [ɪm'prɪzən] *tr* encarcelar
imprisonment [ɪm'prɪzənmənt] *s* encarcelamiento
improbable [ɪm'prɑbəbəl] *adj* improbable
impromptu [ɪm'prɑmptju] o [ɪm'prɑmptu] *adj* improvisado ‖ *adv* de improviso ‖ *s* improvisación; (mus) impromptu *m*
improper [ɪm'prɑpər] *adj* impropio; (*contrary to good taste or decency*) indecoroso
improve [ɪm'pruv] *tr* perfeccionar, mejorar; aprovechar (*la oportunidad*) ‖ *intr* perfeccionarse, mejorar; **to improve on** o **upon** mejorar
improvement [ɪm'pruvmənt] *s* perfeccionamiento, mejoramiento; (*e.g., in health*) mejoría; (*useful employment, e.g., of time*) aprovechamiento
improvident [ɪm'prɑvɪdənt] *adj* imprevisor
improvise ['ɪmprə,vaɪz] *tr & intr* improvisar
imprudent [ɪm'prudənt] *adj* imprudente
impudence ['ɪmpjədəns] *s* insolencia, descaro, impertinencia
impudent ['ɪmpjədənt] *adj* insolente, descarado, impertinente
impugn [ɪm'pjun] *tr* poner en tela de juicio
impulse ['ɪmpʌls] *s* impulso
impulsive [ɪm'pʌlsɪv] *adj* impulsivo
impunity [ɪm'pjunɪti] *s* impunidad
impure [ɪm'pjʊr] *adj* impuro
impuri·ty [ɪm'pjʊrɪti] *s* (*pl* **-ties**) impureza, impuridad
impute [ɪm'pjut] *tr* imputar
in [ɪn] *adj* interior ‖ *adv* dentro; en casa, en la oficina; **in here** aquí dentro; **in there** allí dentro; **to be in** estar en casa; **to be in for** estar expuesto a; **to be in with** gozar del favor de ‖ *prep* en; (*within*) dentro de; (*over, through*) por; (*a period of the day*) en o por; **dressed in . . .** vestido de . . . ; **in so far as** en tanto que; **in that** en que, por cuanto ‖ *s* — **ins and outs** recovecos, pormenores minuciosos
inability [,ɪnə'bɪlɪti] *s* inhabilidad, incapacidad
inaccessible [,ɪnæk'sɛsɪbəl] *adj* inaccesible
inaccura·cy [ɪn'ækjərəsi] *s* (*pl* **-cies**) inexactitud, incorrección
inaccurate [ɪn'ækjərɪt] *adj* inexacto, incorrecto
inaction [ɪn'ækʃən] *s* inacción
inactive [ɪn'æktɪv] *adj* inactivo
inactivity [,ɪnæk'tɪvɪti] *s* inactividad
inadequate [ɪn'ædɪkwɪt] *adj* insuficiente, inadecuado
inadvertent [,ɪnəd'vʌrtənt] *adj* inadvertido
inadvisable [,ɪnəd'vaɪzəbəl] *adj* poco aconsejable, imprudente
inane [ɪn'en] *adj* inane
inanimate [ɪn'ænɪmɪt] *adj* inanimado
inappreciable [,ɪnə'priʃɪ·əbəl] *adj* inapreciable
inappropriate [,ɪnə'proprɪ·ɪt] *adj* no apropiado, no a propósito
inarticulate [,ɪnɑr'tɪkjəlɪt] *adj* (*sounds, words*) inarticulado; (*person*) incapaz de expresarse
inartistic [,ɪnɑr'tɪstɪk] *adj* antiartístico, inartístico
inasmuch as [,ɪnəz'mʌtʃ,æz] *conj* ya que, puesto que; en cuanto, hasta donde
inattentive [,ɪnə'tɛntɪv] *adj* desatento
inaugural [ɪn'ɔgjərəl] *adj* inaugural ‖ *s* discurso inaugural
inaugurate [ɪn'ɔgjə,ret] *tr* inaugurar
inauguration [ɪn,ɔgjə'reʃən] *s* (*formal initiation or opening*) inauguración; (*investiture of a head of government*) toma de posesión
inborn ['ɪn,bɔrn] *adj* innato, ingénito
inbreeding ['ɪn,bridɪŋ] *s* intracruzamiento
inc. *abbr* **inclosure, included, including, incorporated, increase**
Inca ['ɪŋkə] *adj* incaico ‖ *s* inca *mf*
incandescent [,ɪnkən'dɛsənt] *adj* incandescente
incapable [ɪn'kepəbəl] *adj* incapaz
incapacitate [,ɪnkə'pæsɪ,tet] *tr* incapacitar, inhabilitar
incapaci·ty [,ɪnkə'pæsɪti] *s* (*pl* **-ties**) incapacidad
incarcerate [ɪn'kɑrsə,ret] *tr* encarcelar
incarnate [ɪn'kɑrnɪt] o [ɪn'kɑrnet] *adj* encarnado ‖ [ɪn'kɑrnet] *tr* encarnar
incarnation [,ɪnkɑr'neʃən] *s* encarnación
incendiarism [ɪn'sɛndɪ·ə,rɪzəm] *s* incendio intencionado; incitación al desorden
incendiar·y [ɪn'sɛndɪ,ɛri] *adj* incendiario ‖ *s* (*pl* **-ies**) incendiario
incense ['ɪnsɛns] *s* incienso ‖ *tr* (*to burn incense before*) incensar ‖ [ɪn'sɛns] *tr* exasperar, encolerizar
incense burner *s* incensario
incentive [ɪn'sɛntɪv] *adj & s* incentivo
inception [ɪn'sɛpʃən] *s* principio, comienzo
incertitude [ɪn'sʌrtɪ,tjud] o [ɪn'sʌrtɪ,tud] *s* incertidumbre
incessant [ɪn'sɛsənt] *adj* incesante
incest ['ɪnsɛst] *s* incesto
incestuous [ɪn'sɛstʃʊ·əs] *adj* incestuoso
inch [ɪntʃ] *s* pulgada; **to be within an inch of** estar a dos dedos de ‖ *intr* — **to inch ahead** avanzar poco a poco
incidence ['ɪnsɪdəns] *s* incidencia; (*range of occurrence*) extensión
incident ['ɪnsɪdənt] *adj & s* incidente *m*

incidental [ˌɪnsɪˈdɛntəl] *adj* incidente; (*incurred in addition to the regular amount*) obvencional || *s* elemento incidental; **incidentals** gastos menudos
incidentally [ˌɪnsɪˈdɛntəli] *adv* incidentemente; a propósito
incipient [ɪnˈsɪpɪ·ənt] *adj* incipiente
incision [ɪnˈsɪʒən] *s* incisión
incisive [ɪnˈsaɪsɪv] *adj* incisivo
incite [ɪnˈsaɪt] *tr* incitar
incl. *abbr* **inclosure, inclusive**
inclemen·cy [ɪnˈklɛmənsi] *s* (*pl* **-cies**) inclemencia
inclement [ɪnˈklɛmənt] *adj* inclemente
inclination [ˌɪnklɪˈneʃən] *s* inclinación
incline [ˈɪnklaɪn] o [ɪnˈklaɪn] *s* declive *m,* pendiente *f* || [ɪnˈklaɪn] *tr* inclinar || *intr* inclinarse
inclose [ɪnˈkloz] *tr* encerrar; (*in a letter*) adjuntar, incluir; **to inclose herewith** remitir adjunto
inclosure [ɪnˈkloʒər] *s* recinto; cosa inclusa, carta inclusa
include [ɪnˈklud] *tr* incluir, comprender
including [ɪnˈkludɪŋ] *prep* incluso, inclusive
inclusive [ɪnˈklusɪv] *adj* inclusivo; **inclusive of** comprensivo de || *adv* inclusive
incogni·to [ɪnˈkɑgnɪˌto] *adj* incógnito || *adv* de incógnito || *s* (*pl* **-tos**) incógnito
incoherent [ˌɪnkoˈhɪrənt] *adj* incoherente
incombustible [ˌɪnkəmˈbʌstɪbəl] *adj* incombustible
income [ˈɪnkʌm] *s* renta, ingreso, utilidad
income tax *s* impuesto sobre rentas
in′come-tax′ return *s* declaración de impuesto sobre rentas
in′com′ing *adj* de entrada, entrante; (*tide*) ascendente || *s* entrada
incomparable [ɪnˈkɑmpərəbəl] *adj* incomparable
incompatible [ˌɪnkəmˈpætɪbəl] *adj* incompatible
incompetent [ɪnˈkɑmpɪtənt] *adj* incompetente
incomplete [ˌɪnkəmˈplit] *adj* incompleto
incomprehensible [ˌɪnkɑmprɪˈhɛnsɪbəl] *adj* incomprensible
inconceivable [ˌɪnkənˈsivəbəl] *adj* inconcebible
inconclusive [ˌɪnkənˈklusɪv] *adj* inconcluyente
incongruous [ɪnˈkɑŋgrʊ·əs] *adj* incongruo
inconsequential [ɪnˌkɑnsɪˈkwɛnʃəl] *adj* (*lacking proper sequence of thought or speech*) inconsecuente; (*trivial*) de poca importancia
inconsiderate [ˌɪnkənˈsɪdərɪt] *adj* desconsiderado, inconsiderado
inconsisten·cy [ˌɪnkənˈsɪstənsi] *s* (*pl* **-cies**) (*lack of coherence*) inconsistencia; (*lack of logical connection or uniformity*) inconsecuencia
inconsistent [ˌɪnkənˈsɪstənt] *adj* (*lacking coherence of parts*) inconsistente; (*not agreeing with itself or oneself*) inconsecuente
inconsolable [ˌɪnkənˈsoləbəl] *adj* inconsolable
inconspicuous [ˌɪnkənˈspɪkjʊ·əs] *adj* poco impresionante, poco aparente
inconstant [ɪnˈkɑnstənt] *adj* inconstante
incontinent [ɪnˈkɑntɪnənt] *adj* incontinente
incontrovertible [ˌɪnkɑntrəˈvʌrtɪbəl] *adj* incontrovertible
inconvenience [ˌɪnkənˈvinɪ·əns] *s* incomodidad, inconveniencia, molestia || *tr* incomodar, molestar
inconvenient [ˌɪnkənˈvinɪ·ənt] *adj* incómodo, inconveniente, molesto
incorporate [ɪnˈkɔrpəˌret] *tr* incorporar; constituir en sociedad anónima || *intr* incorporarse; constituirse en sociedad anónima
incorporation [ɪnˌkɔrpəˈreʃən] *s* incorporación; constitución en sociedad anónima
incorrect [ˌɪnkəˈrɛkt] *adj* incorrecto
increase [ˈɪnkris] *s* aumento; ganancia, interés *m;* **to be on the increase** ir en aumento || [ɪnˈkris] *tr* aumentar; (*by propagation*) multiplicar || *intr* aumentar; multiplicarse
increasingly [ɪnˈkrisɪŋli] *adv* cada vez más
incredible [ɪnˈkrɛdɪbəl] *adj* increíble
incredulous [ɪnˈkrɛdʒələs] *adj* incrédulo
increment [ˈɪnkrɪmənt] *s* incremento
incriminate [ɪnˈkrɪmɪˌnet] *tr* acriminar, incriminar
incrust [ɪnˈkrʌst] *tr* incrustar
incubate [ˈɪnkjəˌbet] *tr & intr* incubar
incubator [ˈɪnkjəˌbetər] *s* incubadora
inculcate [ɪnˈkʌlket] o [ˈɪnkʌlˌket] *tr* inculcar
incumben·cy [ɪnˈkʌmbənsi] *s* (*pl* **-cies**) incumbencia
incumbent [ɪnˈkʌmbənt] *adj* — **to be incumbent on** incumbir a || *s* titular *m*
incunabula [ˌɪnkjʊˈnæbjələ] *spl* (*beginnings*) orígenes *mpl;* (*early printed books*) incunables *mpl*
in·cur [ɪnˈkʌr] *v* (*pret & pp* **-curred;** *ger* **-curring**) *tr* incurrir en; (*a debt*) contraer
incurable [ɪnˈkjʊrəbəl] *adj & s* incurable *mf*
incursion [ɪnˈkʌrʒən] o [ɪnˈkʌrʃən] *s* incursión, correría
ind. *abbr* **independent, industrial**
indebted [ɪnˈdɛtɪd] *adj* adeudado; obligado
indecen·cy [ɪnˈdisənsi] *s* (*pl* **-cies**) indecencia, deshonestidad
indecent [ɪnˈdisənt] *adj* indecente, deshonesto
indecisive [ˌɪndɪˈsaɪsɪv] *adj* indeciso
indeclinable [ˌɪndɪˈklaɪnəbəl] *adj* (gram) indeclinable
indeed [ɪnˈdid] *adv* verdaderamente, claro || *interj* ¡de veras!
indefatigable [ˌɪndɪˈfætɪgəbəl] *adj* incansable, infatigable

indefensible [ˌɪndɪˈfɛnsɪbəl] *adj* indefendible
indefinable [ˌɪndɪˈfainəbəl] *adj* indefinible
indefinite [ɪnˈdɛfɪnɪt] *adj* indefinido
indelible [ɪnˈdɛlɪbəl] *adj* indeleble
indelicate [ɪnˈdɛlɪkɪt] *adj* indelicado
indemnification [ɪnˌdɛmnɪfɪˈkeʃən] *s* indemnización
indemni·fy [ɪnˈdɛmnɪˌfaɪ] *v* (*pret & pp* **-fied**) *tr* indemnizar
indemni·ty [ɪnˈdɛmnɪti] *s* (*pl* **-ties**) (*security against loss*) indemnidad; (*compensation*) indemnización
indent [ɪnˈdɛnt] *tr* dentar, mellar; (typ) sangrar
indentation [ˌɪndɛnˈteʃən] *s* mella, muesca; (typ) sangría
indenture [ɪnˈdɛntʃər] *s* escritura, contrato; contrato de aprendizaje || *tr* obligar por contrato
independence [ˌɪndɪˈpɛndəns] *s* independencia
independen·cy [ˌɪndɪˈpɛndənsi] *s* (*pl* **-cies**) independencia; país *m* independiente
independent [ˌɪndɪˈpɛndənt] *adj & s* independiente *mf*
indescribable [ˌɪndɪˈskraɪbəbəl] *adj* indescriptible
indestructible [ˌɪndɪˈstrʌktɪbəl] *adj* indestructible
indeterminate [ˌɪndɪˈtʌrmɪnɪt] *adj* indeterminado
index [ˈɪndɛks] *s* (*pl* **indexes** o **indices** [ˈɪndɪˌsiz]) *s* índice *m;* (typ) manecilla || *tr* poner índice a; poner en un índice || **Index** *s* Índice de los libros prohibidos
index card *s* ficha catalográfica
index finger *s* dedo índice
index tab *s* pestaña
India [ˈɪndɪ·ə] *s* la India
India ink *s* tinta china
Indian [ˈɪndɪ·ən] *adj & s* indio
Indian club *s* maza de gimnasia
Indian corn *s* maíz *m*, panizo
Indian file *s* fila india || *adv* en fila india
Indian Ocean *s* mar *m* de las Indias, océano Índico
Indian summer *s* veranillo de San Martín
India paper *s* papel *m* de China
India rubber *s* caucho
indicate [ˈɪndɪˌket] *tr* indicar
indication [ˌɪndɪˈkeʃən] *s* indicación
indicative [ɪnˈdɪkətɪv] *adj & s* indicativo
indicator [ˈɪndɪˌketər] *s* indicador *m*
indict [ɪnˈdaɪt] *tr* (law) acusar, procesar
indictment [ɪnˈdaɪtmənt] *s* acusación, procesamiento; auto de acusación formulado por el gran jurado
indifferent [ɪnˈdɪfərənt] *adj* indiferente; (*not particularly good*) pasadero, mediano
indigenous [ɪnˈdɪdʒɪnəs] *adj* indígena
indigent [ˈɪndɪdʒənt] *adj* indigente
indigestible [ˌɪndɪˈdʒɛstɪbəl] *adj* indigestible
indigestion [ˌɪndɪˈdʒɛstʃən] *s* indigestión
indignant [ɪnˈdɪgnənt] *adj* indignado
indignation [ˌɪndɪgˈneʃən] *s* indignación
indigni·ty [ɪnˈdɪgnɪti] *s* (*pl* **-ties**) indignidad
indi·go [ˈɪndɪˌgo] *adj* azul de añil || *s* (*pl* **-gos** o **-goes**) índigo
indirect [ˌɪndɪˈrɛkt] o [ˌɪndaɪˈrɛkt] *adj* indirecto
indirect discourse *s* estilo indirecto
indiscernible [ˌɪndɪˈzʌrnɪbəl] o [ˌɪndɪˈsʌrnɪbəl] *adj* indiscernible
indiscreet [ˌɪndɪsˈkrit] *adj* indiscreto
indispensable [ˌɪndɪsˈpɛnsəbəl] *adj* indispensable, imprescindible
indispose [ˌɪndɪsˈpoz] *tr* indisponer
indisposed [ˌɪndɪsˈpozd] *adj* (*disinclined*) maldispuesto; (*somewhat ill*) indispuesto
indissoluble [ˌɪndɪˈsɑljəbəl] *adj* indisoluble
indistinct [ˌɪndɪˈstɪŋkt] *adj* indistinto
indite [ɪnˈdaɪt] *tr* redactar, poner por escrito
individual [ˌɪndɪˈvɪdʒʊ·əl] *adj* individual || *s* individuo
individuali·ty [ˌɪndɪˌvɪdʒʊˈælɪti] *s* (*pl* **-ties**) individualidad; (*person of distinctive character*) personaje *m*
Indochina [ˈɪndoˈtʃaɪnə] *s* la Indochina
Indo-Chi·nese [ˈɪndotʃaɪˈniz] *adj* indochino || *s* (*pl* **-nese**) indochino
indoctrinate [ɪnˈdɑktrɪˌnet] *tr* adoctrinar
Indo-European [ˈɪndoˌjʊrəˈpi·ən] *adj & s* indoeuropeo
indolent [ˈɪndələnt] *adj* indolente
Indonesia [ˌɪndoˈniʃə] o [ˌɪndoˈniʒə] *s* la Indonesia
Indonesian [ˌɪndoˈniʃən] o [ˌɪndoˈniʒən] *adj & s* indonesio
indoor [ˈɪnˌdor] *adj* interior, de puertas adentro; (*inclined to stay in the house*) casero
indoors [ˈɪnˈdorz] *adv* dentro, en casa, bajo techado, bajo cubierto
indorse [ɪnˈdɔrs] *tr* endosar; (fig) apoyar, aprobar
indorsee [ˌɪndɔrˈsi] *s* endosatario
indorsement [ɪnˈdɔrsmənt] *s* endoso; (fig) apoyo, aprobación
indorser [ɪnˈdɔrsər] *s* endosante *mf*
induce [ɪnˈdjus] o [ɪnˈdus] *tr* inducir; causar, ocasionar
inducement [ɪnˈdjusmənt] o [ɪnˈdusmənt] *s* aliciente *m*, estímulo, incentivo
induct [ɪnˈdʌkt] *tr* instalar; introducir, iniciar; (mil) quintar
induction [ɪnˈdʌkʃən] *s* instalación; introducción; (elec & log) inducción; (mil) quinta
indulge [ɪnˈdʌldʒ] *tr* gratificar (*p.ej., los deseos de uno*); mimar (*a un niño*) || *intr* abandonar; **to indulge in** entregarse a, permitirse el placer de
indulgence [ɪnˈdʌldʒəns] *s* gusto, inclinación; intemperancia, desenfreno; (*leniency*) indulgencia

indulgent [ɪn'dʌldʒənt] *adj* indulgente
industrial [ɪn'dʌstrɪ·əl] *adj* industrial
industrialist [ɪn'dʌstrɪ·əlɪst] *s* industrial *m*
industrialize [ɪn'dʌstrɪ·ə,laɪz] *tr* industrializar
industrious [ɪn'dʌstrɪ·əs] *adj* industrioso, aplicado
indus·try ['ɪndəstri] *s* (*pl* **-tries**) industria
inebriation [ɪn,ibrɪ'eʃən] *s* embriaguez *f*
inedible [ɪn'ɛdɪbəl] *adj* incomible
ineffable [ɪn'ɛfəbəl] *adj* inefable
ineffective [,ɪnɪ'fɛktɪv] *adj* ineficaz; (*person*) incapaz
ineffectual [,ɪnɪ'fɛktʃʊ·əl] *adj* ineficaz, fútil
inefficacy [ɪn'ɛfɪkəsi] *s* ineficacia
inefficient [,ɪnɪ'fɪʃənt] *adj* de mal rendimiento
ineligible [ɪn'ɛlɪdʒɪbəl] *adj* inelegible
inequali·ty [,ɪnɪ'kwɑlɪti] *s* (*pl* **-ties**) desigualdad
inequi·ty [ɪn'ɛkwɪti] *s* (*pl* **-ties**) inequidad
ineradicable [,ɪnɪ'rædɪkəbəl] *adj* inextirpable
inertia [ɪn'ʌrʃə] *s* inercia
inescapable [,ɪnɛs'kepəbəl] *adj* ineludible
inevitable [ɪn'ɛvɪtəbəl] *adj* inevitable
inexact [,ɪnɛg'zækt] *adj* inexacto
inexcusable [,ɪnɛks'kjuzəbəl] *adj* indisculpable, inexcusable
inexhaustible [,ɪnɛg'zɔstɪbəl] *adj* inagotable
inexorable [ɪn'ɛksərəbəl] *adj* inexorable
inexpedient [,ɪnɛk'spidɪ·ənt] *adj* malaconsejado, inoportuno
inexpensive [,ɪnɛk'spɛnsɪv] *adj* barato, poco costoso
inexperience [,ɪnɛk'spɪrɪ·əns] *s* inexperiencia
inexplicable [ɪn'ɛksplɪkəbəl] *adj* inexplicable
inexpressible [,ɪnɛk'sprɛsɪbəl] *adj* inexpresable
Inf. *abbr* **Infantry**
infallible [ɪn'fælɪbəl] *adj* infalible
infamous ['ɪnfəməs] *adj* infame
infa·my ['ɪnfəmi] *s* (*pl* **-mies**) infamia
infan·cy ['ɪnfənsi] *s* (*pl* **-cies**) infancia
infant ['ɪnfənt] *adj* infantil; (*in the earliest stage*) (fig) naciente || *s* criatura, nene *m*
infantile ['ɪnfən,taɪl] o ['ɪnfəntɪl] *adj* infantil; (*childish*) aniñado
infan·try ['ɪnfəntri] *s* (*pl* **-tries**) infantería
infantry·man ['ɪnfəntrimən] *s* (*pl* **-men** [mən]) infante *m*, soldado de infantería
infatuated [ɪn'fætʃʊ,etɪd] *adj* apasionado, locamente enamorado
infect [ɪn'fɛkt] *tr* inficionar, infectar; influir sobre
infection [ɪn'fɛkʃən] *s* infección
infectious [ɪn'fɛkʃəs] *adj* infeccioso
in·fer [ɪn'fʌr] *v* (*pret & pp* **-ferred**; *ger* **-ferring**) *tr* inferir; (coll) conjeturar, suponer
inferior [ɪn'fɪrɪ·ər] *adj & s* inferior *m*
inferiority [ɪn,fɪrɪ'ɑrɪti] *s* inferioridad
inferiority complex *s* complejo de inferioridad
infernal [ɪn'fʌrnəl] *adj* infernal
infest [ɪn'fɛst] *tr* infestar
infidel ['ɪnfɪdəl] *adj & s* infiel *mf*
infideli·ty [,ɪnfɪ'dɛlɪti] *s* (*pl* **-ties**) infidelidad
in'field' *s* (baseball) cuadro interior
infiltrate [ɪn'fɪltret] o ['ɪnfɪl,tret] *tr* infiltrar; infiltrarse en || *intr* infiltrarse
infinite ['ɪnfɪnɪt] *adj & s* infinito
infinitive [ɪn'fɪnɪtɪv] *adj & s* infinitivo
infini·ty [ɪn'fɪnɪti] *s* (*pl* **-ties**) infinidad; (math) infinito
infirm [ɪn'fʌrm] *adj* infirme, achacoso; (*unsteady*) inestable, inseguro; poco firme, poco sólido
infirma·ry [ɪn'fʌrməri] *s* (*pl* **-ries**) enfermería
infirmi·ty [ɪn'fʌrmɪti] *s* (*pl* **-ties**) achaque *m;* inestabilidad
in'fix *s* (gram) infijo
inflame [ɪn'flem] *tr* inflamar
inflammable [ɪn'flæməbəl] *adj* inflamable
inflammation [,ɪnflə'meʃən] *s* inflamación
inflate [ɪn'flet] *tr* inflar || *intr* inflarse
inflation [ɪn'fleʃən] *s* inflación; (*of a tire*) inflado
inflect [ɪn'flɛkt] *tr* doblar, torcer; modular (*la voz*); (gram) modificar por inflexión
inflection [ɪn'flɛkʃən] *s* inflexión
inflexible [ɪn'flɛksɪbəl] *adj* inflexible
inflict [ɪn'flɪkt] *tr* infligir
influence ['ɪnflu·əns] *s* influencia || *tr* influir sobre, influenciar
influential [,ɪnflu'ɛnʃəl] *adj* influyente
influenza [,ɪnflu'ɛnzə] *s* influenza
inform [ɪn'fɔrm] *tr* informar, avisar, enterar || *intr* informar
informal [ɪn'fɔrməl] *adj* (*not according to established rules*) informal; (*unceremonious; colloquial*) familiar
information [,ɪnfər'meʃən] *s* información, informes *mpl*
informational [,ɪnfər'meʃənəl] *adj* informativo
informed sources *spl* los entendidos
infraction [ɪn'frækʃən] *s* infracción
infrared [,ɪnfrə'rɛd] *adj & s* infrarrojo
infrequent [ɪn'frikwənt] *adj* infrecuente
infringe [ɪn'frɪndʒ] *tr* infringir || *intr* — **to infringe on** o **upon** invadir, abusar de
infringement [ɪn'frɪndʒmənt] *s* infracción
infuriate [ɪn'fjʊrɪ,et] *tr* enfurecer
infuse [ɪn'fjuz] *tr* infundir
infusion [ɪn'fjuʒən] *s* infusión
ingenious [ɪn'dʒinjəs] *adj* ingenioso
ingenui·ty [,ɪndʒɪ'nju·ɪti] o [,ɪndʒɪ'nu·ɪti] *s* (*pl* **-ties**) ingeniosidad
ingenuous [ɪn'dʒɛnjʊ·əs] *adj* ingenuo
ingenuousness [ɪn'dʒɛnjʊ·əsnɪs] *s* ingenuidad
ingest [ɪn'dʒɛst] *tr* injerir
in'go'ing *adj* entrante

ingot ['ɪŋgət] *s* lingote *m*
ingraft [ɪn'græft] o [ɪn'grɑft] *tr* (hort & surg) injertar; (fig) implantar
ingrate ['ɪngret] *s* ingrato
ingratiate [ɪn'greʃɪ,et] *tr* — **to ingratiate oneself with** congraciarse con
ingratiating [ɪn'greʃɪ,etɪŋ] *adj* atrayente, obsequioso
ingratitude [ɪn'grætɪ,tjud] o [ɪn'grætɪ,tud] *s* ingratitud, desagradecimiento
ingredient [ɪn'gridɪ·ənt] *s* ingrediente *m*
in'grow'ing nail *s* uñero
ingulf [ɪn'gʌlf] *tr* hundir, inundar
inhabit [ɪn'hæbɪt] *tr* habitar, poblar
inhabitant [ɪn'hæbɪtənt] *s* habitante *mf*
inhale [ɪn'hel] *tr* aspirar, inspirar || *intr* aspirar, inspirar; tragar el humo
inherent [ɪn'hɪrənt] *adj* inherente
inherit [ɪn'hɛrɪt] *tr & intr* heredar
inheritance [ɪn'hɛrɪtəns] *s* herencia
inheritor [ɪn'hɛrɪtər] *s* heredero
inhibit [ɪn'hɪbɪt] *tr* inhibir, prohibir
inhospitable [ɪn'hɑspɪtəbəl] o [,ɪnhɑs'pɪtəbəl] *adj* inhospitalario; (*affording no shelter or protection*) inhóspito
inhuman [ɪn'hjumən] *adj* inhumano
inhumane [,ɪnhju'men] *adj* inhumano
inhumani·ty [,ɪnhju'mænɪti] *s* (*pl* **-ties**) inhumanidad
inimical [ɪ'nɪmɪkəl] *adj* enemigo
iniqui·ty [ɪ'nɪkwɪti] *s* (*pl* **-ties**) iniquidad
ini·tial [ɪ'nɪʃəl] *adj & s* inicial *f* || *v* (*pret* **-tialed** o **-tialled;** *ger* **-tialing** o **-tialling**) *tr* firmar con sus iniciales; marcar (*p.ej., un pañuelo*)
initiate [ɪ'nɪʃɪ,et] *tr* iniciar
initiation [ɪ,nɪʃɪ'eʃən] *s* iniciación
initiative [ɪ'nɪʃɪ·ətɪv] o [ɪ'nɪʃətɪv] *s* iniciativa
inject [ɪn'dʒɛkt] *tr* inyectar; introducir (*una especie, una advertencia*)
injection [ɪn'dʒɛkʃən] *s* inyección
injudicious [,ɪndʒu'dɪʃəs] *adj* imprudente
injunction [ɪn'dʒʌŋkʃən] *s* admonición, mandato; (law) entredicho
injure ['ɪndʒər] *tr* (*to harm*) dañar, hacer daño a; (*to wound*) herir, lisiar, lastimar; (*to offend*) agraviar
injurious [ɪn'dʒʊrɪ·əs] *adj* dañoso, perjudicial; (*offensive*) agravioso
inju·ry ['ɪndʒəri] *s* (*pl* **-ries**) (*harm*) daño; (*wound*) herida, lesión; (*offense*) agravio
injustice [ɪn'dʒʌstɪs] *s* injusticia
ink [ɪŋk] *s* tinta || *tr* entintar
inkling ['ɪŋklɪŋ] *s* sospecha, indicio, noción vaga, vislumbre *f*
ink'stand' *s* (*cuplike container*) tintero; (*stand for ink, pens, etc.*) portatintero
ink'well' *s* tintero
ink·y ['ɪŋki] *adj* (*comp* **-ier;** *super* **-iest**) entintado; negro
inlaid ['ɪn,led] o [,ɪn'led] *adj* embutido, taraceado
inland ['ɪnlənd] *adj & s* interior *m* || *adv* tierra adentro
in'-law' *s* (coll) pariente político
in·lay ['ɪn,le] *s* embutido || [ɪn'le] o ['ɪn,le] *v* (*pret & pp* **-laid**) *tr* embutir, taracear
in'let *s* ensenada, cala, caleta
in'mate' *s* (*in a hospital or home*) asilado, recluso, acogido; (*in a jail*) presidiario, preso
inn [ɪn] *s* mesón *m,* posada
innate [ɪ'net] o ['ɪnet] *adj* ingénito, innato
inner ['ɪnər] *adj* interior; secreto
in'ner·spring' mattress *s* colchón *m* de muelles interiores
inner tube *s* cámara (de neumático)
inning ['ɪnɪŋ] *s* mano *f,* entrada, turno
inn'keep'er *s* mesonero, posadero
innocence ['ɪnəsəns] *s* inocencia
innocent ['ɪnəsənt] *adj & s* inocente *mf*
innovate ['ɪnə,vet] *tr* innovar
innovation [,ɪnə'veʃən] *s* innovación
innuen·do [,ɪnjʊ'ɛndo] *s* (*pl* **-does**) indirecta, insinuación
innumerable [ɪ'njumərəbəl] o [ɪ'numərəbəl] *adj* innumerable, incontable
inoculate [ɪn'ɑkjə,let] *tr* inocular; (fig) imbuir
inoculation [ɪn,ɑkjə'leʃən] *s* inoculación
inoffensive [,ɪnə'fɛnsɪv] *adj* inofensivo
inopportune [ɪn,ɑpər'tjun] o [ɪn,ɑpər'tun] *adj* inoportuno
inordinate [ɪn'ɔrdɪnɪt] *adj* excesivo; (*unrestrained*) desenfrenado
inorganic [,ɪnɔr'gænɪk] *adj* inorgánico
in'put' *s* gasto, consumo; (elec) entrada; (mech) potencia consumida
inquest ['ɪnkwɛst] *s* encuesta; (*of coroner*) pesquisa judicial, levantamiento del cadáver
inquire [ɪn'kwaɪr] *tr* averiguar, inquirir || *intr* preguntar; **to inquire about, after** o **for** preguntar por; **to inquire into** averiguar, inquirir
inquir·y [ɪn'kwaɪri] o ['ɪnkwɪri] *s* (*pl* **-ies**) averiguación, encuesta; pregunta
inquisition [,ɪnkwɪ'zɪʃən] *s* inquisición
inquisitive [ɪn'kwɪzɪtɪv] *adj* curioso, preguntón
in'road' *s* incursión
ins. *abbr* **insulated, insurance**
insane [ɪn'sen] *adj* loco, insano
insane asylum *s* manicomio, casa de locos
insani·ty [ɪn'sænɪti] *s* (*pl* **-ties**) demencia, locura, insania
insatiable [ɪn'seʃəbəl] *adj* insaciable
inscribe [ɪn'skraɪb] *tr* inscribir; dedicar (*una obra literaria*)
inscription [ɪn'skrɪpʃən] *s* inscripción; (*of a book*) dedicatoria
inscrutable [ɪn'skrutəbel] *adj* inescrutable
insect ['ɪnsɛkt] *s* insecto
insecticide [ɪn'sɛktɪ,saɪd] *adj & s* insecticida *m*
insecure [,ɪnsɪ'kjʊr] *adj* inseguro

inseparable [ɪnˈsɛpərəbəl] *adj* inseparable

insert [ˈɪnsʌrt] *s* inserción || [ɪnˈsʌrt] *tr* insertar

insertion [ɪnˈsʌrʃən] *s* inserción; (*strip of lace*) entredós *m*

in•set [ˈɪn,sɛt] *s* intercalación || [ɪnˈsɛt] o [ˈɪn,sɛt] *v* (*pret & pp* **-set;** *ger* **-setting**) *tr* intercalar, encastrar

in′shore′ *adj* cercano a la orilla || *adv* cerca de la orilla; hacia la orilla

in′side′ *adj* interior; interno; secreto || *adv* dentro, adentro; **inside of** dentro de; **to turn inside out** volver al revés; volverse al revés || *prep* dentro de || *s* interior *m;* **insides** (coll) entrañas; **on the inside** (coll) en el secreto de las cosas

inside information *s* informes *mpl* confidenciales

insider [,ɪnˈsaɪdər] *s* persona enterada

insidious [ɪnˈsɪdɪ·əs] *adj* insidioso

in′sight′ *s* penetración

insigni•a [ɪnˈsɪgnɪ·ə] *s* (*pl* **-a** o **-as**) insignia

insignificant [,ɪnsɪgˈnɪfɪkənt] *adj* insignificante

insincere [,ɪnsɪnˈsɪr] *adj* insincero

insinuate [ɪnˈsɪnjʊ,et] *tr* insinuar

insipid [ɪnˈsɪpɪd] *adj* insípido

insist [ɪnˈsɪst] *intr* insistir

insofar as [,ɪnsoˈfɑr,æz] *conj* en cuanto

insolence [ˈɪnsələns] *s* insolencia

insolent [ˈɪnsələnt] *adj* insolente

insoluble [ɪnˈsɑljəbəl] *adj* insoluble

insolven•cy [ɪnˈsɑlvənsi] *s* (*pl* **-cies**) insolvencia

insomnia [ɪnˈsɑmnɪ·ə] *s* insomnio

insomuch [,ɪnsoˈmʌtʃ] *adv* hasta tal punto; **insomuch as** ya que, puesto que; **insomuch that** hasta el punto que

inspect [ɪnˈspɛkt] *tr* inspeccionar

inspection [ɪnˈspɛkʃən] *s* inspección

inspiration [,ɪnspɪˈreʃən] *s* inspiración

inspire [ɪnˈspaɪr] *tr & intr* inspirar

inspiring [ɪnˈspaɪrɪŋ] *adj* inspirante

inst. *abbr* **instant (***i.e.***, present month)**

Inst. *abbr* **Institute, Institution**

install [ɪnˈstɔl] *tr* instalar

installment [ɪnˈstɔlmənt] *s* instalación; entrega; **in installments** por entregas; a plazos

installment buying *s* compra a plazos

installment plan *s* pago a plazos, compra a plazos; **on the installment plan** con facilidades de pago

instance [ˈɪnstəns] *s* caso, ejemplo; **for instance** por ejemplo

instant [ˈɪnstənt] *adj* instantáneo || *s* instante *m,* momento; mes *m* corriente

instantaneous [,ɪnstənˈtenɪ·əs] *adj* instantáneo

instantly [ˈɪnstəntli] *adv* al instante

instead [ɪnˈstɛd] *adv* preferiblemente; en su lugar; **instead of** en vez de, en lugar de

in′step′ *s* empeine *m*

instigate [ˈɪnstɪ,get] *tr* instigar

in•still′ *tr* instilar

instinct [ˈɪnstɪŋkt] *s* instinto

instinctive [ɪnˈstɪŋktɪv] *adj* instintivo

institute [ˈɪnstɪ,tjut] o [ˈɪnstɪ,tut] *s* instituto || *tr* instituir

institution [,ɪnstɪˈtjuʃən] o [,ɪnstɪˈtuʃən] *s* institución

instruct [ɪnˈstrʌkt] *tr* instruir

instruction [ɪnˈstrʌkʃən] *s* instrucción

instructive [ɪnˈstrʌktɪv] *adj* instructivo

instructor [ɪnˈstrʌktər] *s* instructor *m*

instrument [ˈɪnstrəmənt] *s* instrumento || [ˈɪnstrə,mɛnt] *tr* instrumentar

instrumentalist [,ɪnstrəˈmɛntəlɪst] *s* instrumentista *mf*

instrumentali•ty [,ɪnstrəmənˈtælɪti] *s* (*pl* **-ties**) agencia, mediación

insubordinate [,ɪnsəˈbɔrdɪnɪt] *adj* insubordinado

insufferable [ɪnˈsʌfərəbəl] *adj* insufrible

insufficient [,ɪnsəˈfɪʃənt] *adj* insuficiente

insular [ˈɪnsələr] o [ˈɪnsjulər] *adj* insular; (fig) de miras estrechas

insulate [ˈɪnsə,let] *tr* aislar

insulation [,ɪnsəˈleʃən] *s* aislación

insulator [ˈɪnsə,letər] *s* aislador *m*

insulin [ˈɪnsəlɪn] *s* insulina

insult [ˈɪnsʌlt] *s* insulto || [ɪnˈsʌlt] *tr* insultar

insurance [ɪnˈʃʊrəns] *s* seguro

insure [ɪnˈʃʊr] *tr* asegurar

insurer [ɪnˈʃʊrər] *s* asegurador *m*

insurgent [ɪnˈsʌrdʒənt] *adj & s* insurgente *mf*

insurmountable [,ɪnsərˈmaʊntəbəl] *adj* insuperable

insurrection [,ɪnsəˈrɛkʃən] *s* insurrección

insusceptible [,ɪnsəˈsɛptɪbəl] *adj* insusceptible

int. *abbr* **interest, interior, internal, international**

intact [ɪnˈtækt] *adj* intacto, ileso

in′take′ *s* (*place of taking in*) entrada; (*act or amount*) toma; (mach) admisión

intake manifold *s* múltiple *m* de admisión, colector *m* de admisión

intake valve *s* válvula de admisión

intangible [ɪnˈtændʒɪbəl] *adj* intangible; vago, indefinido

integer [ˈɪntɪdʒər] *s* (arith) entero

integral [ˈɪntɪgrəl] *adj* íntegro; **integral with** solidario de || *s* conjunto

integration [,ɪntɪˈgreʃən] *s* integración

integrity [ɪnˈtɛgrɪti] *s* integridad

intellect [ˈɪntə,lɛkt] *s* intelecto; (*person*) intelectual *mf*

intellectual [,ɪntəˈlɛktʃʊ·əl] *adj & s* intelectual *mf*

intellectuali•ty [,ɪntə,lɛktʃʊˈælɪti] *s* (*pl* **-ties**) intelectualidad

intelligence [ɪnˈtɛlɪdʒəns] *s* inteligencia; información

intelligence bureau *s* departamento de inteligencia

intelligence quotient *s* cociente *m* intelectual

intelligent [ɪnˈtɛlɪdʒənt] *adj* inteligente

intelligentsia [ɪn,tɛlɪˈdʒɛntsɪ·ə] o [ɪn,tɛlɪˈgɛntsɪ·ə] *s* intelectualidad (*con-*

junto de los intelectuales de un país o región)
intelligible [ɪn'tɛlɪdʒɪbəl] *adj* inteligible
intemperance [ɪn'tɛmpərəns] *s* intemperancia
intemperate [ɪn'tɛmpərɪt] *adj* intemperante; (*climate*) riguroso
intend [ɪn'tɛnd] *tr* pensar, proponerse, intentar; (*to mean for a particular purpose*) destinar; (*to signify*) querer decir
intendance [ɪn'tɛndəns] *s* intendencia
intendant [ɪn'tɛndənt] *s* intendente *m*
intended [ɪn'tɛndɪd] *adj & s* (coll) prometido, prometida
intense [ɪn'tɛns] *adj* intenso
intensi•fy [ɪn'tɛnsɪ,faɪ] *v* (*pret & pp* **-fied**) *tr* intensificar, intensar; (phot) reforzar || *intr* intensificarse, intensarse
intensi•ty [ɪn'tɛnsɪti] *s* (*pl* **-ties**) intensidad
intensive [ɪn'tɛnsɪv] *adj* intensivo
intent [ɪn'tɛnt] *adj* atento; resuelto; intenso; **intent on** resuelto a || *s* (*purpose*) intento; (*meaning*) acepción, sentido; **to all intents and purposes** en realidad de verdad
intention [ɪn'tɛnʃən] *s* intención
intentional [ɪn'tɛnʃənəl] *adj* intencional, deliberado
in•ter [ɪn'tʌr] *v* (*pret & pp* **-terred;** *ger* **-terring**) *tr* enterrar
interact ['ɪntər,ækt] *s* (theat) entreacto || [,ɪntər'ækt] *intr* obrar recíprocamente
interaction [,ɪntər'ækʃən] *s* interacción
inter-American [,ɪntərə'mɛrɪkən] *adj* interamericano
inter•breed [,ɪntər'brid] *v* (*pret & pp* **-bred** ['brɛd]) *tr* entrecruzar || *intr* entrecruzarse
intercalate [ɪn'tʌrkə,let] *tr* intercalar
intercede [,ɪntər'sid] *intr* interceder
intercept [,ɪntər'sɛpt] *tr* interceptar
interceptor [,ɪntər'sɛptər] *s* interceptor *m*
interchange ['ɪntər,tʃendʒ] *s* intercambio; (*on a highway*) correspondencia || [,ɪntər'tʃendʒ] *tr* intercambiar || *intr* intercambiarse
intercollegiate [,ɪntərkə'lidʒɪ•ɪt] *adj* interescolar
intercom ['ɪntər,kɑm] *s* interfono
intercourse ['ɪntər,kors] *s* comunicación, trato; (*interchange of products, ideas, etc.*) intercambio; (*copulation*) cópula, comercio; **to have intercourse** juntarse
intercross [,ɪntər'krɔs] o [,ɪntər'krɑs] *tr* entrecruzar || *intr* entrecruzarse
interdict ['ɪntər,dɪkt] *s* entredicho || [,ɪntər'dɪkt] *tr* interdecir
interest ['ɪntərɪst] o ['ɪntrɪst] *s* interés *m;* **the interests** las grandes empresas, el grupo influyente; **to put out at interest** poner a interés || ['ɪntərɪst], ['ɪntrɪst] o ['ɪntə,rɛst] *tr* interesar
interested ['ɪntrɪstɪd] o ['ɪntə,rɛstɪd] *adj* interesado
interesting ['ɪntrɪstɪŋ] o ['ɪntə,rɛstɪŋ] *adj* interesante
interfere [,ɪntər'fɪr] *intr* inmiscuirse, injerirse, interferir; (sport) parar una jugada; **to interfere with** dificultar, impedir, interferir
interference [,ɪntər'fɪrəns] *s* injerencia, interferencia
interim ['ɪntərɪm] *adj* interino || *s* intermedio, intervalo; **in the interim** entretanto
interior [ɪn'tɪrɪ•ər] *adj & s* interior *m*
interject [,ɪntər'dʒɛkt] *tr* interponer || *intr* interponerse
interjection [,ɪntər'dʒɛkʃən] *s* interposición; exclamación; (gram) interjección
interlard [,ɪntər'lɑrd] *tr* interpolar; mechar (*la carne*)
interline [,ɪntər'laɪn] *tr* interlinear; entretelar (*una prenda de vestir*)
interlining ['ɪntər,laɪnɪŋ] *s* (*of a garment*) entretela
interlink [,ɪntər'lɪŋk] *tr* eslabonar
interlock [,ɪntər'lɑk] *tr* trabar || *intr* trabarse
interlope [,ɪntər'lop] *intr* entremeterse; traficar sin derecho
interloper [,ɪntər'lopər] *s* intruso
interlude ['ɪntər,lud] *s* intervalo; (mus) interludio; (theat) intermedio
intermarriage [,ɪntər'mærɪdʒ] *s* casamiento entre parientes; casamiento entre personas de distintas razas, castas, etc.
intermediar•y [,ɪntər'midɪ,ɛri] *adj* intermediario || *s* (*pl* **-ies**) intermediario
intermediate [,ɪntər'midɪ•ɪt] *adj* intermedio
interment [ɪn'tʌrmənt] *s* entierro
intermez•zo [,ɪntər'mɛtso] o [,ɪntər'mɛdzo] *s* (*pl* **-zos** o **-zi** [tsi] o [dzi]) (mus) intermedio, intermezzo
intermingle [,ɪntər'mɪŋgəl] *tr* entremezclar || *intr* entremezclarse
intermittent [,ɪntər'mɪtənt] *adj* intermitente
intermix [,ɪntər'mɪks] *tr* entremezclar || *intr* entremezclarse
intern ['ɪntʌrn] *s* interno de hospital || [ɪn'tʌrn] *tr* internar, recluir
internal [ɪn'tʌrnəl] *adj* interno
inter'nal-combus'tion engine *s* motor *m* de explosión
internal revenue *s* rentas internas
international [,ɪntər'næʃənəl] *adj* internacional
international date line *s* línea internacional de cambio de fecha
internationalize [,ɪntər'næʃənə,laɪz] *tr* internacionalizar
internecine [,ɪntər'nisɪn] *adj* sanguinario
internee [,ɪntʌr'ni] *s* (mil) internado
internist [ɪn'tʌrnɪst] *s* internista *mf*
internment [ɪn'tʌrnmənt] *s* internamiento
internship ['ɪntʌrn,ʃɪp] *s* residencia de un médico en un hospital

interpellate [ˌɪntərˈpɛlet] o [ɪnˈtʌrpɪˌlet] *tr* interpelar
interplay [ˈɪntərˌple] *s* interacción
interpolate [ɪnˈtʌrpəˌlet] *tr* interpolar
interpose [ˌɪntərˈpoz] *tr* interponer
interpret [ɪnˈtʌrprɪt] *tr* interpretar
interpreter [ɪnˈtʌrprɪtər] *s* intérprete *mf*
interrogate [ɪnˈtɛrəˌget] *tr & intr* interrogar
interrogation [ɪnˌtɛrəˈgeʃən] *s* interrogación
interrogation mark o **point** *s* signo de interrogación
interrupt [ˌɪntəˈrʌpt] *tr* interrumpir
interscholastic [ˌɪntərskəˈlæstɪk] *adj* interescolar
intersection [ˌɪntərˈsɛkʃən] *s* (*of streets, roads, etc.*) cruce *m;* (geom) intersección
intersperse [ˌɪntərˈspʌrs] *tr* entremezclar, esparcir
interstice [ɪnˈtʌrstɪs] *s* intersticio
intertwine [ˌɪntərˈtwaɪn] *tr* entrelazar || *intr* entrelazarse
interval [ˈɪntərvəl] *s* intervalo; **at intervals** (*now and then*) de vez en cuando; (*here and there*) de trecho en trecho
intervene [ˌɪntərˈvin] *intr* intervenir
intervening [ˌɪntərˈvinɪŋ] *adj* intermedio
intervention [ˌɪntərˈvɛnʃən] *s* intervención
interview [ˈɪntərˌvju] *s* entrevista, interview *m* || *tr* entrevistarse con
inter•weave [ˌɪntərˈwiv] *v* (*pret* **-wove** [ˈwov] o **-weaved;** *pp* **-wove, woven** o **weaved**) *tr* entretejer
intestate [ɪnˈtɛstet] o [ɪnˈtɛstɪt] *adj & s* intestado
intestine [ɪnˈtɛstɪn] *s* intestino
inthrall [ɪnˈθrɔl] *tr* cautivar, encantar; esclavizar, sojuzgar
inthrone [ɪnˈθron] *tr* entronizar
intima•cy [ˈɪntɪməsi] *s* (*pl* **-cies**) intimidad
intimate [ˈɪntɪmɪt] *adj* íntimo || *s* amigo íntimo || [ˈɪntɪˌmet] *tr* insinuar, intimar
intimation [ˌɪntɪˈmeʃən] *s* insinuación
intimidate [ɪnˈtɪmɪˌdet] *tr* intimidar
intitle [ɪnˈtaɪtəl] *tr* dar derecho a; (*to give a name to; to honor with a title*) intitular
into [ˈɪntu] o [ˈɪntʊ] *prep* en; hacia; hacia el interior de
intolerant [ɪnˈtɑlərənt] *adj & s* intolerante *mf*
intomb [ɪnˈtum] *tr* sepultar
intombment [ɪnˈtummənt] *s* sepultura
intonation [ˌɪntoˈneʃən] *s* entonación
intone [ɪnˈton] *tr* entonar
intoxicant [ɪnˈtɑksɪkənt] *s* bebida alcohólica
intoxicate [ɪnˈtɑksɪˌket] *tr* embriagar, emborrachar; (*to exhilarate*) alegrar, excitar; (*to poison*) envenenar, intoxicar
intoxication [ɪnˌtɑksɪˈkeʃən] *s* embriaguez *f;* alegría, excitación; (*poisoning*) envenenamiento, intoxicación
intractable [ɪnˈtræktəbəl] *adj* intratable
intransigent [ɪnˈtrænsɪdʒənt] *adj & s* intransigente *mf*
intransitive [ɪnˈtrænsɪtɪv] *adj* intransitivo
intrench [ɪnˈtrɛntʃ] *tr* atrincherar || *intr* — **to intrench on** o **upon** infringir, violar
intrepid [ɪnˈtrɛpɪd] *adj* intrépido
intrepidity [ˌɪntrɪˈpɪdɪti] *s* intrepidez *f*
intricate [ˈɪntrɪkɪt] *adj* intrincado
intrigue [ɪnˈtrig] o [ˈɪntrig] *s* intriga; intriga amorosa, enredo amoroso || [ɪnˈtrig] *tr* (*to arouse the curiosity of*) intrigar || *intr* intrigar; tener intrigas amorosas
intrinsic(al) [ɪnˈtrɪnsɪk(əl)] *adj* intrínseco
introd. *abbr* **introduction**
introduce [ˌɪntrəˈdjus] o [ˌɪntrəˈdus] *tr* introducir; (*to make acquainted*) presentar
introduction [ˌɪntrəˈdʌkʃən] *s* introducción; (*of one person to another or others*) presentación
introductory offer [ˌɪntrəˈdʌktəri] *s* ofrecimiento de presentación, oferta preliminar
introit [ˈɪntro·ɪt] *s* (eccl) introito
introspective [ˌɪntrəˈspɛktɪv] *adj* introspectivo
introvert [ˈɪntrəˌvʌrt] *s* introvertido
intrude [ɪnˈtrud] *intr* injerirse, entremeterse
intruder [ɪnˈtrudər] *s* intruso, entremetido
intrusive [ɪnˈtrusɪv] *adj* intruso
intrust [ɪnˈtrʌst] *tr* confiar
intuition [ˌɪntʊˈɪʃən] o [ˌɪntjʊˈɪʃən] *s* intuición
inundate [ˈɪnənˌdet] *tr* inundar
inundation [ˌɪnənˈdeʃən] *s* inundación
inure [ɪnˈjʊr] *tr* acostumbrar, endurecer, aguerrir || *intr* ponerse en efecto; **to inure to** redundar en
inv. *abbr* **inventor, invoice**
invade [ɪnˈved] *tr* invadir
invader [ɪnˈvedər] *s* invasor *m*
invalid [ɪnˈvælɪd] *adj* inválido (*nulo, de ningún valor*) || [ˈɪnvəlɪd] *adj* inválido (*por viejo o por enfermo*) || [ˈɪnvəlɪd] *s* inválido
invalidate [ɪnˈvælɪˌdet] *tr* invalidar
invalidity [ˌɪnvəˈlɪdɪti] *s* invalidez *f*
invaluable [ɪnˈvæljʊ·əbəl] *adj* inestimable, inapreciable
invariable [ɪnˈvɛrɪ·əbəl] *adj* invariable
invasion [ɪnˈveʒən] *s* invasión
invective [ɪnˈvɛktɪv] *s* invectiva
inveigh [ɪnˈve] *intr* — **to inveigh against** lanzar invectivas contra
inveigle [ɪnˈvegəl] o [ɪnˈvigəl] *tr* engatusar
invent [ɪnˈvɛnt] *tr* inventar
invention [ɪnˈvɛnʃən] *s* invención, invento
inventive [ɪnˈvɛntɪv] *adj* inventivo
inventiveness [ɪnˈvɛntɪvnɪs] *s* inventiva

inventor [ɪnˈvɛntər] *s* inventor *m*
invento•ry [ˈɪnvən,tori] *s* (*pl* **-ries**) inventario ‖ *v* (*pret & pp* **-ried**) *tr* inventariar
inverse [ɪnˈvʌrs] *adj* inverso
inversion [ɪnˈvʌrʒən] o [ɪnˈvʌrʃən] *s* inversión
invert [ˈɪnvʌrt] *s* invertido ‖ [ɪnˈvʌrt] *tr* invertir
invertebrate [ɪnˈvʌrtɪ,bret] o [ɪnˈvʌrtɪbrɪt] *adj & s* invertebrado
inverted exclamation point *s* principio de admiración
inverted question mark *s* principio de interrogación
invest [ɪnˈvɛst] *tr* (*to vest, to install*) investir; invertir (*dinero*); (*to besiege*) cercar, sitiar; (*to surround, envelop*) cubrir, envolver
investigate [ɪnˈvɛstɪ,get] *tr* investigar
investigation [ɪn,vɛstɪ•geʃən] *s* investigación
investment [ɪnˈvɛstmənt] *s* (*of money*) inversión; (*with an office or dignity*) investidura; (*siege*) cerco, sitio
investor [ɪnˈvɛstər] *s* inversionista *mf*
inveterate [ɪnˈvɛtərɪt] *adj* inveterado, empedernido
invidious [ɪnˈvɪdɪ•əs] *adj* irritante, odioso, injusto
invigorate [ɪnˈvɪgə,ret] *tr* vigorizar
invigorating [ɪnˈvɪgə,retɪŋ] *adj* vigorizador, vigorizante
invincible [ɪnˈvɪnsɪbəl] *adj* invencible
invisible [ɪnˈvɪzɪbəl] *adj* invisible
invisible ink *s* tinta simpática
invitation [,ɪnvɪˈteʃən] *s* invitación, convite *m*
invite [ɪnˈvaɪt] *tr* invitar, convidar
inviting [ɪnˈvaɪtɪŋ] *adj* atractivo, seductor; (*e.g., food*) apetitoso
invoice [ˈɪnvɔɪs] *s* factura; **as per invoice** según factura ‖ *tr* facturar
invoke [ɪnˈvok] *tr* invocar; evocar, conjurar (*p.ej., los demonios*)
involuntary [ɪnˈvɑlən,tɛri] *adj* involuntario
involution [,ɪnvəˈluʃən] *s* (math) elevación a potencias, potenciación
involve [ɪnˈvɑlv] *tr* envolver, comprometer
invulnerable [ɪnˈvʌlnərəbəl] *adj* invulnerable
inward [ˈɪnwərd] *adj* interior ‖ *adv* interiormente, hacia dentro
iodide [ˈaɪ•ə,daɪd] *s* yoduro
iodine [ˈaɪ•ə,din] *s* yodo ‖ [ˈaɪ•ə,daɪn] *s* tintura de yodo
ion [ˈaɪ•ən] o [ˈaɪ•ɑn] *s* ion *m*
ionize [ˈaɪ•ə,naɪz] *tr* ionizar
IOU [ˈaɪ,oˈju] *s* (letterword) pagaré *m*
I.Q. [ˈaɪˈkju] *abbr & s* (letterword) **intelligence quotient**
Iran [ɪˈrɑn] o [aɪˈræn] *s* el Irán
Iranian [aɪˈrenɪ•ən] *adj & s* iranés *m* o iranio
Iraq [ɪˈrɑk] *s* el Irak
Ira•qi [ɪˈrɑki] *adj* iraqués o iraquiano ‖ *s* (*pl* **-qis**) iraqués *m* o iraquiano
irate [ˈaɪret] o [aɪˈret] *adj* airado
ire [aɪr] *s* ira, cólera
Ireland [ˈaɪrlənd] *s* Irlanda
iris [ˈaɪrɪs] *s* (*of the eye*) iris *m;* (*rainbow*) iris, arco iris; (bot) lirio
Irish [ˈaɪrɪʃ] *adj* irlandés ‖ *s* (*language*) irlandés *m;* whisky *m* de Irlanda; **the Irish** los irlandeses
Irish•man [ˈaɪrɪʃmən] *s* (*pl* **-men** [mən]) irlandés *m*
Irish stew *s* guisado de carne con patatas y cebollas
I′rish•wom′an *s* (*pl* **-wom′en**) irlandesa
irk [ʌrk] *tr* fastidiar, molestar
irksome [ˈʌrksəm] *adj* fastidioso, molesto
iron [ˈaɪ•ərn] *adj* férreo ‖ *s* hierro; (*implement used to press or smooth clothes*) plancha; **irons** (*fetters*) hierros, grilletes *mpl;* **strike while the iron is hot** a hierro caliente batir de repente ‖ *tr* planchar (*la ropa*); **to iron out** allanar (*una dificultad*)
i′ron-bound′ *adj* zunchado con hierro; (*unyielding*) férreo, duro, inflexible; (*rock-bound*) escabroso, rocoso
ironclad [ˈaɪ•ərn,klæd] *adj* acorazado, blindado; inflexible, exigente
iron curtain *s* (fig) telón *m* de hierro, cortina de hierro
iron digestion *s* estómago de avestruz
iron horse *s* (coll) locomotora
ironic(al) [aɪˈrɑnɪk(əl)] *adj* irónico
ironing [ˈaɪ•ərnɪŋ] *s* planchado; ropa planchada; ropa por planchar
ironing board *s* tabla de planchar
iron lung *s* pulmón *m* de acero o de hierro
i′ron•ware′ *s* ferretería
iron will *s* voluntad de hierro
i′ron•work′ *s* herraje *m;* **ironworks** ferrería, herrería
i′ron•work′er *s* herrero de grueso; (*metalworker*) cerrajero
iro•ny [ˈaɪrəni] *s* (*pl* **-nies**) ironía
irradiate [ɪˈredɪ,et] *tr* irradiar; (med) someter a radiación ‖ *intr* irradiar
irrational [ɪˈræʃənəl] *adj* irracional
irrecoverable [,ɪrɪˈkʌvərəbəl] *adj* incobrable, irrecuperable
irredeemable [,ɪrɪˈdiməbəl] *adj* irredimible
irrefutable [,ɪrɪˈfjutəbəl] o [ɪˈrɛfjutəbəl] *adj* irrebatible
irregular [ɪˈrɛgjələr] *adj* irregular ‖ *s* (mil) irregular *m*
irrelevance [ɪˈrɛləvəns] *s* **impertinencia**, inaplicabilidad
irrelevant [ɪˈrɛləvənt] *adj* impertinente, inaplicable
irreligious [,ɪrɪˈlɪdʒəs] *adj* irreligioso
irremediable [,ɪrɪˈmidɪ•əbəl] *adj* irremediable
irremovable [,ɪrɪˈmuvəbəl] *adj* inamovible
irreparable [ɪˈrɛpərəbəl] *adj* irreparable
irreplaceable [,ɪrɪˈplesəbəl] *adj* insubstituíble, irreemplazable
irrepressible [,ɪrɪˈprɛsɪbəl] *adj* irreprimible, incontenible
irreproachable [,ɪrɪˈprotʃəbəl] *adj* irreprochable
irresistible [,ɪrɪˈzɪstɪbəl] *adj* irresistible
irrespective [,ɪrɪˈspɛktɪv] *adj* — **irre-**

spective of sin hacer caso de, independiente de
irresponsible [ˌɪrɪ'spɑnsɪbəl] *adj* irresponsable
irretrievable [ˌɪrɪ'trivəbəl] *adj* irrecuperable
irreverent [ɪ'rɛvərənt] *adj* irreverente
irrevocable [ɪ'rɛvəkəbəl] *adj* irrevocable
irrigate ['ɪrɪˌget] *tr* irrigar
irrigation [ˌɪrɪ'geʃən] *s* irrigación
irritant ['ɪrɪtənt] *adj & s* irritante *m*
irritate ['ɪrɪˌtet] *tr* irritar
irruption [ɪ'rʌpʃən] *s* irrupción
is. *abbr* **island**
isinglass ['aɪzɪŋˌglæs] o ['aɪzɪŋˌglɑs] *s* (*form of gelatine*) cola de pescado, colapez *f;* mica
isl. *abbr* **island**
Islam ['ɪsləm] o [ɪs'lɑm] *s* el Islam
island ['aɪlənd] *adj* isleño ‖ *s* isla
islander ['aɪləndər] *s* isleño
isle [aɪl] *s* isleta
isolate ['aɪsəˌlet] o ['ɪsəˌlet] *tr* aislar
isolation [ˌaɪsə'leʃən] o [ˌɪsə'leʃən] *s* aislamiento
isolationist [ˌaɪsə'leʃənɪst] o [ˌɪsə'leʃənɪst] *s* aislacionista *mf*
isosceles [aɪ'sɑsəˌliz] *adj* isosceles
isotope ['aɪsəˌtop] *s* isótopo
Israe•li [ɪz'reli] *adj* israelí ‖ *s* (*pl* **-lis** [liz]) israelí *mf*
Israelite ['ɪzrɪ•əˌlaɪt] *adj & s* israelita *mf*
issuance ['ɪʃu•əns] *s* emisión, expedición
issue ['ɪʃu] *s* (*outgoing; outlet*) salida; (*result*) consecuencia, resultado; (*offspring*) descendencia, sucesión; (*of a magazine*) edición, impresión, tirada, número; (*e.g., of a bond*) emisión; (*yield, profit*) beneficios, producto; punto en disputa; (pathol) flujo; **at issue** en disputa; **to face the issue** afrontar la situación; **to force the issue** forzar la solución; **to take issue with** llevar la contraria a ‖ *tr* publicar, dar a luz (*un nuevo libro, una revista, etc.*); emitir, expedir (*títulos, obligaciones, etc.*); distribuir (*ropa, alimento*) ‖ *intr* salir; **to issue from** provenir de
isthmus ['ɪsməs] *s* istmo
it [ɪt] *pron pers* (aplícase a cosas inanimadas, a niños de teta, a animales cuyo sexo no se conoce; y muchas veces no se traduce) él, ella; lo, la; **it is I** soy yo; **it is snowing** nieva; **it is three o'clock** son las tres
ital. *abbr* **italics**
Ital. *abbr* **Italian, Italy**
Italian [ɪ'tæljən] *adj & s* italiano
italic [ɪ'tælɪk] *adj* (typ) itálico ‖ **italics** *s* (typ) itálica, bastardilla ‖ **Italic** *adj* itálico
italicize [ɪ'tælɪˌsaɪz] *tr* imprimir en bastardilla; subrayar
Italy ['ɪtəli] *s* Italia
itch [ɪtʃ] *s* comezón *f;* (pathol) sarna; (*eagerness*) (fig) comezón, prurito ‖ *tr* dar comezón a ‖ *intr* picar; **to itch to** tener prurito por
itch•y ['ɪtʃi] *adj* (*comp* **-ier;** *super* **-iest**) picante, hormigoso; (pathol) sarnoso
item ['aɪtəm] *s* artículo; noticia, suelto; (*in an account*) partida
itemize ['aɪtəˌmaɪz] *tr* particularizar, especificar, pormenorizar
itinerant [aɪ'tɪnərənt] o [ɪ'tɪnərənt] *adj* ambulante, errante ‖ *s* viandante *mf*
itinerar•y [aɪ'tɪnəˌrɛri] o [ɪ'tɪnəˌrɛri] *adj* itinerario ‖ *s* (*pl* **-ies**) itinerario
its [ɪts] *adj poss* su ‖ *pron poss* el suyo; suyo
itself [ɪt'sɛlf] *pron pers* mismo; sí, sí mismo; se
ivied ['aɪvid] *adj* cubierto de hiedra
ivo•ry ['aɪvəri] *adj* marfileño ‖ *s* (*pl* **-ries**) marfil *m;* **ivories** (slang) teclas del piano; (slang) bolas de billar; (*dice*) (slang) dados; (slang) dientes *mpl*
ivory tower *s* (fig) torre *f* de marfil
ivy ['aɪvi] *s* (*pl* **ivies**) hiedra

J

J, j [dʒe] décima letra del alfabeto inglés
J. *abbr* **Judge, Justice**
jab [dʒæb] *s* hurgonazo; (*prick*) pinchazo; (*with elbow*) codazo ‖ *v* (*pret & pp* **jabbed;** *ger* **jabbing**) *tr* hurgonear; dar un codazo a ‖ *intr* hurgonear
jabber ['dʒæbər] *s* chapurreo ‖ *tr & intr* chapurrear
jabot [dʒæ'bo] o ['dʒæbo] *s* chorrera
jack [dʒæk] *s* (*for lifting heavy objects*) gato, cric *m;* (*fellow*) mozo, sujeto; (*jackass*) asno, burro; (*in card games*) sota, valet *m;* (*small ball for bowling*) boliche *m;* (*jackstone*) cantillo; (*device for turning a spit*) torno de asador; (*figure which strikes a clock bell*) jaquemar *m;* (*to remove a boot*) sacabotas *m;* marinero; (*flag at the bow*) (naut) yac *m;* (rad & telv) jack *m;* (elec) caja de enchufe; (slang) dinero; **every man Jack** cada hijo de vecino; **jacks** cantillos, juego de los cantillos ‖ *tr* — **to jack up** alzar con el gato; (coll) subir (*sueldos, precios, etc.*); (coll) recordar su obligación a
jackal ['dʒækəl] *s* chacal *m*
jackanapes ['dʒækəˌneps] *s* mequetrefe *m*
jack'ass' *s* asno, burro
jack'daw' *s* corneja
jacket ['dʒækɪt] *s* chaqueta; (*folded*

paper) cubierta, envoltura; (*paper cover of a book*) sobrecubierta; (*metal casing*) camisa
jack'ham'mer *s* martillo perforador
jack'-in-the-box' *s* caja de sorpresa, jugete-sorpresa *m,* muñeco en una caja de resorte
jack'knife' *s* (*pl* **-knives'**) navaja de bolsillo; (*fancy dive*) salto de carpa
jack of all trades *s* hombre que hace toda clase de oficios, dije *m*
jack-o'-lantern ['dʒækə,læntərn] *s* fuego fatuo; linterna hecha con una calabaza cortada de modo que remede una cabeza humana
jack pot *s* — **to hit the jack pot** (slang) ponerse las botas
jack rabbit *s* liebre grande norteamericana
jack'screw' *s* cric *m* o gato de tornillo
jack'stone' *s* cantillo; **jackstones** cantillos, juego de los cantillos
jack'-tar' *s* (coll) marinero
jade [dʒed] *adj* verdoso como el jade || *s* (*ornamental stone*) jade *m;* verde *m* de jade; (*worn-out horse*) jamelgo; picarona, mujerzuela || *tr* cansar, ahitar, saciar
jaded ['dʒedɪd] *adj* ahito, saciado
jag [dʒæg] *s* diente *m,* púa; **to have a jag on** (slang) estar borracho
jagged ['dʒægɪd] *adj* dentado, mellado; rasgado en sietes
jaguar ['dʒægwɑr] *s* jaguar *m*
jail [dʒel] *s* cárcel *f;* **to break jail** escaparse de la cárcel || *tr* encarcelar
jail'bird' *s* (coll) preso, encarcelado; (coll) infractor *m* habitual
jail delivery *s* evasión de la cárcel
jailer ['dʒelər] *s* carcelero
jalop·y [dʒə'lɑpi] *s* (*pl* **-ies**) automóvil viejo y ruinoso
jam [dʒæm] *s* apiñadura, apretura; (*e.g., in traffic*) embotellamiento, bloqueo; (*preserve*) compota, conserva; (*difficult situation*) (coll) aprieto, apuros || *v* (*pret & pp* **jammed;** *ger* **jamming**) *tr* apiñar, apretujar; machucarse (*p.ej., un dedo*); (rad) perturbar, sabotear; **to jam on the brakes** frenar de golpe
Jamaican [dʒə'mekən] *adj & s* jamaicano; jamaiquino (Am)
jamb [dʒæm] *s* jamba
jamboree [,dʒæmbə'ri] *s* (coll) francachela, holgorio; reunión de niños exploradores
jamming ['dʒæmɪŋ] *s* radioperturbación
jam nut *s* contratuerca
jam-packed ['dʒæm'pækt] *adj* (coll) apiñado, apretujado, atestado
jam session *s* reunión de músicos de jazz para tocar improvisaciones
jangle ['dʒæŋgəl] *s* cencerreo; altercado, riña || *tr* hacer sonar con ruido discordante || *intr* cencerrear; reñir
janitor ['dʒænɪtər] *s* portero, conserje *m*
janitress ['dʒænɪtrɪs] *s* portera
January ['dʒænjʊ,ɛri] *s* enero
ja·pan [dʒə'pæn] *s* laca japonesa; obra japonesa laqueada; aceite *m* secante japonés || *v* (*pret & pp* **-panned;** *ger* **-panning**) *tr* barnizar, charolar, laquear con laca japonesa || **Japan** *s* el Japón
Japa·nese [,dʒæpə'niz] *adj* japonés || *s* (*pl* **-nese**) japonés *m*
Japanese beetle *s* escarabajo japonés
Japanese lantern *s* farolillo veneciano
Japanese persimmon *s* caqui *m*
jar [dʒɑr] *s* tarro; (*e.g., of olives*) frasco; (*of a storage battery*) recipiente *m;* (*jolt*) sacudida; ruido desapacible; sorpresa desagradable; **on the jar** (*said of a door*) entreabierto, entornado || *v* (*pret & pp* **jarred;** *ger* **jarring**) *tr* sacudir; chocar; (*with a noise*) traquetear || *intr* sacudirse; traquetear; disputar; **to jar on** irritar
jardiniere [,dʒɑrdɪ'nɪr] *s* (*stand*) jardinera; (*pot, bowl*) florero
jargon ['dʒɑrgən] *s* jerga, jerigonza
jasmine ['dʒæsmɪn] o ['dʒæzmɪn] *s* jazmín *m*
jasper ['dʒæspər] *s* jaspe *m*
jaundice ['dʒɔndɪs] o ['dʒɑndɪs] *s* ictericia; (fig) envidia, celos, negro humor
jaundiced ['dʒɔndɪst] o ['dʒɑndɪst] *adj* ictericiado; (fig) avinagrado
jaunt [dʒɔnt] o [dʒɑnt] *s* caminata, excursión, paseo
jaun·ty ['dʒɔnti] o ['dʒɑnti] *adj* (*comp* **-tier;** *super* **-tiest**) airoso, gallardo, vivo; elegante, de buen gusto
Java·nese [,dʒævə'niz] *adj* javanés || *s* (*pl* **-nese**) javanés *m*
javelin ['dʒævlɪn] o ['dʒævəlɪn] *s* jabalina
jaw [dʒɔ] *s* mandíbula, quijada; **into the jaws of death** a las garras de la muerte; **jaws** boca, garganta || *tr* (slang) regañar || *intr* (slang) regañar; (slang) chacharear, chismear
jaw'bone' *s* mandíbula, quijada
jaw'break'er *s* (*word*) (coll) trabalenguas *m;* (*candy*) (coll) hinchabocas *m;* (mach) trituradora de quijadas
jay [dʒe] *s* (orn) arrendajo; (coll) tonto, necio
jay'walk' *intr* (coll) cruzar la calle descuidadamente
jay'walk'er *s* (coll) peatón descuidado
jazz [dʒæz] *s* (mus) jazz *m;* (coll) animación, viveza || *tr* — **to jazz up** (coll) animar, dar viveza a
jazz band *s* orquesta de jazz
J.C. *abbr* **Jesus Christ, Julius Caesar**
jct. *abbr* **junction**
jealous ['dʒɛləs] *adj* celoso; envidioso; (*watchful in keeping or guarding something*) solícito, vigilante
jealous·y ['dʒɛləsi] *s* (*pl* **-ies**) celosía, celos; envidia; solicitud, vigilancia
jean [dʒin] *s* dril *m;* **jeans** pantalones *mpl* de dril
Jeanne d'Arc [,ʒɑn'dɑrk] *s* Juana de Arco
jeep [dʒip] *s* jip *m,* pequeño automóvil de propulsión total
jeer [dʒɪr] *s* befa, mofa, vaya || *tr*

befar || *intr* mofarse; **to jeer at** befar, mofarse de

jelab [dʒəˈlɑb] *s* chilaba

jell [dʒɛl] *s* jalea || *intr* (*to become jellylike*) cuajarse; (*to take hold, catch on*) (fig) cuajar

jel·ly [ˈdʒɛli] *s* (*pl* **-lies**) jalea || *v* (*pret & pp*) *tr* convertir en jalea || *intr* convertirse en jalea

jel'ly·fish' *s* aguamala, medusa; (*weak person*) (coll) calzonazos *m*

jeopardize [ˈdʒɛpərˌdaɪz] *tr* arriesgar, exponer, poner en peligro

jeopardy [ˈdʒɛpərdi] *s* riesgo, peligro

jeremiad [ˌdʒɛrɪˈmaɪ·æd] *s* jeremiada

Jericho [ˈdʒɛrɪˌko] *s* Jericó

jerk [dʒʌrk] *s* arranque *m*, estirón *m*, tirón *m*; tic *m*, espasmo muscular; **by jerks** a sacudidas || *tr* mover de un tirón; arrojar de un tirón; atasajar (*carne*) || *intr* avanzar a tirones

jerked beef *s* tasajo

jerkin [ˈdʒʌrkɪn] *s* jubón *m*, justillo

jerk'wa'ter train *s* (coll) tren de ferrocarril económico

jerk·y [ˈdʒʌrki] *adj* (*comp* **-ier;** *super* **-iest**) (*road; style*) desigual; que va dando tumbos, que anda a tirones

Jerome [dʒəˈrom] *s* Jerónimo

jersey [ˈdʒʌrsi] *s* jersey *m*, chaqueta de punto

Jerusalem [dʒɪˈrusələm] *s* Jerusalén

jest [dʒɛst] *s* broma, chanza, chiste *m*; cosa de risa; **in jest** en broma || *intr* bromear

jester [ˈdʒɛstər] *s* bromista *mf*, burlón *m*; (*professional fool of medieval rulers*) bufón *m*

Jesuit [ˈdʒɛʒʊ·ɪt] o [ˈdʒɛzjʊ·ɪt] *adj & s* jesuíta *m*

Jesuitic(al) [ˌdʒɛʒʊˈɪtɪk(əl)] o [ˌdʒɛzjʊˈɪtɪk(əl)] *adj* jesuítico

Jesus [ˈdʒizəs] *s* Jesús *m*

Jesus Christ *s* Jesucristo

jet [dʒɛt] *adj* de azabache; azabachado || *s* (*of a fountain*) surtidor *m*; (*of gas*) mechero; (*stream shooting forth from nozzle, etc.*) chorro; avión *m* a reacción, avión de chorro; (*hard black mineral; lustrous black*) azabache *m* || *v* (*pret & pp* **jetted;** *ger* **jetting**) *tr* arrojar en chorro || *intr* chorrear, salir en chorro; volar en avión de chorro

jet age *s* era de los aviones de chorro

jet'-black' *adj* azabachado

jet bomber *s* bombardero de reacción a chorro

jet coal *s* carbón *m* de bujía, carbón de llama larga

jet engine *s* motor *m* a chorro, motor de reacción

jet fighter *s* caza *m* de reacción, cazarreactor *m*

jet'lin'er *s* avión *m* de travesía con propulsión a chorro

jet plane *s* avión *m* de chorro

jet propulsion *s* propulsión a chorro, propulsión de escape

jetsam [ˈdʒɛtsəm] *s* (naut) echazón *f*; cosas desechadas

jet stream *s* escape *m* de un motor cohete; (meteor) chorros de viento (*que soplan de oeste a este a la altura de 10 kilómetros*)

jettison [ˈdʒɛtɪsən] *s* (naut) echazón *f* || *tr* (naut) echar al mar; desechar, rechazar

jettison gear *s* (aer) lanzador *m*

jet·ty [ˈdʒɛti] *s* (*pl* **-ties**) (*structure projecting into sea to protect harbor*) escollera, malecón *m*; (*wharf*) muelle *m*, desembarcadero

Jew [dʒu] *s* judío

jewel [ˈdʒu·əl] *s* piedra preciosa; (*valuable personal ornament*) alhaja, joya; (*of a watch*) rubí *m*; (*article of costume jewelry*) joya de imitación; (*highly prized person or thing*) alhaja, joya

jewel case *s* guardajoyas *m*, estuche *m*, joyero

jeweler o **jeweller** [ˈdʒu·ələr] *s* joyero; relojero

jewelry [ˈdʒu·əlri] *s* joyería, joyas

jewelry shop *s* joyería; relojería

Jewess [ˈdʒu·ɪs] *s* judía

jew'fish' *s* mero

Jewish [ˈdʒu·ɪʃ] *adj* judío

Jew·ry [ˈdʒu·ri] *s* (*pl* **-ries**) judería

jews'-harp o **jew's-harp** [ˈdjuzˌhɑrp] *s* birimbao

jib [dʒɪb] *s* (*of a crane*) aguilón *m*, pescante *m*; (naut) foque *m*

jib boom *s* (naut) botalón *m* de foque

jibe [dʒaɪb] *s* remoque *m*, mofa || *intr* mofarse; (coll) concordar (*dos cosas*); **to jibe at** mofarse de

jif·fy [ˈdʒɪfi] *s* (*pl* **-fies**) — **in a jiffy** (coll) en un santiamén

jig [dʒɪg] *s* (*dance and music*) giga; **the jig is up** (slang) ya se acabó todo, estamos perdidos

jigger [ˈdʒɪgər] *s* (*for fishing*) anzuelo de cuchara; (*for separating ore*) criba de vaivén; (*flea*) nigua; (*gadget*) cosilla, chisme *m*, dispositivo; vasito para medir el licor de un coctel (*onza y media*)

jiggle [ˈdʒɪgəl] *s* zangoloteo || *tr* zangolotear || *intr* zangolotearse

jig saw *s* sierra de vaivén

jig'saw' puzzle *s* rompecabezas *m* (*figura que ha sido cortada caprichosamente en trozos menudos y que hay que recomponer*)

jilt [dʒɪlt] *tr* dar calabazas a (*un novio*)

jim·my [ˈdʒɪmi] *s* (*pl* **-mies**) palanqueta || *v* (*pret & pp* **-mied**) *tr* forzar con palanqueta; **to jimmy open** abrir con palanqueta

jingle [ˈdʒɪŋgəl] *s* (*small bell*) cascabel *m*; (*of tambourine*) sonaja; (*sound*) cascabeleo; rima infantil; (rad) anuncio rimado y cantado || *tr* hacer sonar || *intr* cascabelear

jin·go [ˈdʒɪŋgo] *adj* jingoísta || *s* (*pl* **-goes**) jingoísta *mf*; **by jingo!** (coll) ¡caramba!

jingoism [ˈdʒɪŋgoˌɪzəm] *s* jingoísmo

jinx [dʒɪŋks] *s* gafe *m* || *tr* (coll) traer mala suerte a

jitters [ˈdʒɪtərz] *spl* (coll) inquietud, nerviosidad; **to give the jitters to**

(coll) poner nervioso; **to have the jitters** (coll) ponerse nervioso

jittery [ˈdʒɪtəri] *adj* (coll) nervioso

Joan of Arc [ˈdʒon əv ˈɑrk] *s* Juana de Arco

job [dʒɑb] *s* (*piece of work*) trabajo; (*task, chore*) quehacer *m,* tarea; (*work done by contract*) destajo; (*employment*) empleo, oficio; (coll) robo; **by the job** a destajo; **on the job** trabajando de aprendiz; (slang) vigilante, atento a sus obligaciones; **to be out of a job** estar desocupado, estar sin trabajo; **to lie down on the job** (slang) echarse en el surco, estirar la pierna

job analysis *s* análisis *m* ocupacional

jobber [ˈdʒɑbər] *s* comerciante medianero; (*pieceworker*) destajero; (*dishonest official*) agiotista *m*

job'hold'er *s* empleado; (*in the government*) burócrata *mf*

jobless [ˈjɑblɪs] *adj* desocupado, sin empleo

job lot *s* saldo de mercancías

job printer *s* impresor *m* de remiendos

job printing *s* remiendo

jockey [ˈdʒɑki] *s* jockey *m* ‖ *tr* montar (*un caballo*) en la pista; maniobrar; embaucar

jockstrap [ˈdʒɑk ˌstræp] *s* suspensorio (*para sostener el escroto*)

jocose [dʒoˈkos] *adj* jocoso

jocular [ˈdʒɑkjələr] *adj* jocoso, festivo

jog [dʒɑg] *s* golpecito; (*to the memory*) estímulo; trote corto ‖ *v* (*pret & pp* **jogged;** *ger* **jogging**) *tr* empujar levemente; estimular (*la memoria*) ‖ *intr* — **to jog along** avanzar al trote corto

jog trot *s* trote *m* de perro; (fig) rutina

John [dʒɑn] *s* Juan *m*

John Bull *s* el inglés típico, el pueblo inglés

John Hancock [ˈhænkɑk] *s* (coll) la firma de uno

johnnycake [ˈdʒɑni ˌkek] *s* pan *m* de maíz

John'ny-come'-late'ly *s* (coll) recién llegado

John'ny-jump'-up' *s* (*pansy*) pensamiento, trinitaria; violeta

John'ny-on-the-spot' *s* (coll) el que está siempre presente y listo

John the Baptist *s* San Juan Bautista

join [dʒɔɪn] *tr* juntar, unir, ensamblar; asociarse a, unirse a; incorporarse a, ingresar en; abrazar (*un partido*); hacerse socio de (*una asociación*); alistarse en (*el ejército*); trabar (*batalla*); desaguar en (*el océano*) ‖ *intr* juntarse, unirse; confluir (*p.ej., dos ríos*)

joiner [ˈdʒɔɪnər] *s* carpintero; (coll) el que tiene la manía de incorporarse a muchas asociaciones

joint [dʒɔɪnt] *s* (*in a pipe*) empalme *m,* juntura; (*of bones*) articulación, juntura, coyuntura; (*backbone of book*) nervura; (*hinge of book*) cartivana; (*in woodwork*) emsambladura; (*of meat*) tajada; (elec) empalme *m;* (*gambling den*) (slang) garito; (slang) restaurante *m* de mala muerte; **out of joint** desencajado, descoyuntado; (fig) en desorden, desbarajustado; **to throw out of joint** descoyuntarse (*p.ej., el brazo*)

joint account *s* cuenta en común

Joint Chiefs of Staff *spl* (U.S.A.) Estado mayor conjunto

jointly [ˈdʒɔɪntli] *adv* juntamente, en común

joint owner *s* condueño

joint session *s* sesión conjunta

joint'-stock' company *s* sociedad anónima, compañía por acciones

joist [dʒɔɪst] *s* viga

joke [dʒok] *s* broma, chiste *m;* (*trifling matter*) cosa de reír; (*person laughed at*) bufón *m,* hazmerreír *m;* **no joke** cosa seria; **to tell a joke** contar un chiste; **to play a joke on** gastar una broma a ‖ *tr* — **to joke one's way into** conseguir (*p.ej., un empleo*) burla burlando ‖ *intr* bromear, hablar en broma; **joking aside** o **no joking** burlas aparte

joke book *s* libro de chistes

joker [ˈdʒokər] *s* bromista *mf;* (*wise guy*) sábelotodo; (*playing card*) comodín *m;* (*hidden provision*) cláusula cngañadora

jol·ly [ˈdʒɑli] *adj* (*comp* **-lier;** *super* **-liest**) alegre, festivo ‖ *adv* (coll) muy, harto ‖ *v* (*pret & pp* **-lied**) *tr* (coll) candonguear

jolt [dʒolt] *s* sacudida ‖ *tr* sacudir ‖ *intr* dar tumbos

Jonah [ˈdʒonə] *s* Jonás *m;* (fig) ave *f* de mal agüero

jongleur [ˈdʒɑŋglər] *s* juglar *m,* trovador *m*

jonquil [ˈdʒɑŋkwɪl] *s* junquillo

Jordan [ˈdʒɔrdən] *s* (*country*) Jordania; (*river*) Jordán *m*

Jordan almond *s* almendra de Málaga

Jordanian [dʒɔrˈdenɪ·ən] *adj & s* jordano

josh [dʒɑʃ] *tr* (coll) dar broma a ‖ *intr* dar broma

jostle [ˈdʒɑsəl] *s* empellón *m,* empujón *m* ‖ *tr* empellar, empujar ‖ *intr* chocar, encontrarse; avanzar a fuerza de empujones o codazos

jot [dʒɑt] *s* — **I don't care a jot for** no se me da un bledo de ‖ *v* (*pret & pp* **jotted;** *ger* **jotting**) *tr* — **to jot down** apuntar, anotar

jounce [dʒauns] *s* sacudida ‖ *tr* sacudir ‖ *intr* dar tumbos

journal [ˈdʒʌrnəl] *s* (*newspaper*) periódico; (*magazine*) revista; (*daily record*) diario; (com) libro diario; (naut) cuaderno de bitácora; (mach) gorrón *m,* muñón *m*

journalese [ˌdʒʌrnəˈliz] *s* lenguaje periodístico

journalism [ˈdʒʌrnəˌlɪzəm] *s* periodismo

journalist [ˈdʒʌrnəlɪst] *s* periodista *mf*

journalistic [ˌdʒʌrnəˈlɪstɪk] *adj* periodístico

journey [ˈdʒʌrni] *s* viaje *m* ‖ *intr* viajar

journey•man ['dʒʌrnimən] *s* (*pl* **-men** [mən]) oficial *m*
joust [dʒʌst] o [dʒust] o [dʒaʊst] *s* justa || *intr* justar
jovial ['dʒovɪ·əl] *adj* jovial
joviality [,dʒovɪ'ælɪti] *s* jovialidad
jowl [dʒaʊl] *s* (*cheek*) moflete *m;* (*jawbone*) quijada; (*of cattle*) papada; (*of fowl*) barba
joy [dʒɔɪ] *s* alegría, regocijo; **to leap with joy** saltar de gozo
joyful ['dʒɔɪfəl] *adj* alegre; **joyful over** gozoso con o de
joyless ['dʒɔɪlɪs] *adj* triste, sin alegría
joyous ['dʒɔɪ·əs] *adj* alegre
joy ride *s* (coll) paseo de recreo en coche; (coll) paseo alocado en coche
J.P. *abbr* **Justice of the Peace**
Jr. *abbr* **junior**
jubilant ['dʒubɪlənt] *adj* jubiloso
jubilation [,dʒubɪ'leʃən] *s* júbilo, viva alegría
jubilee ['dʒubɪ,li] *s* (*jubilation*) júbilo; aniversario; quincuagésimo aniversario; (eccl) jubileo
Judaism ['dʒude,ɪzəm] *s* judaísmo
judge [dʒʌdʒ] *s* juez *m;* **to be a good judge of** ser buen juez de o en || *tr & intr* juzgar; **judging by** a juzgar por
judge advocate *s* (*in the army*) auditor *m* de guerra; (*in the navy*) auditor de marina
judgeship ['dʒʌdʒʃɪp] *s* judicatura
judgment ['dʒʌdʒmənt] *s* juicio; (*legal decision*) sentencia, fallo
judgment day *s* día *m* del juicio
judgment seat *s* tribunal *m*
judicature ['dʒudɪkətʃər] *s* judicatura
judicial [dʒu'dɪʃəl] *adj* judicial; (*becoming a judge*) crítico, juicioso
judiciar•y [dʒu'dɪʃɪ,ɛri] *adj* judicial || *s* (*pl* **-ies**) (*judges of a city, country, etc.*) judicatura; (*branch of government that administers justice*) poder *m* judicial
judicious [dʒu'dɪʃəs] *adj* juicioso
jug [dʒʌg] *s* botija, jarra, cántaro; (*jail*) (slang) chirona
juggle ['dʒʌgəl] *s* juego de manos; (*trick, deception*) trampa || *tr* hacer suertes con (*p.ej., bolas*); alterar fraudulentamente, falsear (*cuentas, documentos, etc.*); **to juggle away** escamotear || *intr* hacer suertes; hacer trampas
juggler ['dʒʌglər] *s* malabarista *mf;* impostor *m*
juggling ['dʒʌglɪŋ] *s* juegos malabares
Jugoslav ['jugo'slɑv] *adj & s* yugoeslavo
Jugoslavia ['jugo'slɑvɪ·ə] *s* Yugoeslavia
jugular ['dʒʌgjələr] o ['dʒugjələr] *adj & s* yugular *f*
juice [dʒus] *s* jugo, zumo; (*natural fluid of an animal body*) jugo; (slang) electricidad; (slang) gasolina; **to stew in one's own juice** (coll) freír en su aceite
juic•y ['dʒusi] *adj* (*comp* **-ier;** *super* **-iest**) jugoso, zumoso; (*interesting, spicy*) picante
jukebox ['dʒuk,bɑks] *s* tocadiscos *m* tragamonedas
julep ['dʒulɪp] *s* julepe *m*
julienne [,dʒulɪ'ɛn] *s* sopa juliana
July [dʒu'laɪ] *s* julio
jumble ['dʒʌmbəl] *s* revoltijo, masa confusa || *tr* emburujar, revolver
jum•bo ['dʒʌmbo] *adj* (coll) enorme, colosal || *s* (*pl* **-bos**) (*large clumsy person*) (coll) elefante *m;* (coll) objeto enorme
jump [dʒʌmp] *s* salto; (*in a parachute*) lanzamiento; (*of prices*) alza repentina; **to be always on the jump** (coll) andar siempre de aquí para allí; **to get** o **to have the jump on** (slang) ganar la ventaja a || *tr* saltar; hacer saltar (*a un caballo*); (*in checkers*) comer; salir (*un tren*) fuera de (*el carril*) || *intr* saltar; (*in a parachute from an airplane*) lanzarse; pasar del tope (*el carro de la máquina de escribir*); **to jump at** apresurarse a aceptar (*un convite*); apresurarse a aprovechar (*la oportunidad*); **to jump on** saltar a (*un tren*); (slang) regañar, criticar; **to jump over** saltar por, pasar de un salto; saltar (*la página de un libro*); **to jump to a conclusion** sacar una conclusión precipitadamente
jumper ['dʒʌmpər] *s* saltador *m;* blusa de obrero; **jumpers** traje holgado de juego para niños
jumping jack ['dʒʌmpɪŋ] *s* títere *m*
jump'ing-off' place *s* fin *m* del camino
jump seat *s* estrapontín *m,* traspuntín *m*
jump spark *s* (elec) chispa de entrehierro
jump wire *s* (elec) alambre *m* de cierre
jump•y ['dʒʌmpi] *adj* (*comp* **-ier;** *super* **-iest**) saltón; asustadizo, nervioso
junc. *abbr* **junction**
junction ['dʒʌŋkʃən] *s* juntura, unión; (*of pieces of wood*) ensambladura; (*of two rivers*) confluencia; (*rail connection*) empalme *m;* (rr) estación de empalme
juncture ['dʒʌŋktʃər] *s* juntura, unión; (*time, occasion*) coyuntura; **at this juncture** a esta sazón, a estas alturas
June [dʒun] *s* junio
jungle ['dʒʌŋgəl] *s* jungla, selva; revoltijo, maraña
junior ['dʒunjər] *adj* menor, de menor edad; joven; del penúltimo año; hijo, p.ej., **John Jones, Junior** Juan Jones, hijo || *s* menor *m;* socio menor; alumno del penúltimo año
junior college *s* escuela de estudios universitarios de primero y segundo años
junior high school *s* escuela intermedia entre la primaria y la secundaria
juniper ['dʒunɪpər] *s* enebro; (*red cedar*) cedro de Virginia
juniper berry *s* enebrina
junk [dʒʌŋk] *s* chatarra, hierro viejo; ropa vieja; (*useless stuff*) (coll) trastos viejos, baratijas viejas; (*old cable*) jarcia trozada; (*Chinese ship*) junco; (naut) carne salada || *tr*

(slang) echar a la basura; reducir a hierro viejo
junk dealer *s* chatarrero, chapucero
junket ['dʒʌŋkɪt] *s* manjar *m* de leche, cuajo y azúcar; (*outing*) viaje *m* de recreo; (*trip paid out of public funds*) jira ‖ *intr* hacer un viaje de recreo; ir de jira
junk•man ['dʒʌŋk,mæn] *s* (*pl* **-men** [,mɛn]) chatarrero, chapucero; ropavejero; tripulante *m* de junco
junk room *s* leonera, trastera
junk shop *s* tienda de trastos viejos
junk yard *s* chatarrería
juridical [dʒʊ'rɪdɪkəl] *adj* jurídico
jurisdiction [,dʒʊrɪs'dɪkʃən] *s* jurisdicción
jurisprudence [,dʒʊrɪs'prudəns] *s* jurisprudencia
jurist ['dʒʊrɪst] *s* jurista *mf*
juror ['dʒʊrər] *s* (*individual*) jurado
ju•ry ['dʒʊri] *s* (*pl* **-ries**) (*group*) jurado
jury box *s* tribuna del jurado
jury•man ['dʒʊrimən] *s* (*pl* **-men** [mən]) (*individual*) jurado
Jus. P. *abbr* **justice of the peace**
just [dʒʌst] *adj* justo ‖ *adv* justamente, justo; hace poco, apenas; sólo; (coll) absolutamente; **just** + *pp* acabado de + *inf*, p.ej., **just received** acabado de recibir; recién + *pp*, p.ej., **just arrived** recién llegado; **just as** como; en el momento en que; tal como, lo mismo que; **just beyond** un poco más allá (de); **just now** hace poco; ahora mismo; **just out** acabado de aparecer, recién publicado; **to have just** + *pp* acabar de + *inf*, p.ej., **I have just arrived** acabo de llegar; **I had just arrived** acababa de llegar
justice ['dʒʌstɪs] *s* justicia; (*judge*) juez *m*; (*just deserts*) premio merecido; **to bring to justice** aprehender y condenar por justicia; **to do justice to** hacer justicia a; apreciar debidamente
justice of the peace *s* juez *m* de paz
justifiable ['dʒʌstɪ,faɪ•əbəl] *adj* justificable
justi•fy ['dʒʌstɪ,faɪ] *v* (*pret* & *pp* **-fied**) *tr* justificar; (typ) justificar
justly ['dʒʌstli] *adj* justamente, debidamente
jut [dʒʌt] *v* (*pret* & *pp* **jutted**; *ger* **jutting**) *intr* — **to jut out** resaltar, proyectarse
jute [dʒut] *s* yute *m* ‖ **Jute** *m* juto
Jutland ['dʒʌtlənd] *s* Jutlandia
juvenile ['dʒuvənɪl] o ['dʒuvə,naɪl] *adj* juvenil; para jóvenes ‖ *s* joven *mf*, mocito; libro para niños; (theat) galán *m*, galancete *m*
juvenile court *s* tribunal *m* tutelar de menores
juvenile delinquency *s* delincuencia de menores
juvenile lead [lid] *s* (theat) papel *m* de galancete; (theat) galancete *m*
juvenilia [,dʒuvə'nɪlɪ•ə] *spl* obras de juventud
juxtapose [,dʒʌkstə'poz] *tr* yuxtaponer

K

K, k [ke] undécima letra del alfabeto inglés
k. *abbr* **karat, kilogram**
K. *abbr* **King, Knight**
kale [kel] *s* col *f*, berza; (slang) dinero, pasta
kaleidoscope [kə'laɪdə,skop] *s* calidoscopio
kangaroo [,kæŋgə'ru] *s* canguro
kapok ['kepɑk] *s* capoc *m*, lana de ceiba
katydid ['ketidɪd] *s* saltamontes *m* cuyo macho emite un sonido chillón
kc. *abbr* **kilocycle**
kedge [kɛdʒ] *s* (naut) anclote *m*
keel [kil] *s* quilla ‖ *intr* — **to keel over** (naut) dar de quilla; volcarse; (coll) desmayarse
keelson ['kɛlsən] o ['kilsən] *s* (naut) sobrequilla
keen [kin] *adj* (*having a sharp edge*) agudo, afilado; (*sharp, cutting*) mordaz, penetrante; (*sharp-witted*) sutil, astuto, perspicaz; (*eager, much interested*) entusiasta; intenso, vivo; (slang) maravilloso; **to be keen on** ser muy aficionado a
keep [kip] *s* manutención, subsistencia; (*of medieval castle*) torre *f* del homenaje; **for keeps** (coll) de veras; (coll) para siempre; **to earn one's keep** (coll) ganarse la vida ‖ *v* (*pret* & *pp* **kept** [kɛpt]) *tr* guardar, conservar; (*deciding to make a purchase*) quedarse con; cumplir, guardar (*su palabra, su promesa*); llevar (*cuentas*); apuntar (*los tantos*); tener (*criados, caballos, huéspedes*); cultivar (*una huerta*); dirigir (*un hotel, una escuela*); celebrar (*una fiesta*); hacer tardar (*a una persona*); **to keep away** tener alejado; **to keep back** retener; beberse (*las lágrimas*); reservar, no divulgar; **to keep down** reprimir; reducir (*los gastos*) al mínimo; **to keep** (*a person*) **from** + *ger* no dejarle (*a una persona*) + *inf;* **to keep in** no dejar salir; **to keep off** tener a distancia; no dejar penetrar (*p.ej., la lluvia*); evitar (*p.ej., el polvo*); **to keep out** no dejar entrar; no dejar penetrar; **to keep someone informed (about)** ponerle a uno al corriente (de); **to keep someone waiting** hacerle a uno esperar; **to keep up** mantener, conservar ‖ *intr*

permanecer, quedarse; conservarse, no echarse a perder; **to keep** + *ger* seguir + *ger;* **to keep away** mantenerse a distancia; no dejarse ver; **to keep from** + *ger* abstenerse de + *inf;* **to keep informed (about)** ponerse al corriente (de); **to keep in with** (coll) congraciarse con, no perder el favor de; **to keep off** no acercarse a; no pisar (*el césped*); **to keep on** + *ger* seguir + *ger;* **to keep on with** continuar con; **to keep out** mantenerse fuera, no entrar; **to keep out of** no entrar en; no meterse en; evitar (*el peligro*)*;* **to keep quiet** estarse quieto; **to keep to** seguir por, llevar (*la derecha, la izquierda*); **to keep to oneself** quedarse a solas; **to keep up** continuar; no rezagarse; **to keep up with** correr parejas con; llevar adelante, proseguir

keeper ['kipər] *s* guardián *m,* custodio; (*of a game preserve*) guardabosque *m;* (*of a magnet*) armadura, culata

keeping ['kipɪŋ] *s* custodia, cuidado; (*of a holiday*) celebración; **in keeping with** de acuerdo con, en armonía con; **in safe keeping** en lugar seguro, a buen recaudo; **out of keeping with** en desacuerdo con

keep'sake' *s* recuerdo

keg [kɛg] *s* cuñete *m,* cubeto

ken [kɛn] *s* alcance *m* de la vista, alcance del saber; **beyond the ken of** fuera del alcance de

kennel ['kɛnəl] *s* perrera

kep·i ['kepi] o ['kɛpi] *s* (*pl* **-is**) quepis *m*

kept woman [kɛpt] *s* entretenida, manceba

kerchief ['kʌrtʃɪf] *s* pañuelo, mantón *m*

kerchoo [kər'tʃu] *interj* ¡ah-chís!

kernel ['kʌrnəl] *s* (*inner part of a nut or fruit stone*) almendra, núcleo; (*of wheat or corn*) grano; (fig) medula

kerosene ['kɛrə,sin] o [,kɛrə'sin] *s* keroseno

kerosene lamp *s* lámpara de petróleo

kerplunk [kər'plʌŋk] *interj* ¡pataplún!

ketchup ['kɛtʃəp] *s* salsa de tomate condimentada

kettle ['kɛtəl] *s* caldera, marmita; (*teakettle*) tetera

ket'tle·drum' *s* timbal *m,* tímpano

key [ki] *adj* clave || *s* (*of door, trunk, etc.*) llave *f;* (*of piano, typewriter, etc.*) tecla; (*wedge or cotter used to lock parts together*) clavija, cuña, chaveta; (*reef or low island*) cayo; (bot) sámara; (*tone of voice*) tono; (mus) clave *f* o llave *f;* (telg) manipulador *m;* (*to a puzzle, secret, translation, code*) (fig) clave o llave; (*place giving control to a region*) (fig) llave *f;* (fig) persona principal; **off key** desafinado; desafinadamente || *tr* acuñar, enchavetar; **to key up** alentar, excitar

key'board' *s* teclado

key fruit *s* sámara

key'hole' *s* ojo de la cerradura; (*of a clock*) agujero de cuerda

key'note' *s* (mus) tónica, nota tónica; (fig) idea fundamental

keynote speech *s* discurso de apertura (*en que se expone el programa de un partido político*)

key ring *s* llavero

key'stone' *s* clave *f,* espinazo; (fig) piedra angular

Key West *s* Cayo Hueso

key word *s* palabra clave

kg. *abbr* **kilogram**

K.G. *abbr* **Knight of the Garter**

kha·ki ['kɑki] o ['kæki] *adj* caqui || *s* (*pl* **-kis**) caqui *m*

khedive [kə'div] *s* jedive *m*

kibitz ['kɪbɪts] *intr* (coll) dar consejos molestos a los jugadores

kibitzer ['kɪbɪtsər] *s* (coll) mirón molesto (*de una partida de juego*); (coll) entremetido

kiblah ['kɪblɑ] *s* alquibla

kibosh ['kaɪbɑʃ] o [kɪ'bɑʃ] *s* (coll) música celestial; **to put the kibosh on** (coll) desbaratar, imposibilitar

kick [kɪk] *s* puntapié *m;* (*of an animal*) coz *f;* (*of a gun*) coz, culatazo; (*complaint*) (slang) queja, protesta; (*of liquor*) (slang) fuerza, estímulo; (*thrill*) gusto, placer intenso; **to get a kick out of** (slang) hallar mucho placer en || *tr* acocear, dar de puntapiés a; sacudir (*los pies*); **to kick out** (coll) echar a puntapiés a la calle; (coll) echar, despedir; **to kick up a row** (slang) armar un bochinche || *intr* cocear; dar culetazos (*un arma de fuego*); (coll) quejarse; **to kick about** (coll) quejarse de; **to kick against the pricks** dar coces contra el aguijón; **to kick off** (football) dar el golpe de salida

kick'back' *s* (coll) contragolpe *m;* (slang) devolución a un cómplice de una parte de lo robado

kick'off' *s* (football) golpe *m* de salida, puntapié *m* inicial

kid [kɪd] *s* (*young goat*) cabrito; (*leather*) cabritilla; (coll) chiquillo, chico; **kids** guantes *mpl* o zapatos de cabritilla || *v* (*pret & pp* **kidded;** *ger* **kidding**) *tr* (slang) embromar, tomar el pelo a; **to kid oneself** (slang) forjarse ilusiones || *intr* (slang) decirlo en broma

kidder ['kɪdər] *s* (slang) bromista *mf*

kid gloves *spl* guantes *mpl* de cabritilla; **to handle with kid gloves** tratar con suma discreción o cautela

kid'nap' *s* (*pret & pp* **-naped** o **-napped;** *ger* **-naping** o **-napping**) *tr* secuestrar

kidnaper o **kidnapper** ['kɪd,næpər] *s* secuestrador *m,* ladrón *m* de niños

kidney ['kɪdni] *s* riñón *m;* (coll) clase *f,* especie *f;* (coll) carácter *m*

kidney bean *s* judía

kidney stone *s* cálculo renal

kill [kɪl] *s* matanza; (*of a wild beast, an army, a pack of hounds*) ataque *m* final; (*creek*) arroyo, riachuelo; **for the kill** para el golpe final || *tr* matar; ahogar (*un proyecto de ley*); quitar (*el sabor*); producir una impresión irresistible en

killer ['kɪlər] *s* matador *m*

killer whale *s* orca

killing ['kɪlɪŋ] *adj* matador; (*exhausting*) abrumador; (coll) muy divertido, de lo más ridículo || *s* matanza; (*game killed on a hunt*) cacería, piezas; (coll) gran ganancia; **to make a killing** (coll) enriquecerse de golpe

kill'-joy' *s* aguafiestas *mf*

kiln [kɪl] o [kɪln] *s* horno

kil•o ['kɪlo] o ['kilo] *s* (*pl* **-os**) kilo, kilogramo; kilómetro

kilocycle ['kɪlə,saɪkəl] *s* kilociclo

kilogram ['kɪlə,græm] *s* kilogramo

kilometer ['kɪlə,mitər] o [kɪ'lɑmɪtər] *s* kilómetro

kilometric [,kɪlə'mɛtrɪk] *adj* kilométrico

kilowatt ['kɪlə,wɑt] *s* kilovatio

kilowatt-hour ['kɪlə,wɑt'aur] *s* (*pl* **kilowatt-hours**) kilovatio-hora

kilt [kɪlt] *s* enagüillas, falda corta

kilter ['kɪltər] *s* — **to be out of kilter** (coll) estar descompuesto

kimo•no [kɪ'monə] o [kɪ'mono] *s* (*pl* **-nos**) quimono

kin [kɪn] *s* (*family relationship*) parentesco; (*relatives*) deudos; **near of kin** muy allegado; **of kin** allegado; **the next of kin** el pariente más próximo, los parientes próximos

kind [kaɪnd] *adj* bueno, bondadoso; (*greeting*) afectuoso; **kind to** bueno para con || *s* clase *f*, especie *f*, suerte *f*, género; **a kind of** uno a modo de; **all kinds of** (coll) gran cantidad de; **in kind** en especie; en la misma moneda; **kind of** (coll) algo, más bien; **of a kind** de una misma clase; (*poor, mediocre*) de poco valor, de mala muerte; **of the kind** por el estilo

kindergarten ['kɪndər,gɑrtən] *s* escuela de párvulos, jardín *m* de la infancia

kindergartner ['kɪndər,gɑrtnər] *s* (*child*) párvulo; (*teacher*) parvulista *mf*

kind-hearted ['kaɪnd'hɑrtɪd] *adj* bondadoso, de buen corazón

kindle ['kɪndəl] *tr* encender || *intr* encenderse

kindling ['kɪndlɪŋ] *s* encendajas

kindling wood *s* leña

kind•ly ['kaɪndli] *adj* (*comp* **-lier;** *super* **-liest**) (*kind-hearted*) bondadoso; apacible, benigno; favorable || *adv* bondadosamente; cordialmente; con gusto; por favor; **to not take kindly to** no aceptar de buen grado

kindness ['kaɪndnɪs] *s* bondad; **have the kindness to** tenga Vd. la bondad de

kindred ['kɪndrɪd] *adj* emparentado; afín, semejante || *s* parentela; semejanza, afinidad

kinescope ['kɪnɪ,skop] *s* (trademark) cinescopio, kinescopio

kinetic [kɪ'nɛtɪk] o [kaɪ'nɛtɪk] *adj* cinético || **kinetics** *s* cinética

kinetic energy *s* fuerza viva, energía cinética

king [kɪŋ] *s* rey *m;* (cards, chess, & fig) rey; (checkers) dama

king'bolt' *s* pivote *m* central

kingdom ['kɪŋdəm] *s* reino

king'fish'er *s* martín *m* pescador

king•ly ['kɪŋli] *adj* (*comp* **-lier;** *super* **-liest**) real, regio; (*stately*) majestuoso || *adv* regiamente

king'pin' *s* (bowling) bolo delantero; pivote *m* central; (aut) pivote de dirección; (coll) persona principal

king post *s* pendolón *m*

king's evil *s* escrófula

kingship ['kɪŋʃɪp] *s* dignidad real

king'-size' *adj* de tamaño largo

king's ransom *s* riquezas de Creso

kink [kɪŋk] *s* (*twist, e.g., in a rope*) enroscadura, coca; (*e.g., in Negro's hair*) pasa; (*soreness in neck*) tortícolis *m;* (*flaw, difficulty*) estorbo, traba; (*mental twist*) chifladura, manía || *tr* enroscar || *intr* enroscarse

kink•y ['kɪŋki] *adj* (*comp* **-ier;** *super* **-iest**) encarrujado, ensortijado

kinsfolk ['kɪnz,fok] *s* parentela, familia, deudos

kinship ['kɪnʃɪp] *s* parentesco; semejanza, afinidad

kins•man ['kɪnzmən] *s* (*pl* **-men** [mən]) pariente *m*

kins•woman ['kɪnz,wumən] *s* (*pl* **-women** [,wɪmɪn]) *s* parienta

kipper ['kɪpər] *s* arenque acecinado, salmón acecinado || *tr* acecinar (*el arenque o el salmón*)

kiss [kɪs] *s* beso; (billiards) retruco; (*confection*) dulce *m*, merengue *m* || *tr* besar; **to kiss away** borrar con besos (*las penas de una persona*) || *intr* besar; besarse; (billiards) retrucar

kit [kɪt] *s* cartera de herramientas; (*case and its contents for various purposes*) estuche *m;* (*of a soldier*) equipo, pertrechos; (*of a traveler*) equipaje *m;* (*pail, tub*) balde *m*

kitchen ['kɪtʃən] *s* cocina

kitchenette [,kɪtʃə'nɛt] *s* cocinilla

kitchen garden *s* huerto

kitch'en•maid' *s* ayudanta de cocina, pincha

kitchen police *s* (mil) trabajo de cocina; soldados que están de cocina

kitchen range *s* cocina económica

kitchen sink *s* fregadero

kitch'en•ware' *s* utensilios de cocina

kite [kaɪt] *s* cometa; (orn) milano; **to fly a kite** hacer volar una cometa

kith and kin [kɪθ] *spl* parientes *mpl;* parientes y amigos

kitten ['kɪtən] *s* gatito, minino

kittenish ['kɪtənɪʃ] *adj* juguetón, retozón; (*coy, flirtatious*) coquetón

kit•ty ['kɪti] *s* (*pl* **-ties**) gatito, minino; (*in card games*) polla, puesta || *interj* ¡miz!

kleptomaniac [,klɛptə'menɪ,æk] *s* cleptómano

km. *abbr* **kilometer**

knack [næk] *s* tino, tranquillo, maña

knapsack ['næp,sæk] *s* mochila

knave [nev] *s* bribón *m,* pícaro; (cards) sota
knaver•y ['nevəri] *s* (*pl* **-ies**) bribonería, picardía
knead [nid] *tr* amasar, sobar
knee [ni] *s* rodilla; (*of animal*) codillo; (*e.g., of trousers*) rodillera; (mach) ángulo, codo; **to bring** (*someone*) **to his knees** rendir, vencer; **to go down on one's knees** hincarse de rodillas, caer de rodillas; **to go down on one's kness to** implorar de rodillas
knee breeches ['brɪtʃɪz] *spl* pantalones cortos
knee'cap' *s* rótula; (*protective covering*) rodillera
knee'-deep' *adj* metido hasta las rodillas
knee'-high' *adj* que llega hasta la rodilla
knee'hole' *s* hueco para acomodar las rodillas
knee jerk *s* reflejo rotuliano
kneel [nil] *v* (*pret & pp* **knelt** [nɛlt] o **kneeled**) *intr* arrodillarse; estar de rodillas
knee'pad' *s* rodillera
knee'pan' *s* rótula
knee swell *s* (*of organ*) (mus) rodillera
knell [nɛl] *s* doble *m,* toque *m* de difuntos; mal agüero; **to toll the knell of** anunciar la muerte de, anunciar el fin de || *intr* doblar, tocar a muerto; sonar tristemente
knickers ['nɪkərz] *spl* pantalones *mpl* de media pierna
knickknack ['nɪk,næk] *s* chuchería, bujería, baratija
knife [naɪf] *s* (*pl* **knives** [naɪvz]) cuchillo; (*of a paper cutter or other instrument*) cuchilla; **to go under the knife** (coll) hacerse operar || *tr* acuchillar; (slang) traicionar
knife sharpener *s* afilador *m,* afilón *m*
knife switch *s* (elec) interruptor *m* de cuchilla
knight [naɪt] *s* caballero; (chess) caballo || *tr* armar caballero
knight-errant ['naɪt'ɛrənt] *s* (*pl* **knights-errant**) caballero andante
knight-errant•ry ['naɪt'ɛrəntri] *s* (*pl* **-ries**) caballería andante; (*quixotic behavior*) quijotada
knighthood ['naɪt·hʊd] *s* caballería
knightly ['naɪtli] *adj* caballeroso, caballeresco
Knight of the Rueful Countenance *s* Caballero de la triste figura (*Don Quijote*)
knit [nɪt] *v* (*pret & pp* **knitted** o **knit;** *ger* **knitting**) *tr* tejer a punto de aguja; enlazar, unir; fruncir (*las cejas*), arrugar (*la frente*) || *intr* hacer calceta, hacer malla; trabarse, unirse; soldarse (*un hueso*)
knit goods *spl* géneros de punto
knitting ['nɪtɪŋ] *s* punto de media, trabajo de punto
knitting machine *s* máquina de hacer tejidos de punto
knitting needle *s* aguja de hacer media
knit'wear' *s* géneros de punto
knob [nɑb] *s* (*lump*) bulto, protuberancia; (*of a door*) botón *m,* tirador *m;* (*of a radio set*) botón, perilla; (*ornament on furniture*) manzana; colina o montaña redondeada
knock [nɑk] *s* golpe *m;* (*e.g., on a door*) toque *m,* llamada; (*with a door knocker*) aldabazo; (*of an internal-combustion engine*) pistoneo; (slang) censura, crítica || *tr* golpear; (*repeatedly*) golpetear; (slang) censurar, criticar; **to knock down** (*with a blow, punch, etc.*) derribar; (*to the highest bidder*) rematar; desarmar, desmontar (*un aparato o máquina*); **to knock off** hacer saltar con un golpe; suspender (*el trabajo*); poner fin a; (slang) matar; **to knock out** agotar; (box) poner fuera de combate || *intr* tocar, llamar; golpear, pistonear (*el motor de combustión interna*); (slang) censurar, criticar; **to knock about** andar vagando; **to knock against** dar contra, tropezar con; **to knock at** tocar a, llamar a (*la puerta*); **to knock off** dejar de trabajar
knocker ['nɑkər] *s* (*on a door*) aldaba; (coll) criticón *m*
knock-kneed ['nɑk,nid] *adj* patizambo, zambo
knock'out' *s* golpe decisivo, puñetazo decisivo; (box) (el) fuera de combate; (elec) destapadero; (coll) real moza
knockout drops *spl* (slang) gotas narcóticas
knoll [nol] *s* loma, otero
knot [nɑt] *s* nudo; (*worn as ornament*) lazo; corrillo, grupo; (*difficult matter; bond or tie*) nudo; nudo o lazo de matrimonio; (*protuberance in a fabric*) envoltorio; (naut) nudo; **to tie the knot** (coll) casarse || *v* (*pret & pp* **knotted;** *ger* **knotting**) *tr* anudar; fruncir (*las cejas*) || *intr* anudarse
knot'hole' *s* agujero en la madera (*que deja un nudo al desprenderse*)
knot•ty ['nɑti] *adj* (*comp* **-tier;** *super* **-tiest**) nudoso; (fig) espinoso, difícil
know [no] *s* — **to be in the know** estar enterado, tener informes secretos || *v* (*pret* **knew** [nju] o [nu]; *pp* **known**) *tr & intr* (*by reasoning or learning*) saber; (*by the senses or by perception; through acquaintance or recognition*) conocer; **as far as I know** que yo sepa; **to know about** saber de; **to know best** ser el mejor juez, saber lo que más conviene; **to know how to** + *inf* saber + *inf;* **to know it all** (coll) sabérselo todo; **to know what one is doing** obrar con conocimiento de causa; **to know what's what** (coll) saber cuántas son cinco; **you ought to know better** deberías tener vergüenza
knowable ['no·əbəl] *adj* conocible
know'-how' *s* conocimiento, destreza, habilidad
knowingly ['no·ɪŋli] *adv* a sabiendas,

con conocimiento de causa; (*on purpose*) adrede
know′-it-all′ *adj & s* (coll) sabidillo
knowledge ['nalɪdʒ] *s* (*faculty*) ciencia, conocimientos, el saber; (*awareness, acquaintance, familiarity*) conocimiento; **to have a thorough knowledge of** conocer a fondo; **to my knowledge** que yo sepa; **to the best of my knowledge** según mi leal saber y entender; **with full knowledge** con conocimiento de causa; **without my knowledge** sin saberlo yo
knowledgeable ['nalɪdʒəbəl] *adj* (coll) conocedor, inteligente
know′-noth′ing *s* ignorante *mf*
knuckle ['nʌkəl] *s* nudillo; (*of a quadruped*) jarrete *m;* (mach) junta de charnela; **knuckles** bóxer *m* || *intr* — **to knuckle down** someterse, darse por vencido; aplicarse con empeño al trabajo
knurl [nʌrl] *s* moleteado || *tr* moletear, cerrillar (*p.ej., las piezas de moneda*)
k.o. *abbr* **knockout**
Koran [ko'ran] o [ko'ræn] *s* Corán *m*
Korea [ko'ri·ə] *s* Corea
Korean [ko'ri·ən] *adj & s* coreano
kosher ['koʃər] *adj* autorizado por la ley judía; (coll) genuino
kowtow ['kaʊ'taʊ] o ['ko'taʊ] *intr* arrodillarse y tocar el suelo con la frente; doblegarse servilmente, mostrarse servilmente obsequioso
Kt. *abbr* **Knight**
kudos ['kjudas] o ['kudas] *s* (coll) gloria, renombre *m,* fama
kw. *abbr* **kilowatt**
K.W.H. *abbr* **kilowatt-hour**

L

L, l [ɛl] duodécima letra del alfabeto inglés
l. *abbr* **liter, line, league, length**
L. *abbr* **Latin, Low**
la•bel ['lebəl] *s* etiqueta, marbete *m,* rótulo; (*descriptive word*) calificación || *v* (*pret & pp* **-beled** o **-belled;** *ger* **-beling** o **-belling**) *tr* poner etiqueta o marbete a, rotular; calificar
labial ['lebɪ·əl] *adj & s* labial *f*
labor ['lebər] *adj* obrero || *s* trabajo, labor *f;* (*job, task*) tarea, faena; (*manual work involved in an undertaking; the wages for such work*) mano *f* de obra; (*wage-earning workers as contrasted with capital and management*) los obreros; (*childbirth*) parto; **labors** esfuerzos; **to be in labor** estar de parto || *intr* trabajar; (*to exert oneself*) forcejar; estar de parto; moverse penosamente; cabecear y balancear (*un buque*); **to labor under** ser víctima de
labor and management *spl* los obreros y los patronos
laborato•ry ['læbərə,tori] *s* (*pl* **-ries**) laboratorio
labored ['lebərd] *adj* penoso, dificultoso; artificial, forzado
laborer ['lebərər] *s* trabajador *m,* obrero; (*unskilled worker*) bracero, jornalero, peón *m*
laborious [lə'borɪ·əs] *adj* laborioso
la′bor-man′agement *adj* obrero-patronal
labor union *s* gremio obrero, sindicato
Labourite ['lebə,raɪt] *s* laborista *mf*
Labrador ['læbrə,dər] *s* el Labrador
labyrinth ['læbɪrɪnθ] *s* laberinto
lace [les] *s* encaje *m;* (*string to tie shoe, corset, etc.*) cordón *m,* lazo; (*braid*) galón *m* de oro o plata || *tr* adornar con encaje; atar (*los zapatos, el corsé*); (coll) dar una paliza a
lace trimming *s* randa
lace′work′ *s* encaje *m,* obra de encaje
lachrymose ['lækrɪ,mos] *adj* lacrimoso
lacing ['lesɪŋ] *s* cordón *m;* lazo; galón *m;* (coll) paliza
lack [læk] *s* carencia, falta; (*complete lack*) defecto || *tr* carecer de, necesitar || *intr* (*to be lacking*) faltar
lackadaisical [,lækə'dezɪkəl] *adj* desaprovechado, indiferente
lackey ['læki] *s* lacayo; secuaz *m* servil
lacking ['lækɪŋ] *prep* sin, carente de
lack′lus′ter *adj* deslustrado, deslucido
laconic [lə'kanɪk] *adj* lacónico
lacquer ['lækər] *s* laca || *tr* laquear
lacquer ware *s* lacas, objetos de laca
lacu•na [lə'kjunə] *s* (*pl* **-nas** o **-nae** [ni]) laguna
lac•y ['lesi] *adj* (*comp* **-ier;** *super* **-iest**) de encaje; (fig) diáfano
lad [læd] *s* muchacho, chico
ladder ['lædər] *s* escalera; (*stepladder*) escala, escalera de mano; (*two ladders fastened together at the top with hinges*) escalera de tijera; (*stepping stone*) (fig) escalón *m*
ladder truck *s* carro de escaleras de incendio
ladies' room *s* cuarto tocador
ladle ['ledəl] *s* cazo; (*for soup*) cucharón *m;* (*of tinsmith*) cucharilla || *tr* servir con cucharón; sacar con cucharón
la•dy ['ledi] *s* (*pl* **-dies**) señora, dama
la′dy•bird′ o **la′dy•bug′** *s* mariquita, vaca de San Antón
la′dy•fin′ger *s* melindre *m*
lady in waiting *s* camarera de la reina
la′dy-kil′ler *s* ladrón *m* de corazones
la′dy•like′ *adj* elegante; **to be ladylike** ser muy dama

la'dy·love' *s* amada, amiga querida
lady of the house *s* ama de casa
ladyship ['ledi,ʃɪp] *s* señoría
lady's maid *s* doncella
lady's man *s* perico entre ellas
lag [læg] *s* retraso ‖ *v* (*pret & pp* **lagged;** *ger* **lagging**) *intr* retrasarse; **to lag behind** quedarse atrás, rezagarse
lager beer ['lɑgər] *s* cerveza reposada
laggard ['lægərd] *s* perezoso, rezagado
lagoon [lə'gun] *s* laguna
laid paper [led] *s* papel vergueteado
laid up *adj* almacenado, ahorrado; (naut) inactivo; (coll) encamado por estar enfermo
lair [lɛr] *s* cubil *m*
lai·ty ['le·ɪti] *s* legos
lake [lek] *adj* lacustre ‖ *s* lago
lamb [læm] *s* cordero; carne *f* de cordero; piel *f* de cordero; (*meek person*) (fig) cordero
lambaste [læm'best] *tr* (*to thrash*) (coll) dar una paliza a; (*to reprimand harshly*) (coll) dar una jabonadura a
lamb chop *s* chuleta de cordero
lambkin ['læmkɪn] *s* corderito; (fig) nenito
lamb'skin' *s* piel *f* de cordero, corderina; (*dressed with its wool*) corderillo
lame [lem] *adj* cojo; (*sore*) dolorido; (*e.g., excuse*) débil, pobre ‖ *tr* encojar
lament [lə'mɛnt] *s* lamento; (*dirge*) elegía ‖ *tr* lamentar ‖ *intr* lamentarse
lamentable ['læməntəbəl] *adj* lamentable
lamentation [,læmən'teʃən] *s* lamentación
laminate ['læmɪ,net] *tr* laminar
lamp [læmp] *s* lámpara
lamp'black' *s* negro de humo
lamp chimney *s* tubo de lámpara
lamp'light' *s* luz *f* de lámpara
lamp'light'er *s* farolero
lampoon [læm'pun] *s* pasquín *m*, libelo ‖ *tr* pasquinar
lamp'post' *s* poste *m* de farol
lamp shade *s* pantalla de lámpara
lamp'wick' *s* mecha de lámpara, torcida
lance [læns] o [lɑns] *s* lanza; (surg) lanceta ‖ *tr* alancear; (surg) abrir con lanceta
lance rest *s* ristre *m*
lancet ['lænsɪt] o ['lɑnsɪt] *s* (surg) lanceta
land [lænd] *adj* terrestre; (*wind*) terral ‖ *s* tierra; **on land, on sea, and in the air** en tierra, mar y aire; **to make land** atracar a tierra; **to see how the land lies** medir el terreno, ver el cariz que van tomando las cosas ‖ *tr* desembarcar; conducir (*un avión*) a tierra; coger (*un pez*); (coll) conseguir ‖ *intr* desembarcar; (*to reach land*) arribar, aterrar; aterrizar (*un avión*); (*to arrive or come to rest*) ir a dar, ir a parar; **to land on one's feet** caer de pies; **to land on one's head** caer de cabeza
landau ['lændɔ] o ['lændaʊ] *s* landó *m*
land breeze *s* terral *m*
landed ['lændɪd] *adj* (*owning land*) hacendado; (*real-estate*) inmobiliario; **landed property** bienes *mpl* raíces
land'fall' *s* (*sighting land*) aterrada; (*landing of ship or plane*) aterraje *m;* tierra vista desde el mar; (*landslide*) derrumbe *m*
land grant *s* donación de tierras
land'hold'er *s* terrateniente *mf*, hacendado
landing ['lændɪŋ] *s* (*of ship or plane*) aterraje *m;* (*of passengers*) desembarco; (*place where passengers and goods are landed*) desembarcadero; (*of stairway*) desembarco, descanso
landing beacon *s* (aer) radiofaro de aterrizaje
landing craft *s* (nav) lancha de desembarco
landing field *s* (aer) pista de aterrizaje
landing force *s* (nav) compañía de desembarco
landing gear *s* (aer) tren *m* de aterrizaje
landing stage *s* embarcadero flotante
landing strip *s* (aer) faja de aterrizaje
land'la'dy *s* (*pl* **-dies**) (*e.g., of an apartment*) casera, dueña; (*of a lodging house*) ama, patrona; (*of an inn*) mesonera, posadera
landlocked ['lænd,lɑkt] *adj* rodeado de tierra
land'lord' *s* (*e.g., of an apartment*) casero, dueño; (*of a lodging house*) amo, patrón *m;* (*of an inn*) mesonero, posadero
land'lub'ber *s* (*person unacquainted with the sea*) marinero de agua dulce; (*awkward and unskilled seaman*) marinero matalote
land'mark' *s* (*boundary stone*) mojón *m;* (*feature of landscape that marks a location*) guía; suceso que hace época; (naut) marca de reconocimiento
land office *s* oficina del catastro
land'-of'fice business *s* (coll) negocio de mucho movimiento
land'own'er *s* terrateniente *mf*, hacendado
landscape ['lænd,skep] *s* paisaje *m* ‖ *tr* ajardinar
landscape architect *s* arquitecto paisajista
landscape gardener *s* jardinero adornista, jardinista *mf*
landscape painter *s* paisajista *mf*
landscapist ['lænd,skepɪst] *s* paisajista *mf*
land'slide' *s* derrumbe *m*, derrumbamiento de tierra, corrimiento; (fig) mayoría de votos abrumadora; (fig) victoria arrolladora
landward ['lændwərd] *adv* hacia tierra, hacia la costa
land wind *s* terral *m*
lane [len] *s* (*narrow street or passage*) callejuela; (*path*) carril *m;* (*of an*

automobile highway) faja; (*of an air or ocean route*) derrotero, vía

langsyne [ˈlæŋˈsaɪn] *adv* (Scotch) hace mucho tiempo || *s* (Scotch) tiempo de antaño

language [ˈlæŋgwɪdʒ] *s* idioma *m*, lengua; (*way of speaking or writing, style; figurative or poetic expression; communication of meaning said to be employed by flowers, birds, art, etc.*) lenguaje *m*; (*of a special group of people*) jerga

languid [ˈlæŋgwɪd] *adj* lánguido

languish [ˈlæŋgwɪʃ] *intr* languidecer; afectar languidez

languor [ˈlæŋgər] *s* languidez *f*

languorous [ˈlæŋgərəs] *adj* lánguido; (*causing languor*) enervante

lank [læŋk] *adj* descarnado, larguirucho; (*hair*) lacio

lank•y [ˈlæŋki] *adj* (*comp* **-ier**; *super* **-iest**) descarnado, larguirucho

lantern [ˈlæntərn] *s* linterna

lantern slide *s* diapositiva, tira de vidrio

lanyard [ˈlænjərd] *s* (naut) acollador *m*

lap [læp] *s* (*of human body or clothing*) regazo; (*loose fold*) caída, doblez *f*; (*overlap of garment*) traslapo; (*with the tongue*) lametada; (*of the waves*) chapaleteo; (*in a race*) (sport) etapa, vuelta; **to live in the lap of luxury** llevar una vida regalada || *v* (*pret & pp* **lapped**; *ger* **lapping**) *tr* beber con la lengua; lamer (*las olas la playa*); (*to overlap*) traslapar; juntar a traslapo; **to lap up** tragar a lengüetadas; (coll) aceptar con entusiasmo || *intr* traslapar; traslaparse (*dos o más cosas*); **to lap against** lamer (*las olas la playa*); **to lap over** salir fuera, rebosar

lap'board' *s* tabla faldera

lap dog *s* perro de falda

lapel [ləˈpɛl] *s* solapa

Lap'land' *s* Laponia

Laplander [ˈlæpˌlændər] *s* lapón *m* (*habitante*)

Lapp [læp] *s* lapón *m* (*habitante; idioma*)

lap robe *s* manta de coche

lapse [læps] *s* (*passing of time; slipping into guilt or error*) lapso; (*fall, decline*) caída; caída en desuso; (*e.g., of an insurance policy*) invalidación || *intr* caer en culpa o error; decaer, pasar (*p.ej., el entusiasmo*); caducar (*p.ej., una póliza de seguro*)

lap'wing' *s* ave fría

larce•ny [ˈlɑrsəni] *s* (*pl* **-nies**) hurto, robo

larch [lɑrtʃ] *s* alerce *m*, lárice *m*

lard [lɑrd] *s* cochevira, manteca de puerco || *tr* (culin) mechar

larder [ˈlɑrdər] *s* despensa

large [ˈlɑrdʒ] *adj* grande; **at large** en libertad

large intestine *s* intestino grueso

largely [ˈlɑrdʒli] *adj* por la mayor parte

largeness [ˈlɑrdʒnɪs] *s* grandeza

large'-scale' *adj* en grande escala, grande escala

lariat [ˈlærɪ•ət] *s* (*for catching animals*) lazo; (*for tying grazing animals*) cuerda, soga

lark [lɑrk] *s* alondra; (coll) parranda; **to go on a lark** (coll) andar de parranda, echar una cana al aire

lark'spur' *s* (*rocket larkspur*) espuela de caballero; (*field larkspur*) consuelda real

lar•va [ˈlɑrvə] *s* (*pl* **-vae** [vi]) larva

laryngeal [ləˈrɪndʒɪ•əl] o [ˌlærɪnˈdʒi•əl] *adj* laríngeo

laryngitis [ˌlærɪnˈdʒaɪtɪs] *s* laringitis *f*

laryngoscope [ləˈrɪŋgəˌskop] *s* laringoscopio

larynx [ˈlærɪŋks] *s* (*pl* **larynxes** o **larynges** [ləˈrɪndʒiz]) laringe *f*

lascivious [ləˈsɪvɪ•əs] *adj* lascivo

lasciviousness [ləˈsɪvɪ•əsnɪs] *s* lascivia

lash [læʃ] *s* (*cord on end of whip*) tralla; (*blow with whip; scolding*) latigazo; (*e.g., of animal's tail*) coletazo; (*of waves*) embate *m*; (*eyelash*) pestaña || *tr* (*to beat, whip*) azotar; (*to bind, tie*) atar; (*to shake, to switch*) agitar, sacudir; (*to attack with words*) increpar, reñir || *intr* lanzarse, pasar rápidamente; **to lash out at** azotar; embestir; vituperar

lashing [ˈlæʃɪŋ] *s* atadura; paliza, zurra; (*severe scolding*) latigazo

lass [læs] *s* muchacha, chica; amada

las•so [ˈlæso] o [læˈsu] *s* (*pl* **-sos** o **-soes**) lazo || *tr* lazar

last [læst] o [lɑst] *adj* (*after all others; the only remaining; utmost, extreme*) último; (*most recent*) pasado; **before last** antepasado; **every last one** todos sin excepción; **last but one** penúltimo || *adv* después de todos; por último; por última vez || *s* última persona; última cosa; fin *m*; (*for holding shoe*) horma; **at last** por fin; **at long last** al fin y al cabo; **stick to your last!** ¡zapatero, a tus zapatos!; **the last of the month** a fines del mes; **to breathe one's last** dar el último suspiro; **to see the last of** no volver a ver; **to the last** hasta el fin || *intr* durar; resistir; dar buen resultado (*p.ej., una prenda de vestir*); seguir así

lasting [ˈlæstɪŋ] o [ˈlɑstɪŋ] *adj* perdurable, duradero

lastly [ˈlæstli] o [ˈlɑstli] *adv* finalmente, por último

last'-min'ute news *s* noticias de última hora

last name *s* apellido

last night *adv* anoche

last quarter *s* cuarto menguante

last sleep *s* último sueño

last straw *s* acabóse *m*, colmo

Last Supper, the la Cena

last will and testament *s* última disposición, última voluntad

last word *s* última palabra; (*latest style*) (coll) última palabra

lat. *abbr* **latitude**

Lat. *abbr* **Latin**

latch [lætʃ] *s* picaporte *m* || *tr* cerrar con picaporte
latch'key' *s* llavín *m*
latch'string' *s* cordón *m* de aldaba; **the latchstring is out** ya sabe Vd. que ésta es su casa
late [let] *adj* (*happening after the usual time*) tardío; (*person*) atrasado; (*hour of the night*) avanzado; (*news*) de última hora; (*party, meeting, etc.*) que termina tarde; (*coming toward the end of a period of time*) de fines de; (*incumbent of an office*) anterior; (*deceased*) difunto, fallecido; **of late** recientemente, últimamente; **to be late** ser tarde; tardar (*p.ej., el tren*); **to be late in** + *ger* tardar en + *inf;* **to grow late** hacerse tarde || *adv* tarde; **late in** (*the week, the month, etc.*) a fines de, hacia fines de; **late in life** a una edad avanzada
late-comer ['let ˌkʌmər] *s* recién llegado; (*one who arrives late*) rezagado
lateen sail [læ'tin] *s* vela latina
lateen yard *s* entena
lately ['letli] *adv* recientemente, últimamente
latent ['letənt] *adj* latente
lateral ['lætərəl] *adj* lateral
lath [læθ] o [lɑθ] *s* lata, listón; enlistonado || *tr* enlistonar
lathe [leð] *s* torno (*máquina que sirve para labrar madera, hierro, etc. con un movimiento circular*)
lather ['læðər] *s* espuma de jabón; espuma de sudor || *tr* enjabonar; (coll) tundir, zurrar || *intr* espumar
lathery ['læðəri] *adj* espumoso, jabonoso
lathing ['læθɪŋ] o ['lɑθɪŋ] *s* enlistonado
Latin ['lætɪn] o ['lætən] *adj* latino || *s* (*language*) latín *m;* (*person*) latino
Latin America *s* Latinoamérica, la América Latina
Latin American *s* latinoamericano
Lat'in-Amer'ican *adj* latinoamericano
latitude ['lætɪˌtjud] o ['lætɪˌtud] *s* latitud
latrine [lə'trin] *s* letrina
latter ['lætər] *adj* (*more recent*) posterior; segundo (*de dos*); **the latter** éste; **the latter part of** fines *mpl* de (*p.ej., el siglo*)
lattice ['lætɪs] *s* enrejado || *tr* enrejar
lattice girder *s* viga de celosía
lat'tice•work' *s* enrejado
Latvia ['lætvɪ·ə] *s* Letonia, Latvia
laudable ['lɔdəbəl] *adj* laudable
laudanum ['lɔdənəm] o ['lɔdnəm] *s* láudano
laudatory ['lɔdəˌtori] *adj* laudatorio
laugh [læf] o [lɑf] *s* risa || *tr* — **to laugh away** ahogar en risas; **to laugh off** tomar a risa || *intr* reír, reírse
laughable ['læfəbəl] o ['lɑfəbəl] *adj* risible
laughing ['læfɪŋ] o ['lɑfɪŋ] *adj* reidor; **to be no laughing matter** no ser cosa de risa || *s* risa, (el) reír
laughing gas *s* gas *m* hilarante
laugh'ing•stock' *s* hazmerreír *m*
laughter ['læftər] o ['lɑftər] *s* risa, risas
launch [lɔntʃ] o [lɑntʃ] *s* (*of a ship*) botadura; (*of a rocket*) lanzamiento; (*open motorboat*) lancha automóvil; (nav) lancha || *tr* botar, lanzar (*un buque*); (*to throw; to start, set going, send forth*) lanzar || *intr* lanzarse
launching ['lɔntʃɪŋ] o ['lɑntʃɪŋ] *s* lanzamiento
launching pad *s* plataforma de lanzamiento
launder ['lɔndər] o ['lɑndər] *tr* lavar y planchar || *intr* resistir el lavado
launderer ['lɔndərər] o ['lɑndərər] *s* lavandero
laundress ['lɔndrɪs] o ['lɑndrɪs] *s* lavandera
laun•dry ['lɔndri] o ['lɑndri] *s* (*pl* **-dries**) lavadero; lavado de la ropa; ropa lavada o para lavar
laundry•man ['lɔndrimən] o ['lɑndrimən] *s* (*pl* **-men** [mən]) lavandero
laun'dry•wom'an *s* (*pl* **-wom'en**) lavandera
laureate ['lɔrɪ·ɪt] *adj* laureado || *s* laureado; poeta laureado
lau•rel ['lɔrəl] o ['lɑrəl] *s* laurel *m;* **laurels** laurel (*de la victoria*); **to rest o sleep on one's laurels** dormirse sobre sus laureles || *v* (*pret & pp* **-reled** o **-relled;** *ger* **-reling** o **-relling**) *tr* laurear, coronar de laurel
lava ['lɑvə] o ['lævə] *s* lava
lavato•ry ['lævəˌtori] *s* (*pl* **-ries**) (*room equipped for washing hands and face*) lavabo; (*bowl with running water*) lavamanos *m;* (*toilet*) excusado
lavender ['lævəndər] *s* alhucema, espliego, lavanda
lavender water *s* agua de alhucema, agua de lavanda
lavish ['lævɪʃ] *adj* pródigo || *tr* prodigar
law [lɔ] *s* (*of man, of nature, of science*) ley *f;* (*branch of knowledge concerned with law; body of laws; study of law, profession of law*) derecho; **to enter the law** hacerse abogado; **to go to law** recurrir a la ley; **to lay down the law** dar órdenes terminantes; **to maintain law and order** mantener la paz; **to practice law** ejercer la profesión de abogado; **to read law** estudiar derecho
law-abiding ['lɔ·əˌbaɪdɪŋ] *adj* observante de la ley
law'break'er *s* infractor *m* de la ley
law court *s* tribunal *m* de justicia
lawful ['lɔfəl] *adj* legal, legítimo
lawless ['lɔlɪs] *adj* ilegal; (*unbridled*) desenfrenado, licencioso
law'mak'er *s* legislador *m*
lawn [lɔn] *s* césped *m;* (*fabric*) linón *m*
lawn mower *s* cortacésped *m,* tundidora de césped
law office *s* bufete *m,* despacho de abogado
law of nations *s* derecho de gent[e]
law of the jungle *s* ley *f* de la se[lva]
law student *s* estudiante *mf* de d[erecho]

law'suit' *s* pleito, proceso, litigio
lawyer ['lɔjər] *s* abogado
lax [læks] *adj* (*in morals, discipline, etc.*) laxo, relajado; vago, indeterminado; (*loose, not tense*) laxo, flojo, suelto
laxative ['læksətɪv] *adj & s* laxante *m*
lay [le] *adj* (*not belonging to clergy*) lego, seglar; (*not having special training*) lego, profano || *s* situación, orientación || *v* (*pret & pp* **laid** [led]) *tr* poner, colocar; dejar en el suelo; tender (*un cable*); echar (*los cimientos; la culpa*); situar (*la acción de un drama*); asentar (*el polvo*); poner (*huevos la gallina; la mesa una criada*); formar (*planes*); hacer (*una apuesta*); **to be laid in** ser (*la escena*) en; **to lay aside** echar a un lado; ahorrar; **to lay down** afirmar, declarar; dar (*la vida*); deponer (*las armas*); **to lay low** abatir, derribar; obligar a guardar cama; matar; **to lay off** despedir (*a obreros*); (*to mark off the boundaries of*) marcar, trazar; **to lay open** descubrir, revelar; (*to a risk or danger*) exponer; **to lay out** extender, tender; marcar (*una tarea, un trabajo*); gastar (*dinero*); amortajar (*a un difunto*); **to lay up** obligar a guardar cama; ahorrar; (naut) desarmar || *intr* poner (*las gallinas*); **to lay about** dar palos de ciego; **to lay for** acechar; **to lay off** (coll) dejar de trabajar; (coll) dejar de molestar; **to lay over** detenerse durante un viaje; **to lay to** (naut) capear
lay brother *s* donado, lego
lay day *s* (naut) día *m* de estadía
layer ['le·ər] *s* (*e.g., of paint*) capa; (*e.g., of bricks*) camada; (*e.g., of coal, rocks*) estrato, capa; (hort) codadura || *tr* (hort) acodar
layer cake *s* bizcocho de varias camadas
layette [le'ɛt] *s* canastilla
lay figure *s* maniquí *m*
laying ['le·ɪŋ] *s* colocación; (*of eggs*) postura; (*of a cable*) tendido
lay·man ['lemən] *s* (*pl* **-men** [mən]) (*person who is not a clergyman*) lego, seglar *m;* (*person who has no special training*) lego, profano
lay'off' *s* (*dismissal of workmen*) despido; (*period of unemployment*) paro forzoso
lay of the land *s* cariz *m* que van tomando las cosas
lay'out' *s* plan *m;* (*of tools*) equipo; disposición, organización; (coll) banquete *m,* festín *m*
lay'o'ver *s* parada en un viaje
lay sister *s* donada
laziness ['lezɪnɪs] *s* pereza
la·zy ['lezi] *adj* (*comp* **-zier;** *super* **-ziest**) perezoso
la'zy·bones' *s* (coll) perezoso
lb. *abbr* **pound**
l.c. *abbr* **lower case; loco citato (Lat) in the place cited**
Ld. *abbr* **Lord**
lea [li] *s* prado
lead [lɛd] *adj* plomizo || *s* plomo; (*of lead pencil*) mina; (*for sounding depth*) (naut) escandallo; (typ) interlínea, regleta || [lɛd] *v* (*pret & pp* **leaded;** *ger* **leading**) *tr* emplomar; (typ) interlinear, regletear || *s* [lid] *s* (*foremost place*) primacía; (*guidance*) conducta, guía, dirección; indicación; ejemplo; (cards) salida; (*leash*) traílla; (*of a newspaper article*) primer párrafo; (elec) conductor *m;* (elec & mach) avance *m;* (min) filón *m;* (rad) alambre *m* de entrada; (theat) papel *m* principal; (theat) galán *m;* (theat) dama; **to take the lead** tomar la delantera || [lid] *v* (*pret & pp* **led** [lɛd]) *tr* conducir, llevar; (*to command*) acaudillar, mandar; estar a la cabeza de; dirigir (*p.ej., una orquesta*); llevar (*buena o mala vida*); salir con (*cierto naipe*); (elec & mach) avanzar; **to lead someone to** + *inf* llevar a alguien a + *inf* || *intr* ir delante, enseñar el camino; ser el primero; tener el mando; (cards) salir, ser mano; (mus) llevar la batuta; **to lead up to** conducir a, llevar a; llevar la conversación a
leaden ['lɛdən] *adj* (*of lead; like lead*) plomizo; (*heavy as lead*) plúmbeo; (*sluggish*) tardo, indolente; (*with sleep*) cargado; triste, lóbrego
leader ['lidər] *s* caudillo, jefe *m,* líder *m;* (*ringleader*) cabecilla *m;* (*of an orchestra*) director *m;* (*in a dance; among animals*) guión *m;* (*horse*) guía; (*in a newspaper*) artículo de fondo
leader dog *s* perro-lazarillo
leadership ['lidər,ʃɪp] *s* caudillaje *m,* jefatura; dotes *fpl* de mando
leading ['lidɪŋ] *adj* primero, principal; preeminente; delantero
leading article *s* artículo de fondo
leading edge *s* (aer) borde *m* de ataque
leading lady *s* primera actriz, dama
leading man *s* primer actor *m,* primer galán *m*
leading question *s* pregunta tendenciosa
leading strings *spl* andadores *mpl*
lead-in wire ['lid ,ɪn] *s* (rad) bajada de antena, alambre *m* de entrada
lead pencil [lɛd] *s* lápiz *m*
leaf [lif] *s* (*pl* **leaves** [livz]) hoja; (*of vine*) pámpano; (*hinged leaf of table*) trampilla; **to shake like a leaf** temblar como un azogado; **to turn over a new leaf** hacer libro nuevo || *intr* echar hojas; **to leaf through** hojear, trashojar
leafless ['liflɪs] *adj* deshojado
leaflet ['liflɪt] *s* hoja suelta, hoja volante; (*blade of compound leaf*) hojuela
leaf'stalk' *s* pecíolo
leaf·y ['lifi] *adj* (*comp* **-ier;** *super* **-iest**) hojoso, frondoso
league [lig] *s* (*unit of distance*) legua; (*association, alliance*) liga || *tr* asociar || *intr* asociarse, ligarse

League of Nations *s* Sociedad de las Naciones
leak [lik] *s* (*in a roof*) gotera; (*in a ship*) agua, vía de agua; (*of water, gas, electricity, steam*) escape *m,* fuga, salida; agujero, grieta, raja (*por donde se escapa el agua, etc.*); (*of money, news, etc.*) filtración; **to spring a leak** tener un escape; (naut) empezar a hacer agua || *tr* dejar escapar, dejar salir (*el agua, gas, etc.*); dejar filtrar (*una noticia*) || *intr* rezumarse (*un barril*); escaparse, salirse (*el agua, gas, etc.*); (naut) hacer agua; **to leak away** filtrarse (*el dinero*); **to leak out** rezumarse (*una especie*); trascender (*un hecho que estaba oculto*)
leakage ['likɪdʒ] *s* escape *m,* fuga, salida; (com) merma
leak•y ['liki] *adj* (*comp* **-ier;** *super* **-iest**) agujereado, roto; (*roof*) llovedizo; (naut) que hace agua; (coll) indiscreto
lean [lin] *adj* magro, mollar; (*thin*) flaco; (*gasoline mixture*) pobre; **lean years** años de carestía || *v* (*pret & pp* **leaned** o **leant** [lɛnt]) *tr* inclinar, ladear, arrimar || *intr* inclinarse, ladearse, arrimarse; (fig) inclinarse, tender; **to lean against** arrimarse a, estar arrimado a; **to lean back** retreparse, recostarse; **to lean on** apoyarse en; (*with the elbows*) acodarse sobre; **to lean out (of)** asomarse (a); **to lean over backwards** (coll) extremar la imparcialidad; **to lean toward** (fig) inclinarse a, ladearse a
leaning ['linɪŋ] *adj* inclinado || *s* inclinación; (fig) inclinación, tendencia
lean'-to' *s* (*pl* **-tos**) colgadizo
leap [lip] *s* salto; **by leaps and bounds** a pasos agigantados; **leap in the dark** salto a ciegas, salto en vago || *v* (*pret & pp* **leaped** o **leapt** [lɛpt]) *tr* saltar || *intr* saltar; dar un salto (*el corazón de uno*)
leap day *s* día *m* intercalar
leap'frog' *s* fil derecho, juego del salto; **to play leapfrog** jugar a la una la mula
leap year *s* año bisiesto
learn [lʌrn] *v* (*pret & pp* **learned** o **learnt** [lʌrnt]) *tr* aprender; oír decir; saber (*una noticia*) || *intr* aprender
learned ['lʌrnɪd] *adj* docto, erudito; (*e.g., word*) culto
learned journal *s* revista científica
learned society *s* sociedad de eruditos
learned word *s* cultismo, voz culta
learned world *s* mundo de la erudición
learner ['lʌrnər] *s* principiante *mf,* aprendiz *m,* estudiante *mf*
learning ['lʌrnɪŋ] *s* (*act and time devoted*) aprendizaje *m;* (*scholarship*) erudición
lease [lis] *s* arrendamiento, locación; **to give a new lease on life to** renovar completamente; volver a hacer feliz || *tr* arrendar || *intr* arrendarse
lease'hold' *adj* arrendado || *s* arrendamiento; bienes raíces arrendados
leash [liʃ] *s* traílla; **to strain at the leash** sufrir la sujeción con impaciencia || *tr* atraillar
least [list] *adj* (el) menor, mínimo, más pequeño || *adv* menos || *s* (el) menor; (lo) menos; **at least** o **at the least** al menos, a lo menos, por lo menos; **not in the least** de ninguna manera
leather ['lɛðər] *s* cuero
leath'er•back' turtle *s* laúd *m*
leath'er•neck' *s* (slang) soldado de infantería de marina de los EE.UU.
leathery ['lɛðəri] *adj* correoso, coriáceo
leave [liv] *s* (*permission*) permiso; (*permission to be absent*) licencia; (*farewell*) despedida; **on leave** con licencia; **to give leave to** dar licencia a; **to take leave (of)** despedirse (de) || *v* (*pret & pp* **left** [lɛft]) *tr* (*to let stay; to stop, give up; to disregard*) dejar; (*to go away from*) salir de; (*to bequeath*) legar; **leave it to me!** ¡déjemelo a mí!; **to be left** quedar p.ej., **the letter was left unanswered** la carta quedó sin contestar; **to leave alone** dejar en paz, dejar tranquilo; **to leave no stone unturned** no dejar piedra por mover; **to leave off** dejar; no ponerse (*una prenda de vestir*); **to leave out** omitir; **to leave things as they are** dejarlo como está || *intr* irse, marcharse; salir (*un avión, un tren, un vapor*)
leaven ['lɛvən] *s* levadura; (fig) influencia || *tr* leudar; (fig) transformar
leavening ['lɛvənɪŋ] *s* levadura
leave of absence *s* licencia
leave'-tak'ing *s* despedida
leavings ['livɪŋz] *spl* desperdicios, sobras
Leba•nese [,lɛbə'niz] *adj* libanés || *s* (*pl* **-nese**) libanés *m*
Lebanon ['lɛbənən] *s* el Líbano
Lebanon Mountains *spl* cordillera del Líbano
lecher ['lɛtʃər] *s* libertino, lujurioso
lecherous ['lɛtʃərəs] *adj* lascivo, lujurioso
lechery ['lɛtʃəri] *s* lascivia, lujuria
lectern ['lɛktərn] *s* atril *m*
lecture ['lɛktʃər] *s* conferencia; (*tedious reprimand*) sermoneo || *tr* instruir por medio de una conferencia; sermonear || *intr* dar una conferencia, dar conferencias
lecturer ['lɛktʃərər] *s* conferenciante *mf*
ledge [lɛdʒ] *s* (*projection in a wall*) retallo; cama de roca; arrecife *m*
ledger ['lɛdʒər] *s* (com) libro mayor
ledger line *s* (mus) línea suplementaria
lee [li] *s* (*shelter*) (naut) socaire *m;* (*quarter sheltered from the wind*) sotavento; **lees** heces *fpl*
leech [litʃ] *s* sanguijuela; **to stick like a leech** pegarse como ladilla
leek [lik] *s* puerro
leer [lɪr] *s* mirada de soslayo, mirada lujuriosa || *intr* — **to leer at** mirar de soslayo, mirar lujuriosamente

leery ['lɪri] *adj* (coll) receloso, suspicaz
leeward ['liwərd] o ['lu·ərd] *adj* (naut) de sotavento || *adv* (naut) a sotavento || *s* (naut) sotavento
Leeward Islands ['liwərd] *spl* islas de Sotavento
lee'way' *s* (aer & naut) deriva; (coll) tiempo de sobra, espacio de sobra, dinero de sobra; (coll) libertad de acción
left [lɛft] *adj* izquierdo || *adv* hacia la izquierda || *s* (*left hand*) izquierda; (box) zurdazo; (pol) izquierda; **on the left** a la izquierda
left field *s* (baseball) jardín izquierdo
left'-hand' drive *s* conducción o dirección a la izquierda
left-handed ['lɛft'hændɪd] *adj* (*individual*) zurdo; (*clumsy*) desmañado, torpe; insincero; contrario a las agujas del reloj
leftish ['lɛftɪʃ] *adj* izquierdizante
leftist ['lɛftɪst] *adj* & *s* izquierdista *mf*
left'o'ver *adj* & *s* sobrante *m;* **leftovers** *spl* sobras
left'-wing' *adj* izquierdista
left-winger ['lɛft'wɪŋər] *s* (coll) izquierdista *mf*
leg. *abbr* **legal, legislature**
leg [lɛg] *s* (*of man or animal*) pierna; (*of animal, table, chair, etc.*) pata; (*of boot or stocking*) caña; (*of trousers*) pernera; (*of a cooked fowl*) muslo; (*of a journey*) etapa, trecho; **to be on one's last legs** estar sin recursos; estar en las últimas; **to not have a leg to stand on** (coll) no tener justificación alguna, no tener disculpa alguna; **to pull the leg of** (coll) tomar el pelo a; **to shake a leg** (coll) darse prisa; (*to dance*) (coll) bailar; **to stretch one's legs** estirar las piernas, dar un paseíto
lega·cy ['lɛgəsi] *s* (*pl* **-cies**) legado
legal ['ligəl] *adj* legal
legali·ty [lɪ'gælɪti] *s* (*pl* **-ties**) legalidad
legalize ['ligə,laɪz] *tr* legalizar
legal tender *s* curso legal
legate ['lɛgɪt] *s* legado
legatee [,lɛgə'ti] *s* legatario
legation [lɪ'geʃən] *s* legación
legend ['lɛdʒənd] *s* leyenda
legendary ['lɛdʒən,dɛri] *adj* legendario
legerdemain [,lɛdʒərdɪ'men] *s* juego de manos, prestidigitación; (*cheating, trickery*) trapacería
legging ['lɛgɪŋ] *s* polaina
leg·gy ['lɛgi] *adj* (*comp* **-gier;** *super* **-giest**) zanquilargo; de piernas largas y elegantes
leg'horn' *s* sombrero de paja de Italia || **Leghorn** *s* Liorna
legible ['lɛdʒɪbəl] *adj* legible
legion ['lidʒən] *s* legión
legislate ['lɛdʒɪs,let] *tr* imponer mediante legislación || *intr* legislar
legislation [,lɛdʒɪs'leʃən] *s* legislación
legislative ['lɛdʒɪs,letɪv] *adj* legislativo
legislator ['lɛdʒɪs,letər] *s* legislador *m*
legislature ['lɛdʒɪs,letʃər] *s* asamblea legislativa, cuerpo legislativo
legitimacy [lɪ'dʒɪtɪməsi] *s* legitimidad
legitimate [lɪ'dʒɪtɪmɪt] *adj* legítimo || [lɪ'dʒɪtɪ,met] *tr* legitimar
legitimate drama *s* drama serio (*a distinción del cine o el melodrama*)
legitimize [lɪ'dʒɪtɪ,maɪz] *tr* legitimar
leg'work' *s* (coll) el mucho caminar
leisure ['liʒər] o ['lɛʒər] *s* desocupación, ocio; **at leisure** desocupado, libre; **at one's leisure** a la comodidad de uno, cuando uno pueda
leisure class *s* gente acomodada
leisure hours *spl* horas de ocio, ratos perdidos
leisurely ['liʒərli] o ['lɛʒərli] *adj* lento, pausado || *adv* lentamente, despacio, sin prisa
lemon ['lɛmən] *s* limón *m*
lemonade [,lɛmə'ned] *s* limonada
lemon squeezer *s* exprimidera de limón
lemon verbena *s* luisa
lend [lɛnd] *s* (*pret & pp* **lent** [lɛnt]) *tr* prestar
lending library *s* biblioteca de préstamo
length [lɛŋθ] *s* largura, largo; (*of time*) extensión; (naut) eslora; **at length** por fin; largamente; **to go to any length** hacer cuanto esté de su parte; **to keep at arm's length** mantener a distancia; mantenerse a distancia
lengthen ['lɛŋθən] *tr* alargar || *intr* alargarse
length'wise' *adj* longitudinal || *adv* longitudinalmente
length·y ['lɛŋθi] *adj* (*comp* **-ier;** *super* **-iest**) muy largo, prolongado
leniency ['linɪ·ənsi] *s* clemencia, indulgencia, lenidad
lenient ['linɪ·ənt] *adj* clemente, indulgente
lens [lɛnz] *s* lente *m* & *f;* (*of the eye*) cristalino
Lent [lɛnt] *s* cuaresma *f*
Lenten ['lɛntən] *adj* cuaresmal
lentil ['lɛntəl] *s* lenteja
leopard ['lɛpərd] *s* leopardo
leotard ['li·ə,tɑrd] *s* leotardo
leper ['lɛpər] *s* leproso
leper house *s* leprosería
leprosy ['lɛprəsi] *s* lepra
leprous ['lɛprəs] *adj* leproso; (*covered with scales*) escamoso
Lesbian ['lɛzbɪ·ən] *adj* lesbio || *s* lesbio; (*female homosexual*) lesbia
lesbianism ['lɛzbɪ·ə,nɪzəm] *s* lesbianismo
lese majesty ['liz'mædʒɪsti] *s* delito de lesa majestad
lesion ['liʒən] *s* lesión
less [lɛs] *adj* menor || *adv* menos; **less and less** cada vez menos; **less than** menos que; (*followed by numeral*) menos de; (*followed by verb*) menos de lo que || *s* menos *m*
lessee [lɛs'i] *s* arrendatario
lessen ['lɛsən] *tr* disminuir, reducir a menos; quitar importancia a || *intr*

disminuirse, reducirse; amainar (*el viento*)
lesser ['lɛsər] *adj* menor, más pequeño
lesson ['lɛsən] *s* lección
lessor ['lɛsər] *s* arrendador *m*
lest [lɛst] *conj* no sea que, de miedo que
let [lɛt] *v* (*pret & pp* **let;** *ger* **letting**) *tr* dejar, permitir; alquilar, arrendar; **let** + *inf* que + *subj*, p.ej., **let him come in** que entre; **let alone** y mucho menos; **let good enough alone** bueno está lo bueno; **let us** + *inf* vamos a + *inf*, p.ej., **let us eat** vamos a comer, comamos; **to let** se alquila; **to let alone** dejar en paz, dejar tranquilo; **to let be** no tocar; dejar en paz; **to let by** dejar pasar; **to let down** dejar bajar; desilusionar, traicionar; dejar plantado; **to let fly** disparar; (fig) disparar, soltar (*palabras injuriosas*); **to let go** soltar, desasirse de; vender; **to let in** dejar entrar, dejar entrar en; **to let it go at that** no hacer o decir nada más; **to let know** hacer saber; **to let loose** soltar; **to let on** (coll) dar a entender; **to let out** dejar salir; revelar, publicar; dar, soltar (*p.ej., más cuerda*); dar (*un grito*); ensanchar (*un vestido que aprieta*); dar en arrendamiento; (coll) despedir; **to let through** dejar pasar, dejar pasar por; **to let up** dejar subir; dejar levantarse || *intr* alquilarse, arrendarse; **to let down** (coll) ir más despacio; **to let go** desasirse; **to let go of** desasirse de; **to let on** (coll) fingir; **to let out** (coll) despedirse, cerrarse (*p.ej., la escuela*); **to let up** (coll) desistir; (coll) aflojar, amainar
let'down' *s* disminución; aflojamiento; desilusión, decepción; humillación
lethal ['liθəl] *adj* letal
lethargic [lɪ'θɑrdʒɪk] *adj* (*affected with lethargy*) letárgico; (*producing lethargy*) letargoso
lethar•gy ['lɛθərdʒi] *s* (*pl* **-gies**) letargo
Lett [lɛt] *s* letón *m*
letter ['lɛtər] *s* (*written message*) carta; (*of the alphabet*) letra; (*literal meaning*) (fig) letra; **letters** (*literature*) letras; **to the letter** al pie de la letra || *tr* estampar o marcar con letras
letter box *s* buzón *m* (*caja*)
letter carrier *s* cartero
letter drop *s* buzón *m* (*agujero*)
letter file *s* guardacartas *m*
let'ter•head' *s* membrete *m;* (*paper with printed heading*) memorándum *m*
lettering ['lɛtərɪŋ] *s* inscripción; letras
letter of credit *s* carta de crédito
letter opener ['opənər] *s* abrecartas *m*
letter paper *s* papel *m* de cartas
let'ter•per'fect *adj* que tiene bien aprendido su papel; correcto, exacto
let'ter•press' *s* impresión tipográfica; texto (*a distinción de los grabados*)
letter scales *spl* pesacartas *m*
Lettish ['lɛtɪʃ] *adj* letón || *s* letón *m*
lettuce ['lɛtɪs] *s* lechuga
let'up' *s* (coll) calma, interrupción; **without letup** (coll) sin cesar
leucorrhea [,lukə'ri•ə] *s* leucorrea
leukemia [lu'kimɪ•ə] *s* leucemia
Levant [lɪ'vænt] *s* Levante *m* (*países de la parte oriental del Mediterráneo*)
Levantine ['lɛvən,tin] o [lɪ'væntin] *adj & s* levantino
levee ['lɛvi] *s* (*embankment to hold back water*) ribero; (*reception at court*) besamanos *m*
lev•el ['lɛvəl] *adj* raso, llano; nivelado; (coll) sensato, juicioso; **level with** al nivel de, a flor de, a ras de || *s* (*device for determining horizontal position; degree of elevation*) nivel *m;* (*flat and even area of land*) terreno llano, llanura; (*part of a canal between two locks*) tramo; **to be on the level** obrar sin engaño, decir la pura verdad; **to find one's level** hallar su propio nivel || *v* (*pret & pp* **-eled** o **-elled;** *ger* **-eling** o **-elling**) *tr* nivelar; (*to smooth, flatten out*) arrasar, allanar; (*to bring down*) derribar, echar por tierra; apuntar (*un arma de fuego*); (fig) allanar (*dificultades*) || *intr* — **to level off** (aer) enderezarse para aterrizar
level-headed ['lɛvəl'hɛdɪd] *adj* sensato, juicioso
leveling rod *s* (surv) jalón *m* de mira
lever ['livər] o ['lɛvər] *s* palanca || *tr* apalancar
leverage ['livərɪdʒ] o ['lɛvərɪdʒ] *s* palancada; poder *m* de una palanca; (fig) influencia, poder *m*
leviathan [lɪ'vaɪ•əθən] *s* (Bib & fig) leviatán *m;* buque *m* muy grande
levitation [,lɛvɪ'teʃən] *s* levitación
levi•ty ['lɛvɪti] *s* (*pl* **-ties**) frivolidad; (*fickleness*) ligereza
lev•y ['lɛvi] *s* (*pl* **-ies**) (*of taxes*) exacción, recaudación; dinero recaudado; (mil) leva, enganche *m*, recluta || *v* (*pret & pp* **-ied**) *tr* exigir, recaudar (*impuestos*); (mil) enganchar, reclutar; hacer (*la guerra*)
lewd [lud] *adj* lascivo, lujurioso; obsceno
lewdness ['ludnɪs] *s* lascivia, lujuria; obscenidad
lexical ['lɛksɪkəl] *adj* léxico
lexicographer [,lɛksɪ'kɑgrəfər] *s* lexicógrafo
lexicographic(al) [,lɛksɪkə'græfɪk(əl)] lexicográfico
lexicography [,lɛksɪ'kɑgrəfi] *s* lexicografía
lexicology [,lɛksɪ'kɑlədʒi] *s* lexicología
lexicon ['lɛksɪkən] *s* léxico, lexicón *m*
liabili•ty [,laɪ•ə'bɪlɪti] *s* (*pl* **-ties**) (*e.g., to disease*) propensión; responsabilidad, obligación; desventaja; **liabilities** deudas; (*as detailed in balance sheet*) pasivo
liability insurance *s* seguro de responsabilidad civil
liable ['laɪ•əbəl] *adj* (*e.g., to disease*) propenso, expuesto; responsable; **to**

be liable to + *inf* (coll) amenazar + *inf*

liaison ['li·ə,zɑn] o [li'ezən] *s* enlace *m,* unión; (*illicit relationship between a man and woman*) amancebamiento, enredo, lío; (mil, nav & phonet) enlace *m*

liaison officer *s* (mil) oficial *m* de enlace

liar ['laɪ·ər] *s* mentiroso

lb. *abbr* **librarian, library**

libation [laɪ'beʃən] *s* libación; (*drink*) libación

li·bel ['laɪbəl] *s* calumnia, difamación; (*defamatory writing*) libelo ‖ *v* (*pret & pp* **-beled** o **-belled;** *ger* **-beling** o **-belling)** *tr* calumniar, difamar

libelous ['laɪbələs] *adj* calumniador

liberal ['lɪbərəl] *adj* (*generous; done or given generously*) liberal; (*open-minded*) tolerante, de amplias miras; (*translation*) libre; (pol) liberal ‖ *s* liberal *mf*

liberali·ty [,lɪbə'rælɪti] *s* (*pl* **-ties)** liberalidad

liberal-minded ['lɪbərəl'maɪndɪd] *adj* tolerante, de amplias miras

liberate ['lɪbə,ret] *tr* libertar; (*to disengage from a combination*) (chem) desprender

liberation [,lɪbə'reʃən] *s* liberación; (chem) desprendimiento

liberator ['lɪbə,retər] *s* libertador *m*

libertine ['lɪbər,tin] *adj & s* libertino

liber·ty ['lɪbərti] *s* (*pl* **-ties)** libertad; **to take the liberty to** tomarse la libertad de

liberty-loving ['lɪbərti'lʌvɪŋ] *adj* amante de la libertad

libidinous [lɪ'bɪdɪnəs] *adj* libidinoso

libido [lɪ'bido] o [lɪ'baɪdo] *s* libídine *f,* libido *f*

librarian [laɪ'brɛrɪ·ən] *s* bibliotecario

librar·y ['laɪ,brɛri] o ['laɪbrəri] *s* (*pl* **-ies)** biblioteca

library number *s* signatura

library school *s* escuela de bibliotecarios

library science *s* bibliotecnia

libret·to [lɪ'brɛto] *s* (*pl* **-tos)** (mus) libreto

license ['laɪsəns] *s* licencia ‖ *tr* licenciar

license number *s* número de matrícula

license plate o **tag** *s* chapa de circulación, placa de matrícula

licentious [laɪ'sɛnʃəs] *adj* licencioso, disoluto

lichen ['laɪkən] *s* liquen *m*

lick [lɪk] *s* lamedura; (*place where animals go to lick*) lamedero; (*blow*) (coll) bofetón *m;* (*speed*) (coll) velocidad; (*beating*) (coll) zurra; (*quick cleaning*) (coll) limpión *m;* **to give a lick and a promise to** (coll) hacer rápida y superficialmente ‖ *tr* lamer; lamerse (*p.ej., los dedos*); lamer (*las llamas un tejado*); (*to beat, thrash*) (coll) zurrar; (*to conquer*) (coll) vencer

licorice ['lɪkərɪs] *s* regaliz *m,* orozuz *m;* dulce *m* de regaliz

lid [lɪd] *s* (*of a box, trunk, chest, etc.*) tapa, tapadera; (*of a dish, pot, etc.*) cobertera; (*eyelid*) párpado; (*hat*) (slang) techo

lie [laɪ] *s* mentira; **to catch in a lie** coger en una mentira; **to give the lie to** dar un mentís a ‖ *v* (*pret & pp* **lied;** *ger* **lying)** *tr* — **to lie oneself out of** o **to lie one's way out of** librarse de un aprieto mintiendo ‖ *intr* mentir ‖ *v* (*pret* **lay** [le]; *pp* **lain** [len]; *ger* **lying)** *intr* estar echado; hallarse, estar situado; (*e.g., in the grave*) yacer, estar enterrado; **to lie down** echarse, acostarse

lie detector *s* detector *m* de mentiras

lien [lin] o ['li·ən] *s* gravamen *m,* derecho de retención

lieu [lu] *s* — **in lieu of** en lugar de, en vez de

lieutenant [lu'tɛnənt] *s* lugarteniente *m;* (mil) teniente *m;* (nav) teniente de navío

lieutenant colonel *s* (mil) teniente coronel *m*

lieutenant commander *s* (nav) capitán *m* de corbeta

lieutenant governor *s* (U.S.A.) vicegobernador *m* (*de un Estado*)

lieutenant junior grade *s* (nav) alférez *m* de navío

life [laɪf] *adj* (*animate*) vital; (*lifelong*) perpetuo; (*annuity, income*) vitalicio; (*working from nature*) (fa) del natural ‖ *s* (*pl* **lives** [laɪvz]) vida; (*of an insurance policy*) vigencia; **for life** de por vida; **for the life of me** así me maten; **the life and soul of** (*e.g., a party*) la alegría de; **to come to life** volver a la vida; **to depart this life** partir de esta vida; **to run for one's life** salvarse por los pies

life annuity *s* renta vitalicia

life belt *s* cinturón *m* salvavidas

life'boat' *s* bote *m* de salvamento, bote salvavidas; (*for shore-based rescue services*) lancha de auxilio

life buoy *s* boya salvavidas, guindola

life float *s* balsa salvavidas

life'guard' *s* salvavidas *m,* guardavida *m*

life imprisonment *s* cadena perpetua

life insurance *s* seguro sobre la vida

life jacket *s* chaleco salvavidas

lifeless ['laɪflɪs] *adj* muerto, sin vida; (*in a faint*) desmayado, exánime; (*dull, colorless*) deslucido

life'like' *adj* natural, vivo

life line *s* cuerda salvavidas; cuerda de buzo

life'long' *adj* perpetuo, de toda la vida

life of leisure *s* vida de ocio

life of Riley ['raɪli] *s* (slang) vida regalada

life of the party *s* (coll) alegría de la fiesta, alma de la fiesta

life preserver [prɪ'zʌrvər] *s* chaleco salvavidas

lifer ['laɪfər] *s* (slang) presidiario de por vida

life'sav'er *s* salvador *m* (*de vidas*); (*something that saves a person from* *a predicament*) (coll) tabla de salvación

lifesaving ['laɪf,sevɪŋ] *adj* de salvamento || *s* salvamento (*de vidas*)

life sentence *s* condena a cadena perpetua

life'-size' *adj* de tamaño natural

life'time' *adj* vitalicio || *s* vida, curso de la vida, jornada

life'work' *s* obra principal de la vida de uno

lift [lɪft] *s* elevación, levantamiento; ayuda (*para levantar una carga*); (aer) sustentación; **to give a lift to** invitar (*a un peatón*) a subir a un coche; llevar en un coche; (fig) reanimar || *tr* elevar, levantar; quitarse (*el sombrero*); (naut) izar (*velas, vergas, etc.*); (fig) reanimar, exaltar; (coll) robar; (coll) plagiar || *intr* elevarse, levantarse; disiparse (*las nubes, las nieblas, la obscuridad, etc.*)

lift bridge *s* puente levadizo

lift'-off' *s* despegue *m* vertical

lift truck *s* carretilla elevadora

ligament ['lɪgəmənt] *s* ligamento

ligature ['lɪgətʃər] *s* (mus & surg) ligadura; (mus & typ) ligado

light [laɪt] *adj* (*in weight*) ligero, leve, liviano; (*having illumination; whitish*) claro; (*hair*) blondo, rubio; (*complexion*) blanco; (*oil*) flúido; (*beer*) claro; (*reading*) poco serio; (*heart*) alegre, despreocupado; (*carrying a small cargo or none at all*) (naut) boyante; **light in the head** (*dizzy*) aturdido, mareado; (*simple, silly*) tonto, necio; **to make light of** no dar importancia a, no tomar en serio || *adv* sin carga; sin equipaje || *s* luz *f;* (*to light a cigarette*) lumbre *f*, fuego; (*to control traffic*) luz, señal *f;* (*window or other opening in a wall*) luz, claro, hueco; (*example, shining figure*) lumbrera; **according to one's lights** según Dios le da a uno a entender; **against the light** al trasluz; **in this light** desde este punto de vista; **lights** noticias; (*of sheep, etc.*) bofes *mpl;* **to come to light** salir a luz, descubrirse; **to shed** o **throw light on** echar luz sobre; **to strike a light** echar una yesca; encender un fósforo || *v* (*pret & pp* **lighted** o **lit** [lɪt]) *tr* (*to furnish with illumination*) alumbrar, iluminar; (*to set afire, ignite*) encender; **to light up** iluminar || *intr* alumbrarse; encenderse; posar (*un ave*); (*from an auto*) bajar; **to light into** (*to attack*) (slang) arremeter contra; (*to scold, berate*) (slang) poner de oro y azul; **to light out** (slang) poner pies en polvorosa; **to light upon** tropezar con, hallar por casualidad

light bulb *s* (elec) bombilla

light complexion *s* tez blanca

lighten ['laɪtən] *tr* (*to make lighter in weight*) aligerar; iluminar; (*to cheer up*) alegrar, regocijar || *intr* (*to become less dark*) iluminarse; (*to give off flashes of lightning*) relampaguear; (fig) iluminarse (*los ojos, la cara de una persona*)

lighter ['laɪtər] *s* (*to light a cigarette*) encendedor *m;* (*flat-bottomed barge*) alijador *m*

light-fingered ['laɪt'fɪŋgərd] *adj* largo de uñas, listo de manos

light-footed ['laɪt'futɪd] *adj* ligero de pies

light-headed ['laɪt'hɛdɪd] *adj* (*dizzy*) aturdido, mareado; (*simple, silly*) tonto, necio, ligero de cascos

light-hearted ['laɪt'hɑrtɪd] *adj* alegre, libre de cuidados

light'house' *s* faro

lighting ['laɪtɪŋ] *s* alumbrado, iluminación

lighting fixtures *spl* artefactos de alumbrado

lightly ['laɪtli] *adj* ligeramente

light meter *s* exposímetro

lightness ['laɪtnɪs] *s* (*in weight*) ligereza; (*in illumination*) claridad

lightning ['laɪtnɪŋ] *s* relámpagos, relampagueo || *intr* relampaguear

lightning arrester [ə'rɛstər] *s* pararrayos *m*

lightning bug *s* luciérnaga

lightning rod *s* pararrayos *m*

light opera *s* opereta

light'ship' *s* buque *m* fanal, buque faro

light-struck ['laɪt,strʌk] *adj* velado

light'weight' *adj* ligero; de entretiempo, p.ej., **lightweight coat** abrigo de entretiempo

light'-year' *s* año luz

lignite ['lɪgnaɪt] *s* lignito

lignum vitae ['lɪgnəm'vaɪti] *s* guayaco, palo santo

likable ['laɪkəbəl] *adj* simpático

like [laɪk] *adj* parecido, semejante; parecido a, semejante a, p.ej., **this hat is like mine** este sombrero es parecido al mío; (elec) del mismo nombre; **like father like son** de tal palo tal astilla; **to feel like** + *ger* tener ganas de + *inf;* **to look like** parecerse a; parecer que, p.ej., **it looks like rain** parece que va a llover || *adv* como; **like enough** (coll) probablemente; **nothing like** ni con mucho || *prep* a semejanza de || *conj* (coll) del mismo modo que; (coll) que, p.ej., **it seems like he is right** parece que tiene razón || *s* (*liking*) gusto, preferencia; (*fellow, fellow man*) prójimo, semejante *m;* **and the like** y cosas por el estilo; **to give like for like** pagar en la misma moneda || *tr* gustar de, p.ej., **I like music** gusto de la música; gustar, p.ej., **Mary likes peaches** a María le gustan los melocotones; **to like best** o **better** preferir; **to like it in** encontrarse a gusto en (*p.ej., el campo*); **to like to** + *inf* gustarle a uno + *inf*, p.ej., **I like to travel** me gusta viajar; gustarle a uno que + *subj*, p.ej., **I should like him to come to see me** me gustaría que él viniese a verme ||

intr querer, p.ej., **as you like** como Vd. quiera; **if you like** si Vd. quiere
likelihood ['laɪklɪ,hʊd] *s* probabilidad
like·ly ['laɪkli] *adj* (*comp* **-lier**; *super* **-liest**) probable; a propósito; prometedor; **to be likely to** + *inf* ser probable que + *ind*, p.ej., **Mary is likely to come to see us tomorrow** es probable que María vendrá a vernos mañana || *adv* probablemente
like-minded ['laɪk'maɪndɪd] *adj* del mismo parecer; de natural semejante
liken ['laɪkən] *tr* asemejar, comparar
likeness ['laɪknɪs] *s* (*picture or image*) retrato; (*similarity*) semejanza, parecido; forma, aspecto, apariencia
like'wise' *adv* igualmente, asimismo; **to do likewise** hacer lo mismo
liking ['laɪkɪŋ] *s* gusto, afición, simpatía; **to be to the liking of** ser del gusto de; **to have a liking for** aficionarse a
lilac ['laɪlək] *adj* de color lila || *s* lilac *m*, lila
Lilliputian [,lɪlɪ'pjuʃən] *adj* & *s* liliputiense *mf*
lilt [lɪlt] *s* paso airoso, movimiento airoso; canción cadenciosa, música alegre
lil·y ['lɪli] *s* (*pl* **-ies**) (*Lilium candidum*) azucena, lirio blanco; cala, lirio de agua; (*fleur-de-lis, the royal arms of France*) flor *f* de lis; **to gild the lily** ponerle colores al oro
lily of the valley *s* lirio de los valles, muguete *m*
lily pad *s* hoja de nenúfar
Lima bean ['laɪmə] *s* judía de la peladilla, frijol *m* de media luna
limb [lɪm] *s* (*arm or leg*) miembro; (*of a tree*) rama; (*of a cross; of the sea*) brazo; **to be out on a limb** (coll) estar en un aprieto
limber ['lɪmbər] *adj* ágil; flexible || *intr* — **to limber up** agilitarse
lim·bo ['lɪmbo] *s* (*pl* **-bos**) lugar *m* de olvido; (theol) limbo
lime [laɪm] *s* (*calcium oxide*) cal *f;* (*Citrus aurantifolia*) limero agrio; (*its fruit*) lima agria; (*linden tree*) tila o tilo
lime'kiln' *s* calera, horno de cal
lime'light' *s* — **to be in the limelight** estar a la vista del público
limerick ['lɪmərɪk] *s* quintilla jocosa
lime'stone' *adj* calizo || *s* caliza, piedra caliza
limit ['lɪmɪt] *s* límite *m;* **to be the limit** (slang) ser el colmo; **to go the limit** no dejar piedra por mover || *tr* limitar
lim'ited-ac'cess high'way *s* carretera de vía libre
limited monarchy *s* monarquía constitucional
limitless ['lɪmɪtlɪs] *adj* ilimitado
limousine ['lɪmə,zin] o [,lɪmə'zin] *s* (aut) limusina
limp [lɪmp] *adj* flojo, débil, flexible || *s* cojera || *intr* cojear
limpid ['lɪmpɪd] *adj* diáfano, cristalino
linage ['laɪnɪdʒ] *s* (typ) número de líneas
linchpin ['lɪntʃ,pɪn] *s* pezonera
linden ['lɪndən] *s* tila, tilo
line [laɪn] *s* línea; (*of people, houses, etc.*) hilera; (*rope, string*) cuerda, cordel *m;* (*wrinkle*) arruga; (*for fishing*) sedal *m;* (*written or printed line; line of goods*) renglón *m;* manera (*de pensar*); (*of the spectrum*) (phys) raya; **all along the line** por todas partes; desde cualquier punto de vista; **in line** alineado; dispuesto, preparado; **in line with** de acuerdo con; **out of line** desalineado; en desacuerdo; **to bring into line** poner de acuerdo; **to draw the line at** no ir más allá de; **to fall in line** conformarse; formar cola; alinearse; **to have a line on** (coll) estar enterado de; **to read between the lines** leer entre líneas; **to stand in line** hacer cola; **to toe the line** obrar como se debe; **to wait in line** hacer cola, esperar vez || *tr* alinear, rayar; arrugar (*p.ej., la cara*); formar hilera a lo largo de (*la acera, la calle*); forrar (*un vestido*); guarnecer (*un freno*) || *intr* — **to line up** ponerse en fila; hacer cola
lineage ['lɪnɪ·ɪdʒ] *s* linaje *m*
lineaments ['lɪnɪ·əmənts] *spl* lineamentos
linear ['lɪnɪ·ər] *adj* lineal
line·man ['laɪnmən] *s* (*pl* **-men** [mən]) (elec) celador *m*, recorredor *m* de la línea; (rr) guardavía *m;* (surv) cadenero
linen ['lɪnən] *adj* de lino || *s* (*fabric*) lienzo, lino; (*yarn*) hilo de lino; ropa blanca, ropa de cama
linen closet *s* armario para la ropa blanca
line of battle *s* línea de batalla
line of fire *s* (mil) línea de tiro
line of least resistance *s* ley *f* del menor esfuerzo; **to follow the line of least resistance** seguir la corriente, no oponer resistencia
line of sight *s* visual *f;* (*of firearm*) línea de mira
liner ['laɪnər] *s* vapor *m* de travesía; (baseball) pelota rasa, lineazo
line'-up' *s* agrupación, formación; (*of prisoners*) rueda
linger ['lɪŋgər] *intr* estarse, quedarse; (*to be tardy*) demorar, tardar; tardar en marcharse; tardar en morirse; pasearse con paso lento; **to linger over** contemplar, reflexionar
lingerie [,lænʒə'ri] *s* ropa interior de mujer
lingering ['lɪŋgərɪŋ] *adj* prolongado
lingual ['lɪŋgwəl] *adj* & *s* lingual *f*
linguist ['lɪŋgwɪst] *s* (*person skilled in several languages*) polígloto; (*specialist in linguistics*) lingüista *mf*
linguistic [lɪŋ'gwɪstɪk] *adj* lingüístico || **linguistics** *s* lingüística
liniment ['lɪnɪmənt] *s* linimento
lining ['laɪnɪŋ] *s* (*of a coat*) forro; (*of auto brake*) guarnición; (*of a fur-*

nace) camisa; (*of a wall*) revestimiento
link [lɪŋk] *s* eslabón *m;* **links** campo de golf || *tr* eslabonar || *intr* eslabonarse
linnet [ˈlɪnɪt] *s* pardillo
linoleum [lɪˈnolɪ·əm] *s* linóleo
linotype [ˈlaɪnə,taɪp] (trademark) *adj* linotípico || *s* (*machine*) linotipia; (*matter produced by machine*) linotipo || *tr* componer con linotipia
linotype operator *s* linotipista *mf*
linseed [ˈlɪn,sid] *s* linaza
linseed oil *s* aceite *m* de linaza
lint [lɪnt] *s* borra, pelusa, hilaza; (*used to dress wounds*) hilas
lintel [ˈlɪntəl] *s* dintel *m,* umbral *m*
lion [ˈlaɪ·ən] *s* león *m;* (*man of strength and courage*) (fig) león; (fig) celebridad muy solicitada; **to beard the lion in his den** ir a desafiar la cólera de un jefe; **to put one's head in the lion's mouth** meterse en la boca del lobo
lioness [ˈlaɪ·ənɪs] *s* leona
lion-hearted [ˈlaɪ·ən,hartɪd] *adj* valiente
lionize [ˈlaɪ·ə,naɪz] *tr* agasajar
lions' den *s* (Bib) fosa de los leones
lion's share *s* (la) parte *f* del león
lip [lɪp] *s* labio; (slang) lenguaje *m* insolente; **to hang on the lips of** estar pendiente de las palabras de; **to smack one's lips** chuparse los labios
lip'-read' *v* (*pret & pp* **-read** [,rɛd]) *tr & intr* leer en los labios
lip reading *s* labiolectura
lip service *s* homenaje *m* de boca, jarabe *m* de pico
lip'stick' *s* lápiz *m* de labios, lápiz labial
liq. *abbr* **liquid, liquor**
lique·fy [ˈlɪkwɪ,faɪ] *v* (*pret & pp* **-fied**) *tr* liquidar || *intr* liquidarse
liqueur [lɪˈkʌr] *s* licor *m*
liquid [ˈlɪkwɪd] *adj* líquido || *s* líquido; (phonet) líquida
liquidate [ˈlɪkwɪ,det] *tr & intr* liquidar
liquidity [lɪˈkwɪdɪti] *s* liquidez *f*
liquid measure *s* medida para líquidos
liquor [ˈlɪkər] *s* licor *m*
Lisbon [ˈlɪzbən] *s* Lisboa
lisle [laɪl] *s* hilo fino de algodón, muy retorcido, sedalina
lisp [lɪsp] *s* ceceo || *intr* cecear
lissome [ˈlɪsəm] *adj* flexible, elástico; ágil, ligero
list [lɪst] *s* lista; (*strip*) lista, tira; (*border*) orilla; (*selvage*) orillo; (naut) ladeo; **lists** liza; **to enter the lists** entrar en liza; **to have a list** (naut) irse a la banda || *tr* alistar, listar; registrar || *intr* (naut) irse a la banda
listen [ˈlɪsən] *intr* escuchar; obedecer; **to listen in** escuchar a hurtadillas; escuchar por radio; **to listen to** escuchar; obedecer; **to listen to reason** meterse en razón
listener [ˈlɪsənər] *s* oyente *mf;* radioescucha *mf,* radioyente *mf*
listening post [ˈlɪsənɪŋ] *s* puesto de escucha
listless [ˈlɪstlɪs] *adj* distraído, desatento, indiferente
list price *s* precio de catálogo, precio de tarifa
lit. *abbr* **liter, literal, literature**
lita·ny [ˈlɪtəni] *s* (*pl* **-nies**) letanía; (*repeated series*) (fig) letanía
liter [ˈlitər] *s* litro
literacy [ˈlɪtərəsi] *s* capacidad de leer y escribir; instrucción
literal [ˈlɪtərəl] *adj* literal
literary [ˈlɪtə,rɛri] *adj* literario; (*individual*) literato
literate [ˈlɪtərɪt] *adj* que sabe leer y escribir; (*well-read*) literato, muy leído; (*educated*) instruído || *s* persona que sabe leer y escribir; literato, erudito
literati [,lɪtəˈrati] *spl* literatos
literature [ˈlɪtərətʃər] *s* literatura; impresos, escritos de publicidad
lithe [laiθ] *adj* flexible, cimbreño
lithia [ˈlɪθɪ·ə] *s* (chem) litina
lithium [ˈlɪθɪ·əm] *s* (chem) litio
lithograph [ˈlɪθə,græf] o [ˈlɪθə,graf] *s* litografía || *tr* litografiar
lithographer [lɪˈθagrəfər] *s* litógrafo
lithography [lɪˈθagrəfi] *s* litografía
litigant [ˈlɪtɪgənt] *adj & s* litigante *mf*
litigate [ˈlɪtɪ,get] *tr & intr* litigar
litigation [,lɪtɪˈgeʃən] *s* litigación; (*lawsuit*) litigio
litigious [lɪˈtɪdʒəs] *adj* litigioso
litmus [ˈlɪtməs] *s* tornasol *m*
litmus paper *s* papel *m* de tornasol
litter [ˈlɪtər] *s* desorden *m;* (*scattered rubbish*) basura, papelería; (*young brought forth at one birth*) camada, ventregada; (*bedding for animals*) cama, paja; (*vehicle carried by men or animals*) litera; (*stretcher*) camilla, parihuela || *tr* esparcir papeles por; esparcir (*desechos, papeles, etc.*); cubrir (*el suelo*) con paja || *intr* parir
lit'ter·bug' *s* persona que ensucia las calles tirando papeles rotos
littering [ˈlɪtərɪŋ] *s* — **no littering** se prohibe tirar papeles rotos
little [ˈlɪtəl] *adj* (*in size*) pequeño; (*in amount*) poco, p.ej., **little money** poco dinero; **a little** un poco de, p.ej., **a little money** un poco de dinero || *adv* poco; **little by little** poco a poco || *s* poco; **a little** un poco; (*somewhat*) algo; **to make little of** no dar importancia a, no tomar en serio; **to think little of** tener en poco; no vacilar en
Little Bear *s* Osa menor
Little Dipper *s* Carro menor
little finger *s* dedo auricular, dedo meñique; **to twist around one's little finger** manejar con suma facilidad
lit'tle·neck' *s* almeja redonda (*Venus mercenaria*)
little owl *s* mochuelo (*Athene noctua*)
little people *spl* hadas; gente menuda
Little Red Ridinghood [ˈraɪdɪŋ,hʊd] *s* Caperucita Roja
little slam *s* (bridge) semibola

liturgic(al) [lɪ'tʌrdʒɪk(əl)] *adj* litúrgico
litur·gy ['lɪtərdʒi] *s* (*pl* **-gies**) liturgia
livable ['lɪvəbəl] *adj* habitable, vividero; llevadero, tolerable
live [laɪv] *adj* (*living; full of life; intense*) vivo; (*coals; flame*) ardiente; de actualidad; (elec) cargado || [lɪv] *tr* llevar (*tal o cual vida*); vivir (*una experiencia, una aventura; un actor sus personajes*); **to live down** borrar (*una falta*); **to live out** vivir (*toda la vida*); salir con vida de (*un desastre, una guerra*) || *intr* vivir; **to live and learn** vivir para ver; **to live and let live** vivir y dejar vivir; **to live high** darse buena vida; **to live on** seguir viviendo; vivir de (*p.ej., carne*); vivir a expensas de; **to live up to** cumplir (*lo prometido*); gastar (*todas sus rentas*)
live coal *s* ascua
livelihood ['laɪvlɪ,hʊd] *s* vida; **to earn one's livelihood** ganarse la vida
livelong ['lɪv,lɔŋ] o ['lɪv,lɑŋ] *adj* — **all the livelong day** todo el santo día
live·ly ['laɪvli] *adj* (*comp* **-lier**; *super* **-liest**) animado, vivaz; alegre, festivo; (*active, keen*) vivo; (*resilient*) elástico
liven ['laɪvən] *tr* animar, regocijar || *intr* animarse, regocijarse
liver ['lɪvər] *s* vividor *m;* habitante *mf;* (anat) hígado
liver·y ['lɪvəri] *s* (*pl* **-ies**) librea
livery·man ['lɪvərimən] *s* (*pl* **-men** [mən]) dueño de una cochera; mozo de cuadra
livery stable *s* cochera de carruajes de alquiler
live'stock' *adj* ganadero || *s* ganadería
live wire *s* (elec) alambre cargado; (slang) trafagón *m*
livid ['lɪvɪd] *adj* lívido, amoratado; encolerizado; pálido
living ['lɪvɪŋ] *adj* vivo, viviente || *s* vida; **to earn** o **to make a living** ganarse la vida
living quarters *spl* aposentos, habitaciones
living room *s* sala, sala de estar
living wage *s* jornal *m* suficiente para vivir
lizard ['lɪzərd] *s* lagarto; (slang) holgón *m*
load [lod] *s* carga; **loads** (coll) muchísimo; **loads of** (coll) gran cantidad de; **to get a load of** (slang) escuchar, oír; (slang) mirar; **to have a load on** (slang) estar borracho || *tr* cargar || *intr* cargar; cargarse
loaded ['lodɪd] *adj* cargado; (slang) muy borracho; (slang) muy rico
loaded dice *spl* dados cargados
load'stone' *s* piedra imán; (fig) imán *m*
loaf [lof] *s* (*pl* **loaves** [lovz]) pan *m;* (*of sugar*) pilón *m* || *intr* haraganear
loafer ['lofər] *s* haragán *m*
loam [lom] *s* suelo franco; (*mixture used in making molds*) tierra de moldeo
loamy ['lomi] *adj* franco
loan [lon] *s* (*among individuals*) préstamo; (*between companies or governments*) empréstito; **to hit for a loan** (coll) dar un sablazo a || *tr* prestar
loan shark *s* (coll) usurero
loan word *s* préstamo lingüístico
loath [loθ] *adj* poco dispuesto; **nothing loath** de buena gana
loathe [loð] *tr* abominar, detestar
loathing ['loðɪŋ] *s* abominación, detestación
loathsome ['loðsəm] *adj* abominable, asqueroso
lob [lɑb] *v* (*pret & pp* **lobbed;** *ger* **lobbing**) *tr* (tennis) volear desde muy alto
lob·by ['lɑbi] *s* (*pl* **-bies**) salón *m* de entrada, vestíbulo; cabilderos || *v* (*pret & pp* **-bied**) *intr* cabildear
lobbying ['lɑbɪ·ɪŋ] *s* cabildeo
lobbyist ['lɑbɪ·ɪst] *s* cabildero
lobster ['lɑbstər] *s* (*spiny lobster*) langosta; (*Homarus*) bogavante *m*
lobster pot *s* langostera
local ['lokəl] *adj* local || *s* tren suburbano; (*branch of a union*) junta local; noticia de interés local
locale [lo'kæl] *s* localidad
locali·ty [lo'kælɪti] *s* (*pl* **-ties**) localidad
localize ['lokə,laɪz] *tr* localizar
local option *s* derecho local de legislar sobre la venta de bebidas alcohólicas
locate [lo'ket] o ['loket] *tr* (*to discover the location of*) localizar; (*to place, to settle*) colocar, establecer; (*to ascribe a particular location to*) situar || *intr* establecerse
location [lo'keʃən] *s* (*place, position*) localidad; (*act of placing*) colocación; (*act of finding*) localización; **on location** (mov) en exteriores
loc. cit. *abbr* **loco citato (Lat) in the place cited**
lock [lɑk] *s* cerradura; (*of a canal*) esclusa; (*of hair*) bucle *m;* (*of a firearm*) llave *f;* **lock, stock, and barrel** (coll) del todo, por completo; **under lock and key** bajo llave || *tr* echar la llave a, cerrar con llave; (*to key*) acuñar; hacer pasar (*un buque*) por la esclusa; abrazar, enlazar; **to lock in** encerrar, poner debajo de llave; **to lock out** cerrar la puerta a, dejar en la calle; dejar sin trabajo (*a los obreros*); **to lock up** encerrar, poner debajo de llave; encarcelar
locker ['lɑkər] *s* armario cerrado con llave
locket ['lɑkɪt] *s* guardapelo, medallón *m*
lock'jaw' *s* trismo, oclusión forzosa de la boca
lock nut *s* contratuerca
lock'out' *s* huelga patronal
lock'smith' *s* cerrajero
lock step *s* marcha en fila apretada
lock stitch *s* punto encadenado
lock tender *s* esclusero
lock'up' *s* cárcel *f*
lock washer *s* arandela de seguridad

locomotive [ˌlokəˈmotɪv] *s* locomotora

lo•cus [ˈlokəs] *s* (*pl* **-ci** [saɪ]) sitio, lugar *m;* lugar (geométrico)

locust [ˈlokəst] *s* (ent) langosta (*Pachytylus*); (ent) cigarra (*Cicada*); (bot) acacia falsa

lode [lod] *s* filón *m,* venero, veta

lode′star′ *s* (astr) estrella polar; estrella de guía; (*guide, direction*) guía, norte *m*

lodge [lɑdʒ] *s* casa de guarda; casa de campo; (*e.g., of Masons*) logia || *tr* alojar, hospedar; depositar, colocar; presentar (*una queja*) || alojarse, hospedarse; quedar colgado, ir a parar

lodger [ˈlɑdʒər] *s* inquilino (*en parte de una casa*)

lodging [ˈlɑdʒɪŋ] *s* alojamiento, hospedaje *m;* (*without meals*) cobijo

loft [lɔft] o [lɑft] *s* (*attic*) desván *m,* sobrado; (*hayloft*) henal *m,* pajar *m;* (*in theater or church*) galería; (*in a store or office building*) piso alto

loft•y [ˈlɔfti] o [ˈlɑfti] *adj* (*comp* **-ier;** *super* **-iest**) (*towering; sublime*) encumbrado; (*haughty*) altivo, orgulloso

log. *abbr* **logarithm**

log [lɔg] o [lɑg] *s* leño, tronco; (*log chip*) (naut) barquilla; (*chip and line*) (naut) corredera; (aer) diario de vuelo; **to sleep like a log** dormir como un leño || *v* (*pret & pp* **logged;** *ger* **logging**) *tr* registrar; recorrer (*cierta distancia*)

logarithm [ˈlɔgəˌrɪðəm] o [ˈlɑgəˌrɪðəm] *s* logaritmo

log′book′ *s* (aer) libro de vuelo; (naut) cuaderno de bitácora

log cabin *s* cabaña de troncos

log chip *s* (naut) barquilla

log driver *s* ganchero, maderero

log driving *s* flotaje *m*

logger [ˈlɔgər] o [ˈlɑgər] *s* leñador *m,* maderero; grúa de troncos; tractor *m*

log′ger•head′ *s* mentecato; **at loggerheads** reñidos

loggia [ˈlodʒə] *s* (archit) logia

logic [ˈlɑdʒɪk] *s* lógica

logical [ˈlɑdʒɪkəl] *adj* lógico

logician [loˈdʒɪʃən] *s* lógico

logistic(al) [loˈdʒɪstɪk(əl)] *adj* logístico

logistics [loˈdʒɪstɪks] *s* logística

log′jam′ *s* atasco de rollizos; (fig) estancación

log line *s* (naut) corredera

log′roll′ *intr* trocar favores políticos

log′wood′ *s* campeche *m*

loin [lɔɪn] *s* lomo; **to gird up one's loins** apercibirse para la acción

loin′cloth′ *s* taparrabo

loiter [ˈlɔɪtər] *tr* — **to loiter away** malgastar (*el tiempo*) || *intr* holgazanear, rezagarse

loiterer [ˈlɔɪtərər] *s* holgazán *m,* rezagado

loll [lɑl] *intr* colgar flojamente; arrellanarse, repantigarse

lollipop [ˈlɑliˌpɑp] *s* paleta (*dulce en el extremo de un palito*)

Lombard [ˈlɑmbɑrd] o [ˈlɑmbərd] *adj & s* lombardo

Lombardy [ˈlɑmbərdi] *s* Lombardía

Lombardy poplar *s* álamo de Italia, chopo lombardo

lon. *abbr* **longitude**

London [ˈlʌndən] *adj* londinense || *s* Londres *m*

Londoner [ˈlʌndənər] *s* londinense *mf*

lone [lon] *adj* solo, solitario; (*sole, single*) único

loneliness [ˈlonlinɪs] *s* soledad

lone•ly [ˈlonli] *adj* (*comp* **-lier;** *super* **-liest**) soledoso

lonesome [ˈlonsəm] *adj* soledoso; (*spot, atmosphere*) solitario

lone wolf *s* (fig) lobo solitario

long. *abbr* **longitude**

long [lɔŋ] o [lɑŋ] (*comp* **longer** [ˈlɔŋgər] o [ˈlɑŋgər]; *super* **longest** [ˈlɔŋgɪst] o [ˈlɑŋgɪst]) *adj* largo; de largo, p.ej., **two meters long** dos metros de largo || *adv* mucho tiempo, largo tiempo; **as long as** mientras; (*provided*) con tal de que; (*inasmuch as*) puesto que; **before long** dentro de poco; **how long** cuánto tiempo; **long ago** hace mucho tiempo; **long before** mucho antes; **longer** más tiempo; **long since** desde hace mucho tiempo; **no longer** ya no; **so long!** (coll) ¡hasta luego!; **so long as** con tal de que || *intr* anhelar, suspirar; **to long for** anhelar por, ansiar

long′boat′ *s* (naut) lancha

long′-dis′tance call *s* (telp) llamada a larga distancia

long-distance flight *s* (aer) vuelo a distancia

long′-drawn′-out′ *adj* prolongado, pesado

longeron [ˈlɑndʒərən] *s* larguero

longevity [lɑnˈdʒevɪti] *s* longevidad

long face *s* (coll) cara triste

long′hair′ *adj & s* intelectual *mf;* aficionado a la música clásica

long′hand′ *s* escritura a mano

longing [ˈlɔŋɪŋ] o [ˈlɑŋɪŋ] *adj* anhelante || *s* anhelo, ansia

longitude [ˈlɑndʒɪˌtjud] o [ˈlɑndʒɪˌtud] *s* longitud

long-lived [ˈlɔŋˈlaɪvd], [ˈlɔŋˈlɪvd], [ˈlɑŋˈlaɪvd] o [ˈlɑŋˈlɪvd] *adj* longevo, de larga vida

long-playing record [ˈlɔŋˈple·ɪŋ] o [ˈlɑŋˈple·ɪŋ] *s* disco de larga duración

long primer [ˈprɪmər] *s* (typ) entredós *m*

long′-range′ *adj* de largo alcance

longshore•man [ˈlɔŋˌʃormən] o [ˈlɑŋˌʃormən] *s* (*pl* **-men** [mən]) *s* estibador *m,* portuario

long′-stand′ing *adj* que existe desde hace mucho tiempo

long′-suf′fering *adj* longánimo, sufrido

long suit *s* (cards) palo fuerte; (fig) fuerte *m*

long′-term′ *adj* a largo plazo

long′-wind′ed *adj* difuso, palabrero

look [lʊk] *s* (*appearance*) aspecto, apariencia; (*glance*) mirada; (*search*) búsqueda; **looks** aspecto, apariencia; **to take a look at** echar una mirada a || *tr* expresar con la mirada; representar (*la edad que uno tiene*); **to look daggers at** apuñalar con la mirada; **to look the part** vestir el cargo; **to look up** (*e.g., in a dictionary*) buscar; ir a visitar, venir a ver || *intr* mirar; buscar; parecer; **look out!** ¡cuidado!, ¡ojo!; **to look after** mirar por; ocuparse en; **to look at** mirar; **to look back** mirar hacia atrás; (fig) mirar el pasado; **to look down on** mirar por encima del hombro; **to look for** buscar; creer, p.ej., **I look for rain** creo que va a llover; **to look forward to** esperar con placer anticipado; **to look ill** tener mala cara; **to look in on** pasar por la casa o la oficina de; **to look into** averiguar, estudiar; **to look like** parecerse a; amenazar, p.ej., **it looks like rain** amenaza lluvia, parece que va a llover; **to look oneself** parecer el mismo; tener buena cara; **to look out** tener cuidado; mirar por (*p.ej., la ventana*); **to look out for** mirar por, cuidar de; guardarse de; **to look out on** dar a; **to look through** mirar por; hojear (*un libro*); **to look toward** dar a; **to look up to** admirar, mirar con respeto; **to look well** tener buena cara

looker-on [ˌlukərˈɑn] o [ˌlukərˈɔn] *s* (*pl* **lookers-on**) mirón *m*, espectador *m*

looking glass [ˈlukɪŋ] *s* espejo

look′out′ *s* vigilancia; (*tower*) atalaya; (*person keeping watch*) vigilante *mf;* (*man watching from lookout tower*) atalaya *m;* (*care, concern*) (coll) cuidado; **to be on the lookout for** estar a la mira de

loom [lum] *s* telar *m* || *intr* (*to appear indistinctly*) vislumbrarse; amenazar, parecer inevitable

loon [lun] *s* tonto, bobo; (orn) zambullidor *m*

loon•y [ˈluni] *adj* (*comp* **-ier;** *super* **-iest**) (slang) loco || *s* (*pl* **-ies**) (slang) loco

loop [lup] *s* lazo; (*in a cable or rope*) vuelta; (*of a river*) meandro; (*of a road*) recoveco; (*for fastening a button*) presilla; (aer) rizo; (elec) circuito cerrado; (*part of vibrating body between two nodes*) vientre *m;* **to loop the loop** (aer) rizar el rizo || *tr* hacer lazos en; enlazar || *intr* formar lazo; (aer) hacer el rizo

loop′hole′ *s* (*narrow opening in wall*) lucerna; (*means of evasion*) efugio, escapatoria

loose [lus] *adj* (*dress, tooth, screw, bowels*) flojo; (*fitting, thread, wire, rivet, tongue, bowels*) suelto; (*sleeve*) perdido; (*earth, soil*) desmenuzado; (*unpackaged*) a granel, sin envase; (*unbound papers*) sin encuadernar; (*pulley*) loco; (*translation*) libre; (*life, morals*) relajado; (*woman*) fácil, frágil; **to become loose** desatarse, aflojarse; **to break loose** ponerse en libertad; **to turn loose** soltar || *s* — **to be on the loose** (coll) ser libre, estar sin trabas; (coll) estar de juerga || *tr* soltar; desatar, desencadenar

loose end *s* cabo suelto; **at loose ends** desarreglado, indeciso

loose′-leaf′ notebook *s* cuaderno de hojas cambiables, cuaderno de hojas sueltas

loosen [ˈlusən] *tr* desatar, aflojar, desapretar; aflojar, laxar (*el vientre*) || *intr* desatarse, aflojarse, desapretarse

looseness [ˈlusnɪs] *s* flojedad, soltura; (*in morals*) relajamiento

loose′strife′ *s* lisimaquia; salicaria

loose-tongued [ˈlusˈtʌŋd] *adj* largo de lengua, ligero de lengua

loot [lut] *s* botín *m*, presa || *tr* saquear, pillar

lop [lɑp] *v* (*pret & pp* **lopped;** *ger* **lopping**) *tr* dejar caer (*p.ej., los brazos*); **to lop off** cortar; podar (*un árbol, una vid*) || *intr* colgar

lopsided [ˈlɑpˈsaɪdɪd] *adj* ladeado, sesgado; desproporcionado, asimétrico, patituerto

loquacious [loˈkweʃəs] *adj* locuaz

lord [lɔrd] *s* señor *m;* (Brit) lord *m;* (hum & poet) marido || *tr* — **to lord it over** dominar despóticamente, imponerse a

lord•ly [ˈlɔrdli] *adj* (*comp* **-lier;** *super* **-liest**) señoril; magnífico; despótico, imperioso; altivo, arrogante

Lord's Day, the el domingo

lordship [ˈlɔrdʃɪp] *s* señoría, excelencia

Lord's Prayer *s* oración dominical, padrenuestro

Lord's Supper *s* sagrada comunión; Cena del Señor

lore [lor] *s* ciencia, saber *m;* ciencia popular, saber *m* popular

lorgnette [lɔrnˈjɛt] *s* (*eyeglasses*) impertinentes *mpl;* (*opera glasses*) gemelos de teatro con manija

lor•ry [ˈlɑri] o [ˈlɔri] *s* (*pl* **-ries**) carro de plataforma; (Brit) autocamión *m;* (Brit) vagoneta

lose [luz] *v* (*pret & pp* **lost** [lɔst] o [lɑst]) *tr* perder; no lograr salvar (*el médico al enfermo*); **to lose heart** desalentarse; **to lose oneself** perderse, errar el camino; ensimismarse || *intr* perder; quedar vencido; retrasarse (*el reloj*)

loser [ˈluzər] *s* perdedor *m*

losing [ˈluzɪŋ] *adj* perdedor || **losings** *spl* pérdidas, dinero perdido

loss [lɔs] o [lɑs] *s* pérdida; **to be at a loss** estar perplejo, no saber qué hacer; **to be at a loss to** + *inf* no saber como + *inf;* **to sell at a loss** vender con pérdida

loss of face *s* pérdida de prestigio, desprestigio

lost [lɔst] o [lɑst] *adj* perdido; **lost in thought** ensimismado, abismado; **lost to** perdido para; insensible a

lost′-and-found′ department *s* oficina de objetos perdidos

lost sheep *s* oveja perdida

lot [lɑt] *s* (*for building*) solar *m*, parcela; (*fate, destiny*) suerte *f*; (*portion, parcel*) lote *m*; (*of people*) grupo; (coll) gran cantidad, gran número; (coll) sujeto, tipo; **a lot (of)** o **lots of** (coll) mucho, muchos; **to cast** o **to throw in one's lot with** compartir la suerte de; **to draw** o **to cast lots** echar suertes

lotion [ˈloʃən] *s* loción

lotter•y [ˈlɑtəri] *s* (*pl* **-ies**) lotería

lotto [ˈlɑto] *s* lotería

lotus [ˈlotəs] *s* loto

loud [laʊd] *adj* alto; (*noisy*) ruidoso; (*voice*) fuerte; (*garish*) chillón, llamativo; (*conspicuously vulgar*) charro, cursi; (*foul-smelling*) apestoso, maloliente || *adv* alto, en voz alta; ruidosamente

loudmouthed [ˈlaʊd ˌmaʊθt] o [ˈlaʊd-ˌmaʊðd] *adj* vocinglero

loud′speak′er *s* altavoz *m*

lounge [laʊndʒ] *s* diván *m*, sofá *m* cama; salón *m* de descanso, salón social || *intr* repantigarse a su sabor, recostarse cómodamente; **to lounge around** estar arrimado a la pared, pasearse perezosamente

lounge lizard *s* (slang) holgón *m*

louse [laʊs] *s* (*pl* **lice** [laɪs]) piojo

lous•y [ˈlaʊzi] *adj* (*comp* **-ier**; *super* **-iest**) piojoso; (*mean*) (coll) vil, ruin; (*filthy*) (coll) asqueroso, sucio; (*bungling*) (coll) chapucero; **lousy with** (slang) colmado de (*p.ej., dinero*)

lout [laʊt] *s* patán *m*

louver [ˈluvər] *s* (*opening to let in air and light*) lumbrera; tablilla de persiana; (aut) persiana del radiador

lovable [ˈlʌvəbəl] *adj* amable

love [lʌv] *s* amor *m*; (*tennis*) cero, nada; **not for love nor money** ni a tiros; **to be in love (with)** estar enamorado (de); **to fall in love (with)** enamorarse (de); **to make love to** cortejar, galantear || *tr* amar, querer; gustar de, tener afición a

love affair *s* amores *mpl*, amorío

love′bird′ *s* inseparable *m*; **lovebirds** recién casados muy enamorados

love child *s* hijo del amor

love feast *s* ágape *m*

loveless [ˈlʌvlɪs] *adj* abandonado, sin amor; (*feeling no love*) desamado

lovelorn [ˈlʌv ˌlɔrn] *adj* abandonado por su amor, herido de amor

love•ly [ˈlʌvli] *adj* (*comp* **-lier**; *super* **-liest**) bello, hermoso; adorable, precioso; (coll) encantador, gracioso

love match *s* matrimonio de amor

love potion *s* filtro, filtro de amor

lover [ˈlʌvər] *s* amante *mf*; (*e.g., of hunting, sports*) aficionado; (*e.g., of work*) amigo

love seat *s* confidente *m*

love′sick′ *adj* enfermo de amor

love′sick′ness *s* mal *m* de amor

love song *s* canción de amor

loving [ˈlʌvɪŋ] *adj* amoroso, afectuoso

lov′ing-kind′ness *s* bondad infinita, misericordia

low [lo] *adj* bajo; (*diet; visibility; opinion*) malo; (*dress, waist*) escotado; (*depressed*) abatido; gravemente enfermo; (*fire*) lento; **to lay low** dejar tendido, derribar; matar; **to lie low** no dejarse ver || *adv* bajo || *s* punto bajo; precio más bajo, precio mínimo; (*moo of cow*) mugido; (aut) primera marcha, primera velocidad; (meteor) depresión || *intr* mugir (*la vaca*)

low′born′ *adj* de humilde cuna

low′boy′ *s* cómoda baja con patas cortas

low′brow′ *adj* & *s* (slang) ignorante *mf*

low′-cost′ housing *s* casas baratas

Low Countries, the los Países Bajos

low′-down′ *adj* (coll) bajo, vil, ruin || **low′-down′** *s* (slang) informes *mf* confidenciales, hechos verdaderos

lower [ˈlo·ər] *adj* bajo, inferior || *tr* & *intr* bajar || [ˈlaʊ·ər] *intr* poner mala cara, fruncir el entrecejo; encapotarse (*el cielo*)

lower berth [ˈlo·ər] *s* litera baja, cama baja

Lower California [ˈlo·ər] *s* la Baja California

lower case [ˈlo·ər] *s* (typ) caja baja

lower middle class [ˈlo·ər] *s* pequeña burguesía

lowermost [ˈlo·ər ˌmost] *adj* (el) más bajo

low′-fre′quency *adj* de baja frecuencia

low gear *s* primera marcha, primera velocidad

lowland [ˈlolənd] *s* tierra baja || **Lowlands** *spl* Tierra Baja (*de Escocia*)

low•ly [ˈloli] *adj* (*comp* **-lier**; *super* **-liest**) humilde; (*in growth or position*) bajo

Low Mass *s* misa rezada

low-minded [ˈloˈmaɪndɪd] *adj* vil, ruin

low neck *s* escote *m*, escotado

low-necked [ˈloˈnɛkt] *adj* escotado

low-pitched [ˈloˈpɪtʃt] *adj* (*sound*) grave; (*roof*) de poco declive

low′-pres′sure *adj* de baja presión

low-priced [ˈloˈpraɪst] *adj* barato, de precio bajo

low shoe *s* zapato inglés

low′-speed′ *adj* de baja velocidad

low-spirited [ˈloˈspɪrɪtɪd] *adj* abatido

low spirits *spl* abatimiento

low tide *s* bajamar *f*, marea baja; (fig) punto más bajo

low visibility *s* (aer) poca visibilidad

low water *s* (*of a river*) nivel mínimo; (*because of drought*) estiaje *m*; bajamar *f*, marea baja

loyal [ˈlɔɪ·əl] *adj* leal

loyalist [ˈlɔɪ·əlɪst] *s* leal *m*

loyal•ty [ˈlɔɪ·əlti] *s* (*pl* **-ties**) lealtad

lozenge [ˈlɑzɪndʒ] *s* losange *m*; (*candy cough drop*) pastilla, tableta

LP [ˈɛlˈpi] *s* (letterword) (trademark) disco de larga duración

Ltd. *abbr* **limited**

lubricant [ˈlubrɪkənt] *adj* & *s* lubricante *m*

lubricate [ˈlubrɪ ˌket] *tr* lubricar

lubricous [ˈlubrɪkəs] *adj* (*slippery; lewd*) lúbrico (*resbaladizo; lascivo*); incierto, inconstante

lucerne [lu'sʌrn] *s* mielga
lucid ['lusɪd] *adj* claro, inteligible; (*rational, sane*) lúcido; (*bright, shining*) luciente; (*clear, transparent*) cristalino
Lucifer ['lusɪfər] *s* Lucifer *m*
luck [lʌk] *s* (*good or bad*) suerte *f;* (*good*) suerte, buena suerte; **down on one's luck** de mala suerte, de malas; **in luck** de buena suerte, de buenas; **out of luck** de mala suerte, de malas; **to bring luck** traer buena suerte; **to try one's luck** probar fortuna; **worse luck** desgraciadamente
luckily ['lʌkɪli] *adv* afortunadamente
luckless ['lʌklɪs] *adj* desgraciado
luck•y ['lʌki] *adj* (*comp* **-ier;** *super* **-iest**) afortunado; (*supposed to bring luck*) de buen agüero; **to be lucky** tener suerte
lucky hit *s* (coll) golpe *m* de fortuna
lucrative ['lukrətɪv] *adj* lucrativo
ludicrous ['ludɪkrəs] *adj* absurdo, ridículo
lug [lʌg] *s* orejeta; (*pull, tug*) estirón *m,* esfuerzo || *v* (*pret & pp* **lugged;** *ger* **lugging**) *tr* tirar con fuerza de; (*to bring up irrelevantly*) (coll) traer a colación
luggage ['lʌgɪdʒ] *s* equipaje *m*
lugubrious [lu'gubrɪ•əs] o [lu'gjubrɪ•əs] *adj* lúgubre
lukewarm ['luk,wɔrm] *adj* tibio, templado
lull [lʌl] *s* momento de calma, momento de silencio; (naut) recalmón *m* || *tr* adormecer; calmar, aquietar; apaciguar
lulla•by ['lʌlə,baɪ] *s* (*pl* **-bies**) arrullo, canción de cuna
lumbago [lʌm'bego] *s* lumbago
lumber ['lʌmbər] *s* madera aserrada, madera aserradiza, madera de sierra; trastos viejos || *intr* andar pesadamente
lum'ber•jack' *s* leñador *m,* hachero
lumber•man ['lʌmbərmən] *s* (*pl* **-men** [mən]) (*dealer*) maderero; (*man who cuts down lumber*) leñador *m,* hachero
lumber room *s* leonera, trastera
lum'ber•yard' *s* maderería, depósito de maderas
luminar•y ['lumɪ,nɛri] *s* (*pl* **-ies**) luminar *m,* lumbrera
luminescent [,lumɪ'nɛsənt] *adj* luminiscente
luminous ['lumɪnəs] *adj* luminoso
lummox ['lʌməks] *s* (coll) jergón *m*
lump [lʌmp] *s* terrón *m;* (*swelling*) chichón *m,* bulto, hinchazón *m;* (*stupid person*) (coll) bodoque *m;* **in the lump** en grueso, por junto; **to get a lump in one's throat** hacérsele a (*uno*) un nudo en la garganta || *tr* juntar, mezclar; (*to make into lumps*) aterronar; (coll) aguantar, tragar (*cosa repulsiva*)
lumpish ['lʌmpɪʃ] *adj* hobachón, torpe, pesado
lump sum *s* suma global, suma total
lump•y ['lʌmpi] *adj* (*comp* **-ier;** *super* **-iest**) aterronado, borujoso; torpe, pesado; (*sea*) agitado
luna•cy ['lunəsi] *s* (*pl* **-cies**) demencia, locura
lunar ['lunər] *adj* lunar
lunar landing *s* alunizaje *m*
lunatic ['lunətɪk] *adj & s* lunático, loco
lunatic asylum *s* manicomio
lunatic fringe *s* minoría fanática
lunch [lʌntʃ] *s* (*regular midday meal*) almuerzo; (*light meal*) colación, merienda || *intr* almorzar; merendar, tomar una colación
lunch basket *s* fiambrera
lunch cloth *s* mantelito
luncheon ['lʌntʃən] *s* almuerzo; almuerzo de ceremonia
lunch'room' *s* cantina, merendero
lung [lʌŋ] *s* pulmón *m*
lunge [lʌndʒ] *s* arremetida, embestida; (*with a sword*) estocada || *intr* arremeter, lanzarse; **to lunge at** arremeter contra
lurch [lʌrtʃ] *s* sacudida, tumbo; (naut) bandazo; **to leave in the lurch** dejar en la estacada, dejar colgado || *intr* dar una sacudida, dar un tumbo; (naut) dar un bandazo
lure [lur] *s* (*decoy*) cebo, señuelo; (fig) aliciente *m,* señuelo || *tr* atraer con cebo, atraer con señuelo; (fig) atraer, tentar, seducir; **to lure away** llevarse con señuelo; (*from one's obligations*) desviar
lurid ['lurɪd] *adj* sensacional; (*gruesome*) espeluznante; (*fiery*) ardiente, encendido
lurk [lʌrk] *intr* acechar, andar furtivamente
luscious ['lʌʃəs] *adj* delicioso; lujoso; voluptuoso
lush [lʌʃ] *adj* jugoso, lozano; lujuriante; lujoso
Lusitanian [,lusɪ'tenɪ•ən] *adj & s* lusitano
lust [lʌst] *s* deseo vehemente; (*greed*) codicia; (*strong sexual appetite*) lujuria; entusiasmo || *intr* lujuriar; **to lust after** o **for** codiciar; desear con lujuria
luster ['lʌstər] *s* (*gloss*) lustre *m;* (*of certain fabrics*) viso; (*fame, glory*) (fig) lustre
lus'ter•ware' *s* loza con visos metálicos
lustful ['lʌstfəl] *adj* lujurioso
lustrous ['lʌstrəs] *adj* lustroso
lust•y ['lʌsti] *adj* (*comp* **-ier;** *super* **-iest**) fuerte, robusto, lozano
lute [lut] *s* (mus) laúd *m;* (*substance used to close or seal a joint*) (chem) lodo
Lutheran ['luθərən] *adj & s* luterano
luxuriance [lʌg'ʒurɪ•əns] *s* lozanía
luxuriant [lʌg'ʒurɪ•ənt] *adj* lozano, lujuriante; (*overornamented*) recargado
luxuriate [lʌg'ʒurɪ,et] o [lʌk'ʃurɪ,et] *intr* crecer con lozanía; entregarse al lujo; (*to find keen pleasure*) lozanearse
luxurious [lʌg'ʒurɪ•əs] o [lʌk'ʃurɪ•əs] *adj* lujoso

luxu·ry ['lʌkʃəri] o ['lʌgʒəri] *s* (*pl* **-ries**) lujo
lye [laɪ] *s* lejía
lying ['laɪ·ɪŋ] *adj* mentiroso ‖ *s* el mentir
ly'ing-in' hospital *s* casa de maternidad, clínica de parturientas
lymph [lɪmf] *s* linfa
lymphatic [lɪm'fætɪk] *adj* linfático
lynch [lɪntʃ] *tr* linchar
lynching ['lɪntʃɪŋ] *s* linchamiento
lynch law *s* justicia de la soga
lynx [lɪŋks] *s* lince *m*
lynx-eyed ['lɪŋks,aɪd] *adj* de ojos linces
lyonnaise [,laɪ·ə'nez] *adj* (culin) a la lionesa
lyre [laɪr] *s* (mus) lira
lyric ['lɪrɪk] *adj* lírico ‖ *s* poema lírico; (*words of a song*) (coll) letra
lyrical ['lɪrɪkəl] *adj* lírico
lyricism ['lɪrɪ,sɪzəm] *s* lirismo
lyricist ['lɪrɪsɪst] *s* (*writer of words for songs*) letrista *mf;* (*poet*) poeta lírico

M

M, m [ɛm] decimotercera letra del alfabeto inglés
m. *abbr* **married, masculine, meter, midnight, mile, minute, month**
ma'am [mæm] o [mɑm] *s* (coll) señora
macadam [mə'kædəm] *s* macadán *m*
macadamize [mə'kædə,maɪz] *tr* macadamizar
macaro·ni [,mækə'roni] *s* (*pl* **-nis** o **-nies**) macarrones *mpl*
macaroon [,mækə'run] *s* mostachón *m,* almendrado
macaw [mə'kɔ] *s* aracanga, guacamayo
mace [mes] *s* maza; (*spice*) macis *m*
mace'bear'er *s* macero
machination [,mækɪ'neʃən] *s* maquinación
machine [mə'ʃin] *s* máquina; automóvil *m,* coche *m;* (*of a political party*) camarilla ‖ *tr* trabajar a máquina
machine gun *s* ametralladora
ma·chine'-gun' *tr* ametrallar
ma·chine'-made' *adj* hecho a máquina
machiner·y [mə'ʃinəri] *s* (*pl* **-ies**) maquinaria
machine screw *s* tornillo para metales
machine shop *s* taller mecánico
machine tool *s* máquina-herramienta
machine translation *s* traducción automática
machinist [mə'ʃinɪst] *s* (*person who makes machines*) maquinista *mf;* (*person who operates machines*) mecánico; (naut) segundo maquinista; (theat) maquinista *mf,* tramoyista *mf*
mackerel ['mækərəl] *s* caballa, escombro
mackerel sky *s* cielo aborregado
mackintosh ['mækɪn,tɑʃ] *s* impermeable *m*
mad [mæd] *adj* (*comp* **madder;** *super* **maddest**) (*angry*) enojado, furioso; (*crazy*) loco; (*foolish*) tonto, necio; (*rabid*) rabioso; **to be mad about** (coll) estar loco por; **to drive mad** volver loco; **to go mad** volverse loco; rabiar (*un perro*)
madam ['mædəm] *s* señora
mad'cap' *s* alocado, tarambana *mf*
madden ['mædən] *tr* (*to make angry*) enojar, enfurecer; (*to make insane*) enloquecer
made-to-order ['medtə'ɔrdər] *adj* hecho de encargo; (*clothing*) hecho a la medida
made'-up' *adj* inventado, ficticio; (*artificial*) postizo; (*face*) pintado
mad'house' *s* casa de locos, manicomio
madman ['mæd,mæn] *s* (*pl* **-men** [,mɛn]) loco
madness ['mædnɪs] *s* furia, rabia; locura; (*of a dog*) rabia
Madonna lily. [mə'dɑnə] *s* azucena
maelstrom ['melstrəm] *s* remolino
mag. *abbr* **magazine**
magazine ['mægə,zin] o [,mægə'zin] *s* (*periodical*) revista, magazine *m;* (*warehouse*) almacén *m;* (*for cartridges*) cámara; (*for powder*) polvorín *m;* (naut) santabárbara; (phot) almacén *m*
Magellan [mə'dʒɛlən] *s* Magallanes *m*
maggot ['mægət] *s* cresa
Magi ['medʒaɪ] *spl* magos de Oriente, Reyes Magos
magic ['mædʒɪk] *adj* mágico ‖ *s* magia; ilusionismo, prestidigitación; **as if by magic** como por encanto
magician [mə'dʒɪʃən] *s* (*entertainer with sleight of hand*) ilusionista *mf,* prestidigitador *m;* (*sorcerer*) mágico
magistrate ['mædʒɪs,tret] *s* magistrado
magnanimous [mæg'nænɪməs] *adj* magnánimo
magnesium [mæg'niʃɪ·əm] o [mæg'niʒɪ·əm] *s* magnesio
magnet ['mægnɪt] *s* imán *m*
magnetic [mæg'nɛtɪk] *adj* magnético; (fig) atrayente, cautivador
magnetic curves *spl* fantasma magnético
magnetism ['mægnɪ,tɪzəm] *s* magnetismo
magnetize ['mægnɪ,taɪz] *tr* magnetizar, imanar
magne·to [mæg'nito] *s* (*pl* **-tos**) magneto *m & f*
magnificent [mæg'nɪfɪsənt] *adj* magnífico
magni·fy ['mægnɪ,faɪ] *v* (*pret & pp* **-fied**) *tr* magnificar; exagerar
magnifying glass *s* lupa, vidrio de aumento
magnitude ['mægnɪ,tjud] o ['mægnɪ,tud] *s* magnitud
magpie ['mæg,paɪ] *s* picaza, urraca

Magyar [ˈmægjɑr] *adj & s* magiar *mf*
mahlstick [ˈmɑlˌstɪk] o [ˈmɔlˌstɪk] *s* tiento
mahoga•ny [məˈhɑgəni] *s* (*pl* **-nies**) caoba
Mahomet [məˈhɑmɪt] *s* Mahoma *m*
mahout [məˈhaʊt] *s* naire *m,* cornaca *m*
maid [med] *s* (*female servant*) criada, moza; (*young girl; housemaid*) doncella; (*spinster*) soltera
maiden [ˈmedən] *s* doncella
maid′en•hair′ *s* (bot) cabello de Venus
maid′en•head′ *s* himen *m*
maidenhood [ˈmedənˌhʊd] *s* doncellez *f*
maiden lady *s* soltera
maiden name *s* apellido de soltera
maiden voyage *s* primera travesía
maid′-in-wait′ing *s* (*pl* **maids-in-waiting**) dama
maid of honor *s* (*at a wedding*) primera madrina de boda; (*attendant on a princess*) doncella de honor; (*attendant on a queen*) dama de honor
maid′serv′ant *s* criada, doméstica
mail [mel] *s* correspondencia, correo; (*of armor*) malla; **by return mail** a vuelta de correo || *tr* echar al correo
mail′bag′ *s* valija
mail′boat′ *s* vapor *m* correo
mail′box′ *s* buzón *m*
mail car *s* carro correo, coche-correo, ambulancia de correos
mail carrier *s* cartero
mailing list *s* lista de envío
mailing permit *s* porte concertado
mail•man [ˈmelˌmæn] *s* (*pl* **-men** [ˌmɛn]) cartero
mail order *s* pedido postal
mail′-or′der house *s* casa de ventas por correo
mail′plane′ *s* avión-correo
mail train *s* tren *m* correo
maim [mem] *tr* estropear, mutilar
main [men] *adj* principal, primero, maestro, mayor || *s* cañería maestra; **in the main** mayormente
main clause *s* proposición dominante
main course *s* plato principal, plato fuerte
main deck *s* cubierta principal
mainland [ˈmenˌlænd] o [ˈmenlənd] *s* continente *m,* tierra firme
main line *s* (rr) tronco, línea principal
mainly [ˈmenli] *adv* principalmente, en su mayor parte
mainmast [ˈmenməst], [ˈmenˌmæst] o [ˈmenˌmɑst] *s* palo mayor
mainsail [ˈmensəl] o [ˈmenˌsel] *s* vela mayor
main′spring′ *s* (*of watch*) muelle *m* real; (fig) móvil *m,* origen *m*
main′stay′ *s* (naut) estay *m* mayor; (fig) soporte *m* principal
main street *s* calle *f* mayor
maintain [menˈten] *tr* mantener; (*to support*) (law) manutener
maintenance [ˈmentɪnəns] *s* mantenimiento; (*upkeep*) conservación; gastos de conservación
maître d'hôtel [ˌmetər doˈtɛl] *s* (*butler*) mayordomo; (*headwaiter*) jefe *m* de comedor
maize [mez] *s* maíz *m*
majestic [məˈdʒɛstɪk] *adj* majestuoso
majes•ty [ˈmædʒɪsti] *s* (*pl* **-ties**) majestad
major [ˈmedʒər] *adj* (*greater*) mayor; (*elder*) mayor de edad; (mus) mayor || *s* (educ) especialización; (mil) comandante *m* || *intr* (educ) especializarse
Majorca [məˈdʒɔrkə] *s* Mallorca
Majorcan [məˈdʒɔrkən] *adj & s* mallorquín *m*
major•do•mo [ˌmedʒərˈdomo] *s* (*pl* **-mos**) mayordomo
major general *s* general *m* de división
majori•ty [məˈdʒɑrɪti] o [məˈdʒɔrɪti] *adj* mayoritario || *s* (*pl* **-ties**) (*being of full age; larger number or part*) mayoría; (*full age*) mayoridad; (mil) comandancia
make [mek] *s* (*brand*) marca; (*form, build*) hechura; carácter *m,* natural *m;* **on the make** (slang) buscando provecho || *v* (*pret & pp* **made** [med]) *tr* hacer; cometer (*un error*); efectuar (*un pago*); ganar (*dinero; una baza*); coger (*un tren*); dar (*dinero una empresa*); pronunciar (*un discurso*); cerrar (*un circuito*); poner (*a uno, p.ej., nervioso*); ser, p.ej., **she will make a good wife** será una buena esposa; **to make** + *inf* hacer + *inf,* p.ej., **she made him study** le hizo estudiar; **to make into** convertir en; **to make known** declarar; dar a conocer; **to make of** pensar de; **to make oneself known** darse a conocer; **to make out** distinguir, vislumbrar; descifrar; escribir (*una receta*); llenar (*un cheque*); **to make over** convertir; rehacer (*un traje*); (com) transferir; **to make up** preparar, confeccionar; inventar (*un cuento*); recobrar (*el tiempo perdido*); (theat) maquillar || *intr* estar (*p.ej., seguro*); **to make away with** llevarse; deshacerse de; matar; **to make believe** fingir, p.ej., **he made believe he knew me** fingió conocerme; **to make for** ir hacia; embestir contra; contribuir a (*p.ej., mejores relaciones*); **to make much of** (coll) hacer fiestas a, mostrar cariño a; **to make off** largarse; **to make off with** llevarse, hacerse con; **to make out** arreglárselas; **to make toward** encaminarse a; **to make up** maquillarse, pintarse; componerse, hacer las paces; **to make up for** suplir; compensar por (*una pérdida*); **to make up to** (coll) tratar de congraciarse con
make′-be•lieve′ *adj* simulado || *s* pretexto, simulación, fantasía
maker [ˈmekər] *s* constructor *m,* fabricante *mf*
make′shift′ *adj* de fortuna, provisional || *s* expediente *m;* (*person*) tapagujeros *m*
make′-up′ *s* composición, constitución;

afeite *m*, maquillaje *m;* (typ) imposición
make-up man *s* (theat) maquillador *m*
make'weight' *s* contrapeso; suplente *mf*
making ['mekɪŋ] *s* fabricación; material necesario; causa del éxito; **makings** elementos, materiales *mpl;* (*personal qualities necessary for some purpose*) madera
malachite ['mælə,kaɪt] *s* malaquita
maladjustment [,mælə'dʒʌstmənt] *s* desadaptación
mala•dy ['mælədi] *s* (*pl* **-dies**) dolencia, enfermedad
malaise [mæ'lez] *s* indisposición, malestar *m*
malapropos [,mælæprə'po] *adj* impropio || *adv* fuera de propósito
malaria [mə'lɛrɪ•ə] *s* malaria, paludismo
Malay ['mele] o [mə'le] *adj & s* malayo
malcontent ['mælkən,tɛnt] *adj & s* malcontento
male [mel] *adj* (*sex*) masculino; (*animal, plant, piece of a device*) macho; (*human being*) varón, p.ej., **male child** hijo varón || *s* macho; varón *m*
malediction [,mælɪ'dɪkʃən] *s* maldición
malefactor ['mælɪ,fæktər] *s* malhechor *m*
male nurse *s* enfermero
malevolent [mə'lɛvələnt] *adj* malévolo
malice ['mælɪs] *s* malicia, malevolencia; **to bear malice** guardar rencor; **with malice prepense** [prɪ'pɛns] (law) con malicia y premeditación
malicious [mə'lɪʃəs] *adj* malicioso, malévolo
malign [mə'laɪn] *adj* maligno || *tr* calumniar
malignant [mə'lɪgnənt] *adj* maligno
maligni•ty [mə'lɪgnɪti] *s* (*pl* **-ties**) malignidad
malinger [mə'lɪŋgər] *intr* hacer la zanguanga, fingirse enfermo
mall [mɔl] o [mæl] *s* alameda, paseo de árboles
mallet ['mælɪt] *s* (*wooden hammer*) mazo; (*for croquet and polo*) mallete *m*
mallow ['mælo] *s* malva
malnutrition [,mælnju'trɪʃən] o [,mælnu'trɪʃən] *s* desnutrición
malodorous [mæl'odərəs] *adj* maloliente
malt [mɔlt] *s* malta *m;* (coll) cerveza
maltreat [mæl'trit] *tr* maltratar
mamma ['mɑmə] o [mə'mɑ] *s* mama o mamá *f*
mammal ['mæməl] *s* mamífero
mammalian [mæ'melɪ•ən] *adj & s* mamífero
mammoth ['mæməθ] *adj* gigantesco, enorme || *s* mamut *m*
man [mæn] *s* (*pl* **men** [mɛn]) *s* hombre *m;* (*in chess*) pieza; (*in checkers*) pieza, peón *m;* **a man** uno, p.ej., **a man can't get work in this town** uno no puede obtener empleo en este pueblo; **as one man** unánimemente; **man alive!** ¡hombre!; **man and wife** marido y mujer; **to be one's own man** no depender de nadie || *v* (*pret & pp* **manned;** *ger* **manning)** *tr* dotar, tripular (*un buque*); guarnecer (*una fortaleza*); servir (*los cañones*)
man about town *s* bulevardero, hombre *m* de mucho mundo
manacle ['mænəkəl] *s* manilla; **manacles** esposas || *tr* poner esposas a
manage ['mænɪdʒ] *tr* manejar || *intr* arreglárselas; **to manage to** ingeniarse a o para; **to manage to get along** ingeniarse para ir viviendo
manageable ['mænɪdʒəbəl] *adj* manejable
management ['mænɪdʒmənt] *s* manejo, dirección, gerencia; (*group who manage a business*) la empresa, la parte patronal, los patronos
manager ['mænədʒər] *s* director *m*, administrador *m*, gerente *mf;* empresario; (sport) manager *m*
managerial [,mænə'dʒɪrɪ•əl] *adj* empresarial
mandate ['mændet] *s* mandato || *tr* asignar por mandato
mandolin ['mændəlɪn] *s* mandolina
mandrake ['mændrek] *s* mandrágora
mane [men] *s* (*of horse*) crines *fpl;* (*of lion; of person*) melena
maneuver [mə'nuvər] *s* maniobra || *tr* hacer maniobrar || *intr* maniobrar
manful ['mænfəl] *adj* varonil, resuelto
manganese ['mæŋgə,nis] o ['mæŋgə,niz] *s* manganeso
mange [mendʒ] *s* sarna
manger ['mendʒər] *s* pesebre *m*
mangle ['mæŋgəl] *tr* lacerar, aplastar
man•gy ['mendʒi] *adj* (*comp* **-gier;** *super* **-giest)** sarnoso; (*dirty, squalid*) roñoso
man'han'dle *tr* maltratar
man'hole' *s* caja de registro, pozo de inspección
manhood ['mænhʊd] *s* virilidad; hombres *mpl*
man hunt *s* caza al hombre
mania ['menɪ•ə] *s* manía
maniac ['menɪ,æk] *adj & s* maníaco
manicure ['mænɪ,kjur] *s* (*care of hands*) manicura; (*person*) manicuro, manicura || *tr* hacer la manicura a (*una persona*); hacer (*las manos y las uñas*)
manicurist ['mænɪ,kjʊrɪst] *s* manicuro, manicura
manifest ['mænɪ,fɛst] *adj* manifiesto || *s* (naut) manifiesto || *tr* manifestar
manifes•to [,mænɪ'fɛsto] *s* (*pl* **-toes)** manifiesto
manifold ['mænɪ,fold] *adj* múltiple, vario || *s* copia, ejemplar *m;* (*pipe with outlets or inlets*) colector *m*, múltiple *m*
manikin ['mænɪkɪn] *s* maniquí *m;* (*dwarf*) enano
man in the moon *s* cara o cuerpo de hombre imaginarios en la luna llena
manipulate [mə'nɪpjə,let] *tr* manipular

man'kind' *s* el género humano || **man'kind'** *s* el sexo masculino, los hombres
manliness ['mænlɪnɪs] *s* masculinidad, virilidad
man·ly ['mænli] *adj* (*comp* **-lier;** *super* **-liest**) masculino, varonil
manned spaceship [mænd] *s* astronave tripulada
mannequin ['mænɪkɪn] *s* maniquí *m;* (*young woman employed to exhibit clothing*) maniquí *f*
manner ['mænər] *s* manera; **by all manner of means** de todos modos; **in a manner of speaking** como si dijéramos; **in the manner of** a la manera de; **manners** modales *mpl,* crianza; **to the manner born** avezado desde la cuna
mannish ['mænɪʃ] *adj* hombruno
man of letters *s* hombre *m* de letras
man of means *s* hombre *m* de dinero
man of parts *s* hombre *m* de buenas prendas
man of straw *s* hombre *m* de suposición
man of the world *s* hombre *m* de mundo
man-of-war [,mænəv'wɔr] *s* (*pl* **men-of-war** [,menəv'wɔr]) *s* buque *m* de guerra
manor ['mænər] *s* señorío
manor house *s* casa solariega
man overboard *interj* ¡hombre al agua!
man'pow'er *s* número de hombres; personal *m* competente; (mil) fuerzas nacionales
mansard ['mænsɑrd] *s* mansarda; piso de mansarda
man'serv'ant *s* (*pl* **men'serv'ants**) criado
mansion ['mænʃən] *s* hotel *m,* palacio; (*manor house*) casa solariega
man'slaugh'ter *s* (law) homicidio sin premeditación
mantel ['mæntəl] *s* manto (*de chimenea*); (*shelf above it*) mesilla, repisa de chimenea
man'tel·piece' *s* mesilla, repisa de chimenea
mantle ['mæntəl] *s* capa, manto || *tr* vestir con manto; cubrir, tapar; ocultar || *intr* encenderse (*el rostro*)
manual ['mænjʊ·əl] *adj* manual || *s* (*book*) manual *m;* (mil) ejercicio; (mus) teclado manual
manual training *s* enseñanza de los artes y oficios
manufacture [,mænjə'fæktjər] *s* fabricación; (*thing manufactured*) manufactura || *tr* fabricar, manufacturar
manufacturer [,mænjə'fæktjərər] *s* fabricante *mf*
manure [mə'njʊr] o [mə'nʊr] *s* estiércol *m* || *tr* estercolar
manuscript ['mænjə,skrɪpt] *adj* & *s* manuscrito
many ['meni] *adj* & *pron* muchos; **a good many** o **a great many** un buen número; **as many as** tantos como; hasta, p.ej., **as many as twenty** hasta veinte; **how many** cuántos; **many a** muchos, p.ej., **many a person** muchas personas; **many another** muchos otros; **many more** muchos más; **so many** tantos; **too many** demasiados; **twice as many as** dos veces más que
many-sided ['meni,saɪdɪd] *adj* multilátero; (*having many interests or capabilities*) polifacético
map [mæp] *s* mapa *m;* (*of a city*) plano || *v* (*pret* & *pp* **mapped;** *ger* **mapping**) *tr* trazar el mapa de; indicar en el mapa; **to map out** trazar el plan de
maple ['mepəl] *s* arce *m*
maquette [mɑ'ket] *s* maqueta
Mar. *abbr* **March**
mar [mɑr] *v* (*pret* & *pp* **marred;** *ger* **marring**) *tr* desfigurar, estropear; frustrar
maraud [mə'rɔd] *tr* saquear || *intr* merodear
marauder [mə'rɔdər] *s* merodeador *m*
marble ['mɑrbəl] *adj* marmóreo || *s* mármol *m;* (*little ball of glass, etc.*) canica; **marbles** (*game*) canica || *tr* crispir, jaspear
march [mɑrtʃ] *s* marcha; (*frontier, territory*) marca; **to steal a march on someone** ganarle a uno por la mano || *tr* hacer marchar || *intr* marchar || **March** *s* marzo
marchioness ['mɑrʃənɪs] *s* marquesa
mare [mer] *s* (*female horse*) yegua; (*female donkey*) asna
margarine ['mɑrdʒərɪn] *s* margarina
margin ['mɑrdʒɪn] *s* margen *m* & *f;* (*collateral deposited with a broker*) doble *m*
marginal ['mɑrdʒɪnəl] *adj* marginal
margin release *s* tecla de escape
margin stop *s* fijamárgenes *m,* cierrarrenglón *m,* cortarrenglón *m*
marigold ['mærɪ,gold] *s* clavelón *m;* (*Calendula*) maravilla, flamenquilla
marihuana o **marijuana** [,mɑrɪ'hwɑnə] *s* mariguana
marinate ['mærɪ,net] *tr* escabechar, marinar
marine [mə'rin] *adj* marino, marítimo || *s* marina; soldado de infantería de marina; **marines** infantería de marina; **tell that to the marines** (coll) cuénteselo a su abuela, a otro perro con ese hueso
mariner ['mærɪnər] *s* marino
marionette [,mærɪ·ə'net] *s* marioneta, títere *m*
marital status ['mærɪtəl] *s* estado civil
maritime ['mærɪ,taɪm] *adj* marítimo
marjoram ['mɑrdʒərəm] *s* orégano; mejorana
mark [mɑrk] *s* marca, señal *f;* (*label*) marbete *m;* (*of punctuation*) punto; (*in an examination*) calificación, nota; (*used instead of signature by an illiterate person*) cruz *f,* signo; (*spot, stain*) mancha; (*coin*) marco; (*starting point in a race*) raya; (*target to shoot at*) blanco; **to be beside the mark** no venir al caso; **to hit the mark** dar en el blanco; **to leave one's mark** dejar memoria de sí; **to make one's mark** llegar a ser célebre; **to miss the mark** errar el tiro; **to toe**

the mark ponerse en la raya; obedecer rigurosamente || *tr* marcar, señalar; dar nota a (*un alumno*); calificar (*un examen*); advertir, notar; **to mark down** poner por escrito; rebajar el precio de
mark'down' *s* reducción de precio
market ['markɪt] *s* mercado; **to bear the market** jugar a la baja; **to bull the market** jugar al alza; **to play the market** jugar a la bolsa; **to put on the market** lanzar al mercado || *tr* llevar al mercado; vender
marketable ['markɪtəbəl] *adj* comerciable, vendible
market basket *s* cesta para compras
marketing ['markɪtɪŋ] *s* mercología, mercadotecnia
market place *s* plaza del mercado
market price *s* precio corriente
marking gauge ['markɪŋ] *s* gramil *m*
marks·man ['marksmən] *s* (*pl* **-men** [mən]) tirador *m;* **a good marksman** un buen tiro
marksmanship ['marksmən,ʃɪp] *s* puntería
mark'up' *s* aumento de precio
marl [marl] *s* marga || *tr* margar
marmalade ['marmə,led] *s* mermelada
marmot ['marmət] *s* marmota
maroon [mə'run] *adj & s* marrón *m,* castaño obscuro || *tr* dejar abandonado (*en una isla desierta*)
marquee [mar'ki] *s* marquesina
marquess ['markwɪs] *s* marqués *m*
marque·try ['markətri] *s* (*pl* **-tries**) marquetería (*taracea*)
marquis ['markwɪs] *s* marqués *m*
marquise [mar'kiz] *s* marquesa; (*over the entrance to a hotel*) marquesina
marriage ['mærɪdʒ] *s* casamiento, matrimonio; (*married life; intimate union*) maridaje *m*
marriageable ['mærɪdʒəbəl] *adj* casadero
marriage portion *s* dote *m & f*
marriage rate *s* nupcialidad
married life ['mærid] *s* vida conyugal
marrow ['mæro] *s* médula, tuétano
mar·ry ['mæri] *v* (*pret & pp* **-ried**) *tr* casar (*el sacerdote o el juez a un hombre y una mujer*); (*to take in marriage*) casar con, casarse con; (*to unite intimately*) maridar; **to get married to** casar con, casarse con || *intr* casar, casarse; **to marry into** emparentar con (*p.ej., una familia rica*); **to marry the second time** casarse en segundas nupcias
Mars [marz] *s* Marte *m*
Marseille [mar'sɛ:j] *s* Marsella
marsh [marʃ] *s* ciénaga, pantano
mar·shal ['marʃəl] *s* cursor *m* de procesiones, maestro de ceremonias; (mil) mariscal *m;* (U.S.A.) oficial *m* de justicia || *v* (*pret & pp* **-shaled** o **-shalled;** *ger* **-shaling** o **-shalling**) *tr* conducir con ceremonia; ordenar, reunir (*los hechos de una argumentación*)
marsh mallow *s* (bot) malvavisco
marsh'mal'low *s* bombón *m* de merengue y gelatina; bombón de malvavisco
marsh·y ['marʃi] *adj* (*comp* **-ier;** *super* **-iest**) pantanoso, palúdico
marten ['martən] *s* (*pine marten*) marta; (*beech marten*) garduña
martial ['marʃəl] *adj* marcial
martial law *s* ley *f* marcial; **to be under martial law** estar en estado de guerra
martin ['martɪn] *s* (orn) avión *m*
martinet [,martɪ'nɛt] o ['martɪ,nɛt] *s* ordenancista *mf*
martyr ['martər] *s* mártir *mf*
martyrdom ['martərdəm] *s* martirio
mar·vel ['marvəl] *s* maravilla || *v* (*pret & pp* **-veled** o **-velled;** *ger* **-veling** o **-velling**) *intr* maravillarse; **to marvel at** maravillarse con o de
marvelous ['marvələs] *adj* maravilloso
Marxist ['marksɪst] *adj & s* marxista *mf*
masc. *abbr* **masculine**
mascara [mæs'kærə] *s* tinte *m* para las pestañas
mascot ['mæskat] *s* mascota
masculine ['mæskjəlɪn] *adj & s* masculino
mash [mæʃ] *s* (*crushed mass*) masa; (*to form wort*) masa de cebada || *tr* machacar, majar
mashed potatoes [mæʃt] *spl* puré *m* de patatas
masher ['mæʃər] *s* (*device*) mano *f;* (slang) galanteador atrevido
mask [mæsk] o [mask] *s* máscara; (*of beekeeper*) carilla; (*made from a corpse*) mascarilla; (*person*) máscara *mf;* (phot) desvanecedor *m* || *tr* enmascarar; (phot) desvanecer || *intr* enmascararse
masked ball [mæskt] *s* baile *m* de máscaras
mason ['mesən] *s* albañil *m* || **Mason** *s* masón *m*
mason·ry ['mesənri] *s* (*pl* **-ries**) albañilería || **Masonry** *s* masonería
masquerade [,mæskə'red] o [,maskə'red] *s* mascarada; (*costume, disguise*) máscara; (*false show*) farsa || *intr* enmascararse; **to masquerade as** disfrazarse de
masquerade ball *s* baile *m* de máscaras
mass [mæs] *s* masa; gran cantidad; (*bulk, heap*) mole *f;* (*something glimpsed, e.g., in the fog*) bulto informe; (*big splotch in a painting*) gran mancha; (*celebration of the Eucharist*) misa; **the masses** las masas || *tr* juntar, reunir; enmasar (*tropas*) || *intr* juntarse, reunirse
massacre ['mæsəkər] *s* carnicería, matanza || *tr* degollar, matar
massage [mə'saʒ] *s* masaje *m* || *tr* masar, masajear
masseur [mæ'sœr] *s* masajista *m*
masseuse [mæ'sœz] *s* masajista *f*
massive ['mæsɪv] *adj* macizo; sólido, imponente
mass meeting *s* mitin *m* popular
mass production *s* fabricación en serie
mast [mæst] o [mast] *s* (*for a flag*) palo; (*of a ship*) palo, mástil *m;*

(*food for swine*) bellotas, hayucos; **before the mast** como simple marinero

master ['mæstər] o ['mɑstər] *s* (*employer*) dueño, patrón *m;* (*male head of household*) amo; (*man who possesses some special skill; teacher*) maestro; (*commander of merchant vessel*) capitán *m;* (*title of respect for a boy*) señorito || *tr* dominar

master bedroom *s* alcoba de respeto

master blade *s* hoja maestra (*de una ballesta*)

master builder *s* maestro de obras

masterful ['mæstərfəl] o ['mɑstərfəl] *adj* hábil, experto; dominante, imperioso

master key *s* llave maestra

masterly ['mæstərli] o ['mɑstərli] *adj* magistral || *adv* magistralmente

master mechanic *s* maestro mecánico

mas'ter•mind' *s* mente directora || *tr* dirigir con gran acierto

master of ceremonies *s* maestro de ceremonias; (*in a night club, radio, etc.*) animador *m*

mas'ter•piece' *s* obra maestra

master stroke *s* golpe maestro

mas'ter•work' *s* obra maestra

master•y ['mæstəri] o ['mɑstəri] *s* (*pl* **-ies**) (*command, as of a subject*) dominio; ventaja, superioridad; (*skill*) maestría

mast'head' *s* (*of a newspaper*) cabecera editorial; (naut) tope *m*

masticate ['mæstɪ,ket] *tr* masticar

mastiff ['mæstɪf] o ['mɑstɪf] *s* mastín *m*

masturbate ['mæstər,bet] *intr* masturbarse

mat [mæt] *s* (*for floor*) estera; (*for a cup, vase, etc.*) esterilla, ruedo; (*before a door*) felpudo; (*around a picture*) borde *m* de cartón || *v* (*pret & pp* **matted;** *ger* **matting**) *tr* (*to cover with matting*) esterar; enmarañar || *intr* enmarañarse

match [mætʃ] *s* fósforo; (*wick*) mecha; (*counterpart*) compañero; (*suitable partner in marriage*) partido; (*suitably associated pair*) pareja; (*game, contest*) match *m,* partido; **to be a match for** poder con, poder vencer; **to meet one's match** hallar la horma de su zapato || *tr* igualar; aparear, emparejar; hacer juego con; **to match someone for the drinks** jugarle a uno las bebidas || *intr* hacer juego, correr parejas; **to match** a juego, p.ej., **a chair to match** una silla a juego

match'box' *s* fosforera; (*of wax matches*) cerillera

matchless ['mætʃlɪs] *adj* incomparable, sin par

matchmaker ['mætʃ,mekər] *s* casamentero

mate [met] *s* compañero; (*e.g., of a shoe*) compañero, hermano; (*husband or wife*) cónyuge *mf;* (*to a female*) macho; (*to a male*) hembra; (*in chess*) mate *m;* (naut) piloto || *tr* aparear, casar; (*in chess*) dar jaque mate a; **to be well mated** hacer una buena pareja || *intr* aparearse, casarse

material [mə'tɪrɪ•əl] *adj* material; importante || *s* material *m;* (*what a thing is made of*) materia; (*cloth, fabric*) tela, género

materialism [mə'tɪrɪ•ə,lɪzəm] *s* materialismo

materialize [mə'tɪrɪ•ə,laɪz] *intr* realizarse

matériel [mə,tɪrɪ'ɛl] *s* material *m;* material de guerra

maternal [mə'tʌrnəl] *adj* materno; (*motherly*) maternal

maternity [mə'tʌrnɪti] *s* maternidad

maternity hospital *s* casa de maternidad

math. *abbr* **mathematics**

mathematical [,mæθɪ'mætɪkəl] *adj* matemático

mathematician [,mæθɪmə'tɪʃən] *s* matemático

mathematics [,mæθɪ'mætɪks] *s* matemática, matemáticas

matinée [,mætɪ'ne] *s* matinée *f,* función de tarde

mating season *s* época de celo

matins ['mætɪnz] *spl* maitines *mpl*

matriarch ['metrɪ,ɑrk] *s* matriarca

matricidal [,metrɪ'saɪdəl] o [,mætrɪ'saɪdəl] *adj* matricida

matricide ['metrɪ,saɪd] o ['mætrɪ,saɪd] *s* (*act*) matricidio; (*person*) matricida *mf*

matriculate [mə'trɪkjə,let] *tr* matricular || *intr* matricularse

matrimo•ny ['mætrɪ,moni] *s* (*pl* **-nies**) matrimonio

matron ['metrən] *s* matrona

matronly ['metrənli] *adj* matronal

matter ['mætər] *s* (*physical substance; pus*) materia; (*subject talked or written about*) asunto; (*reason, ground*) motivo; (*copy for printer*) material *m;* (*printed material*) impresos; **a matter of** cosa de, obra de; **for that matter** en cuanto a eso; **in the matter** al respecto; **no matter** no importa; **no matter when** cuando quiera; **no matter where** dondequiera; **what is the matter?** ¿qué hay?; **what is the matter with you?** ¿qué tiene Vd.? || *intr* importar

matter of course *s* cosa de cajón; **as a matter of course** por rutina

matter of fact *s* — **as a matter of fact** en realidad, en honor a la verdad

matter-of-fact ['mætərəv,fækt] *adj* prosaico, práctico, de poca imaginación

mattock ['mætək] *s* zapapico

mattress ['mætrɪs] *s* colchón *m*

mature [mə'tʃur] o [mə'tur] *adj* maduro; (*due*) pagadero, vencido || *tr* madurar || *intr* madurar; (*to become due*) (com) vencer

maturity [mə'tʃurɪti] o [mə'turɪti] *s* madurez *f;* (com) vencimiento

maudlin ['mɔdlɪn] *adj* lacrimoso, sensiblero; chispo y lloroso

maul [mɔl] *tr* aporrear, maltratar

maulstick ['mɔl,stɪk] *s* tiento

maundy ['mɔndi] *s* lavatorio
Maundy Thursday *s* Jueves Santo
mausole·um [,mɔsə'li·əm] *s* (*pl* **-ums** o **-a** [ə]) mausoleo
maw [mɔ] *s* (*of fowl*) buche *m;* (*of fish*) vejiga de aire
mawkish ['mɔkɪʃ] *adj* (*sickening*) empalagoso; (*sentimental*) sensiblero
max. *abbr* **maximum**
maxim ['mæksɪm] *s* máxima
maximum ['mæksɪməm] *adj* & *s* máximo
may *v aux* **it may be** puede ser; **may I come in?** ¿puedo entrar? **may you be happy!** ¡que seas feliz! ‖ **May** *s* mayo
maybe ['mebi] o ['mebɪ] *adv* acaso, quizá, tal vez
May Day *s* primero de mayo; fiesta del primero de mayo
mayhem ['mehɛm] o ['me·əm] *s* (law) mutilación criminal
mayonnaise [,me·ə'nez] *s* mayonesa
mayor ['me·ər] o [mɛr] *s* alcalde *m*
mayoress ['me·ərɪs] o ['mɛrɪs] *s* alcaldesa
May'pole' *s* mayo
Maypole dance *s* danza de cintas
May queen *s* maya
maze [mez] *s* laberinto
M.C. *abbr* **Master of Ceremonies, Member of Congress**
mdse. *abbr* **merchandise**
me [mi] *pron pers* me; mí; **to me** me; a mí; **with me** conmigo
meadow ['mɛdo] *s* prado, vega
mead'ow·land' *s* pradera
meager ['migər] *adj* escaso, pobre; flaco, magro
meal [mil] *s* (*regular repast*) comida; (*edible grain coarsely ground*) harina
meal'time' *s* hora de comer
mean [min] *adj* (*intermediate*) medio; (*low in station or rank*) humilde, obscuro; (*shabby*) andrajoso, raído; (*stingy*) mezquino, tacaño; (*of poor quality*) inferior, pobre; (*small-minded*) vil, ruin, innoble; insignificante; (*vicious, as a horse*) arisco, mal intencionado; (coll) indispuesto; (coll) avergonzado; (coll) de mal genio; **no mean** famoso, excelente ‖ *s* promedio, término medio; **by all means** sí, por cierto, sin falta; **by means of** por medio de; **by no means** de ningún modo, en ningún caso; **means** bienes *mpl* de fortuna; (*agency*) medio, medios; **means to an end** paso para lograr un fin; **to live on one's means** vivir de sus rentas ‖ *v* (*pret & pp* **meant** [mɛnt]) *tr* significar, querer decir; **to mean to** pensar ‖ *intr* — **to mean well** tener buenas intenciones
meander [mɪ'ændər] *s* meandro ‖ *intr* serpentear; vagar
meaning ['minɪŋ] *s* sentido, significado
meaningful ['minɪŋfəl] *adj* significativo
meaningless ['minɪŋlɪs] *adj* sin sentido
meanness ['minnɪs] *s* bajeza, vileza, ruindad; (*stinginess*) mezquindad; (*lowliness*) humildad, pobreza
mean'time' *adv* entretanto, mientras tanto ‖ *s* medio tiempo; **in the meantime** entretanto, mientras tanto
mean'while' *adv* & *s* var de **meantime**
measles ['mizəlz] *s* sarampión *m;* (*German measles*) rubéola
mea·sly ['mizli] *adj* (*comp* **-slier;** *super* **-sliest**) sarampioso; (slang) despreciable, mezquino
measurable ['mɛʒərəbəl] *adj* medible
measure ['mɛʒər] *s* medida; (*step, procedure*) paso, gestión; (*legislative bill*) proyecto de ley; (*of verse*) pie *m;* (mus) compás *m;* **beyond measure** con exceso; **in a measure** hasta cierto punto; **in great measure** en gran parte; (*suit*) **to measure** hecho a la medida; **to take measures** tomar las medidas necesarias; **to take someone's measure** tomarle a uno las medidas ‖ *tr* medir; recorrer (*cierta distancia*); **to measure out** medir; distribuir ‖ *intr* medir
measurement ['mɛʒərmənt] *s* (*act of measuring*) medición; (*measuring; dimension*) medida
measuring glass *s* vaso graduado
meat [mit] *s* carne *f;* (*food in general*) manjar *m,* vianda; (*substance, gist*) meollo
meat ball *s* albóndiga
meat'hook' *s* garabato de carnicero
meat market *s* carnicería
meat·y ['miti] *adj* (*comp* **-ier;** *super* **-iest**) carnoso; (fig) jugoso, substancioso
Mecca ['mɛkə] *s* La Meca
mechanic [mɪ'kænɪk] *s* mecánico
mechanical [mɪ'kænɪkəl] *adj* mecánico, maquinal; (*machinelike*) (fig) maquinal
mechanical toy *s* juguete *m* de movimiento
mechanics [mɪ'kænɪks] *ssg* mecánica
mechanism ['mɛkə,nɪzəm] *s* mecanismo
mechanize ['mɛkə,naɪz] *tr* mecanizar
med. *abbr* **medicine, medieval**
medal ['mɛdəl] *s* medalla
medallion [mɪ'dæljən] *s* medallón *m*
meddle ['mɛdəl] *intr* meterse, entremeterse
meddler ['mɛdlər] *s* entremetido
meddlesome ['mɛdəlsəm] *adj* entremetido
median ['midɪ·ən] *adj* intermedio, medio ‖ *s* punto medio, número medio
median strip *s* faja central o divisoria
mediate ['midɪ,et] *tr* dirimir (*una controversia*); reconciliar ‖ *intr* (*to be in the middle*) mediar; (*to intervene to settle a dispute*) intervenir
mediation [,midɪ'eʃən] *s* mediación
mediator ['midɪ,etər] *s* mediador *m*
medical ['mɛdɪkəl] *adj* médico
medical student *s* estudiante *mf* de medicina
medicine ['mɛdɪsɪn] *s* (*science and art*) medicina; (*remedy, treatment*) medicina, medicamento
medicine cabinet *s* armario botiquín
medicine kit *s* botiquín *m*

medicine man *s* curandero, hechicero (*entre los pieles rojas*)
medieval [ˌmidɪ'ivəl] o [ˌmɛdɪ'ivəl] *adj* medieval
medievalist [ˌmidɪ'ivəlɪst] o [ˌmɛdɪ'ivəlɪst] *s* medievalista *mf*
mediocre ['midɪˌokər] o [ˌmidɪ'okər] *adj* mediocre
mediocri•ty [ˌmidɪ'ɑkrɪti] *s* (*pl* **-ties**) mediocridad
meditate ['mɛdɪˌtet] *tr & intr* meditar
Mediterranean [ˌmɛdɪtə'renɪ·ən] *adj & s* Mediterráneo
medi•um ['midɪ·əm] *adj* intermedio; a medio asar || *s* (*pl* **-ums** o **-a** [ə]) medio; (*in spiritualism*) medio, médium *m;* (*publication*) órgano; **through the medium of** por medio de
me'dium-range' *adj* de alcance medio
medlar ['mɛdlər] *s* (*tree and fruit*) níspero; (*fruit*) níspola
medley ['mɛdli] *s* mescolanza; (mus) popurrí *m*
medul•la [mɪ'dʌlə] *s* (*pl* **-lae** [li]) médula
meek [mik] *adj* dócil, manso
meekness ['miknɪs] *s* docilidad, mansedumbre
meerschaum ['mɪrʃəm] s ['mɪrʃɔm] *s* espuma de mar; pipa de espuma de mar
meet [mit] *adj* conveniente, a propósito || *s* concurso deportivo || *v* (*pret & pp* **met** [mɛt]) *tr* encontrar, encontrarse con; (*to make the acquaintance of*) conocer; empalmar con (*otro tren o autobús*); ir a esperar; honrar, pagar (*una letra*); hacer frente a (*gastos*); cumplir (*sus obligaciones*); batirse con; hallar (*la muerte*); tener (*mala suerte*); aparecer a (*la vista*) || *intr* encontrarse; reunirse; conocerse; **till we meet again** hasta la vista; **to meet with** encontrarse con; reunirse con; empalmar (*un tren*) con (*otro tren*); tener (*un accidente*)
meeting ['mitɪŋ] *s* junta, sesión; reunión; encuentro; (*of two rivers or roads*) confluencia; desafío, duelo
meeting of the minds *s* concierto de voluntades
meeting place *s* lugar *m* de reunión
megacycle ['mɛgəˌsaɪkəl] *s* megaciclo
megaphone ['mɛgəˌfon] *s* megáfono
megohm ['mɛgˌom] *s* megohmio
melancholia [ˌmɛlən'kolɪ·ə] *s* melancolía
melanchol•y ['mɛlənˌkɑli] *adj* melancólico || *s* (*pl* **-ies**) melancolía
melee ['mele] o ['mɛle] *s* refriega, reyerta
mellow ['mɛlo] *adj* maduro, jugoso; suave, meloso; melodioso || *tr* suavizar || *intr* suavizarse
melodious [mɪ'lodɪ·əs] *adj* melodioso
melodramatic [ˌmɛlədrə'mætɪk] *adj* melodramático
melo•dy ['mɛlədi] *s* (*pl* **-dies**) melodía
melon ['mɛlən] *s* melón *m*
melt [mɛlt] *tr* derretir; fundir (*metales*); ablandar, aplacar || *intr* derretirse; fundirse; ablandarse, aplacarse; **to melt away** desvanecerse; **to melt into** convertirse gradualmente en; deshacerse en (*lágrimas*)
melting pot *s* crisol *m;* (fig) caldero de razas
member ['mɛmbər] *s* miembro
membership ['mɛmbərˌʃɪp] *s* asociación; (*e.g., of a club*) personal *m;* número de miembros
membrane ['mɛmbren] *s* membrana
memen•to [mɪ'mɛnto] *s* (*pl* **-tos** o **-toes**) recordatorio, prenda de recuerdo
mem•o ['mɛmo] *s* (*pl* **-os**) (coll) apunte *m,* membrete *m*
memoir ['mɛmwɑr] *s* memoria; biografía; **memoirs** memorias
memoran•dum [ˌmɛmə'rændəm] *s* (*pl* **-dums** o **-da** [də]) apunte *m,* membrete *m*
memorial [mɪ'morɪ·əl] *adj* conmemorativo || *s* monumento conmemorativo; (*petition*) memorial *m*
memorial arch *s* arco triunfal
Memorial Day *s* día *m* de los caídos
memorialize [mɪ'morɪ·əˌlaɪz] *tr* conmemorar
memorize ['mɛməˌraɪz] *tr* aprender de memoria
memo•ry ['mɛməri] *s* (*pl* **-ries**) memoria; **to commit to memory** encomendar a la memoria
menace ['mɛnɪs] *s* amenaza || *tr & intr* amenazar
ménage [me'nɑʒ] *s* casa, hogar *m;* economía doméstica
menagerie [mə'næʒəri] o [mə'nædʒəri] *s* casa de fieras; colección de fieras
mend [mɛnd] *s* remiendo; **to be on the mend** ir mejorando || *tr* (*to repair*) componer, reparar; (*to patch*) remendar; (*to improve*) reformar, mejorar || *intr* mejorar
mendacious [mɛn'deʃəs] *adj* mendaz
mendicant ['mɛndɪkənt] *adj & s* mendicante *mf*
mending ['mɛndɪŋ] *s* remiendo, zurcido
menfolk ['mɛnˌfok] *spl* hombres *mpl*
menial ['minɪ·əl] *adj* bajo, servil || *s* criado, doméstico
menses ['mɛnsiz] *spl* menstruo
men's furnishings *spl* artículos para caballeros
men's room *s* lavabo para caballeros
menstruate ['mɛnstruˌet] *intr* menstruar
mental illness ['mɛntəl] *s* enfermedad mental
mental reservation *s* reserva mental
mental test *s* prueba de inteligencia
mention ['mɛnʃən] *s* mención || *tr* mencionar; **don't mention it** no hay de qué; **not to mention** sin contar
menu ['mɛnju] o ['menju] *s* menú *m,* lista de comidas; comida
meow [mɪ'aʊ] *s* maullido || *intr* maullar
Mephistophelian [ˌmɛfɪstə'filɪ·ən] *adj* mefistofélico
mercantile ['mʌrkənˌtil] o ['mʌrkənˌtaɪl] *adj* mercantil

mercenar•y ['mʌrsə,nɛri] *adj* mercenario || *s* (*pl* **-ies**) mercenario
merchandise ['mʌrtʃən,daɪz] *s* mercancías, mercaderías
merchant ['mʌrtʃənt] *adj* mercante || *s* mercante *m*, mercader *m*
merchant•man ['mʌrtʃəntmən] *s* (*pl* **-men** [mən]) buque *m* mercante
merchant marine *s* marina mercante
merchant vessel *s* buque *m* mercante
merciful ['mʌrsɪfəl] *adj* misericordioso
merciless ['mʌrsɪlɪs] *adj* despiadado, cruel, implacable
mercu•ry ['mʌrkjəri] *s* (*pl* **-ries**) mercurio, azogue *m*; columna de mercurio
mer•cy ['mʌrsi] *s* (*pl* **-cies**) misericordia; (*discretionary power*) merced *f*; **at the mercy of** a merced de
mere [mɪr] *adj* mero, puro; nada más que
meretricious [,mɛrɪ'trɪʃəs] *adj* postizo, de oropel; cursi, llamativo
merge [mʌrdʒ] *tr* enchufar, fusionar || *intr* enchufarse, fusionarse; convergir (*p.ej., dos caminos*); **to merge into** convertirse gradualmente en
merger ['mʌrdʒər] *s* fusión de empresas
meridian [mə'rɪdɪ·ən] *adj* meridiano; (el) más elevado || *s* meridiano; (fig) auge *m*, apogeo
meringue [mə'ræŋ] *s* merengue *m*
meri•no [mə'rino] *adj* merino || *s* (*pl* **-nos**) merino
merit ['mɛrɪt] *s* mérito || *tr* merecer
merlon ['mʌrlən] *s* almena, merlón *m*
mermaid ['mʌr,med] *s* sirena; (*girl who swims well*) ninfa marina
mer•man ['mʌr,mæn] *s* (*pl* **-men** [,mɛn]) tritón *m*; (*good swimmer*) tritón
merriment ['mɛrɪmənt] *s* alegría, regocijo
mer•ry ['mɛri] *adj* (*comp* **-rier;** *super* **-riest**) alegre, regocijado; **to make merry** divertirse
Merry Christmas *interj* ¡Felices Pascuas!, ¡Felices Navidades!
mer'ry-go-round' *s* tiovivo, caballito; serie ininterrumpida (de fiestas, tertulias, etc.)
mer'ry•mak'er *s* fiestero, jaranero
mesh [mɛʃ] *s* (*net, network*) red *f*; (*each open space of net*) malla; (*engagement of gears*) engrane *m*; **meshes** celada, red *f* || *tr* enredar; (mach) engranar || *intr* enredarse; (mach) engranar
mess [mɛs] *s* (*dirty condition*) cochinería; fregado, lío, embrollo; (*meal for a group of people; such a group*) rancho; (*refuse*) bazofia; **to get into a mess** meterse en un lío; **to make a mess of** ensuciar, echar a perder || *tr* ensuciar; desarreglar; estropear, echar a perder || *intr* comer; **to mess around** (coll) ocuparse en fruslerías
message ['mɛsɪdʒ] *s* mensaje *m*; recado
messenger ['mɛsəndʒər] *s* mensajero; (*one who goes on errands*) mandadero; precursor *m*
mess hall *s* sala de rancho; comedor *m* de militares
Messiah [mə'saɪ·ə] *s* Mesías *m*
mess kit *s* utensilios de rancho
mess'mate' *s* comensal *mf*, compañero de rancho
mess of pottage ['pɑtɪdʒ] *s* (Bib) plato de lentejas; cosa de ningún valor
Messrs. ['mɛsərz] *pl* de **Mr.**
mess•y ['mɛsi] *adj* (*comp* **-ier;** *super* **-iest**) desaliñado, desarreglado; sucio
met. *abbr* **metropolitan**
metal ['mɛtəl] *adj* metálico || *s* metal *m*; (fig) brío, ánimo
metallic [mɪ'tælɪk] *adj* metálico
metallurgy ['mɛtə,lʌrdʒi] *s* metalurgia
metal polish *s* limpiametales *m*
met'al•work' *s* metalistería
metamorpho•sis [,mɛtə'mɔrfəsɪs] *s* (*pl* **-ses** [,siz]) metamorfosis *f*
metaphore ['mɛtəfər] o ['mɛtə,fɔr] *s* metáfora
metaphorical [,mɛtə'fɑrɪkəl] o [,mɛtə'fɔrɪkəl] *adj* metafórico
metathe•sis [mɪ'tæθɪsɪs] *s* (*pl* **-ses** [,siz]) metátesis *f*
mete [mit] *tr* — **to mete out** repartir
meteor ['mitɪ·ər] *s* estrella fugaz; (*atmospheric phenomenon*) meteoro
meteorology [,mitɪ·ə'rɑlədʒi] *s* meteorología
meter ['mitər] *s* (*unit of measurement; verse*) metro; (*instrument for measuring gas, electricity, water*) contador *m*; (mus) compás *m*, tiempo || *tr* medir (con contador)
metering ['mitərɪŋ] *s* medición
meter reader *s* lector *m* (del contador)
methane ['mɛθen] *s* metano
method ['mɛθəd] *s* método
methodic(al) [mɪ'θɑdɪk(əl)] *adj* metódico
Methodist ['mɛθədɪst] *adj* & *s* metodista *mf*
Methuselah [mɪ'θuzələ] *s* Matusalén *m*; **to be as old as Methuselah** vivir más años que Matusalén
meticulous [mɪ'tɪkjələs] *adj* meticuloso, minucioso
metric(al) ['mɛtrɪk(əl)] *adj* métrico
metronome ['mɛtrə,nom] *s* metrónomo
metropolis [mɪ'trɑpəlɪs] *s* metrópoli *f*
metropolitan [,mɛtrə'pɑlɪtən] *adj* metropolitano || *s* (eccl) metropolitano
mettle ['mɛtəl] *s* ánimo, brío; **on one's mettle** dispuesto a hacer todo el esfuerzo posible
mettlesome ['mɛtəlsəm] *adj* animoso, brioso
mew [mju] *s* maullido; (orn) gaviota; **mews** (Brit) caballerizas alrededor de un corral
Mexican ['mɛksɪkən] *adj* & *s* mejicano
Mexico ['mɛksɪ,ko] *s* Méjico
mezzanine ['mɛzə,nin] *s* entresuelo
mfr. *abbr* **manufacturer**
mi. *abbr* **mile**
mica ['maɪkə] *s* mica
microbe ['maɪkrob] *s* microbio
microbiology [,maɪkrəbaɪ'ɑlədʒi] *s* microbiología
microcard ['maɪkrə,kɑrd] *s* microficha

microfarad [ˌmaɪkrəˈfæræd] *s* microfaradio
microfilm [ˈmaɪkrəˌfɪlm] *s* microfilm *m,* micropelícula || *tr* microfilmar
microgroove [ˈmaɪkrəˌgruv] *adj* microsurco || *s* microsurco; disco microsurco
microphone [ˈmaɪkrəˌfon] *s* micrófono
microscope [ˈmaɪkrəˌskop] *s* microscopio
microscopic [ˌmaɪkrəˈskɑpɪk] *adj* microscópico
microwave [ˈmaɪkrəˌwev] *s* microonda
mid [mɪd] *adj* medio, p.ej., **in mid course** a medio camino
mid′day′ *adj* del mediodía || *s* mediodía *m*
middle [ˈmɪdəl] *adj* medio || *s* centro, medio; (*of the human body*) cintura; **about the middle of** a mediados de; **in the middle of** en medio de
middle age *s* mediana edad || **Middle Ages** *spl* Edad Media
middle class *s* burguesía, clase media
Middle East *s* Oriente Medio
Middle English *s* el inglés medio
middle finger *s* dedo cordial, de en medio o del corazón
mid′dle•man′ *s* (*pl* **-men** [ˌmɛn]) intermediario
middling [ˈmɪdlɪŋ] *adj* mediano, regular, pasadero || *adv* (coll) medianamente; **fairly middling** (coll) así, así || *s* (*coarsely ground wheat*) cabezuela; **middlings** artículos de calidad o precio medianos
mid•dy [ˈmɪdi] *s* (*pl* **-dies**) (coll) aspirante *m* de marina; (*child's blouse*) marinera
middy blouse *s* marinera
midget [ˈmɪdʒɪt] *s* enano, liliputiense *mf*
midland [ˈmɪdlənd] *adj* de tierra adentro || *s* región central
mid′night′ *adj* de medianoche; **to burn the midnight oil** quemarse las cejas || *s* medianoche *f*
midriff [ˈmɪdrɪf] *s* (anat) diafragma *m;* talle *m*
midship•man [ˈmɪdˌʃɪpmən] *s* (*pl* **-men** [mən]) guardia marina *m,* aspirante *m* de marina
midst [mɪdst] *s* centro; **in the midst of** en medio de; en lo más recio de
mid′stream′ *s* — **in midstream** en pleno río
mid′sum′mer *s* pleno verano
mid′way′ *adj* situado a mitad del camino || *adv* a mitad del camino || *s* mitad del camino; (*of a fair or exposition*) avenida central
mid′week′ *s* mediados de la semana
mid′wife′ *s* (*pl* **-wives**) partera, comadrona
mid′win′ter *s* pleno invierno
mid′year′ *adj* de mediados del año || *s* mediados del año; **midyears** (coll) examen *m* de mediados del año escolar
mien [min] *s* aspecto, semblante *m,* porte *m*
miff [mɪf] *s* (coll) desavenencia || *tr* (coll) ofender
might [maɪt] *s* fuerza, poder *m;* **with might and main** con todas sus fuerzas, a más no poder || *v aux* se emplea para formar el modo potencial, p.ej., **she might not come** es posible que no venga
might•y [ˈmaɪti] *adj* (*comp* **-ier;** *super* **-iest**) potente, poderoso; (*of great size*) grandísimo || *adv* (coll) muy
migrate [ˈmaɪgret] *intr* emigrar
migratory [ˈmaɪgrəˌtori] *adj* migratorio
mil. *abbr* **military, militia**
milch [mɪltʃ] *adj* lechero
mild [maɪld] *adj* blando, suave; dócil, manso; leve, ligero; (*climate*) templado
mildew [ˈmɪlˌdju] o [ˈmɪlˌdu] *s* (*mold*) moho; (*plant disease*) mildeu *m*
mile [maɪl] *s* milla inglesa
mileage [ˈmaɪlɪdʒ] *s* recorrido en millas
mileage ticket *s* billete contado por millas, semejante al billete kilométrico
mile′post′ *s* poste miliario
mile′stone′ *s* piedra miliaria; **to be a milestone** hacer época
milieu [mɪlˈjʊ] *s* ambiente *m,* medio
militancy [ˈmɪlɪtənsi] *s* belicosidad
militant [ˈmɪlɪtənt] *adj* militante, belicoso
militarism [ˈmɪlɪtəˌrɪzəm] *s* militarismo
militarist [ˈmɪlɪtərɪst] *adj & s* militarista *mf*
militarize [ˈmɪlɪtəˌraɪz] *tr* militarizar
military [ˈmɪlɪˌtɛri] *adj* militar || *s* (los) militares
Military Academy *s* (U.S.A.) Academia General Militar
military police *s* policía militar
militate [ˈmɪlɪˌtet] *intr* militar
militia [mɪˈlɪʃə] *s* milicia
militia•man [ˈmɪˈlɪʃəmən] *s* (*pl* **-men** [mən]) miliciano
milk [mɪlk] *adj* lechero, de leche || *s* leche *f* || *tr* ordeñar; chupar (*los bienes de uno*); abusar de, explotar || *intr* dar leche
milk can *s* lechera
milk diet *s* régimen lácteo
milking [ˈmɪlkɪŋ] *s* ordeño
milk′maid′ *s* lechera
milk•man [ˈmɪlkˌmæn] *s* (*pl* **-men** [ˌmɛn]) lechero
milk of human kindness *s* compasión, humanidad
milk pail *s* ordeñadero
milk shake *s* batido de leche
milk′sop′ *s* calzonazos *m,* marica *m*
milk′weed′ *s* algodoncillo, vencetósigo
milk•y [ˈmɪlki] *adj* (*comp* **-ier;** *super* **-iest**) lechoso, lácteo
Milky Way *s* Vía Láctea
mill [mɪl] *s* (*for grinding grain*) molino; (*for making fabrics*) hilandería; (*for cutting wood*) aserradero; (*for refining sugar*) ingenio; (*for produc-*

ing steel) fábrica; (*to grind coffee*) molinillo; (*part of a dollar*) milésima; **to put through the mill** (coll) poner a prueba, someter a un entrenamiento riguroso || *tr* moler (*granos*); acordonar, cerrillar (*monedas*); laminar (*el acero*); triturar (*mena*); (*with a milling cutter*) fresar; batir (*chocolate*) || *intr* — **to mill about** o **around** arremolinarse

mill end *s* retal *m* de hilandería

millennial [mɪˈlɛnɪ·əl] *adj* milenario

millenni·um [mɪˈlɛnɪ·əm] *s* (*pl* **-ums** o **-a** [ə]) milenario, milenio

miller [ˈmɪlər] *s* molinero; (ent) polilla blanca

millet [ˈmɪlɪt] *s* mijo, millo

milliampere [ˌmɪlɪˈæmpɪr] *s* miliamperio

milligram [ˈmɪlɪˌgræm] *s* miligramo

millimeter [ˈmɪlɪˌmitər] *s* milímetro

milliner [ˈmɪlɪnər] *s* modista *mf* de sombreros

millinery [ˈmɪlɪˌnɛri] o [ˈmɪlɪnəri] *s* artículos para sombreros de señora; confección de sombreros de señora; venta de sombreros de señora

millinery shop *s* sombrerería

milling [ˈmɪlɪŋ] *s* (*of grain*) molienda; (*of coins*) acordonamiento, cordoncillo; fresado

milling machine *s* fresadora

million [ˈmɪljən] *adj* millón de, millones de || *s* millón *m*

millionaire [ˌmɪljənˈɛr] *s* millonario

millionth [ˈmɪljənθ] *adj & s* millonésimo

millivolt [ˈmɪlɪˌvolt] *s* milivoltio

mill′pond′ *s* represa de molino

mill′race′ *s* caz *m*

mill′stone′ *s* muela de molino; (fig) carga pesada

mill wheel *s* rueda de molino

mill′work′ *s* carpintería de taller

mime [maɪm] *s* mimo || *tr* remedar

mimeograph [ˈmɪmɪ·əˌgræf] o [ˈmɪmɪ·əˌgrɑf] *s* (trademark) mimeógrafo || *tr* mimeografiar

mim·ic [ˈmɪmɪk] *s* imitador *m*, remedador *m* || *v* (*pret & pp* **-icked**; *ger* **-icking**) *tr* imitar, remedar

mimic·ry [ˈmɪmɪkri] *s* (*pl* **-ries**) mímica, remedo

min. *abbr* **minimum, minute**

minaret [ˌmɪnəˈrɛt] o [ˈmɪnəˌrɛt] *s* alminar *m*, minarete *m*

mince [mɪns] *tr* desmenuzar; picar (*carne*) || *intr* andar remilgadamente; hablar remilgadamente

mince′meat′ *s* cuajado, picadillo

mince pie *s* pastel relleno de carne picada con frutas

mind [maɪnd] *s* mente *f*, espíritu *m*; **to bear in mind** tener presente; **to be not in one's right mind** no estar en sus cabales; **to be of one mind** estar de acuerdo; **to be out of one's mind** estar fuera de juicio; **to change one's mind** mudar de parecer; **to go out of one's mind** volverse loco; **to have a mind to** tener ganas de; **to have in mind to** pensar en; **to have on one's mind** preocuparse con; **to lose one's mind** perder el juicio; **to make up one's mind** resolverse; **to my mind** a mi parecer; **to say whatever comes into one's mind** decir lo que se le viene a la boca; **to set one's mind on** resolverse a; **to slip one's mind** escaparse de la memoria; **to speak one's mind** decir su parecer; **with one mind** unánimamente || *tr* (*to take care of*) cuidar, estar al cuidado de; obedecer; fijarse en; sentir molestia por; **do you mind the smoke?** ¿le molesta el humo?; **mind your own business** no se meta Vd. en lo que no le toca || *intr* tener inconveniente; tener cuidado; **never mind** no se preocupe, no se moleste

mindful [ˈmaɪndfəl] *adj* atento; **mindful of** atento a, cuidadoso de

mind reader *s* adivinador *m* del pensamiento ajeno, lector *m* mental

mind reading *s* adivinación del pensamiento ajeno, lectura de la mente

mine [maɪn] *pron poss* el mío; mío || *s* mina; **to work a mine** beneficiar una mina || *tr* minar; beneficiar (*un terreno*); extraer (*mineral, carbón, etc.*) || *intr* minar; abrir minas

mine field *s* campo de minas

mine layer *s* buque *m* portaminas, lanzaminas *m*

miner [ˈmaɪnər] *s* minero; (mil, nav) minador *m*

mineral [ˈmɪnərəl] *adj & s* mineral *m*

mineralogy [ˌmɪnəˈrælədʒi] *s* mineralogía

mineral wool *s* lana de escorias

mine sweeper *s* dragaminas *m*

mingle [ˈmɪŋgəl] *tr* mezclar, confundir || *intr* mezclarse, confundirse; asociarse

miniature [ˈmɪnɪ·ətʃər] o [ˈmɪnɪtʃər] *s* miniatura; **to paint in miniature** miniar, pintar de miniatura

miniaturization [ˌmɪnɪ·ətʃərɪˈzeʃən] o [ˌmɪnɪtʃərɪˈzeʃən] *s* miniaturización

minimal [ˈmɪnɪməl] *adj* mínimo

minimize [ˈmɪnɪˌmaɪz] *tr* empequeñecer

minimum [ˈmɪnɪməm] *adj & s* mínimo

minimum wage *s* jornal mínimo

mining [ˈmaɪnɪŋ] *adj* minero || *s* mineraje *m*, minería; (nav) minado

minion [ˈmɪnjən] *s* paniaguado

minion of the law *s* esbirro, polizonte *m*

minister [ˈmɪnɪstər] *s* ministro; pastor *m* prostestante || *tr & intr* ministrar

ministerial [ˌmɪnɪsˈtɪrɪ·əl] *adj* ministerial

minis·try [ˈmɪnɪstri] *s* (*pl* **-tries**) ministerio

mink [mɪŋk] *s* visón *m*

minnow [ˈmɪno] *s* pececillo; (ichth) foxino

minor [ˈmaɪnər] *adj* (*smaller*) menor; de menor importancia; (*younger*) menor de edad; (mus) menor || *s* menor *m* de edad; (educ) asignatura secundaria

Minorca [mɪ'nɔrkə] *s* Menorca
Minorcan [mɪ'nɔrkən] *adj & s* menorquín *m*
minori·ty [mɪ'nɑrɪti] o [mɪ'nɔrɪti] *adj* minoritario || *s* (*pl* **-ties**) (*being under age; smaller number or part*) minoría; (*less than full age*) minoridad
minstrel ['mɪnstrəl] *s* (*retainer who sang and played for his lord*) ministril *m;* (*medieval musician and poet*) juglar *m,* trovador *m;* (U.S.A.) cantor cómico disfrazado de negro
minstrel·sy ['mɪnstrəlsi] *s* (*pl* **-sies**) juglaría; compañía de juglares; poesía trovadoresca
mint [mɪnt] *s* casa de moneda; (*plant*) menta, hierbabuena; montón *m* de dinero; fuente *f* inagotable || *tr* acuñar; (fig) inventar
minuet [,mɪnjʊ'ɛt] *s* minué *m,* minuete *m*
minus ['maɪnəs] *adj* menos || *prep* menos; falto de, sin || *s* menos *m*
minute [maɪ'njut] o [maɪ'nut] *adj* diminuto, menudo || ['mɪnɪt] *s* minuto; (*short space of time*) momento; **minutes** acta; **to write up the minutes** levantar acta; **up to the minute** al corriente; de última hora
minute hand ['mɪnɪt] *s* minutero
minutiae [mɪ'njuʃɪ,i] o [mɪ'nuʃɪ,i] *spl* minucias
minx [mɪŋks] *s* moza descarada
miracle ['mɪrəkəl] *s* milagro
miracle play *s* auto
miraculous [mɪ'rækjələs] *adj* milagroso
mirage [mɪ'rɑʒ] *s* espejismo
mire [maɪr] *s* fango, lodo
mirror ['mɪrər] *s* espejo; (aut) retrovisor *m* || *tr* reflejar
mirth [mʌrθ] *s* alegría, regocijo
mir·y ['maɪri] *adj* (*comp* **-ier;** *super* **-iest**) fangoso, lodoso; sucio
misadventure [,mɪsəd'vɛntʃər] *s* desgracia, contratiempo
misanthrope ['mɪsən,θrop] *s* misántropo
misanthropy [mɪs'ænθrəpi] *s* misantropía
misapprehension [,mɪsæprɪ'hɛnʃən] *s* malentendido
misappropriation [,mɪsə,proprɪ'eʃən] *s* malversación
misbehave [,mɪsbɪ'hev] *intr* conducirse mal, portarse mal
misbehavior [,mɪsbɪ'hevɪ·ər] *s* mala conducta, mal comportamiento
misc. *abbr* **miscellaneous, miscellany**
miscalculation [,mɪskælkjə'leʃən] *s* mal cálculo
miscarriage [mɪs'kærɪdʒ] *s* aborto, malparto; fracaso, malogro; (*of a letter*) extravío
miscar·ry [mɪs'kæri] *v* (*pret & pp* **-ried**) *intr* abortar, malparir; malograrse; extraviarse (*una carta*)
miscellaneous [,mɪsə'lenɪ·əs] *adj* misceláneo
miscella·ny ['mɪsə,leni] *s* (*pl* **-nies**) miscelánea
mischief ['mɪstʃɪf] *s* (*harm*) daño, mal *m;* (*disposition to annoy*) malicia; (*prankishness*) travesura
mis'chief-mak'er *s* malsín *m*, cizañero
mischievous ['mɪstʃɪvəs] *adj* dañoso, malo; malicioso; travieso
misconception [,mɪskən'sɛpʃən] *s* concepto erróneo, mala interpretación
misconduct [mɪs'kɑndəkt] *s* mala conducta
misconstrue [,mɪskən'stru] o [mɪs'kɑnstru] *tr* interpretar mal
miscount [mɪs'kaʊnt] *s* cuenta errónea || *tr & intr* contar mal
miscue [mɪs'kju] *s* (*in billiards*) pifia; (*slip*) pifia || *intr* pifiar; (theat) equivocarse de apunte
mis·deal ['mɪs,dil] *s* repartición errónea || [mɪs'dil] *v* (*pret & pp* **-dealt** ['dɛlt]) *tr & intr* repartir mal
misdeed [mɪs'did] o ['mɪs,did] *s* malhecho, fechoría
misdemeanor [,mɪsdɪ'minər] *s* mala conducta; (law) delito de menor cuantía
misdirect [,mɪsdɪ'rɛkt] o [,mɪsdaɪ'rɛkt] *tr* dirigir erradamente; hacer perder el camino
misdoing [mɪs'du·ɪŋ] *s* mala acción
miser ['maɪzər] *s* avaro, verrugo
miserable ['mɪzərəbəl] *adj* miserable; (coll) achacoso, indispuesto
miserly ['maɪzərli] *adj* avariento, mezquino
miser·y ['mɪzəri] *s* (*pl* **-ies**) miseria
misfeasance [mɪs'fizəns] *s* (law) fraude *m*
misfire [mɪs'faɪr] *s* falla de tiro; (*of internal-combustion engine*) falla de encendido || *intr* fallar (*un arma de fuego, el encendido de un motor*)
mis·fit ['mɪs,fɪt] *s* vestido mal cortado; cosa que no encaja bien; persona mal adaptada a su ambiente || [mɪs'fɪt] *v* (*pret & pp* **-fitted;** *ger* **-fitting**) *tr & intr* encajar mal, sentar mal
misfortune [mɪs'fɔrtʃən] *s* desgracia
misgiving [mɪs'gɪvɪŋ] *s* mal presentimiento, rescoldo
misgovern [mɪs'gʌvərn] *tr* desgobernar
misguidance [mɪs'gaɪdəns] *s* error *m,* extravío
misguided [mɪs'gaɪdɪd] *adj* descarriado, malaconsejado
mishap ['mɪshæp] o [mɪs'hæp] *s* accidente *m,* percance *m*
misinform [,mɪsɪn'fɔrm] *tr* dar informes erróneos a
misinterpret [,mɪsɪn'tɛrprɪt] *tr* interpretar mal
misjudge [mɪs'dʒʌdʒ] *tr & intr* juzgar mal
mis·lay [mɪs'le] *v* (*pret & pp* **-laid** [,led]) *tr* extraviar, perder; (*among one's papers*) traspapelar
mis·lead [mɪs'lid] *v* (*pret & pp* **-led** [,lɛd]) *tr* (*to lead astray*) extraviar, descaminar; (*to lead into wrongdoing*) seducir, inducir al mal; (*to deceive*) engañar
misleading [mɪs'lidɪŋ] *adj* engañoso
mismanagement [mɪs'mænɪdʒmənt] *s* mala administración, desgobierno

misnomer [mɪsˈnomər] *s* nombre impropio, mal nombre
misplace [mɪsˈples] *tr* colocar fuera de su lugar; colocar mal; (*to mislay*) (coll) extraviar, perder
misprint [ˈmɪs,prɪnt] *s* errata de imprenta || [mɪsˈprɪnt] *tr* imprimir con erratas
mispronounce [,mɪsprəˈnaʊns] *tr* pronunciar mal
mispronunciation [,mɪsprə,nʌnsɪˈeʃən] o [,mɪsprə,nʌnʃɪˈeʃən] *s* pronunciación incorrecta
misquote [mɪsˈkwot] *tr* citar equivocadamente
misrepresent [,mɪsrɛprɪˈzɛnt] *tr* tergiversar
miss [mɪs] *s* falta, error *m;* fracaso, malogro; tiro errado; jovencita, muchacha || *tr* echar de menos; perder (*el tren, la función, la oportunidad*); errar (*el blanco; la vocación*); no entender, no comprender; omitir; no ver; no dar con, no encontrar; librarse de (*p.ej., la muerte*); escapársele a uno, p.ej., **I missed what you said** se me escapó lo que dijo Vd.; por poco, p.ej., **the car missed hitting me** el coche por poco me atropella || *intr* fallar; errar el blanco; malograrse || **Miss** *s* señorita
missal [ˈmɪsəl] *s* misal *m*
misshapen [mɪsˈʃepən] *adj* deforme, contrahecho
missile [ˈmɪsɪl] *adj* arrojadizo || *s* arma arrojadiza; proyectil *m;* proyectil dirigido
missing [ˈmɪsɪŋ] *adj* extraviado, perdido; desaparecido; ausente; **to be missing** hacer falta; haber desaparecido
missing link *s* hombre *m* mono
missing persons *spl* desaparecidos
mission [ˈmɪʃən] *s* misión; casa de misión
missionar•y [ˈmɪʃən,ɛri] *adj* misional || *s* (*pl* **-ies**) (*one sent to work to propagate his faith*) misionario, misionero; (*on a political or diplomatic mission*) misionario
missive [ˈmɪsɪv] *adj* misivo || *s* misiva
mis•spell [mɪsˈspɛl] *v* (*pret & pp* **-spelled** o **-spelt** [ˈspɛlt]) *tr & intr* deletrear mal, escribir mal
misspelling [mɪsˈspɛlɪŋ] *s* falta de ortografía
misspent [mɪsˈspɛnt] *adj* malgastado
misstatement [mɪsˈstetmənt] *s* relación equivocada, relación falsa
misstep [mɪsˈstɛp] *s* paso falso; (*slip in conduct*) resbalón *m*
miss•y [ˈmɪsi] *s* (*pl* **-ies**) (coll) señorita
mist [mɪst] *s* neblina; (*of tears*) velo; (*fine spray*) vapor *m*
mis•take [mɪsˈtek] *s* error *m,* equivocación; **and no mistake** sin duda alguna; **by mistake** por descuido; **to make a mistake** equivocarse || *v* (*pret* **-took** [ˈtʊk]; *pp* **-taken**) *tr* tomar (*por otro; por lo que no es*); entender mal; **to be mistaken for** equivocarse con
mistaken [mɪsˈtekən] *adj* (*person*) equivocado; (*idea*) erróneo; (*act*) desacertado
mistakenly [mɪsˈtekənli] *adv* equivocadamente, por error
mistletoe [ˈmɪsəl,to] *s* (*Viscum album*) muérdago; (*Phoradendron flavescens, used in Christmas decorations in the U.S.A.*) cabellera
mistreat [mɪsˈtrit] *tr* maltratar
mistreatment [mɪsˈtritmənt] *s* maltratamiento
mistress [ˈmɪstrɪs] *s* (*of a household*) ama, dueña; moza, querida, manceba; (Brit) maestra de escuela
mistrial [mɪsˈtraɪ·əl] *s* pleito viciado de nulidad
mistrust [mɪsˈtrʌst] *s* desconfianza || *tr* desconfiar de || *intr* desconfiar
mistrustful [mɪsˈtrʌstfəl] *adj* desconfiado
mist•y [ˈmɪsti] *adj* (*comp* **-ier;** *super* **-iest**) brumoso, neblinoso; indistinto
misunder•stand [,mɪsʌndərˈstænd] *v* (*pret & pp* **-stood** [ˈstʊd]) *tr* no comprender, entender mal
misunderstanding [,mɪsʌndərˈstændɪŋ] *s* malentendido; (*disagreement*) desavenencia
misuse [mɪsˈjus] *s* abuso, mal uso; (*of funds*) malversación || [mɪsˈjuz] *tr* abusar de, emplear mal; malversar (*fondos*)
misword [mɪsˈwʌrd] *tr* redactar mal
mite [maɪt] *s* (*small contribution*) óbolo; (*small amount*) pizca; (ent) ácaro
miter [ˈmaɪtər] *s* mitra; (carp) inglete *m* || *tr* cortar ingletes en; juntar con junta a inglete
miter box *s* caja de ingletes
mitigate [ˈmɪtɪ,get] *tr* mitigar, atenuar, paliar
mitten [ˈmɪtən] *s* confortante *m,* mitón *m*
mix [mɪks] *tr* mezclar; amasar (*una torta*); aderezar (*ensalada*); **to mix up** equivocar, confundir || *intr* mezclarse; asociarse
mixed [mɪkst] *adj* mixto, mezclado; (*e.g., candy*) variados; (coll) confundido
mixed company *s* reunión de personas de ambos sexos
mixed drink *s* bebida mezclada
mixed feeling *s* concepto vacilante
mixer [ˈmɪksər] *s* (*of concrete*) mezcladora, hormigonera; **to be a good mixer** (coll) tener don de gentes
mixture [ˈmɪkstʃər] *s* mezcla, mixtura
mix′-up′ *s* confusión; enredo, lío; (*of people*) equivocación
mizzen [ˈmɪzən] *s* mesana
mo. *abbr* **month**
M.O. *abbr* **money order**
moan [mon] *s* gemido || *intr* gemir
moat [mot] *s* foso
mob [mɑb] *s* chusma, populacho; (*crowd bent on violence*) muchedumbre airada || *v* (*pret & pp* **mobbed;** *ger* **mobbing**) *tr* asaltar, atropellar
mobile [ˈmobɪl] o [ˈmobil] *adj* móvil
mobility [moˈbɪlɪti] *s* movilidad

mobilization [ˌmobɪlɪˈzeʃən] *s* movilización
mobilize [ˈmobɪˌlaɪz] *tr* movilizar ‖ *intr* movilizar, movilizarse
mob rule *s* gobierno del populacho
mobster [ˈmabstər] *s* (slang) gamberro, pandillero
moccasin [ˈmakəsɪn] *s* mocasín *m*
Mocha coffee [ˈmokə] *s* moca *m*, café *m* de moca
mock [mak] *adj* simulado, fingido ‖ *s* burla, mofa ‖ *tr* burlarse de, mofarse de; despreciar; engañar ‖ *intr* mofarse; **to mock at** mofarse de
mocker·y [ˈmakəri] *s* (*pl* **-ies**) burla, mofa, escarnio; (*subject of derision*) hazmerreír *m;* (*poor imitation*) mal remedo; (*e.g., of justice*) negación
mock'ing·bird' *s* burlón *m*, sinsonte *m*
mock orange *s* jeringuilla, celinda
mock privet *s* olivillo
mock turtle soup *s* sopa de cabeza de ternera
mock'-up' *s* maqueta
mode [mod] *s* modo, manera; (*fashion*) moda; (gram) modo
mod·el [ˈmadəl] *adj* modelo, p.ej., **model city** ciudad modelo ‖ *s* modelo ‖ *v* (*pret & pp* **-eled** o **-elled;** *ger* **-eling** o **-elling**) *tr* (*to fashion in clay, wax, etc.*) modelar ‖ *intr* modelarse; servir de modelo
model airplane *s* aeromodelo
mod'el-air'plane builder *s* aeromodelista *mf*
model-airplane building *s* aeromodelismo
model sailing *s* navegación de modelos a vela
moderate [ˈmadərɪt] *adj* moderado; (*tiempo*) templado; (*precio*) módico ‖ [ˈmadəˌret] *tr* moderar; presidir (*una asamblea*) ‖ *intr* moderarse
moderator [ˈmadəˌretər] *s* (*over an assembly*) presidente *m;* (*mediator*) árbitro; (*for slowing down neutrons*) moderador *m*
modern [ˈmadərn] *adj* moderno
modernize [ˈmadərˌnaɪz] *tr* modernizar
modest [ˈmadɪst] *adj* modesto
modes·ty [ˈmadɪsti] *s* (*pl* **-ties**) modestia
modicum [ˈmadɪkəm] *s* pequeña cantidad
modifier [ˈmadɪˌfaɪ·ər] *s* (gram) modificante *m*
modi·fy [ˈmadɪˌfaɪ] *v* (*pret & pp* **-fied**) *tr* modificar
modish [ˈmodɪʃ] *adj* de moda, elegante
modulate [ˈmadʒəˌlet] *tr & intr* modular
modulation [ˌmadʒəˈleʃən] *s* modulación
mohair [ˈmoˌhɛr] *s* mohair *m* (*pelo de cabra de Angora*)
Mohammedan [moˈhæmɪdən] *adj & s* mahometano
Mohammedanism [moˈhæmɪdəˌnɪzəm] *s* mahometismo
moist [mɔɪst] *adj* húmedo, mojado; (*weather*) lluvioso; (*eyes*) lagrimoso
moisten [ˈmɔɪsən] *tr* humedecer ‖ *intr* humedecerse
moisture [ˈmɔɪstʃər] *s* humedad
molar [ˈmolər] *s* diente *m* molar
molasses [məˈlæsɪz] *s* melaza
molasses candy *s* melcocha
mold [mold] *s* molde *m;* cosa moldeada; (*shape*) forma; (*fungus*) moho; (*humus*) mantillo; (fig) carácter *m*, índole *f* ‖ *tr* amoldar, moldear; (*to make moldy*) enmohecer ‖ *intr* enmohecerse
molder [ˈmoldər] *s* moldeador *m* ‖ *intr* convertirse en polvo, consumirse
molding [ˈmoldɪŋ] *s* moldeado; (*cornice, shaped strip of wood, etc.*) moldura
mold·y [ˈmoldi] *adj* (*comp* **-ier;** *super* **-iest**) (*overgrown with mold*) mohoso; (*stale*) rancio, pasado
mole [mol] *s* (*breakwater*) rompeolas *m;* (*inner harbor*) dársena; (*spot on skin*) lunar *m;* (*small mammal*) topo
molecule [ˈmalɪˌkjul] *s* molécula
mole'hill' *s* topinera
mole'skin' *s* piel *f* de topo, molesquina
molest [məˈlɛst] *tr* molestar; faltar al respeto a (*una mujer*)
moll [mal] *s* (slang) mujer *f* del hampa; (slang) ramera
molli·fy [ˈmalɪˌfaɪ] *v* (*pret & pp* **-fied**) *tr* apaciguar, aplacar
mollusk [ˈmaləsk] *s* molusco
mollycoddle [ˈmalɪˌkadəl] *s* mantecón *m*, marica *m* ‖ *tr* consentir, mimar
molt [molt] *s* muda ‖ *intr* hacer la muda
molten [ˈmoltən] *adj* fundido, derretido; fundido, vaciado
molybdenum [məˈlɪbdɪnəm] o [ˌmalɪbˈdinəm] *s* molibdeno
moment [ˈmomənt] *s* momento; **at any moment** de un momento a otro
momentary [ˈmomənˌtɛri] *adj* momentáneo
momentous [moˈmɛntəs] *adj* importante, grave
momen·tum [moˈmɛntəm] *s* (*pl* **-tums** o **-ta** [tə]) ímpetu *m;* (mech) cantidad de movimiento
monarch [ˈmanərk] *s* monarca *m*
monarchic(al) [məˈnarkɪk(əl)] *adj* monárquico
monarchist [ˈmanərkɪst] *adj & s* monárquico, monarquista *mf*
monar·chy [ˈmanərki] *s* (*pl* **-chies**) monarquía
monaster·y [ˈmanəsˌtɛri] *s* (*pl* **-ies**) monasterio
monastic [məˈnæstɪk] *adj* monástico
monasticism [məˈnæstɪˌsɪzəm] *s* monaquismo
Monday [ˈmʌndi] *s* lunes *m*
monetary [ˈmanɪˌtɛri] *adj* monetario; pecuniario
money [ˈmʌni] *s* dinero; **to make money** ganar dinero; dar dinero (*una empresa*)
mon'ey·bag' *s* monedero, talega; **moneybags** (*wealth*) (coll) talegas; (*wealthy person*) (coll) ricacho

moneychanger ['mʌni,tʃendʒər] *s* cambista *mf*
moneyed ['mʌnid] *adj* adinerado
moneylender ['mʌni,lendər] *s* prestamista *mf*
mon'ey·mak'er *s* acaudalador *m;* (fig) manantial *m* de beneficios
money order *s* giro postal
Mongol ['maŋgəl] o ['maŋgal] *adj & s* mogol *mf*
Mongolian [maŋ'golɪ·ən] *adj & s* mogol *mf*
mon·goose ['maŋgus] *s* (*pl* **-gooses**) mangosta
mongrel ['mʌŋgrəl] o ['maŋgrəl] *adj & s* mestizo
monitor ['manɪtər] *s* monitor *m* || *tr* controlar (*la señal*); escuchar (*radiotransmisiones*); superentender
monk [mʌŋk] *s* monje *m*
monkey ['mʌŋki] *s* mono; **to make a monkey of** tomar el pelo a || *intr* — **to monkey around** haraganear; **to monkey with** ajar, manosear
mon'key·shine' *s* (slang) monería, monada, payasada
monkey wrench *s* llave inglesa
monkhood ['maŋkhud] *s* monacato; los monjes
monkshood ['maŋks·hud] *s* cogulla de fraile
monocle ['manəkəl] *s* monóculo
monogamy [mə'nagəmi] *s* monogamia
monogram ['manə,græm] *s* monograma *m*
monograph ['manə,græf] o ['manə,graf] *s* monografía
monolithic [,manə'lɪθɪk] *adj* monolítico
monologue ['manə,lɔg] o ['manə,lag] *s* monólogo
monomania [,manə'menɪ·ə] *s* monomanía
monomial [mə'nomɪ·əl] *s* monomio
monopolize [mə'napə,laɪz] *tr* monopolizar; acaparar (*p.ej., la conversación*)
monopo·ly [mə'napəli] *s* (*pl* **-lies**) monopolio
monorail ['manə,rel] *s* monorriel *m*
monosyllable ['manə,sɪləbəl] *s* monosílabo
monotheist ['manə,θi·ɪst] *adj & s* monoteísta *mf*
monotonous [mə'natənəs] *adj* monótono
monotony [mə'natəni] *s* monotonía
monotype ['manə,taɪp] *s* (*machine; method*) monotipia; (*machine*) monotipo
monotype operator *s* monotipista *mf*
monoxide [mə'naksaɪd] *s* monóxido
monseigneur [,mansen'jœr] *s* monseñor *m*
monsignor [man'sinjər] *s* (*pl* **monsignors** o **monsignori** [,mɔnsi'njori]) (eccl) monseñor *m*
monsoon [man'sun] *s* monsón *m*
monster ['manstər] *adj* monstruoso || *s* monstruo
monstrance ['manstrəns] *s* custodia, ostensorio
monstrosi·ty [man'strasɪti] *s* (*pl* **-ties**) monstruosidad
monstrous ['manstrəs] *adj* monstruoso
month [mʌnθ] *s* mes *m*
month·ly ['mʌnθli] *adj* mensual || *adv* mensualmente || *s* (*pl* **-lies**) revista mensual; **monthlies** (coll) reglas
monument ['manjəmənt] *s* monumento
moo [mu] *s* mugido || *intr* mugir
mood [mud] *s* humor *m,* genio; (gram) modo; **moods** accesos de mal humor
mood·y ['mudi] *adj* (*comp* **-ier;** *super* **-iest**) triste, hosco, melancólico; caprichoso, veleidoso
moon [mun] *s* luna
moon'beam' *s* rayo lunar
moon'light' *s* claror *m* de luna, luz *f* de la luna
moon'light'ing *s* multiempleo, pluriempleo
moon'sail' *s* (naut) monterilla
moon'shine' *s* luz *f* de la luna; (*idle talk*) cháchara, música celestial; (coll) whisky destilado ilegalmente
moon shot *s* lanzamiento a la Luna
moor [mur] *s* brezal *m,* páramo || *tr* (naut) amarrar || *intr* (naut) echar las amarras || **Moor** *s* moro
Moorish ['murɪʃ] *adj* moro
moor'land' *s* brezal *m*
moose [mus] *s* (*pl* **moose**) alce *m* de América
moot [mut] *adj* discutible, dudoso
mop [map] *s* aljofifa, fregasuelos *m,* estropajo; (*of hair*) espesura || *v* (*pret & pp* **mopped;** *ger* **mopping**) *tr* aljofifar; enjugarse (*la frente con un pañuelo*); **to mop up** limpiar de enemigos
mope [mop] *intr* andar abatido, entregarse a la melancolía
mopish ['mopɪʃ] *adj* abatido, melancólico
moral ['marəl] o ['mɔrəl] *adj* moral || *s* (*of a fable*) moraleja, moral *f;* **morals** (*ethics; conduct*) moral *f*
moral certainty *s* evidencia moral
morale [mə'ræl] o [mə'ral] *s* moral *f* (*estado de ánimo, confianza en sí mismo*)
morali·ty [mə'rælɪti] *s* (*pl* **-ties**) moralidad
morals charge *s* acusación por delito sexual
morass [mə'ræs] *s* pantano
moratori·um [,mɔrə'torɪ·əm] o [,marə'torɪ·əm] *s* (*pl* **-ums** o **-a** [ə]) *s* moratoria
morbid ['mɔrbɪd] *adj* (*feelings, curiosity*) malsano; (*gruesome*) horripilante; (*pertaining to disease; pathologic*) morboso
mordacious [mɔr'deʃəs] *adj* mordaz
mordant ['mɔrdənt] *adj* mordaz || *s* mordiente *m*
more [mor] *adj & adv* más; **more and more** cada vez más; **more than** más que; (*followed by numeral*) más de; (*followed by verb*) más de lo que || *s* más *m*
more·o'ver *adv* además, por otra parte

Moresque [mo'rɛsk] *adj* moro; (archit) árabe ‖ *s* estilo árabe

morgue [mɔrg] *s* depósito de cadáveres

moribund ['mɔrɪ,bʌnd] o ['mɑrɪ,bʌnd] *adj* moribundo

Moris•co [mə'rɪsko] *adj* morisco, moro ‖ *s* (*pl* **-cos** o **-coes**) moro; moro de España; (*offspring of mulatto and Spaniard, in Mexico*) morisco

morning ['mɔrnɪŋ] *adj* matinal ‖ *s* mañana; (*time between midnight and dawn*) madrugada; **in the morning** de mañana, por la mañana

morning coat *s* chaqué *m*

morn'ing-glo'ry *s* (*pl* **-ries**) dondiego de día

morning sickness *s* vómitos del embarazo

morning star *s* lucero del alba

Moroccan [mə'rɑkən] *adj* & *s* marroquí *mf* o marroquín *m*

morocco [mə'rɑko] *s* (*leather*) marroquí *m* o marroquín *m* ‖ **Morocco** *s* Marruecos *m*

moron ['morɑn] *s* (*person of arrested intelligence*) morón *m;* (coll) imbécil *mf*

morose [mə'ros] *adj* adusto, hosco, malhumorado

morphine ['mɔrfin] *s* morfina

morphology [mɔr'fɑlədʒi] *s* morfología

Morris chair ['mɑrɪs] o ['mɔrɪs] *s* poltrona extensible

morrow ['mɑro] o ['mɔro] *s* (*future time*) mañana *m;* (*time following some event*) día *m* siguiente; **on the morrow** en el día de mañana; el día siguiente

morsel ['mɔrsəl] *s* bocadito; pedacito

mortal ['mɔrtəl] *adj* & *s* mortal *m*

mortality [mɔr'tælɪti] *s* mortalidad; (*death or destruction on a large scale*) mortandad

mortar ['mɔrtər] *s* (*bowl used for crushing; mixture of lime, etc.*) mortero; (arti) mortero

mor'tar•board' *s* esparavel *m;* gorro académico cuadrado

mortgage ['mɔrgɪdʒ] *s* hipoteca ‖ *tr* hipotecar

mortgagee [,mɔrgɪ'dʒi] *s* acreedor hipotecario

mortgagor ['mɔrgɪdʒər] *s* deudor hipotecario

mortician [mɔr'tɪʃən] *s* empresario de pompas fúnebres

morti•fy ['mɔrtɪ,faɪ] *v* (*pret* & *pp* **-fied**) *tr* humillar; mortificar (*el cuerpo, las pasiones*); **to be mortified** avergonzarse

mortise ['mɔrtɪs] *s* mortaja, muesca ‖ *tr* amortajar, enmuescar

mortise lock *s* cerradura embutida

mortuar•y ['mɔrtʃʊ,ɛri] *adj* mortuorio ‖ *s* (*pl* **-ies**) depósito de cadáveres; funeraria

mosaic [mo'ze•ɪk] *m* mosaico

Moscow ['mɑskaʊ] o ['mɑsko] *s* Moscú

Moses ['mozɪz] o ['mozɪs] *s* Moisés *m*

Mos•lem ['mɑzləm] o ['mɑsləm] *adj* muslime, musulmán ‖ *s* (*pl* **-lems** o **-lem**) muslime *mf,* musulmán *m*

mosque [mɑsk] *s* mezquita

mosqui•to [məs'kito] *s* (*pl* **-toes** o **-tos**) mosquito

mosquito net *s* mosquitero

moss [mɔs] o [mɑs] *s* musgo

moss'back' *s* (coll) reaccionario; (*old-fashioned person*) (coll) fósil *m*

moss•y ['mɔsi] o ['mɑsi] *adj* (*comp* **-ier;** *super* **-iest**) musgoso

most [most] *adj* más; la mayor parte de, los más de ‖ *adv* más; muy, sumamente; (coll) casi ‖ *s* la mayor parte, el mayor número, los más; **most of** la mayor parte de, el mayor número de; **to make the most of** sacar el mejor partido de

mostly ['mostli] *adv* por la mayor parte, mayormente; casi

moth [mɔθ] o [mɑθ] *s* mariposa nocturna; (*clothes moth*) polilla

moth ball *s* bola de alcanfor, bola de naftalina

moth'-ball' fleet *s* (nav) flota en conserva

moth'-eat'en *adj* apolillado; (fig) anticuado

mother ['mʌðər] *adj* (*love*) maternal; (*tongue*) materno; (*country*) madre; (*church*) metropolitano ‖ *s* madre *f;* (*an elderly woman*) (coll) tía ‖ *tr* servir de madre a

mother country *s* madre patria

Mother Goose *s* supuesta autora o narradora de una colección de cuentos infantiles (in Spain: *Cuentos de Calleja*)

motherhood ['mʌðər,hʊd] *s* maternidad

moth'er-in-law' *s* (*pl* **mothers-in-law**) suegra

moth'er•land' *s* patria

motherless ['mʌðərlɪs] *adj* huérfano de madre, sin madre

motherly ['mʌðərli] *adj* maternal

mother-of-pearl ['mʌðərəv'pʌrl] *adj* nacarado ‖ *s* nácar *m*

Mother's Day *s* día *m* de la madre

mother superior *s* superiora

mother tongue *s* (*language naturally acquired by reason of nationality*) lengua materna; (*language from which another language is derived*) lengua madre, lengua matriz

mother wit *s* gracia natural, chispa

moth hole *s* apolilladura

moth•y ['mɔθi] o ['mɑθi] *adj* (*comp* **-ier;** *super* **-iest**) apolillado

motif [mo'tif] *s* motivo

motion ['moʃən] *s* movimiento; (*signal, gesture*) seña, indicación; (*in a deliberating assembly*) moción ‖ *intr* hacer señas con la mano o la cabeza

motionless ['moʃənlɪs] *adj* inmoble

motion picture *s* película cinematográfica

mo'tion-pic'ture *adj* cinematográfico

motivate ['motɪ,vet] *tr* animar, incitar, mover

motive ['motɪv] *adj* (*promoting action*) motivo; (*producing motion*) motor ‖ *s* motivo

motive power *s* fuerza motriz, potencia

motora o motriz; (rr) conjunto de locomotoras de un ferrocarril
motley ['mɑtli] *adj* abigarrado; mezclado, variado
motor ['motər] *adj* motor || *s* motor *m;* motor eléctrico; automóvil *m* || *intr* viajar en automóvil
mo'tor•boat' *s* gasolinera, canoa automóvil
mo'tor•bus' *s* autobús *m*
motorcade ['motər,ked] *s* caravana de automóviles
mo'tor•car' *s* automóvil *m*
mo'tor•cy'cle *s* motocicleta
motorist ['motərɪst] *s* motorista *mf,* automovilista *mf*
motorize ['motə,raɪz] *tr* motorizar
motor launch *s* lancha automóvil
motor•man ['motərmən] *s* (*pl* **-men** [mən]) conductor *m* de tranvía, conductor de locomotora eléctrica
motor sailer ['selər] *s* motovelero
motor scooter *s* motoneta
motor ship *s* motonave *f*
motor truck *s* autocamión *m*
motor vehicle *s* vehículo motor, autovehículo
mottle ['mɑtəl] *tr* abigarrar, jaspear, motear
mot•to ['mɑto] *s* (*pl* **-toes** o **-tos**) lema *m,* divisa
mould [mold] *s, tr, & intr* var de **mold**
moulder ['moldər] *s & intr* var de **molder**
moulding ['moldɪn] *s* var de **molding**
mouldy ['moldi] *adj* var de **moldy**
mound [maʊnd] *s* montón *m* de tierra; montecillo
mount [maʊnt] *s* (*hill, mountain*) monte *m;* (*horse for riding*) montura; (*setting for a jewel*) montadura; soporte *m;* cartón *m,* tela (*en que está pegada una fotografía*); (mach) montaje *m* || *tr* subir (*una escalera, una cuesta*); subir a (*una plataforma*); escalar (*una muralla*); montar (*un servicio; una piedra preciosa*); poner a caballo; pegar (*vistas, pruebas*); (mil) montar (*la guardia*) || *intr* montar, montarse; aumentar, subir (*los precios*)
mountain ['maʊntən] *s* montaña; **to make a mountain out of a molehill** hacer de una pulga un camello
mountain climbing *s* alpinismo, montañismo
mountaineer [,maʊntə'nɪr] *s* montañés *m*
mountainous ['maʊntənəs] *adj* montañoso
mountain railroad *s* ferrocarril *m* de cremallera
mountain range *s* cordillera, sierra
mountain sickness *s* mal *m* de las montañas
mountebank ['maʊntɪ,bæŋk] *s* saltabanco
mounting ['maʊntɪŋ] *s* (*of a precious stone, of an astronomical instrument*) montura; papel *m* de soporte; papel o tela (*en que está pegada una fotografía*); (mach) montaje *m*
mourn [morn] *tr* llorar (*p.ej., la muerte de una persona*); lamentar (*una desgracia*) || *intr* lamentarse; vestir de luto
mourner ['mornər] *s* doliente *mf;* (*person who makes a public profession of penitence*) penitente *mf;* (*person hired to attend a funeral*) plañidera; **mourners** duelo
mourners' bench *s* banco de los penitentes
mournful ['mornfəl] *adj* (*sorrowful*) doloroso; (*gloomy*) lúgubre
mourning ['mornɪŋ] *s* luto; **to be in mourning** estar de luto
mourning band *s* crespón *m* fúnebre, brazal *m* de luto
mouse [maʊs] *s* (*pl* **mice** [maɪs]) ratón *m*
mouse'hole' *s* ratonera
mouser ['maʊzər] *s* desmurador *m*
mouse'trap' *s* ratonera
moustache [məs'tæʃ] o [məs'tɑʃ] *s* bigote *m,* mostacho
mouth [maʊθ] *s* (*pl* **mouths** [maʊðz]) boca; (*of a river*) desembocadura, embocadura; **by mouth** por vía bucal; **to be born with a silver spoon in one's mouth** nacer de pie; **to make one's mouth water** hacérsele a uno la boca agua; **to not open one's mouth** no decir esta boca es mía
mouthful ['maʊθ,ful] s bocado
mouth organ *s* armónica de boca
mouth'piece' *s* (*of wind instrument*) boquilla; (*of bridle*) embocadura; (*spokesman*) portavoz *m*
mouth'wash' *s* enjuague *m,* enjuagadientes *m*
movable ['muvəbəl] *adj* movible, móvil
move [muv] *s* movimiento; (*démarche*) acción, gestión, paso; (*from one house to another*) mudanza; **on the move** en marcha, en movimiento; **to get a move on** (slang) menearse, darse prisa; **to make a move** dar un paso; hacer una jugada || *tr* mover; evacuar (*el vientre*); (*to stir, excite the feelings of*) conmover, enternecer; **to move up** adelantar (*una fecha*) || *intr* moverse; desplazarse (*un viajante; un planeta*); mudarse, mudar de casa; (*e.g., to another store, to another city*) trasladarse; hacer una jugada; hacer una moción; venderse, tener salida (*una mercancía*); evacuarse, moverse (*el vientre*); **to move away** apartarse; marcharse; mudarse de casa; **to move in** instalarse; alternar con, frecuentar (*la buena sociedad*); **to move off** alejarse
movement ['muvmənt] *s* movimiento; aparato de relojería; (*of the bowels*) evacuación; (*e.g., of a symphony*) tiempo
movie ['muvi] *s* (coll) película, cinta
movie•goer ['movi,go•ər] *s* (coll) aficionado al cine
movie house *s* (coll) cineteatro
mov'ie•land' *s* (coll) cinelandia
moving ['muvɪŋ] *adj* conmovedor, impresionante || *s* movimiento; (*from one house to another*) mudanza

moving picture *s* película cinematográfica
moving spirit *s* alma (*de una empresa*)
moving stairway *s* escalera mecánica, móvil o rodante
mow [mo] *v* (*pret* **mowed;** *pp* **mowed** o **mown**) *tr* segar; **to mow down** matar (*soldados*) con fuego graneado || *intr* segar
mower ['mo·ər] *s* segador *m;* segadora mecánica
mowing machine *s* segadora mecánica
Mozarab [mo'zærəb] *s* mozárabe *mf*
Mozarabic [mo'zærəbɪk] *adj* mozárabe
M.P. *abbr* **Member of Parliament, Military Police**
m.p.h. *abbr* **miles per hour**
Mr. ['mɪstər] *s* (*pl* **Messrs.** ['mɛsərz]) señor *m* (*tratamiento*)
Mrs. ['mɪsɪz] *s* señora (*tratamiento*)
MS. o **ms.** *abbr* **manuscript**
Mt. *abbr* **Mount**
much [mʌtʃ] *adj & pron* mucho; **too much** demasiado || *adv* mucho; **however much** por mucho que; **how much** cuánto; **too much** demasiado; **very much** muchísimo
mucilage ['mjusɪlɪdʒ] *s* goma para pegar; (*gummy secretion in plants*) mucílago
muck [mʌk] *s* estiércol húmedo; suciedad, porquería; (min) zafra
muck'rake' *intr* (coll) exponer ruindades
mucous ['mjukəs] *adj* mucoso
mucus ['mjukəs] *s* moco
mud [mʌd] *s* barro, fango, lodo; **to sling mud at** llenar de fango
muddle ['mʌdəl] *s* confusión, embrollo || *tr* confundir, embrollar; atontar, aturdir || *intr* obrar torpemente; **to muddle through** salir del paso a pesar suyo
mud'dle·head' *s* farraguista *mf,* cajón *m* de sastre
mud·dy ['mʌdi] *adj* (*comp* **-dier;** *super* **-diest**) barroso, fangoso, lodoso; (*obscure*) turbio || *v* (*pret & pp* **-died**) *tr* embarrar, enturbiar
mud'guard' *s* guardabarros *m*
mud'hole' *s* atolladero, ciénaga
mudslinger ['mʌd,slɪŋər] *s* (fig) lanzador *m* de lodo
muezzin [mju'ɛzɪn] *s* almuecín *m,* almuédano
muff [mʌf] *s* manguito || *tr & intr* chapucear
muffin ['mʌfɪn] *s* mollete *m*
muffle ['mʌfəl] *tr* arropar; (*about the face*) embozar; amortiguar (*un ruido*); enfundar (*un tambor*)
muffler ['mʌflər] *s* bufanda, tapaboca; (aut) silenciador *m,* silencioso
mufti ['mʌfti] *s* traje *m* de paisano
mug [mʌg] *s* pichel *m;* (slang) jeta, hocico || *v* (*pret & pp* **mugged;** *ger* **mugging**) *tr* (slang) fotografiar; (slang) atacar || *intr* (slang) hacer muecas
mug·gy ['mʌgi] *adj* (*comp* **-gier;** *super* **-giest**) bochornoso, sofocante
mulat·to [mjʊ'læto] o [mə'læto] *s* (*pl* **-toes**) mulato
mulber·ry ['mʌl,bɛri] *s* (*pl* **-ries**) (*tree*) moral *m;* (*fruit*) mora
mulct [mʌlkt] *tr* defraudar
mule [mjul] *s* mulo, macho; (*slipper*) babucha
mule chair *s* artolas, jamugas
muleteer [,mjulə'tɪr] *s* mulatero
mulish ['mjulɪʃ] *adj* terco, obstinado
mull [mʌl] *tr* calentar (*vino*) con especias || *intr* — **to mull over** reflexionar sobre
mullion ['mʌljən] *s* parteluz *m*
multigraph ['mʌltɪ,græf] o ['mʌltɪ,grɑf] *s* (trademark) multígrafo || *tr* multigrafiar
multilateral [,mʌltɪ'lætərəl] *adj* (*having many sides*) multilátero; (*participated in by more than two nations*) multilateral
multiple ['mʌltɪpəl] *adj* múltiple, múltiplo || *s* (math) múltiplo
multiplici·ty [,mʌltɪ'plɪsɪti] *s* (*pl* **-ties**) multiplicidad
multi·ply ['mʌltɪ,plaɪ] *v* (*pret & pp* **-plied**) *tr* multiplicar || *intr* multiplicar, multiplicarse
multitude ['mʌltɪ,tjud] o ['mʌltɪ,tud] *s* multitud
mum [mʌm] *adj* callado; **mum's the word!** ¡punto en boca!; **to keep mum about** callar || *interj* ¡chitón!
mumble ['mʌmbəl] *tr & intr* mascullar, mascujar
mummer·y ['mʌməri] *s* (*pl* **-ies**) mojiganga
mum·my ['mʌmi] *s* (*pl* **-mies**) momia
mumps [mʌmps] *s* papera
munch [mʌntʃ] *tr* ronzar
mundane ['mʌnden] *adj* mundano
municipal [mju'nɪsɪpəl] *adj* municipal
municipali·ty [mju,nɪsɪ'pælɪti] *s* (*pl* **-ties**) municipio
munificent [mju'nɪfɪsənt] *adj* munífico
munition [mju'nɪʃən] *s* munición || *tr* municionar
munition dump *s* depósito de municiones
mural ['mjʊrəl] *adj* mural || *s* pintura mural; decoración mural
murder ['mʌrdər] *s* asesinato, homicidio || *tr* asesinar; (*to spoil, mar*) (coll) estropear
murderer ['mʌrdərər] *s* asesino
murderess ['mʌrdərɪs] *s* asesina
murderous ['mʌrdərəs] *adj* asesino; cruel, sanguinario
murk·y ['mʌrki] *adj* (*comp* **-ier;** *super* **-iest**) (*hazy*) calinoso; (*gloomy*) lóbrego
murmur ['mʌrmər] *s* murmullo || *tr & intr* murmurar
mus. *abbr* **museum, music**
muscle ['mʌsəl] *s* músculo; (fig) fuerza muscular
muscular ['mʌskjələr] *adj* musculoso
muse [mjuz] *s* musa; **the Muses** las Musas || *intr* meditar, reflexionar; **to muse on** contemplar
museum [mju'zi·əm] *s* museo
mush [mʌʃ] *s* gachas; (coll) sentimentalismo exagerado, sensiblería
mush'room' *s* hongo, seta || *intr* aparecer de la noche a la mañana; **to**

mushroom into convertirse rápidamente en
mushroom cloud *s* nube-hongo *f*
mush·y ['mʌʃi] *adj* (*comp* **-ier;** *super* **-iest**) mollar, pulposo; (coll) sensiblero, sobón; (*with women*) (coll) baboso; **to be mushy** (coll) hacerse unas gachas
music ['mjuzɪk] *s* música; **to face the music** (coll) afrontar las consecuencias; **to set to music** poner en música
musical ['mjuzɪkəl] *adj* musical, músico
musical comedy *s* comedia musical
musicale [,mjuzɪ'kæl] *s* velada musical, concierto casero
music box *s* caja de música
music cabinet *s* musiquero
music hall *s* salón *m* de conciertos; (Brit) teatro de variedades
musician [mju'zɪʃən] *s* músico
musicianship [mju'zɪʃən,ʃɪp] *s* musicalidad
musicologist [,mjuzɪ'kɑlədʒɪst] *s* musicólogo
musicology [,mjuzɪ'kɑlədʒi] *s* musicología
music rack o **music stand** *s* atril *m*
musk [mʌsk] *s* almizcle *m;* olor *m* de almizcle
musk deer *s* almizclero
musket ['mʌskɪt] *s* mosquete *m*
musketeer [,mʌskɪ'tɪr] *s* mosquetero
musk'mel'on *s* melón *m*
musk'rat' *s* almizclera
muslin ['mʌzlɪn] *s* muselina
muss [mʌs] *tr* (*the hair*) (coll) descabellar, desarreglar; (*clothing*) (coll) chafar, arrugar
Mussulman ['mʌsəlmən] *adj* & *s* musulmán *m*
muss·y ['mʌsi] *adj* (*comp* **-ier;** *super* **-iest**) desaliñado, desgreñado
must [mʌst] *s* mosto; (*mold*) moho; cosa que debe hacerse ‖ *v aux* **I must study my lesson** debo estudiar mi lección; **he must work tomorrow** tiene que trabajar mañana; **she must be ill** estará enferma
mustache [məs'tæʃ], [məs'tɑʃ] o ['mʌstæʃ] *s* bigote *m,* mostacho
mustard ['mʌstərd] *s* mostaza
mustard plaster *s* sinapismo, cataplasma *f*
muster ['mʌstər] *s* asamblea; matrícula de revista; **to pass muster** pasar revista; ser aceptable ‖ *tr* llamar a asamblea; reunir para pasar revista; reunir, acumular; **to muster in** alistar; **to muster out** dar de baja a; **to muster up courage** cobrar ánimo
muster roll *s* lista de revista
mus·ty ['mʌsti] *adj* (*comp* **-tier;** *super* **-tiest**) (*moldy*) mohoso; (*stale*) trasnochado; anticuado, pasado de moda
mutation [mju'teʃən] *s* mutación
mute [mjut] *adj* & *s* mudo ‖ *tr* poner sordina a
mutilate ['mjutɪ,let] *tr* mutilar
mutineer [,mjutɪ'nɪr] *s* amotinado
mutinous ['mjutɪnəs] *adj* amotinado
muti·ny ['mjutɪni] *s* (*pl* **-nies**) motín *m* ‖ *v* (*pret* & *pp* **-nied**) *intr* amotinarse
mutt [mʌt] *s* (slang) perro cruzado; (slang) bobo, tonto
mutter ['mʌtər] *tr* & *intr* murmurar
mutton ['mʌtən] *s* carnero, carne *f* de carnero
mutton chop *s* chuleta de carnero
mutual ['mutʃu·əl] *adj* mutual, mutuo
mutual aid *s* apoyo mutuo
mutual benefit association *s* mutualidad
muzzle ['mʌzəl] *s* (*projecting part of head of animal*) hocico; (*device to keep animal from biting*) bozal *m;* (*of firearm*) boca ‖ *tr* abozalar; (*to keep from speaking*) amordazar
my [maɪ] *adj poss* mi
myriad ['mɪrɪ·əd] *s* miríada
myrrh [mʌr] *s* mirra
myrtle ['mʌrtəl] *s* arrayán *m,* mirto
myself [maɪ'sɛlf] *pron pers* yo mismo; mí, mí mismo; me, p.ej., **I enjoyed myself** me divertí; **with myself** conmigo
mysterious [mɪs'tɪrɪ·əs] *adj* misterioso
myster·y ['mɪstəri] *s* (*pl* **-ies**) misterio
mystic ['mɪstɪk] *adj* & *s* místico
mystical ['mɪstɪkəl] *adj* místico
mysticism ['mɪstɪ,sɪzəm] *s* misticismo
mystification [,mɪstɪfɪ'keʃən] *s* confusión, mistificación
mysti·fy ['mɪstɪ,faɪ] *v* (*pret* & *pp* **-fied**) *tr* rodear de misterio; (*to hoax*) confundir, mistificar
myth [mɪθ] *s* mito
mythical ['mɪθɪkəl] *adj* mítico
mythological [,mɪθə'lɑdʒɪkəl] *adj* mitológico
mytholo·gy [mɪ'θɑlədʒi] *s* (*pl* **-gies**) mitología

N

N, n [ɛn] decimocuarta letra del alfabeto inglés
n. *abbr* **neuter, nominative, noon, north, noun, number**
N. *abbr* **Nationalist, Navy, Noon, North, November**
N.A. *abbr* **National Academy, National Army, North America**
nab [næb] *v* (*pret* & *pp* **nabbed;** *ger* **nabbing**) *tr* (slang) agarrar, coger; (slang) poner preso, prender
nag [næg] *s* caballejo, jaco; pequeño caballo de silla ‖ *v* (*pret* & *pp* **nagged;** *ger* **nagging**) *tr* importunar regañando ‖ *intr* regañar
naiad ['ne·æd] o ['naɪ·æd] *s* náyade *f;* (fig) nadadora
nail [nel] *s* (*of finger*) uña; (*to fasten*

wood, etc.) clavo; **to hit the nail on the head** dar en el clavo || *tr* clavar
nail brush *s* cepillo de uñas
nail file *s* lima para las uñas
nail polish *s* esmalte *m* para las uñas, laca de uñas
nailset ['nel,sɛt] *s* contrapunzón *m*
naïve [nɑ'iv] *adj* cándido, ingenuo
naked ['nekɪd] *adj* desnudo; **to go naked** ir desnudo, andar a la cordobana; **to strip naked** desnudar; desnudarse; **with the naked eye** a simple vista
name [nem] *s* nombre *m;* (*first name*) nombre de pila; (*last name*) apellido; fama, reputación, renombre *m;* linaje, *m,* raza; **to call someone names** maltratar a uno de palabra; **to go by the name of** ser conocido por el nombre de; **to make a name for oneself** darse a conocer, hacerse un nombre; **what is your name?** ¿cómo se llama Vd.? || *tr* nombrar; fijar (*un precio*)
name day *s* santo
nameless ['nemlɪs] *adj* sin nombre, anónimo
namely ['nemli] *adv* a saber, es decir
namesake ['nem,sek] *s* homónimo, tocayo
nanny goat ['næni] *s* (coll) cabra
nap [næp] *s* lanilla, flojel *m;* sueñecillo; **to take a nap** descabezar un sueñecillo || *v* (*pret & pp* **napped;** *ger* **napping**) *intr* echar un sueñecillo; estar desprevenido; **to catch napping** coger desprevenido
napalm ['nepɑm] *s* (mil) gelatina incendiaria
nape [nep] *s* cogote *m,* nuca
naphtha ['næfθə] *s* nafta
napkin ['næpkɪn] *s* servilleta; (*of a baby*) (Brit) pañal *m*
napkin ring *s* servilletero
Naples ['nepəlz] *s* Nápoles
Napoleonic [nə,polɪ'ɑnɪk] *adj* napoleónico
narcissus [nɑr'sɪsəs] *s* (bot) narciso || **Narcissus** *s* Narciso
narcotic [nɑr'kɑtɪk] *adj & s* narcótico
narrate [næ'ret] *tr* narrar
narration [næ'reʃən] *s* narración
narrative ['nærətɪv] *adj* narrativo || *s* (*story, tale; art of telling stories*) narrativa
narrator [næ'retər] *s* narrador *m*
narrow ['næro] *adj* angosto, estrecho; intolerante; minucioso; (*sense of a word*) estricto || **narrows** *spl* angostura, paso estrecho || *tr* enangostar, estrechar; reducir, limitar || *intr* enangostarse, estrecharse; reducirse, limitarse
narrow escape *s* trance *m* difícil; **to have a narrow escape** escapar por un pelo, salvarse en una tabla
narrow gauge *s* trocha angosta, vía estrecha
narrow-minded ['næro'maɪndɪd] *adj* intolerante, de miras estrechas, poco liberal
nasal ['nezəl] *adj & s* nasal *f*
nasalize ['nezə,laɪz] *tr* nasalizar || *intr* ganguear
nasturtium [nə'stʌrʃəm] *s* capuchina, espuela de galán
nas·ty ['næsti] o ['nɑsti] *adj* (*comp* **-tier;** *super* **-tiest**) asqueroso, sucio; desagradable; desvergonzado; amenazador; horrible
natatorium [,netə'torɪ·əm] *s* piscina de natación
nation ['neʃən] *s* nación
national ['næʃənəl] *adj & s* nacional *mf*
national anthem *s* himno nacional
national hero *s* benemérito de la patria
national holiday *s* fiesta nacional
nationalism ['næʃənə,lɪzəm] *s* nacionalismo
nationalist ['næʃənəlɪst] *adj & s* nacionalista *mf*
nationali·ty [,næʃən'ælɪti] *s* (*pl* **-ties**) nacionalidad, naturalidad
nationalize ['næʃənə,laɪz] *tr* nacionalizar
na'tion-wide' *adj* de toda la nación
native ['netɪv] *adj* nativo, natural; indígena; (*language*) materno; **to go native** vivir como los indígenas || *s* natural *mf;* indígena *mf*
native land *s* patria
nativi·ty [nə'tɪvɪti] *s* (*pl* **-ties**) nacimiento || **Nativity** *s* (*day; festival; painting*) natividad
Nato ['neto] *s* (acronym) la **O.T.A.N.**
nat·ty ['næti] *adj* (*comp* **-tier;** *super* **-tiest**) elegante, garboso
natural ['nætʃərəl] *adj* natural; (mus) natural || *s* imbécil *mf;* (mus) tono natural, nota natural; (*sign*) (mus) becuadro; (mus) tecla blanca; (coll) cosa de éxito certero
naturalism ['nætʃərə,lɪzəm] *s* naturalismo
naturalist ['nætʃərəlɪst] *s* naturalista *mf*
naturalization [,nætʃərəlɪ'zeʃən] *s* naturalización
naturalization papers *spl* carta de naturaleza
naturalize ['nætʃərə,laɪz] *tr* naturalizar
naturally ['nætʃərəli] *adv* naturalmente; claro, desde luego, por supuesto
nature ['netʃər] *s* naturaleza; **from nature** del natural
naught [nɔt] *s* nada; cero; **to bring to naught** anular, invalidar, destruir; **to come to naught** reducirse a nada, frustrarse
naugh·ty ['nɔti] *adj* (*comp* **-tier;** *super* **-tiest**) desobediente, pícaro; desvergonzado; (*story, tale*) verde
nausea ['nɔʃɪ·ə] o ['nɔsɪ·ə] *s* náusea
nauseate ['nɔʃɪ,et] o ['nɔsɪ,et] *tr* dar náuseas a || *intr* nausear, marearse
nauseating ['nɔʃɪ,etɪŋ] o ['nɔsɪ,etɪŋ] *adj* nauseabundo, asqueroso
nauseous ['nɔʃɪ·əs] o ['nɔsɪ·əs] *adj* nauseabundo
nautical ['nɔtɪkəl] *adj* náutico, marino, naval
nav. *abbr* **naval, navigation**
naval ['nevəl] *adj* naval, naval militar

Naval Academy *s* (U.S.A.) Escuela Naval Militar
naval officer *s* oficial *m* de marina
naval station *s* apostadero
nave [nev] *s* (*of a church*) nave *f* central, nave principal; (*of a wheel*) cubo
navel ['nevəl] *s* ombligo; (*center point, middle*) (fig) ombligo
navel orange *s* navel *f*, naranja de ombligo
navigability [,nævɪgə'bɪlɪti] *s* (*of a river*) navegabilidad; (*of a ship*) buen gobierno
navigable ['nævɪgəbəl] *adj* (*river, canal, etc.*) navegable; (*ship*) marinero, de buen gobierno
navigate ['nævɪ,get] *tr & intr* navegar
navigation [,nævɪ'geʃən] *s* navegación
navigator ['nævɪ,getər] *s* navegador *m*, navegante *m;* (*he who is in charge of course of ship or plane*) oficial *m* de derrota; (Brit) peón *m*
nav•vy ['nævi] *s* (*pl* **-vies**) (Brit) bracero, peón *m*
na•vy ['nevi] *adj* azul oscuro || *s* (*pl* **-vies**) marina de guerra; (*personnel*) marina; azul oscuro
navy bean *s* frijol blanco común
navy blue *s* azul marino, azul oscuro
navy yard *s* arsenal *m* de puerto
Nazarene [,næzə'rin] *adj & s* nazareno
Nazi ['nɑtsi] o ['nætsi] *adj & s* nazi *mf*, nacista *mf*
n.b. *abbr* **nota bene** (Lat) **note well**
N-bomb ['ɛn,bɑm] *s* bomba de neutrones
Neapolitan [,ni•ə'pɑlɪtən] *adj & s* napolitano
neap tide [nip] *s* marea muerta
near [nɪr] *adj* cercano, próximo; íntimo; imitado || *adv* cerca; íntimamente || *prep* cerca de; hacia, por || *tr* acercarse a || *intr* acercarse
nearby ['nɪr,baɪ] *adj* cercano, próximo || *adv* cerca
Near East *s* Cercano Oriente, Próximo Oriente
nearly ['nɪrli] *adv* casi; de cerca; íntimamente; por poco, p.ej., **he nearly fell** por poco se cae
near-sighted ['nɪr'saɪtɪd] *adj* miope
near-sightedness *s* miopía
neat [nit] *adj* aseado, pulcro; pulido; diestro, primoroso; puro, sin mezcla || *ssg* res vacuna || *spl* ganado vacuno
neat's'-foot' oil *s* aceite *m* de pie de buey
Nebuchadnezzar [,nɛbjəkəd'nɛzər] *s* Nabucodonosor *m*
nebu•la ['nɛbjələ] *s* (*pl* **-lae** [,li] o **-las**) nebulosa
nebular ['nɛbjələr] *adj* nebular
nebulous ['nɛbjələs] *adj* nebuloso
necessary ['nɛsɪ,sɛri] *adj* necesario
necessitate [nɪ'sɛsɪ,tet] *tr* necesitar, exigir
necessitous [nɪ'sɛsɪtəs] *adj* necesitado
necessi•ty [nɪ'sɛsɪti] *s* (*pl* **-ties**) necesidad
neck [nɛk] *s* cuello; (*of a bottle*) gollete *m;* (*of violin or guitar*) mástil *m;* istmo, península; estrecho; **neck and neck** parejos; **to break one's neck** (coll) matarse trabajando; **to stick one's neck out** (coll) descubrir el cuerpo || *intr* (slang) acariciarse (*dos enamorados*)
neck'band' *s* tirilla de camisa
necklace ['nɛklɪs] *s* gargantilla, collar *m*
necktie ['nɛk,taɪ] *s* corbata
necktie pin *s* alfiler *m* de corbata
necrology [nɛ'krɑlədʒi] *s* necrología
necromancy ['nɛkrə,mænsi] *s* necromancia, nigromancia
nectarine [,nɛktə'rin] *s* griñón *m*
née o **nee** [ne] *adj* nacida o de soltera, p.ej., **Mary Wilson, née Miller** María Wilson, nacida Miller o María Wilson, de soltera Miller
need [nid] *s* necesidad; pobreza; **in need** necesitado || *tr* necesitar || *intr* estar necesitado; ser necesario || *v aux* — **if need be** si fuere necesario; **to need** + *inf* deber, tener que + *inf*
needful ['nidfəl] *adj* necesario || **the needful** lo necesario; (slang) el dinero
needle ['nidəl] *s* aguja; **to look for a needle in a haystack** buscar una aguja en un pajar || *tr* coser con aguja; (coll) aguijonear, incitar; (coll) añadir alcohol a (*la cerveza o el vino*)
needle bath *s* ducha en alfileres
needle'case' *s* alfiletero
needle point *s* bordado al pasado; encaje *m* de mano
needless ['nidlɪs] *adj* innecesario, inútil
needle'work' *s* costura, labor *f*
needs [nidz] *adv* necesariamente, forzosamente
need•y ['nidi] *adj* (*comp* **-ier;** *super* **-iest**) necesitado, indigente || **the needy** los necesitados
ne'er-do-well ['nɛrdu,wɛl] *adj & s* holgazán, perdido
negation [nɪ'geʃən] *s* negación
negative ['nɛgətɪv] *adj* negativo || *s* negativa; electricidad negativa, borne negativo; (gram) negación; (math) término negativo; (phot) prueba negativa || *tr* desaprobar; anular
neglect [nɪ'glɛkt] *s* negligencia, descuido || *tr* descuidar; **to neglect to** dejar de, olvidarse de
neglectful [nɪ'glɛktfəl] *adj* negligente, descuidado
négligée o **negligee** [,nɛglɪ'ʒe] *s* bata de mujer, traje *m* de casa
negligence ['nɛglɪdʒəns] *s* negligencia, descuido
negligent ['nɛglɪdʒənt] *adj* negligente, descuidado
negligible ['nɛglɪdʒɪbəl] *adj* insignificante, imperceptible
negotiable [nɪ'goʃɪ•əbəl] *adj* negociable; transitable
negotiate [nɪ'goʃɪ,et] *tr* negociar; (coll) salvar, vencer || *intr* negociar
negotiation [nɪ,goʃɪ'eʃən] *s* negociación; trámite *m*

Ne·gro ['nigro] *adj* negro || *s* (*pl* **-groes**) negro
neigh [ne] *s* relincho || *intr* relinchar
neighbor ['nebər] *adj* vecino || *s* vecino; (*fellow man*) prójimo || *tr* ser vecino de; ser amigo de || *intr* estar cercano; tener relaciones amistosas
neighborhood ['nebər ,hʊd] *s* vecindad, vecindario, cercanías; **in the neighborhood of** en las inmediaciones de; (coll) cerca de, aproximadamente
neighboring ['nebərɪŋ] *adj* vecino, colindante
neighborly ['nebərli] *adj* buen vecino, amable, sociable
neither ['niðər] o ['naɪðər] *adj indef* ninguno . . . (de los dos); **neither one** ninguno de los dos || *pron indef* ninguno (de los dos); ni uno ni otro, ni lo uno ni lo otro || *conj* ni; tampoco, ni . . . tampoco, p.ej., **neither do I** yo tampoco, ni yo tampoco; **neither . . . nor** ni . . . ni
neme·sis ['nɛmɪsɪs] *s* (*pl* **-ses** [,siz]) (*someone or something that punishes*) némesis *f* || **Nemesis** *s* Némesis *f*
neologism [ni'ɑlə,dʒɪzəm] *s* neologismo
neomycin [,ni·ə'maɪsɪn] *s* neomicina
neon ['ni·ɑn] *s* neo, neón *m*
neophyte ['ni·ə,faɪt] *s* neófito
Nepal [nɪ'pɔl] *s* el Nepal
Nepa·lese [,nɛpə'liz] *adj* nepalés || *s* (*pl* **-lese**) nepalés *m*
nepenthe [nɪ'pɛnθi] *s* nepente *m*
nephew ['nɛfju] o ['nɛvju] *s* sobrino
Nepos ['nipɑs] o ['nɛpɑs] *s* Nepote *m*
Neptune ['nɛptʃun] o ['nɛptjun] *s* Neptuno
neptunium [nɛp'tʃunɪ·əm] o [nɛp'tjunɪ·əm] *s* neptunio
Nereid ['nɪrɪ·ɪd] *s* nereida
Nero ['nɪro] *s* Nerón *m*
nerve [nʌrv] *adj* (*center; system; tonic; disease; prostration; breakdown*) nervioso || *s* nervio; ánimo, valor *m;* audacia; (coll) descaro; **nerves** excitabilidad nerviosa; **to get on one's nerves** irritar los nervios a uno; **to strain every nerve** esforzarse al máximo
nerve-racking ['nʌrv ,rækɪŋ] *adj* irritante, exasperante
nervous ['nʌrvəs] *adj* nervioso
nervous breakdown *s* colapso nervioso
nervousness ['nʌrvəsnɪs] *s* nerviosidad
nervous shudder *s* muerte chiquita
nerv·y ['nʌrvi] *adj* (*comp* **-ier;** *super* **-iest**) (*strong, vigorous*) nervioso; atrevido, audaz; (coll) descarado
nest [nɛst] *s* nido; (*where hen lays eggs*) nidal *m;* (*birds in a nest*) nidada; (*set of things fitting within each other*) juego; (*of, e.g., thieves*) nido; **to feather one's nest** hacer todo para enriquecerse || *tr* colocar en un nido || *intr* anidar
nest egg *s* (*eggs left in a nest to induce hen to lay more*) nidal *m;* ahorros, hucha
nestle ['nɛsəl] *tr* poner en un nido; arrimar afectuosamente || *intr* anidar; arrimarse cómodamente; **to nestle up to** arrimarse a
net [nɛt] *adj* neto, líquido || *s* red *f;* precio neto, peso neto, ganancia líquida || *v* (*pret & pp* **netted;** *super* **netting**) *tr* enredar, tejer; coger con red; producir (*cierta ganancia líquida*)
nether ['nɛðər] *adj* inferior, más bajo
Netherlander ['nɛðər ,lændər] o ['nɛðərləndər] *s* neerlandés *m*
Netherlandish ['nɛðər ,lændɪʃ] o ['nɛðərləndɪʃ] *adj* neerlandés || *s* neerlandés *m*
Netherlands, The ['nɛðərləndz] los Países Bajos (*Holanda*)
netting ['nɛtɪŋ] *s* red *f*
nettle ['nɛtəl] *s* ortiga || *tr* irritar, provocar
net'work' *s* red *f;* (rad & telv) cadena
neuralgia [njʊ'rældʒə] o [nʊ'rældʒə] *s* neuralgia
neurology [njʊ'rɑlədʒi] o [nʊ'rɑlədʒi] *s* neurología
neuro·sis [njʊ'rosɪs] o [nʊ'rosɪs] *s* (*pl* **-ses** [siz]) neurosis *f*
neurotic [njʊ'rɑtɪk] o [nʊ'rɑtɪk] *adj & s* neurótico
neut. *abbr* **neuter**
neuter ['njutər] o ['nutər] *adj* neutro || *s* género neutro
neutral ['njutrəl] o ['nutrəl] *adj* (*on neither side in a quarrel or war*) neutral; (*having little or no color*) neutro; (bot, chem, elec, phonet, zool) neutro || *s* neutral *mf;* (aut) punto neutral, punto muerto
neutralism ['njutrə ,lɪzəm] o ['nutrə,lɪzəm] *s* neutralismo
neutralist ['njutrəlɪst] o ['nutrəlɪst] *adj & s* neutralista *mf*
neutrality [nju'trælɪti] o [nu'trælɪti] *s* neutralidad
neutralize ['njutrə ,laɪz] o ['nutrə,laɪz] *tr* neutralizar
neutron ['njutrɑn] o ['nutrɑn] *s* neutrón *m*
neutron bomb *s* bomba de neutrones, bomba neutrónica
never ['nɛvər] *adv* nunca; en mi vida; de ningún modo; **never fear** no hay cuidado; **never mind** no importa
nev'er·more' *adv* nunca más
nevertheless [,nɛvərðə'lɛs] *adv* no obstante, sin embargo
new [nju] o [nu] *adj* nuevo; **what's new?** ¿qué hay de nuevo?
new arrival *s* recién llegado; recién nacido
new'born' *adj* recién nacido; renacido
New Castile *s* Castilla la Nueva
New'cas'tle *s* — **to carry coals to Newcastle** echar agua al mar, llevar hierro a Vizcaya, llevar leña al monte
newcomer ['nju ,kʌmər] o ['nu ,kʌmər] *s* recién llegado, recién venido
New England *s* la Nueva Inglaterra
newfangled ['nju ,fæŋgəld] o ['nu,fæŋgəld] *adj* de última moda, recién inventado
Newfoundland ['njufənd ,lænd] o

['nufənd,lænd] *s* (*island and province*) Terranova || [nju'faʊndlənd] o [nu'faʊndlənd] *s* (*dog*) Terranova *m*
newly ['njuli] o ['nuli] *adv* nuevamente; **newly** + *pp* recién + *pp*
new'ly•wed' *s* recién casado
New Mexican *adj* & *s* neomejicano, nuevomejicano
New Mexico *s* Nuevo Méjico
new moon *s* luna nueva, novilunio
news [njuz] o [nuz] *s* noticias; periódico; **a news item** una noticia; **a piece of news** una noticia
news agency *s* agencia de noticias
news beat *s* exclusiva, anticipación de una noticia por un periódico
news'boy' *s* vendedor *m* de periódicos
news'cast' *s* noticiario radiofónico || *tr* radiodifundir (*noticias*) || *intr* radiodifundir noticias
news'cast'er *s* cronista *mf* de radio
news conference *s* var de **press conference**
news coverage *s* reportaje *m*
news•man ['njuzmən] o ['nuzmən] *s* (*pl* **-men** [mən]) noticiero
New South Wales *s* la Nueva Gales del Sur
news'pa'per *adj* periodístico || *s* periódico
newspaper•man ['njuz,pepər,mæn] o ['nuz,pepər,mæn] *s* (*pl* **-men** [,mɛn]) periodista *m*
news'print' *s* papel-prensa *m*
news'reel' *s* actualidades, noticiario cinematográfico
news'stand' *s* quiosco de periódicos, puesto de periódicos
news'week'ly *s* (*pl* **-lies**) semanario de noticias
news'wor'thy *adj* de gran actualidad, de interés periodístico
news•y ['njuzi] o ['nuzi] *adj* (*comp* **-ier;** *super* **-iest**) (coll) informativo
new'-world' *adj* del Nuevo Mundo
New Year's card *s* tarjeta de felicitación de Año Nuevo
New Year's Day *s* el Día de Año Nuevo
New Year's Eve *s* la noche vieja, la víspera de año nuevo
New York [jɔrk] *adj* neoyorkino || *s* Nueva York
New Yorker ['jɔrkər] *s* neoyorkino
New Zealand ['zilənd] *adj* neocelandés || *s* Nueva Zelanda
New Zealander ['ziləndər] *s* neocelandés *m*
next [nɛkst] *adj* próximo, siguiente; de al lado; venidero, que viene || *adv* luego, después; la próxima vez; **next to** junto a; después de; **next to nothing** casi nada; **the next best** lo mejor después de eso; **to come next** venir después, ser el que sigue
next door *s* la casa de al lado; **next door to** en la casa siguiente de; (coll) casi
next'door' *adj* siguiente, de al lado
next of kin *s* (*pl* **next of kin**) pariente más cercano
niacin ['naɪ·əsɪn] *s* niacina
Niagara Falls [naɪ'ægərə] *spl* las Cataratas del Niágara
nibble ['nɪbəl] *s* mordisco || *tr* & *intr* mordiscar; picar (*un pez*); **to nibble at** picar de o en
Nicaraguan [,nɪkə'rɑgwən] *adj* & *s* nicaragüense, nicaragüeño
nice [naɪs] *adj* delicado, fino, sutil; primoroso, pulido, refinado; dengoso, melindroso; atento, cortés, culto; escrupuloso, esmerado; agradable, simpático; decoroso, conveniente; complaciente; preciso; satisfactorio; (*weather*) bueno; (*attractive*) bonito; **nice and . . .** (coll) muy, mucho; **not nice** (coll) feo
nice-looking ['naɪs'lʊkɪŋ] *adj* hermoso, guapo, bien parecido
nicely ['naɪsli] *adv* con precisión; escrupulosamente; satisfactoriamente; (coll) muy bien
nice•ty ['naɪsəti] *s* (*pl* **-ties**) precisión; sutileza; finura; **to a nicety** con la mayor precisión
niche [nɪtʃ] *s* hornacina, nicho; colocación conveniente
Nicholas ['nɪkələs] *s* Nicolás *m*
nick [nɪk] *s* mella, muesca; **in the nick of time** en el momento crítico || *tr* mellar, hacer muescas en; cortar
nickel ['nɪkəl] *s* níquel *m;* (U.S.A.) moneda de cinco centavos || *tr* niquelar
nick'el-plate' *tr* niquelar
nicknack ['nɪk,næk] *s* chuchería, friolera
nick'name' *s* apodo, mote *m* || *tr* apodar
nicotine ['nɪkə,tin] *s* nicotina
niece [nis] *s* sobrina
nif•ty ['nɪfti] *adj* (*comp* **-tier;** *super* **-tiest**) (slang) elegante; (slang) excelente
niggard ['nɪgərd] *adj* & *s* tacaño
night [naɪt] *adj* nocturno || *s* noche *f;* **at** o **by night** de noche o por la noche; **night before last** anteanoche; **to make a night of it** (coll) divertirse hasta muy entrada la noche
night'cap' *s* gorro de dormir; trago antes de acostarse, sosiega
night club *s* cabaret *m,* café *m* cantante, sala de fiestas
night driving *s* conducción de noche
night'fall' *s* anochecer *m,* caída de la noche
night'gown' *s* camisa de dormir
nightingale ['naɪtən,gel] *s* ruiseñor *m*
night latch *s* cerradura de resorte
night letter *s* carta telegráfica nocturna
night'long' *adj* de toda la noche || *adv* durante toda la noche
nightly ['naɪtli] *adj* nocturno; de cada noche || *adv* de noche, por la noche; cada noche
night'mare' *s* pesadilla
nightmarish ['naɪt,mɛrɪʃ] *adj* espeluznante, horroroso
night owl *s* buho nocturno; (coll) anochecedor *m,* trasnochador *m*
night'shirt' *s* camisa de dormir
night'time' *adj* nocturno || *s* noche *f*

night'walk'er *s* vagabundo nocturno; ladrón nocturno; ramera callejera nocturna; sonámbulo
night watch *s* guardia de noche, ronda de noche; sereno; (mil) vigilia
night watchman *s* vigilante nocturno
nihilism ['naɪ·ɪ ,lɪzəm] *s* nihilismo
nihilist ['naɪ·ɪlɪst] *s* nihilista *mf*
nil [nɪl] *s* nada
Nile [naɪl] *s* Nilo
nimble ['nɪmbəl] *adj* ágil, ligero; listo, vivo
nim•bus ['nɪmbəs] *s* (*pl* **-buses** o **-bi** [baɪ]) nimbo
Nimrod ['nɪmrɑd] *s* Nemrod *m*
nincompoop ['nɪnkəm ,pup] *s* badulaque *m,* papirote *m*
nine [naɪn] *adj & pron* nueve || *s* nueve *m;* equipo de béisbol; **nine o'clock** las nueve; **the Nine** las nueve musas
nine hundred *adj & pron* novecientos || *s* novecientos *m*
nineteen ['naɪn'tin] *adj, pron & s* diecinueve *m,* diez y nueve *m*
nineteenth ['naɪn'tinθ] *adj & s* (*in a series*) decimonono; (*part*) diecinueveavo || *s* (*in dates*) diecinueve *m*
ninetieth ['naɪntɪ·ɪθ] *adj & s* (*in a series*) nonagésimo; (*part*) noventavo
nine•ty ['naɪnti] *adj & pron* noventa || *s* (*pl* **-ties**) noventa *m*
ninth [naɪnθ] *adj & s* nono, noveno || *s* (*in dates*) nueve *m*
nip [nɪp] *s* mordisco, pellizco; helada, escarcha; traguito; **nip and tuck** a quién ganará || *v* (*pret & pp* **nipped;** *ger* **nipping**) *tr* mordiscar, pellizcar; helar, escarchar; (slang) asir, coger; **to nip in the bud** atajar en el principio || *intr* beborrotear
nipple ['nɪpəl] *s* (*of female*) pezón *m;* (*of male; of nursing bottle*) tetilla; (mach) tubo roscado de unión, enterrosca
Nippon [nɪ'pɑn] o ['nɪpɑn] *s* el Japón
Nippon•ese [,nɪpə'niz] *adj* nipón || *s* (*pl* **-ese**) nipón *m*
nip•py ['nɪpi] *adj* (*comp* **-pier;** *super* **-piest**) mordaz, picante; frío, helado; (Brit) ágil, ligero
nirvana [nɪr'vɑnə] *s* el nirvana
nit [nɪt] *s* piojito; (*egg of insect*) liendre *f*
niter ['naɪtər] *s* nitro; (agr) nitro de Chile
nitrate ['naɪtret] *s* nitrato; (agr) nitrato de potasio, nitrato de sodio
nitric acid ['naɪtrɪk] *s* ácido nítrico
nitride ['naɪtraɪd] *s* nitruro
nitrogen ['naɪtrədʒən] *s* nitrógeno
nitroglycerin [,naɪtrə'glɪsərɪn] *s* nitroglicerina
nitrous oxide ['naɪtrəs] *s* óxido nitroso
nitwit ['nɪt ,wɪt] *s* (slang) bobalicón *m*
no [no] *adj indef* ninguno; **no admittance** no se permite la entrada; **no matter** no importa; **no parking** se prohibe estacionarse; **no smoking** se prohibe fumar; **no thoroughfare** prohibido el paso; **no use** inútil; **with no** sin || *adv* no; **no good** de ningún valor; ruin, vil; **no longer** ya no; **no sooner** no bien
Noah ['no·ə] *s* Noé *m*
nob•by ['nɑbi] *adj* (*comp* **-bier;** *super* **-biest**) (slang) elegante; (slang) excelente
nobili•ty [no'bɪlɪti] *s* (*pl* **-ties**) nobleza; (*of sentiments, character, etc.*) nobleza, ennoblecimiento
noble ['nobəl] *adj & s* noble *m*
noble•man ['nobəlmən] *s* (*pl* **-men** [mən]) noble *m,* hidalgo
nobod•y ['no ,bɑdi] o ['nobədi] *pron indef* nadie, ninguno; **nobody but** nadie más que; **nobody else** nadie más, ningún otro || *s* (*pl* **-ies**) nadie *m,* don nadie
nocturnal [nɑk'tʌrnəl] *adj* nocturno
nod [nɑd] *s* inclinación de cabeza; seña con la cabeza; (*of a person going to sleep*) cabezada || *v* (*pret & pp* **nodded;** *ger* **nodding**) *tr* inclinar (*la cabeza*); indicar con una inclinación de cabeza || *intr* inclinar la cabeza; (*in going to sleep*) cabecear
node [nod] *s* bulto, protuberancia; nudo, enredo; (astr, med & phys) nodo; (bot) nudo
nohow ['no ,haʊ] *adv* (coll) de ninguna manera
noise [nɔɪz] *s* ruido || *tr* divulgar
noiseless ['nɔɪzlɪs] *adj* silencioso, sin ruido
nois•y ['nɔɪzi] *adj* (*comp* **-ier;** *super* **-iest**) ruidoso; (*boisterous*) estrepitoso
nom. *abbr* **nominative**
nomad ['nomæd] *adj & s* nómada *mf*
nomadic [no'mædɪk] *adj* nomádico
no man's land *s* terreno sin reclamar; (mil) la tierra de nadie
nominal ['nɑmɪnəl] *adj* nominal; (*price*) módico
nominate ['nɑmɪ ,net] *tr* postular como candidato; (*to appoint*) nombrar, designar
nomination [,nɑmɪ'neʃən] *s* postulación
nominative ['nɑmɪnətɪv] *adj & s* nominativo
nominee [,nɑmɪ'ni] *s* propuesto, candidato
nonbelligerent [,nɑnbə'lɪdʒərənt] *adj & s* no beligerante *m*
nonbreakable [nɑn'brekəbəl] *adj* irrompible
nonchalance ['nɑnʃələns] o [,nɑnʃə'lɑns] *s* indiferencia, desenvoltura
nonchalant ['nɑnʃələnt] o [,nɑnʃə'lɑnt] *adj* indiferente, desenvuelto
noncom ['nɑn ,kɑm] *s* (coll) clase, suboficial *m*
noncombatant [nɑn'kɑmbətənt] *adj & s* no combatiente *m*
noncommissioned officer [,nɑnkə'mɪʃənd] *s* clase, suboficial *m*
noncommittal [,nɑnkə'mɪtəl] *adj* evasivo, reticente
noncommitted [,nɑnkə'mɪtɪd] *adj* no empeñado

non compos mentis ['nɑn'kɑmpəs'mɛntɪs] *adj* falto de juicio, loco
nonconformist [,nɑnkən'fɔrmɪst] *s* disidente *mf*
nondelivery [,nɑndɪ'lɪvəri] *s* falta de entrega
nondescript ['nɑndɪ,skrɪpt] *adj* inclasificable, indefinido
none [nʌn] *pron indef* nadie, ninguno, ningunos; **none of** ninguno de; nada de; **none other** ningún otro || *adv* nada, de ninguna manera; **none the less** sin embargo, no obstante
nonenti•ty [nɑn'ɛntɪti] *s* (*pl* **-ties**) cosa inexistente; (*person*) nulidad
nonfiction [nɑn'fɪkʃən] *s* literatura no novelesca
nonfulfillment [,nɑnfʊl'fɪlmənt] *s* incumplimiento
nonintervention [,nɑnɪntər'vɛnʃən] *s* no intervención
nonmetal ['nɑn,mɛtəl] *s* metaloide *m*
nonpayment [nɑn'pemənt] *s* falta de pago
non•plus ['nɑnplʌs] o [nɑn'plʌs] *s* estupefacción || *v* (*pret & pp* **-plused** o **-plussed;** *ger* **-plusing** o **-plussing**) *tr* dejar estupefacto, dejar pegado a la pared
nonprofit [nɑn'prɑfɪt] *adj* sin fin lucrativo
nonrefillable [,nɑnrɪ'fɪləbəl] *adj* irrellenable
nonresident [nɑn'rɛzɪdənt] *s* transeúnte *mf*
nonresidential [nɑn,rɛzɪ'dɛnʃəl] *adj* comercial
nonscientific [nɑn,saɪ·ən'tɪfɪk] *adj* anticientífico
nonsectarian [,nɑnsɛk'tɛrɪ·ən] *adj* no sectario
nonsense ['nɑnsɛns] *s* disparate *m,* tontería
nonsensical [nɑn'sɛnsɪkəl] *adj* disparatado, tonto
nonskid ['nɑn'skɪd] *adj* antideslizante
nonstop ['nɑn'stɑp] *adj & adv* sin parar, sin escala
nonsupport [,nɑnsə'port] *s* falta de manutención
noodle ['nudəl] *s* tallarín *m;* (slang) mentecato, tonto; (slang) cabeza
noodle soup *s* sopa de pastas, sopa de fideos
nook [nʊk] *s* rinconcito
noon [nun] *s* mediodía *m;* **at high noon** en pleno mediodía
no one o **no-one** ['no,wʌn] *pron indef* nadie, ninguno; **no one else** nadie más, ningún otro
noontime ['nun,taɪm] *s* mediodía *m*
noose [nus] *s* lazo corredizo; (*to hang a criminal*) dogal *m;* trampa || *tr* lazar; hacer un lazo corredizo en
nor [nɔr] *conj* ni
Nordic ['nɔrdɪk] *adj & s* nórdico
norm [nɔrm] *s* norma
normal ['nɔrməl] *adj* normal
Norman ['nɔrmən] *adj & s* normando
Normandy ['nɔrməndi] *s* Normandía
Norse [nɔrs] *adj* nórdico; noruego || *s* (*ancient Scandanavian language*) nórdico; (*language of Norway*) noruego; **the Norse** los nórdicos; los noruegos
Norse•man ['nɔrsmən] *s* (*pl* **-men** [mən]) normando
north [nɔrθ] *adj* septentrional, del norte || *adv* al norte, hacia el norte || *s* norte *m*
North America *s* Norteamérica, la América del Norte
North American *adj & s* norteamericano
north'east'er *s* (*wind*) nordestada, nordeste *m* (*viento*)
northern ['nɔrðərn] *adj* septentrional; (*Hemisphere*) boreal
North Korea *s* la Corea del Norte
North Korean *adj & s* norcoreano
northward ['nɔrθwərd] *adv* hacia el norte
north wind *s* norte *m,* aquilón *m*
Norway ['nɔrwe] *s* Noruega
Norwegian [nɔr'widʒən] *adj & s* noruego
nos. *abbr* **numbers**
nose [noz] *s* nariz *f;* (aer) proa; **to blow one's nose** sonarse las narices; **to count noses** averiguar cuántas personas hay; **to follow one's nose** seguir todo derecho; avanzar guiándose por el instinto; **to hold one's nose** tabicarse las narices; **to lead by the nose** llevar por la barba, tener agarrado por las narices; **to look down one's nose at** mirar por encima del hombro; **to pay through the nose** pagar un precio escandaloso; **to pick one's nose** hurgarse las narices; **to poke one's nose into** meter las narices en; **to speak through the nose** ganguear; **to thumb one's nose at** señalar (*a una persona*) poniendo el pulgar sobre la nariz en son de burla; tratar con sumo desprecio; **to turn up one's nose at** mirar con desprecio; **under the nose of** en las narices de, en las barbas de || *tr* olfatear || *intr* ventear; **to nose about** curiosear; **to nose over** capotar (*un avión*); **to nose up** encabritarse (*un buque, un avión*)
nose bag *s* cebadera, morral *m*
nose'band' *s* muserola, sobarba
nose'bleed' *s* hemorragia nasal
nose cone *s* cono de proa
nose dive *s* (aer) descenso de picado; (fig) descenso precipitado
nose'-dive' *intr* (aer) picar; (fig) descender precipidamente
nosegay ['noz,ge] *s* ramillete *m*
nose ring *s* nariguera
no'-show' *s* pasajero no presentado
nostalgia [nɑ'stældʒə] *s* nostalgia
nostril ['nɑstrɪl] *s* nariz *f,* ventana
nos•y ['nozi] *adj* (*comp* **-ier;** *super* **-iest**) (coll) curioso, husmeador
not [nɑt] *adv* no; **not at all** nada, de ningún modo; **not yet** todavía no; **to think not** creer que no; **why not?** ¿cómo no?
notable ['notəbəl] *adj & s* notable *m*
notarize ['notə,raɪz] *tr* abonar con fe notarial
nota•ry ['notəri] *s* (*pl* **-ries**) notario

notch [nɑtʃ] *s* muesca, mella, corte *m;* (U.S.A.) desfiladero, paso; (coll) grado || *tr* hacer muescas en, mellar
note [not] *s* nota; apunte *m;* esquela, cartita; marca, señal *f;* (com) pagaré *m,* vale *m;* canto, melodía; acento, voz *f;* (mus) nota || *tr* notar, apuntar; marcar, señalar
note'book' *s* cuaderno, libro de apuntes
noted ['notɪd] *adj* afamado, conocido
note paper *s* papel *m* de cartas
note'wor'thy *adj* notable, digno de notarse
nothing ['nʌθɪŋ] *pron indef* nada; **for nothing** inútilmente; de balde, gratis; **nothing doing** (slang) ni por pienso; **nothing else** nada más; **that's nothing to me** eso nada me importa; **to make nothing of** no hacer caso de; no aprovecharse de; no entender; despreciar; **to think nothing of** no hacer caso de; tener por fácil; despreciar || *adv* nada, de ninguna manera; **nothing daunted** sin temor alguno || *s* nada; nadería, friolera
notice ['notɪs] *s* atención, reparo, advertencia; aviso, noticia; letrero; mención, reseña; llamada; notificación; **on short notice** con poco tiempo de aviso; **to escape one's notice** pasarle inadvertido a uno; **to serve notice** dar noticia, hacer saber || *tr* notar, observar, reparar, reparar en; mencionar
noticeable ['notɪsəbəl] *adj* sensible, perceptible; notable
noti•fy ['notɪ,faɪ] *v* (*pret & pp* **-fied**) *tr* notificar, avisar, hacer saber
notion ['noʃən] *s* noción; capricho; **notions** mercería, artículos menudos; **to have a notion to** + *inf* pensar + *inf,* tener ganas de + *inf*
notorie•ty [,notə'raɪ·ɪti] *s* (*pl* **-ties**) mala reputación; (*condition of being well known*) notoriedad; (*person*) notable *mf*
notorious [no'torɪ·əs] *adj* reputado, mal reputado; bien conocido
no'-trump' *adj & s* sin triunfo; **a no-trump hand** un sin triunfo
notwithstanding [,nɑtwɪð'stændɪŋ] o [,nɑtwɪθ'stændɪŋ] *adv* no obstante || *prep* a pesar de || *conj* a pesar de que
nougat ['nugət] *s* turrón *m*
noun [naʊn] *s* nombre, nombre sustantivo
nourish ['nʌrɪʃ] *tr* alimentar, nutrir; abrigar (*p.ej., esperanzas*)
nourishing ['nʌrɪʃɪŋ] *adj* alimenticio, nutritivo
nourishment ['nʌrɪʃmənt] *s* alimento, nutrimento
Nov. *abbr* **November**
Nova Scotia ['novə'skoʃə] *s* la Nueva Escocia
Nova Scotian ['novə'skoʃən] *adj & s* neoescocés *m*
novel ['nɑvəl] *adj* nuevo; insólito, extraño, original || *s* novela
novelist ['nɑvəlɪst] *s* novelista *mf*
novel•ty ['nɑvəlti] *s* (*pl* **-ties**) novedad, innovación; **novelties** bisutería, baratijas
November [no'vɛmbər] *s* noviembre *m*
novice ['nɑvɪs] *s* novicio
novocaine ['novə,ken] *s* novocaína
now [naʊ] *adv* ahora; ya; entonces; **from now on** de ahora en adelante; **how now?** ¿cómo?; **just now** hace un momento; **now and again** o **now and then** de vez en cuando; **now . . . now** ora . . . ora, ya . . . ya; **now that** ya que; **now then** ahora bien || *interj* ¡vamos! || *s* actualidad
nowadays ['naʊ·ə,dez] *adv* hoy en día, hoy día
no'way' o **no'ways'** *adv* de ningún modo
no'where' *adv* en ninguna parte, a ninguna parte; **nowhere else** en ninguna otra parte
noxious ['nɑkʃəs] *adj* nocivo
nozzle ['nɑzəl] *s* (*of hose*) lanza; (*of sprinkling can*) rallo, roseta; (*of candlestick*) cubo; (slang) nariz *f*
N.T. *abbr* **New Testament**
nth [ɛnθ] *adj* n^{mo} (*enésimo*); **to the nth degree** elevado a la potencia n; a más no poder
nuance [nju'ɑns] o ['nju·ɑns] *s* matiz *m*
nub [nʌb] *s* protuberancia; pedazo; (coll) meollo
nuclear ['njuklɪ·ər] o ['nuklɪ·ər] *adj* nuclear
nuclear test ban *s* proscripción de las pruebas nucleares
nucle•us ['njuklɪ·əs] o ['nuklɪ·əs] *s* (*pl* **-i** [,aɪ] o **-uses**) núcleo
nude [njud] o [nud] *adj* desnudo || *s* — **in the nude** desnudo; **the nude** el desnudo
nudge [nʌdʒ] *s* codazo suave || *tr* dar un codazo suave a, empujar suavemente
nugget ['nʌgɪt] *s* pedazo; (*of, e.g., gold*) pepita; preciosidad
nuisance ['njusəns] o ['nusəns] *s* molestia, estorbo; persona o cosa fastidiosas
null [nʌl] *adj* nulo; **null and void** nulo, írrito, nulo y sin valor
nulli•fy ['nʌlɪ,faɪ] *v* (*pret & pp* **-fied**) *tr* anular, invalidar
nulli•ty ['nʌlɪti] *s* (*pl* **-ties**) nulidad
numb [nʌm] *adj* entumecido || *tr* entumecer
number ['nʌmbər] *s* número; **a number of** varios || *tr* numerar; ascender a (*cierto número*); **his days are numbered** tiene sus días contados o sus horas contadas; **to be numbered among** hallarse entre; **to number among** contar entre
numberless ['nʌmbərlɪs] *adj* innumerable
numeral ['njumərəl] o ['numərəl] *adj* numeral || *s* número
numerical [nju'mɛrɪkəl] o [nu'mɛrɪkəl] *adj* numérico
numerous ['njumərəs] o ['numərəs] *adj* numeroso
numskull ['nʌm,skʌl] *s* (coll) bodoque *m,* mentecato

nun [nʌn] *s* monja, religiosa
nuptial [ˈnʌpʃəl] *adj* nupcial || **nuptials** *spl* nupcias, bodas
nurse [nʌrs] *s* enfermera; (*to suckle a child*) ama de cría, nodriza; (*to take care of a child*) niñera || *tr* cuidar (*a una persona enferma*); amamantar; alimentar; criar; tratar de curarse de (*p.ej., un resfriado*); abrigar (*p.ej., odio*) || *intr* ser enfermera
nurser·y [ˈnʌrsəri] *s* (*pl* **-ies**) cuarto de los niños; (*of plants*) criadero, plantel *m,* semillero; (fig) semillero
nursery·man [ˈnʌrsərɪmən] *s* (*pl* **-men** [mən]) cultivador *m* de semillero
nursery rhymes *spl* versos para niños
nursery tales *spl* cuentos para niños
nursing bottle *s* biberón *m*
nursing home *s* clínica de reposo
nurture [ˈnʌrtʃər] *s* alimentación, nutrimento; crianza, educación || *tr* alimentar, nutrir; criar, educar; acariciar (*p.ej., una esperanza*)
nut [nʌt] *s* nuez *f;* (*to screw on a bolt*) tuerca; (slang) estrafalario; **a hard nut to crack** (coll) hueso duro de roer
nut'crack'er *s* cascanueces *m*
nutmeg [ˈnʌtˌmɛg] *s* nuez moscada; (*tree*) mirística
nutriment [ˈnjutrɪmənt] o [ˈnutrɪmənt] *s* nutrimento
nutrition [njuˈtrɪʃən] o [nuˈtrɪʃən] *s* nutrición
nutritious [njuˈtrɪʃəs] o [nuˈtrɪʃəs] *adj* nutricioso, nutritivo
nut'shell' *s* cáscara de nuez; **in a nutshell** en pocas palabras
nut·ty [ˈnʌti] *adj* (*comp* **-tier;** *super* **-tiest**) abundante en nueces; que sabe a nueces; (slang) chiflado, loco; **nutty about** (slang) loco por
nuzzle [ˈnʌzəl] *tr* hocicar, hozar || *intr* hocicar; arrimarse cómodamente; arroparse bien
nylon [ˈnaɪlɑn] *s* nilón *m;* **nylons** medias de nilón
nymph [nɪmf] *s* ninfa

O

O, o [o] decimoquinta letra del alfabeto inglés
O *interj* ¡oh!; ¡ay!, p.ej., **O, how pretty she is!** ¡Ay qué linda!; **O that . . . !** ¡Ojalá que . . . !
oaf [of] *s* zoquete *m,* zamacuco; niño contrahecho
oak [ok] *s* roble *m*
oaken [ˈokən] *adj* hecho de roble
oakum [ˈokəm] *s* estopa, estopa de calafatear
oar [or] *s* remo; **to lie** o **rest on one's oars** aguantar los remos; aflojar en el trabajo || *tr* conducir a remo || *intr* remar, bogar
oars·man [ˈorzmən] *s* (*pl* **-men** [mən]) remero
OAS [ˈoˈeˈɛs] *s* (letterword) OEA *f*
oa·sis [oˈesɪs] *s* (*pl* **-ses** [siz]) oasis *m*
oat [ot] *s* avena; **oats** (*edible grain*) avena; **to feel one's oats** (slang) estar fogoso y brioso; (slang) estar muy pagado de sí mismo; **to sow one's wild oats** correrla, pasar las mocedades
oath [oθ] *s* juramento; **on oath** bajo juramento; **to take an oath** prestar juramento
oat'meal' *s* harina de avena; gachas de avena
ob. *abbr* **obiit** (Lat) **died**
obbligato [ˌɑblɪˈgɑto] *adj* & *s* obligado
obduracy [ˈɑbdjərəsi] *s* obduración
obdurate [ˈɑbdjərɪt] *adj* obstinado, terco; empedernido
obedience [oˈbidɪ·əns] *s* obediencia
obedient [oˈbidɪ·ənt] *adj* obediente
obeisance [oˈbesəns] u [oˈbisəns] *s* saludo respetuoso; homenaje *m,* respeto
obelisk [ˈɑbəlɪsk] *s* obelisco
obese [oˈbis] *adj* obeso
obesity [oˈbisɪti] *s* obesidad
obey [oˈbe] *tr* & *intr* obedecer
obfuscate [ɑbˈfʌsket] o [ˈɑbfəsˌket] *tr* ofuscar
obituar·y [oˈbɪtʃʊˌɛri] *adj* necrológico || *s* (*pl* **-ies**) necrología
obj. *abbr* **object, objection, objective**
object [ˈɑbdʒɪkt] *s* objeto || [ɑbˈdʒɛkt] *tr* objetar || *intr* hacer objeciones
objection [ɑbˈdʒɛkʃən] *s* reparo, objeción; **to have no objections to make** no tener nada que objetar
objectionable [ɑbˈdʒɛkʃənəbəl] *adj* desagradable, reprensible; (*causing disapproval*) objetable
objective [ɑbˈdʒɛktɪv] *adj* & *s* objetivo
obl. *abbr* **oblique, oblong**
obligate [ˈɑblɪˌget] *tr* obligar
obligation [ˌɑblɪˈgeʃən] *s* obligación
oblige [əˈblaɪdʒ] *tr* obligar; complacer; **much obliged** muchas gracias
obliging [əˈblaɪdʒɪŋ] *adj* complaciente, condescendiente, servicial
oblique [əˈblik] *adj* oblicuo; indirecto, evasivo
obliterate [əˈblɪtəˌret] *tr* borrar; arrasar, destruir
oblivion [əˈblɪvɪ·ən] *s* olvido
oblivious [əˈblɪvɪ·əs] *adj* olvidadizo
oblong [ˈɑblɔŋ] o [ˈɑblɑŋ] *adj* oblongo
obnoxious [əbˈnɑkʃəs] *adj* detestable, ofensivo
oboe [ˈobo] *s* oboe *m*
oboist [ˈobo·ɪst] *s* oboísta *mf*
obs. *abbr* **obsolete**
obscene [ɑbˈsin] *adj* obsceno

obsceni·ty [ɑb'sɛnɪti] o [ɑb'sinɪti] *s* (*pl* **-ties**) obscenidad
obscure [əb'skjʊr] *adj* obscuro; (*vowel*) relajado, neutro
obscuri·ty [əb'skjʊrɪti] *s* (*pl* **-ties**) obscuridad
obsequies ['ɑbsɪkwiz] *spl* exequias
obsequious [əb'sikwɪ·əs] *adj* obsequioso, servil, rastrero
observance [əb'zʌrvəns] *s* observancia; ceremonia, rito
observant [əb'zʌrvənt] *adj* observador
observation [,ɑbzər'veʃən] *s* observación; observancia
observato·ry [əb'zʌrvə,tori] *s* (*pl* **-ries**) observatorio
observe [əb'zʌrv] *tr* observar; (*a holiday; silence*) guardar
observer [əb'zʌrvər] *s* observador *m*
obsess [əb'sɛs] *tr* obsesionar
obsession [əb'sɛʃən] *s* obsesión
obsolescent [,ɑbsə'lɛsənt] *adj* arcaizante
obsolete ['ɑbsə,lit] *adj* desusado, caído en desuso
obstacle ['ɑbstəkəl] *s* obstáculo
obstetrical [ɑb'stɛtrɪkəl] *adj* obstétrico
obstetrics [ɑb'stɛtrɪks] *ssg* obstetricia
obstina·cy ['ɑbstɪnəsi] *s* (*pl* **-cies**) obstinación
obstinate ['ɑbstɪnɪt] *adj* obstinado
obstruct [əb'strʌkt] *tr* obstruir
obstruction [əb'strʌkʃən] *s* obstrucción
obtain [əb'ten] *tr* obtener || *intr* existir, prevalecer
obtrusive [əb'trusɪv] *adj* entremetido, intruso
obtuse [əb'tjus] o [əb'tus] *adj* obtuso
obviate ['ɑbvɪ,et] *tr* obviar
obvious ['ɑbvɪ·əs] *adj* obvio
occasion [ə'keʒən] *s* ocasión; **to improve the occasion** aprovechar la ocasión
occasional [ə'keʒənəl] *adj* raro, poco frecuente; alguno que otro; de circunstancia
occasionally [ə'keʒənəli] *adv* ocasionalmente, de vez en cuando
occident ['ɑksɪdənt] *s* occidente *m*
occidental [,ɑksɪ'dɛntəl] *adj* occidental
occlusive [ə'klusɪv] *adj* oclusivo || *s* oclusiva
occult [ə'kʌlt] o ['ɑkʌlt] *adj* oculto
occupancy ['ɑkjəpənsi] *s* ocupación
occupant ['ɑkjəpənt] *s* ocupante *mf;* inquilino
occupation [,ɑkjə'peʃən] *s* ocupación
occu·py ['ɑkjə,paɪ] *v* (*pret & pp* **-pied**) *tr* ocupar; habitar
oc·cur [ə'kʌr] *v* (*pret & pp* **-curred;** *ger* **-curring**) *intr* ocurrir, acontecer, suceder; encontrarse; (*to come to mind*) ocurrir
occurrence [ə'kʌrəns] *s* acontecimiento; caso, aparición
ocean ['oʃən] *s* océano
oceanic [,oʃɪ'ænɪk] *adj* oceánico
ocean liner *s* buque transoceánico
o'clock [ə'klɑk] *adv* por el reloj; **it is one o'clock** es la una; **it is two o'clock** son las dos; **what o'clock is it?** ¿qué hora es?
Oct. *abbr* **October**
octave ['ɑktɪv] o ['ɑktev] *s* octava
October [ɑk'tobər] *s* octubre *m*
octo·pus ['ɑktəpəs] *s* (*pl* **-puses** o **-pi** [,paɪ]) pulpo
octoroon [,ɑktə'run] *s* octavo
ocular ['ɑkjələr] *adj & s* ocular *m*
oculist ['ɑkjəlɪst] *s* oculista *mf*
O.D. *abbr* **officer of the day, olive drab**
odd [ɑd] *adj* suelto; (*number*) impar; (*that doesn't match*) dispar; libre, de ocio; sobrante; extraño, raro, singular; y pico, y tantos, p.ej., **two hundred odd** doscientos y pico || **odds** *ssg* o *spl* (*in betting*) ventaja; apuesta desigual; puntos de ventaja; **at odds** de monos, riñendo; **by all odds** muy probablemente, sin duda alguna; **it makes no odds** lo mismo da; **the odds are** lo probable es; la ventaja es de; **to be at odds** estar de punta, estar encontrados; **to set at odds** enemistar, malquistar
oddi·ty ['ɑdɪti] *s* (*pl* **-ties**) rareza, cosa rara
odd jobs *spl* pequeñas tareas
odd lot *s* lote *m* inferior al centenar
odds and ends *spl* pedacitos varios, cajón *m* de sastre
ode [od] *s* oda
odious ['odɪ·əs] *adj* odioso, abominable
odor ['odər] *s* olor *m;* **to be in bad odor** tener mala fama
odorless ['odərlɪs] *adj* inodoro
odorous ['odərəs] *adj* oloroso
Odysseus [o'dɪsjus] u [o'dɪsɪ·əs] *s* Odiseo
Odyssey ['ɑdɪsi] *s* Odisea
Oedipus ['ɛdɪpəs] o ['idɪpəs] *s* Edipo
of [ɑv] o [əv] *prep* de, p.ej., **the top of the mountain** la cima de la montaña; a: **to smell of** oler a; con: **to dream of** soñar con; en: **to think of** pensar en; menos: **a quarter of two** las dos menos un cuarto
off. *abbr* **office, officer, official**
off [ɔf] o [ɑf] *adj* malo, p.ej., **off day** día malo; (*account, sum*) errado; más distante; libre; sin trabajo; quitado; apagado; (*electric current*) cortado; de descuento, de rebaja; de la parte del mar; (*season*) muerto || *adv* fuera, a distancia, lejos; allá; **off of** (coll) de; (coll) a expensas de; **to be off** ponerse en marcha || *prep* de, desde; al lado de, a nivel de; fuera de; libre de; (naut) a la altura de
offal ['ɑfəl] u ['ɔfəl] *s* (*of butchered meat*) carniza; basura, desperdicios
off and on *adv* unas veces sí y otras no
off'beat' *adj* (slang) insólito, chocante, original
off'chance' *s* posibilidad poco probable
off'-col'or *adj* descolorido; indispuesto; (*indecent, risqué*) colorado, subido de color
offend [ə'fɛnd] *tr & intr* ofender
offender [ə'fɛndər] *s* ofensor *m*

offense [ə'fɛns] *s* ofensa; **to take offense (at)** ofenderse (de)
offensive [ə'fɛnsɪv] *adj* ofensivo || *f* ofensiva
offer ['ɔfər] o ['ɑfər] *s* ofrecimiento, oferta || *tr* ofrecer; rezar (*oraciones*); oponer (*resistencia*)
offering ['ɔfərɪŋ] o ['ɑfərɪŋ] *s* ofrecimiento; (*gift, present*) oferta; (*presentation in worship*) ofrenda
off'hand' *adj* hecho de improviso; brusco, desenvuelto || *adv* **de improviso**, súbitamente; bruscamente
office ['ɔfɪs] o ['ɑfɪs] *s* oficina, despacho; función, oficio; cargo, ministerio; (*of a lawyer*) bufete *m;* (*of a doctor*) consultorio
office boy *s* mandadero
office desk *s* escritorio ministro
of'fice·hold'er *s* funcionario, burócrata *m*
office hours *spl* horas de oficina; (*of a doctor*) horas de consultorio
officer ['ɔfɪsər] o ['ɑfɪsər] *s* jefe *m,* director *m;* (*of army, an order, a society, etc.*) oficial *m;* agente *m* de policía
office seeker ['sikər] *s* aspirante *m,* pretendiente *m*
office supplies *spl* suministros para oficinas
official [ə'fɪʃəl] *adj* oficial || *s* jefe *m,* director *m;* (*of a society*) dignatario
officiate [ə'fɪʃɪ,et] *intr* oficiar
officious [ə'fɪʃəs] *adj* oficioso
off'-peak' heater *s* (elec) termos *m* de acumulación
off-peak load *s* (elec) carga de las horas de valle
off'print' *s* sobretiro
off'set' *s* compensación; (typ) offset *m* || **off'set'** *v* (*pret & pp* **-set;** *ger* **-setting**) *tr* compensar; imprimir por offset
off'shoot' *s* (*of plant*) retoño, renuevo; (*of a family or race*) descendiente *mf;* (*branch*) ramal *m;* consecuencia
off'shore' *adj* (*wind*) terral; (*fishing*) de bajura; (*said of islands*) costero || *adv* a lo largo
off'spring' *s* descendencia, sucesión; hijo, hijos
off'-stage' *adj* de entre bastidores
off'-the-rec'ord *adj* extraoficial, confidencial
often ['ɔfən] o ['ɑfən] *adv* a menudo, muchas veces; **how often?** ¿cuántas veces?; **not often** pocas veces
ogive ['odʒaɪv] u [o'dʒaɪv] *s* ojiva
ogle ['ogəl] *tr & intr* ojear; mirar amorosamente
ogre ['ogər] *s* ogro
ohm [om] *s* ohmio
oil [ɔɪl] *adj* (*burner; field; well*) de petróleo; (*pump; stove*) de aceite; (*company; tanker*) petrolero; (*land*) petrolífero || *s* aceite *m;* (*consecrated oil; painting*) óleo; **to burn the midnight oil** quemarse las cejas; **to pour oil on troubled waters** mojar la pólvora; **to strike oil** encontrar una capa de petróleo; (fig) enriquecerse de súbito || *tr* aceitar; lubricar; lisonjear; (*to bribe*) untar || *intr* proveerse de petróleo (*un buque*)
oil'can' *s* aceitera
oil'cloth' *s* encerado, hule *m*
oil gauge indicador *m* del nivel de aceite
oil pan *s* colector *m* de aceite
oil tanker *s* petrolero
oil·y ['ɔɪli] *adj* (*comp* **-ier;** *super* **-iest**) aceitoso; liso, resbaladizo; zalamero
ointment ['ɔɪntmənt] *s* ungüento
O.K. ['o'ke] *adj* (coll) aprobado, conforme || *adv* (coll) muy bien, está bien || *s* (coll) aprobación || *v* (*pret & pp* **O.K.'d;** *ger* **O.K.'ing**) *tr* (coll) aprobar
okra ['okrə] *s* quingombó *m*
old [old] *adj* viejo; antiguo; (*wine*) añejo; **how old is . . . ?** ¿cuántos años tiene . . . ?; **of old** de antaño, antiguamente; **to be . . . years old** tener . . . años
old age *s* ancianidad, vejez *f;* **to die of old age** morir de viejo
old boy *s* viejo; graduado; **the Old Boy** (slang) el diablo
Old Castile *s* Castilla la Vieja
old-clothes·man ['old'kloðz,mæn] *s* (*pl* **-men** [,mɛn]) ropavejero
old country *s* madre patria
old-fashioned ['old'fæʃənd] *adj* chapado a la antigua; anticuado, fuera de moda
old fo·gey u **old fo·gy** ['fogi] *s* (*pl* **-gies**) persona un poco ridícula por sus ideas o costumbres atrasadas
Old Glory *s* la bandera de los Estados Unidos
Old Guard *s* (U.S.A.) bando conservador del partido republicano
old hand *s* practicón *m,* veterano
old maid *s* solterona
old master *s* (paint) gran maestro; obra de un gran maestro
old moon *s* luna menguante
old salt *s* lobo de mar
old school *s* gente chapada a la antigua
old'-time' *adj* del tiempo viejo
old-timer ['old'taɪmər] *s* (coll) antiguo residente, veterano; (coll) persona chapada a la antigua
old wives' tale *s* cuento de viejas
old'-world' *adj* del Viejo Mundo
oleander [,olɪ'ændər] *s* adelfa
oligar·chy ['ɑlɪ,gɑrki] *s* (*pl* **-chies**) oligarquía
olive ['ɑlɪv] *adj* aceitunado || *s* aceituna
olive branch *s* ramo de olivo; (*peace*) oliva; hijo, vástago
olive grove *s* olivar *m*
olive oil *s* aceite *m,* aceite de oliva
olive tree *s* aceituno, olivo
Olympiad [o'lɪmpɪ,æd] *s* Olimpíada
Olympian [o'lɪmpɪ·ən] *adj* olímpico || *s* dios griego
Olympic [o'lɪmpɪk] *adj* olímpico
omelet u **omelette** ['ɑməlɪt] o ['ɑmlɪt] *s* tortilla (de huevos)
omen ['omən] *s* agüero
ominous ['ɑmɪnəs] *adj* ominoso
omission [o'mɪʃən] *s* omisión

omit [o'mɪt] *v* (*pret & pp* **omitted;** *ger* **omitting**) *tr* omitir
omnibus ['ɑmnɪ,bʌs] o ['ɑmnɪbəs] *adj* general; (*volume*) colecticio || *s* ómnibus *m*
omnipotent [ɑm'nɪpətənt] *adj* omnipotente
omniscient [ɑm'nɪʃənt] *adj* omnisciente
omnivorous [ɑm'nɪvərəs] *adj* omnívoro
on [ɑn] u [ɔn] *adj* puesto, p.ej., **with his hat on** con el sombrero puesto; principiando; en funcionamiento; encendido; conectado; **the deal is on** ya está concertado el trato; **the game is on** ya están jugando; **the race is on** allá van los corredores; **what is on at the theater this evening?** ¿qué representan esta noche? || *adv* adelante; encima; **and so on** y así sucesivamente; **come on!** ¡anda, anda!; **farther on** más allá, más adelante; **later on** más tarde, después; **to be on to a person** (coll) conocerle a uno el juego; **to have on** tener puesto; **to . . . on** seguir + *ger,* **he played on** siguió tocando || *prep* en, sobre, encima de; a, p.ej., **on foot** a pie; **on my arrival** a mi llegada; bajo, p.ej., **on my responsibility** bajo mi responsabilidad; contra, p.ej., **an attack on liberty** un ataque contra la libertad; de, p.ej., **on good authority** de buena tinta; **on a journey** de viaje; hacia, p.ej., **to march on the capital** marchar hacia la capital; por, p.ej., **on all sides** por todos lados; tras, p.ej., **defeat on defeat** derrota tras derrota; **on** + *ger* al + *inf,* p.ej., **on arriving** al llegar
on and on *adv* continuamente, sin cesar, sin parar
once [wʌns] *adv* una vez; antes, p.ej., **once so happy** antes tan feliz; alguna vez, p.ej., **if this once becomes known** si esto llega a saberse alguna vez; **all at once** de súbito, de repente; **at once** en seguida; a la vez, en el mismo momento; **for once** una vez por lo menos; **once and again** repetidas veces; **once in a blue moon** cada muerte de obispo; **once in a while** de vez en cuando; **once more** otra vez; una vez más; **once upon a time there was** érase una vez, érase que se era || *conj* una vez que || *s* una vez; vez, p.ej., **this once** esta vez
once'-o'ver *s* (slang) examen rápido; **to give a thing the once-over** (coll) examinar una cosa superficialmente
one [wʌn] *adj* un, uno; un tal, p.ej., **one Smith** un tal Smith; único, p.ej., **one price** precio único || *pron* uno, p.ej., **one does not know what to do here** uno no sabe qué hacer aquí; se, p.ej., **how does one go to the station?** ¿cómo se va a la estación?; **I for one** yo por lo menos; **it's all one and the same to me** me es igual; **my little one** mi chiquito; **of one another** el uno del otro, los unos de los otros, p.ej., **we took leave of one another** nos despedimos el uno del otro; **one and all** todos; **one another** se, p.ej., **they greeted one another** se saludaron; uno a otro, unos a otros, p.ej., **they looked at one another** se miraron uno a otro; **one by one** uno a uno; **one o'clock** la una; **one or two** unos pocos; **one's** su, el . . . de uno; **the blue book and the red one** el libro azul y el rojo; **the one and only** el único; **the one that** el que, la que; **this one** éste; **that one** ése, aquél; **to make one** unir; casar || *s* uno
one'-horse' *adj* de un solo caballo, tirado por un solo caballo; (coll) insignificante, de poca monta
onerous ['ɑnərəs] *adj* oneroso
one'self' *pron* uno mismo; sí, sí mismo; se; **to be oneself** tener dominio de sí mismo; conducirse con naturalidad
one-sided ['wʌn'saɪdɪd] *adj* de un solo lado; injusto, parcial; desigual; unilateral
one'-track' *adj* de carril único; (coll) con un solo interés
one'-way' *adj* de una sola dirección, de dirección única; (*ticket*) sencillo, de ida
onion ['ʌnjən] *s* cebolla
on'ion•skin' *s* papel *m* de seda, papel cebolla
on'look'er *s* mirón *m,* espectador *m*
only ['onlɪ] *adj* solo, único || *adv* solamente, sólo, únicamente; no . . . más que; **not only . . . but also** no sólo . . . sino también || *conj* sólo que, pero
on'set' *s* arremetida, embestida; (*of an illness*) principio
onward ['ɑnwərd] u **onwards** ['ɑnwərdz] *adv* adelante, hacia adelante
onyx ['ɑnɪks] *s* ónice *m* u ónix *m*
ooze [uz] *s* chorro suave; cieno, limo, lama || *tr* rezumar || *intr* rezumar, rezumarse; manar suavemente (*p.ej., la sangre de una herida*); agotarse poco a poco
op. *abbr* **opera, operation, opus, opposite**
opal ['opəl] *s* ópalo
opaque [o'pek] *adj* opaco; (*writer's style*) obscuro; estúpido
open ['opən] *adj* abierto; descubierto, destapado; sin tejado; vacante; (*hour*) libre; discutible, pendiente; (*hand*) liberal; (*hunting season*) legal; **to break** o **to crack open** abrir con violencia, abrir por la fuerza; **to throw open** abrir de par en par || *s* abertura; (*in the woods*) claro; **in the open** al aire libre; a campo raso; en alta mar; abiertamente || *tr* abrir; desbullar (*una ostra*) || *intr* abrir; abrirse; estrenarse (*un drama*); **to open into** desembocar en; **to open on** dar a; **to open up** descubrirse; descubrir el pecho
o'pen-air' *adj* al aire libre, a cielo abierto
open-eyed ['opən ,aɪd] *adj* alerta, vigi-

lante; con ojos asombrados; hecho con los ojos abiertos
open-handed ['opən'hændɪd] *adj* maniabierto, liberal
open-hearted ['opən'hɑrtɪd] *adj* franco, sincero
open house *s* coliche *m;* **to keep open house** recibir a todos, gustar de tener siempre convidados en casa
opening ['opənɪŋ] *s* abertura; (*of, e.g., school*) apertura; (*in the woods*) claro; (*vacancy*) hueco, vacante *f;* (*chance to say something*) ocasión
opening night *s* noche *f* de estreno
opening number *s* primer número
opening price *s* primer curso, precio de apertura
open-minded ['opən'maɪndɪd] *adj* receptivo, razonable, imparcial
open secret *s* secreto a voces
open shop *s* taller franco
o'pen·work' *s* calado
opera ['ɑpərə] *s* ópera
opera glasses *spl* gemelos de teatro
opera hat *s* clac *m,* sombrero de muelles
opera house *s* teatro de la ópera
operate ['ɑpə,ret] *tr* hacer funcionar; dirigir, manejar; explotar || *intr* funcionar; operar; **to operate on** operar (*p.ej., una hernia; a un niño*)
operatic [,ɑpə'rætɪk] *adj* operístico
operating expenses *spl* gastos de explotación
operating room *s* quirófano
operating table *s* mesa operatoria
operation [,ɑpə'reʃən] *s* operación; funcionamiento; explotación
operator ['ɑpə,retər] *s* operador *m,* maquinista *m;* (com) empresario; (coll) corredor *m* de bolsa; (surg, telp) operador *m*
operetta [,ɑpə'rɛtə] *s* opereta
opiate ['opɪ·ɪt] u ['opɪ,et] *adj* & *s* opiato
opinion [ə'pɪnjən] *s* opinión; **in my opinion** a mi parecer; **to have a high opinion of** tener buen concepto de
opinionated [ə'pɪnjə,netɪd] *adj* porfiado en su parecer, dogmático
opium ['opɪ·əm] *s* opio
opium den *s* fumadero de opio
opossum [ə'pɑsəm] *s* zarigüeya
opponent [ə'ponənt] *s* contrario
opportune [,ɑpər'tjun] o [,ɑpər'tun] *adj* oportuno
opportunist [,ɑpər'tjunɪst] o [,ɑpər'tunɪst] *s* oportunista *mf*
opportuni·ty [,ɑpər'tjunɪti] o [,ɑper'tunɪti] *s* (*pl* **-ties**) oportunidad, ocasión
oppose [ə'poz] *tr* oponerse a
opposite ['ɑpəsɪt] *adj* opuesto; de enfrente, p.ej., **the house opposite** la casa de enfrente || *prep* enfrente de || *s* contrario
opposite number *s* igual *mf,* doble *mf*
opposition [,ɑpə'zɪʃən] *s* oposición
oppress [ə'prɛs] *tr* oprimir
oppression [ə'prɛʃən] *s* opresión
oppressive [ə'prɛsɪv] *adj* opresivo; sofocante, bochornoso
opprobrious [ə'probrɪ·əs] *adj* oprobioso
opprobrium [ə'probrɪ·əm] *s* oprobio
optic ['ɑptɪk] *adj* óptico || *s* (coll) ojo; **optics** *ssg* óptica
optical ['ɑptɪkəl] *adj* óptico
optician [ɑp'tɪʃən] *s* óptico
optimism ['ɑptɪ,mɪzəm] *s* optimismo
optimist ['ɑptɪmɪst] *s* optimista *mf*
optimistic [,ɑptɪ'mɪstɪk] *adj* optimístico
option ['ɑpʃən] *s* opción
optional ['ɑpʃənəl] *adj* facultativo, potestativo
optometrist [ɑp'tɑmɪtrɪst] *s* optometrista *mf*
opulent ['ɑpjələnt] *adj* opulento
or [ɔr] *conj* o, u
oracle ['ɑrəkəl] u ['ɔrəkəl] *s* oráculo
oracular [o'rækjələr] *adj* sentencioso; ambiguo, misterioso; fatídico; sabio
oral ['orəl] *adj* oral
orange ['ɑrɪndʒ] u ['ɔrɪndʒ] *adj* anaranjado || *s* naranja
orangeade [,ɑrɪndʒ'ed] u [,ɔrɪndʒ'ed] *s* naranjada
orange blossom *s* azahar *m*
orange grove *s* naranjal *m*
orange juice *s* zumo de naranja
orange squeezer *s* exprimidera de naranjas
orange tree *s* naranjo
orang-outang [o'ræŋu,tæŋ] *s* orangután *m*
oration [o'reʃən] *s* oración, discurso
orator ['ɑrətər] u ['ɔrətər] *s* orador *m*
oratorical [,ɑrə'tɑrɪkəl] u [,ɔrə'tɔrɪkəl] *adj* oratorio
oratori·o [,ɑrə'torɪ,o] u [,ɔrə'torɪ,o] *s* (*pl* **-os**) oratorio
orato·ry ['ɑrə,tori] u ['ɔrə,tori] *s* (*pl* **-ries**) (*art of public speaking*) oratoria; (*small chapel*) oratorio
orb [ɔrb] *s* orbe *m*
orbit ['ɔrbɪt] *s* órbita; **to go into orbit** entrar en órbita || *tr* poner en órbita; moverse en órbita alrededor de || *intr* moverse en órbita
orchard ['ɔrtʃərd] *s* huerto
orchestra ['ɔrkɪstrə] *s* orquesta; (*parquet*) platea
orchestrate ['ɔrkɪs,tret] *tr* orquestar
orchid ['ɔrkɪd] *s* orquídea
ordain [ɔr'den] *tr* (eccl) ordenar; destinar; mandar
ordeal [ɔr'dil] u [ɔr'di·əl] *s* prueba rigurosa o penosa; (hist) juicio de Dios
order ['ɔrdər] *s* (*way one thing follows another; formal or methodical arrangement; peace, quiet; class, category*) orden *m;* (*command; honor society; monastic brotherhood; fraternal organization*) orden *f;* tarea, p.ej., **a big order** una tarea peliaguda; (com) pedido; (com) giro, libranza; (*formation*) (mil) orden *m;* (*command*) (mil) orden *f;* **in order that** para que, a fin de que; **in order to** + *inf* para + *inf,* a fin de + *inf;* **to get out of order** descomponerse; **to give an order** dar una orden; (com) hacer un pedido || *tr* ordenar;

mandar; encargar, pedir; mandar hacer; **to order around** ser muy mandón con; **to order someone away** mandar a uno que se marche
order blank *s* hoja de pedidos
order•ly ['ɔrdərli] *adj* ordenado, gobernoso; tranquilo, obediente || *s* (*pl* **-lies**) asistente *m* en un hospital; (mil) ordenanza *m*
ordinal ['ɔrdɪnəl] *adj & s* ordinal *m*
ordinance ['ɔrdɪnəns] *s* ordenanza
ordinary ['ɔrdɪ,nɛri] *adj* ordinario
ordnance ['ɔrdnəns] *s* artillería, cañones *mpl;* pertrechos de guerra
ore [or] *s* mena, mineral metalífero
organ ['ɔrgən] *s* órgano
organ•dy ['ɔrgəndi] *s* (*pl* **-dies**) organdí *m*
or'gan-grind'er *s* organillero
organic [ɔr'gænɪk] *adj* orgánico
organism ['ɔrgə,nɪzəm] *s* organismo
organist ['ɔrgənɪst] *s* organista *mf*
organize ['ɔrgə,naɪz] *tr* organizar
organ loft *s* tribuna del órgano
or•gy ['ɔrdʒi] *s* (*pl* **-gies**) orgía
orient ['orɪ·ənt] *s* oriente *m* || **Orient** *s* oriente || **orient** ['orɪ,ɛnt] *tr* orientar
oriental [,orɪ'ɛntəl] *adj* oriental
orifice ['ɑrɪfɪs] u ['ɔrɪfɪs] *s* orificio
origin ['ɑrɪdʒɪn] u ['ɔrɪdʒɪn] *s* origen *m*
original [ə'rɪdʒɪnəl] *adj & s* original *m*
originate [ə'rɪdʒɪ,net] *tr* originar || *intr* originarse
oriole ['orɪ,ol] *s* oropéndola
Orkney Islands ['ɔrkni] *spl* Órcadas
ormolu ['ɔrmə,lu] *s* (*gold powder used in gilding*) oro molido; (*alloy of zinc and copper*) similor m; bronce dorado
ornament ['ɔrnəmənt] *s* ornamento || ['ɔrnə,mɛnt] *tr* ornamentar
ornate [ɔr'net] u ['ɔrnet] *adj* muy ornado; (*style*) florido
orphan ['ɔrfən] *adj & s* huérfano || *tr* dejar huérfano
orphanage ['ɔrfənɪdʒ] *s* (*institution*) orfanato; (*state, condition*) orfandad
orphan asylum *s* asilo de huérfanos
Orpheus ['ɔrfjus] u ['ɔrfɪ·əs] *s* Orfeo
orthodox ['ɔrθə,dɑks] *adj* ortodoxo
orthogra•phy [ɔr'θɑgrəfi] *s* (*pl* **-phies**) ortografía
oscillate ['ɑsɪ,let] *intr* oscilar
osier ['oʒər] *s* mimbre *m & f;* sauce mimbrero
ossi•fy ['ɑsɪ,faɪ] *v* (*pret & pp* **-fied**) *tr* osificar || *intr* osificarse
ostensible [ɑs'tɛnsɪbəl] *adj* aparente, pretendido, supuesto
ostentatious [,ɑstɛn'teʃəs] *adj* (*pretentious*) ostentativo; (*showy*) ostentoso
osteopath ['ɑstɪ·ə,pæθ] *s* osteópata *mf*
osteopathy [,ɑstɪ'ɑpəθi] *s* osteopatía
ostracism ['ɑstrə,sɪzəm] *s* ostracismo
ostrich ['ɑstrɪtʃ] *s* avestruz *m*
O.T. *abbr* **Old Testament**
other ['ʌðər] *adj & pron indef* otro || *adv* — **other than** de otra manera que
otherwise ['ʌðər,waɪz] *adv* otramente, de otra manera; en otras circunstancias; fuera de eso; si no, de otro modo
otter ['ɑtər] *s* nutria
ottoman ['ɑtəmən] *s* (*corded fabric*) otomán *m;* (*sofa*) otomana; escañuelo con cojín || **Ottoman** *adj & s* otomano
ouch [autʃ] *interj* ¡ax!
ought [ɔt] *s* alguna cosa; cero; **for ought I know** por lo que yo sepa || *v aux* se emplea para formar el modo potencial, p.ej., **he ought to go at once** debiera salir en seguida
ounce [auns] *s* onza
our [aur] *adj poss* nuestro
ours [aurz] *pron poss* el nuestro; nuestro
ourselves [aur'sɛlvz] *pron pers* nosotros mismos; nos, p.ej., **we enjoyed ourselves** nos divertimos
oust [aust] *tr* echar fuera, desposeer; desahuciar (*al inquilino*)
out [aut] *adj* ausente; apagado; exterior; divulgado; publicado; (*size*) poco común || *adv* afuera, fuera; al aire libre; hasta el fin; **out for** buscando; **out of** de; entre; de entre; fuera de; más allá de; (*kindness, fear, etc.*) por; (*money*) sin; (*a suit of cards*) fallo a; sobre, p.ej., **in nine out of ten cases** en nueve casos sobre diez; **out to** + *inf* esforzándose por + *inf* || *prep* por; allá en || *interj* ¡fuera de aquí! || *s* cesante *mf;* **to be at outs** u **on the outs** estar de monos
out and away *adv* con mucho
out'-and-out' *adj* perfecto, verdadero, rematado || *adv* completamente
out'-and-out'er *s* intransigente *mf;* extremista *mf*
out•bid' *v* (*pret* **-bid;** *pp* **-bid** o **-bidden;** *ger* **-bidding**) *tr* pujar más que (*otra persona*); (bridge) sobrepasar
out'board' motor *s* motor *m* fuera de borda
out'break' *s* tumulto, motín *m;* (*of anger*) arranque *m;* (*of war*) estallido; (*of an epidemic*) brote *m*
out'build'ing *s* dependencia, edificio accesorio
out'burst' *s* explosión, arranque *m;* **outburst of laughter** carcajada
out'cast' *s* proscripto, paria *mf;* vagabundo
out'come' *s* resultado
out'cry' *s* (*pl* **-cries**) grito; gritería, clamoreo
out•dat'ed *adj* fuera de moda, anticuado
out•do' *v* (*pret* **-did;** *pp* **-done**) *tr* exceder; **to outdo oneself** excederse a sí mismo
out'door' *adj* al aire libre
out'doors' *adv* al aire libre, fuera de casa || *s* aire *m* libre, campo raso
outer space ['autər] *s* espacio exterior
out'field' *s* (baseball) jardín *m*
out'field'er *s* (baseball) jardinero
out'fit *s* equipo; traje *m;* juego de herramientas; (*of soldiers*) cuerpo; (*of a bride*) ajuar *m;* (com) compañía ||

v (*pret & pp* **-fitted;** *ger* **-fitting**) *tr* equipar
out'go'ing *adj* de salida; cesante; (*tide*) descendente; (*nature, character*) exteriorista || *s* salida
out•grow' *v* (*pret* **-grew;** *pp* **-grown**) *tr* crecer más que; ser ya grande para; ser ya viejo para; ser ya más apto que; dejar (*las cosas de los niños; a los amigos de la niñez, etc.*) || *intr* extenderse
out'growth' *s* excrecencia, bulto; (*of leaves in springtime*) nacimiento; consecuencia, resultado
outing ['autɪŋ] *s* jira, excursión al campo
outlandish [aut'lændɪʃ] *adj* estrafalario; de aspecto extranjero; de acento extranjero
out•last' *tr* durar más que; sobrevivir a
out'law' *s* forajido, bandido; prófugo, proscrito || *tr* proscribir; declarar ilegal
out'lay' *s* desembolso || **out•lay'** *v* (*pret & pp* **-laid**) *tr* desembolsar
out'let *s* salida; desaguadero; orificio de salida; (elec) caja de enchufe; (*tap*) (elec) toma-corriente *m*
out'line' *s* contorno; trazado; esquema *m;* esbozo, bosquejo; compendio || *tr* contornar; trazar; trazar el esquema de; esbozar, bosquejar; compendiar
out•live' *tr* sobrevivir a; durar más que
out'look' *s* perspectiva; expectativa; concepto de la vida, punto de vista; atalaya
out'ly'ing *adj* remoto, circundante, de las afueras
out•mod'ed *adj* fuera de moda
out•num'ber *tr* exceder en número, ser más numeroso que
out'-of-date' *adj* fuera de moda, anticuado
out'-of-door' *adj* al aire libre
out'-of-doors' *adj* al aire libre || *adv* al aire libre, fuera de casa || *s* aire *m* libre, campo raso
out'-of-print' *adj* agotado
out'-of-the-way' *adj* apartado, remoto; poco usual, poco común
out of tune *adj* desafinado || *adv* desafinadamente
out of work *adj* desempleado, sin trabajo
out'pa'tient *s* paciente *mf* de consulta externa
out'post' *s* avanzada
out'put' *s* rendimiento; (elec) salida; (mech) rendimiento de trabajo, efecto útil
out'rage *s* atrocidad; ultraje *m* || *tr* maltratar; ultrajar; escandalizar
outrageous [aut'redʒəs] *adj* (*grossly offensive*) ultrajoso; (*shocking, fierce*) atroz; (*extreme*) extravagante
out•rank' *tr* exceder en rango o grado
out'rid'er *s* carrerista *m;* (Brit) viajante *m* de comercio
out'right' *adj* cabal, completo; franco, sincero || *adv* enteramente; de una vez; sin rodeos; en seguida
out'run'ner *s* volante *m* (*criado*)
out'set' *s* principio
out'side' *adj* exterior; superficial; ajeno; (*price*) (el) máximo || *adv* fuera, afuera; **outside of** fuera de || *prep* fuera de; más allá de; (coll) a excepción de || *s* exterior *m;* superficie *f;* apariencia
outsider [,aut'saɪdər] *s* forastero; intruso
out'skirts' *spl* afueras
out'spo'ken *adj* boquifresco, franco
out•stand'ing *adj* sobresaliente; prominente; sin pagar, sin cobrar
outward ['autwərd] *adj* exterior; superficial || *adv* exteriormente, hacia fuera
out•weigh' *tr* pesar más que; contrapesar, compensar
out•wit' *v* (*pret & pp* **-witted;** *ger* **-witting**) *tr* burlar, ser más listo que; despistar (*al perseguidor*)
oval ['ovəl] *adj* oval || *s* óvalo
ova•ry ['ovəri] *s* (*pl* **-ries**) ovario
ovation [o'veʃən] *s* ovación
oven ['ʌvən] *s* horno
over ['ovər] *adj* acabado, concluído; superior; adicional; excesivo || *adv* encima; al otro lado, a la otra orilla; hacia abajo; al revés; patas arriba; otra vez, de nuevo; de añadidura; (*at the bottom of a page*) a la vuelta; acá, p.ej., **hand over the money** déme acá el dinero; **over again** una vez más; **over against** enfrente de; a distinción de; en contraste con; **over and over** repetidas veces; **over here** acá; **over in** allá en; **over there** allá || *prep* sobre, encima de, por encima de; por; de un extremo a otro de; al otro lado de; más allá de; desde; (*a certain number*) más de; acerca de; por causa de; durante; **over and above** además de, en exceso de
o'ver•all' *adj* cabal, completo; extremo, total || **overalls** *spl* pantalones *mf* de trabajo
o'ver•bear'ing *adj* altanero, imperioso
o'ver•board' *adv* al agua; **man overboard!** ¡hombre al agua!; **to throw overboard** arrojar, echar o tirar por la borda
o'ver•cast' *adj* encapotado, nublado || *s* cielo encapotado || *v* (*pret & pp* **-cast**) *tr* nublar
o'ver•charge' *s* cargo excesivo; recargo de precio; sobrecarga; (elec) carga excesiva || **o'ver•charge'** *tr* hacer pagar más del valor, cobrar demasiado a; cargar (*p.ej., 50 pesetas*) de más; (elec) poner una carga excesiva a
o'ver•coat' *s* abrigo, gabán *m,* sobretodo
o'ver•come' *v* (*pret* **-came;** *pp* **-come**) *tr* vencer; rendir; superar (*dificultades*)
o'ver•crowd' *tr* atestar, apiñar; poblar con exceso
o'ver•do' *v* (*pret* **-did;** *pp* **-done**) *tr* exagerar; agobiar; asurar, requemar || *intr* cansarse mucho, excederse en el trabajo
o'ver•dose' *s* dosis excesiva

o′ver•draft′ *s* sobregiro, giro en descubierto
o′ver•draw′ *v* (*pret* **-drew;** *pp* **-drawn)** *tr & intr* sobregirar
o′ver•due′ *adj* atrasado; vencido y no pagado
o′ver•eat′ *v* (*pret* **-ate;** *pp* **-eaten)** *tr & intr* comer con exceso
o′ver•exer′tion *s* esfuerzo excesivo
o′ver•expose′ *tr* sobreexponer
o′ver•expo′sure *s* sobreexposición
o′ver•flow′ *s* desbordamiento, rebosamiento, derrame *m;* caño de reboso || **o′ver•flow′** *intr* desbordar, rebosar
o′ver•fly′ *v* (*pret* **-flew;** *pp* **-flown)** *tr* sobrevolar
o′ver•grown′ *adj* demasiado grande para su edad; denso, frondoso
o′ver•hang′ *v* (*pret & pp* **-hung)** *tr* sobresalir por encima de, estar pendiente o colgando sobre, salir fuera del nivel de; amenazar || *intr* estar pendiente, estar colgando
o′ver•haul′ *tr* examinar, registrar, revisar; ir alcanzando, alcanzar; componer, rehabilitar, reacondicionar
o′ver•head′ *adj* de arriba; aéreo, elevado; general, de conjunto || **o′ver•head′** *adv* por encima de la cabeza; arriba, en lo alto || **o′ver•head′** *s* gastos generales
o′ver•hear′ *v* (*pret & pp* **-heard)** *tr* oír por casualidad; acertar a oír, alcanzar a oír
o′ver•heat′ *tr* recalentar || *intr* recalentarse
overjoyed [ˌovərˈdʒɔɪd] *adj* lleno de alegría; **to be overjoyed** no caber de contento
overland [ˈovərˌlænd] u [ˈovərlənd] *adj & adv* por tierra, por vía terrestre
o′ver•lap′ *v* (*pret & pp* **-lapped;** *ger* **-lapping)** *tr* solapar, traslapar || *intr* solapar, traslapar; traslaparse (*dos o más cosas*); suceder (*dos hechos*) en parte al mismo tiempo
o′ver•load′ *s* sobrecarga || **o′ver•load′** *tr* sobrecargar
o′ver•look′ *tr* dominar con la vista; pasar por alto, no hacer caso de; perdonar, tolerar; espiar, vigilar; cuidar de, dirigir; dar a, p.ej., **the window overlooks the garden** la ventana da al jardín
o′ver•lord′ *s* jefe supremo || **o′ver•lord′** *tr* dominar despóticamente, imponerse a
overly [ˈovərli] *adv* (coll) excesivamente, demasiado
o′ver•night′ *adv* toda la noche; de la tarde a la mañana; **to stay overnight** pasar la noche
overnight bag *s* saco de noche
o′ver•pass′ *s* viaducto
o′ver•pop′u•late′ *tr* superpoblar
o′verpow′er *tr* dominar, supeditar, subyugar; colmar, dejar estupefacto
overpowering *adj* abrumador, arrollador, irresistible
o′ver•produc′tion *s* superproducción, sobreproducción
o′ver•rate′ *tr* exagerar el valor de
o′ver•run′ *v* (*pret* **-ran;** *pp* **-run;** *ger* **-running)** *tr* cubrir enteramente; infestar; exceder; **to overrun one's time** quedarse más de lo justo; hablar más de lo justo
o′ver•sea′ u **o′ver•seas′** *adj* de ultramar || **o′ver•sea′** u **o′ver•seas′** *adv* allende los mares, en ultramar
o′ver•seer′ *s* director *m,* superintendente *mf*
o′ver•shad′ow *tr* sombrear; (fig) eclipsar
o′ver•shoe′ *s* chanclo, zapato de goma
o′ver•shoot′ *v* (*pret & pp* **-shot)** *tr* tirar por encima de o más allá de; **to overshoot oneself** pasarse de listo, excederse
o′ver•sight′ *s* inadvertencia, descuido
o′ver•sleep′ *v* (*pret & pp* **-slept)** *intr* dormir demasiado tarde
o′ver•step′ *v* (*pret & pp* **-stepped;** *ger* **-stepping)** *tr* exceder, traspasar
o′ver•stock′ *tr* abarrotar
o′ver•sup•ply′ *s* (*pl* **-plies)** provisión excesiva || **o′ver•sup•ply′** *v* (*pret* **-plied)** *tr* proveer en exceso
overt [ˈovərt] u [oˈvʌrt] *adj* abierto, manifiesto; premeditado
o′ver•take′ *v* (*pret* **-took;** *pp* **-taken)** *tr* alcanzar; sobrepasar; sorprender; sobrevenir a
o′ver-the-count′er *adj* vendido directamente al comprador; vendido en tienda al por mayor
o′ver•throw′ *s* derrocamiento; trastorno || **o′ver•throw′** *v* (*pret* **-threw;** *pp* **-thrown)** *tr* derrocar; trastornar
o′ver•time′ *adj & adv* en exceso de las horas regulares || *s* horas extraordinarias de trabajo
o′ver•trump′ *s* contrafallo || **o′ver•trump′** *tr & intr* contrafallar
overture [ˈovərtʃər] *s* insinuación, proposición; (mus) obertura
o′ver•turn′ *s* vuelco; movimiento de mercancías || **o′ver•turn′** *tr* volcar; trastornar; derrocar || *intr* volcar; trastornarse
overweening [ˌovərˈwinɪŋ] *adj* arrogante, presuntuoso
o′ver•weight′ *adj* excesivamente gordo o grueso || *s* sobrepeso; exceso de peso; peso de añadidura
overwhelm [ˌovərˈhwɛlm] *tr* abrumar; inundar; anonadar; (*with favors, gifts, etc.*) colmar
o′ver•work′ *s* trabajo excesivo, exceso de trabajo; trabajo fuera de las horas regulares || **o′ver•work′** *tr* hacer trabajar demasiado; oprimir con el trabajo || *intr* trabajar demasiado
Ovid [ˈɑvɪd] *s* Ovidio
ow [aʊ] *interj* ¡ax!
owe [o] *tr* deber, adeudar || *intr* tener deudas
owing [ˈo·ɪŋ] *adj* adeudado; debido, pagadero; **owing to** debido a, por causa de
owl [aʊl] *s* buho, lechuza, mochuelo
own [on] *adj* propio, p.ej., **my own brother** mi propio hermano || *s* suyo, lo suyo; **on one's own** (coll) por su propia cuenta; (*without tak-*

ing advice from anyone) por su cabeza; (*without help from anyone*) de su cabeza; **to come into one's own** entrar en posesión de lo suyo; tener el éxito merecido, recibir el honor merecido; **to hold one's own** no aflojar, no cejar, mantenerse firme || *tr* poseer; reconocer || *intr* confesar; **to own up to** (coll) confesar de plano (*una culpa, un delito, etc.*)

owner ['onər] *s* amo, dueño, poseedor *m*, propietario

ownership ['onər,ʃɪp] *s* posesión, propiedad

owner's license *s* permiso de circulación, patente *f* de circulación

ox [ɑks] *s* (*pl* **oxen** ['ɑksən]) buey *m*

ox'cart' *s* carreta de bueyes

oxide ['ɑksaɪd] *s* óxido

oxidize ['ɑksɪ,daɪz] *tr* oxidar || *intr* oxidarse

oxygen ['ɑksɪdʒən] *s* oxígeno

oxygen tent *s* cámara o tienda de oxígeno

oxytone ['ɑksɪ,ton] *adj & s* oxítono

oyster ['ɔɪstər] *adj* ostrero || *s* ostra

oyster bed *s* ostrero

oyster cocktail *s* ostras en su concha

oyster fork *s* desbullador *m*

oys'ter·house' *s* ostrería

oys'ter·knife' *s* abreostras *m*

oyster·man ['ɔɪstərmən] *s* (*pl* **-men** [mən]) ostrero

oyster opener ['opənər] *s* desbullador *m*

oyster shell *s* desbulla, concha de ostra

oyster stew *s* sopa de ostras

oz. *abbr* **ounce, ounces**

ozone ['ozon] *s* ozono; (coll) aire fresco

ozs. *abbr* **ounces**

P

P, p [pi] decimosexta letra del alfabeto inglés

p. *abbr* **page, participle**

P.A. *abbr* **Passenger Agent, power of attorney, Purchasing Agent**

pace [pes] *s* paso; **to keep pace with** ir, andar o avanzar al mismo paso que; **to put through one's paces** poner (*a uno*) a prueba; dar a (*uno*) ocasión de lucirse; **to set the pace** establecer el paso; dar el ejemplo || *tr* establecer el paso para; medir a pasos; recorrer a pasos; **to pace the floor** pasearse desesperadamente por la habitación || *intr* andar a pasos regulares

pace'mak'er *s* (med) marcapaso

pacific [pə'sɪfɪk] *adj* pacífico || **Pacific** *adj & s* Pacífico

pacifier ['pæsɪ,faɪ·ər] *s* pacificador *m*; (*teething ring*) chupador *m*

pacifism ['pæsɪ,fɪzəm] *s* pacifismo

pacifist ['pæsɪfɪst] *adj & s* pacifista *mf*

paci·fy ['pæsɪ,faɪ] *v* (*pret & pp* **-fied**) *tr* pacificar

pack [pæk] *s* lío, fardo; paquete *m*; (*of hounds*) jauría; (*of cattle*) manada; (*of evildoers*) pandilla; (*of lies*) sarta, montón *m*; (*of playing cards*) baraja; (*of cigarettes*) cajetilla; (*of floating ice*) témpano; (med) compresa || *tr* empaquetar; embaular; encajonar; hacer (*el baúl, la maleta*); conservar en latas; apretar, atestar; cargar (*una acémila*); escoger de modo fraudulento (*un jurado*); **to be packed in** (coll) estar como sardinas en banasta || *intr* empaquetarse; hacer el baúl, hacer la maleta; consolidarse, formar masa compacta

package ['pækɪdʒ] *s* paquete *m* || *tr* empaquetar

pack animal *s* acémila, animal *m* de carga

packing box o **case** *s* caja de embalaje

packing house *s* frigorífico

packing slip *s* hoja de embalaje

pack'sad'dle *s* albarda

pack'thread' *s* bramante *m*

pack train *s* recua

pact [pækt] *s* pacto

pad [pæd] *s* cojincillo, almohadilla; (*of writing paper*) bloc *m*; (*for inking*) tampón *m*; (*of an aquatic plant*) hoja; (*for launching a rocket*) plataforma *f*; (*sound of footsteps*) pisada || *v* (*pret & pp* **padded**; *ger* **padding**) *tr* acolchar, rellenar; meter mucho ripio en (*un escrito*) || *intr* andar, caminar; caminar despacio y pesadamente

paddle ['pædəl] *s* (*of a canoe*) canalete *m*; (*of a wheel*) pala, paleta; (*for spanking*) palo || *tr* impulsar con canalete; (*to spank*) apalear || *intr* remar con canalete; remar suavemente; (*to splash*) chapotear

paddle wheel *s* rueda de paletas

paddock ['pædək] *s* dehesa; (*at racecourse*) paddock *m*

pad'lock' *s* candado || *tr* cerrar con candado; (*to lock up officially*) condenar (*una habitación, un teatro*)

pagan ['pegən] *adj & s* pagano

paganism ['pegə,nɪzəm] *s* paganismo

page [pedʒ] *s* (*of a book*) página; (*boy attendant*) paje *m*; (*in a hotel or club*) botones *m* || *tr* paginar; buscar llamando

pageant ['pædʒənt] *s* espectáculo público

pageant·ry ['pædʒəntri] *s* (*pl* **-ries**) pompa, fausto; (*empty display*) bambolla

pail [pel] *s* balde *m*, cubo

pain [pen] *s* dolor *m*; **on pain of** so pena de; **pains** esmero, trabajo; dolores de parto; **to take pains** esmerarse || *tr & intr* doler

painful ['penfəl] *adj* doloroso; penoso
pain'kill'er *s* (coll) remedio contra el dolor
painless ['penlɪs] *adj* sin dolor, indoloro; fácil, sin trabajo
pains'tak'ing *adj* esmerado
paint [pent] *s* pintura; (*rouge*) afeite *m*, colorete *m* || *tr* pintar || *intr* pintar; pintarse, repintarse
paint'box' *s* caja de colores
paint'brush' *s* brocha, pincel *m*
painter ['pentər] *s* pintor *m*
painting ['pentɪŋ] *s* pintura
paint remover [rɪ'muvər] *s* sacapintura *m*, quitapintura *m*
pair [pɛr] *s* par *m;* (*of people*) pareja; (*of cards*) parejas || *tr* aparear || *intr* aparearse
pair of scissors *s* tijeras
pair of trousers *s* pantalones *mpl*
pajamas [pə'dʒɑməz] o [pə'dʒæməz] *spl* pijama
Pakistan [,pɑkɪ'stɑn] *s* el Paquistán
Pakistani [,pɑkɪ'stɑni] *adj & s* paquistano, paquistaní *mf*
pal [pæl] *s* (coll) compañero || *v* (*pret & pp* **palled;** *ger* **palling**) *intr* (coll) ser compañeros
palace ['pælɪs] *s* palacio
palatable ['pælətəbəl] *adj* sabroso, apetitoso
palatal ['pælətəl] *adj & s* palatal *f*
palate ['pælɪt] *s* paladar *m*
pale [pel] *adj* pálido; (*color*) claro || *s* estaca; palizada; límite *m*, término || *intr* palidecer
pale'face' *s* rostropálido
palette ['pælɪt] *s* paleta
palfrey ['pɔlfri] *s* palafrén *m*
palisade [,pælɪ'sed] *s* estaca; estacada; (*line of cliffs*) acantilado
pall [pɔl] *s* paño de ataúd, paño mortuorio; (eccl) palia || *tr* hartar, saciar; quitar el sabor a || *intr* perder el sabor; **to pall on** hartar, saciar
pall'bear'er *s* acompañante *m* de un cadáver; portador *m* del féretro
palliate ['pælɪ,et] *tr* paliar
pallid ['pælɪd] *adj* pálido
pallor ['pælər] *s* palidez *f*, palor *m*
palm [pɑm] *s* (*of the hand*) palma; (*measure*) palmo; (*tree and leaf*) palma; **to carry off the palm** llevarse la palma; **to grease the palm of** (slang) untar la mano a; **to yield the palm to** reconocer por vencedor || *tr* esconder en la mano; escamotear (*una carta*); **to palm off something on someone** encajarle una cosa a uno
palmet·to [pæl'mɛto] *s* (*pl* **-tos** o **-toes**) palmito
palmist ['pɑmɪst] *s* quiromántico
palmistry ['pɑmɪstri] *s* quiromancia
palm leaf *s* palma, hoja de la palmera
palm oil *s* aceite *m* de palma; (slang) propina; (slang) soborno
Palm Sunday *s* domingo de ramos
palpable ['pælpəbəl] *adj* palpable
palpitate ['pælpɪ,tet] *intr* palpitar
pal·sy ['pɔlzi] *s* (*pl* **-sies**) perlesía || *v* (*pret & pp* **-sied**) *tr* paralizar
pal·try ['pɔltri] *adj* (*comp* **-trier;** *super* **-triest**) vil, ruin, mezquino
pamper ['pæmpər] *tr* mimar, consentir
pamphlet ['pæmflɪt] *s* folleto, panfleto
pan [pæn] *s* cacerola, cazuela, sartén *f;* caldera, perol *m* || *v* (*pret & pp* **panned;** *ger* **panning**) *tr* cocer, freír; separar (*el oro*) en la gamella; (coll) criticar ásperamente || *intr* separar el oro en la gamella; dar oro; **to pan out well** (coll) tener éxito, dar buen resultado || **Pan** *s* Pan
panacea [,pænə'si·ə] *s* panacea
Panama Canal ['pænə,mɑ] *s* canal *m* de Panamá
Panama Canal Zone *s* Zona del Canal
Panama hat *s* panamá *m*
Panamanian [,pænə'menɪ·ən] o [,pænə'mɑnɪ·ən] *adj & s* panameño
Pan-American [,pænə'mɛrɪkən] *adj* panamericano
pan'cake' *s* hojuela, panqueque *m* || *intr* (aer) desplomarse
pancake landing *s* aterrizaje aplastado, aterrizaje en desplome
pancreas ['pænkrɪ·əs] *s* páncreas *m*
pander ['pændər] *s* alcahuete *m* || *intr* alcahuetear; **to pander to** gratificar
pane [pen] *s* cristal *m*, vidrio, hoja de vidrio
pan·el ['pænəl] *s* panel *m*, entrepaño, cuarterón *m;* grupo de personas en discusión cara al público; (aut, elec) tablero, panel *m;* (law) lista de personas que pueden servir como jurados || *v* (*pret & pp* **-eled** o **-elled;** *ger* **-eling** o **-elling**) *tr* adornar con cuarterones, labrar en cuarterones; artesonar (*un techo o bóveda*)
panel discussion *s* coloquio cara al público
panelist ['pænəlɪst] *s* coloquiante *mf* cara al público
panel lights *spl* luces *fpl* del tablero
pang [pæŋ] *s* dolor agudo; (*of remorse*) punzada; (*of death*) agonía
pan'han'dle *s* mango de sartén || *intr* (slang) mendigar, pedir limosna
pan·ic ['pænɪk] *adj & s* pánico || *v* (*pret & pp* **-icked;** *ger* **-icking**) *tr* sobrecoger de pánico || *intr* sobrecogerse de pánico
pan'ic-strick'en *adj* muerto de miedo, sobrecogido de terror
pano·ply ['pænəpli] *s* (*pl* **-plies**) panoplia; traje *m* ceremonial
panorama [,pænə'ræmə] o [,pænə'rɑmə] *s* panorama *m*
pan·sy ['pænzi] *s* (*pl* **-sies**) pensamiento
pant [pænt] *s* jadeo; palpitación; **pants** pantalones *mpl;* **to wear the pants** (coll) calzarse los pantalones || *intr* jadear; palpitar
pantheism ['pænθɪ,ɪzəm] *s* panteísmo
pantheon ['pænθɪ,ɑn] o ['pænθɪ·ən] *s* panteón *m*
panther ['pænθər] *s* pantera; puma
panties ['pæntiz] *spl* pantaloncillos de mujer
pantomime ['pæntə,maɪm] *s* pantomima

pan·try ['pæntri] *s* (*pl* **-tries**) despensa
pap [pæp] *s* papilla, papas
papa·cy ['pepəsi] *s* (*pl* **-cies**) papado
paper ['pepər] *s* papel *m;* (*newspaper*) periódico; (*of needles*) paño || *tr* empapelar
pa'per·back' *s* libro en rústica
pa'per·boy' *s* vendedor *m* de periódicos
paper clip *s* sujetapapeles *m*
paper cone *s* cucurucho
paper cutter *s* cortapapeles *m,* guillotina
paper doll *s* muñeca de papel
paper hanger *s* empapelador *m,* papelista *mf*
paper knife *s* cortapapeles *m*
paper mill *s* fábrica de papel
paper money *s* papel *m* moneda
paper profits *spl* ganancias no realizadas sobre valores no vendidos
paper tape *s* cinta perforada
pa'per·weight' *s* pisapapeles *m*
paper work *s* preparación o comprobación de escritos
paprika [pæ'prikə] o ['pæprɪkə] *s* pimentón *m*
papy·rus [pə'paɪrəs] *s* (*pl* **-ri** [raɪ]) papiro
par. *abbr* **paragraph, parallel, parenthesis, parish**
par [pɑr] *adj* a la par; nominal; normal || *s* paridad; valor *m* nominal; **above par** sobre la par; con beneficio, con premio; **below par** o **under par** bajo la par; con pérdida; (coll) indispuesto; **to be on a par with** correr parejas con
parable ['pærəbəl] *s* parábola
parachute ['pærə,ʃut] *s* paracaídas *m* || *intr* lanzarse en paracaídas; **to parachute to safety** salvarse en paracaídas
parachute jump *s* salto en paracaídas
parachutist ['pærə,ʃutɪst] *s* paracaidista *mf*
parade [pə'red] *s* desfile *m;* paseo; ostentación || *tr* ostentar, pasear || *intr* desfilar, pasar por las calles; (mil) formar en parada
paradise ['pærə,daɪs] *s* paraíso
paradox ['pærə,dɑks] *s* paradoja; persona o cosa incomprensibles
paradoxical [,pærə'dɑksɪkəl] *adj* paradójico
paraffin ['pærəfɪn] *s* parafina
paragon ['pærə,gɑn] *s* dechado
paragraph ['pærə,græf] o ['pærə,grɑf] *s* párrafo
Paraguay ['pærə,gwe] o ['pærə,gwaɪ] *s* el Paraguay
Paraguayan [,pærə'gwe·ən] o [,pærə'gwaɪ·ən] *adj* & *s* paraguayano, paraguayo
parakeet ['pærə,kit] *s* perico, periquito
paral·lel ['pærə,lɛl] *adj* paralelo || *s* (línea) paralela; (plano) paralelo; (geog) paralelo; **parallels** (typ) doble raya vertical || *v* (*pret* & *pp* **-leled** o **-lelled;** *ger* **-leling** o **-lelling**) *tr* ser paralelo a; poner en dirección paralela; correr parejas con; (*to compare*) paralelizar
parallel bars *spl* paralelas, barras paralelas
paraly·sis [pə'rælɪsɪs] *s* (*pl* **-ses** [,siz]) parálisis *f*
paralytic [,pærə'lɪtɪk] *adj* & *s* paralítico
paralyze ['pærə,laɪz] *tr* paralizar
paramount ['pærə,maʊnt] *adj* capital, supremo, principalísimo
paranoiac [,pærə'nɔɪ·æk] *adj* & *s* paranoico
parapet ['pærə,pɛt] *s* parapeto
paraphernalia [,pærəfər'nelɪ·ə] *spl* trastos, atavíos
parasite ['pærə,saɪt] *s* parásito
parasitic(al) [,pærə'sɪtɪk(əl)] *adj* parasítico, parasitario
parasol ['pærə,sɔl] o ['pærə,sɑl] *s* quitasol *m,* parasol *m*
pa'ra·troop'er *s* paracaidista *m*
pa'ra·troops' *spl* tropas paracaidistas
parboil ['pɑr,bɔɪl] *tr* sancochar; calentar con exceso
par·cel ['pɑrsəl] *s* paquete *m,* atado, bulto || *v* (*pret* & *pp* **-celed** o **-celled;** *ger* **-celing** o **-celling**) *tr* empaquetar; parcelar (*el terreno*); **to parcel out** repartir
parcel post *s* paquetes *mpl* postales
parch [pɑrtʃ] *tr* abrasar, tostar; **to be parched** tener mucha sed
parchment ['pɑrtʃmənt] *s* pergamino
pardon ['pɑrdən] *s* perdón *m;* (*remission of penalty by the state*) indulto; **I beg your pardon** dispense Vd. || *tr* perdonar, dispensar; indultar
pardonable ['pɑrdənəbəl] *adj* perdonable
pardon board *s* junta de perdones
pare [pɛr] *tr* mondar (*fruta*); pelar (*patatas*); cortar (*callos, uñas*); despalmar (*la palma córnea de los animales*); adelgazar; reducir (*gastos*)
parent ['pɛrənt] *adj* madre, matriz, principal || *s* padre o madre; autor *m,* fuente *f,* origen *m;* **parents** padres *mpl*
parentage ['pɛrəntɪdʒ] *s* paternidad o maternidad; abolengo, linaje *m*
parenthe·sis [pə'rɛnθɪsɪs] *s* (*pl* **-ses** [,siz]) paréntesis *m*
parenthood ['pɛrənt,hʊd] *s* paternidad o maternidad
pariah [pə'raɪ·ə] o ['pɑrɪ·ə] *s* paria *mf*
paring knife ['pɛrɪŋ] *s* cuchillo para mondar
parish ['pærɪʃ] *s* parroquia, feligresía
parishioner [pə'rɪʃənər] *s* parroquiano, feligrés *m*
Parisian [pə'rɪʒən] *adj* & *s* parisiense *mf*
parity ['pærɪti] *s* paridad
park [pɑrk] *s* parque *m* || *tr* estacionar, parquear; (coll) colocar, dejar || *intr* estacionar, parquear
parking ['pɑrkɪŋ] *s* aparcamiento, estacionamiento; **no parking** se prohibe estacionarse
parking lights *spl* (aut) faros de situación
parking lot *s* parque *m* de estacionamiento

parking meter *s* reloj *m* de estacionamiento, parquímetro
parking ticket *s* aviso de multa
park'way' *s* gran vía adornada con árboles
parley ['parli] *s* parlamento ‖ *intr* parlamentar
parliament ['parlɪmənt] *s* parlamento
parlor ['parlər] *s* sala; parlatorio, locutorio
parlor car *s* coche-salón *m*
parlor politics *spl* política de café
Parnassus [par'næsəs] *s* (*collection of poems*) parnaso; el Parnaso; **to try to climb Parnassus** hacer pinos en poesía
parochial [pə'rokɪ·əl] *adj* parroquial; estrecho, limitado
paro•dy ['pærədi] *s* (*pl* **-dies**) parodia ‖ *v* (*pret & pp* **-died**) *tr* parodiar
parole [pə'rol] *s* palabra de honor; libertad bajo palabra ‖ *tr* dejar libre bajo palabra
paroxytone [pær'aksɪ,ton] *adj & s* paroxítono
par•quet [par'ke] *s* entarimado; (theat) platea ‖ *v* (*pret & pp* **-queted** ['ked]; *ger* **-queting** ['ke·ɪŋ]) *tr* entarimar
parricide ['pærɪ,saɪd] *s* (*act*) parricidio; (*person*) parricida *mf*
parrot ['pærət] *s* papagayo, loro; (fig) papagayo ‖ *tr* repetir o imitar como loro
par•ry ['pæri] *s* (*pl* **-ries**) parada, quite *m* ‖ *v* (*pret & pp* **-ried**) *tr* parar; defenderse de
parse [pars] *tr* analizar (*una oración*) gramaticalmente; describir (*una palabra*) gramaticalmente
parsley ['parsli] *s* perejil *m*
parsnip ['parsnɪp] *s* chirivía
parson ['parsən] *s* cura *m*, párroco; clérigo; pastor *m* protestante
part [part] *s* parte *f;* (*of a machine*) pieza; (*of the hair*) raya; (theat) parte *f*, papel *m;* **part and parcel** parte esencial, parte inseparable, elemento esencial; **parts** partes *fpl;* prendas, dotes *fpl;* **to do one's part** cumplir con su obligación; **to look the part** vestir el cargo; **to take the part of** tomar el partido de, defender; desempeñar el papel de ‖ *tr* dividir, partir, separar; **to part the hair** hacerse la raya ‖ *intr* separarse; **to part with** deshacerse de, abandonar; despedirse de
par•take [par'tek] *v* (*pret* **-took** ['tʊk]; *pp* **-taken**) *tr* compartir; comer; beber ‖ *intr* participar
Parthenon ['parθɪ,nan] *s* Partenón *m*
partial ['parʃəl] *adj* parcial; aficionado
participate [par'tɪsɪ,pet] *intr* participar
participle ['partɪ,sɪpəl] *s* participio
particle ['partɪkəl] *s* partícula, corpúsculo
particular [pər'tɪkjələr] *adj* particular; difícil, exigente, quisquilloso; esmerado; minucioso; **a particular . . .** cierto . . . ‖ *s* particular *m*
partisan ['partɪzən] *adj & s* partidario, partidista *mf;* (mil) partisano
partition [par'tɪʃən] *s* partición, distribución; división; porción; tabique *m* ‖ *tr* repartir; dividir en cuartos, aposentos; tabicar
partner ['partnər] *s* compañero; (*wife or husband*) cónyuge *mf;* (*in a dance*) pareja *f;* (*in business*) socio
partnership ['partnər,ʃɪp] *s* asociación; consorcio, vida en común; (com) sociedad, asociación comercial
partridge ['partrɪdʒ] *s* perdiz *f*
part'-time' *adj* por horas, parcial
par•ty ['parti] *adj* de partido; de gala ‖ *s* (*pl* **-ties**) convite *m*, reunión, fiesta, tertulia, recepción; (*for fishing, hunting, etc.*; *of armed men*) partida; cómplice *mf*, interesado; (pol) partido; (coll) persona, individuo
party girl *s* chica de vida alegre
party-goer ['parti,go·ər] *s* tertuliano; fiestero
party line *s* (*between two properties*) linde *m*, lindero; (*of communist party*) línea del partido; (telp) línea compartida
party politics *s* política de partido
pass. *abbr* **passenger, passive**
pass [pæs] o [pas] *s* paso; (*permit; free ticket; movement of hands of mesmerist, of bullfighter*) pase *m;* (*in an examination*) aprobación; nota de aprobación ‖ *tr* pasar; pasar de largo (*una luz roja*); aprobar (*un proyecto de ley; un examen; a un alumno*); ser aprobado en (*un examen*); dejar atrás; cruzarse con; expresar (*una opinión*); pronunciar (*una sentencia*); dar (*la palabra*); dejar sin protestar; no pagar (*un dividendo*); **to pass off** colar, pasar, hacer aceptar (*una moneda falsa*); disimular (*p.ej., una ofensa con una risa*); **to pass over** omitir, pasar por alto; excusar; desdeñar; dejar sin protestar; postergar (*a un empleado*) ‖ *intr* pasar; pasarse (*introducirse*); aprobar; **to bring to pass** llevar a cabo; **to come to pass** suceder; **to pass as** pasar por; **to pass away** pasar, pasar a mejor vida; **to pass off** pasar (*una enfermedad, una tempestad, etc.*); tener lugar; **to pass out** salir; (slang) desmayarse; **to pass over to** pasarse a (*p.ej., el enemigo*)
passable ['pæsəbəl] o ['pasəbəl] *adj* pasadero; (*law*) promulgable
passage ['pæsɪdʒ] *s* pasaje *m;* paso; pasillo; (*of time*) transcurso; (*of bowels*) evacuación
pass'book' *s* cartilla, libreta de banco
passenger ['pæsəndʒər] *adj* de viajeros ‖ *s* pasajero, viajero
passer-by ['pæsər'baɪ] o ['pasər'baɪ] *s* (*pl* **passers-by**) transeúnte *mf*
passing ['pæsɪŋ] o ['pasɪŋ] *adj* pasajero; corriente; de aprobado ‖ *s* (*act of passing; death*) paso; (*in an examination*) aprobación
passion ['pæʃən] *s* pasión
passionate ['pæʃənɪt] *adj* apasionado

passive ['pæsɪv] *adj* pasivo || *s* voz pasiva, verbo pasivo
pass'key' *s* llave *f* de paso
Pass'o'ver *s* pascua (*de los hebreos*)
pass'port' *s* pasaporte *m*
pass'word' *s* santo y seña
past [pæst] o [pɑst] *adj* pasado; último; que fué, p.ej., **past president** presidente que fué; acabado, concluído || *adv* más allá; por delante || *prep* más allá de; más de; por delante de; fuera de; después de, p.ej., **past two o'clock** después de las dos; **past belief** increíble; **past cure** incurable; **past hope** sin esperanza || *s* pasado
paste [pest] *s* (*dough; spaghetti, etc.*) pasta; (*for sticking things together*) engrudo || *tr* engrudar, pegar con engrudo
paste'board' *s* cartón *m*
pasteurize ['pæstə,raɪz] *tr* pasterizar
pastime ['pæs,taɪm] o ['pɑs,taɪm] *s* pasatiempo
pastor ['pæstər] o ['pɑstər] *s* pastor *m*, clérigo, cura *m*
pastoral ['pæstərəl] o ['pɑstərəl] *adj* & *s* pastoral *f*
pas•try ['pestri] *s* (*pl* **-tries**) pastelería
pastry cook *s* pastelero, repostero
pastry shop *s* pastelería, repostería
pasture ['pæstʃər] o ['pɑstʃər] *s* pasto, pastura, dehesa || *tr* apacentar, pacer || *intr* apacentarse, pacer
past•y ['pesti] *adj* (*comp* **-ier;** *super* **-iest**) pastoso; flojo, fofo, pálido
pat [pæt] *s* golpecito, palmadita; ruido de pasos ligeros; (*of butter*) pastelillo || *v* (*pret* & *pp* **patted;** *ger* **patting**) *tr* dar golpecitos a, golpear ligeramente; palmotear, acariciar con la mano; **to pat on the back** elogiar, cumplimentar
patch [pætʃ] *s* remiendo, parche *m;* terreno, pedazo de terreno; mancha; lunar postizo || *tr* remendar; **to patch up** componer (*una desavenencia*); componer lo mejor posible (*una cosa descompuesta*); hacer aprisa y mal
patent ['petənt] *adj* patente; abierto || ['pætənt] *adj* de patentes || *s* patente *f*, patente de invención; propiedad industrial; **patent applied for** se ha solicitado patente || *tr* patentar
patent leather ['pætənt] *s* charol *m*
patent medicine ['pætənt] *s* medicamento de patente
patent rights ['pætənt] *spl* derechos de patente
paternal [pə'tʌrnəl] *adj* paterno; (*affection*) paternal
paternity [pə'tʌrnɪti] *s* paternidad
path [pæθ] o [pɑθ] *s* senda, sendero; trayectoria
pathetic [pə'θɛtɪk] *adj* patético
path'find'er *s* baquiano; explorador *m*
patholo•gy [pə'θɑlədʒi] *s* patología
pathos ['peθɑs] *s* patetismo
path'way' *s* senda, sendero
patience ['peʃəns] *s* paciencia
patient ['peʃənt] *adj* paciente || *s* paciente *mf*, enfermo
patriarch ['petrɪ,ɑrk] *s* patriarca *m*
patrician [pə'trɪʃən] *adj* & *s* patricio
patricide ['pætrɪ,saɪd] *s* (*act*) parricidio; (*person*) parricida *mf*
Patrick ['pætrɪk] *s* Patricio
patrimo•ny ['pætrɪ,moni] *s* (*pl* **-nies**) patrimonio
patriot ['petrɪ•ət] o ['pætrɪ•ət] *s* patriota *mf*
patriotic [,petrɪ'ɑtɪk] o [,pætrɪ'ɑtɪk] *adj* patriótico
patriotism ['petrɪ•ə,tɪzəm] o ['pætrɪ•ə,tɪzəm] *s* patriotismo
pa•trol [pə'trol] *s* patrulla || *v* (*pret* & *pp* **-troled** o **-trolled;** *ger* **-troling** o **-trolling**) *tr* & *intr* patrullar
patrol•man [pə'trolmən] *s* (*pl* **-men** [mən]) guardia *m* municipal, vigilante *m* de policía
patrol wagon *s* camión *m* de policía
patron ['petrən] o ['pætrən] *adj* tutelar || *s* parroquiano; patrocinador *m*
patronize ['petrə,naɪz] o ['pætrə,naɪz] *tr* ser parroquiano de (*un tendero*); comprar de costumbre en; patrocinar; tratar con aire protector
patron saint *s* patrón *m*, santo titular
patter ['pætər] *s* golpeteo; (*of rain*) chapaleteo; charla, parloteo || *intr* golpetear; charlar, parlotear
pattern ['pætərn] *s* patrón *m;* modelo
P.A.U. *abbr* **Pan American Union**
paucity ['pɔsɪti] *s* corto número; falta, escasez *f*, insuficiencia
Paul [pɔl] *s* Pablo; (*name of popes*) Paulo
paunch [pɔntʃ] *s* panza
paunchy ['pɔntʃi] *adj* panzudo
pauper ['pɔpər] *s* pobre *mf*, indigente *mf*
pause [pɔz] *s* pausa; (mus) calderón *m;* **to give pause (to)** dar que pensar (a) || *intr* hacer pausa, detenerse brevemente; vacilar
pave [pev] *tr* pavimentar; (*with flagstones*) enlosar; (*with bricks*) enladrillar; (*with pebbles*) enchinar; **to pave the way (for)** preparar el terreno (para), abrir el camino (a)
pavement ['pevmənt] *s* pavimento; (*of brick*) enladrillado; (*of flagstone*) enlosado; (*sidewalk*) acera
pavilion [pə'vɪljən] *s* pabellón *m*
paw [pɔ] *s* pata; garra, zarpa; (coll) mano *f* || *tr* dar zarpazos a, restregar con las uñas; golpear, patear (*el suelo los caballos*); (coll) manosear; (*to handle overfamiliarly*) (coll) sobar || *intr* piafar (*el caballo*)
pawn [pɔn] *s* (*in chess*) peón *m;* (*security, pledge*) prenda; (*tool of another person*) instrumento; víctima || *tr* empeñar, dar en prenda
pawn'bro'ker *s* prestamista *mf*
pawn'shop' *s* casa de empeños, monte *m* de piedad
pawn ticket *s* papeleta de empeño
pay [pe] *s* paga; recompensa; castigo merecido || *v* (*pret* & *pp* **paid** [ped]) *tr* pagar; prestar o poner (*atención*);

dar (*cumplidos*); dar (*dinero una actividad comercial*); dar dinero a, ser provechoso a; pagar en la misma moneda; pagar con creces; sufrir (*el castigo de una ofensa*); hacer (*una visita*); cubrir (*los gastos*); **to pay back** devolver; pagar en la misma moneda; **to pay off** pagar y despedir (*a un empleado*); pagar todo lo adeudado a; vengarse de; redimir (*una hipoteca*) ‖ *intr* pagar; ser provechoso, valer la pena; **pay as you enter** pague a la entrada; **pay as you go** pagar el impuesto de utilidades con descuentos anticipados; **pay as you leave** pague a la salida

payable [ˈpe·əbəl] *adj* pagadero

pay boost *s* aumento de salario

pay'check' *s* cheque *m* en pago del sueldo; sueldo

pay'day' *s* día *m* de pago

payee [peˈi] *s* portador *m* o tenedor *m* (*de un giro*)

pay envelope *s* sobre *m* con el jornal; jornal *m*, salario

payer [ˈpe·ər] *s* pagador *m*

pay load *s* carga útil

pay'mas'ter *s* pagador *m*

payment [ˈpemənt] *s* pago; castigo

pay roll *s* nómina, hoja de paga

pay station *s* teléfono público

pd. *abbr* **paid**

p.d. *abbr* **per diem, potential difference**

pea [pi] *s* guisante *m*, chícharo

peace [pis] *s* paz *f*; **to make peace with** hacer las paces con

peaceable [ˈpisəbəl] *adj* pacífico

peaceful [ˈpisfəl] *adj* tranquilo, pacífico, sosegado

peace'mak'er *s* iris *m* de paz

peace of mind *s* serenidad del espíritu

peace pipe *s* pipa ceremonial (*de los pieles rojas*)

peach [pitʃ] *s* melocotón *m*; (slang) persona o cosa admirables

peach tree *s* melocotonero

peach·y [ˈpitʃi] *adj* (*comp* **-ier**; *super* **-iest**) (slang) estupendo, magnífico

pea'cock' *s* pavo real, pavón *m*; (fig) pinturero

peak [pik] *s* pico, cima, cumbre *f*; punta, extremo; máximo; (*of a cap*) visera; (*of a curve*) cresta; (elec) pico

peak hour *s* hora punta

peak load *s* (elec) carga de punta

peal [pil] *s* fragor *m*; estruendo; (*of bells*) repique *m*; juego de campanas ‖ *intr* repicar; resonar

peal of laughter *s* carcajada

peal of thunder *s* trueno

pea'nut' *s* cacahuete *m*, aráquida

pear [pɛr] *s* pera

pearl [pʌrl] *s* margarita, perla; (*of running water*) murmullo ‖ *tr* aljofarar

pearl oyster *s* madreperla

pear tree *s* peral *m*

peasant [ˈpɛzənt] *adj* & *s* campesino, rústico

pea'shoot'er *s* cerbatana, bodoquera

pea soup *s* sopa de guisantes; (coll) neblina espesa y amarillenta

peat [pit] *s* turba

pebble [ˈpɛbəl] *s* china, guija ‖ *tr* agranelar (*el cuero*)

peck [pɛk] *s* medida de áridos (*nueve litros*); montón *m*; picotazo; beso dado de mala gana ‖ *tr* picotear ‖ *intr* picotear; (coll) comer melindrosamente; **to peck at** querer picar; regañar constantemente; (coll) comer melindrosamente

peculate [ˈpɛkjəˌlet] *tr* & *intr* malversar

peculiar [pɪˈkjuljər] *adj* peculiar; singular, raro; excéntrico

pedagogue [ˈpɛdəˌgɑg] *s* pedagogo; dómine *m*, pedante *m*

pedagogy [ˈpɛdəˌgodʒi] o [ˈpɛdəˌgɑdʒi] *s* pedagogía

ped·al [ˈpɛdəl] *s* pedal *m* ‖ *v* (*pret* & *pp* **-aled** o **-alled**; *ger* **-aling** o **-alling**) *tr* impulsar pedaleando ‖ *intr* pedalear

pedant [ˈpɛdənt] *s* pedante *mf*

pedantic [pɪˈdæntɪk] *adj* pedantesco

pedant·ry [ˈpɛdəntri] *s* (*pl* **-ries**) pedantería

peddle [ˈpɛdəl] *tr* ir vendiendo de puerta en puerta; traer y llevar (*chismes*); vender (*favores*) ‖ *intr* ser buhonero

peddler [ˈpɛdlər] *s* buhonero

pedestal [ˈpɛdɪstəl] *s* pedestal *m*

pedestrian [pɪˈdɛstrɪ·ən] *adj* pedestre ‖ *s* peatón *m*

pediatrics [ˌpidɪˈætrɪks] o [ˌpɛdɪˈætrɪks] *ssg* pediatría

pedigree [ˈpɛdɪˌgri] *s* árbol genealógico; ascendencia; fuente *f*, origen *m*

pediment [ˈpɛdɪmənt] *s* frontón *m*

peek [pik] *s* mirada rápida y furtiva ‖ *intr* mirar a hurtadillas

peel [pil] *s* cáscara, pellejo ‖ *tr* pelar ‖ *intr* pelarse

peep [pip] *s* mirada a hurtadillas; (*of chickens*) pío ‖ *intr* mirar a hurtadillas; piar (*los pollos*)

peep'hole' *s* atisbadero; (*in a door*) mirilla, ventanillo

peep show *s* mundonuevo; (slang) vistas sicalípticas

peer [pɪr] *s* par *m* ‖ *intr* mirar fijando la vista de cerca; **to peer at** mirar con ojos de miope; **to peer into** mirar hacia lo interior de, escudriñar

peerless [ˈpɪrlɪs] *adj* sin par

peeve [piv] *s* (coll) cojijo ‖ *tr* (coll) enojar, irritar

peevish [ˈpivɪʃ] *adj* cojijoso, displicente

peg [pɛg] *s* clavija, claveta, estaquilla; **to take down a peg** (coll) bajar los humos a ‖ *v* (*pret* & *pp* **pegged**; *ger* **pegging**) *tr* enclavijar; señalar con clavijas; fijar (*precios*) ‖ *intr* trabajar con ahinco; **to peg away at** afanarse en

peg leg *s* pata de palo

peg top *s* peonza; **peg tops** pantalones anchos de caderas y perniles ajustados

Peking [ˈpiˈkɪŋ] *s* Pequín

Peking•ese [ˌpikɪˈniz] *adj* pequinés || *s* (*pl* **-ese**) pequinés *m*
pelf [pɛlf] *s* dinero mal ganado
pell-mell [ˈpɛlˈmɛl] *adj* tumultuoso || *adv* atropelladamente
Peloponnesian [ˌpɛləpəˈniʃən] *adj & s* peloponense *mf*
Peloponnesus [ˌpɛləpəˈnisəs] *s* Peloponeso
Pelops [ˈpilɑps] *s* Pélope *m*
pelota [pɛˈlotə] *s* pelota vasca
pelt [pɛlt] *s* pellejo; golpe violento; (*of a person*) (hum) pellejo || *tr* golpear violentamente; apedrear || *intr* golpear violentamente; caer con fuerza (*el granizo, la lluvia, etc.*); apresurarse
pen. *abbr* **peninsula**
pen [pɛn] *s* pluma; corral *m*, redil *m;* **the pen and the sword** las letras y las armas || *v* (*pret & pp* **penned;** *ger* **penning**) *tr* escribir (*con pluma*); redactar || *v* (*pret & pp* **penned** o **pent** [pɛnt]) *tr* acorralar, encerrar
penalize [ˈpinəˌlaɪz] *tr* penar; (sport) sancionar
penal•ty [ˈpɛnəlti] *s* (*pl* **-ties**) pena; (*for late payment*) recargo; (sport) sanción; **under penalty of** so pena de
penance [ˈpɛnəns] *s* penitencia; **to do penance** hacer penitencia
penchant [ˈpɛnʃənt] *s* afición, inclinación, tendencia
pen•cil [ˈpɛnsəl] *s* lápiz *m;* (*of light*) pincel *m*, haz *m* || *v* (*pret & pp* **-ciled** o **-cilled;** *ger* **-ciling** o **-cilling**) *tr* marcar con lápiz; (med) pincelar
pencil sharpener *s* afilalápices *m*, cortalápices *m*
pendent [ˈpɛndənt] *adj* pendiente; sobresaliente || *s* medallón *m;* (*earring*) pendiente *m*
pending [ˈpɛndɪŋ] *adj* pendiente || *prep* hasta; durante
pendulum [ˈpɛndʒələm] *s* péndulo; (*of a clock*) péndola
pendulum bob *s* lenteja
penetrate [ˈpɛnɪˌtret] *tr & intr* penetrar
penguin [ˈpɛŋgwɪn] *s* pingüino, pájaro bobo
pen'hold'er *s* (*handle*) portaplumas *m;* (*box*) plumero
penicillin [ˌpɛnɪˈsɪlɪn] *s* penicilina
peninsula [pəˈnɪnsələ] *s* península
peninsular [pəˈnɪnsələr] *adj & s* peninsular *mf* || **Peninsular** *adj & s* (*Iberian*) peninsular *mf*
penitence [ˈpɛnɪtəns] *s* penitencia
penitent [ˈpɛnɪtənt] *adj & s* penitente *mf*
pen'knife' *s* (*pl* **-knives**) navaja, cortaplumas *m*
penmanship [ˈpɛnmənˌʃɪp] *s* caligrafía; (*hand of a person*) letra
pen name *s* seudónimo
pennant [ˈpɛnənt] *s* gallardete *m*
penniless [ˈpɛnɪlɪs] *adj* pelón, sin dinero
pennon [ˈpɛnən] *s* pendón *m*
pen•ny [ˈpɛni] *s* (*pl* **-nies**) (**U.S.A.**) centavo || *s* (*pl* **pence** [pɛns]) (**Brit**) penique *m*
pen'ny•weight' *s* peso de 24 granos
pen pal *s* (coll) amigo por correspondencia
pen point *s* punta de la pluma; puntilla de la pluma fuente
pension [ˈpɛnʃən] *s* pensión, jubilación || *tr* pensionar, jubilar
pensioner [ˈpɛnʃənər] *s* pensionista *mf;* **pensioners** clases pasivas
pensive [ˈpɛnsɪv] *adj* pensativo; melancólico
Pentecost [ˈpɛntɪˌkɔst] o [ˈpɛntɪˌkɑst] *s* el Pentecostés
penthouse [ˈpɛntˌhaʊs] *s* alpende *m*, colgadizo; casa de azotea
pent-up [ˈpɛntˌʌp] *adj* contenido, reprimido
penult [ˈpinʌlt] *s* penúltima
penum•bra [pɪˈnʌmbrə] *s* (*pl* **-brae** [bri] o **-bras**) penumbra
penurious [pɪˈnʊrɪ•əs] *adj* (*stingy*) tacaño, mezquino; (*poor*) pobre, indigente
penury [ˈpɛnjəri] *s* tacañería, mezquindad; pobreza, miseria
pen'wip'er *s* limpiaplumas *m*
people [ˈpipəl] *spl* gente *f;* personas; gente del pueblo; se, p.ej., **people say** se dice || *ssg* (*pl* **peoples**) pueblo, nación || *tr* poblar
pep [pɛp] *s* (slang) ánimo, brío, vigor *m* || *v* (*pret & pp* **pepped;** *ger* **pepping**) *tr* — **to pep up** (slang) animar, dar vigor a
pepper [ˈpɛpər] *s* (*spice*) pimienta; (*plant and fruit*) pimiento || *tr* sazonar con pimienta; (*with bullets*) acribillar; salpicar
pep'per•box' *s* pimentero
pep'per•mint' *s* (*plant*) menta piperita; esencia de menta; pastilla de menta
per [pʌr] *prep* por; **as per** según
perambulator [pərˈæmbjəˌletər] *s* cochecillo de niño
per capita [pər ˈkæpɪtə] por cabeza, por persona
perceive [pərˈsiv] *tr* percibir
per cent o **percent** [pərˈsɛnt] por ciento
percentage [pərˈsɛntɪdʒ] *s* porcentaje *m;* (slang) provecho, ventaja
perception [pərˈsɛpʃən] *s* percepción; comprensión, penetración
perch [pʌrtʃ] *s* percha, rama, varilla; sitio o posición elevada; (*fish*) perca || *tr* colocar en un sitio algo elevado || *intr* sentarse en un sitio algo elevado; posar (*un ave*)
percolator [ˈpʌrkəˌletər] *s* cafetera filtradora
per diem [pər ˈdaɪ•əm] por día
perdition [pərˈdɪʃən] *s* perdición
perennial [pəˈrɛnɪ•əl] *adj* perenne; (bot) vivaz || *s* planta vivaz
perfect [ˈpʌrfɪkt] *adj & s* perfecto || [pərˈfɛkt] *tr* perfeccionar
perfidious [pərˈfɪdɪ•əs] *adj* pérfido
perfi•dy [ˈpʌrfɪdi] *s* (*pl* **-dies**) perfidia
perforate [ˈpʌrfəˌret] *tr* perforar
perforce [pərˈfors] *adv* por fuerza, necesariamente

perform [pər'fɔrm] *tr* ejecutar; (theat) representar || *intr* ejecutar; funcionar (*p.ej., una máquina*)
performance [pər'fɔrməns] *s* ejecución; representación; funcionamiento; (theat) función
performer [pər'fɔrmər] *s* ejecutante *mf;* actor *m;* acróbata *mf*
perfume ['pʌrfjum] *s* perfume *m* || [pər'fjum] *tr* perfumar
perfunctory [pər'fʌŋktəri] *adj* hecho sin cuidado, hecho a la ligera; indiferente, negligente
perhaps [pər'hæps] *adv* acaso, tal vez, quizá
per•il ['pɛrəl] *s* peligro || *v* (*pret & pp* **-iled** o **-illed;** *ger* **-iling** o **-illing**) *tr* poner en peligro
perilous ['pɛrɪləs] *adj* peligroso
period ['pɪrɪ•əd] *s* período; (*in school*) hora; (gram) punto; (sport) división
period costume *s* traje *m* de época
periodic [,pɪrɪ'ɑdɪk] *adj* periódico
periodical [,pɪrɪ'ɑdɪkəl] *adj* periódico || *s* periódico, revista periódica
peripher•y [pə'rɪfəri] *s* (*pl* **-ies**) periferia
periscope ['pɛrɪ,skop] *s* periscopio
perish ['pɛrɪʃ] *intr* perecer
perishable ['pɛrɪʃəbəl] *adj* perecedero; (*merchandise*) corruptible
periwig ['pɛrɪ,wɪg] *s* perico
perjure ['pʌrdʒər] *tr* hacer (*a una persona*) quebrantar el juramento; **to perjure oneself** perjurarse
perju•ry ['pʌrdʒəri] *s* (*pl* **-ries**) perjurio
perk [pʌrk] *tr* alzar (*la cabeza*); aguzar (*las orejas*) || *intr* pavonearse; engalanarse; **to perk up** reanimarse, sentirse mejor
permanence ['pʌrmənəns] *s* permanencia
permanen•cy ['pʌrmənənsi] *s* (*pl* **-cies**) permanencia; persona, cosa o posición permanentes
permanent ['pʌrmənənt] *adj* permanente || *s* permanente *f,* ondulación permanente
permanent tenure *s* inamovilidad
permanent way *s* (rr) material fijo
permeate ['pʌrmɪ,et] *tr & intr* penetrar
permission [pər'mɪʃən] *s* permisión
per•mit ['pʌrmɪt] *s* permiso; cédula de aduana || [pər'mɪt] *v* (*pret & pp* **-mitted;** *ger* **-mitting**) *tr* permitir
permute [pər'mjut] *tr* permutar
pernicious [pər'nɪʃəs] *adj* pernicioso
pernickety [pər'nɪkɪti] *adj* (coll) descontentadizo, quisquilloso
perorate ['pɛrə,ret] *intr* perorar
peroration [,pɛrə'reʃən] *s* peroración
peroxide [pər'ɑksaɪd] *s* peróxido; peróxido de hidrógeno
peroxide blonde *s* rubia oxigenada
perpendicular [,pʌrpən'dɪkjələr] *adj & s* perpendicular *f*
perpetrate ['pʌrpɪ,tret] *tr* perpetrar
perpetual [pər'pɛtʃʊ•əl] *adj* perpetuo
perpetuate [pər'pɛtʃʊ,et] *tr* perpetuar
perplex [pər'plɛks] *tr* dejar perplejo
perplexed [pər'plɛkst] *adj* perplejo
perplexi•ty [pər'plɛksɪti] *s* (*pl* **-ties**) perplejidad; problema *m*
per se [pər 'si] por sí mismo, en sí mismo, esencialmente
persecute ['pʌrsɪ,kjut] *tr* perseguir
persecution [,pʌrsɪ'kjuʃən] *s* persecución
persevere [,pʌrsɪ'vɪr] *intr* perseverar
Persian ['pʌrʒən] *adj & s* persa *mf*
persimmon [pər'sɪmən] *s* placaminero
persist [pər'sɪst] o [pər'zɪst] *intr* persistir
persistent [pər'sɪstənt] o [pər'zɪstənt] *adj* persistente; (*insistent*) porfiado; (*e.g., headache*) pertinaz
person ['pʌrsən] *s* persona; **no person** nadie
personage ['pʌrsənɪdʒ] *s* personaje *m;* persona
personal ['pʌrsənəl] *adj* personal; de uso personal || *s* nota de sociedad; (*in a newspaper*) remitido
personali•ty [,pʌrsə'nælɪti] *s* (*pl* **-ties**) personalidad
personality cult *s* culto a la personalidad
personal property *s* bienes *mpl* muebles
personi•fy [pər'sɑnɪ,faɪ] *v* (*pret & pp* **-fied**) *tr* personificar
personnel [,pʌrsə'nɛl] *s* personal *m*
perspective [pər'spɛktɪv] *s* perspectiva
perspicacious [,pʌrspɪ'keʃəs] *adj* perspicaz
perspire [pər'spaɪr] *intr* sudar, transpirar
persuade [pər'swed] *tr* persuadir
persuasion [pər'sweʒən] *s* persuasión; creencia religiosa; creencia fuerte
pert [pʌrt] *adj* atrevido, descarado; (coll) animado, vivo
pertain [pər'ten] *intr* pertenecer; **pertaining to** perteneciente a
pertinacious [,pʌrtɪ'neʃəs] *adj* pertinaz
pertinent ['pʌrtɪnənt] *adj* pertinente
perturb [pər'tʌrb] *tr* perturbar
Peru [pə'ru] *s* el Perú
perusal [pə'ruzəl] *s* lectura cuidadosa
peruse [pə'ruz] *tr* leer con atención
Peruvian [pə'ruvɪ•ən] *adj & s* peruano
pervade [pər'ved] *tr* penetrar, esparcirse por, extenderse por
perverse [pər'vʌrs] *adj* perverso; avieso, díscolo; contumaz
perversion [pər'vʌrʒən] *s* perversión
perversi•ty [pər'vʌrsɪti] *s* (*pl* **-ties**) perversidad; indocilidad; contumacia
pervert ['pʌrvərt] *s* renegado, apóstata; pervertido || [pər'vʌrt] *tr* pervertir; emplear mal (*p.ej., los talentos que uno tiene*)
pes•ky ['pɛski] *adj* (*comp* **-kier;** *super* **-kiest**) (coll) cargante, molesto
pessimism ['pɛsɪ,mɪzəm] *s* pesimismo
pessimist ['pɛsɪmɪst] *s* pesimista *mf*
pessimistic [,pɛsɪ'mɪstɪk] *adj* pesimista
pest [pɛst] *s* peste *f;* insecto nocivo; (*misfortune*) plaga; (*annoying person, bore*) machaca *mf*
pester ['pɛstər] *tr* molestar, importunar

pest'house' *s* lazareto, hospital *m* de contagiosos
pesticide ['pɛstɪ,saɪd] *s* pesticida *m*
pestiferous [pɛs'tɪfərəs] *adj* pestífero; (coll) engorroso, molesto
pestilence ['pɛstɪləns] *s* pestilencia
pestle ['pɛsəl] *s* mano *f* de almirez
pet [pɛt] *s* animal mimado, animal casero; niño mimado; favorito; enojo pasajero || *v* (*pret & pp* **petted**; *ger* **petting**) *tr* acariciar, mimar || *intr* (slang) besuquearse
petal ['pɛtəl] *s* pétalo
petard [pɪ'tɑrd] *s* petardo
pet'cock' *s* llave *f* de desagüe, llave de purga
Peter ['pitər] *s* Pedro; **to rob Peter to pay Paul** desnudar a un santo para vestir a otro
petition [pɪ'tɪʃən] *s* petición; (*formal request signed by a number of people*) memorial *m*, instancia, solicitud || *tr* suplicar; dirigir una instancia a, solicitar
pet name *s* nombre *m* de cariño
Petrarch ['pitrɑrk] *s* Petrarca *m*
petri·fy ['pɛtrɪ,faɪ] *v* (*pret & pp* **-fied**) *tr* petrificar || *intr* petrificarse
petrol ['pɛtrəl] *s* (Brit) gasolina
petroleum [pɪ'trolɪ·əm] *s* petróleo
pet shop *s* pajarería
petticoat ['pɛtɪ,kot] *s* enaguas; (*woman, girl*) (slang) falda
pet·ty ['pɛti] *adj* (*comp* **-tier**; *super* **-tiest**) insignificante, pequeño; mezquino; intolerante
petty cash *s* caja de menores, efectivo para gastos menores
petty larceny *s* ratería, hurto
petty officer *s* (naut) suboficial *m*
petulant ['pɛtjələnt] *adj* malhumorado, enojadizo
pew [pju] *s* banco de iglesia
pewter ['pjutər] *s* peltre *m*; vajilla de peltre
pfd. *abbr* **preferred**
Phaëthon ['fe·ɪθən] *s* Faetón *m*
phalanx ['felæŋks] o ['fælæŋks] *s* falange *f*
phantasm ['fæntæzəm] *s* fantasma *m*
phantom ['fæntəm] *s* fantasma *m*
Pharaoh ['fɛro] *s* Faraón *m*
pharisee ['færɪ,si] *s* fariseo || **Pharisee** *s* fariseo
pharmaceutical [,fɑrmə'sutɪkəl] *adj* farmacéutico
pharmacist ['fɑrməsɪst] *s* farmacéutico
pharma·cy ['fɑrməsi] *s* (*pl* **-cies**) farmacia
pharynx ['færɪŋks] *s* faringe *f*
phase [fez] *s* fase *f* || *tr* poner en fase; llevar a cabo a etapas uniformes; (coll) inquietar, molestar; **to phase out** deshacer paulatinamente
pheasant ['fɛzənt] *s* faisán *m*
phenobarbital [,fino'bɑrbɪ,tæl] *s* fenobarbital *m*
phenomenal [fɪ'nɑmɪnəl] *adj* fenomenal
phenome·non [fɪ'nɑmɪ,nɑn] *s* (*pl* **-na** [nə]) fenómeno
phial ['faɪ·əl] *s* frasco pequeño
Phidias ['fɪdɪ·əs] *s* Fidias *m*
philanderer [fɪ'lændərər] *s* galanteador *m*, tenorio
philanthropist [fɪ'lænθrəpɪst] *s* filántropo
philanthro·py [fɪ'lænθrəpi] *s* (*pl* **-pies**) filantropía
philatelist [fɪ'lætəlɪst] *s* filatelista *mf*
philately [fɪ'lætəli] *s* filatelia
Philip ['fɪlɪp] *s* Felipe *m*; (*of Macedon*) Filipo
Philippine ['fɪlɪ,pin] *adj* filipino || **Philippines** *spl* Islas Filipinas
Philistine [fɪ'lɪstin], ['fɪlɪ,stin] o ['fɪlɪ,staɪn] *adj & s* filisteo
philologist [fɪ'lɑlədʒɪst] *s* filólogo
philology [fɪ'lɑlədʒi] *s* filología
philosopher [fɪ'lɑsəfər] *s* filósofo
philosophic(al) [,fɪlə'sɑfɪk(əl)] *adj* filosófico
philoso·phy [fɪ'lɑsəfi] *s* (*pl* **-phies**) filosofía
philter ['fɪltər] *s* filtro
phlebitis [flɪ'baɪtɪs] *s* flebitis *f*
phlegm [flɛm] *s* flema *f*, gargajo; **to cough up phlegm** gargajear
phlegmatic(al) [flɛg'mætɪk(əl)] *adj* flemático
Phoebe ['fibi] *s* Febe *f*
Phoebus ['fibəs] *s* Febo
Phoenicia [fɪ'nɪʃə] o [fɪ'niʃə] *s* Fenicia
Phoenician [fɪ'nɪʃən] o [fɪ'niʃən] *adj & s* fenicio
phoenix ['finɪks] *s* fénix *m*
phone [fon] *s* (coll) teléfono; **to come** o **to go to the phone** acudir al teléfono, ponerse al aparato || *tr & intr* (coll) telefonear
phone call *s* llamada telefónica
phonetic [fo'nɛtɪk] *adj* fonético
phonograph ['fonə,græf] o ['fonə,grɑf] *s* fonógrafo
phonology [fə'nɑlədʒi] *s* fonología
pho·ny ['foni] *adj* (*comp* **-nier**; *super* **-niest**) falso, contrahecho || *s* (*pl* **-nies**) (slang) farsa; (coll) farsante *mf*
phosphate ['fɑsfet] *s* fosfato
phosphorescent [,fɑsfə'rɛsənt] *adj* fosforescente
phospho·rus ['fɑsfərəs] *s* (*pl* **-ri** [,raɪ]) fósforo
pho·to ['foto] *s* (*pl* **-tos**) foto *f*
photoengraving [,foto·ɛn'grevɪŋ] *s* fotograbado
photo finish *s* (sport) llegada a la meta, determinada mediante el fotofija
pho'to-fin'ish camera *s* fotofija *m*
photogenic [,foto'dʒɛnɪk] *adj* fotogénico
photograph ['fotə,græf] o ['fotə,grɑf] *s* fotografía || *tr & intr* fotografiar
photographer [fə'tɑgrəfər] *s* fotógrafo
photography [fə'tɑgrəfi] *s* fotografía
photojournalism [,fotə'dʒʌrnə,lɪzəm] *s* fotoperiodismo
pho'to·play' *s* fotodrama *m*
photostat ['fotə,stæt] *s* (trademark) fotóstato || *tr & intr* fotostatar
phototube ['fotə,tjub] o ['fotə,tub] *s* fototubo
phrase [frez] *s* frase *f* || *tr* frasear
phrenology [frɪ'nɑlədʒi] *s* frenología

Phyllis ['fɪlɪs] *s* Filis *f*
phys. *abbr* **physical, physician, physics, physiology**
phys·ic ['fɪzɪk] *s* medicamento; purgante *m* || *v* (*pret & pp* **-icked;** *ger* **-icking**) *tr* curar; purgar
physical ['fɪzɪkəl] *adj* físico
physician [fɪ'zɪʃən] *s* médico
physicist ['fɪzɪsɪst] *s* físico
physics ['fɪzɪks] *s* física
physiognomy [ˌfɪzɪ'ɑgnəmi] o [ˌfɪzɪ'ɑnəmi] *s* fisonomía
physiological [ˌfɪzɪ·ə'lɑdʒɪkəl] *adj* fisiológico
physiology [ˌfɪzɪ'ɑlədʒi] *s* fisiología
physique [fɪ'zik] *s* físico, talle *m,* exterior *m*
pi [paɪ] *s* (math) pi *f;* (typ) pastel *m* || *v* (*pret & pp* **pied;** *ger* **piing**) *tr* (typ) empastelar
pian·o [pɪ'æno] *s* (*pl* **-os**) piano
picaresque [ˌpɪkə'rɛsk] *adj* picaresco
picayune [ˌpɪkə'jun] *adj* de poca monta, mezquino
piccadil·ly [ˌpɪkə'dɪli] *s* (*pl* **-lies**) cuello de pajarita
picco·lo ['pɪkəˌlo] *s* (*pl* **-los**) flautín *m*
pick [pɪk] *s* (*tool*) pico; (*choice*) selección; (*choicest*) flor *f* || *tr* escoger; recoger (*p.ej., flores*); recolectar (*p.ej., algodón*); romper (*el hielo*) con un picahielos; escarbarse (*los dientes*); descañonar, desplumar (*un ave*); hurgarse (*la nariz*); rascarse (*una cicatriz, un grano*); roer (*un hueso*); mondar (*las frutas*); falsear, forzar (*una cerradura*); armar (*una pendencia*); herir (*las cuerdas de un instrumento*); buscar (*defectos*); hurtar de (*los bolsillos*); **to pick out** entresacar; **to pick someone to pieces** (coll) no dejarle a uno un hueso sano; **to pick up** recoger; recobrar (*ánimo; velocidad*); descolgar (*el receptor*); hallar por casualidad; aprender con la práctica; aprender de oídas; invitar a subir a un coche; entablar conservación con (*sin presentación previa*); captar (*una señal de radio*) || *intr* comer melindrosamente; escoger esmeradamente; **to pick at** comer melindrosamente; tomarla con, regañar; **to pick on** escoger; (coll) regañar; (coll) molestar; **to pick over** ir revolviendo y examinando; **to pick up** (coll) ir mejor, sentirse mejor; recobrar velocidad
pick'ax' *s* zapapico
picket ['pɪkɪt] *s* (*stake, pale*) piquete *m;* (*of strikers; of soldiers*) piquete *m* || *tr* poner un cordón de piquetes a || *intr* servir de piquete
picket fence *s* cerca de estacas
picket line *s* línea de piquetes
pickle ['pɪkəl] *s* encurtido; escabeche *m,* salmuera; (coll) apuro, aprieto || *tr* encurtir; escabechar
pick-me-up ['pɪkmiˌʌp] *s* (coll) tentempié *m;* (coll) trago fortificante
pick'pock'et *s* carterista *m,* ratero
pick'up' *s* recolección; (*of a motor*) recobro; (*of an automobile*) aceleración; (elec) pick-up, fonocaptor *m*
pic·nic ['pɪknɪk] *s* jira, partida de campo || *v* (*pret & pp* **-nicked;** *ger* **-nicking**) *intr* hacer una jira al campo, merendar en el campo
pictorial [pɪk'torɪ·əl] *adj* gráfico; ilustrado || *s* revista ilustrada
picture ['pɪktʃər] *s* cuadro; retrato; imagen *f;* lámina, grabado; fotografía; película; pintura || *tr* dibujar; pintar; describir; **to picture to oneself** representarse
picture gallery *s* galería de pinturas
picture post card *s* postal ilustrada
picture show *s* exhibición de pinturas; cine *m*
picture signal *s* videoseñal *f*
picturesque [ˌpɪktjə'rɛsk] *adj* pintoresco
picture tube *s* tubo de imagen, tubo de televisión
picture window *s* ventana panorámica
piddling ['pɪdlɪŋ] *adj* de poca monta, insignificante
pie [paɪ] *s* pastel *m;* (*bird*) picaza; (typ) pastel *m* || *v* (*pret & pp* **pied;** *ger* **pieing**) *tr* (typ) empastelar
piece [pis] *s* (*fragment; section of cloth*) pedazo; (*part of a machine; drama; single composition of music; coin; figure or block used in checkers, chess, etc.*) pieza; (*of land*) lote *m,* parcela; **a piece of advice** un consejo; **a piece of baggage** un bulto; **a piece of furniture** un mueble; **to break to pieces** despedazar, hacer pedazos; despedazarse; **to fall to pieces** desbaratarse, caer en ruina; **to give someone a piece of one's mind** decirle a uno su parecer con toda franqueza; **to go to pieces** desvencijarse; darse a la desesperación; ir al desastre (*un negocio*); sufrir un ataque de nervios; perder por completo la salud; **to pick someone to pieces** (coll) no dejarle a uno un hueso sano || *tr* formar juntando piezas; remendar || *intr* (coll) comer a deshora
piece'work' *s* destajo, trabajo a destajo
piece'work'er *s* destajero, destajista *mf*
pier [pɪr] *s* muelle *m;* (*of a bridge*) estribo, sostén *m;* (*of a harbor*) rompeolas *m;* (*wall between two openings*) (archit) entrepaño
pierce [pɪrs] *tr* agujerear, horadar, taladrar; atravesar, traspasar; picar, pinchar, punzar; (fig) traspasar (*de dolor*) || *intr* penetrar, entrar a la fuerza
piercing ['pɪrsɪŋ] *adj* agudo, penetrante, desgarrador; (*pain*) lancinante
pier glass *s* espejo de cuerpo entero
pie·ty ['paɪ·əti] *s* (*pl* **-ties**) piedad, devoción
piffle ['pɪfəl] *s* (coll) disparates *mpl,* música celestial
pig [pɪg] *s* cerdo; (*young hog*) lechón *m;* (*domestic hog*) puerco, cochino; carne *f* de puerco; (metal) lingote *m;* (*person who acts like a pig*) (coll) marrano, cochino
pigeon ['pɪdʒən] *s* paloma

pi'geon•hole' *s* hornilla, casilla de paloma; casilla || *tr* encasillar
pigeon house *s* palomar *m*
piggish ['pɪgɪʃ] *adj* glotón, voraz
pig'gy•back' *adv* a cuestas, en hombros
pig'-head'ed *adj* terco, cabezudo
pig iron *s* arrabio, hierro en lingotes
pigment ['pɪgmənt] *s* pigmento || *tr* pigmentar || *intr* pigmentarse
pig'pen' *s* pocilga; (fig) pocilga, corral *m* de vacas
pig'skin' *s* piel *f* de cerdo; (coll) balón *m* (*con que se juega al fútbol*)
pig'sty' *s* (*pl* **-sties**) pocilga
pig'tail' *s* coleta, trenza; (*of tobacco*) andullo
pike [paɪk] *s* pica; (*of an arrow*) punta; carretera; camino de barrera; (*fish*) lucio
piker ['paɪkər] *s* (slang) persona de poco fuste
Pilate ['paɪlət] *s* Pilatos *m*
pile [paɪl] *s* pila, montón *m;* (*stake*) pilote *m;* lanilla, pelusa; pira; (elec, phys) pila; (coll) caudal *m;* **piles** almorranas || *tr* apilar, amontonar || *intr* apilarse, amontonarse; **to pile in** o **into** entrar atropelladamente en; entrar todos en; subir todos a (*p.ej., un coche*)
pile driver *s* martinete *m*
pilfer ['pɪlfər] *tr & intr* ratear
pilgrim ['pɪlgrɪm] *s* peregrino, romero
pilgrimage ['pɪlgrɪmɪdʒ] *s* peregrinación, romería
pill [pɪl] *s* píldora; mal trago, sinsabor *m;* (coll) persona molesta
pillage ['pɪlɪdʒ] *s* pillaje *m,* saqueo || *tr & intr* pillar, saquear
pillar ['pɪlər] *s* pilar *m;* **from pillar to post** de acá para allá sin objeto determinado
pillo•ry ['pɪləri] *s* (*pl* **-ries**) picota || *v* (*pret & pp* **-ried**) *tr* empicotar; (fig) motejar, poner en ridículo
pillow ['pɪlo] *s* almohada
pil'low•case' o **pil'low•slip'** *s* funda de almohada
pilot ['paɪlət] *s* piloto; (*of a harbor*) práctico; (*of a gas range*) mechero encendedor; (rr) trompa, delantera || *tr* pilotar; conducir
pimp [pɪmp] *s* alcahuete *m*
pimple ['pɪmpəl] *s* barro, grano
pim•ply ['pɪmpli] *adj* (*comp* **-plier;** *super* **-pliest**) granujoso
pin [pɪn] *s* alfiler *m;* (*e.g., for a necktie*) prendedero; (*peg*) clavija; (*e.g., to hold scissors together*) clavillo, clavito; (bowling) bolo; **to be on pins and needles** estar en espinas || *v* (*pret & pp* **pinned;** *ger* **pinning**) *tr* alfilerar; clavar, fijar, sujetar; **to pin something on someone** (coll) acusarle a uno de una cosa; **to pin up** recoger y apuntar con alfileres; fijar en la pared con alfileres
pinafore ['pɪnəˌfor] *s* delantal *m* de niño
pin'ball' *s* billar romano, bagatela
pince-nez ['pænsˌne] *s* lentes *mpl* de nariz, lentes de pinzas
pincers ['pɪnsərz] *ssg* o *spl* pinzas
pinch [pɪntʃ] *s* pellizco; (*of hunger*) tormento; (slang) arresto; (slang) hurto, robo; **in a pinch** en un aprieto; en caso necesario || *tr* pellizcar; cogerse (*los dedos, p.ej., en una puerta*); apretar (*p.ej., el zapato a una persona*); contraer (*el frío la cara de uno*); limitar los gastos de; (slang) arrestar, prender; (slang) hurtar, robar || *intr* apretar; economizar, privarse de lo necesario
pinchers ['pɪntʃərz] *ssg* o *spl* var of **pincers**
pin'cush'ion *s* acerico
Pindar ['pɪndər] *s* Píndaro
pine [paɪn] *s* pino || *intr* languidecer; **to pine away** consumirse; **to pine for** penar por
pine'ap'ple *s* ananás *m,* piña
pine cone *s* piña
pine needle *s* pinocha
ping [pɪŋ] *s* silbido de bala || *intr* silbar (*una bala*); silbar como una bala
pin'head' *s* cabecilla de alfiler; cosa muy pequeña o insignificante; (coll) bobalicón *m*
pink [pɪŋk] *adj* rosado, sonrosado || *s* estado perfecto; comunistoide *mf;* (bot) clavel *m,* clavellina
pin money *s* alfileres *mpl*
pinnacle ['pɪnəkəl] *s* pináculo
pin'point' *adj* exacto, preciso || *s* punta de alfiler || *tr & intr* señalar con precisión
pin'prick' *s* alfilerazo
pinup girl ['pɪnˌʌp] *s* guapa
pin'wheel' *s* rueda de fuego, rueda giratoria de fuegos artificiales; (*child's toy*) rehilandera, ventolera
pioneer [ˌpaɪ·ə'nɪr] *s* pionero; (mil) zapador *m* || *intr* abrir nuevos caminos, explorar
pious ['paɪ·əs] *adj* pío, piadoso; mojigato; respetuoso
pip [pɪp] *s* (*seed*) pepita; (*on a card, dice, etc.*) punto; (vet) pepita
pipe [paɪp] *s* caño, conducto, tubo; (*to smoke tobacco*) pipa; (mus) pipa, caramillo, zampoña; (*of an organ*) cañón *m* || *tr* conducir por medio de tubos o cañerías; proveer de tuberías o cañerías || *intr* tocar el caramillo; **to pipe down** (slang) callarse
pipe cleaner *s* limpiapipas *m*
pipe dream *s* esperanza imposible, castillo en el aire
pipe line *s* cañería, tubería; oleoducto; fuente *f* de informes confidenciales
pipe organ *s* (mus) órgano
piper ['paɪpər] *s* flautista *m;* gaitero; **to pay the piper** pagar los vidrios rotos
pipe wrench *s* llave *f* para tubos
pippin ['pɪpɪn] *s* (*apple*) camuesa; (*tree*) camueso; (slang) real moza
piquancy ['pikənsi] *s* picante *m*
piquant ['pikənt] *adj* picante
pique [pik] *s* pique *m,* resentimiento || *tr* picar, enojar; despertar, excitar
Piraeus [paɪ'ri·əs] *s* el Pireo
pirate ['paɪrɪt] *s* pirata *m* || *tr* pillar,

robar; publicar fraudulentamente || *intr* piratear
pirouette [ˌpɪru'ɛt] *s* pirueta || *intr* piruetear
pistol ['pɪstəl] *s* pistola
piston ['pɪstən] *s* (mach) émbolo, pistón *m;* (mus) pistón *m*
piston displacement *s* cilindrada
piston ring *s* anillo de émbolo, aro de émbolo, segmento de émbolo
piston rod *s* vástago de émbolo
piston stroke *s* carrera de émbolo
pit [pɪt] *s* hoyo; (*in the skin*) cacaraña; (*of certain fruit*) hueso; (*for cockfights, etc.*) cancha, reñidero; (*of the stomach*) boca; abismo, infierno; (min) pozo; (theat) foso || *v* (*pret & pp* **pitted;** *ger* **pitting**) *tr* marcar con hoyos; dejar hoyoso (*el rostro*); deshuesar (*p.ej., una ciruela*)
pitch [pɪtʃ] *s* (*black sticky substance*) pez *f;* echada, lanzamiento; cosa lanzada; pelota lanzada; (*of a boat*) arfada, cabezada; (*of a roof*) pendiente *f;* (*of, e.g., a screw*) paso; (*of a winding*) (elec) paso; (mus) tono, altura; (fig) grado, extremo; (coll) bombo, elogio || *tr* echar, lanzar; elevar (*el heno*) con la horquilla; armar o plantar (*una tienda de campaña*); embrear; (mus) graduar el tono de || *intr* caerse, caer de cabeza; bajar en declive, inclinarse; arfar, cabecear (*un buque*); **to pitch in** (coll) poner manos a la obra; (coll) comenzar a comer
pitch accent *s* acento de altura
pitcher ['pɪtʃər] *s* jarro; (*in baseball*) lanzador *m*
pitch'fork' *s* horca, horquilla; **to rain pitchforks** (coll) llover a cántaros
pitch pipe *s* (mus) diapasón *m*
pit'fall' *s* callejo, trampa; (*danger for the unwary*) escollo, atascadero
pith [pɪθ] *s* médula; (*essential part*) (fig) médula; (fig) fuerza, vigor *m*
pith·y ['pɪθi] *adj* (*comp* **-ier;** *super* **-iest**) medular; enérgico, expresivo
pitiful ['pɪtɪfəl] *adj* lastimoso; compasivo; despreciable
pitiless ['pɪtɪlɪs] *adj* despiadado, empedernido, incompasivo
pit·y ['pɪti] *s* (*pl* **-ies**) piedad, compasión, lástima; **for pity's sake!** ¡por piedad!; **to have** o **to take pity on** tener piedad de, apiadarse de; **what a pity!** ¡qué lástima!, ¡qué pena! || *v* (*pret & pp* **-ied**) *tr* apiadarse de, compadecer
pivot ['pɪvət] *s* pivote *m,* gorrón *m,* eje *m* de rotación; (fig) eje *m* || *intr* pivotar; **to pivot on** girar sobre; depender de
placard ['plækɑrd] *s* cartel *m* || *tr* fijar carteles en; fijar (*un anuncio*) en sitio público; publicar por medio de carteles
place [ples] *s* sitio, lugar *m;* (*of business*) local *m;* (*job*) puesto; grado, rango; **in no place** en ninguna parte; **in place of** en lugar de; **out of place** fuera de su lugar; fuera de propósito; **to be looking for a place to live** buscar piso; **to take place** tener lugar || *tr* poner, colocar; acordarse bien de; dar empleo a; prestar (*dinero*) a interés || *intr* colocarse (*un caballo en las carreras*)
place·bo [plə'sibo] *s* (*pl* **-bos** o **-boes**) placebo
place card *s* tarjetita con el nombre (*que indica la colocación de uno en la mesa*)
placement ['plesmənt] *s* colocación
place name *s* nombre *m* de lugar, topónimo
placid ['plæsɪd] *adj* plácido, tranquilo
plagiarism ['pledʒəˌrɪzəm] *s* plagio
plagiarize ['pledʒəˌraɪz] *tr* plagiar
plague [pleg] *s* peste *f,* plaga; (*great public calamity*) plaga || *tr* apestar, plagar; atormentar, molestar
plaid [plæd] *s* (*cloth*) tartán *m;* cuadros a la escocesa
plain [plen] *adj* llano, claro, evidente; abierto, franco; ordinario; feo; humilde; solo, natural; **in plain English** sin rodeos; **in plain sight** o **view** en plena vista || *s* llano, llanura
plain clothes *spl* traje *m* de calle, traje de paisano
plainclothesman ['plen'kloðzˌmæn] *s* (*pl* **-men** [ˌmɛn]) policía *m* que lleva traje de paisano
plain omelet *s* tortilla a la francesa
plains·man ['plenzmən] *s* (*pl* **-men** [mən]) llanero
plaintiff ['plentɪf] *s* (law) demandante *mf*
plaintive ['plentɪv] *adj* quejumbroso
plan [plæn] *s* plan *m,* intento, proyecto; (*drawing, diagram*) plan *m,* plano; **to change one's plans** cambiar de proyecto || *v* (*pret & pp* **planned;** *ger* **planning**) *tr* planear, planificar; **to plan to** proponerse || *intr* hacer proyectos
plane [plen] *adj* plano || *s* (*surface*) plano; aeroplano, avión *m;* (*of an airplane*) plano; (carp) cepillo; (*tree*) plátano || *tr* cepillar || *intr* viajar en aeroplano
plane sickness *s* mareo del aire, mal *m* de vuelo
planet ['plænɪt] *s* planeta *m*
plane tree *s* plátano
planing mill ['plenɪŋ] *s* taller *m* de cepillado
plank [plæŋk] *s* tabla gruesa, tablón *m;* artículo de un programa político || *tr* entablar, entarimar
plant [plænt] o [plɑnt] *s* fábrica, taller *m;* (*of an automobile*) grupo motor; (*educational establishment*) plantel *m;* (bot) planta || *tr* plantar; sembrar (*semillas*); inculcar (*doctrinas*); (slang) ocultar (*géneros robados*)
plantation [plæn'teʃən] *s* plantación, campo de plantas; (*estate cultivated by workers living on it*) hacienda
planter ['plæntər] *s* plantador *m,* cultivador *m*
plaster ['plæstər] o ['plɑstər] *s* (*gypsum*) yeso; (*mixture of lime, sand,*

water, etc.) argamasa; (*coating*) enlucido; (*poultice*) emplasto || *tr* enyesar; argamasar; enlucir; emplastar; embadurnar; pegar (*anuncios*)
plas'ter•board' *s* cartón *m* de yeso y fieltro
plaster cast *s* (surg) vendaje enyesado; (sculp) yeso
plaster of Paris *s* estuco de París
plastic ['plæstɪk] *adj* plástico || *s* (*substance*) plástico; (*art of modeling*) plástica
plate [plet] *s* (*dish*) plato; (*sheet of metal, etc.*), chapa, placa; vajilla de oro, vajilla de plata; dentadura postiza, base *f* de la dentadura postiza; (baseball) puesto meta, puesto del batter; (anat, elec, electron, phot, zool) placa; (typ) clisé *m* || *tr* chapear, planchear; blindar; platear, dorar, niquelar (*por la galvanoplastia*); (typ) clisar
plateau [plæ'to] *s* meseta
plate glass *s* vidrio o cristal cilindrado
platen ['plætən] *s* rodillo
platform ['plæt,fɔrm] *s* plataforma *f;* (*of passenger station*) andén *m;* (*of freight station*) cargadero; (*of a speaker*) tribuna; (*political program*) plataforma
platform car *s* plataforma *f*
platinum ['plætɪnəm] *s* platino
platinum blonde *s* rubia platino
platitude ['plætɪ,tjud] o ['plætɪ,tud] *s* perogrullada, trivialidad
Plato ['pleto] *s* Platón *m*
platoon [plə'tun] *s* pelotón *m*
platter ['plætər] *s* fuente *f;* (slang) disco de fonógrafo
plausible ['plɔzɪbəl] *adj* aparente, especioso; bien hablado; (coll) creíble
play [ple] *s* juego; (*act or move in a game*) jugada; (*drama*) pieza; (*of water, colors, lights*) juego; (mach) huelgo, juego; **to give full play to** dar rienda suelta a || *tr* jugar (*p.ej., un naipe, una partida de juego*); jugar a (*p.ej., los naipes*); jugar con (*un contrario*); dar (*un chasco*); gastar (*una broma*); hacer (*una mala jugada*); dirigir (*agua, una manguera*); desempeñar (*un papel*); desempeñar el papel de; representar (*una obra dramática, un film*); apostar por (*un caballo*); tocar (*un instrumento, una pieza, un disco de fonógrafo*) || *intr* jugar; desempeñar un papel, representar; correr (*una fuente*); rielar (*la luz en la superficie del agua*); vagar (*p.ej., una sonrisa por los labios*); **to play out** rendirse; agotarse; acabarse; **to play safe** tomar sus precauciones; **to play sick** hacerse el enfermo; **to play up to** hacer la rueda a
play'back' *s* lectura; aparato de lectura
play'bill' *s* (*poster*) cartel *m;* (*of a play*) programa *m*
player piano ['ple•ər] *s* autopiano
playful ['plefəl] *adj* juguetón, retozón; dicho en broma
playgoer ['ple,go•ər] *s* aficionado al teatro
play'ground' *s* campo de juego; patio de recreo
play'house' *s* casita de muñecas; teatro
playing card ['ple•ɪŋ] *s* naipe *m*
playing field *s* campo de deportes
play'mate' *s* compañero de juego
play'-off' *s* partido de desempate
play'pen' *s* parque *m,* corral *m* (*para bebés*)
play'thing' *s* juguete *m*
play'time' *s* hora de recreo, hora de juego
playwright ['ple,raɪt] *s* dramaturgo, autor dramático
play'writ'ing *s* dramaturgia, dramática
plea [pli] *s* ruego, súplica; disculpa, excusa; (law) contestación a la demanda
plead [plid] *v* (*pret & pp* **pleaded** o **pled** [plɛd]) *tr* defender (*una causa*) || *intr* suplicar; abogar; **to plead guilty** confesarse culpable; **to plead not guilty** negar la acusación, declararse inocente
pleasant ['plɛzənt] *adj* agradable; simpático
pleasant•ry ['plɛzəntri] *s* (*pl* **-ries**) broma, chiste *m,* dicho gracioso
please [pliz] *tr & intr* gustar; **as you please** como Vd. quiera; **if you please** si me hace el favor; **please** + *inf* hágame Vd. el favor de + *inf;* **to be pleased to** alegrarse de, complacerse en; **to be pleased with** estar satisfecho de o con
pleasing ['plizɪŋ] *adj* agradable, grato
pleasure ['plɛʒər] *s* placer *m,* gusto; **what is your pleasure?** ¿en qué puedo servirle?, ¿qué es lo que Vd. desea?; **with pleasure** con mucho gusto
pleasure seeker ['sikər] *s* amigo de los placeres
pleat [plit] *s* pliegue *m,* plisado || *tr* plegar, plisar
plebeian [plɪ'bi•ən] *adj & s* plebeyo
pledge [plɛdʒ] *s* empeño, prenda; (*vow*) voto, promesa; (*toast*) brindis *m;* **as a pledge of** en prenda de; **to take the pledge** comprometerse a no tomar bebidas alcohólicas || *tr* empeñar, prendar; dar (*la palabra*); brindar por
plentiful ['plɛntɪfəl] *adj* abundante, copioso
plenty ['plɛnti] *adv* (coll) completamente || *s* abundancia, copia; suficiencia
pleurisy ['plʊrɪsi] *s* pleuresía
pliable ['plaɪ•əbəl] *adj* flexible, plegable; dócil
pliers ['plaɪ•ərz] *ssg* o *spl* alicates *mpl*
plight [plaɪt] *s* estado, situación; apuro, aprieto; compromiso solemne || *tr* dar o empeñar (*su palabra*); **to plight one's troth** prometer fidelidad; dar palabra de casamiento
plod [plɑd] *v* (*pret & pp* **plodded;** *ger* **plodding**) *tr* recorrer (*un camino*) pausada y pesadamente || *intr* caminar pausada y pesadamente; trabajar laboriosamente
plot [plɑt] *s* complot *m,* conspiración; (*of a play or novel*) argumento,

trama; parcela, solar *m;* cuadro de flores; cuadro de hortalizas; plano, mapa *m* || *v* (*pret & pp* **plotted;** *ger* **plotting**) *tr* fraguar, tramar, urdir, maquinar; dividir en parcelas o solares; trazar el plano de; trazar, tirar (*líneas*) || *intr* conspirar

plough [plaʊ] *s, tr & intr* var de **plow**

plover ['plʌvər] o ['plovər] *s* chorlito

plow [plaʊ] *s* arado; quitanieve *m* || *tr* arar; surcar; quitar o barrer (*la nieve*); **to plow back** reinvertir (*ganancias*) || *intr* arar; avanzar como un arado

plow•man ['plaʊmən] *s* (*pl* **-men** [mən]) arador *m,* yuguero

plow'share' *s* reja de arado

pluck [plʌk] *s* ánimo, coraje *m,* valor *m;* tirón *m* || *tr* arrancar; coger (*flores*); desplumar (*un ave*); puntear (*p.ej., una guitarra*) || *intr* dar un tirón; **to pluck up** recobrar ánimo

pluck•y ['plʌki] *adj* (*comp* **-ier;** *super* **-iest**) animoso, valiente

plug [plʌg] *s* taco, tarugo; boca de agua; tableta de tabaco; (*hat*) (slang) chistera; (elec) clavija, toma, ficha; (aut) bujía; (coll) rocín; (slang) elogio incidental || *v* (*pret & pp* **plugged;** *ger* **plugging**) *tr* atarugar; calar (*un melón*); **to plug in** (elec) enchufar || *intr* (coll) trabajar con ahinco

plum [plʌm] *s* (*tree*) ciruelo; (*fruit*) ciruela; (slang) turrón *m,* pingüe destino

plumage ['plumɪdʒ] *s* plumaje *m*

plumb [plʌm] *adj* vertical; (coll) completo || *adv* a plomo; (coll) verticalmente; (coll) directamente || *tr* aplomar; sondear

plumb bob *s* plomada

plumber ['plʌmər] *s* fontanero; (*worker in lead*) plomero

plumbing ['plʌmɪŋ] *s* instalación sanitaria; conjunto de cañerías; (*working in lead*) plomería; sondeo

plumbing fixtures *spl* artefactos sanitarios

plumb line *s* cuerda de plomada

plum cake *s* pastel aderezado con pasas de Corinto y ron

plume [plum] *s* (*of a bird*) pluma; (*tuft of feathers worn as ornament*) penacho || *tr* emplumar; componerse (*las plumas*); **to plume oneself on** enorgullecerse de

plummet ['plʌmɪt] *s* plomada || *intr* caer a plomo, precipitarse

plump [plʌmp] *adj* rechoncho, regordete; brusco, franco || *adv* de golpe; francamente || *s* (coll) caída pesada; (coll) ruido sordo || *intr* caer a plomo

plum pudding *s* pudín *m* inglés con pasas de Corinto, corteza de limón, huevos y ron

plum tree *s* ciruelo

plunder ['plʌndər] *s* pillaje *m;* botín *m* || *tr* pillar, saquear

plunge [plʌndʒ] *s* zambullida; caída a plomo; sacudida violenta; salto; baño de agua fría; (*of a boat*) cabeceo || *tr* zambullir; sumergir; hundir (*p.ej., un puñal*) || *intr* zambullirse; sumergirse; hundirse (*p.ej., en la tristeza*); caer a plomo; arrojarse, precipitarse; cabecear (*un buque*); (slang) entregarse al juego, entregarse a las especulaciones

plunger ['plʌndʒər] *s* zambullidor *m;* émbolo buzo; (*of a tire valve*) obús *m;* (slang) jugador o especulador desenfrenado

plunk [plʌŋk] *adv* (coll) con un golpe seco, con un ruido de golpe seco || *tr* (coll) arrojar, empujar o dejar caer pesadamente || *intr* sonar o caer con un ruido de golpe seco

plural ['plʊrəl] *adj & s* plural *m*

plus [plʌs] *adj* más; y pico; **to be plus** (coll) tener por añadidura || *prep* más || *s* (*sign*) más *m;* añadidura

plush [plʌʃ] *adj* afelpado; (coll) lujoso, suntuoso || *s* felpa

Plutarch ['plutɑrk] *s* Plutarco

plutonium [plu'tonɪ•əm] *s* plutonio

ply [plaɪ] *s* (*pl* **plies**) (*e.g., of a cloth*) capa, doblez *m;* (*of a cable*) cordón *m* || *v* (*pret & pp* **plied**) *tr* manejar (*la aguja, etc.*); ejercer (*un oficio*); batir (*el agua con los remos*); importunar; navegar por (*p.ej., un río*) || *intr* avanzar; **to ply between** hacer (*un barco*) el servicio entre

ply'wood' *s* chapeado, madera laminada

P.M. *abbr* **Postmaster, post meridiem** (Lat) **afternoon**

pneumatic [nju'mætɪk] o [nu'mætɪk] *adj* neumático

pneumatic drill *s* perforadora de aire comprimido

pneumonia [nju'monɪ•ə] o [nu'monɪ•ə] *s* neumonía o pulmonía

P.O. *abbr* **post office**

poach [potʃ] *tr* escalfar (*huevos*) || *intr* cazar o pescar en vedado

poacher ['potʃər] *s* cazador furtivo, pescador furtivo

pock [pɑk] *s* cacaraña, hoyuelo

pocket ['pɑkɪt] *s* bolsillo, faltriquera; (*in billiards*) tronera; (aer) bolsa de aire; (mil) bolsón *m* || *tr* embolsar; entronerar (*una bola de billar*); tragarse (*injurias*)

pock'et•book' *s* portamonedas *m;* (*of a woman*) bolsa

pocket handkerchief *s* pañuelo de bolsillo o de mano

pock'et•knife' *s* (*pl* **-knives**) navaja, cortaplumas *m*

pocket money *s* alfileres *mpl,* dinero de bolsillo

pock'mark' *s* cacaraña, hoyuelo

pod [pɑd] *s* vaina

poem ['po•ɪm] *s* poema *m,* poesía

poet ['po•ɪt] *s* poeta *m*

poetess ['po•ɪtɪs] *s* poetisa

poetic [po'ɛtɪk] *adj* poético || **poetics** *ssg* poética

poetry ['po•ɪtri] *s* poesía

pogrom ['pogrəm] *s* levantamiento contra los judíos

poignancy ['pɔɪnənsi] *s* picante *m,* viveza, intensidad

poignant ['pɔɪnənt] *adj* picante, vivo, intenso
point [pɔɪnt] *s* (*of a sword, pencil; of land*) punta; (*of pen*) pico; (*of fountain pen*) puntilla; (*mark of imperceptible dimensions*) punto; (*of a joke*) gracia; (elec) punta; (math, typ, sport, fig) punto; (coll) indirecta, insinuación; **beside the point** fuera de propósito; **on the point of** a punto de; **to carry one's point** salirse con la suya; **to come to the point** venir al caso o al grano; **to get the point** caer en la cuenta || *tr* aguzar, sacar punta a; apuntar (*p.ej., un arma de fuego*); resanar (*una pared*); **to point one's finger at** señalar con el dedo; **to point out** señalar, indicar, hacer notar || *intr* apuntar; pararse (*el perro de muestra*); **to point at** señalar con el dedo
point'blank' *adj & adv* a quemarropa
pointed ['pɔɪntɪd] *adj* puntiagudo; picante; acentuado, directo
pointer ['pɔɪntər] *s* puntero; indicador *m;* (*of a clock*) manecilla; perro de muestra; (mas) fijador *m;* (coll) indicación, dirección
poise [pɔɪz] *s* aplomo, equilibrio || *tr* equilibrar; considerar || *intr* equilibrarse; estar suspendido
poison ['pɔɪzən] *s* veneno, ponzoña || *tr* envenenar
poison ivy *s* tosiguero
poisonous ['pɔɪzənəs] *adj* venenoso
poke [pok] *s* (*push*) empuje *m,* empujón *m;* (*thrust*) hurgonazo; (*with elbow*) codazo; (*slow person*) tardón *m* || *tr* empujar; hacer (*un agujero*) a empujones; abrirse (*paso*) a empujones; atizar, hurgar (*el fuego*); **to poke fun at** burlarse de; **to poke one's nose into** entremeterse en || *intr* fisgar, husmear; andar perezosamente
poker ['pokər] *s* hurgón *m;* (*card game*) póker *m,* pócar *m*
poker face *s* (coll) cara de jugador de póker; **to keep a poker face** (coll) disfrazar la expresión del rostro, mantener una expresión imperturbable
pok•y ['poki] *adj* (*comp* **-ier;** *super* **-iest**) (coll) tardo, roncero
Poland ['polənd] *s* Polonia
polar bear ['polər] *s* oso blanco
polarize ['polə,raɪz] *tr* polarizar
pole [pol] *s* (*long rod or staff*) pértiga; (*of a flag*) asta; (*upright support*) poste *m;* (*to push a boat*) botador *m;* (astr, biol, elec, geog, math) polo || *tr* impeler (*un barco*) con botador || **Pole** *s* polaco
pole'cat' *s* turón *m,* veso
pole'star' *s* estrella polar; (*guide*) norte *m;* (*center of interest*) miradero
pole vault *s* salto con garrocha o con pértiga
police [pə'lis] *s* policía || *tr* poner o mantener servicio de policía en; (mil) limpiar
police•man [pə'lismən] *s* (*pl* **-men** [mən]) policía *m,* guardia urbano
police state *s* estado-policía *m*
police station *s* cuartel *m* o estación de policía
poli•cy ['palɪsi] *s* (*pl* **-cies**) política; (ins) póliza
polio ['polɪ,o] *s* (coll) polio *f*
polish ['palɪʃ] *s* pulimento; cera de lustrar; (*for shoes*) bola, betún *m,* lustre *m;* elegancia; cultura, urbanidad || *tr* pulimentar, pulir; embolar, dar betún a (*los zapatos*); **to polish off** (coll) terminar de prisa; (slang) engullir (*la comida, un trago*) || **Polish** ['polɪʃ] *adj & s* polaco
polisher ['palɪʃər] *s* pulidor *m;* (*machine*) pulidora; (*for floors, tables, etc.*) enceradora
polite [pə'laɪt] *adj* cortés, fino, urbano; culto
politeness [pə'laɪtnɪs] *s* cortesía, fineza, urbanidad; cultura
politic ['palɪtɪk] *adj* prudente, sagaz; astuto; juicioso
political [pə'lɪtɪkəl] *adj* político
politician [,palɪ'tɪʃən] *s* político; (*politician seeking personal or partisan gain*) politiquero
politics ['palɪtɪks] *ssg* o *spl* política
poll [pol] *s* (*questionnaire to determine opinion*) encuesta; votación; lista electoral; cabeza; **polls** urnas electorales; **to go to the polls** acudir a las urnas; **to take a poll** hacer una encuesta || *tr* dar (*un voto*); recibir (*votos*)
pollen ['palən] *s* polen *m*
pollinate ['palɪ,net] *tr* polinizar
polling booth ['polɪŋ] *s* cabina o caseta de votar
polliwog ['palɪ,wag] *s* renacuajo; (slang) persona que atraviesa el ecuador en un barco por primera vez
poll tax *s* capitación, impuesto por cabeza
pollute [pə'lut] *tr* contaminar, corromper, ensuciar
pollution [pə'luʃən] *s* contaminación
polo ['polo] *s* polo
polo player *s* polista *mf,* jugador *m* de polo
polygamist [pə'lɪgəmɪst] *s* polígamo
polygamous [pə'lɪgəməs] *adj* polígamo
polyglot ['palɪ,glat] *adj & s* poligloto
polygon ['palɪ,gan] *s* polígono
Polyhymnia [,palɪ'hɪmnɪ·ə] *s* Polimnia
polynomial [,palɪ'nomɪ·əl] *s* polinomio
polyp ['palɪp] *s* pólipo
polytheist ['palɪ,θi·ɪst] *s* politeísta *mf*
polytheistic [,palɪθi'ɪstɪk] *adj* politeísta
pomade [pə'med] o [pə'mad] *s* pomada
pomegranate ['pam,grænɪt] *s* (*shrub*) granado; (*fruit*) granada
pom•mel ['pʌməl] o ['paməl] *s* (*on hilt of sword*) pomo; (*on saddle*) perilla || *v* (*pret & pp* **-meled** o

-melled; *ger* **-meling** o **-melling)** *tr* apuñear, aporrear
pomp [pɑmp] *s* pompa, fausto
pompadour [ˈpɑmpəˌdor] o [ˈpɑmpəˌdur] *s* copete *m*
pompous [ˈpɑmpəs] *adj* pomposo, faustoso
pon•cho [ˈpɑntʃo] *s* (*pl* **-chos**) capote *m* de monte, poncho
pond [pɑnd] *s* estanque *m*, charca
ponder [ˈpɑndər] *tr* ponderar || *intr* meditar; **to ponder over** ponderar, considerar con cuidado
ponderous [ˈpɑndərəs] *adj* pesado, inmanejable; tedioso, fastidioso
pond scum *s* lama, verdín *m*
poniard [ˈpɑnjərd] *s* puñal *m*
pontiff [ˈpɑntɪf] *s* pontífice *m*
pontoon [pɑnˈtun] *s* pontón *m*
po•ny [ˈponi] *s* (*pl* **-nies**) jaca, caballito; (*for drinking liquor*) (coll) pequeño vaso; (*translation used dishonestly in school*) (coll) chuleta
poodle [ˈpudəl] *s* perro de lanas
pool [pul] *s* (*small puddle*) charco; (*for swimming*) piscina; (*game*) trucos; (*in certain games*) polla, puesta; combinación de intereses; caudales unidos para un fin || *tr* mancomunar
pool'room' *s* sala de trucos
pool table *s* mesa de trucos
poop [pup] *s* popa; (*deck*) toldilla
poor [pur] *adj* (*having few possessions; arousing pity*) pobre; (*not good, inferior*) malo
poor box *s* cepillo, caja de limosnas
poor'house' *s* asilo de pobres, casa de caridad
poorly [ˈpurli] *adv* mal
poor white *s* pobre *mf* de la raza blanca (*en el sur de los EE.UU.*)
pop. *abbr* **popular, population**
pop [pɑp] *s* estallido, taponazo; bebida gaseosa || *v* (*pret & pp* **popped;** *ger* **popping**) *tr* hacer estallar; **to pop the question** (coll) hacer una declaración de amor || *intr* estallar
pop'corn' *s* rosetas, palomitas (de maíz)
pope [pop] *s* papa *m*
popeyed [ˈpɑpˌaɪd] *adj* de ojos saltones; (*with fear, surprise, etc.*) desorbitado
pop'gun' *s* tirabala
poplar [ˈpɑplər] *s* álamo, chopo
pop•py [ˈpɑpi] *s* (*pl* **-pies**) amapola
pop'py•cock' *s* (coll) necedad, tontería
popsicle [ˈpɑpsɪkəl] *s* polo
populace [ˈpɑpjəlɪs] *s* populacho
popular [ˈpɑpjələr] *adj* popular
popularize [ˈpɑpjələˌraɪz] *tr* popularizar, vulgarizar
populous [ˈpɑpjələs] *adj* populoso
porcelain [ˈpɔrsəlɪn] o [ˈpɔrslɪn] *s* porcelana
porch [portʃ] *s* porche *m*, pórtico
porcupine [ˈpɔrkjəˌpaɪn] *s* puerco espín
pore [por] *s* poro || *intr* — **to pore over** estudiar larga y detenidamente
pork [pork] *s* carne *f* de cerdo
pork chop *s* chuleta de cerdo
porous [ˈporəs] *adj* poroso
porous plaster *s* parche poroso
porphy•ry [ˈpɔrfɪri] *s* (*pl* **-ries**) pórfido
porpoise [ˈpɔrpəs] *s* marsopa, puerco de mar; (*dolphin*) delfín *m*
porridge [ˈpɑrɪdʒ] o [ˈpɔrɪdʒ] *s* gachas
port [port] *adj* portuario || *s* puerto; (*opening in ship's side*) portilla; (*left side of ship or airplane*) babor *m;* oporto, vino de Oporto; (mach) lumbrera
portable [ˈportəbəl] *adj* portátil
portal [ˈportəl] *s* portal *m*
portend [porˈtɛnd] *tr* anunciar de antemano, presagiar
portent [ˈportɛnt] *s* augurio, presagio
portentous [porˈtɛntəs] *adj* portentoso, extraordinario; amenazante, ominoso
porter [ˈportər] *s* (*doorkeeper*) portero, conserje *m;* (*in hotels and trains*) mozo de servicio; pórter *m* (*cerveza de Inglaterra de color obscuro*)
portfoli•o [portˈfolɪˌo] *s* (*pl* **-os**) cartera
port'hole' *s* porta, portilla
porti•co [ˈportɪˌko] *s* (*pl* **-coes** o **-cos**) pórtico
portion [ˈporʃən] *s* porción; (*dowry*) dote *m & f*
port•ly [ˈportli] *adj* (*comp* **-lier;** *super* **-liest**) corpulento; grave, majestuoso
port of call *s* escala
portrait [ˈportret] o [ˈportrɪt] *s* retrato; **to sit for a portrait** retratarse
portray [porˈtre] *tr* retratar
portrayal [porˈtre·əl] *s* representación gráfica; retrato, descripción acertada
Portugal [ˈportʃəgəl] *s* Portugal *m*
Portu•guese [ˈportʃəˌgiz] *adj* portugués || *s* (*pl* **-guese**) portugués *m*
port wine *s* vino de Oporto
pose [poz] *s* pose *f* || *tr* plantear (*una pregunta, cuestión, etc.*) || *intr* posar (*para retratarse; como modelo*); tomar una postura afectada; **to pose as** hacerse pasar por
posh [pɑʃ] *adj* (slang) elegante; (slang) lujoso, suntuoso
position [pəˈzɪʃən] *s* posición; empleo, puesto; opinión; **to be in a position to** estar en condiciones de
positive [ˈpɑzɪtɪv] *adj* positivo || *s* positiva
possess [pəˈzɛs] *tr* poseer
possession [pəˈzɛʃən] *s* posesión
possible [ˈpɑsɪbəl] *adj* posible
possum [ˈpɑsəm] *s* zarigüeya; **to play possum** hacer la mortecina
post [post] *s* (*piece of wood, metal, etc. set upright*) poste *m;* (*position*) puesto; (*job*) puesto, cargo; casa de correos || *tr* fijar (*carteles*); echar al correo; apostar, situar; tener al corriente; **post no bills** se prohibe fijar carteles
postage [ˈpostɪdʒ] *s* porte *m*, franqueo; **postage will be paid by addressee** a franquear en destino
postage meter *s* franqueadora
postage stamp *s* sello de correo; estampilla, timbre *m* (Am)

postal ['postəl] *adj* postal || *s* postal *f*
postal card *s* tarjeta postal
postal permit *s* franqueo concertado
postal savings bank *s* caja postal de ahorros
post card *s* tarjeta postal
post'date' *s* posfecha || **post'date'** *tr* posfechar
poster ['postər] *s* cartel *m,* cartelón *m,* letrero
posterity [pɑs'tɛrɪti] *s* posteridad
postern ['postərn] *s* postigo, portillo
post'haste' *adv* por la posta, a toda prisa
posthumous ['pɑstʃuməs] *adj* póstumo
post•man ['postmən] *s* (*pl* **-men** [mən]) cartero
post'mark' *s* matasellos *m,* timbre *m* de correos || *tr* matasellar, timbrar
post'mas'ter *s* administrador *m* de correos
post-mortem [,post'mɔrtəm] *adj* posterior a la muerte || *s* examen *m* de un cadáver
post office *s* casa de correos
post'-of'fice box *s* apartado de correos, casilla postal
postpaid ['post,ped] *adj* con porte pagado, franco de porte
postpone [post'pon] *tr* aplazar
postscript ['post,skrɪpt] *s* posdata
posttonic [post'tɑnɪk] *adj* postónico
posture ['pɑstʃər] *s* postura || *intr* adoptar una postura
post'war' *adj* de la posguerra
po•sy ['pozi] *s* (*pl* **-sies**) flor *f,* ramillete *m*
pot [pɑt] *s* pote *m;* (*for flowers*) tiesto; (*for the kitchen*) caldera, olla, puchero; vaso de noche, orinal *m;* (*in gambling*) puesta; (slang) mariguana
potash ['pɑt,æʃ] *s* potasa
potassium [pə'tæsɪ•əm] *s* potasio
pota•to [pə'teto] *s* (*pl* **-toes**) patata, papa; (*sweet potato*) batata, buniato
potato omelet *s* tortilla a la española
potbellied ['pɑt,bɛlid] *adj* barrigón, panzudo
poten•cy ['potənsi] *s* (*pl* **-cies**) potencia
potent ['potənt] *adj* potente
potentate ['potən,tet] *s* potentado
potential [pə'tɛnʃəl] *adj* & *s* potencial *m*
pot'hang'er *s* llares *fpl*
pot'hook' *s* garabato
potion ['poʃən] *s* poción
pot'luck' *s* lo que hay de comer; **to take potluck** hacer penitencia
pot shot *s* tiro a corta distancia
potter ['pɑtər] *s* alfarero || *intr* ocuparse en fruslerías
potter's clay *s* arcilla figulina
potter's field *s* cementerio de los pobres, hoyanca
potter's wheel *s* torno de alfarero
potter•y ['pɑtəri] *s* (*pl* **-ies**) alfarería; cacharros (de alfarería)
pouch [pautʃ] *s* bolsa, saquillo; (*of kangaroo*) bolsa; (*for tobacco*) petaca; valija
poulterer ['poltərər] *s* pollero
poultice ['poltɪs] *s* cataplasma *f*
poultry ['poltri] *s* aves *fpl* de corral
pounce [pauns] *intr* — **to pounce on** saltar sobre, precipitarse sobre
pound [paund] *s* (*weight*) libra; (*for stray animals*) corral *m* de concejo || *tr* golpear; machacar, moler; encerrar en el corral de concejo; bombardear incesantemente; (*to keep walking over*) desempedrar || *intr* golpear
pound'cake' *s* pastel *m* en que entra una libra de cada ingrediente; ponqué *m* (Am)
pound sterling *s* libra esterlina
pour [por] *tr* vaciar, verter, derramar; echar, servir (*p.ej., té*); escanciar (*vino*) || *intr* fluir rápidamente; llover a torrentes; **to pour out of** salir a montones de (*p.ej., el teatro*)
pout [paut] *s* mala cara, puchero || *intr* poner mala cara, hacer pucheros
poverty ['pɑvərti] *s* pobreza
POW *abbr* **prisoner of war**
powder ['paudər] *s* polvo; (*for face*) polvos; (*explosive*) pólvora || *tr* pulverizar; (*to sprinkle with powder*) empolvar, polvorear
powder puff *s* borla para empolvarse
powder room *s* cuarto tocador, cuarto de aseo
powdery ['paudəri] *adj* (*like powder*) polvoriento; (*sprinkled with powder*) empolvado; (*crumbly*) quebradizo
power ['pau•ər] *s* (*ability to act or do something; possession*) poder *m;* (*control, influence; wealth*) poderío; (*influential nation; energy, force, strength*) potencia; **the powers that be** las autoridades, los que mandan || *tr* accionar, impulsar
power dive *s* (aer) picado con motor
powerful ['pau•ərfəl] *adj* poderoso
pow'er•house' *s* central eléctrica
powerless ['pau•ərlɪs] *adj* impotente
power line *s* (elec) sector *m* de distribución
power mower *s* motosegadora
power of attorney *s* poder *m*
power plant *s* (aer) grupo motopropulsor; (aut) grupo motor; (elec) central eléctrica, estación generadora
power steering *s* (aut) servodirección
power tool *s* herramienta motriz
pp. *abbr* **pages**
p.p. *abbr* **parcel post, postpaid**
pr. *abbr* **pair, present, price**
practical ['præktɪkəl] *adj* práctico
practically ['præktɪkəli] *adv* poco más o menos
practice ['præktɪs] *s* práctica; uso, costumbre; ensayo; (*of a profession*) ejercicio; (*of a doctor*) clientela || *tr* practicar; ejercitar (*p.ej., la caridad*); ejercer (*una profesión*); estudiar (*p.ej., el piano*); tener por costumbre || *intr* ejercitarse; practicar la medicina; ensayarse; entrenarse, adiestrarse; **to practice as** ejercer de (*p.ej., abogado*)
practitioner [præk'tɪʃənər] *s* (*medical doctor*) práctico
Prague [prɑg] o [preg] *s* Praga

prairie ['prɛri] *s* pradera, llanura, pampa
prairie dog *s* ardilla ladradora
prairie wolf *s* coyote *m*
praise [prez] *s* alabanza, elogio || *tr* alabar, elogiar
praise'wor'thy *adj* laudable, plausible
pram [præm] *s* cochecillo de niño
prance [præns] o [prɑns] *s* cabriola, trenzado || *intr* cabriolar, trenzar
prank [præŋk] *s* travesura
prate [pret] *intr* charlar, parlotear
prattle ['prætəl] *s* charla, parloteo || *intr* charlar, parlotear; balbucear (*un niño*)
pray [pre] *tr* implorar, rogar, suplicar; rezar (*una oración*) || *intr* orar, rezar; **pray tell me** sírvase decirme
prayer [prɛr] *s* ruego, súplica; oración, rezo
prayer book *s* devocionario
preach [pritʃ] *tr* predicar; aconsejar (*p.ej., la paciencia*) || *intr* predicar
preacher ['pritʃər] *s* predicador *m*
preamble ['pri,æmbəl] *s* preámbulo
prebend ['prɛbənd] *s* prebenda
precarious [prɪ'kɛrɪ·əs] *adj* precario
precaution [prɪ'kɔʃən] *s* precaución
precede [prɪ'sid] *tr & intr* preceder
precedent ['prɛsɪdənt] *s* precedente *m*
precept ['prisɛpt] *s* precepto
precinct ['prisɪŋkt] *s* barriada; distrito electoral
precious ['prɛʃəs] *adj* precioso; caro, amado; (coll) considerable || *adv* (coll) muy, p.ej., **precious little** muy poco
precipice ['prɛsɪpɪs] *s* precipicio
precipitate [prɪ'sɪpɪ,tet] *adj & s* precipitado || *tr* precipitar || *intr* precipitarse
precipitous [prɪ'sɪpɪtəs] *adj* empinado, escarpado; (*hurried, reckless*) precipitoso
precise [prɪ'saɪs] *adj* preciso; meticuloso
precision [prɪ'sɪʒən] *s* precisión
preclude [prɪ'klud] *tr* excluir, imposibilitar
precocious [prɪ'koʃəs] *adj* precoz
predatory ['prɛdə,tori] *adj* predatorio
predicament [prɪ'dɪkəmənt] *s* apuro, situación difícil
predict [prɪ'dɪkt] *tr* predecir
prediction [prɪ'dɪkʃən] *s* predicción
predispose [,pridɪs'poz] *tr* predisponer
predominant [prɪ'dɑmɪnənt] *adj* predominante
preëminent [prɪ'ɛmɪnənt] *adj* preeminente
preëmpt [prɪ'ɛmpt] *tr* apropiarse o apropiarse de
preen [prin] *tr* arreglarse (*las plumas*) con el pico; **to preen oneself** componerse, vestirse cuidadosamente
pref. *abbr* **preface, preferred, prefix**
prefabricate [pri'fæbrɪ,ket] *tr* prefabricar
preface ['prɛfɪs] *s* prefacio, advertencia || *tr* introducir, empezar
pre•fer [prɪ'fʌr] *v* (*pret & pp* **-ferred;** *ger* **-ferring**) *tr* preferir; presentar; promover
preferable ['prɛfərəbəl] *adj* preferible
preference ['prɛfərəns] *s* preferencia
prefix ['prifɪks] *s* prefijo || *tr* prefijar
pregnan•cy ['prɛgnənsi] *s* (*pl* **-cies**) preñez *f*, embarazo
pregnant ['prɛgnənt] *adj* preñado
prejudice ['prɛdʒədɪs] *s* prejuicio; (*detriment*) perjuicio; **to the prejudice of** con perjuicio de; **without prejudice** (law) sin detrimento de sus propios derechos || *tr* predisponer, prevenir; (*to harm*) perjudicar
prejudicial [,prɛdʒə'dɪʃəl] *adj* perjudicial
prelate ['prɛlɪt] *s* prelado
pre-Lenten [pri'lɛntən] *adj* carnavalesco
preliminar•y [prɪ'lɪmɪ,nɛri] *adj* preliminar || *s* (*pl* **-ies**) preliminar *m*
prelude ['prɛljud] o ['prilud] *s* preludio || *tr* preludiar
premeditate [pri'mɛdɪ,tet] *tr* premeditar
premier [prɪ'mɪr] o ['primɪ·ər] *s* primer ministro, presidente *m* del consejo
première [prə'mjɛr] o [prɪ'mɪr] *s* estreno; actriz *f* principal
premise ['prɛmɪs] *s* premisa; **on the premises** en el local mismo; **premises** predio, local *m*
premium ['primɪ·əm] *s* premio; (ins) prima
premonition [,primə'nɪʃən] *s* presagio; presentimiento
preoccupancy [pri'ɑkjəpənsi] *s* preocupación
preoccupation [pri,ɑkjə'peʃən] *s* preocupación
preoccu•py [pri'ɑkjə,paɪ] *v* (*pret & pp* **-pied**) *tr* preocupar
prepaid [pri'ped] *adj* pagado por adelantado; con porte pagado
preparation [,prɛpə'reʃən] *s* preparación; (*e.g., for a trip*) preparativo; (pharm) preparado
preparatory [prɪ'pærə,torɪ] *adj* preparativo, preparatorio
prepare [prɪ'pɛr] *tr* preparar || *intr* prepararse
preparedness [prɪ'pɛrɪdnɪs] o [prɪ'pɛrdnɪs] *s* preparación; preparación militar
pre•pay [pri'pe] *v* (*pret & pp* **-paid**) *tr* pagar por adelantado
preponderant [prɪ'pɑndərənt] *adj* preponderante
preposition [,prɛpə'zɪʃən] *s* preposición
prepossessing [,pripə'zɛsɪŋ] *adj* atractivo, simpático
preposterous [prɪ'pɑstərəs] *adj* absurdo, ridículo
prep school [prɛp] *s* (coll) escuela preparatoria
prerecorded [,prirɪ'kɔrdɪd] *adj* (rad & telv) grabado de antemano
prerequisite [pri'rɛkwɪzɪt] *s* requisito previo
prerogative [prɪ'rɑgətɪv] *s* prerrogativa
Pres. *abbr* **Presbyterian, President**

presage ['prɛsɪdʒ] *s* presagio || [prɪ'sedʒ] *tr* presagiar
Presbyterian [,prɛzbɪ'tɪrɪ·ən] *adj & s* presbiteriano
prescribe [prɪ'skraɪb] *tr & intr* prescribir
prescription [prɪ'skrɪpʃən] *s* prescripción; (pharm) receta
presence ['prɛzəns] *s* presencia
present ['prɛzənt] *adj* presente || *s* presente *m,* regalo || [prɪ'zɛnt] *tr* presentar, obsequiar
presentable [prɪ'zɛntəbəl] *adj* bien apersonado
presentation [,prɛzən'teʃən] o [,prizən'teʃən] *s* presentación
presentation copy *s* ejemplar *m* de cortesía con dedicatoria del autor
presentiment [prɪ'zɛntɪmənt] *s* presentimiento
presently ['prɛzəntli] *adv* luego, dentro de poco
preserve [prɪ'zʌrv] *s* conserva, compota; (*for game*) vedado || *tr* conservar; preservar, proteger
preserved fruit *s* dulce *m* de almíbar
preside [prɪ'zaɪd] *intr* presidir; **to preside over** presidir
presiden·cy ['prɛzɪdənsi] *s* (*pl* **-cies**) presidencia
president ['prɛzɪdənt] *s* presidente *m;* (*of a university*) rector *m*
press [prɛs] *s* apretón *m,* empujón *m;* (*e.g., of business*) urgencia; muchedumbre; (*machine for printing, for making wine; newspapers and newspapermen*) prensa; (*printing*) imprenta; (*closet*) armario; **to go to press** entrar en prensa || *tr* apretar (*p.ej., un botón*); (*in a press*) prensar; planchar (*la ropa*); imprimir (*discos de fonógrafo*); oprimir (*una tecla*); apresurar; abrumar; apremiar, instar; insistir en
press agent *s* agente *m* de publicidad
press conference *s* conferencia de prensa
pressing ['prɛsɪŋ] *adj* apremiante, urgente || *s* planchado
press release *s* comunicado de prensa
pressure ['prɛʃər] *s* presión; premura, urgencia
pressure cooker ['kʊkər] *s* olla de presión, cocina de presión
prestige [prɛs'tiʒ] o ['prɛstɪdʒ] *s* prestigio
presumably [prɪ'zuməbli] o [prɪ'zjuməbli] *adv* probablemente, verosímilmente
presume [prɪ'zum] o [prɪ'zjum] *tr* presumir; suponer; **to presume to** tomar la libertad de || *intr* suponer; **to presume on** o **upon** abusar de
presumption [prɪ'zʌmpʃən] *s* presunción; pretensión
presumptuous [prɪ'zʌmptʃʊ·əs] *adj* confianzudo, desenvuelto
presuppose [,prisə'poz] *tr* presuponer
pretend [prɪ'tɛnd] *tr* aparentar, fingir || *intr* fingir; **to pretend to** pretender (*p.ej., el trono*)
pretender [prɪ'tɛndər] *s* pretendiente *mf*
pretense [prɪ'tɛns] o ['pritɛns] *s* pretensión; fingimiento; **under false pretenses** con apariencias fingidas; **under pretense of** so pretexto de
pretentious [prɪ'tɛnʃəs] *adj* pretencioso, aparatoso; ambicioso, vasto
pretonic [prɪ'tɑnɪk] *adj* pretónico
pret·ty ['prɪti] *adj* (*comp* **-tier;** *super* **-tiest**) bonito, lindo; (coll) bastante, considerable || *adv* algo; bastante; muy
prevail [prɪ'vel] *intr* prevalecer, reinar; **to prevail on** o **upon** persuadir
prevailing [prɪ'velɪŋ] *adj* prevaleciente, reinante; común, corriente
prevalent ['prɛvələnt] *adj* común, corriente, en boga
prevaricate [prɪ'værɪ,ket] *intr* mentir
prevent [prɪ'vɛnt] *tr* impedir || *intr* obstar
prevention [prɪ'vɛnʃən] *s* (el) impedir; medidas de precaución
preventive [prɪ'vɛntɪv] *adj & s* preservativo
preview ['pri,vju] *s* vista anticipada; (*private showing*) (mov) preestreno; (*showing of brief scenes for advertising*) (mov) avance *m*
previous ['privɪ·əs] *adj* previo, anterior || *adv* previamente; **previous to** con anterioridad a, antes de
prewar ['pri,wɔr] *adj* prebélico, de preguerra
prey [pre] *s* presa; víctima; **to be prey to** ser presa de || *intr* cazar; **to prey on** o **upon** apresar y devorar; pillar, robar; tener preocupado
price [praɪs] *s* precio || *tr* apreciar, estimar; fijar el precio de, poner precio a; pedir el precio de
price control *s* intervención de precios
price cutting *s* reducción de precios
price fixing *s* fijación de precios
price freezing *s* congelación de precios
priceless ['praɪslɪs] *adj* inapreciable, sin precio; (coll) absurdo, divertido
price war *s* guerra de precios
prick [prɪk] *s* (*pointed weapon or instrument*) espiche *m;* (*sharp point*) púa; (*small hole made with sharp point*) agujerillo; (*spur*) aguijón *m;* (*jab; sharp pain*) pinchazo, punzada; **to kick against the pricks** dar coces contra el aguijón || *tr* pinchar; marcar con agujerillos; dar una punzada a; (*to sting*) punzar; **to prick up** aguzar (*las orejas*)
prick·ly ['prɪkli] *adj* (*comp* **-lier;** *super* **-liest**) espinoso, puado, punzante
prickly heat *s* salpullido causado por el calor
prickly pear *s* (*plant*) chumbera; (*fruit*) higo chumbo
pride [praɪd] *s* orgullo; arrogancia; **the pride of** la flor y nata de || *tr* — **to pride oneself on** o **upon** enorgullecerse de
priest [prist] *s* sacerdote *m*
priesthood ['prist·hʊd] *s* sacerdocio
priest·ly ['pristli] *adj* (*comp* **-lier;** *super* **-liest**) sacerdotal
prig [prɪg] *s* gazmoño, pedante *mf*
prim [prɪm] *adj* (*comp* **primmer;** *super* **primmest**) estirado, relamido

prima·ry ['praɪ,mɛri] o ['praɪməri] *adj* primario || *s* (*pl* **-ries**) elección preliminar; (elec) primario
prime [praɪm] *adj* primero, principal; (*of the best quality*) primo || *s* flor *f*, juventud, primavera; alba, aurora; (la) flor y nata; (*of a degree*) (phys) minuto; (typ) virgulilla; **prime of life** edad viril, flor *f* de edad || *tr* informar de antemano; cebar (*un arma de fuego, una bomba, un carburador*); (*for painting*) imprimar; poner la primera capa o la primera mano a; poner virgulilla a
prime minister *s* primer ministro
primer ['prɪmər] *s* cartilla || ['praɪmər] *s* (*for paint*) aprestado *m;* (mach) cebador *m*
primitive ['prɪmɪtɪv] *adj* primitivo
primp [prɪmp] *tr* acicalar, engalanar || *intr* acicalarse, engalanarse
prim'rose' *s* primavera
primrose path *s* vida dada a los placeres de los sentidos
prin. *abbr* **principal**
prince [prɪns] *s* príncipe *m;* **to live like a prince** portarse como un príncipe
Prince of Wales *s* príncipe *m* de Gales
princess ['prɪnsɪs] *s* princesa
principal ['prɪnsɪpəl] *adj* principal || *s* principal *m,* jefe *m;* (*of a school*) director *m;* criminal *mf;* (*main sum, not interest*) capital *m*
principle ['prɪnsɪpəl] *s* principio
print [prɪnt] *s* marca, impresión; (*printed cloth*) estampado; (*design in printed cloth*) diseño; grabado, lámina; letras de molde; (*act of printing*) impresión; edición, tirada; (phot) impresión; **in print** impreso, publicado; **out of print** agotado || *tr* imprimir; estampar; hacer imprimir; publicar; escribir en caracteres de imprenta; (phot) tirar, imprimir; (fig) imprimir o grabar (*en la memoria*)
printed matter *s* impresos
printer ['prɪntər] *s* impresor *m*
printer's devil *s* aprendiz *m* de imprenta
printer's ink *s* tinta de imprenta
printer's mark *s* pie *m* de imprenta
printing ['prɪntɪŋ] *s* impresión; caracteres impresos; edición, tirada; letras de mano imitación de las impresas; (phot) tiraje *m*
prior ['praɪ·ər] *adj* anterior || *adv* anteriormente; **prior to** antes de
priori·ty [praɪ'ɑrɪti] o [praɪ'ɔrɪti] *s* (*pl* **-ties**) prioridad; **of the highest priority** de máxima prioridad
prism ['prɪzəm] *s* prisma *m*
prison ['prɪzən] *s* cárcel *f*, prisión || *tr* encarcelar
prisoner ['prɪzənər] o ['prɪznər] *s* preso; (mil) prisionero
prison van *s* coche *m* celular
pris·sy ['prɪsi] *adj* (*comp* **-sier;** *super* **-siest**) (coll) remilgado, melindroso
priva·cy ['praɪvəsi] *s* (*pl* **-cies**) aislamiento, retiro; secreto, reserva
private ['praɪvɪt] *adj* particular, privado; confidencial; || *s* soldado raso; **in private** privadamente; en secreto; **privates** partes pudendas
private first class *s* soldado de primera, aspirante *m* a cabo
private hospital *s* clínica, casa de salud
private property *s* bienes *mpl* particulares
private view *s* día *m* de inauguración
privet ['prɪvɪt] *s* aligustre *m*
privilege ['prɪvɪlɪdʒ] *s* privilegio
priv·y ['prɪvi] *adj* privado; **privy to** enterado secretamente de || *s* (*pl* **-ies**) letrina
prize [praɪz] *s* premio; (*something captured*) presa || *tr* apreciar, estimar
prize fight *s* partido de boxeo profesional
prize fighter *s* boxeador *m* profesional
prize ring *s* cuadrilátero de boxeo
pro [pro] *prep* en pro de || *s* (*pl* **pros**) voto afirmativo; (coll) deportista *mf* profesional; **the pros and the cons** el pro y el contra
probabili·ty [,prɑbə'bɪlɪti] *s* (*pl* **-ties**) probabilidad; acontecimiento probable; tiempo probable
probable ['prɑbəbəl] *adj* probable
probation [pro'beʃən] *s* libertad vigilada; período de prueba
probe [prob] *s* encuesta, indagación; (*instrument*) sonda || *tr* indagar; sondar
problem ['prɑbləm] *s* problema *m*
procedure [pro'sidʒər] *s* procedimiento
proceed [pro'sid] *intr* proceder || **proceeds** ['prosidz] *spl* producto, ganancia
proceeding [pro'sidɪŋ] *s* procedimiento; **proceedings** actas; diligencias
process ['prɑsɛs] *s* procedimiento; proceso, progreso; **in the process of time** con el tiempo || *tr* elaborar
process server ['sʌrvər] *s* entregador *m* de la citación
proclaim [pro'klem] *tr* proclamar
proclitic [pro'klɪtɪk] *adj & s* proclítico
procommunist [pro'kɑmjənɪst] *adj & s* filocomunista *mf*
procrastinate [pro'kræstɪ,net] *tr* diferir de un día para otro || *intr* tardar, no decidirse
procure [pro'kjʊr] *tr* conseguir, obtener || *intr* alcahuetear
prod [prɑd] *s* aguijada; empuje *m* || *v* (*pret & pp* **prodded;** *ger* **prodding**) *tr* aguijar, pinchar; aguijonear, estimular
prodigal ['prɑdɪgəl] *adj & s* pródigo
prodigious [pro'dɪdʒəs] *adj* prodigioso, maravilloso; enorme, inmenso
prodi·gy ['prɑdɪdʒi] *s* (*pl* **-gies**) prodigio
produce ['prodjus] o ['produs] *s* producto; productos agrícolas || [pro'djus] o [pro'dus] *tr* producir; presentar (*p.ej., un drama*) al público; (geom) prolongar
product ['prɑdəkt] *s* producto
production [pro'dʌkʃən] *s* producción
profane [pro'fen] *adj* profano; (*lan-*

guage) injurioso, blasfemo || *s* profano || *tr* profanar
profani·ty [pro'fænɪti] *s* (*pl* **-ties**) blasfemia
profess [pro'fɛs] *tr & intr* profesar
profession [pro'fɛʃən] *s* profesión
professor [pro'fɛsər] *s* profesor *m*, catedrático; (coll) profesor, maestro
proffer ['prɑfər] *s* oferta, propuesta || *tr* ofrecer, proponer
proficient [pro'fɪʃənt] *adj* perito, diestro, hábil
profile ['profaɪl] *s* perfil *m* || *tr* perfilar
profit ['prɑfɪt] *s* provecho, beneficio, utilidad, ganancia; **at a profit** con ganancia || *tr* servir, ser de utilidad a || *intr* sacar provecho, ganar; adelantar, mejorar; **to profit by** aprovechar, sacar provecho de
profitable ['prɑfɪtəbəl] *adj* provechoso
profit and loss *s* ganancias y pérdidas
profiteer [,prɑfɪ'tɪr] *s* logrero, explotador *m* || *intr* logrear, explotar
profit taking *s* realización de beneficios
profligate ['prɑflɪgɪt] *adj & s* libertino; pródigo
pro forma invoice [pro 'fɔrmə] *s* factura simulada
profound [pro'faʊnd] *adj* profundo
profuse [prə'fjus] *adj* (*extravagant*) pródigo; (*abundant*) profuso
proge·ny ['prɑdʒəni] *s* (*pl* **-nies**) prole *f*
progno·sis [prɑg'nosɪs] *s* (*pl* **-ses** [siz]) pronóstico
prognostic [prɑg'nɑstɪk] *s* pronóstico
program ['progræm] *s* programa *m* || *tr* programar
progress ['prɑgrɛs] *s* progreso; progresos; **to make progress** hacer progresos || [prə'grɛs] *intr* progresar
progressive [prə'grɛsɪv] *adj* progresivo; (pol) progresista || *s* (pol) progresista *mf*
prohibit [pro'hɪbɪt] *tr* prohibir
project ['prɑdʒɛkt] *s* proyecto || [prə'dʒɛkt] *tr* proyectar || *intr* proyectarse
projectile [prə'dʒɛktɪl] *s* proyectil *m*
projection [prə'dʒɛkʃən] *s* proyección
projector [prə'dʒɛktər] *s* proyector *m*
proletarian [,prolɪ'tɛrɪ·ən] *adj & s* proletario
proletariat [,prolɪ'tɛrɪ·ət] *s* proletariado
proliferate [prə'lɪfə,ret] *intr* proliferar
prolific [prə'lɪfɪk] *adj* prolífico
prolix ['prolɪks] o [pro'lɪks] *adj* difuso, verboso
prologue ['prolɔg] o ['prolɑg] *s* prólogo
prolong [pro'lɔŋ] o [pro'lɑŋ] *tr* prolongar
promenade [,prɑmɪ'ned] o [,prɑmɪ'nɑd] *s* paseo; baile *m* de gala || *intr* pasear o pasearse
promenade deck *s* (naut) cubierta de paseo
prominent ['prɑmɪnənt] *adj* prominente
promise ['prɑmɪs] *s* promesa || *tr & intr* prometer
promising young man *s* joven *m* de esperanzas
promissory ['prɑmɪ,sori] *adj* promisorio
promissory note *s* pagaré *m*
promonto·ry ['prɑmən,tori] *s* (*pl* **-ries**) promontorio
promote [prə'mot] *tr* promover; fomentar
promotion [prə'moʃən] *s* promoción; fomento
prompt [prɑmpt] *adj* pronto, puntual; listo, dispuesto || *tr* incitar, mover; inspirar, sugerir; (theat) apuntar
prompter ['prɑmptər] *s* (theat) apuntador *m*
prompter's box *s* (theat) concha
promulgate ['prɑməl,get] o [pro'mʌlget] *tr* promulgar
prone [pron] *adj* postrado boca abajo; extendido sobre el suelo; dispuesto, propenso
prong [prɔŋ] o [prɑŋ] *s* punta (*de un tenedor, horquilla, etc.*)
pronoun ['pronaʊn] *s* pronombre *m*
pronounce [prə'naʊns] *tr* pronunciar
pronouncement [prə'naʊnsmənt] *s* declaración; decisión, opinión
pronunciamen·to [prə,nʌnsɪ·ə'mɛnto] *s* (*pl* **-tos**) pronunciamiento
pronunciation [prə,nʌnsɪ'eʃən] o [prə,nʌnʃɪ'eʃən] *s* pronunciación
proof [pruf] *adj* de prueba; **proof against** a prueba de || *s* prueba
proof'read'er *s* corrector *m* de pruebas
prop [prɑp] *s* apoyo, puntal *m;* (*to hold up a plant*) rodrigón *m;* **props** (theat) accesorios || *v* (*pret & pp* **propped;** *ger* **propping**) *tr* apoyar, apuntalar; poner un rodrigón a
propaganda [,prɑpə'gændə] *s* propaganda
propagate ['prɑpə,get] *tr* propagar
proparoxytone [,propær'ɑksɪ,ton] *adj & s* proparoxítono
pro·pel [prə'pɛl] *v* (*pret & pp* **-pelled;** *ger* **-pelling**) *tr* propulsar, impeler
propeller [prə'pɛlər] *s* hélice *f*
propensi·ty [prə'pɛnsɪti] *s* (*pl* **-ties**) propensión
proper ['prɑpər] *adj* propio, conveniente; decente, decoroso; exacto, justo
proper·ty ['prɑpərti] *s* (*pl* **-ties**) propiedad; **properties** (theat) accesorios
property owner *s* propietario de bienes raíces
prophe·cy ['prɑfɪsi] *s* (*pl* **-cies**) profecía
prophe·sy ['prɑfɪ,saɪ] *v* (*pret & pp* **-sied**) *tr* profetizar
prophet ['prɑfɪt] *s* profeta *m*
prophetess ['prɑfɪtɪs] *s* profetisa
prophylactic [,profɪ'læktɪk] *adj & s* profiláctico
propitiate [prə'pɪʃɪ,et] *tr* propiciar
propitious [prə'pɪʃəs] *adj* propicio
prop'jet' *s* turbohélice *m*
proportion [prə'porʃən] *s* proporción; **in proportion as** a medida que; **out of proportion** desproporcionado || *tr* proporcionar

proportionate [prə'porʃənɪt] *adj* proporcionado
proposal [prə'pozəl] *s* propuesta; oferta de matrimonio
propose [prə'poz] *tr* proponer || *intr* proponer matrimonio; **to propose to** pedir la mano a; proponerse a + *inf*
proposition [ˌprɑpə'zɪʃən] *s* proposición, propuesta
propound [prə'paʊnd] *tr* proponer
proprietor [prə'praɪ·ətər] *s* propietario
proprietress [prə'praɪ·ətrɪs] *s* propietaria
proprie·ty [prə'praɪ·əti] *s* (*pl* **-ties**) corrección, conducta decorosa, conveniencia; **proprieties** cánones *mpl* sociales, convenciones
propulsion [prə'pʌlʃən] *s* propulsión
prorate [pro'ret] *tr* prorratear
prosaic [pro'ze·ɪk] *adj* prosaico
proscribe [pro'skraɪb] *tr* proscribir
prose [proz] *adj* prosaico || *s* prosa
prosecute ['prɑsɪˌkjut] *tr* llevar a cabo; (law) procesar
prosecutor ['prɑsɪˌkjutər] *s* acusador *m*, demandante *mf*; (*lawyer*) fiscal *m*
proselyte ['prɑsɪˌlaɪt] *s* prosélito
prose writer *s* prosista *mf*
prosody ['prɑsədi] *s* métrica
prospect ['prɑspɛkt] *s* vista; esperanza; probabilidad de éxito; cliente *mf* o comprador *m* probable || *tr* & *intr* prospectar; **to prospect for** buscar (*p.ej., oro, petróleo*)
prosper ['prɑspər] *tr* & *intr* prosperar
prosperi·ty [prɑs'pɛrɪti] *s* (*pl* **-ties**) prosperidad
prosperous ['prɑspərəs] *adj* próspero
prostitute ['prɑstɪˌtjut] o ['prɑstɪˌtut] *s* prostituta || *tr* prostituir
prostrate ['prɑstret] *adj* postrado, prosternado || *tr* postrar
prostration [prɑs'treʃən] *s* postración
Prot. *abbr* **Protestant**
protagonist [pro'tægənɪst] *s* protagonista *mf*
protect [prə'tɛkt] *tr* proteger
protection [prə'tɛkʃən] *s* protección
protégé ['protəˌʒe] *s* protegido
protégée ['protəˌʒe] *s* protegida
protein ['proti·ɪn] o ['protin] *s* proteína
pro-tempore [pro'tɛmpəri] *adj* interino
protest ['protɛst] *s* protesta || [pro'tɛst] *tr* & *intr* protestar
protestant ['prɑtɪstənt] *adj* & *s* protestante *mf* || **Protestant** *adj* & *s* protestante *mf*
prothonotar·y [pro'θɑnəˌtɛri] *s* (*pl* **-ies**) escribano principal (*de un tribunal*)
protocol ['protəˌkɑl] *s* protocolo
protoplasm ['protəˌplæzəm] *s* protoplasma *m*
prototype ['protəˌtaɪp] *s* prototipo
protozoön [ˌprotə'zo·ɑn] *s* protozoo
protract [pro'trækt] *tr* prolongar
protrude [pro'trud] *intr* resaltar
proud [praʊd] *adj* orgulloso; soberbio; glorioso
proud flesh *s* carnosidad, bezo
prov. *abbr* **provincialism**
prove [pruv] *v* (*pret* **proved**; *pp* **proved** o **proven**) *tr* probar || *intr* resultar; **to prove to be** venir a ser, resultar
proverb ['prɑvərb] *s* proverbio
provide [prə'vaɪd] *tr* proporcionar, suministrar || *intr* — **to provide for** proveer a; asegurarse (*el porvenir*)
provided [prə'vaɪdɪd] *conj* a condición (de) que, con tal (de) que
providence ['prɑvɪdəns] *s* providencia
providential [ˌprɑvɪ'dɛnʃəl] *adj* providencial
providing [prə'vaɪdɪŋ] *conj* var de **provided**
province ['prɑvɪns] *s* provincia; (*sphere of activity or knowledge*) competencia
provision [prə'vɪʃən] *s* provisión; condición, estipulación
provi·so [prə'vaɪzo] *s* (*pl* **-sos** o **-soes**) condición, estipulación, salvedad
provoke [prə'vok] *tr* provocar
provoking [prə'vokɪŋ] *adj* provocador, irritante
prow [praʊ] *s* proa
prowess ['praʊ·ɪs] *s* proeza; destreza
prowl [praʊl] *intr* cazar al acecho, rodar, vagabundear
prowler ['praʊlər] *s* rondador *m*; ladrón *m*
proximity [prɑk'sɪmɪti] *s* proximidad
prox·y ['prɑksi] *s* (*pl* **-ies**) poder *m*, poderhabiente *mf*
prude [prud] *s* mojigato, gazmoño
prudence ['prudəns] *s* prudencia
prudent ['prudənt] *adj* prudente
pruder·y ['prudəri] *s* (*pl* **-ies**) mojigatería, gazmoñería
prudish ['prudɪʃ] *adj* mojigato, gazmoño
prune [prun] *s* ciruela pasa || *tr* podar, escamondar
pry [praɪ] *v* (*pret* & *pp* **pried**) *tr* — **to pry open** forzar con la alzaprima o palanca; **to pry out of** arrancar (*p.ej., un secreto*) a (*una persona*) || *intr* entremeterse; **to pry into** entremeterse en
P.S. *abbr* **postscript, Privy Seal**
psalm [sɑm] *s* salmo
Psalter ['sɔltər] *s* Salterio
pseudo ['sudo] o ['sjudo] *adj* supuesto, falso, fingido
pseudonym ['sudənɪm] o ['sjudənɪm] *s* seudónimo
Psyche ['saɪki] *s* Psique *f*
psychiatrist [saɪ'kaɪ·ətrɪst] *s* psiquiatra *mf*
psychiatry [saɪ'kaɪ·ətri] *s* psiquiatría
psychic ['saɪkɪk] *adj* psíquico; mediúmnico || *s* médium *mf*
psychoanalysis [ˌsaɪko·ə'nælɪsɪs] *s* psicoanálisis *m*
psychoanalyze [ˌsaɪko'ænəˌlaɪz] *tr* psicoanalizar
psychologic(al) [ˌsaɪko'lɑdʒɪk(əl)] *adj* psicológico
psychologist [saɪ'kɑlədʒɪst] *s* psicólogo
psychology [saɪ'kɑlədʒi] *s* psicología
psychopath ['saɪkəˌpæθ] *s* psicópata *mf*

psycho·sis [saɪˈkosɪs] *s* (*pl* **-ses** [siz]) psicosis *f;* estado mental
psychotic [saɪˈkɑtɪk] *adj & s* psicótico
pt. *abbr* **part, pint, point**
pub [pʌb] *s* (Brit) taberna
puberty [ˈpjubərti] *s* pubertad
public [ˈpʌblɪk] *adj & s* público
publication [ˌpʌblɪˈkeʃən] *s* publicación
public conveyance *s* vehículo de servicio público
publicity [pʌbˈlɪsɪti] *s* publicidad
publicize [ˈpʌblɪˌsaɪz] *tr* publicar
public library *s* biblioteca municipal
public school *s* (U.S.A.) escuela pública; (Brit) internado privado con dote
public speaking *s* elocución, oratoria
public spirit *s* celo patriótico del buen ciudadano
public toilet *s* quiosco de necesidad
public utility *s* empresa de servicio público; **public utilities** acciones emitidas por empresas de servicio público
publish [ˈpʌblɪʃ] *tr* publicar
publisher [ˈpʌblɪʃər] *s* editor *m*
publishing house *s* casa editorial
pucker [ˈpʌkər] *s* (*small fold*) frunce *m;* pliego mal hecho ‖ *tr* fruncir (*una tela; la frente*); plegar mal ‖ *intr* plegarse mal
pudding [ˈpʊdɪŋ] *s* budín *m,* pudín *m*
puddle [ˈpʌdəl] *s* aguazal *m,* charco
pudg·y [ˈpʌdʒi] *adj* (*comp* **-ier;** *super* **-iest**) gordinflón, rechoncho
puerile [ˈpju·ərɪl] *adj* pueril
puerili·ty [ˌpju·əˈrɪlɪti] *s* (*pl* **-ties**) puerilidad
Puerto Rican [ˈpwɛrto ˈrikən] *adj & s* puertorriqueño
puff [pʌf] *s* soplo vivo; (*of smoke*) bocanada; (*in clothing*) bullón *m;* borla de polvos; pastelillo de crema o jalea; alabanza exagerada; ráfaga, ventolera ‖ *tr* soplar; hinchar; alabar exageradamente ‖ *intr* soplar; hincharse; enorgullecerse exageradamente
puff paste *s* hojaldre *m & f*
pugilism [ˈpjudʒɪˌlɪzəm] *s* pugilismo
pugilist [ˈpjudʒɪlɪst] *s* pugilista *m*
pug-nosed [ˈpʌg ˌnozd] *adj* braco
puke [pjuk] *s* (slang) vómito ‖ *tr & intr* (slang) vomitar
pull [pʊl] *s* estirón *m,* tirón *m;* (*on a cigar*) chupada; (*of a door*) tirador *m;* (slang) enchufe *m,* buenas aldabas ‖ *tr* tirar de; torcer (*un ligamento*); (typ) sacar (*una impresión o prueba*); **to pull down** demoler, derribar; bajar (*p.ej., la cortinilla*); abatir, degradar; **to pull oneself together** componerse, recobrar la calma ‖ *intr* tirar; moverse despacio, moverse con esfuerzo; **to pull at** tirar de (*p.ej., la corbata*); chupar (*p.ej., un cigarro*); **to pull for** (slang) abogar por, ayudar; **to pull for oneself** tirar por su lado; **to pull in** llegar (*un tren*) a la estación; **to pull out** partir (*un tren*) de la estación; **to pull through** salir a flote; recobrar la salud
pullet [ˈpʊlɪt] *s* polla
pulley [ˈpʊli] *s* polea
pulp [pʌlp] *s* pulpa; (*to make paper*) pasta; (*of tooth*) bulbo
pulpit [ˈpʊlpɪt] *s* púlpito
pulsate [ˈpʌlset] *intr* pulsar; vibrar
pulsation [pʌlˈseʃən] *s* pulsación; vibración
pulse [pʌls] *s* pulso; **to feel** o **take the pulse of** tomar el pulso a
pulverize [ˈpʌlvəˌraɪz] *tr* pulverizar
pumice stone [ˈpʌmɪs] *s* pómez *f,* piedra pómez
pum·mel [ˈpʌməl] *v* (*pret & pp* **-meled** o **-melled;** *ger* **-meling** o **-melling**) *tr* apuñear, aporrear
pump [pʌmp] *s* bomba; (*slipperlike shoe*) escarpín *m,* zapatilla ‖ *tr* elevar o sacar (*agua*) por medio de una bomba; (coll) tirar de la lengua a (*una persona*); **to pump up** hinchar, inflar (*un neumático*)
pump handle *s* guimbalete *m*
pumpkin [ˈpʌmpkɪn] o [ˈpuŋkɪn] *s* calabaza común; **some pumpkins** (coll) persona de muchas campanillas
pump-priming [ˈpʌmp ˌpraɪmɪŋ] *s* inyección económica (*por parte del gobierno*)
pun [pʌn] *s* equívoco, retruécano ‖ *v* (*pret & pp* **punned;** *ger* **punning**) *intr* decir equívocos, jugar del vocablo
punch [pʌntʃ] *s* puñetazo; (*tool*) punzón *m;* (*for tickets*) sacabocado; (*drink*) ponche *m* ‖ *tr* dar un puñetazo a; taladrar, perforar (*un billete, una tarjeta*)
punch bowl *s* ponchera
punch card *s* tarjeta perforada
punch clock *s* reloj *m* registrador de tarjetas
punch′-drunk′ *adj* atontado (*p.ej., por una tunda de golpes*); completamente aturdido
punched tape *s* cinta perforada
punching bag *s* punching *m,* boxibalón *m*
punch line *s* broche *m* de oro, colofón *m* del artículo
punctilious [pʌŋkˈtɪlɪ·əs] *adj* puntilloso, pundonoroso
punctual [ˈpʌŋktʃʊ·əl] *adj* puntual
punctuate [ˈpʌŋktʃʊˌet] *tr* puntuar; acentuar, destacar; interrumpir ‖ *intr* puntuar
punctuation [ˌpʌŋktʃʊˈeʃən] *s* puntuación
punctuation mark *s* signo de puntuación
puncture [ˈpʌŋktʃər] *s* puntura; (*of a tire*) picadura, pinchazo ‖ *tr* pinchar, picar, perforar
punc′ture-proof′ *adj* a prueba de pinchazos
pundit [ˈpʌndɪt] *s* erudito, sabio
pungent [ˈpʌndʒənt] *adj* picante; estimulante
punish [ˈpʌnɪʃ] *tr* castigar; (coll) maltratar
punishment [ˈpʌnɪʃmənt] *s* castigo; (coll) maltrato

punk [pʌŋk] *adj* (slang) malo, de mala calidad || *s* yesca, pebete *m;* (*decayed wood*) hupe *m;* (slang) pillo, gamberro
punster [ˈpʌnstər] *s* equivoquista *mf,* vocablista *mf*
pu•ny [ˈpjuni] *adj* (*comp* **-nier;** *super* **-niest**) encanijado, débil; insignificante, mezquino
pup [pʌp] *s* cachorro
pupil [ˈpjupəl] *s* alumno; (*of the eye*) pupila
puppet [ˈpʌpɪt] *s* títere *m;* (*doll*) muñeca; (*person controlled by another*) maniquí *m*
puppet government *s* gobierno de monigotes
puppet show *s* función de títeres
puppy love [ˈpʌpi] *s* (coll) primeros amores
purchase [ˈpʌrtʃəs] *s* compra; agarre *m* firme || *tr* comprar
purchasing power *s* poder adquisitivo
pure [pjʊr] *adj* puro
purgative [ˈpʌrgətɪv] *adj & s* purgante *m*
purge [pʌrdʒ] *s* purga || *tr* purgar
puri•fy [ˈpjʊrɪ‚faɪ] *v* (*pret & pp* **-fied**) *tr* purificar
puritan [ˈpjʊrɪtən] *adj & s* puritano || **Puritan** *adj & s* puritano
purity [ˈpjʊrɪti] *s* pureza
purloin [pərˈlɔɪn] *tr & intr* robar, hurtar
purple [ˈpʌrpəl] *adj* purpurado, rojo morado || *m* púrpura, rojo morado
purport [ˈpʌrport] *s* significado, idea principal || [pərˈport] *tr* significar, querer decir
purpose [ˈpʌrpəs] *s* intención, propósito; fin *m,* objeto; **for the purpose** al efecto; **for what purpose?** ¿con qué fin?; **on purpose** adrede, de propósito; **to good purpose** con buenos resultados; **to no purpose** sin resultado; **to serve one's purpose** servir para el caso
purposely [ˈpʌrpəsli] *adv* adrede, de propósito
purr [pʌr] *s* ronroneo || *intr* ronronear
purse [pʌrs] *s* bolsa; (*money collected for charity*) colecta || *tr* fruncir
purser [ˈpʌrsər] *s* contador *m* de navío, comisario de a bordo
purse snatcher [ˈsnætʃər] *s* carterista *mf*
purse strings *spl* cordones *mpl* de la bolsa; **to hold the purse strings** tener las llaves de la caja
pursue [pərˈsu] o [pərˈsju] *tr* perseguir (*al que huye*); proseguir (*lo empezado*); seguir (*una carrera*); dedicarse a
pursuit [pərˈsut] o [pərˈsjut] *s* persecución; prosecución; (*e.g., of happiness*) busca o búsqueda; empleo
pursuit plane *s* caza *m,* avión *m* de caza
purvey [pərˈve] *tr* proveer, suministrar
pus [pʌs] *s* pus *m*
push [pʊʃ] *s* empuje *m,* empujón *m* || *tr* empujar; pulsar (*un botón*); extender (*p.ej., conquistas*); **to push around** (coll) tratar a empujones; **to push aside** hacer a un lado; **to push through** forzar (*p.ej., una resolución*) || *intr* empujar; **to push off** (coll) irse, salir; (naut) desatracarse
push button *s* botón *m* de llamada, botón interruptor
push'-but'ton control *s* mando por botón
push'cart' *s* carretilla de mano
pushing [ˈpʊʃɪŋ] *adj* emprendedor; entremetido, agresivo
pusillanimous [‚pjusɪˈlænɪməs] *adj* pusilánime
puss [pʊs] *interj* ¡miz! || *s* micho; chica, muchacha; (slang) cara, boca
puss in the corner *s* las cuatro esquinas
puss•y [ˈpʊsi] *s* (*pl* **-ies**) michito
pussy willow *s* sauce norteamericano de amentos muy sedosos
pustule [ˈpʌstʃʊl] *s* pústula
put [pʊt] *v* (*pret & pp* **put;** *ger* **putting**) *tr* poner, colocar; arrojar, echar, lanzar; hacer (*una pregunta*); **to put across** llevar a cabo; hacer aceptar; **to put aside** poner aparte; rechazar; ahorrar (*dinero*); **to put down** anotar, apuntar; sofocar (*una insurrección*); rebajar (*los precios*); **to put off** posponer; deshacerse de; **to put on** ponerse (*la ropa*); poner en escena; llevar (*p.ej., un drama a la pantalla*); accionar (*un freno*); cargar (*impuestos*); fingir; atribuir; **to put oneself out** incomodarse, molestarse; afanarse, desvivirse; **to put out** extender (*la mano*); apagar (*el fuego, la luz*); poner en la calle; dar a luz, publicar; decepcionar; (sport) sacar fuera de la partida; **to put over** o **through** (coll) llevar a cabo; **to put up** construir, edificar; abrir (*un paraguas*); conservar (*fruta, legumbres*); (coll) incitar || *intr* dirigirse; **to put on** fingir; **to put up** parar, hospedarse; **to put up with** aguantar, tolerar
put'-out' *adj* contrariado, enojado
putrid [ˈpjutrɪd] *adj* pútrido; corrompido, perverso
Putsch [pʊtʃ] *s* intentona de sublevación; sublevación
putter [ˈpʌtər] *intr* trabajar sin orden ni sistema; **to putter around** ocuparse en fruslerías, temporizar
put•ty [ˈpʌti] *s* (*pl* **-ties**) masilla || *v* (*pret & pp* **-tied**) *tr* enmasillar
putty knife *s* cuchillo de vidriero, espátula
put'-up' *adj* (coll) premeditado con malicia
puzzle [ˈpʌzəl] *s* enigma *m;* acertijo, rompecabezas *m* || *tr* confundir, poner perplejo; **to puzzle out** descifrar || *intr* estar perplejo; **to puzzle over** tratar de descifrar
puzzler [ˈpʌzlər] *s* quisicosa
PW *abbr* **prisoner of war**
pyg•my [ˈpɪgmi] *adj* pigmeo || *s* (*pl* **-mies**) pigmeo
pylon [ˈpaɪlɑn] *s* pilón *m*
pyramid [ˈpɪrəmɪd] *s* pirámide *f* || *tr* aumentar (*su dinero*) comprando o

vendiendo al crédito y empleando las ganancias para comprar o vender más
pyre [paɪr] *s* pira
Pyrenean [ˌpɪrɪˈni·ən] *adj* pirineo
Pyrenees [ˈpɪrɪˌniz] *spl* Pirineos
pyrites [paɪˈraɪtiz] o [ˈpaɪraɪts] *s* pirita
pyrotechnical [ˌpaɪrəˈtɛknɪkəl] *adj* pirotécnico
pyrotechnics [ˌpaɪrəˈtɛknɪks] *spl* pirotecnia
python [ˈpaɪθɑn] o [ˈpaɪθən] *s* pitón *m*
pythoness [ˈpaɪθənɪs] *s* pitonisa
pyx [pɪks] *s* píxide *f*, copón *m*

Q

Q, q [kju] decimoséptima letra del alfabeto inglés
Q. *abbr* **quarto, queen, question, quire**
Q.M. *abbr* **quartermaster**
qr. *abbr* **quarter, quire**
qt. *abbr* **quantity, quart**
qu. *abbr* **quart, quarter, quarterly, queen, query, question**
quack [kwæk] *adj* falso ‖ *s* graznido del pato; charlatán *m;* medicastro, curandero ‖ *intr* parpar (*el pato*)
quacker·y [ˈkwækəri] *s* (*pl* **-ies**) charlatanismo
quadrangle [ˈkwɑdˌræŋgəl] *s* cuadrángulo; patio cuadrangular
quadrant [ˈkwɑdrənt] *s* cuadrante *m*
quadroon [kwɑdˈrun] *s* cuarterón *m*
quadruped [ˈkwɑdrʊˌpɛd] *adj & s* cuadrúpedo
quadruple [ˈkwɑdrʊpəl] o [kwɑdˈrupəl] *adj & s* cuádruple *m* ‖ *tr* cuadruplicar ‖ *intr* cuadruplicarse
quadruplet [ˈkwɑdrʊˌplɛt] o [kwɑdˈruplɛt] *s* cuatrillizo
quaff [kwɑf] o [kwæf] *s* trago grande ‖ *tr & intr* beber en gran cantidad
quail [kwel] *s* codorniz *f* ‖ *intr* acobardarse
quaint [kwent] *adj* curioso, raro; afectado, rebuscado; fantástico, singular
quake [kwek] *s* temblor *m*, terremoto ‖ *intr* temblar
Quaker [ˈkwekər] *adj & s* cuáquero
Quaker meeting *s* reunión de cuáqueros; reunión en que hay poca conversación
quali·fy [ˈkwɑlɪˌfaɪ] *v* (*pret & pp* **-fied**) *tr* calificar; capacitar, habilitar ‖ *intr* capacitarse, habilitarse
quali·ty [ˈkwɑlɪti] *s* (*pl* **-ties**) (*characteristic; virtue*) calidad; (*property, attribute*) cualidad; (*of a sound*) timbre *m*
qualm [kwɑm] *s* escrúpulo de conciencia; duda, inquietud; (*nausea*) basca
quanda·ry [ˈkwɑndəri] *s* (*pl* **-ries**) incertidumbre, perplejidad
quanti·ty [ˈkwɑntɪti] *s* (*pl* **-ties**) cantidad
quan·tum [ˈkwɑntəm] *adj* cuántico ‖ *s* (*pl* **-ta** [tə]) cuanto, quántum *m*
quantum theory *s* teoría cuántica
quarantine [ˈkwɑrənˌtin] o [ˈkwɔrənˌtin] *s* cuarentena; estación de cuarentena ‖ *tr* poner en cuarentena
quar·rel [ˈkwɑrəl] o [ˈkwɔrəl] *s* disputa, riña, pelea; **to have no quarrel with** no estar en desacuerdo con; **to pick a quarrel with** tomarse con ‖ *v* (*pret & pp* **-reled** o **-relled;** *ger* **-reling** o **-relling**) *intr* disputar, reñir, pelear
quarrelsome [ˈkwɑrəlsəm] o [ˈkwɔrəlsəm] *adj* pendenciero
quar·ry [ˈkwɑri] o [ˈkwɔri] *s* (*pl* **-ries**) cantera, pedrera; caza, presa ‖ *v* (*pret & pp* **-ried**) *tr* sacar de una cantera; extraer, sacar
quart [kwɔrt] *s* cuarto de galón
quarter [ˈkwɔrtər] *adj* cuarto ‖ *s* cuarto, cuarta parte; (*three months*) trimestre *m;* moneda de 25 centavos; cuarto de luna; barrio; región, lugar *m;* (*clemency*) (mil) cuartel *m;* **quarters** morada, vivienda; local *m;* (mil) cuarteles *mpl;* **to take up quarters** alojarse ‖ *tr* descuartizar
quar'ter·deck' *s* alcázar *m*
quar'ter-hour' *s* cuarto de hora; **on the quarter-hour** al cuarto en punto cada cuarto de hora
quarter·ly [ˈkwɔrtərli] *adj* trimestral ‖ *adv* trimestralmente ‖ *s* (*pl* **-lies**) publicación o revista trimestral
quar'ter·mas'ter *s* (mil) comisario; (nav) cabo de brigadas
quartet [kwɔrˈtɛt] *s* cuarteto
quartz [kwɔrts] *s* cuarzo
quasar [ˈkwesɑr] *s* (astr) objeto del espacio, fuente *f* cuasiestelar de radio
quash [kwɑʃ] *tr* sofocar, reprimir; anular, invalidar
quaver [ˈkwevər] *s* temblor *m*, estremecimiento; (mus) trémolo ‖ *intr* temblar, estremecerse
quay [ki] *s* muelle *m*, desembarcadero
queen [kwin] *s* reina; (*in chess*) dama o reina; (*in cards*) dama (*que corresponde al caballo*); abeja reina
queen bee *s* abeja reina, abeja maestra; (slang) marimandona, la que lleva la voz cantante
queen dowager *s* reina viuda
queen·ly [ˈkwinli] *adj* (*comp* **-lier;** *super* **-liest**) de reina; como reina; regio
queen mother *s* reina madre
queen olive *s* aceituna de la reina, aceituna gordal
queen post *s* péndola
queen's English *s* inglés castizo
queer [kwɪr] *adj* curioso, raro; estrambótico, estrafalario; aturdido, indispuesto; (coll) sospechoso, misterioso ‖ *tr* (slang) echar a perder; (slang) comprometer
quell [kwɛl] *tr* sofocar, reprimir; mitigar (*una pena o dolor*)

quench [kwɛntʃ] *tr* apagar (*el fuego; la sed*); sofocar, reprimir; (electron) amortiguar

que·ry ['kwɪri] *s* (*pl* **-ries**) pregunta; signo de interrogación; duda || *v* (*pret & pp* **-ried**) *tr* interrogar; marcar con signo de interrogación; dudar

ques. *abbr* **question**

quest [kwɛst] *s* búsqueda; (*of the Holy Grail*) demanda; **in quest of** en busca de

question ['kwɛstʃən] *s* pregunta; (*problem for discussion*) cuestión; asunto, proposición; **beside the question** que no viene al caso; **beyond question** fuera de duda; **out of the question** imposible, indiscutible; **to ask a question** hacer una pregunta; **to be a question of** tratarse de, ser cuestión de; **to call in question** poner en duda; **without question** sin duda || *tr* interrogar; cuestionar (*poner en tela de juicio*)

questionable ['kwɛstʃənəbəl] *adj* cuestionable

question mark *s* punto interrogante, signo de interrogación

questionnaire [ˌkwɛstʃən'ɛr] *s* cuestionario

queue [kju] *s* (*of hair*) coleta; (*of people*) cola || *intr* hacer cola

quibble [kwɪbəl] *intr* sutilizar

quick [kwɪk] *adj* rápido, veloz; ágil, vivo; despierto, listo; **the quick and the dead** los vivos y los muertos; **to cut** o **to sting to the quick** herir en lo vivo, tocar en la herida

quicken ['kwɪkən] *tr* acelerar, avivar; animar || *intr* acelerarse; animarse

quick'lime' *s* cal viva

quick lunch *s* servicio de la barra, servicio rápido

quick'sand' *s* arena movediza

quick'sil'ver *s* azogue *m*

quiet ['kwaɪ·ət] *adj* (*still*) quieto; silencioso; (*market*) (com) encalmado; **to keep quiet** callarse || *s* quietud; silencio; **on the quiet** a las calladas || *tr* aquietar; acallar || *intr* aquietarse; callarse; **to quiet down** calmarse

quill [kwɪl] *s* pluma de ave; cañón *m* de pluma; (*of hedgehog, porcupine*) púa

quilt [kwɪlt] *s* edredón *m*, colcha || *tr* acolchar

quince [kwɪns] *s* membrillo

quinine ['kwaɪnaɪn] *s* quinina

quinsy ['kwɪnzi] *s* cinanquia, esquinencia

quintessence [kwɪn'tɛsəns] *s* quintaesencia

quintet [kwɪn'tɛt] *s* quinteto

quintuplet [kwɪn'tjuplɛt] o [kwɪn'tuplɛt] *s* quintillizo

quip [kwɪp] *s* chufleta, pulla || *v* (*pret & pp* **quipped;** *ger* **quipping**) *tr* decir en son de burla || *intr* echar pullas

quire [kwaɪr] *s* mano *f* de papel; (bb) alzado

quirk [kwʌrk] *s* excentricidad, rareza; sutileza; vuelta repentina

quit [kwɪt] *adj* libre, descargado; **to be quits** estar desquitados; **to cry quits** pedir treguas || *v* (*pret & pp* **quit** o **quitted;** *ger* **quitting**) *tr* dejar || *intr* irse; (coll) dejar de trabajar

quite [kwaɪt] *adv* enteramente; verdaderamente; (coll) bastante, muy

quitter ['kwɪtər] *s* remolón *m;* (*of a cause*) desertor *m*

quiver ['kwɪvər] *s* temblor *m;* (*to hold arrows*) aljaba, carcaj *m* || *intr* temblar

quixotic [kwɪks'ɑtɪk] *adj* quijotesco

quiz [kwɪz] *s* (*pl* **quizzes**) examen *m;* interrogatorio || *v* (*pret & pp* **quizzed;** *ger* **quizzing**) *tr* examinar; interrogar

quiz game *s* torneo de preguntas y respuestas

quiz program *s* programa *m* de preguntas y respuestas, torneo radiofónico

quiz section *s* grupo de práctica

quizzical ['kwɪzɪkəl] *adj* curioso; cómico; burlón

quoin [kɔɪn] o [kwɔɪn] *s* esquina; piedra angular; (*wedge*) cuña || *tr* (typ) acuñar

quoit [kwɔɪt] o [kɔɪt] *s* herrón *m*, tejo; **quoits** *ssg* hito

quondam ['kwɑndæm] *adj* antiguo, de otro tiempo

quorum ['kworəm] *s* quórum *m*

quota ['kwotə] *s* cuota

quotation [kwo'teʃən] *s* (*from a book*) cita; (*of prices*) cotización

quotation marks *spl* comillas

quote [kwot] *s* (coll) cita; (coll) cotización; **close quote** fin de la cita; **quotes** (coll) comillas || *tr & intr* citar; cotizar; **quote** cito

quotient ['kwoʃənt] *s* cociente *m*

q.v. *abbr* **quod vide** (Lat) **which see**

R

R, r [ɑr] decimoctava letra del alfabeto inglés

r. *abbr* **railroad, railway, road, rod, ruble, rupee**

R. *abbr* **railroad, railway, Regina** (Lat) **Queen; Republican, response, Rex** (Lat) **King; River, Royal**

rabbet ['ræbɪt] *s* barbilla, rebajo || *tr* embarbillar, rebajar

rab·bi ['ræbaɪ] *s* (*pl* **-bis** o **-bies**) rabino

rabbit ['ræbɪt] *s* conejo

rabble ['ræbəl] *s* canalla, gentuza

rabble rouser ['rauzər] *s* populachero, alborotapueblos *mf*

rabies ['rebiz] o ['rebɪˌiz] *s* rabia

raccoon [ræ'kun] *s* mapache *m*, oso lavador

race [res] *s* (*people of same stock*) raza; (*contest in speed, etc.*) carrera; (*channel to lead water*) caz *m* || *tr* competir con, en una carrera; hacer correr de prisa; hacer funcionar (*un motor*) a velocidad excesiva || *intr* correr de prisa; correr en una carrera; competir en una carrera; embalarse (*un motor*); (naut) regatear
race horse *s* caballo de carreras
race riot *s* disturbio racista
race track *s* pista de carreras
racial ['reʃəl] *adj* racial
racing car *s* coche *m* de carreras
rack [ræk] *s* (*sort of shelf*) estante *m;* (*to hang clothes*) percha; (*for fodder for cattle*) pesebre *m;* (*for baggage*) red *f* de equipaje; (*for guns*) armero; (*bar made to gear with a pinion*) cremallera; **to go to rack and ruin** desvencijarse; ir al desastre || *tr* estirar, forzar; atormentar; despedazar; oprimir, agobiar; **to rack off** trasegar (*el vino*); **to rack one's brains** calentarse la cabeza, devanarse los sesos
racket ['rækɪt] *s* raqueta; (*noise*) baraúnda, alboroto; (slang) trapisonda, trapacería; **to raise a racket** armar un alboroto
racketeer [,rækɪ'tɪr] *s* trapisondista *mf,* trapacista *mf* || *intr* trapacear
rack railway *s* ferrocarril *m* de cremallera
rac·y ['resi] *adj* (*comp* **-ier;** *super* **-iest**) espiritoso, chispeante; perfumado; (*somewhat indecent*) picante
radar ['redɑr] *s* radar *m*
radiant ['redɪ·ənt] *adj* radiante, resplandeciente; (*cheerful, smiling*) radiante
radiate ['redɪ,et] *tr* radiar; difundir (*p.ej., felicidad*) || *intr* radiar, irradiar
radiation [,redɪ'eʃən] *s* radiación
radiation sickness *s* enfermedad de radiación, mal *m* de rayos
radiator ['redɪ,etər] *s* radiador *m*
radiator cap *s* tapón *m* de radiador
radical ['rædɪkəl] *adj & s* radical *m*
radi·o ['redɪ,o] *s* (*pl* **-os**) radio *f;* radiograma *m* || *tr* radiodifundir
radioactive [,redɪ·o'æktɪv] *adj* radiactivo
radio amateur *s* radioaficionado
radio announcer *s* locutor *m* de radio
ra'dio·broad'cast'ing *s* radiodifusión
radio frequency *s* radiofrecuencia
radio listener *s* radioescucha *mf,* radioyente *mf*
radiology [,redɪ'ɑlədʒi] *s* radiología
radio network *s* red *f* de emisoras
radio newscaster *s* cronista *mf* de radio
radio receiver *s* radiorreceptor *m*
radio set *s* aparato de radio
radish ['rædɪʃ] *s* rábano
radium ['redɪ·əm] *s* radio
radi·us ['redɪ·əs] *s* (*pl* **-i** [,aɪ] o **-uses**) radio; (*range of operation*) radio; **within a radius of** en . . . a la redonda
raffle ['ræfəl] *s* rifa || *tr & intr* rifar
raft [ræft] o [rɑft] *s* armadía, balsa; (coll) gran número
rafter ['ræftər] o ['rɑftər] *s* cabrio, contrapar *m,* traviesa
rag [ræg] *s* trapo; **to chew the rag** (slang) dar la lengua
ragamuffin ['rægə,mʌfɪn] *s* pelagatos *m;* golfo, chiquillo haraposo
rag baby o **rag doll** *s* muñeca de trapo
rage [redʒ] *s* rabia; **to be all the rage** estar en boga, hacer furor; **to fly into a rage** montar en cólera
ragged ['rægɪd] *adj* andrajoso; (*edge*) cortado en dientes
ragpicker ['ræg,pɪkər] *s* andrajero, trapero
rag'weed' *s* ambrosía
raid [red] *s* incursión, invasión; ataque de sorpresa; ataque aéreo || *tr* invadir; atacar inesperadamente; capturar (*p.ej., la policía un garito*)
rail [rel] *s* carril *m,* riel *m;* (*railing*) barandilla; (*of a bridge*) guardalado; (*at a bar*) apoyo para los pies; palo; **by rail** por ferrocarril; **rails** títulos o valores de ferrocarril || *tr* poner barandilla a || *intr* quejarse amargamente; **to rail at** injuriar, ultrajar
rail fence *s* cerca hecha de palos horizontales
rail'head' *s* (rr) cabeza de línea
railing ['relɪŋ] *s* barandilla, pasamano
rail'road' *adj* ferroviario || *s* ferrocarril *m* || *tr* (coll) llevar a cabo con demasiada precipitación; (slang) encarcelar falsamente || *intr* trabajar en el ferrocarril
railroad crossing *s* paso a nivel
rail'way' *adj* ferroviario || *s* ferrocarril *m*
raiment ['remənt] *s* prendas de vestir, indumentaria
rain [ren] *s* lluvia; **rain or shine** llueva o no, con buen o mal tiempo || *tr & intr* llover
rain'bow' *s* arco iris
rain'coat' *s* impermeable *m*
rain'fall' *s* lluvia repentina; precipitación acuosa
rain·y ['reni] *adj* (*comp* **-ier;** *super* **-iest**) lluvioso
rainy day *s* día lluvioso; tiempo futuro de posible necesidad
raise [rez] *s* aumento || *tr* levantar; aumentar; criar (*a niños, animales*); cultivar (*plantas*); reunir (*dinero*); suscitar (*una duda*); resucitar (*a los muertos*); dejarse (*barba, bigote*); poner (*una objeción*); plantear (*una pregunta*); levantar (*tropas; un sitio*); (math) elevar; (*to come in sight of*) (naut) avistar
raisin ['rezən] *s* pasa, uva seca
rake [rek] *s* rastro, rastrillo; (*person*) calavera *m,* libertino || *tr* rastrillar; **to rake together** acumular (*dinero*)
rake'-off' *s* (slang) dinero obtenido ilícitamente
rakish ['rekɪʃ] *adj* airoso, gallardo; listo, vivo; libertino
ral·ly ['ræli] *s* (*pl* **-lies**) reunión popular, reunión política; recuperación, recobro || *v* (*pret & pp* **-lied**) *tr* reu-

nir; reanimar; recobrar (*la fuerza, la salud, el ánimo*) || *intr* reunirse; recobrarse (*p.ej., los precios en la Bolsa*); recobrar la fuerza, la salud, el ánimo; **to rally to the side of** acudir a, ir en socorro de

ram [ræm] *s* (*male sheep*) morueco, carnero padre; (*device for battering, crushing, etc.*) pisón *m* || *v* (*pret & pp* **rammed;** *ger* **ramming**) *tr* dar contra, chocar en; atestar, rellenar || *intr* chocar; **to ram into** chocar en

ramble ['ræmbəl] *s* paseo || *intr* pasear; serpentear (*p.ej., un río*); extenderse serpenteando (*las enredaderas*); (*to wander aimlessly; to talk in an aimless way*) divagar

rami•fy ['ræmɪ,faɪ] *v* (*pret & pp* **-fied**) *tr* ramificar || *intr* ramificarse

ramp [ræmp] *s* rampa

rampage ['ræmpedʒ] *s* alboroto; **to go on a rampage** alborotar, comportarse como un loco

rampart ['ræmpɑrt] *s* muralla, terraplén *m;* amparo, defensa

ram'rod' *s* atacador *m,* baqueta

ram'shack'le *adj* desvencijado, destartalado

ranch [ræntʃ] *s* granja, hacienda

rancid ['rænsɪd] *adj* rancio

rancor ['ræŋkər] *s* rencor *m*

random ['rændəm] *adj* casual, fortuito; **at random** al azar, a la ventura

range [rendʒ] *s* (*row, line*) fila, hilera; (*scope, reach*) alcance *m;* (*of speeds, prices, etc.*) escala; campo de tiro; terreno de pasto; (*of a boat or airplane*) autonomía; (*of the voice*) extensión; (*of colors*) gama, serie *f;* (*stove*) cocina económica; **within range of** al alcance de || *tr* alinear; recorrer (*un terreno*); ir a lo largo de (*la costa*); arreglar, ordenar || *intr* fluctuar, variar (*entre ciertos límites*); extenderse; divagar, errar; **to range over** recorrer

range finder *s* telémetro

rank [ræŋk] *adj* exuberante, lozano; denso, espeso; grosero; maloliente; excesivo; incorregible, rematado; indecente, vulgar || *s* categoría, rango; condición, posición; distinción; (*line of soldiers standing abreast*) fila; (mil) empleo, grado || *tr* alinear; ordenar; tener grado o posición más alta que || *intr* ocupar el último grado; **to rank high** ocupar alta posición; ser tenido en alta estima; sobresalir; **to rank low** ocupar baja posición; **to rank with** estar al nivel de; tener el mismo grado que

rank and file *s* soldados de fila; pueblo, gente *f* común

rankle ['ræŋkəl] *tr* enconar, irritar || *intr* enconarse

ransack ['rænsæk] *tr* registrar, escudriñar; robar, saquear

ransom ['rænsəm] *s* rescate *m* || *tr* rescatar

rant [rænt] *intr* desvariar, despotricar

rap [ræp] *s* golpe corto y seco; (*noise*) taque *m;* (coll) ardite *m,* bledo; (slang) crítica mordaz; **to take the rap** (slang) pagar la multa; sufrir las consecuencias || *v* (*pret & pp* **rapped;** *ger* **rapping**) *tr* golpear con golpe corto y seco; decir vivamente; (slang) criticar mordazmente || *intr* golpear con golpe corto y seco; **to rap at the door** tocar a la puerta

rapacious [rə'peʃəs] *adj* rapaz

rape [rep] *s* rapto; (*of a woman*) estupro, violación || *tr* raptar; estuprar, violar

rapid ['ræpɪd] *adj* rápido || **rapids** *spl* (*of a river*) rápidos

rap'id-fire' *adj* de tiro rápido; hecho vivamente

rapier ['repɪ·ər] *s* estoque *m,* espadín *m*

rapt [ræpt] *adj* arrebatado, extático, transportado; absorto

rapture ['ræptʃər] *s* embeleso, éxtasis *f,* rapto

rare [rɛr] *adj* raro; (*word*) poco usado; (*meat*) poco asado; (*gem*) precioso

rare bird *s* mirlo blanco

rare•fy ['rɛrɪ,faɪ] *v* (*pret & pp* **-fied**) *tr* enrarecer || *intr* enrarecerse

rarely ['rɛrli] *adv* rara vez

rascal ['ræskəl] *s* bellaco, bribón *m,* pícaro

rash [ræʃ] *adj* temerario || *s* brote *m,* salpullido, **erupción**

rasp [ræsp] o [rɑsp] *s* escofina; (*sound of a rasp*) sonido áspero || *tr* escofinar; irritar, molestar; decir con voz ronca || *intr* hacer sonido áspero

raspber•ry ['ræz,bɛri] o ['rɑz,bɛri] *s* (*pl* **-ries**) frambuesa, sangüesa

raspberry bush *s* frambueso, sangüeso

rat [ræt] *s* rata; (*false hair*) (coll) postizo; **to smell a rat** (coll) olerse una trama, sospechar una intriga

ratchet ['rætʃɪt] *s* trinquete *m*

rate [ret] *s* (*amount or degree measured in proportion to something else*) razón *f;* (*of interest*) tipo; velocidad; precio; **at any rate** de todos modos; **at the rate of** a razón de || *tr* valuar; estimar, juzgar; clasificar || *intr* ser considerado, ser tenido; estar clasificado

rate of exchange *s* tipo de cambio

rather ['ræðər] o ['rɑðər] *adv* algo, un poco; bastante; antes, más bien; mejor dicho; por el contrario; muy, mucho; **rather than** antes que, más bien que || *interj* ¡ya lo creo!

rati•fy ['rætɪ,faɪ] *v* (*pret & pp* **-fied**) *tr* ratificar

ra•tio ['reʃo] o ['reʃɪ,o] *s* (*pl* **-tios**) (math) razón *f;* (math) cociente *m*

ration ['reʃən] o ['ræʃən] *s* ración || *tr* racionar

ration book *s* cartilla de racionamiento

rational ['ræʃənəl] *adj* racional

rat poison *s* matarratas *m*

rattle ['rætəl] *s* (*number of short, sharp sounds*) traqueteo; (*noisemaking device*) carraca, matraca; (*child's toy*) sonajero; baraúnda; (*in the throat*) estertor *m* || *tr* tabletear, traquetear; (*to confuse*) (coll) atortolar, desconcertar; **to rattle off**

decir rápidamente || *intr* tabletear, traquetear
rat'tle·snake' *s* serpiente *f* de cascabel
rat'trap' *s* ratonera; trance apurado, atolladero
raucous ['rɔkəs] *adj* ronco
ravage ['rævɪdʒ] *s* destrucción, estrago, ruina || *tr* destruir, estragar, arruinar
rave [rev] *intr* desvariar, delirar; bramar, enfurecerse; **to rave about** hacerse lenguas de, deshacerse en elogios de
raven ['revən] *s* cuervo
ravenous ['rævənəs] *adj* famélico, hambriento, voraz; rapaz
ravine [rə'vin] *s* cañón *m*, hondonada
ravish ['rævɪʃ] *tr* encantar, entusiasmar; raptar; violar (*a una mujer*)
ravishing ['rævɪʃɪŋ] *adj* encantador
raw [rɔ] *adj* crudo; (*cotton, silk*) en rama; inexperto, principiante; ulceroso; (*weather, day*) crudo
raw deal *s* (slang) mala pasada
raw'hide' *s* cuero en verde; látigo hecho de cuero en verde
raw material *s* primera materia, materia prima
ray [re] *s* (*of light*) rayo; (*fine line; fish*) raya
rayon ['re·ɑn] *s* rayón *m*
raze [rez] *tr* arrasar, asolar
razor ['rezər] *s* navaja de afeitar
razor blade *s* hoja u hojita de afeitar
razor strop *s* asentador *m*, suavizador *m*
razz [ræz] *s* (slang) irrisión || *tr* (slang) mofarse de
R.C. *abbr* **Red Cross, Reserve Corps, Roman Catholic**
R.D. *abbr* **Rural Delivery**
reach [ritʃ] *s* alcance *m*; extensión; **out of reach (of)** fuera del alcance (de); **within reach of** al alcance de || *tr* alcanzar; extender; entregar con la mano; llegar a; ponerse en contacto con; influenciar; cumplir (*cierto número de años*) || *intr* alcanzar; extender la mano o el brazo; **to reach after** o **for** esforzarse por coger
react [rɪ'ækt] *intr* reaccionar
reaction [rɪ'ækʃən] *s* reacción
reactionar·y [rɪ'ækʃən,ɛri] *adj* reaccionario || *s* (*pl* **-ies**) reaccionario
read [rid] *v* (*pret & pp* **read** [rɛd]) *tr* leer; recitar (*poesía*); estudiar (*derecho*); leer en, adivinar (*el pensamiento ajeno*); **to read over** recorrer, repasar || *intr* leer; rezar, p.ej., **this page reads thus** esta página reza así; leerse, p.ej., **this book reads easily** este libro se lee con facilidad; **to read on** seguir leyendo
reader ['ridər] *s* lector *m*; libro de lectura
readily ['rɛdɪli] *adv* de buena gana; fácilmente
reading ['ridɪŋ] *s* lectura; recitación
reading desk *s* atril *m*
reading glass *s* lente *f* para leer, vidrio de aumento; **reading glasses** anteojos para la lectura
reading lamp *s* lámpara de sobremesa
reading room *s* gabinete *m* de lectura; sala de lectura
read·y ['rɛdi] *adj* (*comp* **-ier**; *super* **-iest**) listo, preparado, pronto; ágil, diestro; vivo; disponible; **to make ready** preparar; prepararse || *v* (*pret & pp* **-ied**) *tr* preparar || *intr* prepararse
ready cash *s* dinero a la mano, dinero contante y sonante
read'y-made' clothing *s* ropa hecha
ready-made suit *s* traje hecho
reagent [rɪ'edʒənt] *s* reactivo
real ['ri·əl] *adj* real, verdadero
real estate *s* bienes *mpl* raíces, bienes inmuebles
re'al-es·tate' *adj* inmobiliario
realism ['ri·ə,lɪzəm] *s* realismo
realist ['ri·əlɪst] *s* realista *mf*
reali·ty [rɪ'ælɪti] *s* (*pl* **-ties**) realidad
realize ['ri·ə,laɪz] *tr* darse cuenta de; realizar, llevar a cabo; adquirir (*ganancias*); reportar (*ganancias*) || *intr* (*to sell property for ready money*) realizar
realm [rɛlm] *s* reino
realtor ['ri·əl,tɔr] o ['ri·əltər] *s* corredor *m* de bienes raíces
realty ['ri·əlti] *s* bienes *mpl* raíces, bienes inmuebles
ream [rim] *s* resma; **reams** (coll) montones *mpl* || *tr* escariar
reap [rip] *tr & intr* (*to cut*) segar; (*to gather*) cosechar
reaper ['ripər] *s* (*person*) segador *m*; máquina segadora
reappear [,ri·ə'pɪr] *intr* reaparecer
reapportionment [,ri·ə'porʃənmənt] *s* nuevo prorrateo
rear [rɪr] *adj* posterior, trasero; de atrás || *s* espalda; (*of a room*) fondo; (*of a row; of an automobile*) cola; retaguardia; (slang) culo, trasero || *tr* levantar; edificar; criar, educar || *intr* encabritarse (*un caballo*)
rear admiral *s* contraalmirante *m*
rear drive *s* tracción trasera
rearmament [ri'ɑrməmənt] *s* rearme *m*
rear'-view' mirror *s* retrovisor *m*, espejo de retrovisión
rear window *s* (aut) luneta, luneta posterior
reason ['rizən] *s* razón *f*; **by reason of** con motivo de, a causa de; **to listen to reason** meterse en razón; **to stand to reason** ser razonable || *tr & intr* razonar
reasonable ['rizənəbəl] *adj* razonable
reassessment [,ri·ə'sɛsmənt] *s* nuevo amillaramiento; nueva estimación
reassure [,ri·ə'ʃʊr] *tr* volver a asegurar; tranquilizar
reawaken [,ri·ə'wekən] *tr* volver a despertar || *intr* volver a despertarse
rebate ['ribet] o [rɪ'bet] *s* rebaja || *tr* rebajar
rebel ['rɛbəl] *adj & s* rebelde *mf* || **re·bel** [rɪ'bɛl] *v* (*pret & pp* **-belled**; *ger* **-belling**) *intr* rebelarse
rebellion [rɪ'bɛljən] *s* rebelión
rebellious [rɪ'bɛljəs] *adj* rebelde
re·bind [ri'baɪnd] *v* (*pret & pp* **-bound**

['baund]) *tr* reatar; (*to edge, to border*) ribetear; (bb) reencuadernar
rebirth ['ribʌrθ] o [ri'bʌrθ] *s* renacimiento
rebore [ri'bor] *tr* rectificar
rebound ['ri,baund] o [ri'baund] *s* rebote *m* || [ri'baund] *intr* rebotar
rebroad·cast [ri'brɔd,kæst] o [ri'brɔd,kɑst] *s* retransmisión || *v* (*pret & pp* **-cast** o **-casted**) *tr* retransmitir
rebuff [rɪ'bʌf] *s* desaire *m,* rechazo || *tr* desairar, rechazar
re·build [ri'bɪld] *v* (*pret & pp* **-built** ['bɪlt]) *tr* reconstruir, reedificar
rebuke [rɪ'bjuk] *s* reprensión || *tr* reprender
re·but [rɪ'bʌt] *v* (*pret & pp* **-butted;** *ger* **-butting**) *tr* rebatir, refutar
rebuttal [rɪ'bʌtəl] *s* rebatimiento, refutación
rec. *abbr* **receipt, recipe, record, recorder**
recall [rɪ'kɔl] o ['rikɔl] *s* llamada; recordación; revocación; (*of a diplomat*) retirada || [rɪ'kɔl] *tr* hacer volver, mandar volver; recordar; revocar; retirar (*a un diplomático*)
recant [rɪ'kænt] *tr* retractar || *intr* retractarse
re·cap ['ri,kæp] o [ri'kæp] *v* (*pret & pp* **-capped;** *ger* **-capping**) *tr* recauchutar
recapitalization [ri,kæpɪtəlɪ'zeʃən] *s* recapitalización
recapitulation [,rikə,pɪtʃə'leʃən] *s* recapitulación
re·cast ['ri,kæst] o ['ri,kɑst] *s* refundición; (*of a sentence*) reconstrucción || [ri'kæst] o [ri'kɑst] *v* (*pret & pp* **-cast**) *tr* refundir; reconstruir (*p.ej., una frase*)
recd. o **rec'd.** *abbr* **received**
recede [rɪ'sid] *intr* (*to move back*) retroceder; (*to move away*) alejarse, retirarse; deprimirse (*p.ej., la frente de una persona*)
receipt [rɪ'sit] *s* recepción; (*acknowledgment*) recibo; (*acknowledgment of payment*) recibí *m;* (*recipe*) receta; **receipt in full** finiquito; **receipts** entradas, ingresos || *tr* poner el recibí a
receive [rɪ'siv] *tr* recibir; receptar (*cosas que son materia de delito*); **received payment** recibí || *intr* recibir
receiver [rɪ'sivər] *s* receptor *m;* (*in bankruptcy*) contador *m,* síndico; receptor telefónico
receiving set *s* aparato receptor
receiving teller *s* recibidor *m* (*de un banco*)
recent ['risənt] *adj* reciente
recently ['risəntli] *adv* recientemente; recién, p.ej., **recently arrived** recién llegado
receptacle [rɪ'sɛptəkəl] *s* receptáculo
reception [rɪ'sɛpʃən] *s* recepción; (*welcome*) recibimiento
reception desk *s* recepción
receptionist [rɪ'sɛpʃənɪst] *s* recepcionista *f*
receptive [rɪ'sɛptɪv] *adj* receptivo
recess [rɪ'sɛs] o ['risɛs] *s* intermisión; descanso; hora de recreo; (*in a surface*) depresión; (*in a wall*) hueco, nicho; escondrijo || [rɪ'sɛs] *tr* ahuecar; empotrar; deprimir || *intr* prorrogarse, suspenderse
recession [rɪ'sɛʃən] *s* retroceso, retirada; (*e.g., in a wall*) depresión; procesión de vuelta; contracción económica
recipe ['rɛsɪ,pi] *s* receta (de cocina)
reciprocal [rɪ'sɪprəkəl] *adj* recíproco
reciprocity [,rɛsɪ'prɑsɪti] *s* reciprocidad
recital [rɪ'saɪtəl] *s* narración; (*of music or poetry*) recital *m*
recite [rɪ'saɪt] *tr* narrar; (*formally*) recitar
reckless ['rɛklɪs] *adj* atolondrado, temerario
reckon ['rɛkən] *tr* calcular; considerar; (coll) calcular, conjeturar || *intr* calcular; **to reckon on** contar con; **to reckon with** tener en cuenta
reclaim [rɪ'klem] *tr* hacer utilizable; hacer labrantío (*un terreno*); ganar (*terreno*) a la mar; recuperar (*materiales usados*); conducir, guiar (*a los que hacen mala vida*)
recline [rɪ'klaɪn] *intr* reclinarse
recluse [rɪ'klus] o ['rɛklus] *s* solitario, ermitaño
recognize ['rɛkəg,naɪz] *tr* reconocer
recoil [rɪ'kɔɪl] *s* reculada; (*of a firearm*) reculada, culetazo || *intr* recular, apartarse; recular (*un arma de fuego*)
recollect [,rɛkə'lɛkt] *tr & intr* recordar
recommend [,rɛkə'mɛnd] *tr* recomendar
recompense ['rɛkəm,pɛns] *s* recompensa || *tr* recompensar
reconcile ['rɛkən,saɪl] *tr* reconciliar; **to reconcile oneself** resignarse
reconnaissance [rɪ'kɑnɪsəns] *s* reconocimiento
reconnoiter [,rɛkə'nɔɪtər] o [,rikə'nɔɪtər] *tr & intr* reconocer
reconquest [ri'kɑŋkwɛst] *s* reconquista
reconsider [,rikən'sɪdər] *tr* reconsiderar
reconstruct [,rikən'strʌkt] *tr* reconstruir
reconversion [,rikən'vʌrʒən] o [,rikən'vʌrʃən] *s* reconversión
record ['rɛkərd] *s* anotación; ficha, historial *m,* historia personal; (*of a notary*) protocolo; (*of a phonograph*) disco; (educ) expediente académico; (sport) record *m,* plusmarca; **off the record** confidencialmente; **records** anales *mpl,* memorias; archivo; **to break a record** batir un record; **to make a record** establecer un record; grabar un disco || [rɪ'kɔrd] *tr* asentar; registrar; inscribir; grabar (*un sonido, una canción, un disco fonográfico, etc.*)
record breaker *s* plusmarquista *mf*
record changer ['tʃendʒər] *s* cambiadiscos *m,* tocadiscos automático
record holder *s* (sport) recordman *m*
recording [rɪ'kɔrdɪŋ] *adj* registrador;

(*wire or tape*) magnetofónico || *s* registro; (*of phonograph records*) grabación o grabado
recording secretary *s* secretario escribiente, secretario de actas
record player *s* tocadiscos *m*
recount ['ri ˌkaʊnt] *s* recuento || [ri'kaʊnt] *tr* (*to count again*) recontar || [rɪ'kaʊnt] *tr* (*to narrate*) recontar
recourse [rɪ'kors] o ['rikors] *s* recurso; (*helping hand*) paño de lágrimas; **to have recourse to** recurrir a
recover [rɪ'kʌvər] *tr* recobrar; rescatar; **to recover consciousness** recobrar el conocimiento, volver en sí || *intr* recobrarse; recobrar la salud; ganar un pleito
recover•y [rɪ'kʌvəri] *s* (*pl* **-ies**) recobro, recuperación; **past recovery** sin remedio
recreant ['rɛkrɪ·ənt] *adj* & *s* cobarde *mf*, traidor *m*
recreation [ˌrɛkrɪ'eʃən] *s* recreación
recruit [rɪ'krut] *s* recluta *m* || *tr* reclutar || *intr* alistar reclutas; ganar reclutas; restablecerse, reponerse
rect. *abbr* **receipt, rector, rectory**
rectangle ['rɛk ˌtæŋgəl] *s* rectángulo
recti•fy ['rɛktɪˌfaɪ] *v* (*pret* & *pp* **-fied**) *tr* rectificar
rec•tum ['rɛktəm] *s* (*pl* **-ta** [tə]) recto
recumbent [rɪ'kʌmbənt] *adj* reclinado, recostado
recuperate [rɪ'kjupə ˌret] *tr* recuperar; restablecer, reponer || *intr* recuperarse, recobrarse
re•cur [rɪ'kʌr] *v* (*pret* & *pp* **-curred;** *ger* **-curring**) *intr* volver a ocurrir; volver a presentarse (*a la memoria*); volver (*a un asunto*)
recurrent [rɪ'kʌrənt] *adj* repetido; periódico; (*illness*) recurrente
red [rɛd] *adj* (*comp* **redder;** *super* **reddest**) rojo, colorado; (*wine*) tinto; enrojecido, inflamado || *s* rojo; **in the red** (coll) endeudado; **to see red** (coll) enfurecerse || **Red** *adj* & *s* (*communist*) rojo
red'bait' *tr* motejar (*a uno*) de rojo o comunista
red'bird' *s* cardenal *m;* piranga
red-blooded ['rɛd ˌblʌdɪd] *adj* fuerte, valiente, vigoroso
red'breast' *s* petirrojo
red'bud' *s* ciclamor *m* del Canadá
red'cap' *s* (Brit) policía militar; (U.S.A.) mozo de estación
red cell *s* glóbulo rojo, hematíe *m*
red'coat' *s* (hist) soldado inglés
redden ['rɛdən] *tr* enrojecer || *intr* enrojecerse
redeem [rɪ'dim] *tr* redimir; cumplir (*una promesa*)
redeemer [rɪ'dimər] *s* redentor *m*
redemption [rɪ'dɛmpʃən] *s* redención
red-haired ['rɛd ˌhɛrd] *adj* pelirrojo
red'head' *s* pelirrojo
red herring *s* artificio para distraer la atención del asunto de que se trata
red'-hot' *adj* candente, calentado al rojo; ardiente, entusiasta; fresco, nuevo
rediscount rate [ri'dɪskaʊnt] *s* tipo de redescuento
rediscover [ˌridɪs'kʌvər] *tr* redescubrir
red'-let'ter day *s* día *m* memorable
red'-light' district *s* barrio de los lupanares, barrio de mala vida
red man *s* piel roja *m*
re•do ['ri'du] *v* (*pret* **-did** ['dɪd]; *pp* **-done** ['dʌn]) *tr* rehacer, repetir; refundir; reformar
redolent ['rɛdələnt] *adj* fragante, perfumado; **redolent of** que huele a
redoubt [rɪ'daʊt] *s* (fort) reducto
redound [rɪ'daʊnd] *intr* redundar; **to redound to** redundar en
red pepper *s* pimentón *m*
redress [rɪ'drɛs] o ['ridrɛs] *s* reparación; remedio || [rɪ'drɛs] *tr* reparar; remediar
Red Ridinghood ['raɪdɪŋ ˌhʊd] *s* Caperucita Roja
red'skin' *s* piel roja *m*
red tape *s* expedienteo, papeleo
reduce [rɪ'djus] o [rɪ'dus] *tr* reducir; (mil) degradar || *intr* reducirse; reducir peso
reducing exercises *spl* ejercicios físicos para reducir peso
redundant [rɪ'dʌndənt] *adj* redundante
red'wood' *s* secoya
reed [rid] *adj* (*organ, musical instrument*) de lengüeta || *s* (*stalk*) caña; (*plant*) carrizo, caña; (mus) instrumento de lengüeta; (*of instrument*) lengüeta
reëdit [ri'ɛdɪt] *tr* refundir
reef [rif] *s* arrecife *m*, escollo; (min) filón *m*, veta || *tr* (naut) arrizar
reefer ['rifər] *s* chaquetón *m;* (slang) pitillo de mariguana
reek [rik] *intr* vahear, humear; estar bañado en sudor; estar mojado con sangre; **to reek of** o **with** oler a
reel [ril] *s* (*spool*) carrete *m;* (*of a shuttle*) broca; (*of motion pictures*) cinta; (*sway, staggering*) tambaleo; **off the reel** (coll) fácil y prestamente || *tr* aspar, devanar; **to reel off** (coll) narrar fácil y prestamente || *intr* tambalear; cejar (*p.ej., el enemigo*)
reëlection [ˌri·ɪ'lɛkʃən] *s* reelección
reënlist [ˌri·ɛn'lɪst] *tr* reenganchar || *intr* reengancharse
reën•try [rɪ'ɛntri] *s* (*pl* **-tries**) reingreso, nueva entrada; (*return to earth's atmosphere*) reentrada
reëxamination [ˌri·ɛgˌzæmɪ'neʃən] *s* reexaminación
ref. *abbr* **referee, reference, reformation**
re•fer [rɪ'fʌr] *v* (*pret* & *pp* **-ferred;** *ger* **-ferring**) *tr* referir || *intr* referirse
referee [ˌrɛfə'ri] *s* árbitro || *tr* & *intr* arbitrar
reference ['rɛfərəns] *adj* (*library, book, work*) de consulta || *s* referencia
referen•dum [ˌrɛfə'rɛndəm] *s* (*pl* **-da** [də]) *s* referéndum *m*
refill ['rifɪl] *s* relleno || [ri'fɪl] *tr* rellenar
refine [rɪ'faɪn] *tr* refinar

refinement [rɪˈfaɪnmənt] *s* refinamiento; buena crianza, cultura
refiner•y [rɪˈfaɪnəri] *s* (*pl* **-ies**) refinería
reflect [rɪˈflɛkt] *tr* reflejar || *intr* reflejar; (*to meditate*) reflexionar; **to reflect on** o **upon** reflexionar en o sobre; perjudicar
reflection [rɪˈflɛkʃən] *s* (*thinking*) reflexión; (*reflected light; image*) reflejo
reforestation [ˌrifɑrɪsˈteʃən] o [ˌrifɔrɪsˈteʃən] *s* reforestación
reform [rɪˈfɔrm] *s* reforma || *tr* reformar || *intr* reformarse
reformation [ˌrɛfərˈmeʃən] *s* reformación || **the Reformation** la Reforma
reformato•ry [rɪˈfɔrməˌtori] *s* (*pl* **-ries**) reformatorio
reform school *s* casa de corrección
refraction [rɪˈfrækʃən] *s* refracción
refrain [rɪˈfren] *s* estribillo || *intr* abstenerse
refresh [rɪˈfrɛʃ] *tr* refrescar || *intr* refrescarse
refreshing [rɪˈfrɛʃɪŋ] *adj* confortante, restaurante
refreshment [rɪˈfrɛʃmənt] *s* refresco
refrigerator [rɪˈfrɪdʒəˌretər] *s* heladera, nevera, refrigerador *m*
refrigerator car *s* carro o vagón frigorífico
refuel [riˈfjul] *tr & intr* repostar
refuge [ˈrɛfjudʒ] *s* refugio; expediente *m*, subterfugio; **to take refuge (in)** refugiarse (en)
refugee [ˌrɛfjuˈdʒi] *s* refugiado
refund [ˈrifʌnd] *s* reembolso || [rɪˈfʌnd] *tr* reembolsar || [riˈfʌnd] *tr* consolidar
refurnish [riˈfʌrnɪʃ] *tr* amueblar de nuevo
refusal [rɪˈfjuzəl] *s* negativa
refuse [ˈrɛfjus] *s* basura, desecho, desperdicios || [rɪˈfjuz] *tr* rehusar; rechazar, no querer aceptar; **to refuse to** negarse a
refute [rɪˈfjut] *tr* refutar
reg. *abbr* **register, registrar, registry, regular**
regain [rɪˈgen] *tr* recobrar, recuperar; volver a alcanzar; **to regain consciousness** recobrar el conocimiento, volver en sí
regal [ˈrigəl] *adj* regio
regale [rɪˈgel] *tr* regalar, agasajar
regalia [rɪˈgelɪ·ə] *spl* (*of an office or order*) distintivos; galas, trajes *mpl* de lujo
regard [rɪˈgɑrd] *s* consideración, miramiento; (*esteem*) respeto; (*particular matter*) respecto; (*look*) mirada; **in regard to** respecto a o de; **regards** recuerdos; **without regard to** sin hacer caso de; **with regard to** respecto a o de || *tr* considerar; mirar; tocar a, referirse a; **as regards** en cuanto a
regarding [rɪˈgɑrdɪŋ] *prep* tocante a, respecto a o de
regardless [rɪˈgɑrdlɪs] *adj* desatento, indiferente || *adv* (coll) pese a quien pese, cueste lo que cueste; **regardless of** sin hacer caso de; a pesar de
regenerate [rɪˈdʒɛnəˌret] *tr* regenerar || *intr* regenerarse
regent [ˈridʒənt] *s* regente *mf*
regicide [ˈrɛdʒɪˌsaɪd] *s* (*act*) regicidio; (*person*) regicida *mf*
regime o **régime** [reˈʒim] *s* régimen *m*
regiment [ˈrɛdʒɪmənt] *s* regimiento || [ˈrɛdʒɪˌmɛnt] *tr* regimentar
regimental [ˌrɛdʒɪˈmɛntəl] *adj* regimental || **regimentals** *spl* uniforme *m* militar
region [ˈridʒən] *s* región, comarca
register [ˈrɛdʒɪstər] *s* (*record; book for keeping such a record*) registro; reja regulable de calefacción; (*of the voice or an instrument*) extensión || *tr* (*to indicate by a record; to show, as on a scale*) registrar; empadronar (*los vecinos en el padrón*); manifestar, dar a conocer; certificar (*envíos por correo*); inscribir || *intr* registrarse; empadronarse; inscribirse
registered letter *s* carta certificada
registrar [ˈrɛdʒɪsˌtrɑr] *s* registrador *m*, archivero
registration fee [ˌrɛdʒɪsˈtreʃən] *s* derechos de matrícula
re•gret [rɪˈgrɛt] *s* pesar *m*, sentimiento; pesadumbre, remordimiento; **regrets** excusas || *v* (*pret & pp* **-gretted;** *ger* **-gretting**) *tr* sentir, lamentar; lamentar la pérdida de; arrepentirse de; **to regret to** sentir
regrettable [rɪˈgrɛtəbəl] *adj* lamentable
regular [ˈrɛgjələr] *adj* regular; (coll) cabal, completo, verdadero || *s* obrero permanente; parroquiano regular; **regulars** tropas regulares
regulate [ˈrɛgjəˌlet] *tr* regular
rehabilitate [ˌrihəˈbɪlɪˌtet] *tr* rehabilitar
rehearsal [rɪˈhʌrsəl] *s* ensayo
rehearse [rɪˈhʌrs] *tr* ensayar || *intr* ensayarse
reign [ren] *s* reinado || *intr* reinar
reimburse [ˌri·ɪmˈbʌrs] *tr* reembolsar
rein [ren] *s* rienda; **to give free rein to** dar rienda suelta a || *tr* dirigir por medio de riendas; contener, refrenar, gobernar
reincarnation [ˌri·ɪnkɑrˈneʃən] *s* reencarnación
reindeer [ˈrenˌdɪr] *s* reno
reinforce [ˌri·ɪnˈfors] *tr* reforzar; armar (*el hormigón*)
reinforcement [ˌri·ɪnˈforsmənt] *s* refuerzo
reinstate [ˌri·ɪnˈstet] *tr* reinstalar
reiterate [riˈɪtəˌret] *tr* reiterar
reject [rɪˈdʒɛkt] *tr* rechazar
rejection [rɪˈdʒɛkʃən] *s* rechazamiento
rejoice [rɪˈdʒɔɪs] *intr* regocijarse
rejoinder [rɪˈdʒɔɪndər] *s* contestación; (law) contrarréplica
rejuvenation [rɪˌdʒuvɪˈneʃən] *s* rejuvenecimiento
rel. *abbr* **relating, relative, religion, religious**
relapse [rɪˈlæps] *s* recaída || *intr* recaer
relate [rɪˈlet] *tr* (*to establish relationship between*) relacionar; (*to narrate*) contar, relatar

relation [rɪ'leʃən] *s* (*connection; narration*) relación; (*narration*) relato; (*relative*) pariente *mf;* (*kinship*) parentesco; **in relation to** o **with** tocante a, respecto a o de

relationship [rɪ'leʃən,ʃɪp] *s* (*connection*) relación; (*kinship*) parentesco

relative ['rɛlətɪv] *adj* relativo || *s* deudo, pariente *mf*

relax [rɪ'læks] *tr & intr* relajar

relaxation [,rilæks'eʃən] *s* relajación; despreocupación

relaxation of tension *s* disminución de tensión; disminución de la tirantez internacional

relaxing [rɪ'læksɪŋ] *adj* relajador; despreocupante, tranquilizador

relay ['rile] o [rɪ'le] *s* (elec) relais *m,* relevador *m,* relevo; (mil & sport) relevo; (sport) carrera de relevos || *v* (*pret & pp* **-layed**) *tr* transmitir relevándose; transmitir con un relais; retransmitir (*una emisión*); reexpedir (*un radiotelegrama*) || [rɪ'le] *v* (*pret & pp* **-laid**) *tr* volver a colocar, volver a tender

relay race *s* carrera de relevos

release [rɪ'lis] *s* liberación; (*from jail*) excarcelación; alivio; permiso de publicación, venta, etc.; obra o pieza lista para la publicación, venta, etc.; (aer) lanzamiento; (mach) escape *m,* disparador *m* || *tr* soltar; libertar; excarcelar (*a un preso*); permitir la publicación, venta, etc. de; (aer.) lanzar (*una bomba*)

relent [rɪ'lɛnt] *intr* ablandarse, aplacarse

relentless [rɪ'lɛntlɪs] *adj* implacable

relevant ['rɛlɪvənt] *adj* pertinente

reliable [rɪ'laɪ·əbəl] *adj* confiable, fidedigno

reliance [rɪ'laɪ·əns] *s* confianza

relic ['rɛlɪk] *s* reliquia

relief [rɪ'lif] *s* alivio; caridad; (*projection of figures; elevation*) relieve *m;* (mil) relevo; **in relief** en relieve; **on relief** viviendo de socorro, recibiendo auxilio social

relieve [rɪ'liv] *tr* (*to release from a post*) relevar; aliviar; auxiliar (*a los necesitados*); (mil) relevar

religion [rɪ'lɪdʒən] *s* religión

religious [rɪ'lɪdʒəs] *adj* religioso

relinquish [rɪ'lɪŋkwɪʃ] *tr* abandonar, dejar

relish ['rɛlɪʃ] *s* buen sabor, gusto; condimento, sazón *f;* entremés *m;* buen apetito || *tr* gustar de; comer o beber con placer

reluctance [rɪ'lʌktəns] *s* renuencia, aversión

reluctant [rɪ'lʌktənt] *adj* renuente, maldispuesto

re·ly [rɪ'laɪ] *v* (*pret & pp* **-lied**) *intr* depender, confiar; **to rely on** depender de, confiar en

remain [rɪ'men] *intr* permanecer, quedarse || **remains** *spl* desechos, restos; restos mortales; obra póstuma

remainder [rɪ'mendər] *s* resto, residuo; libro casi invendible || *tr* saldar (*libros que ya no se venden*)

re·make [ri'mek] *v* (*pret & pp* **-made** ['med]) *tr* rehacer

remark [rɪ'mɑrk] *s* observación || *tr & intr* observar; **to remark on** aludir a, comentar

remarkable [rɪ'mɑrkəbəl] *adj* notable, extraordinario

remar·ry [ri'mæri] *v* (*pret & pp* **-ried**) *intr* volver a casarse

reme·dy ['rɛmɪdi] *s* (*pl* **-dies**) remedio || *v* (*pret & pp* **-died**) *tr* remediar

remember [rɪ'mɛmbər] *tr* acordarse de, recordar; dar recuerdos de parte de, p.ej., **remember me to your brother** déle Vd. a su hermano recuerdos de mi parte || *intr* acordarse, recordar; **if I remember correctly** si mal no me acuerdo

remembrance [rɪ'mɛmbrəns] *s* recuerdo

remind [rɪ'maɪnd] *tr* recordar

reminder [rɪ'maɪndər] *s* recordatorio, recordativo

reminisce [,rɛmɪ'nɪs] *intr* entregarse a los recuerdos, contar sus recuerdos

remiss [rɪ'mɪs] *adj* descuidado, negligente

re·mit [rɪ'mɪt] *v* (*pret & pp* **-mitted;** *ger* **-mitting**) *tr* (*to send, to ship; to pardon*) remitir

remittance [rɪ'mɪtəns] *s* remesa

remnant ['rɛmnənt] *s* (*something left over*) remanente *m;* (*of cloth*) retal *m,* retazo; (*piece of cloth to be sold at reduced price*) saldo; vestigio

remod·el [ri'mɑdəl] *v* (*pret & pp* **-eled** o **-elled;** *ger* **-eling** o **-elling**) *tr* modelar de nuevo; rehacer, reconstruir; convertir, transformar

remonstrate [rɪ'mɑnstret] *intr* protestar; **to remonstrate with** reconvenir

remorse [rɪ'mɔrs] *s* remordimiento

remorseful [rɪ'mɔrsfəl] *adj* compungido, arrepentido

remote [rɪ'mot] *adj* remoto

remote control *s* comando a distancia, telecontrol *m*

removable [rɪ'muvəbəl] *adj* amovible

removal [rɪ'muvəl] *s* remoción; mudanza, traslado; (*dismissal*) deposición

remove [rɪ'muv] *tr* remover; quitar de en medio, apartar matando || *intr* removerse

remuneration [rɪ,mjunə'reʃən] *s* remuneración

renaissance [,rɛnə'sɑns] o [rɪ'nesəns] *s* renacimiento

rend [rɛnd] *v* (*pret & pp* **rent** [rɛnt]) *tr* (*to tear*) desgarrar; (*to split*) hender, rajar; estremecer (*un ruido el aire*)

render ['rɛndər] *tr* rendir (*gracias, obsequios, homenaje*); prestar, suministrar (*ayuda*); pagar (*tributo*); desempeñar (*un papel*); traducir (*sentimientos*); (*from one language to another*) verter; hacer (*justicia*); ejecutar (*una pieza de música*); derretir (*cera, manteca*); extraer la grasa o el sebo de; poner, volver

rendezvous ['rɑndə,vu] *s* (*pl* **-vous** [,vuz]) cita; (*in space*) encuentro, reunión || *v* (*pret & pp* **-voused** [ˌvud]; *ger* **-vousing** [ˌvu·ɪŋ]) *intr* reunirse en una cita

rendition [rɛnˈdɪʃən] *s* rendición; traducción; (mus) ejecución

renege [rɪˈnɪg] *s* renuncio || *intr* renunciar; (coll) volverse atrás

renegotiation [ˌrinɪˌgoʃɪˈeʃən] *s* renegociación

renew [rɪˈnju] o [rɪˈnu] *tr* renovar || *intr* renovarse

renewable [rɪˈnju·əbəl] o [rɪˈnu·əbəl] *adj* renovable

renewal [rɪˈnju·əl] o [rɪˈnu·əl] *s* renovación

renounce [rɪˈnaʊns] *tr* renunciar; renunciar a (*p.ej., el mundo*) || *intr* renunciar

renovate [ˈrɛnəˌvet] *tr* renovar; reformar (*p.ej., una tienda, una casa*)

renown [rɪˈnaʊn] *s* renombre *m*

renowned [rɪˈnaʊnd] *adj* renombrado

rent [rɛnt] *adj* desgarrado || *s* alquiler *m*, arriendo; (*tear, slit*) desgarro || *tr* alquilar, arrendar || *intr* alquilarse, arrendarse

rental [ˈrɛntəl] *s* alquiler *m*, arriendo

renunciation [rɪˌnʌnsɪˈeʃən] o [rɪˌnʌnʃɪˈeʃən] *s* renunciación

reopen [riˈopən] *tr* reabrir || *intr* reabrirse

reorganize [riˈɔrgəˌnaɪz] *tr* reorganizar || *intr* reorganizarse

rep. *abbr* **report, reporter, representative, republic**

repair [rɪˈpɛr] *s* reparación; **in repair** en buen estado || *tr* reparar || *intr* dirigirse; volver

repaper [riˈpepər] *tr* empapelar de nuevo

reparation [ˌrɛpəˈreʃən] *s* reparación

repartee [ˌrɛpɑrˈti] *s* respuesta viva; agudeza y gracia en responder

repast [rɪˈpæst] o [rɪˈpɑst] *s* comida, comilona

repatriate [riˈpetrɪˌet] *tr* repatriar

re·pay [rɪˈpe] *v* (*pret & pp* **-paid** [ˈped]) *tr* reembolsar; resarcir (*un daño, una injuria*); compensar

repayment [rɪˈpemənt] *s* reembolso; resarcimiento; compensación

repeal [rɪˈpil] *s* abrogación, revocación || *tr* abrogar, revocar

repeat [rɪˈpit] *s* repetición || *tr & intr* repetir

re·pel [rɪˈpɛl] *v* (*pret & pp* **-pelled**; *ger* **-pelling**) *tr* rechazar, repeler; repugnar

repent [rɪˈpɛnt] *tr* arrepentirse de || *intr* arrepentirse

repentance [rɪˈpɛntəns] *s* arrepentimiento

repentant [rɪˈpɛntənt] *adj* arrepentido

repertory theater [ˈrɛpərˌtori] *s* teatro de repertorio

repetition [ˌrɛpɪˈtɪʃən] *s* repetición

repine [rɪˈpaɪn] *intr* afligirse, quejarse

replace [rɪˈples] *tr* (*to put back*) reponer; (*to take the place of*) reemplazar

replacement [rɪˈplesmənt] *s* reposición; reemplazo; pieza de repuesto; soldado reemplazante

replenish [rɪˈplɛnɪʃ] *tr* rellenar; reaprovisionar

replete [rɪˈplit] *adj* repleto

replica [ˈrɛplɪkə] *s* réplica

re·ply [rɪˈplaɪ] *s* (*pl* **-plies**) contestación, respuesta || *v* (*pret & pp* **-plied**) *tr & intr* contestar, responder

reply coupon *s* vale *m* respuesta

report [rɪˈport] *s* relato, informe *m*; voz *f*, rumor *m*; (*e.g., of a firearm*) detonación, tiro; denuncia || *tr* relatar, informar acerca de; denunciar || *intr* hacer un relato; redactar un informe; ser repórter; presentarse; **to report on** dar cuenta de, notificar

report card *s* certificado escolar

reportedly [rɪˈportɪdli] *adv* según se informa

reporter [rɪˈportər] *s* repórter *m*

reporting [rɪˈportɪŋ] *s* reportaje *m*

repose [rɪˈpoz] *s* descanso || *tr* descansar; poner (*confianza*) || *intr* descansar

reprehend [ˌrɛprɪˈhɛnd] *tr* reprender

represent [ˌrɛprɪˈzɛnt] *tr* representar

representative [ˌrɛprɪˈzɛntətɪv] *adj* representativo || *s* representante *mf*

repress [rɪˈprɛs] *tr* reprimir

reprieve [rɪˈpriv] *s* suspensión temporal de un castigo, suspensión temporal de la pena de muerte; respiro, alivio temporal || *tr* suspender temporalmente el castigo de o la pena de muerte de; aliviar temporalmente

reprimand [ˈrɛprɪˌmænd] o [ˈrɛprɪˌmɑnd] *s* reprimenda || *tr* reconvenir, reprender

reprint [ˈriˌprɪnt] *s* reimpresión; tirada aparte || [riˈprɪnt] *tr* reimprimir

reprisal [rɪˈpraɪzəl] *s* represalia

reproach [rɪˈprotʃ] *s* reproche *m*; oprobio || *tr* reprochar; oprobiar

reproduce [ˌriprəˈdjus] o [ˌriprəˈdus] *tr* reproducir || *intr* reproducirse

reproduction [ˌriprəˈdʌkʃən] *s* reproducción

reproof [rɪˈpruf] *s* reprobación

reprove [rɪˈpruv] *tr* reprobar

reptile [ˈrɛptɪl] *s* reptil *m*

republic [rɪˈpʌblɪk] *s* república

republican [rɪˈpʌblɪkən] *adj & s* republicano

repudiate [rɪˈpjudɪˌet] *tr* repudiar; no reconocer (*p.ej., una deuda*)

repugnant [rɪˈpʌgnənt] *adj* repugnante

repulse [rɪˈpʌls] *s* repulsión, rechazo || *tr* repeler, rechazar

repulsive [rɪˈpʌlsɪv] *adj* repulsivo

reputation [ˌrɛpjəˈteʃən] *s* reputación; buena reputación

repute [rɪˈpjut] *s* reputación; buena reputación || *tr* reputar

reputedly [rɪˈpjutɪdli] *adv* según la opinión común

request [rɪˈkwɛst] *s* petición, solicitud; **at the request of** a petición de || *tr* pedir

require [rɪˈkwaɪr] *tr* exigir, requerir

requirement [rɪˈkwaɪrmənt] *s* requisito; necesidad

requisite [ˈrɛkwɪzɪt] *adj & s* requisito

requital [rɪˈkwaɪtəl] *s* compensación, retorno

requite [rɪˈkwaɪt] *tr* corresponder a (*los beneficios, el amor, etc.*); corresponder con (*el bienhechor*)
re•read [riˈrid] *v* (*pret & pp* **-read** [ˈrɛd]) *tr* releer
resale [ˈriˌsel] o [riˈsel] *s* reventa
rescind [rɪˈsɪnd] *tr* rescindir
rescue [ˈrɛskju] *s* salvación, rescate *m,* liberación; **to go to the rescue of** acudir al socorro de || *tr* salvar, rescatar, libertar
rescue party *s* pelotón *m* de salvamento
research [rɪˈsʌrtʃ] o [ˈrisʌrtʃ] *s* investigación || *intr* investigar
re•sell [riˈsɛl] *v* (*pret & pp* **-sold** [ˈsold]) *tr* revender
resemblance [rɪˈzɛmbləns] *s* parecido, semejanza
resemble [rɪˈzɛmbəl] *tr* parecerse a, asemejarse a
resent [rɪˈzɛnt] *tr* resentirse de o por
resentful [rɪˈzɛntfəl] *adj* resentido
resentment [rɪˈzɛntmənt] *s* resentimiento
reservation [ˌrɛzərˈveʃən] *s* reserva
reserve [rɪˈzʌrv] *s* reserva || *tr* reservar
reservoir [ˈrɛzərˌvwɑr] *s* depósito; (*where water is dammed back*) embalse *m,* pantano; (*of wisdom*) fondo
re•ship [riˈʃɪp] *v* (*pret & pp* **-shipped;** *ger* **-shipping**) *tr* reenviar, reexpedir; (*on a ship*) reembarcar || *intr* reembarcarse
reshipment [riˈʃɪpmənt] *s* reenvío, reexpedición; (*of persons*) reembarco; (*of goods*) reembarque *m*
reside [rɪˈzaɪd] *intr* residir
residence [ˈrɛzɪdəns] *s* residencia
resident [ˈrɛzɪdənt] *adj & s* residente *mf,* vecino
residue [ˈrɛzɪˌdju] o [ˈrɛzɪˌdu] *s* residuo
resign [rɪˈzaɪn] *tr* dimitir, resignar, renunciar || *intr* dimitir; (*to yield, submit*) resignarse; **to resign to** resignarse con (*p.ej., su suerte*)
resignation [ˌrɛzɪgˈneʃən] *s* (*from a job, etc.*) dimisión; (*state of being submissive*) resignación
resin [ˈrɛzɪn] *s* resina
resist [rɪˈzɪst] *tr* resistir (*la tentación*); resistir a (*la violencia; la risa*) || *intr* resistirse
resistance [rɪˈzɪstəns] *s* resistencia
resole [riˈsol] *tr* sobresolar
resolute [ˈrɛzəˌlut] *adj* resuelto
resolution [ˌrɛzəˈluʃən] *s* resolución; **good resolutions** buenos propósitos
resolve [rɪˈzɔlv] *s* resolución || *tr* resolver || *intr* resolverse
resort [rɪˈzɔrt] *s* lugar muy frecuentado; (*e.g., for vacations*) estación; (*for help or support*) recurso; **as a last resort** como último recurso || *intr* recurrir
resound [rɪˈzaʊnd] *intr* resonar
resource [rɪˈsors] o [ˈrisors] *s* recurso
resourceful [rɪˈsorsfəl] *adj* ingenioso
respect [rɪˈspɛkt] *s* (*deference, esteem*) respeto; (*reference, relation; detail*) respecto; **respects** recuerdos, saludos; **to pay one's respects (to)** ofrecer sus respetos (a); **with respect to** respecto a o de || *tr* respetar
respectable [rɪˈspɛktəbəl] *adj* respetable; decente, presentable
respectful [rɪˈspɛktfəl] *adj* respetuoso
respectfully [rɪˈspɛktfəli] *adj* respetuosamente; **respectfully yours** de Vd. atento y seguro servidor
respecting [rɪˈspɛktɪŋ] *prep* con respecto a, respecto de
respective [rɪˈspɛktɪv] *adj* respectivo
respire [rɪˈspaɪr] *tr & intr* respirar
respite [ˈrɛspɪt] *s* (*temporary relief*) respiro; (*postponement, especially of death sentence*) suspensión; **without respite** sin respirar
resplendent [rɪˈsplɛndənt] *adj* resplandeciente
respond [rɪˈspɑnd] *intr* responder
response [rɪˈspɑns] *s* respuesta
responsible [rɪˈspɑnsɪbəl] *adj* responsable; (*job, position*) de confianza; **responsible for** responsable de
rest [rɛst] *s* (*after exertion or work; sleep*) descanso; (*lack of motion*) reposo; (*of the dead*) paz *f;* (*what remains*) resto; (mus) pausa; **at rest** (*not moving*) **en** reposo; tranquilo; dormido; (*dead*) muerto; **the rest** lo demás; los demás; **to come to rest** venir a parar; **to lay to rest** enterrar || *tr* descansar; parar; poner (*p.ej., confianza*) || *intr* descansar; estar, hallarse; **to rest assured (that)** estar seguro, tener la seguridad (de que); **to rest on** descansar en o sobre, estribar en
restaurant [ˈrɛstərənt] o [ˈrɛstəˌrɑnt] *s* restaurante *m*
rest cure *s* cura de reposo
restful [ˈrɛstfəl] *adj* descansado, tranquilo, reposado
resting place *s* lugar *m* de descanso; (*of a staircase*) descansadero; (*of the dead*) última morada
restitution [ˌrɛstɪˈtjuʃən] o [ˌrɛstɪˈtuʃən] *s* restitución
restless [ˈrɛstlɪs] *adj* intranquilo; (*sleepless*) insomne
restock [riˈstɑk] *tr* reaprovisionar; repoblar (*p.ej., un acuario*)
restore [rɪˈstor] *tr* restaurar; (*to give back*) devolver
restrain [rɪˈstren] *tr* contener, refrenar; aprisionar
restraint [rɪˈstrent] *s* restricción; comedimiento, moderación
restrict [rɪˈstrɪkt] *tr* restringir
rest room *s* sala de descanso; excusado, retrete *m;* (*of a theater*) saloncillo
result [rɪˈzʌlt] *s* resultado; **as a result of** de resultas de || *intr* resultar; **to result in** dar por resultado, parar en
resume [rɪˈzum] o [rɪˈzjum] *tr* reasumir; reanudar (*el viaje, el vuelo, etc.*); volver a tomar (*su asiento*) || *intr* continuar; recomenzar; reanudar el hilo del discurso
résumé [ˌrɛzuˈme] o [ˌrɛzjuˈme] *s* resumen *m*
resurface [riˈsʌrfɪs] *tr* dar nueva superficie a || *intr* volver a emerger (*un submarino*)

resurrect [ˌrɛzəˈrɛkt] *tr & intr* resucitar
resurrection [ˌrɛzəˈrɛkʃən] *s* resurrección
resuscitate [rɪˈsʌsɪˌtet] *tr & intr* resucitar
retail [ˈritel] *adj & adv* al por menor ‖ *s* venta al por menor ‖ *tr* detallar, vender al por menor ‖ *intr* vender al por menor; venderse al por menor
retailer [ˈritelər] *s* detallista *mf*, comerciante *mf* al por menor
retain [rɪˈten] *tr* retener; contratar (*a un abogado*)
retaliate [rɪˈtælɪˌet] *intr* desquitarse, vengarse
retaliation [rɪˌtælɪˈeʃən] *s* desquite *m*, venganza
retard [rɪˈtɑrd] *s* retardo ‖ *tr* retardar
retch [rɛtʃ] *tr* vomitar ‖ *intr* arquear, esforzarse por vomitar
retching [ˈrɛtʃɪŋ] *s* arcadas
ret'd. *abbr* **returned**
reticence [ˈrɛtɪsəns] *s* reserva, circunspección, sigilo
reticent [ˈrɛtɪsənt] *adj* reservado, circunspecto
retinue [ˈrɛtɪˌnju] o [ˈrɛtɪˌnu] *s* comitiva, séquito
retire [rɪˈtaɪr] *tr* retirar; jubilar (*a un empleado*) ‖ *intr* retirarse; jubilarse; (*to go to bed*) recogerse; (mil) retirarse
retirement [rɪˈtaɪrmənt] *s* retiro; (*of an employee with pension*) jubilación; (mil) retirada
retirement annuity *s* jubilación
retort [rɪˈtɔrt] *s* respuesta pronta y aguda, réplica; (chem) retorta ‖ *intr* replicar
retouch [riˈtʌtʃ] *tr* retocar
retrace [rɪˈtres] *tr* repasar; **to retrace one's steps** volver sobre sus pasos
retract [rɪˈtrækt] *tr* retractarse de, desdecirse de (*lo que se ha dicho*) ‖ *intr* retractarse, desdecirse
re•tread [ˈriˌtrɛd] *s* neumático recauchutado; neumático ranurado ‖ [riˈtrɛd] *v* (*pret & pp* **-treaded**) *tr* recauchutar; volver a ranurar ‖ *v* (*pret* **-trod** [ˈtrɑd]; *pp* **-trod** o **-trodden**) *tr* desandar ‖ *intr* volverse atrás
retreat [rɪˈtrit] *s* (*act of withdrawing; place of seclusion*) retiro; (eccl) retiro; (mil) retreta, retirada; (*signal*) (mil) retreta; **to beat a retreat** retirarse; (mil) batirse en retirada ‖ *intr* retirarse
retrench [rɪˈtrɛntʃ] *tr* cercenar ‖ *intr* recogerse
retribution [ˌrɛtrɪˈbjuʃən] *s* justo castigo; (theol) juicio final
retrieve [rɪˈtriv] *tr* cobrar; reparar (*p.ej., un daño*); desquitarse de (*una pérdida, una derrota*); (hunt) cobrar, portar ‖ *intr* (hunt) cobrar, portar
retriever [rɪˈtrivər] *s* perro cobrador, perro traedor
retroactive [ˌrɛtroˈæktɪv] *adj* retroactivo
retrofiring [ˌrɛtroˈfaɪrɪŋ] *s* retrodisparo
retrogress [ˈrɛtrəˌgrɛs] *intr* retroceder; empeorar
retrorocket [ˌrɛtroˈrɑkɪt] *s* retrocohete *m*
retrospect [ˈrɛtrəˌspɛkt] *s* retrospección; **in retrospect** retrospectivamente
retrospective [ˌrɛtrəˈspɛktɪv] *adj* retrospectivo
re•try [riˈtraɪ] *v* (*pret & pp* **-tried**) *tr* reensayar; rever (*un caso legal*); procesar de nuevo (*a una persona*)
return [rɪˈtʌrn] *adj* repetido; de vuelta; **by return mail** a vuelta de correo ‖ *s* vuelta; devolución; recompensa; respuesta; informe *m*, noticia; ganancia, beneficio, rédito; (*of an election*) resultado; (*of income tax*) declaración; **in return (for)** en cambio (de); **many happy returns of the day!** ¡que cumpla muchos más! ‖ *tr* devolver; dar en cambio; corresponder a (*un favor*); dar (*una respuesta, las gracias*) ‖ *intr* volver; responder
return address *s* dirección del remitente
return bout o **engagement** *s* (box) combate *m* revancha
return game *s* desquite *m*
return ticket *s* billete *m* de vuelta; billete de ida y vuelta
return trip *s* viaje *m* de vuelta
reunification [riˌjunɪfɪˈkeʃən] *s* reunificación
reunion [riˈjunjən] *s* reunión
reunite [ˌrijuˈnaɪt] *tr* reunir ‖ *intr* reunirse
rev. *abbr* **revenue, reverse, review, revised, revision, revolution**
Rev. *abbr.* **Revelation, Reverend**
rev [rɛv] *s* revolución ‖ *v* (*pret & pp* **revved**; *ger* **revving**) *tr* cambiar la velocidad de; **to rev up** acelerar ‖ *intr* acelerarse
revamp [riˈvæmp] *tr* componer, renovar, remendar
reveal [rɪˈvil] *tr* revelar
reveille [ˈrɛvəli] *s* diana, toque *m* de diana
rev•el [ˈrɛvəl] *s* jarana, regocijo tumultuoso ‖ *v* (*pret & pp* **-eled** o **-elled**; *ger* **-eling** o **-elling**) *intr* jaranear; deleitarse
revelation [ˌrɛvəˈleʃən] *s* revelación
revel•ry [ˈrɛvəlri] *s* (*pl* **-ries**) jarana, diversión tumultuosa
revenge [rɪˈvɛndʒ] *s* venganza ‖ *tr* vengar
revengeful [rɪˈvɛndʒfəl] *adj* vengativo
revenue [ˈrɛvəˌnju] o [ˈrɛvəˌnu] *s* renta, rédito; rentas públicas
revenue cutter *s* escampavía
revenue stamp *s* sello fiscal, timbre *m* del estado
reverberate [rɪˈvʌrbəˌret] *intr* reverberar
revere [rɪˈvɪr] *tr* reverenciar, venerar
reverence [ˈrɛvərəns] *s* reverencia ‖ *tr* reverenciar
reverend [ˈrɛvərənd] *adj & s* reverendo
reverie [ˈrɛvəri] *s* ensueño
reversal [rɪˈvʌrsəl] *s* inversión; (*e.g., of opinion*) cambio
reverse [rɪˈvʌrs] *adj* invertido; con-

trario; de marcha atrás || *s* (*opposite or rear*) revés *m;* contrario; contramarcha, marcha atrás; (*check, defeat*) revés *m,* contratiempo || *tr* invertir; dar vuelta a; poner en marcha atrás; **to reverse oneself** cambiar de opinión; **to reverse the charges** cobrar al destinatario; (telp) cobrar al número llamado || *intr* invertirse

reverse lever *s* palanca de marcha atrás

revert [rɪ'vʌrt] *intr* revertir; saltar atrás; **to revert to one's old tricks** volver a las andadas

review [rɪ'vju] *s* (*reëxamination; survey; magazine; musical show*) revista; (*of a book*) reseña, revista; (*of a lesson*) repaso; (mil) reseña, revista || *tr* rever, revisar; reseñar (*un libro*); repasar (*una lección*); (mil) revistar

revile [rɪ'vaɪl] *tr* ultrajar, vilipendiar

revise [rɪ'vaɪz] *s* revisión; refundición; (typ) segunda prueba || *tr* rever, revisar; refundir (*un libro*); enmendar

revision [rɪ'vɪʒən] *s* revisión; (*of a book*) refundición; enmienda

revisionism [rɪ'vɪʒə,nɪzəm] *s* revisionismo

revisionist [rɪ'vɪʒənɪst] *adj & s* revisionista

revival [rɪ'vaɪvəl] *s* resucitación; reanimación; (*e.g., of learning*) renacimiento; despertamiento religioso; (theat) reestreno, reposición

revive [rɪ'vaɪv] *tr* revivir; (theat) reestrenar, reponer || *intr* revivir; volver en sí, recordar

revoke [rɪ'vok] *tr* revocar

revolt [rɪ'volt] *s* rebelión, sublevación || *tr* dar asco a, repugnar || *intr* rebelarse, sublevarse

revolting [rɪ'voltiŋ] *adj* asqueroso, repugnante; rebelde

revolution [,rɛvə'luʃən] *s* revolución

revolutionar·y [,rɛvə'luʃə,nɛri] *adj* revolucionario || *s* (*pl* **-ies**) revolucionario

revolve [rɪ'vɑlv] *tr* hacer girar; (*in one's mind*) revolver || *intr* girar; revolverse (*un astro en su órbita*)

revolver [rɪ'vɑlvər] *s* revólver *m*

revolving bookcase *s* giratoria

revolving door *s* puerta giratoria

revolving fund *s* fondo rotativo

revue [rɪ'vju] *s* (theat) revista

revulsion [rɪ'vʌlʃən] *s* aversión, repugnancia; reacción fuerte

reward [rɪ'wɔrd] *s* premio, recompensa; (*money used to recapture or recover*) rescate *m;* hallazgo, p.ej., **five dollars reward** cinco dólares de hallazgo || *tr* premiar, recompensar

rewarding [rɪ'wɔrdɪŋ] *adj* remunerador, provechoso, agradecido

re·write [ri'raɪt] *v* (*pret* **-wrote** ['rot]; *pp* **-written** ['rɪtən]) *tr* escribir de nuevo; refundir (*un escrito*); redactar (*un escrito de otra persona*)

R.F. *abbr* **radio frequency**

R.F.D. *abbr* **Rural Free Delivery**

R.H. *abbr* **Royal Highness**

rhapso·dy ['ræpsədi] *s* (*pl* **-dies**) rapsodia

rheostat ['ri·ə,stæt] *s* reóstato

rhesus ['risəs] *s* macaco de la India

rhetoric ['rɛtərɪk] *s* retórica

rhetorical [rɪ'tɑrɪkəl] o [rɪ'tɔrɪkəl] *adj* retórico

rheumatic [ru'mætɪk] *adj & s* reumático

rheumatism ['rumə,tɪzəm] *s* reumatismo

Rhine [raɪn] *s* Rin *m*

Rhineland ['raɪn,lænd] *s* Renania

rhine'stone' *s* diamante de imitación hecho de vidrio

rhinoceros [raɪ'nɑsərəs] *s* rinoceronte *m*

Rhodes [rodz] *s* Rodas *f*

Rhone [ron] *s* Ródano

rhubarb ['rubɑrb] *s* ruibarbo

rhyme [raɪm] *s* rima; **without rhyme or reason** sin ton ni son || *tr & intr* rimar

rhythm ['rɪðəm] *s* ritmo

rhythmic(al) ['rɪðmɪk(əl)] *adj* rítmico

rial·to [rɪ'ælto] *s* (*pl* **-tos**) mercado || **the Rialto** el puente del Rialto; el centro teatral de Nueva York

rib [rɪb] *s* costilla; (*of a fan or umbrella*) varilla; (*of a tire*) cuerda; (*in cloth*) canilla; (*of the wing of an insect*) nervio || *v* (*pret & pp* **ribbed;** *ger* **ribbing**) *tr* proveer de costillas; hacer canillas en; (slang) tomar el pelo a

ribald ['rɪbəld] *adj* grosero y obsceno

ribbon ['rɪbən] *s* cinta

rice [raɪs] *s* arroz *m*

rich [rɪtʃ] *adj* rico; (*color*) vivo; (*voice*) sonoro; (*wine*) generoso; azucarado, condimentado; (coll) divertido; (coll) ridículo; **to strike it rich** descubrir un buen filón || **riches** *spl* riquezas; **the rich** los ricos

rickets ['rɪkɪts] *s* raquitis *f*

rickety ['rɪkɪti] *adj* (*object*) destartalado, desvencijado; (*person*) tambaleante, vacilante; (*suffering from rickets*) raquítico

rid [rɪd] *v* (*pret & pp* **rid;** *ger* **ridding**) *tr* desembarazar; **to get rid of** desembarazarse de, deshacerse de; matar

riddance ['rɪdəns] *s* supresión, libramiento; **good riddance!** ¡adiós, gracias!, ¡de buena me he librado!

riddle ['rɪdəl] *s* acertijo, adivinanza; (*person or thing hard to understand*) enigma *m;* criba gruesa || *tr* acribillar; destruir (*un argumento; la reputación de una persona*); **to riddle with bullets** acribillar a balazos; **to riddle with questions** acribillar a preguntas

ride [raɪd] *s* paseo || *v* (*pret* **rode** [rod]; *pp* **ridden** ['rɪdən]) *tr* montar (*un caballo*); montar sobre (*los hombros de una persona*); recorrer a caballo; flotar sobre (*las olas*); dominar, tiranizar; (coll) burlarse de; **to ride down** atropellar; vencer; **to ride out** luchar felizmente con (*una tempestad*); aguantar con buen éxito (*una desgracia*) || *intr* montar; pa-

sear en coche o carruaje; **to let ride** (slang) dejar correr; **to take riding** llevar de paseo
rider ['raɪdər] *s* jinete *m;* pasajero
ridge [rɪdʒ] *s* (*of a roof; of earth between two furrows*) caballete *m;* (*of a fabric*) cordoncillo; (*of mountains*) cordillera; (*of two plane surfaces*) arista
ridge'pole' *s* parhilera
ridicule ['rɪdɪ,kjul] *s* irrisión; **to expose to ridicule** poner en ridículo || *tr* ridiculizar
ridiculous [rɪ'dɪkjələs] *adj* ridículo
riding academy *s* escuela de equitación
riding boot *s* bota de montar
riding habit *s* amazona, traje *m* de montar
rife [raɪf] *adj* común, corriente, general; abundante, lleno; **rife with** abundante en, lleno de
riffraff ['rɪf,ræf] *s* bahorrina, canalla
rifle ['raɪfəl] *s* rifle *m,* fusil *m* || *tr* hurtar, robar; escudriñar y robar; desnudar, despojar
rift [rɪft] *s* abertura, raja; desacuerdo, desavenencia
rig [rɪg] *s* equipaje *m;* carruaje *m* con caballo o caballos; traje extraño; (naut) aparejo || *v* (*pret & pp* **rigged;** *ger* **rigging**) *tr* equipar; aprestar, disponer; improvisar; vestir de una manera extraña; arreglar de una manera fraudulenta; (naut) aparejar
rigging ['rɪgɪŋ] *s* avíos, instrumentos, equipo; (naut) aparejo, cordaje *m*
right [raɪt] *adj* derecho; verdadero; exacto; conveniente; favorable; sano, normal; bien; correcto; señalado; correspondiente; que se busca, p.ej., **this is the right house** ésta es la casa que se busca; que se necesita, p.ej., **this is the right train** éste es el tren que se necesita; que debe, p.ej., **he is going the right way** sigue el camino que debe; **right or wrong** con razón o sin ella, bueno o malo; **to be all right** estar bien; estar bien de salud; **to be right** tener razón || *adv* derechamente; directamente; correctamente; exactamente; favorablemente; en orden, en buen estado; hacia la derecha; completamente; (coll) muy; mismo, p.ej., **right here** aquí mismo; **all right** muy bien || *interj* ¡bien! || *s* (*justice, reason*) derecho; (*right hand*) derecha; (box) derechazo; (com) derecho; (pol) derecha; **by right** según derecho; **on the right** a la derecha; **to be in the right** tener razón || *tr* enderezar; corregir, rectificar; hacer justicia a; deshacer (*un entuerto*) || *intr* enderezarse
righteous ['raɪtʃəs] *adj* recto, justo; virtuoso
right field *s* (baseball) jardín derecho
rightful ['raɪtfəl] *adj* justo; legítimo
right'-hand' drive *s* conducción o dirección a la derecha
right-hand man *s* mano derecha, brazo derecho
rightist ['raɪtɪst] *adj & s* derechista *mf*
rightly ['raɪtli] *adv* derechamente; correctamente; con razón; convenientemente; **rightly or wrongly** con razón o sin ella; **rightly so** a justo título
right mind *s* entero juicio
right of way *s* derecho de tránsito o de paso; (law) servidumbre de paso; (rr) servidumbre de vía; **to yield the right of way** ceder el paso
rights of man *spl* derechos del hombre
right'-wing' *adj* derechista
right-winger ['raɪt'wɪŋər] *s* (coll) derechista *mf*
rigid ['rɪdʒɪd] *adj* rígido
rigmarole ['rɪgmə,rol] *s* galimatías *m*
rigorous ['rɪgərəs] *adj* riguroso
rile [raɪl] *tr* (coll) exasperar
rill [rɪl] *s* arroyuelo
rim [rɪm] *s* canto, borde *m;* (*of a wheel*) llanta; (*of a tire*) aro
rime [raɪm] *s* (*in verse*) rima; (*frost*) escarcha; **without rime or reason** sin ton ni son || *tr & intr* rimar
rind [raɪnd] *s* cáscara, corteza
ring [rɪŋ] *s* (*circular band, line, or mark*) anillo; (*for the finger*) sortija; (*for curtains; for gymnastics*) anilla; (*for nose of animal*) argolla; (*for fruit jars*) círculo de goma; (*for some sport or exhibition*) circo; (*for boxing*) cuadrilátero, ruedo; (*for bullfight*) redondel *m,* ruedo; boxeo; (*of a group of people*) corro; (*of evildoers*) pandilla; (*under the eyes*) ojera; (*of the anchor*) arganeo; (*sound of a bell, of a clock*) campanada; (*of a small bell; of the glass of glassware*) tintineo; (*to summon a person*) llamada; (*character, nature, spirit*) tono; **to be in the ring (for)** ser candidato (a); **to run rings around** dar cien vueltas a || *v* (*pret & pp* **ringed**) *tr* cercar, rodear; (*to put a ring on*) anillar || *intr* formar círculo o corro || *v* (*pret* **rang** [ræŋ]; *pp* **rung** [rʌŋ]) *tr* tañer, tocar; (*to peal, ring out*) repicar; llamar al timbre; dar (*las horas la campana del reloj*); llamar por teléfono; **to ring up** llamar por teléfono; marcar (*una compra*) con el timbre || *intr* sonar (*una campana, un timbre, el teléfono*); tintinear (*el choque de copas, una campanilla*); resonar, retumbar; llamar; zumbar (*los oídos*); **to ring for** llamar, llamar al timbre; **to ring off** terminar una llamada por teléfono; **to ring up** llamar por teléfono
ring-around-a-rosy ['rɪŋə,raʊndə'rozi] *s* juego del corro
ringing ['rɪŋɪŋ] *adj* resonante, retumbante || *s* anillamiento; campaneo, repique *m;* (*of the glass of glassware*) tintineo; (*in the ears*) retintín *m,* silbido
ring'lead'er *s* cabecilla *m*
ring'mas'ter *s* hombre encargado de los ejercicios ecuestres y acrobáticos de un circo
ring'side' *s* lugar junto al cuadrilátero; lugar desde el cual se puede ver de cerca

ring′worm′ *s* tiña
rink [rɪŋk] *s* patinadero
rinse [rɪns] *s* aclaración, enjuague *m* ‖ *tr* aclarar, enjuagar
riot ['raɪ·ət] *s* alboroto, tumulto; regocijos ruidosos; (*of colors*) exhibición brillante; **to run riot** desenfrenarse; crecer lozanamente (*las plantas*) ‖ *intr* alborotarse, amotinarse
rioter ['raɪ·ətər] *s* alborotador *m,* amotinado
rip [rɪp] *s* rasgón *m,* siete *m;* (*open seam*) descosido ‖ *v* (*pret & pp* **ripped;** *ger* **ripping**) *tr* desgarrar, rasgar; descoser (*lo que estaba cosido*) ‖ *intr* desgarrarse, rasgarse; (coll) adelantar o moverse de prisa o con violencia; **to rip out with** (coll) decir con violencia
ripe [raɪp] *adj* maduro; acabado, hecho; dispuesto, preparado; (*boil, tumor*) madurado; (*olive*) negro
ripen ['raɪpən] *tr & intr* madurar
ripple ['rɪpəl] *s* temblor *m,* rizo; (*sound*) murmullo, susurro ‖ *tr* rizar ‖ *intr* rizarse; murmurar, susurrar
rise [raɪz] *s* (*of temperature, prices, a road*) subida; (*of ground, of the voice*) elevación; (*of a heavenly body*) salida; (*of a step*) altura; (*in one's employment*) ascenso; (*of water*) crecida; (*of a source of water*) nacimiento; (*of a valve*) levantamiento; **to get a rise out of** (slang) sacar una réplica mordaz a; **to give rise to** dar origen a ‖ *v* (*pret* **rose** [roz]; *pp* **risen** ['rɪzən]) *intr* subir; levantarse; salir (*un astro*); asomar (*un peligro*); brotar (*un manantial, una planta*); (*in someone's esteem*) ganar; resucitar; **to rise above** alzarse por encima de; mostrarse superior a; **to rise early** madrugar; **to rise to** ponerse a la altura de
riser ['raɪzər] *s* contraescalón *m,* contrahuella; **early riser** madrugador *m;* **late riser** dormilón *m*
risk [rɪsk] *s* riesgo; **to run** o **take a risk** correr riesgo, correr peligro ‖ *tr* arriesgar; arriesgarse en (*una empresa dudosa*)
risk·y ['rɪski] *adj* (*comp* **-ier;** *super* **-iest**) arriesgado; escabroso
risqué [rɪs'ke] *adj* escabroso
rite [raɪt] *s* rito; **last rites** honras fúnebres
ritual ['rɪtʃʊ·əl] *adj & s* ritual *m*
riv. *abbr* **river**
ri·val ['raɪvəl] *s* rival *mf* ‖ *v* (*pret & pp* **-valed** o **-valled;** *ger* **-valing** o **-valling**) *tr* rivalizar con
rival·ry ['raɪvəlri] *s* (*pl* **-ries**) rivalidad
river ['rɪvər] *s* río; **down the river** río abajo; **up the river** río arriba
river basin *s* cuenca de río
river bed *s* cauce *m*
river front *s* orilla del río
riv′er·side′ *adj* ribereño ‖ *s* ribera
rivet ['rɪvɪt] *s* roblón *m,* remache *m;* (*e.g., to hold scissors together*) clavillo ‖ *tr* remachar; clavar (*p.ej., los ojos en una persona*)
rm. *abbr* **ream, room**
R.N. *abbr* **registered nurse, Royal Navy**
roach [rotʃ] *s* cucaracha
road [rod] *adj* itinerario, caminero ‖ *s* camino; (naut) rada; **to be in the road** estorbar el paso; incomodar; **to get out of the road** quitarse de en medio
road′bed′ *s* (*of a highway*) firme *m;* (rr) infraestructura
road′block′ *s* (mil) barricada; (fig) obstáculo
road′house′ *s* posada en el camino
road laborer *s* peón caminero
road map *s* mapa itinerario
road service *s* auxilio en carretera
road′side′ *s* borde *m* del camino, borde de la carretera
roadside inn *s* posada en el camino
road sign *s* señal *f* de carretera, poste *m* indicador
road′stead′ *s* rada
road′way′ *s* camino, vía
roam [rom] *s* vagabundeo ‖ *tr* vagar por, recorrer a la ventura ‖ *intr* vagar, andar errante
roar [ror] *s* bramido, rugido ‖ *intr* bramar, rugir; reírse a carcajadas
roast [rost] *s* asado; café tostado ‖ *tr* asar; tostar (*café*); (coll) despellejar ‖ *intr* asarse; tostarse
roast beef *s* rosbif *m*
roast of beef *s* carne de vaca asada o para asar
roast pork *s* carne de cerdo asada
rob [rɑb] *v* (*pret & pp* **robbed;** *ger* **robbing**) *tr & intr* robar
robber ['rɑbər] *s* robador *m,* ladrón *m*
robber·y ['rɑbəri] *s* (*pl* **-ies**) robo
robe [rob] *s* manto; abrigo; (*of a woman*) traje *m,* vestido; (*of a professor, judge, etc.*) toga, túnica; (*of a priest*) traje *m* talar; (*dressing gown*) bata; (*for lap in a carriage*) manta ‖ *tr* vestir ‖ *intr* vestirse
robin ['rɑbɪn] *s* (*in Europe*) petirrojo; (*in North America*) primavera
robot ['robɑt] *s* robot *m*
robust [ro'bʌst] *adj* robusto; vigoroso
rock [rɑk] *s* roca; (*sticking out of water*) escollo; (*one that is thrown*) piedra; (slang) diamante *m,* piedra preciosa; **on the rocks** arruinado, en pobreza extrema; (*said of hard liquor*) (coll) sobre hielo ‖ *tr* acunar, mecer; (*to sleep*) arrullar; sacudir; **to rock to sleep** adormecer meciendo ‖ *intr* mecerse; sacudirse
rock′-bot′tom *adj* (el) mínimo, (el) más bajo
rock candy *s* azúcar *m* cande
rock crystal *s* cristal *m* de roca
rocker ['rɑkər] *s* (*chair*) mecedora; (*curved piece at bottom of rocking chair or cradle*) arco; (mach) balancín *m;* (mach) eje *m* de balancín
rocket ['rɑkɪt] *s* cohete *m* ‖ *intr* subir como un cohete
rocket bomb *s* bomba cohete
rocket launcher ['lɔntʃər] o ['lɑntʃər] *s* lanzacohetes *m*
rocket ship *s* aeronave *f* cohete
rock garden *s* jardín *m* entre rocas

rocking chair *s* mecedora, sillón *m* de hamaca
rocking horse *s* caballo mecedor
Rock of Gibraltar [dʒɪˈbrɔltər] *s* peñón *m* de Gibraltar
rock salt *s* sal *f* de compás, sal gema
rock wool *s* lana mineral
rock•y [ˈrɑki] *adj* (*comp* **-ier;** *super* **-iest**) rocoso, roqueño; (slang) débil, poco firme
rod [rɑd] *s* vara; varilla; barra; (*authority*) vara alta; opresión, tiranía; (*of the retina*) bastoncillo; (*elongated microörganism*) bastoncito; (mach) vástago; (surv) jalón *m;* (Bib) linaje *m,* raza, vástago; (slang) revólver *m,* pistola; **to spare the rod** excusar la vara
rodent [ˈrodənt] *adj* & *s* roedor *m*
rod•man [ˈrɑdmən] *s* (*pl* **-men** [mən]) jalonero, portamira *m*
roe [ro] *s* (*deer*) corzo; (*of fish*) hueva
rogue [rog] *s* bribón *m,* pícaro
rogues' gallery *s* colección de retratos de malhechores para uso de la policía
roguish [ˈrogɪʃ] *adj* bribón, pícaro; travieso, retozón
rôle o **role** [rol] *s* papel *m;* **to play a rôle** desempeñar un papel
roll [rol] *s* (*of cloth, film, paper, fat, etc.*) rollo; (*roller*) rodillo; (*cake of bread*) panecillo; (*of dice*) echada; (*of a boat*) balance *m;* (*of a drum*) redoble *m;* (*of thunder*) retumbo; bamboleo; ondulación; rol *m;* lista; (*of paper money*) fajo; **to call the roll** pasar lista || *tr* hacer rodar; empujar hacia adelante; cilindrar, laminar; (*to wrap up with rolling motion*) arrollar; alisar con rodillo; liar (*un cigarrillo*); mover de un lado a otro; poner (*los ojos*) en blanco; tocar redobles con (*el tambor*); vibrar (*la voz; la r*); **to roll one's own** liárselos; **to roll up** arremangar (*p.ej., las mangas*); amontonar (*p.ej., una fortuna*) || *intr* rodar; bambolear; balancear (*un barco*); girar; retumbar (*el trueno*); redoblar (*un tambor*); **to roll around** revolcarse
roll call *s* lista, (el) pasar lista
roller [ˈrolər] *s* rodillo; (*of a piece of furniture*) ruedecilla; (*of a skate*) rueda; ola larga y creciente
roller bearing *s* cojinete *m* de rodillos
roller coaster *s* montaña rusa
roller skate *s* patín *m* de ruedas
roller towel *s* toalla sin fin
rolling mill [ˈrolɪŋ] *s* taller *m* de laminación; tren *m* de laminadores
rolling pin *s* rodillo, hataca
rolling stock *s* (rr) material *m* móvil, material rodante
rolling stone *s* piedra movediza
roll'-top' desk *s* escritorio norteamericano, escritorio de cortina corrediza
roly-poly [ˈroliˈpoli] *adj* regordete, rechoncho
Rom. *abbr* **Roman, Romance**
roman [ˈromən] *adj* (typ) redondo || *s* (typ) letra redonda || **Roman** *adj* & *s* romano
Roman candle *s* vela romana
Roman Catholic *adj* & *s* católico romano
romance [roˈmæns] o [ˈromæns] *s* (*tale of chivalry*) romance *m;* cuento de aventuras; cuento de amor; intriga amorosa; novela sentimental; (mus) romanza || [roˈmæns] *intr* contar o escribir romances, cuentos de aventuras o cuentos de amor; pensar o hablar de un modo romántico; exagerar, mentir || **Romance** [ˈromæns] o [roˈmæns] *adj* (*Neo-Latin*) romance o románico
romance of chivalry *s* libro de caballerías
Roman Empire *s* Imperio romano
Romanesque [ˌromənˈɛsk] *adj* & *s* románico
Roman nose *s* nariz aguileña
romantic [roˈmæntɪk] *adj* romántico; (*spot, place*) encantador
romanticism [roˈmæntɪˌsɪzəm] *s* romanticismo
romp [rɑmp] *intr* corretear, triscar
rompers [ˈrɑmpərz] *spl* traje holgado de juego
roof [ruf] o [rʊf] *s* (*top outer covering of a house*) tejado; (*of a car or bus*) imperial *f,* tejadillo; (*of the mouth*) paladar *m;* (*of heaven*) bóveda; (*home, dwelling*) (fig) techo; **to raise the roof** (slang) poner el grito en el cielo || *tr* techar
roofer [ˈrufər] o [ˈrʊfər] *s* techador *m,* pizarrero
roof garden *s* (*garden on the roof*) pérgola, azotea de baile y diversión
rook [rʊk] *s* (*bird*) grajo; (*in chess*) roque *m* || *tr* trampear
rookie [ˈrʊki] *s* (slang) bisoño, novato
room [rum] o [rʊm] *s* aposento, cuarto, habitación, pieza; espacio, sitio, lugar *m;* ocasión; **to make room** abrir paso, hacer lugar || *intr* alojarse
room and board *s* pensión completa
room clerk *s* empleado en la recepción, encargado de las reservas
roomer [ˈrumər] o [ˈrʊmər] *s* inquilino
rooming house *s* casa donde se alquilan cuartos
room'mate' *s* compañero de cuarto
room•y [ˈrumi] o [ˈrʊmi] *adj* (*comp* **-ier;** *super* **-iest**) amplio, espacioso
roost [rust] *s* percha de gallinero; gallinero; lugar *m* de descanso; **to rule the roost** ser el amo del cotarro, tener el mando y el palo || *intr* descansar (*las aves*) en la percha; estar alojado; pasar la noche
rooster [ˈrustər] *s* gallo
root [rut] o [rʊt] *s* raíz *f;* **to get to the root of** profundizar; **to take root** echar raíces || *tr* hocicar, hozar || *intr* arraigar; **to root for** (slang) gritar alentando
rooter [ˈrutər] o [ˈrʊtər] *s* (slang) hincha *mf*
rope [rop] *s* cuerda; (*of a hangman*)

dogal *m;* (*to catch an animal*) lazo; **to jump rope** saltar a la comba; **to know the ropes** (slang) saber todas las tretas || *tr* atar con una cuerda; coger con lazo; **to rope in** (slang) embaucar, engañar

rope'walk'er *s* funámbulo, volatinero

rosa•ry ['rozəri] *s* (*pl* **-ries**) rosario

rose [roz] *adj* de color de rosa || *s* rosa

rose'bud' *s* pimpollo, capullo de rosa

rose'bush' *s* rosal *m*

rose'-col'ored *adj* rosado; **to see everything through rose-colored glasses** verlo todo de color de rosa

rose garden *s* rosaleda, rosalera

rosemar•y ['roz,mɛri] *s* (*pl* **-ies**) romero

rose of Sharon ['ʃɛrən] *s* granado blanco, rosa de Siria

rose window *s* rosetón *m*

rose'wood' *s* palisandro

rosin ['rɑzɪn] *s* colofonia, brea seca

roster ['rɑstər] *s* catálogo, lista; horario escolar, horas de clase

rostrum ['rɑstrəm] *s* tribuna

ros•y ['rozi] *adj* (*comp* **-ier;** *super* **-iest**) rosado, sonrosado; alegre

rot [rɑt] *s* podredumbre; (slang) tontería || *v* (*pret & pp* **rotted;** *ger* **rotting**) *tr* pudrir || *intr* pudrirse

rotate ['rotet] o [ro'tet] *tr* hacer girar; alternar || *intr* girar; alternar

rote [rot] *s* rutina, repetición maquinal; **by rote** de memoria, maquinalmente

rot'gut' *s* (slang) matarratas *m*

rotogravure [,rotəgrə'vjʊr] o [,rotə'grevjʊr] *s* rotograbado

rotten ['rɑtən] *adj* putrefacto, pútrido; corrompido

rotund [ro'tʌnd] *adj* redondo de cuerpo; (*language*) redondo

rouge [ruʒ] *s* arrebol *m,* colorete *m* || *tr* arrebolar, pintar || *intr* arrebolarse, pintarse

rough [rʌf] *adj* áspero; (*sea*) agitado, picado; (*crude, unwrought*) tosco, grosero; aproximado || *tr* — **to rough it** vivir sin comodidades, hacer vida campestre

rough'cast' *s* modelo tosco; mezcla gruesa || *v* (*pret & pp* **-cast**) *tr* (*to prepare in rough form*) bosquejar; dar a (*la pared*) una capa de mezcla gruesa

rough copy *s* borrador *m*

roughly ['rʌfli] *adv* asperamente; brutalmente; aproximadamente

roulette [ru'lɛt] *s* ruleta

round [raʊnd] *adj* redondo || *adv* redondamente; alrededor; de boca en boca; por todas partes || *prep* alrededor de; (*e.g., the corner*) a la vuelta de; cerca de; acá y allá en || *s* camino, circuito; (*of a policeman; of visits; of drinks or cigars*) ronda; (*of applause; discharge of guns*) salva; (*discharge of a single gun*) disparo, tiro; (*of people*) corro, círculo; (*of golf*) partido; rutina, serie *f,* sucesión; redondez *f;* revolución; (box) asalto; **to go the rounds** ir de boca en boca; ir de mano en mano || *tr* (*to make round*) redondear; cercar, rodear; doblar (*una esquina, un promontorio*); **to round off u out** redondear; acabar, completar, perfeccionar; **to round up** juntar, recoger; rodear (*el ganado*)

roundabout ['raʊndə,baʊt] *adj* indirecto || *s* curso indirecto; (Brit) tío vivo; (Brit) glorieta de tráfico

rounder ['raʊndər] *s* (coll) pródigo; (coll) catavinos *m,* borrachín habitual

round'house' *s* cocherón *m,* casa de máquinas, depósito de locomotoras

round-shouldered ['raʊnd'ʃoldərd] *adj* cargado de espaldas

Round Table *s* Tabla Redonda

round'-trip' ticket *s* billete *m* de ida y vuelta

round'up' *s* (*of cattle*) rodeo; (*of criminals*) redada; (*of old friends*) reunión

rouse [raʊz] *tr* despertar; excitar, provocar; levantar (*la caza*) || *intr* despertarse, despabilarse

rout [raʊt] *s* derrota; fuga desordenada || *tr* derrotar; poner en fuga desordenada; arrancar hozando || *intr* hozar

route [rut] o [raʊt] *s* ruta; itinerario || *tr* encaminar

routine [ru'tin] *adj* rutinario || *s* rutina

rove [rov] *intr* andar errante, vagar

row [raʊ] *s* (coll) camorra, pendencia, riña; (coll) alboroto, bullicio; **to raise a row** (coll) armar camorra || [ro] *s* fila, hilera; (*of houses*) crujía; **in a row** seguidos, p.ej., **five hours in a row** cinco horas seguidas || *intr* remar

rowboat ['ro,bot] *s* bote *m,* bote de remos

row•dy ['raʊdi] *adj* (*comp* **-dier;** *super* **-diest**) gamberro || *s* (*pl* **-dies**) gamberro

rower ['ro•ər] *s* remero

royal ['rɔɪ•əl] *adj* real; (*magnificent, splendid*) regio

royalist ['rɔɪ•əlɪst] *s* realista *mf*

royal•ty ['rɔɪ•əlti] *s* (*pl* **-ties**) realeza; personaje *m* real, personajes reales; derechos de autor; derechos de inventor

r.p.m. *abbr* **revolutions per minute**

R.R. *abbr* **railroad, Right Reverend**

rub [rʌb] *s* frotación, roce *m;* **there's the rub** ahí está el busilis || *v* (*pret & pp* **rubbed;** *ger* **rubbing**) *tr* frotar; **to rub elbows with** rozarse mucho con; **to rub out** borrar; (slang) asesinar || *intr* frotar; **to rub off** quitarse frotando; borrarse

rubber ['rʌbər] *s* caucho, goma; goma de borrar; chanclo, zapato de goma; (*in bridge*) robre *m* || *intr* (slang) estirar el cuello o volver la cabeza para ver

rubber band *s* liga de goma

rubber plant *s* árbol *m* del caucho

rubber plantation *s* cauchal *m*

rubber stamp *s* cajetín *m,* sello de goma; (*with a person's signature*)

estampilla; (coll) persona que aprueba sin reflexionar
rub′ber-stamp′ *tr* estampar con un sello de goma; (*with a person's signature*) estampillar; (coll) aprobar sin reflexionar
rubbish [ˈrʌbɪʃ] *s* basura, desecho, desperdicios; (coll) disparate *m*, tontería
rubble [ˈrʌbəl] *s* (*broken stone*) ripio; (*masonry*) mampostería
rub′down′ *s* masaje *m*, fricción
rube [rub] *s* (slang) isidro, rústico
ru·by [ˈrubi] *s* (*pl* **-bies**) rubí *m*
rudder [ˈrʌdər] *s* timón *m*, gobernalle *m*
rud·dy [ˈrʌdi] *adj* (*comp* **-dier;** *super* **-diest**) coloradote, rubicundo
rude [rud] *adj* rudo
rudiment [ˈrudɪmənt] *s* rudimento
rue [ru] *tr* lamentar, arrepentirse de
rueful [ˈrufəl] *adj* lamentable; triste
ruffian [ˈrʌfɪ·ən] *s* hombre grosero y brutal
ruffle [ˈrʌfəl] *s* arruga; (*of drum*) redoble *m;* (sew) volante *m* ‖ *tr* arrugar; agitar, descomponer; enojar, molestar; confundir; redoblar (*el tambor*); (sew) fruncir un volante en, adornar o guarnecer con volante
rug [rʌg] *s* alfombra; alfombrilla; (*lap robe*) manta
rugged [ˈrʌgɪd] *adj* áspero, rugoso; recio, vigoroso; tempestuoso
ruin [ˈru·ɪn] *s* ruina ‖ *tr* arruinar; estropear; echar a perder
rule [rul] *s* regla; autoridad, mando; regla de imprenta; (*reign*) reinado; (*of a court of law*) decisión, fallo; **as a rule** por regla general; **to be the rule** ser lo que se hace ‖ *tr* gobernar, regir; dirigir, guiar; contener, reprimir; (*to mark with lines*) reglar; (law) decidir, determinar; **to rule out** excluir, rechazar ‖ *intr* gobernar, regir; prevalecer; **to rule over** gobernar, regir
rule of law *s* régimen *m* de justicia
ruler [ˈrulər] *s* gobernante *mf;* soberano; (*for ruling lines*) regla
ruling [ˈrulɪŋ] *adj* gobernante, dirigente, imperante ‖ *s* (*of a court or judge*) decisión, fallo; (*of paper*) rayado
rum [rʌm] *s* ron *m;* (*any alcoholic drink*) (U.S.A.) aguardiente *m*
Rumanian [ruˈmenɪ·ən] *adj* & *s* rumano
rumble [ˈrʌmbəl] *s* retumbo; (*of the intestines*) rugido; (slang) riña entre pandillas ‖ *intr* retumbar; avanzar retumbando
ruminate [ˈrumɪˌnet] *tr* & *intr* rumiar
rummage [ˈrʌmɪdʒ] *tr* & *intr* buscar revolviéndolo todo
rummage sale *s* venta de prendas usadas
rumor [ˈrumər] *s* rumor *m* ‖ *tr* rumorear; **it is rumored that** se rumorea que
rump [rʌmp] *s* anca, nalga; (*cut of beef*) cuarto trasero
rumple [ˈrʌmpəl] *s* arruga ‖ *tr* arrugar, ajar, chafar ‖ *intr* arrugarse
rumpus [ˈrʌmpəs] *s* (coll) batahola, alboroto; **to raise a rumpus** (coll) armar la de San Quintín
run [rʌn] *s* carrera; clase *f*, tipo; arroyo; (*e.g., in a stocking*) carrera; (*on a bank by depositors*) asedio; (*of consecutive performances of a play*) serie *f;* (baseball & mus) carrera; **in the long run** a la larga; **on the run** a escape; en fuga desordenada; **the common run of people** el común de las gentes; **the general run of** la generalidad de; **to have a long run** permanecer en cartel durante mucho tiempo; **to have the run of** hallar el secreto de; tener libertad de ir y venir por ‖ *v* (*pret* **ran** [ræn]; *pp* **run;** *ger* **running**) *tr* hacer funcionar; dirigir, manejar; trazar, tirar (*una línea*); exhibir (*un cine*); hacer (*mandados*); tener como candidato; burlar, violar (*un bloqueo*); tener (*calentura*); correr (*un caballo; un riesgo*); **to run down** cazar y matar; derribar; atropellar (*a un peatón*); (coll) denigrar, desacreditar; **to run in** rodar (*un nuevo coche*); **to run off** tocar (*una pieza de música*); tirar, imprimir; **to run up** (coll) aumentar (*gastos*) ‖ *intr* correr; (*on wheels*) rodar; darse prisa; trepar (*la vid*); ir y venir (*un vapor*); supurar (*una llaga*); colar (*un líquido*); correrse (*un color o tinte*); presentar su candidatura; andar, funcionar, marchar; deshilarse (*las medias*); migrar (*los peces*); estar en fuerza; (*to be worded or written*) rezar; **to run across** dar con, tropezar con; **to run away** correr, huir; desbocarse (*un caballo*); **to run down** escurrir, gotear (*un líquido*); descargarse (*un acumulador*); distenderse (*el muelle de un reloj*); acabarse la cuerda, p.ej., **the watch ran down** se acabó la cuerda; **to run for** presentar su candidatura a; **to run in the family** venir de familia; **to run into** tropezar con; chocar con, topar con; **to run off the track** descarrilar (*un tren*); **to run out** salir; expirar, terminar; acabarse; agotarse; **to run out of** acabársele a uno, e.g., **I have run out of money** se me ha acabado el dinero; **to run over** atropellar (*a un peatón*); registrar a la ligera; pasar por encima; leer rápidamente; rebosar (*un líquido*); **to run through** disipar rápidamente (*una fortuna*); registrar a la ligera; estar difundido en
run′a·way′ *adj* fugitivo; (*horse*) desbocado ‖ *s* fugitivo; caballo desbocado; fuga
run′-down′ *adj* desmedrado; desmantelado; inculto; (*clock spring*) sin cuerda, distendido; (*storage battery*) descargado
rung [rʌŋ] *s* (*of ladder or chair*) travesaño; (*of wheel*) radio, rayo
runner [ˈrʌnər] *s* corredor *m;* caballo

de carreras; mensajero; (*of an ice skate*) cuchilla; (*of a sleigh*) patín *m;* (*long narrow rug*) pasacaminos *m;* (*strip of cloth for table top*) tapete *m;* (*in stockings*) carrera
run'ner-up' *s* (*pl* **runners-up**) subcampeón *m*
running ['rʌnɪŋ] *adj* corredor; (*expenses; water*) corriente; (*knot*) corredizo; (*sore*) supurante; (*writing*) cursivo; continuo; consecutivo; en marcha; (*start*) (sport) lanzado ‖ *s* carrera, corrida; administración, dirección; marcha, funcionamiento; **to be in the running** tener esperanzas o posibilidades de ganar
running board *s* estribo
running head *s* titulillo
running start *s* (sport) salida lanzada
run-of-mine coal ['rʌnəv'maɪn] *s* carbón *m* tal como sale
run'proof' *adj* indesmallable
runt [rʌnt] *s* enano, hombrecillo; (*little child*) redrojo; animal achaparrado
run'way' *s* (*of a stream*) cauce *m;* senda trillada; (aer) pista de aterrizaje
rupture ['rʌptʃər] *s* ruptura; (pathol) quebradura; (*break in relations*) ruptura ‖ *tr* romper; causar una hernia en ‖ *intr* romperse; padecer hernia
rural free delivery ['rurəl] *s* distribución gratuita del correo en el campo
rural police *s* guardia civil
rural policeman *s* guardiacivil *m*
ruse [ruz] *s* astucia, artimaña
rush [rʌʃ] *adj* urgente ‖ *s* prisa grande, precipitación; agolpamiento de gente; (bot) junco; **in a rush** de prisa ‖ *tr* empujar con violencia o prisa; despachar con prontitud; (slang) cortejar insistentemente (*a una mujer*); **to rush through** ejecutar de prisa, despachar rápidamente ‖ *intr* lanzarse, precipitarse; venir de prisa, ir de prisa; actuar con prontitud; **to rush through** lanzarse a través de, lanzarse por entre
rush-bottomed chair ['rʌʃ'bɑtəmd] *s* silla de junco
rush hour *s* hora de aglomeración, horas de punta
rush'light' *s* mariposa, lamparilla
rush order *s* pedido urgente
russet ['rʌsɪt] *adj* canelo
Russia ['rʌʃə] *s* Rusia
Russian ['rʌʃən] *adj & s* ruso
rust [rʌst] *s* orín *m,* moho, herrumbre; (agr) roña, roya; color rojizo o anaranjado ‖ *tr* aherrumbrar ‖ *intr* aherrumbrarse
rustic ['rʌstɪk] *adj* rústico; sencillo, sin artificio ‖ *s* rústico
rustle ['rʌsəl] *s* susurro, crujido ‖ *tr* hacer susurrar, hacer crujir; hurtar (*ganado*) ‖ *intr* susurrar, crujir; (slang) trabajar con ahinco
rust·y ['rʌsti] *adj* (*comp* **-ier;** *super* **-iest**) herrumbroso, mohoso; rojizo; (*out of practice*) empolvado, desusado, remoto
rut [rʌt] *s* (*track, groove in road*) rodada, bache *m;* hábito arraigado; (*sexual excitement in animals*) celo; (*period of this excitement*) brama
ruthless ['ruθlɪs] *adj* despiadado, cruel
Ry. *abbr* **railway**
rye [raɪ] *s* centeno; whisky de centeno

S

S, s [ɛs] decimonona letra del alfabeto inglés
s *abbr* **second, shilling, singular**
Sabbath ['sæbəθ] *s* (*of Jews*) sábado; (*of Christians*) domínica; **to keep the Sabbath** observar el descanso dominical, guardar el domingo
saber ['sebər] *s* sable *m*
sable ['sebəl] *adj* negro ‖ *s* marta cebellina; **sables** vestidos de luto
sabotage ['sæbə,tɑʒ] *s* sabotaje *m* ‖ *tr & intr* sabotear
saccharin ['sækərɪn] *s* sacarina
sachet ['sæʃe] o [sæ'ʃe] *s* polvo oloroso; saquito de perfumes
sack [sæk] *s* saco; vino blanco generoso; (mil) saqueo, saco; (*of an employee*) (slang) despedida ‖ *tr* ensacar; saquear, pillar; (slang) despedir (*a un empleado*)
sack'cloth' *s* harpillera; (*worn for penitence*) cilicio
sacrament ['sækrəmənt] *s* sacramento
sacred ['sekrəd] *adj* sagrado
sacrifice ['sækrɪ,faɪs] *s* sacrificio; **at a sacrifice** con pérdida ‖ *tr* sacrificar; (*to sell at a loss*) malvender ‖ *intr* sacrificar; sacrificarse
Sacrifice of the Mass *s* sacrificio del altar
sacrilege ['sækrɪlɪdʒ] *s* sacrilegio
sacrilegious [,sækrɪ'lɪdʒəs] o [,sækrɪ'lidʒəs] *adj* sacrílego
sacristan ['sækrɪstən] *s* sacristán *m*
sacris·ty ['sækrɪsti] *s* (*pl* **-ties**) sacristía
sad [sæd] *adj* (*comp* **sadder;** *super* **saddest**) triste; (slang) malo
sadden ['sædən] *tr* entristecer ‖ *intr* entristecerse
saddle ['sædəl] *s* silla de montar; (*of a bicycle*) sillín *m* ‖ *tr* ensillar; **to saddle with** echar a cuestas a
sad'dle·bags' *spl* alforjas
sad'dle·bow' [,bo] *s* arzón delantero
sad'dle·tree' *s* arzón *m*
sadist ['sædɪst] o ['sedɪst] *s* sádico
sadistic [sæ'dɪstɪk] o [se'dɪstɪk] *adj* sádico
sadness ['sædnɪs] *s* tristeza
safe [sef] *adj* seguro, ileso, salvo;

cierto, digno de confianza; sin peligro, a salvo; **safe and sound** sano y salvo; **safe from** a salvo de || *s* caja fuerte, caja de caudales
safe'-con'duct *s* salvoconducto
safe'-depos'it box *s* caja de seguridad
safe'guard' *s* salvaguardia, medida de seguridad || *tr* salvaguardar
safe·ty ['sefti] *adj* de seguridad || *s* (*pl* **-ties**) seguridad; **to parachute to safety** lanzarse en paracaídas; **to reach safety** ponerse a salvo, llegar a lugar seguro
safety belt *s* (aer, aut) correa de seguridad; (naut) cinturón *m* salvavidas
safety match *s* fósforo de seguridad
safety pin *s* imperdible *m*, alfiler *m* de seguridad
safety rail *s* guardarriel *m*
safety razor *s* maquinilla de seguridad
safety valve *s* válvula de seguridad
saffron ['sæfrən] *adj* azafranado || *s* azafrán *m* || *tr* azafranar
sag [sæg] *s* comba, combadura; (*e.g.*, *of a cable*) flecha || *v* (*pret & pp* **sagged**; *ger* **sagging**) *intr* combarse; (*to slacken, yield*) aflojar, ceder, doblegarse; bajar (*los precios*)
sagacious [sə'geʃəs] *adj* sagaz
sage [sedʒ] *adj* sabio, cuerdo || *s* sabio; (bot) salvia; (bot) artemisa
sage'brush' *s* (bot) artemisa
sail [sel] *s* vela; barco de vela; paseo en barco de vela; **to set sail** hacerse a la vela; **under full sail** a vela llena || *tr* gobernar (*un barco de vela*); navegar (*un mar, río, etc.*) || *intr* navegar, navegar a la vela; salir, salir de viaje; deslizarse, flotar, volar; **to sail into** (slang) atacar, regañar, reñir
sail'boat' *s* barco de vela, buque *m* de vela, velero
sail'cloth' *s* lona, paño
sailing ['selɪŋ] *adj* de salida || *s* paseo en barco de vela; navegación; salida
sailing vessel *s* buque velero
sailor ['selər] *s* (*one who makes a living sailing*) marinero; (*an enlisted man in the navy*) marino
saint [sent] *adj & s* santo || *tr* (coll) canonizar
saintliness ['sentlɪnɪs] *s* santidad
Saint Vitus's dance ['vaɪtəsəs] *s* (pathol) baile *m* de San Vito
sake [sek] *s* respeto, bien, amor *m*; **for his sake** por su bien; **for the sake of** por, por motivo de, por amor a; **for your own sake** por su propio bien
salaam [sə'lɑm] *s* zalema || *tr* saludar con zalemas, hacer zalemas a
salable ['seləbəl] *adj* vendible
salad ['sæləd] *s* ensalada
salad bowl *s* ensaladera
salad oil *s* aceite *m* de comer
Salamis ['sæləmɪs] *s* Salamina
sala·ry ['sæləri] *s* (*pl* **-ries**) sueldo
sale [sel] *s* venta; (*auction*) almoneda, subasta; **for sale** de venta; se vende(n)
sales'clerk' *s* dependiente *mf* de tienda
sales'la'dy *s* (*pl* **-dies**) vendedora
sales·man ['selzmən] *s* (*pl* **-men** [mən]) vendedor *m*, dependiente *m* de tienda
sales manager *s* gerente *m* de ventas
sales'man·ship' *s* arte de vender
sales'room' *s* salón *m* de ventas; salón de exhibición
sales talk *s* argumento para inducir a comprar
sales tax *s* impuesto sobre ventas
saliva [sə'laɪvə] *s* saliva
sallow ['sælo] *adj* cetrino
sal·ly ['sæli] *s* (*pl* **-lies**) paseo, viaje *m*; ímpetu *m*, arranque *m*; salida, ocurrencia; (mil) salida, surtida || *v* (*pret & pp* **-lied**) *intr* salir, hacer una salida; ir de paseo; **to sally forth** salir, avanzar con denuedo
salmon ['sæmən] *s* salmón *m*
salon [sæ'lɑn] *s* salón *m*
saloon [sə'lun] *s* cantina, taberna; (*on a steamer*) salón *m*
saloon'keep'er *s* tabernero
salt [sɔlt] *s* sal *f*; **to be not worth one's salt** no valer (*uno*) el pan que come || *tr* salar; (*to preserve with salt*) salpresar; marinar (*el pescado*); salgar (*al ganado*); **to salt away** (slang) ahorrar, guardar para uso futuro
salt'cel'lar *s* salero
salted peanuts *spl* saladillos
saltine [sɔl'tin] *s* galletita salada
saltish ['sɔltɪʃ] *adj* salobre
salt lick *s* salero, lamedero
salt of the earth, the lo mejor del mundo
salt'pe'ter *s* (*potassium nitrate*) salitre *m*; (*sodium nitrate*) nitro de Chile
salt'sha'ker *s* salero
salt·y ['sɔlti] *adj* (*comp* **-ier**; *super* **-iest**) salado
salubrious [sə'lubrɪ·əs] *adj* salubre
salutation [ˌsæljə'teʃən] *s* salutación
salute [sə'lut] *s* saludo || *tr* saludar
Salvadoran [ˌsælvə'dorən] o **Salvadorian** [ˌsælvə'dorɪ·ən] *adj & s* salvadoreño
salvage ['sælvɪdʒ] *s* salvamento || *tr* salvar; recobrar
Salvation Army [sæl'veʃən] *s* ejército de Salvación
salve [sæv] o [sɑv] *s* ungüento || *tr* curar con ungüento; preservar; aliviar
sal·vo ['sælvo] *s* (*pl* **-vos** o **-voes**) salva
Samaritan [sə'mærɪtən] *adj & s* samaritano
same [sem] *adj & pron indef* mismo; **it's all the same to me** lo mismo me da; **just the same** lo mismo, sin embargo; **same . . . as** mismo . . . que
samite ['sæmaɪt] o ['semaɪt] *s* jamete *m*
sample ['sæmpəl] *s* muestra || *tr* catar, probar
sample copy *s* ejemplar *m* muestra
sancti·fy ['sæŋktɪˌfaɪ] *v* (*pret & pp* **-fied**) *tr* santificar
sanctimonious [ˌsæŋktɪ'monɪ·əs] *adj* santurrón
sanction ['sæŋkʃən] *s* sanción || *tr* sancionar
sanctuar·y ['sæŋktʃuˌeri] *s* (*pl* **-ies**)

santuario; asilo, refugio; **to take sanctuary** acogerse a sagrado
sand [sænd] *s* arena || *tr* enarenar; lijar con papel de lija
sandal ['sændəl] *s* sandalia
san'dal•wood' *s* (bot) sándalo
sand'bag' *s* saco de arena
sand'bank' *s* banco de arena
sand bar *s* barra de arena
sand'blast' *s* chorro de arena || *tr* limpiar con chorro de arena
sand'box' *s* (rr) arenero
sand dune *s* duna, médano
sand'glass' *s* reloj *m* de arena, ampolleta
sand'pa'per *s* papel *m* de lija || *tr* lijar
sand'stone' *s* piedra arenisca
sand'storm' *s* tempestad de arena
sandwich ['sændwɪtʃ] *s* emparedado, sandwich *m* || *tr* intercalar
sandwich man *s* hombre-anuncio
sand•y ['sændi] *adj* (*comp* **-ier;** *super* **-iest**) arenoso; (*hair*) rufo; cambiante, movible
sane [sen] *adj* cuerdo, sensato; (*principles*) sano
sanguinary ['sæŋgwɪn,ɛri] *adj* sanguinario
sanguine ['sæŋgwɪn] *adj* confiado, esperanzado; (*countenance*) coloradote
sanitary ['sænɪ,tɛri] *adj* sanitario
sanitary napkin *s* compresa higiénica
sanitation [,sænɪ'teʃən] *s* (*sanitary measures*) sanidad; (*drainage*) saneamiento
sanity ['sænɪti] *s* cordura, sensatez *f*
Santa Claus ['sæntə,klɔz] *s* el Papá Noel, San Nicolás
sap [sæp] *s* savia; (mil) zapa; (coll) necio, tonto || *v* (*pret & pp* **sapped;** *ger* **sapping**) *tr* agotar, debilitar; zapar, socavar
sap'head' *s* (coll) cabeza de chorlito
sapling ['sæplɪŋ] *s* árbol *m* muy joven, pimpollo; jovenzuelo, mozuelo
sapphire ['sæfaɪr] *s* zafiro
saraband ['særə,bænd] *s* zarabanda
Saracen ['særəsən] *adj & s* sarraceno
Saragossa [,særə'gɑsə] *s* Zaragoza
sardine [sɑr'din] *s* sardina; **packed in like sardines** como sardinas en banasta o en lata
Sardinia [sɑr'dɪnɪ·ə] *s* Cerdeña
Sardinian [sɑr'dɪnɪ·ən] *adj & s* sardo
sarsaparilla [,sɑrsəpə'rɪlə] *s* zarzaparrilla
sash [sæʃ] *s* banda, faja; (*of a window*) marco
sash window *s* ventana de guillotina
satchel ['sætʃəl] *s* maletín *m;* (*of a schoolboy*) cartapacio
sateen [sæ'tin] *s* satén *m*
satellite ['sætə,laɪt] *s* satélite *m*
satellite country *s* país *m* satélite
satiate ['seʃɪ,et] *adj* ahito, harto || *tr* saciar
satin ['sætən] *s* raso
satinet [,sætɪ'nɛt] *s* rasete *m*
satiric(al) [sə'tɪrɪk(əl)] *adj* satírico
satirist ['sætɪrɪst] *s* satírico
satirize ['sætɪ,raɪz] *tr & intr* satirizar
satisfaction [,sætɪs'fækʃən] *s* satisfacción
satisfactory [,sætɪs'fæktəri] *adj* satisfactorio
satis•fy ['sætɪs,faɪ] *v* (*pret & pp* **-fied**) *tr & intr* satisfacer
saturate ['sætʃə,ret] *tr* saturar
Saturday ['sætərdi] *s* sábado
sauce [sɔs] *s* salsa; (*of fruit*) compota; (*of chocolate*) crema; gracia, viveza; (coll) insolencia, lenguaje descomedido || *tr* condimentar || [sɔs] o [sæs] *tr* (coll) ser respondón con
sauce'pan' *s* cacerola
saucer ['sɔsər] *s* platillo
sau•cy ['sɔsi] *adj* (*comp* **-cier;** *super* **-ciest**) descarado, insolente; gracioso, vivo
sauerkraut ['saʊr,kraʊt] *s* chucruta
saunter ['sɔntər] *s* paseo tranquilo y alegre || *intr* dar un paseo tranquilo y alegre; pasear tranquila y alegremente
sausage ['sɔsɪdʒ] *s* salchicha, embutido
savage ['sævɪdʒ] *adj & s* salvaje *mf*
savant ['sævənt] *s* sabio, erudito
save [sev] *prep* salvo, excepto, menos || *tr* salvar (*p.ej., una vida, un alma*); ahorrar (*dinero*); conservar, guardar; proteger, amparar; **God save the Queen!** ¡Dios guarde a la Reina!; **to save face** salvar las apariencias
saving ['sevɪŋ] *prep* salvo, excepto; con el debido respeto a || *adj* económico || **savings** *spl* ahorros, economías
savings account *s* cuenta de ahorros
savings bank *s* banco de ahorros, caja de ahorros
savior ['sevjər] *s* salvador *m*
Saviour ['sevjər] *s* Salvador *m*
savor ['sevər] *s* sabor *m* || *tr* saborear || *intr* oler; **to savor of** oler a, saber a
savor•y ['sevəri] *adj* (*comp* **-ier;** *super* **-iest**) sabroso; picante; fragante || *s* (*pl* **-ies**) (bot) ajedrea
saw [sɔ] *s* (*tool*) sierra; proverbio, refrán *m* || *tr* aserrar, serrar
saw'buck' *s* cabrilla, caballete *m*
saw'dust' *s* aserrín *m,* serrín *m*
saw'horse' *s* cabrilla, caballete *m*
saw'mill' *s* aserradero, serrería
Saxon ['sæksən] *adj & s* sajón *m*
saxophone ['sæksə,fon] *s* saxofón *m*
say [se] *s* decir *m;* **to have one's say** decir su parecer || *v* (*pret & pp* **said** [sɛd]) *tr* decir; **I should say so!** ¡ya lo creo!; **it is said** se dice; **no sooner said than done** dicho y hecho; **that is to say** es decir, esto es; **to go without saying** caerse de su peso
saying ['se·ɪŋ] *s* dicho; proverbio, refrán *m*
sc. *abbr* **scene, science, scruple, scilicet** (Lat) **namely**
scab [skæb] *s* costra; (*strikebreaker*) esquirol *m;* (slang) bribón *m,* golfo
scabbard ['skæbərd] *s* funda, vaina
scab•by ['skæbi] *adj* (*comp* **-bier;** *super* **-biest**) costroso; (coll) ruin, vil
scabrous ['skæbrəs] *adj* escabroso
scads [skædz] *spl* (slang) montones *mpl*

scaffold ['skæfəld] *s* andamio; (*to execute a criminal*) cadalso, patíbulo
scaffolding ['skæfəldɪŋ] *s* andamiaje *m*
scald [skɔld] *tr* escaldar
scale [skel] *s* escama; balanza; platillo de balanza; (*e.g., of a map*) escala; (mus) escala; **on a scale of** en escala de; **on a large scale** en grande escala; **scales** balanza; **to tip the scales** inclinar la balanza || *tr* escamar; descortezar, descostrar; escalar, subir, trepar; graduar || *intr* descamarse; descortezarse, descostrarse; subir, trepar
scallop ['skɑləp] o ['skæləp] *s* concha de peregrino; (*shell or dish for serving fish*) concha; (*thin slice of meat*) escalope *m;* (*on edge of cloth*) festón *m* || *tr* cocer (*p.ej., ostras*) en su concha; festonear
scalp [skælp] *s* cuero cabelludo || *tr* escalpar; comprar y revender (*billetes de teatro*) a precios extraoficiales
scalpel ['skælpəl] *s* escalpelo
scal•y ['skeli] *adj* (*comp* **-ier;** *super* **-iest**) escamoso
scamp [skæmp] *s* bribón *m,* golfo
scamper ['skæmpər] *intr* escaparse precipitadamente; **to scamper away** escaparse precipitadamente
scan [skæn] *v* (*pret & pp* **scanned;** *ger* **scanning**) *tr* escudriñar; escandir (*versos*); (telv) explorar; (coll) dar un vistazo a
scandal ['skændəl] *s* escándalo
scandalize ['skændə,laɪz] *tr* escandalizar
scandalous ['skændələs] *adj* escandaloso
Scandinavian [,skændɪ'nevɪ•ən] *adj* & *s* escandinavo
scanning ['skænɪŋ] *s* (telv) escansión, exploración
scansion ['skænʃən] *s* escansión
scant [skænt] *adj* escaso, insuficiente; solo, apenas suficiente || *tr* escatimar
scant•y ['skænti] *adj* (*comp* **-ier;** *super* **-iest**) escaso, insuficiente, poco suficiente; (*clothing*) ligero
scape'goat' *s* cabeza de turco, víctima propiciatoria
scar [skɑr] *s* cicatriz *f,* señal *f* || *v* (*pret & pp* **scarred;** *ger* **scarring**) *tr* señalar, marcar || *intr* cicatrizarse
scarce [skɛrs] *adj* escaso, raro; **to make oneself scarce** (coll) no dejarse ver
scarcely ['skɛrsli] *adv* apenas; probablemente no; ciertamente no; **scarcely ever** raramente
scarci•ty ['skɛrsɪti] *s* (*pl* **-ties**) escasez *f,* carestía
scare [skɛr] *s* susto, alarma || *tr* asustar, espantar; **to scare away** espantar, ahuyentar; **to scare up** (coll) juntar, recoger (*dinero*)
scare'crow' *s* espantajo, espantapájaros *m*
scarf [skɑrf] *s* (*pl* **scarfs** o **scarves** [skɑrvz]) bufanda; pañuelo para el cuello; (*cover for a table, bureau, etc.*) tapete *m;* corbata
scarf'pin' *s* alfiler *m* de corbata
scarlet ['skɑrlɪt] *adj* escarlata
scarlet fever *s* escarlata
scar•y ['skɛri] *adj* (*comp* **-ier;** *super* **-iest**) (*easily frightened*) (coll) asustadizo, espantadizo; (*causing fright*) (coll) espantoso
scathing ['skeðɪŋ] *adj* acerbo, duro
scatter ['skætər] *tr* esparcir, dispersar || *intr* esparcirse, dispersarse
scatterbrained ['skætər,brend] *adj* (coll) alegre de cascos, casquivano
scattered showers *spl* lluvias aisladas
scenari•o [sɪ'nɛrɪ,o] o [sɪ'nɑrɪ,o] *s* (*pl* **-os**) guión *m,* escenario
scenarist [sɪ'nɛrɪst] o [sɪ'nɑrɪst] *s* guionista *mf,* escenarista *mf*
scene [sin] *s* (*view*) paisaje *m;* (*in literature, art, the theater, the movie*) escena; escándalo, demostración de pasión; **behind the scenes** entre bastidores; **to make a scene** causar escándalo
scener•y ['sinəri] *s* (*pl* **-ies**) paisaje *m;* (theat) decoraciones
scene shifter ['ʃɪftər] *s* tramoyista *m*
scenic ['sinɪk] o ['sɛnɪk] *adj* pintoresco; (*representing an action graphically*) gráfico; (*pertaining to the stage*) escénico
scent [sɛnt] *s* olor *m;* perfume *m;* (*sense of smell*) olfato; (*trail*) rastro, pista || *tr* oler; perfumar; olfatear, ventear; sospechar
scepter ['sɛptər] *s* cetro
sceptic ['skɛptɪk] *adj* & *s* escéptico
sceptical ['skɛptɪkəl] *adj* escéptico
schedule ['skɛdjul] *s* catálogo, cuadro, lista; plan *m,* programa *m;* (*of trains, planes, etc.*) horario || *tr* catalogar; proyectar; fijar la hora de
scheme [skim] *s* esquema *m;* plan *m,* proyecto; (*trick*) ardid *m,* treta; (*plot*) intriga, trama || *tr* & *intr* proyectar; tramar
schemer ['skimər] *s* proyectista *mf;* intrigante *mf*
scheming ['skimɪŋ] *adj* astuto, mañoso, intrigante || *s* intriga
schism ['sɪzəm] *s* cisma *m;* facción cismática
schist [ʃɪst] *s* esquisto
scholar ['skɑlər] *s* (*pupil*) alumno; (*scholarship holder*) becario; (*learned person*) sabio, erudito
scholarly ['skɑlərli] *adj* sabio, erudito
scholarship ['skɑlər,ʃɪp] *s* erudición; (*grant to study*) beca
school [skul] *s* escuela; (*of a university*) facultad; (*of fish*) banco, cardume *m* || *tr* enseñar, instruir, disciplinar
school age *s* edad escolar
school attendance *s* escolaridad
school board *s* junta de instrucción pública
school'boy' *s* alumno de escuela
school day *s* día lectivo
school'girl' *s* alumna de escuela
school'house' *s* escuela
schooling ['skulɪŋ] *s* instrucción, enseñanza; experiencia
school'mate' *s* compañero de escuela
school'room' *s* aula, sala de clase

school'teach'er *s* maestro de escuela
school year *s* año lectivo
schooner ['skunər] *s* goleta
sci. *abbr* **science, scientific**
science ['saɪ·əns] *s* ciencia
scientific [ˌsaɪ·ən'tɪfɪk] *adj* científico
scientist ['saɪ·əntɪst] *s* científico, sabio, hombre *m* de ciencia
scil. *abbr* **scilicet** (Lat) **namely**
scimitar ['sɪmɪtər] *s* cimitarra
scintillate ['sɪntɪˌlet] *intr* chispear, centellear
scion ['saɪ·ən] *s* vástago
Scipio ['sɪpɪˌo] *s* Escipión *m*
scissors ['sɪzərz] *ssg* o *spl* tijeras
scoff [skɔf] o [skɑf] *s* burla, mofa || *intr* burlarse, mofarse; **to scoff at** burlarse de, mofarse de
scold [skold] *s* regañón *m,* regañona || *tr & intr* regañar
scoop [skup] *s* (*instrument like a spoon*) cuchara, cucharón *m;* (*tool like a shovel*) pala; (*kitchen utensil*) paleta; (*for water*) achicador *m;* cucharada, palada, paletada; (*hollow made by a scoop*) hueco; (*big haul*) (coll) buena ganancia || *tr* sacar con cuchara, pala, paleta; achicar (*agua*); **to scoop out** ahuecar, vaciar
scoot [skut] *s* (coll) carrera precipitada || *intr* (coll) correr precipitadamente
scooter ['skutər] *s* monopatín *m,* patinete *m*
scope [skop] *s* alcance *m,* extensión; campo, espacio; **to give free scope to** dar campo libre a
scorch [skɔrtʃ] *s* chamusco || *tr* chamuscar; (*to dry, wither*) abrasar; criticar acerbamente || *intr* chamuscarse; abrasarse
scorching ['skɔrtʃɪŋ] *adj* abrasador; acerbo, duro, mordaz
score [skor] *s* (*in a game*) cuenta, tantos; (*in an examination*) nota; entalladura, muesca; línea, raya; (*twenty*) veintena; (mus) partitura; **on the score of** a título de; **to keep score** apuntar los tantos || *tr* anotar (*los tantos*); ganar, tantear (*tantos*); rayar, señalar; regañar acerbamente; (mus) instrumentar || *intr* ganar tantos; marcar los tantos
score board *s* marcador *m,* cuadro indicador
scorn [skɔrn] *s* desdén *m,* desprecio || *tr & intr* desdeñar, despreciar; **to scorn to** no dignarse
scornful ['skɔrnfəl] *adj* desdeñoso
scorpion ['skɔrpɪ·ən] *s* alacrán *m,* escorpión *m*
Scot [skɑt] *s* escocés *m*
Scotch [skɑtʃ] *adj* escocés || *s* (*dialect*) escocés *m;* whisky *m* escocés; **the Scotch** los escoceses
Scotch·man ['skɑtʃmən] *s* (*pl* **-men** [mən]) escocés *m*
Scotland ['skɑtlənd] *s* Escocia
Scottish ['skɑtɪʃ] *adj* escocés || *s* (*dialect*) escocés *m;* **the Scottish** los escoceses
scoundrel ['skaʊndrəl] *s* bribón *m,* pícaro
scour [skaʊr] *tr* fregar, estregar; recorrer, explorar detenidamente
scourge [skʌrdʒ] *s* azote *m* || *tr* azotar
scout [skaʊt] *s* (mil) escucha, explorador *m;* niño explorador, niña exploradora; exploración, reconocimiento; (slang) individuo, sujeto, tipo || *tr* explorar, reconocer (*un territorio*); observar (*al enemigo*); negarse a creer
scout'mas'ter *s* jefe *m* de tropa de niños exploradores
scowl [skaʊl] *s* ceño, semblante ceñudo || *intr* mirar con ceño, poner mal gesto, poner mala cara
scramble ['skræmbəl] *s* arrebatiña || *tr* arrebatar; recoger de prisa; revolver; hacer un revoltillo de (*huevos*); trepar || *intr* luchar; trepar
scrambled eggs *spl* revoltillo, huevos revueltos
scrap [skræp] *s* fragmento, pedacito; desecho; chatarra; (slang) riña, contienda; **scraps** desperdicios, desechos; (*from the table*) sobras || *v* (*pret & pp* **scrapped;** *ger* **scrapping**) *tr* desechar, descartar, echar a la basura; reducir a hierro viejo || *intr* (slang) reñir, pelear
scrap'book' *s* álbum *m* de recortes, libro de recuerdos
scrape [skrep] *s* raspadura; (*place scratched*) raspazo; aprieto, enredo; || *tr* raspar; (*to gather together with much difficulty*) arañar || *intr* raspar; **to scrape along** ir tirando; **to scrape through** aprobar justo
scrap heap *s* montón *m* de cachivaches
scrap iron *s* chatarra, desecho de hierro
scrap paper *s* papel *m* para apuntes; papel de desecho
scratch [skrætʃ] *s* arañazo, rasguño; marca, raya, garrapato; (billiards) chiripa; (sport) línea de partida; **to start from scratch** empezar desde el principio; **up to scratch** en buena condición || *tr* arañar, rasguñar; borrar, rasgar (*lo escrito*); garrapatear; (sport) borrar (*a un corredor o caballo*) || *intr* arañar, rasguñar; garrapatear; raspear (*una pluma*)
scratch pad *s* cuadernillo de apuntes
scratch paper *s* papel *m* para apuntes
scrawl [skrɔl] *s* garrapatos || *tr & intr* garrapatear
scraw·ny ['skrɔni] *adj* (*comp* **-nier;** *super* **-niest**) huesudo, flaco
scream [skrim] *s* chillido, grito || *tr* vociferar || *intr* chillar, gritar; reírse a gritos
screech [skritʃ] *s* chillido || *intr* chillar
screech owl *s* buharro; (*barn owl*) lechuza
screen [skrin] *s* mampara, biombo; (*in front of chimney*) pantalla; (*to keep flies out*) alambrera; (*to sift sand*) tamiz *m;* (mov, phys, telv) pantalla; **to put on the screen** llevar a la pantalla, llevar al celuloide || *tr* defender, proteger; cubrir, ocultar; cinematografiar; rodar, proyectar (*una película*); adaptar para el cine; tamizar (*p.ej., arena*)

screen grid *s* (electron) rejilla blindada
screen'play' *s* cinedrama *m*
screw [skru] *s* tornillo; (*internal or female screw*) rosca, tuerca; (*of a boat*) hélice *f;* **to have a screw loose** (slang) tener flojos los tornillos; **to put the screws on** apretar los tornillos a || *tr* atornillar; (*to twist, twist in*) enroscar; **to screw up** torcer (*el rostro*); || *intr* atornillarse
screw'ball' *s* (slang) estrafalario, excéntrico
screw'driv'er *s* destornillador *m*
screw eye *s* armella
screw jack *s* gato de tornillo
screw propeller *s* hélice *f*
scribal error ['skraɪbəl] *s* error *m* de escribiente
scribble ['skrɪbəl] *s* garrapatos || *tr & intr* garrapatear
scribe [skraɪb] *s* (*teacher of Jewish law*) escriba *m;* escribiente *mf;* copista *mf;* autor *m,* escritor *m* || *tr* arañar, rayar; trazar con punzón
scrimp [skrɪmp] *tr & intr* escatimar
script [skrɪpt] *s* escritura, letra cursiva; manuscrito, texto; (*of a play, movie, etc.*) palabras; (rad, telv) guión *m;* (typ) plumilla inglesa
scripture ['skrɪptʃər] *s* escrito sagrado || **Scripture** *s* Escritura
script'writ'er *s* guionista *mf,* cinematurgo
scrofula ['skrɑfjələ] *s* escrófula
scroll [skrol] *s* rollo de papel, rollo de pergamino; (archit) voluta
scroll'work' *s* obra de volutas, adornos de voluta
scrub [skrʌb] *s* chaparral *m,* monte bajo; animal achaparrado; persona de poca monta; (*act of scrubbing*) fregado; (sport) jugador *m* no oficial || *v* (*pret & pp* **scrubbed;** *ger* **scrubbing**) *tr* fregar, restregar
scrub oak *s* chaparro
scrub woman *s* fregona
scruff [skrʌf] *s* nuca; piel *f* que cubre la nuca; capa, superficie *f;* espuma
scruple ['skrupəl] *s* escrúpulo
scrupulous ['skrupjələs] *adj* escrupuloso
scrutinize ['skrutɪ,naɪz] *tr* escudriñar, escrutar
scruti•ny ['skrutɪni] *s* (*pl* **-nies**) escudriñamiento, escrutinio
scuff [skʌf] *s* rascadura, desgaste *m* || *tr* rascar, desgastar
scuffle ['skʌfəl] *s* lucha, sarracina || *intr* forcejear, luchar
scull [skʌl] *s* espadilla || *tr* impulsar con espadilla || *intr* remar con espadilla
sculler•y ['skʌləri] *s* (*pl* **-ies**) trascocina
scullery maid *s* fregona
scullion ['skʌljən] *s* pinche *m*
sculptor ['skʌlptər] *s* escultor *m*
sculptress ['skʌlptrɪs] *s* escultora
sculpture ['skʌlptʃər] *s* escultura || *tr & intr* esculpir
scum [skʌm] *s* espuma, nata; (*on metals*) escoria; (fig) escoria, canalla, gente baja || *v* (*pret & pp* **scummed;** *ger* **scumming**) *tr & intr* espumar
scum•my ['skʌmi] *adj* (*comp* **-mier;** *super* **-miest**) espumoso; (fig) vil, ruin
scurf [skʌrf] *s* (*shed by the skin*) caspa; (*shed by any surface*) costra
scurrilous ['skʌrɪləs] *adj* chocarrero, grosero, insolente, difamatorio
scur•ry ['skʌri] *v* (*pret & pp* **-ried**) *intr* echar a correr, escabullirse; **to scurry around** menearse; **to scurry away** ir respailando
scur•vy ['skʌrvi] *adj* (*comp* **-vier;** *super* **-viest**) despreciable, ruin, vil || *s* escorbuto
scuttle ['skʌtəl] *s* (*bucket for coal*) cubo, balde *m;* (*trap door*) escotillón *m;* fuga, paso acelerado; (naut) escotilla || *tr* barrenar, dar barreno a || *intr* echar a correr
Scylla ['sɪlə] *s* Escila; **between Scylla and Charybdis** entre Escila y Caribdis
scythe [saɪð] *s* dalle *m,* guadaña
sea [si] *s* mar *m & f;* **at sea** en el mar; confuso, perplejo; **by the sea** a la orilla del mar; **to follow the sea** correr los mares, ser marinero; **to put to sea** hacerse a la mar
sea'board' *adj* costanero, costero || *s* costa del mar, litoral *m*
sea breeze *s* brisa de mar
sea'coast' *s* costa marítima, litoral *m*
sea dog *s* (*seal*) foca; (coll) marinero viejo, lobo de mar
seafarer ['si,fɛrər] *s* marinero; viajero por mar
sea'food' *s* mariscos
seagoing ['si,go•ɪŋ] *adj* de alta mar
sea gull *s* gaviota
seal [sil] *s* (*raised design; stamp; mark*) sello; (*sea animal*) foca || *tr* sellar; cerrar herméticamente; decidir irrevocablemente; (*with sealing wax*) lacrar
sea legs *spl* pie marino
sea level *s* nivel *m* del mar
sealing wax *s* lacre *m*
seal'skin' *s* piel *f* de foca
seam [sim] *s* costura; (*edges left after making a seam*) metido; (*mark, line*) arruga; (*scar*) costurón *m;* grieta, juntura; (min) filón *m,* veta
sea•man ['simən] *s* (*pl* **-men** [mən]) marinero; (nav) marino
sea mile *s* milla náutica
seamless ['simlɪs] *adj* inconsútil, sin costura
seamstress ['simstrɪs] *s* costurera; (*dressmaker's helper*) modistilla
seam•y ['simi] *adj* (*comp* **-ier;** *super* **-iest**) lleno de costuras; tosco, burdo; vil, soez; miserable
séance ['se•ɑns] *s* sesión de espiritistas
sea'plane' *s* hidroavión *m,* hidroplano
sea'port' *s* puerto de mar
sea power *s* potencia naval
sear [sɪr] *adj* seco, marchito; gastado, raído || *s* chamusco, socarra || *tr* chamuscar, socarrar; quemar; marchitar; cauterizar
search [sʌrtʃ] *s* busca; pesquisa, in-

dagación; (*frisking a person*) cacheo; **in search of** en busca de || *tr* averiguar, explorar; registrar || *intr* buscar; **to search for** buscar; **to search into** indagar, investigar
search'light' *s* reflector *m,* proyector *m*
search warrant *s* auto de registro domiciliario, orden *f* de allanamiento
sea'scape' *s* vista del mar; (*painting*) marina
sea shell *s* concha marina
sea'shore' *s* costa, playa, ribera del mar
sea'sick' *adj* mareado
sea'sick'ness *s* mareo
sea'side' *s* orilla del mar, ribera del mar, playa
season ['sizən] *s* (*one of four parts of year*) estación; (*period of the year; period marked by certain activities*) temporada; (*opportune time; time of maturity, of ripening*) sazón *f;* **in season** en sazón; **in season and out of season** en tiempo y a destiempo; **out of season** fuera de sazón || *tr* condimentar, sazonar; curar (*la madera*); moderar, templar
seasonal ['sizənəl] *adj* estacional
seasoning ['sizənɪŋ] *s* aderezo, aliño, condimento; (*of wood*) cura; (fig) sal *f,* chiste *m*
season ticket *s* billete *m* de abono
seat [sit] *s* asiento; (*of trousers*) fondillos; morada; sitio, lugar *m;* (*e.g., of government*) sede *f;* (*in parliament*) escaño; (*e.g., of a war*) teatro; (*e.g., of learning*) centro; (*of a saddle*) batalla; (*of human body*) nalgas; (theat) localidad || *tr* sentar; tener asientos para; poner asiento a (*una silla*); echar fondillos a (*pantalones*); arraigar, establecer; **to be seated** estar sentado; **to seat oneself** sentarse
seat belt *s* cinturón *m* de asiento
seat cover *s* funda de asiento, cubreasiento
SEATO ['sito] *s* (acronym) la O.T.A.S.E.
sea wall *s* dique marítimo
sea'way' *s* ruta marítima; avance *m* de un buque por mar; vía de agua interior para buques de alta mar; mar gruesa
sea'weed' *s* alga marina; plantas marinas
sea wind *s* viento que sopla del mar
sea'wor'thy *adj* marinero, en condiciones de navegar
sec. *abbr* **secant, second, secondary, secretary, section, sector**
secede [sɪ'sid] *intr* separarse, retirarse
secession [sɪ'sɛʃən] *s* secesión
seclude [sɪ'klud] *tr* recluir
secluded [sɪ'kludɪd] *adj* aislado, apartado, solitario
seclusion [sɪ'kluʒən] *s* reclusión, soledad
second ['sɛkənd] *adj* segundo; **to be second to none** ser tan bueno como el que más, no tener segundo || *adv* en segundo lugar || *s* segundo; artículo de segunda calidad; (*in dates*) dos *m;* (*in a challenge*) padrino; (aut) segunda (velocidad); (mus) segunda || *tr* secundar; apoyar (*una moción*)
secondar•y ['sɛkən,dɛri] *adj* secundario || *s* (*pl* **-ies**) (elec) secundario
sec'ond-best' *adj* (el) mejor después del primero
sec'ond-class' *adj* de segunda clase
second hand *s* segundero
sec'ond-hand' *adj* de segunda mano, de ocasión
second-hand bookshop *s* librería de viejo
second lieutenant *s* alférez *m,* subteniente *m*
sec'ond-rate' *adj* de segundo orden; de calidad inferior
second sight *s* doble vista
second wind *s* nuevo aliento
secre•cy ['sikrəsi] *s* (*pl* **-cies**) secreto; **in secrecy** en secreto
secret ['sikrɪt] *adj & s* secreto; **in secret** en secreto
secretar•y ['sɛkrɪ,tɛri] *s* (*pl* **-ies**) secretario; (*desk*) secreter *m,* escritorio
secrete [sɪ'krit] *tr* encubrir, esconder; (physiol) secretar
secretive [sɪ'kritɪv] *adj* callado, reservado
sect [sɛkt] *s* secta, comunión
sectarian [sɛk'tɛrɪ·ən] *adj & s* sectario
section ['sɛkʃən] *s* sección; (*of a country*) región; (*of a city*) barrio; (*of a law*) artículo; (*department, bureau*) negociado; (rr) tramo
secular ['sɛkjələr] *adj* secular, seglar || *s* clérigo secular
secularism ['sɛkjələ,rɪzəm] *s* laicismo
secure [sɪ'kjur] *adj* seguro || *tr* asegurar; conseguir, obtener
securi•ty [sɪ'kjurɪti] *s* (*pl* **-ties**) seguridad; (*person*) segurador *m;* **securities** valores *mpl,* obligaciones, títulos
secy. o **sec'y.** *abbr* **secretary**
sedan [sɪ'dæn] *s* silla de manos; (aut) sedán *m*
sedate [sɪ'det] *adj* sentado, sosegado
sedative ['sɛdətɪv] *adj & s* sedativo
sedentary ['sɛdən,tɛri] *adj* sedentario
sedge [sɛdʒ] *s* juncia
sediment ['sɛdɪmənt] *s* sedimento
sedition [sɪ'dɪʃən] *s* sedición
seditious [sɪ'dɪʃəs] *adj* sedicioso
seduce [sɪ'djus] o [sɪ'dus] *tr* seducir
seducer [sɪ'djusər] o [sɪ'dusər] *s* seductor *m*
seduction [sɪ'dʌkʃən] *s* seducción
seductive [sɪ'dʌktɪv] *adj* seductivo
sedulous ['sɛdjələs] *adj* cuidadoso, diligente
see [si] *s* (eccl) sede *f* || *v* (*pret* **saw** [sɔ]; *pp* **seen** [sin]) *tr* ver; **to see off** ir a despedir; **to see through** llevar a cabo; ayudar en un trance difícil || *intr* ver; **see here!** ¡mire Vd.!; **to see into** o **to see through** conocer el juego de
seed [sid] *s* semilla, simiente *f;* **to go to seed** dar semilla; echarse a perder || *tr* sembrar; (*to remove the seeds from*) despepitar || *intr* sembrar; dejar caer semillas
seed'bed' *s* semillero

seedling ['sidlɪŋ] *s* planta de semilla; árbol *m* de pie
seed·y ['sidi] *adj* (*comp* **-ier;** *super* **-iest**) lleno de granos; (coll) andrajoso, raído
seeing ['si·ɪŋ] *adj* vidente ‖ *s* vista, visión ‖ *conj* visto que
Seeing Eye dog *s* perro-lazarillo
seek [sik] *v* (*pret & pp* **sought** [sɔt]) *tr* buscar; recorrer buscando; dirigirse a ‖ *intr* buscar; **to seek after** tratar de obtener; **to seek to** esforzarse por
seem [sim] *intr* parecer
seemingly ['simɪŋli] *adv* aparentemente, al parecer
seem·ly ['simli] *adj* (*comp* **-lier;** *super* **-liest**) decente, decoroso, correcto; bien parecido
seep [sip] *intr* escurrirse, rezumarse
seer [sɪr] *s* profeta *m,* vidente *m*
see'saw' *s* balancín *m,* columpio de tabla; (*motion*) vaivén *m* ‖ *intr* columpiarse; alternar; vacilar
seethe [sið] *intr* hervir
segment ['sɛgmənt] *s* segmento
segregate ['sɛgrɪ,get] *tr* segregar
segregationist [,sɛgrɪ'geʃənɪst] *s* segregacionista *mf*
Seine [sen] *s* Sena *m*
seismograph ['saɪzmə,græf] o ['saɪzme,grɑf] *s* sismógrafo
seismology [saɪz'mɑlədʒi] *s* sismología
seize [siz] *tr* agarrar, asir, coger; atar, prender, sujetar; apoderarse de; comprender; (law) embargar, secuestrar; aprovecharse de (*una oportunidad*)
seizure ['siʒər] *s* prendimiento, prisión; captura, toma; (*of an illness*) ataque *m;* (law) embargo, secuestro
seldom ['sɛldəm] *adv* raramente, rara vez
select [sɪ'lɛkt] *adj* escogido, selecto ‖ *tr* seleccionar
selectee [sɪ,lɛk'ti] *s* (mil) quinto
selection [sɪ'lɛkʃən] *s* selección; trozo escogido; (*of goods for sale*) surtido
self [sɛlf] *adj* mismo ‖ *pron* sí mismo ‖ *s* (*pl* **selves** [sɛlvz]) uno mismo; ser *m;* yo; **all by one's self** sin ayuda de nadie
self'-abuse' *s* abuso de sí mismo; masturbación
self'-addressed' envelope *s* sobre *m* con el nombre y dirección del remitente
self'-cen'tered *adj* egocéntrico
self'-con'scious *adj* cohibido, apocado, tímido
self'-con·trol' *s* dominio de sí mismo
self'-de·fense' *s* autodefensa; **in self-defense** en defensa propia
self'-de·ni'al *s* abnegación
self'-de·ter'mi·na'tion *s* autodeterminación
self'-dis'cipline *s* autodisciplina
self'-ed'u·cat'ed *adj* autodidacto
self'-em·ployed' *adj* que trabaja por su propia cuenta
self'-ev'i·dent *adj* patente, manifiesto
self'-ex·plan'a·tor'y *adj* que se explica por sí mismo
self'-gov'ernment *s* autogobierno, autonomía; dominio sobre sí mismo
self'-im·por'tant *adj* altivo, arrogante
self'-in·dul'gence *s* intemperancia, desenfreno
self'-in'terest *s* egoísmo, interés *m* personal
selfish ['sɛlfɪʃ] *adj* egoísta
selfishness ['sɛlfɪʃnɪs] *s* egoísmo
selfless ['sɛlflɪs] *adj* desinteresado
self'-liq'ui·dat'ing *adj* autoamortizable
self'-love' *s* amor propio, egoísmo
self'-made' man *s* hijo de sus propias obras
self'-por'trait *s* autorretrato
self'-pos·sessed' *adj* dueño de sí mismo
self'-pres'er·va'tion *s* propia conservación
self'-re·li'ant *adj* confiado en sí mismo
self'-re·spect'ing *adj* lleno de dignidad, decoroso
self'-right'eous *adj* santurrón
self'-sac'ri·fice' *s* sacrificio de sí mismo
self'same' *adj* mismísimo
self'-sat'is·fied' *adj* pagado de sí mismo
self'-seek'ing *adj* egoísta ‖ *s* egoísmo
self'-ser'vice restaurant *s* restaurante *m* de libre servicio, restaurante de autoservicio
self'-start'er *s* arranque automático
self'sup·port' *s* mantenimiento económico propio
self'-taught' *adj* autodidacto
self'-willed' *adj* obstinado, terco
self'-wind'ing clock *s* reloj *m* de cuerda automática, reloj de autocuerda
sell [sɛl] *v* (*pret & pp* **sold** [sold]) *tr* vender; **to sell out** realizar, saldar; (*to betray*) vender ‖ *intr* venderse, estar de venta; **to sell for** venderse a o en (*p.ej., cien pesetas*); **to sell off** bajar (*el mercado de valores*); **to sell out** venderlo todo, realizar
seller ['sɛlər] *s* vendedor *m*
sell'out' *s* (slang) realización, saldo; (slang) traición
Seltzer water ['sɛltsər] *s* agua de seltz
selvage ['sɛlvɪdʒ] *s* orillo, vendo
semantic [sɪ'mæntɪk] *adj* semántico ‖ **semantics** *s* semántica
semaphore ['sɛmə,for] *s* semáforo; (rr) disco de señales
semblance ['sɛmbləns] *s* apariencia, imagen *f,* simulacro
semen ['simɛn] *s* semen *m*
semester [sɪ'mɛstər] *adj* semestral ‖ *s* semestre *m*
semester hour *s* hora semestral
sem'ico'lon *s* punto y coma
sem'iconduc'tor *s* semiconductor *m*
sem'icon'scious *adj* semiconsciente
sem'ifi'nal *adj & s* (sport) semifinal *f*
sem'ilearn'ed *adj* semiculto
sem'imonth'ly *adj* quincenal ‖ *s* (*pl* **-lies**) periódico quincenal
seminar ['sɛmɪ,nɑr] o [,sɛmɪ'nɑr] *s* seminario
seminar·y ['sɛmɪ,nɛri] *s* (*pl* **-ies**) seminario
sem'ipre'cious *adj* semiprecioso, fino
Semite ['sɛmaɪt] o ['simaɪt] *s* semita *mf*

Semitic [sɪˈmɪtɪk] *adj* semítico || *s* semita *mf;* (*language*) semita *m*
sem'itrail'er *s* semi-remolque *m*
sem'iweek'ly *adj* bisemanal || *s* (*pl* **-lies**) periódico bisemanal
sem'iyear'ly *adj* semestral
Sen. o **sen.** *abbr* **Senate, Senator, Senior**
senate [ˈsɛnɪt] *s* senado
senator [ˈsɛnətər] *s* senador *m*
senatorship [ˈsɛnətər ˌʃɪp] *s* senaduría
send [sɛnd] *v* (*pret & pp* **sent** [sɛnt]) *tr* enviar, mandar; expedir, remitir; lanzar (*una bola, flecha, etc.*); **to send back** devolver, reenviar; **to send packing** despedir con cajas destempladas || *intr* (rad) transmitir; **to send for** enviar por, enviar a buscar
sender [ˈsɛndər] *s* remitente *mf;* (telg) transmisor *m*
send'-off' *s* (coll) despedida afectuosa
senile [ˈsinaɪl] o [ˈsinɪl] *adj* senil
senility [sɪˈnɪlɪti] *s* senilidad; (pathol) senilismo
senior [ˈsinjər] *adj* mayor, de mayor edad; viejo; del último año; padre, p.ej., **John Jones, Senior** Juan Jones, padre || *s* mayor *m;* socio más antiguo; alumno del último año
senior citizens *spl* gente *f* de edad
seniority [sinˈjɑrɪti] o [sinˈjɔrɪti] *s* antigüedad; precedencia, prioridad
sensation [sɛnˈseʃən] *s* sensación
sense [sɛns] *s* sentido; **to make sense out of** comprender, explicarse || *tr* intuir, sentir, sospechar; (coll) comprender
senseless [ˈsɛnslɪs] *adj* falto de sentido; desmayado; insensato, necio
sense of guilt *s* cargo de conciencia
sense organ *s* órgano sensorio
sensibili·ty [ˌsɛnsɪˈbɪlɪti] *s* (*pl* **-ties**) sensibilidad; **sensibilities** sentimientos delicados
sensible [ˈsɛnsɪbəl] *adj* cuerdo, sensato; perceptible, sensible
sensitive [ˈsɛnsɪtɪv] *adj* sensible; (*of the senses*) sensorio, sensitivo
sensitize [ˈsɛnsɪ ˌtaɪz] *tr* sensibilizar
sensory [ˈsɛnsəri] *adj* sensorio
sensual [ˈsɛnʃu·əl] *adj* sensual, voluptuoso
sensuous [ˈsɛnʃu·əs] *adj* sensual
sentence [ˈsɛntəns] *s* (gram) frase *f,* oración; (law) sentencia || *tr* sentenciar, condenar
sentiment [ˈsɛntɪmənt] *s* sentimiento
sentimentali·ty [ˌsɛntɪmɛnˈtælɪti] *s* (*pl* **-ties**) sentimentalismo
sentinel [ˈsɛntɪnəl] *s* centinela *m* or *f;* **to stand sentinel** estar de centinela, hacer centinela
sen·try [ˈsɛntri] *s* (*pl* **-tries**) centinela *m* or *f*
sentry box *s* garita de centinela
separate [ˈsɛpərɪt] *adj* separado; suelto || [ˈsɛpə ˌret] *tr* separar || *intr* separarse
Sephardic [sɪˈfɑrdɪk] *adj* sefardí, sefardita
Sephardim [sɪˈfɑrdɪm] *spl* sefardíes *mpl*
September [sɛp·tɛmbər] *s* septiembre *m*
septet [sɛpˈtɛt] *s* septeto
septic [ˈsɛptɪk] *adj* séptico
sepulcher [ˈsɛpəlkər] *s* sepulcro
seq. *abbr* **sequentia** (Lat) **the following**
sequel [ˈsikwəl] *s* resultado, secuela; continuación
sequence [ˈsikwəns] *s* serie *f,* sucesión; (cards) secansa, escalera, runfla; (gram, mov & mus) secuencia
sequester [sɪˈkwɛstər] *tr* apartar, separar; (law) secuestrar
sequin [ˈsikwɪn] *s* lentejuela
ser·aph [ˈsɛrəf] *s* (*pl* **-aphs** o **-aphim** [əfɪm]) serafín *m*
Serb [sʌrb] *adj & s* servio
Serbia [ˈsʌrbɪ·ə] *s* Servia
Serbian [ˈsʌrbɪ·ən] *adj & s* servio
Serbo-Croatian [ˌsʌrbokroˈeʃən] *adj & s* servocroata *mf*
sere [sɪr] *adj* seco, marchito
serenade [ˌsɛrəˈned] *s* serenata || *tr* dar serenata a || *intr* dar serenatas
serene [sɪˈrin] *adj* sereno
serenity [sɪˈrɛnɪti] *s* serenidad
serf [sʌrf] *s* siervo de la gleba
serfdom [ˈsʌrfdəm] *s* servidumbre de la gleba
serge [sʌrdʒ] *s* sarga
sergeant [ˈsɑrdʒənt] *s* sargento
ser'geant-at-arms' *s* (*pl* **sergeants-at-arms**) oficial *m* de orden
sergeant major *s* (*pl* **sergeant majors**) sargento mayor
serial [ˈsɪrɪ·əl] *adj* serial; publicado por entregas || *s* cuento o novela por entregas; (rad) serial *m,* serial radiado, emisión seriada
serially [ˈsɪrɪ·əli] *adv* en serie, por series; por entregas
serial number *s* número de serie
se·ries [ˈsɪriz] *s* (*pl* **-ries**) serie *f*
serious [ˈsɪrɪ·əs] *adj* (*e.g., person, face, matter*) serio; (*e.g., condition, illness*) grave
sermon [ˈsʌrmən] *s* sermón *m*
sermonize [ˈsʌrmə ˌnaɪz] *tr & intr* sermonear
serpent [ˈsʌrpənt] *s* serpiente *f*
se·rum [ˈsɪrəm] *s* (*pl* **-rums** o **-ra** [rə]) suero
servant [ˈsʌrvənt] *s* criado, sirviente *m*
servant girl *s* criada, sirvienta
servant problem *s* crisis *f* del servicio doméstico
serve [sʌrv] *s* (*in tennis*) saque *m,* servicio || *tr* servir; (*to supply*) abastecer, proporcionar; cumplir (*una condena*); (*in tennis*) servir; **it serves me right** bien me lo merezco || *intr* servir; **to serve as** servir de
service [ˈsʌrvɪs] *s* servicio; **at your service** para servir a Vd.; **the services** las fuerzas armadas || *tr* instalar; mantener, reparar
serviceable [ˈsʌrvɪsəbəl] *adj* útil; duradero; cómodo
service·man [ˈsʌrvɪs ˌmæn] *s* (*pl* **-men** [ˌmɛn]) reparador *m,* mecánico; militar *m*
service record *s* hoja de servicios

service station *s* estación de servicio, taller *m* de reparaciones
service stripe *s* galón *m* de servicio
servile ['sʌrvɪl] *adj* servil
servitude ['sʌrvɪ,tjud] o ['sʌrvɪ,tud] *s* servidumbre; trabajos forzados
sesame ['sɛsəmi] *s* sésamo; **open sesame** sésamo ábrete
session ['sɛʃən] *s* sesión; **to be in session** sesionar
set [sɛt] *adj* determinado, resuelto; inflexible, obstinado; fijo, firme; estudiado, meditado || *s* (*of books, chairs, etc.*) juego; (*of gears*) tren *m;* (*of horses*) pareja; (*of diamonds*) aderezo; (*of tennis*) partida; (*of dishes*) servicio; (*of kitchen utensils*) batería; clase *f,* grupo; equipo; porte *m,* postura; (*of a garment*) caída, ajuste *m;* (*of glue*) endurecimiento; (*of cement*) fraguado; (*of artificial teeth*) caja; (mov) plató *m;* (rad) aparato; (theat) decoración || *v* (*pret & pp* **set;** *ger* **setting**) *tr* asentar; colocar, poner; establecer, instalar; arreglar, preparar; adornar; apostar; poner (*un reloj*) en hora; (*in bridge*) reenvidar; poner, meter, pegar (*fuego*); fijar (*el precio*); engastar, montar (*una piedra preciosa*); encasar (*un hueso dislocado*); disponer (*los tipos*); triscar (*una sierra*); armar, colocar (*una trampa*); fijar (*el peinado*); poner (*la mesa*); dar (*un ejemplo*); **to set back** parar; poner obstáculos a; hacer retroceder; atrasar, retrasar (*el reloj*); **to set forth** exponer, dar a conocer; **to set one's heart on** tener la esperanza puesta en; **to set store by** dar mucha importancia a; **to set up shop** poner tienda; **to set up the drinks** (coll) convidar a beber || *intr* ponerse (*el Sol, la Luna, etc.*); cuajarse (*un líquido*); endurecerse (*la cola*); fraguar (*el cemento, el yeso*); empollar (*una gallina*); caer, sentar (*una prenda de vestir*); **to set about** ponerse a; **to set out** ponerse en camino; emprender un negocio; **to set out to** ponerse a; **to set to work** poner manos a la obra; **to set upon** acometer, atacar
set'back' *s* revés *m,* contrariedad
set'screw' *s* tornillo de presión
settee [sɛ'ti] *s* sofá *m,* canapé *m*
setting ['sɛtɪŋ] *s* (*environment*) ambiente *m;* (*of a gem*) engaste *m,* montadura; (*of cement*) fraguado; (*e.g., of the sun*) puesta, ocaso; (theat) escena; (theat) puesta en escena, decoración
set'ting-up' exercises *spl* ejercicios sin aparatos, gimnasia sueca
settle ['sɛtəl] *tr* asentar, colocar; asegurar, fijar; componer, conciliar; calmar, moderar; matar (*el polvo*); casar; poblar, colonizar; ajustar, arreglar (*cuentas*) || *intr* asentarse (*un líquido, un edificio*); establecerse; componerse; calmarse, moderarse; solidificarse; **to settle down to work** ponerse seriamente a trabajar; **to settle on** escoger; fijar (*p.ej., una fecha*)
settlement ['sɛtəlmənt] *s* establecimiento; colonia, caserío; decisión; (*of accounts*) arreglo, ajuste *m;* traspaso; casa de beneficencia
settler ['sɛtlər] *s* fundador *m;* poblador *m;* colono; árbitro, conciliador *m*
set'up' *s* porte *m,* postura; (*e.g., of the parts of a machine*) disposición; (coll) organización; (slang) invitación a beber
seven ['sɛvən] *adj & pron* siete || *s* siete *m;* **seven o'clock** las siete
seven hundred *adj & pron* setecientos || *s* setecientos *m*
seventeen ['sɛvən'tin] *adj, pron & s* diecisiete *m,* diez y siete
seventeenth ['sɛvən'tinθ] *adj & s* (*in a series*) decimoséptimo; (*part*) diecisieteavo || *s* (*in dates*) diecisiete *m*
seventh ['sɛvənθ] *adj & s* séptimo || *s* (*in dates*) siete *m*
seventieth ['sɛvəntɪ·ɪθ] *adj & s* (*in a series*) septuagésimo; (*part*) setentavo
seven·ty ['sɛvənti] *adj & pron* setenta || *s* (*pl* **-ties**) setenta *m*
sever ['sɛvər] *tr* desunir, separar; romper (*relaciones*) || *intr* desunirse, separarse
several ['sɛvərəl] *adj* diversos, varios; distintos, respectivos || *spl* varios; algunos
severance pay ['sɛvərəns] *s* indemnización por despido
severe [sɪ'vɪr] *adj* severo; (*weather*) riguroso; recio, violento; (*look*) adusto; (*pain*) agudo; (*illness*) grave
sew [so] *v* (*pret* **sewed;** *pp* **sewed** o **sewn**) *tr & intr* coser
sewage ['su·ɪdʒ] o ['sju·ɪdʒ] *s* agua de albañal, aguas cloacales
sewer ['su·ər] o ['sju·ər] *s* albañal *m,* cloaca, alcantarilla || *tr* alcantarillar
sewerage ['su·ərɪdʒ] o ['sju·ərɪdʒ] *s* desagüe *m;* (*system*) alcantarillado; aguas de albañal
sewing basket ['so·ɪŋ] *s* cesta de costura
sewing machine *s* máquina de coser
sex [sɛks] *s* sexo; **the fair sex** el bello sexo; **the sterner sex** el sexo feo
sex appeal *s* atracción sexual; encanto femenino
sextant ['sɛkstənt] *s* sextante *m*
sextet [sɛks'tɛt] *s* sexteto
sexton ['sɛkstən] *s* sacristán *m*
sexual ['sɛkʃʊ·əl] *adj* sexual
sex·y ['sɛksi] *adj* (*comp* **-ier;** *super* **-iest**) (slang) sicalíptico, erótico
shab·by ['ʃæbi] *adj* (*comp* **-bier;** *super* **-biest**) gastado, raído, usado; andrajoso, desaseado; ruin, vil
shack [ʃæk] *s* casucha, choza
shackle ['ʃækəl] *s* grillete *m;* (*to tie an animal*) maniota; (fig) impedimento, traba; **shackles** cadenas, esposas, grillos || *tr* poner grilletes a, poner esposas a; encadenar; (fig) trabar
shad [ʃæd] *s* sábalo, alosa
shade [ʃed] *s* sombra; (*of a lamp*)

pantalla; (*of a window*) cortina, estor *m*, visillo, cortina de resorte; (*for the eyes*) visera; (*hue; slight difference*) matiz *m;* **the shades** las tinieblas; (*of the dead*) las sombras || *tr* sombrear; obscurecer; rebajar ligeramente (*el precio*)

shadow [ˈʃædo] *s* sombra || *tr* sombrear; simbolizar; acechar, espiar (*a una persona*); **to shadow forth** representar vagamente, representar de un modo profético

shadowy [ˈʃædo·i] *adj* sombroso; ligero, vago; imaginario; simbólico

shad•y [ˈʃedi] *adj* (*comp* **-ier;** *super* **-iest**) sombrío, umbroso; (coll) sospechoso; (coll) de mala fama; (*story*) (coll) verde; **to keep shady** (slang) no dejarse ver

shaft [ʃæft] o [ʃɑft] *s* dardo, flecha, saeta; (*of an arrow; of a feather*) astil *m;* (*of light*) rayo; (*of a wagon*) vara alcándara, limonera; (*of a mine; of an elevator*) pozo; (*of a column*) fuste *m*, caña; (*of a flag*) asta; (*of a motor*) árbol *m;* (*to make fun of someone*) dardo

shag•gy [ˈʃægi] *adj* (*comp* **-gier;** *super* **-giest**) hirsuto, peludo, veludo; lanudo; áspero

shake [ʃek] *s* sacudida; (coll) apretón *m* de manos; (slang) instante *m*, momento || *v* (*pret* **shook** [ʃʊk]; *pp* **shaken**) *tr* sacudir; agitar; apretar, estrechar (*la mano a uno*); inquietar, perturbar; (*to get rid of*) (slang) dar esquinazo a, zafarse de || *intr* sacudirse; agitarse; temblar; inquietarse, perturbarse; (*from cold*) tiritar; **shake!** (coll) ¡choque Vd. esos cinco!, ¡vengan esos cinco!

shake'down' *s* (slang) exacción, concusión

shake'-up' *s* profunda conmoción; cambio de personal, reorganización completa

shak•y [ˈʃeki] *adj* (*comp* **-ier;** *super* **-iest**) trémulo, vacilante, movedizo; indigno de confianza

shall [ʃæl] *v* (*cond* **should** [ʃʊd]) *v aux* empléase para formar (1) el fut de ind, p.ej., **I shall do it** lo haré; (2) el fut perf de ind, p.ej., **I shall have done it** lo habré hecho; (3) el modo potencial, p.ej., **what shall I do?** ¿qué he de hacer?, ¿qué debo hacer?

shallow [ˈʃælo] *adj* bajo, poco profundo; (fig) frívolo, superficial

sham [ʃæm] *adj* falso, fingido; postizo || *s* fingimiento, falsificación, engaño; (*person*) (coll) farsante *mf* || *v* (*pret & pp* **shammed;** *ger* **shamming**) *tr & intr* fingir

sham battle *s* simulacro de combate

shambles [ˈʃæmbəlz] *s* destrucción, ruina; (*confusion, mess*) lío, revoltijo

shame [ʃem] *s* vergüenza; deshonra; **shame on you!** ¡qué vergüenza!; **what a shame!** ¡qué lástima! || *tr* avergonzar; deshonrar

shameful [ˈʃemfəl] *adj* vergonzoso

shameless [ˈʃemlɪs] *adj* descarado, desvergonzado

shampoo [ʃæmˈpu] *s* champú *m* || *tr* lavar (*la cabeza*); lavar la cabeza a

shamrock [ˈʃæmrɑk] *s* trébol *m* irlandés

shanghai [ˈʃæŋhaɪ] o [ʃæŋˈhaɪ] *tr* embarcar emborrachando, embarcar narcotizando; llevarse con violencia, llevarse con engaño

shank [ʃæŋk] *s* (*of the leg*) caña, canilla; (*of an animal*) pierna; (*of a bird*) zanca; (*of an anchor*) caña; (*of the sole of a shoe*) enfranque *m;* astil *m*, caña, fuste *m;* extremidad, remate *m;* **to go** o **to ride on shank's mare** caminar en coche de San Francisco

shan•ty [ˈʃænti] *s* (*pl* **-ties**) chabola, choza

shape [ʃep] *s* forma; **in bad shape** (coll) arruinado; (coll) muy enfermo; **out of shape** deformado; descompuesto || *tr* formar, dar forma a; amoldar || *intr* formarse; **to shape up** tomar forma; desarrollarse bien

shapeless [ˈʃeplɪs] *adj* informe

shape•ly [ˈʃepli] *adj* (*comp* **-lier;** *super* **-liest**) bien formado, esbelto

share [ʃɛr] *s* parte *f*, porción; (*of stock in a company*) acción; **to go shares** ir a la parte || *tr* (*to enjoy jointly*) compartir; (*to apportion*) repartir || *intr* participar, tener parte

share'hold'er *s* accionista *mf*

shark [ʃɑrk] *s* tiburón *m;* (*swindler*) estafador *m;* (slang) experto, perito

sharp [ʃɑrp] *adj* afilado, agudo; anguloso; (*curve, slope, etc.*) fuerte, pronunciado; (*photograph*) nítido; (*hearing*) fino; (*step, gait*) rápido; atento, despierto; picante, mordaz; listo, vivo; (mus) sostenido; (slang) elegante; **sharp features** facciones bien marcadas || *adv* agudamente; en punto, p.ej., **at four o'clock sharp** a las cuatro en punto || *s* (mus) sostenido

sharpen [ˈʃɑrpən] *tr* aguzar; sacar punta a (*un lápiz*) || *intr* afilarse

sharper [ˈʃɑrpər] *s* fullero, jugador *m* de ventaja

sharp'shoot'er *s* tirador certero; (mil) tirador distinguido

shatter [ˈʃætər] *tr* hacer astillas, romper de un golpe; quebrantar (*la salud*); destruir, destrozar; agitar, perturbar || *intr* hacerse pedazos, romperse

shat'ter•proof' *adj* inastillable

shave [ʃev] *s* afeitado; rebanada delgada; **to have a close shave** (coll) escapar en una tabla || *tr* afeitar (*la cara*); raer, raspar; (*to graze; to cut close*) rozar; (*to slice thin*) rebanar; (carp) cepillar || *intr* afeitarse

shaving [ˈʃevɪŋ] *adj* de afeitar, para afeitar, p.ej., **shaving soap** jabón *m* de o para afeitar || *s* afeitado; **shavings** acepilladuras, virutas

shawl [ʃɔl] *s* chal *m*, mantón *m*

she [ʃi] *pron pers* (*pl* **they**) ella || *s* (*pl* **shes**) hembra

sheaf [ʃif] *s* (*pl* **sheaves** [ʃivz]) gavilla; (*of paper*) atado

shear [ʃɪr] *s* hoja de la tijera; **shears** tijeras grandes; (*to cut metal*) cizallas ‖ *v* (*pret* **sheared;** *pp* **sheared** o **shorn** [ʃorn]) *tr* esquilar, trasquilar (*las ovejas*); cizallar; quitar cortando; tundir (*paño*)

sheath [ʃiθ] *s* (**sheaths** [ʃiðz]) envoltura, estuche *m*, funda; (*for a sword*) funda, vaina

sheathe [ʃið] *tr* enfundar, envainar

shed [ʃɛd] *s* cobertizo; (*line from which water flows in two directions*) vertiente *m* & *f* ‖ *v* (*pret* & *pp* **shed;** *ger* **shedding**) *tr* derramar, verter (*p.ej., sangre*); dar, echar, esparcir (*luz*); mudar (*la pluma, el pellejo*)

sheen [ʃin] *s* brillo, lustre *m;* (*of pressed cloth*) prensado

sheep [ʃip] *s* (*pl* **sheep**) carnero; (*female*) oveja; tonto; **to make sheep's eyes (at)** mirar con ojos de carnero degollado

sheep dog *s* perro ovejero, perro de pastor

sheep'fold' *s* aprisco, redil *m*

sheepish ['ʃipɪʃ] *adj* avergonzado, corrido; tímido, tonto

sheep'skin' *s* (*undressed*) zalea; (*dressed*) badana; (coll) diploma *m*

sheer [ʃɪr] *adj* delgado, fino, ligero; casi transparente; escarpado; puro, sin mezcla; completo ‖ *intr* desviarse

sheet [ʃit] *s* (*e.g., for the bed*) sábana; (*of paper*) hoja; (*of metal*) hoja, lámina; (*of water*) extensión; hoja impresa; periódico; (naut) escota

sheet lightning *s* fucilazo

sheet metal *s* metal laminado

sheet music *s* música en hojas sueltas

sheik [ʃik] *s* jeque *m;* (*great lover*) (slang) sultán *m*

shelf [ʃɛlf] *s* (*pl* **shelves** [ʃɛlvz]) estante *m*, anaquel *m;* bajío, banco de arena; **on the shelf** arrinconado, desechado, olvidado

shell [ʃɛl] *s* (*of an egg, nut, etc.*) cáscara; (*of a crustacean*) caparazón *m*, concha; (*of a vegetable*) vaina; (*of a cartridge*) cápsula; (*of a boiler*) cuerpo; armazón *f*, esqueleto; bomba, proyectil *m;* (*long, narrow racing boat*) (sport) yola ‖ *tr* descascarar; desgranar, desvainar (*legumbres*); bombardear, cañonear; **to shell out** (coll) entregar (*dinero*)

shel·lac [ʃə'læk] *s* laca, goma laca ‖ *v* (*pret* & *pp* **-lacked;** *ger* **-lacking**) *tr* barnizar con goma laca; (slang) azotar, zurrar; (slang) derrotar

shell'fish' *s* marisco, mariscos

shell hole *s* (mil) embudo

shell shock *s* neurosis *f* de guerra

shelter ['ʃɛltər] *s* abrigo, asilo, amparo, refugio; **to take shelter** abrigarse, refugiarse ‖ *tr* abrigar, amparar, proteger

shelve [ʃɛlv] *tr* poner sobre un estante; proveer de estantes; arrinconar, dejar a un lado; diferir indefinidamente

shepherd ['ʃɛpərd] *s* pastor *m* ‖ *tr* pastorear (*a las ovejas o los fieles*)

shepherd dog *s* perro ovejero, perro de pastor

shepherdess ['ʃɛpərdɪs] *s* pastora

sherbet ['ʃʌrbət] *s* sorbete *m*

shereef [ʃɛ'rif] *s* jerife *m*

sheriff ['ʃɛrɪf] *s* alguacil *m* mayor

sher·ry ['ʃɛri] *s* (*pl* **-ries**) jerez *m*, vino de Jerez

shield [ʃild] *s* escudo; (*for armpit*) sobaquera; (elec) blindaje *m* ‖ *tr* amparar, defender, escudar; (elec) blindar

shift [ʃɪft] *s* cambio; (*order of work or other activity*) turno; (*group of workmen*) tanda; maña, subterfugio ‖ *tr* cambiar; deshacerse de; echar (*la culpa*); (aut) cambiar de (*marcha*) ‖ *intr* cambiar, cambiar de puesto; mañear; (naut) correrse (*el lastre*); (rr) maniobrar; **to shift for oneself** ayudarse, ingeniarse

shift key *s* tecla de cambio, palanca de mayúsculas

shiftless ['ʃɪftlɪs] *adj* desidioso, perezoso

shift·y ['ʃɪfti] *adj* (*comp* **-ier;** *super* **-iest**) ingenioso, mañoso; evasivo, tramoyista; (*glance*) huyente

shilling ['ʃɪlɪŋ] *s* chelín *m*

shimmer ['ʃɪmər] *s* lúz trémula ‖ *intr* rielar

shin [ʃɪn] *s* espinilla ‖ *v* (*pret* & *pp* **shinned;** *ger* **shinning**) *tr* & *intr* trepar

shin'bone' *s* espinilla

shine [ʃaɪn] *s* brillo, luz *f;* bruñido, lustre *m;* buen tiempo; (*on shoes*) (coll) lustre *m;* **to take a shine to** (slang) tomar simpatía a ‖ *v* (*pret* & *pp* **shined**) *tr* pulir, lustrar; (coll) embolar, limpiar (*el calzado*) ‖ *v* (*pret* & *pp* **shone** [ʃon]) *intr* brillar, lucir, resplandecer; hacer sol, hacer buen tiempo; (*to be distinguished, to stand out*) (fig) brillar, lucir

shingle ['ʃɪŋgəl] *s* ripia, teja de madera; tejamaní *m* (Am); pelo a la garçonne; (coll) letrero de oficina; **shingles** (pathol) zona; **to hang out one's shingle** (coll) abrir una oficina; (coll) abrir un consultorio médico ‖ *tr* cubrir con ripias; cortar (*el pelo*) a la garçonne

shining ['ʃaɪnɪŋ] *adj* brillante, luciente

shin·y ['ʃaɪni] *adj* (*comp* **-ier;** *super* **-iest**) brillante, lustroso; (*paper*) glaseado; (*from much wear*) brilloso

ship [ʃɪp] *s* nave *f*, buque *m*, barco, navío; (*steamer*) vapor *m;* aeronave *f* ‖ *v* (*pret* & *pp* **shipped;** *ger* **shipping**) *tr* embarcar; enviar, remitir, remesar; armar (*los remos*); embarcar (*agua*) ‖ *intr* embarcarse

ship'board' *s* bordo; **on shipboard** a bordo

ship'build'er *s* arquitecto naval, constructor *m* de buques

ship'build'ing *s* arquitectura naval, construcción de buques

ship'mate' *s* camarada *m* de a bordo

shipment ['ʃɪpmənt] *s* embarque *m* (*por agua*); envío, expedición, remesa

shipper ['ʃɪpər] *s* embarcador *m;* expedidor *m,* remitente *mf*
shipping memo ['ʃɪpɪŋ] *s* nota de remisión
ship'shape' *adj & adv* en buen orden
ship'side' *adj & adv* al costado del buque || *s* zona de embarque y desembarque; muelle *m*
ship's papers *spl* documentación del buque
ship's time *s* hora local del buque
ship'wreck' *s* naufragio; barco náufrago || *tr* hacer naufragar || *intr* naufragar
ship'yard' *s* astillero, varadero
shirk [ʃʌrk] *tr* evitar (*el trabajo*)*;* faltar a (*un deber*) || *intr* escurrir el hombro
shirred eggs [ʃʌrd] *spl* huevos al plato
shirt [ʃʌrt] *s* camisa; **to keep one's shirt on** (slang) quedarse sereno; **to lose one's shirt** (slang) perder hasta la camisa
shirt'band' *s* cuello de camisa
shirt front *s* pechera de camisa, camisolín *m*
shirt sleeve *s* manga de camisa; **in shirt sleeves** en mangas de camisa
shirt'tail' *s* faldón *m,* pañal *m*
shirt'waist' *s* blusa (*de mujer*)
shiver ['ʃɪvər] *s* estremecimiento, tiritón *m* || *intr* estremecerse, tiritar
shoal [ʃol] *s* bajío, banco de arena
shock [ʃɑk] *s* (*sudden and violent blow or encounter*) choque *m;* (*sudden agitation of mind or emotions*) sobresalto; temblor *m* de tierra; (*of hair*) greña; (agr) tresnal *m;* (elec) sacudida; (med) choque *m;* (*profound depression*) (pathol) choque *m;* (coll) parálisis *f* || *tr* chocar; sobresaltar; dar una sacudida eléctrica a; chocar, escandalizar
shock absorber [æb'sɔrbər] *s* amortiguador *m*
shocking ['ʃɑkɪŋ] *adj* chocante, escandalizador
shock troops *spl* tropas de asalto
shod·dy ['ʃɑdi] *adj* (*comp* **-dier;** *super* **-diest**) falso, de imitación
shoe [ʃu] *s* (*which goes above the ankle*) bota, botina; (*which does not go above the ankle*) zapato; (*of a tire*) cubierta; **to put on one's shoes** calzarse || *v* (*pret & pp* **shod** [ʃɑd]) *tr* calzar; herrar (*un caballo*)
shoe'black' *s* limpiabotas *m*
shoe'horn' *s* calzador *m*
shoe'lace' *s* cordón *m* de zapato, lazo de zapato
shoe'mak'er *s* zapatero; zapatero remendón
shoe mender ['mendər] *s* zapatero remendón
shoe polish *s* betún *m,* bola
shoe'shine' *s* brillo, lustre *m;* limpiabotas *m*
shoe store *s* zapatería
shoe'string' *s* cordón *m* de zapato, lazo de zapato; **on a shoestring** con muy poco dinero
shoe tree *s* horma
shoo [ʃu] *tr & intr* oxear
shoot [ʃut] *s* (*sprout, twig*) renuevo, vástago; conducto inclinado; (*for grain, sand, etc.*) tolva; tiro al blanco, certamen *m* de tiradores; (*hunting party*) partida de caza || *v* (*pret & pp* **shot** [ʃɑt]) *tr* tirar, disparar (*un arma*); herir o matar con arma; (*to execute with a discharge of rifles*) fusilar; fotografiar; (*to take a moving picture of*) rodar; echar (*los dados*); medir la altura de (*p.ej., el Sol*); **to shoot down** derribar (*un avión*); **to shoot up** (slang) destrozar echando balas a diestra y siniestra || *intr* tirar; nacer, brotar; lanzarse, precipitarse, moverse rápidamente; punzar (*un dolor, una llaga*)*;* **to shoot at** tirar a; (*to strive for*) (coll) poner el tiro en
shooting gallery *s* galería de tiro al blanco
shooting match *s* certamen *m* de tiro al blanco; (slang) conjunto, totalidad
shooting star *s* estrella fugaz, estrella filante
shop [ʃɑp] *s* (*store*) tienda; (*workshop*) taller *m;* **to talk shop** hablar de su oficio, hablar del propio trabajo (*fuera de tiempo*) || *v* (*pret & pp* **shopped;** *ger* **shopping**) *intr* ir de compras, ir de tiendas; **to go shopping** ir de compras, ir de tiendas; **to send shopping** mandar a la compra; **to shop around** ir de tienda en tienda buscando gangas
shop'girl' *s* muchacha de tienda
shop'keep'er *s* tendero
shoplifter ['ʃɑp ˌlɪftər] *s* mechera, ratero de tiendas
shopper ['ʃɑpər] *s* comprador *m*
shopping center *s* centro comercial (*grupo de establecimientos minoristas, con aparcamiento*)
shopping district *s* barrio comercial
shop'win'dow *s* escaparate *m*
shop'work' *s* trabajo de taller
shop'worn' *adj* desgastado con el trajín de la tienda
shore [ʃor] *s* orilla, ribera; costa, playa; **shores** (poet) clima *m,* región || *tr* acodalar, apuntalar
shore dinner *s* comida de pescado y mariscos
shore leave *s* (nav) permiso para ir a tierra
shore line *s* línea de la playa; línea de buques costeros
shore patrol *s* (nav) patrulla en tierra
short [ʃɔrt] *adj* (*in space, time, and quantity*) corto; (*in time*) breve; (*in stature*) bajo; (fig) corto, sucinto; (fig) brusco, seco; **in a short time** dentro de poco; **in short** en fin; **on short notice** con poco tiempo de aviso; **to be short of** estar escaso de; **short of breath** corto de resuello || *adv* brevemente; bruscamente; (*without possessing the stock sold*) al descubierto, p.ej., **to sell short** vender al descubierto; **to run short of** acabársele a uno, p.ej., **I am running short of gasoline** se me acaba la

gasolina; **to stop short** parar de repente || *s* (elec) cortocircuito; (mov) cortometraje *m;* **shorts** calzones cortos, calzoncillos || *tr* (elec) poner en cortocircuito || *intr* (elec) ponerse en cortocircuito

shortage ['ʃɔrtɪdʒ] *s* carestía, escasez *f,* falta; déficit *m;* (*from pilfering*) substracción

short'cake' *s* torta de frutas; torta quebradiza

short'change' *tr* (coll) no devolver la vuelta debida a

short circuit *s* (elec) cortocircuito

short'cir'cuit *tr* (elec) cortocircuitar || *intr* (elec) cortocircuitarse

short'com'ing *s* falta, defecto, desperfecto

short cut *s* atajo; (*method*) remediavagos *m*

shorten ['ʃɔrtən] *tr* acortar, abreviar || *intr* acortarse, abreviarse

short'hand' *adj* taquigráfico || *s* taquigrafía; **to take shorthand** taquigrafiar

short-lived ['ʃɔrt'laɪvd] o ['ʃɔrt'lɪvd] *adj* de breve vida, de breve duración

shortly ['ʃɔrtli] *adv* en breve, luego; descortésmente; **shortly after** poco tiempo después (de)

short'-range' *adj* de poco alcance

short sale *s* (coll) venta al descubierto

short-sighted ['ʃɔrt'saɪtɪd] *adj* miope; (fig) falto de perspicacia

short'stop' *s* (baseball) medio; guardabosque *m,* torpedero (Am)

short story *s* cuento

short-tempered ['ʃɔrt'tɛmpərd] *adj* de mal genio

short'-term' *adj* a corto plazo

shot [ʃɑt] *s* tiro, disparo; (*hit or wound made with a bullet*) balazo; (*distance*) alcance *m;* (*in certain games*) jugada, tirada, golpe *m;* (*of a rocket into space*) lanzamiento; conjetura, tentativa; fotografía, instantánea; (*small pellets of lead*) perdigones *mpl;* munición; (*marksman*) tiro; (*heavy metal ball*) (sport) pesa; (*hypodermic injection*) (slang) jeringazo; (*drink of liquor*) (slang) trago; **not by a long shot** ni con mucho, ni por pienso; **to start like a shot** salir disparado

shot'gun' *s* escopeta

shot'-put' *s* (sport) tiro de la pesa

should [ʃʊd] *v aux* empléase para formar (1) el pres de cond, p.ej., **if I should wait for him, I should miss the train** si yo le esperase, perdería el tren; (2) el perf de cond, p.ej., **if I had waited for him, I should have missed the train** si yo le hubiese esperado, habría perdido el tren; y (3) el modo potencial, p.ej., **he should go at once** debiera salir en seguida; **he should have gone at once** debiera haber salido en seguida

shoulder ['ʃoldər] *s* hombro; (*of slaughtered animal*) brazuelo; (*of a garment*) hombrera; **across the shoulder** en bandolera; **to put one's shoulders to the wheel** arrimar el hombro, echar el pecho al agua; **to turn a cold shoulder to** volver las espaldas a || *tr* cargar sobre las espaldas; tomar sobre sí, hacerse responsable de; empujar con el hombro para abrirse paso

shoulder blade *s* escápula, omóplato

shoulder strap *s* (*of underwear*) presilla; (mil) charretera

shout [ʃaʊt] *s* grito, voz *f* || *tr* gritar, vocear; **to shout down** hacer callar a gritos || *intr* gritar, dar voces

shove [ʃʌv] *s* empujón *m* || *tr* empujar || *intr* dar empujones, avanzar a empujones; **to shove off** alejarse de la costa; (slang) ponerse en marcha, salir

shov·el ['ʃʌvəl] *s* pala || *v* (*pret & pp* **-eled** o **-elled;** *ger* **-eling** o **-elling**) *tr* traspalar; espalar (*p.ej., la nieve*) || *intr* trabajar con pala

show [ʃo] *s* exhibición, exposición, muestra; espectáculo; (*in the theater*) función; (*each performance of a play or movie*) sesión; demostración, prueba; indicación, señal *f,* signo; apariencia; (*e.g., of confidence*) alarde *m;* (coll) ocasión, oportunidad; ostentación; espectáculo ridículo, hazmerreír *m;* **to make a show of** hacer gala de; **to steal the show from** robar la obra a (*otro actor*) || *tr* mostrar, enseñar; demostrar, probar; poner, proyectar (*un film*); (*e.g., to the door*) acompañar; **to show up** (coll) desenmascarar || *intr* mostrarse, aparecer, asomar; salir (*p.ej., las enaguas*); **to show off** fachendear; **to show through** clarearse, transparentarse; **to show up** (coll) presentarse, dejarse ver

show bill *s* cartel *m*

show business *s* comercio de los espectáculos

show'case' *s* vitrina (de exposición)

show'down' *s* cartas boca arriba; (coll) revelación forzosa, arreglo terminante

shower ['ʃaʊ·ər] *s* (*sudden fall of rain*) aguacero, chaparrón *m;* (*shower bath*) ducha; (*e.g., of bullets*) rociada; despedida de soltera || *tr* regar; **to shower with** colmar de || *intr* llover

shower bath *s* ducha, baño de ducha

show girl *s* (theat) corista *f,* conjuntista *f*

show·man ['ʃomən] *s* (*pl* **-men** [mən]) empresario de teatro, empresario de circo

show'-off' *s* (coll) pinturero

show'piece' *s* objeto de arte sobresaliente

show'place' *s* sitio o edificio que se exhibe por su belleza o lujo

show'room' *s* sala de muestras, sala de exhibición

show window *s* escaparate *m* de tienda

show·y ['ʃo·i] *adj* (*comp* **-ier;** *super* **-iest**) aparatoso, cursi, ostentoso

shrapnel ['ʃræpnəl] *s* granada de metralla

shred [ʃrɛd] *s* jirón *m,* tira, triza; frag-

mento, pizca; **to tear to shreds** hacer trizas || *v* (*pret & pp* **shredded** o **shred;** *ger* **shredding**) *tr* desmenuzar, hacer trizas; deshilar (*carne*)
shrew [ʃru] *s* (*nagging woman*) arpía, fierecilla; (*animal*) musaraña
shrewd [ʃrud] *adj* astuto; despierto; listo
shriek [ʃrik] *s* chillido, grito agudo; risotada chillona || *intr* chillar
shrill [ʃrɪl] *adj* agudo, chillón
shrimp [ʃrɪmp] *s* camarón *m;* (*little insignificant person*) renacuajo
shrine [ʃraɪn] *s* relicario; sepulcro de santo; lugar sagrado
shrink [ʃrɪŋk] *v* (*pret* **shrank** [ʃræŋk] o **shrunk** [ʃrʌŋk]; *pp* **shrunk** o **shrunken**) *tr* contraer, encoger || *intr* contraerse, encogerse; moverse hacia atrás; rehuirse, retirarse
shrinkage [ˈʃrɪŋkɪdʒ] *s* contracción, encogimiento; disminución, reducción; merma, pérdida
shriv•el [ˈʃrɪvəl] *v* (*pret & pp* **-eled** o **-elled;** *ger* **-eling** o **-elling**) *tr* arrugar, marchitar, fruncir || *intr* arrugarse, marchitarse, fruncirse; **to shrivel up** avellanarse
shroud [ʃraʊd] *s* mortaja, sudario; cubierta, velo || *tr* amortajar; cubrir, velar
Shrove Tuesday [ʃrov] *s* martes *m* de carnaval
shrub [ʃrʌb] *s* arbusto
shrubber•y [ˈʃrʌbəri] *s* (*pl* **-ies**) arbustos; plantío de arbustos
shrug [ʃrʌg] *s* encogimiento de hombros || *v* (*pret & pp* **shrugged;** *ger* **shrugging**) *tr* contraer; **to shrug one's shoulders** encogerse de hombros || *intr* encogerse de hombros
shudder [ˈʃʌdər] *s* estremecimiento || *intr* estremecerse
shuffle [ˈʃʌfəl] *s* (*of cards*) barajadura; turno de barajar; (*of feet*) arrastramiento; evasiva; recomposición || *tr* barajar (*naipes*); arrastrar (*los pies*); mezclar, revolver || *intr* barajar; caminar arrastrando los pies; bailar arrastrando los pies; moverse rápidamente de un lado a otro; **to shuffle along** ir arrastrando los pies; ir tirando; **to shuffle off** irse arrastrando los pies
shuf′fle•board′ *s* juego de tejo
shun [ʃʌn] *v* (*pret & pp* **shunned;** *ger* **shunning**) *tr* esquivar, evitar, rehuir
shunt [ʃʌnt] *tr* apartar, desviar; (elec) poner en derivación; (rr) desviar
shut [ʃʌt] *adj* cerrado || *v* (*pret & pp* **shut;** *ger* **shutting**) *tr* cerrar; **to shut in** encerrar; **to shut off** cortar (*electricidad, gas, etc.*); **to shut up** cerrar bien; aprisionar; (coll) hacer callar || *intr* cerrarse; **to shut up** (coll) callarse la boca
shut′down′ *s* cierre *m,* paro
shutter [ˈʃʌtər] *s* celosía, persiana; (*outside a window*) contraventana; (*outside a show window*) cierre metálico; (phot) obturador *m*
shuttle [ˈʃʌtəl] *s* (*used in sewing*) lanzadera || *intr* hacer viajes cortos de ida y vuelta
shuttle train *s* tren *m* lanzadera
shy [ʃaɪ] *adj* (*comp* **shyer** o **shier;** *super* **shyest** o **shiest**) arisco, recatado, tímido; (*fearful*) asustadizo; escaso, pobre; **I am shy a dollar** me falta un dólar || *v* (*pret & pp* **shied**) *intr* esquivarse, hacerse a un lado; espantarse, respingar; **to shy away** alejarse asustado
shyster [ˈʃaɪstər] *s* (coll) abogado trampista
Sia•mese [ˌsaɪ·əˈmiz] *adj* siamés || *s* (*pl* **-mese**) siamés *m*
Siamese twins *spl* hermanos siameses
Siberian [saɪˈbɪrɪ·ən] *adj & s* siberiano
sibilant [ˈsɪbɪlənt] *adj & s* sibilante *f*
sibyl [ˈsɪbɪl] *s* sibila
Sicilian [sɪˈsɪljən] *adj & s* siciliano
Sicily [ˈsɪsɪli] *s* Sicilia
sick [sɪk] *adj* enfermo, malo; nauseado; **sick and tired of** (coll) harto y cansado de; **sick at heart** afligido de corazón; **to be sick at one's stomach** tener náuseas; **to take sick** caer enfermo || *tr* azuzar (*a un perro*)
sick′bed′ *s* lecho de enfermo
sicken [ˈsɪkən] *tr & intr* enfermar
sickening [ˈsɪkənɪŋ] *adj* repelente, repugnante, nauseabundo
sick headache *s* jaqueca con náuseas
sickle [ˈsɪkəl] *s* hoz *f*
sick leave *s* licencia por enfermedad
sick•ly [ˈsɪkli] *adj* (*comp* **-lier;** *super* **-liest**) enfermizo
sickness [ˈsɪknɪs] *s* enfermedad; náusea
side [saɪd] *adj* lateral || *s* lado; (*of a solid; of a phonograph record*) cara; (*of a hill*) falda; (*of human body, of a ship*) costado; facción, partido || *intr* tomar partido; **to side with** tomar el partido de
side arms *spl* armas de cinto
side′board′ *s* aparador *m*
side′burns′ *spl* patillas
side dish *s* plato de entrada
side door *s* puerta lateral; puerta excusada
side effect *s* efecto secundario perjudicial (*de ciertos medicamentos*)
side glance *s* mirada de soslayo
side issue *s* cuestión secundaria
side line *s* negocio accesorio; **on the side lines** sin tomar parte
sidereal [saɪˈdɪrɪ·əl] *adj* sidéreo
side′sad′dle *adv* a asentadillas, a mujeriegas
side show *s* función secundaria, espectáculo de atracciones
side′split′ting *adj* desternillante
side′track′ *s* apartadero, desviadero, vía muerta || *tr* desviar (*un tren*); echar a un lado
side view *s* perfil *m,* vista de lado
side′walk′ *s* acera; banqueta (Guat, Mex); vereda (Arg, Cuba, Peru)
sidewalk café *s* terraza, café *m* en la acera
sideward [ˈsaɪdwərd] *adj* oblicuo, sesgado || *adv* de lado, hacia un lado

side′ways′ *adj* oblicuo, sesgado || *adv* de lado, hacia un lado; al través
side whiskers *spl* patillas
side′wise′ *adj* oblicuo, sesgado || *adv* de lado, hacia un lado; al través
siding [ˈsaɪdɪŋ] *s* (rr) apartadero, desviadero, vía muerta
sidle [ˈsaɪdəl] *intr* ir de lado; **to sidle up to** acercarse de lado a (*una persona*) para no ser visto
siege [sidʒ] *s* sitio, cerco; **to lay siege to** poner sitio o cerco a; (fig) asediar (*p.ej., el corazón de una mujer*)
sieve [sɪv] *s* cedazo, tamiz *m* || *tr* cerner, tamizar
sift [sɪft] *tr* cerner, cribar; escudriñar, examinar; (*to screen, separate*) entresacar; (*to scatter with or as with a sieve*) empolvar
sigh [saɪ] *s* suspiro; **to breathe a sigh of relief** respirar || *tr* decir con suspiros || *intr* suspirar; **to sigh for** suspirar por
sight [saɪt] *s* vista; cosa digna de verse; (*of a firearm, telescope, etc.*) mira; (coll) gran cantidad, montón *m;* (coll) horror *m,* atrocidad; **at first sight** a primera vista; **at sight** a primera vista; (*translation*) a libro abierto; (com) a la vista; **out of sight** fuera del alcance de la vista; (*prices*) por las nubes; **to catch sight of** alcanzar a ver; **to know by sight** conocer de vista; **to not be able to stand the sight of** no poder ver ni en pintura; **to see the sights** visitar los puntos de interés || *tr* avistar, alcanzar con la vista || *intr* apuntar con una mira; (arti & surv) visar
sight draft *s* (com) giro a la vista, letra a la vista
sight′-read′ *v* (*pret & pp* **-read** [ˌrɛd]) *tr* leer a libro abierto; (mus) ejecutar a la primera lectura || *intr* leer a libro abierto; (mus) repentizar
sight reader *s* lector *m* a libro abierto; (mus) repentista *mf*
sight′see′ing *s* turismo, visita de puntos de interés; **to go sightseeing** ir a ver los puntos de interés
sightseer [ˈsaɪtˌsi·ər] *s* turista *mf,* excursionista *mf*
sign [saɪn] *s* signo; señal *f,* marca; huella, vestigio; letrero, muestra; **to show signs of** dar muestras de, tener trazas de; **to make the sign of the cross** hacerse la señal de la cruz || *tr* firmar; contratar; ceder, traspasar || *intr* firmar; **to sign off** (rad) terminar la transmisión; **to sign up** (coll) firmar el contrato
sig•nal [ˈsɪgnəl] *adj* señalado, notable || *s* señal *f* || *v* (*pret & pp* **-naled** o **-nalled;** *ger* **-naling** o **-nalling**) *tr* señalar || *intr* hacer señales
signal tower *s* (rr) garita de señales
signato•ry [ˈsɪgnɪˌtori] *s* (*pl* **-ries**) firmante *mf*
signature [ˈsɪgnətʃər] *s* firma; (mus & typ) signatura
sign′board′ *s* cartelón *m,* letrero
signer [ˈsaɪnər] *s* firmante *mf*
signet ring [ˈsɪgnɪt] *s* anillo sigilar, sortija de sello
signi•fy [ˈsɪgnɪˌfaɪ] *v* (*pret & pp* **-fied**) *tr* significar
sign′post′ *s* hito, poste *m* de guía
silence [ˈsaɪləns] *s* silencio || *tr* acallar; (mil) apagar el fuego de; (mil) apagar (*el fuego del enemigo*)
silent [ˈsaɪlənt] *adj* silencioso
silent movie *s* cine mudo
silhouette [ˌsɪluˈɛt] *s* silueta || *tr* siluetear
silk [sɪlk] *adj* sedeño || *s* seda; **to hit the silk** (slang) lanzarse en paracaídas
silken [ˈsɪlkən] *adj* sedeño
silk hat *s* sombrero de copa
silk′-stock′ing *adj* aristocrático || *s* aristócrata *mf*
silk′worm′ *s* gusano de seda
silk•y [ˈsɪlki] *adj* (*comp* **-ier;** *super* **-iest**) sedoso, asedado
sill [sɪl] *s* travesaño; (*of a door*) umbral *m;* (*of a window*) antepecho
sil•ly [ˈsɪli] *adj* (*comp* **-lier;** *super* **-liest**) necio, tonto
si•lo [ˈsaɪlo] *s* (*pl* **-los**) silo || *tr* asilar
silt [sɪlt] *s* cieno, sedimento
silver [ˈsɪlvər] *adj* de plata; (*voice*) argentino; elocuente || *s* plata || *tr* platear; azogar (*un espejo*)
sil′ver•fish′ *s* (ent) pez *m* de plata
silver foil *s* hoja de plata
silver lining *s* aspecto agradable de una condición desgraciada o triste
silver plate *s* vajilla de plata
silver screen *s* pantalla de plata
sil′ver•smith′ *s* platero, orfebre *m*
silver spoon *s* riqueza heredada; **to be born with a silver spoon in one's mouth** nacer de pie
sil′ver-tongue′ *s* (coll) pico de oro
sil′ver•ware′ *s* plata, vajilla de plata
similar [ˈsɪmɪlər] *adj* similar, semejante, análogo
simile [ˈsɪmɪli] *s* (rhet) símil *m*
simmer [ˈsɪmər] *tr* cocer a fuego lento || *intr* cocer a fuego lento; (coll) estar a punto de estallar; **to simmer down** (coll) tranquilizarse lentamente
simoon [sɪˈmun] *s* simún *m*
simper [ˈsɪmpər] *s* sonrisa boba || *intr* sonreír bobamente
simple [ˈsɪmpəl] *adj* simple, sencillo || *s* (*medicinal plant*) simple *m*
simple-minded [ˈsɪmpəlˈmaɪndɪd] *adj* candoroso, ingenuo; idiota, mentecato; estúpido, ignorante
simple substance *s* (chem) cuerpo simple
simpleton [ˈsɪmpəltən] *s* simple *mf,* bobo, mentecato
simulate [ˈsɪmjəˌlet] *tr* simular
simultaneous [ˌsaɪməlˈtenɪ·əs] o [ˌsɪməlˈtenɪ·əs] *adj* simultáneo
sin [sɪn] *s* pecado || *v* (*pret & pp* **sinned;** *ger* **sinning**) *intr* pecar
since [sɪns] *adv* desde entonces, después || *prep* desde; después de || *conj* desde que; después (de) que; ya que, puesto que
sincere [sɪnˈsɪr] *adj* sincero
sincerity [sɪnˈsɛrɪti] *s* sinceridad

sinecure ['saɪnɪ,kjʊr] o ['sɪnɪ,kjʊr] *s* sinecura
sinew ['sɪnju] *s* tendón *m;* (fig) fibra, nervio, vigor *m*
sinful ['sɪnfəl] *adj* (*person*) pecador; (*act, intention, etc.*) pecaminoso
sing [sɪŋ] *v* (*pret* **sang** [sæŋ] o **sung** [sʌŋ]; *pp* **sung**) *tr* cantar; **to sing to sleep** arrullar ‖ *intr* cantar
singe [sɪndʒ] *v* (*ger* **singeing**) *tr* chamuscar, socarrar
singer ['sɪŋər] *s* cantante *mf;* (*in a night club*) vocalista *mf*
single ['sɪŋgəl] *adj* solo, único; simple, sencillo; particular; (*e.g., room in a hotel*) individual; (*copy*) suelto; (*unmarried*) soltero; solteril, de soltero ‖ *tr* escoger, elegir; **to single out** singularizar
single blessedness *s* el bendito celibato
single-breasted ['sɪŋgəl'brɛstɪd] *adj* sin cruzar, de un solo pecho
single entry *s* (com) partida simple
single file *s* fila india; **in single file** de reata
single-handed ['sɪŋgəl'hændɪd] *adj* solo, sin ayuda
single life *s* vida de soltero
sin'gle-track' *adj* de vía única; (coll) de cortos alcances
sing'song' *adj* monótono ‖ *s* sonsonete *m*
singular ['sɪŋgjələr] *adj* & *s* singular *m*
sinister ['sɪnɪstər] *adj* amenazante, ominoso, funesto
sink [sɪŋk] *s* fregadero, pila ‖ *v* (*pret* **sank** [sæŋk] o **sunk** [sʌŋk]; *pp* **sunk**) *tr* hundir, sumergir; echar a pique; abrir, cavar (*un pozo*); hincar (*los dientes*); invertir (*mucho dinero*) perdiéndolo todo ‖ *intr* hundirse; irse a pique; hundirse (*p.ej., el Sol en el horizonte*); descender, desaparecer; decaer (*un enfermo; una llama*); (*e.g., in a chair*) dejarse caer
sinking fund *s* fondo de amortización
sinless ['sɪnlɪs] *adj* impecable
sinner ['sɪnər] *s* pecador *m*
sinuous ['sɪnjʊ·əs] *adj* sinuoso
sinus ['saɪnəs] *s* seno
sip [sɪp] *s* sorbo, trago ‖ *v* (*pret* & *pp* **sipped;** *ger* **sipping**) *tr* sorber, beber a tragos
siphon ['saɪfən] *s* sifón *m* ‖ *tr* sacar con sifón, trasegar con sifón
siphon bottle *s* sifón *m*
sir [sʌr] *s* señor *m;* (*British title*) sir *m;* **Dear Sir** Muy señor mío, Estimado señor
sire [saɪr] *s* padre *m,* semental *m;* caballo padre ‖ *tr* engendrar
siren ['saɪrən] *s* sirena
Sirius ['sɪrɪ·əs] *s* (astr) Sirio
sirloin ['sʌrlɔɪn] *s* solomillo
sirup ['sɪrəp] o ['sʌrəp] *s* var de **syrup**
sissi·fy ['sɪsɪ,faɪ] *v* (*pret* & *pp* **-fied**) *tr* (coll) afeminar
sis·sy ['sɪsi] *s* (*pl* **-sies**) (coll) hermanita; (coll) maricón *m,* santito
sister ['sɪstər] *adj* (*ship*) gemelo; (*language*) hermano ‖ *s* hermana
sis'ter-in-law' *s* (*pl* **sisters-in-law**) cuñada, hermana política; (*wife of one's husband's or wife's brother*) concuñada
Sisyphus ['sɪsɪfəs] *s* Sísifo
sit [sɪt] *v* (*pret* & *pp* **sat** [sæt]; *ger* **sitting**) *intr* estar sentado; sentarse; echarse (*un ave sobre los huevos*); reunirse, celebrar junta; descansar; **to sit down** sentarse; **to sit still** estarse quieto; **to sit up** incorporarse (*el que estaba echado*)
sit'-down' strike *s* huelga de sentados, huelga de brazos caídos
site [saɪt] *s* sitio, paraje *m*
sitting ['sɪtɪŋ] *s* (*period one remains seated*) sentada; (*before a painter*) estadía; (*of a court or legislature*) sesión; **at one sitting** de una sentada
sitting duck *s* pato sentado en el agua (*fácil de matar a tiro de escopeta*); (coll) blanco de fácil alcance
sitting room *s* sala de estar
situate ['sɪtʃʊ,et] *tr* situar
situation [,sɪtʃʊ'eʃən] *s* situación; colocación, puesto
sitz bath [sɪts] *s* baño de asiento
six [sɪks] *adj* & *pron* seis ‖ *s* seis *m;* **at sixes and sevens** en confusión, en desacuerdo; **six o'clock** las seis
six hundred *adj* & *pron* seiscientos ‖ *s* seiscientos *m*
sixteen ['sɪks'tin] *adj, pron* & *s* dieciséis *m,* diez y seis
sixteenth ['sɪks'tinθ] *adj* & *s* (*in a series*) decimosexto; (*part*) dieciseisavo ‖ *s* (*in dates*) dieciséis *m*
sixth [sɪksθ] *adj* & *s* sexto ‖ *s* (*in dates*) seis *m*
sixtieth ['sɪkstɪ·ɪθ] *adj* & *s* (*in a series*) sexagésimo; (*part*) sesentavo
six·ty ['sɪksti] *adj* & *pron* sesenta ‖ *s* (*pl* **-ties**) sesenta *m*
sizable ['saɪzəbəl] *adj* considerable, bastante grande
size [saɪz] *s* tamaño; (*of a person or garment*) talla; (*of a pipe, a wire*) diámetro; (*for gilding*) sisa, cola de retazo; (coll) verdadera situación ‖ *tr* clasificar según tamaño; sisar, encolar; **to size up** enfocar (*un problema*); medir con la vista
sizzle ['sɪzəl] *s* siseo ‖ *intr* sisear
S.J. *abbr* **Society of Jesus**
skate [sket] *s* patín *m;* (slang) adefesio, tipo ‖ *intr* patinar; **to skate on thin ice** buscar el peligro
skating rink *s* patinadero, pista de patinar
skein [sken] *s* madeja; enredo, maraña
skeleton ['skɛlɪtən] *adj* esquelético ‖ *s* esqueleto
skeleton key *s* llave maestra
skeptic ['skɛptɪk] *adj* & *s* escéptico
skeptical ['skɛptɪkəl] *adj* escéptico
sketch [skɛtʃ] *s* boceto, dibujo; bosquejo, esbozo; drama corto, pieza corta ‖ *tr* dibujar; bosquejar, esbozar
sketch'book' *s* libro de bocetos; libro de esbozos literarios
skewer ['skju·ər] *s* broqueta ‖ *tr* espetar; traspasar con aguja

ski [ski] *s* (*pl* **skis** o **ski**) esquí *m* || *intr* esquiar
skid [skɪd] *s* (*of an auto*) resbalón *m;* (*of a wheel*) patinaje *m,* patinazo; calzo || *v* (*pret & pp* **skidded;** *ger* **skidding**) *tr* calzar || *intr* resbalar (*un coche*); patinar (*una rueda*)
skier ['ski·ər] *s* esquiador *m*
skiff [skɪf] *s* esquife *m*
skiing ['ski·ɪŋ] *s* esquiismo
ski jacket *s* plumífero
skijoring [ski'dʒorɪŋ] *s* esquí remolcado
ski jump *s* salto de esquí; cancha de esquiar; trampolín *m*
ski lift *s* telesquí *m*
skill [skɪl] *s* destreza, habilidad, pericia
skilled [skɪld] *adj* hábil, experimentado, experto
skillet ['skɪlɪt] *s* cacerola de mango largo; sartén *f*
skillful ['skɪlfəl] *adj* diestro, hábil
skim [skɪm] *v* (*pret & pp* **skimmed;** *ger* **skimming**) *tr* desnatar (*la leche*); espumar (*el caldo, el almíbar*); (*to graze*) rasar, rozar; examinar ligeramente || *intr* rozar; **to skim over** pasar rozando; examinar a la ligera
ski mask *s* pasamontaña *m*
skimmer ['skɪmər] *s* (*utensil*) espumadera; (*straw hat*) canotié *m*
skim milk *s* leche desnatada
skimp [skɪmp] *tr* escatimar; chapucear || *intr* economizar, apretarse; chapucear
skimp·y ['skɪmpi] *adj* (*comp* **-ier;** *super* **-iest**) escaso; tacaño, mezquino
skin [skɪn] *s* piel *f;* (*of an animal, of fruit*) pellejo; **to be nothing but skin and bones** estar hecho un costal de huesos, estar en los huesos; **to get soaked to the skin** calarse hasta los huesos; **to save one's skin** salvar el pellejo || *v* (*pret & pp* **skinned;** *ger* **skinning**) *tr* pelar, desollar; escoriarse (*p.ej., el codo*); (coll) timar; **to skin alive** (coll) desollar vivo; (coll) vencer completamente
skin'-deep' *adj* superficial
skin diver *s* submarinista *mf*
skin'flint' *s* escasero, avaro
skin game *s* (slang) fullería
skin·ny ['skɪni] *adj* (*comp* **-nier;** *super* **-niest**) flaco, enjuto, magro, seco
skip [skɪp] *s* salto || *v* (*pret & pp* **skipped;** *ger* **skipping**) *tr* saltar || *intr* saltar; saltar espacios (*la máquina de escribir*); moverse saltando; irse precipitadamente
skip bombing *s* (aer) bombardeo de rebote
ski pole *s* bastón *m* de esquiar
skipper ['skɪpər] *s* caudillo, jefe *m;* (*of a boat*) patrón *m;* gusano del queso || *tr* patronear
skirmish ['skʌrmɪʃ] *s* escaramuza || *intr* escaramuzar
skirt [skʌrt] *s* falda; borde *m,* orilla; (*woman*) (slang) falda || *tr* seguir el borde de; moverse a lo largo de
ski run *s* pista de esquí
ski stick *s* bastón *m* de esquiar
skit [skɪt] *s* boceto burlesco, paso cómico
skittish ['skɪtɪʃ] *adj* caprichoso; asustadizo; tímido; (*bull*) abanto
skulduggery [skʌl'dʌgəri] *s* (coll) trampa, embuste *m*
skull [skʌl] *s* cráneo, calavera
skull'cap' *s* casquete *m*
skunk [skʌŋk] *s* mofeta; (*person*) (coll) canalla *m*
sky [skaɪ] *s* (*pl* **skies**) cielo; **to praise to the skies** poner por las nubes, poner en el cielo
sky'lark' *s* alondra || *intr* jaranear
sky'light' *s* tragaluz *m,* claraboya
sky'line' *s* línea del horizonte, línea de los edificios contra el cielo
sky'rock'et *s* cohete *m* || *intr* subir como un cohete
sky'scrap'er *s* rascacielos *m*
sky'writ'ing *s* escritura aérea
slab [slæb] *s* losa; plancha, tabla
slack [slæk] *adj* flojo; perezoso; negligente; inactivo || *s* flojedad; inactividad; estación muerta, temporada inactiva; **slacks** pantalones flojos || *tr* aflojar; apagar (*la cal*) || *intr* atrasarse; descuidarse; **to slack up** aflojar el paso
slacker ['slækər] *s* perezoso; (mil) prófugo
slag [slæg] *s* escoria
slake [slek] *tr* aplacar, calmar; apagar (*la cal*)
slalom ['slɑləm] *s* eslálom *m*
slam [slæm] *s* golpe *m;* (*of a door*) portazo; (coll) crítica acerba || *v* (*pret & pp* **slammed;** *ger* **slamming**) *tr* cerrar de golpe; golpear o empujar estrepitosamente; (coll) criticar acerbamente || *intr* cerrarse de golpe
slam'-bang' *adv* (coll) de golpe y porrazo
slander ['slændər] *s* calumnia, difamación || *tr* calumniar, difamar
slanderous ['slændərəs] *adj* calumnioso, difamatorio
slang [slæŋ] *s* caló *m,* jerigonza
slant [slænt] *s* inclinación; parecer *m,* punto de vista || *tr* inclinar, sesgar; deformar, tergiversar (*un informe*) || *intr* inclinarse, sesgarse
slap [slæp] *s* manazo, palmada; (*in the face*) bofetada; (*in the back*) espaldarazo; desaire *m,* insulto || *v* (*pret & pp* **slapped;** *ger* **slapping**) *tr* dar una palmada a; abofetear
slash [slæʃ] *s* cuchillada || *tr* acuchillar; hacer fuerte rebaja de (*precios, sueldos, etc.*)
slat [slæt] *s* lámina, tablilla
slate [slet] *s* pizarra; candidatura, lista de candidatos || *tr* empizarrar; designar, destinar; poner en la lista de candidatos
slate pencil *s* pizarrín *m*
slate roof *s* empizarrado
slattern ['slætərn] *s* mujer desaliñada, pazpuerca
slaughter ['slɔtər] *s* carnicería, matanza || *tr* matar
slaughter house *s* matadero
Slav [slɑv] o [slæv] *adj & s* eslavo

slave [slev] *adj & s* esclavo || *intr* trabajar como esclavo
slave driver *s* negrero; (fig) negrero
slave'hold'er *s* dueño de esclavos
slavery ['slevəri] *s* esclavitud
slave trade *s* trata de esclavos
slave trader *s* negrero
Slavic ['slɑvɪk] o ['slævɪk] *adj & s* eslavo
slay [sle] *v* (*pret* **slew** [slu]; *pp* **slain** [slen]) *tr* matar
slayer ['sle·ər] *s* matador *m*
sled [slɛd] *s* luge *m* || *v* (*pret & pp* **sledded;** *ger* **sledding**) *intr* deslizarse en luge o trineo
sledge hammer [slɛdʒ] *s* acotillo
sleek [slik] *adj* liso y brillante || *tr* alisar y pulir; suavizar
sleep [slip] *s* sueño; **to be overcome with sleep** caerse de sueño; **to go to sleep** dormirse; dormirse, morirse (*un miembro*); **to put to sleep** adormecer; matar por anestesia || *v* (*pret & pp* **slept** [slɛpt]) *tr* pasar durmiendo; **to sleep it off** dormir la mona; **to sleep it over** consultar con la almohada; **to sleep off** dormir (*p.ej., una borrachera*) || *intr* dormir
sleeper ['slipər] *s* (*person*) durmiente *mf;* (*girder*) durmiente *m*
sleeping bag *s* saco de dormir
sleeping car *s* coche-cama *m*
sleeping pill *s* píldora para dormir
sleepless ['sliplɪs] *adj* insomne, desvelado; pasado en vela
sleep'walk'er *s* sonámbulo
sleep·y ['slipi] *adj* (*comp* **-ier;** *super* **-iest**) soñoliento; **to be sleepy** tener sueño
sleep'y·head' *s* dormilón *m*
sleet [slit] *s* cellisca || *intr* cellisquear
sleeve [sliv] *s* manga; (mach) manguito; **to laugh in** o **up one's sleeve** reírse para sí
sleigh [sle] *s* trineo || *intr* pasearse en trineo
sleigh bell *s* cascabel *m*
sleigh ride *s* paseo en trineo
sleight of hand [slaɪt] *s* juego de manos, prestidigitación
slender ['slɛndər] *adj* esbelto, flaco, delgado; escaso, insuficiente
sleuth [sluθ] *s* sabueso
slew [slu] *s* (coll) montón *m*
slice [slaɪs] *s* rebanada, tajada; (*of an orange*) gajo || *tr* rebanar, tajar; dividir; cortar
slick [slɪk] *adj* liso y brillante; meloso, suave; (coll) astuto, mañoso || *s* lugar aceitoso y lustroso (*en el agua*)
slicker ['slɪkər] *s* impermeable *m* de hule; (coll) embaucador *m*
slide [slaɪd] *s* resbalón *m;* (*slippery place*) resbaladero; (*slippery surface*) desliz *m;* derrumbamiento de tierra; (*image for projection*) diapositiva, transparencia; (*of a microscope*) plaquilla de vidrio; (*piece of a device that slides*) cursor *m;* (*of a trombone*) corredera (tubular) || *v* (*pret & pp* **slid** [slɪd]) *tr* deslizar || *intr* deslizar, resbalar; **to let slide** dejar pasar, no hacer caso de
slide fastener *s* cierre *m* cremallera, cierre relámpago
slide rule *s* regla de cálculo
slide valve *s* corredera, válvula corrediza
sliding contact *s* cursor *m*
sliding door *s* puerta de corredera
sliding scale *s* regla de cálculo; (*of salaries*) escala móvil
slight [slaɪt] *adj* delgado; leve; pequeño; escaso || *s* desatención, descuido; desaire *m,* menosprecio || *tr* desatender, descuidar; desairar
slim [slɪm] *adj* (*comp* **slimmer;** *super* **slimmest**) delgado, esbelto; débil, leve, pequeño, escaso
slime [slaɪm] *s* légamo; (*of snakes, fish, etc.*) baba
slim·y ['slaɪmi] *adj* (*comp* **-ier;** *super* **-iest**) legamoso; baboso, viscoso; puerco, sucio
sling [slɪŋ] *s* (*to shoot stones*) honda; (*to hold up a broken arm*) cabestrillo || *v* (*pret & pp* **slung** [slʌŋ]) *tr* lanzar con una honda; lanzar, tirar; poner en cabestrillo; colgar flojamente
sling'shot' *s* honda
slink [slɪŋk] *v* (*pret & pp* **slunk** [slʌŋk]) *intr* andar furtivamente; **to slink away** escabullirse, salir con el rabo entre piernas
slip [slɪp] *s* resbalón *m,* desliz *m;* falta, error *m,* desliz *m;* lapso; embarcadero; (*cover for a pillow, for furniture*) funda; (*piece of paper*) papeleta; (*cutting from a plant*) sarmiento; (*piece of underclothing*) combinación; (*of a dog*) traílla; huída, evasión; mozuelo, mozuela; **to give the slip to** burlar la vigilancia de || *v* (*pret & pp* **slipped;** *ger* **slipping**) *tr* poner rápidamente; quitar rápidamente; pasar por alto; eludir, evadir; **to slip off** (coll) quitarse de prisa; **to slip on** (coll) ponerse de prisa; **to slip one's mind** olvidársele a uno || *intr* deslizarse; patinar (*el embrague*); errar, equivocarse; (coll) declinar, deteriorarse; **to let slip** dejar pasar; decir inadvertidamente; **to slip away** escurrirse; **to slip by** pasar inadvertido; pasar rápidamente (*el tiempo*); **to slip out of one's hands** escurrirse de entre las manos; **to slip up** (coll) errar, equivocarse
slip cover *s* funda
slip of the pen *s* error *m* de pluma
slip of the tongue *s* error *m* de lengua
slipper ['slɪpər] *s* zapatilla, babucha
slippery ['slɪpəri] *adj* deslizadizo, resbaladizo; astuto, zorro, evasivo
slip'-up' *s* (coll) error *m,* equivocación
slit [slɪt] *s* hendidura, raja; cortada, incisión || *v* (*pret & pp* **slit;** *ger* **slitting**) *tr* hender, rajar; cortar
slob [slɑb] *s* (slang) sujeto desaseado, puerco
slobber ['slɑbər] *s* baba; sensiblería || *intr* babear; hablar con sensiblería
sloe [slo] *s* (*shrub*) endrino; (*fruit*) endrina

slogan [ˈslogən] *s* lema *m,* mote *m;* grito de combate; (*striking phrase used in advertising*) eslogan *m*
sloop [slup] *s* balandra
slop [slɑp] *s* gacha, zupia, agua sucia || *v* (*pret & pp* **slopped;** *ger* **slopping**) *tr* salpicar, ensuciar || *intr* derramarse; chapotear
slope [slop] *s* cuesta, pendiente *f;* (*of a continent or a roof*) vertiente *m & f* || *tr* inclinar || *intr* inclinarse
slop•py [ˈslɑpi] *adj* (*comp* **-pier;** *super* **-piest**) mojado y sucio; (*in one's dress*) desgalichado; (*in one's work*) chapucero
slot [slɑt] *s* ranura; (*for letters*) buzón *m*
sloth [sloθ] o [slɔθ] *s* pereza; (zool) perezoso
slot machine *s* tragamonedas *m,* máquina sacaperras
slot meter *s* contador automático
slouch [slautʃ] *s* postura relajada; persona torpe de movimientos || *intr* agacharse, andar caído de hombros; **to slouch in a chair** repanchigarse
slouch hat *s* sombrero gacho
slough [slau] *s* cenagal *m,* fangal *m;* estado de abandono moral || [slʌf] *s* (*of a snake*) camisa; (pathol) escara || *tr* mudar, echar de sí || *intr* caerse, desprenderse
Slovak [ˈslovæk] o [sloˈvæk] *adj & s* eslovaco
sloven•ly [ˈslʌvənli] *adj* (*comp* **-lier;** *super* **-liest**) desaseado, desaliñado
slow [slo] *adj* lento; (*sluggish*) cachazudo, despacioso; (*clock, watch*) atrasado; (*in understanding*) lerdo, tardo, torpe || *adv* despacio || *tr* retrasar; atrasar (*un reloj*) || *intr* retardarse, ir más despacio; atrasarse (*un reloj*)
slow'down' *s* huelga de brazos caídos
slow'-mo'tion *adj* a cámara lenta
slow'poke' *s* tardón *m*
slug [slʌg] *s* (*heavy piece of metal*) lingote *m;* (*metal disk used as a coin*) ficha; (zool) limaza, babosa; (coll) porrazo, puñetazo || *v* (*pret & pp* **slugged;** *ger* **slugging**) *tr* (coll) aporrear, apuñear
sluggard [ˈslʌgərd] *s* pachón *m,* perezoso
sluggish [ˈslʌgɪʃ] *adj* inactivo, indolente, tardo; pachorrudo, perezoso
sluice [slus] *s* canal *m;* (*floodgate*) compuerta; (*dam; flume*) presa
sluice gate *s* compuerta de presa
slum [slʌm] *s* barrio bajo || *v* (*pret & pp* **slummed;** *ger* **slumming**) *intr* visitar los barrios bajos
slumber [ˈslʌmbər] *s* sueño ligero, sueño tranquilo || *intr* dormir; dormitar
slump [slʌmp] *s* depresión, crisis económica; (*in prices, stocks, etc.*) baja repentina || *intr* hundirse, desplomarse; bajar repentinamente (*los precios, valores, etc.*)
slur [slʌr] *s* pronunciación indistinta; reparo crítico; (mus) ligado || *v* (*pret & pp* **slurred;** *ger* **slurring**) *tr* comerse (*sonidos, sílabas*); despreciar, insultar; (mus) ligar
slush [slʌʃ] *s* fango muy blando, agua nieve fangosa, nieve *f* a medio derretir; sentimentalismo tonto
slut [slʌt] *s* perra; (*slovenly woman*) pazpuerca; ramera, mala mujer
sly [slaɪ] *adj* (*comp* **slyer** o **slier;** *super* **slyest** o **sliest**) furtivo, secreto; astuto, socarrón; travieso; **on the sly** a hurtadillas
smack [smæk] *adv* (coll) de golpe, de sopetón || *s* dejo, gustillo; palmada, manotada; golpe *m;* beso sonado; (*of a whip*) chasquido || *tr* dar una manotada a; golpear; hacer chasquidos con (*un látigo*); besar sonoramente; **to smack one's lips** chuparse los labios || *intr* — **to smack of** saber a, oler a
small [smɔl] *adj* pequeño, chico; (*short in stature*) bajo; pobre, obscuro, humilde; (typ) minúsculo
small arms *spl* armas ligeras
small beer *s* cerveza floja; bagatela; persona de poca monta
small business *s* pequeña empresa
small capital *s* versalilla o versalita
small change *s* suelto, dinero menudo
small fry *s* gente menuda; gente de poca monta
small'-fry' *adj* de niños, para niños; de poca monta
small hours *spl* primeras horas (*de la mañana*)
small intestine *s* intestino delgado
small-minded [ˈsmɔlˈmaɪndɪd] *adj* tacaño, mezquino; intolerante
smallpox [ˈsmɔl,pɑks] *s* viruela
small print *s* tipo menudo
small talk *s* palique *m,* charlas frívolas
small'-time' *adj* de poca monta
small'-town' *adj* lugareño, apegado a cosas lugareñas
smart [smɑrt] *adj* listo, vivo, inteligente; agudo, penetrante; astuto; elegante, majo; picante, punzante; (coll) grande, considerable || *s* escozor *m;* dolor vivo || *intr* escocer, picar; padecer, sufrir
smart aleck [ˈælɪk] *s* (coll) fatuo, sabihondo
smart set *s* gente *f* chic, gente de buen tono
smash [smæʃ] *s* rotura violenta; fracaso, ruina; quiebra, bancarrota; (coll) choque violento, tope violento || *tr* romper con fuerza; arruinar, destrozar; aplastar || *intr* romperse con fuerza; arruinarse, destrozarse; aplastarse; **to smash into** chocar con, topar con
smash hit *s* (coll) éxito rotundo
smash'-up' *s* colisión violenta; ruina, desastre *m;* quiebra, bancarrota
smattering [ˈsmætərɪŋ] *s* barniz *m,* tintura, migaja
smear [smɪr] *s* embarradura; calumnia; (bact) frotis *m* || *tr* embarrar; calumniar || *intr* embarrarse
smear campaign *s* campaña de calumnias
smell [smɛl] *s* olor *m;* (*sense*) olfato;

fragancia, perfume *m* || *v* (*pret & pp* **smelled** o **smelt** [smɛlt]) *tr* oler, olfatear || *intr* oler; heder, oler mal; **to smell of** oler a
smelling salts *spl* sales aromáticas
smell·y ['smɛli] *adj* (*comp* **-ier;** *super* **-iest**) hediondo, maloliente
smelt [smɛlt] *s* (*fish*) eperlano, esperinque *m* || *tr & intr* fundir
smile [smaɪl] *s* sonrisa || *intr* sonreír, sonreírse
smiling ['smaɪlɪŋ] *adj* risueño
smirk [smʌrk] *s* sonrisa fatua y afectada || *intr* sonreír fatua y afectadamente
smite [smaɪt] *v* (*pret* **smote** [smot]; *pp* **smitten** ['smɪtən] o **smit** [smɪt]) *tr* golpear o herir súbitamente y con fuerza; caer con fuerza sobre; apenar, afligir; castigar
smith [smɪθ] *s* forjador *m,* herrero
smith·y ['smɪθi] *s* (*pl* **-ies**) herrería
smitten ['smɪtən] *adj* afligido; (coll) muy enamorado
smock [smɑk] *s* bata
smock frock *s* blusa de obrero
smog [smɑg] *s* (coll) mezcla de humo y niebla
smoke [smok] *s* humo; **to go up in smoke** irse todo en humo || *tr* (*to cure or treat with smoke*) ahumar; fumar (*tabaco*); **to smoke out** ahuyentar con humo, dar humazo a; descubrir || *intr* humear; fumar; hacer humo (*una chimenea dentro de la habitación*)
smoked glasses *spl* gafas ahumadas
smokeless powder ['smoklɪs] *s* pólvora sin humo
smoker ['smokər] *s* fumador *m:* (*room*) fumadero; (rr) coche-fumador *m;* reunión de fumadores
smoke rings *spl* anillos de humo; **to blow smoke rings** sacar humo formando anillos
smoke screen *s* cortina de humo
smoke'stack' *s* chimenea
smoking ['smokɪŋ] *s* el fumar; **no smoking** se prohibe fumar
smoking car *s* coche-fumador *m,* vagón *m* de fumar
smoking jacket *s* batín *m*
smoking room *s* fumadero, saloncito para fumadores
smok·y ['smoki] *adj* (*comp* **-ier;** *super* **-iest**) humoso; (*emitting smoke*) humeante
smolder ['smoldər] *s* fuego lento sin llama y con mucho humo || *intr* arder en rescoldo, arder sin llamas; (fig) estar latente; (*to burn within*) (fig) requemarse; (fig) expresar (*p.ej., los ojos*) una ira latente
smooth [smuð] *adj* liso, terso, suave; plano, llano; igual; acaramelado, afable, blando, meloso; (*water*) tranquilo; (*style*) flúido; **smooth as butter** como manteca || *tr* alisar, suavizar; allanar; facilitar; **to smooth away** quitar (*p.ej., obstáculos*) suavemente; **to smooth down** ablandar, calmar
smooth-faced ['smuð,fest] *adj* barbilampiño
smooth-spoken ['smuθ,spokən] *adj* meloso, lisonjero
smooth·y ['smuði] *s* (*pl* **-ies**) (coll) galante *m;* (coll) elegante *m;* (coll) adulador *m*
smother ['smʌðər] *tr* ahogar, sofocar; suprimir; reprimir
smudge [smʌdʒ] *s* tiznón *m;* mancha || *tr* tiznar; manchar; ahumar, fumigar (*una huerta*)
smug [smʌg] *adj* (*comp* **smugger;** *super* **smuggest**) pagado de sí mismo; compuesto, pulcro; relamido
smuggle ['smʌgəl] *tr* meter de contrabando || *intr* contrabandear
smuggler ['smʌglər] *s* contrabandista *mf*
smuggling ['smʌglɪŋ] *s* contrabando
smut [smʌt] *s* tiznón *m;* obscenidad; (agr) carbón *m,* tizón *m*
smut·ty ['smʌti] *adj* (*comp* **-tier;** *super* **-tiest**) tiznado, manchado; obsceno; (agr) atizonado
snack [snæk] *s* parte *f,* porción; bocadillo, tentempié *m*
snag [snæg] *s* (*of a tree*) tocón *m;* (*of a tooth*) raigón *m;* obstáculo, tropiezo; **to strike** o **to hit a snag** tropezar con un obstáculo
snail [snel] *s* caracol *m;* (*slow person*) pachón *m;* **at a snail's pace** a paso de caracol, a paso de tortuga
snake [snek] *s* culebra, serpiente *f*
snake in the grass *s* traidor *m,* amigo pérfido
snap [snæp] *s* (*crackling sound*) chasquido, estallido; (*of the fingers*) castañetazo; (*bite*) mordisco; (*cracker*) galletita; (*of cold weather*) corto período; (*catch or fastener*) broche *m* de presión; (phot) instantánea; (coll) brío, vigor *m;* (slang) breva, cosa fácil || *v* (*pret & pp* **snapped;** *ger* **snapping**) *tr* asir, cerrar, etc. de golpe; castañetear (*los dedos*); chasquear (*el látigo*); fotografiar instantáneamente; tomar (*una instantánea*); **to snap one's fingers at** tratar con desprecio; **to snap up** aceptar con avidez, comprar con avidez; cortar la palabra a || *intr* chasquear, estallar; (*to crack*) saltar; (*from fatigue*) estallar; **to snap at** querer morder; asir (*una oportunidad*); **to snap out of it** (slang) cambiarse repentinamente; **to snap shut** cerrarse de golpe
snap'drag'on *s* (bot) boca de dragón
snap fastener *s* corchete *m* de presión
snap judgment *s* decisión atolondrada
snap·py ['snæpi] *adj* (*comp* **-pier;** *super* **-piest**) mordaz; (coll) elegante, garboso; (coll) enérgico, vivo; (*food*) acre, picante
snap'shot' *s* instantánea
snap switch *s* (elec) interruptor *m* de resorte
snare [snɛr] *s* lazo, trampa; (*of a drum*) bordón *m,* tirante *m*
snare drum *s* caja clara
snarl [snɑrl] *s* gruñido; regaño; maraña, enredo || *tr* decir con un gru-

ñido; enmarañar, enredar || *intr* gruñir; regañar; enmarañarse, enredarse
snatch [snætʃ] *s* arrebatamiento; pedacito, trocito; ratito || *tr & intr* arrebatar; **to snatch at** tratar de asir o agarrar; **to snatch from** arrebatar a
sneak [snik] *adj* furtivo || *s* sujeto solapado || *tr* mover a hurtadillas || *intr* andar furtivamente, moverse a hurtadillas
sneaker ['snikər] *s* sujeto solapado; (coll) zapato blando, zapato de lona
sneak thief *s* ratero, descuidero
sneak•y ['sniki] *adj* (*comp* **-ier;** *super* **-iest**) solapado, furtivo
sneer [snɪr] *s* expresión de desprecio || *intr* hablar con desprecio, echar una mirada de desprecio; **to sneer at** mofarse de
sneeze [sniz] *s* estornudo || *intr* estornudar; **not to be sneezed at** (coll) no ser despreciable
snicker ['snɪkər] *s* risa tonta || *intr* reírse tontamente
sniff [snɪf] *s* husmeo, venteo; sorbo por las narices || *tr* husmear, ventear; sorber por las narices; (fig) husmear, averiguar; (fig) sospechar || *intr* ventear; **to sniff at** husmear; menospreciar
sniffle ['snɪfəl] *s* resuello fuerte y repetido; **the sniffles** ataque *m* de resoplidos || *intr* resollar fuerte y repetidamente
snip [snɪp] *s* tijeretada; recorte *m*, pedacito; (coll) persona pequeña e insignificante || *v* (*pret & pp* **snipped;** *ger* **snipping**) *tr* tijeretear
snipe [snaɪp] *s* agachadiza, becacín *m* || *intr* paquear, tirar desde un escondite
sniper ['snaɪpər] *s* paco, tirador emboscado
snippet ['snɪpɪt] *s* recorte *m;* (coll) persona pequeña e insignificante
snip•py ['snɪpi] *adj* (*comp* **-pier;** *super* **-piest**) (coll) arrogante, desdeñoso; (coll) acre, brusco
snitch [snɪtʃ] *tr & intr* (slang) escamotear, ratear
sniv•el ['snɪvəl] *s* gimoteo, lloriqueo; moqueo || *v* (*pret & pp* **-eled** o **-elled;** *ger* **-eling** o **-elling**) *intr* gimotear, lloriquear; (*to have a runny nose*) moquear
snob [snɑb] *s* esnob *mf*
snobbery ['snɑbəri] *s* esnobismo
snobbish ['snɑbɪʃ] *adj* esnob, esnobista
snoop [snup] *s* (coll) buscavidas *mf*, curioso || *intr* (coll) curiosear, ventear
snoopy ['snupi] *adj* (coll) curioso, entremetido
snoot [snut] *s* (slang) cara, narices *fpl*
snoot•y ['snuti] *adj* (*comp* **-ier;** *super* **-iest**) (slang) esnob
snooze [snuz] *s* (coll) sueñecito || *intr* echar un sueñecito
snore [snor] *s* ronquido || *intr* roncar
snort [snɔrt] *s* bufido || *intr* bufar
snot [snɑt] *s* (slang) mocarro
snot•ty ['snɑti] *adj* (*comp* **-tier;** *super* **-tiest**) (coll) mocoso; (coll) asqueroso, sucio; (slang) engreído
snout [snaʊt] *s* hocico; (*something shaped like the snout of an animal*) morro; (*of a person*) (coll) hocico
snow [sno] *s* nieve *f* || *intr* nevar
snow'ball' *s* bola de nieve || *tr* lanzar bolas de nieve a || *intr* aumentar rápidamente
snow'-blind' *adj* cegado por reflejos de la nieve
snow-capped ['sno ˌkæpt] *adj* coronado de nieve
snow'drift' *s* ventisquero, masa de nieve
snow'fall' *s* nevada
snow fence *s* valla paranieves
snow'flake' *s* copo de nieve, ampo
snow flurry *s* nevisca
snow line o **limit** *s* límite *m* de las nieves perpetuas
snow man *s* figura de nieve
snow'plow' *s* expulsanieves *m*, quitanieves *m*
snow'shoe' *s* raqueta de nieve
snow'storm' *s* nevasca, fuerte nevada
snow'-white' *adj* blanco como la nieve
snow•y ['sno·i] *adj* (*comp* **-ier;** *super* **-iest**) nevoso
snowy owl *s* lechuza blanca
snub [snʌb] *s* desaire *m* || *v* (*pret & pp* **snubbed;** *ger* **snubbing**) *tr* desairar
snub•by ['snʌbi] *adj* (*comp* **-bier;** *super* **-biest**) (*nose*) respingona
snuff [snʌf] *s* rapé; (*of a candlewick*) moco; **up to snuff** (slang) en buena condición; (slang) difícil de engañar || *tr* husmear, olfatear; sorber por la nariz; despabilar (*una candela*); **to snuff out** apagar, extinguir
snuff'box' *s* tabaquera
snuffers ['snʌfərz] *spl* despabiladeras
snug [snʌg] *adj* (*comp* **snugger;** *super* **snuggest**) cómodo; (*garment*) ajustado, ceñido; (*well-off*) acomodado; (*in hiding*) escondido
snuggle ['snʌgəl] *intr* apretarse, arrimarse; dormir bien abrigado; **to snuggle up to** arrimarse a
so [so] *adv* así; tan + *adj* o *adv;* por tanto; también; **and so** así pues; también, lo mismo; **and so on** y así sucesivamente; **or so** más o menos; **to think so** creer que sí; **so as to** + *inf* para + *inf;* **so far** hasta aquí; hasta ahora; **so long** hasta la vista; **so many** tantos; **so much** tanto; **so so** tal cual, así así; **so that** de modo que, de suerte que, así que; para que; con tal de que; **so to speak** por decirlo así || *conj* así que || *interj* ¡bien!; ¡verdad!
soak [sok] *s* mojada; (*toper*) (coll) potista *mf* || *tr* empapar, remojar; embeber; (slang) aporrear; (slang) hacer pagar un precio exorbitante; **to soak up** absorber, embeber; (fig) entender; **soaked to the skin** calado hasta los huesos || *intr* empaparse, remojarse
so'-and-so' *s* (*pl* **-sos**) fulano, fulano de tal; tal cosa
soap [sop] *s* jabón *m* || *tr* jabonar

soap'box' *s* caja de jabón; tribuna callejera
soapbox orator *s* orador *m* de plazuela
soap bubble *s* burbuja de jabón, pompa de jabón
soap dish *s* jabonera
soap flakes *spl* copos de jabón
soap'mak'er *s* jabonero
soap opera *s* (coll) serial lacrimógeno
soap powder *s* jabón *m* en polvo, polvo de jabón
soap'stone' *s* jaboncillo de sastre
soap'suds' *spl* jabonaduras
soap·y ['sopi] *adj* (*comp* **-ier;** *super* **-iest**) jabonoso
soar [sor] *intr* encumbrarse, subir muy alto, volar a gran altura; aspirar, pretender; (aer) planear
sob [sɑb] *s* sollozo || *v* (*pret & pp* **sobbed;** *ger* **sobbing**) *tr* decir o expresar sollozando || *intr* sollozar
sober ['sobər] *adj* sobrio; no embriagado; grave, serio; cuerdo, sensato; sereno, tranquilo; (*color*) apagado || *tr* poner sobrio; desemborrachar || *intr* volverse sobrio; desemborracharse; **to sober down** calmarse, sosegarse; **to sober up** desemborracharse
sobriety [so'braɪ·əti] *s* sobriedad, moderación; gravedad, seriedad; cordura, sensatez; serenidad
sobriquet ['sobrɪ ,ke] *s* apodo
sob sister *s* (slang) periodista llorona
sob story *s* (slang) historia de lagrimitas
soc. o **Soc.** *abbr* **society**
so'-called' *adj* llamado, así llamado; supuesto
soccer ['sɑkər] *s* fútbol *m* asociación
sociable ['soʃəbəl] *adj* sociable
social ['soʃəl] *adj* social || *s* reunión social
social climber ['klaɪmər] *s* ambicioso de figurar
socialism ['soʃə ,lɪzəm] *s* socialismo
socialist ['soʃəlɪst] *s* socialista *mf*
socialite ['soʃə ,laɪt] *s* (coll) personaje *m* de la buena sociedad
social register *s* guía *m* social, registro de la buena sociedad
socie·ty [sə'saɪ·əti] *s* (*pl* **-ties**) sociedad; (*companionship or company*) compañía; buena sociedad, mundo elegante
society editor *s* cronista *mf* de la vida social
sociology [,sosɪ'ɑlədʒi] o [,soʃɪ'ɑlədʒi] *s* sociología
sock [sɑk] *s* calcetín *m;* (slang) golpe *m* fuerte || *tr* (slang) golpear con fuerza
socket ['sɑkɪt] *s* (*of the eyes*) cuenca; (*of a tooth*) alvéolo; (*of a candlestick*) cañón *m;* (*of a socket wrench*) cubo; (elec) portalámparas; (rad) zócalo
socket wrench *s* llave *f* de caja, llave de cubo
sod [sɑd] *s* césped *m;* terrón *m* de césped || *v* (*pret & pp* **sodded;** *ger* **sodding**) *tr* encespedar
soda ['sodə] *s* soda, sosa; (*drink*) soda
soda fountain *s* fuente *f* de sodas
soda water *s* agua gaseosa
sodium ['sodɪ·əm] *adj* sódico, de sodio || *s* sodio
sofa ['sofə] *s* sofá *m*
soft [sɔft] o [sɑft] *adj* blando, muelle; (*skin*) suave; (*iron*) dulce; (*hat*) flexible; (*solder*) tierno; (coll) fácil
soft-boiled egg ['sɔft'bɔɪld] o ['sɑft'bɔɪld] *s* huevo pasado por agua
soft coal *s* hulla grasa
soft drink *s* bebida no alcohólica, refresco
soften ['sɔfən] o ['sɑfən] *tr* ablandar; **to soften up** (*by bombardment*) ablandar || *intr* ablandarse
soft'-ped'al *tr* (mus) disminuir la intensidad de, por medio del pedal suave; (slang) moderar
soft soap *s* jabón blando o graso; (coll) adulación
soft'-soap' *tr* (coll) enjabonar, dar jabón a
sog·gy ['sɑgi] *adj* (*comp* **-gier;** *super* **-giest**) remojado, ensopado
soil [sɔɪl] *s* suelo; país *m,* región; (*spot, stain*) mancha; (fig) mancha, deshonra || *tr* manchar, ensuciar; manchar, deshonrar; viciar, corromper || *intr* mancharse, ensuciarse
soil pipe *s* tubo de desagüe sanitario
soiree o **soirée** [swɑ're] *s* sarao, velada
sojourn ['sodʒʌrn] *s* estancia, permanencia || ['sodʒʌrn] o [so'dʒʌrn] *intr* estarse, permanecer
sol. *abbr* **soluble, solution**
solace ['sɑlɪs] *s* solaz *m,* consuelo || *tr* solazar, consolar
solar ['solər] *adj* solar
solar battery *s* fotopila
solder ['sɑdər] *s* soldadura || *tr* soldar
soldering iron *s* cautín *m,* soldador *m*
soldier ['soldʒər] *s* (*enlisted man as distinguished from an officer*) soldado; (*man in military service*) militar *m* || *intr* servir como soldado
soldier of fortune *s* aventurero militar
soldier·y ['soldʒəri] *s* (*pl* **-ies**) soldadesca
sold out [sold] *adj* agotado; **the theater is sold out** todas las localidades están vendidas; **we are sold out of those neckties** se nos han agotado esas corbatas
sole [sol] *adj* solo, único; exclusivo || *s* (*of foot*) planta; (*of shoe*) suela; (*fish*) lenguado || *tr* solar
solely ['solli] *adv* solamente, únicamente
solemn ['sɑləm] *adj* solemne
solicit [sə'lɪsɪt] *tr* solicitar; intentar seducir
solicitor [sə'lɪsɪtər] *s* solicitador *m,* agente *m;* (law) procurador *m*
solicitous [sə'lɪsɪtəs] *adj* solícito
solicitude [sə'lɪsɪ ,tjud] o [sə'lɪsɪ ,tud] *s* solicitud
solid ['sɑlɪd] *adj* sólido; unánime; (*sound, good*) sólido, macizo; (*e.g., clouds*) denso; (*without pause or interruption*) entero; (*e.g., gold*) puro || *s* sólido
solid geometry *s* geometría del espacio
solidity [sə'lɪdɪti] *s* (*pl* **-ties**) solidez *f*

solid tire *s* (aut) macizo
solilo·quy [səˈlɪləkwi] *s* (*pl* **-quies**) soliloquio
solitaire [ˈsalɪ,tɛr] *s* (*game and diamond*) solitario; sortija solitario
solitar·y [ˈsalɪ,tɛri] *adj* solitario ‖ *s* (*pl* **-ies**) solitario
solitary confinement *s* incomunicación, aislamiento penal
solitude [ˈsalɪ,tjud] o [ˈsalɪ,tud] *s* soledad
so·lo [ˈsolo] *adj* (*instrument*) solista; a solas, hecho a solas ‖ *s* (*pl* **-los**) (mus) solo
soloist [ˈsolo·ɪst] *s* solista *mf*
solstice [ˈsalstɪs] *s* solsticio
solution [səˈluʃən] *s* solución
solve [salv] *tr* resolver, solucionar; adivinar (*un enigma*)
solvent [ˈsalvənt] *adj* & *s* solvente *m*
somber [ˈsambər] *adj* sombrío
some [sʌm] *adj indef* algún; un poco de; unos; (coll) grande, bueno, famoso ‖ *pron indef pl* algunos, unos
some'bod'y *pron indef* alguien; **somebody else** algún otro, otra persona ‖ *s* (*pl* **-ies**) (coll) personaje *m*
some'day' *adv* algún día
some'how' *adv* de algún modo, de alguna manera; **somehow or other** de un modo u otro
some'one' *pron indef* alguien; **someone else** algún otro, otra persona
somersault [ˈsʌmər,sɔlt] *s* salto mortal ‖ *intr* dar un salto mortal
something [ˈsʌmθɪŋ] *adv* algo, un poco; (coll) muy, excesivamente ‖ *pron indef* alguna cosa, algo; **something else** otra cosa
some'time' *adj* antiguo, de otro tiempo ‖ *adv* alguna vez; antiguamente
some'times' *adv* a veces, algunas veces
some'way' *adv* de algún modo
some'what' *adv* algo, un poco ‖ *s* alguna cosa, algo
some'where' *adv* en alguna parte, a alguna parte; en algún tiempo; **somewhere else** en otra parte, a otra parte
somnambulist [samˈnæmbjəlɪst] *s* sonámbulo
somnolent [ˈsamnələnt] *adj* soñoliento
son [sʌn] *s* hijo
song [sɔŋ] o [saŋ] *s* canción, canto; **for a song** muy barato; **to sing the same old song** volver a la misma canción
song'bird' *s* ave canora
Song of Songs *s* Cantar *m* de los Cantares
sonic [ˈsanɪk] *adj* sónico
sonic boom *s* (aer) estampido sónico
son'-in-law' *s* (*pl* **sons-in-law**) yerno, hijo político
sonnet [ˈsanɪt] *s* soneto
sonneteer [,sanɪˈtɪr] *s* sonetista *mf;* poetastro ‖ *intr* sonetizar
son·ny [ˈsʌni] *s* (*pl* **-nies**) hijito
sonori·ty [səˈnarɪti] o [səˈnɔrɪti] *s* (*pl* **-ties**) sonoridad
soon [sun] *adv* pronto, en breve; temprano; de buena gana; **as soon as** así que, en cuanto, luego que, tan pronto como; **as soon as possible** cuanto antes, lo más pronto posible; **had sooner** preferiría; **how soon?** ¿cuándo?; **soon after** poco después, poco después de; **sooner or later** tarde o temprano
soot [sʊt] o [sut] *s* hollín *m*
soothe [suð] *tr* aliviar, calmar, sosegar
soothsayer [ˈsuθ,se·ər] *s* adivino
soot·y [ˈsʊti] o [ˈsuti] *adj* (*comp* **-ier;** *super* **-iest**) holliniento, tiznado
sop [sap] *s* (*food soaked in milk, etc.*) sopa; regalo (*para acallar, apaciguar o sobornar*) ‖ *v* (*pret* & *pp* **sopped;** *ger* **sopping**) *tr* empapar, ensopar; **to sop up** absorber
sophisticated [səˈfɪstɪ,ketɪd] *adj* mundano, falto de simplicidad, corrido
sophomore [ˈsafə,mor] *s* estudiante *mf* de segundo año
sopping [ˈsapɪŋ] *adj* empapado; **sopping wet** hecho una sopa
sopran·o [səˈpræno] o [səˈprano] *adj* de soprano; para soprano ‖ *s* (*pl* **-os**) soprano *mf*
sorcerer [ˈsɔrsərər] *s* brujo, hechicero
sorceress [ˈsɔrsərɪs] *s* bruja, hechicera
sorcer·y [ˈsɔrsəri] *s* (*pl* **-ies**) brujería, hechicería, sortilegio
sordid [ˈsɔrdɪd] *adj* sórdido
sore [sor] *adj* enrojecido, inflamado; (coll) resentido, picado; **to be sore at** (coll) estar enojado con ‖ *s* llaga, úlcera; pena, dolor *m,* aflicción; **to open an old sore** renovar la herida
sorely [ˈsorli] *adv* penosamente; con urgencia
sore throat *s* dolor *m* de garganta
sorori·ty [səˈrarɪti] o [səˈrɔrɪti] *s* (*pl* **-ties**) hermandad de estudiantas
sorrel [ˈsarəl] o [ˈsɔrəl] *adj* alazán
sorrow [ˈsaro] o [ˈsɔro] *s* dolor *m,* pena pesar *m;* arrepentimiento ‖ *intr* dolerse, apenarse, sentir pena; arrepentirse; **to sorrow for** añorar
sorrowful [ˈsarəfəl] o [ˈsɔrəfəl] *adj* doloroso, pesaroso, acongojado
sor·ry [ˈsari] o [ˈsɔri] *adj* (*comp* **-rier;** *super* **-riest**) afligido, apenado, pesaroso; arrepentido; malo, pésimo; despreciable, ridículo; **to be** o **feel sorry** sentir; arrepentirse; **to be** o **feel sorry for** compadecer; arrepentirse de
sort [sɔrt] *s* clase *f,* especie *f;* modo, manera; **a sort of** uno a modo de; **out of sorts** de mal humor; **sort of** (coll) algo, en cierta medida ‖ *tr* clasificar, separar; escoger, entresacar
so'-so' *adj* mediano, regular, talcualillo ‖ *adv* así así, tal cual
sot [sat] *s* borracho
sotto voce [ˈsato ˈvotʃe] *adv* a sovoz, en voz baja
soubrette [suˈbrɛt] *s* (theat) confidenta de comedia; (theat) doncella coquetona
soul [sol] *s* alma; **upon my soul!** ¡por vida mía!
sound [saund] *adj* sano; sólido, firme; solvente; sonoro; (*sleep*) profundo;

prudente; legal, válido || *adv* profundamente || *s* sonido; ruido; (*passage of water*) estrecho, brazo de mar; (surg) sonda, tienta; **within sound of** al alcance de || *tr* sonar; tocar (*p.ej., campanas*); tantear, sondear; auscultar (*p.ej., los pulmones*); entonar (*p.ej., alabanzas*) || *intr* sonar, resonar; sondar; parecer; **to sound like** sonar a, sonar como

sound film *s* película sonora

soundly ['saʊndli] *adv* sanamente; profundamente; a fondo, completamente

sound'proof' *adj* antisonoro || *tr* insonorizar

soup [sup] *s* sopa

soup kitchen *s* comedor *m* de beneficencia, dispensario de alimentos

soup spoon *s* cuchara de sopa

sour [saʊr] *adj* agrio || *tr* agriar || *intr* agriarse

source [sors] *s* fuente *f*, manantial *m*

source material *s* fuentes *fpl* originales

sour cherry *s* (*tree*) guindo; (*fruit*) guinda

sour grapes *interj* ¡están verdes las uvas!

south [saʊθ] *adj* meridional, del sur || *adv* al sur, hacia el sur || *s* sur *m*, mediodía *m*

South America *s* Sudamérica, la América del Sur

South American *adj & s* sudamericano

southern ['sʌðərn] *adj* meridional

Southern Cross *s* Cruz *f* del Sur

southerner ['sʌðərnər] *s* meridional *mf;* sureño (Am)

South Korea *s* la Corea del Sur

South Korean *adj & s* surcoreano

south'paw' *adj & s* (slang in sport) zurdo

southward ['saʊθwərd] *adv* hacia el sur

south wind *s* austro, noto

souvenir [,suvə'nɪr] o ['suvə,nɪr] *s* recuerdo, memoria

sovereign ['sɑvrɪn] o ['sʌvrɪn] *adj* soberano || *s* (*king; coin*) soberano; (*queen*) soberana

sovereign·ty ['sɑvrɪnti] o ['sʌvrɪnti] *s* (*pl* **-ties**) soberanía

soviet ['sovɪ,ɛt] o [,sovɪ'ɛt] *adj* soviético || *s* soviet *m*

sovietize ['sovɪ·ɛ,taɪz] *tr* sovietizar

Soviet Russia *s* la Rusia Soviética

Soviet Union *s* Unión Soviética

sow [saʊ] *s* puerca || [so] *v* (*pret* **sowed;** *pp* **sown** o **sowed)** *tr* sembrar; (*with mines*) plagar

soybean ['sɔɪ,bin] *s* soja; semilla de soja

sp. *abbr* **special, species, specific, specimen, spelling**

spa [spɑ] *s* caldas, balneario

space [spes] *adj* espacial, del espacio || *s* espacio; **in the space of** por espacio de || *tr* espaciar

space bar *s* espaciador *m*, tecla de espacios

space'craft' *s* astronave *f*

space flight *s* vuelo espacial

space key *s* llave *f* espacial

space·man ['spes,mæn] *s* (*pl* **-men** [,mɛn]) navegador *m* del espacio; visitante *m* a la Tierra del espacio exterior

space'ship' *s* nave *f* del espacio

space suit *s* escafandra espacial

space vehicle *s* vehículo espacial

spacious ['speʃəs] *adj* espacioso

spade [sped] *s* laya; (*playing card*) pique *m;* **to call a spade a spade** llamar al pan pan y al vino vino

spade'work' *s* trabajo preliminar

Spain [spen] *s* España

span [spæn] *s* palmo, cuarta, llave *f* de la mano; espacio, lapso, trecho; (*of horses*) pareja; (*of a bridge*) ojo; (aer) envergadura || *v* (*pret & pp* **spanned;** *ger* **spanning)** *tr* medir a palmos; atravesar, extenderse sobre

spangle ['spæŋgəl] *s* lentejuela || *tr* adornar con lentejuelas; (*to stud with bright objects*) estrellar || *intr* brillar

Spaniard ['spænjərd] *s* español *m*

spaniel ['spænjəl] *s* perro de aguas

Spanish ['spænɪʃ] *adj & s* español *m;* **the Spanish** los españoles

Spanish America *s* la América Española, Hispanoamérica

Spanish broom *s* retama

Spanish fly *s* abadejo, cantárida

Spanish Main *s* Costa Firme, Tierra Firme; mar *m* Caribe

Spanish moss *s* barba española

Spanish omelet *s* tortilla de tomate

Span'ish-speak'ing *adj* de habla española, hispanohablante

spank [spæŋk] *tr* azotar, zurrar

spanking ['spæŋkɪŋ] *adj* rápido; fuerte; (coll) muy grande, muy hermoso, extraordinario || *s* azote *m*

spar *s* (mineral) espato; (naut) mástil *m*, palo, verga || *v* (*pret & pp* **sparred;** *ger* **sparring)** *intr* pelear, reñir; boxear

spare [spɛr] *adj* sobrante; libre, disponible; de repuesto; delgado, enjuto, flaco; parco, sobrio || *tr* pasar sin; perdonar; guardar, salvar; ahorrar; **to have . . . to spare** tener de sobra; **to spare oneself** ahorrarse esfuerzos

spare bed *s* cama de sobra

spare parts *spl* piezas de repuesto o de recambio

spare room *s* cuarto de reserva

sparing ['spɛrɪŋ] *adj* económico; (*scanty*) escaso

spark [spɑrk] *s* chispa; (*e.g., of truth*) centellita || *tr* (coll) cortejar, galantear (*a una mujer*) || *intr* chispear

spark coil *s* bobina de chispas, bobina de encendido

spark gap *s* (*of induction coil*) entrehierro; (*of spark plug*) espacio de chispa

sparkle ['spɑrkəl] *s* chispita, destello; (*wit*) travesura; alegría, viveza || *intr* chispear; ser alegre; espumar, ser efervescente

sparkling ['spɑrklɪŋ] *adj* centelleante, chispeante; (*wine*) espumante, espumoso; (*water*) gaseoso

spark plug *s* bujía
sparrow ['spæro] *s* gorrión *m*
sparse [spɑrs] *adj* (*population*) poco denso; (*hair*) ralo
Spartan ['spɑrtən] *adj* & *s* espartano
spasm ['spæzəm] *s* espasmo; esfuerzo súbito y de breve duración
spasmodic [spæz'mɑdɪk] *adj* espasmódico; intermitente; caprichoso
spastic ['spæstɪk] *adj* espástico
spat [spæt] *s* disputa, riña; botín *m*, polaina corta
spatial ['speʃəl] *adj* espacial
spatter ['spætər] *tr* salpicar; manchar || *intr* chorrear; chapotear
spatula ['spætʃələ] *s* espátula
spavin ['spævɪn] *s* esparaván *m*
spawn [spɔn] *s* freza; prole *f*; producto, resultado || *tr* engendrar || *intr* desovar, frezar (*los peces*)
speak [spik] *v* (*pret* **spoke** [spok]; *pp* **spoken**) *tr* hablar (*un idioma*); decir (*la verdad*) || *intr* hablar; **so to speak** por decirlo así; **speaking!** ¡al habla!; **to speak out** o **up** osar hablar, elevar la voz
speak'-eas'y *s* (*pl* **-ies**) (slang) taberna clandestina
speaker ['spikər] *s* hablante *mf*; orador *m*; (*of a legislative assembly*) presidente *m*; (rad) altavoz *m*
speaking ['spikɪŋ] *adj* hablante; **to be on speaking terms** hablarse || *s* habla; elocuencia
speaking tube *s* tubo acústico
spear [spɪr] *s* lanza; (*for fishing*) arpón *m*; (*of grass*) hoja || *tr* alancear, herir con lanza
spear'head' *s* punta de lanza || *tr* dirigir, conducir; encabezar; dar impulso a
spear'mint' *s* menta verde, menta romana
spec. *abbr* **special**
special ['spɛʃəl] *adj* especial || *s* tren *m* especial
spe'cial-deliv'ery *adj* urgente, de urgencia
specialist ['spɛʃəlɪst] *s* especialista *mf*
speciali•ty [,spɛʃɪ'ælɪti] *s* (*pl* **-ties**) especialidad
specialize ['spɛʃə,laɪz] *tr* especializar || *intr* especializar o especializarse
special•ty ['spɛʃəlti] *s* (*pl* **-ties**) especialidad
spe•cies ['spisiz] *s* (*pl* **-cies**) especie *f*
specific [spɪ'sɪfɪk] *adj* & *s* específico
speci•fy ['spɛsɪ,faɪ] *v* (*pret* & *pp* **-fied**) *tr* especificar
specimen ['spɛsɪmən] *s* espécimen *m*; (coll) tipo, sujeto
specious ['spiʃəs] *adj* especioso, engañoso
speck [spɛk] *s* mota, manchita || *tr* motear, manchar, salpicar de manchas
speckle ['spɛkəl] *s* mota, punto || *tr* motear, puntear
spectacle ['spɛktəkəl] *s* espectáculo; **spectacles** anteojos, gafas
spectator ['spɛktetər] o [spɛk'tetər] *s* espectador *m*
specter ['spɛktər] *s* espectro
spec•trum ['spɛktrəm] *s* (*pl* **-tra** [trə] o **-trums**) espectro
speculate ['spɛkjə,let] *intr* especular
speech [spitʃ] *s* habla; (*of an actor*) parlamento; (*talk before an audience*) conferencia, discurso
speech clinic *s* clínica de la palabra
speech correction *s* rehabilitación del habla
speechless ['spitʃlɪs] *adj* sin habla; estupefacto
speed [spid] *s* velocidad; (aut) marcha, velocidad || *v* (*pret* & *pp* **sped** [spɛd]) *tr* apresurar; despedir; ayudar || *intr* apresurarse; adelantar, progresar; ir con exceso de velocidad
speeding ['spidɪŋ] *s* exceso de velocidad
speed king *s* as *m* del volante
speed limit *s* velocidad permitida
speedometer [spi'dɑmɪtər] *s* (*to indicate speed*) velocímetro; velocímetro y cuentakilómetros unidos
speed record *s* marca de velocidad
speed•y ['spidi] *adj* (*comp* **-ier**; *super* **-iest**) rápido, veloz
spell [spɛl] *s* encanto, hechizo; tanda, turno; rato, poco tiempo; (*e.g., of good weather*) temporada; **to cast a spell on** encantar, hechizar || *v* (*pret* & *pp* **spelled** o **spelt** [spɛlt]) *tr* deletrear; indicar, significar; **to spell out** (coll) explicar detalladamente || *intr* deletrear || *v* (*pret* & *pp* **spelled**) *tr* reemplazar, relevar
spell'bind'er *s* (coll) orador *m* fascinante, orador persuasivo
spelling ['spɛlɪŋ] *adj* ortográfico || *s* (*act*) deletreo; (*subject or study*) ortografía; (*way a word is spelled*) grafía
spelunker [spɪ'lʌŋkər] *s* espeleólogo de afición
spend [spɛnd] *v* (*pret* & *pp* **spent** [spɛnt]) *tr* gastar; pasar (*una hora, un día, etc.*)
spender ['spɛndər] *s* gastador *m*
spending money *s* dinero para gastos menudos
spend'thrift' *s* derrochador *m*, pródigo
sperm [spʌrm] *s* esperma *f*
sperm whale *s* cachalote *m*
spew [spju] *tr* & *intr* vomitar
sp. gr. *abbr* **specific gravity**
sphere [sfɪr] *s* esfera; astro, cuerpo celeste
spherical ['sfɛrɪkəl] *adj* esférico
sphinx [sfɪŋks] *s* (*pl* **sphinxes** o **sphinges** ['sfɪndʒiz]) esfinge *f*
spice [spaɪs] *s* especia; (*zest, piquancy*) sainete *m*; fragancia || *tr* especiar; dar gusto o picante a
spice box *s* especiero
spick-and-span ['spɪkənd'spæn] *adj* flamante; limpio, pulcro
spic•y ['spaɪsi] *adj* (*comp* **-ier**; *super* **-iest**) especiado; picante; aromático; sicalíptico
spider ['spaɪdər] *s* araña
spider web *s* tela de araña, telaraña

spiff·y ['spɪfi] *adj* (*comp* **-ier;** *super* **-iest**) (slang) guapo, elegante
spigot ['spɪgət] *s* grifo; (*plug to stop a vent*) espiche *m*
spike [spaɪk] *s* (*long, heavy nail*) estaca, escarpia; (*sharp projection or part*) punta, pico, púa; (bot) espiga || *tr* empernar; acabar, poner fin a
spill [spɪl] *s* derrame *m;* líquido derramado; (coll) caída, vuelco || *v* (*pret & pp* **spilled** o **spilt** [spɪlt]) *tr* derramar, verter; (coll) hacer caer, volcar || *intr* derramarse, verterse; (coll) caer, volcarse
spill'way' *s* bocacaz *m,* canal *m* de desagüe
spin [spɪn] *s* vuelta, giro muy rápido; (coll) paseo en coche, etc.; **to go into a spin** (aer) entrar en barrena || *v* (*pret & pp* **spun** [spʌn]; *ger* **spinning**) *tr* hacer girar; hilar (*p.ej., lino*); bailar (*un trompo*); **to spin out** extender, prolongar; **to spin yarns** contar cuentos increíbles || *intr* dar vueltas, girar; hilar; bailar (*un trompo*); (aer) entrar en barrena
spinach ['spɪnɪtʃ] o ['spɪnɪdʒ] *s* espinaca; (*leaves used as food*) espinacas
spinal ['spaɪnəl] *adj* espinal
spinal column *s* espina dorsal, columna vertebral
spinal cord *s* médula espinal
spindle ['spɪndəl] *s* (*rounded rod tapering toward each end*) huso; (*small shaft, axle*) eje *m;* (*turned ornament in a baluster*) mazorca
spine [spaɪn] *s* espina, púa; (*rib, ridge*) cordoncillo; loma, cerro; (anat) espina; (bb) lomo; (fig) ánimo, valor *m*
spineless ['spaɪnlɪs] *adj* sin espinas, sin espinazo; sin firmeza de carácter
spinet ['spɪnɪt] *s* espineta
spinner ['spɪnər] *s* hilandero; máquina de hilar
spinning ['spɪnɪŋ] *adj* hilador || *s* (*act*) hila; (*art*) hilandería
spinning wheel *s* torno de hilar
spinster ['spɪnstər] *s* solterona
spi·ral ['spaɪrəl] *adj & s* espiral *f* || *v* (*pret & pp* **-raled** o **-ralled;** *ger* **-raling** o **-ralling**) *intr* dar vueltas como una espiral; (aer) volar en espiral
spiral staircase *s* escalera de caracol
spire [spaɪr] *s* cima, ápice *m;* (*of a steeple*) aguja, chapitel *m;* (*e.g., of grass*) tallo
spirit ['spɪrɪt] *s* espíritu *m;* humor *m,* temple *m;* personaje *m;* licor *m* || *tr* — **to spirit away** llevarse misteriosamente
spirited ['spɪrɪtɪd] *adj* fogoso, espiritoso
spirit lamp *s* lámpara de alcohol
spiritless ['spɪrɪtlɪs] *adj* apocado, tímido, sin ánimo
spirit level *s* nivel *m* de burbuja
spiritual ['spɪrɪtʃu·əl] *adj* espiritual
spiritualism ['spɪrɪtʃuə,lɪzəm] *s* espiritismo; (*belief that all reality is spiritual*) espiritualismo
spirituous liquors ['spɪrɪtʃu·əs] *spl* licores espirituosos
spit [spɪt] *s* esputo, saliva; (*for roasting*) asador *m,* espetón *m;* punta o lengua de tierra; **the spit and image of** la segunda edición de, el retrato de || *v* (*pret & pp* **spat** [spæt] o **spit;** *ger* **spitting**) *tr* escupir || *intr* escupir; lloviznar; neviscar; fufar (*el gato*)
spite [spaɪt] *s* despecho, rencor *m,* inquina; **in spite of** a pesar de, a despecho de; **out of spite** por despecho || *tr* despechar, molestar, picar
spiteful ['spaɪtfəl] *adj* despechado, rencoroso
spit'fire' *s* fierabrás *m;* mujer *f* de mal genio
spittoon [spɪ'tun] *s* escupidera
splash [splæʃ] *s* rociada, salpicadura; (*e.g., with the hands*) chapaleo, chapoteo; **to make a splash** (coll) hacer impresión, llamar la atención || *tr & intr* salpicar; chapotear
splash'down' *s* acuatizaje *m*
spleen [splin] *s* mal humor *m;* (anat) bazo; **to vent one's spleen** descargar la bilis
splendid ['splɛndɪd] *adj* espléndido; (coll) magnífico, maravilloso
splendor ['splɛndər] *s* esplendor *m*
splice [splaɪs] *s* empalme *m,* junta || *tr* empalmar, juntar
splint [splɪnt] *s* (*splinter*) astilla, tablilla; (surg) tablilla || *tr* entablillar (*un hueso roto*)
splinter ['splɪntər] *s* astilla; (*of stone, glass, bone*) esquirla || *tr* astillar || *intr* astillarse, hacerse astillas
splinter group *s* grupo disidente
split [splɪt] *adj* hendido, partido; dividido || *s* división, fractura; (slang) porción || *v* (*pret & pp* **split;** *ger* **splitting**) *tr* dividir, partir; **to split one's sides with laughter** desternillarse de risa || *intr* dividirse a lo largo; **to split away (from)** separarse (de)
split fee *s* dicotomía (*entre médicos*)
split personality *s* personalidad desdoblada
splitting ['splɪtɪŋ] *adj* partidor; fuerte, violento; (*headache*) enloquecedor
splotch [splɑtʃ] *s* borrón *m,* mancha grande || *tr* salpicar, manchar
splurge [splʌrdʒ] *s* (coll) fachenda, ostentación || *intr* (coll) fachendear
splutter ['splʌtər] *s* chisporroteo; (*manner of speaking*) farfulla || *tr* farfullar || *intr* chisporrotear; farfullar
spoil [spɔɪl] *s* botín *m,* presa; **spoils** (*taken from an enemy*) botín, despojos; (*of political victory*) enchufes *mpl* || *v* (*pret & pp* **spoiled** o **spoilt** [spɔɪlt]) *tr* echar a perder, estropear; mimar (*a un niño*); amargar (*una tertulia*) || *intr* echarse a perder
spoiled [spɔɪld] *adj* (*child*) consentido, mimado; (*food*) pasado, podrido
spoils·man ['spɔɪlzmən] *s* (*pl* **-men** [mən]) enchufista *m*
spoils system *s* enchufismo
spoke [spok] *s* (*of a wheel*) radio, rayo; (*of a ladder*) escalón *m*

spokes•man ['spoksmən] *s* (*pl* **-men** [mən]) portavoz *m,* vocero
sponge [spʌndʒ] *s* esponja; **to throw in** (o **up**) **the sponge** (coll) tirar la esponja || *tr* limpiar con esponja; borrar; absorber || *intr* ser absorbente; **to sponge on** (coll) vivir a costa de
sponge cake *s* bizcocho muy ligero
sponger ['spʌndʒər] *s* esponja (*gorrón, parásito*)
sponge rubber *s* caucho esponjoso
spon•gy ['spʌndʒi] *adj* (*comp* **-gier;** *super* **-giest**) esponjoso
sponsor ['spɑnsər] *s* patrocinador *m;* (*godfather*) padrino; (*godmother*) madrina || *tr* patrocinar
sponsorship ['spɑnsər,ʃɪp] *s* patrocinio
spontaneous [spɑn'tenɪ•əs] *adj* espontáneo
spoof [spuf] *s* (slang) mistificación, engaño; (slang) broma || *tr* (slang) mistificar, engañar || *intr* (slang) bromear, burlar; (slang) parodiar
spook [spuk] *s* (coll) aparecido, espectro
spook•y ['spuki] *adj* (*comp* **-ier;** *super* **-iest**) (coll) espectral, espeluznante; (*horse*) (coll) asustadizo
spool [spul] *s* carrete *m,* bobina
spoon [spun] *s* cuchara || *tr* cucharear || *intr* (slang) besuquearse (*los enamorados*)
spoonful ['spun,fʊl] *s* cucharada
spoon•y ['spuni] *adj* (*comp* **-ier;** *super* **-iest**) (coll) baboso, sobón
sporadic(al) [spə'rædɪk(əl)] *adj* esporádico
spore [spor] *s* espora
sport [sport] *adj* deportivo, de deporte || *s* deporte *m;* deportista *mf;* (*person or thing controlled by some power or passion*) juguete *m;* (*laughingstock*) hazmerreír *m;* (*gambler*) (coll) tahur *m,* jugador *m;* (*in gambling or playing games*) (coll) buen perdedor; (*flashy fellow*) (coll) guapo, majo; (biol) mutación; **to make sport of** burlarse de, reírse de || *tr* (coll) lucir (*p.ej., un traje nuevo*) || *intr* divertirse; estar de burla; juguetear
sport clothes *spl* trajes *mpl* de sport
sport fan *s* (slang) aficionado al deporte, deportista *mf*
sporting chance *s* (coll) riesgo de buen perdedor
sporting goods *spl* artículos de deporte
sporting house *s* (coll) casa de juego; (coll) casa de rameras
sports'cast'er *s* locutor deportivo
sports•man ['sportsmən] *s* (*pl* **-men** [mən]) deportista *m;* jugador honrado
sports news *s* noticiario deportivo
sports'wear' *s* trajes deportivos
sports writer *s* cronista deportivo
sport•y ['sporti] *adj* (*comp* **-ier;** *super* **-iest**) (coll) elegante, guapo; (coll) alegre, brillante; (coll) magnánimo; (coll) disipado, libertino
spot [spɑt] *s* mancha; sitio, lugar *m;* (coll) poquito; **on the spot** allí mismo; al punto; (slang) en dificultad; (slang) en peligro de muerte; **to hit the spot** tener razón; (coll) dar completa satisfacción || *v* (*pret & pp* **spotted;** *ger* **spotting**) *tr* manchar; (coll) descubrir, reconocer || *intr* mancharse, tener manchas
spot cash *s* dinero contante
spotless ['spɑtlɪs] *adj* inmaculado, sin manchas
spot'light' *s* proyector *m* orientable; luz concentrada; (aut) faro piloto, faro giratorio; (fig) atención del público
spot remover [rɪ'muvər] *s* (*person*) quitamanchas *mf;* (*material*) quitamanchas *m*
spot welding *s* soldadura por puntos
spouse [spaʊz] o [spaʊs] *s* cónyuge *mf,* consorte *mf*
spout [spaʊt] *s* (*to carry off water from roof*) canalón *m;* (*of a jar, pitcher, etc.*) pico; (*of a sprinkling can*) rallo, roseta; (*jet*) chorro; **up the spout** (slang) acabado, arruinado || *tr* echar en chorro; (coll) declamar || *intr* chorrear; (coll) declamar
sprain [spren] *s* torcedura, esguince *m* || *tr* torcer, torcerse
sprawl [sprɔl] *intr* arrellanarse
spray [spre] *s* rociada; (*of the sea*) espuma; (*device*) pulverizador *m;* (*twig*) ramita || *tr & intr* rociar
sprayer ['spre•ər] *s* rociador *m,* pulverizador *m,* vaporizador *m*
spread [sprɛd] *s* extensión; amplitud, anchura; difusión; diferencia; cubrecama, sobrecama; mantel *m,* tapete *m;* (*of the wings of a bird; of the wings of an airplane*) envergadura; (coll) festín *m,* comilona || *v* (*pret & pp* **spread**) *tr* extender; difundir, propagar; esparcir; escalonar; abrir, separar; poner (*la mesa*) || *intr* extenderse; difundirse; esparcirse; abrirse, separarse
spree [spri] *s* juerga, parranda; borrachera; **to go on a spree** ir de juerga; pillar una mona
sprig [sprɪg] *s* ramita
spright•ly ['spraɪtli] *adj* (*comp* **-lier;** *super* **-liest**) alegre, animado, vivo
spring [sprɪŋ] *adj* primaveral; de manantial; de muelle, de resorte || *s* (*season of the year*) primavera; (*issue of water from earth*) fuente *f,* manantial *m;* (*elastic device*) muelle *m,* resorte *m;* (*of an automobile or wagon*) ballesta; (*leap, jump*) brinco, salto; abertura, grieta; tensión, tirantez *f* || *v* (*pret* **sprang** [spræŋ] o **sprung** [sprʌŋ]; *pp* **sprung**) *tr* soltar (*un muelle o resorte*); torcer, combar, encorvar; hacer saltar (*una trampa, una mina*) || *intr* saltar; saltar de golpe; brotar, nacer, proceder; torcerse, combarse, encorvarse; **to spring at** abalanzarse sobre; **to spring forth** precipitarse; brotar; **to spring up** levantarse de un salto; brotar, nacer; presentarse a la vista
spring'board' *s* trampolín *m*

spring chicken *s* polluelo; (*young person*) (coll) pollita
spring fever *s* (hum) ataque *m* primaveral, galbana
spring mattress *s* colchón *m* de muelles, somier *m*
spring'time' *s* primavera
sprinkle ['sprɪŋkəl] *s* rociada; llovizna; pizca || *tr* regar, rociar; salpicar, sembrar; espolvorear (*p.ej., azucar*) || *intr* rociar; lloviznar, gotear
sprinkling can *s* regadera, rociadera
sprint [sprɪnt] *s* (sport) embalaje *m* || *intr* (sport) embalarse, lanzarse
sprite [spraɪt] *s* duende *m*, trasgo
sprocket ['sprɑkɪt] *s* diente *m* de rueda de cadena; rueda de cadena
sprout [spraʊt] *s* brote *m*, renuevo, retoño || *intr* brotar, germinar, echar renuevos; crecer rápidamente
spruce [sprus] *adj* apuesto, elegante, garboso || *s* abeto del Norte, abeto falso, pícea || *tr* ataviar, componer || *intr* ataviarse, componerse; **to spruce up** emperifollarse
spry [spraɪ] *adj* (*comp* **spryer** o **sprier;** *super* **spryest** o **spriest**) activo, ágil
spud [spʌd] *s* (*chisel*) escoplo; (agr) escoda; (coll) patata
spun glass [spʌn] *s* vidrio hilado, cristal hilado
spunk [spʌŋk] *s* (coll) ánimo, coraje *m*, corazón *m*, valor *m*
spun silk *s* seda cardada o hilada
spur [spʌr] *s* espuela; (*central point of an auger*) gusanillo; (*of a cock, mountain, warship*) espolón *m;* (rr) ramal corto; (*goad, stimulus*) (fig) espuela; **on the spur of the moment** impulsivamente, sin la reflexión debida || *v* (*pret & pp* **spurred;** *ger* **spurring**) *tr* espolear; **to spur on** espolear, aguijonear
spurious ['spjurɪ·əs] *adj* espurio
spurn [spʌrn] desdén *m*, menosprecio || *tr* desdeñar, menospreciar; rechazar con desdén
spurt [spʌrt] *s* chorro repentino; esfuerzo repentino; arranque *m* || *intr* salir en chorro, salir a borbotones
sputter ['spʌtər] *s* (*manner of speaking*) farfulla; (*sizzling*) chisporroteo || *tr* farfullar || *intr* farfullar; chisporrotear
spy [spaɪ] *s* (*pl* **spies**) espía *mf* || *v* (*pret & pp* **spied**) *tr* columbrar, divisar || *intr* espiar; **to spy on** espiar
spy'glass' *s* catalejo, anteojo
sq. *abbr* **square**
squabble ['skwɑbəl] *s* reyerta, riña || *intr* reñir, disputar
squad [skwɑd] *s* escuadra
squadron ['skwɑdrən] *s* (aer) escuadrilla; (*of cavalry*) (mil) escuadrón *m;* (nav) escuadra
squalid ['skwɑlɪd] *adj* escuálido
squall [skwɔl] *s* grupada, turbión *m;* (*quarrel*) (coll) riña; (*upset, commotion*) (coll) chubasco
squalor ['skwɑlər] *s* escualidez *f*
squander ['skwɑndər] *tr* despilfarrar, malgastar
square [skwɛr] *adj* cuadrado, p.ej., **eight square inches** ocho pulgadas cuadradas; en cuadro, de lado, p.ej., **eight inches square** ocho pulgadas en cuadro, ocho pulgadas de lado; rectangular; justo, recto; honrado, leal; saldado; fuerte, sólido; (coll) abundante, completo; **to get square with** (coll) hacérselas pagar a || *adv* en cuadro; en ángulo recto; honradamente, lealmente || *s* cuadrado; (*of checkerboard or chessboard*) casilla, escaque *m;* (*city block*) manzana; (*open area in town or city*) plaza; (*carpenter's tool*) escuadra; **to be on the square** (coll) obrar de buena fe || *tr* cuadrar; dividir en cuadros; ajustar, nivelar, conformar; saldar (*una cuenta*); (carp) escuadrar || *intr* cuadrarse; **to square off** (coll) colocarse en posición de defensa
square dance *s* danza de figuras
square deal *s* (coll) trato equitativo
square meal *s* (coll) comida abundante
square shooter ['ʃutər] *s* (coll) persona leal y honrada
squash [skwɑʃ] *s* aplastamiento; (bot) calabaza; (sport) frontón *m* con raqueta; || *tr* aplastar, despachurrar; confutar (*un argumento*); acallar con un argumento, respuesta, etc. || *intr* aplastarse
squash·y ['skwɑʃi] *adj* (*comp* **-ier;** *super* **-iest**) mojado y blando; (*muddy*) lodoso; (*fruit*) modorro
squat [skwɑt] *adj* en cuclillas; rechoncho || *v* (*pret & pp* **squatted;** *ger* **squatting**) *intr* acuclillarse, agacharse; sentarse en el suelo; establecerse en terreno ajeno sin derecho; establecerse en terreno público para crear un derecho
squatter ['skwɑtər] *s* advenedizo, intruso, colono usurpador
squaw [skwɔ] *s* india norteamericana; mujer, esposa, muchacha
squawk [skwɔk] *s* graznido; (slang) queja chillona || *intr* graznar; (slang) quejarse chillando
squaw man *s* blanco casado con india
squeak [skwik] *s* chillido; chirrido || *intr* dar chillidos; chirriar
squeal [skwil] *s* chillido || *intr* dar chillidos; (slang) delatar, soplar; **to squeal on** (slang) delatar, soplar (*a una persona*)
squealer ['skwilər] *s* (coll) soplón *m*
squeamish ['skwimɪʃ] *adj* escrupuloso, remilgado; excesivamente modesto; (*easily nauseated*) asqueroso
squeeze [skwiz] *s* apretón *m;* **to put the squeeze on someone** (coll) hacer a uno la forzosa, meter en prensa a uno || *tr* apretar; agobiar, oprimir; exprimir || *intr* apretar; **to squeeze through** abrirse paso a estrujones por entre; salir de un aprieto a duras penas
squeezer ['skwizər] *s* exprimidera
squelch [skwɛltʃ] *s* (coll) tapaboca || *tr* apabullar, despachurrar
squid [skwɪd] *s* calamar *m*

squint [skwɪnt] *s* mirada bizca; mirada furtiva; (*strabismus*) bizquera || *tr* achicar, entornar (*los ojos*) || *intr* bizquear; torcer la vista; tener los ojos medio cerrados

squint-eyed [ˈskwɪnt,aɪd] *adj* bisojo, bizco; malévolo, sospechoso

squire [skwaɪr] *s* acompañante *m* (*de una señora*); (Brit) terrateniente *m* de antigua heredad; (U.S.A.) juez *m* de paz, juez local || *tr* acompañar (*a una señora*)

squirm [skwʌrm] *s* retorcimiento || *intr* retorcerse; **to squirm out of** escaparse de (*p.ej., un aprieto*) haciendo mucho esfuerzo

squirrel [ˈskwʌrəl] *s* ardilla

squirt [skwʌrt] *s* chorro; jeringazo; (coll) mono, presuntuoso || *tr* arrojar a chorros || *intr* salir a chorros

Sr. *abbr* **senior, Sir**

S.S. *abbr* **Secretary of State, steamship, Sunday school**

St. *abbr* **Saint, Strait, Street**

stab [stæb] *s* puñalada; (coll) tentativa; **to make a stab at** (slang) esforzarse por hacer || *v* (*pret & pp* **stabbed;** *ger* **stabbing**) *tr* apuñalar; traspasar || *intr* apuñalar

stab in the back *s* puñalada trapera

stable [ˈstebəl] *adj* estable || *s* establo, cuadra, caballeriza

stack [stæk] *s* montón *m,* pila; (*of rifles*) pabellón *m;* (*of books in a library*) estantería, depósito; (*of a chimney*) cañón *m;* (*of straw*) niara; (*of firewood*) hacina; (coll) montón *m,* gran número || *tr* amontonar, apilar; florear (*el naipe*); hacinar (*leña*)

stadi·um [ˈstedɪ·əm] *s* (*pl* **-ums** o **-a** [ə]) estadio

staff [stæf] o [stɑf] *s* bastón *m,* apoyo, sostén *m;* personal *m;* (mil) estado mayor; (mus) pentagrama *m* || *tr* dotar, proveer de personal, nombrar personal para

stag [stæg] *adj* exclusivo para hombres, de hombres solos || *s* (*male deer*) ciervo; varón *m;* varón solo (*no acompañado de mujeres*)

stage [stedʒ] *s* escena; etapa, jornada; (*coach*) diligencia; (*scene of an event*) teatro; (*of a microscope*) portaobjeto; (rad) etapa; **by easy stages** a pequeñas etapas; lentamente; **to go on the stage** hacerse actor || *tr* poner en escena, representar; preparar, organizar

stage'coach' *s* diligencia

stage'craft' *s* arte *f* teatral

stage door *s* (theat) entrada de los artistas

stage fright *s* trac *m,* miedo al público

stage'hand' *s* tramoyista *m,* metemuertos *m,* metesillas *m*

stage manager *s* director *m* de escena

stage'-struck' *adj* loco por el teatro

stage whisper *s* susurro en voz alta

stagger [ˈstægər] *tr* sorprender; asustar; escalonar (*las horas de trabajo*) || *intr* tambalear, hacer eses al andar

staggering *adj* tambaleante; sorprendente

stagnant [ˈstægnənt] *adj* estancado; (fig) estancado, inactivo, paralizado

staid [sted] *adj* grave, serio, formal

stain [sten] *s* mancha; tinte *m,* tintura; materia colorante || *tr* manchar; teñir; colorar || *intr* mancharse; hacer manchas

stained glass *s* vidrio de color

stained'glass' window *s* vidriera de colores, vidriera pintada, vitral *m*

stainless [ˈstenlɪs] *adj* inmanchable; (*steel*) inoxidable; inmaculado

stair [stɛr] *s* escalera; (*step of a series*) escalón *m;* **stairs** escalera

stair'case' *s* escalera

stair'way' *s* escalera

stair well *s* hueco de escalera

stake [stek] *s* estaca; (*of a cart or truck*) telero; (*to hold up a plant*) rodrigón *m;* (*in gambling*) puesta; premio del vencedor; **at stake** en juego; en gran peligro; **to die at the stake** morir en la hoguera; **to pull up stakes** (coll) irse; (coll) mudarse de casa || *tr* estacar; atar a una estaca; rodrigar (*plantas*); apostar; arriesgar, aventurar; **to stake all** jugarse el todo por el todo; **to stake off** o **to stake out** estacar, señalar con estacas

stale [stel] *adj* añejo, rancio, viejo; (*air*) viciado; (*joke*) mohoso; anticuado

stale'mate' *s* mate ahogado; **to reach a stalemate** llegar a un punto muerto || *tr* dar mate ahogado a; estancar, paralizar

stalk [stɔk] *s* tallo || *tr* cazar al acecho; acechar, espiar || *intr* cazar al acecho; andar con paso majestuoso; andar con paso altivo; **to stalk out** salir con paso airado

stall [stɔl] *s* cuadra, establo; pesebre *m;* (*booth in a market*) puesto; (*at a fair*) caseta; (Brit) butaca; (slang) pretexto || *tr* encerrar en un establo; poner trabas a; parar (*un motor*); **to stall off** (coll) eludir, evitar || *intr* atascarse, atollarse; pararse (*un motor*); (slang) eludir para engañar o demorar; **to stall for time** (slang) tardar para ganar tiempo

stallion [ˈstæljən] *s* caballo padre, caballo semental

stalwart [ˈstɔlwərt] *adj* fornido, forzudo; valiente; leal, constante || *s* persona fornida; partidario leal

stamen [ˈstemən] *s* estambre *m*

stamina [ˈstæmɪnə] *s* fuerza, nervio, vigor *m,* resistencia

stammer [ˈstæmər] *s* balbuceo, tartamudeo || *tr* balbucear (*p.ej., excusas*) || *intr* balbucear, tartamudear

stamp [stæmp] *s* (*device used for making an impression; mark made with it; piece of paper or mark used to show payment of postage*) sello; (*tool used for crushing or marking*) pisón *m;* (*tool for stamping coins and medals*) cuño, troquel *m;* marca, impresión; clase *f,* tipo || *tr* sellar; troquelar; estampar, imprimir; hollar,

pisotear; indicar, señalar; poner el sello a; bocartear (*el mineral*); **to stamp out** apagar pateando; extinguir por la fuerza; suprimir; **to stamp the feet** dar patadas || *intr* patalear
stampede [stæm'pid] *s* fuga precipitada; estampida (Am) || *tr* hacer huir en desorden; provocar a pánico || *intr* huir en tropel; obrar por común impulso
stamping grounds *spl* (slang) guarida (*sitio frecuentado por una persona*)
stamp pad *s* tampón *m*
stamp'-vend'ing machine *s* máquina expendedora de sellos
stance [stæns] *s* (sport) postura, planta
stanch [stɑntʃ] *adj* firme, fuerte; constante, leal; (*watertight*) estanco || *tr* estancar; restañar (*la sangre de una herida*)
stand [stænd] *s* parada; alto para defenderse; postura, posición; resistencia; estrado, tribuna; sostén *m*, soporte *m*, pie *m;* puesto, quiosco || *v* (*pret & pp* **stood** [stʊd]) *tr* poner, colocar; poner derecho; soportar, tolerar, resistir; (coll) aguantar (*a una persona*); (coll) sufragar (*un gasto*); **to stand off** tener a raya; **to stand one's ground** mantenerse firme || *intr* estar, estar situado; estar parado; estacionarse; estar de pie, estar derecho; ponerse de pie, levantarse; resultar; persistir; mantenerse; **to stand aloof, apart** o **aside** mantenerse apartado; **to stand back of** respaldar; **to stand for** significar, representar; apoyar, defender; apadrinar; mantener (*p.ej., una opinión*); presentarse como candidato de; navegar hacia; (coll) tolerar; **to stand in line** hacer cola; **to stand out** sobresalir; destacarse, resaltar; **to stand up** ponerse de pie, levantarse; durar; **to stand up to** hacer resueltamente frente a
standard ['stændərd] *adj* normal; (*typewriter keyboard*) universal; corriente, regular; legal; clásico || *s* patrón *m;* norma, regla establecida; bandera, estandarte *m;* emblema *m*, símbolo; soporte *m*, pilar *m*
standardize ['stændər,daɪz] *tr* normalizar, estandardizar
standard of living *s* nivel *m* de vida
standard time *s* hora legal, hora oficial
standee [stæn'di] *s* (coll) espectador *m* que asiste de pie; (coll) pasajero de pie
stand'-in' *s* (theat & mov) doble *mf;* (coll) buenas aldabas
standing ['stændɪŋ] *adj* derecho, en pie; de pie; parado, inmóvil; (*water*) encharcado, estancado; (*army; committee*) permanente; vigente || *s* condición, posición; reputación; parada; **in good standing** en posición acreditada; **of long standing** de mucho tiempo, de antigua fecha
standing army *s* ejército permanente
standing room *s* sitio para estar de pie
stand'point' *s* punto de vista
stand'still' *s* detención, parada; alto; descanso, inactividad; **to come to a standstill** cesar, pararse
stanza ['stænzə] *s* estancia, estrofa
staple ['stepəl] *adj* primero, principal; corriente, establecido || *s* (*to fasten papers*) grapa; artículo o producto de primera necesidad; materia prima; fibra textil || *tr* sujetar con grapas
stapler ['steplər] *s* engrapador *m*, cosepapeles *m*
star [stɑr] *s* (*heavenly body*) astro; (*heavenly body except sun and moon; figure that represents a star*) estrella; (mov & theat) estrella; (*of football*) as *m;* (typ) estrella o asterisco; (*fate, destiny*) (fig) estrella; **to see stars** (coll) ver las estrellas; **to thank one's lucky stars** estar agradecido por su buena suerte || *v* (*pret & pp* **starred;** *ger* **starring**) *tr* estrellar, adornar o señalar con estrellas; marcar con asterisco; presentar como estrella (*a un actor*) || *intr* ser la estrella; lucirse; sobresalir
starboard ['stɑrbərd] o ['stɑr,bord] *adj* de estribor || *adv* a estribor || *s* estribor *m*
starch [stɑrtʃ] *s* almidón *m*, fécula; arrogancia, entono; (slang) fuerza, vigor *m* || *tr* almidonar
stare [stɛr] *s* mirada fija || *intr* mirar fijamente; **to stare at** clavar la vista en, mirar con fijeza
star'fish' *s* estrella de mar, estrellamar *m*
star'gaze' *intr* mirar las estrellas; ser distraído, soñar despierto
stark [stɑrk] *adj* cabal, completo, puro; rígido, tieso; duro, severo || *adv* completamente, enteramente; rígidamente, severamente
stark'-na'ked *adj* en pelota, en cueros
star'light' *s* luz *f* de las estrellas
starling ['stɑrlɪŋ] *s* estornino
Star'-Span'gled Banner *s* bandera estrellada (*bandera de los EE.UU.*)
start [stɑrt] *s* comienzo, principio; salida, partida; lugar *m* de partida; (*scare*) sobresalto; (*sudden start*) arranque *m;* (*advantage*) ventaja || *tr* empezar, principiar; poner en marcha; hacer arrancar; dar la señal de partida a; entablar (*una conversación*); levantar (*la caza*) || *intr* empezar, principiar; ponerse en marcha; arrancar; (*to be startled*) sobresaltar; nacer, provenir; **starting from** o **with** a partir de; **to start after** salir en busca de
starter ['stɑrtər] *s* iniciador *m;* (*of a series*) primero; (aut) arranque *m*, motor *m* de arranque; (sport) juez *m* de salida
starting ['stɑrtɪŋ] *adj* de salida; de arranque || *s* puesta en marcha
starting crank *s* manivela de arranque
starting point *s* punto de partida, arrancadero
startle ['stɑrtəl] *tr* asustar, sorprender, sobrecoger || *intr* asustarse, sorprenderse, sobrecogerse
startling ['stɑrtlɪŋ] *adj* alarmante, asombroso

starvation [stɑr'veʃən] *s* hambre *f,* inanición
starvation diet *s* régimen *m* de hambre, cura de hambre
starvation wages *spl* salario de hambre
starve [stɑrv] *tr* hambrear; hacer morir de hambre; **to starve out** hacer rendirse por hambre || *intr* hambrear; morir de hambre; (coll) tener hambre
starving ['stɑrvɪŋ] *adj* hambriento, famélico
stat. *abbr* **statuary, statute, statue**
state [stet] *adj* de estado; del estado; estatal; público; de gala, de lujo || *s* estado; fausto, ceremonia, pompa; **to lie in state** estar expuesto en capilla ardiente, estar de cuerpo presente; **to live in state** gastar mucho lujo; **to ride in state** pasear en carruaje de lujo || *tr* afirmar, declarar; exponer, manifestar; plantear (*un problema*)
state•ly ['stetli] *adj* (*comp* **-lier;** *super* **-liest**) imponente, majestuoso
statement ['stetmənt] *s* declaración; exposición, informe *m,* relación; (com) estado de cuentas
state of mind *s* estado de ánimo
state'room' *s* camarote *m;* (rr) compartimiento particular
states•man ['stetsmən] *s* (*pl* **-men** [mən]) estadista *m,* hombre *m* de estado
static ['stætɪk] *adj* estático; (rad) atmosférico || *s* (rad) parásitos atmosféricos
station ['steʃən] *s* estación; condición, situación || *tr* estacionar, apostar
station agent *s* jefe *m* de estación
stationary ['steʃən,ɛri] *adj* estacionario
station break *s* (rad) descanso, intermedio
stationer ['steʃənər] *s* papelero
stationery ['steʃən,ɛri] *s* efectos de escritorio; papel *m* para cartas
stationery store *s* papelería
station house *s* cuartelillo de policía
station identification *s* (rad & telv) indicativo de la emisora
sta'tion•mas'ter *s* jefe *m* de estación
station wagon *s* rubia, coche *m* rural, vagoneta
statistical [stə'tɪstɪkəl] *adj* estadístico
statistician [,stætɪs'tɪʃən] *s* estadístico
statistics [stə'tɪstɪks] *ssg* (*science*) estadística; *spl* (*data*) estadística o estadísticas
statue ['stætʃʊ] *s* estatua
statuesque [,stætʃʊ'ɛsk] *adj* escultural
stature ['stætʃər] *s* estatura, talla; carácter *m,* habilidad
status ['stetəs] *s* condición, estado; situación social, legal o profesional; (*prestige or superior rank*) categoría
status seeking *s* esfuerzo por adquirir categoría
status symbol *s* símbolo de categoría social
statute ['stætʃʊt] *s* estatuto, ley *f*
statutory ['stætʃʊ,tori] *adj* estatutario, legal
staunch [stɔntʃ] o [stɑntʃ] *adj & tr* var de **stanch**
stave [stev] *s* (*of a barrel*) duela; (*of a ladder*) peldaño; (mus) pentagrama *m* || *v* (*pret & pp* **staved** o **stove** [stov]) *tr* romper, destrozar; (*to break a hole in*) desfondar; **to stave off** mantener a distancia; evitar, impedir, diferir
stay [ste] *s* morada, permanencia, estancia; suspensión; (*of a corset*) ballena, varilla; apoyo, sostén *m;* (law) espera; (naut) estay *m* || *tr* aplazar, detener; poner freno a || *intr* quedar, quedarse, permanecer; parar, hospedarse; habitar; **to stay up** no acostarse, velar
stay'-at-home' *adj & s* hogareño
stead [stɛd] *s* lugar *m;* **in his stead** en su lugar, en lugar de él; **to stand in good stead** ser de provecho, ser ventajoso
stead'fast' *adj* fijo; resuelto; constante
stead•y ['stɛdi] *adj* (*comp* **-ier;** *super* **-iest**) constante, fijo, firme, seguro; regular, uniforme; resuelto; asentado, serio || *v* (*pret & pp* **-ied**) *tr* estabilizar, reforzar; calmar (*los nervios*) || *intr* estabilizarse; calmarse
steak [stek] *s* lonja, tajada; biftec *m*
steal [stil] *s* (coll) hurto, robo || *v* (*pret* **stole** [stol]; *pp* **stolen**) *tr* hurtar, robar; atraer, cautivar || *intr* hurtar, robar; **to steal away** escabullirse; **to steal into** meterse a hurtadillas en; **to steal upon** aproximarse sin ruido a
stealth [stɛlθ] *s* cautela, recato; **by stealth** a hurtadillas
steam [stim] *adj* de vapor || *s* vapor *m;* vaho, humo; **to get up steam** dar presión; **to let off steam** descargar vapor; (fig) desahogarse || *tr* cocer al vapor; saturar de vapor; empañar (*p.ej., las ventanas*) || *intr* echar vapor, emitir vapor; evaporarse; funcionar o marchar a vapor; **to steam ahead** avanzar por medio del vapor; (fig) hacer grandes progresos
steam'boat' *s* buque *m* de vapor
steamer ['stimər] *s* vapor *m*
steamer rug *s* manta de viaje
steamer trunk *s* baúl *m* de camarote
steam heat *s* calefacción por vapor
steam roller *s* apisonadora movida a vapor; (coll) fuerza arrolladora
steam'ship' *s* vapor *m,* buque *m* de vapor
steam shovel *s* pala mecánica de vapor
steam table *s* plancha caliente
steed [stid] *s* caballo; (*high-spirited horse*) corcel *m*
steel [stil] *adj* acerado; (*business, industry*) siderúrgico; (fig) duro, frío || *s* acero; (*for striking fire from flint; for sharpening knives*) eslabón *m* || *tr* acerar; **to steel oneself** acerarse
steel wool *s* virutillas de acero, estopa de acero
steelyard ['stil,jɑrd] o ['stiljərd] *s* romana
steep [stip] *adj* escarpado, empinado;

(*price*) alto, excesivo || *tr* empapar, remojar; **steeped in** absorbido en
steeple ['stipəl] *s* aguja, campanario
stee'ple•chase' *s* carrera de campanario, carrera de obstáculos
stee'ple•jack' *s* escalatorres *m*
steer [stɪr] *s* buey *m* || *tr* conducir, gobernar, guiar || *intr* conducirse; **to steer clear of** (coll) evitar, eludir
steerage ['stɪrɪdʒ] *s* dirección; (naut) proa, entrepuente *m*
steerage passenger *s* (naut) pasajero de entrepuente
steering wheel *s* (aut) volante *m;* (naut) rueda del timón
stem [stɛm] *s* (*of a goblet*) pie *m;* (*of a pipe, of a feather*) cañón *m;* (*of a column*) fuste *m;* (*of a watch*) botón *m;* (*of a key*) espiga, tija; (*of a word*) tema *m;* (bot) tallo, vástago; **from stem to stern** de proa a popa || *v* (*pret & pp* **stemmed;** *ger* **stemming**) *tr* (*to remove the stem from*) desgranar; (*to check*) detener, refrenar; (*to plug*) estancar; hacer frente a; rendir (*la marea*) || *intr* nacer, provenir; **to stem from** originarse en, provenir de
stem'-wind'er *s* remontuar *m*
stench [stɛntʃ] *s* hedor *m,* hediondez *f*
sten•cil ['stɛnsəl] *s* cartón picado; (*work produced by it*) estarcido || *v* (*pret & pp* **-ciled** o **-cilled;** *ger* **-ciling** o **-cilling**) *tr* estarcir
stenographer [stə'nɑgrəfər] *s* estenógrafo
stenography [stə'nɑgrəfi] *s* estenografía
step [stɛp] *s* paso; (*of staircase*) grada, peldaño; (*footprint*) huella, pisada; (*of carriage*) estribo; (*measure, démarche*) gestión, medida; (mus) intervalo; **step by step** paso a paso; **to watch one's step** proceder con cautela, andarse con tiento || *v* (*pret & pp* **stepped;** *ger* **stepping**) *tr* escalonar; **to step off** medir a pasos || *intr* dar un paso, dar pasos; caminar, ir; (coll) andar de prisa; **to step on it** (coll) acelerar la marcha, darse prisa; **to step on the starter** pisar el arranque
step'broth'er *s* medio hermano, hermanastro
step'child' *s* (*pl* **-children** [,tʃɪldrən]) hijastro
step'daugh'ter *s* hijastra
step'fa'ther *s* padrastro
step'lad'der *s* escala, escalera de tijera
step'moth'er *s* madrastra
steppe [stɛp] *s* estepa
stepping stone *s* estriberón *m,* pasadera; (fig) escalón *m,* escabel *m*
step'sis'ter *s* media hermana, hermanastra
step'son' *s* hijastro
stere•o ['stɛrɪ,o] o ['stɪrɪ,o] *adj* (coll) estereofónico; (coll) estereoscópico || *s* (*pl* **-os**) (coll) música estereofónica, disco estereofónico; (coll) radiodifusión estereofónica; (coll) fotografía estereoscópica
stereotyped ['stɛrɪ·ə,taɪpt] o ['stɪrɪ·ə,taɪpt] *adj* estereotipado
sterile ['stɛrɪl] *adj* estéril
sterilize ['stɛrɪ,laɪz] *tr* esterilizar
sterling ['stʌrlɪŋ] *adj* fino, de ley; verdadero, genuino, puro, excelente || *s* libras esterlinas; plata de ley; vajilla de plata
stern [stʌrn] *adj* austero, severo; decidido, firme || *s* popa
stethoscope ['stɛθə,skop] *s* estetoscopio
stevedore ['stivə,dor] *s* estibador *m*
stew [stju] o [stu] *s* guisado, estofado || *tr* guisar, estofar || *intr* abrasarse; (coll) estar apurado
steward ['stju·ərd] o ['stu·ərd] *s* mayordomo; administrador *m;* (*of ship or plane*) camarero
stewardess ['stju·ərdɪs] o ['stu·ərdɪs] *s* mayordoma; (*of ship or plane*) camarera; (*of plane*) azafata, aeromoza
stewed fruit *s* compota de frutas
stewed tomatoes *spl* puré *m* de tomates
stick [stɪk] *s* palo, palillo; bastón *m,* vara; (*of dynamite*) barra; (naut) mástil *m,* verga; (typ) componedor *m* || *v* (*pret & pp* **stuck** [stʌk]) *tr* picar, punzar; apuñalar; clavar, hincar; pegar; (coll) confundir; **to stick out** asomar (*la cabeza*); sacar (*la lengua*); **to stick up** (*in order to rob*) (slang) asaltar, atracar || *intr* estar prendido, estar hincado; pegarse; agarrarse (*la pintura*); encastillarse (*p.ej., una ventana*); resaltar, sobresalir; continuar, persistir; permanecer; atascarse; **to stick out** salir (*p.ej., el pañuelo del bolsillo*); sobresalir, proyectarse; velar (*un escollo*); resultar evidente; **to stick together** (coll) quedarse unidos, no abandonarse; **to stick up** destacarse; estar de punta (*el pelo*); **to stick up for** (coll) defender
sticker ['stɪkər] *s* etiqueta engomada, marbete engomado; punta, espina; (coll) problema arduo
sticking plaster *s* esparadrapo
stick'pin' *s* alfiler *m* de corbata
stick'-up' *s* (slang) asalto, atraco
stick•y ['stɪki] *adj* (*comp* **-ier;** *super* **-iest**) pegajoso; (coll) húmedo, mojado; (*weather*) bochornoso
stiff [stɪf] *adj* tieso; entorpecido, entumecido; arduo, difícil; (*price*) (coll) excesivo || *s* (slang) cadáver *m*
stiff collar *s* cuello almidonado
stiffen ['stɪfən] *tr* atiesar; endurecer; espesar || *intr* atiesarse; endurecerse; espesarse; obstinarse
stiff neck *s* torticolis *m;* obstinación
stiff-necked ['stɪf,nɛkt] *adj* terco, obstinado
stiff shirt *s* camisola
stifle ['staɪfəl] *tr* ahogar, sofocar; apagar, suprimir
stig•ma ['stɪgmə] *s* (*pl* **-mas** o **-mata** [mətə]) estigma *m*
stigmatize ['stɪgmə,taɪz] *tr* estigmatizar
stilet•to [stɪ'lɛto] *s* (*pl* **-tos**) estilete *m,* puñal *m*
still [stɪl] *adj* inmóvil, quieto, tran-

quilo; callado, silencioso; (*wine*) no espumoso || *adv* tranquilamente; silenciosamente; aún, todavía || *conj* con todo, sin embargo || *s* alambique *m*, destiladera; destilería; fotografía de lo inmóvil; (poet) silencio || *tr* acallar; amortiguar; calmar || *intr* callar; calmarse

still'birth' *s* parto muerto

still'born' *adj* nacido muerto

still life *s* (*pl* **still lifes** o **still lives**) bodegón *m*, naturaleza muerta

stilt [stɪlt] *s* zanco; (*in the water*) pilote *m*

stilted ['stɪltɪd] *adj* elevado; hinchado, pomposo, tieso

stimulant ['stɪmjələnt] *adj & s* estimulante *m*, excitante *m*

stimulate ['stɪmjə,let] *tr* estimular

stimu·lus ['stɪmjələs] *s* (*pl* **-li** [,laɪ]) estímulo

sting [stɪŋ] *s* picadura; aguijón *m* || *v* (*pret & pp* **stung** [stʌŋ]) *tr* picar; aguijonear || *intr* picar

stin·gy ['stɪndʒi] *adj* (*comp* **-gier**; *super* **-giest**) mezquino, tacaño

stink [stiŋk] *s* hedor *m*, mal olor *m* || *v* (*pret* **stank** [stæŋk] o **stunk** [stʌŋk]; *pp* **stunk**) *tr* dar mal olor a || *intr* heder, oler muy mal; **to stink of** heder a; (slang) poseer (*p.ej.*, *dinero*) en un grado que da asco

stint [stɪnt] *s* faena, tarea || *tr* limitar, restringir || *intr* ser económico, ahorrar con mezquindad

stipend ['staɪpənd] *s* estipendio

stipulate ['stɪpjə,let] *tr* estipular

stir [stʌr] *s* agitación, meneo; alboroto, tumulto; **to create a stir** meter ruido || *v* (*pret & pp* **stirred**; *ger* **stirring**) *tr* agitar, mover; revolver; conmover, excitar; atizar, avivar (*el fuego*); remover (*un líquido*); **to stir up** revolver; despertar; conmover; fomentar (*discordias*) || *intr* bullirse, moverse

stirring ['stʌrɪŋ] *adj* conmovedor, emocionante

stirrup ['stʌrəp] o ['stɪrəp] *s* estribo

stitch [stɪtʃ] *s* puntada, punto; pedazo de tela; punzada, dolor *m* punzante; (coll) poquito; **to be in stitches** (coll) desternillarse de risa || *tr* coser, bastear, hilvanar || *intr* coser

stock [stɑk] *adj* común, regular; banal, vulgar; bursátil; ganadero, del ganado; (theat) de repertorio || *s* surtido; capital *f* comercial; acciones, valores *mpl*; (*of meat*) caldo; (*of a tree*) tronco; (*of an anvil*) cepo; (*of a rifle*) caja, culata; (*of a tree; of a family*) cepa; mango, manija; palo, madero; leño; (*livestock*) ganado; (theat) programa *m*, repertorio; **in stock** en existencia; **out of stock** agotado; **to take stock** hacer el inventario; **to take stock in** (coll) dar importancia a, confiar en || *tr* abastecer, surtir; tener existencias de; acopiar, acumular; poblar (*un estanque, una colmena, etc.*)

stockade [stɑ'ked] *s* estacada, empalizada || *tr* empalizar

stock'breed'er *s* criador *m* de ganado

stock'bro'ker *s* bolsista *mf*, corredor *m* de bolsa

stock car *s* (aut) coche *m* de serie; (rr) vagón *m* para el ganado

stock company *s* (com) sociedad anónima; (theat) teatro de repertorio

stock dividend *s* acción liberada

stock exchange *s* bolsa

stock'hold'er *s* accionista *mf*, tenedor *m* de acciones

stockholder of record *s* accionista *mf* que como tal figura en el libro-registro de la compañía

Stockholm ['stɑkhom] *s* Estocolmo

stocking ['stɑkɪŋ] *s* media

stock market *s* bolsa, mercado de valores; **to play the stock market** jugar a la bolsa

stock'pile' *s* reserva de materias primas || *tr* acumular (*materias primas*) || *intr* acumular materias primas

stock raising *s* ganadería

stock'room' *s* almacén *m*; sala de exposición

stock split *s* reparto de acciones gratis

stock·y ['stɑki] *adj* (*comp* **-ier**; *super* **-iest**) bajo, grueso y fornido

stock'yard' *s* corral *m* de concentración de ganado

stoic ['sto·ɪk] *adj & s* estoico

stoke [stok] *tr* atizar, avivar (*el fuego*); alimentar, cebar (*el horno*)

stoker ['stokər] *s* fogonero

stolid ['stɑlɪd] *adj* impasible, insensible

stomach ['stʌmək] *s* estómago; apetito; deseo, inclinación || *tr* tragar; **to not be able to stomach** (coll) no poder tragar

stone [ston] *s* piedra; (*of fruit*) hueso; (pathol) mal *m* de piedra || *tr* lapidar, apedrear; deshuesar (*la fruta*)

stone'-broke' *adj* arrancado, sin blanca

stone'-deaf' *adj* sordo como una tapia

stone'ma'son *s* albañil *m*

stone quarry *s* cantera, pedrera

stone's throw *s* tiro de piedra; **within a stone's throw** a tiro de piedra

ston·y ['stoni] *adj* (*comp* **-ier**; *super* **-iest**) pedregoso; duro, empedernido

stool [stul] *s* escabel *m*, taburete *m*; sillico, retrete *m*; (*bowel movement*) cámara, evacuación

stoop [stup] *s* encorvada, inclinación; escalinata de entrada || *intr* doblarse, inclinarse, encorvarse; andar encorvado; humillarse, rebajarse

stoop-shouldered ['stup'ʃoldərd] *adj* cargado de espaldas

stop [stɑp] *s* parada, alto; estada, estancia; cesación, fin *m*, suspensión; cerradura, tapadura; impedimento, obstáculo; freno; tope *m*, retén *m*; (*in writing; in telegrams*) punto; (*of a guitar*) llave *f*, traste *m*; **to put a stop to** poner fin a || *v* (*pret & pp* **stopped**; *ger* **stopping**) *tr* parar, detener; acabar, terminar; estorbar, obstruir; interceptar; suspender; cerrar, tapar; rechazar (*un golpe*); retener (*un sueldo o parte de él*); **to stop up** cegar, obstruir, tapar || *intr*

parar, pararse, detenerse; quedarse, permanecer; alojarse, hospedarse; acabarse, terminarse; **to stop + ger** cesar de + *inf*, dejar de + *inf*
stop'cock' *s* llave *f* de cierre, llave de paso
stop'gap' *adj* provisional || *s* substituto provisional
stop light *s* luz *f* de parada
stop'o'ver *s* parada intermedia, escala; billete *m* de parada intermedia
stoppage ['stɑpɪdʒ] *s* parada, detención; (*of work*) paro; interrupción; suspensión; obstáculo; (*of wages*) retención; (pathol) obstrucción
stopper ['stɑpər] *s* tapón *m;* taco, tarugo
stop sign o **stop signal** *s* señal *f* de alto, señal de parada
stop watch *s* reloj *m* de segundos muertos, cronómetro
storage ['storɪdʒ] *s* almacenaje *m;* (*costs*) derechos de almacenaje
storage battery *s* (elec) acumulador *m*
store [stor] *s* tienda, almacén *m;* **I know what is in store for you** sé lo que le espera; **to set store by** dar mucha importancia a || *tr* abastecer; tener guardado, almacenar; **to store away** acumular
store'house' *s* almacén *m*, depósito; (*e.g., of wisdom*) (fig) mina
store'keep'er *s* tendero, almacenista *mf*
store'room' *s* cuarto de almacenar; (*for furniture*) guardamuebles *m;* (naut) despensa
stork [stɔrk] *s* cigüeña; **to have a visit from the stork** recibir a la cigüeña
storm [stɔrm] *s* borrasca, tempestad, tormenta; (mil) asalto; (naut) borrasca; (fig) tempestad, tumulto; **to take by storm** tomar por asalto || *tr* asaltar || *intr* tempestear; precipitarse
storm cloud *s* nubarrón *m*
storm door *s* contrapuerta, guardapuerta
storm sash *s* contravidriera
storm troops *spl* tropas de asalto
storm window *s* guardaventana, sobrevidriera
storm·y ['stɔrmi] *adj* (*comp* **-ier;** *super* **-iest**) borrascoso, tempestuoso; (*session, meeting, etc.*) tumultuoso
sto·ry ['stori] *s* (*pl* **-ries**) historia, cuento, anécdota; enredo, trama; (coll) mentira; piso, alto || *v* (*pret & pp* **-ried**) *tr* historiar
sto'ry·tel'ler *s* narrador *m;* (coll) mentiroso
stout [staʊt] *adj* corpulento, gordo, robusto; animoso; leal; terco || *s* cerveza obscura fuerte
stove [stov] *s* (*for heating a house or room*) estufa; (*for cooking*) hornillo, cocina de gas, cocina eléctrica
stove'pipe' *s* tubo de estufa, tubo de hornillo; (*hat*) (coll) chistera, chimenea
stow [sto] *tr* guardar, meter, esconder; (naut) arrumar, estibar || *intr* — **to stow away** embarcarse clandestinamente, esconderse en un barco o avión
stowage ['sto·ɪdʒ] *s* arrumaje *m*, estiba
stow'a·way' *s* llovido, polizón *m*
str. *abbr* **strait, steamer**
straddle ['strædəl] *s* esparrancamiento || *tr* montar a horcajadas; (coll) tratar de favorecer a ambas partes en (*p.ej., un pleito*) || *intr* ponerse a horcajadas; (coll) tratar de favorecer a ambas partes
strafe [strɑf] o [stref] *s* (slang) bombardeo violento || *tr* (slang) bombardear violentamente
straggle ['strægəl] *intr* errar, vagar; andar perdido, extraviarse; separarse; estar esparcido
straight [stret] *adj* derecho; recto; erguido; (*hair*) lacio; continuo, seguido; honrado, sincero; correcto; decidido, intransigente; (*e.g., whiskey*) solo; **to set a person straight** mostrar el camino a una persona; dar consejo a una persona; mostrar a una persona el modo de proceder || *adv* derecho; sin interrupción; sinceramente; exactamente; en seguida; **straight ahead** todo seguido, derecho; **to go straight** (coll) enmendarse
straighten ['stretən] *tr* enderezar; poner en orden || *intr* enderezarse
straight face *s* cara seria
straight'for'ward *adj* franco, sincero; honrado
straight off *adv* luego, en seguida
straight razor *s* navaja barbera
straight'way' *adv* luego, en seguida
strain [stren] *s* tensión, tirantez *f;* esfuerzo muy grande; fatiga excesiva, agotamiento; (*of a muscle*) torcedura; aire *m*, melodía; (*of a family or lineage*) cepa; linaje *m*, raza; rasgo racial; genio, vena; huella, rastro || *tr* estirar; torcer o torcerse (*p.ej., la muñeca*); forzar (*p.ej., los nervios, la vista*); apretar; deformar; colar, tamizar || *intr* esforzarse; deformarse; colarse, tamizarse; filtrarse; exprimirse (*un jugo*); resistirse; **to strain at** hacer grandes esfuerzos por
strained [strend] *adj* (*smile*) forzado; (*friendship*) tirante
strainer ['strenər] *s* colador *m*
strait [stret] *s* estrecho; **straits** estrecho; **to be in dire straits** estar en el mayor apuro, hallarse en gran estrechez
strait jacket *s* camisa de fuerza
strait-laced ['stret,lest] *adj* gazmoño
strand [strænd] *s* playa; filamento; (*of rope or cable*) torón *m*, ramal *m;* (*of pearls*) hilo; pelo || *tr* deshebrar; retorcer, trenzar (*cuerda, cable, etc.*); dejar extraviado; (naut) varar
stranded ['strændɪd] *adj* desprovisto, desamparado; (*ship*) encallado; (*rope or cable*) trenzado, retorcido
strange [strendʒ] *adj* extraño, singular; nuevo, desconocido; novel, no acostumbrado
stranger ['strendʒər] *s* forastero; visi-

tador *m;* intruso; desconocido; principiante *mf*

strangle ['stræŋgəl] *tr* estrangular; reprimir, suprimir || *intr* estrangularse

strap [stræp] *s* (*of leather*) correa; (*of cloth, metal, etc.*) banda, tira; (*to sharpen a razor*) asentador *m* || *v* (*pret & pp* **strapped;** *ger* **strapping**) *tr* atar o liar con correa, banda o tira; azotar con una correa; fajar, vendar; asentar (*una navaja*)

strap'hang'er *s* (coll) pasajero colgado

stratagem ['strætədʒəm] *s* estratagema *f*

strategic(al) [strə'tidʒɪk(əl)] *adj* estratégico

strategist ['strætɪdʒɪst] *s* estratega *m*

strate·gy ['strætɪdʒi] *s* (*pl* **-gies**) estrategia

strati·fy ['strætɪ,faɪ] *v* (*pret & pp* **-fied**) *tr* estratificar || *intr* estratificarse

stratosphere ['strætə,sfɪr] o ['stretə,sfɪr] *s* estratosfera

stra·tum ['stretəm] o ['strætəm] *s* (*pl* **-ta** [tə] o **-tums**) estrato; (*e.g., of society*) clase *f*

straw [strɔ] *adj* pajizo; baladí, de poca importancia; falso; ficticio || *s* paja; (*for drinking*) pajita; **I don't care a straw** no se me da un bledo; **to be the last straw** ser el colmo, no faltar más

straw'ber'ry *s* (*pl* **-ries**) fresa

straw hat *s* sombrero de paja; (*with low flat crown*) canotié *m*

straw man *s* figura de paja; (*figurehead*) testaferro; testigo falso

straw vote *s* voto informativo

stray [stre] *adj* extraviado, perdido; aislado, suelto || *s* animal extraviado o perdido || *intr* extraviarse, perderse

streak [strik] *s* lista, raya; vena, veta; rasgo, traza; (*of light*) rayo; (*of good luck*) racha; (coll) tiempo muy breve; **like a streak** (coll) como un rayo || *tr* listar, rayar; abigarrar || *intr* rayarse; (coll) andar o pasar como un rayo

stream [strim] *s* (*current*) corriente *f;* arroyo, río; chorro, flujo; (*of people*) torrente *m;* (*e.g., of automobiles*) desfile *m* || *intr* correr, manar (*un líquido*); chorrear; flotar, ondear; salir a torrentes

streamer ['strimər] *s* flámula, banderola; cinta ondeante; rayo de luz

streamlined ['strim,laɪnd] *adj* aerodinámico, perfilado

stream'lin'er *s* tren aerodinámico de lujo

street [strit] *adj* callejero || *s* calle *f*

street'car' *s* tranvía *m*

street cleaner *s* basurero; (*device*) barredera

street clothes *spl* traje *m* de calle

street floor *s* piso bajo

street lamp *s* farol *m* (de la calle)

street sprinkler ['sprɪŋklər] *s* carricuba, carro de riego, regadera

street'walk'er *s* cantonera, carrerista

strength [streŋθ] *s* fuerza; intensidad; (*of spirituous liquors*) graduación; (com) tendencia a la subida; (mil) número; **on the strength of** fundándose en, confiando en

strengthen ['streŋθən] *tr* fortificar, reforzar; confirmar || *intr* fortificarse, reforzarse

strenuous ['strenjʊ·əs] *adj* estrenuo, enérgico, vigoroso; arduo, difícil

stress [strɛs] *s* tensión, fuerza; compulsión; acento; (mech) tensión; **to lay stress on** hacer hincapié en || *tr* someter a esfuerzo; hacer hincapié en; acentuar

stress accent *s* acento prosódico

stretch [strɛtʃ] *s* estiramiento, estirón *m;* (*distance in time or space*) trecho; (*section of road*) tramo; extensión; (*of the imagination*) esfuerzo; (*confinement in jail*) (slang) condena; **at a stretch** de un tirón || *tr* estirar; extender; tender; forzar, violentar; (fig) estirar (*el dinero*); **to stretch a point** hacer una concesión; **to stretch oneself** desperezarse || *intr* estirarse; extenderse; tenderse; desperezarse; **to stretch out** (coll) echarse

stretcher ['strɛtʃər] *s* (*for gloves*) ensanchador *m;* (*for a painting*) bastidor *m;* (*to carry sick or wounded*) camilla

stretch'er-bear'er *s* camillero

strew [stru] *v* (*pret* **strewed;** *pp* **strewed** o **strewn**) *tr* derramar, esparcir; sembrar, salpicar; polvorear

stricken ['strɪkən] *adj* afligido; inhabilitado; herido; **stricken in years** debilitado por los años

strict [strɪkt] *adj* estricto, riguroso; (*exacting*) severo

stricture ['strɪktʃər] *s* crítica severa; (pathol) estrictura

stride [straɪd] *s* zancada, tranco; **to hit one's stride** alcanzar la actividad o velocidad acostumbrada; **to make great** (o **rapid**) **strides** avanzar a grandes pasos; **to take in one's stride** hacer sin esfuerzo || *v* (*pret* **strode** [strod]; *pp* **stridden** ['strɪdən]) *tr* cruzar de un tranco; montar a horcajadas || *intr* dar zancadas, caminar a paso largo, andar a trancos

strident ['straɪdənt] *adj* estridente

strife [straɪf] *s* contienda; rivalidad

strike [straɪk] *s* (*blow*) golpe *m;* (*stopping of work*) huelga; (*discovery of ore, oil, etc.*) descubrimiento repentino; golpe *m* de fortuna; **to go on strike** ir a la huelga || *v* (*pret & pp* **struck** [strʌk]) *tr* golpear; pulsar (*una tecla*); herir, percutir; topar, dar con; acuñar (*monedas*); echar (*raíces*); frotar, rayar, encender (*un fósforo*); descubrir repentinamente (*mineral, aceite, etc.*); cerrar (*un trato*); arriar (*las velas*); dar (*la hora*); asumir, tomar (*una postura*); borrar, cancelar; impresionar; atraer (*la atención*); **to strike it rich** descubrir un buen filón, tener un golpe de fortuna || *intr* dar, sonar (*una campana, un reloj*); declararse en huelga;

(mil) dar el asalto; **to strike out** ponerse en marcha, echar camino adelante

strike'break'er *s* rompehuelgas *m,* esquirol *m*

striker ['straɪkər] *s* golpeador *m;* huelguista *mf*

striking ['straɪkɪŋ] *adj* impresionante, llamativo, sorprendente; en huelga

striking power *s* potencia de choque

string [strɪŋ] *s* cuerdecilla; (*of pearls; of lies*) sarta; (*of beans*) hebra; (*of onions or garlic*) ristra; (*row*) hilera; (mus) cuerda; (*limitation, proviso*) (coll) condición; **strings** instrumentos de cuerda; **to pull strings** tocar resortes || *v* (*pret & pp* **strung** [strʌŋ]) *tr* enhebrar, ensartar; atar con cuerdas; proveer de cuerdas; colgar de una cuerda; tender (*un cable, un alambre*); encordar (*un violín, una raqueta*); colocar en fila; (slang) engañar, burlar; **to string along** (slang) traer al retortero; **to string up** (coll) ahorcar

string bean *s* habichuela verde, judía verde

stringed instrument [strɪŋd] *s* instrumento de cuerda

stringent ['strɪndʒənt] *adj* riguroso, severo, estricto; convincente

string quartet *s* cuarteto de cuerdas

strip [strɪp] *s* tira; (*of metal*) lámina; (*of land*) faja || *v* (*pret & pp* **stripped;** *ger* **stripping**) *tr* desnudar; despojar; desforrar; deshacer (*la cama*); estropear (*el engranaje, un tornillo*); desvenar (*tabaco*); descortezar; **to strip of** despojar de || *intr* desnudarse; despojarse; descortezarse

stripe [straɪp] *s* banda, lista, raya; gaya; cinta, franja; (mil & nav) galón *m;* índole *f,* tipo; **to win one's stripes** ganar los entorchados || *tr* listar, rayar; gayar

strip mining *s* mineraje *m* a tajo abierto

strive [straɪv] *v* (*pret* **strove** [strov]; *pp* **striven** ['strɪvən]) *intr* esforzarse; luchar

stroke [strok] *s* golpe *m;* (*of bell or clock*) campanada; (*of pen*) plumada; (*of brush*) pincelada, brochada; (*of arms in swimming*) brazada; (*in a game*) jugada; (*caress with hand*) caricia; (*with a racket*) raquetazo; (*of a piston*) carrera, embolada; (*of a paddle*) palada; (*of an oar*) remada; (*of lightning*) rayo; (*line, mark*) raya; (*of good luck*) golpe *m;* (*of wit*) agudeza, chiste *m;* (*of genius*) rasgo; ataque *m* de parálisis; **at the stroke of** (*e.g., five*) al dar las (*p.ej., cinco*); **to not do a stroke of work** no dar golpe, no levantar paja del suelo || *tr* frotar suavemente, acariciar con la mano

stroll [strol] *s* paseo; **to take a stroll** dar un paseo || *intr* pasear, pasearse; callejear, errar, vagar

stroller ['strolər] *s* paseante *mf;* cochecito para niños

strong [strɔŋ] o [strɑŋ] *adj* fuerte, resistente; recio, robusto; intenso; (*stock market*) firme; enérgico; marcado; picante; rancio

strong'box' *s* cofre *m* fuerte, caja de caudales

strong drink *s* bebida alcohólica, bebida fuerte

strong'hold' *s* plaza fuerte

strong man *s* (*e.g., in a circus*) hércules *m;* (*leader, good planner*) alma, promotor *m;* (*dictator*) hombre *m* fuerte

strong-minded ['strɔŋ,maɪndɪd] o [strɑŋ,maɪndɪd] *adj* independiente; de inteligencia vigorosa; (*e.g., woman*) hombruna

strontium ['strɑnʃɪ·əm] *s* estroncio

strop [strɑp] *s* suavizador *m* || *v* (*pret & pp* **stropped;** *ger* **stropping**) *tr* suavizar, afilar

strophe ['strofi] *s* estrofa

structure ['strʌktʃər] *s* estructura; edificio

struggle ['strʌgəl] *s* lucha; esfuerzo, forcejeo || *intr* luchar; esforzarse, forcejear

strum [strʌm] *v* (*pret & pp* **strummed;** *ger* **strumming**) *tr* arañar (*un instrumento músico*) sin arte || *intr* cencerrear; **to strum on** rasguear

strumpet ['strʌmpɪt] *s* ramera

strut [strʌt] *s* (*brace, prop*) riostra, tornapunta; contoneo, pavoneo || *v* (*pret & pp* **strutted;** *ger* **strutting**) *intr* contonearse, pavonearse

strychnine ['strɪknaɪn] o ['strɪknin] *s* estricnina

stub [stʌb] *s* fragmento, trozo; (*of a cigar*) colilla; (*of a tree*) tocón *m;* (*of a pencil*) cabo; (*of a check*) talón *m* || *v* (*pret & pp* **stubbed;** *ger* **stubbing**) *tr* — **to stub one's toe** dar un tropezón

stubble ['stʌbəl] *s* rastrojo; (*of beard*) cañón *m*

stubborn ['stʌbərn] *adj* terco, testarudo, obstinado; porfiado; intratable

stuc·co ['stʌko] *s* (*pl* **-coes** o **-cos**) estuco || *tr* estucar

stuck'-up' *adj* (coll) estirado, orgulloso

stud [stʌd] *s* tachón *m;* botón *m* de camisa; montante *m,* pie derecho; clavo de adorno; (*bolt*) espárrago; caballeriza; (*of mares*) yeguada || *v* (*pret & pp* **studded;** *ger* **studding**) *tr* tachonar

stud bolt *s* espárrago

stud'book' *s* registro genealógico de caballos

student ['stjudənt] o ['studənt] *adj* estudiantil || *s* estudiante *mf;* (*person who investigates*) estudioso

student body *s* estudiantado, alumnado

stud'horse' *s* caballo padre, caballo semental

studied ['stʌdid] *adj* premeditado, hecho adrede; (*affected*) estudiado

studi·o ['stjudɪ,o] o ['studɪ,o] *s* (*pl* **-os**) estudio, taller *m;* (mov & rad) estudio

studious ['stjudɪ·əs] o ['studɪ·əs] *adj* estudioso; asiduo, solícito

stud·y ['stʌdi] *s* (*pl* **-ies**) estudio; solicitud; meditación profunda; (*e.g.,*

of a professor) gabinete *m*, estudio || *v* (*pret & pp* **-ied**) *tr & intr* estudiar
stuff [stʌf] *s* materia; género, paño, tela; muebles *mpl*, baratijas; medicina; fruslerías; cosa, cosas || *tr* rellenar; henchir, llenar; atascar, cerrar, tapar; embutir; (*with food*) atracar; meter sin orden, llenar sin orden; disecar (*un animal muerto*) || *intr* atracarse, hartarse
stuffed shirt *s* (slang) tragavirotes *m*
stuffing [ˈstʌfɪŋ] *s* relleno
stuff•y [ˈstʌfi] *adj* (*comp* **-ier;** *super* **-iest**) sofocante, mal ventilado; aburrido, sin interés; (*prim*) (coll) relamido
stumble [ˈstʌmbəl] *intr* tropezar, dar un traspié; moverse a tropezones; hablar a tropezones; **to stumble on** o **upon** tropezar con
stumbling block *s* escollo, tropezadero
stump [stʌmp] *s* (*of a tree, arm, etc.*) tocón *m;* (*of an arm*) muñón *m;* (*of a tooth*) raigón *m;* (*of a cigar*) colilla; (*of a tail*) rabo; paso pesado; fragmento, resto; tribuna pública; (*for shading drawings*) esfumino || *tr* recorrer (*el país*) pronunciando discursos políticos; (coll) confundir, dejar sin habla; esfumar
stump speaker *s* orador callejero
stump speech *s* arenga electoral
stun [stʌn] *v* (*pret & pp* **stunned;** *ger* **stunning**) *tr* atolondrar, aturdir
stunning [ˈstʌnɪŋ] *adj* (coll) pasmoso, estupendo, pistonudo, elegante
stunt [stʌnt] *s* atrofia; (*underdeveloped creature*) engendro; (coll) suerte acrobática; (coll) faena, hazaña, proeza || *tr* atrofiar || *intr* (coll) hacer suertes acrobáticas
stunt flying *s* vuelo acrobático
stunt man *s* (mov) doble *m* que hace suertes peligrosas
stupe•fy [ˈstjupɪ,faɪ] o [ˈstupɪ,faɪ] *v* (*pret & pp* **-fied**) *tr* dejar estupefacto, pasmar; causar estupor a
stupendous [stjuˈpɛndəs] o [stuˈpɛndəs] *adj* estupendo; enorme
stupid [ˈstjupɪd] o [ˈstupɪd] *adj* estúpido
stupor [ˈstjupər] o [ˈstupər] *s* estupor *m,* modorra
stur•dy [ˈstʌrdi] *adj* (*comp* **-dier;** *super* **-diest**) fuerte, robusto, fornido; firme, tenaz
sturgeon [ˈstʌrdʒən] *s* esturión *m*
stutter [ˈstʌtər] *s* tartamudeo || *tr* decir tartamudeando || *intr* tartamudear
sty [staɪ] *s* (*pl* **sties**) pocilga, zahurda; (pathol) orzuelo
style [staɪl] *s* estilo; moda; elegancia; **to live in great style** vivir en gran lujo || *tr* intitular, nombrar
stylish [ˈstaɪlɪʃ] *adj* de moda, elegante
styptic pencil [ˈstɪptɪk] *s* lápiz estíptico
Styx [stɪks] *s* Estigia
suave [swɑv] o [swev] *adj* suave; afable, fino, zalamero, pulido
sub. *abbr* **subscription, substitute, suburban**
subaltern [səbˈɔltərn] *adj & s* subalterno
subconscious [səbˈkɑnʃəs] *adj* subconsciente || *s* subconsciencia
subconsciousness [səbˈkɑnʃəsnɪs] *s* subconsciencia
subdeb [ˈsʌb,dɛb] *s* tobillera
subdivide [ˈsʌbdɪ,vaɪd] o [,sʌbdɪˈvaɪd] *tr* subdividir || *intr* subdividirse
subdue [səbˈdju] o [səbˈdu] *tr* sojuzgar, subyugar; amansar, dominar; suavizar
subdued [səbˈdjud] o [səbˈdud] *adj* sojuzgado; sumiso; (*e.g., light*) suave
subheading [ˈsʌb,hɛdɪŋ] *s* subtítulo
subject [ˈsʌbdʒɪkt] *adj* sujeto; súbdito || *s* asunto, materia, tema *m;* (*person in his relationship to a ruler or government*) súbdito; (gram, med, philos) sujeto || [səbˈdʒɛkt] *tr* sujetar, someter, sojuzgar
subject index *s* índice *m* de materias
subjection [səbˈdʒɛkʃən] *s* sumisión, sometimiento
subjective [səbˈdʒɛktɪv] *adj* subjetivo
subject matter *s* asunto, materia
subjugate [ˈsʌbdʒə,get] *tr* subyugar
subjunctive [səbˈdʒʌŋktɪv] *adj & s* subjuntivo
sub•let [sʌbˈlɛt] o [ˈsʌb,lɛt] *v* (*pret & pp* **-let;** *ger* **-letting**) *tr* realquilar, subarrendar
submachine gun [,sʌbməˈʃin] *s* subfusil *m* ametrallador
submarine [ˈsʌbmə,rin] *adj & s* submarino || *tr* (coll) atacar o hundir con un submarino
submarine chaser [ˈtʃesər] *s* cazasubmarinos *m*
submerge [səbˈmʌrdʒ] *tr* sumergir || *intr* sumergirse
submersion [səbˈmʌrʒən] o [səbˈmʌrʃən] *s* sumersión
submission [səbˈmɪʃən] *s* sumisión
submissive [səbˈmɪsɪv] *adj* sumiso
sub•mit [səbˈmɪt] *v* (*pret & pp* **-mitted;** *ger* **-mitting**) *tr* someter; proponer, permitirse decir || *intr* someterse
subordinate [səbˈɔrdɪnɪt] *adj & s* subordinado || [səbˈɔrdɪ,net] *tr* subordinar
subornation of perjury [,sʌbərˈneʃən] *s* (law) soborno de testigo
subplot [ˈsʌb,plɑt] *s* trama secundaria
subpoena o **subpena** [sʌbˈpinə] o [səˈpinə] *s* comparendo || *tr* mandar comparecer
sub rosa [sʌbˈrozə] *adv* en secreto, en confianza
subscribe [səbˈskraɪb] *tr* subscribir || *intr* subscribir; subscribirse, abonarse; **to subscribe to** subscribirse a, abonarse a (*una publicación periódica*); subscribir (*una opinión*)
subscriber [səbˈskraɪbər] *s* abonado
subsequent [ˈsʌbsɪkwənt] *adj* subsiguiente, posterior
subservient [səbˈsʌrvɪ•ənt] *adj* servil; subordinado; útil
subside [səbˈsaɪd] *intr* calmarse; acabarse, cesar; bajar (*el nivel del agua*); amainar (*el viento*)

subsidize ['sʌbsɪ,daɪz] *tr* subsidiar, subvencionar; (*to bribe*) sobornar
subsi·dy ['sʌbsɪdi] *s* (*pl* **-dies**) subsidio, subvención
subsist [səb'sɪst] *intr* subsistir
subsistence [səb'sɪstəns] *s* subsistencia
substance ['sʌbstəns] *s* substancia
substandard [sʌb'stændərd] *adj* inferior al nivel normal
substantial [səb'stænʃəl] *adj* considerable, importante; fuerte, sólido; acomodado, rico; esencial; (*food*) substancial
substantiate [səb'stænʃɪ,et] *tr* comprobar, establecer, verificar
substantive ['sʌbstəntɪv] *adj & s* substantivo
substation ['sʌb,steʃən] *s* (elec) subcentral *f*
substitute ['sʌbstɪ,tjut] o ['sʌbstɪ,tut] *adj* substitutivo || *s* (*person*) substituto; (*thing, substance*) substitutivo; (mil) reemplazo || *tr* poner (*a una persona o cosa*) en lugar de otra || *intr* actuar de substituto; **to substitute for** substituir (with personal a)
substitution [,sʌbstɪ'tjuʃən] o [,sʌbstɪ'tuʃən] *s* empleo o uso (de una persona o cosa en lugar de otra); (chem, law, math) substitución; (coll) imitación fraudulenta
subterranean [,sʌbtə'renɪ·ən] *adj & s* subterráneo
subtitle ['sʌb,taɪtəl] *s* subtítulo || *tr* subtitular
subtle ['sʌtəl] *adj* sutil; astuto; insidioso
subtle·ty ['sʌtəlti] *s* (*pl* **-ties**) sutileza; agudeza; distinción sutil
subtract [səb'trækt] *tr* substraer; (math) substraer, restar
suburb ['sʌbʌrb] *s* suburbio, arrabal *m;* **the suburbs** las afueras, los barrios externos
subvention [səb'vɛnʃən] *s* subvención || *tr* subvencionar
subversive [səb'vʌrsɪv] *adj* subversivo || *s* subversor *m*
subvert [səb'vʌrt] *tr* subvertir
subway ['sʌb,we] *s* galería subterránea; metro, ferrocarril subterráneo
succeed [sək'sid] *tr* suceder (*a una persona o cosa*) || *intr* tener buen éxito
success [sək'sɛs] *s* buen éxito
successful [sək'sɛsfəl] *adj* feliz, próspero; acertado; logrado
succession [sək'sɛʃən] *s* sucesión; **in succession** seguidos, uno tras otro
successive [sək'sɛsɪv] *adj* sucesivo
succor ['sʌkər] *s* socorro || *tr* socorrer
succotash ['sʌkə,tæʃ] *s* guiso de maíz tierno y habas
succumb [sə'kʌm] *intr* sucumbir
such [sʌtʃ] *adj & pron indef* tal, semejante; **such a** tal, semejante; **such a** + *adj* un tan + *adj;* **such as** quienes, los que
suck [sʌk] *s* chupada; mamada || *tr* chupar; mamar; aspirar (*el aire*)
sucker ['sʌkər] *s* chupador *m;* mamón *m;* (bot & mach) chupón *m;* (coll) bobo, primo
suckle ['sʌkəl] *tr* lactar; criar, educar
suckling pig ['sʌklɪŋ] *s* lechón *m,* cerdo de leche
suction ['sʌkʃən] *adj* aspirante || *s* succión
sudden ['sʌdən] *adj* súbito, repentino; **all of a sudden** de repente
suds [sʌdz] *spl* jabonadura; (coll) espuma, cerveza
sue [su] o [sju] *tr* demandar; pedir; (law) procesar || *intr* (law) poner pleito, entablar juicio; **to sue for damages** demandar por daños y perjuicios; **to sue for peace** pedir la paz
suede [swed] *s* gamuza, ante *m*
suet ['su·ɪt] o ['sju·ɪt] *s* sebo
suffer ['sʌfər] *tr & intr* sufrir, padecer
sufferance ['sʌfərəns] *s* tolerancia; paciencia; **on sufferance** por tolerancia
suffering ['sʌfərɪŋ] *adj* doliente || *s* dolencia, sufrimiento
suffice [sə'faɪs] *intr* bastar, ser suficiente
sufficient [sə'fɪʃənt] *adj* suficiente
suffix ['sʌfɪks] *s* sufijo
suffocate ['sʌfə,ket] *tr* sofocar || *intr* sofocarse
suffrage ['sʌfrɪdʒ] *s* sufragio; aprobación, voto favorable
suffragette [,sʌfrə'dʒɛt] *s* sufragista (*mujer*)
suffuse [sə'fjuz] *tr* saturar, bañar
sugar ['ʃugər] *adj* azucarero || *s* azúcar *m* || *tr* azucarar
sugar beet *s* remolacha azucarera
sugar bowl *s* azucarero
sugar cane *s* caña de azúcar
sug'ar-coat' *tr* azucarar; (fig) endulzar, dorar
suggest [səg'dʒɛst] *tr* sugerir
suggestion [səg'dʒɛtʃən] *s* sugestión, sugerencia; sombra, traza ligera
suggestive [səg'dʒɛstɪv] *adj* sugestivo; sicalíptico
suicidal [,su·ɪ'saɪdəl] o [,sju·ɪ'saɪdəl] *adj* suicida
suicide ['su·ɪ,saɪd] o ['sju·ɪ,saɪd] *s* (*act*) suicidio; (*person*) suicida *mf;* **to commit suicide** suicidarse
suit [sut] o [sjut] *s* traje *m,* terno; (*of a lady*) traje *m* sastre; (*group forming a set*) juego; (*of cards*) palo; petición, súplica; cortejo, galanteo; (law) pleito, proceso; **to follow suit** servir del palo; seguir la corriente || *tr* adaptar, ajustar; adaptarse a; sentar, ir o venir bien a; favorecer, satisfacer; **to suit oneself** hacer (*uno*) lo que le guste || *intr* convenir, ser a propósito
suitable ['sutəbəl] o ['sjutəbəl] *adj* apropiado, conveniente, adecuado
suit'case' *s* maleta, valija
suite [swit] *s* comitiva, séquito; (*group forming a set*) juego; serie *f;* (*of rooms*) crujía; habitación salón; (mus) suite *f*
suiting ['sutɪŋ] o ['sjutɪŋ] *s* corte *m* de traje
suit of clothes *s* traje completo (*de hombre*)

suitor ['sutər] o ['sjutər] *s* pretendiente *m;* (law) demandante *mf*
sulfa drugs ['sʌlfə] *spl* medicamentos sulfas
sulfate ['sʌlfet] *s* sulfato
sulfide ['sʌlfaɪd] *s* sulfuro
sulfite ['sʌlfaɪt] *s* sulfito
sulfur ['sʌlfər] *s* (chem) azufre *m;* véase **sulphur**
sulfuric [sʌl'fjʊrɪk] *adj* sulfúrico
sulfur mine *s* azufrera
sulfurous ['sʌlfərəs] *adj* sulfuroso || ['sʌlfərəs] o [sʌl'fjʊrəs] *adj* (chem) sulfuroso
sulk [sʌlk] *s* murria || *intr* amorrarse, enfurruñarse
sulk·y ['sʌlki] *adj* (*comp* **-ier;** *super* **-iest**) enfurruñado, murrio, resentido
sullen ['sʌlən] *adj* hosco, malhumorado, taciturno, triste
sul·ly ['sʌli] *v* (*pret & pp* **-lied**) *tr* empañar, manchar
sulphur ['sʌlfər] *adj* azufrado || *s* azufre *m;* color de azufre || *tr* azufrar
sultan ['sʌltən] *s* sultán *m*
sul·try ['sʌltri] *adj* (*comp* **-trier;** *super* **-triest**) bochornoso, sofocante
sum [sʌm] *s* suma; (coll) problema *m* de aritmética || *v* (*pret & pp* **summed;** *ger* **summing**) *tr* sumar; **to sum up** sumar, resumir
sumac o **sumach** ['ʃumæk] o ['sumæk] *s* zumaque *m*
summarize ['sʌmə,raɪz] *tr* resumir
summa·ry ['sʌməri] *adj* sumario || *s* (*pl* **-ries**) sumario, resumen *m*
summer ['sʌmər] *adj* estival, veraniego || *s* verano, estío || *intr* veranear
summer resort *s* lugar *m* de veraneo
summersault ['sʌmər,sɔlt] *s* salto mortal || *intr* dar un salto mortal
summer school *s* escuela de verano
summery ['sʌməri] *adj* estival, veraniego
summit ['sʌmɪt] *s* cima, cumbre *f*
summit conference *s* conferencia en la cumbre
summon ['sʌmən] *tr* convocar, llamar; evocar; (law) citar, emplazar
summons ['sʌmənz] *s* orden *f,* señal *f;* (law) citación, emplazamiento || *tr* (coll) citar, emplazar
sumptuous ['sʌmptʃʊ·əs] *adj* suntuoso
sun [sʌn] *s* sol *m;* **to have a place in the sun** ocupar su puesto en el mundo || *v* (*pret & pp* **sunned;** *ger* **sunning**) *tr* asolear || *intr* asolearse
sun bath *s* baño de sol
sun'beam' *s* rayo de sol
sun'bon'net *s* papalina
sun'burn' *s* quemadura de sol || *v* (*pret & pp* **-burned** o **burnt**) *tr* quemar al sol || *intr* quemarse al sol
sundae ['sʌndi] *s* helado con frutas, jarabes o nueces
Sunday ['sʌndi] *adj* dominical; (*used or worn on Sunday*) dominguero || *s* domingo
Sunday best *s* (coll) trapos de cristianar, ropa dominguera
Sunday's child *s* niño nacido de pies, niño mimado de la fortuna
Sunday school *s* escuela dominical, doctrina dominical
sunder ['sʌndər] *tr* separar; romper
sun'di'al *s* reloj *m* de sol, cuadrante *m* solar
sun'down' *s* puesta del sol
sundries ['sʌndriz] *spl* artículos diversos
sundry ['sʌndri] *adj* diversos, varios
sun'flow'er *s* girasol *m,* tornasol *m*
sun'glass'es *spl* gafas de sol, gafas para el sol
sunken ['sʌŋkən] *adj* hundido, sumido
sun lamp *s* lámpara de rayos ultravioletas
sun'light' *s* luz *f* del sol
sun'lit' *adj* iluminado por el sol
sun·ny ['sʌni] *adj* (*comp* **-nier;** *super* **-niest**) de sol; asoleado; brillante, resplandeciente; alegre, risueño; **to be sunny** hacer sol
sunny side *s* sol *m;* (fig) lado bueno, lado favorable
sun porch *s* solana
sun'rise' *s* salida del sol; **from sunrise to sunset** de sol a sol
sun'set' *s* puesta del sol
sun'shade' *s* quitasol *m,* sombrilla; toldo; visera contra el sol
sun'shine' *s* claridad del sol; alegría; **in the sunshine** al sol
sun'spot' *s* mancha solar
sun'stroke' *s* insolación
sup. *abbr* **superior, supplement**
sup [sʌp] *v* (*pret & pp* **supped;** *ger* **supping**) *intr* cenar
superannuated [,supər'ænjʊ,etɪd] *adj* jubilado, inhabilitado por ancianidad o enfermedad; fuera de moda
superb [sʊ'pʌrb] o [sə'pʌrb] *adj* soberbio, estupendo, magnífico
supercar·go ['supər,kɑrgo] *s* (*pl* **-goes** o **-gos**) (naut) sobrecargo
supercharge [,supər'tʃɑrdʒ] *tr* sobrealimentar
supercilious [,supər'sɪlɪ·əs] *adj* arrogante, altanero, desdeñoso
superficial [,supər'fɪʃəl] *adj* superficial
superfluous [sʊ'pʌrflʊ·əs] *adj* superfluo
superhuman [,supər'hjumən] *adj* sobrehumano
superimpose [,supərɪm'poz] *tr* sobreponer
superintendent [,supərɪn'tɛndənt] *s* superintendente *mf*
superior [sə'pɪrɪ·ər] o [sʊ'pɪrɪ·ər] *adj* superior; indiferente, sereno; arrogante; (typ) volado || *s* superior *m*
superiority [sə,pɪrɪ'ɑrɪti] o [sʊ,pɪrɪ'ɑrɪti] *s* superioridad; indiferencia, serenidad; arrogancia
superlative [sə'pʌrlətɪv] o [sʊ'pʌrlətɪv] *adj & s* superlativo
super·man ['supər,mæn] *s* (*pl* **-men** [,mɛn]) sobrehombre *m,* superhombre *m*
supermarket ['supər,mɑrkɪt] *s* supermercado
supernatural [,supər'nætʃərəl] *adj* sobrenatural
superpose [,supər'poz] *tr* sobreponer, superponer

supersede [ˌsupərˈsid] *tr* reemplazar; desalojar
supersonic [ˌsupərˈsɑnɪk] *adj* supersónico || **supersonics** *ssg* supersónica
superstitious [ˌsupərˈstɪʃəs] *adj* supersticioso
supervene [ˌsupərˈvin] *intr* sobrevenir
supervise [ˈsupərˌvaɪz] *tr* superintender, supervisar, dirigir
supervisor [ˈsupərˌvaɪzər] *s* superintendente *mf,* supervisor *m,* dirigente *mf*
supp. *abbr* **supplement**
supper [ˈsʌpər] *s* cena
supplant [səˈplænt] *tr* reemplazar
supple [ˈsʌpəl] *adj* flexible; dócil
supplement [ˈsʌplɪmənt] *s* suplemento || [ˈsʌplɪˌmɛnt] *tr* suplir, completar
suppliant [ˈsʌplɪ·ənt] *adj & s* suplicante *mf*
supplication [ˌsʌplɪˈkeʃən] *s* súplica
sup·ply [səˈplaɪ] *s* (*pl* **-plies**) suministro, provisión; surtido, repuesto; oferta, existencia; **supplies** pertrechos, provisiones, víveres *mf;* artículos, efectos || *v* (*pret & pp* **-plied**) *tr* suministrar, aprovisionar; reemplazar
supply and demand *spl* oferta y demanda
support [səˈport] *s* apoyo, soporte *m,* sostén *m;* sustento || *tr* apoyar, soportar, sostener; sustentar; aguantar
supporter [səˈportər] *s* partidario; (*jockstrap*) suspensorio; faja abdominal, faja medical
suppose [səˈpoz] *tr* suponer; creer; **to be supposed to** deber; **to suppose so** creer que sí
supposed [səˈpozd] *adj* supuesto
supposition [ˌsʌpəˈzɪʃən] *s* suposición
supposito·ry [səˈpɑzɪˌtori] *s* (*pl* **-ries**) supositorio
suppress [səˈprɛs] *tr* suprimir
suppression [səˈprɛʃən] *s* supresión
suppurate [ˈsʌpjəˌret] *intr* supurar
supreme [səˈprim] o [sʊˈprim] *adj* supremo
supt. *abbr* **superintendent**
surcharge [ˈsʌrˌtʃɑrdʒ] *s* sobrecarga || [ˌsʌrˈtʃɑrdʒ] o [ˈsʌrˌtʃɑrʒ] *tr* sobrecargar
sure [ʃʊr] *adj* seguro; **to be sure** seguramente, sin duda || *adv* (coll) seguramente, claro; **sure enough** efectivamente
sure thing *adv* (slang) seguramente || *interj* ¡claro!, ¡seguro! || *s* (slang) sacabocados *m*
sure·ty [ˈʃʊrti] o [ˈʃʊrɪti] *s* (*pl* **-ties**) seguridad, garantía, fianza
surf [sʌrf] *s* cachones *mpl,* olas que rompen en la playa
surface [ˈsʌrfɪs] *adj* superficial || *s* superficie *f* || *tr* alisar, allanar; recubrir || *intr* emerger (*p.ej., un submarino*)
surface mail *s* correo por vía ordinaria
surf'board' *s* patín *m* de mar
surfeit [ˈsʌrfɪt] *s* exceso; hartura, hastío; empacho, indigestión || *tr* atracar, hastiar; encebadar (*las bestias*) || *intr* atracarse, hastiarse; encebadarse
surf'-rid'ing *s* patinaje *m* sobre las olas
surge [sʌrdʒ] *s* oleada; (elec) sobretensión || *intr* agitarse, ondular
surgeon [ˈsʌrdʒən] *s* cirujano
surger·y [ˈsʌrdʒəri] *s* (*pl* **-ies**) cirugía; sala de operaciones
surgical [ˈsʌrdʒɪkəl] *adj* quirúrgico
sur·ly [ˈsʌrli] *adj* (*comp* **-lier;** *super* **-liest**) áspero, rudo, hosco, insolente
surmise [sərˈmaɪz] o [ˈsʌrmaɪz] *s* conjetura, suposición || [sərˈmaɪz] *tr & intr* conjeturar, suponer
surmount [sərˈmaʊnt] *tr* levantarse sobre; aventajar, sobrepujar; superar; coronar
surname [ˈsʌrˌnem] *s* apellido; (*added name*) sobrenombre *m* || *tr* apellidar; sobrenombrar
surpass [sərˈpæs] o [sərˈpɑs] *tr* aventajar, sobrepasar
surplice [ˈsʌrplɪs] *s* sobrepelliz *f*
surplus [ˈsʌrplʌs] *adj* sobrante, excedente || *s* sobrante *m,* exceso; (com) superávit *m*
surprise [sərˈpraɪz] *adj* inesperado, improviso || *s* sorpresa; **to take by surprise** coger por sorpresa || *tr* sorprender
surprise package *s* sorpresa
surprise party *s* reunión improvisada para felicitar por sorpresa a una persona
surprising [sərˈpraɪzɪŋ] *adj* sorprendente
surrender [səˈrɛndər] *s* rendición || *tr* rendir || *intr* rendirse
surrender value *s* (ins) valor *m* de rescate
surreptitious [ˌsʌrɛpˈtɪʃəs] *adj* subrepticio
surround [səˈraʊnd] *tr* cercar, rodear, circundar; (mil) sitiar
surrounding [səˈraʊndɪŋ] *adj* circundante, circunstante || **surroundings** *spl* alrededores *mpl,* contornos; ambiente *m,* medio
surtax [ˈsʌrˌtæks] *s* impuesto complementario
surveillance [sərˈveləns] o [sərˈveljəns] *s* vigilancia
survey [ˈsʌrve] *s* estudio, examen *m,* inspección, reconocimiento; agrimensura, medición, plano; levantamiento de planos; (*of opinion*) encuesta; (*of literature*) bosquejo || [sʌrˈve] o [ˈsʌrve] *tr* estudiar, examinar, inspeccionar, reconocer; medir; levantar el plano de || *intr* levantar el plano
surveyor [sərˈve·ər] *s* inspector *m;* agrimensor *m*
survival [sərˈvaɪvəl] *s* supervivencia
survive [sərˈvaɪv] *tr* sobrevivir a (*otra persona; algún acontecimiento*) || *intr* sobrevivir
surviving [sərˈvaɪvɪŋ] *adj* sobreviviente
survivor [sərˈvaɪvər] *s* sobreviviente *mf*
survivorship [sərˈvaɪvərˌʃɪp] *s* (law) sobrevivencia
susceptible [səˈsɛptɪbəl] *adj* susceptible; (*to love*) enamoradizo
suspect [ˈsʌspɛkt] o [səsˈpɛkt] *adj &*

s sospechoso || [səs'pɛkt] *tr* sospechar

suspend [səs'pɛnd] *tr* suspender || *intr* dejar de obrar; suspender pagos

suspenders [səs'pɛndərz] *spl* tirantes *mpl*

suspense [səs'pɛns] *s* suspenso, suspensión; duda, incertidumbre; indecisión, irresolución; ansiedad

suspension bridge [səs'pɛnʃən] *s* puente *m* colgante

suspicion [səs'pɪʃən] *s* sospecha, suspicacia; sombra, traza ligera

suspicious [səs'pɪʃəs] *adj* (*inclined to suspect*) suspicaz; (*subject to suspicion*) sospechoso

sustain [səs'ten] *tr* sostener, sustentar; apoyar, defender; confirmar, probar; sufrir (*p.ej., un daño, una pérdida*)

sustenance ['sʌstɪnəns] *s* sustento, alimentos; sostenimiento

sutler ['sʌtlər] *s* (mil) vivandero

swab [swɑb] *s* escobón *m,* estropajo; (naut) lampazo; (surg) tapón *m* de algodón || *v* (*pret & pp* **swabbed;** *ger* **swabbing**) *tr* fregar, limpiar; (naut) lampacear; (surg) limpiar con algodón

swaddle ['swɑdəl] *tr* empañar, fajar

swaddling clothes *spl* pañales *mpl*

swagger ['swægər] *adj* (coll) muy elegante || *s* fanfarronada; contoneo, paso jactancioso || *intr* fanfarronear; contonear

swain [swen] *s* (*lad*) zagal; galán *m,* amante *m*

swallow ['swɑlo] *s* trago; (orn) golondrina || *tr* tragar, deglutir; (fig) tragar, tragarse || *intr* tragar, deglutir

swallow-tailed coat ['swɑlo ˌteld] *s* frac *m*

swal'low•wort' *s* vencetósigo

swamp [swɑmp] *s* pantano, marisma || *tr* encharcar, inundar; (*e.g., with work*) abrumar

swamp•y ['swɑmpi] *adj* (*comp* **-ier;** *super* **-iest**) pantanoso

swan [swɑn] *s* cisne *m*

swan dive *s* salto de ángel

swank [swæŋk] *adj* (slang) elegante, vistoso || *s* (slang) elegancia vistosa

swan knight *s* caballero del cisne

swan's-down ['swɑnzˌdaʊn] *s* plumón *m* de cisne; moletón *m,* paño de vicuña

swan song *s* canto del cisne

swap [swɑp] *s* (coll) trueque *m,* cambalache *m* || *v* (*pret & pp* **swapped;** *ger* **swapping**) *tr & intr* trocar, cambalachear

swarm [swɔrm] *s* enjambre *m* || *intr* enjambrar; volar en enjambres; hormiguear (*una multitud de gente o animales*)

swarth•y ['swɔrði] o ['swɔrθi] *adj* (*comp* **-ier;** *super* **-iest**) atezado, carinegro, moreno

swashbuckler ['swɑʃˌbʌklər] *s* espadachín *m,* matasiete *m,* valentón *m*

swat [swɑt] *s* (coll) golpe violento || *v* (*pret & pp* **swatted;** *ger* **swatting**) *tr* (coll) golpear con fuerza; (coll) aporrear, aplastar (*una mosca*)

sway [swe] *s* oscilación, vaivén *m;* dominio, imperio || *tr* hacer oscilar; conmover; disuadir; gobernar, dominar || *intr* oscilar; desviarse; tambalear, flaquear

swear [swɛr] *v* (*pret* **swore** [swor]; *pp* **sworn** [sworn]) *tr* jurar; juramentar; prestar (*juramento*); **to swear in** tomar juramento a; **to swear off** jurar renunciar a; **to swear out** obtener mediante juramento || *intr* jurar; **to swear at** maldecir; **to swear by** jurar por; poner toda su confianza en; **to swear to** prestar juramento a; declarar bajo juramento; jurar + *inf*

sweat [swɛt] *s* sudor *m* || *v* (*pret & pp* **sweat** o **sweated**) *tr* sudar (*agua por los poros; la ropa*); (slang) hacer sudar; **to sweat it out** (slang) aguantarlo hasta el fin || *intr* sudar

sweater ['swɛtər] *s* suéter *m*

sweat•y ['swɛti] *adj* (*comp* **-ier;** *super* **-iest**) sudoroso

Swede [swid] *s* sueco

Sweden ['swidən] *s* Suecia

Swedish ['swidɪʃ] *adj & s* sueco

sweep [swip] *s* barrido; alcance *m,* extensión; (*of wind*) soplo; (*of a well*) cigoñal *m* || *v* (*pret & pp* **swept** [swɛpt]) *tr* barrer; arrastrar; rozar, tocar; recorrer con la mirada, los dedos, etc. || *intr* barrer; pasar rápidamente; extenderse; precipitarse; andar con paso majestuoso

sweeper ['swipər] *s* (*person*) barrendero; (*machine for sweeping streets*) barredera; barredera de alfombra; (nav) dragaminas *m*

sweeping ['swipɪŋ] *adj* arrebatador; comprensivo, extenso, vasto || **sweepings** *spl* barreduras

sweep'-sec'ond *s* segundero central

sweep'stakes' *ssg* o *spl* lotería en la cual una persona gana todas las apuestas; carrera que decide todas las apuestas; premio en las carreras de caballos

sweet [swit] *adj* dulce; oloroso; melodioso, grato al oído; fresco; bonito, lindo; amable; querido; **to be sweet on** (coll) estar enamorado de || *adv* dulcemente; **to smell sweet** tener buen olor || **sweets** *spl* dulces *mpl,* golosinas

sweet'bread' *s* lechecillas, mollejas

sweet'bri'er *s* eglantina

sweeten ['switən] *tr* azucarar, endulzar; suavizar; purificar || *intr* azucararse, endulzarse; suavizarse

sweet'heart' *s* enamorado o enamorada; amiga querida; galán *m,* cortejo

sweet marjoram *s* mejorana

sweet'meats' *spl* dulces *mpl,* confites *mpl,* confitura

sweet pea *s* guisante *m* de olor

sweet potato *s* batata, camote *m*

sweet-scented ['switˌsɛntɪd] *adj* oloroso, perfumado

sweet tooth *s* gusto por los dulces

sweet-toothed ['switˌtuθt] *adj* dulcero, goloso

sweet william *s* clavel *m* de ramillete, minutisa

swell [swɛl] *adj* (coll) muy elegante; (slang) de órdago, magnífico ‖ *s* hinchazón *f;* bulto; marejada; oleaje *m;* (*of a crowd of people*) oleada; (coll) petimetre *m,* pisaverde *m* ‖ *v* (*pret* **swelled;** *pp* **swelled** o **swollen** [ˈswolən]) *tr* hinchar, inflar; abultar, aumentar; elevar, levantar; (fig) hinchar, engreír ‖ *intr* hincharse; abultarse, aumentar, crecer; elevarse, levantarse; embravecerse (*el mar*); (fig) hincharse, engreírse

swelled head *s* entono; **to have a swelled head** estar muy pagado de sí mismo, creerse gran cosa

swelter [ˈswɛltər] *intr* sofocarse de sudor

swept'back' wing *s* (aer) ala en flecha

swerve [swʌrv] *s* viraje *m,* desvío brusco ‖ *tr* desviar ‖ *intr* desviarse, torcer

swift [swɪft] *adj* rápido, veloz; pronto; repentino ‖ *adv* rápidamente, velozmente ‖ *s* vencejo

swig [swɪg] *s* (coll) chisguete, tragantada ‖ *v* (*pret & pp* **swigged;** *ger* **swigging**) *tr & intr* (coll) beber a grandes tragos

swill [swɪl] *s* basura, inmundicia; tragantada ‖ *tr* beber a grandes tragos; emborrachar ‖ *intr* beber a grandes tragos; emborracharse

swim [swɪm] *s* natación; **the swim** (*in affairs, society, etc.*) (coll) la corriente ‖ *v* (*pret* **swam** [swæm]; *pp* **swum** [swʌm]; *ger* **swimming**) *tr* pasar a nado ‖ *intr* nadar; deslizarse, escurrirse; padecer vahidos; dar vueltas (*la cabeza*); **to swim across** atravesar a nado

swimmer [ˈswɪmər] *s* nadador *m*

swimming pool *s* piscina

swimming suit *s* traje *m* de baño

swindle [ˈswɪndəl] *s* estafa, timo ‖ *tr & intr* estafar, timar

swine [swaɪn] *s* cerdo, puerco; *spl* ganado porcino

swing [swɪŋ] *s* balance *m,* oscilación, vaivén *m;* (*device used for recreation*) columpio; hamaca; turno, período; fuerza, ímpetu *m;* (*trip*) jira; (box) golpe *m* de lado; (mus) ritmo constantemente repetido; **in full swing** en plena marcha ‖ *v* (*pret & pp* **swung** [swʌŋ]) *tr* blandir (*p.ej., un arma*); menear (*los brazos*); hacer oscilar; columpiar; manejar con éxito ‖ *intr* oscilar; balancearse; columpiar; estar colgado; dar una vuelta; **to swing open** abrirse de pronto (*una puerta*)

swinging door [ˈswɪŋɪŋ] *s* batiente *m* oscilante, puerta de vaivén

swinish [ˈswaɪnɪʃ] *adj* porcuno; (fig) cochino, puerco

swipe [swaɪp] *s* (coll) golpe *m* fuerte ‖ *tr* (coll) dar un golpe fuerte a; (slang) hurtar, robar

swirl [swʌrl] *s* remolino, torbellino ‖ *tr* hacer girar ‖ *intr* arremolinarse, remolinar; girar

swish [swɪʃ] *s* (*e.g., of a whip*) chasquido; (*of a dress*) crujido ‖ *tr* chasquear (*el látigo*) ‖ *intr* chasquear; crujir (*un vestido*)

Swiss [swɪs] *adj & s* suizo

Swiss chard [tʃɑrd] *s* acelga

Swiss cheese *s* Gruyère *m,* queso suizo

Swiss Guards *spl* guardia suiza

switch [swɪtʃ] *s* bastoncillo, latiguillo; latigazo; coletazo; (*false hair*) trenza postiza, moño postizo; (elec) llave *f,* interruptor *m,* conmutador *m;* (rr) agujas ‖ *tr* azotar, fustigar; (elec) conmutar; (rr) desviar; **to switch off** (elec) cortar, desconectar; **to switch on** (elec) cerrar (*el circuito*); (elec) encender, poner (*la luz, la radio, etc.*) ‖ *intr* cambiarse, moverse; desviarse

switch'back' *s* vía en zigzag

switch'board' *s* cuadro de distribución

switching engine *s* locomotora de maniobras

switch·man [ˈswɪtʃmən] *s* (*pl* **-men** [mən]) agujetero, guardagujas *m*

switch'yard' *s* patio de maniobras

Switzerland [ˈswɪtsərlənd] *s* Suiza

swiv·el [ˈswɪvəl] *s* eslabón giratorio ‖ *v* (*pret & pp* **-eled** o **-elled;** *ger* **-eling** o **-elling**) *intr* girar sobre un eje

swivel chair *s* silla giratoria

swoon [swun] *s* desmayo ‖ *intr* desmayarse

swoop [swup] *s* descenso súbito; (*of a bird of prey*) calada ‖ *intr* bajar rápidamente, precipitarse; abatirse (*p.ej., el ave de rapiña*)

sword [sord] *s* espada; **at swords' points** enemistados a sangre y fuego; **to put to the sword** pasar al filo de la espada, pasar a cuchillo

sword belt *s* cinturón *m*

sword'fish' *s* pez *m* espada

sword handler *s* (taur) mozo de estoques

sword rattling *s* fanfarronería

swords·man [ˈsordzmən] *s* (*pl* **-men** [mən]) espada *m;* esgrimidor *m*

sword swallower [ˈswɑlo·ər] *s* tragasable *m*

sword thrust *s* estocada, golpe *m* de espada

sworn [sworn] *adj* (*enemy*) jurado

sycophant [ˈsɪkəfənt] *s* adulador *m;* parásito

sycosis [saɪˈkosɪs] *s* (pathol) sicosis *f*

syll. *abbr* **syllable**

syllable [ˈsɪləbəl] *s* sílaba

syllogism [ˈsɪləˌdʒɪzəm] *s* silogismo

sylph [sɪlf] *s* sílfide *f*

sym. *abbr* **symbol, symmetrical, symphony, symptom**

symbol [ˈsɪmbəl] *s* símbolo

symbolic(al) [sɪmˈbɑlɪk(əl)] *adj* simbólico

symbolize [ˈsɪmbəˌlaɪz] *tr* simbolizar

symmetric(al) [sɪˈmɛtrɪk(əl)] *adj* simétrico

symme·try [ˈsɪmɪtri] *s* (*pl* **-tries**) simetría

sympathetic [ˌsɪmpəˈθɛtɪk] *adj* compasivo; favorablemente dispuesto

sympathize [ˈsɪmpəˌθaɪz] *intr* compa-

decerse; **to sympathize with** compadecerse de; comprender
sympa·thy [ˈsɪmpəθi] *s* (*pl* **-thies**) compasión, conmiseración; **to be in sympathy with** estar de acuerdo con, ser partidario de; **to extend one's sympathy to** dar el pésame a
symphonic [sɪmˈfɑnɪk] *adj* sinfónico
sympho·ny [ˈsɪmfəni] *s* (*pl* **-nies**) sinfonía
symposi·um [sɪmˈpozɪ·əm] *s* (*pl* **-a** [ə]) coloquio
symptom [ˈsɪmptəm] *s* síntoma *m*
syn. *abbr* **synonym, synonymous**
synagogue [ˈsɪnə,gɔg] o [ˈsɪnə,gɑg] *s* sinagoga
synchronize [ˈsɪŋkrə,naɪz] *tr & intr* sincronizar
synchronous [ˈsɪŋkrənəs] *adj* sincrónico
syncope [ˈsɪŋkə,pi] *s* (phonet) síncopa
syndicate [ˈsɪndɪkɪt] *s* sindicato ‖ [ˈsɪndɪ,ket] *tr* sindicar ‖ *intr* sindicarse
synonym [ˈsɪnənɪm] *s* sinónimo
synonymous [sɪˈnɑnɪməs] *adj* sinónimo
synop·sis [sɪˈnɑpsɪs] *s* (*pl* **-ses** [siz]) sinopsis *f*
syntax [ˈsɪntæks] *s* sintaxis *f*
synthe·sis [ˈsɪnθɪsɪs] *s* (*pl* **-ses** [,siz]) síntesis *f*
synthesize [ˈsɪnθɪ,saɪz] *tr* sintetizar
synthetic(al) [sɪnˈθɛtɪk(əl)] *adj* sintético
syphilis [ˈsɪfɪlɪs] *s* sífilis *f*
Syria [ˈsɪrɪ·ə] *s* Siria
Syrian [ˈsɪrɪ·ən] *adj & s* sirio
syringe [sɪˈrɪndʒ] o [ˈsɪrɪndʒ] *s* jeringa; (*fountain syringe*) mangueta; (*syringe fitted with needle for hypodermic injections*) jeringuilla ‖ *tr* jeringar
syrup [ˈsɪrəp] o [ˈsʌrəp] *s* almíbar *m;* (*with fruit juices or medicinal substances*) jarabe *m*
system [ˈsɪstəm] *s* sistema *m*
systematic(al) [,sɪstəˈmætɪk(əl)] *adj* sistemático
systematize [ˈsɪstəmə,taɪz] *tr* sistematizar
systole [ˈsɪstəli] *s* sístole *f*

T

T, t [ti] vigésima letra del alfabeto inglés
t. *abbr* **teaspoon, temperature, tenor, tense, territory, town**
T. *abbr* **Territory, Testament**
tab [tæb] *s* apéndice *m,* proyección; marbete *m;* **to keep tab on** (coll) tener a la vista; **to pick up the tab** (coll) pagar la cuenta
tab·by [ˈtæbi] *s* (*pl* **-bies**) gato atigrado; gata; solterona; chismosa
tabernacle [ˈtæbər,nækəl] *s* tabernáculo
table [ˈtebəl] *s* mesa; (*list, catalogue; index of a book*) tabla; **to set the table** poner la mesa; **to turn the tables** volver las tornas; **under the table** completamente emborrachado ‖ *tr* aplazar la discusión de
tab·leau [ˈtæblo] *s* (*pl* **-leaus** o **-leaux** [loz]) cuadro vivo
ta′ble·cloth′ *s* mantel *m*
table d'hôte [ˈtɑbəlˈdot] *s* mesa redonda; comida a precio fijo
ta′ble·land′ *s* meseta
table linen *s* mantelería
table manners *spl* modales *mpl* que uno tiene en la mesa
table of contents *s* índice *m* de materias, tabla de materias
ta′ble·spoon′ *s* cuchara de sopa
tablespoonful [ˈtebəl,spun,fʊl] *s* cucharada
tablet [ˈtæblɪt] *s* (*writing pad*) bloc *m;* (*slab*) lápida, placa; (*lozenge, pastille*) comprimido, tableta
table talk *s* conversación de sobremesa
table tennis *s* tenis de mesa
ta′ble·ware′ *s* servicio de mesa, artículos para la mesa
tabloid [ˈtæblɔɪd] *s* periódico sensacional
taboo [təˈbu] *adj* prohibido ‖ *s* tabú *m* ‖ *tr* prohibir
tabulate [ˈtæbjə,let] *tr* tabular
tabulator [ˈtæbjə,letər] *s* tabulador *m*
tacit [ˈtæsɪt] *adj* tácito
taciturn [ˈtæsɪ,tʌrn] *adj* taciturno
tack [tæk] *s* tachuela; nuevo plan de acción; (naut) virada; (sew) hilván *m* ‖ *tr* clavar con tachuelas; añadir; unir; (naut) virar; (sew) hilvanar ‖ *intr* cambiar de plan; (naut) virar
tackle [ˈtækəl] *s* avíos, enseres *mpl;* (naut) poleame *m* ‖ *tr* atacar, embestir; emprender
tack·y [ˈtæki] *adj* (*comp* **-ier;** *super* **-iest**) pegajoso; (coll) desaliñado
tact [tækt] *s* tacto, juicio, tino
tactful [ˈtæktfəl] *adj* discreto, político
tactical [ˈtæktɪkəl] *adj* táctico
tactician [tækˈtɪʃən] *s* táctico
tactics [ˈtæktɪks] *ssg* (mil) táctica ‖ *spl* táctica
tactless [ˈtæklɪs] *adj* indiscreto
tad′pole′ *s* renacuajo
taffeta [ˈtæfɪtə] *s* tafetán *m*
taffy [ˈtæfi] *s* arropía, melcocha; (coll) lisonja, zalamería
tag [tæg] *s* etiqueta, marbete *m;* herrete *m;* pingajo; mechón *m;* vedija; (*curlicue in writing*) ringorrango; **to play tag** jugar al tócame tú ‖ *v* (*pret & pp* **tagged;** *ger* **tagging**) *tr* pegar un marbete a; marcar con marbete ‖ *intr* (coll) seguir de cerca
tag end *s* cabo flojo; retal *m,* retazo
Tagus [ˈtegəs] *s* Tajo
tail [tel] *adj* de cola ‖ *s* cola; **tails** (*of a coin*) cruz *f;* (coll) frac *m;* **to turn**

tail mostrar los talones || *tr* atar, juntar || *intr* formar cola; **to tail after** pisar los talones a

tail assembly *s* (aer) empenaje *m,* planos de cola

tail end *s* cola, extremo; conclusión; **at the tail end** al final

tail'light' *s* faro trasero; (rr) disco de cola

tailor ['telər] *s* sastre *m* || *tr* entallar (*un traje*) || *intr* ser sastre

tailoring ['telərıŋ] *s* sastrería, costura

tai'lor-made' suit *s* traje *m* de sastre, traje hecho a la medida

tail'piece' *s* apéndice *m,* cabo; (*of stringed instrument*) (mus) cordal *m;* (typ) florón *m*

tail'race' *s* cauce *m* de salida; (min) canal *m* de desechos

tail spin *s* (aer) barrena picada

tail wind *s* (aer) viento de cola; (naut) viento en popa

taint [tent] *s* mancha; corrupción, infección || *tr* manchar; corromper, inficionar

take [tek] *s* toma; presa, redada; (mov) toma; (slang) entradas, ingresos || *v* (*pret* **took** [tʊk]; *pp* **taken**) *tr* tomar; (*to carry off with one*) llevarse; (*to remove*) quitar; quedarse con (*p.ej., una compra en una tienda*); comer (*una pieza, en el juego de ajedrez y en el de damas*); dar (*un paso, un salto, un paseo*); hacer (*un viaje; ejercicio*); seguir (*un consejo; una asignatura*); sacar (*una fotografía*); calzar, usar (*cierto tamaño de zapatos o guantes*); estudiar (*p.ej., historia, francés, matemáticas*); echar (*una siesta*); tomar (*un tren, autobús, tranvía*); aguantar, tolerar; soportar; **to take amiss** llevar a mal; **to take apart** descomponer, desarmar, desmontar; **to take down** bajar; descolgar; poner por escrito, tomar nota de; desmontar; (*to humble*) quitar los humos a; **to take for** tomar por, p.ej., **I took you for someone else** le tomé por otra persona; **to take from** quitar a; **to take in** acoger, admitir; (*to welcome into one's home, one's company*) recibir; (*to encompass*) abarcar, comprender; ganar (*dinero*); visitar (*los puntos de interés*); (*to win over by flattery or deceit*) cazar; meter (*p.ej., las costuras de una prenda de vestir*); **to take it that** suponer que; **to take off** quitarse (*p.ej., el sombrero*); descontar; (coll) imitar, parodiar; **to take on** tomar, contratar; empezar; cargar con, tomar sobre sí; desafiar; **to take out** sacar; pasear (*p.ej., a un niño, un caballo*); omitir; extraer, separar; **to take place** tener lugar; **to take up** subir; levantar; apretar; coger; recoger; emprender, comenzar; tomar posesión de (*un cargo, un puesto*); tomar, estudiar; ocupar, llenar (*un espacio*) || *intr* arraigar, prender; cuajar; actuar, obrar; salir, resultar; adherirse; pegar; (coll) tener éxito; **to take after** parecerse a; **to take off** levantarse; salir; (aer) despegar; **to take up with** (coll) estrechar amistad con; (coll) vivir con; **to take well** (coll) sacar buen retrato

take'-off' *s* (aer) despegue *m;* (coll) imitación burlesca, parodia

talcum powder ['tælkəm] *s* polvos de talco; talco en polvo

tale [tel] *s* cuento, relato; embuste *m,* mentira

tale'bear'er *s* chismoso, cuentista *mf*

talent ['tælənt] *s* talento; gente *f* de talento

talented ['tæləntıd] *adj* talentoso

talent scout *s* buscador *m* de nuevas figuras

talk [tɔk] *s* charla, plática; (*gossip*) fábula, comidilla; (*lecture*) conferencia; **to cause talk** dar que hablar || *tr* hablar; convencer hablando; **to talk up** ensalzar || *intr* hablar; parlar (*el loro*); **to talk on** discutir (*un asunto*); hablar sin parar; continuar hablando; **to talk up** elevar la voz, osar hablar

talkative ['tɔkətıv] *adj* hablador, locuaz

talker ['tɔkər] *s* hablador *m;* orador *m;* charlatán *m,* parlón *m*

talkie ['tɔki] *s* (coll) cine hablado

talking doll ['tɔkıŋ] *s* muñeca parlante

talking film *s* película hablada

talking machine *s* máquina parlante

talking picture *s* cine hablado, cine parlante

tall [tɔl] *adj* alto; (coll) exagerado

tallow ['tælo] *s* sebo

tal·ly ['tæli] *s* (*pl* **-lies**) cuenta || *v* (*pret & pp* **-lied**) *tr* echar la cuenta de || *intr* echar la cuenta; concordar, corresponder, conformarse

tally sheet *s* hoja en que se anota una cuenta

talon ['tælən] *s* garra

tambourine [,tæmbə'rin] *s* pandereta

tame [tem] *adj* manso, domesticado; dócil, sumiso; insípido || *tr* amansar, domesticar; domar (*a un animal salvaje*); someter; captar (*una caída de agua*)

tamp [tæmp] *tr* atacar (*un barreno*); apisonar

tamper ['tæmpər] *s* (*person*) apisonador *m;* (*ram*) pisón *m* || *intr* entremeterse; **to tamper with** manosear, tocar ajando; tratar de forzar (*una cerradura*); falsificar (*un documento*); corromper (*p.ej., a un testigo*)

tampon ['tæmpɑn] *s* (surg) tapón *m* || *tr* (surg) taponar

tan [tæn] *adj* requemado, tostado; de color de canela; marrón; café (Am) || *v* (*pret & pp* **tanned;** *ger* **tanning**) *tr* adobar, curtir, zurrar; quemar, tostar; (coll) zurrar, dar una paliza a

tang [tæŋ] *s* sabor *m* u olor *m* fuerte y picante; dejo, gustillo; (*ringing sound*) tañido

tangent ['tændʒənt] *adj* tangente || *s* tangente *f;* **to fly off at a tangent** tomar súbitamente nuevo rumbo, cambiar de repente

tangerine [ˌtændʒəˈrin] *s* mandarina
tangible [ˈtændʒɪbəl] *adj* palpable, tangible
Tangier [tænˈdʒɪr] *s* Tánger *f*
tangle [ˈtæŋgəl] *s* enredo, maraña, lío || *tr* enredar, enmarañar || *intr* enredarse, enmarañarse
tank [tæŋk] *s* tanque *m,* depósito; (mil) tanque, carro de combate; (rr) ténder *m;* (*heavy drinker*) (slang) bodega
tank car *s* (rr) carro cuba, vagón *m* tanque
tanker [ˈtæŋkər] *s* barco tanque, buque *m* cisterna; avión-nodriza *m*
tank farming *s* quimicultura, cultivo hidropónico
tank truck *s* camión *m* tanque
tanner [ˈtænər] *s* curtidor *m*
tanner•y [ˈtænəri] *s* (*pl* **-ies**) curtiduría, tenería
tantalize [ˈtæntəˌlaɪz] *tr* atormentar con falsas promesas
tantamount [ˈtæntəˌmaʊnt] *adj* equivalente
tantrum [ˈtæntrəm] *s* berrinche *m,* rabieta
tap [tæp] *s* golpecito, palmadita; canilla, espita; grifo; (elec) toma; (mach) macho de terraja; **on tap** sacado del barril, servido al grifo; listo, a mano; **taps** (*signal to put out lights*) (mil) silencio || *v* (*pret & pp* **tapped;** *ger* **tapping**) *tr* dar golpecitos o un golpecito a o en; espitar, poner la espita a; sacar o tomar (*quitando la espita*); sangrar (*un árbol*); intervenir (*un teléfono*); derivar (*electricidad*); aterrajar (*tuercas*) || *intr* dar golpecitos
tap dance *s* zapateado
tap′-dance′ *intr* zapatear
tape [tep] *s* cinta || *tr* proveer de cinta; medir con cinta; (coll) grabar en cinta magnetofónica
tape measure *s* cinta de medir
taper [ˈtepər] *s* cerilla, velita larga y delgada || *tr* ahusar || *intr* ahusarse; ir disminuyendo
tape′-re•cord′ *tr* grabar sobre cinta
tape recorder [rɪˈkɔrdər] *s* magnetófono, grabadora de cinta
tapes•try [ˈtæpɪstri] *s* (*pl* **-tries**) tapiz *m* || *v* (*pret & pp* **-tried**) *tr* tapizar
tape′worm′ *s* solitaria, lombriz solitaria
tappet [ˈtæpɪt] *s* (aut) alzaválvulas *m,* taqué *m*
tap′room′ *s* bodegón *m,* taberna
tap water *s* agua de grifo
tap wrench *s* volvedor *m* de machos
tar [tɑr] *s* alquitrán *m;* (coll) marinero || *v* (*pret & pp* **tarred;** *ger* **tarring**) *tr* alquitranar; **to tar and feather** embrear y emplumar
tar•dy [ˈtɑrdi] *adj* (*comp* **-dier;** *super* **-diest**) tardío
target [ˈtɑrgɪt] *s* blanco
target area *s* zona a batir
target practice *s* tiro al blanco
tariff [ˈtærɪf] *adj* arancelario || *s* (*duties*) arancel *m;* (*rates in general*) tarifa
tarnish [ˈtɑrnɪʃ] *s* deslustre *m* || *tr* deslustrar || *intr* deslustrarse
tar paper *s* papel alquitranado
tarpaulin [tɑrˈpɔlɪn] *s* alquitranado, encerado, empegado
tar•ry [ˈtɑri] *adj* alquitranado, embreado || [ˈtæri] *v* (*pret & pp* **-ried**) *intr* detenerse, quedarse; tardar
tart [tɑrt] *adj* acre, agrio; (fig) áspero, mordaz || *s* tarta; (coll) puta
task [tæsk] o [tɑsk] *s* tarea; **to bring** o **take to task** llamar a capítulo
task′mas′ter *s* amo, superintendente *mf;* ordenancista *mf,* tirano
tassel [ˈtæsəl] *s* borla; (bot) penacho
taste [test] *s* gusto, sabor *m;* sorbo, trago; muestra; gusto, buen gusto; **in bad taste** de mal gusto; **in good taste** de buen gusto; **to acquire a taste for** tomar gusto a || *tr* gustar; (*to sample*) probar || *intr* saber; **to taste of** saber a
tasteless [ˈtestlɪs] *adj* desabrido, insípido; de mal gusto
tast•y [ˈtesti] *adj* (*comp* **-ier;** *super* **-iest**) (coll) sabroso; (coll) de buen gusto
tatter [ˈtætər] *s* andrajo, harapo, guiñapo || *tr* hacer andrajos
tattered [ˈtætərd] *adj* andrajoso, haraposo
tattle [ˈtætəl] *s* charla; habladuría || *intr* charlar; chismear, murmurar
tat′tle•tale′ *adj* revelador || *s* cuentista *mf,* chismoso
tattoo [tæˈtu] *s* tatuaje *m;* (mil) retreta || *tr* tatuar o tatuarse
taunt [tɔnt] o [tɑnt] *s* mofa, pulla || *tr* provocar con insultos
taut [tɔt] *adj* tieso, tirante
tavern [ˈtævərn] *s* taberna; mesón *m,* posada
taw•dry [ˈtɔdri] *adj* (*comp* **-drier;** *super* **-driest**) cursi, charro, vistoso
taw•ny [ˈtɔni] *adj* (*comp* **-nier;** *super* **-niest**) leonado
tax [tæks] *s* contribución, impuesto || *tr* poner impuestos a (*una persona*); poner impuestos sobre (*la propiedad*); abrumar, cargar; agotar (*la paciencia de uno*)
taxable [ˈtæksəbəl] *adj* imponible
taxation [tækˈseʃən] *s* imposición de contribuciones; contribuciones, impuestos
tax collector *s* recaudador *m* de impuestos
tax cut *s* reducción de impuestos
tax evader [ɪˈvedər] *s* burlador *m* de impuestos
tax′-ex•empt′ *adj* exento de impuesto
tax•i [ˈtæksi] *s* (*pl* **-is**) taxi *m* || *v* (*pret & pp* **-ied;** *ger* **-iing** o **-ying**) *tr* (aer) carretear || *intr* ir en taxi; (aer) carretear, taxear
tax′i•cab′ *s* taxi *m*
taxi dancer *s* taxi *f*
taxi driver *s* taxista *mf*
tax′i•plane′ *s* avioneta de alquiler
taxi stand *s* parada de taxis
tax′pay′er *s* contribuyente *mf*
tax rate *s* tipo impositivo
t.b. *abbr* **tuberculosis**

tbs. o **tbsp.** *abbr* **tablespoon, tablespoons**
tea [ti] *s* té *m;* (*medicinal infusion*) tisana; caldo de carne
tea bag *s* muñeca
tea ball *s* huevo del té
tea'cart' *s* mesita de té (*con ruedas*)
teach [titʃ] *v* (*pret & pp* **taught** [tɔt]) *tr & intr* enseñar
teacher ['titʃər] *s* maestro, instructor *m;* (*such as adversity*) (fig) maestra
teacher's pet *s* alumno mimado
teaching ['titʃɪŋ] *adj* docente || *s* enseñanza; doctrina
teaching aids *spl* material *m* auxiliar de instrucción
teaching staff *s* personal *m* docente
tea'cup' *s* taza para té
tea dance *s* té *m* bailable
teak [tik] *s* teca
tea'ket'tle *s* tetera
team [tim] *s* (*e.g., of horses*) tiro, tronco; (*of oxen*) yunta; (sport) equipo || *tr* enganchar, uncir, enyugar || *intr* — **to team up** asociarse, unirse; formar un equipo
team'mate' *s* compañero de equipo, equipier *m*
teamster ['timstər] *s* (*of horses*) tronquista *m;* (*of a truck*) camionista *m*
team'work' *s* espíritu de equipo; trabajo de equipo
tea'pot' *s* tetera
tear [tɪr] *s* lágrima; **to burst into tears** romper a llorar; **to fill with tears** arrasarse (*los ojos*) de o en lágrimas; **to hold back one's tears** beberse las lágrimas; **to laugh away one's tears** convertir las lágrimas en risas || [tɛr] *s* desgarro, rasgón *m* || [tɛr] *v* (*pret* **tore** [tor]; *pp* **torn** [torn]) *tr* desgarrar, rasgar; acongojar, afligir; mesarse (*los cabellos*); **to tear apart** romper en dos; **to tear down** derribar (*un edificio*); desarmar (*una máquina*); **to tear off** desgajar; **to tear up** romper (*p.ej., un papel*) || *intr* desgarrarse, rasgarse; **to tear along** correr a toda velocidad
tear bomb [tɪr] *s* bomba lacrimógena
tearful ['tɪrfəl] *adj* lacrimoso
tear gas [tɪr] *s* gas lacrimógeno
tear-jerker ['tɪr,dʒʌrkər] *s* (slang) drama *m* o cine *m* que arrancan lágrimas
tear-off ['tɛr,ɔf] o ['tɛr,ɑf] *adj* exfoliador
tea'room' *s* salón *m* de té
tear sheet [tɛr] *s* hoja del anunciante
tease [tiz] *tr* embromar, azuzar
tea'spoon' *s* cucharilla, cucharita
teaspoonful ['ti,spun,fʊl] *s* cucharadita
teat [tit] *s* teta, pezón *m*
tea time *s* hora del té
technical ['tɛknɪkəl] *adj* técnico
technicali•ty [,tɛknɪ'kælɪti] *s* (*pl* **-ties**) detalle técnico
technician [tɛk'nɪʃən] *s* técnico
technics ['tɛknɪks] *ssg* técnica
technique [tɛk'nik] *s* técnica
Teddy bear ['tɛdi] *s* oso de juguete, oso de trapo
tedious ['tidɪ·əs] o ['tidʒəs] *adj* tedioso, enfadoso
teem [tim] *intr* hormiguear; llover a cántaros; **to teem with** hervir de
teeming ['timɪŋ] *adj* hormigueante; (*rain*) torrencial
teen age [tin] *s* edad de 13 a 19 años
teen-ager ['tin,edʒər] *s* joven *mf* de 13 a 19 años de edad
teens [tinz] *spl* números ingleses que terminan en **-teen** (de 13 a 19); edad de 13 a 19 años; **to be in one's teens** tener de 13 a 19 años
tee•ny ['tini] *adj* (*comp* **-nier;** *super* **-niest**) (coll) diminuto, pequeñito
teeter ['titər] *s* vaivén *m,* balanceo || *intr* balancear, oscilar
teethe [tið] *intr* endentecer
teething ['tiðɪŋ] *s* dentición
teething ring *s* chupador *m*
teetotaler [ti'totələr] *s* teetotalista *mf,* nefalista *mf,* abstemio
tel. *abbr* **telegram, telegraph, telephone**
tele•cast ['tɛlɪ,kæst] o ['tɛlɪ,kɑst] *s* teledifusión || *v* (*pret & pp* **-cast** o **-casted**) *tr & intr* teledifundir
telegram ['tɛlɪ,græm] *s* telegrama *m*
telegraph ['tɛlɪ,græf] o ['tɛlɪ,grɑf] *s* telégrafo || *tr & intr* telegrafiar
telegrapher [tɪ'lɛgrəfər] *s* telegrafista *mf*
telegraph pole *s* poste *m* de telégrafo
Telemachus [tɪ'lɛməkəs] *s* Telémaco
telemeter [tɪ'lɛmɪtər] *s* telémetro || *tr* telemetrar
telemetry [tɪ'lɛmɪtri] *s* telemetría
telephone ['tɛlɪ,fon] *s* teléfono || *tr & intr* telefonear
telephone booth *s* locutorio, cabina telefónica
telephone call *s* llamada telefónica
telephone directory *s* anuario telefónico, guía telefónica
telephone exchange *s* estación telefónica, central *f* de teléfonos
telephone operator *s* telefonista *mf*
telephone receiver *s* receptor telefónico
telephone table *s* mesita portateléfono
teleprinter ['tɛlɪ,prɪntər] *s* teleimpresor *m*
telescope ['tɛlɪ,skop] *s* telescopio || *tr* telescopar || *intr* telescoparse
teletype ['tɛlɪ,taɪp] *s* teletipo || *tr & intr* transmitir por teletipo
teleview ['tɛlɪ,vju] *tr & intr* ver por televisión
televiewer ['tɛlɪ,vju·ər] *s* televidente *mf,* telespectador *m*
televise ['tɛlɪ,vaɪz] *tr* televisar
television ['tɛlɪ,vɪʒən] *adj* televisor || *s* televisión
television screen *s* pantalla televisora
television set *s* televisor *m,* telerreceptor *m*
tell [tɛl] *v* (*pret & pp* **told** [told]) *tr* decir; (*to narrate; to count*) contar; determinar; conocer, distinguir; **I told you so!** ¡por algo te lo dije!; **to tell someone to** + *inf* decirle a uno que + *subj* || *intr* hablar; surtir efecto; **to tell on** dejarse ver en (*p.ej., la salud de uno*); (coll) denunciar

teller ['tɛlər] *s* narrador *m;* (*of a bank*) cajero; (*of votes*) escrutador *m*
temper ['tɛmpər] *s* temple *m,* natural *m,* genio; cólera, mal genio; (*of steel, glass, etc.*) temple *m;* **to keep one's temper** dominar su mal genio; **to lose one's temper** encolerizarse, perder la paciencia || *tr* templar || *intr* templarse
temperament ['tɛmpərəmənt] *s* disposición; temperamento sensible o excitable
temperamental [,tɛmpərə'mɛntəl] *adj* temperamental
temperance ['tɛmpərəns] *s* templanza
temperate ['tɛmpərɪt] *adj* templado
temperature ['tɛmpərətʃər] *s* temperatura
tempest ['tɛmpɪst] *s* tempestad
tempestuous [tɛm'pɛstʃu·əs] *adj* tempestuoso
temple ['tɛmpəl] *s* (*place of worship*) templo; (*side of forehead*) sien *f;* (*sidepiece of spectacles*) gafa
tem·po ['tɛmpo] *s* (*pl* **-pos** o **-pi** [pi]) (mus) tiempo; (fig) ritmo (*p.ej., de la vida*)
temporal ['tɛmpərəl] *adj* temporal
temporary ['tɛmpə,rɛri] *adj* temporáneo, temporario, provisional, interino
temporize ['tɛmpə,raɪz] *intr* contemporizar, temporizar
tempt [tɛmpt] *tr* tentar
temptation [tɛmp'teʃən] *s* tentación
tempter ['tɛmptər] *s* tentador *m*
tempting ['tɛmptɪŋ] *adj* tentador
ten [tɛn] *adj & pron* diez || *s* diez *m;* **ten o'clock** las diez
tenable ['tɛnəbəl] *adj* defendible
tenacious [tɪ'neʃəs] *adj* tenaz
tenacity [tɪ'næsɪti] *s* tenacidad
tenant ['tɛnənt] *s* arrendatario, inquilino; morador *m,* residente *mf*
tend [tɛnd] *tr* cuidar, vigilar; servir || *intr* tender, dirigirse; **to tend to** atender a; **to tend to** + *inf* tender a + *inf*
tenden·cy ['tɛndənsi] *s* (*pl* **-cies**) tendencia
tender ['tɛndər] *adj* tierno; (*painfully sensitive*) dolorido || *n* oferta; (naut) alijador *m,* falúa; (rr) ténder *m* || *tr* ofrecer, tender
tender-hearted ['tɛndər ,hɑrtɪd] *adj* compasivo, tierno de corazón
ten'der·loin' *s* filete *m* || **Tenderloin** *s* barrio de mala vida
tenderness ['tɛndərnɪs] *s* ternura, terneza; sensibilidad
tendon ['tɛndən] *s* tendón *m*
tendril ['tɛndrɪl] *s* zarcillo
tenement ['tɛnɪmənt] *s* habitación, vivienda; casa de vecindad
tenement house *s* casa de vecindad
tenet ['tɛnɪt] *s* dogma *m,* credo, principio
tennis ['tɛnɪs] *s* tenis *m*
tennis court *s* campo de tenis
tennis player *s* tenista *mf*
tenor ['tɛnər] *s* tenor *m,* carácter *m,* curso, tendencia; (mus) tenor
tense [tɛns] *adj* tenso, tieso; (*person; situation*) (fig) tenso; (*relations*) tirante || *s* (gram) tiempo
tension ['tɛnʃən] *s* tensión; ansia, congoja, esfuerzo mental; (*in personal or diplomatic relations*) tirantez *f*
tent [tɛnt] *s* tienda; tienda de campaña
tentacle ['tɛntəkəl] *s* tentáculo
tentative ['tɛntətɪv] *adj* tentativo
tenth [tɛnθ] *adj & s* décimo || *s* (*in dates*) diez *m*
tenuous ['tɛnju·əs] *adj* tenue; (*thin in consistency*) raro
tenure ['tɛnjər] *s* (*of property*) tenencia; (*of an office*) ejercicio; (*protection from dismissal*) inamovilidad
tepid ['tɛpɪd] *adj* tibio
tercet ['tʌrsɪt] *s* terceto
term [tʌrm] *s* término; (*of imprisonment*) condena; semestre *m,* período escolar; (*of the presidency of the U.S.A.*) mandato, período; **terms** condiciones || *tr* llamar, nombrar
termagant ['tʌrməgənt] *s* mujer regañona, mujer de mal genio
terminal ['tʌrmɪnəl] *adj* terminal || *s* término, fin *m;* (elec) terminal *m;* (rr) estación de fin de línea
terminate ['tʌrmɪ,net] *tr & intr* terminar
termination [,tʌrmɪ'neʃən] *s* terminación
terminus ['tʌrmɪnəs] *s* término; (rr) estación de cabeza, estación extrema
termite ['tʌrmaɪt] *s* termite *m,* comején *m*
terrace ['tɛrəs] *s* terraza; (*flat roof of a house*) azotea
terra firma ['tɛrə 'fʌrmə] *s* tierra firme; **on terra firma** sobre suelo firme
terrain [tɛ'ren] *s* terreno
terrestrial [tə'rɛstrɪ·əl] *adj* terrestre
terrible ['tɛrɪbəl] *adj* terrible; muy desagradable
terrific [tə'rɪfɪk] *adj* terrífico; (coll) enorme, intenso, brutal
terri·fy ['tɛrɪ,faɪ] *v* (*pret & pp* **-fied**) *tr* aterrorizar, atemorizar
territo·ry ['tɛrɪ,tori] *s* (*pl* **-ries**) territorio
terror ['tɛrər] *s* terror *m*
terrorize ['tɛrə,raɪz] *tr* aterrorizar; imponerse a, mediante el terror
terry cloth ['tɛri] *s* albornoz *m*
terse [tʌrs] *adj* breve, sucinto
tertiary ['tʌrʃɪ,ɛri] o ['tʌrʃəri] *adj* terciario
Test. *abbr* **Testament**
test [tɛst] *s* prueba, ensayo; examen *m* || *tr* probar, poner a prueba; examinar
testament ['tɛstəmənt] *s* testamento
test flight *s* vuelo de ensayo
testicle ['tɛstɪkəl] *s* testículo
testi·fy ['tɛstɪ,faɪ] *v* (*pret & pp* **-fied**) *tr & intr* testificar
testimonial [,tɛstɪ'monɪ·əl] *s* recomendación, certificado; (*expression of esteem, gratitude, etc.*) homenaje *m*
testimo·ny ['tɛstɪ,moni] *s* (*pl* **-nies**) testimonio
test pilot *s* (aer) piloto de pruebas
test tube *s* probeta, tubo de ensayo

tether ['tɛðər] *s* atadura, traba; **at the end of one's tether** al límite de las posibilidades o la paciencia de uno || *tr* apersogar
tetter ['tɛtər] *s* empeine *m*
text [tɛkst] *s* texto; tema *m*, lema *m*
text'book' *s* libro de texto
textile ['tɛkstɪl] o ['tɛkstaɪl] *adj & s* textil *m*
texture ['tɛkstʃər] *s* textura
Thai ['tɑ·i] o ['taɪ] *adj & s* tailandés *m*
Thailand ['taɪlənd] *s* Tailandia
Thales ['θeliz] *s* Tales *m*
Thalia [θə'laɪ·ə] *s* Talía
Thames [tɛmz] *s* Támesis *m*
than [ðæn] *conj* que, p.ej., **he is richer than I** es más rico que yo; (*before a numeral*) de, p.ej., **more than twenty** más de veinte; (*before a verb*) de lo que, p.ej., **the crop is larger than was expected** la cosecha es mayor de lo que se esperaba; (*before a verb with direct object understood*) del (de la, de los, de las) que, p.ej., **they sent us more coffee than we ordered** nos enviaron más café del que pedimos
thank [θæŋk] *tr* agradecer, dar las gracias a; **to thank someone for something** agradecerle a uno una cosa || **thanks** *spl* gracias; **thanks to** gracias a, merced a || **thanks** *interj* ¡gracias!
thankful ['θæŋkfəl] *adj* agradecido
thankless ['θæŋklɪs] *adj* ingrato
thanksgiving [,θæŋks'gɪvɪŋ] *s* acción de gracias
Thanksgiving Day *s* (**U.S.A.**) día *m* de acción de gracias
that [ðæt] *adj dem* (*pl* **those**) ese; aquel; **that one** ése; aquél || *pron dem* (*pl* **those**) ése; aquél; eso; aquello || *pron rel* que, quien, el cual, el que || *adv* tan; **that far** tan lejos; hasta allí; **that many** tantos; **that much** tanto || *conj* que; para que
thatch [θætʃ] *s* barda, paja; techo de paja || *tr* cubrir de paja, techar con paja, bardar
thaw [θɔ] *s* deshielo, derretimiento || *tr* deshelar, derretir || *intr* deshelarse, derretirse
the [ðə], [ðɪ] o [ði] *art def* el || *adv* cuanto, p.ej., **the more the merrier** cuanto más mejor; **the more . . . the more** cuanto más . . . tanto más
theater ['θi·ətər] *s* teatro
the'ater-go'er *s* teatrero
theater news *s* actualidad escénica
theater page *s* noticiario teatral
theatrical [θɪ'ætrɪkəl] *adj* teatral
Thebes [θibz] *s* Tebas *f*
thee [ði] *pron pers* (archaic, poet, **Bib**) te; ti; **with thee** contigo
theft [θɛft] *s* hurto, robo
their [ðɛr] *adj poss* su; el . . . de ellos
theirs [ðɛrz] *pron poss* el suyo, el de ellos
them [ðɛm] *pron pers* los; ellos; **to them** les; a ellos
theme [θim] *s* tema *m*; (mus) tema *m*
theme song *s* (mus) tema *m* central; (rad) sintonía
them·selves' *pron pers* ellos mismos; sí, sí mismos; se, p.ej., **they enjoyed themselves** se divirtieron; **with themselves** consigo
then [ðɛn] *adv* entonces; después, luego, en seguida; además, también; **by then** para entonces; **from then on** desde entonces, de allí en adelante; **then and there** ahí mismo
thence [ðɛns] *adv* desde allí; desde entonces; por eso
thence'forth' *adv* de allí en adelante; desde entonces
theolo·gy [θi'ɑlədʒi] *s* (*pl* **-gies**) teología
theorem ['θi·ərəm] *s* teorema *m*
theo·ry ['θi·əri] *s* (*pl* **-ries**) teoría
therapeutic [,θɛrə'pjutɪk] *adj* terapéutico || **therapeutics** *ssg* terapéutica
thera·py ['θɛrəpi] *s* (*pl* **-pies**) terapia
there [ðɛr] *adv* allí, allá; **there is** o **there are** hay; aquí tiene Vd.
there'a·bouts' *adv* por allí; cerca, aproximadamente
there·af'ter *adv* de allí en adelante, después de eso
there·by' *adv* con eso; así, de tal modo; por allí cerca
therefore ['ðɛrfor] *adv* por lo tanto, por consiguiente
there·in' *adv* en esto, en eso; en ese respecto
there·of' *adv* de ello, de eso
Theresa [tə'risə] o [tə'rɛsə] *s* Teresa
there'u·pon' *adv* sobre eso, encima de eso; por consiguiente; en seguida
thermistor [θər'mɪstər] *s* (elec) termistor *m*
thermocouple ['θʌrmo,kʌpəl] *s* (elec) termopar *m*
thermodynamic [,θʌrmodaɪ'næmɪk] *adj* termodinámico || **thermodynamics** *ssg* termodinámica
thermometer [θər'mɑmɪtər] *s* termómetro
thermonuclear [,θʌrmo'njuklɪ·ər] o [,θʌrmo'nuklɪ·ər] *adj* termonuclear
Thermopylae [θər'mɑpɪ,li] *s* las Termópilas
thermos bottle ['θʌrməs] *s* termos *m*, botella termos
thermostat ['θʌrmə,stæt] *s* termóstato
thesau·rus [θɪ'sɔrəs] *s* (*pl* **-ri** [raɪ]) tesoro; (*dictionary or the like*) tesauro, tesoro
these [ðiz] *pl de* **this**
the·sis ['θisɪs] *s* (*pl* **-ses** [siz]) tesis *f*
Thespis ['θɛspɪs] *s* Tespis *m*
Thessaly ['θɛsəli] *s* la Tesalia
they [ðe] *pron pers* ellos, ellas
thick [θɪk] *adj* espeso; grueso; denso; (coll) estúpido; (coll) íntimo || *s* espesor *m*; **the thick of** (*e.g., a crowd*) lo más denso de; (*e.g., a battle*) lo más reñido de; **through thick and thin** contra viento y marea
thicken ['θɪkən] *tr* espesar || *intr* espesarse; complicarse (*el enredo*)
thicket ['θɪkɪt] *s* espesura, matorral *m*, soto
thick-headed ['θɪk'hɛdɪd] *adj* (coll) torpe, estúpido
thick'-set' *adj* grueso, rechoncho

thief [θif] *s* (*pl* **thieves** [θivz]) ladrón *m*
thieve [θiv] *intr* hurtar, robar
thiever•y [ˈθivəri] *s* (*pl* **-ies**) latrocinio, hurto, robo
thigh [θaɪ] *s* muslo
thigh′bone′ *s* hueso del muslo, fémur *m*
thimble [ˈθɪmbəl] *s* dedal *m*
thin [θɪn] *adj* (*comp* **thinner;** *super* **thinnest**) delgado, flaco, tenue; (*cloth, paper, sole of shoe, etc.*) fino; (*hair*) ralo; (*broth*) aguado; (*excuse*) débil; claro, ligero, escaso || *v* (*pret & pp* **thinned;** *ger* **thinning**) *tr* adelgazar, enflaquecer; enrarecer; aclarar; aguar; desleír (*los colores*) || *intr* adelgazarse, enflaquecerse; enrarecerse; **to thin out** ralear (*el pelo*)
thine [ðaɪn] *adj poss* (archaic & poet) tu || *pron poss* (archaic & poet) tuyo; el tuyo
thing [θɪŋ] *s* cosa; **of all things!** ¡qué sorpresa!; **to be the thing** ser la última moda; **to be the thing to do** ser lo que debe hacerse; **to see things** ver visiones, padecer alucinaciones
think [θɪŋk] *v* (*pret & pp* **thought** [θɔt]) *tr* pensar; **to think it over** pensarlo; **to think nothing of** tener en poco; creer fácil; no dar importancia a; **to think of** pensar de, p.ej., **what do you think of this book?** ¿qué piensa Vd. de este libro?; **to think up** imaginar; inventar (*p.ej., una excusa*) || *intr* pensar; **to think not** creer que no; **to think of** (*to turn one's thoughts to*) pensar en; pensar (*un número, un naipe, etc.*); **to think so** creer que sí; **to think well of** tener buena opinión de
thinker [ˈθɪŋkər] *s* pensador *m*
third [θʌrd] *adj* tercero || *s* (*in a series*) tercero; (*one of three equal parts*) tercio; (*in dates*) tres *m*
third degree *s* (coll) interrogatorio bajo tortura
third rail *s* (rr) tercer carril *m*, carril de toma
thirst [θʌrst] *s* sed *f* || *intr* tener sed; **to thirst for** tener sed de
thirst•y [ˈθʌrsti] *adj* (*comp* **-ier;** *super* **-iest**) sediento; **to be thirsty** tener sed
thirteen [ˈθʌrˈtin] *adj, pron & s* trece *m*
thirteenth [ˈθʌrˈtinθ] *adj & s* (*in a series*) decimotercero; (*part*) trezavo || *s* (*in dates*) trece *m*
thirtieth [ˈθʌrtɪ·ɪθ] *adj & s* (*in a series*) trigésimo; (*part*) treintavo || *s* (*in dates*) treinta *m*
thir•ty [ˈθʌrti] *adj & pron* treinta || *s* (*pl* **-ties**) treinta *m*
this [ðɪs] *adj dem* (*pl* **these**) este; **this one** éste || *pron dem* (*pl* **these**) éste; esto || *adv* tan
thistle [ˈθɪsəl] *s* cardo
thither [ˈθɪðər] o [ˈðɪðər] *adv* allá, hacia allá
Thomas [ˈtɑməs] *s* Tomás *m*
thong [θɔŋ] o [θɑŋ] *s* correa
tho•rax [ˈθoræks] *s* (*pl* **-raxes** o **-races** [rəˌsiz]) tórax *m*
thorn [θɔrn] *s* espina
thorn•y [ˈθɔrni] *adj* (*comp* **-ier;** *super* **-iest**) espinoso; (*difficult*) (fig) espinoso
thorough [ˈθʌro] *adj* cabal, completo; concienzudo, cuidadoso
thor′ough•bred′ *adj* de pura sangre; bien nacido || *s* pura sangre *m;* persona bien nacida
thor′ough•fare′ *s* vía pública; **no thoroughfare** se prohibe el paso
thor′ough•go′ing *adj* cabal, completo, esmerado, perfecto
thoroughly [ˈθʌroli] *adv* a fondo
those [ðoz] *pl de* **that**
thou [ðaʊ] *pron pers* (archaic, poet & Bib) tú || *tr & intr* tutear
though [ðo] *adv* sin embargo || *conj* aunque, bien que; **as though** como si
thought [θɔt] *s* pensamiento
thoughtful [ˈθɔtfəl] *adj* pensativo; atento, considerado
thoughtless [ˈθɔtlɪs] *adj* irreflexivo; descuidado; inconsiderado
thought transference *s* transmisión del pensamiento
thousand [ˈθaʊzənd] *adj & s* mil *m;* **a thousand** u **one thousand** mil *m*
thousandth [ˈθaʊzəndθ] *adj & s* milésimo
thralldom [ˈθrɔldəm] *s* esclavitud, servidumbre
thrash [θræʃ] *tr* (agr) trillar; azotar, zurrar; **to thrash out** decidir después de una discusión cabal || *intr* trillar; agitarse, menearse
thread [θrɛd] *s* hilo; (mach) filete *m,* rosca; (*of a speech, of life*) hilo; **to lose the thread of** perder el hilo de || *tr* enhebrar, enhilar; ensartar (*p.ej., cuentas*); (mach) aterrajar, filetear
thread′bare′ *adj* raído; gastado, usado, viejo
threat [θrɛt] *s* amenaza
threaten [ˈθrɛtən] *tr & intr* amenazar
threatening [ˈθrɛtənɪŋ] *adj* amenazante
three [θri] *adj & pron* tres || *s* tres *m;* **three o'clock** las tres
three′-cor′nered *adj* triangular; (*hat*) de tres picos
three hundred *adj & pron* trescientos || *s* trescientos *m*
threepence [ˈθrɛpəns] o [ˈθrɪpəns] *s* suma de tres peniques; moneda de tres peniques
three′-ply′ *adj* de tres capas
three R's [ɑrz] *spl* lectura, escritura y aritmética, primeras letras
three′score′ *adj* tres veintenas de
threno•dy [ˈθrɛnədi] *s* (*pl* **-dies**) treno
thresh [θrɛʃ] *tr* (agr) trillar; **to thresh out** decidir después de una discusión cabal || *intr* trillar; agitarse, menearse
threshing machine *s* máquina trilladora
threshold [ˈθrɛʃold] *s* umbral *m;* (physiol, psychol & fig) umbral, limen *m;* **to be on the threshold of** estar en los umbrales de; **to cross the threshold** atravesar o pisar los umbrales
thrice [θraɪs] *adv* tres veces; repetidamente, sumamente

thrift [θrɪft] *s* economía, parquedad

thrift•y [ˈθrɪfti] *adj* (*comp* **-ier;** *super* **-iest**) económico, parco; próspero

thrill [θrɪl] *s* emoción viva ‖ *tr* emocionar, conmover ‖ *intr* emocionarse, conmoverse

thriller [ˈθrɪlər] *s* cuento o pieza de teatro espeluznante

thrilling [ˈθrɪlɪŋ] *adj* emocionante; espeluznante

thrive [θraɪv] *v* (*pret* **thrived** o **throve** [θrov]; *pp* **thrived** o **thriven** [ˈθrɪvən]) *intr* medrar, prosperar

throat [θrot] *s* garganta; **to clear one's throat** aclarar la voz

throb [θrɑb] *s* latido, palpitación, pulsación ‖ *v* (*pret & pp* **throbbed;** *ger* **throbbing**) *intr* latir, palpitar, pulsar

throe [θro] *s* congoja, dolor *m;* **throes** angustia, agonía; esfuerzo penoso

throne [θron] *s* trono

throng [θrɔŋ] o [θrɑŋ] *s* gentío, tropel *m,* muchedumbre ‖ *intr* agolparse, apiñarse

throttle [ˈθrɑtəl] *s* válvula reguladora; (*of a locomotive*) regulador *m;* (*of an automobile*) acelerador *m* ‖ *tr* ahogar, sofocar; impedir, suprimir; (mach) regular; **to throttle down** reducir la velocidad de

through [θru] *adj* directo, sin paradas; acabado, terminado; **to be through with** haber terminado; no querer ocuparse más de ‖ *adv* a través, de un lado a otro; completamente ‖ *prep* por, a través de; por medio de; a causa de; todo lo largo de

through•out′ *adv* por todas partes; en todos respectos; desde el principio hasta el fin ‖ *prep* por todo . . .; durante todo . . .; a lo largo de

through′way′ *s* carretera de peaje de acceso limitado

throw [θro] *s* echada, tirada, lance *m;* cobertor ligero ‖ *v* (*pret* **threw** [θru]; *pp* **thrown**) *tr* arrojar, echar, lanzar; tirar (*los dados*); lanzar (*una mirada*); desarzonar (*a un jinete*); proyectar (*una sombra*); tender (*un puente*); perder con premeditación (*un juego, una carrera*); **to throw away** tirar; malgastar; perder, no aprovechar; **to throw in** añadir, dar de más; **to throw out** arrojar, botar, desechar; echar a la calle; **to throw over** abandonar, dejar ‖ *intr* arrojar, echar, lanzar; **to throw up** vomitar

thrum [θrʌm] *v* (*pret & pp* **thrummed;** *ger* **thrumming**) *intr* teclear; zangarrear; **to thrum on** rasguear

thrush [θrʌʃ] *s* tordo

thrust [θrʌst] *s* empuje *m;* acometida; (*with horns*) cornada; (*with dagger*) puñalada; (*with sword*) estocada; (*with knife*) cuchillada ‖ *v* (*pret & pp* **thrust**) *tr* empujar; acometer; clavar, hincar; atravesar, traspasar

thud [θʌd] *s* baque *m,* ruido sordo ‖ *v* (*pret & pp* **thudded;** *ger* **thudding**) *tr & intr* golpear con ruido sordo

thug [θʌg] *s* ladrón *m,* asesino

thumb [θʌm] *s* pulgar *m,* dedo gordo; **all thumbs** (coll) desmañado, chapucero, torpe; **to twiddle one's thumbs** menear ociosamente los pulgares; no hacer nada; **under the thumb of** bajo la férula de ‖ *tr* manosear sin cuidado; ensuciar con los dedos; hojear (*un libro*) con el pulgar; **to thumb a ride** pedir ser llevado en automóvil indicando la dirección con el pulgar; **to thumb one's nose at** (coll) señalar (*a una persona*) poniendo el pulgar sobre la nariz en son de burla; (coll) tratar con sumo desprecio

thumb index *s* escalerilla, índice *m* con pestañas

thumb′print′ *s* impresión del pulgar ‖ *tr* marcar con impresión del pulgar

thumb′screw′ *s* tornillo de mariposa, tornillo de orejas

thumb′tack′ *s* chinche *m*

thump [θʌmp] *s* golpazo, porrazo ‖ *tr* golpear, aporrear ‖ *intr* caer con golpe pesado; andar con pasos pesados; latir (*el corazón*) con golpes pesados

thumping [ˈθʌmpɪŋ] *adj* (coll) enorme, pesado

thunder [ˈθʌndər] *s* trueno; (*of applause*) estruendo; amenaza ‖ *tr* fulminar (*p.ej., censuras, amenazas*) ‖ *intr* tronar; **to thunder at** tronar contra

thun′der•bolt′ *s* rayo

thun′der•clap′ *s* tronido

thunderous [ˈθʌndərəs] *adj* atronador, tronitoso

thun′der•show′er *s* chubasco con truenos

thun′der•storm′ *s* tronada

thun′der•struck′ *adj* atónito, estupefacto, pasmado

Thursday [ˈθʌrsdi] *s* jueves *m*

thus [ðʌs] *adv* así; **thus far** hasta aquí, hasta ahora

thwack [θwæk] *s* golpe *m,* porrazo ‖ *tr* golpear, pegar

thwart [θwɔrt] *adj* transversal, oblicuo ‖ *adv* de través ‖ *tr* desbaratar, impedir, frustrar

thy [ðaɪ] *adj poss* (archaic & poet) tu

thyme [taɪm] *s* tomillo

thyroid gland [ˈθaɪrɔɪd] *s* glándula tiroides

thyself [ðaɪˈsɛlf] *pron* (archaic & poet) tú mismo; ti mismo; te; ti

tiara [taɪˈɑrə] o [taɪˈɛrə] *s* (*papal miter*) tiara; (*female adornment*) diadema *f*

tick [tɪk] *s* tictac *m;* funda (*de almohada o colchón*); (coll) crédito; (ent) garrapata; **on tick** (coll) al fiado ‖ *intr* hacer tictac; latir (*el corazón*)

ticker [ˈtɪkər] *s* teleimpresor *m* de cinta; (slang) reloj *m;* (slang) corazón *m*

ticker tape *s* cinta de teleimpresor

ticket [ˈtɪkɪt] *s* billete *m;* boleto (Am); (theat) entrada, localidad; (*for wrong parking*) (coll) aviso de multa; (*of a political party*) (U.S.A.) lista de candidatos; **that's the ticket** (coll) eso es, eso es lo que se necesita

ticket agent *s* taquillero
ticket collector *s* revisor *m*
ticket office *s* taquilla, despacho de billetes
ticket scalper ['skælpər] *s* revendedor *m* de billetes de teatro
ticket window *s* taquilla, ventanilla
ticking ['tɪkɪŋ] *s* cutí *m*, terliz *m*
tickle ['tɪkəl] *s* cosquillas ‖ *tr* cosquillear; gustar, satisfacer; divertir ‖ *intr* cosquillear
ticklish ['tɪklɪʃ] *adj* cosquilloso; difícil, delicado; inseguro
tick-tock ['tɪk ˌtɑk] *s* tictac *m*
tidal wave ['taɪdəl] *s* aguaje *m*, ola de marea; (*e.g., of popular indignation*) ola
tidbit ['tɪdˌbɪt] *s* buen bocado, bocadito
tiddlywinks ['tɪdliˌwɪŋks] *s* juego de la pulga
tide [taɪd] *s* marea; temporada; **to go against the tide** ir contra la corriente; **to stem the tide** rendir la marea ‖ *tr* llevar, hacer flotar; **to tide over** ayudar un poco; superar (*una dificultad*)
tide'wa'ter *adj* costanero ‖ *s* agua de marea; orilla del mar
tidings ['taɪdɪŋz] *spl* noticias, informes *mpl*
ti·dy ['taɪdi] *adj* (*comp* **-dier;** *super* **-diest**) aseado, limpio, pulcro, ordenado ‖ *s* (*pl* **-dies**) pañito bordado, cubierta de respaldar ‖ *v* (*pret & pp* **-died**) *tr* asear, limpiar, arreglar, poner en orden ‖ *intr* asearse
tie [taɪ] *s* atadura; lazo, nudo; (*worn on neck*) corbata; (*in games and elections*) empate *m;* (mus) ligado; (rr) traviesa ‖ *v* (*pret & pp* **tied;** *ger* **tying**) *tr* atar, liar; enlazar; hacer (*la corbata*); confinar, limitar; empatar (*p.ej., una elección*); empatársela a (*una persona*); **to be tied up** estar ocupado; **to tie down** confinar, limitar; **to tie up** atar; envolver; obstruir (*el tráfico*) ‖ *intr* atar; empatar o empatarse (*dos candidatos, dos equipos*)
tie'pin' *s* alfiler *m* de corbata
tier [tɪr] *s* fila, ringlera; (theat) fila de palcos
tiger ['taɪgər] *s* tigre *m*
tiger lily *s* azucena atigrada
tight [taɪt] *adj* apretado, estrecho, ajustado; bien cerrado, hermético; compacto, denso; fijo, firme, sólido; (com) escaso; (sport) casi igual; (coll) agarrado, tacaño; (slang) borracho ‖ *adv* firmemente; **to hold tight** mantener fijo; agarrarse bien ‖ **tights** *spl* traje *m* de malla
tighten ['taɪtən] *tr* apretar; atiesar, estirar ‖ *intr* apretarse; atiesarse, estirarse
tight-fisted ['taɪt'fɪstɪd] *adj* agarrado, tacaño
tight'-fit'ting *adj* ceñido, muy ajustado
tight'rope' *s* cuerda tirante
tight squeeze *s* (coll) brete *m*, aprieto
tigress ['taɪgrɪs] *s* tigresa
tile [taɪl] *s* azulejo; (*for floors*) baldosa; (*for roofs*) teja ‖ *tr* azulejar; embaldosar; tejar
tile roof *s* tejado (de tejas)
till [tɪl] *prep* hasta ‖ *conj* hasta que ‖ *s* cajón *m* o gaveta del dinero ‖ *tr* labrar, cultivar
tilt [tɪlt] *s* inclinación; justa, torneo; **full tilt** a toda velocidad ‖ *tr* inclinar; asestar (*una lanza*) ‖ *intr* inclinarse; justar, tornear; luchar; **to tilt at** luchar con, arremeter contra; protestar contra
timber ['tɪmbər] *s* madera de construcción; madero, viga; bosque *m*, árboles *mpl* de monte
tim'ber·land' *s* bosque *m* maderable
timber line *s* límite *m* de la vegetación, límite del bosque maderable
timbre ['tɪmbər] *s* (phonet & phys) timbre *m*
time [taɪm] *s* tiempo; hora, p.ej., **time to eat** hora de comer; vez, p.ej., **five times** cinco veces; rato, p.ej., **a nice time** un buen rato; (*period for payment*) plazo; horas de trabajo; sueldo; tiempo de parir, término del embarazo; última hora; (phot) tiempo de exposición; **for the time being** por ahora, por el momento; **on time** a tiempo, a la hora debida; (*in installments*) a plazos; **to bide one's time** esperar la hora propicia; **to do time** (coll) cumplir una condena; **to have a good time** darse buen tiempo; **to have no time for** no poder tolerar; **to lose time** atrasarse (*el reloj*); **to make time** avanzar con rapidez; **to pass the time of day** saludarse (*dos personas*); **to take one's time** no darse prisa, ir despacio; **what time is it?** ¿qué hora es? ‖ *tr* calcular el tiempo de; medir el tiempo de; (sport) cronometrar
time bomb *s* bomba-reloj *f*
time'card' *s* hoja de presencia, tarjeta registradora
time clock *s* reloj *m* registrador
time exposure *s* exposición de tiempo
time fuse *s* espoleta de tiempos
time'keep'er *s* alistador *m* de tiempo; reloj *m;* (sport) cronometrador *m*, juez *m* de tiempo
time·ly ['taɪmli] *adj* (*comp* **-lier;** *super* **-liest**) oportuno
time'piece' *s* reloj *m*
time signal *s* señal horaria
time'ta'ble *s* horario, itinerario
time'work' *s* trabajo a jornal
time'worn' *adj* gastado por el tiempo
time zone *s* huso horario
timid ['tɪmɪd] *adj* tímido
timing gears ['taɪmɪŋ] *spl* engranaje *m* de distribución, mando de las válvulas
timorous ['tɪmərəs] *adj* tímido, miedoso
tin [tɪn] *s* (*element*) estaño; (*tin plate*) hojalata; (*cup, box, etc.*) lata ‖ *v* (*pret & pp* **tinned;** *ger* **tinning**) *tr* estañar; (*to pack in cans*) enlatar; recubrir de hojalata
tin can *s* lata, envase *m* de hojalata
tincture ['tɪŋktʃər] *s* tintura

tin cup *s* taza de hojalata
tinder ['tɪndər] *s* yesca
tin'der•box' *s* lumbres *fpl,* yesquero; persona muy excitable; semillero de violencia
tin foil *s* hojuela de estaño, papel *m* de estaño
ting-a-ling ['tɪŋə,lɪŋ] *s* tilín *m*
tinge [tɪndʒ] *s* matiz *m,* tinte *m;* dejo, gustillo || *v* (*ger* **tingeing** o **tinging**) *tr* matizar, teñir; dar gusto o sabor a
tingle ['tɪŋgəl] *s* comezón *f,* picazón *f* || *intr* sentir comezón; zumbar (*los oídos*); (*e.g., with enthusiasm*) estremecerse
tin hat *s* (coll) yelmo de acero
tinker ['tɪŋkər] *s* calderero remendón; chapucero || *intr* ocuparse vanamente
tinkle ['tɪŋkəl] *s* retintín *m* || *tr* hacer retiñir || *intr* retiñir
tin plate *s* hojalata
tin roof *s* tejado de hojalata
tinsel ['tɪnsəl] *s* oropel *m;* (*e.g., for a Christmas tree*) lentejuelas de hojas de estaño
tin'smith' *s* hojalatero
tin soldier *s* soldadito de plomo
tint [tɪnt] *s* tinte *m,* matiz *m* || *tr* teñir, matizar, colorar ligeramente
tin'type' *s* ferrotipo
tin'ware' *s* objetos de hojalata
ti•ny ['taɪni] *adj* (*comp* **-nier;** *super* **-niest**) diminuto, menudo, pequeñito
tip [tɪp] *s* extremo, extremidad; (*of shoestring*) herrete *m;* (*of arrow*) casquillo; (*of umbrella*) regatón *m;* (*of tongue*) punta; (*of shoe*) puntera; (*of cigarette*) embocadura; inclinación; golpecito; soplo, aviso confidencial; (*fee*) propina || *v* (*pret & pp* **tipped;** *ger* **tipping**) *tr* herretear; inclinar, ladear; volcar; golpear ligeramente; dar propina a; informar por debajo de cuerda; tocarse (*el sombrero*) con los dedos; quitarse (*el sombrero en señal de cortesía*); **to tip in** (typ) encañonar (*un pliego*) || *intr* dar una propina o propinas; inclinarse, ladearse; volcarse
tip'cart' *s* volquete *m*
tip'-off' *s* (coll) informe dado por debajo de cuerda
tipped'-in' *adj* (bb) fuera de texto
tipple ['tɪpəl] *intr* beborrotear
tip'staff' *s* vara de justicia; alguacil *m* de vara
tip•sy ['tɪpsi] *adj* (*comp* **-sier;** *super* **-siest**) achispado
tip'toe' *s* punta del pie; **on tiptoe** de puntillas; alerta; furtivamente || *v* (*pret & pp* **-toed;** *ger* **-toeing**) *intr* andar de puntillas
tirade ['taɪred] *s* diatriba, invectiva
tire [taɪr] *s* neumático, llanta de goma; (*of metal*) calce *m,* llanta || *tr* cansar; aburrir, fastidiar || *intr* (*to be tiresome*) cansar; (*to get tired*) cansarse; aburrirse, fastidiarse
tire chain *s* cadena de llanta, cadena antirresbaladiza
tired [taɪrd] *adj* cansado, rendido
tire gauge *s* indicador *m* de presión de inflado
tireless ['taɪrlɪs] *adj* incansable, infatigable
tire pressure *s* presión de inflado
tire pump *s* bomba para inflar neumáticos
tiresome ['taɪrsəm] *adj* cansado, aburrido, pesado
tissue ['tɪsjʊ] *s* tejido fino; papel *m* de seda; (biol & fig) tejido
tissue paper *s* papel *m* de seda
titanium [tai'tenɪ•əm] o [tɪ'tenɪ•əm] *s* titanio
tithe [taɪð] *s* décimo, décima parte; (*tax paid to church*) diezmo || *tr* diezmar
Titian ['tɪʃən] *adj* castaño rojizo || *s* el Ticiano
title ['taɪtəl] *s* título; (sport) campeonato || *tr* titular
title deed *s* título de propiedad
ti'tle•hold'er *s* titulado; (sport) campeón *m*
title page *s* portada, frontispicio
title rôle *s* (theat) papel *m* principal (*el que corresponde al título de la obra*)
titter ['tɪtər] *s* risita ahogada, risita disimulada || *intr* reír a medias, reír con disimulo
titular ['tɪtʃələr] *adj* titular; nominal
tn. *abbr* **ton**
to [tu], [tʊ] o [tə] *adv* hacia adelante; **to and fro** de una parte a otra, de aquí para allá; **to come to** volver en sí || *prep* a, p.ej., **he is going to Madrid** va a Madrid; **they gave something to the beggar** dieron algo al pobre; **we are learning to dance** aprendemos a bailar; para, p.ej., **he is reading to himself** lee para sí; por, p.ej., **work to do** trabajo por hacer; hasta, p.ej., **to a certain extent** hasta cierto punto; en, p.ej., **from door to door** de puerta en puerta; con, p.ej., **kind to her** amable con ella; segun, p.ej., **to my way of thinking** según mi modo de pensar; menos, p.ej., **five minutes to ten** las diez menos cinco
toad [tod] *s* sapo
toad'stool' *s* agárico, seta; seta venenosa
to-and-fro ['tu•ənd'fro] *adj* alternativo, de vaivén
toast [tost] *s* tostadas; (*drink*) brindis *m;* **a piece of toast** una tostada || *tr* tostar; brindar a o por || *intr* tostarse; brindar
toaster ['tostər] *s* (*of bread*) tostador *m;* brindador *m*
toast'mas'ter *s* el que presenta a los oradores en un banquete, maestro de ceremonias
tobac•co [tə'bæko] *s* (*pl* **-cos**) tabaco
tobacco pouch *s* petaca
toboggan [tə'bɑgən] *s* tobogán *m* || *intr* deslizarse en tobogán
tocsin ['tɑksɪn] *s* campana de alarma; campanada de alarma
today [tʊ'de] *adv & s* hoy
toddle ['tɑdəl] *s* pasitos vacilantes || *intr* andar con pasitos vacilantes; hacer pinitos (*un niño o un enfermo*)

tod·dy ['tadi] *s* (*pl* **-dies**) ponche *m*
to-do [tə'du] *s* (coll) alharaca, alboroto
toe [to] *s* dedo del pie; (*of stocking*) punta || *v* (*pret & pp* **toed;** *ger* **toeing**) *tr* — **to toe the line** o **the mark** ponerse a la raya; obrar como se debe
toe'nail' *s* uña del dedo del pie
tog [tag] *s* (coll) prenda de vestir
together [tʊ'gɛðər] *adv* juntamente; juntos; al mismo tiempo; sin interrupción; de acuerdo; **to bring together** reunir; confrontar; reconciliar; **to call together** convocar; **to go together** ir juntos; ser novios; hacer juego; **to stick together** (coll) quedarse unidos, no abandonarse
toil [tɔɪl] *s* afán *m*, fatiga; faena, obra laboriosa; **toils** red *f*, lazo || *intr* atrafagar; moverse con fatiga
toilet ['tɔɪlɪt] *s* tocado, atavío; (*dressing table*) tocador *m;* retrete *m*, inodoro, excusado; **to make one's toilet** asearse, acicalarse
toilet articles *spl* artículos de tocador
toilet paper *s* papel higiénico
toilet powder *s* polvos de tocador
toilet soap *s* jabón *m* de olor, jabón de tocador
toilet water *s* agua de tocador
token ['tokən] *s* señal *f*, prueba; prenda, recuerdo; (*used as money*) ficha, tanto; **by the same token** por el mismo motivo; **in token of** en señal de
tolerance ['talərəns] *s* tolerancia
tolerate ['talə,ret] *tr* tolerar
toll [tol] *s* (*of bells*) doble *m;* (*to pass along a road or over a bridge*) peaje *m;* (*to use a canal*) derechos de paso; (*to use a telephone*) tarifa; (*number of victims*) baja, mortalidad || *tr* tocar a muerto (*una campana*); llamar con toque de difuntos || *intr* doblar
toll bridge *s* puente *m* de peaje
toll call *s* (telp) llamada a larga distancia
toll'gate' *s* barrera de peaje
toma·to [tə'meto] o [tə'mato] *s* (*pl* **-toes**) (*plant*) tomatera o tomate *m;* (*fruit*) tomate
tomb [tum] *s* tumba, sepulcro
tomboy ['tam,bɔɪ] *s* moza retozona, muchacha traviesa
tomb'stone' *s* piedra o lápida sepulcral
tomcat ['tam,kæt] *s* gato macho
tome [tom] *s* tomo; libro grueso
tomorrow [tʊ'maro] o [tʊ'mɔro] *adv* mañana || *s* mañana *m;* **the day after tomorrow** pasado mañana
tom-tom ['tam,tam] *s* tantán *m*
ton [tʌn] *s* tonelada; **tons** (coll) montones *mpl*
tone [ton] *s* tono || *tr* entonar || *intr* armonizar; **to tone down** moderarse; **to tone up** reforzarse
tone poem *s* poema sinfónico
tongs [tɔŋz] o [taŋz] *spl* tenazas; (*e.g., for sugar*) tenacillas
tongue [tʌŋ] *s* (anat) lengua; (*of a wagon*) vara, lanza; (*of a belt buckle*) tarabilla; (*of shoe*) lengua, lengüeta; (*language*) lengua, idioma *m;* **to hold one's tongue** morderse la lengua
tongue twister ['twɪstər] *s* trabalenguas *m*
tonic ['tanɪk] *adj & s* tónico
tonic accent *s* acento prosódico
tonight [tʊ'naɪt] *adv & s* esta noche
tonnage ['tʌnɪdʒ] *s* tonelaje *m*
tonsil ['tansəl] *s* tonsila, amígdala
tonsillitis [,tansɪ'laɪtɪs] *s* tonsilitis *f*, amigdalitis *f*
ton·y ['toni] *adj* (*comp* **-ier;** *super* **-iest**) (slang) elegante, aristocrático
too [tu] *adv* (*also*) también; (*more than enough*) demasiado; **too bad!** ¡qué lástima!; **too many** demasiados; **too much** demasiado
tool [tul] *s* herramienta; (*person used for one's own ends*) instrumento || *tr* trabajar con herramienta; (bb) filetear, estampar
tool bag *s* bolsa de herramientas
tool'mak'er *s* tallador *m* de herramientas, herrero de herramientas
toot [tut] *s* (*of horn*) toque *m;* (*of klaxon*) bocinazo; (*of locomotive*) pitazo; (coll) parranda || *tr* sonar; **to toot one's own horn** cantar sus propias alabanzas || *intr* sonar
tooth [tuθ] *s* (*pl* **teeth** [tiθ]) diente *m*
tooth'ache' *s* dolor *m* de muelas
tooth'brush' *s* cepillo de dientes
toothless ['tuθlɪs] *adj* desdentado
tooth paste *s* pasta dentífrica
tooth'pick' *s* limpiadientes *m*, mondadientes *m*, palillo
tooth powder *s* polvo dentífrico
top [tap] *s* (*of a mountain, tree, etc.*) cima; (*of a mountain; high point*) cumbre *f;* (*of a tree*) copa; (*of a barrel, box, etc.*) tapa; (*of a page*) principio; (*of a table*) tablero; (*of a wall*) coronamiento; (*of a bathing suit*) camiseta; (*of a carriage or auto*) capota; (*toy*) peón *m*, peonza; (naut) cofa; **at the top of** en lo alto de; (*e.g., one's class*) a la cabeza de; **at the top of one's voice** a voz en grito; **from top to bottom** de arriba abajo; de alto a bajo; completamente; **on top of** en lo alto de; encima de; **the tops** (slang) la flor de la canela; **to sleep like a top** dormir como un leño || *v* (*pret & pp* **topped;** *ger* **topping**) *tr* coronar, rematar; cubrir; aventajar, superar; descopar (*p.ej., un árbol*)
topaz ['topæz] *s* topacio
top billing *s* cabecera de cartel
top'coat' *s* sobretodo; abrigo de entretiempo
toper ['topər] *s* borrachín *m*
top hat *s* chistera, sombrero de copa
top'-heav'y *adj* más pesado arriba que abajo
topic ['tapɪk] *s* asunto, materia, tema *m*
top'knot' *s* moño
top'mast' *s* (naut) mastelero
top'most *adj* (el) más alto
topogra·phy [tə'pagrəfi] *s* (*pl* **-phies**) topografía
topple ['tapəl] *tr* derribar, volcar ||

intr derribarse, volcarse; caerse, venirse abajo
top priority *s* máxima prioridad
topsail ['tɑpsəl] o ['tɑp,sel] *s* (naut) gavia
top'soil' *s* capa superficial del suelo
topsy-turvy ['tɑpsi'tʌrvi] *adj* desbarajustado || *adv* en cuadro, patas arriba || *s* desbarajuste *m*
torch [tɔrtʃ] *s* antorcha; lámpara de bolsillo; **to carry the torch for** (slang) amar desesperadamente
torch'bear'er *s* hachero; (fig) adicto, partidario
torch'light' *s* luz *f* de antorcha
torch song *s* canción lenta y melancólica de amor no correspondido
torment ['tɔrmɛnt] *s* tormento || [tɔr'mɛnt] *tr* atormentar
torna•do [tɔr'nedo] *s* (*pl* **-does** o **-dos**) tornado, tromba terrestre
torpe•do [tɔr'pido] *s* (*pl* **-does**) torpedo || *tr* torpedear
torrent ['tɑrənt] o ['tɔrənt] *s* torrente *m*
torrid ['tɑrɪd] o ['tɔrɪd] *adj* tórrido
tor•so ['tɔrso] *s* (*pl* **-sos**) torso
tortoise ['tɔrtəs] *s* tortuga
tortoise shell *s* carey *m*
torture ['tɔrtʃər] *s* tortura || *tr* torturar, atormentar
toss [tɔs] o [tɑs] *s* echada; alcance *m* de una echada || *tr* arrojar, echar; lanzar al aire; agitar, menear; levantar airosamente (*la cabeza*); lanzar (*p.ej., un comentario*); echar a cara o cruz; **to toss off** hacer muy rápidamente; tragar de un golpe || *intr* agitarse, menearse; **to toss and turn** (*in bed*) revolverse, dar vueltas
toss'-up' *s* cara o cruz; probabilidad igual
tot [tɑt] *s* párvulo, peque *m*, chiquitín *m*
to•tal ['totəl] *adj* total; (*e.g., loss*) completo || *s* total *m* || *v* (*pret & pp* **-taled** o **-talled;** *ger* **-taling** o **-talling**) *tr* ascender a, sumar
totter ['tɑtər] *s* tambaleo || *intr* tambalear; estar para desplomarse
touch [tʌtʃ] *s* (*act*) toque *m;* (*sense*) tacto, tiento; (*of piano, pianist, typewriter, typist*) tacto; (*of an illness*) ramo, ataque ligero; pizca, poquito; **to get in touch with** ponerse en comunicación o contacto con; **to lose one's touch** perder el tiento || *tr* tocar; conmover, enternecer; probar (*vino, licor*); (*for a loan*) (slang) pedir prestado a, dar un sablazo a; **to touch up** retocar || *intr* tocar; **to touch at** tocar en (*un puerto*)
touching ['tʌtʃɪŋ] *adj* conmovedor, enternecedor || *prep* tocante a
touch typewriting *s* escritura al tacto
touch•y ['tʌtʃi] *adj* (*comp* **-ier;** *super* **-iest**) quisquilloso, enojadizo
tough [tʌf] *adj* correoso; tenaz; difícil; gamberro; (*e.g., luck*) malo || *s* gamberro, guapetón *m*
toughen ['tʌfən] *tr* hacer correoso; hacer tenaz; dificultar || *intr* ponerse correoso; hacerse tenaz; hacerse difícil
tour [tur] *s* jira, paseo, vuelta; viaje largo; **on tour** de jira, de viaje || *tr* viajar por, recorrer || *intr* viajar por distracción o diversión
touring car ['turɪŋ] *s* coche *m* de turismo
tourist ['turɪst] *adj* turístico || *s* turista *mf*
tournament ['turnəmənt] o ['tʌrnəmənt] *s* torneo
tourney ['turni] o ['tʌrni] *s* torneo || *intr* tornear
tourniquet ['turnɪ,kɛt] o ['tʌrnɪ,ke] *s* torniquete *m*
tousle ['tauzəl] *tr* despeinar, enmarañar
tow [to] *s* remolque *m;* (*e.g., of hemp*) estopa; **to take in tow** dar remolque a; (fig) encargarse de || *tr* remolcar
towage ['to•ɪdʒ] *s* remolque *m;* derechos de remolque
toward(s) [tord(z)] o [tə'wɔrd(z)] *prep* (*in the direction of*) hacia; (*with regard to*) para con; (*a certain hour*) cerca de, a eso de
tow'boat' *s* remolcador *m*
tow•el ['tau•əl] *s* toalla || *v* (*pret & pp* **-eled** o **-elled;** *ger* **-eling** o **-elling**) *tr* secar con toalla
towel rack *s* toallero
tower ['tau•ər] *s* torre *f* || *intr* encumbrarse, empinarse
towering ['tau•ərɪŋ] *adj* encumbrado; sobresaliente; excesivo
towing service ['to•ɪŋ] *s* servicio de grúa
tow'line' *s* cable *m* de remolque, sirga
town [taun] *s* población, pueblo, villa; **in town** a la ciudad, en la ciudad
town clerk *s* escribano municipal
town council *s* concejo municipal
town crier *s* pregonero público
town hall *s* ayuntamiento, casa de ayuntamiento
towns'folk' *spl* vecinos del pueblo
township ['taunʃɪp] *s* sexmo; terreno público de seis millas en cuadro
towns•man ['taunzmən] *s* (*pl* **-men** [mən]) ciudadano, vecino; conciudadano, paisano
towns'peo'ple *spl* vecinos del pueblo
town talk *s* comidilla o hablillas del pueblo
tow'path' *s* camino de sirga
tow plane *s* avión *m* de remolque
tow'rope' *s* cuerda de remolque
tow truck *s* camión-grúa *m*
toxic ['tɑksɪk] *adj & s* tóxico
toy [tɔɪ] *adj* de juguete || *s* juguete *m;* (*trifle*) bagatela; (*trinket*) dije *m*, bujería || *intr* jugar; divertirse; **to toy with** jugar con (*los sentimientos de una persona*); acariciar (*una idea*)
toy bank *s* alcancía, hucha
toy soldier *s* soldado de juguete
trace [tres] *s* huella, rastro; indicio, vestigio; (*of harness*) tirante *m;* pizca || *tr* rastrear; trazar (*p.ej., una curva; los rasgos de una persona o cosa*); averiguar el paradero de; remontar al origen de

trache•a ['trekɪ•ə] *s* (*pl* **-ae** [ˌi]) tráquea

track [træk] *s* (*of foot*) huella; (*of a wheel*) rodada, carril *m;* (*of a boat*) estela; (*of railroad*) vía; (*of an airplane, a hurricane*) trayectoria; (*of a tractor*) llanta de oruga; camino, senda; (*course followed by a boat*) derrota; (*of ideas, events, etc.*) sucesión; (sport) pista; **to keep track of** no perder de vista; no olvidar; **to lose track of** perder de vista; olvidar; **to make tracks** dejar pisadas; irse muy de prisa || *tr* rastrear; seguir la huella o la pista de; dejar pisadas en, manchar pisando; **to track down** seguir y capturar; averiguar el origen de

tracking ['trækɪŋ] *s* seguimiento (*de vehículos espaciales*)

tracking station *s* estación de seguimiento

trackless trolley ['træklɪs] *s* filobús *m,* trolebús *m*

track meet *s* concurso de carreras y saltos

track'walk'er *s* guardavía *m*

tract [trækt] *s* espacio, tracto; folleto; (anat) canal *m,* sistema *m*

traction ['trækʃən] *s* tracción

traction company *s* empresa de tranvías

tractor ['træktər] *s* tractor *m*

trade [tred] *s* comercio; negocio, trato; trueque *m,* canje *m;* (*calling, job*) oficio; clientela, parroquia; (*e.g., in slaves*) trata || *tr* cambiar, trocar; **to trade in** dar como parte del pago; **to trade off** cambalachear; || *intr* comerciar; comprar; **to trade in** comerciar en; **to trade on** aprovecharse de

trade'mark' *s* marca de fábrica, marca registrada

trade name *s* nombre *m* comercial, razón *f* social; nombre de fábrica

trader ['tredər] *s* traficante *mf*

trade school *s* escuela de artes y oficios

trades•man ['tredzmən] *s* (*pl* **-men** [mən]) tendero; comerciante *m;* (Brit) artesano

trades union o **trade union** *s* sindicato, gremio de obreros

trade unionist *s* sindicalista *mf*

trade winds *spl* vientos alisios

trading post ['tredɪŋ] *s* factoría; (*in stock exchange*) puesto de compraventa

trading stamp *s* sello de premio, sello de descuento

tradition [trə'dɪʃən] *s* tradición

traduce [trə'djus] o [trə'dus] *tr* calumniar

traf•fic ['træfɪk] *s* tráfico, comercio; tráfico, circulación; (*e.g., in slaves*) trata || *v* (*pret & pp* **-ficked;** *ger* **-ficking**) *intr* traficar

traffic circle *s* glorieta de tráfico

traffic court *s* juzgado de tráfico

traffic jam *s* embotellamiento, tapón *m* de tráfico

traffic light *s* luz *f* de tráfico, semáforo

traffic sign o **signal** *s* señal *f* de tráfico

traffic ticket *s* aviso de multa

tragedian [trə'dʒidɪ•ən] *s* trágico

trage•dy ['trædʒɪdi] *s* (*pl* **-dies**) tragedia

tragic ['trædʒɪk] *adj* trágico

trail [trel] *s* rastro, huella, pista; (*path through rough country*) trocha, senda, vereda; (*of a gown*) cola; (*of smoke, a rocket, etc.*) estela || *tr* arrastrar; seguir la pista de; andar detrás de; llevar (*p.ej., barro*) con los pies || *intr* arrastrar; rezagarse; arrastrarse, trepar (*una planta*); **to trail off** desaparecer poco a poco

trailer ['trelər] *s* remolque *m,* coche-habitación *m,* casa rodante; planta rastrera

trailing arbutus ['trelɪŋ] *s* epigea rastrera

train [tren] *s* (*of railway cars; of waves*) tren *m;* (*of thought*) hilo || *tr* adiestrar; guiar (*las plantas*); (sport) entrenar || *intr* adiestrarse; (sport) entrenarse

trained nurse *s* enfermera graduada

trainer ['trenər] *s* (sport) entrenador *m*

training ['trenɪŋ] *s* adiestramiento; instrucción; (sport) entrenamiento

training school *s* escuela práctica; reformatorio

training ship *s* buque *m* escuela

trait [tret] *s* característica, rasgo

traitor ['tretər] *s* traidor *m*

traitress ['tretrɪs] *s* traidora

trajecto•ry [trə'dʒɛktəri] *s* (*pl* **-ries**) trayectoria

tramp [træmp] *s* vagabundo; marcha pesada, ruido de pisadas || *tr* pisar con fuerza; recorrer a pie || *intr* andar a pie; vagabundear

trample ['træmpəl] *tr* pisotear || *intr* — **to trample on** o **upon** pisotear

tramp steamer *s* vapor volandero

trance [træns] o [trɑns] *s* arrobamiento, rapto; estado hipnótico

tranquil ['træŋkwɪl] *adj* tranquilo

tranquilize ['træŋkwɪˌlaɪz] *tr & intr* tranquilizar

tranquilizer ['træŋkwɪˌlaɪzər] *s* tranquilizante *m*

tranquillity [træŋ'kwɪlɪti] *s* tranquilidad

transact [træn'zækt] o [træns'ækt] *tr* tramitar; llevar a cabo

transaction [træn'zækʃən] o [træns'ækʃən] *s* tramitación, transacción

transatlantic [ˌtrænsət'læntɪk] *adj & s* transatlántico

transcend [træn'sɛnd] *tr* exceder, superar || *intr* sobresalir

transcribe [træn'skraɪb] *tr* transcribir

transcript ['trænskrɪpt] *s* trasunto, traslado; (educ) hoja de estudios, certificado de estudios

transcription [træn'skrɪpʃən] *s* transcripción

transept ['trænsɛpt] *s* crucero, transepto

trans•fer ['trænsfər] *s* traslado; transbordo; contraseña o billete *m* de transferencia || [træns'fʌr] o ['trænsfər] *v* (*pret & pp* **-ferred;** *ger*

-ferring) *tr* trasladar, transferir; transbordar || *intr* cambiar de tren, tranvía, etc.
transfix [træns'fɪks] *tr* espetar, traspasar; dejar atónito
transform [træns'fɔrm] *tr* transformar || *intr* transformarse
transformer [træns'fɔrmər] *s* transformador *m*
transfusion [træns'fjuʃən] *s* transfusión; (med) transfusión de la sangre
transgress [træns'grɛs] *tr* transgredir, violar; exceder, traspasar (*p.ej., los límites de la prudencia*) || *intr* pecar, prevaricar
transgression [træns'grɛʃən] *s* transgresión; pecado, prevaricación
transient ['trænʃənt] *adj* pasajero, transitorio; de tránsito || *s* transeúnte *mf*
transistor [træn'zɪstər] *s* transistor *m*
transit ['trænsɪt] o ['trænzɪt] *s* tránsito
transitive ['trænsɪtɪv] *adj* transitivo || *s* verbo transitivo
transitory ['trænsɪ,tori] *adj* transitorio
translate [træns'let] o ['trænslet] *tr* (*from one language to another*) traducir; (*from one place to another*) trasladar || *intr* traducirse
translation [træns'leʃən] *s* traducción; traslación
translator [træns'letər] *s* traductor *m*
transliterate [træns'lɪtə,ret] *tr* transcribir
translucent [træns'lusənt] *adj* translúcido
transmission [træns'mɪʃən] *s* transmisión; (aut) cambio de marchas, cambio de velocidades
transmis'sion-gear' box *s* caja de cambio de marchas, caja de velocidades
trans•mit [træns'mɪt] *v* (*pret & pp* **-mitted;** *ger* **-mitting**) *tr & intr* transmitir
transmitter [træns'mɪtər] *s* transmisor *m*
transmitting set *s* aparato transmisor
transmitting station *s* estacion transmisora, emisora
transmute [træns'mjut] *tr & intr* transmutar
transom [trænsəm] *s* (*crosspiece*) travesaño; (*window over door*) montante *m;* (*of ship*) yugo de popa
transparen•cy [træns'pɛrənsi] *s* (*pl* **-cies**) transparencia
transparent [træns'pɛrənt] *adj* transparente
transpire [træns'paɪr] *intr* transpirar; (*to become known, leak out*) transpirar; (coll) acontecer, tener lugar
transplant [træns'plænt] o [træns'plɑnt] *tr* transplantar || *intr* transplantarse
transport ['trænsport] *s* transporte *m;* (aer & naut) transporte *m;* rapto, éxtasis *m,* transporte *m* || [træns'port] *tr* transportar
transportation [,trænspor'teʃən] *s* transporte *m;* (U.S.A.) pasaje *m,* billete *m* de viaje
transport worker *s* transportista *mf*
transpose [træns'poz] *tr* transponer; (mus) transportar
trans•ship [træns'ʃɪp] *v* (*pret & pp* **-shipped;** *ger* **-shipping**) *tr* transbordar
transshipment [træns'ʃɪpmənt] *s* transbordo
trap [træp] *s* trampa; (*double-curved pipe*) sifón *m;* coche ligero de dos ruedas; (sport) lanzaplatos *m* || *v* (*pret & pp* **trapped;** *ger* **trapping**) *tr* entrampar; atrapar (*a un ladrón*)
trap door *s* escotillón *m,* trampa; (theat) escotillón *m,* pescante *m*
trapeze [trə'piz] *s* trapecio
trapezoid ['træpɪ,zɔɪd] *s* trapecio
trapper ['træpər] *s* cazador *m* de alforja
trappings ['træpɪŋz] *spl* (*adornments*) adornos, atavíos; (*of a horse's harness*) jaeces *mpl*
trap'shoot'ing *s* tiro al vuelo
trash [træʃ] *s* broza, basura, desecho; (*junk*) cachivaches *mpl;* (*nonsense*) disparates *mpl;* (*worthless people*) gentuza
trash can *s* basurero
travail ['trævel] o [trə'vel] *s* afán *m,* labor *f,* pena; dolores *mpl* del parto
trav•el ['trævəl] *s* viaje *m;* el viajar; (mach) recorrido || *v* (*pret & pp* **-eled** o **-elled;** *ger* **-eling** o **-elling**) *tr* viajar por; recorrer || *intr* viajar; andar, recorrer
travel bureau *s* oficina de turismo
traveler ['trævələr] *s* viajero; (*salesman*) viajante *m*
traveler's check *s* cheque *m* de viajeros
traveling expenses *spl* gastos de viaje
traveling salesman *s* viajante *m,* agente viajero
traverse ['trævərs] o [trə'vʌrs] *tr* atravesar; recorrer, pasar por
traves•ty ['trævɪsti] *s* (*pl* **-ties**) parodia || *v* (*pret & pp* **-tied**) *tr* parodiar
trawl [trɔl] *s* red barredera, espinel *m,* palangre *m* || *tr & intr* pescar a la rastra
tray [tre] *s* bandeja; (chem & phot) cubeta
treacherous ['trɛtʃərəs] *adj* traicionero, traidor; incierto, poco seguro
treacher•y ['trɛtʃəri] *s* (*pl* **-ies**) traición, alevosía
tread [trɛd] *s* (*stepping*) pisada; (*of stairs*) grada, huella, peldaño; (*of stilts*) horquilla; (*of a tire*) banda de rodamiento; (*of shoe*) suela; (*of an egg*) meaje, galladura || *v* (*pret* **trod** [trɑd]; *pp* **trodden** ['trɑdən] o **trod**) *tr* pisar, pisotear; abrumar, agobiar || *intr* andar, caminar
treadle ['trɛdəl] *s* pedal *m*
tread'mill' *s* rueda de andar; (*futile drudgery*) noria
treas. *abbr* **treasurer, treasury**
treason ['trizən] *s* traición
treasonable ['trizənəbəl] *adj* traicionero, traidor
treasure ['trɛʒər] *s* tesoro || *tr* atesorar
treasurer ['trɛʒərər] *s* tesorero
treasur•y ['trɛʒəri] *s* (*pl* **-ies**) tesorería; tesoro

treat [trit] *s* convite *m;* (*to a drink*) convidada; (*something providing particular enjoyment*) regalo, deleite *m* || *tr* tratar; convidar, regalar; curar (*a un enfermo*) || *intr* tratar; convidar, regalar; **to treat of** tratar de
treatise ['tritɪs] *s* tratado
treatment ['tritmənt] *s* tratamiento
trea·ty ['triti] *s* (*pl* **-ties**) tratado
treble ['trɛbəl] *adj* (*threefold*) tresdoble, triple; sobreagudo; (mus) atiplado; (mus) de tiple || *s* (*person*) tiple *mf;* (*voice*) tiple *m* || *tr* triplicar || *intr* triplicarse
tree [tri] *s* árbol *m*
tree farm *s* monte *m* tallar
treeless ['trilɪs] *adj* pelado, sin árboles
tree'top' *s* copa, cima de árbol
trellis ['trɛlɪs] *s* enrejado, espaldera; emparrado
tremble ['trɛmbəl] *s* temblor *m,* estremecimiento || *intr* temblar, estremecerse
tremendous [trɪ'mɛndəs] *adj* tremendo
tremor ['trɛmər] o ['trimər] *s* temblor *m*
trench [trɛntʃ] *s* foso, zanja; (*for irrigation*) acequia; (mil) trinchera
trenchant ['trɛntʃənt] *adj* mordaz, punzante; enérgico, bien definido
trench coat *s* trinchera
trench mortar *s* (mil) lanzabombas *m*
trench'-plow' *tr* (agr) desfondar
trend [trɛnd] *s* curso, dirección, tendencia || *intr* dirigirse, tender
trespass ['trɛspəs] *s* entrada sin derecho; infracción, violación; culpa, pecado || *intr* entrar sin derecho; pecar; **no trespassing** prohibida la entrada; **to trespass against** pecar contra; **to trespass on** entrar sin derecho en; infringir, violar; abusar de (*p.ej., la paciencia de uno*)
tress [trɛs] *s* (*braid of hair*) trenza; (*curl*) bucle *m,* rizo
trestle ['trɛsəl] *s* caballete *m;* puente *m* o viaducto de caballetes
trial ['traɪ·əl] *s* ensayo, prueba; aflicción, desgracia; (law) juicio, proceso, vista; **on trial** a prueba; (law) en juicio; **to bring to trial** encausar
trial and error *s* método de tanteos
trial balloon *s* globo sonda; **to send up a trial balloon** (fig) lanzar un globo sonda
trial by jury *s* juicio por jurado
trial jury *s* jurado procesal
trial order *s* (com) pedido de ensayo
triangle ['traɪ,æŋgəl] *s* triángulo
tribe [traɪb] *s* tribu *f*
tribunal [trɪ'bjunəl] o [traɪ'bjunəl] *s* tribunal *m*
tribune ['trɪbjun] *s* tribuna
tributar·y ['trɪbjə,tɛri] *adj* tributario || *s* (*pl* **-ies**) tributario
tribute ['trɪbjut] *s* tributo
trice [traɪs] *s* momento, instante *m;* **in a trice** en un periquete
trick [trɪk] *s* ardid *m,* artimaña; (*knack*) maña; (*feat*) suerte *f;* (*prank*) travesura, burla, chasco; tanda, turno; ilusión; (*feat with cards*) truco; (*cards in one round*) baza; (coll) chiquita; **to be up to one's old tricks** hacer de las suyas; **to play a dirty trick on** hacer una mala jugada a || *tr* trampear; burlar, engañar; ataviar
tricker·y ['trɪkəri] *s* (*pl* **-ies**) trampería, malas mañas
trickle ['trɪkəl] *s* chorro delgado, goteo || *intr* escurrir, gotear; pasar gradual e irregularmente
trickster ['trɪkstər] *s* tramposo, embustero
trick·y ['trɪki] *adj* (*comp* **-ier;** *super* **-iest**) tramposo, engañoso; difícil; (*animal*) vicioso; (*ticklish to deal with*) delicado
tricorn ['traɪkɔrn] *adj & s* tricornio
tried [traɪd] *adj* fiel, probado, seguro
trifle ['traɪfəl] *s* bagatela, friolera, fruslería; (*trinket*) bagatela, baratija || *tr* — **to trifle away** malgastar || *intr* estar ocioso, holgar; **to trifle with** manosear; jugar con, burlarse de
trifling ['traɪflɪŋ] *adj* frívolo, fútil, ligero; insignificante, trivial
trifocal [traɪ'fokəl] *adj* trifocal || *s* lente *f* trifocal; **trifocals** anteojos trifocales
trig. *abbr* **trigonometric, trigonometry**
trigger ['trɪgər] *s* (*e.g., of a gun*) disparador *m,* gatillo; (*of any device*) disparador || *tr* poner en movimiento, provocar
trigonometry [,trɪgə'nɑmɪtri] *s* trigonometría
trill [trɪl] *s* trinado, trino; (*made with voice, esp. of birds*) gorjeo; (phonet) vibración || *tr* decir o cantar gorjeando; pronunciar con vibración || *intr* trinar; gorjear
trillion ['trɪljən] *s* (U.S.A.) billón *m;* (Brit) trillón *m*
trilo·gy ['trɪlədʒi] *s* (*pl* **-gies**) trilogía
trim [trɪm] *adj* (*comp* **trimmer;** *super* **trimmest**) acicalado, compuesto, elegante || *s* condición, estado; buena condición; adorno, atavío; traje *m,* vestido; (*of sails*) orientación || *v* (*pret & pp* **trimmed;** *ger* **trimming**) *tr* ajustar, adaptar; arreglar, componer; adornar, decorar; decorar, enguirnaldar (*el árbol de Navidad*); recortar; cortar ligeramente (*el pelo*); despabilar (*una lámpara o vela*); mondar, podar (*árboles, plantas*); acepillar, desbastar; (naut) orientar (*las velas*); (coll) derrotar, vencer; (coll) regañar
trimming ['trɪmɪŋ] *s* adorno, guarnición; franja, orla; (coll) paliza, zurra; (coll) derrota; **trimmings** accesorios, arrequives *mpl;* recortes *mpl*
trini·ty ['trɪnɪti] *s* (*pl* **-ties**) (*group of three*) trinca || **Trinity** *s* Trinidad
trinket ['trɪŋkɪt] *s* (*small ornament*) dije *m;* (*trivial object*) baratija, bujería, chuchería
tri·o ['tri·o] *s* (*pl* **-os**) (*group of three*) terna, trío; (mus) trío
trip [trɪp] *s* viaje *m;* jira, recorrido;

(*stumble*) tropiezo; (*act of causing a person to stumble*) traspié *m*, zancadilla; (*blunder*) desliz *m* || *v* (*pret & pp* **tripped;** *ger* **tripping**) *tr* trompicar, echar la zancadilla a; detener, estorbar; inclinar; coger en falta; coger en una mentira || *intr* ir con paso rápido y ligero; brincar, saltar, correr; tropezar; **to trip over** tropezar con, contra o en

tripe [traɪp] *s* callos, mondongo; (slang) disparate *m*, barbaridad

trip'ham'mer *s* martillo pilón

triphthong ['trɪfθɔŋ] o ['trɪfθɑŋ] *s* triptongo

triple ['trɪpəl] *adj & s* triple *m* || *tr* triplicar || *intr* triplicarse

triplet ['trɪplɪt] *s* (*offspring*) trillizo; (*stanza of three lines*) terceto; (mus) terceto, tresillo

triplicate ['trɪplɪkɪt] *adj & s* triplicado; **in triplicate** por triplicado || ['trɪplɪ,ket] *tr* triplicar

tripod ['traɪpɑd] *m* trípode *m*

triptych ['trɪptɪk] *s* tríptico

trite [traɪt] *adj* gastado, trillado, trivial

triumph ['traɪ·əmf] *s* triunfo || *intr* triunfar; **to triumph over** triunfar de

triumphal arch [traɪ'ʌmfəl] *s* arco triunfal

triumphant [traɪ'ʌmfənt] *adj* triunfante

trivia ['trɪvɪ·ə] *spl* bagatelas, trivialidades

trivial ['trɪvɪ·əl] *adj* trivial, insignificante

triviali·ty [,trɪvɪ'ælɪti] *s* (*pl* **-ties**) trivialidad

Trojan ['trodʒən] *adj & s* troyano

Trojan horse *s* caballo de Troya

Trojan War *s* guerra de Troya

troll [trol] *tr & intr* pescar a la cacea

trolley ['trɑli] *s* polea o arco de trole; tranvía *m*

trolley bus *s* trolebús *m*

trolley car *s* coche *m* de tranvía

trolley pole *s* trole *m*

trolling ['trolɪŋ] *s* cacea, pesca a la cacea

trollop ['trɑləp] *s* (*slovenly woman*) cochina; mujer *f* de mala vida

trombone ['trɑmbon] *s* trombón *m*

troop [trup] *s* tropa; (*of actors*) compañía; (*of cavalry*) escuadrón *m* || *intr* agruparse; marcharse en tropel

trooper ['trupər] *s* soldado de caballería; corcel *m* de guerra; policía *m* de a caballo; (*ship*) transporte *m;* **to swear like a trooper** jurar como un carretero

tro·phy ['trofi] *s* (*pl* **-phies**) trofeo; (*any memento*) recuerdo

tropic ['trɑpɪk] *adj* tropical || *s* trópico

tropical ['trɑpɪkəl] *adj* tropical

tropics o **Tropics** ['trɑpɪks] *spl* zona tropical

troposphere ['trɑpə,sfɪr] *s* troposfera

trot [trɑt] *s* trote *m* || *v* (*pret & pp* **trotted;** *ger* **trotting**) *tr* hacer trotar; **to trot out** (slang) sacar para mostrar || *intr* trotar

troth [trɔθ] o [troθ] *s* fe *f;* verdad; esponsales *mpl;* **in troth** en verdad; **to plight one's troth** prometer fidelidad; dar palabra de casamiento

troubadour ['trubə,dor] o ['trubə,dʊr] *adj* trovadoresco || *s* trovador *m*

trouble ['trʌbəl] *s* apuro, dificultad; confusión, estorbo; conflicto; inquietud, preocupación; pena, molestia; mal *m*, enfermedad; (*of a mechanical nature*) avería, falla, pana; **not to be worth the trouble** no valer la pena; **that's the trouble** ahí está el busilis; **the trouble is that . . .** lo malo es que . . .; **to be in trouble** estar en un aprieto; **to be looking for trouble** buscar tres pies al gato; **to get into trouble** enredarse, meterse en líos; **to take the trouble to** tomarse la molestia de || *tr* apurar; confundir, estorbar; inquietar, preocupar; apenar, afligir; incomodar, molestar; dar que hacer a; **to be troubled with** padecer de; **to trouble oneself** molestarse || *intr* apurarse; inquietarse, preocuparse; molestarse, darse molestia; **to trouble to** molestarse en

trouble lamp *s* lámpara de socorro

trou'ble·mak'er *s* perturbador *m*, alborotador *m*

troubleshooter ['trʌbəl,ʃutər] *s* localizador *m* de averías; (*in disputes*) componedor *m*

troubleshooting ['trʌbəl,ʃutɪŋ] *s* localización de averías; (*of disputes*) composición, arbitraje *m*

troublesome ['trʌbəlsəm] *adj* molesto, pesado, gravoso; impertinente; perturbador

trouble spot *s* lugar *m* de conflicto

trough [trɔf] o [trɑf] *s* (*e.g., to knead bread*) artesa; (*for water for animals*) abrevadero; (*for feeding animals*) comedero; (*under eaves*) canal *f;* (*between two waves*) seno

troupe [trup] *s* compañía de actores o de circo

trousers ['traʊzərz] *spl* pantalones *mpl*

trous·seau [tru'so] o ['truso] *s* (*pl* **-seaux** o **-seaus**) ajuar *m* de novia, equipo de novia

trout [traʊt] *s* trucha

trouvère [tru'vɛr] *s* trovero

trowel ['traʊ·əl] *s* paleta, llana

Troy [trɔɪ] *s* Troya

truant ['tru·ənt] *s* novillero; **to play truant** hacer novillos

truce [trus] *s* tregua

truck [trʌk] *s* carro; vagoneta; camión *m;* autocamión *m;* (*to be moved by hand*) carretilla; (*of locomotive or car*) carretón *m;* hortalizas para el mercado; (coll) desperdicios; (coll) negocio, relaciones || *tr* acarrear

truck driver *s* camionista *mf*

truck garden *s* huerto de hortalizas (*para el mercado*)

truculent ['trʌkjələnt] o ['trukjələnt] *adj* truculento

trudge [trʌdʒ] *intr* caminar, ir a pie; **to trudge along** marchar con pena y trabajo

true [tru] *adj* verdadero; exacto; constante, uniforme; fiel, leal; alineado; a plomo, a nivel; **to come true** hacerse realidad; **true to life** conforme a la realidad
true copy *s* copia fiel
true-hearted ['tru ,hartɪd] *adj* fiel, leal, sincero
true'love' *s* fiel amante *mf;* (bot) hierba de París
truelove knot *s* lazo de amor
truffle ['trʌfəl] o ['trufəl] *s* trufa
truism ['tru·ɪzəm] *s* perogrullada, verdad trillada
truly ['truli] *adv* verdaderamente; efectivamente; fielmente; **truly yours** de Vd. atto. y S.S., su seguro servidor
trump [trʌmp] *s* triunfo; (coll) buen chico, buena chica; **no trump** sin triunfo || *tr* matar con un triunfo; aventajar, sobrepujar; **to trump up** forjar, inventar (*para engañar*) || *intr* triunfar
trumpet ['trʌmpɪt] *s* trompeta; trompeta acústica; **to blow one's own trumpet** cantar sus propias alabanzas || *tr* pregonar a son de trompeta || *intr* trompetear
truncheon ['trʌntʃən] *s* cachiporra; bastón *m* de mando
trunk [trʌŋk] *s* (*of living body, tree, family, railroad*) tronco; (*chest for clothes, etc.*) baúl *m;* (*of an automobile*) portaequipaje *m;* (*of elephant*) trompa; **trunks** taparrabo
trunk hose *spl* trusas
truss [trʌs] *s* (*framework*) armadura; haz *m*, paquete *m*, lío; (*for holding back a hernia*) braguero || *tr* armar; empaquetar; espetar; apretar (*barriles*)
trust [trʌst] *s* confianza; esperanza; cargo, custodia; depósito; crédito; obligación; (econ) trust *m*, cartel *m;* (law) fideicomiso; **in trust** en confianza; en depósito; **on trust** a crédito, al fiado || *tr* confiar; confiar en; vender a crédito a || *intr* confiar; fiar; **to trust in** fiarse a o de
trust company *s* banco fideicomisario, banco de depósitos
trustee [trʌs'ti] *s* administrador *m*, comisario; regente (universitario); (*of an estate*) fideicomisario
trusteeship [trʌs'tiʃɪp] *s* cargo de administrador, fideicomisario; (*of the UN*) fideicomiso
trustful ['trʌstfəl] *adj* confiado
trust'wor'thy *adj* confiable, fidedigno
trust·y ['trʌsti] *adj* (*comp* **-ier**; *super* **-iest**) honrado, fidedigno || *s* (*pl* **-ies**) presidiario fidedigno (*que se ha merecido ciertos privilegios*)
truth [truθ] *s* verdad; **in truth** a la verdad, en verdad
truthful ['truθfəl] *adj* verídico, veraz
try [traɪ] *s* (*pl* **tries**) ensayo, intento, prueba || *v* (*pret & pp* **tried**) *tr* ensayar, intentar, probar; comprobar, verificar; cansar; exasperar, irritar; (law) procesar (*a una persona*); (law) ver (*un pleito*); **to try on** probarse (*una prenda de vestir*) || *intr* ensayar, probar; esforzarse; **to try to** tratar de, intentar
trying ['traɪ·ɪŋ] *adj* cansado, molesto, irritante; penoso
tryst [trɪst] o [traɪst] *s* cita; lugar *m* de cita
tub [tʌb] *s* cuba, tina; (coll) baño; (*clumsy boat*) (coll) carcamán *m*, trompo; (*fat person*) (coll) cuba
tube [tjub] o [tub] *s* tubo; túnel *m;* (*of a tire*) cámara; (coll) ferrocarril subterráneo
tuber ['tjubər] o ['tubər] *s* tubérculo
tubercle ['tjubərkəl] o ['tubərkəl] *s* tubérculo
tuberculosis [tju,bʌrkjə'losɪs] o [tu,bʌrkjə'losɪs] *s* tuberculosis *f*
tuck [tʌk] *s* alforza || *tr* alforzar; **to tuck away** encubrir, ocultar; **to tuck in** arropar, enmantar; remeter (*p.ej., la ropa de cama*); **to tuck up** arremangar (*un vestido*); guarnecer (*la cama*)
tucker ['tʌkər] *s* escote *m* || *tr* — **to tucker out** (coll) agotar, cansar
Tuesday ['tjuzdi] o ['tuzdi] *s* martes *m*
tuft [tʌft] *s* (*of feathers, hair, etc.*) penacho, copete *m;* manojo, racimo, ramillete *m;* borla || *tr* empenachar || *intr* crecer formando mechones
tug [tʌg] *s* estirón *m*, tirón *m;* (*boat*) remolcador *m* || *v* (*pret & pp* **tugged;** *ger* **tugging**) *tr* arrastrar, tirar con fuerza de; remolcar (*un barco*) || *intr* tirar con fuerza; esforzarse, luchar
tug'boat' *s* remolcador *m*
tug of war *s* lucha de la cuerda
tuition [tju'ɪʃən] o [tu'ɪʃən] *s* enseñanza; precio de la enseñanza
tulip ['tjulɪp] o ['tulɪp] *s* tulipán *m*
tumble ['tʌmbəl] *s* caída, tumbo; (*somersault*) voltereta, tumba; confusión, desorden *m* || *intr* caerse, rodar; voltear; derribarse, volcarse; brincar, dar saltos; (*into bed*) echarse; (*to catch on*) (slang) caer, comprender; **to tumble down** desplomarse, hundirse, venirse abajo
tum'ble-down' *adj* destartalado, desvencijado
tumbler ['tʌmblər] *s* (*for drinking*) vaso; (*person who performs bodily feats*) volatinero; (*self-righting toy*) dominguillo, tentemozo
tumor ['tjumər] o ['tumər] *s* tumor *m*
tumult ['tjumʌlt] o ['tumʌlt] *s* tumulto
tun [tʌn] *s* barril *m*, tonel *m;* (*measure of capacity for wine*) tonelada
tuna ['tunə] *s* atún *m*
tune [tjun] o [tun] *s* tonada, aire *m;* (*manner of acting or speaking*) tono; **in tune** afinado; afinadamente; **out of tune** desafinado; desafinadamente; **to change one's tune** mudar de tono || *tr* acordar, afinar; (rad) sintonizar; **to tune in** (rad) sintonizar; **to tune out** (rad) desintonizar; **to tune up** poner a punto; poner a tono (*un motor de automóvil*)
tungsten ['tʌŋstən] *s* tungsteno
tunic ['tjunɪk] o ['tunɪk] *s* túnica
tuning coil *s* (rad) bobina de sintonía

tuning fork *s* diapasón *m*
Tunis ['tjunɪs] o ['tunɪs] *s* Túnez (*ciudad*)
Tunisia [tju'niʒə] o [tu'niʒə] *s* Túnez (*país*)
Tunisian [tju'niʒən] o [tu'niʒən] *adj & s* tunecino
tun•nel ['tʌnəl] *s* túnel *m;* (min) galería ‖ *v* (*pret & pp* **-neled** o **-nelled;** *ger* **-neling** o **-nelling**) *tr* construir un túnel a través de o debajo de
turban ['tʌrbən] *s* turbante *m*
turbid ['tʌrbɪd] *adj* turbio
turbine ['tʌrbɪn] o ['tʌrbaɪn] *s* turbina
turbojet ['tʌrbo,dʒɛt] *s* turborreactor *m;* avión *m* de turborreacción
turboprop ['tʌrbo,prɑp] *s* turbopropulsor *m;* avión *m* de turbopropulsión
turbulent ['tʌrbjələnt] *adj* turbulento
tureen [tʊ'rin] o [tjʊ'rin] *s* sopera
turf [tʌrf] *s* (*surface layer of grassland*) césped *m;* terrón *m* de césped; (*peat*) turba; **the turf** el hipódromo; las carreras de caballos
turf•man ['tʌrfmən] *s* (*pl* **-men** [mən]) turfista *m*
Turk [tʌrk] *s* turco
turkey ['tʌrki] *s* pavo ‖ **Turkey** *s* Turquía
turkey vulture *s* aura
Turkish ['tʌrkɪʃ] *adj & s* turco
Turkish towel *s* toalla rusa
turmoil ['tʌrmɔɪl] *s* alboroto, disturbio, tumulto
turn [tʌrn] *s* vuelta; (*time of action*) turno; (*change of direction*) virada; (*bend*) recodo; (*walk*) paseo corto; (*of a spiral, roll of wire, etc.*) espira; aspecto; inclinación; vahido, vértigo; giro, expresión; servicio; (coll) sacudida, susto; **at every turn** a cada paso; **in turn** por turno; **to be one's turn** tocarle a uno, p.ej., **it's your turn** le toca a Vd.; **to take turns** alternar, turnar; **to wait one's turn** aguardar turno, esperar vez ‖ *tr* volver; dar vuelta a (*p.ej., una llave*); torcer (*p.ej., el tobillo*); doblar (*la esquina*); dirigir (*p.ej., los ojos*); (*to make sour*) agriar; (*on a lathe*) tornear; tener (*p.ej., veinte años cumplidos*); **to turn against** predisponer en contra de; **to turn around** volver; voltear; torcer (*las palabras de una persona*); **to turn aside** desviar; **to turn away** desviar; despedir; **to turn back** devolver; hacer retroceder; retrasar (*el reloj*); **to turn down** doblar hacia abajo; invertir; rechazar, rehusar; bajar (*p.ej., el gas*); **to turn in** doblar hacia adentro; entregar; **to turn off** apagar (*la luz, la radio*); cortar (*el agua, gas, etc.*); cerrar (*la llave del agua, gas, etc.; la radio, la televisión*); interrumpir (*la corriente eléctrica*); **to turn on** encender (*la luz*); poner (*la luz, la radio, etc.*); abrir (*la llave del agua, gas, etc.*); establecer (*la corriente eléctrica*); **to turn out** despedir; echar al campo (*a los animales*); volver al revés; apagar (*la luz*); hacer, fabricar; **to turn up** doblar hacia arriba; levantar; arremangar (*p.ej., las mangas*); volver (*un naipe*); poner más alto o más fuerte (*la radio*); abrir la llave de (*p.ej., el gas*) ‖ *intr* volver, p.ej., **the road turns to the right** el camino vuelve a la derecha; virar (*un automóvil, un avión, etc.*); (*to revolve*) girar; volverse (*p.ej., la conversación; la opinión; ciertos licores*); **to turn against** cobrar aversión a; rebelarse contra; **to turn around** dar vuelta; **to turn aside** o **away** desviarse; alejarse; **to turn back** volver, regresar; retroceder; **to turn down** doblarse hacia abajo; invertirse; **to turn in** doblarse hacia adentro; replegarse; recogerse, volver a casa; (coll) recogerse, acostarse; **to turn into** entrar en; convertirse en; **to turn on** volverse contra; depender de; versar sobre; ocuparse de; **to turn out badly** salir mal; **to turn out right** acabar bien; **to turn out to be** venir a ser; resultar, salir; **to turn over** volcar, derribarse (*un vehículo*); **to turn up** doblarse hacia arriba; levantarse; acontecer; aparecer
turn'coat' *s* tránsfuga *mf,* apóstata *mf,* renegado; **to become a turncoat** volver la casaca, cambiarse la camisa
turn'down' *adj* (*collar*) caído ‖ *s* rechazamiento
turning point *s* punto de transición, punto decisivo
turnip ['tʌrnɪp] *s* nabo; (*cheap watch*) (slang) calentador *m;* (slang) tipo
turn'key' *s* carcelero, llavero de cárcel
turn of life *s* menopausia
turn of mind *s* natural *m,* inclinación
turn'out' *s* (*gathering of people*) concurrencia; (*number attending a show, etc.*) entrada; (*side track or passage*) apartadero; (*amount produced*) producción; (*array, outfit*) equipaje *m;* carruaje *m* de lujo
turn'o'ver *s* (*spill, upset*) vuelco; cambio de personal; movimiento de mercancías; ciclo de compra y venta
turn'pike' *s* carretera de peaje
turnstile ['tʌrn,staɪl] *s* torniquete *m*
turn'ta'ble *s* (*of phonograph*) placa giratoria, plato giratorio; (rr) placa giratoria, plataforma giratoria
turpentine ['tʌrpən,taɪn] *s* trementina
turpitude ['tʌrpɪ,tjud] o ['tʌrpɪ,tud] *s* torpeza, infamia, vileza
turquoise ['tʌrkɔɪz] o ['tʌrkwɔɪz] *s* turquesa
turret ['tʌrɪt] *s* torrecilla; (archit) torreón *m;* (nav) torreta
turtle ['tʌrtəl] *s* tortuga; **to turn turtle** derribarse patas arriba
tur'tle•dove' *s* tórtola
Tuscan ['tʌskən] *adj & s* toscano
Tuscany ['tʌskəni] *s* la Toscana
tusk [tʌsk] *s* colmillo
tussle ['tʌsəl] *s* agarrada ‖ *intr* agarrarse, asirse, reñir
tutor ['tjutər] o ['tutər] *s* maestro particular; (*guardian*) tutor *m* ‖ *tr* dar enseñanza particular a ‖ *intr*

dar enseñanza particular; (coll) tomar lecciones particulares
tuxe·do [tʌk'sido] *s* (*pl* **-dos**) esmoquin *m*, smoking *m*
TV *abbr* **television**
twaddle ['twɑdəl] *s* charla, tonterías, música celestial || *intr* charlar, decir tonterías
twang [twæŋ] *s* (*of musical instrument*) tañido; (*of voice*) timbre *m* nasal || *tr* tocar con un tañido; decir con timbre nasal || *intr* hablar por la nariz
twang·y [twæŋi] *adj* (*comp* **-ier;** *super* **-iest**) (*device*) tañente; (*person, voice*) gangoso
tweed [twid] *s* mezcla de lana; traje *m* de mezcla de lana; **tweeds** ropa de mezcla de lana
tweet [twit] *s* pío || *intr* piar
tweeter ['twitər] *s* altavoz *m* para audiofrecuencias elevadas
tweezers ['twizərz] *spl* bruselas, pinzas, tenacillas
twelfth [twɛlfθ] *adj* & *s* (*in a series*) duodécimo; (*part*) dozavo || *s* (*in dates*) doce *m*
Twelfth'-night' *s* la víspera del día de Reyes; la noche del día de Reyes
twelve [twɛlv] *adj* & *pron* doce || *s* doce *m;* **twelve o'clock** las doce
twentieth ['twɛntɪ·ɪθ] *adj* & *s* (*in a series*) vigésimo; (*part*) veintavo || *s* (*in dates*) veinte *m*
twen·ty ['twɛnti] *adj* & *pron* veinte || *s* (*pl* **-ties**) veinte *m*
twice [twaɪs] *adv* dos veces
twice'-told' *adj* dicho dos veces; trillado, sabido
twiddle ['twɪdəl] *tr* menear o revolver ociosamente
twig [twɪg] *s* ramito; **twigs** leña menuda
twilight ['twaɪ,laɪt] *adj* crepuscular || *s* crepúsculo
twill [twɪl] *s* tela cruzada; (*pattern of weave*) cruzado || *tr* cruzar
twin [twɪn] *adj* & *s* gemelo
twine [twaɪn] *s* guita, cuerda, bramante *m* || *tr* enroscar, retorcer || *intr* enroscarse, retorcerse
twinge [twɪndʒ] *s* punzada, dolor agudo
twin'jet' plane *s* avión *m* birreactor
twinkle ['twɪŋkəl] *s* centelleo; (*of eye*) pestañeo; instante *m* || *intr* centellear; pestañear; moverse rápidamente
twin'-screw' *adj* (naut) de doble hélice
twirl [twʌrl] *s* vuelta, giro || *tr* hacer girar; (baseball) lanzar (*la pelota*) || *intr* dar vueltas, girar; piruetear
twist [twɪst] *s* torcedura; enroscadura; curva, recodo; giro, vuelta; propensión, prejuicio; (*of mind or disposition*) sesgo || *tr* torcer; retorcer; enroscar; hacer girar; entrelazar; desviar; (*to give a different meaning to*) torcer || *intr* torcerse; retorcerse; enroscarse; dar vueltas; entrelazarse; desviarse; serpentear; **to twist and turn** (*in bed*) dar vueltas
twit [twɪt] *v* (*pret* & *pp* **twitted;** *ger* **twitting**) *tr* reprender (*a uno*) recordando algo desagradable o poniéndole en ridículo
twitch [twɪtʃ] *s* crispatura; ligero temblor || *intr* crisparse; temblar (*p.ej., los párpados*)
twitter ['twɪtər] *s* gorjeo; risita sofocada; inquietud || *intr* gorjear; reír sofocadamente; temblar de inquietud
two [tu] *adj* & *pron* dos || *s* dos *m;* **to put two and two together** atar cabos, sacar la conclusión evidente; **two o'clock** las dos
two'-cy'cle *adj* (mach) de dos tiempos
two'-cyl'inder *adj* (mach) de dos cilindros
two-edged ['tu,ɛdʒd] *adj* de dos filos
two hundred *adj* & *pron* doscientos || *s* doscientos *m*
twosome ['tusəm] *s* pareja; pareja de jugadores; juego de dos
two'-time' *tr* (slang) engañar en amor, ser infiel a (*una persona del otro sexo*)
tycoon [taɪ'kun] *s* (coll) magnate *m*
type [taɪp] *s* tipo; (*piece*) (typ) tipo, letra; (*pieces collectively*) (typ) letra; letras impresas, letras escritas a máquina || *tr* escribir a máquina, tipiar; representar, simbolizar || *intr* escribir a máquina
type'face' *s* tipo de letra
type'script' *s* material escrito a máquina
typesetter ['taɪp,sɛtər] *s* (typ) cajista *mf;* (typ) máquina de componer
type'write' *v* (*pret* **-wrote** [,rot]; *pp* **-written** [,rɪtən]) *tr* & *intr* escribir a máquina, tipiar
type'writ'er *s* máquina de escribir; tipista *mf*
typewriter ribbon *s* cinta para máquinas de escribir
type'writ'ing *s* mecanografía; trabajo hecho con máquina de escribir
typhoid fever ['taɪfɔɪd] *s* fiebre tifoidea
typhoon [taɪ'fun] *s* tifón *m*
typical ['tɪpɪkəl] *adj* típico
typi·fy ['tɪpɪ,faɪ] *v* (*pret* & *pp* **-fied**) *tr* simbolizar; ser ejemplo o modelo de
typist ['taɪpɪst] *s* mecanógrafo, tipista *mf*
typographic(al) [,taɪpə'græfɪk(əl)] *adj* tipográfico
typographical error *s* error *m* de imprenta
typography [taɪ'pɑgrəfi] *s* tipografía
tyrannic(al) [tɪ'rænɪk(əl)] o [taɪ'rænɪk(əl)] *adj* tiránico
tyrannous ['tɪrənəs] *adj* tirano
tyran·ny ['tɪrəni] *s* (*pl* **-nies**) tiranía
tyrant ['taɪrənt] *s* tirano
ty·ro ['taɪro] *s* (*pl* **-ros**) tirón *m*, novicio

U

U, u [ju] vigésima primera letra del alfabeto inglés
U. *abbr* **University**
ubiquitous [ju'bɪkwɪtəs] *adj* ubicuo
udder ['ʌdər] *s* ubre *f*
ugliness ['ʌglɪnɪs] *s* fealdad; (coll) malhumor *m*
ug·ly ['ʌgli] *adj* (*comp* **-lier;** *super* **-liest**) feo; (coll) malhumorado
ugly mug *s* (slang) carantamaula
Ukraine ['jukren] o [ju'kren] *s* Ucrania
Ukrainian [ju'krenɪ·ən] *adj & s* ucraniano, ucranio
ulcer ['ʌlsər] *s* llaga, úlcera; (*corrupting influence*) (fig) llaga
ulcerate ['ʌlsə,ret] *tr* ulcerar ‖ *intr* ulcerarse
ulterior [ʌl'tɪrɪ·ər] *adj* ulterior; (*concealed*) escondido, oculto
ultimate ['ʌltɪmɪt] *adj* último
ultima·tum [,ʌltɪ'metəm] *s* (*pl* **-tums** o **-ta** [tə]) ultimátum *m*
ultimo ['ʌltɪ,mo] *adv* de o en el mes próximo pasado
ultrahigh [,ʌltrə'haɪ] *adj* (electron) ultraelevado
ultraviolet [,ʌltrə'vaɪ·əlɪt] *adj & s* ultravioleta, ultraviolado
umbilical cord [ʌm'bɪlɪkəl] *s* cordón *m* umbilical
umbrage ['ʌmbrɪdʒ] *s* — **to take umbrage at** resentirse de o por
umbrella [ʌm'brɛlə] *s* paraguas *m;* (mil) sombrilla protectora
umbrella man *s* paragüero
umbrella stand *s* paragüero
umlaut ['ʊmlaʊt] *s* inflexión vocálica, metafonía; (*mark*) diéresis *f* ‖ *tr* inflexionar; escribir con diéresis
umpire ['ʌmpaɪr] *s* árbitro ‖ *tr & intr* arbitrar
UN ['ju'ɛn] *s* (letterword) ONU *f*
unable [ʌn'ebəl] *adj* incapaz, imposibilitado; **to be unable to** no poder
unabridged [,ʌnə'brɪdʒd] *adj* sin abreviar, íntegro
unaccented [ʌn'æksɛntɪd] o [,ʌnæk'sɛntɪd] *adj* inacentuado
unaccountable [,ʌnə'kaʊntəbəl] *adj* inexplicable; irresponsable
unaccounted-for [,ʌnə'kaʊntɪd,fɔr] *adj* inexplicado; no hallado
unaccustomed [,ʌnə'kʌstəmd] *adj* (*unusual*) desacostumbrado; inhabituado
unafraid [,ʌnə'fred] *adj* sin miedo
unaligned [,ʌnə'laɪnd] *adj* no empeñado
unanimity [,junə'nɪmɪti] *s* unanimidad
unanimous [jʊ'nænɪməs] *adj* unánime
unanswerable [ʌn'ænsərəbəl] *adj* incontestable; (*argument*) incontrastable
unappreciative [,ʌnə'priʃɪ,etɪv] *adj* ingrato, desagradecido
unapproachable [,ʌnə'protʃəbəl] *adj* inabordable; incomparable, único
unarmed [ʌn'ɑrmd] *adj* desarmado, inerme
unascertainable [ʌn,æsər'tenəbəl] *adj* inaveriguable
unasked [ʌn'æskt] o [ʌn'ɑskt] *adj* no solicitado; no convidado
unassembled [,ʌnə'sɛmbəld] *adj* desmontado, desarmado
unassuming [,ʌnə'sumɪŋ] o [,ʌnə'sjumɪŋ] *adj* modesto, sencillo
unattached [,ʌnə'tætʃt] *adj* independiente; (*loose*) suelto; (*not engaged to be married*) no prometido; (law) no embargado; (mil & nav) de reemplazo
unattainable [,ʌnə'tenəbəl] *adj* inasequible, inalcanzable
unattractive [,ʌnə'træktɪv] *adj* poco atrayente, desairado
unavailable [,ʌnə'veləbəl] *adj* indisponible
unavailing [,ʌnə'velɪŋ] *adj* ineficaz, inútil, vano
unavoidable [,ʌnə'vɔɪdəbəl] *adj* inevitable, ineluctable
unaware [,ʌnə'wɛr] *adj* — **to be unaware of** no estar al corriente de ‖ *adv* de improviso; sin saberlo
unawares [,ʌnə'wɛrz] *adv* (*unexpectedly*) de improviso; (*unknowingly*) sin saberlo
unbalanced [ʌn'bælənst] *adj* desequilibrado
unbandage [ʌn'bændɪdʒ] *tr* desvendar
un·bar [ʌn'bɑr] *v* (*pret & pp* **-barred;** *ger* **-barring**) *tr* desatrancar
unbearable [ʌn'bɛrəbəl] *adj* inaguantable
unbeatable [ʌn'bitəbəl] *adj* imbatible
unbecoming [,ʌnbɪ'kʌmɪŋ] *adj* inconveniente, indecente; que sienta mal
unbelievable [,ʌnbɪ'livəbəl] *adj* increíble
unbending [ʌn'bɛndɪŋ] *adj* inflexible
unbiased o **unbiassed** [ʌn'baɪ·əst] *adj* imparcial
un·bind [ʌn'baɪnd] *v* (*pret & pp* **-bound** ['baʊnd]) *tr* desatar
unbleached [ʌn'blitʃt] *adj* sin blanquear
unbolt [ʌn'bolt] *tr* desatrancar (*p.ej., una puerta*); (*to remove the bolts from*) desempernar
unborn [ʌn'bɔrn] *adj* no nacido, por nacer, futuro
unbosom [ʌn'bʊzəm] *tr* confesar, descubrir (*sus pensamientos, sus secretos*); **to unbosom oneself** abrir su pecho, desahogarse
unbound [ʌn'baʊnd] *adj* (*book*) sin encuadernar
unbreakable [ʌn'brekəbəl] *adj* irrompible
unbuckle [ʌn'bʌkəl] *tr* deshebillar
unburden [ʌn'bʌrdən] *tr* descargar; **to unburden oneself of** desahogarse de
unburied [ʌn'bɛrid] *adj* insepulto
unbutton [ʌn'bʌtən] *tr* desabotonar
uncalled-for [ʌn'kɔld,fɔr] *adj* inne-

cesario, no justificado; insolente
uncanny [ʌn'kæni] *adj* espectral, misterioso; extraordinario, maravilloso
uncared-for [ʌn'kɛrd ˌfɔr] *adj* desamparado, descuidado, abandonado
unceasing [ʌn'sisɪŋ] *adj* incesante
unceremonious [ˌʌnsɛrɪ'monɪ·əs] *adj* inceremonioso
uncertain [ʌn'sʌrtən] *adj* incierto
uncertain·ty [ʌn'sʌrtənti] *s* (*pl* **-ties**) incertidumbre
unchain [ʌn'tʃen] *tr* desencadenar
unchangeable [ʌn'tʃendʒəbəl] *adj* incambiable, inmutable
uncharted [ʌn'tʃartɪd] *adj* inexplorado
unchecked [ʌn'tʃɛkt] *adj* no verificado; no refrenado; desenfrenado
uncivilized [ʌn'sɪvɪ ˌlaɪzd] *adj* incivilizado
unclad [ʌn'klæd] *adj* desvestido
unclaimed [ʌn'klemd] *adj* sin reclamar; (*mail*) rechazado, sobrante
unclasp [ʌn'klæsp] o [ʌn'klɑsp] *tr* desabrochar
unclassified [ʌn'klæsɪ ˌfaɪd] *adj* no clasificado; no clasificado como secreto
uncle ['ʌŋkəl] *s* tío
unclean [ʌn'klin] *adj* desaseado, sucio
un·clog [ʌn'klɑg] *v* (*pret & pp* **-clogged;** *ger* **-clogging**) *tr* desatrancar
unclouded [ʌn'klaʊdɪd] *adj* despejado
uncollectible [ˌʌnkə'lɛktɪbəl] *adj* incobrable
uncomfortable [ʌn'kʌmfərtəbəl] *adj* incomodo
uncommitted [ˌʌnkə'mɪtɪd] *adj* no empeñado, no comprometido
uncommon [ʌn'kɑmən] *adj* raro, poco común
uncompromising [ʌn'kɑmprə ˌmaɪzɪŋ] *adj* intransigente
unconcerned [ˌʌnkən'sʌrnd] *adj* despreocupado, indiferente
unconditional [ˌʌnkən'dɪʃənəl] *adj* incondicional
uncongenial [ˌʌnkən'dʒinɪ·əl] *adj* antipático; incompatible; desagradable
unconquerable [ʌn'kɑŋkərəbəl] *adj* inconquistable
unconquered [ʌn'kɑŋkərd] *adj* invicto
unconscionable [ʌn'kɑnʃənəbəl] *adj* inescrupuloso; desrazonable, excesivo
unconscious [ʌn'kɑnʃəs] *adj* inconsciente; (*temporarily deprived of consciousness*) desmayado; (*unintentional*) involuntario
unconsciousness [ʌn'kɑnʃəsnɪs] *s* inconsciencia; desmayo
unconstitutional [ˌʌnkɑnstɪ'tjuʃənəl] o [ˌʌnkɑnstɪ'tuʃənəl] *adj* inconstitucional
uncontrollable [ˌʌnkən'troləbəl] *adj* ingobernable; (*laughter*) inextinguible
unconventional [ˌʌnkən'vɛnʃənəl] *adj* no convencional
uncork [ʌn'kɔrk] *tr* destapar, descorchar
uncouth [ʌn'kuθ] *adj* desgarbado, torpe, rústico
uncover [ʌn'kʌvər] *tr* descubrir
unction ['ʌŋkʃən] *s* (*anointing*) unción; suavidad hipócrita
unctuous ['ʌŋktʃʊ·əs] *adj* untuoso; zalamero
uncultivated [ʌn'kʌltɪ ˌvetɪd] *adj* inculto (*que no está cultivado; rústico, grosero*)
uncultured [ʌn'kʌltʃərd] *adj* inculto, rústico, grosero
uncut [ʌn'kʌt] *adj* sin cortar; (*book or magazine*) intonso
undamaged [ʌn'dæmɪdʒd] *adj* indemne, ileso
undaunted [ʌn'dɔntɪd] *adj* impávido, denodado
undecided [ˌʌndɪ'saɪdɪd] *adj* indeciso
undefeated [ˌʌndɪ'fitɪd] *adj* invicto
undefended [ˌʌndɪ'fɛndɪd] *adj* indefenso
undefiled [ˌʌndɪ'faɪld] *adj* inmaculado, impoluto
undeniable [ˌʌndɪ'naɪ·əbəl] *adj* innegable
under ['ʌndər] *adj* inferior; (*clothing*) interior ‖ *adv* debajo; más abajo; **to go under** hundirse; (*to fail*) fracasar ‖ *prep* bajo, debajo de; inferior a; **under full sail** a vela llena; **under lock and key** bajo llave; **under oath** bajo juramento; **under penalty of death** so pena de muerte; **under sail** a vela; **under separate cover** por separado, bajo cubierta separada; **under steam** bajo presión; **under the hand and seal of** firmado y sellado por; **under the nose of** (coll) en las barbas de; **under the weather** (coll) algo indispuesto; **under way** en camino
un'der·age' *adj* menor de edad
un'der·bid' *v* (*pret & pp* **-bid;** *ger* **-bidding**) *tr* ofrecer menos que
un'der·brush' *s* maleza
un'der·car'riage *s* carro inferior; (aer) tren *m* de aterrizaje
un'der·clothes' *s* ropa interior
un'der·con·sump'tion *s* infraconsumo
un'der·cov'er *adj* secreto
underdeveloped [ˌʌndərdɪ'vɛləpt] *adj* subdesarrollado
un'der·dog' *s* víctima, perdidoso; **the underdogs** los de abajo
underdone ['ʌndər ˌdʌn] *adj* a medio asar, soasado
un'der·es'ti·mate' *tr* subestimar
un'der·gar'ment *s* prenda de vestir interior
un'der·go' *v* (*pret* **-went;** *pp* **-gone**) *tr* experimentar; sufrir, padecer
un'der·grad'uate *adj* no graduado; (*course*) para el bachillerato ‖ *s* alumno no graduado de universidad
un'der·ground' *adj* subterráneo; clandestino ‖ *adv* bajo tierra; ocultamente ‖ *s* ferrocarril subterráneo; movimiento de resistencia
un'der·growth' *s* maleza
underhanded ['ʌndər'hændɪd] *adj* clandestino, taimado, disimulado
un'der·line' o **un'der·line'** *tr* subrayar
underling ['ʌndərlɪŋ] *s* subordinado, secuaz *m* servil
un'der·mine' *tr* socavar, minar

underneath [ˌʌndərˈniθ] *adj* inferior, más bajo || *adv* debajo || *prep* debajo de || *s* parte baja, superficie *f* inferior
undernourished [ˌʌndərˈnʌrɪʃt] *adj* desnutrido
un'der•nour'ish•ment *s* desnutrición
un'der•pass' *s* paso inferior
un'der•pay' *s* pago insuficiente || *v* (*pret & pp* **-paid**) *tr & intr* pagar insuficientemente
un'der•pin' *v* (*pret & pp* **-pinned;** *ger* **-pinning**) *tr* apuntalar, socalzar
underprivileged [ˌʌndərˈprɪvɪlɪdʒd] *adj* desheredado, desamparado
un'der•rate' *tr* menospreciar
un'der•score' *tr* subrayar
un'der•sea' *adj* submarino || **un'der•sea'** *adv* debajo de la superficie del mar
un'der•sec're•tar'y *s* (*pl* **-ies**) subsecretario
un'der•sell' *v* (*pret & pp* **-sold**) *tr* vender a menor precio que; (*for less than the actual value*) malbaratar
un'der•shirt' *s* camiseta
undersigned [ˈʌndərˌsaɪnd] *adj* infrascrito, subscrito
un'der•skirt' *s* enaguas, refajo
un'der•stand' *v* (*pret & pp* **-stood**) *tr* entender, comprender; sobrentender, subentender (*una cosa que no está expresa*) || *intr* entender, comprender
understandable [ˌʌndərˈstændəbəl] *adj* comprensible
understanding [ˌʌndərˈstændɪŋ] *adj* entendedor; (*tolerant, sympathetic*) comprensivo || *s* comprensión; (*intellectual faculty, mind*) entendimiento; (*agreement*) acuerdo; **to come to an understanding** llegar a un acuerdo
un'der•stud'y *s* (*pl* **-ies**) sobresaliente *mf*
un'der•take' *v* (*pret* **-took;** *pp* **-taken**) *tr* emprender; (*to agree to perform*) comprometerse a
undertaker [ˌʌndərˈtekər] o [ˈʌndərˌtekər] *s* empresario || [ˈʌndərˌtekər] *s* empresario de pompas fúnebres, director *m* de funeraria
undertaking [ˌʌndərˈtekɪŋ] *s* (*task*) empresa; (*pledge*) empeño || [ˈʌndərˌtekɪŋ] *s* (*business of funeral director*) funeraria
un'der•tak'ing establishment *s* funeraria, empresa de pompas fúnebres
un'der•tone' *s* voz baja; (*background sound*) fondo; color apagado
un'der•tow' *s* (*countercurrent below surface*) contracorriente *f;* (*on the beach*) resaca
un'der•wear' *s* ropa interior
un'der•world' *s* (*criminal world*) inframundo, bajos fondos sociales; (*the earth*) mundo terrenal; (*pagan world of the dead*) averno, infierno; (*world under the water*) mundo submarino; (*opposite side of earth*) antípodas
un'der•write' o **un'der•write'** *v* (*pret* **-wrote;** *pp* **-written**) *tr* subscribir; (*to insure*) asegurar
un'der•writ'er *s* subscritor *m;* asegurador *m;* compañía aseguradora
undeserved [ˌʌndɪˈzʌrvd] *adj* inmerecido
undesirable [ˌʌndɪˈzaɪrəbəl] *adj & s* indeseable *mf*
undetachable [ˌʌndɪˈtætʃəbəl] *adj* inamovible
undignified [ʌnˈdɪgnɪˌfaɪd] *adj* poco digno, poco grave, indecoroso
undiscernible [ˌʌndɪˈzʌrnɪbəl] o [ˌʌndɪˈsʌrnəbəl] *adj* imperceptible, invisible
un•do' *v* (*pret* **-did;** *pp* **-done**) *tr* deshacer; anular, borrar; arruinar
undoing [ʌnˈdu·ɪŋ] *s* destrucción, pérdida, ruina
undone [ʌnˈdʌn] *adj* sin hacer, por hacer; **to come undone** deshacerse, desatarse; **to leave nothing undone** no dejar nada por hacer
undoubtedly [ʌnˈdaʊtɪdli] *adv* indudablemente, sin duda
undramatic [ˌʌndrəˈmætɪk] *adj* poco dramático
undress [ˈʌnˌdrɛs] o [ʌnˈdrɛs] *s* traje *m* de casa; vestido de calle; (mil) traje de cuartel || [ʌnˈdrɛs] *tr* desnudar; desvendar (*una herida*) || desnudarse
undrinkable [ʌnˈdrɪŋkəbəl] *adj* impotable
undue [ʌnˈdju] o [ʌnˈdu] *adj* indebido
undulate [ˈʌndjəˌlet] *intr* ondular
unduly [ʌnˈdjuli] o [ʌnˈduli] *adv* indebidamente
undying [ʌnˈdaɪ·ɪŋ] *adj* imperecedero
unearned increment [ʌnˈʌrnd] *s* plusvalía
unearth [ʌnˈʌrθ] *tr* desenterrar
unearthly [ʌnˈʌrθli] *adj* sobrenatural; fantástico, espectral; extraordinario
uneasy [ʌnˈizi] *adj* (*worried*) inquieto; (*constrained*) encogido, embarazado
uneatable [ʌnˈitəbəl] *adj* incomible
uneconomic(al) [ˌʌnikəˈnɑmɪk(əl)] o [ˌʌnɛkəˈnɑmɪk(əl)] *adj* antieconómico
uneducated [ʌnˈɛdjəˌketɪd] *adj* ineducado, sin instrucción
unemployed [ˌʌnɛmˈplɔɪd] *adj* desocupado, desempleado; improductivo
unemployment [ˌʌnɛmˈplɔɪmənt] *s* desocupación, desempleo
unemployment insurance *s* seguro de desempleo o desocupación, seguro contra el paro obrero
unending [ʌnˈɛndɪŋ] *adj* interminable
unequal [ʌnˈikwəl] *adj* desigual; **to be unequal to** (*a task*) no estar a la altura de
unequaled o **unequalled** [ʌnˈikwəld] *adj* inigualado
unerring [ʌnˈʌrɪŋ] o [ʌnˈɛrɪŋ] *adj* infalible, seguro
unessential [ˌʌnɛˈsɛnʃəl] *adj* no esencial
uneven [ʌnˈivən] *adj* desigual; (*number*) impar
unexceptionable [ˌʌnɛkˈsɛpʃənəbəl] *adj* intachable, irreprensible
unexpected [ˌʌnɛkˈspɛktɪd] *adj* inesperado
unexplained [ˌʌnɛkˈsplend] *adj* inexplicado

unexplored [ˌʌnɛkˈsplord] *adj* inexplorado
unexposed [ˌʌnɛkˈspozd] *adj* (phot) inexpuesto
unfading [ʌnˈfedɪŋ] *adj* inmarcesible
unfailing [ʌnˈfelɪŋ] *adj* indefectible; (*inexhaustible*) inagotable
unfair [ʌnˈfɛr] *adj* injusto; desleal, doble, falso; (sport) sucio
unfaithful [ʌnˈfeθfəl] *adj* infiel
unfamiliar [ˌʌnfəˈmɪljər] *adj* poco familiar; poco familiarizado
unfasten [ʌnˈfæsən] o [ʌnˈfɑsən] *tr* desatacar, desatar, soltar
unfathomable [ʌnˈfæðəməbəl] *adj* insondable
unfavorable [ʌnˈfevərəbəl] *adj* desfavorable
unfeathered [ʌnˈfɛðərd] *adj* implume
unfeeling [ʌnˈfilɪŋ] *adj* insensible
unfetter [ʌnˈfɛtər] *tr* desencadenar
unfilled [ʌnˈfɪld] *adj* no lleno; por cumplir, pendiente
unfinished [ʌnˈfɪnɪʃt] *adj* sin acabar; imperfecto, mal acabado; (*business*) pendiente
unfit [ʌnˈfɪt] *adj* impropio, incapaz, inhábil; inservible, inútil
unfold [ʌnˈfold] *tr* desplegar ‖ *intr* desplegarse
unforeseeable [ˌʌnforˈsi·əbəl] *adj* imprevisible
unforeseen [ˌʌnforˈsin] *adj* imprevisto
unforgettable [ˌʌnfərˈgɛtəbəl] *adj* inolvidable
unforgivable [ˌʌnfərˈgɪvəbəl] *adj* imperdonable
unfortunate [ʌnˈfɔrtjənɪt] *adj & s* desgraciado
unfounded [ʌnˈfaʊndɪd] *adj* infundado
unfreeze [ʌnˈfriz] *tr* deshelar; desbloquear (*el crédito*)
unfriendly [ʌnˈfrɛndli] *adj* inamistoso; desfavorable
unfruitful [ʌnˈfrutfəl] *adj* infructuoso
unfulfilled [ˌʌnfəlˈfɪld] *adj* incumplido
unfurl [ʌnˈfʌrl] *tr* desplegar, extender
unfurnished [ʌnˈfʌrnɪʃt] *adj* desamueblado
ungainly [ʌnˈgenli] *adj* desgarbado, desmañado
ungentlemanly [ʌnˈdʒɛntəlmənli] *adj* poco caballeroso, descortés
ungird [ʌnˈgʌrd] *tr* desceñir
ungodly [ʌnˈgɑdli] *adj* impío, irreligioso; (*dreadful*) (coll) atroz
ungracious [ʌnˈgreʃəs] *adj* descortés; desagradable
ungrammatical [ˌʌngrəˈmætɪkəl] *adj* ingramatical
ungrateful [ʌnˈgretfəl] *adj* ingrato, desagradecido
ungrudgingly [ʌnˈgrʌdʒɪŋli] *adj* de buena gana, sin quejarse
unguarded [ʌnˈgɑrdɪd] *adj* indefenso; descuidado; (*moment*) de inadvertencia
unguent [ˈʌŋgwənt] *s* ungüento
unhandy [ʌnˈhændi] *adj* inmanejable; (*awkward*) desmañado
unhappiness [ʌnˈhæpɪnɪs] *s* infelicidad
unhap·py [ʌnˈhæpi] *adj* (*comp* **-pier;** *super* **-piest**) infeliz; (*unlucky*) desgraciado; (*fateful*) aciago
unharmed [ʌnˈhɑrmd] *adj* indemne
unharmonious [ˌʌnhɑrˈmonɪ·əs] *adj* inarmónico
unharness [ʌnˈhɑrnɪs] *tr* desenjaezar, desguarnecer; desenganchar
unhealthy [ʌnˈhɛlθi] *adj* malsano
unheard-of [ʌnˈhʌrd ˌɑv] *adj* inaudito
unhinge [ʌnˈhɪndʒ] *tr* desgonzar; (fig) desequilibrar, trastornar
unhitch [ʌnˈhɪtʃ] *tr* desenganchar
unho·ly [ʌnˈholi] *adj* (*comp* **-lier;** *super* **-liest**) impío, malo, profano
unhook [ʌnˈhʊk] *tr* desabrochar; desenganchar; (*to take down from a hook*) descolgar
unhoped-for [ʌnˈhoptˌfɔr] *adj* inesperado, no esperado
unhorse [ʌnˈhɔrs] *tr* desarzonar
unhurt [ʌnˈhʌrt] *adj* incólume, ileso
unicorn [ˈjunɪˌkɔrn] *s* unicornio
unification [ˌjunɪfɪˈkeʃən] *s* unificación
uniform [ˈjunɪˌfɔrm] *adj & s* uniforme *m* ‖ *tr* uniformar
uniformi·ty [ˌjunɪˈfɔrmɪti] *s* (*pl* **-ties**) uniformidad
uni·fy [ˈjunɪˌfaɪ] *v* (*pret & pp* **-fied**) *tr* unificar
unilateral [ˌjunɪˈlætərəl] *adj* unilateral
unimpeachable [ˌʌnɪmˈpitʃəbəl] *adj* irrecusable, intachable
unimportant [ˌʌnɪmˈpɔrtənt] *adj* poco importante
uninhabited [ˌʌnɪnˈhæbɪtɪd] *adj* inhabitado
uninspired [ˌʌnɪnˈspaɪrd] *adj* sin inspiración; aburrido, fastidioso
unintelligent [ˌʌnɪnˈtɛlɪdʒənt] *adj* ininteligente
unintelligible [ˌʌnɪnˈtɛlɪdʒɪbəl] *adj* ininteligible
uninterested [ʌnˈɪntrɪstɪd] o [ʌnˈɪntəˌrɛstɪd] *adj* desinteresado
uninteresting [ʌnˈɪntrɪstɪŋ] o [ʌnˈɪntəˌrɛstɪŋ] *adj* poco interesante
uninterrupted [ˌʌnɪntəˈrʌptɪd] *adj* ininterrumpido
union [ˈjunjən] *s* unión; (*organization of workmen*) gremio obrero, sindicato; unión matrimonial
unionize [ˈjunjəˌnaɪz] *tr* agremiar ‖ *intr* agremiarse
union shop *s* taller *m* de obreros agremiados
union suit *s* traje *m* interior de una sola pieza
unique [jʊˈnik] *adj* único
unison [ˈjunɪsən] o [ˈjunɪzən] *s* unisonancia; **in unison (with)** al unísono (de)
unit [ˈjunɪt] *adj* unitario ‖ *s* unidad; (mach & elec) grupo
unite [jʊˈnaɪt] *tr* unir ‖ *intr* unirse
united [jʊˈnaɪtɪd] *adj* unido
United Kingdom *s* Reino Unido
United Nations *spl* Naciones Unidas
United States *adj* estadounidense ‖ **the United States** *s* los Estados Unidos *mpl;* Estados Unidos *msg*
uni·ty [ˈjunɪti] *s* (*pl* **-ties**) unidad
univ. *abbr* **universal, university**

universal [ˌjunɪˈvʌrsəl] *adj* universal
universal joint *s* cardán *m*, junta universal
universe [ˈjunɪˌvʌrs] *s* universo
universi·ty [ˌjunɪˈvʌrsɪti] *adj* universitario || *s* (*pl* **-ties**) universidad
unjust [ʌnˈdʒʌst] *adj* injusto
unjustified [ʌnˈdʒʌstɪˌfaɪd] *adj* injustificado
unkempt [ʌnˈkɛmpt] *adj* despeinado
unkind [ʌnˈkaɪnd] *adj* poco amable; duro, despiadado
unknowable [ʌnˈno·əbəl] *adj* inconocible, insabible
unknowingly [ʌnˈno·ɪŋli] *adv* desconocidamente, sin saberlo
unknown [ʌnˈnon] *adj* desconocido, ignoto, incógnito || *s* desconocido; (math) incógnita
unknown quantity *s* (math & fig) incógnita
unknown soldier *s* soldado desconocido
unlace [ʌnˈles] *tr* desenlazar; desatar (*los cordones del zapato*)
unlatch [ʌnˈlætʃ] *tr* abrir levantando el picaporte
unlawful [ʌnˈlɔfəl] *adj* ilegal
unleash [ʌnˈliʃ] *tr* destraillar; soltar, desencadenar
unleavened [ʌnˈlɛvənd] *adj* ázimo
unless [ʌnˈlɛs] *conj* a menos que, a no ser que
unlettered [ʌnˈlɛtərd] *adj* iletrado, indocto; sin rotular; (*illiterate*) analfabeto
unlike [ʌnˈlaɪk] *adj* desemejante; desemejante de; (*poles of a magnet*) (elec) de nombres contrarios; (elec) de signo contrario || *prep* a diferencia de
unlikely [ʌnˈlaɪkli] *adj* improbable
unlimber [ʌnˈlɪmbər] *tr* preparar para la acción || *intr* prepararse para la acción
unlined [ʌnˈlaɪnd] *adj* (*coat*) sin forro; (*paper*) sin rayar; (*face*) sin arrugas
unload [ʌnˈlod] *tr* descargar; (coll) deshacerse de || *intr* descargar
unloading [ʌnˈlodɪŋ] *s* descarga, descargue *m*
unlock [ʌnˈlɑk] *tr* abrir (*p.ej., una puerta*); (typ) desapretar
unloose [ʌnˈlus] *tr* aflojar, soltar, desatar
unloved [ʌnˈlʌvd] *adj* desamado
unlovely [ʌnˈlʌvli] *adj* desgraciado
unluck·y [ʌnˈlʌki] *adj* (*comp* **-ier;** *super* **-iest**) desgraciado, desdichado; aciago, nefasto; de mala suerte
un·make [ʌnˈmek] *v* (*pret & pp* **-made** [ˈmed]) *tr* deshacer; destruir
unmanageable [ʌnˈmænɪdʒəbəl] *adj* inmanejable
unmanly [ʌnˈmænli] *adj* afeminado; bajo, cobarde
unmannerly [ʌnˈmænərli] *adj* descortés, malcriado
unmarketable [ʌnˈmɑrkɪtəbəl] *adj* incomerciable
unmarriageable [ʌnˈmærɪdʒəbəl] *adj* incasable
unmarried [ʌnˈmærid] *adj* soltero
unmask [ʌnˈmæsk] o [ʌnˈmɑsk] *tr* desenmascarar || *intr* desenmascararse
unmatchable [ʌnˈmætʃəbəl] *adj* incomparable, sin igual; (*price*) incompetible
unmerciful [ʌnˈmʌrsɪfəl] *adj* despiadado, inclemente
unmesh [ʌnˈmɛʃ] *tr* desengranar || *intr* desengranarse
unmindful [ʌnˈmaɪndfəl] *adj* desatento, descuidado; **to be unmindful of** olvidar, no pensar en
unmistakable [ˌʌnmɪsˈtekəbəl] *adj* inequívoco, inconfundible
unmixed [ʌnˈmɪkst] *adj* puro, sin mezcla
unmoor [ʌnˈmur] *tr* desamarrar (*un buque*); desaferrar (*las áncoras*)
unmoved [ʌnˈmuvd] *adj* fijo, inmoto; impasible
unmuzzle [ʌnˈmʌzəl] *tr* desbozalar
unnatural [ʌnˈnætʃərəl] *adj* innatural; (*artificial, forced*) afectado; anormal; inhumano
unnecessary [ʌnˈnɛsəˌsɛri] *adj* innecesario
unnerve [ʌnˈnʌrv] *tr* acobardar, trastornar
unnoticeable [ʌnˈnotɪsəbəl] *adj* imperceptible
unnoticed [ʌnˈnotɪst] *adj* inadvertido
unobliging [ˌʌnəˈblaɪdʒɪŋ] *adj* poco servicial, poco amable
unobserved [ˌʌnəbˈzʌrvd] *adj* inadvertido, sin ser visto
unobtainable [ˌʌnəbˈtenəbəl] *adj* inencontrable, inasequible
unobtrusive [ˌʌnəbˈtrusɪv] *adj* discreto, reservado
unoccupied [ʌnˈɑkjəˌpaɪd] *adj* libre, vacante; (*not busy*) desocupado
unofficial [ˌʌnəˈfɪʃəl] *adj* extraoficial, oficioso
unopened [ʌnˈopənd] *adj* sin abrir; (*book*) no cortado
unorthodox [ʌnˈɔrθəˌdɑks] *adj* inortodoxo
unpack [ʌnˈpæk] *tr* desembalar, desempaquetar
unpalatable [ʌnˈpælətəbəl] *adj* desabrido, ingustable
unparalleled [ʌnˈpærəˌlɛld] *adj* incomparable, sin par, sin igual
unpardonable [ʌnˈpɑrdənəbəl] *adj* imperdonable
unpatriotic [ˌʌnpetrɪˈɑtɪk] o [ˌʌnpætrɪˈɑtɪk] *adj* antipatriótico
unperceived [ˌʌnpərˈsivd] *adj* inadvertido
unperturbable [ˌʌnpərˈtʌrbəbəl] *adj* infracto, imperturbable
unpleasant [ʌnˈplɛzənt] *adj* antipático, desagradable
unpopular [ʌnˈpɑpjələr] *adj* impopular
unpopularity [ʌnˌpɑpjəˈlærɪti] *s* impopularidad
unprecedented [ʌnˈprɛsɪˌdɛntɪd] *adj* sin precedente, inaudito
unprejudiced [ʌnˈprɛdʒədɪst] *adj* sin prejuicios, imparcial
unpremeditated [ˌʌnprɪˈmɛdɪˌtetɪd] *adj* impremeditado

unprepared [ˌʌnprɪˈpɛrd] *adj* desprevenido; falto de preparación
unprepossessing [ˌʌnpripəˈzɛsɪŋ] *adj* poco atrayente
unpresentable [ˌʌnprɪˈzɛntəbəl] *adj* impresentable
unpretentious [ˌʌnprɪˈtɛnʃəs] *adj* modesto, sencillo
unprincipled [ʌnˈprɪnsɪpəld] *adj* sin principios, sin conciencia
unproductive [ˌʌnprəˈdʌktɪv] *adj* improductivo
unprofitable [ʌnˈprɑfɪtəbəl] *adj* no provechoso, inútil
unpronounceable [ˌʌnprəˈnaʊnsəbəl] *adj* impronunciable
unpropitious [ˌʌnprəˈpɪʃəs] *adj* impropicio
unpublished [ʌnˈpʌblɪʃt] *adj* inédito
unpunished [ʌnˈpʌnɪʃt] *adj* impune
unpurchasable [ʌnˈpʌrtʃəsəbəl] *adj* incomprable
unquenchable [ʌnˈkwɛntʃəbəl] *adj* inextinguible
unquestionable [ʌnˈkwɛstʃənəbəl] *adj* incuestionable
unrav•el [ʌnˈrævəl] *v* (*pret & pp* **-eled** o **-elled;** *ger* **-eling** o **-elling**) *tr* deshebrar; desenredar, desenmarañar || *intr* desenredarse, desenmarañarse
unreachable [ʌnˈritʃəbəl] *adj* inalcanzable
unreal [ʌnˈri·əl] *adj* irreal
unreali•ty [ˌʌnrɪˈælɪti] *s* (*pl* **-ties**) irrealidad
unreasonable [ʌnˈrizənəbəl] *adj* irrazonable, desrazonable
unrecognizable [ʌnˈrɛkəgˌnaɪzəbəl] *adj* irreconocible
unreel [ʌnˈril] *tr* desenrollar || *intr* desenrollarse
unrefined [ˌʌnrɪˈfaɪnd] *adj* no refinado, impuro; grosero, rudo, tosco
unrelenting [ˌʌnrɪˈlɛntɪŋ] *adj* inexorable, inflexible, implacable
unreliable [ˌʌnrɪˈlaɪ·əbəl] *adj* indigno de confianza, informal
unremitting [ˌʌnrɪˈmɪtɪŋ] *adj* constante, incesante; infatigable
unrenewable [ˌʌnrɪˈnju·əbəl] o [ˌʌnrɪˈnu·əbəl] *adj* irrenovable; (com) improrrogable
unrented [ʌnˈrɛntɪd] *adj* desalquilado
unrepentant [ˌʌnrɪˈpɛntənt] *adj* impenitente
unrequited love [ˌʌnrɪˈkwaɪtɪd] *s* amor no correspondido
unresponsive [ˌʌnrɪˈspɑnsɪv] *adj* insensible, frío, desinteresado
unrest [ʌnˈrɛst] *s* intranquilidad, inquietud; alboroto, desorden *m*
un•rig [ʌnˈrɪg] *v* (*pret & pp* **-rigged;** *ger* **-rigging**) *tr* (naut) desaparejar
unrighteous [ʌnˈraɪtʃəs] *adj* injusto, malvado, vicioso
unripe [ʌnˈraɪp] *adj* inmaturo, verde; prematuro, precoz
unrivaled o **unrivalled** [ʌnˈraɪvəld] *adj* sin rival, sin par
unroll [ʌnˈrol] *tr* desenrollar, desplegar
unromantic [ˌʌnroˈmæntɪk] *adj* poco romántico
unruffled [ʌnˈrʌfəld] *adj* tranquilo, sereno
unruly [ʌnˈruli] *adj* ingobernable, indómito, revoltoso
unsaddle [ʌnˈsædəl] *tr* desensillar (*un caballo*); desarzonar (*al jinete*)
unsafe [ʌnˈsef] *adj* inseguro, peligroso
unsaid [ʌnˈsɛd] *adj* callado, no dicho
unsalable [ʌnˈseləbəl] *adj* invendible
unsanitary [ʌnˈsænɪˌtɛri] *adj* antihigiénico, insalubre
unsatisfactory [ʌnˌsætɪsˈfæktəri] *adj* insatisfactorio, poco satisfactorio
unsatisfied [ʌnˈsætɪsˌfaɪd] *adj* insatisfecho
unsavory [ʌnˈsevəri] *adj* desabrido; (fig) infame, deshonroso
unscathed [ʌnˈskeðd] *adj* ileso, sano y salvo
unscientific [ˌʌnsaɪ·ənˈtɪfɪk] *adj* anticientífico
unscrew [ʌnˈskru] *tr* destornillar || *intr* destornillarse
unscrupulous [ʌnˈskrupjələs] *adj* inescrupuloso
unseal [ʌnˈsil] *tr* desellar; (fig) abrir
unseasonable [ʌnˈsizənəbəl] *adj* intempestivo, inoportuno
unseaworthy [ʌnˈsiˌwʌrði] *adj* innavegable
unseemly [ʌnˈsimli] *adj* impropio, indecoroso, indigno
unseen [ʌnˈsin] *adj* invisible, oculto
unselfish [ʌnˈsɛlfɪʃ] *adj* desinteresado, generoso, altruísta
unsettled [ʌnˈsɛtəld] *adj* inhabitado, despoblado; sin residencia fija; indeciso; descompuesto; (*bills*) por pagar
unshackle [ʌnˈʃækəl] *tr* desherrar, desencadenar
unshaken [ʌnˈʃekən] *adj* imperturbado
unshapely [ʌnˈʃepli] *adj* desproporcionado, mal formado
unshatterable [ʌnˈʃætərəbəl] *adj* inastillable
unshaven [ʌnˈʃevən] *adj* sin afeitar
unsheathe [ʌnˈʃið] *tr* desenvainar
unshod [ʌnˈʃɑd] *adj* descalzo; (*horse*) desherrado
unshrinkable [ʌnˈʃrɪŋkəbəl] *adj* inencogible
unsightly [ʌnˈsaɪtli] *adj* feo, de aspecto malo, repugnante
unsinkable [ʌnˈsɪŋkəbəl] *adj* insumergible
unskilled [ʌnˈskɪld] *adj* inexperto
unskilled laborer *s* bracero, peón *m*
unskillful [ʌnˈskɪlfəl] *adj* desmañado
unsnarl [ʌnˈsnɑrl] *tr* desenredar
unsociable [ʌnˈsoʃəbəl] *adj* insociable, huraño
unsold [ʌnˈsold] *adj* invendido
unsolder [ʌnˈsɑdər] *tr* desoldar; (fig) desunir, separar
unsophisticated [ˌʌnsəˈfɪstɪˌketɪd] *adj* ingenuo, natural, sencillo
unsound [ʌnˈsaʊnd] *adj* poco firme; falso, erróneo; (*decayed*) podrido; (*sleep*) ligero
unsown [ʌnˈson] *adj* yermo, no sembrado
unspeakable [ʌnˈspikəbəl] *adj* indeci-

ble, inefable; (*atrocious, infamous*) incalificable
unsportsmanlike [ʌn'sportsmən,laɪk] *adj* antideportivo
unstable [ʌn'stebəl] *adj* inestable
unsteady [ʌn'stɛdi] *adj* inseguro, inestable; irresoluto, inconstante; poco juicioso
unstinted [ʌn'stɪntɪd] *adj* no escatimado, generoso, liberal
unstitch [ʌn'stɪtʃ] *tr* descoser
un•stop [ʌn'stɑp] *v* (*pret & pp* **-stopped;** *ger* **-stopping**) *tr* destaponar
unstressed [ʌn'strɛst] *adj* sin énfasis; (*syllable*) inacentuado
unstrung [ʌn'strʌŋ] *adj* nervioso, trastornado
unsuccessful [,ʌnsək'sɛsfəl] *adj* (*person*) desairado; (*undertaking*) impróspero; **to be unsuccessful** no tener éxito
unsuitable [ʌn'sutəbəl] o [ʌn'sjutəbəl] *adj* inadecuado, inconveniente
unsurpassable [,ʌnsər'pæsəbəl] o [,ʌnsər'pɑsəbəl] *adj* insuperable
unsuspected [,ʌnsəs'pɛktɪd] *adj* insospechado
unswerving [ʌn'swʌrvɪŋ] *adj* firme, inmutable, resoluto
unsymmetrical [,ʌnsɪ'mɛtrɪkəl] *adj* asimétrico, disimétrico
unsympathetic [,ʌnsɪmpə'θɛtɪk] *adj* incompasivo, indiferente
unsystematic(al) [,ʌnsɪstə'mætɪk(əl)] *adj* poco sistemático, sin sistema
untactful [ʌn'tæktfəl] *adj* indiscreto, falto de tacto
untamed [ʌn'temd] *adj* indomado, bravío
untangle [ʌn'tæŋgəl] *tr* desenredar, desenmarañar
unteachable [ʌn'titʃəbəl] *adj* indócil
untenable [ʌn'tɛnəbəl] *adj* insostenible
unthankful [ʌn'θæŋkfəl] *adj* ingrato, desagradecido
unthinkable [ʌn'θɪŋkəbəl] *adj* impensable
unthinking [ʌn'θɪŋkɪŋ] *adj* irreflexivo, desatento; irracional, instintivo
untidy [ʌn'taɪdi] *adj* desaseado, desaliñado
un•tie [ʌn'taɪ] *v* (*pret & pp* **-tied;** *ger* **-tying**) *tr* desatar; deshacer (*un nudo, una cuerda*); (*to free from restraint*) soltar; resolver || *intr* desatarse
until [ʌn'tɪl] *prep* hasta || *conj* hasta que; **to wait until** aguardar a que, esperar a que
untillable [ʌn'tɪləbəl] *adj* incultivable
untimely [ʌn'taɪmli] *adj* intempestivo
untiring [ʌn'taɪrɪŋ] *adj* incansable
untold [ʌn'told] *adj* nunca dicho; (*uncounted*) innumerable, incalculable
untouchable [ʌn'tʌtʃəbəl] *adj* intangible || *s* intocable *mf*
untouched [ʌn'tʌtʃt] *adj* intacto; íntegro; impasible; no mencionado
untoward [ʌn'tord] *adj* desfavorable; indecoroso
untrammeled o **untrammelled** [ʌn'træməld] *adj* libre, sin trabas
untried [ʌn'traɪd] *adj* no probado, no ensayado
untroubled [ʌn'trʌbləd] *adj* tranquilo, sosegado
untrue [ʌn'tru] *adj* falso; infiel
untrustworthy [ʌn'trʌst,wʌrði] *adj* indigno de confianza
untruth [ʌn'truθ] *s* falsedad, mentira
untruthful [ʌn'truθfəl] *adj* falso, mentiroso
untwist [ʌn'twɪst] *tr* destorcer || *intr* destorcerse
unused [ʌn'juzd] *adj* inutilizado, no usado; nuevo; **unused to** [ʌn'juzdtʊ] o [ʌn'justʊ] *adj* no acostumbrado a
unusual [ʌn'juʒʊ·əl] *adj* inusual, insólito
unutterable [ʌn'ʌtərəbəl] *adj* indecible, inexpresable
unvanquished [ʌn'væŋkwɪʃt] *adj* invicto
unvarnished [ʌn'vɑrnɪʃt] *adj* sin barnizar; (fig) sencillo, sin adornos
unveil [ʌn'vel] *tr* quitar el velo a; descubrir, develar, inaugurar (*una estatua*) || *intr* quitarse el velo
unveiling [ʌn'velɪŋ] *s* develación, inauguración
unventilated [ʌn'vɛntɪ,letɪd] *adj* sin ventilar
unvoice [ʌn'vɔɪs] *tr* afonizar, ensordecer || *intr* afonizarse, ensordecerse
unwanted [ʌn'wɑntɪd] *adj* indeseado
unwarranted [ʌn'wɑrəntɪd] *adj* injustificado; no autorizado; sin garantía
unwary [ʌn'wɛri] *adj* incauto, imprudente
unwavering [ʌn'wevərɪŋ] *adj* firme, determinado, resuelto
unwelcome [ʌn'wɛlkəm] *adj* mal acogido; importuno, molesto
unwell [ʌn'wɛl] *adj* indispuesto, enfermo; (coll) menstruante
unwholesome [ʌn'holsəm] *adj* insalubre
unwieldy [ʌn'wildi] *adj* inmanejable, abultado, pesado
unwilling [ʌn'wɪlɪŋ] *adj* desinclinado, maldispuesto, renuente
unwillingly [ʌn'wɪlɪŋli] *adv* de mala gana
un•wind [ʌn'waɪnd] *v* (*pret & pp* **-wound** ['waʊnd]) *tr* desenvolver || *intr* desenvolverse; distenderse (*el muelle del reloj*)
unwise [ʌn'waɪz] *adj* indiscreto, malaconsejado
unwished-for [ʌn'wɪʃt,fɔr] *adj* indeseado
unwitting [ʌn'wɪtɪŋ] *adj* inadvertido, inconsciente
unwonted [ʌn'wʌntɪd] *adj* poco común, raro, insólito
unworldly [ʌn'wʌrldli] *adj* no terrenal, no mundano, espiritual
unworthy [ʌn'wʌrði] *adj* indigno, desmerecedor
un•wrap [ʌn'ræp] *v* (*pret & pp* **-wrapped;** *ger* **-wrapping**) *tr* desenvolver, desempapelar
unwrinkle [ʌn'rɪŋkəl] *tr* desarrugar || *intr* desarrugarse

unwritten [ʌnˈrɪtən] *adj* no escrito; (*blank*) en blanco; oral
unyielding [ʌnˈjildɪŋ] *adj* firme, inflexible; terco, reacio
unyoke [ʌnˈjok] *tr* desuncir
up [ʌp] *adj* ascendente; alto, elevado; derecho, en pie; terminado; cumplido; levantado de la cama; **to be up and about** estar levantado (*el que estaba enfermo*) ‖ *s* subida; **ups and downs** altibajos, vicisitudes ‖ *adv* arriba; en el aire; hacia arriba; al norte; **to be up** estar levantado; vencer (*un plazo*); **to be up in arms** estar sobre las armas; protestar vehementemente; **to be up to a person** tocarle a una persona; **to get up** levantarse; **to go up** subir; **to keep up** mantener; continuar; mantenerse firme; **to keep up with** correr parejas con; **up above** allá arriba; **up against it** (slang) en apuros; **up to** hasta; (*capable of*) a la altura de; (*informed of*) al corriente de; (*scheming*) armando, tramando; **what is up?** ¿qué pasa? ‖ *prep* subiendo; **up the river** río arriba; **up the street** calle arriba
up-and-coming [ˈʌpənˈkʌmɪŋ] *adj* (coll) prometedor
up-and-doing [ˈʌpənˈdu·ɪŋ] *adj* (coll) emprendedor
up-and-up [ˈʌpənˈʌp] *s* — **on the up-and-up** (coll) mejorándose; (coll) abiertamente, sin dolo
up•braid′ *tr* regañar, reprender
upbringing [ˈʌpˌbrɪŋɪŋ] *s* educación, crianza
up′coun′try *adv* (coll) hacia el interior, tierra adentro ‖ *s* (coll) interior *m* del país
up•date′ *tr* poner al día
upheaval [ʌpˈhivəl] *s* trastorno, cataclismo
up′hill′ *adj* ascendente; arduo, difícil, penoso ‖ **up′hill′** *adv* cuesta arriba
up•hold′ *v* (*pret & pp* **-held**) *tr* levantar; apoyar, sostener; defender
upholster [ʌpˈholstər] *tr* tapizar
upholsterer [ʌpˈholstərər] *s* tapicero
upholster•y [ʌpˈholstəri] *s* (*pl* **-ies**) tapicería
up′keep′ *s* conservación, manutención; gastos de conservación, gastos de entretenimiento
upland [ˈʌplənd] o [ˈʌplænd] *adj* alto, elevado ‖ *s* tierra alta, terreno elevado
up′lift′ *s* (*lifting*) elevación, levantamiento; mejora social; (*moral or spiritual improvement*) edificación ‖ **up•lift′** *tr* elevar, levantar; edificar
upon [əˈpɑn] *prep* en, sobre, encima de; **upon** + *ger* al + *inf*, p.ej., **upon arriving** al llegar; **upon my word!** ¡por mi palabra!
upper [ˈʌpər] *adj* alto, superior; (*country*) interior; (*clothing*) exterior ‖ *s* (*of shoe*) pala; **on one's uppers** con las suelas gastadas; (coll) andrajoso, pobre, sin blanca
upper berth *s* litera alta, cama alta
upper case *s* (typ) caja alta
upper classes *spl* altas clases
upper hand *s* dominio, ventaja; **to have the upper hand** tener vara alta
upper middle class *s* alta burguesía
up′per•most′ *adj* (el) más alto; (el) principal ‖ *adv* en lo más alto; primero, en primer lugar
uppish [ˈʌpɪʃ] *adj* (coll) copetudo, arrogante
up•raise′ *tr* levantar
up′right′ *adj* derecho, vertical; probo, recto ‖ *adv* verticalmente ‖ *s* montante *m*
uprising [ʌpˈraɪzɪŋ] o [ˈʌpˌraɪzɪŋ] *s* insurrección, levantamiento
up′roar′ *s* alboroto, conmoción, tumulto
uproarious [ʌpˈrorɪ·əs] *adj* tumultuoso; (*noisy*) ruidoso; (*funny*) muy cómico
up•root′ *tr* desarraigar
up•set′ o **up′set′** *adj* (*overturned*) volcado; trastornado; indispuesto ‖ **up′set′** *s* (*overturn*) vuelco; (*unexpected defeat*) contratiempo; (*disturbance*) trastorno; (*illness*) indisposición, enfermedad ‖ **up•set′** *v* (*pret & pp* **-set;** *ger* **-setting**) *tr* volcar; trastornar; indisponer ‖ *intr* volcar
upset price *s* precio mínimo fijado en una subasta
upsetting [ʌpˈsɛtɪŋ] *adj* desconcertante
up′shot′ *s* conclusión, resultado; esencia, quid *m*
up′side′ *s* parte *f* superior, lado superior; **on the upside** (*said of prices*) subiendo
upside down *adv* al revés, lo de arriba abajo, patas arriba; en confusión, revuelto; **to turn upside down** volcar; trastornar; volcarse; trastornarse
up′stage′ *adj* situado al fondo de la escena; (coll) altanero, arrogante ‖ *adv* al fondo de la escena ‖ **up′stage′** *tr* (coll) mirar por encima del hombro, desairar
up′stairs′ *adj* de arriba ‖ *adv* arriba ‖ *s* piso superior, pisos superiores
upstanding [ʌpˈstændɪŋ] *adj* derecho; gallardo; probo, recto
up′start′ *adj & s* advenedizo
up′stream′ *adv* aguas arriba, río arriba
up′stroke′ *s* carrera ascendente
up′swing′ *s* movimiento hacia arriba; mejora notable; **on the upswing** mejorando notablemente
up′-to-date′ *adj* corriente; reciente, moderno; de última hora, de última moda
up′-to-the-min′ute *adj* al día, de actualidad
up′town′ *adj* de la parte alta de la ciudad ‖ *adv* en la parte alta de la ciudad
up train *s* tren *m* ascendente
up′trend′ *s* tendencia al alza
up′turn′ *s* alza, subida, mejora
upturned [ʌpˈtʌrnd] *adj* revuelto; (*part of clothing*) arremangado; (*nose*) respingada
upward [ˈʌpwərd] *adj* ascendente ‖ *adv* hacia arriba; **upward of** más de

Ural ['jurəl] *adj* ural || **Urals** *spl* Urales *mpl*
uranium [ju'renɪ·əm] *s* uranio
urban ['ʌrbən] *adj* urbano (*perteneciente a la ciudad*)
urbane [ʌr'ben] *adj* urbano (*atento, cortés*)
urbanite ['ʌrbə,naɪt] *s* ciudadano
urbanity [ʌr'bænɪti] *s* urbanidad
urbanize ['ʌrbə,naɪz] *tr* urbanizar
urchin ['ʌrtʃɪn] *s* pilluelo, galopín *m*
ure•thra [ju'riθrə] *s* (*pl* **-thras** o **-thrae** [θri]) uretra
urge [ʌrdʒ] *s* impulso, estímulo || *tr* apremiar, impeler, estimular; pedir instantemente; (*to try to persuade*) instar || *intr* instar
urgen•cy ['ʌrdʒənsi] *s* (*pl* **-cies**) urgencia; instancia, apremio
urgent ['ʌrdʒənt] *adj* urgente; apremiante
urinal ['jurɪnəl] *s* (*receptacle*) orinal *m;* (*place*) urinario
urinary ['jurɪ,neri] *adj* urinario
urinate ['jurɪ,net] *tr* orinar (*p.ej., sangre*) || *intr* orinar, orinarse
urine ['jurɪn] *s* orina, orines *mpl*
urn [ʌrn] *s* (*decorative vase*) jarrón *m;* cafetera o tetera con grifo; (*to hold ashes of the dead after cremation*) urna
urology [ju'rɑlədʒi] *s* urología
Uruguay ['jurə,gwe] o ['jurə,gwaɪ] *s* el Uruguay
Uruguayan [,jurə'gwe·ən] o [,jurə'gwaɪ·ən] *adj & s* uruguayo
us [ʌs] *pron pers* nos; nosotros; **to us** nos; a nosotros
U.S.A. *abbr* **United States of America, United States Army, Union of South Africa**
usable ['juzəbəl] *adj* aprovechable, utilizable
usage ['jusɪdʒ] o ['juzɪdʒ] *s* usanza; (*e.g., of a language*) uso
use [jus] *s* uso, empleo; utilidad; **in use** en uso; **out of use** desusado; **to be of no use** no servir para nada; **to have no use for** no necesitar; no servirse de; (coll) tener en poco; **to make use of** servirse de || [juz] *tr* usar, emplear, servirse de; **to use badly** maltratar; **to use up** agotar, consumir || *intr* (empléase sólo en el pretérito y se traduce al español con el pretérito imperfecto o el verbo **soler**), p.ej., **I used to go out for a walk every evening** salía de paseo todas las tardes o solía salir de paseo todas las tardes
used [juzd] *adj* (*customarily employed; worn, partly worn-out; accustomed*) usado; **used to** ['juzdtu] o ['justu] acostumbrado a
useful ['jusfəl] *adj* útil
usefulness ['jusfəlnɪs] *s* utilidad
useless ['juslɪs] *adj* inservible, inútil
user ['juzər] *s* usuario
usher ['ʌʃər] *s* (*in a theater*) acomodador *m;* (*doorkeeper*) ujier *m,* portero || *tr* acomodar; **to usher in** anunciar, introducir
U.S.S.R. *abbr* **Union of Soviet Socialist Republics**
usual ['juʒu·əl] *adj* usual, acostumbrado; **as usual** como de costumbre
usually ['juʒu·əli] *adj* usualmente, de ordinario
usurp [ju'zʌrp] *tr* usurpar
usu•ry ['juʒəri] *s* (*pl* **-ries**) usura
utensil [ju'tensɪl] *s* utensilio
uter•us ['jutərəs] *s* (*pl* **-i** [,aɪ]) útero
utilitarian [,jutɪlɪ'terɪ·ən] *adj* utilitario
utili•ty [ju'tɪlɪti] *s* (*pl* **-ties**) utilidad; empresa de servicio público
utilize ['jutɪ,laɪz] *tr* utilizar
utmost ['ʌt,most] *adj* sumo, extremo, último; más grande, mayor posible; más lejano || *s* — **the utmost** lo sumo, lo mayor, lo más; **to the utmost** a lo sumo, a más no poder; **to do one's utmost** hacer todo lo posible
utopia [ju'topɪ·ə] *s* utopía
utopian [ju'topɪ·ən] *adj* utópico, utopista || *s* utopista *mf*
utter ['ʌtər] *adj* total, absoluto || *tr* proferir, pronunciar; dar (*un suspiro*)
utterance ['ʌtərəns] *s* expresión, pronunciación; declaración
utterly ['ʌtərli] *adj* completamente, totalmente, absolutamente
uxoricide [ʌk'sorɪ,saɪd] *s* (*husband*) uxoricida *m;* (*act*) uxoricidio
uxorious [ʌk'sorɪ·əs] *adj* uxorio

V

V, v [vi] vigésima segunda letra del alfabeto inglés
v. *abbr* **verb, verse, versus, vide** (Lat) **see, voice, volt, volume**
V. *abbr* **Venerable, Vice, Viscount, Volunteer**
vacan•cy ['vekənsi] *s* (*pl* **-cies**) (*emptiness; gap, opening*) vacío; (*unfilled position or job*) vacancia, vacante *f,* vacío; piso vacante; cargo vacante
vacant ['vekənt] *adj* (*empty*) vacío; (*having no occupant; untenanted*) vacante; (*expression, look*) vago; distraído
vacate ['veket] *tr* dejar vacante; anular, invalidar, revocar || *intr* (*to move out*) desalojar; (coll) irse, marcharse
vacation [ve'keʃən] *s* vacaciones; **on vacation** de vacaciones || *intr* tomar vacaciones
vacationist [ve'keʃənɪst] *s* vacacionista *mf*
vacation with pay *s* vacaciones retribuídas

vaccinate ['væksɪ,net] *tr* vacunar
vaccination [,væksɪ'neʃən] *s* vacunación
vaccine [væk'sin] *s* vacuna
vacillate ['væsɪ,let] *intr* vacilar
vacillating ['væsɪ,letɪŋ] *adj* vacilante
vacui·ty [væ'kju·ɪti] *s* (*pl* **-ties**) vacuidad
vacu·um ['vækjʊ·əm] *s* (*pl* **-ums** o **-a** [ə]) vacío || *tr* (coll) limpiar
vacuum cleaner *s* aspirador *m* de polvo
vacuum tank *s* (aut) aspirador *m* de gasolina, nodriza
vacuum tube *s* tubo de vacío
vagabond ['vægə,bɑnd] *adj* & *s* vagabundo
vagar·y [və'gɛri] *s* (*pl* **-ies**) capricho
vagran·cy ['vegrənsi] *s* (*pl* **-cies**) vagabundaje *m*
vagrant ['vegrənt] *adj* & *s* vagabundo
vague [veg] *adj* vago
vain [ven] *adj* vano; (*conceited*) vanidoso; **in vain** en vano
vainglorious [ven'glorɪ·əs] *adj* vanaglorioso
valance ['væləns] *s* (*across the top of a window*) guardamalleta; (*drapery*) doselera
vale [vel] *s* valle *m*
valedictorian [,vælɪdɪk'torɪ·ən] *s* alumno que pronuncia el discurso de despedida al fin del curso
valedicto·ry [,vælɪ'dɪktəri] *adj* de despedida || *s* (*pl* **-ries**) discurso de despedida
valence ['veləns] *s* (chem) valencia
valentine ['vælən,taɪn] *s* tarjeta amorosa o jocosa del día de San Valentín
Valentine Day *s* día *m* de los corazones, día de los enamorados (*14 de febrero*)
vale of tears *s* valle *m* de lágrimas
valet ['vælɪt] o ['væle] *s* ayuda *m*, paje *m*
valiant ['væljənt] *adj* valiente, valeroso
valid ['vælɪd] *adj* válido, valedero
validate ['vælɪ,det] *tr* validar; (sport) homologar
validation [,vælɪ'deʃən] *s* validación; (sport) homologación
validi·ty [və'lɪdɪti] *s* (*pl* **-ties**) validez *f*
valise [və'lis] *s* maleta
valley ['væli] *s* valle *m*; (*of roof*) lima hoya
valor ['vælər] *s* valor *m*, ánimo
valorous ['vælərəs] *adj* valeroso
valuable ['vælju·əbəl] o ['væljəbəl] *adj* (*having monetary value*) valioso; (*highly thought of*) estimable || **valuables** *spl* alhajas, objetos de valor
value ['vælju] *s* valor *m*; (*return for one's money in a purchase*) (coll) adquisición, inversión, p.ej., **an excellent value** una adquisición excelente || *tr* (*to think highly of*) estimar; (*to set a price for*) valorar, valuar
valueless ['væljulɪs] *adj* sin valor
valve [vælv] *s* válvula; (*of mollusk*) valva; (mus) llave *f*
valve cap *s* capuchón *m*
valve gears *spl* distribución
valve'-in-head' engine *s* motor *m* con válvulas en cabeza
valve lifter ['lɪftər] *s* levantaválvulas *m*
valve seat *s* asiento de válvula
valve spring *s* muelle *m* de válvula
valve stem *s* vástago de válvula
vamp [væmp] *s* (*of shoe*) empella; (*patchwork*) remiendo; (*woman who preys on men*) (slang) mujer *f* fatal, vampiresa || *tr* poner empella a (*un zapato*); remendar; (*to concoct*) componer, enmendar; (jazz) improvisar (*un acompañamiento*); (slang) seducir (*una mujer mundana a un hombre*)
vampire ['væmpaɪr] *s* vampiro; (*woman who preys on men*) mujer *f* fatal, vampiresa
van [væn] *s* carro de carga, camión *m* de mudanzas; (mil & fig) vanguardia; (Brit) furgón *m* de equipajes
vanadium [və'nedɪ·əm] *s* vanadio
vandal ['vændəl] *adj* & *s* vándalo || **Vandal** *adj* & *s* vándalo
vandalism ['vændə,lɪzəm] *s* vandalismo
vane [ven] *s* (*weathervane*) veleta; (*of windmill*) aspa; (*of propeller or turbine*) paleta; (*of feather*) barba
vanguard ['væn,gɑrd] *s* (mil & fig) vanguardia; **in the vanguard** a vanguardia
vanilla [və'nɪlə] *s* vainilla
vanish ['vænɪʃ] *intr* desvanecerse
vanishing cream ['vænɪʃɪŋ] *s* crema desvanecedora
vani·ty ['vænɪti] *s* (*pl* **-ties**) vanidad; (*dressing table*) tocador *m*; (*vanity case*) estuche *m* de afeites
vanity case *s* estuche *m* de afeites, neceser *m* de belleza
vanquish ['væŋkwɪʃ] *tr* vencer, rendir
vantage ground ['væntɪdʒ] *s* posición ventajosa
vapid ['væpɪd] *adj* insípido
vapor ['vepər] *s* vapor *m* (*el visible; exhalación, vaho, niebla, etc.*)
vaporize ['vepə,raɪz] *tr* vaporizar || *intr* vaporizarse
vaporous ['vepərəs] *adj* vaporoso
vapor trail *s* (aer) estela de vapor, rastro de condensación
var. *abbr* **variant**
variable ['vɛrɪ·əbəl] *adj* & *s* variable *f*
variance ['vɛrɪ·əns] *s* diferencia, variación; **at variance with** en desacuerdo con
variant ['vɛrɪ·ənt] *adj* & *s* variante *f*
variation [,vɛrɪ'eʃən] *s* variación
varicose ['værɪ,kos] *adj* varicoso
varicose vein *s* (pathol) varice *f*
varied ['vɛrid] *adj* variado, vario
variegated ['vɛrɪ·ə,getɪd] o ['vɛrɪ,getɪd] *adj* abigarrado, variado
varie·ty [və'raɪ·ɪti] *s* (*pl* **-ties**) variedad
variety show *s* variedades
variola [və'raɪ·ələ] *s* (pathol) viruela
various ['vɛrɪ·əs] *adj* (*several; of different kinds*) varios; (*many-sided; many-colored*) vario
varnish ['vɑrnɪʃ] *s* barniz *m*; (fig) capa, apariencia || *tr* barnizar; (fig) dar apariencia falsa a
varsi·ty ['vɑrsɪti] *adj* (sport) universi-

tario || *s* (*pl* **-ties**) (sport) equipo principal de la universidad
var•y ['vɛri] *v* (*pret & pp* **-ied**) *tr & intr* variar
vase [ves] o [vez] *s* florero, jarrón *m*
vaseline ['væsə,lin] *s* (trademark) vaselina
vassal ['væsəl] *adj & s* vasallo
vast [væst] o [vɑst] *adj* vasto
vastly ['væstli] o ['vɑstli] *adv* enormemente
vastness ['væstnɪs] o ['vɑstnɪs] *s* vastedad
vat [væt] *s* cuba, tina
vaudeville ['vodvɪl] o ['vɔdəvɪl] *s* variedades; (*light theatrical piece interspersed with songs*) zarzuela
vault [vɔlt] *s* (*underground chamber*) bodega; (*of a bank*) cámara acorazada; (*burial chamber*) sepultura, tumba; (*firmament*) bóveda celeste; (*leap*) salto; (archit) bóveda || *tr* abovedar; saltar || *intr* saltar
vaunt [vɔnt] o [vɑnt] *s* jactancia || *tr* jactarse de || *intr* jactarse
veal [vil] *s* ternera, carne *f* de ternera
veal chop *s* chuleta de ternera
vedette [vɪ'dɛt] *s* buque *m* escucha; centinela *m* de avanzada
veer [vɪr] *s* viraje *m* || *tr* virar || *intr* virar; (naut) llamar (*el viento*)
vegetable ['vɛdʒɪtəbəl] *adj* vegetal || *s* (*plant*) vegetal *m;* (*edible part of plant*) hortaliza, legumbre *f*
vegetable garden *s* huerto de hortalizas, huerto de verduras
vegetable soup *s* menestra, sopa de hortalizas
vegetarian [,vɛdʒɪ'tɛrɪ·ən] *adj & s* vegetariano
vehemence ['vi·ɪməns] *s* vehemencia
vehement ['vi·ɪmənt] *adj* vehemente
vehicle ['vi·ɪkəl] *s* vehículo
vehicular traffic [vɪ'hɪkjələr] *s* circulación rodada
veil [vel] *s* velo; **to take the veil** tomar el velo || *tr* velar (*cubrir con un velo; cubrir, disimular*)
vein [ven] *s* vena; (*streak*) veta; (*distinctive quality*) rasgo || *tr* vetear
velar ['vilər] *adj & s* velar *f*
vellum ['vɛləm] *s* vitela; papel *m* vitela
veloci•ty [vɪ'lɑsɪti] *s* (*pl* **-ties**) velocidad
velvet ['vɛlvɪt] *adj* de terciopelo || *s* terciopelo; (slang) ganancia limpia
velveteen [,vɛlvɪ'tin] *s* velludillo
velvety ['vɛlvɪti] *adj* aterciopelado
Ven. *abbr* **Venerable**
vend [vɛnd] *tr* vender como buhonero
vending machine *s* distribuidor automático
vendor ['vɛndər] *s* vendedor *m,* buhonero
veneer [və'nɪr] *s* chapa, enchapado; (fig) apariencia || *tr* enchapar
venerable ['vɛnərəbəl] *adj* venerable
venerate ['vɛnə,ret] *tr* venerar
venereal [vɪ'nɪrɪ·əl] *adj* venéreo
Venetia [vɪ'niʃɪ·ə] o [vɪ'niʃə] *s* Venecia (*provincia*)
Venetian [vɪ'niʃən] *adj & s* veneciano
Venetian blind *s* persiana
Venezuela [,vɛnɪ'zwilə] *s* Venezuela
Venezuelan [,vɛnɪ'zwilən] *adj & s* venezolano
vengeance ['vɛndʒəns] *s* venganza; **with a vengeance** con furia, con violencia; excesivamente, con creces
vengeful ['vɛndʒfəl] *adj* vengativo
Venice ['vɛnɪs] *s* Venecia (*ciudad*)
venire [vɪ'naɪri] *s* (law) auto de convocación del jurado
venison ['vɛnɪsən] o ['vɛnɪzən] *s* carne *f* de venado
venom ['vɛnəm] *s* veneno
venomous ['vɛnəməs] *adj* venenoso
vent [vɛnt] *s* agujero, orificio; (*outlet*) salida; **to give vent to** dar libre curso a || *tr* proveer de abertura; desahogar, expresar; **to vent one's spleen** descargar la bilis
vent'hole' *s* respiradero
ventilate ['vɛntɪ,let] *tr* ventilar
ventilator ['vɛntɪ,letər] *s* ventilador *m*
ventricle ['vɛntrɪkəl] *s* ventrículo
ventriloquism [vɛn'trɪlə,kwɪzəm] *s* ventriloquia
ventriloquist [vɛn'trɪləkwɪst] *s* ventrílocuo
venture ['vɛntʃər] *s* empresa arriesgada; **at a venture** a la buena ventura || *tr* aventurar || *intr* aventurarse; **to venture on** arriesgarse en
venturesome ['vɛntʃərsəm] *adj* (*bold, daring*) aventurero; (*hazardous*) aventurado
venturous ['vɛntʃərəs] *adj* (*bold, daring*) aventurero; (*hazardous*) aventurado, arriesgado
venue ['vɛnju] *s* (law) lugar *m* del crimen; (law) lugar donde se reúne el jurado; **change of venue** (law) traslado de jurisdicción
Venus ['vinəs] *s* (astr) Venus *m;* (myth) Venus *f;* (*very beautiful woman*) Venus *f*
veracious [vɪ'reʃəs] *adj* veraz
veraci•ty [vɪ'ræsɪti] *s* (*pl* **-ties**) veracidad
veranda o **verandah** [və'rændə] *s* terraza, veranda, galería
verb [vʌrb] *adj* verbal || *s* verbo
verbatim [vər'betɪm] *adj* textual || *adv* palabra por palabra, al pie de la letra
verbena [vər'binə] *s* (bot) verbena
verbiage ['vʌrbɪ·ɪdʒ] *s* palabrería, verbosidad
verbose [vər'bos] *adj* verboso
verdant ['vʌrdənt] *adj* verde; cándido, sencillo
verdict ['vʌrdɪkt] *s* veredicto, fallo
verdigris ['vʌrdɪ,gris] *s* verdete *m*
verdure ['vʌrdʒər] *s* verdor *m*
verge [vʌrdʒ] *s* borde *m,* límite *m;* (*of a column*) fuste *m;* báculo; (eccl) cetro; **on the verge of** al borde de; a punto de; **within the verge of** al alcance de || *intr* — **to verge on** o **upon** llegar casi hasta, rayar en
verification [,vɛrɪfɪ'keʃən] *s* verificación
veri•fy ['vɛrɪ,faɪ] *v* (*pret & pp* **-fied**) *tr* verificar, comprobar; (law) afirmar bajo juramento

verily ['vɛrɪli] *adv* verdaderamente, en verdad
veritable ['vɛrɪtəbəl] *adj* verdadero
vermicelli [ˌvʌrmɪ'sɛli] *s* fideos
vermilion [vər'mɪljən] *adj* bermejo || *s* bermellón *m*
vermin ['vʌrmɪn] *ssg* (*objectionable person*) sabandija || *spl* (*objectionable animals or persons*) sabandijas
vermouth [vər'muθ] o ['vʌrmuθ] *s* vermú *m*
vernacular [vər'nækjələr] *adj* vernáculo || *s* lenguaje vernáculo; idioma *m* corriente; (*language peculiar to a class or profession*) jerga
veronica [və'rɑnɪkə] *s* (bot & taur) verónica; lienzo de la Verónica
Versailles [vɛr'saɪ] *s* Versalles
versatile ['vʌrsətɪl] *adj* (*person*) de muchas habilidades; (*informed on many subjects*) polifacético, universal; (*device or tool*) útil para muchas cosas
verse [vʌrs] *s* verso; (*in the Bible*) versículo
versed [vʌrst] *adj* versado; **to become versed in** versarse en
versification [ˌvʌrsɪfɪ'keʃən] *s* versificación
versi•fy ['vʌrsɪˌfaɪ] *v* (*pret & pp* **-fied**) *tr & intr* versificar
version ['vʌrʒən] *s* versión
ver•so ['vʌrso] *s* (*pl* **-sos**) (*e.g., of a coin*) reverso; (typ) verso
versus ['vʌrsəs] *prep* contra
verte•bra ['vʌrtɪbrə] *s* (*pl* **-brae** [ˌbri] o **-bras**) vértebra
vertebrate ['vʌrtɪˌbret] *adj & s* vertebrado
ver•tex ['vʌrtɛks] *s* (*pl* **-texes** o **-tices** [tɪˌsiz]) (*top, summit*) ápice *m;* (geom) vértice *m*
vertical ['vʌrtɪkəl] *adj & s* vertical *f*
vertical hold *s* (telv) bloqueo vertical
vertical rudder *s* (aer) timón *m* de dirección
verti•go ['vʌrtɪˌgo] *s* (*pl* **-gos** o **-goes**) vértigo
verve [vʌrv] *s* brío, ánimo, vigor *m*
very ['vɛri] *adj* mismísimo; (*sheer, utter*) mero, puro; (*actual*) verdadero || *adv* muy; mucho, p.ej., **to be very hungry** tener mucha hambre
vesicle ['vɛsɪkəl] *s* vesícula
vesper ['vɛspər] *s* tarde *f,* caída de la tarde; oración de la tarde; canción de la tarde; **vespers** (eccl) vísperas || **Vesper** *s* Véspero
vesper bell *s* campana que llama a vísperas
vessel ['vɛsəl] *s* vasija, recipiente *m;* (*ship*) bajel *m,* embarcación, buque *m;* (anat) vaso
vest [vɛst] *s* (*of man's suit*) chaleco; (*jabot*) chorrera; (*undershirt*) camiseta || *tr* vestir; **to vest in** conceder (*p.ej., poder*) a; **to vest with** investir de || *intr* vestirse; **to vest in** pasar a
vested interests *spl* intereses creados
vestibule ['vɛstɪˌbjul] *s* vestíbulo, zaguán *m*
vestige ['vɛstɪdʒ] *s* vestigio
vestment ['vɛstmənt] *s* vestidura
vest'-pock'et *adj* de bolsillo, en miniatura; diminuto
ves•try ['vɛstri] *s* (*pl* **-tries**) sacristía; (*chapel*) capilla; junta parroquial; reunión de la junta parroquial
vestry•man ['vɛstrimən] *s* (*pl* **-men** [mən]) miembro de la junta parroquial
Vesuvius [vɪ'suvɪ•əs] o [vɪ'sjuvɪ•əs] *s* el Vesubio
vet. *abbr* **veteran, veterinary**
vetch [vɛtʃ] *s* arveja, veza; (*grass pea*) almorta
veteran ['vɛtərən] *adj & s* veterano
veterinarian [ˌvɛtərɪ'nɛrɪ•ən] *s* veterinario
veterinar•y ['vɛtərɪˌnɛri] *adj* veterinario || *s* (*pl* **-ies**) veterinario
veterinary medicine *s* veterinaria, medicina veterinaria
ve•to ['vito] *s* (*pl* **-toes**) veto || *tr* vetar
vex [vɛks] *tr* vejar, molestar
vexation [vɛk'seʃən] *s* vejación, molestia
v.g. *abbr* **verbi gratia** (Lat) **for example**
via ['vaɪ•ə] *prep* vía, p.ej., **via Lisbon** vía Lisboa
viaduct ['vaɪ•əˌdʌkt] *s* viaducto
vial ['vaɪ•əl] *s* redoma, frasco pequeño
viati•cum [vaɪ'ætɪkəm] *s* (*pl* **-cums** o **-ca** [kə]) (eccl) viático
viand ['vaɪ•ənd] *s* vianda, manjar *m*
vibrate ['vaɪbret] *tr & intr* vibrar
vibration [vaɪ'breʃən] *s* vibración
vicar ['vɪkər] *s* vicario
vicarage ['vɪkərɪdʒ] *s* casa del vicario; (*duties of vicar*) vicaría
vicarious [vaɪ'kɛrɪ•əs] o [vɪ'kɛrɪ•əs] *adj* substituto; (*punishment*) sufrido por otro; (*power, authority*) delegado; (*enjoyment*) reflejado
vice [vaɪs] *s* vicio
vice'-ad'miral *s* vicealmirante *m*
vice'-pres'ident *s* vicepresidente *m*
viceroy ['vaɪsrɔɪ] *s* virrey *m*
vice versa ['vaɪsi 'vʌrsə] o ['vaɪs 'vʌrsə] *adv* viceversa
vicini•ty [vɪ'sɪnɪti] *s* (*pl* **-ties**) vecindad
vicious ['vɪʃəs] *adj* vicioso; (*dog*) bravo; (*horse*) arisco
victim ['vɪktɪm] *s* víctima
victimize ['vɪktɪˌmaɪz] *tr* hacer víctima; engañar, estafar
victor ['vɪktər] *s* vencedor *m*
victorious [vɪk'torɪ•əs] *adj* victorioso
victo•ry ['vɪktəri] *s* (*pl* **-ries**) victoria
victuals ['vɪtəlz] *spl* vituallas, provisiones de boca
vid. *abbr* **vide** (Lat) **see**
video signal ['vɪdɪˌo] *s* señal *f* de vídeo
video tape *s* cinta grabada de televisión
vid'eo-tape' recording *s* videograbación
vie [vaɪ] *v* (*pret & pp* **vied;** *ger* **vying**) *intr* competir, emular, rivalizar
Vien•nese [ˌvi•ə'niz] *adj* vienés || *s* (*pl* **-nese**) vienés *m*
Vietnam•ese [vɪˌɛtnə'miz] *adj* vietnamés || *s* (*pl* **-ese**) vietnamés *m*
view [vju] *s* vista; (*purpose*) intento, propósito, vista; **to be on view** estar expuesto (*p.ej., un cadáver*); **to keep in view** no perder de vista; no olvi-

dar, tener presente; **to take a dim view of** no entusiasmarse por, mirar escépticamente; **with a view to** con vistas a || *tr* ver, mirar; considerar, contemplar; examinar, inspeccionar
viewer ['vju·ər] *s* espectador *m;* telespectador *m,* televidente *mf;* proyector *m* de transparencias; mirador *m* de transparencias
view finder *s* (phot) visor *m*
view'point' *s* punto de vista
vigil ['vɪdʒɪl] *s* vigilia; **to keep vigil** velar
vigilance ['vɪdʒɪləns] *s* vigilancia
vigilant ['vɪdʒɪlənt] *adj* vigilante
vignette [vɪn'jɛt] *s* viñeta
vigor ['vɪgər] *s* vigor *m*
vigorous ['vɪgərəs] *adj* vigoroso
vile [vaɪl] *adj* vil; (*disgusting*) asqueroso, repugnante; (*weather*) muy malo
vili·fy ['vɪlɪ,faɪ] *v* (*pret & pp* **-fied**) *tr* difamar, denigrar
villa ['vɪlə] *s* villa, quinta
village ['vɪlɪdʒ] *s* aldea
villager ['vɪlɪdʒər] *s* aldeano
villain ['vɪlən] *s* malvado; (*of a play*) malo, traidor *m*
villainous ['vɪlənəs] *adj* malvado
villain·y ['vɪləni] *s* (*pl* **-ies**) maldad, perfidia
vim [vɪm] *s* fuerza, brío, vigor *m*
vinaigrette [,vɪnə'grɛt] *s* vinagrera
vinaigrette sauce *s* vinagreta
vindicate ['vɪndɪ,ket] *tr* vindicar, exculpar
vindictive [vɪn'dɪktɪv] *adj* vengativo
vine [vaɪn] *s* (*creeping or climbing plant*) enredadera; (*grape plant*) vid *f,* parra
vine'dress'er *s* viñador *m,* viticultor *m*
vinegar ['vɪnɪgər] *s* vinagre *m*
vinegarish ['vɪnɪgərɪʃ] *adj* avinagrado
vinegary ['vɪnɪgəri] *adj* vinagroso
vineyard ['vɪnjərd] *s* viña, viñedo
vineyardist ['vɪnjərdɪst] *s* viñador *m,* viticultor *m*
vintage ['vɪntɪdʒ] *s* vendimia; vino de buena cosecha; (coll) categoría, clase *f*
vintager ['vɪntɪdʒər] *s* vendimiador *m*
vintage wine *s* vino de buena cosecha
vintage year *s* año de buen vino
vintner ['vɪntnər] *s* vinatero
vinyl ['vaɪnɪl] o ['vɪnɪl] *s* vinilo
violate ['vaɪ·ə,let] *tr* violar
violence ['vaɪ·ələns] *s* violencia
violent ['vaɪ·ələnt] *adj* violento
violet ['vaɪ·əlɪt] *adj* violado || *s* (*color*) violeta *m,* violado; (*dye*) violeta *m;* (bot) violeta *f*
violin [,vaɪ·ə'lɪn] *s* violín *m*
violinist [,vaɪ·ə'lɪnɪst] *s* violinista *mf*
violoncellist [,vaɪ·ələn'tʃɛlɪst] o [,vi·ələn'tʃɛlɪst] *s* violoncelista *mf*
violoncel·lo [,vaɪ·ələn'tʃɛlo] o [,vi·ələn'tʃɛlo] *s* (*pl* **-los**) violoncelo
viper ['vaɪpər] *s* víbora
vira·go [vɪ'rego] *s* (*pl* **-goes** o **-gos**) mujer de mal genio
virgin ['vʌrdʒɪn] *adj & s* virgen *f*
virgin birth *s* parto virginal de María Santísima; (zool) partenogénesis *f*
Virginia creeper [vər'dʒɪnɪ·ə] *s* (bot) guau *m*
virginity [vər'dʒɪnɪti] *s* virginidad
virility [vɪ'rɪlɪti] *s* virilidad
virology [vaɪ'rɑlədʒi] *s* virología
virtual ['vʌrtʃu·əl] *adj* virtual
virtue ['vʌrtʃu] *s* virtud
virtuosi·ty [,vʌrtʃu'ɑsɪti] *s* (*pl* **-ties**) virtuosismo
virtuo·so [,vʌrtʃu'oso] *s* (*pl* **-sos** o **-si** [si]) virtuoso
virtuous ['vʌrtʃu·əs] *adj* virtuoso
virulence ['vɪrjələns] *s* virulencia
virulent ['vɪrjələnt] *adj* virulento
virus ['vaɪrəs] *s* virus *m*
Vis. *abbr* **Viscount**
visa ['vizə] *s* visa || *tr* visar
visage ['vɪzɪdʒ] *s* cara, semblante *m;* aspecto, apariencia
vis-à-vis [,vizə'vi] *adj* enfrentados || *adv* frente a frente || *prep* enfrente de; respecto de
viscera ['vɪsərə] *spl* vísceras
viscount ['vaɪkaunt] *s* vizconde *m*
viscountess ['vaɪkauntɪs] *s* vizcondesa
viscous ['vɪskəs] *adj* viscoso
vise [vaɪs] *s* tornillo, torno
visé ['vize] o [vi'ze] *s & tr* var de **visa**
visible ['vɪzɪbəl] *adj* visible
Visigoth ['vɪzɪ,gɑθ] *s* visigodo
vision ['vɪʒən] *s* visión; (*sense of sight*) vista
visionar·y ['vɪʒə,nɛri] *adj* visionario || *s* (*pl* **-ies**) visionario
visit ['vɪzɪt] *s* visita || *tr* visitar; afligir, acometer; enviar (*p.ej., castigo, venganza*) || *intr* hacer visitas; visitarse (*dos o más personas*)
visitation [,vɪzɪ'teʃən] *s* visitación; gracia del cielo, castigo del cielo
visiting card *s* tarjeta de visita
visiting hours *spl* horas de visita
visiting nurse *s* enfermera ambulante
visitor ['vɪsɪtər] *s* visitante *mf*
visor ['vaɪzər] *s* visera; (*disguise*) máscara
vista ['vɪstə] *s* vista, panorama *m*
visual ['vɪʒu·əl] *adj* visual
visual acuity *s* agudeza visual
visualize ['vɪʒu·ə,laɪz] *tr* representarse en la mente; hacer visible
vital ['vaɪtəl] *adj* vital; (*deadly*) mortal || **vitals** *spl* partes *fpl* vitales, órganos vitales
vitality [vaɪ'tælɪti] *s* vitalidad
vitalize ['vaɪtə,laɪz] *tr* vitalizar
vitamin ['vaɪtəmɪn] *s* vitamina
vitiate ['vɪʃɪ,et] *tr* viciar
vitreous ['vɪtrɪ·əs] *adj* vítreo
vitriolic [,vɪtrɪ'ɑlɪk] *adj* (chem) vitriólico; (fig) cáustico, mordaz
vituperable [vaɪ'tupərəbəl] o [vaɪ'tjupərəbəl] *adj* vituperable
vituperate [vaɪ'tupə,ret] o [vaɪ'tjupə,ret] *tr* vituperar
viva ['vivə] *interj* ¡viva! || *s* viva *m*
vivacious [vɪ'veʃəs] o [vaɪ'veʃəs] *adj* vivaz, vivaracho
vivaci·ty [vɪ'væsɪti] o [vaɪ'væsɪti] *s* (*pl* **-ties**) vivacidad, animación
viva voce ['vaɪvə 'vosi] *adv* de viva voz

vivid ['vɪvɪd] *adj* vivo (*intenso; brillante; expresivo*)
vivi•fy ['vɪvɪ,faɪ] *v* (*pret & pp* **-fied**) *tr* vivificar
vivisection [,vɪvɪ'sɛkʃən] *s* vivisección
vixen [vɪksən] *s* vulpeja; mujer regañona y colérica
viz. *abbr* **videlicet** (Lat) **namely, to wit**
vizier [vɪ'zɪr] o ['vɪzjər] *s* visir *m*
vocabular•y [vo'kæbjə,lɛri] *s* (*pl* **-ies**) vocabulario
vocal ['vokəl] *adj* vocal; (*inclined to express oneself freely*) expresivo
vocalist ['vokəlɪst] *s* vocalista *mf*
vocation [vo'keʃən] *s* vocación; empleo, ocupación
vocative ['vɑkətɪv] *s* vocativo
vociferate [vo'sɪfə,ret] *intr* vociferar
vociferous [vo'sɪfərəs] *adj* clamoroso, vocinglero
vogue [vog] *s* boga, moda; **in vogue** en boga, de moda
voice [vɔɪs] *s* voz *f;* **in a loud voice** en alta voz; **in a low voice** en voz baja; **with one voice** a una voz || *tr* expresar; sonorizar (*una consonante sorda*) || *intr* sonorizarse
voiceless ['vɔɪslɪs] *adj* sin voz; mudo; silencioso; (phonet) sordo
void [vɔɪd] *adj* (*empty*) vacío; (*useless*) vano; (law) inválido, nulo; **void of** desprovisto de || *s* vacío; (*gap*) hueco || *tr* vaciar; evacuar (*el vientre*); anular || *intr* excretar
voile [vɔɪl] *s* espumilla
vol. *abbr* **volume**
volatile ['vɑlətɪl] *adj* volátil
volatilize ['vɑlətɪ,laɪz] *tr* volatilizar || *intr* volatilizarse
volcanic [vɑl'kænɪk] *adj* volcánico
volca•no [vɑl'keno] *s* (*pl* **-noes** o **-nos**) volcán *m*
volition [və'lɪʃən] *s* voluntad; **of one's own volition** por su propia voluntad
volley ['vɑli] *s* (*of stones, bullets, etc.*) descarga, lluvia; (mil) descarga; (tennis) voleo || *tr & intr* volear
vol'ley•ball' *s* volibol *m*
volplane ['vɑl,plen] *s* vuelo planeado || *intr* planear
volt [volt] *s* voltio
voltage ['voltɪdʒ] *s* voltaje *m*
voltage divider *s* (rad) divisor *m* de voltaje
voltaic [vɑl'te·ɪk] *adj* voltaico
volte-face [vɔlt'fɑs] *s* cambio de dirección; cambio de opinión
volt'me'ter *s* voltímetro
voluble ['vɑljəbəl] *adj* locuaz, hablador
volume ['vɑljəm] *s* (*book; bulk; mass, e.g., of water*) volumen *m;* (*each book in a set*) tomo; (*degree of loudness*) volumen sonoro; (geom) volumen *m;* **to speak volumes** ser muy significativo; ser muy expresivo
voluminous [və'lumɪnəs] *adj* voluminoso
voluntar•y ['vɑlən,tɛri] *adj* voluntario || *s* (*pl* **-ies**) (eccl) solo de órgano
volunteer [,vɑlən'tɪr] *adj & s* voluntario || *tr* ofrecer (*sus servicios*) || *intr* ofrecerse; servir como voluntario; **to volunteer to** + *inf* ofrecerse a + *inf*
voluptuar•y [və'lʌptʃʊ,ɛri] *adj* voluptuoso || *s* (*pl* **-ies**) voluptuoso, sibarita *mf*
voluptuous [və'lʌptʃʊ·əs] *adj* voluptuoso
volute [və'lut] *s* voluta
vomit ['vɑmɪt] *s* vómito; (*emetic*) vomitivo || *tr & intr* vomitar
voodoo ['vudu] *adj* voduísta || *s* (*practice*) vodú *m;* (*person*) voduísta *mf*
voracious [və'reʃəs] *adj* voraz
voracity [və'ræsɪti] *s* voracidad
vor•tex ['vɔrtɛks] *s* (*pl* **-texes** o **-tices** [tɪ,siz]) vórtice *m*
vota•ry ['votəri] *s* (*pl* **-ries**) persona ligada por votos solemnes; aficionado, partidario
vote [vot] *s* (*formal expression of choice; right to vote; person who votes*) voto; (*act of voting; votes considered together*) votación; **to put to the vote** poner a votación; **to tally the votes** regular los votos || *tr* votar (*sí, no*); **to vote down** derrotar por votación; **to vote in** elegir por votación || *intr* votar
vote getter ['gɛtər] *s* acaparador *m* de votos; (*slogan*) consigna que gana votos
voter ['votər] *s* votante *mf*
voting machine ['votɪŋ] *s* máquina registradora de votos
votive ['votɪv] *adj* votivo
votive offering *s* voto, exvoto
vouch [vaʊtʃ] *tr* garantizar || *intr* — **to vouch for** responder de (*una cosa*); responder por (*una persona*)
voucher ['vaʊtʃər] *s* garante *mf;* (*certificate*) comprobante *m*
vouch•safe' *tr* conceder, otorgar; permitir || *intr* — **to vouchsafe to** + *inf* dignarse + *inf*
voussoir [vu'swɑr] *s* dovela
vow [vaʊ] *s* voto; **to take vows** tomar el hábito religioso || *tr* votar (*p.ej., un cirio a la Virgen*); jurar (*venganza*) || *intr* votar; **to vow to** hacer votos de
vowel ['vaʊ·əl] *s* vocal *f*
voyage ['vɔɪ·ɪdʒ] *s* travesía, trayecto; (*any journey*) viaje *m* || *tr* atravesar (*p.ej., el mar*) || *intr* viajar
voyager ['vɔɪ·ɪdʒər] *s* pasajero, navegante *mf,* viajero
V.P. *abbr* **Vice-President**
vs. *abbr* **versus**
Vul. *abbr* **Vulgate**
vulcanize ['vʌlkə,naɪz] *tr* vulcanizar
vulg. *abbr* **vulgar**
Vulg. *abbr* **Vulgate**
vulgar ['vʌlgər] *adj* grosero; (*popular, common; vernacular*) vulgar
vulgari•ty [vʌl'gærɪti] *s* (*pl* **-ties**) grosería
Vulgar Latin *s* latín vulgar, latín rústico
Vulgate ['vʌlget] *s* Vulgata
vulnerable ['vʌlnərəbəl] *adj* vulnerable
vulture ['vʌltʃər] *s* buitre *m;* (*American vulture*) catartes *m,* aura (*buitre americano*)

W

W, w ['dʌbəl ˌju] vigésima tercera letra del alfabeto inglés
w *abbr* **watt**
w. *abbr* **week, west, wide, wife**
W. *abbr* **Wednesday, west**
wad [wɑd] *s* (*of cotton*) bolita, tapón *m;* (*of papers*) fajo, lío; (*in a gun*) taco ‖ *v* (*pret & pp* **wadded;** *ger* **wadding**) *tr* emborrar, rellenar; atacar (*una escopeta*)
waddle ['wɑdəl] *s* anadeo ‖ *intr* anadear
wade [wed] *intr* andar sobre terreno cubierto de agua; andar descalzo por la orilla; chapotear (*los niños*) con los pies desnudos; **to wade into** (coll) embestir con violencia; (coll) meter el hombro a; **to wade through** (coll) avanzar con dificultad por; (coll) leer con dificultad
wading bird ['wedɪŋ] *s* ave zancuda
wafer ['wefər] *s* (*for sealing letters; pill*) oblea; (*thin, crisp cake*) hostia; (eccl) hostia
waffle ['wɑfəl] *s* barquillo
wafflle iron *s* barquillero
waft [wæft] o [wɑft] *tr* llevar por el aire; llevar por encima del agua ‖ *intr* flotar
wag [wæg] *s* (*of head*) meneo; (*of tail*) coleada; (*jester*) bromista *mf* ‖ *v* (*pret & pp* **wagged;** *ger* **wagging**) *tr* menear (*la cabeza, la cola*) ‖ *intr* menearse
wage [wedʒ] *s* salario; **wages** galardón *m,* premio ‖ *tr* hacer (*la guerra*)
wage earner ['ʌrnər] *s* asalariado
wager ['wedʒər] *s* apuesta; **to lay a wager** hacer una apuesta ‖ *tr & intr* apostar
wage'work'er *s* asalariado
waggish ['wægɪʃ] *adj* divertido, gracioso; (*person*) bromista
Wagnerian [vɑg'nɪrɪ·ən] *adj & s* vagneriano
wagon ['wægən] *s* carro, furgón *m,* carretón *m;* **on the wagon** (slang) sin tomar bebidas alcohólicas; **to hitch one's wagon to a star** poner el tiro muy alto
wag'tail' *s* aguanieves *m,* aguzanieves *m*
waif [wef] *s* (*foundling*) expósito; animal extraviado o abandonado; (*stray child*) granuja *m*
wail [wel] *s* gemido, lamento ‖ *intr* gemir, lamentar
wain•scot ['wenskət] o ['wenskɑt] *s* arrimadillo, friso de madera ‖ *v* (*pret & pp* **-scoted** o **-scotted;** *ger* **-scoting** o **-scotting**) *tr* poner arrimadillo o friso de madera a
waist [west] *s* (*of human body; corresponding part of garment*) talle *m,* cintura; (*garment*) corpiño, jubón *m,* blusa
waist'band' *s* pretina
waist'cloth' *s* taparrabo
waistcoat ['west ˌkot] o ['wɛskət] *s* chaleco
waist'line' *s* cintura
wait [wet] *s* espera; **to have a good wait** (coll) esperar sentado; **to lie in wait for** acechar emboscado ‖ *tr* — **to wait one's turn** esperar vez ‖ *intr* esperar, aguardar; **to wait for** esperar, aguardar; **to wait on** atender, despachar (*a los parroquianos en una tienda*); servir (*a una persona a la mesa*); **to wait until** esperar a que
waiter ['wetər] *s* camarero, mozo de restaurante; (*tray*) bandeja
waiting list *s* lista de espera
waiting room *s* (*of station*) sala de espera; (*of doctor's office*) antesala
waitress ['wetrɪs] *s* camarera, moza de restaurante
waive [wev] *tr* renunciar a (*un derecho*); diferir, poner a un lado
waiver ['wevər] *s* renuncia
wake [wek] *s* (*watch by the body of a dead person*) velatorio; (*of a boat or other moving object*) estela; **in the wake of** siguiendo inmediatamente; de resultas de ‖ *v* (*pret* **waked** o **woke** [wok]; *pp* **waked**) *tr* despertar ‖ *intr* — **to wake to** darse cuenta de; **to wake up** despertar
wakeful ['wekfəl] *adj* desvelado
wakefulness ['wekfəlnɪs] *s* desvelo
waken ['wekən] *tr & intr* despertar
wale [wel] *s* verdugón *m*
Wales [welz] *s* Gales, el país de Gales
walk [wɔk] *s* (*act*) paseo; (*distance*) caminata; (*way of walking, bearing*) andar *m,* paso; (*of a horse*) andadura; (*place to walk animals*) cercado; empleo, cargo, carrera; **at a walk** al paso de una persona; **to go for a walk** salir a pasear; **to take a walk** dar un paseo ‖ *tr* pasear (*a un niño, un caballo*); caminar (*recorrer caminando*); hacer ir al paso (*un caballo*); **to walk off** quitarse (*p.ej., un dolor de cabeza*) caminando ‖ *intr* andar, caminar, ir a pie; (*to stroll*) pasear; **to walk away from** alejarse caminando de; **to walk off with** cargar con, llevarse; **to walk out** salir repentinamente; declararse en huelga; **to walk out on** (coll) dejar airadamente
walkaway ['wɔkə ˌwe] *s* (coll) triunfo fácil
walker ['wɔkər] *s* caminante *mf;* (*pedestrian*) peatón *m;* (*gocart*) andaderas
walkie-talkie ['wɔki'tɔki] *s* (rad) transmisor-receptor *m* portátil
walking papers *spl* (coll) despedida de un empleo
walking stick *s* bastón *m*
walk'-on' *s* (theat) parte *f* de por medio
walk'out' *s* (coll) huelga
walk'o'ver *s* (coll) triunfo fácil
wall [wɔl] *s* muro; (*between rooms; of a pipe, boiler, etc.*) pared *f;* (*of a*

fortification) muralla; **to drive to the wall** poner entre la espada y la pared; **to go to the wall** rendirse; fracasar || *tr* murar, amurallar (*una ciudad, un castillo*); emparedar (*a un criminal*); **to wall up** cerrar con muro
wall'board' *s* cartón *m* tabla
wallet ['wɑlɪt] *s* cartera de bolsillo
wall'flow'er *s* alhelí *m;* **to be a wallflower** (coll) comer pavo, planchar el asiento
Walloon [wɑ'lun] *adj & s* valón *m*
wallop ['wɑləp] *s* (coll) golpazo, puñetazo || *tr* (coll) golpear fuertemente; (coll) vencer cabalmente
wallow ['wɑlo] *s* revuelco; (*place*) revolcadero || *intr* revolcarse; (*e.g., in wealth*) nadar
wall'pa'per *s* papel *m* de empapelar, papel pintado || *tr* empapelar
walnut ['wɔlnət] *s* (*tree and wood*) nogal *m;* nuez *f* de nogal
walrus ['wɔlrəs] o ['wɑlrəs] *s* morsa
Walter ['wɔltər] *s* Gualterio
waltz [wɔlts] *s* vals *m* || *tr* hacer valsar; (coll) conducir directamente || *intr* valsar
wan [wɑn] *adj* (*comp* **wanner;** *super* **wannest**) pálido, macilento; débil
wand [wɑnd] *s* vara; (*of deviner or magician*) varilla de virtudes
wander ['wɑndər] *tr* recorrer a la ventura || *intr* errar, vagar; extraviarse, perderse; **to wander around** errar de una parte a otra
wanderer ['wɑndərər] *s* vagabundo; peregrino
wan'der•lust' *s* ansia de viajar
wane [wen] *s* decadencia, declinación; menguante *f* de la luna; **on the wane** decayendo, declinando; menguando (*la luna*) || *intr* decaer, declinar; menguar (*la luna*)
wangle ['wæŋgəl] *tr* (*to obtain by scheming*) (coll) mamar o mamarse; (coll) adulterar, falsear (*cuentas*); **to wangle one's way out of** (coll) salir con maña de || *intr* (*to get along by scheming*) (coll) sacudirse
want [wɑnt] o [wɔnt] *s* deseo; necesidad; carencia; **for want of** a falta de; **to be in want** pasar necesidad || *tr* desear; necesitar; carecer de || *intr* desear; **to want for** necesitar; carecer de
want ad *s* anuncio clasificado
wanton ['wɑntən] *adj* inconsiderado, desconsiderado; insensible, perverso; disoluto, licencioso; lascivo; cabezudo
war [wɔr] *s* guerra; **to go to war** declarar la guerra; (*as a soldier*) ir a la guerra; **to wage war** hacer la guerra || *v* (*pret & pp* **warred;** *ger* **warring**) *intr* guerrear; **to war on** guerrear con, hacer la guerra a
warble ['wɔrbəl] *s* gorjeo, trino || *intr* gorjear, trinar
warbler ['wɔrblər] *s* pájaro cantor; curruca de cabeza negra
war cloud *s* amenaza de guerra
ward [wɔrd] *s* (*person, usually a minor, under protection of another*) pupilo; (*guardianship*) custodia, tutela; (*of a city*) barrio, distrito; (*of a hospital*) cuadra, crujía; (*of a lock*) guarda || *tr* — **to ward off** parar, desviar
warden ['wɔrdən] *s* guardián *m;* (*of a jail*) alcaide *m,* carcelero; (*of a church*) capiller *m;* (*in charge of fire prevention*) vigía *m*
ward heeler *s* muñidor *m*
ward'robe' *s* (*closet or cabinet for holding clothes*) guardarropa *m;* (*stock of clothing for a person*) vestuario; (theat) guardarropía
wardrobe trunk *s* baúl ropero
ward'room' *s* (nav) cámara de oficiales
ware [wɛr] *s* loza; **wares** efectos, artículos de comercio, mercancías
war effort *s* esfuerzo bélico
ware'house' *s* almacén *m;* (*for furniture*) guardamuebles *m*
warehouse•man ['wɛr,hausmən] *s* (*pl* **-men** [mən]) almacenista *m;* guardaalmacén *m*
war'fare' *s* guerra
war'head' *s* punta de combate
war horse *s* corcel *m* de guerra; (coll) veterano
warily ['wɛrɪli] *adv* cautelosamente
wariness ['wɛrɪnɪs] *s* cautela
war'like' *adj* guerrero
war loan *s* empréstito de guerra
war lord *s* jefe *m* militar
warm [wɔrm] *adj* (*being moderately hot*) caliente; (*neither hot nor cold*) templado; (*clothing*) abrigador; (*climate, region*) caluroso; (*color*) cálido; (fig) caluroso, cordial; **to be warm** (*said of a person*) tener calor; (*said of the weather*) hacer calor || *tr* calentar, acalorar; (fig) animar, acalorar; **to warm up** recalentar (*p.ej., la comida*); hacer más amistoso || *intr* calentarse; **to warm up** templar (*el tiempo*); (*with work or exercise*) acalorarse; **to warm up to** cobrar afecto a
warm-blooded ['wɔrm'blʌdɪd] *adj* apasionado, ardiente; (*animals*) de sangre caliente
war memorial *s* monumento a los caídos
warmer ['wɔrmər] *s* calentador *m*
warm-hearted ['wɔrm'hɑrtɪd] *adj* afectuoso, de buen corazón
warming pan *s* mundillo
warmonger ['wɔr,mʌŋgər] *s* belicista *mf*
war mother *s* madrina de guerra
warmth [wɔrmθ] *s* calor *m;* ardor *m,* entusiasmo; cordialidad
warm'-up' *s* calentón *m*
warn [wɔrn] *tr* advertir, avisar; (*to exhort*) amonestar; (*to advise*) aconsejar
warning *adj* de aviso || *s* advertencia, aviso
War of the Roses *s* guerra de las dos Rosas
warp [wɔrp] *s* (*of a fabric*) urdimbre *f;* (*of a board*) comba, alabeo; aberración mental; (naut) espía || *tr* combar, alabear; pervertir (*el juicio*

de una persona); (naut) mover con espía || *intr* combarse, alabearse; (naut) espiar

war'path' *s* — **to be on the warpath** prepararse para la guerra; estar buscando pendencia

war'plane' *s* avión *m* de guerra

warrant ['warənt] o ['wɔrənt] *s* garantía, promesa; (*for arrest*) orden *f* de prisión; (*before a judge*) citación; cédula, certificado || *tr* garantizar, prometer; autorizar; justificar

warrantable ['warəntəbəl] o ['wɔrəntəbəl] *adj* garantizable; justificable

warrant officer *s* suboficial *m* de las clases

warren ['warən] o ['wɔrən] *s* (*where rabbits breed*) conejera; barrio densamente poblado

warrior ['wɔrjər] o ['warjər] *s* guerrero

Warsaw ['wɔrsɔ] *s* Varsovia

war'ship' *s* buque *m* de guerra

wart [wɔrt] *s* verruga

war'time' *s* tiempo de guerra

war'-torn' *adj* devastado por la guerra

war to the death *s* guerra a muerte

war•y ['weri] *adj* (*comp* **-ier;** *super* **-iest**) cauteloso

wash [waʃ] o [wɔʃ] *s* lavado; (*clothes washed or to be washed*) jabonado; (*dirty water*) lavazas; loción; (*place where surf breaks*) batiente *m;* (aer) estela turbulenta || *tr* lavar; fregar (*los platos*); bañar, mojar; **to wash away** quitar lavando; derrubiar (*las aguas corrientes la tierra de las riberas*) || *intr* lavarse; lavar la ropa; batir (*el agua*); derrubiarse

washable ['waʃəbəl] o ['wɔʃəbəl] *adj* lavable

wash and wear *adj* de lava y pon

wash'ba'sin *s* jofaina, palangana

wash'bas'ket *s* cesto de la colada

wash'board' *s* lavadero, tabla de lavar; (*baseboard*) rodapié *m*

wash'bowl' *s* jofaina, palangana

wash'cloth' *s* paño para lavarse

wash'day' *s* día *m* de la colada

washed-out ['waʃt ˌaut] o ['wɔʃt ˌaut] *adj* desteñido; (coll) debilitado, rendido

washed-up ['waʃt ˌʌp] o ['wɔʃt ˌʌp] *adj* (coll) agotado, deslomado

washer ['waʃər] o ['wɔʃər] *s* lavador *m;* (*machine*) lavadora; (*ring of metal placed under head of bolt*) arandela; (*ring of rubber, etc. to keep a spigot from leaking*) zapatilla; (phot) lavador

wash'er•wom'an *s* (*pl* **-wom'en**) lavandera

wash goods *spl* tejidos lavables

washing ['waʃɪŋ] o ['wɔʃɪŋ] *s* (*act of washing; washed clothes or clothes to be washed*) lavado; **washings** (*dirty water; abraded material*) lavadura

washing machine *s* lejiadora, lavadora mecánica

washing soda *s* sal *f* de sosa

wash'out' *s* derrubio; derrumbe *m;* (coll) desilusión, fracaso

wash'rag' *s* paño para lavarse; paño de cocina

wash'room' *s* gabinete *m* de aseo, lavabo

wash'stand' *s* lavamanos *m*

wash'tub' *s* cuba de colada, tina de lavar

wash water *s* lavazas

wasp [wasp] *s* avispa

waste [west] *s* derroche *m,* desgaste *m;* (*garbage*) basura, despojo; (*wild region*) despoblado, yermo; (*of time*) pérdida; (*useless by-products*) desperdicios; excremento; (*for wiping machinery*) hilacha de algodón; **to lay waste** devastar, poner a fuego y sangre || *tr* malgastar, perder || *intr* — **to waste away** consumirse

waste'bas'ket *s* papelera

wasteful ['westfəl] *adj* derrochador, manirroto; devastador, destructivo

waste paper *s* papeles usados, papel de desecho, papel viejo

waste pipe *s* tubo de desagüe

waste products *spl* desperdicios; materia excretada

wastrel ['westrəl] *s* derrochador *m,* malgastador *m;* pródigo, perdido

watch [watʃ] *s* reloj *m* (*de bolsillo o de pulsera*); (*lookout*) vigía *m;* (mil) vigilia; (naut) guardia; **to be on the watch for** estar a la mira de; **to keep watch over** velar || *tr* (*to look at*) mirar; (*to oversee*) velar, vigilar; guardar; tener cuidado con || *intr* mirar; (*to keep awake*) velar; **to watch for** acechar; **to watch out** tener cuidado; **to watch out for** estar a la mira de; tener cuidado con; guardarse de; **to watch over** velar, vigilar

watch'case' *s* caja de reloj

watch charm *s* dije *m*

watch crystal *s* cristal *m* de reloj

watch'dog' *s* perro de guarda, perro guardián; (fig) guardián *m* fiel

watchful ['watʃfəl] *adj* desvelado, vigilante

watchfulness ['watʃfəlnɪs] *s* desvelo, vigilancia

watch'mak'er *s* relojero

watch•man ['watʃmən] *s* (*pl* **-men** [mən]) vigilante *m,* velador *m*

watch night *s* noche vieja; oficio de noche vieja

watch pocket *s* relojera

watch strap *s* pulsera

watch'tow'er *s* atalaya, vigía

watch'word' *s* santo y seña; (*slogan*) lema *m*

water ['wɔtər] o ['watər] *s* agua; **of the first water** de lo mejor; **to back water** ciar; **to carry water on both shoulders** nadar entre dos aguas; **to fish in troubled waters** pescar en río revuelto; **to hold water** (coll) ser bien fundado; **to make water** (*to urinate*) hacer aguas; (naut) hacer agua; **to pour** o **throw cold water on** echar un jarro de agua (fría) a || *tr* regar, rociar; abrevar (*el ganado*); aguar (*el vino*); proveer de agua || *intr*

abrevarse (*el ganado*); tomar agua (*una locomotora*); llorar (*los ojos*)
water carrier *s* aguador *m*
water closet *s* excusado, retrete *m*, váter *m*
water color *s* acuarela
wa′ter·course′ *s* corriente *f* de agua; lecho de corriente
water cress *s* berzo
water cure *s* cura de aguas
wa′ter·fall′ *s* cascada, caída de agua
water front *s* terreno ribereño
water gap *s* garganta, hondonada
water hammer *s* golpe *m* de ariete
water heater *s* calentador *m* de agua
water ice *s* sorbete *m*
watering can *s* regadera
watering place *s* aguadero; balneario
watering pot *s* regadera
watering trough *s* abrevadero
water jacket *s* camisa de agua
water lily *s* ninfea, nenúfar *m*
water line *s* línea de agua, línea de flotación; nivel *m* de agua
water main *s* cañería de agua
wa′ter·mark′ *s* (*in paper*) filigrana; marca de nivel de agua
wa′ter·mel′on *s* sandía
water meter *s* contador *m* de agua
water pipe *s* cañería de agua
water polo *s* polo de agua
water power *s* fuerza de agua, hulla blanca
wa′ter·proof′ *adj & s* impermeable *m*
wa′ter·shed′ *s* divisoria de aguas; (*drainage area*) cuenca
water ski *s* esquí acuático
wa′ter·spout′ *s* (*to carry water from roof*) canalón *m;* (*funnel of wet air extending from cloud to surface of water*) manga de agua, tromba marina
wa′ter-sup·ply′ system *s* fontanería
wa′ter·tight′ *adj* estanco, hermético; (fig) seguro
water tower *s* arca de agua
water wagon *s* (mil) carro de agua; **on the water wagon** (slang) sin tomar bebidas alcohólicas
wa′ter·way′ *s* vía de agua, vía fluvial; (naut) canalizo
water wheel *s* rueda de agua; turbina de agua; (*of steamboat*) rueda de paletas
water wings *spl* nadaderas
wa′ter·works′ *s* estación de bombas
watery [ˈwɔtəri] o [ˈwɑtəri] *adj* acuoso; (*said of the eyes*) lagrimoso, lloroso; insípido; húmedo, mojado
watt [wɑt] *s* vatio
wattage [ˈwɑtɪdʒ] *s* vatiaje *m*
watt′-hour′ *s* (*pl* **watt-hours**) vatio-hora
wattle [ˈwɑtəl] *s* (*of bird*) barba; (*of fish*) barbilla
watt′me′ter *s* vatímetro
wave [wev] *s* onda; (*of hair*) onda, ondulación; (*e.g., of heat or cold*) ola; (*e.g., of strikes*) oleaje *m;* señal hecha con la mano ‖ *tr* blandir (*la espada*); ondear, ondular (*el cabello*); hacer señal con (*la mano*); decir (*adiós*) con la mano; **to wave aside** rechazar ‖ *intr* ondear u ondearse; hacer señal con la mano
wave motion *s* movimiento ondulatorio
waver [ˈwevər] *intr* oscilar; (*to hesitate*) vacilar, titubear; (*to totter*) tambalear
wav·y [ˈwevi] *adj* (*comp* **-ier;** *super* **-iest**) undoso, ondoso; (*water*) ondulado; (*hair*) ondeado
wax [wæks] *s* cera; **to be wax in one's hands** ser como una cera ‖ *tr* encerar; cerotear (*el hilo*) ‖ *intr* hacerse, volverse; crecer (*la luna*)
wax paper *s* papel encerado, papel parafinado
wax taper *s* cerilla
wax′works′ *s* museo de cera
way [we] *s* vía, camino; dirección, sentido; manera, modo; costumbre, hábito; **across the way** enfrente; **a good way** un buen trecho; **all the way** hasta el fin del camino; **any way** de cualquier modo; **by the way** a propósito; **in a way** hasta cierto punto; **in every way** en todos respectos; **in this way** de este modo; **on the way to** camino de, rumbo a; **on the way out** saliendo; desapareciendo; **out of the way** hecho, despachado; inconveniente, impropio; a un lado, apartado; fuera de lo común; **that way** por allí; de ese modo; **this way** por aquí; de este modo; **to be in the way** estorbar; **to feel one's way** tantear el camino; proceder con tiento; **to force one's way** abrirse paso por fuerza; **to get out of the way** quitarse de en medio; (*to finish*) quitarse de encima; **to give way** ceder, retroceder; romperse (*una cuerda*); fracasar; **to give way to** entregarse a; **to go out of one's way** dar un rodeo; dar un rodeo innecesario; darse molestia; **to have one's way** salirse con la suya; **to keep out of the way** no obstruir el paso; **to know one's way around** saber entendérselas; **to know one's way to** conocer el camino a, saber ir a; **to lead the way** enseñar el camino; ir o entrar primero; **to lose one's way** perder el camino, extraviarse; **to make one's way** avanzar; hacer carrera, acreditarse; **to make way for** dar paso a, hacer lugar para; **to mend one's ways** mudar de vida; **to not know which way to turn** no saber dónde meterse; **to put out of the way** alejar, apartar; quitar de en medio; **to see one's way to** ver el modo de; **to take one's way** irse, marcharse; **to wend one's way** seguir camino; **to wind one's way through** serpentear por; **to wing one's way** ir volando; **under way** en marcha, en camino; **way in** entrada; **way out** salida; **ways** maneras, modales *mpl;* (*for launching a ship*) anguilas; **which way?** ¿por dónde?; ¿cómo?
way′bill′ *s* hoja de ruta
wayfarer [ˈweˌfɛrər] *s* caminante *mf*
way′lay′ *v* (*pret & pp* **-laid′**) *tr* detener de improviso; (*to attack from ambush*) insidiar, asaltar

way'side' *s* borde *m* del camino; **to fall by the wayside** (*to disappear*) caer en el camino; fracasar
way station *s* apeadero
way train *s* tren *m* ómnibus
wayward ['wewərd] *adj* díscolo, voluntarioso; voltario, caprichoso
w.c. *abbr* **water closet, without charge**
we [wi] *pron pers* nosotros
weak [wik] *adj* débil, flaco; (*vowel; verb*) débil
weaken ['wikən] *tr* debilitar, enflaquecer || *intr* debilitarse, enflaquecerse
weakling ['wiklɪŋ] *s* alfeñique *m*, canijo
weak-minded ['wik'maɪndɪd] *adj* irresoluto; simple, mentecato
weakness ['wiknɪs] *s* debilidad, flaqueza; lado débil; afición, gusto
weal [wil] *s* verdugón *m*
wealth [wɛlθ] *s* riqueza
wealth·y ['wɛlθi] *adj* (*comp* **-ier;** *super* **-iest**) rico
wean [win] *tr* destetar; **to wean away from** apartar gradualmente de
weanling ['winlɪŋ] *adj* & *s* destetado
weapon ['wɛpən] *s* arma
wear [wɛr] *s* (*act of wearing*) uso; (*clothing*) ropa; estilo, moda; (*wasting away from use*) desgaste *m*, deterioro; (*lasting quality*) durabilidad; **for all kinds of wear** a todo llevar; **for everyday wear** para todo trote || *v* (*pret* **wore** [wor]; *pp* **worn** [worn]) *tr* llevar, traer, llevar puesto; calzar (*cierto tamaño de zapato o guante*); (*to waste away by use*) desgastar, deteriorar; (*to tire*) agotar, cansar; **to wear out** consumir, gastar; agotar, cansar; abusar de (*la hospitalidad de una persona*) || *intr* desgastarse, deteriorarse; **to wear off** pasar, desaparecer; **to wear out** gastarse, usarse; **to wear well** durar, ser duradero
wear and tear *s* uso y desgaste
weariness ['wɪrɪnɪs] *s* cansancio; aburrimiento
wearing apparel ['wɛrɪŋ] *s* ropaje *m*, prendas de vestir
wearisome ['wɪrɪsəm] *adj* aburrido, cansado, fastidioso
wea·ry ['wɪri] *adj* (*comp* **-rier;** *super* **-riest**) cansado || *v* (*pret* & *pp* **-ried**) *tr* cansar || *intr* cansarse
weasel ['wizəl] *s* comadreja
weaseler ['wizələr] *s* pancista *mf*
weasel words *spl* palabras ambiguas
weather ['wɛðər] *s* tiempo; mal tiempo; **to be under the weather** (coll) no estar muy católico; (coll) estar borracho || *tr* aguantar (*el temporal, la adversidad*)
weather-beaten ['wɛðər ,bitən] *adj* curtido por la intemperie
weather bureau *s* meteo *f*, servicio meteorológico
weath'er·cock' *s* veleta; (*fickle person*) (fig) veleta
weather forecasting *s* pronóstico del tiempo, previsión del tiempo
weather·man ['wɛðər ,mæn] *s* (*pl* **-men** [,mɛn]) meteorologista *m*, pronosticador *m* del tiempo
weather report *s* parte meteorológico
weather stripping ['strɪpɪŋ] *s* burlete *m*, cierre hermético
weather vane *s* veleta
weave [wiv] *s* tejido || *v* (*pret* **wove** [wov] o **weaved;** *pp* **wove** o **woven** ['wovən]) *tr* tejer; **to weave one's way** avanzar zigzagueando || *intr* tejer; zigzaguear
weaver ['wivər] *s* tejedor *m*
web [wɛb] *s* tejido, tela; (*of spider*) tela; (*between toes of birds and other animals*) membrana; (*of an iron rail*) alma; (fig) tejido, tela, enredo
web-footed ['wɛb ,futɪd] *adj* palmípedo, de pie palmeado
wed [wɛd] *v* (*pret* & *pp* **wed** o **wedded;** *ger* **wedding**) *tr* (*to join in marriage*) casar; casarse con || *intr* casarse
wedding ['wɛdɪŋ] *adj* nupcial || *s* bodas, nupcias, matrimonio
wedding cake *s* pastel *m* de boda
wedding day *s* día *m* de bodas
wedding march *s* marcha nupcial
wedding night *s* noche *f* de bodas
wedding ring *s* anillo nupcial
wedge [wɛdʒ] *s* cuña || *tr* acuñar, apretar con cuña
wed'lock' *s* matrimonio
Wednesday ['wɛnzdi] *s* miércoles *m*
wee [wi] *adj* pequeñito, diminuto
weed [wid] *s* mala hierba; (coll) tabaco; **weeds** ropa de luto (*especialmente, de una viuda*) || *tr* desherbar, escardar
weeding hoe *s* escardillo
weed killer *s* matamalezas *m*, herbicida *m*
week [wik] *s* semana; **week in week out** semana tras semana
week'day' *s* día *m* laborable
week'end' *s* fin *m* de semana || *intr* pasar el fin de semana
week·ly ['wikli] *adj* semanal || *adv* cada semana || *s* (*pl* **-lies**) revista semanal, semanario
weep [wip] *v* (*pret* & *pp* **wept** [wɛpt]) *tr* llorar (*p.ej., la muerte de una persona*); derramar (*lágrimas*) || *intr* llorar
weeper ['wipər] *s* llorón *m;* (*hired mourner*) llorona, plañidera
weeping willow *s* sauce *m* llorón
weep·y ['wipi] *adj* (*comp* **-ier;** *super* **-iest**) (coll) lloroso
weevil ['wivəl] *s* gorgojo
weft [wɛft] *s* (*yarns running across warp*) trama; (*fabric*) tejido
weigh [we] *tr* pesar; (naut) levantar (*el ancla*) || *intr* pesar; **to weigh in** pesarse (*un jockey*)
weight [wet] *s* peso; (*of scales, clock, gymnasium, etc.*) pesa; **to lose weight** rebajar de peso; **to put on weight** ponerse gordo; **to throw one's weight around** (coll) hacer valer su poder || *tr* cargar, gravar; (*statistically*) ponderar
weightless ['wetlɪs] *adj* ingrávido
weightlessness ['wetlɪsnɪs] *s* ingravidez *f*
weight·y ['weti] *adj* (*comp* **-ier;** *super*

-iest) (*heavy*) pesado; (*troublesome*) gravoso; importante, influyente
weir [wɪr] *s* presa, vertedero; (*for catching fish*) pescadera
weird [wɪrd] *adj* misterioso, sobrenatural, espectral; extraño, raro
welcome ['wɛlkəm] *adj* bienvenido; grato, agradable; **you are welcome** (*i.e., gladly received*) sea Vd. bienvenido; (*in answer to thanks*) no hay de qué; **you are welcome to it** está a la disposición de Vd.; **you are welcome to your opinion** piense Vd. lo que quiera || *interj* ¡bienvenido! || *s* bienvenida, buena acogida || *tr* dar la bienvenida a; acoger con gusto, recibir con amabilidad
weld [wɛld] *s* autógena; (bot) gualda || *tr* soldar con autógena; (fig) unir || *intr* soldarse
welder ['wɛldər] *s* soldador *m;* (*machine*) soldadora
welding ['wɛldɪŋ] *s* autógena, soldadura autógena
wel'fare' *s* bienestar *m;* (*effort to improve living conditions of the underprivileged*) asistencia, beneficencia; **to be on welfare** vivir de la asistencia pública
welfare state *s* gobierno socializante, estado de beneficencia
well [wɛl] *adj* bien; bien de salud || *adv* bien; pues; pues bien; **as well** también; **as well as** así como; además de || *interj* ¡vaya! || *s* pozo; (*natural source of water*) fuente *f,* manantial *m* || *intr* — **to well up** salir a borbotones
well-appointed ['wɛlə'pɔɪntɪd] *adj* bien amueblado, bien equipado
well-attended ['wɛlə'tɛndɪd] *adj* muy concurrido
well-behaved ['wɛlbɪ'hevd] *adj* de buena conducta
well'-be'ing *s* bienestar *m*
well'born' *adj* bien nacido
well-bred ['wɛl'brɛd] *adj* cortés, bien criado
well-disposed ['wɛldɪs'pozd] *adj* bien dispuesto
well-done ['wɛl'dʌn] *adj* bien hecho; (*meat*) bien asado
well-fixed ['wɛl'fɪkst] *adj* (coll) acaudalado
well-formed ['wɛl'fɔrmd] *adj* bien formado; (*nose*) perfilado
well-founded ['wɛl'faʊndɪd] *adj* bien fundado
well-groomed ['wɛl'grumd] *adj* de mucho aseo, atildado
well-heeled ['wɛl'hild] *adj* (coll) acomodado; **to be well-heeled** (coll) tener bien cubierto el riñón
well-informed ['wɛlɪn'fɔrmd] *adj* versado, bien enterado
well-intentioned ['wɛlɪn'tɛnʃənd] *adj* bien intencionado
well-kept ['wɛl'kɛpt] *adj* bien cuidado, bien atendido; (*secret*) bien guardado
well-known ['wɛl'non] *adj* bien conocido; familiar
well-meaning ['wɛl'minɪŋ] *adj* bien intencionado
well-nigh ['wɛl'naɪ] *adv* casi
well'-off' *adj* adinerado, acaudalado
well-preserved ['wɛlprɪ'zʌrvd] *adj* bien conservado
well-read ['wɛl'rɛd] *adj* leído, muy leído
well-spent ['wɛl'spɛnt] *adj* (*money, youth, life*) bien empleado
well-spoken ['wɛl'spokən] *adj* (*person*) bienhablado; (*word*) bien dicho
well'spring' *s* fuente *f,* manantial *m;* fuente inagotable
well sweep *s* cigoñal *m*
well-tempered ['wɛl'tɛmpərd] *adj* bien templado
well-thought-of ['wɛl'θɔt,ɑv] *adj* bien mirado
well-timed ['wɛl'taɪmd] *adj* oportuno
well-to-do ['wɛltə'du] *adj* adinerado, acaudalado
well-wisher ['wɛl'wɪʃər] *s* amigo, favorecedor *m*
well-worn ['wɛl'worn] *adj* trillado, vulgar
welsh [wɛlʃ] *intr* (slang) dejar de cumplir; **to welsh on** (slang) dejar de cumplir con || **Welsh** *adj* galés || *s* (*language*) galés *m;* **the Welsh** los galeses
Welsh·man ['wɛlʃmən] *s* (*pl* **-men** [mən]) galés *m*
Welsh rabbit o **rarebit** ['rɛrbɪt] *s* tostada cubierta de queso derretido en cerveza
welt [wɛlt] *s* (*finish along a seam*) ribete *m;* (*of a shoe*) vira; (*wale from a blow*) verdugón *m*
welter ['wɛltər] *s* confusión, conmoción; (*a tumbling about*) revuelco || *intr* revolcar
wel'ter·weight' *s* (box) peso mediano ligero
wen [wɛn] *s* lobanillo
wench [wɛntʃ] *s* muchacha, jovencita; moza, criada
wend [wɛnd] *tr* — **to wend one's way** dirigir sus pasos, seguir su camino
west [wɛst] *adj* occidental, del oeste || *adv* al oeste, hacia el oeste || *s* oeste *m*
western ['wɛstərn] *adj* occidental || *s* película del Oeste
West Indies ['ɪndiz] *spl* Indias Occidentales
westward ['wɛstwərd] *adv* hacia el oeste
wet [wɛt] *adj* (*comp* **wetter;** *super* **wettest**) mojado; (*damp*) húmedo; (*paint*) fresco; (*weather*) lluvioso; (coll) antiprohibicionista || *s* (coll) antiprohibicionista *mf* || *v* (*pret & pp* **wet** o **wetted;** *ger* **wetting**) *tr* mojar || *intr* mojarse
wet'back' *s* mojado
wet battery *s* pila húmeda
wet blanket *s* aguafiestas *mf*
wet goods *spl* caldos
wet nurse *s* ama de cría o de leche
w.f. *abbr* **wrong font**
w.g. *abbr* **wire gauge**
whack [hwæk] *s* (coll) golpe ruidoso;

(coll) prueba, tentativa || *tr* (coll) golpear ruidosamente
whale [hwel] *s* ballena; (*sperm whale*) cachalote *m;* **a whale at** (coll) un as de; **a whale for** (coll) un genio para; **a whale of a difference** (coll) una enorme diferencia; **a whale of a meal** (coll) una comida brutal || *tr* (coll) azotar || *intr* pescar ballenas
whale'bone' *s* ballena
wharf [hwɔrf] *s* (*pl* **wharves** [hwɔrvz] o **wharfs**) muelle *m,* embarcadero
what [hwɑt] *pron interr* qué; cuál; **what else?** ¿qué más?; **what if . . .?** ¿y si . . .?, ¿qué le parece si?; **what of it?** ¿qué importa? || *pron rel* lo que; **what's what** lo que hay, toda la verdad || *adj interr* qué || *adj rel* el . . . que, la . . . que, etc. || *interj* qué; **what a . . .!** qué . . . más o tan, p.ej., **what a beautiful day!** ¡qué día más (o tan) hermoso!
what•ev'er *pron* cualquiera; todo lo que || *adj* cualquier; cualquier . . . que
what'not' *s* juguetero
what's-his-name ['hwɑtsɪz,nem] *s* (coll) el señor fulano
wheal [hwil] *s* roncha
wheat [hwit] *s* trigo
wheedle ['hwidəl] *tr* engatusar; conseguir por medio de halagos
wheel [hwil] *s* rueda; (coll) bicicleta; **at the wheel** en el volante || *tr* pasear (*a un niño*) en un cochecito; conducir (*a un enfermo*) en una silla de ruedas || *intr* (coll) ir en bicicleta; **to wheel about** o **around** dar una vuelta; cambiar de opinión
wheelbarrow ['hwil,bæro] *s* carretilla
wheel base *s* batalla, paso, distancia entre ejes
wheel chair *s* silla de ruedas, cochecillo para inválidos
wheeler-dealer ['hwilər'dilər] *s* (slang) negociante *m* de gran influencia e independencia
wheel horse *s* caballo de varas; (fig) esclavo (*el que trabaja mucho y cumple con sus obligaciones*)
wheelwright ['hwil,raɪt] *s* carpintero de carretas
wheeze [hwiz] *s* resuello ruidoso || *intr* resollar produciendo un silbido
whelp [hwɛlp] *s* cachorro || *intr* parir
when [hwɛn] *adv* cuándo || *conj* cuando
whence [hwɛns] *adv* de dónde; por lo tanto || *conj* de donde
when•ev'er *conj* siempre que, cada vez que
where [hwɛr] *adv* dónde; adónde || *conj* donde; adonde
whereabouts ['hwɛrə,baʊts] *s* paradero
whereas [hwɛr'æz] *conj* mientras que, al paso que; considerando || *s* considerando
where•by' *adv* por medio del cual
wherefore ['hwɛrfor] *adv* por qué, para qué; por eso, por tanto || *conj* por lo cual || *s* motivo, razón *f*
where•from' *adv* de donde
where•in' *adv* dónde, en qué || *conj* donde; en el que; en lo cual
where•of' *adv* de qué || *conj* de que; de lo cual
where'up•on' *adv* con lo cual, después de lo cual
wherever [hwɛr'ɛvər] *conj* dondequiera que
wherewithal ['hwɛrwɪð,ɔl] *s* cumquibus *m,* medios
whet [hwɛt] *v* (*pret & pp* **whetted;** *ger* **whetting**) *tr* afilar, aguzar; despertar, estimular; abrir (*el apetito*)
whether ['wɛðər] *conj* si; **whether or no** en todo caso, de todas maneras; **whether or not** si . . . o no, ya sea que . . . o no
whet'stone' *s* piedra de afilar
whey [hwe] *s* suero de la leche
which [hwɪtʃ] *pron interr* cuál; **which is which** cuál es el uno y cuál el otro || *pron rel* que, el (la, etc.) que || *adj interr* qué; cuál, cuál de los (las) || *adj rel* el (la, etc.) . . . que
which•ev'er *pron rel* cualquiera || *adj rel* cualquier; **whichever ones** cualesquiera
whiff [hwɪf] *s* soplo; fumada; olorcillo; acceso, arranque *m;* **to get a whiff of** percibir un olor fugaz de || *intr* soplar (*el viento*); echar bocanadas (*el que fuma*)
while [hwaɪl] *conj* mientras, mientras que || *s* rato; **a long while** largo rato; **a while ago** hace un rato; **between whiles** de vez en cuando || *tr* — **to while away** entretener (*el tiempo*); pasar (*p.ej., la tarde*) de un modo entretenido
whim [hwɪm] *s* capricho, antojo
whimper ['hwɪmpər] *s* lloriqueo || *tr* decir lloriqueando || *intr* lloriquear
whimsical ['hwɪmzɪkəl] *adj* caprichoso, extravagante, fantástico
whine [hwaɪn] *s* gimoteo, quejido || *intr* gimotear, quejarse
whin•ny ['hwɪni] *s* (*pl* **-nies**) relincho || *v* (*pret & pp* **-nied**) *intr* relinchar
whip [hwɪp] *s* látigo, zurriago; huevos batidos con nata || *v* (*pret & pp* **whipped** o **whipt;** *ger* **whipping**) *tr* azotar, zurriagar, fustigar; batir (*huevos y nata*); (coll) derrotar, vencer; **to whip off** (coll) escribir de prisa; **to whip out** sacar de repente; **to whip up** (coll) preparar de prisa; (coll) avivar, excitar
whip'cord' *s* tralla; tejido fuerte con costurones diagonales
whip hand *s* mano *f* del látigo; (*upper hand*) vara alta
whip'lash' *s* tralla
whipped cream *s* nata, crema batida
whipper-snapper ['hwɪpər,snæpər] *s* arrapiezo, mequetrefe *m*
whippet ['hwɪpɪt] *s* perro lebrel
whipping boy ['hwɪpɪŋ] *s* cabeza de turco, víctima inocente
whipping post *s* poste *m* de flagelación
whippoorwill [,hwɪpər'wɪl] *s* chotacabras norteamericano (*Caprimulgus vociferus*)
whir [hwʌr] *s* zumbido || *v* (*pret & pp*

whirred; *ger* **whirring)** *intr* girar zumbando

whirl [hwʌrl] *s* vuelta, giro; remolino; (*of events, parties, etc.*) serie *f* interminable || *tr & intr* remolinear; **my head whirls** siento vértigo

whirligig ['hwʌrlɪ,gɪg] *s* (ent) escribano del agua; tíovivo; (*pinwheel*) rehilandera, molinete *m;* peonza

whirl'pool' *s* remolino, vorágine *f*

whirl'wind' *s* torbellino, manga de viento

whirlybird ['hwʌrli,bʌrd] *s* (coll) helicóptero

whish [hwɪʃ] *s* zumbido suave || *intr* zumbar suavemente

whisk [hwɪsk] *s* escobilla; toque ligero || *tr* barrer, cepillar; **to whisk out of sight** escamotear || *intr* moverse rápidamente

whisk broom *s* escobilla

whiskers ['hwɪskərz] *spl* barbas; (*on side of face*) patillas; (*of cat*) bigotes *mpl*

whiskey ['hwɪski] *adj* (*voice*) (coll) aguardentoso || *s* whisky *m*

whisper ['hwɪspər] *s* cuchicheo; (*of leaves*) susurro; **in a whisper** en voz baja || *tr* susurrar, decir al oído || *intr* cuchichear, hablar al oído; susurrar (*p.ej., las hojas*); (*to gossip*) susurrar, murmurar

whisperer ['hwɪspərər] *s* susurrón *m*

whispering ['hwɪspərɪŋ] *adj & s* (*gossiping*) susurrón *m*

whist [hwɪst] *s* whist *m* (*juego de naipes*)

whistle ['hwɪsəl] *s* (*sound*) silbido, silbo; (*device*) silbato, pito; **to wet one's whistle** (coll) remojar la palabra || *tr* silbar (*p.ej., una canción*) || *intr* silbar; **to whistle for** llamar con un silbido; (coll) tener que componérselas sin

whistle stop *s* apeadero, pueblecito

whit [hwɪt] *s* — **not a whit** ni pizca; **to not care a whit** no importarle a (*uno*) un bledo

white [hwaɪt] *adj* blanco || *s* blanco; (*of an egg*) clara; **whites** (pathol) pérdidas blancas, flujo blanco

white'caps' *spl* cabrillas, palomas

white coal *s* hulla blanca

white'-col'lar *adj* oficinesco

white feather *s* — **to show the white feather** mostrarse cobarde

white goods *spl* tejidos de algodón; ropa blanca; aparatos electrodomésticos

white-haired ['hwaɪt,hɛrd] *adj* de pelo blanco; (*gray-haired*) cano; (coll) favorito, predilecto

white heat *s* blanco, calor blanco; (fig) viva agitación

white lead [lɛd] *s* albayalde *m*

white lie *s* mentirilla, mentira inocente u oficiosa

white meat *s* pechuga, carne *f* de la pechuga del ave

whiten ['hwaɪtən] *tr* blanquear, emblanquecer || *intr* blanquear, emblanquecerse; palidecer

whiteness ['hwaɪtnɪs] *s* blancura

white plague *s* peste blanca (*tuberculosis*)

white slavery *s* trata de blancas

white tie *s* corbatín blanco; traje *m* de etiqueta

white'wash' *s* jalbegue *m*, lechada; (*e.g., of a scandal*) encubrimiento || *tr* jalbegar, enjalbegar, encalar; absolver sin justicia; encubrir (*un escándalo*)

whither ['hwɪðər] *adv* adónde || *conj* adonde

whitish ['hwaɪtɪʃ] *adj* blanquecino, blancuzco

whitlow ['hwɪtlo] *s* panadizo, uñero

Whitsuntide ['hwɪtsən,taɪd] *s* semana de Pentecostés

whittle ['hwɪtəl] *tr* sacar pedazos a (*un trozo de madera*); **to whittle away** o **down** reducir poco a poco

whiz o **whizz** [hwɪz] *s* silbido, zumbido; (slang) perito, fenómeno || *v* (*pret & pp* **whizzed;** *ger* **whizzing)** *intr* — **to whiz by** rehilar, silbar; pasar como una flecha

who [hu] *pron interr* quién; **who else?** ¿quién más?; **who goes there?** (mil) ¿quién vive?; **who's who** quién es el uno y quién el otro; quiénes son gente de importancia || *pron rel* que, quien; el (la, etc.) que

whoa [hwo] o [wo] *interj* ¡so!

who•ev'er *pron rel* quienquiera que, cualquiera que

whole [hol] *adj* todo, entero; (*intact*) ileso; (*not scattered or dispersed*) único, p.ej., **the whole interest for him was the child he was raising** el único interés para él era el niño que educaba; **made out of the whole cloth** enteramente falso o imaginario || *s* conjunto, todo; **as a whole** en conjunto; **on the whole** en general; por la mayor parte

wholehearted ['hol,hɑrtɪd] *adj* sincero, cordial

whole note *s* (mus) semibreve *f*

whole'sale' *adj & adv* al por mayor || *s* venta al por mayor || *tr* vender al por mayor || *intr* vender al por mayor; venderse al por mayor

wholesaler ['hol,selər] *s* comerciante *mf* al por mayor

wholesome ['holsəm] *adj* (*conducive to good health*) saludable; (*in good health*) fresco, rollizo

wholly ['holi] *adv* enteramente, completamente

whom [hum] *pron interr* a quién || *pron rel* que, a quien; al (a la, etc.) que

whom•ev'er *pron rel* a quienquiera que

whoop [hup] o [hwup] *s* ululato || *tr* — **to whoop it up** (slang) armar una gritería || *intr* ulular

whooping cough ['hupɪŋ] o ['hupɪŋ] *s* tos ferina, tos convulsiva

whopper ['hwɑpər] *s* (coll) enormidad; (coll) mentirón *m*

whopping ['hwɑpɪŋ] *adj* (coll) enorme, grandísimo

whore [hor] *s* puta || *intr* — **to whore around** putañear, putear

whortleber•ry ['hwʌrtəl,bɛri] *s* (*pl* **-ries**) arándano
whose [huz] *pron interr* de quién || *pron rel* de quien, cuyo
why [hwaɪ] *adv* por qué; **why not?** ¿cómo no? || *s* (*pl* **whys**) porqué *m* || *interj* ¡toma!; **why, certainly!** ¡desde luego!, ¡por supuesto!; **why, yes!** ¡claro!, ¡pues sí!
wick [wɪk] *s* mecha, pabilo
wicked ['wɪkɪd] *adj* malo; (*mischievous*) travieso, revoltoso; (*vicious*) arisco; ofensivo
wicker ['wɪkər] *adj* mimbroso || *s* mimbre *m* & *f*
wicket ['wɪkɪt] *s* (*small door in a larger one*) portillo, postigo; (*small opening in a door*) ventanillo; (*ticket window*) taquilla; (*gate to regulate flow of water*) compuerta; (cricket) meta; (croquet) aro
wide [waɪd] *adj* ancho; de ancho; (*sense of a word*) amplio, lato || *adv* de par en par; enteramente; lejos; **wide of the mark** lejos del blanco; fuera de propósito
wide'-an'gle *adj* granangular
wide'-a•wake' *adj* despabilado
widen ['waɪdən] *tr* ensanchar || *intr* ensancharse
wide'-o'pen *adj* abierto de par en par; **to be wide-open** estar (*p.ej., una ciudad*) abierta a los jugadores
wide'spread' *adj* (*arms, wings*) extendido; difundido, extenso
widow ['wɪdo] *s* viuda; (cards) baceta || *tr* dejar viuda
widower ['wɪdo•ər] *s* viudo
widowhood ['wɪdo,hʊd] *s* viudez *f*
widow's mite *s* limosna que da un pobre
widow's pension *s* viudedad
widow's weeds *spl* luto de viuda
width [wɪdθ] *s* anchura
wield [wild] *tr* esgrimir, manejar (*la espada*); ejercer (*el poder*)
wife [waɪf] *s* (*pl* **wives** [waɪvz]) esposa, mujer *f*
wig [wɪg] *s* peluca
wiggle ['wɪgəl] *s* meneo rápido || *tr* menear rápidamente || *intr* menearse rápidamente
wig'wag' *s* comunicación con banderas || *v* (*pret & pp* **-wagged;** *ger* **-wagging**) *tr* menear; mandar (*informes*) moviendo banderas || *intr* menearse; señalar con banderas
wigwam ['wɪgwɑm] *s* choza cónica (*de los pieles rojas*)
wild [waɪld] *adj* (*not domesticated; growing without cultivation; uncivilized*) salvaje; (*unrestrained*) descabellado; (*frantic, mad*) frenético; (*riotous*) desenfrenado, revoltoso; extravagante; (*bullet, shot*) perdido; **wild about** loco por || *adv* disparatadamente; **to run wild** crecer locamente; estar sin gobierno || *s* desierto, yermo; **wilds** monte *m*, despoblado
wild boar *s* jabalí *m*
wild card *s* comodín *m*
wild'cat' *s* gato montés; lince *m;* empresa arriesgada
wildcat strike *s* huelga no autorizada por el sindicato
wilderness ['wɪldərnɪs] *s* desierto, yermo
wild'fire' *s* fuego fatuo; fucilazo; **to spread like wildfire** ser un reguero de pólvora, correr como pólvora en reguero
wild flower *s* flor *f* del campo
wild goose *s* ganso bravo
wild'-goose' chase *s* caza de grillos
wild'life' *s* animales *mf* salvajes
wild oats *spl* excesos de la juventud, mocedad; **to sow one's wild oats** llevar (*los mozos*) una vida de excesos
wild olive *s* acebuche *m*
wile [waɪl] *s* ardid *m*, engaño; (*cunning*) astucia || *tr* engatusar; **to wile away** entretener (*el tiempo*); pasar (*p.ej., la tarde*)
will [wɪl] *s* voluntad; (law) testamento; **at will** a voluntad || *tr* querer; (*to bequeath*) legar || *intr* querer; **do as you will** haga Vd. lo que quiera || *v* (*pret & cond* **would**) *v aux* **he will arrive at six o'clock** llegará a las seis; **he will go for days without smoking** pasa días enteros sin fumar
willful ['wɪlfəl] *adj* voluntarioso
willfulness ['wɪlfəlnɪs] *s* voluntariedad
William ['wɪljəm] *s* Guillermo
willing ['wɪlɪŋ] *adj* dispuesto; gustoso, pronto; espontáneo; **willing or unwilling** que quiera, que no quiera
willingly ['wɪlɪŋli] *adv* de buena gana, de buena voluntad
willingness ['wɪlɪŋnɪs] *s* buena gana, buena voluntad
will-o'-the-wisp ['wɪləðə'wɪsp] *s* fuego fatuo; ilusión, quimera
willow ['wɪlo] *s* sauce *m*
willowy ['wɪlo•i] *adj* (*pliant*) juncal, mimbreño; (*slender, graceful*) juncal, cimbreño, esbelto; lleno de sauces
will power *s* fuerza de voluntad
willy-nilly ['wɪli'nɪli] *adv* de grado o por fuerza
wilt [wɪlt] *tr* marchitar || *intr* marchitarse
wil•y ['waɪli] *adj* (*comp* **-ier;** *super* **-iest**) artero, engañoso; astuto
wimple ['wɪmpəl] *s* griñón *m*, impla
win [wɪn] *s* (coll) éxito, triunfo || *v* (*pret & pp* **won** [wʌn]; *ger* **winning**) *tr* ganar; **to win over** ganar, conquistar || *intr* ganar; **to win out** ganar; (coll) tener éxito
wince [wɪns] *s* sobresalto || *intr* sobresaltarse
winch [wɪntʃ] *s* maquinilla, torno; (*handle, crank*) manubrio
wind [wɪnd] *s* viento; (*gas in intestines*) (coll) viento; (*breath*) respiración, resuello; **to break wind** ventosear; **to get wind of** saber de, tener noticia de; **to sail close to the wind** (naut) ceñir el viento; **to take the wind out of one's sails** apagarle a uno los fuegos || *tr* dejar sin aliento || [waɪnd] *v* (*pret & pp* **wound**

[waund]) *tr* (*to coil; to wrap up*) arrollar, envolver; devanar (*alambre*); ovillar (*hilo*); torcer (*hebras*); hacer girar (*un manubrio*); dar cuerda a (*un reloj*); **to wind one's way through** serpentear por; **to wind up** arrollar, envolver; (coll) poner punto final a || *intr* serpentear (*un camino*)

windbag ['wɪnd,bæg] *s* (*of bagpipe*) odre *m;* (coll) charlatán *m,* palabrero

windbreak ['wɪnd,brek] *s* guardavientos *m*

wind cone [wɪnd] *s* (aer) cono de viento

winded ['wɪndɪd] *adj* falto de respiración, sin resuello

windfall ['wɪnd,fɔl] *s* fruta caída del árbol; fortunón *m,* cosa llovida del cielo

winding sheet ['waɪndɪŋ] *s* sudario, mortaja

winding stairs *spl* escalera de caracol

wind instrument [wɪnd] *s* (mus) instrumento de viento

windlass ['wɪndləs] *s* maquinilla, torno

windmill ['wɪnd,mɪl] *s* (*mill operated by wind*) molino de viento; (*modern wind-driven source of power*) aeromotor *m;* (*pinwheel*) molinete *m;* **to tilt at windmills** luchar con los molinos de viento

window ['wɪndo] *s* ventana; (*of ticket office; of envelope*) ventanilla; (*of coach, automobile*) ventanilla, portezuela

window dresser *s* escaparatista *mf*

window dressing *s* adorno de escaparates

window frame *s* marco de ventana

win'dow•pane' *s* cristal *m* o vidrio de ventana

window screen *s* alambrera, sobrevidriera

window shade *s* visillo, transparente *m* de resorte

win'dow-shop' *v* (*pret & pp* **-shopped;** *ger* **-shopping**) *intr* mirar los escaparates sin comprar

window shutter *s* contraventana

window sill *s* repisa de ventana

windpipe ['wɪnd,paɪp] *s* tráquea

windshield ['wɪnd,ʃild] *s* parabrisa *m*

windshield washer *s* lavaparabrisas *m*

windshield wiper *s* limpiaparabrisas *m*

wind sock *s* (aer) cono de viento

windstorm ['wɪnd,stɔrm] *s* ventarrón *m*

wind-up ['waɪnd,ʌp] *s* conclusión; (sport) final *f* de partido

windward ['wɪndwərd] *s* barlovento; **to turn to windward** barloventear

Windward Islands *spl* islas de Barlovento

Windward Passage *s* paso de los Vientos

wind•y ['wɪndi] *adj* (*comp* **-ier;** *super* **-iest**) ventoso; (*unsubstantial*) vacío; palabrero, ampuloso; **it is windy** hace viento

wine [waɪn] *s* vino || *tr* obsequiar con vino || *intr* beber vino

wine cellar *s* bodega

wine'glass' *s* copa para vino

winegrower ['waɪn,gro•ər] *s* vinicultor *m*

winegrowing ['waɪn,gro•ɪŋ] *s* vinicultura

wine press *s* lagar *m*

winer•y ['waɪnəri] *s* (*pl* **-ies**) lagar *m*

wine'skin' *s* odre *m*

winetaster ['waɪn,testər] *s* catavinos *m*

wing [wɪŋ] *s* ala; facción, bando; (theat) bastidor *m;* **to take wing** alzar el vuelo || *tr* herir en el ala; **to wing one's way** avanzar volando

wing chair s sillón *m* de orejas

wing collar *s* cuello de pajarita

wing nut *s* tuerca de aletas

wing'spread' *s* envergadura

wink [wɪŋk] *s* guiño; **to not sleep a wink** no pegar los ojos; **to take forty winks** (coll) descabezar el sueño || *tr* guiñar (*el ojo*) || *intr* guiñar; (*to blink*) parpadear, pestañear; **to wink at** guiñar el ojo a; fingir no ver

winner ['wɪnər] *s* ganador *m,* vencedor *m;* premiado

winning ['wɪnɪŋ] *adj* triunfante, victorioso; atrayente, simpático || **winnings** *spl* ganancias

winnow ['wɪno] *tr* aventar; entresacar || *intr* aletear

winsome ['wɪnsəm] *adj* atrayente, simpático, engañador; alegre

winter ['wɪntər] *adj* invernal || *s* invierno || *intr* invernar

win'ter•green' *s* gaulteria, té *m* del Canadá; esencia de gaulteria

win•try ['wɪntri] *adj* (*comp* **-trier;** *super* **-triest**) invernal, invernizo; helado, frío

wipe [waɪp] *tr* frotar para limpiar; enjugar (*la cara, el sudor, las manos*); **to wipe away** enjugar (*lágrimas*); **to wipe off** quitar frotando; **to wipe out** (coll) borrar, cancelar; (coll) aniquilar, destruir; (coll) enjugar (*deudas, un déficit*)

wiper ['waɪpər] *s* paño, trapo; (elec) contacto deslizante

wire [waɪr] *s* (*thread of metal*) alambre *m;* telégrafo; telegrama *m;* teléfono; **to pull wires** (coll) tocar resortes || *tr* alambrar; telegrafiar || *intr* telegrafiar

wire cutter *s* cortaalambres *m*

wire entanglement *s* (mil) alambrado

wire gauge *s* calibrador *m* de alambre

wire-haired ['waɪr,hɛrd] *adj* de pelo áspero

wireless ['waɪrlɪs] *adj* inalámbrico, sin hilos

wire nail *s* punta de París, clavo de alambre

wire pulling ['pulɪŋ] *s* (coll) empleo de resortes

wire recorder *s* grabadora de alambre

wire screen *s* alambrera, tela de alambre

wire'tap' *v* (*pret & pp* **-tapped;** *ger* **-tapping**) *tr* intervenir (*una conversación telefónica*)

wiring ['waɪrɪŋ] *s* (elec) alambraje *m*

wir•y ['waɪri] *adj* (*comp* **-ier;** *super*

-iest) alambrino; cimbreante; nervudo; vibrante
wisdom ['wɪzdəm] *s* sabiduría, cordura
wisdom tooth *s* muela cordal, muela del juicio
wise [waɪz] *adj* sabio, cuerdo; (*step, decision*) acertado, juicioso; **to be wise to** (slang) conocer el juego de; **to get wise** (coll) caer en el chiste ‖ *s* modo, manera; **in no wise** de ningún modo
wiseacre ['waɪz,ekər] *s* sabihondo
wise'crack' *s* (slang) cuchufleta ‖ *intr* (slang) cuchufletear
wise guy *s* (slang) sabelotodo
wish [wɪʃ] *s* deseo; **to make a wish** pensar algo que se desea ‖ *tr* desear; dar (*los buenos días*) ‖ *intr* desear; **to wish for** desear, anhelar
wish'bone' *s* espoleta, hueso de la suerte
wishful ['wɪʃfəl] *adj* deseoso
wishful thinking *s* optimismo a ultranza; **to indulge in wishful thinking** forjarse ilusiones
wistful ['wɪstfəl] *adj* melancólico, tristón, pensativo
wit [wɪt] *s* agudeza; (*person*) chistoso; (*keen mental power*) juicio; **to be at one's wits' end** no saber qué hacer; **to have the wit to** tener el tino de; **to live by one's wits** vivir del cuento
witch [wɪtʃ] *s* bruja, hechicera; (*old hag*) bruja
witch'craft' *s* brujería
witches' Sabbath *s* aquelarre *m*
witch hazel *s* (*shrub*) nogal *m* de la brujería, planta del sortilegio; (*liquid*) hamamelina, hazelina
with [wɪð] o [wɪθ] *prep* con; de
with·draw' *v* (*pret* **-drew;** *pp* **-drawn)** *tr* retirar ‖ *intr* retirarse
withdrawal [wɪð'drɔ·əl] o [wɪθ'drɔ·əl] *s* retirada
wither ['wɪðər] *tr* marchitar; (fig) aplastar, confundir ‖ *intr* marchitarse; confundirse
with·hold' *v* (*pret & pp* **-held)** *tr* retener; suspender (*pago*); negar (*un permiso*)
withholding tax *s* impuesto deducido del sueldo
with·in' *adv* dentro ‖ *prep* dentro de; al alcance de; poco menos de; con un margen de
with·out' *adv* fuera ‖ *prep* fuera de; (*lacking, not with*) sin; **to do without** pasar sin; **without** + *ger* sin + *inf,* p.ej., **he left without saying goodbye** salió sin despedirse; sin que + *subj,* p.ej., **he came in without anyone seeing him** entró sin que nadie le viese
with·stand' *v* (*pret & pp* **-stood)** *tr* aguantar, resistir
witness ['wɪtnɪs] *s* testigo *mf;* **in witness whereof** en fe de lo cual; **to bear witness** dar testimonio ‖ *tr* (*to be present at*) presenciar; (*to attest*) atestiguar, testimoniar; firmar como testigo
witness stand *s* banquillo o estrado de los testigos
witticism ['wɪtɪ,sɪzəm] *s* agudeza, dicho agudo, ocurrencia
wittingly ['wɪtɪŋli] *adv* a sabiendas
wit·ty ['wɪti] *adj* (*comp* **-tier;** *super* **-tiest)** agudo, ingenioso; (*person*) ocurrente, chistoso
wizard ['wɪzərd] *s* brujo, hechicero; (coll) as *m,* experto
wizardry ['wɪzərdri] *s* hechicería, magia
wizened ['wɪzənd] *adj* acartonado, arrugado
wk. *abbr* **week**
w.l. *abbr* **wave length**
woad [wod] *s* hierba pastel
wobble ['wɑbəl] *s* bamboleo, tambaleo ‖ *intr* bambolear, tambalear; bailar (*una silla*); (fig) vacilar, ser inconstante
wob·bly ['wɑbli] *adj* (*comp* **-blier;** *super* **-bliest)** bamboleante, inseguro; vacilante
woe [wo] *s* aflicción, miseria, infortunio ‖ *interj* — **woe is me!** ¡ay de mí!
woebegone ['wobɪ,gɔn] o ['wobɪ,gɑn] *adj* cariacontecido, triste
woeful ['wofəl] *adj* triste, miserable; (*of poor quality*) malo, pésimo
wolf [wʊlf] *s* (*pl* **wolves** [wʊlvz]) lobo; persona cruel, persona mañosa; (coll) tenorio; **to cry wolf** dar falsa alarma; **to keep the wolf from the door** ponerse a cubierto del hambre ‖ *tr & intr* comer vorazmente, engullir
wolf'hound' *s* galgo lobero
wolfram ['wʊlfrəm] *s* (*element*) volframio; (*mineral*) volframita
wolf's-bane o **wolfsbane** ['wʊlfs,ben] *s* matalobos *m*
woman ['wʊmən] *s* (*pl* **women** ['wɪmɪn]) mujer *f*
womanhood ['wʊmən,hʊd] *s* el sexo femenino; las mujeres
womanish ['wʊmənɪʃ] *adj* mujeril; (*effeminate*) afeminado
wom'an·kind' *s* el sexo femenino
womanly ['wʊmənli] *adj* (*comp* **-lier;** *super* **-liest)** femenil, mujeriego
woman suffrage *s* sufragismo
woman-suffragist ['wʊmən'sʌfrədʒɪst] *s* sufragista *mf*
womb [wum] *s* útero; (fig) seno
womenfolk ['wɪmɪn,fok] *spl* las mujeres
wonder ['wʌndər] *s* (*something strange or surprising*) maravilla; (*feeling of surprise*) admiración; (*something strange, miracle*) milagro; **for a wonder** cosa extraña; **no wonder that . . .** no es mucho que . . .; **to work wonders** hacer milagros ‖ *tr* preguntarse ‖ *intr* admirarse, maravillarse; **to wonder at** admirarse de, maravillarse con o de
wonder drugs *spl* drogas milagrosas
wonderful ['wʌndərfəl] *adj* maravilloso
won'der·land' *s* tierra de las maravillas; reino de las hadas
wonderment ['wʌndərmənt] *s* asombro, sorpresa
wont [wʌnt] o [wɔnt] *adj* acostum-

brado; **to be wont to** acostumbrar || *s* costumbre, hábito
wonted [ˈwʌntɪd] o [ˈwɔntɪd] *adj* acostumbrado, habitual
woo [wu] *tr* cortejar (*a una mujer*); tratar de conquistar; tratar de persuadir
wood [wʊd] *s* madera; (*for making a fire*) leña; barril *m* de madera; **out of the woods** (coll) fuera de peligro; (coll) libre de dificultades; **to take to the woods** andar a monte; **woods** bosque *m*
woodbine [ˈwʊdˌbaɪn] *s* (*honeysuckle*) madreselva; (*Virginia creeper*) guau *m*
wood carving *s* labrado de madera
wood'chuck' *s* marmota de América
wood'cock' *s* becada, coalla, chocha
wood'cut' *s* (typ) grabado en madera
wood'cut'ter *s* leñador *m*
wooded [ˈwʊdɪd] *adj* arbolado, enselvado
wooden [ˈwʊdən] *adj* de madera, hecho de madera; torpe, estúpido; sin ánimo
wood engraving *s* (typ) grabado en madera
wooden-headed [ˈwʊdənˌhɛdɪd] *adj* (coll) torpe, estúpido
wooden leg *s* pata de palo
wooden shoe *s* zueco
wood grouse *s* gallo de bosque
woodland [ˈwʊdlənd] *adj* selvático || *s* bosque *m*, monte *m*
woodland scene *s* (paint) boscaje *m*
wood·man [ˈwʊdmən] *s* (*pl* **-men** [mən]) leñador *m*
woodpecker [ˈwʊdˌpɛkər] *s* carpintero, pájaro carpintero; (*green woodpecker*) picamaderos *m*
wood'pile' *s* montón *m* de leña
wood screw *s* tirafondo
wood'shed' *s* leñero
woods·man [ˈwʊdzmən] *s* (*pl* **-men** [mən]) leñador *m*
wood'wind' *s* (mus) instrumento de viento de madera
wood'work' *s* (*working in wood*) ebanistería, obra de carpintería; (*things made of wood*) maderaje *m*
wood'work'er *s* ebanista *mf*, carpintero
wood'worm' *s* carcoma
wood·y [ˈwʊdi] *adj* (*comp* **-ier**; *super* **-iest**) arbolado, enselvado; (*like wood*) leñoso
wooer [ˈwu·ər] *s* pretendiente *m*, galán *m*
woof [wuf] *s* (*yarns running across warp*) trama; (*fabric*) tejido
woofer [ˈwʊfər] *s* altavoz *m* para audiofrecuencias bajas
wool [wʊl] *s* lana
woolen [ˈwʊlən] *adj* de lana, hecho de lana || *s* tejido de lana; **woolens** lanerías
woolgrower [ˈwʊlˌgro·ər] *s* criador *m* de ganado lanar
wool·ly [ˈwʊli] *adj* (*comp* **-lier**; *super* **-liest**) lanoso, lanudo; borroso, confuso
word [wʌrd] *s* palabra; **to be as good as one's word** cumplir lo prometido; **to have a word with** hablar cuatro palabras con; **to have word from** recibir noticias de; **to keep one's word** cumplir su palabra; **to leave word** dejar dicho; **to send word that** mandar decir que; **words** (*a quarrel*) palabras mayores; (*text of a song*) letra || *tr* redactar, formular || **Word** *s* (theol) Verbo
word count *s* recuento de vocabulario
word formation *s* (gram) formación de palabras
wording [ˈwʌrdɪŋ] *s* fraseología, estilo
word order *s* (gram) orden *m* de colocación
word'stock' *s* vocabulario, léxico
word·y [ˈwʌrdi] *adj* (*comp* **-ier**; *super* **-iest**) verboso
work [wʌrk] *s* (*exertion; labor, toil*) trabajo; (*result of exertion; human output; engineering structure*) obra; (sew) labor *f*; **at work** trabajando; (*not at home*) en la oficina, en el taller, en la tienda; **out of work** sin trabajo, desempleado; **to shoot the works** (slang) echar el resto; **works** fábrica; mecanismo; (*of clock*) movimiento || *tr* hacer trabajar; trabajar, obrar (*la madera, el hierro*); obrar (*un milagro*); explotar (*una mina*); **to work up** preparar; estimular, excitar || *intr* trabajar; funcionar, marchar (*un aparato, un motor*); obrar (*p.ej., un remedio*); **to work loose** aflojarse; **to work out** resolverse
workable [ˈwʌrkəbəl] *adj* (*feasible*) practicable; (*that can be worked*) laborable
work'bench' *s* banco de trabajo, banco de taller
work'book' *s* (*manual of instructions*) libro de reglas; libro de ejercicios
work'box' *s* caja de herramientas; (*for needlework*) caja de labor
work'day' *adj* de cada día; ordinario, vulgar || *s* día *m* de trabajo; (*number of hours of work*) jornada
worked-up [ˈwʌrktˈʌp] *adj* muy conmovido, sobreexcitado, exaltado
worker [ˈwʌrkər] *s* trabajador *m*, obrero
work force *s* mano *f* de obra, personal obrero
work'horse' *s* caballo de carga; (*tireless worker*) yunque *m*
work'house' *s* taller penitenciario; (Brit) asilo de pobres
working class *s* clase obrera
work'ing·girl' *s* trabajadora joven
working hours *spl* horas de trabajo
working·man [ˈwʌrkɪŋˌmæn] *s* (*pl* **-men** [ˌmɛn]) *s* obrero, trabajador *m*
working·woman [ˈwʌrkɪŋˌwʊmən] *s* (*pl* **-women** [ˌwɪmɪn]) obrera, trabajadora
work·man [ˈwʌrkmən] *s* (*pl* **-men** [mən]) obrero, trabajador *m*; (*skilled worker*) artífice *m*
workmanship [ˈwʌrkmənˌʃɪp] *s* destreza en el trabajo; (*work executed*) hechura, obra
work of art *s* obra de arte

work'out' *s* ensayo, prueba; (*physical exercise*) ejercicio

work'room' *s* (*for manual work*) obrador *m,* taller *m;* (*study*) gabinete *m* de trabajo

work'shop' *s* obrador *m,* taller *m*

work stoppage *s* paro

world [wʌrld] *adj* mundial || *s* mundo; **a world of** la mar de; **half the world** (*a lot of people*) medio mundo; **since the world began** desde que el mundo es mundo; **the other world** el otro mundo; **to bring into the world** echar al mundo; **to see the world** ver mundo; **to think the world of** tener un alto concepto de

world affairs *spl* asuntos internacionales

world·ly ['wʌrldli] *adj* (*comp* **-lier;** *super* **-liest**) mundano

world'ly-wise' *adj* que tiene mucho mundo

world's fair *s* exposición mundial

World War *s* Guerra Mundial

world'-wide' *adj* global, mundial

worm [wʌrm] *s* gusano; **worms** (pathol) lombrices *fpl* || *tr* limpiar de lombrices; **to worm a secret out of a person** arrancar mañosamente un secreto a una persona; **to worm one's way into** insinuarse en

worm-eaten ['wʌrm ,itən] *adj* carcomido; (fig) decaído, desgastado

worm gear *s* engranaje *m* de tornillo sin fin

worm'wood' *s* (*Artemisia*) ajenjo; (*Artemisia absinthium*) ajenjo del campo o ajenjo mayor; (*something bitter or grievous*) (fig) ajenjo

worm·y ['wʌrmi] *adj* (*comp* **-ier;** *super* **-iest**) gusaniento, gusanoso; (*worm-eaten*) carcomido; (*groveling*) rastrero, servil

worn [worn] *adj* roto, raído, gastado

worn'-out' *adj* muy gastado, inservible; (*by toil, illness*) consumido, rendido

worrisome ['wʌrisəm] *adj* inquietante; (*inclined to worry*) aprensivo, inquieto

wor·ry ['wʌri] *s* (*pl* **-ries**) inquietud, preocupación; (*cause of anxiety*) molestia || *v* (*pret & pp* **-ried**) *tr* inquietar, preocupar; (*to harass, pester*) acosar, molestar; **to be worried** estar inquieto || *intr* inquietarse, preocuparse; **don't worry** pierda Vd. cuidado

worse [wʌrs] *adj & adv comp* peor; **worse and worse** de mal en peor

worsen ['wʌrsən] *tr & intr* empeorar

wor·ship ['wʌrʃɪp] *s* adoración, culto; **your worship** vuestra merced || *v* (*pret & pp* **-shiped** o **-shipped;** *ger* **-shiping** o **-shipping**) *tr & intr* adorar, venerar

worshiper o **worshipper** ['wʌrʃɪpər] *s* adorador *m,* devoto

worst [wʌrst] *adj & adv super* peor || *s* (lo) peor; **at worst** en las peores circunstancias; **if worst comes to worst** si pasa lo peor; **to get the worst of** llevar la peor parte, salir perdiendo

worsted ['wʊstɪd] *adj* de estambre || *s* estambre *m;* tela de estambre

wort [wʌrt] *s* (bot) hierba, planta; mosto de cerveza

worth [wʌrθ] *adj* del valor de; digno de; **to be worth** valer; tener una fortuna de; **to be worth** + *ger* valer la pena de + *inf;* **to be worth while** valer la pena; ser de mérito || *s* valor *m;* mérito; **a dollar's worth of** un dólar de

worthless ['wʌrθlɪs] *adj* sin valor, inútil, inservible; (*person*) despreciable

worth'while' *adj* de mérito, digno de atención

wor·thy ['wʌrði] *adj* (*comp* **-thier;** *super* **-thiest**) digno; benemérito, meritorio || *s* (*pl* **-thies**) benemérito; (*hum & iron*) personaje *m*

would [wʊd] *v aux* **she said she would do it** dijo que lo haría; **he would come if he could** vendría si pudiese; **he would go for days without smoking** pasaba días enteros sin fumar; **would that . . .!** ¡ojalá que . . .!

would'-be' *adj* llamado; supuesto || *s* presumido

wound [wund] *s* herida || *tr* herir

wounded ['wundɪd] *adj* herido || **the wounded** los heridos

wow [waʊ] *s* (*of phonograph record*) ululación; (slang) éxito rotundo || *tr* (slang) entusiasmar

wrack [ræk] *s* naufragio; vestigio; (*fucaceous seaweed*) varec *m;* **to go to wrack and ruin** desvencijarse; ir al desastre

wraith [reθ] *s* fantasma *m,* espectro

wrangle ['ræŋgəl] *s* pendencia, riña || *intr* pelotear, reñir

wrap [ræp] *s* abrigo, manto || *v* (*pret & pp* **wrapped;** *ger* **wrapping**) *tr* envolver; **to be wrapped up in** (fig) estar prendado de; **to wrap up** envolver; (*in clothing*) arropar; (coll) concluir || *intr* — **to wrap up** arroparse

wrapper ['ræpər] *s* bata, peinador *m;* (*of newspaper or magazine*) faja; (*of tobacco*) capa

wrapping paper ['ræpɪŋ] *s* papel *m* de envolver, papel de embalar

wrath [ræθ] o [rɑθ] *s* cólera, ira; venganza

wrathful ['ræθfəl] o ['rɑθfəl] *adj* colérico, iracundo

wreak [rik] *tr* descargar (*la cólera*); infligir (*venganza*)

wreath [riθ] *s* (*pl* **wreaths** [riðz]) guirnalda; corona funeraria; (*worn as a mark of honor or victory*) corona de laurel; (*of smoke*) espiral *f*

wreathe [rið] *tr* enguirnaldar; ceñir, envolver; tejer (*una guirnalda*) || *intr* elevarse en espirales (*el humo*)

wreck [rɛk] *s* destrucción, ruina; naufragio; catástrofe *f,* desastre *m;* despojos, restos; (*of one's hopes*) naufragio; **to be a wreck** estar hecho un cascajo, estar hecho una ruina || *tr* destruir, arruinar; hacer

naufragar; hacer chocar, descarrilar (*un tren*)
wrecking ball *s* bola rompedora
wrecking car *s* (aut) camión *m* de auxilio; (rr) carro de grúa
wrecking crane *s* grúa de auxilio
wren [rɛn] *s* buscareta, coletero, rey *m* de zarza
wrench [rɛntʃ] *s* llave *f;* (*pull*) arranque *m,* tirón *m;* (*twist of a joint*) esguince *m* || *tr* torcerse (*p.ej., la muñeca*); (fig) torcer (*el sentido de una oración*)
wrest [rɛst] *tr* arrebatar, arrancar violentamente
wrestle ['rɛsəl] *s* lucha; partido de lucha || *intr* luchar
wrestling match ['rɛslɪŋ] *s* partido de lucha
wretch [rɛtʃ] *s* miserable *mf*
wretched ['rɛtʃɪd] *adj* miserable; (*poor, worthless*) malísimo, pésimo
wriggle ['rɪgəl] *s* culebreo, meneo serpentino || *tr* menear rápidamente || *intr* culebrear, ondular; **to wriggle out of** escabullirse de
wrig·gly ['rɪgli] *adj* (*comp* **-glier;** *super* **-gliest**) retorciéndose; (fig) evasivo, tramoyista
wring [rɪŋ] *v* (*pret & pp* **wrung** [rʌŋ]) *tr* torcer; retorcer (*las manos*); exprimir (*el zumo, la ropa, etc.*); sacar por fuerza (*la verdad*); arrancar (*dinero*); **to wring out** exprimir (*la ropa*)
wringer ['rɪŋər] *s* exprimidor *m*
wrinkle ['rɪŋkəl] *s* arruga; (*clever trick or idea*) (coll) ardid *m,* truco || *tr* arrugar || *intr* arrugarse
wrin·kly ['rɪŋkli] *adj* (*comp* **-klier;** *super* **-kliest**) arrugado
wrist [rɪst] *s* muñeca
wrist'band' *s* bocamanga, puño
wrist watch *s* reloj *m* de pulsera
writ [rɪt] *s* escrito, escritura; (law) mandato, orden *f*
write [raɪt] *v* (*pret* **wrote** [rot]; *pp* **written** ['rɪtən]) *tr* escribir; **to write down** poner por escrito; bajar el precio de; **to write off** cancelar (*una deuda*); **to write up** describir extensamente por escrito; (*to ballyhoo*) dar bombo a || *intr* escribir; **to write back** contestar por carta
writer ['raɪtər] *s* escritor *m*
writer's cramp *s* grafospasmo
write'-up' *s* (*favorable report*) bombo; (com) valoración excesiva
writhe [raɪð] *intr* contorcerse, retorcerse
writing ['raɪtɪŋ] *s* el escribir; (*something written*) escrito; profesión de escritor; **at this writing** al escribir ésta; **in one's own writing** de su puño y letra; **to put in writing** poner por escrito
writing desk *s* escritorio
writing materials *spl* recado de escribir
writing paper *s* papel *m* de escribir, papel de cartas
written accent ['rɪtən] *s* acento ortográfico
wrong [rɔŋ] o [rɑŋ] *adj* injusto; malo; erróneo, equivocado; impropio; no . . . que se busca, p.ej., **this is the wrong house** ésta no es la casa que se busca; no . . . que se necesita, p.ej., **this is the wrong train** éste no es el tren que se necesita; no . . . que debe, p.ej., **he is going the wrong way** no sigue el camino que debe; **in the wrong place** mal colocado; **to be wrong** no tener razón; tener la culpa; **to be wrong with** pasar algo a, p.ej., **something is wrong with the motor** algo le pasa al motor || *adv* mal; sin razón; al revés; **to go wrong** ir por mal camino; darse a la mala vida || *s* daño, perjuicio; agravio, injusticia; error *m;* **to be in the wrong** no tener razón; tener la culpa; **to do wrong** obrar mal || *tr* agraviar, hacer daño a, ofender, ser injusto con
wrongdoer ['rɔŋ,du·ər] o ['rɑŋ,du·ər] *s* malhechor *m*
wrongdoing ['rɔŋ,du·ɪŋ] o ['rɑŋ,du·ɪŋ] *s* malhecho, maldad
wrong number *s* (telp) número equivocado
wrong side *s* contrahaz *f,* revés *m;* (*of the street*) lado contrario; **to get out of bed on the wrong side** levantarse del lado izquierdo; **wrong side out** al revés
wrought iron [rɔt] *s* hierro dulce
wrought'-up' *adj* muy conmovido, sobreexcitado, exaltado
wry [raɪ] *adj* (*comp* **wrier;** *super* **wriest**) torcido; desviado, pervertido; irónico, burlón
wry'neck' *s* (orn) torcecuello; (pathol) torticolis *m*
wt. *abbr* **weight**

X

X, x [ɛks] vigésima cuarta letra del alfabeto inglés
Xanthippe [zæn'tɪpi] *s* Jantipa
Xavier ['zævɪ·ər] o ['zevɪ·ər] *s* Javier *m*
xebec ['zibɛk] *s* (naut) jabeque *m*
xenia ['zinɪ·ə] *s* xenia
xenon ['zinɑn] o ['zɛnɑn] *s* xenón *m*
xenophobe ['zɛnə,fob] *s* xenófobo
xenophobia [,zɛnə'fobɪ·ə] *s* xenofobia
Xenophon ['zɛnəfən] *s* Jenofonte *m*
Xerxes ['zʌrksiz] *s* Jerjes *m*
Xmas ['krɪsməs] *s* Navidad

X ray *s* rayo X; (*photograph*) radiograma *m*
X-ray ['ɛks,re] *adj* radiográfico || ['ɛks're] *tr* radiografiar; tratar por medio de los rayos X
xylograph ['zaɪlə,græf] o ['zaɪlə,grɑf] *s* xilografía
xylography [zaɪ'lɑgrəfi] *s* xilografía
xylophone ['zaɪlə,fon] *s* (mus) xilófono

Y

Y, y [waɪ] vigésima quinta letra del alfabeto inglés
y. *abbr* **yard, year**
yacht [jɑt] *s* yate *m*
yacht club *s* club náutico
yak [jæk] *s* (zool) yac *m*
yam [jæm] *s* ñame *m;* (*sweet potato*) boniato, camote *m*
yank [jæŋk] *s* (coll) tirón *m* || *tr* (coll) sacar de un tirón || *intr* (coll) dar un tirón
Yankee ['jæŋki] *adj & s* yanqui *mf*
Yankeedom ['jæŋkidəm] *s* Yanquilandia; los yanquis
yap [jæp] *s* ladrido corto; (slang) charla necia y ruidosa || *v* (*pret & pp* **yapped;** *ger* **yapping**) *intr* ladrar con ladrido corto; (slang) charlar necia y ruidosamente
yard [jɑrd] *s* cercado, patio; (*measure*) yarda; (naut) verga; (rr) patio
yard'arm' *s* (naut) penol *m*
yard goods *spl* géneros de pieza
yard'mas'ter *s* (rr) superintendente *m* de patio
yard'stick' *s* yarda, vara de medir; (fig) criterio, norma
yarn [jɑrn] *s* hilado, hilaza; (coll) cuento increíble, burlería
yarrow ['jæro] *s* milenrama
yaw [jɔ] *s* (naut) guiñada; **yaws** (pathol) frambesia || *intr* (naut) guiñar
yawl [jɔl] *s* (naut) bote *m;* (naut) queche *m*
yawn [jɔn] *s* bostezo || *intr* bostezar; abrirse desmesuradamente
yd. *abbr* **yard**
yea [je] *adv & s* sí *m*
yean [jin] *intr* parir (*la oveja, la cabra, etc.*)
year [jɪr] *s* año; **to be . . . years old** cumplir . . . años; **year in, year out** año tras año
year'book' *s* anuario
yearling ['jɪrlɪŋ] *adj & s* primal *m*
yearly ['jɪrli] *adj* anual || *adv* anualmente
yearn [jʌrn] *intr* suspirar; **to yearn for** suspirar por, anhelar por
yearning ['jʌrnɪŋ] *s* anhelo, deseo ardiente
yeast [jist] *s* levadura
yeast cake *s* levadura comprimida, pastilla de levadura
yell [jɛl] *s* grito, voz *f* || *tr* decir a gritos || *intr* gritar, dar voces
yellow ['jɛlo] *adj* amarillo; (*cowardly*) (coll) blanco; (*journalism*) sensacional || *s* amarillo; yema de huevo || *intr* amarillecer
yellowish ['jɛlo·ɪʃ] *adj* amarillento
yellow jacket *s* avispón *m*
yellowness ['jɛlonɪs] *s* amarillez *f*
yellow streak *s* vena de cobarde
yelp [jɛlp] *s* gañido || *intr* gañir
yeo•man ['jomən] *s* (*pl* **-men** [mən]) (naut) pañolero; (naut) oficinista *m* de a bordo; (Brit) labrador acomodado
yeoman of the guard *s* (Brit) alabardero de palacio, continuo
yeoman's service *s* ayuda leal
yes [jɛs] *adv* sí || *s* sí *m;* **to say yes** dar el sí || *v* (*pret & pp* **yessed;** *ger* **yessing**) *tr* decir sí a || *intr* decir sí
yes man *s* (coll) sacristán *m* de amén
yesterday ['jɛstərdi] o ['jɛstər,de] *adj & s* ayer *m*
yet [jɛt] *adv* todavía, aún; **as yet** hasta ahora; **not yet** todavía no || *conj* sin embargo
yew tree [ju] *s* tejo
yield [jild] *s* producción, rendimiento; (*crop*) cosecha; (*income produced*) rédito || *tr* producir, rendir, redituar || *intr* entregarse, rendirse, someterse; acceder, ceder, consentir; producir
yodeling o **yodelling** ['jodəlɪŋ] *s* tirolesa
yoke [jok] *s* (*pair of draft animals*) yunta; (*device to join a pair of draft animals*) yugo; (fig) yugo; (*of a shirt*) hombrillo; (elec) culata; **to throw off the yoke** sacudir el yugo || *tr* uncir
yokel ['jokəl] *s* patán *m*
yolk [jok] *s* yema
yonder ['jɑndər] *adj* aquel, de más allá || *adv* allá, más allá
yore [jor] *s* — **of yore** antaño, antiguamente
you [ju] *pron pers* usted, ustedes; le, la, les; **with you** consigo || *pron indef se,* p.ej., **you go in this way** se entra por aquí
young [jʌŋ] *adj* (*comp* **younger** ['jʌŋgər]; *super* **youngest** ['jʌŋgɪst]) joven || **the young** los jóvenes, la gente joven
young hopeful *s* joven *m* de esperanzas
young people *spl* jóvenes *mpl,* gente *f* joven
youngster ['jʌŋstər] *s* jovencito; (*child*) chico, chiquillo
your [jur] *adj poss* su, el (o su) de Vd. o de Vds.
yours [jurz] *pron poss* suyo; de Vd., de Vds.; el suyo; el de Vd., el de Vds.; **of yours** suyo; de Vd., de

Vds.; **yours truly** su seguro servidor; (coll) este cura (*yo*)
your·self [jʊr'sɛlf] *pron pers* (*pl* **-selves** ['sɛlvz]) usted mismo; sí, sí mismo; se, p.ej., **you enjoyed yourself** se divirtió Vd.
youth [juθ] *s* (*pl* **youths** [juθs] o [juðz]) juventud; (*person*) jovenzuelo; jovenzuelos, jóvenes *mpl*
youthful ['juθfəl] *adj* juvenil, mocil
yowl [jaʊl] *s* aullido, alarido ‖ *intr* aullar, dar alaridos
yr. *abbr* **year**
Yugoslav ['jugo'slɑv] *adj & s* yugoeslavo
Yugoslavia ['jugo'slɑvɪ·ə] *s* Yugoeslavia
Yule [jul] *s* la Navidad; la pascua de Navidad
Yule log *s* nochebueno, leño de nochebuena
Yuletide ['jul,taɪd] *s* la pascua de Navidad

Z

Z, z [zi] vigésima sexta letra del alfabeto inglés
za·ny ['zeni] *adj* (*comp* **-nier;** *super* **-niest**) cómico, gracioso, chiflado ‖ *s* (*pl* **-nies**) bufón *m*, payaso; mentecato
zeal [zil] *s* celo, entusiasmo
zealot ['zɛlət] *s* fanático, entusiasta *mf*
zealotry ['zɛlətri] *s* fanatismo
zealous ['zɛləs] *adj* celoso, entusiasta
zebra ['zibrə] *s* cebra
zebu ['zibju] *s* cebú *m*
zenith ['zinɪθ] *s* cenit *m*
zephyr ['zɛfər] *s* céfiro
zeppelin ['zɛpəlɪn] *s* zepelín *m*
ze·ro ['zɪro] *s* (*pl* **-ros** o **-roes**) cero
zero gravity *s* gravedad nula
zest [zɛst] *s* entusiasmo; (*agreeable and piquant flavor*) gusto, sabor *m*
Zeus [zus] *s* Zeus *m*
zig·zag ['zɪg,zæg] *adj & adv* en zigzag ‖ *s* zigzag *m*, ziszas *m* ‖ *v* (*pret & pp* **-zagged;** *ger* **-zagging**) *intr* zigzaguear
zinc [zɪŋk] *s* cinc *m*
zinc etching *s* cincograbado
zinnia ['zɪnɪ·ə] *s* rascamoño
Zionism ['zaɪ·ə,nɪzəm] *s* sionismo
zip [zɪp] *s* (coll) silbido, zumbido; (coll) energía, brío ‖ *v* (*pret & pp* **zipped;** *ger* **zipping**) *tr* cerrar con cierre relámpago, abrir con cierre relámpago; (coll) llevar con rapidez; **to zip up** dar gusto a ‖ *intr* silbar, zumbar; (coll) moverse con energía; **to zip by** (coll) pasar rápidamente
zipper ['zɪpər] *s* cierre *m* relámpago, cierre cremallera; chanclo con cierre relámpago
zircon ['zʌrkɑn] *s* circón *m*
zirconium [zər'konɪ·əm] *s* circonio
zither ['zɪθər] *s* (mus) cítara
zodiac ['zodɪ,æk] *s* zodíaco
zone [zon] *s* zona; distrito postal ‖ *tr* dividir en zonas
zoölogic(al) [,zo·ə'lɑdʒɪk(əl)] *adj* zoológico
zoölogist [zo'ɑlədʒɪst] *s* zoólogo
zoölogy [zo'ɑlədʒi] *s* zoología
zoom [zum] *s* zumbido; (aer) empinada ‖ *tr* (aer) empinar ‖ *intr* zumbar; (aer) empinarse
zoöphyte ['zo·ə,faɪt] *s* zoófito
Zu·lu ['zulu] *adj* zulú ‖ *s* (*pl* **-lus**) zulú *mf*